TEXT, CASES AND MATERIALS ON
SEX–BASED DISCRIMINATION

Fourth Edition

By

Herma Hill Kay
Dean and Richard W. Jennings Professor of Law
University of California, Berkeley

Martha S. West
Professor of Law
University of California, Davis

AMERICAN CASEBOOK SERIES®

WEST PUBLISHING CO.
ST. PAUL, MINN., 1996

American Casebook Series, the key symbol appearing on the front
cover and the WP symbol are registered trademarks of West Publishing
Co. Registered in the U.S. Patent and Trademark Office.

COPYRIGHT © 1974, 1981, 1988 WEST PUBLISHING CO.

COPYRIGHT © 1996 By WEST PUBLISHING CO.
                        610 Opperman Drive
                        P.O. Box 64526
                        St. Paul, MN 55164–0526
                        1–800–328–9352

Library of Congress Cataloging-in-Publication Data

Kay, Herma Hill.
    Text, cases and materials on sex-based discrimination / by Herma
Hill Kay, Martha S. West. — 4th ed.
        p.   cm. — (American casebook series)
    Includes index.
    ISBN 0–314–09633–7 (hc)
    1. Sex discrimination—Law and legislation—United States—Cases.
I. West, Martha S., 1946–   .   II. Title.   III. Series.
KF4758.A7K39   1996
342.73 ' 0878—dc20
[347.302878]   96–23279
                                                          CIP

ISBN 0–314–09633–7

 TEXT IS PRINTED ON 10% POST CONSUMER RECYCLED PAPER

Preface

The fourth edition of these materials appears at a time when questions once thought settled are being reopened and new questions, some posing previously unimagined issues, are emerging. Because many of those questions ultimately will find their way to the docket of the United States Supreme Court, that Court's attitude toward equality between women and men, while always important, is critical to the development of the law in this area.

Since their appearance in 1974, these materials have both reflected and critiqued the Supreme Court's views of how the law — both constitutional and statutory — should respond to the efforts of individual women and men to break free of social, economic, and legal constraints that have embodied our cultural image of who the two sexes are and how they should behave in relationship to each other in varied contexts. As this edition demonstrates, the Court has moved over time from an early willingness to sustain laws prohibiting women from entering the legal profession and denying men the opportunity to nurture their children. In the 1970s, the Court recognized that sex-based classifications were sufficiently troublesome to require a heightened level of scrutiny. One of the questions thought settled, if not resolved, at that time — whether sex, like race, should be categorized as a suspect classification deserving of the highest level of strict scrutiny — is once again on the Court's open agenda.

The Court's calendar was dominated for nearly twenty years — between 1973 and 1992 — by the regulation of abortion. The contentious struggle to locate a coherent body of law on the unstable basis of an emerging right to privacy stood in sharp contrast to the Court's more principled development of the equality doctrine in the areas of family law, employment discrimination, and education. Now that the majority's approach to abortion is being nudged away from privacy rationales toward considerations of equality, a less combative, if not harmonious, bench may emerge in this area as well.

Other questions receiving fresh analysis include the constitutional limits to be imposed on affirmative action both as a remedy for past discrimination and as a voluntary initiative to create a more racially and sexually balanced society; the propriety of single-sex education in the context of military academies; and the proof necessary to establish intentional discrimination. In the sphere of family life, a renewed effort to legalize same-sex marriage is gaining momentum, even as Congress moves to encourage states to deny recognition to such unions, should the effort succeed. No-fault divorce laws, currently in force in all states, are being attacked in the name of family values, while rapid discoveries in the field of reproductive technology are changing the very concept of family life.

The final resolution of these and other issues cannot be foreseen. But whatever the outcome of these specific contentions, the ideal of equality between women and men is an enduring one that has taken vigorous root in our culture. As this Fourth Edition goes to press, I welcome the addition of Professor Martha S. West of the University of California, Davis, law faculty as my co-author and respected colleague in this field.

HERMA HILL KAY
BERKELEY, CALIFORNIA

Authors' Note and Acknowledgements

This Fourth Edition continues the practice of earlier Editions in presenting lightly edited cases in order to preserve the flavor of judicial reasoning about sex differences and their relevance in the context of Constitutional and statutory challenges to differential treatment of women and men. The Text Notes are intended to provide relevant background material that can serve as the basis for more general discussion.

We gratefully acknowledge the permission extended by the authors and publishers of copyrighted works excerpted in the First, Second, and Third Editions, as well as in this Fourth Edition. Specific acknowledgements are found in the Acknowledgements and Permission section.

Personal thanks are due to Priscilla MacDougal, for her generous help in preparing the material on names included in the Text Note on The Married Woman's Loss of Identity in Chapter One; to Dr. David Truman, who wrote the letter included in the Text Note on Women's Colleges in Chapter Four; to Professor Christine Littleton, who co-authored with Herma Hill Kay the Text Note on Feminist Jurisprudence in Chapter Five; and to Nicole G. Berner, Herma Hill Kay's excellent research assistant, who wrote the section on Woman Abuse in Chapter Five in addition to her other help in revising Chapters One and Two.

Herma Hill Kay gives special thanks to the Law Library Research Staff at U.C. Berkeley, who were always ready to help out with an obscure reference or a missing book, and to her able secretary, Nancy Anvari. Martha West gives special thanks to her research assistant, Tracy Knorr, for help in updating the notes in Chapters Three, Four, and Five; to Saralee Buck, for her tireless efforts on the computer in reorganizing Chapter Three; and to Deborah Dubroff, research assistant, for help in finalizing the manuscript for publication.

Finally, we are both grateful to our students, whose reflections on the issues presented in this casebook have contributed greatly to our own thinking and writing on this subject.

*

Acknowledgements and Permission

We are grateful for permission to reprint the following copyrighted material:

Dorothy Sue Cobble, Women and Unions. Reprinted from *Women and Unions: Forging a New Partnership*, ed. Dorothy Sue Cobble, pp. 5-10, 70-2, & 103, Copyright (©) 1993 by Cornell University. Used by permission of the publisher, Cornell University Press.

Sheila Cronan, Marriage. Reprinted from Notes From The Third Year: Women's Liberation 62-65 (1971).

Lori S. Kornblum, Women Warriors in a Men's World: The Combat Exclusion. Reprinted from 2 Law & Inequality 351, 358–59, 395, 442--443 (1984).

Charles R. Lawrence III, The Id, the Ego, and Equal Protection: Reckoning with Unconscious Racism. Reprinted from 39 Stanford Law Review 317, 322, 324, 355–56, 370, 373, 375 (1987). Copyright 1987 by the Board of Trustees of the Leland Stanford Junior University.

Pat Mainardi, The Politics of Housework. Reprinted from Notes From The Second Year: Women's Liberation 28–31 (1970).

Catharine A. MacKinnon, Feminism Unmodified: Discourses on Life and Law. Reprinted from Feminism Unmodified: Discourses on Life and Law 210–211 (Harvard University Press 1987). Copyright © 1987 by the President and Fellows of Harvard College.

Catharine A. MacKinnon, Pornography, Civil Rights and Speech. Reprinted from 20 Harvard Civil Rights—Civil Liberties Law Review 1, 22–23 (1985).

Deborah L. Rhode, Equal Rights in Retrospect. Reprinted from 1 Law & Inequality 1, 4–8 (1983).

Jean Yarbrough, The Feminist Mistake: Sexual Equality and the Decline of the American Military. Reprinted from 33 Policy Review 48, 52 (Summer 1985). *The Feminist Mistake: Sexual Equality and the Decline of the American Military* by Jean Yarbrough is reprinted from POLICY REVIEW, the flagship quarterly of The Heritage Foundation, Summer 1985.

*

Summary of Contents

*

Table of Contents

Page

Table of Cases

The principal cases are in bold type. Cases cited or discussed in the text are roman type. References are to pages. Cases cited in principal cases and within other quoted materials are not included.

TEXT, CASES AND MATERIALS ON
SEX–BASED DISCRIMINATION

Fourth Edition

*

INTRODUCTION

WHAT IS EQUALITY BETWEEN THE SEXES?

In October 1995, the ACLU and the Columbia Women's Law Association sponsored a bake sale that charged women less than men for cake. "To highlight gender inequalities in pay," the flyer read, "women will be charged 75 cents to men's charge of a dollar." Is a feminist bake sale with differential pricing based on sex an act of revolutionary self-help, or a misguided policy that buys into the stereotype that women are less capable than men? Are the bakers overcharging men or undercharging women? If you agree that reparations are appropriate, do you think women workers should be paid more than men? Would such a policy help to achieve equality between the sexes? Would it violate the Equal Pay Act, a 1963 statute designed to prevent employers from paying women less than men for doing equal jobs?

In November 1995, black male students at the College of the Holy Cross—many of them recruited as athletes—boycotted sports and other extracurricular activities to protest the Student Government Association's decision to delete a clause in the Constitution of the Black Students' Union limiting elected officers of the group to students "of African descent."[1] The BSU does not limit its membership to African–Americans, merely its elected leadership. Three days later, the campus administration ended the boycott by overruling the SGA, indicating that the constitutional restriction would "preserve the integrity of the group." Did the BSU think that its white members would out vote its black members to elect white officers? Or did they fear that black members, given the opportunity, would choose white leaders? Justice Clarence Thomas, a graduate of Holy Cross and a secretary-treasurer of BSU in 1969–70, has stated in a concurring opinion that even "benign" affirmative action designed to improve the employment position of blacks competing for federal contracts is paternalistic, immoral, and unconstitutional.[2] What would he think of the Holy Cross boycott? Of the pricing policy at the Columbia bake sale? Why do you think the Holy Cross administration sided with the black athletes?

What do these two unrelated events have in common, and what is their significance for a law school course on sex discrimination? Consider this:

1. The New York Times, Nov. 19, 1995, at 19–Y, cols. 1–5.

2. Adarand Construction Co. v. Pena, ___ U.S. ___, 115 S.Ct. 2097, 2119, 132 L.Ed.2d 158, 190–91 (1995) (Thomas, J., concurring in part and concurring in the judgment.)

1

More than two hundred years after the Declaration of Independence was signed in 1776, over one hundred years since President Lincoln signed the Emancipation Proclamation in 1863 abolishing slavery, and seventy-five years since the suffrage amendment was added to the U.S. Constitution in 1920, neither women nor blacks are fully "equal before the law" in the United States. The history, sources, and present socio-economic characteristics of the condition of these two groups are quite different, and the situation of individuals within each group varies perhaps as much as their external difference from each other. Yet their common struggle for legal equality is inextricably intertwined, if only because their respective constitutional arguments are are drawn from a single text, and their ultimate appeals are argued to the same High Court. Moreover, the national political community within which they seek to make their voices heard provides not only a context for their present situation and a measure of their power to achieve change, but also will judge the fairness of the remedies they seek.

This book aims to examine the legal aspects of the struggle for equality between women and men. In doing so, it will necessarily consider a wide range of factors that bear crucially on the purpose, the process, and the possible outcomes of that struggle. This brief introduction identifies some underlying themes that accompany and inform the legal analysis undertaken throughout the course.

A quest for "equality," whether between races or sexes, begins with the question: "equal to what?" In the case of blacks, the primary comparison group has been whites, while for women, it has been men. But, of course, the group of whites and of men differs as widely among itself as does the group of blacks and women: and stressing the polarity between both groups serves to obscure, if not to ignore, the unique situation of black women and other women of color.[3] The second definitional question follows hard on the heels of the first: "what do you mean by 'equality' "? Formal equality of opportunity ("everyone should start the race from the same point and the playing field should be level") or substantive equality of outcome (recall Aesop's fox and stork, who cannot drink as easily from the same vessel)?

Once inequality, however defined, is shown to exist, the question of remedy takes precedence. Here the advocates of racial equality initially began with a claim of formal equality: end the intentional oppression of blacks by whites. Their agenda varied over time, but their thrust remained the same: abolish slavery; end segregation; guarantee access to the ballot; stop discrimination in jobs, housing, the military, sports, in short, in all facets of society. Only after it became clear in the mid–1960s that these measures had not been sufficient to remedy the substantial social, economic, and political differences between blacks and whites—that is, had not achieved equality of outcome—did advocates of racial equality turn to affirmative action policies designed to speed the remedial process. Today, these policies are themselves under attack both as unfair to whites and as stigmatizing to blacks. As we approach the next century, the agenda of racial equality remains unfinished.

---

3. See Angela Harris, Race and Essentialism in Feminist Legal Theory, 42 Stan.L.Rev. 581 (1990); Trina Grillo and Stephanie M. Wildman, Obscuring the Importance of Race: The Implication of Making Comparisons Between Racism and Sexism (or Other -Isms), 1991 Duke L.J. 397.

The early advocates of equality between women and men, many of whom were abolitionists, initially claimed the same high ground: witness Sarah Grimké's bold assertion of formal equality in the face of male domination:[4]

> I ask no favors for my sex. I surrender not our claim to equality. All I ask of our brethren is that they will take their feet from off our necks, and permit us to stand upright on the ground which God has designed us to occupy.

Similarly, the suffragists' quest for votes for women[5] and the later demand for Equal Pay for Equal Work were claims for formal equality. But the Equal Rights Amendment, first introduced into Congress in 1923 and finally approved by that body and sent to the states for adoption in 1972, was never ratified.[6] And despite the 1855 "Protest" signed by Henry Blackwell and Lucy Stone upon their marriage,[7] there was no general feminist demand that marriage be abolished.[8] Instead, women began to reform marriage, successfully claiming their property,[9] their earnings,[10] and their legal identity as independent of their husbands.[11]

Having accomplished that much, however, once women began to reassess the meaning of the biological differences that defined them as women, together with the social conditioning built on the foundation of those differences, they discovered a formidable barrier to the theory of formal equality.[12] The fierce political struggle that continues to rage in the wake of the Supreme Court's 1973 decision legalizing abortion[13] is ample proof that women have not yet been able to claim full control over their bodies.[14] The most divisive recent confrontation between the legal advocates of women's equality occurred over the treatment of pregnancy in the workforce,[15] followed closely in intensity by the treatment of pornography.[16] These confrontations reflect a

4. Sarah Grimké, The Equality of the Sexes and the Condition of Women 9–10 (1838).

5. See Eleanor Flexner, Century of Struggle (1959).

6. See Deborah L. Rhode, Equal Rights in Retrospect, 1 J.L. & Inequality 1 (1983).

7. See p. 246, infra.

8. The Redstockings put forth such a demand in 1971. See Sheila Cronan, Marriage, in Notes from the Third Year: Women's Liberation 62 (1971), reprinted at p. 248, infra.

9. Richard H. Chused, Married Women's Property Law: 1800–1850, 71 Geo.L.J. 1359 (1983).

10. Reva B. Siegel, Home As Work: The First Woman's Rights Claims Concerning Wives' Household Labor, 1850–1880, 103 Yale L.J. 1073 (1994).

11. See Text Note: The Married Woman's Loss of Identity, Chapter II, infra.

12. Richard Epstein, Two Challenges for Feminist Thought, 18 Harv.J.L. & Pub.Pol. 331 (1995); compare Herma Hill Kay, Perspectives on Sociobiology, Feminism, and the Law, in Theoretical Perspectives on Sexual Difference 74 (Deborah L. Rhode ed., 1990).

13. Roe v. Wade, 410 U.S. 113, 93 S.Ct. 705, 35 L.Ed.2d 147 (1973).

14. See Reva B. Siegel, Reasoning from the Body: A Historical Perspective on Abortion Regulation and Questions of Equal Protection, 44 Stan.L.Rev. 261 (1992).

15. California Federal Savings & Loan Ass'n v. Guerra, 479 U.S. 272, 107 S.Ct. 683, 93 L.Ed.2d 613 (1987). Compare Herma Hill Kay, Equality and Difference: The Case of Pregnancy, 1 Berkeley Wom.L.J. 1 (1985) with Wendy Webster Williams, Equality's Riddle: Pregnancy and the Equal Treatment/Special Treatment Debate, 13 N.Y.U.Rev.L. & Soc. Change 325 (1984–85).

16. American Booksellers Ass'n, Inc. v. Hudnut, 771 F.2d 323 (7th Cir.1985), aff'd mem. 475 U.S. 1001, 106 S.Ct. 1172, 89 L.Ed.2d 291, rehearing den. 475 U.S. 1132, 106 S.Ct. 1664, 90 L.Ed.2d 206 (1986). Compare Catharine A. MacKinnon, Pornography, Civil Rights, and Speech, 20 Harv.Civ.Rts.Civ.Lib. L.Rev. 1 (1985), id., Pornography Left and Right, 30 Harv.Civ.Rts.–Civ.Lib.L.Rev. 143 (1995), with Nadine Strossen, A Feminist Critique of "The" Feminist Critique of Pornography, 79 Va.L.Rev. 1099 (1993). See also Kathryn Abrams, Sex Wars Redux: Agency and Coercion in Feminist Legal Theory, 95 Colum.L.Rev. 304 (1995) (critiqueing the "dominance feminism" of MacKinnon and others and

lack of clarity in the philosophical foundations of women's equality, and until they are resolved, the legal strategy available to women's rights advocates is in danger of becoming blurred. A brief overview of the conceptual basis for equality between women and men is therefore in order.

Philosophers have disagreed over how the differences between women and men should be viewed in the good, or just, society. If the proposition offered is that women and men should be viewed as equals in such a society, what does that proposition entail, given the different reproductive capacities of women and men? Several models have been offered. Thus, Richard Wasserstrom [17] explains that the assimilationist ideal posits that a nonsexist society would be like a nonracist society: sex, like race, would be a "wholly unimportant characteristic of individuals," having no greater significance than the color of one's eyes has in our own society. According to Alison Jaggar,[18] this has been the traditional feminist position:

> * * * [A] sexually egalitarian society is one in which virtually no public recognition is given to the fact that there is a physiological sex difference between persons. This is not to say that the different reproductive function of each sex should be unacknowledged in such a society nor that there should be no physicians specializing in female and male complaints, etc. But it is to say that, except in this sort of context, the question whether someone is female or male should have no significance.

But as Wasserstrom notes,[19] "the assimilationist ideal in respect to sex does not seem to be as readily plausible and obviously attractive * * * as it is in the case of race." George Rutherglen agrees with this observation: [20]

> * * * any prohibition against sexual classifications must be flexible enough to accommodate two legitimate sources of distinctions on the basis of sex: biological differences between the sexes and the prevailing heterosexual ethic of American society.

While today many would challenge Rutherglen's assumption that the "prevailing heterosexual ethic" is legitimate insofar as it is directed against gays and lesbians,[21] he notes that the heterosexual ethic is reflected in laws regulating the family as a legal and social unit, sexual practices both inside and outside marriage, and sex-specific dress codes imposed by employers as part of general grooming standards.[22] Rutherglen further contends that the reason why governmental regulation is so easily accepted in the context of sex differences but is typically rejected in the context of racial differences [23]

offering a vision of woman's "agency"—the capacity to develop and act on unforced conceptions of the self).

17. Richard Wasserstrom, Racism and Sexism, in Philosophy and Social Issues 11, 24 (1980).

18. Alison M. Jaggar, On Sexual Equality, 84 Ethics 275, 276 (1974).

19. Wasserstrom, supra note 17, at 25.

20. George Rutherglen, Sexual Equality in Fringe–Benefit Plans, 65 Va.L.Rev. 199, 206–09 (1979).

21. See Patricia A. Cain, Litigating for Lesbian and Gay Rights: A Legal History, 79 Va.L.Rev. 1551 (1993); Mary Eaton, At the Intersection of Gender and Sexual Orientation: Toward Lesbian Jurisprudence, 3 So.Cal.Rev.L. & Wom.St. 183 (1994); Francisco Valdes, Queers, Sissies, Dykes, and Tomboys: Deconstructing the Conflation of "Sex," "Gender," and "Sexual Orientation" in Euro–American Law and Society, 83 Calif.L.Rev. 1 (1995).

22. Rutherglen, supra note 20, at 206–09.

23. Id., at 209–10 (footnote omitted).

* * * draws support from contemporary morality, both in the descriptive sense of the moral consensus prevalent today and in the normative sense of the justifiability of that consensus. At the descriptive level, sexual classifications are valued for their own sake within an important area of human life, namely sexual conduct, whereas racial classifications are neither so widely nor so openly valued in everyday life. * * *

At the normative level, however, it might be argued that contemporary morality is wrong and that distinctions on the basis of sex should be condemned as forcefully as distinctions on the basis of race. For instance, it has been argued that oppression of women is inseparably tied to the existence of sexual roles and that the value of individual self-realization must take precedence over the limitations of choice entailed by such roles. These arguments, however, fail as moral arguments because they do not explain how abolition of sexual roles can be accomplished and why abolition is superior to reform of sexual roles to eliminate sexist practices.

Accordingly, other models have emerged. Wasserstrom identifies for discussion another ideal, drawn from our present treatment of religious differences: [24]

There is, for instance, another one that is closely related to, but distinguishable from that of the assimilationist ideal. It can be understood by considering how religion rather than eye color tends to be thought about in our culture today and incorporated within social life today. If the good society were to match the present state of affairs in respect to one's religious identity, rather than the present state of affairs in respect to one's eye color, the two societies would be different, but not very greatly so. In neither would we find that the allocation of basic political rights and duties ever took an individual's religion into account. And there would be a comparable indifference to religion even in respect to most important institutional benefits and burdens—for example, access to employment in the desirable vocations, the opportunity to live where one wished to live, and the like. Nonetheless, in the good society in which religious differences were to some degree socially relevant, it would be deemed appropriate to have some institutions (typically those which are connected in an intimate way with these religions) which did in a variety of ways properly take the religion of members of the society into account. For example, it would be thought both permissible and appropriate for members of a religious group to join together in collective associations which have religious, educational, and social dimensions, and when it came to the employment of persons who were to be centrally engaged in the operation of those religious institutions (priests, rabbis and ministers, for example), it would be unobjectionable and appropriate explicitly to take the religion of job applicants into account. On the individual, interpersonal level, it might also be thought natural and possibly even admirable, were persons to some significant degree to select their associates, friends, and mates on the basis of their religious orientation. So there is another possible and plausible ideal of what the good society would look like in respect to a particular characteristic in which

24. Wasserstrom, supra note 17, at 26–27.

differences based upon that characteristic would be to some degree maintained in some aspects of institutional and interpersonal life. The diversity of the religious beliefs of individuals would be reflected in the society's institutional and ideological fabric in a way in which the diversity of eye color would not be in the assimilationist society. The picture is a more complex, somewhat less easily describable one than that of the assimilationist ideal.

Elizabeth Wolgast defends yet another model, the anti-assimilationist ideal, which posits that sexual differences between women and men should be institutionalized and valued. She writes: [25]

What is needed is another model, more complicated but also more useful to our deliberations about justice. We need a model that acknowledges many kinds of relations among people, and many kinds of social roles, and other kinds of interest than self-interest. In that model, what is fair will not derive from a sense in which games are fair but will appear fundamental to the game conception. In that model, competition will be only one of the relations among people where determinations of justice apply.

How will women fit in this better model? They will fit in a variety of ways and roles, depending on what real roles and functions need to be represented. Many forms of life will appear there: the career woman, married and unmarried; the wife and mother who does not want a career; the woman who wants both career and family simultaneously, without wanting two full-time jobs; the woman who seeks a career after her children are grown; the divorced woman who must combine the responsibilities of both parents. * * *

The rights needed by women in different life forms will differ. The wife and homemaker will need some special provisions for her old age; the career woman will not need these, but will need equal rights with respect to work. The woman who pursues a part-time career will need both kinds of rights less urgently; the woman whose career begins late will have a special set of needs again; while the divorced mother's needs are probably the greatest of all. The difficult problem is to formulate a program that takes cognizance of all these needs within the framework of some reasonable social cost. To acknowledge only the claims of one group and to pursue only that set of rights is just another Procrustean bed.

To acknowledge the legitimacy of these different life forms requires a different vision of society. And though it is not recognized, this may be the most important mission of the movement for women's rights. For since their demands cannot fit into the framework ready at hand, it is up to them to help create a new one. Nor does it make sense for women to refuse this responsibility, since without their participation, the old problem of perspectives is introduced again. The perspectives of both sexes need representing, not just in the political arena, but in the very conception of what society is. It is an appropriate challenge for women of spirit and imagination.

I have spoken throughout as if rights can, and often do, derive from needs. But of course not just any need will justify a right. The particular needs that I mention are not trivial or negligible; the needs of the blind and the disabled may be counted a plausible basis for special rights, though costs and competing needs may restrict them. But the question may arise, why should the needs of women—who are not disabled or weak or ill—count as justifying rights for them? The answer to that does not seem to me difficult. It involves reference to a fact that individualism obscures, that one of society's chief and rudimentary concerns is that the children in it, and the families who care for the children, and the mothers who are their primary parents, have the best support it can provide.

Although Wolgast's model could be viewed as embraced within the pluralist ideal, her conception seems to put more weight on the fact that humans are a "two-sexed species" than the pluralist ideal would accommodate. She appears not merely to want sex differences recognized and valued for the variation and richness they add to human society, but also to want to use those differences as the basis for the assignment of social roles. Here lies a fundamental difference between the views of Wolgast and Rutherglen, on the one hand, and those of Wasserstrom and Jaggar on the other: the extent to which, in the good or just society, social roles ought to be assigned purely on the basis of sex. Wasserstrom defends his ideal of the assimilationist society in part because he believes that sex roles are inherently oppressive. He reasons,[26]

[O]ne thing that distinguishes sex roles from many other roles is that they are wholly involuntarily assumed. One has no choice about whether one shall be born a male or female. And if it is a consequence of one's being born a male or a female that one's subsequent emotional, intellectual, and material development will be substantially controlled by this fact, then it is necessarily the case that substantial, permanent, and involuntarily assumed restraints have been imposed on some of the most central factors concerning the way one will shape and live one's life. The point to be emphasized is that this would necessarily be the case, even in the unlikely event that substantial sexual differentiation could be maintained without one sex or the other becoming dominant and developing oppressive institutions and an ideolgy [sic] to support that dominance and oppression. Absent some far stronger showing than seems either reasonable or possible that potential talents, abilities, interests, and the like are inevitably and irretrievably distributed between the sexes in such a way that the sex roles of the society are genuinely congruent with and facilitative of the development of those talents, abilities, interests, and the like that individuals can and do possess, sex roles are to this degree incompatible with the kind of respect which the good or the just society would accord to each of the individual persons living within it. It seems to me, therefore, that there are persuasive reasons to believe that no

26. Wasserstrom, supra note 17, at 41.

society which maintained what I have been describing as *substantial* sexual differentiation could plausibly be viewed as a good or just society.

Rutherglen and Wolgast both accept the utility of social roles and reply that what is needed in the case of sex roles is not abolition but, in Rutherglen's words, "reform to eliminate the oppressive aspects of existing sexual roles." [27] Wasserstrom appears to admit that this might be possible, in the passage quoted above, but points out the "difficulty * * * of specifying what will be preserved and what will not, and * * * of preventing the reappearance of the type of systemic dominance and subservience that produces the injustice of oppression." [28]

Wolgast's fuller response to these objections appears to be: women will decide for themselves what roles will be preserved and what protections ("special" rights) will be provided for women who choose self-limiting roles. Forecasting her argument in the Introduction to her book, Wolgast writes,[29]

> [i]t is my thesis that a profound difficulty for the advance of women's rights is conceptual. We need an alternative to egalitarian reasoning. One such alternative would be a bivalent form of thinking, a form that distinguishes between the interests of men and the interests of women. Women, it could be argued, need to represent their own concerns and should not expect them to be represented by men. This is clearest in matters of family and maternity care, but a case could also be made in regard to the economic dependence of women, their opportunities for employment, and provisions for their later years. Such a bivalent view provides a justification for affirmative action policies because it rejects a neutral perspective from which the concerns of both sexes can be seen "objectively." It supports the idea that women contribute distinctively to their professions and fields of interest, to the diversity of our culture and the richness of its values. And it casts suspicion on the idea that women's qualifications for various endeavors should be judged exclusively by men.

> But I do not think this bivalent view can give the full solution to the problems raised by the atomistic-egalitarian model. For an adequate solution, it would be necessary to replace this model by one that gives emphasis to human connections, to forms of human interdependence, and to the needs that lead to them. Many important facts should be taken into account: that a baby needs someone's time-consuming love and care; that elderly persons are unable to compete for their sustenance; that childbearing and childnurturing are not primarily ways to satisfy self-oriented desires; that families are not associations of individuals who join together for their mutual benefit. A model that cannot reasonably represent these facts is just not an acceptable model of human society.

Which of these models do the legal advocates of equality between women and men have in mind? Like philosophers, their visions differ: ranging from the formal equality that Ruth Bader Ginsburg sought as an advocate before

---

27. Rutherglen, supra note 20, at 210. See Wolgast, supra note 25, at 121–25.

28. Wasserstrom, supra note 17, at 42.

29. Wolgast, supra note 25, at 16–17.

the United States Supreme Court [30] while she argued many of the cases discussed in Chapter I; through the critiques of formal equality put forward by Catherine A. MacKinnon,[31] Christine Littleton,[32] and Mary Becker;[33] to the more pragmatic approaches of Deborah L. Rhode [34] and Margaret Radin.[35] As you study the materials that follow and encounter the work of these and other feminist legal theorists, consider how they might have responded, had they been consulted, to the differential sex-based pricing at the Columbia bake sale and to the voting policy adopted by the Holy Cross BSU. Consider, as well, the challenge posed by Owen Fiss, as he exposes what he sees as a conflict within feminist legal theory: [36]

> Feminism is as varied as any body of thought. It presents a special difficulty, however, because it encompasses not one theory, but two. On one level feminism is a theory about equality. Yet on another, more abstract or general level, it is a theory about the objectivity of law. Each of these strands of feminism represents a profound challenge to established political and legal traditions. At the same time they are in conflict with each other. Feminism's egalitarianism is at war with its radical epistemology, and we should acknowledge that in the end one will have to give way to the other.

How might one approach the resolution of this conflict, if, indeed, it is a conflict? What is your vision of sexual equality? What are the methods that will accomplish its goals? [37]

30. Ruth Bader Ginsburg and Barbara Flagg, Some Reflections on the Feminist Legal Thought of the 1970s, 1989 U.Chi.L.Forum 9; see also Wendy Webster Williams, The Equality Crisis: Some Reflections on Culture, Courts, and Feminism, 7 Wom.Rts.L.Rep. 175 (1982).

31. Catharine A. MacKinnon, Sexual Harassment of Working Women (1979); id., Feminism Unmodified (1987).

32. Christine Littleton, Reconstructing Sexual Equality, 75 Calif.L.Rev. 1279 (1987).

33. Mary Becker, Prince Charming: Abstract Equality, 1987 Supreme Court Review 201 (1988).

34. Deborah L. Rhode, Justice and Gender (1990).

35. Margaret Radin, The Pragmatist and the Feminist, 63 So.Cal.L.Rev. 1699 (1990).

36. Owen Fiss, What is Feminism? 26 Ariz.L.St.L.J. 413, 415 (1994).

37. See Katharine T. Bartlett, Feminist Legal Methods, 103 Harv.L.Rev. 829 (1990).

Chapter I

CONSTITUTIONAL LIMITS ON SEX–BASED DISCRIMINATION

A. THE TRADITION

1. TEXT NOTE: LEGISLATIVE AND JUDICIAL PERSPECTIVES ON AMERICAN WOMANHOOD

The notion that men and women stand as equals before the law was not the original understanding. Thomas Jefferson put it this way:

> Were our state a pure democracy there would still be excluded from our deliberations women, who, to prevent depravation of morals and ambiguity of issues, should not mix promiscuously in gatherings of men.[1]

Alexis de Tocqueville, some years later, included this observation among his commentaries on life in the young United States:

> In no country has such constant care been taken as in America to trace two clearly distinct lines of action for the two sexes, and to make them keep pace one with the other, but in two pathways which are always different. American women never manage the outward concerns of the family, or conduct a business, or take a part in political life.[2]

During the long debate over women's suffrage the prevailing view of the natural subordination of women to men was rehearsed frequently in the press and in legislative chambers. For example, an editorial in the New York Herald in 1852 asked:

> How did woman first become subject to man as she now is all over the world? By her nature, her sex, just as the negro, is and always will be, to the end of time, inferior to the white race, and, therefore, doomed to subjection; but happier than she would be in any other condition, just because it is the law of her nature. The women themselves would not have this law reversed * * *.[3]

Mid-nineteenth century feminists, many of them diligent workers in the cause of abolition, looked to Congress after the Civil War for an express

1. Martin Gruberg, Women in American Politics 4 (1968).

2. Democracy in America, pt. 2 (Reeves tr. 1840), in World's Classics Series at 400 (Galaxy ed. 1947).

3. Aileen S. Kraditor, Up From the Pedestal: Selected Writings in the History of American Feminism 190 (1968).

guarantee of equal rights for men and women. Viewed in historical perspective, their expectations appear unrealistic. A problem of far greater immediacy faced the nation. Moreover, the common law heritage, ranking the married woman in relationship to her husband as "something better than his dog, a little dearer than his horse," [4] was just beginning to erode. Nonetheless, the text of the fourteenth amendment appalled the proponents of a sex equality guarantee. Their concern centered on the abortive second section of the amendment, which placed in the Constitution for the first time the word "male." Threefold use of the word "male," always in conjunction with the term "citizens," [5] caused concern that the grand phrases of the first section of the fourteenth amendment would have, at best, qualified application to women.[6]

For more than a century after the adoption of the fourteenth amendment, the judiciary, with rare exceptions, demonstrated utmost deference to sex lines drawn by the legislature. The pattern is most easily illustrated by a brief review of the cases decided during this period by the United States Supreme Court.[7]

The Court's initial examination of a woman's claim to full participation in society through entry into a profession traditionally reserved to men came in 1873 in Bradwell v. Illinois.[8] Myra Bradwell's application for a license to practice law had been denied by the Illinois Supreme Court solely because she was a female. The Supreme Court affirmed this judgment with only one dissent, recorded but not explained, by Chief Justice Chase. Justice Miller's opinion for the majority was placed on two grounds: (1) since petitioner was a citizen of Illinois, the privileges and immunities clause of article IV, section 2 of the Federal Constitution [9] was inapplicable to her claim; and (2) since admission to the bar of a state is not one of the privileges and immunities of United States citizenship, the fourteenth amendment did not secure the asserted right.[10] Justice Bradley, speaking for himself and Justices Swayne

---

4. Alfred Lord Tennyson, Locksley Hall (1842); see John D. Johnston, Sex and Property: The Common Law Tradition, The Law School Curriculum, and Developments Toward Equality, 47 N.Y.U.L.Rev. 1033, 1044–1070 (1972); pp. 191–207 infra.

5. Section 2 of the fourteenth amendment reads: "Representatives shall be apportioned among the several States according to their respective numbers, counting the whole number of persons in each State, excluding Indians not taxed. But when the right to vote at any election for the choice of electors for President and Vice President of the United States, Representatives in Congress, the Executive and Judicial officers of a State, or the members of the Legislature thereof, is denied to any of the male inhabitants of such State, being twenty-one years of age, and citizens of the United States, or in any way abridged, except for participation in rebellion, or other crime, the basis of representation therein shall be reduced in the proportion which the number of such male citizens shall bear to the whole number of male citizens twenty-one years of age in such State."

6. Eleanor Flexner, Century of Struggle 142–55 (1959).

7. This discussion draws heavily on Ruth Bader Ginsburg, Gender and the Constitution, 44 Cinn.L.Rev. 1, 4–8 (1975).

8. 83 U.S. (16 Wall.) 130, 21 L.Ed. 442 (1872). See Frances Olsen, From False Paternalism to False Equality: Judicial Assaults on Feminist Community, Illinois 1869–1895, 84 Mich.L.Rev. 1518, 1523–29 (1986) (characterizing Myra Bradwell's case as an example of false paternalism).

9. Article IV, section 2 reads: "The Citizens of each State shall be entitled to all Privileges and Immunities of Citizens in the several States."

10. No consideration was given to the application of the due process and equal protection clauses of the fourteenth amendment. With respect to the latter clause, the Court had said in the Slaughter–House Cases, 83 U.S. (16 Wall.) 36, 81, 21 L.Ed. 394, 410 (1872), a decision handed down just prior to Bradwell, "We doubt very much whether any action of a State not directed by way of discrimination

and Field, chose to place his concurrence in the judgment on broader grounds. He wrote: [11]

> [T]he civil law, as well as nature herself, has always recognized a wide difference in the respective spheres and destinies of man and woman. Man is, or should be, woman's protector and defender. The natural and proper timidity and delicacy which belongs to the female sex evidently unfits it for many of the occupations of civil life. The constitution of the family organization, which is founded in the divine ordinance, as well as in the nature of things, indicates the domestic sphere as that which properly belongs to the domain and functions of womanhood. The harmony, not to say identity, of interests and views which belong, or should belong, to the family institution is repugnant to the idea of a woman adopting a distinct and independent career from that of her husband. So firmly fixed was this sentiment in the founders of the common law that it became a maxim of that system of jurisprudence that a woman had no legal existence separate from her husband, who was regarded as her head and representative in the social state and, notwithstanding some recent modifications of this civil status, many of the special rules of law flowing from and dependent upon this cardinal principle still exist in full force in most States. One of these is, that a married woman is incapable, without her husband's consent, of making contracts which shall be binding on her or him. This very incapacity was one circumstance which the Supreme Court of Illinois deemed important in rendering a married woman incompetent fully to perform the duties and trusts that belong to the office of an attorney and counsellor.

> It is true that many women are unmarried and not affected by any of the duties, complications, and incapacities arising out of the married state, but these are exceptions to the general rule. The paramount destiny and mission of woman are to fulfil the noble and benign offices of wife and mother. This is the law of the Creator. And the rules of civil society must be adapted to the general constitution of things, and cannot be based upon exceptional cases.

> The humane movements of modern society, which have for their object the multiplication of avenues for woman's advancement, and of occupations adapted to her condition and sex, have my heartiest concurrence. But I am not prepared to say that it is one of her fundamental rights and privileges to be admitted into every office and position, including those which require highly special qualifications and demanding special responsibilities. In the nature of things it is not every citizen of every age, sex, and condition that is qualified for every calling and position. It is the prerogative of the legislator to prescribe regulations founded on nature, reason, and experience for the due admission of qualified persons to professions and callings demanding special skill and confidence. This fairly belongs to the police power of the State; and, in my opinion, in view of the peculiar characteristics, destiny, and mission of woman, it is within the province of the legislature to ordain what offices,

against the negroes as a class, or on account of their race, will ever be held to come within the purview of this (equal protection) provision. It is so clearly a provision for that race and that emergency, that a strong case would be necessary for its application to any other."

11.   83 U.S. (16 Wall.) at 141–42.

positions, and callings shall be filled and discharged by men, and shall receive the benefit of those energies and responsibilities, and that decision and firmness which are presumed to predominate in the sterner sex.

Although the method of communication between the Creator and the judge is never disclosed, "divine ordinance" has been a dominant theme in decisions justifying laws establishing sex-based classifications.[12] Well past the middle of the twentieth century laws delineating "a sharp line between the sexes"[13] were sanctioned by the judiciary on the basis of lofty inspiration as well as restrained constitutional interpretation.

Bradwell was followed in In re Lockwood,[14] in which the Supreme Court refused to issue a writ of mandamus ordering Virginia to admit to practice a woman who had already been admitted to the bars of the Supreme Court and the District of Columbia. Virginia's statute provided that any "person" admitted to practice in any state or in the District of Columbia could also practice in Virginia; the Supreme Court of Appeals of Virginia, construing this statute, defined "person" to mean "male."[15] Contrast the advantaged treatment sanctioned when the employment was regarded as more appropriate for women. In Quong Wing v. Kirkendall,[16] the Supreme Court upheld license fee exemption for women operators of hand laundries where no man and not more than two women were employed.

It is now established that an arbitrary denial of admission to the bar of a state violates the due process and equal protection guarantees of the fourteenth amendment.[17] Although the *Bradwell* and *Lockwood* decisions qualify as museum pieces, a century after *Bradwell,* equality of opportunity for women in the legal profession remained unfinished business.[18]

A year after *Bradwell,* in Minor v. Happersett[19] the Supreme Court ruled that the right to vote was not among the "privileges and immunities of United States citizenship," hence states were not inhibited by the Constitution from committing "that important trust to men alone."[20] But the Court

12. E.g., State v. Heitman, 105 Kan. 139, 146–47, 181 P. 630, 633–34 (1919); State v. Bearcub, 1 Or.App. 579, 580, 465 P.2d 252, 253 (1970).

13. Goesaert v. Cleary, 335 U.S. 464, 466, 69 S.Ct. 198, 199, 93 L.Ed. 163, 165 (1948). *Goesaert* was disapproved in Craig v. Boren, 429 U.S. 190, 210 n. 23, 97 S.Ct. 451, 463, 50 L.Ed.2d 397, 414 (1976).

14. 154 U.S. 116, 14 S.Ct. 1082, 38 L.Ed. 929 (1894).

15. British judges as well as their American counterparts resorted to interpretations of the statutory term "person" to exclude women from public office, male professions, and access to the ballot. See Albie Sachs & Joan Hoff Wilson, Sexism and the Law 22–35 (Free Press 1979).

16. 223 U.S. 59, 32 S.Ct. 192, 56 L.Ed. 350 (1912). The suggestion that the legislation discriminated against Chinese hand laundry operators was not pursued by the Court since plaintiff had not initially challenged the statute on that account.

17. In re Griffiths, 413 U.S. 717, 93 S.Ct. 2851, 37 L.Ed.2d 910 (1973); Konigsberg v. State Bar, 353 U.S. 252, 262, 77 S.Ct. 722, 727, 1 L.Ed.2d 810, 819 (1957); Schware v. Board of Bar Examiners, 353 U.S. 232, 238–39, 77 S.Ct. 752, 755, 1 L.Ed.2d 796, 801 (1957).

18. See Report of the New York Task Force on Women in the Courts 205–49 (Office of Court Administration, New York, March 1986) (discussing the status of women attorneys). See also Joan E. Baker, The Impact of Title VII of the 1964 Civil Rights Act on Employment of Women Lawyers, 59 A.B.A.J. 1029 (1973); Shirley Raissi Bysiewicz, 1972 Association of American Law Schools Questionnaire on Women in Legal Education, 25 J.Legal Ed. 503 (1973); Bradley Soule & Kay Standley, Lawyers' Perceptions of Sex Discrimination in Their Profession, 59 A.B.A.J. 1144 (1973).

19. 88 U.S. (21 Wall.) 162, 22 L.Ed. 627 (1874).

20. Cf. the British forerunner, Chorlton v. Lings, (1868–69) L.R. 4 C.P. 374 (Court of Common Pleas denied claim of women in Man-

emphasized that, beyond doubt, women are "persons" and may be "citizens" within the meaning of the fourteenth amendment. The Court also pointed out that children qualify under both headings.

In 1920, after a century's effort by suffragists,[21] the nineteenth amendment accorded to women citizens the right to vote:

> The right of citizens of the United States to vote shall not be denied or abridged by the United States or by any State on account of sex.

* * *

Compare the text of the fifteenth amendment:

> The right of citizens of the United States to vote shall not be denied or abridged by the United States or by any State on account of race, color, or previous condition of servitude.

* * *

Even after the suffrage amendment, male voters in a state that had not ratified required instruction. In Leser v. Garnett,[22] the Maryland Court of Appeals and, on appeal, the United States Supreme Court, rejected the complaint that the amendment denied to the state its autonomy as a political body. Compare Senator Ervin's assertion fifty years later that if the equal rights amendment is adopted, "it will come near to abolishing the States * * * as viable governmental bodies."[23]

A law review comment relating Minor v. Happersett and the amendment that overruled it to the *Dred Scott*[24] decision and the post-Civil War amendments, interprets the nineteenth amendment as a mandate of full equality for women.[25] But judicial construction focused on the very specific purpose and language of the amendment.[26] Recognizing the limitations of an amendment confined to the franchise, the National Women's Party proposed in 1923 an equal rights amendment.[27] The proponents explained:

> [A]s we were working for the national suffrage amendment * * * it was borne very emphatically in upon us that we were not thereby going to gain full equality for the women of this country, but that we were merely taking a step, but a very important step, it seemed to us, toward gaining this equality.[28]

chester to a common law right to have their names placed on the register of voters).

21. On the suffrage campaigns, see generally Eleanor Flexner, Century of Struggle (1959).

22. 139 Md. 46, 114 A. 840 (1921), aff'd sub nom. Leser v. Garnett, 258 U.S. 130, 42 S.Ct. 217, 66 L.Ed. 505 (1922).

23. 118 Cong.Rec. S4580 (daily ed. March 22, 1972).

24. Dred Scott v. Sandford, 60 U.S. (19 How.) 393, 15 L.Ed. 691 (1856).

25. William W. Hodes, Women and the Constitution: Some Legal History and a New Approach to the Nineteenth Amendment, 25 Rutgers L.Rev. 26 (1970).

26. See, e.g., State v. Mittle, 120 S.C. 526, 113 S.E. 335, writ of error dismissed for want

of jurisdiction 260 U.S. 705, 43 S.Ct. 164, 67 L.Ed. 473, cert. denied 260 U.S. 744, 43 S.Ct. 164, 67 L.Ed. 473 (1922) (right to jury service by women is not implicit in the nineteenth amendment).

27. S.J.Res. 21, 68th Cong., 1st Sess., 65 Cong.Rec. 150 (1923).

28. Statement of Mabel Vernon, Executive Secretary of the National Women's Party, Hearings on H.R.J.Res. 75 Before the House Comm. on the Judiciary, 68th Cong., 2d Sess. 2 (1925). Comprehensive statement of the view of the early proponents appears in Burnita Shelton Matthews, Women Should Have Equal Rights With Men, A Reply, 12 A.B.A.J. 117 (1926).

Differential treatment of men and women citizens was upheld in Breed-love v. Suttles,[29] where the Court rejected a constitutional challenge to a Georgia statute providing that each inhabitant of the state between the ages of 21 and 60 was subject to a poll tax of one dollar, except for blind persons and women who did not register to vote. The specific issue is now moot; in Harper v. Virginia Board of Elections,[30] the Court held that the exercise of the franchise may not be conditioned on the payment of a poll tax. Since women generally earn less than men, and have fewer income-producing opportunities, is economic legislation that benefits women more or burdens them less constitutionally tolerable? Should it be? Would it be under an equal rights amendment?

The Court's refusal to ascribe to the fourteenth amendment privileges and immunities clause the breadth urged by Myra Bradwell and Virginia Minor was predictable without regard to any sexist assumptions indulged by the justices. In the *Slaughter–House Cases* (1872),[31] the Court virtually ruled out any independent range of application for the clause. The *Slaughter–House Cases* also dimmed prospects for resort to the equal protection clause. But *faute de mieux,* that clause became the prime constitutional testing ground in twentieth century sex discrimination cases.

Three of the Supreme Court's twentieth century gender discrimination cases deserve particular comment: all were equal protection challenges decided before 1971. The first, Muller v. Oregon,[32] was once a celebrated landmark, long noted in Constitutional Law texts as the initiation of the Brandeis brief, and as the occasion for a significant step in the Court's retreat from a due process/liberty-to-contract doctrine that left scant room for state economic regulation. But from a contemporary perspective, *Muller* has been described as a "roadblock to the full equality of women." [33]

At issue in *Muller* was the constitutionality of an Oregon statute prohibiting employment of women in any mechanical establishment, or factory, or laundry more than ten hours per day. Muller, a laundry owner, had been convicted of a violation of this statute. Three years earlier, in Lochner v. New York,[34] the Court had declared inconsistent with liberty to contract a New York law setting maximum hours of work at ten per day and sixty per week for all bakery employees, men as well as women. Not yet prepared to overrule *Lochner,* the Court distinguished it in an opinion reflecting the differences in the station occupied by men and women in the society of that day (208 U.S. at 421–23, 28 S.Ct. at 326–27, 52 L.Ed.2d at 556):

> That woman's physical structure and the performance of maternal functions place her at a disadvantage in the struggle for subsistence is obvious. This is especially true when the burdens of motherhood are

29. 302 U.S. 277, 58 S.Ct. 205, 82 L.Ed. 252 (1937).

30. 383 U.S. 663, 86 S.Ct. 1079, 16 L.Ed.2d 169 (1966).

31. 83 U.S. (16 Wall.) 36, 71, 77–79, 21 L.Ed. 394, 407, 409 (1872).

32. 208 U.S. 412, 28 S.Ct. 324, 52 L.Ed. 551 (1908). Although *Muller* was argued and decided principally under the due process clause, appellant also raised an equal protec-

tion objection, asserting that the statute constituted impermissible "class legislation."

33. Pauli Murray, The Rights of Women, in The Rights of Americans 521, 525 (N.Dorsen ed. 1971). For criticism at a time when the decision was generally regarded in a favorable light, see Blanche Crozier, Regulations of Conditions of Employment of Women. A Critique of Muller v. Oregon, 13 B.U.L.Rev. 276 (1933).

34. 198 U.S. 45, 25 S.Ct. 539, 49 L.Ed. 937 (1905).

upon her. Even when they are not, by abundant testimony of the medical fraternity continuance for a long time on her feet at work, repeating this from day to day, tends to injurious effects upon the body, and as healthy mothers, are essential to vigorous offspring, the physical well-being of woman becomes an object of public interest and care in order to preserve the strength and vigor of the race.

Still again, history discloses the fact that woman has always been dependent upon man. He established his control at the outset by superior physical strength, and this control in various forms, with diminishing intensity, has continued to the present. As minors, though not to the same extent, she has been looked upon in the courts as needing especial care that her rights may be preserved. Education was long denied her, and while now the doors of the school room are opened and her opportunities for acquiring knowledge are great, yet even with that and the consequent increase of capacity for business affairs it is still true that in the struggle for subsistence she is not an equal competitor with her brother. Though limitations upon personal and contractual rights may be removed by legislation, there is that in her disposition and habits of life which will operate against a full assertion of those rights. She will still be where some legislation to protect her seems necessary to secure a real equality of right. Doubtless there are individual exceptions, and there are many respects in which she has an advantage over him; but looking at it from the viewpoint of the effort to maintain an independent position in life, she is not upon an equality. Differentiated by these matters from the other sex, she is properly placed in a class by herself, and legislation designed for her protection may be sustained, even when like legislation is not necessary for men and could not be sustained. It is impossible to close one's eyes to the fact that she still looks to her brother and depends upon him. Even though all restrictions on political, personal and contractual rights were taken away, and she stood, so far as statutes are concerned, upon an absolutely equal plane with him, it would still be true that she is so constituted that she will rest upon and look to him for protection; that her physical structure and a proper discharge of her maternal functions—having in view not merely her own health, but the well-being of the race—justify legislation to protect her from the greed as well as the passion of man. The limitations which this statute places upon her contractual powers, upon her right to agree with her employer as to the time she shall labor, are not imposed solely for her benefit, but also largely for the benefit of all. Many words cannot make this plainer. The two sexes differ in structure of body, in the functions to be performed by each, in the amount of physical strength, in the capacity for long-continued labor, particularly when done standing, the influence of vigorous health upon the future well-being of the race, the self-reliance which enables one to assert full rights, and in the capacity to maintain the struggle for subsistence. This difference justifies a difference in legislation and upholds that which is designed to compensate for some of the burdens which rest upon her.

We have not referred in this discussion to the denial of the elective franchise in the State of Oregon, for while it may disclose a lack of political equality in all things with her brother, that is not of itself decisive. The reason runs deeper, and rests in the inherent difference between the two sexes, and in the different functions in life which they perform.

The *Muller* Court, to escape from the *Lochner* holding, placed men and women in different categories. Benign preference is the main theme of its opinion. Following *Muller,* state statutes restricting the number of hours women were permitted to work in various establishments were consistently upheld. But by 1917, the Court had departed from *Lochner,* approving hours regulation for both sexes.[35] In 1941, *Lochner's* reasoning was further eroded and the constitutionality of protective laws for all workers was solidly established.[36] Nevertheless, many states retained their women-only "protective" laws. Protection was not extended to men. Why do you think these states remained content with half the loaf—protection for women only—after the whole was available? As the twelve hour day went to eight, and the sixty hour week to forty, women workers became increasingly skeptical of the "favor" thrust on them by *Muller.* Some complained that hours and other limitations applicable to "women only" operated to deny women's access to better-paying positions and promotions, thus protecting men's jobs from women's competition.[37]

Next in the pre–1971 twentieth century trilogy is the Court's 1948 opinion in Goesaert v. Cleary.[38] The Michigan statute challenged in *Goesaert* allowed women to serve as waitresses in taverns, but barred them from the more lucrative job of bartender. An exception was provided for the wives and daughters of male tavern owners. In contrast to the benign protective motive apparently present in *Muller,* suspicion lurked in *Goesaert* that "an unchivalrous desire of male bartenders to try to monopolize the calling," [39] stimulated the measure's enactment. Yet even this outright exclusion was tendered in a protective wrapping. The opinion of the court below, which had declined to enjoin the enforcement of the statute, spoke of the "grave social problems" that could be created by the presence of female bartenders, contrasting the "wholesome atmosphere" that a male owner would maintain if his wife or daughter tended bar. Hence the statute constituted a "special provision for the protection of women." [40]

Wary of challenging the gender differential head-on, appellant's counsel focused her Supreme Court argument on the exception for wives and daughters rather than the general exclusion. Justice Frankfurter's opinion for the majority, which upheld the Michigan statute, indicates that counsel understood her audience. His starting point was, "Michigan could, beyond question, forbid all women from working behind a bar." [41] His conclusion was

35. Bunting v. Oregon, 243 U.S. 426, 37 S.Ct. 435, 61 L.Ed. 830 (1917).

36. United States v. Darby, 312 U.S. 100, 61 S.Ct. 451, 85 L.Ed. 609 (1941).

37. See generally Judith A. Baer, The Chains of Protection (1978). The impact of Title VII of the Civil Rights Act of 1964 (42 U.S.C.A. § 2000e et seq.) on state protective laws will be considered in Chapter Three, infra.

38. 335 U.S. 464, 69 S.Ct. 198, 93 L.Ed. 163 (1948).

39. Id., 335 U.S. at 467, 69 S.Ct. at 200, 93 L.Ed. at 166.

40. 74 F.Supp. 735, 739 (E.D.Mich.1947) (three judge court).

41. Goesaert v. Cleary, 335 U.S. 464, 465, 69 S.Ct. 198, 199, 93 L.Ed. 163, 165 (1948).

that the exception for wives and daughters was not "without a basis in reason" [42] (335 U.S. at 466, 69 S.Ct. at 200, 93 L.Ed. at 166):

> Since bartending by women may, in the allowable legislative judgment, give rise to moral and social problems against which it may devise preventive measures, the legislature need not go to the full length of prohibition if it believes that as to a defined group of females other factors are operating which either eliminate or reduce the moral and social problems otherwise calling for prohibition. Michigan evidently believes that the oversight assured through ownership of a bar by a barmaid's husband or father minimizes hazards that may confront a barmaid without such protecting oversight. This Court is certainly not in a position to gainsay such belief by the Michigan legislature.

Three dissenters thought the relevant discrimination was not between wives and daughters of tavern owners and all other women, but rather between male and female tavern owners (335 U.S. at 468, 69 S.Ct. at 201, 93 L.Ed. at 167):

> The statute arbitrarily discriminates between male and female owners of liquor establishments. A male owner, although he himself is always absent from his bar, may employ his wife and daughter as barmaids. A female owner may neither work as a barmaid herself nor employ her daughter in that position, even if a man is always present in the establishment to keep order. This inevitable result of the classification belies the assumption that the statute was motivated by a legislative solicitude for the moral and physical well-being of women who, but for the law, would be employed as barmaids. Since there could be no other conceivable justification for such discrimination against women owners of liquor establishments, the statute should be held invalid as a denial of equal protection.

The third and last case in the trilogy is Hoyt v. Florida,[43] a prosecution for second degree murder of a woman charged with killing her husband by assaulting him with a baseball bat during an altercation in which she claimed he had insulted and humiliated her to the breaking point. In the belief that female peers might better comprehend her state of mind and her defense of temporary insanity, Hoyt claimed that her conviction by an all-male jury deprived her of her rights under the Fourteenth Amendment. The Florida statute involved required both males and females to serve on juries, but provided, as to women, that "the name of no female person shall be taken for jury service unless said person has registered with the clerk of the circuit court her desire to be placed on the jury list." [44] Observing that "woman is still the center of home and family life," [45] a unanimous Court concluded that the Florida legislature had not transgressed constitutional limitations by according her advantageous treatment. A woman had the right, but not the corresponding duty, to serve.[46] More than thirty years after *Hoyt*, the Court

---

42. Id., 335 U.S. at 466, 69 S.Ct. at 200, 93 L.Ed. at 166.

43. 368 U.S. 57, 82 S.Ct. 159, 7 L.Ed.2d 118 (1961).

44. Id., 368 U.S. at 58, 82 S.Ct. at 161, 7 L.Ed.2d at 120, quoting Fla.Stat. 1959, § 40.01(1).

45. Id., 368 U.S. at 62, 82 S.Ct. at 162, 7 L.Ed.2d at 122.

46. In Taylor v. Louisiana, 419 U.S. 522, 95 S.Ct. 692, 42 L.Ed.2d 690 (1975), the Court effectively overturned *Hoyt*. Acting at the behest of a male complainant charged with rape, the Court held Louisiana's "volunteers only"

struck down a prosecutor's use of peremptory challenges to select an all-female jury to decide a paternity case.[47] Did this holding expand or contract women's right to equal treatment as jurors?

By the middle of the twentieth century, the home-centered economic activity that occupied women in an earlier age had disappeared and, increasingly, the possibility opened to women to determine whether and when to bear children. These developments and their significance to the traditional sex-role division eventually impelled a more dynamic approach by jurists. New directions in constitutional interpretation began to appear in the late 1960s and early 1970s. But traditional attitudes die hard, as indicated in this comment by two law professors who evaluated the judicial record up to 1971: [48]

> Each of us is a middle-aged, white male—some might characterize us as fairly typical WASPs * * *. Neither of us has ever been radicalized, brutalized, politicized or otherwise leaned on by the Establishment in any of the ways that in recent years have led many to adopt heretical views of various kinds.

> Each of us, however, was led last year * * * to begin to investigate the ways in which American judges have responded to various types of

provision for female jury service a violation of defendant's Sixth Amendment right to a jury drawn from a fair cross-section of the community. *Hoyt* was formally distinguished as not resting on Sixth Amendment grounds. This distinction was carefully preserved by the majority in Duren v. Missouri, 439 U.S. 357, 99 S.Ct. 664, 58 L.Ed.2d 579 (1979), which extended *Taylor's* reasoning to invalidate a Missouri statute that permitted women to opt out of jury service and which had, in practice, produced jury venires averaging less than 15% female. Disdainfully labelling the opinion a "half-hearted effort" to maintain the fiction that *Taylor* and *Duren* involved Sixth Amendment rights and were distinguishable from *Hoyt* and other equal protection cases, Justice Rehnquist in dissent challenged the majority either to "insist that women be treated identically to men for purposes of jury selection * * * or [to] discover some peculiar magic in the number 15 that will enable it to distinguish between such a percentage and higher percentages less than 50." 439 U.S. at 374, 99 S.Ct. at 673–74, 58 L.Ed.2d at 593.

In United States v. Daly, 573 F.Supp. 788, 793–94 (N.D.Tex.1983), affirmed on other grounds 756 F.2d 1076 (5th Cir.1985), rehearing denied 763 F.2d 416 (5th Cir.1985), cert. denied 474 U.S. 1022, 106 S.Ct. 574, 88 L.Ed.2d 558 (1985), the court upheld against defendant's fair-cross-section challenge the following policy of exemption from federal jury service:

> Persons having active care and custody of a child or children under 10 years of age whose health and/or safety would be jeopardized by

their absence for jury service; or a person who is essential to the care of aged or infirm persons.

The *Duren* majority had observed that an exemption "appropriately tailored" to the state's interest in "assuring that those members of the family responsible for the care of children are available to do so" would, it thought, "survive a fair-cross-section challenge." Id., 439 U.S. at 370, 99 S.Ct. at 671, 58 L.Ed.2d at 590. The district judge thought the provision "clearly sets forth a 'reasonable exemption' under the *Duren* test." Id., at 794. Do you agree? Even if it turns out that the bulk of the prospective jurors who apply for the so-called "child care exemption" are women? Does the phrasing of the exemption suggest that children under 10 need a caretaker at home? Would the exemption excuse a paid child care worker from jury service?

Does the "fair cross-section" rationale assume that women who serve on juries participate in the deliberations to the same extent as men? Research done on mock juries challenges such an assumption and suggests that women's participation rate is lower than that of men. See Nancy S. Marder, Note, Gender Dynamics and Jury Deliberations, 96 Yale L.J. 593 (1987).

47. J.E.B. v. Alabama ex rel. T.B., 511 U.S. 127, 114 S.Ct. 1419, 128 L.Ed.2d 89 (1994), excerpted at p. 77, infra.

48. John D. Johnston & Charles L. Knapp, Sex Discrimination by Law: A Study in Judicial Perspective, 46 N.Y.U.L.Rev. 675–76 (1971).

sex discrimination. Our research has been of the most traditional kind: finding, analyzing, attacking and defending judicial opinions. * * *

Our conclusion, independently reached, but completely shared, is that by and large the performance of American judges in the area of sex discrimination can be succinctly described as ranging from poor to abominable. With some notable exceptions, they have failed to bring to sex discrimination cases those judicial virtues of detachment, reflection and critical analysis which have served them so well with respect to other sensitive social issues. * * * Judges have largely freed themselves from patterns of thought that can be stigmatized as "racist" * * *. [But] "sexism"—the making of unjustified (or at least unsupported) assumptions about individual capabilities, interests, goals and social roles solely on the basis of sex differences—is as easily discernible in contemporary judicial opinions as racism ever was.

The judges who produced the decisions that these professors analyzed were almost entirely white men.[49] Now that women are entering the judiciary in increasing numbers,[50] do you expect judicial performance to improve in sex discrimination cases? Analyzing "the uneasy case for binding judicial review" from the perspective of women, Mary Becker observes that an influx of women judges would not make the case more secure because "[e]ven were women present today in the judiciary at appropriate levels, they would be bound by precedent developed by men."[51] As a general matter, do women judges have a different perception of what constitutes sex discrimination than their male colleagues?[52]

Useful references on sex discrimination and traditional constitutional interpretation include Leo Kanowitz, Women and the Law: The Unfinished Revolution (1969); Blanche Crozier, Constitutionality of Discrimination Based on Sex, 15 B.U.L.Rev. 723 (1935); Ruth Bader Ginsburg, Gender and the Constitution, 44 Cinn.L.Rev. 1 (1975); John D. Johnston & Charles L. Knapp, Sex Discrimination by Law: A Study in Judicial Perspective, 46 N.Y.U.L.Rev. 675 (1971); Pauli Murray & Mary O. Eastwood, Jane Crow and the Law: Sex Discrimination and Title VII, 34 Geo.Wash.L.Rev. 232 (1965); Note, Sex, Discrimination, and the Constitution, 2 Stan.L.Rev. 691 (1950). Supreme Court decisions prior to 1971 are collected in Annot., 27 L.Ed.2d 935.

2. MEN AS VICTIMS?

In a statement opposing the equal rights amendment as a "potentially destructive and self-defeating blunderbuss," Senator Sam Ervin of North Carolina offered his view of the Creator's plan:

49. See Susan Maloney Smith, Comment, "Diversifying the Judiciary: The Influence of Gender and Race on Judging," 28 U.Richmond L.Rev. 179, 179–80 (1993).

50. Ruth Bader Ginsburg and Laura W. Brill, "Women in the Federal Judiciary: Three Way Pavers and the Exhilarating Change President Carter Wrought," 64 Fordham L.Rev. 281, 287–88 (1995).

51. Mary Becker, "Conservative Free Speech and the Uneasy Case for Judicial Review," 64 U.Colo.L.Rev. 975, 976 (1993).

52. See Suzanna Sherry, "Civic Virtue and the Feminine Voice in Constitutional Adjudication," 72 Va.L.Rev. 543 (1986).

When he created them, God made physiological and functional differences between men and women. These differences confer upon men a greater capacity to perform arduous and hazardous physical tasks. Some wise people even profess the belief that there may be psychological differences between men and women. To justify their belief, they assert that women possess an intuitive power to distinguish between wisdom and folly, good and evil.

* * *

The physiological and functional differences between men and women empower men to beget and women to bear children, who enter life in a state of utter helplessness and ignorance, and who must receive nurture, care, and training at the hands of adults throughout their early years if they and the race are to survive, and if they are to grow mentally and spiritually. From time whereof the memory of mankind runneth not to the contrary, custom and law have imposed upon men the primary responsibility for providing a habitation and a livelihood for their wives and children to enable their wives to make the habitations homes, and to furnish nurture, care and training to their children during their early years.

* * *

The physiological and functional differences between men and women constitute earth's important reality. Without them human life could not exist.

For this reason, any country which ignores these differences when it fashions its institutions and makes its law is woefully lacking in rationality. 116 Cong.Rec. 29670, 29672 (1970).

See also S.Rep.No. 92–689, Senate Comm. on the Judiciary, 92d Cong., 2d Sess. 48–49 (1972) and 118 Cong.Rec. S4251, S4531 (daily ed. March 20, 22, 1972).

UNITED STATES v. ST. CLAIR

United States District Court, Southern District of New York, 1968.
291 F.Supp. 122.

Bonsal, District Judge.

On March 28, 1968, defendant James St. Clair was charged in a three-count Grand Jury indictment with violating the Military Selective Service Act of 1967 (formerly the Universal Military Training and Service Act, as amended), 50 U.S.C.A.App. § 451 et seq. (the Act). The three counts of the indictment charge that defendant failed and refused (1) to submit to registration, (2) to have his Registration Certificate in his possession at all times, and (3) to complete the questionnaire which had been mailed to him by his Selective Service Local Board.

Defendant moves * * * to dismiss the indictment on the grounds that:

* * *

2) the Act is unconstitutional in that it makes an invidious discrimination on the basis of sex in violation of the defendant's right under the Fifth Amendment to due process of law; * * *

VIOLATION OF DUE PROCESS

Defendant contends that the Act makes an invidious discrimination based upon sex in violation of his right to due process of law under the Fifth Amendment. Defendant argues that men are denied equal protection of the laws in being compelled to serve in the Armed Forces when women are not so compelled. See Bolling v. Sharpe, 347 U.S. 497, 74 S.Ct. 693, 98 L.Ed. 884 (1954). Defendant points out that Congress has established women's corps in the various branches of the Armed Forces and therefore urges that Congress has treated the sexes equally with respect to their ability to serve in the Armed Forces.

In the Act and its predecessors, Congress made a legislative judgment that men should be subject to involuntary induction but that women, presumably because they are "still regarded as the center of home and family life" (Hoyt v. State of Florida, 368 U.S. 57, 62, 82 S.Ct. 159, 162, 7 L.Ed.2d 118 (1961)), should not. Women may constitutionally be afforded "special recognition" (cf. Gruenwald v. Gardner, 390 F.2d 591, 592 (2d Cir.1968)), particularly since women are not excluded from service in the Armed Forces. Compare Hoyt v. State of Florida, supra, with White v. Crook, 251 F.Supp. 401 (M.D.Ala.1966).

In providing for involuntary service for men and voluntary service for women, Congress followed the teachings of history that if a nation is to survive, men must provide the first line of defense while women keep the home fires burning. Moreover, Congress recognized that in modern times there are certain duties in the Armed Forces which may be performed by women volunteers. For these reasons, the distinction between men and women with respect to service in the Armed Forces is not arbitrary, unreasonable or capricious. See generally Goesaert v. Cleary, 335 U.S. 464, 69 S.Ct. 198, 93 L.Ed. 163 (1948); West Coast Hotel Co. v. Parrish, 300 U.S. 379, 57 S.Ct. 578, 81 L.Ed. 703 (1937).

* * *

Defendant's motion for a jury hearing and to dismiss the indictment is denied.

It is so ordered.

Notes on **St. Clair:**

1. Judge Bonsal's view that Congress might appropriately rely on the traditional division of responsibilities between women and men to sustain the Selective Service Act against constitutional attack was amply grounded in the decisions of the United States Supreme Court summarized in the Text Note on Legislative and Judicial Perspectives on American Womanhood, at pp. 10–20, supra. But this legally-sanctioned protection of women has as its other side the legally-compelled exposure of men to inconvenience, hardship, danger and death. The unfairness of this differential treatment to both sexes was pointed out by Judge Murray in the only decision prior to the termination of the draft in 1973 that held the Selective Service Act unconstitutional. Writing in U.S. v. Reiser, 394 F.Supp. 1060, 1062 (D.Mont.1975), rev'd 532 F.2d 673 (9th Cir.1976), certiorari denied 429 U.S. 838, 97 S.Ct. 108, 50 L.Ed.2d 105 (1976), he observed,

> [t]he draft, resulting in compulsory military service, is one of the most serious and onerous duties of citizenship. The Supreme Court has stated that "the

duty of citizens by force of arms to defend our government against all enemies whenever necessity arises is a fundamental principle of the Constitution." United States v. Schwimmer, 279 U.S. 644, 650, 49 S.Ct. 448, 450, 73 L.Ed. 889 (1929). Although women have made great strides in removing the vestiges of sex discrimination in many areas of the law, they will never accomplish total equality unless they are allowed to accept the concomitant obligations of citizenship. Brown, Emerson, Falk & Freedman, The Equal Rights Amendment: A Constitutional Basis for Equal Rights for Women, 80 Yale L.J. 871, 873–74 (1971). Discriminatory treatment in one area of the law is bound to be reflected in other areas. Indeed, the drafting of women into the military has been the worst of the "parade of horribles" utilized as grounds for denial of sexual equality in considering the proposed Equal Rights Amendment. Although military service can provide a number of benefits, the requirements of serving in the armed forces will undoubtedly be an unpleasant experience for many women; but it is an equally unattractive experience for many men. Such men have a vital interest in sexual equality, as the addition of women to the draft pool substantially decreases the statistical likelihood of individual men being subject to the draft.

2. The constitutional validity of the male-only draft became moot after President Ford terminated registration for the draft in 1975, see Proclamation No. 4360, 3 C.F.R. 460 (1975), and chose to rely on volunteers to staff America's peacetime military forces. The issue was revived in 1980 by President Carter's recommendation that the Selective Service Act be amended to confer authority upon the President to order both sexes to register for military service. His initiative, and its fate at the hands of Congress and the Supreme Court, will be considered at pp. 110–28, infra.

B. THE NEW DIRECTION

1. THE TURNING POINT

REED v. REED

Supreme Court of the United States, 1971.
404 U.S. 71, 92 S.Ct. 251, 30 L.Ed.2d 225.

MR. CHIEF JUSTICE BURGER delivered the opinion of the Court.

Richard Lynn Reed, a minor, died intestate in Ada County, Idaho, on March 29, 1967. His adoptive parents, who had separated sometime prior to his death, are the parties to this appeal. Approximately seven months after Richard's death, his mother, appellant Sally Reed, filed a petition in the Probate Court of Ada County, seeking appointment as administratrix of her son's estate.[1] Prior to the date set for a hearing on the mother's petition, appellee Cecil Reed, the father of the decedent, filed a competing petition seeking to have himself appointed administrator of the son's estate. The probate court held a joint hearing on the two petitions and thereafter ordered that letters of administration be issued to appellee Cecil Reed upon his taking the oath and filing the bond required by law. The court treated §§ 15–312 and 15–314 of the Idaho Code as the controlling statutes and read those sections as compelling a preference for Cecil Reed because he was a male.

---

1. In her petition, Sally Reed alleged that her son's estate, consisting of a few items of personal property and a small savings account, had an aggregate value of less than $1,000.

Section 15–312[2] designates the persons who are entitled to administer the estate of one who dies intestate. In making these designations, that section lists 11 classes of persons who are so entitled and provides, in substance, that the order in which those classes are listed in the section shall be determinative of the relative rights of competing applicants for letters of administration. One of the 11 classes so enumerated is "[t]he father or mother" of the person dying intestate. Under this section, then, appellant and appellee, being members of the same entitlement class, would seem to have been equally entitled to administer their son's estate. Section 15–314 provides, however, that

> "[o]f several persons claiming and equally entitled [under § 15–312] to administer, males must be preferred to females, and relatives of the whole to those of the half blood."

In issuing its order, the probate court implicitly recognized the equality of entitlement of the two applicants under § 15–312 and noted that neither of the applicants was under any legal disability; the court ruled, however, that appellee, being a male, was to be preferred to the female appellant "by reason of Section 15–314 of the Idaho Code." In stating this conclusion, the probate judge gave no indication that he had attempted to determine the relative capabilities of the competing applicants to perform the functions incident to the administration of an estate. It seems clear the probate judge considered himself bound by statute to give preference to the male candidate over the female, each being otherwise "equally entitled."

Sally Reed appealed from the probate court order, and her appeal was treated by the District Court of the Fourth Judicial District of Idaho as a constitutional attack on § 15–314. In dealing with the attack, that court held that the challenged section violated the Equal Protection Clause of the Fourteenth Amendment[3] and was, therefore, void; the matter was ordered "returned to the Probate Court for its determination of which of the two parties" was better qualified to administer the estate.

This order was never carried out, however, for Cecil Reed took a further appeal to the Idaho Supreme Court, which reversed the District Court and reinstated the original order naming the father administrator of the estate. In reaching this result, the Idaho Supreme Court first dealt with the governing statutory law and held that under § 15–312 "a father and mother are 'equally entitled' to letters of administration," but the preference given to

2. Section 15–312 provides as follows:

"Administration of the estate of a person dying intestate must be granted to some one or more of the persons hereinafter mentioned, and they are respectively entitled thereto in the following order:

"1. The surviving husband or wife or some competent person whom he or she may request to have appointed.

"2. The children.

"3. The father or mother.

"4. The brothers.

"5. The sisters.

"6. The grandchildren.

"7. The next of kin entitled to share in the distribution of the estate.

"8. Any of the kindred.

"9. The public administrator.

"10. The creditors of such person at the time of death.

"11. Any person legally competent.

"If the decedent was a member of a partnership at the time of his decease, the surviving partner must in no case be appointed administrator of his estate."

3. The court also held that the statute violated Art. I, § 1 of the Idaho Constitution.

males by § 15–314 is "mandatory" and leaves no room for the exercise of a probate court's discretion in the appointment of administrators. Having thus definitively and authoritatively interpreted the statutory provisions involved, the Idaho Supreme Court then proceeded to examine, and reject, Sally Reed's contention that § 15–314 violates the Equal Protection Clause by giving a mandatory preference to males over females, without regard to their individual qualifications as potential estate administrators. 93 Idaho 511, 465 P.2d 635.

Sally Reed thereupon appealed for review by this Court pursuant to 28 U.S.C.A. § 1257(2), and we noted probable jurisdiction. 401 U.S. 934, 91 S.Ct. 917, 28 L.Ed.2d 213. Having examined the record and considered the briefs and oral arguments of the parties, we have concluded that the arbitrary preference established in favor of males by § 15–314 of the Idaho Code cannot stand in the face of the Fourteenth Amendment's command that no State deny the equal protection of the laws to any person within its jurisdiction.[4]

Idaho does not, of course, deny letters of administration to women altogether. Indeed, under § 15–312, a woman whose spouse dies intestate has a preference over a son, father, brother, or any other male relative of the decedent. Moreover, we can judicially notice that in this country, presumably due to the greater longevity of women, a large proportion of estates, both intestate and under wills of decedents, are administered by surviving widows.

Section 15–314 is restricted in its operation to those situations where competing applications for letters of administration have been filed by both male and female members of the same entitlement class established by § 15–312. In such situations, § 15–314 provides that different treatment be accorded to the applicants on the basis of their sex; it thus establishes a classification subject to scrutiny under the Equal Protection Clause.

In applying that clause, this Court has consistently recognized that the Fourteenth Amendment does not deny to States the power to treat different classes of persons in different ways. Barbier v. Connolly, 113 U.S. 27, 5 S.Ct. 357, 28 L.Ed. 923 (1885); Lindsley v. Natural Carbonic Gas Co., 220 U.S. 61, 31 S.Ct. 337, 55 L.Ed. 369 (1911); Railway Express Agency, Inc. v. New York, 336 U.S. 106, 69 S.Ct. 463, 93 L.Ed. 533 (1949); McDonald v. Board of Election Commissioners, 394 U.S. 802, 89 S.Ct. 1404, 22 L.Ed.2d 739 (1968). The Equal Protection Clause of that Amendment does, however, deny to States the power to legislate that different treatment be accorded to persons placed by a statute into different classes on the basis of criteria wholly unrelated to the objective of that statute. A classification "must be reasonable, not arbitrary, and must rest upon some ground of difference having a fair and substantial relation to the object of the legislation, so that all persons similarly circumstanced shall be treated alike." Royster Guano Co. v. Virginia, 253 U.S. 412, 415, 40 S.Ct. 560, 561, 64 L.Ed. 989 (1920). The question

---

4. We note that § 15–312, set out in n. 2, supra, appears to give a superior entitlement to brothers of an intestate (class 4) than is given to sisters (class 5). The parties now before the Court are not affected by the operation of § 15–312 in this respect, however, and appellant has made no challenge to that section.

We further note that on March 12, 1971, the Idaho Legislature adopted the Uniform Probate Code, effective July 1, 1972. Ch. 111 (1971) Idaho Session Laws 233. On that date, §§ 15–312 and 15–314 of the present code will, then, be effectively repealed, and there is in the new legislation no mandatory preference for males over females as administrators of estates.

presented by this case, then, is whether a difference in the sex of competing applicants for letters of administration bears a rational relationship to a state objective that is sought to be advanced by the operation of §§ 15–312 and 15–314.

In upholding the latter section, the Idaho Supreme Court concluded that its objective was to eliminate one area of controversy when two or more persons, equally entitled under § 15–312, seek letters of administration and thereby present the probate court "with the issue of which one should be named." The court also concluded that where such persons are not of the same sex, the elimination of females from consideration "is neither an illogical nor arbitrary method devised by the legislature to resolve an issue that would otherwise require a hearing as to the relative merits * * * of the two or more petitioning relatives. * * * " 93 Idaho, at 514, 465 P.2d, at 638.

Clearly the objective of reducing the workload on probate courts by eliminating one class of contests is not without some legitimacy. The crucial question, however, is whether § 15–314 advances that objective in a manner consistent with the command of the Equal Protection Clause. We hold that it does not. To give a mandatory preference to members of either sex over members of the other, merely to accomplish the elimination of hearings on the merits, is to make the very kind of arbitrary legislative choice forbidden by the Equal Protection Clause of the Fourteenth Amendment; and whatever may be said as to the positive values of avoiding intrafamily controversy, the choice in this context may not lawfully be mandated solely on the basis of sex.

We note finally that if § 15–314 is viewed merely as a modifying appendage to § 15–312 and as aimed at the same objective, its constitutionality is not thereby saved. The objective of § 15–312 clearly is to establish degrees of entitlement of various classes of persons in accordance with their varying degrees and kinds of relationship to the intestate. Regardless of their sex, persons within any one of the enumerated classes of that section are similarly situated with respect to that objective. By providing dissimilar treatment for men and women who are thus similarly situated, the challenged section violates the Equal Protection Clause. Royster Guano Co. v. Virginia, supra.

The judgment of the Idaho Supreme Court is reversed and the case remanded for further proceedings not inconsistent with this opinion.

Notes on Reed

1. On March 28, 1973, after an evidentiary hearing, the probate court in Boise, Idaho issued letters of administration to Sally Reed and Cecil Reed as co-administrators of the estate of Richard Lynn Reed.

2. Sally Reed's brief in the United States Supreme Court sought to establish a strict standard of review for gender discrimination cases. In her summary of argument, she said (at p. 5):

The sex line drawn by Sec. 15–314, mandating subordination of women to men without regard to individual capacity, creates a "suspect classification" requiring close judicial scrutiny. Although the legislature may distinguish between individuals on the basis of their need or ability, it is presumptively impermissible to distinguish on the basis of an unalterable identifying trait over which the individual has no control and for which he or she should not be disadvantaged by the law. Legislative discrimination grounded on sex, for purposes unrelated to any biological difference between the sexes, ranks with legislative discrimination based on race, another congenital, unalterable trait of birth, and merits no greater judicial deference.

Are you persuaded by the analogy between sex and race discrimination? Why did the *Reed* court fail to embrace its logic? Appellant's alternate position was that the line drawn by the Idaho legislature "lacks the constitutionally required fair and reasonable relation to any legitimate state interest" (Appellant's Brief at 10). Was this a sounder position?

3. The *Reed* opinion received mixed reviews from commentators. Professor Gerald Gunther suggests that the quite brief opinion, handed down just one month after argument, may not have received the fullest deliberate attention of the Court. The Supreme Court 1971 Term, Foreword: In Search of Evolving Doctrine on a Changing Court: A Model for a Newer Equal Protection, 86 Harv.L.Rev. 1, 36 (1972). However, he discerns in the decision a significant departure from the Court's traditionally deferential approach to legislative lines of the kind drawn in *Reed:*

> It is difficult to understand [the *Reed*] result without an assumption that some special sensitivity to sex as a classifying factor entered into the analysis. * * * Only by importing some special suspicion of sex-related means * * * can the result be made entirely persuasive. Id. at 34.

Contrast the view expressed in W. William Hodes, A Disgruntled Look at Reed v. Reed, 1 Women's Rights Law Reporter 9, 12 (1972):

> [T]here is a real danger that *Reed* will be used in the future to *deny* the claims of women plaintiffs. For *Reed* reaffirms the heavy burden of proof that the plaintiff must meet, and may well demonstrate that only in the most blatant cases will relief be granted. The Court specifically refused—although urged—to hold that classification by sex is inherently suspect.

4. Although judicial interpretation of *Reed* was far from uniform, a number of courts recognized that something new was in the wind. Compare Green v. Waterford Board of Education, 473 F.2d 629, 633–34 (2d Cir.1973) (*Reed* and other cases decided during the Court's 1971 term call for more rigorous rational relationship review), Eslinger v. Thomas, 476 F.2d 225, 230–31 (4th Cir.1973) ("*Reed,* in a case of invidious sex discrimination, prescribed as a test of validity the presence of a 'fair and substantial' relation between the basis of the classification and the object of the classification. A classification based upon sex is less than suspect; a validating relationship must be more than minimal. What emerges is an 'intermediate approach' between rational basis and compelling interest as a test of validity under the equal protection clause."), and Brenden v. Independent School District, 477 F.2d 1292, 1296 (8th Cir.1973) ("There is no longer any doubt that sex-based classifications are subject to scrutiny * * * and will be struck down when they provide dissimilar treatment for men and women who are similarly situated with respect to the object of the classification."), with Robinson v. Board of Regents of Eastern Kentucky University, 475 F.2d 707, 710–11 (6th Cir.1973), cert. denied 416 U.S. 982, 94 S.Ct. 2382, 40 L.Ed.2d 758 (1974) (*Reed* calls for application of the traditional standard of equal protection review under which classifications based on sex are presumptively valid).

Text Note
An Overview of Equal Protection Analysis

The guarantee of equal protection that is explicitly contained in the Fourteenth Amendment (applicable to the states) and implicitly found to exist within the due process clause of the Fifth Amendment (applicable to the federal government) is a promise that persons subject to the law will be treated equally by those who make and administer the laws. Yet as Tussman and tenBroek have noted,[1]

> [h]ere, then, is a paradox: The equal protection of the laws is a "pledge of the protection of equal laws." But laws may classify. And "the very idea of classification is that of inequality." In tackling this paradox, the Court has neither abandoned the demand for equality nor denied the legislative right to classify. It has taken a middle course. It has resolved the contradictory demands of legislative specialization and constitutional generality by a doctrine of reasonable classification.
>
> The essence of that doctrine can be stated with deceptive simplicity. The Constitution does not require that things different in fact be treated in law as though they were the same. But it does require, in its concern for equality, that those who are similarly situated be similarly treated. The measure of the reasonableness of a classification is the degree of its success in treating similarly those similarly situated.

As we have seen,[2] at one time in our history, legislators and judges thought it reasonable to classify persons according to their sex. Sex-based lines were perceived as natural; conversely, men and women were thought not to be similarly situated for purposes of admission to the legal profession, voting, holding public office, or serving on juries or even behind bars. But the fact that all women are members of a rather easily identifiable class[3] does not end the inquiry under the equal protection guarantee. In order to determine whether a classification is reasonable, the courts must examine the purpose for which it is used: "A reasonable classification is one which includes all persons who are similarly situated with respect to the purpose of the law."[4]

It is not always clear what the purpose of a given law is or was at the time of its enactment. In an effort to give the legislature the widest possible constitutional scope in enacting general economic and social legislation, the United States Supreme Court at one time was willing to accord extreme deference to legislative purpose in such cases. Thus, in his opinion for the Court holding that Maryland's "blue laws", which generally forbade commercial activities on Sunday while permitting the sale of certain items of merchandise, did not violate the equal protection clause, Chief Justice Warren said:[5]

1. Joseph Tussman & Jacobus tenBroek, The Equal Protection of the Laws, 37 Calif.L.Rev. 341, 344 (1949).

2. See Text Note: Legislative and Judicial Perspectives on American Womanhood, at pp. 1–11, supra.

3. Like all other lines, that between the sexes becomes fluid at the edges. See Lisa M. Bassis, The Psychological Test of Sex and the Transsexual: A Legal Response, 7 J.Psych. & Law 211 (1979), discussing the case of Richards v. United States Tennis Ass'n, 93 Misc.2d 713, 400 N.Y.S.2d 267 (1977). But see Regents of the University of California v. Bakke, 438 U.S. 265, 302–03, 98 S.Ct. 2733, 2755, 57 L.Ed.2d 750, 779 (1978) (opinion of Justice Powell) ("Gender-based distinctions are less likely to create the analytical and practical problems present in preferential programs premised on racial or ethnic criteria. With respect to gender there are only two possible classifications. The incidence of the burdens imposed by preferential classifications is clear. There are no rival groups who can claim that they, too, are entitled to preferential treatment. Classwide questions as to the group suffering previous injury and groups which fairly can be burdened are relatively manageable for reviewing courts.")

4. Tussman & tenBroek, supra note 1, at 346.

5. McGowan v. Maryland, 366 U.S. 420, 425–26, 81 S.Ct. 1101, 1105, 6 L.Ed.2d 393, 399 (1961). See generally, Edward L. Barrett, The Rational Basis Standard For Equal Protection Review of Ordinary Legislative Classifications, 68 Ky.L.J. 845 (1979–80).

Although no precise formula has been developed, the Court has held that the Fourteenth Amendment permits the States a wide scope of discretion in enacting laws which affect some groups of citizens differently than others. The constitutional safeguard is offended only if the classification rests on grounds wholly irrelevant to the achievement of the State's objective. State legislatures are presumed to have acted within their constitutional power despite the fact that, in practice, their laws result in some inequality. A statutory discrimination will not be set aside if any state of facts reasonably may be conceived to justify it.

This standard of review, known as the "rational relationship" test, is very lenient. In practice, it permits the use of most legislative classifications. All of the sex discrimination cases decided on equal protection grounds up to 1971 were decided under the rational relationship test. Using one of these cases to illustrate the Court's unwillingness to inquire carefully into the legislature's real purpose when following the rational relationship test, a notewriter commented: [6]

In Goesaert v. Cleary the Supreme Court was confronted with a Michigan statute which denied bartending licenses to all women except the wives or daughters of male bar owners. One might well have argued that the most probable purpose of this statute was the impermissible one of monopolizing the jobs for men. Yet, exercising considerable restraint, and according a strong presumption of constitutionality to the action of the legislature, the Court refused to inquire into discriminatory purpose. Instead, it attributed to the legislature the conceivable, though perhaps less probable, purpose of avoiding social and moral problems which might attend the employment of women in bars.

The attributed legislative purpose—maintaining decorum in bars—is thus found to be rationally related to the class of persons permitted to work as bartenders: all men, or women who are related by blood or marriage to a male bar owner. The leniency of this standard is shown by the lack of any requirement that the male bar owner actually be present to preserve order or that he have the desire or capacity to protect the female bartender in the event of trouble.

The rational relationship test for many years formed the lower level of a two-tier standard of review used by the United States Supreme Court in equal protection cases. The top level was occupied by cases accorded "strict scrutiny" of the fit between legislative purpose and classification. The highest level of review was reserved for "suspect classifications" such as race or national origin, or for cases where "fundamental rights", such as voting, were involved. If strict scrutiny was invoked, the Court would not defer to legislative judgments as it did under the rational relationship standard. Instead, the government would be required to show [7]

that it is pursuing a "compelling" or "overriding" end—one whose value is so great that it justifies the limitation of fundamental constitutional values. Even if the government can demonstrate such an end, the Court will not uphold the classification unless the justices have independently reached the conclusion that the classification is necessary to promote that compelling interest.

6. Developments in the Law—Equal Protection, 82 Harv.L.Rev. 1065, 1079 (1969).

7. John E. Nowak, Ronald D. Rotunda & J. Nelson Young, Constitutional Law 524 (West, 1978).

As Professor Gunther has noted, during the years of the Warren Court, the two-tier standard was characterized by an upper-level "scrutiny that was 'strict' in theory and fatal in fact" and a lower-level test exhibiting "minimal scrutiny in theory and virtually none in fact."[8] In trying to bring her case within the strict scrutiny standard, therefore, Sally Reed was attempting to secure for her cause and that of other women almost certain victory. Although that strategy did not succeed in *Reed,* it was considered so important that it was renewed in later cases. In the meantime, as we have seen in the Notes on *Reed,* supra at pp. 26–27, for the first time in a gender discrimination case a step was taken in *Reed* towards dismantling the two-tier equal protection standard.

More recently, the Court has strengthened its review of legislative purpose in the lowest tier of cases, requiring that, in addition to a tighter fit between ends and means, the government's ends themselves must not be impermissible. See City of Cleburne v. Cleburne Living Center, 473 U.S. 432, 105 S.Ct. 3249, 87 L.Ed.2d 313 (1985) (invalidating a zoning ordinance that, as applied, required a special use permit in residential areas for institutions housing mentally retarded persons under circumstances suggesting that their exclusion rested on an irrational prejudice against the mentally retarded). This development is discussed at pp. 55–58, infra.

In Quinn v. Millsap, 491 U.S. 95, 109 S.Ct. 2324, 105 L.Ed.2d 74 (1989), the Court invalidated a Missouri state constitutional provision authorizing a "board of freeholders" composed only of property owners to draft a governmental reorganization plan to be submitted to voters, explaining that the provision constituted invidious discrimination against non-property owners that could not survive review under the rational basis standard. The Court also rejected the Missouri Supreme Court's view that the provision was not subject to scrutiny under the Equal Protection clause because the board exercised no general governmental powers, noting that this rationale "would render the Equal Protection Clause inapplicable even to a requirement that all members of the board be white males." Id., 491 U.S. at 106, 109 S.Ct. at 2331, 105 L.Ed.2d at 88.

In Wauchope v. U.S. Department of State, 756 F.Supp. 1277 (N.D.Cal.1991), affirmed 985 F.2d 1407 (9th Cir.1993), Judge Peckham invalidated an 1894 U.S. citizenship law, repealed in 1934, that had allowed male but not female citizens married to non-citizen spouses to confer U.S. citizenship on their children born in foreign countries. Peckham tested the law, which was invoked to deny citizenship to the Canadian-born daughter of an American mother married to a Canadian man, under a rational basis standard rather than an intermediate standard because the subject matter of the case "touches on areas, like immigration and alienage, where Congress's power is at its zenith. Fiallo v. Bell, 430 U.S. 787, 792, 97 S.Ct. 1473, 1477, 52 L.Ed.2d 50 (1977)." The use of a lower standard, however, did not save the statute. Invoking a Congressional concern over dual citizenship, the government noted that distinctions between male and female citizens for this purpose were common at the time the statute was enacted. Judge Peckham was not impressed:

> That other countries had similarly discriminatory laws, though, does not justify Section 1993's own arbitrary distinctions. The mimicry of external prejudices cannot itself constitute a legitimate purpose. It matters not that congressmen bore no particular animus toward citizen-mothers in crafting the limitations of § 1993, so long as they were motivated—as the government

8. Gerald Gunther, Foreword: In Search of Evolving Doctrine on a Changing Court: A Model for a Newer Equal Protection, 86 Harv. L.Rev. 1, 8 (1972).

apparently concedes—by the prejudices and stereotypes suffered by women at that time. Put most plainly, the government may not justify a discriminatory law by relying on the prejudices of others.

Id., 756 F.Supp. at 1285. Plaintiff Valerie Wauchope must have particularly relished this passage because she was asserting the constitutional claims of her deceased mother.

2. SEX AS A "SUSPECT" CLASSIFICATION

FRONTIERO v. RICHARDSON

Supreme Court of the United States, 1973.
411 U.S. 677, 93 S.Ct. 1764, 36 L.Ed.2d 583.

MR. JUSTICE BRENNAN announced the judgment of the Court and an opinion in which MR. JUSTICE DOUGLAS, MR. JUSTICE WHITE, and MR. JUSTICE MARSHALL join.

The question before us concerns the right of a female member of the uniformed services [1] to claim her spouse as a "dependent" for the purposes of obtaining increased quarters allowances and medical and dental benefits under 37 U.S.C.A. §§ 401, 403, and 10 U.S.C.A. §§ 1072, 1076, and an equal footing with male members. Under these statutes, a serviceman may claim his wife as a "dependent" without regard to whether she is in fact dependent upon him for any part of her support. * * * A servicewoman, on the other hand, may not claim her husband as a "dependent" under these programs unless he is in fact dependent upon her for over one-half of his support. * * * [2] Thus, the question for decision is whether this difference in treatment constitutes an unconstitutional discrimination against servicewomen in violation of the Due Process Clause of the Fifth Amendment. A three-judge District Court for the Middle District of Alabama, one judge dissenting, rejected this contention and sustained the constitutionality of the provisions of the statutes making this distinction. * * * We reverse.

I

In an effort to attract career personnel through reenlistment, Congress established * * * a scheme for the provision of fringe benefits to members of the uniformed services on a competitive basis with business and industry. Thus, * * * a member of the uniformed services with dependents is entitled to an increased "basic allowance for quarters" and, * * * a member's dependents are provided comprehensive medical and dental care.

1. The "uniformed services" include the Army, Navy, Air Force, Marine Corps, Coast Guard, Environmental Science Services Administration, and Public Health Service. 37 U.S.C.A. § 101(3); 10 U.S.C.A. § 1072(1).

2. 37 U.S.C.A. § 401 provides in pertinent part:

"In this chapter, 'dependent,' with respect to a member of a uniformed service, means—

"(1) his spouse;

* * *

"However, a person is not a dependent of a female member unless he is in fact depen-

dent on her for over one-half of his support. * * * "

10 U.S.C.A. § 1072(2) provides in pertinent part:

" 'Dependent,' with respect to a member * * * of a uniformed service, means—

"(A) the wife;

* * *

"(C) the husband, if he is in fact dependent on the member * * * for over one-half of his support. * * * "

Appellant Sharron Frontiero, a lieutenant in the United States Air Force, sought increased quarters allowances, and housing and medical benefits for her husband, appellant Joseph Frontiero, on the ground that he was her "dependent." Although such benefits would automatically have been granted with respect to the wife of a male member of the uniformed services, appellant's application was denied because she failed to demonstrate that her husband was dependent on her for more than one-half of his support.[4] Appellants then commenced this suit, contending that, by making this distinction, the statutes unreasonably discriminate on the basis of sex in violation of the Due Process Clause of the Fifth Amendment.[5] In essence, appellants asserted that the discriminatory impact of the statutes is twofold: first, as a procedural matter, a female member is required to demonstrate her spouse's dependency, while no such burden is imposed upon male members; and second, as a substantive matter, a male member who does not provide more than one-half of his wife's support receives benefits, while a similarly situated female member is denied such benefits. Appellants therefore sought a permanent injunction against the continued enforcement of these statutes and an order directing the appellees to provide Lieutenant Frontiero with the same housing and medical benefits that a similarly situated male member would receive.

Although the legislative history of these statutes sheds virtually no light on the purposes underlying the differential treatment accorded male and female members,[6] a majority of the three-judge District Court surmised that Congress might reasonably have concluded that since the husband in our society is generally the "breadwinner" in the family—and the wife typically the "dependent" partner—"it would be more economical to require married female members claiming husbands to prove actual dependency than to extend the presumption of dependency to such members." * * * Indeed, given the fact that approximately 99% of all members of the uniformed services are male, the District Court speculated that such differential treat-

---

4. Appellant Joseph Frontiero is a full-time student at Huntingdon College in Montgomery, Alabama. According to the agreed stipulation of facts, his living expenses, including his share of the household expenses, total approximately $354 per month. Since he receives $205 per month in veterans' benefits it is clear that he is not dependent upon appellant Sharron Frontiero for more than one-half of his support.

5. "[W]hile the Fifth Amendment contains no equal protection clause, it does forbid discrimination that is 'so unjustifiable as to be violative of due process.'" Schneider v. Rusk, 377 U.S. 163, 168, 84 S.Ct. 1187, 1190, 12 L.Ed.2d 218 (1964); see Shapiro v. Thompson, 394 U.S. 618, 641–642, 89 S.Ct. 1322, 1335, 22 L.Ed.2d 600 (1969); Bolling v. Sharpe, 347 U.S. 497, 74 S.Ct. 693, 98 L.Ed. 884 (1954).

6. The housing provisions, set forth in 37 U.S.C.A. § 701 et seq., were enacted as part of the Career Compensation Act of 1949, which established a uniform pattern of military pay and allowances, consolidating and revising the piecemeal legislation that had been developed over the previous 40 years. See H.R.Rep. No. 779, 81st Cong., 1st Sess.; S.Rep. No. 733, 81st Cong., 1st Sess. The Act apparently retained in substance the dependency definitions of § 4 of the Pay Readjustment Act of 1942 (56 Stat. 361), as amended by § 6 of the Act of September 7, 1944 (58 Stat. 730), which required a female member of the service to demonstrate her spouse's dependency. It appears that this provision was itself derived from unspecified earlier enactments. See S.Rep. No. 917, 78th Cong., 2d Sess., 4.

The medical benefits legislation, 47 U.S.C.A. § 401 et seq., was enacted as the Dependents' Medical Care Act of 1956. As such, it was designed to revise and make uniform the existing law relating to medical services for military personnel. It, too, appears to have carried forward, without explanation, the dependency provisions found in other military pay and allowance legislation. See H.R.Rep. No. 1805, 84th Cong., 2d Sess.; S.Rep. No. 1878, 84th Cong., 2d Sess.

ment might conceivably lead to a "considerable saving of administrative expense and manpower."

II

At the outset, appellants contend that classifications based upon sex, like classifications based upon race, alienage, and national origin, are inherently suspect and must therefore be subjected to close judicial scrutiny. We agree and, indeed, find at least implicit support for such an approach in our unanimous decision only last Term in Reed v. Reed.

* * *

* * * [T]he Court held the statutory preference for male applicants unconstitutional. In reaching this result, the Court implicitly rejected appellee's apparently rational explanation of the statutory scheme, and concluded that, by ignoring the individual qualifications of particular applicants, the challenged statute provided "dissimilar treatment for men and women who are * * * similarly situated." * * * The Court therefore held that, even though the State's interest in achieving administrative efficiency "is not without some legitimacy," "[t]o give a mandatory preference to members of either sex over members of the other, merely to accomplish the elimination of hearings on the merits, is to make the very kind of arbitrary legislative choice forbidden by the [Constitution]. * * *". * * * This departure from "traditional" rational basis analysis with respect to sex-based classifications is clearly justified.

There can be no doubt that our Nation has had a long and unfortunate history of sex discrimination.[13] Traditionally, such discrimination was rationalized by an attitude of "romantic paternalism" which, in practical effect, put women not on a pedestal, but in a cage. Indeed, this paternalistic attitude became so firmly rooted in our national consciousness that, exactly 100 years ago, a distinguished member of this Court was able to proclaim:

> "Man is, or should be, woman's protector and defender. The natural and proper timidity and delicacy which belongs to the female sex evidently unfits it for many of the occupations of civil life. The constitution of the family organization, which is founded in the divine ordinance, as well as in the nature of things, indicates the domestic sphere as that which properly belongs to the domain and functions of womanhood. The harmony, not to say identity, of interests and views which belong, or should belong, to the family institution is repugnant to the ideas of a woman adopting a distinct and independent career from that of her husband. * * *

> " * * * The paramount destiny and mission of woman are to fulfil the noble and benign offices of wife and mother. This is the law of the Creator." Bradwell v. Illinois, 83 U.S. [16 Wall.] 130, 141, 21 L.Ed. 442 (1873) (Bradley, J., concurring).

---

13. Indeed, the position of women in this country at its inception is reflected in the view expressed by Thomas Jefferson that women should be neither seen nor heard in society's decisionmaking councils. See M. Gruberg, Women in American Politics 4 (1968). See also A. de Tocqueville, Democracy in America, pt. 2 (Reeves tr. 1840), in World's Classic Series 400 (Galaxy ed. 1947).

As a result of notions such as these, our statute books gradually became laden with gross, stereotypical distinctions between the sexes and, indeed, throughout much of the 19th century the position of women in our society was, in many respects, comparable to that of blacks under the pre-Civil War slave codes.   Neither slaves nor women could hold office, serve on juries, or bring suit in their own names, and married women traditionally were denied the legal capacity to hold or convey property or to serve as legal guardians of their own children.   See generally L. Kanowitz, Women and the Law: The Unfinished Revolution 5–6 (1969); G. Myrdal, An American Dilemma 1073 (2d ed. 1962).   And although blacks were guaranteed the right to vote in 1870, women were denied even that right—which is itself "preservative of other basic civil and political rights"—until adoption of the Nineteenth Amendment half a century later.

It is true, of course, that the position of women in America has improved markedly in recent decades.[15]   Nevertheless, it can hardly be doubted that, in part because of the high visibility of the sex characteristic,[16] women still face pervasive, although at times more subtle, discrimination in our educational institutions, on the job market and, perhaps most conspicuously, in the political arena.[17]   See generally K. Amundsen, The Silenced Majority: Women and American Democracy (1971); The President's Task Force on Women's Rights and Responsibilities, A Matter of Simple Justice (1970).

Moreover, since sex, like race and national origin, is an immutable characteristic determined solely by the accident of birth, the imposition of special disabilities upon the members of a particular sex because of their sex would seem to violate "the basic concept of our system that legal burdens should bear some relationship to individual responsibility.   * * *"   Weber v. Aetna Casualty & Surety Co., 406 U.S. 164, 175, 92 S.Ct. 1400, 1407, 31 L.Ed.2d 768 (1972).   And what differentiates sex from such nonsuspect statutes as intelligence or physical disability, and aligns it with the recognized suspect criteria, is that sex characteristic frequently bears no relation to ability to perform or contribute to society.[18]   As a result, statutory distinctions between the sexes often have the effect of invidiously relegating the entire class of females to inferior legal status without regard to the actual capabilities of its individual members.

We might also note that, over the past decade, Congress has itself manifested an increasing sensitivity to sex-based classifications.   In Tit. VII of the Civil Rights Act of 1964, for example, Congress expressly declared that no

15. See generally, The President's Task Force on Women's Rights and Responsibilities, A Matter of Simple Justice (1970); L. Kanowitz, Women and the Law: The Unfinished Revolution (1969); A. Montagu, Man's Most Dangerous Myth (4th ed. 1964); The President's Commission on the Status of Women, American Women (1963).

16. See, e.g., Note, Sex Discrimination and Equal Protection: Do We Need a Constitutional Amendment?, 84 Harv.L.Rev. 1499, 1507 (1971).

17. It is true, of course, that when viewed in the abstract, women do not constitute a small and powerless minority.   Nevertheless, in part because of past discrimination, women are vastly underrepresented in this Nation's decisionmaking councils.   There has never been a female President, nor a female member of this Court.   Not a single woman presently sits in the United States Senate, and only 14 women hold seats in the House of Representatives.   And, as appellants point out, this underrepresentation is present throughout all levels of our State and Federal Government.   See Joint Reply Brief of Appellants and American Civil Liberties Union (Amicus Curiae) 9.

18. See, e.g., Developments in the Law—Equal Protection, 82 Harv.L.Rev. 1065, 1173–1174 (1969).

employer, labor union, or other organization subject to the provisions of the Act shall discriminate against any individual on the basis of "race, color, religion, *sex,* or national origin." [19] Similarly, the Equal Pay Act of 1963 provides that no employer covered by the Act "shall discriminate * * * between employees on the basis of sex." [20] And § 1 of the Equal Rights Amendment, passed by Congress on March 22, 1972, and submitted to the legislatures of the States for ratification, declares that "[e]quality of rights under the law shall not be denied or abridged by the United States or by any State on account of sex." [21] Thus, Congress has itself concluded that classifications based upon sex are inherently invidious, and this conclusion of a coequal branch of Government is not without significance to the question presently under consideration. * * *

With these considerations in mind, we can only conclude that classifications based upon sex, like classifications based upon race, alienage, or national origin, are inherently suspect, and must therefore be subjected to strict judicial scrutiny. Applying the analysis mandated by that stricter standard of review, it is clear that the statutory scheme now before us is constitutionally invalid.

III

The sole basis of the classification established in the challenged statutes is the sex of the individuals involved. * * * [A] female member of the uniformed services seeking to obtain housing and medical benefits for her spouse must prove his dependency in fact, whereas no such burden is imposed upon male members. In addition, the statutes operate so as to deny benefits to a female member, such as appellant Sharron Frontiero, who provides less than one-half of her spouse's support, while at the same time granting such benefits to a male member who likewise provides less than one-half of his spouse's support. Thus, to this extent at least, it may fairly be said that these statutes command "dissimilar treatment for men and women who are * * * similarly situated." Reed v. Reed, * * *

Moreover, the Government concedes that the differential treatment accorded men and women under these statutes serves no purpose other than mere "administrative convenience." In essence, the Government maintains that, as an empirical matter, wives in our society frequently are dependent upon their husbands, while husbands rarely are dependent upon their wives. Thus, the Government argues that Congress might reasonably have concluded that it would be both cheaper and easier simply conclusively to presume that

19. 42 U.S.C.A. § 2000e–2(a), (b), (c). (Emphasis added.) See generally, Sape & Hart, Title VII Reconsidered: The Equal Employment Opportunity Act of 1972, 40 Geo. Wash.L.Rev. 824 (1972); Developments in the Law—Employment Discrimination and Title VII of the Civil Rights Act of 1964, 84 Harv. L.Rev. 1109 (1971).

20. 29 U.S.C.A. § 206(d). (Emphasis added). See generally, Murphy, Female Wage Discrimination: A Study of the Equal Pay Act 1963–1970, 39 U.Cin.L.Rev. 615 (1970).

21. H.J.Res. No. 208, 92d Cong., 2d Sess. (1972). In conformity with these principles, Congress in recent years has amended various statutory schemes similar to those presently under consideration so as to eliminate the differential treatment of men and women. See 5 U.S.C.A. § 2108, as amended, 85 Stat. 644; 5 U.S.C.A. § 7152, as amended, 85 Stat. 644; 5 U.S.C.A. § 8341, as amended, 84 Stat. 1961; 38 U.S.C.A. § 102(b), as amended, 86 Stat. 1074.

wives of male members are financially dependent upon their husbands, while burdening female members with the task of establishing dependency in fact.[22]

The Government offers no concrete evidence, however, tending to support its view that such differential treatment in fact saves the Government any money. In order to satisfy the demands of strict judicial scrutiny, the Government must demonstrate, for example, that it is actually cheaper to grant increased benefits with respect to *all* male members, than it is to determine which male members are in fact entitled to such benefits and to grant increased benefits only to those members whose wives actually meet the dependency requirement. Here, however, there is substantial evidence that, if put to the test, many of the wives of male members would fail to qualify for benefits.[23] And in light of the fact that the dependency determination with respect to the husbands of female members is presently made solely on the basis of affidavits, rather than through the more costly hearing process, the Government's explanation of the statutory scheme is, to say the least, questionable.

In any case, our prior decisions make clear that, although efficacious administration of governmental programs is not without some importance, "the Constitution recognizes higher values than speed and efficiency." Stanley v. Illinois, 405 U.S. 645, 656, 92 S.Ct. 1208, 1215, 31 L.Ed.2d 551 (1972). And when we enter the realm of "strict judicial scrutiny," there can be no doubt that "administrative convenience" is not a shibboleth, the mere recitation of which dictates constitutionality. See Shapiro v. Thompson, 394 U.S. 618, 89 S.Ct. 1322, 22 L.Ed.2d 600 (1969); Carrington v. Rash, 380 U.S. 89, 85 S.Ct. 775, 13 L.Ed.2d 675 (1965). On the contrary, any statutory scheme which draws a sharp line between the sexes, *solely* for the purpose of achieving administrative convenience, necessarily commands "dissimilar treatment for men and women who are * * * similarly situated," and therefore involves the "very kind of arbitrary legislative choice forbidden by the [Constitution]. * * *" Reed v. Reed, * * *. We therefore conclude that, by according differential treatment to male and female members of the uniformed services for the sole purpose of achieving administrative convenience,

---

22. It should be noted that these statutes are not in any sense designed to rectify the effects of past discrimination against women. See Gruenwald v. Gardner, 390 F.2d 591 (C.A.2 1968), cert. denied 393 U.S. 982, 89 S.Ct. 456, 21 L.Ed.2d 445 (1968); cf. Jones v. Alfred H. Mayer Co., 392 U.S. 409, 88 S.Ct. 2186, 20 L.Ed.2d 1189 (1968); South Carolina v. Katzenbach, 383 U.S. 301, 86 S.Ct. 803, 15 L.Ed.2d 769 (1966). On the contrary, these statutes seize upon a group—women—who have historically suffered discrimination in employment, and rely on the effects of this past discrimination as a justification for heaping on additional economic disadvantages. Cf. Gaston County v. United States, 395 U.S. 285, 296–297, 89 S.Ct. 1720, 1725–1726, 23 L.Ed.2d 309 (1969).

23. In 1971, 43% of all women over the age of 16 were in the labor force, and 18% of all women worked fulltime 12 months per year. See U.S. Women's Bureau, Dept. of Labor, Highlights of Women's Employment & Education 1 (W.B.Pub. No. 71–191, March 1972). Moreover, 41.5% of all married women are employed. See U.S. Bureau of Labor Statistics, Dept. of Labor, Work Experience of the Population in 1971 4 (Summary Special Labor Force Report, August 1972). It is also noteworthy that, while the median income of a male member of the armed forces is approximately $3,686, see The Report of the President's Commission on an All Volunteer Armed Force 51, 181 (1970), the median income for all women over the age of 14, including those who are not employed, is approximately $2,237. See U.S. Dept. of Commerce, Bureau of the Census, Statistical Abstract of the United States Table No. 535 (1972). Applying the statutory definition of "dependency" to these statistics, it appears that, in the "median" family, the wife of a male member must have personal expenses of approximately $4,474, or about 75% of the total family income, in order to qualify as a "dependent."

the challenged statutes violate the Due Process Clause of the Fifth Amendment insofar as they require a female member to prove the dependency of her husband.[25]

Reversed.

Mr. Justice Stewart concurs in the judgment, agreeing that the statutes before us work an invidious discrimination in violation of the Constitution. Reed v. Reed, * * *.

Mr. Justice Rehnquist dissents for the reasons stated by Judge Rives in his opinion for the District Court, Frontiero v. Laird, 341 F.Supp. 201 (1972).

––––––––––

Mr. Justice Powell with whom The Chief Justice and Mr. Justice Blackmun join concurring in the judgment.

I agree that the challenged statutes constitute an unconstitutional discrimination against service women in violation of the Due Process Clause of the Fifth Amendment, but I cannot join the opinion of Mr. Justice Brennan, which would hold that all classifications based upon sex, "like classifications based upon race, alienage, and national origin," are "inherently suspect and must therefore be subjected to close judicial scrutiny." Supra at 5. It is unnecessary for the Court in this case to characterize sex as a suspect classification, with all of the far-reaching implications of such a holding. Reed v. Reed, * * *, which abundantly supports our decision today, did not add sex to the narrowly limited group of classifications which are inherently suspect. In my view, we can and should decide this case on the authority of *Reed* and reserve for the future any expansion of its rationale.

There is another, and I find compelling, reason for deferring a general categorizing of sex classifications as invoking the strictest test of judicial scrutiny. The Equal Rights Amendment, which if adopted will resolve the substance of this precise question, has been approved by the Congress and submitted for ratification by the States. If this Amendment is duly adopted, it will represent the will of the people accomplished in the manner prescribed by the Constitution. By acting prematurely and unnecessarily, as I view it, the Court has assumed a decisional responsibility at the very time when state legislatures, functioning within the traditional democratic process, are debating the proposed Amendment. It seems to me that this reaching out to preempt by judicial action a major political decision which is currently in process of resolution does not reflect appropriate respect for duly prescribed legislative processes.

There are times when this Court, under our system, cannot avoid a constitutional decision on issues which normally should be resolved by the elected representatives of the people. But democratic institutions are weak-

---

25. As noted earlier, the basic purpose of these statutes was to provide fringe benefits to members of the uniformed services in order to establish a compensation pattern which would attract career personnel through reenlistment. * * * Our conclusion in no wise invalidates the statutory schemes except insofar as they require a female member to prove the dependency of her spouse. See Weber v. Aetna Casualty & Surety Co., 406 U.S. 164, 92 S.Ct. 1400, 31 L.Ed.2d 768 (1972); Levy v. Louisiana, 391 U.S. 68, 88 S.Ct. 1509, 20 L.Ed.2d 436 (1968); Moritz v. Commissioner of Internal Revenue, 469 F.2d 466 (C.A.10 1972) cert. denied, 412 U.S. 906, 93 S.Ct. 2291, 36 L.Ed.2d 971 (1973). See also 1 U.S.C.A. § 1.

ened, and confidence in the restraint of the Court is impaired, when we appear unnecessarily to decide sensitive issues of broad social and political importance at the very time they are under consideration within the prescribed constitutional processes.

Notes on Frontiero

1. After *Frontiero,* what standard of review applies to sex-based classifications? What standard did Justice Stewart apply? In Justice Brennan's view, is sex the suspect criterion or female sex? What standard would he apply to a statute "designed to rectify the effects of past discrimination against women"? (See *Frontiero* opinion n. 22.) What kind of statute does that? Suppose the legislative history of the statutes at issue in *Frontiero* indicated a congressional interest in improving the lot of service wives because they encountered sex-based discrimination when they sought employment. Could the statutes then be viewed as measures favoring women? Compare Kahn v. Shevin, 416 U.S. 351, 94 S.Ct. 1734, 40 L.Ed.2d 189 (1974) with Califano v. Webster, 430 U.S. 313, 97 S.Ct. 1192, 51 L.Ed.2d 360 (1977). See Ruth Bader Ginsburg, Some Thoughts on Benign Classification in the Context of Sex, 10 Conn.L.Rev. 813 (1978).

2. Justice Powell refers to the plurality opinion as action of "the Court." Is it? See Comment, Supreme Court No–Clear Majority Decisions: A Study in Stare Decisis, 24 U.Chi.L.Rev. 99 (1956). In Aiello v. Hansen, 359 F.Supp. 792, 796 (N.D.Cal.1973), rev'd 417 U.S. 484, 94 S.Ct. 2485, 41 L.Ed.2d 256 (1974), the court said:

> Although four members of the *Frontiero* Court were willing to hold that sex is a "suspect" classification, the majority refused to put sex in this category, at least until a case is presented that requires consideration of this extension of *Reed.* In view of the Supreme Court's intentional restraint, this court similarly does not consider whether sex discrimination is "suspect," because the challenged statute is invalid even under the *Reed* test.

3. A review of Supreme Court decisions handed down in 1972–73, appearing in 42 U.S.Law Week 3057 (July 17, 1973), comments with respect to *Frontiero:* "The Court came within a vote of rendering state ratification of the Equal Rights Amendment superfluous." Do you agree? See Leo Kanowitz, The ERA: The Task Ahead, 6 Hast.Const.L.Q. 637, 655–60 (1979), arguing that the Supreme Court's "changed jurisprudence" in gender discrimination cases was prompted in large part by the pro–ERA campaign. Has the argument that sex should be deemed a suspect classification for equal protection purposes been foreclosed by the defeat of the ERA in 1982?

Justice Ginsburg, in her first concurring opinion after her appointment as the Court's second female Justice, pointedly observed that the issue "remains an open question." Harris v. Forklift Systems, Inc., 510 U.S. 17, ___ n.*, 114 S.Ct. 367, 373 n.*, 126 L.Ed.2d 295, 304 n. 1 (1993). Her observation was accepted by the Court in J.E.B. v. Alabama ex rel. T.B., 511 U.S. 127, ___ n. 6, 114 S.Ct. 1419, 1425 n. 6, 128 L.Ed.2d 89, 102 n. 6 (1994). Whether and, if so, how, this "open question" should be resolved was argued to the Court in two amicus briefs filed by women's rights groups in the Virginia Military Institute case, United States v. Commonwealth of Virginia, cert. granted ___ U.S. ___, 116 S.Ct. 281, 133 L.Ed.2d 201 (1995). Compare the briefs of The Women's Legal Defense Fund (strict scrutiny should apply to all claims of sex discrimination) and The Employment Law Center and Equal Rights Advocates, Inc. (strict scrutiny should apply only to harmful sex-based classifications which exclude or stigmatize, not to classifications that seek to assist members of one sex who are disproportionately burdened). Which of these formulations will better advance the goal of equality between the sexes?

4. Do you agree with Justice Brennan that "throughout much of the 19th century the position of women in our society was, in many respects, comparable to that of blacks under the pre-Civil War slave codes"? Compare George Rutherglen, Sexual Equality in Fringe–Benefit Plans, 65 Va.L.Rev. 199, 205–12 (1979) (concluding that "any close analogy between the constitutional treatment of racial and sexual classifications must be abandoned") with Richard A. Wasserstrom, Racism, Sexism, and Preferential Treatment: An Approach to the Topics, 24 U.C.L.A.L.Rev. 581 (1977) (comparing the social and legal treatment of women and blacks). Is it necessary to conclude that women have been disadvantaged in the same ways and for the same reasons as blacks in order to justify placing sex in the "suspect" category? See Kenneth L. Karst, Foreword: Equal Citizenship Under the Fourteenth Amendment, 91 Harv.L.Rev. 1, 22–26 (1977).

5. Other courts, however, were not reluctant to place sex-based classifications on the same level of constitutional scrutiny as that accorded to racial ones. Six months earlier than *Reed,* and two years before *Frontiero,* the California Supreme Court had already declared sex to be a suspect classification for purposes of the equal protection clauses of both the federal and state constitutions. The statute challenged in Sail'er Inn, Inc. v. Kirby, 5 Cal.3d 1, 95 Cal.Rptr. 329, 485 P.2d 529 (1971), prohibited women from working as bartenders, except women who held on-sale liquor licenses, who were wives of licensees, or were, singly or with their husbands, sole shareholders of a liquor license. Anticipating Justice Brennan's analysis in the *Frontiero* plurality, Justice Peters fashioned the following constitutional standard that he then applied to invalidate the statute:

> Sex, like race and lineage, is an immutable trait, a status into which the class members are locked by the accident of birth. What differentiates sex from nonsuspect statuses, such as intelligence or physical disability, and aligns it with the recognized suspect classifications is that the characteristic frequently bears no relation to ability to perform or contribute to society. (See Note: Developments in the Law—Equal Protection (1969), 82 Harv. L.Rev. 1065, 1173–1174). The result is that the whole class is relegated to an inferior legal status without regard to the capabilities or characteristics of its individual members. (See Karczewski v. Baltimore and Ohio Railroad Company (D.C., 1967) 274 F.Supp. 169, 179.) Where the relation between characteristic and evil to be prevented is so tenuous, courts must look closely at classifications based on that characteristic lest outdated social stereotypes result in invidious laws or practices.
>
> Another characteristic which underlies all suspect classifications is the stigma of inferiority and second class citizenship associated with them. (See Note: Developments in the Law—Equal Protection, supra, 82 Harv.L.Rev. 1065, 1125–1127.) Women, like Negroes, aliens, and the poor have historically labored under severe legal and social disabilities. Like black citizens, they were, for many years, denied the right to vote and, until recently, the right to serve on juries in many states. They are excluded from or discriminated against in employment and educational opportunities. Married women in particular have been treated as inferior persons in numerous laws relating to property and independent business ownership and the right to make contracts.

> Laws which disable women from full participation in the political, business and economic arenas are often characterized as "protective" and beneficial. Those same laws applied to racial or ethnic minorities would readily be recognized as invidious and impermissible. The pedestal upon which women have been placed has all too often, upon closer inspection, been revealed as a cage. We conclude that the sexual classifications are properly treated as suspect, particularly when those classifications are made with respect to a fundamental interest such as employment.

Id., 5 Cal.3d at 18–20, 95 Cal.Rptr. at 340–41, 485 P.2d at 540–41 (footnotes omitted). That wasn't so hard to do, was it? Why has the United States Supreme Court failed to accept a similar analysis? Since it has not yet done so, however, is Justice Peters's holding confined to the California State Constitution? See also Matter of Compensation of Williams, 294 Or. 33, 653 P.2d 970 (1982), interpreting the privileges and immunities clause of the Oregon State Constitution to embody an inherently suspect prohibition against sex-based discrimination.

6. Did Justices Powell and Blackmun, and Chief Justice Burger follow the course of judicial restraint they espoused in *Frontiero* in the abortion cases decided some months earlier? (See pp. 477–88, infra.) Or did they on that occasion "reach out to pre-empt by judicial action a major political decision"? Compare John Hart Ely, The Wages of Crying Wolf: A Comment on Roe v. Wade, 82 Yale L.J. 920 (1973), with Laurence Tribe, Foreward: Toward a Model of Roles in the Due Process of Life and Law, 87 Harv.L.Rev. 1 (1973). Does the absence of a pending constitutional amendment that would have controlled the abortion cases distinguish the proper role of judicial restraint in the two situations? More recently, in her Madison Lecture, Justice Ginsburg contrasted the Court's general approach in the post–1970 sex discrimination cases, in which it "approved the direction of change through a temperate brand of decisionmaking, one that was not extravagant or decisive" with its decision in *Roe,* which "halted a political process that was moving in a reform direction and thereby, I believe, prolonged divisiveness and deferred stable settlement of the issue." Ruth Bader Ginsburg, Speaking in a Judicial Voice, 67 N.Y.U.L.Rev. 1185, 1208 (1992).

7. Justice Brennan pointed out in footnote 17 of his opinion in *Frontiero* that no woman had ever been appointed to the United States Supreme Court. Since that observation was written, both Justices Sandra Day O'Connor and Ruth Bader Ginsburg have joined the Court. Professor Suzanna Sherry, after reviewing Justice O'Connor's work during her first four years on the Court, concluded that her presence there has contributed a distinctive feminine perspective in that her work tends toward a classical jurisprudence that values the rights belonging to individuals as members of communities, rather than the dominant modern jurisprudence that prized individual rights, autonomy, and separation. Sherry also finds that O'Connor emphasizes contextual decisionmaking and the virtues of the decisionmaker. See Suzanna Sherry, Civic Virtue and the Feminine Voice in Constitutional Adjudication, 72 Va.L.Rev. 543 (1986). How would Sherry analyze Justice Ginsburg's work? As you read the Court's cases decided since the October 1993 Term that are included in these materials, consider how you would compare the perspectives of Justices O'Connor and Ginsburg on questions of sex-based discrimination.

3. AN INTERMEDIATE APPROACH

CRAIG v. BOREN

Supreme Court of the United States, 1976.
429 U.S. 190, 97 S.Ct. 451, 50 L.Ed.2d 397.

MR. JUSTICE BRENNAN delivered the opinion of the Court.

The interaction of two sections of an Oklahoma statute, Tit. 37 Okl.Stat. §§ 241 and 245 (1958 and Supp.1976),[1] prohibits the sale of "nonintoxicating" 3.2% beer to males under the age of 21 and to females under the age of 18. The question to be decided is whether such a gender-based differential constitutes a denial to males 18–20 years of age of the equal protection of the laws in violation of the Fourteenth Amendment.

This action was brought in the District Court for the Western District of Oklahoma on December 20, 1972, by appellant Craig, a male then between 18 and 21 years of age, and by appellant Whitener, a licensed vendor of 3.2% beer. The complaint sought declaratory and injunctive relief against enforcement of the gender-based differential on the ground that it constituted invidious discrimination against males 18–20 years of age. A three-judge court convened under 28 U.S.C. § 2281 sustained the constitutionality of the statutory differential and dismissed the action. * * * We reverse.

* * *

[The Court first determined (1) the controversy had been rendered moot as to Craig, because he had attained the age of 21, but (2) vendor Whitener had standing to raise relevant equal protection challenges.]

II

A

* * *

Analysis may appropriately begin with the reminder that *Reed* emphasized that statutory classifications that distinguish between males and females are "subject to scrutiny under the Equal Protection Clause." * * * To withstand constitutional challenge, previous cases establish that classifications by gender must serve important governmental objectives and must be substantially related to achievement of those objectives. Thus, in *Reed,* the objectives of "reducing the workload on probate courts," * * * and "avoiding intrafamily controversy," * * * were deemed of insufficient importance to sustain use of an overt gender criterion in the appointment of administrators of intestate decedents' estates. Decisions following *Reed* similarly have rejected administrative ease and convenience as sufficiently important objectives to justify gender-based classifications. * * * And only two Terms ago,

---

1. Sections 241 and 245 provide in pertinent part:

§ 241. "It shall be unlawful for any person who holds a license to sell and dispense beer * * * to sell, barter or give to any minor any beverage containing more than one-half of one per cent of alcohol measured by volume and not more than three and two-tenths (3.2) per cent alcohol measured by weight.

§ 245. "A 'minor,' for the purposes of Section * * * 241 * * * is defined as a female under the age of eighteen (18) years, and a male under the age of twenty-one (21) years."

Stanton v. Stanton, 421 U.S. 7, 95 S.Ct. 1373, 43 L.Ed.2d 688 (1975), expressly stating that Reed v. Reed was "controlling," * * * held that *Reed* required invalidation of a Utah differential age-of-majority statute, notwithstanding the statute's coincidence with and furtherance of the State's purpose of fostering "old notions" of role typing and preparing boys for their expected performance in the economic and political worlds. * * * [6]

Reed v. Reed has also provided the underpinning for decisions that have invalidated statutes employing gender as an inaccurate proxy for other, more germane bases of classification. Hence, "archaic and overbroad" generalizations, Schlesinger v. Ballard, * * * concerning the financial position of servicewomen, Frontiero v. Richardson, * * * and working women, Weinberger v. Wiesenfeld, * * * could not justify use of a gender line in determining eligibility for certain governmental entitlements. Similarly, increasingly outdated misconceptions concerning the role of females in the home rather than in the "marketplace and world of ideas" were rejected as loose-fitting characterizations incapable of supporting state statutory schemes that were premised upon their accuracy. Stanton v. Stanton, * * *; Taylor v. Louisiana, * * *. In light of the weak congruence between gender and the characteristic or trait that gender purported to represent, it was necessary that the legislatures choose either to realign their substantive laws in a gender-neutral fashion, or to adopt procedures for identifying those instances where the sex-centered generalization actually comported with fact. * * *

In this case, too, "*Reed,* we feel, is controlling * * *," We turn then to the question whether, under *Reed,* the difference between males and females with respect to the purchase of 3.2% beer warrants the differential in age drawn by the Oklahoma statute. We conclude that it does not.

B

The District Court recognized that Reed v. Reed was controlling. In applying the teachings of that case, the court found the requisite important governmental objective in the traffic-safety goal proffered by the Oklahoma Attorney General. It then concluded that the statistics introduced by the appellees established that the gender-based distinction was substantially related to achievement of that goal.

C

We accept for purposes of discussion the District Court's identification of the objective underlying §§ 241 and 245 as the enhancement of traffic safety.[7]

---

6. Kahn v. Shevin, 416 U.S. 351, 94 S.Ct. 1734, 40 L.Ed.2d 189 (1974) and Schlesinger v. Ballard, 419 U.S. 498, 95 S.Ct. 572, 42 L.Ed.2d 610 (1975), upholding the use of gender-based classifications, rested upon the Court's perception of the laudatory purposes of those laws as remedying disadvantageous conditions suffered by women in economic and military life. * * * Needless to say, in this case Oklahoma does not suggest that the age-sex differential was enacted to ensure the availability of 3.2% beer for women as compensation for previous deprivations.

7. That this was the true purpose is not at all self-evident. The purpose is not apparent from the face of the statute and the Oklahoma Legislature does not preserve statutory history materials capable of clarifying the objectives served by its legislative enactments. The District Court acknowledged the nonexistence of materials necessary "to reveal what the actual purpose of the legislature was," but concluded that "we feel it apparent that a major purpose of the legislature was to promote the safety of the young persons affected and the public generally." 399 F.Supp., at 1311 n. 6. Similarly, the attorney for Oklahoma, while proposing traffic safety as a legitimate rationale for the 3.2% beer law, candidly acknowledged at oral argument that he is unable to assert that traf-

Clearly, the protection of public health and safety represents an important function of state and local governments. However, appellees' statistics in our view cannot support the conclusion that the gender-based distinction closely serves to achieve that objective and therefore the distinction cannot under *Reed* withstand equal protection challenge.

The appellees introduced a variety of statistical surveys. First, an analysis of arrest statistics for 1973 demonstrated that 18–20–year–old male arrests for "driving under the influence" and "drunkenness" substantially exceeded female arrests for that same age period.[8] Similarly, youths aged 17–21 were found to be overrepresented among those killed or injured in traffic accidents, with males again numerically exceeding females in this regard.[9] Third, a random roadside survey in Oklahoma City revealed that young males were more inclined to drive and drink beer than were their female counterparts.[10] Fourth, Federal Bureau of Investigation nationwide statistics exhibited a notable increase in arrests for "driving under the influence."[11] Finally, statistical evidence gathered in other jurisdictions, particularly Minnesota and Michigan, was offered to corroborate Oklahoma's experience by indicating the pervasiveness of youthful participation in motor vehicle accidents following the imbibing of alcohol. Conceding that "the case is not free from doubt," 399 F.Supp., at 1314, the District Court nonetheless concluded that this statistical showing substantiated "a rational basis for the legislative judgment underlying the challenged classification." Id., at 1307.

Even were this statistical evidence accepted as accurate, it nevertheless offers only a weak answer to the equal protection question presented here. The most focused and relevant of the statistical surveys, arrests of 18–20–year–olds for alcohol-related driving offenses, exemplifies the ultimate unpersuasiveness of this evidentiary record. Viewed in terms of the correlation between sex and the actual activity that Oklahoma seeks to regulate—driving while under the influence of alcohol—the statistics broadly establish that .18% of females and 2% of males in that age group were arrested for that offense. While such a disparity is not trivial in a statistical sense, it hardly can form the basis for employment of a gender line as a classifying device. Certainly if maleness is to serve as a proxy for drinking and driving, a

fic safety is "indeed the reason" for the gender line contained in § 245. Tr. of Oral Arg. 27. For this appeal we find adequate the appellee's representation of legislative purpose, leaving for another day consideration of whether the statement of the State's Assistant Attorney General should suffice to inform this Court of the legislature's objectives, or whether the Court must determine if the litigant simply is selecting a convenient, but false *post hoc* rationalization.

8. The disparities in 18–20–year–old male-female arrests were substantial for both categories of offenses: 427 versus 24 for driving under the influence of alcohol, and 966 versus 102 for drunkenness. Even if we assume that a legislature may rely on such arrest data in some situations, these figures do not offer sup-

port for a differential age line, for the disproportionate arrests of males persisted at older ages; indeed, in the case of arrests for drunkenness, the figures for all ages indicated "even more male involvement in such arrests at later ages." 399 F.Supp., at 1309. See also n. 14, infra.

9. This survey drew no correlation between the accident figures for any age group and levels of intoxication found in those killed or injured.

10. For an analysis of the results of this exhibit, see n. 16, infra.

11. The FBI made no attempt to relate these arrest figures either to beer drinking or to an 18–21 age differential, but rather found that male arrests for all ages exceeded 90% of the total.

correlation of 2% must be considered an unduly tenuous "fit." [12]   Indeed, prior cases have consistently rejected the use of sex as a decisionmaking factor even though the statutes in question certainly rested on far more predictive empirical relationships than this.[13]

Moreover, the statistics exhibit a variety of other shortcomings that seriously impugn their value to equal protection analysis. Setting aside the obvious methodological problems,[14] the surveys do not adequately justify the salient features of Oklahoma's gender-based traffic-safety law. None purports to measure the use and dangerousness of 3.2% beer as opposed to alcohol generally, a detail that is of particular importance since, in light of its low alcohol level, Oklahoma apparently considers the 3.2% beverage to be "nonintoxicating." Tit. 37 Okl.Stat. § 163.1 (1958); see State ex rel. Springer v. Bliss, 199 Okl. 198, 185 P.2d 220 (1947). Moreover, many of the studies, while graphically documenting the unfortunate increase in driving while under the influence of alcohol, make no effort to relate their findings to age-sex differentials as involved here.[15] Indeed, the only survey that explicitly centered its attention upon young drivers and their use of beer—albeit apparently not of the diluted 3.2% variety—reached results that hardly can be viewed as impressive in justifying either a gender or age classification.[16]

---

12. Obviously, arrest statistics do not embrace all individuals who drink and drive. But for purposes of analysis, this "underinclusiveness" must be discounted somewhat by the shortcomings inherent in this statistical sample, see n. 14, infra. In any event, we decide this case in light of the evidence offered by Oklahoma and know of no way of extrapolating these arrest statistics to take into account the driving and drinking population at large, including those who avoided arrest.

13. For example, we can conjecture that in *Reed,* Idaho's apparent premise that women lacked experience in formal business matters (particularly compared to men) would have proved to be accurate in substantially more than 2% of all cases. And in both *Frontiero* and *Wiesenfeld,* we expressly found appellees' empirical defense of mandatory dependency tests for men but not women to be unsatisfactory, even though we recognized that husbands are still far less likely to be dependent on their wives than vice versa. * * *

14. The very social stereotypes that find reflection in age-differential laws, see Stanton v. Stanton, 421 U.S. 7, 14–15, 95 S.Ct. 1373, 1378 (1975), are likely substantially to distort the accuracy of these comparative statistics. Hence "reckless" young men who drink and drive are transformed into arrest statistics, whereas their female counterparts are chivalrously escorted home. See, e.g., W. Reckless & B. Kay, The Female Offender 4, 7, 13, 16–17 (Report to Presidential Commission on Law Enforcement and Administration of Justice, 1967). Moreover, the Oklahoma surveys, gathered under a regime where the age-differential law in question has been in effect, are lacking in controls necessary for appraisal of the actual effectiveness of the male 3.2% beer prohibition.

In this regard, the disproportionately high arrest statistics for young males—and, indeed, the growing alcohol-related arrest figures for all ages and sexes—simply may be taken to document the relative futility of controlling driving behavior by the 3.2% beer statute and like legislation, although we obviously have no means of estimating how many individuals, if any, actually were prevented from drinking by these laws.

15. See, e.g., nn. 9 and 11, supra. See also n. 16, infra.

16. The random roadside survey of drivers conducted in Oklahoma City during August 1972 found that 78% of drivers under 20 were male. Turning to an evaluation of their drinking habits and factoring out nondrinkers, 84% of the males versus 77% of the females expressed a preference for beer. Further 16.5% of the men and 11.4% of the women had consumed some alcoholic beverage within two hours of the interview. Finally, a blood alcohol concentration greater than .01% was discovered in 14.6% of the males compared to 11.5% of the females. "The 1973 figures, although they contain some variations, reflect essentially the same pattern." 399 F.Supp., at 1309. Plainly these statistical disparities between the sexes are not substantial. Moreover, when the 18–20 age boundaries are lifted and all drivers analyzed, the 1972 roadside survey indicates that male drinking rose slightly whereas female exposure to alcohol remained relatively constant. Again, in 1973, the survey established that "compared to all drivers interviewed, * * * the under–20 age group generally showed a lower involvement with alcohol in terms of having drunk within the past two hours or having a significant BAC

There is no reason to belabor this line of analysis. It is unrealistic to expect either members of the judiciary or state officials to be well versed in the rigors of experimental or statistical technique. But this merely illustrates that proving broad sociological propositions by statistics is a dubious business, and one that inevitably is in tension with the normative philosophy that underlies the Equal Protection Clause. Suffice to say that the showing offered by the appellees does not satisfy us that sex represents a legitimate, accurate proxy for the regulation of drinking and driving. In fact, when it is further recognized that Oklahoma's statute prohibits only the selling of 3.2% beer to young males and not their drinking the beverage once acquired (even after purchase by their 18–20–year–old female companions), the relationship between gender and traffic safety becomes far too tenuous to satisfy *Reed's* requirement that the gender-based difference be substantially related to achievement of the statutory objective.

We hold, therefore, that under *Reed,* Oklahoma's 3.2% beer statute invidiously discriminates against males 18–20 years of age.

D

[The Court next determined that the twenty-first amendment did not insulate Oklahoma's "near beer" sex/age differential from constitutional infirmity.]

We conclude that the gender-based differential contained in Tit. 37 Okl.Stat. § 245 (1976 Supp.) constitutes a denial of the equal protection of the laws to males aged 18–20 [23] and reverse the judgment of the District Court.[24]

Mr. Justice Powell, concurring.

I join the opinion of the Court as I am in general agreement with it. I do have reservations as to some of the discussion concerning the appropriate standard for equal protection analysis and the relevance of the statistical evidence. Accordingly, I add this concurring statement.

With respect to the equal protection standard, I agree that Reed v. Reed, * * * is the most relevant precedent. But I find it unnecessary, in deciding this case, to read that decision as broadly as some of the Court's language may imply. *Reed* and subsequent cases involving gender-based classifications make clear that the Court subjects such classifications to a more critical examination than is normally applied when "fundamental" constitutional rights and "suspect classes" are not present.*

(blood alcohol content)." Ibid. In sum, this survey provides little support for a gender line among teenagers and actually runs counter to the imposition of drinking restrictions based upon age.

23. Insofar as Goesaert v. Cleary, 335 U.S. 464, 69 S.Ct. 198, 93 L.Ed. 163 (1948), may be inconsistent, that decision is disapproved. Undoubtedly reflecting the view that *Goesaert's* equal protection analysis no longer obtains, the District Court made no reference to that decision in upholding Oklahoma's statute. Similarly, the opinions of the federal and state courts cited earlier in the text invalidating gender lines with respect to alcohol regulation

uniformly disparaged the contemporary vitality of *Goesaert.*

24. As noted in Stanton v. Stanton, * * * the Oklahoma Legislature is free to redefine any cutoff age for the purchase and sale of 3.2% beer that it may choose, provided that the redefinition operates in a gender-neutral fashion.

* As is evident from our opinions, the Court has had difficulty in agreeing upon a standard of equal protection analysis that can be applied consistently to the wide variety of legislative classifications. There are valid reasons for dissatisfaction with the "two-tier" approach that has been prominent in the Court's decisions in

I view this as a relatively easy case. No one questions the legitimacy or importance of the asserted governmental objective: the promotion of highway safety. The decision of the case turns on whether the state legislature, by the classification it has chosen, has adopted a means that bears a " 'fair and substantial relation' " to this objective. Id., * * * quoting Royster Guano Co. v. Virginia, 253 U.S. 412, 415, 40 S.Ct. 560, 561, 64 L.Ed. 989 (1920).

It seems to me that the statistics offered by appellees and relied upon by the District Court do tend generally to support the view that young men drive more, possibly are inclined to drink more, and—for various reasons—are involved in more accidents than young women. Even so, I am not persuaded that these facts and the inferences fairly drawn from them justify this classification based on a three-year age differential between the sexes, and especially one that is so easily circumvented as to be virtually meaningless. Putting it differently, this gender-based classification does not bear a fair and substantial relation to the object of the legislation.

MR. JUSTICE STEVENS, concurring.

There is only one Equal Protection Clause. It requires every State to govern impartially. It does not direct the courts to apply one standard of review in some cases and a different standard in other cases. Whatever criticism may be leveled at a judicial opinion implying that there are at least three such standards applies with the same force to a double standard.

I am inclined to believe that what has become known as the two-tiered analysis of equal protection claims does not describe a completely logical method of deciding cases, but rather is a method the Court has employed to explain decisions that actually apply a single standard in a reasonably consistent fashion. I also suspect that a careful explanation of the reasons motivating particular decisions may contribute more to an identification of that standard than an attempt to articulate it in all-encompassing terms. It may therefore be appropriate for me to state the principal reasons which persuaded me to join the Court's opinion.

In this case, the classification is not as obnoxious as some the Court has condemned,[1] nor as inoffensive as some the Court has accepted. It is objectionable because it is based on an accident of birth,[2] because it is a mere

---

the past decade. Although viewed by many as a result-oriented substitute for more critical analysis, that approach—with its narrowly limited "upper-tier"—now has substantial precedential support. As has been true of Reed and its progeny, our decision today will be viewed by some as a "middle-tier" approach. While I would not endorse that characterization and would not welcome a further subdividing of equal protection analysis, candor compels the recognition that the relatively deferential "rational basis" standard of review normally applied takes on a sharper focus when we address a gender-based classification. So much is clear from our recent cases. For thoughtful discussions of equal protection analysis, see, e.g., Gunther, The Supreme Court, 1971 Term—Foreword: In Search of Evolving Doctrine on a Changing Court: A Model for A Newer Equal Protection, 86 Harv.L.Rev. 1 (1972); Wilkin-

son, The Supreme Court, the Equal Protection Clause, and the Three Faces of Constitutional Equality, 61 Va.L.Rev. 945 (1975).

1. Men as a general class have not been the victims of the kind of historic, pervasive discrimination that has disadvantaged other groups.

2. "[S]ince sex, like race and national origin, is an immutable characteristic determined solely by the accident of birth, the imposition of special disabilities upon the members of a particular sex because of their sex would seem to violate 'the basic concept of our system that legal burdens should bear some relationship to individual responsibility * * *,' Weber v. Aetna Casualty & Surety Co., 406 U.S. 164, 175, 92 S.Ct. 1400, 1407, 31 L.Ed.2d 768." Frontiero v. Richardson, 411 U.S. 677, 686, 93 S.Ct. 1764, 1770, 36 L.Ed.2d 583.

remnant of the now almost universally rejected tradition of discriminating against males in this age bracket,[3] and because, to the extent it reflects any physical difference between males and females, it is actually perverse.[4] The question then is whether the traffic safety justification put forward by the State is sufficient to make an otherwise offensive classification acceptable.

The classification is not totally irrational. For the evidence does indicate that there are more males than females in this age bracket who drive and also more who drink. Nevertheless, there are several reasons why I regard the justification as unacceptable. It is difficult to believe that the statute was actually intended to cope with the problem of traffic safety,[5] since it has only a minimal effect on access to a not very intoxicating beverage and does not prohibit its consumption.[6] Moreover, the empirical data, submitted by the State accentuate the unfairness of treating all 18–20-year-old males as inferior to their female counterparts. The legislation imposes a restraint on 100% of the males in the class allegedly because about 2% of them have probably violated one or more laws relating to the consumption of alcoholic beverages.[7] It is unlikely that this law will have a significant deterrent effect either on that 2% or on the law-abiding 98%. But even assuming some such slight benefit, it does not seem to me that an insult to all of the young men of the State can be justified by visiting the sins of the 2% on the 98%.

Mr. Justice Blackmun, concurring in part.

I join the Court's opinion except Part II–D thereof. I agree, however, that the Twenty-first Amendment does not save the challenged Oklahoma statute.

3. Apparently Oklahoma is the only State to permit this narrow discrimination to survive the elimination of the disparity between the age of majority for males and females.

4. Because males are generally heavier than females, they have a greater capacity to consume alcohol without impairing their driving ability than do females.

5. There is no legislative history to indicate that this was the purpose, and several features of the statutory scheme indicate the contrary. The statute exempts license holders who dispense 3.2% beer to their own children, and a related statute makes it unlawful for 18-year-old men (but not women), to work in establishments in which 3.2% beer accounts for over 25% of gross sales. Okla.Stat., Tit. 37, §§ 241, 243, 245 (1953 and Supp.1976). There is, of course, no way of knowing what actually motivated this discrimination, but I would not be surprised if it represented nothing more than the perpetuation of a stereotyped attitude about the relative maturity of the members of the two sexes in this age bracket. If so, the following comment is relevant:

"[A] traditional classification is more likely to be used without pausing to consider its justification than is a newly created classification. Habit, rather than analysis, makes it seem acceptable and natural to distinguish between male and female, alien and citizen, legitimate and illegitimate; for too much of our history there was the same inertia in distinguishing between black and white. But that sort of stereotyped reaction may have no rational relationship—other than pure prejudicial discrimination—to the stated purpose for which the classification is being made." Mathews v. Lucas, 427 U.S. 495, 520–521, 96 S.Ct. 2755, 2769, 49 L.Ed.2d 651 (Stevens, J., dissenting).

6. It forbids the sale of 3.2% beer to 18–20-year–old men without forbidding possession, or preventing them from obtaining it from other sources, such as friends who are either older or female. Thus, the statute only slightly impedes access to 3.2% beer.

7. The only direct evidence submitted by the State concerning use of beer by young drivers indicates that there is no substantial difference between the sexes. In a random roadside survey of drivers, 16.5% of the male drivers under 20 had consumed alcohol within two hours of the interview as opposed to 11.4% of the women. Over three-fourths of the non-abstainers in both groups expressed a preference for beer. And 14.6% of the men, as opposed to 11.5% of the women, had blood alcohol concentrations over .01%. See [Court's Opinion] n. 16.

Mr. Justice Stewart, concurring in the judgment.

* * *

The disparity created by these Oklahoma statutes amounts to total irrationality. For the statistics upon which the State now relies, whatever their other shortcomings, wholly fail to prove or even suggest that 3.2% beer is somehow more deleterious when it comes into the hands of a male aged 18–20 than of a female of like age. The disparate statutory treatment of the sexes here, without even a colorably valid justification or explanation, thus amounts to invidious discrimination. See Reed v. Reed, * * *

Mr. Chief Justice Burger, dissenting.

[The Chief Justice first explained his disagreement with the Court's holding "that appellant Whitener has standing arising from her status as a saloonkeeper to assert the constitutional rights of her customers."]

On the merits, we have only recently recognized that our duty is not "to create substantive constitutional rights in the name of guaranteeing equal protection of the laws." San Antonio School Dist. v. Rodriguez, 411 U.S. 1, 33, 93 S.Ct. 1278, 1297, 36 L.Ed.2d 16 (1973). Thus, even interests of such importance in our society as public education and housing do not qualify as "fundamental rights" for equal protection purposes because they have no textually independent constitutional status. * * * Though today's decision does not go so far as to make gender-based classifications "suspect," it makes gender a disfavored classification. Without an independent constitutional basis supporting the right asserted or disfavoring the classification adopted, I can justify no substantive constitutional protection other than the normal McGowan v. Maryland, * * * protection afforded by the Equal Protection Clause.

The means employed by the Oklahoma Legislature to achieve the objectives sought may not be agreeable to some judges, but since eight Members of the Court think the means not irrational, I see no basis for striking down the statute as violative of the Constitution simply because we find it unwise, unneeded, or possibly even a bit foolish.

With Mr. Justice Rehnquist, I would affirm the judgment of the District Court.

Mr. Justice Rehnquist, dissenting.

The Court's disposition of this case is objectionable on two grounds. First is its conclusion that *men* challenging a gender-based statute which treats them less favorably than women may invoke a more stringent standard of judicial review than pertains to most other types of classifications. Second is the Court's enunciation of this standard, without citation to any source, as being that "classifications by gender must serve *important* government objectives and must be *substantially* related to achievement of those objectives" (emphasis added). The only redeeming feature of the Court's opinion, to my mind, is that it apparently signals a retreat by those who joined the plurality opinion in Frontiero v. Richardson, * * * from their view that sex is a "suspect" classification for purposes of equal protection analysis. I think the Oklahoma statute challenged here need pass only the "rational basis" equal protection analysis expounded in cases such as McGowan v. Maryland, * * *

and Williamson v. Lee Optical Co., * * * and I believe that it is constitutional under that analysis.

I

In Frontiero v. Richardson, supra, the opinion for the plurality sets forth the reasons of four Justices for concluding that sex should be regarded as a suspect classification for purposes of equal protection analysis. These reasons center on our Nation's "long and unfortunate history of sex discrimination," * * * which has been reflected in a whole range of restrictions on the legal rights of women, not the least of which have concerned the ownership of property and participation in the electoral process. Noting that the pervasive and persistent nature of the discrimination experienced by women is in part the result of their ready identifiability, the plurality rested its invocation of strict scrutiny largely upon the fact that "statutory distinctions between the sexes often have the effect of invidiously relegating the entire class of females to inferior legal status without regard to the actual capabilities of its individual members." * * * See Stanton v. Stanton, * * *.

Subsequent to *Frontiero,* the Court has declined to hold that sex is a suspect class, Stanton v. Stanton, * * * and no such holding is imported by the Court's resolution of this case. However, the Court's application here of an elevated or "intermediate" level scrutiny, like that invoked in cases dealing with discrimination against females, raises the question of why the statute here should be treated any differently from countless legislative classifications unrelated to sex which have been upheld under a minimum rationality standard. * * *

Most obviously unavailable to support any kind of special scrutiny in this case, is a history or pattern of past discrimination, such as was relied on by the plurality in *Frontiero* to support its invocation of strict scrutiny. There is no suggestion in the Court's opinion that males in this age group are in any way peculiarly disadvantaged, subject to systematic discriminatory treatment, or otherwise in need of special solicitude from the courts.

The Court does not discuss the nature of the right involved, and there is no reason to believe that it sees the purchase of 3.2% beer as implicating any important interest, let alone one that is "fundamental" in the constitutional sense of invoking strict scrutiny. Indeed, the Court's accurate observation that the statute affects the selling but not the drinking of 3.2% beer further emphasizes the limited effect that it has on even those persons in the age group involved. There is, in sum, nothing about the statutory classification involved here to suggest that it affects an interest, or works against a group, which can claim under the Equal Protection Clause that it is entitled to special judicial protection.

It is true that a number of our opinions contain broadly phrased dicta implying that the same test should be applied to all classifications based on sex, whether affecting females or males. E.g., Frontiero v. Richardson, * * * Reed v. Reed, * * *. However, before today, no decision of this Court has applied an elevated level of scrutiny to invalidate a statutory discrimination harmful to males, except where the statute impaired an important personal interest protected by the Constitution.[1] There being no such interest here,

---

1. In Stanley v. Illinois, * * * the Court struck down a statute allowing separation of illegitimate children from a surviving father but not a surviving mother, without any show-

and there being no plausible argument that this is a discrimination against females,[2] the Court's reliance on our previous sex-discrimination cases is ill-founded. It treats gender classification as a talisman which—without regard to the rights involved or the persons affected—calls into effect a heavier burden of judicial review.

The Court's conclusion that a law which treats males less favorably than females "must serve important governmental objectives and must be substantially related to achievement of those objectives" apparently comes out of thin air. The Equal Protection Clause contains no such language, and none of our previous cases adopt that standard. I would think we have had enough difficulty with the two standards of review which our cases have recognized—the norm of "rational basis," and the "compelling state interest" required where a "suspect classification" is involved—so as to counsel weightily against the insertion of still another "standard" between those two. How is this Court to divine what objectives are important? How is it to determine whether a particular law is "substantially" related to the achievement of such objective, rather than related in some other way to its achievement? Both of the phrases used are so diaphanous and elastic as to invite subjective judicial preferences or prejudices relating to particular types of legislation, masquerading as judgments whether such legislation is directed at "important" objectives or, whether the relationship to those objectives is "substantial" enough.

I would have thought that if this Court were to leave anything to decision by the popularly elected branches of the Government, where no constitutional claim other than that of equal protection is invoked, it would be the decision as to what governmental objectives to be achieved by law are "important," and which are not. As for the second part of the Court's new test, the Judicial Branch is probably in no worse position than the Legislative or Executive Branches to determine if there is *any* rational relationship between a classification and the purpose which it might be thought to serve. But the introduction of the adverb "substantially" requires courts to make subjective judgments as to operational effects, for which neither their expertise nor their access to data fits them. And even if we manage to avoid both confusion and the mirroring of our own preferences in the development of this new doctrine,

ing of parental unfitness. The Court stated that "the interest of a parent in the companionship, care, custody, and management of his or her children 'come[s] to this Court with a momentum for respect lacking when appeal is made to liberties which derive merely from shifting economic arrangements.' "

In Kahn v. Shevin, * * * the Court upheld Florida's $500 property tax exemption for widows only. The opinion of the Court appears to apply a rational-basis test, and is so understood by the dissenters. * * *

In Weinberger v. Wiesenfeld, * * * the Court invalidated § 202(g) of the Social Security Act, which allowed benefits to mothers but not fathers of minor children, who survive the wage earner. This statute was treated, in the opinion of the Court, as a discrimination against female wage earners, on the ground that it minimizes the financial security which their work efforts provide for their families. * * *

2. I am not unaware of the argument from time to time advanced, that all discriminations between the sexes ultimately redound to the detriment of females, because they tend to reinforce "old notions" restricting the roles and opportunities of women. As a general proposition applying equally to all sex categorizations, I believe that this argument was implicitly found to carry little weight in our decisions upholding gender-based differences. See Schlesinger v. Ballard, * * * Kahn v. Shevin. * * * Seeing no assertion that it has special applicability to the situation at hand, I believe it can be dismissed as an insubstantial consideration.

the thousands of judges in other courts who must interpret the Equal Protection Clause may not be so fortunate.

II

The applicable rational-basis test is one which

"permits the States a wide scope of discretion in enacting laws which affect some groups of citizens differently than others. The constitutional safeguard is offended only if the classification rests on grounds wholly irrelevant to the achievement of the State's objective. State legislatures are presumed to have acted within their constitutional power despite the fact that, in practice, their laws result in some inequality. A statutory discrimination will not be set aside if any state of facts reasonably may be conceived to justify it." McGowan v. Maryland, * * *.

Our decisions indicate that application of the Equal Protection Clause in a context not justifying an elevated level of scrutiny does not demand "mathematical nicety" or the elimination of all inequality. Those cases recognize that the practical problems of government may require rough accommodations of interests, and hold that such accommodations should be respected unless no reasonable basis can be found to support them. Dandridge v. Williams, * * *. Whether the same ends might have been better or more precisely served by a different approach is no part of the judicial inquiry under the traditional minimum rationality approach. Richardson v. Belcher, * * *.

The Court "accept[s] for purposes of discussion" the District Court's finding that the purpose of the provisions in question was traffic safety, and proceeds to examine the statistical evidence in the record in order to decide if "the gender-based distinction *closely* serves to achieve that objective." * * * (Whether there is a difference between laws which "closely [serve]" objectives and those which are only "substantially related" to their achievement, * * * we are not told.) I believe that a more traditional type of scrutiny is appropriate in this case, and I think that the Court would have done well here to heed its own warning that "[i]t is unrealistic to expect * * * members of the judiciary * * * to be well versed in the rigors of experimental or statistical technique." * * * One need not immerse oneself in the fine points of statistical analysis, however, in order to see the weaknesses in the Court's attempted denigration of the evidence at hand.

* * *

The Court's criticism of the statistics relied on by the District Court conveys the impression that a legislature in enacting a new law is to be subjected to the judicial equivalent of a doctoral examination in statistics. Legislatures are not held to any rules of evidence such as those which may govern courts or other administrative bodies, and are entitled to draw factual conclusions on the basis of the determination of probable cause which an arrest by a police officer normally represents. In this situation, they could reasonably infer that the incidence of drunk driving is a good deal higher than the incidence of arrest.

And while, as the Court observes, relying on a report to a Presidential Commission which it cites in a footnote, such statistics may be distorted as a result of stereotyping, the legislature is not required to prove before a court that its statistics are perfect. In any event, if stereotypes are as pervasive as the Court suggests, they may in turn influence the conduct of the men and women in question, and cause the young men to conform to the wild and reckless image which is their stereotype.

* * *

Quite apart from these alleged methodological deficiencies in the statistical evidence, the Court appears to hold that that evidence, on its face, fails to support the distinction drawn in the statute. The Court notes that only 2% of males (as against .18% of females) in the age group were arrested for drunk driving, and that this very low figure establishes "an unduly tenuous 'fit' " between maleness and drunk driving in the 18–20–year–old group. On this point the Court misconceives the nature of the equal protection inquiry.

The rationality of a statutory classification for equal protection purposes does not depend upon the statistical "fit" between the class and the trait sought to be singled out. It turns on whether there may be a sufficiently higher incidence of the trait within the included class than in the excluded class to justify different treatment. Therefore the present equal protection challenge to this gender-based discrimination poses only the question whether the incidence of drunk driving among young men is sufficiently greater than among young women to justify differential treatment. Notwithstanding the Court's critique of the statistical evidence, that evidence suggests clear differences between the drinking and driving habits of young men and women. Those differences are grounds enough for the State reasonably to conclude that young males pose by far the greater drunk-driving hazard, both in terms of sheer numbers and in terms of hazard on a per-driver basis. The gender-based difference in treatment in this case is therefore not irrational.

The Court's argument that a 2% correlation between maleness and drunk driving is constitutionally insufficient therefore does not pose an equal protection issue concerning discrimination between males and females. The clearest demonstration of this is the fact that the precise argument made by the Court would be equally applicable to a flat bar on such purchases by *anyone,* male or female, in the 18–20 age group; in fact it would apply *a fortiori* in that case given the even more "tenuous 'fit' " between drunk-driving arrests and femaleness. The statistics indicate that about 1% of the age group population as a whole is arrested. What the Court's argument is relevant to is not equal protection, but due process—whether there are enough persons in the category who drive while drunk to justify a bar against purchases by all members of the group.

Cast in those terms, the argument carries little weight, in light of our decisions indicating that such questions call for a balance of the State's interest against the harm resulting from any overinclusiveness or underinclusiveness. Vlandis v. Kline, 412 U.S. 441, 448–452, 93 S.Ct. 2230, 2234–2236, 37 L.Ed.2d 63 (1973). The personal interest harmed here is very minor—the present legislation implicates only the right to purchase 3.2% beer, certainly a far cry from the important personal interests which have on occasion supported this Court's invalidation of statutes on similar reasoning. Cleveland Board of Education v. LaFleur, 414 U.S. 632, 640, 94 S.Ct. 791, 796, 39 L.Ed.2d 52 (1974); Stanley v. Illinois, 405 U.S. 645, 651, 92 S.Ct. 1208, 1212,

31 L.Ed.2d 551 (1972). And the state interest involved is significant—the prevention of injury and death on the highways.

This is not a case where the classification can only be justified on grounds of administrative convenience. Vlandis v. Kline, supra, * * * Stanley v. Illinois, supra, * * *. There being no apparent way to single out persons likely to drink and drive, it seems plain that the legislature was faced here with the not atypical legislative problem of legislating in terms of broad categories with regard to the purchase and consumption of alcohol. I trust, especially in light of the Twenty-first Amendment, that there would be no due process violation if no one in this age group were allowed to purchase 3.2% beer. Since males drink and drive at a higher rate than the age group as a whole, I fail to see how a statutory bar with regard only to them can create any due process problem.

The Oklahoma Legislature could have believed that 18–20–year–old males drive substantially more, and tend more often to be intoxicated than their female counterparts; that they prefer beer and admit to drinking and driving at a higher rate than females; and that they suffer traffic injuries out of proportion to the part they make up of the population. Under the appropriate rational-basis test for equal protection, it is neither irrational nor arbitrary to bar them from making purchases of 3.2% beer, which purchases might in many cases be made by a young man who immediately returns to his vehicle with the beverage in his possession. The record does not give any good indication of the true proportion of males in the age group who drink and drive (except that it is no doubt greater than the 2% who are arrested), but whatever it may be I cannot see that the mere purchase right involved could conceivably raise a due process question. There being no violation of either equal protection or due process, the statute should accordingly be upheld.

Notes on Craig

1. Prior to *Craig,* a bemused federal district judge commented that lower courts searching for guidance in 1970s Supreme Court sex discrimination precedent have "an uncomfortable feeling"—like players at a shell game who are "not absolutely sure there is a pea." Newcomer, J., in Vorchheimer v. School Dist. of Philadelphia, 400 F.Supp. 326, 340–41 (E.D.Pa.1975), reversed 532 F.2d 880 (3d Cir.1976) (2–1), affirmed by an equally divided Court, 430 U.S. 703, 97 S.Ct. 1671, 51 L.Ed.2d 750 (1977). Does the intermediate standard acknowledged in *Craig* reveal the pea? Try to identify governmental objectives appropriately labeled "permissible," but not "important." The alleged legislative objective in *Craig*—enhancement of traffic safety—was identified in the Court's opinion as clearly important. Is pursuit of administrative convenience (*Reed, Frontiero*) unimportant? How should a lower court go about determining the "substantiality" of the relationship between legislative ends and means? Cf. Laurence Tribe, American Constitutional Law 1082–89 (1978).

2. In footnote 2 to his dissenting opinion, Justice Rehnquist comments on a position taken by sex equality advocates in virtually every case of explicit gender classification to reach the High Court in the 1970s, that discrimination by gender generally cuts with two edges. In *Craig,* appellants argued that the legislation reflected a familiar set of assumptions: young women are (usually) more "mature" than young men and are (inclined to be) passive, unassertive, "settled,"

while young men are (generally) boys at heart, (apt to be) adventurous, daring, even reckless. A brief amicus curiae filed by the American Civil Liberties Union (at 19–20, 22) elaborated:

> [T]he purported rationale is protection, ironically, protection of [young men] and the public against the vulnerabilities of the dominant sex. But the acknowledged basis for the once pervasive 18 female/21 male age of majority differential suggests another perspective. Is it not probable that Oklahoma's legislators had in view likely coupling at the beer parlor—the 21 year old male paired with a female two or three years his junior?

* * *

> On its face, Oklahoma's 3.2 beer differential accords young women a liberty withheld from young men. Upon deeper inspection, however, the discrimination is revealed as simply another manifestation of traditional attitudes and prejudices about the expected behavior and roles of the two sexes in our society, part of the myriad signals and messages that daily underscore the notion of men as society's active members, women as men's quiescent companions.

For the first time in *Craig,* Justice Rehnquist objected to application of "an elevated level of scrutiny to invalidate a statutory classification harmful to males." On his analysis, and that of Chief Justice Burger, how would a statute fare that permitted boys to purchase "near beer" at 18, but required girls to wait until 21? Compare the view expressed by the Chief Justice in *Craig* with Justice Jackson's position in Fay v. New York, 332 U.S. 261, 290, 67 S.Ct. 1613, 1628, 91 L.Ed. 2043 (1947).

3. Professor Gunther characterizes the *Craig* standard as " 'intermediate' with respect to both ends and means: where ends must be 'compelling' to survive strict scrutiny, 'important' objectives are enough here; and where means must be 'necessary' under the new equal protection, and merely rationally related under the old equal protection, they must be 'substantially related' to survive the intermediate level of review." Gerald Gunther, Cases and Materials on Constitutional Law 674 (10th ed. 1980). In Ginsburg's formulation, after *Craig*

> [c]lassification by gender fails unless the legislative objective is *important* (a word stronger than *legitimate,* but weaker than *compelling*). Moreover, the classification must relate *substantially* to the important objective. (Again, *substantial* has a more stringent tone than *rational,* but implies a connection less tight than a *necessary* one.)

Ruth Bader Ginsburg, Sex Equality and the Constitution, 52 Tul.L.Rev. 451, 468–69 (1978). Are these two interpretations the same? If so, how are they to be applied to future cases?

4. How would you apply the *Craig* standard to the following cases? (a) A Board of Education rule forbids male high school students from wearing gang symbols or jewelry, including earrings, to school; female students are not prohibited from wearing earrings (see Olesen v. Board of Education of School Dist. No. 228, 676 F.Supp. 820, 823 (N.D.Ill.1987)); (b) A National Park Service regulation prohibits the public exposure of female breasts, but not male chests, at the Cape Cod National Seashore (see Craft v. Hodel, 683 F.Supp. 289, 299–301 (D.Mass. 1988)); (c) a former provision of the Immigration and Nationality Act that conferred citizenship upon children born abroad whose fathers, but not mothers, were United States citizens (see Elias v. United States Department of State, 721 F.Supp. 243 (N.D.Cal.1989)).

5. In City of Cleburne v. Cleburne Living Center, 473 U.S. 432, 105 S.Ct. 3249, 87 L.Ed.2d 313 (1985), the Court expressed its continuing disagreement over the appropriate standard of review in equal protection cases. The Court agreed that a zoning ordinance interpreted to require a special use permit for a proposed group home for thirteen mentally retarded persons, but which had not been invoked to forbid institutional housing for other groups of persons, violated the Equal Protection Clause. It disagreed, however, on the standard of review that led to its result. Justice White, joined by Justices Rehnquist, Powell, and O'Connor, declined to identify the mentally retarded as a "quasi-suspect" classification, arguing instead that the ordinance, as applied, could not pass the rational relationship standard of review used to test the validity of economic and social legislation. Justice White thus described the Court's prior decisions:

II

The Equal Protection Clause of the Fourteenth Amendment commands that no State shall "deny to any person within its jurisdiction the equal protection of the laws," which is essentially a direction that all persons similarly situated should be treated alike. Plyler v. Doe, 457 U.S. 202, 216, 102 S.Ct. 2382, 2394, 72 L.Ed.2d 786 (1982). Section 5 of the Amendment empowers Congress to enforce this mandate, but absent controlling congressional direction, the courts have themselves devised standards for determining the validity of state legislation or other official action that is challenged as denying equal protection. The general rule is that legislation is presumed to be valid and will be sustained if the classification drawn by the statute is rationally related to a legitimate state interest. Schweiker v. Wilson, 450 U.S. 221, 230, 101 S.Ct. 1074, 1080, 67 L.Ed.2d 186 (1981); United States Railroad Retirement Board v. Fritz, 449 U.S. 166, 174–175, 101 S.Ct. 453, 459, 66 L.Ed.2d 368 (1980); Vance v. Bradley, 440 U.S. 93, 97, 99 S.Ct. 939, 943, 59 L.Ed.2d 171 (1979); New Orleans v. Dukes, 427 U.S. 297, 303, 96 S.Ct. 2513, 2516, 49 L.Ed.2d 511 (1976). When social or economic legislation is at issue, the Equal Protection Clause allows the States wide latitude, United States Railroad Retirement Board v. Fritz, supra, at 174; New Orleans v. Dukes, supra, at 303, and the Constitution presumes that even improvident decisions will eventually be rectified by the democratic processes.

The general rule gives way, however, when a statute classifies by race, alienage, or national origin. These factors are so seldom relevant to the achievement of any legitimate state interest that laws grounded in such considerations are deemed to reflect prejudice and antipathy—a view that those in the burdened class are not as worthy or deserving as others. For these reasons and because such discrimination is unlikely to be soon rectified by legislative means, these laws are subjected to strict scrutiny and will be sustained only if they are suitably tailored to serve a compelling state interest. McLaughlin v. Florida, 379 U.S. 184, 192, 85 S.Ct. 283, 288, 13 L.Ed.2d 222 (1964); Graham v. Richardson, 403 U.S. 365, 91 S.Ct. 1848, 29 L.Ed.2d 534 (1971). Similar oversight by the courts is due when state laws impinge on personal rights protected by the Constitution. Kramer v. Union Free School District No. 15, 395 U.S. 621, 89 S.Ct. 1886, 23 L.Ed.2d 583 (1969); Shapiro v. Thompson, 394 U.S. 618, 89 S.Ct. 1322, 22 L.Ed.2d 600 (1969); Skinner v. Oklahoma ex rel. Williamson, 316 U.S. 535, 62 S.Ct. 1110, 86 L.Ed. 1655 (1942).

Legislative classifications based on gender also call for a heightened standard of review. That factor generally provides no sensible ground for differential treatment. "[W]hat differentiates sex from such nonsuspect statuses as intelligence or physical disability * * * is that the sex characteristic frequently bears no relation to ability to perform or contribute to society." Frontiero v. Richardson, 411 U.S. 677, 686, 93 S.Ct. 1764, 1770, 36 L.Ed.2d 583 (1973) (plurality opinion). Rather than resting on meaningful considerations, statutes distributing benefits and burdens between the sexes in different ways very likely reflect out-moded notions of the relative capabilities of men and women. A gender classification fails unless it is substantially related to a sufficiently important governmental interest. Mississippi University for Women v. Hogan, 458 U.S. 718, 102 S.Ct. 3331, 73 L.Ed.2d 1090 (1982); Craig v. Boren, 429 U.S. 190, 97 S.Ct. 451, 50 L.Ed.2d 397 (1976). Because illegitimacy is beyond the individual's control and bears "no relation to the individual's ability to participate in and contribute to society," Mathews v. Lucas, 427 U.S. 495, 505, 96 S.Ct. 2755, 2762, 49 L.Ed.2d 651 (1976), official discriminations resting on that characteristic are also subject to somewhat heightened review. Those restrictions "will survive equal protection scrutiny to the extent they are substantially related to a legitimate state interest." Mills v. Habluetzel, 456 U.S. 91, 99, 102 S.Ct. 1549, 1554, 71 L.Ed.2d 770 (1982).

We have declined, however, to extend heightened review to differential treatment based on age:

> "While the treatment of the aged in this Nation has not been wholly free of discrimination, such persons, unlike, say, those who have been discriminated against on the basis of race or national origin, have not experienced a 'history of purposeful unequal treatment' or been subjected to unique disabilities on the basis of stereotyped characteristics not truly indicative of their abilities." Massachusetts Board of Retirement v. Murgia, 427 U.S. 307, 313, 96 S.Ct. 2562, 2566, 49 L.Ed.2d 520 (1976).

The lesson of *Murgia* is that where individuals in the group affected by a law have distinguishing characteristics relevant to interests the State has the authority to implement, the courts have been very reluctant, as they should be in our federal system and with our respect for the separation of powers, to closely scrutinize legislative choices as to whether, how, and to what extent those interests should be pursued. In such cases, the Equal Protection Clause requires only a rational means to serve a legitimate end.

Id., 473 U.S. at 439–42, 105 S.Ct. at 3254–55, 87 L.Ed.2d at 320–21. Justice Stevens and Chief Justice Burger, concurring, joined the Court in using a rational basis test, but disavowed the existence of a clearly-defined standard of review in equal protection cases. Citing his concurring opinion in *Craig,* Justice Stevens thus spelled out his own approach:

> In my own approach to these cases, I have always asked myself whether I could find a "rational basis" for the classification at issue. The term "rational," of course, includes a requirement that an impartial lawmaker could logically believe that the classification would serve a legitimate public purpose that transcends the harm to the members of the disadvantaged class. Thus, the word "rational"—for me at least—includes elements of legitimacy and neutrality that must always characterize the performance of the sovereign's duty to govern impartially.

> The rational-basis test, properly understood, adequately explains why a law that deprives a person of the right to vote because his skin has a different pigmentation than that of other voters violates the Equal Protection Clause.

It would be utterly irrational to limit the franchise on the basis of height or weight; it is equally invalid to limit it on the basis of skin color. None of these attributes has any bearing at all on the citizen's willingness or ability to exercise that civil right. We do not need to apply a special standard, or to apply "strict scrutiny," or even "heightened scrutiny," to decide such cases.

In every equal protection case, we have to ask certain basic questions. What class is harmed by the legislation, and has it been subjected to a "tradition of disfavor" by our laws?[6] What is the public purpose that is being served by the law? What is the characteristic of the disadvantaged class that justifies the disparate treatment? In most cases the answer to these questions will tell us whether the statute has a "rational basis." The answers will result in the virtually automatic invalidation of racial classifications and in the validation of most economic classifications, but they will provide differing results in cases involving classifications based on alienage, gender, or illegitimacy. But that is not because we apply an "intermediate standard of review" in these cases; rather it is because the characteristics of these groups are sometimes relevant and sometimes irrelevant to a valid public purpose, or, more specifically, to the purpose that the challenged laws purportedly intended to serve.[11]

Every law that places the mentally retarded in a special class is not presumptively irrational. The differences between mentally retarded persons and those with greater mental capacity are obviously relevant to certain legislative decisions. An impartial lawmaker—indeed, even a member of a class of persons defined as mentally retarded—could rationally vote in favor of a law providing funds for special education and special treatment for the mentally retarded. A mentally retarded person could also recognize that he is a member of a class that might need special supervision in some situations, both to protect himself and to protect others. Restrictions on his right to drive cars or to operate hazardous equipment might well seem rational even though they deprived him of employment opportunities and the kind of freedom of travel enjoyed by other citizens. "That a civilized and decent society expects and approves such legislation indicates that governmental consideration of those differences in the vast majority of situations is not only legitimate but also desirable." * * *

Even so, the Court of Appeals correctly observed that through ignorance and prejudice the mentally retarded "have been subjected to a history of unfair and often grotesque mistreatment." * * * The discrimination against

---

6. The Court must be especially vigilant in evaluating the rationality of any classification involving a group that has been subjected to a "tradition of disfavor [for] a traditional classification is more likely to be used without pausing to consider its justification than is a newly created classification. Habit, rather than analysis, makes it seem acceptable and natural to distinguish between male and female, alien and citizen, legitimate and illegitimate; for too much of our history there was the same inertia in distinguishing between black and white. But that sort of stereotyped reaction may have no rational relationship—other than pure prejudicial discrimination—to the stated purpose for which the classification is being made." Mathews v. Lucas, 427 U.S. 495, 520–521, 96 S.Ct. 2755, 2769, 49 L.Ed.2d 651 (1976) (Ste-

vens, J., dissenting). See also New York Transit Authority v. Beazer, 440 U.S. 568, 593, 99 S.Ct. 1355, 1370, 59 L.Ed.2d 587 (1979).

11. See Michael M. v. Superior Court of Sonoma County, 450 U.S. 464, 497–498, and n. 4, 101 S.Ct. 1200, 1218–19, 67 L.Ed.2d 437 (1981) (Stevens, J., dissenting). See also Caban v. Mohammed, 441 U.S. 380, 406–407, 99 S.Ct. 1760, 1775–76, 60 L.Ed.2d 297 (1979) (Stevens, J., dissenting) ("But as a matter of equal protection analysis, it is perfectly obvious that at the time and immediately after a child is born out of wedlock, differences between men and women justify some differential treatment of the mother and father in the adoption process").

the mentally retarded that is at issue in this case is the city's decision to require an annual special use permit before property in an apartment house district may be used as a group home for persons who are mildly retarded. The record convinces me that this permit was required because of the irrational fears of neighboring property owners, rather than for the protection of the mentally retarded persons who would reside in respondent's home.[12]

Although the city argued in the Court of Appeals that legitimate interests of the neighbors justified the restriction, the court unambiguously rejected that argument. In this Court, the city has argued that the discrimination was really motivated by a desire to protect the mentally retarded from the hazards presented by the neighborhood. Zoning ordinances are not usually justified on any such basis, and in this case, for the reasons explained by the Court, I find that justification wholly unconvincing. I cannot believe that a rational member of this disadvantaged class could ever approve of the discriminatory application of the city's ordinance in this case.

Id., 473 U.S. at 452–55, 105 S.Ct. at 3261–63, 87 L.Ed.2d at 328–30 (Concurring opinion of Stevens, J.).

JUSTICES MARSHALL, BRENNAN, and BLACKMUN, dissenting, thought an elevated standard appropriate, and accused the Court of using a "second order rational basis review." Does Justice Stevens's "rational basis" approach provide the same level of scrutiny to classifications based on sex as the intermediate standard presently does? What kind of sex-based distinctions would a "rational" woman approve?

6. Commentators have identified *Cleburne* and other cases decided during the 1984 Term as establishing a stricter scrutiny for the lowest level of equal protection review, one that forbids the government from acting out of impermissible purposes. See Brenda Swierenga, Comment, Still Newer Equal Protection: Impermissible Purpose Review in the 1984 Term, 53 U.Chi.L.Rev. 1454, 1474–83 (1986) (suggesting that content of the new inquiry can be made more intelligible by analogizing it to racial classifications, and identifying two categories of legislation that are generally invidious in the same way racial classifications are invidious—those based on unfounded stereotypes that stem from prejudice, asthetic distaste, or moral disapproval of the majority, and those that discriminate against the politically powerless); Melanie E. Meyers, Note, Impermissible Purposes and the Equal Protection Clause, 86 Columb.L.Rev. 1184, 1195–1204 (1986) (arguing that impermissible purpose analysis is not limited to minimal scrutiny review, but rather provides "a determinative element throughout equal protection review that uniformly condemns governmental countenance of societal prejudice.") Are these interpretations of the scope of impermissible purpose review confirmed by the Court's subsequent expansion of the coverage of 42 U.S.C. § 1981 in Saint Francis College v. Al–Khazraji, 481 U.S. 604, 107 S.Ct. 2022, 95 L.Ed.2d 582 (1987) rehearing denied 483 U.S. 1011, 107 S.Ct. 3244, 97 L.Ed.2d 749 (1987)?

7. The Court's evolving formulation and application of its intermediate level equal protection scrutiny in sex discrimination cases has itself received increasing scrutiny from commentators since its initial announcement in *Craig*. For example, Professor Ann Freedman offers a trenchant critique of the philosophical alignment of the individual Justices in sex discrimination cases. She contrasts

---

12. In fact, the ordinance provides that each applicant for a special use permit "shall be required to obtain the signatures of the property owners within two hundred (200) feet of the property to be used." App. 63.

the Rehnquist–Stewart approach, which narrowly conceives sex discrimination to consist of the use of sex classifications when no "real" differences between men and women are involved, with the Brennan–Marshall approach, which perceives sex discrimination more broadly as a pervasive and morally troubling phenomenon. In Freedman's view, this latter moral critique serves two preliminary functions: it rejects the encouragement of traditional sex roles as a legitimate governmental goal and it creates a presumption against the validity of all sex classifications. Brennan and Marshall then use that presumption as follows in applying the Court's intermediate standard. First, they use a means-ends analysis to determine the actual purpose of a challenged classification, and whether that purpose is an important one. Secondly, they decide whether the classification is substantially related to the asserted end. In making this determination, they ask whether sex is an accurate proxy for the characteristics that are related to the end, and whether a sex-neutral rule would be equally effective in achieving the government's goal. Freedman prefers the Brennan–Marshall approach to the Rehnquist–Stewart formulation, but believes neither is ultimately satisfactory. She calls instead for the formulation of a more compelling sex discrimination jurisprudence, one that would make its moral choices explicit rather than value neutral, and that would attempt to promote equality between the sexes by describing in concrete terms the harmful consequences of sexism while considering which alternative social arrangements are desirable. See Ann E. Freedman, Sex Equality, Sex Differences, and the Supreme Court, 92 Yale L.J. 913 (1983).

Another writer suggests that the Court's requirement that a gender-based classification must be "substantially related" to its objective is susceptible to two interpretations: either that there is a significant difference between men and women, related to the purpose of the legislation, that provides a reason for treating them differently (the "similarly situated" test), or that the state must also show that there is a good reason for not treating men and women identically (the "gender-neutral" test). The author suggests that the gender-neutral test might be imposed in addition to the similarly-situated test, and that it might represent a new approach to equal protection doctrine which rests on a conception of sexual equality as an affirmative value in itself. The writer does not claim that the Court has adopted a gender-neutral test in sex discrimination cases, but he points to *Michael M.* (set forth at p. 1131, infra) and *Rostker*(set forth at p. 110, infra) as cases in which the Court openly debated its application. See William R. Engles, Comment, The "Substantial Relation" Question in Gender Discrimination Cases, 52 U.Chi.L.Rev. 149 (1985). How closely does this writer's "similarly-situated" test correspond to Freedman's description of the Rehnquist–Stewart approach, and his "gender-neutral" test to her analysis of the Brennan–Marshall approach? Would a gender-neutral standard forbid the legislative recognition of biological reproductive sex differences between men and women? See generally, Sylvia A. Law, Rethinking Sex and the Constitution, 132 U.Pa.L.Rev. 955 (1984).

Both Freedman and the Chicago commentator seem willing to continue to work within, while refining, the general equal protection framework. Professor Stephanie Wildman, however, proposes that we abandon the antidiscrimination principle, with its inherent comparison between men and women, because she believes that it perpetuates sex discrimination. She proposes instead a "participatory perspective" to eliminate sex discrimination against women by ensuring their full societal participation. See Stephanie M. Wildman, The Legitimation of Sex Discrimination: A Critical Response to Supreme Court Jurisprudence, 63 Or. L.Rev. 265 (1984).

C. IDENTIFYING THE VICTIMS OF DISCRIMINATION

1. DISCRIMINATION AS THE "ACCIDENTAL BY–PRODUCT OF A TRADITIONAL WAY OF THINKING ABOUT FEMALES"

CALIFANO v. GOLDFARB

Supreme Court of the United States, 1977.
430 U.S. 199, 97 S.Ct. 1021, 51 L.Ed.2d 270.

MR. JUSTICE BRENNAN announced the judgment of the Court and delivered an opinion in which MR. JUSTICE WHITE, MR. JUSTICE MARSHALL, and MR. JUSTICE POWELL joined.

Under the Federal Old–Age, Survivors, and Disability Insurance Benefits (OASDI) program, 42 U.S.C.A. §§ 401–431, survivors' benefits based on the earnings of a deceased husband covered by the Act are payable to his widow. Such benefits on the basis of the earnings of a deceased wife covered by the Act are payable to the widower, however, only if he "was receiving at least one-half of his support" from his deceased wife. The question in this case is whether this gender-based distinction violates the Due Process Clause of the Fifth Amendment.

A three-judge District Court for the Eastern District of New York held that the different treatment of men and women mandated by § 402(f)(1)(D) constituted invidious discrimination against female wage earners by affording them less protection for their surviving spouses than is provided to male employees, 396 F.Supp. 308 (1975).[2] * * *. We affirm.

I

Hannah Goldfarb worked as a secretary in the New York City public school system for almost 25 years until her death in 1968. During that entire time she paid in full all social security taxes required by the Federal Insurance Contributions Act, 26 U.S.C. §§ 3101–3126. She was survived by her husband, Leon Goldfarb, now age 72, a retired federal employee. Leon duly applied for widower's benefits. The application was denied with the explanation:

> "You do not qualify for a widower's benefit because you do not meet one of the requirements for such entitlement. This requirement is that you must have been receiving at least one half support from your wife when she died."

* * *

II

The gender-based distinction drawn by § 402(f)(1)(D)—burdening a widower but not a widow with the task of proving dependency upon the deceased

2. The decision also applied to § 402(c)(1)(C), which imposes a dependency requirement on husbands of covered female wage earners applying for old-age benefits; wives applying for such benefits are not required to prove dependency, § 402(b). These gender-based classifications have been uniformly held [by lower courts] to be unconstitutional. [Citations omitted.]

spouse—presents an equal protection question indistinguishable from that decided in Weinberger v. Wiesenfeld, [420 U.S. 636, 95 S.Ct. 1225, 43 L.Ed.2d 514 (1975)]. That decision and the decision in Frontiero v. Richardson, supra, plainly require affirmance of the judgment of the District Court.[4]

The statutes held unconstitutional in *Frontiero* provided increased quarters allowance and medical and dental benefits to a married male member of the uniformed armed services whether or not his wife in fact depended on him, while a married female service member could only receive the increased benefits if she in fact provided over one-half of her husband's support. To justify the classification, the Secretary of Defense argued that "as an empirical matter, wives in our society frequently are dependent upon their husbands, while husbands rarely are dependent upon their wives. Thus, * * * Congress might reasonably have concluded that it would be both cheaper and easier simply conclusively to presume that wives of male members are financially dependent upon their husbands, while burdening female members with the task of establishing dependency in fact." * * *. But *Frontiero* concluded that by according such differential treatment to male and female members of the uniformed services for the sole purpose of achieving administrative convenience, the challenged statute violated the Fifth Amendment. See Reed v. Reed, * * *.

Weinberger v. Wiesenfeld, like the instant case, presented the question in the context of the OASDI program. There the Court held unconstitutional a provision that denied father's insurance benefits to surviving widowers with children in their care, while authorizing similar mother's benefits to similarly situated widows. Paula Wiesenfeld, the principal source of her family's support, and covered by the Act, died in childbirth, survived by the baby and her husband Stephen. Stephen applied for survivors' benefits for himself and his infant son. Benefits were allowed the baby under 42 U.S.C.A. § 402(d), but denied the father on the ground that "mother's benefits" under § 402(g) were available only to women. The Court reversed, holding that the gender-based distinction made by § 402(g) was "indistinguishable from that invalidated in *Frontiero,*" * * * and therefore:

> "[While] the notion that men are more likely than women to be the primary supporters of their spouses and children is not entirely without empirical support, * * * such a gender-based generalization cannot suffice to justify the denigration of the efforts of women who do work and whose earnings contribute significantly to their families' support.

> "Section 402(g) clearly operates, as did the statutes invalidated by our judgment in *Frontiero,* to deprive women of protection for their families which men receive as a result of their employment. Indeed, the classification here is in some ways more pernicious. * * * [I]n this case social security taxes were deducted from Paula's salary during the years

---

4. The dissent maintains that this sentence "overstates [the] relevance" of *Wiesenfeld* and *Frontiero*. It is sufficient to answer that the principal propositions argued by appellant and in the dissent—namely, the focus on discrimination between surviving, rather than insured, spouses; the reliance on Kahn v. Shevin, 416 U.S. 351, 94 S.Ct. 1734, 40 L.Ed.2d 189 (1974); the argument that the presumption of female dependence is empirically supportable; and the emphasis on the special deference due to classifications in the Social Security Act—were all asserted and rejected in one or both of those cases as justifications for statutes substantially similar in effect to § 402(f)(1)(D).

in which she worked. Thus, she not only failed to receive for her family the same protection which a similarly situated male worker would have received, but she also was deprived of a portion of her own earnings in order to contribute to the fund out of which benefits would be paid to others." * * *

Precisely the same reasoning condemns the gender-based distinction made by § 402(f)(1)(D) in this case. For that distinction, too, operates "to deprive women of protection for their families which men receive as a result of their employment": social security taxes were deducted from Hannah Goldfarb's salary during the quarter century she worked as a secretary, yet, in consequence of § 402(f)(1)(D), she also "not only failed to receive for her [spouse] the same protection which a similarly situated male worker would have received [for his spouse] but she also was deprived of a portion of her own earnings in order to contribute to the fund out of which benefits would be paid to others." *Wiesenfeld* thus inescapably compels the conclusion reached by the District Court that the gender-based differentiation created by § 402(f)(1)(D)—that results in the efforts of female workers required to pay social security taxes producing less protection for their spouses than is produced by the efforts of men—is forbidden by the Constitution, at least when supported by no more substantial justification than "archaic and overbroad" generalizations, Schlesinger v. Ballard, * * * or " 'old notions,' " Stanton v. Stanton, * * *, such as "assumptions as to dependency," Weinberger v. Wiesenfeld, * * * that are more consistent with "the role-typing society has long imposed," Stanton v. Stanton, * * * than with contemporary reality. Thus § 402(f)(1)(D) " '[b]y providing dissimilar treatment for men and women who are * * * similarly situated * * * violates the [Fifth Amendment].' Reed v. Reed, * * *." Weinberger v. Wiesenfeld, * * *

III

Appellant, however, would focus equal protection analysis, not upon the discrimination against the covered wage earning female, but rather upon whether her surviving widower was unconstitutionally discriminated against by burdening him but not a surviving widow with proof of dependency. The gist of the argument is that, analyzed from the perspective of the widower, "the denial of benefits reflected the congressional judgment that aged widowers as a class were sufficiently likely not to be dependent upon their wives that it was appropriate to deny them benefits unless they were in fact dependent." * * *

But Weinberger v. Wiesenfeld rejected the virtually identical argument when appellant's predecessor argued that the statutory classification there attacked should be regarded from the perspective of the prospective beneficiary and not from that of the covered wage earner. The Secretary in that case argued that the "pattern of legislation reflects the considered judgment of Congress that the 'probable need' for financial assistance is greater in the case of a widow, with young children to maintain, than in the case of similarly situated males." * * *. The Court, however, analyzed the classification from the perspective of the wage earner and concluded that the classification was unconstitutional because "benefits must be distributed according to classifications which do not without sufficient justification differentiate among covered employees solely on the basis of sex." * * * Thus contrary to appellant's insistence, * * * *Wiesenfeld* is "dispositive here."

From its inception, the social security system has been a program of social insurance. Covered employees and their employers pay taxes into a fund administered distinct from the general federal revenues to purchase protection against the economic consequences of old age, disability, and death. But under § 402(f)(1)(D) female insureds received less protection for their spouses solely because of their sex. Mrs. Goldfarb worked and paid social security taxes for 25 years at the same rate as her male colleagues, but because of § 402(f)(1)(D) the insurance protection received by the males was broader than hers. Plainly then § 402(f)(1)(D) disadvantages women contributors to the social security system as compared to similarly situated men.[5] The section then "impermissibly discriminates against a female wage earner because it provides her family less protection than it provides that of a male wage earner, even though the family needs may be identical." [*Wiesenfeld*] (Powell, J., concurring). In a sense, of course, both the female wage earner and her surviving spouse are disadvantaged by operation of the statute, but this is because "Social Security is designed * * * for the protection of the *family*," [*Wiesenfeld*] (Powell, J., concurring), and the section discriminates against one particular category of family—that in which the female spouse is a wage earner covered by social security. Therefore decision of the equal protection challenge in this case cannot focus solely on the distinction drawn between widowers and widows but, as *Wiesenfeld* held, upon the gender-based discrimination against covered female wage earners as well.[8]

IV

Appellant's emphasis upon the sex-based distinction between widow and widower as recipients of benefits rather than that between covered female and covered male employees also emerges in his other arguments. These arguments have no merit.

A

We accept as settled the proposition argued by appellant that Congress has wide latitude to create classifications that allocate noncontractual benefits

---

5. The disadvantage to the woman wage earner is even more pronounced in the case of old-age benefits, to which a similarly unequal dependency requirement applies. 42 U.S.C.A. §§ 402(b), (c)(1)(C). See n. 2, supra. In that situation, where the insured herself is still living, she is denied not only "the dignity of knowing [during her working career] that her social security tax would contribute to their joint welfare when the couple or one of them retired and to her husband's welfare should she predecease him," 396 F.Supp. 308, 309 (E.D.N.Y.1975) (opinion below), but also the more tangible benefit of an increase in the income of the family unit of which she remains a part.

8. In any event, gender-based discriminations against men have been invalidated when they do not "serve important governmental objectives and [are not] substantially related to the achievement of those objectives." Craig v. Boren, * * *. Neither Kahn v. Shevin, * * *

nor Schlesinger v. Ballard, * * * relied on by appellant, supports a contrary conclusion. The gender-based distinctions in the statutes involved in *Kahn* and *Ballard* were justified because the only discernible purpose of each was the permissible one of redressing our society's long-standing disparate treatment of women. Craig v. Boren, * * *

But "the mere recitation of a benign, compensatory purpose is not an automatic shield which protects against any inquiry into the actual purposes underlying a statutory scheme." Weinberger v. Wiesenfeld, * * *. That inquiry in this case demonstrates that § 402(f)(1)(D) has no such remedial purpose. * * * Moreover, the classifications challenged in *Wiesenfeld* and in this case rather than advantaging women to compensate for past wrongs compounds those wrongs by penalizing women "who do work and whose earnings contribute significantly to their families' support." *Wiesenfeld,* * * *

under a social welfare program. Weinberger v. Salfi, 422 U.S. 749, 776–777, 95 S.Ct. 2457, 2472, 45 L.Ed.2d 522 (1975); Flemming v. Nestor, 363 U.S. 603, 609–610, 80 S.Ct. 1367, 1371–1372, 4 L.Ed.2d 1435 (1960). * * *

* * *

But this "does not, of course, immunize [social welfare legislation] from scrutiny under the Fifth Amendment." * * * The Social Security Act is permeated with provisions that draw lines in classifying those who are to receive benefits. Congressional decisions in this regard are entitled to deference as those of the institution charged under our scheme of government with the primary responsibility for making such judgments in light of competing policies and interests. But "[t]o withstand constitutional challenge, * * * classifications by gender must serve important governmental objectives and must be substantially related to the achievement of those objectives." Craig v. Boren, * * *.[9] Such classifications, however, have frequently been revealed on analysis to rest only upon "old notions" and "archaic and overbroad" generalizations, * * * and so have been found to offend the prohibitions against denial of equal protection of the law. * * *

Therefore, *Wiesenfeld,* * * * expressly rejected the argument of appellant's predecessor, relying on Flemming v. Nestor, that the "noncontractual" interest of a covered employee in future social security benefits precluded any claim of denial of equal protection. Rather, *Wiesenfeld* held that the fact that the interest is "noncontractual" does not mean that "a covered employee has no right whatever to be treated equally with other employees as regards the benefits which flow from his or her employment," nor does it "sanction differential protection for covered employees which is solely gender based." * * * On the contrary, benefits "directly related to years worked and amount earned by a covered employee, and not to the need of the beneficiaries directly," like the employment-related benefits in *Frontiero,* "must be distributed according to classifications which do not without sufficient justification differentiate among covered employees solely on the basis of sex." * * *

B

Appellant next argues that *Frontiero* and *Wiesenfeld* should be distinguished as involving statutes with different objectives from § 402(f)(1)(D). Rather than merely enacting presumptions designed to save the expense and trouble of determining which spouses are really dependent, providing benefits to all widows, but only to such widowers as prove dependency, § 402(f)(1)(D), it is argued, rationally defines different standards of eligibility because of the differing social welfare needs of widowers and widows. That is, the argument runs, Congress may reasonably have presumed that nondependent widows,

---

9. Thus, justifications that suffice for non-gender-based classifications in the social welfare area do not necessarily justify gender discriminations. For example, Weinberger v. Salfi, 422 U.S. 749, 95 S.Ct. 2457, 45 L.Ed.2d 522 (1975), sustained a discrimination designed to weed out collusive marriages without making case-by-case determinations between marriages of less than nine months' duration and longer ones on the ground:

"While such a limitation doubtless proves in particular cases to be 'under-inclusive' or 'over-inclusive' in light of its presumed purpose, it is nonetheless a widely accepted response to legitimate interests in administrative economy and certainty of coverage for those who meet its terms." * * *.

Yet administrative convenience and certainty of result have been found inadequate justifications for gender-based classifications. Reed v. Reed, * * *

who receive benefits, are needier than nondependent widowers, who do not, because of job discrimination against women (particularly older women), see Kahn v. Shevin, 416 U.S. 351, 353–354, 94 S.Ct. 1734, 1736–1737, 40 L.Ed.2d 189 (1974), and because they are more likely to have been more dependent on their spouses. * * *

But "inquiry into the actual purposes" of the discrimination, * * * proves the contrary. First, § 402(f)(1)(D) itself is phrased in terms of *dependency,* not *need.* Congress chose to award benefits, not to widowers who could prove that they are needy, but to those who could prove that they had been dependent on their wives for more than one-half of their support. On the face of the statute, dependency, not need, is the criterion for inclusion.

Moreover, the general scheme of OASDI shows that dependence on the covered wage earner is the critical factor in determining beneficiary categories.[11] OASDI is intended to insure covered wage earners and their families against the economic and social impact on the family normally entailed by loss of the wage earner's income due to retirement, disability, or death, by providing benefits to replace the lost wages. Cf. Jimenez v. Weinberger, 417 U.S. 628, 633–634, 94 S.Ct. 2496, 2500, 41 L.Ed.2d 363 (1974). Thus, benefits are not paid, as under other welfare programs, simply to categories of the population at large who need economic assistance, but only to members of the family of the insured wage earner. Moreover, every family member other than a wife or widow is eligible for benefits only if a dependent of the covered wage earner. This accords with the system's general purpose; one who was not dependent to some degree on the covered wage earner suffers no economic loss when the wage earner leaves the work force. Thus the overall statutory scheme makes actual dependency the general basis of eligibility for OASDI benefits, and the statute, in omitting that requirement for wives and widows, reflects only a presumption that they are ordinarily dependent. At all events, nothing whatever suggests a reasoned congressional judgment that nondependent widows should receive benefits because they are more likely to be needy than nondependent widowers.

Finally, the legislative history of § 402(f)(1)(D) refutes appellant's contention. The old-age provisions of the original Social Security Act, 49 Stat. 622, provided pension benefits only to the wage earner himself, with a lump-sum payment to his estate under certain circumstances. Wives' and widows' benefits were first provided when coverage was extended to other family members in 1939. Social Security Act Amendments of 1939, 53 Stat. 1360, 1364–1366. The general purpose of the amendments was "to afford more adequate protection to the *family* as a unit." * * *. There is no indication whatever in any of the legislative history that Congress gave any attention to the specific case of nondependent widows, and found that they were in need of benefits despite their lack of dependency, in order to compensate them for disadvantages caused by sex discrimination. There is every indication that, as *Wiesenfeld* recognized, * * * "the framers of the Act legislated on the 'then

11. Although presumed need has been a factor in determining the amounts of social security benefits, in addition to the extent of contributions made to the system, the primary determinants of the benefits received are the years worked and amount earned by the covered worker. 42 U.S.C.A. §§ 414, 415. * * *. In any event, need is not a requirement for inclusion in any beneficiary category, 42 U.S.C.A. § 402, and from the beginning was intended to be irrelevant to the right to receive benefits. * * *

generally accepted presumption that a man is responsible for the support of his wife and children.' D. Hoskins & L. Bixby, Women and Social Security: Law and Policy in Five Countries, Social Security Administration Research Report No. 42, p. 77 (1973)."

Survivors' and old-age benefits were not extended to husbands and widowers until 1950. 64 Stat. 483, 485. The legislative history of this provision also demonstrates that Congress did not create the disparity between nondependent widows and widowers with a compensatory purpose. The impetus for change came from the Advisory Council on Social Security, which recommended benefits for "the aged, dependent husband * * * [and] widower." The purpose of this recommendation was *"[t]o equalize the protection given to the dependents of women and men"* because *"[u]nder the present program, insured women lack some of the rights which insured men can acquire."* * * * It is clear from the report that the Advisory Council assumed that the provision of benefits to dependent husbands and widowers was the equivalent of the provision of benefits to wives and widows under the previous statute, and not a lesser protection deliberately made because of lesser need. Although the original bill, H.R. 6000, that became the Social Security Act Amendments of 1950 did not contain a provision for husbands' and widowers' benefits, the Senate Finance Committee added it, because "the committee believes that protection given to dependents of women and men should be made more comparable." * * * In 1950, as in 1939, there was simply no indication of an intention to create a differential treatment for the benefit of nondependent wives.

We conclude, therefore, that the differential treatment of nondependent widows and widowers results not, as appellant asserts, from a deliberate congressional intention to remedy the arguably greater needs of the former, but rather from an intention to aid the dependent spouses of deceased wage earners, coupled with a presumption that wives are usually dependent. This presents precisely the situation faced in *Frontiero* and *Wiesenfeld.* The only conceivable justification for writing the presumption of wives' dependency into the statute is the assumption, not verified by the Government in *Frontiero,* * * * or here, but based simply on "archaic and overbroad" generalizations, * * * that it would save the Government time, money, and effort simply to pay benefits to all widows, rather than to require proof of dependency of both sexes.[18] We held in *Frontiero,* and again in *Wiesenfeld,* and therefore hold again here, that such assumptions do not suffice to justify a gender-based discrimination in the distribution of employment-related benefits.

MR. JUSTICE STEVENS, concurring in the judgment.

Although my conclusion is the same, my appraisal of the relevant discrimination and my reasons for concluding that it is unjustified, are somewhat different from those expressed by Mr. Justice Brennan.

First, I agree with Mr. Justice Rehnquist that the constitutional question raised by this plaintiff requires us to focus on his claim for benefits rather than his deceased wife's tax obligation. She had no contractual right to

---

18. In fact, the legislative history suggests that Congress proceeded casually on a "then generally accepted" stereotype and did not fo- cus on the possible expense of determining dependence in every case.

receive benefits or to control their payment; moreover, the payments are not a form of compensation for her services.[1] At the same salary level, all workers must pay the same tax, whether they are male or female, married or single, old or young, the head of a large family or a small one. The benefits which may ultimately become payable to them or to a wide variety of beneficiaries—including their families, their spouses, future spouses, and even their ex-wives—vary enormously, but such variations do not convert a uniform tax obligation into an unequal one. The discrimination against this plaintiff would be the same if the benefits were funded from general revenues. In short, I am persuaded that the relevant discrimination in this case is against surviving male spouses, rather than against deceased female wage earners.[2]

Second, I also agree with Mr. Justice Rehnquist that a classification which treats certain aged widows[3] more favorably than their male counterparts is not "invidious." Such a classification does not imply that males are inferior to females, cf. Mathews v. Lucas, * * * (Stevens, J., dissenting); does not condemn a large class on the basis of the misconduct of an unrepresentative few, cf. Craig v. Boren, * * *, Stevens, J., concurring); and does not add to the burdens of an already disadvantaged discrete minority. Cf. Hampton v. Mow Sun Wong, 426 U.S. 88, 102, 96 S.Ct. 1895, 1904, 48 L.Ed.2d 495. It does, however, treat similarly situated persons differently solely because they are not of the same sex.

Third, Mr. Justice Rehnquist correctly identifies two hypothetical justifications for this discrimination that are comparable to those the Court found acceptable in Mathews v. Lucas, * * *, and Kahn v. Shevin, * * * Neither the "administrative convenience" rationale of *Lucas,* nor the "policy of cushioning the financial impact of spousal loss upon the sex for which that loss imposes a disproportionately heavy burden," Kahn v. Shevin, * * *, can be described as wholly irrational. Nevertheless, I find both justifications unacceptable in this case.

The administrative-convenience rationale rests on the assumption that the cost of providing benefits to nondependent widows is justified by eliminating the burden of requiring those who are dependent to establish that fact. Mr. Justice Rehnquist's careful analysis of the relevant data demonstrates that at present only about 10% of the married women in the relevant age bracket are nondependent. Omitting any requirement that widows establish dependency therefore expedites the processing of about 90% of the applica-

---

1. For this reason this case is not controlled by Frontiero v. Richardson, * * *.

2. The contrary analysis in Weinberger v. Wiesenfeld, * * *, was not necessary to the decision of that case. * * *

3. In most cases the statutory scheme for the distribution of benefits to the surviving spouses of deceased persons who paid FICA taxes on their earnings does not involve any discrimination on account of sex. Dependent spouses of both sexes are eligible; also, nondependent surviving spouses of both sexes are ineligible if their own social security retire-ment benefits are as large as those of their deceased spouses. There is, however, a narrow area in which the eligibility of nondependent spouses depends solely on their sex: Those who received between 50% and 75% of their support from their deceased spouses are eligible for benefits if they are female, but not if they are male. Similarly, if their earnings were not covered by the Social Security Act, as was true of the plaintiff in this case, and their earnings were less than 75% of the decedent's, they are eligible if they are female, but not if they are male.

tions. This convenience must be regarded as significant even though procedures could certainly be developed to minimize the burden.

But what is the offsetting cost that Congress imposed on the Nation in order to achieve this administrative convenience? Assuming that Congress intended only to benefit dependent spouses, and that it has authorized payments to nondependent widows to save the cost of administering a dependency requirement for widows, it has paid a truly staggering price for a relatively modest administrative gain: the cost of payments to the hundreds of thousands of widows who are not within the described purpose of the statute is perhaps $750 million a year. The figures for earlier years were presumably smaller, but must still have been large in relation to the possible administrative savings. It is inconceivable that Congress would have authorized such large expenditures for an administrative purpose without the benefit of any cost analysis, or indeed, without even discussing the problem. I am therefore convinced that administrative convenience was not the actual reason for the discrimination.

It is also clear that the disparate treatment of widows and widowers is not the product of a conscious purpose to redress the "legacy of economic discrimination" against females. Kahn v. Shevin, * * *, (Brennan, J., dissenting). The widows who benefit from the disparate treatment are those who were sufficiently successful in the job market to become nondependent on their husbands. Such a widow is the least likely to need special benefits. The widow most in need is the one who is "suddenly forced into a job market with which she is unfamiliar, and in which, because of her former economic dependency, she will have fewer skills to offer." Kahn v. Shevin, supra, * * *. To accept the *Kahn* justification we must presume that Congress deliberately gave a special benefit to those females least likely to have been victims of the historic discrimination discussed in *Kahn*. Respect for the legislative process precludes the assumption that the statutory discrimination is the product of such irrational lawmaking.

The step-by-step evolution of this statutory scheme included a legislative decision to provide benefits for all widows and a separate decision to provide benefits for dependent widowers. Admittedly, each of these separate judgments has a rational and benign purpose. But I consider it clear that Congress never focused its attention on the question whether to divide nondependent surviving spouses into two classes on the basis of sex. The history of the statute is entirely consistent with the view that Congress simply assumed that all widows should be regarded as "dependents" in some general sense, even though they could not satisfy the statutory support test later imposed on men. It is fair to infer that habit, rather than analysis or actual reflection, made it seem acceptable to equate the terms "widow" and "dependent surviving spouse." That kind of automatic reflex is far different from either a legislative decision to favor females in order to compensate for past wrongs, or a legislative decision that the administrative savings exceed the cost of extending benefits to nondependent widows.

I am therefore persuaded that this discrimination against a group of males is merely the accidental byproduct of a traditional way of thinking about females. I am also persuaded that a rule which effects an unequal distribution of economic benefits solely on the basis of sex is sufficiently questionable that "due process requires that there be a legitimate basis for presuming that the rule was actually intended to serve [the] interest" put forward by the government as its justification. See Hampton v. Mow Sun Wong, 426 U.S. 88, 103, 96 S.Ct. 1895, 1905, 48 L.Ed.2d 495.[9] In my judgment, something more than accident is necessary to justify the disparate treatment of persons who have as strong a claim to equal treatment as do similarly situated surviving spouses.

But if my judgment is correct, what is to be said about Kahn v. Shevin? For that case involved a discrimination between surviving spouses which originated in 1885; a discrimination of that vintage cannot reasonably be supposed to have been motivated by a decision to repudiate the 19th century presumption that females are inferior to males. It seems clear, therefore, that the Court upheld the Florida statute on the basis of a hypothetical justification for the discrimination which had nothing to do with the legislature's actual motivation. On this premise, I would be required to regard *Kahn* as controlling in this case, were it not for the fact that I believe precisely the same analysis applies to Weinberger v. Wiesenfeld, * * *.

In *Wiesenfeld,* the Court rejected an attempt to use "mere recitation of a benign, compensatory purpose" as "an automatic shield," * * *, for a statute which was actually based on " 'archaic and overbroad' generalization[s]," * * *. In *Wiesenfeld,* as in this case, the victims of the statutory discrimination were widowers. They were totally excluded from eligibility for benefits available to similarly situated widows, just as in this case nondependent widowers are totally excluded from eligibility for benefits payable to nondependent widows. The exclusion in *Wiesenfeld* was apparently the accidental byproduct of the same kind of legislative process that gave rise to *Kahn* and to this case. If there is inconsistency between *Kahn* and *Wiesenfeld,* as I believe there is, it is appropriate to follow the later unanimous holding rather than the earlier, sharply divided decision. And if the cases are distinguishable, *Wiesenfeld* is closer on its facts to this case than is *Kahn.*

For these reasons, and on the authority of the *holding* in *Wiesenfeld,* I concur in the Court's judgment.

Mr. Justice Rehnquist, with whom The Chief Justice, Mr. Justice Stewart, and Mr. Justice Blackmun join, dissenting.

In light of this Court's recent decisions beginning with Reed v. Reed, * * *, one cannot say that there is no support in our cases for the result reached by the Court. One can, however, believe as I do that careful consideration of these cases affords more support for the opposite result than it does for that reached by the Court. Indeed, it seems to me that there are two largely separate principles which may be deduced from these cases which indicate that the Court has reached the wrong result.

The first of these principles is that cases requiring heightened levels of scrutiny for particular classifications under the Equal Protection Clause, which have originated in areas of the law outside of the field of social

---

9. In the absence of evidence to the contrary, we might presume that Congress had such an interest in mind, see Hampton v. Mow Sun Wong, 426 U.S., at 103, 96 S.Ct., at 1905, but here that presumption is untenable. Perhaps an actual, considered legislative choice would be sufficient to allow this statute to be upheld, but that is a question I would reserve until such a choice has been made.

insurance legislation, will not be uncritically carried over into that field. This does not mean that the phrase "social insurance" is some sort of magic phrase which automatically mutes the requirements of the equal protection component of the Fifth Amendment. But it does suggest that in a legislative system which distributes benefit payments among literally millions of people there are at least two characteristics which are not found in many other types of statutes. The first is that the statutory scheme will typically have been expanded by amendment over a period of years so that it is virtually impossible to say that a particular amendment fits with mathematical nicety into a carefully conceived overall plan for payment of benefits. The second is that what in many other areas of the law will be relatively low-level considerations of "administrative convenience" will in this area of the law bear a much more vital relation to the overall legislative plan because of congressional concern for certainty in determination of entitlement and promptness in payment of benefits.

The second principle upon which I believe this legislative classification should be sustained is that set forth in our opinion in Kahn v. Shevin, * * *. The effect of the statutory scheme is to make it easier for widows to obtain benefits than it is for widowers, since the former qualify automatically while the latter must show proof of need. Such a requirement in no way perpetuates or exacerbates the economic disadvantage which has led the Court to conclude that gender-based discrimination must meet a different test from other types of classifications. It is, like the property tax exemption to widows in *Kahn,* supra, a differing treatment which " 'rest[s] upon some ground of difference having a fair and substantial relation to the object of the legislation.' " * * *.

I

Both Weinberger v. Wiesenfeld, * * *, and Frontiero v. Richardson, * * *, are undoubtedly relevant to the decision of this case, but the plurality overstates that relevance when it says that these two cases "plainly require affirmance of the judgment of the District Court." The disparate treatment of widows and widowers by this Act is undoubtedly a gender-based classification, but this is the beginning and not the end of the inquiry. In the case of classifications based on legitimacy, and in the case of irrebuttable presumptions, constitutional doctrine which would have invalidated the same distinctions in other contexts has been held not to require that result when they were used within comprehensive schemes for social insurance. The same result should obtain in the case of constitutional principles dealing with gender-based distinctions.

* * *

Two observations about *Wiesenfeld* are pertinent. First, the provision of the Social Security Act held unconstitutional there flatly denied surviving widowers the possibility of obtaining benefits no matter what showing of need might be made. The section under attack in the instant case does not totally foreclose widowers, but simply requires from them a proof of dependency which is not required from similarly situated widows. Second, *Wiesenfeld* was decided before either Weinberger v. Salfi, supra, or Mathews v. Lucas, supra. Each of those decisions refused uncritically to extend into the field of social security law constitutional proscriptions against distinctions based on illegitimacy and irrebuttable presumptions which had originated in other areas of the law. While the holding of *Wiesenfeld* is not inconsistent with *Salfi* or *Lucas,* its reasoning is not in complete harmony with the recognition in those cases of the special characteristics of social insurance plans.

II

* * *

The provisions at issue in this case, relating to widows' and widowers' benefits, display all the earmarks of their origins in the oft-repeated process of legislative reconsideration and expansion of beneficiary groups. As originally enacted in 1935, the Social Security Act provided for old-age benefits only to the wage earner. 49 Stat. 623. In 1939, additional provisions were made for benefits to the wage earner's family, including wives and widows, but not including husbands and widowers. The widow's benefit was in an amount larger by one-half than that for the wife, and was available notwithstanding the widow's primary entitlement to benefits in an amount greater than permissible in the case of a wife. All things considered, the 1939 amendments reflect a legislative judgment that elderly wives and widows of Social Security recipients were needy groups, and that of the two, the plight of widows was especially severe. I agree with the plurality's statement that "[t]here is no indication whatever in any of the legislative history that Congress gave any attention to the specific case of nondependent widows, and found that they were in need of benefits despite their lack of dependency * * *." But neither is there any reason to doubt that it singled out the group of aged widows for especially favorable treatment, because it saw prevalent throughout that group a characteristically high level of need.

* * *

The second legislative judgment implicit in the widow's and widower's provisions is that widows, as a practical matter, are much more likely to be without adequate means of support than are widowers. The plurality opinion makes much of establishing this point, that the absence of any dependency prerequisite to the award of widow's benefits reflects a judgment, resting on "administrative convenience," that dependence among aged widows is frequent enough to justify waiving the requirement entirely. I differ not with the recognition of this administrative convenience purpose but with the conclusion that such a purpose *necessarily* invalidates the resulting classification. Our decisions dealing with social welfare legislation indicate that our inquiry must go further. For rational classifications aimed at distributing funds to beneficiaries under social insurance legislation weigh a good deal more heavily on the governmental interest side of the equal protection balance than they may in other legislative contexts. The "administrative convenience" which is afforded by such classifications in choosing the administrator of a decedent's estate, see Reed v. Reed, supra, is significantly less important to the effectiveness of the legislative scheme than is the "convenience" afforded by classifications in administering an Act designed to provide benefits to millions upon millions of beneficiaries with promptness and certainty. For this reason, the plurality errs in merely dispatching this statute with an incantation of "administrative convenience." It should go further and consider the governmental interest advanced by the statutory classification in a social insurance statute such as this, in light of the claimed injury to appellee.

* * *

IV

Perhaps because the reasons asserted for "heightened scrutiny" of gender-based distinctions are rooted in the fact that women have in the past been victims of unfair treatment, see Frontiero v. Richardson, * * *, the plurality says that the difference in treatment here is not only between a widow and a widower, but between the respective deceased spouses of the two. It concludes that wage-earning wives are deprived " 'of protection for their families which men receive as a result of their employment.' "

But this is a questionable tool of analysis which can be used to prove virtually anything. It might just as well have been urged in Kahn v. Shevin, supra, where we upheld a Florida property tax exemption redounding to the benefit of widows but not widowers, that the real discrimination was between the deceased spouses of the respective widow and widower, who had doubtless by their contributions to the family or marital community helped make possible the acquisition of the property which was now being disparately taxed.

Since the claim to social security benefits is noncontractual in nature, * * *, the contributions of the deceased spouse cannot be regarded as creating any sort of contractual entitlement on the part of either the deceased wife or the surviving husband. Here the female wage earner has gotten the degree of protection for her family which Congress was concerned to extend to all. Neither she nor her surviving husband has any constitutional claim to more, simply because Congress has chosen, for administrative reasons, to give benefits to widows without requiring proof of dependency.

* * *

In Weinberger v. Wiesenfeld, * * *, the Court again invalidated OASDI provisions which denied one group any opportunity to show themselves proper beneficiaries given the apparent statutory purpose. A widow not qualifying for widow's benefits was entitled to a mother's benefit if she had in her care a minor child qualifying for a child's benefit, and if she did not receive more than a certain amount of primary benefits in her own right. No such provision was made, however, for a widower in a parallel position. The Court found a purpose in the statute to allow a single parent to stay home and care for the minor child * * * and struck down the denial of benefits to fathers similarly situated. The defect of that statute was its conclusive exception of widowers from the benefited class, solely on the basis of their sex, and in contravention of the legislative purpose to allow parents with deceased spouses to provide personal parental care. There is no plausible claim to be made here that a statutory objective is being thwarted by underinclusiveness of the classes of beneficiaries.

This case is also distinguishable from Frontiero v. Richardson, supra, in the sense that social insurance differs from compensation for work done. While there is no basis for assessing the propriety of a given allocation of funds within a social insurance program apart from an identifiable legislative purpose, a compensatory scheme may be evaluated under the principle of equal pay for equal work done. This case is therefore unlike *Frontiero,* where the Court invalidated sex discrimination among military personnel in their entitlement to increased quarters allowances on account of marriage, and in the eligibility of their spouses for dental and medical care. These compensatory fringe benefits were available to male employees as a matter of course, but were unavailable to females except on proof that their husbands depended on them for over one-half of their support. Since males got such compensatory benefits even though their wives were not so dependent, females with nondependent husbands were effectively denied equal compensation for equal efforts. The same is not true here, where the benefit payments to survivors are neither contractual nor compensatory for work done, and where there is thus no comparative basis for evaluating the propriety of a given benefit apart from the legislative purpose.

* * *

V

The very most that can be squeezed out of the facts of this case in the way of cognizable "discrimination" is a classification which favors aged widows. Quite apart from any considerations of legislative purpose and "administrative convenience" which may be advanced to support the classification, this is scarcely an invidious discrimination. Two of our recent cases have rejected efforts by men to challenge similar classifications. We have held that it is not improper for the military to formulate "up-or-out" rules taking into account sex-based differences in employment opportunities in a way working to the benefit of women, Schlesinger v. Ballard, 419 U.S. 498, 95 S.Ct. 572, 42 L.Ed.2d 610 (1975), or to grant solely to widows a property tax exemption in recognition of their depressed plight. Kahn v. Shevin, supra. A waiver of the dependency prerequisite for benefits, in the case of this same class of aged widows, under a program explicitly aimed at the assistance of needy groups, appears to be well within the holding of the *Kahn* case, which upheld a flat $500 exemption to widows, without any consideration of need.

VI

The classification challenged here is "overinclusive" only in the sense that widows over 62 may obtain benefits without a showing of need, whereas widowers must demonstrate need. Because this over-inclusion is rationally justifiable, given available empirical data, on the basis of "administrative convenience," Mathews v. Lucas, supra, is authority for upholding it. The differentiation in no way perpetuates the economic discrimination which has been the basis for heightened scrutiny of gender-based classifications, and is, in fact, explainable as a measure to ameliorate the characteristically depressed condition of aged widows. Kahn v. Shevin, supra, is therefore also authority for upholding it. For both of these reasons, I would reverse the judgment of the District Court.

Notes on Goldfarb

1. What turns on whether the discrimination in *Goldfarb* was against men or women? Pointing out at oral argument that Leon Goldfarb was a man who complained of discrimination against his deceased wife, the government suggested

three possible reasons for this strategy. First, it contended, Goldfarb sought to divert attention from the fact that he would obtain a windfall if he won: already covered by his own civil service pension as a retired federal employee, Goldfarb would receive double payments by collecting as a surviving widower under Social Security; second, the cause of women's rights was currently fashionable, and Goldfarb hoped to be swept to victory by its skirts; and third, Goldfarb wanted to avail himself of the heightened constitutional standard of review applicable to cases involving discrimination against women. The last point was the most significant. *Goldfarb* and Craig v. Boren, p. 41, supra, were both argued on October 5, 1976; at that time, the Court had not yet formally acknowledged its "intermediate" equal protection standard for gender discrimination cases, nor had the elevated standard been applied to the case of a male plaintiff complaining of discrimination against himself. Technically, this did not occur even in *Craig*. The controversy had become moot as to Curtis Craig, who had become 21 prior to oral argument, and Carolyn Whitener, a vendor of near-beer, was permitted to assert the constitutional rights of her thirsty male customers. Accordingly, interest in the formulation of the relevant standard was high.

Questioning then–Professor Ginsburg, who appeared on behalf of Leon Goldfarb, Justice Stewart probed the government's position. Does it matter, he asked, whether the Court views this case as a discrimination against men or against women? Would the constitutional standard be any different? In reply, Ginsburg suggested that gender discrimination works against both sexes, but this perception has been blurred because the bulk of anti-male discrimination is disguised as protection for women. How did the Court resolve this issue in *Craig* and *Goldfarb?* Compare Justice Stevens's concurring opinions in the two cases, and note the rejection, in both cases, by Justice Rehnquist of Ginsburg's argument that discrimination against either sex harms the members of both.

2. Justice Brennan's opinion in *Goldfarb* was that of a plurality of the Court. Justice Stevens's concurring vote was necessary to the result. But three years later, when Wengler v. Druggists Mut. Ins. Co., 446 U.S. 142, 100 S.Ct. 1540, 64 L.Ed.2d 107 (1980), was decided, seven votes were present for the proposition that a Missouri statute that granted worker's compensation death benefits to widows, but not widowers, without proof of actual dependency "discriminates against both men and women." (446 U.S. at 147, 100 S.Ct. at 1544, 64 L.Ed.2d at 113). Unpersuaded by the state's attempt to justify the law on the ground that, at the time of its passage in 1925, the legislature had believed that "a widow was more in need of prompt payment of death benefits upon her husband's death without drawn-out proceedings to determine the amount of dependency than was a widower" (446 U.S. at 150, 100 S.Ct. at 1546, 64 L.Ed.2d at 115), the majority held the classification invalid. Justice Rehnquist, continuing to believe that *Goldfarb* was wrongly decided, dissented. Justice Stevens concurred. His opinion reads as follows (446 U.S. at 154–55, 100 S.Ct. at 1547–48, 64 L.Ed.2d at 117–18):

> Nothing has happened since the decision in Califano v. Goldfarb, 430 U.S. 199, 97 S.Ct. 1021, 51 L.Ed.2d 270, to persuade me that this kind of gender-based classification can simultaneously disfavor the male class and the female class.

> To illustrate my difficulty with the analysis in Part II of the Court's opinion, it should be noted that there are three relevant kinds of marriages: (1) those in which the husband is dependent on the wife; (2) those in which the wife is dependent on the husband; and (3) those in which neither spouse is dependent on the other.

Under the Missouri statute, in either of the first two situations, if the dependent spouse survives, a death benefit will be paid regardless of whether the survivor is male or female; conversely, if the working spouse survives, no death benefit will be paid. The only difference in the two situations is that the surviving male, unlike the surviving female, must undergo the inconvenience of proving dependency. That surely is not a discrimination against females.

In the third situation, if one spouse dies, benefits are payable to a surviving female but not to a surviving male. In my view, that is a rather blatant discrimination against males. While both spouses remain alive, the prospect of receiving a potential death benefit upon the husband's demise reduces the wife's need for insurance on his life, whereas the prospect of *not* receiving a death benefit upon the wife's demise increases the husband's need for insurance on her life. That difference again places the husband at a disadvantage.*

No matter how the statute is viewed, the class against which it discriminates is the male class. I therefore cannot join Part II of the Court's opinion. I do, however, agree that Missouri has failed to justify the disparate treatment of persons who have as strong a claim to equal treatment as do similarly situated surviving spouses, see Califano v. Goldfarb, 430 U.S. 199, 223, 97 S.Ct. 1021, 1035, 51 L.Ed.2d 270 (Stevens, J., concurring), and that its statute violates the Equal Protection Clause of the Fourteenth Amendment. For that reason I concur in the Court's judgment.

Is there any answer to Justice Stevens's demonstration that the discrimination in *Wengler* is only against males? Can you think of a case where his perception of the victimized group would affect his vote?

3. Which group is the target of discrimination in the following cases? A provision of the Aid to Families with Dependent Children program grants benefits to needy and intact families whose dependent children have been deprived of parental support because of the unemployment of the father, but not if the mother loses her job (Califano v. Westcott, 443 U.S. 76, 99 S.Ct. 2655, 61 L.Ed.2d 382 (1979)). A state statute provides that husbands, but not wives, may be required to pay alimony to a former spouse upon divorce (Orr v. Orr, 440 U.S. 268, 99 S.Ct. 1102, 59 L.Ed.2d 306 (1979)). In *Westcott,* a unanimous court held the statute (§ 407 of the Social Security Act, 42 U.S.C.A. § 607) violative of the equal protection component of the Fifth Amendment. Speaking for himself and four others, Justice Blackmun rejected the government's argument that, although the statute was "gender-based", it was not "gender-biased", since the ultimate discrimination was against the family unit. Relying on the *Frontiero–Wiesenfeld–Goldfarb* line of cases, Blackmun pointed out that "this Court has not hesitated to strike down gender classifications that result in benefits being granted or denied to family units on the basis of the sex of the qualifying parent." (443 U.S. at 84, 99 S.Ct. at 2660, 61 L.Ed.2d at 390). In *Orr,* it was clear to the Court that "the classification expressly discriminates against men rather than women", but that fact "does not protect it from scrutiny." (440 U.S. at 279, 99 S.Ct. at 1111, 59 L.Ed.2d at 319). The *Craig* heightened standard of review was applied and the statute found invalid. How does the argument that gender discrimination harms

---

* There is no claim that the wage earner's take home pay is affected by the Missouri statute. Whether the wage earner is single or married, and, if married, whether the other spouse is male or female, dependent or independent, the wage earner's pay is the same.

both sexes (see Note 1, supra) apply to *Orr?* Justice Blackmun concurred, with the following reservations (440 U.S. at 284, 99 S.Ct. at 1114, 59 L.Ed.2d at 322):

> On the assumption that the Court's language concerning discrimination "in the sphere" of the relevant preference statute, * * *, does not imply that society-wide discrimination is always irrelevant, and on the further assumption that the language in no way cuts back on the Court's decision in Kahn v. Shevin, * * *, I join the opinion and judgment of the Court.

What does that mean? *Orr* is considered further at p. 290, infra.

4. In 1977 Congress responded to some of the Supreme Court decisions striking down gender discrimination in the Social Security Act and reserved others for future resolution. The dependency requirement for widowers challenged by Leon Goldfarb, together with the equivalent dependency requirement for husbands, was repealed by striking out 42 U.S.C.A. §§ 402(f)(1)(D) and 402(c)(1)(C). But a "set off" was added in the same section for pensions received through noncovered employment by wives, widows, husbands and widowers who were employed by the federal or state governments. A man in Leon Goldfarb's position in the future will not be required to establish dependency, but he will be required to subtract his own pension as a federal employee from any entitlement he might acquire through his wife's social security earnings record. Due to the concern of the House managers of the bill that the set off would be unfair if applied immediately to women public employees who could have reasonably expected to receive both their own pensions based on noncovered employment and their social security benefits as wives or widows, the set off provision was postponed as to them for five years from the effective date of the amendments. P.L. 95–216 § 334(g)(1), 91 Stat. 1546–47 (Dec. 20, 1977); see also House Conference Report No. 95–937, pp. 71–72, 12 U.S.Code Cong. & Adm.News 6525–26 (1978). As to future Leon Goldfarbs, does the failure to "phase in" the set off for widowers and husbands constitute a denial of equal protection? The court held in Heckler v. Mathews, 465 U.S. 728, 104 S.Ct. 1387, 79 L.Ed.2d 646 (1984), that the set off was constitutional. Speaking for a unanimous Court, Justice Brennan reasoned that the Secretary had carried her burden of showing a legitimate and exceedingly persuasive justification for the sex-based classification contained in the offset provision by pointing to the governmental purpose of protecting the reliance upon former law by persons, both men and women, who had planned their retirements based on the pre-January 1977 law. The means employed by the statute were substantially related to the achievement of that objective because the five-year revival of the eligibility criteria in effect in January 1977 was narrowly tailored to protect only those individuals who had made retirement plans prior to the subsequent changes in the law. Moreover, the solution finally chosen distinguishes Social Security applicants according to the law in effect at the time when they planned their retirements, not according to archaic generalizations about the roles and abilities of men and women. Do you agree with this reasoning?

The House version of the bill also would have formally extended the mother's insurance benefit that was the subject of litigation in Weinberger v. Wiesenfeld to fathers and would have added a divorced husband's benefit comparable to that now provided for divorced wives. These and other proposals not concurred in by the Senate which would bring about equal treatment for men and women under the program were referred to the Secretary for study in consultation with others. The mandated report, "Social Security and the Changing Roles of Men and

Women", appeared in 1979. Its proposals are discussed in the Text Note on Support of Spouse and Children During Marriage at p. 221, infra.

2. PURPOSEFUL DISCRIMINATION

J.E.B. v. ALABAMA EX REL. T.B.

Supreme Court of the United States, 1994.
511 U.S. 127, 114 S.Ct. 1419, 128 L.Ed.2d 89.

JUSTICE BLACKMUN delivered the opinion of the Court.

In *Batson v. Kentucky,* 476 U.S. 79 (1986), this Court held that the Equal Protection Clause of the Fourteenth Amendment governs the exercise of peremptory challenges by a prosecutor in a criminal trial. The Court explained that although a defendant has "no right to a 'petit jury composed in whole or in part of persons of his own race,' " * * * quoting *Strauder v. West Virginia,* 100 U.S. 303, 305 (1880), the "defendant does have the right to be tried by a jury whose members are selected pursuant to nondiscriminatory criteria." * * * Since *Batson,* we have reaffirmed repeatedly our commitment to jury selection procedures that are fair and nondiscriminatory. We have recognized that whether the trial is criminal or civil, potential jurors, as well as litigants, have an equal protection right to jury selection procedures that are free from state-sponsored group stereotypes rooted in, and reflective of, historical prejudice. * * *

Although premised on equal protection principles that apply equally to gender discrimination, all our recent cases defining the scope of *Batson* involved alleged racial discrimination in the exercise of peremptory challenges. Today we are faced with the question whether the Equal Protection Clause forbids intentional discrimination on the basis of gender, just as it prohibits discrimination on the basis of race. We hold that gender, like race, is an unconstitutional proxy for juror competence and impartiality.

I

On behalf of relator T.B., the mother of a minor child, respondent State of Alabama filed a complaint for paternity and child support against petitioner J.E.B. in the District Court of Jackson County, Alabama. On October 21, 1991, the matter was called for trial and jury selection began. The trial court assembled a panel of 36 potential jurors, 12 males and 24 females. After the court excused three jurors for cause, only 10 of the remaining 33 jurors were male. The State then used 9 of its 10 peremptory strikes to remove male jurors; petitioner used all but one of his strikes to remove female jurors. As a result, all the selected jurors were female.

Before the jury was empaneled, petitioner objected to the State's peremptory challenges on the ground that they were exercised against male jurors solely on the basis of gender, in violation of the Equal Protection Clause of the Fourteenth Amendment. * * * Petitioner argued that the logic and reasoning of *Batson v. Kentucky,* which prohibits peremptory strikes solely on the basis of race, similarly forbids intentional discrimination on the basis of gender. The court rejected petitioner's claim and empaneled the all-female jury. * * * The jury found petitioner to be the father of the child and the court entered an order directing him to pay child support. On post-judgment motion, the court reaffirmed its ruling that *Batson* does not extend to gender-based peremptory challenges. * * *

We granted certiorari, * * * to resolve a question that has created a conflict of authority—whether the Equal Protection Clause forbids peremptory challenges on the basis of gender as well as on the basis of race. Today we reaffirm what, by now, should be axiomatic: Intentional discrimination on the basis of gender by state actors violates the Equal Protection Clause, particularly where, as here, the discrimination serves to ratify and perpetuate invidious, archaic, and overbroad stereotypes about the relative abilities of men and women. * * *

II

Discrimination on the basis of gender in the exercise of peremptory challenges is a relatively recent phenomenon. Gender-based peremptory strikes were hardly practicable for most of our country's existence, since, until the 19th century, women were completely excluded from jury service.[2] So well-entrenched was this exclusion of women that in 1880 this Court, while finding that the exclusion of African–American men from juries violated the Fourteenth Amendment, expressed no doubt that a State "may confine the selection [of jurors] to males." *Strauder v. West Virginia,* 100 U.S. 303, 310; see also *Fay v. New York,* 332 U.S. 261, 289–290 (1947).

Many States continued to exclude women from jury service well into the present century, despite the fact that women attained suffrage upon ratification of the Nineteenth Amendment in 1920.[3] States that did permit women to serve on juries often erected other barriers, such as registration requirements and automatic exemptions, designed to deter women from exercising their right to jury service. See, *e.g., Fay v. New York,* * * * ("[I]n 15 of the 28 states which permitted women to serve [on juries in 1942], they might claim exemption because of their sex"); *Hoyt v. Florida,* * * * (upholding affirmative registration statute that exempted women from mandatory jury service).

The prohibition of women on juries was derived from the English common law which, according to Blackstone, 'rightfully excluded women from juries under "the doctrine of *propter defectum sexus,* literally, the 'defect of sex.'" *United States v. DeGross,* 960 F.2d 1433, 1438 (C.A.9 1992) (en banc), quoting 2 W. Blackstone, Commentaries * * *.[4] In this country, supporters

---

2. There was one brief exception. Between 1870 and 1871, women were permitted to serve on juries in Wyoming Territory. They were no longer allowed on juries after a new chief justice who disfavored the practice was appointed in 1871. See Abrahamson, Justice and Juror, 20 Ga.L.Rev. 257, 263–264 (1986).

3. In 1947, women still had not been granted the right to serve on juries in 16 States. See Rudolph, Women on the Jury—Voluntary or Compulsory?, 44 J.Am.Jud.Soc. 206 (1961). As late as 1961, three States, Alabama, Mississippi, and South Carolina, continued to exclude women from jury service. See *Hoyt v. Florida,* * * *. Indeed, Alabama did not recognize women as a "cognizable group" for jury-service purposes until after the 1966 decision in *White*

v. Crook, 251 F.Supp. 401 (M.D.Ala.) (three-judge court).

4. In England there was at least one deviation from the general rule that only males could serve as jurors. If a woman was subject to capital punishment, or if a widow sought postponement of the disposition of her husband's estate until birth of a child, a *writ de ventre inspiciendo* permitted the use of a jury of matrons to examine the woman to determine whether she was pregnant. But even when a jury of matrons was used, the examination took place in the presence of 12 men, who also composed part of the jury in such cases. The jury of matrons was used in the United States during the Colonial period, but apparently fell into disuse when the medical profes-

of the exclusion of women from juries tended to couch their objections in terms of the ostensible need to protect women from the ugliness and depravity of trials. Women were thought to be too fragile and virginal to withstand the polluted courtroom atmosphere. See *Bailey v. State,* 215 Ark. 53, 61, 219 S.W.2d 424, 428 (1949) ("Criminal court trials often involve testimony of the foulest kind, and they sometimes require consideration of indecent conduct, the use of filthy and loathsome words, references to intimate sex relationships, and other elements that would prove humiliating, embarrassing and degrading to a lady"); *In re Goodell,* 39 Wis. 232, 245–246 (1875) (endorsing statutory ineligibility of women for admission to the bar because "[r]everence for all womanhood would suffer in the public spectacle of women * * * so engaged"). *Bradwell v. State,* 16 Wall. 130, 141 (1872) (concurring opinion) ("[T]he civil law, as well as nature herself, has always recognized a wide difference in the respective spheres and destinies of man and woman. Man is, or should be, woman's protector and defender. The natural and proper timidity and delicacy which belongs to the female sex evidently unfits it for many of the occupations of civil life.... The paramount destiny and mission of woman are to fulfil the noble and benign offices of wife and mother. This is the law of the Creator"). Cf. *Frontiero v. Richardson,* * * * (plurality opinion) (This "attitude of 'romantic paternalism' * * * put women, not on a pedestal, but in a cage").

This Court in *Ballard v. United States,* 329 U.S. 187 (1946), first questioned the fundamental fairness of denying women the right to serve on juries. Relying on its supervisory powers over the federal courts, it held that women may not be excluded from the venire in federal trials in States where women were eligible for jury service under local law. In response to the argument that women have no superior or unique perspective, such that defendants are denied a fair trial by virtue of their exclusion from jury panels, the Court explained:

> "It is said * * * that an all male panel drawn from the various groups within a community will be as truly representative as if women were included. The thought is that the factors which tend to influence the action of women are the same as those which influence the action of men—personality, background, economic status—and not sex. Yet it is not enough to say that women when sitting as jurors neither act nor tend to act as a class. Men likewise do not act like a class. * * * The truth is that the two sexes are not fungible; a community made up exclusively of one is different from a community composed of both; the subtle interplay of influence one on the other is among the imponderables. To insulate the courtroom from either may not in a given case make an iota of difference. Yet a flavor, a distinct quality is lost if either sex is excluded."* * *

Fifteen years later, however, the Court still was unwilling to translate its appreciation for the value of women's contribution to civic life into an enforceable right to equal treatment under state laws governing jury service. In *Hoyt v. Florida,* * * * the Court found it reasonable, "despite the enlight-

---

sion began to perform that function. See   224–225 (1959).
Note, Jury Service for Women, 12 U.Fla.L.Rev.

ened emancipation of women," to exempt women from mandatory jury service by statute, allowing women to serve on juries only if they volunteered to serve. The Court justified the differential exemption policy on the ground that women, unlike men, occupied a unique position "as the center of home and family life."* * *

In 1975, the Court finally repudiated the reasoning of *Hoyt* and struck down, under the Sixth Amendment, an affirmative registration statute nearly identical to the one at issue in *Hoyt*. See *Taylor v. Louisiana,* 419 U.S. 522 (1975).[5]

We explained: "Restricting jury service to only special groups or excluding identifiable segments playing major roles in the community cannot be squared with the constitutional concept of jury trial." * * * The diverse and representative character of the jury must be maintained "partly as assurance of a diffused impartiality and partly because sharing in the administration of justice is a phase of civic responsibility.'" *Id.,* * * *. quoting *Thiel v. Southern Pacific Co.,* 328 U.S. 217, 227 (1946) (Frankfurter, J., dissenting). See also *Duren v. Missouri,* 439 U.S. 357 (1979).

III

Taylor relied on Sixth Amendment principles, but the opinion's approach is consistent with the heightened equal protection scrutiny afforded gender-based classifications. * * *

Despite the heightened scrutiny afforded distinctions based on gender, respondent argues that gender discrimination in the selection of the petit jury should be permitted, though discrimination on the basis of race is not. Respondent suggests that "gender discrimination in this country * * * has never reached the level of discrimination" against African–Americans, and therefore gender discrimination, unlike racial discrimination, is tolerable in the courtroom. * * *

While the prejudicial attitudes toward women in this country have not been identical to those held toward racial minorities, the similarities between the experiences of racial minorities and women, in some contexts, "overpower those differences." Note, Beyond *Batson:* Eliminating Gender–Based Peremptory Challenges, 105 Harv.L.Rev. 1920, 1921 (1992). As a plurality of this Court observed in *Frontiero v. Richardson,* * * *:

> "[T]hroughout much of the 19th century the position of women in our society was, in many respects, comparable to that of blacks under the pre-Civil War slave codes. Neither slaves nor women could hold office, serve on juries, or bring suit in their own names, and married women traditionally were denied the legal capacity to hold or convey property or to serve as legal guardians of their own children. * * * And although blacks were guaranteed the right to vote in 1870, women were denied even that right—which is itself 'preservative of other basic civil and political rights'—until adoption of the Nineteenth Amendment half a century later." * * *

---

5. *Taylor* distinguished *Hoyt* by explaining that that case "did not involve a defendant's Sixth Amendment right to a jury drawn from a fair cross section of the community," * * *. The Court now, however, has stated that *Taylor* "in effect" overruled *Hoyt*. See *Payne v. Tennessee,* 501 U.S. 808, 828, n. 1 (1991).

Certainly, with respect to jury service, African–Americans and women share a history of total exclusion, a history which came to an end for women many years after the embarrassing chapter in our history came to an end for African–Americans.

We need not determine, however, whether women or racial minorities have suffered more at the hands of discriminatory state actors during the decades of our Nation's history. It is necessary only to acknowledge that "our Nation has had a long and unfortunate history of sex discrimination," * * * a history which warrants the heightened scrutiny we afford all gender-based classifications today. Under our equal protection jurisprudence, gender-based classifications require "an exceedingly persuasive justification" in order to survive constitutional scrutiny. * * * Thus, the only question is whether discrimination on the basis of gender in jury selection substantially furthers the State's legitimate interest in achieving a fair and impartial trial.[6] In making this assessment, we do not weigh the value of peremptory challenges as an institution against our asserted commitment to eradicate invidious discrimination from the courtroom.[7] Instead, we consider whether peremptory challenges based on gender stereotypes provide substantial aid to a litigant's effort to secure a fair and impartial jury.[8]

Far from proffering an exceptionally persuasive justification for its gender-based peremptory challenges, respondent maintains that its decision to strike virtually all the males from the jury in this case "may reasonably have been based upon the perception, supported by history, that men otherwise totally qualified to serve upon a jury might be more sympathetic and receptive to the arguments of a man alleged in a paternity action to be the father of an out-of-wedlock child, while women equally qualified to serve upon a jury might be more sympathetic and receptive to the arguments of the complaining witness who bore the child." * * * [9]

6. Because we conclude that gender-based peremptory challenges are not substantially related to an important government objective, we once again need not decide whether classifications based on gender are inherently suspect. See *Mississippi University for Women,* 458 U.S., at 724, n. 9; *Stanton v. Stanton,* 421 U.S. 7, 13 (1975); *Harris v. Forklift Systems,* 510 U.S. __, __ (1993) (GINSBURG, J., concurring) ("[I]t remains an open question whether 'classifications based on gender are inherently suspect' ") (citations omitted).

7. Although peremptory challenges are valuable tools in jury trials, they "are not constitutionally protected fundamental rights; rather they are but one state-created means to the constitutional end of an impartial jury and a fair trial." *Georgia v. McCollum,* 505 U.S. 42, 57 (1992).

8. Respondent argues that we should recognize a special state interest in this case: the State's interest in establishing the paternity of a child born out of wedlock. Respondent contends that this interest justifies the use of gender-based peremptory challenges, since illegitimate children are themselves victims of historical discrimination and entitled to height-

ened scrutiny under the Equal Protection Clause.

What respondent fails to recognize is that the only legitimate interest it could possibly have in the exercise of its peremptory challenges is securing a fair and impartial jury. See *Edmonson v. Leesville Concrete Co.,* 500 U.S. 614, __ (1991) (slip op. 5) ("[T]he sole purpose [of the peremptory challenge] is to permit litigants to assist the government in the selection of an impartial trier of fact"). This interest does not change with the parties or the causes. The State's interest in *every* trial is to see that the proceedings are carried out in a fair, impartial, and nondiscriminatory manner.

9. Respondent cites one study in support of its quasi-empirical claim that women and men may have different attitudes about certain issues justifying the use of gender as a proxy for bias. See R. Hastie, S. Penrod & N. Pennington, Inside the Jury 140 (1983). The authors conclude: "Neither student nor citizen judgments for typical criminal case material have revealed differences between male and female verdict preferences. * * * The picture differs [only] for rape cases, where female jurors ap-

We shall not accept as a defense to gender-based peremptory challenges "the very stereotype the law condemns." *Powers v. Ohio,* 499 U.S. 400, 410 (1991). Respondent's rationale, not unlike those regularly expressed for gender-based strikes, is reminiscent of the arguments advanced to justify the total exclusion of women from juries.[10] Respondent offers virtually no support for the conclusion that gender alone is an accurate predictor of juror's attitudes; yet it urges this Court to condone the same stereotypes that justified the wholesale exclusion of women from juries and the ballot box.[11] Respondent seems to assume that gross generalizations that would be deemed impermissible if made on the basis of race are somehow permissible when made on the basis of gender.

Discrimination in jury selection, whether based on race or on gender, causes harm to the litigants, the community, and the individual jurors who are wrongfully excluded from participation in the judicial process. The

pear to be somewhat more conviction-prone than male jurors". The majority of studies suggest that gender plays no identifiable role in jurors' attitudes. See, *e.g.,* V. Hans & N. Vidmar, Judging the Jury 76 (1986) ("[I]n the majority of studies there are no significant differences in the way men and women perceive and react to trials; yet a few studies find women more defense-oriented, while still others show women more favorable to the prosecutor"). Even in 1956, before women had a constitutional right to serve on juries, some commentators warned against using gender as a proxy for bias. See 1 F. Busch, Law and Tactics in Jury Trials § 143, p. 207 (1949) ("In this age of general and specialized education, availed of generally by both men and women, it would appear unsound to base a peremptory challenge in any case upon the sole ground of sex * * *.").

10. A manual formerly used to instruct prosecutors in Dallas, Texas, provided the following advice: "I don't like women jurors because I can't trust them. They do, however, make the best jurors in cases involving crimes against children. It is possible that the 'women's intuition' can help you if you can't win your case with the facts." Alschuler, The Supreme Court and the Jury: Voir Dire, Peremptory Challenges, and the Review of Jury Verdicts, 56 U.Chi.L.Rev. 153, 210 (1989). Another widely circulated trial manual speculated:

"If counsel is depending upon a clearly applicable rule of law and if he wants to avoid a verdict of 'intuition' or 'sympathy,' if his verdict in amount is to be proved by clearly demonstrated blackboard figures for example, generally he would want a male juror. * * *

"[But women] are desired jurors when the plaintiff is a man. A woman juror may see a man impeached from the beginning of the case to the end, but there is at least the chance with the woman juror (particularly if the man happens to be handsome or appeal-

ing) [that] the plaintiff's derelictions in and out of court will be overlooked. A woman is inclined to forgive sin in the opposite sex; but definitely not her own. * * *" 3 M. Belli, Modern Trials §§ 51.67 and 51.68, pp. 446–447 (2d ed.1982).

11. Even if a measure of truth can be found in some of the gender stereotypes used to justify gender-based peremptory challenges, that fact alone cannot support discrimination on the basis of gender in jury selection. We have made abundantly clear in past cases that gender classifications that rest on impermissible stereotypes violate the Equal Protection Clause, even when some statistical support can be conjured up for the generalization. See, *e.g., Weinberger v. Wiesenfeld,* (holding unconstitutional a Social Security Act classification authorizing benefits to widows but not to widowers despite the fact that the justification for the differential treatment was "not entirely without empirical support"); *Craig v. Boren,* (invalidating an Oklahoma law that established different drinking ages for men and women, although the evidence supporting the age differential was "not trivial in a statistical sense"). The generalization advanced by Alabama in support of its asserted right to discriminate on the basis of gender is, at the least, overbroad, and serves only to perpetuate the same "outmoded notions of the relative capabilities of men and women," *Cleburne v. Cleburne Living Center, Inc.,* 473 U.S. 432, 441 (1985), that we have invalidated in other contexts. See *Frontiero v. Richardson,* * * *; *Stanton v. Stanton,* * * * 421 U.S. 7 (1975); *Craig v. Boren,* * * *; *Mississippi University for Women v. Hogan.* The Equal Protection Clause, as interpreted by decisions of this Court, acknowledges that a shred of truth may be contained in some stereotypes, but requires that state actors look beyond the surface before making judgments about people that are likely to stigmatize as well as to perpetuate historical patterns of discrimination.

litigants are harmed by the risk that the prejudice which motivated the discriminatory selection of the jury will infect the entire proceedings. See *Edmonson,* * * * (discrimination in the courtroom "raises serious questions as to the fairness of the proceedings conducted there"). The community is harmed by the State's participation in the perpetuation of invidious group stereotypes and the inevitable loss of confidence in our judicial system that state-sanctioned discrimination in the courtroom engenders.

When state actors exercise peremptory challenges in reliance on gender stereotypes, they ratify and reinforce prejudicial views of the relative abilities of men and women. Because these stereotypes have wreaked injustice in so many other spheres of our country's public life, active discrimination by litigants on the basis of gender during jury selection "invites cynicism respecting the jury's neutrality and its obligation to adhere to the law." *Powers v. Ohio* * * *. The potential for cynicism is particularly acute in cases where gender-related issues are prominent, such as cases involving rape, sexual harassment, or paternity. Discriminatory use of peremptory challenges may create the impression that the judicial system has acquiesced in suppressing full participation by one gender or that the "deck has been stacked" in favor of one side. * * * ("The verdict will not be accepted or understood [as fair] if the jury is chosen by unlawful means at the outset").

In recent cases we have emphasized that individual jurors themselves have a right to nondiscriminatory jury selection procedures.[12] See *Powers, Edmonson,* and *McCollum,* all *supra.* Contrary to respondent's suggestion, this right extends to both men and women. See *Mississippi University for Women v. Hogan,* * * * (that a state practice "discriminates against males rather than against females does not exempt it from scrutiny or reduce the standard of review"); cf. Brief for Respondent * * * (arguing that men deserve no protection from gender discrimination in jury selection because they are not victims of historical discrimination). All persons, when granted the opportunity to serve on a jury, have the right not to be excluded summarily because of discriminatory and stereotypical presumptions that reflect and reinforce patterns of historical discrimination.[13] Striking individu-

---

12. Given our recent precedent, the doctrinal basis for Justice Scalia's dissenting opinion is a mystery. Justice Scalia points out that the discrimination at issue in this case was directed at men, rather than women, but then acknowledges that the Equal Protection Clause protects both men and women from intentional discrimination on the basis of gender. See *post,* * * * citing *Mississippi University for Women v. Hogan,* * * *. He also appears cognizant of the fact that classifications based on gender must be more than merely rational, * * * they must be supported by an "exceedingly persuasive justification." *Hogan,* * * *. Justice Scalia further admits that the Equal Protection Clause, as interpreted by decisions of this Court, governs the exercise of peremptory challenges in every trial, and that potential jurors, as well as litigants, have an equal protection right to nondiscriminatory jury selection procedures. See *post,* * * * citing *Batson, Powers, Edmonson,* and *McCollum.* Justice Scalia does not suggest that we overrule

these cases, nor does he attempt to distinguish them. He intimates that discrimination on the basis of gender in jury selection may be rational, * * * but offers no "exceedingly persuasive justification" for it. Indeed, Justice Scalia fails to advance *any* justification for his apparent belief that the Equal Protection Clause, while prohibiting discrimination on the basis of race in the exercise of peremptory challenges, allows discrimination on the basis of gender. His dissenting opinion thus serves as a tacit admission that, short of overruling a decade of cases interpreting the Equal Protection Clause, the result we reach today is doctrinally compelled.

13. It is irrelevant that women, unlike African–Americans, are not a numerical minority and therefore are likely to remain on the jury if each side uses its peremptory challenges in an equally discriminatory fashion. Cf. *United States v. Broussard,* 987 F.2d 215, 220 (C.A.5 1993) (declining to extend *Batson* to gender;

al jurors on the assumption that they hold particular views simply because of their gender is "practically a brand upon them, affixed by law, an assertion of their inferiority." *Strauder v. West Virginia,* 100 U.S. 303, 308 (1880). It denigrates the dignity of the excluded juror, and, for a woman, reinvokes a history of exclusion from political participation.[14] The message it sends to all those in the courtroom, and all those who may later learn of the discriminatory act, is that certain individuals, for no reason other than gender, are presumed unqualified by state actors to decide important questions upon which reasonable persons could disagree.[15]

IV

Our conclusion that litigants may not strike potential jurors solely on the basis of gender does not imply the elimination of all peremptory challenges. Neither does it conflict with a State's legitimate interest in using such challenges in its effort to secure a fair and impartial jury. Parties still may remove jurors whom they feel might be less acceptable than others on the panel; gender simply may not serve as a proxy for bias. Parties may also exercise their peremptory challenges to remove from the venire any group or class of individuals normally subject to "rational basis" review. See *Cleburne v. Cleburne Living Center, Inc.,* * * *; *Clark v. Jeter,* 486 U.S. 456, 461 (1988). Even strikes based on characteristics that are disproportionately associated with one gender could be appropriate, absent a showing of pretext.[16]

If conducted properly, *voir dire* can inform litigants about potential jurors, making reliance upon stereotypical and pejorative notions about a particular gender or race both unnecessary and unwise. *Voir dire* provides a

noting that "[w]omen are not a numerical minority," and therefore are likely to be represented on juries despite the discriminatory use of peremptory challenges). Because the right to nondiscriminatory jury selection procedures belongs to the potential jurors, as well as to the litigants, the possibility that members of both genders will get on the jury despite the intentional discrimination is beside the point. The exclusion of even one juror for impermissible reasons harms that juror and undermines public confidence in the fairness of the system.

14. The popular refrain is that *all* peremptory challenges are based on stereotypes of some kind, expressing various intuitive and frequently erroneous biases. * * * But where peremptory challenges are made on the basis of group characteristics other than race or gender (like occupation, for example), they do not reinforce the same stereotypes about the group's competence or predispositions that have been used to prevent them from voting, participating on juries, pursuing their chosen professions, or otherwise contributing to civic life. See B. Babcock, A Place in the Palladium, Women's Rights and Jury Service, 61 U.Cinn. L.Rev. 1139, 1173 (1993).

15. Justice Scalia argues that there is no "discrimination and dishonor" in being subject to a race- or gender-based peremptory strike. * * * Justice Scalia's argument has been rejected many times, see, *e.g., Powers,* 499 U.S., at 410, and we reject it once again. The only support Justice Scalia offers for his conclusion is the fact that race- and gender-based peremptory challenges have a long history in this country. * * * (discriminatory peremptory challenges "have co-existed with the Equal Protection Clause for 120 years"); * * * (there was a "106–year interlude between our holding that exclusion from juries on the basis of race was unconstitutional, [*Strauder, supra*], and our holding that peremptory challenges on the basis of race were unconstitutional, [*Batson, supra*]"). We do not dispute that this Court long has tolerated the discriminatory use of peremptory challenges, but this is not a reason to continue to do so. Many of "our people's traditions," * * * such as *de jure* segregation and the total exclusion of women from juries, are now unconstitutional even though they once co-existed with the Equal Protection Clause.

16. For example, challenging all persons who have had military experience would disproportionately affect men at this time, while challenging all persons employed as nurses would disproportionately affect women. Without a showing of pretext, however, these challenges may well not be unconstitutional, since they are not gender- or race-based. See *Hernandez v. New York,* 500 U.S. 352 (1991).

means of discovering actual or implied bias and a firmer basis upon which the parties may exercise their peremptory challenges intelligently. * * *

The experience in the many jurisdictions that have barred gender-based challenges belies the claim that litigants and trial courts are incapable of complying with a rule barring strikes based on gender.[17] * * *

As with race-based *Batson* claims, a party alleging gender discrimination must make a prima facie showing of intentional discrimination before the party exercising the challenge is required to explain the basis for the strike. * * *. When an explanation is required, it need not rise to the level of a "for cause" challenge; rather, it merely must be based on a juror characteristic other than gender, and the proffered explanation may not be pretextual. See *Hernandez v. New York,* 500 U.S. 352 (1991).

Failing to provide jurors the same protection against gender discrimination as race discrimination could frustrate the purpose of *Batson* itself. Because gender and race are overlapping categories, gender can be used as a pretext for racial discrimination.[18] Allowing parties to remove racial minorities from the jury not because of their race, but because of their gender, contravenes well-established equal protection principles and could insulate effectively racial discrimination from judicial scrutiny.

V

Equal opportunity to participate in the fair administration of justice is fundamental to our democratic system.[19] It not only furthers the goals of the

---

17. Respondent argues that Alabama's method of jury selection would make the extension of *Batson* to gender particularly burdensome. In Alabama, the "struck-jury" system is employed, a system which requires litigants to strike alternately until 12 persons remain, who then constitute the jury. See Ala.Rule Civ.Proc. 47 (1990). Respondent suggests that, in some cases at least, it is necessary under this system to continue striking persons from the venire after the litigants no longer have an articulable reason for doing so. As a result, respondent contends, some litigants may be unable to come up with gender-neutral explanations for their strikes.

We find it worthy of note that Alabama has managed to maintain its struck-jury system even after the ruling in *Batson,* despite the fact that there are counties in Alabama that are predominately African–American. In those counties, it presumably would be as difficult to come up with race-neutral explanations for peremptory strikes as it would be to advance gender-neutral explanations. No doubt the *voir dire* process aids litigants in their ability to articulate race-neutral explanations for their peremptory challenges. The same should be true for gender. Regardless, a State's choice of jury-selection methods cannot insulate it from the strictures of the Equal Protection Clause. Alabama is free to adopt whatever jury-selection procedures it chooses so long as they do not violate the Constitution.

18. The temptation to use gender as a pretext for racial discrimination may explain why the majority of the lower court decisions extending *Batson* to gender involve the use of peremptory challenges to remove minority women. All four of the gender-based peremptory cases to reach the federal courts of appeals * * * involved the striking of minority women.

19. This Court almost a half century ago stated:

The American tradition of trial by jury, considered in connection with either criminal or civil proceedings, necessarily contemplates an impartial jury drawn from a cross-section of the community. * * * This does not mean, of course, that every jury must contain representatives of all the economic, social, religious, racial, political and geographical groups of the community; frequently such complete representation would be impossible. But it does mean that prospective jurors shall be selected by court officials without systematic and intentional exclusion of any of these groups. Recognition must be given to the fact that those eligible for jury service are to be found in every stratum of society. Jury competence is an individual rather than a group or class matter. That fact lies at the very heart of the jury system. To disregard it is to open the door to class distinctions and discriminations which are abhorrent to the democratic ideals of trial by jury." *Thiel v. Southern Pacific Co.,* 328 U.S. 217, 220 (1946).

jury system. It reaffirms the promise of equality under the law—that all citizens, regardless of race, ethnicity, or gender, have the chance to take part directly in our democracy. *Powers v. Ohio,* * * * ("Indeed, with the exception of voting, for most citizens the honor and privilege of jury duty is their most significant opportunity to participate in the democratic process"). When persons are excluded from participation in our democratic processes solely because of race or gender, this promise of equality dims, and the integrity of our judicial system is jeopardized.

In view of these concerns, the Equal Protection Clause prohibits discrimination in jury selection on the basis of gender, or on the assumption that an individual will be biased in a particular case for no reason other than the fact that the person happens to be a woman or happens to be a man. As with race, the "core guarantee of equal protection, ensuring citizens that their State will not discriminate * * *, would be meaningless were we to approve the exclusion of jurors on the basis of such assumptions, which arise solely from the jurors' [gender]." *Batson,* * * *.

The judgment of the Court of Civil Appeals of Alabama is reversed and the case is remanded to that court for further proceedings not inconsistent with this opinion.

It is so ordered.

————

JUSTICE O'CONNOR, concurring.

I agree with the Court that the Equal Protection Clause prohibits the government from excluding a person from jury service on account of that person's gender. * * * The State's proffered justifications for its gender-based peremptory challenges are far from the "exceedingly persuasive" showing required to sustain a gender-based classification. * * * I therefore join the Court's opinion in this case. But today's important blow against gender discrimination is not costless. I write separately to discuss some of these costs, and to express my belief that today's holding should be limited to the *government's* use of gender-based peremptory strikes.

Batson * * * itself was a significant intrusion into the jury selection process. *Batson* mini-hearings are now routine in state and federal trial courts, and *Batson* appeals have proliferated as well. Demographics indicate that today's holding may have an even greater impact than did *Batson* itself. In further constitutionalizing jury selection procedures, the Court increases the number of cases in which jury selection—once a sideshow—will become part of the main event.

For this same reason, today's decision further erodes the role of the peremptory challenge. * * *. "Peremptory challenges, by enabling each side to exclude those jurors it believes will be most partial toward the other side, are a means of eliminat[ing] extremes of partiality on both sides, thereby assuring the selection of a qualified and unbiased jury." *Holland v. Illinois,* 493 U.S. 474, 484 (1990) * * * The peremptory's importance is confirmed by its persistence: it was well established at the time of Blackstone and continues to endure in all the States. * * *

Moreover, "[t]he essential nature of the peremptory challenge is that it is one exercised without a reason stated, without inquiry and without being subject to the court's control." * * * Our belief that experienced lawyers will often correctly intuit which jurors are likely to be the least sympathetic, and our understanding that the lawyer will often be unable to explain the intuition, are the very reason we cherish the peremptory challenge. But, as we add, layer by layer, additional constitutional restraints on the use of the peremptory, we force lawyers to articulate what we know is often inarticulable.

* * * Because I believe the peremptory remains an important litigator's tool and a fundamental part of the process of selecting impartial juries, our increasing limitation of it gives me pause.

Nor is the value of the peremptory challenge to the litigant diminished when the peremptory is exercised in a gender-based manner. We know that like race, gender matters. A plethora of studies make clear that in rape cases, for example, female jurors are somewhat more likely to vote to convict than male jurors. See R. Hastie, S. Penrod, & N. Pennington, Inside the Jury 140–141 (1983) (collecting and summarizing empirical studies). Moreover, though there have been no similarly definitive studies regarding, for example, sexual harassment, child custody, or spousal or child abuse, one need not be a sexist to share the intuition that in certain cases a person's gender and resulting life experience will be relevant to his or her view of the case. " 'Jurors are not expected to come into the jury box and leave behind all that their human experience has taught them.' " *Beck v. Alabama*, 447 U.S. 625, 642 (1980). Individuals are not expected to ignore as jurors what they know as men—or women.

Today's decision severely limits a litigant's ability to act on this intuition, for the import of our holding is that any correlation between a juror's gender and attitudes is irrelevant as a matter of constitutional law. But to say that gender makes no difference as a matter of law is not to say that gender makes no difference as a matter of fact. I previously have said with regard to *Batson:* "That the Court will not tolerate prosecutors' racially discriminatory use of the peremptory challenge, in effect, is a special rule of relevance, a statement about what this Nation stands for, rather than a statement of fact." *Brown v. North Carolina,* 479 U.S. 940, 941–942 (1986) (O'Connor, J., concurring in denial of certiorari). Today's decision is a statement that, in an effort to eliminate the potential discriminatory use of the peremptory, * * * gender is now governed by the special rule of relevance formerly reserved for race. Though we gain much from this statement, we cannot ignore what we lose. In extending *Batson* to gender we have added an additional burden to the state and federal trial process, taken a step closer to eliminating the peremptory challenge, and diminished the ability of litigants to act on sometimes accurate gender-based assumptions about juror attitudes.

These concerns reinforce my conviction that today's decision should be limited to a prohibition on the government's use of gender-based peremptory challenges. The Equal Protection Clause prohibits only discrimination by state actors. In *Edmonson, supra,* we made the mistake of concluding that private civil litigants were state actors when they exercised peremptory challenges; in *Georgia v. McCollum,* 505 U.S. 42, ___ (1992), we compounded the mistake by holding that criminal defendants were also state actors. Our commitment to eliminating discrimination from the legal process should not allow us to forget that not all that occurs in the courtroom is state action. Private civil litigants are just that—*private* litigants. * * *

Clearly, criminal defendants are not state actors. "From arrest, to trial, to possible sentencing and punishment, the antagonistic relationship between government and the accused is clear for all to see * * *. [T]he unique relationship between criminal defendants and the State precludes attributing defendants' actions to the State * * *." * * * The peremptory challenge is " 'one of the most important of the rights secured to the *accused.*' " *Swain,* * * *; Goldwasser, Limiting a Criminal Defendant's Use of Peremptory Challenges: On Symmetry and the Jury in a Criminal Trial, 102 Harv.L.Rev. 808, 826–833 (1989). Limiting the accused's use of the peremptory is "a serious misordering of our priorities," for it means "we have exalted the right of citizens to sit on juries over the rights of the criminal defendant, even though it is the defendant, not the jurors, who faces imprisonment or even death." *McCollum,* * * * (Thomas, J., concurring in judgment) * * *

Accordingly, I adhere to my position that the Equal Protection Clause does not limit the exercise of peremptory challenges by private civil litigants and criminal defendants. This case itself presents no state action dilemma, for here the State of Alabama itself filed the paternity suit on behalf of petitioner. But what of the next case? Will we, in the name of fighting gender discrimination, hold that the battered wife—on trial for wounding her abusive husband—is a state actor? Will we preclude her from using her peremptory challenges to ensure that the jury of her peers contains as many women members as possible? I assume we will, but I hope we will not.

————

JUSTICE KENNEDY, concurring in the judgment.

I am in full agreement with the Court that the Equal Protection Clause prohibits gender discrimination in the exercise of peremptory challenges. I write to explain my understanding of why our precedents lead to that conclusion.

* * *

There is no doubt under our precedents, * * * that the Equal Protection Clause prohibits sex discrimination in the selection of jurors. *Duren v. Missouri,* 439 U.S. 357 (1979); *Taylor v. Louisiana,* 419 U.S. 5226 (1975). The only question is whether the Clause also prohibits peremptory challenges based on sex. The Court is correct to hold that it does. The Equal Protection Clause and our constitutional tradition are based on the theory that an individual possesses rights that are protected against lawless action by the government. The neutral phrasing of the Equal Protection Clause, extending its guarantee to "any person," reveals its concern with rights of individuals, not groups (though group disabilities are sometimes the mechanism by which the State violates the individual right in question). * * * For purposes of the Equal Protection Clause, an individual denied jury service because of a peremptory challenge exercised against her on account of her sex is no less injured than the individual denied jury service because of a law banning members of her sex from serving as jurors. * * * The injury is to personal dignity and to the individual's right to participate in the political process. * * * The neutrality of the Fourteenth Amendment's guarantee is confirmed by the fact that the Court has no difficulty in finding a constitutional wrong in this case, which involves males excluded from jury service because of their gender.

The importance of individual rights to our analysis prompts a further observation concerning what I conceive to be the intended effect of today's decision. We do not prohibit racial and gender bias in jury selection only to encourage it in jury deliberations. Once seated, a juror should not give free rein to some racial or gender bias of his or her own. The jury system is a kind of compact by which power is transferred from the judge to jury, the jury in turn deciding the case in accord with the instructions defining the relevant issues for consideration. The wise limitations on the authority of courts to inquire into the reasons underlying a jury's verdict does not mean that a jury ought to disregard the court's instructions. A juror who allows racial or gender bias to influence assessment of the case breaches the compact and renounces his or her oath.

In this regard, it is important to recognize that a juror sits not as a representative of a racial or sexual group but as an individual citizen. Nothing would be more pernicious to the jury system than for society to presume that persons of different backgrounds go to the jury room to voice prejudice. * * * The jury pool must be representative of the community, but that is a structural mechanism for preventing bias, not enfranchising it. * * * "Jury competence is an individual rather than a group or class matter. That fact lies at the very heart of the jury system." * * * Thus, the Constitution guarantees a right only to an impartial jury, not to a jury composed of members of a particular race or gender. * * *

* * *

For these reasons, I concur in the judgment of the Court holding that peremptory strikes based on gender violate the Equal Protection Clause.

———

CHIEF JUSTICE REHNQUIST, dissenting.

I agree with the dissent of JUSTICE SCALIA, which I have joined. I add these words in support of its conclusion. Accepting *Batson* * * * as correctly decided, there are sufficient differences between race and gender discrimination such that the principle of *Batson* should not be extended to peremptory challenges to potential jurors based on sex.

That race and sex discrimination are different is acknowledged by our equal protection jurisprudence, which accords different levels of protection to the two groups. Classifications based on race are inherently suspect, triggering "strict scrutiny," while gender-based classifications are judged under a heightened, but less searching standard of review. *Mississippi Univ. for Women v. Hogan,* * * *. Racial groups comprise numerical minorities in our society, warranting in some situations a greater need for protection, whereas the population is divided almost equally between men and women. Furthermore, while substantial discrimination against both groups still lingers in our society, racial equality has proved a more challenging goal to achieve on many fronts than gender equality. See, *e.g.,* D. Kirp, M. Yudof, M. Franks, Gender Justice 137 (1986).

Batson, which involved a black defendant challenging the removal of black jurors, announced a sea-change in the jury selection process. In balancing the dictates of equal protection and the historical practice of peremptory challenges, long recognized as securing fairness in trials, the Court concluded that the command of the Equal Protection Clause was superior. But the Court was careful that its rule not "undermine the contribution the challenge generally makes to the administration of justice." * * * *Batson* is best understood as a recognition that race lies at the core of the commands of the Fourteenth Amendment. Not surprisingly, all of our post-*Batson* cases have dealt with the use of peremptory strikes to remove black or racially identified venirepersons, and all have described *Batson* as fashioning a rule aimed at preventing purposeful discrimination against a cognizable racial group. As Justice O'Connor once recognized, *Batson* does not apply "[o]utside the uniquely sensitive area of race." *Brown v. North Carolina,* 479 U.S. 940, 942 (1986) (opinion concurring in denial of certiorari).

Under the Equal Protection Clause, these differences mean that the balance should tilt in favor of peremptory challenges when sex, not race, is the issue. Unlike the Court, I think the State has shown that jury strikes on the basis of gender "substantially further" the State's legitimate interest in achieving a fair and impartial trial through the venerable practice of peremptory challenges. * * * The two sexes differ, both biologically and, to a diminishing extent, in experience. It is not merely "stereotyping" to say that these differences may produce a difference in outlook which is brought to the jury room. Accordingly, use of peremptory challenges on the basis of sex is generally not the sort of derogatory and invidious act which peremptory challenges directed at black jurors may be.

Justice O'Connor's concurrence recognizes several of the costs associated with extending *Batson* to gender-based peremptory challenges—lengthier trials, an increase in the number and complexity of appeals addressing jury selection, and a "diminished * * * ability of litigants to act on sometimes accurate gender-based assumptions about juror attitudes." * * * These costs are, in my view, needlessly imposed by the Court's opinion, because the Constitution simply does not require the result which it reaches.

JUSTICE SCALIA, with whom THE CHIEF JUSTICE and JUSTICE THOMAS join, dissenting.

Today's opinion is an inspiring demonstration of how thoroughly up-to-date and right-thinking we Justices are in matters pertaining to the sexes (or as the Court would have it, the genders), and how sternly we disapprove the male chauvinist attitudes of our predecessors. The price to be paid for this display—a modest price, surely—is that most of the opinion is quite irrelevant to the case at hand. The hasty reader will be surprised to learn, for example, that this lawsuit involves a complaint about the use of peremptory challenges to exclude *men* from a petit jury. To be sure, petitioner, a man, used all but one of *his* peremptory strikes to remove *women* from the jury (he used his last challenge to strike the sole remaining male from the pool), but the validity of *his* strikes is not before us. Nonetheless, the Court treats itself to an extended discussion of the historic exclusion of women not only from jury service, but also from service at the bar (which is rather like jury service, in that it involves going to the courthouse a lot). * * * All this, as I say, is irrelevant, since the case involves state action that allegedly discriminates against men. The parties do not contest that discrimination on the basis of sex [1] is subject to what our cases call "heightened scrutiny," and the citation of one of those cases (preferably one involving men rather than women, see, *e.g., Mississippi Univ. for Women v. Hogan,* * * *) is all that was needed.

The Court also spends time establishing that the use of sex as a proxy for particular views or sympathies is unwise and perhaps irrational. The opinion stresses the lack of statistical evidence to support the widely held belief that, at least in certain types of cases, a juror's sex has some statistically significant predictive value as to how the juror will behave. See *ante,* * * * n. 9. This assertion seems to place the Court in opposition to its earlier Sixth Amendment "fair cross-section" cases. See, *e.g., Taylor v. Louisiana,* 419 U.S. 522, 532, n. 12 (1975) ("Controlled studies * * * have concluded that women bring to juries their own perspectives and values that influence both jury deliberation and result"). But times and trends do change, and unisex is unquestionably in fashion. Personally, I am less inclined to demand statistics, and more inclined to credit the perceptions of experienced litigators who have had money on the line. But it does not matter. The Court's fervent defense of the proposition *il n'y a pas de différence entre les hommes et les femmes* (it stereotypes the opposite view as hateful "stereotyping") turns out to be, like its recounting of the history of sex discrimination against women, utterly irrelevant. Even if sex was a remarkably good predictor in certain cases, the Court would find its use in peremptories unconstitutional. See *ante,* at * n. 11; * * *.

Of course the relationship of sex to partiality *would have been* relevant if the Court had demanded in this case what it ordinarily demands: that the complaining party have suffered some injury. Leaving aside for the moment the reality that the defendant himself had the opportunity to strike women from the jury, the defendant would have some cause to complain about the prosecutor's striking male jurors if male jurors tend to be more favorable towards defendants in paternity suits. But if men and women jurors are (as the Court thinks) fungible, then the only arguable injury from the prosecutor's "impermissible" use of male sex as the basis for his peremptories is injury to the stricken juror, not to the defendant. Indeed, far from having suffered harm, petitioner, a state actor under our precedents, * * * has

---

1. Throughout this opinion, I shall refer to the issue as sex discrimination rather than (as the Court does) gender discrimination. The word "gender" has acquired the new and useful connotation of cultural or attitudinal characteristics (as opposed to physical characteristics) distinctive to the sexes. That is to say, gender is to sex as feminine is to female and masculine to male. The present case does not involve peremptory strikes exercised on the basis of femininity or masculinity (as far as it appears, effeminate men did not survive the prosecution's peremptories). The case involves, therefore, sex discrimination plain and simple.

himself actually *inflicted* harm on female jurors.[2] The Court today presumably supplies petitioner with a cause of action by applying the uniquely expansive third-party standing analysis of *Powers v. Ohio,* 499 U.S. 400, 415 (1991), according petitioner a remedy because of the wrong done to male jurors. This case illustrates why making restitution to Paul when it is Peter who has been robbed is such a bad idea. Not only has petitioner, by implication of the Court's own reasoning, suffered no harm, but the scientific evidence presented at trial established petitioner's paternity with 99.92% accuracy. Insofar as petitioner is concerned, this is a case of harmless error if there ever was one; a retrial will do nothing but divert the State's judicial and prosecutorial resources, allowing either petitioner or some other malefactor to go free.

The core of the Court's reasoning is that peremptory challenges on the basis of any group characteristic subject to heightened scrutiny are inconsistent with the guarantee of the Equal Protection Clause. That conclusion can be reached only by focusing unrealistically upon individual exercises of the peremptory challenge, and ignoring the totality of the practice. Since all groups are subject to the peremptory challenge (and will be made the object of it, depending upon the nature of the particular case) it is hard to see how any group is denied equal protection. * * * That explains why peremptory challenges coexisted with the Equal Protection Clause for 120 years. This case is a perfect example of how the system as a whole is even-handed. While the only claim before the Court is petitioner's complaint that the prosecutor struck male jurors, for every man struck by the government petitioner's own lawyer struck a woman. To say that men were singled out for discriminatory treatment in this process is preposterous. The situation would be different if both sides systematically struck individuals of one group, so that the strikes evinced group-based animus and served as a proxy for segregated venire lists. See *Swain v. Alabama,* 380 U.S. 202, 223–224 (1965). The pattern here, however, displays not a systemic sex-based animus but each side's desire to get a jury favorably disposed to its case. That is why the Court's characterization of respondent's argument as "reminiscent of the arguments advanced to justify the total exclusion of women from juries," * * * is patently false. Women were categorically excluded from juries because of doubt that they were competent; women are stricken from juries by peremptory challenge because of doubt that they are well disposed to the striking party's case. * * * There is discrimination and dishonor in the former, and not in the latter—which explains the 106–year interlude between our holding that exclusion from juries on the basis of race was unconstitutional, *Strauder* * * * and our holding that peremptory challenges on the basis of race were unconstitutional, *Batson* * * *.

2. I continue to agree with Justice O'Connor that *McCollum* and *Edmondson* erred in making civil litigants and criminal defendants state actors for purposes of the Equal Protection Clause. I do not, however, share her belief that correcting that error while continuing to consider the exercise of peremptories by prosecutors a denial of equal protection will make things right. If, in accordance with common perception but contrary to the Court's unisex creed, women really will decide some cases differently from men, allowing defendants alone to strike jurors on the basis of sex will produce—and will be seen to produce—juries intentionally weighted in the defendant's favor: no women jurors, for example, in a rape prosecution. That is not a desirable outcome.

Although the Court's legal reasoning in this case is largely obscured by anti-male-chauvinist oratory, to the extent such reasoning is discernible it invalidates much more than sex-based strikes. After identifying unequal treatment (by separating individual exercises of peremptory challenge from the process as a whole), the Court applies the "heightened scrutiny" mode of equal-protection analysis used for sex-based discrimination, and concludes that the strikes fail heightened scrutiny because they do not substantially further an important government interest. The Court says that the only important government interest that could be served by peremptory strikes is "securing a fair and impartial jury," *ante,* at * * * n. 8.[3] It refuses to accept respondent's argument that these strikes further that interest by eliminating a group (men) which may be partial to male defendants, because it will not accept any argument based on " 'the very stereotype the law condemns.' "

* * * This analysis, entirely eliminating the only allowable argument, implies that sex-based strikes do not even rationally further a legitimate government interest, let alone pass heightened scrutiny. That places *all* peremptory strikes based on *any* group characteristic at risk, since they can all be denominated "stereotypes." Perhaps, however (though I do not see why it should be so), only the stereotyping of groups entitled to heightened or strict scrutiny constitutes "the very stereotype the law condemns"—so that other stereotyping (*e.g.,* wide-eyed blondes and football players are dumb) remains OK. Or perhaps when the Court refers to "impermissible stereotypes," *ante,* at * * * n. 11, it means the adjective to be limiting rather than descriptive—so that we can expect to learn from the Court's peremptory/stereotyping jurisprudence in the future which stereotypes the Constitution frowns upon and which it does not.

Even if the line of our later cases guaranteed by today's decision limits the theoretically boundless *Batson* principle to race, sex, and perhaps other classifications subject to heightened scrutiny (which presumably would include religious belief, see *Larson v. Valente,* 456 U.S. 228, 244–246 (1982)), much damage has been done. It has been done, first and foremost, to the peremptory challenge system, which loses its whole character when (in order to defend against "impermissible stereotyping" claims) "reasons" for strikes must be given. The right of peremptory challenge " 'is, as Blackstone says, an arbitrary and capricious right; and it must be exercised with full freedom, or it fails of its full purpose.' " * * *

The loss of the real peremptory will be felt most keenly by the criminal defendant, * * * whom we have until recently thought "should not be held to accept a juror, apparently indifferent, whom he distrusted for any reason or for no reason." * * * And make no mistake about it: there really is no substitute for the peremptory. Voir dire (though it can be expected to expand as a consequence of today's decision) cannot fill the gap. The biases that go along with group characteristics tend to be biases that the juror himself does not perceive, so that it is no use asking about them. It is fruitless to inquire

3. It does not seem to me that even this premise is correct. Wise observers have long understood that the appearance of justice is as important as its reality. If the system of peremptory strikes affects the actual impartiality of the jury not a bit, but gives litigants a greater belief in that impartiality, it serves a most important function. See, *e.g.,* 4 W. Blackstone, Commentaries * * * In point of fact, that may well be its greater value.

of a male juror whether he harbors any subliminal prejudice in favor of unwed fathers.

And damage has been done, secondarily, to the entire justice system, which will bear the burden of the expanded quest for "reasoned peremptories" that the Court demands. The extension of *Batson* to sex, and almost certainly beyond, * * * will provide the basis for extensive collateral litigation, which especially the criminal defendant (who litigates full-time and cost-free) can be expected to pursue. While demographic reality places some limit on the number of cases in which race-based challenges will be an issue, every case contains a potential sex-based claim. Another consequence, as I have mentioned, is a lengthening of the voir dire process that already burdens trial courts.

The irrationality of today's strike-by-strike approach to equal protection is evident from the consequences of extending it to its logical conclusion. If a fair and impartial trial is a prosecutor's only legitimate goal; if adversarial trial stratagems must be tested against that goal in abstraction from their role within the system as a whole; and if, so tested, sex-based stratagems do not survive heightened scrutiny—then the prosecutor presumably violates the Constitution when he selects a male or female police officer to testify because he believes one or the other sex might be more convincing in the context of the particular case, or because he believes one or the other might be more appealing to a predominantly male or female jury. A decision to stress one line of argument or present certain witnesses before a mostly female jury—for example, to stress that the defendant victimized women—becomes, under the Court's reasoning, intentional discrimination by a state actor on the basis of gender.

* * *

In order, it seems to me, not to eliminate any real denial of equal protection, but simply to pay conspicuous obeisance to the equality of the sexes, the Court imperils a practice that has been considered an essential part of fair jury trial since the dawn of the common law. The Constitution of the United States neither requires nor permits this vandalizing of our people's traditions.

For these reasons, I dissent.

PERSONNEL ADM'R OF MASSACHUSSETS v. FEENEY

Supreme Court of the United States, 1979.
442 U.S. 256, 99 S.Ct. 2282, 60 L.Ed.2d 870.

MR. JUSTICE STEWART delivered the opinion of the Court.

This case presents a challenge to the constitutionality of the Massachusetts veterans' preference statute, Mass.Gen.Laws Ann., ch. 31, § 23, on the ground that it discriminates against women in violation of the Equal Protection Clause of the Fourteenth Amendment. Under ch. 31, § 23, all veterans who qualify for state civil service positions must be considered for appointment ahead of any qualifying nonveterans. The preference operates overwhelmingly to the advantage of males.

* * *

I

A

The Federal Government and virtually all of the States grant some sort of hiring preference to veterans.[6] The Massachusetts preference, which is loosely termed an "absolute lifetime" preference, is among the most generous.[7] It applies to all positions in the State's classified civil service, which constitute approximately 60% of the public jobs in the State. It is available to "any person, male or female, including a nurse," who was honorably discharged from the United States Armed Forces after at least 90 days of active service, at least one day of which was during "wartime." Persons who are deemed veterans and who are otherwise qualified for a particular civil service job may exercise the preference at any time and as many times as they wish.

Civil service positions in Massachusetts fall into two general categories, labor and official. For jobs in the official service, with which the proofs in this action were concerned, the preference mechanics are uncomplicated. All applicants for employment must take competitive examinations. Grades are based on a formula that gives weight both to objective test results and to training and experience. Candidates who pass are then ranked in the order of their respective scores on an "eligible list." Chapter 31, § 23, requires, however, that disabled veterans, veterans, and surviving spouses and surviving parents of veterans be ranked—in the order of their respective scores— above all other candidates.

Rank on the eligible list and availability for employment are the sole factors that determine which candidates are considered for appointment to an official civil service position. When a public agency has a vacancy, it requisitions a list of "certified eligibles" from the state personnel division. Under formulas prescribed by civil service rules, a small number of candidates from the top of an appropriate list, three if there is only one vacancy, are certified. The appointing agency is then required to choose from among these candidates. Although the veterans' preference thus does not guarantee that a veteran will be appointed, it is obvious that the preference gives to veterans who achieve passing scores a well-nigh absolute advantage.

---

6. The first comprehensive federal veterans' statute was enacted in 1944. Veterans' Preference Act of 1944, 58 Stat. 387. The Federal Government has, however, engaged in preferential hiring of veterans, through official policies and various special laws, since the Civil War. See, e.g., Res. of Mar. 3, 1865, No. 27, 13 Stat. 571 (hiring preference for disabled veterans). See generally House Committee on Veterans' Affairs, The Provision of Federal Benefits for Veterans, An Historical Analysis of Major Veterans' Legislation, 1862–1954, 84th Cong., 1st Sess., 258–265 (Comm.Print 1955). For surveys of state veterans' preference laws, many of which also date back to the late 19th century, see State Veterans' Laws, Digests of State Laws Regarding Rights, Benefits, and Privileges of Veterans and Their Dependents, House Committee on Veterans' Affairs, 91st Cong., 1st Sess. (1969); Fleming & Shanor,

Veterans Preferences in Public Employment: Unconstitutional Gender Discrimination?, 26 Emory L.J. 13 (1977).

7. The forms of veterans' hiring preferences vary widely. The Federal Government and approximately 41 States grant veterans a point advantage on civil service examinations, usually 10 points for a disabled veteran and 5 for one who is not disabled. See Fleming & Shanor, supra n. 6, at 17, and n. 12 (citing statutes). A few offer only tie-breaking preferences. Id., at n. 14 (citing statutes). A very few States, like Massachusetts, extend absolute hiring or positional preferences to qualified veterans. Id., at n. 13. See, e.g., N.J.Stat. Ann. § 11:27–4 (West 1976); S.D.Comp.Laws Ann. § 3–3–1 (1974); Utah Code Ann. § 34–30–11 (1953); Wash.Rev.Code §§ 41.04.010, 73.16.010 (1976).

B

The appellee has lived in Dracut, Mass., most of her life. She entered the work force in 1948, and for the next 14 years worked at a variety of jobs in the private sector. She first entered the state civil service system in 1963, having competed successfully for a position as Senior Clerk Stenographer in the Massachusetts Civil Defense Agency. There she worked for four years. In 1967, she was promoted to the position of Federal Funds and Personnel Coordinator in the same agency. The agency, and with it her job, was eliminated in 1975.

During her 12–year tenure as a public employee, Ms. Feeney took and passed a number of open competitive civil service examinations. On several she did quite well, receiving in 1971 the second highest score on an examination for a job with the Board of Dental Examiners, and in 1973 the third highest on a test for an Administrative Assistant position with a mental health center. Her high scores, however, did not win her a place on the certified eligible list. Because of the veterans' preference, she was ranked sixth behind five male veterans on the Dental Examiner list. She was not certified, and a lower scoring veteran was eventually appointed. On the 1973 examination, she was placed in a position on the list behind 12 male veterans, 11 of whom had lower scores. Following the other examinations that she took, her name was similarly ranked below those of veterans who had achieved passing grades.

Ms. Feeney's interest in securing a better job in state government did not wane. Having been consistently eclipsed by veterans, however, she eventually concluded that further competition for civil service positions of interest to veterans would be futile. In 1975, shortly after her civil defense job was abolished, she commenced this litigation.

C

The veterans' hiring preference in Massachusetts, as in other jurisdictions, has traditionally been justified as a measure designed to reward veterans for the sacrifice of military service, to ease the transition from military to civilian life, to encourage patriotic service, and to attract loyal and well-disciplined people to civil service occupations.[12] See, e.g., Hutcheson v. Director of Civil Service, 361 Mass. 480, 281 N.E.2d 53 (1972). The Massachusetts law dates back to 1884, when the State, as part of its first civil service legislation, gave a statutory preference to civil service applicants who were Civil War veterans if their qualifications were equal to those of nonveterans. 1884 Mass.Acts, ch. 320, § 14 (sixth). This tie-breaking provision blossomed into a truly absolute preference in 1895, when the State enacted its first general veterans' preference law and exempted veterans from all merit selection requirements. 1895 Mass.Acts, ch. 501, § 2. In response to a challenge brought by a male nonveteran, this statute was declared violative of

---

12. Veterans' preference laws have been challenged so often that the rationale in their support has become essentially standardized. See, e.g., Koelfgen v. Jackson, 355 F.Supp. 243 (Minn.1972), summarily aff'd, 410 U.S. 976, 93 S.Ct. 1502, 36 L.Ed.2d 173; August v. Bronstein, supra; Rios v. Dillman, 499 F.2d 329 (C.A.5 1974); cf. Mitchell v. Cohen, 333 U.S. 411, 419 n. 12, 68 S.Ct. 518, 522 n. 12, 92 L.Ed. 774. See generally Blumberg, De Facto and De Jure Sex Discrimination Under the Equal Protection Clause: A Reconsideration of the Veterans' Preference in Public Employment, 26 Buffalo L.Rev. 3 (1977). For a collection of early cases, see Annot., Veterans' Preference Laws, 161 A.L.R. 494 (1946).

state constitutional provisions guaranteeing that government should be for the "common good" and prohibiting hereditary titles. Brown v. Russell, 166 Mass. 14, 43 N.E. 1005 (1896).

The current veterans' preference law has its origins in an 1896 statute, enacted to meet the state constitutional standards enunciated in Brown v. Russell. That statute limited the absolute preference to veterans who were otherwise qualified.[13] A closely divided Supreme Judicial Court, in an advisory opinion issued the same year, concluded that the preference embodied in such a statute would be valid. Opinion of the Justices, 166 Mass. 589, 44 N.E. 625 (1896). In 1919, when the preference was extended to cover the veterans of World War I, the formula was further limited to provide for a priority in eligibility, in contrast to an absolute preference in hiring.[14] See Corliss v. Civil Service Comm'rs, 242 Mass. 61, 136 N.E. 356 (1922). In Mayor of Lynn v. Commissioner of Civil Service, 269 Mass. 410, 414, 169 N.E. 502, 503–504 (1929), the Supreme Judicial Court, adhering to the views expressed in its 1896 advisory opinion, sustained this statute against a state constitutional challenge.

Since 1919, the preference has been repeatedly amended to cover persons who served in subsequent wars, declared or undeclared. See 1943 Mass.Acts, ch. 194; 1949 Mass.Acts, ch. 642, § 2 (World War II); 1954 Mass.Acts, ch. 627 (Korea); 1968 Mass.Acts, ch. 531, § 1 (Vietnam).[15] The current preference formula in ch. 31, § 23, is substantially the same as that settled upon in 1919. This absolute preference—even as modified in 1919—has never been universally popular. Over the years it has been subjected to repeated legal challenges, see Hutcheson v. Director of Civil Service, supra (collecting cases), to criticism by civil service reform groups, see, e.g., Report of the Massachusetts Committee on Public Service on Initiative Bill Relative to Veterans' Preference, S. No. 279 (1926); Report of Massachusetts Special Commission on Civil Service and Public Personnel Administration 37–43 (June 15, 1967) (hereinafter 1967 Report), and, in 1926 to a referendum in which it was reaffirmed by a majority of 51.9%. See id., at 38. The present case is apparently the first to challenge the Massachusetts veterans' preference on the simple ground that it discriminates on the basis of sex.[16]

13. 1896 Mass.Acts, ch. 517, § 2. The statute provided that veterans who passed examinations should "be preferred in appointment to all persons not veterans * * *." A proviso stated: "But nothing herein contained shall be construed to prevent the certification and employment of women."

14. 1919 Mass.Acts, ch. 150, § 2. The amended statute provided that "the names of veterans who pass examinations * * * shall be placed upon the * * * eligible lists in the order of their respective standing, above the names of all other applicants," and further provided that "upon receipt of a requisition not especially calling for women, names shall be certified from such lists * * *." The exemption for "women's requisitions" was retained in substantially this form in subsequent revisions, see, e.g., 1954 Mass.Acts, ch. 627, § 5. It was eliminated in 1971, 1971 Mass.Acts, ch. 219, when the State made all single-sex examina-

tions subject to the prior approval of the Massachusetts Commission Against Discrimination, 1971 Mass.Acts, ch. 221.

15. A provision requiring public agencies to hire disabled veterans certified as eligible was added in 1922. 1922 Mass.Acts, ch. 463. It was invalidated as applied in Hutcheson v. Director of Civil Service, 361 Mass. 480, 281 N.E.2d 53 (1972) (suit by veteran arguing that absolute preference for disabled veterans was arbitrary on facts). It has since been eliminated and replaced with a provision giving disabled veterans an absolute preference in retention. See Mass.Gen.Laws Ann., ch. 31, § 26 (West 1979). * * *

16. For cases presenting similar challenges to the veterans' preference laws of other States, see Ballou v. State Department of Civil Service, 75 N.J. 365, 382 A.2d 1118 (1978) (sustaining New Jersey absolute preference);

D

The first Massachusetts veterans' preference statute defined the term "veterans" in gender-neutral language. See 1896 Mass.Acts, ch. 517, § 1 ("a person" who served in the United States Army or Navy), and subsequent amendments have followed this pattern, see, e.g., 1919 Mass.Acts, ch. 150, § 1 ("any person who has served * * * "); 1954 Mass.Acts, ch. 627, § 1 ("any person, male or female, including a nurse"). Women who have served in official United States military units during wartime, then, have always been entitled to the benefit of the preference. In addition, Massachusetts, through a 1943 amendment to the definition of "wartime service", extended the preference to women who served in unofficial auxiliary women's units. 1943 Mass.Acts, ch. 194.

When the first general veterans' preference statute was adopted in 1896, there were no women veterans. The statute however, covered only Civil War veterans. Most of them were beyond middle age, and relatively few were actively competing for public employment. Thus, the impact of the preference upon the employment opportunities of nonveterans as a group and women in particular was slight.

Notwithstanding the apparent attempts by Massachusetts to include as many military women as possible within the scope of the preference, the statute today benefits an overwhelmingly male class. This is attributable in some measure to the variety of federal statutes, regulations, and policies that have restricted the number of women who could enlist in the United States Armed Forces, and largely to the simple fact that women have never been subjected to a military draft. See generally Binkin and Bach 4–21.

When this litigation was commenced, then, over 98% of the veterans in Massachusetts were male; only 1.8% were female. And over one-quarter of the Massachusetts population were veterans. During the decade between 1963 and 1973 when the appellee was actively participating in the State's merit selection system, 47,005 new permanent appointments were made in the classified official service. Forty-three percent of those hired were women, and 57% were men. Of the women appointed, 1.8% were veterans, while 54% of the men had veteran status. A large unspecified percentage of the female appointees were serving in lower paying positions for which males traditionally had not applied.[22] On each of 50 sample eligible lists that are part of the

Feinerman v. Jones, 356 F.Supp. 252 (M.D.Pa. 1973) (sustaining Pennsylvania point preference); Branch v. Du Bois, 418 F.Supp. 1128 (N.D.Ill.1976) (sustaining Illinois modified point preference); Wisconsin Nat. Organization for Women v. Wisconsin, 417 F.Supp. 978 (W.D.Wis.1976) (sustaining Wisconsin point preference).

22. The former exemption for "women's requisitions," see nn. 13, 14, supra, may have operated in the 20th century to protect these types of jobs from the impact of the preference. However, the statutory history indicates that this was not its purpose. The provision dates back to the 1896 veterans' preference law and was retained in the law substantially unchanged until it was eliminated in 1971. See

n. 14, supra. Since veterans in 1896 were a small but an exclusively male class, such a provision was apparently included to ensure that the statute would not be construed to outlaw a pre-existing practice of single-sex hiring explicitly authorized under the 1884 Civil Service statute. See Rule XIX.3, Massachusetts Civil Service Law and Rules and Regulations of the Commissioners (1884) ("In case the request for any * * * certification, or any law or regulation, shall call for persons of one sex, those of that sex shall be certified; otherwise sex shall be disregarded in certification"). The veterans' preference statute at no point endorsed this practice. Historical materials indicate, however, that the early preference law may have operated to encourage the employment of women in positions from which

record in this case, one or more women who would have been certified as eligible for appointment on the basis of test results were displaced by veterans whose test scores were lower.

At the outset of this litigation appellants conceded that for "many of the permanent positions for which males and females have competed" the veterans' preference has "resulted in a substantially greater proportion of female eligibles than male eligibles" not being certified for consideration. The impact of the veterans' preference law upon the public employment opportunities of women has thus been severe. This impact lies at the heart of the appellee's federal constitutional claim.

II

The sole question for decision on this appeal is whether Massachusetts, in granting an absolute lifetime preference to veterans, has discriminated against women in violation of the Equal Protection Clause of the Fourteenth Amendment.

A

The equal protection guarantee of the Fourteenth Amendment does not take from the States all power of classification. * * *

Certain classifications, however, in themselves supply a reason to infer antipathy. Race is the paradigm. A racial classification, regardless of purported motivation, is presumptively invalid and can be upheld only upon an extraordinary justification. * * * This rule applies as well to a classification that is ostensibly neutral but is an obvious pretext for racial discrimination. * * * But, as was made clear in Washington v. Davis, 426 U.S. 229, 96 S.Ct. 2040, 48 L.Ed.2d 597, and Arlington Heights v. Metropolitan Housing Dev. Corp., 429 U.S. 252, 97 S.Ct. 555, 50 L.Ed.2d 450, even if a neutral law has a disproportionately adverse effect upon a racial minority, it is unconstitutional under the Equal Protection Clause only if that impact can be traced to a discriminatory purpose.

Classifications based upon gender, not unlike those based upon race, have traditionally been the touchstone for pervasive and often subtle discrimination. * * * This Court's recent cases teach that such classifications must bear a close and substantial relationship to important governmental objectives, Craig v. Boren, * * * and are in many settings unconstitutional. Reed v. Reed, * * *. Although public employment is not a constitutional right, * * * and the States have wide discretion in framing employee qualifications, * * * these precedents dictate that any state law overtly or covertly designed to prefer males over females in public employment would require an exceedingly persuasive justification to withstand a constitutional challenge under the Equal Protection Clause of the Fourteenth Amendment.

B

The cases of Washington v. Davis, supra, and Arlington Heights v. Metropolitan Housing Dev. Corp., supra, recognize that when a neutral law has a disparate impact upon a group that has historically been the victim of

they previously had been excluded. See Thirteenth Annual Report, supra n. 20, at 5, 6; Third Annual Report, supra n. 19, at 23.

discrimination, an unconstitutional purpose may still be at work. But those cases signaled no departure from the settled rule that the Fourteenth Amendment guarantees equal laws, not equal results. *Davis* upheld a job-related employment test that white people passed in proportionately greater numbers than Negroes, for there had been no showing that racial discrimination entered into the establishment or formulation of the test. *Arlington Heights* upheld a zoning board decision that tended to perpetuate racially segregated housing patterns, since, apart from its effect, the board's decision was shown to be nothing more than an application of a constitutionally neutral zoning policy. Those principles apply with equal force to a case involving alleged gender discrimination.

When a statute gender-neutral on its face is challenged on the ground that its effects upon women are disproportionably [sic] adverse, a twofold inquiry is thus appropriate. The first question is whether the statutory classification is indeed neutral in the sense that it is not gender based. If the classification itself, covert or overt, is not based upon gender, the second question is whether the adverse effect reflects invidious gender-based discrimination. See Arlington Heights v. Metropolitan Housing Dev. Corp., supra. In this second inquiry, impact provides an "important starting point," * * * but purposeful discrimination is "the condition that offends the Constitution." Swann v. Charlotte–Mecklenburg Board of Education, 402 U.S. 1, 16, 91 S.Ct. 1267, 1276, 28 L.Ed.2d 554.

It is against this background of precedent that we consider the merits of the case before us.

III

A

The question whether ch. 31, § 23, establishes a classification that is overtly or covertly based upon gender must first be considered. The appellee has conceded that ch. 31, § 23, is neutral on its face. She has also acknowledged that state hiring preferences for veterans are not *per se* invalid, for she has limited her challenge to the absolute lifetime preference that Massachusetts provides to veterans. The District Court made two central findings that are relevant here: first, that ch. 31, § 23, serves legitimate and worthy purposes; second, that the absolute preference was not established for the purpose of discriminating against women. The appellee has thus acknowledged and the District Court has thus found that the distinction between veterans and nonveterans drawn by ch. 31, § 23, is not a pretext for gender discrimination. The appellee's concession and the District Court's finding are clearly correct.

If the impact of this statute could not be plausibly explained on a neutral ground, impact itself would signal that the real classification made by the law was in fact not neutral. See Washington v. Davis, supra, * * *; Arlington Heights v. Metropolitan Housing Dev. Corp., * * *. But there can be but one answer to the question whether this veteran preference excludes significant numbers of women from preferred state jobs because they are women or because they are nonveterans. Apart from the fact that the definition of "veterans" in the statute has always been neutral as to gender and that Massachusetts has consistently defined veteran status in a way that has been inclusive of women who have served in the military, this is not a law that can plausibly be explained only as a gender-based classification. Indeed, it is not a law that can rationally be explained on that ground. Veteran status is not uniquely male. Although few women benefit from the preference, the nonveteran class is not substantially all female. To the contrary, significant numbers of nonveterans are men, and all nonveterans—male as well as female—are placed at a disadvantage. Too many men are affected by ch. 31, § 23, to permit the inference that the statute is but a pretext for preferring men over women.

Moreover, as the District Court implicitly found, the purposes of the statute provide the surest explanation for its impact. Just as there are cases in which impact alone can unmask an invidious classification, cf. Yick Wo v. Hopkins, * * * there are others, in which—notwithstanding impact—the legitimate noninvidious purposes of a law cannot be missed. This is one. The distinction made by ch. 31, § 23, is, as it seems to be, quite simply between veterans and nonveterans, not between men and women.

B

The dispositive question, then, is whether the appellee has shown that a gender-based discriminatory purpose has, at least in some measure, shaped the Massachusetts veterans' preference legislation. As did the District Court, she points to two basic factors which in her view distinguish ch. 31, § 23, from the neutral rules at issue in the Washington v. Davis and *Arlington Heights* cases. The first is the nature of the preference, which is said to be demonstrably gender-biased in the sense that it favors a status reserved under federal military policy primarily to men. The second concerns the impact of the absolute lifetime preference upon the employment opportunities of women, an impact claimed to be too inevitable to have been unintended. The appellee contends that these factors, coupled with the fact that the preference itself has little if any relevance to actual job performance, more than suffice to prove the discriminatory intent required to establish a constitutional violation.

1

The contention that this veterans' preference is "inherently non-neutral" or "gender-biased" presumes that the State, by favoring veterans, intentionally incorporated into its public employment policies the panoply of sex-based and assertedly discriminatory federal laws that have prevented all but a handful of women from becoming veterans. There are two serious difficulties with this argument. First, it is wholly at odds with the District Court's central finding that Massachusetts has not offered a preference to veterans for the purpose of discriminating against women. Second, it cannot be reconciled with the assumption made by both the appellee and the District Court that a more limited hiring preference for veterans could be sustained. Taken together, these difficulties are fatal.

To the extent that the status of veteran is one that few women have been enabled to achieve, every hiring preference for veterans, however modest or extreme, is inherently gender-biased. If Massachusetts by offering such a preference can be said intentionally to have incorporated into its state employment policies the historical gender-based federal military personnel practices, the degree of the preference would or should make no constitutional difference. Invidious discrimination does not become less so because the discrimination accomplished is of a lesser magnitude.[23] Discriminatory intent is simply not amenable to calibration. It either is a factor that has influenced the legislative choice or it is not. The District Court's conclusion that the absolute veterans' preference was not originally enacted or subsequently reaffirmed for the purpose of giving an advantage to males as such necessarily compels the conclusion that the State intended nothing more than to prefer "veterans." Given this finding, simple logic suggests that an intent to exclude women from significant public jobs was not at work in this law. To reason that it was, by describing the preference as "inherently nonneutral" or "gender-biased," is merely to restate the fact of impact, not to answer the question of intent.

To be sure, this case is unusual in that it involves a law that by design is not neutral. The law overtly prefers veterans as such. As opposed to the written test at issue in *Davis,* it does not purport to define a job-related characteristic. To the contrary, it confers upon a specifically described group—perceived to be particularly deserving—a competitive headstart. But the District Court found, and the appellee has not disputed, that this legislative choice was legitimate. The basic distinction between veterans and nonveterans, having been found not gender-based, and the goals of the preference having been found worthy, ch. 31 must be analyzed as is any other neutral law that casts a greater burden upon women as a group than upon men as a group. The enlistment policies of the Armed Services may well have discriminated on the basis of sex. * * * But the history of discrimination against women in the military is not on trial in this case.

2

The appellee's ultimate argument rests upon the presumption, common to the criminal and civil law, that a person intends the natural and foreseeable consequences of his voluntary actions. Her position was well stated in the concurring opinion in the District Court:

"Conceding * * * that the goal here was to benefit the veteran, there is no reason to absolve the legislature from awareness that the means chosen to achieve this goal would freeze women out of all those state jobs actively sought by men. To be sure, the legislature did not wish to harm women. But the cutting-off of women's opportunities was an inevitable concomitant of the chosen scheme—as inevitable as the proposition that if tails is up, heads must be down. Where a law's consequences are *that* inevitable, can they meaningfully be described as unintended?" 451 F.Supp., at 151.

This rhetorical question implies that a negative answer is obvious, but it is not. The decision to grant a preference to veterans was of course "intentional." So, necessarily, did an adverse impact upon nonveterans follow from that decision. And it cannot seriously be argued that the Legislature of Massachusetts could have been unaware that most veterans are men. It would thus be disingenuous to say that the adverse consequences of this

23. This is not to say that the degree of impact is irrelevant to the question of intent. But it is to say that a more modest preference, while it might well lessen impact and, as the State argues, might lessen the effectiveness of the statute in helping veterans, would not be any more or less "neutral" in the constitutional sense.

legislation for women were unintended, in the sense that they were not volitional or in the sense that they were not foreseeable.

"Discriminatory purpose," however, implies more than intent as volition or intent as awareness of consequences. See United Jewish Organizations v. Carey, 430 U.S. 144, 179, 97 S.Ct. 996, 1016, 51 L.Ed.2d 229 (concurring opinion) [24] It implies that the decisionmaker, in this case a state legislature, selected or reaffirmed a particular course of action at least in part "because of," not merely "in spite of," its adverse effects upon an identifiable group.[25] Yet nothing in the record demonstrates that this preference for veterans was originally devised or subsequently re-enacted because it would accomplish the collateral goal of keeping women in a stereotypic and predefined place in the Massachusetts Civil Service.

To the contrary, the statutory history shows that the benefit of the preference was consistently offered to "any person" who was a veteran. That benefit has been extended to women under a very broad statutory definition of the term veteran. The preference formula itself, which is the focal point of this challenge, was first adopted—so it appears from this record—out of a perceived need to help a small group of older Civil War veterans. It has since been reaffirmed and extended only to cover new veterans.[27] When the totality of legislative actions establishing and extending the Massachusetts veterans' preference are considered, see Washington v. Davis, 426 U.S., at 242, 96 S.Ct., at 2049, the law remains what it purports to be: a preference for veterans of either sex over nonveterans of either sex, not for men over women.

IV

Veterans' hiring preferences represent an awkward—and, many argue, unfair—exception to the widely shared view that merit and merit alone should prevail in the employment policies of government. After a war, such laws have been enacted virtually without opposition. During peacetime, they inevitably have come to be viewed in many quarters as undemocratic and

24. Proof of discriminatory intent must necessarily usually rely on objective factors, several of which were outlined in Arlington Heights v. Metropolitan Housing Dev. Corp., 429 U.S. 252, 266, 97 S.Ct. 555, 564, 50 L.Ed.2d 450. The inquiry is practical. What a legislature or any official entity is "up to" may be plain from the results its actions achieve, or the results they avoid. Often it is made clear from what has been called, in a different context, "the give and take of the situation." Cramer v. United States, 325 U.S. 1, 32–33, 65 S.Ct. 918, 934, 89 L.Ed. 1441 (Jackson, J.).

25. This is not to say that the inevitability or foreseeability of consequences of a neutral rule has no bearing upon the existence of discriminatory intent. Certainly, when the adverse consequences of a law upon an identifiable group are as inevitable as the gender-based consequences of ch. 31, § 23, a strong inference that the adverse effects were desired can reasonably be drawn. But in this inquiry—made as it is under the Constitution—an inference is a working tool, not a synonym for proof. When as here, the impact is essentially

an unavoidable consequence of a legislative policy that has in itself always been deemed to be legitimate, and when, as here, the statutory history and all of the available evidence affirmatively demonstrate the opposite, the inference simply fails to ripen into proof.

27. The appellee has suggested that the former statutory exception for "women's requisitions," see nn. 13, 14, supra, supplies evidence that Massachusetts, when it established and subsequently reaffirmed the absolute-preference legislation, assumed that women would not or should not compete with men. She has further suggested that the former provision extending the preference to certain female dependents of veterans, see n. 10, supra, demonstrates that ch. 31, § 23, is laced with "old notions" about the proper roles and needs of the sexes. See Califano v. Goldfarb, * * * Weinberger v. Wiesenfeld, * * *. But the first suggestion is totally belied by the statutory history, see supra, at 267–271, and nn. 19, 20, and the second fails to account for the consistent statutory recognition of the contribution of women to this Nation's military efforts.

unwise. Absolute and permanent preferences, as the troubled history of this law demonstrates, have always been subject to the objection that they give the veteran more than a square deal. But the Fourteenth Amendment "cannot be made a refuge from ill-advised * * * laws." District of Columbia v. Brooke, 214 U.S. 138, 150, 29 S.Ct. 560, 563, 53 L.Ed. 941. The substantial edge granted to veterans by ch. 31, § 23, may reflect unwise policy. The appellee, however, has simply failed to demonstrate that the law in any way reflects a purpose to discriminate on the basis of sex.

The judgment is reversed, and the case is remanded for further proceedings consistent with this opinion.

It is so ordered.

MR. JUSTICE STEVENS, with whom MR. JUSTICE WHITE joins, concurring.

While I concur in the Court's opinion, I confess that I am not at all sure that there is any difference between the two questions posed ante, at 274. [See p. 101, supra—ed.] If a classification is not overtly based on gender, I am inclined to believe the question whether it is covertly gender based is the same as the question whether its adverse effects reflect invidious gender-based discrimination. However the question is phrased, for me the answer is largely provided by the fact that the number of males disadvantaged by Massachusetts' veterans' preference (1,867,000) is sufficiently large—and sufficiently close to the number of disadvantaged females (2,954,000)—to refute the claim that the rule was intended to benefit males as a class over females as a class.

MR. JUSTICE MARSHALL, with whom MR. JUSTICE BRENNAN joins, dissenting.

Although acknowledging that in some circumstances, discriminatory intent may be inferred from the inevitable or foreseeable impact of a statute, ante, at n. 25, the Court concludes that no such intent has been established here. I cannot agree. In my judgment, Massachusetts' choice of an absolute veterans' preference system evinces purposeful gender-based discrimination. And because the statutory scheme bears no substantial relationship to a legitimate governmental objective, it cannot withstand scrutiny under the Equal Protection Clause.

I

The District Court found that the "prime objective" of the Massachusetts veterans' preference statute, * * * was to benefit individuals with prior military service. * * *. Under the Court's analysis, this factual determination "necessarily compels the conclusion that the State intended nothing more than to prefer 'veterans.' Given this finding, simple logic suggests that an intent to exclude women from significant public jobs was not at work in this law." * * * I find the Court's logic neither simple nor compelling.

That a legislature seeks to advantage one group does not, as a matter of logic or of common sense, exclude the possibility that it also intends to disadvantage another. * * * Thus, the critical constitutional inquiry is not whether an illicit consideration was the primary or but-for cause of a decision, but rather whether it had an appreciable role in shaping a given legislative enactment. Where there is "proof that a discriminatory purpose has been *a* motivating factor in the decision, * * * judicial deference is no longer justified." Arlington Heights v. Metropolitan Housing Dev. Corp., * * *.

Moreover, since reliable evidence of subjective intentions is seldom obtainable, resort to inference based on objective factors is generally unavoidable. * * * To discern the purposes underlying facially neutral policies, this Court has therefore considered the degree, inevitability, and foreseeability of any disproportionate impact as well as the alternatives reasonably available. * * *

In the instant case, the impact of the Massachusetts statute on women is undisputed. Any veteran with a passing grade on the civil service exam must be placed ahead of a nonveteran, regardless of their respective scores. The District Court found that, as a practical matter, this preference supplants test results as the determinant of upper level civil service appointments. * * * Because less than 2% of the women in Massachusetts are veterans, the absolute preference formula has rendered desirable state civil service employment an almost exclusively male prerogative. * * *

As the District Court recognized, this consequence follows foreseeably, indeed inexorably, from the long history of policies severely limiting women's participation in the military. Although neutral in form, the statute is anything but neutral in application. It inescapably reserves a major sector of public employment to "an already established class which, as a matter of historical fact, is 98% male." * * * Where the foreseeable impact of a facially neutral policy is so disproportionate, the burden should rest on the State to establish that sex-based considerations played no part in the choice of the particular legislative scheme. Cf. Castaneda v. Partida, 430 U.S. 482, 97 S.Ct. 1272, 51 L.Ed.2d 498 (1977); Washington v. Davis, 426 U.S. 229, 241, 96 S.Ct. 2040, 2048, 48 L.Ed.2d 597 (1976); Alexander v. Louisiana, 405 U.S. 625, 632, 92 S.Ct. 1221, 1226, 31 L.Ed.2d 536 (1972); see generally Brest, Palmer v. Thompson: An Approach to the Problem of Unconstitutional Legislative Motive, 1971 Sup.Ct.Rev. 95, 123.

Clearly, that burden was not sustained here. The legislative history of the statute reflects the Commonwealth's patent appreciation of the impact the preference system would have on women, and an equally evident desire to mitigate that impact only with respect to certain traditionally female occupations. Until 1971, the statute and implementing civil service regulations exempted from operation of the preference any job requisitions "especially calling for women." * * * In practice, this exemption, coupled with the absolute preference for veterans, has created a gender-based civil service hierarchy, with women occupying low-grade clerical and secretarial jobs and men holding more responsible and remunerative positions. * * *

Thus, for over 70 years, the Commonwealth has maintained, as an integral part of its veterans' preference system, an exemption relegating female civil service applicants to occupations traditionally filled by women. Such a statutory scheme both reflects and perpetuates precisely the kind of archaic assumptions about women's roles which we have previously held invalid. * * * Particularly when viewed against the range of less discriminatory alternatives available to assist veterans,[2] Massachusetts' choice of a

2. Only four States afford a preference comparable in scope to that of Massachusetts. See Fleming & Shanor, Veterans' Preferences and Public Employment: Unconstitutional Gender Discrimination?, 26 Emory L.J. 13, 17 n. 13 (1977) (citing statutes). Other States and the Federal Government grant point or

formula that so severely restricts public employment opportunities for women cannot reasonably be thought gender-neutral. * * * The Court's conclusion to the contrary—that "nothing in the record" evinces a "collateral goal of keeping women in a stereotypic and predefined place in the Massachusetts Civil Service," * * *—displays a singularly myopic view of the facts established below.[3]

II

To survive challenge under the Equal Protection Clause, statutes reflecting gender-based discrimination must be substantially related to the achievement of important governmental objectives. * * * Appellants here advance three interests in support of the absolute preference system: (1) assisting veterans in their readjustment to civilian life; (2) encouraging military enlistment; and (3) rewarding those who have served their country. * * * Although each of those goals is unquestionably legitimate, the "mere recitation of a benign, compensatory purpose" cannot of itself insulate legislative classifications from constitutional scrutiny. * * * And in this case, the Commonwealth has failed to establish a sufficient relationship between its objectives and the means chosen to effectuate them.

With respect to the first interest, facilitating veterans' transition to civilian status, the statute is plainly overinclusive. * * * By conferring a permanent preference, the legislation allows veterans to invoke their advantage repeatedly, without regard to their date of discharge. As the record demonstrates, a substantial majority of those currently enjoying the benefits of the system are not recently discharged veterans in need of readjustment assistance.[4]

Nor is the Commonwealth's second asserted interest, encouraging military service, a plausible justification for this legislative scheme. In its original and subsequent re-enactments, the statute extended benefits retroactively to veterans who had served during a prior specified period. * * * If the Commonwealth's "actual purpose" is to induce enlistment, this legislative design is hardly well suited to that end. * * * For I am unwilling to assume what appellants made no effort to prove, that the possibility of obtaining an *ex post facto* civil service preference significantly influenced the enlistment decisions of Massachusetts residents. Moreover, even if such influence could be presumed, the statute is still grossly overinclusive in that it bestows benefits on men drafted as well as those who volunteered.

Finally, the Commonwealth's third interest, rewarding veterans, does not "adequately justify the salient features" of this preference system. * * * Where a particular statutory scheme visits substantial hardship on a class long subject to discrimination, the legislation cannot be sustained unless

tie-breaking preferences that do not foreclose opportunities for women. * * *

3. Although it is relevant that the preference statute also disadvantages a substantial group of men, see ante, * * * (Stevens, J., concurring), it is equally pertinent that 47% of Massachusetts men over 18 are veterans, as compared to 0.8% of Massachusetts women. * * * Given this disparity, and the indicia of intent noted supra, * * * the absolute number of men denied preference cannot be dispositive, especially since they have not faced the barriers to achieving veteran status confronted by women. * * *

4. The eligibility lists for the positions Ms. Feeney sought included 95 veterans for whom discharge information was available. Of those 95 males, 64 (67%) were discharged prior to 1960. * * *

" 'carefully tuned to alternative considerations.' " Trimble v. Gordon, * * *. Here, there are a wide variety of less discriminatory means by which Massachusetts could effect its compensatory purposes. For example, a point preference system, such as that maintained by many States and the Federal Government, see n. 2, supra, or an absolute preference for a limited duration, would reward veterans without excluding all qualified women from upper level civil service positions. Apart from public employment, the Commonwealth can, and does, afford assistance to veterans in various ways, including tax abatements, educational subsidies, and special programs for needy veterans. * * * Unlike these and similar benefits, the costs of which are distributed across the taxpaying public generally, the Massachusetts statute exacts a substantial price from a discrete group of individuals who have long been subject to employment discrimination, and who, "because of circumstances totally beyond their control, have [had] little if any chance of becoming members of the preferred class." * * *

In its present unqualified form, the veterans' preference statute precludes all but a small fraction of Massachusetts women from obtaining any civil service position also of interest to men. * * * Given the range of alternatives available, this degree of preference is not constitutionally permissible.

I would affirm the judgment of the court below.

Notes on J.E.B. and Feeney

1. Which sex was subjected to intentional discrimination in *J.E.B.?* Does the majority ever answer Justice Scalia's charge that its discussion of the historic exclusion of women from jury service is irrelevant to the matter at hand? Why should state action striking male jurors from service receive heightened scrutiny?

2. Do you share Justice O'Connor's "hope" that a female defendant charged with harming her male batterer could constitutionally avail herself of peremptory challenges to eliminate men from her jury? Is O'Connor indulging in stereotypical thinking by assuming that a female juror would be more likely to acquit?

3. If Justice Scalia's prediction is correct that other groups will come forward in the wake of *J.E.B.* to challenge the use of peremptory strikes to eliminate their members, does that mean that the practice has become a cloak for prejudice rather than an avenue for sound prosecutorial instinct? If so, why shouldn't the peremptory challenge simply be eliminated? Otherwise, won't trials have to be extended to receive proof of neutral "reasons" for dismissing jurors? Compare Christy Chandler, Race, Gender and the Peremptory Challenge: A Postmodern Feminist Approach, 7 Yale J.L. & Fem. 173 (1995) with Nancy S. Marder, Beyond Gender: Peremptory Challenges and the Roles of the Jury, 73 Tex.L.Rev. 1041 (1995).

4. Unlike those considered so far, the statutory classification at issue in *Feeney* was not expressly phrased in terms of sex. The benefits of the Massachusetts law were extended to "any person, male or female, including a nurse" who met specified requirements, including honorable discharge and length and condition of service. Why, then, did Helen Feeney claim that the statute discriminated against her because she was a woman, rather than because she was a nonveteran? Did she hope thereby to gain a stricter standard of constitutional review than the "rational relationship" test otherwise applicable? Recall that, although Craig v. Boren, p. 41, supra, had not been decided when the initial decision of the

three-judge court in *Feeney* was handed down on March 29, 1976, predictions that the Court was using a heightened standard in gender discrimination cases had been in the air since the *Reed* decision in 1971. Or was it simply that, since earlier challenges by non-veterans to the veterans' preference laws had been largely unsuccessful, see Justice Stewart's opinion at note 12, p. 96, supra, the women non-veterans in *Feeney* had chosen to try a new approach? Following her defeat at the hands of the Supreme Court, Feeney did attempt to raise the argument that the statute constituted a denial of due process to all non-veterans, men as well as women. A majority of the three-judge court refused to entertain this argument, treating it as a "newly-tendered" legal theory. Feeney v. Commonwealth of Massachusetts, 475 F.Supp. 109, 111 (D.Mass.1979), affirmed mem. 445 U.S. 901, 100 S.Ct. 1075, 63 L.Ed.2d 317 (1980). Had Feeney been allowed to raise this new argument, would it have been successful?

5. As Justice Stewart notes, at least since its 1976 decision in Washington v. Davis, infra, the Court has held that a classification that is facially neutral with respect to a group normally protected by a heightened standard of review does not violate the Equal Protection Clause even if it has a disproportionately adverse effect upon that group, unless the "impact can be traced to a discriminatory purpose". Washington v. Davis involved a classification that disadvantaged blacks. In *Feeney,* the Court made clear that the same discriminatory purpose requirement applies to a neutral statute that disadvantages women. Presumably, had a discriminatory purpose been shown either in Washington v. Davis or *Feeney,* the result would have been use of the relevant higher standard of review: strict scrutiny in race cases, intermediate scrutiny in sex cases. Since practically no cases survive strict scrutiny and few (except those viewed as "benign" classifications) survive even the intermediate level of review, the requirement of discriminatory purpose has been characterized as a way of permitting more leeway to the legislative branch in cases where its classification is facially neutral than would otherwise be the case. See Bruce E. Rosenblum, Note, Discriminatory Purpose and Disproportionate Impact: An Assessment After *Feeney,* 79 Colum.L.Rev. 1376, 1382–85 (1979).

6. Do you agree with the majority that no discriminatory purpose was present in *Feeney?* Professor Blumberg has argued that the veterans' preference laws must be viewed in light of the deliberate exclusion of women from military service, thus preventing them from achieving veterans' status. She goes further:

> It should not be deemed significant that some parts of the armed forces may be starting to abandon their discriminatory policies. The effect of prior de jure discrimination on the operation of the preference will persist until all those women denied equal armed services opportunity have departed from the labor force.

Grace Blumberg, De Facto and De Jure Sex Discrimination Under the Equal Protection Clause: A Reconsideration of the Veterans' Preference in Public Employment, 26 Buff.L.Rev. 3, 47 (1977). Was this argument accepted by Justices Marshall and Brennan? Why does the majority refuse to give it serious consideration?

Attacking the view that the relevant comparison for equal protection purposes is between veterans and female non-veterans, one commentator offers the following analogy:

> If a person with flat feet were to challenge a state's veterans' preference statute, it would not be appropriate to compare the "non-veteran" subclassification of "flat-footed people" with the major classification of "veterans."

Clearly, it would be incorrect to do so since the subclassification of "flat-footed people" does not include all persons similarly situated with respect to the purpose of the law. So, just as flat-footed people must be considered as part of the larger class of non-veterans, so must women. Actually, since there are no flat-footed veterans, the argument on behalf of flat-footed people would be even stronger than that for women, because the "veteran" class would include some females but would not include any individuals with flat feet. Thus, the systematic exclusion argument is not sufficient to raise an inference of discriminatory intent: the veterans' preference classification is not a mere pretext for "invidious" sex discrimination.

Pat Labbadia III, Comment, The Veterans' Preference Statutes: Do They Really Discriminate Against Women? 18 Duq.L.Rev. 653, 674 (1980). Does this nail it down? Persons with flat feet were rejected by the Army only if their conditions were pathological: either pronounced or spastic, according to Army Regulation 40–501. Such persons obviously suffered from a disabling condition related to military duties. What disabilities are inherent in the condition of being female that are related to military service? Is it relevant that flat-footed persons are not otherwise subject to societal discrimination because of that characteristic? Blumberg suggests that, regardless of the military's justifications for limiting the number of women allowed to serve, these attitudes should not be "permitted to spill over into the civil sector, as it does in the case of the veterans' preference." (Blumberg, id., at 51). Does that mean that a state legislature, wishing to compensate veterans, cannot do so if the federal government, which controls matters of national defense, has purposefully excluded certain protected groups?

7. Rejecting arguments based on analogies to tort law—that the Massachusetts Legislature must be held to have intended the necessary and foreseeable consequences of its preferential treatment of veterans—Justice Stewart defined "discriminatory purpose" as implying "that the decisionmaker, * * * selected or reaffirmed a particular course of action at least in part 'because of,' not merely 'in spite of,' its adverse effects upon an identifiable group." See p. 78, supra. The Court reaffirmed *Feeney* on this point in McCleskey v. Kemp, 481 U.S. 279, 107 S.Ct. 1756, 95 L.Ed.2d 262 reh'g denied, 482 U.S. 920, 107 S.Ct. 3199, 96 L.Ed.2d 686 (1987), in which it rejected McCleskey's argument that Georgia had denied him the equal protection of the laws by allowing its capital punishment statute to remain in force despite his statistical demonstration that black defendants charged with killing white victims were 4.3 times as likely to be sentenced to death as defendants charged with killing blacks. After citing *Feeney,* Justice Powell said for the Court, "[f]or this claim to prevail, McCleskey would have to prove that the Georgia Legislature enacted or maintained the death penalty statute *because of* an anticipated racially discriminatory effect." Id., 481 U.S. at 298, 107 S.Ct. at 1769, 95 L.Ed.2d at 282 (emphasis in original). What kind of proof does this standard require? A notewriter, while approving the Court's "refusal to equate foreseeability with intent" in *Feeney,* is critical of Stewart's formulation if it requires proof of "a very particular kind of gender-based motivation—animus, or desire to harm." See Note, supra Note 2, 79 Colum.L.Rev. at 1392, 1397. Such a holding, it is suggested, is inconsistent with prior cases finding gender discrimination to be "invidious" when it stems, not from malice, but from archaic generalizations about women's place in society: "Such discrimination is likely to be a product not of animus toward women but of a genuine, if misplaced, solicitude." (Id., at 1398.) What, then, would be a sufficient showing of discriminatory purpose? The notewriter concludes:

The gender cases suggest that to demonstrate discriminatory purpose it would be sufficient to show that the framing of a disputed policy was premised on archaic and outmoded notions about women; for example, that it is not important for women to find employment, or that it is not essential for women to go to college. Even proof of *indifference* to the fate of women might be considered relevant if it reflects stereotypic thinking about "women's place." Although it seems reasonable under this analysis to require that plaintiffs demonstrate that a law would not have been enacted *but for* this kind of stereotypic thinking, it goes too far to suggest that plaintiffs must show that the law would not have been enacted but for legislative desire to achieve harmful effects.

Id., at 1398. But the previous gender cases have all involved express classifications using sex as the distinguishing factor. Are they susceptible to being used as the foundation for a critical appraisal of the Court's definition of discriminatory purpose in a case where the statute is neutral toward the disadvantaged group? It may not be enough to show that the Massachusetts Legislature was indifferent to the impact of its preference for veterans upon women; it may first be necessary to show that the Legislature had women in mind at all. Does *McCleskey* bear out this interpretation? The Court held in Hunter v. Underwood, 471 U.S. 222, 228, 105 S.Ct. 1916, 1920, 85 L.Ed.2d 222, 228 (1985), however, that "[o]nce racial discrimination is shown to have been a 'substantial' or 'motivating factor' behind enactment of the law, the burden shifts to the law's defenders to demonstrate that the law would have been enacted without this factor." *Hunter* invalidated a provision of the Alabama Constitution of 1901 which disenfranchised persons convicted of a "crime involving moral turpitude," a law found to disenfranchise approximately ten times as many black voters as whites within two years of its operative date and 1.7 times as many even in modern times. Would the *Hunter* test have made Helen Feeney's task any easier?

8.   While *Feeney* was pending, the Massachusetts Legislature substituted an "interim" point system for the absolute preference favoring veterans. After the decision became final, the absolute preference went back into effect. See Mass. Gen.Laws Ann. ch. 31, § 26 (West, 1980). Helen Feeney thereupon challenged the revived preference under the Massachusetts state Equal Rights Amendment, which provides that "[e]quality under the law shall not be denied or abridged because of sex, race, color, creed or national origin." Mass. Const., pt. 1, art. I. See Feeney v. Commonwealth of Massachusetts, Supreme Judicial Court No. 80–206 (May 21, 1980). Will this attack fare better than that based on the Equal Protection Clause of the Federal Constitution? Even under the state provision, the plaintiff is required to prove that the classification is based on "sex", isn't she? Is that hurdle any different from the one she faced in federal court?

9. See also Commonwealth of Pennsylvania v. Flaherty, 983 F.2d 1267 (3d Cir.1993), refusing to infer sex discrimination despite the unrefuted finding that the City of Pittsburg's use of add-on veterans' preference points disadvantaged women in being hired as police officers because *Feeney* meant that the practice was constitutional. Is this a correct interpretation of *Feeney* ?

ROSTKER v. GOLDBERG

Supreme Court of the United States, 1981.
453 U.S. 57, 101 S.Ct. 2646, 69 L.Ed.2d 478.

JUSTICE REHNQUIST delivered the opinion of the Court.

The question presented is whether the Military Selective Service Act, 50 U.S.C.App. § 451 et seq. (1976 ed. and Supp. III), violates the Fifth Amendment to the United States Constitution in authorizing the President to require the registration of males and not females.

* * *

II

Whenever called upon to judge the constitutionality of an Act of Congress—"the gravest and most delicate duty that this Court is called upon to perform," Blodgett v. Holden, 275 U.S. 142, 148, 48 S.Ct. 105, 107, 72 L.Ed. 206 (1927) (Holmes, J.)—the Court accords "great weight to the decisions of Congress." * * * The customary deference accorded the judgments of Congress is certainly appropriate when, as here, Congress specifically considered the question of the Act's constitutionality. * * *

This is not, however, merely a case involving the customary deference accorded congressional decisions. The case arises in the context of Congress' authority over national defense and military affairs, and perhaps in no other area has the Court accorded Congress greater deference. * * *

Not only is the scope of Congress' constitutional power in this area broad, but the lack of competence on the part of the courts is marked. * * *

The operation of a healthy deference to legislative and executive judgments in the area of military affairs is evident in several recent decisions of this Court. * * *

In Schlesinger v. Ballard, 419 U.S. 498, 95 S.Ct. 572, 42 L.Ed.2d 610 (1975), the Court considered a due process challenge, brought by males, to the navy policy of according females a longer period than males in which to attain promotions necessary to continued service. The Court distinguished previous gender-based discriminations held unlawful in Reed v. Reed, * * * and Frontiero v. Richardson, * * *. In those cases, the classifications were based on "overbroad generalizations." * * * In the case before it, however, the Court noted:

> "the different treatment of men and women naval officers * * * reflects, not archaic and overbroad generalizations, but, instead, the demonstrable fact that male and female line officers in the Navy are not similarly situated with respect to opportunities for professional service. Appellee has not challenged the current restrictions on women officers' participation in combat and in most sea duty." * * *

In light of the combat restrictions, women did not have the same opportunities for promotion as men, and therefore it was not unconstitutional for Congress to distinguish between them.

None of this is to say that Congress is free to disregard the Constitution when it acts in the area of military affairs. In that area as any other Congress remains subject to the limitations of the Due Process Clause, * * * but the tests and limitations to be applied may differ because of the military context. We of course do not abdicate our ultimate responsibility to decide the constitutional question, but simply recognize that the Constitution itself requires such deference to congressional choice. * * * In deciding the question before us we must be particularly careful not to substitute our judgment of what is desirable for that of Congress, or our own evaluation of evidence for a reasonable evaluation by the Legislative Branch.

The District Court purported to recognize the appropriateness of deference to Congress when that body was exercising its constitutionally delegated authority over military affairs, * * * but it stressed that "[w]e are not here concerned with military operations or day-to-day conduct of the military into which we have no desire to intrude." * * * Appellees also stress that this case involves civilians, not the military, and that "the impact of registration on the military is only indirect and attenuated." * * * We find these efforts to divorce registration from the military and national defense context, with all the deference called for in that context, singularly unpersuasive. * * * Registration is not an end in itself in the civilian world but rather the first step in the induction process into the military one, and Congress specifically linked its consideration of registration to induction, * * * Congressional judgments concerning registration and the draft are based on judgments concerning military operations and needs, see, e.g., id., at 157, U.S.Code Cong. & Admin.News 1980, 2647 ("the starting point for any discussion of the appropriateness of registering women for the draft is the question of the proper role of women in combat"), and the deference unquestionably due the latter judgments is necessarily required in assessing the former as well. Although the District Court stressed that it was not intruding on military questions, its opinion was based on assessments of military need and flexibility in a time of mobilization. * * * It would be blinking reality to say that our precedents requiring deference to Congress in military affairs are not implicated by the present case.

The Solicitor General argues, largely on the basis of the foregoing cases emphasizing the deference due Congress in the area of military affairs and national security, that this Court should scrutinize the MSSA only to determine if the distinction drawn between men and women bears a rational relation to some legitimate government purpose, see United States Railroad Retirement Board v. Fritz, 449 U.S. 166, 101 S.Ct. 453, 66 L.Ed.2d 368 (1980), and should not examine the Act under the heightened scrutiny with which we have approached gender-based discrimination, see Michael M. v. Superior Court of Sonoma County, 450 U.S. 464, 101 S.Ct. 1200, 67 L.Ed.2d 437 (1981); Craig v. Boren, supra; Reed v. Reed, supra.[7] We do not think that the substantive guarantee of due process or certainty in the law will be advanced by any further "refinement" in the applicable tests as suggested by the Government. Announced degrees of "deference" to legislative judgments, just as levels of "scrutiny" which this Court announces that it applies to particular classifications made by a legislative body, may all too readily become facile abstractions used to justify a result. In this case the courts are called upon to decide whether Congress, acting under an explicit constitutional grant of authority, has by that action transgressed an explicit guarantee of individual rights which limits the authority so conferred. Simply labelling the legislative decision "military" on the one hand or "gender-based" on the other does not automatically guide a court to the correct constitutional result.

No one could deny that under the test of Craig v. Boren, supra, the Government's interest in raising and supporting armies is an "important

---

7. It is clear that "[g]ender has never been rejected as an impermissible classification in all instances." Kahn v. Shevin, 416 U.S. 351, 356, n. 10, 94 S.Ct. 1734, 1737–1738, n. 10, 40 L.Ed.2d 189 (1974). In making this observation the Court noted that "Congress has not so far drafted women into the Armed Services, 50 U.S.C.App. § 454." Ibid.

governmental interest." Congress and its committees carefully considered and debated two alternative means of furthering that interest: the first was to register only males for potential conscription, and the other was to register both sexes. Congress chose the former alternative. When that decision is challenged on equal protection grounds, the question a court must decide is not which alternative it would have chosen, had it been the primary decision-maker, but whether that chosen by Congress denies equal protection of the laws.

Nor can it be denied that the imposing number of cases from this Court previously cited suggest that judicial deference to such congressional exercise of authority is at its apogee when legislative action under the congressional authority to raise and support armies and make rules and regulations for their governance is challenged. * * *

* * *

Schlesinger v. Ballard did not purport to apply a different equal protection test because of the military context, but did stress the deference due congressional choices among alternatives in exercising the congressional authority to raise and support armies and make rules for their governance. In light of the floor debate and the report of the Senate Armed Services Committee hereinafter discussed, it is apparent that Congress was fully aware not merely of the many facts and figures presented to it by witnesses who testified before its committees, but of the current thinking as to the place of women in the Armed Services. In such a case, we cannot ignore Congress' broad authority conferred by the Constitution to raise and support armies when we are urged to declare unconstitutional its studied choice of one alternative in preference to another for furthering that goal.

III

This case is quite different from several of the gender-based discrimination cases we have considered in that, despite appellees' assertions, Congress did not act "unthinkingly" or "reflexively and not for any considered reason." Brief for Appellees 35. The question of registering women for the draft not only received considerable national attention and was the subject of wide-ranging public debate, but also was extensively considered by Congress in hearings, floor debate, and in committee. Hearings held by both Houses of Congress in response to the President's request for authorization to register women adduced extensive testimony and evidence concerning the issue. * * *

* * *

The foregoing clearly establishes that the decision to exempt women from registration was not the "accidental by-product of a traditional way of thinking about women." * * * The issue was considered at great length, and Congress clearly expressed its purpose and intent. Contrast Califano v. Westcott, 443 U.S. 76, 87, 99 S.Ct. 2655, 2662, 61 L.Ed.2d 382 (1979) ("The gender qualification * * * escaped virtually unnoticed in the hearings and floor debate").[11]

---

11. Nor can we agree with the characterization of the MSSA in the Brief for National   Organization for Women as Amicus Curiae as a law which "coerce[s] or preclude[s] women as a

For the same reasons we reject appellees' argument that we must consider the constitutionality of the MSSA solely on the basis of the views expressed by Congress in 1948, when the MSSA was first enacted in its modern form.   Contrary to the suggestions of appellees and various *amici,* reliance on the legislative history of Joint Resolution 521 and the activity of the various committees of the 96th Congress considering the registration of women does not violate sound principles that appropriations legislation should not be considered as modifying substantive legislation.   Congress did not change the MSSA in 1980, but it did thoroughly reconsider the question of exempting women from its provisions, and its basis for doing so.   The 1980 legislative history is, therefore, highly relevant in assessing the constitutional validity of the exemption.

The MSSA established a plan for maintaining "adequate armed strength * * * to ensure the security of [the] nation."   * * * Registration is the first step "in a united and continuous process designed to raise an army speedily and efficiently," Falbo v. United States, 320 U.S. 549, 553, 64 S.Ct. 346, 348, 88 L.Ed. 305 (1944), * * * and Congress provided for the reactivation of registration in order to "provid[e] the means for the early delivery of inductees in an emergency."   * * *   Although the three-judge District Court often tried to sever its consideration of registration from the particulars of induction, * * * Congress rather clearly linked the need for renewed registration with its views on the character of a subsequent draft.   The Senate Report specifically found that "[a]n ability to mobilize rapidly is essential to the preservation of our national security.   A functioning registration system is a vital part of any mobilization plan."   * * * Such an approach is certainly logical, since under the MSSA induction is interlocked with registration: only those registered may be drafted, and registration serves no purpose beyond providing a pool for the draft.   Any assessment of the congressional purpose and its chosen means must therefore consider the registration scheme as a prelude to a draft in a time of national emergency.   Any other approach would not be testing the Act in light of the purposes Congress sought to achieve.

Congress determined that any future draft, which would be facilitated by the registration scheme, would be characterized by a need for combat troops. * * * Congress' determination that the need would be for combat troops if a draft took place was sufficiently supported by testimony adduced at the hearings so that the courts are not free to make their own judgment on the question.   * * * The purpose of registration, therefore, was to prepare for a draft *of combat troops.*

Women as a group, however, unlike men as a group, are not eligible for combat.   The restrictions on the participation of women in combat in the Navy and Air Force are statutory.   Under 10 U.S.C. § 6015 "women may not be assigned to duty on vessels or in aircraft that are engaged in combat missions," and under 10 U.S.C. § 8549 female members of the Air Force "may not be assigned to duty in aircraft engaged in combat missions."   The Army and Marine Corps preclude the use of women in combat as a matter of established policy.   * * * Congress specifically recognized and endorsed the

class from performing tasks or jobs of which they are capable," or the suggestion that this case involves "[t]he exclusion of women from the military."   * * * Nothing in the MSSA restricts in any way the opportunities for women to volunteer for military service.

exclusion of women from combat in exempting women from registration. In the words of the Senate Report:

> "The principle that women should not intentionally and routinely engage in combat is fundamental, and enjoys wide support among our people. It is universally supported by military leaders who have testified before the Committee. * * * Current law and policy exclude women from being assigned to combat in our military forces, and the Committee reaffirms this policy." S.Rep. No. 96–826, supra, at 157, U.S.Code Cong. & Admin.News 1980, 2641.

The Senate Report specifically found that "Women should not be intentionally or routinely placed in combat positions in our military services." * * * [12] The President expressed his intent to continue the current military policy precluding women from combat, * * * and appellees present their argument concerning registration against the background of such restrictions on the use of women in combat.[13] Consistent with the approach of this Court in Schlesinger v. Ballard, supra, we must examine appellees' constitutional claim concerning registration with these combat restrictions firmly in mind.

The existence of the combat restrictions clearly indicates the basis for Congress' decision to exempt women from registration. The purpose of registration was to prepare for a draft of combat troops. Since women are excluded from combat, Congress concluded that they would not be needed in the event of a draft, and therefore decided not to register them. Again turning to the Senate Report:

> "In the Committee's view, the starting point for any discussion of the appropriateness of registering women for the draft is the question of the proper role of women in combat. * * * The policy precluding the use of women in combat is, in the Committee's view, the most important reason for not including women in a registration system." * * * [14]

The District Court stressed that the military need for women was irrelevant to the issue of their registration. As that court put it: "Congress could not constitutionally require registration under MSSA of only black citizens or only white citizens, or single out any political or religious group simply because those groups contained sufficient persons to fill the needs of the Selective Service System." * * * This reasoning is beside the point. The reason women are exempt from registration is not because military needs can be met by drafting men. This is not a case of Congress arbitrarily choosing to burden one of two similarly situated groups, such as would be the case with an all-black or all-white, or an all-Catholic or all-Lutheran, or an all-Republican or all-Democratic registration. Men and women, because of the combat

12. No major country has women in combat jobs in their standing army. See J.A. 143.

13. See Brief for Appellees 1–2, n. 2 (denying any concession of the validity of combat restrictions, but submitting restrictions are irrelevant to the present case). * * *

14. Justice Marshall's suggestion that since Congress focused on the need for combat troops in authorizing male-only registration the Court could "be forced to declare the male-only registration program unconstitutional,"

* * * in the event of a peace-time draft misreads our opinion. The perceived need for combat or combat-eligible troops in the event of a draft was not limited to a wartime draft. See, e.g., S.Rep. No. 96–826, * * * (considering problems associated with "[r]egistering women for assignment to combat *or assigning women to combat positions in peace-time*.") (emphasis supplied); * * * (need for rotation between combat and non-combat positions "[i]n peace and war").

restrictions on women, are simply not similarly situated for purposes of a draft or registration for a draft.

Congress' decision to authorize the registration of only men, therefore, does not violate the Due Process Clause. The exemption of women from registration is not only sufficiently but closely related to Congress' purpose in authorizing registration. See *Michael M.,* 450 U.S., at 472–473, 101 S.Ct., at 1204 (plurality opinion); Craig v. Boren, * * *; Reed v. Reed, * * *. The fact that Congress and the Executive have decided that women should not serve in combat fully justifies Congress in not authorizing their registration, since the purpose of registration is to develop a pool of potential combat troops. As was the case in Schlesinger v. Ballard, supra, "the gender classification is not invidious, but rather realistically reflects the fact that the sexes are not similarly situated" in this case. * * * The Constitution requires that Congress treat similarly situated persons similarly, not that it engage in gestures of superficial equality.

In holding the MSSA constitutionally invalid the District Court relied heavily on the President's decision to seek authority to register women and the testimony of members of the Executive Branch and the military in support of that decision. * * * As stated by the Administration's witnesses before Congress, however, the President's "decision to ask for authority to register women is based on equity." * * * The Senate Report, evaluating the testimony before the Committee, recognized that "the argument for registration and induction of women * * * is not based on military necessity, but on considerations of equity." * * * Congress was certainly entitled, in the exercise of its constitutional powers to raise and regulate armies and navies, to focus on the question of military need rather than "equity." [15] * * * See also House Hearings 20 (Rep. Holt) ("You are talking about equity. I am talking about military.").[16]

Although the military experts who testified in favor of registering women uniformly opposed the actual drafting of women, * * * there was testimony that in the event of a draft of 650,000 the military could absorb some 80,000 female inductees. * * * The 80,000 would be used to fill noncombat positions, freeing men to go to the front. In relying on this testimony in striking down the MSSA, the District Court palpably exceeded its authority when it ignored Congress' considered response to this line of reasoning.

In the first place, assuming that a small number of women could be drafted for noncombat roles, Congress simply did not consider it worth the added burdens of including women in draft and registration plans. "It has been suggested that all women be registered, but only a handful actually be

15. The grant of constitutional authority is, after all, to Congress and not to the Executive or military officials.

16. The District Court also focused on what it termed Congress' "inconsistent positions" in encouraging women to volunteer for military service and expanding their opportunities in the service, on the one hand, and exempting them from registration and the draft on the other. * * * This reasoning fails to appreciate the different purposes served by encouraging women volunteers and registration for the draft. Women volunteers do not occupy com- bat positions, so encouraging women to volunteer is not related to concerns about the availability of combat troops. In the event of a draft, however, the need would be for combat troops or troops which could be rotated into combat. * * * Congress' positions are clearly not inconsistent and in treating them as such the District Court failed to understand Congress' purpose behind registration as distinguished from its purpose in encouraging women volunteers.

inducted in an emergency. The Committee finds this a confused and ultimately unsatisfactory solution." * * * As the Senate Committee recognized a
year before, "training would be needlessly burdened by women recruits who
could not be used in combat." * * * ("Other administrative problems such
as housing and different treatment with regard to dependency, hardship and
physical standards would also exist."). It is not for this Court to dismiss such
problems as insignificant in the context of military preparedness and the
exigencies of a future mobilization.

Congress also concluded that whatever the need for women for noncombat roles during mobilization, whether 80,000 or less, it could be met by
volunteers. * * *

Most significantly, Congress determined that staffing non-combat positions with women during a mobilization would be positively detrimental to
the important goal of military flexibility.

"   * * * [T]here are other military reasons that preclude very large
numbers of women from serving. Military flexibility requires that a
commander be able to move units or ships quickly. Units or ships not
located at the front or not previously scheduled for the front nevertheless
must be able to move into action if necessary. In peace and war,
significant rotation of personnel is necessary. We should not divide the
military into two groups—one in permanent combat and one in permanent support. Large numbers of non-combat positions must be available
to which combat troops can return for duty before being redeployed."
S.Rep. No. 96–826, supra, at 158, U.S.Code Cong. & Admin.News 1980,
2648.

* * * In sum, Congress carefully evaluated the testimony that 80,000 women
conscripts could be usefully employed in the event of a draft and rejected it in
the permissible exercise of its constitutional responsibility. * * * The District Court was quite wrong in undertaking an independent evaluation of this
evidence, rather than adopting an appropriately deferential examination of
Congress' evaluation of that evidence.

In light of the foregoing, we conclude that Congress acted well within its
constitutional authority when it authorized the registration of men, and not
women, under the Military Selective Service Act. The decision of the District
Court holding otherwise is accordingly reversed.

JUSTICE WHITE, with whom JUSTICE BRENNAN joins, dissenting.

I assume what has not been challenged in this case—that excluding
women from combat positions does not offend the Constitution. Granting
that, it is self evident that if during mobilization for war, all noncombat
military positions must be filled by combat-qualified personnel available to be
moved into combat positions, there would be no occasion whatsoever to have
any women in the Army, whether as volunteers or inductees. The Court
appears to say, * * * that Congress concluded as much and that we should
accept that judgment even though the serious view of the Executive Branch,
including the responsible military services, is to the contrary. The Court's
position in this regard is most unpersuasive. I perceive little, if any, indication that Congress itself concluded that every position in the military, no
matter how far removed from combat, must be filled with combat-ready men.

Common sense and experience in recent wars, where women volunteers were employed in substantial numbers, belie this view of reality. It should not be ascribed to Congress, particularly in the face of the testimony of military authorities, hereafter referred to, that there would be a substantial number of positions in the services that could be filled by women both in peacetime and during mobilization, even though they are ineligible for combat.

I would also have little difficulty agreeing to a reversal if all the women who could serve in wartime without adversely affecting combat readiness could predictably be obtained through volunteers. In that event, the equal protection component of the Fifth Amendment would not require the United States to go through, and a large segment of the population to be burdened with, the expensive and essentially useless procedure of registering women. But again I cannot agree with the Court, * * * that Congress concluded or that the legislative record indicates that each of the services could rely on women volunteers to fill all the positions for which they might be eligible in the event of mobilization. On the contrary, the record as I understand it, supports the District Court's finding that the services would have to conscript at least 80,000 persons to fill positions for which combat-ready men would not be required. The consistent position of the Defense Department representatives was that their best estimate of the number of women draftees who could be used productively by the Services in the event of a major mobilization would be approximately 80,000 over the first six months. * * * This number took into account the estimated number of women volunteers, Except for a single, unsupported, and ambiguous statement in the Senate Report to the effect that "women volunteers would fill the requirements for women," there is no indication that Congress rejected the Defense Department's figures or relied upon an alternative set of figures.

Of course, the division among us indicates that the record in this respect means different things to different people, and I would be content to vacate the judgment below and remand for further hearings and findings on this crucial issue. Absent that, however, I cannot agree that the record supports the view that all positions for which women would be eligible in war time could and would be filled by female volunteers.

The Court also submits that because the primary purpose of registration and conscription is to supply combat troops and because the great majority of noncombat positions must be filled by combat-trained men ready to be rotated into combat, the absolute number of positions for which women would be eligible is so small as to be *de minimis* and of no moment for equal protection purposes, especially in light of the administrative burdens involved in registering all women of suitable age. There is some sense to this; but at least on the record before us, the number of women who could be used in the military without sacrificing combat-readiness is not at all small or insubstantial, and administrative convenience has not been sufficient justification for the kind of outright gender-based discrimination involved in registering and conscripting men but no women at all.

As I understand the record, then, in order to secure the personnel it needs during mobilization, the Government cannot rely on volunteers and must register and draft not only to fill combat positions and those noncombat positions that must be filled by combat-trained men, but also to secure the personnel needed for jobs that can be performed by persons ineligible for combat without diminishing military effectiveness. The claim is that in providing for the latter category of positions, Congress is free to register and draft only men. I discern no adequate justification for this kind of discrimination between men and women. Accordingly, with all due respect, I dissent.

JUSTICE MARSHALL, with whom JUSTICE BRENNAN joins, dissenting.

The Court today places its imprimatur on one of the most potent remaining public expressions of "ancient canards about the proper role of women," Phillips v. Martin Marietta Corp., 400 U.S. 542, 545, 91 S.Ct. 496, 498, 27 L.Ed.2d 613 (1971) (Marshall, J., concurring). It upholds a statute that requires males but not females to register for the draft, and which thereby categorically excludes women from a fundamental civic obligation. Because I believe the Court's decision is inconsistent with the Constitution's guarantee of equal protection of the laws, I dissent.

I

A

* * * It bears emphasis * * * that the only question presented by this case is whether the exclusion of women from registration under the Military Selective Service Act, * * * contravenes the equal protection component of the Due Process Clause of the Fifth Amendment. Although the purpose of registration is to assist preparations for drafting civilians into the military, *we are not asked to rule on the constitutionality of a statute governing conscription.* With the advent of the All–Volunteer Armed Forces, the MSSA was specifically amended to preclude conscription as of July 1, 1973, * * * and reactivation of the draft would therefore require a legislative amendment. * * * Consequently, we are not called upon to decide whether either men or women can be drafted at all, whether they must be drafted in equal numbers, in what order they should be drafted, or once inducted, how they are to be trained for their respective functions. In addition, this case does not involve a challenge to the statutes or policies that prohibit female members of the Armed Forces from serving in combat.[2] It is with this understanding that I turn to the task at hand.

B

By now it should be clear that statutes like the MSSA, which discriminate on the basis of gender, must be examined under the "heightened" scrutiny mandated by Craig v. Boren, * * *.[3] Under this test, a gender-based classification cannot withstand constitutional challenge unless the classification is substantially related to the achievement of an important governmental objective. * * * This test applies whether the classification discriminates against

2. By statute, female members of the Air Force and the Navy may not be assigned to vessels or aircraft engaged in combat missions. See 10 U.S.C. §§ 6015 and 8549. Although there are no statutory restrictions on the assignment of women to combat in the Army and the Marine Corps, both services have established policies that preclude such assignment.

Appellees do not concede the constitutional validity of these restrictions on women in com-

bat, but they have taken the position that their validity is irrelevant, for purposes of this case.

3. I join the Court, * * * in rejecting the Solicitor General's suggestion that the gender-based classification employed by the MSSA should be scrutinized under the "rational relationship" test used in reviewing challenges to certain types of social and economic legislation. * * *

males or females. Caban v. Mohammed, * * *.[4] The party defending the challenged classification carries the burden of demonstrating both the importance of the governmental objective it serves and the substantial relationship between the discriminatory means and the asserted end. See Wengler v. Druggist Mutual Insurance Co., supra, 446 U.S., at 151, 100 S.Ct., at 1546; Caban v. Mohammed, supra, 441 U.S., at 393, 99 S.Ct., at 1769; Craig v. Boren, supra, 429 U.S., at 204, 97 S.Ct., at 460. Consequently, before we can sustain the MSSA, the Government must demonstrate that the gender-based classification it employs bears "a close and substantial relationship to [the achievement of] important governmental objectives." Personnel Administrator of Massachusetts v. Feeney, 442 U.S. 256, 273, 99 S.Ct. 2282, 2293, 60 L.Ed.2d 870 (1979).

C

The MSSA states that "an adequate armed strength must be achieved and maintained to insure the security of this Nation." * * * I agree with the majority, * * * that "none could deny that * * * the Government's interest in raising and supporting armies is an 'important governmental interest.'" Consequently, the first part of the Craig v. Boren, test is satisfied. But the question remains whether the discriminatory means employed itself substantially serves the statutory end. * * *

II

A

The Government does not defend the exclusion of women from registration on the ground that preventing women from serving in the military is substantially related to the effectiveness of the Armed Forces. Indeed, the successful experience of women serving in all branches of the Armed Services would belie any such claim. Some 150,000 women volunteers are presently on active service in the military, and their number is expected to increase to over 250,000 by 1985. * * * At the congressional hearings, representatives of both the Department of Defense and the Armed Services testified that the participation of women in the All–Volunteer Armed Forces has contributed substantially to military effectiveness. * * * Congress has never disagreed with the judgment of the military experts that women have made significant contributions to the effectiveness of the military. On the contrary, Congress has repeatedly praised the performance of female members of the Armed Forces, and has approved efforts by the Armed Services to expand their role. * * * These statements thus make clear that Congress' decision to exclude women from registration—and therefore from a draft drawing on the pool of registrants—cannot rest on a supposed need to prevent women from serving in the Armed Forces. The justification for the MSSA's gender-based discrimination must therefore be found in considerations that are peculiar to the objectives of registration.

* * *

4. Consequently, it is of no moment that the constitutional challenge in this case is pressed by men who claim that the MSSA's gender classification discriminates against them.

B

According to the Senate Report, "[t]he policy precluding the use of women in combat is * * * the most important reason for not including women in a registration system." * * * Had appellees raised a constitutional challenge to the prohibition against assignment of women to combat, this discussion in the Senate Report might well provide persuasive reasons for upholding the restrictions. But the validity of the combat restrictions is not an issue we need decide in this case. Moreover, since the combat restrictions on women have already been accomplished through statutes and policies that remain in force whether or not women are required to register or be drafted, including women in registration and draft plans will not result in their being assigned to combat roles. Thus, even assuming that precluding the use of women in combat is an important governmental interest in its own right, there can be no suggestion that the exclusion of women from registration and a draft is substantially related to the achievement of this goal.

The Court's opinion offers a different though related explanation of the relationship between the combat restrictions and Congress' decision not to require registration of women. The majority states that "Congress * * * clearly linked the need for renewed registration with its views of the character of a subsequent draft." * * * The Court also states that "Congress determined that any future draft, which would be facilitated by the registration scheme, would be characterized by a need for combat troops." * * * The Court then reasons that since women are not eligible for assignment to combat, Congress' decision to exclude them from registration is not unconstitutional discrimination inasmuch as "[m]en and women, because of the combat restrictions on women, are simply not similarly situated for purposes of a draft or registration for a draft." * * * There is a certain logic to this reasoning, but the Court's approach is fundamentally flawed.

In the first place, although the Court purports to apply the Craig v. Boren test, the "similarly situated" analysis the Court employs is in fact significantly different from the Craig v. Boren approach. * * * The Court essentially reasons that the gender classification employed by the MSSA is constitutionally permissible because nondiscrimination is not necessary to achieve the purpose of registration to prepare for a draft of combat troops. In other words, the majority concludes that women may be excluded from registration because they will not be needed in the event of a draft.[10]

This analysis, however, focuses on the wrong question. The relevant inquiry under the Craig v. Boren test is not whether a *gender-neutral* classification would substantially advance important governmental interests. Rather, the question is whether the gender-based classification is itself substantially related to the achievement of the asserted governmental interest. Thus, the Government's task in this case is to demonstrate that excluding women from registration substantially furthers the goal of preparing for a draft of combat troops. Or to put it another way, the Government must show that registering women would substantially impede its efforts to prepare for such a draft. Under our precedents, the Government cannot meet

10. I would have thought the logical conclusion from this reasoning is that there is in fact no discrimination against women, in which case one must wonder why the Court feels compelled to pledge its purported fealty to the Craig v. Boren test.

this burden without showing that a gender neutral statute would be a less effective means of attaining this end. See Wengler v. Druggists Mutual Ins. Co., 446 U.S., at 151, 100 S.Ct., at 1546. As the Court explained in Orr v. Orr, 440 U.S., at 283, 99 S.Ct., at 1113 (emphasis added):

> "Legislative classifications which distribute benefits and burdens on the basis of gender *carry the inherent risk of reinforcing sexual stereotypes about the 'proper place' of women and their need for special protection.* * * * Where, as here, the [Government's] * * * purposes are as well served by a gender-neutral classification as one that gender classifies and therefore carries with it the baggage of sexual stereotypes, the [Government] cannot be permitted to classify on the basis of sexual stereotypes."

In this case, the Government makes no claim that preparing for a draft of combat troops cannot be accomplished just as effectively by *registering* both men and women but *drafting* only men if only men turn out to be needed.[11] Nor can the Government argue that this alternative entails the additional cost and administrative inconvenience of registering women. This Court has repeatedly stated that the administrative convenience of employing a gender classification is not an adequate constitutional justification under the Craig v. Boren test. * * *

The fact that registering women in no way obstructs the governmental interest in preparing for a draft of combat troops points up a second flaw in the Court's analysis. The Court essentially reduces the question of the constitutionality of male-only *registration* to the validity of a hypothetical program for *conscripting* only men. The Court posits a draft in which *all* conscripts are either assigned to those specific combat posts presently closed to women or must be available for rotation into such positions. By so doing, the Court is able to conclude that registering women would be no more than a "gestur[e] of superficial equality," * * * since women are necessarily ineligible for every position to be filled in its hypothetical draft. If it could indeed be guaranteed in advance that conscription would be reimposed by Congress only in circumstances where, and in a form under which, all conscripts would have to be trained for and assigned to combat or combat rotation positions from which women are categorically excluded, then it could be argued that registration of women would be pointless.

But of course, no such guarantee is possible. Certainly, nothing about the MSSA limits Congress to reinstituting the draft only in such circumstances. For example, Congress may decide that the All–Volunteer Armed Forces are inadequate to meet the Nation's defense needs even in times of peace and reinstitute peacetime conscription. In that event, the hypothetical draft the Court relied on to sustain the MSSA's gender-based classification would presumably be of little relevance, and the Court could then be forced to declare the male-only registration program unconstitutional. This difficulty comes about because both Congress[12] and the Court have lost sight of the

---

11. Alternatively, the Government could employ a classification that is related to the statutory objective but is not based on gender, for example, combat eligibility. Under the current scheme, large subgroups of the male population who are ineligible for combat because of physical handicaps or conscientious objector status are nonetheless required to register.

12. The Court quotes Senator Warner's comment: " 'I equate registration with the draft,' " * * * The whole of Senator Warner's statement merits quotation because it explains

important distinction between *registration* and *conscription*. Registration provides "an inventory of what the available strength is within the military qualified pool in this country." * * * Conscription supplies the military with the personnel needed to respond to a particular exigency. The fact that registration is a first step in the conscription process does not mean that a registration law expressly discriminating between men and women may be justified by a valid conscription program which would, in retrospect, make the current discrimination appear functionally related to the program that emerged.

But even addressing the Court's reasoning on its own terms, its analysis is flawed because the entire argument rests on a premise that is demonstrably false. As noted, the majority simply assumes that registration prepares for a draft in which *every* draftee must be available for assignment to combat. But the majority's draft scenario finds no support in either the testimony before Congress, or more importantly, in the findings of the Senate Report. Indeed, the scenario appears to exist only in the Court's imagination, for even the Government represents only that "in the event of mobilization, *approximately two-thirds* of the demand on the induction system would be for *combat skills.*" Brief for Appellant, at 29 (emphasis added). For my part, rather than join the Court in imagining hypothetical drafts, I prefer to examine the findings in the Senate Report and the testimony presented to Congress.

C

Nothing in the Senate Report supports the Court's intimation that women must be excluded from registration because combat eligibility is a prerequisite for *all* the positions that would need to be filled in the event of a draft. The Senate Report concluded only that "[i]f mobilization were to be ordered in a wartime scenario, the *primary* manpower need would be for combat replacements." * * *

This review of the findings contained in the Senate Report and the testimony presented at the congressional hearings demonstrates that there is no basis for the Court's representation that women are ineligible for *all* the positions that would need to be filled in the event of a draft. Testimony about personnel requirements in the event of a draft established that women could fill at least 80,000 of the 650,000 positions for which conscripts would be inducted. Thus, with respect to these 80,000 or more positions, the statutes and policies barring women from combat do not provide a reason for distinguishing between male and female potential conscripts; the two groups are, in the majority's parlance, "similarly situated." As such, the combat restrictions cannot by themselves supply the constitutionally required justification for the MSSA's gender-based classification. Since the classification precludes women from being drafted to fill positions for which they would be qualified and useful, the Government must demonstrate that excluding women from those positions is substantially related to the achievement of an important governmental objective.

why Congress refused to acknowledge the distinction between registration and the draft. Senator Warner stated: "Frankly I equate registration with the draft because there is no way you can establish a registration law on a co-

equal basis and then turn right around and establish a draft on a nonequal basis. I think the court would knock that down right away." * * *

III

The Government argues, however, that the "consistent testimony before Congress was to the effect that there is *no military need* to draft women." Brief for Appellant, at 31 (emphasis in original). And the Government points to a statement in the Senate Report that "[b]oth the civilian and military leadership agreed that there was no military need to draft women. * * * The argument for registration and induction of women * * * is not based on military necessity, but on considerations of equity." * * * In accepting the Government's contention, the Court asserts that the President's decision to seek authority to register women was based on "equity," and concludes that "Congress was certainly entitled, in the exercise of its constitutional powers to raise and regulate armies and navies, to focus on the question of military need rather than 'equity.' " * * * In my view, a more careful examination of the concepts of "equity" and "military need" is required.

* * *

By "considerations of equity," the military experts acknowledged that female conscripts can perform as well as male conscripts in certain positions, and that there is therefore no reason why one group should be totally excluded from registration and a draft. Thus, what the majority so blithely dismisses as "equity" is nothing less than the Fifth Amendment's guarantee of equal protection of the laws which "requires that Congress treat similarly situated persons similarly," * * * Moreover, whether Congress could subsume this constitutional requirement to "military need," in part depends on precisely what the Senate Report meant by "military need."

The Report stated that "[b]oth the civilian and military leadership agreed that there was no military need to draft women." * * * An examination of what the "civilian and military leadership" meant by "military need" should therefore provide an insight into the Report's use of the term. Several witnesses testified that because personnel requirements in the event of a mobilization could be met by drafting men, including women in draft plans is not a military necessity. * * *

To be sure, there is no "military need" to draft women in the sense that a war could be waged without their participation. This fact is, however, irrelevant to resolving the constitutional issue. As previously noted, * * * it is not appellees' burden to prove that registration of women substantially furthers the objectives of the MSSA.[17] Rather, because eligibility for combat is not a requirement for some of the positions to be filled in the event of a draft, it is incumbent on the Government to show that excluding women from a draft to fill those positions substantially furthers an important governmental objective.

It may be, however, that the Senate Report's allusion to "military need" is meant to convey Congress' expectation that women volunteers will make it unnecessary to draft any women. The majority apparently accepts this meaning when it states: "Congress also concluded that whatever the need for

17. If we were to assign appellees this burden, then all of the Court's prior "mid-level" scrutiny equal protection decisions would be drawn into question. For the Court would be announcing a new approach under which the party challenging a gender-based classification has the burden of showing that *elimination* of the classification substantially furthers an important governmental interest.

women for noncombat roles during mobilization, whether 80,000 or less, it could be met by volunteers." * * * But since the purpose of registration is to protect against unanticipated shortages of volunteers, it is difficult to see how excluding women from registration can be justified by conjectures about the expected number of female volunteers. I fail to see why the exclusion of a pool of persons who would be conscripted only *if needed* can be justified by reference to the current supply of volunteers. In any event, the Defense Department's best estimate is that in the event of a mobilization requiring reinstitution of the draft, there will not be enough women volunteers to fill the positions for which women would be eligible. The Department told Congress:

> "If we had a mobilization, our present best projection is that we could use women in some 80,000 of the jobs we would be *inducting* people for." 1980 Senate Hearings, supra, at 1688 (Principal Deputy Assistant Secretary of Defense Danzig) (emphasis added).

Thus, however the "military need" statement in the Senate Report is understood, it does not provide the constitutionally required justification for the total exclusion of women from registration and draft plans.

IV

Recognizing the need to go beyond the "military need" argument, the Court asserts that "Congress determined that staffing noncombat positions with women during a mobilization would be positively detrimental to the important goal of military flexibility." * * * None would deny that preserving "military flexibility" is an important governmental interest. But to justify the exclusion of women from registration and the draft on this ground, there must be a further showing that staffing even a limited number of noncombat positions with women would impede military flexibility. I find nothing in the Senate Report, to provide any basis for the Court's representation that Congress believed this to be the case.

* * *

Similarly, there is no reason why induction of a limited number of female draftees should any more divide the military into "permanent combat" and "permanent support" groups than is presently the case with the All–Volunteer Armed Forces. The combat restrictions that would prevent a female draftee from serving in a combat or combat rotation position also apply to the 150,000–250,000 women volunteers in the Armed Services. If the presence of increasing but controlled numbers of female volunteers has not unacceptably "divide[d] the military into two groups," it is difficult to see how the induction of a similarly limited additional number of women could accomplish this result. In these circumstances, I cannot agree with the Court's attempt to "interpret" the Senate Report's conclusion that drafting *very large numbers* of women would impair military flexibility, as proof that Congress reached the entirely different conclusion that drafting a limited number of women would adversely affect military flexibility.

V

The Senate Report itself recognized that the "military flexibility" objective speaks only to the question whether "very large numbers" of women should be drafted. * * *

The Senate Report simply failed to consider the possibility that a limited number of women could be drafted because of its conclusion that § 5(a)(1) of the MSSA does not authorize drafting different numbers of men and women and its speculation on judicial reaction to a decision to register women. But since Congress was free to amend § 5(a)(1), and indeed would have to undertake new legislation to authorize any draft, the matter cannot end there. Furthermore, the Senate Report's speculation that a statute authorizing differential induction of male and female draftees would be vulnerable to constitutional challenge is unfounded. The unchallenged restrictions on the assignment of women to combat, the need to preserve military flexibility, and the other factors discussed in the Senate Report provide more than ample grounds for concluding that the discriminatory means employed by such a statute would be substantially related to the achievement of important governmental objectives. Since Congress could have amended § 5(a)(1) to authorize differential induction of men and women based on the military's personnel requirements, the Senate Report's discussion about "added burdens" that would result from drafting equal numbers of male and female draftees provides no basis for concluding that the total exclusion of women from registration and draft plans is substantially related to the achievement of important governmental objectives.

In sum, neither the Senate Report itself nor the testimony presented at the congressional hearings provides any support for the conclusion the Court seeks to attribute to the Report—that drafting a limited number of women, with the number and the timing of their induction and training determined by the military's personnel requirements, would burden training and administrative facilities.

VI

After reviewing the discussion and findings contained in the Senate Report, the most I am able to say of the Report is that it demonstrates that drafting *very large numbers* of women would frustrate the achievement of a number of important governmental objectives that relate to the ultimate goal of maintaining "an adequate armed strength * * * to insure the security of this Nation," 50 U.S.C.App. § 451(b). Or to put it another way, the Senate Report establishes that induction of a large number of men but only a limited number of women, as determined by the military's personnel requirements, would be substantially related to important governmental interests. But the discussion and findings in the Senate Report do not enable the Government to carry its burden of demonstrating that *completely* excluding women from the draft by excluding them from registration substantially furthers important governmental objectives.

In concluding that the Government has carried its burden in this case, the Court adopts "an appropriately deferential examination of *Congress'* evaluation of [the] evidence," * * *. The majority then proceeds to supplement Congress' actual findings with those the Court apparently believes Congress could (and should) have made. Beyond that, the Court substitutes hollow shibboleths about "deference to legislative decisions" for constitutional analysis. It is as if the majority has lost sight of the fact that "it is the responsibility of this Court to act as the ultimate interpreter of the Constitution." * * * Congressional enactments in the area of military affairs must, like all other laws, be *judged* by the standards of the Constitution. For the Constitution is the supreme law of the land and *all* legislation must conform to the principles it lay down. As the Court has pointed out, "the phrase 'war power' cannot be invoked as a talismanic incantation to support any exercise of congressional power which can be brought within its ambit." * * *

Furthermore, "[w]hen it appears that an Act of Congress conflicts with [a constitutional] provisio[n], we have no choice but to enforce the paramount commands of the Constitution. We are sworn to do no less. We cannot push back the limits of the Constitution merely to accommodate challenged legislation." * * * In some 106 instances since this Court was established it has determined that congressional action exceeded the bounds of the Constitution. I believe the same is true of this statute. In an attempt to avoid its constitutional obligation, the Court today "pushes back the limits of the Constitution" to accommodate an Act of Congress.

I would affirm the judgment of the District Court.

Notes on Goldberg

1. Can you explain why gender-based combat restrictions justify gender-based registration provisions? If Congress decided that blacks should not engage in combat, would a white-only draft pass muster under the Fifth Amendment? Is the classification suggested by Justice Marshall in footnote 11 of his dissenting opinion—that only combat-eligible persons be registered—any better? As Marshall notes, the class of non-combat-eligible persons contains both male and female members, and is therefore gender neutral. As we will learn in Chapter 3, infra, the same is true of another well-known class, non-pregnant persons. Does the facial neutrality of either class make it less objectionable? * * * At the time *Goldberg* was decided, were there any more combat-eligible persons who are female than there were pregnant persons who are male?

2. Why did the *Goldberg* plaintiffs refrain from challenging the combat exclusion for women? Judge Sirica had earlier held 10 U.S.C.A. § 6015 unconstitutional as applied to prevent Navy women from serving at sea in Owens v. Brown, 455 F.Supp. 291 (D.D.C.1978), discussed at p. 129 n. 9, infra. What remains of *Owens* after *Goldberg?* Is the female combat exclusion constitutional?

3. Which group is the target of discrimination in *Goldberg?* Males, because the absence of females in the registration pool increases the chance of being drafted? Females, because, as Justice Marshall points out, they are excluded from performing a "fundamental civic obligation"? If the discrimination is truly against women, why does Justice Marshall think it necessary to point out in footnote 4 of his dissenting opinion that "it is of no moment that the constitutional challenge in this case is pressed by men who claim that the MSSA's gender classification discriminates against them"? The strategy adopted in Frontiero v. Richardson, set forth at p. 31, supra, and followed in subsequent cases, of having male plaintiffs complain of discrimination against their wives rather than against themselves, was discarded in *Goldberg*. Was this a sound choice? Would it have been convincing for male registrants to argue that females were being subjected to discrimination? Why were there no female plaintiffs in *Goldberg?* Do women have standing to challenge their exclusion from the draft? Compare Kenneth L. Karst, Woman's Constitution, 1984 Duke L.J. 447, 471 (no), with Lori S. Kornblum, Women Warriors in a Men's World: The Combat Exclusion, 2 Law & Inequality 351, 430–32 (1984) (arguing that women have standing to challenge the

combat exclusion). Since women can volunteer for military service, but are excluded from combat jobs, aren't both Karst and Kornblum right?

4. Did the *Goldberg* majority use the *Craig* standard? When he was called upon to review the validity of an Army enlistment policy that permits men who have not graduated from high school but who have obtained a General Educational Development (GED) certificate to enlist but prohibits women from so doing, Judge Newcomer inferred from *Goldberg* and two Court of Appeal decisions, Jaffee v. United States, 663 F.2d 1226 (3d Cir.1981), cert. denied 456 U.S. 972, 102 S.Ct. 2234, 72 L.Ed.2d 845 (1982) and Katcoff v. Marsh, 755 F.2d 223 (2d Cir.1985), that "the standard outlined in *Craig* is not applicable to gender-based equal protection claims raised in the context of military affairs." Lewis v. United States Army, 697 F.Supp. 1385, 1390 n. 5 (E.D.Pa.1988). Instead, Judge Newcomer tested the Army policy "using a standard of review that asks whether the regulations are reasonably relevant and necessary to the national defense, with any doubt as to constitutionality resolved in favor of deference to the military's exercise of its discretion." Id., at 1390. The Army relied on studies showing that high school graduates are more likely than GED holders to complete their initial enlistment term and to reenlist; thus, it would prefer to impose the high school diploma requirement on all recruits. Because of its policy barring women from combat, however, the Army felt it needed to enlist a "much greater number of men than women" and accordingly could not afford to impose the high school diploma restriction on men. Not surprisingly, under Judge Newcomer's standard plaintiff Vivian Lewis lost her case. Would she have won under *Craig?*

Text Note
Women in the Military

Cultural attitudes, as well as history, dictate that in times of war, to use Judge Bonsal's words, "men must provide the first line of defense while women keep the home fires burning." [1] History also discloses, however, that women have served as combatants since ancient times. Lori Kornblum thus summarizes the known record: [2]

> Herodotus reported long ago that women in African Zaveces drove war chariots and that the Scythian women of classical Greece were so "warlike" that they inspired the legend of the Amazons. In the Niger and Chad, traditional Hausa territory, women "founded cities, led migrations and conquered kingdoms." More recently, mid-nineteenth century Dahomeian women formed a large part of the King's army; six thousand women fought during the kingdom's last battle in 1851.

Small numbers of women, disguised as men, have served in combat roles in every war in which the United States was involved before the Twentieth Century.[3] During the First World War, women were employed without full military status as nurses by both the Army and Navy and, by the Navy, in shore-based clerical positions that did carry full military rank and status.

Not until World War II, however, were women involved in large numbers in military service. Special women's corps, designed, as their names indicated, to be

---

1. U.S. v. St. Clair, 291 F.Supp. 122, 125 (S.D.N.Y.1968), reprinted at p. 21 supra.

2. Lori S. Kornblum, Women Warriors in a Men's World: The Combat Exclusion, 2 Law & Inequality 351, 395 (1984) (footnotes omitted;

quotations are from John Laffin, Women in Battle (1967)).

3. This discussion draws heavily on Martin Binkin & Shirley J. Bach, Women and the Military (Brookings Institution, 1977).

temporary, were established in 1942: the Women's Army Auxiliary Corps (WAAC); Women Accepted for Voluntary Emergency Service (WAVES); and the U.S. Marine Corps and Coast Guard Women's Reserve, called by their motto: "Sempter Paratus, Always Ready" (SPARs). Another unit of approximately 800 women, called the Women's Airforce Service Pilots (WASPs), was used to ferry all types of military aircraft, including combat aircraft.[4] A total of 350,000 women were active in the four services, performing a variety of traditional as well as non-traditional tasks. After World War II, the continuing presence of a small number of women in the military was authorized by the Women's Armed Services Integration Act of 1948.[5] This legislation, however, contained several highly restrictive provisions: a ceiling on enlistment (no more than 2% of total enlisted strength could be women[6]); disparate enlistment requirements (women could enlist at 18, but needed parental consent if they were under 21; the respective ages for men were 17 and 18[7]); career limitations (no women could serve in command positions or hold a permanent grade above Lieutenant Colonel in the Army or Commander in the Navy[8]); restrictions on deployment (women could not be used in combat nor could they serve aboard aircraft engaged in combat missions or be assigned to duty on vessels of the Navy except hospital ships or transports[9]); and less valuable benefits for their families than those enjoyed by servicemen (spouses of servicemen were presumed dependent for purposes of quarters allowances and medical benefits, but spouses of servicewomen had to prove actual dependency[10]).

Not until the decision to move toward a volunteer force was taken in the wake of the Vietnam War did it become apparent to military planners that an increase in women volunteers might be needed to offset a possible shortage of male recruits once the draft was terminated. Accordingly, a number of changes were implemented between 1972 and 1976 in military personnel policies, some of them compelled by litigation, others the product of plans designed to make military life more attractive to women. In the view of two knowledgeable

---

4. The WASPs received retroactive recognition, together with Veteran's Benefits, in 1977. 38 U.S.C.A. § 106n, Pub.L. No. 95–202, Title IV § 401, 91 Stat. 1449 (Nov. 23, 1977). For a fictionalized account of the experiences of some of these women, see Mardo Crane, Fly–Down of the WASP (1967).

5. Ch. 449, § 101, 62 Stat. 356 (June 12, 1948).

6. Id., § 102, 62 Stat. 357 (Army); § 202, 62 Stat. at 363 (Navy); § 302, 62 Stat. at 371 (Air Force). The 2% ceiling was never attained. It was removed by Pub.L. No. 90–130, 81 Stat. 374 (November 8, 1967).

7. Id., § 106, 62 Stat. 360 (Army). The age differential was challenged in Beatty v. Brown, # 79 Civil 0512 (D.D.C.1979); the suit was dismissed on June 29, 1979, after the Army changed its regulations to permit women to enlist under the same rules applicable to men. Army Regulation 601.210 (1979).

8. Ch. 449, § 104(d)(6), 62 Stat. 358 (June 12, 1948) (Army); § 203, 62 Stat. at 363 (Navy). This restriction was also removed by Pub.L. No. 90–130, 81 Stat. 374 (November 8, 1967).

9. Ch. 449, § 210, 62 Stat. 368 (Navy and Marines); Id., § 307, 62 Stat. at 373 (Air Force). The prohibition against Navy women serving at sea was successfully challenged in Owens v. Brown, 455 F.Supp. 291 (D.D.C. 1978). Judge Sirica held that 10 U.S.C.A. § 6015, the successor to 62 Stat. 368, violated the equal protection component of the Fifth Amendment because of its overbreadth. Even if the provision had been "within the bounds of congressional power" at the time of its enactment in 1948, said Sirica, "over a generation later, when Congress carved out the disputed exception to the Navy's ability to use women aboard Navy vessels, it acted without serious deliberation, against the expressed judgment of the military and, by foreclosing the Navy's discretion regarding women well beyond the legitimate demands of military preparedness and efficiency, it acted arbitrarily." Id., 455 F.Supp. at 309.

10. Ch. 449, § 107, 62 Stat. 361 (June 12, 1948). This distinction was declared unconstitutional in Frontiero v. Richardson, 411 U.S. 677, 93 S.Ct. 1764, 36 L.Ed.2d 583 (1973), set out at p. 20, supra.

observers, the most notable of these were [11]

- Permitting women to command organizations composed of both men and women;

- Allowing women to enter aviation training and military academies;

- Eliminating policies that require the automatic discharge of pregnant women and those with minor dependents;

- Equalizing family entitlements for married servicemen and servicewomen;

- Giving women access to a wider range of training opportunities (for example, Army women can be trained to use light antitank weapons, the M–16 rifle, the grenade launcher, the Claymore mine, and the M–60 machine gun).

These changes had their effects: in 1972, one of every 30 enlisted recruits was female, while in 1976, one of every 13 was a woman. Women numbered about 8 percent of total enlisted strength in the four services by 1980 [12]. The service academies graduated their first class of women in 1980, producing a total of 229 female officers who comprised 8 percent of their classes.[13] By 1986, women comprised 10 percent of the 2.1 million people in the armed forces.[14] For the first time in its 32–year history, the Air Force named a woman, Terrie Ann McLaughlin, as its Top Cadet.[15] Several months later, the Air Force decided to open more than 1600 jobs to women that involved crew assignments to RC–135 reconnaissance aircraft and EC–130 electronic warfare planes.[16] The growth rate has slowed somewhat: by 1994, women made up 11.8 percent of the active duty force, and accounted for 199,043 of the total 1,692,541 positions.[17]

What has been the impact on the military establishment and on American society of this higher prominence of women in military life? At one level, as the increasing sophistication of military technology and the need for more highly trained personnel tend to equate many military jobs with those available in the civilian sector, it becomes apparent that there are many such jobs that women can perform as effectively as men. Binkin and Bach note: [18]

> [I]n occupations in which women have traditionally been employed, there is little question that they can perform at least on a par with men. Included are a wide range of technical and administrative positions for which the principal requirements are general intelligence and academic ability, characteristics that women, on average, are as likely to possess as men. In these occupations, which are analogous to white-collar jobs in the civilian sector, physical strength is relatively unimportant. For example, jobs in administration, health care, communications, intelligence, and other technical occupations (photography, mapping, weather) are largely sedentary or, at most, involve

11. M. Binkin & S.J. Bach, supra note 3, at 17.

12. Id., at 15; Presidential Recommendations for Selective Service Reform: A Report to Congress Pursuant to P.L. 96–107, at 42 (Feb. 11, 1980), 1 U.S.Code Cong. & Ad.News 261, 296 (March, 1980).

13. The New York Times, May 25, 1980, at 1, col. 4; at 42, col. 1.

14. The New York Times, Aug. 25, 1986, at 1, col. 2; at 12, col. 4.

15. San Francisco Chronicle, May 29, 1986, at 2, col. 1. Kristin M. Baker, the daughter of

an Army colonel who describes herself as an "Army brat," became the First Captain of the Corps of Cadets at West Point in 1989. The New York Times, August 9, 1989, at A1, col. 2.

16. San Francisco Chronicle, Dec. 13, 1986, at 7, col. 4.

17. James Kitfield, "Women Warriors," 26 Government Executive 22, 22 & 24 (Graph) (March, 1994).

18. M. Binkin & S.J. Bach, supra note 3, at 98–99.

light work. Some 540,000 enlisted jobs, or about one out of every three, are in this category; about 11 percent are now filled by women. * * * By contrast, of approximately 18 million jobs in similar categories in the civilian sector, some 10 million, about 55 percent, are held by women. With few exceptions, women could be at least as effective in these jobs as men.

How effective women would be in the remaining jobs is less clear and in need of further study. Included are those positions roughly comparable to blue-collar jobs in the private sector: equipment repair, crafts (metalworker, machinist, carpenter), and service and supply handlers. Along with the so-called combat skills, these positions require physical capabilities and attitudes now more often found in males than in females. * * * Although most are now "open" to women (the combat skills are the principal exception), approximately 17,000, or only about 1.7 percent of the blue-collar jobs, are currently filled by women. In contrast, close to 21 percent of comparable civilian jobs have a female incumbent.

At the level of physical strength and endurance, the performance record of the women graduates from the service academies is notable. Rear Admiral William P. Lawrence, the Superintendent at Annapolis, was quoted in the press as having stated that the academies chose not to alter the programs to accommodate the women, except where changes were "absolutely necessary." [19] Changes that were made included allowing women an extra minute to run the mile, permitting them to carry the 8–pound M–16 rifle in simulated combat rather than the 11–pound M–14 carried by men, and giving them an extra 30 seconds to complete the obstacle course.[20] The military has also managed to adjust to another inherent difference between the sexes: the capacity of women to become pregnant. Once grounds for compulsory discharge,[21] and still the basis for voluntary termination, pregnancy now is regarded as a temporary physical disability that entitles the mother to up to six weeks of paid postpartum convalescent leave.[22] The services will also have to adjust to dual career marriages between officers: according to The New York Times,[23] roughly half of the 62 women who graduated from West Point in 1980 married within a week of graduation, most of them to other West Point graduates, while the comparable figure for the Air Force Academy was one-third.

As *Goldberg* suggests, the major remaining restriction on women's full participation in the military is the policy that excludes them from combat and combat-related service. Binkin and Bach estimated in 1977 that, unless these restrictions were removed, women could never total more than 22 percent of the nation's military force.[24] Controversy surrounds the idea of using women in combat. At the root of the controversy lies the unknown effects of integrating the sexes in fighting units. Social scientists have explained the behavior of men in combat as motivated by their dependence on primary groups for their own personal survival: the soldier's identification with and solidarity toward his fellow

19. The New York Times, supra note 13, at 42, col. 1.

20. Id. See also Newsweek Magazine, Feb. 18, 1980, at 36, cols. 2–3. Newsweek quoted the views of James Webb, an ex-Marine and author of the combat novel, Fields of Fire, on these adaptations in the training of women: "You can take football and modify the rules so women can play. That's fine—until they face the Dallas Cowboys and get slaughtered." Is

there a satisfactory response to this observation?

21. M. Binkin & S.J. Bach, supra note 3, at 44.

22. Id., at 61.

23. The New York Times, supra note 13, at 42, col. 4.

24. M. Binkin & S.J. Bach, supra note 3, at 109.

squad and platoon members, rather than his loyalty to his commanders or his commitment to serving his country, is the stimulus for his actions in battle.[25] Would the introduction of women into this situation prevent or hamper the formation of this identification and thus decrease the military effectiveness of the combat unit? The expectation that this might occur, combined with fears of conducting experiments to discover results while the nation is at war, have led military observers to oppose the use of women in combat.[26] Although there are obvious differences between wartime and peacetime conditions, one commentator has urged that the military should "be expected to test the effectiveness of integrated units in a variety of situations during the present peacetime environment and to produce empirical evidence establishing the necessity for any desired segregation to the satisfaction of the courts." [27]

The problem is complicated by the fact that, as Kornblum notes,[28] the meaning of "combat" is far from precise:

> * * * When Congress adopted the combat exclusion in 1948, the Army did not have a definition of "combat." The Navy's definition of "combat" was codified as service aboard ships, and the Air Force's definition as service aboard aircraft engaged in combat missions. * * *
>
> Thirty years after enactment of the combat exclusion, the Defense Department defined "combat." Since 1978, the Defense Department has had a three-factor definition of "close combat." "Close combat" exists when (1) a person engages an enemy with individual or crew-served weapons while exposed to direct enemy fire, (2) the person is subject to a high probability of direct physical contact with the enemy's personnel, and (3) the person is subject to a substantial risk of capture. The Army's definition of "direct combat" substantially repeats the Defense Department's three-factor definition and adds that "direct combat" takes place while the person "clos[es] with the enemy by fire, maneuver, and shock effect to destroy or capture him or while repelling his assault by fire, close combat, or counterattack."

In practice, Kornblum observes,[29] the new definition has done little to resolve either the question of which military jobs are off-limits to women or what risks they will bear in time of war. Thus, the Army's list of "combat" positions includes some, such as carpentry and masonry specialist, plumber, and interior electrician, that do not appear to involve any of the three factors contained in the

25. See Charles Moskos, The American Enlisted Man 144 (1970), reporting studies of combat behavior of American soldiers during World War II. Based on his own studies of men serving in Vietnam, Moskos concluded that a more individualistic self-interest in survival was the primary motivational factor. Id., at 145–56.

26. See M. Binkin & S.J. Bach, supra note 3, at 89–92; Note, The Equal Rights Amendment and the Military, 82 Yale L.J. 1533, 1547–52 (1973); Owens v. Brown, supra note 9, at 305–8.

27. Note, The Equal Rights Amendment and the Military, 82 Yale L.J. 1533, 1551–52 (1973). See also M. Binkin & S.J. Bach, supra note 3, at 93–95, discussing some empirical data on the effect of introducing women into male-dominated groups.

28. Kornblum, supra note 2, at 358–59 (footnotes omitted).

29. Id., at 360–65. Nor are the laws always observed. Quoting "senior Air Force officials," the Los Angeles Times reported that "[d]espite federal laws barring women from combat duties, several female pilots, flight engineers and load masters flew missions to Grenada during the initial phases of the 1983 invasion * * *". The explanation, attributed to "sources within the Air Force's Military Airlift Command," was that "[i]nvasion planning was so swift * * * that there was no time to handpick the crews of airlift aircraft." San Francisco Chronicle, Jan. 27, 1986, at p. 5, col. 6.

Defense Department's definition. And in war theaters, medical women are routinely exposed both to enemy fire and to capture.

The presence of military women in the Persian Gulf during Operation Desert Storm in 1991 provided the force that changed the combat exclusion for women. President George Bush signed the National Defense Authorization Act for Fiscal Years 1992 and 1993 on December 5, 1991.[30] Section 531 of the Act repealed the combat exclusion formerly contained in 10 U.S.C. § 8549 (Air Force) and 10 U.S.C. § 6015 (Navy and Marine Corps).

In addition, the Act established a Commission on the Assignment of Women in the Armed Forces to assess the laws and policies restricting the assignment of female service members and make findings on such matters.

The Commission recommended that the combat exclusion be reimposed, with only slight modifications. Specifically, it recommended that women should be excluded from direct land combat units and positions, and that these exclusions should be codified.[31] The Commission summarized its reasoning as follows:[32]

> The case against women in ground combat is compelling and conclusive. The physiological differences between men and women are most stark when compared to ground combat tasks. This is underscored by the evidence that there are few women, especially enlisted women, interested in serving in ground combat specialties. The overriding importance of small unit cohesion to ground military success, and the unknown but probably negative effect that the presence of women would have in those units were of critical concern to most Commissioners. Several polls revealed in most convincing terms that the public and military, especially the military people most familiar with its rigors, were fundamentally opposed to women in ground combat. The weight of international experience with women in ground combat units provides no conclusive evidence supporting the assignment of women in ground combat units. Finally, the legal implications of lifting the ground combat exclusion policy for the possible registration and conscription of women for ground combat were considered. The current ground combat exclusion policies, which are derived from Congressional intent to restrict the assignment of women in other Services, would be vulnerable if the remaining statute was repealed. The Commission therefore recommends that the ground exclusion policies be enacted into law for consistency and sound public policy.

The Commission adopted this recommendation by a vote of 10–0, with two abstentions. By a narrower vote (8–7), it went on to recommend that women not be assigned to combat aircraft.[33] This recommendation would require the re-enactment of 10 U.S.C.A. § 8549 and 10 U.S.C.A. § 6015. The Commission did, however, vote 8 to 6 with 1 abstention to recommend the repeal of existing laws and modification of Service policies which prevent women from serving on combatant vessels, except submarines and amphibious vessels.[34] Why the difference between aircraft and ships? Fourteen years of positive experience with Navy women serving aboard tenders and service craft. Why the exclusion for submarines? Too costly to modify ($1 million per submarine, depending on the number

---

30. (Pub.L. 102–190).

31. The Presidential Commission on the Assignment of Women in the Armed Forces: Report to the President, November 15, 1992, Recommendation K: Ground Combat, at p. 24 [hereafter cited as "Report"].

32. Id., at 26–27.

33. Report, Recommendation L: Combat Aircraft, at p. 28.

34. Report, Recommendation M: Combatant Vessels, at p. 31.

and mix of women assigned). The modification cost per ship was estimated to range between $66,000 and $4 million.

The Commission also recommended that women not be made subject to a military draft.[35] The major purpose of conscription is to produce combat troops, and since the Commission had recommended that women be excluded from ground combat units, it opposed drafting women even for positions open to them. The Commission did recommend, however, that quotas limiting women's access to the military services be removed.[36]

The Report contains other recommendations, among them such matters as Basic Training Standards, Gender–Related Occupational Standards, Parental and Family Policies, and Pregnancy and Deployability Policies. There is also a minority report, filed by five Commissioners, concluding that the Armed Forces should not assign women to combat.

The Report was referred to the Congressional Committee on Armed Forces on January 5, 1993.[37] The Clinton administration left the Report to gather dust while adopting policies that contradict many of its recommendations. Thus, in April, 1993, then-Defense Secretary Les Aspin issued a directive repealing the exclusion of women from combat aircraft and ships.[38] On January 13, 1994, Secretary Aspin announced that the Department of Defense "risk rule", which prohibited requiring women in administrative or medical positions to serve in or near the front lines, would be repealed, and the definition of "close combat" with respect to land operations would be relaxed.[39] These policies became effective on October 1, 1994; their immediate result was to open new positions to women, including air cavalry units and some combat engineer, bridge crew and Marine explosive ordinance officer positions. At the same time, a policy became effective that allows women to fly combat helicopters in support of tank operations.

Critics of these policies, including Elaine Donnelly, President of the Center for Military Readiness,[40] point out that they will be implemented on an involuntary basis: like their male counterparts, women will be unable to reject "close combat" duty.[41]

Should the combat exclusion be attacked by feminists? Kornblum concludes that "eliminating the combat exclusion is a necessary step for changing the position of women in American social institutions." [42] She explores both legisla-

---

35. Report, Recommendation O: Conscription, at p. 40.

36. Report, Recommendation A: Quotas and Goals, at p. 1: "DoD should establish a policy to ensure that no person who is best qualified is denied access on the basis of gender to an assignment that is open to both men and women. As far as it is compatible with the above policy, the Secretary of Defense should retain discretion to set goals that encourage the recruitment and optimize the utilization of women in the Services, allowing for the requirements of each Service."

37. 103rd Congress, 1st Session Vol. 139 § 71.

38. Kitfield, supra note 17, at 22.

39. Memorandum from the Secretary of Defense to the [Service Secretaries], the Chairman of the Joint Chiefs of Staff, Assistant Secretary of Defense [Personnel and Readiness], and Assistant Secretary of Defense [Reserve Affairs], "Direct Ground Combat Definition and Assignment Rule," January 13, 1994.

40. Roni Galgano, Q & A: Elaine Donnelly, President, Center for Military Readiness, The San Diego Union–Tribune, September 14, 1995, at G–5, col. 2.

41. Ibid.

42. Kornblum, supra note 2, at 357. Compare Sara Ruddick, Pacifying the Forces: Drafting Women in the Interests of Peace, 8 SIGNS 471 (1983) (exploring the tension between feminism and antimilitarism, but rejecting as improbable a proposal to undermine militarism by conscripting "peaceful women").

tive and judicial avenues to change, and argues that an equal protection challenge to the combat exclusion should be successful.[43]

Could such a constitutional challenge survive the traditional judicial posture of deference to legislative and executive judgments in the area of military affairs exhibited in Rostker v. Goldberg?[44] Kornblum notes that the Court could not claim that women and men are not similarly situated with respect to combat in a direct challenge to that exclusion as it was able to do in the more limited context of compulsory registration. She thus summarizes her argument:[45]

A court should not simply defer to Congressional and military judgments that women should not be in combat. Women and men are similarly situated with respect to combat. A court has as much expertise in determining whether women should be combatants as Congress, and a court reviewing the constitutionality of the combat exclusion would only need to follow its traditional decision-making function in balancing the constitutional rights of individuals against the evidence advanced to justify abrogation of those rights. Finally, the legal concerns that underlie the *Rostker* "healthy deference" standard are not relevant to a case involving the combat exclusion. A court could and should determine that the combat exclusion denies both women and men equal protection of the laws.

Political scientist Jean Yarbrough takes a different view. Characterizing the effort to open combat to women as a "feminist mistake,"[46] she argues that:[47]

The demand for equity has widespread appeal because it is simple and reflects the egalitarian principle of American society. But when applied to military affairs, it is wrong and dangerous. The military cannot and should not try to mirror exactly the principles of democratic society. The military is not a "civic instrument" that reflects social progress. Nor is it a social welfare agency. The relationship between the military and civilian spheres is more complicated. Although the military defends the principles of democratic society, it cannot fully embody them. Its end is victory, not equity; its virtue is courage, not justice; its structure is authoritarian, not pluralistic. In short, although the military defends democratic principles and is shaped by the regime of which it is a part, it is not simply a microcosm of the larger society. The requirements of military life clash with the democratic commitment to equality, natural rights, and consent.

This does not mean that the military can or ought to ignore democratic principles altogether. The demands of black soldiers are a case in point. Until after World War II, racial segregation was official military policy. Beginning in 1948, and prior to the great court decisions outlawing discrimination in civil society, the services sought to eliminate racial segregation. But the situation of blacks and women is not the same. The arguments for segregating blacks was based on longstanding and irrational white prejudice,

43. Kornblum, supra note 2, at 430–43. See also Kenneth L. Karst, The Pursuit of Manhood and the Desegregation of the Armed Forces, 38 U.C.L.A.L.Rev. 499, 523–45 (1991); G. Sidney Buchanan, Women in Combat: An Essay on Ultimate Rights and Responsibilities, 28 Houston L.Rev. 503 (1991). Note, Women and the Draft: The Constitutionality of All–Male Registration, 94 Harv.L.Rev. 406 (1980).

44. 453 U.S. 57, 101 S.Ct. 2646, 69 L.Ed.2d 478 (1981), set out at p. 110, supra. See generally, John C. Roberts, Gender–Based

Draft Registration, Congressional Policy and Equal Protection: A Proposal for Deferential Middle–Tier Review, 27 Wayne L.Rev. 35 (1980).

45. Kornblum, supra note 2, at 442–43.

46. Jean Yarbrough, The Feminist Mistake: Sexual Equality and the Decline of the American Military, 33 Policy Review 48 (Summer 1985).

47. Id., at 52.

whereas the case against women in combat is rooted in recognition of genuine physical and psychological differences that are important in battle, such as strength, aggressiveness, and sexual attraction. To the extent that the prejudice against women is based on an appreciation of these natural and desirable differences, it is valid and should influence military policy.

How do you evaluate these arguments? Consider the critique that Professor Wendy Williams has provided of *Rostker:*[48]

Suppose you could step outside our culture, rise above its minutiae, and look at its great contours. Having done so, speculate for a moment about where society might draw the line and refuse to proceed further with gender equality. What does our culture identify as quintessentially masculine? Where is the locus of traditional masculine pride and self-identity? What can we identify in men's cultural experience that most divides it from women's cultural experience? Surely, one rather indisputable answer to that question is "war": physical combat and its modern equivalents.

* * *

Not surprisingly, the Court in *Rostker* didn't come right out and say, "We've reached our cultural limits." * * * When Congress considered whether women should be drafted, it was much more forthright about its reasons and those reasons support my thesis. * * * To translate, Congress was worried that (1) sexually mixed units would not be able to function—perhaps because of sex in the foxhole? (2) if women were assigned to combat, the nation might be reluctant to go to war, presumably because the specter of women fighting would deter a protective and chivalrous populace; and (3) the idea that mom could go into battle and dad keep the home fires burning is simply beyond the cultural pale. In short, current notions of acceptable limits on sex-role behavior would be surpassed by putting women into combat.

Yet if military women cannot hold combat assignments, their usefulness as military officers is open to question. As the Women Midshipmen Study Group put it in a Report to Superintendent Maryott,[49]

[t]he combat exclusion law results in many male midshipmen undervaluing the contributions women midshipmen will make as officers and serves as justification for those who believe women should not be at the Naval Academy. This attitude is so pervasive that some women midshipmen have come to see their Naval Academy training as incongruent with the career options presently open to them.

The lack of respect for women in the military was demonstrated for many observers by the rowdy activities of naval aviators assembled in Las Vegas in September 1991 for their Tailhook convention at which 83 women, including naval officers and guests, were assaulted. This conclusion was confirmed when it became clear, nearly three years later, that no one would stand trial for the lewd conduct that the Navy admitted had occurred. The Navy decided not to appeal a military court's dismissal of the last three cases arising from the incident, despite the judge's statement that Admiral Frank B. Kelso, the Chief of Naval Operations,

48. Wendy W. Williams, The Equality Crisis: Some Reflections on Culture, Courts, and Feminism, 7 Women's Rights L.Rep. 175, 182–85 (1982) (footnotes omitted).

49. Report to the Superintendent on the Integration of Women in the Brigade of Midshipmen, Executive Summary, p. v (Nov.1987).

had lied to obstruct the Navy's investigation. Admiral Kelso denied the charge[50] but later agreed to resign two months early in exchange for a tribute that would clear his name.[51] That took care of the matter, right? Well, just barely. Despite a determined effort by all seven women Senators to strip away two of his stars, the full Senate voted 54–43 to permit Admiral Kelso to retire with full honors and all four stars.[52] At a hearing held by the House Armed Services Committee on March 9, 1994, four military women (representing each of the armed forces) testified that they, not their harassers, were punished by the services for complaining about sexual harassment.[53]

3. "BENIGN" CLASSIFICATIONS

MISSISSIPPI UNIVERSITY FOR WOMEN v. HOGAN

Supreme Court of the United States, 1982.
458 U.S. 718, 102 S.Ct. 3331, 73 L.Ed.2d 1090.

JUSTICE O'CONNOR delivered the opinion of the Court.

This case presents the narrow issue of whether a state statute that excludes males from enrolling in a state-supported professional nursing school violates the Equal Protection Clause of the Fourteenth Amendment.

I

The facts are not in dispute. In 1884, the Mississippi Legislature created the Mississippi Industrial Institute and College for the Education of White Girls of the State of Mississippi, now the oldest state-supported all-female college in the United States. 1884 Miss.Gen.Laws, Ch. 30, § 6. The school, known today as Mississippi University for Women (MUW), has from its inception limited its enrollment to women.[1]

In 1971, MUW established a School of Nursing, initially offering a 2–year associate degree. Three years later, the school instituted a 4–year baccalaureate program in nursing and today also offers a graduate program. The School of Nursing has its own faculty and administrative officers and establishes its own criteria for admission.

50. The New York Times, February 12, 1994, at A–1, cols. 5–6.

51. The New York Times, February 20, 1994, at E–2, col. 2.

52. The New York Times, April 20, 1994, at A–1, cols. 2–3.

53. The New York Times, March 10, 1994, at A–1, cols. 4–5. See Maya Murray, Sexual Harassment in the Military, 3 So.Cal.Rev.L. & Wom.St. 279 (1994) (urging extension of Title VII, discussed in chapter III, infra, to the uniformed services). Would this be an effective solution for military women?

1. The charter of MUW, basically unchanged since its founding, now provides:

"The purpose and aim of the Mississippi State College for Women is the moral and intellectual advancement of the girls of the state by the maintenance of a first-class institution for their education in the arts and sciences, for their training in normal school methods and kindergarten, for their instruction in bookkeeping, photography, stenography, telegraphy, and typewriting, and in designing, drawing, engraving, and painting, and their industrial application, and for their instruction in fancy, general, and practical needlework, and in such other industrial branches as experience, from time to time, shall suggest as necessary or proper to fit them for the practical affairs of life." Miss. Code Ann. § 37–117–3 (1972).

Mississippi maintains no other single-sex public university or college. Thus, we are not faced with the question of whether States can provide "separate but equal" undergraduate institutions for males and females. Cf. Vorchheimer v. School District of Philadelphia, 532 F.2d 880 (C.A.3 1976), aff'd by an equally divided court, 430 U.S. 703, 97 S.Ct. 1671, 51 L.Ed.2d 750 (1977).

Respondent, Joe Hogan, is a registered nurse but does not hold a baccalaureate degree in nursing. Since 1974, he has worked as a nursing supervisor in a medical center in Columbus, the city in which MUW is located. In 1979, Hogan applied for admission to the MUW School of Nursing's baccalaureate program.[3] Although he was otherwise qualified, he was denied admission to the School of Nursing solely because of his sex. School officials informed him that he could audit the courses in which he was interested, but could not enroll for credit. * * *[4]

Hogan filed an action in the United States District Court for the Northern District of Mississippi, claiming the single-sex admissions policy of MUW's School of Nursing violated the Equal Protection Clause of the Fourteenth Amendment. Hogan sought injunctive and declaratory relief, as well as compensatory damages.

Following a hearing, the District Court denied preliminary injunctive relief. * * *

The Court of Appeals for the Fifth Circuit reversed, * * *

We granted certiorari, * * * and now affirm the judgment of the Court of Appeals.[7]

II

We begin our analysis aided by several firmly established principles. Because the challenged policy expressly discriminates among applicants on the basis of gender, it is subject to scrutiny under the Equal Protection Clause of the Fourteenth Amendment. Reed v. Reed, * * *. That this statutory policy discriminates against males rather than against females does not exempt it from scrutiny or reduce the standard of review.[8] Caban v. Mohammed, * * *; Orr v. Orr, * * *. Our decisions also establish that the party seeking to uphold a statute that classifies individuals on the basis of their gender must carry the burden of showing an "exceedingly persuasive justification" for the classification. Kirchberg v. Feenstra, * * *; Personnel

3. With a baccalaureate degree, Hogan would be able to earn a higher salary and would be eligible to obtain specialized training as an anesthetist. * * *

4. Dr. James Strobel, President of MUW, verified that men could audit the equivalent of a full classload in either night or daytime classes. * * *.

7. Although some statements in the Court of Appeals' decision refer to all schools within MUW, see 646 F.2d, at 1119, the factual underpinning of Hogan's claim for relief involved only his exclusion from the nursing program, * * * and the Court of Appeals' holding applies only to Hogan's individual claim for relief. * * * Additionally, during oral argument, counsel verified that Hogan sought only admission to the School of Nursing. * * * Because Hogan's claim is thus limited, and because we review judgments, not statements in opinions, Black v. Cutter Laboratories, 351 U.S. 292, 76 S.Ct. 824, 100 L.Ed. 1188 (1956), we decline to address the question of whether MUW's admissions policy, as applied to males seeking admission to schools other than the School of Nursing, violates the Fourteenth Amendment.

8. Without question, MUW's admissions policy worked to Hogan's disadvantage. Although Hogan could have attended classes and received credit in one of Mississippi's state-supported coeducational nursing programs, none of which was located in Columbus, he could attend only by driving a considerable distance from his home. * * * A similarly situated female would not have been required to choose between foregoing credit and bearing that inconvenience. Moreover, since many students enrolled in the School of Nursing hold full-time jobs, deposition of Dean Annette K. Barrar 29–30, Hogan's female colleagues had available an opportunity, not open to Hogan, to obtain credit for additional training. The policy of denying males the right to obtain credit toward a baccalaureate degree thus imposed upon Hogan "a burden he would not bear were he female." Orr v. Orr, 440 U.S. 268, 273, 99 S.Ct. 1102, 1108, 59 L.Ed.2d 306 (1979).

Administrator of Massachusetts v. Feeney, * * *. The burden is met only by showing at least that the classification serves "important governmental objectives and that the discriminatory means employed" are "substantially related to the achievement of those objectives." Wengler v. Druggists Mutual Insurance Co., 446 U.S. 142, 150, 100 S.Ct. 1540, 1545, 64 L.Ed.2d 107 (1980).[9]

Although the test for determining the validity of a gender-based classification is straightforward, it must be applied free of fixed notions concerning the roles and abilities of males and females. Care must be taken in ascertaining whether the statutory objective itself reflects archaic and stereotypic notions. Thus, if the statutory objective is to exclude or "protect" members of one gender because they are presumed to suffer from an inherent handicap or to be innately inferior, the objective itself is illegitimate. See Frontiero v. Richardson, * * * (plurality opinion).[10]

If the State's objective is legitimate and important, we next determine whether the requisite direct, substantial relationship between objective and means is present. The purpose of requiring that close relationship is to assure that the validity of a classification is determined through reasoned analysis rather than through the mechanical application of traditional, often inaccurate, assumptions about the proper roles of men and women.[11] The

9. In his dissenting opinion, Justice Powell argues that a less rigorous test should apply because Hogan does not advance a "serious equal protection claim. * * *" * * * Justice Blackmun, without proposing an alternative test, labels the test applicable to gender-based discrimination as "rigid" and productive of "needless conformity." * * * Our past decisions establish, however, that when a classification expressly discriminates on the basis of gender, the analysis and level of scrutiny applied to determine the validity of the classification do not vary simply because the objective appears acceptable to individual Members of the Court. While the validity and importance of the objective may affect the outcome of the analysis, the analysis itself does not change.

Thus, we apply the test previously relied upon by the Court to measure the constitutionality of gender-based discrimination. Because we conclude that the challenged statutory classification is not substantially related to an important objective, we need not decide whether classifications based upon gender are inherently suspect. See Stanton v. Stanton, 421 U.S. 7, 13, 95 S.Ct. 1373, 1377, 43 L.Ed.2d 688 (1975).

10. History provides numerous examples of legislative attempts to exclude women from particular areas simply because legislators believed women were less able than men to perform a particular function. In 1873, this Court remained unmoved by Myra Bradwell's argument that the Fourteenth Amendment prohibited a State from classifying her as unfit to practice law simply because she was female. Bradwell v. Illinois, 16 Wall. 130, 21 L.Ed. 442 (1873). In his opinion concurring in the judgment, Justice Bradley described the reasons underlying the State's decision to determine which positions only men could fill:

"It is the prerogative of the legislator to prescribe regulations founded on nature, reason, and experience for the due admission of qualified persons to professions and callings demanding special skill and confidence. This fairly belongs to the police power of the State; and, in my opinion, in view of the peculiar characteristics, destiny, and mission of woman, it is within the province of the legislature to ordain what offices, positions, and callings shall be filled and discharged by men, and shall receive the benefit of those energies and responsibilities, and that decision and firmness which are presumed to predominate in the sterner sex." Id., 16 Wall., at 142.

In a similar vein, the Court in Goesaert v. Cleary, 335 U.S. 464, 466, 69 S.Ct. 198, 199, 93 L.Ed. 163 (1948), upheld a legislature's right to preclude women from bartending, except under limited circumstances, on the ground that the legislature could devise preventive measures against "moral and social problems" that result when women, but apparently not men, tend bar. Similarly, the many protective labor laws enacted in the late 19th and early 20th centuries often had as their objective the protection of weaker workers, which the laws assumed meant females. See generally, B. Brown, A. Freedman, H. Katz, & A. Price, Women's Rights and the Law 209–210 (1977).

11. For instance, in Stanton v. Stanton, supra, this Court invalidated a state statute that specified a greater age of majority for males than for females and thereby affected

need for the requirement is amply revealed by reference to the broad range of statutes already invalidated by this Court, statutes that relied upon the simplistic, outdated assumption that gender could be used as a "proxy for other, more germane bases of classification," Craig v. Boren, * * *, to establish a link between objective and classification.[12]

Applying this framework, we now analyze the arguments advanced by the State to justify its refusal to allow males to enroll for credit in MUW's School of Nursing.

III

A

The State's primary justification for maintaining the single-sex admissions policy of MUW's School of Nursing is that it compensates for discrimination against women and, therefore, constitutes educational affirmative action. * * *.[13] As applied to the School of Nursing, we find the State's argument unpersuasive.

the period during which a divorced parent was responsible for supporting his children. We did not question the importance or validity of the State's interest in defining parents' obligation to support children during their minority. On analysis, however, we determined that the purported relationship between that objective and the gender-based classification was based upon traditional assumptions that "the female [is] destined solely for the home and the rearing of the family, and only the male for the marketplace and the world of ideas * * *. If a specified age of minority is required for the boy in order to assure him parental support while he attains his education and training, so, too, is it for the girl." * * * Once those traditional notions were abandoned, no basis for finding a substantial relationship between classification and objective remained.

12. See, e.g., Kirchberg v. Feenstra, * * * (statute granted only husbands the right to manage and dispose of jointly owned property without the spouse's consent); Wengler v. Druggists Mutual Insurance Co., * * * (statute required a widower, but not a widow, to show he was incapacitated from earning to recover benefits for a spouse's death under workers' compensation laws); Orr v. Orr, * * * (only men could be ordered to pay alimony, following divorce); Craig v. Boren, * * * (women could purchase "nonintoxicating" beer at a younger age than could men); Stanton v. Stanton, supra (women reached majority at an earlier age than did men); Weinberger v. Wiesenfeld, * * * (widows, but not widowers, could collect survivors' benefits under the Social Security Act); Frontiero v. Richardson, * * * (determination of spouse's dependency based upon gender of member of armed forces claiming dependency benefits); Reed v. Reed, * * * (statute preferred men to women as administrators of estates).

13. In its Reply Brief, the State understandably retreated from its contention that MUW was founded to provide opportunities for women which were not available to men. * * * Apparently, the impetus for founding MUW came not from a desire to provide women with advantages superior to those offered men, but rather from a desire to provide white women in Mississippi access to state-supported higher learning. In 1856, Sally Reneau began agitating for a college for white women. Those initial efforts were unsuccessful, and, by 1870, Mississippi provided higher education only for white men and black men and women. E. Mayes, History of Education in Mississippi 178, 228, 245, 259, 266, 270 (1899) (hereinafter Mayes). See also S. Neilson, The History of Mississippi State College for Women 4–5 (unpublished manuscript, 1952) (hereinafter Neilson). In 1882, two years before MUW was chartered, the University of Mississippi opened its doors to women. However, the institution was in those early years not "extensively patronized by females; most of those who come being such as desire to qualify themselves to teach." Mayes, at 178. By 1890, the largest number of women in any class at the University had been 23, while nearly 350 women enrolled in the first session of MUW. Mayes, at 178, 253. Because the University did not solicit the attendance of women until after 1920, and did not accept women at all for a time between 1907 and 1920, most Mississippi women who attended college attended MUW. Neilson, at 86. Thus, in Mississippi, as elsewhere in the country, women's colleges were founded to provide some form of higher education for the academically disenfranchised. See generally 2 T. Woody, A History of Women's Education in the United States 137–223 (1929); L. Baker, I'm Radcliffe! Fly Me! The Seven Sisters and the Failure of Women's Education 22, 136–141 (1976).

In limited circumstances, a gender-based classification favoring one sex can be justified if it intentionally and directly assists members of the sex that is disproportionately burdened. See Schlesinger v. Ballard, 419 U.S. 498, 95 S.Ct. 572, 42 L.Ed.2d 610 (1975). However, we consistently have emphasized that "the mere recitation of a benign, compensatory purpose is not an automatic shield which protects against any inquiry into the actual purposes underlying a statutory scheme." Weinberger v. Wiesenfeld, 420 U.S. 636, 648, 95 S.Ct. 1225, 1233, 43 L.Ed.2d 514 (1975). The same searching analysis must be made, regardless of whether the State's objective is to eliminate family controversy, Reed v. Reed, * * * to achieve administrative efficiency, Frontiero v. Richardson, * * * or to balance the burdens borne by males and females.

It is readily apparent that a State can evoke a compensatory purpose to justify an otherwise discriminatory classification only if members of the gender benefited by the classification actually suffer a disadvantage related to the classification. We considered such a situation in Califano v. Webster, 430 U.S. 313, 97 S.Ct. 1192, 51 L.Ed.2d 360 (1977), which involved a challenge to a statutory classification that allowed women to eliminate more low-earning years than men for purposes of computing Social Security retirement benefits. Although the effect of the classification was to allow women higher monthly benefits than were available to men with the same earning history, we upheld the statutory scheme, noting that it took into account that women "as such have been unfairly hindered from earning as much as men" and "work[ed] directly to remedy" the resulting economic disparity. * * *

A similar pattern of discrimination against women influenced our decision in Schlesinger v. Ballard, * * *. There, we considered a federal statute that granted female Naval officers a 13–year tenure of commissioned service before mandatory discharge, but accorded male officers only a 9–year tenure. We recognized that, because women were barred from combat duty, they had had fewer opportunities for promotion than had their male counterparts. By allowing women an additional four years to reach a particular rank before subjecting them to mandatory discharge, the statute directly compensated for other statutory barriers to advancement.

In sharp contrast, Mississippi has made no showing that women lacked opportunities to obtain training in the field of nursing or to attain positions of leadership in that field when the MUW School of Nursing opened its door or that women currently are deprived of such opportunities. In fact, in 1970, the year before the School of Nursing's first class enrolled, women earned 94 percent of the nursing baccalaureate degrees conferred in Mississippi and 98.6 percent of the degrees earned nationwide. * * * That year was not an aberration; one decade earlier, women had earned all the nursing degrees conferred in Mississippi and 98.9 percent of the degrees conferred nationwide. * * * As one would expect, the labor force reflects the same predominance of women in nursing. When MUW's School of Nursing began operation, nearly 98 percent of all employed registered nurses were female.[14] * * *.

---

14. Relatively little change has taken place during the past 10 years. In 1980, women received more than 94 percent of the baccalau- reate degrees conferred nationwide, * * * and constituted 96.5 percent of the registered nurs- es in the labor force. * * *.

Rather than compensate for discriminatory barriers faced by women, MUW's policy of excluding males from admission to the School of Nursing tends to perpetuate the stereotyped view of nursing as an exclusively woman's job.[15] By assuring that Mississippi allots more openings in its state-supported nursing schools to women than it does to men, MUW's admissions policy lends credibility to the old view that women, not men, should become nurses, and makes the assumption that nursing is a field for women a self-fulfilling prophecy. * * * Thus, we conclude that, although the State recited a "benign, compensatory purpose," it failed to establish that the alleged objective is the actual purpose underlying the discriminatory classification.[16]

The policy is invalid also because it fails the second part of the equal protection test, for the State has made no showing that the gender-based classification is substantially and directly related to its proposed compensatory objective. To the contrary, MUW's policy of permitting men to attend classes as auditors fatally undermines its claim that women, at least those in the School of Nursing, are adversely affected by the presence of men.

MUW permits men who audit to participate fully in classes. Additionally, both men and women take part in continuing education courses offered by the School of Nursing, in which regular nursing students also can enroll. * * * The uncontroverted record reveals that admitting men to nursing classes does not affect teaching style, * * * that the presence of men in the classroom would not affect the performance of the female nursing students, * * * and that men in coeducational nursing schools do not dominate the classroom. * * * In sum, the record in this case is flatly inconsistent with the claim that excluding men from the School of Nursing is necessary to reach any of MUW's educational goals.

Thus, considering both the asserted interest and the relationship between the interest and the methods used by the State, we conclude that the State has fallen far short of establishing the "exceedingly persuasive justification" needed to sustain the gender-based classification. Accordingly, we hold that MUW's policy of denying males the right to enroll for credit in its School of Nursing violates the Equal Protection Clause of the Fourteenth Amendment.[17]

* * *

15. Officials of the American Nurses Association have suggested that excluding men from the field has depressed nurses' wages. * * * To the extent the exclusion of men has that effect, MUW's admissions policy actually penalizes the very class the State purports to benefit. Cf. Weinberger v. Wiesenfeld, supra.

16. Even were we to assume that discrimination against women affects their opportunity to obtain an education or to obtain leadership roles in nursing, the challenged policy nonetheless would be invalid, for the State has failed to establish that the legislature intended the single-sex policy to compensate for any perceived discrimination. Cf. Califano v. Webster, 430 U.S. 313, 318, 97 S.Ct. 1192, 1195, 51 L.Ed.2d 360 (1977) (legislative history of the compensatory statute revealed that Congress "directly addressed the justification for differing treatment of men and women" and "purposely en-

acted the more favorable treatment for female wage earners. * * * "). The State has provided no evidence whatever that the Mississippi legislature has ever attempted to justify its differing treatment of men and women seeking nurses' training. Indeed, the only statement of legislative purpose is that in § 37–117–3 of the Mississippi Code, see n. 1, supra, a statement that relies upon the very sort of archaic and overbroad generalizations about women that we have found insufficient to justify a gender-based classification. E.g., Orr v. Orr, supra; Stanton v. Stanton, supra.

17. Justice Powell's dissent suggests that a second objective is served by the gender-based classification in that Mississippi has elected to provide women a choice of educational environments. * * * Since any gender-based classification provides one class a benefit or choice not

IV

Because we conclude that the State's policy of excluding males from MUW's School of Nursing violates the Equal Protection Clause of the Fourteenth Amendment, we affirm the judgment of the Court of Appeals.

It is so ordered.

CHIEF JUSTICE BURGER, dissenting.

I agree generally with Justice Powell's dissenting opinion. I write separately, however, to emphasize that the Court's holding today is limited to the context of a professional nursing school. * * * Since the Court's opinion relies heavily on its finding that women have traditionally dominated the nursing profession, * * * it suggests that a State might well be justified in maintaining, for example, the option of an all-women's business school or liberal arts program.

JUSTICE BLACKMUN, dissenting.

Unless Mississippi University for Women wished to preserve an historical anachronism, one only states the obvious when he observes that the University long ago should have replaced its original statement of purpose and brought its corporate papers into the 20th century. It failed to do so and, perhaps in partial consequence, finds itself in this litigation, with the Court's opinion, * * * n. 1, * * * now taking full advantage of that failure, to MUW's embarrassment and discomfiture.

Despite that failure, times have changed in the intervening 98 years. What was once an "Institute and College" is now a genuine university, with a 2–year School of Nursing established 11 years ago and then expanded to a 4–year baccalaureate program in 1974. But respondent Hogan "wants in" at this particular location in his home city of Columbus. It is not enough that his State of Mississippi offers baccalaureate programs in nursing open to males at Jackson and at Hattiesburg. Mississippi thus has not closed the doors of its educational system to males like Hogan. Assuming that he is qualified—and I have no reason whatsoever to doubt his qualifications—those doors are open and his maleness alone does not prevent his gaining the additional education he professes to seek.

I have come to suspect that it is easy to go too far with rigid rules in this area of claimed sex discrimination, and to lose—indeed destroy—values that mean much to some people by forbidding the State to offer them a choice while not depriving others of an alternate choice. Justice Powell in his separate opinion, * * * advances this theme well.

While the Court purports to write narrowly, declaring that it does not decide the same issue with respect to "separate but equal" undergraduate institutions for females and males, * * * n. 1, * * * or with respect to units of MUW other than its School of Nursing, * * * n. 7, there is inevitable spillover from the Court's ruling today. That ruling, it seems to me, places in constitutional jeopardy any state-supported educational institution that confines its student body in any area to members of one sex, even though the

available to the other class, however, that argument begs the question. The issue is not whether the benefited class profits from the classification, but whether the State's decision to confer a benefit only upon one class by means of a discriminatory classification is substantially related to achieving a legitimate and substantial goal.

State elsewhere provides an equivalent program to the complaining applicant. The Court's reasoning does not stop with the School of Nursing of the Mississippi University for Women.

I hope that we do not lose all values that some think are worthwhile (and are not based on differences of race or religion) and relegate ourselves to needless conformity. The ringing words of the Equal Protection Clause of the Fourteenth Amendment—what Justice Powell aptly describes as its "liberating spirit," * * *—do not demand that price.

JUSTICE POWELL, with whom JUSTICE REHNQUIST joins, dissenting.

The Court's opinion bows deeply to conformity. Left without honor—indeed, held unconstitutional—is an element of diversity that has characterized much of American education and enriched much of American life. The Court in effect holds today that no State now may provide even a single institution of higher learning open only to women students. It gives no heed to the efforts of the State of Mississippi to provide abundant opportunities for young men and young women to attend coeducational institutions, and none to the preferences of the more than 40,000 young women who over the years have evidenced their approval of an all-women's college by choosing Mississippi University for Women (MUW) over seven coeducational universities within the State. The Court decides today that the Equal Protection Clause makes it unlawful for the State to provide women with a traditionally popular and respected choice of educational environment. It does so in a case instituted by one man, who represents no class, and whose primary concern is personal convenience.

It is undisputed that women enjoy complete equality of opportunity in Mississippi's public system of higher education. Of the State's 8 universities and 16 junior colleges, all except MUW are coeducational. At least two other Mississippi universities would have provided respondent with the nursing curriculum that he wishes to pursue.[1] No other male has joined in his complaint. The only groups with any personal acquaintance with MUW to file *amicus* briefs are female students and alumnae of MUW. And they have emphatically rejected respondent's arguments, urging that the State of Mississippi be allowed to continue offering the choice from which they have benefited.

Nor is respondent significantly disadvantaged by MUW's all-female tradition. His constitutional complaint is based upon a single asserted harm: that he must *travel* to attend the state-supported nursing schools that concededly are available to him. The Court characterizes this injury as one of "inconvenience." * * * This description is fair and accurate, though somewhat embarrassed by the fact that there is, of course, no constitutional right to attend a state-supported university in one's home town. Thus the Court, to redress respondent's injury of inconvenience, must rest its invalidation of MUW's single-sex program on a mode of "sexual stereotype" reasoning that has no application whatever to the respondent or to the "wrong" of which he complains. At best this is anomalous. And ultimately the anomaly reveals

---

1. "[T]wo other Mississippi universities offered coeducational programs leading to a Bachelor of Science in Nursing—the University of Southern Mississippi in Hattiesburg, 178 miles from Columbus; and the University of Mississippi in Jackson, 147 miles from Columbus * * *."

legal error—that of applying a heightened equal protection standard, developed in cases of genuine sexual stereotyping, to a narrowly utilized state classification that provides an *additional* choice for women. Moreover, I believe that Mississippi's educational system should be upheld in this case even if this inappropriate method of analysis is applied.

I

Coeducation, historically, is a novel educational theory. From grade school through high school, college, and graduate and professional training, much of the nation's population during much of our history has been educated in sexually segregated classrooms. At the college level, for instance, until recently some of the most prestigious colleges and universities—including most of the Ivy League—had long histories of single-sex education. As Harvard, Yale, and Princeton remained all-male colleges well into the second half of this century, the "Seven Sister" institutions established a parallel standard of excellence for women's colleges. Of the Seven Sisters, Mount Holyoke opened as a female seminary in 1837 and was chartered as a college in 1888. Vassar was founded in 1865, Smith and Wellesley in 1875, Radcliffe in 1879, Bryn Mawr in 1885, and Barnard in 1889. Mount Holyoke, Smith, and Wellesley recently have made considered decisions to remain essentially single-sex institutions. See Carnegie Commission on Higher Education, Opportunities for Women in Higher Education 70–75 (1973) (Carnegie Report), excerpted in B. Babcock, A. Freedman, E. Norton, & S. Ross, Sex Discrimination and the Law 1013, 1014 (1975) (Babcock). Barnard retains its independence from Columbia, its traditional coordinate institution. Harvard and Radcliffe maintained separate admissions policies as recently as 1975.[2]

The sexual segregation of students has been a reflection of, rather than an imposition upon, the preference of those subject to the policy. It cannot be disputed, for example, that the highly qualified women attending the leading women's colleges could have earned admission to virtually any college of their choice.[3] Women attending such colleges have chosen to be there, usually expressing a preference for the special benefits of single-sex institutions. Similar decisions were made by the colleges that elected to remain open to women only.[4]

2. The history, briefly summarized above, of single-sex higher education in the Northeast is duplicated in other States. I mention only my State of Virginia, where even today Hollins College, Mary Baldwin College, Randolph Macon Woman's College, and Sweet Briar College remain all women's. Each has a proud and respected reputation of quality education.

3. It is true that historically many institutions of higher education—particularly in the East and South—were single-sex. To these extents, choices were by no means universally available to all men and women. But choices always were substantial, and the purpose of relating the experience of our country with single-sex colleges and universities is to document what should be obvious: generations of Americans, including scholars, have thought—wholly without regard to any discriminatory

animus—that there were distinct advantages in this type of higher education.

4. In announcing Wellesley's decision in 1973 to remain a women's college, President Barbara Newell said that "[t]he research we have clearly demonstrates that women's colleges produce a disproportionate number of women leaders and women in responsible positions in society; it does demonstrate that the higher proportion of women on the faculty the higher the motivation for women students." Carnegie Report, supra, in Babcock, at 1014. Similarly rejecting coeducation in 1971, the Mount Holyoke Trustees Committee on Coeducation reported that "the conditions that historically justified the founding of women's colleges" continued to justify their remaining in that tradition. Ibid.

The arguable benefits of single-sex colleges also continue to be recognized by students of higher education. The Carnegie Commission on Higher Education has reported that it "favor[s] the continuation of colleges for women. They provide an element of diversity * * * and [an environment in which women] generally * * * speak up more in their classes, * * * hold more positions of leadership on campus, * * * and * * * have more role models and mentors among women teachers and administrators." Carnegie Report, quoted in K. Davidson, R. Ginsburg, & H. Kay, Sex–Based Discrimination 814 (1975 ed.). A 10–year empirical study by the Cooperative Institutional Research Program of the American Counsel of Education and the University of California, Los Angeles, also has affirmed the distinctive benefits of single-sex colleges and universities. As summarized in A. Astin, Four Critical Years 232 (1977), the data established that

> "[b]oth [male and female] single-sex colleges facilitate student involvement in several areas: academic, interaction with faculty, and verbal aggressiveness * * *. Men's and women's colleges also have a positive effect on intellectual self-esteem. Students at single-sex colleges are more satisfied than students at coeducational colleges with virtually all aspects of college life * * *. The only area where students are less satisfied is social life." [5]

Despite the continuing expressions that single-sex institutions may offer singular advantages to their students, there is no doubt that coeducational institutions are far more numerous. But their numerical predominance does not establish—in any sense properly cognizable by a court—that individual preferences for single-sex education are misguided or illegitimate, or that a State may not provide its citizens with a choice.[6]

II

The issue in this case is whether a State transgresses the Constitution when—within the context of a public system that offers a diverse range of campuses, curricula, and educational alternatives—it seeks to accommodate the legitimate personal preferences of those desiring the advantages of an all-women's college. In my view, the Court errs seriously by assuming—without argument or discussion—that the equal protection standard generally applica-

---

5. In this Court the benefits of single-sex education have been asserted by the students and alumnae of MUW. One would expect the Court to regard their views as directly relevant to this case:

"[I]n the aspect of life known as courtship or mate-pairing, the American female remains in the role of the pursued sex, expected to adorn and groom herself to attract the male. Without comment on the equities of this social arrangement, it remains a sociological fact.

"An institution of collegiate higher learning maintained exclusively for women is uniquely able to provide the education atmosphere in which some, but not all, women can best attain maximum learning potential. It can serve to overcome the historic repression of the past and can orient a woman to function and achieve in the still male domi-

nated economy. It can free its students of the burden of playing the mating game while attending classes, thus giving academic rather than sexual emphasis. Consequently, many such institutions flourish and their graduates make significant contributions to the arts, professions and business." Brief for Mississippi University for Women Alumnae Assn. as *Amicus Curiae* 2–3.

6. "[T]he Constitution does not require that a classification keep abreast of the latest in educational opinion, especially when there remains a respectable opinion to the contrary * * *. Any other rule would mean that courts and not legislatures would determine all matters of public policy." Williams v. McNair, 316 F.Supp. 134, 137 (D.S.C.1970), aff'd mem., 401 U.S. 951, 91 S.Ct. 976, 28 L.Ed.2d 235 (1971) (quotations and footnotes omitted).

ble to sex discrimination is appropriate here. That standard was designed to free women from "archaic and overbroad generalizations * * *." Schlesinger v. Ballard, * * * In no previous case have we applied it to invalidate state efforts to *expand* women's choices. Nor are there prior sex discrimination decisions by this Court in which a male plaintiff, as in this case, had the choice of an equal benefit.

The cases cited by the Court therefore do not control the issue now before us. In most of them women were given no opportunity for the same benefit as men.[7] Cases involving male plaintiffs are equally inapplicable. In Craig v. Boren, * * * a male under 21 was not permitted to buy beer anywhere in the State, and women were afforded no choice as to whether they would accept the "statistically measured but loose-fitting generalities concerning the drinking tendencies of aggregate groups." * * * A similar situation prevailed in Orr v. Orr, * * * where men had no opportunity to seek alimony from their divorced wives, and women had no escape from the statute's stereotypical announcement of "the State's preference for an allocation of family responsibilities under which the wife plays a dependent role * * *."[8]

By applying heightened equal protection analysis to this case,[9] the Court frustrates the liberating spirit of the Equal Protection Clause. It prohibits the States from providing women with an opportunity to choose the type of university they prefer. And yet it is these women whom the Court regards as the *victims* of an illegal, stereotyped perception of the role of women in our society. The Court reasons this way in a case in which no woman has complained, and the only complainant is a man who advances no claims on behalf of anyone else. His claim, it should be recalled, is not that he is being denied a substantive educational opportunity, or even the right to attend an all-male or a coeducational college. See Brief for Respondent 24.[10] It is *only*

---

7. See Kirchberg v. Feenstra, * * * (invalidating statute "that gave husband, as 'head and master' of property jointly owned with his wife, the unilateral right to dispose of such property without his spouse's consent"); Wengler v. Druggist Mutual Ins. Co., * * * (invalidating law under which the benefits "that the working woman can expect to be paid to her spouse in the case of her work-related death are less than those payable to the spouse of the deceased male wage earner"); Stanton v. Stanton, * * * (invalidating statute that provided a shorter period of parental support obligation for female children than for male children); Weinberger v. Wiesenfeld, * * * (invalidating statute that failed to grant a woman worker "the same protection which a similarly situated male worker would have received"); Frontiero v. Richardson, * * * (invalidating statute containing a "mandatory preference for male applicants"); Reed v. Reed, * * * (invalidating an "arbitrary preference established in favor of males" in the administration of decedent's estates).

8. See also Caban v. Mohammed, * * * (invalidating law that both denied men the opportunity—given to women—of blocking the adoption of his illegitimate child by means of withholding his consent, and that did not per-

mit women to counter the statute's generalization that the maternal role is more important to women than the paternal role is to men).

9. Even the Court does not argue that the appropriate standard here is "strict scrutiny"—a standard that none of our "sex discrimination" cases ever has adopted. Sexual segregation in education differs from the tradition, typified by the decision in Plessy v. Ferguson, 163 U.S. 537, 16 S.Ct. 1138, 41 L.Ed. 256 (1896), of "separate but equal" *racial* segregation. It was characteristic of racial segregation that segregated facilities were offered, not as alternatives to increase the choices available to blacks, but as the *sole* alternative. MUW stands in sharp contrast. Of Mississippi's 8 public universities and 16 public junior colleges, only MUW considers sex as a criterion for admission. Women consequently are free to select a coeducational education environment for themselves if they so desire; their attendance of MUW is not a matter of coercion.

10. The Court says that "any gender-based classification provides one class a benefit or choice not available to the other class * * *." * * * n. 17. It then states that the issue "is not whether the benefited class profits from the classification, but whether the state's deci-

that the colleges open to him are located at inconvenient distances.[11]

III

The Court views this case as presenting a serious equal protection claim of sex discrimination. I do not, and I would sustain Mississippi's right to continue MUW on a rational basis analysis. But I need not apply this "lowest tier" of scrutiny. I can accept for present purposes the standard applied by the Court: that there is a gender-based distinction that must serve an important governmental objective by means that are substantially related to its achievement. * * * The record in this case reflects that MUW has a historic position in the State's educational system dating back to 1884. More than 2,000 women presently evidence their preference for MUW by having enrolled there. The choice is one that discriminates invidiously against no one.[12] And the State's purpose in preserving that choice is legitimate and substantial. Generations of our finest minds, both among educators and students, have believed that single-sex, college-level institutions afford distinctive benefits. There are many persons, of course, who have different views. But simply because there are these differences is no reason—certainly none of constitutional dimension—to conclude that no substantial state interest is served when such a choice is made available.

In arguing to the contrary, the Court suggests that the MUW is so operated as to "perpetuate the stereotyped view of nursing as an exclusively women's job." * * * But as the Court itself acknowledges, * * * MUW's School of Nursing was not created until 1971—about 90 years after the single-sex campus itself was founded. This hardly supports a link between nursing as a woman's profession and MUW's single-sex admission policy. Indeed, MUW's School of Nursing was not instituted until more than a decade *after* a separate School of Nursing was established at the coeducational University of Mississippi at Jackson. * * * The School of Nursing makes up only one part—a relatively small part—of MUW's diverse modern university campus and curriculum. The other departments on the MUW campus offer a typical range of degrees and a typical range of subjects. There is no indication that

sion to confer a benefit *only* upon *one* class by means of a discriminatory classification is substantially related to achieving a legitimate and substantial goal." * * * This is *not* the issue in this case. Hogan is not complaining about any benefit conferred upon women. Nor is he claiming discrimination because Mississippi offers no all-male college. As his brief states: "Joe Hogan does not ask to attend an all-male college which offers a Bachelor of Science in nursing; he asks only to attend MUW." * * * And he asks this only for his personal convenience.

11. Students in respondent's position, in "being denied the right to attend the State college in their home town, are treated no differently than are other students who reside in communities many miles distant from any State supported college or university. The location of any such institution must necessarily inure to the benefit of some and to the detri-

ment of others, depending upon the distance the affected individuals reside from the institution." Heaton v. Bristol, 317 S.W.2d 86, 99 (Tex.Civ.App.1958), cert. denied, 359 U.S. 230, 79 S.Ct. 802, 3 L.Ed.2d 765 (1959), quoted in Williams v. McNair, 316 F.Supp. 134, 137 (D.S.C.1970), aff'd mem., 401 U.S. 951, 91 S.Ct. 976, 28 L.Ed.2d 235 (1971).

12. "Such a plan (i.e., giving the student a choice of a 'single-sex' and coeducational institutions) exalts neither sex at the expense of the other, but to the contrary recognizes the equal rights of both sexes to the benefit of the best, most varied system of higher education that the State can supply." Williams v. McNair, 316 F.Supp. 134, 138 n. 15 (D.S.C. 1970), aff'd mem., 401 U.S. 951, 91 S.Ct. 976, 28 L.Ed.2d 235 (1971), quoting Heaton v. Bristol, 317 S.W.2d 86, 100 (Tex.Civ.App.1958), cert. denied, 359 U.S. 230, 79 S.Ct. 802, 3 L.Ed.2d 765 (1959).

women suffer fewer opportunities at other Mississippi state campuses because of MUW's admission policy.

In sum, the practice of voluntarily chosen single-sex education is an honored tradition in our country, even if it now rarely exists in state colleges and universities. Mississippi's accommodation of such student choices is legitimate because it is completely consensual and is important because it permits students to decide for themselves the type of college education they think will benefit them most. Finally, Mississippi's policy is substantially related to its long-respected objective.[17]

IV

A distinctive feature of America's tradition has been respect for diversity. This has been characteristic of the peoples from numerous lands who have built our country. It is the essence of our democratic system. At stake in this case as I see it is the preservation of a small aspect of this diversity. But that aspect is by no means insignificant, given our heritage of available choice between single-sex and coeducational institutions of higher learning. The Court answers that there is discrimination—not just that which may be tolerable, as for example between those candidates for admission able to contribute most to an educational institution and those able to contribute less—but discrimination of constitutional dimension. But, having found "discrimination," the Court finds it difficult to identify the victims. It hardly can claim that women are discriminated against. A constitutional case is held to exist solely because one man found it inconvenient to travel to any of the other institutions made available to him by the State of Mississippi. In essence he insists that he has a right to attend a college in his home community. This simply is not a sex discrimination case. The Equal Protection Clause was never intended to be applied to this kind of case.[18]

17. The Court argues that MUW's means are not sufficiently related to its goal because it has allowed men to audit classes. The extent of record information is that men have audited 138 courses in the last 10 years. * * * On average, then, men have audited 14 courses a year. MUW's current annual catalog lists 913 courses offered in *one* year. * * *

It is understandable that MUW might believe that it could allow men to audit courses without materially affecting its environment. MUW charges tuition but gives no academic credit for auditing. The University evidently is correct in believing that few men will choose to audit under such circumstances. This deviation from a perfect relationship between means and ends is insubstantial.

18. The Court, in the opening and closing sentences and note 7 of its opinion, states the issue in terms only of a "professional nursing school" and "decline[s] to address the question of whether MUW's admissions policy, as applied to males seeking admission to schools other than the School of Nursing, violates the Fourteenth Amendment." This would be a welcome limitation if, in fact, it leaves MUW free to remain an all-women's university in each of its other schools and departments—

which include four schools and more than a dozen departments. * * * The question the Court does not answer is whether MUW may remain a women's university in every respect except its School of Nursing. This is a critical question for this University and its responsible board and officials. The Court holds today that they have deprived Hogan of constitutional rights because MUW is adjudged guilty of sex discrimination. The logic of the Court's entire opinion, apart from its statements mentioned above, appears to apply sweepingly to the entire University. The exclusion of men from the School of Nursing is repeatedly characterized as "gender-based discrimination," subject to the same standard of analysis applied in previous sex discrimination cases of this Court. Nor does the opinion anywhere deny that this analysis applies to the entire University.

The Court nevertheless purports to decide this case "narrow[ly]." Normally and properly we decide only the question presented. It seems to me that in fact the issue properly before us is the single-sex policy of the University, and it is this issue that I have addressed in this dissent. The Court of Appeals so viewed this case, and unambiguously held that

Notes on **Hogan**

1. If Mississippi can't exclude men from nursing school, can Virginia exclude women from military school? * Can Mississippi open an all-male nursing school? How about an all-female law school? What is the impact of the *Hogan* decision on MUW's undergraduate liberal arts program? Can it remain available only to women? The arguments for and against single sex education are considered in Chapter IV, infra.

2. Note Justice O'Connor's insistence that the party seeking to uphold a statute drawing a gender-based line carry the burden of justifying the classification. That's a change from the Court's willingness in *Craig* to assume for purposes of discussion a likely-sounding justification for the statute, isn't it? See p. 42, n. 7, supra. The change came in Kirchberg v. Feenstra, 450 U.S. 455, 101 S.Ct. 1195, 67 L.Ed.2d 428 (1981), where the Court declined to speculate about the possible justifications for a gender-based classification. The point seems to have been made: in Cimaglia v. Schweiker, 555 F.Supp. 710 (S.D.Fla.1983), the Secretary admitted that he had no "knowledge of factors which tend either to support or to invalidate" a provision of the Social Security Act which terminated eligibility for Child's Disability Insurance Benefits for a woman, but not a man, upon marriage to another recipient of Child's Disability Insurance Benefits. The Court held the gender based distinction in violation of the equal protection component of the Fifth Amendment, noting that "[a]pparently, the Secretary has done extensive research into the legislative history of these provisions and has found no rationale for this distinction based upon gender—much less facts or statistics to support any valid rationale." Id., 555 F.Supp. at 712. It is a sign of progress that no one suggested the husband's duty of support as a possible rationale. Obligations of support during marriage are discussed in Chapter Two.

Does the Court's unwillingness to give the legislator the benefit of the doubt further differentiate the level of judicial scrutiny used in sex discrimination cases from that used in cases examining social and economic legislation under the rational relationship standard?

3. What is the justification for using the *Craig* standard in *Hogan?* Does Justice Powell use that standard correctly in his dissent? What do you make of his distinction between state statutes that expand options for women and those that curtail women's opportunities? Do men need encouragement to attend secretarial school?

4. In Kahn v. Shevin, 416 U.S. 351, 94 S.Ct. 1734, 40 L.Ed.2d 189 (1974), the Court upheld a Florida statute, originally enacted in 1885, that granted an annual $500 exemption from property tax to widows. Widowers did not receive a like exemption. Writing for the Court, Justice Douglas observed that "[t]here can be no dispute that the financial difficulties confronting a lone woman in Florida or in any other State exceed those facing the man." After comparing the income of working women to those of working men, he concluded that " * * * Florida's

a single-sex state institution of higher education no longer is permitted by the Constitution. I see no principled way—in light of the Court's rationale—to reach a different result with respect to other MUW schools and departments. But given the Court's insistence that its decision applies only to the School of Nursing, it is my view that the Board and officials of MUW may continue to operate the remainder of the University on a single-sex basis

without fear of personal liability. The standard of such liability is whether the conduct of the official "violate[s] clearly established statutory or constitutional rights of which a reasonable person would have known". Harlow v. Fitzgerald, 457 U.S. 800, 818, 102 S.Ct. 2727, 2738, 73 L.Ed.2d 396 (1982). The Court today leaves in doubt the reach of its decision.

* See U.S. v. Virginia (AMI) in the Appendix.

differing treatment of widows and widowers 'rest[s] upon some ground of difference having a fair and substantial relation to the object of the legislation.' [citing *Reed*]." He also justified the result by invoking the Court's traditional deference to state tax legislation, noting that "[w]e deal here with a state tax law reasonably designed to further the state policy of cushioning the financial impact of spousal loss upon the sex for whom that loss imposes a disproportionately heavy burden." Justices Brennan and Marshall, dissenting, applied the strict scrutiny standard of review they had urged the Court to adopt in Frontiero v. Richardson, set out at p. 20, supra. They concluded that the state's failure to prove that its compelling objective could not have been achieved by a more precisely tailored statute or a less drastic means required reversal. Justice White, also dissenting, found the Florida statute "invidious." He was not persuaded by the majority's income statistics:

> It may be suggested that the State is entitled to prefer widows over widowers because their assumed need is rooted in past and present economic discrimination against women. But this is not a credible explanation of Florida's tax exemption; for if the State's purpose was to compensate for past discrimination against females, surely it would not have limited the exemption to women who are widows. Moreover, even if past discrimination is considered to be the criterion for current tax exemption, the State nevertheless ignores all those widowers who have felt the effects of economic discrimination, whether as a member of a racial group or as one of the many who cannot escape the cycle of poverty. It seems to me that the State in this case is merely conferring an economic benefit in the form of a tax exemption and has not adequately explained why women should be treated differently than men.

Kahn v. Shevin, id., 416 U.S. at 361–62, 94 S.Ct. at 1740, 40 L.Ed.2d at 197 (dissenting opinion of Justice White). Why do you suppose Justice O'Connor did not mention *Kahn* in her opinion in *Hogan*?

5. Justice O'Connor cites with approval the case of Califano v. Webster, 430 U.S. 313, 97 S.Ct. 1192, 51 L.Ed.2d 360 (1977). See her opinion in *Hogan* at p. 137, supra. Compare this appraisal of *Webster* and consider whether the writer's prediction is confirmed by Heckler v. Mathews, 465 U.S. 728, 104 S.Ct. 1387, 79 L.Ed.2d 646 (1984), noted following *Goldfarb* at p. 76, supra.

> *Webster* * * * underscores that, in contrast to *Goldfarb, Wiesenfeld* and *Frontiero,* the provision at issue involved no "romantically paternalistic" view of women as men's dependents or appendages. Two points are stressed in the opinion. First, when—as in *Webster*—legislation directly addresses discrimination and serves to remedy it, disparate treatment of the sexes, at least as an interim measure, is constitutional. Second, when—as in *Goldfarb*— disparate treatment is rooted in traditional role-typing and is not deliberately and specifically aimed at redressing past injustice, disparate treatment based on sex is unconstitutional. If the Court adheres to the *Webster* synthesis, it will uphold a gender classification justified as compensatory only if in fact adopted by the legislature for remedial reasons rather than out of prejudice about "the way women (or men) are," and even then, only if the classification neatly matches the remedial end.

> *Webster* thus attempts to preserve and bolster a general rule of equal treatment while leaving a corridor open for genuinely compensatory classifications. The line between impermissible adverse discrimination and permissible rectification for past injustice sketched in *Webster* may well be elaborated

in the Court's resolution of more heated "affirmative action" controversies
* * *.

Ruth Bader Ginsburg, Women, Equality, & The Bakke Case, 4 Civil Liberties
Review No. 4, at 8, 13–14 (November/December 1977). Would it be better just to
abolish "benign" discrimination altogether—at least in cases dealing with sex,
rather than race, discrimination? Professor Kanowitz thinks so. See Leo Kanowitz, "Benign" Sex Discrimination: Its Troubles and Their Cure, 31 Hast.L.J. 1379
(1980).

 6. Does Justice O'Connor's statement of the intermediate scrutiny standard
in *Hogan* appreciably tighten its application? Recall the discussion of "impermissible purpose analysis" at p. 58, supra. Does *Cleburne* do more than apply the
Hogan interpretation of the intermediate scrutiny standard to the rational relationship test?

D. FIRST AMENDMENT CONSTRAINTS ON SEX DISCRIMINATION CLAIMS

1. PRIVATE CLUBS

BOARD OF DIRECTORS OF ROTARY INTERNATIONAL v. ROTARY CLUB

Supreme Court of the United States, 1987.
481 U.S. 537, 107 S.Ct. 1940, 95 L.Ed.2d 474.

JUSTICE POWELL delivered the opinion of the Court.

We must decide whether a California statute that requires California
Rotary Clubs to admit women members violates the First Amendment.

I

A

 Rotary International (International) is a nonprofit corporation founded in
1905, with headquarters in Evanston, Illinois. It is "an organization of
business and professional men united worldwide who provide humanitarian
service, encourage high ethical standards in all vocations, and help build
goodwill and peace in the world." * * * Individual members belong to a local
Rotary Club rather than to International. In turn, each local Rotary Club is a
member of International. * * * In August 1982, shortly before the trial in
this case, International comprised 19,788 Rotary Clubs in 157 countries, with
a total membership of about 907,750. * * *

 Individuals are admitted to membership in a Rotary Club according to a
"classification system." The purpose of this system is to ensure "that each
Rotary Club includes a representative of every worthy and recognized business, professional, or institutional activity in the community." * * * Each
active member must work in a leadership capacity in his business or profession. The general rule is that "one active member is admitted for each
classification, but he, in turn, may propose an additional active member, who
must be in the same business or professional classification." [1] * * * Thus,

---

 1. Rotary Clubs may establish separate
classifications for subcategories of a business
 or profession as long as the classification "describe[s] the member's principal and recog-

each classification may be represented by two active members. In addition, "senior active" and "past service" members may represent the same classifications as active members. * * * There is no limit to the number of clergymen, journalists, or diplomats who may be admitted to membership. * * *

Subject to these requirements, each local Rotary Club is free to adopt its own rules and procedures for admitting new members. * * * International has promulgated Recommended Club By-laws providing that candidates for membership will be considered by both a "classifications committee" and a "membership committee." The classifications committee determines whether the candidate's business or profession is described accurately and fits an "open" classification. The membership committee evaluates the candidate's "character, business and social standing, and general eligibility." * * * If any member objects to the candidate's admission, the final decision is made by the club's board of directors.

Membership in Rotary Clubs is open only to men. * * * Herbert A. Pigman, the General Secretary of Rotary International, testified that the exclusion of women results in an "aspect of fellowship * * * that is enjoyed by the present male membership," * * * and also allows Rotary to operate effectively in foreign countries with varied cultures and social mores. Although women are not admitted to membership, they are permitted to attend meetings, give speeches, and receive awards. Women relatives of Rotary members may form their own associations, and are authorized to wear the Rotary lapel pin. Young women between 14 and 28 years of age may join Interact or Rotaract, organizations sponsored by Rotary International.

B

In 1977 the Rotary Club of Duarte, California admitted Donna Bogart, Mary Lou Elliott, and Rosemary Freitag to active membership. International notified the Duarte Club that admitting women members is contrary to the Rotary constitution. After an internal hearing, International's board of directors revoked the charter of the Duarte Club and terminated its membership in Rotary International. The Duarte Club's appeal to the International Convention was unsuccessful.

The Duarte Club and two of its women members filed a complaint in the California Superior Court for the County of Los Angeles. The complaint alleged, *inter alia,* that appellants' actions violated the Unruh Civil Rights Act, Cal.Civ.Code Ann. § 51 (West 1982).[2] Appellees sought to enjoin International from enforcing its restrictions against admitting women members, revoking the Duarte Club's charter, or compelling delivery of the charter to any representative of International. Appellees also sought a declaration that the appellants' actions had violated the Unruh Act. After a bench trial, the

---

nized professional activity * * *." For example, a single Rotary Club may admit categories and subcategories of lawyers: *e.g.,* trial, corporate, tax, labor, and so on.

2. The Unruh Civil Rights Act provides, in part:

"All persons within the jurisdiction of this state are free and equal, and no matter what

their sex, race, color, religion, ancestry, or national origin are entitled to the full and equal accommodations, advantages, facilities, privileges, or services in all business establishments of every kind whatsoever." Cal. Civ.Code Ann. § 51 (West 1982).

court concluded that neither Rotary International nor the Duarte Club is a "business establishment" within the meaning of the Unruh Act.

* * *

The California Court of Appeal reversed. It held that both Rotary International and the Duarte Rotary Club are business establishments subject to the provisions of the Unruh Act. For purposes of the Act, a " 'business' embraces everything about which one can be employed," and an "establishment" includes "not only a fixed location, * * * but also a permanent 'commercial force or organization' or a 'permanent settled position (as in life or business).' "

* * *

We * * * affirm the judgment of the Court of Appeal.

II

In *Roberts v. United States Jaycees,* 468 U.S. 609, 104 S.Ct. 3244, 82 L.Ed.2d 462 (1984), we upheld against First Amendment challenge a Minnesota statute that required the Jaycees to admit women as full voting members. *Roberts* provides the framework for analyzing appellants' constitutional claims. As we observed in *Roberts,* our cases have afforded constitutional protection to freedom of association in two distinct senses. First, the Court has held that the Constitution protects against unjustified government interference with an individual's choice to enter into and maintain certain intimate or private relationships. Second, the Court has upheld the freedom of individuals to associate for the purpose of engaging in protected speech or religious activities. In many cases, government interference with one form of protected association will also burden the other form of association. In *Roberts* we determined the nature and degree of constitutional protection by considering separately the effect of the challenged state action on individuals' freedom of private association and their freedom of expressive association. We follow the same course in this case.[4]

A

The Court has recognized that the freedom to enter into and carry on certain intimate or private relationships is a fundamental element of liberty protected by the Bill of Rights. Such relationships may take various forms, including the most intimate. See *Moore v. East Cleveland,* 431 U.S. 494, 503–504, 97 S.Ct. 1932, 1937–1938, 52 L.Ed.2d 531 (1977) (plurality opinion). We have not attempted to mark the precise boundaries of this type of constitutional protection. The intimate relationships to which we have accorded constitutional protection include marriage, *Zablocki v. Redhail,* 434 U.S. 374, 383–386, 98 S.Ct. 673, 679–681, 54 L.Ed.2d 618 (1978); the begetting and bearing of children, *Carey v. Population Services International,* 431 U.S. 678, 684–686, 97 S.Ct. 2010, 2015–2016, 52 L.Ed.2d 675 (1977); child rearing and education, *Pierce v. Society of Sisters,* 268 U.S. 510, 534–535, 45 S.Ct. 571, 573, 69 L.Ed. 1070 (1925); and cohabitation with relatives, *Moore v. East*

---

4. International, an association of thousands of local Rotary Clubs, can claim no constitutionally protected right of private association. Moreover, its expressive activities are quite limited. * * * Because the Court of Appeal held that the Duarte Rotary Club also is a business establishment subject to the provisions of the Unruh Act, we proceed to consider whether application of the Unruh Act violates the rights of members of local Rotary Clubs.

Cleveland, supra, 431 U.S., at 503–504, 97 S.Ct., at 1937–1938. Of course, we have not held that constitutional protection is restricted to relationships among family members. We have emphasized that the First Amendment protects those relationships, including family relationships, that presuppose "deep attachments and commitments to the necessarily few other individuals with whom one shares not only a special community of thoughts, experiences, and beliefs but also distinctively personal aspects of one's life." *Roberts v. United States Jaycees,* * * * But in *Roberts* we observed that "[d]etermining the limits of state authority over an individual's freedom to enter into a particular association * * * unavoidably entails a careful assessment of where that relationship's objective characteristics locate it on a spectrum from the most intimate to the most attenuated of personal attachments." * * * (citing *Runyon v. McCrary,* 427 U.S. 160, 187–189, 96 S.Ct. 2586, 2602–2603, 49 L.Ed.2d 415 (1976) (Powell, J., concurring)). In determining whether a particular association is sufficiently personal or private to warrant constitutional protection, we consider factors such as size, purpose, selectivity, and whether others are excluded from critical aspects of the relationship. * * *

The evidence in this case indicates that the relationship among Rotary Club members is not the kind of intimate or private relation that warrants constitutional protection. The size of local Rotary Clubs ranges from fewer than 20 to more than 900. * * * There is no upper limit on the membership of any local Rotary Club. About ten percent of the membership of a typical club moves away or drops out during a typical year. * * * The clubs therefore are instructed to "keep a flow of prospects coming" to make up for the attrition and gradually to enlarge the membership. * * * The purpose of Rotary "is to produce an inclusive, not exclusive, membership, making possible the recognition of all useful local occupations, and enabling the club to be a true cross section of the business and professional life of the community." * * * The membership undertakes a variety of service projects designed to aid the community, to raise the standards of the members' businesses and professions and to improve international relations.[5] Such an inclusive "fellowship for service based on diversity of interest," * * * however, beneficial to the members and to those they serve, does not suggest the kind of private or personal relationship to which we have accorded protection under the First Amendment. To be sure, membership in Rotary Clubs is not open to the general public. But each club is instructed to include in its membership "all fully qualified prospective members located within its territory," to avoid "arbitrary limits on the number of members in the club," and to "establish and maintain a membership growth pattern." * * *

Many of the Rotary Clubs' central activities are carried on in the presence of strangers. Rotary Clubs are required to admit any member of any other Rotary Club to their meetings. Members are encouraged to invite business associates and competitors to meetings. At some Rotary Clubs, the visitors number "in the tens and twenties each week." * * * Joint meetings with the members of other organizations, and other joint activities, are permitted.

---

5. We of course recognize that Rotary Clubs, like similar organizations, perform useful and important community services. Rotary Clubs in the vicinity of the Duarte Club have provided meals and transportation to the elderly, vocational guidance for high school students, a swimming program for handicapped children, and international exchange programs, among many other service activities. * * *

The clubs are encouraged to seek coverage of their meetings and activities in local newspapers. In sum, Rotary Clubs, rather than carrying on their activities in an atmosphere of privacy, seek to keep their "windows and doors open to the whole world," * * *. We therefore conclude that application of the Unruh Act to local Rotary Clubs does not interfere unduly with the members' freedom of private association.[6]

B

The Court also has recognized that the right to engage in activities protected by the First Amendment implies "a corresponding right to associate with others in pursuit of a wide variety of political, social, economic, educational, religious, and cultural ends." *Roberts v. United States Jaycees, supra,* at 622, 104 S.Ct., at 3251–3252. See *NAACP v. Claiborne Hardware Co.,* 458 U.S. 886, 907–909, 932–933, 102 S.Ct. 3409, 3422–3424, 3435–3436, 73 L.Ed.2d 1215 (1982). For this reason, "[i]mpediments to the exercise of one's right to choose one's associates can violate the right of association protected by the First Amendment. * * * " *Hishon v. King & Spalding,* 467 U.S. 69, 80, n. 4, 104 S.Ct. 2229, 2236, n. 4, 81 L.Ed.2d 59 (1984) (POWELL, J., concurring) (citing *NAACP v. Button,* 371 U.S. 415, 83 S.Ct. 328, 9 L.Ed.2d 405 (1963); *NAACP v. Alabama ex rel. Patterson,* 357 U.S. 449, 78 S.Ct. 1163, 2 L.Ed.2d 1488 (1958)). In this case, however, the evidence fails to demonstrate that admitting women to Rotary Clubs will affect in any significant way the existing members' ability to carry out their various purposes.

As a matter of policy, Rotary Clubs do not take positions on "public questions," including political or international issues. * * * To be sure, Rotary Clubs engage in a variety of commendable service activities that are protected by the First Amendment. But the Unruh Act does not require the clubs to abandon or alter any of these activities. It does not require them to abandon their basic goals of humanitarian service, high ethical standards in all vocations, goodwill, and peace. Nor does it require them to abandon their classification system or admit members who do not reflect a cross-section of the community. Indeed, by opening membership to leading business and professional women in the community, Rotary Clubs are likely to obtain a more representative cross-section of community leaders with a broadened capacity for service.[7]

6. Appellants assert that we "approved" a distinction between the Jaycees and the Kiwanis Club in *Roberts v. United States Jaycees,* 468 U.S. 609, 630, 104 S.Ct. 3244, 3256, 82 L.Ed.2d 462 (1984). Brief for Appellants 21. Appellants misconstrue *Roberts.* In that case we observed that the Minnesota court had suggested Kiwanis Clubs were outside the scope of the State's public accommodations law. We concluded that this refuted the Jaycees' arguments that the Minnesota statute was vague and overbroad. We did not consider whether the relationship among members of the Kiwanis Club was sufficiently intimate or private to warrant constitutional protection. Similarly, we have no occasion in this case to consider the extent to which the First Amendment protects the right of individuals to associate in the many clubs and other entities with selective membership that are found throughout the country. Whether the "zone of privacy" established by the First Amendment extends to a particular club or entity requires a careful inquiry into the objective characteristics of the particular relationships at issue. *Roberts v. United States Jaycees, supra,* at 620, 104 S.Ct., at 3250. Cf. *Moose Lodge No. 107 v. Irvis,* 407 U.S. 163, 179–180, 92 S.Ct. 1965, 1974–1975, 32 L.Ed.2d 627 (1972) (Douglas, J., dissenting).

7. In 1980 women were reported to make up 40.6 percent of the managerial and professional labor force in the United States. U.S. Department of Commerce, Statistical Abstract of the United States 400 (1986).

Even if the Unruh Act does work some slight infringement on Rotary members' right of expressive association, that infringement is justified because it serves the State's compelling interest in eliminating discrimination against women. See *Buckley v. Valeo,* 424 U.S. 1, 25, 96 S.Ct. 612, 637, 46 L.Ed.2d 659 (1976) (*per curiam*) (right of association may be limited by state regulations necessary to serve a compelling interest unrelated to the suppression of ideas). On its face the Unruh Act, like the Minnesota public accommodations law we considered in *Roberts,* makes no distinctions on the basis of the organization's viewpoint. Moreover, public accommodations laws "plainly serv[e] compelling state interests of the highest order." * * * In *Roberts* we recognized that the State's compelling interest in assuring equal access to women extends to the acquisition of leadership skills and business contacts as well as tangible goods and services. * * * The Unruh Act plainly serves this interest. We therefore hold that application of the Unruh Act to California Rotary Clubs does not violate the right of expressive association afforded by the First Amendment.[8]

* * *

IV

The judgment of the Court of Appeal of California is affirmed.

It is so ordered.

JUSTICE SCALIA concurs in the judgment.

JUSTICE BLACKMUN and JUSTICE O'CONNOR took no part in the decision or consideration of this case.

Notes on Rotary International

1. Women have frequently sought to dismantle admission barriers that prevent their membership in men's clubs where valuable business contacts are often made. See generally, Michael M. Burns, The Exclusion of Women from Influential Men's Clubs: The Inner Sanctum and the Myth of Full Equality, 18 Harv.Civ.Rts.Civ.Lib.L.Rev. 321 (1983).

An early target was the United States Jaycees, a civic and service organization which excluded women as regular members. Repeated efforts to change the national organization's membership policy were defeated, and early equal protection challenges foundered on plaintiffs' inability to show state action. See, e.g., Junior Chamber of Commerce of Rochester, Inc. v. United States Jaycees, 495 F.2d 883 (10th Cir.1974), certiorari denied 419 U.S. 1026, 95 S.Ct. 505, 42 L.Ed.2d 301 (1974) (receipt of federal funds does not make Jaycees a governmental actor for purposes of the Fifth Amendment) [the Jaycees subsequently ceased to receive federal funds—Ed.]. In 1974, in defiance of the national policy, the Minneapolis and St. Paul, Minnesota, local chapters began accepting women as regular members. Faced with a threat from the U.S. Jaycees to revoke their charter, the local chapters sought a declaration from the Minnesota Department of Human Rights that the exclusion of women violated the public accommodations provisions

8. Appellants assert that admission of women will impair Rotary's effectiveness as an international organization. This argument is undercut by the fact that the legal effect of the judgment of the California Court of Appeal is limited to the State of California. See *supra,* at 1945. Appellants' argument also is undermined by the fact that women already attend the Rotary Clubs' meetings and participate in many of its activities.

of the Minnesota Human Rights Act. When the state agency found probable cause to believe that the Act had been violated, the national organization sought protection of its asserted First Amendment rights of speech and association from the federal courts.

In Roberts v. United States Jaycees, 468 U.S. 609, 104 S.Ct. 3244, 82 L.Ed.2d 462 (1984), the Supreme Court rejected the First Amendment claim, and sustained the Minnesota statute as applied. Four members of the Court joined Justice Brennan in an opinion that distinguished between the right to freedom of intimate association—such as that accorded to highly personal relationships like family groups—and freedom of expressive association. Relationships that are entitled to the former protection, Brennan reasoned, "[a]mong other things, * * * are distinguished by such attributes as relative smallness, a high degree of selectivity in decisions to begin and maintain the affiliation, and seclusion from others in critical aspects of the relationship." Id., 468 U.S. at 620, 104 S.Ct. at 3250, 82 L.Ed.2d at 472. The Jaycees, which are large, basically unselective, and which routinely admit new members with no inquiry into their backgrounds, did not fit the described model. Brennan admitted, however, that the Jaycees' freedom of expressive association was infringed by Minnesota's attempt to interfere with the group's internal organization or affairs, but he concluded that the infringement was justified, on balance, by the state's policy against sex discrimination.

Justice O'Connor, concurring in part and concurring in the judgment, placed her First Amendment analysis on a different basis. She preferred to distinguish between the freedom of expressive association and that of commercial association. Noting that the "outcome of this case" should not change if, for example, the Jaycees' membership had a history of opposing public issues thought by the Court to be favored by women, which their admission as members would presumably affect, she concluded that "[w]hether an association is or is not constitutionally protected in the selection of its membership should not depend on what the association says or why its members say it." Id., 468 U.S. at 633, 104 S.Ct. at 3258, 82 L.Ed.2d at 481. Since Justice O'Connor did not participate in *Rotary International* (can you imagine why she did not?), her separate opinion in *Roberts* is quoted in part here:

> In my view, an association should be characterized as commercial, and therefore subject to rationally related state regulation of its membership and other associational activities, when, and only when, the association's activities are not predominantly of the type protected by the First Amendment. It is only when the association is predominantly engaged in protected expression that state regulation of its membership will necessarily affect, change, dilute, or silence one collective voice that would otherwise be heard. An association must choose its market. Once it enters the marketplace of commerce in any substantial degree it loses the complete control over its membership that it would otherwise enjoy if it confined its affairs to the marketplace of ideas.

> Determining whether an association's activity is predominantly protected expression will often be difficult, if only because a broad range of activities can be expressive. It is easy enough to identify expressive words or conduct that are strident, contentious, or divisive, but protected expression may also take the form of quiet persuasion, inculcation of traditional values, instruction of the young and community service. Cf. Pierce v. Society of Sisters, 268 U.S. 510, 45 S.Ct. 571, 69 L.Ed. 1070 (1925); Meyer v. Nebraska, 262 U.S. 390, 43 S.Ct. 625, 67 L.Ed. 1042 (1923). The purposes of an association, and

the purposes of its members in adhering to it, are doubtless relevant in determining whether the association is primarily engaged in protected expression. Lawyering to advance social goals may be speech, NAACP v. Button, 371 U.S. 415, 429–430, 83 S.Ct. 328, 335–336, 9 L.Ed.2d 405 (1963), but ordinary commercial law practice is not, see Hishon v. King and Spalding, 467 U.S. 69, 104 S.Ct. 2229, 81 L.Ed.2d 59 (1984). A group boycott or refusal to deal for political purposes may be speech, NAACP v. Claiborne Hardware Co., 458 U.S. 886, 912–915, 102 S.Ct. 3409, 3425–3427, 73 L.Ed.2d 1215 (1982), though a similar boycott for purposes of maintaining a cartel is not. Even the training of outdoor survival skills or participation in community service might become expressive when the activity is intended to develop good morals, reverence, patriotism, and a desire for self-improvement.*

The considerations that may enter into the determination of when a particular association of persons is predominantly engaged in expression are therefore fluid and somewhat uncertain. But the Court has recognized the need to draw similar lines in the past. Two examples, both addressed in cases decided this Term, stand out.

The first concerns claims of First Amendment protection made by lawyers. On the one hand, some lawyering activity is undoubtedly protected by the First Amendment. "[C]ollective activity undertaken to obtain meaningful access to the courts is a fundamental right within the protection of the First Amendment." In re Primus, 436 U.S. 412, 426, 98 S.Ct. 1893, 1901, 56 L.Ed.2d 417 (1978); see NAACP v. Button, supra, 371 U.S., at 429–430, 83 S.Ct., at 335–336. On the other hand, ordinary law practice for commercial ends has never been given special First Amendment protection. "A lawyer's procurement of remunerative employment is a subject only marginally affected with First Amendment concerns." Ohralik v. Ohio State Bar Assn., 436 U.S. 447, 459, 98 S.Ct. 1912, 1920, 56 L.Ed.2d 444 (1978). We emphasized this point only this Term in *Hishon v. King and Spalding,* supra, where we readily rejected a large commercial law firm's claim to First Amendment protection for alleged gender-based discriminatory partnership decisions for associates of the firm. We found no need to inquire into any connection between gender as a condition of partnership and the speech of the law firm, and we undertook no weighing of "compelling" state interests against the speech interests of the law firm. As a commercial enterprise, the law firm could claim no First Amendment immunity from employment discrimination laws, and that result would not have been altered by a showing that the firm engaged even in a substantial amount of activity entitled to First Amendment protection.

We have adopted a similar analysis in our cases concerning association with a labor union. A State is free to impose rational regulation of the membership of a labor union representing "the general *business* needs of employees." Railway Mail Assn. v. Corsi, 326 U.S. 88, 94, 65 S.Ct. 1483, 1487, 89 L.Ed. 2072 (1945) (emphasis added). The State may not, on the other hand, compel association with a union engaged in ideological activities. Abood v. Detroit Board of Education, 431 U.S. 209, 236, 97 S.Ct. 1782, 1800,

* See, *e.g.,* Girl Scouts of the U.S.A., You Make the Difference (1980); W. Hillcourt, The Official Boy Scout Handbook (1979); P. Fussell, The Boy Scout Handbook and Other Observations 7–8 (1982) ("The Official Boy Scout Handbook, for all its focus on Axmanship, Backpacking, Cooking, First Aid, Flowers, Hiking, Map and Compass, Semaphore, Trees, and Weather, is another book about goodness. No home, and certainly no government office, should be without a copy").

52 L.Ed.2d 261 (1977). The Court has thus ruled that a State may compel association for the commercial purposes of engaging in collective bargaining, administering labor contracts, and adjusting employment-related grievances, but it may not infringe on associational rights involving ideological or political associations. Ibid. We applied this distinction in Ellis v. Railway Clerks, 466 U.S. 435, 104 S.Ct. 1883, 80 L.Ed.2d 428 (1984), decided this Term. Again, the constitutional inquiry is not qualified by any analysis of governmental interests and does not turn on an individual's ability to establish disagreement with the particular views promulgated by the union. It is enough if the individual simply expresses unwillingness to be associated with the union's ideological activities.

In summary, this Court's case law recognizes radically different constitutional protections for expressive and non-expressive associations. The First Amendment is offended by direct state control of the membership of a private organization engaged exclusively in protected expressive activity, but no First Amendment interest stands in the way of a State's rational regulation of economic transactions by or within a commercial association. The proper approach to analysis of First Amendment claims of associational freedom is, therefore, to distinguish non-expressive from expressive associations and to recognize that the former lack the full constitutional protections possessed by the latter.

II

Minnesota's attempt to regulate the membership of the Jaycees chapters operating in that State presents a relatively easy case for application of the expressive-commercial dichotomy. Both the Minnesota Supreme Court and the United States District Court, which expressly adopted the state court's findings, made findings of fact concerning the commercial nature of the Jaycees activities. The Court of Appeals, which disagreed with the District Court over the legal conclusions to be drawn from the facts, did not dispute any of those findings. United States Jaycees v. McClure, 709 F.2d 1560 (C.A.8 1983). "The Jaycees is not a political party, or even primarily a political pressure group, but the advocacy of political and public causes, selected by the membership, is a not insubstantial part of what it does * * *. [A] good deal of what the [Jaycees] does indisputably comes within the right of association * * * in pursuance of the specific ends of speech, writing, belief, and assembly for redress of grievances." Id., at 1570.

There is no reason to question the accuracy of this characterization. Notwithstanding its protected expressive activities, the Jaycees—otherwise known as the Junior Chamber of Commerce—is, first and foremost, an organization that, at both the national and local levels, promotes and practices the art of solicitation and management. The organization claims that the training it offers its members gives them an advantage in business, and business firms do indeed sometimes pay the dues of individual memberships for their employees. Jaycees members hone their solicitation and management skills, under the direction and supervision of the organization, primarily through their active recruitment of new members. "One of the major activities of the Jaycees is the sale of memberships in the organization. It encourages continuous recruitment of members with the expressed goal of increasing membership.... The Jaycees itself refers to its members as customers and membership as a product it is selling. More than 80 percent of the national officers' time is dedicated to recruitment, and more than half of the available achievement awards are in part conditioned on achievement in recruitment." United States Jaycees v. McClure, 534 F.Supp. 766, 769 (D.Minn.1982). The organization encourages record-breaking performance in selling memberships: the current records are 348 for most memberships sold in a year by one person, 134 for most sold in a month, and 1,586 for most sold in a lifetime.

Recruitment and selling are commercial activities, even when conducted for training rather than for profit. The "not insubstantial" volume of protected Jaycees activity found by the Court of Appeals is simply not enough to preclude state regulation of the Jaycees' commercial activities. The State of Minnesota has a legitimate interest in ensuring nondiscriminatory access to the commercial opportunity presented by membership in the Jaycees. The members of the Jaycees may not claim constitutional immunity from Minnesota's antidiscrimination law by seeking to exercise their First Amendment rights through this commercial organization.

For these reasons, I agree with the Court that the Jaycees' First Amendment challenge to the application of Minnesota's public accommodations law is meritless. I therefore concur in Parts I and III of the Court's opinion and in the judgment.

Id., 468 U.S. at 635–40, 104 S.Ct. at 3258–3261, 82 L.Ed.2d at 481–486.

Both *Roberts* and *Rotary International* underscore the fact that state public accommodations laws provide the legal basis for attacks on the sex-based membership policies of private clubs. Accordingly, an interpretation of state law is the first order of business in such cases. In Kiwanis International v. Ridgewood Kiwanis Club, 806 F.2d 468 (3d Cir.1986), rehearing denied 811 F.2d 247 (3d Cir.1987), certiorari dismissed 483 U.S. 1050, 108 S.Ct. 362, 97 L.Ed.2d 812 (1987), Judge Garth interpreted New Jersey law as inapplicable to the Kiwanis Club. The New Jersey statute provided an exception for "any institution, bona fide club, or place of accommodation, which is in its nature distinctly private; * * *". Relying on National Organization for Women v. Little League Baseball, Inc., 127 N.J.Super. 522, 318 A.2d 33 (1974), affirmed mem. 67 N.J. 320, 338 A.2d 198 (1974), Judge Garth used a selectivity standard to determine that the Kiwanis Club of Redwood was "distinctly private." The Third Circuit adhered to that interpretation *en banc* by denying a petition for rehearing, despite the presence of an *amicus curiae* brief filed by the State of New Jersey disputing the panel's understanding of state law. The New York City Council took a more aggressive approach than the New Jersey legislature had done to ending discrimination in "distinctly private" clubs. On October 9, 1984, the Council enacted Local Law No. 63, which states that a club "shall not be considered in its nature distinctly private if it [1] has more than four hundred members, [2] provides regular meal service, and [3] regularly receives payment for dues, fees, use of space, facilities, services, meals or beverages directly or indirectly from or on behalf of nonmembers for the furtherance of trade or business." The United States Supreme Court rejected a facial constitutional attack on this provision in New York State Club Ass'n v. City of New York, 487 U.S. 1, 108 S.Ct. 2225, 101 L.Ed.2d 1 (1988). Writing for the Court, Justice White stressed that to prevail on a facial attack, the plaintiff must demonstrate that the challenged law either could never be applied in a valid manner, or that even though it may be validly applied to the plaintiff and others, it nevertheless is so broad that it may inhibit the constitutionally protected speech of third parties. Given the range of clubs represented by the appellant, and the Court's previous holdings in *Roberts* and *Rotary International*,

Justice White easily concluded that appellant could not succeed on either point. Clubs with 400 members which provide regular meal service and receive regular payments directly or indirectly from or on behalf of nonmembers for the further-ance of trade or business do not fit the definition of "intimate association" protected by the First Amendment. Nor did Local Law 63 on its face affect in any significant way the ability of individuals to form associations to advocate public or private viewpoints, under the standard announced in *Rotary International*. Nor, on the showing made, was the Court willing to assume that the law was "substantially overbroad." Appellant had not identified those clubs for whom the antidiscrimination provisions will impair their ability to associate together or to advocate public or private viewpoints. Absent such a showing, the Court could not conclude that the Law threatens to undermine the associational or expressive purposes of any club, and instead must assume that whatever overbreadth may exist should be cured through a case-by-case analysis of the fact situations to which its sanctions might be applied.

Justice O'Connor, joined by Justice Kennedy, concurred in order to note that she found nothing in the Court's opinion that in any way undermined or denigrated the importance of the associational interest at stake. She emphasized the Court's observation that the three factors identified by the Law to determine whether a particular club is "distinctly private" are not conclusive, but are to be considered along with other considerations, including size, purpose, policies, selectivity, and congeniality. Noting that " * * * there may well be organizations whose expressive purposes would be substantially undermined if they were unable to confine their membership to those of the same sex, race, religion, or ethnic background, or who share some other such common bond"; id., 487 U.S. at 19, 108 S.Ct. at 2237, 101 L.Ed.2d at 20, she pointed out that such clubs are provided with an adequate opportunity to raise any any constitutional claims in the administrative proceeding through which Local Law 63 is applied.

Did *N.Y. State Club Ass'n* correctly apply the standards developed in *Roberts* and *Rotary International*? Is there any magic in the number 400? Would a provision that set a limit of, say, 200 members also survive a facial attack under the First Amendment? What kinds of groups does Justice O'Connor think might pass muster under the New York City law? Several other cities, including San Francisco, Chicago, Los Angeles, the District of Columbia, and Buffalo, have followed New York City's lead. See N.Y. Times, June 21, 1988, at p. A–1, col. 3. Should stronger laws now be attempted? See also Isbister v. Boys' Club of Santa Cruz, Inc., 40 Cal.3d 72, 219 Cal.Rptr. 150, 707 P.2d 212 (1985), applying the Unruh Act (quoted in footnote 2 of *Rotary International*,) to require the Boys' Club of Santa Cruz, Inc., to admit girls as members. The Boys' Club was established by private gift, was chartered as a private nonprofit corporation, and was affiliated with the Boys' Clubs of America, Inc., a congressionally chartered organization. The Boys' Club of Santa Cruz owned and operated a building which included such recreational facilities as a gymnasium, an indoor competition-sized swimming pool, a snack bar, and a craft and game area. Its membership was open to all Santa Cruz boys between the ages of eight and eighteen, upon payment of a $3.25 annual fee. Reasoning that the Club was a place of public accommoda-tion and amusement, with unrestrictive membership policies (except for the ban on females), the Court held it was covered by the Unruh Act. Further, the Court interpreted the statutory phrase "business establishment" to include nonprofit places of public accommodation. Finally, it relied on *Roberts* to reject the club members' asserted first amendment claim. Was *Isbister* correctly decided as a matter of state law? Of Federal law?

See also State v. Burning Tree Club, Inc., 315 Md. 254, 554 A.2d 366 (1989), certiorari denied 493 U.S. 816, 110 S.Ct. 66, 107 L.Ed.2d 33 (1989), noted 49 Md.L.Rev. 509, 549–63 (1990), upholding the state's denial of preferential "open space" tax treatment to the Burning Tree Country Club in Montgomery County, Maryland, because of its exclusion of women as members. The court rejected Burning Tree's first amendment arguments on the grounds that withdrawing a tax benefit would not appear to burden unconstitutionally any rights of intimate association that might inhere in a sizable, all-male organization devoted to playing golf, and that Maryland's compelling state interest in achieving equal rights for women outweighed whatever burden the full tax assessment may have imposed on the club's associational rights.

2. What do you make of the "size and selectivity" test developed in *Roberts* and applied in *Rotary International* for determining whether the male club members enjoy the kind of intimate or private relationships that warrant constitutional protection? Is the numerical limit used by the New York City Council, see Note 1, supra, any better? Professor Deborah Rhode said of *Roberts:*

> If hard cases make bad law, easy cases sometimes do no better, and *Jaycees* is a good example. The organizational practices at issue were not typical of most sex-segregated clubs, and neither Justice Brennan's balancing approach nor Justice O'Connor's commercial/expressive dichotomy adequately captures the competing values. Most separatist associations do not fit comfortably within the public/private categories of constitutional legal frameworks.

Deborah L. Rhode, Association and Assimilation, 81 Nw.U.L.Rev. 106, 117 (1986). Would Professor Rhode give *Rotary International* a higher grade? Her own view of the problem suggests that:

> An alternative theoretical framework for evaluating separatist associations should neither minimize the values at issue nor assume their primacy for all selective organizations. Such an approach requires a greater sensitivity to context, to the varying cultural functions, meanings, and consequences of particular social relationships.

Rhode, id., at 124. Rhode has indicated more recently that she finds the holdings in *Roberts, Rotary,* and *New York Clubs* "quite limited." She points out that these cases

> * * * permitted states to bar gender discrimination by certain organizations, but fell short of creating a constitutional remedy for such discrimination or of clarifying the organizations subject to regulation. These limitations in the Court's approach reflect more fundamental limitations in its public-private dichotomy. Such an approach obscures how women's exclusion from spheres conventionally classified as private contributes to their exclusion from spheres uniformly understood as public.

Deborah L. Rhode, Justice and Gender 283 (1990).

3. Zonta International is a women's service club that uses a classified membership scheme not unlike that described in *Rotary International*. Are Zonta's local California clubs also subject to the Unruh Act? If so, can you make a constitutional argument upholding Zonta's membership practices after *Rotary International?* Would you want to make such an argument? Professor Rhode suggests that, if her approach to single-sex clubs is adopted, "men's and women's groups frequently will stand on different footing. The point is not that values of choice and intimacy have less social importance for men than women, but rather

that the social costs are different." Rhode, supra Note 2, at 124. See also Chai R. Feldblum, Virginia G. Krent & Nancy Fredman Watkin, Legal Challenges to All–Female Organizations, 21 Harv.Civ.Rts. Civ.Lib.L.Rev. 171 (1986), arguing that challenges to single-sex organizations are less compelling when made against all-female organizations that counteract the societal disadvantages that women have suffered and that are designed to aid women in achieving equality with men. Do women's service clubs fit that description? One of the stated purposes of Zonta International is to advance the legal status of women. Does that help the argument? What about women's "networking" organizations that accept as members only successful female entrepreneurs, business executives, highly placed professional women, and prominent women politicians?

2. PORNOGRAPHY

AMERICAN BOOKSELLERS ASS'N, INC. V. HUDNUT

United States Court of Appeals, Seventh Circuit, 1985.
771 F.2d 323, affirmed mem. 475 U.S. 1001, 106 S.Ct. 1172, 89 L.Ed.2d 291,
1986. Rehearing denied 475 U.S. 1132, 106 S.Ct. 1664, 90 L.Ed.2d 206.

EASTERBROOK, CIRCUIT JUDGE.

Indianapolis enacted an ordinance defining "pornography" as a practice that discriminates against women. "Pornography" is to be redressed through the administrative and judicial methods used for other discrimination. The City's definition of "pornography" is considerably different from "obscenity," which the Supreme Court has held is not protected by the First Amendment.

To be "obscene" under *Miller v. California,* 413 U.S. 15, 93 S.Ct. 2607, 37 L.Ed.2d 419 (1973), "a publication must, taken as a whole, appeal to the prurient interest, must contain patently offensive depictions or descriptions of specified sexual conduct, and on the whole have no serious literary, artistic, political, or scientific value." *Brockett v. Spokane Arcades, Inc.,* 472 U.S. 491, 105 S.Ct. 2794, 2800, 86 L.Ed.2d 394 (1985). Offensiveness must be assessed under the standards of the community. Both offensiveness and an appeal to something other than "normal, healthy sexual desires" (*Brockett, supra,* 105 S.Ct. at 2799) are essential elements of "obscenity."

"Pornography" under the ordinance is "the graphic sexually explicit subordination of women, whether in pictures or in words, that also includes one or more of the following:

(1) Women are presented as sexual objects who enjoy pain or humiliation; or

(2) Women are presented as sexual objects who experience sexual pleasure in being raped; or

(3) Women are presented as sexual objects tied up or cut up or mutilated or bruised or physically hurt, or as dismembered or truncated or fragmented or severed into body parts; or

(4) Women are presented as being penetrated by objects or animals; or

(5) Women are presented in scenarios of degradation, injury, abasement, torture, shown as filthy or inferior, bleeding, bruised, or hurt in a context that makes these conditions sexual; or

(6) Women are presented as sexual objects for domination, conquest, violation, exploitation, possession, or use, or through postures or positions of servility or submission or display."

Indianapolis Code § 16–3(q). The statute provides that the "use of men, children, or transsexuals in the place of women in paragraphs (1) through (6) above shall also constitute pornography under this section." The ordinance as passed in April 1984 defined "sexually explicit" to mean actual or simulated intercourse or the uncovered exhibition of the genitals, buttocks or anus. An amendment in June 1984 deleted this provision, leaving the term undefined.

The Indianapolis ordinance does not refer to the prurient interest, to offensiveness, or to the standards of the community. It demands attention to particular depictions, not to the work judged as a whole. It is irrelevant under the ordinance whether the work has literary, artistic, political, or scientific value. The City and many amici point to these omissions as virtues. They maintain that pornography influences attitudes, and the statute is a way to alter the socialization of men and women rather than to vindicate community standards of offensiveness. And as one of the principal drafters of the ordinance has asserted, "if a woman is subjected, why should it matter that the work has other value?" Catharine A. MacKinnon, *Pornography, Civil Rights, and Speech,* 20 Harv.Civ.Rts.—Civ.Lib.L.Rev. 1, 21 (1985).

Civil rights groups and feminists have entered this case as amici on both sides. Those supporting the ordinance say that it will play an important role in reducing the tendency of men to view women as sexual objects, a tendency that leads to both unacceptable attitudes and discrimination in the workplace and violence away from it. Those opposing the ordinance point out that much radical feminist literature is explicit and depicts women in ways forbidden by the ordinance and that the ordinance would reopen old battles. It is unclear how Indianapolis would treat works from James Joyce's *Ulysses* to Homer's *Iliad;* both depict women as submissive objects for conquest and domination.

We do not try to balance the arguments for and against an ordinance such as this. The ordinance discriminates on the ground of the content of the speech. Speech treating women in the approved way—in sexual encounters "premised on equality" (MacKinnon, *supra,* at 22)—is lawful no matter how sexually explicit. Speech treating women in the disapproved way—as submissive in matters sexual or as enjoying humiliation—is unlawful no matter how significant the literary, artistic, or political qualities of the work taken as a whole. The state may not ordain preferred viewpoints in this way. The Constitution forbids the state to declare one perspective right and silence opponents.

I

The ordinance contains four prohibitions. People may not "traffic" in pornography, "coerce" others into performing in pornographic works, or "force" pornography on anyone. Anyone injured by someone who has seen or read pornography has a right of action against the maker or seller.

Trafficking is defined in § 16–3(g)(4) as the "production, sale, exhibition, or distribution of pornography." The offense excludes exhibition in a public or educational library, but a "special display" in a library may be sex discrimination. Section 16–3(g)(4)(C) provides that the trafficking paragraph "shall not be construed to make isolated passages or isolated parts actionable."

"Coercion into pornographic performance" is defined in § 16–3(g)(5) as "[c]oercing, intimidating or fraudulently inducing any person * * * into performing for pornography * * *." The ordinance specifies that proof of any of the following "shall not constitute a defense: I. That the person is a woman; * * * VI. That the person has previously posed for sexually explicit pictures * * * with anyone * * *; * * * VIII. That the person actually consented to a use of the performance that is changed into pornography; * * * IX. That the person knew that the purpose of the acts or events in question was to make pornography; * * * XI. That the person signed a contract, or made statements affirming a willingness to cooperate in the production of pornography; XII. That no physical force, threats, or weapons were used in the making of the pornography; or XIII. That the person was paid or otherwise compensated."

"Forcing pornography on a person," according to § 16–3(g)(5), is the "forcing of pornography on any woman, man, child, or transsexual in any place of employment, in education, in a home, or in any public place." The statute does not define forcing, but one of its authors states that the definition reaches pornography shown to medical students as part of their education or given to language students for translation. MacKinnon, *supra,* at 40–41.

Section 16–3(g)(7) defines as a prohibited practice the "assault, physical attack, or injury of any woman, man, child, or transsexual in a way that is directly caused by specific pornography."

For purposes of all four offenses, it is generally "not * * * a defense that the respondent did not know or intend that the materials were pornography * * *." Section 16–3(g)(8). But the ordinance provides that damages are unavailable in trafficking cases unless the complainant proves "that the respondent knew or had reason to know that the materials were pornography." It is a complete defense to a trafficking case that all of the materials in question were pornography only by virtue of category (6) of the definition of pornography. In cases of assault caused by pornography, those who seek damages from "a seller, exhibitor or distributor" must show that the defendant knew or had reason to know of the material's status as pornography. By implication, those who seek damages from an author need not show this.

A woman aggrieved by trafficking in pornography may file a complaint "as a woman acting against the subordination of women" with the office of equal opportunity. Section 16–17(b). A man, child, or transsexual also may protest trafficking "but must prove injury in the same way that a woman is injured. * * * " *Ibid.* Subsection (a) also provides, however, that "any person claiming to be aggrieved" by trafficking, coercion, forcing, or assault may complain against the "perpetrators." We need not decide whether § 16–17(b) qualifies the right of action in § 16–17(a).

The office investigates and within 30 days makes a recommendation to a panel of the equal opportunity advisory board. The panel then decides whether there is reasonable cause to proceed (§ 16–24(2)) and may refer the dispute to a conciliation conference or to a complaint adjudication committee for a hearing (§§ 16–24(3), 16–26(a)). The committee uses the same procedures ordinarily associated with civil rights litigation. It may make findings and enter orders, including both orders to cease and desist and orders "to take further affirmative action * * * including but not limited to the power to restore complainant's losses. * * *" Section 16–26(d). Either party may appeal the committee's decision to the board, which reviews the record before the committee and may modify its decision.

Under Indiana law an administrative decision takes effect when rendered, unless a court issues a stay. Ind.Stat. § 4–22–1–13. The board's decisions are subject to review in the ordinary course. Ind.Stat. § 4–22–1–14. Judicial review in pornography cases is to be de novo, Indianapolis Code § 16–27(e), which provides a second complete hearing. When the board finds that a person has engaged in trafficking or that a seller, exhibitor, or distributor is responsible for an assault, it must initiate judicial review of its own decision, *ibid.*, and the statute prohibits injunctive relief in these cases in advance of the court's final decision. (This is unlike the usual procedure under state law, which permits summary enforcement. Ind.Stat. §§ 4–22–1–18 and 4–22–1–27.)

The district court held the ordinance unconstitutional. 598 F.Supp. 1316 (S.D.Ind.1984). * * *

II

The plaintiffs are a congeries of distributors and readers of books, magazines, and films. * * * Collectively the plaintiffs (or their members, whose interests they represent) make, sell, or read just about every kind of material that could be affected by the ordinance, from hard-core films to W.B. Yeats's poem "Leda and the Swan" (from the myth of Zeus in the form of a swan impregnating an apparently subordinate Leda), to the collected works of James Joyce, D.H. Lawrence, and John Cleland.

* * *

III

"If there is any fixed star in our constitutional constellation, it is that no official, high or petty, can prescribe what shall be orthodox in politics, nationalism, religion, or other matters of opinion or force citizens to confess by word or act their faith therein." *West Virginia State Board of Education v. Barnette,* 319 U.S. 624, 642, 63 S.Ct. 1178, 1187, 87 L.Ed. 1628 (1943). Under the First Amendment the government must leave to the people the evaluation of ideas. Bald or subtle, an idea is as powerful as the audience allows it to be. A belief may be pernicious—the beliefs of Nazis led to the death of millions, those of the Klan to the repression of millions. A pernicious belief may prevail. Totalitarian governments today rule much of the planet, practicing suppression of billions and spreading dogma that may enslave others. One of the things that separates our society from theirs is our absolute right to propagate opinions that the government finds wrong or even hateful.

* * *

Under the ordinance graphic sexually explicit speech is "pornography" or not depending on the perspective the author adopts. Speech that "subordinates" women and also, for example, presents women as enjoying pain, humiliation, or rape, or even simply presents women in "positions of servility or submission or display" is forbidden, no matter how great the literary or political value of the work taken as a whole. Speech that portrays women in positions of equality is lawful, no matter how graphic the sexual content. This is thought control. It establishes an "approved" view of women, of how they may react to sexual encounters, of how the sexes may relate to each other. Those who espouse the approved view may use sexual images; those who do not, may not.

Indianapolis justifies the ordinance on the ground that pornography affects thoughts. Men who see women depicted as subordinate are more likely to treat them so. Pornography is an aspect of dominance.[1] It does not persuade people so much as change them. It works by socializing, by establishing the expected and the permissible. In this view pornography is not an idea; pornography is the injury.

There is much to this perspective. Beliefs are also facts. People often act in accordance with the images and patterns they find around them. People raised in a religion tend to accept the tenets of that religion, often without independent examination. People taught from birth that black people are fit only for slavery rarely rebelled against that creed; beliefs coupled with the self-interest of the masters established a social structure that inflicted great harm while enduring for centuries. Words and images act at the level of the subconscious before they persuade at the level of the conscious. Even the truth has little chance unless a statement fits within the framework of beliefs that may never have been subjected to rational study.

Therefore we accept the premises of this legislation. Depictions of subordination tend to perpetuate subordination. The subordinate status of women in turn leads to affront and lower pay at work, insult and injury at home, battery and rape on the streets.[2] In the language of the legislature,

---

1. "Pornography constructs what a woman is in terms of its view of what men want sexually * * *. Pornography's world of equality is a harmonious and balanced place. Men and women are perfectly complementary and perfectly bipolar * * *. All the ways men love to take and violate women, women love to be taken and violated. * * * What pornography *does* goes beyond its content: It eroticizes hierarchy, it sexualizes inequality. It makes dominance and submission sex. Inequality is its central dynamic; the illusion of freedom coming together with the reality of force is central to its working. * * * [P]ornography is neither harmless fantasy nor a corrupt and confused misrepresentation of an otherwise neutral and healthy sexual situation. It institutionalizes the sexuality of male supremacy, fusing the erotization of dominance and submission with the social construction of male and female. * * * Men treat women as who they see women as being. Pornography constructs who that is. Men's power over women

means that the way men see women defines who women can be. Pornography * * * is a sexual reality." MacKinnon, *supra*, at 17–18 (note omitted, emphasis in original). See also Andrea Dworkin, *Pornography: Men Possessing Women* (1981). A national commission in Canada recently adopted a similar rationale for controlling pornography. Special Commission on Pornography and Prostitution, 1 *Pornography and Prostitution in Canada* 49–59 (Canadian Government Publishing Centre 1985).

2. MacKinnon's article collects empirical work that supports this proposition. The social science studies are very difficult to interpret, however, and they conflict. Because much of the effect of speech comes through a process of socialization, it is difficult to measure incremental benefits and injuries caused by particular speech. Several psychologists have found, for example, that those who see violent, sexually explicit films tend to have more violent thoughts. But how often does this lead to actual violence? National commis-

"[p]ornography is central in creating and maintaining sex as a basis of discrimination. Pornography is a systematic practice of exploitation and subordination based on sex which differentially harms women. The bigotry and contempt it produces, with the acts of aggression it fosters, harm women's opportunities for equality and rights [of all kinds]." Indianapolis Code § 16–1(a)(2).

Yet this simply demonstrates the power of pornography as speech. All of these unhappy effects depend on mental intermediation. Pornography affects how people see the world, their fellows, and social relations. If pornography is what pornography does, so is other speech. Hitler's orations affected how some Germans saw Jews. Communism is a world view, not simply a *Manifesto* by Marx and Engels or a set of speeches. Efforts to suppress communist speech in the United States were based on the belief that the public acceptability of such ideas would increase the likelihood of totalitarian government. Religions affect socialization in the most pervasive way. * * *

Racial bigotry, anti-semitism, violence on television, reporters' biases— these and many more influence the culture and shape our socialization. None is directly answerable by more speech, unless that speech too finds its place in the popular culture. Yet all is protected as speech, however insidious. Any other answer leaves the government in control of all of the institutions of culture, the great censor and director of which thoughts are good for us.

Sexual responses often are unthinking responses, and the association of sexual arousal with the subordination of women therefore may have a substantial effect. But almost all cultural stimuli provoke unconscious responses. Religious ceremonies condition their participants. Teachers convey messages by selecting what not to cover; the implicit message about what is off limits or unthinkable may be more powerful than the messages for which they present rational argument. Television scripts contain unarticulated assumptions. People may be conditioned in subtle ways. If the fact that speech plays a role in a process of conditioning were enough to permit governmental regulation, that would be the end of freedom of speech.

It is possible to interpret the claim that the pornography is the harm in a different way. Indianapolis emphasizes the injury that models in pornographic films and pictures may suffer. The record contains materials depicting sexual torture, penetration of women by red-hot irons and the like. These concerns have nothing to do with written materials subject to the statute, and physical injury can occur with or without the "subordination" of women. As we discuss in Part IV, a state may make injury in the course of producing a film unlawful independent of the viewpoint expressed in the film.

sions on obscenity here, in the United Kingdom, and in Canada have found that it is not possible to demonstrate a direct link between obscenity and rape or exhibitionism. The several opinions in *Miller v. California* discuss the U.S. commission. See also *Report of the Committee on Obscenity and Film Censorship* 61–95 (Home Office, Her Majesty's Stationery Office, 1979); Special Committee on Pornography and Prostitution, 1 *Pornography and Prostitution in Canada* 71–73, 95–103 (Canadian Government Publishing Centre 1985). In saying that we accept the finding that pornography as the ordinance defines it leads to unhappy consequences, we mean only that there is evidence to this effect, that this evidence is consistent with much human experience, and that as judges we must accept the legislative resolution of such disputed empirical questions. See *Gregg v. Georgia*, 428 U.S. 153, 184–87, 96 S.Ct. 2909, 2930–31, 49 L.Ed.2d 859 (1976) (opinion of Stewart, Powell, and Stevens, JJ.).

The more immediate point, however, is that the image of pain is not necessarily pain. In *Body Double,* a suspense film directed by Brian DePalma, a woman who has disrobed and presented a sexually explicit display is murdered by an intruder with a drill. The drill runs through the woman's body. The film is sexually explicit and a murder occurs—yet no one believes that the actress suffered pain or died. In *Barbarella* a character played by Jane Fonda is at times displayed in sexually explicit ways and at times shown "bleeding, bruised, [and] hurt in a context that makes these conditions sexual"—and again no one believes that Fonda was actually tortured to make the film. In *Carnal Knowledge* a woman grovels to please the sexual whims of a character played by Jack Nicholson; no one believes that there was a real sexual submission, and the Supreme Court held the film protected by the First Amendment. *Jenkins v. Georgia,* 418 U.S. 153, 94 S.Ct. 2750, 41 L.Ed.2d 642 (1974). And this works both ways. The description of women's sexual domination of men in *Lysistrata* was not real dominance. Depictions may affect slavery, war, or sexual roles, but a book about slavery is not itself slavery, or a book about death by poison a murder.

Much of Indianapolis's argument rests on the belief that when speech is "unanswerable," and the metaphor that there is a "marketplace of ideas" does not apply, the First Amendment does not apply either. The metaphor is honored; Milton's *Aeropagitica* and John Stewart Mill's *On Liberty* defend freedom of speech on the ground that the truth will prevail, and many of the most important cases under the First Amendment recite this position. The Framers undoubtedly believed it. As a general matter it is true. But the Constitution does not make the dominance of truth a necessary condition of freedom of speech. To say that it does would be to confuse an outcome of free speech with a necessary condition for the application of the amendment.

A power to limit speech on the ground that truth has not yet prevailed and is not likely to prevail implies the power to declare truth. At some point the government must be able to say (as Indianapolis has said): "We know what the truth is, yet a free exchange of speech has not driven out falsity, so that we must now prohibit falsity." If the government may declare the truth, why wait for the failure of speech? Under the First Amendment, however, there is no such thing as a false idea, *Gertz v. Robert Welch, Inc.,* 418 U.S. 323, 339, 94 S.Ct. 2997, 3006, 41 L.Ed.2d 789 (1974), so the government may not restrict speech on the ground that in a free exchange truth is not yet dominant.

At any time, some speech is ahead in the game; the more numerous speakers prevail. Supporters of minority candidates may be forever "excluded" from the political process because their candidates never win, because few people believe their positions. This does not mean that freedom of speech has failed.

The Supreme Court has rejected the position that speech must be "effectively answerable" to be protected by the Constitution. For example, in *Buckley v. Valeo, supra,* 424 U.S. at 39–54, 96 S.Ct. at 644–51, the Court held unconstitutional limitations on expenditures that were neutral with regard to the speakers' opinions and designed to make it easier for one person to answer another's speech. See also *FEC v. National Conservative PAC,* 470 U.S. 480, 105 S.Ct. 1459, 84 L.Ed.2d 455 (1985). In *Mills v. Alabama,* 384

U.S. 214, 86 S.Ct. 1434, 16 L.Ed.2d 484 (1966), the Court held unconstitutional a statute prohibiting editorials on election day—a statute the state had designed to prevent speech that came too late for answer. In cases from *Eastern Railroad Presidents Conference v. Noerr Motor Freight, Inc.,* 365 U.S. 127, 81 S.Ct. 523, 5 L.Ed.2d 464 (1961), through *NAACP v. Claiborne Hardware Co.,* 458 U.S. 886, 102 S.Ct. 3409, 73 L.Ed.2d 1215 (1982), the Court has held that the First Amendment protects political stratagems—obtaining legislation through underhanded ploys and outright fraud in *Noerr,* obtaining political and economic ends through boycotts in *Claiborne Hardware* —that may be beyond effective correction through more speech.

We come, finally, to the argument that pornography is "low value" speech, that it is enough like obscenity that Indianapolis may prohibit it. Some cases hold that speech far removed from politics and other subjects at the core of the Framers' concerns may be subjected to special regulation. E.g., *FCC v. Pacifica Foundation,* 438 U.S. 726, 98 S.Ct. 3026, 57 L.Ed.2d 1073 (1978); *Young v. American Mini Theatres, Inc.,* 427 U.S. 50, 67–70, 96 S.Ct. 2440, 2450–52, 49 L.Ed.2d 310 (1976) (plurality opinion); *Chaplinsky v. New Hampshire,* 315 U.S. 568, 571–72, 62 S.Ct. 766, 768–69, 86 L.Ed. 1031 (1942). These cases do not sustain statutes that select among viewpoints, however. In *Pacifica* the FCC sought to keep vile language off the air during certain times. The Court held that it may; but the Court would not have sustained a regulation prohibiting scatological descriptions of Republicans but not scatological descriptions of Democrats, or any other form of selection among viewpoints. See *Planned Parenthood Ass'n v. Chicago Transit Authority,* 767 F.2d 1225, 1232–33 (7th Cir.1985).

At all events, "pornography" is not low value speech within the meaning of these cases. Indianapolis seeks to prohibit certain speech because it believes this speech influences social relations and politics on a grand scale, that it controls attitudes at home and in the legislature. This precludes a characterization of the speech as low value. True, pornography and obscenity have sex in common. But Indianapolis left out of its definition any reference to literary, artistic, political, or scientific value. The ordinance applies to graphic sexually explicit subordination in works great and small.[3] The Court sometimes balances the value of speech against the costs of its restriction, but it does this by category of speech and not by the content of particular works. See John Hart Ely, *Flag Desecration: A Case Study in the Roles of Categorization and Balancing in First Amendment Analysis,* 88 Harv.L.Rev. 1482 (1975); Geoffrey R. Stone, *Restrictions of Speech Because of its Content: The Strange Case of Subject–Matter Restrictions,* 46 U.Chi.L.Rev. 81 (1978). Indianapolis has created an approved point of view and so loses the support of these cases.

---

3. Indianapolis briefly argues that *Beauharnais v. Illinois,* 343 U.S. 250, 72 S.Ct. 725, 96 L.Ed. 919 (1952), which allowed a state to penalize "group libel," supports the ordinance. In *Collin v. Smith, supra,* 578 F.2d at 1205, we concluded that cases such as *New York Times v. Sullivan* had so washed away the foundations of *Beauharnais* that it could not be considered authoritative. If we are wrong in this, however, the case still does not support the ordinance. It is not clear that depicting women as subordinate in sexually explicit ways, even combined with a depiction of pleasure in rape, would fit within the definition of a group libel. The well received film *Swept Away* used explicit sex, plus taking pleasure in rape, to make a political statement, not to defame. Work must be an insult or slur for its own sake to come within the ambit of *Beauharnais,* and a work need not be scurrilous at all to be "pornography" under the ordinance.

Any rationale we could imagine in support of this ordinance could not be limited to sex discrimination. Free speech has been on balance an ally of those seeking change. Governments that want stasis start by restricting speech. Culture is a powerful force of continuity; Indianapolis paints pornography as part of the culture of power. Change in any complex system ultimately depends on the ability of outsiders to challenge accepted views and the reigning institutions. Without a strong guarantee of freedom of speech, there is no effective right to challenge what is.

IV

The definition of "pornography" is unconstitutional. No construction or excision of particular terms could save it.

* * *

No amount of struggle with particular words and phrases in this ordinance can leave anything in effect. The district court came to the same conclusion. Its judgment is therefore

AFFIRMED.

Notes on Hudnut

1. In *N.Y. State Club Ass'n, Rotary International,* and *Roberts,* the first amendment claim was asserted defensively by all-male clubs seeking to continue their traditional exclusion of women as members. That claim was rejected because the state's interest in ending sex discrimination outweighed the associational interests of the members in the types of organizations involved. In *Hudnut* the first amendment claim was asserted defensively by book publishers, dealers and readers seeking to preserve their access to material with literary, artistic, political, or scientific value traditionally protected under the amendment. That claim was upheld because the City's interest in defining pornography as sex discrimination did not permit it to control the content of protected speech. Are these two applications of the first amendment consistent? Do both strive to place men and women on an equal footing of mutual respect? Is the first amendment designed to perform that function?

2. The Indianapolis ordinance invalidated in *Hudnut* was based on a measure enacted earlier by the Minneapolis City Council and vetoed by the Mayor. The feminist struggle that culminated in the Minneapolis ordinance is described in detail by Dean Paul Brest and Amy Vanderbilt in Politics, Feminism, and the Constitution: The Anti–Pornography Movement in Minneapolis, 39 Stan.L.Rev. 607 (1987). Professor Catharine A. MacKinnon, who, with Andrea Dworkin, drafted the Minneapolis Ordinance, has explained that "[o]ur law is designed to further the equality of the sexes, to help make sex equality real," Catherine A. MacKinnon, Pornography, Civil Rights, and Speech, 20 Harv.Civ.Rts. Civ.Lib. L.Rev. 1, 26–27 (1985). She thus summarized the theory underlying the Ordinance:

> * * * We defined pornography as a practice of sex discrimination, a violation of women's civil rights, the opposite of sexual equality. Its point is to hold accountable, to those who are injured, those who profit from and benefit from that injury. It means that women's injury—our damage, our pain, our enforced inferiority, should outweigh their pleasure and their profits, or sex equality is meaningless.

We defined pornography as the graphic sexually explicit subordination of women through pictures or words that also includes women dehumanized as sexual objects, things, or commodities, enjoying pain or humiliation or rape, being tied up, cut up, mutilated, bruised, or physically hurt, in postures of sexual submission or servility or display, reduced to body parts, penetrated by objects or animals, or presented in scenarios of degradation, injury, torture, shown as filthy or inferior, bleeding, bruised, or hurt in a context that makes these conditions sexual. Erotica, defined by distinction as not this, might be sexually explicit materials premised on equality. We also provide that the use of men, children or transsexuals in the place of women is pornography. The definition is substantive in that it is sex-specific, but it covers everyone in a sex-specific way, so is gender neutral in overall design.

There is a buried issue within sex discrimination law about what sex, meaning gender, is. If sex is a *difference,* social or biological, one looks to see if a challenged practice occurs along the same lines; if it does, or if it is done to both sexes, the practice is not discrimination, not inequality. If, by contrast, sex inequality is a matter of *dominance,* the issue is not the gender difference but the difference gender makes. In this more substantive, less abstract approach, the concern is whether a practice *subordinates* on the basis of sex. The first approach implies that marginal correction is needed; the second suggests social change. Equality to the first centers on abstract symmetry between equivalent categories; the asymmetry that occurs when categories are not equivalent is not inequality, it is treating unlikes differently. To the second approach, inequality centers on the substantive, cumulative disadvantagement of social hierarchy. Equality to the first is nondifferentiation; to the second, equality is nonsubordination. Although it is consonant with both approaches, our anti-pornography statute emerges largely from an analysis of the problem under the second approach.

Id., at 22–23 (emphasis in original) (footnotes omitted). See also Andrea Dworkin, Against the Male Flood: Censorship, Pornography, and Equality, 8 Harv. Women's L.J. 1 (1985). As you might expect, Hustler Magazine did not stand idly by while MacKinnon and Dworkin waged their battle on one of its steady sources of income, the pornography industry. In its February, March, and December, 1984 issues, Hustler published features that mentioned Dworkin's name in a derogatory manner. Dworkin sued Hustler for libel, invasion of privacy, intentional infliction of emotional injury, and outrage, but Hustler won a motion for summary judgment. See Dworkin v. Hustler Magazine, Inc., 668 F.Supp. 1408 (C.D.Cal.1987), affirmed 867 F.2d 1188 (9th Cir.1989), certiorari denied 493 U.S. 812, 110 S.Ct. 59, 107 L.Ed.2d 26 (1989).

3. Law review commentary published prior to the Seventh Circuit opinion, while on the whole presenting a sympathetic account of the feminist anti-pornography position, was critical of the ordinance on both doctrinal and political grounds. Thus, one observer recognizes that the analysis presented by Dworkin and others injects a new perspective into the old debate over pornography between liberals (who champion non-regulation in the name of liberty) and conservatives (who defend regulation in the name of virtue):

* * * the focal point of the feminist view is neither virtue nor liberty but instead, equality. This different focus produces a crucial insight: only from a male perspective, whether liberal or conservative, does pornography seem to be primarily about sex. Feminists emphasize equality in sexual relations and

evaluate sexually-oriented materials in that light. Pornography, so viewed, is not so much about sex as it is about power.

Eric Hoffman, Feminism, Pornography, and Law, 133 U.Pa.L.Rev. 497, 510 (1985). Hoffman argues that "insofar as the law plays a role in defining and shaping social values, pursuit of feminist anti-pornography laws may well have some value", but he nevertheless concludes that "[f]rom a political perspective, however, feminists should probably avoid endorsing state regulation of pornography." He explains,

> Feminists have reasons for being suspicious of the power of the state, which has historically been, and seems likely to remain, male-dominated. Thus the potential value of feminist antipornography laws may well be offset by considerations of political strategy as well as first amendment principles.

Id., at 499. Another writer, after reviewing the traditional exceptions to first amendment protection—speech that incites others to illegal action, obscenity, and libel—and rejecting efforts to justify an anti-pornography measure by manipulating these recognized categories, is willing to support limited state intervention on a different basis:

> * * * some images arguably harmful to the rights of women are so devoid of value under the first amendment that the Supreme Court should grant the publication of such images only minimal constitutional protection. * * * in light of the minimal first amendment protection appropriate for pornography, * * * a legislative determination [that at least some kinds of pornography harm women] is adequate to justify prohibitions on certain pornographic materials.

Note, Anti–Pornography Laws and First Amendment Values, 98 Harv.L.Rev. 460, 463 (1984). The Seventh Circuit rejected the "low value" speech argument. Did it do so correctly?

4. Commentary published after the *Hudnut* decision is more sharply divided. Judge Easterbrook's opinion for the Seventh Circuit is defended by Dean Geoffrey Stone in Comment: Anti–Pornography Legislation as Viewpoint–Discrimination, 9 Harv.J.L. & Pub. Policy 461 (1986), and criticized by Professor Elizabeth Spahn in her Symposium Introduction, entitled On Sex and Violence, 20 New England L.Rev. 629, 638–42 (1984–85). Professor Robert Post sheds a different and interesting light on the debate by his suggestion that the pornography ordinance can usefully be seen as a current example of the historical tension between individualism and pluralism. See Robert C. Post, Cultural Heterogeneity and Law: Pornography, Blasphemy, and the First Amendment, 76 Calif.L.Rev. 297 (1988). MacKinnon herself roundly denounces the Supreme Court's summary affirmance in *Hudnut:*

> On a direct appeal, the Supreme Court invalidated a local ordinance by summary affirmance—no arguments, no briefs on the merits, no victims, no opinion, not so much as a single line of citation to controlling precedent. One is entitled to think that they would have put one there if they had had one.

Her criticism of the Seventh Circuit opinion is scarcely less biting:

> The Court of Appeals opinion * * * expressly concedes that pornography violates women in all the ways Indianapolis found it did. * * *
>
> Now we are told that pornography, which, granted, does the harm we say it does, this pornography as we define it is protected speech. It has speech value. You can tell it has value as speech because it is so effective in doing

the harm that it does. * * * The more harm, the more protection. This is now apparently the law of the First Amendment, at least where harm to women is the rationale. * * * [I]t is now clear that whatever the value of pornography is—and it is universally conceded to be low—the value of women is lower.

It is a matter of real interest to me exactly what the viewpoint element in our law is, according to Easterbrook's opinion. My best guess is that our law takes the point of view that women do not enjoy and deserve rape, and he saw that as just one point of view among many. * * * Another possible rendering is that our law takes the position that women should not be subordinated to men on the basis of sex, that women are or should be equal, and he regards relief to that end as the enforcement of a prohibited viewpoint.

Catharine A. MacKinnon, Feminism Unmodified: Discourses on Life and Law 210–211 (1987) (footnote omitted). Is this criticism justified?

Other writers have offered a more general defense of anti-pornography legislation, see Cass R. Sunstein, Pornography and the First Amendment, 1986 Duke L.J. 589, or have proposed less sweeping legislative approaches, see Angela A. Liston, Note, Pornography and the First Amendment: The Feminist Balance, 27 Ariz.L.Rev. 415 (1985) (proposing a private cause of action based on a criminal obscenity law for "hard core" pornography that is unprotected by the first amendment). Can you think of other ways to counter the view of women presented through pornography apart from legislation? See Christina Spaulding, Anti–Pornography Laws as a Claim for Equal Respect: Feminism, Liberalism & Community, 4 Berkeley Wom.L.J. 128 (1988–89) (a thoughtful re-examination of the pornography debate from the perspective of the feminist as social critic, which offers a broader notion of equal respect as membership in the sense of belonging and acceptance); see generally, Symposium, 21 U.Mich.J. of L.Reform 1 (1987–88).

5. MacKinnon's view of pornography received a more sympathetic hearing from the Supreme Court of Canada. In Butler v. The Queen (1992), 89 D.L.R. (4th) 449, 70 C.C.C. (3d) 129, Justice Sopinka upheld the constitutionality of section 163(8) of the Canadian Criminal Code, R.S.C., 1985, c. C–46, which provides that "For the purposes of this Act, any publication a dominant character-istic of which is the undue exploitation of sex, or of sex and any one or more of the following subjects, namely, crime, horror, cruelty and violence, shall be deemed to be obscene." Justice Sopinka explained that

In order for the work or material to qualify as "obscene", the exploitation of sex must not only be its dominant characteristic, but such exploitation must be "undue". In determining when the exploitation of sex will be considered "undue", the courts have attempted to formulate workable tests. The most important of these is the "community standard of tolerance" test.

* * *

* * * the community standards test is concerned not with what Canadi-ans would not tolerate being exposed to themselves, but what they would not tolerate *other* Canadians being exposed to.

Id., 89 D.L.R. (4th) at 464–65, 70 C.C.C. (3d) at 144–46. He added that the standard refers to a national community standard of tolerance, one which does not vary depending on the manner, time, and place in which the material is presented as well as the audience to whom it is directed. Dividing pornography into three categories, (1) explicit sex with violence, (2) explicit sex without violence but which subjects people to treatment that is degrading or dehumanizing, and (3) explicit sex without violence that is neither degrading nor dehumanizing, Justice Sopinka noted that the third category was not criminalized by the code unless it employs children in its production. He held that because both the purpose and effect of section 163(8) as applied to categories one and two is specifically to restrict the communication of certain types of materials based on their content, the section violates the freedom of expression guaranteed under section 2(b) of the Canadian Charter of Rights and Freedoms, but is nevertheless constitutional because it is justified under section 1 of the Charter as a reasonable limit prescribed by law. He accepted the overriding objective of the obscenity law as "avoidance of harm to society" not as "moral disapprobation," and went on to quote a description of the harm found in the Report on Pornography by the Standing Committee on Justice and Legal Affairs (MacGuigan Report) (1978), at p. 18:4:

> The clear and unquestionable danger of this type of material is that it reinforces some unhealthy tendencies in Canadian society. The effect of this type of material is to reinforce male-female stereotypes to the detriment of both sexes. It attempts to make degradation, humiliation, victimization, and violence in human relationships appear normal and acceptable. A society which holds that egalitarianism, non-violence, consensualism, and mutuality are basic to any human interaction, whether sexual or other, is clearly justified in controlling and prohibiting any medium of depiction, description or advocacy which violates these principles.

Id., 89 D.L.R. (4th) at 477, 70 C.C.C. (3d) at 157. Justice Sopinka concluded this part of the Court's opinion with the following statement:

> Finally, it should be noted that the burgeoning pornography industry renders the concern even more pressing and substantial than when the impugned provisions were first enacted. I would therefore conclude that the objective of avoiding the harm associated with the dissemination of pornography in this case is sufficiently pressing and substantial to warrant some restriction on full exercise of the right to freedom of expression. The analysis of whether the measure is proportional to the objective must, in my view, be undertaken in light of the conclusion that the objective of the impugned section is valid only insofar as it relates to the harm to society associated with obscene materials. Indeed, the section as interpreted in previous decisions and in these reasons is fully consistent with that objective. The objective of maintaining conventional standards of propriety, independently of any harm to society, is no longer justified in light of the values of individual liberty which underlie the *Charter*. This, then, being the objective of s. 163, which I have found to be pressing and substantial, I must now determine whether the section is rationally connected and proportional to this objective. As outlined above, s. 163(8) criminalizes the exploitation of sex and sex and violence, when, on the basis of the community test, it is undue. The determination of when such exploitation is undue is directly related to the immediacy of a risk of harm to society which is reasonably perceived as arising from its dissemination.

Id., 89 D.L.R. (4th) at 480, 70 C.C.C. (3d) at 160. Justice Sopinka went on to determine that despite the difficulty of proving a direct link between obscenity and harm to society, "there is a sufficiently rational link between the criminal sanction, which demonstrates our community's disapproval of the dissemination of materials which potentially victimize women and which restricts the negative influence which such materials have on changes in attitudes and behavior, and the objective." Id., 89 D.L.R. (4th) at 484, 70 C.C.C. (3d) at 164. Next, he found that the provision minimally impairs the freedom of expression which is infringed, since it proscribes only material that creates a risk of harm to society; it does not apply to materials that have scientific, artistic or literary merit; it is better designed than earlier legislative attempts to control obscenity; and it applies only to the public distribution and exhibition of obscene materials. Finally, Justice Sopinka concluded that the restriction on freedom of expression involved does not outweigh the importance of the legislative objective. His reasoning on this point is as follows:

> The final question to be answered in the proportionality test is whether the effects of the law so severely trench on a protected right that the legislative objective is outweighed by the infringement. The infringement on freedom of expression is confined to a measure designed to prohibit the distribution of sexually explicit materials accompanied by violence, and those without violence that are degrading or dehumanizing. As I have already concluded, this kind of expression lies far from the core of the guarantee of freedom of expression. It appeals only to the most base aspect of individual fulfilment, and it is primarily economically motivated.

> The objective of the legislation, on the other hand, is of fundamental importance in a free and democratic society. It is aimed at avoiding harm, which Parliament has reasonably concluded will be caused directly or indirectly, to individuals, groups such as women and children, and consequently to society as a whole, by the distribution of these materials. It thus seeks to enhance respect for all members of society, and non-violence and equality in their relations with each other.

Id., 89 D.L.R. (4th) at 487–88, 70 C.C.C. (3d) at 167–68. How does Judge Easterbrook's interpretation of the First Amendment compare to Justice Sopinka's analysis of the Canadian Charter? Would you expect Canadian feminists to be as divided over the issue posed in *Butler v. The Queen* as American feminists were over *Hudnut?* What about civil libertarians? See generally, Cass Sunstein, Neutrality in Constitutional Law (With Special Reference to Pornography, Abortion, and Surrogacy), 92 Colum.L.Rev. 1 (1992).

ACLU President and Professor of Law Nadine Strossen notes that "one of the first targets of the new [Canadian] law was a lesbian and gay bookstore, Glad Day Bookstore, and a magazine produced by lesbians for lesbians," adding that Canadian customs officials confiscated several feminist works that Canadian bookstores sought to import from the United States, including two books written by Andrea Dworkin. Nadine Strossen, A Feminist Critique of "The" Feminist Critique of Pornography, 79 Va.L.Rev. 1099, 1145–46 (1993). She concludes that "[t]he speculative, attenuated benefits of censoring 'pornography,' in terms of reducing violence and discrimination against women, are far outweighed by the substantial, demonstrable costs of such a censorship regime in terms of women's rights." Id., at 1186. Do you agree? See generally, Joan Kennedy Taylor, Does Sexual Speech Harm Women? The Split Within Feminism, 5 Stan.L. & Pol.Rev. 49 (1994). Catharine A. MacKinnon, Pornography Left and Right, 30 Harv.Civ. Rts.—Civ.Lib.L.Rev. 143 (1995).

At the moment of her untimely death, Professor Mary Joe Frug was working on a manifesto focusing on the relationship of the law to the female body. Her reflections on the lessons to be drawn from the politics of the pornography struggle are especially pertinent here. See Mary Joe Frug, Commentary: A

Postmodern Feminist Legal Manifesto (An Unfinished Draft), 105 Harv.L.Rev. 1045, 1067–75 (1992).

6. Does the First Amendment permit a state university to adopt a policy subjecting persons to discipline for engaging in "[a]ny behavior, verbal or physical, that stigmatizes or victimizes an individual on the basis of race, ethnicity, religion, sex, sexual orientation, creed, national origin, ancestry, age, marital status, handicap or Vietnam-era veteran status, and that (a) involves an express or implied threat to an individual's academic efforts, employment, participation in University sponsored extra-curricular activities or personal safety; or (b) has the purpose or reasonably foreseeable effect of interfering with an individual's academic efforts, employment, participation in University sponsored extra-curricular activities or personal safety"? See Doe v. University of Michigan, 721 F.Supp. 852 (E.D.Mich.1989). Compare R.A.V. v. City of St. Paul, 505 U.S. 377, 112 S.Ct. 2538, 120 L.Ed.2d 305 (1992). See Steven H. Shiffrin, Racist Speech, Outsider Jurisprudence, and the Meaning of America, 80 Cornell L.J. 43 (1994) (critiqueing R.A.V.).

See also Iota XI Chapter v. George Mason University, 993 F.2d 386 (4th Cir.1993), holding that the First Amendment's protection of expressive conduct extended to a fraternity's "ugly woman" contest in which fraternity members dressed as caricatures of different types of women, including one offensively caricaturing a black woman. The University's subsequent disciplinary measures were held to discriminate on the basis of viewpoint and were thus invalid.

E.   STATE EQUAL RIGHTS AMENDMENTS

MARCHIORO v. CHANEY

Supreme Court of Washington, 1978.
90 Wash.2d 298, 582 P.2d 487.

DOLLIVER, JUSTICE.

This is an action for declaratory and injunctive relief brought by plaintiffs who are active in the affairs of the Democratic Party in the State of Washington. Included are the chairwoman of the King County Democratic Central Committee, the chairmen of the Pierce County and Spokane County Democratic Central Committees, and several members of the Democratic Party of the State of Washington. Defendants are the incumbent chairman and the members of the Washington State Democratic Committee, established in conformity with RCW 29.42.020.

The bases of plaintiffs' action are that (1) RCW 29.42.020 and .030, which provide the two members of the State Democratic Committee elected by the county central committees be of the opposite sex and the chairman and vice chairman of the State Democratic Committee be of the opposite sex, violate Const. art. 31, the equal rights amendment (ERA); * * *

The trial court granted summary judgment for plaintiffs on each of these claims. We reverse on issues (1) * * *

The state committee * * * was created by laws enacted in 1909. * * * At that time, the state committee was composed of one member elected by the county committee from each county. In 1927, the composition from each county to the state committee was changed to one committee-man and one committee-woman. * * * In 1939, the requirement was enacted which provided for officers of the state and county committees and the further mandate that they must include a chairman and vice chairman who shall be of the opposite sex. * * * Regulation by statute of political parties in this state has been in effect since 1907. * * * State committees, whose size and composition were mandated by statute, have been in effect since 1909; equal representation by sex of the governing body of the state committee has been required since 1927; and a state committee chairman and vice chairman of the opposite sex have been required since 1939.

* * *

I

THE EQUAL RIGHTS AMENDMENT

* * *

* * * Const. art. 31, § 1, approved in 1972, reads as follows:

> Equality of rights and responsibility under the law shall not be denied or abridged on account of sex.

In memoranda to the trial court and briefs to this court, plaintiffs assert the equal rights amendment forbids any classification based on sex. They cite Darrin v. Gould, 85 Wash.2d 859, 540 P.2d 882 (1975), in support of this view. This is not, however, what *Darrin* said. The determination that classification by sex is suspect, which is the key to the analysis used under equal protection (Hanson v. Hutt, 83 Wash.2d 195, 517 P.2d 599 (1973)), has been replaced by the new demands of the equal rights amendment. As we said in Darrin v. Gould, supra, 85 Wash.2d at 871, 540 P.2d at 889:

> Const. art. 31, provided the latest expression of the constitutional law of the state, dealing with sex discrimination, as adopted by the people themselves. Presumably the people in adopting Const. art. 31 intended to do more than repeat what was already contained in the otherwise governing constitutional provisions, federal and state, by which discrimination based on sex was permissible under the rational relationship and strict scrutiny tests. Any other view would mean the people intended to accomplish no change in the existing constitutional law governing sex discrimination, except possibly to make the validity of a classification based on sex come within the suspect class under Const. art. 1, § 12. See footnote 7, supra. Had such a limited purpose been intended, there would have been no necessity to resort to the broad, sweeping, mandatory language of the Equal Rights Amendment. See Comment, Sex Discrimination in Interscholastic High School Athletics, 25 Syracuse L.Rev. 535, 570–74 (1974).

Darrin makes clear that the old approach of sex as a suspect class, strict scrutiny and proof of compelling state interest enunciated in Hanson v. Hutt, supra, has been swept away by the equal rights amendment. See Brown, Emerson, Falk & Freedman, The Equal Rights Amendment: A Constitutional Basis for Equal Rights for Women, 80 Yale L.J. 871, 904 (1971).

Under the equal rights amendment, the equal protection/suspect classification test is replaced by the single criterion: Is the classification by sex discriminatory? or, in the language of the amendment, Has equality been denied or abridged on account of sex? In the language of Darrin v. Gould at page 877, 540 P.2d at page 893, "under our ERA *discrimination* on account of sex is forbidden". (Italics ours.) See Singer v. Hara, 11 Wash.App. 247, 257, 522 P.2d 1187 (1974).

The thrust of the equal rights amendment (see e.g., 80 Yale L.J. 871 (1971), supra; Comment, Equal Rights Provisions: The Experience Under State Constitutions, 65 Cal.L.Rev. 1086 (1977)), is to end special treatment for or discrimination against either sex. As stated in California Comm'n on the Status of Women, Impact ERA: Limitations and Possibilities (1976) at page 8: "[P]ower need not imply hierarchy; power can be shared, and ERA advocates desire female equality not superiority." See also Official Voters Pamphlet, November 7, 1972, House Joint Resolution No. 61, at 52–53, especially "Statement for" at page 52.

The Yale Law Journal analysis, contrary to the views of plaintiffs, does not forbid the type of legislation found in RCW 29.42.020 and .030. As the article states, at page 904, "This does not mean, however, that the government would be powerless to take measures designed to assure women actual as well as theoretical equality of rights." This is precisely the purpose of this legislation.

What are the rights involved here? They are (1) the right to run for a position on the state committee of a major political party and to run for the position of chairman or vice chairman of the state committee; and (2) the right as a member of the state committee or as one of the two statutory officers of the state committee to play a role in the leadership of a major political party. What has been done to assure women actual as well as theoretical equality of these rights? The legislature has found that in the conduct of the offices of state committees there shall be an absolute equality of rights between the sexes. An equal number of both sexes must be elected to the committee and as chairman and vice chairman of the state committee. Neither sex may predominate. Neither may discriminate or be discriminated against. There is an equality of numbers and an equality of rights to be in office and to control the affairs of the state committee. The ironic result of plaintiffs' theory would be to abolish a statute which mandates equality by invoking a provision of the constitution passed to guarantee equality.

The major objection of plaintiffs seems to be the mandate by statute that one of the positions on the state committee from each county is reserved for a female and the other for a male and that this violates the equal rights amendment. But if the statute simply said, "The state committee of each major political party shall be composed of an equal number of women and men" there clearly would be no abridgment or denial on account of sex of any equality of rights under the law. We have found no case or any literature which suggests mandated equality by statute would violate the equal rights amendment.

If equality under the statute is not offensive to the equal rights amendment, then certainly, as here, the state may adopt a rational means—one male and one female state committee member from each county—to achieve the equality required.

As commentators have consistently stated (see 80 Yale L.J. 871, 920, et seq.), the equal rights amendment does not permit special exemptions or exceptions because of sex, e.g., "protective" labor legislation applicable to women only. These laws generally provided special benefits, excluded women from particular occupations or from employment under certain conditions, or restricted conditions of employment. They are exclusionary statutes which apply to one sex only and are in no way comparable to the statutory scheme considered here. See Hanson v. Hutt, supra; see also Official Voters Pamphlet, November 7, 1972, supra.

The marital community and the community property statutes in this state are in some ways analogous to the situation in this case. The "governing parties" in a marriage must be male and female—one of each. RCW 26.04; Singer v. Hara, supra. The persons in the marital community are vested with equal power to manage the affairs of the community and its property. RCW 26.16.030. Thus, while there is certainly a classification, there is equality of treatment and this is sufficient to meet the requirements of the equal rights amendment. Singer v. Hara, supra.

There is another aspect of Const. art. 31 which is not mentioned by either party, is not referred to in any case involving the equal rights amendment, and is not the subject of any article or comment. There are 16 states which have some kind of equal rights provisions in their constitutions. See 65 Cal.L.Rev. 1086 at 1111–1112 (1977), supra. In only one does the word "responsibility" appear—the Constitution of the State of Washington.

The legislative history is scanty. The phrase "and responsibility" was placed in the proposed equal rights amendment by the House committee and was approved apparently without question by the legislature and by the people. Although no reference to the phrase "and responsibility" is made anywhere, we must presume the legislature and the people did not intend the phrase to be mere surplusage but that it was to have meaning. Chlopeck Fish Co. v. Seattle, 64 Wash. 315, 117 P. 232 (1911).

The most obvious and we believe correct meaning is on the face of the amendment: "Equality of * * * responsibility under the law shall not be denied or abridged on account of sex." The "Equality of * * * responsibility under the law" involved here is for each sex equally to conduct the affairs of major political parties through the statutory instrumentalities required by RCW 29.42.020 and .030—the state committees. This is an equal responsibility mandated by law and which, under the equal rights amendment, "shall not be denied or abridged on account of sex." When the state, by statute, mandates an equality of responsibility, it is hardly appropriate for this court to hold this statutory mandate to be stricken by the very constitutional provisions which approve it. Neither RCW 29.42.020 nor RCW 29.42.030 violate Const. art. 31, the equal rights amendment.

* * *

The judgment of the trial court as to the applicability of Const. art. 31 to RCW 29.42.020 and .030 * * * is reversed. With the exception of article 4(G)(4), the judgment that the State Democratic Charter is binding on the Democratic State Committee is affirmed.

RosELLINI, HAMILTON, BRACHTENBACH and HICKS, JJ., concur.

HOROWITZ, JUSTICE (dissenting).

The majority opinion denies the State Democratic Party the right to control the size and composition of its own state committee, the body charged with governing the statewide operations of the Party between conventions, through the means of a Charter duly adopted by the Party's own convention. First the majority holds sex is to be a criterion for membership on the committee, despite the Party members' expressed will that ability—not sex—be the relevant criterion, and despite the mandate of the people of Washington, expressed in their adoption of the Equal Rights Amendment to our state constitution, that sex not be a criterion in creating classifications affecting rights and responsibilities.

* * *

In reaching its result, the majority has seriously undermined the strength of the Equal Rights Amendment. * * *

I. THE EQUAL RIGHTS AMENDMENT

The Equal Rights Amendment adopted by the people of the State of Washington in 1972 (Const. art. 31, § 1) absolutely forbids any classification of persons based on sex. Darrin v. Gould, 85 Wash.2d 859, 540 P.2d 882 (1975). The majority concedes the amendment's broad language is not to be construed under the judicial standards adopted by the United States Supreme Court for the Equal Protection Clause of the Fourteenth Amendment, which permit classifications based on sex where the requirements of the rational relationship or strict scrutiny test have been met. Moreover, the majority correctly points out that the thrust of the Equal Rights Amendment is to end discrimination against either sex. The majority wrongly concludes, however, that the equality of rights and responsibilities guaranteed by the amendment is the same as equality of numbers, an interpretation which is obviously at odds with both the language and the spirit of the amendment. Equality of the *right* to seek and hold Party offices cannot be guaranteed when these offices are to be allocated on the basis of sex so as to achieve equality of *numbers*. Furthermore, the majority approves, and thereby perpetuates, the use of sex as a criterion for classification, the very evil sought to be eliminated by the amendment.

In Darrin v. Gould, supra, this court adopted a standard for application of the new constitutional amendment, namely, outright prohibition of classifications on the basis of sex, even where such a classification would have been permissible under the Equal Protection Clause. *All* classifications based on sex are prohibited. The only exceptions, we pointed out, are where the function of the classification is to regulate cohabitation in sexual activity between unmarried persons, protect fundamental rights of privacy, or allow dissimilar treatment because of characteristics unique to one sex. Darrin v. Gould, supra, at 872, n. 8, 540 P.2d 882. The majority even quotes the rationale adopted for this far-reaching standard: that the Equal Rights Amendment must have been intended to prohibit sex classifications allowable under other constitutional provisions. The majority fails to state the rule adopted in Darrin v. Gould, though, that is that a classification cannot be based on sex alone, with no relation to the individuals' ability to perform the activity regulated. In *Darrin* the activity regulated was participation in high school football, and we held that, under the facts of that case, a classification based on sex did not relate to the ability of the individual to play football.

Here the activity regulated is representation of a constituency on the Democratic Party's county or state committees. It should be obvious that sex is completely unrelated to the ability of an individual to perform these duties. This classification based on sex is also prohibited by the Equal Rights Amendment.

The majority argues, however, that RCW 29.42.020 and .030, which require delegations to the state committee to consist of one man and one woman from each county, and that the chairman and vice-chairman of the state and county committees be of opposite sexes, breathe the *spirit* of equality and therefore conform to the requirements of the Equal Rights Amendment. The error in this argument is easily demonstrated. The sex related provisions of the statutes have the effect that once a woman is chosen to represent her county on the state committee, or to be chairman or vice-chairman of one of the committees, no other woman is eligible for the remaining position, even though she may be the best qualified candidate and the person who would receive the most votes in a free election. A man must be chosen, even though that man may not possess the same qualities. All women desiring to seek and hold the remaining office are denied the right to do so *merely because of their sex*. Obviously, the same inequity applies to men seeking office under these statutes. Furthermore, contrary to the assertion of the majority, this inequity would exist, and be equally repulsive to the Equal Rights Amendment, even if the statutory language required "an equal number of women and men." Clearly the majority opinion prevents the Equal Rights Amendment from achieving its purpose of making sex a neutral factor, one to be disregarded in favor of ability and performance.

The majority argues that the use of the word "responsibility" in the Amendment is ignored by this interpretation. On the contrary, the use of the word "responsibility" in the amendment emphasizes its aim that appropriate criteria, such as excellence in the activity regulated, be applied in creating necessary classifications, instead of the inappropriate criterion of sex. Talent is to be the guide, not sex.

I believe the Equal Rights Amendment was intended to aid a political party, including the Democratic Party, in its effort to set ability as the criterion for election of its officials, not to hamstring it. The majority's interpretation distorts the amendment's very purpose. The Democratic Party in convention assembled decided the welfare of the Party would be best served by the use of criterion of ability, rather than sex, in choosing its officials. It is supported in its effort to employ that criterion by the language and spirit of the Equal Rights Amendment. The majority's distortion of the Amendment stymies the efforts of both the Democratic Party and the people of Washington to make sex a completely neutral factor in the creation of classifications affecting rights and responsibilities in this state.

* * *

I dissent.

WRIGHT, C.J., and UTTER, J., concur.

STAFFORD, JUSTICE.

I concur in the dissent except insofar as it appears to elevate footnote 8 in Darrin v. Gould, 85 Wash.2d 859, 540 P.2d 882 (1975) to the status of a *holding.* In the footnote we merely commented that "three *possible* exceptions" (italics mine) to the federal Equal Rights Amendment were discussed in Brown, Emerson, Falk & Freedman, The Equal Rights Amendment: A Constitutional Basis of Equal Rights for Women, 80 Yale L.J. 871, 904 (1971). We did not hold that there were in fact three exceptions to the absolute ban of classifications based upon sex under the Equal Rights Amendment (Const. art. 31, § 1). Further, none of the three *possible* exceptions applied in Darrin v. Gould, supra, and none apply here. Thus, we should follow the lead of *Darrin* and again refrain from deciding either whether such exceptions exist or whether they are absolutes, until the issue is properly before us.

Notes on Marchioro

1. Plaintiffs' claim that the Washington statute violated their First Amendment right to freedom of association, also rejected by the Washington Supreme Court, was pursued to the United States Supreme Court, which affirmed the Washington judgment. Marchioro v. Chaney, 442 U.S. 191, 99 S.Ct. 2243, 60 L.Ed.2d 816 (1979). Compare Bachur v. Democratic National Party, 836 F.2d 837 (4th Cir.1987) (rejecting a voter's challenge to the "equal division" rule that required each state in selecting its delegates for the 1984 Democratic National Convention to "provide for equal division between delegate men and delegate women and alternate men and alternate women" on the ground that the private associational rights of the party to give shape to its goals through a measure designed to ensure the equal participation of women at the national convention outweighed the indirect limitation imposed on Bachur's right to vote for a candidate of his choice regardless of sex).Plaintiffs in *Marchioro* did not seek review of the "one man and one woman" requirement of the statute at the United States Supreme Court level, nor did they raise any claim based on the Equal Protection Clause of the Fourteenth Amendment. See 442 U.S. at 194–95 n. 8, 99 S.Ct. at 2245–46, 60 L.Ed.2d at 820. Would the United States Supreme Court have had jurisdiction to review the Washington Supreme Court's interpretation of the state Equal Rights Amendment? If not, what significance would a contrary determination under the Equal Protection Clause have had?

2. Does the Washington ERA prohibit classifications based on sex or only discriminatory classifications? If the former is the correct interpretation, would the standard of review be more stringent than that under "strict scrutiny" equal protection analysis? If the latter is correct, how do you decide which classifications are discriminatory? The majority in *Marchioro* accepts that the ERA requires a standard of review stricter than that formerly applied to suspect classifications, but nevertheless allows classifications to be made. Does this make sense? The majority seems to be saying that neither sex is subject to discrimination if both must be represented on the state committee in equal numbers. Are they suggesting that this result would be required under the state ERA? Must the composition of, say, all local public school boards in Washington now be made mathematically equal in numbers of men and women by command of the state ERA? Is the analogy to the "governance" in a marriage and in matters affecting marital property a convincing one? See Note, 15 Gonzaga L.Rev. 1093, 1100–1101 (1980), criticizing *Marchioro* on this point.

3. In Franklin County Sheriff's Office v. Sellers, 97 Wash.2d 317, 646 P.2d 113 (1982), the Washington Supreme Court applied its state statute prohibiting discrimination in employment rather than its Equal Rights Amendment to a plan by the Sheriff of Franklin County to staff a work release program for inmates of

the county jail with two counselors, a male and a female. Plaintiff, Betty Sellers, was not considered for the open position since the Sheriff's Office already had a female counselor. The Court held that this rejection violated the Law Against Discrimination:

> The County's decision to achieve a sexual balance by providing a male counselor and female counselor resulted in the County refusing to hire Sellers because of her sex. As such, the action was prohibited by the statute unless it was based upon a bona fide occupational qualification. [The Court affirmed the determination of the administrative tribunal that no BFOQ existed.]

Id., 97 Wn.2d at 328–329, 646 P.2d at 119. The Court noted that, since the statutory violation disposed of the case, it need not reach the question whether the County's actions violated the State Equal Rights Amendment, citing *Marchioro* as an example of a case dealing with the constitutional claims. Id., 97 Wn.2d at 329 n. 2, 646 P.2d at 119 n. 2. Are *Sellers* and *Marchioro* inconsistent? As a matter of state law, which should prevail?

4. What do you suppose was the reason for the 1927 and 1939 amendments to the Washington laws challenged in *Marchioro?* Emily Newell Blair, who served as Vice–Chair of the Democratic National Committee from 1921 until 1928, gave the following account of the mood at the national level:

> When it became evident that the passage of the suffrage amendment was imminent, the women who wished to enter political life realized that they must break the precedent of male eligibility to party committees. At the same time, the political organizations were faced with the problem of winning the woman's vote. Mrs. George Bass, chairman of the Women's Bureau of the Democratic National Committee, saw an opportunity to use this necessity in order to break the precedent, and devised a plan which she hoped would do both. She persuaded the Democratic National Committee to increase its membership so as to provide for a national committeewoman as well as a national committeeman from each state, this committeewoman to be named by the national committeeman. At the same time, in her position as national organizer of the women's vote, she urged state committees to follow this example. The Republican National Committee, no less eager to win the approval of the women, adopted the same plan.

* * *

> At its National Convention in 1920 the Democratic Party adopted a resolution formulated by Mrs. Bass to the effect that, thereafter, the National Committee be composed of a man and a woman from each state, and that the national committeewoman be elected in the same manner as the man. This meant that, thereafter, the national committeewoman would have the same authority as the national committeeman, would be in every way equal to the men members of the committee. What had been given the appointees by courtesy now became theirs by authority. In 1924 the Republican National Convention adopted the same plan.
>
> Various state committees followed their example. This was called the fifty-fifty plan. In some states, especially those where the committee was a matter constituted by law, this fifty-fifty plan was written into law and it was obligatory to have a man and a woman member from each unit of representation. Some states went further and provided that when the chairman of said committee was a man, the vice chairman should be a woman, and vice versa. In some states, it was provided that at least two of the officers be women.

Between the years 1920 and 1928 there was agitation in many states for this kind of a law.

There was, naturally, objection to this plan. Some women felt that it limited their activities. They preferred, so their argument ran, to go into the primaries or caucuses and defeat some man and so serve on the committees, not as women, but as citizens. To this, those favoring the law replied that it would be many years before women would be powerful enough in politics to defeat men for places in the political organization, and that it was essential both to party success and to the participation of women in party politics that a special place be made for women. Men would not give up the places they already held, but they might admit women to a place beside them. Therefore, it was wiser to get "in" by the only way they could get in. Once in, the men would grow accustomed to having women about, and women would have an opportunity to learn the ropes. As a matter of logic, of course, it was ridiculous. If the women were citizens and there was to be no sex line in politics, they should run and be elected to political committees as individuals and not as men or as women. But as a practicality the men held the citadel. The only way women could get in was by making a place for women. It was a case of logic against practicality. And practicality won. It won the men as it did the women. The bait to which the men rose was women's votes. * * *

Although this system is what might be called the "model" established by the national organizations, it has not been adopted by all the state organizations. In a few of the southern states there is no provision made for women as women on the state committees. And, incidentally, there are no women on these state committees. The "model" has not proved popular with the western states that had woman suffrage before the passage of the Nineteenth Amendment, and in other states women are still either ignored, or taken care of on subsidiary or auxiliary committees. It is interesting to note that in no states where the "model" has not been adopted, as far as I can discover, has a woman displaced a man member of a committee—far less risen to any position of importance in any party organization.

Emily Newell Blair, Women in the Political Parties, 143 The Annals of the American Academy of Political and Social Science 217, 217–19 (1929). Does the dispute Blair recounts between "logic" and "practicality" strike you as familiar? Karen Marchioro's later challenge to the statute grew out of an unsuccessful effort to amend the state law to provide greater representation in party governance for the more populous counties. Seattle Sun, June 13, 1979, at p. 3, col. 1.

5. The interpretation of state equal rights amendments has varied widely, and has ranged from the "rational basis" equal protection standard through "strict scrutiny" to interpretations that suggest an absolute prohibition on sex-based classifications is being employed. See Lujuana W. Treadwell & Nancy W. Page, Comment, Equal Rights Provisions: The Experience under State Constitutions, 65 Calif.L.Rev. 1086 (1977). For example, Pennsylvania's provision ("Equality of rights under the law shall not be denied or abridged in the Commonwealth of Pennsylvania because of the sex of the individual", Art. I, Sec. 27) has been interpreted to prohibit classifications based on sex. Thus, in Henderson v. Henderson, 458 Pa. 97, 101, 327 A.2d 60, 62 (1974), the Pennsylvania Supreme Court held unconstitutional a statute providing for temporary support during the pendency of divorce proceedings for wives only, saying

[t]he thrust of the Equal Rights Amendment is to insure equality of rights under the law and to eliminate sex as a basis for distinction. The sex of

citizens of this Commonwealth is no longer a permissible factor in the determination of their legal rights and legal responsibilities.

The Massachusetts Supreme Judicial Court, interpreting art. 1, Part I of its Constitution ("Equality under the law shall not be denied or abridged because of sex, race, color, creed or national origin") has adopted a strict scrutiny approach for all the listed classifications. Thus, in Lowell v. Kowalski, 380 Mass. 663, 405 N.E.2d 135, 139 (1980), in performing a salvage operation on a statute that permitted illegitimate children to inherit from mothers but not from fathers, the court thus phrased the relevant standard:

> A statutory classification based on sex is subject to strict judicial scrutiny under the State ERA and will be upheld only if a compelling interest justifies the classification and if the impact of the classification is limited as narrowly as possible consistent with its proper purpose.

Based on its earlier decision in Darrin v. Gould, 85 Wash.2d 859, 540 P.2d 882 (1975), the Washington Supreme Court appeared to be tending in the direction of adopting an absolute prohibition against classifications based on sex similar to that used in Pennsylvania. The majority opinion in *Marchioro* laid that prediction to rest, didn't it? What standard would you say Washington is using after *Marchioro*? The authors of the Comment cited earlier proposed an "ideal standard" for an equal rights amendment, one that "would lie between strict scrutiny and an absolute ban." 65 Calif.L.Rev. at 1109. Is that the standard adopted by the majority in *Marchioro*? Explaining their standard further, the authors write:

> Such a test could establish a strong presumption that any sex-based classification was unconstitutional. In order to sustain the sex-based classification, the state would have to show that no other basis of classification would achieve the purpose behind the statutory distinction. Such a standard would require a closer match between the sex classification and the purpose of the distinction than strict scrutiny now requires.

Id., 65 Calif.L.Rev. at 1109. Do you agree that this is the ideal standard for interpreting an equal rights amendment?

6. Are state equal rights provisions limited by a state action requirement as is the federal equal protection clause? Two states have so held, interpreting the phrase "under the law" in their state equal rights amendments as requiring state action. See Murphy v. Harleysville Mutual Insurance Co., 282 Pa.Super. 244, 422 A.2d 1097 (1980), certiorari denied 454 U.S. 896, 102 S.Ct. 395, 70 L.Ed.2d 211 (1981) (suit challenging automobile insurance rates that varied with sex, marital status, and age failed to show sufficient state involvement through regulation of insurance companies); and Lincoln v. Mid–Cities Pee Wee Football Association, 576 S.W.2d 922 (Tex.Civ.App.1979) (remanded to allow proof of state action through use of state property for football facilities). Compare Hartford Accident & Indemnity v. Insurance Commissioner of Commonwealth of Pennsylvania, 65 Pa.Cmwlth. 249, 442 A.2d 382 (1982), affirmed 505 Pa. 571, 482 A.2d 542 (1984), holding that Commissioner did not exceed his authority to set insurance rates when he disapproved the use of sex as a basis for classification for automobile insurance rate differentials. The Commissioner was permitted to read the Casualty and Surety Rate Regulatory Act in light of the state Equal Rights Amendment. One commentator argues that no sex discrimination existed in *Hartford:* the court failed "to recognize that for nondiscriminatory treatment to exist, different prices on insurance should be charged to young men and women; the coverage is provided at different costs, because there are basic differences in

accident history between the two groups." Richard A. Miller, Discrimination by Gender in Automobile Insurance: A Note on Hartford Accident and Indemnity Co. v. Insurance Commissioner, 23 Duquesne L.Rev. 621, 626 (1985). Do you agree?

7. When a court invalidates, under an equal rights or equal protection provision, a classification that is under-inclusive, what is the proper remedy? Simple invalidation of the statute, with the repair job left to the legislature? Or extension of the benefit provided or burden imposed to the omitted group? The United States Supreme Court makes this decision itself for federal laws, but remands to state courts to choose the remedy in cases challenging state legislation. Compare, e.g., Califano v. Westcott, 443 U.S. 76, 99 S.Ct. 2655, 61 L.Ed.2d 382 (1979) (using extension for a provision of the Aid to Families with Dependent Children program granting benefits to families with unemployed fathers, but not unemployed mothers) with Orr v. Orr, 440 U.S. 268, 99 S.Ct. 1102, 59 L.Ed.2d 306 (1979) (invalidating and remanding a state alimony statute providing alimony for wives only). The Pennsylvania legislature has come to the rescue of Pennsylvania courts struggling with this issue in the wake of the state equal rights amendment by declaring its intent that

> where in any statute heretofore enacted there is a designation restricted to a single sex, the designation shall be deemed to refer to both sexes unless the designation does not operate to deny or abridge equality of rights under the law of this Commonwealth because of the sex of the individual.

1 Pa.Com.St.Ann. § 2301 (1979 Supp.). The Pennsylvania Supreme Court has treated this statute as meaning that a finding of unconstitutionality without more is "an alternative no longer available". George v. George, 487 Pa. 133, 136, 409 A.2d 1, 2 (1979). See generally, Ruth Bader Ginsburg, Some Thoughts on Judicial Authority to Repair Unconstitutional Legislation, 28 Clev.St.L.Rev. 301 (1979); see also Candace S. Kovacic, Remedying Underinclusive Statutes, 33 Wayne L.Rev. 39 (1986).

———

Chapter II

SEXUAL INTERACTION WITHIN
THE FAMILY

A. MARRIAGE AND FAMILY LIFE

1. THE MARRIAGE CONTRACT

a. *Traditional Marriage and Its Consequences for Women*

i. Age at Marriage, Married Name, Domicile

BOBB v. MUNICIPAL COURT

California Court of Appeal, 1983.
143 Cal.App.3d 860, 192 Cal.Rptr. 270.

MILLER, J.—Carolyn Bobb appeals from the superior court's judgment denying her petition for writ of certiorari and affirming respondent court's judgment of contempt.

The facts of this case are not in dispute. On January 26, 1982, appellant, an attorney, was called and appeared for jury duty on a criminal case in municipal court. When appellant was called to take her place in the jury box as a prospective juror the following voir dire examination was conducted by the trial judge:

"THE COURT: Miss Bobb, what is your occupation?

"MISS BOBB: I'm an attorney.

"THE COURT: And in your practice do you practice criminal law as well as civil law?

"MISS BOBB: No, I practice entirely bankruptcy law.

"THE COURT: All right. Is there a Mr. Bobb?

"MISS BOBB: I have some difficulty with that question because I've noticed only the women have been asked to answer that.

"THE COURT: Yes, I know. Do you have a Mr. Bobb—is there a Mr. Bobb?

"MISS BOBB: Are you going to pool [sic] the men to see if they care to disclose—

"THE COURT: No, I'm just going to ask you if you have a husband or not. Do you have a husband?

"MISS BOBB: I don't care to answer it then. What's relative to women is relative to men.

"THE COURT: Yes, I know. What is your husband's occupation?

"MISS BOBB: I don't care to answer that.

"THE COURT: I instruct you to answer.

"MISS BOBB: I don't think I should.

"THE COURT: I've got—you understand that you'll be in contempt of Court—jury—you're an attorney, you understand these rules, don't you?

"MISS BOBB: No, I do not understand why only the women are asked certain questions and the men aren't asked the same questions.

"THE COURT: The question to you, Mrs. Bobb—you're an attorney at law, you understand the rules and regulations of—of—of being an attorney. And the question to you now simply is: What is your husband's occupation?

"MISS BOBB: I refuse to answer.

"THE COURT: You're held in contempt of Court, Mrs. Bobb."

Immediately thereafter appellant was taken to a holding facility to await transfer to the county jail. After spending approximately 15 minutes at the holding facility, appellant was ordered released on her own recognizance on condition that she return at 3 p.m. that afternoon for sentencing by respondent court.

At the sentencing hearing appellant requested a continuance in order to obtain counsel and to do further research. The court denied the continuance. After appellant further explained her objection to the voir dire questioning, the court acknowledged her sincerity but repeated its conviction that the questions posed were valid and that refusal to answer them constituted contempt of court. Appellant was then sentenced to one day in jail, with credit for her time served.

Appellant petitioned the superior court for a writ of certiorari requesting that the orders made by respondent court be annulled and set aside. The superior court affirmed respondent court's judgment of contempt finding that the cases cited by appellant regarding the United States and California Constitutions' prohibition against racial discrimination did not apply to the facts in the present action.

On appeal appellant concedes that the questions put to her, when administered in a gender-neutral context, were constitutionally valid. However, she contends that when the questions are posed as part of a discriminatory pattern they constitute a denial of equal protection. (*Yick Wo v. Hopkins* (1886) 118 U.S. 356 [30 L.Ed. 220, 6 S.Ct. 1064].)

Citing *Hamilton v. Alabama* (1964) 376 U.S. 650 [11 L.Ed.2d 979, 84 S.Ct. 982], *Johnson v. Virginia* (1963) 373 U.S. 61 [10 L.Ed.2d 195, 83 S.Ct. 1053] and *In re Berry* (1968) 68 Cal.2d 137 [65 Cal.Rptr. 273, 436 P.2d 273], appellant maintains that a court which issues an unconstitutional order acts in excess of its jurisdiction and, accordingly, there is no contempt of court on the part of one who refuses to obey such an order. The facts in *Hamilton* are the most analogous to the instant action.

In *Hamilton* a black woman who was called as a witness refused to answer questions on cross-examination so long as she was referred to as "Mary" instead of "Mrs. Hamilton." [1] The trial court held her in contempt of court. However, the contempt conviction was annulled per curiam by the United States Supreme Court. Although the Monterey Superior Court found *Hamilton* and appellant's other cited cases inapposite to the present action, it appears that the cases are directly on point.

Equal protection provisions of the California Constitution "while 'substantially the equivalent of' the guarantees contained in the Fourteenth Amendment to the United States Constitution, are possessed of an independent vitality which, in a given case, may demand an analysis different from that which would obtain if only the federal standard were applicable." (*Serrano v. Priest* (1976) 18 Cal.3d 728, 764 [135 Cal.Rptr. 345, 557 P.2d 929].) It can be seen that this state has applied a standard of review different from that applied by federal courts under the Fourteenth Amendment in cases which involve classifications based on gender. * * *

* * *

For example, in *Sail'er Inn, Inc. v. Kirby* (1971) 5 Cal.3d 1 [95 Cal.Rptr. 329, 485 P.2d 529, 46 A.L.R.3d 351], a woman challenged the constitutionality of a California law prohibiting females from tending bar unless they or their husbands held a liquor license on equal protection grounds. Our Supreme Court applied the strict scrutiny standard of review * * *.

* * *

Since *Sail'er Inn* our Supreme Court has consistently reaffirmed its holding that gender-based differentials are to be treated as "suspect classifications" subject to strict scrutiny. (See, *Arp v. Workers' Comp. Appeals Bd.* (1977) 19 Cal.3d 395, 400 [138 Cal.Rptr. 293, 563 P.2d 849]; *Hardy v. Stumpf* (1978) 21 Cal.3d 1, 7 [145 Cal.Rptr. 176, 576 P.2d 1342].)

In light of *Sail'er Inn*'s pronouncement, no significant difference can be seen between ordering a witness to submit to an attorney's imposition of a "relic of slavery" such as addressing blacks only by their first names, and ordering only female prospective jurors to announce their marital status and husbands' occupations which is likewise a relic of a bygone age when women

---

1. The *Hamilton* record was quoted in *Bell v. Maryland* (1964) 378 U.S. 226, 248–249, footnote 4 [12 L.Ed.2d 822, 871, 84 S.Ct. 1814]:

" 'Cross examination by Solicitor Rayburn:

" 'Q. What is your name, please?

" 'A. Miss Mary Hamilton.

" 'Q. Mary, I believe—you were arrested—who were you arrested by?

" 'A. My name is Miss Hamilton. Please address me correctly.

" 'Q. Who were you arrested by, Mary?

" 'A. I will not answer a question—

" 'By Attorney Amaker: The witness's name is Miss Hamilton.

" 'A. —your question until I am addressed correctly.

" 'The Court: Answer the question.

" 'The Witness: I will not answer them unless I am addressed correctly.

" 'The Court: You are in contempt of court—

" 'Attorney Conley: Your Honor—your Honor,

" 'The Court: You are in contempt of this court, and you are sentenced to five days in jail and a fifty dollar fine.' "

Justice Douglas characterized this exchange as one of the " 'relics of slavery.' "

were presumed incapable of independent thought. Both orders reinforce a stigma of inferiority and second-class citizenship.

* * *

Applying the strict scrutiny standard to the case at bench, respondent does not suggest and we cannot think of any compelling governmental interest for posing one set of questions to female jurors but not to male jurors. Clearly, administrative convenience cannot justify a suspect classification in the face of the strict scrutiny test. (*Inmates of Sybil Brand Inst. for Women v. County of Los Angeles, supra,* 130 Cal.App.3d 89, 102.) The fact that counsel was free to ask the men the same questions as were put to the women does not alter the fact that the judge initiated and reinforced the practice of special treatment for female jurors.

Appellant found herself in a situation identical to the one faced by Mary Hamilton some 20 years earlier. Just as Mary Hamilton was justified in disobeying the court's order to respond to discriminatory questioning, so was appellant justified in her refusal to comply with equally discriminatory questioning.

* * *

The judgment accordingly is reversed.

KLINE, P.J.—I concur.

Justice Miller has in my view reached the right result for the wrong reason. I think it unnecessary to reach the constitutional issue, for on the unique facts of this case I would not sustain the judgment even if persuaded the court's questioning were constitutionally valid. Moreover, I believe the most significant issue raised by this case relates more to the proper treatment of jurors than the rights of women.

* * *

Because petitioner was a prospective juror and the record demonstrates she acted during voir dire on the basis of a moral principle asserted respectfully and in good faith, I concur in the judgment setting aside the judgment of contempt.

ROUSE, J.—I respectfully dissent.

At oral argument, counsel for appellant conceded that, if the questions were proper, then she would not challenge the trial judge's right to hold that appellant's refusal to answer was an act of contempt. Therefore, in my view, the only issue before this court is whether appellant had the right to refuse to answer the questions "Do you have a husband?" and "What is [his] occupation?"

I cannot accept appellant's assertion that her refusal to answer such innocuous questions is a matter of constitutional dimension. Both as a trial lawyer and a trial judge, I have asked similar questions of prospective jurors on many occasions, blissfully unaware of the sinister nature of the inference now ascribed to them by appellant. Clearly, it is a proper area of inquiry, generally addressed to both male and female members of a venire, but, until I read Justice Miller's opinion, I was unaware of any requirement that such questions be put to each or to none. It seems to me that the matter of one's marital status and occupation is a common subject of inquiry and discussion at any gathering of two or more persons, in a variety of settings, including (but certainly not confined to) social affairs, various agencies in the private and public sectors, and even in the courtroom.

The *Hamilton* case, relied upon by Justice Miller in his opinion (i.e., *Hamilton v. Alabama* (1964) 376 U.S. 650 [11 L.Ed.2d 979, 84 S.Ct. 982]) is readily distinguishable from the facts of this case. There the court's behavior toward Mrs. Hamilton was personally demeaning with racial overtones. Here, there was nothing demeaning to appellant, either in the questions themselves or in the manner in which they were asked.

* * *

Obviously, appellant views this matter as a manifestation of sexual bias and one of constitutional magnitude. She has successfully persuaded one of my colleagues on that point. Unfortunately, I cannot agree with either of my colleague's resolution of the matter.

I would affirm the judgment.

The petition of defendant and respondent for a hearing by the Supreme Court was denied August 11, 1983. Grodin, J., did not participate therein.

IN RE LAURA BETH LAMB ON DISBARMENT

Supreme Court of California, 1989.
49 Cal.3d 239, 260 Cal.Rptr. 856, 776 P.2d 765.

BY THE COURT:

Petitioner Laura Beth Lamb was admitted to practice in December 1983. She has no prior record of discipline. On November 13, 1986, she pled nolo contendere to two felony counts of false personation to obtain a benefit. (Pen.Code, § 529, subd. 3.) The charges arose from allegations that petitioner took the July 1985 bar examination for her husband.

Upon receiving the record of conviction, we referred the matter to the State Bar for a determination whether the misconduct involved moral turpitude and, if so, what discipline should be imposed. Among other things, the parties stipulated before the State Bar Court that moral turpitude was involved. The hearing officer proposed disbarment, and the review department concurred. Petitioner sought review.

Petitioner's case has sympathetic aspects, and her expressions of contrition seem genuine. Nonetheless, her deceitful crime was exceptionally serious. Considering the public danger inherent in bar exam cheating, and the criminal dishonesty and moral turpitude involved, "[o]nly * * * the most compelling mitigating circumstances" could prevent disbarment. * * * Moreover, despite her intellectual promise, the psychological problems which led to petitioner's moral misjudgment cast continuing doubt upon her fitness to practice law. Under the circumstances, we adopt the State Bar Court's proposal and disbar petitioner.

* * *

DISCUSSION

The only issue is the appropriate discipline. On that score we must examine the record independently and exercise our own judgment. * * *

* * *

As the State Bar suggests on review, because petitioner's criminal breach of professional standards was so morally serious and so dangerous, only the most overwhelming evidence of mitigation could prevent her disbarment in the public interest. Petitioner fails to sustain that heavy burden.

* * *

Petitioner emphasizes that she has ended the marriage which contributed to her acute stress. She also points out that diabetes, though sometimes controllable, cannot be cured. Thus, she urges, she has done everything possible to eliminate the causes of her misconduct.

However, the consensus of mental health professionals was that petitioner suffered a *chronic emotional disability, independent* of her marital and physical problems, which contributed substantially to her disastrous misjudgment. As noted, we have no convincing evidence that her susceptibility in this regard has ended.

* * *

Despite our sympathetic feelings, our paramount duty is to protect the public, the courts, and the profession. Accordingly we, like the State Bar Court, believe that reinstatement proceedings are the means by which petitioner should demonstrate her clear rehabilitation after "the passage of considerable time." (Std. 1.2(e)(viii).) We therefore adopt the State Bar Court's recommendation that petitioner be disbarred.

* * *

KAUFMAN, JUSTICE, dissenting.

I dissent.

There was public danger inherent in petitioner's serious misconduct, but the circumstances that gave rise to that misconduct were unique and no longer exist. Contrary to the majority's premise, there is no danger to the public or anyone else from petitioner's one-time, aberrational conduct stemming from circumstances that no longer exist and as to which there is not the slightest possibility of recurrence. Thus, while disbarment in this case will doubtlessly be applauded in some circles, it is wholly unwarranted. It serves only to punish an apparently talented lawyer whose misconduct resulted from the most desperate, life-threatening circumstances. Indeed, such drastic discipline serves the public interest *less* well than would a long period of probation on appropriate conditions, including proof of fitness before returning to the practice of law.

The record discloses the following uncontroverted facts: After adamantly refusing several times her then-husband's insistent demands that she take the bar examination for him, petitioner eventually did so only when she was so desperately physically ill and overwhelmingly mentally intimidated by his barbaric threats and conduct that she felt she had no alternative but to do so, or lose the unborn child with which she was then many months pregnant. The child has long since been born and petitioner's marriage to her former husband has been dissolved. The circumstances were absolutely unique and could not possibly recur.

Petitioner is an insulin-dependent diabetic. When she became pregnant, her physician advised her the pregnancy and its anticipated complications would be life threatening and recommended that she have the pregnancy aborted. She refused. What ensued was nightmarish.

* * *

In addition to the overwhelming physical and emotional problems of her pregnancy, petitioner's marriage and home life had become nothing short of a disaster.

Petitioner had met Morgan Lamb in law school. In 1983, after their graduation from law school, Morgan accepted employment at a prestigious law firm in Houston. Petitioner joined Morgan in Houston and they were married in October 1983. After passing the California bar examination, petitioner was hired as an attorney in the Houston office of the Securities and Exchange Commission (SEC). Soon after, however, things began to fall apart.

Morgan failed the Texas bar examination. He began to act depressed and moody. He would cry, hide in bed, or watch television. He also became violently argumentative.

Morgan retook the Texas bar examination. He was so convinced he would fail again that he became hysterical. Although he did pass, he was fired by his law firm. His reactions became more extreme, violent and unpredictable. He would shout and throw things, and even abused petitioner physically.

After these setbacks, petitioner and her husband attempted a new start. They moved to Los Angeles where Morgan had secured a position with a prominent law firm. Petitioner was able to transfer to the Los Angeles office of the SEC.

Morgan sat for the February 1985 California bar examination. By this time, petitioner was pregnant and already so ill she had to take a leave of absence from her job. Then, within a short space of time, Morgan was fired from his position with the Los Angeles law firm and he received a letter notifying him that he had failed the California bar examination. After that, he lost any semblance of self-control. He threw heavy objects and furniture. He smashed large lamps and tore down the curtain rods. He screamed at petitioner and pushed her violently. He threatened to kill himself. He threatened to kill petitioner and the baby. Petitioner was so frightened she removed a gun he kept near the bed. Members of petitioner's family who visited her saw broken glass on the floor, smashed lamps, holes in the wall and bits of food plastered on the wall. Petitioner lived in fear of her husband's violent tantrums.

Petitioner desperately wanted to save her marriage and the lives of herself and her baby. The stress of her home situation placed an intolerable stress on the unborn baby because of petitioner's extremely high blood pressure and physical illnesses. Her doctors told her she had to alleviate the stress or risk the life of her baby or herself. Petitioner was required to lie still because of her dangerous protein deficiency. At times, however, Morgan would shake her and force her to get up and do housework and take care of him.

Morgan became convinced he could not pass the bar examination and repeatedly importuned petitioner to take it for him. She refused numerous times, although she was afraid of what he might do to her or to himself if she did not relent. Each time she refused he would fly into a rage. Finally, in her weak and confused state, petitioner gave in to her husband's demands that she take the exam for him because she could not think of any way to refuse without endangering herself or the baby. She submitted her photograph with his application to take the July 1985 bar examination. Even thereafter, she attempted to convince her husband to take the examination himself and studied with him so that he would be prepared for the examination. For a short time, that plan seemed to be working, but then Morgan began to find more and more excuses not to study. Ultimately, petitioner succumbed to the overwhelming pressures and took the examination posing as her husband.

Immediately upon completing the bar examination, petitioner entered the hospital, where her doctors urged her to have the baby delivered at once or risk the death of both herself and her baby. Petitioner refused because the baby's lungs were too underdeveloped for it to survive outside her body. Petitioner underwent experimental treatments to help the baby's lungs develop. She herself was on the verge of death and required intensive care. After ten days, labor was induced and a healthy baby girl was born, two months prematurely.

DISCUSSION

Petitioner does not claim that her conduct was justified or legally excused by these circumstances. She in fact stipulated her conduct involved moral turpitude and accepts responsibility for it. Rather, the issue is what discipline is appropriate for petitioner's conduct.

In fastening upon disbarment as the appropriate discipline the majority give insufficient consideration to the mitigating circumstances in this case. * * *

Petitioner's "long term" psychological problems relate to her childhood in a dysfunctional family where one parent abused drugs and all the family members became withdrawn and isolated. Yet it is uncontroverted that, despite the psychological shortcomings attributable to her past, petitioner had always been able to conform her conduct to the highest ethical standards. The record shows that the conduct leading to this offense was completely aberrational and out of character. It was only in the unique combination of situational circumstances here, in which she was on the verge of complete physical, mental and emotional collapse, that she engaged in these bizarre acts.

Petitioner has shown, not only clearly and convincingly, but beyond question, that she has done everything possible to eliminate the extreme emotional and physical difficulties that led to the misconduct. She is, of course, no longer pregnant and no longer suffers the dire complications brought on by the combination of pregnancy and her diabetes. She has ended her marriage to Morgan Lamb. Though she cannot change the fact of her diabetes, she has brought it under control. And she has committed to voluntary, long-term therapy to overcome her problems. * * *

* * *

* * * Disbarment here serves only to punish petitioner. An alternative is available which would, in my view, far better serve the public, the profession and the courts. To the extent necessary, we may impose conditions of probation which will ensure that the attorney is rehabilitated and the public is protected. I would impose a lengthy probation, with a substantial term of actual suspension and with appropriate probationary conditions, including continued therapy and a demonstration of fitness before returning to the practice of law.

Notes on Bobb and Lamb

1. Which of the three opinions in *Bobb* do you find most persuasive? Judge Miller stresses Ms. Bobb's right as a woman not to respond to discriminatory questioning; Presiding Judge Kline vindicates the right of all prospective jurors, acting respectfully and in good faith, to decline to answer questions because of an articulated moral principle; and Judge Rouse fails to recognize either right. Ms. Bobb was represented by staff attorneys of the ACLU of Northern California. Should their litigation strategy have been aimed at unmasking and declaring unacceptable the trial judge's stereotypical notions about married women, or designed instead to obtain greater freedom for all prospective jurors? If their aim was to achieve greater respect for women jurors in the courtroom, which strategy is more likely to be successful?

2. Do you agree with Judge Rouse that the questions put to Ms. Bobb were not "personally demeaning"? Why do you suppose she chose this time and place to assert her independence as a woman? Here is what she said during the sentencing hearing:

> What I was objecting to * * * was the inference * * * that women would be influenced by their spouse and the men, on the other hand * * * wouldn't be influenced by their spouses because you had no questions of any man * * * as to what their spouses did. And, I felt this line drawn between the men and women prospective jurors this morning very, very strongly. And I was hoping I wouldn't be called * * * to the jury box because I knew I would have to object. * * * [U]nfortunately, when my name was called and I had to go forth and answer the questions, I had to decide whether I was going to participate in this or not and I elected not to and I don't feel as a citizen I have to. * * * I did not come in here to make a statement. I'm not known for my espousal of erratical [sic] causes. All I know is it just hurt my gut. And that's why I took the stand I did.

Id., 163 Cal.App.3d at 871, 192 Cal.Rptr. at 277. *Bobb* is discussed in Karen A. Wells, Note, 12 Hastings Con.L.Q. 315 (1985), and in Randy Riddle, Note and Comment, 14 Golden Gate Univ.L.Rev. 769 (1984).

3. Do you think that Laura Beth Lamb should have been disbarred? What would Justice Kaufman have done if she had remained married to Morgan Lamb?

4. Do the facts of *Lamb* lend support to the *Bobb* Trial Court's voir dire examination of Carolyn Bobb?

Text Note
The Married Woman's Loss of Identity

In his Commentaries on the Law of England,[1] Blackstone summarized the position of the married woman at common law as follows:

By marriage, the husband and wife are one person in law: that is, the very being or legal existence of the woman is suspended during the marriage, or at least is incorporated and consolidated into that of the husband; under whose wing, protection, and *cover,* she performs every thing; and is therefore called in our law-French a *feme-covert, foemina viro co-operta;* is said to be *covert-baron,* or under the protection and influence of her husband, her *baron,* or lord; and her condition during her marriage is called her *coverture.* Upon this principle, of a union of person in husband and wife, depend almost all the legal rights, duties, and disabilities, that either of them acquire by the marriage. I speak not at present of the rights of property, but of such as are merely *personal.* For this reason, a man cannot grant anything to his wife, or enter into covenant with her: for the grant would be to suppose her separate existence; and to covenant with her, would be only to covenant with himself: and therefore it is also generally true, that all compacts made between husband and wife, when single, are voided by the intermarriage. A woman indeed may be attorney for her husband; for that implies no separation from, but is rather a representation of, her lord. And a husband may also bequeath any thing to his wife by will; for that cannot take effect till the coverture is determined by his death. The husband is bound to provide his wife with necessaries by law, as much as himself; and, if she contracts debts for them, he is obliged to pay them; but for anything besides necessaries he is not chargeable. Also if a wife elopes, and lives with another man, the husband is not chargeable even for necessaries; at least if the person who furnishes them is sufficiently apprized of her elopement. If the wife be indebted before marriage, the husband is bound afterwards to pay the debt; for he has adopted her and her circumstances together. If the wife be injured in her person or her property, she can bring no action for redress without her husband's concurrence, and in his name, as well as her own: neither can she be sued without making the husband a defendant. There is indeed one case where the wife shall sue and be sued as a feme sole, viz. where the husband has abjured the realm, or is banished, for then he is dead in law; and the husband being thus disabled to sue for or defend the wife, it would be most unreasonable if she had no remedy, or could make no defence at all. In criminal prosecutions, it is true, the wife may be indicted and punished separately; for the union is only a civil union. But in trials of any sort they are not allowed to be evidence for, or against, each other: partly because it is impossible their testimony should be indifferent, but principally because of the union of person; and therefore, if they were admitted to be witnesses *for* each other, they would contradict one maxim of law, *"nemo in propria causa testis esse debet"*; and if *against* each other, they would contradict another maxim, *"nemo tenetur seipsum accusare."* But, where the offence is directly against the person of the wife, this rule has been usually dispensed with; and therefore, by statute 3 Hen. VII, c. 2, in case a woman be forcibly taken away, and married, she may be a witness against such her husband, in order to convict him of felony. For in this case she can with no propriety be reckoned his wife; because a main ingredient, her consent, was wanting to the

1. I Blackstone, Commentaries 442–445
(1765).

contract: and also there is another maxim of law, that no man shall take advantage of his own wrong; which the ravisher here would do, if, by forcibly marrying a woman, he could prevent her from being a witness, who is perhaps the only witness to that very fact.

In the civil law the husband and the wife are considered as two distinct persons, and may have separate estates, contracts, debts, and injuries; and therefore in our ecclesiastical courts, a woman may sue and be sued without her husband.

But though our law in general considers man and wife as one person, yet there are some instances in which she is separately considered; as inferior to him, and acting by his compulsion. And therefore all deeds executed, and acts done, by her, during her coverture, are void; except it be a fine, or the like manner of record, in which case she must be solely and secretly examined, to learn if her act be voluntary. She cannot by will devise lands to her husband, unless under special circumstances; for at the time of making it she is supposed to be under his coercion. And in some felonies, and other inferior crimes, committed by her, through constraint of her husband, the law excuses her: but this extends not to treason or murder.

The husband also, by the old law, might give his wife moderate correction. For, as he is to answer for her misbehaviour, the law thought it reasonable to intrust him with this power of restraining her, by domestic chastisement, in the same moderation that a man is allowed to correct his apprentices or children; for whom the master or parent is also liable in some cases to answer. But this power of correction was confined within reasonable bounds, and the husband was prohibited from using any violence to his wife, *aliter quam ad virum, ex causa regiminis et castigationis uxoris suae, licite et rationabiliter pertinet.* The civil law gave the husband the same, or a larger, authority over his wife: allowing him, for some misdemeanors, *flagellis et fustibus acriter verberare uxorem;* for others, only *modicam castigationem adhibere.* But with us, in the politer reign of Charles the second, this power of correction began to be doubted; and a wife may now have security of the peace against her husband; or, in return, a husband against his wife. Yet the lower rank of people, who were always fond of the old common law, still claim and exert their ancient privilege: and the courts of law will still permit a husband to restrain a wife of her liberty, in case of any gross misbehaviour.

These are the chief legal effects of marriage during the coverture; upon which we may observe, that even the disabilities which the wife lies under are for the most part intended for her protection and benefit: so great a favourite is the female sex of the laws of England.

It may seem an unwarranted conceit to speak of a woman's loss of identity upon marriage. The law has relaxed its repressive grip since Blackstone's time when a married woman literally surrendered control of her property, her right to sue and be sued, in short, her entire legal personality to her husband. In our day, social custom restricts the independence of both spouses more firmly than do legal injunctions, yet both types of restrictions fall more heavily on women than men in several particulars. First, there is the matter of *marriageable age*. Writing in 1969, Professor Leo Kanowitz noted that only eleven states prescribed the same minimum age at marriage for males and females, while the remaining thirty-nine permitted females to marry from two to three years earlier than males, the most common arrangement being that in which males could marry at 21, females at 18 without parental consent.[2]

Kanowitz persuasively argued that these laws suggest to young women that marriage is their proper life choice and that only men should postpone marriage while devoting themselves to acquiring the education necessary for their future careers.[3]

These laws have changed dramatically. By 1987, all states and the District of Columbia had equalized the age for marriage without parental consent at 18 for both sexes.[4] The Uniform Marriage and Divorce Act had taken this position in 1971,[5] basing its choice of the lower age in part on the federal and state trend to lower the voting age to 18.[6] Was this a wise choice? The Marriage and Family Committee of the National Organization for Women criticized this decision, urging that both men and women should be encouraged to postpone marriage during their teens in order to spend this time in education and preparation for jobs.[7] The decisions of young people, if not of their legislators, have favored the Committee's position. Since the middle 1970s young adults of both sexes have postponed marriage until they are well into their twenties. The median age at marriage for males in 1975 was 23.5, for females 21.1, compared to 26.5 and 24.5 in 1993.[8]

What accounts for this shift? One important factor is the larger percentage of women who postpone marriage to enter college. In the Fall of 1979, the largest group of eighteen-year olds that the country has ever had swelled college and university enrollments by 2.5 million—a 5 per cent increase over 1978, and the largest single year increase since 1975.[9] And, for the first time, a majority of all college students were women. In 1979, women outnumbered men on the campus by 5.9 million to 5.7 million; and by 7.8 million to 6.2 million in 1992.[10] Women,

2. Leo Kanowitz, Women and the Law 10 (1969) [hereafter cited as Kanowitz].

3. Id., at 11–13.

4. Were the earlier statutes constitutional? Lower courts in New York had disagreed over whether a provision permitting females to marry without parental consent at 18, males at 21 violated equal protection guarantees when the legislature resolved the matter by lowering the minimum age for males to 18. Compare Friedrich v. Katz, 73 Misc.2d 663, 341 N.Y.S.2d 932 (1973) (statute valid) reversed as moot in light of change in statute 34 N.Y.2d 987, 360 N.Y.S.2d 415, 318 N.E.2d 606 with Berger v. Adornato, 76 Misc.2d 122, 350 N.Y.S.2d 520 (1973) (invalid). The Illinois Supreme Court struck down a statute of this type under the state equal rights amendment. Phelps v. Bing, 58 Ill.2d 32, 316 N.E.2d 775 (1974). See also Moe v. Dinkins, 533 F.Supp. 623 (S.D.N.Y. 1981), affirmed 669 F.2d 67 (2d Cir.), certiorari denied sub nom. Axelrod v. Coe, 459 U.S. 827, 103 S.Ct. 61, 74 L.Ed.2d 64 (1982), upholding against an attack based on due process (but not equal protection) a New York statute requiring parental consent for the marriage of males aged 16–18 and females aged 14–18; the statute also required judicial approval for the marriage of females aged 14–16. See Lynn D. Wardle, Rethinking Marital Age Restrictions, 22 J.Fam.L. 1 (1983–84).

5. Uniform Marriage and Divorce Act § 203 (1971); see Note, Uniform Marriage and Divorce Act—Marital Age Provisions, 57 Minn. L.Rev. 179 (1972).

6. Uniform Marriage and Divorce Act, Comment to Section 203.

7. Report of the Marriage and Family Committee of the National Organization for Women, Suggested Guidelines in Studying and Comments on the Uniform Marriage and Divorce Act 1–2 (April 11, 1971).

8. U.S.Bur.Cen., Current Population Reports, Ser. P–20, No. 478, "Marital Status and Living Arrangements: March 1993," VII (May 1994).

9. Chronicle of Higher Education, May 12, 1980, at 1, col. 2.

10. Ibid. Women enrolled in college continued to outnumber men in 1985, by 5.5 million to 5.3 million. U.S.Bur.Cen., Current Population Reports, Ser. P–20, No. 409, "School Enrollment—Social and Economic Characteristics of Students: October 1985" (Advance Report), Table 3, at p. 5 (Sept. 1986). By 1992, 6.2 million men and 7.8 million women enrolled in college. Ibid. No. 231 "Enrollment by Sex and Level: 1960–1992," p. 156.

who had formerly seemed content with high school diplomas, are now more likely to go on to college than men.

Taking account of these and similar trends, the United States Supreme Court in Stanton v. Stanton [11] struck down, in the context of parental liability for child support, a Utah statute that specified 21 as the age of majority for males, 18 for females. As applied in *Stanton,* the statute would have ended a father's obligation to support his daughter at 18, but continued his support duty to his son until 21. The statute had been upheld by the Utah Supreme Court in reliance on traditional attitudes: [12]

> It may be that our ancestors for generations before us have been misguided in their belief that there are some fundamental differences between the sexes. But it is remarkable how some of those old notions do continue to prevail as to numerous interesting differences. Included among them is the belief held by many that generally it is the man's primary responsibility to provide a home and its essentials for the family; and that however many exceptions and whatever necessary and proper variations therefrom may exist in differing circumstances, it is a salutary thing for him to get a good education and/or training before he undertakes those responsibilities.

> Perhaps more important than this, there is another widely accepted idea: that girls tend generally to mature physically, emotionally and mentally before boys, and that they generally tend to marry earlier. We realize that as a court made up of men, there is a possibility of masculine bias, which we should endeavor to guard against in considering matters of this character. But we do not regard it as our judicial function to pass upon the soundness or the unsoundness of the ideas just mentioned above. What we do note is our knowledge of their existence; and that they have played an essential role in the history of the development of the law as declared in the statute under attack.

But in the controlling judgment of the United States Supreme Court, these "old notions" were insufficient to sustain the Utah statute.[13]

III

The appellant argues that Utah's statutory prescription establishing different ages of majority for males and females denies equal protection; that it is a classification based solely on sex and affects a child's "fundamental right" to be fed, clothed, and sheltered by its parents; that no compelling state interest supports the classification; and that the statute can withstand no judicial scrutiny, "close" or otherwise, for it has no relationship to any ascertainable legislative objective. The appellee contends that the test is that of rationality and that the age classification has a rational basis and endures any attack based on equal protection.

We find it unnecessary in this case to decide whether a classification based on sex is inherently suspect. * * *

Reed, we feel, is controlling here.

* * *

11. 421 U.S. 7, 95 S.Ct. 1373, 43 L.Ed.2d 688 (1975).

12. Stanton v. Stanton, 30 Utah 2d 315, 318–19, 517 P.2d 1010, 1012–13 (1974).

13. Stanton v. Stanton, supra note 11, 421 U.S. at 13–17, 95 S.Ct. at 1377–79, 43 L.Ed.2d at 694–96.

The test here, then, is whether the difference in sex between children warrants the distinction in the appellee's obligation to support that is drawn by the Utah statute. We conclude that it does not. It may be true, as the Utah court observed and as is argued here, that it is the man's primary responsibility to provide a home and that it is salutary for him to have education and training before he assumes that responsibility; that girls tend to mature earlier than boys; and that females tend to marry earlier than males. The last mentioned factor, however, under the Utah statute loses whatever weight it otherwise might have, for the statute states that "all minors obtain their majority by marriage"; thus minority, and all that goes with it, is abruptly lost by marriage of a person of either sex at whatever tender age the marriage occurs.

Notwithstanding the "old notions" to which the Utah court referred, we perceive nothing rational in the distinction drawn by § 15–2–1 which, when related to the divorce decree, results in the appellee's liability for support for Sherri only to age 18 but for Rick to age 21. This imposes "criteria wholly unrelated to the objective of that statute." A child, male or female, is still a child. No longer is the female destined solely for the home and the rearing of the family, and only the male for the marketplace and the world of ideas. See Taylor v. Louisiana, 419 U.S. 522, 535 n. 17, 95 S.Ct. 692, 700, 42 L.Ed.2d 690 (1975). Women's activities and responsibilities are increasing and expanding. Coeducation is a fact, not a rarity. The presence of women in business, in the professions, in government and, indeed, in all walks of life where education is a desirable, if not always a necessary antecedent, is apparent and a proper subject of judicial notice. If a specified age of minority is required for the boy in order to assure him parental support while he attains his education and training, so, too, it is for the girl. To distinguish between the two on educational grounds is to be self-serving: if the female is not to be supported so long as the male, she hardly can be expected to attend school as long as he does, and bringing her education to an end earlier coincides with the role-typing society has long imposed. And if any weight remains in this day in the claim of earlier maturity of the female, with a concomitant inference of absence of need for support beyond 18, we fail to perceive its unquestioned truth or its significance, particularly when marriage, as the statute provides, terminates minority for a person of either sex.

Only Arkansas, so far as our investigation reveals, remains with Utah in fixing the age of majority for females at 18 and for males at 21. Ark.Stat. Ann. § 57–103. See Petty v. Petty, 252 Ark. 1032, 482 S.W.2d 119 (1972). Furthermore, Utah itself draws the 18–21 distinction only in § 15–2–1 defining minority, and in § 30–1–9 relating to marriage without the consent of parent or guardian. See also § 30–1–2(4) making void a marriage where the male is under 16 or the female under 14. Elsewhere, in the State's present constitutional and statutory structure, the male and the female appear to be treated alike. The State's Constitution provides that the rights of Utah citizens to vote and hold office "shall not be denied or abridged on account of sex," and that "[b]oth male and female citizens * * * shall enjoy equally all civil, political and religious rights and privileges," Art. IV, § 1, and, since long before the Nation's adoption of the Twenty-sixth Amendment in 1971, did provide that every citizen "of the age of twenty-one years and upwards," who satisfies durational requirements, "shall be entitled to vote." Art. IV, § 2. Utah's statutes provide that any citizen over the age of 21 who meets specified nonsex qualifications is "competent to act as a juror," U.C.A.

§ 78–46–8, may be admitted to the practice of law, § 78–51–10, and may act as an incorporator, § 16–10–48, and, if under 21 and in need, may be entitled to public assistance, § 55–15a–17. The ages at which persons may serve in legislative, executive, and judicial offices are the same for males and females. Utah Const., Art. VI, § 5, Art. VII, § 3, and Art. VIII, § 2. Tobacco may not be sold, purchased or possessed by persons of either sex under 19 years of age. §§ 76–10–104 and 76–10–105. No age differential is imposed with respect to the issuance of motor vehicle licenses. § 41–2–10. State adult education programs are open to every person 18 years of age or over. § 53–30–5. The Uniform Gifts to Minors Act is in effect in Utah and defines a minor, for its purposes, as any person "who has not attained the age of twenty-one years." § 75–15–2.11. Juvenile court jurisdiction extends to persons of either sex under a designated age. §§ 55–10–64 and 55–10–77. Every person over the age of 18 and of sound mind may dispose of his property by will. § 74–1–1. And the Uniform Civil Liability for Support Act, noted above and in effect in Utah since 1957, imposes on each parent an obligation of support of both sons and daughters until age 21. §§ 78–45–2(4), 78–45–3 and 78–45–4.

This is not to say that § 15–2–1 does not have important effect in application. A "minor" may disaffirm his contracts. § 15–2–2. An "infant" must appear in court by guardian or guardian *ad litem*. Rule 17(b), Utah Rules of Civ.Proc. A parent has a right of action for injury to, or wrongful death of, "a minor child." § 78–11–6. A person "[u]nder the age of majority" is not competent or entitled to serve as an administrator of a decedent's estate, § 75–4–4, or as the executor of a decedent's will. § 75–3–15(1). The statute of limitations is tolled while a person entitled to bring an action is "[u]nder the age of majority." § 78–12–36. Thus, the distinction drawn by § 15–2–1 affects other rights and duties. It has pervasive effect, both direct and collateral.

We therefore conclude that under any test—compelling state interest, or rational basis, or something in between—§ 15–2–1 in the context of child support, does not survive an equal protection attack. In that context, no valid distinction between male and female may be drawn.

* * *

Having found the Utah statute invalid, the Court remanded to permit the state courts to resolve the remaining state law issue of whether the inequality should be remedied by treating males as adults at age 18 or by withholding majority status from females until age 21. The Utah legislature amended the statute, after *Stanton,* to read: "The period of minority extends in males and females to the age of eighteen years; * * *." [14] This amendment applied only after its passage in 1975. As to Sherri Lyn, the Utah lower court, on remand, equalized up and awarded three years' support payments for her. A divided Utah Supreme Court reversed, the majority declining to "legislate a bit * * * and say that the age of majority * * * for the one sex is also the age of majority for the other sex." Instead, it declared the male/female stipulations in § 15–2–1, pre-amendment, "obviously separable" and, viewing the female stipulation in isolation, held 18 a constitutional majority age.[15] On second appeal, the United States Supreme Court again vacated the judgment and remanded, instructing that

14. Utah Code Ann.1953, § 15–2–1 (Supp. 1977).

15. Stanton v. Stanton, 552 P.2d 112 (Utah 1976). The Utah court also commented, "One looks in vain for some provision of the Constitution which says a girl does not become of age at age 18, and so we must hold that a girl does reach her majority at that age." (Id., at 113.)

the starting point for the Utah court must be that "males and females cannot be treated differently for child support purposes consistently with the Equal Protection Clause of the United States Constitution."[16]

Would it surprise you to learn that the provision of the Utah constitution quoted in *Stanton* at p. 202, supra, which was part of that state's original constitution of 1896, is credited with being an equal rights provision?[17] Needless to say, the provision has never been construed expansively.

Although both men and women have postponed their first marriage,[18] it remains accurate to observe that women marry at an earlier age than men, usually by two or three years.[19] Still, the implications of delayed marriage have yet to be felt. The proportion of women between ages 20 to 24 who had never been married in 1993 was over two-thirds (66.8 per cent): not quite double that of women aged 20 to 24 in 1970 (35.8 per cent never married).[20] In 1993, all but 5.4 per cent of women had married by the time they reached the age range between 45 to 54 years; whether today's young women will follow that path is unknown. Cynthia Epstein observed in 1970:[21]

> All arrows direct the girl to marriage. We do not need to document this or back it up with opinion polls or attitude studies. In fact, there is probably no society in the world which does not stress marriage as the primary objective of the overwhelming majority of its young women, exception made for the small number of women recruited into religious orders. Men face the marriage mandate too, but, though marriage is implicitly emphasized as a requisite for manhood, marriage itself is not seen as a goal, a limiting factor, or a state excluding the man's other role commitments. Men marry and seek happiness by challenging the world; for women, however, it is enough to marry and to live happily ever after. The emphasis on being a wife first and foremost has many consequences for the girl's behavior at all stages of development and at all points in her preparation for a career when a decision must be made.

Whether this observation remains accurate today will be explored in the Text Note on The Legal Structure of Family Life, at p. 440, infra.

Second, a woman customarily exchanges her *surname* for that of her husband upon marriage. That this widely-followed practice is based on social custom alone, and is not required by law, now is well established.[22] Recent examinations by American courts[23] of the English common law regarding surnames have noted

---

16. Stanton v. Stanton, 429 U.S. 501, 503, 97 S.Ct. 717, 718, 50 L.Ed.2d 723, 726 (1977). On remand the Utah Supreme Court grudgingly reinterpreted its prior decision as recognizing 18 as the age of majority for both sexes. Stanton v. Stanton, 564 P.2d 303 (Utah 1977), reh. denied 567 P.2d 625.

17. Lujuana Wolfe Treadwell & Nancy Wallace Page, Comment, Equal Rights Provisions: The Experience Under State Constitutions, 65 Calif.L.Rev. 1086, 1092 n. 40 (1977). Utah, along with Louisiana and Virginia, was identified as a state whose equal rights provision had been "ineffectual in eliminating sex stereotypes embodied in the law." (Id., at 1095). None of these three states ratified the proposed Equal Rights Amendment to the United States Constitution.

18. See text at note 8, supra.

19. U.S.Bur.Cen., supra note 8, at VII (Table B).

20. Id., at Table C, p. VIII.

21. Cynthia Fuchs Epstein, Woman's Place 62 (1970).

22. See William C. Matthews, Comment, Married Women and the Name Game, 11 U.Rich.L.Rev. 121, 132 (1976); Priscilla Ruth MacDougall, Women's, Men's, Children's Names: An Outline and Bibliography, 7 Fam. L.Rep. 4013 (Mar. 17, 1981).

23. E.g., Secretary of Commonwealth v. City Clerk of Lowell, 373 Mass. 178, 366 N.E.2d 717 (1977); Dunn v. Palermo, 522 S.W.2d 679 (Tenn.1975); Kruzel v. Podell, 67 Wis.2d 138, 226 N.W.2d 458 (1975); Stuart v. Board of Supervisors, 266 Md. 440, 295 A.2d

that earlier judicial assertions to the effect that a woman is required to take her husband's surname upon marriage [24] were based on a misunderstanding of the common law.[25] As Justice Heffernan put it, in his especially well-reasoned opinion for the Wisconsin Supreme Court in Kruzel v. Podell,[26]

> a woman upon marriage adopts the surname of her husband by thereafter customarily using that name, but no law requires that she do so. If she continues to use her anti-nuptial [sic] surname, her name is unchanged by the fact that marriage has occurred.

In states where the common law has been interpreted to require that a married woman take her husband's surname, are her constitutional rights infringed? "No," according to Forbush v. Wallace,[27] which upheld against constitutional attack an unwritten regulation of the Alabama Department of Public Safety requiring a married woman to use her husband's surname in applying for a driver's license. Apart from its summary affirmance in *Forbush*,[28] the United States Supreme Court has not spoken on the question. In Whitlow v. Hodges,[29] the Court denied certiorari to the Sixth Circuit's decision upholding the constitutionality of an unwritten Kentucky regulation which required a married woman to apply for a driver's license in her husband's surname despite a showing that she had consistently used her birth name for all purposes. The Sixth Circuit deemed itself bound as to the constitutional issue by the Court's summary affirmance in *Forbush*. Judge McCree urged in dissent that the court must first determine whether the common law of Kentucky, like that of Alabama in *Forbush*, required a married woman to adopt her husband's name.[30] Wasn't he right? See Com-

---

223 (1972); State ex rel. Krupa v. Green, 114 Ohio App. 497, 177 N.E.2d 616 (1961).

24. See, e.g., Chapman v. Phoenix Nat'l Bank, 85 N.Y. 437, 449 (1881), in which the court stated in dictum that "[f]or several centuries, by the common law among all English-speaking people, a woman, upon her marriage, takes her husband's surname. That becomes her legal name, and she ceases to be known by her maiden name." *Chapman* held that notice of a judicial proceeding given to a married woman in her pre-marital name which she had not used for many years was insufficient.

25. Dunn v. Palermo, supra note 23, 522 S.W.2d at 683–84; Kruzel v. Podell, supra note 23, 67 Wis.2d at 144–46, 226 N.W.2d at 461–62; Stuart v. Board of Supervisors, supra note 23, 266 Md. at 445–48, 295 A.2d at 225–27. All three cases reject the reasoning of People ex rel. Rago v. Lipsky, 327 Ill.App. 63, 63 N.E.2d 642 (1945), which had relied on Chapman v. Phoenix Nat'l Bank, supra note 24. As the *Dunn* court notes, id., 522 S.W.2d at 681–85, *Rago* was subsequently repudiated as bad law by the Illinois Attorney General.

26. Supra note 23, 67 Wis.2d at 140, 226 N.W.2d at 459.

27. 341 F.Supp. 217 (M.D.Ala.1971), affirmed mem. 405 U.S. 970, 92 S.Ct. 1197, 31 L.Ed.2d 246 (1972). A Hawaiian statute requiring a married woman to assume her husband's name as a "family name" was repealed after Hawaii adopted a state equal rights amendment. The new statute provides that

"[u]pon marriage each of the parties to a marriage shall declare the surname each will use as a married person. The surname chosen may be the person's own, that of the person's spouse alone or that of the person's spouse placed before or after the person's own surname and separated by a hyphen." Haw.Rev. Stat. § 574–1 (1976).

28. See note 27, supra. The plaintiff, who conceded the existence of the so-called "common law rule" in her pleadings, did not challenge the accuracy of the lower court's interpretation of Alabama common law. In State v. Taylor, 415 So.2d 1043, 1048 (Ala.1982), the Supreme Court of Alabama repudiated the interpretation of Alabama common law on married women's names adopted in *Forbush* and endorsed the reading of English common law (held to be in force in Alabama) found in *Kruzel;* the Alabama court concluded that "[e]ven though the State is correct in stating that most married women customarily assume the surnames of their husbands, and register to vote in the surnames of their husbands, we hold that they are not legally required to do so."

29. 429 U.S. 1029, 97 S.Ct. 654, 50 L.Ed.2d 632 (1976).

30. Whitlow v. Hodges, 539 F.2d 582, 584–85 (6th Cir.1976) (dissenting opinion). Subsequent to its decision in *Whitlow,* the Sixth Circuit held in Allen v. Lovejoy, 553 F.2d 522 (6th Cir.1977), that an employer's policy requiring female, but not male, employees to

ment, The Constitutionality of Requiring Use of Husband's Name in Driver's License: Whitlow v. Hodges,[31] arguing that the cases are distinguishable on this point. In view of the threshold state common law question, would you have advised the plaintiffs in *Forbush* and *Whitlow* to pursue their claims in state rather than federal court?[32] In any event, how should the constitutional claim be resolved?

If a woman has voluntarily changed her surname to that of her husband upon marriage and thereafter, during the marriage, proceeds under a general name change statute to resume her birth or former name, the case law supports her right to do so.[33] The common practice whereby a married woman uses her own name for business or professional purposes while using her husband's name socially has been specifically recognized in some states.[34]

A woman who has used her husband's surname during marriage and who wishes to resume her birth or former name upon divorce may do so.[35] The fact that the woman has been awarded custody of the couple's children, who will continue to bear the father's name, is not in itself a sufficient basis for refusing to allow her name change.

Should the courts take account of the views of a married woman's husband about her surname? In name retention cases, no special point has been made about whether he consented to her continued use of her birth or former name. But in cases where she wished to resume a former name after having voluntarily assumed her husband's name at marriage, many courts have noted his consent, or at least his lack of objection, to the name change.[36] A few courts[37] have noted the views of the children as well. Why should the husband's views be treated as relevant in name change, but not in name retention, cases? Are the courts simply

change their surnames on personnel forms following marriage constituted a discrimination based on sex in violation of Title VII of the 1964 Civil Rights Act. *Whitlow* was distinguished on the basis that the United States Supreme Court's summary affirmance in *Forbush* was not controlling in employment situations, which are governed by Title VII.

31. 38 Ohio St.L.J. 157, 160–63 (1977).

32. Priscilla Ruth MacDougall, A Lesson From Whitlow v. Hodges: Stay In The State Courts, 3 Marriage, Divorce & The Family Newsletter 4 (March 1977).

33. E.g., In re Mullinix, 152 Ga.App. 215, 262 S.E.2d 540 (1979); In re Miller, 218 Va. 939, 243 S.E.2d 464 (1978); In re Erickson, 547 S.W.2d 357 (Tex.Civ.App.1977); In re Reben, 342 A.2d 688 (Me.1975); In re Strikwerda, 216 Va. 470, 220 S.E.2d 245 (1975); In re Lawrence, 133 N.J.Super. 408, 337 A.2d 49 (1975); Petition of Hauptly, 262 Ind. 150, 312 N.E.2d 857 (1974).

34. See, e.g., Secretary of Com. v. City Clerk of Lowell, supra note 23, 373 Mass. at 187, 366 N.E.2d at 723–24, Op.Atty.Gen.Wis. No. 7–77 (Jan. 30, 1977). See M. Hannah Leavitt, Comment, Surname Alternatives in Pennsylvania, 82 Dick.L.Rev. 101, 110–13 (1977) (defending the "two name" practice for women against a potential challenge under the state equal rights amendment); Patricia J. Go-

rence, Comment, Women's Name Rights, 59 Marq.L.Rev. 876 (1976); Priscilla Ruth Mac-Dougall, The Right of Women To Determine Their Own Names Irrespective of Marital Status, 1 Fam.L.Rep. 4005, 4008–09 (BNA, 1974).

35. She may resume her former name by common law usage, e.g., Traugott v. Petit, 122 R.I. 60, 404 A.2d 77 (1979); pursuant to an order made part of the divorce proceedings, e.g., Sneed v. Sneed, 585 P.2d 1363 (Okl.1978); Klein v. Klein, 36 Md.App. 177, 373 A.2d 86 (1977); Piotrowski v. Piotrowski, 71 Mich.App. 213, 247 N.W.2d 354 (1976); Egner v. Egner, 133 N.J.Super. 403, 337 A.2d 46 (1975); Marriage of Banks, 42 Cal.App.3d 631, 117 Cal. Rptr. 37 (1974); Elwell v. Elwell, 132 Vt. 73, 313 A.2d 394 (1973); or by proceeding under a general name change statute, e.g., Ogle v. Circuit Court, 89 S.D. 18, 227 N.W.2d 621 (1975); In re Harris, 160 W.Va. 422, 236 S.E.2d 426 (1977). She may also retain her ex-husband's surname after divorce, despite his objection. E.g., Welcker v. Welcker, 342 So.2d 251 (La. App.) certiorari denied 343 So.2d 1077 (La. 1977).

36. See cases cited in note 35, supra.

37. E.g., In re Mullinix, supra note 33, 152 Ga.App. at 215, 262 S.E.2d at 540. In both In re Miller and In re Strikwerda, supra note 33, the couple assured the Virginia court that, should they have children, the children would

reflecting the fact that the woman or her attorney has chosen to make this information available? What should the result be in a name change case if the husband were to oppose the wife's petition?

It is traditional for the children of a married couple to be given the surname of the father at birth. Several courts and State Attorneys General have, however, recognized the common law and constitutional rights of parents to choose a name for their children different from that of the father.[38] What happens if the parents disagree over what surname the child will bear? Little case law exists, perhaps because the issue is not often raised. Not surprisingly, there is no reported case law where the parents are living together in an intact marriage. Case law is beginning to develop where the parents are divorced or separated at the time of the child's birth and disagree about its surname. In Webber v. Parker,[39] the court rejected a father's claim that he had an absolute legal right to have his son, born after the parties had separated, bear his first name as well as his family surname, where the mother had used her own choice of first name and had omitted a lineal designation. Had the parties brought a proceeding to have the child named before the mother had chosen a name, the court reasoned,[40]

> there is no question that the court would have had the exclusive right to decide the issue, since it affected the present and future welfare of the child.

The effect of dismissal of the father's demand to have the child's name changed "was tantamount to the court's approving the name given by the wife-mother".[41] The father did not seek custody; the mother had continued to use his surname as her own following the separation.

The traditional approach to choosing surnames for infants when the parents disagree was examined and rejected as inconsistent with recent legislative and social developments in a bold opinion by Justice Frank Newman for the California Supreme Court in Marriage of Schiffman.[42] Patricia Herdman and Jason Schiffman were married on January 15, 1977 and separated six months later. Ms. Herdman was four months pregnant at the time of separation. The child was born on November 2, 1977 and was named by her mother, Aita Marie Herdman. When the father learned of the mother's action, he objected. The divorce court, in recognition of the father's primary right to have the child bear his surname,

be given the father's surname. Why was this relevant?

38. E.g., Sydney v. Pingree, 564 F.Supp. 412 (S.D.Fla.1983), (invalidating on Fourteenth Amendment grounds a Florida statute requiring that a child conceived and born in wedlock be given the father's name on the birth certificate; the parents, Chris Ledbetter and Dean Skylar, wished to name their son "Sidney Skybetter"); O'Brien v. Tilson, 523 F.Supp. 494 (E.D.N.C.1981) (holding similar North Carolina law violated both due process and equal protection; the former because it interfered with the privacy rights of parents and children, the latter because it created invalid classifications based on sex (mothers versus fathers) and birth status (legitimate versus illegitimate children)). Jech v. Burch, 466 F.Supp. 714 (D.Hawai'i 1979) (fused name); Secretary of Com. v. City Clerk of Lowell, supra note 23; Op.Atty.Gen.Mich. (April 14, 1980); Op.Atty.Gen.Md. (Nov. 9, 1978); Op. Atty.Gen.Me. (Aug. 18, 1976); Op.Atty.Gen. Me. (May 5, 1976); Op.Atty.Gen.Alaska (May 5, 1976); Op.Atty.Gen.Conn. (Jan. 23, 1975); Op.Atty.Gen.Wis. (Oct. 7, 1974).

39. 167 So.2d 519 (La.App.1964), writ refused 246 La. 886, 168 So.2d 269 (1964) (mother had named child Michael Quinn Webber— father wanted child named Absalom Theodore Webber, III). Compare In re Wilcox, No. 80D–18624 (Cook County, Ill.1980) (court ruled, on father's suit to compel use of his surname brought just prior to child's birth, that mother might name child if it were born female; if born male, court would decide what child's name should be). Should the naming right depend on the sex of the child? Is the court just pairing like-sexed parents and children, or is it making the unjustified assumption that daughters will not continue to bear their father's name after marriage?

40. Id., 167 So.2d at 522.

41. Id., at 523.

42. 28 Cal.3d 640, 169 Cal.Rptr. 918, 620 P.2d 579 (1980).

ordered the child's name changed to "Schiffman" and enjoined both parents from changing the child's name without the court's permission. Custody was granted to the mother, who appealed that portion of the interlocutory decree determining the child's name.

Justice Newman characterized the father's common law right to name his child as "part of that system, wherein he was sole legal representative of the marriage, its property, and its children." [43] Reviewing the changes that have occurred in the traditional system in California and elsewhere, including the enactment of Married Women's Property Acts, the adoption of no-fault divorce, the equalization of parental rights to custody, the elimination of sex-specific differences in property rights, and the adoption in California of the Uniform Parentage Act, Newman concluded that [44]

> [t]he Legislature clearly has articulated the policy that irrational, sex-based differences in marital and parental rights should end and that parental disputes about children should be resolved in accordance with each child's best interest.

Do you agree that the best interests standard gives adequate guidance to the trial court in cases like *Schiffman?* Justice Mosk, concurring in the judgment, would have preferred to establish a rebuttable presumption that the parent having custody had acted in the child's best interests in selecting a surname. Is that a better test? What happens if a joint custody award is made? Chief Justice Rose Bird, concurring in the judgment, questioned the jurisdiction of the divorce court to change the child's surname in the absence of specific statutory authority to do so, and suggested that legislative attention to the matter would be appropriate.[45]

---

43. Id., 28 Cal.3d at 643, 169 Cal.Rptr. at 920, 620 P.2d at 581.

44. Id., 28 Cal.3d at 645, 169 Cal.Rptr. at 921, 620 P.2d at 582. *Schiffman's* "best interests" test was adopted by the Court of Appeals of Maryland in Lassiter–Geers v. Reichenbach, 303 Md. 88, 492 A.2d 303 (Md.), certiorari denied 474 U.S. 1019, 106 S.Ct. 568, 88 L.Ed.2d 553 (1985). Appellant Linda Lassiter-Geers was pregnant in June, 1980, when she separated from her husband, George Richard Reichenbach. Without her husband's knowledge, the mother named her daughter Jamie Lauren Lassiter at the time of her birth on January 17, 1981. At the divorce hearing, on March 30, 1982, the mother was permitted to resume her birth name, Lassiter, but the issue of the child's surname was reserved for future determination. Still later, the mother remarried and assumed the name Lassiter–Geers. On April 9, 1984, the father petitioned the court that the child be named Reichenbach. Treating the case as one to determine the child's surname, rather than a petition to change the child's surname, the court adopted the best interests standard as appropriate for cases in which the parents had been unable to agree upon a surname for their child. Applying that standard, it affirmed the Chancellor's decision that the child bear her father's surname, approving the following reasoning as appropriate:

> [A]s this child gets older, starts going to school, making friends and so on, the child is

going to find herself in a situation where someone says, what is your name. My name is Lassiter. The person says, well, your mother's name is Geers. I guess your father's name is Lassiter. What is your father's name? My father's name is Reichenbach. Where did Lassiter come from? Some people and a lot of people may well infer this child was born out of wedlock. Where did Lassiter come from? She was not married to anybody named Lassiter. The father's name is Reichenbach. It just doesn't seem right to me that it puts the child in a very good position at all. As far as the child is concerned it lends itself to the child being put in an embarrassing position; and I don't think that is in the best interest of the child.

Id., 492 A.2d at 307. Is this how the California Supreme Court would have applied the best interests test? One writer advocates a rebuttable presumption favoring compound names for children under 14 in disputed cases; see Note, Like Father, Like Child: The Rights of Parents in Their Children's Surnames, 70 Va. L.Rev. 1303, 1346–54 (1984). Is that a good idea? Does it mean that, unless the presumption were overcome, Jamie's surname would be Lassiter–Reichenbach? Or Reichenbach–Lassiter? Or, perhaps, Lassiter–Geers–Reichenbach?

45. A similar objection was used as the basis for reversing the divorce court's order changing a child's surname from that of the

Schiffman was extended to apply to a case where the mother and father disagreed about what surname should be recorded on the child's birth certificate. In In re Douglass,[46] Cynthia Lesher and Bruce S. Douglass married on July 18, 1986; Cynthia assumed her husband's surname as her marital name. They separated one month later, on August 21, 1986. Cynthia was pregnant at the time of separation. After the separation, she resumed her birth name of Lesher (also the name used by her two sons by a prior marriage who were in her custody). Bruce had physical custody of two children by a prior marriage; their surname was Douglass. Their son, David Thomas, was born on March 19, 1987, and was placed in the temporary custody of his mother. Bruce wanted their son's surname to be recorded on the birth certificate as Douglass; Cynthia wanted it to be Lesher. The trial court ordered the child's surname entered on the birth certificate as David Thomas Douglass–Lesher, but provided that he shall be known as Lesher for all other purposes. Bruce appealed, arguing that *Schiffman* was limited to name changes because the California Supreme Court had indicated that it had no intention of changing the "established practice" and "prevalent custom" of giving a child born in wedlock the paternal surname on the birth certificate. The appellate court dismissed this argument as "a distinction without a difference," going on to hold that the *Schiffman* best interest standard applied to parental disputes over initial naming as well as name changes. The best interests standard led the court to affirm the trial judge's "Solomon-like determination that the birth certificate should state both surnames in a hyphenated form" on the ground that "[i]t meets and satisfies the concerns of both parents in establishing an identity with both parents and their respective family members."[47]

Compare Henne v. Wright,[48] refusing to recognize the fundamental right of two different mothers to give a child the surname at birth of a person with whom the child had no legally established parental connection at the time. Debra Henne wanted to name her daughter Alicia after the child's biological father, Gary Brinton, rather than Debra's husband, Robert Henne, from whom she was obtaining a divorce. Linda Spidell wanted to give her daughter Quintessa the same surname, McKenzie, held by her two other children, rather than her surname or that of the child's biological father, Ray Duffer, with whom she was living in nonmarital cohabitation. The court pointed out that each mother could ultimately succeed in giving her child the desired name: Debra Henne could name her daughter Alicia Brinton once the child's biological father, Gary Brinton, rather than the mother's former husband, Robert Henne, had been legally declared to be her father; and Linda Spidell could accomplish her aim if she were willing to change her own surname to McKenzie. None of the three affected men, Robert Henne, Gary Brinton and Ray Duffer, had any objection to the proposed surnames. Judge Bright, however, was unable to discern the existence of a fundamental right, "grounded in the tradition and history of this nation" to support a parent's decision "to give a child a surname with which that child has no legally recognized parental connection."[49] Does this way of asking the ques-

mother to that of the father on facts virtually indistinguishable from those in *Schiffman* in Hurta v. Hurta, 25 Wash.App. 95, 605 P.2d 1278 (1979). Should a guardian ad litem or an attorney be appointed to represent the child in such cases? See Note, Family Law—Change of Name Proceedings—Failure to Appoint Guardian Ad Litem for Minor Not Fundamental Error, 22 Sw.L.J. 649 (1968) (discussing Newman v. King, 433 S.W.2d 420 (Tex.1968).)

46. 205 Cal.App.3d 1046, 252 Cal.Rptr. 839 (1988).

47. Id., 205 Cal.App.3d at 1055, 252 Cal. Rptr. at 844–45.

48. 904 F.2d 1208 (8th Cir.1990), certiorari denied 498 U.S. 1032, 111 S.Ct. 692, 112 L.Ed.2d 682 (1991).

49. Id., 904 F.2d at 1214–15.

tion make the best interests standard irrelevant? Judge Arnold, dissenting on this point, was of the view that since there was no identifiable tradition denying what the mothers proposed, the court should hold that their right as adults to change their own names without permission of the government should extend to their right to change their children's names. Does this argument also make the best interests standard irrelevant?

Children born to unmarried women have usually taken their mother's surname. This practice, too, is currently being challenged, both in situations where the parents are living together in nonmarital cohabitation and object to state laws compelling use of the mother's name as well as in cases where the father, after having legitimated the child or having been identified in a paternity suit, insists that the child use his surname.[50]

Litigation is frequent over the right of a divorced mother who has custody of the children to change their surname from that of the father to that of their step-father if she remarries and adopts his name as her own. In general, if the father objects to the name change and if he has maintained contact with his children after the divorce, his wishes have been allowed to prevail.[51] Less often litigated is the question whether a custodial mother who has resumed her birth or former name may change the child's surname to her own or to a combination of hers and that of the father.[52] Should cases of this kind, especially where the children have used a particular surname for a long period, be decided under the general "best interests of the child" standard adopted in *Schiffman,* rather than attempting to piece out which parent has the primary legal right? If so, what factors should be taken into account in determining what the child's "best interests" might be? *Schiffman* identified several: the length of time that the child has used the surname; the effect of a name change on preservation of the father-child relationship; the strength of the mother-child relationship; and the identification of the child as part of a family unit. Can you think of others? Priscilla Ruth MacDou-

50. E.g., Donald J. v. Evna M., 81 Cal. App.3d 929, 147 Cal.Rptr. 15 (1978) (applying the Uniform Parentage Act); Roe v. Conn, 417 F.Supp. 769 (M.D.Ala.1976) (statute requiring that father's name be given to child after legitimation held unconstitutional). See also Bobo v. Jewell, 38 Ohio St.3d 330, 528 N.E.2d 180 (1988), following *Schiffman* in adopting a best interests standard to reverse an order changing the name of an illegitimate child in the custody of his mother from her surname to that of his father in the context of a proceeding to establish the father's paternity.

51. E.g., Norton v. Norton, 268 Ark. 791, 595 S.W.2d 709 (App.1980); Firman v. Firman, 187 Mont. 465, 610 P.2d 178 (1980); Burke v. Hammonds, 586 S.W.2d 307 (Ky.App.1979); Ward v. Faw, 219 Va. 1120, 253 S.E.2d 658 (1979); In re Spatz, 199 Neb. 332, 258 N.W.2d 814 (1977); Flowers v. Cain, 218 Va. 234, 237 S.E.2d 111 (1977); Hall v. Hall, 30 Md.App. 214, 351 A.2d 917 (1976); Robinson v. Hansel, 302 Minn. 34, 223 N.W.2d 138 (1974); cf. Carroll v. Johnson, 263 Ark. 280, 565 S.W.2d 10 (1978) (failure to notify father of petition to change child's name to that of step-father violates due process; citing cases).

52. See, e.g., In re Harris, supra note 35; Laks v. Laks, 25 Ariz.App. 58, 540 P.2d 1277

(1975). In Matter of Saxton, 309 N.W.2d 298, 301 (Minn.1981), certiorari denied sub nom. Saxton v. Dennis, 455 U.S. 1034, 102 S.Ct. 1737, 72 L.Ed.2d 152 (1982), the Minnesota Supreme Court adhered to the best interests standard for change of name cases announced in Robinson v. Hansel, supra note 47; it made clear, however, that "neither parent has a superior right to determine the initial name their child shall bear." The court noted appropriate factors that the trial court should consider in determining whether the proposed name change would be in the child's best interests, including the child's preference; the effect of the change on the child's relationship with both parents; the length of time the child had used the surname; the degree of community respect accorded the surnames; and the "difficulties, harassment or embarrassment" attendant upon the use of either surname. The mother's constitutional arguments were rejected. See generally, Kathryn R. Urbanya, Note, No Judicial Dyslexia: The Custodial Parent Presumption Distinguishes The Paternal From The Parental Right to Name a Child, 58 No.Dak.L.Rev. 793 (1982).

gall concludes in her authoritative article [53] that *Schiffman* "should become a guiding light for the future in order for women to have any bona fide right to name their children." Do you think this will happen?

The wealth of recent case law, opinions of State Attorneys General, and legislative activity concerning names is eloquent testimony that the traditional status of wife and/or mother is insufficient to confer personal identity.[54] Although the married woman's customary change of name is unobjectionable to many, it is resented by the woman who wishes to retain her birth name, or whatever surname she has chosen to use, in order to establish a continuity of identity throughout her life. And a woman in public or professional life stands to suffer a real loss of recognition if she alters her name upon marriage. With few exceptions,[55] American common and statutory law has now developed to the point where all adults, regardless of sex or marital status, have the right to choose what surname they will bear at any given stage of their lives. Cultural attitudes have changed less swiftly: the married woman who insists upon using her birth or former name for all purposes, including social occasions, may still encounter difficulties, depending on where she lives. Where children are involved, both judicial and cultural acceptance of change is less rapid still. But the accumulated law in this field has gone far toward freeing married women of one symbol of their traditional dependence.

Third, marriage has traditionally deprived a woman, but not a man, of the privilege accorded all other responsible adults, that of choosing her own *legal domicile*. In most states when a woman marries, her husband's domicile automatically supersedes her own.[56] If her husband's legal domicile was different from her pre-marital domicile, she must re-register to vote; she may be subjected to unfavorable state income tax consequences; she may lose the right to attend a university in her home state as a resident student; and she may lose the privilege of running for public office in her home state. In 1971, the Restatement of Conflict of Laws (Second) suggested a limited exception to the traditional rule that would allow a married woman living with her husband to maintain her own domicile when "special circumstances" make it "unreasonable" for her to acquire

53. The Right of Women to Name Their Children, 3 Law & Inequality 91, 159 (1985).

54. See generally, Kenneth L. Karst, "A Discrimination So Trivial": A Note on Law and the Symbolism of Women's Dependency, 35 Ohio St.L.J. 546, 549–54 (1974) (primarily concerns use of the title "Ms.", but also discusses lack of judicial sensitivity in relevant ways). Discussion of legislative change is found in Richard H. Thornton, Comment, The Controversy Over Children's Surnames: Familial Autonomy, Equal Protection and the Child's Best Interests, 1979 Utah L.Rev. 303 (see especially the chart of statutes relating to naming newborn children and minors); Priscilla Ruth MacDougall, Divorce/Dissolution Name Change—Ripe for Legislative Reform, 2 Marriage, Divorce & The Family Newsletter (September 1976) (contains an outline of how divorce name change statutes should be worded so as to be nondiscretionary and accord name change rights to both spouses as well as a survey of divorce name change statutes).

55. See Application of Dengler, 287 N.W.2d 637 (Minn.1979), appeal dism'd sub nom. Dengler v. Atty. Gen., 446 U.S. 949, 100 S.Ct. 2913, 64 L.Ed.2d 806 (1980) (a name is not a number under the common law or name change statute; not unconstitutional to deny request to change petitioner's name from Michael Herbert Dengler to 1069, although request to change name to Ten Sixty–Nine or One Zero Six Nine would be approved); None of the Above v. Hardy, 377 So.2d 385 (La.App. 1979) (refusing to permit candidate for public office, who had obtained judicial change of name to "None of the Above", to run for public office in that name where candidate admits his campaign is not serious and name was adopted only to arouse interest in a "None of the Above" option on ballot; proposed action would be fraudulent and deceptive use of a name).

56. Kanowitz 46–52; Homer Harrison Clark, The Law of Domestic Relations 149–51 (1968).

his domicile.[57]   Examples given are those of a woman holding public office at the time of her marriage who continues to serve as an officeholder and remains chiefly in her home state after marriage, and a woman who owns a home at her premarital domicile where both spouses spend "by far the greater part of each year."[58]   More sweeping change was accepted by the 1988 Revisions to Restatement Second, which abandoned the common law position to provide in section 21 that "[t]he rules for the acquisition of a domicile of choice are the same in the case of a married woman." Comment *a* explains, correctly, that "[t]he common law rule * * * is clearly inconsistent with contemporary views relating to the legal position of married women." It goes on to point out, however, that since most married couples live in the same place, they will continue to have the same domicile. Comment *b* opines that the couple may have separate domiciles when, for example, a wife who owned a house in her premarital domicile executes a written agreement with her husband prior to their marriage indicating that she wishes to retain her premarital domicile and when both spouses live together in the wife's house "by far the greater part of the year" after marriage. If a married woman's domicile is now governed by the same rule as that of a married man, why is a premarital agreement necessary? Marriage had no effect on a man's domicile under the common law rule, did it? As noted above, a different question arises when the wife abandons her premarital domicile to live with her husband in another state.

A different analysis has been attempted by a Maryland court. In Blair v. Blair,[59] the court suggested that where the wife is the breadwinner, her income providing the main support of the family, she need not take her husband's domicile and thus was not guilty of desertion when she returned from his home at college to the home where they had lived together while she worked. The court reasoned[60] that the rule imposing a husband's domicile upon his wife was

> based upon the fact that the husband earned the money for the support of the family, and, therefore, had the right to decide where the family should live, so that he could best fulfill this obligation, but where the wife also works, and where in some cases, as in the one before us, she earns more than he does, the reason for the rule no longer exists, and it cannot be equitably enforced.

Does the court imply that under these circumstances the husband takes the wife's domicile? Or merely that the two have different domiciles? Which result is preferable? Why? Do you agree that, in cases where the husband is the chief breadwinner, he therefore should have the right to decide where the family should live? George Berkwitt has reported a growing revolt by corporate wives who refuse to go along when the corporation wants to relocate their husbands.[61] The result is that many executives refuse to be relocated, even at the price of having to quit their jobs.

But what is needed is a different approach, not exceptions to an arbitrary rule. Professor Weintraub supports a limited change. Relying on cases dealing

57. Restatement, Second, Conflict of Laws § 21 (1971).

58. Id. Comment to § 21, at p. 85. See also McKinney's N.Y.Dom.Rel.Law § 61 (1964) (allowing a married woman to establish her own domicile for the purposes of voting and office-holding); Ashmore v. Ashmore, 251 So.2d 15 (Fla.App.1971), certiorari dismissed 256 So.2d 513 (Fla.1972), facts reported in Ashmore v. Ashmore, 241 So.2d 424 (Fla.App. 1970) (holding the wife did not acquire her husband's domicile in England since the spouses had never lived there together but had lived at the wife's home in Florida).

59. 199 Md. 9, 85 A.2d 442 (1952).

60. 199 Md. at 14, 85 A.2d at 445.

61. George J. Berkwitt, Corporate Wives: The Third Party, Dun's Review, Vol. 100, No. 2, p. 61 (August, 1972).

with such diverse issues as the diversity jurisdiction of the federal courts, tuition for state institutions of higher education, divorce jurisdiction, and voting rights, he thus traces the modern development of the married woman's domicile rule: [62]

> In the United States, the concept of the domicile of a wife has evolved from (1) a wife may acquire a separate domicile if she has justifiably left her husband, to (2) she may acquire a separate domicile if in fact she is separated from her husband, and now seems to be, at least in some states, (3) a rebuttable presumption that the wife's domicile is the same as her husband's. In the light of the status of women as equal participants in all aspects of modern society, the preferable presumption is simply that spouses have the same domicile.

Why not simply provide that all competent adults, regardless of sex or marital status, may choose their own domicile? What would such a rule mean in practice? Consider the following situations:

1. Robert Wheeler and Bonnie Wheeler, husband and wife, live together in Cleveland (where he teaches history at Cleveland State University) from Thursday evening until Monday evening each week. On Monday, Bonnie boards a plane for New York City (where she teaches English at Columbia University). She rents a New York apartment and lives there from Monday evening through Thursday afternoon, when she returns to Ohio.[63]

2. Nancy Schmidt, a United States citizen born in Washington State, presently lives in the Federal Republic of Germany with her husband, Hans Schmidt, a German citizen and a non-resident alien of the United States. Ms. Schmidt works in Germany as an employee of the United States government. As a government employee, her income is not subject to the exemption from taxation provided by section 911 of the Internal Revenue Code for other American citizens residing abroad. But if any of her income can be attributed to her husband, it would be exempt from taxation under § 861(a)(3) and 871 of the Code as compensation for personal services performed outside the United States by a non-resident alien. Washington is a community property state. The Internal Revenue Service takes the position in its booklet "Tax Guide for U.S. Citizens Abroad" (IRS R6 #54, p. 21, Rev. 10–70) that a *husband* domiciled in a community property state who is employed abroad and married to a non-resident alien *wife* may report only half of his income earned abroad since the half belonging to his wife by virtue of the community property laws of his domicile is exempt from tax. Relying on this provision, Ms. Schmidt claimed a domicile in Washington State and sought to attribute one-half of her income to her husband. This was disallowed by the IRS on the ground that Ms. Schmidt's marriage had terminated her Washington domicile.[64]

3. Representative Andrew Jacobs Jr. (Dem.—Ind.) and Representative Martha Keys (Dem.—Kan.), both Members of the United States House of Representa-

62. Russell J. Weintraub, Commentary on the Conflict of Laws 19 (2d Ed.1980) (footnotes omitted).

63. The New York Times, Nov. 13, 1972, at 42, C, col. 1. See Herma Hill Kay, Legal and Social Impediments to Dual Career Marriages, 12 U.C. Davis L.Rev. 207, 211–12 (1979).

64. See Lane–Burslem v. Commissioner, 72 T.C. 849 (1979), affirmed on other grounds 659 F.2d 209 (D.C.Cir.1981), rejecting a similar claim by a woman who had been domiciled in Louisiana prior to her marriage to an Englishman. The court reasoned that even if it held unconstitutional the Louisiana law requiring a married woman to take her husband's domicile, petitioner would not be able to attribute half her earnings to her husband, for in that case, the court would determine her marital domicile on a factual basis and would conclude that it was in England.

tives, were married in January, 1976. Both were reelected in November, 1976; only Representative Jacobs remained in office after the 1978 election.

In a perceptive article [65] describing the European notion of "habitual residence" currently being used in several Hague Conventions as an alternative to both the civil-law concept of "nationality" and the common-law concept of "domicile," Professor David Cavers suggests its usefulness as a factual description of the connection between a person and a particular territory that may exist quite apart from the more formal ties a person is deemed to have to his domicile. Referring specifically to the marital situation, he argues that although it has seemed necessary to recognize only one domicile—in the Holmesian sense of a single legal headquarters [66]—for both husband and wife during the marriage,[67] the new concept would permit a wife to "have her habitual residence apart from her husband even though their relations remained conjugal." [68] The state of habitual residence could then attach legal consequences on a case-by-case basis to that factual status without further definition as long as the residence remained habitual.

Does the concept of "habitual residence" offer a solution for the domicile problems of the married woman? Where is Nancy Schmidt's "habitual residence?" The wife who teaches at Columbia would have two "habitual residences," would she not? If she could choose her own domicile, and if domicile as a legal concept is based on a person's physical presence in a particular place plus the intention to "make that place his home for the time at least" [69] where would she be domiciled? Ohio or New York? Is the suggestion that, regardless of where her technical domicile is located, both New York and Ohio have sufficient interests in her based on her factual connections with both states to be able to assert the application of their laws in given circumstances? What circumstances? Are Representatives Jacobs and Keys protected by the 1971 Restatement's exception, noted earlier, for women holding public office at the time of marriage? What if Representative Keys had not run for public office until after her marriage? Is a premarital agreement necessary?

Is the traditional rule requiring a married woman to assume her husband's domicile vulnerable to constitutional attack? Two courts have so held, in limited contexts. In Samuel v. University of Pittsburgh,[70] a class of married female students challenged the tuition regulations of three universities which determined the residence of married women based on the residence of their husbands. The court thus characterized the issue before it: [71]

65. David F. Cavers, "Habitual Residence": A Useful Concept?, 21 Am.U.L.Rev. 475 (1972).

66. The reference is to Holmes' opinion in Williamson v. Osenton, 232 U.S. 619, 625, 34 S.Ct. 442, 443, 58 L.Ed. 758, 761 (1914).

67. Cavers, supra note 65 at 482.

68. Id. at 483–484.

69. Restatement, Second, Conflict of Laws § 18 (1971). See also Id. §§ 15, 16.

70. 375 F.Supp. 1119 (W.D.Pa.1974), appeal dismissed, 506 F.2d 355 (3d Cir.1974), decision to decertify class vacated 538 F.2d 991 (3d Cir.1976).

71. Id., 375 F.Supp. at 1131. See also West's Ann.Cal.Govt.Code § 244(g), which provides that "A married person shall have the

right to retain his or her legal residence in the State of California notwithstanding the legal residence or domicile of his or her spouse." This provision was originally enacted to apply only to women. In that form it effectively protected the tuition privileges of California women who married nonresidents against the harm complained of in Samuel. Does it have any other effect? A commentator noted that "[i]t does not appear that any of the * * * changes will have significant practical effect." 4 Pac.L.J. 422, 423 (1973). Do you agree? Section 244 was made gender-neutral as part of an overall effort to eliminate sex references from the California codes. Does it make any sense as applied to married men?

But, the singularly striking aspect of the application of residency rules at the defendant universities is the fact that no rule, rebuttable or irrebuttable, has ever existed to tie the residency classification of any group other than married women to the classification of someone else. Married men, single men and single women must indeed submit residency classification information to the registrars of their respective universities, but in their case no formal or informal rule has ever existed to tie their classification to that of another group, be it wives, parents, roommates or whomever. During the period in question, the policy of the three defendant universities, following the guidelines of the defendant state officials, has been to presume that a woman married to an out-of-state resident is herself an out-of-state resident, while a man married to an out-of-state resident was not presumed to be an out-of-state resident.

Applying the *Reed* standard,[72] the court held that the residency rules violated the equal protection clause.[73] And in Craig v. Craig,[74] the Supreme Court of Louisiana applied its state equal rights amendment to hold unconstitutional article 39 of its Civil Code, insofar as that provision allowed husbands to bring an action for annulment of marriage, separation from bed and board, or divorce in a parish not that of the matrimonial domicile without offering proof of his wife's misconduct, but which demanded proof of the husband's misconduct from a wife seeking to sue in a parish other than that of the matrimonial domicile. Stressing the limited nature of its holding, the court rejected the suggestion that the classification was adopted as part of an overall attempt to protect the "marriage, home and family."[75] The sole effect of article 39, as it affected the venue of matrimonial actions, was to give husbands a procedural advantage that wives lacked: wider choice of venue without an accompanying proof of marital misconduct. That classification was arbitrary, capricious and unreasonable; therefore it violated the state equal rights provision.

Does *Craig* suggest that the provisions of article 39, which state in part that "a married woman has no other domicile than that of her husband", in contexts apart from venue of matrimonial actions, are justified by the state's interest in protecting marriage, homes, and families? In what way does article 39 do this? The Louisiana legislature in 1979, as part of a general revision of its community property laws, repealed that part of La.Civ.Code Ann. art. 2404 which had provided that "the husband is the head and master of the partnership or community of gains; he administers its effects * * * without the consent and permission of his wife."[76] Why didn't the Louisiana legislature discard article 39 while it was at it?

Have the laws affecting age at marriage, married name, and domicile of married women changed so greatly that it is now not only an "unwarranted conceit", but inaccurate as well, to continue to speak of a woman's loss of identity upon marriage?

---

72. Reed v. Reed, 404 U.S. 71, 92 S.Ct. 251, 30 L.Ed.2d 225 (1971), discussed in Chapter I, supra.

73. Samuel v. University of Pittsburgh, supra note 70, 375 F.Supp. at 1133–34.

74. 365 So.2d 1298 (La.1978).

75. Id., at 1300.

76. See generally La.Civ.Code Ann. arts. 2325–2376 (West 1985 & Cum. Pocket Part 1995). Compare former Cal.Civ.Code § 5101: "The husband is the head of the family. He may choose any reasonable place or mode of living, and the wife must conform thereto." Section 5101 was repealed by Stats.1973, c. 987, p. 1898, § 2, operative January 1, 1975.

ii. Support of Spouse and Children

COMMONWEALTH EX REL. GOLDSTEIN v. GOLDSTEIN

Superior Court of Pennsylvania, 1979.
271 Pa.Super. 389, 413 A.2d 721.

Before CERCONE, PRESIDENT JUDGE, and WATKINS and HOFFMAN, JJ.

CERCONE, PRESIDENT JUDGE:

This is an appeal from the order of the Court of Common Pleas of Philadelphia County denying support to appellant, Charlotte Goldstein. We affirm the decision of the lower court.

The parties, Charlotte and Gilbert Goldstein, were married in 1972 and reside in a fashionable condominium in Rittenhouse Square, Philadelphia. In the summer of 1977, Charlotte was staying in Atlantic City while Gilbert was ill and living with his mother. Gilbert asked Charlotte to return home but she refused. Gilbert then announced that the parties were separated, and upon Charlotte's return, they no longer shared a common bedroom. However, Gilbert made repeated attempts toward a reconciliation, the parties consulting a marriage counselor once with Charlotte refusing to return for additional counselling. The parties continued to reside in the same condominium, but in separate bedrooms, when Charlotte sued Gilbert for support alleging that he had discontinued her monthly allowance of $1000 and, therefore, was not supporting her in the manner in which she was accustomed during their marriage.

* * * After a thorough review of the evidence on depositions, the lower court judge concluded that the case of Commonwealth v. George, 358 Pa. 118, 56 A.2d 228 (1948) was applicable in the instant matter and that Gilbert was supplying Charlotte with all the essentials required to maintain her standard of living. This finding coupled with the fact of Charlotte's independent assets as disclosed in the depositions did not permit the court to enter a support award. Finally, the trial judge concluded that even if Commonwealth v. George, supra, did not apply, Charlotte has no grounds for support based on her contention that the parties were separated merely on her husband's separation statement of 1977, despite his repeated attempts to reconcile.

Although appellant raises three issues in her brief,[1] all three revolve around the question of whether appellant has a right to support while living under the same roof with her husband. Our appellate review of such an issue is narrowly defined, and we will not disturb the findings of the lower court absent a clear abuse of discretion. * * * We find that the lower court judge

---

1. The three issues as stated by appellant are:

"(1) Whether the principle set forth in Commonwealth v. George should be applied in a broken marriage situation where the parties are no longer living together as husband and wife although they continue to reside physically under the same roof.

"(2) Whether, after the breakdown of marital relations, a husband is required to continue to support his dependent spouse in the same manner and lifestyle in which he had been supporting her and as to which she had become accustomed prior to the breakdown of marital relations absent a finding that she lacks entitlement to receive support and notwithstanding the fact that the parties physically occupy the same residence.

"(3) Whether the Court below erred in refusing to consider evidence of husband's income, earnings, earning capacity, assets, and business interests in connection with its finding that husband is adequately supporting his wife."

did not abuse his discretion in this case, but made a well-reasoned decision based on the evidence before him.

In Commonwealth v. George, * * * a wife brought a criminal support action alleging that she and her children were being neglected even though they resided within the same home with the husband-father. The wife admitted that they lived well, had maid service three days each week and that she could entertain guests in the home when she pleased. Her major objection was that her husband controlled the expenditure of his income too strictly. * * * In answer to the wife's allegations, the court said:

> "This record established that appellant has provided adequate shelter, food, clothing and reasonable medical attention. It presents conflicting concepts of family financial management. Prosecutrix does not suggest that appellant cease his present performance but desires to secure in addition thereto a monthly allowance for herself of $300. Her charges of 'neglect to maintain' are general and their weight greatly lessened by her testimony in cross-examination. That the wife is not receiving that degree of control over her husband's income to which she feels entitled does not establish 'neglect' within the meaning of the law."

In construing the relevant statute [2] further, the court said:

> "The arm of the court is not empowered to reach into the home and to determine the manner in which the earnings of a husband shall be expended where he has neither deserted his wife without cause nor neglected to support her and their children. In the absence of evidence legally sufficient to support a finding of either essentials the court is without power to enter an order upon the husband directing payment to the wife of any amount. The statute was never intended to constitute a court a sounding board for domestic financial disagreements, nor a board of arbitration to determine the extent to which a husband is required to recognize the budget suggested by the wife or her demands for control over the purse strings." * * *

Based on the facts of the case, the *George* court denied the right of support to the wife and concluded:

> "We decide only that where, as here, the husband provides a home, food, clothing and reasonable medical attention, he cannot be directed to pay a given stipend to the wife so that she may have it available for her own personal disposition. The method whereby a husband secures to his wife and family the necessities of life is not a proper subject for judicial consideration and determination in the absence of proof of desertion without cause or neglect to maintain." * * *

Since the *George* case was decided, our courts have cited its rule with approval. For example, in Scuro v. Scuro, 226 Pa.Super. 592, 323 A.2d 49 (1974), a husband and wife were living together in a jointly owned home. The husband was paying all the bills and giving the wife $20.00 per week. Our court decided that the case was controlled by Commonwealth v. George and

2. The statute construed in Commonwealth v. George, supra, was the Act of 1939, P.L. 872, § 733, 18 P.S. § 4733, which has since been repealed. See now, Crimes Code, 18 Pa.C.S. § 4322 (1973) for similar provisions presently in effect. See also Scuro v. Scuro, 226 Pa.Super. 592, 594, 323 A.2d 49 (1974).

held that "[u]nder those circumstances, the appellant was not neglecting to maintain his wife and could not be subjected to an order."   * * *

The same reasoning is applicable to the instant case. Gilbert Goldstein pays for all the household expenses including food, rent, utilities, maid service, clothing,[3] medical expenses and insurance. Charlotte has credit at two food stores, three of the finest restaurants in Philadelphia, and three large department stores, the bills from which Gilbert continues to pay.[4] Based on these facts, we conclude that Gilbert is not neglecting to support his wife in any way upon which we could grant relief.

Appellant argues that although she is receiving these items from Gilbert, she still is not being supported in the manner to which she has grown accustomed. However, in light of the funds she presently receives from Gilbert, plus the additional income she collects from her independent assets,[5] it is impossible to conclude that Charlotte is "neglected" under the statute. It is true that some of our cases have allowed a support order where the parties are living in the same home. DiPadova v. DiPadova, 223 Pa.Super. 408, 302 A.2d 510 (19732); Commonwealth ex rel. Turner v. Turner, 192 Pa.Super. 502, 161 A.2d 922 (1960). However, these cases involved extreme neglect where the wife and children were not receiving adequate food and housing. To the contrary, appellant lives in one of the best residential neighborhoods in Philadelphia and receives all the conveniences and services necessary to maintain her living there. In Scuro v. Scuro, supra, we invoked the *George* rule and held that no support order would issue where the wife received all the necessities plus $20.00 per week. The *George* rule is applicable here. The appellant in this case is not entitled to an order of support, because she is receiving more than adequate comfort.

Finally, we agree with the reasoning of the lower court that appellant has not made out a case for support even absent the *George* rule. The law in this area states that although a wife attempting to procure a support order following a nonconsensual, voluntary withdrawal from the common abode need not present grounds for leaving her husband that would entitle her to a divorce, she must at least show she withdrew for a reasonable cause. Commonwealth ex rel. Halderman v. Halderman, 230 Pa.Super. 125, 326 A.2d 908 (1974). In the instant case, appellant has not deemed it necessary to leave the marital domicile, but only to leave the marital bedroom based on the "separation" conversation the parties had in August, 1977. This "separation" statement alone is not sufficient evidence to prove a reasonable cause upon which Charlotte based her claim to a support order, especially in light of Gilbert's repeated attempts at reconciliation. Charlotte's refusal to accept Gilbert's bona fide offers of reconciliation[6] is enough to deny her right of support.   * * *

3. Gilbert has insisted that the clothing bills be reasonable and therefore refused to pay for a suit purchased by Charlotte for her son by a prior marriage.

4. The lower court opinion insists that Charlotte is being paid $100.00 per week spending money in addition to the necessities she receives. However, our review of the record reveals these payments ceased as of August 12, 1977.

5. The lower court judge calculated appellant's annual independent income from the dividends and interest on her assets and other sources to be in excess of $5,000.00, free of taxes which Gilbert pays.

6. Conversely, Charlotte said she would only reconcile if the following monetary demands were met by Gilbert to which he would not agree:

Order of the lower court dismissing appellant's petition for support affirmed.

Notes on **Goldstein**

1. Why do you suppose appellant's statement of the issues in *Goldstein* (see footnote 1 to the court's opinion) stressed her view that the parties' marital relations had "broken down"? Would a court refuse to order a husband to support his wife (or a wife her husband) if their marital relations had not broken down? In what way had Mr. Goldstein refused to support his wife?

2. As long as the spouses are living together and the providing spouse is furnishing support to the dependent spouse, even if the level of support provided is meager compared to the funds available, courts have tended to refuse to intervene in the governance of the marital unit by ordering that a specified allowance be paid to the dependent spouse. A case frequently cited for this proposition is McGuire v. McGuire, 157 Neb. 226, 59 N.W.2d 336 (1953), where a 66–year-old wife complained that her 80–year-old husband refused to give her any spending money and, although he purchased groceries, set a standard of living far below that which he could afford. She testified

> that she was a dutiful and obedient wife, worked and saved, and cohabited with the defendant until the last 2 or 3 years. She worked in the fields, did outside chores, cooked, and attended to her household duties such as cleaning the house and doing the washing. For a number of years she raised as high as 300 chickens, sold poultry and eggs, and used the money to buy clothing, things she wanted, and for groceries. She further testified that the defendant was the boss of the house and his word was law; that he would not tolerate any charge accounts and would not inform her as to his finances or business; and that he was a poor companion. The defendant did not complain of her work, but left the impression to her that she had not done enough. On several occasions the plaintiff asked the defendant for money. He would give her very small amounts, and for the last 3 or 4 years he had not given her any money nor provided her with clothing, except a coat about 4 years previous. The defendant had purchased the groceries the last 3 or 4 years, and permitted her to buy groceries, but he paid for them by check. There is apparently no complaint about the groceries the defendant furnished. The defendant had not taken her to a motion picture show during the past 12 years. They did not belong to any organizations or charitable institutions, nor did he give her money to make contributions to any charitable institutions. The defendant belongs to the Pleasant Valley Church which occupies about 2 acres of his farm land. At the time of trial there was no minister for this church so there were no services. For the past 4 years or more, the defendant had not given the plaintiff money to purchase furniture or other household necessities. Three years ago he did purchase an electric, wood-and-cob combination stove which was installed in the kitchen, also linoleum floor covering for the kitchen. The plaintiff further testified that the house is

"$400 a week spending money

A $50,000.00 annuity

$20,000.00 for furniture

That he continue to support Diane at college and generally

That he will allow her wide use of various credit cards (Some paid totally by him; some paid partially out of her allowance)

Ten overnight trips a year to New York at her discretion

Unlimited trips, at her discretion to Florida

Purchase a wedding ring"

not equipped with a bathroom, bathing facilities, or inside toilet. The kitchen is not modern. She does not have a kitchen sink. Hard and soft water is obtained from a well and cistern. She has a mechanical Servel refrigerator, and the house is equipped with electricity. There is a pipeless furnace which she testified had not been in good working order for 5 or 6 years, and she testified she was tired of scooping coal and ashes. She had requested a new furnace but the defendant believed the one they had to be satisfactory. She related that the furniture was old and she would like to replenish it, at least to be comparable with some of her neighbors; that her silverware and dishes were old and were primarily gifts, outside of what she purchased; that one of her daughters was good about furnishing her clothing, at least a dress a year, or sometimes two; that the defendant owns a 1929 Ford coupé equipped with a heater which is not efficient, and on the average of every 2 weeks he drives the plaintiff to Wayne to visit her mother; and that he also owns a 1927 Chevrolet pickup which is used for different purposes on the farm. The plaintiff was privileged to use all of the rent money she wanted to from the 80–acre farm, and when she goes to see her daughters, which is not frequent, she uses part of the rent money for that purpose, the defendant providing no funds for such use. The defendant ordinarily raised hogs on his farm, but the last 4 or 5 years has leased his farm land to tenants, and he generally keeps up the fences and the buildings. At the present time the plaintiff is not able to raise chickens and sell eggs. She has about 25 chickens. The plaintiff has had three abdominal operations for which the defendant has paid. She selected her own doctor, and there were no restrictions placed in that respect. When she has requested various things for the home or personal effects, defendant has informed her on many occasions that he did not have the money to pay for the same. She would like to have a new car. * * *

The plaintiff further testified that she had very little funds, possibly $1,500 in the bank which was chicken money and money which her father furnished her, he having departed this life a few years ago; and that use of the telephone was restricted, indicating that defendant did not desire that she make long distance calls, otherwise she had free access to the telephone.

157 Neb. at 228–30, 59 N.W.2d at 337–38. Mr. McGuire's assets, including real estate, bonds, and bank accounts, exceeded $200,000; his income was between $8,000 and $9,000 per year. Ms. McGuire had a bank account containing approximately $5,960.00. The trial court's order requiring Mr. McGuire to pay his wife $50.00 per month and to permit her to use his credit for household improvements was reversed on appeal. After reviewing cases, the Nebraska Supreme Court held that the wife could not maintain an action against her husband for support unless she was living separate and apart from him. The court explained:

> The living standards of a family are a matter of concern to the household, and not for the courts to determine, even though the husband's attitude toward his wife, according to his wealth and circumstances, leaves little to be said in his behalf. As long as the home is maintained and the parties are living as husband and wife it may be said that the husband is legally supporting his wife and the purpose of the marriage relation is being carried out. Public policy requires such a holding.

157 Neb. at 238, 59 N.W.2d at 342. Do *McGuire* and *Goldstein* raise the same issue? Note that in both cases the wives had property of their own. Did that

influence the courts? Would the cases have been decided any differently if neither wife had had private resources?

3. If a wife can enforce her husband's legal obligation to support her only by leaving him, what good is her right to be supported during marriage? An indirect method of enforcing the husband's duty of support, once more widely available than it is today, was for the wife to obtain "necessaries" of life on credit and to have the providing merchant sue the husband for reimbursement. According to Professor Clark, the doctrine of necessaries became hedged about with so many restrictions that few merchants were willing to rely on it. See H. Clark, The Law of Domestic Relations 189–92 (1968). At any event, according to the Supreme Court of Florida, " * * * because a wife was deemed legally incapable of incurring an obligation independent of her husband and because the husband was legally, and exclusively, responsible for providing the necessaries for the entire family unit, there was no reciprocal liability on the part of the wife to a third party for providing the necessaries of the husband." Shands Teaching Hosp. & Clinics, Inc. v. Smith, 497 So.2d 644, 645 (Fla.1986). Leaving to the legislature the task of reforming the common law and refusing to reach an asserted equal protection claim for lack of standing, the Florida court declined to hold a wife liable for medical services provided to her deceased husband. See also Sharpe Furniture, Inc. v. Buckstaff, 99 Wis.2d 114, 299 N.W.2d 219 (1980), applying the common law doctrine of necessaries to hold a husband primarily liable for household furnishings (a sofa) sold to his wife on credit. The husband earned a substantial income; his wife did not work outside the home and had no property in her own name. Justice Abrahamson concurred in the judgment, but argued that the majority's general rule that the husband's duty of support was always primary to that of the wife was inconsistent with the Wisconsin statutes which placed the obligation of support on both spouses on the basis of their respective economic resources rather than gender, and was invalid under the state and federal constitutional guarantees of equal protection since it discriminated against men. Was she right? Today, creditors may sue the wife directly for necessaries furnished to her during the marriage. See, e.g., Sillery v. Fagan, 120 N.J.Super. 416, 294 A.2d 624 (1972) (hospital that had furnished medical services to wife at the time of the birth of her sixth child could sue her directly for reimbursement). See also Memorial Hospital v. Hahaj, 430 N.E.2d 412, 416 (Ind.App.1982) (placing primary liability for medical expenses upon whichever spouse incurred the expenses, with the "financial resources of the marital relationship" being secondarily liable). Is that the right result?

Text Note
Support of Spouse and Children During Marriage

Conundrum: When a wife who is supporting herself actually being supported by her husband? *Answer:* When her earnings are community property under the management and control of her husband. See Washburn v. Washburn,[1] an 1858 case where wife was denied a divorce on the ground of her husband's willful neglect to provide the common necessaries of life. The husband was described[2] as "an able-bodied man, a seaman by occupation, of idle habits, and an occasional tippler * * * " who had not "made any provision for the support of his wife for the last four years" during which time she had supported herself from her own earnings. But, since he had never interfered with her use of her earnings for her support, he was actually supporting her with funds over which he had the legal

1. 9 Cal. 475 (1858).   2. Id., at 476.

power of management and control. This situation was corrected in California in 1951 by the enactment of a statute [3] allowing wives to manage their own earnings. That statute, in turn, was repealed in favor of a more extensive power conferred on wives in 1975 to share with their husbands the right to manage the entire community.[4] Does this mean that *Washburn* has been revived? Or did California's adoption of a no-fault divorce law [5] in 1970 make *Washburn* obsolete?

At the end of the 1960s, the general law of spousal and family support during marriage was fairly clear. Virtually all American states placed the primary obligation of family support upon the husband, requiring the wife to support her husband only if he was disabled and her children only if her husband was unwilling or unable to do so.[6] Writing in 1968, Professor Homer Clark [7] described the rules governing spousal behavior as characterized by "extraordinary conservatism"; specifically, they

> describe the traditional roles of husband and wife. The husband is to provide the family with food, clothing, shelter and as many of the amenities of life as he can manage, either (in earlier days) by the management of his estates or (more recently) by working for wages or a salary. The wife is to be mistress of the household, maintaining the home with the resources furnished by the husband, and caring for the children. A reading of contemporary judicial opinions leaves the impression that these roles have not changed over the last two hundred years, in spite of the changes in the legal position of the married woman carried through in the Nineteenth Century and in her social economic position in this century.

The different obligations for spousal support placed upon men and women are reflected by the Uniform Civil Liability for Support Act,[8] which requires (in section two) that

> Every man shall support his wife, and his child; [and his parent when in need];

but in section three only that

> Every woman shall support her child; and her husband [and her parent] when in need.

In practice, however,[9]

> The rights to support of women and children are much more limited than is generally known and enforcement is very inadequate. A married woman living with her husband can in practice get only what he chooses to give her.

3. Former Cal.Civ.Code § 171c, renumbered § 5124, repealed by Stats.1973, c. 987, p. 1901, § 13, operative Jan. 1, 1975.

4. Cal.Stats.1973, c. 987, operative Jan. 1, 1980. See Text Note, Position of the Wife in Common Law and Community Property States, at p. 234, infra.

5. Cal.Stats.1969, c. 1608, operative Jan. 1, 1970. See Text Note, The Statutory Basis for Marriage Dissolution, at p. 288, infra.

6. Homer Harrison Clark, The Law of Domestic Relations 181–192 (West, 1968).

7. Id., at 181. More recently, Professor Clark noted that "[S]ince the late 1960s, however, changes in statutory and constitutional law accompanying the influence of the women's rights movement and the changes in the

economic position of women have been reflected in new legal rules governing support obligations of husbands and wives." Homer H. Clark, The Law of Domestic Relations in the United States, 251 (West 1988).

8. The Uniform Civil Liability for Support Act, which was promulgated in 1954, has been adopted in only three states: Maine, New Hampshire, and Utah. See 9 U.L.A. 189 (1968 & 1995 Cum. Annual Pocket Part).

9. Report of the Citizen's Advisory Council on the Status of Women, Women in 1971, Appendix C, "The Equal Rights Amendment and Alimony and Child Support Laws," 38 (1972).

The legal obligation to support can generally be enforced only through an action for separation or divorce, and the data available, although scant, indicates that in practically all cases the wife's ability to support herself is a factor in determining the amount of alimony; that alimony is granted in only a very small percentage of cases; that fathers, by and large, are contributing less than half the support of the children in divided families; and that alimony and child support awards are very difficult to collect.

Although the continued viability of laws differentiating support obligations during marriage on the basis of sex was questioned during the debate over ratification of the Equal Rights Amendment,[10] few actual cases can be cited in which such laws have been challenged under equal protection provisions or state equal rights amendments while the spouses are living together. Challenges to sex-based alimony and child support laws at the time of divorce or separation have been more frequent and are often successful.[11] Sparse as they are, however, a few cases do question sex-based support obligations during marriage. For example, in State v. Barton,[12] a statute that defined as criminal neglect a husband's desertion or intentional nonsupport of his wife but did not place a corresponding duty upon a wife was attacked as invalid under the Louisiana equal rights amendment and the equal protection clauses of both state and federal constitutions. A majority of the court found the statute valid, relying on its belief that "[d]espite the increasing activities of women in the marketplace of commerce, it presently remains a fact of life that, between two spouses, the husband is invariably the means of support for the couple."[13] A dissenting judge pointed out that "[e]very economic publication dealing with the employment of sexes refutes that statement."[14] Is the majority implicitly invoking wage discrimination against working women as the basis for holding the classification valid? Would such a showing be enough to justify criminal liability for men only? The dissent argues not: the law applies only to husbands who leave their wives destitute without means of support. It should also apply to a wife who leaves her husband in such a situation.[15] Which side has the best of this argument?

More cases have arisen in the context of child support obligations. Three courts have upheld statutes placing the primary obligation of child support on fathers;[16] in two of these states, the statute was subsequently amended to place

10. The potential impact of the ERA on family support laws was one of the "emotionally-charged" issues that surfaced during the debate over ratification. See Leo Kanowitz, The ERA: The Task Ahead, 6 Hast.Con.L.Q. 637, 647–49 (1979).

11. See, e.g., Orr v. Orr, 440 U.S. 268, 99 S.Ct. 1102, 59 L.Ed.2d 306 (1979), set out at p. 290, infra (state statute providing alimony for wives only violates equal protection clause).

12. 315 So.2d 289 (La.1975).

13. Id., at 291.

14. Id., at 293 (dissenting opinion).

15. Ibid.

16. People v. Elliott, 186 Colo. 65, 525 P.2d 457 (1974) (relying on Kahn v. Shevin, 416 U.S. 351, 94 S.Ct. 1734, 40 L.Ed.2d 189 (1974), set out at p. 72, supra); Dill v. Dill, 232 Ga. 231, 206 S.E.2d 6 (1974) (also relying on *Kahn*); People v. Olague, 31 Cal.App.3d Supp.

5, 9–10, 106 Cal.Rptr. 612, 615 (1973) ("The court will judicially notice that Penal Code section 270 in substantially its present form was enacted in 1923; that although, during the ensuing 50 years the structure of our society has undergone far-reaching changes of many kinds, the family remains the basic social unit; that children still must be fed and nurtured by their parents; that serious and increasing strains have developed in the family unit due to a variety of causes, including the phenomenon of working mothers and the proliferation of divorce; that these centrifugal forces have resulted, in many cases, in division of the family and establishment of multiple households; that, despite current efforts to minimize the fact, mothers generally do not compete in the labor market on terms of equality with fathers; that the compensation of mothers in employment is generally lower than for fathers and opportunities for advancement and for business independence are less for mothers; that working mothers frequently are required to place

the obligation on both parents.[17]   One court held such a statute in violation of the equal protection clause; [18] another held that case law presumptions that fathers were primarily liable for the support of their children could not stand in light of the adoption of a state equal rights amendment.[19] Is it somehow easier for judges to conclude that both parents ought to support their children than it is to decide that wives should support their husbands? For legislators?

What implications do traditional support laws carry for the position of women in marriage? At least three stand out. First, the support laws embody the legal view that a married woman is an economically nonproductive person dependent upon others for the necessities of life. That almost 60% (59.4%) of married women living with their husbands in 1993 participated in the labor force [20] indicates the gross inaccuracy of this view. Yet the married woman continues to be treated as a legal dependent, like the children and insane persons with whom the law formerly classified her. At the same time, as we have seen,[21] the law refuses to permit the married woman any effective means of enforcing her right to support during the marriage. It has been persuasively argued that these laws are misleading to young women contemplating marriage, inequitable as applied to the on-going marriage, and demeaning since they obscure the value of the homemaker's contributions to society.[22] Even the United States Supreme Court has recognized that the presumption of dependency works to the disadvantage of married women and their husbands when its effect is to deny the working woman the same financial protection for her family that is available to a similarly-situated working man.[23] Still, apart from constitutional challenges in the context of benefits provided to workers as part of the pay package,[24] little effort has been made to revise the dependency presumption as it affects women who do not work outside the home. Is this because the presumption is thought to be beneficial to women whose primary identification is that of wife and mother? Is this perception accurate?

spend a substantial part of their earnings for care of their children by others; and that, despite the changes in social life during the past half-century, young children still are largely regarded and treated as the special concern of their mothers, who devote a major share of otherwise employable time to the care of children.'').

17.   Cal.Pen.C. § 270 was amended in 1974 to make it gender-neutral. See West's 1980 Supp. for the current language. The Colorado statute had been amended in 1973; the extension of the duty formerly imposed on men to women was discussed in the *Elliott* opinion. See People v. Elliott, supra note 16, 186 Colo. at 69, 525 P.2d at 459.

18.   Cotton v. Municipal Court, 59 Cal. App.3d 601, 130 Cal.Rptr. 876 (1976) (applying the "strict scrutiny" standard adopted for gender discrimination cases by the California Supreme Court in Sail'er Inn, Inc. v. Kirby, 5 Cal.3d 1, 95 Cal.Rptr. 329, 485 P.2d 529 (1971), discussed at p. 28, supra; disapproving People v. Olague, supra note 16).

19.   Conway v. Dana, 456 Pa. 536, 318 A.2d 324 (1974) (post-divorce litigation over amount of child support father ordered to pay).

20. U.S. Bureau of the Census, Statistical Abstract of the United States, Table 626, at 402 (1994). This is compared to just over 50% (50.1%) in 1980. Ibid.

21. See *Goldstein* and *McGuire* discussed at pp. 216–21 supra.

22. Joan M. Krauskopf & Rhonda Carr Thomas, Partnership Marriage: The Solution to an Ineffective and Inequitable Law of Support, 35 Ohio St.L.J. 558, 577–84 (1974). See also Randall M. Chastain, James B. Henry & B. Perry Woodside, Determination of Property Rights Upon Divorce in South Carolina: An Exploration and Recommendation, 33 So.Car. L.Rev. 227, 250–260 (1981), discussing methods of valuing indirect contributions, particularly homemaker's services.

23. E.g., Wengler v. Druggists Mut. Ins. Co., 446 U.S. 142, 100 S.Ct. 1540, 64 L.Ed.2d 107 (1980); Califano v. Goldfarb, 430 U.S. 199, 97 S.Ct. 1021, 51 L.Ed.2d 270 (1977); Frontiero v. Richardson, 411 U.S. 677, 93 S.Ct. 1764, 36 L.Ed.2d 583 (1973), all discussed in Chapter 1.

24. Ibid. These cases dealt with worker's compensation laws, social security benefits, and military allotments, respectively.

A second implication of placing the primary obligation of support upon husbands is that the wife's work in the home continues to be seen as a service she owes to the husband, rather than as a job deserving the dignity of economic return. It was in response to this situation that the NOW Marriage and Family Committee, commenting on the Uniform Marriage and Divorce Act, stated: [25]

> We are greatly disappointed that the proposed act does not deal with the structure of marriage and with the necessary reforms to make housewife a bona fide occupation, and to lessen the dependency status and inferior economic status of the housewife or dependent spouse. We refer to compensation and fringe benefits normally occurring in any career. A defined work week, paid vacations, workmen's compensation, health and medical insurance, full coverage under social security, pension plans, and the partnership concept of the assets of the marriage are a few of the working conditions that need to be incorporated in the law to insure good labor standards for those going into marriage as a full-time career.

The Task Force on Family Law and Policy observed in its 1968 Report [26] to the Citizens' Advisory Council on the Status of Women:

> If marriage is viewed as a partnership between a man and a woman, then each spouse should be responsible for the other in accordance with need and ability to support. This general principle should be reflected in State laws dealing with support obligations for spouses. Some of the task force members believed that a husband should only be liable for the support of a wife who is unable to support herself due to physical handicap, acute stage of family responsibility or unemployability on other grounds. Other task force members believed that other factors may need to be considered in light of the general equities of the situation. A wife should be responsible for the support of her husband if he is unable to support himself and she is able to furnish such support.
>
>   * * *
>
> As an extension of the equal partnership principle of marriage, both parents should be liable for the support of their offspring, not merely the father. No distinction should be made in the rights of legitimate and "illegitimate" children to parental support. * * * No distinction should be made in the rights of boys and girls to parental support.

It has been suggested [27] that although passage of the equal rights amendment "would *not* require mathematically equal contributions to family support from husband and wife in any given family," nevertheless "if husband and wife had equal resources and earning capacity, neither would have a claim for support against the other" and, moreover, "if one spouse were a wage earner and the other spouse performed uncompensated domestic labor for the family, the wage-earning spouse would owe a duty of support to the spouse who worked in the home."

25. Report of the Marriage and Family Committee of the National Organization for Women, Suggested Guidelines in Studying and Comments on the Uniform Marriage and Divorce Act, 2 (April 11, 1971). See also Res. 151, Sixth National Conference of NOW, 6 NOW Acts # 1, 10–11 (1973).

26. Report of the Task Force on Family Law and Policy to the Citizens' Advisory Council on the Status of Women 9–10 (1968).

27. Barbara A. Brown, Thomas I. Emerson, Gail Falk & Ann E. Freedman, The Equal Rights Amendment: A Constitutional Basis for Equal Rights for Women, 80 Yale L.J. 871, 946 (1971).

Should there be a sharing of the obligation of support by husband and wife? When the wife is employed outside the home, is it not clear that in fact she does share the burden of family support? If the husband is to act as her employer when she is a full-time homemaker, as the NOW Committee suggests, should the result differ? Is it unfair to ask that the husband earn enough money to support himself, his wife and the children while still being required to compensate his wife for her work in the home? But is it fair to permit the spouse with outside employment, whether it be husband or wife, to determine the cost of supporting the homemaking spouse and to deduct that cost from the compensation? Or should the housekeeper be paid and given the opportunity to manage the income, subject only to the obligation to share in the family support? Would a practical approach be to deduct the agreed-upon family expenses from the weekly or monthly paycheck and divide the excess? What if both spouses hold outside jobs and both share in the housework? Is it self-evident that either should compensate the other? Should the support obligation still be shared? Suppose the working wife is also a homemaker in the traditional style: can it be argued that she holds two jobs and should be paid for her "moonlighting" in the home? Do you agree that being a housewife should become a paying job? Does NOW's proposal rest partly on the prospect of government benefits, such as worker's compensation and social security, being available to the housewife? What if a woman wishes to marry a man who cannot afford to hire her as his housewife? Should the occupation of househusband be available to men? What implications do these proposals carry for the structure of marriage?

A third implication of the present support laws is that the housewife cannot provide for her old age. Since she is not compensated for her work, she is not entitled to contribute to social security and has no pension or retirement plan of her own. When the Social Security Act was amended in 1939 [28] to provide family protection for dependents and survivors of insured workers, the amendments were expressly limited to wives, widows, children and dependent parents. In order to avoid the need for detailed investigations into family financial relationships, wives, widows and minor children were presumed to be dependent on the husband and father for support.[29] The result was a continuation of the treatment of housewives as legal dependents. By the end of 1976, the number of wives and widows drawing social security based on their husbands' earning record approximated 3.4 million and 5 million respectively.[30]

The husbands, widowers and children of married working women were not covered by Social Security until 1950; [31] even then no presumption of dependency was extended to them. Instead, a showing was required that at least one-half of the necessary support was provided by the female worker.[32] By the end of 1971, fewer than 9,000 men qualified for benefits as dependent husbands and slightly more than 3,000 qualified as dependent widowers.[33]

The United States Supreme Court held the dependency test for widowers

28. Social Security Act Amendments of 1939, ch. 666, § 202, 53 Stat. 1363–1366.

29. Report of the Task Force on Social Insurance and Taxes, 67, Citizens' Advisory Council on the Status of Women (1968).

30. U.S. Dept. of Health, Educ., and Welfare, Social Security and the Changing Roles of Men and Women, 4 (February 1979) (hereinafter cited as "HEW Report").

31. Social Security Act Amendments of 1950, ch. 809, § 101, 64 Stat. 483–484.

32. Ibid. The Act was further amended in 1967 to equalize the criteria for determining a child's dependency upon its mother. P.L. 90–248 § 152 (Jan. 2, 1968), 81 Stat. 860.

33. Bixby, Women and Social Security in the United States, 35 Soc.Sec.Bull. 3, 8 (1972).

invalid in 1977.[34]   As we have seen, Congress responded by eliminating the dependency test for husbands as well and by adding a "set off" for pensions earned in employment not covered by social security,[35] a provision aimed primarily at federal civilian employees.[36]   Beyond that, Congress mandated a study of ways to eliminate dependency as a factor in entitlement to spouse's benefits and to end sex discrimination in the social security program.

Proposals to eliminate dependency, more accurately, the presumption of dependency that arises from marital status or prior marital status of at least 10 years' duration,[37] will have a major impact on social security coverage for women. This is because a wife who works is theoretically eligible for *two* benefits: her own as an insured worker, and a wife's benefit based on her husband's earnings record.   Because of the prohibitive cost,[38] however, giving the working wife the full amount of both her old-age benefit *and* her wife's benefit has not been considered a serious possibility.[39]   Present law permits a married woman to draw a benefit based either on her own or her husband's earnings record, whichever is larger, but not on both.[40]   Since women's earnings are generally lower than those of men, the frequent result is that the working wife receives a benefit no larger than that paid to the housewife who has not worked in paid employment at all.[41] The earnings gap between men and women will generally mean as well that, even with the dependency test for husbands eliminated, a working husband will be limited to his own earned benefit since it will be higher than that attributable to him as a spouse.[42]

Questions of equity between single earner families and two-earner families are also raised by proposals to change the dependency presumption.   Under present law, as a result of the provision of spouse's benefits and of the "dual entitlement" doctrine which requires an election between spouse's and worker's benefits, two couples with the same earnings records can receive different benefit amounts.   Single earner couples may receive higher benefits than two-earner families.[43]

The 1979 report issued by the Department of Health, Education and Welfare in response to the Congressional mandate proposed two options for dealing with

34. Califano v. Goldfarb, 430 U.S. 199, 97 S.Ct. 1021, 51 L.Ed.2d 270 (1977), set out at p. 60, supra.

35. Pub.L. No. 95–216, § 334(g)(1), 91 Stat. 1546–47, codified at 42 U.S.C.A. § 402(b)(4)(A), (c)(2)(A), (e)(8)(A), (f)(2)(A). The Supreme Court upheld this provision against the claim that it constituted an unconstitutional discrimination against men in Heckler v. Mathews, 465 U.S. 728, 104 S.Ct. 1387, 79 L.Ed.2d 646 (1984).

36. See Wilbur J. Cohen, Social Security: Current Myths and Reality—The Need for Its Preservation and Reform, 25 Wayne L.Rev. 1419, 1437–38 (1979).

37. For a discussion of the arbitrary way in which the marital status test works in practice, see Peter W. Martin, Social Security Benefits for Spouses, 63 Cornell L.Rev. 789, 816–24 (1978).

38. Report of the Task Force on Social Insurance and Taxes, supra note 29, at 74.

39. In 1963, the Committee on Social Insurance and Taxes recommended that the working wife be paid part of both benefits, but

that her wife's benefit be reduced on a sliding scale in proportion to her own benefits.   The specific suggestion was that a wife's benefit based on her husband's earnings should be reduced by $1.00 for every $2.00 in benefits based on her own wages.   This recommendation was not adopted by the President's Commission on the Status of Women. Id., at 74.

40. Bixby, supra note 33, at 9.

41. Report of the Task Force on Social Insurance and Taxes, supra, note 29, at 70–71; Bixby, supra note 33, at 9.

42. In *Goldfarb,* the Government claimed that the total initial year cost of covering husbands, widowers and disabled widowers would be $447 million.   Appellee responded that this figure represented about 0.67% of annual social security benefits.   Brief for Appellee, Califano v. Goldfarb, 430 U.S. 199, 97 S.Ct. 1021, 51 L.Ed.2d 270 (1977), at 45 n. 46.

43. See H.E.W. Report, supra note 30, at 11.

the dependency presumption and other issues: an "earnings-sharing" plan and a "double-decker" plan.[44] The double-decker plan would establish a two-tier benefit system. Tier I would provide a flat-dollar payment to all U.S. residents at age 65, or upon disability, regardless of whether they had covered earnings.[45] Tier II would provide a benefit based upon covered employment equal to 30% of current benefits.[46] This proposal combines the goals of social adequacy (Tier I's fixed payment regardless of employment) and equity among workers (Tier II's amount depends on the worker's average indexed monthly earnings, or AIME, as do present benefits). It is anticipated that Tier I benefits would be paid out of general revenues, while Tier II payments would be financed from employer and employee contributions as is the present system.[47]

The earnings sharing plan is a scheme whereby each person's social security protection would be based on his or her earnings while unmarried and, when married, on one-half of the total earnings credits of the married couple.[48] The annual credits acquired by the couple would be divided between them during the marriage for purposes of computing retirement benefits; upon divorce, or when one spouse reached age 62, the earnings would be divided.[49] The effect of this scheme would be to lower the benefits of the higher-paid spouse and to increase those of the lower-paid spouse upon divorce. It would also provide lower total benefits for single earner families than are available under present law.[50] Both options contemplate the phased elimination of aged spouse's and surviving spouse's benefits in favor of giving each person his or her own primary benefit.[51]

The HEW report took no position on which of these options it preferred; indeed, neither was proposed as a recommendation for legislative action, only as a basis for discussion.[52] Professor Grace Blumberg,[53] in her comprehensive review of these and other proposals for social security reform, endorses the income-splitting approach and offers a proposal of her own which would maintain two accounts for married persons: one that measures personal earnings subject to social security tax, the other that records earnings attributed to the spouse's account on the basis of a 50–50 income splitting plan. At retirement, if both spouses retire at the same time, each receives benefits as an individual based on the attributed earnings account. If the spouses reach retirement age at different times, the first to retire would receive benefits based on his or her actual earnings account until both retire. At death, the survivor would retain two-thirds of the

44. Id., at 35.

45. Id., at 71. The flat-dollar figure was set, for purposes of calculation, at $122 per month (the minimum benefit available under present law).

46. Ibid. The combination of $122 for Tier I and 30% of AIME was chosen because it would approximate benefit levels under present law.

47. Id., at 36.

48. Id., at 39.

49. An alternative to earnings sharing, known as AIME averaging, might be applied to couples who are married at retirement. This plan would not split earnings in half at retirement, but would compute an individual retirement benefit for each spouse based on their averaged AIME, divided in proportion to their benefits under present law. Under this plan, a lifelong homemaker would get one-third and

the earner two-thirds of the couple's total benefit. Survivors of all retired couples would get two-thirds of the couple's total benefit as do present survivors in one-earner families. Id., at 41–42.

50. Id., at 48–55.

51. Id., at 39 (earnings sharing); 71–2 (double-decker plan). Some modifications were proposed in the double-decker plan to deal with the issue of protection for homemakers. Id., at 71–72.

52. Id., at 35. See Mary E. Becker, Obscuring the Struggle: Sex Discrimination, Social Security, and Stone, Seidman, Sunstein & Tushnet's *Constitutional Law,* 89 Colum.L.Rev. 264, 276–88 (1989).

53. Grace Ganz Blumberg, Adult Derivative Benefits in Social Security, 32 Stan.L.Rev. 233, 284–90 (1980).

combined attributed earnings account. And if there is a divorce, each spouse would take away his or her attributed earnings account, as well as the capacity for adding future credits to the actual earnings account. This proposal, too, envisages the gradual elimination of all adult derivative benefits.[54]

Which, if any, of these proposals seems sensible to you? As is the case with most questions of basic social policy, the choice cannot be placed on purely objective grounds. Blumberg cautions,[55]

> [i]n the final analysis, the proposed measures reflect the values of their proponents. Those who would establish independent social insurance for women who are predominantly or exclusively homemakers place a very high value on homemaking and the preservation of this option for married women. Those who propose child care credits and who would alter the worklife norms of social security so as to include female as well as male workers are primarily concerned that women not be shortchanged by the system when their domestic roles curtail an otherwise substantial role in gainful employment. Those who propose partnership plans take a relatively neutral view toward female roles but strongly espouse the position that, as an ethical matter, marriage should be treated as a sharing partnership. * * * Those who, in contrast, value individual autonomy and the freedom of women not to marry tend to prefer alteration of worklife norms and child care credits for all mothers, whether married or not.

Where, on that spectrum, do your values lie? Congress has not acted on either of these proposals. It seems instructive to compare the observations made on a similar topic by Professor Paul Sayre [56] over thirty years ago. Characterizing the duty of the husband to support the wife and her duty to render services as the two particular property interests growing out of marriage during its existence, Sayre pointed out:

> The striking thing about these two duties is that they are perhaps the most significant examples of rights or duties in the law that are enforceable only indirectly or, in large measure, not enforceable at all. The husband's duty to support is enforceable mainly by the wife's power to buy necessaries (if she can find a merchant who will run the risk of selling them to her) upon her husband's credit. * * * But she has no claim for as much as 5 cents in money and no definite share in his income. Under the community property system, which obtains in only eight of our states, the wife does have an ultimate share in all the property gained after marriage, but the management of the husband's income remains with him, and so far as her claim to actual money goes for her own spending purposes, she is as badly off as under the common law system.

> As for her husband, he has a legal right to his wife's services, but no legal way under heaven to compel them. The duty to support is not dependent on the performance of the duty to render services.

> * * * under modern statutes indeed the wife is entitled to receive for herself wages for her own labor outside the home, and this right to keep her wages is absolute in her, and the duty to support her continues in the husband, even though she renders no services whatever at home and keeps all

54. Id., at 290. See also Martin, supra note 37, at 828–40, supporting a split-earnings model based on community property notions.

55. Blumberg, supra note 53, at 291–92.

56. Paul Sayre, Property Rights of Husband and Wife, 6 Marr. & Family Living 17, 17–18 (1944); Selected Essays on Family Law 503, 504 (A.A.L.S., 1950).

the wages. On the other hand, if she works in the most generous way at home in special emergencies, far beyond any reasonable interpretation of her duty to render services, and if on top of this her husband promises to pay her for this extra labor, still she cannot collect. Whatever labor she performs at home, in theory of the law, is her absolute duty anyway, and hence she has no basis for claim if she does more than could reasonably be expected.

* * * Surely what we need is a workable, dignified scheme of mutual rights in the earnings of both spouses * * * and this in addition: that these rights in earnings of each spouse shall be considered in terms of equal duty of each to support the family which they have formed by their marriage. Each spouse is perfectly capable of supporting himself or herself if it were not for the family which they have formed by their marriage. The duty in marriage properly, therefore, should be one of supporting the family. This is in keeping with the facts of marriage, and it is in support of the proper dignity and freedom of the husband as well as of the wife.

iii. Marital Property Regimes

KIRCHBERG v. FEENSTRA

Supreme Court of the United States, 1981.
450 U.S. 455, 101 S.Ct. 1195, 67 L.Ed.2d 428.

JUSTICE MARSHALL delivered the opinion of the Court.

In this appeal we consider the constitutionality of a now superseded Louisiana statute that gave a husband, as "head and master" of property jointly owned with his wife, the unilateral right to dispose of such property without his spouse's consent. Concluding that the provision violates the Equal Protection Clause of the Fourteenth Amendment, we affirm the judgment of the Court of Appeals for the Fifth Circuit invalidating the statute.

I

In 1974, appellee Joan Feenstra filed a criminal complaint against her husband, Harold Feenstra, charging him with molesting their minor daughter. While incarcerated on that charge, Mr. Feenstra retained appellant Karl Kirchberg, an attorney, to represent him. Mr. Feenstra signed a $3,000 promissory note in prepayment for legal services to be performed by appellant Kirchberg. As security on this note, Mr. Feenstra executed a mortgage in favor of appellant on the home he jointly owned with his wife. Mrs. Feenstra was not informed of the mortgage, and her consent was not required because a state statute, former Art. 2404 of the Louisiana Civil Code, gave her husband exclusive control over the disposition of community property.[1]

Mrs. Feenstra eventually dropped the charge against her husband. He did not return home, but instead obtained a legal separation from his wife and moved out of the State. Mrs. Feenstra first learned of the existence of the mortgage in 1976, when appellant Kirchberg threatened to foreclose on her

---

1. Article 2404, in effect at the time Mr. Feenstra executed the mortgage on behalf of appellant, provided in pertinent part:

"The husband is the head and master of the partnership or community of gains; he administers its effects, disposes of the reve-

nues which they produce, and may alienate them by an onerous title, without the consent and permission of his wife."

This provision has been repealed. See infra, at 1198, and nn. 3 and 4.

home unless she paid him the amount outstanding on the promissory note executed by her husband. After Mrs. Feenstra refused to pay the obligation, Kirchberg obtained an order of executory process directing the local sheriff to seize and sell the Feenstra home.

Anticipating Mrs. Feenstra's defense to the foreclosure action, Kirchberg in March 1976 filed this action in the United States District Court for the Eastern District of Louisiana, seeking a declaratory judgment against Mrs. Feenstra * * *. In her answer to Kirchberg's complaint, Mrs. Feenstra alleged * * * a second counterclaim challenging the constitutionality of the statutory scheme that empowered her husband unilaterally to execute a mortgage on their jointly owned home. The State of Louisiana and its Governor were joined as third party defendants on the constitutional counterclaim. The governmental parties, joined by appellant, moved for summary judgment on this claim. The District Court, characterizing Mrs. Feenstra's counterclaim as an attack on "the bedrock of Louisiana's community property system," granted the State's motion for summary judgment. * * *

While Mrs. Feenstra's appeal from the District Court's order was pending before the Court of Appeals for the Fifth Circuit, the Louisiana Legislature completely revised its code provisions relating to community property. In so doing, the State abandoned the "head and master" concept embodied in Art. 2404, and instead granted spouses equal control over the disposition of community property. La.Civ.Code Ann. Art. 2346 (West Cum. Pamphlet 1980).[3] The new code also provided that community immovables could not be alienated, leased or otherwise encumbered without the concurrence of both spouses. La.Civ.Code Ann. Art. 2347 (West Cum. Pamphlet 1980).[4] These provisions, however, did not take effect until January 1, 1980, and the Court of Appeals was therefore required to consider whether Art. 2404, the civil code provision which had authorized Mr. Feenstra to mortgage his home in 1974 without his wife's knowledge or consent, violated the Equal Protection Clause of the Fourteenth Amendment.

Because this provision explicitly discriminated on the basis of gender, the Court of Appeals properly inquired whether the statutory grant to the husband of exclusive control over disposition of community property was substantially related to the achievement of an important governmental objective. See, e.g., Wengler v. Druggists Mutual Insurance Co., 446 U.S. 142, 100 S.Ct. 1540, 64 L.Ed.2d 107 (1980); Craig v. Boren, 429 U.S. 190, 97 S.Ct. 451, 50 L.Ed.2d 397 (1976). The court noted that the State had advanced only one justification for the provision—that "[o]ne of the two spouses has to be designated as the manager of the community." The court agreed that the State had an interest in defining the manner in which community property was to be managed, but found that the State had failed to show why the mandatory designation of the husband as manager of the property was necessary to further that interest. The court therefore concluded that Art. 2404 violated the Equal Protection Clause. * * * Only Kirchberg appealed the judgment of this Court of Appeals to this Court. * * *

---

3. Article 2346 provides that "Each spouse acting alone may manage, control, or dispose of community property unless otherwise provided by law."

4. However, either spouse may renounce his or her right to concur in the disposition of community immovables. La.Civ.Code Ann. Art. 2348 (West's Cum.Pamphlet 1980).

II

By granting the husband exclusive control over the disposition of community property, Art. 2404 clearly embodies the type of express gender-based discrimination that we have found unconstitutional absent a showing that the classification is tailored to further an important governmental interest. In defending the constitutionality of Art. 2404, appellant Kirchberg does not claim that the provision serves any such interest.[7] Instead, appellant attempts to distinguish this Court's decisions in cases such as Craig v. Boren, supra, and Orr v. Orr, 440 U.S. 268, 99 S.Ct. 1102, 59 L.Ed.2d 306 (1979), which struck down similar gender-based statutory classifications, by arguing that appellee Feenstra, as opposed to the disadvantaged individuals in those cases, could have taken steps to avoid the discriminatory impact of Art. 2404. Appellant notes that under Art. 2334 of the Louisiana Civil Code, in effect at the time Mr. Feenstra executed the mortgage, Mrs. Feenstra could have made a "declaration by authentic act" prohibiting her husband from executing a mortgage on her home without her consent.[8] By failing to take advantage of this procedure, Mrs. Feenstra, in appellant's view, became the "architect of her own predicament" and therefore should not be heard to complain of the discriminatory impact of Art. 2404.

By focusing on steps that Mrs. Feenstra could have taken to preclude her husband from mortgaging their home without her consent, however, appellant overlooks the critical question: whether Art. 2024 substantially furthers an important government interest. As we have previously noted, the "absence of an insurmountable barrier" will not redeem an otherwise unconstitutionally discriminatory law. Trimble v. Gordon, 430 U.S. 762, 774, 97 S.Ct. 1459, 1467, 52 L.Ed.2d 31 (1977). * * *. Instead the burden remains on the party seeking to uphold a statute that expressly discriminates on the basis of sex to advance an "exceedingly persuasive justification" for the challenged classification. Personnel Administrator of Massachusetts v. Feeney, 442 U.S. 256, 273, 99 S.Ct. 2282, 2293, 60 L.Ed.2d 870 (1979). * * * Because appellant has failed to offer such a justification, and because the State, by declining to appeal from the decision below, has apparently abandoned any claim that an important government objective was served by the statute, we affirm the judgment of the Court of Appeals invalidating Art. 2404.[9]

* * *

7. Nor will this Court speculate about the existence of such a justification. "The burden * * * is on those defending the discrimination to make out the claimed justification. * * * " Wengler v. Druggist Mutual Insurance Co., supra, 446 U.S., at 151, 100 S.Ct., at 1546. We note, however, that the failure of the State to appeal from the decision of the Court of Appeals and the decision of the Louisiana Legislature to replace Art. 2404 with a gender-neutral statute, suggest that appellant would be hardpressed to show that the challenged provision substantially furthered an important governmental interest.

8. Article 2334, as it existed in 1974, provided:

"Where the title to immovable property stands in the names of both the husband and the wife, it may not be leased, mortgaged or sold by the husband without the wife's consent where she has made a declaration by authentic act that her authority and consent are required for such lease, sale or mortgage and has filed such a declaration in the mortgage and conveyance records of the parish in which the property is located."

This Article has been replaced with a new code provision prohibiting either spouse from alienating or encumbering community immovables without the consent of the other spouse. See n. 3, supra.

9. In so ruling, we also reject appellant's secondary argument that the constitutional challenge to Art. 2404 should be rejected because the provision was an integral part of the

Accordingly, the judgment of the Court of Appeals is affirmed.

So ordered.

JUSTICE STEWART, with whom JUSTICE REHNQUIST joins, concurring in the result.

Since men and women were similarly situated for all relevant purposes with respect to the management and disposition of community property, I agree that Art. 2404 of the Louisiana Civil Code, which allowed husbands but not wives to execute mortgages on jointly owned real estate without spousal consent, violated the Equal Protection Clause of the Fourteenth Amendment. See Michael M. v. Superior Court, 450 U.S. 464, 477–479, 101 S.Ct. 1200, 1204, 67 L.Ed.2d 437 (Stewart, J., concurring).

* * *

Notes on Kirchberg

1. The United States Supreme Court noted probable jurisdiction in *Kirchberg* at a time when the critical issue raised by the case—the constitutionality of male management of property owned by both spouses—had been resolved by the legislatures of all eight American community property states. Although the question was not moot to Joan Feenstra, who remained in danger of losing her home because of her husband's unilateral mortgage, for all practical purposes the matter had been settled by extending management and control to wives. Did the Court's opinion in *Kirchberg* go beyond preventing foreclosure on Ms. Feenstra's home? Does it, for example, afford support for an argument that the non-wage earning spouse in a community property state is entitled to an accounting of the nature and extent of property owned by the community?

2. The origins of the community property system, its transplantation in Europe, and some speculations on why it flourished in France but not in England are discussed in Charles Donahue, What Causes Fundamental Legal Ideas? Marital Property in England and France in the Thirteenth Century, 78 Mich. L.Rev. 59 (1979). An account of the reception of the community property regime in California is provided by Susan Westerberg Prager, The Persistence of Separate Property Concepts in California's Community Property System, 1849–1975, 24 U.C.L.A.L.Rev. 1 (1976). Apart from a brief period in the late 1930s and 1940s, when five common law states adopted community property laws in order to secure the tax benefits of income-splitting that the United States Supreme Court had extended to spouses in community property states, the community regime has largely been regarded by other states as a mildly interesting oddity. When Congress enacted an optional income-splitting provision for all married couples in 1948, the number of community property states was again reduced to eight. See J.W. Riehm, Jr., The Impact of Community Property Law on Federal Taxation, 4 Sw.L.J. 161 (1950). But with the promulgation of the Uniform Marriage and Divorce Act in 1970, which contained in § 307 a deferred community model for purposes of property division on divorce, and in the wake of no-fault divorce laws, community property concepts are once again being considered by common law states. In 1984, Wisconsin became the first, and so far the only, common law

State's community property law and its invalidation would call into question the constitutionality of related provisions of the Louisiana Civil Code. The issue before us is not whether the State's community property law, as it existed in 1974, could have functioned without Art. 2404, but rather whether that provision unconstitutionally discriminated on the basis of sex.

state to adopt a community property regime. A brief comparison of the chief features of the two systems follows.

Text Note
Position of the Wife in Common Law and Community Property States

Although the differences among states within each system are great, two contrasting approaches to the ownership of property during marriage still co-exist in the United States. Forty-one states follow some version of the common law, which in general recognizes the separate property rights of the two individuals who compose a marriage. Nine states—Arizona, California, Idaho, Louisiana, Nevada, New Mexico, Texas, Washington and Wisconsin—have a variation of the civil law concept of community property, which emphasizes the rights of each spouse in the acquisitions of the other and thus is primarily concerned with the interests created by the marriage. No attempt will be made here to describe either system in detail. Rather the discussion will focus on raising issues that must be considered in deciding what arrangement of property ownership and control might best serve the interests of both spouses in an egalitarian marriage.

Addressing himself to this issue more than fifty years ago, Professor Richard Powell came to an unambiguous conclusion. After a careful survey of the laws of two common law states—Oregon and New York—and two community property states—California and Washington—he found the common law system preferable to the community property system, which he characterized as highly complex, injecting "useless uncertainty and unjustifiable barriers" into dealings between the marital unit and outsiders, and submerging the two individual spouses "in a purely imaginary third entity—the family, in a fashion promoting the ultimate welfare of no one except those parasites who live on litigation breeding rules of law and have no care for the social implications of the statutes and decisions of their jurisdiction." [1] In 1969 Professor Leo Kanowitz, after comparing the two systems, concluded that "the property rights of married women under both systems are not fundamentally dissimilar." [2] In 1971, the authors of a survey article on the equal rights amendment predicted that both systems "contain sex discriminatory aspects which would be changed under the Equal Rights Amendment." [3] In 1973 Professor Judith Younger, exploring the legal rights of women in community property states, concluded that when judged by the standard of its treatment of women, the community property system is deficient: although "[a]ttractive in theory, it disappoints in practice by failing to produce equality of result between spouses." [4]

Underlying these specific assessments of relative merit is an ambivalence about ultimate goals. Professor Mary Ann Glendon states the dilemma as follows: [5]

> [C]urrent changes [in matrimonial property systems] * * * are related to changes in the ideology of marriage and in the economic and social roles of

1. Richard R.B. Powell, Community Property—A Critique of its Regulation of Intra-Family Relations, 11 Wash.L.Rev. 12, 38 (1936).

2. Leo Kanowitz, Women and the Law 60 (1969).

3. Barbara A. Brown, Thomas I. Emerson, Gail Falk & Ann E. Freedman, The Equal Rights Amendment: A Constitutional Basis for Equal Rights for Women, 80 Yale L.J. 871, 946 (1971).

4. Judith T. Younger, Community Property, Women, and Curriculum, 48 N.Y.U.L.Rev. 211, 258 (1973).

5. Mary Ann Glendon, Matrimonial Property: A Comparative Study of Law and Social Change, 49 Tul.L.Rev. 21, 23 (1974).

women, especially of married women, which are having an impact on this, as well as many other areas of the law. The peculiar difficulty with which all systems of marital property are presently struggling arises from the fact that the idea of the independent and equal individuality of each spouse coexists in modern industrialized and urbanized societies with the idea that marriage is somehow a community of interest of those independent and equal individuals. The coexistence is uneasy because these two ideas are always in tension.

After surveying the matrimonial property systems of England, France, and the community property states of the United States, Glendon concludes: [6]

> Thus it can be said that the common law systems are searching for a way to introduce more sharing into a regime where equality has been realized at the same time that the community property systems are trying to introduce more equality into a regime where sharing has been achieved.

In 1983, the Commissioners on Uniform State Laws proposed the Uniform Marital Property Act (UMPA) for adoption by all American states.[7] UMPA is based on community property principles, but it attempts to avoid most of these earlier criticisms. Wisconsin was the first common law state to enact UMPA, effective January 1, 1986.[8]

In order to compare the two systems as a prelude to evaluating these judgments, let us construct a hypothetical couple—John and Mary Jones—and follow their course through married life, death, or divorce first in a community property state (California), then in a common law state (New York). We will assume that at the time of their marriage, on January 1, 1988, both John and Mary were employed, Mary as a lawyer and John as a high school music teacher. Mary had a checking account in a local bank containing a balance of $900; a savings account of $9000; a 1987 BMW; personal property consisting of clothing, books, records, a few household effects, and her grandmother's jewels (valued at $10,000). John had $400,000 worth of stocks and bonds, which were acquired by inheritance from his father, the family home (also inherited from his father) valued at $875,000, and furnished with antiques appraised at $200,000, a checking account containing $500, a bicycle on which he rides to work, clothing, records, books, and his own paintings. John's salary as a high school music teacher is $12,500; Mary's as a junior associate in a San Francisco law firm is $65,000. Both spouses intend to continue working after marriage.

What is the impact of their marriage upon their property interests? All property owned by either spouse prior to marriage, and all property acquired afterwards by gift, bequest, devise, or descent, is separate property.[9] The marriage itself has absolutely no impact on this property. Moreover, in California, the rents, issues and profits of separate property continue to be separate property.[10] Thus, the annual income from John's stocks and bonds—assume $24,000 per year—will remain his separate property after marriage. And if Mary uses her $9,000 savings account to make a down payment on a vacation home in Lake Tahoe (California), taking title in her name alone, that, too, would be her separate

---

6. Id., at 39.

7. Uniform Marital Property Act, 9A U.L.A. 97 (1987).

8. Wisconsin Marital Property Act codified as amended at Wis.Stat.Ann. §§ 766.001–766.97 (West 1994 and 1995 Cum. Pocket Part).

9. West's Ann.Cal.Fam.Code § 770 (1994).

10. Ibid. Idaho, Louisiana and Texas by statute, and Arizona by judicial decision, follow the Spanish principle that the rents, issues and profits of separate property feed the community. William Quinby de Funiak & Michael J. Vaughn, Principles of Community Property 161–62 (2d ed. 1971).

property. Her husband would acquire no interest in the property rights attributable to the down payment.

At the beginning of their life together, then, the community property will consist of the salary earned by both John and Mary after marriage. Both spouses have "present, existing, and equal" interests in this property.[11] Since 1975, either spouse has had management and control of the community real and personal property.[12] Both spouses must join in the sale, conveyance, encumbrance, or lease for longer than one year of the community realty. When managing the community personalty, each spouse is enjoined to "act in good faith with respect to the other spouse in the management and control of the community property in accordance with the general rules which control the actions of persons having relationships of personal confidence as specified in Section 721, until such time as the assets and liabilities have been divided by the parties or by a court."[13] A spouse operating or managing a community personal property business is given the "primary management and control of the business or interest." [14] The managing spouse is obliged "to make full disclosure to the other spouse of the existence of assets in which the community has an interest and debts for which the community may be liable, upon request"; a spouse is given a claim against the other spouse for breach of these duties, if the breach "results in impairment to the claimant spouse's present undivided one-half interest in the community estate." [15]

A few years after the marriage, Mary and John decide to start their family. Mary's pregnancy turns out to be a difficult one. A miscarriage is threatened, and she is unable to work for the last six months. Since no maternity leave is provided by her law firm, Mary's income ceases and John supports the family from his earnings and the income from his separate property. The baby is born with brain damage. John is profoundly affected by this event, and feels responsible because there is a history of mental instability in his family. Mary is unable to reason with him, and John gives up his job to spend full time with their child. Mary returns to work.

As the years pass, John's condition deteriorates. The child died at the age of ten, causing John to regress even more. Medical bills consume most of John's income from his separate estate, and Mary becomes the main support of the family. She is very successful in her work and opens her own law office. After twenty years of marriage essentially without companionship, Mary decides to get a divorce. She brings suit for dissolution on the ground of irremediable breakdown of the marriage, caused by irreconcilable differences.[16] A guardian is appointed for John, who does not contest the dissolution, but who asks for a division of the community property and spousal support for John.[17]

At the hearing, the judge finds that the community property consists of Mary's savings account of $25,000, the goodwill in her law practice (valued at $150,000),[18] the vacation home at Lake Tahoe, valued at $130,000 of which $5,000

11. West's Ann.Cal.Fam.Code § 751 (1994).

12. West's Ann.Cal.Fam.Code §§ 1100, 1102 (1994).

13. West's Ann.Cal.Fam.Code § 1100 (1994).

14. West's Ann.Cal.Fam.Code § 1100 (1994).

15. West's Ann.Cal.Fam.Code § 1101(a), (1994).

16. West's Ann.Cal.Fam.Code § 2310 (1994).

17. West's Ann.Cal.Fam.Code § 4320 (1994) allows alimony to be awarded to either spouse.

18. Although a professional degree is not considered property subject to division in California, see West's Ann.Cal.Fam.Code § 2641 (1994) as interpreted in Marriage of Sullivan, 37 Cal.3d 762, 691 P.2d 1020, 209 Cal.Rptr.

is Mary's separate property attributable to the down payment from her premarital savings, and her car, valued at $2,500. In fulfilling its statutory obligation to divide the community property equally,[19] the court awards Mary the goodwill of her law practice, her car, and $1250 cash. John is given the remaining $23,750 from Mary's savings and the Tahoe property, subject to a lien worth $5,000 given to Mary. John's separate property, which has nearly doubled in value during the marriage due to the expert management of the bank handling the funds under John's father's will,[20] is not subject to division on divorce.[21] The court took its value into account, however, in refusing to grant John a support order.

If John's death, rather than divorce, had dissolved the marriage, Mary would have found that half the community property is subject to his testamentary disposition,[22] plus all of his separate property. Had John died intestate, Mary would have inherited his entire separate estate provided there was no issue, parent, brother, sister nor any descendants of deceased siblings.[23]

Assuming that John and Mary had married and lived together in New York, these results would follow: As in California, Mary's premarital property would be her separate property; but unlike California, all the property she acquired after marriage, together with its rents, issues, proceeds and profits, would also be her sole and separate property.[24] She would, of course, have full rights of management over her earnings.[25] Dower and curtesy have been abolished.[26] Mary and John may hold real property as tenants by the entirety; the Married Woman's Property Acts have been construed to end the husband's common law right to the control and management of such property.[27]

Until 1980, when New York's "equitable distribution" law became effective,[28] John would not have been entitled to a share of Mary's property upon divorce, nor she to his. New York was a "title" state in which only jointly owned property

354 (1984), the goodwill of a professional practice acquired during the marriage is community property. Marriage of Foster, 42 Cal.App.3d 577, 117 Cal.Rptr. 49 (1974).

19. West's Ann.Cal.Fam.Code § 2550 (1994).

20. If John had actually managed the funds himself, the community would have been entitled to the value of his services. See generally, Vol. I Barbara Nachtrieb Armstrong, California Family Law 475–82 (1953); Beam v. Bank of America, 6 Cal.3d 12, 98 Cal.Rptr. 137, 490 P.2d 257 (1971); Brigette M. Bodenheimer, The Community without Community Property: The Need for Legislative Attention to Separate–Property Marriages Under Community Property Laws, 8 Cal.West.L.Rev. 381 (1972).

21. Fox v. Fox, 18 Cal.2d 645, 646, 117 P.2d 325, 326 (1941).

22. West's Ann.Cal.Prob.Code § 100 (1991).

23. West's Ann.Cal.Prob.Code § 6401 (1991)

24. N.Y.Dom.Rel.Law § 50 (McKinney 1988) See also William Tucker Dean, Economic Relations Between Husband and Wife in New York, 41 Cornell L.Q. 175 (1956).

25. N.Y.Gen.Obl.Law §§ 3–301, 3–315 (McKinney 1989). For an historical analysis of

the treatment of married women's property rights at common law, see John D. Johnston, Sex and Property: The Common Law Tradition, The Law School Curriculum, and Developments Toward Equality, 47 N.Y.U.L.Rev. 1033 (1972).

26. N.Y.Real Property Law §§ 189, 190 (McKinney 1986).

27. Hiles v. Fisher, 144 N.Y. 306, 39 N.E. 337 (1895). See generally Hilary P. Bradford, Comment, Tenancies by the Entirety in New York, 1 Buf.L.Rev. 279 (1952); Johnston, supra note 1, at 1061–70.

28. 1980 N.Y.Laws c. 281 (approved June 19, 1980). On approving c. 281, Governor Hugh L. Carey stated that "[t]he bill recognizes that the marriage relationship is also an economic partnership. Upon its dissolution, property accumulated during the marriage should be distributed in a manner which reflects the individual needs and circumstances of the parties regardless of the name in which such property is held." 5 McKinney's Sess. L.News, A–249 (July 1980). For a general description of the equitable distribution law, see Henry H. Foster, An Explanation of the New York 1980 Equitable Distribution Law, 6 F.L.R. 2651 (1980).

could be divided.[29] As part of a support order, however, the divorce court had authority to make such orders "concerning the possession of property, as in the court's discretion justice requires having regard to the circumstances of the case and of the respective parties." [30] Thus, the court was able to permit the wife and children to live in the family home,[31] even though title was held by the husband.

Present New York law distinguishes between marital property [32] and separate property.[33] Upon divorce, unless the parties have agreed upon a different disposition, the court will set aside to each party his or her separate property and will distribute the marital property "equitably between the parties, considering the circumstances of the case and of the respective parties." [34] Although the New York statute permits the same property distribution to John and Mary that was arrived at under the California equal division rule, the New York court has authority to take account of ten factors listed in the statute in arriving at an equitable distribution.[35] Since the listed factors include the health of both parties,

---

29. Id., Foster, 6 F.L.R. at 2652.

30. N.Y.Dom.Rel.Law § 234 (McKinney 1986). Section 234 was not affected by the equitable distribution law. See note 28 supra.

31. E.g., King v. King, 100 Misc.2d 98, 418 N.Y.S.2d 531 (Fam.Ct.1979) (Family Court has jurisdiction, on referral from Supreme Court, to continue its order allowing wife and children to reside in family home even though husband had, in violation of Family Court order, conveyed the home to third parties).

32. N.Y.Laws 1980, c. 281, § 9, amending N.Y.Dom.Rel.Law § 236. Section 236, Part B, 1(c) (McKinney 1986 and 1995 Cum. Pocket Part) provides:

c. The term "marital property" shall mean all property acquired by either or both spouses during the marriage and before the execution of a separation agreement or the commencement of a matrimonial action, regardless of the form in which title is held, except as otherwise provided in agreement pursuant to subdivision three of this part. Marital property shall not include separate property as hereinafter defined.

33. Id. Section 236, Part B, 1(d) (McKinney 1986) provides:

d. The term separate property shall mean:

(1) property acquired before marriage or property acquired by bequest, devise, or descent, or gift from a party other than the spouse;

(2) compensation for personal injuries;

(3) property acquired in exchange for or the increase in value of separate property, except to the extent that such appreciation is due in part to the contributions or efforts of the other spouse;

(4) property described as separate property by written agreement of the parties pursuant to subdivision three of this part.

In California compensation for personal injuries is community property if the cause of

action arose during the marriage (West's Ann. Cal.Fam.Code § 780) (1994), except where the other spouse is the tortfeasor (Id., § 781(c)). Upon dissolution of the marriage, the injured spouse will be awarded the community personal injury damages, unless the court finds that "the interests of justice require another disposition", in which case the injured spouse must get at least one-half of the damages. West's Ann.Cal.Fam.Code § 2603(b) (1994).

34. N.Y.Laws 1980, c. 281, § 9, amending N.Y.Dom.Rel.Law § 236. Section 236, Part B, 5(a), (b) and (c) (McKinney 1986).

35. Id., § 236, Part B, 5(d) provides:

d. In determining an equitable disposition of property under paragraph c, the court shall consider:

(1) the income and property of each party at the time of marriage, and at the time of the commencement of the action;

(2) the duration of the marriage and the age and health of both parties;

(3) the need of a custodial parent to occupy or own the marital residence and to use or own its household effects;

(4) the loss of inheritance and pension rights upon dissolution of the marriage as of the date of dissolution;

(5) any award of maintenance under subdivision six of this part;

(6) any equitable claim to, interest in, or direct or indirect contribution made to the acquisition of such marital property by the party not having title, including joint efforts or expenditures and contributions and services as a spouse, parent, wage earner and homemaker, and to the career or career potential of the other party;

(7) the liquid or non-liquid character of all marital property;

(8) the probable future financial circumstances of each party;

their separate property, the direct or indirect contributions of each party to the acquisition of the marital property, and the probable future financial circumstances of each party, it seems likely that the court in New York might take into account the disparate property holdings of the spouses by awarding the bulk of the marital property to Mary.[36] It seems unlikely that either John or Mary would be granted maintenance.[37]

If John had died intestate during the marriage leaving no issue, Mary would inherit his entire property.[38] And, since 1966, she would be protected against the possibility that he might try to disinherit her by will or by will substitutes. In either event Mary would have the right to elect to take against the will [39] or testamentary substitutes: [40] she could take one-third of the estate if there were issue or one-half if there were not.[41] The statute counts as part of the decedent's estate property disposed of *inter vivos* through the use of testamentary substitutes such as gifts *causa mortis*, Totten trusts, joint bank accounts, and revocable gifts.[42] If John had left Mary an income trust for life, she may withdraw up to $10,000 in cash.[43] But if she is given more than $10,000 by the will plus an income trust equal to or in excess of the difference between that bequest and her

---

(9) the impossibility or difficulty of evaluating any component asset or any interest in a business, corporation or profession, and the economic desirability of retaining such asset or interest intact and free from any claim or interference by the other party;

(10) the tax consequences to each party;

(11) the wasteful dissipation of assets by either spouse;

(12) any transfer or encumbrance made in contemplation of a matrimonial action without fair consideration;

(13) any other factor which the court shall expressly find to be just and proper.

36. It is not clear whether the court may award all of the marital property to one spouse, although a literal reading of § 236, Part B, 5(a) and (c) appears to exclude that result. Under 5(a) the court "shall determine the respective rights of the parties in their separate or marital property, and shall provide for the disposition thereof in the final judgment", while under 5(c) the court is instructed that "[m]arital property shall be distributed equitably *between* the parties, considering the circumstances of the case and of the respective parties." The point may be of little practical significance, since in a proper case the court could, by using the considerations enumerated in 5(d), quoted in note 35 supra, award $1.00 of the marital property to a spouse. Would such an award to John be appropriate? Section 236, Part B, 5(e) authorizes a "distributive award" defined as

"payments provided for in a valid agreement between the parties or awarded by the court, in lieu of or to supplement, facilitate or effectuate the division or distribution of property where authorized in a matrimonial action, and payable either in a lump sum or over a period of time in fixed amounts. Dis-

tributive awards shall not include payments which are treated as ordinary income to the recipient under the provisions of the United States Internal Revenue Code." N.Y.Dom. Rel.Law § 236, Part B (1)(b) (McKinney 1986).

in lieu of an equitable distribution in situations where such a distribution would be

"impractical or burdensome or where the distribution of an interest in a business, corporation or profession would be contrary to law, the court in lieu of such equitable distribution shall make a distributive award in order to achieve equity between the parties. The court in its discretion, also may make a distributive award to supplement, facilitate or effectuate a distribution of marital property."

Foster says this section is an effort to avoid requiring one spouse to dissolve a law partnership or making the other spouse a "silent partner" in the firm. See note 28 supra, 6 F.L.R. at 2653.

37. See, N.Y.Laws 1980, c. 281, § 9, amending N.Y.Dom.Rel.Law § 236. Section 236, Part B, 6(a) (McKinney 1986) provides for maintenance.

38. N.Y.E.P.T.Law § 4–1.1(a)(2) (McKinney 1995 Cum. Pocket Part).

39. N.Y.E.P.T.Law § 5–1.1(c) (McKinney 1981). See generally Miles B. Amend, The Surviving Spouse and the Estates, Powers, and Trusts Law, 33 Brook.L.Rev. 530 (1967).

40. Ibid.

41. Ibid.

42. N.Y.E.P.T.Law § 5–1.1(b) (McKinney 1981).

43. N.Y.E.P.T.Law § 5–1.1(c)(D) (McKinney 1981) See Amend, supra note 39, at 541.

statutory share upon election, she is deprived of the right to elect.[44]

The case of John and Mary indicates some of the pitfalls the California community property system holds for a working wife who divorces a wealthy husband. Not only must she surrender half of the community assets attributable to her efforts if her husband insists on a division,[45] but she is unlikely to receive any spousal support where there are no children and she has a history of working during the marriage. The situation is not a great deal better for a housekeeping wife. There is still no community property to divide, but she will have a better chance of getting spousal support, particularly if the marriage has been one of long duration.[46] The situation in New York is better only because there Mary might be allowed to keep her post-marital acquisitions.[47] She would still not be entitled to any of her husband's separate property on divorce.[48]

Not surprisingly, it has been suggested that California law be changed "to reflect a policy of greater protection to the wife who marries a wealthy man." [49] The recommended changes include charging the family living expenses ratably against the community and separate property to prevent the husband from using up the community assets in family support and adopting the Texas rule that the income from separate property is community property. Would either of these proposals have helped Mary? What is your evaluation of them apart from Mary's case?

If we move from considering the situation of the working wife to that of the homemaking wife, other problems of the community system become apparent. Assume a marriage between Tom and Jane Smith, also on January 1, 1988. Tom is a medical student and Jane works as a receptionist in a medical clinic. Both are agreed that Jane will stop working when Tom completes his residency. During the marriage Tom amasses a large estate from his medical practice. He is very outgoing and has many friends. Much of his income is spent on entertaining, travel and a showplace home. Jane spends her time caring for the couple's four children and promoting her husband's career. When Tom is 44 and Jane is 46, he finds that she is no longer able to keep up with his social position.[50] He wishes to divorce her and marry Alice, who is 35 and a prominent socialite.

How will Jane fare upon divorce? Leaving aside the matters of alimony and child support, which will be discussed in a subsequent section,[51] let us focus on the marital property aspects of the case. The facts establish that everything Tom has acquired during the marriage is attributable to his professional work and is therefore community property in California, marital property for purposes of

---

44. N.Y.E.P.T.Law § 5–1.1(c)(F) (McKinney 1981).

45. The parties may agree to an unequal property division. West's Ann.Cal.Fam.Code § 2550 (1994). The equal division requirement applies only to court-ordered divisions.

46. West's Ann.Cal.Fam.Code § 4320(f) (1994). See also Marriage of Morrison, 20 Cal.3d 437, 143 Cal.Rptr. 139, 573 P.2d 41 (1978).

47. See note 36 supra.

48. N.Y.Laws 1980, c. 281, § 9, amending N.Y.Dom.Rel.Law § 236. Section 236, Part B, 5(b) (McKinney 1986) provides: "Separate property shall remain such."

49. Kenna J. Helms, Comment, Never Marry a Rich Man: The Lesson of Beam v. Bank of America, 13 Santa Clara L.Rev. 121, 139 (1972); see also Bodenheimer, supra note 20, at 407–18.

50. Cf. Irving Rosow and K. Daniel Rose, Divorce Among Doctors, 34 J. Marriage & Family 587, 592 (1972), making the point that California physicians who become divorced do so when their "careers are already well-established and they are at the height of their professional powers." The peak number of divorces were filed when the physicians were between the ages of 35–44.

51. See Text Note, Spousal Support and Division of Property Following Divorce, at p. 316, infra.

equitable distribution in New York. At the end of the marriage, very little cash or investments are available for division or distribution. The community's chief assets are the family home, with its furnishings appraised at $300,000, and the goodwill of Tom's medical practice. Under the equal division rule, a California court could award the house to both parties as tenants in common, directing that it be sold when the children all reach majority,[52] and order Tom to pay Jane one-half of the community interest in the goodwill of his medical practice.[53] Or, if the value of the goodwill equals that of the house, Jane could keep the house while Tom took his goodwill.[54] Not limited by an equal division principle, a New York court might be able to award the house to Jane while at the same time giving her a distributive award in lieu of part of the marital interest in Tom's practice.[55]

The major theoretical difference between the legal rights of Jane in California and New York appears during the marriage, not at divorce. Since 1975, California wives in Jane's position have had the same right to manage the community property as their husbands. In New York, the sharing principle of the marital property concept is deferred until the marriage has ended. Marriage is a partnership in New York only when it is terminated by divorce. But what rights does Jane have in California as a practical matter? She has no access to Tom's earnings if he chooses to keep them in a bank account in his name alone.[56] She cannot sell the house without his consent.[57] She can make contracts binding on the community property,[58] and can obtain credit in her own name.[59]

Effective July 1, 1987, California wives like Jane acquired important new remedies against their husbands' mismanagement; the same remedies are available to husbands against wives.[60] They have a claim for violations of the duty to deal in good faith that results in substantial impairment to the community estate, as well as rights to an accounting of the property and obligations of the community, and the right to petition to have their name added to community property held in the name of the other spouse alone, with specified exceptions for business assets. These new rights, if they are interpreted broadly enough to afford adequate protection to nonmanaging spouses, will go far toward making marriage in California a true economic partnership.

It may seem strange that so much uncertainty surrounds the implementation of the wife's newly-acquired powers of management in California. In part, the explanation is that the topic is still relatively new and there have been few cases interpreting the statutory language. Nor is the problem confined to California. Although joint management of the community property was proposed in Louisiana

---

52. E.g., In re Marriage of Duke, 101 Cal. App.3d 152, 161 Cal.Rptr. 444 (1980). See also West's Ann.Cal.Fam.Code § 3800–10 (1994), authorizing a "deferred sale of home order" that permits a party with custody of minor children or disabled children to have the temporary use of the family home.

53. See note 18 supra.

54. See In re Marriage of Fink, 25 Cal.3d 877, 160 Cal.Rptr. 516, 603 P.2d 881 (1979) (West's Ann.Cal.Fam.Code § 2550 does not require an equal division of each asset in kind; the asset distribution method of division complies with the statute). In New York, unlike California, see note 18 supra, Tom's medical degree is considered marital property subject to distribution. See O'Brien v. O'Brien, 66

N.Y.2d 576, 489 N.E.2d 712, 498 N.Y.S.2d 743 (1985). Jane would thus be entitled to claim a portion of that asset.

55. See note 36 supra.

56. West's Ann.Cal.Fin.Code § 851 (1989).

57. West's Ann.Cal.Fam.Code § 1102 (1994).

58. West's Ann.Cal.Fam.Code § 910 (1994).

59. West's Ann.Cal.Civ.Code § 112.30 (1995 Cum. Pocket Part).

60. West's Ann.Cal.Fam.Code § 1101 (1994). See generally Carol S. Bruch, Management Powers and Duties Under California's Community Property Laws: Recommendations for Reform, 34 Hastings L.J. 227 (1982).

as early as 1936,[61] the final version of an equal management bill did not emerge until 1979, effective January 1, 1980,[62] making Louisiana the last of the eight original community property states to effect changes in the male management model.[63] Without attempting to treat any of these revisions in detail, a comparison of the general approach taken by each may prove instructive in assessing the practical impact of the wife's new powers.

The Texas law,[64] the first to be enacted, falls short of achieving a true marital partnership. Although the partnership approach, giving each spouse acting alone power to deal with the entire community and to incur liabilities binding on the community, was favored by some of the women's groups participating in the revision, this proposal was objectionable to men because it would give wives too much power over the husband's earnings.[65] Instead, the new law divides the community property into three parts, giving (1) the wife control of her earnings and the income from her separate property, (2) the husband control over his earnings and the income from his separate property, and (3) both spouses joint control over "mixed or combined" community property—property that each spouse would have controlled separately had its source been identifiable.[66] The extent of joint control in Texas will thus depend in part on how carefully the first two categories of property are kept segregated. If no "mixed" property exists, and if the wife neither owns any separate property nor works outside the home, she will acquire no managerial powers under the Texas law.

The 1972 Washington law apparently attempted to achieve a partnership notion. The statute expressly gives either spouse, acting alone, power to manage and control the entire community property to the same extent each now controls his or her separate property. Exceptions to this provision apply to both spouses and forbid devises of more than half the community property as well as engaging in certain transactions without the consent or joinder of the other spouse: these include gifts; sales, conveyances, or encumbrances of community realty; purchases of community realty; creation of security interests; sales of household goods or furnishings; and sale or encumbrance of the assets of a business if both spouses participate in its management.[67] The wife's statutory power to control

61. Harriet S. Daggett, Is Joint Control of Community Property Possible? 10 Tul.L.Rev. 589 (1936).

62. La.Civ.Code Ann. arts. 2346–2355.1 (West 1985 and 1995 Cum. Pocket Part). See Katherine Shaw Spaht & Cynthia A. Samuel, Equal Management Revisited: 1979 Legislative Modifications of the 1978 Matrimonial Regimes Law, 40 La.L.Rev. 83 (1979).

63. The rapidity with which this change took place is impressive. As recently as 1971 the generalization could be made that, in the main, statutes in the eight community property states

give the husband the managerial control of the community personal property, with the like power of disposition (other than testamentary) as he has of his separate estate; and give him the managerial control of the community real property, but with the condition that the husband and wife must both join in the execution and acknowledgment of any instrument by which it is sought to

convey, transfer or encumber it. In some of the states, however, the husband has the same power to dispose of the community realty as he does of the community personalty without the joinder of the wife, except where homestead property is involved.

William Quinby de Funiak & Michael J. Vaughn, Principles of Community Property 277–78 (2d ed. 1971) (footnotes omitted).

64. Tex.Fam. Code Ann. §§ 5.01–5.27 (West 1993).

65. Joseph W. McKnight, Texas Community Property Law—Its Course of Development and Reform, 8 Calif.West.L.Rev. 117, 130 (1971). See also, Ronald G. Williams, Comment, Section 5.22 of the Texas Family Code: Control and Management of the Marital Estate, 27 Sw.L.J. 837 (1973).

66. Id., 8 Calif.West.L.Rev. at 137–42.

67. Wash.Laws, 1972, 1st Ex.Sess., ch. 108 § 3, p. 245, amending Wash.Rev. Code Ann. § 26.16.030 (West 1986).

her earnings was repealed.[68] The statute leaves a great deal to individual initiative, doesn't it? What happens if one spouse moves swiftly to assert control over the entire community, including the earnings of the other spouse? Can an employer be ordered to pay over a spouse's wages to the self-designated community "manager"? Are the rights of a homemaking spouse substantially greater in Washington than in Texas?

An astonishingly limited interpretation of the wife's newly-acquired powers of management and control has been suggested by one Washington commentator. Noting that prior to 1972, the standard by which the husband was adjudged to be meeting his managerial responsibilities was merely his "good faith," rather than his "good judgment," the writer questions whether the wife's new status as equal manager of the community should give her the right to question her husband's judgment as well. Surprisingly, the answer is "No": [69]

> If the answer were otherwise, courts would be asked to choose between alternative business decisions and thus would undertake to decide what is in the best interests of the community. This is impractical and undesirable. Absent some evidence of bad faith, a dispute over what is best for the community is nothing more than an internal disagreement between husband and wife. A contrary conclusion would be inconsistent with the traditional community property concept that only a few important transactions should require participation by both spouses. As a practical matter, if either spouse could contest the judgment of the other, joint participation by the spouses always would be necessary before a third party could safely transact business with the community.

But wasn't the whole purpose of the amendments that of changing traditional community property concepts? If this interpretation is followed, what will wives have gained in terms of real power to participate in the management and control of community property in Washington?

As between the Texas model and the Washington approach, revisions in Arizona, California, Idaho, Louisiana, Nevada, and New Mexico all favor the Washington partnership notion by affirming the power of either spouse to manage the property, with restrictions similar to those contained in the Washington statute.[70] In adopting this approach, both California and Idaho repealed statutes giving the working wife control of her earnings; in Arizona, Louisiana, and New Mexico, a wife's earnings were previously controlled by her husband.[71] An important statutory limitation on the partnership approach in several states relates to the management of a community business.[72] California gives "primary management and control" of the business or interest in the business to the managing spouse.[73] Louisiana permits a spouse to renounce the right to partici-

68. Id. § 8, p. 247, repealing Wash.Rev. Code Ann. § 26.16.130.

69. Harry M. Cross, Equality for Spouses in Washington Community Property Law—1972 Statutory Changes, 48 Wash.L.Rev. 527, 542–43 (1973).

70. Ariz.Rev.Stat. § 25–214(B) and (C) (1976); West's Ann.Cal.Fam.Code §§ 910–11, 1100–02 (1994); Idaho Code § 32–912 (1995 Cum.Pocket Supp.); La.Civ.Code Ann. arts. 2346–2355.1 (West 1985 and 1995 Cum.Pocket Part); Nev.Rev.Stat.Ann. § 123.230 (Mitchie

1993); N.M.Stat.Ann. §§ 40–3–13, 40–3–14 (Mitchie 1994).

71. Wives in Nevada had the power to manage their earnings only when the earnings were "used for the care and maintenance of the family." Former Nev.Rev.Stat. § 123–230.

72. See generally, James S. Macdonald, The Impact of Equal Management Upon Community Property Businesses, 13 Idaho L.Rev. 191 (1977).

73. West's Ann.Cal.Fam.Code § 1101(d) (1994).

pate in a community business.[74] In New Mexico, in the absence of a written and filed assertion of her managerial rights, the wife initially was presumed to have acquiesced in management by the husband.[75] Washington has a less-than-clear provision about "participation" in the management of a community business.[76] More is at stake here than the rights of husbands and wives between themselves; the rights of creditors are involved as well.[77]

What have these statutory changes accomplished? Very little, according to Professor Judith Younger,[78] who reports responses from practicing lawyers in six states, all suggesting that male management of community property remains the normal pattern. Professor Bingaman, herself also a practitioner, offers a hypothetical case and an explanation: [79]

> A wife in an equal management community property state does not work outside the home for compensation. Her husband does work and receives a paycheck every two weeks drawn in his name alone. He alone can endorse that check, and he regularly deposits it in a bank account held in his name alone, upon which his wife cannot draw. In what sense can it be said that this wife has "equal" management rights to the community property earnings in which she has a vested one-half ownership interest? Similarly, if the husband chooses to invest his paycheck in stocks held in his name alone, or in an insurance policy of which he is the only named owner, in what manner may his wife "manage" the community property which she technically owns?

> In any such situation the legal right to manage community property has little practical significance during the continuance of the marriage. In fact, wives in equal management community property states who do not themselves work and earn their own paychecks, to deposit in their own bank accounts, are generally in no better legal position during marriage than are wives in separate property states, or than were they themselves under the old "husband management" statutes.

Does this mean that Jane is no better off in California than she is in New York? What further changes are needed to improve her situation? For housewives in equal management community property states, Bingaman thinks the federal Equal Credit Opportunity Act[80] holds some promise: since the wife is entitled to credit on the basis of the community's rating if the husband would be, she may manage the property independently of her husband's consent or coopera-

74. La.Civ.Code Ann. art. 2348 (West 1985). See Janet Mary Riley, Analysis of the 1980 Revision of the Matrimonial Regimes Law of Louisiana, 26 Loyola L.Rev. 453, 455 (1980) ("Without overt sex discrimination, Louisiana's new system favors the breadwinner over the homemaker, and favors creditors of the debtor spouse over the non-debtor spouse.").

75. 1973 Laws of New Mexico, ch. 320 § 9, p. 1366–67. See generally, Anne K. Bingaman, The Community Property Act of 1973: A Commentary and Quasi–Legislative History, 5 N.Mex.L.Rev. 1, 35–47 (1974). With certain exceptions, both spouses have the power to manage community real property and "either" spouse has the full power to manage community personal property. N.M.Stat.Ann., §§ 40–3–13, 40–3–14 (Mitchie 1994).

76. Wash.Rev.Code § 26.16.030(6) (1986). See Harry M. Cross, Community Property: A

Comparison of the Systems in Washington and Louisiana, 39 La.L.Rev. 479, 482 (1979).

77. See generally, Alan Pedlar, The Implications of the New Community Property Laws for Creditors' Remedies and Bankruptcy, 63 Calif.L.Rev. 1610 (1975); Alan Pedlar, Community Property and the Bankruptcy Reform Act of 1978, 11 St. Mary's L.J. 349 (1979).

78. Judith T. Younger, Not Equal Yet, 13 Idaho L.Rev. 227, 240–43 (1977).

79. Anne K. Bingaman, Equal Management of Community Property and Equal Credit Opportunity, 13 Idaho L.Rev. 161, 161–62 (1977).

80. 15 U.S.C.A. §§ 1691–1691e (West 1981 and 1995 Cum.Pocket Part). See generally, James A. Burns, Jr., An Empirical Analysis of the Equal Credit Opportunity Act, 13 Univ. of Mich.J. Law Reform 102 (1979).

tion through the creation of debts binding on the community.[81]   This avenue is presumably closed to wives in Texas, who have no general power to bind the community, and to wives in common law states who are not independently creditworthy.

Professor Younger wants to go further.   She thinks the "ideal marital regime" is one that [82]

> eliminates distinctions between husbands and wives yet recognizes that one of the spouses may be dependent during marriage.   For him or her, it provides extra protections designed to put both spouses on a par economically and thus, through different treatment, to achieve equality of result between them. It further attempts to end the dependence of the dependent spouse on dissolution of the marriage.

Among the improvements necessary to achieve this ideal marital regime are joint, rather than equal, management of community property, and enactment of a provision that specifically authorizes courts "to set standards of support in the ongoing marriage while the spouses are living together, and to enforce agreements between spouses reducing the support obligation to cash in the same kind of situation." [83]

Responding to these and other proposals to embody in property law the concept of marriage as an economic partnership, the National Conference of Commissioners on Uniform State Laws promulgated the Uniform Marital Property Act in 1983.[84]   The drafting committee chose two principles that informed its work: that a sharing principle should characterize the spouses' relationship toward their property, and that the sharing principle should be operative at the inception of the marriage, rather than being deferred until divorce.[85]   The Uniform Marital Property Act has been generally well-received by commentators.[86] In 1984, Wisconsin became the first common-law state to adopt a version of UMPA.[87]

Have you formed your own opinion about the question posed at the beginning of this Text Note—whether the common law system or community property best serves the interests of both spouses in an egalitarian marriage?   Your answer may depend in part on the future social and economic conditions you foresee affecting marriage.[88]   If, as Mary Ann Glendon has suggested,[89] housewife marriage is becoming less prevalent, spouses who view themselves as economically self-sufficient individuals may object to marital property regimes that force division of earned assets at dissolution.   But if it is socially desirable to encourage couples to

---

81.   Bingaman, supra note 79, at 164.   See also, Judy Gray, Comment, Credit for Women in California, 22 U.C.L.A.L.Rev. 873 (1975).

82.   Younger, supra note 78, at 243–44.

83.   Id., at 244–45.

84.   9A U.L.A. 97 (1987).

85.   William P. Cantwell, The Uniform Marital Property Act: Origin and Intent, 68 Marq. L.Rev. 383 (1985).

86.   See, e.g., Patrick N. Parkinson, Who Needs the Uniform Marital Property Act?, 55 U.Cin.L.Rev. 677 (1987); William A. Reppy, The Uniform Marital Property Act: Some Suggested Revisions for a Basically Sound Act, 21 Houston L.Rev. 679 (1984).

87.   Act of April 4, 1984, ch. 186, § 47, 1983 Wis.Laws 1153, 1163–75 (codified at Wis.Stat.

Ann. §§ 766.001–766.97 (West 1993 and 1994 Cum.Pocket Part).   See generally, June Miller Weisberger, The Wisconsin Marital Property Act: Highlights of the Wisconsin Experience in Developing a Model for Comprehensive Common Law Property Reform, 1 Wis. Women's L.J. 5 (1985).

88.   For a statistical portrait of the "new marriage, American style," see Mary Ann Glendon, Modern Marriage Law and Its Underlying Assumptions: The New Marriage and the New Property, 13 Fam.L.Q. 441, 448–49 (1980).

89.   Mary Ann Glendon, Is There a Future for Separate Property?   8 Fam.L.Q. 315 (1974).

make the accommodations necessary to enable them to enjoy an intimate family life while furthering their individual development, as Susan Prager suggests it is,[90] then the sharing principle inherent in community property systems may be a better choice.

It has, however, been suggested [91] that the equal management schemes have seriously endangered marriage as an institution. Perhaps, then, we should postpone our final evaluation of marital property reforms until after we have reassessed the modern significance of marriage.

b. *Rethinking the Marriage Contract*

i. *Feminists and Marriage*

PROTEST

While we acknowledge our mutual affection by publicly assuming the relationship of husband and wife, yet in justice to ourselves and a great principle, we deem it a duty to declare that this act on our part implies no sanction of, nor promise of voluntary obedience to such of the present laws of marriage as refuse to recognize the wife as an independent, rational being, while they confer upon the husband an injurious and unnatural superiority, investing him with legal powers which no honorable man would exercise and which no man should possess. We protest especially against the laws which give the husband:

1. The custody of the wife's person.

2. The exclusive control and guardianship of their children.

3. The sole ownership of her personal and use of her real estate, unless previously settled upon her, or placed in the hands of trustees, as in the case of minors, lunatics and idiots.

4. The absolute right to the product of her industry.

5. Also against laws which give to the widower so much larger and more permanent an interest in the property of his deceased wife than they give to the widow in that of the deceased husband.

6. Finally, against the whole system by which "the legal existence of the wife is suspended during marriage" so that, in most States, she neither has a legal part in the choice of her residence, nor can she make a will, nor sue or be sued in her own name, nor inherit property.

We believe that personal independence and equal human rights can never be forfeited except for crime; that marriage should be an equal and permanent partnership, and so recognized by law; that until it is so recognized, married partners should provide against the radical injustice of present laws, by every means in their power.

We believe that where domestic difficulties arise, no appeal should be made to legal tribunals under existing laws but that all difficulties should be submitted to the equitable adjustment of arbitrators mutually chosen.

---

90. Susan Prager, Sharing Principles and the Future of Marital Property Law, 25 U.C.L.A.L.Rev. 1 (1977); see also Herma Hill Kay, Legal and Social Impediments to Dual Career Marriages, 12 U.C.Davis L.Rev. 207, 214–15 (1979).

91. W.T. Tête, A Critique of the Equal Management Act of 1978, 39 La.L.Rev. 491, 525–26 (1979).

Thus reverencing law, we enter our protest against rules and customs which are unworthy of the name, since they violate justice, the essence of law.

Worcester Spy, 1855   (Signed) Henry B. Blackwell
                                                          Lucy Stone

———

PROCLAMATION 4786 OF AUGUST 29, 1980

By the President of the United States.
45 Federal Register 58325 (Sept. 3, 1980).

WORKING MOTHERS' DAY, 1980

A Proclamation

In greater numbers than ever before, American mothers are taking on important job responsibilities outside the home. In workplaces across our Nation and in every occupation, more than 16 million employed mothers are contributing their valuable skills to the labor force. In fact, more than half of all the mothers in this country have taken on jobs outside the home, and it is estimated that by 1990, 75% of all two-parent families will have both parents in the work force.

On the job and in the home, working mothers are making a vital contribution to the national economy and to the strength of the American family. Working mothers do not shed homemaking and parental responsibilities; they merely add the demands of a job to those of wife and mother. As we recognize the hard work and dedication of these women, we also acknowledge the many special problems they confront in meeting their dual responsibilities. We have an obligation to reinforce and support them in their endeavors.

To give special recognition to working mothers for fulfilling their exceptional responsibilities in the home and in the world of commerce, the House of Representatives (House Joint Resolution 379) has requested that I designate August 31, 1980, as Working Mothers' Day. I fully support this Resolution.

NOW THEREFORE, I, JIMMY CARTER, President of the United States of America, do hereby designate August 31, 1980, as Working Mothers' Day and call upon families, individual citizens, labor and civic organizations, and the business community to recognize publicly the unique contributions of mothers currently in the work force, and to honor former generations of working mothers for their important role in building American society.

IN WITNESS WHEREOF, I have hereunto set my hand this twenty-ninth day of August, in the year of our Lord nineteen hundred and eighty, and of the Independence of the United States of America the two hundred and fifth.

JIMMY CARTER

———

MARRIAGE

Sheila Cronan. Reprinted from *Notes From the Third Year:*
Women's Liberation 62–65 (1971).

[Sheila Cronan was a founding member of Redstockings and was active in The Feminists for more than two years. In 1974, she graduated from law school at the University of California, Berkeley.]

Marriage has been a subject which has generated considerable controversy in the Women's Movement. So far as I know, no group other than The Feminists has publicly taken a stand against marriage, although I'm sure it has been a topic of discussion in most.

One widely held view in the Movement is represented in the following statement:

We women can use marriage as the "dictatorship of the proletariat" in the family revolution. When male supremacy is completely eliminated, marriage, like the state, will wither away.[1]

The basic assumption behind this concept, and one that I myself shared at one time, is that marriage benefits women. This idea is very much part of the male culture and is always being reinforced by men's complaints about marriage and by the notion that women are the ones who want to get married. We've all heard plenty of jokes about how women "snare" husbands, and popular songs with lines like "the boy chases the girl until she catches him." Mothers give their daughters advice on how to get their boy friends to marry them, etc. The propaganda tells us that marriage laws are operating in the interest of women and in fact exist to provide protection for the woman. From this assumption it is logical to conclude that we must retain the institution of marriage until such time as discrimination against women no longer exists and consequently "protection" is no longer necessary.

The Feminists decided to examine the institution of marriage as it is set up by law in order to find out whether or not it did operate in women's favor. It became increasingly clear to us that the institution of marriage "protects" women in the same way that the institution of slavery was said to "protect" blacks—that is, that the word "protection" in this case is simply a euphemism for oppression.

We discovered that women are not aware of what marriage is really about. We are given the impression that love is the purpose of marriage—after all, in the ceremony, the wife promises to "love, honor, and cherish" her husband and the husband promises to "love, honor, and protect" his wife. This promise, which women believe to be central to the marriage contract, is viewed as irrelevant by the courts. For example, in a well-known case here in New York State, a woman attempted to obtain an annulment on the grounds that her husband had told her that he loved her prior to the marriage and then afterward admitted that he did not and never would. This was held *not*

---

1. Kathie Sarachild, "Hot and Cold Flashes," in The Newsletter, Vol. I, No. 3, May 1, 1969.

to give grounds for annulment,[2] despite the fact that the man committed fraud, which is normally grounds for nullifying any contract.

There is nothing in most marriage ceremonies specifically referring to sex, yet the courts have held that "the fact that a party agrees to and does enter into the marriage implies a promise to consummate the marriage by cohabitation, so that failure to do so gives grounds for annulment on the basis of fraud in the inducement."[3] An annulment was granted a New York man on the grounds that his wife was unable to have sex with him due to an incurable nervous condition.[4]

But then, one might ask, how is this particularly oppressive to women? After all, men also enter into marriage with the understanding that love is central. Many of us, examining our personal histories, however, have suspected that "love" has a different meaning for men than it does for women. This has been substantiated by a study done by a man, Clifford R. Adams of Penn State University, who spent thirty years researching the subconscious factors involved in mate selection, studying 4000 couples. His conclusion was:

> When a man and a woman gaze into each other's eyes with what they think are love and devotion, they are not seeing the same thing. * * * For the woman, the first things she seeks are love, affection, sentiment. She has to feel loved and wanted. The second is security, then companionship, home and family, community acceptance, and sixth, sex. But for the man sex is at the top of the list, not at the bottom. It's second only to companionship. The single category of love-affection-sentiment is *below* sex.[5]

Sex is compulsory in marriage. A husband can legally force his wife to have sexual relations with him against her will, an act which if committed against any other woman would constitute the crime of rape. Under law, "a husband cannot be guilty of raping his own wife by forcing her to have sexual intercourse with him. By definition, the crime [of rape] is ordinarily that of forcing intercourse on someone other than the wife of the person accused."[6] Thus the threat of force is always present even if it is not necessary for the man to exert it—after all, most women are aware of the " 'right' of the husband to insist on and the 'duty' of the wife to 'submit' "[7] to sexual intercourse.

It is clear that the compulsory nature of sex in marriage operates to the advantage of the male. The husband theoretically has the duty to have intercourse with his wife also, but this normally cannot occur against his will. Furthermore, as far as the enjoyment of the sex act is concerned, figures show that men (with the exception of impotent men who generally cannot have sex at all) nearly always experience orgasm when they have sex. Women, however, are not so fortunate. Surveys have shown that:

2. Schaeffer v. Schaeffer, 160 App.Div. 48, 144 N.Y.S. 774.

3. Eugene R. Canudo, Law of Marriage, Divorce and Adoption (Gould Publications, 1966), p. 20.

4. Hiebink v. Hiebink, 56 N.Y.S.2d 394, aff'd 269 App.Div. 786, 56 N.Y.S.2d 397.

5. Reported in Glamour Magazine, November, 1969, p. 214.

6. Harriet F. Pilpel and Theodora Zavin, Your Marriage and the Law (New York: Collier Books, 1964), p. 215.

7. Ibid., p. 64.

fifteen to twenty percent of all [American] married women have never had an orgasm. About fifty percent reach orgasm on a "now and then" basis, meaning that they experience full culmination about one sex act out of three. Thirty to thirty-five percent of American wives say that they "usually" reach orgasm, meaning that they get there two out of three times or thereabouts. Only a very few women can claim that they have an orgasm every time they take part in sexual activities.[8]

Thus sex as practiced in American marriages clearly benefits the male far more than the female. Despite the emphasis that has recently been put on the husband's duty to give pleasure to his wife, this is not happening most of the time, and we all know that intercourse without orgasm is at best a waste of time. From the above figures we see that 70 percent of American wives have this boring and often painful experience over two-thirds of the time.

In Alabama's legal code of 1852 two clauses, standing in significant juxtaposition, recognized the dual character of the slave.

The first clause confirmed his status as property—the right of the owner to his "time, labor and services" and to his obedient compliance with all lawful commands. * * *

The second clause acknowledged the slave's status as a person. The law required that masters be humane to their slaves, furnish them adequate food and clothing, and provide care for them during sickness and in old age. In short, the state endowed masters with obligations as well as rights and assumed some responsibility for the welfare of the bondsmen.[9]

The following is a description of marital responsibilities:

The legal responsibilities of a wife are to live in the home established by her husband; to perform the domestic chores (cleaning, cooking, washing, etc.) necessary to help maintain that home; to care for her husband and children.

The legal responsibilities of a husband are to provide a home for his wife and children; to support, protect and maintain his wife and children.[10]

The word "slave" is usually defined as a person owned by another and forced to work without pay for, and obey, the owner. Although wives are not bought and sold openly, I intend to show that marriage is a form of slavery. We are told that marriage is an equitable arrangement entered into freely by both husband and wife. We have seen above that this is not true with regard to the sexual aspect of marriage—that in this respect marriage is clearly set up to benefit the male. It also is not true with regard to the rest of the marital responsibilities.

Women believe that they are voluntarily giving their household services, whereas the courts hold that the husband is legally entitled to his wife's domestic services and, further, that she *cannot be paid* for her work.

8. L.T. Woodward, M.D., Sophisticated Sex Techniques in Marriage (New York: Lancer Books, 1967), p. 18.

9. Kenneth M. Stampp, The Peculiar Institution (New York: Vintage Books, 1956), p. 192.

10. Richard T. Gallen, Wives' Legal Rights (New York: Dell Publishing Co., 1967), pp. 4–5.

As part of the rights of consortium, the husband is entitled to the services of his wife. If the wife works outside the home for strangers she is usually entitled to her own earnings. But domestic services or assistances which she gives the husband are generally considered part of her wifely duties. The wife's services and society are so essential a part of what the law considers the husband is entitled to as part of the marriage that it will not recognize any agreement between the spouses which provides that the husband is to pay for such services or society. In a Texas case David promised his wife, Fannie, that he would give her $5000 if she would stay with him while he lived and continue taking care of his house and farm accounts, selling his butter and doing all the other tasks which she had done since their marriage. After David's death, Fannie sued his estate for the money which had been promised her. The court held that the contract was unenforceable since Fannie had agreed to do nothing which she was not already legally and morally bound to do as David's wife.[11]

Whereas the legal responsibilities of the wife include providing all necessary domestic services—that is maintaining the home (cleaning, cooking, washing, purchasing food and other necessities, etc.), providing for her husband's personal needs and taking care of the children—the husband in return is obligated only to provide her with basic maintenance—that is, bed and board. Were he to employ a live-in servant in place of a wife, he would have to pay the servant a salary, provide her with her own room (as opposed to "bed"), food, and the necessary equipment for doing her job. She would get at least one day a week off and probably would be required to do considerably less work than a wife and would normally not be required to provide sexual services.

Thus, being a wife is a full-time job for which one is not entitled to pay. Does this not constitute slavery? Furthermore, slavery implies a lack of freedom of movement, a condition which also exists in marriage. The husband has the right to decide where the couple will live. If he decides to move, his wife is obligated to go with him. If she refuses, he can charge her with desertion. This has been held up by the courts even in certain cases where the wife would be required to change her citizenship.[12] In states where desertion is grounds for divorce (forty-seven states plus the District of Columbia), the wife would be the "guilty party" and would therefore be entitled to no monetary settlement.

The enslavement of women in marriage is all the more cruel and inhumane by virtue of the fact that it appears to exist with the consent of the enslaved group. Part of the explanation for this phenomenon lies in the fact that marriage has existed for so many thousands of years—the female role has been internalized in so many successive generations. If people are forced into line long enough, they will begin to believe in their own inferiority and to accept as natural the role created for them by their oppressor. Furthermore, the society has been so structured that there is no real alternative to marriage for women. Employment discrimination, social stigma, fear of attack, sexual

---

11. Pilpel and Zavin, op. cit., p. 65. For a New York case similar to the Texas one cited, see Garlock v. Garlock, 279 N.Y. 337, 18 N.E.2d 521 (1939).

12. Gallen, op. cit. p. 6.

exploitation are only a few of the factors that make it nearly impossible for women to live as single people. Furthermore, women are deceived as to what the nature of marriage really is. We have already seen how we are made to believe that it is in our interest. Also, marriage is so effectively disguised in glowing, romantic terms that young girls rush into it excitedly, only to discover too late what the real terms of the marriage contract are.

The marriage contract is the only important legal contract in which the terms are not listed. It is in fact a farce created to give women the illusion that they are consenting to a mutually beneficial relationship when in fact they are signing themselves into slavery.

The fact that women sign themselves into slavery instead of being purchased has significance from another point of view. A purchased slave is valuable property who would not be merely cast aside if the master no longer liked him, but would be sold to someone else who would be obligated to care for him. Furthermore, the necessity for purchasing slaves ensured that only people with money could be slave masters, whereas almost any man can have a wife.

Given the existence of marriage and the fact that women work for no pay but with the expectation of security—that is, that their husbands will continue to "support" them—divorce is against the interests of women. Many of us have suspected this for some time because of the eagerness with which men have taken up the cause of divorce reform (i.e., making it easier to get one). When a man "takes a wife" he is obtaining her unpaid labor in return for providing her with basic maintenance. After twenty years of marriage in which she has provided him with domestic and sexual services, given birth to and raised his children, and perhaps even put him through medical school and helped him build a thriving practice, he is free to cast her aside in order to replace her with someone more exciting. If there are minor children involved, he will probably be required to provide child support—which is only fair since they are his children. If he is well off financially and the judge is sympathetic to the woman, he may be required to pay alimony; if this occurs you can be sure that he will complain bitterly and claim that it constitutes oppression for him. But what is alimony after all? Isn't it ridiculous to require an employer to give his employee severance pay when he in fact owes him twenty years' back wages?

Very few women get alimony anyway. Often child support payments are camouflaged as alimony because it is beneficial to the man tax-wise to do so.[13]

It is hardly necessary to go into the situation a woman finds herself in after the divorce, particularly if the marriage has lasted any length of time. Her productive years have been devoted to her husband's interests rather than her own and she is consequently in no position to fend for herself in this society. She is not trained for any job besides that of domestic servant. Her only hope is to find another husband, and if she is past a certain age this may be very difficult. In other forms of slavery this tragic situation would not occur as the monetary value of the slave would ensure his security.

---

13. Report of the Task Force on Family Law and Policy to the Citizens' Advisory Council on the Status of Women, April, 1968, p. 7.

While wives are "owned" by their husbands in the same sense that slaves are owned by their masters—that is, that the master is entitled to free use of the slave's labor, to deny the slave his human right to freedom of movement and control over his own body—the scarcity of slaves resulted in their monetary value. Any man can take a wife and although he is legally required to support her, there is very little anyone can do if he is unable to fulfill this responsibility. Thus many women are forced to work outside the home because their husbands are unemployed or are not making enough money to support the family. This in no way absolves us from our domestic and child care duties, however.[14]

Since marriage constitutes slavery for women, it is clear that the Women's Movement must concentrate on attacking this institution. Freedom for women cannot be won without the abolition of marriage. Attack on such issues as employment discrimination is superfluous; as long as women are working for nothing in the home we cannot expect our demands for equal pay outside the home to be taken seriously.

Furthermore, marriage is the model for all other forms of discrimination against women. The relationships between men and women outside of marriage follow this basic pattern. Although the law does not officially sanction the right of a man to force his sweetheart to have sex with him, she would find it very difficult to prove rape in the courts, especially if they have had a regular sexual relationship. Also, it is not unusual for a man to expect his girl friend to type his term papers, iron his shirts, cook dinner for him, and even clean his apartment. This oppressive relationship carries over into employment and is especially evident in the role of the secretary, also known as the "office wife."

One of the arguments in the Movement against our attacking marriage has been that most women are married. This has always seemed strange to me as it is like saying we should not come out against oppression since all women are oppressed. Clearly of all the oppressive institutions, marriage is the one that affects the most women. It is logical, then, that if we are interested in building a mass movement of women, this is where we should begin.

Another argument against attacking marriage has been that it is dying out anyway. The evidence cited for this is usually the growing rate of divorce. But the high rate of remarriage among divorced persons show that divorce is not evidence for the decline of marriage. We have seen that divorce is in fact a further abuse so far as women's interests are concerned. And the fact is that marriage rates have been on the increase. From 1900 to 1940 approximately one half of all American women over twenty years of age were married at any given time. After 1940 the figure began to rise noticeably: by 1960 it had reached the rate of two-thirds of all women over twenty.[15]

The Women's Movement must address itself to the marriage issue from still another point of view. The marriage relationship is so physically and emotionally draining for women that we must extricate ourselves if for no

14. Gallen, op. cit., p. 7.

15. American Women: Report of the President's Commission on the Status of Women, 1963, p. 6.

other reason than to have the time and energy to devote ourselves to building a feminist revolution.

The Feminists have begun to work on the issue of marriage. It is only a beginning, however; all women must join us in this fight.

THE POLITICS OF HOUSEWORK

Pat Mainardi: Originally published in *Notes From The Second Year: Women's Liberation* 28–31 (1970).

[Pat Mainardi is a housewife and a member of the Redstockings.]

Though women do not complain of the power of husbands each complains of her own husband, or of the husbands of her friends. It is the same in all other cases of servitude; at least in the commencement of the emancipatory movement. The serfs did not at first complain of the power of the lords, but only of their tyranny.

—John Stuart Mill,

On the Subjection of Women

Liberated women—very different from Women's Liberation! The first signals all kinds of goodies, to warm the hearts (not to mention other parts) of the most radical men. The other signals—HOUSEWORK. The first brings sex without marriage, sex before marriage, cozy housekeeping arrangements ("I'm living with this chick") and the self-content of knowing that you're not the kind of man who wants a doormat instead of a woman. That will come later. After all, who wants that old commodity anymore, the Standard American Housewife, all husband, home and kids. The New Commodity, the Liberated Woman, has sex a lot and has a Career, preferably something that can be fitted in with the household chores—like dancing, pottery, or painting.

On the other hand is Women's Liberation—and housework. What? You say this is all trivial? Wonderful! That's what I thought. It seemed perfectly reasonable. We both had careers, both had to work a couple of days a week to earn enough to live on, so why shouldn't we share the housework? So I suggested it to my mate and he agreed—most men are too hip to turn you down flat. You're right, he said. It's only fair.

Then an interesting thing happened. I can only explain it by stating that we women have been brainwashed more than even we can imagine. Probably too many years of seeing television women in ecstacy over their shiny waxed floors or breaking down over their dirty shirt collars. Men have no such conditioning. They recognize the essential fact of housework right from the very beginning. Which is that it stinks.

Here's my list of dirty chores: buying groceries, carting them home and putting them away; cooking meals and washing dishes and pots; doing the laundry, digging out the place when things get out of control; washing floors. The list could go on but the sheer necessities are bad enough. All of us have to do these things, or get someone else to do them for us. The longer my husband contemplated these chores, the more repulsed he became, and so proceeded the change from the normally sweet considerate Dr. Jekyll into the crafty Mr. Hyde who would stop at nothing to avoid the horrors of—housework. As he felt himself backed into a corner laden with dirty dishes, brooms, mops and reeking garbage, his front teeth grew longer and pointier, his fingernails haggled and his eyes grew wild. Housework trivial? Not on your life! Just try to share the burden.

So ensued a dialogue that's been going on for several years. Here are some of the high points:

"I don't mind sharing the housework, but I don't do it very well. We should each do the things we're best at." MEANING: Unfortunately I'm no good at things like washing dishes or cooking. What I do best is a little light carpentry, changing light bulbs, moving furniture (how often do *you* move furniture?) ALSO MEANING: Historically the lower classes (black men and us) have had hundreds of years experience doing menial jobs. It would be a waste of manpower to train someone else to do them now. ALSO MEANING: I don't like the dull stupid boring jobs, so you should do them.

"I don't mind sharing the work, but you'll have to show me how to do it." MEANING: I ask a lot of questions and you'll have to show me everything every time I do it because I don't remember so good. Also don't try to sit down and read while I'M doing my jobs because I'm going to annoy hell out of you until it's easier to do them yourself.

"We used to be so happy!" (Said whenever it was his turn to do something.) MEANING: I used to be so happy. MEANING: Life without housework is bliss. No quarrel here. Perfect Agreement.

"We have different standards, and why should I have to work to your standards? That's unfair." MEANING: If I begin to get bugged by the dirt and crap I will say, "This place sure is a sty" or "How can anyone live like this?" and wait for your reaction. I know that all women have a sore called "Guilt over a messy house" or "Household work is ultimately my responsibility." I know that men have caused that sore—if anyone visits and the place *is* a sty, they're not going to leave and say, "He sure is a lousy housekeeper." You'll take the rap in any case. I can outwait you. ALSO MEANING: I can provoke innumerable scenes over the housework issue. Eventually doing all the housework yourself will be less painful to you than trying to get me to do half. Or I'll suggest we get a maid. She will do my share of the work. You will do yours. It's women's work.

"I've got nothing against sharing the housework, but you can't make me do it on your schedule." MEANING: Passive resistance. I'll do it when I damned well please, if at all. If my job is doing dishes, it's easier to do them once a week. If taking out laundry, once a month. If washing the floors, once a year. If you don't like it, do it yourself oftener, and then I won't do it at all.

"I hate it more than you. You don't mind it so much." MEANING: Housework is garbage work. It's the worst crap I've ever done. It's degrading and humiliating for someone of *my* intelligence to do it. But for someone of *your* intelligence.   * * *

"Housework is too trivial to even talk about." MEANING: It's even more trivial to do. Housework is beneath my status. My purpose in life is to deal with matters of significance. Yours is to deal with matters of insignificance. You should do the housework.

"This problem of housework is not a man-woman problem. In any relationship between two people one is going to have a stronger personality and dominate." MEANING: That stronger personality had better be *me*.

"In animal societies, wolves, for example, the top animal is usually a male even where he is not chosen for brute strength but on the basis of cunning and intelligence. Isn't that interesting?" MEANING: I have historical, psychological, anthropological and biological justification for keeping you down. How can you ask the top wolf to be equal?

"Women's Liberation isn't really a political movement." MEANING: The Revolution is coming too close to home. ALSO MEANING: I am only interested in how I am oppressed, not how I oppress others. Therefore the war, the draft and the university are political. Women's Liberation is not.

"Man's accomplishments have always depended on getting help from other people, mostly women. What great man would have accomplished what he did if he had to do his own housework?" MEANING: Oppression is built into the system and I, as the white American male, receive the benefits of this system. I don't want to give them up.

* * *

Participatory democracy begins at home. If you are planning to implement your politics, there are certain things to remember:

1. He *is* feeling it more than you. He's losing some leisure and you're gaining it. The measure of your oppression is his resistance.

2. A great many American men are not accustomed to doing monotonous repetitive work which never issues in any lasting, let alone important, achievement. This is why they would rather repair a cabinet than wash dishes. If human endeavors are like a pyramid with man's highest achievements at the top, then keeping oneself alive is at the bottom. Men have always had servants (us) to take care of this bottom strata of life while they have confined their efforts to the rarefied upper regions. It is thus ironic when they ask of women—where are your great painters, statesmen, etc. Mme Matisse ran a millinery shop so he could paint. Mrs. Martin Luther King kept his house and raised his babies.

3. It is a traumatizing experience for someone who has always thought of himself as being against any oppression or exploitation of one human being by another to realize that in his daily life he has been accepting and implementing (and benefiting from) this exploitation; that his rationalization is little different from that of the racist who says "Black people don't feel pain" (women don't mind doing the shitwork); and that the oldest form of oppression in history has been the oppression of 50% of the population by the other 50%.

4. Arm yourself with some knowledge of the psychology of oppressed peoples everywhere, and a few facts about the animal kingdom. I admit playing top wolf or who runs the gorillas is silly but as a last resort men bring it up all the time. Talk about bees. If you feel really hostile bring up the sex life of spiders. They have sex. She bites off his head.

The psychology of oppressed peoples is not silly. Jews, immigrants, black men and all women have employed the same psychological mechanisms to survive: admiring the oppressor, glorifying the oppressor, wanting to be like the oppressor, wanting the oppressor to like them, mostly because the oppressor held all the power.

5. In a sense, all men everywhere are slightly schizoid—divorced from the reality of maintaining life. This makes it easier for them to play games with it. It is almost a cliché that women feel greater grief at sending a son off to a war or losing him to that war because they bore him, suckled him, and raised him. The men who foment those wars did none of those things and have a more superficial estimate of the worth of human life. One hour a day is a low estimate of the amount of time one has to spend "keeping" oneself. By foisting this off on others, man has seven hours a week—one working day more to play with his mind and not his human needs. Over the course of generations it is easy to see whence evolved the horrifying abstractions of modern life.

6. With the death of each form of oppression, life changes and new forms evolve. English aristocrats at the turn of the century were horrified at the idea of enfranchising working men—were sure that it signalled the death of civilization and a return to barbarism. Some workingmen were even deceived by this line. Similarly with the minimum wage, abolition of slavery, and female suffrage. Life changes but it goes on. Don't fall for any line about the death of everything if men take a turn at the dishes. They will imply that you are holding back the Revolution (their Revolution). But you are advancing it (your Revolution).

7. Keep checking up. Periodically consider who's actually *doing* the jobs. These things have a way of backsliding so that a year later once again the woman is doing everything. After a year make a list of jobs the man has rarely if ever done. You will find cleaning pots, toilets, refrigerators and ovens high on the list. Use time sheets if necessary. He will accuse you of being petty. He is above that sort of thing (housework). Bear in mind what the worst jobs are, namely the ones that have to be done every day or several times a day. Also the ones that are dirty—it's more pleasant to pick up books, newspapers, etc., than to wash dishes. Alternate the bad jobs. It's the daily grind that gets you down. Also make sure that you don't have the responsibility for the housework with occasional help from him. "I'll cook dinner for you tonight" implies it's really your job and isn't he a nice guy to do some of it for you.

8. Most men had a rich and rewarding bachelor life during which they did not starve or become encrusted with crud or buried under the litter. There is a taboo that says women mustn't strain themselves in the presence of men—we haul around 50 lbs of groceries if we have to but aren't allowed to open a jar if there is someone around to do it for us. The reverse side of the

coin is that men aren't supposed to be able to take care of themselves without a woman. Both are excuses for making women do the housework.

9. Beware of the double whammy. He won't do the little things he always did because you're now a "Liberated Woman," right? Of course he won't do anything else either. * * *

I was just finishing this when my husband came in and asked what I was doing. Writing a paper on housework. Housework? he said, *Housework?* Oh my god how trivial can you get. A paper on housework.

THE FAMILY: PRESERVING AMERICA'S FUTURE

A Report of the Working Group on the Family.
November, 1986.

[The Working Group was appointed by Attorney General Edwin Meese in February, 1986, acting in his capacity as Chairman of the White House Domestic Policy Council. The Report was sent to President Reagan on December 2, 1986, by its Chairman, Undersecretary of Education Gary L. Bauer. The following excerpt is from the opening section of the Report.]

THE AMERICAN FAMILY

The American people have reached a new consensus about the family. Common sense has prevailed. After two decades of unprecedented attacks upon it, the family's worth—indeed, its essential role—in our free society has become the starting point in a national effort to reclaim a precious part of our heritage.

We are all "pro-family" now, but it was not always so. Only a few years ago, the American household of persons related by blood, marriage or adoption—the traditional definition of the family—seemed to be in peril. In academia, in the media, and even in government, radical critiques of family life were conspicuous. It was trendy to advocate "open marriage," "creative divorce," "alternate lifestyles," and to consider family life as a cause of "neurotic individualism."

Some experts taught that parenthood was too important for amateurs, that children should be raised in State-approved clinics, that a license should be required for procreation, that tax penalties should be levied against those with large families. Husbands and wives were urged to kick "the togetherness habit." A radical redefinition of "family" was underway. It reached its peak of confusion in 1980, when the White House Conference on Families foundered on the fundamental question of what constitutes a family and what makes for good family life.

This hostility toward the family was new to Americans, even as we experienced its devastating impact upon our communities, our neighborhoods, our circles of friends and relations, and in many cases, our own homes. But it was not entirely new. It was merely a manifestation during a period of domestic strife and social dislocation, of an animus long at war with the values and beliefs of democratic capitalism.

It is no accident that every totalitarian movement of the 20th Century has tried to destroy the family. Marx and Engels viewed family life as Cato viewed Carthage: it was to be destroyed. Their disciples in state socialism, from the Petrograd Soviet to the Third Reich, from Hanoi to Havana, have sought to crush family life. The essence of modern totalitarianism has been to substitute the power of the State for the rights, responsibilities, and authority of the family.

Everywhere the equation holds true: Where there are strong families, the freedom of the individual expands and the reach of the State contracts. Where family life weakens and fails, government advances, intrudes, and ultimately compels.

That was the anti-family agenda of many in the 1960s and 1970s: a governmental solution to every problem government had caused in the first place. Because government had fostered welfare dependency, more government programs were needed. Because government imposed crushing economic burdens upon families, more governmental redistribution of income was required. Somehow the bottom line was always the same: government would take resources from the families of America in order to "help" them.

That approach came to a crashing halt in 1980, when the American people gave an unprecedented electoral mandate to a new president. He trusted them to manage their own lives. He sought to empower them anew, with all the promise of a growing economy, safer communities, a more decent way of life.

By lightening the heavy hand of government—through historic tax cuts, regulatory reform, respect for State and local authority—he unleashed their energy and initiative. *The result has been the greatest period of expansion and job creation in modern times.*

By standing firm for neglected verities—law and order, a depoliticized judiciary, parental rights, and plain civility—he sparked a social renewal that is bringing reform to our schools, our courts, our safer streets and more decent neighborhoods.

His defense of the family is now widely imitated. Indeed, it has become fashionable to recognize that the restoration of family life is vital to our society's future. But some have learned only part of his lesson. They finally see the import of the family, but they do not yet understand the basics of a pro-family policy.

That we need such a policy is clear. The statistics on the pathology impacting many American families are overwhelming. Consider the following statistical portrait of the 3.6 million children who began their formal schooling in the United States in September of 1986.

- 14 percent were children of unmarried parents.
- 40 percent will live in a broken home before they reach 18.
- Between one-quarter and one-third are latchkey children with no one to greet them when they come home from school.

Other trends are equally disturbing. For example:

- In 1960, there were 393,000 divorces in America; by 1985, that number had increased more than threefold to 1,187,000.

- Births out of wedlock, as a percentage of all births, increased more than 450 percent in just 30 years.

The family needs help!

That is the reason for this report: to attempt to distill the essentials of what government should, and should not do concerning the family. To individuals and organizations of all shades of opinion earlier this year, we posed a question: "What can we do to help America's families?" The response was overwhelming; and while the specific suggestions differed greatly, it became clear that there is a new awareness among the American people of a basic truth many had forgotten or overlooked. *It is as simple as this: private choices have public effects. The way our fellow citizens choose to live affects many other lives. For example, there is no such thing as private drug abuse. The abandonment of spouse and children hurts far beyond the home. Illegitimacy exacts a price from society as well as from the individuals involved. Child Pornography and obscenity degrade the community, especially its women and children, as well as those who patronize it. The casual disregard of human life ultimately imperils all those who are weak, infirm, and dependent upon the compassion and resources of others.*

It simply is not true that what we do is our business only. For in the final analysis, the kind of people we are—the kind of nation we will be for generations hence—is the sum of what millions of Americans do in their otherwise private lives. If increasing numbers of our children are born or raised outside of marriage and if youth drug and alcohol abuse remains at current levels, there will be staggering consequences for us all: greater poverty, more crime, a less educated workforce, mounting demands for government spending, higher taxes, worsening deficits, and crises we have only begun to anticipate.

If an ever larger percentage of adults choose not to marry or choose to remain without children, there will be public policy implications. For example, the withering of the American family has already had unexpected demographic consequences. With current fertility levels and without immigration, our population will decline a problem we share with much of the western world. We can forsee the graying of America, with new strains on social security, the manpower needs of the economy, and the viability of the volunteer armed forces. For another example, our entire society is now confronted with the fallout from the sexual revolution of the last quarter-century. Was it really just a matter of private choice that has ravaged the country with an epidemic of sexually transmitted diseases, many of them new and virulent? Is it a private matter that results in staggering medical bills distributed among consumers (through higher insurance premiums) and among taxpayers (through taxes to support medical research and care)?

Who pays the bills? In this as in so many other cases, the American family pays, even when it stands apart from the pathologies that inflict such costs, economic and social, upon the body politic.

The family has paid too much. It has lost too much of its authority to courts and rule-writers, too much of its voice in education and social policy, too much of its resources to public officials at all levels. We have made dramatic progress, during the past six years of economic reform, in turning back those resources to the men and women who earn them through labor, invention, and investment. Now we face the unfinished agenda: turning back to the households of this land the autonomy that once was theirs, in a society stable and secure, where the family can generate and nurture what no government can ever produce—Americans who will responsibly exercise their freedom and, if necessary, defend it.

It is time to reaffirm some "home truths" and to restate the obvious. Intact families are good. Families who choose to have children are making a desirable decision. Mothers and fathers who then decide to spend a good deal of time raising those children themselves rather than leaving it to others are demonstrably doing a good thing for those children. Countless Americans do these things every day. They ask for no special favors—they do these things naturally out of love, loyalty and a commitment to the future. They are the bedrock of our society. Public policy and the culture in general must support and reaffirm these decisions—not undermine and be hostile to them or send a message that we are neutral. [Report of the Working Group on the Family, pp. 1–3; footnotes omitted; emphasis in original.]

CONTRACT WITH THE AMERICAN FAMILY

Christian Coalition, May 1995.

INTRODUCTION

In the 1994 midterm elections, the American people elected the first Republican Congress in 40 years. The message of the election was clear: the American people want lower taxes, less government, strong families, protection of innocent human life, and traditional values.

The 104th Congress devoted its first hundred days to the Contract with America, including a Balanced Budget Amendment, tax relief for families, welfare reform, and term limits. * * *

But the problems our nation faces are not all economic. The American people are increasingly concerned about the breakup of the family and a general moral decay. * * *

The Contract with the American Family is a bold agenda for Congress intended to strengthen families and restore traditional values. Congress would be well advised to act with all deliberate speed. The provisions in the Contract enjoy support from 60 to 90 percent of the American people.

These items do not represent the pro-family movement's entire agenda. This contract is designed to be the first word, not the last word, in developing a bold and incremental start to strengthening the family and restoring values.

1. *Restoring Religious Equality:* A constitutional amendment to protect the religious liberties of Americans. * * *

2. *Returning Education Control to the Local Level:* Transfer funding of the federal Department of Education to families and local school boards. * * *

3. *Promoting School Choice:* Enactment of legislation that will enhance parents' choice of schools for their children. * * *

4. *Protecting Parental Rights:* Enactment of a Parental Rights Act and defeat of the U.N. Convention on the Rights of the Child. * * *

5. *Family–Friendly Tax Relief:* Reduce the tax burden on the American family, eliminate the marriage penalty, and pass the *Mothers and Homemakers' Rights Act* to remedy the unequal treatment that homemakers receive under the Internal Revenue Service Code with respect to saving for retirement. * * *

6. *Restoring Respect for Human Life:* Protecting innocent human life and ending funds to organizations that promote and perform abortions. * * *

7. *Encouraging Support of Private Charities:* Enactment of legislation to enhance contributions to private charities as a first step toward transforming the bureaucratic welfare state into a system of private and faith-based compassion. * * *

8. *Restricting Pornography:* Protecting children from exposure to pornography and from sexual exploitation by pornographers. * * *

9. *Privatizing the Arts:* The National Endowment for the Arts, National Endowment for the Humanities, Corporation for Public Broadcasting, and Legal Services Corporation should become voluntary organizations funded through private contributions. * * *

10. *Crime Victim Restitution:* Funds given to states to build prisons should require work and drug testing for prisoners and restitution to victims. * * *

CONCLUSION

The *Contract With The American Family* is the first word, not the last word, on a cultural agenda for the 104th Congress during the post–100–day period. The ideas included in this document are designed to help Congress fulfill its mandate for dramatic change. * * *

The American people now have a Congress that is receptive to their desire for religious liberty, stronger families, lower taxes, local control of education, and tougher laws against crime. With the *Contract with the American Family,* the nation now has an agenda with broad support that addresses time-honored values for the 104th Congress and beyond.

Notes on Feminists *and* Marriage

1. Are Cronan's criticisms of the laws regulating sexual interaction in marriage valid today? Wives still are not paid for household services and, in the absence of an agreement for compensation, may not even be entitled to reimbursement for their services in the family business. See, e.g., Leatherman v. Leatherman, 297 N.C. 618, 256 S.E.2d 793 (1979), discussed in Peter McLean III, Note, Domestic Relations—The Presumption of Gratuitous Services—Must a Wife Work for Free?, 16 Wake Forest L.Rev. 235, 246 (1980) ("The significance of *Leatherman* lies not in any major change in established law, but rather in its affirmation of an outdated rule."). Did North Carolina's enactment of an Equitable Distribution Law in 1981 cure the harsh effect of *Leatherman*? See White v. White, 312 N.C. 770, 776–77, 324 S.E.2d 829, 832–33 (1985), set out at p. 299 infra. As we have seen, housewives continue to experience difficulties in enforcing their legal right to be supported by their husbands during marriage and prior to separation, or in obtaining actual control over property legally subject to their management

and control in community property states. But we have also noted rapid change in laws governing a married woman's name, and some change in laws determining her legal domicile. As we will learn in Chapter Five, some states have enacted laws prohibiting rape in marriage (e.g., West's Ann.Cal.Pen.Code § 262 (1980)), and efforts are being made to control domestic violence (e.g., West's Ann.Cal.Civ. Proc.Code §§ 540–553, effective July 1, 1980). Are these modest reforms enough to negate Cronan's thesis?

2. Is Mainardi's account of the politics of housework exaggerated? Alice Rossi noted in 1972 that "women devote to household chores four times as many hours as they do to interaction with their husbands, and three times as many hours as they do to interaction with their children." (Alice S. Rossi, Family Development in a Changing World, 128 Amer.J.Psychiat. 1057, 1059 (1972)). Jessie Bernard pointed out in the same year that men and women have very different experiences in marriage and that "being a housewife makes women sick." (Jessie Shirley Bernard, The Future of Marriage 3–53, at 48 (1972)). Ann Oakley, who interviewed forty London housewives in 1971, found that seventy percent were dissatisfied with house*work,* even though nearly half valued the autonomy of being "one's own boss" that they enjoyed as house*wives.* (Ann Oakley, The Sociology of Housework 182–84 (1974)). Is true equality between men and women possible as long as women continue to accept the social division of labor that makes women primarily responsible for child rearing and housework?

3. What do you make of the following sentence in President Carter's Proclamation of Working Mothers' Day, 1980, quoted at p. 247 supra: "[w]orking mothers do not shed homemaking and parental responsibilities; they merely add the demands of a job to those of wife and mother." Is this sentence intended as a factual description or as the statement of a normative obligation? Do working fathers shed homemaking and parental responsibilities when they leave for the office or plant? Perhaps it is more significant to ask whether most men have ever placed their duties as husband and father on a par with the demands of their jobs. When both parents work, who takes care of the children? See generally Sheila B. Kamerman, Alfred J. Kahn & Paul Kingston, Maternity Policies and Working Women (1983).

4. Are the members of Attorney General Meese's Working Group on the Family for or against government intervention in the family? The Working Group seems particularly anxious to prevent federal judicial intervention into the family. In a later section of its report entitled "Legal Status of the Family," the Working Group criticizes a series of United States Supreme Court cases that it characterizes as having a "common thread" of repudiating "State or Federal statutes or regulations based upon traditional relationships between spouses and between parents and children." These cases include several[1] that struck down state or federal laws limiting welfare benefits or food stamps to persons living in nonmarital cohabitation or communal homes (characterized as having "gutted attempts to enforce the moral order of the family as the basis for public assistance"); equalized some rights of illegitimate children with those accorded

1. King v. Smith, 392 U.S. 309, 88 S.Ct. 2128, 20 L.Ed.2d 1118 (1968) (invalidating Alabama's "substitute father" regulation, which denied welfare benefits to children of a mother who cohabited with a man outside of marriage, whether or not he had a legal obligation to support her children); New Jersey Welfare Rights Organization v. Cahill, 411 U.S. 619, 93 S.Ct. 1700, 36 L.Ed.2d 543 (1973) (invalidating a New Jersey statute that denied public assistance to illegitimate children); and United States Department of Agriculture v. Moreno, 413 U.S. 528, 93 S.Ct. 2821, 37 L.Ed.2d 782 (1973) (invalidating a Food Stamp Act provision that based eligibility for food stamps in part on whether an individual lived in a household with related or unrelated members).

legitimate children [2] (characterized as having "put an end to legal preference for the intact family"); recognized a woman's right to choose whether to have an abortion [3] (characterized as having struck down "State attempts to protect the life of children in utero, to protect paternal interest in the life of the child before birth, and to respect parental authority over minor children in abortion decisions"); and a case striking down a zoning law that limited the right of members of an extended family to live in the same household [4] (characterized as a case which "in effect forbade any community in America to define 'family' in a traditional way"). How can this "fatally flawed line of court decisions" be corrected? While stating that "we do not presume to endorse or oppose" any such suggestion in the Report, the Working Group notes that others have proposed the use of "mechanisms created by the Constitution itself." What mechanisms? "These include the appointment of new judges and their confirmation by the Senate, the limitation of the jurisdiction of Federal courts, and, in extreme cases, amendment of the Constitution itself." Report of the Working Group on the Family, "The Family: Preserving America's Future," at 10–12 (November 1986). Professor Frances Olsen, discussing the nineteenth century doctrine of family privacy, argues that nonintervention functioned at that time as legal support for the hierarchical family. See Frances E. Olsen, The Myth of State Intervention in the Family, 18 U.Mich.J.L.Reform 835, 845–55 (1985). Does the Working Group want to return to the nineteenth century?

5. What do you make of the Christian Coalition's "Contract with the American Family"? Unlike the Meese Working Group's document, the Coalition takes a broad view of issues that are necessary to strengthen the family, ranging as it does from an endorsement of voluntary prayer in the public schools to IRAs for homemakers. Leaving aside its predictable opposition to abortion, the Coalition is quite sophisticated in some of its proposals. Thus, its opposition to pornography is aimed at banning sexually explicit material from the Internet. Its encouragement for private charities includes support for legislation giving taxpayers "the choice between having their tax dollars subsidize government welfare programs or helping a charity." Contract With The American Family 20 (1995). Its desire to privatize the Arts expresses disapproval of the NEA's funding of "controversial works that denigrate the religious beliefs and moral values of

2. Levy v. Louisiana, 391 U.S. 68, 88 S.Ct. 1509, 20 L.Ed.2d 436, rehearing denied 393 U.S. 898, 89 S.Ct. 65, 21 L.Ed.2d 185 (1968) (invalidating a Louisiana statute that prevented an illegitimate child from recovering for the wrongful death of its mother when such recoveries were authorized for legitimate children); Glona v. American Guarantee and Liability Insurance Co., 391 U.S. 73, 88 S.Ct. 1515, 20 L.Ed.2d 441, rehearing denied 393 U.S. 898, 89 S.Ct. 66, 21 L.Ed.2d 185 (1968) (upholding right of natural mother to recover for the wrongful death of her illegitimate child); Gomez v. Perez, 409 U.S. 535, 93 S.Ct. 872, 35 L.Ed.2d 56 (1973) (invalidating a Texas statute that required a father to support his legitimate, but not illegitimate, children); and Weber v. Aetna Cas. & Sur. Co., 406 U.S. 164, 92 S.Ct. 1400, 31 L.Ed.2d 768 (1972) (invalidating a Louisiana statute that prevented dependent, unacknowledged illegitimate children from recovering workers' compensation death benefits for the death of their natural father on an equal basis with dependent legitimate children).

3. Roe v. Wade, 410 U.S. 179, 93 S.Ct. 756, 35 L.Ed.2d 147 (1973) (recognizing woman's right, in consultation with her physician, to choose whether to terminate her pregnancy; right must be balanced over course of pregnancy against state's competing interests in her health and potential life of the fetus); Planned Parenthood of Central Missouri v. Danforth, 428 U.S. 52, 96 S.Ct. 2831, 49 L.Ed.2d 788 (1976) (invalidating a Missouri statute that required the consent of a pregnant woman's spouse to an abortion performed during the first 12 weeks of pregnancy, unless a physician had certified that the procedure was necessary to save the woman's life; also invalidating a similar provision in the same statute that required parental consent to an abortion performed on an unmarried woman under the age of 18).

4. Moore v. City of East Cleveland, 431 U.S. 494, 97 S.Ct. 1932, 52 L.Ed.2d 531 (1977).

mainstream Americans." Id., at 23. When, by the way, did the Legal Services Corporation become one of the "Arts"? The Coalition's explanation of this part of the Contract is a thinly-disguised attack on divorce:

> What many Americans don't realize is that divorce proceedings are a high priority for many legal services grantees. The LSC alone paid for 210,000 divorces in 1990, at an estimated cost to taxpayers of $50 million. Yet, as study after study has revealed, divorce is not helping our nation's poor break out of poverty. Rather, as historian Barbara Dafoe Whitehead has pointed out: "Children in single-parent families are six times as likely to be poor. * * *." Therefore, an agency that was established to help ameliorate poverty is instead fostering it through its financing of divorce actions.

Id., at 25 (footnotes omitted). How successful do you think the Coalition will be in getting its Contract enacted? If this Contract represents only the entering wedge of the Coalition's cultural agenda, what items do you expect will be among its subsequent proposals?

6. Do shared household arrangements offer a way for women to achieve equality in the family and lessen their traditional burdens of housework and child care? During the history of American society, such options have included religious communities in the sixteenth century, agricultural and utopian communes in the eighteenth and nineteenth centuries, and student and counter-culture urban and rural communes in the twentieth century. Do all of these alternatives to the traditional nuclear family have the same capacity to foster equality between men and women in family life? Are some of them more repressive than traditional marriage? Unmarried and unrelated persons who wish to share a household may encounter various legal obstacles, including zoning ordinances, that limit their choices. See, e.g., Village of Belle Terre v. Boraas, 416 U.S. 1, 94 S.Ct. 1536, 39 L.Ed.2d 797 (1974) (upholding an ordinance limiting the number of unmarried and unrelated persons who could share a household to two); compare City of Santa Barbara v. Adamson, 27 Cal.3d 123, 164 Cal.Rptr. 539, 610 P.2d 436 (1980) (striking down, as violative of the right to privacy contained in the California State Constitution, a similar ordinance limiting the number to five persons). See generally, Jonathan Shor, Comment, All in the "Family": Legal Problems of Communes, 7 Harv.Civ.Rights–Civ.Lib.L.Rev. 393 (1972). Betty Friedan has proposed the creation of new housing forms that would provide shared cooking, dining, and child care facilities for several families with separate private apartments for other functions. See Betty Friedan, The Second Stage 286–87 (1981). Is this proposal a more promising alternative than those described above? Would it be acceptable to the members of the Working Group on the Family? To the Christian Coalition?

ii. Same–Sex Marriage

BAKER v. NELSON

Supreme Court of Minnesota, en banc, 1971.
291 Minn. 310, 191 N.W.2d 185, appeal dismissed 409
U.S. 810, 93 S.Ct. 37, 34 L.Ed.2d 65 (1972).

PETERSON, JUSTICE. The questions for decision are whether a marriage of two persons of the same sex is authorized by state statutes and, if not, whether state authorization is constitutionally compelled.

Petitioners, Richard John Baker and James Michael McConnell, both adult male persons, made application to respondent, Gerald R. Nelson, clerk of Hennepin County District Court, for a marriage license, pursuant to Minn.St. 517.08. Respondent declined to issue the license on the sole ground that petitioners were of the same sex, it being undisputed that there were otherwise no statutory impediments to a heterosexual marriage by either petitioner.

The trial court, quashing an alternative writ of mandamus, ruled that respondent was not required to issue a marriage license to petitioners and specifically directed that a marriage license not be issued to them. This appeal is from those orders. We affirm.

1. Petitioners contend, first, that the absence of an express statutory prohibition against same-sex marriages evinces a legislative intent to authorize such marriages. We think, however, that a sensible reading of the statute discloses a contrary intent.

Minn.St. c. 517, which governs "marriage," employs that term as one of common usage, meaning the state of union between persons of the opposite sex.[1] It is unrealistic to think that the original draftsmen of our marriage statutes, which date from territorial days, would have used the term in any different sense. The term is of contemporary significance as well, for the present statute is replete with words of heterosexual import such as "husband and wife" and "bride and groom" (the latter words inserted by L.1969, c. 1145, § 3, subd. 3).

We hold, therefore, that Minn.St. c. 517 does not authorize marriage between persons of the same sex and that such marriages are accordingly prohibited.

2. Petitioners contend, second, that Minn.St. c. 517, so interpreted, is unconstitutional. There is a dual aspect to this contention: The prohibition of a same-sex marriage denies petitioners a fundamental right guaranteed by the Ninth Amendment to the United States Constitution, arguably made applicable to the states by the Fourteenth Amendment, and petitioners are deprived of liberty and property without due process and are denied the equal protection of the laws, both guaranteed by the Fourteenth Amendment.[2]

These constitutional challenges have in common the assertion that the right to marry without regard to the sex of the parties is a fundamental right of all persons and that restricting marriage to only couples of the opposite sex is irrational and invidiously discriminatory. We are not independently persuaded by these contentions and do not find support for them in any decisions of the United States Supreme Court.

The institution of marriage as a union of man and woman, uniquely involving the procreation and rearing of children within a family, is as old as the book of Genesis. Skinner v. Oklahoma ex rel. Williamson, 316 U.S. 535, 541, 62 S.Ct. 1110, 1113, 86 L.Ed. 1655, 1660 (1942), which invalidated

---

1. Webster's Third New International Dictionary (1966) p. 1384 gives this primary meaning to marriage: "1 a: the state of being united to a person of the opposite sex as husband or wife."

Black, Law Dictionary (4 ed.) p. 1123 states this definition: "Marriage * * * is the civil status, condition, or relation of one man and one women united in law for life, for the discharge to each other and the community of the duties legally incumbent on those whose association is founded on the distinction of sex."

2. We dismiss without discussion petitioners' additional contentions that the statute contravenes the First Amendment and Eighth Amendment of the United States Constitution.

Oklahoma's Habitual Criminal Sterilization Act on equal protection grounds, stated in part: "Marriage and procreation are fundamental to the very existence and survival of the race." This historic institution manifestly is more deeply founded than the asserted contemporary concept of marriage and societal interests for which petitioners contend. The due process clause of the Fourteenth Amendment is not a charter for restructuring it by judicial legislation.

Griswold v. Connecticut, 381 U.S. 479, 85 S.Ct. 1678, 14 L.Ed.2d 510 (1965), upon which petitioners rely, does not support a contrary conclusion. A Connecticut criminal statute prohibiting the use of contraceptives by married couples was held invalid, as violating the due process clause of the Fourteenth Amendment. The basic premise of that decision, however, was that the state, having authorized marriage, was without power to intrude upon the right of privacy inherent in the marital relationship. Mr. Justice Douglas, author of the majority opinion, wrote that this criminal statute "operates directly on an intimate relation of husband and wife," 381 U.S. 482, 85 S.Ct. 1680, 14 L.Ed.2d 513, and that the very idea of its enforcement by police search of "the sacred precincts of marital bedrooms for telltale signs of the use of contraceptives * * * is repulsive to the notions of privacy surrounding the marriage relationship," 381 U.S. 485, 85 S.Ct. 1682, 14 L.Ed.2d 516. In a separate opinion for three justices, Mr. Justice Goldberg similarly abhorred this state disruption of "the traditional relation of the family—a relation as old and as fundamental as our entire civilization." 381 U.S. 496, 85 S.Ct. 1688, 14 L.Ed.2d 522.[3]

The equal protection clause of the Fourteenth Amendment, like the due process clause, is not offended by the state's classification of persons authorized to marry. There is no irrational or invidious discrimination. Petitioners note that the state does not impose upon heterosexual married couples a condition that they have a proved capacity or declared willingness to procreate, posing a rhetorical demand that this court must read such condition into the statute if same-sex marriages are to be prohibited. Even assuming that such a condition would be neither unrealistic nor offensive under the *Griswold* rationale, the classification is no more than theoretically imperfect. We are reminded, however, that "abstract symmetry" is not demanded by the Fourteenth Amendment.[4]

Loving v. Virginia, 388 U.S. 1, 87 S.Ct. 1817, 18 L.Ed.2d 1010 (1967), upon which petitioners additionally rely, does not militate against this conclusion. Virginia's antimiscegenation statute, prohibiting interracial marriages, was invalidated solely on the grounds of its patent racial discrimination. As

3. The difference between the majority opinion of Mr. Justice Douglas and the concurring opinion of Mr. Justice Goldberg was that the latter wrote extensively concerning this right of marital privacy as one preserved to the individual by the Ninth Amendment. He stopped short, however, of an implication that the Ninth Amendment was made applicable against the states by the Fourteenth Amendment.

4. See, Patsone v. Pennsylvania, 232 U.S. 138, 144, 34 S.Ct. 281, 282, 58 L.Ed. 539, 543 (1914). As stated in Tigner v. Texas, 310 U.S. 141, 147, 60 S.Ct. 879, 882, 84 L.Ed. 1124, 1128, 130 A.L.R. 1321, 1324 (1940), and reiterated in Skinner v. Oklahoma ex rel. Williamson, 316 U.S. 535, 540, 62 S.Ct. 1110, 1113, 86 L.Ed. 1655, 1659, "[t]he Constitution does not require things which are different in fact or opinion to be treated in law as though they were the same."

Mr. Chief Justice Warren wrote for the court (388 U.S. 12, 87 S.Ct. 1824, 18 L.Ed.2d 1018):

> "Marriage is one of the 'basic civil rights of man,' fundamental to our very existence and survival. Skinner v. Oklahoma, 316 U.S. 535, 541, 62 S.Ct. 1110, 86 L.Ed. 1655 (1942). See also Maynard v. Hill, 125 U.S. 190, 8 S.Ct. 723, 31 L.Ed. 654 (1888). To deny this fundamental freedom on so unsupportable a basis as the racial classifications embodied in these statutes, classifications so directly subversive of the principle of equality at the heart of the Fourteenth Amendment, is surely to deprive all the State's citizens of liberty without due process of law. The Fourteenth Amendment requires that the freedom of choice to marry not be restricted by invidious racial discriminations.[5] "

Loving does indicate that not all state restrictions upon the right to marry are beyond reach of the Fourteenth Amendment. But in commonsense and in a constitutional sense, there is a clear distinction between a marital restriction based merely upon race and one based upon the fundamental difference in sex.

We hold, therefore, that Minn.St. c. 517 does not offend the First, Eighth, Ninth, or Fourteenth Amendments to the United States Constitution.

Affirmed.

BAEHR v. LEWIN

Supreme Court of Hawaii, 1993.
74 Hawaii 530, 852 P.2d 44.

[Plaintiffs, three same-sex couples (two female and one male) alleged that in December 1990 each had applied to the Hawaii Department of Health for a license to enter into a civil marriage; that the license had been denied on the sole basis that the applicant couples were of the same sex; and that in all other respects, the applicants were free to marry. These allegations were not disputed. The defendant Lewin, Director of the Department of Health, responded that the Department had indicated in a letter sent to each couple its view that the law of Hawaii does not treat a union between persons of the same sex as a valid marriage; that, accordingly, the Department declined to issue a license to these applicants; and that, even if the Department were to issue a license, the resulting union would not be a valid marriage under Hawaii law.

[On May 1, 1991, plaintiffs filed a complaint for injunctive and declaratory relief, alleging that defendant's interpretation and application of the marriage statute violated their right to privacy and their right to equal protection and due process of the law under the Hawaii Constitution. Plaintiffs did not allege a violation of the United States Constitution.

[On July 9, 1991, Director Lewin filed a motion for judgment on the pleadings. In response, plaintiffs argued that their complaint could not be

---

5. See, also, McLaughlin v. Florida, 379 U.S. 184, 85 S.Ct. 283, 13 L.Ed.2d 222 (1964), in which the United States Supreme Court, for precisely the same reason of classification based only upon race, struck down a Florida criminal statute which proscribed and punished habitual cohabitation only if one of an unmarried couple was white and the other black.

dismissed for failure to state a claim unless it appeared beyond doubt that they could prove no set of facts that would entitle them to the relief sought.

[The circuit court heard argument on defendant's motion on September 3, 1991, and filed its order granting the motion and dismissing plaintiff's complaint with prejudice on October 1, 1991. Plaintiffs appealed, and on May 5, 1993, the Hawaii Supreme Court sustained the judgment on the grounds of privacy and due process, reversed the judgment on the equal protection claim, and remanded the matter for trial on that issue.

[There is no majority opinion in *Baehr*. The Court that heard the appeal was composed of two Justices of the Hawaii Supreme Court, Acting Chief Justice Moon and Justice Levinson; two Intermediate Court of Appeals Judges appointed *pro tem*, Chief Judge Burns and Judge Heen; and a retired Supreme Court Justice, Justice Hayashi, appointed to fill the vacant seat on the Court. The panel filed three opinions: a plurality opinion written by Justice Levinson and signed by Acting Chief Justice Moon; a concurring opinion by Chief Judge Burns; and a dissenting opinion by Judge Heen with which Justice Hayashi (whose appointment had expired before the decision was filed) expressed agreement. Only the equal protection issue is set out in the following excerpt.]

LEVINSON, JUDGE, in which MOON, CHIEF JUDGE, joins.

* * *

II.   JUDGMENT ON THE PLEADINGS WAS ERRONEOUSLY GRANTED

* * *

C.   *Inasmuch as the Applicant Couples Claim That the Express Terms of HRS § 572–1, which Discriminates against Same–Sex Marriages, Violate Their Rights under the Equal Protection Clause of the Hawaii Constitution, the Applicant Couples Are Entitled to an Evidentiary Hearing to Determine Whether Lewin Can Demonstrate that HRS § 572–1 Furthers Compelling State Interests and Is Narrowly Drawn to Avoid Unnecessary Abridgments of Constitutional Rights.*

In addition to the alleged violation of their constitutional rights to privacy and due process of law, the applicant couples contend that they have been denied the equal protection of the laws as guaranteed by article I, section 5 of the Hawaii Constitution. On appeal, the plaintiffs urge and, on the state of the bare record before us, we agree that the circuit court erred when it concluded, *as a matter of law*, that: (1) homosexuals do not constitute a "suspect class" for purposes of equal protection analysis under article I, section 5 of the Hawaii Constitution; [17] (2) the classification created by HRS

---

17. For the reasons stated *infra* in this opinion, it is irrelevant, for purposes of the constitutional analysis germane to this case, whether homosexuals constitute a "suspect class" because it is immaterial whether the plaintiffs, or any of them, are homosexuals. *See supra* note 14. [Footnote 14 reads as follows]:

  14. For the reasons stated *infra* in this opinion, it is irrelevant, for purposes of the

constitutional analysis germane to this case, whether homosexuality constitutes "an immutable trait" because it is immaterial whether the plaintiffs, or any of them, are homosexuals. Specifically, the issue is not material to the equal protection analysis set forth in section II.C of this opinion. * * * Its resolution is unnecessary to our ruling that HRS § 572–1, both on its face as applied, denies same-sex couples access to the

§ 572–1 is not subject to "strict scrutiny," but must satisfy only the "rational relationship" test; and (3) HRS § 572–1 satisfies the rational relationship test because the legislature "obviously designed [it] to promote the general welfare interests of the community by sanctioning traditional man-woman family units and procreation."

1.   Marriage is a state-conferred legal partnership status, the existence of which gives rise to a multiplicity of rights and benefits reserved exclusively to that particular relation.

The power to regulate marriage is a sovereign function reserved exclusively to the respective states.   * * * By its very nature, the power to regulate the marriage relation includes the power to determine the requisites of a valid marriage contract and to control the qualifications of the contracting parties, the forms and procedures necessary to solemnize the marriage, the duties and obligations it creates, its effect upon property and other rights, and the grounds for marital dissolution.   * * *

* * *

The applicant couples correctly contend that the DOH's refusal to allow them to marry on the basis that they are members of the same sex deprives them of access to a multiplicity of rights and benefits that are contingent upon that status.   * * * For present purposes, it is not disputed that the applicant couples would be entitled to all of these marital rights and benefits, but for the fact that they are denied access to the state-conferred legal status of marriage.

2.   HRS § 572–1, on its face, discriminates based on sex against the applicant couples in the exercise of the civil right of marriage, thereby implicating the equal protection clause of article I, section 5 of the Hawaii Constitution.

Notwithstanding the state's acknowledged stewardship over the institution of marriage, the extent of permissible state regulation of the right of access to the marital relationship is subject to constitutional limitations or constraints.   * * *   It has been held that a state may deny the right to marry only for compelling reasons.   * * *

The equal protection clauses of the United States and Hawaii Constitutions are not mirror images of one another.   The fourteenth amendment to the United States Constitution somewhat concisely provides, in relevant part, that a state may not "deny to any person within its jurisdiction the equal protection of the laws."   Hawaii's counterpart is more elaborate.   Article I,

marital status and its concomitant rights and benefits.   Its resolution is also unnecessary to our conclusion that it is the state's regulation of access to the marital status, on the basis of the applicants' sex, that gives rise to the question whether the applicant couples have been denied the equal protection of the laws in violation of article I, section 5 of the Hawaii Constitution.

And, in particular, it is immaterial to the exercise of "strict scrutiny" review, * * * inasmuch as we are unable to perceive any conceivable relevance of the issue to the ultimate conclusion of law—which, in the absence of further evidentiary proceedings, we cannot reach at this time—regarding whether HRS § 572–1 furthers compelling state interests and is narrowly drawn to avoid unnecessary abridgements of constitutional rights.   * * *

In light of the above, we disagree with Chief Judge Burns's position that "questions whether heterosexuality, homosexuality, bisexuality, and asexuality are 'biologically fated' are relevant questions of fact."   * * * This preoccupation seems simply to restate the immaterial question whether sexual orientation is an "immutable trait."

section 5 of the Hawaii Constitution provides in relevant part that "[n]o person shall * * * be denied the equal protection of the laws, *nor be denied the enjoyment of the person's civil rights or be discriminated against in the exercise thereof because of* race, religion, *sex,* or ancestry." (Emphasis added.) Thus, by its plain language, the Hawaii Constitution prohibits state-sanctioned discrimination against any person in the exercise of his or her civil rights on the basis of sex.

"The freedom to marry has long been recognized as one of the vital personal rights essential to the orderly pursuit of happiness by free [people]." *Loving,* * * *. So "fundamental" does the United States Supreme Court consider the institution of marriage that it has deemed marriage to be "one of the 'basic civil rights of [men and women.]' " * * *.

Black's Law Dictionary (6th ed. 1990) defines "civil rights" as synonymous with "civil liberties." * * * "Civil liberties" are defined, *inter alia,* as "[p]ersonal, natural rights guaranteed and protected by Constitution; *e.g.,* * * * freedom from discrimination * * *. Body of law dealing with natural liberties * * * which invade equal rights of others. Constitutionally, they are restraints on government." This court has held, in another context, that such "privilege[s] of citizenship * * * cannot be taken away [on] any of the prohibited bases of race, religion, *sex* or ancestry" enumerated in article I, section 5 of the Hawaii Constitution and that to do so violates the right to equal protection of the laws as guaranteed by that constitutional provision. *State v. Levinson,* 71 Haw. 492, 499, 795 P.2d 845, 849–50 (1990) (exclusion of female jurors solely because of their sex denies them equal protection under Hawaii Constitution) (emphasis added).

Rudimentary principles of statutory construction render manifest the fact that, by its plain language, HRS § 572–1 restricts the marital relation to a male and a female.

* * * Accordingly, on its face and (as Lewin admits) as applied, HRS § 572–1 denies same-sex couples access to the marital status and its concomitant rights and benefits. It is the state's regulation of access to the status of married persons, on the basis of the applicants' sex, that gives rise to the question whether the applicant couples have been denied the equal protection of the laws in violation of article I, section 5 of the Hawaii Constitution.

Relying primarily on four decisions construing the law of other jurisdictions,[21] Lewin contends that "the fact that homosexual [sic—actually, same-sex] [22] partners cannot form a state-licensed marriage is not the product of

21. The four decisions are *Jones v. Hallahan,* 501 S.W.2d 588 (Ky.1973); *Baker v. Nelson,* 291 Minn. 310, 191 N.W.2d 185 (1971), *appeal dismissed,* 409 U.S. 810, 93 S.Ct. 37, 34 L.Ed.2d 65 (1972); *De Santo v. Barnsley, supra;* and *Singer v. Hara,* 11 Wash.App. 247, 522 P.2d 1187, *review denied,* 84 Wash.2d 1008 (1974).

22. *See supra* note 11.

[Footnote 11 reads as follows]:

11. "Homosexual" and "same-sex" marriages are not synonymous; by the same token, a "heterosexual" same-sex marriage is, in theory, not oxymoronic. A "homosexu-

al" person is defined as "[o]ne sexually attracted to another of the same sex." *Taber's Cyclopedic Medical Dictionary* 839 (16th ed. 1989). "Homosexuality" is "sexual desire or behavior directed toward a person or persons of one's own sex." *Webster's Encyclopedic Unabridged Dictionary of the English Language* 680 (1989). Conversely, "heterosexuality" is "[s]exual attraction for one of the opposite sex," *Taber's Cyclopedic Medical Dictionary* at 827, or "sexual feeling or behavior directed toward a person or persons of the opposite sex." *Webster's Encyclopedic Unabridged Dictionary of the English Lan-*

impermissible discrimination" implicating equal protection considerations, but rather "a function of their biologic inability as a couple to satisfy the definition of the status to which they aspire." * * * Put differently, Lewin proposes that "the right of persons of the same sex to marry one another does not exist because marriage, by definition and usage, means a special relationship between a man and a woman." * * * We believe Lewin's argument to be circular and unpersuasive.

Two of the decisions upon which Lewin relies are demonstrably inapposite to the appellant couples' claim. In *Baker v. Nelson,* 291 Minn. 310, 191 N.W.2d 185 (1971), *appeal dismissed,* 409 U.S. 810, 93 S.Ct. 37, 34 L.Ed.2d 65 (1972), the questions for decision were whether a marriage of two persons of the same sex was authorized by state statutes and, if not, whether state authorization was compelled by various provisions of the United States Constitution, including the fourteenth amendment. Regarding the first question, the *Baker* court arrived at the same conclusion as have we with respect to HRS § 572–1: by their plain language, the Minnesota marriage statutes precluded same-sex marriages. Regarding the second question, however, the court merely held that the United States Constitution was not offended; apparently, no state constitutional questions were raised and none were addressed.

De Santo v. Barnsley, 328 Pa.Super. 181, 476 A.2d 952 (1984), is also distinguishable. In *De Santo,* the court held only that common law same-sex marriage did not exist in Pennsylvania, a result irrelevant to the present case. The appellants sought to assert that denial of same-sex common law marriages violated the state's equal rights amendment, but the appellate court expressly declined to reach the issue because it had not been raised in the trial court.

Jones v. Hallahan, 501 S.W.2d 588 (Ky.1973), and *Singer v. Hara,* 11 Wash.App. 247, 522 P.2d 1187, *review denied,* 84 Wash.2d 1008 (1974), warrant more in-depth analysis. In *Jones,* the appellants, both females, sought review of a judgment that held that they were not entitled to have a marriage license issued to them, contending that refusal to issue the license deprived them of the basic constitutional rights to marry, associate, and exercise religion freely. In an opinion acknowledged to be "a case of first impression in Kentucky," the Court of Appeals summarily affirmed, ruling as follows:

> Marriage was a custom long before the state commenced to issue licenses for that purpose * * *. [M]arriage has always been considered as a union of a man and a woman * * *.

> It appears to us that appellants are prevented from marrying, not by the statutes of Kentucky or the refusal of the County Clerk * * * to issue them a license, but rather by their own incapability of entering into a marriage as that term is defined.

* * *

guage at 667. Parties to "a union between a man and a woman" may or may not be homosexuals. Parties to a same-sex marriage could theoretically be either homosexuals or heterosexuals.

In substance, the relationship proposed by the appellants does not authorize the issuance of a marriage license because what they propose is not a marriage.

* * *

Significantly, the appellants' equal protection rights—federal or state—were not asserted in *Jones,* and, accordingly, the appeals court was relieved of the necessity of addressing and attempting to distinguish the decision of the United States Supreme Court in *Loving. Loving* involved the appeal of a black woman and a caucasian man (the Lovings) who were married in the District of Columbia and thereafter returned to their home state of Virginia to establish their marital abode.   * * * The Lovings were duly indicted for and convicted of violating Virginia's miscegenation laws, which banned interracial marriages.   In his sentencing decision, the trial judge stated, in substance, that Divine Providence had not intended that the marriage state extend to interracial unions:

"Almighty God created the races white, black, yellow, malay and red, and he placed them on separate continents.   And but for the interference with his arrangement there would be no cause for such marriages.   The fact that he separated the races shows that *he did not intend for the races to mix.*"

* * *

The Lovings appealed the constitutionality of the state's miscegenation laws to the Virginia Supreme Court of Appeals, which, *inter alia,* upheld their constitutionality and affirmed the Lovings' convictions.   * * * The Lovings then pressed their appeal to the United States Supreme Court.

In a landmark decision, the United States Supreme Court, through Chief Justice Warren, struck down the Virginia miscegenation laws on both equal protection and due process grounds.   The Court's holding as to the former is pertinent for present purposes:

* * *

There can be no question but that Virginia's miscegenation statutes rest solely upon distinctions drawn according to race. *The statutes proscribe generally accepted conduct* if engaged in by members of different races * * *.   At the very least, the Equal Protection Clause demands that racial classifications * * * be subjected to the "most rigid scrutiny," * * * and, if they are ever to be upheld, *they must be shown to be necessary to the accomplishment of some permissible state objective, independent of the racial discrimination which it was the object of the Fourteenth Amendment to eliminate* * * *.

There is patently no legitimate overriding purpose independent of invidious discrimination which justifies this classification * * *.   We have consistently denied the constitutionality of measures which restrict the rights of citizens on account of race.   There can be no doubt that restricting the freedom to marry solely because of racial classifications violates the central meaning of the Equal Protection Clause.

* * *

The facts in *Loving* and the respective reasoning of the Virginia courts, on the one hand, and the United States Supreme Court, on the other, both discredit the reasoning of *Jones* and unmask the tautological and circular nature of Lewin's argument that HRS § 572–1 does not implicate article I, section 5 of the Hawaii Constitution because same sex marriage is an innate impossibility. Analogously to Lewin's argument and the rationale of the *Jones* court, the Virginia courts declared that interracial marriage simply could not exist because the Deity had deemed such a union intrinsically unnatural, * * * and, in effect, because it had theretofore never been the "custom" of the state to recognize mixed marriages, marriage "always" having been construed to presuppose a different configuration. With all due respect to the Virginia courts of a bygone era, we do not believe that trial judges are the ultimate authorities on the subject of Divine Will, and, as *Loving* amply demonstrates, constitutional law may mandate, like it or not, that customs change with an evolving social order.

Singer v. Hara, 11 Wash.App. 247, 522 P.2d 1187, *review denied,* 84 Wash.2d 1008 (1974), suffers the same fate as does *Jones.* In *Singer,* two males appealed from a trial court's order denying their motion to show cause by which they sought to compel the county auditor to issue them a marriage license. On appeal, the unsuccessful applicants argued that: (1) the trial court erred in concluding that the Washington state marriage laws prohibited same-sex marriages; (2) the trial court's order violated the equal rights amendment to the state constitution; and (3) the trial court's order violated various provisions of the United States Constitution, including the fourteenth amendment.

The Washington Court of Appeals affirmed the trial court's order, rejecting all three of the appellants' contentions. Predictably, and for the same reasons that we have reached the identical conclusion regarding HRS § 572–1, the *Singer* court determined that it was "apparent from a plain reading of our marriage statutes that the legislature has not authorized same-sex marriages." * * * Regarding the appellants' federal and state claims, the court specifically "[did] not take exception to the proposition that *the Equal Protection Clause of the Fourteenth Amendment requires strict judicial scrutiny of legislative attempts at sexual discrimination.*" * * * Nevertheless, the *Singer* court found no defect in the state's marriage laws, under either the United States Constitution or the state constitution's equal rights amendment, based upon the rationale of *Jones:* "[a]ppellants were not denied a marriage license because of their sex; rather, they were denied a marriage license because of the nature of marriage itself." * * * As in *Jones,* we reject this exercise in tortured and conclusory sophistry.

3. *Equal Protection Analysis under Article I, Section 5 of the Hawaii Constitution.*

* * *

As we have indicated, HRS § 572–1, on its face and as applied, regulates access to the marital status and its concomitant rights and benefits on the basis of the applicants' sex. * * * As such, HRS § 572–1 establishes a sex-based classification.

HRS § 572–1 is not the first sex-based classification with which this court has been confronted. In *Holdman v. Olim, supra,* [59 Haw. 346, 581 P.2d 1164 (1978).] a woman prison visitor (Holdman) brought an action against prison officials seeking injunctive, monetary, and declaratory relief arising from a prison matron's refusal to admit Holdman entry when she was not wearing a brassiere. The matron's refusal derived from a directive, promulgated by the Acting Prison Administrator, that "visitors will be properly dressed. *Women* visitors are asked to be fully clothed, including undergarments. Provocative attire is discouraged." * * * (emphasis added). Holdman proceeded to trial, and the circuit court dismissed her action at the close of her case in chief. * * *

On appeal, this court affirmed the dismissal of Holdman's complaint. * * *

* * *

Our decision in *Holdman* is key to the present case in several respects. First, we clearly and unequivocally established, for purposes of equal protection analysis under the Hawaii Constitution, that sex-based classifications are subject, as a *per se* matter, to some form of "heightened" scrutiny, be it "strict" or "intermediate," rather than mere "rational basis" analysis. Second, we assumed, *arguendo,* that such sex-based classifications were subject to "strict scrutiny." Third, we reaffirmed the longstanding principle that this court is free to accord greater protections to Hawaii's citizens under the state constitution than are recognized under the United States Constitution. And fourth, we looked to the *then current* case law of the United States Supreme Court for guidance.

Of the decisions of the United States Supreme Court cited in *Holdman, Frontiero v. Richardson, supra,* was by far the most significant. * * *

* * *

Particularly noteworthy in *Frontiero,* however, was the concurring opinion of Justice Powell, joined by the Chief Justice and Justice Blackmun (the Powell group). The Powell group agreed that "the challenged statutes constitute[d] an unconstitutional discrimination against servicewomen," but deemed it "unnecessary for the Court *in this case* to characterize sex as a suspect classification, with all of the far-reaching implications of such a holding." * * *

The Powell group's concurring opinion * * * permits but one inference: had the Equal Rights Amendment been incorporated into the United States Constitution, at least seven members (and probably eight) of the *Frontiero* Court would have subjected statutory sex-based classifications to "strict" judicial scrutiny.

In light of the interrelationship between the reasoning of the Brennan plurality and the Powell group in *Frontiero,* on the one hand, and the presence of article I, section 3—the Equal Rights Amendment—in the Hawaii Constitution, on the other, it is time to resolve once and for all the question left dangling in *Holdman.* Accordingly, we hold that sex is a "suspect category" for purposes of equal protection analysis under article I, section 5 of the Hawaii Constitution [33] and that HRS § 572–1 is subject to the "strict scrutiny" test. It therefore follows, and we so hold, that (1) HRS § 572–1 is presumed to be unconstitutional (2) unless Lewin, as an agent of the State of Hawaii, can show that (a) the statute's sex-based classification is justified by compelling state interests and (b) the statute is narrowly drawn to avoid unnecessary abridgements of the applicant couples' constitutional rights.

   4. The dissenting opinion misconstrues the holdings and reasoning of the plurality.

   We would be remiss if we did not address certain basic misconstructions of this opinion appearing in Judge Heen's dissent. First, we have *not* held, as Judge Heen seems to imply, that (1) the appellants "have a 'civil right' to a same sex marriage[,]" (2) "the civil right to marriage must be accorded to same sex couples[,]" and (3) the applicant couples "have a right to a same sex marriage[.]" * * * These conclusions would be premature. We have, however, noted that the United States Supreme Court has recognized for over fifty years that marriage is a basic civil right. * * * That proposition is relevant to the prohibition set forth in article I, section 5 of the Hawaii Constitution against discrimination in the exercise of a person's civil rights, *inter alia,* on the basis of sex. * * *

   Second, we have *not* held, as Judge Heen also seems to imply, that HRS § 572–1 "unconstitutionally discriminates against [the applicant couples] who seek a license to enter into a same sex marriage[.]" * * * Such a holding would likewise be premature at this time. What we *have* held is that, on its face and as applied, HRS § 572–1 denies same-sex couples access to the marital status and its concomitant rights and benefits, thus implicating the equal protection clause of article I, section 5. * * *

   We understand that Judge Heen disagrees with our view in this regard based on his belief that "HRS § 572–1 treats everyone alike and applies equally to both sexes[,]" with the result that "neither sex is being *granted* a right or benefit the other does not have, and neither sex is being *denied* a right or benefit that the other has." * * * The rationale underlying Judge Heen's belief, however, was expressly considered and rejected in *Loving:*

> Thus, the State contends that, because its miscegenation statutes punish equally both the white and the Negro participants in an interracial marriage, these statutes, despite their reliance on racial classifications do not constitute an invidious discrimination based upon race * * *. [W]e reject the notion that the mere "equal application" of a statute containing racial classifications is enough to remove the classifications from the Fourteenth Amendment's proscriptions of all invidious discriminations * * *. In the case at bar, * * * we deal with statutes containing racial classifications, and the fact of equal application does not immunize the statute from the very heavy burden of justification which the Fourteenth Amendment has traditionally required of state statutes drawn according to race.

33. Our holding in this regard is *not,* as the dissent suggests, "[t]hat Appellants are a 'suspect class.' " * * *

* * * Substitution of "sex" for "race" and article I, section 5 for the fourteenth amendment yields the precise case before us together with the conclusion that we have reached.

As a final matter, we are compelled to respond to Judge Heen's suggestion that denying the appellants access to the multitude of statutory benefits "conferred upon spouses in a legal marriage * * * is a matter for the legislature, which can express the will of the populace in deciding whether such benefits should be extended to persons in [the applicant couples'] circumstances." * * * In effect, we are being accused of engaging in judicial legislation. We are not. The result we reach today is in complete harmony with the *Loving* Court's observation that any state's powers to regulate marriage are subject to the constraints imposed by the constitutional right to the equal protection of the laws. * * * If it should ultimately be determined that the marriage laws of Hawaii impermissibly discriminate against the appellants, based on the suspect category of sex, then that would be the result of the interrelation of existing legislation.

* * *

III. CONCLUSION

Because, for the reasons stated in this opinion, the circuit court erroneously granted Lewin's motion for judgment on the pleadings and dismissed the plaintiffs' complaint, we vacate the circuit court's order and judgment and remand this matter for further proceedings consistent with this opinion. On remand, in accordance with the "strict scrutiny" standard, the burden will rest on Lewin to overcome the presumption that HRS § 572–1 is unconstitutional by demonstrating that it furthers compelling state interests and is narrowly drawn to avoid unnecessary abridgements of constitutional rights. * * *

Vacated and remanded.

JAMES S. BURNS, INTERMEDIATE COURT OF APPEALS CHIEF JUDGE, concurring.

I concur that the circuit court's October 1, 1991 order erroneously granted the State's motion for judgment on the pleadings and erroneously dismissed the plaintiffs' complaint with prejudice. My concurrence is based on my conclusion that this case involves genuine issues of material fact. * * *

* * *

As used in the Hawaii constitution, to what does the word "sex" refer? In my view, the Hawaii constitution's reference to "sex" includes all aspects of each person's "sex" that are "biologically fated." The decision whether a person when born will be a male or a female is "biologically fated." Thus, the word "sex" includes the male-female difference. Is there any other aspect of a person's "sex" that is "biologically fated"?

In March 1993, the *Cox News Service* reported in relevant part as follows:

> The issue of whether people become homosexuals because of "nature or nurture" is one of the most controversial subjects scientists have confronted in recent years.

* * * * * *

Until the middle 1980s, the prevailing view among most scientists was that homosexual "tendencies" were mostly the result of upbringing * * *.

* * * * * *

Later, researchers at the Salk Institute in San Diego found anatomical differences between homosexual and heterosexual men in parts of the brain noted for differences between men and women.

Theories gravitate to the role of male sex hormones.

* * * * * *

The Honolulu Advertiser, March 9, 1993, at A8, col. 1.

In March 1993, the *Associated Press* reported in relevant part as follows:

CHICAGO—Genes appear to play an important role in determining whether women are lesbians, said a researcher who found similar results among gay men.

* * * * * *

"I think we're dealing with something very complex, perhaps the interaction between hormones, the environment and genetic components," [Roger] Gorski [an expert in biological theories of homosexuality] said yesterday.

* * * * * *

The Honolulu Advertiser, March 12, 1993, at A–24, col. 1.

On the other hand, columnist Charles Krauthammer reports as follows:

It is natural, therefore, that just as parents have the inclination and right to wish to influence the development of a child's character, they have the inclination and right to try to influence a child's sexual orientation. Gay advocates argue, however, that such influence is an illusion. Sexual orientation, they claim, is biologically fated and thus entirely impervious to environmental influence.

Unfortunately, as E.L. Pattullo, former director of Harvard's Center for the Behavioral Sciences, recently pointed out in Commentary magazine, the scientific evidence does not support such a claim * * *.

* * * * * *

The Honolulu Advertiser, May 2, 1993, at B2, cols. 3, 4 and 5.

If heterosexuality, homosexuality, bisexuality, and asexuality are "biologically fated[,]" then the word "sex" also includes those differences. Therefore, the questions whether heterosexuality, homosexuality, bisexuality, and asexuality are "biologically fated" are relevant questions of fact which must be determined before the issue presented in this case can be answered. If the answers are yes, then each person's "sex" includes both the "biologically fated" male-female difference and the "biologically fated" sexual orientation difference, and the Hawaii constitution probably bars the State from discriminating against the sexual orientation difference by permitting opposite-sex Hawaii Civil Law Marriages and not permitting same-sex Hawaii Civil Law Marriages. If the answers are no, then each person's "sex" does not include the sexual orientation difference, and the Hawaii constitution may permit the State to encourage heterosexuality and discourage homosexuality, bisexuality, and asexuality by permitting opposite-sex Hawaii Civil Law Marriages and not permitting same-sex Hawaii Civil Law Marriages.

WALTER M. HEEN, INTERMEDIATE COURT OF APPEALS JUDGE, dissenting.

I dissent.[1] Although the lower court judge may have engaged in "verbal overkill" in arriving at his decision, the result he reached was correct and should be affirmed. * * *

I agree with the plurality's holding that Appellants do not have a fundamental right to a same sex marriage protected by article I, § 6 of the Hawaii State Constitution.

However, I cannot agree with the plurality that (1) Appellants have a "civil right" to a same sex marriage; (2) Hawaii Revised Statutes (HRS) § 572–1 unconstitutionally discriminates against Appellants who seek a license to enter into a same sex marriage; (3) Appellants are entitled to an evidentiary hearing that applies a "strict scrutiny" standard of review to the statute; and (4) HRS § 572–1 is presumptively unconstitutional. Moreover, in my view, Appellants' claim that they are being discriminatorily denied statutory benefits accorded to spouses in a legalized marriage should be addressed to the legislature.

1.

Citing *Loving v. Virginia*, * * * the plurality holds that Appellants have a civil right to marriage. I disagree. * * *

Loving is simply not authority for the plurality's proposition that the civil right to marriage must be accorded to same sex couples. *Loving* points out that the right to marriage occupies an extremely venerated position in our society. So does every other case discussing marriage. However, the plaintiff in *Loving* was not claiming a right to a same sex marriage. *Loving* involved a marriage between a white male and a black female whose marriage, which took place in Washington, D.C., was refused recognition in Virginia under that state's miscegenation laws. * * *

* * *

Although appellants suggest an analogy between the racial classification involved in *Loving* and *Perez* and the alleged sexual classification involved in the case at bar, we do not find such an analogy. The operative distinction lies in the relationship which is described by the term "marriage" itself, and that relationship is the legal union of one man and one woman. Washington statutes, specifically those relating to marriage * * * and marital (community) property * * *, are clearly

1. Retired Associate Justice Yoshimi Hayashi, whose appointment as a substitute justice in this case expired before this dissent was filed, concurs with this dissent.

founded upon the presumption that marriage, as a legal relationship, may exist only between one man and one woman who are otherwise qualified to enter that relationship.

*   *   *   *   *   *

[A]ppellants are not being denied entry into the marriage relationship because of their sex; rather, they are being denied entry into the marriage relationship because of the recognized definition of that relationship as one which may be entered into only by two persons who are members of the opposite sex.

Singer v. Hara, 11 Wash.App. 247, 253–55, 522 P.2d 1187, 1191–92, *review denied,* 84 Wash.2d 1008 (1974) (footnotes omitted).

The issue of a right to a same sex marriage has been considered by the courts in four other states. Those courts arrive at the opposite conclusion from the plurality here. * * * I do not agree with the plurality's contention that those cases are not precedent for this case. The basic issue in each of those four cases, as in this one, was whether any person has the right to legally marry another person of the same sex. Neither do I agree with the plurality that *Loving* refutes the reasoning of the courts in those four cases.

2.

HRS § 572–1 treats everyone alike and applies equally to both sexes. The effect of the statute is to prohibit same sex marriages on the part of professed or nonprofessed heterosexuals, homosexuals, bisexuals, or asexuals, and does not effect an invidious discrimination.[3]

The constitutional guarantee of equal protection of the laws means that no person or class of persons shall be denied the same privileges and benefits under the laws that are enjoyed by other persons or other classes of persons in like circumstances. *Mahiai v. Suwa,* 69 Haw. 349, 742 P.2d 359 (1987).

HRS § 572–1 does not establish a "suspect" classification based on gender because all males and females are treated alike. A male cannot obtain a license to marry another male, and a female cannot obtain a license to marry another female. Neither sex is being *granted* a right or benefit the other does not have, and neither sex is being *denied* a right or benefit that the other has.

My thesis is well illustrated by the case of *Phillips v. Wisconsin Personnel Comm'n,* 167 Wis.2d 205, 482 N.W.2d 121 (Ct.App.1992). In that case, the plaintiff, an unmarried female, was denied medical benefits for her unmarried female "dependent" lesbian companion because Phillips' state health plan defined "dependent" as spouse or children. Phillips appealed the commission's dismissal of her gender discrimination complaint and the Wisconsin Court of Appeals, in striking down her claim, stated that

> dependent insurance coverage is unavailable to unmarried companions of both male *and* female employees. A statute is only subject to a challenge

---

3. Appellants' sexual preferences or lifestyles are completely irrelevant. Although the plurality appears to recognize the irrelevance, the real thrust of the plurality opinion disregards the true import of the statute. The statute treats everyone alike and applies equally to both sexes.

for gender discrimination under the equal protection clause when it discriminates on its face, or in effect, between males and females.

* * *

Similarly, HRS § 572–1 does not discriminate on the basis of gender. The statute applies equally to *all* unmarried persons, both male and female, who desire to enter into a legally recognized marriage.[5] Thus, no evidentiary hearing is required.

The cases cited by the plurality to support its holding that Appellants are a "suspect class" are inapposite.[6] Unlike the instant case, the facts in both cases show government regulations preferring one gender (class) over another. In *Holdman v. Olim,* 59 Haw. 346, 581 P.2d 1164 (1978), the prison regulation requiring female visitors to wear proper undergarments clearly affected only female visitors to the state prison system. Male visitors to the prison were not subject to such a regulation. The supreme court explicitly referred to the regulation as being a sex-based classification. While the reasoning in *Holdman* is very interesting, it does not support the plurality's conclusion in this case that HRS § 572–1 creates a suspect class.

Likewise, in *Frontiero v. Richardson,* 411 U.S. 677, 93 S.Ct. 1764, 36 L.Ed.2d 583 (1973), the federal statutes required that female members of the military service, but not male members, prove that they provided over one-half of their spouse's support in order to have the spouses classified as "dependents." The statutes were clearly discriminatory, since male members of the military were favored over female members.

3.

Since HRS § 572–1 is not invidiously discriminatory and Appellants are not members of a suspect class, this court should not require an evidentiary hearing.[7] Neither should this court mandate that HRS § 572–1 be subjected to the "strict scrutiny" test. If anything, Appellants' challenge subjects the statute only to the "rational basis" test. *Estate of Coates v. Pacific Engineering,* 71 Haw. 358, 791 P.2d 1257 (1990). Thus, the issue is whether the statute rationally furthers a legitimate state interest. *Id.* There is no question that such a rational relationship exists; therefore, the statute is a constitutional exercise of the legislature's authority.

5. Indeed, it may be said that the statute establishes one classification: *unmarried persons.*

6. The plurality does not define "suspect class." A suspect classification exists where the class of individuals formed by a statute, on its face or as administered, has been " * * * saddled with such disabilities, or subjected to such a history of purposeful unequal treatment or relegated to such a position of political powerlessness as to command extraordinary protection from the majoritarian political process." *San Antonio Independent School District v. Rodriguez,* 411 U.S. 1, 28, 93 S.Ct. 1278, 1294, 36 L.Ed.2d 16, 40, *reh'g denied,* 411 U.S. 959, 93 S.Ct. 1919, 36 L.Ed.2d 418 (1973).

7. The apparent result of the plurality opinion is that Appellants do not have any

burden of proof on remand. According to the plurality opinion, all Appellants need to do is appear in court and say, "Here we are. The statute discriminates against us on the basis of our sex (whether male or female) and sex is a suspect class." Even in cases alleging racial discrimination (a suspect class), "the invidious quality of a law claimed to be racially discriminatory must ultimately be traced to a racially discriminatory purpose[,]" and the burden is on the plaintiff to prove that discriminatory purpose. *Washington v. Davis,* 426 U.S. 229, 240, 96 S.Ct. 2040, 2048, 48 L.Ed.2d 597, 607–08 (1976); *see State v. Tookes,* 67 Haw. 608, 699 P.2d 983 (1985). The plurality opinion has eliminated the need for Appellants to prove purposeful discrimination.

In my view, the purpose of HRS § 572–1 is analogous to the purpose of Washington's marriage license statute as stated in *Singer, supra.*

In the instant case, it is apparent that the *state's refusal to grant a license allowing the appellants to marry one another is not based upon appellants' status as males, but rather it is based upon the state's recognition that our society as a whole views marriage as the appropriate and desirable forum for procreation and the rearing of children * * *. [M]arriage exists as a protected legal institution primarily because of societal values associated with the propagation of the human race. Further, it is apparent that no same-sex couple offers the possibility of the birth of children by their union. Thus the refusal of the state to authorize same sex marriage results from such impossibility of reproduction rather than from an invidious discrimination "on account of sex."* Therefore, the definition of marriage as the legal union of one man and one woman is permissible as applied to appellants, notwithstanding the prohibition contained in the ERA, because it is founded upon the unique physical characteristics of the sexes and appellants are not being discriminated against because of their status as males per se.[8]

* * * The court in *Singer* was considering the case in the light of that state's Equal Rights Amendment (identical to article I, § 3 of the Hawaii State Constitution). The Washington court's reasoning is pertinent, in my view, to Appellants' claim in the case at hand and supports the constitutionality of the statute.

4.

Furthermore, I cannot agree with the plurality that HRS § 572–1 is presumptively unconstitutional.

* * *

In my view, the statute's classification is clearly designed to promote the legislative purpose of fostering and protecting the propagation of the human race through heterosexual marriages and bears a reasonable relationship to that purpose. I find nothing unconstitutional in that.

5.

Appellants complain that because they are not allowed to legalize their relationships, they are denied a multitude of statutory benefits conferred upon spouses in a legal marriage. However, redress for those deprivations is a matter for the legislature, which can express the will of the populace in deciding whether such benefits should be extended to persons in Appellants' circumstances. Those benefits can be conferred without rooting out the very essence of a legal marriage.[10] This court should not manufacture a civil right which is unsupported by any precedent, and whose legal incidents—the entitlement to those statutory benefits—will reach beyond the right to enter

8. Since, in my view, the purpose of HRS § 572–1 is to promote and protect propagation, the concern expressed in Chief Judge Burns' concurring opinion as to whether the statute discriminates against persons who may be genetically impelled to homosexuality does not cause the statute to be invidiously discriminatory.

10. I note that a number of municipalities across the country have adopted domestic partnership ordinances that confer such benefits on the domestic partners as the municipalities have authority to grant. Note: *A More Perfect Union: A Legal And Social Analysis Of Domestic Partnership Ordinances,* 92 Colum.L.Rev. 1164 (1992).

into a legal marriage and overturn long standing public policy encompassing other areas of public concern. This decision will have far-reaching and grave repercussions on the finances and policies of the governments and industry of this state and all the other states in the country.

MOTION FOR RECONSIDERATION OR CLARIFICATION

Before MOON, C.J., LEVINSON, J., NAKAYAMA, J.,* JAMES S. BURNS, INTERMEDI-ATE COURT OF APPEALS CHIEF JUDGE, in place of LUM, FORMER C.J., recused,** WALTER M. HEEN, INTERMEDIATE COURT OF APPEALS JUDGE, in place of KLEIN, J., recused.

Defendant–Appellee's motion for reconsideration, or, in the alternative, for clarification, and suggestion of the appropriateness of rebriefing and reargument having been filed in the above-captioned matter on May 17, 1993, the motion is hereby granted in part, and the mandate on remand is hereby clarified as follows:

> Because, for the reasons stated in the plurality opinion filed in the above-captioned matter on May 5, 1993, the circuit court erroneously granted Lewin's motion for judgment on the pleadings and dismissed the plaintiffs' complaint, the circuit court's order and judgment are vacated and the matter is remanded for further proceedings consistent with the plurality opinion. On remand, in accordance with the "strict scrutiny" standard, the burden will rest on Lewin to overcome the presumption that HRS § 572-1 is unconstitutional by demonstrating that it furthers compelling state interests and is narrowly drawn to avoid unnecessary abridgments of constitutional rights. * * *

Defendant–Appellee's motion is denied in all other respects.

INTERMEDIATE COURT OF APPEALS JUDGE HEEN, having filed a dissenting opinion in this matter, does not concur.

JAMES S. BURNS, INTERMEDIATE COURT OF APPEALS CHIEF JUDGE, concurring.

There are three opinions in this case: (1) Levinson–Moon; (2) Burns; and (3) Heen–Hayashi. Appellee Lewin disagrees with the Levinson–Moon and Burns opinions and seeks reconsideration of both. With respect to the Levinson–Moon opinion, I concur with the decision by Justice Levinson and Chief Justice Moon to grant the motion in part. With respect to the Burns opinion, I deny the request.

Alternatively, appellee Lewin seeks clarification of this court's mandate. The only agreement by a majority of this court is that this case involves genuine issues of material fact. In my view, that is this court's mandate. Thus far, there is no majority agreement as to what these issues are or which side has the burden to prove them. Presented with this chance to write more than I have already written in the Burns opinion about these issues and burdens, I choose to wait for the next appeal. At that time, hopefully, there will be: a complete record of a trial in which the parties have presented their evidence and arguments and the trial court has made its decisions of fact and

---

* In place of Substitute Justice Hayashi, whose term of Substitution expired on October 30, 1992. * * *

** Chief Justice Lum retired March 31, 1993. * * *

law; and opening, answering and reply briefs fully discussing the issues and the applicable law.

Notes on Baker *and* Baehr

1. Does the Minnesota court deal adequately with petitioners' constitutional arguments? If the state permits (as it does) marriages between a man and a woman unable or unwilling to have children, how can it be said that procreation is essential to the concept of marriage? Could the state deny a marriage license to a heterosexual couple who refused to have children?

2. As long as all men can marry only women and all women can marry only men, why is a man who wishes to marry another man or a woman who wishes to marry another woman denied equal protection? Is the argument that all members of one sex are denied a right accorded to all members of the opposite sex, namely, that of marrying a member of their own sex? Is this argument valid? Does petitioners' reliance upon Loving v. Virginia help their argument? How? Does the *Baehr* plurality do a better job of interpreting *Loving* than the Minnesota Supreme Court? How do you answer the *Baehr* dissent's argument that *Loving* is limited to heterosexual interracial marriages? Is it as easy as the plurality suggests simply to substitute "sex" for "race" in the *Loving* analysis? Professor Kenneth Karst rejects the "simple" sex discrimination argument— "Jenny is free to marry Arthur, but Lance is not"—as "unhelpful," noting that "[w]hat makes a miscegenation law invalid, after all, is not merely that it classifies on the basis of race, but that it is designed to promote white supremacy." He also characterizes as a "makeweight" the "more sophisticated" attack that claims the denial of marriage to lesbians invokes historical assumptions about the need for a male-headed nuclear family, and, by extension, argues that the denial of marriage to homosexual men also supports the traditional nuclear family. In Karst's view,

> * * * the heart of the constitutional problem lies in the freedom of intimate association. What homosexuals lack is a formalized legal status that recognizes their union and commitment. Such a status would mean not only that they would have the same opportunity as heterosexual couples to make the public self-identifying statements implicit in marriage, but also that the state recognized their status as an acceptable one in society rather than one deserving of stigma.

Kenneth L. Karst, The Freedom of Intimate Association, 89 Yale L.J. 624, 683–84 (1980) (footnotes omitted). Which constitutional provision guarantees the freedom of intimate association? See also William N. Eskridge, A History of Same– Sex Marriage, 79 Va.L.Rev. 1419 (1993); Herma Hill Kay, Private Choices and Public Policy: Confronting the Limitations of Marriage, 5 Australian J.Fam.L. 69 (1991); Claudia A. Lewis, From This Day Forward: A Feminine Moral Discourse on Homosexual Marriage, 97 Yale L.J. 1783, 1797 (1988) (arguing that a feminine vision of equality "mandates that if marriage is a primary unit of community and that community strives to treat all individuals with equal care, then homosexuals have an equal right to establish a connection to the community as a whole through the institution of marriage").

3. The Uniform Marriage and Divorce Act provides in Section 201 that "a marriage between a man and a woman, licensed, solemnized, and registered as provided in this Act is valid in this state" and the Comment adds that "in accordance with established usage, marriage is required to be between a man and

a woman." The Uniform Act does not, however, include same-sex marriages among its list of prohibited marriages in Section 207, and no position is taken on any of the constitutional issues. How should the constitutional questions be resolved?

4. The Hawaii Legislature lost no time repudiating *Baehr*. It enacted HRS § 572–1 (Mitchie 1994) which states plainly that " * * * the marriage contract * * * shall be only between a man and a woman * * *." A lengthy statement of legislative findings and purpose accompany the Act, indicating the Legislature's strong feeling that the Supreme Court plurality had impermissibly invaded its province:

> The legislature finds that Hawaii's marriage licensing laws were original-ly and are presently intended to apply only to male-female couples, not same-sex couples. This determination is one of policy. Any change in these laws must come from either the legislature or a constitutional convention, not the judiciary. The Hawaii supreme court's recent plurality opinion in Baehr * * * effaces the recognized tradition of marriage in this State and, in so doing, impermissibly negates the constitutionally mandated role of the legisla-ture as a co-equal, coordinate branch of government.

But just a minute: didn't the Court agree that the plain meaning of the marriage statute prohibited same-sex marriages, go on to measure that provision against the equal protection clause of the Hawaii constitution, and find it constitutionally infirm unless the state could show that it furthers a compelling interest and is narrowly drawn to avoid unnecessary abridgements of constitution-al rights? Isn't that what high courts are supposed to do in their exercise of judicial review of statutory enactments? In its zeal to obliterate *Baehr,* the legislature interpreted the constitution for itself:

> Although the Hawaii supreme court has the right to pass on the constitu-tionality of section 572–1, * * * the question before the court in Baehr was and is essentially one of policy, thereby rendering it inappropriate for judicial response. * * *

> The legislature finds that the prohibition against discrimination on the basis of sex in Article I, section 5 of the Hawaii Constitution is for the purpose of protecting gender equality. In other words, "sex" means gender, not sexual orientation, for purposes of both the marriage licensing statutes and Article I of the Hawaii Constitution. The court in Baehr, in analyzing the equal protection issue presented in that case in terms of sexual orienta-tion or preference classifications rather than gender classifications, impermis-sibly expanded the intention of that word as it appears both in the marriage statutes and the Constitution.

Now who is invading whose province? Does the 1994 amendment, which inserted the words "man" and "woman" in the marriage statute in two places for good measure, resolve the constitutional question? Is the Hawaii supreme court bound by the legislature's interpretation of Article I of the Constitution?

5. The claim that the Equal Rights Amendment would require states to permit same-sex marriage was raised by opponents during the ratification debate. See Paul M. Kurtz, The State Equal Rights Amendments and Their Impact on Domestic Relations Law, 11 Fam.L.Q. 101, 115 (1977). The issue has been litigated in Washington under a state equal rights amendment. In Singer v. Hara, 11 Wash.App. 247, 522 P.2d 1187 review denied, 84 Wash.2d 1008 (1974), the court upheld a prohibition against homosexual marriage, reasoning that the

equal rights amendment did not itself create any new rights or responsibilities; it merely insured that existing ones or those to be created in the future would be equally available to all persons regardless of sex. In the course of its opinion, the court expressly rejected the reasoning of a Yale notewriter, see Note, The Legality of Homosexual Marriage, 82 Yale L.J. 573, 583–88 (1973). Do you agree with the *Singer* court's interpretation of an equal rights provision? If applied to the equal protection clause, would it be unduly restrictive? In the context of same-sex marriages, the analysis suggests that since the members of neither sex have the right to marry like-sexed persons under existing law, the equal rights amendment cannot, by its own force, create such a right. Are there other constitutional provisions that might support a right to a homosexual marriage? Kurtz, id., at 117–18, discusses and rejects three possible independent sources: the right to privacy, the Ninth Amendment, and the due process clause.

6. See also Adams v. Howerton, 673 F.2d 1036 (9th Cir.1982), certiorari denied 458 U.S. 1111, 102 S.Ct. 3494, 73 L.Ed.2d 1373 (1982), declining to classify a male alien as a "spouse" of a male American citizen following their having obtained a marriage license in Boulder, Colorado, and having gone through a marriage ceremony performed by a minister. Regardless of the validity of the "marriage" under Colorado law, the court reasoned, Congress had established its own definition of what marriages would confer the status of "spouse" for immigration purposes. The court concluded that Congress had not intended to go beyond the common dictionary meaning of "marriage" as a relationship between a man and a woman, and a "spouse" as one of the parties to a heterosexual marriage, in enacting the Immigration and Nationality Act. The Ninth Circuit subsequently affirmed the decision of the Board of Immigration Appeals to deny Anthony Sullivan's application for suspension of deportation on grounds of extreme hardship to him and Richard Adams. Judge Pregerson dissented, charging that the BIA had treated Sullivan's application in abstract terms, failing to evaluate his special circumstances realistically. Sullivan v. Immigration and Naturalization Service, 772 F.2d 609 (9th Cir.1985).

7. In an action for a declaratory judgment as to marital status, a New York court has held that a man who married another man under the mistaken belief that he was a woman did not contract a valid marriage because "the law makes no provision for a 'marriage' between persons of the same sex." The parties had separated immediately upon plaintiff's discovery, on the morning after the wedding, that his spouse was really a man. Anonymous v. Anonymous, 325 N.Y.S.2d 499, 67 Misc.2d 982 (1971).

8. In Anonymous v. Anonymous, supra Note 7, the court did not pass on the significance of a surgical sex change undergone by defendant after the parties had separated. The relevant time was said to be that of the marriage ceremony. Why should this be so? Couldn't the operation act to ratify the marriage in much the same way as a common law marriage acts to cure the impediment of a prior existing marriage once that marriage has terminated in death or divorce? See Homer H. Clark, The Law of Domestic Relations in the United States 52–53 (1988) for a discussion of the curative impact of common law marriage. An English court, deciding that a sex change operation did not alter the "true" legal sex of the individual concerned, annulled a 14 day marriage between a male transsexual and her transvestite husband. Corbett v. Corbett, [1970] 2 W.L.R. 1306, 2 All E.R. 33 (P.D.A.). The case is discussed in Douglass K. Smith, Comment, Transsexualism, Sex Reassignment Surgery, and the Law, 56 Corn. L.Rev. 963, 1004–1008 (1971).

See also B. v. B., 78 Misc.2d 112, 118, 355 N.Y.S.2d 712, 717 (1974), annulling a marriage between a woman and a female-to-male transsexual who had represented himself to be male. ("While it is possible that defendant may function as a male in other situations and other relationships, defendant cannot function as a husband by assuming male duties and obligations inherent in the marriage relationship. As plaintiff asserts, defendant 'does not have male sexual organs, does not possess a normal penis * * *'.") But see M.T. v. J.T., 140 N.J.Super. 77, 355 A.2d 204, certificate denied 71 N.J. 345, 364 A.2d 1076 (1976), upholding a marriage between a male-to-female transsexual and a male who had helped his wife obtain the sex change operation. See generally, Meredith Gould, Sex, Gender, and the Need for Legal Clarity: The Case of Transsexualism, 13 Val. U.L.Rev. 423 (1979).

9. What would be the effect of a statute allowing homosexual marriages in a state where sexual relationships between consenting adults of the same sex are prohibited? Could sexual interaction be inferred from the fact of the marriage? If so, would the marriage ceremony serve as an invitation to zealous law enforcement officers to arrest the newlyweds? Or would the marriage be a defense to the criminal charge? If not, wouldn't the statutory authorization to marry itself be a sort of entrapment for persons taking advantage of its terms?

10. Why do homosexuals want to be able to contract a legal marriage? According to Del Martin and Phyllis Lyon the reasons include the following:

> For some, marriage means a religious sacrament and commitment. For others it may also take on a legal significance in terms of community property, the filing of joint income tax returns and inheritance rights. Recognition of a Lesbian union might also serve to validate the couple who wished to take on the legal responsibility of adopting homeless, unwanted children. It would also simplify insurance problems, making the couple eligible for family policies, for family rates on airlines travel and for that matter, for "couple" entry to entertainment functions, too.

Del Martin and Phyllis Lyon, Lesbian/Woman 103 (Glide 1972). In Maryland, a gay account executive who won a company-paid vacation for two in Hawaii was told that he could take along a wife or female companion, but not his male companion with whom he had lived since 1984. After the ACLU filed suit on the executive's behalf under the Montgomery County Human Relations Act, however, the company agreed to pay the expenses of both men. The New York Times, November 3, 1989, at A8, col. 4. See generally Alissa Friedman, The Necessity for State Recognition of Same–Sex Marriage: Constitutional Requirements and Evolving Notions of Family, 3 Berkeley Wom.L.J. 134 (1987–88).

Even if laws prohibiting homosexual marriages do not discriminate between the sexes, they may nevertheless discriminate against both sexes by reinforcing traditional mores concerning the roles of men and women in our society. Should not the law undertake to provide room for experimentation by those who seek alternatives to the dominant-male/submissive-female relationship, even though dominance and submissiveness also occur in same-sex relationships? Is this not the proper subject of laws prohibiting sex-based discrimination? See William N. Estridge, The Many Faces of Sexual Consent, 37 Wm. & Mary L.Rev. 47 (1995).

11. In 1973, Jack Baker and Jim McConnell obtained a marriage license in another Minnesota county and went through a wedding ceremony. San Francisco Chronicle, January 8, 1973, p. 20, col. 6. Subsequently, Baker's application for increased VA educational benefits on account of his "dependent spouse" was rejected. McConnell v. Nooner, 547 F.2d 54 (8th Cir.1976).

12.   Does the plurality in *Baehr* significantly expand the boundaries of what we think of as sex discrimination?   Is that why Judge Burns wants to know whether homosexuality is "biologically fated"?   What impact would an affirmative answer to that question have on the outcome in *Baehr*?   How might it influence our thinking in other cases, such as those to be considered in Chapter Three?

2.   DISSOLUTION OF MARRIAGE

a.   *Grounds*

Text Note
The Statutory Basis for Marriage Dissolution

The question of what grounds are sufficient to permit dissolution of a valid marriage is not primarily a problem of sex-based discrimination.   Rather, the modern debate over divorce reform has concerned itself with the impact of strict divorce laws on marital stability and other issues of private morality and public policy.[1]   But, as Sheila Cronan suggested, some social observers contend that as long as married women work within the home not for pay but with the expectation of security, liberalization of divorce is against the interests of women.[2]   Thus it is not surprising that America's first true no-fault divorce law, that enacted in California in 1969,[3] was attacked by a married woman as unconstitutional. Norma Janet Walton contended that the basis for divorce specified in the California statute, "irreconcilable differences which have caused the irremediable breakdown of the marriage," [4] impaired the obligation of the marriage contract; retroactively deprived her of a vested interest in her marital status in violation of due process of law; and was vague and ambiguous.[5]   Nor is it surprising, given the state's vast powers to regulate marriage and divorce, that she lost.   Nevertheless, her additional complaint, that the impact of no-fault divorce is unfair and unjust to wives,[6] has been echoed by others.[7]   At bottom, however, these complaints seem addressed to the financial consequences of divorce, rather than to the statutory basis of the action.

At any event, the debate over no-fault divorce in the United States seems to have been settled, at least for the time being.   All American states have adopted some form of a no-fault standard for the dissolution of marriage.   Fifteen states have "pure" no-fault laws that abolish all fault-based grounds for divorce and substitute a judicial finding of marriage breakdown; twenty-one states have added a no-fault provision based either on "irreconcilable differences" or some form of marriage breakdown to their list of fault-based grounds; and fourteen states and the District of Columbia provide a no-fault ground based on separation or incompatibility in addition to their fault-based grounds.[8]

1.   See, e.g., Max Rheinstein, Marriage Stability, Divorce, and the Law (1972); Brigette M. Bodenheimer, Reflections on the Future of Grounds for Divorce, 8 J.Fam.L. 179 (1968).

2.   Sheila Cronan, Marriage, in Notes from the Third Year: Women's Liberation 62, 64 (1971), set out at p. 248, supra.

3.   Cal.Stats.1969, c. 1608, operative Jan. 1, 1970.

4.   West's   Ann.Cal.Civ.Code   § 4506(1) (1970); now West's Ann.Cal.Fam.Code § 2310 (1994).

5.   In re Marriage of Walton, 28 Cal.App.3d 108, 111, 104 Cal.Rptr. 472, 475 (1972).

6.   Ibid.

7.   E.g., Reilley v. Reilley, 409 U.S. 1003, 93 S.Ct. 440, 34 L.Ed.2d 294 (1972) (dismissing an appeal challenging the constitutional validity of West Virginia's no-fault divorce law).

8.   See Herma Hill Kay, Equality and Difference: A Perspective on No–Fault Divorce and Its Aftermath, 56 U.Cin.L.Rev. 1, 5–6, 26–55 (1987).   Compare Elizabeth S. Scott, Rational Decisionmaking About Marriage and Divorce, 76 Va.L.Rev. 9 (1990) (applying "precommitment theory" to the marital relationship and reexamining the role of fault from that perspective).   See also, J. Herbie DiFonzo, No–Fault Marital Dissolution: The Bitter

A lively debate still rages, however, over the financial provisions that should accompany no-fault divorce. Wisconsin adopted the Uniform Marital Property Act following its enactment of a no-fault divorce law, in part to provide better financial protection to divorced spouses.[9] Equitable distribution laws have been enacted both in Pennsylvania and New York: the underlying proposals were received quite differently by affected groups in the two states, as Freed and Foster report: [10]

> [O]ne of the interesting political aspects of the Pennsylvania campaign for divorce law reform was the full support received from various women's groups who fought for *equitable* distribution. They were opposed by men's groups who lobbied for *equal* distribution. In New York, precisely opposite positions were taken in that N.O.W. demanded *equal* distribution and other groups *equitable* distribution. The men's groups in Pennsylvania were concerned that "equitable" might mean more than "equal," and N.O.W. in New York was concerned that "equitable" might mean less than "equal."

These differing perceptions go to the heart of many family law disputes. California attorney Riane Eisler comments,[11]

> despite all this variety and complexity, in a very practical sense, family law has not really changed that much. It can still be summed up in one phrase: judicial discretion. * * *

> In practical terms, judicial discretion means that judges sitting in family-law cases have vast power. * * * Of course, family-law judges are supposed to exercise this discretion equitably. And it is precisely in connection with what is equitable that most of the problems in family law arise.

> What is considered equitable is more an issue of social values than it is of law; of individual attitudes rather than of statutes and rules of legal procedure. In short, it is, more often than not, a function of the personal and social circumstances and background and sometimes even mood of the individual judge.

Family law cases are handled in state, not federal courts.[12] The majority of judges sitting in these courts are still white males, most of them without prior experience in the handling of family law cases. As the following materials suggest, the law that is being developed at the trial court level in many states is shaped in important ways by the attitudes of these judges to emerging lifestyles and changing roles for both women and men. Predictably, correction has been required at the appellate level.

Triumph of Naked Divorce, 31 San Diego L.Rev. 519 (1994); Lynn D. Wardle, No–Fault Divorce and the Divorce Conundrum, 1991 B.Y.U.L.Rev. 79, 98 ("It appears that none of the purposes which led to the adoption of no-fault grounds for divorce have been fully achieved."). But see Robert J. Levy, A Reminiscence About the Uniform Marriage and Divorce Act—and Some Reflections About Its Critics and Its Policies, 1991 B.Y.U.L.Rev. 43.

9. See generally June M. Weisberger, The Wisconsin Marital Property Act: Highlights of the Wisconsin Experience in Developing a Model for Comprehensive Common Law Property Reform, 1 Wis.Women's L.J. 5 (1985).

10. Henry H. Foster, Jr. & Doris Jonah Freed, Divorce in the Fifty States: An Overview as of August 1, 1980, 6 Family Law Reporter 4043 (Sept. 2, 1980).

11. Riane T. Eisler, Dissolution: No–Fault Divorce, Marriage, and the Future of Women 17–18 (1977).

12. E.g., Barber v. Barber, 62 U.S. (21 How.) 582, 584, 16 L.Ed. 226 (1858) ("We disclaim altogether any jurisdiction in the courts of the United States upon the subject of divorce, or for the allowance of alimony, either as an original proceeding in chancery or as an incident to divorce *a vinculo*, or to one from bed and board.").

b. ***Financial Provisions***

ORR v. ORR

Supreme Court of the United States, 1979.
440 U.S. 268, 99 S.Ct. 1102, 59 L.Ed.2d 306.

MR. JUSTICE BRENNAN delivered the opinion of the Court.

The question presented is the constitutionality of Alabama alimony statutes which provide that husbands, but not wives, may be required to pay alimony upon divorce.[1]

On February 26, 1974, a final decree of divorce was entered, dissolving the marriage of William and Lillian Orr. That decree directed appellant, Mr. Orr, to pay appellee, Mrs. Orr, $1,240 per month in alimony. On July 28, 1976, Mrs. Orr initiated a contempt proceeding in the Circuit Court of Lee County, Ala., alleging that Mr. Orr was in arrears in his alimony payments. On August 19, 1976, at the hearing on Mrs. Orr's petition, Mr. Orr submitted in his defense a motion requesting that Alabama's alimony statutes be declared unconstitutional because they authorize courts to place an obligation of alimony upon husbands but never upon wives. * * * We now hold the challenged Alabama statutes unconstitutional and reverse.

* * *

[The Court's discussion of three preliminary issues not raised below—whether Mr. Orr had standing to challenge the constitutionality of the Alabama statutes since he did not seek alimony for himself; whether, if so, his challenge was timely; and whether he was, at any event, bound by contract under state law to support his wife—is omitted.]

II

In authorizing the imposition of alimony obligations on husbands, but not on wives, the Alabama statutory scheme "provides that different treatment be accorded * * * on the basis of * * * sex; it thus establishes a classification subject to scrutiny under the Equal Protection Clause," Reed v. Reed, * * *. The fact that the classification expressly discriminates against men rather than women does not protect it from scrutiny. Craig v. Boren, * * *. "To withstand scrutiny" under the Equal Protection Clause, " 'classifications by

---

1. The statutes, Ala.Code, Tit. 30 (1975), provide that:

"§ 30–2–51. * * * If the wife has no separate estate or if it be insufficient for her maintenance, the judge, upon granting a divorce, at his discretion, may order to the wife an allowance out of the estate of the husband, taking into consideration the value thereof and the condition of his family.

"§ 30–2–52. * * * If the divorce is in favor of the wife for the misconduct of the husband, the judge trying the case shall have the right to make an allowance to the wife out of the husband's estate, or not make her an allowance as the circumstances of the case may justify, and if an allowance is made, it must be as liberal as the estate of the husband will permit, regard being had to the condition of his family and to all the circumstances of the case.

"§ 30–2–53. * * * If the divorce is in favor of the husband for the misconduct of the wife and if the judge in his discretion deems the wife entitled to an allowance, the allowance must be regulated by the ability of the husband and the nature of the misconduct of the wife."

The Alabama Supreme Court has held that "there is no authority in this state for awarding alimony against the wife in favor of the husband. * * * The statutory scheme is to provide alimony only in favor of the wife." Davis v. Davis, 279 Ala. 643, 644, 189 So.2d 158, 160 (1966).

gender must serve important governmental objectives and must be substantially related to achievement of those objectives.'" Califano v. Webster, * * *. We shall, therefore, examine the three governmental objectives that might arguably be served by Alabama's statutory scheme.

Appellant views the Alabama alimony statutes as effectively announcing the State's preference for an allocation of family responsibilities under which the wife plays a dependent role, and as seeking for their objective the reinforcement of that model among the State's citizens. * * *. We agree, as he urges, that prior cases settle that this purpose cannot sustain the statutes.[9] Stanton v. Stanton, * * * held that the "old notio[n]" that "generally it is the man's primary responsibility to provide a home and its essentials," can no longer justify a statute that discriminates on the basis of gender. "No longer is the female destined solely for the home and the rearing of the family, and only the male for the marketplace and the world of ideas," * * *. If the statute is to survive constitutional attack, therefore, it must be validated on some other basis.

The opinion of the Alabama Court of Civil Appeals suggests other purposes that the statute may serve. Its opinion states that the Alabama statutes were "designed" for "the wife of a broken marriage who needs financial assistance," * * *. This may be read as asserting either of two legislative objectives. One is a legislative purpose to provide help for needy spouses, using sex as a proxy for need. The other is a goal of compensating women for past discrimination during marriage, which assertedly has left them unprepared to fend for themselves in the working world following divorce. We concede, of course, that assisting needy spouses is a legitimate and important governmental objective. We have also recognized "[r]eduction of the disparity in economic condition between men and women caused by the long history of discrimination against women * * * as * * * an important governmental objective," * * *. It only remains, therefore, to determine whether the classification at issue here is "substantially related to achievement of those objectives." Ibid.[10]

Ordinarily, we would begin the analysis of the "needy spouse" objective by considering whether sex is a sufficiently "accurate proxy," Craig v. Boren, * * * for dependency to establish that the gender classification rests " 'upon some ground of difference having a fair and substantial relation to the object

9. Appellee attempts to buttress the importance of this objective by arguing that while "[t]he common law stripped the married woman of many of her rights and most of her property, * * * it attempted to partially compensate by giving her the assurance that she would be supported by her husband." Brief for Appellee 11–12. This argument, that the "support obligation was imposed by the common law to compensate the wife for the discrimination she suffered at the hands of the common law," id., at 11, reveals its own weakness. At most it establishes that the alimony statutes were part and parcel of a larger statutory scheme which invidiously discriminated against women, removing them from the world of work and property and "compensating" them by making their designated place "se-

cure." This would be reason to invalidate the entire discriminatory scheme—not a reason to uphold its separate invidious parts. But appellee's argument is even weaker when applied to the facts of this case, as Alabama has long ago removed, by statute, the elements of the common law appellee points to as justifying further discrimination. See Ala. Const., Art. X, § 209 (married women's property rights).

10. Of course, if upon examination it becomes clear that there is no substantial relationship between the statutes and their purported objectives, this may well indicate that these objectives were not the statutes' goals in the first place. See Ely, The Centrality and Limits of Motivation Analysis, 15 San Diego L.Rev. 1155 (1978).

of the legislation,' " Reed v. Reed, * * *. Similarly, we would initially approach the "compensation" rationale by asking whether women had in fact been significantly discriminated against in the sphere to which the statute applied a sex-based classification, leaving the sexes *"not* similarly situated with respect to opportunities" in that sphere, Schlesinger v. Ballard, * * *. Compare Califano v. Webster, * * * and Kahn v. Shevin * * * with Weinberger v. Wiesenfeld, * * *.[11]

But in this case, even if sex were a reliable proxy for need, and even if the institution of marriage did discriminate against women, these factors still would "not adequately justify the salient features of" Alabama's statutory scheme, Craig v. Boren, * * *. Under the statute, individualized hearings at which the parties' relative financial circumstances are considered *already* occur. See Russell v. Russell, 247 Ala. 284, 286, 24 So.2d 124, 126 (1945); Ortman v. Ortman, 203 Ala. 167, 82 So. 417 (1919). There is no reason, therefore, to use sex as a proxy for need. Needy males could be helped along with needy females with little if any additional burden on the State. In such circumstances, not even an administrative-convenience rationale exists to justify operating by generalization or proxy.[12] Similarly, since individualized hearings can determine which women were in fact discriminated against vis-à-vis their husbands, as well as which family units defied the stereotype and left the husband dependent on the wife, Alabama's alleged compensatory purpose may be effectuated without placing burdens solely on husbands. Progress toward fulfilling such a purpose would not be hampered, and it would cost the State nothing more, if it were to treat men and women equally by making alimony burdens independent of sex. "Thus, the gender-based distinction is gratuitous; without it, the statutory scheme would only provide benefits to those men who are in fact similarly situated to the women the statute aids," Weinberger v. Wiesenfeld, * * * and the effort to help those women would not in any way be compromised.

Moreover, use of a gender classification actually produces perverse results in this case. As compared to a gender-neutral law placing alimony obligations on the spouse able to pay, the present Alabama statutes give an advantage only to the financially secure wife whose husband is in need. Although such a wife might have to pay alimony under a gender-neutral statute, the present statutes exempt her from that obligation. Thus, "[t]he [wives] who benefit from the disparate treatment are those who were * * * nondependent on their husbands," Califano v. Goldfarb, 430 U.S. 199, 221, 97 S.Ct. 1021, 1034, 51 L.Ed.2d 270 (1977) (Stevens, J., concurring in judgment). They are

11. We would also consider whether the purportedly compensatory "classifications in fact penalized women," and whether "the statutory structure and its legislative history revealed that the classification was not enacted as compensation for past discrimination." Califano v. Webster, 430 U.S. 313, 317, 97 S.Ct. 1192, 1194, 51 L.Ed.2d 360 (1977).

12. It might be argued that Alabama's rule at least relieves the State of the administrative burden of actions by husbands against their wives for alimony. However, when the wife is also seeking alimony, no savings will occur, as a hearing will be required in any event. But even when the wife is willing to forgo alimony, it appears that under Alabama law savings will still not accrue, as Alabama courts review the financial circumstances of the parties to a divorce despite the parties' own views—even when settlement is reached. See Russell v. Russell, 247 Ala. 284, 286, 24 So.2d 124, 126 (1945). Even were this not true, and some administrative time and effort were conserved, "[t]o give a mandatory preference to members of either sex * * * merely to accomplish the elimination of hearings on the merits, is to make the very kind of arbitrary legislative choice forbidden by the Equal Protection Clause," Reed v. Reed, 404 U.S. 71, 76, 92 S.Ct. 251, 254, 30 L.Ed.2d 225 (1971).

precisely those who are not "needy spouses" and who are "least likely to have been victims of * * * discrimination," ibid., by the institution of marriage. A gender-based classification which, as compared to a gender-neutral one, generates additional benefits only for those it has no reason to prefer cannot survive equal protection scrutiny.

Legislative classifications which distribute benefits and burdens on the basis of gender carry the inherent risk of reinforcing stereotypes about the "proper place" of women and their need for special protection. Cf. United Jewish Organizations v. Carey, 430 U.S. 144, 173–174, 97 S.Ct. 996, 1013–1014, 51 L.Ed.2d 229 (1977) (opinion concurring in part). Thus, even statutes purportedly designed to compensate for and ameliorate the effects of past discrimination must be carefully tailored. Where, as here, the State's compensatory and ameliorative purposes are as well served by a gender-neutral classification as one that gender classifies and therefore carries with it the baggage of sexual stereotypes, the State cannot be permitted to classify on the basis of sex. And this is doubly so where the choice made by the State appears to redound—if only indirectly—to the benefit of those without need for special solicitude.

III

Having found Alabama's alimony statutes unconstitutional, we reverse the judgment below and remand the cause for further proceedings not inconsistent with this opinion. That disposition, of course, leaves the state courts free to decide any questions of substantive state law not yet passed upon in this litigation. * * * Therefore, it is open to the Alabama courts on remand to consider whether Mr. Orr's stipulated agreement to pay alimony, or other grounds of gender-neutral state law, bind him to continue his alimony payments.

Reversed and remanded.

Mr. Justice Blackmun, concurring.

On the assumption that the Court's language concerning discrimination "in the sphere" of the relevant preference statute, * * * does not imply that society-wide discrimination is always irrelevant, and on the further assumption that that language in no way cuts back on the Court's decision in Kahn v. Shevin, * * * I join the opinion and judgment of the Court.

Mr. Justice Stevens, concurring.

Whether Mr. Orr has a continuing contractual obligation to pay alimony to Mrs. Orr is a question of Alabama law that the Alabama courts have not yet decided. In Part I–B of his opinion, Mr. Justice Rehnquist seems to be making one of two alternative suggestions:

    (1) that we should decide the state-law issue; or

    (2) that we should direct the Supreme Court of Alabama to decide that issue before deciding the federal constitutional issue.

In my judgment the Court has correctly rejected both of these alternatives. To accept either—or a rather confused blend of the two—would violate principles of federalism that transcend the significance of this case. I therefore join the Court's opinion.

Mr. Justice Powell, dissenting.

I agree with Mr. Justice Rehnquist that the Court, in its desire to reach the equal protection issue in this case, has dealt too casually with the difficult Art. III problems which confront us. Rather than assume the answer to questions of state law on which the resolution of the Art. III issue should depend, and which well may moot the equal protection question in this case, I would abstain from reaching either of the constitutional questions at the present time.

* * *

MR. JUSTICE REHNQUIST, with whom THE CHIEF JUSTICE joins, dissenting.

In Alabama only wives may be awarded alimony upon divorce. In Part I of its opinion, the Court holds that Alabama's alimony statutes may be challenged in this Court by a divorced male who has never sought alimony, who is demonstrably not entitled to alimony even if he had, and who contractually bound himself to pay alimony to his former wife and did so without objection for over two years. I think the Court's eagerness to invalidate Alabama's statutes has led it to deal too casually with the "case and controversy" requirement of Art. III of the Constitution.

* * *

IN RE MARRIAGE OF MORRISON

Supreme Court of California, 1978.
20 Cal.3d 437, 143 Cal.Rptr. 139, 573 P.2d 41.

BIRD, CHIEF JUSTICE.

Appellant, Patricia R. Morrison appeals from an interlocutory judgment of dissolution of marriage from respondent David E. Morrison. She contends that the trial court erred (1) in terminating jurisdiction to award spousal support to her after 11 years; (2) in limiting her spousal support to $400 a month; * * *

I

The parties were married in New York in 1947. At that time the husband was in military service, and the wife was also employed. However, shortly after the marriage and at her husband's insistence, the wife quit her job. Although the wife did hold a few part-time jobs in the early years of the marriage, she devoted her time principally to maintaining the home and raising two children, who are now adults.

In 1975, the husband petitioned the court for dissolution of the 28–year marriage. At that time he was 52 years old, and the wife was 54. At the dissolution hearing the wife testified, and the husband agreed, that she had no job skills or training and was then employed part time as a newspaper collator. She received $2.25 an hour for this work, with monthly earnings of approximately $100. The wife testified that she was being treated for a low blood sugar condition, that she had little energy as a result of this condition, and that she did not know whether or not she would be able to work full time. A financial declaration, which listed the wife's estimated monthly expenses at $946, was filed, and she testified she might be able to "make it" if she received $700 or $800 a month in spousal support.

At the time of the dissolution, the husband had retired from military service and was employed in private industry as a quality control supervisor. His gross monthly salary for his work as a supervisor was $1,500, and he received $394 a month in military pension benefits. His net monthly income from these two sources was $1,456. In his financial declaration, the husband claimed monthly expenses of $1,367.

During the marriage, community property was acquired which consisted of equity in the family home, two automobiles, the cash surrender value of various insurance policies, stocks, a coin collection, household furnishings, and numerous other items of personal property. The trial court awarded $10,066.47 of the community property to the husband, and the house and other property with a value of $38,197.88 to the wife. Additionally, the husband was ordered to pay community obligations in the amount of $3,342.10. In order that the property and the obligations might be equally apportioned, the wife was required to execute a secured note in favor of the husband in the amount of $15,736.55 with interest at 7 percent per annum. The note was payable three years after the interlocutory decree or immediately if the residence were sold, refinanced, or abandoned.

The court awarded the wife a 42.5 percent interest in the husband's military pension or approximately $167 a month. The wife had also listed the husband's nonvested pension rights with his present employer as property subject to disposition by the court, but the court made no mention of that pension in its order. Finally, the court ordered spousal support to the wife in the amount of $400 a month "for a period of eight years, thereafter jurisdiction shall be reserved for three years, thereafter spousal support is to terminate absolutely."

II

The wife contends that the trial court abused its discretion in failing to retain jurisdiction to award spousal support to her after 11 years.

At the time of the interlocutory judgment in this case, Civil Code section 4801, subdivision (a), provided in pertinent part: "[T]he court may order a party to pay for the support of the other party any amount, and for such period of time, as the court may deem just and reasonable having regard for the circumstances of the respective parties, including the duration of the marriage, and the ability of the supported spouse to engage in gainful employment without interfering with the interests of the children of the parties in the custody of such spouse." (Stats.1971, ch. 1675, § 3, p. 3602.) Subdivision (d) of that section provided: "An order for payment of an allowance for the support of one of the parties shall terminate at the end of the period specified in the order and shall not be extended unless the court in its original order retains jurisdiction." (Id., at p. 3603.)

The courts of appeal are in disagreement as to the guidelines to be followed by a trial court in determining whether or not to retain jurisdiction to extend a spousal support order. * * *

The guidelines set forth in the *Rosan–Dennis* line of cases prohibit a trial court from terminating jurisdiction over spousal support after a lengthy marriage unless the record contains evidence that the supported spouse will be able to adequately support himself or herself at the time selected for termination of jurisdiction. The opposite is true if *Patrino* and *Lopez* are followed, since those cases permit a trial court to terminate jurisdiction over spousal support after a lengthy marriage even though no such showing of self-sufficiency has been made. The *Patrino* and *Lopez* courts claim that the Legislature, in passing the Family Law Act of 1969 (Stats.1969, ch. 1608, p. 3314, eff. Jan. 1, 1970), endorsed a policy of encouraging the termination of jurisdiction to reduce the number of future modification proceedings and to provide the parties with some degree of "post-dissolution economic stability."

However, a review of the legislative history does not support the thesis that the Legislature intended to authorize trial courts to disregard the parties' circumstances and terminate jurisdiction for either of these reasons.

* * *

The enactment of the Family Law Act in 1969 did nothing to change this requirement that a court be guided by the circumstances of the parties in resolving issues relating to spousal support. * * * The major differences between former section 139 and the new section were that the new section eliminated consideration of the comparative marital fault of the parties in setting support, and listed two specific factors to be considered by the court in setting support—the duration of the marriage and the ability of the supported spouse to engage in gainful employment. * * * [T]he trial court was, as with the old statutory scheme, to be guided by the "circumstances of the respective parties" in determining the amount and duration of spousal support. * * *

* * *

As noted ante, former section 4801, subdivision (a), which was enacted as part of the Family Law Act, did expressly direct that in determining the amount and duration of spousal support, a court was to consider the supported spouse's ability to engage in gainful employment. It certainly may be inferred that by specifically setting forth this factor, the Legislature intended that all supported spouses who were able to do so should seek employment. It also appears the Legislature expected that courts would issue orders encouraging these spouses to seek employment and to work toward becoming self-supporting. * * * However, * * * the courts in *Patrino* and *Lopez* misconstrue the intent of the Legislature. They conclude that to promote such self-sufficiency, a court may set a termination date for spousal support without retaining jurisdiction to extend that date, even though the record does not indicate that the supported spouse will be financially independent at that time. This conclusion finds no support in the legislative history of section 4801, subdivision (d), or any other provision of the Family Law Act.

In 1969, the Assembly Committee on the Judiciary issued a report setting forth its intent in approving the Family Law Act. On the issue of support, that report states: "In awarding alimony or modifying a previous award, the court is directed to consider the duration of the marriage and the ability of the supported spouse to engage in gainful employment with due regard to the interests of any children of the parties. [¶] When our divorce law was originally drawn, woman's role in society was almost totally that of mother and homemaker. She could not even vote. Today, increasing numbers of married women are employed, even in the professions. In addition, they have long been accorded full civil rights. Their approaching equality with the male should be reflected in the law governing marriage dissolution and in the decisions of courts with respect to matters incident to dissolution." * * *

This report indicates that in those cases in which the supported spouse is working, the amount and duration of support, if any, should reflect this fact. The report also sets forth the Legislature's intent that courts should encourage supported spouses to seek employment. However, the report does not in any way suggest that when the supported spouse is unemployed or is earning only a small salary, a court should set a jurisdictional termination date based on the mere hope that this will induce that spouse to become self-supporting. Nor does it suggest that a court is justified in setting a jurisdictional termination date simply to relieve the supporting spouse of a long-term obligation. In short, while a court is to consider a supported spouse's employment in setting the amount and duration of support and is to encourage a supported spouse to seek employment, there is nothing in this report (or any other legislative history) to indicate that the Family Law Act was intended to be "some sort of mandate by the Legislature to the courts to relieve [the supporting spouse in every case] of any long, continuing obligation for spousal support." (In re Marriage of Rosan, supra, 24 Cal.App.3d at p. 897, 101 Cal.Rptr. at p. 304.)

Limiting the duration of support so that both parties can develop their own lives, free from obligations to each other, is a commendable goal. However, if courts were to award support with a set termination date simply for this reason and without any evidence as to the ability of the supported spouse to support himself or herself, great injustices could result. Although increasing numbers of married women today are employed, many others have devoted their time, with their spouse's approval, to maintaining the home and raising the children, leaving them no time for employment outside the home. This willingness of the wife to remain at home limits her ability to develop a career of her own. If the marriage is later dissolved, the wife may be unable, despite her greatest efforts, to enter the job market. As the Legislature has recognized, "displaced homemakers * * * are subject to the highest unemployment rate of any sector of the work force; they face continuing discrimination in employment because they are older and have no recent paid work experience * * *." (Gov.Code, § 7300.) If a court has encouraged the wife's self-sufficiency by ordering a limited period of support without retaining jurisdiction, it cannot provide additional support despite her continuing need and her efforts to become financially independent.

Based on this review of the legislative history of former section 139.7 and the Family Law Act, this court agrees with the reasoning in *Rosan* and *Dennis* concerning the retention of jurisdiction. A trial court should not terminate jurisdiction to extend a future support order after a lengthy marriage, unless the record clearly indicates that the supported spouse will be able to adequately meet his or her financial needs at the time selected for termination of jurisdiction. In making its decision concerning the retention of jurisdiction, the court must rely only on the evidence in the record and the reasonable inferences to be drawn therefrom. It must not engage in speculation. If the record does not contain evidence of the supported spouse's ability to meet his or her future needs, the court should not "burn its bridges" and fail to retain jurisdiction. (In re Marriage of Dennis, supra, 35 Cal.App.3d at p. 285, 110 Cal.Rptr. 619.) To the extent that the *Patrino* and *Lopez* decisions contain language contrary to the views expressed in this opinion, they are disapproved.

These standards will not require a trial court to retain jurisdiction in every case involving a lengthy marriage. In some instances the record will indicate that both spouses are employed, an increasingly prevalent situation today, or that there are sufficient assets available to enable each to provide for his or her needs. In that event, no support or support for only a limited time, without a retention of jurisdiction, would be appropriate. (Civ.Code, §§ 4801, subd. (a), 4806.) Where jurisdiction has been retained in the original order, future modification hearings may well reveal that the supported spouse has found adequate employment, has delayed seeking employment, or has refused available employment. At that time, the court may appropriately consider such factors in deciding whether or not to modify its original order. * * *

In some cases the supported spouse may never be able to adequately provide for his or her needs. A wife who has spent her married years as a homemaker and mother may, despite her best efforts, find it impossible to reenter the job market. In such a case "the husband simply has to face up to the fact that his support responsibilities are going to be of extended duration—perhaps for life. This has nothing to do with feminism, sexism, male chauvinism * * *. It is ordinary common-sense, basic decency and simple justice." (In re Marriage of Brantner, supra, 67 Cal.App.3d at p. 420, 136 Cal.Rptr. at p. 637.) The same will, of course, be expected of a wife in those cases in which a husband has devoted his time to maintaining the home and raising the children while the wife has pursued a career outside the home.

In the present case, no showing was made that the wife would be self-supporting at the end of 11 years. All the evidence in the record is to the contrary. The wife has no significant job skills or work history and has been able to secure only relatively low paying part-time employment. Further, the record indicates the wife's ability to obtain full-time employment may be hampered by medical problems. At the time the court's jurisdiction terminates in 11 years, the wife will have reached the customary retirement age of 65. The record does not indicate what, if any, retirement benefits she will be eligible to receive at that time.

The trial court abused its discretion by divesting itself of jurisdiction to award future spousal support after 11 years without any evidence in the record that the wife would be able to provide for herself at that time. Accordingly, the portion of the judgment which fails to retain jurisdiction after 11 years must be reversed.

III

Next, the wife contends that the trial court abused its discretion in limiting her spousal support to $400 a month.

* * *

The financial information contained in the record of this case indicates that the wife's monthly income will be approximately $667 under the challenged order—$400 from spousal support, $167 from her share of the military pension benefits, and $100 from her part-time employment. This amount is less than the wife's claimed expenses, but under the terms of the interlocutory decree, the husband's income is also less than his anticipated expenses.

Although the husband's claimed monthly expenses are $1,367, his net monthly income will be reduced to approximately $900 due to the division of his military pension benefits and to the spousal support payments.

The husband's and wife's incomes, which were sufficient to cover their expenses when they were living together, are not sufficient to sustain the expenses of two separate households. Under these circumstances, the trial court was unable to provide fully for the financial needs of both parties. In attempting to fairly allocate the funds that were available, the court did not abuse its discretion in setting the wife's spousal support at $400 a month.

* * *

The judgment is reversed and the cause remanded for further proceedings consistent with the views expressed herein.

TOBRINER, J., MOSK, J., CLARK, J., MANUEL, J., and NEWMAN, J., concurred.

WHITE v. WHITE

Supreme Court of North Carolina, 1985.
312 N.C. 770, 324 S.E.2d 829.

MITCHELL, JUSTICE.

This case presents fundamental questions arising under the Equitable Distribution Act concerning the proper distribution of marital property when a couple is divorced.

The litigants in this action were married on September 8, 1951. In July, 1980, the plaintiff husband abandoned the home of the parties. On November 23, 1981, he filed an action for divorce based on one year's separation. The defendant wife counterclaimed for equitable distribution of the marital property under N.C.G.S. 50–20.

* * *

With regard to the wife's claim for equitable distribution the trial court made findings of fact which may be summarized as follows:

Prior to the marriage, the plaintiff had received a Bachelor of Science degree in agricultural engineering from North Carolina State University. The defendant had obtained her certification as a registered nurse and was working at Rex Hospital in Raleigh at the time of the marriage.

The plaintiff was employed as a salesman of heavy equipment and was transferred to Charlotte shortly after the marriage. The defendant gave up her job and moved to Charlotte with him. Soon thereafter, she became pregnant with their first child which was born in September, 1952. A second child was born of the marriage in February, 1954. The parties agreed that the defendant wife would not pursue a nursing career, but would instead devote her time and energy to the rearing of the children. During the first twenty-four years of the marriage, the plaintiff husband traveled extensively in connection with his sales job. During this period the defendant attended to the needs of the children and managed the home. She also contributed substantially to the career of her husband by acquiescing in several job transfers that he made. The defendant wife also worked part-time, often at night and on weekends, in various communities in which the family resided.

In June, 1970, the defendant began work full time as an Occupational Health Nurse with the Postal Service. She has continued in that position to the present.

During the course of the marriage, the plaintiff invested in securities in his separate name. He purchased the majority of his holdings during the early 1970's. He was employed through 1975, but from 1975 until 1978 he had no full time employment. During this period the defendant's earnings and contributions to the home were $63,471, or more than three times the $19,505 earned and contributed by the plaintiff husband. Her earnings permitted him to devote his full attention to the management of his individual investments.

In 1978, the plaintiff husband obtained a position with the Postal Service and is presently so employed. He is 55, earns $20,500 per year and has the opportunity to earn salary increases in his present employment. The defendant wife is 52, earns $23,000 per year and has reached the maximum salary level which can be earned in her present employment. He has bursitis. She suffers from arthritis and osteoporosis and has had periods of depression which on two occasions interfered with her work. He has vested pension rights of $3,300. She has vested pension rights of $8,900. The plaintiff husband also has prospects of inheriting a substantial estate.

The parties, either individually or jointly, owned the following marital property: (1) a house, lot and greenhouse valued at $57,900; (2) automobiles valued at $2,500; (3) securities valued at $72,408.86; (4) banking and savings accounts in the amount of $1,478; and (5) furniture and household goods valued at $1,000. Since 1975 the defendant wife has made the regular mortgage payments on the house. The trial court also found that the defendant had contributed services as a spouse, mother, homemaker and wage earner which exceeded in value the total fair market value of her interest in the jointly held property and her separately held property.

The trial court concluded that the contributions of the parties entitled each to an equal share of the marital property and ordered the property distributed accordingly. The order was affirmed by the Court of Appeals. This Court allowed the defendant wife's petition for discretionary review.

The defendant wife contends that the trial court erred in ordering an equal division of the marital property. She argues that her contributions to the marital estate vastly exceeded those of her husband, and that she should be awarded a greater share of the property.

This case involves the Equitable Distribution Act. 1981 N.C.Sess.Laws, ch. 815. Though touched upon in *Mims v. Mims,* 305 N.C. 41, 286 S.E.2d 779 (1982), this is our first opportunity to expressly address the Act. Therefore, it is appropriate to briefly examine the purposes of the Act.

The theory of husband-wife unity which existed at early common law gave the wife virtually no legal status or property rights. Upon marriage the wife's personal property vested absolutely in her husband. When the wife brought any real property into the marriage, the husband became seized of an estate in it which gave him the right of possession and control. He could sell and convey the land for a period not exceeding the coverture, and he was entitled to rents received from her real property. Though the wife retained her interest in the real property, she could not convey during coverture even with the consent of the husband. Also, the wife's personal estate and the husband's interest in her real property were subject to levy under execution for his debts. 2 R. Lee, *N.C. Family Law* § 107 (4th ed. 1980) [hereinafter cited as *Lee*].

In the 1830's and 1840's the North Carolina General Assembly enacted several statutes which accorded married women greater control over their property. Under these provisions a conveyance of the wife's land was required to be jointly executed by the husband and wife, and the wife was privately questioned as to the voluntary nature of the transfer. * * * The wife was also permitted to have and retain property acquired by her following a divorce. * * * Another statutory provision prohibited the husband from leasing the wife's real property for a term of years or for life without her joining in the lease following a privy examination. * * * A fourth provision prevented the sale under execution of the husband's interest in his wife's real property. * * * These enactments paved the way for a constitutional provision which established a woman's right to keep as her separate estate all property she brought into the marriage or acquired during coverture and which exempted her separate estate from liability for the husband's debts. N.C. Const. of 1868, art. X, § 6 (now N.C. Const. art. X, § 4). Chapter 52 of the North Carolina General Statutes and N.C.G.S. 39–7 *et seq.* carry forward the intent of those early statutory provisions.

Despite the enlightened views evidenced by these enactments, our courts continued to adhere to the common law rules based on title when confronted with the task of dividing marital property upon divorce. *See 2 Lee,* §§ 107–27; L. Kelso, *North Carolina Divorce, Alimony and Child Custody,* § 8–1 (1983); *Survey of Developments In North Carolina Law,* 60 N.C.L.Rev. 1159 (1982); Marschall, *Proposed Reforms In North Carolina Divorce Law,* 8 N.C.Cent.L.J. 35 (1976). The allocation of marital property to the party who held title thereto tended to reward the spouse directly responsible for its acquisition, while overlooking the contribution of the homemaking spouse. L. Golden, *Equitable Distribution of Property,* § 1.03 (1983) [hereinafter cited as *Golden*]. Though the title theory approach made property distribution relatively simple, the result was often harsh for the homemaker. *See e.g., Leatherman v. Leatherman,* 297 N.C. 618, 256 S.E.2d 793 (1979).

In 1981, the General Assembly sought to alleviate the unfairness of the common law rule by enacting our Equitable Distribution Act which is now codified as N.C.G.S. 50–20 and 21. As early as the 1930's, a third of the states had some form of equitable distribution. By the early 1980's, forty-one states and the District of Columbia had adopted the concept. *Golden,* § 1.02. Equitable distribution reflects the idea that marriage is a partnership enterprise to which both spouses make vital contributions and which entitles the homemaker spouse to a share of the property acquired during the relationship. *See In Re Marriage of Komnick,* 84 Ill.2d 89, 49 Ill.Dec. 291, 417 N.E.2d 1305 (1981); *Rothman v. Rothman,* 65 N.J. 219, 320 A.2d 496 (1974); *D'Agostino v. D'Agostino,* 463 A.2d 200 (R.I.1983); *LaRue v. LaRue,* 304 S.E.2d 312 (W.Va.1983); Sharp, *Equitable Distribution of Property In North Carolina: A Preliminary Analysis,* 61 N.C.L.Rev. 247 (1983).

With this background information in mind, we now turn to the specific issues raised by this appeal. Our first task is to determine whether the trial court was correct in its view that the Equitable Distribution Act creates a presumption that an equal division of the marital property is equitable and therefore appropriate. N.C.G.S. 50–20(c) provides:

> There shall be an equal division by using net value of marital property unless the court determines that an equal division is not equitable. If the court determines that an equal division is not equitable, the court shall divide the marital property equitably. Factors the court shall consider under this subsection are as follows:
>
> (1) The income, property, and liabilities of each party at the time the division of property is to become effective;
>
> (2) Any obligation for support arising out of a prior marriage;
>
> (3) The duration of the marriage and the age and physical and mental health of both parties;
>
> (4) The need of a parent with custody of a child or children of the marriage to occupy or own the marital residence and to use or own its household effects;
>
> (5) The expectation of nonvested pension or retirement rights, which is separate property;
>
> (6) Any equitable claim to, interest in, or direct or indirect contribution made to the acquisition of such marital property by the party not having title, including joint efforts or expenditures and contributions and services, or lack thereof, as a spouse, parent, wage earner or homemaker;
>
> (7) Any direct or indirect contribution made by one spouse to help educate or develop the career potential of the other spouse;
>
> (8) Any direct contribution to an increase in value of separate property which occurs during the course of the marriage;
>
> (9) The liquid or nonliquid character of all marital property;
>
> (10) The difficulty of evaluating any component asset or any interest in a business, corporation or profession, and the economic desirability of retaining such asset or interest, intact and free from any claim or interference by the other party;
>
> (11) The tax consequences to each party; and
>
> (12) Any other factor the court finds to be just and proper.

The trial court in the present case indicated that "pursuant to G.S. 50–20, an equal division of the marital property of the parties is presumed appropriate." The statute in fact does more. It does not create a "presumption" in any of the senses that term has been used to express "the common idea of assuming or inferring the existence of one fact from another fact or combination of facts." 2 Brandis on North Carolina Evidence, § 215 (2d ed. 1982). Instead, the statute is a legislative enactment of public policy so strongly favoring the equal division of marital property that an equal division is made *mandatory* "unless the court determines that an equal division is not equitable." N.C.G.S. 50–20(c). The clear intent of the legislature was that a party desiring an unequal division of marital property bear the burden of producing evidence concerning one or more of the twelve factors in the statute and the burden of proving by a preponderance of the evidence that an equal division would not be equitable. Therefore, if no evidence is admitted tending to show that an equal division would be inequitable, the trial court *must* divide the marital property equally.

When evidence tending to show that an equal division of marital property would not be equitable is admitted, however, the trial court must exercise its discretion in assigning the weight each factor should receive in any given case. It must then make an equitable division of the marital property by balancing the evidence presented by the parties in light of the legislative policy which favors equal division.

In the present case evidence was admitted tending to show that an equal division would not be equitable. We turn then to consider the proper standard of review of equitable distribution awards in such cases. Historically our trial courts have been granted wide discretionary powers concerning domestic law cases. * * * The legislature also clearly intended to vest trial courts with discretion in distributing marital property under N.C.G.S. 50–20, but guided always by the public policy expressed therein favoring an equal division. The legislative intent to vest our trial courts with such broad discretion is emphasized by the inclusion of the catchall factor codified in N.C.G.S. 50–20(c)(12).

It is well established that where matters are left to the discretion of the trial court, appellate review is limited to a determination of whether there was a clear abuse of discretion. * * * A ruling committed to a trial court's discretion is to be accorded great deference and will be upset only upon a showing that it was so arbitrary that it could not have been the result of a reasoned decision.

Turning to the facts of this case, we are unable to say that the trial court abused its discretion in concluding that each party was entitled to an equal share of the marital property. The findings of fact show that the trial court admitted and considered evidence relating to several of the twelve factors contained in N.C.G.S. 50–20(c). The defendant wife does not allege that the trial court failed to consider the evidence relevant to such factors. Instead she claims that in reaching a decision on the division of the marital property, the trial court failed to give proper weight to her nonfinancial contributions to the marriage and to the fact that her income significantly exceeded that of her husband from 1975 to 1978.

The trial court found as a fact that she had contributed nonfinancial services and wages to the marriage which exceeded in value the total fair market value of her interest in the jointly held property and her separately held property. The trial court, however, also found facts favorable to the plaintiff including that he was employed during the early part of the marriage, that his present salary was less than the defendant's, and that the defendant's vested pension rights exceeded his. The trial court perhaps could have weighed the evidence differently and awarded the defendant wife more than an equal share of the property. However, when coupled with the legislative policy favoring equal division, we cannot say that the evidence fails to show any rational basis for the distribution ordered by the court. Therefore, we detect no abuse of discretion.

In this case the trial court did not expressly state in its order that an equal division of the marital property would be equitable. The defendant argues that a specific determination to this effect was required. We disagree. The task of a trial court when faced with an action under N.C.G.S. 50–20 is to equitably distribute the marital property between the litigants. This is evident from the language and the title of the Act. Once the trial court orders a distribution, it has held *sub silentio* that such distribution is fair and equitable. A specific statement that the distribution ordered is equitable is not required.

As modified herein, the decision of the Court of Appeals affirming the order of the trial court is affirmed.

MODIFIED AND AFFIRMED.

VAUGHN, J., took no part in the consideration or decision of this case.

PETERSEN v. PETERSEN

Court of Appeals of Utah, 1987.
737 P.2d 237.

ORME, JUDGE:

The appellant seeks a reversal or readjustment of the property division and alimony awarded to his former wife upon their divorce. His challenge focuses on a $120,000 property settlement given to his ex-wife to reflect her interest in his medical degree. We affirm the trial court's basic disposition, but require amendment of the decree insofar as the $120,000 award is concerned.

* * *

The parties were married in September 1963 when they were both entering their senior year of college. Both graduated with Bachelor's degrees. Dr. Petersen continued his education and obtained a Master's degree, while Mrs. Petersen worked as an elementary school teacher to help finance her husband's education. After receiving his Master's degree, Dr. Petersen entered medical school. During medical school, Dr. Petersen earned approximately $1,000 per year in income. The couple also took out a student loan and received some money from Mrs. Petersen's parents. While her husband was in medical school, Mrs. Petersen worked one year on a full time basis and three years part time.

When Dr. Petersen began his internship, Mrs. Petersen stopped working to stay at home with their child. During the next fifteen years, Mrs. Petersen was not employed outside the home and her teaching certification expired.

By the time of their divorce, the parties had been married twenty years and had six children under the age of 18. The decree gave Mrs. Petersen custody of the six minor children, the family residence subject to the first mortgage, most of the family furniture, and two automobiles. She was awarded $300 per month per child as child support, $1,000 per month alimony, and the cash property settlement of $120,000, which Dr. Petersen was to pay in installments of $1,000 per month without interest.

Under the decree, Dr. Petersen received his professional corporation, the total interest in his pension and profit sharing plan, two condominiums, a boat, an undivided one-seventh interest in a cabin near Bear Lake, and other rental property. He also was given the right to claim all six children as dependents for income tax purposes.

The trial court explained the $120,000 cash settlement as follows:

> The Court believes that this case is classic, in that defendant is entitled to a property award reflecting an ownership interest of the defendant in plaintiff's medical degree. It is abundantly clear that defendant helped plaintiff earn that degree during their marriage, and that plaintiff's ability to earn is based upon that degree. Further, that following the earning of the degree and the entry into the medical practice, by mutual agreement, defendant undertook the raising and nurturing of the children as her responsibility to the marital partnership, while plaintiff practiced medicine. It is difficult to find in the evidence presented any system for the measurement of the value of the degree, and the Court must therefore deal with the case mostly upon an alimony basis. To deal with the case fully upon an alimony basis is not fair to the defendant, inasmuch as any effort to restructure her life by seeking to better her employment opportunities or to remarry will operate against her alimony rights. Defendant is therefore awarded $1,000 per month permanent alimony and a lump sum property award in respect to the medical degree in the amount of $120,000, payable in installments of $1,000 per month from the date of the decree.

On appeal, Dr. Petersen argues that the division of marital property was inequitable, particularly the $120,000 property settlement given to his wife. Dr. Petersen argues that it was error to characterize "his" medical degree as marital property and require him to cash out Mrs. Petersen's interest therein over a 10-year period.

* * *

Generally, the trial court is permitted considerable discretion in adjusting the financial and property interests of the parties to a divorce action and its determinations are entitled to a presumption of validity. * * *

In the present case, the trial court appropriately attempted to equalize the parties' respective standards of living. *See Olson v. Olson,* 704 P.2d 564, 566 (Utah 1985). Dr. Petersen was found capable of earning $100,000 per year while Mrs. Petersen's ability to obtain recertification and secure a teaching contract was found to be speculative at best. Even if she succeeded, she would earn only one-fourth to one-fifth of what Dr. Petersen would earn annually. The trial court spoke of the difficulty of measuring the value of Dr. Petersen's degree. The court chose to balance the inequalities between the parties partly with the alimony award. However, the trial court did not want Mrs. Petersen to lose all of her entitlement upon remarriage, so the trial court provided for an additional $120,000 as a property award, payable in $1,000 monthly installments. Characterization of these payments as a property award created the main issue for appeal.

* * *

The question of whether an advanced degree is a property interest subject to division upon divorce is one of first impression at the appellate level in Utah. However, the majority of jurisdictions that have considered the issue have held that advanced degrees or professional licenses are not property. *Wisner v. Wisner,* 129 Ariz. 333, 631 P.2d 115, 122 (Ariz.App.1981) (husband's medical license and board certificate are not property subject to division, but education is a factor to be considered in arriving at equitable property division, maintenance, and child support); *In re Marriage of Aufmuth,* 89 Cal.App.3d 446, 152 Cal.Rptr. 668, 677 (1979) (legal education not a property right); *In re Marriage of Graham,* 194 Colo. 429, 574 P.2d 75, 77 (1978) (MBA degree not marital property subject to division); *In re Marriage of Horstmann,* 263 N.W.2d 885, 891 (Iowa 1978) (law degree is not a distributable asset upon divorce; future earnings are); *Olah v. Olah,* 135 Mich.App. 404, 354 N.W.2d 359, 361 (Mich.App.1984) (medical degree not property or marital asset); *Mahoney v. Mahoney,* 91 N.J. 488, 453 A.2d 527, 536 (1982) (courts may not make any permanent distribution of the value of professional degrees and licenses, whether based on estimated worth or cost); *Ruben v. Ruben,* 123 N.H. 358, 461 A.2d 733, 735 (1983) (graduate degree acquired by one spouse during the marriage is not an asset subject to division upon divorce); *Muckleroy v. Muckleroy,* 84 N.M. 14, 498 P.2d 1357, 1358 (1972) (medical license is not community property); *Hubbard v. Hubbard,* 603 P.2d 747, 750–751 (Okl.1979) (medical license not property but wife entitled to compensation for her investment).

These cases and others are consistent with our understanding of what "property" is and what an educational degree is. Property can be bought, sold, and devised. Bona fide degrees cannot be bought; they are earned. They cannot be sold; they are personal to the named recipient. Upon the death of the named recipient, the certificate commemorating award of the degree might be passed along and treasured as a family heirloom, but the recipient may not, on the strength of that degree, practice law or medicine. In this case, the court awarded the parties' home to Mrs. Petersen. But it might have awarded the home to Dr. Petersen or it might have ordered the home sold and the net proceeds divided. The court had no such alternatives with the medical degree, precisely because the degree is not property.

* * *

The same issue arose as to an M.B.A. degree earned by the husband in *In re Marriage of Graham,* 194 Colo. 429, 574 P.2d 75 (1978). Again, the concept of an advanced degree being property was rejected:

> An educational degree, such as an M.B.A., is simply not encompassed even by the broad views of the concept of "property." It does not have an exchange value or any objective transferable value on an open market. It is personal to the holder. It terminates on death of the holder and is not inheritable. It cannot be assigned, sold, transferred, conveyed, or pledged. An advanced degree is a cumulative product of many years of previous education, combined with diligence and hard work. It may not be acquired by the mere expenditure of money. It is simply an intellectual achievement that may potentially assist in the future acquisition of

property.   In our view, it has none of the attributes of property in the usual sense of that term.

* * *

The wife in *Graham* had worked full time throughout the couple's six-year marriage, and had contributed 70 percent of the family income in addition to most of the household work while her husband was acquiring his degree.   * * * The fact that the decision left Mrs. Graham with nothing to show for her six years of labor prompted a three judge dissent which strongly urged that the husband's increased earning power represented by the degree should be considered marital property, where there was no accumulated property and the spouse who subsidized the degree was ineligible for maintenance.[3]   * * *

The equitable concerns addressed in the *Graham* dissent are reflected in the few cases that have found an advanced degree or professional license to be marital property.

* * *

Recently, in *O'Brien v. O'Brien,* 66 N.Y.2d 576, 489 N.E.2d 712, 498 N.Y.S.2d 743 (1985), the New York Court of Appeals affirmed the trial court's holding that a license to practice medicine acquired during the marriage is marital property subject to division.   In *O'Brien,* the wife was held entitled to a 40 percent interest in her husband's medical license.   The wife had contributed approximately 76 percent of the couples' total income while the husband obtained his license.   The breakdown of the marriage occurred shortly after the husband completed his schooling, and the only tangible asset existing after their nine-year marriage was the husband's medical license.

The New York court distinguished its analysis in *O'Brien* from that of other jurisdictions which have found a license or advanced degree not to be marital property.   As the *O'Brien* court explained:

> Plaintiff does not contend that his license is excluded from distribution because it is separate property; rather, he claims that it is not property at all but represents a personal attainment in acquiring knowledge. He rests his argument on decisions in similar cases from other jurisdictions and on his view that a license does not satisfy common-law concepts of property. Neither contention is controlling because decisions in other States rely principally on their own statutes, and the legislative history underlying them, and because the New York Legislature deliberately went beyond traditional property concepts when it formulated the Equitable Distribution Law.

* * * New York's highest court acknowledged in *O'Brien* that their statute creates a new species of property previously unknown at common law or under prior statutes.   * * * Critical portions of the New York Equitable Distribution Law provide that in making an equitable distribution of marital property, the court shall consider the efforts one spouse made to the other spouse's career or career potential and the difficulty of evaluating an interest

---

3. In *Graham,* the wife did not request alimony because a Colorado statute, Colo.Rev. Stat. § 14–10–114 (1973), restricted the court's power to award maintenance to cases where the spouse seeking it was unable to support himself or herself.   574 P.2d at 79.

in a profession. * * * Thus, the analysis in *O'Brien*, although illustrative of the equitable concerns for the working spouse who supports the other through an advanced degree, * * * is limited in application because of the pivotal role of the unusual and expansive distribution statute enacted in New York.

We agree with the majority opinion in *Graham* that an advanced degree is or confers an intangible right which, because of its character, cannot properly be characterized as property subject to division between the spouses. No special statute, as in New York, permits us to treat the degree as though it were property. On the other hand, criteria for an award of support in Utah are not so rigid as in Colorado, preventing the harsh result of *Graham*. In this state, traditional alimony analysis is the appropriate and adequate method for making adjustments between the parties in cases of this type.[4]

* * *

As indicated, the trial court was in error when it awarded Mrs. Petersen the $120,000 cash settlement to reflect her share of the value of her husband's medical degree. Nonetheless, the court's basic disposition was fair and can be sustained if the $1,000 monthly payments which Dr. Petersen was to make in satisfaction of that obligation are recharacterized as additional alimony, a result which is readily supported by the trial court's findings.

* * *

As for the cash settlement payable in monthly installments of $1,000, it is properly affirmed as alimony, making Mrs. Petersen's entire alimony award $2,000 per month. Criteria considered in determining a reasonable award of support must include the financial conditions and needs of the spouse in need of support, the ability of that spouse to produce sufficient income for his or her own support, and the ability of the other spouse to provide support. *Jones v. Jones*, 700 P.2d 1072, 1075 (Utah 1985).

In this case, then, the first factor to be considered is the financial condition and needs of Mrs. Petersen. For over ten years, Mrs. Petersen and her family enjoyed a very comfortable lifestyle. She now must make mortgage payments on the home and pay for the ordinary expenses of food, clothing and transportation. Other than the one-half interest in the investment corporation, Mrs. Petersen was awarded none of the income-producing assets. She has no outside income.

4. In cases like the instant one, life patterns have largely been set, the earning potential of both parties can be predicted with some reliability, and the contributions and sacrifices of the one spouse in enabling the other to attain a degree have been compensated by many years of the comfortable lifestyle which the degree permitted. Traditional alimony analysis works nicely to assure equity in such cases.

In another kind of recurring case, typified by *Graham*, where divorce occurs shortly after the degree is obtained, traditional alimony analysis would often work hardship because, while both spouses have modest incomes at the time of divorce, the one is on the threshold of a significant increase in earnings. Moreover, the spouse who sacrificed so the other could attain a degree is precluded from enjoying the anticipated dividends the degree will ordinarily provide. Nonetheless, such a spouse is typically not remote in time from his or her previous education and is otherwise better able to adjust and to acquire comparable skills, given the opportunity and the funding. In such cases, alimony analysis must become more creative to achieve fairness, and an award of "rehabilitative" or "reimbursement" alimony, not terminable upon remarriage, may be appropriate. *See, e.g., Haugan v. Haugan*, 117 Wis.2d 200, 343 N.W.2d 796 (1984); *Mahoney v. Mahoney*, 91 N.J. 488, 453 A.2d 527 (1982).

The second factor to be considered is Mrs. Petersen's ability to produce a sufficient income for herself. Although Mrs. Petersen is a college graduate with a Bachelor's degree and is trained as a school teacher, she is not currently certified. She would require additional training to become certified and, even if certified, her ability to produce income would be one fourth to one fifth of what Dr. Petersen's income has provided the family. The trial court found that the chance of her being able to secure a teaching contract was "speculative." During most of the marriage, Mrs. Petersen was not employed outside the home. She stopped working, primarily at the urging of her husband, and devoted her time to raising their six children. It is unreasonable to assume that she will be able immediately to enter the job market and support herself in the style in which she had been living before the divorce. *See Jones v. Jones,* 700 P.2d 1072, 1075 (Utah 1985).

The final factor to be considered is the ability of Dr. Petersen to provide support. This is the proper realm in which to consider advanced degrees or professional licenses. An advanced degree is ordinarily an indicator of potential future earnings. In addition, the attainment of a degree by one spouse often results in a disparity of income that is likely to last for a great time, particularly in cases like the present one. Dr. Petersen has a history of earning more than $100,000 a year and Mrs. Petersen has not worked for the past fifteen. But it is the discrepancy in their earning power which is the basis for alimony, not the discrepancy in their educations. There is no logical reason, for example, for treating differently a self-trained artist without formal education who earns and will earn $100,000 a year and a doctor with a medical degree who earns and will earn $100,000 a year. Other things being equal, if such an artist divorces his or her spouse, he or she should pay alimony comparable to that paid by such a doctor. Whether a spouse's ability to provide support is the result of an advanced degree or professional license is irrelevant to the analysis. The key is the spouse's *ability.*

In *Savage v. Savage,* 658 P.2d 1201 (Utah 1983), the Supreme Court explained:

> Where a marriage is of long duration and the earning capacity of one spouse greatly exceeds that of the other, as here, it is appropriate to order alimony and child support at a level which will insure that the supported spouse and children may maintain a standard of living not unduly disproportionate to that which they would have enjoyed had the marriage continued.

658 P.2d at 1205. * * *

In *Savage,* the parties had enjoyed a high standard of living during the marriage and the court upheld an award of $2,000 per month alimony and child support of $500 per month per child. * * * In *Yelderman v. Yelderman,* 669 P.2d 406 (Utah 1983), the Supreme Court upheld an alimony award of $2,500 per month as not excessive. * * * We agree that $2,000 per month alimony to Mrs. Petersen is sufficient to help her maintain a standard of living not unduly disproportionate to that which she would have enjoyed if the marriage had continued.[5]

---

5. It is clear the court viewed the payments to Mrs. Petersen, both those it specifically called alimony and the additional $1,000 monthly payments, as appropriate for her sup-

Accordingly, this case is remanded to District Court to amend the decree to provide that Mrs. Petersen receive $2,000 per month alimony and, correspondingly, to delete the $120,000 cash award. * * *

Notes on Orr, Morrison, White, *and* Petersen

1. On remand in *Orr,* the Alabama courts chose to cure the underinclusiveness of the alimony statute by extending its benefits to needy husbands. Orr v. Orr, 374 So.2d 895 (Ala.Civ.App.1979), writ denied 374 So.2d 898 (Ala.), appeal dismissed, cert. denied 444 U.S. 1060, 100 S.Ct. 993, 62 L.Ed.2d 738 (1980). Accord, Beal v. Beal, 388 A.2d 72 (Me.1978).

2. The husbands in *Orr* and *Beal* did not seek alimony for themselves. Instead, they attempted to avoid the obligation to support their former wives by challenging the alimony statutes. What standards should govern the award of alimony to husbands? Addressing this issue in 1972, a Florida court said, "no matter which direction the flow of alimony may take, its basic nature and purpose remains the same as heretofore, i.e., to provide nourishment, sustenance and the necessities of life to a former spouse who has neither the resources nor ability to be self-sustaining." Lefler v. Lefler, 264 So.2d 112, 113–14 (Fla.App.1972). The court went on to hold that "just as heretofore the wife's entitlement to alimony depended upon a showing of her need and the husband's ability to pay * * * so now the husband's entitlement to alimony depends upon a showing of his need and the wife's ability to pay." (Id., at 114.) The trial court's award of one-half the marital domicile to the husband as lump sum alimony was found erroneous because the evidence did not sustain the finding that the husband lacked the ability to provide for his own support.

3. Under what circumstances should a wife be required to pay alimony to her husband following divorce? Only when she had had primary responsibility for supporting the family during marriage? Suppose both spouses were professionally trained and the husband can show that the couple made the moves and took the job opportunities that enhanced the wife's professional advancement at the expense of the husband's career: Should the wife be required to reimburse her husband for his lost opportunities? Would she be entitled to similar reimbursement if the roles had been reversed? In a pre-*Orr* decision, a New York court was called upon to consider the validity of an agreement between the husband and wife that the wife was to pay the husband "as and for his support and maintenance, in the form of alimony, if you will, the sum of $125 per week". The parties were married in 1953 and divorced in 1974. At the insistence of his wife, the

port. It utilized the "property" label in characterizing some of the monthly total as a means to preclude termination of the payments to Mrs. Petersen upon her remarriage. Although the court provided that the $1,000 per month payments not called alimony would terminate in ten years, nothing in the court's findings establishes any particular significance to that point in time. We accordingly see no basis, now that the entire monthly payment is properly characterized as alimony, to require that half of the $2,000 monthly total automatically and arbitrarily terminate at the end of ten years. *Cf. Olson v. Olson,* 704 P.2d 564, 567 (Utah 1985) (court modified divorce decree to delete provision that alimony would terminate after two years where monthly amount was reasonable but two-year limit was not). Of course, it would be proper for the district court to readjust the amount of alimony awarded to Mrs. Petersen if at *any* point in time there develops a material change of circumstances, such as Mrs. Petersen securing gainful employment or if Dr. Petersen's salary drops dramatically through no fault of his own. *See, e.g., Naylor v. Naylor,* 700 P.2d 707, 710 (Utah 1985); *Haslam v. Haslam,* 657 P.2d 757, 758 (Utah 1982). The district court retains continuing jurisdiction in divorce actions to amend alimony. Utah Code Ann. § 30–3–5 (1986). In addition, the alimony awarded to Mrs. Petersen automatically terminates under certain circumstances. *Id.*

husband stopped working in 1955. During the remainder of the marriage the wife, a successful business woman, supported the family. Claiming that his unemployment rendered him "unable to work" and left him without funds to support himself, the husband sought alimony. The agreement, subsequently incorporated into the court's judgment, was arrived at after the case had been called for trial as part of a settlement. The wife's later claim that the agreement was void because she was under no obligation to pay alimony to her husband was rejected. The court reasoned that "[w]hile it is against public policy for a husband and wife to enter into an agreement whereby one relieves the other of the mutual obligation to support each other * * * it is not against public policy for a party not legally liable to pay alimony to agree to do so, particularly when that agreement is part of a settlement of a matrimonial dispute." Cheatham v. Cheatham, 93 Misc.2d 576, 581, 405 N.Y.S.2d 878, 881–82 (Sup.Ct.1976), affirmed mem. 44 N.Y.2d 823, 406 N.Y.S.2d 456, 377 N.E.2d 987 (1978). See generally, Isabel Marcus, Locked In and Locked Out: Reflections on the History of Divorce Law Reform in New York State, 37 Buff.L.Rev. 375 (1989).

Either party to a matrimonial action in New York may now be ordered to pay "maintenance" to the other under proper circumstances. See N.Y.Dom.Rel.Law § 236(6) (McKinney, 1986 & 1995 Cum.Ann. Pocket Part). Would Mr. Cheatham be awarded alimony by a court today? The governing statute provides:

6. Maintenance. a. Except where the parties have entered into an agreement pursuant to subdivision three of this part providing for maintenance, in any matrimonial action the court may order temporary maintenance or maintenance in such amount as justice requires, having regard for the standard of living of the parties established during the marriage, whether the party in whose favor maintenance is granted lacks sufficient property and income to provide for his or her reasonable needs and whether the other party has sufficient property or income to provide for the reasonable needs of the other and the circumstances of the case and of the respective parties. Such order shall be effective as of the date of the application therefor, and any retroactive amount of maintenance due shall be paid in one sum or periodic sums, as the court shall direct, taking into account any amount of temporary maintenance which has been paid. In determining the amount and duration of maintenance the court shall consider:

(1) the income and property of the respective parties including marital property distributed pursuant to subdivision five of this part;

(2) the duration of the marriage and the age and health of both parties;

(3) the present and future earning capacity of both parties;

(4) the ability of the party seeking maintenance to become self-supporting and, if applicable, the period of time and training necessary therefor;

(5) reduced or lost lifetime earning capacity of the party seeking maintenance as a result of having foregone or delayed education, training, employment, or career opportunities during the marriage;

(6) the presence of children of the marriage in the respective homes of the parties;

(7) the tax consequences to each party;

(8) contributions and services of the party seeking maintenance as a spouse, parent, wage earner and homemaker, and to the career or career potential of the other party;

(9) the wasteful dissipation of marital property by either spouse;

(10) any transfer or encumbrance made in contemplation of a matrimonial action without fair consideration; and

(11) any other factor which the court shall expressly find to be just and proper.

b. In any decision made pursuant to this subdivision, the court shall set forth the factors it considered and the reasons for its decision and such may not be waived by either party or counsel.

c. The court may award permanent maintenance, but an award of maintenance shall terminate upon the death of either party or upon the recipient's valid or invalid marriage, or upon modification pursuant to paragraph (b) of subdivision nine of section two hundred thirty-six of this part or section two hundred forty-eight of this chapter.

d. In any decision made pursuant to this subdivision the court shall, where appropriate, consider the effect of a barrier to remarriage, as defined in subdivision six of section two hundred fifty-three of this article, on the factors enumerated in paragraph a of this subdivision.

4. *Marriage of Morrison* presents the case of the "displaced homemaker" in its most typical form. At the time of the marriage in 1947, the wife was 26, the husband 24. At her husband's request, Ms. Morrison did not work outside the home during their 28 year marriage. By the time of the divorce in 1975, she was 54 years old and lacked both job skills and training. Alimony has been the traditional way of providing for women in Ms. Morrison's situation, but observers have noted that awards of "spousal support" had grown smaller in amount and shorter in duration following the enactment of California's no-fault divorce law in 1969. See Wendell H. Goddard, A Report on California's New Divorce Law: Progress and Problems, 6 Fam.L.Q. 405 (1972); Marvin A. Freeman, Should Spousal Support Be Abolished?, 48 L.A.Bar Bull. 236 (1973). Similar trends had been noted in other states where no-fault divorce laws had taken effect. See, e.g., Daniel E. Murray, Twelfth Survey of Florida Law: Family Law, 30 U.Miami L.Rev. 107, 108 (1976). A Florida court, reversing as insufficient an award of nine months "rehabilitative" alimony to another displaced homemaker after a marriage of 26 years, pointedly observed, "[t]here is apparently a feeling in some circles that the passage of the 'no-fault' divorce law in 1971 had the effect of abolishing permanent alimony except where the wife (or the husband, as the case may be) is unable to get a job. We know of no controlling decision to this effect and do not believe it to be the law." Lash v. Lash, 307 So.2d 241, 242 (Fla.App.1975).

Judicial perception of the effect to be given the "women's movement" may be as influential as no-fault divorce on the tendency to reduce alimony awards. An amicus curiae brief filed in *Marriage of Morrison* informed the California Supreme Court that judges frequently discussed the "movement" during settlement conferences; their attitude was thought to be a factor in the alimony decision. Brief of Queen's Bench as Amicus Curiae in *Marriage of Morrison*, at 7.

Will decisions like *Marriage of Morrison* and *Lash* be effective in persuading trial court judges to consider only economic factors when awarding spousal support? What is the underlying rationale for alimony, regardless of who pays it, once the fault-based grounds for divorce have been abolished? See generally, Ira Mark Ellman, The Theory of Alimony, 77 Calif.L.Rev. 1 (1989); Mary E. O'Connell, Alimony After No–Fault; A Practice in Search of a Theory, 23 N.E.L.Rev. 437 (1988); June Carbone, Economics, Feminism, and the Reinvention of Alimony: A Reply to Ira Ellman, 43 Vanderbilt L.Rev. 1463 (1990). Carl Schneider, Rethinking Alimony: Marital Decisions and Moral Discourse, 1991 B.Y.U.L.Rev. 197; Ira Ellman, Should *The Theory* of *Alimony* Include Nonfinancial Losses and Motivations? 1991 B.Y.U.L.Rev. 259; Jana B. Singer, Alimony and Efficiency: The Gendered Costs and Benefits of the Economic Justification for Alimony, 82 Geo.L.J. 2423 (1994); Margaret F. Brinig, Comment on Jana Singer's *Alimony and Efficiency,* 82 Geo.L.J. 2461 (1994).

5. The legislative shift recounted in *White* from property allocation at divorce based on title to the concept of equitable distribution grounded in the trial court's discretion is typical of many common law states. Justice Mitchell's observation that the title system had a harsh impact on homemakers finds support among scholars. See, e.g., Joan M. Krauskopf, A Theory for "Just" Division of Marital Property in Missouri, 41 Mo.L.Rev. 165, 167–71 (1976) (criticizing common law title approach). By 1987, all of the forty-two common law states had adopted one form or another of equitable distribution of marital assets upon divorce. Doris J. Freed & Timothy B. Walker, Family Law in the Fifty States: An Overview, 22 Fam.L.Q. 439, 476 (1987). As *White* demonstrates, however, the enactment of these provisions started another debate between advocates of "equal" versus "equitable" distribution. See, e.g., Mary Ann Glendon, Family Law Reform in the 1980's, 44 La.L.Rev. 1553, 1555–57 (1984) (criticizing equitable distribution as unwieldy, unpredictable, and often perceived as unfair); Mildred W. Levin, Virtue Does Not Have its Reward for Women in California, 61 Women Law.J. 55, 57 (1975) (criticizing California's law requiring equal division of community property). Do you agree with the *White* court's interpretation of the North Carolina statute? Compare Rodgers v. Rodgers, 98 A.D.2d 386, 390–91, 470 N.Y.S.2d 401, 404–405 (A.D. 2 Dept.1983), in which the court warned that "it is a mistake to suggest that equitable distribution and community property are synonymous," and emphasized the following difference between equal division and equitable distribution: "[u]nlike a community property regime, fairness, not mathematical precision, is the guidepost. Under equitable distribution, a court possesses flexibility and elasticity to mold an appropriate decree because what is fair and just in one circumstance may not be so in another * * *". See Marsha Garrison, Good Intentions Gone Awry: The Impact of New York's Equitable Distribution Law on Divorce Outcomes, 57 Brooklyn L.Rev. 621 (1991). When is an equal division unfair?

6. Lenore Weitzman, who supports equal, rather than equitable, division of property following divorce, is nevertheless critical of the limited legal definition of property offered in many states. Specifically, she charges that "[t]he omission of the career assets from the pool of marital property makes *a mockery of the equal division rule.*" Lenore J. Weitzman, The Divorce Revolution 388 (1985) (emphasis in original). In her view, career assets include pensions and other employment-related benefits; the goodwill of a business or a professional practice; and a professional degree and license to practice, together with the holder's enhanced capacity of producing a higher stream of future income. The trend favors recognition of pensions as property subject to division on divorce. See Freed & Walker, supra Note 5, at 510–16. As the *Petersen* case indicates, however, only a few states have chosen to define a professional degree or a license to practice as property subject to division on divorce. What is the theoretical basis for such a

definition? See Joan M. Krauskopf, Recompense for Financing Spouse's Education: Legal Protection for the Marital Investor in Human Capital, 28 U.Kan. L.Rev. 379 (1980), grounding her theory of compensation for a wife who works to put the husband through school on an extension of the economic concept of investment in human capital to the context of divorce. Krauskopf does not, however, support Weitzman in defining the investment as a right to property; she prefers to recognize the wife's investment through an award of gross maintenance. Krauskopf, id., at 417. Do you think the professional degree and license should be defined as property for purposes of distribution upon divorce? If so, in states where only marital property or community property can be divided on divorce, should these assets be classified as community or separate property? See, e.g., Allen M. Parkman, The Recognition of Human Capital as Property in Divorce Settlements, 40 Ark.L.Rev. 439 (1987) (arguing that the courts have obscured the issue by focussing on the degree and license; these items are not themselves human capital, but merely evidence of an investment in human capital; whether human capital should be classified as separate or community property depends on whether the investment made after marriage is more substantial than that made prior to marriage; but even if the facts of a particular case support a classification as separate property, reimbursement is proper if the investment was funded in part by the non-student spouse); Bruce H. Rhodes, Comment, Half a Loaf is Better Than None: *Sullivan* Revisited, 15 Golden Gate U.L.Rev. 527, 569–70 (1985) (suggesting that the degree and license be classified as separate property even if acquired after marriage, but that the community be reimbursed for the student spouse's time, effort, and energy devoted to studying, the reimbursement to be measured by the increase in the student's earning capacity attributable to the degree). This proposal goes beyond that adopted by the California legislature in 1984, when it provided that "the community," not the supporting spouse, "shall be reimbursed for community contributions to education or training of a party that substantially enhances the earning capacity of the party". West's Ann.Cal.Fam.Code § 2641 (1994) Subsection (c) allows the reimbursement to be reduced or modified if "circumstances render such a disposition unjust", including three specified circumstances: (1) the community has "substantially benefitted" from its investment; (2) offsetting community contributions have been made to the other party's education or training; or (3) the education or training received "substantially reduces" the party's need for spousal support. The statute creates a presumption that the community has substantially benefitted from education or training received more than 10 years before commencement of a dissolution proceeding. Note that, under California's statutory requirement that community property be divided equally in dissolution proceedings, the result of § 2641 is to return the reimbursement to the general community pool for division. Subsection (b)(2) mitigates the impact of this factor somewhat, however, by providing that loans incurred for education or training will be assigned to the spouse receiving the education or training for repayment, rather than be added to the community's liabilities. In view of this legislative action, the California Supreme Court reversed and remanded for further proceedings under the statute a case in which it had granted a hearing to determine whether a spouse, who had made economic sacrifices to enable the other spouse to obtain an education, is entitled to compensation upon dissolution of the marriage. In Re Marriage of Sullivan, 37 Cal.3d 762, 209 Cal.Rptr. 354, 691 P.2d 1020 (1984).

7. If you decide that a professional degree and license should be defined as property and classified as the sort of property that may be divided upon divorce, a second problem awaits you. How are these assets to be valued? Professor

Mullenix asserts that precise monetary valuation is impossible. See Linda Susan Mullenix, The Valuation of an Educational Degree at Divorce, 16 Loy.L.A.L.Rev. 227, 259–74 (1983) (reviewing and rejecting proposed methods of valuation). Do you agree? Parkman, supra Note 6, at 454–57, prefers not to attempt to place a value on the husband's degree and license, but rather to focus on the concrete situation of the supporting spouse, and either to reimburse her for investment in her husband's human capital or to compensate her for her sacrifice of human capital to the marriage, whichever is appropriate under the circumstances. See also Herma Hill Kay, An Appraisal of California's No–Fault Divorce Law, 75 Calif.L.Rev. 291, 315 (1987) ("Rather than focus on the gain enjoyed by the student spouse and attempt to enable the supporting spouse to participate in that gain as a co-owner, I suggest that we emphasize instead the loss incurred by the supporting spouse and devise rules that require the student spouse to make up that loss.") But if these solutions must be implemented by a spousal support order, rather than a property award, they are subject in many states to termination if the wife remarries or dies. This is what the trial court was trying to avoid in the *Petersen* case, wasn't it? Are you satisfied with Judge Orme's solution? Compare footnotes 4 and 5 of his opinion to determine what Mrs. Petersen has actually received. The Colorado Supreme Court, reaffirming its holding in *Graham* that an educational degree is not marital property, broadened its earlier interpretation of the Colorado maintenance statute to recognize that the phrase "appropriate employment" means "specially suitable" or "proper," noting that such an interpretation "limits the otherwise harsh results of denying a spouse maintenance if any kind of employment is attainable." In re Marriage of Olar, 747 P.2d 676, 681 (Colo.1987). In Mahoney v. Mahoney, 91 N.J. 488, 453 A.2d 527 (1982), cited in footnote 4 of the *Petersen* case, the New Jersey Supreme Court introduced the concept of "reimbursement" alimony, designed to reimburse one spouse for monetary contributions to the other spouse's professional education when the contributions were "made with the mutual and shared expectation that both parties to the marriage will derive increased income and material benefits" from the educated spouse's professional practice. Reimbursement alimony is contrasted with "rehabilitative" alimony, ordered in a lump sum or for a temporary period to provide for the supporting spouse's own education. The Supreme Court of South Carolina followed *Mahoney* to adopt the concept of reimbursement alimony in Donahue v. Donahue, 299 S.C. 353, 384 S.E.2d 741, 747–48 (1989). In Reiss v. Reiss, 195 N.J.Super. 150, 478 A.2d 441 (Ch.1984), a wife who had put her husband through medical school was awarded $46,706.50 in reimbursement alimony, payable in monthly installments of $1,500. After receiving two monthly installments, the wife remarried. The husband moved to have the reimbursement alimony terminated. This motion was denied by the court, which pointed out that "reimbursement" alimony was something of a misnomer. Unlike true alimony, which looks to the future needs of the recipient and the ability of the obligor to pay, reimbursement alimony involves a determination of what was paid in the past. Accordingly, the court reasoned, under most circumstances reimbursement alimony should not terminate upon remarriage. Reiss v. Reiss, 200 N.J.Super. 122, 490 A.2d 378 (Ch.1984), affirmed in part and reversed in part 205 N.J.Super. 41, 500 A.2d 24 (1985).

The Utah Court of Appeals, struggling with the *Reiss* termination problem, extended *Petersen* to create an "equitable restitution" award that may be granted in addition to alimony, but that does not terminate on divorce. Martinez v. Martinez, 754 P.2d 69 (Utah App.1988), reversed 818 P.2d 538 (Utah 1991). In disapproving the concept of "equitable restitution," the Utah Supreme Court cited three reasons for its action: first, it rejected the idea that a failed marriage was comparable to a commercial partnership, noting that "[t]he efforts each spouse makes for the other and for their common marital interests cannot be quantified in monetary terms, their respective contributions netted out, and a balance struck at the termination of a marriage." Second, an award of equitable restitution would be "extraordinarily speculative." Third, the Court of Appeals' concept of equitable restitution is "essentially indistinguishable" from defining a profession-al degree as property and awarding the nonprofessional spouse an interest in it. How would you respond to these objections? Justice Christine Durham dissented from the Court's rejection of the concept of equitable restitution, given its failure to fashion a "new and more flexible theory of alimony." She went on to observe that:

> * * * My criticism of the majority opinion is that it makes no effort to guide the trial courts in fashioning a realistic remedy for what is a realistic loss. It rejects the effort of the court of appeals to do precisely that and offers no alternative. The legal status quo is unacceptable, in my view, and I hope that the majority will be willing in the future to make good on its representa-tion that the concept of alimony (or property distribution when there is any property) can be accommodated to the need for equity. Unless and until that happens, any woman (or man, for that matter) who sacrifices her own education, earning capacity, or career development so that a spouse may advance and the marriage may prosper as a joint venture will inevitably suffer the full cost of that decision at divorce, while the advantaged spouse will continue to walk away from the marriage with all of the major financial gain. That is unfair, and in this area at least, the responsibility of the law is to seek fairness.

Id., 818 P.2d at 545–46 (dissenting opinion).

Text Note
Spousal Support and Division of Property Following Divorce

In its beginnings in English law, alimony was administered by the ecclesiasti-cal courts and was granted in cases of legal separation (divorce *a mensa et thoro*), not in cases of nullity (divorce *a vinculo matrimonii*).[1] Absolute divorce, in the sense of a decree terminating a valid marriage, did not exist except by Private Act of Parliament.[2] Alimony was not granted to husbands by the ecclesiastical courts, only to wives.[3] In its inception, therefore, alimony was a judicial order entered during the existence of the marriage fixing a husband's duty to support his wife while they were living apart due to his fault. Two by-products of the transfer of divorce jurisdiction from the ecclesiastical courts to the civil courts by the Divorce Act of 1857 in England[4] and earlier in America[5] were that the grounds for legal separation became the grounds for divorce and that alimony was extended to provide support for an ex-wife following divorce.

Despite the dramatic shift in the nature of alimony from an allowance paid during marriage to one payable after divorce, its theoretical justification continued

1. Chester G. Vernier & John B. Hurlbut, The Historical Background of Alimony Law and its Present Statutory Structure, 6 Law & Cont.Prob. 197, 197–201 (1939).

2. Id., at 198. See also Oliver Ross McGre-gor, Divorce in England 10–11 (1957).

3. Vernier & Hurlbut, supra note 1, at 200.

4. McGregor, supra note 2, at 17–19.

5. Vernier & Hurlbut, supra note 1, at 198, 201–202.

to be its function as a substitute for the common law duty of support.[6] Accordingly, as women have continued to make legal, social, and economic progress towards the capacity for being self-supporting, persistent arguments have been made for reducing or terminating their right to alimony. Thus, as early as 1939, reformers relied on the improved legal status of women to argue that alimony should no longer be used as a device to punish guilty husbands, but rather that it should reflect the wife's needs and should certainly end upon her remarriage.[7] In 1956, the New York Appellate Division proclaimed that the wife's "role as a frail, sheltered, ineffectual person—if ever authentic—is as much a thing of the past as her crinoline and whalebone"[8] and asserted its right to take account of the wife's assets in fixing the amount of alimony to the end of allocating "the economic burdens fairly, so that members of the former family group, including the husband, are not individually destroyed by crushing economic and psychological pressures."[9]

The emergence of no-fault divorce in the 1980s as the universally available American basis for marriage dissolution may have facilitated the demise of alimony as the preferred vehicle for financial transfers between the spouses. Professor Robert Levy, Co–Reporter for the Uniform Marriage and Divorce Act, recommended that property division, rather than spousal support, be used as the primary economic tool upon dissolution. He proposed that alimony be abolished, except in cases meeting three conditions: the spouses have no unemancipated children, the wife's circumstances make it unlikely she will remarry or become self-supporting, and the property available for disposition to the wife does not fairly reflect her economic and/or other contributions to the marriage.[10] While this suggestion was not accepted, the Uniform Act did make clear that the property disposition should be made first, and that any support order should be contingent on the inadequacy of that award to provide for the reasonable needs of the dependent spouse.[11] Professor Mary Ann Glendon is critical of this effort to achieve a "clean break" between the spouses, objecting that " * * * no legal system has been able to achieve this result on a widespread basis because, in most divorce cases, children are present and there is insufficient property."[12]

In her study of the impact of the California no-fault divorce law, Professor Lenore Weitzman found that "[d]ivorce has radically different economic consequences for men and women."[13] In particular, she concluded that "[j]ust one year after legal divorce, [m]en experience a 42 percent improvement in their postdivorce standard of living, while women experience a 73 percent decline."[14] She points to several factors, including insufficient pools of property to provide for

6. Id., at 206. Because this duty was not owed by a wife to her husband, the authors argue that using the term "alimony" to refer to an allowance paid by a wife to her husband following divorce is a misnomer.

7. Robert W. Kelso, The Changing Social Setting of Alimony Law, 6 Law & Cont.Prob. 186, 192–93 (1939).

8. Phillips v. Phillips, 1 A.D.2d 393, 394–95, 150 N.Y.S.2d 646, 649, affirmed 2 N.Y.2d 742, 157 N.Y.S.2d 378, 138 N.E.2d 738 (1956).

9. Id., 150 N.Y.S.2d at 651.

10. Robert J. Levy, Uniform Marriage and Divorce Legislation: A Preliminary Analysis 140–47 (1969).

11. UMDA, § 308(a)(1), (2), 9A U.L.A. 348 (1987).

12. Mary Ann Glendon, Family Law Reform in the 1980's, 44 La.L.Rev. 1553, 1558 (1984).

13. Lenore J. Weitzman, The Divorce Revolution 323 (1985).

14. Id., at 339 (emphasis omitted). Saul D. Hoffman and Greg J. Duncan claim that Weitzman's findings on this point "are almost certainly in error." See Hoffman & Duncan, What Are The Economic Consequences of Divorce?, 25 Demography, No. 4, at 641 (November, 1988). After a reanalysis of Weitzman's data, sociologist Richard R. Peterson concluded that the correct numbers were a 27 percent

the needs of both spouses, inadequate spousal and child support awards, the presence of children in the divorced mother's household, and the greater earning capacity of divorced men over divorced women, to explain her finding.[15] Weitzman's claim that this striking sex-based difference in the economic consequences of divorce was caused by the enactment of no-fault divorce laws has been disputed by others.[16] Still, the assessment of blame may be pointless: the more pressing problem is how to achieve economic justice between women and men at divorce, especially in cases where the marriage was a traditional one that featured the man as breadwinner, the woman as mother and homemaker. Although the percentage of households composed of a married couple and their children under age 18 has decreased from 40 percent in 1970 to 25.8 percent in 1994,[17] the problem of housewife dependency created by that traditional lifestyle continues to be a significant one if the marriage is dissolved by divorce. Is the California Supreme Court's solicitude for Ms. Morrison, who was divorced after 28 years of marriage during which she did not work outside the home and who lacked adequate job training,[18] an example of misplaced protectionism or a realistic evaluation of her situation? Even assuming that in the future all young women will be rigorously counselled from infancy to prepare themselves to be self-supporting both during and after marriage (how likely is that?), what of the so-called "transitional woman" like Ms. Morrison? Do any helpful devices—short of meager public support—exist for her?

Commenting on *Morrison,* a California lawyer has suggested that the theory underlying alimony has evolved from punishment of a guilty spouse to rehabilitation of a dependent spouse so that the spouse can become "a self-functioning, economically self-sufficient unit".[19] Another writer, recognizing that "[a]bandonment of the fault theory has left the courts without a comprehensive theoretical framework in which to consider the award of spousal support",[20] suggests several theories on which such awards might be based. Those advanced are (a) *contract:* "the wife clearly could claim a reasonable expectation of support in exchange for her assumption of the homemaker role and for foregoing employment outside the home during marriage";[21] (b) *back pay:* "[v]iewing spousal support as payment for homemaking services * * * would acknowledge the importance of the homemaking spouse's services, add prestige and dignity to those services, and perhaps benefit the nuclear family by providing security and encouragement to those spouses, including men, inclined to devote themselves to a homemaking career";[22] and (c) *return on investment:* "[s]pousal support might also be viewed as a fair

decline for women and a 10 percent increase for men. His study is forthcoming in the American Sociological Review. San Francisco Chronicle, May 17, 1996, at A–9, 61.3.

15. Id., at 340–43.

16. See, e.g., Robert J. Levy, A Reminiscence About the Uniform Marriage and Divorce Act—and Some Reflections About Its Critics and Its Policies, 1991 B.Y.U.L.Rev. 43; Herma Hill Kay, Equality and Difference: A Perspective on No–Fault Divorce and its Aftermath, 56 U.Cin.L.Rev. 1, 66–77 (1987); Nora Jane Lauerman, Book Review, 2 Berkeley Women's L.J. 246, 249–52 (1986); Marygold S. Melli, Constructing a Social Problem: The Post–Divorce Plight of Women and Children, 1986 Am.B.F.Res.J. 759, 768–70; Herbert Jacob, Faulting No–Fault, 1986 Am.B.F.Res.J. 773, 776–79.

17. U.S.Bur.Cen., Current Population Reports, Ser. P–20, No. 483, "Household and Family Characteristics: March 1994", vii (1994).

18. In re Marriage of Morrison, 20 Cal.3d 437, 143 Cal.Rptr. 139, 573 P.2d 41 (1978), opinion excerpted at p. 268 supra.

19. Jack Gillman, Alimony/Spousal Support: From Punishment to Rehabilitation, 7 Community Property Journal 135, 138 (1980).

20. Bianca G. Larson, Equity and Economics: A Case for Spousal Support, 8 Golden Gate Univ.L.Rev. 443, 469 (Women's Law Forum, Spring, 1979).

21. Id., at 470.

22. Id., at 472–73.

return to the wife on her investment in or contribution to her ex-husband's career".[23]

Which, if any, of these theories do you find acceptable? Are there others that might be suggested? See the suggestions advanced by the authors cited in *Notes on Orr, Morrison, White*, and *Petersen*, Note 4, supra. Are different approaches required to justify spousal support orders and property awards to "displaced homemakers" like Ms. Morrison, Ms. White, and Ms. Petersen, women in dual career marriages who may have helped put their husbands through school before going back for their own education, and women whose former husbands can barely support their second families?[24] As the economic participation of women in the work force increases, will these same questions be raised with respect to financial settlements for husbands?

c.   *Custody and Support of Children*

PIKULA v. PIKULA

Supreme Court of Minnesota, 1985.
374 N.W.2d 705.

WAHL, JUSTICE.

This matter concerns the propriety of the custody award of two minor children in the judgment and decree dissolving the marriage of Kelly Jo Pikula and Dana David Pikula. Both parents sought custody of their daughters, aged 4 and 2. After a two day trial, the trial court awarded custody to Dana, the father. On Kelly's appeal, the Court of Appeals reversed, 349 N.W.2d 322, concluding that the evidence, considered in light of the statutory factors set forth in Minn.Stat. § 518.17, subd. 1 (1984), was insufficient to support the award of custody. The Court of Appeals remanded the matter with direction to the trial court to enter judgment granting custody to the mother. We granted discretionary review.

Kelly and Dana Pikula were married on March 29, 1980, when Kelly was 17 and Dana 20. At the time of their marriage, their older daughter, Tiffany, was 8 months old. Prior to Tiffany's birth, Kelly and Dana had lived with Kelly's sister, Denise, in St. Paul. After the baby was born, the family moved to Brainerd, Dana's hometown, where they had frequent contact with Dana's parents and sisters. The Pikula family is closely knit, with Dana's parents at the center of the family. The family members visit each other frequently and spend holidays together. Two of the three adult Pikula children work for their father, and the parents continue to assist the adult children financially. Dana took a job with his father's trucking company, working a split shift as a driver. Kelly had a second daughter, Tanisha, in 1981, and finished high school while taking care of the children and managing the home.

As the Court of Appeals observed, it appears from the evidence that both Kelly and Dana were imperfect parents. Dana and members of his family testified Kelly occasionally had trouble controlling her temper with the two girls, was somewhat ambivalent about her role as mother, and was a poor housekeeper. Kelly did not dispute she was sometimes dissatisfied and frustrated, but by her own account and by the testimony of Dana and his

---

23. Id., at 473.

24. Cf. Zablocki v. Redhail, 434 U.S. 374, 98 S.Ct. 673, 54 L.Ed.2d 618 (1978).

family, she was a good mother. She testified her dissatisfactions were rooted in her relationship with Dana and in Dana's problems with alcohol which at times resulted in physical displays of temper and verbal abuse. These problems persisted throughout the marriage and became particularly severe after Tanisha, their second child, was born. Dana was hospitalized during this period after injuring his hand by putting his fist through a door. He initially agreed to undergo counseling at that time, but soon stopped attending because he "didn't feel he had a problem with other people." He did attend AA meetings for a period, but began drinking again after five or six months. According to the report prepared by the custody evaluator, Dana continues to have problems with chemical dependency.

Kelly and her sisters also testified Dana's drinking in part precipitated the couple's separation. At the time Dana began drinking again, Dana forced Kelly and the children to leave her sister Renee's home in St. Paul where Kelly had been visiting with the children. Dana appeared at the house at around 9 p.m. and insisted Kelly and the girls leave immediately with him. When Kelly resisted, he took the children, put them in the car, and then dragged Kelly out of the house. In the meantime, Renee's boyfriend came out of the house and hit Dana on the arm with a baseball bat. Kelly said the children were watching this scene from the car, and once they were underway, Dana drove recklessly, shouted at her, and prevented her from comforting the children. Dana denies he used physical force, had trouble operating the car, or kept Kelly from the children. Kelly's sisters stated, though, they were sufficiently concerned to report the incident to the police.

Kelly did not remain in the home long after their return from St. Paul. She said Dana told her he was going to keep her there and he intended to take the children away so she would know what it was like to be alone. He was angry at her for not taking his side against her sister's boyfriend. Kelly then left the home and moved into the Women's Center of Mid–Minnesota, a shelter for battered women, where she continued to live until the time of the trial.

During this time, the couple agreed to a joint custody arrangement until custody was judicially determined. The arrangement was an uneasy one. For a time, the children remained in the family home while Kelly and Dana alternated living there on a four-day rotation schedule. Kelly began bringing the children to the shelter for her custody period, however, when tensions between Kelly and Dana escalated.

The recommendations of three professional social workers were also before the trial court. All three recommended that custody be awarded to Kelly. Social worker Jean Remke met with Kelly and Dana together or separately four times. In her view, both Kelly and Dana are somewhat emotionally immature. In Remke's opinion Kelly is "decidedly the most functional parent," because she seemed more capable of "putting herself aside to attend to the physical and emotional needs of others," while Dana "repeatedly used the children in efforts to control their mother," and showed "no signs of really understanding this and no signs of altering his behavior."

Social worker Louise Seliski had extensive contact with Kelly at the shelter, both through individual counseling and observation. Seliski also found Kelly had been a fit mother to the two girls and believed she would continue to provide a loving and supportive environment for them. She said she observed affection between Kelly and the children, that Kelly never used excessive discipline, and that the children were always clean. Seliski terminated therapy with Kelly because Kelly was "handling her life as well as anyone could expect her to handle it" and had no significant psychological problems or chemical dependency. It was Seliski's recommendation that custody be given to Kelly.

The reports prepared by Remke and Seliski were included in the custody evaluation prepared by social worker Nancy Archibald. The evaluation also included reports of interviews with the parties, their families, neighbors and friends, a church premarital evaluation, and letters of recommendation. In Archibald's opinion, the views expressed by Remke and Seliski were supported by her interviews with Kelly and Dana. She also recommended, based on all the data, that custody be awarded to Kelly with reasonable visitation provided to Dana.

Evidence was also introduced at trial concerning the custodial environment each parent would provide the children. Kelly testified she intended to move with the children to her sister's home in Maplewood until she could find employment and move into her own apartment. Dana objected to this plan, and testified that Kelly's sister had used marijuana and characterized some of her sister's friends as "bikers." Dana testified that he intended to remain in Brainerd if he were awarded custody of the girls. He continued to work a split shift at the time of trial, and his schedule required him to leave Brainerd at 3:00 a.m. for Wadena, lay over in Wadena from 7:00 a.m. until 3:00 p.m., and return to Brainerd at 7:00 p.m. Occasionally, he would return to Brainerd during his layover, permitting him to spend several hours at home. The child care responsibilities were principally borne by Dana's mother, however, and the children frequently spent the night with her and were cared for by her during the day.

Based on this record, the trial court * * * made two key findings of fact in awarding custody to Dana. These findings stated as follows:

* * *

Amended Finding 11. That there is a strong, stable, religious family group relationship within the Pikula family, including respondent and the children, that has been developed, nurtured and cultivated over the years. It has stood like a bedrock through the depression years and post-war years of plenty and permissiveness. This environment has inbred in the family, including respondent, a unity, respect, loyalty and love that for the most part has been destroyed and lost in most modern American families. It is in the best interests and welfare of the children that their custody be awarded to respondent, who shares these attributes and who will assure that these children will be raised in the present cultural, family, religious and community environment of which they have been and are integral parts, which environment affords them stability, appropriate socializing and family orientation. The children are properly adjusted to their current home situation, broadly defined, and to the greater community within which they have lived virtually their entire lives, the children behave well and have extensive and qualitative contacts with significant persons within this environment, respondent's personal environment continues to stabilize and improve and is presently satisfactory, as well as gives indications of continuing stability, and it is desirable that the children's continuity with respondent and significant other persons and institutions here be maintained, respondent offering a permanent, well-established, concerned and involved, as well as supporting home for the children, the overall health of those who likely will here affect the mental, physical, emotional, educational, cultural and religious growth of the children is good, and respondent is inclined to, has and likely will continue to care for the children and raise them in their religion, creed and culture.

Amended Finding 12. That the environment in which petitioner finds herself is almost the exact opposite of that in which respondent lives and will raise the children, it would subject the children to considerable uncertainty and instability in home, community, culture, persons and religion, should custody be awarded to petitioner, and further, such an award would disrupt, curtail and likely end the children's nurturing and constant contacts with the environment, persons and institutions now significantly and positively affecting their lives, petitioner's behavior and practices of child rearing as well as her interest in her children are at least subject to serious question and doubt, and it would not be in the children's best interest to award their custody to petitioner.

The Court of Appeals, in reversing, held that the trial court had abused its discretion in awarding custody of the children to Dana on the facts of this case. * * *

* * *

2. The trial court's findings must be sustained unless clearly erroneous. The trial court's first finding describes the custodial environment provided by Dana and his family. The court found that the extended Pikula family surrounded the girls with a social milieu imbued with the "traditional" values, shared and fostered by Dana. The court further found that the girls were significantly attached to that environment, so as to be afforded "stability, appropriate socializing and family orientation," and that Dana would continue to raise them within "their religion, creed and culture." Given the close knit and interdependent character of the Pikula family, these findings appear reasonably supported by the evidence, although they do emphasize the desirability of the environment that would be provided by the paternal grandparents and the extended family rather than that of the proposed custodian, the father.

The trial court's findings regarding Kelly's fitness as a custodial parent are troubling in light of the whole record. The court found Kelly's environment would "subject the children to considerable uncertainty and instability in home, community, culture, persons and religion," that granting Kelly custody would sever the children's relationship with the Pikula family, and that Kelly's "behavior and practices of child rearing as well as her interest in her children are at least subject to serious question." Each of these findings was contradicted by evidence submitted by Kelly, and inconsistent with testimony from Dana and his family that Kelly was a good mother. In fashioning these findings, the trial court also discredited the custody evaluator's report and the recommendations of two other professional counsellors.

The trial court is not, however, bound to adhere to such expert testimony if it believes it is outweighed by other evidence. While the grounds for the trial court's failure to consider this evidence are not apparent, given our limited scope of review we cannot conclude there was not sufficient evidence on the record to outweigh it. We therefore hold that the evidence was adequate to support the findings which the trial court did make.

3. We conclude, however, that the trial court erred in determining that custody of the children should be awarded to Dana on the basis of the facts that were found. Minn.Stat. § 518.17, subd. 3 (1984) provides that "[i]n determining custody, the court shall consider the best interests of the child * * *." The statute further defines "best interests of the child" as "all relevant factors" to be considered and evaluated by the court, including:

(a) The wishes of the child's parent or parents as to his custody;

(b) The reasonable preference of the child, if the court deems the child to be of sufficient age to express preference;

(c) The interaction and interrelationship of the child with his parent or parents, his siblings, and any other person who may significantly affect the child's best interests;

(d) The child's adjustment to his home, school, and community;

(e) The length of time the child has lived in a stable, satisfactory environment and the desirability of maintaining a continuity;

(f) The permanence, as a family unit, of the existing or proposed custodial home;

(g) The mental and physical health of all individuals involved;

(h) The capacity and disposition of the parties to give the child love, affection, and guidance, and to continue educating and raising the child in his culture and religion or creed, if any; and

(i) The child's cultural background.

The court shall not consider conduct of a proposed custodian that does not affect his relationship to the child.

Minn.Stat. § 518.17, subd. 1 (1984). In *Berndt v. Berndt*, 292 N.W.2d 1 (Minn.1980), we held the enumerated statutory criteria, even absent consideration of other relevant factors, mandate that, when the evidence indicates that both parents would be suitable custodians, the intimacy of the relationship between the primary parent and the child should not be disrupted "without strong reasons which relate specifically to the [primary] parent's capacity to provide and care for the child." *Berndt*, 292 N.W.2d at 2. Awarding custody to the non-primary parent without such strong reasons, when the primary parent has given the child good care, may constitute reversible error. *Id.*

The guiding principle in all custody cases is the best interest of the child. *Berndt*, 292 N.W.2d at 2, *citing* Minn.Stat. § 518.17, subd. 1 (1976); *Rosenfeld v. Rosenfeld*, 311 Minn. 76, 249 N.W.2d 168 (1976); *LaBelle v. LaBelle*, 296 Minn. 173, 207 N.W.2d 291 (1973). The importance of emotional and psychological stability to the child's sense of security, happiness, and adaptation that we deemed dispositive in *Berndt* is a postulate embedded in the statutory factors [1] and about which there is little disagreement within the profession of child psychology. *See* J. Goldstein, A. Freud and A. Solnit, Before the Best Interests of the Child 31–35 (1979); Leonard & Provence, *The Development of Parent–Child Relationships and the Psychological Parent,* 53 Conn.B.J. 320, 326 (1979); Okpaku, *Psychology: Impediment or Aid in Child Custody Cases?* 29 Rutgers L.Rev. 1117, 1121–22 (1976) *cited in* Klaff, *The Tender Years Doctrine: A Defense,* 70 Cal.L.Rev. 335, 348 (1982). For younger children in particular, that stability is most often provided by and through the child's relationship to his or her primary caretaker—the person who provides the child with daily nurturence, care and support. As we further noted in *Berndt,* a court order separating a child from the primary parent could thus rarely be deemed in the child's best interests. Courts in three other states have reached similar conclusions in construing their custody statutes and rules.[2] *Garska v. McCoy,* 278 S.E.2d 357 (W.Va.1981); *In re Maxwell,* 8 Ohio App.3d 302, 456 N.E.2d 1218 (1982); *Van Dyke v. Van Dyke,* 48 Or.App. 965, 618 P.2d 465 (1980); *see also Commonwealth ex rel. Jordan,* 302 Pa.Super. 421, 448 A.2d 1113 (1982). We follow the reasoning of those states in adopting the rule that when both parents seek custody of a child too young to express a preference, and one parent has been the primary caretaker of the child, custody should be awarded to the primary caretaker absent a showing that that parent is unfit to be the custodian.

Continuity of care with the primary caretaker is not only central and crucial to the best interest of the child, but is perhaps the single predicator of a child's well-being about which there is agreement, and which can be competently evaluated by judges. The other indicia of a child's best interests set forth in section 518.17, while plainly relevant to a child's wellbeing and security, are, by contrast, both inherently resistant of evaluation and difficult to apply in any particular case. Subdivision[s] 1(g) and (h) require judges to assess the proposed custodians' "mental and physical health," and "capacity and disposition" to give the child "love, affection, and guidance." A trial court is further required to consider all other "relevant factors" in reaching

1. Four of the nine statutory criteria rest on the centrality of continuity of care and environment to the best interest of the child. *See* Minn.Stat. § 518.17, subd. 1(c), (d), (e), (f) (1984).

2. Historically, similar but not identical considerations supported the "tender years" doctrine, the legal rule that when a child is of a young age, custody should ordinarily be awarded to the mother. That doctrine, unlike the rule we announce today, was premised on a presumed natural capacity of women to selflessly and instinctively raise children, often articulated in terms such as:

> [N]othing can be an adequate substitute for mother love—for that constant ministration required during the period of nurture that only a mother can give because in her alone is duty swallowed up in desire; in her alone is service expressed in terms of love.

Jenkins v. Jenkins, 173 Wis. 592, 593, 181 N.W. 826, 827 (1921). While at one time the tender years doctrine was universally adopted in the state courts, most jurisdictions have repudiated the doctrine as sex discriminatory.

A recent survey of state laws lists 38 states which have rejected the presumption, four which retain "tie-breaker" versions, and eight states with doubtful or unique laws. Freed & Foster, *Divorce in Fifty States: An Overview as of August 1, 1981,* 7 Fam.L.Rep. 4049, 4063 (1981).

The primary parent preference, while in accord with the tender years doctrine insofar as the two rules recognize the importance of the bond formed between a primary parent and a child, differs from the tender years doctrine in significant respects. Most importantly, the primary parent rule is gender neutral. Either parent may be the primary parent; the rule does not incorporate notions of biological gender determinism or sex stereotyping. In addition, the rule we fashion today we believe will encourage co-parenting in a marriage unlike the tender years doctrine which, for fathers, meant that whatever function they assumed in the rearing of their children would be deemed irrelevant in a custody contest.

its decision. We are mindful that trial courts, seeking to apply these factors to reach an intelligent determination of relative degrees of fitness, must aspire to a "precision of measurement which is not possible given the tools available to the judges." *Garska,* 278 S.E.2d at 361. Moreover, as one author has observed, "[e]mpirical findings directly or indirectly relevant to questions for which judges deciding difficult [custody] cases need answers are virtually non-existent." Okpaku, *supra* at 1140. The legislature, in enacting Minn.Stat. § 518.167 (1984), which permits trial courts to order professional custody evaluations, has recognized the special needs of judges in that regard. That custody evaluations may not adequately provide a judge with such needed insight in particular cases, however, is embedded in the rule that such evaluations may be disregarded when outweighed by other evidence.

This inherent lack of objective standards aside from primary parent status in custody determinations has several related effects which are not in the best interests of children. Imprecision in the application of the law may result in "wrong" results, and in unpredictability of outcome. Parents already estranged may be tempted to use a threatened custody contest strategically when neither parent can predict with any certainty which parent will ultimately be awarded custody. The availability of such strategies cannot in any sense be viewed as in the best interests of the children involved. *See generally* Mnookin & Kornhauser, *Bargaining in the Shadow of the Law: The Case of Divorce,* 88 Yale L.J. 950 (1979).

This situation is exacerbated by the fact that the two parents may be unequally situated with respect to other matters at issue in the negotiation process. A parent who has remained at home throughout a marriage to raise the children will often have sacrificed economic and educational opportunities in order to perform that role, and he or she will likely be in greater need of economic support upon dissolution of a marriage. A spouse in that position has only one issue available to "concede" in the division of marital assets: custody of the children. At the same time, as the *Garska* court observed, "uncertainty of outcome is very destructive of the position of the primary caretaker parent because he or she will be willing to sacrifice everything in order to avoid the terrible prospect of losing the child in the unpredictable process of litigation." *Garska,* 278 S.E.2d 357 at 360 (W.Va.1981). Moreover, in practical fact, many primary caretakers may simply be unable to afford the expense of litigation at all, further weakening their bargaining position when the uncertainty in the outcome of a trial is necessarily high. The rule we fashion today should largely remove the issue of custody from the arena of dispute over such matters, and prevent the custody determination from being used in an abusive way to affect the level of support payments and the outcome of other issues in the proceeding.

The inherent imprecision heretofore present in our custody law has, in turn, diminished meaningful appellate review. * * * We recognize the inherent difficulty of principled decisionmaking in this area of the law. Legal rules governing custody awards have generally incorporated evaluations of parental fitness replete with ad hoc judgments on the beliefs, lifestyles, and perceived credibility of the proposed custodian. *See, e.g., Jarrett v. Jarrett,* 78 Ill.2d 337, 36 Ill.Dec. 1, 400 N.E.2d 421 (1979), *cert. den.* 449 U.S. 927, 101 S.Ct. 329, 66 L.Ed.2d 155 (1980) (mother's cohabitation contrary to the moral standards of the state). It is in these circumstances that the need for effective appellate review is most necessary to ensure fairness to the parties and to maintain the legitimacy of judicial decisionmaking.

For these reasons—the recognized need for stability in children's lives, the uncertainty of other indicia of a child's best interests in custody decisions, and the pressing need for coherent decisionmaking on the trial court level and for effective appellate review—we hold the factors set forth in section 518.17, subd. 1, require that when both parents seek custody of a child too young to express a preference for a particular parent and one parent has been the primary caretaker, custody be awarded to the primary parent absent a showing that that parent is unfit to be the custodian. We adopt the indicia of primary parenthood set forth in *Garska* to aid trial courts in determining which, if either, parent is the primary caretaker:

> While it is difficult to enumerate all of the factors which will contribute to a conclusion that one or the other parent was the primary caretaker parent, nonetheless, there are certain obvious criteria to which a court must initially look. In establishing which natural or adoptive parent is the primary caretaker, the trial court shall determine which parent has taken primary responsibility for, *inter alia,* the performance of the following caring and nurturing duties of a parent: (1) preparing and planning of meals; (2) bathing, grooming and dressing; (3) purchasing, cleaning, and care of clothes; (4) medical care, including nursing and trips to physicians; (5) arranging for social interaction among peers after school, i.e. transporting to friends' houses or, for example, to girl or boy scout meetings; (6) arranging alternative care, i.e. babysitting, day-care, etc.; (7) putting child to bed at night, attending to child in the middle of the night, waking child in the morning; (8) disciplining, i.e. teaching general manners and toilet training; (9) educating, i.e., religious, cultural, social, etc.; and, (10) teaching elementary skills, i.e., reading, writing and arithmetic.

Garska, 278 S.E.2d at 363. When the facts demonstrate that responsibility for and performance of child care was shared by both parents in an entirely equal way, then no preference arises and the court must limit its inquiry to other indicia of parental fitness. Once the preference does arise, however, the primary parent should be given custody unless it is shown that the child's physical or emotional health is likely to be endangered or impaired by being placed in the primary parent's custody.

The indicia of primary parenthood set forth above make plain that a parent who has performed the traditional role of homemaker will ordinarily be able to establish primary parent status in a custody proceeding involving young children. That this is so reflects no judgment by this court on the competence or fitness of parents who choose or are compelled to fashion less traditional divisions of labor within a family. Our decision today merely encompasses our understanding of the traumatic impact on children of separation from the primary caretaker parent. Nor do we mean to suggest that a parent who works outside the home may not be deemed the primary parent. We would expect that, as between any two parents, one will be the primary parent even if neither conforms to the more traditional pattern of one parent working outside the home and one within it. *See Wagoner v.*

Wagoner, 310 S.E.2d 204 (W.Va.1983) (both parents employed, mother found primary caretaker).

Turning to the facts of this case, we conclude that the matter must be remanded for a determination of which, if either, parent was the primary caretaker of the children at the time the dissolution proceeding was commenced.[3] Any disruption in the relationships between the children and their parents occasioned by the events leading to the divorce is irrelevant to that determination. If either parent was the primary caretaker, custody should be awarded to that parent absent a strong showing of unfitness.

The Court of Appeals is affirmed in part in reversing the trial court's award of custody to the father, reversed in part in awarding custody to the mother, and the matter is remanded for proceedings consistent with the rule set out in this opinion.

KELLEY, J., took no part in the consideration of this case.

SCHUSTER v. SCHUSTER

Supreme Court of Washington, 1978.
90 Wash.2d 626, 585 P.2d 130.

BRACHTENBACH, JUSTICE.

These consolidated cases involve factually related divorces. The respondent women separated from their husbands and lived together in a lesbian relationship with their children of their marriages. The appellant fathers filed for divorces from their respective spouses. Each mother was given custody of her children. However, the mothers were ordered to live separate and apart and were prohibited from removing the children from the state. *Those decrees were not appealed.*

Later, each of the fathers filed modification petitions seeking custody of their children. Subsequently, motions for contempt were filed charging violations of the original decrees. The alleged violations by the mothers were: (1) renting separate apartments in the same building but in fact living together along with all the children; and (2) taking the children out of state. The mothers filed counter petitions seeking modification of the original decrees by deleting the prohibition against their living together.

The two modification proceedings were joined for hearing. An attorney was appointed to represent the children's interests. The findings and conclusions resulted in the custody of the children remaining with the mothers and

---

3. The phrase "at the time the dissolution proceeding was commenced" is used to indicate the point in time at which the family relationships were physically disrupted by events leading to the dissolution of the marriage, e.g., at the time of the parties' separation or the interruption of the functioning full family unit. In a hearing on remand to determine which, if either, parent was the primary caretaker at that time, and whether that parent was a fit custodian, the trial court would, of course, use the record developed at trial and available to the court when the initial custody determination was made. While it would be inappropriate to permit factual consequences caused by an improper initial decision to determine on remand which parent is found to have been the primary caretaker, the trial court must look at present circumstances to determine the limited issue of the proposed custodian's fitness. After an award of custody on remand, subsequent changes in circumstances of the children or custodian would be addressed by the non-custodial parent in a motion for modification of custody under Minn.Stat. sec. 518.18.

the deletion of the prohibition against the mothers living together in an open and publicized lesbian relationship. We affirm in part and reverse in part.

At the outset we emphasize that these cases do not involve the question of whether it was proper to award custody of the children to lesbian mothers. That question was litigated in the original divorce actions. No appeal was taken by any party. There being no appeal, the original award of custody with all limitations contained therein is binding on all parties and upon this court. The issue is simply not before us.

The only question presented by this appeal is whether any modification of the original decrees was proper. When is a modification of the custody provisions of an original divorce decree justified? We have long held that a modification will not be granted unless there has been a subsequent substantial change in circumstances which requires a modification of custody in the best interests of the children. Peugh v. Peugh, 67 Wash.2d 469, 408 P.2d 10 (1965).

The policy is obvious. Children and their parents should not be subjected to repeated relitigation of the custody issues determined in the original action. Stability of the child's environment is of utmost concern. If an error was allegedly made in the original custody award, the remedy is by appeal. We repeat that the fathers did not appeal from the award of custody to the mothers; the mothers did not appeal from the prohibition against their living together.

This philosophy of stability in custody matters has been adopted by the legislature. In the marriage dissolution act of 1973, it prohibited a modification of a prior custody decree unless the court finds, upon the basis of facts that have arisen since the prior decree or that were unknown to the court at the time of the prior decree, that a change has occurred in the circumstances of the child or his custodian and that a modification is necessary to serve the best interests of the child. RCW 26.09.260(1).

Under these guidelines, the fathers must lose their modification petitions. Their circumstances have changed; each has remarried. They were found by the trial court to be good and capable fathers, vitally interested in their children. But the statute requires a change in the circumstances of either child or the custodian, the mothers in this case.

Has there been any change in the circumstances of the mothers to warrant a modification of the custody decree to allow them to live together?

In their modification petitions, the respondent mothers did not allege any change of circumstances and the findings and conclusions evidence absolutely none. At best the respondents established that it was preferable for their own personal circumstances, both financially and in pursuit of their relationship, to live together. That issue had been tried, they lost and did not appeal. They did not meet the judicial or statutory standards to change it. Therefore it was error to modify that aspect of the decrees.

Respondents make a belated effort to raise constitutional questions of freedom of association, equal protection and due process from the requirement that they live separate and apart. First, there is more involved than the rights of these two women. The lives of six children are at stake. Second, neither side has briefed nor argued the constitutional issues as they relate to this requirement. Though the amicus curiae brief did discuss the issue, appellate courts will not pass upon points raised only by amicus. Long v. Odell, 60 Wash.2d 151, 372 P.2d 548 (1962).

Finally, we turn to the fathers' argument that the trial court erred in failing to find the mothers in contempt for alleged violations of the original divorce decrees. As we noted in State v. Caffrey, 70 Wash.2d 120, 122–23, 422 P.2d 307, 308–09 (1966):

> Punishment for contempt of court is within the sound discretion of the judge so ruling. Unless there is abuse of a trial court's exercise of discretion, it will not be disturbed on appeal.

(Citations omitted.)

It appears that the fathers seek to use violation of the decrees as a basis to justify a change of custody. Suffice it to say that even if the trial court had found the mothers in contempt, that alone would not justify a change in custody. Punishment of the parent for contempt may not be visited upon the child in custody cases. The custody of a child is not to be used as a reward or punishment for the conduct of the parents. "The court shall not consider conduct of a proposed guardian that does not affect the welfare of the child." RCW 26.09.190. The best interests of the child are the paramount and controlling considerations. Thompson v. Thompson, 56 Wash.2d 244, 352 P.2d 179 (1960).

The trial court is affirmed except for its deletion of the requirement that the respondent mothers live separate and apart. As to that, it is reversed. The matter is remanded for entry of decrees in accordance with this opinion.

STAFFORD, HOROWITZ and HICKS, JJ., concur.

DOLLIVER, JUSTICE (concurring in part; dissenting in part).

I concur with the reasoning of the majority in its affirmance of the award of custody to the defendants. I dissent on the modification of the decree relating to the defendants' living arrangements.

* * *

In the findings at the time of the dissolutions, the trial court specifically found Sandra Schuster and Madeleine Isaacson were cohabiting and that "such living arrangements are not in the best interest of the children." However, the court in the modification proceedings which are now before us found:

> That since the time of the Divorce Decree the respondents at first lived separate and apart and then moved into adjoining apartments where they in fact lived together as one household and that the living arrangement did not prove to be against the best interests of the children, except it added a financial burden.

Thus, contrary to the assertion of the majority, a change of circumstances is contained in the findings. This change went far beyond the personal convenience of the defendants and was not to be found against the best interests of the children. The crucial question, then, is not whether the trial court made a finding of changed circumstances but whether there is evidence in the record to support the findings.

During the trial, voluminous testimony was taken on the living environment in which the children of the parties were being raised. According to expert testimony, since the divorce decrees the Isaacsons and Schusters had come to regard themselves as a family of eight; the Isaacson and Schuster children would refer to one another as brother or sister. Testimony established that there was a "crossover of the parent roles" between Ms. Isaacson and Ms. Schuster for the nurturing and assistance of the children. This development of a family unit and the strengthening of the relationships among the eight family members presents a significant change of circumstances which may appropriately be recognized and was recognized by the trial court in its findings.

Furthermore, in its oral opinion, the trial court stated that living apart for the sake of appearances was imposing a financial burden on the parties and their children. This circumstance was also recognized in the findings. Where the funds of the parties are limited, the children would naturally be affected adversely by an unnecessary expenditure of household resources.

The trial court should be given broad discretion in matters dealing with the welfare of the children. A finding was made of changed circumstances. Substantial evidence is in the record to support this finding. The disposition of this case should not be disturbed except for a manifest abuse of discretion. Lambert v. Lambert, 66 Wash.2d 503, 403 P.2d 664 (1965); Selivanoff v. Selivanoff, 12 Wash.App. 263, 266, 529 P.2d 486 (1974). No abuse has been shown.

The change of circumstances which occurred here may have developed while Ms. Schuster and Ms. Isaacson were in violation of the original decree, an act which this court need not approve. Nevertheless, it occurred. The trial court chose not to punish the parties for contempt and, finding no abuse of discretion, we have agreed. The majority rightly states that "Punishment of the parent for contempt may not be visited upon the child in custody cases. The custody of the child is not to be used as a reward or punishment for the conduct of the parents." This is a salutary rule. Having so held, we should not now punish the parties backhandedly by refusing to recognize an unquestionable change of circumstances found by the trial court and established by ample evidence.

UTTER, J., concurs.

ROSELLINI, JUSTICE (dissenting).

In awarding custody of children, the primary or paramount consideration is the welfare of the children. Pierce v. Pierce, 52 Wash. 679, 101 P. 358 (1909); Thompson v. Thompson, 56 Wash.2d 244, 352 P.2d 179 (1960).

Granting that a change of circumstances needs to be found to modify a custody decree, such change of circumstances exists. In the finding at the time of the dissolution, the trial court specifically found that Sandra Schuster and Madeleine Isaacson were cohabiting and that such living arrangements were not in the best interest of the children.

This finding was made to insulate the children from the harmful atmosphere of living together in the same household where evidence of cohabitation would be apparent.

Since that time the respondents have in fact lived together in one household and have publicly espoused on radio, television and in lectures the superiority of the homosexual lifestyle. They have involved their children in these activities. This is a change of circumstances that requires the court to reexamine the correctness of its previous custody order.

In Gaylord v. Tacoma School Dist. 10, 88 Wash.2d 286, 559 P.2d 1340 (1977), this court held that a teacher was "guilty" of immorality because of his status of being a homosexual. Also, the evidence in the case did not involve any known homosexual acts. Nevertheless, this court assumed that his effectiveness as a teacher would be impaired. Mr. Gaylord was an excellent teacher. His superior's evaluation of his teaching effectiveness stated: "Mr. Gaylord continues his high standards and thorough teaching performance. He is both a teacher and student in his field."

* * *

In the instant case, Sandra Schuster and Madeleine Isaacson were and are living together in a homosexual relationship. The respondents are living together with their children as a family unit.

The respondents have been engaged in publicizing the homosexual cause in general and their lesbian relationship. They have given a series of lectures and granted interviews where they discussed their own homosexual lifestyle. The children have accompanied respondents at some of these engagements, and the respondents and their children participated in making a movie which depicts the lifestyle of two families bound together by homosexual parents.

They have advertised in a brochure entitled "The Gay Family A Valid Life–Style?" in which they offered interested persons a booklet, "Love is for All", and information about a film entitled "Sandy and Madeleine's Family", and also offer to make personal appearances. An article in the San Francisco Chronicle with the headline "The Lesbian Love of Two Mothers" explained the appearance of the two women visiting in the Bay Area publicizing their film.

From such publicizing it can be readily seen that they are not content to pursue their lifestyle but are also using their children for the purpose of advocating and proselytizing that style.

I am unable to understand how the court can declare that a school teacher who only admitted to his preference as a homosexual and did not engage in any overt act, is guilty of immorality, and yet, in the instant case, can find perfectly moral the conduct of the respondents.

The State does have an interest in the matter of heterosexual acts versus homosexual acts. Professors J. Harvie Wilkinson III and G. Edward White, writing in 62 Cornell L.Rev. 563, 595–96 (1977), in an article entitled "Constitutional Protection for Personal Lifestyles", state that

> [t]he most threatening aspect of homosexuality is its potential to become a viable alternative to heterosexual intimacy. This argument is premised upon the belief that the practice of an alternative mode of sexual relations will inimically affect the predominant mode. Thus, any recognition of a constitutional right to practice homosexuality would undermine

the value of heterosexuality and the institutions and practices—conventional marriage and childrearing—associated with it.

This state concern, in our view, should not be minimized. The nuclear, heterosexual family is charged with several of society's most essential functions. It has served as an important means of educating the young; it has often provided economic support and psychological comfort to family members; and it has operated as the unit upon which basic governmental policies in such matters as taxation, conscription, and inheritance have been based. Family life has been a central unifying experience throughout American society. Preserving the strength of this basic, organic unit is a central and legitimate end of the police power. The state ought to be concerned that if allegiance to traditional family arrangements declines, society as a whole may well suffer.

Disapproving sexual conduct that might threaten traditional family life is arguably a means related to this end. Criminal law provides perhaps the strongest vehicle for expressing such disapproval. On the other hand, it is not the only vehicle for enforcing conventional mores; community disapproval of errant behavior is arguably a more potent enforcement mechanism than the law. Moreover, the criminal law's effectiveness will be reduced if social practices and attitudes run counter to its underlying assumptions. Yet criminalization, whatever its lack of perfection as a deterrent, is a dramatic symbol of social disapprobation. Decriminalization means, quite literally, the removal of disapproval, the recasting of the state's posture as one of neutrality.

In seeking to regulate homosexuality, the state takes as a basic premise that social and legal attitudes play an important and interdependent role in the individual's formation of his or her sexual destiny. A shift on the part of the law from opposition to neutrality arguably makes homosexuality appear a more acceptable sexual lifestyle, particularly to younger persons whose sexual preferences are as yet unformed. Young people form their sexual identity partly on the basis of models they see in society. If homosexual behavior is legalized, and thus partly legitimized, an adolescent may question whether he or she should "choose" heterosexuality. At the time their sexual feelings begin to develop, many young people have more interests in common with members of their own sex; sexual attraction rather than genuine interest often first draws adolescents to members of the opposite sex. If society accorded more legitimacy to expressions of homosexual attraction, attachment to the opposite sex might be postponed or diverted for some time, perhaps until after the establishment of sexual patterns that would hamper development of traditional heterosexual family relationships. For those persons who eventually choose the heterosexual model, the existence of conflicting models might provide further sexual tension destructive to the traditional marital unit.

(Footnotes omitted.) These arguments were endorsed by one of the authors, Professor Wilkinson.

The Superior Court of New Jersey held in In the Matter of J.S. & C., 129 N.J.Super. 486, 324 A.2d 90 (1974), that granting a father, who was deeply involved in the movement to further homosexuality, the right to unrestricted visitation would not be in the best interest of the children, and that such visitation right should extend to the daytime hours only. And in Chaffin v. Frye, 45 Cal.App.3d 39, 119 Cal.Rptr. 22 (1975), where a mother was a homosexual living with a female companion in the same apartment that the children would occupy, the trial court's implied finding that an award of custody to the mother would be detrimental to the children was sustained.

In this case the trial court found, in the original trial, that both parents were fit and proper persons to have the custody of the children. The fathers have since remarried and have established good homes. Where should the scale of justice be tipped? In favor of the mothers who are living in a lesbian relationship? Or on the side of the fathers whose lifestyles and relationships are considered normal and moral?

On the state of this record, the primary and paramount consideration in awarding the children to a parent is the welfare of the children. I would hold that the mothers are not morally fit to have the custody of the children, and I would award the children to the fathers.

WRIGHT, C.J., and HAMILTON, J., concur.

GREENFIELD v. GREENFIELD

Supreme Court of Nebraska, 1977.
199 Neb. 648, 260 N.W.2d 493.

C. THOMAS WHITE, JUSTICE.

The parties to this action were divorced on March 5, 1976. The decree approved a property settlement and child custody agreement providing that Lorraine Greenfield, petitioner and appellee here, should have custody of the parties' two minor children, Shane, the adopted child of appellant and the natural child of appellee, now age 10, and Jay, the natural child of the parties, now age 4. The appellant had suffered a severe business reversal in a service station and was not able nor required to pay child support.

Appellant filed an application for change of custody on November 26, 1976, alleging a change of circumstances and that appellee Lorraine Greenfield was not a fit and proper person to have the custody of the minor children. The trial court denied the application and confirmed the custody of the appellee with reasonable visitation to appellant. Appellant appeals.

All parties agree that the care for the physical needs of the children by Lorraine has been exemplary within her means; nor has any complaint been raised against the appellant Marlin who has contributed to the children's needs by purchases of clothing and toys and occasional modest support payments although not under court order to do so. Marlin has been faithful in visitation, and the older son Shane, a witness, testified he would like to live with both of them and loved each of them.

Each has an adequate income and support from relatives and friends although Marlin's work history is less stable than that of Lorraine.

The circumstances which gave rise to this application are easily stated, but difficult to resolve. About the latter part of September 1976, a Donny Ring moved into the home Lorraine was sharing with her children and lived with her in the one bedroom shared by all. Sexual relations between Donny and Lorraine were observed by Shane. Donny Ring was unemployed, drank a good deal, but was not unkind to the children or abusive toward them. He did not contribute to the household expenses and used whatever money he received to maintain a trailer, his car, and his drinking expense which ran approximately $100 to $150 a month. Upon notice to Lorraine of the application for change of custody, Donny moved out and, according to Lorraine, will remain out until such time as they marry, which is contemplated but not definitely planned.

Marlin also lived out of wedlock with a woman for a month although the children did not visit him at her home while he was doing so. The children were once brought to the woman's home for a visit.

The trial court obviously believed Lorraine's declaration that she would not again live with Donny outside of marriage nor live with him in marriage in the same bedroom with the children.

We have long passed the point where sexual misconduct automatically disqualifies a mother from obtaining custody of her minor children. See Lockard v. Lockard, 193 Neb. 400, 227 N.W.2d 581. We are further aware of the drastically changing life styles and the casualness with which intimate relations are entered and ended. We are, however, unaware of a case involving this type of action where custody was not changed or at least severely modified.

In child custody cases, this court gives great weight to the findings of the trial court in determining the best interests of a minor child. Reynek v. Reynek, 193 Neb. 404, 227 N.W.2d 578.

The trial court's findings will not ordinarily be disturbed on appeal unless there is a clear abuse of discretion or the decision is against the weight of the evidence. Boyles v. Boyles, 191 Neb. 66, 213 N.W.2d 729.

We cannot condone the appellee's actions nor can we approve the appellant's life style. In view of the otherwise satisfactory care of the children and the trial court's belief that the objectionable conduct has ended, we only modify the trial court's order to the extent that physical custody of the minor children remain with appellee. Legal custody is placed in the District Court, with the suggestion that the court require periodic visits in the home by the welfare department of the county. Appellant shall continue to have reasonable rights of visitation. We affirm, as modified, the decision of the District Court. No costs are allowed to either party.

Affirmed as modified.

Notes on Pikula, Schuster, and Greenfield

1. Is the primary caretaker rule adopted in *Pikula* an improvement over the presumption favoring mothers as custodians for children of "tender years?" As Justice Rosalie Wahl points out in footnote 2 of her opinion, the "tender years" doctrine has fallen into disfavor because it overtly discriminated against fathers. Does adoption of the primary caretaker rule substantially improve a father's chances of obtaining custody of a child? Chief Justice Richard Neely, who announced the primary caretaker rule in Garska v. McCoy, 167 W.Va. 59, 278 S.E.2d 357 (1981), admits that "[o]ur rule inevitably involves some injustice to fathers who, as a group, are usually not primary caretakers." Richard Neely, The

Primary Caretaker Parent Rule: Child Custody and the Dynamics of Greed, 3 Yale L. & Pol.Rev. 168, 180 (1984). He insists, however, that because the rule itself is phrased in gender neutral terms, it can take account of non-traditional lifestyles: "[i]n West Virginia we have women who pursue lucrative and successful careers while their husbands take care of the children; those husbands receive the benefit of the presumption as strongly as do traditional mothers." Ibid. Nancy Polikoff characterized *Garska* as "a landmark decision which realistically examined the larger picture of custody disputes and also developed a standard which preserves sex neutrality, encourages paternal involvement in childrearing, and guarantees that the child's bond with the parent providing daily care and nurturance will be maintained." Nancy D. Polikoff, Why Are Mothers Losing: A Brief Analysis of Criteria Used in Child Custody Determinations, 7 Women's Rights L.Rep. 235, 241 (1982). Do you agree with this evaluation? Does it extend to *Pikula?* See Dan O'Hanlon & Margaret Workman, Beyond the Best Interest of the Child: The Primary Caretaker Doctrine in West Virginia, 92 W.Va.L.Rev. 355, 380–88 (1990), detailing West Virginia's experience with the doctrine. See also Davis v. Davis, 749 P.2d 647 (Utah 1988), awarding custody of a three-year-old boy to his father under the primary caretaker rule in a case where the boy had lived with the father in the family home for one year pursuant to a divorce decree that was set aside three days after its entry because of the mother's emotional instability. The Utah Supreme Court disregarded the mother's argument that the trial court's order was improper because it had the effect of rewarding the father's exploitative conduct in securing the earlier hurried divorce and custody order, pointing out that the mother's difficulties in caring for the child were in part responsible for the divorce. Is *Davis* a proper application of the primary caretaker doctrine?

2. Is joint custody preferable to sole custody in either parent as a way of ending sex discrimination in custody awards? Does it elevate the rights of the separating parents over the best interests of the children? The impetus for joint or shared custody legislation seems to have come primarily from father's rights groups. Commentators have noted the influence of such groups on the country's most far-reaching joint custody statute, California Civil Code Sections 4600 and 4600.5, which became effective January 1, 1980. See Billy G. Mills & Steven P. Belzer, Joint Custody As A Parenting Alternative, 9 Pepperdine L.Rev. 853 (1982); Nancy K. Lemon, Joint Custody as a Statutory Presumption: California's New Civil Code Sections 4600 and 4600.5, 11 Golden Gate U.L.Rev. 485 (1981). Is joint custody detrimental to mothers? Feminists disagree. Compare Katharine T. Bartlett & Carol B. Stack, Joint Custody, Feminism, and the Dependency Dilemma, 2 Berkeley Women's L.J. 9 (1986) (arguing that joint custody is an alternative that promises greater independence to women) with Joanne Schulman & Valerie Pitt, Second Thoughts on Joint Custody: Analysis of Legislation and Its Implications for Women and Children, 12 Golden Gate U.L.Rev. 539 (1982) (arguing that joint custody may be detrimental to women and children). Is it in the best interests of the children? Courts have rejected joint custody in cases where such an order appears not to serve the children's interests: see, e.g., Turner v. Turner, 455 So.2d 1374, 1380–81 (La.1984) (reversing award of joint custody where parents disagree about how the twin boys should be reared); Elebash v. Elebash, 450 So.2d 1268, 1270 (Fla.App.1984) (affirming trial court's refusal to award joint custody despite parental request because planned rotation of children, almost on a daily basis, between parents' homes was presumptively not in children's best interests). Nor do the experts agree about whether joint custody is in the best interests of children. Compare, e.g., Frederick W. Ilfeld,

Holly Zingale Ilfeld & John R. Alexander, Does Joint Custody Work? A First Look at Outcome Data of Relitigation, 139 Am.J.Psychiatry 62 (1982) with Elissa P. Benedek & Richard S. Benedek, Joint Custody: Solution or Illusion? 136 Am.J.Psychiatry 1540 (1979). A symposium on joint custody appears in 16 U.C. Davis L.Rev. 739 (1983). See generally, Jay Folberg, ed., Joint Custody and Shared Parenting (1984); Jay Folberg, Joint Custody Law: The Second Wave, 23 Fam.L.J. 1 (1984).

3. Do working mothers need something like a "tender years" doctrine or a primary caretaker rule to protect their interests as mothers against trial court judges who disapprove of nontraditional roles for women? In Marriage of Tresnak, 297 N.W.2d 109 (Iowa 1980), both parents sought custody of two boys, aged 9 and 11. Except for a one-year stint when she worked in a nursing home, Linda Tresnak had been a full time homemaker during the 14 year marriage. Jim Tresnak had been the sole breadwinner, earning the family living by teaching business courses in high school. Linda, who had had only one year of college previously, earned her degree in psychology during the marriage. Her proposal to enter law school in 1979 apparently broke up the marriage. Looking at Linda's plans from the perspective of custody of the children, the trial court judge thought her ambition to study law was "commendable", but "not necessarily for the best interest and welfare of her minor children", primarily because of the time-consuming nature of legal studies and the necessity of doing much of one's work in the law library. Custody of the boys was awarded to the father.

On appeal, this judgment was reversed and the trial court was ordered to award custody to Linda. The Iowa Supreme Court noted that the trial court's observations about the necessity of extensive library study for law students were not properly the subject of judicial notice and were not otherwise supported by the record. It also disregarded the lower court's view that the father would be better equipped than the mother to participate with the boys in activities such as athletic events, fishing, hunting, and mechanical training, as the product of "a stereotypical view of sexual roles which has no place in child custody adjudication." Addressing the merits of the case de novo, the court held that custody should be awarded to the mother. Its opinion on that issue follows:

Because either parent would be a good custodian of the children, the decision on the merits is difficult. Linda and Jim are stable and responsible persons who love their children and are capable of giving them adequate care.

Prior to returning to school, Linda fulfilled a traditional role as housewife and mother while Jim was the breadwinner. Until Linda moved to Kirksville in January 1978, she continued to have primary responsibility for the day-to-day parenting of the children. This was true even when she was attending junior college full-time. Although Jim had primary responsibility for the children from January through May 1978, Linda came home each weekend to clean house, help with the laundry, cook meals, and prepare foods to be served during the following week. During that period Rick required assistance at home with his spelling. After first agreeing to help, Jim later asserted he was too busy to do so. Linda provided the assistance during her weekends at home. She has had primary care of the children since the fall of 1978.

Linda is a fastidious housekeeper and obviously a highly-motivated and organized person. She has been active in school affairs. She plays with the children and has counseled with them concerning their development as adolescents.

Jim likes his work and keeps busy with it. He is not as concerned about household cleanliness as Linda. Nor did he display her concern about the children's meals and clothing during the period he had their primary care. He has not been active in their school affairs, and he was not aware of several of their allergies. Although this is explained in part by the necessity of devoting his time and energy to making a living, the record shows that even when he had primary responsibility for the care of the children, he was not as attentive as Linda to the details of their lives. Moreover, she maintained her attentiveness even during the times when her studies were demanding as much time as Jim's work.

A psychologist who interviewed the children testified in Linda's behalf. He said the children were exceptionally well-adjusted and would not suffer from moving with their mother to Iowa City. He reasoned that the stability of their relationship with their mother was more important than continuity in their place of residence. The children are normal, although Rick has had problems with spelling and underachievement at school. Linda has worked with him on these problems. The children are close, well-mannered and disciplined.

The trial court believed Linda's pursuit of a legal education would be detrimental to the children's interests. We do not think the record bears out this concern. She very capably cared for the children during her undergraduate studies. During that time Jim did not complain of her ability to do so. Moreover, the children did not suffer when, by agreement of the parties, they lived with Linda and attended the Kirksville schools in the 1978–79 school year. No question existed about their moving again. The only issue was whether they would return to Chariton or accompany Linda to Iowa City.

Furthermore, no basis exists for characterizing Linda's law school years as unstable. She has demonstrated she can control the time she spends on her studies as well as Jim can control the time he spends on his work. Although she may move again when she finishes law school, this prospect differs little from Jim's readiness to move to a junior college teaching position if an opportunity arises.

It is common knowledge that in many homes today both parents have demanding out-of-home activities, whether in employment, school or community affairs. Neither should necessarily be penalized in child custody cases for engaging in such activities. In this case, Linda seeks a legal education for self-fulfillment and as a means of achieving financial independence. These goals are not inimical to the children's best interests. Because the record shows she is capable of continuing to provide the children with the same high quality of care she has given them in the past, her attendance at law school should not disqualify her from having their custody. We perceive no reason for believing she will not give the children excellent care during her law school years and thereafter.

Id., 297 N.W.2d at 113–14. See also Ireland v. Smith, Docket # 93–0385–DS, Macomb County Circuit Court, Michigan (1994), in which a Michigan Family Court judge awarded custody to a father rather than a mother in part because the mother's plan to attend the University of Michigan would require placing the three-year old girl in child care for most of the day, while the father, also a student, would place her with his parents. In considering the list of statutory factors provided for child custody cases by Michigan Comp.Laws Ann. § 722.23

(West 1995 Cum.Ann.Pocket Part), set out at p. 349, infra, the Court made the following finding of fact on factor (e):

> (e) The permanence, as a family unit, of the existing or proposed custodial home or homes. Defendant proposes that the child would be raised in the paternal grandparent's home. * * * The defendant is now a student at Macomb County Community College and at the same time maintains part time employment. * * * His parents would welcome the minor child to their home for whatever length of time it takes for the defendant to eventually establish his own residence. * * * The plaintiff is academically bright and has been accorded a scholarship at the University of Michigan. * * * She would contemplate living at the U of M and placing the child in appropriate day care or schooling, whichever is appropriate to the child's development and in off-school times or on weekends, etc., she would return to her mother's home. * * * The mother's program would require that the child be in day care. * * * The mother's academic pursuits, although laudable, are demanding and in order to complete her program it necessitates the leaving of the child for a considerable portion of its life in the care of strangers. There is no way that a single parent, attending an academic program at an institution as prestigious as the University of Michigan, can do justice to their studies and the raising of an infant child. There are not that many hours in the day. Parents do raise children in a college setting but it is hoped that the cooperation and the efforts of both parents negate parental neglect. The plaintiff's situation is entirely different, however, she must rely upon other people to take care of this child while she is in class and it is pretty clear that the demands of academia are such that her time for her youngster would be circumscribed. The permanence of a regular home and a regular program far out weigh the multitude of changes in housing, day care, etc., that one would necessarily experience year-to-year while being a student at a university. It would appear to the Court that this paragraph weighs heavily in favor of the defendant.

In weighing the various factors, the Court gave "supreme importance" to (e):

> * * * Paragraph (e) above, very succinctly states the elements which will impact most heavily upon the life of the child. Under the future plans of the mother, the minor child will be in essence raised and supervised a great part of the time by strangers. Under the future plans of the father, the minor child will be raised and supervised by blood relatives. Under the mother's plan, the child will not have a specific residence, being moved periodically between the University of Michigan and the maternal grandmother's home. Under the father's plan, the child will reside in the paternal grandparent's home for an indefinite period. A child gains the feeling of security, a safe place, by virtue of permanency. * * * Our goal must be to create and insure in the child as great a feeling of stability and permanency as can be consistent with the circumstances that exist. * * *

Would the court have come to the same conclusion if the mother had gotten a job in an office or store, and had planned to place her daughter in child care during her nine to five working day? On appeal, the matter was reversed and remanded for reevaluation of factor (e) by a different judge. Ireland v. Smith, Court of Appeals of Michigan, 214 Mich.App. 235, 542 N.W.2d 344 (1995).

Compare Gulyas v. Gulyas, 75 Mich.App. 138, 254 N.W.2d 818 (1977), where both parents worked full time. The mother, a regional manager for H & R Block, testified that she worked about 40 to 50 hours per week during the income tax season (about four months of the year) and 10 to 30 hours per week during the rest of the year. The father, whose occupation was not revealed, testified that he worked a "standard 40–hour week". Both parents sought custody of their 6 year old daughter, Tiffany. The father proposed to care for her in the home of his parents, where the paternal grandmother could assume Tiffany's care during the working day. The mother, who had remarried a co-worker, had been using day care homes in the past. She testified, however, that she would give up her job if Tiffany were awarded to her. The trial court characterized the mother as "an energetic and ambitious career woman," and viewed the father as more of a "homebody" than she. Custody was awarded to the father; this order was affirmed on appeal. Judge Riley, dissenting, thought the trial court judge had given undue weight to the mother's career. Although he concluded that this preoccupation with the mother's job status was probably not enough to amount to an abuse of discretion, Judge Riley nonetheless warned that "the best interests of the child * * * should not be used as a screen with which to hide outmoded notions of a woman's rule being near hearth and home." (75 Mich.App. at 151, 254 N.W.2d at 823.) Is this warning well taken? Judge Riley also noted that, given the seasonal characteristics of the mother's job, she probably worked fewer hours per year than the father. What weight should be given to this fact? Is it significant that the mother was willing to give up her job if she was given custody? Do you suppose she made that offer because she thought Tiffany would be better off if her custodial parent stayed home, or because she believed it necessary to obtain a favorable ruling from the trial court judge? Note that the father made no comparable offer. What would happen if the mother did give up her job, obtained custody of Tiffany, and later went back to work at that job or another? Should Tiffany then be shifted to her father?

4. In Hammett v. Hammett, 46 Ala.App. 206, 239 So.2d 778 (1970), custody of three children ranging in age from 11 to 14 was awarded to the father over the mother's objection. The father was retired from military service, where he had been a cook and NCO in charge of the general mess. The mother was a beautician. At the time of the decree the father was unemployed and stayed home doing all the cooking for the family. The mother worked six days a week in Montgomery. The children, particularly the twelve-year-old boy, were in need of discipline. All the children had expressed a preference for living with the father. In reversing the trial court, which had awarded custody to the mother, the appellate court said (46 Ala.App. at 208–209, 239 So.2d at 780):

> To summarize the evidence which forces us to our decision—The children prefer to live with their father. The father has prepared their meals almost exclusively since their birth. He is free to be at home with them at all times. He is undisputedly fitted morally and financially to provide them with a good home. The mother, whether from necessity or inclination, has worked throughout the children's lives, all day and every day, except Sunday, leaving their care to someone else. She, admittedly, cannot cook for them as well as the father. The children are enrolled in schools near the home of appellant. The children are in need of parental discipline.

> It really matters not whether our determination of error in the decree is stated to be based upon a wrong conclusion of facts, or a wrong application of governing principles of law. In any event, it is clear that to serve the best interest of the children the decree in respect to custody must be reversed.

> In the event there is not involved a child of such tender years as to be peculiarly dependent upon the mother, there is no rule requiring that custody

be granted to the mother rather than the father, when either is a fit and proper custodian. From the facts in the instant case, it rather appears that the children are peculiarly dependent upon the father. In making such statement and in rendering this decision, we do not intend to appear derogatory to the appellee as a mother. We are certain she has attempted to do her best for her children under difficult circumstances. We are further certain that the trial court will insure that she has every opportunity, consonant with the welfare of the children, to be with them and have them with her.

The trial court is hereby directed to amend its decree wherein it granted to appellee the permanent care, custody and control of the children, and grant such custody to the appellant, granting appellee such reasonable rights of visitation as is deemed proper in the premises. It follows that the portion of the decree as to payment of support for the children to appellee by appellant, be amended to conform with this decision.

Is the court unduly influenced by the role-reversal that exists in *Hammett?* If the father were a beautician and the mother a retired military mess officer who prepared the family meals, would custody have been given to her? See also McCreery v. McCreery, 218 Va. 352, 237 S.E.2d 167 (1977), affirming an order awarding custody to a father. Both parents worked outside the home, but while the mother seemed to the trial court to have "perhaps unconsciously, relegated these two little girls to a position secondary to her job and her relationship with Mr. Short [her supervisor and fellow employee]", the father impressed several witnesses as being a mother figure to his daughters. And recall that the trial court in *Gulyas,* Note 3, supra, commented favorably that the father, unlike the mother, was something of a "homebody." Do these cases, together with *Hammett,* suggest that fathers who are comfortable in traditional mothering roles have a better chance of being awarded custody? If so, is this a desirable trend?

5. *Schuster* is one of the early published cases confirming custody in a lesbian mother. While at least one court had held that a mother's homosexuality was not enough, as a matter of law, to form the basis of a decision denying custody to her, Nadler v. Superior Court, 255 Cal.App.2d 523, 63 Cal.Rptr. 352 (1967), not very much more in the way of evidence was required to support a negative result. Even in *Nadler,* the court on remand again awarded custody to the heterosexual father after hearing testimony from a psychiatrist that the mother would have greater difficulty than a heterosexual person in encouraging her children to seek heterosexual relationships and that she would be impaired in teaching them a "traditional concept of morality." This testimony was elicited on cross-examination; the psychiatrist, Dr. George Gross, had stated in his direct testimony that the mother was a "reasonable, sensible, sensitive, aware person * * * who is interested in her children" and had ventured the opinion that her homosexual activity would not have any adverse effect upon the children. See Del Martin & Phyllis Lyon, Lesbian/Woman 137–39 (1972).

What, by the way, was the final outcome in *Schuster?* Can Sandra Schuster and Madeleine Isaacson live together with their children or not? Professor Rhonda Rivera, reviewing recent cases (many of them unpublished in official reports), notes that limitations on the visitation or custodial rights of homosexual parents are common. See Rhonda Rivera, Our Straight–Laced Judges: The Legal Position of Homosexual Persons in the United States, 30 Hastings L.J. 799, 891 (1979). Do these limitations reflect the sound exercise of judicial discretion? Are they even constitutional? See Marilyn Riley, Law Note, The Avowed Lesbian

Mother and Her Right to Child Custody: A Constitutional Challenge That Can No Longer Be Denied, 12 San Diego L.Rev. 799, 821–64 (1975).

6.   Do gay fathers who seek custody or visitation with their children face legal restrictions similar to those placed on lesbian mothers? If so, do these cases pose questions of sex-based discrimination or a problem of divergent life-styles common to homosexual persons regardless of sex? Compare A. v. A., 15 Or.App. 353, 514 P.2d 358, reh'g denied, 15 Or.App. 353, 515 P.2d 730 (1973), permitting a father who had been awarded custody of two boys by a divorce decree eleven years earlier to retain custody as against the mother despite his admission on cross-examination that "he believed he 'might have possible homosexual traits and tendencies' but categorically denied actively carrying on any homosexual activity." Despite the father's denials, the trial court conditioned its custody order upon having his male business partner move out of the home and prohibiting any other man from moving in, presumably in order "to safeguard the home environment against possible pernicious influences." (514 P.2d at 359.) For good measure, the Appellate Court, in affirming the order, modified it to include a requirement that supervision of the home be provided by the Clackamas County Juvenile Department. (514 P.2d at 361.) What do you suppose would have happened if the father in A., like the mothers in Schuster, had admitted being an active homosexual? See also In re J.S. & C., 129 N.J.Super. 486, 324 A.2d 90 (1974), affirmed 142 N.J.Super. 499, 362 A.2d 54 (1976), granting visitation rights to a homosexual father active in the Gay Liberation Movement with the following restrictions: No overnight visits except for a period of 3 weeks during the summer; the 3 week visit to be at an address other than the father's present apartment in a building occupied almost entirely by homosexuals; during the visits, the father cannot "cohabit or sleep with any individual other than a lawful spouse" or be in the presence of his lover; and he cannot involve the children in any activities or publicity related to homosexuality nor take them to a particular meeting hall. See generally Nan D. Hunter & Nancy D. Polikoff, Custody Rights of Lesbian Mothers: Legal Theory and Litigation Strategy, 25 Buff.L.Rev. 691 (1976).

7.   How should custody of four minor children be awarded—to their "cold and aloof" father or to their mother, now a transsexual married to another woman? The original Nevada divorce decree had given custody to the mother, but that judgment later was modified in Colorado to change custody to the father. By the time of the third hearing, the children had run away from their father to return to their mother/father and his wife. Taking into account the desire of all four girls to remain with their mother and resolving the conflict with his "personal beliefs and opinions" posed by the decision, Judge Frank Gregory returned the children to their mother, noting that (Randall v. Christian, No. 32964, Carson City Dist.Ct., Nov. 14, 1973):

> [t]he girls have been taught of their former mother's change of sex and they understand it, and appreciate it for the fact that it is. We feel, that despite social mores and old-fashioned attitudes, the welfare of the children will be best served by placing them with their former mother, and now the father-image, Mark Randall.

Mark Randall also obtained a reversal of the Colorado judgment that had modified the Nevada divorce decree to award the children to their father. See Christian v. Randall, 33 Colo.App. 129, 133, 516 P.2d 132, 134 (1973), holding, under Colorado's version of the Uniform Marriage and Divorce Act, that the court could not consider conduct of a proposed custodian that does not affect his or her relationship with the child. Since there was no evidence that Mark Randall's sex change, his change of name, or his remarriage to a woman had affected his relationship with the children in an adverse way, custody should not have been changed to the father.

8. How much weight did the court in *Greenfield* give to the trial court's reliance on the mother's statement that she would not continue to live in nonmarital cohabitation with Donny Ring? While *Greenfield* was pending, the mother sought modification of the child support provisions of the decree, alleging that the father's circumstances had improved sufficiently so that he was able to contribute to the support of the children. In response, the father admitted his improved financial condition, but sought once again to obtain custody of the children. Although his cross-application was dismissed because he failed to appear at the hearing, the court noted that the mother was still living with Donny Ring in nonmarital cohabitation, "under circumstances which may be harmful to the morals of the two minor children." The court, on its own motion, ordered the district court to hold a further hearing on the custody issue. Greenfield v. Greenfield, 200 Neb. 608, 611, 264 N.W.2d 675, 677 (1978). A hearing date was set, but the parties settled before any testimony was given.

Compare with the *Greenfield* court's approach the decision in Parrillo v. Parrillo, 554 A.2d 1043 (R.I.1989), certiorari denied 493 U.S. 954, 110 S.Ct. 364, 107 L.Ed.2d 351 (1989). Carla Parrillo divorced Justin Parrillo in mid-May 1986. She was given custody of the three children. In early June, she sought to fix Justin's visitation schedule; he responded with a request for an order restraining Carla from permitting unrelated males to stay overnight at her residence. Carla admitted that she was dating Joseph DiPippo, and that occasionally he stayed overnight in the family home. The opinion indicates how the trial court handled the dispute:

> Carla told the trial justice that Justin began to harass her once he learned she was dating Joseph. Carla acknowledged that Joseph would remain overnight "[o]nce or twice a week behind closed doors." Carla saw no risk to the children, who were present when Joseph was staying overnight, because, she explained, the daughters slept in separate bedrooms about twenty feet away from her bedroom and the son's bedroom was downstairs. When asked if Joseph wore his pajamas in front of the children, Carla explained that when Joseph stayed overnight, he wore a jogging suit. She explained to the trial justice that the children liked Joseph but that she had no intention of marrying him in the near future.

> Justin began to reduce his support payments once he learned that Joseph was making his nocturnal visitations.

> With the consent and in the presence of counsel, the trial justice met with the three children in his chambers. All the children said they got along well with Joseph, although the son did say that there were times when he did not like him.

> In a bench decision given immediately after the presentation of the evidence, the trial justice stated that the children "appear to be well cared for" and that he could not fault the mother's care of her children. However, he did observe that Joseph's overnight visits, in the presence of the children, were not conducive to their general wellbeing, at least in terms of their psychological welfare. The trial justice did observe that if Carla married

Joseph, he would become the children's stepfather and the cohabitation [1] issue would become moot.

The trial justice directed Carla to refrain from allowing any "unrelated males" to stay overnight at her residence when the children were present. Id., 554 A.2d at 1044. On appeal, Justice Kelleher affirmed the trial court's order, pointing out that:

This court, in Vieira v. Vieira, 98 R.I. 454, 204 A.2d 431 (1964), approved a change of custody from the mother to the father because six days after granting the father's petition for a divorce on the grounds of gross misbehavior, the mother and the children spent the night at a New Hampshire motor lodge. Present at the lodge was the male whose association with the mother caused the divorce. This court, in commenting on the trial justice's action, observed "it cannot seriously be questioned that the best interests of these children could no longer be served by continuing their custody in their mother. The harmful effect of her conduct on children of tender years and at impressionable ages cannot be doubted." Id. at 458, 204 A.2d at 433.

However, in this dispute no change in custody has been ordered by the Family Court. In entering the order that was without question directed at Joseph, the trial justice, in simple and direct language, ordered the mother to forgo any overnight visitations with Joseph on those occasions when the children are present. We cannot fault the trial justice's actions. Joseph may still visit the marital domicile overnight, with the exception of those times when the children are with their mother. Notwithstanding the views of Carla's appellate counsel to the contrary, we see no great constitutional issue in this controversy.

Id., 554 A.2d at 1045. Justice Kelleher was right about the absence of any "great constitutional issue" in the case, wasn't he? Do you think the United States Supreme Court should have granted certiorari? If so, how and why should the case have been decided?

What weight ought to be given to the fact that the custodial parent lives in nonmarital cohabitation in the presence of the children? See Jarrett v. Jarrett, 78 Ill.2d 337, 36 Ill.Dec. 1, 400 N.E.2d 421 (1979), cert. den., 449 U.S. 927, 101 S.Ct. 329, 66 L.Ed.2d 155 reh'g denied, 449 U.S. 1067, 66 L.Ed.2d 612, 101 S.Ct. 797 (1980), set out at p. 365, infra.

9. What weight, if any, should be given to the sexual activity of the custodial parent? In Marriage of Wellman, 104 Cal.App.3d 992, 164 Cal.Rptr. 148 (1980), the mother had custody of three children, aged 8, 10, and 13, by agreement of the parties. It developed at the hearing that she had an intimate relationship with Mr. Randolph Silver, a marriage counselor, and that he visited the mother and her children on some weekends, occasionally staying at their home from Thursday evening until Sunday. He slept alone in a room downstairs. The mother testified that she and Mr. Silver never "had relations" except when they were certain the children were asleep. The trial court granted custody of the three children to the mother, but ordered that "[p]etitioner shall have no overnight visitation with a member of the opposite sex, in the presence of the children, until or unless she is married to that individual." On appeal, this restriction was removed from the judgment. Noting the lack of any evidence in the record about the impact of the relationship on the children (Mr. Silver's offer to testify as an expert witness was rejected by the trial court), as well as possible constitutional issues surrounding

---

1. In using the term "cohabitation," we are referring to sexual relations.

the mother's right to privacy, the court held that "the order in question * * * is so intrusive upon the privacy and associational interests of the mother and so lacking in evidentiary support in terms of the interests of the children that it cannot be sustained." (Id., 104 Cal.App.3d at 999, 164 Cal.Rptr. at 152.) Is this the right result? Since the parents had agreed that the mother should have custody of the children, did the court have jurisdiction to enter the restrictive order in the first place?

Text Note
Child Custody and Support

1. *Child Custody*

The choice between parents of a proper custodian for their children has nearly always been sex-determined in Anglo–American law. At common law, the father's right to custody of his legitimate children was virtually absolute, regardless of whether the issue arose via *habeas corpus* proceedings in the law courts or by petition to the Chancellor in Equity.[1] The mother's right to custody arose only after the father's death, but after 1660 he could defeat her claim by appointing a testamentary guardian.[2] So great were the father's powers that we are told "he could lawfully claim from [the mother] the possession even of a child at the breast."[3]

The common law rule was altered by statutory changes in England culminating in the Guardianship of Infants Act 1925, which expressly provided that neither parent had any right superior to the other to the custody or upbringing of their child, to the administration of its property, or the application of its income.[4]

Statutes and case law in the United States generally recognize that both parents are equally entitled to the custody of their children.[5] When the issue of custody arises between parents in divorce cases, courts apply a vague standard centering around the "best interests" or "welfare" of the child.[6] California, long one of the few states to establish an express statutory preference for mother custody of young children in divorce cases,[7] amended its law in 1972 to abolish any priority between parents.[8] Despite the surface neutrality of the law, however,

1. Joseph Warren Madden, Persons and Domestic Relations 369–70 (1931). The mother's right to custody of illegitimate children was primary. Id. at 372. See Text Note, Illegitimacy and Sex–Based Discrimination, at p. 375, infra.

2. Peter M. Bromley, Family Law 306 (5th ed. 1976). The Guardianship of Infants Act 1886 ended this practice by making the mother joint guardian with the father's testamentary appointee. Id. at 307.

3. Id. at 306.

4. This provision has been carried over without change into section 1 of the Guardianship of Minors Act 1971. See Bromley, supra note 2, at 308.

5. Homer H. Clark, The Law of Domestic Relations 584–85 (1968). See also, summarizing recent statutory and judicial developments, Ralph J. Podell, Harry F. Peck & Curry First, Custody—To Which Parent? 56 Marquette L.Rev. 51 (1972).

6. Herma Hill Kay and Irving Philips, Poverty and the Law of Child Custody, 54 Calif.L.Rev. 717, 719–22 (1966).

7. Cal.Civ.Code § 4600 formerly provided that "[a]s between parents adversely claiming the custody, neither parent is entitled to it as of right; but other things being equal, if the child is of tender years, it should be given to the mother; if it is of an age to require education and preparation for labor and business, then to the father." Cal.Stats.1931, c. 930, p. 1928 § 1. The father preference clause was dropped and the maternal preference seemingly made nearly mandatory in 1969, when the statute directed that custody be awarded "to either parent according to the best interests of the child, but, other things being equal, custody *shall* be given to the mother if the child is of tender years." Cal.Stats.1969, c. 1608, p. 3330 § 8. In 1970, the word "shall" was changed back to "should". Cal.Stats.1970, c. 1545, p. 3139 § 2. See also note 8, infra.

8. Cal.Stats.1972, Ch. 1007, § 1 (amending Civ.Code § 4600) and § 2 (amending Prob.C.

there exists a well-recognized judicial penchant for finding that the welfare of young children is served best by awarding their custody to the mother.[9] Moreover, this preference is said to be "psychologically sound provided that the mother is emotionally capable." [10]

The "tender years" presumption, as the maternal preference is often called, has survived constitutional challenge by fathers in several traditionally-minded courts. For example, the Supreme Court of Utah brushed aside an equal protection attack on a statute directing judges to consider "the natural presumption that the mother is best suited to care for young children" with the statement that "[t]he contention might have some merit to it in a proper case if the father was equally gifted in lactation as is the mother." [11] The Oklahoma Supreme Court in Gordon v. Gordon [12] went to greater lengths to justify its reversal of an order awarding custody of a three year old boy to his father. The relevant statute provided that "[a]s between parents adversely claiming the custody or guardianship, neither parent is entitled to it as of right, but, other things being equal, if the child be of tender years, it should be given to the mother; if it be of an age to require education and preparation for labor or business, then to the father." The court interpreted this statute to require the award of a young child to the mother if she is not unfit. Applying the standard established in Craig v. Boren [13] to the father's argument that the statutory maternal preference was an unconstitutional discrimination based on sex, the court found the "gender-based means" chosen by the Legislature to be "substantially related to the important objective" of placing children in the custody of "that parent most apt to provide them with the best care and protection." The opinion continues: [14]

> It is indeed an old notion that a child of tender years needs a mother more than a father, but defendant has not persuaded us that this notion is either unsound or unconstitutional. We believe that consideration of the cultural, psychological and emotional characteristics that are gender related make this custodial preference one of "those instances where the sex-centered generalization actually [comports] to fact." Craig v. Boren, supra, 50 L.Ed.2d, at 408. The statute's additional provision that children who are of an age to require education and preparation for labor or business should be placed in the father's custody further reinforces our decision. This provision makes clear the essential fact that this statute is not concerned entirely with the "rights" of parents to their children. In addition to, and far beyond, their rights, the paramount purpose of the statute is to serve the welfare and best interests of children.

Contrast the reasoning of Judge Sybil Hart Kooper in State ex rel. Watts v. Watts,[15] justifying her award of the custody of three infants to their father:

§ 1408), Deering's Adv.Leg.Ser. 446–47 (1972). In 1979, § 4600 was amended to provide that "[i]n making an order for custody to either parent, the court * * * shall not prefer a parent as custodian because of that parent's sex." Cal.Stats.1979, c. 915, p. 3149, § 3.

9. Clark, supra note 5, at 585.

10. Andrew S. Watson, The Children of Armageddon: Problems of Custody Following Divorce, 21 Syracuse L.Rev. 55, 70 (1969).

11. Arends v. Arends, 30 Utah 2d 328, 329, 517 P.2d 1019, 1020 (1974), cert. denied 419 U.S. 881, 95 S.Ct. 146, 42 L.Ed.2d 121. See

also Cox v. Cox, 532 P.2d 994, 996 (Utah, 1975) (upholding mother preference against attack based on the Utah state equal rights amendment).

12. 577 P.2d 1271 (Okl.1978) cert. denied 439 U.S. 863, 99 S.Ct. 185, 58 L.Ed.2d 172.

13. 429 U.S. 190, 97 S.Ct. 451, 50 L.Ed.2d 397 (1976), set forth at p. 41, supra.

14. Gordon v. Gordon, supra note 12, at 1277.

15. 77 Misc.2d 178, 181, 350 N.Y.S.2d 285, 288–89 (Fam.Ct., N.Y.Cty.1973).

[T]he "tender years presumption" should be discarded because it is based on outdated social stereotypes rather than on rational and up-to-date consideration of the welfare of the children involved.

The simple fact of being a mother does not, by itself, indicate a capacity or willingness to render a quality of care different from that which the father can provide. The traditional and romantic view, at least since the turn of the century, has been that nothing can be an adequate substitute for mother love.

* * *

Later decisions have recognized that this view is inconsistent with informed application of the best interests of the child doctrine and out of touch with contemporary thought about child development and male and female stereotypes.

Judge Kooper was aided in reaching her decision by the language of the New York statute which still provides in part that "[i]n all cases there shall be no prima facie right to the custody of the child in either parent." [16] Reading the tender years presumption into this provision, she warned, would constitute error and would probably violate the equal protection clause.[17]

Other judges, confronted with equally plain legislative mandates to disregard sex as a criterion in awarding custody, have not shared Judge Kooper's fidelity to the statutory language. Thus, in Erickson v. Erickson,[18] the court interpreted a statute requiring the trial court to "consider all facts in the best interest of the children" and forbidding it to "prefer one parent over the other solely on the basis of the sex of the parent" merely to prohibit according mothers an "absolute or arbitrary preference." Quoting with approval from its earlier decisions, the court saw no conflict between the statute and its own statement that "although * * * normally, other things being equal, the interests of young children are better served by placing them in their mother's custody rather than their father's custody, the paramount and overriding consideration must be the welfare of the children".[19] Following Minnesota's lead, the Wisconsin Supreme Court interpreted its identical statutory language as consistent with a "slight" but not an "irrebuttable" presumption favoring the mother. In Scolman v. Scolman,[20] the court reversed and remanded a custody award to a mother, stating that the statute

does not strike down the holdings of this court indicating that, other things being equal, there is usually a preference for the mother. The trial court may properly find that young children are better off with their mother. The statute merely decrees what the law in Wisconsin is already, that the trial court's decision cannot solely be based on the sex of the parent.

But, as Justice Heffernan pointed out in his concurring opinion, since the majority went on to reaffirm its earlier statement in Jenkins v. Jenkins,[21] to the effect that a mother's love and nurture are unique, it is a bit difficult to conclude

---

16. Id., 77 Misc.2d at 179, 350 N.Y.S.2d at 287, quoting Domestic Relations Law sections 240 and 70.

17. Id., 77 Misc.2d at 182–84, 350 N.Y.S.2d at 290–91. Judge Kooper's constitutional analysis is flawed by a misreading of Frontiero v. Richardson, 411 U.S. 677, 93 S.Ct. 1764, 36 L.Ed.2d 583 (1973) to require a strict scrutiny standard in gender discrimination cases. See also Ex parte Devine, 398 So.2d 686 (Ala.1981)

(holding maternal presumption unconstitutional).

18. 300 Minn. 559, 220 N.W.2d 487 (1974).

19. Id., 300 Minn. at 560–61, 220 N.W.2d at 489.

20. 66 Wis.2d 761, 766, 226 N.W.2d 388, 390 (1975).

21. 173 Wis. 592, 595, 181 N.W. 826, 827 (1921).

that the trial judge had actually committed error by voicing his belief that "the sociological impact of the mother's care, of a mother's interest in a four year old child overcome the other considerations, both [the Court Counsel and the guardian *ad litem*] used in arriving at the conclusions." Are you tempted to agree with Justice Heffernan that the majority "gives lip service to the statute, but seeks to circumvent it"? [22]

Does the outcome in these cases turn as much on the sex of the judge as on the sex of the parent? Justice Heffernan, at least, recognizes that under the traditional approach [23]

> child rearing and child care, by and large, have worked out very nicely for the males. A substantial portion of parental responsibility has thus been transferred with good conscience to the female, because by it she is "rewarded" and "ennobled."

Do you agree with Judge Kooper that the "tender years" presumption should be discarded? One writer concludes that the tender years presumption fails the equal protection test enunciated in Craig v. Boren [24] because none of three generally asserted justifications (the mother's capacity for breastfeeding; the value of preserving the mother-infant bond; and the mother's superior knowledge and skill in the child's daily care) are substantially related to the state's interest in promoting the welfare of children.[25] Another writer, who sets out to defend the presumption as sound child welfare policy, gives away much of his case when he concedes that the person identified by the presumption is that parent who has actually performed the primary caregiving function.[26]

One of the chief values of the "tender years" presumption has been to discourage litigation over the issue of child custody, a process thought to be disruptive to children.[27] Professor Robert Mnookin,[28] who opposes the maternal preference rule in part because it is based on "value judgments and sexual stereotypes that our society is in the process of rejecting", nevertheless recognizes that [29]

> [a] standard providing for maternal preference * * * does more than affect the outcome of the small number of disputes that are actually litigated. It also gives mothers as a class more bargaining power than fathers in negotiations over custody.

Will the primary caretaker rule perform the same function of equalizing bargaining power between mothers and fathers? Justice Wahl, citing the Mnookin and Kornhauser study, concluded that it would.[30] Do you agree? Rena Uviller was

---

22. Scolmon v. Scolmon, supra note 20, 66 Wis.2d at 771, 226 N.W.2d at 393.

23. Id., 66 Wis.2d at 770, 226 N.W.2d at 392.

24. 429 U.S. 190, 97 S.Ct. 451, 50 L.Ed.2d 397 (1976), set forth at p. 30, supra.

25. Rob Strom, Comment, The Tender Years Presumption: Is It Presumably Unconstitutional? 21 San Diego L.Rev. 861 (1984).

26. Ramsay L. Klaff, The Tender Years Doctrine: A Defense, 70 Calif.L.Rev. 333, 343–44 (1982).

27. See, e.g., Watson, supra note 10. A perceptive study of the impact of divorce on children is found in Judith S. Wallerstein & Joan B. Kelly, Surviving the Breakup: How Children and Parents Cope With Divorce (1980).

28. Robert Mnookin, Child–Custody Adjudication: Judicial Functions in the Face of Indeterminacy, 39 Law & Contemp.Prob. 226 (1975).

29. Id., at 284.

30. Pikula v. Pikula, 374 N.W.2d 705, 712 (Minn.1985), set out at p. 319, supra.

prepared to retain the maternal presumption to maintain the legal position of mothers in custody disputes: [31]

> [t]he maternal presumption in divorce proceedings is anathema to most feminists. The legal presumption that children belong with their mothers absent maternal unfitness reinforces the enduring stereotype of women as instinctive child rearers, inherently unsuited for worldly pursuits. * * *

> Yet giving fathers an equal footing with mothers in custody disputes is a feminist goal that bears reconsideration. Discarding the maternal preference before women as a class have made any substantial headway in the non-domestic world may just be a case of the proverbial cart and horse; under the guise of sex-neutrality, women who want their children may be at a distinct disadvantage in custody disputes due to their inferior earning capacity and an enduring social bias against working mothers. In addition, despite their feminist and child welfare rhetoric, rapidly proliferating "fathers' rights" groups are ringing an unmistakable note of sexist backlash.

Should Uviller now support the primary caretaker rule?

Another important function of the "tender years" doctrine was that of discouraging protracted child custody litigation by giving judges a relatively simple rule to decide disputed cases without the need to resort to expensive and time-consuming expert opinion. Chief Justice Neely says the primary caretaker rule is well-designed to perform this task, despite some shortcomings: [32]

> * * * There are instances where the primary caretaker will not be the better custodian in the long run. Yet there is no guarantee that the courts will be able to know, in advance and based on the deliberately distorted evidence that characterizes courtroom custody proceedings, when such is the case.

What percent of the cases will the primary caretaker rule decide? Justice Wahl in *Pikula* limited its use to cases where the child was too young to express a preference for a particular parent.[33] Chief Justice Neely asserts that the rule is absolute where both parents are fit in cases involving children under the age of six, but a child between six and fourteen may offer his or her own testimony to rebut the rule.[34] Children over fourteen may choose their own custodian in West Virginia if both parents are fit.[35] Does Chief Justice Neely really mean to exclude expert testimony offered by a parent to rebut the primary caretaker rule? On what issue would such testimony be relevant?

Are you persuaded that Chief Justice Neely has solved the problem of contested child custody cases in a way that is fair to both parents and adequately provides for the welfare of their children? Professor David Chambers, after a painstaking survey of social and behavioral science studies touching on this matter, tentatively concludes that he is willing to support a presumption favoring the primary caretaker, but only for children under the age of five.[36]

Apart from efforts to formulate specific rules, such as the primary caretaker rule, the present thrust in child custody statutory reform appears to lie in devising

31. Rena K. Uviller, Fathers' Rights and Feminism: The Maternal Presumption Revisited, 1 Harv.Women's L.J. 107, 108–09 (1978).

32. Richard Neely, The Primary Caretaker Rule: Child Custody and the Dynamics of Greed, 3 Yale L. & Pol.Rev. 168, 180 (1984).

33. 374 N.W.2d at 713, quoted at p. 326, supra.

34. Neely, supra note 32, at 182.

35. Ibid.

36. David L. Chambers, Rethinking the Substantive Rules for Custody in Divorce, 83 Mich.L.Rev. 477, 558–65 (1984).

ways to make the vague "best interests" test more concrete. Both the Uniform Marriage and Divorce Act and the Michigan Legislature have followed this course. The Uniform Marriage and Divorce Act [37] asks the court, in determining the best interests of the child, to consider

* * * all relevant factors including

(1) the wishes of the child's parent or parents as to his custody;

(2) the wishes of the child as to his custodian;

(3) the interaction and interrelationship of the child with his parents, his siblings, and any other person who may significantly affect the child's best interest;

(4) the child's adjustment to his home, school, and community; and

(5) the mental and physical health of all individuals involved.

The Michigan Legislature's list [38] is somewhat similar, but more heavily weighted with psychological considerations perhaps because of the participation of behavioral scientists in the drafting process.[39] It asks the court to take account of these factors:

(a) The love, affection and other emotional ties existing between the parties involved and the child.

(b) The capacity and disposition of the parties involved to give the child love, affection and guidance and to continue the education and raising of the child in his or her religion or creed, if any.

(c) The capacity and disposition of the parties involved to provide the child with food, clothing, medical care or other remedial care recognized and permitted under the laws of this state in place of medical care, and other material needs.

(d) The length of time the child has lived in a stable, satisfactory environment, and the desirability of maintaining continuity.

(e) The permanence, as a family unit, of the existing or proposed custodial home or homes.

(f) The moral fitness of the parties involved.

(g) The mental and physical health of the parties involved.

(h) The home, school, and community record of the child.

(i) The reasonable preference of the child, if the court considers the child to be of sufficient age to express preference.

(j) The willingness and ability of each of the parties to facilitate and encourage a close and continuing parent-child relationship between the child and the other parent, or the child and the parents.

(k) Domestic violence, regardless of whether the violence was directed against or witnessed by the child.

(l) Any other factor considered by the court to be relevant to a particular child custody dispute.

37. Uniform Marriage and Divorce Act § 402, 9A U.L.A. 348 (1987).

38. Mich.Comp.Laws Ann. § 722.23 (1995 Cum.Ann.Pocket Part).

39. Elissa P. Benedek, Child Custody Laws: Their Psychiatric Implications, 129 Amer.J.Psychiatry 326, 327–28 (1972).

Will the use of these factors tend to diminish or support the judicial preference for mother custody? The Comment to section 402 of the Uniform Act points out that "[t]he preference for the mother as custodian of young children when all things are equal * * * is simply a shorthand method of expressing the best interest of children—and this section enjoins judges to decide custody cases according to that general standard." [40] Dr. Watson, an advisor for both the Uniform Act and the Michigan statute, suggests a more precise use of sex-linked characteristics in awarding custody: while generally supporting mother custody for pre-adolescent children, he notes that [41]

> with the onset of adolescence, however, the like-sexed parent becomes more important since learning to become male or female is the principal psychological task for that age group. This means that with boys there should be a higher incidence of placement with fathers if the needs of male children are to be met.

Courts interpreting these provisions have not appreciably curtailed the exercise of their discretion. Thus, in Casale v. Casale,[42] a Kentucky court interpreting a version of the Uniform Act relied on the quoted Comment to reverse an award of custody to the father. In a case where the evidence was "close", the father should not obtain custody unless he was able to overcome the maternal preference. The Minnesota statute quoted in *Pikula* combines the Uniform Act and the Michigan lists. How does the Minnesota court reconcile its adoption of the primary caretaker rule with the Minnesota statute? One observer finds the court's action "unjustified" and argues that it essentially instructed trial courts to "substitute a list of homemaking duties for the best interests factors expressly provided by the Minnesota Legislature in section 518.17." [43]

How do you assess Watson's proposal for open use of the sex of children and parent at different stages of development as the basis for the custody decision? Care must be taken that this approach does not create its own stereotypes. See, for example, Marriage of Carney,[44] in which the California Supreme Court reversed an order awarding custody of two boys, aged 6 and 8, to their mother. The parents had separated five years earlier, and they had agreed that the father would take the boys with him. During that period the mother had not seen the boys and had kept up minimal contact with them by mail and telephone. The father, who ultimately moved to California, was living in nonmarital cohabitation with Lori Rivera and the two boys lived with them and their daughter. One year before the father filed for divorce, he was injured in a car accident. He became a quadriplegic. At the time of trial, he was recuperating and had bought a van equipped with a wheelchair lift and hand controls to permit him to drive. The trial court recognized that the family relationship had been a good one prior to the father's accident, but questioned the expert witnesses sharply about whether it wouldn't be advantageous to the boys to have a parent who "was able to actively go places with them, take them places, play Little League baseball, go fishing?" [45] The judge stated his views for the record: [46]

40. Uniform Marriage and Divorce Act. Comment to Section 402, p. 46 (1971).

41. Watson, supra note 10, at 70.

42. 549 S.W.2d 805, 806 (Ky.1977).

43. Sheri A. Ahl, Minnesota Developments, A Step Backward: The Minnesota Supreme Court Adopts a "Primary Caretaker" Presumption in Child Custody Cases: Pikula v. Pikula, 70 Minn.L.Rev. 1344 (1986).

44. 24 Cal.3d 725, 157 Cal.Rptr. 383, 598 P.2d 36 (1979).

45. Id., 24 Cal.3d at 734, 157 Cal.Rptr. at 387, 598 P.2d at 40.

46. Id., 24 Cal.3d at 735, 157 Cal.Rptr. at 388, 598 P.2d at 41.

I think it would be detrimental to the boys to grow up until age 18 in the custody of their father. It wouldn't be a normal relationship between father and boys. * * * It's unfortunate he has to have help bathing and dressing and undressing. He can't do anything for the boys himself except maybe talk to them and teach them, be a tutor, which is good, but it's not enough. I feel that it's in the best interests of the two boys to be with the mother even though she hasn't had them for five years.

Is this decision the product of the maternal preference or of a belief that a handicapped father who cannot interact with his sons in traditional manly pursuits has nothing to offer them as a parent? How would Watson decide this case? Speaking for a unanimous court, Justice Mosk reversed the judgment. On the question of the father's impairment, he said,[47]

the court's belief that there could be no "normal relationship between father and boys" unless William engaged in vigorous sporting activities with his sons is a further example of the conventional sex-stereotyped thinking that we condemned in another context in Sail'er Inn v. Kirby. * * * For some, the court's emphasis on the importance of a father's "playing baseball" or "going fishing" with his sons may evoke nostalgic memories of a Norman Rockwell cover on the old Saturday Evening Post. But it has at last been understood that a boy need not prove his masculinity on the playing fields of Eton, nor must a man compete with his son in athletics in order to be a good father: their relationship is no less "normal" if it is built on shared experiences in such fields of interest as science, music, arts and crafts, history or travel, or in pursuing such classic hobbies as stamp or coin collecting. In short, an afternoon that a father and son spend together at a museum or the zoo is surely no less enriching than an equivalent amount of time spent catching either balls or fish.

Justice Mosk added in a footnote [48] that

[t]he sex stereotype, of course, cuts both ways. If the trial court's approach herein were to prevail, in the next case a divorced mother who became physically handicapped could be deprived of her young daughters because she is unable to participate with them in embroidery, *haute cuisine,* or the fine arts of washing and ironing. To state the proposition is to refute it.

Despite the strong preference for mother custody of young children, courts have not been loath to deny custody to mothers guilty of loose sexual behavior,

47. Id., 24 Cal.3d at 736–37, 157 Cal.Rptr. at 389, 598 P.2d at 42. See also Marriage of Tresnak, 297 N.W.2d 109 (Iowa 1980), discussed in Note 3 at p. 336, supra, where the trial court had indulged in similar notions about appropriate father-son activities. It turned out, however, that the boys in *Tresnak* enjoyed fishing, reading, baking cookies, bicycling, swimming, soccer, and basketball. They did not play baseball or football. Both parents swam with the children; their mother took them fishing and joined them in bicycling and baking cookies; their father played soccer with them about fifteen minutes at a time, within the limits established by his age and his habit of smoking. The Iowa Supreme Court concluded from this testimony that

[n]o evidence was received that these boys were interested in hunting or mechanical

training, that the enumerated pursuits are more appropriate to males, that "other activities" exist in which males have a necessary interest, or that these children will necessarily have the same interests as other males. Nor does the record contain any evidence that Jim was capable of participating in any activities with the children that Linda could not participate in with them equally well.

Id., 297 N.W.2d at 112.

48. Id., 24 Cal.3d at 737 n. 9, 157 Cal.Rptr. at 389, 598 P.2d at 42. Justice Mosk's prediction very nearly came true. See Marriage of Levin, 102 Cal.App.3d 981, 162 Cal.Rptr. 757 (1980) (reversing the trial court's award of a 2 year old daughter to the father rather than to the handicapped mother).

particularly adultery.[49] Nor have the "no-fault" divorce statutes, successful in some states in eradicating fault as the basis for alimony and property division,[50] been able to eliminate fault from consideration in the custody award. The California Family Law Act which initially excluded evidence of "specific acts of misconduct" from all pleadings or proceedings "except where child custody is in issue and such evidence is relevant to that issue", now admits such evidence "as otherwise provided by statute," with a comment referencing child abuse and domestic violence statutes.[51] But the Uniform Act expressly forbids the trial court to consider "conduct of a proposed custodian that does not affect his relationship to the child," [52] and the Comment pointedly observes that "there is no reason to encourage parties to spy on each other in order to discover marital (most commonly, sexual) misconduct for use in a custody contest." [53] How effective will this provision be? As *Greenfield* indicates, the spying does not stop when the initial award of custody is announced.[54] For a mother with young children whose former husband is determined to regain their custody, the spying may continue until the children reach majority—a steady source of pressure forcing the mother to conform to a conventional life-style. Far from resolving the parents' emotional involvement with each other, the divorce decree and its custody provisions may only intensify it, leaving the children to become pawns in yet another "spectacular" legal battle.[55]

Overcoming the maternal preference has also been relatively simple if it could be shown that the mother seeking custody was a practicing lesbian. As *Schuster* indicates, some progress has been made in persuading judges to look beyond the labels to the parent-child relationship itself. Still, the trial court's attitude in Nadler v. Superior Court,[56] that a lesbian is unfit to have custody as a matter of law, appears not uncommon.[57] Indeed, Nan Hunter and Nancy Polikoff, the authors of a widely-cited article on lesbian mother custody cases, state frankly in their discussion of strategy and trial tactics that [58]

> [w]e begin this section with the premise that a judge is often likely to be predisposed against a lesbian mother and that, therefore, an attorney can usually best serve his or her client by making every attempt to keep a case from going to trial.

They go on to advise that, if litigation cannot be avoided, "the primary goal of the mother's attorney should be to prevent the mother's sexual preference from becoming the central issue of the case." [59] Donna Hitchins and Barbara Price

49. H. Clark, supra note 5, at 585–86 (1968). See also Bunim v. Bunim, 298 N.Y. 391, 83 N.E.2d 848 reh'g denied, 298 N.Y. 923, 85 N.E.2d 65 (1949).

50. E.g., In re Marriage of Williams, 199 N.W.2d 339 (Iowa 1972).

51. West's Ann.Cal.Fam.Code § 2335 (1994), replacing former West's Ann.Cal.Civ. Code § 4509. The comment states that no "substantive change" has been made. Do you agree?

52. Uniform Marriage and Divorce Act § 402.

53. Id., Comment to Section 402, pp. 46–47.

54. See also Marriage of Russo, 21 Cal. App.3d 72, 98 Cal.Rptr. 501 (1971).

55. Watson, supra note 10, at 55.

56. 255 Cal.App.2d 523, 63 Cal.Rptr. 352 (1967), discussed in Note 5, at p. 340, supra.

57. See Del Martin & Phyllis Lyon, Lesbian/Woman 132–34 (1972). See also Rhonda Rivera, Our Straight–Laced Judges: The Legal Position of Homosexual Persons in the United States, 30 Hastings L.J. 799, 883–904 (1979). See also Jacobson v. Jacobson, 314 N.W.2d 78 (N.D.1981), holding that where both parents are fit custodians, the mother's homosexuality is the "overriding factor", given her plan to live with her lesbian lover and the children.

58. Nan D. Hunter & Nancy D. Polikoff, Custody Rights of Lesbian Mothers: Legal Theory and Litigation Strategy, 25 Buffalo L.Rev. 691, 715 (1976).

59. Id., at 720–21.

have observed, however, that [60]

> once the mother's lesbianism has been brought to the attention of the court, it must be dealt with directly and forcefully. The alternative is to seek a ruling that the mother's sexual preference is irrelevant and, therefore, testimony on the issue should be prohibited or limited. The risk of such an approach is that the mother's attorney will be prohibited from presenting evidence that rebuts commonly held prejudices about homosexuals. Since the judge will know the mother is a lesbian, whatever biases and assumptions the judge holds about the propriety of lesbians raising children will never be confronted and may play a major role in the outcome of the case.

Both sets of authors have valuable suggestions to offer about the use of expert witnesses and how to deal with those testifying for the other side.[61] In addition, Hitchins and Price review the use of psychological and social science data in lesbian custody cases.[62]

Reliable work on the impact on children of living with homosexual parents is just beginning to be published.[63] As more data become available, the tasks of judges and lawyers in these cases will become less difficult.[64] What may emerge, however, is that the legal obstacles faced by lesbian mothers do not stem from sex-based discrimination. Gay fathers, if they are encouraged to seek custody of their children, will also confront the same problems.[65] What avenues of legal attack are available to homosexual parents?[66] What are the rights of their children?[67]

60. Donna J. Hitchins & Barbara Price, Trial Strategy in Lesbian Mother Custody Cases: The Use of Expert Testimony, 9 Golden Gate Univ.L.Rev. 451, 452 (Women's Law Forum, 1978–79).

61. Id., at 471–79; Hunter & Polikoff, supra note 58, at 724–32.

62. Hitchins & Price, supra note 60, at 461–71. See also, Donna J. Hitchins & Ann G. Thomas, Lesbian Mothers and Their Children: An Annotated Bibliography of Legal and Psychological Materials (Lesbian Rights Project, 2d ed. 1983).

63. E.g., Richard Green, Sexual Identity of 37 Children Raised by Homosexual or Transsexual Parents, 135 Am.J. Psychiatry 692 (June, 1978) (36 of the children appeared to have a "typical" psychosexual development).

64. See the exchange between a judge and attorneys who have represented lesbian mothers in court: Ross W. Campbell, Child Custody: When One Parent is a Homosexual, 17 The Judges' Journal 38 (Spring, 1978); Donna Hitchins, Del Martin & Mary Morgan, Child Custody and the Homosexual Parent, 18 The Judges' Journal 33 (Fall, 1979). Compare the weight given to expert testimony in Bezio v. Patenaude, 381 Mass. 563, 410 N.E.2d 1207 (1980) (where experts for both parties testified that a mother's sexual preference per se is irrelevant to her parenting skills), and in M.J.P. v. J.G.P., 640 P.2d 966 (Okl.1982), noted, 35 Okla.L.Rev. 633 (1982) (mother's expert witness testified on cross-examination that the children might have "severe problems" in the future because of the conflict between social norms and their mother's sexual conduct). An

order changing custody from the mother to the father was affirmed in *M.J.P.;* in *Bezio,* denial of custody to the mother was reversed and the case remanded for a determination of her current fitness to advance the best interests of the children.

65. In Roe v. Roe, 228 Va. 722, 324 S.E.2d 691 (1985), the Virginia Supreme Court reversed an award of custody to a gay father as an abuse of discretion. The parents were divorced in 1976, and the mother was given custody. In 1978, when the mother was ill with cancer, the father took the child into his home. In 1979, the parents agreed to shift custody to the father. Later, the mother sought to regain custody, alleging that the daughter, then aged nine, had seen her father and his male lover "hugging and kissing and sleeping in bed together." The trial court granted joint custody to both parents, with the child to live with the father during the school year, and with the mother during summer vacations. The father was ordered not to share a bed or bedroom with his lover. The Virginia Supreme Court held that "[t]he father's continuous exposure of the child to his immoral and illicit relationship renders him an unfit and improper custodian as a matter of law." Id., at 694.

66. See Mary C. Dunlap, The Constitutional Rights of Sexual Minorities: A Crisis of the Male/Female Dichotomy, 30 Hastings L.J. 1131 (1979).

67. See Steve Susoeff, Comment, Assessing Children's Best Interests When a Parent is Gay or Lesbian: Toward a Rational Custody Standard, 32 U.C.L.A.L.Rev. 852 (1985).

Despite the controversy over the presumption that children of tender years should be placed with their mothers and the disagreement about whether it should be abandoned, little evidence exists that fathers are seeking custody of their children in larger percentages even in those states where the statutory presumption favoring mothers has been repealed. Thus, sociologists Lenore Weitzman and Ruth Dixon, who have studied the California experience with no-fault divorce, report that "there was no statistically significant increase in the percentage of fathers who either asked for or were awarded custody of their children between 1972 [when the statutory presumption was repealed] and 1977 [when the data were gathered]." [68] Analysis of the few cases in which fathers did request, and receive, custody of their children produced this profile: [69] in more than half the cases, there was an agreement between the parents that the father should be given custody; fathers who were awarded custody tended to be slightly older, better educated, and have a higher occupational status than most divorcing men. Watson's correlation between age and sex was not borne out by the data: although husbands were more likely to seek custody of teenagers than of preschoolers, the age of the child made no difference in whether custody was obtained. Fathers were, however, more likely to receive custody of sons than of daughters,[70] as Watson proposed.

Weitzman and Dixon conclude,[71]

[t]oday, the vast majority of divorced fathers are not really interested in obtaining custody of their children after divorce, while the vast majority of divorced women are. And until these preferences and the social patterns on which these preferences are based change, mothers will continue to have custody of most children after divorce. Thus the legal system serves primarily as a means of formalizing the custodial arrangements that have already been agreed upon by divorcing fathers and mothers.

2. *Child Support*

The child support order in a divorce decree is essentially a remedy to enforce the obligation of support which parents owe their children.[72] Since the remedy reflects the obligation, this duty has traditionally been placed primarily on men with mothers being liable only if the father is unable to provide adequate support.[73] As a practical matter, however, since noncompliance with support orders is quite common, observers have noted that most child support following divorce is "actually carried by the mother or by the state." [74]

As in the case of spousal support, the modern tendency is to draft statutes that make the child support obligation fall neutrally upon both parents. Thus, Section 309 of the Uniform Marriage and Divorce Act provides:

Section 309. [Child Support.] In a proceeding for dissolution of marriage, legal separation, maintenance, or child support, the court may order

---

68. Lenore J. Weitzman & Ruth B. Dixon, Child Custody Awards: Legal Standards and Empirical Patterns for Child Custody, Support and Visitation After Divorce, 12 U.C.Davis L.Rev. 473, 502–03 (1979). See also Lenore J. Weitzman, The Divorce Revolution 223–28 (1985).

69. Id., at 515–17.

70. Id., at 517.

71. Id., at 521. See also Henry J. Friedman, The Father's Parenting Experience in Divorce, 137 Am.J. Psychiatry 1177 (October, 1980) (suggesting that both mothers and fathers need to be helped to recognize the father's potential as an adequate caretaker and his capacity for nurturance).

72. H. Clark, supra note 5, at 488.

73. Id. at 488–89.

74. Stuart S. Nagle and Lenore J. Weitzman, Women as Litigants, 23 Hastings L.J. 171, 190–91 (1971).

either or both parents owing a duty of support to a child of the marriage to pay an amount reasonable or necessary for his support, without regard to marital misconduct, after considering all relevant factors including:

(1) the financial resources of the child;

(2) the financial resources of the custodial parent;

(3) the standard of living the child would have enjoyed had the marriage not been dissolved;

(4) the physical and emotional condition of the child, and his educational needs; and

(5) the financial resources and needs of the non-custodial parent.

The Comment adds that Section 309 "does not set forth the conditions under which a parent owes a duty of support to a child * * * the intent is merely to indicate the factors which a court should consider in setting the amount of support to be paid by either the mother or the father or both." [75] No position is taken as to whether either parent has a primary obligation of support, or whether both parents share an equal burden following a divorce.

Compare the list of factors contained in the New York statute: [76]

7. Child support. a. In any matrimonial action, or in an independent action for child support, the court as provided in section two hundred forty of this chapter shall order either or both parents to pay temporary child support or child support without requiring a showing of immediate or emergency need. Such order shall be effective as of the date of the application therefor, and any retroactive amount of child support due shall be paid in one sum or periodic sums, as the court shall direct, taking into account any amount of temporary child support which has been paid. The court shall not consider the misconduct of either party but shall make its award for child support after consideration of all relevant factors, including:

(1) the financial resources of the custodial and non-custodial parent, and those of the child;

(2) the physical and emotional health of the child, and his or her educational or vocational needs and aptitudes;

(3) where practical and relevant, the standard of living the child would have enjoyed had the marriage not been dissolved;

(4) where practical and relevant, the tax consequences to the parties; and

(5) the non-monetary contributions that the parents will make toward the care and well-being of the child.

b. In any decision made pursuant to this subdivision the court shall set forth the factors it considered and the reasons for its decision and such may not be waived by either party or counsel.

What is the significance of subdivision (a)(5)? Does it provide an adequate response to the charges of opponents of the equal rights amendment that its ratification would force women out of the home in order to meet their child support obligations?

---

75. Uniform Marriage and Divorce Act, Comment to Section 309, 9A U.L.A. 400 (1987).

76. New York Dom.Rel.Law, § 236 (McKinney 1986).

Is the equal protection clause violated by placing the primary obligation of child support following divorce upon fathers? In Dill v. Dill,[77] the Supreme Court of Georgia upheld a statute that placed this duty upon fathers, holding the mother responsible only if the father "is dead, or cannot be found, or is incapable of support of such child or children." Relying on Kahn v. Shevin,[78] the court held that "[t]he different treatment of male and female parents here has a fair and substantial relation to the object of the legislation."[79] Can this decision stand after Orr v. Orr?[80]

Compare Carter v. Carter,[81] interpreting a prior New York statute containing language virtually identical to that considered in *Dill*. In order to sustain its constitutionality the court read this language in light of the court's authority to "apportion" the costs of child support between the parents "according to their respective means and responsibilities" to mean[82]

> that both the father and the mother are equally responsible for the support of their children and that it is within the power of the Family Court, and it is its duty, to apportion the costs of such support between them in accordance with their respective means and responsibilities, without regard to the sex of the parent.

Other courts have recognized the mother's obligation of support under sex-neutral statutes without reaching constitutional issues. Thus in Marriage of Muldrow,[83] the trial court was reversed for its failure to consider the mother's ability to contribute to the support of the children: it had made the "antiquated assumption" that the responsibilities of male and female parents, if similarly situated, were not the same. Should the mother's "non-monetary contributions" to the child's care and well-being, mentioned in subsection 7(a)(5) of the New York statute quoted above, be considered only when she is the custodial parent?

B. FAMILY LIFE WITHOUT MARRIAGE

1. BARRIERS AGAINST THE UNWED FAMILY

PARHAM v. HUGHES

Supreme Court of the United States, 1979.
441 U.S. 347, 99 S.Ct. 1742, 60 L.Ed.2d 269.

MR. JUSTICE STEWART announced the judgment of the Court and delivered an opinion in which the THE CHIEF JUSTICE, MR. JUSTICE REHNQUIST, and MR. JUSTICE STEVENS join.

77. 232 Ga. 231, 206 S.E.2d 6 (1974).

78. 416 U.S. 351, 94 S.Ct. 1734, 40 L.Ed.2d 189 (1974), noted at p. 150, supra.

79. Dill v. Dill, supra note 77, 232 Ga. at 233, 206 S.E.2d at 7. See also Agg v. Flanagan, 855 F.2d 336 (6th Cir.1988), rejecting the equal protection claims of a class of male litigants who were or would be subjected to wage assignments, garnishments, or wage attachments under Ohio child support procedures. Characterizing the argument as "essentially a 'reverse discrimination' claim, based on the disparate impact on men of Ohio's child support procedures", the court held that plaintiffs were required to prove intentional discrimination to make out their case. Judge Kennedy pointed out that "[i]t is fairly obvious that the disparate impact on men, insofar as we may characterize the law's effect in that way, is a

result of the fact that men generally have higher incomes than women, and that society wants some of that income used to support their children. * * * Ohio, like other states, has attempted to redress the unequal burden of supporting the children of divorced parents between the custodial and non-custodial parents, according to their ability to pay." Id., 855 F.2d at 342.

80. 440 U.S. 268, 99 S.Ct. 1102, 59 L.Ed.2d 306 (1979), set out at p. 290, supra.

81. 58 A.D.2d 438, 397 N.Y.S.2d 88 (Sup. Ct.1977).

82. Id., 58 A.D.2d at 447, 397 N.Y.S.2d at 93–94.

83. 61 Cal.App.3d 327, 132 Cal.Rptr. 48 (1976).

Under § 105–1307 of the Georgia Code (1978) (hereinafter Georgia statute),[1] the mother of an illegitimate child can sue for the wrongful death of that child. A father who has legitimated a child can also sue for the wrongful death of the child if there is no mother. A father who has not legitimated a child, however, is precluded from maintaining a wrongful-death action. The question presented in this case is whether this statutory scheme violates the Equal Protection or Due Process Clause of the Fourteenth Amendment by denying the father of an illegitimate child who has not legitimated the child the right to sue for the child's wrongful death.

I

The appellant was the biological father of Lemuel Parham, a minor child who was killed in an automobile collision. The child's mother, Cassandra Moreen, was killed in the same collision. The appellant and Moreen were never married to each other, and the appellant did not legitimate the child as he could have done under Georgia law.[2] The appellant did, however, sign the child's birth certificate and contribute to his support.[3] The child took the appellant's name and was visited by the appellant on a regular basis.

After the child was killed in the automobile collision, the appellant brought an action seeking to recover for the allegedly wrongful death. The complaint named the appellee (the driver of the other automobile involved in the collision) as the defendant, and charged that negligence on the part of the appellee had caused the death of the child. The child's maternal grandmother, acting as administratrix of his estate, also brought a lawsuit against the appellee to recover for the child's wrongful death.

The appellee filed a motion for summary judgment in the present case, asserting that under the Georgia statute the appellant was precluded from recovering for his illegitimate child's wrongful death. * * *

II

State laws are generally entitled to a presumption of validity against attack under the Equal Protection Clause. * * *

---

1. Section 105–1307 provides:

"A mother, or, if no mother, a father, may recover for the homicide of a child, minor or sui juris, unless said child shall leave a wife, husband or child. The mother or father shall be entitled to recover the full value of the life of such child. *In suits by the mother the illegitimacy of the child shall be no bar to a recovery.*" (Emphasis added.)

2. Under Ga.Code § 74–103 (1978), a natural father can have his child legitimated by court order. Section 74–103 provides:

"A father of an illegitimate child may render the same legitimate by petitioning the superior court of the county of his residence, setting forth the name, age, and sex of such

child, and also the name of the mother; and if he desires the name changed, stating the new name, and praying the legitimation of such child. Of this application the mother, if alive, shall have notice. Upon such application, presented and filed, the court may pass an order declaring said child to be legitimate, and capable of inheriting from the father in the same manner as if born in lawful wedlock, and the name by which he or she shall be known."

3. Under Ga.Code § 74–202 (1978), a father is required to support an illegitimate child until the child reaches 18, marries, or becomes self-supporting, whichever occurs first.

In the absence of invidious discrimination, however, a court is not free under the aegis of the Equal Protection Clause to substitute its judgment for the will of the people of a State as expressed in the laws passed by their popularly elected legislatures. * * * The threshold question, therefore, is whether the Georgia statute is invidiously discriminatory. If it is not, it is entitled to a presumption of validity and will be upheld "unless the varying treatment of different groups or persons is so unrelated to the achievement of any combination of legitimate purposes that we can only conclude that the legislature's actions were irrational." * * *

III

The appellant relies on decisions of the Court that have invalidated statutory classifications based upon illegitimacy and upon gender to support his claim that the Georgia statute is unconstitutional. Both of these lines of cases have involved laws reflecting invidious discrimination against a particular class. We conclude, however, that neither line of decisions is applicable in the present case.

A

The Court has held on several occasions that state legislative classifications based upon illegitimacy—i.e., that differentiate between illegitimate children and legitimate children—violate the Equal Protection Clause. E.g., Trimble v. Gordon, 430 U.S. 762, 97 S.Ct. 1459, 52 L.Ed.2d 31; Weber v. Aetna Casualty & Surety Co., 406 U.S. 164, 92 S.Ct. 1400, 31 L.Ed.2d 768.[5] The basic rationale of these decisions is that it is unjust and ineffective for society to express its condemnation of procreation outside the marital relationship by punishing the illegitimate child who is in no way responsible for his situation and is unable to change it. As Mr. Justice Powell stated for the Court in the *Weber* case:

> "The status of illegitimacy has expressed through the ages society's condemnation of irresponsible liaisons beyond the bonds of marriage. But visiting this condemnation on the head of an infant is illogical and unjust. Moreover, imposing disabilities on the illegitimate child is contrary to the basic concept of our system that legal burdens should bear some relationship to individual responsibility or wrongdoing. Obviously, no child is responsible for his birth and penalizing the illegitimate child is an ineffectual—as well as an unjust—way of deterring the parent."
> * * *

It is apparent that this rationale is in no way applicable to the Georgia statute now before us. The statute does not impose differing burdens or award differing benefits to legitimate and illegitimate children. It simply denies a natural father the right to sue for his illegitimate child's wrongful death. The appellant, as the natural father, was responsible for conceiving an illegitimate child and had the opportunity to legitimate the child but failed to do so. Legitimation would have removed the stigma of bastardy and allowed the child to inherit from the father in the same manner as if born in lawful

5. In cases where statutory classifications affecting illegitimates are so precisely structured as to further a sufficiently adequate state interest, however, the Court has upheld the validity of the statutes. Lalli v. Lalli, 439 U.S. 259, 99 S.Ct. 518, 58 L.Ed.2d 503; Mathews v. Lucas, 427 U.S. 495, 96 S.Ct. 2755, 49 L.Ed.2d 651; Labine v. Vincent, 401 U.S. 532, 91 S.Ct. 1017, 28 L.Ed.2d 288.

wedlock. Ga.Code § 74–103 (1978). Unlike the illegitimate child for whom the status of illegitimacy is involuntary and immutable, the appellant here was responsible for fostering an illegitimate child and for failing to change its status. It is thus neither illogical nor unjust for society to express its "condemnation of irresponsible liaisons beyond the bounds of marriage" by not conferring upon a biological father the statutory right to sue for the wrongful death of his illegitimate child. The justifications for judicial sensitivity to the constitutionality of differing legislative treatment of legitimate and illegitimate children are simply absent when a classification affects only the fathers of deceased illegitimate children.

B

The Court has also held that certain classifications based upon sex are invalid under the Equal Protection Clause, e.g., Reed v. Reed, supra; * * * Underlying these decisions is the principle that a State is not free to make overbroad generalizations based on sex which are entirely unrelated to any differences between men and women or which demean the ability or social status of the affected class. * * *

In cases where men and women are not similarly situated, however, and a statutory classification is realistically based upon the differences in their situations, this Court has upheld its validity. In Schlesinger v. Ballard, 419 U.S. 498, 95 S.Ct. 572, 42 L.Ed.2d 610, for example, the Court upheld the constitutionality of a federal statute which provided that male naval officers who were not promoted within a certain length of time were subject to mandatory discharge while female naval officers who were not promoted within the same length of time could continue as officers. Because of restrictions on women officers' seagoing service, their opportunities to compile records entitling them to promotion were more restricted than were those of their male counterparts. Thus, unlike the *Reed* and *Frontiero* cases where the gender-based classifications were based solely on administrative convenience and outworn cliches, the different treatment in the *Schlesinger* case reflected "not archaic and overbroad generalizations, but, instead, the demonstrable fact that male and female line officers in the Navy are *not* similarly situated with respect to opportunities for professional service." * * * (emphasis in original).

With these principles in mind, it is clear that the Georgia statute does not invidiously discriminate against the appellant simply because he is of the male sex. The fact is that mothers and fathers of illegitimate children are not similarly situated. Under Georgia law, only a father can by voluntary unilateral action make an illegitimate child legitimate.[6] Unlike the mother of an illegitimate child whose identity will rarely be in doubt, the identity of the father will frequently be unknown. Lalli v. Lalli, 439 U.S. 259, 99 S.Ct. 518, 58 L.Ed.2d 503.[7] By coming forward with a motion under

---

6. The constitutionality of the legitimation provision of the Georgia statute has not been challenged and is not at issue in this case.

7. As Mr. Justice Powell stated for the plurality in the *Lalli* case:

"That the child is the child of a particular woman is rarely difficult to prove. Proof of

paternity, by contrast, frequently is difficult when the father is not part of a formal family unit. The putative father often goes his way unconscious of the birth of a child. Even if conscious, he is very often totally unconcerned because of the absence of any ties to the mother. Indeed the mother may

Thus, the conferral of the right of a natural father to sue for the wrongful death of his child only if he has previously acted to identify himself, undertake his paternal responsibilities, and make his child legitimate, does not reflect any overbroad generalizations about men as a class, but rather the reality that in Georgia only a father can by unilateral action legitimate an illegitimate child. Since fathers who do legitimate their children can sue for wrongful death in precisely the same circumstances as married fathers whose children were legitimate *ab initio*, the statutory classification does not discriminate against fathers as a class but instead distinguishes between fathers who have legitimated their children and those who have not. Such a classification is quite unlike those condemned in the *Reed, Frontiero,* and *Stanton* cases which were premised upon overbroad generalizations and excluded all members of one sex even though they were similarly situated with members of the other sex.

IV

Having concluded that the Georgia statute does not invidiously discriminate against any class, we still must determine whether the statutory classification is rationally related to a permissible state objective.

This Court has frequently recognized that a State has a legitimate interest in the maintenance of an accurate and efficient system for the disposition of property at death. * * * Of particular concern to the State is the existence of some mechanism for dealing with "the often difficult problem of proving the paternity of illegitimate children and the related danger of spurious claims against intestate estates." Lalli v. Lalli, supra, * * *.

This same state interest in avoiding fraudulent claims of paternity in order to maintain a fair and orderly system of decedent's property disposition is also present in the context of actions for wrongful death. If paternity has not been established before the commencement of a wrongful-death action, a defendant may be faced with the possibility of multiple lawsuits by individuals all claiming to be the father of the deceased child. Such uncertainty would make it difficult if not impossible for a defendant to settle a wrongful-death action in many cases, since there would always exist the risk of a subsequent suit by another person claiming to be the father. The State of Georgia has chosen to deal with this problem by allowing only fathers who have established their paternity by legitimating their children to sue for wrongful death,

not know *who* is responsible for her pregnancy." * * *

In Glona v. American Guarantee & Liability Ins. Co., 391 U.S. 73, 88 S.Ct. 1515, 20 L.Ed.2d 441, the Court held that a Louisiana statute that did not allow a natural mother of an illegitimate child to sue for its wrongful death violated the Equal Protection Clause. That cause was quite different from this one. The invidious discrimination perceived in that case was between married and unmarried mothers. There thus existed no real problem of identity or of fraudulent claims. See Part IV, infra. Moreover, the statute in Glona excluded every mother of an illegitimate child from bringing a wrongful-death action while the Georgia stat-

ute at issue here excludes only those fathers who have not legitimated their children. Thus, the Georgia statute has in effect adopted "a middle ground between the extremes of complete exclusion and case-by-case determination of paternity." Trimble v. Gordon, 430 U.S. 762, 771, 97 S.Ct. 1459, 1465, 52 L.Ed.2d 31. Cf. Lalli v. Lalli, supra. We need not decide whether a statute which completely precluded fathers, as opposed to mothers, of illegitimate children from maintaining a wrongful-death action would violate the Equal Protection Clause. § 74–103 of the Georgia Code, however, a father can both establish his identity and make his illegitimate child legitimate.

and we cannot say that this solution is an irrational one. Cf. Lalli v. Lalli, supra.[11]

The appellant argues, however, that whatever may be the problem with establishing paternity generally, there is no question in this case that he is the father. This argument misconceives the basic principle of the Equal Protection Clause. The function of that provision of the Constitution is to measure the validity of classifications created by state laws.[12] Since we have concluded that the classification created by the Georgia statute is a rational means for dealing with the problem of proving paternity, it is constitutionally irrelevant that the appellant may be able to prove paternity in another manner.

* * *

For these reasons, the judgment of the Supreme Court of Georgia is affirmed.

It is so ordered.

MR. JUSTICE POWELL, concurring in the judgment.

I agree that the gender-based distinction of Ga.Code § 105–1307 (1978) does not violate equal protection.* I write separately, however, because I arrive at this conclusion by a route somewhat different from that taken by Mr. Justice Stewart.

To withstand judicial scrutiny under the Equal Protection Clause, gender-based distinctions must "serve important governmental objectives and must be substantially related to achievement of those objectives." * * * We have recognized in various contexts the importance of a State's interest in minimizing potential problems in identifying the natural father of an illegitimate child. * * * Indeed, we have sought to avoid "impos[ing] on state court systems a greater burden" in determining paternity for purposes of wrongful-death actions. Weber v. Aetna Casualty & Surety Co., * * *.

The question, therefore, is whether the gender-based distinction at issue in the present case is substantially related to achievement of the important state objective of avoiding difficult problems in proving paternity after the death of an illegitimate child. In Ga.Code § 74–103 (1978), the State has provided a simple, convenient mechanism by which the father of an illegitimate child can eliminate all questions concerning the child's parentage. Under that statute, a father can legitimate his child simply by filing a petition in state court identifying the child and its mother and requesting an order of legitimation. After notice has been served on the mother, the state court can enter an order declaring the child legitimate for all purposes of Georgia law.

11. We thus need not decide whether the classification created by the Georgia statute is rationally related to the State's interests in promoting the traditional family unit or in setting a standard of morality.

12. It cannot seriously be argued that a statutory entitlement to sue for the wrongful death of another is itself a "fundamental" or constitutional right.

* I also agree with Mr. Justice Stewart that the classification of § 105–1307 affects only fathers of illegitimates—not the illegitimates themselves—and therefore that this case differs substantially from those in which we have found classifications based upon illegitimacy to be unconstitutional. See, e.g., Trimble v. Gordon, * * *.

It is clear that the Georgia statute is substantially related to the State's objective. It lies entirely within a father's power to remove himself from the disability that only he will suffer. The father is required to declare his intentions at a time when both the child and its mother are likely to be available to provide evidence. The mother, on the other hand, is given the opportunity to appear and either support or rebut the father's claim of paternity. The marginally greater burden placed upon fathers is no more severe than is required by the marked difference between proving paternity and proving maternity—a difference we have recognized repeatedly. * * *

I find the present case to be quite different from others in which the Court has found unjustified a State's reliance upon a gender-based classification. In several cases, the Court has confronted a state law under which the burdened individual (whether a child born out of wedlock or the father of such a child) has been powerless to remove himself from the statutory burden—regardless of the proof of paternity. See, e.g., Caban v. Mohammed, supra; Trimble v. Gordon, supra. To require marriage between the father and mother often is tantamount to a total exclusion of fathers, as marriage is possible only with the consent of the mother. In the present case, however, no such requirement is imposed upon the father under Georgia law. In sum, therefore, I conclude that the Georgia statute challenged in this case, unlike the statutes reviewed in our prior decisions, is substantially related to the State's objective of avoiding difficult problems of proof of paternity.

MR. JUSTICE WHITE, with whom MR. JUSTICE BRENNAN, MR. JUSTICE MARSHALL, and MR. JUSTICE BLACKMUN join, dissenting.

Appellant is the father, rather than the mother, of a deceased illegitimate child. It is conceded that for this reason alone he may not bring an action for the wrongful death of his child. Yet four Members of the Court conclude that appellant is not discriminated against "simply" because of his sex, * * * because Georgia provides a means by which fathers can legitimate their children. The dispositive point is that only a father may avail himself of this process. Therefore, we are told, "[t]he fact is that mothers and fathers of illegitimate children are not similarly situated," ibid.

There is a startling circularity in this argument. The issue before the Court is whether Georgia may require unmarried fathers, but not unmarried mothers, to have pursued the statutory legitimization procedure in order to bring suit for the wrongful death of their children. Seemingly, it is irrelevant that as a matter of state law mothers may not legitimate their children,[1] for they are not required to do so in order to maintain a wrongful-death action. That only fathers *may* resort to the legitimization process cannot dissolve the sex discrimination in *requiring* them to.[2] Under the plurality's bootstrap

1. Although Ga.Code § 74–103 (1978) provides that a father may petition, with notice to the mother, to legitimate his child, mothers are not given a similar right. At least one State provides that either parent, or both, may legitimate a child. La.Civ.Code Ann., Art. 203 (West 1952).

2. The plurality not only fails to examine whether required resort by fathers to the legitimization procedure bears more than a rational relationship to any state interest, but also fails even to address the constitutionality of the sex discrimination in allowing fathers but not mothers to legitimate their children. It is anomalous, at least, to assert that sex discrimination in one statute is constitutionally invisible because it is tied to sex discrimination in another statute, without subjecting *either* of these classifications on the basis of sex to an appropriate level of scrutiny.

rationale, a State could require that women, but not men, pass a course in order to receive a taxi license, simply by limiting admission to the course to women.[3]

The plain facts of the matter are that the statute conferring the right to recovery for the wrongful death of a child discriminates between unmarried mothers and unmarried fathers, and that this discrimination is but one degree greater than the statutory discrimination between married mothers and married fathers.[4] In order to withstand scrutiny under the Equal Protection Clause, gender-based discrimination " 'must serve important governmental objectives and must be substantially related to achievement of those objectives.' " * * * Because none of the interests urged by the State warrant the sex discrimination in this case, I would reverse the judgment below.

I

The Georgia Supreme Court suggested that the state legislature may have denied a right of action to fathers of illegitimate children because of its interests in "promoting a legitimate family unit" and "setting a standard of morality." 241 Ga. 198, 200, 243 S.E.2d 867, 869–870 (1978). But the actual relationship between these interests and the particular classification chosen is far too tenuous to justify the sex discrimination involved. Cf. Trimble v. Gordon, * * *.

Unmarried mothers and those fathers who legitimate their children but remain unmarried presumably also defy the state interest in "the integrity of the family unit." In any event, it is untenable to conclude that denying parents a right to recover when their illegitimate children die will further the asserted state interests. In Glona v. American Guarantee & Liability Ins. Co., * * * we were faced with the same argument in the context of an unmarried mother's attempt to recover for her child's death in a State allowing wrongful-death suits by parents of legitimate children. Even though that mother—like appellant in this case—had not pursued a statutory procedure whereby she could have unilaterally legitimated her child and thereby become eligible to sue for the child's death, we held that it was impermissible to prevent her from seeking to recover. What we said in *Glona* about unmarried mothers applies equally to unmarried fathers:

> "[W]e see no possible rational basis * * * for assuming that if the natural mother is allowed recovery for the wrongful death of her illegitimate child, the cause of illegitimacy will be served. It would, indeed, be farfetched to assume that women have illegitimate children so that they can be compensated in damages for their death." * * *

II

Another interest suggested by the Georgia Supreme Court, which a majority of the Court today finds pervasive, is that of "forestalling potential

---

3. Men and women would therefore not be "similarly situated." Yet requiring a course for women but not for men is quite obviously a classification on the basis of sex.

4. The opinion of Mr. Justice Stewart shunts aside the readily apparent classification on the basis of sex in Georgia's wrongful-death scheme by stressing that appellant's child was never made legitimate, but it is only the fortuitous event of the mother's death in this case that makes legitimacy even relevant. In the case of parents of legitimate children, only the mother may sue if she is alive; the father is allowed to sue only "if [there is] no mother." Ga. Code § 105–1307 (1978). * * *

problems of proof of paternity," 241 Ga., at 200, 243 S.E.2d at 869. Whatever may be the evidentiary problems associated with proof of parenthood where a father, but presumably not a mother, is involved, I am sure that any interest the State conceivably has in simplifying the determination of liability in wrongful-death actions does not justify the outright gender discrimination in this case.

The Court has shown due respect for a State's undoubted interest in effecting a sound system of inheritance that will not unduly tie up the assets of the deceased, including his real estate, and prevent its transmission to and utilization by his heirs and the upcoming generation. Formal documentation of entitlement to inherit may be significant in avoiding unending litigation inimical to this interest. But the State has no comparable interest in protecting a tortfeasor from having his liability litigated and determined in the usual way. * * *

Much the same is true of the rather lame suggestion that keeping fathers such as this appellant out of court will protect wrongdoers and their insurance companies from multiple recoveries. This claimed danger is but one of many potential hazards in personal injury litigation, and it is very doubtful that it would be exacerbated if the Georgia statute in this case were stricken down. * * *

III

The fourth and final interest suggested by the Supreme Court of Georgia as a reason that the state legislature may have denied the wrongful-death action to fathers such as appellant is that "more often than not the father of an illegitimate child who has elected neither to marry the mother nor to legitimate the child pursuant to proper legal proceedings suffers no real loss from the child's wrongful death." 241 Ga., at 200, 243 S.E.2d, at 870. Unlike the previous hypothesized state interests, this last does at least provide a plausible explanation for the classification at issue. Yet such a legislative conception about fathers of illegitimate children is an unacceptable basis for a blanket discrimination against all such fathers. Whatever may be true with respect to certain of these parents, we have recognized that at least some of them maintain as close a relationship to their children as do unmarried mothers. * * *

Nor does the discrimination against fathers of illegitimate children on the basis of their presumed lack of affection for their children become any more permissible simply because a father who is aware of the State's legitimization procedure may resort to it and thereby become eligible to recover for the wrongful death of his children. Particularly given the facts of this case—where it is conceded that appellant signed his child's birth certificate, continuously contributed to the child's financial support, and maintained daily contact with him—it is unrealistic to presume that unmarried fathers (or mothers) having real interest in their children and suffering palpable loss if their children die will, as a general rule, have pursued a statutory legitimization procedure. * * *

Moreover, it is clear that the discrimination at issue in this case does not proceed from merely a considered legislative determination, however unjustified, that parents such as appellant do not suffer loss when their children die. Rather, the particular discrimination in this case is but part of the pervasive sex discrimination in the statute conferring the right to sue for the wrongful death of a child. Even where the deceased is legitimate, the father is absolutely prohibited from bringing a wrongful-death action if the mother is still alive, even if the mother does not desire to bring suit and even if the parents are separated or divorced. The incredible presumption that fathers, but not mothers, of illegitimate children suffer no injury when they lose their children is thus only a more extreme version of the underlying and equally untenable presumption that fathers are less deserving of recovery than are mothers.

If Georgia would prefer that the amount of wrongful-death recovery be based upon the mental anguish and loss of future income suffered when a child dies—rather than on the "full value of the life of such child," as the statute now provides—it may amend the statute. But it may not categorically eliminate on the basis of sex any recovery by those parents it deems uninjured or undeserving.

JARRETT v. JARRETT

Supreme Court of Illinois, 1979.
78 Ill.2d 337, 36 Ill.Dec. 1, 400 N.E.2d 421, cert. denied 449 U.S. 927, 101 S.Ct. 329, 66 L.Ed.2d 155 rehearing denied 449 U.S. 1067, 101 S.Ct. 797, 66 L.Ed.2d 612 (1980).

UNDERWOOD, JUSTICE:

On December 6, 1976, Jacqueline Jarrett received a divorce from Walter Jarrett in the circuit court of Cook County on grounds of extreme and repeated mental cruelty. The divorce decree, by agreement, also awarded Jacqueline custody of the three Jarrett children subject to the father's right of visitation at reasonable times. Seven months later, alleging changed conditions, Walter petitioned the circuit court to modify the divorce decree and award him custody of the children. The circuit court granted his petition subject to the mother's right of visitation at reasonable times, but a majority of the appellate court reversed (64 Ill.App.3d 932, 21 Ill.Dec. 718, 382 N.E.2d 12) and we granted leave to appeal.

During their marriage, Walter and Jacqueline had three daughters, who, at the time of the divorce, were 12, 10 and 7 years old. In addition to custody of the children, the divorce decree also awarded Jacqueline the use of the family home, and child support; Walter received visitation rights at all reasonable times and usually had the children from Saturday evening to Sunday evening. In April 1977, five months after the divorce, Jacqueline informed Walter that she planned to have her boyfriend, Wayne Hammon, move into the family home with her. Walter protested, but Hammon moved in on May 1, 1977. Jacqueline and Hammon thereafter cohabited in the Jarrett home but did not marry.

The children, who were not "overly enthused" when they first learned that Hammon would move into the family home with them, asked Jacqueline if she intended to marry Hammon, but Jacqueline responded that she did not know. At the modification hearing Jacqueline testified that she did not want to remarry because it was too soon after her divorce; because she did not believe that a marriage license makes a relationship; and because the divorce decree required her to sell the family home within six months after remarriage. She did not want to sell the house because the children did not want to move and she could not afford to do so. Jacqueline explained to the children that some people thought it was wrong for an unmarried man and woman to live together but she thought that what mattered was that they loved each other. Jacqueline testified that she told some neighbors that Hammon would move in with her but that she had not received any adverse comments. Jacqueline further testified that the children seemed to develop an affectionate relationship with Hammon, who played with them, helped them with their homework, and verbally disciplined them. Both Jacqueline and Hammon testified at the hearing that they did not at that time have any plans to marry. In oral argument before this court Jacqueline's counsel conceded that she and Hammon were still living together unmarried.

Walter Jarrett testified that he thought Jacqueline's living arrangements created a moral environment which was not a proper one in which to raise three young girls. He also testified that the children were always clean, healthy, well dressed and well nourished when he picked them up, and that when he talked with his oldest daughter, Kathleen, she did not object to Jacqueline's living arrangement.

The circuit court found that it was "necessary for the moral and spiritual well-being and development" of the children that Walter receive custody. In reversing, the appellate court reasoned that the record did not reveal any negative effects on the children caused by Jacqueline's cohabitation with Hammon, and that the circuit court had not found Jacqueline unfit. It declined to consider potential future harmful effects of the cohabitation on the children. 64 Ill.App.3d 932, 937, 21 Ill.Dec. 718, 382 N.E.2d 12.

Both parties to this litigation have relied on sections 602 and 610 of the new Illinois Marriage and Dissolution of Marriage Act (Ill.Rev.Stat.1977, ch. 40, pars. 602, 610), * * *

The chief issue in this case is whether a change of custody predicated upon the open and continuing cohabitation of the custodial parent with a member of the opposite sex is contrary to the manifest weight of the evidence in the absence of any tangible evidence of contemporaneous adverse effect upon the minor children. Considering the principles previously enunciated, and the statutory provisions, and prior decisions of the courts of this State, we conclude that under the facts in this case the trial court properly transferred custody of the Jarrett children from Jacqueline to Walter Jarrett.

The relevant standards of conduct are expressed in the statutes of this State: Section 11–8 of the Criminal Code of 1961 (Ill.Rev.Stat.1977, ch. 38, par. 11–8) provides that "[a]ny person who cohabits or has sexual intercourse with another not his spouse commits fornication if the behavior is open and notorious." In Hewitt v. Hewitt (1979), 77 Ill.2d 49, 61–62, 31 Ill.Dec. 827, 394 N.E.2d 1204, we emphasized the refusal of the General Assembly in enacting the new Illinois Marriage and Dissolution of Marriage Act (Ill.Rev. Stat.1977, ch. 40, par. 101 et seq.) to sanction any nonmarital relationships and its declaration of the purpose to "strengthen and preserve the integrity of marriage and safeguard family relationships" (Ill.Rev.Stat.1977, ch. 40, par. 102(2)).

Jacqueline argues, however, that her conduct does not affront public morality because such conduct is now widely accepted, and cites 1978 Census Bureau statistics that show 1.1 million households composed of an unmarried man and woman, close to a quarter of which also include at least one child. This is essentially the same argument we rejected last term in Hewitt v. Hewitt (1979), 77 Ill.2d 49, 31 Ill.Dec. 827, 394 N.E.2d 1204, and it is equally unpersuasive here. The number of people living in such households forms only a small percentage of the adult population, but more to the point, the statutory interpretation urged upon us by Jacqueline simply nullifies the fornication statute. The logical conclusion of her argument is that the statutory prohibitions are void as to those who believe the proscribed acts are not immoral, or, for one reason or another, need not be heeded. So stated, of course, the argument defeats itself. The rules which our society enacts for the governance of its members are not limited to those who agree with those rules—they are equally binding on the dissenters. The fornication statute and the Illinois Marriage and Dissolution of Marriage Act evidence the relevant moral standards of this State, as declared by our legislature. The open and notorious limitation on the former's prohibitions reflects both a disinclination to criminalize purely private relationships and a recognition that open fornication represents a graver threat to public morality than private violations. Conduct of that nature, when it is open, not only violates the statutorily expressed moral standards of the State, but also encourages others to violate those standards, and debases public morality. While we agree that the statute does not penalize conduct which is essentially private and discreet (People v. Cessna (1976), 42 Ill.App.3d 746, 749, 1 Ill.Dec. 433, 356 N.E.2d 621), Jacqueline's conduct has been neither, for she has discussed this relationship and her rationalization of it with at least her children, her former husband and her neighbors. It is, in our judgment, clear that her conduct offends prevailing public policy. Lyman v. People (1902), 198 Ill. 544, 549–50, 64 N.E. 974; Searls v. People (1852), 13 Ill. 597, 598; People v. Potter (1943), 319 Ill.App. 409, 410–11, 416, 49 N.E.2d 307.

Jacqueline's disregard for existing standards of conduct instructs her children, by example, that they, too, may ignore them (see Stark v. Stark (1973), 13 Ill.App.3d 35, 299 N.E.2d 605; Brown v. Brown (1977), 218 Va. 196, 237 S.E.2d 89), and could well encourage the children to engage in similar activity in the future. That factor, of course, supports the trial court's conclusion that their daily presence in that environment was injurious to the moral well-being and development of the children.

It is true that, as Jacqueline argues, the courts have not denied custody to every parent who has violated the community's moral standards, nor do we now intimate a different rule. Rather than mechanically denying custody in every such instance, the courts of this State appraise the moral example currently provided and the example which may be expected by the parent in the future. We held in Nye v. Nye (1952), 411 Ill. 408, 415, 105 N.E.2d 300, that past moral indiscretions of a parent are not sufficient grounds for denying custody if the parent's present conduct establishes the improbability of such lapses in the future. This rule focuses the trial court's attention on the moral values which the parent is actually demonstrating to the children.

Since the decision in *Nye*, the appellate courts of this State have repeatedly emphasized this principle, particularly when the children were unaware of their parent's moral indiscretion. * * *

At the time of this hearing, however, and even when this case was argued orally to this court, Jacqueline continued to cohabit with Wayne Hammon and had done nothing to indicate that this relationship would not continue in the future. Thus the moral values which Jacqueline currently represents to her children, and those which she may be expected to portray to them in the future, contravene statutorily declared standards of conduct and endanger the children's moral development.

* * *

Jacqueline also argues, and the appellate court agreed * * *, that the trial court's decision to grant custody of the children to Walter Jarrett was an improper assertion by the trial judge of his own personal moral beliefs. She further argues that the assertion of moral values in this case, as in Hewitt v. Hewitt * * * is a task more appropriately carried out by the legislature. As pointed out earlier, however, it is the legislature which has established the standards she has chosen to ignore, and the action of the trial court merely implemented principles which have long been followed in this State.

The mother argues, too, that section 610 of the Illinois Marriage and Dissolution of Marriage Act (Ill.Rev.Stat.1977, ch. 40, par. 610) requires the trial court to refrain from modifying a prior custody decree unless it finds that the children have suffered actual tangible harm. The statute, however, directs the trial court to determine whether "the child's present environment *endangers* seriously his physical, mental, moral or emotional health." (Emphasis added.) (Ill.Rev.Stat.1977, ch. 40, par. 610(b)(3).) In some cases, particularly those involving physical harm, it may be appropriate for the trial court to determine whether the child is endangered by considering evidence of actual harm. In cases such as this one, however, such a narrow interpretation of the statute would defeat its purpose. At the time of the hearing the three Jarrett children, who were then 12, 10 and 7 years old, were obviously incapable of emulating their mother's moral indiscretions. To wait until later years to determine whether Jacqueline had inculcated her moral values in the children would be to await a demonstration that the very harm which the statute seeks to avoid had occurred. Measures to safeguard the moral well-being of children, whose lives have already been disrupted by the divorce of their parents, cannot have been intended to be delayed until there are tangible manifestations of damage to their character.

While our comments have focused upon the moral hazards, we are not convinced that open cohabitation does not also affect the mental and emotional health of the children. Jacqueline's testimony at the hearing indicated that when her children originally learned that Wayne Hammon would move in with them, they initially expected that she would marry him. It is difficult to predict what psychological effects or problems may later develop from their efforts to overcome the disparity between their concepts of propriety and their mother's conduct. (Gehn v. Gehn (1977), 51 Ill.App.3d 946, 949, 10 Ill.Dec. 120, 367 N.E.2d 508.) Nor will their attempts to adjust to this new environment occur in a vacuum. Jacqueline's domestic arrangements are known to her neighbors and their children; testimony at the hearing indicated that Wayne Hammon played with the Jarrett children and their friends at the Jarrett home and also engaged in other activities with them. If the Jarrett children remained in that situation, they might well be compelled to try to explain Hammon's presence to their friends and, perhaps, to endure their taunts and jibes. In a case such as this the trial judge must also weigh these imponderables, and he is not limited to examining the children for current physical manifestations of emotional or mental difficulties.

Finally, we do not believe that the United States Supreme Court's opinion in Stanley v. Illinois * * * requires a different result. In *Stanley* the Supreme Court found that Illinois statutes created a presumption that an unwed father is unfit to exercise custody over his children. The court held that depriving an unwed father of his illegitimate children without a prior hearing to determine his actual rather than presumptive unfitness, when the State accords that protection to other parents, deprives him of equal protection of the law.

The case before us is fundamentally different. The trial court did not presume that Jacqueline was not an adequate parent, as the juvenile court in effect did in *Stanley*. Rather the trial court recognized that the affection and care of a parent do not alone assure the welfare of the child if other conduct of the parent threatens the child's moral development. Since the evidence indicated that Jacqueline had not terminated the troublesome relationship and would probably continue it in the future, the trial court transferred custody to Walter Jarrett, an equally caring and affectionate parent whose conduct did not contravene the standards established by the General Assembly and earlier judicial decisions. Its action in doing so was not contrary to the manifest weight of the evidence.

Accordingly, we reverse the judgment of the appellate court and affirm the judgment of the circuit court of Cook County.

Appellate court reversed; circuit court affirmed.

GOLDENHERSH, CHIEF JUSTICE, with whom THOMAS J. MORAN, JUSTICE, joins, dissenting:

The majority states, "The chief issue in this case is whether a change of custody predicated upon the open and continuing cohabitation of the custodial parent with a member of the opposite sex is contrary to the manifest weight of the evidence in the absence of any tangible evidence of contemporaneous adverse effect upon the minor children." * * * An examination of the opinions fails to reveal any other issue, and the effect of the decision is that the plaintiff's cohabitation with Hammon *per se* was sufficient grounds for changing the custody order previously entered. This record shows clearly that the children were healthy, well adjusted, and well cared for, and it should be noted that both the circuit and appellate courts made no finding that plaintiff was an unfit mother. The majority, too, makes no such finding and based its decision on a nebulous concept of injury to the children's "moral well-being and development." * * * I question that any competent sociologist would attribute the increase of "live in" unmarried couples to parental example.

The fragility of its conclusion concerning "prevailing public policy" is demonstrated by the majority's reliance on cases decided by this court in 1852 * * * and 1902 * * *, and an appellate court decision * * * (1943), * * * which, rather than "prevailing public policy," more clearly indicates the prejudice extant in that period against interracial sexual relations.

As the appellate court pointed out, the courts should not impose the personal preferences and standards of the judiciary in the decision of this case. Courts are uniquely equipped to decide legal issues and are well advised to leave to the theologians the question of the morality of the living arrangement into which the plaintiff had entered.

As a legal matter, simply stated, the majority has held that on the basis of her presumptive guilt of fornication, a Class B misdemeanor, plaintiff, although not declared to be an unfit mother, has forfeited the right to have the custody of her children. This finding flies in the face of the established rule that, in order to modify or amend an award of custody, the evidence must show that the parent to whom custody of the children was originally awarded is unfit to retain custody, or that a change of conditions makes a change of custody in their best interests. This record fails to show either. Mr. Justice Moran and I dissent and would affirm the decision of the appellate court.

MORAN, JUSTICE, with whom GOLDENHERSH, CHIEF JUSTICE, joins, dissenting:

I join in the dissent of the chief justice, but also dissent separately. My primary disagreement with the majority lies with its countenancing a change of custody based solely on a *conclusive presumption* that harm to the Jarrett children stemmed from Jacqueline's living arrangements. The majority purports to follow the Illinois Marriage and Dissolution of Marriage Act. Yet, under that act, only on the basis of fact can there be a finding that a change in circumstances has occurred and that modification of the prior custody judgment is necessary to serve the best interest of the children. (Ill.Rev.Stat. 1977, ch. 40, par. 610(b).) The court is not to consider conduct of a custodian if that conduct does not affect his relationship to the child. (Ill.Rev.Stat.1977, ch. 40, par. 602(b).) In this case, not one scintilla of actual or statistical evidence of harm or danger to the children has been presented. To the contrary, all of the evidence of record, as related by the majority, indicates that under Jacqueline's custodianship the children's welfare and needs were met. Also, the trial court expressly declined to find Jacqueline unfit. Nevertheless, the majority's finding of a violation of the seldom-enforced fornication [sic] statute effectively foreclosed any further consideration of the custody issue. Instead of focusing solely on the best interest of the children—the "guiding star" (Nye v. Nye (1952), 411 Ill. 408, 415, 105 N.E.2d 300)—the majority has utilized child custody as a vehicle to punish Jacqueline for her "misconduct." Such selective enforcement of a statute is inappropriate and, especially in the child-custody context, unfortunate.

The majority decision also is at odds with the principle of Stanley v. Illinois * * * The constitutional infirmity of the statutory presumption in *Stanley* casts doubt on the validity of the judicially created conclusive presumption in this case. After *Stanley,* an unwed father may not be deprived of his illegitimate children without a prior hearing to determine his actual fitness. Similarly, Jacqueline should not be deprived of the children in the absence of evidence that a change is necessary to serve the best interest of the children. A hearing at which custody is determined on the basis of the conclusive presumption sanctioned by the majority amounts to no hearing at all.

BOWERS v. HARDWICK

Supreme Court of the United States, 1986.
478 U.S. 186, 106 S.Ct. 2841, 92 L.Ed.2d 140.

JUSTICE WHITE delivered the opinion of the Court.

In August 1982, respondent was charged with violating the Georgia statute criminalizing sodomy [1] by committing that act with another adult male in the bedroom of respondent's home. After a preliminary hearing, the District Attorney decided not to present the matter to the grand jury unless further evidence developed.

Respondent then brought suit in the Federal District Court, challenging the constitutionality of the statute insofar as it criminalized consensual sodomy.[2] He asserted that he was a practicing homosexual, that the Georgia sodomy statute, as administered by the defendants, placed him in imminent danger of arrest, and that the statute for several reasons violates the Federal Constitution. The District Court granted the defendants' motion to dismiss for failure to state a claim, relying on *Doe v. Commonwealth's Attorney for the City of Richmond,* 403 F.Supp. 1199 (E.D.Va.1975), which this Court summarily affirmed, 425 U.S. 901, 96 S.Ct. 1489, 47 L.Ed.2d 751 (1976).

A divided panel of the Court of Appeals for the Eleventh Circuit reversed. 760 F.2d 1202 (1985). * * * We agree with the State that the Court of Appeals erred, and hence reverse its judgment.

This case does not require a judgment on whether laws against sodomy between consenting adults in general, or between homosexuals in particular, are wise or desirable. It raises no question about the right or propriety of state legislative decisions to repeal their laws that criminalize homosexual sodomy, or of state court decisions invalidating those laws on state constitutional grounds. The issue presented is whether the Federal Constitution confers a fundamental right upon homosexuals to engage in sodomy and hence invalidates the laws of the many States that still make such conduct illegal and have done so for a very long time. The case also calls for some judgment about the limits of the Court's role in carrying out its constitutional mandate.

---

1. Ga.Code Ann. § 16–6–2 (1984) provides, in pertinent part, as follows:

"(a) A person commits the offense of sodomy when he performs or submits to any sexual act involving the sex organs of one person and the mouth or anus of another. * * *

"(b) A person convicted of the offense of sodomy shall be punished by imprisonment for not less than one nor more than 20 years. * * * "

2. John and Mary Doe were also plaintiffs in the action. They alleged that they wished to engage in sexual activity proscribed by § 16–6–2 in the privacy of their home, App. 3, and that they had been "chilled and deterred" from engaging in such activity by both the existence of the statute and Hardwick's arrest.

Id., at 5. The District Court held, however, that because they had neither sustained, nor were in immediate danger of sustaining, any direct injury from the enforcement of the statute, they did not have proper standing to maintain the action. *Id.,* at 18. The Court of Appeals affirmed the District Court's judgment dismissing the Does' claim for lack of standing, 760 F.2d 1202, 1206–1207 (1985), and the Does do not challenge that holding in this Court.

The only claim properly before the Court, therefore, is Hardwick's challenge to the Georgia statute as applied to consensual homosexual sodomy. We express no opinion on the constitutionality of the Georgia statute as applied to other acts of sodomy.

We first register our disagreement with the Court of Appeals and with respondent that the Court's prior cases have construed the Constitution to confer a right of privacy that extends to homosexual sodomy and for all intents and purposes have decided this case. The reach of this line of cases was sketched in *Carey v. Population Services International,* 431 U.S. 678, 685, 97 S.Ct. 2010, 2016, 52 L.Ed.2d 675 (1977). *Pierce v. Society of Sisters,* 268 U.S. 510, 45 S.Ct. 571, 69 L.Ed. 1070 (1925), and *Meyer v. Nebraska,* 262 U.S. 390, 43 S.Ct. 625, 67 L.Ed. 1042 (1923), were described as dealing with child rearing and education; *Prince v. Massachusetts,* 321 U.S. 158, 64 S.Ct. 438, 88 L.Ed. 645 (1944), with family relationships; *Skinner v. Oklahoma ex rel. Williamson,* 316 U.S. 535, 62 S.Ct. 1110, 86 L.Ed. 1655 (1942), with procreation; *Loving v. Virginia,* 388 U.S. 1, 87 S.Ct. 1817, 18 L.Ed.2d 1010 (1967), with marriage; *Griswold v. Connecticut, supra,* and *Eisenstadt v. Baird, supra,* with contraception; and *Roe v. Wade,* 410 U.S. 113, 93 S.Ct. 705, 35 L.Ed.2d 147 (1973), with abortion. The latter three cases were interpreted as construing the Due Process Clause of the Fourteenth Amendment to confer a fundamental individual right to decide whether or not to beget or bear a child. *Carey v. Population Services International, supra,* 431 U.S., at 688–689, 97 S.Ct., at 2017–2018.

Accepting the decisions in these cases and the above description of them, we think it evident that none of the rights announced in those cases bears any resemblance to the claimed constitutional right of homosexuals to engage in acts of sodomy that is asserted in this case. No connection between family, marriage, or procreation on the one hand and homosexual activity on the other has been demonstrated, either by the Court of Appeals or by respondent. Moreover, any claim that these cases nevertheless stand for the proposition that any kind of private sexual conduct between consenting adults is constitutionally insulated from state proscription is unsupportable. Indeed, the Court's opinion in *Carey* twice asserted that the privacy right, which the *Griswold* line of cases found to be one of the protections provided by the Due Process Clause, did not reach so far. * * *

Precedent aside, however, respondent would have us announce, as the Court of Appeals did, a fundamental right to engage in homosexual sodomy. This we are quite unwilling to do. It is true that despite the language of the Due Process Clauses of the Fifth and Fourteenth Amendments, which appears to focus only on the processes by which life, liberty, or property is taken, the cases are legion in which those Clauses have been interpreted to have substantive content, subsuming rights that to a great extent are immune from federal or state regulation or proscription. Among such cases are those recognizing rights that have little or no textual support in the constitutional language. *Meyer, Prince,* and *Pierce* fall in this category, as do the privacy cases from *Griswold* to *Carey.*

Striving to assure itself and the public that announcing rights not readily identifiable in the Constitution's text involves much more than the imposition of the Justices' own choice of values on the States and the Federal Government, the Court has sought to identify the nature of the rights qualifying for heightened judicial protection. In *Palko v. Connecticut,* 302 U.S. 319, 325, 326, 58 S.Ct. 149, 151, 152, 82 L.Ed. 288 (1937), it was said that this category includes those fundamental liberties that are "implicit in the concept of ordered liberty," such that "neither liberty nor justice would exist if [they] were sacrificed." A different description of fundamental liberties appeared in *Moore v. East Cleveland,* 431 U.S. 494, 503, 97 S.Ct. 1932, 1937, 52 L.Ed.2d 531 (1977) (opinion of Powell, J.), where they are characterized as those liberties that are "deeply rooted in this Nation's history and tradition." * * *

It is obvious to us that neither of these formulations would extend a fundamental right to homosexuals to engage in acts of consensual sodomy. Proscriptions against that conduct have ancient roots. See generally, Survey on the Constitutional Right to Privacy in the Context of Homosexual Activity, 40 U.Miami L.Rev. 521, 525 (1986). Sodomy was a criminal offense at common law and was forbidden by the laws of the original thirteen States when they ratified the Bill of Rights. In 1868, when the Fourteenth Amendment was ratified, all but 5 of the 37 States in the Union had criminal sodomy laws. In fact, until 1961, all 50 States outlawed sodomy, and today, 24 States and the District of Columbia continue to provide criminal penalties for sodomy performed in private and between consenting adults. Survey, U.Miami L.Rev., *supra,* at 524, n. 9. Against this background, to claim that a right to engage in such conduct is "deeply rooted in this Nation's history and tradition" or "implicit in the concept of ordered liberty" is, at best, facetious.

Nor are we inclined to take a more expansive view of our authority to discover new fundamental rights imbedded in the Due Process Clause. The Court is most vulnerable and comes nearest to illegitimacy when it deals with judge-made constitutional law having little or no cognizable roots in the language or design of the Constitution. That this is so was painfully demonstrated by the face-off between the Executive and the Court in the 1930's, which resulted in the repudiation of much of the substantive gloss that the Court had placed on the Due Process Clause of the Fifth and Fourteenth Amendments. There should be, therefore, great resistance to expand the substantive reach of those Clauses, particularly if it requires redefining the category of rights deemed to be fundamental. Otherwise, the Judiciary necessarily takes to itself further authority to govern the country without express constitutional authority. The claimed right pressed on us today falls far short of overcoming this resistance.

Respondent, however, asserts that the result should be different where the homosexual conduct occurs in the privacy of the home. He relies on *Stanley v. Georgia,* 394 U.S. 557, 89 S.Ct. 1243, 22 L.Ed.2d 542 (1969), where the Court held that the First Amendment prevents conviction for possessing and reading obscene material in the privacy of his home: "If the First Amendment means anything, it means that a State has no business telling a man, sitting alone in his house, what books he may read or what films he may watch." * * *

Stanley did protect conduct that would not have been protected outside the home, and it partially prevented the enforcement of state obscenity laws; but the decision was firmly grounded in the First Amendment. The right pressed upon us here has no similar support in the text of the Constitution, and it does not qualify for recognition under the prevailing principles for construing the Fourteenth Amendment. Its limits are also difficult to discern. Plainly enough, otherwise illegal conduct is not always immunized whenever it occurs in the home. Victimless crimes, such as the possession and use of illegal drugs do not escape the law where they are committed at home. *Stanley* itself recognized that its holding offered no protection for the possession in the home of drugs, firearms, or stolen goods. * * * And if respondent's submission is limited to the voluntary sexual conduct between consenting adults, it would be difficult, except by fiat, to limit the claimed right to homosexual conduct while leaving exposed to prosecution adultery, incest, and other sexual crimes even though they are committed in the home. We are unwilling to start down that road.

Even if the conduct at issue here is not a fundamental right, respondent asserts that there must be a rational basis for the law and that there is none in this case other than the presumed belief of a majority of the electorate in Georgia that homosexual sodomy is immoral and unacceptable. This is said to be an inadequate rationale to support the law. The law, however, is constantly based on notions of morality, and if all laws representing essentially moral choices are to be invalidated under the Due Process Clause, the courts will be very busy indeed. Even respondent makes no such claim, but insists that majority sentiments about the morality of homosexuality should be declared inadequate. We do not agree, and are unpersuaded that the sodomy laws of some 25 States should be invalidated on this basis.[8]

Accordingly, the judgment of the Court of Appeals is

Reversed.

CHIEF JUSTICE BURGER, concurring.

I join the Court's opinion, but I write separately to underscore my view that in constitutional terms there is no such thing as a fundamental right to commit homosexual sodomy.

As the Court notes, the proscriptions against sodomy have very "ancient roots." Decisions of individuals relating to homosexual conduct have been subject to state intervention throughout the history of Western Civilization. Condemnation of those practices is firmly rooted in Judaeo–Christian moral and ethical standards. Homosexual sodomy was a capital crime under Roman law. See Code Theod. 9.7.6; Code Just. 9.9.31. See also D. Bailey, Homosexuality in the Western Christian Tradition 70–81 (1975). During the English Reformation when powers of the ecclesiastical courts were transferred to the King's Courts, the first English statute criminalizing sodomy was passed. 25 Hen. VIII, c. 6. Blackstone described "the infamous crime against nature" as an offense of "deeper malignity" than rape, an heinous act "the very mention of which is a disgrace to human nature," and "a crime not fit to be named." Blackstone's Commentaries *215. The common law of England, including its prohibition of sodomy, became the received law of Georgia and the other Colonies. In 1816 the Georgia Legislature passed the statute at issue here, and that statute has been continuously in force in one form or another since that time. To hold that the act of homosexual sodomy is somehow protected as a fundamental right would be to cast aside millennia of moral teaching.

This is essentially not a question of personal "preferences" but rather of the legislative authority of the State. I find nothing in the Constitution depriving a State of the power to enact the statute challenged here.

---

8. Respondent does not defend the judgment below based on the Ninth Amendment, the Equal Protection Clause or the Eighth Amendment.

JUSTICE POWELL, concurring.

I join the opinion of the Court. I agree with the Court that there is no fundamental right—*i.e.,* no substantive right under the Due Process Clause—such as that claimed by respondent, and found to exist by the Court of Appeals. This is not to suggest, however, that respondent may not be protected by the Eighth Amendment of the Constitution.

* * *

JUSTICE BLACKMUN, with whom JUSTICE BRENNAN, JUSTICE MARSHALL, and JUSTICE STEVENS join, dissenting.

This case is no more about "a fundamental right to engage in homosexual sodomy," as the Court purports to declare, * * * than *Stanley v. Georgia,* 394 U.S. 557, 89 S.Ct. 1243, 22 L.Ed.2d 542 (1969), was about a fundamental right to watch obscene movies, or *Katz v. United States,* 389 U.S. 347, 88 S.Ct. 507, 19 L.Ed.2d 576 (1967), was about a fundamental right to place interstate bets from a telephone booth. Rather, this case is about "the most comprehensive of rights and the right most valued by civilized men," namely, "the right to be let alone." *Olmstead v. United States,* 277 U.S. 438, 478, 48 S.Ct. 564, 572, 72 L.Ed. 944 (1928) (Brandeis, J., dissenting).

* * *

II

"Our cases long have recognized that the Constitution embodies a promise that a certain private sphere of individual liberty will be kept largely beyond the reach of government." *Thornburgh v. American Coll. of Obst. & Gyn.,* 476 U.S. 747, 772, 106 S.Ct. 2169, 2184, 90 L.Ed.2d 779 (1986). In construing the right to privacy, the Court has proceeded along two somewhat distinct, albeit complementary, lines. First, it has recognized a privacy interest with reference to certain *decisions* that are properly for the individual to make. *E.g., Roe v. Wade,* * * *; *Pierce v. Society of Sisters,* * * *. Second, it has recognized a privacy interest with reference to certain *places* without regard for the particular activities in which the individuals who occupy them are engaged. *E.g., United States v. Karo,* 468 U.S. 705, 104 S.Ct. 3296, 82 L.Ed.2d 530 (1984); *Payton v. New York,* 445 U.S. 573, 100 S.Ct. 1371, 63 L.Ed.2d 639 (1980); *Rios v. United States,* 364 U.S. 253, 80 S.Ct. 1431, 4 L.Ed.2d 1688 (1960). The case before us implicates both the decisional and the spatial aspects of the right to privacy.

A

The Court concludes today that none of our prior cases dealing with various decisions that individuals are entitled to make free of governmental interference "bears any resemblance to the claimed constitutional right of homosexuals to engage in acts of sodomy that is asserted in this case." * * * While it is true that these cases may be characterized by their connection to protection of the family, * * * the Court's conclusion that they extend no further than this boundary ignores the warning in *Moore v. East Cleveland,* * * * (plurality opinion), against "clos[ing] our eyes to the basic reasons why certain rights associated with the family have been accorded shelter under the Fourteenth Amendment's Due Process Clause." We protect those rights not because they contribute, in some direct and material way, to the general public welfare, but because they form so central a part of an individual's life. "[T]he concept of privacy embodies the 'moral fact that a person belongs to himself and not others nor to society as a whole.' " *Thornburgh v. American Coll. of Obst. & Gyn.,* 476 U.S., at 777, n. 5, 106 S.Ct., at 2187, n. 5 (Stevens, J., concurring), quoting Fried, Correspondence, 6 Phil. & Pub. Affairs 288–289 (1977).   And so we protect the decision whether to marry precisely because marriage "is an association that promotes a way of life, not causes; a harmony in living, not political faiths; a bilateral loyalty, not commercial or social projects." *Griswold v. Connecticut,* * * * We protect the decision whether to have a child because parenthood alters so dramatically an individual's self-definition, not because of demographic considerations or the Bible's command to be fruitful and multiply. Cf. *Thornburgh v. American Coll. of Obst. & Gyn.,* * * * (Stevens, J., concurring). And we protect the family because it contributes so powerfully to the happiness of individuals, not because of a preference for stereotypical households. Cf. *Moore v. East Cleveland,* * * * (plurality opinion). The Court recognized in *Roberts,* 468 U.S., at 619, 104 S.Ct., at 3250, that the "ability independently to define one's identity that is central to any concept of liberty" cannot truly be exercised in a vacuum; we all depend on the "emotional enrichment of close ties with others." *Ibid.*

Only the most willful blindness could obscure the fact that sexual intimacy is "a sensitive, key relationship of human existence, central to family life, community welfare, and the development of human personality," *Paris Adult Theatre I v. Slaton,* * * * The fact that individuals define themselves in a significant way through their intimate sexual relationships with others suggests, in a Nation as diverse as ours, that there may be many "right" ways of conducting those relationships, and that much of the richness of a relationship will come from the freedom an individual has to *choose* the form and nature of these intensely personal bonds. See Karst, The Freedom of Intimate Association, 89 Yale L.J. 624, 637 (1980); * * *

* * *   The Court claims that its decision today merely refuses to recognize a fundamental right to engage in homosexual sodomy; what the Court really has refused to recognize is the fundamental interest all individuals have in controlling the nature of their intimate associations with others.

B

The behavior for which Hardwick faces prosecution occurred in his own home, a place to which the Fourth Amendment attaches special significance. The Court's treatment of this aspect of the case is symptomatic of its overall refusal to consider the broad principles that have informed our treatment of privacy in specific cases. Just as the right to privacy is more than the mere aggregation of a number of entitlements to engage in specific behavior, so too, protecting the physical integrity of the home is more than merely a means of protecting specific activities that often take place there. * * *

The Court's interpretation of the pivotal case of *Stanley v. Georgia,* * * * is entirely unconvincing. * * *

The central place that *Stanley* gives Justice Brandeis' dissent in *Olmstead,* a case raising *no* First Amendment claim, shows that *Stanley* rested as much on the Court's understanding of the Fourth Amendment as it did on the First. * * *   "The right of the people to be secure in their * * * houses," expressly guaranteed by the Fourth Amendment, is perhaps the most "textual" of the various constitutional provisions that inform our understanding of the right to privacy, and thus I cannot agree with the Court's statement that "[t]he right pressed upon us here has no * * * support in the text of the Constitution," * * *. Indeed, the right of an individual to conduct intimate relationships in the intimacy of his or her own home seems to me to be the heart of the Constitution's protection of privacy.

III

The Court's failure to comprehend the magnitude of the liberty interests at stake in this case leads it to slight the question whether petitioner, on behalf of the State, has justified Georgia's infringement on these interests.

* * *

I cannot agree that either the length of time a majority has held its convictions or the passions with which it defends them can withdraw legislation from this Court's scrutiny. See, *e.g., Roe v. Wade,* * * *; *Loving v. Virginia,* * * *; *Brown v. Board of Education,* * * *.[5]

* * *

The assertion that "traditional Judeo–Christian values proscribe" the conduct involved, Brief for Petitioner 20, cannot provide an adequate justification for § 16–6–2. * * * A State can no more punish private behavior because of religious intolerance than it can punish such behavior because of racial animus. * * *

Nor can § 16–6–2 be justified as a "morally neutral" exercise of Georgia's power to "protect the public environment," *Paris Adult Theatre I,* * * *. Petitioner and the Court fail to see the difference between laws that protect public sensibilities and those that enforce private morality. Statutes banning public sexual activity are entirely consistent with protecting the individual's liberty interest in decisions concerning sexual relations: the same recognition that those decisions are intensely private which justifies protecting them from governmental interference can justify protecting individuals from unwilling exposure to the sexual activities of others. But the mere fact that intimate behavior may be punished when it takes place in public cannot dictate how

5. The parallel between *Loving* and this case is almost uncanny. There, too, the State relied on a religious justification for its law. Compare 388 U.S., at 3, 87 S.Ct., at 1819 (quoting trial court's statement that "Almighty God created the races white, black, yellow, malay and red, and he placed them on separate continents. . . . The fact that he separated the races shows that he did not intend for the races to mix"), with Brief for Petitioner 20–21 (relying on the Old and New Testaments and the writings of St. Thomas Aquinas to show that "traditional Judeo–Christian values proscribe such conduct"). There, too, defenders of the challenged statute relied heavily on the fact that when the Fourteenth Amendment was ratified, most of the States had similar prohibitions. Compare Brief for Appellee in *Loving v. Virginia,* O.T.1966, No. 395, pp. 28–29, with *ante,* at 2844–2845 and n. 6. There, too, at the time the case came before the Court, many of the States still had criminal statutes concerning the conduct at issue. Compare 388 U.S., at 6, n. 5, 87 S.Ct., at 1820, n. 5 (noting that 16 States still outlawed interracial marriage), with *ante,* 2845–2846 (noting that 24 States and the District of Columbia have sodomy statutes). Yet the Court held, not only that the invidious racism of Virginia's law violated the Equal Protection Clause, see 388 U.S., at 7–12, 87 S.Ct., at 1821–1823, but also that the law deprived the Lovings of due process by denying them the "freedom of choice to marry" that had "long been recognized as one of the vital personal rights essential to the orderly pursuit of happiness by free men." *Id.,* at 12, 87 S.Ct., at 1824.

States can regulate intimate behavior that occurs in intimate places. See *Paris Adult Theatre I, supra,* * * * ("marital intercourse on a street corner or a theater stage" can be forbidden despite the constitutional protection identified in *Griswold v. Connecticut,* 381 U.S. 479, 85 S.Ct. 1678, 14 L.Ed.2d 510 (1965)).

This case involves no real interference with the rights of others, for the mere knowledge that other individuals do not adhere to one's value system cannot be a legally cognizable interest, cf. *Diamond v. Charles,* 476 U.S. 54, 62, 106 S.Ct. 1697, 1703, 90 L.Ed.2d 48 (1986), let alone an interest that can justify invading the houses, hearts, and minds of citizens who choose to live their lives differently.

* * *

JUSTICE STEVENS, with whom JUSTICE BRENNAN and JUSTICE MARSHALL join, dissenting.

Like the statute that is challenged in this case, the rationale of the Court's opinion applies equally to the prohibited conduct regardless of whether the parties who engage in it are married or unmarried, or are of the same or different sexes. Sodomy was condemned as an odious and sinful type of behavior during the formative period of the common law. That condemnation was equally damning for heterosexual and homosexual sodomy. Moreover, it provided no special exemption for married couples. The license to cohabit and to produce legitimate offspring simply did not include any permission to engage in sexual conduct that was considered a "crime against nature."

The history of the Georgia statute before us clearly reveals this traditional prohibition of heterosexual, as well as homosexual, sodomy. Indeed, at one point in the 20th century, Georgia's law was construed to permit certain sexual conduct between homosexual women even though such conduct was prohibited between heterosexuals. The history of the statutes cited by the majority as proof for the proposition that sodomy is not constitutionally protected, * * * similarly reveals a prohibition on heterosexual, as well as homosexual, sodomy.

Because the Georgia statute expresses the traditional view that sodomy is an immoral kind of conduct regardless of the identity of the persons who engage in it, I believe that a proper analysis of its constitutionality requires consideration of two questions: First, may a State totally prohibit the described conduct by means of a neutral law applying without exception to all persons subject to its jurisdiction? If not, may the State save the statute by announcing that it will only enforce the law against homosexuals? The two questions merit separate discussion.

I

Our prior cases make two propositions abundantly clear. First, the fact that the governing majority in a State has traditionally viewed a particular practice as immoral is not a sufficient reason for upholding a law prohibiting the practice; neither history nor tradition could save a law prohibiting miscegenation from constitutional attack. Second, individual decisions by married persons, concerning the intimacies of their physical relationship, even when not intended to produce offspring, are a form of "liberty" protected by the Due Process Clause of the Fourteenth Amendment. *Griswold v. Connect-*

icut, 381 U.S. 479, 85 S.Ct. 1678, 14 L.Ed.2d 510 (1965). Moreover, this protection extends to intimate choices by unmarried as well as married persons. *Carey v. Population Services International,* 431 U.S. 678, 97 S.Ct. 2010, 52 L.Ed.2d 675 (1977); *Eisenstadt v. Baird,* 405 U.S. 438, 92 S.Ct. 1029, 31 L.Ed.2d 349 (1972).

* * *

Society has every right to encourage its individual members to follow particular traditions in expressing affection for one another and in gratifying their personal desires. It, of course, may prohibit an individual from imposing his will on another to satisfy his own selfish interests. It also may prevent an individual from interfering with, or violating, a legally sanctioned and protected relationship, such as marriage. And it may explain the relative advantages and disadvantages of different forms of intimate expression. But when individual married couples are isolated from observation by others, the way in which they voluntarily choose to conduct their intimate relations is a matter for them—not the State—to decide.[10] The essential "liberty" that animated the development of the law in cases like *Griswold, Eisenstadt,* and *Carey* surely embraces the right to engage in nonreproductive, sexual conduct that others may consider offensive or immoral.

Paradoxical as it may seem, our prior cases thus establish that a State may not prohibit sodomy within "the sacred precincts of marital bedrooms," *Griswold,* 381 U.S., at 485, 85 S.Ct., at 1682, or, indeed, between unmarried heterosexual adults. *Eisenstadt,* 405 U.S., at 453, 92 S.Ct., at 1038. In all events, it is perfectly clear that the State of Georgia may not totally prohibit the conduct proscribed by § 16–6–2 of the Georgia Criminal Code.

II

If the Georgia statute cannot be enforced as it is written—if the conduct it seeks to prohibit is a protected form of liberty for the vast majority of Georgia's citizens—the State must assume the burden of justifying a selective application of its law. Either the persons to whom Georgia seeks to apply its statute do not have the same interest in "liberty" that others have, or there must be a reason why the State may be permitted to apply a generally applicable law to certain persons that it does not apply to others.

The first possibility is plainly unacceptable. Although the meaning of the principle that "all men are created equal" is not always clear, it surely must mean that every free citizen has the same interest in "liberty" that the members of the majority share. From the standpoint of the individual, the homosexual and the heterosexual have the same interest in deciding how he will live his own life, and, more narrowly, how he will conduct himself in his personal and voluntary associations with his companions. State intrusion into the private conduct of either is equally burdensome.

The second possibility is similarly unacceptable. A policy of selective application must be supported by a neutral and legitimate interest—some-

---

10. Indeed, the Georgia Attorney General concedes that Georgia's statute would be unconstitutional if applied to a married couple. See Tr. of Oral Arg. 8 (stating that application of the statute to a married couple "would be unconstitutional" because of the "right of marital privacy as identified by the Court in Griswold"). Significantly, Georgia passed the current statute three years after the Court's decision in *Griswold.*

thing more substantial than a habitual dislike for, or ignorance about, the disfavored group. Neither the State nor the Court has identified any such interest in this case. The Court has posited as a justification for the Georgia statute "the presumed belief of a majority of the electorate in Georgia that homosexual sodomy is immoral and unacceptable." *Ante,* at 2846. But the Georgia electorate has expressed no such belief—instead, its representatives enacted a law that presumably reflects the belief that *all sodomy* is immoral and unacceptable. Unless the Court is prepared to conclude that such a law is constitutional, it may not rely on the work product of the Georgia Legislature to support its holding. For the Georgia statute does not single out homosexuals as a separate class meriting special disfavored treatment.

Nor, indeed, does the Georgia prosecutor even believe that all homosexuals who violate this statute should be punished. This conclusion is evident from the fact that the respondent in this very case has formally acknowledged in his complaint and in court that he has engaged, and intends to continue to engage, in the prohibited conduct, yet the State has elected not to process criminal charges against him. As Justice Powell points out, moreover, Georgia's prohibition on private, consensual sodomy has not been enforced for decades. The record of nonenforcement, in this case and in the last several decades, belies the Attorney General's representations about the importance of the State's selective application of its generally applicable law.

Both the Georgia statute and the Georgia prosecutor thus completely fail to provide the Court with any support for the conclusion that homosexual sodomy, *simpliciter,* is considered unacceptable conduct in that State, and that the burden of justifying a selective application of the generally applicable law has been met.

III

The Court orders the dismissal of respondent's complaint even though the State's statute prohibits all sodomy; even though that prohibition is concededly unconstitutional with respect to heterosexuals; and even though the State's *post hoc* explanations for selective application are belied by the State's own actions. At the very least, I think it clear at this early stage of the litigation that respondent has alleged a constitutional claim sufficient to withstand a motion to dismiss.

I respectfully dissent.

Notes on **Parham, Jarrett,** *and* **Hardwick**

1. Can you explain why, since *Parham* involved a state statute that allowed mothers, but not fathers, to sue for the wrongful death of their illegitimate child, the Court's prior decisions governing gender discrimination are not applicable? Is it less difficult to understand why cases concerning the rights of illegitimate children are not in point? Will the outcome of *Parham* provide an incentive for fathers of illegitimate children in Georgia to utilize the statutory legitimation procedure in order to become eligible to bring wrongful death suits? What other consequences follow from compliance with the statutory procedure?

2. The Georgia legitimation statute, quoted in footnote 2 of the Court's opinion, appears to give the father the right, upon legitimation, to have the child's name changed. Is this provision constitutional? See Text Note on the Married

Woman's Loss of Identity at p. 198, supra. The mother has the statutory right to notice of the father's proceeding. Does she have the right to contest legitimation, if the father can prove his paternity of the child? Can she object to the name change? In Jones v. McDowell, 53 N.C.App. 434, 281 S.E.2d 192 (1981), the court held unconstitutional as a denial of equal protection to the mother of an illegitimate child the requirement of the North Carolina legitimation statute that the child's surname be changed from that of the mother to that of the father upon legitimation.

3.   The Court has recognized the right of illegitimate children to sue for the wrongful death of their mother, Levy v. Louisiana, 391 U.S. 68, 88 S.Ct. 1509, 20 L.Ed.2d 436 rehearing denied 393 U.S. 898, 21 L.Ed.2d 185, 89 S.Ct. 65 (1968); and to share in a worker's compensation death benefit arising from the work-related death of their father, Weber v. Aetna Cas. & Sur. Co., 406 U.S. 164, 92 S.Ct. 1400, 31 L.Ed.2d 768 (1972). These cases live in uneasy constitutional tension with the Court's treatment of the rights of illegitimate children to inherit from their father. Three cases are in point. In Labine v. Vincent, 401 U.S. 532, 91 S.Ct. 1017, 28 L.Ed.2d 288 (1971), rehearing denied 402 U.S. 990, 29 L.Ed.2d 156, 91 S.Ct. 1672 (1971), the Court upheld a Louisiana statute that permitted acknowledged illegitimate children to inherit from the father only if he died without legitimate descendants, parents, grandparents, or collateral relatives. A plurality of the Court, speaking through Justice Black, reasoned that Louisiana might in this way prefer legal family units to illegal ones:

> The social difference between a wife and a concubine is analogous to the difference between a legitimate and an illegitimate child. One set of relationships is socially sanctioned, legally recognized, and gives rise to various rights and duties. The other set of relationships is illicit and beyond the recognition of the law.

Id., 401 U.S. at 538, 91 S.Ct. at 1021, 28 L.Ed.2d at 293–94.

Six years later, in Trimble v. Gordon, 430 U.S. 762, 97 S.Ct. 1459, 52 L.Ed.2d 31 (1977), an Illinois statute which allowed illegitimate children to inherit only from their mothers, while permitting legitimate children to inherit from both parents was held to violate the equal protection clause. Illinois's interest in protecting legitimate family relationships was insufficient to sustain the statute, for the Court had learned in the intervening years that states may not "attempt to influence the actions of men and women by imposing sanctions on the children born of their illegitimate relationships." Id., 430 U.S. at 769, 97 S.Ct. at 1464, 52 L.Ed.2d at 39. Nor could the state's interest in the orderly distribution of property after death suffice to sustain the law in a case where the decedent had been found to be the child's father in a paternity action brought during his lifetime. Did *Trimble* overrule *Labine*? The illegitimate daughter in *Labine* had been formally acknowledged by her parents in a proceeding that made her a "natural child" under Louisiana law and thus entitled to support from them. The paternity action in *Trimble* had also produced a support order against the father. Would *Labine* be decided differently on its facts after *Trimble*?

The Court performed another seeming about-face in Lalli v. Lalli, 439 U.S. 259, 99 S.Ct. 518, 58 L.Ed.2d 503 (1978). At issue was a New York statute that permitted an illegitimate child to inherit from the father only if "a court of competent jurisdiction has, during the lifetime of the father, made an order of filiation declaring paternity in a proceeding instituted during the pregnancy of the mother or within two years from the birth of the child." The New York Court of Appeals had stressed that the purpose of the statute was not to "discourage illegitimacy, to mold human conduct or to set societal norms", but merely to provide for the just and orderly disposition of property at death. Accepting this statement of purpose, the Court upheld the statute. *Trimble* was distinguished: under the Illinois scheme an illegitimate child could inherit only if he was legitimated by the father through marriage with the mother and acknowledgment. New York's scheme was less rigid, while maintaining a clear means of identification; it satisfied the constitutional scrutiny. Did *Lalli* overrule *Trimble?* If so, did it resurrect *Labine?* Justice Blackmun thought so, and applauded the Court's gratifying reversion to the principles of *Labine.* Id., 439 U.S. at 276–77, 99 S.Ct. at 529, 58 L.Ed.2d at 516.

The cases are ably discussed in Homer H. Clark, Constitutional Protection of the Illegitimate Child?, 12 U.C. Davis L.Rev. 383, 385–92 (1979).

4.   The Court's scrutiny of the treatment of illegitimate children by the Social Security Act has produced equally puzzling results. Compare Jimenez v. Weinberger, 417 U.S. 628, 94 S.Ct. 2496, 41 L.Ed.2d 363 (1974) (unconstitutional to exclude from child's benefits extended to children of disabled workers illegitimate, but not legitimate, children born after the father became disabled) with Mathews v. Lucas, 427 U.S. 495, 96 S.Ct. 2755, 49 L.Ed.2d 651 (1976) (constitutional to exclude unacknowledged illegitimate children not living with or being supported by wage earner at the time of his death) and Califano v. Boles, 443 U.S. 282, 99 S.Ct. 2767, 61 L.Ed.2d 541 (1979) (constitutional to restrict mother's benefits to women who were married to wage earner at some time during his life). Professor Clark thinks that *Jimenez* and *Mathews* are irreconcilable. Clark, supra Note 3, at 397–98. Do you agree?

The "mother's benefits" at issue in *Boles* were designed to permit women who had been dependent on the wage earner for support to elect not to work but rather to stay home and care for their children after loss of the wage earner's support. The benefits were extended to fathers in Weinberger v. Wiesenfeld, 420 U.S. 636, 95 S.Ct. 1225, 43 L.Ed.2d 514 (1975). Under the compulsion of further litigation, these benefits have been extended as well to young husbands and to surviving divorced husbands who have the care of the wage earner's child. See 45 Federal Register 68931 (Oct. 17, 1980). As a result of *Boles,* they will not be available for unwed mothers, or, presumably, unwed fathers. The child, if eligible, will receive a child's benefit. The majority and the dissent disagreed in *Boles* over whether the relevant discrimination was against the mothers or their children. Justice Rehnquist, writing for the majority, repudiated his earlier view of the legislative history which had led him to conclude in *Wiesenfeld* that the only purpose of the benefit was to make it possible for the children of the deceased worker to have the personal care of a surviving parent. See Weinberger v. Wiesenfeld, supra, 420 U.S. at 655, 95 S.Ct. at 1236, 43 L.Ed.2d at 529 (Rehnquist, J., concurring). In *Boles,* he perceived that the focus of the mother's benefit was to alleviate the economic plight of the surviving or former spouse; the child's needs were addressed through the separate child's insurance benefit. Califano v. Boles, supra, 443 U.S. at 294, 99 S.Ct. at 2775, 61 L.Ed.2d at 551. But since the mother or father is not eligible unless a child under 18 or disabled needs care, wasn't he right the first time? If so, can this distinction between the parents of legitimate and illegitimate children survive constitutional scrutiny? See Barbera Levitan, Comment, Califano v. Boles: Unequal Protection for Illegitimate Children and Their Mothers, 9 N.Y.U.Rev.L. & Soc.Change 241 (1979–1980).

5.   How do you evaluate the following arguments put forward by fathers in paternity actions seeking support for illegitimate children when paternity is

established, but the claim is made that the mother falsely represented that she was using birth control pills: (a) Since the United States Constitution guarantees to both men and women the freedom to choose whether to begat a child, the imposition of a support order on a father under these circumstances would interfere with his right to avoid procreation together with its burdens; or (b) The mother is liable to the father in tort for the "wrongful birth" of the child; damages include compensation for his mental agony and distress as well as punitive damages for the mother's oppression, fraud and malice. The latter argument was rejected on public policy and privacy grounds in Stephen K. v. Roni L., 105 Cal.App.3d 640, 164 Cal.Rptr. 618 (1980); the former argument was accepted in Matter of Pamela P., 110 Misc.2d 978, 443 N.Y.S.2d 343 (Family Ct.1981). The father in *Pamela P.* was represented by Karen DeCrow, the former President of the National Organization for Women and author of SEXIST JUS- TICE (Random House, 1974). In an interview with the New York Times, she is quoted as having said, "Men should not automatically have to pay for a child they don't want: It's the only logical feminist position to take." The New York Times, Nov. 6, 1981, p. B 6, col. 1. Judge Nanette Dembitz apparently agreed, for she held that the father would not be ordered to pay child support unless the mother's financial means were insufficient to satisfy the child's fair and reasonable needs. Do you agree that this result is right? Higher courts did not. Judge Dembitz's order was modified to strike the father's defense of fraud as irrelevant to the statutory factors controlling the amount of support awarded: the needs of the child and the financial means of both parents. Pamela P. v. Frank S., 88 A.D.2d 865, 451 N.Y.S.2d 766 (1982). In affirming the modification, the Court of Appeals observed:

> The interest asserted by the father on this appeal is not, strictly speak- ing, his freedom to choose to avoid procreation, because the mother's conduct in no way limited his right to use contraception. Rather, he seeks to have his choice regarding procreation fully respected by other individuals and effectu- ated to the extent that he should be relieved of his obligation to support a child that he did not voluntarily choose to have. But respondent's constitu- tional entitlement to avoid procreation does not encompass a right to avoid a child support obligation simply because another private person has not fully respected his desires in this regard. However unfairly respondent may have been treated by petitioner's failure to allow him an equal voice in the decision to conceive a child, such a wrong does not rise to the level of a constitutional violation.

Pamela P. v. Frank S., 59 N.Y.2d 1, 6–7, 462 N.Y.S.2d 819, 822, 449 N.E.2d 713, 716 (1983). Is this an adequate response to the father's argument? The holding is approved in Recent Developments, 29 Villanova L.Rev. 185 (1983–84); the writer observes that the court's recognition of its "inability to remedy all human wrongs without engendering further social damage" would be "a policy ground sufficient to bar any claim or defense of fraud and deceit." Id., at 206. See also Paula Murray & Brenda Winslett, The Constitutional Right to Privacy and Emerging Tort Liability for Deceit in Interpersonal Relationships, 1986 U.Ill. L.Rev. 799.

6. Would the Jarrett children have been removed from their home if Wayne Hammon had been their natural father and he and Jacqueline Jarrett had been living together in nonmarital cohabitation? Who would have raised the issue of the children's custody in such a case? The district attorney, in a prosecution under the fornication statute? A school teacher, learning of the parents' lifestyle? A neighbor, observing the family situation? Why does the non-custodial parent

have the right to check up on the mother's activities? Because of his concern for the welfare of their children? Are you persuaded that the children are endangered by the presence of Hammon in the home? Lower courts in Illinois have tried to limit *Jarrett* as narrowly as possible. See, e.g., Brandt v. Brandt, 99 Ill.App.3d 1089, 55 Ill.Dec. 78, 425 N.E.2d 1251 (1981) (rejecting father's argument that *Jarrett* established a *per se* rule requiring a change of custody whenever the custodial parent cohabits, in the children's presence, with a person to whom she is not married and does so openly and continuously); In re Marriage of Olson, 98 Ill.App.3d 316, 53 Ill.Dec. 751, 424 N.E.2d 386 (1981) (no change of custody where mother and her friend maintained separate residences and the trial court found that the 4 year old boy in her custody had not been adversely affected by her sexual relationship). Custody of one of the two daughters was changed from the mother to the father in *Brandt,* but the modification was based on the daughter's wish to live with her father stemming from her hostility toward her mother, not on the mother's living arrangements. Is *Jarrett* a dead letter? See Mary Beth Cyze, Judicial Treatment of Parental Cohabitation After Jarrett v. Jarrett, 15 Loyola Univ. of Chi.L.J. 337 (1984).

7. Has the Illinois Supreme Court nullified the provision of the Illinois Marriage and Dissolution of Marriage Act, which is based on the Uniform Marriage and Divorce Act, that states, "[t]he court shall not consider conduct of a present or proposed custodian that does not affect his relationship to the child"? The Reporter's Comment to Section 402 of the Uniform Act reads in part as follows:

> The last sentence of the section changes the law in those states which continue to use fault notions in custody adjudication. There is no reason to encourage parties to spy on each other in order to discover marital (most commonly, sexual) misconduct for use in a custody contest. This provision makes it clear that unless a contestant is able to prove that the parent's behavior in fact affects his relationship to the child (a standard which could seldom be met if the parent's behavior has been circumspect or unknown to the child), evidence of such behavior is irrelevant.

Does this Comment fit the *Jarrett* facts? Is what worries the Illinois court most the fact that the mother's conduct is *not* circumspect and is certainly known to the children? Would the children have been left with the mother if she had been willing to confess the error of her ways, tell Hammon to leave (or marry him), and instruct her children not to follow her earlier example? Why do you suppose she refused to follow this course? Did the requirement of the divorce decree that Jacqueline sell the family home within six months of her remarriage have a major influence on her decision? Is such a provision wise?

8. Would the *Hardwick* majority have upheld the Georgia sodomy law if it had been applied to a heterosexual couple living in nonmarital cohabitation? As Justice Stevens points out in footnote 10 of his dissenting opinion, Georgia conceded that the statute would be unconstitutional if enforced against a married couple. Since homosexual couples are not permitted to marry, see discussion at pp. 265–88 supra, does *Hardwick* permit states with sodomy laws also to deny such couples the right to live in family relationships? Would Stevens uphold a sodomy law expressly limited to homosexuals?

9. What state purposes are furthered by sodomy laws? One commentator, noting that the country is about evenly divided between states that have decriminalized sodomy (21 states) and those that have retained such prohibitions (24 states), argues on the basis of original intent that courts lack a sufficient warrant

in the history, structure, or language of the Constitution to invalidate sodomy laws:

> A state's decision to prohibit sodomy, however, does not violate any constitutional limitation on majoritarian morality. Sodomy laws, at the very least, manifest society's displeasure with homosexual conduct and reinforce social values. The law provides citizens with the moral gratification of living in a state which prohibits behavior they feel is morally wrong. The Constitution is silent on the question of the social propriety of homosexuality, and therefore the Court has no mandate to intervene. No principle identifiable in the text or history of the Constitution makes homosexuals' sexual gratification more important than other citizens' moral gratification.

Alan J. Wertjes Note, Behind the Facade: Understanding the Potential Extension of the Constitutional Right to Privacy to Homosexual Conduct, 64 Wash. U.L.Q. 1233, 1246–47 (1986) (citing Bork, Neutral Principles and Some First Amendment Problems, 47 Ind.L.Rev. 1, 10 (1971); other footnotes omitted). Professor Kenneth Karst, on the other hand, finds important First Amendment values implicated in the prohibition on sodomy:

> [W]hatever may have been the original purposes of laws forbidding homosexual sex, it seems clear that today one of the chief concerns underlying the maintenance of those laws is a concern to regulate the content of messages about sexual preference. It is said that the state, by repealing its prohibition on homosexual conduct, will itself be seen as making a statement approving the conduct. The selective enforcement of these laws lends credence to the notion that one of the main policies being pursued is the suppression of expression. The laws are rarely enforced against behavior carried on entirely in private; it is those persons who advertise their sexual preferences by frequenting gay bars and the like, or who openly display their homosexual affections, who are likely to be punished. The immediate practical effect of such a law's enforcement is thus to penalize public expression. And that public expression itself, as I have said, may be a political act.

Kenneth L. Karst, The Freedom of Intimate Association, 89 Yale L.J. 624, 658 (1980) (footnotes omitted). In Fricke v. Lynch, 491 F.Supp. 381 (D.R.I.1980), the Principal of Cumberland High School was enjoined from denying Aaron Fricke the right to attend the senior prom with a male escort, Paul Guilbert. Basing its decision on the first amendment, the court found that the proposed activity had significant expressive content (Fricke had testified that he was sincerely committed to a homosexual orientation and that he felt attending the dance with another young man would be a political statement for equal rights and human rights) and that the school's interest in student safety and the prevention of violence could be achieved by a less restrictive means than suppression of free expression: a firm administrative prohibition against disturbance, backed up by adequate security measures. Is the first amendment argument available in the same sex marriage cases? See also, Sylvia A. Law, Homosexuality and the Social Meaning of Gender, 1988 Wis.L.Rev. 187, defending the thesis "that contemporary legal and cultural contempt for lesbian women and gay men serves primarily to preserve and reinforce the social meaning attached to gender."

10. Homosexual couples have tried other avenues of obtaining legal recognition of their family relationship, with varying success. Several lower court decisions in New York, which had recognized the right of a surviving "gay life partner" to continue to occupy the rent stabilized or rent controlled apartment leased by his deceased lover and in which they had lived together in a family

relationship, were reversed on appeal. See, e.g., Two Associates v. Brown, 131 Misc.2d 986, 502 N.Y.S.2d 604 (Sup.1986) reversed summ. judgment granted, 127 A.D.2d 173, 513 N.Y.S.2d 966 (1st Dept. 1987) (applying the Rent Stabilization Law); Yorkshire Towers Co. v. Harpster, 134 Misc.2d 384, 510 N.Y.S.2d 976 (N.Y.City Civ.Ct.1986) reversed 141 Misc.2d 516, 538 N.Y.S.2d 703 (App.Term 1988) (applying Real Property Law section 235–f, popularly known as the "room-mate law"); but see Gelman v. Castaneda, 13 Family L. Reporter 1044 (1986) (N.Y.Surr.Ct. N.Y.Cty.) (applying the New York City Rent Control Law). See generally, Lawrence A. Kanushes, Note, All in the Family: Succession Rights and Rent Stabilized Apartments, 53 Brooklyn L.Rev. 213, 235–36 (1987). In Braschi v. Stahl Associates Co., 74 N.Y.2d 201, 544 N.Y.S.2d 784, 543 N.E.2d 49 (1989), the New York Court of Appeals upheld a preliminary injunction preventing the eviction of Miguel Braschi from the rent-controlled apartment he had shared with Leslie Blanchard for eleven years. A plurality of the court, led by Judge Titone and joined by Judges Kaye and Alexander, interpreted New York City Rent and Eviction Regulations § 2204.6(d), which provides that "[n]o occupant of housing accommodations shall be evicted under this section where the occupant is either the surviving spouse of the deceased tenant or some other member of the deceased tenant's family who has been living with the tenant," to include same-sex couples. Judge Titone reasoned that:

> * * * we conclude that the term family, as used in 9 NYCRR 2204.6(d), should not be rigidly restricted to those people who have formalized their relationship by obtaining, for instance, a marriage certificate or an adoption order. The intended protection against sudden eviction should not rest on fictitious legal distinctions or genetic history, but instead should find its foundation in the reality of family life. In the context of eviction, a more realistic, and certainly equally valid, view of a family includes two adult lifetime partners whose relationship is long term and characterized by an emotional and financial commitment and interdependence. This view comports both with our society's traditional concept of "family" and with the expectations of individuals who live in such nuclear units (see, also, 829 Seventh Ave. Co. v. Reider, 67 N.Y.2d 930, 931–932, 502 N.Y.S.2d 715, 493 N.E.2d 939 [interpreting 9 NYCRR 2204.6(d)'s additional "living with" re-quirement to mean living with the named tenant "in a *family unit,* which in turn connotes an arrangement, whatever its duration, bearing some indicia of permanence or continuity" (emphasis supplied)]). In fact, Webster's Dictio-nary defines "family" *first* as "a group of people united by certain convictions or common affiliation" (Webster's Ninth New Collegiate Dictionary 448 [1984]; see, Ballantine's Law Dictionary 456 [3d ed. 1969] ["family" defined as "(p)rimarily, the collective body of persons who live in one house and under one head or management"]; Black's Law Dictionary 543 [Special Deluxe 5th ed. 1979]). Hence, it is reasonable to conclude that, in using the term "family," the Legislature intended to extend protection to those who reside in households having all of the normal familial characteristics. Appel-lant Braschi should therefore be afforded the opportunity to prove that he and Blanchard had such a household.

This definition of "family" is consistent with both of the competing purposes of the rent-control laws: the protection of individuals from sudden dislocation and the gradual transition to a free market system. Family members, whether or not related by blood, or law who have always treated the apartment as their family home will be protected against the hardship of eviction following the death of the named tenant, thereby furthering the Legislature's goals of preventing dislocation and preserving family units which might otherwise be broken apart upon eviction. This approach will foster the transition from rent control to rent stabilization by drawing a distinction between those individuals who are, in fact, genuine family members, and those who are mere roommates (see, Real Property Law § 235–f; Yorkshire Towers Co. v. Harpster, 134 Misc.2d 384, 510 N.Y.S.2d 976) or newly discovered relatives hoping to inherit the rent-controlled apartment after the existing tenant's death.

Id., 74 N.Y.2d at 211, 544 N.Y.S.2d at 788–89, 543 N.E.2d at 53–54. Judge Bellacosa, concurring, saw no reason to choose between the differing definitions of "family" advocated by the plurality and the dissent. In his view, it was enough that irreparable harm would result from the eviction:

> The plurality opinion favors the petitioner's side by invoking the nomenclature of "nuclear"/"normal"/"genuine" family versus the "traditional"/"legally recognizable" family selected by the dissenting opinion in favor of the landlord. I eschew both polar camps because I see no valid reason for deciding so broadly; indeed, there are cogent reasons not to yaw towards either end of the spectrum.

> The application of the governing word and statute to reach a decision in this case can be accomplished on a narrow and legitimate jurisprudential track. The enacting body has selected an unqualified word for a socially remedial statute, intended as a protection against one of the harshest decrees known to the law—eviction from one's home. Traditionally, in such circumstances, generous construction is favored. Petitioner has made his shared home in the affected apartment for 10 years. The only other occupant of that rent-controlled apartment over that same extended period of time was the tenant-in-law who has now died, precipitating this battle for the apartment. The best guidance available to the regulatory agency for correctly applying the rule in such circumstances is that it would be irrational not to include this petitioner and it is a more reasonable reflection of the intention behind the regulation to protect a person such as petitioner as within the regulation's class of "family". In that respect, he qualifies as a tenant in fact for purposes of the interlocking provisions and policies of the rent-control law. Therefore, under CPLR 6301, there would unquestionably be irreparable harm by not upholding the preliminary relief Supreme Court has decreed; the likelihood of success seems quite good since four Judges of this court, albeit by different rationales, agree at least that petitioner fits under the beneficial umbrella of the regulation; and the balance of equities would appear to favor petitioner.

Id., 74 N.Y.2d at 215, 544 N.Y.S.2d at 791, 543 N.E.2d at 56. Judges Simons and Hancock, in dissent, interpreted the regulation as limited to persons related to the decedent by blood, marriage, or adoption:

> Central to any interpretation of the regulatory language is a determination of its purpose. There can be little doubt that the purpose of section 2204.6(d) was to create succession rights to a possessory interest in real property where the tenant of record has died or vacated the apartment * * *. It creates a new tenancy for every surviving family member living with decedent at the time of death who then becomes a new statutory tenant until death or until he or she vacates the apartment. The State concerns underlying this provision include the orderly and just succession of property interests (which includes protecting a deceased's spouse and family from loss of their

longtime home) and the professed State objective that there be a gradual transition from government regulation to a normal market of free bargaining between landlord and tenant. Those objectives require a weighing of the interests of certain individuals living with the tenant of record at his or her death and the interests of the landlord in regaining possession of its property and rerenting it under the less onerous rent-stabilization laws. The interests are properly balanced if the regulation's exception is applied by using objectively verifiable relationships based on blood, marriage and adoption, as the State has historically done in the estate succession laws, family court acts and similar legislation * * *. The distinction is warranted because members of families, so defined, assume certain legal obligations to each other and to third persons, such as creditors, which are not imposed on unrelated individuals and this legal interdependency is worthy of consideration in determining which individuals are entitled to succeed to the interest of the statutory tenant in rent-controlled premises. Moreover, such an interpretation promotes certainty and consistency in the law and obviates the need for drawn out hearings and litigation focusing on such intangibles as the strength and duration of the relationship and the extent of the emotional and financial interdependency * * *. So limited, the regulation may be viewed as a tempered response, balancing the rights of landlords with those of the tenant. To come within that protected class, individuals must comply with State laws relating to marriage or adoption. Plaintiff cannot avail himself of these institutions, of course, but that only points up the need for a legislative solution, not a judicial one * * *.

Id., 74 N.Y.2d at 218–19, 544 N.Y.S.2d at 793, 543 N.E.2d at 58. Which of the three opinions has it right? The New York Times editorialized that:

> Judge Titone's view is humane; it is also impractical and illustrates how a warm heart can sometimes turn the law upside down. There may be strong reasons for legislators to broaden the legal definition of family. But absent such change, case-by-case judicial redefinition risks unanticipated grief. In this case, for instance, Judge Titone risks turning more landlords into spies.

The New York Times, July 11, 1989, at A18, col. 1. Do you agree? Should New York City "broaden the legal definition of family" by permitting gay and lesbian couples to register as domestic partners? Denmark created the status of domestic partnership, a legal relationship that is said to be the functional equivalent of marriage, except that adoption is not permitted, and the State Lutheran Church is not required to recognize it. San Francisco Chronicle, May 27 1989, at A15, col. 3. Eleven gay couples were "married" under the new law on October 1, 1989. San Francisco Chronicle, October 2, 1989, at A14, col. 1. San Francisco approved a domestic partners ordinance in 1991. In 1996, the Board of Supervisors authorized wedding ceremonies for gay and lesbian couples in City Hall. San Francisco Chronicle, January 30, 1996, at A1, col. 5.

"Domestic Partnership" Ordinances, such as Ordinance No. 22, enacted by the City of West Hollywood on February 21, 1985, provide limited legal recognition for homosexual couples, and some California trial court cases have extended employee benefits to homosexual partners. See Roberta Achtenberg, Partner Benefits Litigation: Expanding Definitions of the Family, 2 Cal.Fam.L. Monthly 351 (1968). But see Hinman v. Department of Personnel Administraton, 167 Cal.App.3d 516, 213 Cal.Rptr. 410 (1985), in which the court rejected the argument that a limitation of dental benefits to family members of state employees, where "family members" excluded persons living in nonmarital cohabitation, constituted a discrimination against homosexual employees. Plaintiffs' suggested distinction of their situation from that of nonmarital heterosexual couples, that those couples could marry if they liked but plaintiffs could not legally marry their "family partners," was brushed aside with the comment that relief should be sought in an amendment to the state marriage laws. Was that response adequate? The couple, Boyce Hinman and Larry Beaty, subsequently lost their challenge to an insurance company's practice of limiting "umbrella" policies for a single premium to married couples. Beaty v. Truck Insurance Exchange, 6 Cal.App.4th 1455, 8 Cal.Rptr.2d 593 (1992).

2. THE UNWED PARENT

LEHR v. ROBERTSON

Supreme Court of the United States, 1983.
463 U.S. 248, 103 S.Ct. 2985, 77 L.Ed.2d 614.

JUSTICE STEVENS delivered the opinion of the Court.

The question presented is whether New York has sufficiently protected an unmarried father's inchoate relationship with a child whom he has never supported and rarely seen in the two years since her birth. The appellant, Jonathan Lehr, claims that the Due Process and Equal Protection Clauses of the Fourteenth Amendment, as interpreted in *Stanley v. Illinois,* 405 U.S. 645 (1972), and *Caban v. Mohammed,* 441 U.S. 380 (1979), give him an absolute right to notice and an opportunity to be heard before the child may be adopted. We disagree.

Jessica M. was born out of wedlock on November 9, 1976. Her mother, Lorraine Robertson, married Richard Robertson eight months after Jessica's birth. On December 21, 1978, when Jessica was over two years old, the Robertsons filed an adoption petition in the Family Court of Ulster County, New York. The court heard their testimony and received a favorable report from the Ulster County Department of Social Services. On March 7, 1979, the court entered an order of adoption. In this proceeding, appellant contends that the adoption order is invalid because he, Jessica's putative father, was not given advance notice of the adoption proceeding.

The State of New York maintains a "putative father registry." A man who files with that registry demonstrates his intent to claim paternity of a child born out of wedlock and is therefore entitled to receive notice of any proceeding to adopt that child. Before entering Jessica's adoption order, the Ulster County Family Court had the putative father registry examined. Although appellant claims to be Jessica's natural father, he had not entered his name in the registry.

In addition to the persons whose names are listed on the putative father registry, New York law requires that notice of an adoption proceeding be given to several other classes of possible fathers of children born out of wedlock—those who have been adjudicated to be the father, those who have been identified as the father on the child's birth certificate, those who live openly with the child and the child's mother and who hold themselves out to be the father, those who have been identified as the father by the mother in a sworn written statement, and those who were married to the child's mother before the child was six months old. Appellant admittedly was not a member of any of those classes. He had lived with appellee prior to Jessica's birth and visited her in the hospital when Jessica was born, but his name does not appear on Jessica's birth certificate. He did not live with appellee or Jessica after Jessica's birth, he has never provided them with any financial support, and he has never offered to marry appellee. Nevertheless, he contends that the following special circumstances gave him a constitutional right to notice and a hearing before Jessica was adopted.

On January 30, 1979, one month after the adoption proceeding was commenced in Ulster County, appellant filed a "visitation and paternity petition" in the Westchester County Family Court. In that petition, he asked for a determination of paternity, an order of support, and reasonable visitation privileges with Jessica. Notice of that proceeding was served on appellee on February 22, 1979. Four days later appellee's attorney informed the Ulster County Court that appellant had commenced a paternity proceeding in Westchester County; the Ulster County judge then entered an order staying appellant's paternity proceeding until he could rule on a motion to change the venue of that proceeding to Ulster County. On March 3, 1979, appellant received notice of the change of venue motion and, for the first time, learned that an adoption proceeding was pending in Ulster County.

On March 7, 1979, appellant's attorney telephoned the Ulster County judge to inform him that he planned to seek a stay of the adoption proceeding pending the determination of the paternity petition. In that telephone conversation, the judge advised the lawyer that he had already signed the adoption order earlier that day. According to appellant's attorney, the judge stated that he was aware of the pending paternity petition but did not believe he was required to give notice to appellant prior to the entry of the order of adoption.

Thereafter, the Family Court in Westchester County granted appellee's motion to dismiss the paternity petition, holding that the putative father's right to seek paternity "must be deemed severed so long as an order of adoption exists." App. 228. Appellant did not appeal from that dismissal. On June 22, 1979, appellant filed a petition to vacate the order of adoption on the ground that it was obtained by fraud and in violation of his constitutional rights. The Ulster County Family Court received written and oral argument on the question whether it had "dropped the ball" by approving the adoption without giving appellant advance notice. Tr. 53. After deliberating for several months, it denied the petition, explaining its decision in a thorough written opinion. *In re Adoption of Martz,* 102 Misc.2d 102, 423 N.Y.S.2d 378 (1979).

The Appellate Division of the Supreme Court affirmed. *In re Adoption of Jessica "XX,"* 77 App.Div.2d 381, 434 N.Y.S.2d 772 (1980).

* * *

Appellant has now invoked our appellate jurisdiction. He offers two alternative grounds for holding the New York statutory scheme unconstitutional. First, he contends that a putative father's actual or potential relationship with a child born out of wedlock is an interest in liberty which may not be destroyed without due process of law; he argues therefore that he had a constitutional right to prior notice and an opportunity to be heard before he was deprived of that interest. Second, he contends that the gender-based classification in the statute, which both denied him the right to consent to Jessica's adoption and accorded him fewer procedural rights than her mother, violated the Equal Protection Clause.

THE DUE PROCESS CLAIM

* * *

I

The intangible fibers that connect parent and child have infinite variety. They are woven throughout the fabric of our society, providing it with strength, beauty, and flexibility. It is self-evident that they are sufficiently vital to merit constitutional protection in appropriate cases. In deciding whether this is such a case, however, we must consider the broad framework that has traditionally been used to resolve the legal problems arising from the parent-child relationship.

* * *

This Court has examined the extent to which a natural father's biological relationship with his child receives protection under the Due Process Clause in precisely three cases: *Stanley v. Illinois,* 405 U.S. 645 (1972), *Quilloin v. Walcott,* 434 U.S. 246 (1978), and *Caban v. Mohammed,* 441 U.S. 380 (1979).

Stanley involved the constitutionality of an Illinois statute that conclusively presumed every father of a child born out of wedlock to be an unfit person to have custody of his children. The father in that case had lived with his children all their lives and had lived with their mother for 18 years. There was nothing in the record to indicate that Stanley had been a neglectful father who had not cared for his children. * * * Under the statute, however, the nature of the actual relationship between parent and child was completely irrelevant. Once the mother died, the children were automatically made wards of the State. Relying in part on a Michigan case [14] recognizing that the preservation of "a subsisting relationship with the child's father" may better serve the child's best interest than "uprooting him from the family which he knew from birth," * * * the Court held that the Due Process Clause was violated by the automatic destruction of the custodial relationship without giving the father any opportunity to present evidence regarding his fitness as a parent.

Quilloin involved the constitutionality of a Georgia statute that authorized the adoption, over the objection of the natural father, of a child born out of wedlock. The father in that case had never legitimated the child. It was only after the mother had remarried and her new husband had filed an adoption petition that the natural father sought visitation rights and filed a petition for legitimation. The trial court found adoption by the new husband to be in the child's best interests, and we unanimously held that action to be consistent with the Due Process Clause.

Caban involved the conflicting claims of two natural parents who had maintained joint custody of their children from the time of their birth until they were respectively two and four years old. The father challenged the

14. *In re Mark T.,* 8 Mich.App. 122, 154 N.W.2d 27 (1967).

validity of an order authorizing the mother's new husband to adopt the children; he relied on both the Equal Protection Clause and the Due Process Clause. Because this Court upheld his equal protection claim, the majority did not address his due process challenge. * * *

The difference between the developed parent-child relationship that was implicated in *Stanley* and *Caban,* and the potential relationship involved in *Quilloin* and this case, is both clear and significant. When an unwed father demonstrates a full commitment to the responsibilities of parenthood by "com[ing] forward to participate in the rearing of his child," *Caban,* * * * his interest in personal contact with his child acquires substantial protection under the Due Process Clause. At that point it may be said that he "act[s] as a father toward his children." * * * But the mere existence of a biological link does not merit equivalent constitutional protection. The actions of judges neither create nor sever genetic bonds. "[T]he importance of the familial relationship, to the individuals involved and to the society, stems from the emotional attachments that derive from the intimacy of daily association, and from the role it plays in 'promot[ing] a way of life' through the instruction of children * * * as well as from the fact of blood relationship." *Smith v. Organization of Foster Families for Equality and Reform,* 431 U.S. 816, 844 (1977) (quoting *Wisconsin v. Yoder,* 406 U.S. 205, 231–233 (1972)).

The significance of the biological connection is that it offers the natural father an opportunity that no other male possesses to develop a relationship with his offspring. If he grasps that opportunity and accepts some measure of responsibility for the child's future, he may enjoy the blessings of the parent-child relationship and make uniquely valuable contributions to the child's development. If he fails to do so, the Federal Constitution will not automatically compel a State to listen to his opinion of where the child's best interests lie.

In this case, we are not assessing the constitutional adequacy of New York's procedures for terminating a developed relationship. Appellant has never had any significant custodial, personal, or financial relationship with Jessica, and he did not seek to establish a legal tie until after she was two years old. We are concerned only with whether New York has adequately protected his opportunity to form such a relationship.

II

The most effective protection of the putative father's opportunity to develop a relationship with his child is provided by the laws that authorize formal marriage and govern its consequences. But the availability of that protection is, of course, dependent on the will of both parents of the child. Thus, New York has adopted a special statutory scheme to protect the unmarried father's interest in assuming a responsible role in the future of his child.

After this Court's decision in *Stanley,* the New York Legislature appointed a special commission to recommend legislation that would accommodate both the interests of biological fathers in their children and the children's interest in prompt and certain adoption procedures. The commission recommended, and the legislature enacted, a statutory adoption scheme that automatically provides notice to seven categories of putative fathers who are likely to have assumed some responsibility for the care of their natural children. If this scheme were likely to omit many responsible fathers, and if qualification for notice were beyond the control of an interested putative father, it might be thought procedurally inadequate. Yet, as all of the New York courts that reviewed this matter observed, the right to receive notice was completely within appellant's control. By mailing a postcard to the putative father registry, he could have guaranteed that he would receive notice of any proceedings to adopt Jessica. The possibility that he may have failed to do so because of his ignorance of the law cannot be a sufficient reason for criticizing the law itself. The New York Legislature concluded that a more open-ended notice requirement would merely complicate the adoption process, threaten the privacy interests of unwed mothers, create the risk of unnecessary controversy, and impair the desired finality of adoption decrees. Regardless of whether we would have done likewise if we were legislators instead of judges, we surely cannot characterize the State's conclusion as arbitrary.

Appellant argues, however, that even if the putative father's opportunity to establish a relationship with an illegitimate child is adequately protected by the New York statutory scheme in the normal case, he was nevertheless entitled to special notice because the court and the mother knew that he had filed an affiliation proceeding in another court. This argument amounts to nothing more than an indirect attack on the notice provisions of the New York statute. The legitimate state interests in facilitating the adoption of young children and having the adoption proceeding completed expeditiously that underlie the entire statutory scheme also justify a trial judge's determination to require all interested parties to adhere precisely to the procedural requirements of the statute. The Constitution does not require either a trial judge or a litigant to give special notice to nonparties who are presumptively capable of asserting and protecting their own rights. Since the New York statutes adequately protected appellant's inchoate interest in establishing a relationship with Jessica, we find no merit in the claim that his constitutional rights were offended because the Family Court strictly complied with the notice provisions of the statute.

THE EQUAL PROTECTION CLAIM

* * *

The legislation at issue in this case, N.Y.Dom.Rel.Law §§ 111 and 111–a (McKinney 1977 and Supp. 1982–1983), is intended to establish procedures for adoptions. Those procedures are designed to promote the best interests of the child, to protect the rights of interested third parties, and to ensure promptness and finality. To serve those ends, the legislation guarantees to certain people the right to veto an adoption and the right to prior notice of any adoption proceeding. The mother of an illegitimate child is always within that favored class, but only certain putative fathers are included. Appellant contends that the gender-based distinction is invidious.

As we have already explained, the existence or nonexistence of a substantial relationship between parent and child is a relevant criterion in evaluating both the rights of the parent and the best interests of the child. In *Quilloin v. Walcott,* we noted that the putative father, like appellant, "ha[d] never shouldered any significant responsibility with respect to the daily supervision, education, protection, or care of the child. Appellant does not complain of his exemption from these responsibilities * * *." We therefore found that a Georgia statute that always required a mother's consent to the adoption of a child born out of wedlock, but required the father's consent only if he had legitimated the child, did not violate the Equal Protection Clause. Because appellant, like the father in *Quilloin,* has never established a substantial relationship with his daughter, * * * the New York statutes at issue in this case did not operate to deny appellant equal protection.

We have held that these statutes may not constitutionally be applied in that class of cases where the mother and father are in fact similarly situated with regard to their relationship with the child. In *Caban v. Mohammed,* * * * the Court held that it violated the Equal Protection Clause to grant the mother a veto over the adoption of a 4–year-old girl and a 6–year-old boy, but not to grant a veto to their father, who had admitted paternity and had participated in the rearing of the children. The Court made it clear, however, that if the father had not "come forward to participate in the rearing of his child, nothing in the Equal Protection Clause [would] preclud[e] the State from withholding from him the privilege of vetoing the adoption of that child." * * *

Jessica's parents are not like the parents involved in *Caban.* Whereas appellee had a continuous custodial responsibility for Jessica, appellant never established any custodial, personal, or financial relationship with her. If one parent has an established custodial relationship with the child and the other parent has either abandoned or never established a relationship, the Equal Protection Clause does not prevent a State from according the two parents different legal rights.

The judgment of the New York Court of Appeals is

Affirmed.

JUSTICE WHITE, with whom JUSTICE MARSHALL and JUSTICE BLACKMUN join, dissenting.

The question in this case is whether the State may, consistent with the Due Process Clause, deny notice and an opportunity to be heard in an adoption proceeding to a putative father when the State has actual notice of his existence, whereabouts, and interest in the child.

I

* * *

According to Lehr, he and Jessica's mother met in 1971 and began living together in 1974. The couple cohabited for approximately two years, until Jessica's birth in 1976. Throughout the pregnancy and after the birth, Lorraine acknowledged to friends and relatives that Lehr was Jessica's father; Lorraine told Lehr that she had reported to the New York State Department of Social Services that he was the father. Lehr visited Lorraine and Jessica in the hospital every day during Lorraine's confinement. According to Lehr, from the time Lorraine was discharged from the hospital until August 1978, she concealed her whereabouts from him. During this time Lehr never ceased his efforts to locate Lorraine and Jessica and achieved sporadic success until August 1977, after which time he was unable to locate them at all. On those occasions when he did determine Lorraine's location, he visited with her and her children to the extent she was willing to permit it. When Lehr, with the aid of a detective agency, located Lorraine and Jessica in August 1978, Lorraine was already married to Mr. Robertson. Lehr asserts that at this time he offered to provide financial assistance and to set up a trust fund for Jessica, but that Lorraine refused. Lorraine threatened Lehr with arrest unless he stayed away and refused to permit him to see Jessica. Thereafter Lehr retained counsel who wrote to Lorraine in early December 1978, requesting that she permit Lehr to visit Jessica and threatening legal action on Lehr's behalf. On December 21, 1978, perhaps as a response to Lehr's threatened legal action, appellees commenced the adoption action at issue here.

* * *

Lehr's version of the "facts" paints a far different picture than that portrayed by the majority. The majority's recitation, that "[a]ppellant has never had any significant custodial, personal, or financial relationship with Jessica, and he did not seek to establish a legal tie until after she was two years old," obviously does not tell the whole story. Appellant has never been afforded an opportunity to present his case. The legitimation proceeding he instituted was first stayed, and then dismissed, on appellees' motions. Nor could appellant establish his interest during the adoption proceedings, for it is the failure to provide Lehr notice and an opportunity to be heard there that is at issue here. We cannot fairly make a judgment based on the quality or substance of a relationship without a complete and developed factual record. This case requires us to assume that Lehr's allegations are true—that but for the actions of the child's mother there would have been the kind of significant relationship that the majority concedes is entitled to the full panoply of procedural due process protections.

I reject the peculiar notion that the only significance of the biological connection between father and child is that "it offers the natural father an opportunity that no other male possesses to develop a relationship with his offspring." A "mere biological relationship" is not as unimportant in determining the nature of liberty interests as the majority suggests.

"[T]he usual understanding of 'family' implies biological relationships, and most decisions treating the relation between parent and child have stressed this element." *Smith v. Organization of Foster Families,* [431 U.S. 816], at 843. The "biological connection" is itself a relationship that creates a protected interest. Thus the "nature" of the interest is the parent-child relationship; how well developed that relationship has become goes to its "weight," not its "nature." [4] Whether Lehr's interest is entitled to constitutional protection does not entail a searching inquiry into the quality of the relationship but a simple determination of the *fact* that the relationship exists—a fact that even the majority agrees must be assumed to be established.

* * *

4. The majority's citation of *Quilloin* and *Caban* as examples that the Constitution does not require the same procedural protections for the interests of all unwed fathers is disingenu-

ous. Neither case involved notice and opportunity to be heard. In both, the unwed fathers were notified and participated as parties in the adoption proceedings. * * *

II

In this case, of course, there was no question about either the identity or the location of the putative father. The mother knew exactly who he was and both she and the court entering the order of adoption knew precisely where he was and how to give him actual notice that his parental rights were about to be terminated by an adoption order.

* * *

The State concedes this much but insists that Lehr has had all the process that is due to him.

* * *

I am unpersuaded by the State's position. In the first place, § 111–a defines six categories of unwed fathers to whom notice must be given even though they have not placed their names on file pursuant to the section. Those six categories, however, do not include fathers such as Lehr who have initiated filiation proceedings, even though their identity and interest are as clearly and easily ascertainable as those fathers in the six categories. Initiating such proceedings necessarily involves a formal acknowledgment of paternity, and requiring the State to take note of such a case in connection with pending adoption proceedings would be a trifling burden, no more than the State undertakes when there is a final adjudication in a paternity action. Indeed, there would appear to be more reason to give notice to those such as Lehr who acknowledge paternity than to those who have been adjudged to be a father in a contested paternity action.

The State asserts that any problem in this respect is overcome by the seventh category of putative fathers to whom notice must be given, namely, those fathers who have identified themselves in the putative fathers' register maintained by the State. Since Lehr did not take advantage of this device to make his interest known, the State contends, he was not entitled to notice and a hearing even though his identity, location, and interest were known to the adoption court prior to entry of the adoption order. I have difficulty with this position. First, it represents a grudging and crabbed approach to due process. The State is quite willing to give notice and a hearing to putative fathers who have made themselves known by resorting to the putative fathers' register. It makes little sense to me to deny notice and hearing to a father who has not placed his name in the register but who has unmistakably identified himself by filing suit to establish his paternity and has notified the adoption court of his action and his interest. I thus need not question the statutory scheme on its face. Even assuming that Lehr would have been foreclosed if his failure to utilize the register had somehow disadvantaged the State, he effectively made himself known by other means, and it is the sheerest formalism to deny him a hearing because he informed the State in the wrong manner.

No state interest is substantially served by denying Lehr adequate notice and a hearing. The State no doubt has an interest in expediting adoption proceedings to prevent a child from remaining unduly long in the custody of the State or foster parents. But this is not an adoption involving a child in the custody of an authorized state agency. Here the child is in the custody of the mother and will remain in her custody. Moreover, had Lehr utilized the putative fathers' register, he would have been granted a prompt hearing, and there was no justifiable reason, in terms of delay, to refuse him a hearing in the circumstances of this case.

The State's undoubted interest in the finality of adoption orders likewise is not well served by a procedure that will deny notice and a hearing to a father whose identity and location are known. As this case well illustrates, denying notice and a hearing to such a father may result in years of additional litigation and threaten the reopening of adoption proceedings and the vacation of the adoption. Here, the Family Court's unseemly rush to enter an adoption order after ordering that cause be shown why the filiation proceeding should not be transferred and consolidated with the adoption proceeding can hardly be justified by the interest in finality. To the contrary, the adoption order entered in March 1979 has remained open to question until this very day.

Because in my view the failure to provide Lehr with notice and an opportunity to be heard violated rights guaranteed him by the Due Process Clause, I need not address the question whether § 111–a violates the Equal Protection Clause by discriminating between categories of unwed fathers or by discriminating on the basis of gender.

Respectfully, I dissent.

MICHAEL H. v. GERALD D.

Supreme Court of the United States, 1989.
491 U.S. 110, 109 S.Ct. 2333, 105 L.Ed.2d 91,
rehearing denied 492 U.S. 937, 110 S.Ct. 22, 106 L.Ed.2d 634 (1989).

JUSTICE SCALIA announced the judgment of the Court and delivered an opinion, in which THE CHIEF JUSTICE joins, and in all but note 6 of which JUSTICE O'CONNOR and JUSTICE KENNEDY join.

Under California law, a child born to a married woman living with her husband is presumed to be a child of the marriage. Cal.Evid.Code Ann. § 621 (West Supp.1989). The presumption of legitimacy may be rebutted only by the husband or wife, and then only in limited circumstances. *Ibid.* The instant appeal presents the claim that this presumption infringes upon the due process rights of a man who wishes to establish his paternity of a child born to the wife of another man, and the claim that it infringes upon the constitutional right of the child to maintain a relationship with her natural father.

I

The facts of this case are, we must hope, extraordinary. On May 9, 1976, in Las Vegas, Nevada, Carole D., an international model, and Gerald D., a top executive in a French oil company, were married. The couple established a home in Playa del Rey, California in which they resided as husband and wife when one or the other was not out of the country on business. In the summer of 1978, Carole became involved in an adulterous affair with a neighbor, Michael H. In September 1980, she conceived a child, Victoria D., who was born on May 11, 1981. Gerald was listed as father on the birth certificate and has always held Victoria out to the world as his daughter.

Soon after delivery of the child, however, Carole informed Michael that she believed he might be the father.

In the first three years of her life, Victoria remained always with Carole, but found herself within a variety of quasi-family units. In October 1981, Gerald moved to New York City to pursue his business interests, but Carole chose to remain in California. The end of that month, Carole and Michael had blood tests of themselves and Victoria, which showed a 98.07% probability that Michael was Victoria's father. In January 1982, Carole visited Michael in St. Thomas, where his primary business interests were based. There Michael held Victoria out as his child. In March, however, Carole left Michael and returned to California, where she took up residence with yet another man, Scott K. Later that spring, and again in the summer, Carole and Victoria spent time with Gerald in New York City, as well as on vacation in Europe. In the fall, they returned to Scott in California.

In November 1982, rebuffed in his attempts to visit Victoria, Michael filed a filiation action in California Superior Court to establish his paternity and right to visitation. In March 1983, the court appointed an attorney and guardian ad litem to represent Victoria's interests. Victoria then filed a cross-complaint asserting that if she had more than one psychological or *de facto* father, she was entitled to maintain her filial relationship, with all of the attendant rights, duties, and obligations, with both. In May 1983, Carole filed a motion for summary judgment. During this period, from March through July of 1983, Carole was again living with Gerald in New York. In August, however, she returned to California, became involved once again with Michael, and instructed her attorneys to remove the summary judgment motion from the calendar.

For the ensuing eight months, when Michael was not in St. Thomas he lived with Carole and Victoria in Carole's apartment in Los Angeles, and held Victoria out as his daughter. In April 1984, Carole and Michael signed a stipulation that Michael was Victoria's natural father. Carole left Michael the next month, however, and instructed her attorneys not to file the stipulation. In June 1984, Carole reconciled with Gerald and joined him in New York, where they now live with Victoria and two other children since born into the marriage.

In May 1984, Michael and Victoria, through her guardian ad litem, sought visitation rights for Michael *pendente lite*. To assist in determining whether visitation would be in Victoria's best interests, the Superior Court appointed a psychologist to evaluate Victoria, Gerald, Michael, and Carole. The psychologist recommended that Carole retain sole custody, but that Michael be allowed continued contact with Victoria pursuant to a restricted visitation schedule. The court concurred and ordered that Michael be provided with limited visitation privileges *pendente lite*.

On October 19, 1984, Gerald, who had intervened in the action, moved for summary judgment on the ground that under Cal.Evid.Code § 621 there were no triable issues of fact as to Victoria's paternity. This law provides that "the issue of a wife cohabiting with her husband, who is not impotent or sterile, is conclusively presumed to be a child of the marriage." Cal.Evid.Code Ann. § 621(a) (Supp.1989). The presumption may be rebutted by blood tests, but only if a motion for such tests is made, within two years from the date of the child's birth, either by the husband or, if the natural father has filed an affidavit acknowledging paternity, by the wife. § 621(c) and (d).

On January 28, 1985, having found that affidavits submitted by Carole and Gerald sufficed to demonstrate that the two were cohabiting at conception and birth and that Gerald was neither sterile nor impotent, the Superior Court granted Gerald's motion for summary judgment, rejecting Michael's and Victoria's challenges to the constitutionality of § 621. The court also denied their motions for continued visitation pending the appeal under Cal.Civ.Code § 4601, which provides that a court may, in its discretion, grant "reasonable visitation rights * * * to any * * * person having an interest in the welfare of the child." Cal.Civ.Code Ann. § 4601 (West Supp.1989). It found that allowing such visitation would "violat[e] the intention of the Legislature by impugning the integrity of the family unit."

* * * After submission of briefs and a hearing, the California Court of Appeal affirmed the judgment of the Superior Court and upheld the constitutionality of the statute. * * *

* * * Before us, Michael and Victoria both raise equal protection and due process challenges. We do not reach Michael's equal protection claim, however, as it was neither raised nor passed upon below. * * *

II

The California statute that is the subject of this litigation is, in substance, more than a century old. * * * In their present form, the substantive provisions of the statute are as follows:

"§ 621. Child of the marriage; notice of motion for blood tests

"(a) Except as provided in subdivision (b), the issue of a wife cohabiting with her husband, who is not impotent or sterile, is conclusively presumed to be a child of the marriage.

"(b) Notwithstanding the provisions of subdivision (a), if the court finds that the conclusions of all the experts, as disclosed by the evidence based upon blood tests * * * are that the husband is not the father of the child, the question of paternity of the husband shall be resolved accordingly.

"(c) The notice of motion for blood tests under subdivision (b) may be raised by the husband not later than two years from the child's date of birth.

"(d) The notice of motion for blood tests under subdivision (b) may be raised by the mother of the child not later than two years from the child's date of birth if the child's biological father has filed an affidavit with the court acknowledging paternity of the child.

"(e) The provisions of subdivision (b) shall not apply to any case [dealing with artificial insemination] or to any case in which the wife, with the consent of the husband, conceived by means of a surgical procedure."

III

We address first the claims of Michael. At the outset, it is necessary to clarify what he sought and what he was denied. California law, like nature itself, makes no provision for dual fatherhood. Michael was seeking to be declared *the* father of Victoria. The immediate benefit he evidently sought to obtain from that status was visitation rights. * * * But if Michael were successful in being declared the father, other rights would follow—most importantly, the right to be considered as the parent who should have custody, * * *. All parental rights, including visitation, were automatically denied by denying Michael status as the father. While Cal.Civ.Code Ann. § 4601 places it within the discretionary power of a court to award visitation rights to a nonparent, the Superior Court here, affirmed by the Court of Appeal, held that California law denies visitation, against the wishes of the mother, to a putative father who has been prevented by § 621 from establishing his paternity. * * *

Michael raises two related challenges to the constitutionality of § 621. * * * We * * * reject Michael's procedural due process challenge and proceed to his substantive claim.

Michael contends as a matter of substantive due process that because he has established a parental relationship with Victoria, protection of Gerald's and Carole's marital union is an insufficient state interest to support termination of that relationship. This argument is, of course, predicated on the assertion that Michael has a constitutionally protected liberty interest in his relationship with Victoria.

* * * As we have put it, the Due Process Clause affords only those protections "so rooted in the traditions and conscience of our people as to be ranked as fundamental." *Snyder v. Massachusetts,* 291 U.S. 97, 105, 54 S.Ct. 330, 332, 78 L.Ed. 674 (1934) (Cardozo, J.). Our cases reflect "continual insistence upon respect for the teachings of history [and] solid recognition of the basic values that underlie our society * * *." *Griswold v. Connecticut,* 381 U.S. 479, 501, 85 S.Ct. 1678, 1690, 14 L.Ed.2d 510 (1965) (Harlan, J., concurring in judgment).

This insistence that the asserted liberty interest be rooted in history and tradition is evident, as elsewhere, in our cases according constitutional protection to certain parental rights. Michael reads the landmark case of *Stanley v. Illinois,* * * * and the subsequent cases of *Quilloin v. Walcott,* * * * *Caban v. Mohammed,* * * * and *Lehr v. Robertson,* * * * as establishing that a liberty interest is created by biological fatherhood plus an established parental relationship—factors that exist in the present case as well. We think that distorts the rationale of those cases. As we view them, they rest not upon such isolated factors but upon the historic respect—indeed, sanctity would not be too strong a term—traditionally accorded to the relationships that develop within the unitary family.[3] * * *

3. Justice Brennan asserts that only "a pinched conception of 'the family'" would exclude Michael, Carole and Victoria from protection. * * * We disagree. The family unit accorded traditional respect in our society, which we have referred to as the "unitary family," is typified, of course, by the marital family, but also includes the household of unmarried parents and their children. Perhaps the concept can be expanded even beyond this, but it will bear no resemblance to traditionally respected relationships—and will thus cease to have any constitutional significance—if it is stretched so far as to include the relationship established between a married woman, her lover and their child, during a three-month sojourn in St. Thomas, or during a subsequent 8-month period when, if he happened to be in Los Angeles, he stayed with her and the child.

Thus, the legal issue in the present case reduces to whether the relationship between persons in the situation of Michael and Victoria has been treated as a protected family unit under the historic practices of our society, or whether on any other basis it has been accorded special protection. We think it impossible to find that it has. In fact, quite to the contrary, our traditions have protected the marital family (Gerald, Carole, and the child they acknowledge to be theirs) against the sort of claim Michael asserts.[4]

The presumption of legitimacy was a fundamental principle of the common law. H. Nicholas, Adulturine Bastardy 1 (1836). Traditionally, that presumption could be rebutted only by proof that a husband was incapable of procreation or had had no access to his wife during the relevant period. *Id.,* at 9–10 (citing Bracton, De Legibus et Consuetudinibus Angliae, bk. i, ch. 9, p. 6; bk. ii, ch. 29, p. 63, ch. 32, p. 70 (1569)). As explained by Blackstone, nonaccess could only be proved "if the husband be out of the kingdom of England (or, as the law somewhat loosely phrases it, *extra quatuor maria* [beyond the four seas]) for above nine months * * *." 1 Blackstone's Commentaries 456 (Chitty ed.1826). And, under the common law both in England and here, "neither husband nor wife [could] be a witness to prove access or nonaccess." J. Schouler, Law of the Domestic Relations § 225, p. 306 (3d ed.1882); R. Graveson & F. Crane, A Century of Family Law: 1857–1957, p. 158 (1957). The primary policy rationale underlying the common law's severe restrictions on rebuttal of the presumption appears to have been an aversion to declaring children illegitimate, see Schouler, *supra,* § 225, at 306–307; M. Grossberg, Governing the Hearth 201 (1985), thereby depriving them of rights of inheritance and succession, 2 Kent's Commentaries 175 (1827), and likely making them wards of the state. A secondary policy concern was the interest in promoting the "peace and tranquillity of States and families," Schouler, *supra,* § 225, at 304, quoting Boullenois, Traité des Status, bk. 1, p. 62, a goal that is obviously impaired by facilitating suits against husband and wife asserting that their children are illegitimate. Even though, as bastardy laws became less harsh, "[j]udges in both [England and the United States] gradually widened the acceptable range of evidence that could be offered by spouses, and placed restraints on the 'four seas rule' * * * [,] the law retained a strong bias against ruling the children of married women illegitimate." Grossberg, *supra,* at 202.

We have found nothing in the older sources, nor in the older cases, addressing specifically the power of the natural father to assert parental rights over a child born into a woman's existing marriage with another man. Since it is Michael's burden to establish that such a power (at least where the natural father has established a relationship with the child) is so deeply embedded within our traditions as to be a fundamental right, the lack of evidence alone might defeat his case. But the evidence shows that even in

---

4. Justice Brennan insists that in determining whether a liberty interest exists we must look at Michael's relationship with Victoria in isolation, without reference to the circumstance that Victoria's mother was married to someone else when the child was conceived, and that that woman and her husband wish to raise the child as their own. * * * We cannot imagine what compels this strange procedure of looking at the act which is assertedly the subject of a liberty interest in isolation from its effect upon other people—rather like inquiring whether there is a liberty interest in firing a gun where the case at hand happens to involve its discharge into another person's body. The logic of Justice Brennan's position leads to the conclusion that if Michael had begotten Victoria by rape, that fact would in no way affect his possession of a liberty interest in his relationship with her.

modern times—when, as we have noted, the rigid protection of the marital family has in other respects been relaxed—the ability of a person in Michael's position to claim paternity has not been generally acknowledged. For example, a 1957 annotation on the subject: "Who may dispute presumption of legitimacy of child conceived or born during wedlock," 53 ALR2d 572, shows three States (including California) with statutes limiting standing to the husband or wife and their descendants, one State (Louisiana) with a statute limiting it to the husband, two States (Florida and Texas) with judicial decisions limiting standing to the husband, and two States (Illinois and New York) with judicial decisions denying standing even to the mother. Not a single decision is set forth specifically according standing to the natural father, and "express indications of the nonexistence of any * * * limitation" upon standing were found only "in a few jurisdictions." * * *

Moreover, even if it were clear that one in Michael's position generally possesses, and has generally always possessed, standing to challenge the marital child's legitimacy, that would still not establish Michael's case. As noted earlier, what is at issue here is not entitlement to a state pronouncement that Victoria was begotten by Michael. It is no conceivable denial of constitutional right for a State to decline to declare facts unless some legal consequence hinges upon the requested declaration. What Michael asserts here is a right to have himself declared the natural father *and thereby to obtain parental prerogatives.* [5] What he must establish, therefore, is not that our society has traditionally allowed a natural father in his circumstances to establish paternity, but that it has traditionally accorded such a father parental rights, or at least has not traditionally denied them. Even if the law in all States had always been that the entire world could challenge the marital presumption and obtain a declaration as to who was the natural father, that would not advance Michael's claim. Thus, it is ultimately irrelevant, even for purposes of determining *current* social attitudes towards the alleged substantive right Michael asserts, that the present law in a number of States appears to allow the natural father—including the natural father who has not established a relationship with the child—the theoretical power to rebut the marital presumption, see Note, Rebutting the Marital Presumption: A Developed Relationship Test, 88 Col.L.Rev. 369, 373 (1988). What counts is whether the States in fact award substantive parental rights to the natural father of a child conceived within and born into an extant marital union that wishes to embrace the child. We are not aware of a single case, old or new, that has done so. This is not the stuff of which fundamental rights qualifying as liberty interests are made.[6]

5. According to Justice Brennan, Michael does not claim—and in order to prevail here need not claim—a substantive right to maintain a parental relationship with Victoria, but merely the right to "a hearing on the issue" of his paternity. *Post,* at * * * n. 12. "Michael's challenge * * * does not depend," we are told, "on his ability ultimately to obtain visitation rights." * * * To be sure it does not depend upon his ability ultimately to *obtain* those rights, but it surely depends upon his *asserting a claim* to those rights, which is precisely what Justice Brennan denies. We cannot grasp the concept of a "right to a hearing" on the part of

a person who claims no substantive entitlement that the hearing will assertedly vindicate.

6. Justice Brennan criticizes our methodology in using historical traditions specifically relating to the rights of an adulterous natural father, rather than inquiring more generally "whether parenthood is an interest that historically has received our attention and protection." * * * There seems to us no basis for the contention that this methodology is "nove[l]," * * *. For example, in *Bowers v. Hardwick,* 478 U.S. 186, 106 S.Ct. 2841, 92 L.Ed.2d 140 (1986), we noted that at the time

In *Lehr v. Robertson,* a case involving a natural father's attempt to block his child's adoption by the unwed mother's new husband, we observed that "[t]he significance of the biological connection is that it offers the natural father an opportunity that no other male possesses to develop a relationship with his offspring," * * * and we assumed that the Constitution might require some protection of that opportunity, * * *. Where, however, the child is born into an extant marital family, the natural father's unique opportunity conflicts with the similarly unique opportunity of the husband of the marriage; and it is not unconstitutional for the State to give categorical preference to the latter. In *Lehr* we quoted approvingly from Justice Stewart's dissent in *Caban v. Mohammed,* * * * to the effect that although " '[i]n some circumstances the actual relationship between father and child may suffice to create in the unwed father parental interests comparable to those of the married father,' " " 'the absence of a legal tie with the mother may in such circumstances appropriately place a limit on whatever substantive constitutional claims might otherwise exist.' " * * *   In accord with our tradi-

the Fourteenth Amendment was ratified all but 5 of the 37 States had criminal sodomy laws, that all 50 of the States had such laws prior to 1961, and that 24 States and the District of Columbia continued to have them; and we concluded from that record, regarding that very specific aspect of sexual conduct, that "to claim that a right to engage in such conduct is 'deeply rooted in this Nation's history and tradition' or 'implicit in the concept of ordered liberty' is, at best, facetious." *Id.,* at 194, 106 S.Ct. at 2845. In *Roe v. Wade,* 410 U.S. 113, 93 S.Ct. 705, 35 L.Ed.2d 147 (1973), we spent about a fifth of our opinion negating the proposition that there was a long-standing tradition of laws proscribing abortion. *Id.,* at 129–141, 93 S.Ct., at 715–721.

We do not understand why, having rejected our focus upon the societal tradition regarding the natural father's rights vis-à-vis a child whose mother is married to another man, Justice Brennan would choose to focus instead upon "parenthood." Why should the relevant category not be even more general—perhaps "family relationships"; or "personal relationships"; or even "emotional attachments in general"? Though the dissent has no basis for the level of generality it would select, we do: We refer to the most specific level at which a relevant tradition protecting, or denying protection to, the asserted right can be identified. If, for example, there were no societal tradition, either way, regarding the rights of the natural father of a child adulterously conceived, we would have to consult, and (if possible) reason from, the traditions regarding natural fathers in general. But there is such a more specific tradition, and it unqualifiedly denies protection to such a parent.

One would think that Justice Brennan would appreciate the value of consulting the most specific tradition available, since he acknowledges that "[e]ven if we can agree * * * that 'family' and 'parenthood' are part of the good

life, it is absurd to assume that we can agree on the content of those terms and destructive to pretend that we do." * * * Because such general traditions provide such imprecise guidance, they permit judges to dictate rather than discern the society's views. The need, if arbitrary decision-making is to be avoided, to adopt the most specific tradition as the point of reference—or at least to announce, as Justice Brennan declines to do, some other criterion for selecting among the innumerable relevant traditions that could be consulted—is well enough exemplified by the fact that in the present case Justice Brennan's opinion and Justice O'Connor's opinion, which disapproves this footnote, *both* appeal to tradition, but on the basis of the tradition they select reach opposite results. Although assuredly having the virtue (if it be that) of leaving judges free to decide as they think best when the unanticipated occurs, a rule of law that binds neither by text nor by any particular, identifiable tradition, is no rule of law at all.

Finally, we may note that this analysis is not inconsistent with the result in cases such as *Griswold v. Connecticut,* 381 U.S. 479, 85 S.Ct. 1678, 14 L.Ed.2d 510 (1965), or *Eisenstadt v. Baird,* 405 U.S. 438, 92 S.Ct. 1029, 31 L.Ed.2d 349 (1972). None of those cases acknowledged a longstanding and still extant societal tradition withholding the very right pronounced to be the subject of a liberty interest and then rejected it. Justice Brennan must do so here. In this case, the existence of such a tradition, continuing to the present day, refutes any possible contention that the alleged right is "so rooted in the traditions and conscience of our people as to be ranked as fundamental," *Snyder v. Massachusetts,* 291 U.S. 97, 105, 54 S.Ct. 330, 332, 78 L.Ed. 674 (1934), or "implicit in the concept of ordered liberty," *Palko v. Connecticut,* 302 U.S. 319, 325, 58 S.Ct. 149, 152, 82 L.Ed. 288 (1937).

tions, a limit is also imposed by the circumstance that the mother is, at the time of the child's conception and birth, married to and cohabiting with another man, both of whom wish to raise the child as the offspring of their union.[7] It is a question of legislative policy and not constitutional law whether California will allow the presumed parenthood of a couple desiring to retain a child conceived within and born into their marriage to be rebutted.

We do not accept Justice Brennan's criticism that this result "squashes" the liberty that consists of "the freedom not to conform," * * *. It seems to us that reflects the erroneous view that there is only one side to this controversy—that one disposition can expand a "liberty" of sorts without contracting an equivalent "liberty" on the other side. Such a happy choice is rarely available. Here, to *provide* protection to an adulterous natural father is to *deny* protection to a marital father, and vice versa. If Michael has a "freedom not to conform" (whatever that means), Gerald must equivalently have a "freedom to conform." One of them will pay a price for asserting that "freedom"—Michael by being unable to act as father of the child he has adulterously begotten, or Gerald by being unable to preserve the integrity of the traditional family unit he and Victoria have established. Our disposition does not choose between these two "freedoms," but leaves that to the people of California. Justice Brennan's approach chooses one of them as the constitutional imperative, on no apparent basis except that the unconventional is to be preferred.

IV

* * *

The judgment of the California Court of Appeal is

Affirmed.

JUSTICE O'CONNOR, with whom JUSTICE KENNEDY joins, concurring in part.

I concur in all but footnote 6 of Justice Scalia's opinion. This footnote sketches a mode of historical analysis to be used when identifying liberty interests protected by the Due Process Clause of the Fourteenth Amendment that may be somewhat inconsistent with our past decisions in this area. See *Griswold v. Connecticut*, 381 U.S. 479, 85 S.Ct. 1678, 14 L.Ed.2d 510 (1965); *Eisenstadt v. Baird*, 405 U.S. 438, 92 S.Ct. 1029, 31 L.Ed.2d 349 (1972). On occasion the Court has characterized relevant traditions protecting asserted rights at levels of generality that might not be "the most specific level" available. * * * See *Loving v. Virginia*, 388 U.S. 1, 12, 87 S.Ct. 1817, 1823,

---

7. Justice Brennan chides us for thus limiting our holding to situations in which, as here, the husband and wife wish to raise her child jointly. The dissent believes that without this limitation we would be unable to "rely on the State's asserted interest in protecting the 'unitary family' in denying that Michael and Victoria have been deprived of liberty." * * *. As we have sought to make clear, however, and as the dissent elsewhere seems to understand, * * * we rest our decision not upon our independent "balancing" of such interests, but upon the absence of any constitutionally protected right to legal parentage on the part of an adulterous natural father in Michael's situation, as evidenced by long tradition. That tradition reflects a "balancing" that has already been made by society itself. We limit our pronouncement to the relevant facts of this case because it is at least possible that our traditions lead to a different conclusion with regard to adulterous fathering of a child whom the marital parents do not wish to raise as their own. It seems unfair for those who disagree with our holding to include among their criticisms that we have not extended the holding more broadly.

18 L.Ed.2d 1010 (1967); *Turner v. Safley,* 482 U.S. 78, 94, 107 S.Ct. 2254, 2265, 96 L.Ed.2d 64 (1987); cf. *United States v. Stanley,* 483 U.S. 669, 709, 107 S.Ct. 3054, ___, 97 L.Ed.2d 550 (1987) (opinion concurring in part and dissenting in part). I would not foreclose the unanticipated by the prior imposition of a single mode of historical analysis. *Poe v. Ullman,* 367 U.S. 497, 542, 544, 81 S.Ct. 1752, 1776, 1777, 6 L.Ed.2d 989 (1961) (Harlan, J., dissenting).

JUSTICE STEVENS, concurring in the judgment.

As I understand this case, it raises two different questions about the validity of California's statutory scheme. First, is Cal.Evid.Code Ann. § 621 (West Supp.1989) unconstitutional because it prevents Michael and Victoria from obtaining a judicial determination that he is her biological father—even if no legal rights would be affected by that determination? Second, does the California statute deny appellants a fair opportunity to prove that Victoria's best interests would be served by granting Michael visitation rights?

On the first issue I agree with Justice Scalia that the Federal Constitution imposes no obligation upon a State to "declare facts unless some legal consequence hinges upon the requested declaration." * * * "The actions of judges neither create nor sever genetic bonds." *Lehr v. Robertson,* 463 U.S. 248, 261, 103 S.Ct. 2985, 2993, 77 L.Ed.2d 614 (1983).

On the second issue I do not agree with Justice Scalia's analysis. He seems to reject the possibility that a natural father might ever have a constitutionally protected interest in his relationship with a child whose mother was married to and cohabiting with another man at the time of the child's conception and birth. I think cases like *Stanley v. Illinois,* * * * (1972) and *Caban v. Mohammed,* * * * demonstrate that enduring "family" relationships may develop in unconventional settings. I therefore would not foreclose the possibility that a constitutionally protected relationship between a natural father and his child might exist in a case like this. Indeed, I am willing to assume for the purpose of deciding this case that Michael's relationship with Victoria is strong enough to give him a constitutional right to try to convince a trial judge that Victoria's best interest would be served by granting him visitation rights. I am satisfied, however, that the California statute, as applied in this case, gave him that opportunity.

Section 4601 of the California Civil Code Annotated (West Supp.1989) provides:

> "[R]easonable visitation rights [shall be awarded] to a parent unless it is shown that the visitation would be detrimental to the best interests of the child. In the discretion of the court, reasonable visitation rights may be granted *to any other person having an interest in the welfare of the child.*" (Emphasis added.)

The presumption established by § 621 denied Michael the benefit of the first sentence of § 4601 because, as a matter of law, he is not a "parent." It does not, however, prevent him from proving that he is an "other person having an interest in the welfare of the child." On its face, therefore, the statute plainly gave the trial judge the authority to grant Michael "reasonable visitation rights."

I recognize that my colleagues have interpreted § 621 as creating an absolute bar that would prevent a California trial judge from regarding the natural father as either a "parent" within the meaning of the first sentence of § 4601 *or* as "any other person" within the meaning of the second sentence. * * * (BRENNAN, J., dissenting). That is not only an unnatural reading of the statute's plain language, but it is also not consistent with the California courts' reading of the statute. * * *

* * * [I]n this case, the trial judge not only found the conclusive presumption applicable, but also separately considered the effect of § 4601 and expressly found "that, at the present time, it is not in the best interests of the child that the Plaintiff have visitation. The Court believes that the existence of two (2) 'fathers' as male authority figures will confuse the child and be counter-productive to her best interests." * * *

Under the circumstances of the case before us, Michael was given a fair opportunity to show that he is Victoria's natural father, that he had developed a relationship with her, and that her interests would be served by granting him visitation rights. On the other hand, the record also shows that after its rather shaky start, the marriage between Carole and Gerald developed a stability that now provides Victoria with a loving and harmonious family home. In the circumstances of this case, I find nothing fundamentally unfair about the exercise of a judge's discretion that, in the end, allows the mother to decide whether her child's best interest would be served by allowing the natural father visitation privileges. Because I am convinced that the trial judge had the authority under state law both to hear Michael's plea for visitation rights and to grant him such rights if Victoria's best interests so warranted, I am satisfied that the California statutory scheme is consistent with the Due Process Clause of the Fourteenth Amendment.

I therefore concur in the Court's judgment of affirmance.

JUSTICE BRENNAN, with whom JUSTICE MARSHALL and JUSTICE BLACKMUN join, dissenting.

In a case that has yielded so many opinions as has this one, it is fruitful to begin by emphasizing the common ground shared by a majority of this Court. Five Members of the Court refuse to foreclose "the possibility that a natural father might ever have a constitutionally protected interest in his relationship with a child whose mother was married to and cohabiting with another man at the time of the child's conception and birth." * * * (Stevens, J., concurring in judgment). Five Justices agree that the flaw inhering in a conclusive presumption that terminates a constitutionally protected interest without any hearing whatsoever is a *procedural* one. * * * (White, J., dissenting); * * * (Stevens, J., concurring in judgment). Four Members of the Court agree that Michael H. has a liberty interest in his relationship with Victoria, * * * (White, J., dissenting), and one assumes for purposes of this case that he does, * * * (Stevens, J., concurring in judgment).

In contrast, only two Members of the Court fully endorse Justice Scalia's view of the proper method of analyzing questions arising under the Due Process Clause. * * * (O'Connor, J., concurring in part). Nevertheless, because the plurality opinion's exclusively historical analysis portends a significant and unfortunate departure from our prior cases and from sound constitutional decisionmaking, I devote a substantial portion of my discussion to it.

I

Once we recognized that the "liberty" protected by the Due Process Clause of the Fourteenth Amendment encompasses more than freedom from bodily restraint, today's plurality opinion emphasizes, the concept was cut loose from one natural limitation on its meaning. This innovation paved the way, so the plurality hints, for judges to substitute their own preferences for those of elected officials. Dissatisfied with this supposedly unbridled and uncertain state of affairs, the plurality casts about for another limitation on the concept of liberty.

It finds this limitation in "tradition." Apparently oblivious to the fact that this concept can be as malleable and as elusive as "liberty" itself, the plurality pretends that tradition places a discernible border around the Constitution. The pretense is seductive; it would be comforting to believe that a search for "tradition" involves nothing more idiosyncratic or complicated than poring through dusty volumes on American history. Yet, as Justice White observed in his dissent in *Moore v. East Cleveland,* * * * : "What the deeply rooted traditions of the country are is arguable." Indeed, wherever I would begin to look for an interest "deeply rooted in the country's traditions," one thing is certain: I would not stop (as does the plurality) at Bracton, or Blackstone, or Kent, or even the American Law Reports in conducting my search. Because reasonable people can disagree about the content of particular traditions, and because they can disagree even about which traditions are relevant to the definition of "liberty," the plurality has not found the objective boundary that it seeks.

Even if we could agree, moreover, on the content and significance of particular traditions, we still would be forced to identify the point at which a tradition becomes firm enough to be relevant to our definition of liberty and the moment at which it becomes too obsolete to be relevant any longer. The plurality supplies no objective means by which we might make these determinations. Indeed, as soon as the plurality sees signs that the tradition upon which it bases its decision (the laws denying putative fathers like Michael standing to assert paternity) is crumbling, it shifts ground and says that the case has nothing to do with that tradition, after all. "What is at issue here," the plurality asserts after canvassing the law on paternity suits, "is not entitlement to a state pronouncement that Victoria was begotten by Michael." * * * But that is precisely what is at issue here, and the plurality's last-minute denial of this fact dramatically illustrates the subjectivity of its own analysis.

* * *

It is not that tradition has been irrelevant to our prior decisions. Throughout our decisionmaking in this important area runs the theme that certain interests and practices—freedom from physical restraint, marriage, childbearing, childrearing, and others—form the core of our definition of "liberty." Our solicitude for these interests is partly the result of the fact that the Due Process Clause would seem an empty promise if it did not protect them, and partly the result of the historical and traditional importance of these interests in our society. In deciding cases arising under the Due Process Clause, therefore, we have considered whether the concrete limitation under consideration impermissibly impinges upon one of these more generalized interests.

Today's plurality, however, does not ask whether parenthood is an interest that historically has received our attention and protection; the answer to that question is too clear for dispute. Instead, the plurality asks whether the specific variety of parenthood under consideration—a natural father's relationship with a child whose mother is married to another man— has enjoyed such protection.

If we had looked to tradition with such specificity in past cases, many a decision would have reached a different result. Surely the use of contraceptives by unmarried couples, *Eisenstadt v. Baird,* * * * or even by married couples, *Griswold v. Connecticut,* * * * the freedom from corporal punishment in schools, *Ingraham v. Wright,* * * * the freedom from an arbitrary transfer from a prison to a psychiatric institution, *Vitek v. Jones,* * * * and even the right to raise one's natural but illegitimate children, *Stanley v. Illinois,* * * * were not "interest[s] traditionally protected by our society," * * * at the time of their consideration by this Court. If we had asked, therefore, in *Eisenstadt, Griswold, Ingraham, Vitek,* or *Stanley* itself whether the specific interest under consideration had been traditionally protected, the answer would have been a resounding "no." That we did not ask this question in those cases highlights the novelty of the interpretive method that the plurality opinion employs today.

The plurality's interpretive method is more than novel; it is misguided. It ignores the good reasons for limiting the role of "tradition" in interpreting the Constitution's deliberately capacious language. In the plurality's constitutional universe, we may not take notice of the fact that the original reasons for the conclusive presumption of paternity are out of place in a world in which blood tests can prove virtually beyond a shadow of a doubt who sired a particular child and in which the fact of illegitimacy no longer plays the burdensome and stigmatizing role it once did. Nor, in the plurality's world, may we deny "tradition" its full scope by pointing out that the rationale for the conventional rule has changed over the years, as has the rationale for Cal.Evid.Code Ann. § 621 (West Supp.1989);[1] instead, our task is simply to identify a rule denying the asserted interest and not to ask whether the basis for that rule—which is the true reflection of the values undergirding it—has changed too often or too recently to call the rule embodying that rationale a "tradition." Moreover, by describing the decisive question as whether Michael and Victoria's interest is one that has been "traditionally *protected by our society,*" * * * (emphasis added), rather than one that society traditionally has thought important (with or without protecting it), and by suggesting that our sole function is to "*discern* the society's views," * * *, n. 6 (emphasis added), the plurality acts as if the only purpose of the Due Process Clause is to confirm the importance of interests already protected by a majority of the

---

1. See *In re Marriage of Stephen and Sharyne B.,* 124 Cal.App.3d 524, 528–531, 177 Cal. Rptr. 429, 431–433 (1981) (noting that California courts initially justified conclusive presumption of paternity on the ground that biological paternity was impossible to prove, but that the preservation of family integrity became the rule's paramount justification when paternity tests became reliable).

States. Transforming the protection afforded by the Due Process Clause into a redundancy mocks those who, with care and purpose, wrote the Fourteenth Amendment.

In construing the Fourteenth Amendment to offer shelter only to those interests specifically protected by historical practice, moreover, the plurality ignores the kind of society in which our Constitution exists. We are not an assimilative, homogeneous society, but a facilitative, pluralistic one, in which we must be willing to abide someone else's unfamiliar or even repellant practice because the same tolerant impulse protects our own idiosyncracies. Even if we can agree, therefore, that "family" and "parenthood" are part of the good life, it is absurd to assume that we can agree on the content of those terms and destructive to pretend that we do. In a community such as ours, "liberty" must include the freedom not to conform. The plurality today squashes this freedom by requiring specific approval from history before protecting anything in the name of liberty.

The document that the plurality construes today is unfamiliar to me. It is not the living charter that I have taken to be our Constitution; it is instead a stagnant, archaic, hidebound document steeped in the prejudices and superstitions of a time long past. *This* Constitution does not recognize that times change, does not see that sometimes a practice or rule outlives its foundations. I cannot accept an interpretive method that does such violence to the charter that I am bound by oath to uphold.

II

The plurality's reworking of our interpretive approach is all the more troubling because it is unnecessary. This is not a case in which we face a "new" kind of interest, one that requires us to consider for the first time whether the Constitution protects it. On the contrary, we confront an interest—that of a parent and child in their relationship with each other— that was among the first that this Court acknowledged in its cases defining the "liberty" protected by the Constitution, * * * and I think I am safe in saying that no one doubts the wisdom or validity of those decisions. Where the interest under consideration is a parent-child relationship, we need not ask, over and over again, whether that interest is one that society traditionally protects.

* * *

On four prior occasions, we have considered whether unwed fathers have a constitutionally protected interest in their relationships with their children. See *Stanley v. Illinois,* * * * *Quilloin v. Walcott,* * * * *Caban v. Mohammed,* * * * and *Lehr v. Robertson,* * * *. Though different in factual and legal circumstances, these cases have produced a unifying theme: although an unwed father's biological link to his child does not, in and of itself, guarantee him a constitutional stake in his relationship with that child, such a link combined with a substantial parent-child relationship will do so.[2] "When an unwed father demonstrates a full commitment to the responsibilities of

---

2. The plurality's claim that "the logic of [my] position leads to the conclusion that if Michael had begotten Victoria by rape, that fact would in no way affect his possession of a liberty interest in his relationship with her," *ante,* at * * * n. 4, ignores my observation that a mere biological connection is insufficient to establish a liberty interest on the part of an unwed father.

parenthood by 'com[ing] forward to participate in the rearing of his child,' * * * his interest in personal contact with his child acquires substantial protection under the Due Process Clause. At that point it may be said that he 'act[s] as a father toward his children.' " *Lehr v. Robertson,* * * * quoting *Caban v. Mohammed,* * * *. This commitment is why Mr. Stanley and Mr. Caban won; why Mr. Quilloin and Mr. Lehr lost; and why Michael H. should prevail today. Michael H. is almost certainly Victoria D.'s natural father, has lived with her as her father, has contributed to her support, and has from the beginning sought to strengthen and maintain his relationship with her.

Claiming that the intent of these cases was to protect the "unitary family," * * * the plurality waves *Stanley, Quilloin, Caban,* and *Lehr* aside. In evaluating the plurality's dismissal of these precedents, it is essential to identify its conception of the "unitary family." If, by acknowledging that *Stanley, et al.,* sought to protect "the relationships that develop within the unitary family," * * * the plurality meant only to describe the kinds of relationships that develop when parents and children live together (formally or informally) as a family, then the plurality's vision of these cases would be correct. But that is not the plurality's message. Though it pays lip service to the idea that marriage is not the crucial fact in denying constitutional protection to the relationship between Michael and Victoria, *ante,* at * * * n. 3, the plurality cannot mean what it says.

The evidence is undisputed that Michael, Victoria, and Carole did live together as a family; that is, they shared the same household, Victoria called Michael "Daddy," Michael contributed to Victoria's support, and he is eager to continue his relationship with her. Yet they are not, in the plurality's view, a "unitary family," whereas Gerald, Carole, and Victoria do compose such a family. The only difference between these two sets of relationships, however, is the fact of marriage. The plurality, indeed, expressly recognizes that marriage is the critical fact in denying Michael a constitutionally protected stake in his relationship with Victoria: no fewer than six times, the plurality refers to Michael as the "*adulterous* natural father." * * * However, the very premise of *Stanley* and the cases following it is that marriage is not decisive in answering the question whether the Constitution protects the parental relationship under consideration. These cases are, after all, important precisely because they involve the rights of *unwed* fathers. * * *

The plurality has wedged itself between a rock and a hard place. If it limits its holding to those situations in which a wife and husband wish to raise the child together, then it necessarily takes the State's interest into account in defining "liberty"; yet if it extends that approach to circumstances in which the marital union already has been dissolved, then it may no longer rely on the State's asserted interest in protecting the "unitary family" in denying that Michael and Victoria have been deprived of liberty.

The plurality's confusion about the proper analysis of claims involving procedural due process also becomes obvious when one examines the plurality's shift in emphasis from the putative father's standing to his ability to obtain parental prerogatives. * * * In announcing that what matters is not the father's ability to claim paternity, but his ability to obtain "substantive parental rights," * * * the plurality turns procedural due process upside down. Michael's challenge in this Court does not depend on his ability ultimately to obtain visitation rights; it would be strange indeed if, before one could be granted a hearing, one were required to prove that one would prevail on the merits. The point of procedural due process is to give the litigant a fair chance at prevailing, not to ensure a particular substantive outcome. Nor does Michael's challenge depend on the success of fathers like him in obtaining parental rights in past cases; procedural due process is, by and large, an individual guarantee, not one that should depend on the success or failure of prior cases having little or nothing to do with the claimant's own suit.

* * *

IV

The atmosphere surrounding today's decision is one of make-believe. Beginning with the suggestion that the situation confronting us here does not repeat itself every day in every corner of the country, * * * moving on to the claim that it is tradition alone that supplies the details of the liberty that the Constitution protects, and passing finally to the notion that the Court always has recognized a cramped vision of "the family," today's decision lets stand California's pronouncement that Michael—whom blood tests show to a 98 percent probability to be Victoria's father—is not Victoria's father. When and if the Court awakes to reality, it will find a world very different from the one it expects.

JUSTICE WHITE, with whom JUSTICE BRENNAN joins, dissenting.

California law, as the plurality describes it, * * * tells us that, except in limited circumstances, California declares it to be *"irrelevant* for paternity purposes whether a child conceived during and born into a lawful marriage was begotten by someone other than the husband," (emphasis in original). This I do not accept, for the fact that Michael H. is the biological father of Victoria is to me highly relevant to whether he has rights, as a father or otherwise, with respect to the child. Because I believe that Michael H. has a liberty interest that cannot be denied without due process of the law, I must dissent.

I

Like Justices Brennan, Marshall, Blackmun and Stevens, I do not agree with the plurality opinion's conclusion that a natural father can never "have a constitutionally protected interest in his relationship with a child whose mother was married to and cohabiting with another man at the time of the child's conception and birth." * * * Prior cases here have recognized the liberty interest of a father in his relationship with his child. In none of these cases did we indicate that the fathers' rights were dependent on the marital status of the mother or biological father. The basic principle enunciated in the Court's unwed father cases is that an unwed father who has demonstrated a sufficient commitment to his paternity by way of personal, financial, or custodial responsibilities has a protected liberty interest in a relationship with his child.

* * *

In the case now before us, Michael H. is not a father unwilling to assume his responsibilities as a parent. To the contrary, he is a father who has asserted his interests in raising and providing for his child since the very time of the child's birth. In contrast to the father in *Lehr,* Michael H. had begun to develop a relationship with his daughter. There is no dispute on this point. * * * It is clear enough that Michael H. more than meets the mark in establishing the constitutionally protected liberty interest discussed in *Lehr* and recognized in *Stanley v. Illinois, supra,* and *Caban v. Mohammed, supra.* He therefore has a liberty interest entitled to protection under the Due Process Clause of the Fourteenth Amendment.

II

California plainly denies Michael this protection, by refusing him the opportunity to rebut the State's presumption that the mother's husband is the father of the child. California law not only deprives Michael H. of a legal parent-child relationship with his daughter Victoria but even denies him the opportunity to introduce blood-test evidence to rebut the demonstrable fiction that Gerald is Victoria's father. Unlike *Lehr,* Michael H. has not been denied notice. He has, most definitely, however, been denied any real opportunity to be heard. * * * The Court gives its blessing to § 621 by relying on the State's asserted interests in the integrity of the family (defined as Carole and Gerald) and in protecting Victoria from the stigma of illegitimacy and by balancing away Michael's interest in establishing that he is the father of the child.

The interest in protecting a child from the social stigma of illegitimacy lacks any real connection to the facts of a case where a father is seeking to establish, rather than repudiate, paternity. * * *

The State's professed interest in the preservation of the existing marital unit is a more significant concern. To be sure, the intrusion of an outsider asserting that he is the father of a child whom the husband believes to be his own would be disruptive to say the least. On the facts of this case, however, Gerald was well aware of the liaison between Carole and Michael. The conclusive presumption of evidentiary rule § 621 virtually eliminates the putative father's chances of succeeding in his effort to establish paternity, but it by no means prevents him from asserting the claim. It may serve as a deterrent to such claims but does not eliminate the threat. Further, the argument that the conclusive presumption preserved the sanctity of the marital unit had more sway in a time when the husband was similarly prevented from challenging paternity.

* * *

As the Court has said: "The significance of the biological connection is that it offers the natural father an opportunity that no other male possesses to develop a relationship with his offspring. If he grasps that opportunity and accepts some measure of responsibility for the child's future, he may enjoy the blessings of the parent-child relationship and make uniquely valuable contributions to the child's development." *Lehr,* 463 U.S., at 262, 103 S.Ct., at 2993. It is as if this passage was addressed to Michael H. Yet the plurality today recants. Michael H. eagerly grasped the opportunity to have a relationship with his daughter (he lived with her; he declared her to be his child; he provided financial support for her) and still, with today's opinion, his opportunity has vanished. He has been rendered a stranger to his child.

Because Cal.Evid.Code Ann. § 621, as applied, should be held unconstitutional under the Due Process Clause of the Fourteenth Amendment, I respectfully dissent.

Notes on Lehr *and* Michael H.

1. Stanley v. Illinois, 405 U.S. 645, 92 S.Ct. 1208, 31 L.Ed.2d 551 (1972), was the first United States Supreme Court case to recognize that an unwed father had a constitutionally-protected private interest in "the children he has sired and raised." The case represented a victory for fathers' rights advocates, and caught state adoption agencies, among others, by surprise. Thus, Professor Clark criticizes *Stanley* for its failure to attach any value to the "state's interest in distinguishing between those parents willing to make the social, personal, financial commitments attendant upon a legal marriage from those unwilling to make such commitments" and notes that it has had "a profound effect upon adoption procedure." Homer H. Clark, Constitutional Protection of the Illegitimate Child?, 12 U.C.Davis L.Rev. 383, 403 (1979). Concern was expressed in the wake of *Stanley* that recognition of the father's rights would interfere with the early and smooth placement of illegitimate children for adoption. See Nora L. Freeman, Remodeling Adoption Statutes After Stanley v. Illinois, 15 J.Fam.L. 385 (1977). As Justice Stevens notes, the New York statute challenged in *Lehr* was drafted in response to *Stanley*. Do you agree that it was adequate to protect the rights of the natural father?

2. The United States Supreme Court first addressed the implications of *Stanley* for the adoption process in Quilloin v. Walcott, 434 U.S. 246, 98 S.Ct. 549, 54 L.Ed.2d 511 (1978). In *Quilloin,* the court upheld, as applied, a Georgia law that permitted the adoption of illegitimate children upon the sole consent of the mother. The case involved the stepparent adoption of an 11–year–old boy who had never lived with the natural father, although they had visited each other on "many occasions." The father had never attempted to legitimate his son, nor did he oppose the adoption in order to gain the boy's custody. Instead, he sought only visitation rights. Justice Marshall, speaking for a unanimous Court, held that rejection of the father's efforts to block the adoption did not violate due process because the procedure would give full recognition to an existing family unit and was therefore in the child's best interests. Nor was the father denied equal protection when his situation was compared to that of married, but divorced, fathers, since unlike them he had never at any time shouldered the obligation of "daily supervision, education, protection, or care of the child." The father failed to raise in a timely manner any equal protection claims arising from the disparate treatment accorded to unwed fathers as compared to unwed mothers. How do *Quilloin* and *Stanley* fit together? A notewriter suggests that Leon Quilloin's relationship with his son more closely resembled that of an uncle and nephew than a father and son; his failure to undertake parenting responsibility was fatal to his constitutional claim. See Robert S. Rausch, Note, Unwed Fathers and the Adoption Process, 22 Wm. & Mary L.Rev. 85, 98–99 (1980). Clark, noting that this distinction may just be a factual variation without general application, comments that "[i]t is * * * impossible to determine from its opinion whether the Court was overruling *Stanley,* beating a partial retreat from *Stanley,* or just emphasizing a factual difference in the cases." Clark, supra Note 1, at 404.

3. Seven years after *Stanley* implicitly raised the question whether fathers of illegitimate children might constitutionally be treated differently from their mothers, Caban v. Mohammed, 441 U.S. 380, 99 S.Ct. 1760, 60 L.Ed.2d 297 (1979)

squarely decided the sex discrimination issue in the context of the adoption of older children. Was the matter resolved correctly? The Pennsylvania Supreme Court had come to the same conclusion two years earlier in a case applying the state equal rights amendment. In Adoption of Walker, 468 Pa. 165, 360 A.2d 603 (1976), the answer seemed simple: since the "only differences between unwed fathers and unwed mothers are those based on sex", the statute that permitted only mothers to consent to the adoption of an illegitimate child rested on an impermissible basis and must be struck down. Justice Stevens, the author of the *Lehr* opinion, dissented in *Caban,* taking explicit account of the biological differences between mothers and fathers of newborn infants as the basis for distinguishing their constitutional rights:

> Men and women are different, and the difference is relevant to the question whether the mother may be given the exclusive right to consent to the adoption of a child born out of wedlock. Because most adoptions involve newborn infants or very young children, it is appropriate at the outset to focus on the significance of the difference in such cases.

> Both parents are equally responsible for the conception of the child out of wedlock. But from that point on through pregnancy and infancy, the differences between the male and the female have an important impact on the child's destiny. Only the mother carries the child; it is she who has the constitutional right to decide whether to bear it or not. In many cases, only the mother knows who sired the child, and it will often be within her power to withhold that fact, and even the fact of her pregnancy, from that person. If during pregnancy the mother should marry a different partner, the child will be legitimate when born, and the natural father may never even know that his "rights" have been affected. On the other hand, only if the natural mother agrees to marry the natural father during that period can the latter's actions have a positive impact on the status of the child; if he instead should marry a different partner during that time, the only effect on the child is negative, for the likelihood of legitimacy will be lessened.

> These differences continue at birth and immediately thereafter. During that period, the mother and child are together;[10] the mother's identity is known with certainty. The father, on the other hand, may or may not be present; his identity may be unknown to the world and may even be uncertain to the mother. These natural differences between unmarried fathers and mothers make it probable that the mother, and not the father or both parents, will have custody of the newborn infant.

> In short, it is virtually inevitable that from conception through infancy the mother will constantly be faced with decisions about how best to care for the child, whereas it is much less certain that the father will be confronted with comparable problems. There no doubt are cases in which the relationship of the parties at birth makes it appropriate for the State to give the father a voice of some sort in the adoption decision. But as a matter of equal protection analysis, it is perfectly obvious that at the time and immediately after a child is born out of wedlock, differences between men and women

10. In fact, there is some sociological and anthropological research indicating that by virtue of the symbiotic relationship between mother and child during pregnancy and the initial contact between mother and child directly after birth a physical and psychological bond immediately develops between the two that is not then present between the infant and the father or any other person. E.g., 1 & 2 John Bowlby, Attachment and Loss (1969, 1973); Margaret S. Mahler, The Psychological Birth of the Human Infant (1975).

justify some differential treatment of the mother and father in the adoption process.

Most particularly, these differences justify a rule that gives the mother of the newborn infant the exclusive right to consent to its adoption. Such a rule gives the mother, in whose sole charge the infant is often placed anyway, the maximum flexibility in deciding how best to care for the child. It also gives the loving father an incentive to marry the mother, and has no adverse impact on the disinterested father. Finally, it facilitates the interests of the adoptive parents, the child, and the public at large by streamlining the often traumatic adoption process and allowing the prompt, complete, and reliable integration of the child into a satisfactory new home at as young an age as is feasible. Put most simply, it permits the maximum participation of interested natural parents without so burdening the adoption process that its attractiveness to potential adoptive parents is destroyed.

This conclusion is borne out by considering the alternative rule proposed by appellant. If the State were to require the consent of both parents, or some kind of hearing to explain why either's consent is unnecessary or unobtainable, it would unquestionably complicate and delay the adoption process. Most importantly, such a rule would remove the mother's freedom of choice in her own and the child's behalf without also relieving her of the unshakable responsibility for the care of the child. Furthermore, questions relating to the adequacy of notice to absent fathers could invade the mother's privacy, cause the adopting parents to doubt the reliability of the new relationship, and add to the expense and time required to conclude what is now usually a simple and certain process. While it might not be irrational for a State to conclude that these costs should be incurred to protect the interest of natural fathers, it is nevertheless plain that those costs, which are largely the result of differences between the mother and the father, establish an imposing justification for *some* differential treatment of the two sexes in this type of situation.

Id., 441 U.S. at 404–09, 99 S.Ct. at 1774–77, 60 L.Ed.2d at 314–17 (dissenting opinion of Justice Stevens). Do you agree with this analysis? Does it reappear in *Lehr*?

4. Does *Lehr* resolve the question left open in *Caban* about the respective constitutional rights of the natural parents when the mother wishes to place the child for adoption by strangers immediately after its birth? The Court had agreed to hear a case raising this question, but the case was vacated and remanded before oral argument because of a newly-raised issue of state law, the application of Texas Fam.Code §§ 13.01–13.09, that might afford the father the relief he sought without resort to constitutional aid. In In re Baby Girl S., 628 S.W.2d 261 (Tex.App.1982), vacated and remanded sub nom. Kirkpatrick v. Christian Homes, 460 U.S. 1074, 103 S.Ct. 1760, 76 L.Ed.2d 337 (1983), the natural mother was sixteen and the natural father twenty-five at the time of the hearing. The mother, whose parents had opposed her marriage to the father, decided to place the infant for adoption immediately upon its birth. Christian Homes of Abilene, Inc., the adoption agency, filed suit to terminate the mother's parental rights preparatory to placing the child for adoption. The father appeared in these proceedings and sought to legitimate the child and to be granted her custody. Under Texas Family Code section 13.21, (the Voluntary Legitimation subchapter), if the mother failed to consent to the father's petition, he could legitimate the child only if the court found that legitimation was in the child's best interest.

The court did not make that finding, and the father's petition for legitimation was denied. The father's argument that the statutory distinction between mothers and fathers violated the equal protection and due process clauses of the United States Constitution as well as the Texas state equal rights amendment was rejected. The state's objective of protecting children born out of wedlock by assuring the mother that her plans for the child's future will not, absent her consent or a court finding that the child's best interests require a contrary result, be disrupted by the veto of the natural father, was held to be "important" and substantially related to the achievement of that objective for federal constitutional purposes and a "compelling reason" for drawing a gender based line when measured by the higher state constitutional requirement. Had the United States Supreme Court reached the constitutional issue in *Kirkpatrick*, how should it have been decided? Was the case decided correctly under the Texas state equal rights amendment?

An *amicus curiae* brief prepared by Professor Nancy Erickson and filed on behalf of unwed mothers in *Kirkpatrick* argued that, even assuming the unwed father whose biological paternity resulted from an unintended contraceptive failure had due process rights, the Texas statutory scheme which allows the mother to prevent him from legitimating the child is supported by four compelling state interests. These are: the interest in encouraging mothers to make plans for the future of their children that will be in the best interests of those children; the interest in preserving a woman's right to choose whether or not to bear the child; the interest in safeguarding the unwed mother's right to anonymity and her right not to have a relationship with the child by placing it for adoption by strangers; and the interest in preventing the exploitation of women as unwilling breeders of children for males who desire children, but who have not found women able and willing to bear those children. How do you assess the validity of these arguments?

On remand, a state court held that petitioner could not have obtained and may not now obtain a decree designating him as the father of Baby Girl S. under V.T.C.A.Fam.Code §§ 13.01–13.09 (the Paternity Suit subchapter). In re Baby Girl S., 658 S.W.2d 794, 796 (Tex.App.1983). His constitutional claim, presumably, remains to be determined.

How would Professor Erickson decide the following case? The natural parents had been living together in nonmarital cohabitation in California when the mother became pregnant. She came back to Utah to give birth, living there with members of her family. They disapproved of the natural father, and urged her to give the child up for adoption. The natural father, in reliance on the mother's plans to live in Arizona with him and the child, found a job in Arizona and began moving their household belongings to a new home. The child was unexpectedly born early, while the father was en route to Arizona. Three days after the child's birth, the father learned that the mother had relinquished her parental rights and that an adoption petition had been filed. See Baby Boy Doe, 717 P.2d 686 (Utah 1986), noted, 1986 Brigham Young Univ.L.Rev. 1081 (1986). How should the case be decided in light of *Stanley, Quilloin, Caban,* and *Lehr?*

5. Has the Supreme Court satisfactorily resolved the inherent conflict between unmarried mothers and fathers in the context of adoption? Several feminist theorists have offered thoughtful critiques of the problem; most conclude that giving clear priority to either parent is not a satisfactory solution. See, e.g., Deborah L. Forman, Unwed Fathers and Adoption: A Theoretical Analysis in Context, 72 Tex.L.Rev. 967 (1994); Mary L. Shanley, Unwed Fathers' Rights,

Adoption, and Sex Equality: Gender–Neutrality and the Perpetuation of Patriarchy, 85 Colum.L.Rev. 60 (1994); Karen Czapanskiy, Volunteers and Draftees: The Struggle for Parental Equality, 38 U.C.L.A. L.Rev. 1415 (1991).

6. All of the United States Supreme Court cases dealing with the rights of natural fathers prior to *Michael H.* involved children born out of wedlock. Victoria D., by contrast, was born during the marriage of her mother, Carole D., to Gerald D. Should this single fact make a constitutional difference in the rights of her natural father, Michael H.? What weight does Justice Scalia give to the fact that, as he points out in distinguishing *Lehr,* Victoria was "born into an extant marital family"? Does Justice Stevens concur in this distinction? Does Justice Brennan give it any significance at all? What is Justice White's position? What are the rights of natural fathers of children born to married women cohabiting with their husbands after *Michael H.*? In Ex Parte Presse, 554 So.2d 406 (Ala.1989), the Alabama Supreme Court cited *Michael H.* in support of its interpretation of the Uniform Parentage Act (UPA) to deny a natural father the right to challenge the husband's paternity even though the father had subsequently married the child's mother after she divorced her first husband and the child, who was in her mother's custody, lived in their home. Justice Jones reasoned as follows:

> Admittedly, this case and the case of *Michael H. v. Gerald D., supra,* have some factual differences, notably the fact that Michael was not married to and living with the mother and child when he brought his suit seeking visitation rights. Nevertheless, the applicable rules of law are the same. In this case, as in *Michael H.,* the legal question is whether a man has standing to bring an action seeking to declare a child illegitimate and to have himself declared the father of that child. This is not permitted under the UPA, as long as there is a presumed father, pursuant to § 26–17–5(a)(1), who has not disclaimed his status as the child's father, consequently, another man, though he later marries the mother and lives with the mother and child, has no standing to challenge the presumed paternity of that child. Put another way, so long as the presumed father persists in maintaining his paternal status, not even the subsequent marriage of the child's mother to another man can create standing in the other man to challenge the presumed father's parental relationship.

> The record before us shows that despite divorce, physical separation, and painful assertions that he is not the true father of Shelly, Norman J. Presse has provided her with unconditional love, financial support, and companionship. The Court, therefore, is of the opinion that to sever or curtail this father-child relationship would frustrate the benevolent purpose of the legislative expression of public policy. Koenemann's interest in judicially establishing his claimed biological relationship is outweighed by the substantial state interest in the psychological stability and general welfare of the child and the state's overriding interest in affording legitimacy to children whenever possible, all of which are obvious objectives of Alabama's UPA.

Id., 554 So.2d at 417–18. Justice Maddox, in dissent, charged the majority with creating an irrebuttable presumption favoring the mother's husband that "sets back the law regarding paternity issues 100 years" and asked the majority to answer the following question:

> Why does a biological father not have standing to establish his paternity of a child when the mother of the child says he is the father, when the

scientific tests show that he is the father, and when he is now married to the child's mother and the child lives in his home and calls him "Daddy." Id., at 418 (dissenting opinion of Justice Maddox). Do you agree that *Michael H.* supports the majority's interpretation of the Uniform Parentage Act?

7. When the natural father's responsibility for child support, rather than his right to visit the child is at stake, however, the shoe appears to be on the other foot. In Smith v. Cole, 553 So.2d 847 (La.1989), the Louisiana Supreme Court held that its doctrine of dual paternity meant that a child conceived and born during the mother's marriage but after she separated from her husband was the husband's legitimate daughter, a fact that did not excuse the biological father from being ordered to support the child. As Justice Cole put it, "[l]egitimate children cannot be bastardized by succeeding proof of actual parentage." Id., at 854. Is this result consistent with *Michael H.*? Note that the California statute applied in *Michael H.* would not have required a different result, since the conclusive presumption of legitimacy applies only when the child is conceived during the mother's cohabitation with her husband, and when he is not impotent or sterile. Under Justice Scalia's analysis, are these distinctions relevant?

8. What do you make of the historical "methodology" that Justice Scalia announces in footnote 6 of his opinion in *Michael H.*? If this methodology is accepted by a majority of the Court, what would be its likely impact on the future development of sex discrimination claims? See The Supreme Court—1988 Term: Leading Cases, 103 Harv.L.Rev. 137, 183 (1989):

> The plurality's due process methodology dramatically departs from past due process decisions, which relied on general principles rather than specific historical practices supporting or proscribing the particular interest alleged. By abandoning the attempt to effectuate general rights when challenged by specific historical practices, the plurality's analysis chips away at the already shaky foundations of substantive due process jurisprudence. Moreover, although packaged as an objectively precise method of avoiding judicial arbitrariness, the plurality's approach is prone to the same problems of judicial subjectivity that Justice Scalia so vigorously decries.

See also Cass R. Sunstein, Sexual Orientation and the Constitution: A Note on the Relationship Between Due Process and Equal Protection, 55 U.Chi.L.Rev. 1161 (1988), discussing the different functions performed by the two clauses.

3. TEXT NOTE: ILLEGITIMACY AND SEX–BASED DISCRIMINATION

a. *The Relative Rights of the Natural Parents*

In contrast to the position of the legitimate child whose custody was entrusted exclusively to his father,[1] at common law the illegitimate child was denied even the protection of his mother. He had neither family nor kin; he was *filius nullius,* the child of nobody, or *filius populi,* the child of everybody.[2] Despite these phrases, the common law did not ignore the biological relationship between the child and his natural parents; rather, the relationship itself did not confer status. Thus when the phrase *filius nullius* was used, after the Norman Conquest, it signified merely that the illegitimate child was a stranger in blood to his kin in the sense that he could not inherit property

---

1. See Text Note: Child Custody and Support, at p. 316, supra.

2. Sir William Blackstone, Commentaries on the Law of England 459 (1765). See also id. at 454–58.

from them.[3] Rather than being nobody's child, he was nobody's heir.[4] At common law, however, the right to inherit carried with it more than the chance of sharing the family property. Because he could not inherit, the illegitimate was excluded from entry to the trade guilds and corporations that were open only to the sons of freemen.[5] By the same token, disabilities were not inherited: the illegitimate child of a bondsman was free.[6]

One consequence of the logic of the concept of *filius nullius* was that the natural parents of an illegitimate child had no right to his custody and no duty to support him.[7] Their consent to his marriage was neither required nor permitted; a court-appointed guardian performed this parental function.[8] Commentators agree that when the law saw fit to give nobody's child a family, its primary motivation was fiscal, not humanitarian: it desired merely to relieve the public of its duty to support the poor.[9] Thus, the Poor Law Act of 1576 authorized the parish where the child was born to impose a weekly charge for his support upon the mother or reputed father,[10] and the poor law authorities commonly placed the child with the mother for nurture until the age of seven.[11] The Poor Law Amendment Act, 1834, placed upon the mother the duty of supporting her illegitimate children until the age of sixteen, and this was taken to imply a correlative right to custody.[12] The Bastardy Act, 1872, allowed the mother to proceed against the putative father for an allowance, not exceeding 5 shillings a week, for the maintenance and support of their illegitimate child, but the proceeding was not thought to entitle the father to custody.[13]

In light of this common law background, statements of American law prior to the decision in *Stanley* have indicated that the mother has the primary right to custody of an illegitimate child.[14] Her claim would of course be open to dispute if she was not a suitable custodian, for the child's welfare is the ultimate test,[15] but normally her rights to guide the child's upbringing were viewed as equivalent to those shared by both parents of a legitimate child. The father's chief relationship to his illegitimate child was limited to the duty of support.[16]

The father's duty of support, however, was not seen as sufficient to accord him other parental rights. In most states, a finding of paternity did not confer the status of legitimacy upon the child[17] and did not diminish the mother's parental rights. Moreover, the mother has had the sole right to

---

3. The right to inherit remains one of the tests for status as a "child" under the Social Security Act. See 42 U.S.C.A. § 416(h)(2)(A), discussed in Davis v. Richardson, 342 F.Supp. 588 (D.Conn., 1972) (three-judge court), affirmed mem. 409 U.S. 1069, 93 S.Ct. 678, 34 L.Ed.2d 659.

4. Wilfrid Hooper, The Law of Illegitimacy 24–25 (1911).

5. Id., at 31–33.

6. Harry D. Krause, Illegitimacy: Law and Social Policy 3–4 (1971).

7. Hooper, supra note 4, at 124–38.

8. Id., at 138–40.

9. Id., at 102–103; Jacobus tenBroek, California's Dual System of Family Law: Its Origin, Development, and Present Status, Part I, 16 Stan.L.Rev. 257, 284 (1964).

10. Hooper, supra note 4, at 102, tenBroek, supra note 9, at 284.

11. Hooper, supra note 4, at 125.

12. Id., at 128.

13. Id., at 138.

14. Krause, supra note 6, at 28–29; Homer H. Clark, The Law of Domestic Relations 176 (1968); Joseph Warren Madden, Persons and Domestic Relations 348–51 (1931).

15. Ibid.

16. Clark, supra note 14, at 162–67; Krause, supra note 6, at 22.

17. H. Clark, supra note 14, at 159.

consent to the child's adoption by strangers; the father has not been given even the courtesy of notice, let alone the power to object.[18] If the mother chose to keep the child with her, courts were divided as to whether the father was entitled to visitation rights even when he was supporting the child.[19]

Clear sex-based discrimination has existed, therefore, between parents as to their rights of custody and control over their illegitimate children. What is the impact of the Court's decisions in *Stanley, Quilloin, Caban, Lehr,* and *Michael H.* on this body of law? What about *Parham, Levy,* and the triad of cases dealing with inheritance rights: *Labine, Trimble,* and *Lalli?* Professor Clark does not find the outcome of this judicial activity entirely reassuring. He comments,[20]

> [t]en years of Supreme Court litigation have undeniably eliminated many of the legal disabilities formerly afflicting the illegitimate child. The cases seem to rest on the rationale, often articulated more precisely by lower courts than by the Supreme Court, that the illegitimate child, by virtue of a status for which he is not responsible and which has no relation to his worth as an individual, has been the object of discriminatory legal doctrines having no substantial social purpose. The implication, seldom spelled out, is that the recognition by the law of the special position of the traditional family, composed of a married man and woman and their offspring, is not a social purpose which could warrant the discrimination.

As Clark notes,[21] this rationale should have been sufficient to justify the elimination of all forms of discrimination against illegitimate children. Indeed, the authors of appellants' brief in the United States Supreme Court in *Levy* hailed that decision, and its companion case, Glona v. American Guar. & Liab. Ins. Co.,[22] as providing "a basis from which all the major legal disadvantages suffered by reason of illegitimacy can be challenged successfully."[23] Things haven't quite turned out that way, have they? Given the uncertainty that has resulted from the Court's decisions and writing prior to *Lehr,* Clark concludes[24]

> it would have been preferable for the Supreme Court to abstain entirely. The position of the illegitimate child could have been more effectively, and more efficiently, protected by state statutes which were coming to be passed before the Court decided the *Levy* case and are now exemplified by the Uniform Parentage Act. As matters now stand, it is unclear to what extent some states' statutes are valid. It will remain unclear until we have another round of Supreme Court pronouncements, and perhaps even beyond that point.

Has *Lehr* resolved the uncertainty? The Uniform Parentage Act has been adopted in eighteen states.[25] But were the Court's decisions necessary to

---

18. Id., at 625–26; H. Krause, supra note 6, at 32.

19. Id., Krause at 30–31.

20. Homer H. Clark, Constitutional Protection of the Illegitimate Child?, 12 U.C.Davis L.Rev. 383, 410 (1979).

21. Ibid.

22. 391 U.S. 73, 88 S.Ct. 1515, 20 L.Ed.2d 441 (1968).

23. John C. Gray & David Rudovsky, The Court Acknowledges the Illegitimate, 118 U.Pa.L.Rev. 1, 2 (1969).

24. Clark, supra note 20, at 411.

25. Alabama, California, Colorado, Delaware, Hawaii, Illinois, Kansas, Minnesota, Mis-

make equal the respective rights of the natural parents? Have they succeeded in doing that?

b. Illegitimacy and the Social Status of Women

Although illegitimate children have been singled out for social disapproval over the centuries, public opinion has apparently gradually shifted its censure from the child to the mother and quite recently has encompassed the father as well.[26] Drawing upon cross-cultural data, Malinowski in 1930 formulated a Principle of Legitimacy which held that "no child should be brought into the world without a man—and one man at that—assuming the role of sociological father, that is, guardian and protector, the male link between the child and the rest of the community."[27] In 1939, Davis equated legitimacy with marriage and argued that social disapproval for illegitimacy was necessary to maintain marriage as the preferred institutional setting for reproduction.[28] Scoffing at attempts to abolish illegitimacy by granting equal rights to all children, Davis took the unequivocal position that—short of abolishing marriage—illegitimacy could be ended only by eliminating the birth of children out of wedlock through a four-point program consisting of compulsory sex education, free contraceptives distributed by the government, free (and perhaps compulsory) abortion for unmarried women, and criminal penalties for both parents.[29] Since public opinion would not have supported—or even taken seriously—such a "bizarre plan",[30] the import of Davis's analysis was that less drastic legal reforms were useless. Sex education, birth control and abortion are more widely available in 1988 than in 1940, but these services are by no means free to all and the matter of compulsion remains controversial.[31] The percentage of live births occurring out of wedlock stood at 28% in 1991.[32] But, while courts still seek to deal with the social problems arising from illegitimacy by decisions reducing the burdens placed on illegitimate children,[33] the Uniform Parentage Act has proposed a sweeping legislative approach to the matter. Attempting what Davis dismissed as impossible, the Act abandons all distinctions between legitimate and illegitimate children. A child has a legal parent and child relationship to its mother at birth, and to its father if he is married to the mother, has attempted to marry her, has received the child into his home and held it out as his natural child, has acknowledged his paternity in a writing filed with the appropriate authority, or has been identified as the father in a court proceeding.[34] The Act abandons

souri, Montana, Nevada, New Jersey, New Mexico, North Dakota, Ohio, Rhode Island, Washington, and Wyoming. 9B Uniform Laws Ann. 287 (Supp.1995).

26. Clark E. Vincent, Illegitimacy, 7 Int. Ency.Soc.Sci. 85, 88 (1968).

27. Bronislaw Malinowski, Parenthood: The Basis of Social Structure, in Victor F. Calverton & Samuel D. Schmalhausen eds., The New Generation: The Intimate Problems of Modern Parents and Children 113, 137 (1930).

28. Kingsley Davis, Illegitimacy and the Social Structure, 45 Am.J.Sociol. 215 (1939).

29. Id., at 231–32.

30. Id., at 232–33.

31. E.g., Anthony M. Dileo, Directions and Dimensions of Population Policy in the United States: Alternatives for Legal Reform, 46 Tul. L.Rev. 184 (1971); Note, Legal Analysis and Population Control: The Problem of Coercion, 84 Harv.L.Rev. 1856 (1971).

32. U.S. Bureau of the Census, Statistical Abstract of the United States at 79, Table 97 (1994).

33. E.g., Levy v. Louisiana, 391 U.S. 68, 88 S.Ct. 1509, 20 L.Ed.2d 436 (1968); Trimble v. Gordon, 430 U.S. 762, 97 S.Ct. 1459, 52 L.Ed.2d 31 (1977); but see Lalli v. Lalli, 439 U.S. 259, 99 S.Ct. 518, 58 L.Ed.2d 503 (1978).

34. Uniform Parentage Act §§ 1–4.

the premise of the earlier Proposed Uniform Legitimacy Act that would have conditioned legitimacy on a court order identifying the father.[35]   Under the Uniform Parentage Act, the child is the legitimate offspring of its mother at birth.

The underlying premise of the Proposed Uniform Legitimacy Act has been attacked sharply by Tenoso and Wallach,[36] who argued that the law's primary goal should not be a search for the father whose identification would serve to legitimate the child.   Rather, they proposed that the law recognize that a woman and her children constitute a legitimate family unit.[37]   This "woman-centered and defined family" [38] should be allowed to develop as a viable alternative to the existing nuclear family dominated by the male.[39]   Toward that end, the authors proposed a broad legislative program that would recognize all children as legitimate at birth regardless of whether the father can be identified; allow the mother to choose whether the father should be identified at all; require the payment of state support as a substitute for the father's duty rather than as welfare; and provide social welfare resources for all children regardless of the support received from either parent.[40]   To what extent has this approach been embodied in the Uniform Parentage Act? [41]   As we have seen, the mother-child relationship is recognized by the Act as a legal parent-child relationship regardless of the mother's marital status.   If the father is not a "presumed" father under section 4, he cannot bring an action to have himself declared the father unless the mother chooses to place the child for adoption and there is no other presumed father.[42]   The authors' support proposals are not addressed by the Uniform Parentage Act.

What would be the social impact of legislation forthrightly declaring all children to be legitimate?   Exactly that pronouncement was made by the French revolutionary government in 1794; the ensuing reaction that such a

---

35.   Krause, supra note 6, at 235–39.

36.   Patricia Tenoso & Aleta Wallach, Book Review, 19 U.C.L.A.L.Rev. 845 (1972).

37.   Id., at 851–52. See also Carol A. Donovan, The Uniform Parentage Act and Nonmarital Motherhood-by-Choice, 11 N.Y.U.Rev.L. & Soc. Ch. 193 (1983), proposing an amendment to the Uniform Parentage Act that would permit pre-conception agreements between mothers and fathers that the father will not act as the child's social or legal father after its birth.

38.   Id., at 859.

39.   Id., at 865. See also Kristine Roszak, Comment, Mother Knows Best: A Constitutional Perspective on Single Motherhood by Choice, 1984 So.Ill.U.L.J. 329, 348 (1984), arguing that "[t]he right of the single mother-by-choice to structure her family in a nontraditional manner cannot be overcome either by the parental rights of the biological father, the equal protection rights of the child, or the right of the state to protect the traditional family." Do you agree?

40.   Id., at 858–59. The last two suggestions are attributed to Norwegian practice.

41.   In a subsequent article, Wallach and Tenoso recognize that the Uniform Parentage Act is an improvement over the Proposed Uni-

form Legitimacy Act. They criticize the Parentage Act, however, for its failure to go beyond constitutional requirements, and suggest that the Act be modified to make clear its concern with equal status for illegitimate children, not merely equality of legal relationships. They propose that a new section one be adopted that would read as follows:

Section 1.   Status Equality Among All Children and Among All Parents.

It is the intent of this Act to abolish the institution of illegitimacy and differential family status based thereon and to provide equality of legal status to (1) all children by virtue of the fact of birth and regardless of the ability to determine parentage and to (2) all parents by virtue of the fact of parentage.

Aleta Wallach & Patricia Tenoso, A Vindication of the Rights of Unmarried Mothers and Their Children: An Analysis of the Institution of Illegitimacy, Equal Protection, and The Uniform Parentage Act, 23 U.Kan.L.Rev. 23, 68 (1974). Other modifications are suggested at id., 69–70.

42.   Uniform Parentage Act § 24. This provision was held unconstitutional in R. McG. v. J.W., 200 Colo. 345, 615 P.2d 666 (1980).

doctrine would destroy marriage plus Napoleon's opposition led to the abolition of the paternity action in 1803 and left the mother and her illegitimate child in a worse position than they had held before.[43] The Russians, perhaps inadvertently, approached illegitimacy initially by very nearly abolishing marriage: in 1917, religious marriage was prohibited and in 1926 de facto cohabitation was equated with marriage for most purposes so that distinctions between legal and non-legal cohabitation were blurred.[44] The need to replace the war-decimated population as quickly as possible [45] led to the prohibition of abortion in 1936 [46] and to the abolition in 1944 of unregistered marriage and divorce and the reestablishment of distinctions between legitimate and illegitimate children.[47] As in France, the paternity action was abolished; [48] the Russian government itself assumed the burden of support. The repressive laws of 1944 rested most heavily upon women both in terms of financial hardship and social stigma, the latter being particularly strong in rural Russia.[49] Consequently, women were active in seeking legislative change.[50] Some measure of relief was afforded by the liberalization of abortion laws in 1955 and by the 1968 Basic Principles of Legislation on Marriage and the Family,[51] which permitted a father to acknowledge his illegitimate child with the mother's agreement and to be identified as the father by a court if his joint cohabitation with the mother could be shown or if satisfactory evidence established that he had acknowledged paternity.[52]

What conclusions can be drawn from the experience of France in the late eighteenth and early nineteenth centuries and Russia in the twentieth? Would legislation abolishing illegitimacy in the United States in the 1980's produce such an unstable social situation that marriage would be threatened? Professor Krause thinks not.[53]

> We still have adultery and we still have families. Indeed, if we did not still have families, there would be no legitimacy, and consequently no illegitimacy. If equal legal rights are sought for the child without a family, it is only on the assumption that the family will remain.

Does this comment do more than restate the question? Must the experience of France and Russia be explained by the upheavals of a revolutionary society? If not, should feminists take the tack of advocating the abolition of illegitimacy *because* to do so would tend to weaken marriage? If bastardy and marriage are really the only alternatives (are they?) which is least detrimental to women and their children?

43. Crane Brinton, French Revolutionary Legislation on Illegitimacy, 1789–1804 (1936).

44. Jan Gorecki, Communist Family Pattern: Law as an Implement of Change, 1972 U.Ill.L.F. 121, 122–23 (1972); Alice Eh–Soon Tay, The Status of Women in the Soviet Union, 20 Am.J.Comp.L. 662, 668–73 (1972).

45. Max Rheinstein, Marriage Stability, Divorce and the Law 231–32 (1972).

46. Tay, supra note 44, at 674–75.

47. Gorecki, supra note 44, at 126–27.

48. Rheinstein, supra note 45, at 229–30; Tay, supra note 44, at 678.

49. Gorecki, supra note 44, at 134–36.

50. O.M. Stone, The New Fundamental Principles of Soviet Family Law and Their Social Background, 18 Int. & Comp.L.Q. 392, 396–97 (1969).

51. Id., at 410–23; Tay, supra note 44, at 679–81.

52. Id., at 399–400. See also Gorecki, supra note 44, at 135.

53. Krause, supra note 6, at 104.

What is the likelihood that an unmarried mother and her children will be socially accepted as a legitimate family unit? Goode has questioned whether societies with high illegitimacy rates may not have rejected Malinowski's Principle of [male] Legitimacy.[54] He suggests that in many New World societies, from the Southern United States through South America and including the Caribbean, the high illegitimacy rates—approaching seventy percent in some cultures—reflect harsh conditions of settlement and discrimination that weakened both the earlier social norms against illegitimacy and the effectiveness of social controls erected to prevent it.[55] In the United States, high illegitimacy[56] and divorce rates, female-headed families, and increasing welfare dependency among lower-class blacks have been interpreted by the Moynihan Report as indicative of the collapse of the lower-class black family[57] and by Billingsley as proof of its amazing resilience in the face of "oppression and sharply restricted economic and social support."[58] In a discussion of comparative family structure, Smith concludes that the matrifocal family in low-status ethnic groups is a "useful adaptation to conditions of economic insecurity."[59] One study of low-income blacks in American urban centers has found that the black community does not stigmatize illegitimate children or their mothers.[60]

What about support for the mother-centered family? As we have seen, some writers have proposed both children's allowances and public support in lieu of the father's duty to provide for illegitimate children.[61] But others doubt that such schemes for circumventing the welfare bureaucracy are presently viable.[62] Without going into detail on the subject of women and welfare,[63] it may be relevant here to note that receipt of public support— particularly for illegitimate children—is itself a stigma in the United States. A severe tension exists between the desire that all children be supported and the disinclination to encourage sexual promiscuity at the public expense. As a result, traditional notions of morality combined with an effort to reduce the relief rolls have produced restrictions on eligibility unrelated to the needs of

54. William Josiah Goode, The Family 28 (Prentice–Hall Foundations of Modern Sociology Series, 1964).

55. Id., at 27–30. See also William Josiah Goode, Illegitimacy in the Caribbean Social Structure, 25 Am.Soc.Rev. 21 (1960).

56. In 1965, the illegitimacy rate was 97.6 live births per 1,000 unmarried black and other nonwhite women aged 15–44 in the U.S. The comparable white illegitimacy rate was 11.6. Series 21, Vital and Health Statistics # 15, Trends in Illegitimacy United States 1940–1965, p. 26 (Pub. Health Service, U.S. Dept. H.E.W., 1968). In 1984, the illegitimacy rate for black and other nonwhite women was 71.4, for black women 76.8, and for white women 20.1. U.S. Bureau of the Census, Statistical Abstract of the United States at 61, Table 86 (1987). By 1991, the illegitimacy rate among white women was 18, among black women 68.2, and among women of Hispanic origin 38.5. U.S. Bureau of the Census, Statis-

tical Abstract of the United States at 79, Table 97 (1994).

57. Office of Policy Planning and Research, The Negro Family: The Case for National Action 5–14 (U.S. Dept. Labor, 1965).

58. Andrew Billingsley, Black Families in White America 21 (1968).

59. Raymond T. Smith, Family: Comparative Structure, 5 Int.Ency.Soc.Sci. 301, 311 (1968). See also Paul L. Adams, Functions of the Lower–Class Partial Family, 130 Am.J.Psychiatry 200 (1973).

60. Joyce A. Ladner, Tomorrow's Tomorrow: The Black Woman 214 (1972).

61. Tenoso & Wallach, supra note 36, at 858–59.

62. Krause, supra note 6, at 282–84.

63. See generally, Martha Minow, The Welfare of Single Mothers and their Children, 26 Conn.L.Rev. 817 (1994), and accompanying commentary at id., 843–911.

either mothers or children.[64] The courts have struck down or limited restrictions based on the presence in the home of a "substitute father",[65] but restrictions based on a mother's refusal to allow scheduled home visits by a welfare caseworker[66] have been upheld, as have maximum grants regardless of family size.[67] These restrictions and the burden of resisting them add to the difficulties faced by a mother who must rely upon public support for her children. Moreover, when legislative relief is offered, it may contain sex-based discriminations such as those implicitly present in the Work Incentive (WIN) program.[68]

Is public opinion more supportive of mother-centered families when public financial support is not a factor? Reports have indicated that unwed mothers with independent incomes and their own homes are currently tending to keep their children rather than surrender them for adoption.[69] The example of prominent women, including Catherine Deneuve, Vanessa Redgrave and Bernadette Devlin, who did not hide the birth of a child out of wedlock may have influenced others. And artificial insemination of unmarried women who want to have children without legally-designated fathers is not unknown.[70] But does this conclusion imply a class distinction which allows the financially independent woman to have children out of wedlock while denying that privilege to poor women? In view of the Supreme Court's refusal to hold that there is either a statutory or constitutional basis for requiring the state to shoulder the cost of medically necessary abortions for poor women,[71] isn't that the wrong question? Why should the choice of whether to give birth to an unwanted child, whether conceived within or without wedlock, be limited to women who are financially secure?

4. PROPERTY RIGHTS OF COUPLES LIVING IN NONMARITAL COHABITATION

WATTS v. WATTS

Supreme Court of Wisconsin, 1987.
137 Wis.2d 506, 405 N.W.2d 303.

SHIRLEY S. ABRAHAMSON, JUSTICE.

This is an appeal from a judgment of the circuit court for Dane County, William D. Byrne, Judge, dismissing Sue Ann Watts' amended complaint,

64. Roger E. Kohn, Comment, AFDC Eligibility Requirements Unrelated to Need: The Impact of King v. Smith, 118 U.Penn.L.Rev. 1219 (1970). See also Krause, supra note 6, at 267–84. A more general discussion is found in Andrea M. Pearldaughter & Vivian Schneider, Women and Welfare: The Cycle of Female Poverty, 10 Golden Gate Univ.L.Rev. 1043 (Women's Law Forum, 1980).

65. King v. Smith, 392 U.S. 309, 88 S.Ct. 2128, 20 L.Ed.2d 1118 (1968). Recall the criticism of this case offered by the Reagan administration's Working Group on the Family, discussed at p. 254, supra.

66. Wyman v. James, 400 U.S. 309, 91 S.Ct. 381, 27 L.Ed.2d 408 (1971).

67. Dandridge v. Williams, 397 U.S. 471, 90 S.Ct. 1153, 25 L.Ed.2d 491 reh'g denied 398 U.S. 914, 26 L.Ed.2d 80, 90 S.Ct. 1684 (1970).

68. Colquitt M. Walker, Sex Discrimination in Government Benefit Programs, 23 Hastings L.J. 277, 286–89 (1971).

69. Trudy Bradley Festinger, Unwed Mothers and Their Decisions to Keep or Surrender Children, 50 Child Welfare 253 (1971).

70. See generally, Sheila M. O'Rourke, Family Law in a Brave New World: Private Ordering of Parental Rights and Responsibilities for Donor Insemination, 1 Berkeley Women's L.J. 140 (1985).

71. Harris v. McRae, 448 U.S. 297, 100 S.Ct. 2671, 65 L.Ed.2d 784 (1980).

pursuant to sec. 802.06(2)(f), Stats. 1985–86, for failure to state a claim upon which relief may be granted.

* * *

We test the sufficiency of the plaintiff's amended complaint by first setting forth the facts asserted in the complaint and then analyzing each of the five legal theories upon which the plaintiff rests her claim for relief.

I.

The plaintiff commenced this action in 1982. The plaintiff's amended complaint alleges the following facts, which for purposes of this appeal must be accepted as true. The plaintiff and the defendant met in 1967, when she was 19 years old, was living with her parents and was working full time as a nurse's aide in preparation for a nursing career. Shortly after the parties met, the defendant persuaded the plaintiff to move into an apartment paid for by him and to quit her job. According to the amended complaint, the defendant "indicated" to the plaintiff that he would provide for her.

Early in 1969, the parties began living together in a "marriage-like" relationship, holding themselves out to the public as husband and wife. The plaintiff assumed the defendant's surname as her own. Subsequently, she gave birth to two children who were also given the defendant's surname. The parties filed joint income tax returns and maintained joint bank accounts asserting that they were husband and wife. The defendant insured the plaintiff as his wife on his medical insurance policy. He also took out a life insurance policy on her as his wife, naming himself as the beneficiary. The parties purchased real and personal property as husband and wife. The plaintiff executed documents and obligated herself on promissory notes to lending institutions as the defendant's wife.

During their relationship, the plaintiff contributed childcare and home-making services, including cleaning, cooking, laundering, shopping, running errands, and maintaining the grounds surrounding the parties' home. Additionally, the plaintiff contributed personal property to the relationship which she owned at the beginning of the relationship or acquired through gifts or purchases during the relationship. She served as hostess for the defendant for social and business-related events. The amended complaint further asserts that periodically, between 1969 and 1975, the plaintiff cooked and cleaned for the defendant and his employees while his business, a landscaping service, was building and landscaping a golf course.

From 1973 to 1976, the plaintiff worked 20–25 hours per week at the defendant's office, performing duties as a receptionist, typist, and assistant bookkeeper. From 1976 to 1981, the plaintiff worked 40–60 hours per week at a business she started with the defendant's sister-in-law, then continued and managed the business herself after the dissolution of that partnership. The plaintiff further alleges that in 1981 defendant made their relationship so intolerable that she was forced to move from their home and their relationship was irretrievably broken. Subsequently, the defendant barred the plaintiff from returning to her business.

The plaintiff alleges that during the parties' relationship, and because of her domestic and business contributions, the business and personal wealth of the couple increased. Furthermore, the plaintiff alleges that she never received any compensation for these contributions to the relationship and that the defendant indicated to the plaintiff both orally and through his conduct that he considered her to be his wife and that she would share equally in the increased wealth.

The plaintiff asserts that since the breakdown of the relationship the defendant has refused to share equally with her the wealth accumulated through their joint efforts or to compensate her in any way for her contributions to the relationship.

II.

The plaintiff's first legal theory to support her claim against the property accumulated during the cohabitation is that the plaintiff, defendant, and their children constitute a "family," thus entitling the plaintiff to bring an action for property division under sec. 767.02(1)(h), Stats. 1985–86, and to have the court "divide the property of the parties and divest and transfer the title of any such property" pursuant to sec. 767.255, 1985–86.

* * *

The plaintiff relies on *Warden v. Warden,* 36 Wash.App. 693, 676 P.2d 1037 (1984), to support her claim for relief under secs. 767.02(1)(h) and 767.255. In *Warden,* the Washington court of appeals held that the statute providing guidelines for property division upon dissolution of marriage, legal separation, etc., could also be applied to divide property acquired by unmarried cohabitants in what was "tantamount to a marital family except for a legal marriage." *Warden,* 36 Wash.App. at 698, 676 P.2d at 1039. *Warden* is remarkably similar on its facts to the instant case. The parties in *Warden* had lived together for 11 years, had two children, held themselves out as husband and wife, acquired property together, and filed joint tax returns. On those facts, the Washington court of appeals held that the trial court correctly treated the parties as a "family" within the meaning of the Washington marriage dissolution statute. In addition, the trial court had considered such statutory factors as the length and purpose of the parties' relationship, their two children, and the contributions and future prospects of each in determining their respective shares of the property.

Although the *Warden* case provides support for the plaintiff's argument, most courts which have addressed the issue of whether marriage dissolution statutes provide relief to unmarried cohabitants have either rejected or avoided application of a marriage dissolution statute to unmarried cohabitants. *See, e.g., Marvin v. Marvin,* 18 Cal.3d 660, 681, 134 Cal.Rptr. 815, 557 P.2d 106 (1976); *Metten v. Benge,* 366 N.W.2d 577, 579–80 (Iowa 1985); *Glasgo v. Glasgo,* 410 N.E.2d 1325, 1331 (Ind.Ct.App.1980); *Kozlowski v. Kozlowski,* 80 N.J. 378, 383, 403 A.2d 902, 905 (1979).

* * *

On the basis of our analysis of sec. 767.255 and the Family Code which revealed no clear evidence that the legislature intended sec. 767.255 to apply to unmarried persons, we decline the invitation to extend the application of sec. 767.255 to unmarried cohabitants. We therefore hold that the plaintiff has not stated a claim for property division under sec. 767.255.

III.

The plaintiff urges that the defendant, as a result of his own words and conduct, be estopped from asserting the lack of a legal marriage as a defense against the plaintiff's claim for property division under sec. 767.255.

* * *

Although the defendant has not discussed this legal theory, we conclude that the doctrine of "marriage by estoppel" should not be applied in this case. We reach this result primarily because we have already concluded that the legislature did not intend sec. 767.255 to govern property division between unmarried cohabitants. We do not think the parties' conduct should place them within the ambit of a statute which the legislature did not intend to govern them.

IV.

The plaintiff's third legal theory on which her claim rests is that she and the defendant had a contract to share equally the property accumulated during their relationship. The essence of the complaint is that the parties had a contract, either an express or implied in fact contract, which the defendant breached.

Wisconsin courts have long recognized the importance of freedom of contract and have endeavored to protect the right to contract. A contract will not be enforced, however, if it violates public policy. A declaration that the contract is against public policy should be made only after a careful balancing, in the light of all the circumstances, of the interest in enforcing a particular promise against the policy against enforcement. Courts should be reluctant to frustrate a party's reasonable expectations without a corresponding benefit to be gained in deterring "misconduct" or avoiding inappropriate use of the judicial system. * * *

The defendant appears to attack the plaintiff's contract theory on three grounds. First, the defendant apparently asserts that the court's recognition of plaintiff's contract claim for a share of the parties' property contravenes the Wisconsin Family Code. Second, the defendant asserts that the legislature, not the courts, should determine the property and contract rights of unmarried cohabiting parties. Third, the defendant intimates that the parties' relationship was immoral and illegal and that any recognition of a contract between the parties or plaintiff's claim for a share of the property accumulated during the cohabitation contravenes public policy.

The defendant rests his argument that judicial recognition of a contract between unmarried cohabitants for property division violates the Wisconsin Family Code on *Hewitt v. Hewitt,* 77 Ill.2d 49, 31 Ill.Dec. 827, 394 N.E.2d 1204, 3 A.L.R. 4th 1 (1979). In *Hewitt* the Illinois Supreme Court concluded that judicial recognition of mutual property rights between unmarried cohabitants would violate the policy of the Illinois Marriage and Dissolution Act because enhancing the attractiveness of a private arrangement contravenes the Act's policy of strengthening and preserving the integrity of marriage. The Illinois court concluded that allowing such a contract claim would weaken the sanctity of marriage, put in doubt the rights of inheritance, and open the door to false pretenses of marriage. *Hewitt,* 77 Ill.2d at 65, 31 Ill.Dec. at 834, 394 N.E.2d at 1211.

We agree with Professor Prince and other commentators that the *Hewitt* court made an unsupportable inferential leap when it found that cohabitation agreements run contrary to statutory policy and that the *Hewitt* court's approach is patently inconsistent with the principle that public policy limits are to be narrowly and exactly applied.[14]

Furthermore, the Illinois statutes upon which the Illinois supreme court rested its decision are distinguishable from the Wisconsin statutes. The Illinois supreme court relied on the fact that Illinois still retained "fault" divorce and that cohabitation was unlawful. By contrast, Wisconsin abolished "fault" in divorce in 1977 and abolished criminal sanctions for nonmarital cohabitation in 1983.[15]

The defendant has failed to persuade this court that enforcing an express or implied in fact contract between these parties would in fact violate the Wisconsin Family Code. The Family Code, chs. 765–768 Stats. 1985–86, is intended to promote the institution of marriage and the family. We find no indication, however, that the Wisconsin legislature intended the Family Code to restrict in any way a court's resolution of property or contract disputes between unmarried cohabitants.

* * *

We turn to the defendant's third point, namely, that any contract between the parties regarding property division contravenes public policy because the contract is based on immoral or illegal sexual activity. The defendant does not appear to make this argument directly. It is not well developed in the brief, and at oral argument defendant's attorney indicated that he did not find this argument persuasive in light of the current community mores, the substantial number of unmarried people who cohabit, and the legislature's abolition of criminal sanctions for cohabitation. Although the parties in the instant case cohabited at a time when cohabitation was illegal, the defendant's counsel at oral argument thought that the present law should govern this aspect of the case. Because illegal sexual activity has posed a problem for courts in contract actions, we discuss this issue even though the defendant did not emphasize it.

Courts have generally refused to enforce contracts for which the sole consideration is sexual relations, sometimes referred to as "meretricious" relationships. *See In Matter of Estate of Steffes,* 95 Wis.2d 490, 514, 290 N.W.2d 697 (1980), *citing* Restatement of Contracts Section 589 (1932). Courts distinguish, however, between contracts that are explicitly and inseparably founded on sexual services and those that are not. This court, and numerous other courts, have concluded that "a bargain between two people is not illegal merely because there is an illicit relationship between the two so

14. Prince, *Public Policy Limitations in Cohabitation Agreements: Unruly Horse or Circus Pony,* 70 Minn.L.Rev. 163, 189–205 (1985).

15. Both Illinois and Wisconsin have abolished common law marriages. In our view this abolition does not invalidate a private cohabitation contract. Cohabitation agreements differ in effect from common law marriage. There is a significant difference between the consequences of achieving common law marriage status and of having an enforceable cohabitation agreement.

In *Latham v. Latham,* 274 Or. 421, 426–27, 547 P.2d 144, 147 (1976), the Oregon supreme court found that the Legislature's decriminalization of cohabitation represented strong evidence that enforcing agreements made by parties during cohabitation relationships would not be contrary to Oregon public policy.

long as the bargain is independent of the illicit relationship and the illicit relationship does not constitute any part of the consideration bargained for and is not a condition of the bargain." *Steffes,* * * *.

While not condoning the illicit sexual relationship of the parties, many courts have recognized that the result of a court's refusal to enforce contract and property rights between unmarried cohabitants is that one party keeps all or most of the assets accumulated during the relationship, while the other party, no more or less "guilty," is deprived of property which he or she has helped to accumulate. *See e.g., Glasgo v. Glasgo,* 410 N.E.2d 1325, 1330 (Ind.App.1980); *Latham v. Latham,* 274 Or. 421, 426, 547 P.2d 144 (1976); *Marvin v. Marvin, supra,* 18 Cal.3d at 682, 134 Cal.Rptr. at 830, 557 P.2d at 121; *West v. Knowles,* 50 Wash.2d 311, 315–16, 311 P.2d 689 (1957).

The *Hewitt* decision, which leaves one party to the relationship enriched at the expense of the other party who had contributed to the acquisition of the property, has often been criticized by courts and commentators as being unduly harsh.[18] Moreover, courts recognize that their refusal to enforce what are in other contexts clearly lawful promises will not undo the parties' relationship and may not discourage others from entering into such relationships. *Tyranski v. Piggins,* 44 Mich.App. 570, 577, 205 N.W.2d 595 (1973). A harsh, *per se* rule that the contract and property rights of unmarried cohabiting parties will not be recognized might actually encourage a partner with greater income potential to avoid marriage in order to retain all accumulated assets, leaving the other party with nothing. *See Marvin v. Marvin, supra,* 18 Cal.3d at 683, 134 Cal.Rptr. at 831, 557 P.2d at 122.

* * *

The plaintiff has alleged that she quit her job and abandoned her career training upon the defendant's promise to take care of her. A change in one party's circumstances in performance of the agreement may imply an agreement between the parties. *Steffes,* * * * Tyranski * * *.

In addition, the plaintiff alleges that she performed housekeeping, childbearing, childrearing, and other services related to the maintenance of the parties' home, in addition to various services for the defendant's business and her own business, for which she received no compensation. Courts have recognized that money, property, or services (including housekeeping or childrearing) may constitute adequate consideration independent of the parties' sexual relationship to support an agreement to share or transfer property. *See Tyranski,* * * * *Carlson v. Olson,* 256 N.W.2d 249, 253–254 (1977); *Carroll v. Lee,* 148 Ariz. 10, 14, 712 P.2d 923, 927 (1986); *Steffes.* * * * [19]

---

18. *See* Prince, *Public Policy Limitations on Cohabitation Agreements: Unruly Horse or Circus Pony,* 70 Minn.L.Rev. 163, 189–205 (1985); Oldham & Caudill, *A Reconnaissance of Public Policy Restrictions upon Enforcement of Contracts between Cohabitants,* 18 Fam.L.Q. 93, 132 (Spring 1984); Comment, *Marvin v. Marvin: Five Years Later,* 65 Marq.L.Rev. 389, 414 (1982).

19. Until recently, the prevailing view was that services performed in the context of a "family or marriage relationship" were presumed gratuitous. However, that presumption was rebuttable. See *Steffes,* * * *. In *Steffes,* we held the presumption to be irrelevant where the plaintiff can show either an express or implied agreement to pay for those services, even where the plaintiff has rendered them "with a sense of affection, devotion and duty." * * *. For a discussion of the evolution of thought regarding the economic value of homemaking services by cohabitants, *see* Bruch, *Property Rights of De Facto Spouses Including Thoughts on the Value of Homemakers' Services,* 10 Fam.L.Q. 101, 110–14 (Summer 1976).

According to the plaintiff's complaint, the parties cohabited for more than twelve years, held joint bank accounts, made joint purchases, filed joint income tax returns, and were listed as husband and wife on other legal documents. Courts have held that such a relationship and "joint acts of a financial nature can give rise to an inference that the parties intended to share equally." *Beal v. Beal,* 282 Or. 115, 122, 577 P.2d 507, 510 (1978). The joint ownership of property and the filing of joint income tax returns strongly implies that the parties intended their relationship to be in the nature of a joint enterprise, financially as well as personally. * * *

Having reviewed the complaint and surveyed the law in this and other jurisdictions, we hold that the Family Code does not preclude an unmarried cohabitant from asserting contract and property claims against the other party to the cohabitation. We further conclude that public policy does not necessarily preclude an unmarried cohabitant from asserting a contract claim against the other party to the cohabitation so long as the claim exists independently of the sexual relationship and is supported by separate consideration. Accordingly, we conclude that the plaintiff in this case has pleaded the facts necessary to state a claim for damages resulting from the defendant's breach of an express or an implied in fact contract to share with the plaintiff the property accumulated through the efforts of both parties during their relationship. Once again, we do not judge the merits of the plaintiff's claim; we merely hold that she be given her day in court to prove her claim.

V.

The plaintiff's fourth theory of recovery involves unjust enrichment. Essentially, she alleges that the defendant accepted and retained the benefit of services she provided knowing that she expected to share equally in the wealth accumulated during their relationship. She argues that it is unfair for the defendant to retain all the assets they accumulated under these circumstances and that a constructive trust should be imposed on the property as a result of the defendant's unjust enrichment. In his brief, the defendant does not attack specifically either the legal theory or the factual allegations made by the plaintiff.

Unlike claims for breach of an express or implied in fact contract, a claim of unjust enrichment does not arise out of an agreement entered into by the parties. Rather, an action for recovery based upon unjust enrichment is grounded on the moral principle that one who has received a benefit has a duty to make restitution where retaining such a benefit would be unjust. *Puttkammer v. Minth,* 83 Wis.2d 686, 689, 266 N.W.2d 361, 363 (1978).

Because no express or implied in fact agreement exists between the parties, recovery based upon unjust enrichment is sometimes referred to as "quasi contract," or contract "implied in law" rather than "implied in fact." Quasi contracts are obligations created by law to prevent injustice. *Shulse v. City of Mayville,* 223 Wis. 624, 632, 271 N.W. 643 (1937).

In Wisconsin, an action for unjust enrichment, or quasi contract, is based upon proof of three elements: (1) a benefit conferred on the defendant by the plaintiff, (2) appreciation or knowledge by the defendant of the benefit, and (3) acceptance or retention of the benefit by the defendant under circumstances making it inequitable for the defendant to retain the benefit. *Putt-*

kammer, supra, 83 Wis.2d at 689, 266 N.W.2d 361; Wis.J.I.Civil No. 3028 (1981).

* * *

As we have discussed previously, allowing no relief at all to one party in a so-called "illicit" relationship effectively provides total relief to the other, by leaving that party owner of all the assets acquired through the efforts of both. Yet it cannot seriously be argued that the party retaining all the assets is less "guilty" than the other. Such a result is contrary to the principles of equity. Many courts have held, and we now so hold, that unmarried cohabitants may raise claims based upon unjust enrichment following the termination of their relationships where one of the parties attempts to retain an unreasonable amount of the property acquired through the efforts of both.

In this case, the plaintiff alleges that she contributed both property and services to the parties' relationship. She claims that because of these contributions the parties' assets increased, but that she was never compensated for her contributions. She further alleges that the defendant, knowing that the plaintiff expected to share in the property accumulated, "accepted the services rendered to him by the plaintiff" and that it would be unfair under the circumstances to allow him to retain everything while she receives nothing. We conclude that the facts alleged are sufficient to state a claim for recovery based upon unjust enrichment.

As part of the plaintiff's unjust enrichment claim, she has asked that a constructive trust be imposed on the assets that the defendant acquired during their relationship. A constructive trust is an equitable device created by law to prevent unjust enrichment. *Wilharms v. Wilharms,* 93 Wis.2d 671, 678, 287 N.W.2d 779, 783 (1980). To state a claim on the theory of constructive trust the complaint must state facts sufficient to show (1) unjust enrichment and (2) abuse of a confidential relationship or some other form of unconscionable conduct. The latter element can be inferred from allegations in the complaint which show, for example, a family relationship, a close personal relationship, or the parties' mutual trust. These facts are alleged in this complaint or may be inferred. *Gorski v. Gorski,* 82 Wis.2d 248, 254–55, 262 N.W.2d 120 (1978). Therefore, we hold that if the plaintiff can prove the elements of unjust enrichment to the satisfaction of the circuit court, she will be entitled to demonstrate further that a constructive trust should be imposed as a remedy.

VI.

The plaintiff's last alternative legal theory on which her claim rests is the doctrine of partition.

* * *

In Wisconsin partition is a remedy under both the statutes and common law. Partition applies generally to all disputes over property held by more than one party.

* * *

Apart from citing the partition statutes, the plaintiff relies heavily on *Carlson v. Olson, supra* 256 N.W.2d at 255, in which the Minnesota supreme court approved the application of common law partition principles to augment partition statutes on facts very similar to those in this case.[22] *Carlson* is one of a number of cases similar to the fact situation in the case at bar in which the court used the partition remedy to protect the interests of both parties to a nonmarital cohabitation relationship in the property acquired during their relationship. *See, e.g., Carroll v. Lee,* 148 Ariz. 10, 14, 712 P.2d 923 (1986) (partition allowed where parties acquired property in joint title through joint common effort and for a common purpose and parties had implied partnership or joint enterprise agreement).

The defendant refutes the plaintiff's claim for partition on two grounds. First, the defendant cites generally to *Slocum v. Hammond,* 346 N.W.2d 485, 494–95 (Iowa 1984), a case involving nonmarital cohabitation in which the Iowa supreme court denied the plaintiff's partition claim. *Slocum* is inapposite. In *Slocum* the court denied partition simply because the woman had failed to establish through evidence the requisite "joint venture," not because the partition action was an improper remedy in nonmarital cohabitation cases. *Slocum* was recently distinguished in *Metten v. Benge,* 366 N.W.2d 577, 579–80 (Iowa 1985), in which the Iowa supreme court upheld the trial court's application of equitable partition principals to settle a dispute over property by unmarried cohabitants.

Second, as we have previously said, the defendant relying on *Hewitt* groups all of the plaintiff's claims together, including the partition claim, labels them "marriage-like claims," and argues that the court should not grant relief relating to the parties' accumulated property in cases of nonmarital cohabitation. We have already discussed the defendant's position and concluded that we are not persuaded by it.

In this case, the plaintiff has alleged that she and the defendant were engaged in a joint venture or partnership, that they purchased real and personal property as husband and wife, and that they intended to share all the property acquired during their relationship. In our opinion, these allegations, together with other facts alleged in the plaintiff's complaint (*e.g.,* the plaintiff's contributions to the acquisition of their property) and reasonable inferences therefrom, are sufficient under Wisconsin's liberal notice pleading rule to state a claim for an accounting of the property acquired during the parties' relationship and partition. We do not, of course, presume to judge the merits of the plaintiff's claim. Proof of her allegations must be made to the circuit court. We merely hold that the plaintiff has alleged sufficient facts in her complaint to state a claim for relief statutory or common law partition.

In summary, we hold that the plaintiff's complaint has stated a claim upon which relief may be granted. We conclude that her claim may not rest on sec. 767.255, Stats. 1985–86, or the doctrine of "marriage by estoppel," but that it may rest on contract, unjust enrichment or partition. Accordingly, we

---

22. In *Carlson,* as in the instant case, the parties held themselves out to be married. The parties filed joint income tax returns and maintained joint bank accounts. The major difference between *Carlson* and the instant case is that in *Carlson,* the plaintiff's contribution was limited to homemaking and childcare. That contribution was found sufficient to imply an agreement to share all the property accumulated during the parties' relationship. In this case, the plaintiff allegedly contributed business services and personal property as well as homemaking and childcare services.

reverse the judgment of the circuit court, and remand the cause to the circuit court for further proceedings consistent with this opinion.

The judgment of the circuit court is reversed and the cause remanded.

Notes on Watts

1. What rights, if any, do persons who live together in nonmarital cohabitation obtain in the property acquired by each during the relationship? In California, prior to the decision in the leading case of Marvin v. Marvin, 18 Cal.3d 660, 134 Cal.Rptr. 815, 557 P.2d 106 (1976), cited in *Watts,* a relatively clear line could be drawn between married and unmarried cohabiting couples: married couples enjoyed community property rights in the assets acquired by either during the marriage, but unmarried couples obtained property rights only through participating in the acquisition of the property through the contribution of funds or other property, not through the contribution of services. Thus, in rejecting a woman's claim of co-ownership in property acquired by her male cohabitant based on her contribution of unpaid services in the home, the California Supreme Court denied that "a woman living with a man as his wife but with no genuine belief that she is legally married to him acquires by reason of cohabitation alone the rights of a cotenant in his earnings and accumulations during the period of their relationship." Vallera v. Vallera, 21 Cal.2d 681, 684–85, 134 P.2d 761, 762–63 (1943). Similarly, a man who contributed his services as a gardener and carpenter acquired no rights in property owned and operated as a saloon and bar by the woman with whom he lived in nonmarital cohabitation. Gjurich v. Fieg, 164 Cal. 429, 432, 129 Pac. 464, 466 (1913). If property rights were not available, however, contract was an alternative basis for recovery. The California cases had recognized and enforced an express agreement between nonmarried cohabitants that they would live together as husband and wife, that the woman would contribute her services as a homemaker, that the man would invest all monies acquired by either, and that the property acquired by those funds would be the joint property of both. Trutalli v. Meraviglia, 215 Cal. 698, 12 P.2d 430 (1932). Contracts based on the rendition of sexual services, however, were rejected as immoral, so that a woman was unable to recover from the estate of her cohabitant for living with him "as a concubine" and bearing their children. Hill v. Westbrook's Estate, 39 Cal.2d 458, 247 P.2d 19 (1952). *Marvin* reshaped this body of case law to abolish the distinction between the contribution of funds and services to the acquisition of property, and to ground the rights of nonmarital cohabitants doctrinally in contract, trust, and equity, rather than community property law. In making this choice, the *Marvin* court followed the suggestions of Professor Carol Bruch in her article, Property Rights of De Facto Spouses Including Thoughts on the Value of Homemakers' Services, 10 Fam.L.Q. 101 (1976). The *Marvin* opinion is analyzed in Herma Hill Kay & Carol Amyx, Marvin v. Marvin: Preserving the Options, 65 Calif.L.Rev. 937 (1977).

2. Does Justice Abrahamson accept the *Marvin* distinction between marital property and contract as the appropriate basis for recovery in her opinion for the Wisconsin Supreme Court in *Watts?* Under what conditions would she decline to enforce a contract based on the rendition of sexual services? The Illinois Supreme Court in Hewitt v. Hewitt, 77 Ill.2d 49, 31 Ill.Dec. 827, 394 N.E.2d 1204 (1979), cited by the defendant in *Watts,* refused to limit the question to the contract rights of the individual parties; instead, Justice Underwood focused on the broader issue of public policy:

The issue of unmarried cohabitants' mutual property rights, however, as we earlier noted, cannot appropriately be characterized solely in terms of contract law, nor is it limited to considerations of equity or fairness as between the parties to such relationships. There are major public policy questions involved in determining whether, under what circumstances, and to what extent it is desirable to accord some type of legal status to claims arising from such relationships. Of substantially greater importance than the rights of the immediate parties is the impact of such recognition upon our society and the institution of marriage. Will the fact that legal rights closely resembling those arising from conventional marriages can be acquired by those who deliberately choose to enter into what have heretofore been commonly referred to as "illicit" or "meretricious" relationships encourage formation of such relationships and weaken marriage as the foundation of our family-based society? In the event of death shall the survivor have the status of a surviving spouse for purposes of inheritance, wrongful death actions, workmen's compensation, etc.? And still more importantly: what of the children born of such relationships? What are their support and inheritance rights and by what standards are custody questions resolved? What of the sociological and psychological effects upon them of that type of environment? Does not the recognition of legally enforceable property and custody rights emanating from nonmarital cohabitation in practical effect equate with the legalization of common law marriage—at least in the circumstances of this case?

Id., 77 Ill.2d at 57–58, 394 N.E.2d at 1207–08. Does Justice Abrahamson ignore these larger matters? On what basis does she reject the *Hewitt* approach? Can you tell from her opinion whether the trend in American case law favors *Marvin* or *Hewitt?* The New York Court of Appeals, while reaffirming earlier cases recognizing express contracts between persons living in nonmarital cohabitation, also declined to follow *Marvin's* recognition of implied contracts on the ground that the *Marvin* doctrine is "conceptually so amorphous as practically to defy equitable enforcement, and inconsistent with the legislative policy enunciated in 1933 when common-law marriages were abolished in New York". Morone v. Morone, 50 N.Y.2d 481, 484, 429 N.Y.S.2d 592, 593, 413 N.E.2d 1154, 1155 (1980).

3. Do cases like *Watts* and *Marvin* offer adequate protection to women living in nonmarital cohabitation? Professor Grace Blumberg is critical of these approaches as applied to cohabitants who have achieved the kind of stable economic integration of their affairs that suggests the existence of "an intimate personal relationship in which the boundaries of self are expanded to include the needs and interests of another." Grace Ganz Blumberg, Cohabitation Without Marriage: A Different Perspective, 28 U.C.L.A.L.Rev. 1125, 1134 (1981). She rejects contract theories in favor of a legally-imposed status akin to marriage as the basis of property and support claims between the cohabitants. Contract theory, she argues is inadequate to protect the woman in either marital or nonmarital relationships; publicly created status is a more suitable vehicle for this purpose. Blumberg proposes that cohabitants be treated as though they were married for purposes of maintenance and divorce-style property divisions if they have cohabited for a period of two or more years or if they have had a child. Cohabitants who wish to contract out of this assigned status would be permitted to do so, but one gathers that the mere failure to enter a formal marriage would not be effective to achieve this end. Are women in such an inferior bargaining position as compared to men with regard to intimate relationships that such legal devices are required to prevent unfair or unconscionable results? If so, is it better to build in mandatory legal protections for women, or to change the social and

economic conditions that produce the inequality? Blumberg also proposes analogous solutions, with some variation in the duration requirement, to other issues involving the cohabitants in relation to third parties, such as former spouses, or governmental benefit programs, such as workers' compensation. Special solutions are suggested for social security coverage, eligibility for such state programs as AFDC and SSI, and income tax treatment.

Despite her victory in the California Supreme Court, Michelle Triola Marvin did not succeed against actor Lee Marvin at trial before the Los Angeles Superior Court. Judge Marshall found no contract, either express or implied, between the parties, and he refused to apply the equitable remedies of resulting trust, constructive trust, or division of property acquired through "mutual effort." Judge Marshall, mindful of the Supreme Court's directive in footnote 25 of its opinion that trial court judges employ "additional equitable remedies" if "existing remedies prove inadequate" to protect the expectations of the parties, did award Ms. Marvin $104,000 for purposes of "rehabilitation". The sum was said to be the approximate equivalent of the highest pay she had ever earned as a singer, $1,000 per week, for two years. Marvin v. Marvin, No. C 23303 (Superior Court of Los Angeles County, April 17, 1979). This award, immediately dubbed "palimony" by the press, was subsequently reversed on appeal. Marvin v. Marvin, 122 Cal. App.3d 871, 176 Cal.Rptr. 555 (1981). Hearing was denied by the California Supreme Court. See generally, Noel Myricks, "Palimony": The Impact of Marvin v. Marvin, 29 Fam.Rel. 210 (1980).

4. In Smith v. Shalala, 5 F.3d 235 (7th Cir.1993), certiorari denied ___ U.S. ___, 114 S.Ct. 1309, 127 L.Ed.2d 660 (1994), petitioner Charles Smith, a disabled man, contested his classification for SSI benefits as an "eligible spouse" of Cindy Smith, the disabled woman with whom he was living in nonmarital cohabitation. At the time Charles was notified of his eligibility, Cindy was notified that her benefits would be reduced: as an eligible couple, they would share a monthly benefit of $504, while as unmarried individuals they would each receive $336 per month. The Department "deemed" the pair to be married for purposes of SSI benefits because they lived together and held themselves out to the community as husband and wife. Mr. Smith argued that the "deemed married" classification infringed his fundamental right to choose whether to marry and denied him the equal protection of the laws. The court rejected both arguments, pointing out as to the first that the classification " * * * does not bar them from entering other intimate relationships because each is free to marry or to live with whomever they choose; the classification does nothing to abridge such choices"; and as to the second that "Congress has determined that two people can live together more cheaply than one and, therefore, in furthering the apportionment and distribution of supplemental security income and assessing the financial needs of potential claimants, has determined that marriage or 'deemed marriage' is a reasonable indicator of economies of scale and a lowered cost of living." Id., 5 F.3d at 238, 240. Do you agree with this reasoning? The Court also brushed aside the claim that the classification was underinclusive, since Congress does not "deem" married either heterosexual housemates who do not hold themselves out as husband and wife or same-sex couples who do. If the Court had followed the approach taken by the plurality in *Baehr v. Lewin,* set out at p. 268, supra, would it have taken this argument more seriously?

5. The question of whether landlords who believe that unmarried heterosexual cohabitation is sinful may refuse to rent housing to unmarried couples has arisen in several state courts. In California the asserted conflict was between the state Fair Employment and Housing Act (FEHA), which prohibits discrimination

based on marital status, and the owner's First Amendment free exercise rights as well as the federal Religious Freedom Restoration Act of 1993 (RFRA). In Smith v. Fair Employment and Housing Commission, ___ Cal.3d ___, 51 Cal.Rptr.2d 700, ___ P.2d ___ (1996), the California Supreme Court held that FEHA protects unmarried couples, not merely unmarried individuals, against discrimination in housing. In deciding whether Smith should be exempt from FEHA's provisions because of her religious beliefs, Justice Werdegar reasoned for a plurality of the Court that:

> Smith's religion does not require her to rent apartments, nor is investment in rental units the only available income-producing use of her capital. Thus, she can avoid the burden on her religious exercise without violating her beliefs or threatening her livelihood. * * * The asserted burden is the result not of a law directed against religious exercise, but of a religion-neutral law that happens to operate in a way that makes Smith's religious exercise more expensive. * * * Finally, to grant the requested accommodation would not affect Smith alone, but would necessarily impair the rights and interests of third parties. * * *
>
> This set of facts does not, under the relevant case law, support Smith's argument that requiring her to comply with FEHA's antidiscrimination provisions substantially burdens her religious exercise. Accordingly, we have no occasion to determine whether application of the statute to her furthers a compelling state interest or is the least restrictive means to further such an interest. * * *

Justice Mosk, concurring, concluded that RFRA violates the constitutional principle of separation of powers. Justice Kennard, concurring and dissenting, agreed that FEHA protects unmarried couples, but disagreed with Mosk that RFRA was unconstitutional. She was of the view that the state, in requiring Smith to comply with FEHA by renting to such a couple, had substantially burdened her exercise of her religious beliefs in violation of RFRA. In view of this conflict, she believed the state was required (but had failed) to show that there is no less restrictive alternative to enforcing FEHA, such as granting individual exemptions from the Act to Smith and others similarly situated. Justice Baxter, joined by Chief Justice Lucas, concurring and dissenting, was persuaded that RFRA superseded FEHA under the Supremacy Clause. He preferred to remand the case to permit the Commission to apply the compelling governmental interest test consistent with the mandate of RFRA.

Why is this question so difficult? Of the three other state high court cases addressing similar issues, only the Alaska Supreme Court has agreed with the result in the *Smith*. See Swanner v. Anchorage Equal Rights Com'n, 874 P.2d 274 (Alaska 1994), certiorari denied ___ U.S. ___, 115 S.Ct. 460, 130 L.Ed.2d 368 (1994). The Supreme Court of Minnesota avoided the issue by interpreting its state law to permit discrimination in housing against unmarried couples. See State ex rel. Cooper v. French, 460 N.W.2d 2 (Minn.1990). The Supreme Court of Massachusetts found the issue inappropriate for resolution on summary judgment. See Attorney General v. Desilets, 418 Mass. 316, 636 N.E.2d 233 (1994).

6. Both the Illinois court in *Hewitt* and the New York court in *Morone*, discussed in Note 2 supra, rejected the *Marvin* approach in part because of fears that its acceptance would resurrect the doctrine of common law marriage which had been abolished in Illinois in 1905 and in New York in 1933. What was so terrible about common law marriage that these two courts should be so unwilling to disturb its permanent repose? *Hewitt* referred to cases from other states

commenting on the doctrine as a "fruitful source of perjury and fraud" and as a means of weakening "the public estimate of the sanctity of the marriage relation." Hewitt v. Hewitt, 77 Ill.2d 49, 65, 31 Ill.Dec. 827, 834, 394 N.E.2d 1204, 1211 (1979). *Morone* cited legislative history surrounding the abolition of common law marriage in New York, to the effect that attempts "to collect from decedents' estates" under the doctrine "were a fruitful source of litigation." The consensus of those favoring abolition was that "while the doctrine of common-law marriage could work substantial justice in certain cases, there was no built-in method for distinguishing between valid and specious claims". Morone v. Morone, 50 N.Y.2d 481, 489, 429 N.Y.S.2d 592, 596, 413 N.E.2d 1154, 1158 (1980). Common law marriage has also been abolished in California and in Wisconsin, but the fears that troubled the judges in Illinois and New York were given short shrift in both states. How can this difference in attitude be explained?

The specter of reviving common law marriage by granting relief to a woman who, attempting reconciliation with her husband following divorce, lived with him in nonmarital cohabitation for five years, did not deter the Indiana Court of Appeals. In Glasgo v. Glasgo, 410 N.E.2d 1325, 1329 (Ind.App.1980), it upheld an order awarding the woman one-half of the property the parties had accumulated during the five year period. *Hewitt* was rejected as "unduly harsh and unnecessary" since the woman had based her claim on contractual or equitable grounds, not on being a common law wife.

7. Divorced women who are receiving alimony from a former husband and who choose to live in nonmarital cohabitation with another man face special dangers of losing their payments. In some states, the result is made possible by statute. See, e.g., New York Domestic Relations Law § 248, which provides in part:

> The Court in its discretion upon application of the husband on notice, upon proof that the wife is habitually living with another man and holding herself out as his wife, although not married to such man, may modify such final judgment and any orders made with respect thereto by annulling the provisions of such final judgment or orders or of both, directing payment of money for the support of such wife.

This statute has been interpreted to apply only when the wife is receiving "double support" from her husband and her male companion, Krawczuk v. Krawczuk, 49 A.D.2d 1003, 374 N.Y.S.2d 70 (1975). The "living with" and "holding out" requirements have been read disjunctively, so that a mere showing that the former wife lived with a male companion for six months was not sufficient to terminate her alimony in the absence of any evidence that she had represented herself, orally or by conduct, to be his wife. Northrup v. Northrup, 43 N.Y.2d 566, 402 N.Y.S.2d 997, 373 N.E.2d 1221 (1978). See also Stern v. Stern, 88 Misc.2d 860, 389 N.Y.S.2d 265 (1976) and Citron v. Citron, 91 Misc.2d 785, 398 N.Y.S.2d 624 (1977), both refusing to terminate alimony where the ex-wife and her companion went to great lengths to assure the world at large that they were not actually married.

See also In the Matter of Anonymous, 90 Misc.2d 801, 395 N.Y.S.2d 1000 (Sup.Ct.1977) (sub-titled by the judge after a late 1960s movie, "Bob and Carol and Ted and Alice"), where the court refused to terminate support payments provided for "Carol" in her separation agreement with "Bob"; both couples had divorced, "Bob" and "Alice" had married, while "Carol" and "Ted" were merely living together. To apply section 248 to this situation, said the judge, would be a "travesty of justice." And see, construing a California statute that ordered revocation of support upon proof that the supported spouse "is living with a person of the opposite sex and holding himself or herself out as the spouse of the person for a total of 30 days or more, either consecutive or nonconsecutive, although not married to the person," Lang v. Superior Court, 53 Cal.App.3d 852, 126 Cal.Rptr. 122 (1975). The statute was subsequently amended to provide a rebuttable presumption of "decreased need for support if the supported party is cohabiting with a person of the opposite sex." West's Ann.Cal.Fam.Code 4323. In Marriage of Leib, 80 Cal.App.3d 629, 145 Cal.Rptr. 763 (1978), a husband who had been unsuccessful in terminating his ex-wife's spousal support under the earlier version of this statute because she and her male companion were not "holding themselves out" as married, won under the new amendment. Holding out was no longer required, reasoned the court, and the ex-wife had failed to overcome the presumption of decreased need. Was this what the legislature intended?

Compare Sims v. Sims, 245 Ga. 680, 682, 266 S.E.2d 493, 495 (1980), which upheld against constitutional attack Georgia's "live-in lover" law, commenting that "[i]f the law ensures the continuation of alimony payments subsequent to the formation of a relationship akin to marriage while providing that such payments would cease upon remarriage, it would tend to discourage marriage. * * * Code Ann. § 30–220(b), therefore, fosters the legitimate government objective of encouraging the stability of marriage and the family." The court subsequently made clear that the Georgia statute applies both when the cohabitants live together openly, even though there is no economic benefit to the supported former spouse, and when the former spouse shares expenses of the cohabitation, even though there is no proof of sexual intercourse. See Hathcock v. Hathcock, 249 Ga. 74, 287 S.E.2d 19 (1982). In Marriage of Sappington, 106 Ill.2d 456, 88 Ill.Dec. 61, 478 N.E.2d 376 (1985), the Illinois Supreme Court applied its statute terminating maintenance "if the party receiving maintenance cohabits with another person on a resident, continuing conjugal basis" to a woman who was living with a man who testified that he was impotent. Sexual intercourse, the court reasoned, was not essential to a conjugal relationship. Isn't this carrying things too far? Does the statute apply to a woman who shares the marital home with another woman, but who does not have a sexual relationship with her? See generally, Comment, Alimony, Cohabitation, and the Wages of Sin: A Statutory Analysis, 33 Ala.L.Rev. 577 (1982).

In the absence of a specific statute, the husband's motion to terminate alimony when his former wife is living with another man must be measured against the general standard for modification, whether the circumstances of the parties have changed since the original award. Several courts have ruled that the changed circumstances must be financial, not sexual: if the male companion is not contributing to the ex-wife's support, no modification will be granted. See, e.g., Gayet v. Gayet, 92 N.J. 149, 456 A.2d 102 (1983) (the test for whether cohabiting spouse's alimony award should be modified is whether the relationship has reduced the financial needs of the dependent former spouse); Van Gorder v. Van Gorder, 110 Wis.2d 188, 327 N.W.2d 674 (1983) (rejecting former husband's contention that cohabitation alone is a sufficient change of circumstances that justifies the termination of maintenance payments; cohabitation is only a factor to consider in so far as it may change the former spouse's economic status); Mitchell v. Mitchell, 418 A.2d 1140 (Me.1980), (refusing to terminate or reduce an ex-husband's support payments to his 60 year old former wife who had moved in with a 57 year old "gentleman friend" because of her fears of living alone when she suffered from eye trouble that might lead to blindness: the court reasoned that the fact of cohabitation without more did not indicate that the ex-wife's need for alimony had ended, and there were no other facts shown that established a substantial change in her financial resources); Myhre v. Myhre, 296 N.W.2d 905 (S.D.1980) (ordering former husband to resume alimony payments to 60 year old former wife who shared a household, but not sleeping quarters, with another man; rejecting the holdings of other states that termination should be automatic regardless of need). Is this the better approach? See generally Walter Wadlington, Sexual Relations After Separation or Divorce: The New Morality and the Old and New Divorce Laws, 63 Va.L.Rev. 249, 265–77 (1977).

8. Useful discussion is contained in John M. Eekelaar and Sanford N. Katz, Marriage and Cohabitation in Contemporary Societies (1980).

C. TEXT NOTE: THE LEGAL STRUCTURE OF FAMILY LIFE

Why is it necessary or desirable to have laws governing family life?[1] Marriage laws determine which persons are eligible to marry, the permissible range of their choice of partners, and the number of partners they may have at a given time. Divorce laws control the duration of the relationship and the conditions under which it can be dissolved. Family support and property laws establish the framework within which the on-going relationship is carried out, although, as we have seen, very little direct enforcement of these provisions occurs during the existence of the relationship. Laws governing child labor, child abuse and neglect, and domestic violence set limits to parental control of children as well as spousal interaction. Laws governing testamentary disposition and intestate succession control the intergenerational transfer of property among persons identified as family members. Eligibility for social security benefits may depend on which family relationships are legally recognized, as do inheritance tax laws that treat transferees classed as family members more favorably than strangers. Income tax laws presently discriminate between types of marriages, favoring the single-earner couple over the two-earner family. After centuries of neglect, the criminal law is beginning to assert control over marital rape.

What would happen if this vast legal apparatus were dismantled? If marriage were abolished as a civil ceremony, leaving its regulation as a religious sacrament in the hands of the various religious groups? If all legal sanctions against voluntary cohabitation were withdrawn? If divorce, as a civil procedure, no longer existed? If property and support rights between adults were governed by contract? If the duty of child support once more became a moral, not a legal, obligation? If parental disputes over children upon the termination of a relationship were settled by agreement or informal mediation? If all children were treated alike, regardless of the living arrangements of their parents? If, in the absence of testamentary disposition (from which forced shares were eliminated), all of a decedent's property escheated to the state? If violence within the home were handled like violence in the community at large? If the social security system were shorn of its concepts of adult dependency and its benefits were not conditioned on family status?

1. Another exploration of this theme is carried out by E.M. Clive, Marriage: An Unnecessary Legal Concept? in [John M. Eekelaar & Sanford N. Katz, eds.] Marriage and Cohabitation in Contemporary Societies at 71–81 (1980).

If tax laws treated all individuals alike, regardless of their living arrangements?

If, in short, the legal structure surrounding family life were withdrawn, what would happen? Would society collapse? Would the family disappear? Both results seem unlikely. For many people, religious doctrine or moral values would continue to define proper conduct in family life. For others, sexual attraction, mutual interests, and the economies of scale derived from shared living arrangements would continue to make cohabitation agreeable. The reciprocal bonds of love and duty that develop from the parent-child relationship would not disappear.

If family life might be expected to survive in the absence of legal regulation, or even legal definition, why does so much controversy surround the content of laws presently governing family arrangements? It may be suggested that what is in dispute is not the legal definition of the family, but more basic underlying value judgments about what forms of family life are socially and ethically appropriate today.[2] It is unlikely that the outcome of this debate will be decided by judges or even determined by legislators; rather, their future decisions will be molded by the debate and will reflect its ultimate resolution.

Academic concern about the role, function, and appropriate form of family life is by no means new. Social scientists have identified various causes for what is perceived as the reduction of functions formerly ascribed to the family, leading to its decline as a useful and respected social institution. These include the industrial revolution, with its accompanying separation of the home from the workplace; the emancipation of women, which made possible a broader choice of lifestyles; the relinquishment of child-rearing to the experts in medicine and in education; and the liberalization of divorce laws, which itself was seen as a response to some of the earlier trends.[3] Even the family's capacity to perform its seemingly unique function of providing a private sanctuary for its members from the outside world has been questioned.[4] The accumulated effects of these and other trends, as reflected in sociological data, are used by Weitzman to show that the social assumptions on which current legal regulation of the family rests no longer conform to social reality.[5] Her conclusion, however, is not that laws governing family life should be abolished, but rather that they should be changed to accommodate current social forms including serial family formation resulting from divorce and remarriage; marriage among the elderly; childless marriage; egalitarian and dual career marriage; plural marriage; and same-sex marriage.

Weitzman's proposals would allow an almost unrestricted choice of lifestyle and living arrangement. They depend for legal protection, not on alterations in the law governing marriage and the family, but on an expansion

2. Compare, e.g., Brigette Berger & Peter L. Berger, The War Over the Family: Capturing the Middle Ground (1983) with Letty Cottin Pogrebin, Family Politics: Love and Power on an Intimate Frontier (1983).

3. See generally, Carl N. Degler, At Odds: Women and the Family in America From the Revolution to the Present (1980).

4. Christopher Lasch, Haven in a Heartless World: The Family Besieged (1979).

5. Lenore J. Weitzman, Legal Regulation of Marriage: Tradition and Change, 62 Calif.L.Rev. 1169 (1974).

of the law of contract to permit recognition and enforcement of what she calls "contracts within and in lieu of marriage".[6] Students of traditional contract law may wonder whether such an expansion is possible. But, as Marjorie Shultz has convincingly demonstrated, the private contract is a tool with sufficient flexibility and sensitivity to be used in structuring intimate relationships.[7]

Feminists have been in the forefront of the most recent re-examination of laws governing the family. Apart from those who would like to abolish marriage as a social as well as a legal institution,[8] their efforts have been primarily concerned with eliminating legal reinforcement of the social assignment of family functions on the basis of sex. The Uniform Marriage and Divorce Act has served as a partial model in this effort. But, as Prager has noted, "the achievement of equality does not necessarily spell the end of division of functions within a family; it simply ends the assignment of function based upon sex." [9] But even that modest statement of the feminist position is fraught with controversy. If women are not accepted as equals in the marketplace, one argument runs, why should they relinquish their primacy in the home? This argument ignores the work of those, like Bernard,[10] who have shown that traditional married life is a very different experience for men and women: healthy for men, damaging for women. But when women, to seek for themselves the rewards available in the world of affairs long the province of men, undertake demanding responsibilities outside the home, they are reproached for abandoning their primary duty to their children.[11] Is this not the assignment of function on the basis of sex? Rossi, who, with the help of new learning in biology, now sees that women and men are situated differently with respect to their innate attachment to infants,[12] once, saw, with equal clarity, that women could never attain social, economic or legal equality as long as child care remained the primary duty of mothers.[13] Must anatomy once again become destiny?

The ongoing academic exploration into the appropriate form and function of the modern family was transformed into a public debate by the unsuccessful struggle for ratification of an Equal Rights Amendment to the United States Constitution between 1972 and 1982. Both opponents and proponents of the ERA believed that its ratification would require fundamental changes in traditional family life. Professor Lenore J. Weitzman, a proponent, saw

---

6. Id., at 1249–76.

7. Marjorie Maguire Shultz, Contractual Ordering of Marriage: A New Model For State Policy, 70 Calif.L.Rev. 204 (1982).

8. Sheila Cronan, Marriage, Notes From the Third Year: Women's Liberation 62 (1971), reprinted at p. 248, supra.

9. Susan W. Prager, Sharing Principles and the Future of Marital Property Law, 25 U.C.L.A.L.Rev. 1, 13–14 (1977).

10. Jessie Shirley Bernard, The Future of Marriage 3–53 (1972).

11. Lasch, supra note 4, at xvi–xvii. ("While defenders of the family need to acknowledge the justice of the central feminist demands, feminists, for their part need to ac-

knowledge the deterioration of care for the young and the justice of the demand that something be done to arrest it. Feminists have not answered the argument that day care provides no substitute for the family.")

12. Alice S. Rossi, Gender and Parenthood, 49 Am.Soc.Rev. 1 (1984).

13. Alice S. Rossi, Equality Between the Sexes: An Immodest Proposal, 93 Daedalus 607 (1964). See also Herma Hill Kay, Equality and Difference: A Perspective on No–Fault Divorce and its Aftermath, 56 U.Cin.L.Rev. 1, 77–89 (1987) (episodic analysis supports shared parenting of children by emphasizing the analytic distinction between childbearing and child-rearing).

the ERA as a necessary tool for restructuring an outmoded institution: [14]

> The Equal Rights Amendment provides a unique opportunity to bring the structure of legal marriage into line with social reality. The present structure of legal marriage is archaic: it continues to enforce outmoded and inflexible roles on husbands and wives. These roles are based on sex stereotypes and strongly contradict the living reality of most marriages. The passage of the Equal Rights Amendment will necessitate fundamental changes in family law to make legal marriage more closely reflect an egalitarian partnership between husband and wife. In this way the Equal Rights Amendment will revitalize and strengthen marriage by making it a more viable and equal relationship, a structure more in accord with the needs and family patterns of most people in our society.

Compare the remarks of Barbara B. Smith, General President, Relief Society, "The Mormon Woman Looks at ERA", delivered at Weber State Institute on April 20, 1978:

> I think there is reason to be deeply concerned about the possible effect on the family. We believe that the basic unit of society, eternally, as well as temporally, is the family. The family pattern which has served best over the centuries provides some preferential treatment for the woman in the home. The husband is designated by the law as the provider.

> The law as we know it today in the United States makes the husband liable for the support of his wife and children. This concept is found in the laws of each of the fifty states. Under the ERA this kind of a legal assumption would not be allowed. I think this would definitely work a hardship on the woman who has elected to stay at home and rear a family. All preferential treatment would be gone from the law under ERA. I do not find this to be in the best interest of women.

Were the hopes and fears of both proponents and opponents overdrawn? It seems clear that concern over the ERA's potential harm to American homemakers contributed to its defeat.[15] Yet feminists may not be well-advised to place great reliance on the law as an instrument for social change in matters affecting the family. A more open-textured, contextual, and non-judgmental legal framework may afford more leeway for individual growth and social accommodation.[16]

Others, however, appear to believe that the American family is in need of additional legislative protection. Senator Laxalt introduced his "Family Protection Act" in 1979 for the purpose of strengthening the American family and removing "those Federal Governmental policies which inhibit its strength

---

14. Lenore J. Weitzman, Legal Equality in Marriage and Divorce: The ERA's Mandate, in Impact ERA: Limitations and Possibilities at 184 (Calif.Comm. on the Status of Women) (1976).

15. See Jane J. Mansbridge, Why We Lost the ERA 90–117 (1986).

16. See generally, David L. Chambers, The "Legalization" of the Family: Toward a Policy of Supportive Neutrality, 18 U.Mich.J.L.Reform 805 (1985); Martha Minow, "Forming Underneath Everything That Grows:" Toward a History of Family Law, 1985 Wis.L.Rev. 819; Carl Schneider, Moral Discourse and the

and prosperity." [17]   The policies that need to be removed, in the Senator's view, include restrictions on prayer in public buildings; on the right of parents to inspect their children's school records, and to review textbooks selected for use in public school classrooms; and on the right of parents and school boards to limit or prohibit the "intermingling of sexes" in sports or other school-related activities.[18]   The bill also contained a variety of measures dealing with tax assistance, grants to local schools and educational agencies, and the right of parents to be notified of the provision to their minor children of contraceptive devices, abortion counseling, or treatment for veneral disease. We have already noted the criticism directed toward the decisions of the United States Supreme Court that have prevented some state legislatures from enacting a conservative family program.[19]

Ellen Ross [20] identifies the hidden agenda behind many of these efforts to preserve the traditional family:

> [T]oday's predictions of family decay serve undiluted right-wing purposes. American voters are being mobilized nationally not only against abortion, affirmative action, and the Equal Rights Amendment, but also for bigger defense budgets, massive cutbacks in social services, and removal of restraints on corporate profits—all in the name of the "love, trust, and fulfillment" of traditional marriage and the family. * * *

If the family is to provide the institutional battleground on which opposing political groups choose to test their strength, it is not surprising that some feminists have found it necessary to provide elaborate explanations of their own decisions to marry.[21]   It would, however, be surprising and even a bit disheartening if, having married, they and their spouses were to lose interest in a continued critical examination of marriage and family life.

D. FAMILY PLANNING: WHO CONTROLS THE REPRODUCTIVE PROCESS?

1. CONTRACEPTION

CAREY v. POPULATION SERVS. INT'L

Supreme Court of the United States, 1977.
431 U.S. 678, 97 S.Ct. 2010, 52 L.Ed.2d 675.

MR. JUSTICE BRENNAN delivered the opinion of the Court (Parts I, II, III, and V), together with an opinion (Part IV), in which MR. JUSTICE STEWART, MR. JUSTICE MARSHALL, and MR. JUSTICE BLACKMUN joined.

Transformation of American Family Law, 83 Mich.L.Rev. 1803 (1985).

17. S. 1808, 96th Cong., 1st Sess., § 2(b) 1979.

18. Id., § 101.

19. See Report of the Working Group on the Family, The Family: Preserving America's Future (U.S. Dept. of Education, 1986), quoted in part at p. 258, supra; The Contract with the American Family (1995), quoted in part at p. 261, supra.

20. Ellen Ross, "The Love Crisis": Couples Advice Books of the Late 1970s, 6 Signs 109, 122 (1980).

21. Esther Margolis, Jane Pauley, Michele Shay, Lynn Sherr, Lucia Staniels, Carol Tavris & Marlo Thomas, Why We Decided to Marry Now—And Not Before, Ms. Magazine, 47–51, March 1981. See also Sally Quinn, Why I, Too, Finally Had to Get Married, San Francisco Chronicle, February 9, 1981, at 16, col. 1.

Under New York Educ.Law § 6811(8) (McKinney 1972) it is a crime (1) for any person to sell or distribute any contraceptive of any kind to a minor under the age of 16 years; (2) for anyone other than a licensed pharmacist to distribute contraceptives to persons 16 or over; and (3) for anyone, including licensed pharmacists, to advertise or display contraceptives. A three-judge District Court for the Southern District of New York declared § 6811(8) unconstitutional in its entirety under the First and Fourteenth Amendments of the Federal Constitution insofar as it applies to nonprescription contraceptives, and enjoined its enforcement as so applied. 398 F.Supp. 321 (1975). * * *

We affirm.

* * *

II

Although "[t]he Constitution does not explicitly mention any right of privacy," the Court has recognized that one aspect of the "liberty" protected by the Due Process Clause of the Fourteenth Amendment is "a right of personal privacy, or a guarantee of certain areas or zones of privacy." Roe v. Wade, 410 U.S. 113, 152, 93 S.Ct. 705, 726, 35 L.Ed.2d 147 (1973). This right of personal privacy includes "the interest in independence in making certain kinds of important decisions." Whalen v. Roe, 429 U.S. 589, 599–600, 97 S.Ct. 869, 876, 51 L.Ed.2d 64 (1977). While the outer limits of this aspect of privacy have not been marked by the Court, it is clear that among the decisions that an individual may make without unjustified government interference are personal decisions "relating to marriage, Loving v. Virginia, 388 U.S. 1, 12, 87 S.Ct. 1817, 1823, 18 L.Ed.2d 1010 (1967); procreation, Skinner v. Oklahoma ex rel. Williamson, 316 U.S. 535, 541–542, 62 S.Ct. 1110, 1113–1114, 86 L.Ed. 1655 (1942); contraception, Eisenstadt v. Baird, 405 U.S., at 453–454, 92 S.Ct., at 1038–1039; id., at 460, 463–465, 92 S.Ct., at 1042, 1043–1044 (White, J., concurring in result); family relationships, Prince v. Massachusetts, 321 U.S. 158, 166, 64 S.Ct. 438, 442, 88 L.Ed. 645 (1944); and child rearing and education, Pierce v. Society of Sisters, 268 U.S. 510, 535, 45 S.Ct. 571, 573, 69 L.Ed. 1070 (1925); Meyer v. Nebraska, [262 U.S. 390, 399, 43 S.Ct. 625, 67 L.Ed. 1042 (1923)]." Roe v. Wade, supra, at 152–153, 93 S.Ct., at 726. See also Cleveland Board of Education v. LaFleur, 414 U.S. 632, 639–640, 94 S.Ct. 791, 796–797, 39 L.Ed.2d 52 (1974).

The decision whether or not to beget or bear a child is at the very heart of this cluster of constitutionally protected choices. That decision holds a particularly important place in the history of the right of privacy, a right first explicitly recognized in an opinion holding unconstitutional a statute prohibiting the use of contraceptives, Griswold v. Connecticut, supra, and most prominently vindicated in recent years in the contexts of contraception, Griswold v. Connecticut, supra; Eisenstadt v. Baird, supra; and abortion, Roe v. Wade, supra; Doe v. Bolton, 410 U.S. 179, 93 S.Ct. 739, 35 L.Ed.2d 201 (1973); Planned Parenthood of Central Missouri v. Danforth, 428 U.S. 52, 96 S.Ct. 2831, 49 L.Ed.2d 788 (1976). This is understandable, for in a field that by definition concerns the most intimate of human activities and relationships, decisions whether to accomplish or to prevent conception are among the most private and sensitive. "If the right of privacy means anything, it is the right of the individual, married or single, to be free of unwarranted governmental intrusion into matters so fundamentally affecting a person as the decision whether to bear or beget a child." Eisenstadt v. Baird, supra, 405 U.S., at 453, 92 S.Ct., at 1038. (Emphasis omitted.)

That the constitutionally protected right of privacy extends to an individual's liberty to make choices regarding contraception does not, however, automatically invalidate every state regulation in this area. The business of manufacturing and selling contraceptives may be regulated in ways that do not infringe protected individual choices. And even a burdensome regulation may be validated by a sufficiently compelling state interest. * * * "Compelling" is of course the key word; where a decision as fundamental as that whether to bear or beget a child is involved, regulations imposing a burden on it may be justified only by compelling state interests, and must be narrowly drawn to express only those interests. * * *.

With these principles in mind, we turn to the question whether the District Court was correct in holding invalid the provisions of § 6811(8) as applied to the distribution of nonprescription contraceptives.

III

We consider first the wider restriction on access to contraceptives created by § 6811(8)'s prohibition of the distribution of nonmedical contraceptives to adults except through licensed pharmacists.

Appellants argue that this Court has not accorded a "right of access to contraceptives" the status of a fundamental aspect of personal liberty. They emphasize that Griswold v. Connecticut struck down a state prohibition of the *use* of contraceptives, and so had no occasion to discuss laws "regulating their manufacture or sale." * * * *Griswold* may no longer be read as holding only that a State may not prohibit a married couple's use of contraceptives. Read in light of its progeny, the teaching of *Griswold* is that the Constitution protects individual decisions in matters of childbearing from unjustified intrusion by the State.

Restrictions on the distribution of contraceptives clearly burden the freedom to make such decisions. A total prohibition against sale of contraceptives, for example, would intrude upon individual decisions in matters of procreation and contraception as harshly as a direct ban on their use. Indeed, in practice, a prohibition against all sales, since more easily and less offensively enforced, might have an even more devastating effect upon the freedom to choose contraception. Cf. Poe v. Ullman, 367 U.S. 497, 81 S.Ct. 1752, 6 L.Ed.2d 989 (1961).

* * *

There remains the inquiry whether the provision serves a compelling state interest. Clearly "interests * * * in maintaining medical standards, and in protecting potential life," Roe v. Wade, * * * cannot be invoked to justify this statute. Insofar as § 6811(8) applies to nonhazardous contraceptives, it bears no relation to the State's interest in protecting health. Eisenstadt v. Baird, * * *. Nor is the interest in protecting potential life implicated in state regulation of contraceptives. Roe v. Wade, supra, at 163–164, 93 S.Ct., at 731–732.

Appellants therefore suggest that § 6811(8) furthers other state interests. But none of them is comparable to those the Court has heretofore recognized as compelling. Appellants argue that the limitation of retail sales of nonmedical contraceptives to pharmacists (1) expresses "a proper concern that young people not sell contraceptives"; (2) "allows purchasers to inquire as to the relative qualities of the varying products and prevents anyone from tampering with them"; and (3) facilitates enforcement of the other provisions of the statute. * * * The first hardly can justify the statute's incursion into constitutionally protected rights, and in any event the statute is obviously not substantially related to any goal of preventing young people from selling contraceptives. Nor is the statute designed to serve as a quality control device. Nothing in the record suggests that pharmacists are particularly qualified to give advice on the merits of different nonmedical contraceptives, or that such advice is more necessary to the purchaser of contraceptive products than to consumers of other nonprescription items. Why pharmacists are better able or more inclined than other retailers to prevent tampering with prepackaged products, or, if they are, why contraceptives are singled out for this special protection, is also unexplained. As to ease of enforcement, the prospect of additional administrative inconvenience has not been thought to justify invasion of fundamental constitutional rights. * * *

IV [12]

A

The District Court also held unconstitutional, as applied to nonprescription contraceptives, the provision of § 6811(8) prohibiting the distribution of contraceptives to those under 16 years of age. Appellants contend that this provision of the statute is constitutionally permissible as a regulation of the morality of minors, in furtherance of the State's policy against promiscuous sexual intercourse among the young.

* * *

Of particular significance to the decision of this case, the right to privacy in connection with decisions affecting procreation extends to minors as well as to adults. Planned Parenthood of Central Missouri v. Danforth, supra, held that a State "may not impose a blanket provision * * * requiring the consent of a parent or person *in loco parentis* as a condition for abortion of an unmarried minor during the first 12 weeks of her pregnancy." * * *

Since the State may not impose a blanket prohibition, or even a blanket requirement of parental consent, on the choice of a minor to terminate her pregnancy, the constitutionality of a blanket prohibition of the distribution of contraceptives to minors is *a fortiori* foreclosed. The State's interests in protection of the mental and physical health of the pregnant minor, and in protection of potential life are clearly more implicated by the abortion decision than by the decision to use a nonhazardous contraceptive.

Appellants argue, however, that significant state interests are served by restricting minors' access to contraceptives, because free availability to minors of contraceptives would lead to increased sexual activity among the young, in

---

12. This part of the opinion expresses the views of Justices Brennan, Stewart, Marshall, and Blackmun.

violation of the policy of New York to discourage such behavior. The argument is that minors' sexual activity may be deterred by increasing the hazards attendant on it. The same argument, however, would support a ban on abortions for minors, or indeed support a prohibition on abortions, or access to contraceptives, for the unmarried, whose sexual activity is also against the public policy of many States. Yet, in each of these areas, the Court has rejected the argument, noting in Roe v. Wade, that "no court or commentator has taken the argument seriously." * * * The reason for this unanimous rejection was stated in Eisenstadt v. Baird: "It would be plainly unreasonable to assume that [the State] has prescribed pregnancy and the birth of an unwanted child [or the physical and psychological dangers of an abortion] as punishment for fornication." * * * We remain reluctant to attribute any such "scheme of values" to the State.

* * *

B

Appellants argue that New York does not totally prohibit distribution of contraceptives to minors under 16, and that accordingly § 6811(8) cannot be held unconstitutional. Although § 6811(8) on its face is a flat unqualified prohibition, Educ.Law § 6807(b) (McKinney, Supp.1976–1977), see nn. 1, 7, and 13, supra, provides that nothing in Education Law §§ 6800–6826 shall be construed to prevent "[a]ny physician * * * from supplying his patients with such drugs as [he] * * * deems proper in connection with his practice." This narrow exception, however, does not save the statute. * * *

V

The District Court's holding that the prohibition of any "advertisement or display" of contraceptives is unconstitutional was clearly correct. * * *

Affirmed.

THE CHIEF JUSTICE dissents.

MR. JUSTICE WHITE, concurring in part and concurring in the result.

I join Parts I, III, and V of the Court's opinion and concur in the result with respect to Part IV.

Although I saw no reason in Eisenstadt v. Baird, * * * to reach "the novel constitutional question whether a State may restrict or forbid the distribution of contraceptives to the unmarried," * * *, four of the seven Justices participating in that case held that in this respect the rights of unmarried persons were equal to those of the married. Given Eisenstadt and given the decision of the Court in the abortion case, Roe v. Wade, * * * the result reached by the Court in Part III of its opinion appears warranted. I do not regard the opinion, however, as declaring unconstitutional any state law forbidding extramarital sexual relations. On this assumption I join Part III.

I concur in the result in Part IV primarily because the State has not demonstrated that the prohibition against distribution of contraceptives to minors measurably contributes to the deterrent purposes which the State advances as justification for the restriction. Again, however, the legality of state laws forbidding premarital intercourse is not at issue here; and, with Mr. Justice Stevens, "I would describe as 'frivolous' appellees' argument that a minor has the constitutional right to put contraceptives to their intended use, notwithstanding the combined objection of both parents and the State," * * *.

In joining Part V of the Court's opinion, I should also say that I agree with the views of Mr. Justice Stevens expressed in Part II of his separate opinion.

MR. JUSTICE POWELL, concurring in part and concurring in the judgment.

* * *

I

The Court apparently would subject all state regulation affecting adult sexual relations to the strictest standard of judicial review. Under today's decision, such regulation "may be justified only by compelling state interests, and must be narrowly drawn to express only those interests." * * * Even regulation restricting only the sexual activity of the young must now be justified by a "significant state interest," a standard that is "apparently less rigorous" than the standard the Court would otherwise apply. * * * In my view, the extraordinary protection the Court would give to all personal decisions in matters of sex is neither required by the Constitution nor supported by our prior decisions.

* * *

In sum, the Court quite unnecessarily extends the reach of cases like *Griswold* and *Roe*. Neither our precedents nor sound principles of constitutional analysis require state legislation to meet the exacting "compelling state interest" standard whenever it implicates sexual freedom. In my view, those cases make clear that that standard has been invoked only when the state regulation entirely frustrates or heavily burdens the exercise of constitutional rights in this area. See Bellotti v. Baird, 428 U.S. 132, 147, 96 S.Ct. 2857, 2866, 49 L.Ed.2d 844 (1976). This is not to say that other state regulation is free from judicial review. But a test so severe that legislation rarely can meet it should be imposed by courts with deliberate restraint in view of the respect that properly should be accorded legislative judgments.

B

There is also no justification for subjecting restrictions on the sexual activity of the young to heightened judicial review. * * *

II

With these considerations in mind, I turn to the specific provisions of the New York statute limiting the distribution of contraceptives.

A

New York has made it a crime for anyone other than a physician to sell or distribute contraceptives to minors under the age of 16 years. Educ.Law § 6811(8) (McKinney 1972). This element of New York's program of regulation for the protection of its minor citizens is said to evidence the State's judgment that the health and well-being of minors would be better assured if they are not encouraged to engage in sexual intercourse without guidance. Although I have no doubt that properly framed legislation serving this purpose would meet constitutional standards, the New York provision is defective in two respects. First, it infringes the privacy interests of married females between the ages of 14 and 16, * * * in that it prohibits the distribution of contraceptives to such females except by a physician. In authorizing marriage at that age, the State also sanctions sexual intercourse between the partners and expressly recognizes that once the marriage relationship exists the husband and wife are presumed to possess the requisite understanding and maturity to make decisions concerning sex and procreation. Consequently, the state interest that justifies a requirement of prior counseling with respect to minors in general simply is inapplicable with respect to minors for whom the State has affirmatively approved marriage.

Second, this provision prohibits parents from distributing contraceptives to their children, a restriction that unjustifiably interferes with parental interests in rearing their children. * * *

But in my view there is considerably more room for state regulation in this area than would be permissible under the plurality's opinion. It seems clear to me, for example, that the State would further a constitutionally permissible end if it encouraged adolescents to seek the advice and guidance of their parents before deciding whether to engage in sexual intercourse. * * * The State justifiably may take note of the psychological pressures that might influence children at a time in their lives when they generally do not possess the maturity necessary to understand and control their responses. Participation in sexual intercourse at an early age may have both physical and psychological consequences. These include the risks of venereal disease and pregnancy, and the less obvious mental and emotional problems that may result from sexual activity by children. Moreover, society has long adhered to the view that sexual intercourse should not be engaged in promiscuously, a judgment that an adolescent may be less likely to heed than an adult.

MR. JUSTICE STEVENS, concurring in part and concurring in the judgment.

* * *

I

There are two reasons why I do not join Part IV. First, the holding in Planned Parenthood of Missouri v. Danforth, 428 U.S. 52, 72–75, 96 S.Ct. 2831, 2842–2844, 49 L.Ed.2d 788, that a minor's decision to abort her pregnancy may not be conditioned on parental consent, is not dispositive here. The options available to the already pregnant minor are fundamentally different from those available to nonpregnant minors. The former must bear a child unless she aborts; but persons in the latter category can and generally will avoid childbearing by abstention. Consequently, even if I had joined that part of *Planned Parenthood,* I could not agree that the Constitution provides the same measure of protection to the minor's right to use contraceptives as to the pregnant female's right to abort.

Second, I would not leave open the question whether there is a significant state interest in discouraging sexual activity among unmarried persons under 16 years of age. Indeed, I would describe as "frivolous" appellees' argument that a minor has the constitutional right to put contraceptives to their intended use, notwithstanding the combined objection of both parents and the State.

For the reasons explained by Mr. Justice Powell, I agree that the statute may not be applied to married females between the ages of 14 and 16, or to distribution by parents. I am not persuaded, however, that these glaring defects alone justify an injunction against other applications of the statute. Only one of the three plaintiffs in this case is a parent who wishes to give contraceptives to his children. The others are an Episcopal minister who sponsors a program against venereal disease, and a mail-order firm, which presumably has no way to determine the age of its customers. I am satisfied, for the reasons that follow, that the statute is also invalid as applied to them.

The State's important interest in the welfare of its young citizens justifies a number of protective measures. * * * Such special legislation is premised on the fact that young persons frequently make unwise choices with harmful consequences; the State may properly ameliorate those consequences by providing, for example, that a minor may not be required to honor his bargain. It is almost unprecedented, however, for a State to require that an ill-advised act by a minor give rise to greater risk of irreparable harm than a similar act by an adult.

Common sense indicates that many young people will engage in sexual activity regardless of what the New York Legislature does; and further, that the incidence of venereal disease and premarital pregnancy is affected by the availability or unavailability of contraceptives. Although young persons theoretically may avoid those harms by practicing total abstention, inevitably many will not. The statutory prohibition denies them and their parents a choice which, if available, would reduce their exposure to disease or unwanted pregnancy.

The State's asserted justification is a desire to inhibit sexual conduct by minors under 16. Appellants do not seriously contend that if contraceptives are available, significant numbers of minors who now abstain from sex will cease abstaining because they will no longer fear pregnancy or disease. Rather appellants' central argument is that the statute has the important *symbolic* effect of communicating disapproval of sexual activity by minors. In essence, therefore, the statute is defended as a form of propaganda, rather than a regulation of behavior.

Although the State may properly perform a teaching function, it seems to me that an attempt to persuade by inflicting harm on the listener is an unacceptable means of conveying a message that is otherwise legitimate. The propaganda technique used in this case significantly increases the risk of unwanted pregnancy and venereal disease. It is as though a State decided to dramatize its disapproval of motorcycles by forbidding the use of safety helmets. One need not posit a constitutional right to ride a motorcycle to characterize such a restriction as irrational and perverse.

Even as a regulation of behavior, such a statute would be defective. Assuming that the State could impose a uniform sanction upon young persons who risk self-inflicted harm by operating motorcycles, or by engaging in sexual activity, surely that sanction could not take the form of deliberately injuring the cyclist or infecting the promiscuous child. If such punishment may not be administered deliberately, after trial and a finding of guilt, it manifestly cannot be imposed by a legislature, indiscriminately and at ran-

Kay Sex Based Discrim 4th —11

dom. This kind of government-mandated harm, is, in my judgment, appropriately characterized as a deprivation of liberty without due process of law.

* * *

I concur in the judgment and in Parts I, II, III, and V of the Court's opinion.

Mr. Justice Rehnquist, dissenting.

Those who valiantly but vainly defended the heights of Bunker Hill in 1775 made it possible that men such as James Madison might later sit in the first Congress and draft the Bill of Rights to the Constitution. The post-Civil War Congresses which drafted the Civil War Amendments to the Constitution could not have accomplished their task without the blood of brave men on both sides which was shed at Shiloh, Gettysburg, and Cold Harbor. If those responsible for these Amendments, by feats of valor or efforts of draftsmanship, could have lived to know that their efforts had enshrined in the Constitution the right of commercial vendors of contraceptives to peddle them to unmarried minors through such means as window displays and vending machines located in the men's room of truck stops, notwithstanding the considered judgment of the New York Legislature to the contrary, it is not difficult to imagine their reaction.

I do not believe that the cases discussed in the Court's opinion require any such result, but to debate the Court's treatment of the question on a case-by-case basis would concede more validity to the result reached by the Court than I am willing to do. There comes a point when endless and ill-considered extension of principles originally formulated in quite different cases produces such an indefensible result that no logic chopping can possibly make the fallacy of the result more obvious. The Court here in effect holds that the First and Fourteenth Amendments not only guarantee full and free debate *before* a legislative judgment as to the moral dangers to which minors within the jurisdiction of the State should not be subjected, but goes further and absolutely prevents the representatives of the majority from carrying out such a policy *after* the issues have been fully aired.

No questions of religious belief, compelled allegiance to a secular creed, or decisions on the part of married couples as to procreation, are involved here. New York has simply decided that it wishes to discourage unmarried minors under 16 from having promiscuous sexual intercourse with one another. Even the Court would scarcely go so far as to say that this is not a subject with which the New York Legislature may properly concern itself.

That legislature has not chosen to deny to a pregnant woman, after the *fait accompli* of pregnancy, the one remedy which would enable her to terminate an unwanted pregnancy. It has instead sought to deter the conduct which will produce such *faits accomplis*. The majority of New York's citizens are in effect told that however deeply they may be concerned about the problem of promiscuous sex and intercourse among unmarried teenagers, they may not adopt this means of dealing with it. The Court holds that New York may not use its police power to legislate in the interests of its concept of the public morality as it pertains to minors. The Court's denial of a power so fundamental to self-government must, in the long run, prove to be but a temporary departure from a wise and heretofore settled course of adjudication to the contrary. I would reverse the judgment of the District Court.

Notes on Carey

1. Compare with *Carey* the case of Doe v. Planned Parenthood Ass'n of Utah, 29 Utah 2d 356, 510 P.2d 75 (1973), appeal dismissed and cert. denied 414 U.S. 805, 94 S.Ct. 138, 38 L.Ed.2d 42. *Doe* was a class action brought by a 16 year old unmarried woman who wished to compel Planned Parenthood to provide her with contraceptive information despite the fact that she did not have the consent of her parents to receive the requested services. The trial court ruled that the services must be furnished; the Utah Supreme Court reversed, stating in part that:

> The [trial] court reasoned that in family planning there was no reason to distinguish between married people and single people.

> We cannot agree with his reasoning. We think there is a vast difference between married people as a class who plan the number of children they wish to raise, and single people as a class who may likewise wish to plan the number of children which they do not wish to procreate.

> To give information and contraceptives to married people so as to control the size of their families is one thing. To deny it to single minor children is not a denial of the equal protection of the law, as they are not in the same class with married people.

> The law has ever been jealous of the rights of minors; and statutes for their benefit and protection (like the right to rescind a contract) have never been thought of as denying the equal protection of the law to adults.

> The law which makes sexual relations lawful between spouses and unlawful between others has never been considered to deny the equal protection of the law to single people who may want to satisfy their lusts on each other.

> If refusing the requests of this plaintiff here denies to her and her class the equal protection of the law, then the statutes which provide a punishment for fornication and carnal knowledge are such a denial.

Id., 29 Utah 2d at 359, 510 P.2d at 76–77. Is this case distinguishable from *Carey?* The Utah court's opinion has been criticized for its assumption that preventing access to contraceptives by minors would tend to deter them from engaging in premarital sex, and for its failure to give adequate consideration to the fundamental nature of the minor's right to privacy as applied to the contraceptive decision. See Note, Parental Consent Requirements and Privacy Rights of Minors: The Contraceptive Controversy, 88 Harv.L.Rev. 1001, 1011 n. 73 (1975); Richard A. Koch, Comment, Doe v. Planned Parenthood Association of Utah—The Constitutional Right of Minors to Obtain Contraceptives Without Parental Consent, 1974 Utah L.Rev. 433, 439–40. Note that the Utah court's rhetoric is not restricted to single persons who are minors. Given the facts of the case, however, presumably the holding must be so limited. After *Griswold, Eisenstadt,* and *Carey,* is it still open for a state to prohibit the sale of contraceptives to everyone, regardless of marital status or condition of minority?

2. Note Justice Brennan's reference, in Part IV of his plurality opinion, to the Court's statement in *Eisenstadt* that "[i]t would be plainly unreasonable to assume that Massachusetts has prescribed pregnancy and the birth of an unwant-

ed child as punishment for fornication." But, since the Massachusetts statute under consideration had been construed to mean that unmarried persons could obtain contraceptives only to prevent the spread of disease, not to prevent pregnancy, isn't it clear that Massachusetts intended exactly that? If so, doesn't the "punishment for fornication" fall unequally on the two persons who participated equally in the "crime"? Or is the father's duty to support the child considered to be *his* punishment?

3. Does the State have a valid interest in preventing sexual associations outside marriage? Why? If the interest centers around providing a stable family life for children, isn't that interest thwarted by a ban on contraceptives for the unmarried? Can't a stable family life be achieved without marriage? How stable *is* marriage, anyway? If the state's interest is directed towards the protection of public morality, is it relevant to ask whether contemporary moral standards condemn pre-marital and extra-marital sexuality? Do they? For both men and women? In either event, is the right of privacy as expressed in *Griswold* and *Eisenstadt* a defense against the assertion of these and other possible state interests? Does the right of privacy extend to homosexual acts between consenting adults? See Bowers v. Hardwick, set forth at p. 343, supra. What has been the impact of the AIDS epidemic on public attitudes toward contraception?

4. Doe v. Irwin, 615 F.2d 1162 (6th Cir.1980), cert. denied 449 U.S. 829, 101 S.Ct. 95, 66 L.Ed.2d 33, presented the reverse situation to that involved in Doe v. Planned Parenthood Association of Utah, Note 1 supra. In *Irwin,* the Tri–County Family Planning Center offered its family planning services to minors without parental knowledge or consent. A class of parents challenged this practice as violative of their constitutional rights. The course taken by this litigation indicates the difficulty of perceiving the correct constitutional result, given the lack of unanimity on the Supreme Court. The district court first held that dispensation of contraceptives to minors without adequate notice to their parents was unconstitutional. Doe v. Irwin, 428 F.Supp. 1198 (W.D.Mich.1977). This opinion was vacated for reconsideration in light of *Carey.* Doe v. Irwin, 559 F.2d 1219 (6th Cir.1977). On remand, the district court adhered to its prior position, reasoning that

> a close reading of *Carey* indicates a majority of the Supreme Court would support a state statute requiring prior parental notice and consultation before *non-prescriptive* contraceptives are distributed to unemancipated minors. * * * *Carey* provides additional support for the position previously reached by this court. The instant case involves the distribution of *prescriptive* contraceptives and the many dangerous medical complications attendant thereto. The result reached in the instant case in no way would prevent unemancipated minors from obtaining contraceptives—it would only require prior parental notification and the opportunity for consultation before that civil right, which surely implicates the capacity of the minor, is exercised.

Doe v. Irwin, 441 F.Supp. 1247, 1260 (W.D.Mich.1977). This judgment was reversed on appeal. The court noted that, whereas the prior Supreme Court decisions setting out the rights of parents to determine the upbringing of their children had all involved efforts by a state to require or prohibit some activity, *Irwin* involved only a voluntary service provided by the state. Since the minors were not required to participate in the Center's services, nor were the parents excluded from its program if they inquired about it, the latter remained "free to exercise their traditional care, custody and control over their unemancipated children." Accordingly, the court was unable to find any deprivation of the liberty interest of parents in the practice of not notifying them of their children's voluntary decisions to participate in the activities of the Center.

Id., 615 F.2d at 1168. *Carey* did not support the district court's decision: "[t]here was no majority opinion on this particular issue" and

> [t]he various opinions of the Justices do not indicate a belief that parents have a constitutional right to be notified by a public facility which distributes contraceptives to unemancipated minors.

Id., 615 F.2d at 1169. Which court is right about the implications of *Carey?* A majority of the Supreme Court was able to uphold the validity of a Utah statute requiring that notice be given, "if possible", to the parents of a minor who seeks an abortion, but only as applied to a minor who

> (a) * * * is living with and dependent upon her parents,
>
> (b) when she is not emancipated by marriage or otherwise, and
>
> (c) when she has made no claim or showing as to her maturity or as to her relations with her parents.

H.L. v. Matheson, 450 U.S. 398, 407, 101 S.Ct. 1164, 1170, 67 L.Ed.2d 388, 397 (1981). Justices Powell and Stewart, concurring, made clear that *Matheson* left open the question of whether the Utah statute unconstitutionally burdens the right of a mature minor or a minor whose best interests would not be served by parental notification. Those issues were not reached because neither the plaintiff nor any member of her class had standing to raise them. Justices Marshall, Brennan, and Blackmun dissented. Only Justice Stevens would have upheld the statute as applied to all minors, whether or not mature or emancipated. What remains of *Irwin* after *Matheson? Matheson* is discussed further at pp. 538–39, infra.

5. Research and development leading to new and innovative approaches to contraception has slowed in the United States since the birth control pill was introduced in the early 1960s. According to Stanford professor Carl Djerassi, this situation is the result of a combination of factors: social and political opposition to new postcoital birth control techniques; the reluctance of the pharmaceutical industry to incur litigation risks associated with the introduction of new products; and the shift of medical research interests from contraception to infertility. Djerassi, The Bitter Pill, 245 Science 356 (28 July 1989). One bright exception to this forecast is RU 486, the drug developed in France by Dr. Etienne–Emile and manufactured by Roussel–Uclaf. Djerassi calls RU 486 "the most significant research achievement of the 1980s in new practical fertility control." Id., at 359. RU 486 taken in conjunction with prostaglandins terminates pregnancy within the first nine weeks of gestation. See Stopping the Process of Pregnancy, 245 Science 1320 (22 September 1989). The drug provides an alternative to surgical abortion that can be self-administered in the privacy of a woman's home. As Djerassi notes, "[s]uch a method would not be acceptable or suitable for every woman, but to many such a one-pill regimen would represent an enormous improvement: at a maximum, a woman would be taking 12 pills annually, rather than the present 250 or more." Id., at 359. Anti-choice activists view RU 486 as "the death pill" and they have so far lobbied successfully to prevent its importation into the United States. In early 1990, the Feminist Majority Foundation launched a counter-offensive to bring RU 486 to this country. Will RU 486, if made freely available in the United States, effectively silence the abortion controversy?

6.   On January 26, 1983, the Department of Health and Human Services announced new rules governing projects that provide family planning services pursuant to Title X of the Public Health Service Act.   The rules were designed to implement Pub.L. 97–35, section 931(b)(1) (1981), which added the following language to section 1001(a) of the Act:

> To the extent practical, entities which receive grants or contracts under this subsection shall encourage family participation in projects assisted under this subsection.

The Department's rule, known in the media as the "squeal rule", amended 42 CFR 59.5 to require that the project must notify a parent or guardian that prescription drugs or devices had been provided to an unemancipated minor within 10 working days after the drugs or devices were initially provided.   The minor must be informed about the notification requirement before receiving the services; an exception is made for cases in which the project director determines that notification will result in "physical harm" to the minor from a parent or guardian.

The new rule was immediately challenged in the courts.   Its implementation was permanently enjoined on statutory, rather than constitutional grounds.   In Planned Parenthood Federation of America v. Schweiker, 559 F.Supp. 658 (D.D.C.), affirmed 712 F.2d 650 (D.C.Cir.1983), Judge Flannery held that the regulation was inconsistent with Congressional intent in enacting Title X.   Noting that Title X's original passage in 1970 had been motivated by Congressional concern over the increasing numbers of adolescent pregnancies, and that Congress had rejected in 1978 an amendment proposed by Representative Volker that would have required parental notification before prescriptive contraceptive drugs or devices were furnished to unemancipated minors on the ground that such a requirement would undermine the intent of Title X, the court concluded that nothing in the 1981 amendment was intended to reverse this longstanding assurance of confidentiality in the services provided to clients under Title X. Judge Flannery therefore held that the parental notification regulations were outside the scope of the Agency's authorizing legislation and, accordingly, invalid. Accord: State of New York v. Heckler, 719 F.2d 1191 (2d Cir.1983).

Do you agree with this reasoning?   What sort of regulations are authorized by this reading of the legislative history?   Judge Flannery pointed out that the General Counsel of the Department had advised the Secretary that any regulation implementing the 1981 amendment should "be limited to requiring Title X grantees to encourage unemancipated minors seeking counselling, or other services, to involve their family, to the maximum extent possible, in these activities." Id., 559 F.Supp. at 668, n. 17.   Is this what the Congressional proponents of the 1981 amendment had in mind?

If the squeal rule had survived statutory scrutiny, would it have been subject to constitutional attack as an infringement on the minor's right to privacy?   Does *Carey* support such an attack?   Note that *Carey* applied only to nonprescription contraceptives, while the new rules were limited to prescription drugs and devices, defined as including birth control pills, the IUD, and the diaphragm.   Can it be argued that because there are no prescription drugs or devices covered by the regulation that are used by men, the rule can be challenged as an unconstitutional discrimination based on gender?   If the *Craig* test is applied, what would be the result?

2. GESTATIONAL SURROGACY

JOHNSON v. CALVERT

Supreme Court of California, 1993.
5 Cal.4th 84, 19 Cal.Rptr.2d 494, 851 P.2d 776.

PANELLI, JUSTICE.

In this case we address several of the legal questions raised by recent advances in reproductive technology. When, pursuant to a surrogacy agreement, a zygote [1] formed of the gametes [2] of a husband and wife is implanted in the uterus of another woman, who carries the resulting fetus to term and gives birth to a child not genetically related to her, who is the child's "natural mother" under California law? Does a determination that the wife is the child's natural mother work a deprivation of the gestating woman's constitutional rights? And is such an agreement barred by any public policy of this state?

We conclude that the husband and wife are the child's natural parents, and that this result does not offend the state or federal Constitution or public policy.

FACTS

Mark and Crispina Calvert are a married couple who desired to have a child. Crispina was forced to undergo a hysterectomy in 1984. Her ovaries remained capable of producing eggs, however, and the couple eventually considered surrogacy. In 1989 Anna Johnson heard about Crispina's plight from a coworker and offered to serve as a surrogate for the Calverts.

On January 15, 1990, Mark, Crispina, and Anna signed a contract providing that an embryo created by the sperm of Mark and the egg of Crispina would be implanted in Anna and the child born would be taken into Mark and Crispina's home "as their child." Anna agreed she would relinquish "all parental rights" to the child in favor of Mark and Crispina. In return, Mark and Crispina would pay Anna $10,000 in a series of installments, the last to be paid six weeks after the child's birth. Mark and Crispina were also to pay for a $200,000 life insurance policy on Anna's life.[4]

The zygote was implanted on January 19, 1990. Less than a month later, an ultrasound test confirmed Anna was pregnant.

Unfortunately, relations deteriorated between the two sides. Mark learned that Anna had not disclosed she had suffered several stillbirths and miscarriages. Anna felt Mark and Crispina did not do enough to obtain the required insurance policy. She also felt abandoned during an onset of premature labor in June.

In July 1990, Anna sent Mark and Crispina a letter demanding the balance of the payments due her or else she would refuse to give up the child. The following month, Mark and Crispina responded with a lawsuit, seeking a

---

1. An organism produced by the union of two gametes. (McGraw–Hill Dict. of Scientific and Technical Terms (4th ed. 1989) p. 783.)

2. A cell that participates in fertilization and development of a new organism, also

known as a germ cell or sex cell. (McGraw–Hill Dict. of Scientific and Technical Terms, *supra*, p. 2087.)

4. At the time of the agreement, Anna already had a daughter, Erica, born in 1987.

declaration they were the legal parents of the unborn child. Anna filed her own action to be declared the mother of the child, and the two cases were eventually consolidated. The parties agreed to an independent guardian ad litem for the purposes of the suit.

The child was born on September 19, 1990, and blood samples were obtained from both Anna and the child for analysis. The blood test results excluded Anna as the genetic mother. The parties agreed to a court order providing that the child would remain with Mark and Crispina on a temporary basis with visits by Anna.

At trial in October 1990, the parties stipulated that Mark and Crispina were the child's genetic parents. After hearing evidence and arguments, the trial court ruled that Mark and Crispina were the child's "genetic, biological and natural" father and mother, that Anna had no "parental" rights to the child, and that the surrogacy contract was legal and enforceable against Anna's claims. The court also terminated the order allowing visitation. Anna appealed from the trial court's judgment. The Court of Appeal for the Fourth District, Division Three, affirmed. We granted review.

DISCUSSION

DETERMINING MATERNITY UNDER THE UNIFORM PARENTAGE ACT

The Uniform Parentage Act (the Act) was part of a package of legislation introduced in 1975 as Senate Bill No. 347. The legislation's purpose was to eliminate the legal distinction between legitimate and illegitimate children. * * *

* * *

Passage of the Act clearly was not motivated by the need to resolve surrogacy disputes, which were virtually unknown in 1975. Yet it facially applies to *any* parentage determination, including the rare case in which a child's maternity is in issue. We are invited to disregard the Act and decide this case according to other criteria, including constitutional precepts and our sense of the demands of public policy. We feel constrained, however, to decline the invitation. Not uncommonly, courts must construe statutes in factual settings not contemplated by the enacting legislature. * * * Similarly, the Act offers a mechanism to resolve this dispute, albeit one not specifically tooled for it. We therefore proceed to analyze the parties' contentions within the Act's framework.

These contentions are readily summarized. Anna, of course, predicates her claim of maternity on the fact that she gave birth to the child. The Calverts contend that Crispina's genetic relationship to the child establishes that she is his mother. Counsel for the minor joins in that contention and argues, in addition, that several of the presumptions created by the Act dictate the same result. As will appear, we conclude that presentation of blood test evidence is one means of establishing maternity, as is proof of having given birth, but that the presumptions cited by minor's counsel do not apply to this case.

We turn to those few provisions of the Act directly addressing the determination of maternity. "Any interested party," presumably including a genetic mother, "may bring an action to determine the existence * * * of a mother and child relationship." (Civ.Code, § 7015.) Civil Code section 7003 provides, in relevant part, that between a child and the natural mother a parent and child relationship "*may* be established by proof of her having given birth to the child, or under [the Act]." (Civ.Code, § 7003, subd. (1), emphasis added.) Apart from Civil Code section 7003, the Act sets forth no specific means by which a natural mother can establish a parent and child relationship. However, it declares that, insofar as practicable, provisions applicable to the father and child relationship apply in an action to determine the existence or nonexistence of a mother and child relationship. (Civ.Code, § 7015.) Thus, it is appropriate to examine those provisions as well.

A man can establish a father and child relationship by the means set forth in Civil Code section 7004. (Civ.Code, §§ 7006, 7004.) Paternity is presumed under that section if the man meets the conditions set forth in section 621 of the Evidence Code. (Civ.Code, § 7004, subd. (a).) The latter statute applies, by its terms, when determining the questioned paternity of a child born to a married woman, and contemplates reliance on evidence derived from blood testing. * * *

Alternatively, Civil Code section 7004 creates a presumption of paternity based on the man's conduct toward the child (e.g., receiving the child into his home and openly holding the child out as his natural child) or his marriage or attempted marriage to the child's natural mother under specified conditions.

In our view, the presumptions contained in Civil Code section 7004 do not apply here. They describe situations in which substantial evidence points to a particular man as the natural father of the child. (9B West's U.Laws Ann. (1987) Unif. Parentage Act, com. foll. § 4, p. 299.) In this case, there is no question as to who is claiming the mother and child relationship, and the factual basis of each woman's claim is obvious. Thus, there is no need to resort to an evidentiary presumption to ascertain the identity of the natural mother. Instead, we must make the purely legal determination as between the two claimants.

Significantly for this case, Evidence Code section 892 provides that blood testing may be ordered in an action when paternity is a relevant fact. When maternity is disputed, genetic evidence derived from blood testing is likewise admissible. (Evid.Code, § 892; see Civ.Code, § 7015.) The Evidence Code further provides that if the court finds the conclusions of all the experts, as disclosed by the evidence based on the blood tests, are that the alleged father is not the father of the child, the question of paternity is resolved accordingly. (Evid.Code, § 895.) By parity of reasoning, blood testing may also be dispositive of the question of maternity. Further, there is a rebuttable presumption of paternity (hence, maternity as well) on the finding of a certain number of genetic markers. (Evid.Code, § 895.5.)

Disregarding the presumptions of paternity that have no application to this case, then, we are left with the undisputed evidence that Anna, not Crispina, gave birth to the child and that Crispina, not Anna, is genetically related to him. Both women thus have adduced evidence of a mother and child relationship as contemplated by the Act. (Civ.Code, §§ 7003, subd. (1), 7004, subd. (a), 7015; Evid.Code, §§ 621, 892.) Yet for any child California law recognizes only one natural mother, despite advances in reproductive technology rendering a different outcome biologically possible.[8]

We see no clear legislative preference in Civil Code section 7003 as between blood testing evidence and proof of having given birth. "May" indicates that proof of having given birth is a permitted method of establishing a mother and child relationship, although perhaps not the exclusive one. The disjunctive "or" indicates that blood test evidence, as prescribed in the Act, constitutes an alternative to proof of having given birth. It may be that the language of the Uniform Parentage Act merely reflects "the ancient dictum *mater est quam [gestation] demonstrat* (by gestation the mother is demonstrated). This phrase, by its use of the word 'demonstrated,' has always reflected an ambiguity in the meaning of the presumption. It is arguable that, while gestation may demonstrate maternal status, it is not the sine qua non of motherhood. Rather, it is possible that the common law viewed genetic consanguinity as the basis for maternal rights. Under this latter interpretation, gestation simply would be irrefutable evidence of the more fundamental genetic relationship." (Hill, *What Does It Mean to Be a "Parent"? The Claims of Biology As the Basis for Parental Rights* (1991) 66 N.Y.U.L.Rev. 353, 370, fns. omitted.) This ambiguity, highlighted by the problems arising from the use of artificial reproductive techniques, is nowhere explicitly resolved in the Act.

Because two women each have presented acceptable proof of maternity, we do not believe this case can be decided without enquiring into the parties' intentions as manifested in the surrogacy agreement. Mark and Crispina are a couple who desired to have a child of their own genetic stock but are physically unable to do so without the help of reproductive technology. They affirmatively intended the birth of the child, and took the steps necessary to effect in vitro fertilization. But for their acted-on intention, the child would not exist. Anna agreed to facilitate the procreation of Mark's and Crispina's child. The parties' aim was to bring Mark's and Crispina's child into the world, not for Mark and Crispina to donate a zygote to Anna. Crispina from the outset intended to be the child's mother. Although the gestative function Anna performed was necessary to bring about the child's birth, it is safe to say that Anna would not have been given the opportunity to gestate or deliver the child had she, prior to implantation of the zygote, manifested her own intent to be the child's mother. No reason appears why Anna's later change of heart should vitiate the determination that Crispina is the child's natural mother.

We conclude that although the Act recognizes both genetic consanguinity and giving birth as means of establishing a mother and child relationship, when the two means do not coincide in one woman, she who intended to procreate the child—that is, she who intended to bring about the birth of a

---

8. We decline to accept the contention of amicus curiae the American Civil Liberties Union (ACLU) that we should find the child has two mothers. Even though rising divorce rates have made multiple parent arrangements common in our society, we see no compelling reason to recognize such a situation here. The Calverts are the genetic and intending parents of their son and have provided him, by all accounts, with a stable, intact, and nurturing home. To recognize parental rights in a third party with whom the Calvert family has had little contact since shortly after the child's birth would diminish Crispina's role as mother.

child that she intended to raise as her own—is the natural mother under California law.[10]

Our conclusion finds support in the writings of several legal commentators. (See Hill, *What Does It Mean to Be a "Parent"? The Claims of Biology As the Basis for Parental Rights, supra,* 66 N.Y.U.L.Rev. 353; Shultz, *Reproductive Technology and Intent–Based Parenthood: An Opportunity for Gender Neutrality* (1990) Wis.L.Rev. 297 [Shultz]; Note, *Redefining Mother: A Legal Matrix for New Reproductive Technologies* (1986) 96 Yale L.J. 187, 197–202 [note].) Professor Hill, arguing that the genetic relationship *per se* should not be accorded priority in the determination of the parent-child relationship in the surrogacy context, notes that "while all of the players in the procreative arrangement are necessary in bringing a child into the world, *the child would not have been born but for the efforts of the intended parents* * * * [¶] * * * [T]he intended parents are the first cause, or the prime movers, of the procreative relationship." (Hill, *op. cit. supra,* at p. 415, emphasis in original.)

Similarly, Professor Shultz observes that recent developments in the field of reproductive technology "dramatically extend affirmative intentionality * * *. Steps can be taken to bring into being a child who would not otherwise have existed." (Shultz, *op. cit. supra,* p. 309.) "Within the context of artificial reproductive techniques," Professor Shultz argues, "intentions that are voluntarily chosen, deliberate, express and bargained-for ought presumptively to determine legal parenthood." (*Id.,* at p. 323, fn. omitted.)

Another commentator has cogently suggested, in connection with reproductive technology, that "[t]he mental concept of the child is a controlling factor of its creation, and the originators of that concept merit full credit as conceivers. The mental concept must be recognized as independently valuable; it creates expectations in the initiating parents of a child, and it creates expectations in society for adequate performance on the part of the initiators as parents of the child." (Note, *op. cit. supra,* 96 Yale L.J. at p. 196.)

Moreover, as Professor Shultz recognizes, the interests of children, particularly at the outset of their lives, are "[un]likely to run contrary to those of adults who choose to bring them into being." (Shultz, *op. cit. supra,* at p. 397.) Thus, "[h]onoring the plans and expectations of adults who will be responsible for a child's welfare is likely to correlate significantly with positive outcomes for parents and children alike." (*Ibid.*) Under Anna's interpreta-

10. Thus, under our analysis, in a true "egg donation" situation, where a woman gestates and gives birth to a child formed from the egg of another woman with the intent to raise the child as her own, the birth mother is the natural mother under California law.

The dissent would decide *parentage* based on the best interests of the child. Such an approach raises the repugnant specter of governmental interference in matters implicating our most fundamental notions of privacy, and confuses concepts of parentage and custody. Logically, the determination of parentage must precede, and should not be dictated by, eventual custody decisions. The implicit assumption of the dissent is that a recognition of the genetic intending mother as the natural mother may sometimes harm the child. This assumption overlooks California's dependency laws, which are designed to protect *all* children irrespective of the manner of birth or conception. Moreover, the best interest standard poorly serves the child in the present situation: it fosters instability during litigation and, if applied to recognize the gestator as natural mother, results in a split of custody between the natural father and the gestator, an outcome not likely to benefit the child. Further, it may be argued that, by voluntarily contracting away any rights to the child, the gestator has, in effect, conceded the best interest of the child is not with her.

tion of the Act, by contrast, a woman who agreed to gestate a fetus genetically related to the intending parents would, contrary to her expectations, be held to be the child's natural mother, with all the responsibilities that ruling would entail, if the intending mother declined to accept the child after its birth. In what we must hope will be the extremely rare situation in which neither the gestator nor the woman who provided the ovum for fertilization is willing to assume custody of the child after birth, a rule recognizing the intending parents as the child's legal, natural parents should best promote certainty and stability for the child.

In deciding the issue of maternity under the Act we have felt free to take into account the parties' intentions, as expressed in the surrogacy contract, because in our view the agreement is not, on its face, inconsistent with public policy.

* * *

Anna urges that surrogacy contracts violate several social policies. Relying on her contention that she is the child's legal, natural mother, she cites the public policy embodied in Penal Code section 273, prohibiting the payment for consent to adoption of a child. She argues further that the policies underlying the adoption laws of this state are violated by the surrogacy contract because it in effect constitutes a prebirth waiver of her parental rights.

We disagree. Gestational surrogacy differs in crucial respects from adoption and so is not subject to the adoption statutes. The parties voluntarily agreed to participate in in vitro fertilization and related medical procedures before the child was conceived; at the time when Anna entered into the contract, therefore, she was not vulnerable to financial inducements to part with her own expected offspring. As discussed above, Anna was not the genetic mother of the child. The payments to Anna under the contract were meant to compensate her for her services in gestating the fetus and undergoing labor, rather than for giving up "parental" rights to the child. Payments were due both during the pregnancy and after the child's birth. We are, accordingly, unpersuaded that the contract used in this case violates the public policies embodied in Penal Code section 273 and the adoption statutes. For the same reasons, we conclude these contracts do not implicate the policies underlying the statutes governing termination of parental rights. (See Welf. & Inst.Code, § 202.)

It has been suggested that gestational surrogacy may run afoul of prohibitions on involuntary servitude. (See U.S. Const., Amend. XIII; Cal. Const., art. I, § 6; Pen.Code, § 181.) Involuntary servitude has been recognized in cases of criminal punishment for refusal to work. * * * We see no potential for that evil in the contract at issue here, and extrinsic evidence of coercion or duress is utterly lacking. We note that although at one point the contract purports to give Mark and Crispina the sole right to determine whether to abort the pregnancy, at another point it acknowledges: "All parties understand that a pregnant woman has the absolute right to abort or not abort any fetus she is carrying. Any promise to the contrary is unenforceable." We therefore need not determine the validity of a surrogacy contract purporting to deprive the gestator of her freedom to terminate the pregnancy.

Finally, Anna and some commentators have expressed concern that surrogacy contracts tend to exploit or dehumanize women, especially women of lower economic status. Anna's objections center around the psychological harm she asserts may result from the gestator's relinquishing the child to whom she has given birth. Some have also cautioned that the practice of surrogacy may encourage society to view children as commodities, subject to trade at their parents' will.

We are all too aware that the proper forum for resolution of this issue is the Legislature, where empirical data, largely lacking from this record, can be studied and rules of general applicability developed. However, in light of our responsibility to decide this case, we have considered as best we can its possible consequences.

We are unpersuaded that gestational surrogacy arrangements are so likely to cause the untoward results Anna cites as to demand their invalidation on public policy grounds. Although common sense suggests that women of lesser means serve as surrogate mothers more often than do wealthy women, there has been no proof that surrogacy contracts exploit poor women to any greater degree than economic necessity in general exploits them by inducing them to accept lower-paid or otherwise undesirable employment. We are likewise unpersuaded by the claim that surrogacy will foster the attitude that children are mere commodities; no evidence is offered to support it. The limited data available seem to reflect an absence of significant adverse effects of surrogacy on all participants.[12]

The argument that a woman cannot knowingly and intelligently agree to gestate and deliver a baby for intending parents carries overtones of the reasoning that for centuries prevented women from attaining equal economic rights and professional status under the law. To resurrect this view is both to foreclose a personal and economic choice on the part of the surrogate mother, and to deny intending parents what may be their only means of procreating a child of their own genetic stock. Certainly in the present case it cannot seriously be argued that Anna, a licensed vocational nurse who had done well in school and who had previously borne a child, lacked the intellectual wherewithal or life experience necessary to make an informed decision to enter into the surrogacy contract.

CONSTITUTIONALITY OF THE DETERMINATION THAT ANNA JOHNSON IS NOT THE NATURAL MOTHER

Anna argues at length that her right to the continued companionship of the child is protected under the federal Constitution.

* * *

Anna's argument depends on a prior determination that she is indeed the child's mother. Since Crispina is the child's mother under California law because she, not Anna, provided the ovum for the in vitro fertilization procedure, intending to raise the child as her own, it follows that any constitutional interests Anna possesses in this situation are something less than those of a mother. As counsel for the minor points out, the issue in this

---

12. See Andrews and Douglass, *Alternative Reproduction* (1991) 65 So.Cal.L.Rev. 623, 673–678.

case is not whether Anna's asserted rights as a natural mother were unconstitutionally violated, but rather whether the determination that she is not the legal natural mother at all is constitutional.

Anna relies principally on the decision of the United States Supreme Court in *Michael H. v. Gerald D.* (1989) 491 U.S. 110, 109 S.Ct. 2333, 105 L.Ed.2d 91, to support her claim to a constitutionally protected liberty interest in the companionship of the child, based on her status as "birth mother." In that case, a plurality of the court held that a state may constitutionally deny a man parental rights with respect to a child he fathered during a liaison with the wife of another man, since it is the marital family that traditionally has been accorded a protected liberty interest, as reflected in the historic presumption of legitimacy of a child born into such a family. (491 U.S. at pp. 124–125, 109 S.Ct. at pp. 2342–2343 (plur. opn. by Scalia, J.).) The reasoning of the plurality in *Michael H.* does not assist Anna. Society has not traditionally protected the right of a woman who gestates and delivers a baby pursuant to an agreement with a couple who supply the zygote from which the baby develops and who intend to raise the child as their own; such arrangements are of too recent an origin to claim the protection of tradition. To the extent that tradition has a bearing on the present case, we believe it supports the claim of the couple who exercise their right to procreate in order to form a family of their own, albeit through novel medical procedures.

Moreover, if we were to conclude that Anna enjoys some sort of liberty interest in the companionship of the child, then the liberty interests of Mark and Crispina, the child's natural parents, in their procreative choices and their relationship with the child would perforce be infringed. Any parental rights Anna might successfully assert could come only at Crispina's expense. As we have seen, Anna has no parental rights to the child under California law, and she fails to persuade us that sufficiently strong policy reasons exist to accord her a protected liberty interest in the companionship of the child when such an interest would necessarily detract from or impair the parental bond enjoyed by Mark and Crispina.

Amicus curiae ACLU urges that Anna's right of privacy, embodied in the California Constitution (Cal. Const., art. I, § 1), requires recognition and protection of her status as "birth mother." We cannot agree. Certainly it is true that our state Constitution has been construed to provide California citizens with privacy protections encompassing procreative decisionmaking— broader, indeed, than those recognized by the federal Constitution.   * * * However, amicus curiae fails to articulate persuasively how Anna's claim falls within even the broad parameters of the state right of privacy. Amicus curiae appears to assume that the choice to gestate and deliver a baby to its genetic parents pursuant to a surrogacy agreement is the equivalent, in constitutional weight, of the decision whether to bear a child of one's own. We disagree. A woman who enters into a gestational surrogacy arrangement is not exercising her own right to make procreative choices; she is agreeing to provide a necessary and profoundly important service without (by definition) any expectation that she will raise the resulting child as her own.

Drawing an analogy to artificial insemination, Anna argues that Mark and Crispina were mere genetic donors who are entitled to no constitutional protection. That characterization of the facts is, however, inaccurate. Mark and Crispina never intended to "donate" genetic material to anyone. Rather, they intended to procreate a child genetically related to them by the only available means. Civil Code section 7005, governing artificial insemination, has no application here.

Finally, Anna argues that the Act's failure to address novel reproductive techniques such as in vitro fertilization indicates legislative disapproval of such practices. Given that the Act was drafted long before such techniques were developed, we cannot agree. Moreover, we may not arrogate to ourselves the power to disapprove them. It is not the role of the judiciary to inhibit the use of reproductive technology when the Legislature has not seen fit to do so; any such effort would raise serious questions in light of the fundamental nature of the rights of procreation and privacy. Rather, our task has been to resolve the dispute before us, interpreting the Act's use of the term "natural mother" (Civ.Code, § 7003, subd. (1)) when the biological functions essential to bringing a child into the world have been allocated between two women.

DISPOSITION

The judgment of the Court of Appeal is affirmed.

LUCAS, C.J., and MOSK, BAXTER and GEORGE, JJ., concur.

ARABIAN, JUSTICE, concurring to opinion by PANELLI, JUSTICE.

I concur in the decision to find under the Uniform Parentage Act that Crispina Calvert is the natural mother of the child she at all times intended to parent and raise as her own with her husband Mark, the child's natural father. That determination answers the question on which this court granted review, and in my view sufficiently resolves the controversy between the parties to warrant no further analysis. I therefore decline to subscribe to the dictum in which the majority find surrogacy contracts "not * * * inconsistent with public policy." * * *

* * *

Clearly, this court should not avoid proper resolution of the issue before it. "[T]he law, equity and justice must not themselves quail and be helpless in the face of modern technological marvels presenting questions hitherto unthought of." (*In re Quinlan* (1976) 70 N.J. 10, 44, 355 A.2d 647, 665, cert. den. *sub nom. Garger v. New Jersey,* 429 U.S. 922, 97 S.Ct. 319, 50 L.Ed.2d 289.) Nevertheless, I would not move beyond the available legal mechanism into such socially and morally uncharted waters. The implications of addressing the general soundness of surrogacy contracts are vast and profound. To date, the legislative process has failed to produce a satisfactory answer. This court should be chastened and not emboldened by that failure.

KENNARD, JUSTICE, dissenting.

When a woman who wants to have a child provides her fertilized ovum to another woman who carries it through pregnancy and gives birth to a child, who is the child's legal mother? Unlike the majority, I do not agree that the determinative consideration should be the intent to have the child that originated with the woman who contributed the ovum. In my view, the woman who provided the fertilized ovum and the woman who gave birth to the child both have substantial claims to legal motherhood. Pregnancy entails a unique commitment, both psychological and emotional, to an unborn child. No less substantial, however, is the contribution of the woman from whose egg the child developed and without whose desire the child would not exist.

For each child, California law accords the legal rights and responsibilities of parenthood to only one "natural mother." When, as here, the female reproductive role is divided between two women, California law requires courts to make a decision as to which woman is the child's natural mother, but provides no standards by which to make that decision. The majority's resort to "intent" to break the "tie" between the genetic and gestational mothers is unsupported by statute, and in the absence of appropriate protections in the law to guard against abuse of surrogacy arrangements, it is ill-advised. To determine who is the legal mother of a child born of a gestational surrogacy arrangement, I would apply the standard most protective of child welfare—the best interests of the child.

* * *

II. THIS OPINION'S APPROACH

The determination of a question of parental rights to a child born of a surrogacy arrangement was before the New Jersey Supreme Court in *Matter of Baby M.* (1988) 109 N.J. 396, 537 A.2d 1227, a case that received worldwide attention. But in the surrogacy arrangement at issue there the woman who gave birth to the child, Marybeth Whitehead, had been impregnated by artificial insemination with the sperm of the intending father, William Stern. Whitehead thus provided the genetic material and carried the fetus to term. This case is different, because here those two aspects of the female role in reproduction were divided between two women. This process is known as "gestational" surrogacy, to distinguish it from the surrogacy arrangement involved in *Baby M.*[1]

In this opinion, I first discuss gestational surrogacy in light of the medical advances that have made it a reality. I next consider the wider social and philosophical implications of using gestational surrogacy to give birth to a child, and set out some of the suggested models for deciding the child's parentage in this situation. I then review a comprehensive model legislative scheme, not enacted in California, designed to accommodate the interests of all participants in surrogacy arrangements. I next turn to California's Uniform Parentage Act, and critique the majority's reliance on "intent" as the determinative factor under that act in deciding who is the "natural," and thus legal, mother of a child born of a gestational surrogacy arrangement.

---

1. The terms "surrogacy" and "surrogate" have been criticized as being inaccurate, particularly when applied to the type of arrangement involved in *Baby M.,* in which the child a woman bears, intending to relinquish the child at birth, was formed from her own egg. (See Capron & Radin, *Choosing Family Law Over Contract Law as a Paradigm for Surrogate Motherhood,* in Surrogate Motherhood (Gostin edit. 1990) p. 72, fn. 2; Annas, *Fairy Tales Surrogate Mothers Tell,* in Surrogate Motherhood, *supra,* at p. 46 [suggesting that the phrase "surrogate mother" derives from Har-

low's monkey studies, in which the responses of newborn monkeys were tested by isolating them in cages with cloth or wire "surrogate mothers."].)

Because "gestational surrogacy" is now widely used to describe the situation in which one woman agrees to be impregnated with an embryo formed from another woman's fertilized egg, I use the phrase throughout this opinion and occasionally also refer to the woman who gestates the fetus as the "surrogate."

Finally, I explain why, in the absence of legislation designed to address the unique problems of gestational surrogacy, courts deciding who is the legal mother of a child born of gestational surrogacy should look to the best interests of that child.

III.　GESTATIONAL SURROGACY

Recent advances in medical technology have dramatically expanded the means of human reproduction. Among the new technologies are in vitro fertilization, embryo and gamete freezing and storage, gamete intra-fallopian transfer, and embryo transplantation. (Shultz, *Reproductive Technology and Intent–Based Parenthood: An Opportunity for Gender Neutrality,* 1990 Wis. L.Rev. 297, 299 fn. 5 [hereafter *Reproductive Technology*].) Gestational surrogacy is the result of two of these techniques: in vitro fertilization and embryo transplantation. (See Shalev, Birth Power: The Case for Surrogacy (Yale U. Press 1989) p. 115.)

In vitro fertilization or IVF is the fertilization of a human egg outside the human body in a laboratory. Children that have been conceived this way are often called "test tube babies," because their actual conception took place in a petri dish. The first live birth of a child conceived in vitro occurred in 1979 in Great Britain after 20 years of research by a British team. (Shalev, Birth Power: The Case for Surrogacy, *supra,* at p. 105.)

To facilitate the retrieval or "harvesting" of eggs for in vitro fertilization, a woman ingests fertility hormones to induce "superovulation" or the production of multiple eggs. The eggs are then removed through aspiration, a nonsurgical technique, or through an invasive surgical procedure known as laparoscopy. (See generally *Developments in the Law: Medical Technology and the Law* (1990) 103 Harv.L.Rev. 1519, 1537–1542 [hereafter *Medical Technology*].) To undergo superovulation and egg retrieval is taxing, both physically and emotionally; the hormones used for superovulation produce bodily changes similar to those experienced in pregnancy, while the surgical removal of mature eggs has been likened to caesarian-section childbirth. (*Id.,* at p. 1540; Shalev, Birth Power: The Case for Surrogacy, *supra,* at pp. 117–118.)

After removal, eggs are exposed to live sperm in a petri dish. If an egg is fertilized, the resulting zygote is allowed to divide and become multicellular before uterine implantation. The expense and low success rate of in vitro fertilization demonstrate just how much prospective parents are willing to endure to achieve biological parenthood. (*Medical Technology, supra,* 103 Harv.L.Rev. at p. 1539.)

Generally, an egg fertilized in vitro is implanted in the uterus of the woman who produced it. The technique, however, allows for embryo transplantation, which is the transfer of an embryo formed from one woman's egg to the uterus of another woman who will gestate the fetus to term. This can take place in at least three different situations: (1) a woman may donate an egg that, when fertilized, will be implanted in the uterus of a woman who intends to raise the child; (2) the woman who provides the egg may herself intend to raise the child carried to term by a gestational surrogate; or (3) a couple desiring a child may arrange for a surrogate to gestate an embryo produced from an egg and sperm, both donated (perhaps by close relatives of the couple). (Goodwin, *Determination of Legal Parentage in Egg Donation,*

Embryo Transplantation, and Gestational Surrogacy Arrangements (1992) 26 Fam.L.Q. 275, 276–277 [hereafter *Determination of Legal Parentage*].)

The division of the female reproductive role in gestational surrogacy points up the three discrete aspects of motherhood: genetic, gestational and social. The woman who contributes the egg that becomes the fetus has played the genetic role of motherhood; the gestational aspect is provided by the woman who carries the fetus to term and gives birth to the child; and the woman who ultimately raises the child and assumes the responsibilities of parenthood is the child's social mother. (Shalev, Birth Power: The Case for Surrogacy, *supra,* at p. 115; see also Macklin, *Artificial Means of Reproduction and Our Understanding of the Family* (1991) 21 Hastings Center Rep. 5, 6.)

IV.   Policy Considerations

The ethical, moral and legal implications of using gestational surrogacy for human reproduction have engendered substantial debate. A review of the scholarly literature that addresses gestational surrogacy reveals little consensus on the desirability of surrogacy arrangements, particularly those involving paid surrogacy, or on how best to decide questions of the parentage of children born of such arrangements.

Surrogacy proponents generally contend that gestational surrogacy, like the other reproductive technologies that extend the ability to procreate to persons who might not otherwise be able to have children, enhances "individual freedom, fulfillment and responsibility." (Shultz, *Reproductive Technology, supra,* 1990 Wis.L.Rev. 297, 303.) Under this view, women capable of bearing children should be allowed to freely agree to be paid to do so by infertile couples desiring to form a family. (Shalev, Birth Power: The Case for Surrogacy, *supra,* at p. 145 [arguing for a "free market in reproduction" in which the "reproducing woman" operates as an "autonomous moral and economic agent"]; see also Posner, Economic Analysis of Law (3 ed. 1986) p. 139; Landes & Posner, *The Economics of the Baby Shortage* (1978) 7 J.Legal Stud. 323 [proposing a "market in babies"].) The "surrogate mother" is expected "to weigh the prospective investment in her birthing labor" before entering into the arrangement, and if her "autonomous reproductive decision" is "voluntary," she should be held responsible for it so as "to fulfill the expectations of the other parties * * *." (Shalev, Birth Power: The Case for Surrogacy, *supra,* at p. 96.)

One constitutional law scholar argues that the use of techniques such as gestational surrogacy is constitutionally protected and should be restricted only on a showing of a compelling state interest. (Robertson, *Procreative Liberty and the Control of Conception, Pregnancy, and Childbirth* (1983) 69 Va.L.Rev. 405; Robertson, *Procreative Liberty and the State's Burden of Proof in Regulating Noncoital Reproduction,* in Surrogate Motherhood, *supra,* pp. 24–26, 35; Robertson, *Embryos, Families, and Procreative Liberty: The Legal Structure of the New Reproduction* (1986) 59 So.Cal.L.Rev. 939, 960.) * * *

* * *

Surrogacy critics, however, maintain that the payment of money for the gestation and relinquishment of a child threatens the economic exploitation of poor women who may be induced to engage in commercial surrogacy arrangements out of financial need. (Capron & Radin, *Choosing Family Law Over Contract Law as a Paradigm for Surrogate Motherhood,* in Surrogate Motherhood, *supra,* p. 62.) Some fear the development of a "breeder" class of poor women who will be regularly employed to bear children for the economically advantaged. (See *Women and Children Used in Systems of Surrogacy: Position Statement of the Institute on Women and Technology,* in Surrogate Motherhood, *supra,* at p. 322; and Corea, *Junk Liberty,* testimony before Cal.Assem. Judiciary Com., April 5, 1988, in Surrogate Motherhood, *supra,* at pp. 325, 335.) Others suggest that women who enter into surrogacy arrangements may underestimate the psychological impact of relinquishing a child they have nurtured in their bodies for nine months. (See Macklin, *Artificial Means of Reproduction and Our Understanding of the Family, supra,* 21 Hastings Center Rep. 5, 10.)

Gestational surrogacy is also said to be "dehumanizing" (Capron & Radin, *Choosing Family Law Over Contract Law as a Paradigm for Surrogate Motherhood,* in Surrogate Motherhood, *supra,* at p. 62) and to "commodify" women and children by treating the female reproductive capacity and the children born of gestational surrogacy arrangements as products that can be bought and sold (Radin, *Market–Inalienability* (1987) 100 Harv.L.Rev. 1849, 1930–1932). The commodification of women and children, it is feared, will reinforce oppressive gender stereotypes and threaten the well-being of all children. (*Medical Technology, supra,* 103 Harv.L.Rev. 1519, 1550; Annas, *Fairy Tales Surrogate Mothers Tell,* in Surrogate Motherhood, *supra,* p. 50.) Some critics foresee promotion of an ever-expanding "business of surrogacy brokerage." (E.g., Goodwin, *Determination of Legal Parentage, supra,* 26 Fam.L.Q. at p. 283.)

Whether surrogacy contracts are viewed as personal service agreements or agreements for the sale of the child born as the result of the agreement, commentators critical of contractual surrogacy view these contracts as contrary to public policy and thus not enforceable. (Radin, *Market–Inalienability, supra,* 100 Harv.L.Rev. at p. 1924, fn. 261; Capron & Radin, *Choosing Family Law Over Contract Law as a Paradigm for Surrogate Motherhood, supra,* in Surrogate Motherhood, at pp. 62–63; see also Krimmel, *Can Surrogate Parenting Be Stopped? An Inspection of the Constitutional and Pragmatic Aspects of Outlawing Surrogate Mother Arrangements* (1992) 27 Val.U.L.Rev. 1, 4–5.)

* * *

Proponents and critics of gestational surrogacy propose widely differing approaches for deciding who should be the legal mother of a child born of a gestational surrogacy arrangement. Surrogacy advocates propose to enforce pre-conception contracts in which gestational mothers have agreed to relinquish parental rights, and, thus, would make "bargained-for intentions determinative of legal parenthood." (Shultz, *Reproductive Technology, supra,* 1990 Wis.L.Rev. at p. 323.) Professor Robertson, for instance, contends that "The right to noncoital, collaborative reproduction also includes the right of the parties to agree how they should allocate their obligations and entitlements with respect to the child. Legal presumptions of paternity and maternity would be overridden by this agreement of the parties." (Robertson, *Procreative Liberty and the Control of Conception, Pregnancy, and Childbirth, supra,*

69 Va.L.Rev. 405, 436; see also Shalev, Birth Power: The Case for Surrogacy, *supra,* at p. 141 [arguing for enforcing the parties' legal expectations].)

Surrogacy critics, on the other hand, consider the unique female role in human reproduction as the determinative factor of questions of legal parentage. They reason that although males and females both contribute genetic material for the child, the act of gestating the fetus falls only on the female. (See Radin, *Market–Inalienability, supra,* 100 Harv.L.Rev. 1849, 1932, fn. 285 [pointing out the "asymmetrical" interests of males and females in human reproduction].) Accordingly, in their view, a woman who, as the result of gestational surrogacy, is not genetically related to the child she bears is like any other woman who gives birth to a child. In either situation the woman giving birth is the child's mother. (See Capron & Radin, *Choosing Family Law Over Contract Law as a Paradigm for Surrogate Motherhood,* in Surrogate Motherhood, *supra,* at pp. 64–65.) Under this approach, the laws governing adoption should govern the parental rights to a child born of gestational surrogacy. Upon the birth of the child, the gestational mother can decide whether or not to relinquish her parental rights in favor of the genetic mother. (*Ibid.*)

V. MODEL LEGISLATION

The debate over whom the law should recognize as the legal mother of a child born of a gestational surrogacy arrangement prompted the National Conference of Commissioners on Uniform State Laws to propose the Uniform Status of Children of Assisted Conception Act. (9B West's U.Laws Ann. (1992 Supp.) Uniform Status of Children of Assisted Conception Act (1988 Act) pp. 122–137 [hereafter USCACA].) This model legislation addresses many of the concerns discussed above.

The commissioners gave careful consideration to the competing interests of the various participants in assisted conception arrangements, and sought to accommodate those interests in the model legislation. Their overriding concern, however, was the well-being of children born of gestational surrogacy and other types of assisted conception. As the foreword to the model legislation notes, the extraordinary circumstances of these children's births deprive them of parentage in the traditional sense. (9B West's U.Laws Ann. (1992 Supp.) USCACA, *supra,* at p. 123.) Thus, the intent of the proposed legislation was to define with precision the legal status of these children as well as to codify the rights of the other participants in a surrogacy arrangement. The commissioners proposed alternative versions of the USCACA: one that would disallow gestational surrogacy and another that would permit it only under court supervision.

In its key components, the proposed legislation provides that "a woman who gives birth to a child is the child's mother" (USCACA, § 2) unless a court has approved a surrogacy agreement before conception (USCACA, §§ 5, 6). In the absence of such court approval, any surrogacy agreement would be void. (USCACA, § 5, subd. (b).) If, however, the arrangement for gestational surrogacy has court approval, "the intended parents are the parents of the child." (USCACA, § 8, subd. (a)(1).)

To obtain court approval, the parties to the surrogacy arrangement must file a petition. (USCACA, § 6, subd. (a).) The model legislation provides for the court to appoint a guardian ad litem for the intended child and legal counsel for the surrogate mother. (*Ibid.*) Before approving a surrogacy arrangement, the trial court must conduct a hearing and enter detailed findings, including the following: medical evidence shows the intended mother's inability to bear a child or that for her to do so poses an unreasonable risk to the unborn child or to the physical or mental health of the intended mother; all parties to the surrogacy agreement (including the surrogate's husband if she has one) meet the standards of fitness of adoptive parents; the agreement was voluntary and all parties understand its terms; the surrogate mother has undergone at least one successful pregnancy and medical evidence shows that another pregnancy will not endanger her physical or mental health or pose an unreasonable risk to the unborn child; and all parties have received professional mental health counseling pertaining to the effect of the surrogacy arrangement. (USCACA, § 6, subd. (b).) These provisions serve to minimize the potential for overreaching and to ensure that all parties to a surrogacy arrangement understand their respective roles and obligations.

The USCACA offers predictability in delineating the parentage of children born of gestational surrogacy arrangements. Under the model legislation, if enacted, there would never be a question as to who has the legal responsibility for a child born of a gestational surrogacy arrangement: If the couple who initiated the surrogacy had complied with the provisions of the legislation, they would be the child's legal parents. If they had not, the rights and responsibilities of parenthood would go to the woman who gave birth to the child and her spouse.

Because California Legislature has not enacted the Uniform Status of Children of Assisted Conception Act, its provisions were not followed in this case.

* * *

VII. ANALYSIS OF THE MAJORITY'S "INTENT" TEST

Faced with the failure of current statutory law to adequately address the issue of who is a child's natural mother when two women qualify under the UPA, the majority breaks the "tie" by resort to a criterion not found in the UPA—the "intent" of the genetic mother to be the child's mother.

This case presents a difficult issue. The majority's resolution of that issue deserves serious consideration. Ultimately, however, I cannot agree that "intent" is the appropriate test for resolving this case.

The majority offers four arguments in support of its conclusion to rely on the intent of the genetic mother as the exclusive determinant for deciding who is the natural mother of a child born of gestational surrogacy. Careful examination, however, demonstrates that none of the arguments mandates the majority's conclusion.

The first argument that the majority uses in support of its conclusion that the intent of the genetic mother to bear a child should be dispositive of the question of motherhood is "but-for" causation. Specifically, the majority relies on a commentator who writes that in a gestational surrogacy arrangement, " 'the child would not have been born *but for* the efforts of the intended parents.' " (Maj. opn., * * * quoting Hill, *What Does It Mean to Be a "Parent"? The Claims of Biology as the Basis for Parental Rights* (1991) 66 N.Y.U.L.Rev. 353, 415, original italics omitted, italics added.)

The majority's resort to "but-for" causation is curious. The concept of "but-for" causation is a "test used in determining tort liability * * *." (Black's Law Dict. (6th ed. 1990) p. 200.) In California, the test for causation is whether the conduct was a "substantial factor" in bringing about the event. (*Mitchell v. Gonzales* (1991) 54 Cal.3d 1041, 1049, 1054, 1056 [disapproving "but-for" jury instruction in tort cases].) Neither test for causation assists the majority, as I shall discuss.

The proposition that a woman who gives birth to a child after carrying it for nine months is a "substantial factor" in the child's birth cannot reasonably be debated. Nor can it reasonably be questioned that "but for" the gestational mother, there would not be a child. Thus, the majority's reliance on principles of causation is misplaced. Neither the "but for" nor the "substantial factor" test of causation provides any basis for preferring the genetic mother's intent as the determinative factor in gestational surrogacy cases: Both the genetic and the gestational mothers are indispensable to the birth of a child in a gestational surrogacy arrangement.

Behind the majority's reliance on "but-for" causation as justification for its intent test is a second, closely related argument. The majority draws its second rationale from a student note: " 'The mental concept of the child is a controlling factor of its creation, and the originators of that concept merit full credit as conceivers.' " (Maj. opn., * * * quoting Note, *Redefining Mother: A Legal Matrix for New Reproductive Technologies* (1986) 96 Yale L.J. 187, 196.)

The "originators of the concept" rationale seems comfortingly familiar. The reason it seems familiar, however, is that it is a rationale that is frequently advanced as justifying the law's protection of intellectual property. As stated by one author, "an idea belongs to its creator because the idea is a manifestation of the creator's personality or self." (Hughes, *The Philosophy of Intellectual Property* (1988) 77 Geo.L.J. 287, 330.) Thus, it may be argued, just as a song or invention is protected as the property of the "originator of the concept," so too a child should be regarded as belonging to the originator of the concept of the child, the genetic mother.

The problem with this argument, of course, is that children are not property. Unlike songs or inventions, rights in children cannot be sold for consideration, or made freely available to the general public. Our most fundamental notions of personhood tell us it is inappropriate to treat children as property. Although the law may justly recognize that the originator of a concept has certain property rights in that concept, the originator of the concept of a child can have no such rights, because children cannot be owned as property. Accordingly, I cannot endorse the majority's "originators of the concept" or intellectual property rationale for employing intent to break the "tie" between the genetic mother and the gestational mother of the child.

Next, the majority offers as its third rationale the notion that bargained-for expectations support its conclusion regarding the dispositive significance of the genetic mother's intent. Specifically, the majority states that " 'intentions that are voluntarily chosen, deliberate, express and bargained-for ought presumptively to determine legal parenthood.' " (Maj. opn., * * * quoting Schultz, *Reproductive Technology, supra,* 1990 Wis.L.Rev. at p. 323.)

It is commonplace that, in real or personal property transactions governed by contracts, "intentions that are voluntarily chosen, deliberate, express and bargained-for" ought presumptively to be enforced and, when one party seeks to escape performance, the court may order specific performance. (See, e.g., § 3384 et seq.; 11 Witkin, Summary of Cal. Law (9th ed. 1990), Equity, § 21, p. 698.) But the courts will not compel performance of all contract obligations. For instance, even when a party to a contract for personal services (such as employment) has wilfully breached the contract, the courts will not order specific enforcement of an obligation to perform that personal service. (§ 3390; see 11 Witkin, Summary of Cal. Law, *supra,* Equity, § 59, p. 736.) The unsuitability of applying the notion that, because contract intentions are "voluntarily chosen, deliberate, express and bargained-for," their performance ought to be compelled by the courts is even more clear when the concept of specific performance is used to determine the course of the life of a child. Just as children are not the intellectual property of their parents, neither are they the personal property of anyone, and their delivery cannot be ordered as a contract remedy on the same terms that a court would, for example, order a breaching party to deliver a truckload of nuts and bolts.

Thus, three of the majority's four arguments in support of its exclusive reliance on the intent of the genetic mother as determinative in gestational surrogacy cases cannot withstand analysis. And, as I shall discuss shortly, the majority's fourth rationale has merit, but does not support the majority's conclusion. But before turning to the majority's fourth rationale, I shall discuss two additional considerations, not noted by the majority, that in my view also weigh against utilizing the intent of the genetic mother as the sole determinant of the result in this case and others like it.

First, in making the intent of the genetic mother who wants to have a child the dispositive factor, the majority renders a certain result preordained and inflexible in every such case: as between an intending genetic mother and a gestational mother, the genetic mother will, under the majority's analysis, always prevail. The majority recognizes no meaningful contribution by a woman who agrees to carry a fetus to term for the genetic mother beyond that of mere employment to perform a specified biological function.

The majority's approach entirely devalues the substantial claims of motherhood by a gestational mother such as Anna. True, a woman who enters into a surrogacy arrangement intending to raise the child has by her intent manifested an assumption of parental responsibility in addition to her biological contribution of providing the genetic material. (See *Adoption of Kelsey S., supra,* 1 Cal.4th at pp. 838, 849, 4 Cal.Rptr.2d 615, 823 P.2d 1216.) But the gestational mother's biological contribution of carrying a child for nine months and giving birth is likewise an assumption of parental responsibility. (See Dolgin, *Just a Gene: Judicial Assumptions About Parenthood* (1993) 40 UCLA L.Rev. 637, 659.) A pregnant woman's commitment to the unborn child she carries is not just physical; it is psychological and emotional as well. * * * A pregnant woman intending to bring a child into the world is more than a mere container or breeding animal; she is a conscious agent of creation no less than the genetic mother, and her humanity is implicated on a deep level. Her role should not be devalued.

To summarize, the woman who carried the fetus to term and brought a child into the world has, like the genetic mother, a substantial claim to be the natural mother of the child. The gestational mother has made an indispensable and unique biological contribution, and has also gone beyond biology in an intangible respect that, though difficult to label, cannot be denied. Accordingly, I cannot agree with the majority's devaluation of the role of the gestational mother.

* * *

The majority's final argument in support of using the intent of the genetic mother as the exclusive determinant of the outcome in gestational surrogacy cases is that preferring the intending mother serves the child's interests, which are " '[u]nlikely to run contrary to those of adults who choose to bring [the child] into being.' " (Maj. opn., * * * quoting Schultz, *Reproductive Technology, supra,* 1990 Wis.L.Rev. at p. 397.)

I agree with the majority that the best interests of the child is an important goal; indeed, as I shall explain, the best interests of the child, rather than the intent of the genetic mother, is the proper standard to apply in the absence of legislation. The problem with the majority's rule of intent is that application of this inflexible rule will not serve the child's best interests in every case.

I express no view on whether the best interests of the child in this case will be served by determining that the genetic mother is or is not the natural mother under California's UPA. It may be that in this case the child's interests will be best served by recognizing Crispina as the natural mother. But this court is not just making a rule to resolve this case. Because the UPA does not adequately address the situation of gestational surrogacy, this court is of necessity making a rule that, unless new legislation is enacted, will govern all future cases of gestational surrogacy in California. And all future cases will not be alike. * * * It requires little imagination to foresee cases in which the genetic mothers are, for example, unstable or substance abusers, or in which the genetic mothers' life circumstances change dramatically during the gestational mothers' pregnancies, while the gestational mothers, though of a less advantaged socioeconomic class, are stable, mature, capable and willing to provide a loving family environment in which the child will flourish. Under those circumstances, the majority's rigid reliance on the intent of the genetic mother will not serve the best interests of the child.

VIII. THE BEST INTERESTS OF THE CHILD

* * *

[A]s I have pointed out, we are not deciding a case involving the commission of a tort, the ownership of intellectual property, or the delivery of goods under a commercial contract; we are deciding the fate of a child. In the absence of legislation that is designed to address the unique problems of gestational surrogacy, this court should look not to tort, property or contract law, but to family law, as the governing paradigm and source of a rule of decision.

The allocation of parental rights and responsibilities necessarily impacts the welfare of a minor child. And in issues of child welfare, the standard that courts frequently apply is the best interests of the child. * * * This "best interests" standard serves to assure that in the judicial resolution of disputes affecting a child's well-being, protection of the minor child is the foremost consideration. Consequently, I would apply "the best interests of the child" standard to determine who can best assume the social and legal responsibilities of motherhood for a child born of a gestational surrogacy arrangement.[4]

The determination of a child's best interests does not depend on the parties' relative economic circumstances, which in a gestational surrogacy situation will usually favor the genetic mother and her spouse. (See *Matter of Baby M., supra,* 537 A.2d at p. 1249.) As this court has recognized, however, superior wealth does not necessarily equate with good parenting. (See *Burchard v. Garay* (1986) 42 Cal.3d 531, 540, 229 Cal.Rptr. 800, 724 P.2d 486.)

Factors that are pertinent to good parenting, and thus that are in a child's best interests, include the ability to nurture the child physically and psychologically (Cahill, *The Ethics of Surrogate Motherhood: Biology, Freedom, and Moral Obligation,* in Surrogate Motherhood, *supra,* at p. 160), and to provide ethical and intellectual guidance (see *In re Marriage of Carney* (1979) 24 Cal.3d 725, 739, 157 Cal.Rptr. 383, 598 P.2d 36). Also crucial to a child's best interests is the "well recognized right" of every child "to stability and continuity." (*Burchard v. Garay, supra,* 42 Cal.3d at p. 546, 229 Cal.Rptr. 800, 724 P.2d 486 (conc. opn. of Mosk, J.).) The intent of the genetic mother to procreate a child is certainly relevant to the question of the child's best interests; alone, however, it should not be dispositive.

Here, the child born of the gestational surrogacy arrangement between Anna Johnson and Mark and Crispina Calvert has lived continuously with Mark and Crispina since his birth in September 1990. The trial court awarded parental rights to Mark and Crispina, concluding that as a matter of law they were the child's "genetic, biological and natural" parents. In reaching that conclusion, the trial court did not treat Anna's statutory claim to be the child's legal mother as equal to Crispina's, nor did the trial court consider the child's best interests in deciding between those two equal statutory claims. Accordingly, I would remand the matter to the trial court to undertake that evaluation.

4. In a footnote responding to this opinion, the majority confuses questions of custody, which I do not address, with the issue of maternal parentage, which I do address. (See maj. opn., *ante,* at p. 500, fn. 10 of 19 Cal. Rptr.2d, p. 782, fn. 10 of 851 P.2d.) The majority suggests that it is somehow inappropriate for a court to look to the child's best interests when deciding a question of parentage under the UPA; this is refuted by the express terms of the UPA itself, which, as noted above, requires the court to consider the child's best interests in deciding another question of parentage. (§ 7017, subd. (d)(2).)

The majority is also wrong when it suggests that the "best interests" approach for resolving the disputed issue of parentage, more than the majority's "intent" approach, raises the "specter of governmental interference" in fundamentally private matters. * * * This court's grant of review to decide who is the

natural mother of the child placed one branch of government squarely in the middle of this controversy—as did the parties' decisions to resort to the court system in the first place. Judicial resolution of family law matters, by its nature, necessarily involves some governmental interference in what would otherwise be private concerns.

On another point, the majority writes that the gestational mother could "voluntarily contract[ ] away any rights to the child," and that this would represent a "concession" as to the child's best interests. * * * It is questionable whether the parentage of children is a proper subject of contract. But even assuming that a parent could contract away parental rights to a child—for instance, by selling the child into slavery—this would not logically amount to a binding "concession" that such a sale would be in the child's best interests.

CONCLUSION

Recent advances in medical technology have made it possible for the human female reproductive role to be divided between two women, the genetic mother and the gestational mother. Such gestational surrogacy arrangements call for sensitivity to each of the adult participants. But the paramount concern must be the well-being of the child that gestational surrogacy has made possible.

The model legislation proposed by the National Conference of Commissioners on Uniform Laws would protect such children's well-being by precisely defining their parentage. Such precision is not possible using a "best interests of the child" standard, which requires a case-by-case evaluation after the birth of the child. But that evaluation would afford many protections similar to those set out in USCACA, such as judicial oversight, legal counsel, and an opportunity for the court to determine who best can provide for the child.

I recognize that, for couples such as Mark and Crispina, gestational surrogacy offers the only hope of raising a child who is genetically related to both. But the desire for a genetically related child does not diminish the substantial concerns expressed by a broad spectrum of commentators that surrogacy left unregulated poses a fundamental threat to the well-being of women and children. This threat could largely be allayed by legislation permitting gestational surrogacy, but under court supervision and with the type of procedural requirements proposed in the USCACA that serve to protect all of those affected by a gestational surrogacy arrangement, particularly the child. In my view, the Legislature should turn its attention to the complex issues posed by gestational surrogacy.

In this opinion, I do not purport to offer a perfect solution to the difficult questions posed by gestational surrogacy; perhaps there can be no perfect solution. But in the absence of legislation specifically designed to address the complex issues of gestational surrogacy and to protect against potential abuses, I cannot join the majority's uncritical validation of gestational surrogacy.

I would reverse the judgment of the Court of Appeal, and remand the case to the trial court for a determination of disputed parentage on the basis of the best interests of the child.

Notes on Johnson

1. Should gestational surrogacy arrangements of the type featured in *Johnson* be encouraged or discouraged as a matter of public policy? How would the result reached under the Uniform Status of Children of Assisted Conception Act (discussed in Part V of Justice Kennard's opinion) differ from that in *Johnson*?

2. What is your assessment of the relative merits of the "intent" test adopted by the majority and the "best interests" approach favored by Justice Kennard? Is one more empowering for women? Which one? Is one more sensitive to the developmental needs of children? Which one? Are these the right questions?

3. How does Professor Marjorie Maguire Shultz's "intent" standard, adopted in *Johnson,* apply to a case where neither the intended parents nor the surrogate are the genetic parents of the child? In Jaycee B. v. Superior Court, 42

Cal.App.4th 718, 49 Cal.Rptr.2d 694 (1996), six people were involved in the gestational surrogacy process: the four contracting parties, who were the intended parents and the surrogate and her husband, and the two genetic parents, who donated the sperm and egg anonymously. The intended parents had separated and the husband had filed a petition for divorce before the child was born. After birth, Jaycee lived with the intended mother. The husband, who concededly had signed the surrogacy contract, denied that Jaycee was a "child of the marriage" for purposes of the divorce proceeding since there had been no adoption, and argued that the Family Court lacked jurisdiction to order him to pay temporary child support. The court accepted this argument, and its order ruling that it had no jurisdiction to award support was reviewed in the Court of Appeals by peremptory writ. Following *Johnson,* the appellate court held that the Family Court had jurisdiction to award temporary support because the husband's act of signing the surrogacy contract was enough to show, by a preponderance of the evidence, that on remand he will likely be held to be Jaycee's father. Do you agree with this result? If the Family Court does find that the husband is Jaycee's legal father, but he refuses to agree to an adoption, will Jaycee be his illegitimate child?

4. Should Mary Beth Whitehead and Anna Johnson stand on the same legal footing in their efforts to gain custody of the children they birthed? What differences seem to you relevant? Why?

5. If you support gestational surrogacy when the intended mother is incapable of sustaining a pregnancy and giving birth, do you also support it when the intended mother is capable of doing both, but prefers to avoid the inconvenience or disruption of pregnancy and childbirth? Would the fears of opponents of gestational surrogacy be lessened if the government set a nonexploitative price for the surrogate's services?

6. Professor Mary Becker applies four feminist theories to surrogacy in Mary Becker, Four Feminist Theoretical Approaches and the Double Bind of Surrogacy, 69 Chi.–Kent L.Rev. 303 (1993).

3. ABORTION

ROE v. WADE

Supreme Court of the United States, 1973.
410 U.S. 113, 93 S.Ct. 705, 35 L.Ed.2d 147.

MR. JUSTICE BLACKMUN delivered the opinion of the Court.

This Texas federal appeal and its Georgia companion, Doe v. Bolton, post, 410 U.S. 179, 93 S.Ct. 739, 35 L.Ed.2d 201, present constitutional challenges to state criminal abortion legislation. * * *

I

The Texas statutes that concern us here are Arts. 1191–1194 and 1196 of the State's Penal Code. These make it a crime to "procure an abortion," as therein defined, or to attempt one, except with respect to "an abortion procured or attempted by medical advice for the purpose of saving the life of the mother." Similar statutes are in existence in a majority of the States.

* * *

II

Jane Roe, a single woman who was residing in Dallas County, Texas, instituted this federal action in March 1970 against the District Attorney of the county. She sought a declaratory judgment that the Texas criminal abortion statutes were unconstitutional on their face, and an injunction restraining the defendant from enforcing the statutes.

Roe alleged that she was unmarried and pregnant; that she wished to terminate her pregnancy by an abortion "performed by a competent, licensed physician under safe, clinical conditions"; that she was unable to get a "legal" abortion in Texas because her life did not appear to be threatened by the continuation of her pregnancy; and that she could not afford to travel to another jurisdiction in order to secure a legal abortion under safe conditions. She claimed that the Texas statutes were unconstitutionally vague and that they abridged her right of personal privacy, protected by the First, Fourth, Fifth, Ninth, and Fourteenth Amendments. By an amendment to her complaint Roe purported to sue "on behalf of herself and all other women" similarly situated.

* * *

V

The principal thrust of appellant's attack on the Texas statutes is that they improperly invade a right, said to be possessed by the pregnant woman, to choose to terminate her pregnancy. Appellant would discover this right in the concept of personal "liberty" embodied in the Fourteenth Amendment's Due Process Clause; or in personal, marital, familial, and sexual privacy said to be protected by the Bill of Rights or its penumbras, see Griswold v. Connecticut, 381 U.S. 479, 85 S.Ct. 1678, 14 L.Ed.2d 510 (1965); Eisenstadt v. Baird, 405 U.S. 438 (1972); id., at 460, 92 S.Ct. 1029, at 1042, 31 L.Ed.2d 349 (White, J., concurring); or among those rights reserved to the people by the Ninth Amendment, Griswold v. Connecticut, 381 U.S., at 486, 85 S.Ct. at 1682 (Goldberg, J., concurring).

* * *

VII

Three reasons have been advanced to explain historically the enactment of criminal abortion laws in the 19th century and to justify their continued existence.

It has been argued occasionally that these laws were the product of a Victorian social concern to discourage illicit sexual conduct. Texas, however, does not advance this justification in the present case, and it appears that no court or commentator has taken the argument seriously. The appellants and *amici* contend, moreover, that this is not a proper state purpose at all and suggest that, if it were, the Texas statutes are overbroad in protecting it since the law fails to distinguish between married and unwed mothers.

A second reason is concerned with abortion as a medical procedure. When most criminal abortion laws were first enacted, the procedure was a hazardous one for the woman. This was particularly true prior to the development of antisepsis. Antiseptic techniques, of course, were based on discoveries by Lister, Pasteur, and others first announced in 1867, but were not generally accepted and employed until about the turn of the century. Abortion mortality was high. Even after 1900, and perhaps until as late as the development of antibiotics in the 1940's, standard modern techniques such as dilation and curettage were not nearly so safe as they are today. Thus it has been argued that a State's real concern in enacting a criminal abortion law was to protect the pregnant woman, that is, to restrain her from submitting to a procedure that placed her life in serious jeopardy.

Modern medical techniques have altered this situation. Appellants and various *amici* refer to medical data indicating that abortion in early pregnancy, that is, prior to the end of first trimester, although not without its risk, is now relatively safe. Mortality rates for women undergoing early abortions, where the procedure is legal, appear to be as low as or lower than the rates for normal childbirth. Consequently, any interest of the State in protecting the woman from an inherently hazardous procedure, except when it would be equally dangerous for her to forgo it, has largely disappeared. Of course, important state interests in the area of health and medical standards do remain. The State has a legitimate interest in seeing to it that abortion, like any other medical procedure, is performed under circumstances that insure maximum safety for the patient. This interest obviously extends at least to the performing physician and his staff, to the facilities involved, to the availability of aftercare and to adequate provision for any complication or emergency that might arise. The prevalence of high mortality rates at illegal "abortion mills" strengthens, rather than weakens, the State's interest in regulating the conditions under which abortions are performed. Moreover, the risk to the woman increases as her pregnancy continues. Thus the State retains a definite interest in protecting the woman's own health and safety when an abortion is proposed at a late stage of pregnancy.

The third reason is the State's interest—some phrase it in terms of duty—in protecting prenatal life. Some of the argument for this justification rests on the theory that a new human life is present from the moment of conception. The State's interest and general obligation to protect life then extends, it is argued, to prenatal life. Only when the life of the pregnant mother herself is at stake, balanced against the life she carries within her, should the interest of the embryo or fetus not prevail. Logically, of course, a legitimate state interest in this area need not stand or fall on acceptance of the belief that life begins at conception or at some other point prior to live birth. In assessing the State's interest, recognition may be given to the less rigid claim that as long as at least *potential* life is involved, the State may assert interests beyond the protection of the pregnant woman alone.

Parties challenging state abortion laws have sharply disputed in some courts the contention that a purpose of these laws, when enacted, was to protect prenatal life. Pointing to the absence of legislative history to support the contention, they claim that most state laws were designed solely to protect the woman. Because medical advances have lessened this concern, at least with respect to abortion in early pregnancy, they argue that with respect to such abortions the laws can no longer be justified by any state interest. There is some scholarly support for this view of original purpose. The few state courts called upon to interpret their laws in the late 19th and early 20th centuries did focus on the State's interest in protecting the woman's health rather than in preserving the embryo and fetus. Proponents of this view point out that in many States, including Texas, by statute or judicial interpretation, the pregnant woman herself could not be prosecuted for self-abortion or for cooperating in an abortion performed upon her by another. They claim that adoption of the "quickening" distinction through received common law and state statutes tacitly recognizes the greater health hazards inherent in late abortion and impliedly repudiates the theory that life begins at conception.

It is with these interests, and the weight to be attached to them, that this case is concerned.

VIII

The Constitution does not explicitly mention any right of privacy. In a line of decisions, however, going back, perhaps as far as Union Pacific R. Co. v. Botsford, 141 U.S. 250, 251, 11 S.Ct. 1000, 1001, 35 L.Ed. 734 (1891), the Court has recognized that a right of personal privacy, or a guarantee of certain areas or zones of privacy, does exist under the Constitution. In varying contexts the Court or individual Justices have indeed found at least the roots of that right in the First Amendment, Stanley v. Georgia, 394 U.S. 557, 564, 89 S.Ct. 1243, 1247, 22 L.Ed.2d 542 (1969); in the Fourth and Fifth Amendments, Terry v. Ohio, 392 U.S. 1, 8–9, 88 S.Ct. 1868, 1872–1873, 20 L.Ed.2d 889 (1968), Katz v. United States, 389 U.S. 347, 350, 88 S.Ct. 507, 510, 19 L.Ed.2d 576 (1967), Boyd v. United States, 116 U.S. 616, 6 S.Ct. 524, 29 L.Ed. 746 (1886), see Olmstead v. United States, 277 U.S. 438, 478, 48 S.Ct. 564, 572, 72 L.Ed. 944 (1928) (Brandeis, J., dissenting); in the penumbras of the Bill of Rights, Griswold v. Connecticut, 381 U.S. 479, 484–485, 85 S.Ct., at 1681–1682; in the Ninth Amendment, id., at 486, 85 S.Ct., at 1682 (Goldberg, J., concurring); or in the concept of liberty guaranteed by the first section of the Fourteenth Amendment, see Meyer v. Nebraska, 262 U.S. 390, 399, 43 S.Ct. 625, 626, 67 L.Ed. 1042 (1923). These decisions make it clear that only personal rights that can be deemed "fundamental" or "implicit in the concept of ordered liberty," Palko v. Connecticut, 302 U.S. 319, 325, 58 S.Ct. 149, 152, 82 L.Ed. 288 (1937), are included in this guarantee of personal privacy. They also make it clear that the right has some extension to activities relating to marriage, Loving v. Virginia, 388 U.S. 1, 12, 87 S.Ct. 1817, 1823, 18 L.Ed.2d 1010 (1967), procreation, Skinner v. Oklahoma, 316 U.S. 535, 541–542, 62 S.Ct. 1110, 1113–1114, 86 L.Ed. 1655 (1942), contraception, Eisenstadt v. Baird, 405 U.S. 438, 453–454, 92 S.Ct., at 1038–1039; id., at 460, 463–465, 92 S.Ct. at 1042, 1043–1044 (White, J., concurring), family relationships, Prince v. Massachusetts, 321 U.S. 158, 166, 64 S.Ct. 438, 442, 88 L.Ed. 645 (1944), and child rearing and education, Pierce v. Society of Sisters, 268 U.S. 510, 535, 45 S.Ct. 571, 573, 69 L.Ed. 1070 (1925), Meyer v. Nebraska, supra.

This right of privacy, whether it be founded in the Fourteenth Amendment's concept of personal liberty and restrictions upon state action, as we feel it is, or, as the District Court determined, in the Ninth Amendment's reservation of rights to the people, is broad enough to encompass a woman's decision whether or not to terminate her pregnancy. The detriment that the State would impose upon the pregnant woman by denying this choice altogether is apparent. Specific and direct harm medically diagnosable even in early pregnancy may be involved. Maternity, or additional offspring, may force upon the woman a distressful life and future. Psychological harm may be imminent. Mental and physical health may be taxed by child care. There is also the distress, for all concerned, associated with the unwanted child, and there is the problem of bringing a child into a family already unable, psychologically and otherwise, to care for it. In other cases, as in this one, the additional difficulties and continuing stigma of unwed motherhood may be involved. All these are factors the woman and her responsible physician necessarily will consider in consultation.

On the basis of elements such as these, appellants and some *amici* argue that the woman's right is absolute and that she is entitled to terminate her pregnancy at whatever time, in whatever way, and for whatever reason she alone chooses. With this we do not agree. Appellants' arguments that Texas either has no valid interest at all in regulating the abortion decision, or no interest strong enough to support any limitation upon the woman's sole determination, is unpersuasive. The Court's decisions recognizing a right of privacy also acknowledge that some state regulation in areas protected by that right is appropriate. As noted above, a state may properly assert important interests in safeguarding health, in maintaining medical standards, and in protecting potential life. At some point in pregnancy, these respective interests become sufficiently compelling to sustain regulation of the factors that govern the abortion decision. The privacy right involved, therefore, cannot be said to be absolute. In fact, it is not clear to us that the claim asserted by some *amici* that one has an unlimited right to do with one's body as one pleases bears a close relationship to the right of privacy previously articulated in the Court's decisions. The Court has refused to recognize an unlimited right of this kind in the past. Jacobson v. Massachusetts, 197 U.S. 11, 25 S.Ct. 358, 49 L.Ed. 643 (1905) (vaccination); Buck v. Bell, 274 U.S. 200, 47 S.Ct. 584, 71 L.Ed. 1000 (1927) (sterilization).

We therefore conclude that the right of personal privacy includes the abortion decision, but that this right is not unqualified and must be considered against important state interests in regulation.

* * *

IX

The District Court held that the appellee failed to meet his burden of demonstrating that the Texas statute's infringement upon Roe's rights was necessary to support a compelling state interest, and that, although the defendant presented "several compelling justifications for state presence in the area of abortions," the statutes outstripped these justifications and swept "far beyond any areas of compelling state interest." 314 F.Supp., at 1222–1223. Appellant and appellee both contest that holding. Appellant, as has been indicated, claims an absolute right that bars any state imposition of criminal penalties in the area. Appellee argues that the State's determination to recognize and protect prenatal life from and after conception constitutes a compelling state interest. As noted above, we do not agree fully with either formulation.

A. The appellee and certain *amici* argue that the fetus is a "person" within the language and meaning of the Fourteenth Amendment. In support of this they outline at length and in detail the well-known facts of fetal development. If this suggestion of personhood is established, the appellant's case, of course, collapses, for the fetus' right to life is then guaranteed specifically by the Amendment. The appellant conceded as much on reargument. On the other hand, the appellee conceded on reargument that no case could be cited that holds that a fetus is a person within the meaning of the Fourteenth Amendment.

The Constitution does not define "person" in so many words. Section 1 of the Fourteenth Amendment contains three references to "person." The first, in defining "citizens," speaks of "persons born or naturalized in the United States." The word also appears both in the Due Process Clause and in the Equal Protection Clause. "Person" is used in other places in the Constitution: in the listing of qualifications for representatives and senators, Art. I, § 2, cl. 2, and § 3, cl. 3; in the Apportionment Clause, Art. I, § 2, cl. 3; in the Migration and Importation provision, Art. I, § 9, cl. 1; in the Emolument Clause, Art. I, § 9, cl. 8; in the Electors provisions, Art. II, § 1, cl. 2, and the superseded cl. 3; in the provision outlining qualifications for the office of President, Art. II, § 1, cl. 5; in the Extradition provisions, Art. IV, § 2, cl. 2, and the superseded Fugitive Slave cl. 3; and in the Fifth, Twelfth, and Twenty-second Amendments as well as in §§ 2 and 3 of the Fourteenth Amendment. But in nearly all these instances, the use of the word is such that it has application only post-natally. None indicates, with any assurance, that it has any possible pre-natal application.

All this together with our observation, supra, that throughout the major portion of the 19th century prevailing legal abortion practices were far freer than they are today, persuades us that the word "person," as used in the Fourteenth Amendment, does not include the unborn. This is in accord with the results reached in those few cases where the issue has been squarely presented. * * * Indeed, our decision in United States v. Vuitch, 402 U.S. 62, 91 S.Ct. 1294, 28 L.Ed.2d 601 (1971), inferentially is to the same effect, for we there would not have indulged in statutory interpretation favorable to abortion in specified circumstances if the necessary consequence was the termination of life entitled to Fourteenth Amendment protection.

This conclusion, however, does not of itself fully answer the contentions raised by Texas, and we pass on to other considerations.

B. The pregnant woman cannot be isolated in her privacy. She carries an embryo and, later, a fetus, if one accepts the medical definitions of the developing young in the human uterus. See Dorland's Illustrated Medical Dictionary, 478–479, 547 (24th ed. 1965). The situation therefore is inherently different from marital intimacy, or bedroom possession of obscene material, or marriage, or procreation, or education, with which *Eisenstadt, Griswold, Stanley, Loving, Skinner, Pierce,* and *Meyer* were respectively concerned. As we have intimated above, it is reasonable and appropriate for a State to decide that at some point in time another interest, that of health of the mother or that of potential human life, becomes significantly involved. The woman's privacy is no longer sole and any right of privacy she possesses must be measured accordingly.

Texas urges that, apart from the Fourteenth Amendment, life begins at conception and is present throughout pregnancy, and that, therefore, the State has a compelling interest in protecting that life from and after conception. We need not resolve the difficult question of when life begins. When those trained in the respective disciplines of medicine, philosophy, and theology are unable to arrive at any consensus, the judiciary, at this point in the development of man's knowledge, is not in a position to speculate as to the answer. * * *

In areas other than criminal abortion the law has been reluctant to endorse any theory that life, as we recognize it, begins before live birth or to accord legal rights to the unborn except in narrowly defined situations and except when the rights are contingent upon live birth. For example, the traditional rule of tort law had denied recovery for prenatal injuries even though the child was born alive. That rule has been changed in almost every jurisdiction. In most States recovery is said to be permitted only if the fetus is viable, or at least quick, when the injuries were sustained, though few courts have squarely so held. In a recent development, generally opposed by the commentators, some States permit the parents of a stillborn child to maintain an action for wrongful death because of prenatal injuries. Such an action, however, would appear to be one to vindicate the parents' interest and is thus consistent with the view that the fetus, at most, represents only the potentiality of life. Similarly, unborn children have been recognized as acquiring rights or interests by way of inheritance or other devolution of property, and have been represented by guardians *ad litem*. Perfection of the interests involved, again, has generally been contingent upon live birth. In short, the unborn have never been recognized in the law as persons in the whole sense.

X

In view of all this, we do not agree that, by adopting one theory of life, Texas may override the rights of the pregnant woman that are at stake. We repeat, however, that the State does have an important and legitimate interest in preserving and protecting the health of the pregnant woman, whether she be a resident of the State or a nonresident who seeks medical consultation and treatment there, and that it has still *another* important and legitimate interest in protecting the potentiality of human life. These interests are separate and distinct. Each grows in substantiality as the woman approaches term and, at a point during pregnancy, each becomes "compelling."

With respect to the State's important and legitimate interest in the health of the mother, the "compelling" point, in the light of present medical knowledge, is at approximately the end of the first trimester. This is so because of the now established medical fact, referred to above at p. 34, 93 S.Ct., at 725, that until the end of the first trimester mortality in abortion is less than mortality in normal childbirth. It follows that, from and after this point, a State may regulate the abortion procedure to the extent that the regulation reasonably relates to the preservation and protection of maternal health. Examples of permissible state regulation in this area are requirements as to the qualifications of the person who is to perform the abortion; as to the licensure of that person; as to the facility in which the procedure is to be performed, that is, whether it must be a hospital or may be a clinic or some other place of less-than-hospital status; as to the licensing of the facility; and the like.

This means, on the other hand, that, for the period of pregnancy prior to this "compelling" point, the attending physician, in consultation with his patient, is free to determine, without regulation by the State, that in his medical judgment the patient's pregnancy should be terminated. If that decision is reached, the judgment may be effectuated by an abortion free of interference by the State.

With respect to the State's important and legitimate interest in potential life, the "compelling" point is at viability. This is so because the fetus then presumably has the capability of meaningful life outside the mother's womb. State regulation protective of fetal life after viability thus has both logical and biological justifications. If the State is interested in protecting fetal life after viability, it may go so far as to proscribe abortion during that period except when it is necessary to preserve the life or health of the mother.

Measured against these standards, Art. 1196 of the Texas Penal Code, in restricting legal abortions to those "procured or attempted by medical advice for the purpose of saving the life of the mother," sweeps too broadly. The statute makes no distinction between abortions performed early in pregnancy and those performed later, and it limits to a single reason, "saving" the mother's life, the legal justification for the procedure. The statute, therefore, cannot survive the constitutional attack made upon it here.

This conclusion makes it unnecessary for us to consider the additional challenge to the Texas statute asserted on grounds of vagueness. See United States v. Vuitch, 402 U.S. 62, 67–72, 91 S.Ct., at 1296–1299 (1971).

XI

To summarize and to repeat:

1. A state criminal abortion statute of the current Texas type, that excepts from criminality only *a life saving* procedure on behalf of the mother, without regard to pregnancy stage and without recognition of the other interests involved, is violative of the Due Process Clause of the Fourteenth Amendment.

(a) For the stage prior to approximately the end of the first trimester, the abortion decision and its effectuation must be left to the medical judgment of the pregnant woman's attending physician.

(b) For the stage subsequent to approximately the end of the first trimester, the State, in promoting its interest in the health of the mother, may, if it chooses, regulate the abortion procedure in ways that are reasonably related to maternal health.

(c) For the stage subsequent to viability the State, in promoting its interest in the potentiality of human life, may, if it chooses, regulate, and even proscribe, abortion except where it is necessary, in appropriate medical judgment, for the preservation of the life or health of the mother.

2. The State may define the term "physician," as it has been employed in the preceding numbered paragraphs of this Part XI of this opinion, to mean only a physician currently licensed by the State, and may proscribe any abortion by a person who is not a physician as so defined.

In Doe v. Bolton, 410 U.S. 179, 93 S.Ct. 739, 35 L.Ed.2d 201, procedural requirements contained in one of the modern abortion statutes are considered. That opinion and this one, of course, are to be read together.[67]

---

67. Neither in this opinion nor in Doe v. Bolton, 410 U.S. 179, 93 S.Ct. 739, 35 L.Ed.2d 201, do we discuss the father's rights, if any exist in the constitutional context, in the abor-

This holding, we feel, is consistent with the relative weights of the respective interests involved, with the lessons and example of medical and legal history, with the lenity of the common law, and with the demands of the profound problems of the present day. The decision leaves the State free to place increasing restrictions on abortion as the period of pregnancy lengthens, so long as those restrictions are tailored to the recognized state interests. The decision vindicates the right of the physician to administer medical treatment according to his professional judgment up to the points where important state interests provide compelling justifications for intervention. Up to those points the abortion decision in all its aspects is inherently, and primarily, a medical decision, and basic responsibility for it must rest with the physician. If an individual practitioner abuses the privilege of exercising proper medical judgment, the usual remedies, judicial and intra-professional, are available.

XII

Our conclusion that Art. 1196 is unconstitutional means, of course, that the Texas abortion statutes, as a unit, must fall. * * *

The judgment of the District Court * * * is affirmed. * * *

It is so ordered.

Mr. Justice Stewart, concurring.

In 1963, this Court, in Ferguson v. Skrupa, 372 U.S. 726, 83 S.Ct. 1028, 10 L.Ed.2d 93, purported to sound the death knell for the doctrine of substantive due process, a doctrine under which many state laws had in the past been held to violate the Fourteenth Amendment. As Mr. Justice Black's opinion for the Court in *Skrupa* put it: "We have returned to the original constitutional proposition that courts do not substitute their social and economic beliefs for the judgment of legislative bodies, who are elected to pass laws." Id., at 730, 83 S.Ct., at 1031.

Barely two years later, in Griswold v. Connecticut, 381 U.S. 479, 85 S.Ct. 1678, 14 L.Ed.2d 510 the Court held a Connecticut birth control law unconstitutional. In view of what had been so recently said in *Skrupa,* the Court's opinion in *Griswold* understandably did its best to avoid reliance on the Due Process Clause of the Fourteenth Amendment as the ground for decision. Yet, the Connecticut law did not violate any provision of the Bill of Rights, nor any other specific provision of the Constitution. So it was clear to me then, and it is equally clear to me now, that the *Griswold* decision can be rationally understood only as a holding that the Connecticut statute substantively invaded the "liberty" that is protected by the Due Process Clause of the Fourteenth Amendment. As so understood, *Griswold* stands as one in a long line of pre-*Skrupa* cases decided under the doctrine of substantive due process, and I now accept it as such.

tion decision. No paternal right has been asserted in either of the cases, and the Texas and the Georgia statutes on their face take no cognizance of the father. We are aware that some statutes recognize the father under certain circumstances. North Carolina, for example, 1B N.C.Gen.Stat. § 14–45.1 (Supp.1971), requires written permission for the abortion from the husband when the woman is a married minor, that is, when she is less than 18 years of age, 41 N.C.A.G. 489 (1971); if the woman is an unmarried minor, written permission from the parents is required. We need not now decide whether provisions of this kind are constitutional.

"In a Constitution for a free people, there can be no doubt that the meaning of 'liberty' must be broad indeed." Board of Regents v. Roth, 408 U.S. 564, 572, 92 S.Ct. 2701, 2707, 33 L.Ed.2d 548. The Constitution nowhere mentions a specific right of personal choice in matters of marriage and family life, but the "liberty" protected by the Due Process Clause of the Fourteenth Amendment covers more than those freedoms explicitly named in the Bill of Rights. [Citations omitted.]

* * *

Several decisions of this Court make clear that freedom of personal choice in matters of marriage and family life is one of the liberties protected by the Due Process Clause of the Fourteenth Amendment. * * *

Clearly, therefore, the Court today is correct in holding that the right asserted by Jane Roe is embraced within the personal liberty protected by the Due Process Clause of the Fourteenth Amendment.

It is evident that the Texas abortion statute infringes that right directly. Indeed, it is difficult to imagine a more complete abridgment of a constitutional freedom than that worked by the inflexible criminal statute now in force in Texas. The question then becomes whether the state interests advanced to justify this abridgment can survive the "particularly careful scrutiny" that the Fourteenth Amendment here requires.

The asserted state interests are protection of the health and safety of the pregnant woman, and protection of the potential future human life within her. These are legitimate objectives, amply sufficient to permit a State to regulate abortions as it does other surgical procedures, and perhaps sufficient to permit a State to regulate abortions more stringently or even to prohibit them in the late stages of pregnancy. But such legislation is not before us, and I think the Court today has thoroughly demonstrated that these state interests cannot constitutionally support the broad abridgment of personal liberty worked by the existing Texas law. Accordingly, I join the Court's opinion holding that that law is invalid under the Due Process Clause of the Fourteenth Amendment.

Mr. Justice Rehnquist, dissenting.

The Court's opinion brings to the decision of this troubling question both extensive historical fact and a wealth of legal scholarship. While its opinion thus commands my respect, I find myself nonetheless in fundamental disagreement with those parts of it which invalidate the Texas statute in question, and therefore dissent.

* * *

II

Even if there were a plaintiff in this case capable of litigating the issue which the Court decides, I would reach a conclusion opposite to that reached by the Court. I have difficulty in concluding, as the Court does, that the right of "privacy" is involved in this case. Texas by the statute here challenged bars the performance of a medical abortion by a licensed physician on a plaintiff such as Roe. A transaction resulting in an operation such as this is not "private" in the ordinary usage of that word. Nor is the "privacy" which the Court finds here even a distant relative of the freedom from searches and seizures protected by the Fourth Amendment to the Constitution which the Court has referred to as embodying a right to privacy. Katz v. United States, 389 U.S. 347, 88 S.Ct. 507, 19 L.Ed.2d 576 (1967).

If the Court means by the term "privacy" no more than that the claim of a person to be free from unwanted state regulation of consensual transactions may be a form of "liberty" protected by the Fourteenth Amendment, there is no doubt that similar claims have been upheld in our earlier decisions on the basis of that liberty. I agree with the statement of Mr. Justice Stewart in his concurring opinion that the "liberty," against deprivation of which without due process the Fourteenth Amendment protects, embraces more than the rights found in the Bill of Rights. But that liberty is not guaranteed absolutely against deprivation, but only against deprivation without due process of law. The test traditionally applied in the area of social and economic legislation is whether or not a law such as that challenged has a rational relation to a valid state objective. Williamson v. Lee Optical Co., 348 U.S. 483, 491, 75 S.Ct. 461, 466, 99 L.Ed. 563 (1955). The Due Process Clause of the Fourteenth Amendment undoubtedly does place a limit on legislative power to enact laws such as this, albeit a broad one. If the Texas statute were to prohibit an abortion even where the mother's life is in jeopardy, I have little doubt that such a statute would lack a rational relation to a valid state objective under the test stated in *Williamson,* supra. But the Court's sweeping invalidation of any restrictions on abortion during the first trimester is impossible to justify under that standard, and the conscious weighing of competing factors which the Court's opinion apparently substitutes for the established test is far more appropriate to a legislative judgment than to a judicial one.

* * *

The fact that a majority of the States reflecting, after all, the majority sentiment in those States, have had restrictions on abortions for at least a century is a strong indication, it seems to me, that the asserted right to an abortion is not "so rooted in the traditions and conscience of our people as to be ranked as fundamental," Snyder v. Massachusetts, 291 U.S. 97, 105, 54 S.Ct. 330, 332, 78 L.Ed. 674 (1934). Even today, when society's views on abortion are changing, the very existence of the debate is evidence that the "right" to an abortion is not so universally accepted as the appellants would have us believe.

* * *

There apparently was no question concerning the validity of this provision or of any of the other state statutes when the Fourteenth Amendment was adopted. The only conclusion possible from this history is that the drafters did not intend to have the Fourteenth Amendment withdraw from the States the power to legislate with respect to this matter.

III

Even if one were to agree that the case which the Court decides were here, and that the enunciation of the substantive constitutional law in the Court's opinion were proper, the actual disposition of the case by the Court is still difficult to justify. The Texas statute is struck down *in toto,* even though the Court apparently concedes that at later periods of pregnancy Texas might impose these selfsame statutory limitations on abortion. My understanding of past practice is that a statute found to be invalid as applied to a particular plaintiff, but not unconstitutional as a whole, is not simply "struck down" but is, instead, declared unconstitutional as applied to the fact situation before the Court. Yick Wo v. Hopkins, 118 U.S. 356, 6 S.Ct. 1064, 30 L.Ed. 220 (1886); Street v. New York, 394 U.S. 576, 89 S.Ct. 1354, 22 L.Ed.2d 572 (1969).

For all of the foregoing reasons, I respectfully dissent.

PLANNED PARENTHOOD OF SOUTHEASTERN PENNSYLVANIA v. CASEY

Supreme Court of the United States, 1992.
505 U.S. 833, 112 S.Ct. 2791, 120 L.Ed.2d 674.

JUSTICE O'CONNOR, JUSTICE KENNEDY, and JUSTICE SOUTER announced the judgment of the Court and delivered the opinion of the Court with respect to Parts I, II, III, V–A, V–C, and VI, an opinion with respect to Part V–E, in which JUSTICE STEVENS joins, and an opinion with respect to Parts IV, V–B, and V–D.

I

Liberty finds no refuge in a jurisprudence of doubt. Yet 19 years after our holding that the Constitution protects a woman's right to terminate her pregnancy in its early stages, *Roe v. Wade,* 410 U.S. 113 (1973), that definition of liberty is still questioned. Joining the respondents as *amicus curiae,* the United States, as it has done in five other cases in the last decade, again asks us to overrule *Roe.*   * * *

At issue in these cases are five provisions of the Pennsylvania Abortion Control Act of 1982 as amended in 1988 and 1989. * * * The Act requires that a woman seeking an abortion give her informed consent prior to the abortion procedure, and specifies that she be provided with certain information at least 24 hours before the abortion is performed. § 3205. For a minor to obtain an abortion, the Act requires the informed consent of one of her parents, but provides for a judicial bypass option if the minor does not wish to or cannot obtain a parent's consent. § 3206. Another provision of the Act requires that, unless certain exceptions apply, a married woman seeking an abortion must sign a statement indicating that she has notified her husband of her intended abortion. § 3209. The Act exempts compliance with these three requirements in the event of a "medical emergency," which is defined in § 3203 of the Act. See §§ 3203, 3205(a), 3206(a), 3209(c). In addition to the above provisions regulating the performance of abortions, the Act imposes certain reporting requirements on facilities that provide abortion services. §§ 3207(b), 3214(a), 3214(f).

Before any of these provisions took effect, the petitioners, who are five abortion clinics and one physician representing himself as well as a class of physicians who provide abortion services, brought this suit seeking declaratory and injunctive relief. Each provision was challenged as unconstitutional on its face. The District Court entered a preliminary injunction against the enforcement of the regulations, and, after a 3–day bench trial, held all the provisions at issue here unconstitutional, entering a permanent injunction against Pennsylvania's enforcement of them. 744 F.Supp. 1323 (E.D.Pa.

1990). The Court of Appeals for the Third Circuit affirmed in part and reversed in part, upholding all of the regulations except for the husband notification requirement. 947 F.2d 682 (1991). * * *

* * * [A]t oral argument in this Court, the attorney for the parties challenging the statute took the position that none of the enactments can be upheld without overruling *Roe v. Wade.* * * * We disagree with that analysis; but we acknowledge that our decisions after *Roe* cast doubt upon the meaning and reach of its holding. Further, the CHIEF JUSTICE admits that he would overrule the central holding of *Roe* and adopt the rational relationship test as the sole criterion of constitutionality. * * * State and federal courts as well as legislatures throughout the Union must have guidance as they seek to address this subject in conformance with the Constitution. Given these premises, we find it imperative to review once more the principles that define the rights of the woman and the legitimate authority of the State respecting the termination of pregnancies by abortion procedures.

After considering the fundamental constitutional questions resolved by *Roe,* principles of institutional integrity, and the rule of *stare decisis,* we are led to conclude this: the essential holding of *Roe v. Wade* should be retained and once again reaffirmed.

It must be stated at the outset and with clarity that *Roe*'s essential holding, the holding we reaffirm, has three parts. First is a recognition of the right of the woman to choose to have an abortion before viability and to obtain it without undue interference from the State. Before viability, the State's interests are not strong enough to support a prohibition of abortion or the imposition of a substantial obstacle to the woman's effective right to elect the procedure. Second is a confirmation of the State's power to restrict abortions after fetal viability, if the law contains exceptions for pregnancies which endanger a woman's life or health. And third is the principle that the State has legitimate interests from the outset of the pregnancy in protecting the health of the woman and the life of the fetus that may become a child. These principles do not contradict one another; and we adhere to each.

II

Constitutional protection of the woman's decision to terminate her pregnancy derives from the Due Process Clause of the Fourteenth Amendment. It declares that no State shall "deprive any person of life, liberty, or property, without due process of law." The controlling word in the case before us is "liberty." Although a literal reading of the Clause might suggest that it governs only the procedures by which a State may deprive persons of liberty, for at least 105 years, at least since *Mugler v. Kansas,* 123 U.S. 623, 660–661 (1887), the Clause has been understood to contain a substantive component as well, one "barring certain government actions regardless of the fairness of the procedures used to implement them." *Daniels v. Williams,* 474 U.S. 327, 331 (1986). * * *

The most familiar of the substantive liberties protected by the Fourteenth Amendment are those recognized by the Bill of Rights. * * *

It is * * * tempting, * * * to suppose that the Due Process Clause protects only those practices, defined at the most specific level, that were protected against government interference by other rules of law when the

Fourteenth Amendment was ratified. See *Michael H. v. Gerald D.,* 491 U.S. 110, 127–128, n. 6 (1989) (opinion of SCALIA, J.). But such a view would be inconsistent with our law. It is a promise of the Constitution that there is a realm of personal liberty which the government may not enter. We have vindicated this principle before. Marriage is mentioned nowhere in the Bill of Rights and interracial marriage was illegal in most States in the 19th century, but the Court was no doubt correct in finding it to be an aspect of liberty protected against state interference by the substantive component of the Due Process Clause in *Loving v. Virginia,* 388 U.S. 1, 12 (1967) (relying, in an opinion for eight Justices, on the Due Process Clause). * * *

The inescapable fact is that adjudication of substantive due process claims may call upon the Court in interpreting the Constitution to exercise that same capacity which by tradition courts always have exercised: reasoned judgment. Its boundaries are not susceptible of expression as a simple rule. That does not mean we are free to invalidate state policy choices with which we disagree; yet neither does it permit us to shrink from the duties of our office. * * *

Men and women of good conscience can disagree, and we suppose some always shall disagree, about the profound moral and spiritual implications of terminating a pregnancy, even in its earliest stage. Some of us as individuals find abortion offensive to our most basic principles of morality, but that cannot control our decision. Our obligation is to define the liberty of all, not to mandate our own moral code. The underlying constitutional issue is whether the State can resolve these philosophic questions in such a definitive way that a woman lacks all choice in the matter, except perhaps in those rare circumstances in which the pregnancy is itself a danger to her own life or health, or is the result of rape or incest.

* * *

Our law affords constitutional protection to personal decisions relating to marriage, procreation, contraception, family relationships, child rearing, and education. *Carey v. Population Services International,* 431 U.S., at 685. Our cases recognize "the right of the *individual,* married or single, to be free from unwarranted governmental intrusion into matters so fundamentally affecting a person as the decision whether to bear or beget a child." *Eisenstadt v. Baird, supra,* at 453 (emphasis in original). Our precedents "have respected the private realm of family life which the state cannot enter." *Prince v. Massachusetts,* 321 U.S. 158, 166 (1944). These matters, involving the most intimate and personal choices a person may make in a lifetime, choices central to personal dignity and autonomy, are central to the liberty protected by the Fourteenth Amendment. At the heart of liberty is the right to define one's own concept of existence, of meaning, of the universe, and of the mystery of human life. Beliefs about these matters could not define the attributes of personhood were they formed under compulsion of the State.

These considerations begin our analysis of the woman's interest in terminating her pregnancy but cannot end it, for this reason: though the abortion decision may originate within the zone of conscience and belief, it is more than a philosophic exercise. Abortion is a unique act. It is an act fraught with consequences for others: for the woman who must live with the implications of her decision; for the persons who perform and assist in the procedure; for the spouse, family, and society which must confront the knowledge that these procedures exist, procedures some deem nothing short of an act of violence against innocent human life; and, depending on one's beliefs, for the life or potential life that is aborted. Though abortion is conduct, it does not follow that the State is entitled to proscribe it in all instances. That is because the liberty of the woman is at stake in a sense unique to the human condition and so unique to the law. The mother who carries a child to full term is subject to anxieties, to physical constraints, to pain that only she must bear. That these sacrifices have from the beginning of the human race been endured by woman with a pride that ennobles her in the eyes of others and gives to the infant a bond of love cannot alone be grounds for the State to insist she make the sacrifice. Her suffering is too intimate and personal for the State to insist, without more, upon its own vision of the woman's role, however dominant that vision has been in the course of our history and our culture. The destiny of the woman must be shaped to a large extent on her own conception of her spiritual imperatives and her place in society.

It should be recognized, moreover, that in some critical respects the abortion decision is of the same character as the decision to use contraception, to which *Griswold v. Connecticut, Eisenstadt v. Baird,* and *Carey v. Population Services International,* afford constitutional protection. We have no doubt as to the correctness of those decisions. They support the reasoning in *Roe* relating to the woman's liberty because they involve personal decisions concerning not only the meaning of procreation but also human responsibility and respect for it. As with abortion, reasonable people will have differences of opinion about these matters. One view is based on such reverence for the wonder of creation that any pregnancy ought to be welcomed and carried to full term no matter how difficult it will be to provide for the child and ensure its well-being. Another is that the inability to provide for the nurture and care of the infant is a cruelty to the child and an anguish to the parent. These are intimate views with infinite variations, and their deep, personal character underlay our decisions in *Griswold, Eisenstadt,* and *Carey.* The same concerns are present when the woman confronts the reality that, perhaps despite her attempts to avoid it, she has become pregnant.

It was this dimension of personal liberty that *Roe* sought to protect, and its holding invoked the reasoning and the tradition of the precedents we have discussed, granting protection to substantive liberties of the person. *Roe* was, of course, an extension of those cases and, as the decision itself indicated, the separate States could act in some degree to further their own legitimate interests in protecting pre-natal life. The extent to which the legislatures of the States might act to outweigh the interests of the woman in choosing to terminate her pregnancy was a subject of debate both in *Roe* itself and in decisions following it.

While we appreciate the weight of the arguments made on behalf of the State in the case before us, arguments which in their ultimate formulation conclude that *Roe* should be overruled, the reservations any of us may have in reaffirming the central holding of *Roe* are outweighed by the explication of individual liberty we have given combined with the force of *stare decisis.* We turn now to that doctrine.

III

A

The obligation to follow precedent begins with necessity, and a contrary necessity marks its outer limit. With Cardozo, we recognize that no judicial system could do society's work if it eyed each issue afresh in every case that raised it. See B. Cardozo, The Nature of the Judicial Process 149 (1921). Indeed, the very concept of the rule of law underlying our own Constitution requires such continuity over time that a respect for precedent is, by definition, indispensable. See Powell, Stare Decisis and Judicial Restraint, 1991 Journal of Supreme Court History 13, 16. At the other extreme, a different necessity would make itself felt if a prior judicial ruling should come to be seen so clearly as error that its enforcement was for that very reason doomed.

* * *

So in this case we may inquire whether *Roe*'s central rule has been found unworkable; whether the rule's limitation on state power could be removed without serious inequity to those who have relied upon it or significant damage to the stability of the society governed by the rule in question; whether the law's growth in the intervening years has left *Roe's* central rule a doctrinal anachronism discounted by society; and whether *Roe*'s premises of fact have so far changed in the ensuing two decades as to render its central holding somehow irrelevant or unjustifiable in dealing with the issue it addressed.

* * *

4

We have seen how time has overtaken some of *Roe*'s factual assumptions: advances in maternal health care allow for abortions safe to the mother later in pregnancy than was true in 1973, * * * and advances in neonatal care have advanced viability to a point somewhat earlier. * * * But these facts go only to the scheme of time limits on the realization of competing interests, and the divergences from the factual premises of 1973 have no bearing on the validity of *Roe*'s central holding, that viability marks the earliest point at which the State's interest in fetal life is constitutionally adequate to justify a legislative ban on nontherapeutic abortions. The soundness or unsoundness of that constitutional judgment in no sense turns on whether viability occurs at approximately 28 weeks, as was usual at the time of *Roe,* at 23 to 24 weeks, as it sometimes does today, or at some moment even slightly earlier in pregnancy, as it may if fetal respiratory capacity can somehow be enhanced in the future. Whenever it may occur, the attainment of viability may continue to serve as the critical fact, just as it has done since *Roe* was decided; which is to say that no change in *Roe*'s factual underpinning has left its central holding obsolete, and none supports an argument for overruling it.

5

The sum of the precedential inquiry to this point shows *Roe*'s underpinnings unweakened in any way affecting its central holding. While it has engendered disapproval, it has not been unworkable. An entire generation has come of age free to assume *Roe*'s concept of liberty in defining the capacity of women to act in society, and to make reproductive decisions; no erosion of principle going to liberty or personal autonomy has left *Roe*'s central holding a doctrinal remnant; *Roe* portends no developments at odds with other precedent for the analysis of personal liberty; and no changes of fact have rendered viability more or less appropriate as the point at which the balance of interests tips. Within the bounds of normal *stare decisis* analysis, then, and subject to the considerations on which it customarily turns, the stronger argument is for affirming *Roe*'s central holding, with whatever degree of personal reluctance any of us may have, not for overruling it.

* * *

C

* * *

Our analysis would not be complete, however, without explaining why overruling *Roe*'s central holding would not only reach an unjustifiable result under principles of *stare decisis,* but would seriously weaken the Court's capacity to exercise the judicial power and to function as the Supreme Court of a Nation dedicated to the rule of law. To understand why this would be so it is necessary to understand the source of this Court's authority, the conditions necessary for its preservation, and its relationship to the country's understanding of itself as a constitutional Republic.

* * * The Court's power lies, * * * in its legitimacy, a product of substance and perception that shows itself in the people's acceptance of the Judiciary as fit to determine what the Nation's law means and to declare what it demands.

* * *

* * * Where, in the performance of its judicial duties, the Court decides a case in such a way as to resolve the sort of intensely divisive controversy reflected in *Roe* and those rare, comparable cases, its decision has a dimension that the resolution of the normal case does not carry. It is the dimension present whenever the Court's interpretation of the Constitution calls the contending sides of a national controversy to end their national division by accepting a common mandate rooted in the Constitution.

The Court is not asked to do this very often, having thus addressed the Nation only twice in our lifetime, in the decisions of *Brown* and *Roe*. But when the Court does act in this way, its decision requires an equally rare precedential force to counter the inevitable efforts to overturn it and to thwart its implementation. Some of those efforts may be mere unprincipled emotional reactions; others may proceed from principles worthy of profound respect. But whatever the premises of opposition may be, only the most convincing justification under accepted standards of precedent could suffice to demonstrate that a later decision overruling the first was anything but a surrender to political pressure, and an unjustified repudiation of the principle on which the Court staked its authority in the first instance. So to overrule under fire in the absence of the most compelling reason to reexamine a watershed decision would subvert the Court's legitimacy beyond any serious question. Cf. *Brown v. Board of Education,* 349 U.S. 294, 300 (1955) (*Brown II*) ("[I]t should go without saying that the vitality of th[e] constitutional principles [announced in *Brown v. Board of Education,* 347 U.S. 483 (1954),] cannot be allowed to yield simply because of disagreement with them").

* * *

The Court's duty in the present case is clear. In 1973, it confronted the already-divisive issue of governmental power to limit personal choice to undergo abortion, for which it provided a new resolution based on the due process guaranteed by the Fourteenth Amendment. Whether or not a new social consensus is developing on that issue, its divisiveness is no less today than in 1973, and pressure to overrule the decision, like pressure to retain it, has grown only more intense. A decision to overrule *Roe*'s essential holding under the existing circumstances would address error, if error there was, at the cost of both profound and unnecessary damage to the Court's legitimacy, and to the Nation's commitment to the rule of law. It is therefore imperative to adhere to the essence of *Roe*'s original decision, and we do so today.

IV

From what we have said so far it follows that it is a constitutional liberty of the woman to have some freedom to terminate her pregnancy. We conclude that the basic decision in *Roe* was based on a constitutional analysis which we cannot now repudiate. The woman's liberty is not so unlimited, however, that from the outset the State cannot show its concern for the life of the unborn, and at a later point in fetal development the State's interest in life has sufficient force so that the right of the woman to terminate the pregnancy can be restricted.

* * *

We conclude the line should be drawn at viability, so that before that time the woman has a right to choose to terminate her pregnancy. We adhere to this principle for two reasons. First, as we have said, is the doctrine of *stare decisis.* Any judicial act of line-drawing may seem somewhat arbitrary, but *Roe* was a reasoned statement, elaborated with great care. We have twice reaffirmed it in the face of great opposition. See *Thornburgh v. American College of Obstetricians & Gynecologists,* * * * *Akron I,* * * *. Although we must overrule those parts of *Thornburgh* and *Akron I* which, in our view, are inconsistent with *Roe*'s statement that the State has a legitimate interest in promoting the life or potential life of the unborn, * * * the central premise of those cases represents an unbroken commitment by this Court to the essential holding of *Roe.* It is that premise which we reaffirm today.

The second reason is that the concept of viability, as we noted in *Roe,* is the time at which there is a realistic possibility of maintaining and nourishing a life outside the womb, so that the independent existence of the second life can in reason and all fairness be the object of state protection that now overrides the rights of the woman. * * * Consistent with other constitutional norms, legislatures may draw lines which appear arbitrary without the necessity of offering a justification. But courts may not. We must justify the lines we draw. And there is no line other than viability which is more workable. To be sure, as we have said, there may be some medical developments that affect the precise point of viability, * * * but this is an imprecision within tolerable limits given that the medical community and all those who must apply its discoveries will continue to explore the matter. The viability line also has, as a practical matter, an element of fairness. In some broad sense it might be said that a woman who fails to act before viability has consented to the State's intervention on behalf of the developing child.

The woman's right to terminate her pregnancy before viability is the most central principle of *Roe v. Wade*. It is a rule of law and a component of liberty we cannot renounce.

On the other side of the equation is the interest of the State in the protection of potential life. The *Roe* Court recognized the State's "important and legitimate interest in protecting the potentiality of human life." * * * The weight to be given this state interest, not the strength of the woman's interest, was the difficult question faced in *Roe*. We do not need to say whether each of us, had we been Members of the Court when the valuation of the State interest came before it as an original matter, would have concluded, as the *Roe* Court did, that its weight is insufficient to justify a ban on abortions prior to viability even when it is subject to certain exceptions. The matter is not before us in the first instance, and coming as it does after nearly 20 years of litigation in *Roe's* wake we are satisfied that the immediate question is not the soundness of *Roe's* resolution of the issue, but the precedential force that must be accorded to its holding. And we have concluded that the essential holding of *Roe* should be reaffirmed.

Yet it must be remembered that *Roe v. Wade* speaks with clarity in establishing not only the woman's liberty but also the State's "important and legitimate interest in potential life." * * * That portion of the decision in *Roe* has been given too little acknowledgement and implementation by the Court in its subsequent cases. Those cases decided that any regulation touching upon the abortion decision must survive strict scrutiny, to be sustained only if drawn in narrow terms to further a compelling state interest. See, *e.g., Akron I,* * * *. Not all of the cases decided under that formulation can be reconciled with the holding in *Roe* itself that the State has legitimate interests in the health of the woman and in protecting the potential life within her. In resolving this tension, we choose to rely upon *Roe,* as against the later cases.

Roe established a trimester framework to govern abortion regulations. Under this elaborate but rigid construct, almost no regulation at all is permitted during the first trimester of pregnancy; regulations designed to protect the woman's health, but not to further the State's interest in potential life, are permitted during the second trimester; and during the third trimester, when the fetus is viable, prohibitions are permitted provided the life or health of the mother is not at stake. * * * Most of our cases since *Roe* have involved the application of rules derived from the trimester framework. See, *e.g., Thornburgh v. American College of Obstetricians and Gynecologists, supra; Akron I, supra.*

The trimester framework no doubt was erected to ensure that the woman's right to choose not become so subordinate to the State's interest in promoting fetal life that her choice exists in theory but not in fact. We do not agree, however, that the trimester approach is necessary to accomplish this objective. A framework of this rigidity was unnecessary and in its later interpretation sometimes contradicted the State's permissible exercise of its powers.

Though the woman has a right to choose to terminate or continue her pregnancy before viability, it does not at all follow that the State is prohibited from taking steps to ensure that this choice is thoughtful and informed. Even in the earliest stages of pregnancy, the State may enact rules and regulations designed to encourage her to know that there are philosophic and social arguments of great weight that can be brought to bear in favor of continuing the pregnancy to full term and that there are procedures and institutions to allow adoption of unwanted children as well as a certain degree of state assistance if the mother chooses to raise the child herself. " '[T]he Constitution does not forbid a State or city, pursuant to democratic processes, from expressing a preference for normal childbirth.' " *Webster v. Reproductive Health Services,* 492 U.S., at 511 (opinion of the Court) (quoting *Poelker v. Doe,* 432 U.S. 519, 521 (1977)). It follows that States are free to enact laws to provide a reasonable framework for a woman to make a decision that has such profound and lasting meaning. This, too, we find consistent with *Roe's* central premises, and indeed the inevitable consequence of our holding that the State has an interest in protecting the life of the unborn.

We reject the trimester framework, which we do not consider to be part of the essential holding of *Roe.* * * * Measures aimed at ensuring that a woman's choice contemplates the consequences for the fetus do not necessarily interfere with the right recognized in *Roe,* although those measures have been found to be inconsistent with the rigid trimester framework announced in that case. A logical reading of the central holding in *Roe* itself, and a necessary reconciliation of the liberty of the woman and the interest of the State in promoting prenatal life, require, in our view, that we abandon the trimester framework as a rigid prohibition on all previability regulation aimed at the protection of fetal life. The trimester framework suffers from these basic flaws: in its formulation it misconceives the nature of the pregnant woman's interest; and in practice it undervalues the State's interest in potential life, as recognized in *Roe.*

As our jurisprudence relating to all liberties save perhaps abortion has recognized, not every law which makes a right more difficult to exercise is, *ipso facto,* an infringement of that right. An example clarifies the point. We have held that not every ballot access limitation amounts to an infringement of the right to vote. Rather, the States are granted substantial flexibility in establishing the framework within which voters choose the candidates for whom they wish to vote. *Anderson v. Celebrezze,* 460 U.S. 780, 788 (1983); *Norman v. Reed,* 502 U.S. 279 (1992).

The abortion right is similar. Numerous forms of state regulation might have the incidental effect of increasing the cost or decreasing the availability of medical care, whether for abortion or any other medical procedure. The fact that a law which serves a valid purpose, one not designed to strike at the right itself, has the incidental effect of making it more difficult or more expensive to procure an abortion cannot be enough to invalidate it. Only where state regulation imposes an undue burden on a woman's ability to make this decision does the power of the State reach into the heart of the liberty protected by the Due Process Clause. * * *

For the most part, the Court's early abortion cases adhered to this view. In *Maher v. Roe,* 432 U.S. 464, 473–474 (1977), the Court explained: *"Roe* did not declare an unqualified 'constitutional right to an abortion,' as the District Court seemed to think. Rather, the right protects the woman from unduly burdensome interference with her freedom to decide whether to terminate her pregnancy." See also *Doe v. Bolton,* 410 U.S. 179, 198 (1973) ("[T]he interposition of the hospital abortion committee is unduly restrictive of the patient's rights"); *Bellotti I, supra,* at 147 (State may not "impose undue burdens upon a minor capable of giving an informed consent"); *Harris v. McRae,* 448 U.S. 297, 314 (1980) (citing *Maher, supra*). Cf. *Carey v. Population Services International,* 431 U.S., at 688 ("[T]he same test must be applied to state regulations that burden an individual's right to decide to prevent conception or terminate pregnancy by substantially limiting access to the means of effectuating that decision as is applied to state statutes that prohibit the decision entirely").

These considerations of the nature of the abortion right illustrate that it is an overstatement to describe it as a right to decide whether to have an abortion "without interference from the State," *Planned Parenthood of Central Mo. v. Danforth,* 428 U.S. 52, 61 (1976). All abortion regulations interfere to some degree with a woman's ability to decide whether to terminate her pregnancy. It is, as a consequence, not surprising that despite the protestations contained in the original *Roe* opinion to the effect that the Court was not recognizing an absolute right, * * * the Court's experience applying the trimester framework has led to the striking down of some abortion regulations which in no real sense deprived women of the ultimate decision. Those decisions went too far because the right recognized by *Roe* is a right "to be free from unwarranted governmental intrusion into matters so fundamentally affecting a person as the decision whether to bear or beget a child." *Eisenstadt v. Baird,* 405 U.S., at 453. Not all governmental intrusion is of necessity unwarranted; and that brings us to the other basic flaw in the trimester framework: even in *Roe's* terms, in practice it undervalues the State's interest in the potential life within the woman.

Roe v. Wade was express in its recognition of the State's "important and legitimate interest[s] in preserving and protecting the health of the pregnant woman [and] in protecting the potentiality of human life." * * * The trimester framework, however, does not fulfill *Roe's* own promise that the State has an interest in protecting fetal life or potential life. *Roe* began the contradiction by using the trimester framework to forbid any regulation of abortion designed to advance that interest before viability. * * * Before viability, *Roe* and subsequent cases treat all governmental attempts to influence a woman's decision on behalf of the potential life within her as unwarranted. This treatment is, in our judgment, incompatible with the recognition that there is a substantial state interest in potential life throughout pregnancy. Cf. *Webster,* 492 U.S., at 519 (opinion of REHNQUIST, * * *.

The very notion that the State has a substantial interest in potential life leads to the conclusion that not all regulations must be deemed unwarranted. Not all burdens on the right to decide whether to terminate a pregnancy will be undue. In our view, the undue burden standard is the appropriate means of reconciling the State's interest with the woman's constitutionally protected liberty.

The concept of an undue burden has been utilized by the Court as well as individual members of the Court, including two of us, in ways that could be considered inconsistent. * * * Because we set forth a standard of general application to which we intend to adhere, it is important to clarify what is meant by an undue burden.

A finding of an undue burden is a shorthand for the conclusion that a state regulation has the purpose or effect of placing a substantial obstacle in the path of a woman seeking an abortion of a nonviable fetus. A statute with this purpose is invalid because the means chosen by the State to further the interest in potential life must be calculated to inform the woman's free choice, not hinder it. And a statute which, while furthering the interest in potential life or some other valid state interest, has the effect of placing a substantial obstacle in the path of a woman's choice cannot be considered a permissible means of serving its legitimate ends. To the extent that the opinions of the Court or of individual Justices use the undue burden standard in a manner that is inconsistent with this analysis, we set out what in our view should be the controlling standard. * * * In our considered judgment, an undue burden is an unconstitutional burden. * * * Understood another way, we answer the question, left open in previous opinions discussing the undue burden formulation, whether a law designed to further the State's interest in fetal life which imposes an undue burden on the woman's decision before fetal viability could be constitutional. * * * The answer is no.

Some guiding principles should emerge. What is at stake is the woman's right to make the ultimate decision, not a right to be insulated from all others in doing so. Regulations which do no more than create a structural mechanism by which the State, or the parent or guardian of a minor, may express profound respect for the life of the unborn are permitted, if they are not a substantial obstacle to the woman's exercise of the right to choose. See *infra,* at * * * (addressing Pennsylvania's parental consent requirement). Unless it has that effect on her right of choice, a state measure designed to persuade her to choose childbirth over abortion will be upheld if reasonably related to that goal. Regulations designed to foster the health of a woman seeking an abortion are valid if they do not constitute an undue burden.

Even when jurists reason from shared premises, some disagreement is inevitable. * * * That is to be expected in the application of any legal standard which must accommodate life's complexity. We do not expect it to be otherwise with respect to the undue burden standard. We give this summary:

(a) To protect the central right recognized by *Roe v. Wade* while at the same time accommodating the State's profound interest in potential life, we will employ the undue burden analysis as explained in this opinion. An undue burden exists, and therefore a provision of law is invalid, if its purpose or effect is to place a substantial obstacle in the path of a woman seeking an abortion before the fetus attains viability.

(b) We reject the rigid trimester framework of *Roe v. Wade.* To promote the State's profound interest in potential life, throughout pregnancy the State may take measures to ensure that the woman's choice is informed, and measures designed to advance this interest will not be invalidated as long as their purpose is to persuade the woman to choose childbirth over abortion. These measures must not be an undue burden on the right.

(c) As with any medical procedure, the State may enact regulations to further the health or safety of a woman seeking an abortion. Unnecessary health regulations that have the purpose or effect of presenting a substantial obstacle to a woman seeking an abortion impose an undue burden on the right.

(d) Our adoption of the undue burden analysis does not disturb the central holding of *Roe v. Wade,* and we reaffirm that holding. Regardless of whether exceptions are made for particular circumstances, a State may not prohibit any woman from making the ultimate decision to terminate her pregnancy before viability.

(e) We also reaffirm *Roe's* holding that "subsequent to viability, the State in promoting its interest in the potentiality of human life may, if it chooses, regulate, and even proscribe, abortion except where it is necessary, in appropriate medical judgment, for the preservation of the life or health of the mother." * * *

These principles control our assessment of the Pennsylvania statute, and we now turn to the issue of the validity of its challenged provisions.

V

The Court of Appeals applied what it believed to be the undue burden standard and upheld each of the provisions except for the husband notification requirement. We agree generally with this conclusion, but refine the undue burden analysis in accordance with the principles articulated above. We now consider the separate statutory sections at issue.

A

Because it is central to the operation of various other requirements, we begin with the statute's definition of medical emergency. Under the statute, a medical emergency is

"[t]hat condition which, on the basis of the physician's good faith clinical judgment, so complicates the medical condition of a pregnant woman as to necessitate the immediate abortion of her pregnancy to avert her death or for which a delay will create serious risk of substantial and irreversible impairment of a major bodily function." 18 Pa.Cons.Stat. (1990). § 3203.

Petitioners argue that the definition is too narrow, contending that it forecloses the possibility of an immediate abortion despite some significant health risks. If the contention were correct, we would be required to invalidate the restrictive operation of the provision, for the essential holding of *Roe* forbids a State from interfering with a woman's choice to undergo an abortion procedure if continuing her pregnancy would constitute a threat to her health. * * *.

The District Court found that there were three serious conditions which would not be covered by the statute: preeclampsia, inevitable abortion, and premature ruptured membrane. * * *. Yet, as the Court of Appeals observed, * * * it is undisputed that under some circumstances each of these conditions could lead to an illness with substantial and irreversible consequences. While the definition could be interpreted in an unconstitutional manner, the Court of Appeals construed the phrase "serious risk" to include those circumstances. * * *. It stated: "we read the medical emergency exception as intended by the Pennsylvania legislature to assure that compliance with its abortion regulations would not in any way pose a significant threat to the life or health of a woman." * * * As we said in *Brockett v. Spokane Arcades, Inc.,* 472 U.S. 491, 499–500 (1985): "Normally, * * * we defer to the construction of a state statute given it by the lower federal courts." * * * We adhere to that course today, and conclude that, as construed by the Court of Appeals, the medical emergency definition imposes no undue burden on a woman's abortion right.

B

We next consider the informed consent requirement. * * * Except in a medical emergency, the statute requires that at least 24 hours before performing an abortion a physician inform the woman of the nature of the procedure, the health risks of the abortion and of childbirth, and the "probable gestational age of the unborn child." The physician or a qualified nonphysician must inform the woman of the availability of printed materials published by the State describing the fetus and providing information about medical assistance for childbirth, information about child support from the father, and a list of agencies which provide adoption and other services as alternatives to abortion. An abortion may not be performed unless the woman certifies in writing that she has been informed of the availability of these printed materials and has been provided them if she chooses to view them.

Our prior decisions establish that as with any medical procedure, the State may require a woman to give her written informed consent to an abortion. See *Planned Parenthood of Central Mo. v. Danforth,* 428 U.S., at 67. In this respect, the statute is unexceptional. Petitioners challenge the statute's definition of informed consent because it includes the provision of specific information by the doctor and the mandatory 24–hour waiting period. The conclusions reached by a majority of the Justices in the separate opinions filed today and the undue burden standard adopted in this opinion require us to overrule in part some of the Court's past decisions, decisions driven by the trimester framework's prohibition of all previability regulations designed to further the State's interest in fetal life.

In *Akron I,* 462 U.S. 416 (1983), we invalidated an ordinance which required that a woman seeking an abortion be provided by her physician with specific information "designed to influence the woman's informed choice between abortion or childbirth." * * * As we later described the *Akron I* holding in *Thornburgh v. American College of Obstetricians and Gynecologists,* 476 U.S., at 762, there were two purported flaws in the Akron ordinance: the information was designed to dissuade the woman from having an abortion and the ordinance imposed "a rigid requirement that a specific body of information be given in all cases, irrespective of the particular needs of the patient * * *."

To the extent *Akron I* and *Thornburgh* find a constitutional violation when the government requires, as it does here, the giving of truthful, nonmisleading information about the nature of the procedure, the attendant health risks and those of childbirth, and the "probable gestational age" of the fetus, those cases go too far, are inconsistent with *Roe's* acknowledgment of an important interest in potential life, and are overruled. This is clear even on the very terms of *Akron I* and *Thornburgh*. Those decisions, along with *Danforth*, recognize a substantial government interest justifying a requirement that a woman be apprised of the health risks of abortion and childbirth. * * * It cannot be questioned that psychological well-being is a facet of health. Nor can it be doubted that most women considering an abortion would deem the impact on the fetus relevant, if not dispositive, to the decision. In attempting to ensure that a woman apprehend the full consequences of her decision, the State furthers the legitimate purpose of reducing the risk that a woman may elect an abortion, only to discover later, with devastating psychological consequences, that her decision was not fully informed. If the information the State requires to be made available to the woman is truthful and not misleading, the requirement may be permissible.

We also see no reason why the State may not require doctors to inform a woman seeking an abortion of the availability of materials relating to the consequences to the fetus, even when those consequences have no direct relation to her health. An example illustrates the point. We would think it constitutional for the State to require that in order for there to be informed consent to a kidney transplant operation the recipient must be supplied with information about risks to the donor as well as risks to himself or herself. A requirement that the physician make available information similar to that mandated by the statute here was described in *Thornburgh* as "an outright attempt to wedge the Commonwealth's message discouraging abortion into the privacy of the informed-consent dialogue between the woman and her physician." * * * We conclude, however, that informed choice need not be defined in such narrow terms that all considerations of the effect on the fetus are made irrelevant. As we have made clear, we depart from the holdings of *Akron I* and *Thornburgh* to the extent that we permit a State to further its legitimate goal of protecting the life of the unborn by enacting legislation aimed at ensuring a decision that is mature and informed, even when in so doing the State expresses a preference for childbirth over abortion. In short, requiring that the woman be informed of the availability of information relating to fetal development and the assistance available should she decide to carry the pregnancy to full term is a reasonable measure to insure an informed choice, one which might cause the woman to choose childbirth over abortion. This requirement cannot be considered a substantial obstacle to obtaining an abortion, and, it follows, there is no undue burden.

Our prior cases also suggest that the "straitjacket," * * * of particular information which must be given in each case interferes with a constitutional right of privacy between a pregnant woman and her physician. * * *

Whatever constitutional status the doctor-patient relation may have as a general matter, in the present context it is derivative of the woman's position. The doctor-patient relation does not underlie or override the two more general rights under which the abortion right is justified: the right to make family decisions and the right to physical autonomy. On its own, the doctor-patient relation here is entitled to the same solicitude it receives in other contexts. Thus, a requirement that a doctor give a woman certain information as part of obtaining her consent to an abortion is, for constitutional purposes, no different from a requirement that a doctor give certain specific information about any medical procedure.

All that is left of petitioners' argument is an asserted First Amendment right of a physician not to provide information about the risks of abortion, and childbirth, in a manner mandated by the State. To be sure, the physician's First Amendment rights not to speak are implicated, see *Wooley v. Maynard,* 430 U.S. 705 (1977), but only as part of the practice of medicine, subject to reasonable licensing and regulation by the State. Cf. *Whalen v. Roe,* 429 U.S. 589, 603 (1977). We see no constitutional infirmity in the requirement that the physician provide the information mandated by the State here.

The Pennsylvania statute also requires us to reconsider the holding in *Akron I* that the State may not require that a physician, as opposed to a qualified assistant, provide information relevant to a woman's informed consent. * * * Since there is no evidence on this record that requiring a doctor to give the information as provided by the statute would amount in practical terms to a substantial obstacle to a woman seeking an abortion, we conclude that it is not an undue burden. Our cases reflect the fact that the Constitution gives the States broad latitude to decide that particular functions may be performed only by licensed professionals, even if an objective assessment might suggest that those same tasks could be performed by others. See *Williamson v. Lee Optical of Oklahoma, Inc.,* 348 U.S. 483 (1955). Thus, we uphold the provision as a reasonable means to insure that the woman's consent is informed.

Our analysis of Pennsylvania's 24–hour waiting period between the provision of the information deemed necessary to informed consent and the performance of an abortion under the undue burden standard requires us to reconsider the premise behind the decision in *Akron I* invalidating a parallel requirement. In *Akron I* we said: "Nor are we convinced that the State's legitimate concern that the woman's decision be informed is reasonably served by requiring a 24–hour delay as a matter of course." * * * We consider that conclusion to be wrong. The idea that important decisions will be more informed and deliberate if they follow some period of reflection does not strike us as unreasonable, particularly where the statute directs that important information become part of the background of the decision. The statute, as construed by the Court of Appeals, permits avoidance of the waiting period in the event of a medical emergency and the record evidence shows that in the vast majority of cases, a 24–hour delay does not create any appreciable health risk. In theory, at least, the waiting period is a reasonable measure to implement the State's interest in protecting the life of the unborn, a measure that does not amount to an undue burden.

Whether the mandatory 24–hour waiting period is nonetheless invalid because in practice it is a substantial obstacle to a woman's choice to terminate her pregnancy is a closer question. The findings of fact by the District Court indicate that because of the distances many women must travel to reach an abortion provider, the practical effect will often be a delay of much more than a day because the waiting period requires that a woman seeking an abortion make at least two visits to the doctor. The District Court also found that in many instances this will increase the exposure of women seeking abortions to "the harassment and hostility of anti-abortion protestors demonstrating outside a clinic." * * *. As a result, the District Court found that for those women who have the fewest financial resources, those who must travel long distances, and those who have difficulty explaining their whereabouts to husbands, employers, or others, the 24–hour waiting period will be "particularly burdensome." * * *

These findings are troubling in some respects, but they do not demonstrate that the waiting period constitutes an undue burden. We do not doubt that, as the District Court held, the waiting period has the effect of "increasing the cost and risk of delay of abortions," * * * but the District Court did not conclude that the increased costs and potential delays amount to substantial obstacles. Rather, applying the trimester framework's strict prohibition of all regulation designed to promote the State's interest in potential life before viability, * * * the District Court concluded that the waiting period does not further the state "interest in maternal health" and "infringes the physician's discretion to exercise sound medical judgment." * * * Yet, as we have stated, under the undue burden standard a State is permitted to enact persuasive measures which favor childbirth over abortion, even if those measures do not further a health interest. And while the waiting period does limit a physician's discretion, that is not, standing alone, a reason to invalidate it. In light of the construction given the statute's definition of medical emergency by the Court of Appeals, and the District Court's findings, we cannot say that the waiting period imposes a real health risk.

We also disagree with the District Court's conclusion that the "particularly burdensome" effects of the waiting period on some women require its invalidation. A particular burden is not of necessity a substantial obstacle. Whether a burden falls on a particular group is a distinct inquiry from whether it is a substantial obstacle even as to the women in that group. And the District Court did not conclude that the waiting period is such an obstacle even for the women who are most burdened by it. Hence, on the record before us, and in the context of this facial challenge, we are not convinced that the 24–hour waiting period constitutes an undue burden.

We are left with the argument that the various aspects of the informed consent requirement are unconstitutional because they place barriers in the way of abortion on demand. Even the broadest reading of *Roe,* however, has not suggested that there is a constitutional right to abortion on demand. * * * Rather, the right protected by *Roe* is a right to decide to terminate a pregnancy free of undue interference by the State. Because the informed consent requirement facilitates the wise exercise of that right it cannot be classified as an interference with the right *Roe* protects. The informed consent requirement is not an undue burden on that right.

C

Section 3209 of Pennsylvania's abortion law provides, except in cases of medical emergency, that no physician shall perform an abortion on a married woman without receiving a signed statement from the woman that she has notified her spouse that she is about to undergo an abortion. The woman has the option of providing an alternative signed statement certifying that her husband is not the man who impregnated her; that her husband could not be located; that the pregnancy is the result of spousal sexual assault which she has reported; or that the woman believes that notifying her husband will cause him or someone else to inflict bodily injury upon her. A physician who performs an abortion on a married woman without receiving the appropriate signed statement will have his or her license revoked, and is liable to the husband for damages.

The District Court heard the testimony of numerous expert witnesses, and made detailed findings of fact regarding the effect of this statute. These included:

"273. The vast majority of women consult their husbands prior to deciding to terminate their pregnancy * * *.

* * *

"281. Studies reveal that family violence occurs in two million families in the United States. This figure, however, is a conservative one that substantially understates (because battering is usually not reported until it reaches life-threatening proportions) the actual number of families affected by domestic violence. In fact, researchers estimate that one of every two women will be battered at some time in their life. * * *

* * *

"288. In a domestic abuse situation, it is common for the battering husband to also abuse the children in an attempt to coerce the wife. * * *

"289. Mere notification of pregnancy is frequently a flashpoint for battering and violence within the family. The number of battering incidents is high during the pregnancy and often the worst abuse can be associated with pregnancy * * *. The battering husband may deny parentage and use the pregnancy as an excuse for abuse. * * *

"290. Secrecy typically shrouds abusive families. Family members are instructed not to tell anyone, especially police or doctors, about the abuse and violence. Battering husbands often threaten their wives or her children with further abuse if she tells an outsider of the violence and tells her that nobody will believe her. A battered woman, therefore, is highly unlikely to disclose the violence against her for fear of retaliation by the abuser. * * *

"291. Even when confronted directly by medical personnel or other helping professionals, battered women often will not admit to the battering because they have not admitted to themselves that they are battered. * * *

* * *

"298. Because of the nature of the battering relationship, battered women are unlikely to avail themselves of the exceptions to section 3209 of the Act, regardless of whether the section applies to them." 744 F.Supp., at 1360–1362.

These findings are supported by studies of domestic violence. * * *

* * *

The limited research that has been conducted with respect to notifying one's husband about an abortion, although involving samples too small to be representative, also supports the District Court's findings of fact. The vast majority of women notify their male partners of their decision to obtain an abortion. In many cases in which married women do not notify their husbands, the pregnancy is the result of an extramarital affair. Where the husband is the father, the primary reason women do not notify their husbands is that the husband and wife are experiencing marital difficulties, often accompanied by incidents of violence. Ryan & Plutzer, When Married Women Have Abortions: Spousal Notification and Marital Interaction, 51 J. Marriage & the Family 41, 44 (1989).

This information and the District Court's findings reinforce what common sense would suggest. In well-functioning marriages, spouses discuss important intimate decisions such as whether to bear a child. But there are millions of women in this country who are the victims of regular physical and psychological abuse at the hands of their husbands. Should these women become pregnant, they may have very good reasons for not wishing to inform their husbands of their decision to obtain an abortion. Many may have justifiable fears of physical abuse, but may be no less fearful of the consequences of reporting prior abuse to the Commonwealth of Pennsylvania. Many may have a reasonable fear that notifying their husbands will provoke further instances of child abuse; these women are not exempt from § 3209's notification requirement. Many may fear devastating forms of psychological abuse from their husbands, including verbal harassment, threats of future violence, the destruction of possessions, physical confinement to the home, the withdrawal of financial support, or the disclosure of the abortion to family and friends. These methods of psychological abuse may act as even more of a deterrent to notification than the possibility of physical violence, but women who are the victims of the abuse are not exempt from § 3209's notification requirement. And many women who are pregnant as a result of sexual assaults by their husbands will be unable to avail themselves of the exception for spousal sexual assault, § 3209(b)(3), because the exception requires that the woman have notified law enforcement authorities within 90 days of the assault, and her husband will be notified of her report once an investigation begins. § 3128(c). If anything in this field is certain, it is that victims of spousal sexual assault are extremely reluctant to report the abuse to the government; hence, a great many spousal rape victims will not be exempt from the notification requirement imposed by § 3209.

The spousal notification requirement is thus likely to prevent a significant number of women from obtaining an abortion. It does not merely make abortions a little more difficult or expensive to obtain; for many women, it will impose a substantial obstacle. We must not blind ourselves to the fact that the significant number of women who fear for their safety and the safety of their children are likely to be deterred from procuring an abortion as surely as if the Commonwealth had outlawed abortion in all cases.

Respondents attempt to avoid the conclusion that § 3209 is invalid by pointing out that it imposes almost no burden at all for the vast majority of women seeking abortions. They begin by noting that only about 20 percent of the women who obtain abortions are married. They then note that of these women about 95 percent notify their husbands of their own volition.

Thus, respondents argue, the effects of § 3209 are felt by only one percent of the women who obtain abortions. Respondents argue that since some of these women will be able to notify their husbands without adverse consequences or will qualify for one of the exceptions, the statute affects fewer than one percent of women seeking abortions. For this reason, it is asserted, the statute cannot be invalid on its face. * * * We disagree with respondents' basic method of analysis.

The analysis does not end with the one percent of women upon whom the statute operates; it begins there. Legislation is measured for consistency with the Constitution by its impact on those whose conduct it affects. For example, we would not say that a law which requires a newspaper to print a candidate's reply to an unfavorable editorial is valid on its face because most newspapers would adopt the policy even absent the law. See *Miami Herald Publishing Co. v. Tornillo,* 418 U.S. 241 (1974). The proper focus of constitutional inquiry is the group for whom the law is a restriction, not the group for whom the law is irrelevant.

Respondents' argument itself gives implicit recognition to this principle, at one of its critical points. Respondents speak of the one percent of women seeking abortions who are married and would choose not to notify their husbands of their plans. By selecting as the controlling class women who wish to obtain abortions, rather than all women or all pregnant women, respondents in effect concede that § 3209 must be judged by reference to those for whom it is an actual rather than irrelevant restriction. Of course, as we have said, § 3209's real target is narrower even than the class of women seeking abortions identified by the State: it is married women seeking abortions who do not wish to notify their husbands of their intentions and who do not qualify for one of the statutory exceptions to the notice requirement. The unfortunate yet persisting conditions we document above will mean that in a large fraction of the cases in which § 3209 is relevant, it will operate as a substantial obstacle to a woman's choice to undergo an abortion. It is an undue burden, and therefore invalid.

This conclusion is in no way inconsistent with our decisions upholding parental notification or consent requirements. * * * Those enactments, and our judgment that they are constitutional, are based on the quite reasonable assumption that minors will benefit from consultation with their parents and that children will often not realize that their parents have their best interests at heart. We cannot adopt a parallel assumption about adult women.

We recognize that a husband has a "deep and proper concern and interest * * * in his wife's pregnancy and in the growth and development of the fetus she is carrying." * * * With regard to the children he has fathered and raised, the Court has recognized his "cognizable and substantial" interest in their custody. *Stanley v. Illinois,* 405 U.S. 645, 651–652 (1972); see also *Quilloin v. Walcott,* 434 U.S. 246 (1978); *Caban v. Mohammed,* 441 U.S. 380 (1979); *Lehr v. Robertson,* 463 U.S. 248 (1983). If this case concerned a State's ability to require the mother to notify the father before taking some action with respect to a living child raised by both, therefore, it would be reasonable to conclude as a general matter that the father's interest in the welfare of the child and the mother's interest are equal.

Before birth, however, the issue takes on a very different cast. It is an inescapable biological fact that state regulation with respect to the child a woman is carrying will have a far greater impact on the mother's liberty than on the father's. The effect of state regulation on a woman's protected liberty is doubly deserving of scrutiny in such a case, as the State has touched not only upon the private sphere of the family but upon the very bodily integrity of the pregnant woman. Cf. *Cruzan v. Director, Missouri Dept. of Health,* 497 U.S., at 281. The Court has held that "when the wife and the husband disagree on this decision, the view of only one of the two marriage partners can prevail. Inasmuch as it is the woman who physically bears the child and who is the more directly and immediately affected by the pregnancy, as between the two, the balance weighs in her favor." * * * This conclusion rests upon the basic nature of marriage and the nature of our Constitution: "[T]he marital couple is not an independent entity with a mind and heart of its own, but an association of two individuals each with a separate intellectual and emotional makeup. If the right of privacy means anything, it is the right of the *individual,* married or single, to be free from unwarranted governmental intrusion into matters so fundamentally affecting a person as the decision whether to bear or beget a child." *Eisenstadt v. Baird,* 405 U.S., at 453 (emphasis in original). The Constitution protects individuals, men and women alike, from unjustified state interference, even when that interference is enacted into law for the benefit of their spouses.

There was a time, not so long ago, when a different understanding of the family and of the Constitution prevailed. In *Bradwell v. Illinois,* 16 Wall. 130 (1873), three Members of this Court reaffirmed the common-law principle that "a woman had no legal existence separate from her husband, who was regarded as her head and representative in the social state; and, notwithstanding some recent modifications of this civil status, many of the special rules of law flowing from and dependent upon this cardinal principle still exist in full force in most States." * * * (BRADLEY J., joined by SWAYNE and FIELD, JJ., concurring in judgment). Only one generation has passed since this Court observed that "woman is still regarded as the center of home and family life," with attendant "special responsibilities" that precluded full and independent legal status under the Constitution. *Hoyt v. Florida,* 368 U.S. 57, 62 (1961). These views, of course, are no longer consistent with our understanding of the family, the individual, or the Constitution.

In keeping with our rejection of the common-law understanding of a woman's role within the family, the Court held in *Danforth* that the Constitution does not permit a State to require a married woman to obtain her husband's consent before undergoing an abortion. * * * The principles that guided the Court in *Danforth* should be our guides today. For the great many women who are victims of abuse inflicted by their husbands, or whose children are the victims of such abuse, a spousal notice requirement enables the husband to wield an effective veto over his wife's decision. Whether the prospect of notification itself deters such women from seeking abortions, or whether the husband, through physical force or psychological pressure or economic coercion, prevents his wife from obtaining an abortion until it is too late, the notice requirement will often be tantamount to the veto found unconstitutional in *Danforth*. The women most affected by this law—those who most reasonably fear the consequences of notifying their husbands that they are pregnant—are in the gravest danger.

The husband's interest in the life of the child his wife is carrying does not permit the State to empower him with this troubling degree of authority over his wife. The contrary view leads to consequences reminiscent of the common law. A husband has no enforceable right to require a wife to advise him before she exercises her personal choices. If a husband's interest in the potential life of the child outweighs a wife's liberty, the State could require a married woman to notify her husband before she uses a postfertilization contraceptive. Perhaps next in line would be a statute requiring pregnant married women to notify their husbands before engaging in conduct causing risks to the fetus. After all, if the husband's interest in the fetus' safety is a sufficient predicate for state regulation, the State could reasonably conclude that pregnant wives should notify their husbands before drinking alcohol or smoking. Perhaps married women should notify their husbands before using contraceptives or before undergoing any type of surgery that may have complications affecting the husband's interest in his wife's reproductive organs. And if a husband's interest justifies notice in any of these cases, one might reasonably argue that it justifies exactly what the *Danforth* Court held it did not justify—a requirement of the husband's consent as well. A State may not give to a man the kind of dominion over his wife that parents exercise over their children.

Section 3209 embodies a view of marriage consonant with the common-law status of married women but repugnant to our present understanding of marriage and of the nature of the rights secured by the Constitution. Women do not lose their constitutionally protected liberty when they marry. The Constitution protects all individuals, male or female, married or unmarried, from the abuse of governmental power, even where that power is employed for the supposed benefit of a member of the individual's family. These considerations confirm our conclusion that § 3209 is invalid.

D

We next consider the parental consent provision. Except in a medical emergency, an unemancipated young woman under 18 may not obtain an abortion unless she and one of her parents (or guardian) provides informed consent as defined above. If neither a parent nor a guardian provides consent, a court may authorize the performance of an abortion upon a determination that the young woman is mature and capable of giving informed consent and has in fact given her informed consent, or that an abortion would be in her best interests.

We have been over most of this ground before. Our cases establish, and we reaffirm today, that a State may require a minor seeking an abortion to obtain the consent of a parent or guardian, provided that there is an adequate judicial bypass procedure. * * * Under these precedents, in our view, the one-parent consent requirement and judicial bypass procedure are constitutional.

* * *

E

Under the recordkeeping and reporting requirements of the statute, every facility which performs abortions is required to file a report stating its name and address as well as the name and address of any related entity, such as a controlling or subsidiary organization. In the case of state-funded institutions, the information becomes public.

For each abortion performed, a report must be filed identifying: the physician (and the second physician where required); the facility; the referring physician or agency; the woman's age; the number of prior pregnancies and prior abortions she has had; gestational age; the type of abortion procedure; the date of the abortion; whether there were any pre-existing medical conditions which would complicate pregnancy; medical complications with the abortion; where applicable, the basis for the determination that the abortion was medically necessary; the weight of the aborted fetus; and whether the woman was married, and if so, whether notice was provided or the basis for the failure to give notice. Every abortion facility must also file quarterly reports showing the number of abortions performed broken down by trimester. * * * In all events, the identity of each woman who has had an abortion remains confidential.

In *Danforth,* * * * we held that recordkeeping and reporting provisions "that are reasonably directed to the preservation of maternal health and that properly respect a patient's confidentiality and privacy are permissible." We think that under this standard, all the provisions at issue here except that relating to spousal notice are constitutional. Although they do not relate to the State's interest in informing the woman's choice, they do relate to health. The collection of information with respect to actual patients is a vital element of medical research, and so it cannot be said that the requirements serve no purpose other than to make abortions more difficult. Nor do we find that the requirements impose a substantial obstacle to a woman's choice. At most they might increase the cost of some abortions by a slight amount. While at some point increased cost could become a substantial obstacle, there is no such showing on the record before us.

Subsection (12) of the reporting provision requires the reporting of, among other things, a married woman's "reason for failure to provide notice" to her husband. § 3214(a)(12). This provision in effect requires women, as a condition of obtaining an abortion, to provide the Commonwealth with the precise information we have already recognized that many women have pressing reasons not to reveal. Like the spousal notice requirement itself, this provision places an undue burden on a woman's choice, and must be invalidated for that reason.

VI

Our Constitution is a covenant running from the first generation of Americans to us and then to future generations. It is a coherent succession. Each generation must learn anew that the Constitution's written terms embody ideas and aspirations that must survive more ages than one. We accept our responsibility not to retreat from interpreting the full meaning of the covenant in light of all of our precedents. We invoke it once again to define the freedom guaranteed by the Constitution's own promise, the promise of liberty.

* * *

The judgment in No. 91–902 is affirmed. The judgment in No. 91–744 is affirmed in part and reversed in part, and the case is remanded for proceedings consistent with this opinion, including consideration of the question of severability.

It is so ordered.

JUSTICE BLACKMUN, concurring in part, concurring in the judgment in part, and dissenting in part.

I join parts I, II, III, V–A, V–C, and VI of the joint opinion of JUSTICES O'CONNOR, KENNEDY, and SOUTER, * * *.

Three years ago, in *Webster v. Reproductive Health Serv.,* 492 U.S. 490 (1989), four Members of this Court appeared poised to "cas[t] into darkness the hopes and visions of every woman in this country" who had come to believe that the Constitution guaranteed her the right to reproductive choice. *Id.,* at 557 (BLACKMUN, J., dissenting). See *id.,* at 499 (opinion of REHNQUIST, C.J.); *id.,* at 532 (opinion of SCALIA, J.). All that remained between the promise of *Roe* and the darkness of the plurality was a single, flickering flame. Decisions since *Webster* gave little reason to hope that this flame would cast much light. See, *e.g., Ohio v. Akron Center for Reproductive Health,* 497 U.S. 502, 524 (1990) (opinion of BLACKMUN, J.). But now, just when so many expected the darkness to fall, the flame has grown bright.

I do not underestimate the significance of today's joint opinion. Yet I remain steadfast in my belief that the right to reproductive choice is entitled to the full protection afforded by this Court before *Webster.* And I fear for the darkness as four Justices anxiously await the single vote necessary to extinguish the light.

I

Make no mistake, the joint opinion of JUSTICES O'CONNOR, KENNEDY, and SOUTER is an act of personal courage and constitutional principle. In contrast to previous decisions in which JUSTICES O'CONNOR and KENNEDY postponed reconsideration of *Roe v. Wade,* * * * the authors of the joint opinion today join JUSTICE STEVENS and me in concluding that "the essential holding of *Roe* should be retained and once again reaffirmed." * * * In brief, five Members of this Court today recognize that "the Constitution protects a woman's right to terminate her pregnancy in its early stages." * * *

II

Today, no less than yesterday, the Constitution and decisions of this Court require that a State's abortion restrictions be subjected to the strictest of judicial scrutiny. Our precedents and the joint opinion's principles require us to subject all non-*de minimis* abortion regulations to strict scrutiny. Under this standard, the Pennsylvania statute's provisions requiring content-based counseling, a 24–hour delay, informed parental consent, and reporting of abortion-related information must be invalidated.

A

The Court today reaffirms the long recognized rights of privacy and bodily integrity. * * *

State restrictions on abortion violate a woman's right of privacy in two ways. First, compelled continuation of a pregnancy infringes upon a woman's right to bodily integrity by imposing substantial physical intrusions and significant risks of physical harm. * * *

Further, when the State restricts a woman's right to terminate her pregnancy, it deprives a woman of the right to make her own decision about reproduction and family planning—critical life choices that this Court long has deemed central to the right to privacy. * * *

A State's restrictions on a woman's right to terminate her pregnancy also implicate constitutional guarantees of gender equality. State restrictions on abortion compel women to continue pregnancies they otherwise might terminate. By restricting the right to terminate pregnancies, the State conscripts women's bodies into its service, forcing women to continue their pregnancies, suffer the pains of childbirth, and in most instances, provide years of maternal care. The State does not compensate women for their services; instead, it assumes that they owe this duty as a matter of course. This assumption—that women can simply be forced to accept the "natural" status and incidents of motherhood—appears to rest upon a conception of women's role that has triggered the protection of the Equal Protection Clause. See, *e.g., Mississippi Univ. for Women v. Hogan*, 458 U.S. 718, 724–726 (1982); *Craig v. Boren*, 429 U.S. 190, 198–199 (1976).[4] The joint opinion recognizes that these assumptions about women's place in society "are no longer consistent with our understanding of the family, the individual, or the Constitution." * * *

B

The Court has held that limitations on the right of privacy are permissible only if they survive "strict" constitutional scrutiny—that is, only if the governmental entity imposing the restriction can demonstrate that the limitation is both necessary and narrowly tailored to serve a compelling governmental interest. *Griswold v. Connecticut*, 381 U.S. 479, 485 (1965). We have applied this principle specifically in the context of abortion regulations. *Roe v. Wade*, * * *.[5]

Roe implemented these principles through a framework that was designed "to insure that the woman's right to choose not become so subordinate to the

---

4. A growing number of commentators are recognizing this point. See, *e.g.,* L. Tribe, American Constitutional Law, § 15–10, pp. 1353–1359 (2d ed. 1988); Siegel, Reasoning from the Body: A Historical Perspective on Abortion Regulation and Questions of Equal Protection, 44 Stan.L.Rev. 261, 350–380 (1992); Sunstein, Neutrality in Constitutional Law (With Special Reference to Pornography, Abortion, and Surrogacy), 92 Colum.L.Rev. 1, 31–44 (1992); cf. Rubenfeld, The Right of Privacy, 102 Harv.L.Rev. 737, 788–791 (1989) (similar analysis under the rubric of privacy).

5. To say that restrictions on a right are subject to strict scrutiny is not to say that the

right is absolute. Regulations can be upheld if they have no significant impact on the woman's exercise of her right and are justified by important state health objectives. See, *e.g., Planned Parenthood of Central Mo. v. Danforth*, 428 U.S. 52, 65–67, 79–81 (1976) (upholding requirements of a woman's written consent and record keeping). But the Court today reaffirms the essential principle of *Roe* that a woman has the right "to choose to have an abortion before viability and to obtain it without undue interference from the State." * * * Under *Roe*, any more than *de minimis* interference is undue.

State's interest in promoting fetal life that her choice exists in theory but not in fact," * * * *Roe* identified two relevant State interests: "an interest in preserving and protecting the health of the pregnant woman" and an interest in "protecting the potentiality of human life." * * * With respect to the State's interest in the health of the mother, "the 'compelling' point * * * is at approximately the end of the first trimester," because it is at that point that the mortality rate in abortion approaches that in childbirth. *Roe,* * * *. With respect to the State's interest in potential life, "the 'compelling' point is at viability," because it is at that point that the fetus "presumably has the capability of meaningful life outside the mother's womb." * * * In order to fulfill the requirement of narrow tailoring, "the State is obligated to make a reasonable effort to limit the effect of its regulations to the period in the trimester during which its health interest will be furthered." * * *

In my view, application of this analytical framework is no less warranted than when it was approved by seven Members of this Court in *Roe.* Strict scrutiny of state limitations on reproductive choice still offers the most secure protection of the woman's right to make her own reproductive decisions, free from state coercion. No majority of this Court has ever agreed upon an alternative approach. The factual premises of the trimester framework have not been undermined, * * * and the *Roe* framework is far more administrable, and far less manipulable, than the "undue burden" standard adopted by the joint opinion.

Nonetheless, three criticisms of the trimester framework continue to be uttered. First, the trimester framework is attacked because its key elements do not appear in the text of the Constitution. My response to this attack remains the same as it was in *Webster:*

"Were this a true concern, we would have to abandon most of our constitutional jurisprudence. [T]he 'critical elements' of countless constitutional doctrines nowhere appear in the Constitution's text * * *. The Constitution makes no mention, for example, of the First Amendment's 'actual malice' standard for proving certain libels, see *New York Times Co. v. Sullivan,* * * *. Similarly, the Constitution makes no mention of the rational-basis test, or the specific verbal formulations of intermediate and strict scrutiny by which this Court evaluates claims under the Equal Protection Clause. The reason is simple. Like the *Roe* framework, these tests or standards are not, and do not purport to be, rights protected by the Constitution. Rather, they are judge-made methods for evaluating and measuring the strength and scope of constitutional rights or for balancing the constitutional rights of individuals against the competing interests of government." * * *.

The second criticism is that the framework more closely resembles a regulatory code than a body of constitutional doctrine. Again, my answer remains the same as in *Webster.*

"[I]f this were a true and genuine concern, we would have to abandon vast areas of our constitutional jurisprudence. * * * Are [the distinctions entailed in the trimester framework] any finer, or more 'regulatory,' than the distinctions we have often drawn in our First Amendment jurisprudence, where, for example, we have held that a 'release time' program permitting public-school students to leave school grounds during school hours to receive religious instruction does not violate the Establishment Clause, even though a release-time program permitting religious instruction on school grounds does violate the Clause? Compare *Zorach v. Clauson*, 343 U.S. 306 (1952), with *Illinois ex rel. McCollum v. Board of Education of School Dist. No. 71, Champaign County*, 333 U.S. 203 (1948). * * * Similarly, in a Sixth Amendment case, the Court held that although an overnight ban on attorney-client communication violated the constitutionally guaranteed right to counsel, *Geders v. United States*, 425 U.S. 80 (1976), that right was not violated when a trial judge separated a defendant from his lawyer during a 15–minute recess after the defendant's direct testimony. *Perry v. Leeke*, 488 U.S. 272 (1989). That numerous constitutional doctrines result in narrow differentiations between similar circumstances does not mean that this Court has abandoned adjudication in favor of regulation." * * *

The final, and more genuine, criticism of the trimester framework is that it fails to find the State's interest in potential human life compelling throughout pregnancy. No member of this Court—nor for that matter, the Solicitor General, * * *—has ever questioned our holding in *Roe* that an abortion is not "the termination of life entitled to Fourteenth Amendment protection." * * * Accordingly, a State's interest in protecting fetal life is not grounded in the Constitution. Nor, consistent with our Establishment Clause, can it be a theological or sectarian interest. * * * It is, instead, a legitimate interest grounded in humanitarian or pragmatic concerns. * * *

But while a State has "legitimate interests from the outset of the pregnancy in protecting the health of the woman and the life of the fetus that may become a child," * * * legitimate interests are not enough. To overcome the burden of strict scrutiny, the interests must be compelling. The question then is how best to accommodate the State's interest in potential human life with the constitutional liberties of pregnant women. Again, I stand by the views I expressed in *Webster:*

> "I remain convinced, as six other Members of this Court 16 years ago were convinced, that the *Roe* framework, and the viability standard in particular, fairly, sensibly, and effectively functions to safeguard the constitutional liberties of pregnant women while recognizing and accommodating the State's interest in potential human life. The viability line reflects the biological facts and truths of fetal development; it marks that threshold moment prior to which a fetus cannot survive separate from the woman and cannot reasonably and objectively be regarded as a subject of rights or interests distinct from, or paramount to, those of the pregnant woman. At the same time, the viability standard takes account of the undeniable fact that as the fetus evolves into its postnatal form, and as it loses its dependence on the uterine environment, the State's interest in the fetus' potential human life, and in fostering a regard for human life in general, becomes compelling. As a practical matter, because viability follows 'quickening'—the point at which a woman feels movement in her womb—and because viability occurs no earlier than 23 weeks gestational age, it establishes an easily applicable standard for regulating abortion while providing a pregnant woman ample time to exercise her fundamental right with her responsible physician to terminate her pregnancy." * * *

Roe's trimester framework does not ignore the State's interest in prenatal life. Like JUSTICE STEVENS, I agree that the State may take steps to ensure that a woman's choice "is thoughtful and informed," * * * and that "States are free to enact laws to provide a reasonable framework for a woman to make a decision that has such profound and lasting meaning." * * *

As the joint opinion recognizes, "the means chosen by the State to further the interest in potential life must be calculated to inform the woman's free choice, not hinder it." * * *

In sum, *Roe*'s requirement of strict scrutiny as implemented through a trimester framework should not be disturbed. No other approach has gained a majority, and no other is more protective of the woman's fundamental right. Lastly, no other approach properly accommodates the woman's constitutional right with the State's legitimate interests.

C

Application of the strict scrutiny standard results in the invalidation of all the challenged provisions. Indeed, as this Court has invalidated virtually identical provisions in prior cases, *stare decisis* requires that we again strike them down.

* * *

III

At long last, THE CHIEF JUSTICE admits it. Gone are the contentions that the issue need not be (or has not been) considered. There, on the first page, for all to see, is what was expected: "We believe that *Roe* was wrongly decided, and that it can and should be overruled consistently with our traditional approach to *stare decisis* in constitutional cases." * * * If there is much reason to applaud the advances made by the joint opinion today, there is far more to fear from THE CHIEF JUSTICE's opinion.

THE CHIEF JUSTICE's criticism of *Roe* follows from his stunted conception of individual liberty. While recognizing that the Due Process Clause protects more than simple physical liberty, he then goes on to construe this Court's personal-liberty cases as establishing only a laundry list of particular rights, rather than a principled account of how these particular rights are grounded in a more general right of privacy. * * * This constricted view is reinforced by THE CHIEF JUSTICE's exclusive reliance on tradition as a source of fundamental rights. He argues that the record in favor of a right to abortion is no stronger than the record in *Michael H. v. Gerald D.*, 491 U.S. 110 (1989), where the plurality found no fundamental right to visitation privileges by an adulterous father, or in *Bowers v. Hardwick*, 478 U.S. 186 (1986), where the Court found no fundamental right to engage in homosexual sodomy, or in a case involving the "firing of a gun * * * into another person's body." * * * In THE CHIEF JUSTICE's world, a woman considering whether to terminate a pregnancy is entitled to no more protection than adulterers, murderers, and so-called "sexual deviates." [11] Given THE CHIEF JUSTICE's exclusive reliance on

---

11. Obviously, I do not share the plurality's views of homosexuality as sexual deviance. See *Bowers,* 478 U.S., at 202–03 n. 2.

tradition, people using contraceptives seem the next likely candidate for his list of outcasts.

Even more shocking than THE CHIEF JUSTICE's cramped notion of individual liberty is his complete omission of any discussion of the effects that compelled childbirth and motherhood have on women's lives. The only expression of concern with women's health is purely instrumental—for THE CHIEF JUSTICE, only women's *psychological* health is a concern, and only to the extent that he assumes that every woman who decides to have an abortion does so without serious consideration of the moral implications of their decision. * * * In short, THE CHIEF JUSTICE's view of the State's compelling interest in maternal health has less to do with health than it does with compelling women to be maternal.

Nor does THE CHIEF JUSTICE give any serious consideration to the doctrine of *stare decisis*. For THE CHIEF JUSTICE, the facts that gave rise to *Roe* are surprisingly simple: "women become pregnant, there is a point somewhere, depending on medical technology, where a fetus becomes viable, and women give birth to children." * * * This characterization of the issue thus allows THE CHIEF JUSTICE quickly to discard the joint opinion's reliance argument by asserting that "reproductive planning could take * * * virtually immediate account of a decision overruling *Roe*." * * * (internal quotations omitted).

THE CHIEF JUSTICE's narrow conception of individual liberty and *stare decisis* leads him to propose the same standard of review proposed by the plurality in *Webster*. "States may regulate abortion procedures in ways rationally related to a legitimate state interest. *Williamson v. Lee Optical Co.*, 348 U.S. 483, 491 (1955); cf. *Stanley v. Illinois*, 405 U.S. 645, 651–653 (1972)." * * * THE CHIEF JUSTICE then further weakens the test by providing an insurmountable requirement for facial challenges: petitioners must " 'show that no set of circumstances exists under which the [provision] would be valid.' " * * * In short, in his view, petitioners must prove that the statute cannot constitutionally be applied to *anyone*. Finally, in applying his standard to the spousal-notification provision, THE CHIEF JUSTICE contends that the record lacks any "hard evidence" to support the joint opinion's contention that a "large fraction" of women who prefer not to notify their husbands involve situations of battered women and unreported spousal assault. * * * Yet throughout the explication of his standard, THE CHIEF JUSTICE never explains what hard evidence is, how large a fraction is required, or how a battered woman is supposed to pursue an as-applied challenge.

* * *

Even if it is somehow "irrational" for a State to require a woman to risk her life for her child, what protection is offered for women who become pregnant through rape or incest? Is there anything arbitrary or capricious about a State's prohibiting the sins of the father from being visited upon his offspring? [12]

---

12. JUSTICE SCALIA urges the Court to "get out of this area" and leave questions regarding abortion entirely to the States. * * * Putting aside the fact that what he advocates is nothing short of an abdication by the Court of its constitutional responsibilities, JUSTICE SCA-LIA is uncharacteristically naive if he thinks that overruling *Roe* and holding that restrictions on a woman's right to an abortion are subject only to rational-basis review will enable the Court henceforth to avoid reviewing abortion-related issues. State efforts to regu-

But, we are reassured, there is always the protection of the democratic process. While there is much to be praised about our democracy, our country since its founding has recognized that there are certain fundamental liberties that are not to be left to the whims of an election. A woman's right to reproductive choice is one of those fundamental liberties. Accordingly, that liberty need not seek refuge at the ballot box.

IV

In one sense, the Court's approach is worlds apart from that of THE CHIEF JUSTICE and JUSTICE SCALIA. And yet, in another sense, the distance between the two approaches is short—the distance is but a single vote.

I am 83 years old. I cannot remain on this Court forever, and when I do step down, the confirmation process for my successor well may focus on the issue before us today. That, I regret, may be exactly where the choice between the two worlds will be made.

JUSTICE STEVENS, concurring in part and dissenting in part.

The portions of the Court's opinion that I have joined are more important than those with which I disagree. I shall therefore first comment on significant areas of agreement, and then explain the limited character of my disagreement.

I

The Court is unquestionably correct in concluding that the doctrine of *stare decisis* has controlling significance in a case of this kind, notwithstanding an individual justice's concerns about the merits.[1] The central holding of *Roe v. Wade,* * * * has been a "part of our law" for almost two decades. * * * It was a natural sequel to the protection of individual liberty established in *Griswold v. Connecticut,* * * *. The societal costs of overruling *Roe* at this late date would be enormous. *Roe* is an integral part of a correct understanding of both the concept of liberty and the basic equality of men and women.

Stare decisis also provides a sufficient basis for my agreement with the joint opinion's reaffirmation of *Roe*'s post-viability analysis. Specifically, I accept the proposition that "[i]f the State is interested in protecting fetal life after viability, it may go so far as to proscribe abortion during that period, except when it is necessary to preserve the life or health of the mother." * * *

---

late and prohibit abortion in a post-*Roe* world undoubtedly would raise a host of distinct and important constitutional questions meriting review by this Court. For example, does the Eighth Amendment impose any limits on the degree or kind of punishment a State can inflict upon physicians who perform, or women who undergo, abortions? What effect would differences among States in their approaches to abortion have on a woman's right to engage in interstate travel? Does the First Amendment permit States that choose not to criminalize abortion to ban all advertising providing information about where and how to obtain abortions?

1. It is sometimes useful to view the issue of *stare decisis* from a historical perspective. In the last nineteen years, fifteen Justices have confronted the basic issue presented in *Roe*. Of those, eleven have voted as the majority does today: Chief Justice Burger, Justices Douglas, Brennan, Stewart, Marshall, and Powell, and Justices Blackmun, O'Connor, Kennedy, Souter, and myself. Only four—all of whom happen to be on the Court today— have reached the opposite conclusion.

I also accept what is implicit in the Court's analysis, namely, a reaffirmation of *Roe*'s explanation of *why* the State's obligation to protect the life or health of the mother must take precedence over any duty to the unborn. The Court in *Roe* carefully considered, and rejected, the State's argument "that the fetus is a 'person' within the language and meaning of the Fourteenth Amendment." * * *. After analyzing the usage of "person" in the Constitution, the Court concluded that that word "has application only postnatally." * * * Commenting on the contingent property interests of the unborn that are generally represented by guardians ad litem, the Court noted: "Perfection of the interests involved, again, has generally been contingent upon live birth. In short, the unborn have never been recognized in the law as persons in the whole sense." * * * Accordingly, an abortion is not "the termination of life entitled to Fourteenth Amendment protection." * * * From this holding, there was no dissent, * * *indeed, no member of the Court has ever questioned this fundamental proposition. Thus, as a matter of federal constitutional law, a developing organism that is not yet a "person" does not have what is sometimes described as a "right to life."[2] This has been and, by the Court's holding today, remains a fundamental premise of our constitutional law governing reproductive autonomy.

II

My disagreement with the joint opinion begins with its understanding of the trimester framework established in *Roe*. Contrary to the suggestion of the joint opinion, * * * it is not a "contradiction" to recognize that the State may have a legitimate interest in potential human life and, at the same time, to conclude that that interest does not justify the regulation of abortion before viability (although other interests, such as maternal health, may). The fact that the State's interest is legitimate does not tell us when, if ever, that interest outweighs the pregnant woman's interest in personal liberty. It is appropriate, therefore, to consider more carefully the nature of the interests at stake.

First, it is clear that, in order to be legitimate, the State's interest must be secular; consistent with the First Amendment the State may not promote a theological or sectarian interest. * * * Moreover, as discussed above, the state interest in potential human life is not an interest *in loco parentis,* for the fetus is not a person.

2. Professor Dworkin has made this comment on the issue:

"The suggestion that states are free to declare a fetus a person * * * assumes that a state can curtail some persons' constitutional rights by adding new persons to the constitutional population. The constitutional rights of one citizen are of course very much affected by who or what else also has constitutional rights, because the rights of others may compete or conflict with his. So any power to increase the constitutional population by unilateral decision would be, in effect, a power to decrease rights the national Constitution grants to others.

"If a state could declare trees to be persons with a constitutional right to life, it could prohibit publishing newspapers or books in spite of the First Amendment's guarantee of free speech, which could not be understood as a license to kill * * *. Once we understand that the suggestion we are considering has that implication, we must reject it. If a fetus is not part of the constitutional population, under the national constitutional arrangement, then states have no power to overrule that national arrangement by themselves declaring that fetuses have rights competitive with the constitutional rights of pregnant women." Dworkin, Unenumerated Rights: Whether and How *Roe* Should be Overruled, 59 U.Chi.L.Rev. 381, 400–401 (1992).

Identifying the State's interests—which the States rarely articulate with any precision—makes clear that the interest in protecting potential life is not grounded in the Constitution. It is, instead, an indirect interest supported by both humanitarian and pragmatic concerns. Many of our citizens believe that any abortion reflects an unacceptable disrespect for potential human life and that the performance of more than a million abortions each year is intolerable; many find third-trimester abortions performed when the fetus is approaching personhood particularly offensive. The State has a legitimate interest in minimizing such offense. The State may also have a broader interest in expanding the population,[3] believing society would benefit from the services of additional productive citizens—or that the potential human lives might include the occasional Mozart or Curie. These are the kinds of concerns that comprise the State's interest in potential human life.

In counterpoise is the woman's constitutional interest in liberty. One aspect of this liberty is a right to bodily integrity, a right to control one's person. * * * This right is neutral on the question of abortion: The Constitution would be equally offended by an absolute requirement that all women undergo abortions as by an absolute prohibition on abortions. "Our whole constitutional heritage rebels at the thought of giving government the power to control men's minds." * * * The same holds true for the power to control women's bodies.

The woman's constitutional liberty interest also involves her freedom to decide matters of the highest privacy and the most personal nature. * * * The authority to make such traumatic and yet empowering decisions is an element of basic human dignity. As the joint opinion so eloquently demonstrates, a woman's decision to terminate her pregnancy is nothing less than a matter of conscience.

Weighing the State's interest in potential life and the woman's liberty interest, I agree with the joint opinion that the State may " 'expres[s] a preference for normal childbirth,' " that the State may take steps to ensure that a woman's choice "is thoughtful and informed," and that "States are free to enact laws to provide a reasonable framework for a woman to make a decision that has such profound and lasting meaning." * * * Serious questions arise, however, when a State attempts to "persuade the woman to choose childbirth over abortion." * * * Decisional autonomy must limit the State's power to inject into a woman's most personal deliberations its own views of what is best. The State may promote its preferences by funding childbirth, by creating and maintaining alternatives to abortion, and by espousing the virtues of family; but it must respect the individual's freedom to make such judgments.

---

3. The state interest in protecting potential life may be compared to the state interest in protecting those who seek to immigrate to this country. A contemporary example is provided by the Haitians who have risked the perils of the sea in a desperate attempt to become "persons" protected by our laws. Humanitarian and practical concerns would support a state policy allowing those persons unrestricted entry; countervailing interests in population control support a policy of limiting the entry of these potential citizens. While the state interest in population control might be sufficient to justify strict enforcement of the immigration laws, that interest would not be sufficient to overcome a woman's liberty interest. Thus, a state interest in population control could not justify a state-imposed limit on family size or, for that matter, state-mandated abortions.

This theme runs throughout our decisions concerning reproductive freedom. In general, *Roe's* requirement that restrictions on abortions before viability be justified by the State's interest in *maternal* health has prevented States from interjecting regulations designed to influence a woman's decision. Thus, we have upheld regulations of abortion that are not efforts to sway or direct a woman's choice but rather are efforts to enhance the deliberative quality of that decision or are neutral regulations on the health aspects of her decision. We have, for example, upheld regulations requiring written informed consent, see *Planned Parenthood of Central Mo. v. Danforth,* 428 U.S. 52 (1976); limited recordkeeping and reporting, see *ibid.*; and pathology reports, see *Planned Parenthood Assn. of Kansas City, Mo., Inc. v. Ashcroft,* 462 U.S. 476 (1983); as well as various licensing and qualification provisions, see *e.g., Roe,* 410 U.S., at 150; *Simopoulos v. Virginia,* 462 U.S. 506 (1983). Conversely, we have consistently rejected state efforts to prejudice a woman's choice, either by limiting the information available to her, see *Bigelow v. Virginia,* 421 U.S. 809 (1975), or by "requir[ing] the delivery of information designed 'to influence the woman's informed choice between abortion or childbirth.'" *Thornburgh,* 476 U.S., at 760; see also *Akron v. Akron Center for Reproductive Health, Inc.,* 462 U.S. 416, 442–449 (1983).

In my opinion, the principles established in this long line of cases and the wisdom reflected in Justice Powell's opinion for the Court in *Akron* (and followed by the Court just six years ago in *Thornburgh*) should govern our decision today. Under these principles, §§ 3205(a)(2)(i)–(iii) of the Pennsylvania statute are unconstitutional. Those sections require a physician or counselor to provide the woman with a range of materials clearly designed to persuade her to choose not to undergo the abortion. While the State is free, pursuant to § 3208 of the Pennsylvania law, to produce and disseminate such material, the State may not inject such information into the woman's deliberations just as she is weighing such an important choice.

Under this same analysis, §§ 3205(a)(1)(i) and (iii) of the Pennsylvania statute are constitutional. Those sections, which require the physician to inform a woman of the nature and risks of the abortion procedure and the medical risks of carrying to term, are neutral requirements comparable to those imposed in other medical procedures. Those sections indicate no effort by the State to influence the woman's choice in any way. If anything, such requirements *enhance,* rather than skew, the woman's decisionmaking.

III

The 24–hour waiting period required by §§ 3205(a)(1)–(2) of the Pennsylvania statute raises even more serious concerns. Such a requirement arguably furthers the State's interests in two ways, neither of which is constitutionally permissible.

First, it may be argued that the 24–hour delay is justified by the mere fact that it is likely to reduce the number of abortions, thus furthering the State's interest in potential life. But such an argument would justify any form of coercion that placed an obstacle in the woman's path. The State cannot further its interests by simply wearing down the ability of the pregnant woman to exercise her constitutional right.

Second, it can more reasonably be argued that the 24–hour delay furthers the State's interest in ensuring that the woman's decision is informed and thoughtful. But there is no evidence that the mandated delay benefits women or that it is necessary to enable the physician to convey any relevant information to the patient. The mandatory delay thus appears to rest on outmoded and unacceptable assumptions about the decisionmaking capacity of women. While there are well-established and consistently maintained reasons for the State to view with skepticism the ability of minors to make decisions, see *Hodgson v. Minnesota,* 497 U.S. 417, 449 (1990), none of those reasons applies to an adult woman's decisionmaking ability. Just as we have left behind the belief that a woman must consult her husband before undertaking serious matters, * * * so we must reject the notion that a woman is less capable of deciding matters of gravity. Cf. *Reed v. Reed,* 404 U.S. 71 (1971).

In the alternative, the delay requirement may be premised on the belief that the decision to terminate a pregnancy is presumptively wrong. This premise is illegitimate. Those who disagree vehemently about the legality and morality of abortion agree about one thing: The decision to terminate a pregnancy is profound and difficult. No person undertakes such a decision lightly—and States may not presume that a woman has failed to reflect adequately merely because her conclusion differs from the State's preference. A woman who has, in the privacy of her thoughts and conscience, weighed the options and made her decision cannot be forced to reconsider all, simply because the State believes she has come to the wrong conclusion.[5]

Part of the constitutional liberty to choose is the equal dignity to which each of us is entitled. A woman who decides to terminate her pregnancy is entitled to the same respect as a woman who decides to carry the fetus to term. The mandatory waiting period denies women that equal respect.

IV

In my opinion, a correct application of the "undue burden" standard leads to the same conclusion concerning the constitutionality of these requirements. A state-imposed burden on the exercise of a constitutional right is measured both by its effects and by its character: A burden may be "undue"

5. The joint opinion's reliance on the indirect effects of the regulation of constitutionally protected activity, * * * is misplaced; what matters is not only the effect of a regulation but also the reason for the regulation. As I explained in *Hodgson*:

"In cases involving abortion, as in cases involving the right to travel or the right to marry, the identification of the constitutionally protected interest is merely the beginning of the analysis. State regulation of travel and of marriage is obviously permissible even though a State may not categorically exclude nonresidents from its borders, *Shapiro v. Thompson,* 394 U.S. 618, 631 (1969), or deny prisoners the right to marry, *Turner v. Safley,* 482 U.S. 78, 94–99 (1987). But the regulation of constitutionally protected decisions, such as where a person shall reside or whom he or she shall marry, must be predicated on legitimate state concerns other than disagreement with the choice the individual has made. Cf. *Turner v. Safley, supra; Loving v. Virginia,* 388 U.S. 1

(1967). In the abortion area, a State may have no obligation to spend its own money, or use its own facilities, to subsidize nontherapeutic abortions for minors or adults. See, e.g., *Maher v. Roe,* 432 U.S. 464 (1977); cf. *Webster v. Reproductive Health Services,* 492 U.S. 490, 508–511 (1989) (plurality opinion); *id.,* at 523–524 (O'CONNOR, J., concurring in part and concurring in judgment). A State's value judgment favoring childbirth over abortion may provide adequate support for decisions involving such allocation of public funds, but not for simply substituting a state decision for an individual decision that a woman has a right to make for herself. Otherwise, the interest in liberty protected by the Due Process Clause would be a nullity. A state policy favoring childbirth over abortion is not in itself a sufficient justification for overriding the woman's decision or for placing 'obstacles—absolute or otherwise—in the pregnant woman's path to an abortion.'" *Hodgson,* 497 U.S., at 435.

either because the burden is too severe or because it lacks a legitimate, rational justification.[6]

The 24–hour delay requirement fails both parts of this test. The findings of the District Court establish the severity of the burden that the 24–hour delay imposes on many pregnant women. Yet even in those cases in which the delay is not especially onerous, it is, in my opinion, "undue" because there is no evidence that such a delay serves a useful and legitimate purpose. As indicated above, there is no legitimate reason to require a woman who has agonized over her decision to leave the clinic or hospital and return again another day. While a general requirement that a physician notify her patients about the risks of a proposed medical procedure is appropriate, a rigid requirement that all patients wait 24 hours or (what is true in practice) much longer to evaluate the significance of information that is either common knowledge or irrelevant is an irrational and, therefore, "undue" burden.

The counseling provisions are similarly infirm. Whenever government commands private citizens to speak or to listen, careful review of the justification for that command is particularly appropriate. In this case, the Pennsylvania statute directs that counselors provide women seeking abortions with information concerning alternatives to abortion, the availability of medical assistance benefits, and the possibility of child-support payments. §§ 3205(a)(2)(i)–(iii). The statute requires that this information be given to *all* women seeking abortions, including those for whom such information is clearly useless, such as those who are married, those who have undergone the procedure in the past and are fully aware of the options, and those who are fully convinced that abortion is their only reasonable option. Moreover, the statute requires physicians to inform all of their patients of "the probable gestational age of the unborn child." § 3205(a)(1)(ii). This information is of little decisional value in most cases, because 90% of all abortions are performed during the first trimester[7] when fetal age has less relevance than when the fetus nears viability. Nor can the information required by the statute be justified as relevant to any "philosophic" or "social" argument, * * * either favoring or disfavoring the abortion decision in a particular case. In light of all of these facts, I conclude that the information requirements in § 3205(a)(1)(ii) and §§ 3205(a)(2)(i)–(iii) do not serve a useful purpose and thus constitute an unnecessary—and therefore undue—burden on the woman's constitutional liberty to decide to terminate her pregnancy.

Accordingly, while I disagree with Parts IV, V–B, and V–D of the joint opinion,[8] I join the remainder of the Court's opinion.

6. The meaning of any legal standard can only be understood by reviewing the actual cases in which it is applied. For that reason, I discount both Justice Scalia's comments on past descriptions of the standard, * * * and the attempt to give it crystal clarity in the joint opinion. The several opinions supporting the judgment in *Griswold v. Connecticut*, 381 U.S. 479 (1965), are less illuminating than the central holding of the case, which appears to have passed the test of time. The future may also demonstrate that a standard that analyzes both the severity of a regulatory burden and the legitimacy of its justification will provide a fully adequate framework for the review of abortion legislation even if the contours of the standard are not authoritatively articulated in any single opinion.

7. U.S. Dept. of Commerce, Bureau of the Census, Statistical Abstract of the United States 71 (111th ed. 1991).

8. Although I agree that a parental-consent requirement (with the appropriate bypass) is constitutional, I do not join Part V–D of the joint opinion because its approval of Pennsylvania's informed parental-consent requirement

CHIEF JUSTICE REHNQUIST, with whom JUSTICE WHITE, JUSTICE SCALIA, and JUSTICE THOMAS join, concurring in the judgment in part and dissenting in part.

The joint opinion, following its newly-minted variation on *stare decisis,* retains the outer shell of *Roe v. Wade,* * * * but beats a wholesale retreat from the substance of that case. We believe that *Roe* was wrongly decided, and that it can and should be overruled consistently with our traditional approach to *stare decisis* in constitutional cases. We would adopt the approach of the plurality in *Webster v. Reproductive Health Services,* 492 U.S. 490 (1989), and uphold the challenged provisions of the Pennsylvania statute in their entirety.

I

* * *

In arguing that this Court should invalidate each of the provisions at issue, petitioners insist that we reaffirm our decision in *Roe v. Wade, supra,* in which we held unconstitutional a Texas statute making it a crime to procure an abortion except to save the life of the mother. We agree with the Court of Appeals that our decision in *Roe* is not directly implicated by the Pennsylvania statute, which does not prohibit, but simply regulates, abortion. But, as the Court of Appeals found, the state of our post-*Roe* decisional law dealing with the regulation of abortion is confusing and uncertain, indicating that a reexamination of that line of cases is in order. Unfortunately for those who must apply this Court's decisions, the reexamination undertaken today leaves the Court no less divided than beforehand. Although they reject the trimester framework that formed the underpinning of *Roe,* Justices O'Connor, Kennedy, and Souter adopt a revised undue burden standard to analyze the challenged regulations. We conclude, however, that such an outcome is an unjustified constitutional compromise, one which leaves the Court in a position to closely scrutinize all types of abortion regulations despite the fact that it lacks the power to do so under the Constitution.

* * *

In *Roe v. Wade,* the Court recognized a "guarantee of personal privacy" which "is broad enough to encompass a woman's decision whether or not to terminate her pregnancy." * * * We are now of the view that, in terming this right fundamental, the Court in *Roe* read the earlier opinions upon which it based its decision much too broadly. Unlike marriage, procreation and contraception, abortion "involves the purposeful termination of potential life." *Harris v. McRae,* 448 U.S. 297, 325 (1980). The abortion decision must therefore "be recognized as *sui generis,* different in kind from the others that the Court has protected under the rubric of personal or family privacy and autonomy." * * * One cannot ignore the fact that a woman is not isolated in her pregnancy, and that the decision to abort necessarily involves the destruction of a fetus. See *Michael H. v. Gerald D., supra,* at * * * n. 4 (To look "at the act which is assertedly the subject of a liberty interest in isolation from its effect upon other people [is] like inquiring whether there is

is based on the reasons given in Part V–B, with which I disagree.

FAMILY PLANNING

a liberty interest in firing a gun where the case at hand happens to involve its discharge into another person's body'').

Nor do the historical traditions of the American people support the view that the right to terminate one's pregnancy is "fundamental." The common law which we inherited from England made abortion after "quickening" an offense. At the time of the adoption of the Fourteenth Amendment, statutory prohibitions or restrictions on abortion were commonplace; in 1868, at least 28 of the then–37 States and 8 Territories had statutes banning or limiting abortion. J. Mohr, Abortion in America 200 (1978). By the turn of the century virtually every State had a law prohibiting or restricting abortion on its books. By the middle of the present century, a liberalization trend had set in. But 21 of the restrictive abortion laws in effect in 1868 were still in effect in 1973 when *Roe* was decided, and an overwhelming majority of the States prohibited abortion unless necessary to preserve the life or health of the mother. * * * On this record, it can scarcely be said that any deeply rooted tradition of relatively unrestricted abortion in our history supported the classification of the right to abortion as "fundamental" under the Due Process Clause of the Fourteenth Amendment.

We think, therefore, both in view of this history and of our decided cases dealing with substantive liberty under the Due Process Clause, that the Court was mistaken in *Roe* when it classified a woman's decision to terminate her pregnancy as a "fundamental right" that could be abridged only in a manner which withstood "strict scrutiny." In so concluding, we repeat the observation made in *Bowers v. Hardwick,* 478 U.S. 186 (1986):

> "Nor are we inclined to take a more expansive view of our authority to discover new fundamental rights imbedded in the Due Process Clause. The Court is most vulnerable and comes nearest to illegitimacy when it deals with judge-made constitutional law having little or no cognizable roots in the language or design of the Constitution." * * *

We believe that the sort of constitutionally imposed abortion code of the type illustrated by our decisions following *Roe* is inconsistent "with the notion of a Constitution cast in general terms, as ours is, and usually speaking in general principles, as ours does." *Webster v. Reproductive Health Services,* * * * (plurality opinion). The Court in *Roe* reached too far when it analogized the right to abort a fetus to the rights involved in *Pierce, Meyer, Loving,* and *Griswold,* and thereby deemed the right to abortion fundamental.

II

The joint opinion of JUSTICES O'CONNOR, KENNEDY, and SOUTER cannot bring itself to say that *Roe* was correct as an original matter, but the authors are of the view that "the immediate question is not the soundness of *Roe*'s resolution of the issue, but the precedential force that must be accorded to its holding." * * * Instead of claiming that *Roe* was correct as a matter of original constitutional interpretation, the opinion therefore contains an elaborate discussion of *stare decisis.* This discussion of the principle of *stare decisis* appears to be almost entirely dicta, because the joint opinion does not apply that principle in dealing with *Roe. Roe* decided that a woman had a fundamental right to an abortion. The joint opinion rejects that view. *Roe* decided that abortion regulations were to be subjected to "strict scrutiny" and could be justified only in the light of "compelling state interests." The joint opinion rejects that view.   * * * *Roe* analyzed abortion regulation under a rigid trimester framework, a framework which has guided this Court's decisionmaking for 19 years.   The joint opinion rejects that framework.   * * *

Stare decisis is defined in Black's Law Dictionary as meaning "to abide by, or adhere to, decided cases."   * * *   Whatever the "central holding" of *Roe* that is left after the joint opinion finishes dissecting it is surely not the result of that principle.   While purporting to adhere to precedent, the joint opinion instead revises it.   *Roe* continues to exist, but only in the way a storefront on a western movie set exists: a mere facade to give the illusion of reality.   Decisions following *Roe,* such as *Akron v. Akron Center for Reproductive Health, Inc.,* 462 U.S. 416 (1983), and *Thornburgh v. American College of Obstetricians and Gynecologists,* 476 U.S. 747 (1986), are frankly overruled in part under the "undue burden" standard expounded in the joint opinion. * * *

In our view, authentic principles of *stare decisis* do not require that any portion of the reasoning in *Roe* be kept intact.   * * *

The joint opinion discusses several *stare decisis* factors which, it asserts, point toward retaining a portion of *Roe.*   Two of these factors are that the main "factual underpinning" of *Roe* has remained the same, and that its doctrinal foundation is no weaker now than it was in 1973.   * * * Of course, what might be called the basic facts which gave rise to *Roe* have remained the same—women become pregnant, there is a point somewhere, depending on medical technology, where a fetus becomes viable, and women give birth to children.   But this is only to say that the same facts which gave rise to *Roe* will continue to give rise to similar cases.   It is not a reason, in and of itself, why those cases must be decided in the same incorrect manner as was the first case to deal with the question.   And surely there is no requirement, in considering whether to depart from *stare decisis* in a constitutional case, that a decision be more wrong now than it was at the time it was rendered.   If that were true, the most outlandish constitutional decision could survive forever, based simply on the fact that it was no more outlandish later than it was when originally rendered.

Nor does the joint opinion faithfully follow this alleged requirement.   The opinion frankly concludes that *Roe* and its progeny were wrong in failing to recognize that the State's interests in maternal health and in the protection of unborn human life exist throughout pregnancy.   * * * But there is no indication that these components of *Roe* are any more incorrect at this juncture than they were at its inception.

The joint opinion also points to the reliance interests involved in this context in its effort to explain why precedent must be followed for precedent's sake.   * * *

The joint opinion thus turns to what can only be described as an unconventional—and unconvincing—notion of reliance, a view based on the surmise that the availability of abortion since *Roe* has led to "two decades of economic and social developments" that would be undercut if the error of *Roe* were recognized.   * * * The joint opinion's assertion of this fact is undeveloped and totally conclusory.   In fact, one can not be sure to what economic and social developments the opinion is referring.   Surely it is dubious to suggest that women have reached their "places in society" in reliance upon

Roe, rather than as a result of their determination to obtain higher education and compete with men in the job market, and of society's increasing recognition of their ability to fill positions that were previously thought to be reserved only for men. * * *

In the end, having failed to put forth any evidence to prove any true reliance, the joint opinion's argument is based solely on generalized assertions about the national psyche, on a belief that the people of this country have grown accustomed to the *Roe* decision over the last 19 years and have "ordered their thinking and living around" it. * * * As an initial matter, one might inquire how the joint opinion can view the "central holding" of *Roe* as so deeply rooted in our constitutional culture, when it so casually uproots and disposes of that same decision's trimester framework. Furthermore, at various points in the past, the same could have been said about this Court's erroneous decisions that the Constitution allowed "separate but equal" treatment of minorities, see *Plessy v. Ferguson,* 163 U.S. 537 (1896), or that "liberty" under the Due Process Clause protected "freedom of contract." See *Adkins v. Children's Hospital of D.C.,* 261 U.S. 525 (1923); *Lochner v. New York,* 198 U.S. 45 (1905). The "separate but equal" doctrine lasted 58 years after *Plessy,* and *Lochner*'s protection of contractual freedom lasted 32 years. However, the simple fact that a generation or more had grown used to these major decisions did not prevent the Court from correcting its errors in those cases, nor should it prevent us from correctly interpreting the Constitution here. * * *

Apparently realizing that conventional *stare decisis* principles do not support its position, the joint opinion advances a belief that retaining a portion of *Roe* is necessary to protect the "legitimacy" of this Court. * * * Because the Court must take care to render decisions "grounded truly in principle," and not simply as political and social compromises, * * * the joint opinion properly declares it to be this Court's duty to ignore the public criticism and protest that may arise as a result of a decision. Few would quarrel with this statement, although it may be doubted that Members of this Court, holding their tenure as they do during constitutional "good behavior," are at all likely to be intimidated by such public protests.

But the joint opinion goes on to state that when the Court "resolve[s] the sort of intensely divisive controversy reflected in *Roe* and those rare, comparable cases," its decision is exempt from reconsideration under established principles of *stare decisis* in constitutional cases. * * * This is a truly novel principle, one which is contrary to both the Court's historical practice and to the Court's traditional willingness to tolerate criticism of its opinions. Under this principle, when the Court has ruled on a divisive issue, it is apparently prevented from overruling that decision for the sole reason that it was incorrect, *unless opposition to the original decision has died away.*

The first difficulty with this principle lies in its assumption that cases which are "intensely divisive" can be readily distinguished from those that are not. The question of whether a particular issue is "intensely divisive" enough to qualify for special protection is entirely subjective and dependent on the individual assumptions of the members of this Court. In addition, because the Court's duty is to ignore public opinion and criticism on issues that come before it, its members are in perhaps the worst position to judge whether a decision divides the Nation deeply enough to justify such uncommon protection. Although many of the Court's decisions divide the populace to a large degree, we have not previously on that account shied away from applying normal rules of *stare decisis* when urged to reconsider earlier decisions. Over the past 21 years, for example, the Court has overruled in whole or in part 34 of its previous constitutional decisions. * * *

There is also a suggestion in the joint opinion that the propriety of overruling a "divisive" decision depends in part on whether "most people" would now agree that it should be overruled. Either the demise of opposition or its progression to substantial popular agreement apparently is required to allow the Court to reconsider a divisive decision. How such agreement would be ascertained, short of a public opinion poll, the joint opinion does not say. But surely even the suggestion is totally at war with the idea of "legitimacy" in whose name it is invoked. The Judicial Branch derives its legitimacy, not from following public opinion, but from deciding by its best lights whether legislative enactments of the popular branches of Government comport with the Constitution. The doctrine of *stare decisis* is an adjunct of this duty, and should be no more subject to the vagaries of public opinion than is the basic judicial task.

There are other reasons why the joint opinion's discussion of legitimacy is unconvincing as well. In assuming that the Court is perceived as "surrender[ing] to political pressure" when it overrules a controversial decision, * * * the joint opinion forgets that there are two sides to any controversy. The joint opinion asserts that, in order to protect its legitimacy, the Court must refrain from overruling a controversial decision lest it be viewed as favoring those who oppose the decision. But a decision to *adhere* to prior precedent is subject to the same criticism, for in such a case one can easily argue that the Court is responding to those who have demonstrated in favor of the original decision. The decision in *Roe* has engendered large demonstrations, including repeated marches on this Court and on Congress, both in opposition to and in support of that opinion. A decision either way on *Roe* can therefore be perceived as favoring one group or the other. But this perceived dilemma arises only if one assumes, as the joint opinion does, that the Court should make its decisions with a view toward speculative public perceptions. If one assumes instead, as the Court surely did in both *Brown* and *West Coast Hotel,* that the Court's legitimacy is enhanced by faithful interpretation of the Constitution irrespective of public opposition, such self-engendered difficulties may be put to one side.

* * *

The end result of the joint opinion's paeans of praise for legitimacy is the enunciation of a brand new standard for evaluating state regulation of a woman's right to abortion—the "undue burden" standard. As indicated above, *Roe v. Wade* adopted a "fundamental right" standard under which state regulations could survive only if they met the requirement of "strict scrutiny." While we disagree with that standard, it at least had a recognized basis in constitutional law at the time *Roe* was decided. The same cannot be said for the "undue burden" standard, which is created largely out of whole cloth by the authors of the joint opinion. It is a standard which even today does not command the support of a majority of this Court. And it will not, we believe, result in the sort of "simple limitation," easily applied, which the joint opinion anticipates. * * * In sum, it is a standard which is not built to last.

In evaluating abortion regulations under that standard, judges will have to decide whether they place a "substantial obstacle" in the path of a woman seeking an abortion. * * * In that this standard is based even more on a judge's subjective determinations than was the trimester framework, the standard will do nothing to prevent "judges from roaming at large in the constitutional field" guided only by their personal views. *Griswold v. Connecticut*, 381 U.S., at 502 (HARLAN, J., concurring in judgment). Because the undue burden standard is plucked from nowhere, the question of what is a "substantial obstacle" to abortion will undoubtedly engender a variety of conflicting views. For example, in the very matter before us now, the authors of the joint opinion would uphold Pennsylvania's 24–hour waiting period, concluding that a "particular burden" on some women is not a substantial obstacle. * * * But the authors would at the same time strike down Pennsylvania's spousal notice provision, after finding that in a "large fraction" of cases the provision will be a substantial obstacle. * * * And, while the authors conclude that the informed consent provisions do not constitute an "undue burden," Justice Stevens would hold that they do. * * *

Furthermore, while striking down the spousal *notice* regulation, the joint opinion would uphold a parental *consent* restriction that certainly places very substantial obstacles in the path of a minor's abortion choice. The joint opinion is forthright in admitting that it draws this distinction based on a policy judgment that parents will have the best interests of their children at heart, while the same is not necessarily true of husbands as to their wives. * * * This may or may not be a correct judgment, but it is quintessentially a legislative one. The "undue burden" inquiry does not in any way supply the distinction between parental consent and spousal consent which the joint opinion adopts. Despite the efforts of the joint opinion, the undue burden standard presents nothing more workable than the trimester framework which it discards today. Under the guise of the Constitution, this Court will still impart its own preferences on the States in the form of a complex abortion code.

The sum of the joint opinion's labors in the name of *stare decisis* and "legitimacy" is this: *Roe v. Wade* stands as a sort of judicial Potemkin Village, which may be pointed out to passersby as a monument to the importance of adhering to precedent. But behind the facade, an entirely new method of analysis, without any roots in constitutional law, is imported to decide the constitutionality of state laws regulating abortion. Neither *stare decisis* nor "legitimacy" are truly served by such an effort.

We have stated above our belief that the Constitution does not subject state abortion regulations to heightened scrutiny. Accordingly, we think that the correct analysis is that set forth by the plurality opinion in *Webster*. A woman's interest in having an abortion is a form of liberty protected by the Due Process Clause, but States may regulate abortion procedures in ways rationally related to a legitimate state interest. *Williamson v. Lee Optical of Okla., Inc.*, 348 U.S. 483, 491 (1955); cf. *Stanley v. Illinois*, 405 U.S. 645, 651–

653 (1972).   With this rule in mind, we examine each of the challenged provisions.

III

A

Section 3205 of the Act imposes certain requirements related to the informed consent of a woman seeking an abortion. * * *

We conclude that this provision of the statute is rationally related to the State's interest in assuring that a woman's consent to an abortion be a fully informed decision.

Section 3205(a)(1) requires a physician to disclose certain information about the abortion procedure and its risks and alternatives. This requirement is certainly no large burden, as the Court of Appeals found that "the record shows that the clinics, without exception, insist on providing this information to women before an abortion is performed." * * * We are of the view that this information "clearly is related to maternal health and to the State's legitimate purpose in requiring informed consent." * * *

Section 3205(a)(2) compels the disclosure, by a physician or a counselor, of information concerning the availability of paternal child support and state-funded alternatives if the woman decides to proceed with her pregnancy. Here again, the Court of Appeals observed that "the record indicates that most clinics already require that a counselor consult in person with the woman about alternatives to abortion before the abortion is performed." * * * And petitioners do not claim that the information required to be disclosed by statute is in any way false or inaccurate; indeed, the Court of Appeals found it to be "relevant, accurate, and non-inflammatory." * * * We conclude that this required presentation of "balanced information" is rationally related to the State's legitimate interest in ensuring that the woman's consent is truly informed, * * * and in addition furthers the State's interest in preserving unborn life. That the information might create some uncertainty and persuade some women to forgo abortions does not lead to the conclusion that the Constitution forbids the provision of such information. Indeed, it only demonstrates that this information might very well make a difference, and that it is therefore relevant to a woman's informed choice. * * * We acknowledge that in *Thornburgh* this Court struck down informed consent requirements similar to the ones at issue here. * * * It is clear, however, that while the detailed framework of *Roe* led to the Court's invalidation of those informational requirements, they "would have been sustained under any traditional standard of judicial review, * * * or for any other surgical procedure except abortion." * * * id. In light of our rejection of *Roe*'s "fundamental right" approach to this subject, we do not regard *Thornburgh* as controlling.

For the same reason, we do not feel bound to follow this Court's previous holding that a State's 24–hour mandatory waiting period is unconstitutional. * * * Petitioners are correct that such a provision will result in delays for some women that might not otherwise exist, therefore placing a burden on their liberty. But the provision in no way prohibits abortions, and the informed consent and waiting period requirements do not apply in the case of a medical emergency. * * * We are of the view that, in providing time for reflection and reconsideration, the waiting period helps ensure that a woman's decision to abort is a well-considered one, and reasonably furthers the State's legitimate interest in maternal health and in the unborn life of the fetus.   * * *

B

In addition to providing her own informed consent, before an unemancipated woman under the age of 18 may obtain an abortion she must either furnish the consent of one of her parents, or must opt for the judicial procedure that allows her to bypass the consent requirement.   * * *

This provision is entirely consistent with this Court's previous decisions involving parental consent requirements.   * * *

We think it beyond dispute that a State "has a strong and legitimate interest in the welfare of its young citizens, whose immaturity, inexperience, and lack of judgment may sometimes impair their ability to exercise their rights wisely." *Hodgson v. Minnesota,* 497 U.S., at 444 (opinion of STEVENS, J.).   A requirement of parental consent to abortion, like myriad other restrictions placed upon minors in other contexts, is reasonably designed to further this important and legitimate state interest.   * * * We thus conclude that Pennsylvania's parental consent requirement should be upheld.

C

Section 3209 of the Act contains the spousal notification provision.   * * *

We first emphasize that Pennsylvania has not imposed a spousal *consent* requirement of the type the Court struck down in *Planned Parenthood of Central Mo. v. Danforth,* 428 U.S., at 67–72.   Missouri's spousal consent provision was invalidated in that case because of the Court's view that it unconstitutionally granted to the husband "a veto power exercisable for any reason whatsoever or for no reason at all." *Id.,* at 71.   But this case involves a much less intrusive requirement of spousal *notification,* not consent.   * * * *Danforth* thus does not control our analysis.   * * * Furthermore, because this is a facial challenge to the Act, it is insufficient for petitioners to show that the notification provision "might operate unconstitutionally under some conceivable set of circumstances." *United States v. Salerno,* 481 U.S. 739, 745 (1987).   Thus, it is not enough for petitioners to show that, in some "worst-case" circumstances, the notice provision will operate as a grant of veto power to husbands. *Ohio v. Akron Center for Reproductive Health,* 497 U.S., at 514.   Because they are making a facial challenge to the provision, they must "show that no set of circumstances exists under which the [provision] would be valid."   * * *   This they have failed to do.[2]

---

2. The joint opinion of JUSTICES O'CONNOR, KENNEDY, and SOUTER appears to ignore this point in concluding that the spousal notice provision imposes an undue burden on the abortion decision.   * * *

The joint opinion puts to one side these situations where the regulation imposes no obstacle at all, and instead focuses on the group of married woman who would not otherwise notify their husbands and who do not qualify for one of the exceptions.   Having narrowed the focus, the joint opinion concludes that in a

"large fraction" of those cases, the notification provision operates as a substantial obstacle, * * * and that the provision is therefore invalid.   There are certainly instances where a woman would prefer not to notify her husband, and yet does not qualify for an exception.   For example, there are the situations of battered women who fear psychological abuse or injury to their children as a result of notification; because in these situations the women do not fear bodily injury, they do not qualify for an exception.   And there are situations where a

The question before us is therefore whether the spousal notification requirement rationally furthers any legitimate state interests. We conclude that it does. First, a husband's interests in procreation within marriage and in the potential life of his unborn child are certainly substantial ones. * * * The State itself has legitimate interests both in protecting these interests of the father and in protecting the potential life of the fetus, and the spousal notification requirement is reasonably related to advancing those state interests. By providing that a husband will usually know of his spouse's intent to have an abortion, the provision makes it more likely that the husband will participate in deciding the fate of his unborn child, a possibility that might otherwise have been denied him. This participation might in some cases result in a decision to proceed with the pregnancy. * * *

The State also has a legitimate interest in promoting "the integrity of the marital relationship." * * * This Court has previously recognized "the importance of the marital relationship in our society." * * * In our view, the spousal notice requirement is a rational attempt by the State to improve truthful communication between spouses and encourage collaborative decisionmaking, and thereby fosters marital integrity. * * * The Pennsylvania Legislature was in a position to weigh the likely benefits of the provision against its likely adverse effects, and presumably concluded, on balance, that the provision would be beneficial. Whether this was a wise decision or not, we cannot say that it was irrational. We therefore conclude that the spousal notice provision comports with the Constitution. * * *

D

The Act also imposes various reporting requirements. * * * We further conclude that these reporting requirements rationally further the State's legitimate interests in advancing the state of medical knowledge concerning maternal health and prenatal life, in gathering statistical information with respect to patients, and in ensuring compliance with other provisions of the Act.

* * *

E

Finally, petitioners challenge the medical emergency exception provided for by the Act. The existence of a medical emergency exempts compliance with the Act's informed consent, parental consent, and spousal notice requirements. * * *

* * *

woman has become pregnant as a result of an unreported spousal sexual assault; when such an assault is unreported, no exception is available. But, as the District Court found, there are also instances where the woman prefers not to notify her husband for a variety of other reasons. * * * For example, a woman might desire to obtain an abortion without her husband's knowledge because of perceived economic constraints or her husband's previously expressed opposition to abortion. The joint opinion concentrates on the situations involving battered women and unreported spousal assault, and assumes, without any support in the record, that these instances constitute a "large fraction" of those cases in which women prefer not to notify their husbands (and do not qualify for an exception). * * * This assumption is not based on any hard evidence, however. And were it helpful to an attempt to reach a desired result, one could just as easily assume that the battered women situations form 100 percent of the cases where women desire not to notify, or that they constitute only 20 percent of those cases. But reliance on such speculation is the necessary result of adopting the undue burden standard.

We find that the interpretation of the Court of Appeals in this case is eminently reasonable, and that the provision thus should be upheld. When a woman is faced with any condition that poses a "significant threat to [her] life or health," she is exempted from the Act's consent and notice requirements and may proceed immediately with her abortion.

IV

For the reasons stated, we therefore would hold that each of the challenged provisions of the Pennsylvania statute is consistent with the Constitution. It bears emphasis that our conclusion in this regard does not carry with it any necessary approval of these regulations. Our task is, as always, to decide only whether the challenged provisions of a law comport with the United States Constitution. If, as we believe, these do, their wisdom as a matter of public policy is for the people of Pennsylvania to decide.

JUSTICE SCALIA, with whom THE CHIEF JUSTICE, JUSTICE WHITE, and JUSTICE THOMAS join, concurring in the judgment in part and dissenting in part.

My views on this matter are unchanged from those I set forth in my separate opinions in *Webster v. Reproductive Health Services,* 492 U.S. 490, 532 (1989) (SCALIA, J., concurring in part and concurring in judgment), and *Ohio v. Akron Center for Reproductive Health,* 497 U.S. 502, 520 (1990) (*Akron II*) (SCALIA, J., concurring). The States may, if they wish, permit abortion-on-demand, but the Constitution does not *require* them to do so. The permissibility of abortion, and the limitations upon it, are to be resolved like most important questions in our democracy: by citizens trying to persuade one another and then voting. As the Court acknowledges, "where reasonable people disagree the government can adopt one position or the other." * * * The Court is correct in adding the qualification that this "assumes a state of affairs in which the choice does not intrude upon a protected liberty," * * *—but the crucial part of that qualification is the penultimate word. A State's choice between two positions on which reasonable people can disagree is constitutional even when (as is often the case) it intrudes upon a "liberty" in the absolute sense. Laws against bigamy, for example—which entire societies of reasonable people disagree with—intrude upon men and women's liberty to marry and live with one another. But bigamy happens not to be a liberty specially "protected" by the Constitution.

That is, quite simply, the issue in this case: not whether the power of a woman to abort her unborn child is a "liberty" in the absolute sense; or even whether it is a liberty of great importance to many women. Of course it is both. The issue is whether it is a liberty protected by the Constitution of the United States. I am sure it is not. I reach that conclusion not because of anything so exalted as my views concerning the "concept of existence, of meaning, of the universe, and of the mystery of human life." * * * Rather, I reach it for the same reason I reach the conclusion that bigamy is not constitutionally protected—because of two simple facts: (1) the Constitution says absolutely nothing about it, and (2) the longstanding traditions of American society have permitted it to be legally proscribed.[1] *Akron II, supra,* at 520 (SCALIA, J., concurring).

1. The Court's suggestion, * * * that adherence to tradition would require us to uphold laws against interracial marriage is entirely wrong. Any tradition in that case was

The Court destroys the proposition, evidently meant to represent my position, that "liberty" includes "only those practices, defined at the most specific level, that were protected against government interference by other rules of law when the Fourteenth Amendment was ratified," * * * (citing *Michael H. v. Gerald D.,* 491 U.S. 110, 127, n. 6 (1989) (opinion of SCALIA, J.). That is not, however, what *Michael H.* says; it merely observes that, in defining "liberty," we may not disregard a specific, "relevant tradition protecting, or denying protection to, the asserted right," 491 U.S., at 127, n. 6. But the Court does not wish to be fettered by any such limitations on its preferences. The Court's statement that it is "tempting" to acknowledge the authoritativeness of tradition in order to "cur[b] the discretion of federal judges," *ante,* at 5, is of course rhetoric rather than reality; no government official is "tempted" to place restraints upon his own freedom of action, which is why Lord Acton did not say "Power tends to purify." The Court's temptation is in the quite opposite and more natural direction—towards systematically eliminating checks upon its own power; and it succumbs.

Beyond that brief summary of the essence of my position, I will not swell the United States Reports with repetition of what I have said before; and applying the rational basis test, I would uphold the Pennsylvania statute in its entirety. * * *

[The remainder of Justice Scalia's dissenting opinion is omitted.]

Notes on Roe and Casey

1. The decisions in *Roe* and its companion case, Doe v. Bolton, 410 U.S. 179, 93 S.Ct. 739, 35 L.Ed.2d 201 (1973), were handed down on January 22, 1973. On January 30, 1973, Representative Hogan of Maryland introduced H.J.Res. 261, which proposed the following amendment to the U.S. Constitution:

> Section 1. Neither the United States nor any State shall deprive any human being, from the moment of conception, of life without due process of law; nor deny to any human being, from the moment of conception, within its jurisdiction, the equal protection of the laws.

> Section 2. Neither the United States nor any State shall deprive any human being of life on account of illness, age, or incapacity.

> Section 3. Congress and the several states shall have the power to enforce this article by appropriate legislation.

By late summer, 1973, sixteen proposed anti-abortion amendments were pending before the House Judiciary Subcommittee No. 4, and one such proposal, S.J.Res.

contradicted *by a text*—an Equal Protection Clause that explicitly establishes racial equality as a constitutional value. See *Loving v. Virginia,* 388 U.S. 1, 9 (1967) ("In the case at bar, * * * we deal with statutes containing racial classifications, and the fact of equal application does not immunize the statute from the very heavy burden of justification which the Fourteenth Amendment has traditionally required of state statutes drawn according to race"); see also *id.,* at 13 (STEWART, J., concurring in judgment). The enterprise launched in *Roe,* by contrast, sought to *establish*—in the teeth of a clear, contrary tradition—a value found nowhere in the constitutional text.

There is, of course, no comparable tradition barring recognition of a "liberty interest" in carrying one's child to term free from state efforts to kill it. For that reason, it does not follow that the Constitution does not protect childbirth simply because it does not protect abortion. The Court's contention, * * * that the only way to protect childbirth is to protect abortion shows the utter bankruptcy of constitutional analysis deprived of tradition as a validating factor. It drives one to say that the only way to protect the right to eat is to acknowledge the constitutional right to starve oneself to death.

119, had been introduced into the Senate by Senator Buckley and six of his colleagues. S.J.Res. 119 provided:

Section 1. With respect to the right to life, the word "person", as used in this article and in the fifth and fourteenth articles of amendment to the Constitution of the United States, applies to all human beings, including their unborn offspring at every stage of their biological development, irrespective of age, health, function, or condition of dependency.

Section 2. This article shall not apply in an emergency when a reasonable medical certainty exists that continuation of the pregnancy will cause the death of the mother.

Section 3. Congress and the several States shall have power to enforce this article by appropriate legislation within their respective jurisdictions.

Compare the constitutional amendment proposed by the National Right to Life Committee:

Section 1. With respect to the right to life, the word "person", as used in this article and in the fifth and fourteenth articles of amendment to the Constitution of the United States, applies to all human beings, irrespective of age, health, function, or condition of dependency, including their unborn offspring at every stage of their biological development.

Section 2. No unborn person shall be deprived of life by any person: Provided, however, That nothing in this article shall prohibit a law permitting only those medical procedures required to prevent the death of the mother.

Section 3. Congress and the several States shall have the power to enforce this article by appropriate legislation within their respective jurisdictions.

If a "right to life" amendment is passed by Congress and ratified by three-fourths of the states, what would be its impact on *Roe*? Note Mr. Justice Blackmun's statement that if the fetus had enjoyed the status of a person within the meaning of the fourteenth amendment, appellant's case would collapse, "for the fetus' right to life is then guaranteed specifically by the Amendment." Roe v. Wade, 410 U.S. 113, 155, 93 S.Ct. 705, 728, 35 L.Ed.2d 147, 179. Is this argument persuasive? Imagine a case where continuance of the pregnancy threatened the woman's life, not merely her health: isn't her life, too, protected under the Constitution? How is this conflict to be resolved? Is section 2 of S.J.R. 119, which would allow an abortion to prevent the mother's death, significantly more restrictive than the Texas statute held unconstitutional in *Roe,* which permitted abortions to save the mother's life? See generally, Sarah Weddington, A Question of Choice (1992).

What obligations would the proposed amendments place upon the states? Would the enactment of criminal statutes making abortion murder be constitutionally compelled? If not, would state abortion laws generally reflecting the time-table in *Roe* be unconstitutional? What if a state simply repealed its abortion law altogether? What impact would the amendment have in that case? Does the performance of an abortion by a private doctor in a private hospital or clinic constitute state action? Under what conditions of due process could the fetus be deprived of its life? What is added by the equal protection requirement? How is section 2 of the H.J.R. 261 to be interpreted? Is abortion of a fetus during the first trimester, after due process considerations have been met, an impermissible deprivation of life on account of age? Or does this section apply only to the elderly? Finally, when, exactly, does the "moment of conception" occur? When the sperm is united with the egg? Not until implantation on the wall of the uterus? This decision will be critical, will it not, for the future legality under this proposal of such birth control devices as the IUD, the morning-after pill, and the suction tube (endometrial aspiration)? On February 1, 1973, Representative Zwach of Maine introduced H.J.R. 284, which is identical to H.J.R. 261 except that it uses the phrase "from conception" rather than "from the moment of conception." Does this make any difference? Buckley's phrasing, "at every stage of their biological development," covers all the possibilities, doesn't it?

2. A statute enacted by the Rhode Island legislature in March, 1973 (73–S287 Substitute "A"), creating a conclusive presumption "that human life commences at the instant of conception and that said human life at said instant of conception is a person within the language and meaning of the fourteenth amendment of the Constitution of the United States * * * " was declared unconstitutional in Doe v. Israel, 358 F.Supp. 1193 (D.R.I.1973), affirmed mem. 482 F.2d 156 (1st Cir.), cert. denied 416 U.S. 993, 94 S.Ct. 2406, 40 L.Ed.2d 772 (1974). The court found the claim of constitutionality "frivolous" and reminded the Rhode Island Legislature that it had no authority to overturn Supreme Court decisions interpreting the Constitution by the simple device of creating evidentiary presumptions. 358 F.Supp. at 1199–1202. A congressional interpretation of the fourteenth amendment, however, could not be disposed of so easily, could it? This point seems to have been recognized by two writers who, although recommending a variety of possible state legislative actions directed toward minimizing the impact of *Roe* nevertheless conclude that a right to life amendment to the U.S. Constitution is " * * * the best course of action to pursue." Patrick T. Conley & Robert J. McKenna, The Supreme Court on Abortion—A Dissenting View, 19 Catholic Lawyer 19, 27–28 (1973).

Professor Joseph Witherspoon, one of the two principal draftsmen of the National Right to Life Committee proposal, has discussed the strategy underlying the Rhode Island legislation at issue in Doe v. Israel. He also suggested several courses of action that Congress and the state legislatures might pursue while waiting for the gathering of sufficient political force to enact and ratify a right to life amendment. Among his proposals was the use of nonregulatory governmental powers, including "the appropriative or spending power, the property control and disposition power, and the contract power." Joseph P. Witherspoon, The New Pro–Life Legislation: Patterns and Recommendations, 7 St. Mary's L.J. 637, 672 (1976). The success of the Hyde Amendment in the United States Supreme Court in *McRae* is the proof of Witherspoon's strategy. Nor was he loath to state his own interpretation of the meaning of such legislative efforts: "[t]his is not to say that the [regulatory] legislation does not aim at preventing the performance of abortions. That is very much its aim and its effect." Ibid.

The drawback of a constitutional amendment, of course, is the necessity of mustering a two-thirds vote in Congress in order to propose it for ratification. Counting noses shortly after the opening of the first session of the 97th Congress, Senator Jesse Helms and Representative Henry Hyde found themselves short of the desired goal. Casting about for appropriate action requiring only a simple majority vote, they hit upon a Congressional interpretation of the 14th Amendment. S. 158, 97th Cong., 1st Sess. § 1 (1981) reads:

> Section 1. The Congress finds that present day scientific evidence indicates a significant likelihood that actual human life exists from conception.

> The Congress further finds that the Fourteenth Amendment to the Constitution of the United States was intended to protect all human beings.

Upon the basis of these findings, and in the exercise of the powers of the Congress, including its power under Section 5 of the Fourteenth Amendment to the Constitution of the United States, the Congress hereby declares that for the purpose of enforcing the obligation of the States under the Fourteenth Amendment not to deprive persons of life without due process of law, human life shall be deemed to exist from conception, without regard to race, sex, age, health, defect, or condition of dependency; and for this purpose "person" shall include all human life as defined herein.

Will that do the trick?

3. During the years following the announcement of its opinions in *Roe* and *Doe,* the Supreme Court has had many opportunities to explore the implications of its holdings in those cases. Its actions have been taken against a background of growing political opposition to the results obtained in those cases, including not only efforts to move a "right to life" amendment through Congress and to call a Constitutional Convention to consider "the rights of the family and the life of the unborn," but also to press for adoption of restrictive laws and practices at the state and local levels. Some of the more significant issues that have been considered by the Court are mentioned here.

a. Consent to abortion by the father. In Planned Parenthood of Central Missouri v. Danforth, 428 U.S. 52, 96 S.Ct. 2831, 49 L.Ed.2d 788 (1976), the Court struck down a Missouri statute that required the consent of the woman's spouse to an abortion performed during the first 12 weeks of pregnancy unless a physician had certified that the procedure was necessary to preserve the mother's life. Speaking for himself and Justices Marshall, Brennan, and Stevens, Justice Blackmun reasoned that since *Roe* had prohibited the State from regulating or proscribing first trimester abortions, the State is also prohibited from delegating that authority to husbands. He added a second basis for the holding, acceptable to Justices Stewart and Powell, that since the view of only one marital partner could prevail in cases of disagreement, the woman should have the last word because it is she who physically bears the child and is the more directly and immediately affected by the pregnancy. Justices White and Rehnquist, joined by Chief Justice Burger, would have upheld the statute: the father is entitled to vindicate his own interest, not that of the State, in having the child born alive.

The *Danforth* case did not raise the rights, if any, of the father of an illegitimate child in the abortion decision. Would his case be decided by an *a fortiori* application of *Danforth?* Judge Lester of New Jersey thinks so: see Rothenberger v. Doe, 149 N.J.Super. 478, 374 A.2d 57 (1977). Do you agree?

b. Consent to abortion by the parents of an unmarried minor. The Missouri statute construed in *Danforth* also required parental consent to an abortion performed on an unmarried woman under the age of 18 during the first 12 weeks of pregnancy unless a physician had certified that the procedure was necessary to preserve the mother's life. This time the Court split 5–4. Justices Stewart and Powell joined Justices Blackmun, Marshall, and Brennan to hold that state delegation of a blanket prohibition to parents, who might exercise the veto in an arbitrary fashion, was impermissible. Justice Stevens joined the three *Danforth* dissenters in urging recognition of a state's power to ensure that the minor pregnant woman exercise her right to consent in a knowledgeable manner by requiring parental consultation and consent. On the same day, a unanimous court, in Bellotti v. Baird, 428 U.S. 132, 96 S.Ct. 2857, 49 L.Ed.2d 844 (1976), withheld decision pending authoritative construction by the Supreme Judicial Court of a Massachusetts statute requiring parental consent to the abortion of an unmarried woman under the age of 18, but providing for court-ordered consent "for good cause shown" if one or both parents refused to consent. Abstention was proper because the state officials charged with enforcement of the statute suggested an interpretation of the statute that preferred parental consultation and consent, but permitted ready access to the court both by "a mature minor capable of giving informed consent" as well as by a minor incapable of giving such consent where there was a showing that the abortion would be in her best interests.

The Supreme Judicial Court of Massachusetts construed the statute as requiring prior parental consultation in nonemergency cases where at least one parent or person with parental responsibilities is available as a condition to recourse to the court or, at the very least, "as much parental consultation as is permissible constitutionally." Baird v. Attorney General, 371 Mass. 741, 360 N.E.2d 288 (1977). In determining whether to give consent, both parents and the court must use a "best interests of the pregnant minor" standard, eschewing other considerations. The court found that the "mature minor" exception urged in the United States Supreme Court by the Massachusetts Attorney General was foreclosed by the statute in abortion cases. But the exception was adopted for other situations, and contingently for abortion cases as well, should the Supreme Court hold unconstitutional the statutory requirement of parental consultation. Following receipt of this opinion, a three-judge federal court stayed the operation of the Massachusetts statute pending a determination of its constitutionality, in part because the opinion of the Massachusetts court had seemingly interpreted the statute to "mean whatever the Supreme Court determines that, constitutionally, it ought to mean." Baird v. Bellotti, 428 F.Supp. 854 (D.Mass.1977). After further hearings, the court held the statute unconstitutional and enjoined its enforcement. Baird v. Bellotti, 450 F.Supp. 997 (D.Mass.1978). This judgment was affirmed by the Supreme Court in Bellotti v. Baird, 443 U.S. 622, 99 S.Ct. 3035, 61 L.Ed.2d 797 (1979). Once again, the Court was badly fragmented. Justice Powell, joined by the Chief Justice and Justices Stewart and Rehnquist, found two constitutional flaws in the Massachusetts statute as construed by the Massachusetts court:

> First, it permits judicial authorization for an abortion to be withheld from a minor who is found by the superior court to be mature and fully competent to make this decision independently. Second, it requires parental consultation or notification in every instance, without affording the pregnant minor an opportunity to receive an independent judicial determination that she is mature enough to consent or that an abortion would be in her best interests.

Id., 443 U.S. at 651, 99 S.Ct. at 3052, 61 L.Ed.2d at 818. Justice Rehnquist concurred in the opinion and judgment, but made clear his willingness to reconsider *Danforth*. Justice Stevens, joined by Justices Brennan, Marshall and Blackmun, concurred in the judgment on the ground that *Danforth* was controlling. They declined, however, to join in the opinion of Justice Powell because it discussed "the constitutionality of an abortion statute that Massachusetts has not enacted". Justice White dissented as he had done in *Danforth,* but noted that *Bellotti* went beyond *Danforth:*

> Until now, I would have thought inconceivable a holding that the United States Constitution forbids even notice to parents when their minor child who seeks surgery objects to such notice and is able to convince a judge that the parents should be denied participation in the decision.

Id., 443 U.S. at 657, 99 S.Ct. at 3055, 61 L.Ed.2d at 822.

In that part of his opinion labelled "advisory" by Stevens, Justice Powell had volunteered that if a state wished to require a pregnant minor to obtain parental consent for an abortion, it must also provide an alternative procedure to secure such consent. He continued,

> [a] pregnant minor is entitled in such a proceeding to show either: (1) that she is mature enough and well enough informed to make her abortion decision, in consultation with her physician, independently of her parents' wishes; or (2) that even if she is not able to make this decision independently, the desired abortion would be in her best interests. The proceeding in which this showing is made must assure that a resolution of the issue, and any appeals that may follow, will be completed with anonymity and sufficient expedition to provide an effective opportunity for an abortion to be obtained. In sum, the procedure must ensure that the provision requiring parental consent does not in fact amount to the "absolute, and possibly arbitrary, veto" that was found impermissible in *Danforth.*

Id., 443 U.S. at 643–44, 99 S.Ct. at 3048–49, 61 L.Ed.2d at 813–14.

The Massachusetts Legislature was quick to act on this advice. Chapter 240 of the 1980 Acts of the General Court amends the section construed in *Bellotti.* In relevant part, Chapter 112, § 12S of the Massachusetts General Laws now reads:

> If a pregnant woman less than eighteen years of age has not married and if one or both of her parents or guardians refuse to consent to the performance of an abortion, or if she elects not to seek the consent of one or both of her parents or guardians, a judge of the superior court department of the trial court shall, upon petition, or motion, and after an appropriate hearing, authorize a physician to perform the abortion if said judge determines that the pregnant woman is mature and capable of giving informed consent to the proposed abortion or, if said judge determines that she is not mature, that the performance of an abortion upon her would be in her best interests. A pregnant woman less than eighteen years of age may participate in proceedings in the superior court department of the trial court on her own behalf, and the court may appoint a guardian ad litem for her. The court shall, however, advise her that she has a right to court appointed counsel, and shall, upon her request, provide her with such counsel. Proceedings in the superior court department of the trial court under this section shall be confidential and shall be given such precedence over other pending matters that the court may reach a decision promptly and without delay so as to serve the best interests of the pregnant woman. A judge of the superior court department of the trial court who conducts proceedings under this section shall make in writing specific factual findings and legal conclusions supporting his decision and shall order a record of the evidence to be maintained including his own findings and conclusions.

Does this draft capture Justice Powell's intent? Is it constitutional? The new provision survived a motion for preliminary injunction at the district court level, see Planned Parenthood League of Massachusetts v. Bellotti, 499 F.Supp. 215 (D.Mass.1980) affirmed on this point 641 F.2d 1006, 1009–13 (1st Cir.1981), but the First Circuit thought an injunction was proper to restrain enforcement of sections of the Act (not quoted here) requiring that the consent form contain a description of the state of development of the fetus and that a 24 hour waiting period elapse between the woman's signing the consent form and the performance of the abortion. See Planned Parenthood League of Massachusetts v. Bellotti, 641 F.2d 1006 (1st Cir.1981).

The Supreme Court sustained the validity of the parental notification provisions of a Utah statute that requires a physician to "notify, if possible, the parents or guardian of the woman upon whom the abortion is to be performed, if she is a minor or the husband of the woman, if she is married." (1953 Utah Code Ann. § 76–7–304(2).) This provision is part of Utah's criminal laws: a physician who fails to comply is subject to a one-year prison term and a $1000 fine. Because plaintiff was an unemancipated 15–year–old living with her parents, the Court declined to address the broad question whether the Utah statute was facially invalid as applied to all unmarried minor girls, including those who are mature and emancipated. Limiting its holding to the constitutionality of the statute as applied only to a girl living with and dependent upon her parents, who is not emancipated by marriage or otherwise, and who made no claim or showing respecting her individual maturity or her relationship with her parents, the majority concluded that the statute served important state interests that were sufficient to sustain its constitutionality, including the preservation of family integrity and the protection of adolescents as well as enabling the parents to supply essential medical and other information to the treating physician. H.L. v. Matheson, 450 U.S. 398, 101 S.Ct. 1164, 67 L.Ed.2d 388 (1981). Justice Stevens, concurring in the judgment, would have upheld the notification requirement as applied to all minor pregnant women. Justices Marshall, Brennan and Blackmun, dissenting, were persuaded that the notice requirement unduly burdened the minor woman's fundamental right to choose, in consultation with her physician, whether to terminate her pregnancy.

Can a state constitutionally combine a parental notification requirement with a waiting period, thus maximizing a parent's opportunity to dissuade a minor from obtaining an abortion? In Zbaraz v. Hartigan, 763 F.2d 1532 (7th Cir.1985), affirmed by an equally divided Court 484 U.S. 171, 108 S.Ct. 479, 98 L.Ed.2d 478 (1987), rehearing denied 484 U.S. 1082, 108 S.Ct. 1064, 98 L.Ed.2d 1026 (1988), the Seventh Circuit struck down a provision of the Illinois Parental Notice Abortion Act of 1983 that imposed a twenty-four hour waiting period following actual notice to both parents that an unemancipated minor was seeking an abortion. A similar provision is under challenge in Minnesota. See Hodgson v. Minnesota, 827 F.2d 1191 (8th Cir.1987), rehearing en banc granted 835 F.2d 1545, order rescinded 835 F.2d 1546 (8th Cir.1987).

The *Bellotti* opinions are discussed in Gary D. Abel Lozano, Comment, Abortions for Minors After Bellotti II: An Analysis of State Law and Proposal, 11 St. Mary's L.J. 946 (1980), and Note, Restrictions on the Abortion Rights of Minors: Bellotti v. Baird, 3 Harv.Women's L.J. 119 (1980). For a defense of parental notice provisions written prior to the Court's decision in *H.L.*, see Note, Parental Notice Statutes: Permissible State Regulation of A Minor's Abortion Decision, 49 Fordham L.Rev. 81 (1980). A persuasive case against such provisions is made by Judge Nanette Dembitz, who points out that "a minor's very decision to seek an abortion shows deliberation, a sense of responsibility and foresight as to consequences—qualities lacking in numerous teenagers, who ignore their pregnancies, fantasizing that they will magically disappear." Nanette Dembitz, The Supreme Court and a Minor's Abortion Decision, 80 Columb.L.Rev. 1251, 1255–56 (1980).

Note that *H.L.* did not raise the validity of that part of the Utah statute requiring notification of the pregnant woman's husband. Is it constitutional?

See Planned Parenthood of R.I. v. Board of Medical Review, 598 F.Supp. 625 (D.R.I.1984) (invalidating a similar provision).

c. Funding abortions at public expense. In Maher v. Roe, 432 U.S. 464, 97 S.Ct. 2376, 53 L.Ed.2d 484 (1977), the Court upheld a Connecticut welfare regulation under which Medicaid recipients received payments for medical services incident to childbirth, but not for medical services incident to nontherapeutic abortions. The Court reasoned that *Roe* and its progeny did not prevent Connecticut from making "a value judgment favoring childbirth over abortion." It elaborated:

> The Connecticut regulation before us is different in kind from the laws invalidated in our previous abortion decisions. The Connecticut regulation places no obstacles—absolute or otherwise—in the pregnant woman's path to an abortion. An indigent woman who desires an abortion suffers no disadvantage as a consequence of Connecticut's decision to fund childbirth; she continues as before to be dependent on private sources for the service she desires. The State may have made childbirth a more attractive alternative, thereby influencing the woman's decision, but it has imposed no restriction on access to abortions that was not already there. The indigency that may make it difficult—and in some cases, perhaps, impossible—for some women to have abortions is neither created nor in any way affected by the Connecticut regulation.

Id., 432 U.S. at 464, 97 S.Ct. at 2382–83. Perhaps taking a leaf from Connecticut's book, Congress, beginning in 1976, has prohibited the use of any federal funds to reimburse the cost of abortions under the Medicaid program except under certain specified circumstances, usually where the life of the mother would be endangered if the fetus were carried to term, sometimes as well where the pregnancy was caused by rape or incest, if the rape or incest was reported promptly to a law enforcement agency, and occasionally if two physicians determined that long-lasting physical health damage to the mother would result from carrying the pregnancy to term. The funding restriction, in any of its various forms, is commonly known as the "Hyde Amendment," after its original sponsor, Representative Henry J. Hyde. The Court upheld the first Hyde Amendment in Harris v. McRae, 448 U.S. 297, 100 S.Ct. 2671, 65 L.Ed.2d 784 (1980), finding a federal refusal to fund medically necessary abortions no more contravened the pregnant woman's constitutionally-protected liberty interests than Connecticut's refusal to fund elective abortions had done. Justice Stewart, writing for the Court, conceded that "[b]ecause even the compelling interest of the State in protecting potential life after fetal viability was held to be insufficient to outweigh a woman's decision to protect her life or health, it could be argued that the freedom of a woman to decide whether to terminate her pregnancy for health reasons does in fact lie at the core of the constitutional liberty identified in *Wade*." He went on, however, to reject the argument:

> But, regardless of whether the freedom of a woman to choose to terminate her pregnancy for health reasons lies at the core or the periphery of the due process liberty recognized in *Wade,* it simply does not follow that a woman's freedom of choice carried with it a constitutional entitlement to the financial resources to avail herself of the full range of protected choices. The reason why was explained in *Maher:* although government may not place obstacles in the path of a woman's exercise of her freedom of choice, it need not remove those not of its own creation. Indigency falls in the latter category. * * * Although Congress has opted to subsidize medically neces-

sary services generally, but not certain medically necessary abortions, the fact remains that the Hyde Amendment leaves an indigent woman with at least the same range of choice in deciding whether to obtain a medically necessary abortion as she would have had if Congress had chosen to subsidize no health care costs at all. We are thus not persuaded that the Hyde Amendment impinges on the constitutionally protected freedom of choice recognized in *Wade*.

Id., 448 U.S. at 316–17, 100 S.Ct. at 2688, 65 L.Ed.2d at 804.

The Court's opinions in *Maher* and *McRae* make clear that neither a state legislature nor the Congress is required to provide funding for abortions. The Court also upheld the right of a municipality to refuse to perform abortions in city hospitals except where a threat exists of grave physiological injury or death to the mother and to implement its policy by staffing the obstetrics-gynecology clinic exclusively with doctors and medical students from a medical school operated by Jesuits. Poelker v. Doe, 432 U.S. 519, 97 S.Ct. 2391, 53 L.Ed.2d 528 (1977). Thus foreclosed from challenging funding restrictions on federal constitutional grounds, proponents of public funding for abortion have turned to challenges based on the state constitution. In several states, including California, Massachusetts, and New Jersey, the state's highest court has gone beyond the federal command in requiring state funding for abortions. In Committee to Defend Reproductive Rights v. Myers, 29 Cal.3d 252, 625 P.2d 779, 172 Cal.Rptr. 866 (1981), the California court rested on the California constitutional provision that lists "privacy" as among the "inalienable rights" of Californians as well as its prior decisions holding that when the state implements a general public benefit program, it cannot offer those benefits in a fashion that discriminates against the exercise of a constitutional right. Taken together, these precedents and constitutional provisions were read to mean that the state cannot condition a poor woman's exercise of her right of procreative choice upon whether she chooses to give birth rather than to have an abortion. The Supreme Judicial Court of Massachusetts, declining to consider a challenge based on the Massachusetts state Equal Rights Amendment, held instead that its prior decisions under the state constitution's due process clause were more expansive than those of the United States Supreme Court interpreting the comparable federal clause. Like the California court, the Massachusetts court held that funding of medically necessary abortions was required to protect a woman's fundamental interest in reproductive choice. See Moe v. Secretary of Administration and Finance, 382 Mass. 629, 417 N.E.2d 387 (1981). In Right to Choose v. Byrne, 91 N.J. 287, 450 A.2d 925 (1982), the New Jersey Supreme Court held that a limitation of funding for elective, nontherapeutic abortions violated the right of pregnant women to equal protection of the laws under Art. I, par. 1 of the New Jersey Constitution. Can the application of these decisions be limited to pregnant women who are residents of California, Massachusetts and New Jersey? Cf. Doe v. Bolton, 410 U.S. 179, 200, 93 S.Ct. 739, 751–52, 35 L.Ed.2d 201, 217 (1973).

d. Protection of fetal life and the definition of viability. In Colautti v. Franklin, 439 U.S. 379, 99 S.Ct. 675, 58 L.Ed.2d 596 (1979), the Court held void for vagueness a provision of the Pennsylvania Abortion Control Act which specified that if the person performing an abortion determined that the fetus was viable, or if there was sufficient reason to believe that the fetus might be viable, the person was required to

exercise that degree of professional skill, care and diligence to preserve the life and health of the fetus which such person would be required to exercise in order to preserve the life and health of any fetus intended to be born and not aborted and the abortion technique employed shall be that which would provide the best opportunity for the fetus to be aborted alive so long as a different technique would not be necessary in order to preserve the life or health of the mother.

Id., 439 U.S. at 380 n. 1, 99 S.Ct. at 678, 58 L.Ed.2d at 599. Regarding viability, the majority had this to say:

In these three cases [i.e., *Roe, Doe,* and *Danforth*], then, this Court has stressed viability, has declared its determination to be a matter for medical judgment, and has recognized that differing legal consequences ensue upon the near and far sides of that point in the human gestation period. We reaffirm these principles. Viability is reached when, in the judgment of the attending physician on the particular facts of the case before him, there is a reasonable likelihood of the fetus' sustained survival outside the womb, with or without artificial support. Because this point may differ with each pregnancy, neither the legislature nor the courts may proclaim one of the elements entering into the ascertainment of viability—be it weeks of gestation or fetal weight or any other single factor—as the determinant of when the State has a compelling interest in the life or health of the fetus. Viability is the critical point. And we have recognized no attempt to stretch the point of viability one way or the other.

Id., 439 U.S. at 388–89, 99 S.Ct. at 682, 58 L.Ed.2d at 605. Justice White, joined by Chief Justice Burger and Justice Rehnquist dissented, believing that the majority had withdrawn from the states a "substantial measure of the power to protect fetal life that was reserved to them" in *Roe* and *Danforth*. Id., 439 U.S. at 401, 99 S.Ct. at 689, 58 L.Ed.2d at 613. Do you agree? See generally, Mary Anne Wood & Lisa Bolin Hawkins, State Regulation of Late Abortion and the Physician's Duty of Care to the Viable Fetus, 45 Mo.L.Rev. 394 (1980).

4. Is it possible to take seriously the Court's assertion in *McRae* that "the Hyde Amendment does not impinge on the due process liberty recognized in *Wade* "? Professor Michael J. Perry thinks not; in his view, *McRae* is fundamentally inconsistent with even the narrowest possible reading of *Roe*. See Perry, Why the Supreme Court Was Plainly Wrong in the Hyde Amendment Case: A Brief Comment on Harris v. McRae, 32 Stan.L.Rev. 1113 (1980). His point is that since the necessary rationale for *Roe* was that a woman's interest in terminating her pregnancy outweighed the state's interest in preventing the taking of fetal life during the previability period, it must follow that the state may not take any action during that period predicated on the view that abortion, because it consists of the taking of fetal life, is a morally objectionable act. The crucial issue in *McRae,* not discussed by the Court, should have been whether the Hyde Amendment was predicated on the view that abortion was morally objectionable. How would that issue have been resolved? Is it different from the question, which the Court did resolve against the challengers, of whether the Hyde Amendment violated the Establishment Clause? Was that question correctly resolved? See Elizabeth Symonds, The Denial of Medi–Cal Funds for Abortion: An Establishment of Religion, 9 Golden Gate Univ.L.Rev. 421 (Women's Law Forum, 1978–1979).

5. Answer the following questions, true or false:

(a) States cannot prohibit abortions prior to viability.

(b) The legitimacy of the Supreme Court is damaged less by reversing specific rulings reached in its prior cases (e.g., the validity of a 24–hour waiting period) than by overruling the constitutional interpretation that supported those rulings.

(c) States are free to permit and to fund abortions at any point during pregnancy.

(d) The "essential holding" of *Roe v. Wade* is still the law.

6. Now that the right to privacy has been gutted as an effective basis for the federal constitution's protection of a woman's right to control her reproductive capacity, what other doctrinal sources might be developed? Is Justice Blackmun's invocation of "constitutional guarantees of gender equality" a promising alternative? Professor Reva Siegel, cited by Blackmun in footnote 4, demonstrates how such an argument might be built:

> Abortion-restrictive regulation can be analyzed as an expression of sex discrimination: as legislation that reflects traditional sex-role assumptions about women and presents problems of gender bias discernible in other forms of sex-based state action. But to perform this analysis, it is necessary to break out of the physiological paradigms in which the Court reasons about reproductive regulation in *both* privacy and equal protection law. More than any doctrinal factor, it is the physiological framework in which the Court reasons about reproductive regulation that obscures the gender-based judgments that may animate such regulations and the gender-based injuries they can inflict on women. When abortion-restrictive regulation is analyzed in physiological paradigms, as past cases have shown, the inquiry focuses on questions concerning gestation. By contrast, if restrictions on abortion are analyzed in a social framework, they present questions concerning the regulation of motherhood, and, thus, value judgments concerning women's roles.

> This article employs historical analysis to situate abortion-restrictive regulation in a social framework, building its argument from an account of the original campaign to criminalize abortion during the nineteenth century. Those who advocated restricting women's access to abortion in the nineteenth century were interested in enforcing women's roles, an objective they justified with arguments concerning women's bodies. Analyzing the historical record reveals how social discourses concerning women's roles have converged with physiological discourses concerning women's bodies, as two distinct but compatible ways of reasoning about women's obligations as mothers. When issues which we habitually conceptualize in terms of women's bodies are reconsidered in light of this history, it is possible to see that they in fact involve questions concerning women's roles. Considered from this perspective, abortion-restrictive regulation presents many of the concerns that have traditionally triggered heightened equal protection scrutiny.

Reva Siegel, Reasoning from the Body: A Historical Perspective on Abortion Regulation and Questions of Equal Protection, 44 Stan.L.Rev. 261, 265 (1992) (footnote omitted). Stunning, isn't it? See also Sylvia A. Law, Rethinking Sex and the Constitution, 132 U.Pa.L.Rev. 955, 1002–1028 (1984); Kathryn Holmes Snedaker, Reconsidering Roe v. Wade; Equal Protection Analysis as an Alternative Approach, 17 N.Mex.L.Rev. 115 (1987).

7. Is *Casey's* abandonment of the "trimester" analysis adopted in *Roe* unjustified? The Court's "three stage" approach was not warmly received, even by those contemporary writers who agreed, on political grounds, with its outcome.

Thus, Ely, who noted that "[w]ere I a legislator I would vote for a statute very much like the one the Court ends up drafting", nevertheless went on to reject the decision itself: "It is bad because it is bad constitutional law, or rather because it is *not* constitutional law and gives almost no sense of an obligation to try to be." John Hart Ely, The Wages of Crying Wolf: A Comment on Roe v. Wade, 82 Yale L.J. 920, 926, 947 (1973). In a published discussion of the case among three feminist law professors and litigators, the gap between what had been sought—total decriminalization of abortion—and what the opinion recognized was summed up by Rhonda Copelon Schoenbrod:

> Put it this way: they went far enough basically to effectuate our rights because there are not a whole lot of women who are going to seek abortions in their third trimester. Philosophically, they didn't go all the way with us, and they still left abortion to be treated differently under the law from the way any other medical procedure is to be treated, even an extremely dangerous one like heart transplant.

Janice Goodman, Rhonda Copelon Schoenbrod & Nancy Stearns, Doe and Roe: Where Do We Go From Here? 1 Wom.Rts.L.Rptr. 20, 26–27 (Spring 1973). Would the holding in *Roe* have been more easily defended if it had been placed on grounds of sexual equality, focusing on a woman's right to exercise autonomous choice over her full life's course, rather than based, as it was, on a medical model which highlights the physician's role in collaboration with that of the woman? Justice Ginsburg believes that it would. See Ruth Bader Ginsburg, Some Thoughts on Autonomy and Equality in Relation to Roe v. Wade, 63 No.Car. L.Rev. 375 (1985).

8. *Casey* reaffirmed the constitutionality of a parental consent requirement, coupled with a judicial bypass procedure, for an unemancipated pregnant minor who chooses to have an abortion. The Court had previously upheld the constitutionality of a two-parent notification requirement coupled with a judicial bypass procedure for unemancipated minors, but had left open the question whether the Fourteenth Amendment requires notification statutes to contain bypass procedures. See Hodgson v. Minnesota, 497 U.S. 417, 110 S.Ct. 2926, 111 L.Ed.2d 344 (1990); Ohio v. Akron Center for Reproductive Health, 497 U.S. 502, 110 S.Ct. 2972, 111 L.Ed.2d 405 (1990). Does *Casey* shed any light on that question?

9. The Third Circuit held, on remand in *Casey,* that the invalidated spousal notice provisions were severable from the rest of the Pennsylvania abortion law, despite the Clinics' argument that these provisions formed the "centerpiece" of the Act. Planned Parenthood v. Casey, 978 F.2d 74 (3d Cir.1992).

10. Did *Casey* miss an opportunity to put *Roe* on a stronger basis directly upholding the woman's right to choose whether to terminate her pregnancy, rather than the existing medical model that highlights the role of the physician in determining appropriate medical care? Professor Susan Appleton makes a persuasive case for such a theoretical restructuring of the underlying justification for the constitutional holding. See Susan Frelich Appleton, Doctors, Patients and the Constitution: A Theoretical Analysis of the Physician's Role in "Private" Reproductive Decisions, 63 Wash.U.L.Q. 183 (1985).

11. Does the pregnant woman have a constitutional right to refuse to accept medical attention directed toward preservation of fetal life? Does she have a right to a dead fetus? Or does the state's interest in preserving potential life mean that it can require that transplantation of an unwanted fetus to a willing patient or an artificial womb, should the necessary medical technology be perfected? See Mark A. Goldstein, Note, Choice Rights and Abortion: The Begetting Choice Right and

State Obstacles to Choice in Light of Artificial Womb Technology, 51 So.Cal.L.Rev. 877 (1978). This general problem has attracted the attention of philosophers: see Steven L. Ross, Abortion and the Death of the Fetus, 11 Philosophy and Public Affairs 232 (1982), defending the claim that "the fetus is the only thing that someone—a parent—may with equal comprehensibility and legitimacy care for or want dead", but leaving open the more specific question whether the parent's desire to see the fetus killed "translates into a *right*." Id., at 237, 245 (emphasis in original).

BRAY v. ALEXANDRIA WOMEN'S HEALTH CLINIC

Supreme Court of the United States, 1993.
506 U.S. 263, 113 S.Ct. 753, 122 L.Ed.2d 34.

JUSTICE SCALIA delivered the opinion of the Court.

This case presents the question whether the first clause of Rev.Stat. § 1980, 42 U.S.C. § 1985(3)—the surviving version of § 2 of the Civil Rights Act of 1871—provides a federal cause of action against persons obstructing access to abortion clinics. Respondents are clinics that perform abortions, and organizations that support legalized abortion and that have members who may wish to use abortion clinics. Petitioners are Operation Rescue, an unincorporated association whose members oppose abortion, and six individuals. Among its activities, Operation Rescue organizes antiabortion demonstrations in which participants trespass on, and obstruct general access to, the premises of abortion clinics. The individual petitioners organize and coordinate these demonstrations.

Respondents sued to enjoin petitioners from conducting demonstrations at abortion clinics in the Washington, D.C., metropolitan area. Following an expedited trial, the District Court ruled that petitioners had violated § 1985(3) by conspiring to deprive women seeking abortions of their right to interstate travel. * * * As relief * * *, the court enjoined petitioners from trespassing on, or obstructing access to, abortion clinics in specified Virginia counties and cities in the Washington, D.C., metropolitan area. *National Organization for Women v. Operation Rescue*, 726 F.Supp. 1483 (E.D.Va. 1989). Based on its § 1985(3) ruling and pursuant to 42 U.S.C. § 1988, the court also ordered petitioners to pay respondents $27,687.55 in attorney's fees and costs.

The Court of Appeals for the Fourth Circuit affirmed, *National Organization for Women v. Operation Rescue*, 914 F.2d 582 (C.A.4 1990) * * *.

I

Our precedents establish that in order to prove a private conspiracy in violation of the first clause of § 1985(3),[1] a plaintiff must show, *inter alia*, (1)

---

1. Section 1985(3) provides as follows:

"If two or more persons in any State or Territory conspire or go in disguise on the highway or on the premises of another, for the purpose of depriving, either directly or indirectly, any person or class of persons of the equal protection of the laws, or of equal privileges and immunities under the laws; or for the purpose of preventing or hindering the constituted authorities of any State of Territory from giving or securing to all persons within such State or Territory the equal protection of the laws; or if two or more persons conspire to prevent by force, intimidation, or threat, any citizen who is lawfully entitled to vote, from giving his support or advocacy in a legal manner, toward or in favor of the election of any lawfully qualified

that "some racial, or perhaps otherwise class-based, invidiously discriminatory animus [lay] behind the conspirators' action," *Griffin v. Breckenridge,* 403 U.S. 88, 102, 91 S.Ct. 1790, 1798, 29 L.Ed.2d 338 (1971), and (2) that the conspiracy "aimed at interfering with rights" that are "protected against private, as well as official, encroachment," *Carpenters v. Scott,* 463 U.S. 825, 833, 103 S.Ct. 3352, 3358, 77 L.Ed.2d 1049 (1983). We think neither showing has been made in the present case.

A

In *Griffin* this Court held, reversing a 20–year–old precedent, see *Collins v. Hardyman,* 341 U.S. 651, 71 S.Ct. 937, 95 L.Ed. 1253 (1951), that § 1985(3) reaches not only conspiracies under color of state law, but also purely private conspiracies. In finding that the text required that expanded scope, however, we recognized the "constitutional shoals that would lie in the path of interpreting § 1985(3) as a general federal tort law." * * * That was to be avoided, we said, "by requiring, as an element of the cause of action, the kind of invidiously discriminatory motivation stressed by the sponsors of the limiting amendment,"—citing specifically Representative Shellabarger's statement that the law was restricted " 'to the prevention of deprivations which shall attack the equality of rights of American citizens; that any violation of the right, the *animus* and effect of which is to strike down the citizen, to the end that he may not enjoy equality of rights as contrasted with his and other citizens' rights, shall be within the scope of the remedies * * *.' " *Id.,* * * * (emphasis in original), quoting Cong.Globe, 42d Cong., 1st Sess., App. 478 (1871). We said that "[t]he language [of § 1985(3)] requiring intent to deprive of *equal* protection, or *equal* privileges and immunities, means that there must be some racial, or perhaps otherwise class-based, invidiously discriminatory animus behind the conspirators' action." * * *

We have not yet had occasion to resolve the "perhaps"; only in *Griffin* itself have we addressed and upheld a claim under § 1985(3), and that case involved race discrimination. Respondents assert that there qualifies alongside race discrimination, as an "otherwise class-based, invidiously discriminatory animus" covered by the 1871 law, opposition to abortion. Neither common sense nor our precedents support this.

To begin with, we reject the apparent conclusion of the District Court (which respondents make no effort to defend) that opposition to abortion constitutes discrimination against the "class" of "women seeking abortion." Whatever may be the precise meaning of a "class" for purposes of *Griffin's* speculative extension of § 1985(3) beyond race, the term unquestionably connotes something more than a group of individuals who share a desire to engage in conduct that the § 1985(3) defendant disfavors. Otherwise, innumerable tort plaintiffs would be able to assert causes of action under § 1985(3) by simply defining the aggrieved class as those seeking to engage in

person as an elector for President or Vice President, or as a Member of Congress of the United States; or to injure any citizen in person or property on account of such support or advocacy; in any case of conspiracy set forth in this section, if one or more persons engaged therein do, or cause to be done, any act in furtherance of the object of such conspiracy, whereby another is injured in his person or property, or deprived of having and exercising any right or privilege of a citizen of the United States, the party so injured or deprived may have an action for the recovery of damages occasioned by such injury or deprivation, against one or more of the conspirators." 42 U.S.C. § 1985(3).

the activity the defendant has interfered with. This definitional ploy would convert the statute into the "general federal tort law" it was the very purpose of the animus requirement to avoid. As Justice Blackmun has cogently put it, the class "cannot be defined simply as the group of victims of the tortious action." *Carpenters, supra,* * * * (BLACKMUN, J., dissenting). "Women seeking abortion" is not a qualifying class.

Respondents' contention, however, is that the alleged class-based discrimination is directed not at "women seeking abortion" but at women in general. We find it unnecessary to decide whether *that* is a qualifying class under § 1985(3), since the claim that petitioners' opposition to abortion reflects an animus against women in general must be rejected. We do not think that the "animus" requirement can be met only by maliciously motivated, as opposed to assertedly benign (though objectively invidious), discrimination against women. It does demand, however, at least a purpose that focuses upon women *by reason of their sex* —for example (to use an illustration of assertedly benign discrimination), the purpose of "saving" women *because they are women* from a combative, aggressive profession such as the practice of law. The record in this case does not indicate that petitioners' demonstrations are motivated by a purpose (malevolent *or* benign) directed specifically at women as a class; to the contrary, the District Court found that petitioners define their "rescues" not with reference to women, but as physical intervention " 'between abortionists and the innocent victims,' " and that "all [petitioners] share a deep commitment to the goals of stopping the practice of abortion and reversing its legalization." * * * Given this record, respondents' contention that a class-based animus has been established can be true only if one of two suggested propositions is true: (1) that opposition to abortion can reasonably be presumed to reflect a sex-based intent, or (2) that intent is irrelevant, and a class-based animus can be determined solely by effect. Neither proposition is supportable.

As to the first: Some activities may be such an irrational object of disfavor that, if they are targeted, and if they also happen to be engaged in exclusively or predominantly by a particular class of people, an intent to disfavor that class can readily be presumed. A tax on wearing yarmulkes is a tax on Jews. But opposition to voluntary abortion cannot possibly be considered such an irrational surrogate for opposition to (or paternalism towards) women. Whatever one thinks of abortion, it cannot be denied that there are common and respectable reasons for opposing it, other than hatred of or condescension toward (or indeed any view at all concerning) women as a class—as is evident from the fact that men and women are on both sides of the issue, just as men and women are on both sides of petitioners' unlawful demonstrations. See *Planned Parenthood of Southeastern Pennsylvania v. Casey,* 505 U.S. 833, ___, 112 S.Ct. 2791, ___, 120 L.Ed.2d 674 (1992).

Respondents' case comes down, then, to the proposition that intent is legally irrelevant; that since voluntary abortion is an activity engaged in only by women,[2] to disfavor it is *ipso facto* to discriminate invidiously against

2. Petitioners and their *amici* argue that the intentional destruction of human fetuses, which is the target of their protests, is engaged in not merely by the women who seek and receive abortions, but by the medical and support personnel who provide abortions, and even by the friends and relatives who escort the women to and from the clinics. Many of

women as a class. Our cases do not support that proposition. In *Geduldig v. Aiello,* 417 U.S. 484, 94 S.Ct. 2485, 41 L.Ed.2d 256 (1974), we rejected the claim that a state disability insurance system that denied coverage to certain disabilities resulting from pregnancy discriminated on the basis of sex in violation of the Equal Protection Clause of the Fourteenth Amendment. "While it is true," we said, "that only women can become pregnant, it does not follow that every legislative classification concerning pregnancy is a sex-based classification." *Id.,* at * * *, n. 20, * * *. We reached a similar conclusion in *Personnel Administrator of Mass. v. Feeney,* 442 U.S. 256, 99 S.Ct. 2282, 60 L.Ed.2d 870 (1979), sustaining against an Equal Protection Clause challenge a Massachusetts law giving employment preference to military veterans, a class which in Massachusetts was over 98% male, *id.,* at 270, 99 S.Ct., at 2291. " 'Discriminatory purpose,' " we said, "implies more than intent as volition or intent as awareness of consequences. It implies that the decisionmaker * * * selected or reaffirmed a particular course of action at least in part 'because of,' not merely 'in spite of,' its adverse effects upon an identifiable group." * * *[3] The same principle applies to the "class-based, invidiously discriminatory animus" requirement of § 1985(3).[4] Moreover,

those in the latter categories, petitioners point out, are men, and petitioners block their entry to the clinics no less than the entry of pregnant women. Respondents reply that the essential object of petitioners' conspiracy is to prevent women from intentionally aborting their fetuses. The fact that the physical obstruction targets some men, they say, does not render it any less "class-based" against women—just as a racial conspiracy against blacks does not lose that character when it targets in addition white supporters of black rights, see *Carpenters v. Scott,* 463 U.S. 825, 836, 103 S.Ct. 3352, 3360, 77 L.Ed.2d 1049 (1983). We need not resolve this dispute, but assume for the sake of argument that respondents' characterization is correct.

3. Justice Stevens asserts that, irrespective of intent or motivation, a classification is sex-based if it has a sexually discriminatory effect. * * * The cases he puts forward to confirm this revisionist reading of *Geduldig v. Aiello,* 417 U.S. 484, 94 S.Ct. 2485, 41 L.Ed.2d 256 (1974), in fact confirm the opposite. *Nashville Gas Co., v. Satty,* 434 U.S. 136, 98 S.Ct. 347, 54 L.Ed.2d 356 (1977), cited *Geduldig* only once, in *endorsement* of *Geduldig's* ruling that a facially neutral benefit plan is not sex-based unless it is shown that " 'distinctions involving pregnancy are mere pretexts designed to effect an invidious discrimination against the members of one sex or the other.' " (quoting *Geduldig, supra,* * * * at * * * n. 20). *Satty* said that the Court "need not decide" whether "it is necessary to prove intent to establish a prima facie violation of § 703(a)(1)," * * * because "[r]espondent failed to prove *even* a discriminatory *effect,*". It is clear from this that sex-based discriminatory intent is something beyond sexually discriminatory effect. The Court found liability in *Satty* "[n]otwithstand-

ing *Geduldig,*" * * * *not* (as Justice STEVENS suggests) because *Geduldig* is compatible with the belief that effects alone constitute the requisite intent, but rather because § 703(a)(2) of Title VII *has no intent requirement.* * * * In his discussion of the (inapplicable) Pregnancy Discrimination Act, 92 Stat. 2076, Justice Stevens acknowledges that *Congress* understood *Geduldig* as we do, see *post,* at * * * nn. 29–30. As for the cases Justice STEVENS relegates to footnotes: *Turner v. Department of Employment Security of Utah,* 423 U.S. 44, 96 S.Ct. 249, 46 L.Ed.2d 181 (1975), was not even a discrimination case; *General Electric Co. v. Gilbert,* 429 U.S. 125, 135, 97 S.Ct. 401, 407, 50 L.Ed.2d 343 (1976), describes the holding of *Geduldig* precisely as we do; and *Newport News Shipbuilding & Dry Dock Co. v. EEOC,* 462 U.S. 669, 103 S.Ct. 2622, 77 L.Ed.2d 89 (1983), casts no doubt on the continuing vitality of *Geduldig.*

4. We think this principle applicable to § 1985(3) *not* because we believe that Equal Protection Clause jurisprudence is automatically incorporated into § 1985(3), but rather because it is inherent in the requirement of a class-based animus, *i.e.,* an *animus based on class.* We do not dispute Justice Stevens' observation * * * that Congress "may offer relief from discriminatory effects," without evidence of intent. The question is whether it has done so, and if we are faithful to our precedents we must conclude that it has not.

Justice Stevens and Justice O'Connor would replace discriminatory purpose with a requirement of intentionally class-specific (or perhaps merely disparate) impact. * * * It is enough for these dissenters that members of a protected class are "targeted" for unlawful action "by virtue of their class characteristics," * * * (O'Connor, J., dissenting), * * * regardless of

two of our cases deal specifically with the disfavoring of abortion, and establish conclusively that it is not *ipso facto* sex discrimination. In *Maher v. Roe,* 432 U.S. 464, 97 S.Ct. 2376, 53 L.Ed.2d 484 (1977), and *Harris v. McRae,* 448 U.S. 297, 100 S.Ct. 2671, 65 L.Ed.2d 784 (1980), we held that the constitutional test applicable to government abortion-funding restrictions is not the heightened-scrutiny standard that our cases demand for sex-based discrimination, see *Craig v. Boren,* 429 U.S. 190, 197–199, 97 S.Ct. 451, 456–458, 50 L.Ed.2d 397 (1976), but the ordinary rationality standard. * * *

The nature of the "invidiously discriminatory animus" *Griffin* had in mind is suggested both by the language used in that phrase ("invidious * * * [t]ending to excite odium, ill will, or envy; likely to give offense; esp., unjustly and irritatingly discriminating," Webster's Second International Dictionary 1306 (1954)) and by the company in which the phrase is found ("there must be *some racial, or perhaps otherwise class-based,* invidiously discriminatory animus," *Griffin,* 403 U.S., at 102, 91 S.Ct., at 353 (emphasis added)). Whether one agrees or disagrees with the goal of preventing abortion, that goal in itself (apart from the use of unlawful means to achieve it, which is not relevant to our discussion of animus) does not remotely qualify for such harsh description, and for such derogatory association with racism. To the contrary, we have said that "a value judgment favoring childbirth over abortion" is proper and reasonable enough to be implemented by the allocation of public funds, see *Maher, supra,* * * * and Congress itself has, with our approval, discriminated against abortion in its provision of financial support for medical procedures, see *Harris, supra,* * * *. This is not the stuff out of which a § 1985(3) "invidiously discriminatory animus" is created.

B

Respondents' federal claim fails for a second, independent reason: A § 1985(3) private conspiracy "for the purpose of depriving * * * any person or class of persons of the equal protection of the laws, or of equal privileges and immunities under the laws," requires an intent to deprive persons of a right guaranteed against private impairment. See *Carpenters,* 463 U.S., at 833, 103 S.Ct., at 3358. No intent to deprive of such a right was established here.

Respondents, like the courts below, rely upon the right to interstate travel—which we have held to be, in at least some contexts, a right constitu-

what the motivation or animus underlying that unlawful action might be. Accord, * * * (Stevens, J., dissenting). This approach completely eradicates the distinction, apparent in the statute itself, between purpose and effect. Under Justice Stevens' approach, petitioners' admitted purpose of preserving fetal life (a *"legitimate and nondiscriminatory goal,"* * * * (emphasis added)) becomes the *"indirect consequence* of petitioners' blockade," while the discriminatory effect on women seeking abortions is now "the conspirators' *immediate purpose. " Ibid* (emphasis added). Justice O'Connor acknowledges that petitioners' "target[ing]" is motivated by "opposition to the practice of abortion." * * *

In any event, the characteristic that formed the basis of the targeting here was not woman-

hood, but the seeking of abortion—so that the class the dissenters identify is the one we have rejected earlier: women seeking abortion. The approach of equating opposition to an activity (abortion) that can be engaged in only by a certain class (women) with opposition to that class leads to absurd conclusions. On that analysis, men and women who regard rape with revulsion harbor an invidious antimale animus. Thus, if state law should provide that convicted rapists must be paroled so long as they attend weekly counseling sessions; and if persons opposed to such lenient treatment should demonstrate their opposition by impeding access to the counseling centers; those protesters would, on the dissenters' approach, be liable under § 1985(3) because of their antimale animus.

tionally protected against private interference. See *Griffin, supra,* 403 U.S., at 105–106, 91 S.Ct., at 1799–1800. But all that respondents can point to by way of connecting petitioners' actions with that particular right is the District Court's finding that "[s]ubstantial numbers of women seeking the services of [abortion] clinics in the Washington Metropolitan area travel interstate to reach the clinics." 726 F.Supp., at 1489. That is not enough. As we said in a case involving 18 U.S.C. § 241, the criminal counterpart of § 1985(3):

> "[A] conspiracy to rob an interstate traveler would not, of itself, violate § 241. But if the predominant purpose of the conspiracy is to impede or prevent the exercise of the right of interstate travel, or to oppress a person because of his exercise of that right, then * * * the conspiracy becomes a proper object of the federal law under which the indictment in this case was brought." *United States v. Guest,* 383 U.S. 745, 760, 86 S.Ct. 1170, 1179, 16 L.Ed.2d 239 (1966).[5]

Our discussion in *Carpenters* makes clear that it does not suffice for application of § 1985(3) that a protected right be incidentally affected. A conspiracy is not "for the purpose" of denying equal protection simply because it has an effect upon a protected right. The right must be *"aimed at,"* 463 U.S., at 833, 103 S.Ct., at 3358 (emphasis added); its impairment must be a conscious objective of the enterprise. Just as the "invidiously discriminatory animus" requirement, discussed above, requires that the defendant have taken his action "at least in part 'because of,' not merely 'in spite of,' its adverse effects upon an identifiable group," *Feeney,* 442 U.S., at 279, 99 S.Ct., at 2296, so also the "intent to deprive of a right" requirement demands that the defendant do more than merely be aware of a deprivation of right that he causes, and more than merely accept it; he must act at least in part for the very purpose of producing it. That was not shown to be the case here, and is on its face implausible. Petitioners oppose abortion, and it is irrelevant to their opposition whether the abortion is performed after interstate travel.

* * *

The other right alleged by respondents to have been intentionally infringed is the right to abortion. The District Court declined to rule on this contention, relying exclusively upon the right-of-interstate-travel theory; in our view it also is an inadequate basis for respondents' § 1985(3) claim. Whereas, unlike the right of interstate travel, the asserted right to abortion was assuredly "aimed at" by the petitioners, deprivation of that federal right (whatever its contours) cannot be the object of a purely private conspiracy. In *Carpenters,* we rejected a claim that an alleged private conspiracy to infringe First Amendment rights violated § 1985(3). The statute does not apply, we said, to private conspiracies that are "aimed at a right that is by

---

5. Justice Stevens finds "most significant * * * the dramatic difference between the language of 18 U.S.C. § 241" and that of § 1985(3), in that the former "includes an unequivocal 'intent' requirement." * * * He has it precisely backwards. The *second* paragraph of § 241 does contain an explicit "intent" requirement, but the *first* paragraph, which was the only one at issue in *Guest,* see 383 U.S., at 747, 86 S.Ct., at 1172, does not; whereas § 1985(3) does explicitly require a "purpose." As for Justice Stevens' emphasis upon the fact that § 1985(3), unlike § 241, embraces "a purpose to deprive another of a protected privilege 'either directly or indirectly'," * * * that in no way contradicts a specific intent requirement. The phrase "either directly or indirectly" modifies "depriving," not "purpose." The deprivation, whether direct or indirect, must still have been the *purpose* of the defendant's action.

definition a right only against state interference," but applies only to such conspiracies as are "aimed at interfering with rights * * * protected against private, as well as official, encroachment." 463 U.S., at 833, 103 S.Ct., at 3358. There are few such rights (we have hitherto recognized only the Thirteenth Amendment right to be free from involuntary servitude, *United States v. Kozminski,* 487 U.S. 931, 942, 108 S.Ct. 2751, 2759, 101 L.Ed.2d 788 (1988), and, in the same Thirteenth Amendment context, the right of interstate travel, see *United States v. Guest, supra,* 383 U.S., at 759, n. 17, 86 S.Ct., at 1179, n. 17). The right to abortion is not among them. It would be most peculiar to accord it that preferred position, since it is much less explicitly protected by the Constitution than, for example, the right of free speech rejected for such status in *Carpenters.* Moreover, the right to abortion has been described in our opinions as one element of a more general right of privacy, see *Roe v. Wade,* 410 U.S. 113, 152–153, 93 S.Ct. 705, 726–727, 35 L.Ed.2d 147 (1973), or of Fourteenth Amendment liberty, see *Planned Parenthood of Southeastern Pennsylvania,* 505 U.S., at __, 112 S.Ct., at __; and the other elements of those more general rights are obviously *not* protected against private infringement. (A burglar does not violate the Fourth Amendment, for example, nor does a mugger violate the Fourteenth.) Respondents' § 1985(3) "deprivation" claim must fail, then, because they have identified no right protected against private action that has been the object of the alleged conspiracy.

* * *

III

* * *

Justice Stevens' dissent observes that this is "a case about the exercise of federal power to control an interstate conspiracy to commit illegal acts," * * * and involves "no ordinary trespass," or "picketing of a local retailer," but "the kind of zealous, politically motivated, lawless conduct that led to the enactment of the Ku Klux Act in 1871 and gave it its name," * * *. Those are certainly evocative assertions, but as far as the point of law we have been asked to decide is concerned, they are irrelevant. We construe the statute, not the views of "most members of the citizenry." * * * By its terms, § 1985(3) covers concerted action by as few as two persons, and does not require even interstate (much less nationwide) scope. It applies no more and no less to completely local action by two part-time protesters than to nationwide action by a full-time force of thousands.[17] And under our precedents it simply does not apply to the sort of action at issue here.

Trespassing upon private property is unlawful in all States, as is, in many States and localities, intentionally obstructing the entrance to private premises. These offenses may be prosecuted criminally under state law, and may also be the basis for state civil damages. They do not, however, give rise to a

17. Justice Stevens chides us for invoking text here, whereas (he says) we rely instead upon "statutory purpose" for our class-based animus requirement—"selectively employ[ing] both approaches to give [§ 1985(3)] its narrowest possible construction." * * * That is not so. For our class-based animus require- ment we rely, plainly and simply, upon our holding in *Griffin, whatever* approach *Griffin* may have used. That holding is (though Justice Stevens might wish otherwise) an integral part of our jurisprudence extending § 1985(3) to purely private conspiracies.

federal cause of action simply because their objective is to prevent the performance of abortions, any more than they do so (as we have held) when their objective is to stifle free speech.

The judgment of the Court of Appeals is reversed in part and vacated in part, and the case is remanded for further proceedings consistent with this opinion.

It is so ordered.

JUSTICE KENNEDY, concurring.

In joining the opinion of the Court, I make these added observations.

The three separate dissenting opinions in this case offer differing interpretations of the statute in question, 42 U.S.C. § 1985(3). Given the difficulty of the question, this is understandable, but the dissenters' inability to agree on a single rationale confirms, in my view, the correctness of the Court's opinion. As all recognize, essential considerations of federalism are at stake here. The federal balance is a fragile one, and a false step in interpreting § 1985(3) risks making a whole catalog of ordinary state crimes a concurrent violation of a single congressional statute passed more than a century ago.

* * *

JUSTICE SOUTER, concurring in the judgment in part and dissenting in part.

I

* * *

Prior cases giving the words "equal protection of the laws" in the deprivation clause an authoritative construction have limited liability under that clause by imposing two conditions not found in the terms of the text. An actionable conspiracy must have some racial or perhaps other class-based motivation, *Griffin v. Breckenridge,* 403 U.S. 88, 102, 91 S.Ct. 1790, 1798, 29 L.Ed.2d 338 (1971), and, if it is "aimed at" the deprivation of a constitutional right, the right must be one secured not only against official infringement, but against private action as well. *Carpenters v. Scott,* 463 U.S. 825, 833, 103 S.Ct. 3352, 3358, 77 L.Ed.2d 1049 (1983). The Court follows these cases in applying the deprivation clause today, and to this extent I take no exception to its conclusion. I know of no reason that would exempt us from the counsel of *stare decisis* in adhering to this settled statutory construction, see *Hilton v. South Carolina Public Railways Comm'n,* 502 U.S. 197, 112 S.Ct. 560, 116 L.Ed.2d 560 (1991), which Congress is free to change if it should think our prior reading unsound.

* * *

[Justice Souter's analysis of the hindrance clause, which the majority ruled was not before the Court, is omitted.]

JUSTICE STEVENS, with whom JUSTICE BLACKMUN joins, dissenting.

After the Civil War, Congress enacted legislation imposing on the Federal Judiciary the responsibility to remedy both abuses of power by persons acting under color of state law and lawless conduct that state courts are neither fully competent, nor always certain, to prevent. The Ku Klux Act of 1871, 17 Stat. 13, was a response to the massive, organized lawlessness that infected our

Southern States during the post-Civil War era. When a question concerning this statute's coverage arises, it is appropriate to consider whether the controversy has a purely local character or the kind of federal dimension that gave rise to the legislation.

* * *

It is unfortunate that the Court has analyzed this case as though it presented an abstract question of logical deduction rather than a question concerning the exercise and allocation of power in our federal system of government. The Court ignores the obvious (and entirely constitutional) congressional intent behind § 1985(3) to protect this Nation's citizens from what amounts to the theft of their constitutional rights by organized and violent mobs across the country.

The importance of the issue warrants a full statement of the facts found by the District Court before reaching the decisive questions in this case.

I

Petitioners are dedicated to a cause that they profoundly believe is far more important than mere obedience to the laws of the Commonwealth of Virginia or the police power of its cities. To achieve their goals, the individual petitioners "have agreed and combined with one another and with defendant Operation Rescue to organize, coordinate and participate in 'rescue' demonstrations at abortion clinics in various parts of the country, including the Washington Metropolitan area. The purpose of these 'rescue' demonstrations is to disrupt operations at the target clinic and indeed ultimately to cause the clinic to cease operations entirely."

The scope of petitioners' conspiracy is nationwide; it far exceeds the bounds or jurisdiction of any one State. They have blockaded clinics across the country, and their activities have been enjoined in New York, Pennsylvania, Washington, Connecticut, California, Kansas, and Nevada, as well as the District of Columbia metropolitan area. They have carried out their "rescue" operations in the District of Columbia and Maryland in defiance of federal injunctions.

Pursuant to their overall conspiracy, petitioners have repeatedly engaged in "rescue" operations that violate local law and harm innocent women. Petitioners trespass on clinic property and physically block access to the clinic, preventing patients, as well as physicians and medical staff, from entering the clinic to render or receive medical or counseling services. Uncontradicted trial testimony demonstrates that petitioners' conduct created a "substantial risk that existing or prospective patients may suffer physical or mental harm." Petitioners make no claim that their conduct is a legitimate form of protected expression.

Petitioners' intent to engage in repeated violations of law is not contested. They trespass on private property, interfere with the ability of patients to obtain medical and counseling services, and incite others to engage in similar unlawful activity. They also engage in malicious conduct, such as defacing clinic signs, damaging clinic property, and strewing nails in clinic parking lots and on nearby public streets. This unlawful conduct is "vital to [petitioners'] avowed purposes and goals." They show no signs of abandoning their chosen method for advancing their goals.

Rescue operations effectively hinder and prevent the constituted authorities of the targeted community from providing local citizens with adequate protection. The lack of advance warning of petitioners' activities, combined with limited police department resources, makes it difficult for the police to prevent petitioners' ambush by "rescue" from closing a clinic for many hours at a time. The trial record is replete with examples of petitioners overwhelming local law enforcement officials by sheer force of numbers. In one "rescue" in Falls Church, Virginia, the demonstrators vastly outnumbered the police department's complement of 30 deputized officers. The police arrested 240 rescuers, but were unable to prevent the blockade from closing the clinic for more than six hours. Because of the large-scale, highly organized nature of petitioners' activities, the local authorities are unable to protect the victims of petitioners' conspiracy.

Petitioners' conspiracy had both the purpose and effect of interfering with interstate travel. The number of patients who cross state lines to obtain an abortion obviously depends, to some extent, on the location of the clinic and the quality of its services. In the Washington Metropolitan area, where interstate travel is routine, 20 to 30 percent of the patients at some clinics were from out of State, while at least one clinic obtained over half its patients from other States. * * *

To summarize briefly, the evidence establishes that petitioners engaged in a nationwide conspiracy; to achieve their goal they repeatedly occupied public streets and trespassed on the premises of private citizens in order to prevent or hinder the constituted authorities from protecting access to abortion clinics by women, a substantial number of whom traveled in interstate commerce to reach the destinations blockaded by petitioners. The case involves no ordinary trespass, nor anything remotely resembling the peaceful picketing of a local retailer. It presents a striking contemporary example of the kind of zealous, politically motivated, lawless conduct that led to the enactment of the Ku Klux Act in 1871 and gave it its name.

II

The text of the statute makes plain the reasons Congress considered a federal remedy for such conspiracies both necessary and appropriate. * * *

The plain language of the statute is surely broad enough to cover petitioners' conspiracy. Their concerted activities took place on both the public "highway" and the private "premises of another." The women targeted by their blockade fit comfortably within the statutory category described as "any person or class of persons." Petitioners' interference with police protection of women seeking access to abortion clinics "directly or indirectly" deprived them of equal protection of the laws and of their privilege of engaging in lawful travel. Moreover, a literal reading of the second clause of the statute describes petitioners' proven "purpose of preventing or hindering the constituted authorities of any State or Territory" from securing "to all persons within such State or Territory the equal protection of the laws."

No one has suggested that there would be any constitutional objection to the application of this statute to petitioners' nationwide conspiracy; it is obvious that any such constitutional claim would be frivolous. Accordingly, if, as it sometimes does, the Court limited its analysis to the statutory text, it would certainly affirm the judgment of the Court of Appeals. For both the first clause and the second clause of § 1985(3) plainly describe petitioners' conspiracy.

III

The Court bypasses the statute's history, intent, and plain language in its misplaced reliance on prior precedent. * * *

For present purposes, it is important to note that in each of these cases the Court narrowly construed § 1985(3) to avoid what it perceived as serious constitutional problems with the statute itself. Because those problems are not at issue here, it is even more important to note a larger point about our precedent. In the course of applying Civil War era legislation to civil rights issues unforeseeable in 1871, the Court has adopted a flexible approach, interpreting the statute to reach current concerns without exceeding the bounds of its intended purposes or the constitutional powers of Congress. We need not exceed those bounds to apply the statute to these facts.

The facts and decision in *Griffin* are especially instructive here. In overruling an important part of *Collins,* the Court found that the conduct the plaintiffs alleged—a Mississippi highway attack on a white man suspected of being a civil rights worker and the two black men who were passengers in his car—was emblematic of the antiabolitionist violence that § 1985(3) was intended to prevent. A review of the legislative history demonstrated, on the one hand, that Congress intended the coverage of § 1985(3) to reach purely private conspiracies, but on the other hand, that it wanted to avoid the "constitutional shoals" that would lie in the path of a general federal tort law punishing an ordinary assault and battery committed by two or more persons. The racial motivation for the battery committed by the defendants in the case before the Court placed their conduct "close to the core of the coverage intended by Congress." * * *

* * *

The concerns that persuaded the Court to adopt a narrow reading of the text of § 1985(3) in *Griffin* are not presented in this case. Giving effect to the plain language of § 1985(3) to provide a remedy against the violent interference with women exercising their privilege—indeed, their right—to engage in interstate travel to obtain an abortion presents no danger of turning the statute into a general tort law. Nor does anyone suggest that such relief calls into question the constitutional powers of Congress. * * * Once concerns about the constitutionality of § 1985(3) are properly put aside, we can focus more appropriately on giving the statute its intended effect. On the facts disclosed by this record, I am convinced that both the text of the statute and its underlying purpose support the conclusion that petitioners' conspiracy was motivated by a discriminatory animus and violated respondents' protected right to engage in interstate travel.

IV

The question left open in *Griffin*—whether the coverage of § 1985(3) is limited to cases involving racial bias—is easily answered. The text of the statute provides no basis for excluding from its coverage any cognizable class of persons who are entitled to the equal protection of the laws. This Court has repeatedly and consistently held that gender-based classifications are subject to challenge on constitutional grounds, see, *e.g., Reed v. Reed,* 404 U.S. 71, 92 S.Ct. 251, 30 L.Ed.2d 225 (1971); *Mississippi University for Women v. Hogan,* 458 U.S. 718, 102 S.Ct. 3331, 73 L.Ed.2d 1090 (1982). A parallel construction of post-Civil War legislation that, in the words of Justice Holmes, "dealt with Federal rights and with all Federal rights, and protected them in the lump," *United States v. Mosley,* 238 U.S. 383, 387, 35 S.Ct. 904, 905, 59 L.Ed. 1355 (1915), is obviously appropriate.

The legislative history of the Act confirms the conclusion that even though it was primarily motivated by the lawless conduct directed at the recently emancipated citizens, its protection extended to "all the thirty-eight millions of the citizens of this nation." Cong.Globe, 42d Cong., 1st Sess., 484 (1871). Given then prevailing attitudes about the respective roles of males and females in society, it is possible that the enacting legislators did not anticipate protection of women against class-based discrimination. That, however, is not a sufficient reason for refusing to construe the statutory text in accord with its plain meaning, particularly when that construction fulfills the central purpose of the legislation. See *Union Bank v. Wolas,* 502 U.S. 151, ___, 112 S.Ct. 527, 530, 116 L.Ed.2d 514 (1991).

The gloss that Justice Stewart placed on the statute in *Griffin,* then, did not exclude gender-based discrimination from its coverage. But it does require us to resolve the question whether a conspiracy animated by the desire to deprive women of their right to obtain an abortion is "class-based."

V

The terms "animus" and "invidious" are susceptible to different interpretations. The Court today announces that it could find class-based animus in petitioners' mob violence "only if one of two suggested propositions is true: (1) that opposition to abortion can reasonably be presumed to reflect a sex-based intent, or (2) that intent is irrelevant, and a class-based animus can be determined solely by effect." * * *

The first proposition appears to describe a malevolent form of hatred or ill-will. When such an animus defends itself as opposition to conduct that a given class engages in exclusively or predominantly, we can readily unmask it as the intent to discriminate against the class itself.

Griffin itself, for instance, involved behavior animated by the desire to keep African–American citizens from exercising their constitutional rights. The defendants were no less guilty of a class-based animus because they *also* opposed the cause of desegregation or rights of African–American suffrage, and the Court did not require the plaintiffs in *Griffin* to prove that their beatings were motivated by hatred for African–Americans. Similarly, a decision disfavoring female lawyers,[15] female owners of liquor establish-

---

15. See *Bradwell v. Illinois,* 16 Wall. 130, 21 L.Ed. 442 (1873). The reasoning of the concurring Justices surely evidenced invidious animus, even though it rested on traditional views about a woman's place in society, rather than on overt hostility toward women. These Justices wrote:

"[T]he civil law, as well as nature herself, has always recognized a wide difference in the respective spheres and destinies of man and woman. Man is, or should be, woman's protector and defender. The natural and proper timidity and delicacy which belongs to the female sex evidently unfits it for many of the occupations of civil life. The constitution of the family organization, which is founded in the divine ordinance, as well as in the nature of things, indicates the domestic

ments,[16] or pregnant women [17] may appropriately be characterized as "invidiously discriminatory" even if the decisionmakers have goals other than—or in addition to—discrimination against individual women.

The second proposition deserves more than the Court's disdain. It plausibly describes an assumption that intent lies behind the discriminatory effects from which Congress intended § 1985(3) to protect American citizens. Congress may obviously offer statutory protections against behavior that the Constitution does not forbid, including forms of discrimination that undermine § 1985(3)'s guarantee of equal treatment under the law. Regardless of whether the examples of paternalistic discrimination given above involve a constitutional violation, as a matter of statutory construction it is entirely appropriate to conclude that each would satisfy the class-based animus requirement because none of them poses any danger of converting § 1985(3) into a general tort law or creating concerns about the constitutionality of the statute.

Both forms of class-based animus that the Court proposes are present in this case.

Sex–Based Discrimination

It should be noted that a finding of class-based animus in this case does not require finding that to disfavor abortion is "ipso facto" to discriminate invidiously against women. * * * Respondents do not take that position, and they do not rely on abstract propositions about "opposition to abortion" *per se,* * * *. Instead, they call our attention to a factual record showing a particular lawless conspiracy employing force to prevent women from exercising their constitutional rights. Such a conspiracy, in the terms of the Court's first proposition, may "reasonably be presumed to reflect a sex-based intent." * * *

To satisfy the class-based animus requirement of § 1985(3), the conspirators' conduct need not be motivated by hostility toward individual women. As women are unquestionably a protected class, that requirement—as well as the central purpose of the statute—is satisfied if the conspiracy is aimed at

sphere as that which properly belongs to the domain and functions of womanhood. The harmony, not to say identity, of interests and views which belong, or should belong, to the family institution is repugnant to the idea of a woman adopting a distinct and independent career from that of her husband. So firmly fixed was this sentiment in the founders of the common law that it became a maxim of that system of jurisprudence that a woman had no legal existence separate from her husband, who was regarded as her head and representative in the social state; and, notwithstanding some recent modifications of this civil status, many of the special rules of law flowing from and dependent upon this cardinal principle still exist in full force in most States. One of these is, that a married woman is incapable, without her husband's consent, of making contracts which shall be binding on her or him * * *.

" * * * The paramount destiny and mission of woman are to fulfil the noble and benign offices of wife and mother. This is the law of the Creator." *Id.,* at 141 (Bradley, J., joined by Swayne and Field, JJ., concurring in judgment).

The Justices who subscribed to those views were certainly not misogynists, but their basic attitude—or animus—toward women is appropriately characterized as "invidiously discriminatory."

16. See *Goesaert v. Cleary,* 335 U.S. 464, 69 S.Ct. 198, 93 L.Ed. 163 (1948). In a prescient dissenting opinion written in 1948 that accords with our current understanding of the idea of equality, Justice Rutledge appropriately selected the word "invidious" to characterize a statutory discrimination between male and female owners of liquor establishments. *Id.,* at 468, 69 S.Ct., at 200–201 (Rutledge, J., dissenting).

17. See *Nashville Gas Co. v. Satty,* 434 U.S. 136, 98 S.Ct. 347, 54 L.Ed.2d 356 (1977).

conduct that only members of the protected class have the capacity to perform. It is not necessary that the intended effect upon women be the sole purpose of the conspiracy. It is enough that the conspiracy be motivated "at least in part" by its adverse effects upon women. * * * The immediate and intended effect of this conspiracy was to prevent women from obtaining abortions. Even assuming that the ultimate and indirect consequence of petitioners' blockade was the legitimate and non-discriminatory goal of saving potential life, it is undeniable that the conspirators' immediate purpose was to affect the conduct of women.[19] Moreover, petitioners target women *because of* their sex, specifically, because of their capacity to become pregnant and to have an abortion.[20]

It is also obvious that petitioners' conduct was motivated "at least in part" by the invidious belief that individual women are not capable of deciding whether to terminate a pregnancy, or that they should not be allowed to act on such a decision. Petitioners' blanket refusal to allow any women access to an abortion clinic overrides the individual class member's choice, no matter whether she is the victim of rape or incest, whether the abortion may be necessary to save her life,[21] or even whether she is merely seeking advice or information about her options. Petitioners' conduct is designed to deny *every* woman the opportunity to exercise a constitutional right that *only* women possess. Petitioners' conspiracy, which combines massive defiance of the law with violent obstruction of the constitutional

19. In *Personnel Administrator of Mass. v. Feeney,* 442 U.S. 256, 99 S.Ct. 2282, 60 L.Ed.2d 870 (1979), we inquired whether the challenged conduct was undertaken "at least in part 'because of,' not merely 'in spite of,' its adverse effects upon an identifiable group." *Id.,* at 279, 99 S.Ct., at 2296. It would be nonsensical to say that petitioners blockaded clinics "in spite of" the effect of the blockades on women.

20. The Court mischaracterizes this analysis by ignoring the distinction between a classification that is sex-based and a classification that constitutes sexual discrimination prohibited by the Constitution or by statute. See *ante,* at * * * n. 3. A classification is sex-based if it classifies on the basis of sex. As the capacity to become pregnant is a characteristic necessarily associated with one sex, a classification based on the capacity to become pregnant is a classification based on sex.

See Sunstein, Neutrality in Constitutional Law (With Special Reference to Pornography, Abortion, and Surrogacy), 92 Colum.L.Rev. 1, 32–33 (1992) (footnotes omitted):

"The first point is that restrictions on abortion should be seen as a form of sex discrimination. The proper analogy here is to a law that is targeted solely at women, and thus contains a de jure distinction on the basis of sex. A statute that is explicitly addressed to women is of course a form of sex discrimination. A statute that involves a defining characteristic or a biological correlate of being female should be treated in

precisely the same way. If a law said that 'no woman' may obtain an abortion, it should readily be seen as a sex-based classification. A law saying that 'no person' may obtain an abortion has the same meaning.

"The fact that some men may also be punished by abortion laws—for example, male doctors—does not mean that restrictions on abortion are sex-neutral. Laws calling for racial segregation make it impermissible for whites as well as blacks to desegregate, and this does not make such laws race-neutral. Nor would it be correct to say that restrictions on abortion merely have a discriminatory impact on women, and that they should therefore be treated in the same way as neutral weight and height requirements having disproportionate effects on women. With such requirements, men and women are on both sides of the legal line; but abortion restrictions exclusively target women. A law that prohibited pregnant women, or pregnant people, from appearing on the streets during daylight would readily be seen as a form of de jure sex discrimination. A restriction on abortion has the same sex-based features."

21. The Court refers to petitioners' opposition to "voluntary" abortion. * * * It is not clear what the Court means by "voluntary" in this context, but petitioners' opposition is certainly not limited to "elective" abortions. Petitioners' conduct evidences a belief that it is better for a woman to die than for the fetus she carries to be aborted. * * *

rights of their fellow citizens, represents a paradigm of the kind of conduct that the statute was intended to cover.[22]

The Court recognizes that the requisite animus may "readily be presumed" on the basis of the relationship between the targeted activity and membership in the targeted class. * * * But the Court insists that opposition to an act engaged in exclusively by members of a protected class does not involve class-based animus unless the act itself is an "irrational object of disfavor." * * * The Court's view requires a subjective judicial interpretation inappropriate in the civil rights context, where what seems rational to an oppressor seems equally irrational to a victim. Opposition to desegregation, and opposition to the voting rights of both African–Americans and women, were certainly at one time considered "rational" propositions. But such propositions were never free of the class-based discrimination from which § 1985(3) protects the members of both classes.

The activity of traveling to a clinic to obtain an abortion is, of course, exclusively performed by women. Opposition to that activity may not be "irrational," but violent interference with it is unquestionably "aimed at" women. The Court offers no justification for its newly crafted suggestion that *deliberately* imposing a burden on an activity exclusively performed by women is not class-based discrimination unless opposition to the activity is also irrational. The Court is apparently willing to presume discrimination only when opposition to the targeted activity is—in its eyes—wholly pretextual: that is, when it thinks that no rational person would oppose the activity, except as a means of achieving a separate and distinct goal.[23] The Court's analysis makes sense only if every member of a protected class exercises all of her constitutional rights, or if no rational excuse remains for otherwise invidious discrimination. Not every member of every protected class chooses to exercise all of his or her constitutional rights; not all of them want to. That many women do not obtain abortions—that many women *oppose* abortion—does not mean that those who violently prevent the exercise of that right by women who do exercise it are somehow cleansed of their discriminatory intent. In enacting a law such as § 1985(3) for federal courts to enforce, Congress asked us to see through the excuses—the "rational" motives—that will always disguise discrimination. Congress asked us to foresee, and speed, the day when such discrimination, no matter how well disguised, would be unmasked.

Statutory Relief From Discriminatory Effects

As for the second definition of class-based animus, disdainfully proposed by the Court, * * * there is no reason to insist that a statutory claim under § 1985(3) must satisfy the restrictions we impose on constitutional claims

22. The Court's discussion of the record suggests that the District Court made a finding that petitioners were not motivated by a purpose directed at women as a class. * * * The District Court made no such finding, and such a finding would be inconsistent with the District Court's conclusion that petitioners' gender-based animus satisfied the class-based animus requirement of § 1985(3), see 726 F.Supp., at 1492.

23. The limitations of this analysis are apparent from the example the Court invokes: "A tax on wearing yarmulkes is a tax on Jews." * * *. The yarmulke-tax would not become less of a tax on Jews if the taxing authorities really did wish to burden the wearing of yarmulkes. And the fact that many Jews do not wear yarmulkes—like the fact that many women do not seek abortions—would not prevent a finding that the tax—like petitioners' blockade—targeted a particular class.

under the Fourteenth Amendment. A congressional statute may offer relief from discriminatory effects even if the Fourteenth Amendment prevents only discriminatory intent.

The Court attempts to refute the finding of class-based animus by relying on our cases holding that the governmental denial of either disability benefits for pregnant women or abortion funding does not violate the Constitution. That reliance is misplaced for several reasons. Cases involving constitutional challenges to governmental plans denying financial benefits to pregnant women, and cases involving Equal Protection challenges to facially neutral statutes with discriminatory effects, involve different concerns and reach justifiably different results than a case involving citizens' statutory protection against burdens imposed on their constitutional rights.

* * *

Geduldig, of course, did not purport to establish that, as a matter of logic, a classification based on pregnancy is gender-neutral. As an abstract statement, that proposition is simply false; a classification based on pregnancy is a sex-based classification, just as, to use the Court's example, a classification based on the wearing of yarmulkes is a religion-based classification. Nor should *Geduldig* be understood as holding that, as a matter of law, pregnancy-based classifications never violate the Equal Protection Clause. In fact, as the language of the opinion makes clear, what *Geduldig* held was that not every legislative classification based on pregnancy was equivalent, for equal protection purposes, to the explicitly gender-based distinctions struck down in *Frontiero* * * * and *Reed* * * *. That *Geduldig* must be understood in these narrower terms is apparent from the sentence which the Court quotes in part: "While it is true that only women can become pregnant, it does not follow that every legislative classification concerning pregnancy is a sex-based classification *like those considered in Reed,* * * * *and Frontiero,* * * * "

Central to the holding in *Geduldig* was the Court's belief that the disability insurance system before it was a plan that conferred benefits evenly on men and women. Later cases confirmed that the holding in *Geduldig* depended on an analysis of the insurance plan as a benefit program with an overall nondiscriminatory effect. *Nashville Gas Co. v. Satty,* 434 U.S. 136, 98 S.Ct. 347, 54 L.Ed.2d 356 (1977), applied a statute without an intent requirement to an employer's policy denying accumulated seniority to employees returning from pregnancy leave. Notwithstanding *Geduldig,* the Court found that the policy burdened only women, and therefore constituted discrimination on the basis of sex. The Court stated that "petitioner has not merely refused to extend to women a benefit that men cannot and do not receive, but has imposed on women a substantial burden that men need not suffer. The distinction between benefits and burdens is more than one of semantics." 434 U.S., at 142, 98 S.Ct., at 351. The distinction between those who oppose abortion, and those who physically threaten women and obstruct their access to abortion clinics, is also more than semantic. Petitioners in this case form a mob that seeks to impose a burden on women by forcibly preventing the exercise of a right that only women possess. The discriminatory effect of petitioners' conduct is beyond doubt.

Geduldig is inapplicable for another reason. The issue of class-based animus in this case arises in a statutory, not a constitutional, context. There are powerful reasons for giving § 1985(3) a reading that is broader than the constitutional holdings on which the Court relies. In our constitutional cases, we apply the intent standard to determine whether a constitutional violation has occurred. In cases under § 1985(3), we apply the class-based animus test not to determine whether a constitutional violation has occurred—the violation is independently established—but to determine whether that violation can be remedied. Given the differing roles the intent standard and the class-based animus requirement play in our jurisprudence, there is no justification for applying the same stringent standards in the context of § 1985(3) as in our constitutional cases.

As a matter of statutory interpretation, I have always believed that rules that place special burdens on pregnant women discriminate on the basis of sex, for the capacity to become pregnant is the inherited and immutable characteristic that "primarily differentiates the female from the male." *General Electric Co. v. Gilbert,* 429 U.S. 125, 162, 97 S.Ct. 401, 421, 50 L.Ed.2d 343 (1976) (STEVENS, J., dissenting). I continue to believe that that view should inform our construction of civil rights legislation.

That view was also the one affirmed by Congress in the Pregnancy Discrimination Act, 92 Stat. 2076, which amended Title VII of the Civil Rights Act of 1964, 42 U.S.C. § 2000e *et seq.* The Act categorically expressed Congress' view that "discrimination based on a woman's pregnancy is, on its face, discrimination because of her sex." * * * In the Pregnancy Discrimination Act, Congress rejected *Geduldig* 's focus on benefits and overall impact, instead insisting that discrimination on the basis of pregnancy necessarily constitutes prohibited sex discrimination. * * *

* * *

VI

Respondents' right to engage in interstate travel is inseparable from the right they seek to exercise. * * *

The District Court's conclusion that petitioners intended to interfere with the right to engage in interstate travel is well-supported by the record. Interference with a woman's ability to visit another State to obtain an abortion is essential to petitioners' achievement of their ultimate goal—the complete elimination of abortion services throughout the United States. No lesser purpose can explain their multi-state "rescue" operations.

Even in a single locality, the effect of petitioners' blockade on interstate travel is substantial. Between 20 and 30 percent of the patients at a targeted clinic in Virginia were from out of State and over half of the patients at one of the Maryland clinics were interstate travelers. * * * Making their destination inaccessible to women who have engaged in interstate travel for a single purpose is unquestionably a burden on that travel. That burden was not only a foreseeable and natural consequence of the blockades, but indeed was also one of the intended consequences of petitioners' conspiracy.

Today the Court advances two separate reasons for rejecting the District Court's conclusion that petitioners deliberately deprived women seeking abortions of their right to interstate travel. First, relying on an excerpt from our opinion in *United States v. Guest,* * * * the Court assumes that " 'the predominant purpose' " or "the very purpose" of the conspiracy must be to impede interstate travel. * * * Second, the Court assumes that even an intentional restriction on out-of-state travel is permissible if it imposes an equal burden on intrastate travel. The first reason reflects a mistaken understanding of *Guest* and *Griffin,* and the second is unsupported by precedent or reason.

* * *

The implausibility of the Court's readings of *Griffin* and *Guest* is matched by its conclusion that a burden on interstate travel is permissible as long as an equal burden is imposed on local travelers. The Court has long recognized that a burden on interstate commerce may be invalid even if the same burden is imposed on local commerce. See *Pike v. Bruce Church, Inc.,* 397 U.S. 137, 90 S.Ct. 844, 25 L.Ed.2d 174 (1970); *Dean Milk Co. v. Madison,* 340 U.S. 349, 354, n. 4, 71 S.Ct. 295, 298, n. 4, 95 L.Ed. 329 (1951); *Southern Pacific Co. v. Arizona ex rel. Sullivan,* 325 U.S. 761, 65 S.Ct. 1515, 89 L.Ed. 1915 (1945). The fact that an impermissible burden is most readily identified when it discriminates against nonresidents does not justify immunizing conduct that even-handedly disrupts both local and interstate travel. The defendants in *Griffin,* for example, could not have refuted the claim that they interfered with the right to travel by demonstrating that they indiscriminately attacked local civil rights activists as well as nonresidents.

In this case petitioners have deliberately blockaded access to the destinations sought by a class of women including both local and interstate travelers. Even though petitioners may not have known which of the travelers had crossed the state line, petitioners unquestionably knew that many of them had. * * *

Discrimination is a necessary element of the class-based animus requirement, not of the abridgement of a woman's right to engage in interstate travel. Perhaps nowhere else in its opinion does the Court reject such obvious assumptions of the authors of § 1985(3). The Reconstruction Congress would have been startled, I think, to learn that § 1985(3) protected freed slaves and their supporters from Klan violence not covered by the Thirteenth Amendment only if the Klan members spared *local* African–Americans and abolitionists their wrath. And it would have been shocked to learn that its law offered relief from a Klan lynching of an out-of-state abolitionist only if the plaintiff could show that the Klan specifically intended to prevent his travel between the States. Yet these are the impossible requirements the Court imposes on a § 1985(3) plaintiff who has shown that her right to travel has been deliberately and significantly infringed. It is difficult to know whether the Court is waiting until only a few States have abortion clinics before it finds that petitioners' behavior violates the right to travel, or if it believes that petitioners could never violate that right as long as they oppose the abortion a woman seeks to obtain as well as the travel necessary to obtain it.

* * *

VIII

In sum, it is irrelevant whether the Court is correct in its assumption that "opposition to abortion" does not necessarily evidence an intent to disfavor women. Many opponents of abortion respect both the law and the rights of others to make their own decisions on this important matter. Petitioners, however, are not mere opponents of abortion; they are defiant lawbreakers who have engaged in massive concerted conduct that is designed to prevent all women from making up their own minds about not only the issue of abortion in general, but also whether they should (or will) exercise a right that all women—and only women—possess.

Indeed, the error that infects the Court's entire opinion is the unstated and mistaken assumption that this is a case about opposition to abortion. It is not. It is a case about the exercise of Federal power to control an interstate conspiracy to commit illegal acts. I have no doubt that most opponents of abortion, like most members of the citizenry at large, understand why the existence of federal jurisdiction is appropriate in a case of this kind.

The Court concludes its analysis of § 1985(3) by suggesting that a contrary interpretation would have condemned the massive "sit-ins" that were conducted to promote desegregation in the 1960's—a "wildly improbable result." * * * This suggestion is profoundly misguided. It assumes that we must totally reject the class-based animus requirement to affirm the District Court, when, in fact, we need only construe that requirement to satisfy its purpose. Moreover, the demonstrations in the 1960's were motivated by a desire to extend the equal protection of the laws to all classes—not to impose burdens on any disadvantaged class. Those who engaged in the nonviolent "sit-ins" to which the Court refers were challenging "a political and economic system that had denied them the basic rights of dignity and equality that this country had fought a Civil War to secure." *NAACP v. Claiborne Hardware Co.*, 458 U.S. 886, 918, 102 S.Ct. 3409, 3428, 73 L.Ed.2d 1215 (1982). The suggestion that there is an analogy between their struggle to achieve equality and these petitioners' concerted efforts to deny women equal access to a constitutionally protected privilege may have rhetorical appeal, but it is insupportable on the record before us, and does not justify the majority's parsimonious construction of an important federal statute.

I respectfully dissent.

JUSTICE O'CONNOR, with whom JUSTICE BLACKMUN joins, dissenting.

Petitioners act in organized groups to overwhelm local police forces and physically blockade the entrances to respondents' clinics with the purpose of preventing women from exercising their legal rights. Title 42 U.S.C. § 1985(3) provides a federal remedy against private conspiracies aimed at depriving any person or class of persons of the "equal protection of the laws," or of "equal privileges and immunities under the laws." In my view, respondents' injuries and petitioners' activities fall squarely within the ambit of this statute.

I

The Reconstruction Congress enacted the Civil Rights Act of 1871, also known as the Ku Klux Act (Act), 17 Stat. 13, to combat the chaos that paralyzed the post-War South. * * * Section 2 of the Act extended the protection of federal courts to those who effectively were prevented from exercising their civil rights by the threat of mob violence. Although the immediate purpose of § 1985(3) was to combat animosity against blacks and their supporters, * * * the language of the Act, like that of many Reconstruction statutes, is more expansive than the historical circumstances that inspired it. * * *

The Court's approach to Reconstruction Era civil rights statutes has been to "accord [them] a sweep as broad as [their] language." * * * Today, the Court does just the opposite, precluding application of the statute to a situation that its language clearly covers. There is no dispute that petitioners have "conspired" through their concerted and unlawful activities. The record shows that petitioners' "purpose" is "directly" to "depriv[e]" women of their ability to obtain the clinics' services, see *National Organization for Women v. Operation Rescue,* 726 F.Supp. 1483, 1488 (E.D.Va.1989), as well as "indirectly" to infringe on their constitutional privilege to travel interstate in seeking those services. *Id.,* at 1489. The record also shows that petitioners accomplish their goals by purposefully "preventing or hindering" local law enforcement authorities from maintaining open access to the clinics. See *ibid.,* and n. 4. In sum, petitioners' activities fit precisely within the language of both clauses of § 1985(3).

Yet the Court holds otherwise, and it does so primarily on the basis of an "element" of the § 1985(3) cause of action that does not appear on the face of the statute. Adhering adamantly to our choice of words in *Griffin v. Breckenridge, supra,* the Court holds that petitioners did not exhibit a "class-based, invidiously discriminatory animus" against the clinics or the women they serve. I would not parse *Griffin* so finely as to focus on that phrase to the exclusion of our reasons for adopting it as an element of a § 1985(3) civil action.

A

* * *

Griffin's requirement of class-based animus is a reasonable shorthand description of the type of actions the 42d Congress was attempting to address. Beginning with *Carpenters v. Scott,* 463 U.S. 825, 103 S.Ct. 3352, 77 L.Ed.2d 1049 (1983), however, that shorthand description began to take on a life of its own. In that case, a majority of the Court held that conspiracies motivated by bias toward others on account of their economic views or activities did not constitute class-based discrimination within the reach of the statute. * * * I agreed with the dissent, however, that "[i]nstead of contemplating a list of actionable class traits, * * * Congress had in mind a functional definition of the scope of [§ 1985(3)]," and intended to "provide a federal remedy for all classes that seek to exercise their legal rights in unprotected circumstances similar to those of the victims of Klan violence." * * * (BLACKMUN, J., dissenting) (emphasis deleted). Accordingly, I would have found that § 1985(3) provided a remedy to non-union employees injured by mob violence in a "self-professed union town" whose residents resented nonunion activities. * * *

For the same reason, I would find in this case that the statute covers petitioners' conspiracy against the clinics and their clients. Like the Klan conspiracies Congress tried to reach in enacting § 1985(3), "[p]etitioners intended to hinder a particular group in the exercise of their legal rights because of their membership in a specific class." * * * The controversy associated with the exercise of those rights, although legitimate, makes the clinics and the women they serve especially vulnerable to the threat of mob violence. The women seeking the clinics' services are not simply "the group of victims of the tortious action," * * * as was the case in *Carpenters,* petitioners' intended targets are clearly identifiable—by virtue of their affiliation and activities—before any tortious action occurs.

B

Even if I had not dissented in *Carpenters,* I would still find in today's case that § 1985(3) reaches conspiracies targeted at a gender-based class and that petitioners' actions fall within that category. I agree with Justice Stevens that "[t]he text of the statute provides no basis for excluding from its coverage any cognizable class of persons who are entitled to the equal protection of the laws." * * * At the very least, the classes protected by § 1985(3) must encompass those classifications that we have determined merit a heightened scrutiny of state action under the Equal Protection Clause of the Fourteenth Amendment. Classifications based on gender fall within that narrow category of protected classes. * * * Not surprisingly, the seven federal courts of appeals to have addressed the question have all reached the conclusion that the class of "women" falls within the protection of the statute. * * *

If women are a protected class under § 1985(3), and I think they are, then the statute must reach conspiracies whose motivation is directly related to characteristics unique to that class. The victims of petitioners' tortious actions are linked by their ability to become pregnant and by their ability to terminate their pregnancies, characteristics unique to the class of women. Petitioners' activities are directly related to those class characteristics and therefore, I believe, are appropriately described as class based within the meaning of our holding in *Griffin.*

Petitioners assert that, even if their activities are class based, they are not motivated by any *discriminatory* animus but only by their profound opposition to the practice of abortion. I do not doubt the sincerity of that opposition. But in assessing the motivation behind petitioners' actions, the sincerity of their opposition cannot surmount the manner in which they have chosen to express it. Petitioners are free to express their views in a variety of ways, including lobbying, counseling, and disseminating information. Instead, they have chosen to target women seeking abortions and to prevent them from exercising their equal rights under law. Even without relying on the federally protected right to abortion, petitioners' activities infringe on a number of state-protected interests, including the state laws that make abortion legal, Va.Code Ann. §§ 18.2–72, 18.2–73 (1988), and the state laws that protect against force, intimidation, and violence, *e.g.,* Va.Code Ann. § 18.2–119 (Supp.1992) (trespassing), § 18.2–120 (1988) (instigating trespass to prevent the rendering of services to persons lawfully on the premises), § 18.2–404 (obstructing free passage of others), § 18.2–499 (conspiring to injure another in his business or profession). It is undeniably petitioners' purpose to target a protected class, on account of their class characteristics, and to prevent them from the equal enjoyment of these personal and property rights under law. The element of class-based discrimination that *Griffin* read into § 1985(3) should require no further showing.

I cannot agree with the Court that the use of unlawful means to achieve one's goal "is not relevant to [the] discussion of animus." * * * To the contrary, the deliberate decision to isolate members of a vulnerable group and physically prevent them from conducting legitimate activities cannot be irrelevant in assessing motivation. * * * The clinics at issue are lawful operations; the women who seek their services do so lawfully. In my opinion, petitioners' unlawful conspiracy to prevent the clinics from serving those women, who are targeted by petitioners by virtue of their class characteristics, is a group-based, private deprivation of the "equal protection of the laws" within the reach of § 1985(3).

The Court finds an absence of discriminatory animus by reference to our decisions construing the scope of the Equal Protection Clause, and reinforces its conclusion by recourse to the dictionary definition of the word "invidious." * * * The first step would be fitting if respondents were challenging state action; they do not. The second would be proper if the word "invidious" appeared in the statute we are construing; it does not. As noted above, *Griffin*'s requirement of "class-based, invidiously discriminatory animus" was a shorthand description of the congressional purpose behind the legislation that became § 1985(3). Microscopic examination of the language we chose in *Griffin* should not now substitute for giving effect to Congress' intent in enacting the relevant legislative language, *i.e.*, "that any violation of the right, the *animus* and effect of which is to strike down the citizen, to the end that he [or she] may not enjoy equality of rights as contrasted with * * * other citizens' rights, shall be within the scope of the remedies of this section." Cong.Globe, 42d Cong., 1st Sess. 478 (1871) (Rep. Shellabarger).

Because § 1985(3) is a statute that was designed to address deprivations caused by *private* actors, the Court's invocation of our cases construing the reach of the Equal Protection Clause of the Fourteenth Amendment is misplaced. * * *

In today's case, I see no reason to hold a § 1985(3) plaintiff to the constitutional standard of invidious discrimination that we have employed in our Fourteenth Amendment jurisprudence. To be sure, the language of that Amendment's Equal Protection Clause and § 1985(3) are similar, and "[a] century of Fourteenth Amendment adjudication has * * * made it understandably difficult to conceive of what might constitute a deprivation of the equal protection of the laws by private persons." *Griffin*, 403 U.S., at 97, 91 S.Ct., at 1796. The Court resolves that difficulty by construing the two provisions in tandem, although there surely is no requirement that we do so. Cf. *Romero v. International Terminal Operating Co.*, 358 U.S. 354, 378–379, 79 S.Ct. 468, 484–485, 3 L.Ed.2d 368 (1959) (explaining that statutory grant of "arising under" jurisdiction need not mirror the reach of Art. III "arising under" jurisdiction).

I would focus not on the similarities of the two provisions, but on their differences. The Equal Protection Clause guarantees that no State shall "*deny* to any person within its jurisdiction the equal protection of the laws." U.S. Const., Amdt. 14, § 1 (emphasis added). In my view, § 1985(3) does not simply repeat that guarantee, but provides a complement to it: no private actor may conspire with the purpose of "*depriving* * * * any person or class of persons of the equal protection of the laws." (Emphasis added.) Unlike "deny," which connotes a withholding, the word "deprive" indicates an intent to prevent private actors from taking away what the State has seen fit to bestow.

The distinction in choice of words is significant in light of the interrelated objectives of the two provisions. The Fourteenth Amendment protects against state action, but it "erects no shield against merely private conduct, however discriminatory or wrongful." *Shelley v. Kraemer,* 334 U.S. 1, 13, 68 S.Ct. 836, 842, 92 L.Ed. 1161 (1948). Section 1985(3), by contrast, was "meant to reach private action." *Griffin, supra,* 403 U.S., at 101, 91 S.Ct., at 1798. Given that difference in focus, I would not interpret "discriminatory animus" under the statute to establish the same high threshold that must be met before this Court will find that a State has engaged in invidious discrimination in violation of the Constitution. As the 42d Congress well appreciated, private actors acting in groups can be as devastating to the exercise of civil rights as hostile state actors, and they pose an even greater danger because they operate in an unregulated realm divorced from the responsibilities and checking functions of government. In recognition of that danger, I would hold that *Griffin's* element of class-based discrimination is met whenever private conspirators target their actions at members of a protected class, by virtue of their class characteristics, and deprive them of their equal enjoyment of the rights accorded them under law.

This case is not about abortion. It most assuredly is not about "the disfavoring of abortions" by state legislatures. *Ante,* * * * (discussing *Maher v. Roe,* 432 U.S. 464, 97 S.Ct. 2376, 53 L.Ed.2d 484 (1977); *Harris v. McRae,* 448 U.S. 297, 100 S.Ct. 2671, 65 L.Ed.2d 784 (1980)). Rather, this case is about whether a private conspiracy to deprive members of a protected class of legally protected interests gives rise to a federal cause of action. In my view, it does, because that is precisely the sort of conduct that the 42d Congress sought to address in the legislation now codified at § 1985(3). Our precedents construing the scope of gender discrimination under the Fourteenth Amendment should not distract us from properly interpreting the scope of the statutory remedy.

II

The second reason the majority offers for reversing the decision below is that petitioners' activities did not intentionally deprive the clinics and their clients of a right guaranteed against private impairment, a requirement that the Court previously has grafted onto the *first* clause of § 1985(3). See *Carpenters,* 463 U.S., at 833, 103 S.Ct., at 3358–3359. I find it unnecessary to address the merits of this argument, however, as I am content to rest my analysis solely on the basis that respondents are entitled to invoke the protections of a federal court under the *second* clause of § 1985(3). * * *

Respondents attempted to brief the issue for the Court in a supplemental brief on reargument, but the effort was rejected by a majority of the Court. * * * Although the issue is open to be decided on remand, I agree with Justice Stevens that "[r]espondents have unquestionably established a claim under the second clause of § 1985(3), the state hindrance provision." * * *

III

In *Griffin,* this Court "resurrect[ed]" § 1985(3) "from its interment under *Collins v. Hardyman,* 341 U.S. 651, 71 S.Ct. 937, 95 L.Ed. 1253

(1951)," to hold that the statute provided a federal remedy for those injured by purely private conspiracies. *Novotny, supra,* 442 U.S., at 395, n. 19, 99 S.Ct., at 2361, n. 19 (WHITE, J., dissenting). That resurrection proved a false hope indeed. The statute was intended to provide a federal means of redress to the targets of private conspiracies seeking to accomplish their political and social goals through unlawful means. Today the Court takes yet another step in restricting the scope of the statute, to the point where it now cannot be applied to a modern-day paradigm of the situation the statute was meant to address. I respectfully dissent.

Notes on Bray

1. If, as Justice Scalia reasons in *Bray,* "a tax on wearing yarmulkes is a tax on Jews," why does it not follow that an attack on abortion is an attack on women? True, not all women have abortions. Do all Jews wear yarmulkes? Justice Scalia relies on *Geduldig* for the proposition that not all classifications based on pregnancy constitute discrimination based on sex, but he fails to quote the famous (and much ridiculed) distinction drawn by then-Justice Rehnquist in *Geduldig's* footnote 20:

> "The lack of identity between the excluded disability and gender as such under this insurance program becomes clear upon the most cursory analysis. The program divides potential recipients into two groups—pregnant women and nonpregnant persons. While the first group is exclusively female, the second includes members of both sexes."

As discussed in Chapter Three, infra, the Court later applied this distinction to the provision of Title VII of the Civil Rights Act prohibiting discrimination in employment based on sex. Congress subsequently amended the statute to repeal that application of the Court's analysis. But Congress, acting alone, cannot change the Court's interpretation of the Constitution. Does *Bray* lay the basis for a revival of *Geduldig?* Professor Cass Sunstein's view of this matter (cited by Justice Stevens in footnote 20) is that "If a law said that 'no woman' may obtain an abortion, it should readily be seen as a sex-based classification. A law saying that 'no person' may obtain an abortion has the same meaning." Cass R. Sunstein, Neutrality in Constitutional Law (With Special Reference to Pornography, Abortion, and Surrogacy), 92 Colum.L.Rev. 1, 32–33 (1992). Does Justice Scalia have a satisfactory response to that argument?

2. Another effort to use the Ku Klux Act against Operation Rescue arose in California. National Abortions Federation v. Operation Rescue, 8 F.3d 680 (9th Cir.1993) accepted *Bray* as foreclosing the plaintiffs' claims under the "deprivation" clause of the statute, but went on to decide that injunctive and declaratory relief might issue under the second ("hindrance") clause of the statute—a question left open by the Supreme Court. Judge Hug, trying to read the tea leaves in *Bray,* noted that Justice White's resignation left the Court composed of "four justices [who] have indicated in dictum that the hindrance clause should be interpreted with the same restrictions as the deprivation clause and four justices [who] interpret the hindrance clause more broadly." Id., at 683. He concluded:

> There is a significant distinction between the clauses. The deprivation clause concerns conspiracies of some private persons to commit tortious actions against other private persons. The restrictions of *Griffin* and *Carpenters* leave most of such activity to be handled by state enforcement. The

hindrance clause, on the other hand, concerns conspiracies to thwart state law enforcement from protecting against such tortious activities.

Id., at 685. This distinction enabled the court to

> * * * conclude that a conspiracy to prevent or hinder state law enforcement officers from securing the constitutional right to an abortion for women, a class exclusively seeking to exercise that right, is actionable under the hindrance clause of section 1985(3) * * *. The allegations of the complaint state the type of nationwide conspiracy to prevent or hinder state law enforcement from securing and protecting women in the exercise of a constitutional right that is analogous to the type of conspiracy to hinder state law enforcement that brought about the original enactment of the hindrance clause of section 1985(3).

Id., at 687. Judge Trott concurred in the holding that *Bray* foreclosed any claim under the "deprivation" clause, but he agreed with Justice Scalia's dictum that the same result would follow under the "hindrance" clause, and therefore dissented from that part of the judgment. Noting that the court faced "a practical dilemma caused by a new justice on the court who has yet to be heard on this contentious issue", he added that "an already well-informed Supreme Court will surely decide this issue in short order." Id., at 687, 688 (concurring and dissenting opinion). How do you think Justice Ruth Bader Ginsburg would decide this issue?

3.   Justice Ginsburg voted with a unanimous court in National Organization for Women, Inc. v. Scheidler, 510 U.S. 249, 114 S.Ct. 798, 127 L.Ed.2d 99 (1994), in holding that the Racketeer Influenced and Corrupt Organizations (RICO) chapter of the Organized Crime Control Act of 1970 does not require proof that either the racketeering enterprise or the predicate acts of racketeering were motivated by an economic motive. Accordingly, NOW's suit against a coalition of antiabortion groups called the Pro–Life Action Network (PLAN), Scheidler and other individuals, alleging that respondents were members of a nationwide conspiracy to shut down abortion clinics through a pattern of racketeering activity including extortion, was allowed to proceed to trial. Noting that the statute nowhere expressly required any economic motive, Chief Justice Rehnquist pointed out that "predicate acts, such as the alleged extortion, may not benefit the protestors financially but still may drain money from the economy by harming businesses such as the clinics which are petitioners in this case." Id., 114 S.Ct. at 805, 127 L.Ed.2d at ___.

4.   As *Bray* makes clear, the public confrontation over abortion is being fought at the clinic door. The challenge of balancing women's constitutionally-protected rights to privacy in reproductive health matters against the First Amendment rights of abortion protesters was recently on the agenda of Congress.

S. 636, the Freedom of Access to Clinic Entrances Act of 1994, is a measure establishing Federal criminal penalties (fines ranging from $10,000 to $25,000 and imprisonment from six months to three years; if death results, for an unlimited term or for life) and civil remedies (including injunctive relief, and compensatory and punitive damages) against anyone who commits violent, threatening, obstructive and destructive conduct that is intended to injure, intimidate or interfere with persons seeking to obtain or provide reproductive health services. The measure expressly applies only to conduct occurring on or after its effective date. Opponents of the bill charged that, because it levies heavy fines on some nonviolent acts—such as chaining protesters to clinic doorways—the measure would have prevented the civil rights demonstrations against segregated lunch counters in the

South during the 1960s. The New York Times, May 13, 1994, at A11, col. 6. Do you agree? Does the measure create serious First Amendment problems? To date, the "Access Act" has uniformly been upheld as constitutional. See, e.g., American Life League, Inc. v. Reno, 47 F.3d 642 (4th Cir.1995), certiorari denied ___ U.S. ___, 116 S.Ct. 55, 133 L.Ed.2d 19 (1995); United States v. Wilson, 73 F.3d 675 (7th Cir.1995), petition for certiorari filed March 20, 1996 (No. 95–1523).

5. Does Justice Scalia fail to appreciate the extent to which the anti-abortionists' "blockades reflected and perpetuated stereotypical notions about women's proper roles"? See David H. Gans, Note: Stereotyping and Difference: *Planned Parenthood v. Casey* and the Future of Sex Discrimination Law, 104 Yale L. J. 1875 (1995), proposing a new analysis based on stereotyping.

4. STERILIZATION

WALKER v. PIERCE

United States Court of Appeals, Fourth Circuit, 1977.
560 F.2d 609, certiorari denied 434 U.S. 1075, 98 S.Ct. 1266, 55 L.Ed.2d 782 (1978).

ALBERT V. BRYAN, SENIOR CIRCUIT JUDGE:

Violation of their civil rights was laid, in this action for damages and declaratory and injunctive relief by Virgil Walker and Shirley Brown, black females, to Clovis H. Pierce, the attending obstetrician at the Aiken County Hospital in South Carolina for sterilizing them, or threatening to do so, solely on account of their race and number of their children, while they were receiving medical assistance under the Medicaid program. The other defendants, the Chairman of the Board of Trustees of the Hospital, its Administrator, the Director of the Department of Social Services of Aiken County, the State Commissioner of the Department of Social Services of South Carolina and the Hospital, are charged with conspiring or acting in concert with Dr. Pierce in the unlawful acts imputed to him.

Verdicts, those directed and those returned by the jury, went for the defendants except Pierce, against whom the jury assessed damages of $5.00 in favor of Shirley Brown. Judgments were passed accordingly, including denial of declaratory and injunctive relief. On plaintiffs' appeals we affirm; on the obstetrician's we reverse.

THE COMPLAINT

As faultlessly put in the plaintiffs' brief: "The essence of the complaint was that Medicaid recipients were being required to consent to undergo a tubal ligation if they were delivering a third living child."

Centering the controversy is the policy previously announced and constantly pursued in practice by the doctor, testified to by him as follows:

> "My policy was with people who were unable to financially support themselves, whether they be on Medicaid or just unable to pay their own bills, if they were having a third child, to request they voluntarily submit to sterilization following the delivery of the third child. If they did not wish this as a condition for my care, then I requested that they seek another physician other than myself."

There is no question of his professional qualifications or experience.

As drawn by the plaintiffs, he is the arch-offender. The accusation is incursion upon their Constitutional rights of privacy, due process of law and equal protection of the law as well as of their statutory privileges against discrimination on account of their race and color, all by subjecting or threatening the plaintiffs as citizens of the United States with involuntary sterilization. These deprivations, they further say, are the result of the effectuation of Pierce's policy under color of State law, that is, under the Medicaid program administered by South Carolina. His codefendants, to repeat, are impleaded for conspiring and acting in concert with him, and for acquiescing in his unlawful conduct. 42 U.S.C.A. §§ 1981, 1983, 1985(3) and 2000d. Personal injury has been suffered, each plaintiff asserts, as a direct consequence of acts of the defendants under this policy.

Now to follow are the facts as elicited by the plaintiffs from their evidence, but denied by the defendants as inculpations of them.

PLAINTIFF WALKER

Virgil Walker had completed the seventh grade, was separated from her husband and was receiving Aid to Families with Dependent Children and Medicaid benefits. Expecting her fourth child, she first went to Pierce on January 7, 1972. During this consultation, he discussed family planning and his sterilization policy. Walker refused to consent. The issue again came up at the second visit and she again declined. Walker testified that Pierce threatened to have her State assistance terminated unless she cooperated. She called another doctor, but he was not taking new patients.

On February 4, 1972, Spears, a Department of Social Services caseworker assigned to Walker, received a note from Pierce's office asking that he talk with Walker about sterilization. Thereupon, Spears, according to his testimony, spoke with her on February 17th, offering to get her a second doctor. On the other hand, Walker stated that Spears had said there was nothing he could do. Then she returned to Pierce and subsequently signed a consent form for sterilization.

Her fourth child was delivered at the Aiken County Hospital April 16, 1972 by Dr. Billy Burke, an obstetrician who substituted for Pierce on occasion. Burke discussed tubal ligation with Walker. Her response was that she did not want additional children and understood that it would be a permanent sterilization. Two more consent forms were then signed. Pierce performed the operation April 17, 1972. She protested no further because, she said, it would have been futile.

Walker's hospital bills and doctor's fees were paid by Medicaid. Under the South Carolina plan operated by the Department of Social Services, the patient-physician relationship is one of free choice for both parties. The physician, under no contract with the State, simply submits his bill when treatment is concluded to the Medicaid insurance carrier instead of the patient.

PLAINTIFF BROWN

Shirley Brown consulted Pierce regarding her third pregnancy. She, too, was separated from her husband and had taken job maternity leave from Seminole Mills. On her initial visit, Brown paid Pierce $50.00. Sterilization was not discussed. A $250.00 balance due on his fee was satisfied in part by Brown and her husband and partially by the health insurance plan at the mill.

At the end of August 1973, Brown qualified for Medicaid benefits. She was delivered of her third child at the Hospital September 2, 1973 by a doctor other than Pierce. The hospital bills, not Pierce's fees, were to be paid by Medicaid. After the delivery, Pierce requested his nurse to obtain Brown's consent to sterilization. Brown refused. Upon word of her refusal, Pierce saw no necessity for further hospitalization and ordered her discharge and release from the Hospital.

Her mother intervened, offering to pay the hospital bill, but Brown left September 3, 1973, "afraid something might happen to her." Protest was made to the defendant Nesbit, Hospital Administrator, who suggested she file a complaint with the Board of Trustees since he had no control over a doctor's discharge of patients. At trial, Brown's attorney conceded that she sustained no actual damages in leaving the Hospital.

The Defendants

Defendant Nesbit stated that he first learned of Pierce's policy in July, 1973 from newspaper accounts appearing in the local papers. He reported it to the Chief of Obstetrics and Gynecology at the Hospital but at that time he received no answer as to anything he should do.

Defendant Poore, Director of the Aiken County Department of Social Services since March 23, 1972, testified that he also originally learned of Pierce's policy from press items on July 17, 1973. He called a staff meeting and arranged for a doctor in Augusta, Georgia to see obstetric patients. Transportation for them was provided by the Department.

Defendant Ellis, State Commissioner of DSS, became aware of the sterilization policy through July, 1973 news accounts. He fixed a meeting for July 26 between Pierce, a Medicaid deputy and a State attorney general. An investigation included a review of records of Pierce's patients and interviews with Medicaid recipients sterilized at the Hospital in the first six months of 1973.[4] Early September, Ellis and a State attorney general met with Pierce and his attorney. Ellis asked Pierce to sign an affidavit stating that he would not discriminate against Medicaid patients. Pierce declined. Finally Ellis wrote Pierce September 27, 1973 that his continued refusal to sign the affidavit forced the Department to impose a non-payment sanction for Pierce's submitted Medicaid bills. Pierce no longer treated Medicaid patients. From January 1, 1972 to June 30, 1973 the doctor had received $60,000 in Medicaid fees.

The Verdicts and Judgments

The claims against Poda, Chairman of the Board of the Hospital, were withdrawn. In the Walker action under section 1981 verdicts were directed for all of the defendants except Dr. Pierce, Nesbit individually and as Administrator of the Hospital and the Hospital itself, but the jury returned a

---

4. The investigation revealed 50 Medicaid deliveries and 18 Medicaid tubal ligations during this period. Forty of the deliveries and 17 of the ligations were done by Pierce. Of the 50 deliveries, 42 women were black, 32 single, nine separated, eight married and one widowed. Sixteen women sterilized were black and either single or separated; one was white and separated and one was black and married.

verdict for the latter defendants; in the Walker action under section 1983, verdicts were directed for all defendants except Dr. Pierce and Nesbit, but the verdict acquitted these two. In Brown's action under section 1981, directed verdicts were granted for all defendants, except Pierce, Poore and the Hospital, but the jury found for them. In Brown's action under section 1983, verdicts were instructed for all defendants except Dr. Pierce and Poore. However, the jury found for Poore but against Dr. Pierce assessing damages at $5.00 "Nominal Damages".

As weighed by the Court, the evidence was not sufficient to permit a finding of a conspiracy under section 1985(3), and, therefore, the case was not submitted to the jury on that count, directed verdicts going for all the defendants. Judgments, with costs, went accordingly. Motions for new trials were denied, as was a motion for judgment n.o.v. by Dr. Pierce. Previously the Court had denied plaintiffs' request for a class action under Rule 23(a), (b)(1) and (b)(2) F.R.Civ.P.

The claim for a class action was not argued before the court but the plaintiffs noted that they reserved the point. The Court did not abuse its discretion in refusing the request and the record confirms the soundness of this resolution. Nor is error apparent in the directed verdicts. The proof was not adequate to establish discrimination, racial or otherwise, conspiracy, or recklessness or want of good faith, as to those favored by the directions, and the jury found none save against Pierce under 1983. Therefore, without further discussion we affirm as to all defendants in each case save as to the verdict against Dr. Pierce. In his instance we reverse and enter final judgment.

The Case Against Dr. Pierce

We perceive no reason why Dr. Pierce could not establish and pursue the policy he has publicly and freely announced. Nor are we cited to judicial precedent or statute inhibiting this personal economic philosophy. Particularly is this so when all persons coming to him as patients are seasonably made fully aware of his professional attitude toward the increase in offspring and his determination to see it prevail. At no time is he shown to have forced his view upon any mother. Indeed, quite the opposite appears. In the single occasion in this case of a sterilization by this doctor, not just one but three formal written consents were obtained—the first before delivery of the fourth child and two afterwards.

But if his conduct is nevertheless to be judged by the factors of section 1983, Dr. Pierce was not a violator. He was not acting under color of State law when treating the only successful plaintiff, Brown. His fee for her delivery was paid by her and her employer's insurance plan; there was no use of Medicaid money. Incidentally, he did not sterilize her; the tort charged to him is his discharge and release of her from the Hospital, an accepted procedure there. Receipt by the Hospital of Hill–Burton funds, 42 U.S.C. 291 et seq. did not convert Dr. Pierce into a participant in a Federal program and thus in State action. Ascherman v. Presbyterian Hospital, 507 F.2d 1103, 1105 (9 Cir.1974). No decision has been advanced holding that a physician by simply practicing in such an institution acts under color of State law. Certainly the Fourth Circuit did not do so in its line of decisions on the question terminating in Doe v. Charleston Area Medical Center, Inc., 529 F.2d 638 (1975).

The judgments of the District Court are affirmed except that granted Shirley Brown against Clovis H. Pierce, which is reversed with final judgment for the defendant.

Affirmed in part; reversed in part; and final judgment.

BUTZNER, CIRCUIT JUDGE, concurring in part and dissenting in part:

I join in affirming the judgments in favor of the hospital, its officers, and the state and county officials. The evidence did not prove them to be willful participants in Dr. Pierce's practice of sterilizing Medicaid patients.

I dissent from the reversal of the judgment against Dr. Pierce. The facts and the law fully justify the district judge's ruling that Dr. Pierce was acting under color of state law within the meaning of 42 U.S.C.A. § 1983.

At the outset, it is necessary to note the distinction between Dr. Pierce's professional role as a physician treating Medicaid patients and his role as a participant in the fiscal and administrative aspects of the Medicaid program. Title 42 U.S.C.A. § 1396a, dealing with state plans for the Medicaid program, is designed to avoid governmental intrusion in the doctor-patient relationship. "[T]he very heart of the congressional scheme is that the physician and patient should have complete freedom to choose those medical procedures for a given condition which are best suited to the needs of the patient." Beal v. Doe, 432 U.S. 438, 450, 97 S.Ct. 2366, 2374, 53 L.Ed.2d 464 (1977) (Brennan, J., dissenting). Thus, a physician paid by Medicaid does not act as an agent of the state or under color of its laws when he decides what medical care and services his patient's health requires. Cf. Byrne v. Kysar, 347 F.2d 734, 736 (7th Cir.1965); Duzynski v. Nosal, 324 F.2d 924, 929 (7th Cir.1963). Consequently, it is necessary to ascertain whether Dr. Pierce's policy of sterilizing Medicaid patients was based on considerations of their health.

When Dr. Pierce treated a patient who could pay for delivery of her child, he did not exact consent for sterilization regardless of the number of her children. If, however, the patient already had more than two children and her bill was to be paid by Medicaid, he refused to treat her unless she consented to sterilization. One witness testified:

> He came in and he hadn't examined me or anything. I was laying on the table. And, he said, "Listen here young lady." He said, "This is my tax money paying for something like this." He said, "I am tired of people going around here having babies and my tax money paying for it." He said, "So, if you don't want this done, you go and find yourself another doctor."

Dr. Pierce's policy of requiring sterilization of Medicaid patients is also illustrated by his treatment of Mrs. Shirley Brown. As long as it appeared that her expenses were being paid from private funds, Dr. Pierce was content to accept her as a patient without conditioning either his services or her hospitalization on her consent to sterilization. When he learned from hospital records that her hospital bill was being paid by Medicaid, he directed a nurse to obtain her consent to sterilization. Upon Mrs. Brown's refusal, he ordered her discharged from the hospital.

Had Dr. Pierce's decisions to sterilize his patients been based on their medical needs, he would not have acted under color of state law within the meaning of § 1983. See e.g., Byrne v. Kysar, 347 F.2d 734 (7th Cir.1965); Duzynski v. Nosal, 324 F.2d 924 (7th Cir.1963). However, the foregoing evidence establishes beyond doubt that Dr. Pierce's policy pertaining to sterilization was based on economic factors instead of the health of his Medicaid patients. It is clear that he undertook to grant or deny Medicaid benefits for reasons unrelated to his patients' health. It therefore becomes necessary to determine next whether Dr. Pierce's policy of sterilization for economic reasons establishes that he was acting under color of state law.

There is no litmus test for ascertaining whether an ostensibly private person is in fact acting under color of state law. "Only by sifting facts and weighing circumstances can the nonobvious involvement of the State in private conduct be attributed its true significance." Burton v. Wilmington Parking Authority, 365 U.S. 715, 722, 81 S.Ct. 856, 860, 6 L.Ed.2d 45 (1961). This inquiry must determine "whether there is a sufficiently close nexus between the State and the challenged action of * * * [the person under scrutiny] so that the action of the latter may be fairly treated as that of the State itself." Jackson v. Metropolitan Edison Co., 419 U.S. 345, 351, 95 S.Ct. 449, 453, 42 L.Ed.2d 477 (1974). Action under color of law may be found when (A) the state is involved in the questioned activity, or (B) the private actor has assumed a state or public function. See Greco v. Orange Memorial Hospital Corp., 513 F.2d 873, 878 (5th Cir.1975). Among the significant factors to be considered are the private person's operation as an integral part of a comprehensive governmental program and his consequent receipt of substantial public funds. Sams v. Ohio Valley General Hospital Assoc., 413 F.2d 826, 828 (4th Cir.1969); Simkins v. Moses H. Cone Memorial Hospital, 323 F.2d 959, 967 (4th Cir.1963). Applying these principles, I believe Dr. Pierce acted under color of state law.

In this case, the state's involvement is readily apparent. The questioned activity is the grant or denial of Medicaid benefits for fiscal reasons unrelated to a patient's health. Under the Medicaid statute, the state is responsible for ascertaining which women are entitled to receive Medicaid benefits for the delivery of their children. Because the state is involved in the activity under scrutiny, one criterion for applying § 1983 is satisfied.

Furthermore, the evidence discloses that Dr. Pierce assumed a state function. South Carolina does not contract directly with physicians to participate in Medicaid; rather, qualified doctors are free to accept Medicaid patients, if they choose. Under this arrangement, a pregnant woman can select a participating doctor of her choice, and the doctor can accept or reject the patient. Freedom of choice on the part of both physician and patient is assured as an essential part of the program. When a physician accepts a Medicaid patient, the state is not made aware of the relationship until the doctor's bill is presented to the state's agent (a private insurance company) for processing and payment. By these procedures the state delegates much of its administrative responsibility for the operation of the Medicaid program to individual doctors. Therefore, a doctor who represents himself to the public as a qualified Medicaid practitioner assumes a state or public administrative function when he conditions the grant or denial of Medicaid benefits on requirements not connected with the patient's health.

Dr. Pierce was free to decline to treat any or all persons dependent on Medicaid. He opted to participate in the program and accepted patients entitled to receive Medicaid. He undertook an administrative function when he insisted for economic reasons unrelated to health that a patient otherwise entitled to the delivery of her child by the physician of her choice at Medicaid expense should be sterilized. Finally, as further indication of his operation as an integral part of a comprehensive governmental program, Medicaid paid Dr. Pierce more than $60,000 during the time when the events giving rise to this suit occurred.

These facts and circumstances fully warrant the district judge's conclusion that Dr. Pierce was acting under color of state law. The nexus between the state and Dr. Pierce was sufficient to establish that his sterilization of Medicaid patients for economic reasons not related to their health can be fairly treated as the action of the state. In fact, Dr. Pierce was his patients' most important contact with the state program. Therefore, I would affirm the district judge's ruling that Dr. Pierce was acting under color of law within the meaning of 42 U.S.C.A. § 1983.

Notes on Walker

1. Why is Dr. Pierce permitted to establish his own eligibility test for Medicaid benefits? Is it sufficient to say, as the majority suggest, that his patients were free to consult other physicians? What if no other physician is readily available? Apart from your opinion of Dr. Pierce's "personal economic philosophy", what do you make of the dissent's characterization of his practice as an action "under color of state law"? Compare Downs v. Sawtelle, 574 F.2d 1 (1st Cir.1978), cert. denied 439 U.S. 910, 99 S.Ct. 278, 58 L.Ed.2d 255 (1978), holding that the physician who sterilized plaintiff without her consent was acting under color of state law because he was the Chief of Staff of defendant Milo Community Hospital. Was *Walker* correctly decided?

2. Is sterilization psychologically more damaging to men than to women? Dr. Peter Forbes thinks it is, finding that while women "usually do not confuse the feminine role with reproductive capacity after they have given birth to a number of children," men, who confuse "fertility, virility and masculinity," are "often emotionally unstrung by the surgery." Peter R. Forbes, Voluntary Sterilization of Women as a Right, 18 De Paul L.Rev. 560, 561 (1969). But what about the depression of many women occasioned by their loss of fertility at menopause?

3. Since sterilization for birth control reasons is entirely lawful in most states, and civil liability can be prevented by execution of proper consent forms coupled with a clear understanding on the part of doctor and patient alike that the success of the operation is not guaranteed, see Linda K. Champlin & Mark E. Winslow, Note, Elective Sterilization, 113 U.Penn.L.Rev. 415, 427–39 (1965), why has access to the procedure been so restricted? A Philadelphia survey found that doctors were concerned about the quality of their patients' request for sterilization: had they adequately considered the possibility of remarriage or the desire to replace a child who might die? But apart from these factors, the doctors were also concerned with loss of reputation that might accompany a conspicuously large sterilization practice and with potential legal liability. Id., at 421–27. One physician who also has a law degree has warned his colleagues that, medical complications aside, the legal consequences of a vasectomy may include such issues as "informed consent, failure of the operation to achieve its purpose,

residual sperm storage, pregnancy, paternity, adequate advice, and laboratory follow-up visits." John R. Feegel, How To Stay Out of Court If You Do Vasectomies, 49 Medical Economics 200, 201 (Nov. 6, 1972). The article gives advice on how to avoid these problems, and on how to build a solid defense case by holding on to such items as "excised segments of vas—cross-sectioned, stained and mounted under delicate glass for the whole jury to see." Id., at 206. See also, James F. McKenzie Note, Contraceptive Sterilization: The Doctor, The Patient, and the United States Constitution, 25 U.Fla.L.Rev. 327 (1973).

4. Should the consent of the patient's spouse to the sterilization be required? Hospital practice is uniform: the consent is a necessary prerequisite to the procedure. But although new research promises to develop procedures for female sterilization that do not require abdominal surgery with its accompanying hospitalization, see Jean L. Marx, Birth Control: Current Technology, Future Prospects, 179 Science 1222, 1224 (March 23, 1973), female tubal ligation is presently a hospital procedure while male vasectomy is commonly performed in a urologist's office. Nevertheless, most physicians also demand the wife's consent. See John R. Feegel, Note 3 above at 201. The most common reason given for this practice is that it protects the physician and hospital against civil suits based on interference with the marital relationship. Is this practice an interference with the individual's right of privacy? It has been suggested that, regardless of the physician's potential liability, the spouse's consent should be required to prevent possible future actions for divorce or annulment against the sterile spouse. Linda K. Champlin & Mark E. Winslow, Note, Elective Sterilization, 113 U.Penn.L.Rev. 415, 437–39 (1965). But what concern is this of the doctor? See generally American Public Health Association Recommended Program Guide For Voluntary Sterilization, 62 Am.J.Pub.H. 1265 (1972).

In Ponter v. Ponter, 135 N.J.Super. 50, 342 A.2d 574 (1975), the court issued a declaratory judgment to the effect that a married woman had a constitutional right to be sterilized without the consent of her husband. The parties had been living separate and apart for six years at the time of the court's decision; would the same result have been proper if the couple were living together? The court reasoned that:

> Women have emerged in our law from the status of their husband's chattels to the position of "frail vessels" and now finally to the recognition that women are individual persons with certain and absolute constitutional rights. Included within those rights is the right to procure an abortion or other operation without her husband's consent. A natural and logical corollary of those rights is a right to be sterilized without her husband's consent.

Id., 135 N.J.Super. at 56, 342 A.2d at 577–78.

5. Is compulsory sterilization after two children constitutionally permissible, given the magnitude of present concerns about the population crisis and the quality of life? If your answer is "yes," how do you decide which sex is to be sterilized? Men, because vasectomy is a simpler surgical procedure that requires no hospitalization? Women, because the performance of a salpingectomy immediately after the birth of a second child would make enforcement easier? Or should there be a lottery, with couples drawing lots to see who is to be designated the "sterilized" spouse? Does the Constitution require the sterilization of both spouses? See Jan Charles Gray, Compulsory Sterilization in a Free Society: Choices and Dilemmas, 41 U.Cinn.L.Rev. 529, 535–36 (1972). What will be the impact of the improved techniques for female sterilization?

The practice of compulsory sterilization for eugenic purposes has been greatly curtailed in recent years, perhaps because of the modern disbelief that mental illness and mental retardation are hereditary. But there is growing reason to believe that sterilization may be taken up by those whose primary interest lies in reducing the welfare rolls. As you might expect, the reported cases all involve welfare mothers. See generally Elyce Zenoff Ferster, Eliminating the Unfit—Is Sterilization the Answer?, 27 Ohio St.L.J. 591 (1966); Angela R. Holder, Compulsory Sterilization, in Law and Medicine, 221 J.A.M.A. 229 (July 10, 1972).

6. Dr. Pierce is not the sole adherent of the view that sterilization of poor women is an effective way to reduce the welfare rolls. Relf v. Weinberger, 372 F.Supp. 1196 (D.D.C.1974), permanently enjoined the use of federal funds for involuntary sterilizations and declared arbitrary and unreasonable regulations that had permitted such funding. The suit was subsequently dismissed as moot when H.E.W. withdrew the regulations. See Relf v. Weinberger, 565 F.2d 722 (D.C.Cir.1977). New regulations were proposed in final form on November 8, 1978. See 43 Fed.Reg. 52,165 (1978). Plaintiffs in *Relf* were two black girls, aged 12 and 14, who were surgically sterilized after their mother signed a consent form with an "X". The parents alleged that they did not understand the consequences of the surgery. See, generally, Dick Grosboll, Sterilization Abuse: Current State of the Law and Remedies for Abuse, 10 Golden Gate Univ.L.Rev. 1147 (Women's Law Forum, 1980).

7. After the Supreme Court decisions in *Roe* and *Doe,* is it unconstitutional for a municipal hospital established pursuant to state law to deny the use of its facilities for the performance of voluntary sterilizations for both men and women? In Hathaway v. Worcester City Hospital, 475 F.2d 701 (1st Cir.1973), appellant Hathaway, who had had twelve pregnancies resulting in the birth of eight children, challenged as unconstitutional such an anti-sterilization policy adopted by defendant Worcester City Hospital. The facts disclosed that appellant was a married woman aged 36 at the time of the complaint, that she suffered from high blood pressure and an umbilical hernia which, in addition to the sheer number of past pregnancies, rendered future pregnancies a risk to her life. Due to her high blood pressure and heavy, irregular menstrual flow, she had been advised not to use birth control pills, intrauterine devices, or other methods of birth control. Her physician recommended a therapeutic sterilization, but the hospital administrator specifically refused to permit her physician to perform a tubal ligation at the time of delivery of her eighth child in 1971. Nor was the procedure permitted at a later time, although the request was apparently renewed. The First Circuit, reversing a district court judgment dismissing plaintiff's complaint, held the hospital's policy unconstitutional in reliance on *Roe* and *Doe.* See Lewis Olshin, Comment, Hathaway v. Worcester City Hospital—The Right to be Sterilized, 47 Temp.L.Q. 403 (1974).

Chapter III

WOMEN AND EMPLOYMENT

Introductory Note

The movement of American women from the home into the workforce has been one of the most dramatic economic developments of the past forty years. The number of women workers almost doubled between 1960 and 1980.[1] This dramatic increase continued throughout the 1980s, and by 1993 women composed 45.6 percent of the workforce: 58.4 million women were employed or seeking employment, compared to 69.6 million men.[2] Women's labor force participation rate is approaching that of men. In 1990, 58 percent of all women age 20 or above were in the labor force, compared to 78 percent of all men 20 years or older.[3] This trend has been due largely to the dramatic increase in the labor force participation of married women.[4] The sharpest increase has occurred among married mothers of young children: in 1960, 18.6 percent of married women with children under the age of 6 were working. By 1993, 59.6 percent of these women were in the labor force.[5] Among married women with school-age children, 75 percent were working or seeking work in 1993.[6] The proportion of women working full time has increased as well; three out of four employed adult women (20 years old and over) worked full time in 1990.[7] The number of women in a traditional housekeeping role has declined sharply. In 1962, the majority of women 25 to 54 years old kept house full time, while only 43 percent worked or sought work; by 1990 74 percent of women in this age group were in the workforce, and the number of full time homemakers dropped to 21 per cent.[8] Among all families in 1990, less than 20 percent met the traditional description of employed husband with wife at home.[9]

1. Statistical Abstract of the United States: 1994 (Table No. 616), U.S. Department of Commerce, Bureau of the Census (114th ed., 1994). In 1960, 23 million women were working or seeking work. By 1980, 45.5 million women were in the labor force. Id.

2. Id. at Table No. 615.

3. Working Women: A Chartbook (Table No. A–2), U.S. Department of Labor, Bureau of Labor Statistics, Bulletin 2385, August 1991. By the year 2005, the Bureau of Labor Statistics estimates that the gap between women and men will have narrowed to less than 12 points: 74.7% of men over 16 will be working and 63.2% of women. Statistical Abstract, supra note 1, at Table No. 615.

4. Statistical Abstract, supra note 1, Table No. 624. In 1960, 32% of married women worked. By 1993, 60% of all married women were working. Id.

5. Id. at Table No. 626.

6. Id. Among single mothers with school-age children, between the ages of 6 and 17, 70% were in the labor force. Among mothers of school-age children who were divorced, separated, or widowed, over 78% were in the labor force in 1993. Id.

7. Chartbook, supra note 3, at 14.

8. Id., at 31.

9. Chartbook, supra note 3, at Table No. A–17.

Despite women's significant contribution to the labor force, women earn less than men,[10] and find barriers to advancement into and within many professions.[11] In 1990, about 59 percent of employed women continued to work in just three broad occupational groupings: clerical, service, or sales. This represented a decline of only 5 percent since 1972 when 64 percent of women were employed in these relatively low paid job categories.[12] On the other hand, from 1972 to 1990, the proportion of employed women who were working in executive, administrative, or managerial jobs increased from 5 to 11 percent, and in professional specialty occupations, such as doctor or lawyer, the proportion of women so employed rose from 12 to 15 percent.[13]

The social, economic, and political implications of these developments have been subjected to intense study.[14] Our concern here with the results of such studies is only peripheral: what occupies the bulk of the materials that follow is an examination of the conceptual basis and practical implementation of laws designed to control the response of the labor market to the entry of large numbers of women workers. As we shall see, that response has largely been to segregate women into low-paying jobs that lack possibilities for advancement. Because the market has responded in essentially the same way to minority group workers, the history of antidiscrimination laws designed to improve the lot of minority group persons and women is inextricably intertwined.

A variety of laws has developed, at the state and federal level, to combat employment discrimination. One of these laws, Title VII of the Civil Rights Act of 1964, has had a greater impact than the others on job discrimination. It is given greatest attention here. It is an ironic accident of history, however, that women were included at all in Title VII in 1964. The Equal Pay Act, designed specifically to give women equal pay for equal work, had been enacted just a year earlier in 1963. On the last day of debate on the Civil Rights bill in the House of Representatives, a southern congressman and principal opponent of the legislation moved to amend the bill to add the word "sex" to the list of "race, color, religion, and national origin," as characteristics which employers would no longer be able to use as a basis for discriminatory action. The congressman's apparent purpose was to defeat the entire bill; even Congresswoman Edith Green, a supporter of

10. In 1990, women on average earned 71.8% of the median weekly earnings of men. Chartbook, supra note 3, at Table No. A–11. See also Susan McGee Bailey and Patricia B. Campbell, Gender Equality: The Unexamined Basic of School Reform, 4 Stan. L. & Pol'y Rev. 73 (1993)(the average women still earns only slightly more than two-thirds of a man's salary, but women's wages make a critically important contribution to family income. Wives contribute 50% of African American family income, 40% of Hispanic family income and 35% of white family income.)

11. Federal Glass Ceiling Commission, Good For Business: Making Full Use of the Nation's Human Capital, U.S. Departure of Labor (1995).

12. Chartbook, supra note 3, at 15 and Table A–8. In 1990, 27% of employed men worked in these job categories. Id.

13. Among men in the labor force in 1990, 14% worked in executive, administrative, or managerial jobs; 12% of men had a profession-al specialty occupation. A significant portion of men, 40%, were employed in production, craft, operator, fabrication, or laborer occupations, compared to only 11% of employed women. Id.

14. E.g., Barbara Reskin & Patricia A. Roos, Job Queues, Gender Queues: Explaining Women's Inroads into Male Occupations (1990); Clair Brown & Joseph A. Pechman, Gender in the Workplace (Brookings Institution 1987); Karen Shallcross Koziara, Michael H. Moskow, & Lucretia Dewey Tanner, Working Women: Past—Present—Future (Industrial Relations Research Association Series, BNA 1987); Karen Wolk Feinstein (ed.), Working Women and Families (1979); Juanita Morris Kreps (ed.), Women and the American Economy (The American Assembly, 1976); Elizabeth Janeway, Man's World, Woman's Place: A Study in Social Mythology (1971); Cynthia Fuchs Epstein, Woman's Place: Options and Limits in Professional Careers (1970); Valerie Kincade Oppenheimer, The Female Labor Force in the United States (1970).

women's rights, voted against the amendment. The landmark civil rights legislation, however, was enacted with the word "sex" included, but with no legislative history to assist in the statute's interpretation.[15] In 1991, as discussed below, Title VII was amended in significant ways, primarily in response to a variety of Supreme Court interpretations restricting the scope of the statute. It has now been thirty years since Title VII first went into effect in July 1965. Sufficient time has passed to ask ourselves what role the law has played or is able to play in changing the patterns of women's employment.

A. TITLE VII OF THE CIVIL RIGHTS ACT OF 1964

[Excerpts from Title VII appear in the Statutory Appendix]

1. THE LEGAL FRAMEWORK FOR TITLE VII LITIGATION

a. *Disparate Impact*

GRIGGS v. DUKE POWER CO.

Supreme Court of the United States, 1971.
401 U.S. 424, 91 S.Ct. 849, 28 L.Ed.2d 158.

MR. CHIEF JUSTICE BURGER delivered the opinion of the Court.

We granted the writ in this case to resolve the question whether an employer is prohibited by the Civil Rights Act of 1964, Title VII, from requiring a high school education or passing of a standardized general intelligence test as a condition of employment in or transfer to jobs when (a) neither standard is shown to be significantly related to successful job performance, (b) both requirements operate to disqualify Negroes at a substantially higher rate than white applicants, and (c) the jobs in question formerly had been filled only by white employees as part of a longstanding practice of giving preference to whites.

Congress provided, in Title VII of the Civil Rights Act of 1964, for class actions for enforcement of provisions of the Act and this proceeding was brought by a group of incumbent Negro employees against Duke Power Company. All the petitioners are employed at the Company's Dan River Steam Station, a power generating facility located at Draper, North Carolina. At the time this action was instituted, the Company had 95 employees at the Dan River Station, 14 of whom were Negroes; 13 of these are petitioners here.

The District Court found that prior to July 2, 1965, the effective date of the Civil Rights Act of 1964, the Company openly discriminated on the basis of race in the hiring and assigning of employees at its Dan River plant. The plant was organized into five operating departments: (1) Labor, (2) Coal Handling, (3) Operations, (4) Maintenance, and (5) Laboratory and Test. Negroes were employed only in the Labor Department where the highest paying jobs paid less than the lowest paying jobs in the other four "operating"

---

15. For accounts of this peculiar legislative history, see Leo Kanowitz, Women and the Law: the Unfinished Revolution 104–105 (1969); Caroline Bird, "Ladies Day in the House," in Born Female 1–15 (1969). See also Developments in the Law—Employment Discrimination and Title VII of the Civil Rights Act of 1964, 84 Harvard L. Rev. 1109, 1167 (1971).

departments in which only whites were employed.[2] Promotions were normally made within each department on the basis of job seniority. Transferees into a department usually began in the lowest position.

In 1955 the Company instituted a policy of requiring a high school education for initial assignment to any department except Labor, and for transfer from the Coal Handling to any "inside" department (Operations, Maintenance, or Laboratory). When the Company abandoned its policy of restricting Negroes to the Labor Department in 1965, completion of high school also was made a prerequisite to transfer from Labor to any other department. From the time the high school requirement was instituted to the time of trial, however, white employees hired before the time of the high school education requirement continued to perform satisfactorily and achieve promotions in the "operating" departments. Findings on this score are not challenged.

The Company added a further requirement for new employees on July 2, 1965, the date on which Title VII became effective. To qualify for placement in any but the Labor Department it became necessary to register satisfactory scores on two professionally prepared aptitude tests, as well as to have a high school education. Completion of high school alone continued to render employees eligible for transfer to the four desirable departments from which Negroes had been excluded if the incumbent had been employed prior to the time of the new requirement. In September 1965 the Company began to permit incumbent employees who lacked a high school education to qualify for transfer from Labor or Coal Handling to an "inside" job by passing two tests—the Wonderlic Personnel Test, which purports to measure general intelligence, and the Bennett Mechanical Comprehension Test. Neither was directed or intended to measure the ability to learn to perform a particular job or category of jobs. The requisite scores used for both initial hiring and transfer approximated the national median for high school graduates.[3]

The District Court had found that while the Company previously followed a policy of overt racial discrimination in a period prior to the Act, such conduct had ceased. The District Court also concluded that Title VII was intended to be prospective only and, consequently, the impact of prior inequities was beyond the reach of corrective action authorized by the Act.

The Court of Appeals was confronted with a question of first impression, as are we, concerning the meaning of Title VII. After careful analysis a majority of that court concluded that a subjective test of the employer's intent should govern, particularly in a close case, and that in this case there was no showing of a discriminatory purpose in the adoption of the diploma and test requirements. * * *

* * * In so doing, the Court of Appeals rejected the claim that because these two requirements operated to render ineligible a markedly dispropor-

---

2. A Negro was first assigned to a job in an operating department in August 1966, five months after charges had been filed with the Equal Employment Opportunity Commission. The employee, a high school graduate who had begun in the Labor Department in 1953, was promoted to a job in the Coal Handling Department.

3. The test standards are thus more stringent than the high school requirement, since they would screen out approximately half of all high school graduates.

tionate number of Negroes, they were unlawful under Title VII unless shown to be job related. * * *

The objective of Congress in the enactment of Title VII is plain from the language of the statute. It was to achieve equality of employment opportunities and remove barriers that have operated in the past to favor an identifiable group of white employees over other employees. Under the Act, practices, procedures, or tests, neutral on their face, and even neutral in terms of intent, cannot be maintained if they operate to "freeze" the status quo of prior discriminatory employment practices.

The Court of Appeals' opinion, and the partial dissent, agreed that, on the record in the present case, "whites register far better on the Company's alternative requirements" than Negroes.[6] 420 F.2d 1225, 1239 n. 6. This consequence would appear to be directly traceable to race. Basic intelligence must have the means of articulation to manifest itself fairly in a testing process. Because they are Negroes, petitioners have long received inferior education in segregated schools and this Court expressly recognized these differences in Gaston County v. United States, 395 U.S. 285, 89 S.Ct. 1720, 23 L.Ed.2d 309 (1969). There, because of the inferior education received by Negroes in North Carolina, this Court barred the institution of a literacy test for voter registration on the ground that the test would abridge the right to vote indirectly on account of race. Congress did not intend by Title VII, however, to guarantee a job to every person regardless of qualifications. In short, the Act does not command that any person be hired simply because he was formerly the subject of discrimination, or because he is a member of a minority group. Discriminatory preference for any group, minority or majority, is precisely and only what Congress has proscribed. What is required by Congress is the removal of artificial, arbitrary, and unnecessary barriers to employment when the barriers operate invidiously to discriminate on the basis of racial or other impermissible classification.

Congress has now provided that tests or criteria for employment or promotion may not provide equality of opportunity merely in the sense of the fabled offer of milk to the stork and the fox. On the contrary, Congress has now required that the posture and condition of the job-seeker be taken into account. It has—to resort again to the fable—provided that the vessel in which the milk is proffered be one all seekers can use. The Act proscribes not only overt discrimination but also practices that are fair in form, but discriminatory in operation. The touchstone is business necessity. If an employment practice which operates to exclude Negroes cannot be shown to be related to job performance, the practice is prohibited.

On the record before us, neither the high school completion requirement nor the general intelligence test is shown to bear a demonstrable relationship to successful performance of the jobs for which it was used. Both were

6. In North Carolina, 1960 census statistics show that, while 34% of white males had completed high school, only 12% of Negro males had done so. U.S. Bureau of the Census, U.S. Census of Population: 1960, Vol. 1, Characteristics of the Population, Part 35, Table 47.

Similarly, with respect to standardized tests, the EEOC in one case found that use of a battery of tests, including the Wonderlic and Bennett tests used by the Company in the instant case, resulted in 58% of whites passing the tests, as compared with only 6% of the blacks. Decision of EEOC, CCH Empl.Prac. Guide, ¶ 17,304.53 (Dec. 2, 1966). See also Decision of EEOC 70–552, CCH Empl.Prac. Guide, ¶ 6139 (Feb. 19, 1970).

adopted, as the Court of Appeals noted, without meaningful study of their relationship to job-performance ability. Rather, a vice president of the Company testified, the requirements were instituted on the Company's judgment that they generally would improve the overall quality of the work force.

The evidence, however, shows that employees who have not completed high school or taken the tests have continued to perform satisfactorily and make progress in departments for which the high school and test criteria are now used. The promotion record of present employees who would not be able to meet the new criteria thus suggests the possibility that the requirements may not be needed even for the limited purpose of preserving the avowed policy of advancement within the Company. In the context of this case, it is unnecessary to reach the question whether testing requirements that take into account capability for the next succeeding position or related future promotion might be utilized upon a showing that such long-range requirements fulfill a genuine business need. In the present case the Company has made no such showing.

The Court of Appeals held that the Company had adopted the diploma and test requirements without any "intention to discriminate against Negro employees." 420 F.2d, at 1232. We do not suggest that either the District Court or the Court of Appeals erred in examining the employer's intent; but good intent or absence of discriminatory intent does not redeem employment procedures or testing mechanisms that operate as "built-in headwinds" for minority groups and are unrelated to measuring job capability.

The Company's lack of discriminatory intent is suggested by special efforts to help the undereducated employees through Company financing of two-thirds the cost of tuition for high school training. But Congress directed the thrust of the Act to the *consequences* of employment practices, not simply the motivation. More than that, Congress has placed on the employer the burden of showing that any given requirement must have a manifest relationship to the employment in question.

The facts of this case demonstrate the inadequacy of broad and general testing devices as well as the infirmity of using diplomas or degrees as fixed measures of capability. History is filled with examples of men and women who rendered highly effective performance without the conventional badges of accomplishment in terms of certificates, diplomas, or degrees. Diplomas and tests are useful servants, but Congress has mandated the commonsense proposition that they are not to become masters of reality.

The Company contends that its general intelligence tests are specifically permitted by § 703(h) of the Act.[8] That section authorizes the use of "any professionally developed ability test" that is not "designed, intended *or used* to discriminate because of race.　* * *" (Emphasis added.)

The Equal Employment Opportunity Commission, having enforcement responsibility, has issued guidelines interpreting § 703(h) to permit only the use of job-related tests.[9] The administrative interpretation of the Act by the

8. Section 703(h) applies only to tests. It has no applicability to the high school diploma requirement.

9. EEOC Guidelines on Employment Testing Procedures, issued August 24, 1966, provide:

enforcing agency is entitled to great deference. See, e.g., United States v. City of Chicago, 400 U.S. 8, 91 S.Ct. 18, 27 L.Ed.2d 9 (1970); Udall v. Tallman, 380 U.S. 1, 85 S.Ct. 792, 13 L.Ed.2d 616 (1965); Power Reactor Co. v. Electricians, 367 U.S. 396, 81 S.Ct. 1529, 6 L.Ed.2d 924 (1961). Since the Act and its legislative history support the Commission's construction, this affords good reason to treat the guidelines as expressing the will of Congress.

Section 703(h) was not contained in the House version of the Civil Rights Act but was added in the Senate during extended debate. For a period, debate revolved around claims that the bill as proposed would prohibit all testing and force employers to hire unqualified persons simply because they were part of a group formerly subject to job discrimination. Proponents of Title VII sought throughout the debate to assure the critics that the Act would have no effect on job-related tests. Senators Case of New Jersey and Clark of Pennsylvania, comanagers of the bill on the Senate floor, issued a memorandum explaining that the proposed Title VII "expressly protects the employer's right to insist that any prospective applicant, Negro or white, *must meet the applicable job qualifications. Indeed, the very purpose of title VII is to promote hiring on the basis of job qualifications, rather than on the basis of race or color.*" 110 Cong.Rec. 7247. (Emphasis added.) Despite these assurances, Senator Tower of Texas introduced an amendment authorizing "professionally developed ability tests." Proponents of Title VII opposed the amendment because, as written, it would permit an employer to give any test, "whether it was a good test or not, so long as it was professionally designed. Discrimination could actually exist under the guise of compliance with the statute." 110 Cong. Rec. 13504 (remarks of Sen. Case).

The amendment was defeated and two days later Senator Tower offered a substitute amendment which was adopted verbatim and is now the testing provision of § 703(h). Speaking for the supporters of Title VII, Senator Humphrey, who had vigorously opposed the first amendment, endorsed the substitute amendment, stating: "Senators on both sides of the aisle who were deeply interested in title VII have examined the text of this amendment and have found it to be in accord with the intent and purpose of that title." 110 Cong. Rec. 13724. The amendment was then adopted. From the sum of the legislative history relevant in this case, the conclusion is inescapable that the EEOC's construction of § 703(h) to require that employment tests be job related comports with congressional intent.

Nothing in the Act precludes the use of testing or measuring procedures; obviously they are useful. What Congress has forbidden is giving these devices and mechanisms controlling force unless they are demonstrably a

---

"The Commission accordingly interprets 'professionally developed ability test' to mean a test which fairly measures the knowledge or skills required by the particular job or class of jobs which the applicant seeks, or which fairly affords the employer a chance to measure the applicant's ability to perform a particular job or class of jobs. The fact that a test was prepared by an individual or organization claiming expertise in test preparation does not, without more, justify its use within the meaning of Title VII."

The EEOC position has been elaborated in the New Guidelines on Employee Selection Procedures, 29 CFR § 1607, 35 Fed.Reg. 12333 (August 1, 1970). These guidelines demand that employers using tests have available "data demonstrating that the test is predictive of or significantly correlated with important elements of work behavior which comprise or are relevant to the job or jobs for which candidates are being evaluated." Id., at § 1607.4(c).

reasonable measure of job performance. Congress has not commanded that the less qualified be preferred over the better qualified simply because of minority origins. Far from disparaging job qualifications as such, Congress has made such qualifications the controlling factor, so that race, religion, nationality, and sex become irrelevant. What Congress has commanded is that any tests used must measure the person for the job and not the person in the abstract.

The judgment of the Court of Appeals is, as to that portion of the judgment appealed from, reversed.

Notes on Griggs

1. Does *Griggs* invalidate the high school diploma requirement for all employees of the Duke Power Company, or only for its black employees? Could the latter position be justified under an affirmative action rationale? See Kenneth M. Davidson, Preferential Treatment and Equal Opportunity, 55 Or.L.Rev. 53, 56 (1976)("The decision striking down the criterion did not create preferential treatment for uneducated blacks; it merely eliminated a non-functional device which had the effect of giving whites preferred treatment.") Can the same be said of an employer requirement that college and university professors hold the Ph.D. degree? See Campbell v. Ramsay, 484 F.Supp. 190 (E.D.Ark.1980), affirmed 631 F.2d 597 (8th Cir.1980), finding that the requirement had a disparate impact on women, but holding that the University of Arkansas had shown it to be a business necessity for professors of mathematics. See also Aguilera v. Cook County Police and Corrections Merit Board, 760 F.2d 844, 847–48 (7th Cir.1985), cert. denied 474 U.S. 907, 106 S.Ct. 237, 88 L.Ed.2d 238 (1985), in which Judge Posner upheld the employer's right to insist that its corrections officers have a high school diploma or a high-school-equivalence certificate, despite the disproportionate impact that requirement had on Hispanics, and observed:

> It is an ideal of our profession, if all too often an unattainable one, to make law certain; and there has now been enough judicial and professional experience with educational requirements in law enforcement to establish a presumption in civil rights cases that a high school education is an appropriate requirement for anyone who is going to be a policeman, or we add, a corrections officer (jail or prison guard), and therefore to excuse civil rights defendants from having to prove, over and over again, that such requirements really are necessary for such jobs.

Is Judge Posner's suggested presumption consistent with *Griggs*? See generally, for a penetrating criticism of "credentialism", David M. White and Richard L. Francis, Title VII and the Masters of Reality: Eliminating Credentialism in the American Labor Market, 64 Geo.L.J. 1213 (1976).

2. Did *Griggs* expand the coverage of Title VII in its adoption of disparate impact analysis? Professor Alfred W. Blumrosen, who immediately hailed the opinion in his article, Strangers in Paradise: Griggs v. Duke Power Co., and the Concept of Employment Discrimination, 71 Mich.L.Rev. 59 (1972), credits it fifteen years later with having "paved the way for the massive improvement in the occupational position of minorities and women * * *". Blumrosen, The Legacy of *Griggs:* Social Progress and Subjective Judgments, 63 Chicago–Kent L.Rev. 1, 3 (1987). Others, critical of the expansion, wish to return to the "original intent" of Congress in enacting Title VII. See Michael Evan Gold, *Griggs'* Folly: An Essay on the Theory, Problems, and Origin of the Adverse

Impact Definition of Employment Discrimination and a Recommendation for Reform, 7 Ind.Rel.L.J. 429 (1985). Professor George Rutherglen finds statutory support for the disparate impact doctrine in the very redundancy of the two main prohibitory sections of Title VII: §§ 703(a)(1) and 703(a)(2). The function of that redundancy, he argues, is to prevent avoidance, evasion and pretextual discrimination as well as overt discrimination. He concludes that:

> Both title VII and its legislative history reveal that Congress was aware of the problem of pretextual discrimination, but that it left this problem to be resolved by the federal courts. It was in *Griggs* that the Supreme Court—far from engaging in folly—devised a solution to the problem of pretextual discrimination.

Rutherglen, Disparate Impact Under Title VII: An Objective Theory of Discrimination, 73 Va.L.Rev. 1297, 1309 (1987). Who has it right?

3. Height and weight requirements frequently have a disparate impact on women. The Supreme Court addressed itself to this problem in Dothard v. Rawlinson, 433 U.S. 321, 97 S.Ct. 2720, 53 L.Ed.2d 786 (1977). The Alabama Board of Corrections had established a 120 pound minimum weight and a 5'2" minimum height for the position of prison guard. Plaintiffs convinced the district court that the height requirement would exclude 33.29% of American women between the ages of 18–79, while excluding only 1.28% of men between the same ages, and that the weight requirement would exclude 22.29% of the women and 2.35% of the men in the same age group. Combined, the requirements would exclude 41.13% of women, but less than 1% of men. The Court held that a prima facie case of unlawful sex discrimination had been established:

> The appellants argue that a showing of disproportionate impact on women based on generalized national statistics should not suffice to establish a prima facie case. They point in particular to Rawlinson's failure to adduce comparative statistics concerning actual applicants for correctional counselor positions in Alabama. There is no requirement, however, that a statistical showing of disproportionate impact must always be based on analysis of the characteristics of actual applicants. See Griggs v. Duke Power Co., 401 U.S., at 430, 91 S.Ct., at 853. The application process might itself not adequately reflect the actual potential applicant pool, since otherwise qualified people might be discouraged from applying because of a self-recognized inability to meet the very standards challenged as being discriminatory. See International Brotherhood of Teamsters v. United States, 431 U.S. 324, 363–365, 367–368, 97 S.Ct. 1843, 1869–1871, 52 L.Ed.2d 396. A potential applicant could easily measure her height and weight and conclude that to make an application would be futile. Moreover, reliance on general population demographic data was not misplaced where there was no reason to suppose that physical height and weight characteristics of Alabama men and women differ markedly from those of the national population.

> For these reasons, we cannot say that the District Court was wrong in holding that the statutory height and weight standards had a discriminatory impact on women applicants. The plaintiffs in a case such as this are not required to exhaust every possible source of evidence, if the evidence actually presented on its face conspicuously demonstrates a job requirement's grossly discriminatory impact. If the employer discerns fallacies or deficiencies in the data offered by the plaintiff, he is free to adduce countervailing evidence of his own. In this case no such effort was made.

Id., 433 U.S. at 330–31, 97 S.Ct. at 2727–28, 53 L.Ed.2d at 798.

See also Boyd v. Ozark Air Lines, Inc., 568 F.2d 50 (8th Cir.1977), holding defendant's height requirement of 5′7″ for airline pilots discriminatory to female applicants. The court found a height requirement of 5′5″ would be less discriminatory and would still permit defendant to satisfy its objective of hiring pilots who could reach all the instruments in the cockpit and meet the design eye reference point set by the manufacturer of its aircraft. Since plaintiff was approximately 5′2″, the altered standards did not benefit her. Boyd illustrates a set of problems arising from the fact that equipment used in the industrial workplace has been designed and engineered for the average male rather than the average person. Women attempting to operate this equipment may be unable to do so or able to do so only at the risk of physical strain. Does this mean that the employer must retool his shop to accommodate women workers? See Ellen Shapiro, Remedies for Sex–Discriminatory Health and Safety Conditions in Male–Dominated Industrial Jobs, 10 Golden Gate Univ.L.Rev. 1087 (Women's Law Forum, 1980). What bearing, if any, does the discussion in the Text Note on Ensuring Non–Discrimination, at pp. 767–777, infra, have on equipment design?

4. Does plaintiff make out a disparate impact claim under Title VII by showing that an employer compensates employees in jobs where females predominate at lower pay rates than employees in jobs where males predominate, if these jobs, although dissimilar, were identified by a job evaluation study to be of comparable worth to the employer? Such an argument was rejected in American Fed. of State, County, & Mun. Emp. v. State of Washington, 770 F.2d 1401 (9th Cir.1985). Justice Kennedy, then on the Ninth Circuit, reasoned as follows:

> The trial court erred in ruling that liability was established under a disparate impact analysis. The precedents do not permit the case to proceed upon that premise. AFSCME's disparate impact argument is based on the contention that the State of Washington's practice of taking prevailing market rates into account in setting wages has an adverse impact on women, who, historically, have received lower wages than men in the labor market. Disparate impact analysis is confined to cases that challenge a specific, clearly delineated employment practice applied at a single point in the job selection process. Atonio v. Wards Cove Packing Co., 768 F.2d 1120, 1130 (9th Cir.1985); see also *Dothard,* 433 U.S. at 328–29, 97 S.Ct. at 2726–27 (height and weight requirement disproportionately excluded women); *Griggs,* 401 U.S. at 430–31, 91 S.Ct. at 853–54 (requirement of high school diploma or satisfactory performance on standardized tests disproportionately affected minorities); Harriss v. Pan American World Airways, Inc., 649 F.2d 670, 674 (9th Cir.1980)(policy mandating maternity leave immediately upon learning of pregnancy had an adverse impact on women); Gregory v. Litton Systems, 472 F.2d 631, 632 (9th Cir.1972)(policy excluding applicants with arrest records adversely affected minorities). The instant case does not involve an employment practice that yields to disparate impact analysis. As we noted in an earlier case, the decision to base compensation on the competitive market, rather than on a theory of comparable worth, involves the assessment of a number of complex factors not easily ascertainable, an assessment too multifaceted to be appropriate for disparate impact analysis. *Spaulding,* 740 F.2d at 708. In the case before us, the compensation system in question resulted from surveys, agency hearings, administrative recommendations, budget proposals, executive actions, and legislative enactments. A compensation system that is responsive to supply and demand and other market forces is not the type of specific, clearly delineated employment policy contemplated by *Dothard* and *Griggs;* such a compensation system, the result of a complex of

market forces, does not constitute a single practice that suffices to support a claim under disparate impact theory. See *Spaulding,* 740 F.2d at 708; see also *Atonio,* at 1129 (broad scale attacks against a wide range of ill-defined employment practices are inappropriate for disparate impact analysis); Pouncy v. Prudential Insurance Co., 668 F.2d 795, 800–01 (5th Cir.1982)(disparate impact model is ill-suited for application to wide-ranging challenges to general compensation policies). Such cases are controlled by disparate treatment analysis. Under these principles and precedents, we must reverse the district court's determination of liability under the disparate impact theory of discrimination.

Id., 770 F.2d at 1405–06. Do you agree? Justice Kennedy's reasoning is criticized in Diana Stone, Comparable Worth in the Wake of *AFSCME v. State of Washington*, 1 Berkeley Women's L.J. 78, 101–112 (1985). Comparable worth is considered further at pp. 966–972, infra.

5. The issue of whether disparate impact analysis could be used to attack subjective decision making systems in employment continued to split the federal circuits. The panel opinion in *Atonio,* cited by Justice Kennedy in *AFSCME,* was subsequently withdrawn and the case was heard *en banc.* The Ninth Circuit held that disparate impact analysis is not limited to objective criteria such as the testing and diploma requirements involved in *Griggs,* or the height and weight requirements analyzed in *Dothard,* discussed in Note 3, supra, but may also be applied to judge the validity of subjective employer practices. In Atonio v. Wards Cove Packing Co., Inc., 810 F.2d 1477 (9th Cir.1987) *(en banc),* Judge Tang thus stated the new Ninth Circuit approach:

> We now hold that disparate impact analysis may be applied to challenge subjective employment practices or criteria provided the plaintiffs have proved a causal connection between those practices and the demonstrated impact on members of a protected class. The three elements of the plaintiffs' prima facie case are that they must (1) show a significant disparate impact on a protected class, (2) identify specific employment practices or selection criteria and (3) show the causal relationship between the identified practices and the impact. We are persuaded that this holding comports with the express language of the statute, the intent of Congress as revealed in its discussions of the 1972 amendments, the enforcement agencies' interpretation, and the broad prophylactic purposes of Title VII.

Id., 810 F.2d at 1482.

The United States Supreme Court resolved this matter in Watson v. Fort Worth Bank & Trust, 487 U.S. 977 (1988), adopting the approach outlined above by the Ninth Circuit. Clara Watson, a black woman, was hired by the Bank in August, 1973, as a proof operator. She was promoted to teller in 1976, and to commercial teller in 1980. During 1980 she unsuccessfully applied for four different promotions. The Fifth Circuit rejected her effort to apply disparate impact analysis to the Bank's allegedly discretionary promotion system that she claimed disadvantaged blacks. Watson's unrebutted statistical evidence indicated that a black applicant has one-fourth the chance of a white applicant to get the job; should the black be hired, her performance is apt to be evaluated thirty points lower and she is apt to be paid $46.00 per month less than an identically qualified white; and the Bank is likely to advance her at a rate six-tenths of a pay grade per year more slowly than an equally qualified white person. Justice O'Connor, writing for the Court, held this disparate impact analysis could be applied to subjective employer practices, in addition to litigating the case under disparate treatment theory:

> The District Court addressed Watson's individual claims under the evidentiary standards that apply in a discriminatory treatment case. See McDonnell Douglas Corp. v. Green, 411 U.S. 792 (1973), and Texas Department of Community Affairs v. Burdine, 450 U.S. 248 (1981). It concluded, on the evidence presented at trial, that Watson had established a prima facie case of employment discrimination, but that the Bank had met its rebuttal burden by presenting legitimate and nondiscriminatory reasons for each of the challenged promotion decisions. The court also concluded that Watson had failed to show that these reasons were pretexts for racial discrimination. Accordingly, the action was dismissed. * * *

> Watson argued that the District Court had erred in failing to apply "disparate impact" analysis to her claims of discrimination in promotion. Relying on Fifth Circuit precedent, the majority of the Court of Appeals panel held that "a Title VII challenge to an allegedly discretionary promotion system is properly analyzed under the disparate treatment model rather than the disparate impact model." * * *

> Several of our decisions have dealt with the evidentiary standards that apply when an individual alleges that an employer has treated that particular person less favorably than others because of the plaintiff's race, color, religion, sex, or national origin. In such "disparate treatment" cases, which involve "the most easily understood type of discrimination," Teamsters v. United States, 431 U.S. 324, 335, n. 15 (1977), the plaintiff is required to prove that the defendant had a discriminatory intent or motive. In order to facilitate the orderly consideration of relevant evidence, we have devised a series of shifting evidentiary burdens that are "intended progressively to sharpen the inquiry into the elusive factual question of intentional discrimination." Texas Department of Community Affairs v. Burdine, 450 U.S., at 255, n.8 * * *

> In Griggs v. Duke Power Co., 401 U.S. 424 (1971), this Court held that a plaintiff need not necessarily prove intentional discrimination in order to establish that an employer has violated section 703. In certain cases, facially neutral employment practices that have a significant adverse effect on protected groups have been held to violate the Act without proof that the employer adopted those practices with a discriminatory intent. The factual issues and the character of the evidence are inevitably somewhat different when the plaintiff is exempted from the need to prove intentional discrimination. * * * The evidence in these "disparate impact" cases usually focuses on statistical disparities, rather than specific incidents, and on competing explanations for those disparities.

> The distinguishing features of the factual issues that typically dominate in disparate impact cases do not imply that the ultimate legal issue is different than in cases where disparate treatment analysis is used. See, e.g., Washington v. Davis, 426 U.S. 229, 253–254 (1976)(Stevens, J., concurring). Nor do we think it is appropriate to hold a defendant liable for unintentional discrimination on the basis of less evidence than is required to prove intentional discrimination. Rather, the necessary premise of the disparate impact approach is that some employment practices, adopted without a deliberately

discriminatory motive, may in operation be functionally equivalent to intentional discrimination.

* * *

This Court has repeatedly reaffirmed the principle that some facially neutral employment practices may violate Title VII even in the absence of a demonstrated discriminatory intent. We have not limited this principle to cases in which the challenged practice served to perpetuate the effects of pre-Act intentional discrimination. Each of our subsequent decisions, however, like *Griggs* itself, involved standardized employment tests or criteria. See, e.g., Albemarle Paper Co. v. Moody, 422 U.S. 405 (1975)(written aptitude tests); Washington v. Davis, supra, (written test of verbal skills); Dothard v. Rawlinson, 433 U.S. 321 (1977)(height and weight requirements); New York City Transit Authority v. Beazer, 440 U.S. 568 (1979)(rule against employing drug addicts); Connecticut v. Teal, 457 U.S. 440 (1982)(written examination). In contrast, we have consistently used conventional disparate-treatment theory, in which proof of intent to discriminate is required, to review hiring and promotion decisions that were based on the exercise of personal judgment or the application of inherently subjective criteria. See, e.g., McDonnell Douglas Corp. v. Green, supra, (discretionary decision not to rehire individual who engaged in criminal acts against employer while laid off); Furnco Construction Corp., v. Waters, 438 U.S. 567 (1978)(hiring decisions based on personal knowledge of candidates and recommendations); Texas Department of Community Affairs v. Burdine, 450 U.S. 248 (1981)(discretionary decision to fire individual who said not to get along with co-workers); United States Postal Service Bd of Governors v. Aikens, 460 U.S., at 715 (discretionary promotion decision).

* * *

The parties present us with stark and uninviting alternatives. Petitioner contends that subjective selection methods are at least as likely to have discriminatory effects as are the kind of objective tests at issue in *Griggs* and our other disparate impact cases. Furthermore, she argues, if disparate impact analysis is confined to objective tests, employers will be able to substitute subjective criteria having substantially identical effects, and *Griggs* will become a dead letter. Respondent and the United States (appearing as amicus curiae) argue that conventional disparate treatment analysis is adequate to accomplish Congress' purpose in enacting Title VII. They also argue that subjective selection practices would be so impossibly difficult to defend under disparate impact analysis that employers would be forced to adopt numerical quotas in order to avoid liability.

We are persuaded that our decisions in *Griggs* and succeeding cases could largely be nullified if disparate impact analysis were applied only to standardized selection practices. However one might distinguish "subjective" from "objective" criteria, it is apparent that selection systems that combine both types would generally have to be considered subjective in nature. Thus, for example, if the employer in *Griggs* had consistently preferred applicants who had a high school diploma and who passed the company's general aptitude test, its selection system could nonetheless have been considered "subjective" if it also included brief interviews with the candidates. So long as an employer refrained from making standardized criteria absolutely determinative, it would remain free to give such tests almost as much weight as it chose without risking a disparate impact challenge. If we announced a rule that allowed employers so easily to insulate themselves from liability under *Griggs*, disparate impact analysis might effectively be abolished.

We are also persuaded that disparate impact analysis is in principle no less applicable to subjective employment criteria than to objective or standardized tests. In either case, a facially neutral practice, adopted without discriminatory intent, may have effects that are indistinguishable from intentionally discriminatory practices. It is true, to be sure, that an employer's policy of leaving promotion decisions to the unchecked discretion of lower level supervisors should itself raise no inference of discriminatory conduct. Especially in relatively small businesses like respondent's, it may be customary and quite reasonable simply to delegate employment decisions to those employees who are most familiar with the jobs to be filled and with the candidates for those jobs. It does not follow, however, that the particular supervisors to whom this discretion is delegated always act without discriminatory intent. Furthermore, even if one assumed that any such discrimination can be adequately policed through disparate treatment analysis, the problem of subconscious stereotypes and prejudices would remain. In this case, for example, petitioner was apparently told at one point that the teller position was a big responsibility with "a lot of money * * * for blacks to have to count." Such remarks may not prove discriminatory intent, but they do suggest a lingering form of the problem that Title VII was enacted to combat. If an employer's undisciplined system of subjective decisionmaking has precisely the same effects as a system pervaded by impermissible intentional discrimination, it is difficult to see why Title VII's proscription against discriminatory actions should not apply. In both circumstances, the employer's practices may be said to "adversely affect (an individual's) status as an employee, because of such individual's race, color, religion, sex, or national origin." 42 U.S.C. section 2000e–2(a)(2). We conclude, accordingly, that subjective or discretionary employment practices may be analyzed under the disparate impact approach in appropriate cases.

After holding that plaintiff could use disparate impact analysis to attack the bank's subjective promotion system, Justice O'Connor proceeded to substantially modify the *Griggs* burdens of proof, making the plaintiff's prima facie case of impact more difficult to prove and removing the burden of persuasion from the defendant employer on the "business necessity" or "job relatedness" defense. In *Watson*, this portion of her opinion garnered only three additional votes. The next Term, however, a majority of the Court agreed with her and restructured disparate impact litigation in *Ward's Cove*, set out on p. 596 infra.

6. The "business necessity" defense created by the Court in *Griggs* was initially used in race discrimination cases to respond to a showing of disparate impact. See Note, Business Necessity Under Title VII of the Civil Rights Act of 1964: A No–Alternative Approach, 84 Yale L.J. 98 (1974). The Court in *Griggs* used the term "business necessity" to identify a potential defense that an employer might offer in a case where the discrimination had resulted from its use of a facially-neutral job requirement that had a disparate impact on members of a racial minority group. The courts have interpreted the business necessity test quite narrowly in disparate impact race discrimination cases. In a widely-followed formulation, the Fourth Circuit articulated the standard in Robinson v. Lorillard Corp., 444 F.2d 791, 798 (4th Cir.1971), cert. dismissed 404 U.S. 1006, 92 S.Ct. 573, 30 L.Ed.2d 655:

[T]he applicable test is not merely whether there exists a business purpose for adhering to a challenged practice. The test is whether there exists an overriding legitimate business purpose such that the practice is necessary to the safe and efficient operation of the business. Thus, the business purpose must be sufficiently compelling to override any racial impact; the challenged practice must effectively carry out the business purpose it is alleged to serve; and there must be available no acceptable alternative policies or practices which would better accomplish the business purpose advanced, or accomplish it equally well with a lesser differential racial impact.

It has been suggested that this formulation is excessively restrictive and that a more generous approach to the business necessity test would better accomplish the Congressional goal of achieving fair treatment for individuals rather than parity for groups. See Comment, The Business Necessity Defense to Disparate–Impact Liability Under Title VII, 46 U.Chi.L.Rev. 911 (1979). Do you agree?

The business necessity defense applies to disparate impact sex discrimination cases as well as race cases. In *Dothard*, as we have seen, the Supreme Court dealt with two employer rules that prevented women from obtaining positions as prison guards in Alabama: the height and weight requirements and the express gender disqualification contained in Regulation 204. While the Court treated Regulation 204 as intentional discrimination based on sex subject to the bona fide occupational qualification (BFOQ) defense, discussed at p. 777 infra, it analyzed the height and weight requirements as a neutral rule subject to the business necessity defense. As in *Griggs*, the employer was required to show that the employment practice which operated to exclude women was related to job performance. In the view of a majority of the Court, the employer failed to make this showing:

We turn therefore, to the appellants' argument that they have rebutted the prima facie case of discrimination by showing that the height and weight requirements are job related. These requirements, they say, have a relationship to strength, a sufficient but unspecified amount of which is essential to effective job performance as a correctional counselor. In the District Court, however, the appellants produced no evidence correlating the height and weight requirements with the requisite amount of strength thought essential to good job performance. Indeed, they failed to offer evidence of any kind in specific justification of the statutory standards.

If the job-related quality that the appellants identify is bona fide, their purpose could be achieved by adopting and validating a test for applicants that measures strength directly. Such a test, fairly administered, would fully satisfy the standards of Title VII because it would be one that "measure[s] the person for the job and not the person in the abstract." Griggs v. Duke Power Co., 401 U.S., at 436, 91 S.Ct., at 856. But nothing in the present record even approaches such a measurement.

For the reasons we have discussed, the District Court was not in error in holding that Title VII of the Civil Rights Act of 1964, as amended, prohibits application of the statutory height and weight requirements to Rawlinson and the class she represents.

433 U.S. at 331–32, 97 S.Ct. at 2728, 53 L.Ed.2d at 798–99. Justice Rehnquist, joined by Chief Justice Berger and Justice Blackmun, had some reservations:

While I also agree with the Court's conclusion in Part II of its opinion, holding that the District Court was "not in error" in holding the statutory height and weight requirements in this case to be invalidated by Title VII, the issues with which that part deals are bound to arise so frequently that I feel obliged to separately state the reasons for my agreement with its result. I view affirmance of the District Court in this respect as essentially dictated by the peculiarly limited factual and legal justifications offered below by appellants on behalf of the statutory requirements. For that reason, I do not believe—and do not read the Court's opinion as holding—that all or even many of the height and weight requirements imposed by States on applicants for a multitude of law enforcement agency jobs are pretermitted by today's decision.

* * *

Appellants, in order to rebut the prima facie case under the statute, had the burden placed on them to advance job-related reasons for the qualification. McDonnell Douglas Corp. v. Green, 411 U.S. 792, at 802, 93 S.Ct. 1817, at 1824, 36 L.Ed.2d 668 (1973). This burden could be shouldered by offering evidence or by making legal arguments not dependent on any new evidence. The District Court was confronted, however, with only one suggested job-related reason for the qualification—that of strength. Appellants argued only the job-relatedness of actual physical strength; they did not urge that an equally job-related qualification for prison guards is the *appearance* of strength. As the Court notes, the primary job of correctional counselor in Alabama prisons "is to maintain security and control of the inmates * * *," a function that I at least would imagine is aided by the psychological impact on prisoners of the presence of tall and heavy guards. If the appearance of strength had been urged upon the District Court here as a reason for the height and weight minima, I think that the District Court would surely have been entitled to reach a different result than it did. For, even if not perfectly correlated, I would think that Title VII would not preclude a State from saying that anyone under 5'2" or 120 pounds, no matter how strong in fact, does not have a sufficient appearance of strength to be a prison guard.

But once the burden has been placed on the defendant, it is then up to the defendant to articulate the asserted job-related reasons underlying the use of the minima. * * * As appellants did not even present the "appearance of strength" contention to the District Court as an asserted job-related reason for the qualification requirements, I agree that their burden was not met. The District Court's holding thus did not deal with the question of whether such an assertion could or did rebut appellee's prima facie case.

433 U.S. at 337–40, 97 S.Ct. at 2731–32, 53 L.Ed.2d at 802–04.

7. Women have challenged physical ability tests used for police and firefighter jobs under disparate impact theory. In light of *Dothard,* do you agree with the California Supreme Court that a physical agility test requiring Oakland police officer candidates to run 300 feet, scale a 6–foot wall (the height limit for Oakland fences), walk across a balance beam, run another 300 feet, register 75 pounds on a grip dynamometer device, and drag a 140–pound dummy for 50 feet, raising it to a 2–foot platform, all within 2 1/2 minutes, passes muster under the constitution and Title VII even though the test eliminated 85% of female but only 15% of male applicants? Plaintiff, a 27 year old, 5'4", 118–pound female, failed twice to scale the wall. Her challenge to the test was rejected in Hardy v. Stumpf, 21 Cal.3d 1, 145 Cal.Rptr. 176, 576 P.2d 1342 (1978). The dissent pointed out that several currently-employed Oakland officers also had failed to scale the wall; that it was questionable whether the smooth plywood wall used in the test was representative of Oakland fences; and that defendant had not shown that females, once hired,

could not easily be trained to scale 6–foot walls. The physical agility test was based on a "job analysis survey" and had been devised after Oakland's height and weight requirements for police officers had been declared invalid. Hardy v. Stumpf, 37 Cal.App.3d 958, 112 Cal.Rptr. 739 (1974). See also Smith v. Troyan, 520 F.2d 492 (6th Cir.1975), cert. denied 426 U.S. 934, 96 S.Ct. 2646, 49 L.Ed.2d 385 (1976)(upholding a requirement that police officers be over five feet, eight inches tall, but striking down a weight requirement of 150 pounds).

Compare with *Hardy,* Berkman v. City of New York, 536 F.Supp. 177 (E.D.N.Y.1982), affirmed 705 F.2d 584 (2d Cir.1983), invalidating a physical ability test administered to firefighter candidates which eliminated all of the women and more than half of the men who took it. Plaintiffs Brenda Berkman and Zaida Gonzalez thereafter passed the qualifying exam and were appointed as firefighters, only to be terminated at the end of their probationary period. Holding this action to have been in retaliation for their having filed the original lawsuit, the district court ordered both women reinstated. Berkman v. City of New York, 580 F.Supp. 226 (E.D.N.Y.1983). New York City subsequently prepared and administered a new entry-level firefighter test: 95.42% of the men who took its physical test passed, but only 46.47% of women did so. The City's eligibility list, based on an equal weighting of the written and physical tests, showed 6,500 applicants who received a combined score of 94.5 and who would be offered jobs over the four-year life of the list in order to recruit 2,800 new firefighters: only two women are members of this group. Judge Newman upheld the validity of the test and permitted the City to begin hiring from the combined eligibility list, supplemented with the combined scores of any women who passed the written test and accepted the City's offer to participate in a training program and take the physical test again. Rejecting plaintiff's argument that the test discriminated against women because it "measures an applicant's anaerobic energy system, as applied to firefighters' tasks, and substantially ignores the aerobic energy system," Judge Newman reasoned in part as follows:

> We do not doubt the plaintiff's basic point that stamina, a function of a person's aerobic energy system, is important in the performance of a firefighter's tasks. The evidence of senior officials of the Fire Department acknowledged that stamina was an important attribute for successful job performance. It does not follow, however, that a physical test of the ability to perform simulated job tasks of firefighters, without a specific measurement of stamina, lacks validity to a degree that renders it vulnerable to a Title VII challenge. Obviously, firefighters frequently face situations where their anaerobic abilities determine whether or not they will save the lives of fire victims. The firefighter arriving on the scene of a fire will frequently be obliged to use strength and speed in a short amount of time. Abundant evidence in the record supports this point, which in any event would be self-evident. It may well be that the effectiveness of a person with minimal stamina will decline if called upon to perform firefighting tasks over a considerable period of time. Perhaps a person with greater stamina would perform the tasks better after protracted activity than the firefighter who might excel in the first few minutes of activity. But the Fire Department is entitled to select those who are endowed with the physical abilities to act effectively in the first moments of arrival at a fire scene, where immediate speed and strength literally concern matters of life and death. If a person with limited stamina tires during the course of firefighting duties, that person can be replaced with a fresh firefighter. However, if the first firefighters on the scene are deficient in the speed and strength necessary to handle their

tasks, those in need of immediate rescue will not be comforted by the fact that those first on the scene might be able to sustain their modest energy levels for a prolonged period of time. See Spurlock v. United Airlines, Inc., 475 F.2d 216, 219 (10th Cir.1972)(employer's burden to justify employment criteria correspondingly lighter where "human risks involved").

In an ideal world, a fire department might first select those applicants with a high degree of speed and strength and from that group make a second selection of those with relatively greater stamina. There is nothing in this record, however, to show that such a selection process would have a less adverse effect upon women. Indeed, since only seven women placed in the top 15,316 applicants on the physical test, which primarily measured speed and strength in the performance of firefighters' tasks, a further selection from among these applicants, giving priority to those with relatively greater stamina, would at most have placed only these seven women applicants somewhat higher on the eligibility list, an outcome by no means certain.

In sum, the District Court's conclusion that the written and physical tests of Exam 1162 are appropriate for use to select entry-level firefighters is entitled to be approved.

Berkman v. City of New York, 812 F.2d 52, 59–60 (2d Cir.1987). Can New York City women forget about working as firefighters?

Things may be better in San Francisco. After the City refused to defend selection and promotion tests that had a disparate impact on minorities and women, Judge Marilyn Patel granted partial summary judgment and injunctive relief against the City. See United States v. City and County of San Francisco, 656 F.Supp. 276 (N.D.Cal.1987). Nine months later, the City signed a consent agreement providing that the San Francisco Fire Department will reach a goal of 40% minority firefighters and 10% women by 1994, compared to its present 14% minorities and 1% women. The predominantly white S.F. Firefighters' Union appealed the consent decree. In addition to the United States, the plaintiffs in the San Francisco case included Blacks, Asians, Hispanics, and women. The consent agreement provided that half of the women hired as firefighters would be minority women. The Ninth Circuit affirmed Judge Patel's order confirming the consent decree, holding that it passed muster both when measured against "some level of elevated scrutiny" required by the Equal Protection clause and the showing of "manifest imbalance" required for voluntary race-based affirmative action plans under Title VII. See Davis v. City and County of San Francisco, 890 F.2d 1438, 1445–48 (Equal Protection), 1448–49 (Title VII) (9th Cir.1989).

See also Brunet v. City of Columbus, 642 F.Supp. 1214 (S.D.Ohio 1986), appeal dismissed 826 F.2d 1062 (6th Cir.1987), cert. denied 485 U.S. 1034, 108 S.Ct. 1593, 99 L.Ed.2d 908 (1988), invalidating the City's 1984 firefighter physical test because it did not represent the physical demands of the job and there was no evidence that higher scores on the test varied directly with job performance to justify ranking. Consequently, the City discriminated against women on the basis of their sex when it used the 1984 examination to hire firefighters.

In a case decided after passage of the 1991 Civil Rights Act amendments discussed in Note 3, p. 609 infra, a federal district court in New Hampshire found that plaintiff proved likelihood of success on the merits in seeking a preliminary injunction against a fire department's physical ability tests that screened out 5 of 35 male applicants and all 11 of the female applicants. Legault v. aRusso, 842 F.Supp. 1479 (D.N.H.1994). The trial court found that "whether the yardstick is intuition, the EEOC's 'four-fifths rule,' or some other measure, this discrepancy is 'substantial' for Title VII purposes." Id. at 1486. The physical test's designer admitted that the test was not gender-neutral, in that the hose-pull portion of the test put a premium on men's physical abilities and required a degree of upper arm and body strength not possessed by average women. The fire department failed to make any showing that it had validated the tests by analyzing fire fighting jobs and relating test performance to job performance. Id. at 1489. The district court ordered the department to hire plaintiff immediately as an entry-level firefighter, pending a trial on the merits, noting that plaintiff had finished second in the fire department's training program. Id. at 1492.

WARDS COVE PACKING CO., INC. v. ATONIO

Supreme Court of the United States, 1989.
490 U.S. 642, 109 S.Ct. 2115, 104 L.Ed.2d 733.

JUSTICE WHITE delivered the opinion of the Court.

Title VII of the Civil Rights Act of 1964 * * * makes it an unfair employment practice for an employer to discriminate against any individual with respect to hiring or the terms and condition of employment because of such individual's race, color, religion, sex, or national origin; or to limit, segregate or classify his employees in ways that would adversely affect any employee because of the employee's race, color, religion, sex, or national origin. *Griggs v. Duke Power Co.* * * * construed Title VII to proscribe "not only overt discrimination but also practices that are fair in form but discriminatory in practice." Under this basis for liability, which is known as the "disparate impact" theory and which is involved in this case, a facially neutral employment practice may be deemed violative of Title VII without evidence of the employer's subjective intent to discriminate that is required in a "disparate treatment" case.

I

The claims before us are disparate-impact claims, involving the employment practices of petitioners, two companies that operate salmon canneries in remote and widely separated areas of Alaska. The canneries operate only during the salmon runs in the summer months. They are inoperative and vacant for the rest of the year. In May or June of each year, a few weeks before the salmon runs begin, workers arrive and prepare the equipment and facilities for the canning operation. Most of these workers possess a variety of skills. When salmon runs are about to begin, the workers who will operate the cannery lines arrive, remain as long as there are fish to can, and then depart. The canneries are then closed down, winterized, and left vacant until the next spring. During the off season, the companies employ only a small number of individuals at their headquarters in Seattle and Astoria, Oregon, plus some employees at the winter shipyard in Seattle.

The length and size of salmon runs vary from year to year and hence the number of employees needed at each cannery also varies. Estimates are made as early in the winter as possible; the necessary employees are hired, and when the time comes, they are transported to the canneries. Salmon must be processed soon after they are caught, and the work during the canning season is therefore intense. For this reason, and because the canneries are located in remote regions, all workers are housed at the canneries and have their meals in company-owned mess halls.

Jobs at the canneries are of two general types: "cannery jobs" on the cannery line, which are unskilled positions; and "noncannery jobs," which fall into a variety of classifications. Most noncannery jobs are classified as skilled positions. Cannery jobs are filled predominantly by nonwhites, Filipinos and Alaska Natives. The Filipinos are hired through and dispatched by Local 37 of the International Longshoremen Workers Union pursuant to a hiring hall agreement with the Local. The Alaska Natives primarily reside in villages near the remote cannery locations. Noncannery jobs are filled with predominantly white workers, who are hired during the winter months from the companies' offices in Washington and Oregon. Virtually all of the noncannery jobs pay more than cannery positions. The predominantly white noncannery workers and the predominantly nonwhite cannery employees live in separate dormitories and eat in separate mess halls.

In 1974, respondents, a class of nonwhite cannery workers who were (or had been) employed at the canneries, brought this Title VII action against petitioners. Respondents alleged that a variety of petitioners' hiring/promotion practices—e.g., nepotism, a rehire preference, a lack of objective hiring criteria, separate hiring channels, a practice of not promoting from within—were responsible for the racial stratification of the work force, and had denied them and other nonwhites employment as noncannery workers on the basis of race. Respondents also complained of petitioners' racially segregated housing and dining facilities. All of respondents' claims were advanced under both the disparate-treatment and disparate-impact theories of Title VII liability.

The District Court held a bench trial, after which it * * * rejected all of respondents' disparate-treatment claims. It also rejected the disparate-impact challenges involving the subjective employment criteria used by petitioners to fill these noncannery positions, on the ground that those criteria were not subject to attack under a disparate-impact theory. * * * Petitioner's "objective" employment practices (e.g., an English language requirement, alleged nepotism in hiring, failure to post noncannery openings, the rehire preference, etc.) were found to be subject to challenge under the disparate-impact theory, but these claims were rejected for failure of proof. Judgment was entered for petitioners.

On appeal, * * * the Court of Appeals held—as this Court subsequently ruled in *Watson v. Fort Worth Bank & Trust,* 487 U.S. 977, 108 S.Ct. 2777, 101 L.Ed.2d 827 (1988)—that disparate-impact analysis could be applied to subjective hiring practices. * * * The Ninth Circuit also concluded that in such a case, "[o]nce the plaintiff class has shown disparate-impact caused by specific, identifiable employment practices or criteria, the burden shifts to the employer," * * * to "prov[e the] business necessity" of the challenged practice. * * * Because the en banc holding on subjective employment practices reversed the District Court's contrary ruling, the en banc Court of Appeals remanded the case to a panel for further proceedings.

* * * Neither the en banc court nor the panel disturbed the District Court's rejection of the disparate-treatment claims.[4]

4. The fact that neither the District Court, nor the Ninth Circuit *en banc,* nor the subsequent Court of Appeals panel ruled for respondents on their disparate treatment claims—*i.e.,* their allegations of intentional racial discrimination—warrants particular attention in light of the dissents' comment that the canneries "bear an unsettling resemblance to aspects of a

Petitioners sought review of the Court of Appeals' decision in this Court, challenging it on several grounds. Because some of the issues raised by the decision below were matters on which this Court was evenly divided in *Watson v. Fort Worth Bank & Trust Co.,* * * * we granted certiorari, * * * for the purpose of addressing these disputed questions of the proper application of Title VII's disparate-impact theory of liability.

II

In holding that respondents had made out a prima facie case of disparate impact, the court of appeals relied solely on respondents' statistics showing a high percentage of nonwhite workers in the cannery jobs and a low percentage of such workers in the noncannery positions. Although statistical proof can alone make out a prima facie case, see *Teamsters v. United States,* * * * *Hazelwood School Dist. v. United States,* * * * the Court of Appeals' ruling here misapprehends our precedents and the purposes of Title VII, and we therefore reverse.

"There can be no doubt," as there was when a similar mistaken analysis had been undertaken by the courts below in *Hazelwood,* * * * "that the * * * comparison * * * fundamentally misconceived the role of statistics in employment discrimination cases." The "proper comparison [is] between the racial composition of [the at-issue jobs] and the racial composition of the qualified * * * population in the relevant labor market." * * * It is such a comparison—between the racial composition of the qualified persons in the labor market and the persons holding at-issue jobs—that generally forms the proper basis for the initial inquiry in a disparate impact case. Alternatively, in cases where such labor market statistics will be difficult if not impossible to ascertain, we have recognized that certain other statistics—such as measures indicating the racial composition of "otherwise-qualified applicants" for at-issue jobs—are equally probative for this purpose. See, *e.g., New York City Transit Authority v. Beazer,* * * *.[6]

It is clear to us that the Court of Appeals' acceptance of the comparison between the racial composition of the cannery work force and that of the noncannery work force, as probative of a prima facie case of disparate impact in the selection of the latter group of workers, was flawed for several reasons. Most obviously, with respect to the skilled noncannery jobs at issue here, the cannery work force in no way reflected "the pool of *qualified* job applicants"

plantation economy." * * * (Stevens, J., dissenting); * * * (Blackmun, J., dissenting).

Whatever the "resemblance," the unanimous view of the lower courts in this litigation has been that respondents did not prove that the canneries practice intentional racial discrimination. Consequently, Justice Blackmun's hyperbolic allegation that our decision in this case indicates that this Court no longer "believes that race discrimination * * * against nonwhites * * * is a problem in our society," * * * is inapt. Of course, it is unfortunately true that race discrimination exists in our country. That does not mean, however, that it exists at the canneries—or more precisely, that it has been proven to exist at the canneries.

Indeed, Justice Stevens concedes that respondents did not press before us the legal theories under which the aspects of cannery life that he finds to most resemble a "plantation economy" might be unlawful. * * * Thus, the question here is not whether we "approve" of petitioners' employment practices or the society that exists at the canneries, but rather, whether respondents have properly established that these practices violate Title VII.

6. In fact, where "figures for the general population might * * * accurately reflect the pool of qualified job applicants," cf. *Teamsters v. United States,* * * * we have even permitted plaintiffs to rest their prima facie cases on such statistics as well. *See,* e.g., Dothard v. Rawlinson, * * *.

or the "*qualified* population in the labor force." Measuring alleged discrimination in the selection of accountants, managers, boat captains, electricians, doctors, and engineers—and the long list of other "skilled" noncannery positions found to exist by the District Court, * * *—by comparing the number of nonwhites occupying these jobs to the number of nonwhites filling cannery worker positions is nonsensical. If the absence of minorities holding such skilled positions is due to a dearth of qualified nonwhite applicants (for reasons that are not petitioners' fault),[7] petitioners' selection methods or employment practices cannot be said to have had a "disparate impact" on nonwhites.

One example illustrates why this must be so. Respondents' own statistics concerning the noncannery work force at one of the canneries at issue here indicate that approximately 17% of the new hires for medical jobs, and 15% of the new hires for officer worker positions, were nonwhite. * * * If it were the case that less than 15–17% of the applicants for these jobs were nonwhite and that nonwhites made up a lower percentage of the relevant qualified labor market, it is hard to see how respondents, without more, cf. *Connecticut v. Teal,* * * * would have made out a prima facie case of disparate impact. Yet, under the Court of Appeals' theory, simply because nonwhites comprise 52% of the cannery workers at the cannery in question, * * * respondents would be successful in establishing a prima facie case of racial discrimination under Title VII.

Such a result cannot be squared with our cases or with the goals behind the statute. The Court of Appeals' theory, at the very least, would mean that any employer who had a segment of his work force that was—for some reason—racially imbalanced, could be haled into court and forced to engage in the expensive and time-consuming task of defending the "business necessity" of the methods used to select the other members of his work force. The only practicable option for many employers will be to adopt racial quotas, insuring that no portion of his work force deviates in racial composition from the other portions thereof; this is a result that Congress expressly rejected in drafting Title VII. See 42 U.S.C. § 2000e–2(j); see also *Watson v. Fort Worth Bank & Trust Co.,* * * * at n. 2, * * * (opinion of O'Connor, J.). The Court of Appeals' theory would "leave the employer little choice * * * but to engage in a subjective quota system of employment selection. This, of course, is far from the intent of Title VII." *Albemarle Paper Co. v. Moody,* * * * (BLACK-MUN, J., concurring in judgment).

* * *

Consequently, we reverse the Court of Appeals' ruling that a comparison between the percentage of cannery workers who are nonwhite and the percentage of noncannery workers who are nonwhite makes out a prima facie case of disparate impact. Of course, this leaves unresolved whether the record made in the District Court will support a conclusion that a prima facie case of disparate impact has been established on some basis other than the racial disparity between cannery and noncannery workers. This is an issue

7. Obviously, the analysis would be different if it were found that the dearth of qualified nonwhite applicants was due to practices on petitioner's part which—expressly or implicit-ly—deterred minority group members from applying for noncannery positions. See, *e.g., Teamsters v. United States,* * * *.

that the Court of Appeals or the District Court should address in the first instance.

III

Since the statistical disparity relied on by the Court of Appeals did not suffice to make out a prima facie case, any inquiry by us into whether the specific challenged employment practices of petitioners caused that disparity is pretermitted, as is any inquiry into whether the disparate impact that any employment practice may have had was justified by business considerations.[9] Because we remand for further proceedings, however, on whether a prima facie case of disparate impact has been made in defensible fashion in this case, we address two other challenges petitioners have made to the decision of the Court of Appeals.

A

First is the question of causation in a disparate-impact case. The law in this respect was correctly stated by Justice O'Connor's opinion last Term in *Watson v. Fort Worth Bank & Trust,* * * *:

> "* * * The plaintiff must begin by identifying the specific employment practice that is challenged * * *. Especially in cases where an employer combines subjective criteria with the use of more rigid standardized rules or tests, the plaintiff is in our view responsible for isolating and identifying the specific employment practices that are allegedly responsible for any observed statistical disparities."

* * *

Our disparate-impact cases have always focused on the impact of *particular* hiring practices on employment opportunities for minorities. Just as an employer cannot escape liability under Title VII by demonstrating that, "at the bottom line," his work force is racially balanced (where particular hiring practices may operate to deprive minorities of employment opportunities), see *Connecticut v. Teal,* * * * a Title VII plaintiff does not make out a case of disparate impact simply by showing that, "at the bottom line," there is racial *imbalance* in the work force. As a general matter, a plaintiff must demonstrate that it is the application of a specific or particular employment practice that has created the disparate impact under attack. Such a showing is an integral part of the plaintiff's prima facie case in a disparate-impact suit under Title VII.

Here, respondents have alleged that several "objective" employment practices (*e.g.,* nepotism, separate hiring channels, rehire preferences), as well as the use of "subjective decision making" to select noncannery workers, have had a disparate impact on nonwhites. Respondents base this claim on statistics that allegedly show a disproportionately low percentage of non-

---

9. As we understand the opinions below, the specific employment practices were challenged only insofar as they were claimed to have been responsible for the overall disparity between the number of minority cannery and noncannery workers. The Court of Appeals did not purport to hold that any specified employment practice produced its own disparate impact that was actionable under Title VII.

This is not to say that a specific practice, such as nepotism, if it were proved to exist, could not itself be subject to challenge if it had a disparate impact on minorities. Nor is it to say that segregated dormitories and eating facilities in the work-place may not be challenged under 42 U.S.C. § 2000e–2(a)(2) without showing a disparate impact on hiring or promotion.

whites in the at-issue positions. However, even if on remand respondents can show that nonwhites are underrepresented in the at-issue jobs in a manner that is acceptable under the standards set forth in Part II, *supra,* this alone will *not* suffice to make out a prima facie case of disparate impact. Respondents will also have to demonstrate that the disparity they complain of is the result of one or more of the employment practices that they are attacking here, specifically showing that each challenged practice has a significantly disparate impact on employment opportunities for whites and nonwhites. To hold otherwise would result in employers being potentially liable for "the myriad of innocent causes that may lead to statistical imbalances in the composition of their work forces." *Watson v. Fort Worth Bank & Trust,* * * *.

Some will complain that this specific causation requirement is unduly burdensome on Title VII plaintiffs. But liberal civil discovery rules give plaintiffs broad access to employers' records in an effort to document their claims. Also, employers falling within the scope of the Uniform Guidelines on Employee Selection Procedures, 29 CFR § 1607.1 *et seq.* (1988), are required to "maintain * * * records or other information which will disclose the impact which its tests and other selection procedures have upon employment opportunities of persons by identifiable race, sex, or ethnic group[s.]" See § 1607.4(A). This includes records concerning "the individual components of the selection process" where there is a significant disparity in the selection rates of whites and nonwhites. See § 1607.4(C). Plaintiffs as a general matter will have the benefit of these tools to meet their burden of showing a causal link between challenged employment practices and racial imbalances in the work force; respondents presumably took full advantage of these opportunities to build their case before the trial in the District Court was held.[10]

Consequently, on remand, the courts below are instructed to require, as part of respondents' prima facie case, a demonstration that specific elements of the petitioners' hiring process have a significantly disparate impact on nonwhites.

B

If, on remand, respondents meet the proof burdens outlined above, and establish a prima facie case of disparate impact with respect to any of petitioners' employment practices, the case will shift to any business justification petitioners offer for their use of these practices. This phase of the disparate-impact case contains two components: first, a consideration of the justifications an employer offers for his use of these practices; and second, the availability of alternate practices to achieve the same business ends, with less racial impact. See, *e.g., Albemarle Paper Co. v. Moody,* * * *. We consider these two components in turn.

(1)

Though we have phrased the query differently in different cases, it is generally well-established that at the justification stage of such a disparate impact case, the dispositive issue is whether a challenged practice serves, in a

---

10. Of course, petitioners' obligation to collect or retain any of these data may be limited by the Guidelines themselves. See 29 CFR § 1602.14(b) (1988)(exempting "seasonal" jobs from certain record-keeping requirements).

significant way, the legitimate employment goals of the employer. * * * The touchstone of this inquiry is a reasoned review of the employer's justification for his use of the challenged practice. A mere insubstantial justification in this regard will not suffice, because such a low standard of review would permit discrimination to be practiced through the use of spurious, seemingly neutral employment practices. At the same time, though, there is no requirement that the challenged practice be "essential" or "indispensable" to the employer's business for it to pass muster: this degree of scrutiny would be almost impossible for most employers to meet, and would result in a host of evils we have identified above.

In this phase, the employer carries the burden of producing evidence of a business justification for his employment practice. The burden of persuasion, however, remains with the disparate-impact plaintiff. To the extent that the Ninth Circuit held otherwise in its en banc decision in this case, * * * or in the panel's decision on remand, * * *—suggesting that the persuasion burden should shift to the petitioners once the respondents established a prima facie case of disparate impact—its decisions were erroneous. "[T]he ultimate burden of proving that discrimination against a protected group has been caused by a specific employment practice remains with the plaintiff *at all times." Watson, * * * *(O'Connor, J.)(emphasis added). This rule conforms with the usual method for allocating persuasion and production burdens in the federal courts, see Fed.Rule.Evid. 301, and more specifically, it conforms to the rule in disparate-treatment cases that the plaintiff bears the burden of disproving an employer's assertion that the adverse employment action or practice was based solely on a legitimate neutral consideration. See *Texas Dept. of Community Affairs v. Burdine, * * *. We acknowledge that some of our earlier decisions can be read as suggesting otherwise. See *Watson, * * * (BLACKMUN, J., concurring). But to the extent that those cases speak of an employers' "burden of proof" with respect to a legitimate business justification defense, see, e.g., *Dothard v. Rawlinson, * * * they should have been understood to mean an employer's production—but not persuasion—burden. Cf., e.g., *NLRB v. Transportation Management Corp., * * *. The persuasion burden here must remain with the plaintiff, for it is he who must prove that it was "because of such individual's race, color," etc., that he was denied a desired employment opportunity. See 42 U.S.C. § 2000e–2(a).

(2)

Finally, if on remand the case reaches this point, and respondents cannot persuade the trier of fact on the question of petitioners' business necessity defense, respondents may still be able to prevail. To do so, respondents will have to persuade the factfinder that "other tests or selection devices, without a similarly undesirable racial effect, would also serve the employer's legitimate [hiring] interest[s];" by so demonstrating, respondents would prove that "[petitioners were] using [their] tests merely as a 'pretext' for discrimination." *Albemarle Paper Co., * * *; see also *Watson, * * *. If respondents, having established a prima facie case, come forward with alternatives to petitioners' hiring practices that reduce the racially-disparate impact of practices currently being used, and petitioners refuse to adopt these alternatives, such a refusal would belie a claim by petitioners that their incumbent practices are being employed for nondiscriminatory reasons.

Of course, any alternative practices which respondents offer up in this respect must be equally effective as petitioners' chosen hiring procedures in achieving petitioners' legitimate employment goals. Moreover, "[f]actors such as the cost or other burdens of proposed alternative selection devices are relevant in determining whether they would be equally as effective as the challenged practice in serving the employer's legitimate business goals." *Watson,* * * * (O'Connor, J.). "Courts are generally less competent than employers to restructure business practices," *Furnco Construction Corp. v. Waters,* * * *; consequently, the judiciary should proceed with care before mandating that an employer must adopt a plaintiff's alternate selection or hiring practice in response to a Title VII suit.

IV

For the reasons given above, the judgment of the Court of Appeals is reversed, and the case is remanded for further proceedings consistent with this opinion.

It is so ordered.

Justice Stevens, with whom Justice Brennan, Justice Marshall, and Justice Blackmun join, dissenting.

Fully 18 years ago, this Court unanimously held that Title VII of the Civil Rights Act of 1964 prohibits employment practices that have discriminatory effects as well as those that are intended to discriminate. *Griggs v. Duke Power Co.,* * * *. Federal courts and agencies consistently have enforced that interpretation, thus promoting our national goal of eliminating barriers that define economic opportunity not by aptitude and ability but by race, color, national origin, and other traits that are easily identified but utterly irrelevant to one's qualification for a particular job. Regrettably, the Court retreats from these efforts in its review of an interlocutory judgment respecting the "peculiar facts" of this lawsuit.[3] Turning a blind eye to the meaning and purpose of Title VII, the majority's opinion perfunctorily rejects a longstanding rule of law and underestimates the probative value of evidence of a racially stratified work force.[4] I cannot join this latest sojourn into judicial activism.

3. The majority purports to reverse the Court of Appeals but in fact directs the District Court to make additional findings, some of which had already been ordered by the Court of Appeals. * * * Furthermore, nearly half the majority's opinion is devoted to two questions not fairly raised at this point: "the question of causation in a disparate impact case," and the nature of the employer's defense. Because I perceive no urgency to decide "these disputed questions," at an interlocutory stage of such a factually complicated case, I believe the Court should have denied certiorari and allowed the District Court to make the additional findings directed by the Court of Appeals.

4. Respondents comprise a class of present and former employees of petitioners, two Alaskan salmon canning companies. The class members, described by the parties as "nonwhite," include persons of Samoan, Chinese, Filipino, Japanese, and Alaska Native descent, all but one of whom are United States citizens. * * * Fifteen years ago they commenced this suit, alleging that petitioners engage in hiring, job assignment, housing, and messing practices that segregate nonwhites from whites, in violation of Title VII. Evidence included this response in 1971 by a foreman to a college student's inquiry about cannery employment:

" 'We are not in a position to take many young fellows to our Bristol Bay canneries as they do not have the background for our type of employees. Our cannery labor is either Eskimo or Filipino and we do not have the facilities to mix others with these groups.' "

Some characteristics of the Alaska salmon industry described in this litigation—in particular, the segregation of housing and dining facilities and the stratification of jobs along racial and ethnic lines—bear an unsettling re-

I

I would have thought it superfluous to recount at this late date the development of our Title VII jurisprudence, but the majority's facile treatment of settled law necessitates such a primer. This Court initially considered the meaning of Title VII in *Griggs v. Duke Power Co.,* * * * in which a class of utility company employees challenged the conditioning of entry into higher paying jobs upon a high school education or passage of two written tests. Despite evidence that "these two requirements operated to render ineligible a markedly disproportionate number of Negroes," the Court of Appeals had held that because there was no showing of an intent to discriminate on account of race, there was no Title VII violation. Chief Justice Burger's landmark opinion established that an employer may violate the statute even when acting in complete good faith without any invidious intent. * * *

The opinion in *Griggs* made it clear that a neutral practice that operates to exclude minorities is nevertheless lawful if it serves a valid business purpose. "The touchstone is business necessity," the Court stressed. Because "Congress directed the thrust of the Act to the *consequences* of employment practices, not simply the motivation[,] * * * Congress has placed on the employer the burden of showing that any given requirement must have a manifest relationship to the employment in question." (emphasis in original). * * *

The *Griggs* framework, with its focus on ostensibly neutral qualification standards, proved inapposite for analyzing an individual employee's claim, brought under § 703(a)(1), that an employer intentionally discriminated on account of race. The means for determining intent absent direct evidence was outlined in *McDonnell Douglas Corp. v. Green,* * * * and *Texas Dept. of Community Affairs v. Burdine,* * * * two opinions written by Justice Powell for unanimous Courts. In such a "disparate treatment" case, * * * the plaintiff's initial burden, which is "not onerous," * * * is to establish "a prima facie case of racial discrimination," * * * that is, to create a presumption of unlawful discrimination by "eliminat[ing] the most common nondiscriminatory reasons for the plaintiff's rejection." * * * "The burden then must shift to the employer to articulate some legitimate, nondiscriminatory reason for the employee's rejection." * * * Finally, because "Title VII does not * * * permit [the employer] to use [the employee's] conduct as a pretext for the sort of discrimination prohibited by § 703(a)(1)," the employee "must be given a full and fair opportunity to demonstrate by competent evidence that the presumptively valid reasons for his rejection were in fact a coverup for a racially discriminatory decision." * * * While the burdens of producing evidence thus shift, the "ultimate burden of persuading the trier of fact that the defendant intentionally discriminated against the plaintiff remains at all times with the plaintiff." * * *

semblance to aspects of a plantation economy. See generally Plantation, Town, and County, Essays on the Local History of American Slave Society 163–334 (E. Miller & E. Genovese eds. 1974). Indeed the maintenance of inferior, segregated facilities for housing and feeding nonwhite employees, * * * strikes me as a form of discrimination that, although it does not necessarily fit neatly into a disparate impact or disparate treatment mold, nonetheless violates Title VII. See generally Brief for National Association for the Advancement of Colored People as *Amicus Curiae.* Respondents, however, do not press this theory before us.

Decisions of this Court and other federal courts repeatedly have recognized that while the employer's burden in a disparate treatment case is simply one of coming forward with evidence of legitimate business purpose, its burden in a disparate impact case is proof of an affirmative defense of business necessity. Although the majority's opinion blurs that distinction, thoughtful reflection on common-law pleading principles clarifies the fundamental differences between the two types of "burdens of proof." In the ordinary civil trial, the plaintiff bears the burden of persuading the trier of fact that the defendant has harmed her. * * * The defendant may undercut plaintiff's efforts both by confronting plaintiff's evidence during her case in chief and by submitting countervailing evidence during its own case. But if the plaintiff proves the existence of the harmful act, the defendant can escape liability only by persuading the factfinder that the act was justified or excusable. * * * The plaintiff in turn may try to refute this affirmative defense. Although the burdens of producing evidence regarding the existence of harm or excuse thus shift between the plaintiff and the defendant, the burden of proving either proposition remains throughout on the party asserting it.

In a disparate treatment case there is no "discrimination" within the meaning of Title VII unless the employer intentionally treated the employee unfairly because of race. Therefore, the employee retains the burden of proving the existence of intent at all times. If there is direct evidence of intent, the employee may have little difficulty persuading the factfinder that discrimination has occurred. But in the likelier event that intent has to be established by inference, the employee may resort to the *McDonnell/Burdine* inquiry. In either instance, the employer may undermine the employee's evidence but has no independent burden of persuasion.

In contrast, intent plays no role in the disparate impact inquiry. The question, rather, is whether an employment practice has a significant, adverse effect on an identifiable class of workers—regardless of the cause or motive for the practice. The employer may attempt to contradict the factual basis for this effect; that is, to prevent the employee from establishing a prima facie case. But when an employer is faced with sufficient proof of disparate impact, its only recourse is to justify the practice by explaining why it is necessary to the operation of business. Such a justification is a classic example of an affirmative defense.

Failing to explore the interplay between these distinct orders of proof, the Court announces that our frequent statements that the employer shoulders the burden of proof respecting business necessity "should have been understood to mean an employer's production—but not persuasion—burden."[18] Our opinions always have emphasized that in a disparate impact case the employer's burden is weighty. "The touchstone," the Court said in *Griggs,* "is business necessity." * * * Later, we held that prison administrators had failed to "rebu[t] the prima facie case of discrimination by showing that the height and weight requirements are * * * essential to effective job perfor-

---

18. The majority's only basis for this proposition is the plurality opinion in *Watson v. Fort Worth Bank & Trust,* * * *, which in turn cites no authority. As Justice Blackmun explained in *Watson,* * * * (concurring in part and concurring in judgment), and as I have shown here, the assertion profoundly misapprehends the difference between disparate impact and disparate treatment claims.

mance," *Dothard v. Rawlinson,* * * *. I am thus astonished to read that the "touchstone of this inquiry is a reasoned review of the employer's justification for his use of the challenged practice * * *. [T]here is no requirement that the challenged practice be * * * 'essential,' * * * ". This casual—almost summary—rejection of the statutory construction that developed in the wake of *Griggs* is most disturbing. I have always believed that the *Griggs* opinion correctly reflected the intent of the Congress that enacted Title VII. Even if I were not so persuaded, I could not join a rejection of a consistent interpretation of a federal statute. Congress frequently revisits this statutory scheme and can readily correct our mistakes if we misread its meaning. * * *

Also troubling is the Court's apparent redefinition of the employees' burden of proof in a disparate impact case. No prima facie case will be made, it declares, unless the employees " 'isolat[e] and identif[y] the specific employment practices that are allegedly responsible for any observed statistical disparities.' " (quoting *Watson v. Fort Worth Bank & Trust,* * * * (plurality opinion)). This additional proof requirement is unwarranted. It is elementary that a plaintiff cannot recover upon proof of injury alone; rather, the plaintiff must connect the injury to an act of the defendant in order to establish prima facie that the defendant is liable. * * * Although the causal link must have substance, the act need not constitute the sole or primary cause of the harm. * * * Thus in a disparate impact case, proof of numerous questionable employment practices ought to fortify an employee's assertion that the practices caused racial disparities.[20] Ordinary principles of fairness require that Title VII actions be tried like "any lawsuit." * * * The changes the majority makes today, tipping the scales in favor of employers, are not faithful to those principles.

II

Petitioners seek reversal of the Court of Appeals and dismissal of this suit on the ground that respondents' statistical evidence failed to prove a prima facie case of discrimination. * * * The District Court concluded "there were 'significant disparities' " between the racial composition of the cannery workers and the noncannery workers, but it "made no precise numerical findings" on this and other critical points. Given this dearth of findings and the Court's newly articulated preference for individualized proof of causation, it would be manifestly unfair to consider respondents' evidence in the aggregate and deem it insufficient. Thus the Court properly rejects petitioners' request for a final judgment and remands for further determination of the strength of respondents' prima facie case. Even at this juncture, however, I believe that respondents' evidence deserves greater credit than the majority allows.

* * *

Evidence that virtually all the employees in the major categories of at-issue jobs were white, whereas about two-thirds of the cannery workers were

20. The Court discounts the difficulty its causality requirement presents for employees, reasoning that they may employ "liberal civil discovery rules" to obtain the employer's statistical personnel records. * * * Even assuming that this generally is true, it has no bearing in this litigation, since it is undisputed that

nonwhite,[25] may not by itself suffice to establish a prima facie case of discrimination. But such evidence of racial stratification puts the specific employment practices challenged by respondents into perspective. Petitioners recruit employees for at-issue jobs from outside the work force rather than from lower-paying, overwhelmingly nonwhite, cannery worker positions. Information about availability of at-issue positions is conducted by word of mouth; therefore, the maintenance of housing and mess halls that separate the largely white noncannery work force from the cannery workers, * * *, coupled with the tendency toward nepotistic hiring,[28] are obvious barriers to employment opportunities for nonwhites. Putting to one side the issue of business justifications, it would be quite wrong to conclude that these practices have no discriminatory consequence.[29] Thus I agree with the Court of Appeals, that when the District Court makes the additional findings prescribed today, it should treat the evidence of racial stratification in the work force as a significant element of respondents' prima facie case.

III

The majority's opinion begins with recognition of the settled rule that "a facially neutral employment practice may be deemed violative of Title VII without evidence of the employer's subjective intent to discriminate that is required in a 'disparate treatment' case." * * * It then departs from the body of law engendered by this disparate impact theory, reformulating the order of proof and the weight of the parties' burdens. Why the Court undertakes these unwise changes in elementary and eminently fair rules is a mystery to me.

I respectfully dissent.

JUSTICE BLACKMUN, with whom JUSTICE BRENNAN and JUSTICE MARSHALL join, dissenting.

I fully concur in Justice Stevens' analysis of this case. Today a bare majority of the Court takes three major strides backwards in the battle against race discrimination. It reaches out to make last Term's plurality opinion in *Watson v. Fort Worth Bank & Trust*, * * * the law, thereby upsetting the longstanding distribution of burdens of proof in Title VII disparate-impact cases. It bars the use of internal workforce comparisons in

petitioners did not preserve such records. * * *

25. The Court points out that nonwhites are "overrepresented" among the cannery workers. * * * Such an imbalance will be true in any racially stratified work force; its significance becomes apparent only upon examination of the pattern of segregation within the work force. In the cannery industry nonwhites are concentrated in positions offering low wages and little opportunity for promotion. Absent any showing that the "underrepresentation" of whites in this stratum is the result of a barrier to access, the "overrepresentation" of nonwhites does not offend Title VII.

28. The District Court found but downplayed the fact that relatives of employees are given preferential consideration. * * * But "of 349 nepotistic hires in four upper-level

departments during 1970–75, 332 were of whites, 17 of nonwhites," the Court of Appeals noted. "If nepotism exists, it is by definition a practice of giving preference to relatives, and where those doing the hiring are predominantly white, the practice necessarily has an adverse impact on nonwhites." * * *

29. The Court suggests that the discrepancy in economic opportunities for white and nonwhite workers does not amount to disparate impact within the meaning of Title VII unless respondents show that it is "petitioners' fault." * * * This statement distorts the disparate impact theory, in which the critical inquiry is whether an employer's practices *operate* to discriminate. *E.g., Griggs,* * * *. Whether the employer intended such discrimination is irrelevant.

the making of a prima facie case of discrimination, even where the structure of the industry in question renders any other statistical comparison meaningless. And it requires practice-by-practice statistical proof of causation, even where, as here, such proof would be impossible.

The harshness of these results is well demonstrated by the facts of this case. The salmon industry as described by this record takes us back to a kind of overt and institutionalized discrimination we have not dealt with in years: a total residential and work environment organized on principles of racial stratification and segregation, which, as Justice Stevens points out, resembles a plantation economy. * * * This industry long has been characterized by a taste for discrimination of the old-fashioned sort: a preference for hiring nonwhites to fill its lowest-level positions, on the condition that they stay there. The majority's legal rulings essentially immunize these practices from attack under a Title VII disparate-impact analysis.

Sadly, this comes as no surprise. One wonders whether the majority still believes that race discrimination—or, more accurately, race discrimination against non-whites—is a problem in our society, or even remembers that it ever was. Cf. *City of Richmond v. J.A. Croson Co.,* 488 U.S. 469, 109 S.Ct. 706, 102 L.Ed.2d 854 (1989).

Notes on Wards Cove

1. Commenting on *Watson,* a Harvard notewriter said:

[T]he Court's discussion of the evidentiary standards to be applied in such challenges blurred the Court's prior distinctions between disparate treatment and disparate impact, and threatened to increase the hurdles for plaintiffs bringing disparate impact challenges against objective as well as subjective hiring practices. The Court's general uneasiness about the proper evidentiary standards to be applied to Watson's claim on remand may indicate that the Court is reconsidering altogether the principles underlying disparate impact doctrine, as originally articulated in *Griggs* itself.

The Supreme Court, 1987 Term—Leading Cases, 102 Harv.L.Rev. 143, 309–10 (1988). Does *Wards Cove* vindicate this forecast? A different Harvard notewriter, while admitting that the Court had "stiffened the requirements for the use of disparate-impact analysis," nevertheless stoutly denied that "the *Wards Cove* decision eliminated the disparate-impact model introduced in *Griggs*":

The case does not * * * reach that far: title VII plaintiffs retain the weapon of disparate impact, although the Court has stripped it of some power. *Wards Cove,* rather, reshapes the disparate-impact law in accordance with a theory of equality based on equal treatment and color blindness, and thus resolves a great deal of the ambiguity present in *Griggs*. In addition, by adopting this theory of equal treatment as its guide, the Court shapes title VII doctrine in a manner more consistent with congressional intent, and reaffirms the validity of merit and ability as criteria in employment decisions.

The Supreme Court, 1988 Term—Leading Cases, 103 Harv.L.Rev. 137, 351, 356 (1989). Do you agree with this analysis?

2. *Wards Cove* was one of six Supreme court cases handed down in 1989 that made it harder for plaintiffs to win job discrimination suits. Because *Wards Cove* was widely perceived as having eviscerated the disparate impact standard enunciated in *Griggs*, by forcing plaintiffs to identify the specific employer practices that

caused the disparate impact, and by redefining business necessity and shifting the burden of proof on business necessity from the employer to the plaintiff, it became the centerpiece of a struggle between Congress and the Bush Administration over the Civil Rights Act of 1990. The dispute focused on alternate definitions of "business necessity." The final Congressional version required that the employment practice or practices "must bear a significant relationship to successful performance of the job," while the Administration preferred language that distinguished between employment practices defended as a measure of job performance and other employment practices: the former "must bear a significant relationship to successful performance of the job" while the latter "must bear a significant relationship to a significant business objective of the employer." Congress enacted its version of the definition as part of the Civil Rights Act of 1990; President Bush vetoed the bill, and his veto was sustained by a one-vote margin in the Senate. For a compelling account of the politics behind this struggle, see Andrew M. Dansicker, A Sheep in Wolf's Clothing: Affirmative Action, Disparate Impact, Quotas and the Civil Rights Act, 25 Colum.J.L. & Soc.Probs. 1 (1991).

3. One year later, the Civil Rights Act of 1991 neatly avoided the fatal struggle over a definition of business necessity by the simple expedient of using the term but leaving it undefined. For the new disparate impact provisions, see § 703(k) of the amended Title VII, 42 U.S.C. 2000e–2, in the Statutory Appendix. In addition, the 1991 Civil Rights Act limited the use of any legislative history on this issue in section 105(b):

(b) No statements other than the interpretive memorandum appearing at Vol. 137 Congressional Record S 15276 (daily ed. Oct. 25, 1991) shall be considered legislative history of, or relied upon in any way as legislative history in construing or applying, any provision of this Act that relates to Wards Cove—Business necessity/cumulation/alternative business practice.

The "interpretative memorandum" referred to reads, in its entirety, as follows:

INTERPRETIVE MEMORANDUM

The final compromise on S. 1745 agreed to by several Senate sponsors, including Senators Danforth, Kennedy, and Dole, and the Administration states that with respect to Wards Cove—Business necessity/cumulation/alternative business practice—the exclusive legislative history is as follows:

The terms "business necessity" and "job related" are intended to reflect the concepts enunciated by the Supreme Court in Griggs v. Duke Power Co., 401 U.S. 424 (1971), and in the other Supreme Court decisions prior to Wards Cove Packing Co. v. Atonio, 490 U.S. 642 (1989).

When a decision-making process includes particular, functionally-integrated practices which are components of the same criterion, standard, method of administration, or test, such as the height and weight requirements designed to measure strength in Dothard v. Rawlinson, 433 U.S. 321 (1977), the particular, functionally-integrated practices may be analyzed as one employment practice.

137 Cong.Rec. S 15276 (daily ed. Oct. 25, 1991). What does this mean? *Griggs* offered two phrasings of the standard. At one point, Chief Justice Burger said:

The Act proscribes not only overt discrimination but also practices that are fair in form, but discriminatory in operation. The touchstone is business necessity. If an employment practice which operates to exclude Negroes cannot be shown to be related to job performance, the practice is prohibited.

Griggs v. Duke Power Co. supra at p. 582. A few paragraphs later, he said "* * * Congress has placed on the employer the burden of showing that any given requirement must have a manifest relationship to the employment in question." (supra at 583). Are these two standards the same? How did *Wards Cove* change either statement? Look carefully at Justice White's language in part III–B(1) of the *Wards Cove* opinion. Has the language of the Civil Rights Act of 1991 done what the "interpretative memorandum" claims? Does § 703(k)(A)(i) reinstate the *Griggs* standard for a showing of disparate impact? Does subsection (B)(i) overturn *Wards Cove?* What is the significance of subsections (A)(ii) and (C)? Is anything left of *Wards Cove?*

Despite Congress' resurrection of the *Griggs* formulation in the 1991 amendments, current disparate impact theory has built-in limitations. As explained by Professor Barbara Flagg in Fashioning a Title VII Remedy for Transparently White Subjective Decisionmaking, 104 Yale L. J. 2009 (1995), facially neutral policies or practices, particularly subjective decisionmaking systems, are often transparent forms of "whiteness:" behaviors and characteristics associated with white culture which take on an aura of race neutrality. Id. at 2013. She has argued that rather than adopt an "assimilationist" approach to equal opportunity, interpretation of Title VII should expand to incorporate a pluralist model, allowing plaintiffs to prove the "foreseeable impact" of decisionmaking systems and the existence of pluralist alternatives. Id. at 2038–2051.

4. The Wards Cove employees, by the way, did not benefit from the 1991 Act. Title IV, section 402(b) of the Act exempts from its terms "any disparate impact case for which a complaint was filed before March 1, 1975, and for which an initial decision was rendered after October 30, 1983." That description just happens to apply to the *Wards Cove* case. On remand, the Ninth Circuit upheld this statutory exemption against the employees' charges that it violated the separation of powers, denied their rights to due process and equal protection, and constituted a bill of attainder. See Atonio v. Wards Cove Packing Co., Inc., 10 F.3d 1485, 1492–96 (9th Cir.1993). Applying the law governing Title VII disparate impact claims as it stood prior to the 1991 Civil Rights Act, the court proceeded to hold that the employees had not made out their claim of disparate impact caused by subjective hiring criteria, nepotism, and messing arrangements. It remanded the case, however, for the district court to determine whether a disparate impact arose from race-labelling or the impression that separate hiring channels were used, as well as for a determination of the feasibility of the workers' suggested alternatives to segregated housing at the cannery. How would *Wards Cove* have been decided absent the statutory exemption?

5. In returning to *Griggs* and the pre-*Wards Cove* standards, defendant employers will again carry the burden of persuasion on the job-relatedness, business necessity defense, if plaintiffs are able to carry their burden of proving discriminatory impact. In Johnston v. City of Philadelphia, 863 F.Supp. 231 (E.D.Pa.1994), plaintiffs were able to survive a summary judgment motion by presenting evidence of a disparate impact on women in the police department's selection of police officer recruits from three eligibility lists in 1990 and 1991. The eligibility lists were based on written examinations. The average rates of selection from the lists did not show a great disparity—12.1% of male applicants were hired and 10.9% of female applicants. The trial court, however, pointed out that the rate of selection for women had declined significantly from the first list to the third list: from the first list, 14% of the women had been selected and 11% of the men. From the third list, 7% of the women were selected and 13% of the

men. Id. at 236. The trial court held this was a sufficient showing to make a prima facie case of disparate impact, requiring a trial on the merits.

In Bradley v. Pizzaco of Nebraska, Inc., 7 F.3d 795 (8th Cir.1993), the Eighth Circuit reaffirmed the defendant's burden of proving business justification under the 1991 amendments restoring *Griggs*. In a race discrimination case, the EEOC established that Domino's Pizza's no-beard policy for its delivery drivers had disparate impact on African American men because of a skin condition affecting up to 50% of black men, many of whom cannot shave at all. Id. at 796. The Eighth Circuit described Domino's burden of proving business justification as a "heavy one," requiring Domino's to show a "compelling need" to maintain its practice, and that "there is no alternative to the challenged practice." Id. at 798. The court rejected the Vice President's testimony that "the better our people look, the better our sales will be" as "largely speculative and conclusory." "Such testimony, without more, does not prove the business necessity of maintaining a strict no-beard policy." Arguments about customer preference were also rejected by the court: "The existence of a beard on the face of a delivery man does not affect in any manner Domino's ability to make or deliver pizzas to their customers." The Eighth Circuit reversed the trial court's finding of business justification and held that the burden on Domino's would be minimal to create an alternative policy and recognize a narrow medical exception for African American men who cannot shave. Id. at 799.

b. *Disparate Treatment*

i. *The Prima Facie Case*

McDONNELL DOUGLAS CORP. v. GREEN

Supreme Court of the United States, 1973.
411 U.S. 792, 93 S.Ct. 1817, 36 L.Ed.2d 668.

Mr. Justice Powell delivered the opinion of the Court.

The case before us raises significant questions as to the proper order and nature of proof in actions under Title VII of the Civil Rights Act of 1964, 78 Stat. 253, 42 U.S.C.A. § 2000e et seq.

Petitioner, McDonnell Douglas Corp., is an aerospace and aircraft manufacturer headquartered in St. Louis, Missouri, where it employs over 30,000 people. Respondent, a black citizen of St. Louis, worked for petitioner as a mechanic and laboratory technician from 1956 until August 28, 1964 when he was laid off in the course of a general reduction in petitioner's work force.

Respondent, a long-time activist in the civil rights movement, protested vigorously that his discharge and the general hiring practices of petitioner were racially motivated. As part of this protest, respondent and other members of the Congress on Racial Equality illegally stalled their cars on the main roads leading to petitioner's plant for the purpose of blocking access to it at the time of the morning shift change. The District Judge described the plan for, and respondent's participation in, the "stall-in" as follows:

"[F]ive teams, each consisting of four cars would 'tie up' five main access roads into McDonnell at the time of the morning rush hour. The drivers of the cars were instructed to line up next to each other completely blocking the intersections or roads. The drivers were also instructed to stop their cars, turn off the engines, pull the emergency brake, raise all windows, lock the doors, and remain in their cars until the police arrived. The plan was to have the cars remain in position for one hour.''

"Acting under the 'stall in' plan, plaintiff [respondent in the present action] drove his car onto Brown Road, a McDonnell access road, at approximately 7:00 a.m., at the start of the morning rush hour. Plaintiff was aware of the traffic problems that would result. He stopped his car with the intent to block traffic. The police arrived shortly and requested plaintiff to move his car. He refused to move his car voluntarily. Plaintiff's car was towed away by the police, and he was arrested for obstructing traffic. Plaintiff pleaded guilty to the charge of obstructing traffic and was fined." 318 F.Supp. 846, 849.

On July 2, 1965, a "lock-in" took place wherein a chain and padlock were placed on the front door of a building to prevent the occupants, certain of petitioner's employees, from leaving. Though respondent apparently knew beforehand of the "lock-in," the full extent of his involvement remains uncertain.

Some three weeks following the "lock-in," on July 25, 1965, petitioner publicly advertised for qualified mechanics, respondent's trade, and respondent promptly applied for re-employment. Petitioner turned down respondent, basing its rejection on respondent's participation in the "stall-in" and "lock-in." * * *

II

The critical issue before us concerns the order and allocation of proof in a private, non-class action challenging employment discrimination. The language of Title VII makes plain the purpose of Congress to assure equality of employment opportunities and to eliminate those discriminatory practices and devices which have fostered racially stratified job environments to the disadvantage of minority citizens. * * *

There are societal as well as personal interests on both sides of this equation. The broad, overriding interest, shared by employer, employee, and consumer, is efficient and trustworthy workmanship assured through fair and racially neutral employment and personnel decisions. In the implementation of such decisions, it is abundantly clear that Title VII tolerates no racial discrimination, subtle or otherwise.

In this case respondent, the complainant below, charges that he was denied employment "because of his involvement in civil rights activities" and "because of his race and color." Petitioner denied discrimination of any kind, asserting that its failure to re-employ respondent was based upon and justified by his participation in the unlawful conduct against it. Thus, the issue at the trial on remand is framed by those opposing factual contentions. The two opinions of the Court of Appeals and the several opinions of the three judges of that court attempted, with a notable lack of harmony, to state the applicable rules as to burden of proof and how this shifts upon the making of a prima facie case. We now address this problem.

The complainant in a Title VII trial must carry the initial burden under the statute of establishing a prima facie case of racial discrimination. This may be done by showing (i) that he belongs to a racial minority; (ii) that he applied and was qualified for a job for which the employer was seeking applicants; (iii) that, despite his qualifications, he was rejected; and (iv) that, after his rejection, the position remained open and the employer continued to seek applicants from persons of complainant's qualifications.[13]   In the instant case, we agree with the Court of Appeals that respondent proved a prima facie case.   463 F.2d 337, 353.   Petitioner sought mechanics, respondent's trade, and continued to do so after respondent's rejection.   Petitioner, moreover, does not dispute respondent's qualifications and acknowledges that his past work performance in petitioner's employ was "satisfactory."

The burden then must shift to the employer to articulate some legitimate, nondiscriminatory reason for the employee's rejection.   We need not attempt in the instant case to detail every matter which fairly could be recognized as a reasonable basis for a refusal to hire.   Here petitioner has assigned respondent's participation in unlawful conduct against it as the cause for his rejection.   We think that this suffices to discharge petitioner's burden of proof at this stage and to meet respondent's prima facie case of discrimination.

The Court of Appeals intimated, however, that petitioner's stated reason for refusing to rehire respondent was a "subjective" rather than objective criterion which "carr[ies] little weight in rebutting charges of discrimination," 463 F.2d, at 352.   This was among the statements which caused the dissenting judge to read the opinion as taking "the position that such unlawful acts as Green committed against McDonnell would not legally entitle McDonnell to refuse to hire him, even though no racial motivation was involved * * *."   Id., at 355.   Regardless of whether this was the intended import of the opinion, we think the court below seriously underestimated the rebuttal weight to which petitioner's reasons were entitled.   Respondent admittedly had taken part in a carefully planned "stall-in," designed to tie up access to and egress from petitioner's plant at a peak traffic hour.[16]   Nothing in Title VII compels an employer to absolve and rehire one who has engaged in such deliberate, unlawful activity against it.[17]   In upholding, under the National Labor Relations Act, the discharge of employees who had seized and forcibly retained an employer's factory building in an illegal sit-down strike, the Court noted pertinently:

> "We are unable to conclude that Congress intended to compel employers to retain persons in their employ regardless of their unlawful conduct,— to invest those who go on strike with an immunity from discharge for acts of trespass or violence against the employer's property * * *.   Apart from the question of the constitutional validity of an enactment of that sort, it is enough to say that such a legislative intention should be found in some definite and unmistakable expression."   NLRB v. Fansteel Corp., 306 U.S. 240, 255, 59 S.Ct. 490, 496, 83 L.Ed. 627 (1939).

13. The facts necessarily will vary in Title VII cases, and the specification above of the prima facie proof required from respondent is not necessarily applicable in every respect to differing factual situations.

16. The trial judge noted that no personal injury or property damage resulted from the "stall-in" due "solely to the fact that law enforcement officials had obtained notice in advance of plaintiff's [here respondent's] demonstration and were at the scene to remove plaintiff's car from the highway."   318 F.Supp. 846, 851.

17. The unlawful activity in this case was directed specifically against petitioner.   We need not consider or decide here whether, or under what circumstances, unlawful activity not directed against the particular employer may be a legitimate justification for refusing to hire.

Petitioner's reason for rejection thus suffices to meet the prima facie case, but the inquiry must not end here. While Title VII does not, without more, compel rehiring of respondent, neither does it permit petitioner to use respondent's conduct as a pretext for the sort of discrimination prohibited by § 703(a)(1). On remand, respondent must, as the Court of Appeals recognized, be afforded a fair opportunity to show that petitioner's stated reason for respondent's rejection was in fact pretext. Especially relevant to such a showing would be evidence that white employees involved in acts against petitioner of comparable seriousness to the "stall-in" were nevertheless retained or rehired. Petitioner may justifiably refuse to rehire one who was engaged in unlawful, disruptive acts against it, but only if this criterion is applied alike to members of all races.

Other evidence that may be relevant to any showing of pretext includes facts as to the petitioner's treatment of respondent during his prior term of employment; petitioner's reaction, if any, to respondent's legitimate civil rights activities; and petitioner's general policy and practice with respect to minority employment.[18] On the latter point, statistics as to petitioner's employment policy and practice may be helpful to a determination of whether petitioner's refusal to rehire respondent in this case conformed to a general pattern of discrimination against blacks. Jones v. Lee Way Motor Freight, Inc., 431 F.2d 245 (C.A.10 1970); Blumrosen, Strangers in Paradise: *Griggs v. Duke Power Co.,* and the Concept of Employment Discrimination, 71 Mich.L.Rev. 59, 91–94 (1972).[19] In short, on the retrial respondent must be given a full and fair opportunity to demonstrate by competent evidence that the presumptively valid reasons for his rejection were in fact a coverup for a racially discriminatory decision.

The court below appeared to rely upon Griggs v. Duke Power Co., supra, in which the Court stated: "If an employment practice which operates to exclude Negroes cannot be shown to be related to job performance, the practice is prohibited." 401 U.S., at 431, 91 S.Ct., at 853, 28 L.Ed.2d 158. But *Griggs* differs from the instant case in important respects. It dealt with standardized testing devices which, however neutral on their face, operated to exclude many blacks who were capable of performing effectively in the desired positions. *Griggs* was rightly concerned that childhood deficiencies in the education and background of minority citizens, resulting from forces beyond their control, not be allowed to work a cumulative and invidious burden on such citizens for the remainder of their lives. Id., at 430, 91 S.Ct., at 853.

18. We are aware that some of the above factors were, indeed, considered by the District Judge in finding under § 704(a), that "defendant's [here petitioner's] reasons for refusing to rehire the plaintiff were motivated solely and simply by the plaintiff's participation in the 'stall in' and 'lock in' demonstrations." 318 F.Supp., at 850. We do not intimate that this finding must be overturned after consideration on remand of respondent's § 703(a)(1) claim. We do, however, insist that respondent under § 703(a)(1) must be given a full and fair opportunity to demonstrate by competent evidence that whatever the stated reasons for his rejection, the decision was in reality racially premised.

19. The District Court may, for example, determine, after reasonable discovery that "the [racial] composition of defendant's labor force is itself reflective of restrictive or exclusionary practices." See Blumrosen, supra, at 92. We caution that such general determinations, while helpful, may not be in and of themselves controlling as to an individualized hiring decision, particularly in the presence of an otherwise justifiable reason for refusing to rehire. See generally United States v. Bethlehem Steel Corp., 312 F.Supp. 977, 992 (W.D.N.Y.1970), order modified, 446 F.2d 652 (C.A.2 1971). Blumrosen, supra, n. 19, at 93.

Respondent, however, appears in different clothing. He had engaged in a seriously disruptive act against the very one from whom he now seeks employment. And petitioner does not seek his exclusion on the basis of a testing device which overstates what is necessary for competent performance, or through some sweeping disqualification of all those with any past record of unlawful behavior, however remote, insubstantial, or unrelated to applicant's personal qualifications as an employee. Petitioner assertedly rejected respondent for unlawful conduct against it and, in the absence of proof of pretext or discriminatory application of such a reason, this cannot be thought the kind of "artificial, arbitrary, and unnecessary barriers to employment" which the Court found to be the intention of Congress to remove. Id., at 431, 91 S.Ct., at 853.[21]

III

In sum, respondent should have been allowed to pursue his claim under § 703(a)(1). If the evidence on retrial is substantially in accord with that before us in this case, we think that respondent carried his burden of establishing a prima facie case of racial discrimination and that petitioner successfully rebutted that case. But this does not end the matter. On retrial, respondent must be afforded a fair opportunity to demonstrate that petitioner's assigned reason for refusing to re-employ was a pretext or discriminatory in its application. If the District Judge so finds, he must order a prompt and appropriate remedy. In the absence of such a finding, petitioner's refusal to rehire must stand.

The judgment is vacated and the cause is hereby remanded to the District Court for further proceedings consistent with this opinion.

So ordered.

Notes on McDonnell Douglas

1. On remand, Percy Green failed to persuade the court that he had been discriminated against because of his race. See Green v. McDonnell Douglas Corp., 390 F.Supp. 501 (E.D.Mo.1975). But, while he himself did not prevail on the merits, the standard established in his case for the order and burden of proof in Title VII cases has become the accepted rule for all individual disparate treatment cases. Despite the Court's express use of the words "racial minority" in its statement of the test, the *McDonnell Douglas* standard has been used in individual cases of sex discrimination, see East v. Romine, Inc., 518 F.2d 332, 337 n. 4 (5th Cir.1975); national origin discrimination, see Banerjee v. Board of Trustees of Smith College, 495 F.Supp. 1148, 1153 (D.Mass.1980), affirmed 648 F.2d 61 (1st Cir.1981), cert. denied 454 U.S. 1098, 102 S.Ct. 671, 70 L.Ed.2d 639 (1981); and age discrimination, see Loeb v. Textron, Inc., 600 F.2d 1003 (1st Cir.1979).

---

21. It is, of course, a predictive evaluation, resistant to empirical proof, whether "an applicant's past participation in unlawful conduct directed at his prospective employer might indicate the applicant's lack of a responsible attitude toward performing work for that employer." 463 F.2d, at 353. But in this case, given the seriousness and harmful potential of respondent's participation in the "stall-in" and the accompanying inconvenience to other em-ployees, it cannot be said that petitioner's refusal to employ lacked a rational and neutral business justification. As the Court has noted elsewhere: "Past conduct may well relate to present fitness; past loyalty may have a reasonable relationship to present and future trust." Garner v. Los Angeles Board, 341 U.S. 716, 720, 71 S.Ct. 909, 912, 95 L.Ed. 1317 (1951).

2. Normally, it is not difficult to establish the first of the four *McDonnell Douglas* prima facie case factors. Kenneth Robinson, a black male, failed to make out a prima facie case, however, because he was unable to prove that the employer knew he was black. The job application form that Robinson filled out placed the information he supplied about his race and other demographic characteristics on a "tear-off form." The employer testified that this part of the application was not sent to the application screener, or that the flap was folded so that it was not visible. All of the application screeners who rejected Robinson's job applications for employment with defendant Orange County testified that they were unaware of Robinson's race when they reviewed his applications. The Ninth Circuit affirmed the district court's summary judgment against Robinson; Judge Wallace reasoned that "[a]n employer cannot intentionally discriminate against a job applicant based on race unless the employer knows the applicant's race." Robinson v. Adams, 830 F.2d 128, 129 (9th Cir.1987). Is that conclusion self-evident?

3. The distinction between "disparate treatment" and "disparate impact" cases for Title VII purposes was first articulated in footnote 15 of the Court's opinion in International Broth. of Teamsters v. United States, 431 U.S. 324, 97 S.Ct. 1843, 52 L.Ed.2d 396 (1977), a systemic disparate treatment case in which the Government proved a systemwide pattern or practice of intentional discrimination against minority truckers who sought positions as line drivers. The Court said:

> Consideration of the question whether the company engaged in a pattern or practice of discriminatory hiring practices involves controlling legal principles that are relatively clear. The Government's theory of discrimination was simply that the company, in violation of § 703(a) of Title VII, regularly and purposefully treated Negroes and Spanish-surnamed Americans less favorably than white persons. The disparity in treatment allegedly involved the refusal to recruit, hire, transfer, or promote minority group members on an equal basis with white people, particularly with respect to line-driving positions. The ultimate factual issues are thus simply whether there was a pattern or practice of such disparate treatment and, if so, whether the differences were "racially premised." McDonnell Douglas Corp. v. Green, 411 U.S. 792, 805 n. 18, 93 S.Ct. 1817, 1825, 36 L.Ed.2d 668.[15]

15. "Disparate treatment" such as alleged in the present case is the most easily understood type of discrimination. The employer simply treats some people less favorably than others because of their race, color, religion, sex, or national origin. Proof of discriminatory motive is critical, although it can in some situations be inferred from the mere fact of differences in treatment. See, e.g., Village of Arlington Heights v. Metropolitan Housing Dev. Corp., 429 U.S. 252, 265–266, 97 S.Ct. 555, 563–565, 50 L.Ed.2d 450. Undoubtedly disparate treatment was the most obvious evil Congress had in mind when it enacted Title VII. See, e.g., 110 Cong.Rec. 13088 (1964)(remarks of Sen. Humphrey)("What the bill does * * * is simply to make it an illegal practice to use race as a factor in denying employment. It provides that men and women shall be employed on the basis of their qualifications, not as Catholic citizens, not as protestant citizens, not as Jewish citizens, not as colored citizens, but as citizens of the United States").

Claims of disparate treatment may be distinguished from claims that stress "disparate impact." The latter involve employment practices that are facially neutral in their treatment of different groups but that in fact fall more harshly on one group than another and cannot be justified by business necessity. Proof of discriminatory motive, we have held, is not required under a disparate impact theory. Compare, e.g., Griggs v. Duke Power Co., 401 U.S. 424, 430–432, 91 S.Ct. 849, 853–854, 28 L.Ed.2d 158, with McDonnell Douglas Corp. v. Green, 411 U.S. 792, 802–806, 93 S.Ct. 1817, 1824–1826, 36 L.Ed.2d 668. See generally Schlei & Grossman, Employment Discrimination Law 1–12 (1976); Blumrosen, Strangers in Paradise: Griggs v. Duke Power Co. and the Concept of Employment Discrimination, 71 Mich.L.Rev. 59 (1972). Either theory may, of course, be applied to a particular set of facts.

Id., 431 U.S. at 334–36, 97 S.Ct. at 1854–55, 52 L.Ed.2d at 415. Does plaintiff have the choice of which theory to use? Can both be pleaded? *Watson* and *Wards Cove* are examples of attempting to litigate employment decisions under both theories, with significantly mixed results.

4. Disparate treatment theory requires that plaintiff prove the employer's adverse action was motivated by discriminatory intent. In an individual disparate treatment case, such intent may be inferred from all the factual circumstances, including proof that the plaintiff was treated differently than another similarly situated employee of the opposite sex. In a systemic disparate treatment case, such as the "pattern and practice" case of *Teamsters*, the necessary showing of "intentional" discrimination is proven by a combination of statistical proof and individual examples of disparate treatment. Systemic disparate treatment cases are discussed at pp. 698–714, infra.

If an employer uses a rule or policy that is facially discriminatory, or if the employer admits it does not hire women (or men), or only some types of women (or men), then "intent" does not need to be inferred from the circumstances. Consequently, the proof structure of *McDonnell Douglas* is not followed. Instead, the employer must seek to establish that sex is a bona fide occupational qualification (BFOQ) justifying its overt sex discrimination. Such sex classification and the BFOQ defense are discussed at pp. 777–789, infra.

ii. Articulating Legitimate and Nondiscriminatory Reasons

TEXAS DEPARTMENT OF COMMUNITY AFFAIRS v. BURDINE

Supreme Court of the United States, 1981.
450 U.S. 248, 101 S.Ct. 1089, 67 L.Ed.2d 207.

Justice Powell delivered the opinion of the Court.

This case requires us to address again the nature of the evidentiary burden placed upon the defendant in an employment discrimination suit brought under Title VII of the Civil Rights Act of 1964, 42 U.S.C.A. § 2000e et seq. The narrow question presented is whether, after the plaintiff has proved a prima facie case of discriminatory treatment, the burden shifts to the defendant to persuade the court by a preponderance of the evidence that legitimate, nondiscriminatory reasons for the challenged employment action existed.

I

Petitioner, the Texas Department of Community Affairs (TDCA), hired respondent, a female, in January 1972, for the position of accounting clerk in the Public Service Careers Division (PSC). PSC provided training and employment opportunities in the public sector for unskilled workers. When hired, respondent possessed several years' experience in employment training. She was promoted to Field Services Coordinator in July 1972. Her supervisor resigned in November of that year, and respondent was assigned additional duties. Although she applied for the supervisor's position of Project Director, the position remained vacant for six months.

PSC was funded completely by the United States Department of Labor. The Department was seriously concerned about inefficiencies at PSC. In February, 1973, the Department notified the Executive Director of TDCA,

B.R. Fuller, that it would terminate PSC the following month. TDCA officials, assisted by respondent, persuaded the Department to continue funding the program, conditioned upon PSC reforming its operations. Among the agreed conditions were the appointment of a permanent Project Director and a complete reorganization of the PSC staff.

After consulting with personnel within TDCA, Fuller hired a male from another division of the agency as Project Director. In reducing the PSC staff, he fired respondent along with two other employees, and retained another male, Walz, as the only professional employee in the division. It is undisputed that respondent had maintained her application for the position of Project Director and had requested to remain with TDCA. Respondent soon was rehired by TDCA and assigned to another division of the agency. She received the exact salary paid to the Project Director at PSC, and the subsequent promotions she has received have kept her salary and responsibility commensurate with what she would have received had she been appointed Project Director.

Respondent filed this suit * * *. She alleged that the failure to promote and the subsequent decision to terminate her had been predicated on gender discrimination in violation of Title VII. After a bench trial, the District Court held that neither decision was based on gender discrimination. The court relied on the testimony of Fuller that the employment decisions necessitated by the commands of the Department of Labor were based on consultation among trusted advisers and a nondiscriminatory evaluation of the relative qualifications of the individuals involved. He testified that the three individuals terminated did not work well together and that TDCA thought that eliminating this problem would improve PSC's efficiency. The court accepted this explanation as rational and, in effect, found no evidence that the decisions not to promote and to terminate respondent were prompted by gender discrimination.

The Court of Appeals for the Fifth Circuit reversed in part.

* * *

II

In McDonnell Douglas Corp. v. Green, 411 U.S. 792, 93 S.Ct. 1817, 36 L.Ed.2d 668 (1973), we set forth the basic allocation of burdens and order of presentation of proof in a Title VII case alleging discriminatory treatment. First, the plaintiff has the burden of proving by the preponderance of the evidence a prima facie case of discrimination. Second, if the plaintiff succeeds in proving the prima facie case, the burden shifts to the defendant "to articulate some legitimate, nondiscriminatory reason for the employee's rejection." * * * Third, should the defendant carry this burden, the plaintiff must then have an opportunity to prove by a preponderance of the evidence that the legitimate reasons offered by the defendant were not its true reasons, but were a pretext for discrimination. * * *

The nature of the burden that shifts to the defendant should be understood in light of the plaintiff's ultimate and intermediate burdens. The ultimate burden of persuading the trier of fact that the defendant intentionally discriminated against the plaintiff remains at all times with the plaintiff. See, Board of Trustees of Keene State College v. Sweeney, 439 U.S. 24, 25, n.

2, 99 S.Ct. 295, 296, n. 2, 58 L.Ed.2d 216 (1978); id., at 29, 99 S.Ct., at 297 (Stevens, J., dissenting). See generally 9 Wigmore, Evidence § 2489 (3d ed. 1940)(the burden of persuasion "never shifts"). The *McDonnell Douglas* division of intermediate evidentiary burdens serves to bring the litigants and the court expeditiously and fairly to this ultimate question.

The burden of establishing a prima facie case of disparate treatment is not onerous. The plaintiff must prove by a preponderance of the evidence that she applied for an available position, for which she was qualified, but was rejected under circumstances which give rise to an inference of unlawful discrimination.[6] The prima facie case serves an important function in the litigation: it eliminates the most common nondiscriminatory reasons for the plaintiff's rejection. See Teamsters v. United States, 431 U.S. 324, 358 & n. 44, * * * (1977). As the Court explained in Furnco Construction Co. v. Waters, 438 U.S. 567, 577 * * *, (1978), the prima facie case "raises an inference of discrimination only because we presume these acts, if otherwise unexplained, are more likely than not based on the consideration of impermissible factors." Establishment of the prima facie case in effect creates a presumption that the employer unlawfully discriminated against the employee. If the trier of fact believes the plaintiff's evidence, and if the employer is silent in the face of the presumption, the court must enter judgment for the plaintiff because no issue of fact remains in the case.[7]

The burden that shifts to the defendant, therefore, is to rebut the presumption of discrimination by producing evidence that the plaintiff was rejected, or someone else was preferred, for a legitimate, nondiscriminatory reason. The defendant need not persuade the court that it was actually motivated by the proffered reasons. See *Sweeney,* supra, at 25, 99 S.Ct., at 296. It is sufficient if the defendant's evidence raises a genuine issue of fact as to whether it discriminated against the plaintiff.[8] To accomplish this, the defendant must clearly set forth, through the introduction of admissible evidence, the reasons for the plaintiff's rejection.[9] The explanation provided must be legally sufficient to justify a judgment for the defendant. If the defendant carries this burden of production, the presumption raised by the

6. * * * In the instant case, it is not seriously contested that respondent has proved a prima facie case. She showed that she was a qualified woman who sought an available position, but the position was left open for several months before she finally was rejected in favor of a male who had been under her supervision.

7. The phrase "prima facie case" may denote not only the establishment of a legally mandatory, rebuttable presumption, but also may be used by courts to describe the plaintiff's burden of producing enough evidence to permit the trier of fact to infer the fact at issue. 9 Wigmore, Evidence § 2494 (3d ed. 1940). *McDonnell Douglas* should have made it apparent that in the Title VII context we use "prima facie case" in the former sense.

8. This evidentiary relationship between the presumption created by a prima facie case and the consequential burden of production placed on the defendant is a traditional feature of the common law. "The word 'presumption'

properly used refers only to a device for allocating the production burden." F. James & G. Hazard, Civil Procedure § 7.9, at 255 (2d ed. 1977)(footnote omitted). See Fed.Rule Evid. 301. See generally 9 Wigmore, Evidence § 2491 (3d Ed.1940). Cf. J. Maguire, Evidence, Common Sense and Common Law, 185–186 (1947). Usually, assessing the burden of production helps the judge determine whether the litigants have created an issue of fact to be decided by the jury. In a Title VII case, the allocation of burdens and the creation of a presumption by the establishment of a prima facie case is intended progressively to sharpen the inquiry into the elusive factual question of intentional discrimination.

9. An articulation not admitted into evidence will not suffice. Thus, the defendant cannot meet its burden merely through an answer to the complaint or by argument of counsel.

prima facie case is rebutted,[10] and the factual inquiry proceeds to a new level of specificity. Placing this burden of production on the defendant thus serves simultaneously to meet the plaintiff's prima facie case by presenting a legitimate reason for the action and to frame the factual issue with sufficient clarity so that the plaintiff will have a full and fair opportunity to demonstrate pretext. The sufficiency of the defendant's evidence should be evaluated by the extent to which it fulfills these functions.

The plaintiff retains the burden of persuasion. She now must have the opportunity to demonstrate that the proffered reason was not the true reason for the employment decision. This burden now merges with the ultimate burden of persuading the court that she has been the victim of intentional discrimination. She may succeed in this either directly by persuading the court that a discriminatory reason more likely motivated the employer or indirectly by showing that the employer's proffered explanation is unworthy of credence. See *McDonnell Douglas,* supra, at 804–805, 93 S.Ct., at 1825–1826.

III

In reversing the judgment of the District Court that the discharge of respondent from PSC was unrelated to her sex, the Court of Appeals adhered to two rules it had developed to elaborate the defendant's burden of proof. First, the defendant must prove by a preponderance of the evidence that legitimate, nondiscriminatory reasons for the discharge existed. 608 F.2d, at 567. See Turner v. Texas Instruments, Inc., 555 F.2d 1251, 1255 (C.A.5 1977). Second, to satisfy this burden, the defendant "must prove that those he hired * * * were somehow *better* qualified than was plaintiff; in other words, comparative evidence is needed." 608 F.2d, at 567 (emphasis in original). See East v. Romine, Inc., 518 F.2d 332, 339–340 (C.A.5 1975).

A

The Court of Appeals has misconstrued the nature of the burden that *McDonnell Douglas* and its progeny place on the defendant. See Part II, supra. We stated in *Sweeney* that "the employer's burden is satisfied if he simply 'explains what he has done' or 'produc[es] evidence of legitimate nondiscriminatory reasons.' " 439 U.S., at 25, n. 2, 99 S.Ct., at 296 n. 2, quoting id., at 28, 29, 99 S.Ct., at 297–298 (Stevens, J., dissenting). It is plain that the Court of Appeals required much more: it placed on the defendant the burden of persuading the court that it had convincing, objective reasons for preferring the chosen applicant above the plaintiff.[11]

---

10. See generally J. Thayer, Preliminary Treatise on Evidence 346 (1898). In saying that the presumption drops from the case, we do not imply that the trier of fact no longer may consider evidence previously introduced by the plaintiff to establish a prima facie case. A satisfactory explanation by the defendant destroys the legally mandatory inference of discrimination arising from the plaintiff's initial evidence. Nonetheless, this evidence and inferences properly drawn therefrom may be considered by the trier of fact on the issue of whether the defendant's explanation is pretextual. Indeed, there may be some cases where

the plaintiff's initial evidence, combined with effective cross-examination of the defendant, will suffice to discredit the defendant's explanation.

11. The court reviewed the defendant's evidence and explained its deficiency:

"Defendant failed to introduce comparative factual data concerning Burdine and Walz. Fuller merely testified that he discharged and retained personnel in the spring shakeup at TDCA primarily on the recommendations of subordinates and that he considered Walz qualified for the position he was retained to do. Fuller failed to specify

The Court of Appeals distinguished *Sweeney* on the ground that the case held only that the defendant did not have the burden of proving the absence of discriminatory intent. But this distinction slights the rationale of *Sweeney* and of our other cases. We have stated consistently that the employee's prima facie case of discrimination will be rebutted if the employer articulates lawful reasons for the action; that is, to satisfy this intermediate burden, the employer need only produce admissible evidence which would allow the trier of fact rationally to conclude that the employment decision had not been motivated by discriminatory animus. The Court of Appeals would require the defendant to introduce evidence which, in the absence of any evidence of pretext, would *persuade* the trier of fact that the employment action was lawful. This exceeds what properly can be demanded to satisfy a burden of production.

The court placed the burden of persuasion on the defendant apparently because it feared that "[i]f an employer need only *articulate,* not prove a legitimate, nondiscriminatory reason for his action, he may compose fictitious, but legitimate, reasons for his actions." Turner v. Texas Instruments, Inc., supra, at 1255 (emphasis in original). We do not believe, however, that limiting the defendant's evidentiary obligation to a burden of production will unduly hinder the plaintiff. First, as noted above, the defendant's explanation of its legitimate reasons must be clear and reasonably specific. Supra, at 5–6. See Loeb v. Textron, Inc., 600 F.2d 1003, 1011–1012, n. 5 (C.A.1 1979). This obligation arises both from the necessity of rebutting the inference of discrimination arising from the prima facie case and from the requirement that the plaintiff be afforded "a full and fair opportunity" to demonstrate pretext. Second, although the defendant does not bear a formal burden of persuasion, the defendant nevertheless retains an incentive to persuade the trier of fact that the employment decision was lawful. Thus, the defendant normally will attempt to prove the factual basis for its explanation. Third, the liberal discovery rules applicable to any civil suit in federal court are supplemented in a Title VII suit by the plaintiff's access to the Equal Employment Opportunity Commission's investigatory files concerning her complaint. See EEOC v. Associated Dry Goods Corp., 449 U.S. 590, 101 S.Ct. 817, 66 L.Ed.2d 762 (1981). Given these factors, we are unpersuaded that the plaintiff will find it particularly difficult to prove that a proffered explanation lacking a factual basis is a pretext. We remain confident that the *McDonnell Douglas* framework permits the plaintiff meriting relief to demonstrate intentional discrimination.

B

The Court of Appeals also erred in requiring the defendant to prove by objective evidence that the person hired or promoted was more qualified than the plaintiff. *McDonnell Douglas* teaches that it is the plaintiff's task to demonstrate that similarly situated employees were not treated equally. 411

any objective criteria on which he based the decision to discharge Burdine and retain Walz. He stated only that the action was in the best interest of the program and that there had been some friction within the department that might be alleviated by Burdine's discharge. Nothing in the record indi-

cates whether he examined Walz' ability to work well with others. This court in *East* found such unsubstantiated assertions of 'qualification' and 'prior work record' insufficient absent data that will allow a true *comparison* of the individuals hired and rejected." 608 F.2d, at 568.

U.S., at 804, 93 S.Ct., at 1825. The Court of Appeals' rule would require the employer to show that the plaintiff's objective qualifications were inferior to those of the person selected. If it cannot, a court would, in effect, conclude that it has discriminated.

The court's procedural rule harbors a substantive error. Title VII prohibits all discrimination in employment based upon race, sex and national origin. "The broad, overriding interest, shared by employer, employee, and consumer, is efficient and trustworthy workmanship assured through fair and * * * neutral employment and personnel decisions." *McDonnell Douglas,* supra, at 801, 93 S.Ct., at 1823. Title VII, however, does not demand that an employer give preferential treatment to minorities or women. 42 U.S.C.A. § 2000e–2(j). See Steelworkers v. Weber, 443 U.S. 193, 205–206, 99 S.Ct. 2721, 2728–2729, 61 L.Ed.2d 480 (1979). The statute was not intended to "diminish traditional management prerogatives." Id., at 207, 99 S.Ct., at 2729. It does not require the employer to restructure his employment practices to maximize the number of minorities and women hired. Furnco Construction Co. v. Waters, 438 U.S., at 577–578 * * *.

The views of the Court of Appeals can be read, we think, as requiring the employer to hire the minority or female applicant whenever that person's objective qualifications were equal to those of a white male applicant. But Title VII does not obligate an employer to accord this preference. Rather, the employer has discretion to choose among equally qualified candidates, provided the decision is not based upon unlawful criteria. The fact that a court may think that the employer misjudged the qualifications of the applicants does not in itself expose him to Title VII liability, although this may be probative of whether the employer's reasons are pretexts for discrimination. Loeb v. Textron, Inc., supra, at 1012, n. 6; see Lieberman v. Gant, 630 F.2d 60, 65 (C.A.2 1980).

IV

In summary, the Court of Appeals erred by requiring the defendant to prove by a preponderence of the evidence the existence of nondiscriminatory reasons for terminating the respondent and that the person retained in her stead had superior objective qualifications for the position. When the plaintiff has proved a prima facie case of discrimination, the defendant bears only the burden of explaining clearly the nondiscriminatory reasons for its actions. The judgment of the Court of Appeals is vacated and the case is remanded for further proceedings consistent with this opinion.

It is so ordered

Notes on Burdine

1. The burden on a plaintiff who claims that she was not hired because of her sex is to show intentional discrimination against her by the employer: disparate treatment requires proof of illegal motive. Not all potential employers, however, are cooperative enough to write the plaintiff a letter of rejection stating that the job she desires can be filled only by a man. See Davis v. Passman, 442 U.S. 228, 99 S.Ct. 2264, 60 L.Ed.2d 846 (1979)(Congressman Passman fired plaintiff because it was "essential" that the understudy to his Administrative Assistant "be a man.") The *McDonnell Douglas* test is designed to permit the

plaintiff to make out a prima facie case by showing four objective facts that are sufficient to raise an inference that it is more likely than not that she was rejected because of her sex. The burden of explanation then shifts to the employer. Under this format, the first tender of evidence concerning motive or intent comes from the defendant. What is the significance of the Court's statement in *Burdine* that "[t]he defendant need not persuade the court that it was actually motivated by the proffered reasons"? In Board of Trustees of Keene State College v. Sweeney, 439 U.S. 24, 99 S.Ct. 295, 58 L.Ed.2d 216 (1978), the Court rejected the suggestion that the defendant must prove the absence of discriminatory motive in order to rebut the plaintiff's prima facie case. Does *Burdine,* read in light of *Sweeney,* mean that the defendant need not prove that it acted out of nondiscriminatory motives either?

What constitutes a "legitimate, nondiscriminatory reason" for the employer's action? This issue is usually combined on appeal with the question of whether plaintiff has shown the employer's explanation to be pretextual. As Judge Martin explained in one of the rare cases that did focus on whether defendant had sustained its burden of production,

> [b]ecause the burden of *producing* is much lighter than the burden of *persuading,* most Title VII disparate treatment cases are decided on the pretext issue, on which the plaintiff has the burden of persuasion.

Burton v. State of Ohio, Adult Parole Authority, 798 F.2d 164, 166 (6th Cir.1986), affirmed after remand 830 F.2d 193 (6th Cir.1987)(Table) cert. denied 485 U.S. 964, 108 S.Ct. 1232, 99 L.Ed.2d 432 (1988)(emphasis in original). In *Burton,* plaintiff was a black man who alleged he had been denied promotion because of his race; John Severn, a white man, had been chosen instead. The employer's proffered explanation was that E.H. Harris, the Superintendent who made the final selection, had relied on the recommendation of Valerian Kostyk, who had supervised both Burton and Severn and who recommended Severn. Harris did not testify at trial because of ill health, but Kostyk appeared and was extensively cross-examined concerning his reasons for recommending Severn. Rejecting Burton's charge that the employer had failed to articulate a legitimate, nondiscriminatory reason for Burton's dismissal, the Sixth Circuit reasoned as follows:

> Testimony of the actual appointing authority is highly desirable in a Title VII case, because through direct and cross-examination the court may learn information bearing on the ultimate issue of intentional discrimination. However, * * * a district court cannot require a defendant to prove its legitimate, nondiscriminatory reason, but merely to produce it. Therefore, the production of John Severn's recommendation by Supervisor Kostyk, bolstered by his stated reasons for the recommendation, is sufficient to satisfy the Parole Authority's burden of *producing* a legitimate, nondiscriminatory reason for its actions. * * *

Id., 798 F.2d at 167 (emphasis in original). The matter was remanded for analysis of the issue of pretext. Has the Parole Authority shown that Harris's reasons for accepting Kostyk's recommendation were the same as Kostyk's reasons for making the recommendation?

2. In its restatement of the three-stage structure of proof of a disparate treatment case, the *Burdine* Court began the process of separating individual disparate treatment cases into two types: (1) single motive, "pretext" cases and (2) dual motive or "mixed" motive cases. The Court suggests these categories when it instructs plaintiff on how she can meet her burden of persuasion at the

third stage, after the employer has produced evidence of its legitimate business reason:

> She now must have the opportunity to demonstrate that the proffered reason was not the true reason for the employment decision. * * * She may succeed in this either directly by persuading the court that a discriminatory reason *more likely* motivated the employer or indirectly by showing that the employer's proffered explanation is unworthy of credence.

Burdine, supra at p. 620 (emphasis added). A single motive, pretext case results when plaintiff rebuts the employer's legitimate reason in its entirety, showing it "unworthy of credence." A dual or mixed motive case results when the trier of fact must choose between several surviving motivations, when the plaintiff is attempting to prove that the discriminatory motive "more likely" motivated the employer, even though non-discriminatory motives existed as well. For a discussion of mixed motive cases, see Price Waterhouse v. Hopkins, at p. 664, infra.

3. Under *Burdine's* three-part structure, once the defendant has offered an alternative legitimate non-discriminatory reason for refusing to hire plaintiff, she has the opportunity to show that the stated reason was merely a pretext. How is this done? Is the plaintiff, at this third stage, required to prove that defendant's true intent was a discriminatory one?

Cases holding that plaintiff failed to prove pretext include Yowell v. United States Postal Service, 810 F.2d 644 (7th Cir.1987)(black male, ostensibly discharged for poor attendance and insubordination, unable to prove pretext); Conner v. Fort Gordon Bus Co., 761 F.2d 1495 (11th Cir.1985)(female bus driver, ostensibly fired after President of company saw her make an illegal left turn that he believed endangered the safety of bus passengers, unable to prove pretext); Holden v. Commission Against Discrimination, 671 F.2d 30 (1st Cir.1982), certiorari denied 459 U.S. 843, 103 S.Ct. 97, 74 L.Ed.2d 88 (1982) (black woman discharged as public information officer failed to show that employer's reasons for her discharge, which included inability to accept direction from supervisors, incompetence in the performance of duties, failure to supervise personnel assigned to her, and inability to work within the agency rules, were pretextual); Kenyatta v. Bookey Packing Co., 649 F.2d 552 (8th Cir.1981)(black male discharged, ostensibly because of chronic absenteeism, was unable to prove pretext); Correa v. Nampa School District No. 131, 645 F.2d 814 (9th Cir.1981)(Mexican–American woman not rehired as curriculum supervisor, on grounds that she was unable to function effectively in her job due to her inability to get along with co-workers, including other Mexican–Americans, was unable to prove pretext); Akins v. Medical Environmental Systems, Inc., 513 F.Supp. 686 (E.D.Mo.1981), affirmed 676 F.2d 704 (8th Cir.1981)(black woman fired as cleaning technician at hospital charged race discrimination; employer's articulated reason for her discharge was that she stole food from the cafeteria; plaintiff was unable to prove pretext).

Compare the following cases, where plaintiff did establish that the employer's articulated reason was a pretext for discrimination: Thorne v. City of El Segundo, 726 F.2d 459 (9th Cir.1983), cert. denied 469 U.S. 979, 105 S.Ct. 380, 83 L.Ed.2d 315 (1984), opinion on remand 802 F.2d 1131 (9th Cir.1986). Plaintiff Deborah Lynn Thorne applied for a position as a police officer. She received the second highest score on the written test, passed the agility test, and passed the psychological test. The first sign of trouble developed during the polygraph test, when she disclosed in response to questioning about a miscarriage that she had been pregnant as the result of an affair with a married police officer formerly a member of the department to which she was applying. The interviewing officer decided that she lacked "sufficient aggressiveness, self-assuredness or probable physical ability to presently handle herself in stress situations." After further investigation, the department recommended that she be disqualified, citing three reasons: first, her poor record of tardiness and sick time at prior jobs; second, she had "barely passed" the physical agility test and was "a very feminine type person who is apparently very weak in the upper body"; and third, her interest in police work was very recent. The trial court's judgment that plaintiff had failed to make out a prima facie case under Title VII and that, even if she had, the defendant had rejected her for nondiscriminatory reasons that were not pretextual was reversed on appeal. Judge Betty Fletcher wrote for the court:

> The district court's finding that defendants did not reject Thorne because of the information they uncovered regarding her sexual history also flies in the face of the overwhelming weight of the evidence. * * *

> The nondiscriminatory reasons offered by the City and accepted by the district court to justify the refusal to hire appellant are simply incredible and clearly pretextual. * * *

> The evidence in the record is more than sufficient to justify the legal conclusion that, in fact, Thorne was rejected because of intentional discrimination in violation of Title VII. A refusal to hire a woman because of a sex-stereotyped view of her physical abilities is the kind of invidious discrimination that violates Title VII. * * * Similarly, application to women of a standard of moral integrity that is not applied equally to men violates Title VII. * * * Thorne's evidence was sufficient to prove that sex-stereotyping and unequal job standards were applied to her.

Id., 726 F.2d at 466–68. See also Chaline v. KCOH, Inc., 693 F.2d 477 (5th Cir.1982)(white male discharged as production manager of black-oriented radio station ostensibly because he was not qualified to assume new position of part-time disc jockey since he did not have a characteristic black "voice"; court's finding that plaintiff's idiom and voice quality were sufficiently similar to those of black disc jockeys to make the proffered reason a mere pretext for discrimination was affirmed); United States EEOC v. Minneapolis Electric Steel Casting Co., 552 F.Supp. 957 (D.Minn.1982)(white woman discharged from her job as a chipper-grinder in a steel foundry ostensibly because she violated a safety rule that required workers to operate the large grinder with both feet on the ground; she proved that several male employees also regularly violated the safety rule and that she had been watched more closely than other employees because of her sex); Furr v. Goodwill Industries Rehabilitation Center, 513 F.Supp. 161 (W.D.Tenn. 1981)(white woman rejected as truck driver because black helper who was delegated to accompany her was afraid to be seen riding in a truck with a white woman on the streets of Memphis at night; the employer's articulated reason of safety and the plaintiff's inability to learn the route without a helper was rejected as pretextual). Compare Jackson v. University of Pittsburgh, 826 F.2d 230 (3d Cir.1987)(reversing summary judgment against black male lawyer fired from his position as staff attorney ostensibly because of poor performance; remanded for trial on issue of pretext).

Can any patterns be discerned in these cases? Has plaintiff's proof of "pretext" become more difficult following the Supreme Court's decision in St. Mary's Honor Center v. Hicks, set out at p. 648, infra.

4. Note the Court's statement in *Burdine,* made in the process of rejecting the Fifth Circuit's requirement that the employer prove that the person hired or promoted was more qualified than the plaintiff, that "the employer has discretion

to choose among equally qualified candidates, provided the decision is not based upon unlawful criteria." The evidence offered below to justify the employer's decision to hire a man rather than Burdine was that he had a college degree and had done advanced work and that he had administrative experience and worked well with others. Burdine had attended college for only one year and had no degree; she was perceived as having had some interpersonal difficulty with her co-workers. The employer admitted that a college degree was not required for the position of Project Director. If the employer nonetheless relies on the degree to select among candidates otherwise equally qualified, does it thereby base its decision on "unlawful criteria" if fewer women than men have college degrees? Does Griggs v. Duke Power Co., set forth at p. 580, supra, require this result? See also Schulte v. Wilson Industries, Inc., 547 F.Supp. 324, 341 (S.D.Tex.1982), holding in a case brought under Title VII and the Equal Pay Act that an employer may not rebut a prima facie case by "purporting to rely on criteria [here, a college degree—Ed.] which measures attributes unrelated to probable job performance." See also Lewis v. Central Piedmont Community College, 689 F.2d 1207 (4th Cir.1982) cert. denied 460 U.S. 1040, 103 S.Ct. 1433, 75 L.Ed.2d 792 (1983) (examining the educational backgrounds of the black woman plaintiff and the white woman who was hired for the job of accounting lab instructor, including a comparison of their grades, and concluding that the person hired was so much more qualified than plaintiff that the inference of discriminatory racial intent had disappeared from the case).

5. Are largely subjective reasons "lawful criteria," or "legitimate, non-discriminatory" reasons? On remand, the Fifth Circuit upheld the district court's finding that Burdine "was terminated for the good of the agency and because she and two others also terminated did not work well together and had disagreements," rather than because of her sex. Burdine v. Texas Department of Community Affairs, 647 F.2d 513, 514 (5th Cir.1981). Does this determination reflect an accurate understanding of the Supreme Court's holding in *Burdine?* Reread footnote 11 in *Burdine* in the context of the Court's opinion.

The existence of subjective evaluations has often made it easier for a plaintiff to prove pretext and existence of an employer's illegal intent. In Miles v. M.N.C. Corp., 750 F.2d 867 (11th Cir.1985), the Eleventh Circuit noted: "Subjective evaluation involving white supervisors provide a ready mechanism for racial discrimination." 750 F.2d at 871. Most of the cases criticizing an employer's use of subjective standards, however, involve lower level jobs or non-professional employees. See Elizabeth Bartholet, Application of Title VII to Jobs in High Places, 95 Harv. L. Rev. 947, 973–78 (1982). For more recent blue or pink collar cases, see Mozee v. American Commercial Marine Serv. Co., 940 F.2d 1036, 1050 (7th Cir.1991), (ruling that employer who gave foremen complete discretion to choose leadmen from lower level employees has burden of proving subjective requirements it used in choosing leadmen); cert. denied 113 S.Ct. 207 (1992); Hill v. Seaboard Coast Line R.R., 885 F.2d 804, 809 (11th Cir.1989)(finding that although district court properly considered employer's subjective qualifications, plaintiffs were unable to prove race discrimination in promotion of railroad journeymen from carmen to foreman); Green v. USX Corp., 843 F.2d 1511, 1527 (3d Cir.1988)(finding discrimination where black man was denied position as laborer which required no education or work experience, and where employer was aware of significant racial disparity in hiring and decisions were predicated on unguided and unvalidated subjective criteria), cert. granted and vacated 490 U.S. 1103 (1989); Pitre v. Western Elec. Inc., 843 F.2d 1262, 1272 (10th Cir.1988)(finding district court properly considered employer's reliance on subjective evaluations as evidence of gender discrimination where women clustered in lower plant positions and where layoff and promotion policies discriminated against women).

For scrutiny of subjective evaluations in semi-professional jobs, see Mallory v. Booth Refrigeration Supply Co., 882 F.2d 908, 910–11 (4th Cir.1989)(holding use of subjective criteria, while relevant to allegations of racial discrimination, does not, standing alone, prove Title VII violation; thus, no discrimination where two blacks denied promotion to data entry supervisor based on employer's personal observations); Jauregui v. City of Glendale, 852 F.2d 1128, 1135–36 (9th Cir.1988)(determining use of subjective factors had potential for manipulation where city failed to promote Hispanic police officer allegedly lacking strong interpersonal skills, while promoting white officer with lower objective exam scores and same lack of interpersonal skills).

There are a few cases, however, where courts criticize subjective evaluations in professional jobs. See Farber v. Massillon Bd. of Educ., 917 F.2d 1391, 1399 (6th Cir.1990)(holding use of subjective criteria was "merely a poor disguise for discriminatory action" where school board selected man as director of instruction for subjective reasons when female teacher met board's written appointee qualifications policy while man selected did not), cert. denied 498 U.S. 1082 (1991); Bruhwiler v. University of Tenn., 859 F.2d 419, 421 (6th Cir.1988)(affirming district court's careful scrutiny of employer's proffered reasons for non-promotion of white female employee and finding of gender discrimination where white male employees trained by white female plaintiff were promoted to positions supervising her); Willis v. Watson Chapel Sch. Dist., 703 F.Supp. 1381, 1386–88 (E.D.Ark.1988)(finding male superintendent's subjective reasons for recommending only men to fill six school administrator positions were pretextual, where female applicant met stated education and experience qualifications and none of the male applicants did), affirmed in part and reversed in part 899 F.2d 745 (8th Cir.1990).

For an example of continuing deference to professional jobs, however, see Ross v. William Beaumont Hosp., 678 F.Supp. 655, 677 (E.D.Mich.1988) (stating that courts have traditionally shown greater deference to subjective job appraisals for "white collar" or professional positions because such positions are more difficult to evaluate objectively than "blue collar" jobs).

6. Can an employer defend against a charge of race or sex discrimination by showing that the person chosen instead of plaintiff was also of plaintiff's race or sex? The Fifth Circuit thinks so: it held in Adams v. Reed, 567 F.2d 1283, 1286–87 (5th Cir.1978), rehearing *en banc* denied 572 F.2d 320 (5th Cir.1978), that an employer who hired another woman after refusing to hire the female plaintiff had not discriminated against plaintiff because of her sex. Similarly, it held in Jefferies v. Harris County Community Action Ass'n, 615 F.2d 1025, 1030 (5th Cir.1980), that a black woman who was not promoted to the position of Field Representative failed to prove race discrimination because the person who was promoted was also black. Is this a correct interpretation of the Act? Compare Gutzwiller v. Fenik, 860 F.2d 1317 (6th Cir.1988), where Sixth Circuit affirmed jury finding of sex discrimination under § 1983 in denial of tenure for woman, despite fact that another woman received tenure by the same department at the same time. The United States Supreme Court noted in Furnco Constr. Corp. v. Waters, 438 U.S. 567, 579, 98 S.Ct. 2943, 2950–51, 57 L.Ed.2d 957, 969 (1978), that "[a] racially balanced work force cannot immunize an employer from liability for specific acts of discrimination."

In Connecticut v. Teal, 457 U.S. 440, 102 S.Ct. 2525, 73 L.Ed.2d 130 (1982), a majority of the Court rejected an employer's attempt to assert a "bottom line" theory of defense to a disparate impact case. The employer had administered a written examination as the first step in a selection process for the position of Welfare Eligibility Supervisor. Only 54.17% of black applicants, as compared to 79.54% of white applicants, passed the test. When the time came to promote applicants based on eligibility lists generated by the written test, however, defendant chose to promote 46 persons, 11 of whom were black and 35 of whom were white. The "bottom line" of the selection process was that the actual promotion rate of blacks was close to 170% of that of whites, for of 48 black candidates, 22.9% were promoted, while of 259 white candidates, only 13.5% were promoted. Defendant urged this "bottom line" result as a defense to plaintiffs' charge that the written test had improperly excluded them. Characterizing this argument as one in which "petitioners seek simply to justify discrimination against respondents on the basis of their favorable treatment of other members of respondents' racial group", id., 457 U.S. at 454, 102 S.Ct. at 2534, 73 L.Ed.2d at 142, Justice Brennan held it impermissible:

> Title VII does not permit the victim of a facially discriminatory policy to be told that he has not been wronged because other persons of his or her race or sex were hired. That answer is no more satisfactory when it is given to victims of a policy that is facially neutral but practically discriminatory. Every *individual* employee is protected against both discriminatory treatment and against "practices that are fair in form, but discriminatory in operation." [citing *Griggs*].

Id., 457 U.S. at 455–456, 102 S.Ct. at 2535, 73 L.Ed.2d at 142–143 (emphasis in original). Justice Powell, Chief Justice Burger, Justice Rehnquist, and Justice O'Connor, dissenting, asserted that "while disparate-*treatment* cases focus on the way in which an individual has been treated, disparate-*impact* cases are concerned with the protected group." Id., 457 U.S. at 440, 102 S.Ct. at 2436, 73 L.Ed.2d at 144 (emphasis in original). They concluded that respondents were trying to have it both ways:

> The respondents, as individuals, are entitled to the full personal protection of Title VII. But, having undertaken to prove a violation of their rights by reference to group figures, respondents cannot deny petitioner the opportunity to rebut their evidence by introducing figures of the same kind. Having pleaded a disparate impact case, the plaintiffs cannot deny the defendant the opportunity to show that there was no disparate impact.

Id., 457 U.S. at 460, 102 S.Ct. at 2537, 73 L.Ed.2d at 145.

Does *Teal* mean that the Fifth Circuit's analysis in *Adams* and *Jefferies* was misguided?

7. Having taken the view of Title VII defenses outlined in Note 6, supra, the Fifth Circuit concluded in *Jefferies* that plaintiff had not proven race discrimination. After reviewing and remanding her sex discrimination claim, however, the court took an additional step and considered a third claim, one based on a combination of both race and sex: possible discrimination against Jefferies as a black woman. It found that black women were not adequately protected by the Act. It agreed with plaintiff Dafro Jefferies that "discrimination against black females can exist even in the absence of discrimination against black men or white women." *Jefferies*, Note 6, supra, 615 F.2d at 1032. Its solution to this problem was to expand the protection of Title VII by recognizing a subclass of black women

who could allege a cause of action based on the "combination discrimination" of race and sex:

> Recognition of black females as a distinct protected subgroup for purposes of the prima facie case and proof of pretext is the only way to identify and remedy discrimination directed toward black females. Therefore, we hold that when a Title VII plaintiff alleges that an employer discriminates against black females, the fact that black males and white females are not subject to discrimination is irrelevant and must not form any part of the basis for a finding that the employer did not discriminate against the black female plaintiff. Thus, the fact that Jones, who won the promotion Jefferies sought, was black does not bring him within Jefferies' protected class for purposes of her prima facie case. Similarly, when pretext is at issue—that is, when Jefferies attempts to show that the employer's purported reason for the adverse employment action is merely a mask for discrimination by showing that persons outside her class were treated differently than herself—black males and white females must be treated as persons outside Jefferies' class.

> Because the district court did not consider Jefferies' claim of discrimination on the basis of both race and sex, and because its treatment of HCCAA's defensive evidence impermissibly placed Jefferies in the same class as black males and white females, we must remand the issue to the district court so it may make appropriate findings of fact and conclusions of law in light of this opinion concerning Jefferies' claim of discrimination in promotion based on both race and sex. On remand, the district court should make findings on whether the evidence Jefferies presented was sufficient to establish a violation of Title VII under the standards that govern Title VII claims which we discussed above.

Id., 615 F.2d at 1034. The court justified its result expanding Title VII's protection by invoking the sex-plus cases, like Phillips v. Martin Marietta, set out at p. 714, infra (holding that an employer's refusal to hire mothers of pre-school aged children violated Title VII), and Sprogis v. United Air Lines, Inc., discussed at p. 722, infra (invalidating employer's no-marriage rule for stewardesses). The court reasoned that:

> * * * An employer may not apply different standards of treatment to women with young children, to married women, or to women who are single and pregnant. It is beyond belief that, while an employer may not discriminate against these subclasses of women, he could be allowed to discriminate against black females as a class. This would be a particularly illogical result, since the "plus" factors in the former categories are ostensibly "neutral" factors, while race itself is prohibited as a criterion for employment. As this court stated in Willingham, distinctions in employment practices between men and women on the basis of immutable or protected characteristics inhibit employment opportunity in violation of Section 703(a). 507 F.2d at 1091.

Id., 615 F.2d at 1034. Despite the Fifth Circuit's expansive approach in *Jefferies*, on remand, the district court dismissed the suit. Its action was affirmed on appeal without further discussion of the combination discrimination theory. Jefferies v. Harris County Community Action Ass'n, 693 F.2d 589 (5th Cir.1982).

At least two federal district judges have followed the Fifth Circuit in *Jefferies* in recognizing black women as a special subclass for Title VII purposes. In both cases, however, the black female plaintiff lost her Title VII claim. See Chambers v. Omaha Girls Club, 629 F.Supp. 925, 944 & n. 34 (D.Neb.1986), affirmed 834 F.2d 697 (8th Cir.1987), rehearing denied 840 F.2d 583 (8th Cir.1988), discussed at p. 766, infra (expressly adopting the reasoning in *Jefferies*); Judge v. Marsh, 649 F.Supp. 770, 779–80 (D.D.C.1986)(plaintiff was unable to prove that her nonselection as EEO Officer was based on her status as a black woman).

Professor Kimberle Crenshaw has criticized antidiscrimination doctrine for its failure to take account of the "intersectionality" that represents the experience of Black women. She argues that

> Black women are sometimes excluded from feminist theory and antiracist policy discourse because both are predicated on a discrete set of expectations that often does not accurately reflect the interaction of race and gender. These problems cannot be solved simply by including Black women within an already established analytical structure. Because the intersectional experience is greater than the sum of racism and sexism, any analysis that does not take intersectionality into account cannot sufficiently address the particular manner in which Black women are subordinated. Thus, for feminist theory and antiracist policy discourse to embrace the experiences and concerns of Black women, the entire framework that has been used as a basis for translating "women's experience" or "the Black experience" into concrete policy demands must be rethought and recast.

Crenshaw, Demarginalizing the Intersection of Race and Sex: A Black Feminist Critique of Antidiscrimination Doctrine, Feminist Theory and Antiracist Politics, 1989 U.Chi.L.F. 139, 140 (1989). Applying this critique to the question of compound discrimination claims brought by Black women, Crenshaw argues that the consequence of rejecting such claims is that "the employment experiences of white women obscured the distinct discrimination that Black women experienced." Id., at 148 (discussing DeGraffenreid v. General Motors, 413 F.Supp. 142 (E.D.Mo.1976) affirmed in part on other grounds, reversed in part, and remanded 558 F.2d 480 (8th Cir.1977)). She also criticizes Moore v. Hughes Helicopters, 708 F.2d 475 (9th Cir.1983) for its failure to certify a Black woman as a class representative in a case challenging sex discrimination against all women, pointing out that the court's action "left Moore with the task of supporting her race and sex discrimination claims with statistical evidence of discrimination against Black females alone." Id., at 145. Crenshaw recognizes that critics might respond that she is trying to have the argument both ways by insisting that Black women are harmed both by being treated differently than other protected groups and by being treated the same as they are. Id., at 148–49. She responds, "The point is that Black women can experience discrimination in any number of ways and that the contradiction arises from our assumptions that their claims of exclusion must be unidirectional." Id., at 149. Can a similar argument be made by Black men? See Note, Invisible Man: Black and Male Under Title VII, 104 Harv.L.Rev. 749 (1991).

Does Crenshaw's critique mean that *Jefferies* is right? Cathy Scarborough argues that the "sex plus" rationale offered in *Jefferies* and limited in *Judge* to only one "plus" factor is inadequate to redress the multi-factored discrimination often experienced by women of color. She believes that both *Jefferies* and *Judge* should be rejected in favor of a "category-plus" approach that would recognize Black women as a single class for Title VII purposes, and would permit "plus" factors to be added that are not themselves protected categories under the statute. A "category plus" case might then be a claim that a Black woman or another woman of color was discriminated against because she is married, has children, or speaks with an accent. Note, Conceptualizing Black Women's Employment

Experiences, 98 Yale L.J. 1457 (1989). Does this approach expand Title VII beyond the intent of Congress?

Consider the more recent case of Lam v. University of Hawaii, 40 F.3d 1551 (9th Cir.1994). In *Lam*, the Ninth Circuit reversed a summary judgment against plaintiff, an Asian woman, who claimed sex, race, and national origin discrimination in her failure to be hired for a position at the U. of Hawaii Law School. Judge Reinhardt wrote:

> The district court's second justification for granting summary judgment was based on the defendants' favorable consideration of two other candidates for the PALS [Pacific Asian Legal Studies] position: one an Asian man, the other a white woman. In assessing the significance of these candidates, the court seemed to view racism and sexism as separate and distinct elements amenable to almost mathematical treatment, so that evaluating discrimination against an Asian woman became a simple matter of performing two separate tasks: looking for racism "alone" and looking for sexism "alone," with Asian men and white women as the corresponding model victims. The court questioned Lam's claim of racism in light of the fact that the Dean had been interested in the late application of an Asian male.[16] Similarly, it concluded that the faculty's subsequent offer of employment to a white woman indicated a lack of gender bias.[17] We conclude that in relying on these facts as a basis for its summary judgment decision, the district court misconceived important legal principles.

> To begin with, even the Law School's favorable treatment of other Asian women would not necessarily defeat Lam's claim at trial. See *Gutzwiller*, 860 F.2d at 1320–21 (tenure position denied one white female professor in favor of another). Certainly it could not do so at summary judgment, for such evidence creates at most a genuine dispute as to a material factual question.[18] At least equally significant is the error committed by the court in its separate treatment of race and and sex discrimination. As other courts have recognized, where two bases for discrimination exist, they cannot be neatly reduced

---

16. Aside from the difference in gender, it is significant that Lam and the Asian male candidate were of different national origins— Lam being Vietnamese–French, the male candidate, Chinese. Lam alleged not only race discrimination but also national origin discrimination, thereby raising the distinction as relevant under Title VII. Moreover, the particular geographical consciousness of the PALS program means that the distinction might be more salient than it otherwise might be.

17. The district court should have noted, besides the difference in race, the chronological considerations that preclude reliance on this fact to defeat Lam's discrimination claim. The offer of employment to the female applicant was made long after Lam had complained of discrimination both publicly and by filing the present discrimination action. By that time, the Law School was on notice that its employment actions would be subject to scrutiny. Given the obvious incentive in such circumstances for an employer to take corrective action in an attempt to shield itself from liability, it is clear that nondiscriminatory employer actions occurring subsequent to the filing of a

discrimination complaint will rarely even be relevant as circumstantial evidence in favor of the employer. Gonzales v. Police Dept. of San Jose, 901 F.2d 758, 761–62 (9th Cir.1990).

18. Since the district court is barred from weighing conflicting evidence in ruling on a motion for summary judgment, we need not decide if such evidence might be deemed relevant to, though not determinative of, a claim of race and sex discrimination. We note, nonetheless, that in Jefferies v. Harris County Community Action Ass'n, 615 F.2d 1025 (5th Cir. 1980), the Fifth Circuit held that evidence of nondiscriminatory treatment of black males and white females is wholly irrelevant to the question of discrimination against a black female plaintiff claiming bias on both racial and gender grounds. Id. at 1034. On the other hand, evidence of *discriminatory* treatment of, for example, a black male clearly is relevant to the discrimination claim of a black woman. See, e.g., EEOC v. Beverage Canners, Inc., 897 F.2d 1067, 1072 (11th Cir.1990). We express no view on whether such a one-way bar is justified in either some or all cases.

to distinct components. See *Jefferies*, 615 F.2d at 1032–34; Graham v. Bendix Corp., 585 F.Supp. 1036, 1047 (N.D.Ind.1984); Chambers v. Omaha Girls Club, 629 F.Supp. 925, 946 n. 34 (D.Neb.1986), aff'd, 834 F.2d 697 (8th Cir.1987).[19] Rather than aiding the decisional process, the attempt to bisect a person's identity at the intersection of race and gender often distorts or ignores the particular nature of their experiences.[20] Cf. Moore v. Hughes Helicopters, Inc., 708 F.2d 475, 480 (9th Cir.1983)(black female not necessarily representative of interests of black males and white females). Like other subclasses under Title VII, Asian women are subject to a set of stereotypes and assumptions shared neither by Asian men nor by white women.[21] In consequence, they may be targeted for discrimination "even in the absence of discrimination against [Asian] men or white women." *Jefferies*, 615 F.2d at 1032 (discussing black women); Hicks v. Gates Rubber Co., 833 F.2d 1406, 1416 (10th Cir.1987)(same). Accordingly, we agree with the *Jefferies* court that, when a plaintiff is claiming race *and* sex bias, it is necessary to determine whether the employer discriminates on the basis of that *combination* of factors, not just whether it discriminates against people of the same race or of the same sex. Cf. Connecticut v. Teal, 457 U.S. 440, 455, 102 S.Ct. 2525, 2535, 73 L.Ed.2d 130 (1982)("Title VII does not permit the victim of a facially discriminatory policy to be told that he has not been wronged because other persons of his or her race or sex were hired.").

iii. Discriminatory Motive as a Finding of Fact

UNITED STATES POSTAL SERVICE BOARD OF GOVERNORS v. AIKENS

Supreme Court of the United States, 1983.
460 U.S. 711, 103 S.Ct. 1478, 75 L.Ed.2d 403.

JUSTICE REHNQUIST delivered the opinion of the Court.

Respondent Louis Aikens filed suit under Title VII of the Civil Rights Act of 1964, as amended, 42 U.S.C. § 2000e et seq., claiming that petitioner, the United States Postal Service, discriminated against him on account of his race. Aikens, who is black, claimed that the Postal Service had discriminatorily refused to promote him to higher positions in the Washington, D.C. Post Office where he had been employed since 1937. After a bench trial, the District Court entered judgment in favor of the Postal Service, but the Court of Appeals reversed. 642 F.2d 514 (C.A.D.C.1980). We vacated the Court of Appeals' judgment and remanded for reconsideration in light of Texas Department of Community Affairs v. Burdine, 450 U.S. 248 * * * (1981). * * *

On remand, the Court of Appeals reaffirmed its earlier holding that the District Court had erred in requiring Aikens to offer direct proof of discrimi-

---

19. In essence, the district court's approach reduces discrimination against Asian women to discrimination against Asian men plus discrimination against white women. The inherent fallacy of this approach is obvious when one considers that discrimination against white men could be similarly analyzed, using the same models: Asian men plus white women.

20. See K. Crenshaw, Demarginalizing the Intersection of Race and Sex: A Black Feminist Critique of Antidiscriminatory Doctrine,

Feminist Theory and Antiracist Politics, 1989 U. Chi. Legal F. 139; J. Winston, Mirror, Mirror on the Wall: Title VII, Section 1981 and the Intersection of Race and Gender in the Civil Rights Act of 1990, 79 Cal. L. Rev. 775 (1991).

21. See, e.g., J. Hagedorn, Asian Women in Film: No Joy, No Luck, Ms. Jan./Feb. 1994, at 74 (listing stereotypes of Asian women such as geisha, dragon lady, concubine, lotus blossom).

natory intent. It also held that the District Court erred in requiring Aikens to show, as part of his *prima facie* case, that he was "as qualified or more qualified" than the people who were promoted. 665 F.2d 1057, 1058, 1059 (C.A.D.C.1981)(Per Curiam). We granted certiorari.[1] 455 U.S. 1015 * * * (1982).

The Postal Service argues that an employee who has shown only that he was black, that he applied for a promotion for which he possessed the minimum qualifications, and that the employer selected a non-minority applicant has not established a *"prima facie"* case of employment discrimination under Title VII. Aikens argues that he submitted sufficient evidence that the Postal Service discriminated against him to warrant a finding of a *prima facie* case.[2] Because this case was fully tried on the merits, it is surprising to find the parties and the Court of Appeals still addressing the question whether Aikens made out a *prima facie* case. We think that by framing the issue in these terms, they have unnecessarily evaded the ultimate question of discrimination *vel non*.[3]

By establishing a *prima facie* case, the plaintiff in a Title VII action creates a rebuttable "presumption that the employer unlawfully discriminated against" him. Texas Department of Community Affairs v. Burdine * * *. See McDonnell Douglas Corp. v. Green * * *. To rebut this presumption, "the defendant must clearly set forth, through the introduction of admissible evidence, the reasons for the plaintiff's rejection." *Burdine,* supra, * * *. In other words, the defendant must "produc[e] evidence that the plaintiff was rejected, or someone else was preferred, for a legitimate, nondiscriminatory reason." * * *

But when the defendant fails to persuade the district court to dismiss the action for lack of a *prima facie* case,[4] and responds to the plaintiff's proof by

1. We have consistently distinguished disparate treatment cases from cases involving facially neutral employment standards that have disparate impact on minority applicants. See, e.g., Texas Department of Community Affairs v. Burdine, 450 U.S. 248, 252 n. 5 * * * (1981); McDonnell Douglas Corp. v. Green, 411 U.S. 792, 802 n. 14, 93 S.Ct. 1817, 1824 n. 14 * * * (1973).

2. Aikens showed that white persons were consistently promoted and detailed over him and all other black persons between 1966 and 1974. Aikens has been rated as "an outstanding supervisor whose management abilities are far above average." App. 8. There was no derogatory or negative information in his Personnel Folder. He had more supervisory seniority and training and development courses than all but one of the white persons who were promoted above him. He has a master's degree and has completed three years of residence towards a Ph.D. Aikens had substantially more education than the white employees who were advanced ahead of him; of the 12, only 2 had any education beyond high school and none had a college degree. He introduced testimony that the person responsible for the promotion decisions at issue had made numer-

ous derogatory comments about blacks in general and Aikens in particular. If the District Court were to find, on the basis of this evidence, that the Postal Service did discriminate against Aikens, we do not believe that this would be reversible error.

3. As in any lawsuit, the plaintiff may prove his case by direct or circumstantial evidence. The trier of fact should consider all the evidence, giving it whatever weight and credence it deserves. Thus, we agree with the Court of Appeals that the District Court should not have required Aikens to submit direct evidence of discriminatory intent. See International Brotherhood of Teamsters v. United States, 431 U.S. 324, 358 n. 44, 97 S.Ct. 1843, 1866 n. 44, 52 L.Ed.2d 396 (1977)("[T]he *McDonnell Douglas* formula does not require direct proof of discrimination").

4. It appears that at one point in the trial the District Court decided that Aikens had made out a *prima facie* case. When Aikens concluded his case in chief, the Postal Service moved to dismiss on the ground that there was no *prima facie* case. Tr. 256. The District Court denied this motion. Tr. 259. See Pet. App. 47a.

offering evidence of the reason for the plaintiff's rejection, the factfinder must then decide whether the rejection was discriminatory within the meaning of Title VII. At this stage, the *McDonnell–Burdine* presumption "drops from the case," id., at 255, n. 10, * * * and "the factual inquiry proceeds to a new level of specificity." Id., at 255 * * *. After Aikens presented his evidence to the District Court in this case, the Postal Service's witnesses testified that he was not promoted because he had turned down several lateral transfers that would have broadened his Postal Service experience. See Tr. 311–313, 318–320, 325; Pet.App. 53a. The District Court was then in a position to decide the ultimate factual issue in the case.

The "factual inquiry" in a Title VII case is "whether the defendant intentionally discriminated against the plaintiff." *Burdine,* supra, * * *. In other words, is "the employer * * * treating 'some people less favorably than others because of their race, color, religion, sex, or national origin.' " Furnco Construction Corp. v. Waters, 438 U.S. 567, 577 * * * (1978), quoting Int'l Brotherhood of Teamsters v. United States, 431 U.S. 324, 335, n. 15, * * * (1977). The *prima facie* case method established in *McDonnell Douglas* was "never intended to be rigid, mechanized, or ritualistic. Rather, it is merely a sensible, orderly way to evaluate the evidence in light of common experience as it bears on the critical question of discrimination." *Furnco,* supra, 438 U.S., at 577, 98 S.Ct., at 2949. Where the defendant has done everything that would be required of him if the plaintiff had properly made out a *prima facie* case, whether the plaintiff really did so is no longer relevant. The district court has before it all the evidence it needs to decide whether "the defendant intentionally discriminated against the plaintiff." *Burdine,* supra, * * *.

On the state of the record at the close of the evidence, the District Court in this case should have proceeded to this specific question directly, just as district courts decide disputed questions of fact in other civil litigation.[5] As we stated in *Burdine:*

> "The plaintiff retains the burden of persuasion. [H]e may succeed in this either directly by persuading the court that a discriminatory reason more likely motivated the employer or indirectly by showing that the employer's proffered explanation is unworthy of credence." 450 U.S., at 256, 101 S.Ct., at 1095.

In short, the district court must decide which party's explanation of the employer's motivation it believes.

All courts have recognized that the question facing triers of fact in discrimination cases is both sensitive and difficult. The prohibitions against discrimination contained in the Civil Rights Act of 1964 reflect an important national policy. There will seldom be "eyewitness" testimony as to the employer's mental processes. But none of this means that trial courts or reviewing courts should treat discrimination differently from other ultimate questions of fact. Nor should they make their inquiry even more difficult by applying legal rules which were devised to govern "the basic allocation of burdens and order of presentation of proof," *Burdine,* 450 U.S., at 252, 101

---

5. Of course, the plaintiff must have an adequate "opportunity to demonstrate that the proffered reason was not the true reason for the employment decision," but rather a pre- text. *Burdine,* supra, at 256, 101 S.Ct., at 1095. There is no suggestion in this case that Aikens did not have such an opportunity.

S.Ct., at 1093, in deciding this ultimate question. The law often obliges finders of fact to inquire into a person's state of mind. As Lord Justice Bowen said in treating this problem in an action for misrepresentation nearly a century ago:

> "The state of a man's mind is as much a fact as the state of his digestion. It is true that it is very difficult to prove what the state of a man's mind at a particular time is, but if it can be ascertained it is as much a fact as anything else." Edgington v. Fitzmaurice, 29 Ch.Div. 459, 483 (1885).

The District Court erroneously thought that respondent was required to submit direct evidence of discriminatory intent, see n. 3, supra, and erroneously focused on the question of *prima facie* case rather than directly on the question of discrimination. Thus we cannot be certain that its findings of fact in favor of the Postal Service were not influenced by its mistaken view of the law. We accordingly vacate the judgment of the Court of Appeals, and remand the case to the District Court so that it may decide on the basis of the evidence before it whether the Postal Service discriminated against Aikens.

It is so ordered.

Justice Marshall concurs in the judgment.

Justice Blackmun, with whom Justice Brennan joins, concurring.

I join the Court's opinion. I write to stress the fact, however, that, as I read its opinion, the Court today reaffirms the framework established by McDonnell Douglas Corp. v. Green * * * for Title VII cases. Under that framework, once a Title VII plaintiff has made out a prima facie case and the defendant-employer has articulated a legitimate, nondiscriminatory reason for the employment decision, the plaintiff bears the burden of demonstrating that the reason is pretextual, that is, it is "not the true reason for the employment decision." Texas Dept. of Community Affairs v. Burdine * * *. As the Court's opinion today implies, * * * this burden "merges with the ultimate burden of persuading the court that [the plaintiff] has been the victim of intentional discrimination." * * *

This ultimate burden may be met in one of two ways. First, as the Court notes, a plaintiff may persuade the court that the employment decision more likely than not was motivated by a discriminatory reason. * * * In addition, however, this burden is also carried if the plaintiff shows "that the employer's proffered explanation is unworthy of credence." *Burdine,* 450 U.S., at 256, 101 S.Ct., at 1095, citing *McDonnell Douglas* * * *. While the Court is correct that the ultimate determination of factual liability in discrimination cases should be no different from that in other types of civil suits, * * * the *McDonnell Douglas* framework requires that a plaintiff prevail when at the third stage of a Title VII trial he demonstrates that the legitimate, nondiscriminatory reason given by the employer is in fact not the true reason for the employment decision.

Notes on Aikens

1. *Aikens* was widely perceived as a test case for the application of Title VII to higher level jobs. See Elizabeth Bartholet, Proof of Discriminatory Intent Under Title VII: United States Postal Service Board of Governors v. Aikens, 70

Calif.L.Rev. 1201 (1982). Qualifications for the managerial positions for which Aikens had applied were not easily defined. As Judge Wilkey put it in his dissent from the first panel opinion,

> [t]o be "qualified" for any managerial position at this level requires above all that one have managerial ability—an ability to supervise, direct, and cooperate with others; a personal sense of responsibility and initiative; an ability to motivate other persons; and a familiarity with the substantive area of activity for which one is responsible. Such traits of managerial ability are intangible and defy measurement by "objective" means using figures or paper credentials.

Aikens v. United States Postal Service, 642 F.2d 514, 522 (D.C.Cir.1980)(dissenting opinion), vacated 453 U.S. 902, 101 S.Ct. 3135, 69 L.Ed.2d 989 (1981). The district court had addressed this problem by requiring Aikens to show, apparently as part of his prima facie case, that he was as qualified or more qualified than the individuals who were promoted or detailed in his stead. Judge Harry Edwards, writing for the first panel majority, rejected this proposition as "plainly at odds with the test enunciated in *McDonnell Douglas* ", id., 642 F.2d at 519, and observed that Aikens had demonstrated his qualifications to perform the work he sought by showing his record of accomplishments, including his educational background and his experience with the Post Office.

After this buildup, the opinion itself rather fizzled, didn't it? Does it serve as anything more than a reminder that the only way to test the sufficiency of a prima facie case is by a motion for summary judgment? Can you tell whether a plaintiff must prove that he or she is "as qualified or more qualified" than other candidates as part of the prima facie case? Recall that the Court had rejected, in *Burdine,* the Fifth Circuit's rule that the employer must prove at the second stage that the person hired or promoted was more qualified than the plaintiff. See pp. 627, 631 supra. Does this mean that neither party is required to produce evidence of comparable qualifications? Or does *Aikens,* read in light of *Burdine,* mean that this burden rests with plaintiff at the final stage?

2. What is the significance of Justice Blackmun's concurring opinion? Does the majority opinion require more of a plaintiff at the third stage than a showing that "the legitimate, nondiscriminatory reason given by the employer is in fact not the true reason for the employment decision"? Is anything more suggested by Justice Rehnquist's statement, not about what the plaintiff must show, but about what the district court must determine: "In short, the district court must decide which party's explanation of the employer's motivation it believes"? In light of the quotation in the Court's opinion of Lord Bowen's observations about the factual nature of the state of a person's mind, is the plaintiff being given the task of proving that the employer affirmatively intended to discriminate against him? Is this different than a showing of pretext? If so, is it foreclosed by the Court's agreement with the appellate court in footnote 3 that the district court should not have required Aikens to submit direct evidence of discriminatory intent? Or was that limited to the prima facie case stage? The Court also quotes *Burdine* for the proposition that the "factual inquiry" in Title VII cases is "whether the defendant intentionally discriminated against the plaintiff." Has the Court left the plaintiff's burden at the prima facie case stage relatively easy, only to increase substantially its difficulty at the final stage? Further discussion of these issues is found in St. Mary's Honor Center v. Hicks, set forth at p. 648 infra.

3.   While *Aikens* was pending, the argument that a Title VII plaintiff has the burden of proving relative qualifications for higher level jobs as part of the prima facie case was rejected by several courts. See, e.g., Hawkins v. Anheuser–Busch, Inc., 697 F.2d 810, 813–14 (8th Cir.1983)(citing Bartholet's article as well as Note, Relative Qualifications and the Prima Facie Case in Title VII Litigation, 82 Colum.L.Rev. 533 (1982), in support of its holding); Cavallari v. Stetson, 555 F.Supp. 561, 564 (D.Mass.1982). Defendants in both *Hawkins* and *Cavallari* defended the person chosen as more qualified than the plaintiff at the second stage of articulating a legitimate, nondiscriminatory reason for the employment action. In *Hawkins,* but not *Cavallari,* plaintiff was successful in proving pretext. As a practical matter, is the employer compelled to offer such evidence at the second stage in cases involving managerial jobs?

What do you make of the Court's open invitation in footnote 2 of its opinion to the district court to find on remand that Aikens had suffered job discrimination? If the court so finds, can the Supreme Court identify *Aikens* in subsequent cases as a situation where plaintiff did, in fact, prove that his qualifications were as good as, or superior to, those of the persons chosen in his stead?

4.   In a Title VII disparate treatment case, what is a finding of fact and what is a conclusion of law? In *Burdine,* the Court told us that plaintiff's "ultimate burden" was to persuade the court that "she has been the victim of intentional discrimination." Is this a conclusion of law? A finding of fact?

In *Aikens,* the Court tells us "the 'factual inquiry' in a Title VII case is 'whether the defendant intentionally discriminated against the plaintiff.'" The Court explains that this issue of "discrimination" should not be treated any differently by reviewing courts than other "ultimate questions of fact." (supra at p. 634). The Court then quotes from Lord Justice Bowen: "The state of a man's mind is as much a fact as the state of his digestion." Does this mean the determination of whether a plaintiff has been discriminated against is solely a question of fact? Under the language of § 703(a)(1), an unlawful employment practice is defined as any adverse action taken by an employer against any individual "because of" the individual's race or sex. Under the structure of a disparate treatment case, is this final determination a question of fact or law?

iv.   The "Clearly Erroneous" Standard of Review

ANDERSON v. CITY OF BESSEMER CITY

Supreme Court of the United States, 1985.
470 U.S. 564, 105 S.Ct. 1504, 84 L.Ed.2d 518.

JUSTICE WHITE delivered the opinion of the Court.

In Pullman–Standard v. Swint, 456 U.S. 273, 102 S.Ct. 1781, 72 L.Ed.2d 66 (1982), we held that a District Court's finding of discriminatory intent in an action brought under Title VII of the Civil Rights Act of 1964, 78 Stat. 253, as amended, 42 U.S.C. § 2000e *et seq.,* is a factual finding that may be overturned on appeal only if it is clearly erroneous. In this case, the Court of Appeals for the Fourth Circuit concluded that there was clear error in a District Court's finding of discrimination and reversed. Because our reading of the record convinces us that the Court of Appeals misapprehended and misapplied the clearly-erroneous standard, we reverse.

I

Early in 1975, officials of respondent City of Bessemer City, North Carolina, set about to hire a new Recreation Director for the city. Although the duties that went with the position were not precisely delineated, the new Recreation Director was to be responsible for managing all of the city's recreational facilities and for developing recreational programs—athletic and otherwise—to serve the needs of the city's residents. A five-member committee selected by the Mayor was responsible for choosing the Recreation Director. Of the five members, four were men; the one woman on the committee, Mrs. Auddie Boone, served as the chairperson.

Eight persons applied for the position of Recreation Director. Petitioner, at the time a 39–year–old schoolteacher with college degrees in social studies and education, was the only woman among the eight. The selection committee reviewed the resumes submitted by the applicants and briefly interviewed each of the jobseekers. Following the interviews, the committee offered the position to Mr. Donald Kincaid, a 24–year–old who had recently graduated from college with a degree in physical education. All four men on the committee voted to offer the job to Mr. Kincaid; Mrs. Boone voted for petitioner.

Believing that the committee had passed over her in favor of a less qualified candidate solely because she was a woman, petitioner filed discrimination charges with the Charlotte District Office of the Equal Employment Opportunity Commission. In July 1980 (five years after petitioner filed the charges), the EEOC's District Director found that there was reasonable cause to believe that petitioner's charges were true and invited the parties to attempt a resolution of petitioner's grievance through conciliation proceedings. The EEOC's efforts proved unsuccessful, and in due course, petitioner received a right-to-sue letter.

Petitioner then filed this Title VII action in the United States District Court for the Western District of North Carolina. After a 2–day trial during which the court heard testimony from petitioner, Mr. Kincaid, and the five members of the selection committee, the court issued a brief memorandum of decision setting forth its finding that petitioner was entitled to judgment because she had been denied the position of Recreation Director on account of her sex.

* * *

As set forth in the formal findings of fact and conclusions of law, the court's finding that petitioner had been denied employment by respondent because of her sex rested on a number of subsidiary findings. First, the court found that at the time the selection committee made its choice, petitioner had been better qualified than Mr. Kincaid to perform the range of duties demanded by the position. The court based this finding on petitioner's experience as a classroom teacher responsible for supervising schoolchildren in recreational and athletic activities, her employment as a hospital recreation director in the late 1950's, her extensive involvement in a variety of civic organizations, her knowledge of sports acquired both as a high school athlete and as a mother of children involved in organized athletics, her skills as a public speaker, her experience in handling money (gained in the course of her community activities and in her work as a bookkeeper for a group of physicians), and her knowledge of music, dance, and crafts. The court found that Mr. Kincaid's principal qualifications were his experience as a student teacher and as a coach in a local youth basketball league, his extensive knowledge of team and individual sports, acquired as a result of his lifelong involvement in athletics, and his formal training as a physical education major in college. Noting that the position of Recreation Director involved more than the management of athletic programs, the court concluded that petitioner's greater breadth of experience made her better qualified for the position.

Second, the court found that the male committee members had in fact been biased against petitioner because she was a woman. The court based this finding in part on the testimony of one of the committee members that he believed it would have been "real hard" for a woman to handle the job and that he would not want his wife to have to perform the duties of the Recreation Director. The finding of bias found additional support in evidence that another male committee member had told Mr. Kincaid, the successful applicant, of the vacancy and had also solicited applications from three other men, but had not attempted to recruit any women for the job.

Also critical to the court's inference of bias was its finding that petitioner, alone among the applicants for the job, had been asked whether she realized the job would involve night work and travel and whether her husband approved of her applying for the job. The court's finding that the committee had pursued this line of inquiry only with petitioner was based on the testimony of petitioner that these questions had been asked of her and the testimony of Mrs. Boone that similar questions had not been asked of the other applicants. Although Mrs. Boone also testified that during Mr. Kincaid's interview, she had made a "comment" to him regarding the reaction of his new bride to his taking the position of Recreation Director, the court concluded that this comment was not a serious inquiry, but merely a "facetious" remark prompted by Mrs. Boone's annoyance that only petitioner had been questioned about her spouse's reaction. The court also declined to credit the testimony of one of the male committee members that Mr. Kincaid had been asked about his wife's feelings "in a way" and the testimony of another committeeman that all applicants had been questioned regarding their willingness to work at night and their families' reaction to night work. The court concluded that the finding that only petitioner had been seriously questioned about her family's reaction suggested that the male committee members believed women had special family responsibilities that made certain forms of employment inappropriate.

Finally, the court found that the reasons offered by the male committee members for their choice of Mr. Kincaid were pretextual. The court rejected the proposition that Mr. Kincaid's degree in physical education justified his choice, as the evidence suggested that where male candidates were concerned, the committee valued experience more highly than formal training in physical education.[1] The court also rejected the claim of one of the committeemen that Mr. Kincaid had been hired because of the superiority of the recreational programs he planned to implement if selected for the job. The court credited the testimony of one of the other committeemen who had voted for Mr.

---

1. The evidence established that the committee members had initially favored a third candidate, Bert Broadway, and had decided not to hire him only because he stated that he was unwilling to move to Bessemer City. Mr. Broadway had two years of experience as a community recreation director; but like petitioner, he lacked a college degree in physical education.

Kincaid that the programs outlined by petitioner and Mr. Kincaid were substantially identical.

On the basis of its findings that petitioner was the most qualified candidate, that the committee had been biased against hiring a woman, and that the committee's explanations for its choice of Mr. Kincaid were pretextual, the court concluded that petitioner had met her burden of establishing that she had been denied the position of Recreation Director because of her sex. Petitioner having conceded that ordering the city to hire her would be an inappropriate remedy under the circumstances, the court awarded petitioner backpay in the amount of $30,397.00 and attorney fees of $16,971.59.

The Fourth Circuit reversed the District Court's finding of discrimination. 717 F.2d 149 (1983). In the view of the Court of Appeals, three of the District Court's crucial findings were clearly erroneous: the finding that petitioner was the most qualified candidate, the finding that petitioner had been asked questions that other applicants were spared, and the finding that the male committee members were biased against hiring a woman. Having rejected these findings, the Court of Appeals concluded that the District Court had erred in finding that petitioner had been discriminated against on account of her sex.

* * *

III

Because a finding of intentional discrimination is a finding of fact, the standard governing appellate review of a district court's finding of discrimination is that set forth in Federal Rule of Civil Procedure 52(a): "Findings of fact shall not be set aside unless clearly erroneous, and due regard shall be given to the opportunity of the trial court to judge of the credibility of the witnesses." The question before us, then, is whether the Court of Appeals erred in holding the District Court's finding of discrimination to be clearly erroneous.

Although the meaning of the phrase "clearly erroneous" is not immediately apparent, certain general principles governing the exercise of the appellate court's power to overturn findings of a district court may be derived from our cases. The foremost of these principles, as the Fourth Circuit itself recognized, is that "a finding is 'clearly erroneous' when although there is evidence to support it, the reviewing court on the entire evidence is left with the definite and firm conviction that a mistake has been committed." United States v. United States Gypsum Co., 333 U.S. 364, 395, 68 S.Ct. 525, 542, 92 L.Ed. 746 (1948). This standard plainly does not entitle a reviewing court to reverse the finding of the trier of fact simply because it is convinced that it would have decided the case differently. The reviewing court oversteps the bounds of its duty under Rule 52 if it undertakes to duplicate the role of the lower court. "In applying the clearly erroneous standard to the findings of a district court sitting without a jury, appellate courts must constantly have in mind that their function is not to decide factual issues de novo." Zenith Radio Corp. v. Hazeltine Research, Inc., 395 U.S. 100, 123, 89 S.Ct. 1562, 1576, 23 L.Ed.2d 129 (1969). If the district court's account of the evidence is plausible in light of the record viewed in its entirety, the court of appeals may not reverse it even though convinced that had it been sitting as the trier of fact, it would have weighed the evidence differently. Where there are two permissible views of the evidence, the fact-finder's choice between them cannot be clearly erroneous. United States v. Yellow Cab Co., 338 U.S. 338, 342, 70 S.Ct. 177, 179, 94 L.Ed. 150 (1949); see also Inwood Laboratories, Inc. v. Ives Laboratories, Inc., 456 U.S. 844, 102 S.Ct. 2182, 72 L.Ed.2d 606 (1982).

This is so even when the district court's findings do not rest on credibility determinations, but are based instead on physical or documentary evidence or inferences from other facts. To be sure, various Courts of Appeals have on occasion asserted the theory that an appellate court may exercise *de novo* review over findings not based on credibility determinations. See, e.g., Orvis v. Higgins, 180 F.2d 537 (C.A.2 1950); Lydle v. United States, 635 F.2d 763, 765, n. 1 (C.A.6 1981); Swanson v. Baker Industries, Inc., 615 F.2d 479, 483 (C.A.8 1980). This theory has an impressive genealogy, having first been articulated in an opinion written by Judge Frank and subscribed to by Judge Augustus Hand, see *Orvis v. Higgins,* supra, but it is impossible to trace the theory's lineage back to the text of Rule 52, which states straightforwardly that "findings of fact shall not be set aside unless clearly erroneous." That the Rule goes on to emphasize the special deference to be paid credibility determinations does not alter its clear command: Rule 52 "does not make exceptions or purport to exclude certain categories of factual findings from the obligation of a court of appeals to accept a district court's findings unless clearly erroneous." Pullman–Standard v. Swint, 456 U.S., at 287, 102 S.Ct., at 1789.

The rationale for deference to the original finder of fact is not limited to the superiority of the trial judge's position to make determinations of credibility. The trial judge's major role is the determination of fact, and with experience in fulfilling that role comes expertise. Duplication of the trial judge's efforts in the court of appeals would very likely contribute only negligibly to the accuracy of fact determination at a huge cost in diversion of judicial resources. In addition, the parties to a case on appeal have already been forced to concentrate their energies and resources on persuading the trial judge that their account of the facts is the correct one; requiring them to persuade three more judges at the appellate level is requiring too much. As the Court has stated in a different context, the trial on the merits should be "the 'main event' * * * rather than a 'tryout on the road.'" Wainwright v. Sykes, 433 U.S. 72, 90, 97 S.Ct. 2497, 2508, 53 L.Ed.2d 594 (1977). For these reasons, review of factual findings under the clearly-erroneous standard—with its deference to the trier of fact—is the rule, not the exception.

When findings are based on determinations regarding the credibility of witnesses, Rule 52 demands even greater deference to the trial court's findings; for only the trial judge can be aware of the variations in demeanor and tone of voice that bear so heavily on the listener's understanding of and belief in what is said. See Wainwright v. Witt, 469 U.S. 412, 105 S.Ct. 844, 83 L.Ed.2d 841 (1985). This is not to suggest that the trial judge may insulate his findings from review by denominating them credibility determinations, for factors other than demeanor and inflection go into the decision whether or not to believe a witness. Documents or objective evidence may contradict the witness' story; or the story itself may be so internally inconsistent or implausible on its face that a reasonable factfinder would not credit it. Where such factors are present, the court of appeals may well find clear error even in a finding purportedly based on a credibility determination. See, e.g., United States v. United States Gypsum Co., supra, 333 U.S., at 396, 68 S.Ct., at 542. But when a trial judge's finding is based on his decision to credit the testimony of one of two or more witnesses, each of whom has told a coherent and facially plausible story that is not contradicted by extrinsic evidence, that finding, if not internally inconsistent, can virtually never be clear error. Cf. United States v. Aluminum Co. of America, 148 F.2d 416, 433 (C.A.2 1945); Orvis v. Higgins, supra, at 539–540.

IV

Application of the foregoing principles to the facts of the case lays bare the errors committed by the Fourth Circuit in its employment of the clearly-erroneous standard. In detecting clear error in the District Court's finding that petitioner was better qualified than Mr. Kincaid, the Fourth Circuit improperly conducted what amounted to a *de novo* weighing of the evidence in the record. The District Court's finding was based on essentially undisputed evidence regarding the respective backgrounds of petitioner and Mr. Kincaid and the duties that went with the position of Recreation Director. The District Court, after considering the evidence, concluded that the position of Recreation Director in Bessemer City carried with it broad responsibilities for creating and managing a recreation program involving not only athletics, but also other activities for citizens of all ages and interests. The court determined that petitioner's more varied educational and employment background and her extensive involvement in a variety of civic activities left her better qualified to implement such a rounded program than Mr. Kincaid, whose background was more narrowly focused on athletics.

The Fourth Circuit, reading the same record, concluded that the basic duty of the Recreation Director was to implement an athletic program, and that the essential qualification for a successful applicant would be either education or experience specifically related to athletics.[2] Accordingly, it seemed evident to the Court of Appeals that Mr. Kincaid was in fact better qualified than petitioner.

Based on our own reading of the record, we cannot say that either interpretation of the facts is illogical or implausible. Each has support in inferences that may be drawn from the facts in the record; and if either interpretation had been drawn by a district court on the record before us, we would not be inclined to find it clearly erroneous. The question we must answer, however, is not whether the Fourth Circuit's interpretation of the facts was clearly erroneous, but whether the District Court's finding was clearly erroneous. See McAllister v. United States, 348 U.S. 19, 20–21, 75 S.Ct. 6, 7–8, 99 L.Ed. 20 (1954). The District Court determined that petitioner was better qualified, and, as we have stated above, such a finding is entitled to deference notwithstanding that it is not based on credibility determinations. When the record is examined in light of the appropriately deferential

---

2. The Fourth Circuit thus saw no inconsistency between the statement of the male committee members that they preferred Bert Broadway because of his experience and their claim that they had selected Mr. Kincaid over petitioner because of his formal training. See n. 1, supra. In the view of the Court of Appeals, this demonstrated only that Mr. Broadway had relevant experience and Mr. Kincaid had relevant education, while petitioner had neither.

standard, it is apparent that it contains nothing that mandates a finding that the District Court's conclusion was clearly erroneous.

Somewhat different concerns are raised by the Fourth Circuit's treatment of the District Court's finding that petitioner, alone among the applicants for the position of Recreation Director, was asked questions regarding her spouse's feelings about her application for the position. Here the error of the Court of Appeals was its failure to give due regard to the ability of the District Court to interpret and discern the credibility of oral testimony. The Court of Appeals rested its rejection of the District Court's finding of differential treatment on its own interpretation of testimony by Mrs. Boone—the very witness whose testimony, in the view of the District Court, supported the finding. In the eyes of the Fourth Circuit, Mrs. Boone's testimony that she had made a "comment" to Mr. Kincaid about the feelings of his wife (a comment judged "facetious" by the District Court) conclusively established that Mr. Kincaid, and perhaps other male applicants as well, had been questioned about the feelings of his spouse.

Mrs. Boone's testimony on this point, which is set forth in the margin,[3] is certainly not free from ambiguity. But Mrs. Boone several times stated that other candidates had not been questioned about the reaction of their wives— at least, "not in the same context" as had petitioner. And even after recalling and calling to the attention of the court that she had made a comment on the subject to Mr. Kincaid, Mrs. Boone denied that she had "asked" Mr. Kincaid about his wife's reaction. Mrs. Boone's testimony on these matters is not inconsistent with the theory that her remark was not a serious inquiry into whether Mr. Kincaid's wife approved of his applying for the position. Whether the judge's interpretation is actually correct is impossible to tell from the paper record, but it is easy to imagine that the tone of voice in which the witness related her comment, coupled with her immediate denial that she had questioned Mr. Kincaid on the subject, might have conclusively established that the remark was a facetious one. We therefore

---

3. "Q: Did the committee members ask that same kind of question of the other applicants?

"A: Not that I recall.

"Q: Do you deny that the other applicants, aside from the plaintiff, were asked about the prospect of working at night in that position?

"A: Not to my knowledge.

"Q: Are you saying they were not asked that?

"A: They were not asked, not in the context that they were asked of Phyllis. I don't know whether they were worried because Jim wasn't going to get his supper or what. You know, that goes both ways.

"Q: Did you tell Phyllis Anderson that Donnie Kincaid was not asked about night work?

"A: He wasn't asked about night work.

"Q: That answers one question. Now, let's answer the other one. Did you tell Phyllis Anderson that, that Donnie Kincaid was not asked about night work?

"A: Yes, after the interviews—I think the next day or sometime, and I know—may I answer something?

"Q: If it's a question that has been asked; otherwise, no. It's up to the Judge to say.

"A: You asked if there was any question asked about—I think Donnie was just married, and I think I made the comment to him personally—and your new bride won't mind.

"Q: So, you asked him yourself about his own wife's reaction?

"A: No, no.

"Q: That is what you just said.

"Mr. Gibson: Objection, Your Honor.

"[The] Court: Sustained. You don't have to rephrase the answer."

* * *

cannot agree that the judge's conclusion that the remark was facetious was clearly erroneous.

Once the trial court's characterization of Mrs. Boone's remark is accepted, it is apparent that the finding that the male candidates were not seriously questioned about the feelings of their wives cannot be deemed clearly erroneous. The trial judge was faced with the testimony of three witnesses, one of whom (Mrs. Boone) stated that none of the other candidates had been so questioned, one of whom (a male committee member) testified that Mr. Kincaid had been asked such a question "in a way," and one of whom (another committeeman) testified that all the candidates had been subjected to similar questioning. None of these accounts is implausible on its face, and none is contradicted by any reliable extrinsic evidence. Under these circumstances, the trial court's decision to credit Mrs. Boone was not clearly erroneous.

The Fourth Circuit's refusal to accept the District Court's finding that the committee members were biased against hiring a woman was based to a large extent on its rejection of the finding that petitioner had been subjected to questioning that the other applicants were spared. Given that that finding was not clearly erroneous, the finding of bias cannot be termed erroneous: it finds support not only in the treatment of petitioner in her interview, but also in the testimony of one committee member that he believed it would have been difficult for a woman to perform the job and in the evidence that another member solicited applications for the position only from men.[4]

Our determination that the findings of the District Court regarding petitioner's qualifications, the conduct of her interview, and the bias of the male committee members were not clearly erroneous leads us to conclude that the court's finding that petitioner was discriminated against on account of her sex was also not clearly erroneous. The District Court's findings regarding petitioner's superior qualifications and the bias of the selection committee are sufficient to support the inference that petitioner was denied the position of Recreation Director on account of her sex. Accordingly, we hold that the Fourth Circuit erred in denying petitioner relief under Title VII.

In so holding, we do not assert that our knowledge of what happened 10 years ago in Bessemer City is superior to that of the Court of Appeals; nor do we claim to have greater insight than the Court of Appeals into the state of mind of the men on the selection committee who rejected petitioner for the position of Recreation Director. Even the trial judge, who has heard the witnesses directly and who is more closely in touch than the appeals court with the milieu out of which the controversy before him arises, cannot always be confident that he "knows" what happened. Often, he can only determine whether the plaintiff has succeeded in presenting an account of the facts that is more likely to be true than not. Our task—and the task of appellate tribunals generally—is more limited still: we must determine whether the

4. The Fourth Circuit's suggestion that any inference of bias was dispelled by the fact that each of the male committee members was married to a woman who had worked at some point in the marriage is insufficient to establish that the finding of bias was clearly erroneous. Although we decline to hold that a man's attitude toward his wife's employment is irrelevant to the question whether he may be found to have a bias against working women, any relevance the factor may have in a particular case is a matter for the district court to weigh in its consideration of bias, not the court of appeals.

trial judge's conclusions are clearly erroneous. On the record before us, we cannot say that they are. Accordingly, the judgment of the Court of Appeals is

Reversed.

* * *

The concurring opinions of JUSTICE POWELL and JUSTICE BLACKMUN are omitted.

Notes on Anderson

1. Do you agree that Phyllis Anderson was not hired as Recreation Director because of her sex? Would her case have been weaker if Bert Broadway, the selection committee's first choice, had moved to Bessemer City to accept the job? Did the trial court judge and the Fourth Circuit agree on what qualifications were appropriate for the position?

On remand, Phyllis Anderson received her full back pay award, plus interest on the award for attorneys fees and expenses from the date of the original judgment. Anderson v. City of Bessemer City, 619 F.Supp. 153 (W.D.N.C.1985).

2. What impact does the "clearly erroneous" standard of review have on plaintiffs in disparate treatment sex discrimination cases? Does it increase or decrease their chances for ultimate success in litigation? Does it apply to disparate impact cases?

The "clearly erroneous" standard will become less significant over time because of the jury trial amendment to Title VII made by the Civil Rights Act of 1991. For the first time, most plaintiffs under Title VII, particularly women asserting gender bias, will be able to demand a jury trial. The Civil Rights Act of 1991 provides that "[i]f a complaining party seeks compensatory or punitive damages under this section any party may demand a trial by jury." § 102(c)(1)(codified at 42 U.S.C. § 1981A (Supp. III 1991)) in Appendix at p. 1248, infra. The benefit for women is emphasized because persons of color were able to obtain a jury trial on most issues prior to 1991, if they joined a race or color discrimination claim under 42 U.S.C. § 1981 with their Title VII claim. Because there was a right to jury trial under § 1981, any jury findings of fact on questions common to both claims were binding on the trial judge in making findings under Title VII. See Brown v. Boston University, 891 F.2d 337, 344 (1st Cir.1989), p. 838, infra. We assume that Title VII plaintiffs will take advantage of this opportunity in a large number of cases. Consequently, the trier of fact in a disparate treatment case will no longer be a federal judge, but a jury. Disparate impact cases will continue to be tried by judges, because compensatory damages are available only for intentional discrimination.

If the case is tried to a jury, instead of to a judge, the standard of judicial review is even more deferential to the jury as trier of fact than the "clearly erroneous" standard of Rule 52(a). Rule 52 applies only to actions tried before the court without a jury. If the case is tried to a jury, the trial judge may enter judgment for a party as a matter of law only if there is "no legally sufficient evidentiary basis for a reasonable jury to have found for that party * * *." Fed. R. Civ. P. 50. The U.S. Constitution provides in the Seventh Amendment: "No fact tried by a jury, shall be otherwise re-examined in any Court of the United States, than according to the rules of the common law." In practice, the right to jury trial means that a plaintiff's jury verdict will be sustained on appeal as long as legally sufficient evidence has been presented upon which a "jury could reasonably find for the plaintiff." Anderson v. Liberty Lobby, Inc., 477 U.S. 242, 252 (1986). Phrased another way, jury findings of fact, and inferences upon which the findings are based, must be viewed in the light most favorable to the winning side. The findings of fact must be upheld if reasonable minds could differ, and a reasonable person could have reached the same decision as the jury. See Stephan Alan Childress & Martha S. Davis, Federal Standards of Review, §§ 3.01—3.02. Under this standard, jury findings, at least in theory, will be more insulated from judicial review than findings by the district court.

Historically, juries have been viewed as more sympathetic to employee claims than judges. See discussion in Martha S. West, The Case Against Reinstatement in Wrongful Discharge, 1988 U. Ill. L. Rev. 1, 48 (1988). In discussing the value of requesting a jury in § 1981 litigation, one attorney commented that judges tend to be jaded by their experiences and "may have limited empathy for victims of race discrimination." Jurors, on the other hand may "understand better than judges appointed for life the anguish caused by loss of a job." Jonathan Wallas, Race Discrimination: Who Should Decide?, Trial, July 1987, 44, 49. Jonathan Wallas successfully represented the plaintiff before the Supreme Court in Anderson v. Bessemer City. The success rates for plaintiffs in employment cases that have gone to a jury in California have been high, averaging above 60%. Orrick, Herrington & Sutcliffe, Labor and Employment Department, Employment Law Verdicts (1992). Success rates for plaintiffs from 1981–1992 were highest in wrongful discharge claims under state law, 65%, and on sexual harassment claims, also 65%. Success rates dropped, however, on race claims, 39%, and on non-harassment sex discrimination claims, 38%. The number of these cases reported were small: 61 race discrimination cases and 21 sex discrimination cases, out of a total of 610 cases. Success rates may be similar in Title VII jury cases. If juries are, in fact, more sympathetic to employee's claims than federal judges, the 1991 amendments will work in favor of Title VII plaintiffs.

3. A rare example of reversal under the "clearly erroneous" standard occurred in Ezold v. Wolf, Block, Schorr and Solis–Cohen, 983 F.2d 509 (3d Cir.1992), certiorari denied __ U.S. __, 114 S.Ct. 88, 126 L.Ed.2d 56 (1993). Plaintiff Nancy O'Mara Ezold charged that Wolf, Block had discriminated against her on the basis of her sex by refusing to admit her to the firm's partnership. The district court granted judgment in her favor, holding that the firm's articulated nondiscriminatory reason for rejecting her candidacy—that her legal analytical ability failed to meet the firm's partnership standard—was a pretext. On appeal, the Third Circuit reversed, indicating that:

> The district court first impermissibly substituted its own subjective judgment for that of Wolf in determining that Ezold met the firm's partnership standards. Then, with its view improperly influenced by its own judgment of what Wolf should have done, it failed to see that the evidence could not support a finding that Wolf's decision to deny Ezold admission to the partnership was based upon a sexually discriminatory motive rather than the firm's assessment of her legal qualifications. Accordingly, we hold not only that the district court analyzed the evidence improperly and that its resulting finding of pretext is clearly erroneous, but also that the evidence, properly analyzed, is insufficient to support that finding and therefore its ultimate conclusion of discrimination cannot stand.

Id., at 512–13. At the time she was hired by Wolf, Block, Nancy Ezold was warned that her credentials—graduation from Villanova University Law School in the top third of her class—were not up to the firm's standards. She was told during an interview that things would not be easy for her because "she was a woman, had not attended an Ivy League law school, and had not been on law review." Id., at 514. The Third Circuit nevertheless concluded that Ezold did not make partner because the firm decided that she did not possess sufficient legal analytical skills to handle the responsibilities of partner in the firm's complex litigation practice. At the time she was informed of this decision, she was told that she would have a better chance of making partner if she transferred to the firm's domestic relations department because of the positive evaluations of her skills with clients and in the courtroom and because this practice area did not require the same complex analysis as the firm's commercial litigation practice. Id., at 521. In reversing the district court, the Third Circuit found that the trial judge had relied on his own subjective judgment regarding partnership standards, thereby interfering with the law firm's control over its selection of partners. Note how close this approach comes to the deference federal courts traditionally accord universities in reviewing faculty tenure decisions. See the text note on Title VII in academe, p. 871 infra.

Perhaps reversal under the "clearly erroneous" standard is not so rare after all. Another trial victory for a Title VII plaintiff was reversed by the Second Circuit in Fisher v. Vassar College, 852 F.Supp. 1193 (S.D.N.Y.1994), reversed, 70 F.3d 1420 (2d Cir.1995). District Court Judge Constance Baker Motley had found that Vassar College discriminated against Cynthia Fisher on the basis of sex plus marital status in denying her tenure. Judge Motley found that Vassar had not tenured a married woman in the "hard" sciences for over a 30–year period and that Vassar's evaluation of the plaintiff's qualifications for tenure was pretextual and made in bad faith. Plaintiff had left academia for 8 years in order to raise a family, prior to her hire by Vassar in 1977 as a lecturer and then as assistant professor. When she went up for tenure in 1985, the trial court found that the Biology Department tenure committee held her earlier absence from academia against her, and that the "persistent fixation" of the senior faculty on "a married woman's pre-Vassar family choices reflects the acceptance of a stereotype and bias." 852 F.Supp. at 1216. A panel of the Second Circuit, after reciting the "clearly erroneous" standard of judicial review, agreed with the trial court that Vassar's tenure evaluation of Fisher was pretextual and made in bad faith, but reversed the ultimate findings of discrimination. Instead of being motivated by sex discrimination, the Second Circuit found that the senior members of the Biology Department "simply did not like Fisher and did not wish to establish a career-long professional association with her. It is arguable that such grounds alone justified the department's recommendation against tenure." 68 FEP Cases at 1548. In reversing the finding of sex discrimination based on the "family" gap in Fisher's career, the Second Circuit found this absence from academia *relevant* to the tenure decision made eight years later: "This is a telling fact for a tenure decision, because (among other things) it has obvious bearing on the level of professional commitment the department could expect once the pressure of tenure scrutiny was over." Id. at 1551. In December 1995 the court amended its slip opinion to delete this particular sentence and make additional changes. Fisher v. Vassar College, 70 F.3d 1420 (2d Cir.1995) Order Amending Opinion, ¶ 4, (2d Cir. Dec. 14, 1995). It did not, however, delete language later in the opinion finding that employers are justified in taking into account such a prolonged absence from a career. The Second Circuit panel held that a policy that discriminates between employees who take off long periods of time in order to raise children "is not inherently sex specific and does not give rise to a claim under Title VII." Id. at

1557. In February 1996 the Second Circuit granted plaintiff's petition for a rehearing en banc.

What is going on in these cases? Hasn't the Court said that findings of intent and motivation are findings of fact? Aren't factual inferences also findings of fact? Isn't the trial court in the best position to judge credibility and determine motivation based on live testimony and demeanor? Are both *Wolf* and *Fisher* examples of appellate courts improperly substituting their own assessment of the facts for the trial courts' inferences?

4. The "clearly erroneous" standard of review, coupled with the emphasis in *Aikens,* set forth at p. 632, supra, on the ultimate finding of discrimination has stimulated several courts of appeal to collapse their review of the *McDonnell–Douglas–Burdine* three-step process of proof in disparate treatment cases into one stage on appeal: they focus on whether plaintiff has established intentional discrimination. See, e.g., Johnson v. Allyn & Bacon, Inc., 731 F.2d 64, 70 (1st Cir.1984), certiorari denied 469 U.S. 1018, 105 S.Ct. 433, 83 L.Ed.2d 359 (1984)(affirming judgment holding that woman failed to prove sex discrimination in being denied promotion); Wall v. National Railroad Passenger Corp., 718 F.2d 906, 908–909 (9th Cir.1983)(affirming judgment holding that black male failed to prove race discrimination in being fired by the railroad); Williams v. Southwestern Bell Telephone Co., 718 F.2d 715, 717 (5th Cir.1983)(affirming judgment holding that a black woman failed to prove race discrimination in being fired as a telephone bill teller); Sweeney v. Research Foundation of State University of New York, 711 F.2d 1179, 1184–85 (2d Cir.1983)(affirming judgment holding that woman failed to prove sex discrimination in being denied appointment as Systems Analyst). Compare Griffin v. City of Omaha, 785 F.2d 620 (8th Cir.1986)(reversing as clearly erroneous a trial court's finding that two black female police recruits were terminated because of their failure to meet minimum firearm proficiency standards, not because of their race and sex). Has *Aikens* obviated the three-step process of proof at the trial court stage as well? If so, is there any meaningful way for an appellate court to review on the merits an adverse finding after *Anderson?* Reconsider these questions after reading St. Mary's Honor Center v. Hicks, the next case set forth below.

v.   Proof of Pretext

ST. MARY'S HONOR CENTER v. HICKS

Supreme Court of the United States, 1993.
509 U.S. 502, 113 S.Ct. 2742, 125 L.Ed.2d 407.

JUSTICE SCALIA delivered the opinion of the Court.

We granted certiorari to determine whether, in a suit against an employer alleging intentional racial discrimination in violation of § 703(a)(1) of Title VII * * * the trier of fact's rejection of the employer's asserted reasons for its actions mandates a finding for the plaintiff.

I

Petitioner St. Mary's Honor Center (St. Mary's) is a halfway house operated by the Missouri Department of Corrections and Human Resources (MDCHR). Respondent Melvin Hicks, a black man, was hired as a correctional officer at St. Mary's in August 1978 and was promoted to shift commander, one of six supervisory positions, in February 1980.

In 1983 MDCHR conducted an investigation of the administration of St. Mary's, which resulted in extensive supervisory changes in January 1984. Respondent retained his position, but John Powell became the new chief of custody (respondent's immediate supervisor) and petitioner Steve Long the new superintendent. Prior to these personnel changes respondent had enjoyed a satisfactory employment record, but soon thereafter became the subject of repeated, and increasingly severe, disciplinary actions. He was suspended for five days for violations of institutional rules by his subordinates on March 3, 1984. He received a letter of reprimand for alleged failure to conduct an adequate investigation of a brawl between inmates that occurred during his shift on March 21. He was later demoted from shift commander to correctional officer for his failure to ensure that his subordinates entered their use of a St. Mary's vehicle into the official log book on March 19, 1984. Finally, on June 7, 1984, he was discharged for threatening Powell during an exchange of heated words on April 19.

Respondent brought this suit in the United States District Court for the Eastern District of Missouri, alleging that petitioner St. Mary's violated § 703(a)(1) of Title VII * * * and that petitioner Long violated Rev.Stat. § 1979, 42 U.S.C. § 1983, by demoting and then discharging him because of his race. After a full bench trial, the District Court found for petitioners. 756 F.Supp. 1244 (E.D.Mo.1991). The United States Court of Appeals for the Eighth Circuit reversed and remanded, 970 F.2d 487 (1992), and we granted certiorari, * * *.

II

* * *

With the goal of "progressively * * * sharpen[ing] the inquiry into the elusive factual question of intentional discrimination," *Texas Dept. of Community Affairs v. Burdine,* * * * (1981), our opinion in *McDonnell Douglas Corp. v. Green,* (1973), established an allocation of the burden of production and an order for the presentation of proof in Title VII discriminatory-treatment cases.[1] The plaintiff in such a case, we said, must first establish, by a preponderance of the evidence, a "prima facie" case of racial discrimination. * * * Petitioners do not challenge the District Court's finding that respondent satisfied the minimal requirements of such a prima facie case * * * by proving (1) that he is black, (2) that he was qualified for the position of shift commander, (3) that he was demoted from that position and ultimately discharged, and (4) that the position remained open and was ultimately filled by a white man. * * *

Under the *McDonnell Douglas* scheme, "[e]stablishment of the prima facie case in effect creates a presumption that the employer unlawfully discriminated against the employee." *Burdine, supra,* * * *. To establish a "presumption" is to say that a finding of the predicate fact (here, the prima facie case) produces "a required conclusion in the absence of explanation"

---

1. The Court of Appeals held that the purposeful-discrimination element of respondent's § 1983 claim against petitioner Long is the same as the purposeful-discrimination element of his Title VII claim against petitioner St. Mary's. * * * Neither side challenges that proposition, and we shall assume that the *McDonnell Douglas* framework is fully applicable to racial-discrimination-in-employment claims under 42 U.S.C. § 1983. Cf. *Patterson v. McLean Credit Union,* * * * (1989)(applying framework to claims under 42 U.S.C. § 1981).

(here, the finding of unlawful discrimination). 1 D. Louisell & C. Mueller, Federal Evidence § 67, p. 536 (1977). Thus, the *McDonnell Douglas* presumption places upon the defendant the burden of producing an explanation to rebut the prima facie case—*i.e.,* the burden of "producing evidence" that the adverse employment actions were taken "for a legitimate, nondiscriminatory reason." *Burdine,* * * *. "[T]he defendant must clearly set forth, through the introduction of admissible evidence," reasons for its actions which, *if believed by the trier of fact,* would support a finding that unlawful discrimination was not the cause of the employment action. *Id.,* at 254–255, and n. 8, 101 S.Ct., at 1094–1095, and n. 8. It is important to note, however, that although the *McDonnell Douglas* presumption shifts the burden of *production* to the defendant, "[t]he ultimate burden of persuading the trier of fact that the defendant intentionally discriminated against the plaintiff remains at all times with the plaintiff," * * *. In this regard it operates like all presumptions, * * *.

Respondent does not challenge the District Court's finding that petitioners sustained their burden of production by introducing evidence of two legitimate, nondiscriminatory reasons for their actions: the severity and the accumulation of rules violations committed by respondent. * * * Our cases make clear that at that point the shifted burden of production became irrelevant: "If the defendant carries this burden of production, the presumption raised by the prima facie case is rebutted," *Burdine,* * * * and "drops from the case," * * *. The plaintiff then has "the full and fair opportunity to demonstrate," through presentation of his own case and through cross-examination of the defendant's witnesses, "that the proffered reason was not the true reason for the employment decision," * * * and that race was. He retains that "ultimate burden of persuading the [trier of fact] that [he] has been the victim of intentional discrimination." * * *

The District Court, acting as trier of fact in this bench trial, found that the reasons petitioners gave were not the real reasons for respondent's demotion and discharge. It found that respondent was the only supervisor disciplined for violations committed by his subordinates; that similar and even more serious violations committed by respondent's coworkers were either disregarded or treated more leniently; and that Powell manufactured the final verbal confrontation in order to provoke respondent into threatening him. * * * It nonetheless held that respondent had failed to carry his ultimate burden of proving that *his race* was the determining factor in petitioners' decision first to demote and then to dismiss him.[2] In short, the District Court concluded that "although [respondent] has proven the existence of a crusade to terminate him, he has not proven that the crusade was racially rather than personally motivated." * * *

The Court of Appeals set this determination aside on the ground that "[o]nce [respondent] proved all of [petitioners'] proffered reasons for the adverse employment actions to be pretextual, [respondent] was entitled to judgment as a matter of law." * * * The Court of Appeals reasoned:

2. Various considerations led it to this conclusion, including the fact that two blacks sat on the disciplinary review board that recommended disciplining respondent, that respondent's black subordinates who actually committed the violations were not disciplined, and that "the number of black employees at St. Mary's remained constant." 756 F.Supp. 1244, 1252 (E.D.Mo.1991).

"Because all of defendants' proffered reasons were discredited, defendants were in a position of having offered no legitimate reason for their actions. In other words, defendants were in no better position than if they had remained silent, offering no rebuttal to an established inference that they had unlawfully discriminated against plaintiff on the basis of his race." * * *

That is not so. By producing *evidence* (whether ultimately persuasive or not) of nondiscriminatory reasons, petitioners sustained their burden of production, and thus placed themselves in a "better position than if they had remained silent."

In the nature of things, the determination that a defendant has met its burden of production (and has thus rebutted any legal presumption of intentional discrimination) can involve no credibility assessment. For the burden-of-production determination necessarily *precedes* the credibility-assessment stage. At the close of the defendant's case, the court is asked to decide whether an issue of fact remains for the trier of fact to determine. None does if, on the evidence presented, (1) any rational person would have to find the existence of facts constituting a prima facie case, and (2) the defendant has failed to meet its burden of production—*i.e.,* has failed to introduce evidence which, *taken as true,* would *permit* the conclusion that there was a nondiscriminatory reason for the adverse action. In that event, the court must award judgment to the plaintiff as a matter of law under Federal Rule of Civil Procedure 50(a)(1)(in the case of jury trials) or Federal Rule of Civil Procedure 52(c)(in the case of bench trials). See F. James & G. Hazard, Civil Procedure § 7.9, p. 327 (3d ed. 1985); 1 Louisell & Mueller, Federal Evidence § 70, at 568. If the defendant has failed to sustain its burden but reasonable minds could *differ* as to whether a preponderance of the evidence establishes the facts of a prima facie case, then a question of fact *does* remain, which the trier of fact will be called upon to answer.

If, on the other hand, the defendant has succeeded in carrying its burden of production, the *McDonnell Douglas* framework—with its presumptions and burdens—is no longer relevant. To resurrect it later, after the trier of fact has determined that what was "produced" to meet the burden of production is not credible, flies in the face of our holding in *Burdine* that to rebut the presumption "[t]he defendant need not persuade the court that it was actually motivated by the proffered reasons." * * * The presumption, having fulfilled its role of forcing the defendant to come forward with some response, simply drops out of the picture. * * * The defendant's "production" (whatever its persuasive effect) having been made, the trier of fact proceeds to decide the ultimate question: whether plaintiff has proven "that the defendant intentionally discriminated against [him]" because of his race. * * * The factfinder's disbelief of the reasons put forward by the defendant (particularly if disbelief is accompanied by a suspicion of mendacity) may, together with the elements of the prima facie case, suffice to show intentional discrimination. Thus, rejection of the defendant's proffered reasons, will *permit* the trier of fact to infer the ultimate fact of intentional discrimination, and the Court of Appeals was correct when it noted that, upon such rejection, "[n]o additional proof of discrimination is *required,*" * * * (emphasis added). But the Court of Appeals' holding that rejection of the defendant's proffered reasons *compels* judgment for the plaintiff disregards the fundamental principle of Rule 301 that a presumption does not shift the burden of proof, and ignores our repeated admonition that the Title VII plaintiff at all times bears the "ultimate burden of persuasion." * * *

III

Only one unfamiliar with our case-law will be upset by the dissent's alarum that we are today setting aside "settled precedent," * * *.

The principal case on which the dissent relies is *Burdine*. While there are some statements in that opinion that could be read to support the dissent's position, all but one of them bear a meaning consistent with our interpretation, and the one exception is simply incompatible with other language in the case. *Burdine* describes the situation that obtains after the employer has met its burden of adducing a nondiscriminatory reason as follows: "Third, should the defendant carry this burden, the plaintiff must then have an opportunity to prove by a preponderance of the evidence that the legitimate reasons offered by the defendant were not its true reasons, but were a pretext for discrimination." * * * The dissent takes this to mean that if the plaintiff proves the asserted reason to be *false,* the plaintiff wins. But a reason cannot be proved to be "a pretext *for discrimination*" unless it is shown *both* that the reason was false, *and* that discrimination was the real reason. *Burdine's* later allusions to proving or demonstrating simply "pretext," *e.g., id.,* at 258, 101 S.Ct., at 1096, are reasonably understood to refer to the previously described pretext, *i.e.,* "pretext for discrimination."[6]

Burdine also says that when the employer has met its burden of production "the factual inquiry proceeds to a new level of specificity." *Id.,* at 255 * * *. The dissent takes this to mean that the factual inquiry reduces to whether the employer's asserted reason is true or false—if false, the defendant loses. But the "new level of specificity" may also (as we believe) refer to the fact that the inquiry now turns from the few generalized factors that establish a prima facie case to the specific proofs and rebuttals of discriminatory motivation the parties have introduced.

In the next sentence, *Burdine* says that "[p]lacing this burden of production on the defendant thus serves * * * to frame the factual issue with sufficient clarity so that the plaintiff will have a full and fair opportunity to demonstrate pretext." *Id.,* at 255–256, 101 S.Ct., at 1095. The dissent thinks this means that the only factual issue remaining in the case is whether the employer's reason is false. But since in our view "pretext" means "pretext for discrimination," we think the sentence must be understood as addressing the form rather than the substance of the defendant's production burden: The requirement that the employer "clearly set forth" its reasons, *id.,* at 255, 101 S.Ct., at 1094, gives the plaintiff a "full and fair" rebuttal opportunity.

A few sentences later, *Burdine* says: "[The plaintiff] now must have the opportunity to demonstrate that the proffered reason was not the true reason

---

6. The same is true of *McDonnell Douglas's* concluding summary of the framework it created (relied upon by the dissent, *post,* at 2759) to the effect that if the plaintiff fails to show "pretext," the challenged employment action "must stand." 411 U.S., at 807, 93 S.Ct., at 1827. There, as in *Burdine,* "pretext" means the pretext required earlier in the opinion, *viz.,* "pretext for the sort of discrimination prohibited by [Title VII]," 411 U.S., at 804, 93 S.Ct., at 1825.

for the employment decision. This burden now merges with the ultimate burden of persuading the court that she has been the victim of intentional discrimination." *Id.,* at 256, 101 S.Ct., at 1095. The dissent takes this "merger" to mean that "the ultimate burden of persuading the court that she has been the victim of intentional discrimination" is *replaced* by the mere burden of "demonstrat[ing] that the proffered reason was not the true reason for the employment decision." But that would be a merger in which the little fish swallows the big one. Surely a more reasonable reading is that proving the employer's reason false becomes part of (and often considerably assists) the greater enterprise of proving that the real reason was intentional discrimination.

Finally, in the next sentence *Burdine* says: "[The plaintiff] may succeed in this [*i.e.,* in persuading the court that she has been the victim of intentional discrimination] either directly by persuading the court that a discriminatory reason more likely motivated the employer or indirectly by showing that the employer's proffered explanation is unworthy of credence. See *McDonnell Douglas,* 411 U.S., at 804–805 [93 S.Ct., at 1825–1827]." *Ibid.* We must agree with the dissent on this one: The words bear no other meaning but that the falsity of the employer's explanation is *alone enough* to compel judgment for the plaintiff. The problem is, that that dictum contradicts or renders inexplicable numerous other statements, both in *Burdine* itself and in our later case-law—commencing with the very citation of authority *Burdine* uses to support the proposition. *McDonnell Douglas* does *not* say, at the cited pages or elsewhere, that all the plaintiff need do is disprove the employer's asserted reason. In fact, it says just the opposite: "[O]n the retrial respondent must be given a full and fair opportunity to demonstrate by competent evidence that the presumptively valid reasons for his rejection *were in fact a coverup for a racially discriminatory decision.*" 411 U.S., at 805, 93 S.Ct., at 1826 (emphasis added). "We * * * insist that respondent under § 703(a)(1) must be given a full and fair opportunity to demonstrate by competent evidence *that whatever the stated reasons for his rejection, the decision was in reality racially premised.*" *Id.,* at 805, n. 18, 93 S.Ct., at 1825, n. 18 (emphasis added). The statement in question also contradicts *Burdine*'s repeated assurance (indeed, its holding) regarding the burden of persuasion: "The ultimate burden of persuading the trier of fact that the defendant intentionally discriminated against the plaintiff remains at all times with the plaintiff." * * * "The plaintiff retains the burden of persuasion." *Id.,* at 256, 101 S.Ct., at 1095.[7] And lastly, the statement renders inexplicable *Burdine* 's explicit reliance, in describing the shifting burdens of *McDonnell Douglas,* upon authorities setting forth the classic law of presumptions we have described earlier, * * *. In light of these inconsistencies, we think that the dictum at issue here must be regarded as an inadvertence, to the extent that it describes disproof of the defendant's reason as a totally independent, rather than an auxiliary, means of proving unlawful intent.

---

7. The dissent's reading leaves *some* burden of persuasion on the plaintiff, to be sure: the burden of persuading the factfinder that the employer's explanation is not true. But it would be beneath contempt for this Court, in a unanimous opinion no less, to play such word-games with the concept of "leaving the burden of persuasion upon the plaintiff." By parity of analysis, it could be said that holding a criminal defendant guilty unless he comes forward with a credible alibi does not shift the ultimate burden of persuasion, so long as the Government has the burden of persuading the factfinder that the alibi is *not* credible.

In sum, our interpretation of *Burdine* creates difficulty with one sentence; the dissent's interpretation causes many portions of the opinion to be incomprehensible or deceptive. But whatever doubt *Burdine* might have created was eliminated by *Aikens*. There we said, in language that cannot reasonably be mistaken, that "the ultimate question [is] discrimination *vel non*." 460 U.S., at 714, 103 S.Ct., at 1481. Once the defendant "responds to the plaintiff's proof by offering evidence of the reason for the plaintiff's rejection, the factfinder must then decide" *not* (as the dissent would have it) whether that evidence is credible, but "whether the rejection was discriminatory within the meaning of Title VII." *Id.*, at 714–715, 103 S.Ct., at 1481. At that stage, we said, "[t]he District Court was * * * in a position to decide the ultimate factual issue in the case," which is "whether the defendant intentionally discriminated against the plaintiff." *Id.*, at 715, 103 S.Ct. at 1482 (brackets and internal quotation marks omitted). The *McDonnell Douglas* methodology was "'never intended to be rigid, mechanized, or ritualistic.'" 460 U.S., at 715, 103 S.Ct., at 1482 (quoting *Furnco Construction Corp. v. Waters* * * *). Rather, once the defendant has responded to the plaintiff's prima facie case, "the district court has before it all the evidence it needs to decide" *not* (as the dissent would have it) whether defendant's response is credible, but "whether the defendant intentionally discriminated against the plaintiff." 460 U.S., at 715, 103 S.Ct., at 1482 (internal quotation marks omitted). "On the state of the record at the close of the evidence, the District Court in this case should have proceeded to this specific question directly, just as district courts decide disputed questions of fact in other civil litigation." *Id.*, at 715–716, 103 S.Ct., at 1482. *In confirmation of this* (rather than in contradiction of it), the Court then quotes the problematic passage from *Burdine,* which says that the plaintiff may carry her burden either directly "'or indirectly by showing that the employer's proffered explanation is unworthy of credence.'" 460 U.S., at 716, 103 S.Ct., at 1482. It then characterizes that passage as follows: "In short, the district court must decide which party's explanation of the employer's motivation it believes." *Ibid.* It is not enough, in other words, to *dis*believe the employer; the factfinder must *believe* the plaintiff's explanation of intentional discrimination. It is noteworthy that Justice Blackmun, although joining the Court's opinion in *Aikens,* wrote a separate concurrence for the sole purpose of saying that he understood the Court's opinion to be saying what the dissent today asserts. That concurrence was joined only by Justice Brennan. Justice Marshall would have none of that, but simply refused to join the Court's opinion, concurring without opinion in the judgment. We think there is little doubt what *Aikens* meant.

IV

We turn, finally, to the dire practical consequences that the respondents and the dissent claim our decision today will produce. What appears to trouble the dissent more than anything is that, in its view, our rule is adopted "for the benefit of employers who have been found to have given false evidence in a court of law," whom we "favo[r]" by "exempting them from responsibility for lies." * * * As we shall explain, our rule in no way gives special favor to those employers whose evidence is disbelieved. But initially we must point out that there is no justification for assuming (as the dissent repeatedly does) that those employers whose evidence is disbelieved are perjurers and liars.   * * *   Even if these were typically cases in which an individual defendant's sworn assertion regarding a physical occurrence was pitted against an individual plaintiff's sworn assertion regarding the same physical occurrence, surely it would be imprudent to call the party whose assertion is (by a mere preponderance of the evidence) disbelieved, a perjurer and a liar. And in these Title VII cases, the defendant is ordinarily *not* an individual but a company, which must rely upon the statement of an employee—often a relatively low-level employee—as to the central fact; and that central fact is *not* a physical occurrence, but rather that employee's state of mind. To say that the company which in good faith introduces such testimony, or even the testifying employee himself, becomes a liar and a perjurer when the testimony is not believed, is nothing short of absurd.

* * *

The dissent repeatedly raises a procedural objection that is impressive only to one who mistakes the basic nature of the *McDonnell Douglas* procedure. It asserts that "the Court now holds that the further enquiry [*i.e.,* the inquiry that follows the employer's response to the prima facie case] is wide open, not limited at all by the scope of the employer's proffered explanation." * * * The plaintiff cannot be expected to refute "reasons not articulated by the employer, but discerned in the record by the factfinder." * * * Of course it does not work like that. The reasons the defendant sets forth are set forth "through the introduction of admissible evidence." *Burdine,* 450 U.S., at 255, 101 S.Ct., at 1094. In other words, the defendant's "articulated reasons" *themselves* are to be found "lurking in the record." It thus makes no sense to contemplate "the employer who is caught in a lie, but succeeds in *injecting* into the trial an *unarticulated* reason for its actions." * * * (emphasis added). There is a "lurking-in-the-record" problem, but it exists not for us but for the dissent. *If,* after the employer has met its preliminary burden, the plaintiff need not prove discrimination (and therefore need not disprove *all* other reasons suggested, no matter how vaguely, in the record) there must be some device for determining which particular portions of the record represent "articulated reasons" set forth with sufficient clarity to satisfy *McDonnell Douglas*—since it is only *that* evidence which the plaintiff must refute. But of course our *McDonnell Douglas* framework makes no provision for such a determination, which would have to be made not at the close of the trial but *in medias res,* since otherwise the plaintiff would not know what evidence to offer. It makes no sense.

Respondent contends that "[t]he litigation decision of the employer to place in controversy only * * * particular explanations eliminates from further consideration the alternative explanations that the employer chose not to advance." * * * The employer should bear, he contends, "the responsibility for its choices and the risk that plaintiff will disprove any pretextual reasons *and therefore prevail.*" * * * (emphasis added). It is the "therefore" that is problematic. Title VII does not award damages against employers who cannot prove a nondiscriminatory reason for adverse employment action, but only against employers who are proven to have taken adverse employment action by reason of (in the context of the present case) race. That the employer's proffered reason is unpersuasive, or even obviously contrived, does not necessarily establish that the plaintiff's proffered reason of race is correct.

That remains a question for the factfinder to answer, subject, of course, to appellate review—which should be conducted on remand in this case under the "clearly erroneous" standard of Federal Rule of Civil Procedure 52(a), see, *e.g., Anderson v. Bessemer City,* 470 U.S. 564, 573–576 * * * (1985).

Finally, respondent argues that it "would be particularly ill-advised" for us to come forth with the holding we pronounce today "just as Congress has provided a right to jury trials in Title VII" cases. * * * See § 102 of the Civil Rights Act of 1991, 105 Stat. 1073, 42 U.S.C. § 1981a(c)(1988 ed., Supp. III)(providing jury trial right in certain Title VII suits). We think quite the opposite is true. Clarity regarding the requisite elements of proof becomes all the more important when a jury must be instructed concerning them, and when detailed factual findings by the trial court will not be available upon review.

* * *

We reaffirm today what we said in *Aikens:*

"[T]he question facing triers of fact in discrimination cases is both sensitive and difficult. The prohibitions against discrimination contained in the Civil Rights Act of 1964 reflect an important national policy. There will seldom be 'eyewitness' testimony as to the employer's mental processes. But none of this means that trial courts or reviewing courts should treat discrimination differently from other ultimate questions of fact. Nor should they make their inquiry even more difficult by applying legal rules which were devised to govern 'the basic allocation of burdens and order of presentation of proof' * * * in deciding this ultimate question." * * *

The judgment of the Court of Appeals is reversed, and the case is remanded for further proceedings consistent with this opinion.

It is so ordered.

JUSTICE SOUTER, with whom JUSTICE WHITE, JUSTICE BLACKMUN, and JUSTICE STEVENS join, dissenting.

Twenty years ago, in *McDonnell Douglas Corp. v. Green,* 411 U.S. 792, 93 S.Ct. 1817, 36 L.Ed.2d 668 (1973), this Court unanimously prescribed a "sensible, orderly way to evaluate the evidence" in a Title VII disparate-treatment case, giving both plaintiff and defendant fair opportunities to litigate "in light of common experience as it bears on the critical question of discrimination." * * * We have repeatedly reaffirmed and refined the *McDonnell Douglas* framework, * * *. But today, after two decades of stable law in this Court and only relatively recent disruption in some of the Circuits, * * * the Court abandons this practical framework together with its central purpose, which is "to sharpen the inquiry into the elusive factual question of intentional discrimination." * * * Ignoring language to the contrary in both *McDonnell Douglas* and *Burdine,* the Court holds that, once a Title VII plaintiff succeeds in showing at trial that the defendant has come forward with pretextual reasons for its actions in response to a prima facie showing of discrimination, the factfinder still may proceed to roam the record, searching for some nondiscriminatory explanation that the defendant has not raised and that the plaintiff has had no fair opportunity to disprove. Because the majority departs from settled precedent in substituting a scheme of proof for disparate-treatment actions that promises to be unfair and unworkable, I respectfully dissent.

* * *

Under *McDonnell Douglas* and *Burdine,* however, proof of a prima facie case not only raises an inference of discrimination; in the absence of further evidence, it also creates a mandatory presumption in favor of the plaintiff. * * *

Obviously, it would be unfair to bar an employer from coming forward at this stage with a nondiscriminatory explanation for its actions, since the lack of an open position and the plaintiff's lack of qualifications do not exhaust the set of nondiscriminatory reasons that might explain an adverse personnel decision. If the trier of fact could not consider other explanations, employers' autonomy would be curtailed far beyond what is needed to rectify the discrimination identified by Congress. Cf. *Furnco,* * * * (Title VII "does not impose a duty to adopt a hiring procedure that maximizes hiring of minority employees"). On the other hand, it would be equally unfair and utterly impractical to saddle the victims of discrimination with the burden of either producing direct evidence of discriminatory intent or eliminating the entire universe of possible nondiscriminatory reasons for a personnel decision. The Court in *McDonnell Douglas* reconciled these competing interests in a very sensible way by requiring the employer to "articulate," through the introduction of admissible evidence, one or more "legitimate, nondiscriminatory reason[s]" for its actions. * * * Proof of a prima facie case thus serves as a catalyst obligating the employer to step forward with an explanation for its actions. St. Mary's, in this case, used this opportunity to provide two reasons for its treatment of Hicks: the severity and accumulation of rule infractions he had allegedly committed. * * *

The Court emphasizes that the employer's obligation at this stage is only a burden of production, * * * and that, if the employer meets the burden, the presumption entitling the plaintiff to judgment "drops from the case." * * * This much is certainly true,[2] but the obligation also serves an important function neglected by the majority, in requiring the employer "to frame the factual issue with sufficient clarity so that the plaintiff will have a full and fair opportunity to demonstrate pretext." * * * The employer, in other words, has a "burden of production" that gives it the right to choose the scope of the factual issues to be resolved by the factfinder. But investing the employer with this choice has no point unless the scope it chooses binds the employer as well as the plaintiff. Nor does it make sense to tell the employer, as this Court has done, that its explanation of legitimate reasons "must be clear and reasonably specific," if the factfinder can rely on a reason not clearly articulated, or on one not articulated at all, to rule in favor of the employer.[3] * * *

2. The majority contends that it would "fl[y] in the face of our holding in *Burdine*"to "resurrect" this mandatory presumption at a later stage, in cases where the plaintiff proves that the employer's proffered reasons are pretextual. * * * Hicks does not argue to the contrary. * * * The question presented in this case is not whether the mandatory presumption is resurrected (everyone agrees that it is not), but whether the factual enquiry is narrowed by the *McDonnell Douglas* framework to the question of pretext.

3. The majority is simply wrong when it suggests that my reading of *McDonnell Douglas* and *Burdine* proceeds on the assumption

Once the employer chooses the battleground in this manner, "the factual inquiry proceeds to a new level of specificity." *Id.,* at 255, 101 S.Ct., at 1095. During this final, more specific enquiry, the employer has no burden to prove that its proffered reasons are true; rather, the plaintiff must prove by a preponderance of the evidence that the proffered reasons are pretextual. *Id.,* at 256, 101 S.Ct., at 1095. *McDonnell Douglas* makes it clear that if the plaintiff fails to show "pretext," the challenged employment action "must stand." 411 U.S., at 807, 93 S.Ct., at 1827. If, on the other hand, the plaintiff carries his burden of showing "pretext," the court "must order a prompt and appropriate remedy." *Ibid.* Or, as we said in *Burdine:* "[The plaintiff] now must have the opportunity to demonstrate that the proffered reason was not the true reason for the employment decision. This burden now merges with the ultimate burden of persuading the court that [the plaintiff] has been the victim of intentional discrimination."[6] 450 U.S., at 256, 101 S.Ct., at 1095. *Burdine* drives home the point that the case has proceeded to "a new level of specificity" by explaining that the plaintiff can meet his burden of persuasion in either of two ways: "either directly by persuading the court that a discriminatory reason more likely motivated the employer or indirectly by showing that the employer's proffered explanation is unworthy of credence."[7] *Ibid.;* see *Aikens,* 460 U.S., at 716, 103 S.Ct., at 1482 (quoting this language from *Burdine*); *id.,* at 717–718, 103 S.Ct., at 1482–1483 (BLACKMUN, J., joined by Brennan, J., concurring); see also *Price Waterhouse v. Hopkins,* 490 U.S. 228, 287–289, 109 S.Ct. 1775, 1810–1811, 104 L.Ed.2d 268 (1989)(KENNEDY, J., dissenting)(discussing these "two alternative methods" and relying on Justice Blackmun's concurrence in *Aikens*).

that the employer's reasons must be stated "apart from the record." * * * As I mentioned above, and I repeat here, such reasons must be set forth "through the introduction of admissible evidence." *Supra,* at 2758; see *Burdine,* 450 U.S., at 255, 101 S.Ct., at 1094. Such reasons cannot simply be found "lurking in the record," as the Court suggests, * * * for *Burdine* requires the employer to articulate its reasons through testimony or other admissible evidence that is "clear and reasonably specific," 450 U.S., at 258, 101 S.Ct., at 1096. Accordingly, the plaintiff need not worry about waiting for the court to identify the employer's reasons at the end of trial, or in this case six months after trial, because *McDonnell Douglas* and *Burdine* require the employer to articulate its reasons clearly during trial. No one, for example, had any trouble in this case identifying the two reasons for Hicks's dismissal that St. Mary's articulated during trial.

6. The majority puts forward what it calls "a more reasonable reading" of this passage, * * * but its chosen interpretation of the "merger" that occurs is flatly contradicted by the very next sentence in *Burdine,* which indicates, as the majority subsequently admits, * * * that the burden of persuasion is limited to the question of pretext. It seems to me "more reasonable" to interpret the "merger" language in harmony with, rather than in contradiction to, its immediate context in *Burdine.*

7. The majority's effort to rewrite *Burdine* centers on repudiating this passage, * * * which has provided specific, concrete guidance to courts and Title VII litigants for more than a decade, and on replacing "pretext" wherever it appears with "pretext for discrimination," as defined by the majority. * * * These two efforts are intertwined, for *Burdine* tells us specifically how a plaintiff can prove either "pretext" or "pretext for discrimination": "*either* directly or persuading the court that a discriminatory reason more likely motivated the employer *or* indirectly by showing that the employer's proffered explanation is unworthy of credence." 450 U.S., at 256, 101 S.Ct., at 1095 (emphasis supplied). The majority's chosen method of proving "pretext for discrimination" changes *Burdine'*s "either * * * or" into a "both * * * and": "[A] reason cannot be proved to be 'a pretext for discrimination' unless it is shown both that the reason was false, and that discrimination was the real reason." * * * The majority thus takes a shorthand phrase from *Burdine* ("pretext for discrimination"), discovers requirements in the phrase that are directly at odds with the specific requirements actually set out in *Burdine,* and then rewrites *Burdine* in light of this "discovery." No one "[f]amiliar with our case-law," * * * will be persuaded by this strategy.

That the plaintiff can succeed simply by showing that "the employer's proffered explanation is unworthy of credence" indicates that the case has been narrowed to the question whether the employer's proffered reasons are pretextual.[8] Thus, because Hicks carried his burden of persuasion by showing that St. Mary's proffered reasons were "unworthy of credence," the Court of Appeals properly concluded that he was entitled to judgment. * * *

The Court today decides to abandon the settled law that sets out this structure for trying disparate-treatment Title VII cases, only to adopt a scheme that will be unfair to plaintiffs, unworkable in practice, and inexplicable in forgiving employers who present false evidence in court. Under the majority's scheme, once the employer succeeds in meeting its burden of production, "the *McDonnell Douglas* framework * * * is no longer relevant." * * * Whereas we said in *Burdine* that if the employer carries its burden of production, "the factual inquiry proceeds to a new level of specificity," 450 U.S., at 255, * * * the Court now holds that the further enquiry is wide open, not limited at all by the scope of the employer's proffered explanation. Despite the Court's assiduous effort to reinterpret our precedents, it remains clear that today's decision stems from a flat misreading of *Burdine* and ignores the central purpose of the *McDonnell Douglas* framework, which is "progressively to sharpen the inquiry into the elusive factual question of intentional discrimination." *Id.,* at 255, n. 8 * * *. We have repeatedly identified the compelling reason for limiting the factual issues in the final stage of a *McDonnell Douglas* case as "the requirement that the plaintiff be afforded a full and fair opportunity to demonstrate pretext." * * * The majority fails to explain how the plaintiff, under its scheme, will ever have a "full and fair opportunity" to demonstrate that reasons not articulated by the employer, but discerned in the record by the factfinder, are also unworthy of credence. The Court thus transforms the employer's burden of production from a device used to provide notice and promote fairness into a misleading and potentially useless ritual.

The majority's scheme greatly disfavors Title VII plaintiffs without the good luck to have direct evidence of discriminatory intent. The Court repeats the truism that the plaintiff has the "ultimate burden" of proving discrimination, * * * without ever facing the practical question of how the plaintiff without such direct evidence can meet this burden. *Burdine* provides the answer, telling us that such a plaintiff may succeed in meeting his ultimate burden of proving discrimination "indirectly by showing that the employer's proffered explanation is unworthy of credence." * * * The possibility of some practical procedure for addressing what *Burdine* calls indirect proof is crucial to the success of most Title VII claims, for the simple reason that employers who discriminate are not likely to announce their discriminatory motive. And yet, under the majority's scheme, a victim of discrimination

---

8. That the sole, and therefore determinative, issue left at this stage is pretext is further indicated by our discussion in *McDonnell Douglas* of the various types of evidence "that may be relevant to any showing of pretext," 411 U.S., at 804, 93 S.Ct., at 1825, by our decision to reverse in *Furnco* because the Court of Appeals "did not conclude that the [challenged] practices were a pretext for dis- crimination," 438 U.S., at 578, * * * and by our reminder in *Burdine* that even after the employer meets the plaintiff's prima facie case, the "evidence previously introduced by the plaintiff to establish a prima facie case" and the "inferences properly drawn therefrom may be considered by the trier of fact on the issue of whether the [employer's] explanation is pretextual," 450 U.S., at 255, n. 10 * * *.

lacking direct evidence will now be saddled with the tremendous disadvantage of having to confront, not the defined task of proving the employer's stated reasons to be false, but the amorphous requirement of disproving all possible non-discriminatory reasons that a factfinder might find lurking in the record. * * *

While the Court appears to acknowledge that a plaintiff will have the task of disproving even vaguely suggested reasons, and while it recognizes the need for "[c]larity regarding the requisite elements of proof," * * * it nonetheless gives conflicting signals about the scope of its holding in this case. In one passage, the Court states that although proof of the falsity of the employer's proffered reasons does not "compe[l] judgment for the plaintiff," such evidence, without more, "will permit the trier of fact to infer the ultimate fact of intentional discrimination." * * * The same view is implicit in the Court's decision to remand this case, * * * keeping Hicks's chance of winning a judgment alive although he has done no more (in addition to proving his prima facie case) than show that the reasons proffered by St. Mary's are unworthy of credence. But other language in the Court's opinion supports a more extreme conclusion, that proof of the falsity of the employer's articulated reasons will not even be sufficient to sustain judgment for the plaintiff. For example, the Court twice states that the plaintiff must show "*both* that the reason was false, *and* that discrimination was the real reason." * * * In addition, in summing up its reading of our earlier cases, the Court states that "[i]t is not enough * * * to disbelieve the employer." * * * This "pretext-plus" approach would turn *Burdine* on its head, see n. 7, *supra,* and it would result in summary judgment for the employer in the many cases where the plaintiff has no evidence beyond that required to prove a prima facie case and to show that the employer's articulated reasons are unworthy of credence. Cf. *Carter v. Duncan–Huggins, Ltd.,* 234 U.S.App.D.C. 126, 146, 727 F.2d 1225, 1245 (1984)(Scalia, J., dissenting)("[I]n order to get to the jury the plaintiff would * * * have to introduce some evidence * * * that the *basis* for [the] discriminatory treatment was *race*")(emphasis in original). See generally Lanctot, The Defendant Lies and the Plaintiff Loses: The Fallacy of the "Pretext–Plus" Rule in Employment Discrimination Cases, 43 Hastings L.J. 57 (1991)(criticizing the "pretext-plus" approach).

The Court's final attempt to neutralize the force of our precedents comes in its claim that *Aikens* settled the question presented today. This attempt to rest on *Aikens* runs into the immediate difficulty, however, that *Aikens* repeats what we said earlier in *Burdine:* the plaintiff may succeed in meeting his ultimate burden of persuasion "'either directly by persuading the court that a discriminatory reason more likely motivated the employer or indirectly by showing that the employer's proffered explanation is unworthy of credence.'" *Aikens,* 460 U.S., at 716, 103 S.Ct., at 1482 (quoting *Burdine,* 450 U.S., at 256, 101 S.Ct., at 1095). Although the *Aikens* Court quoted this statement approvingly, the majority here projects its view that the latter part of the statement is "problematic," * * * arguing that the next sentence in *Aikens* takes care of the "problem." The next sentence, however, only creates more problems for the majority, as it directs the District Court to "decide *which party's* explanation of the employer's motivation it believes." 460 U.S., at 716, 103 S.Ct., at 1482 (emphasis supplied). By requiring the factfinder to choose between the employer's explanation and the plaintiff's claim of discrimination (shown either directly or indirectly), *Aikens* flatly bars the Court's conclusion here that the factfinder can choose a third explanation, never offered by the employer, in ruling against the plaintiff. Because *Aikens* will not bear the reading the majority seeks to place upon it, there is no hope of projecting into the past the abandonment of precedent that occurs today.

I cannot join the majority in turning our back on these earlier decisions. * * * It is not as though Congress is unaware of our decisions concerning Title VII, and recent experience indicates that Congress is ready to act if we adopt interpretations of this statutory scheme it finds to be mistaken. See Civil Rights Act of 1991, 105 Stat. 1071. Congress has taken no action to indicate that we were mistaken in *McDonnell Douglas* and *Burdine*.

* * *

The enhancement of a Title VII plaintiff's burden wrought by the Court's opinion is exemplified in this case. Melvin Hicks was denied any opportunity, much less a full and fair one, to demonstrate that the supposedly nondiscriminatory explanation for his demotion and termination, the personal animosity of his immediate supervisor, was unworthy of credence. In fact, the District Court did not find that personal animosity (which it failed to recognize might be racially motivated) was the true reason for the actions St. Mary's took; it adduced this reason simply as a possibility in explaining that Hicks had failed to prove "that the crusade [to terminate him] was racially rather than personally motivated." 756 F.Supp. 1244, 1252 (E.D.Mo.1991). It is hardly surprising that Hicks failed to prove anything about this supposed personal crusade, since St. Mary's never articulated such an explanation for Hicks's discharge, and since the person who allegedly conducted this crusade denied at trial any personal difficulties between himself and Hicks. App. 46. While the majority may well be troubled about the unfair treatment of Hicks in this instance and thus remands for review of whether the District Court's factual conclusions were clearly erroneous, * * * the majority provides Hicks with no opportunity to produce evidence showing that the District Court's hypothesized explanation, first articulated six months after trial, is unworthy of credence. Whether Melvin Hicks wins or loses on remand, many plaintiffs in a like position will surely lose under the scheme adopted by the Court today, unless they possess both prescience and resources beyond what this Court has previously required Title VII litigants to employ.

Because I see no reason why Title VII interpretation should be driven by concern for employers who are too ashamed to be honest in court, at the expense of victims of discrimination who do not happen to have direct evidence of discriminatory intent, I respectfully dissent.

Notes on Hicks

1. How do you answer the questions posed in Note 2, after *Aikens* at p. 636, supra, in light of *Hicks*? Did *Aikens* forecast the *Hicks* result? Note Justice Scalia's insinuation, at the end of Part III, that Justice Blackmun, by joining the Court's opinion in *Aikens*, had not been as wary as Justice Marshall, who merely concurred in the judgment. Is this an implicit confession that *Aikens* was crafted as a stepping stone toward the *Hicks* result?

2. What options are open to Melvin Hicks on remand? The Eighth Circuit, remanding to the District Court, suggested that:

In particular, the district court may decide to hold an evidentiary hearing in order to permit the parties to present additional evidence on the now-critical question of personal animosity. For example, Hicks may be able to demonstrate that defendants were not motivated by personal animosity or that defendants' personal animosity was itself racially motivated.

Hicks v. St. Mary's Honor Center, 2 F.3d 265, 267 (8th Cir.1993). How will it help Hicks to refute a point the employer never articulated? Does Title VII prohibit personal animosity in the workplace, even if race-based, so long as the employer's work-related decisions are not discriminatory?

3. The Court in *Hicks* adopted a modified version of what had become known as the "pretext plus" rule: at the pretext stage the plaintiff must prove not only that the employer's motivation was pretextual, false or not relied upon, but in addition, that discrimination was the true motivation for the action at issue. For a comprehensive pre-*Hicks* analysis, see Catherine J. Lanctot, The Defendant Lies and the Plaintiff Loses: The Fallacy of the "Pretext–Plus" Rule in Employment Discrimination Cases, 43 Hastings L.J. 57 (1991).

Hicks does not actually require that a plaintiff present more evidence than that required to prove the prima facie case and "pretext." *Hicks* holds that at the pretext stage, the trier of fact is *permitted*, but not required, to find for plaintiff, if the jury (or judge) is convinced the employer was motivated by discriminatory intent. As Justice Scalia says, "The factfinder's disbelief of the reasons put forward by the defendant (particularly if disbelief is accompanied by a suspicion of mendacity) may, together with the elements of the prima facie case, suffice to show intentional discrimination." *Hicks*, at p. 651 supra.

Hicks may not be an insurmountable barrier for a plaintiff whose case actually goes to trial. In Barbour v. Merrill, 48 F.3d 1270 (D.C.Cir. 1995), reh'g en banc denied (May 16, 1995), petition for certiorari filed (Jul 03, 1995)(No. 95–27), plaintiff, an African American, applied for a management position within the company, made the final round of interviews, but was eventually passed over in favor of an "outside" white candidate. When this candidate refused the position, the employer reopened the search, without considering the other final candidates including Barbour. On Barbour's protest, he was considered a second time, but again the position was offered to a white applicant. The employer's rationale was that it sought an applicant with "multi-system private sector experience," an attribute that plaintiff did not possess. Id. at 1274. The jury found in plaintiff's favor on his race discrimination claim, awarding him compensatory and punitive damages. The employer appealed the district court's failure to grant a post-trial motion for judgment as a matter of law. The D.C. Circuit affirmed the jury's verdict:

> Although defendants argue that Barbour was not qualified because he lacked significant private-sector experience, the jury reasonably could have determined, from the evidence before it, including the original job description and the fact that Barbour progressed to the final round of interviews, that private sector experience was not an absolute prerequisite.

> Similarly, after hearing testimony about Barbour's background and experience, about Merrill's assessments of Barbour's abilities, and about Medlantic's decision to hire Shoup notwithstanding his lack of the educational prerequisites Medlantic initially described as required for the job, the jury reasonably could have rejected Medlantic's proffered nondiscriminatory reasons for not hiring Barbour.

Id. at 1276. The court rejected the defendants' argument that Barbour's evidentiary showing was not enough after *Hicks*: "According to Hicks, a plaintiff need only establish a prima facie case and introduce evidence sufficient to discredit the defendant's proffered nondiscriminatory reasons; at that point, the factfinder, if so persuaded, may infer discrimination." The appellate court found that Barbour had introduced sufficient evidence for the jury to conclude "both that he had proven a prima facie case * * * and that Medlantic's reasons were pretextual[.] [T]he jury could have reasonably concluded that Barbour had proven unlawful discrimination." Id. at 1277.

On the other hand, it remains to be seen how often plaintiffs will prevail after *Hicks* without a "smoking gun." The Seventh Circuit, in Anderson v. Baxter Healthcare Corp., 13 F.3d 1120 (7th Cir. 1994), (an age discrimination case using *Hicks*), cautions plaintiffs that they "might be well advised to present additional evidence of discrimination, because the factfinder is not required to find in [their] favor simply because [they] establish a prima facie case and show that the employer's proffered reasons are false." Id. at 1124.

Commentators Victoria A. Cundiff & Ann E. Chiatovitz in St. Mary's Honor Center v. Hicks: Lots of Sound and Fury But What Does it Signify?, 19 Employee Rel. L.J. 147 (Winter 1993), note that some have said "from now on job-bias victims 'may be able to prevail only when a boss sends a racist note along with a pink slip'." They characterize *Hicks* as a "hybrid approach," and note that decisions "issued by lower courts show that the St. Mary's decision has not created a uniformly applied test." Id. at 149–50. They predict, that the helpful "smoking gun" may come in an increasing reliance by plaintiffs on statistics to prove "pretext-plus." Id. at 160.

4. The major difficulty for plaintiffs after *Hicks* will arise at the summary judgment stage. How much of a showing will plaintiffs have to make to survive a summary judgment motion? Even before *Hicks*, plaintiffs were having difficulty making a sufficient showing of discriminatory intent at the summary judgment stage, largely as a result of the Supreme Court's summary judgment "trilogy" in 1986: Matsushita Electrical Industrial Co. v. Zenith Radio Corp., 475 U.S. 574, 106 S.Ct. 1348, 89 L.Ed.2d 538 (1986); Anderson v. Liberty Lobby, 477 U.S. 242 (1986); Celotex v. Catrett, 477 U.S. 317 (1986). For a detailed analysis, see Ann C. McGinley, Credulous Courts and the Tortured Trilogy: The Improper Use of Summary Judgment in Title VII and ADEA Cases, 34 B.C. L. Rev. 203 (1993), (documenting a "gradual and continuing erosion of the factfinder's role in federal employment discrimination cases [through] increasing use of summary judgment," Id. at 206. "Courts must avoid automatically crediting defendants' reasons, drawing inferences in defendants' favor, deciding witnesses' credibility on paper and requiring plaintiffs to prove their cases at the summary judgment stage." Id. at 256.).

Lanctot, Note 3 supra, cautioned that under the "pretext plus" approach, a defendant's summary judgment motion will most likely be granted where a "plaintiff has shown only that he may be able to prove that he may be able to refute the defendant's explanation, but has no additional evidence to prove that the false explanation conceals discriminatory animus. The 'pretext plus' rule effectively prevents the plaintiff from presenting live testimony and having the factual question of 'mistake' versus 'intent' resolved at trial." Lanctot, supra at 91. See also Phyllis Tropper Baumann, et. al., Substance in the Shadow of Procedure: The Integration of Substantive and Procedural Law in Title VII Cases, 33 B.C. L. Rev. 211 (1992); Michael J. Lambert, St. Mary's Honor Center v.

Hicks: The "Pretext Maybe" Approach, 29 N.Engl. L.Rev. 163 (1994); and Jody H. Odell, Case Comment: Between Pretext Only and Pretext Plus: Understanding St. Mary's Honor Center v. Hicks and its Application to Summary Judgment, 69 Notre Dame L. Rev. 1251, (1994).

In Walker v. NationsBank of Florida N.A., 53 F.3d 1548, (11th Cir.1995), a directed verdict case, not a summary judgment case, Senior Circuit Judge Johnson concurred specially and commented that in *Hicks* the Supreme Court rejected both the pretext only and pretext plus positions, creating a "middle ground * * * leav[ing] unresolved whether, where the plaintiff has supplied sufficient evidence for a jury to disbelieve the reasons proffered by the employer, a judge may find as a matter of law that the evidence is insufficient for a reasonable jury to infer discriminatory intent." Id. at 1561. He also pointed to the "uncertainty * * * generated [by *Hicks*] in the lower federal courts," citing the division over the "propriety of granting summary judgment where there is a genuine issue of fact regarding the truth of the legitimate reasons proffered by the employer." Id.

In Anderson v. Baxter Healthcare, Note 3 supra, the Seventh Circuit restated its rule on summary judgments after Hicks:

> "[Plaintiff] must only 'produce evidence from which a rational factfinder could infer that the company lied' about its proffered reasons for his dismissal. * * * 'If the only reason an employer offers for firing an employee is a lie, the inference that the real reason was a forbidden one * * * may rationally be drawn.' "

13 F.3rd at 1124. As characterized by one district court, this "pretext only" summary judgment standard means that if plaintiff can prove her prima facie case and demonstrate that the employer's reasons are false, she is entitled to submit her case to a jury, even though, after *Hicks*, she is not entitled to judgment as a matter of law. See Waldron v. SL Industries Inc., 849 F.Supp. 996 n. 11 at 1005 (D.N.J.1994). The district court in *Waldron*, however, adopted a "pretext plus" rule at the summary judgment stage, holding that plaintiff not only must produce evidence of pretext, that the employer's decision was false or not relied upon, but also that discrimination was the real reason for the adverse action. It should be noted, however, that *Waldron*, like *Baxter*, was an age discrimination case. Summary judgment has always seemed easier for employers to obtain under the ADEA than under Title VII.

Most federal courts have recognized that under *Hicks*, a prima facie case, coupled with proof of pretext and the factfinder's disbelief of the employer's stated reasons, *permits* but does not mandate a decision in favor of the plaintiff. The question remains whether a plaintiff with some evidence that the employer's "legitimate" reasons may have been false, or not relied upon, will survive summary judgment because she has been able to create a genuine issue of material fact regarding the employer's credibility.

vi. "Mixed Motives" As Disparate Treatment

PRICE WATERHOUSE v. HOPKINS

Supreme Court of the United States, 1989.
490 U.S. 228, 109 S.Ct. 1775, 104 L.Ed.2d 268.

JUSTICE BRENNAN announced the judgment of the Court and delivered an opinion, in which JUSTICE MARSHALL, JUSTICE BLACKMUN, and JUSTICE STEVENS join.

Ann Hopkins was a senior manager in an office of Price Waterhouse when she was proposed for partnership in 1982. She was neither offered nor denied admission to the partnership; instead, her candidacy was held for reconsideration the following year. When the partners in her office later refused to repropose her for partnership, she sued Price Waterhouse under Title VII, * * * charging that the firm had discriminated against her on the basis of sex in its decisions regarding partnership. Judge Gesell in the District Court for the District of Columbia ruled in her favor on the question of liability, * * * and the Court of Appeals for the District of Columbia Circuit affirmed. * * * We granted certiorari to resolve a conflict among the Courts of Appeals concerning the respective burdens of proof of a defendant and plaintiff in a suit under Title VII when it has been shown that an employment decision resulted from a mixture of legitimate and illegitimate motives. * * *

I

At Price Waterhouse, a nationwide professional accounting partnership, a senior manager becomes a candidate for partnership when the partners in her local office submit her name as a candidate. All of the other partners in the firm are then invited to submit written comments on each candidate—either on a "long" or a "short" form, depending on the partner's degree of exposure to the candidate. Not every partner in the firm submits comments on every candidate. After reviewing the comments and interviewing the partners who submitted them, the firm's Admissions Committee makes a recommendation to the Policy Board. This recommendation will be either that the firm accept the candidate for partnership, put her application on "hold," or deny her the promotion outright. The Policy Board then decides whether to submit the candidate's name to the entire partnership for a vote, to "hold" her candidacy, or to reject her. The recommendation of the Admissions Committee, and the decision of the Policy Board, are not controlled by fixed guidelines: a certain number of positive comments from partners will not guarantee a candidate's admission to the partnership, nor will a specific quantity of negative comments necessarily defeat her application. Price Waterhouse places no limit on the number of persons whom it will admit to the partnership in any given year.

Ann Hopkins had worked at Price Waterhouse's Office of Government Services in Washington, D.C., for five years when the partners in that office proposed her as a candidate for partnership. Of the 662 partners at the firm at that time, 7 were women. Of the 88 persons proposed for partnership that year, only 1—Hopkins—was a woman. Forty-seven of these candidates were admitted to the partnership, 21 were rejected, and 20—including Hopkins—were "held" for reconsideration the following year.[1] Thirteen of the 32 partners who had submitted comments on Hopkins supported her bid for

---

1. Before the time for reconsideration came, two of the partners in Hopkins' office withdrew their support for her, and the office informed her that she would not be reconsidered for partnership. Hopkins then resigned. Price Waterhouse does not challenge the Court of Appeals' conclusion that the refusal to repropose her for partnership amounted to a constructive discharge. That court remanded the case to the District Court for further pro-

ceedings to determine appropriate relief, and those proceedings have been stayed pending our decision. * * * We are concerned today only with Price Waterhouse's decision to place Hopkins' candidacy on hold. Decisions pertaining to advancement to partnership are, of course, subject to challenge under Title VII. *Hishon v. King & Spalding,* 467 U.S. 69, 104 S.Ct. 2229, 81 L.Ed.2d 59 (1984).

partnership. Three partners recommended that her candidacy be placed on hold, eight stated that they did not have an informed opinion about her, and eight recommended that she be denied partnership.

In a jointly prepared statement supporting her candidacy, the partners in Hopkins' office showcased her successful 2–year effort to secure a $25 million contract with the Department of State, labeling it "an outstanding performance" and one that Hopkins carried out "virtually at the partner level." * * * Despite Price Waterhouse's attempt at trial to minimize her contribution to this project, Judge Gesell specifically found that Hopkins had "played a key role in Price Waterhouse's successful effort to win a multi-million dollar contract with the Department of State." * * * Indeed, he went on, "[n]one of the other partnership candidates at Price Waterhouse that year had a comparable record in terms of successfully securing major contracts for the partnership." * * *

The partners in Hopkins' office praised her character as well as her accomplishments, describing her in their joint statement as "an outstanding professional" who had a "deft touch," a "strong character, independence and integrity." * * * Clients appear to have agreed with these assessments. At trial, one official from the State Department described her as "extremely competent, intelligent," "strong and forthright, very productive, energetic and creative." * * * Another high-ranking official praised Hopkins' decisiveness, broadmindedness, and "intellectual clarity"; she was, in his words, "a stimulating conversationalist." * * * Evaluations such as these led Judge Gesell to conclude that Hopkins "had no difficulty dealing with clients and her clients appear to have been very pleased with her work" and that she "was generally viewed as a highly competent project leader who worked long hours, pushed vigorously to meet deadlines and demanded much from the multidisciplinary staffs with which she worked." * * *

On too many occasions, however, Hopkins' aggressiveness apparently spilled over into abrasiveness. Staff members seem to have borne the brunt of Hopkins' brusqueness. Long before her bid for partnership, partners evaluating her work had counseled her to improve her relations with staff members. Although later evaluations indicate an improvement, Hopkins' perceived shortcomings in this important area eventually doomed her bid for partnership. Virtually all of the partners' negative remarks about Hopkins— even those of partners supporting her—had to do with her "interpersonal skills." Both "[s]upporters and opponents of her candidacy," stressed Judge Gesell, "indicated that she was sometimes overly aggressive, unduly harsh, difficult to work with and impatient with staff." * * *

There were clear signs, though, that some of the partners reacted negatively to Hopkins' personality because she was a woman. One partner described her as "macho"; * * * another suggested that she "overcompensated for being a woman"; * * * a third advised her to take "a course at charm school". * * * Several partners criticized her use of profanity; in response, one partner suggested that those partners objected to her swearing only "because it[']s a lady using foul language." * * * Another supporter explained that Hopkins "ha[d] matured from a tough-talking somewhat masculine hardnosed mgr to an authoritative, formidable, but much more appealing lady ptr candidate." * * * But it was the man who, as Judge Gesell found,

bore responsibility for explaining to Hopkins the reasons for the Policy Board's decision to place her candidacy on hold who delivered the *coup de grace:* in order to improve her chances for partnership, Thomas Beyer advised, Hopkins should "walk more femininely, talk more femininely, dress more femininely, wear make-up, have her hair styled, and wear jewelry."
* * *

Dr. Susan Fiske, a social psychologist and Associate Professor of Psychology at Carnegie–Mellon University, testified at trial that the partnership selection process at Price Waterhouse was likely influenced by sex stereotyping. Her testimony focused not only on the overtly sex-based comments of partners but also on gender-neutral remarks, made by partners who knew Hopkins only slightly, that were intensely critical of her. One partner, for example, baldly stated that Hopkins was "universally disliked" by staff, * * * and another described her as "consistently annoying and irritating"; * * * yet these were people who had had very little contact with Hopkins. According to Fiske, Hopkins' uniqueness (as the only woman in the pool of candidates) and the subjectivity of the evaluations made it likely that sharply critical remarks such as these were the product of sex stereotyping—although Fiske admitted that she could not say with certainty whether any particular comment was the result of stereotyping. Fiske based her opinion on a review of the submitted comments, explaining that it was commonly accepted practice for social psychologists to reach this kind of conclusion without having met any of the people involved in the decisionmaking process.

In previous years, other female candidates for partnership also had been evaluated in sex-based terms. As a general matter, Judge Gesell concluded, "[c]andidates were viewed favorably if partners believed they maintained their femin[in]ity while becoming effective professional managers"; in this environment, "[t]o be identified as a 'women's lib[b]er' was regarded as [a] negative comment." * * * In fact, the judge found that in previous years "[o]ne partner repeatedly commented that he could not consider any woman seriously as a partnership candidate and believed that women were not even capable of functioning as senior managers—yet the firm took no action to discourage his comments and recorded his vote in the overall summary of the evaluations." * * *

Judge Gesell found that Price Waterhouse legitimately emphasized interpersonal skills in its partnership decisions, and also found that the firm had not fabricated its complaints about Hopkins' interpersonal skills as a pretext for discrimination. Moreover, he concluded, the firm did not give decisive emphasis to such traits only because Hopkins was a woman; although there were male candidates who lacked these skills but who were admitted to partnership, the judge found that these candidates possessed other, positive traits that Hopkins lacked.

The judge went on to decide, however, that some of the partners' remarks about Hopkins stemmed from an impermissibly cabined view of the proper behavior of women, and that Price Waterhouse had done nothing to disavow reliance on such comments. He held that Price Waterhouse had unlawfully discriminated against Hopkins on the basis of sex by consciously giving credence and effect to partners' comments that resulted from sex stereotyping. Noting that Price Waterhouse could avoid equitable relief by proving by clear and convincing evidence that it would have placed Hopkins' candidacy on hold even absent this discrimination, the judge decided that the firm had not carried this heavy burden.

The Court of Appeals affirmed the District Court's ultimate conclusion, but departed from its analysis in one particular: it held that even if a plaintiff proves that discrimination played a role in an employment decision, the defendant will not be found liable if it proves, by clear and convincing evidence, that it would have made the same decision in the absence of discrimination. * * * Under this approach, an employer is not deemed to have violated Title VII if it proves that it would have made the same decision in the absence of an impermissible motive, whereas under the District Court's approach, the employer's proof in that respect only avoids equitable relief. We decide today that the Court of Appeals had the better approach, but that both courts erred in requiring the employer to make its proof by clear and convincing evidence.

II

The specification of the standard of causation under Title VII is a decision about the kind of conduct that violates that statute. According to Price Waterhouse, an employer violates Title VII only if it gives decisive consideration to an employee's gender, race, national origin, or religion in making a decision that affects that employee. On Price Waterhouse's theory, even if a plaintiff shows that her gender played a part in an employment decision, it is still her burden to show that the decision would have been different if the employer had not discriminated. In Hopkins' view, on the other hand, an employer violates the statute whenever it allows one of these attributes to play any part in an employment decision. Once a plaintiff shows that this occurred, according to Hopkins, the employer's proof that it would have made the same decision in the absence of discrimination can serve to limit equitable relief but not to avoid a finding of liability. We conclude that, as often happens, the truth lies somewhere in-between.

A

In passing Title VII, Congress made the simple but momentous announcement that sex, race, religion, and national origin are not relevant to the selection, evaluation, or compensation of employees.[3] Yet, the statute does not purport to limit the other qualities and characteristics that employers *may* take into account in making employment decisions. The converse, therefore, of "for cause" legislation, Title VII eliminates certain bases for distinguishing among employees while otherwise preserving employers' freedom of choice. This balance between employee rights and employer prerogatives turns out to be decisive in the case before us.

Congress' intent to forbid employers to take gender into account in making employment decisions appears on the face of the statute. In now-familiar language, the statute forbids an employer to "fail or refuse to hire or to discharge any individual, or otherwise to discriminate with respect to his compensation, terms, conditions, or privileges of employment," or to "limit, segregate, or classify his employees or applicants for employment in any way which would deprive or tend to deprive any individual of employment oppor-

---

3. We disregard, for purposes of this discussion, the special context of affirmative action.

tunities or otherwise adversely affect his status as an employee, *because of* such individual's * * * sex." * * * We take these words to mean that gender must be irrelevant to employment decisions. To construe the words "because of" as colloquial shorthand for "but-for causation," as does Price Waterhouse, is to misunderstand them.[6]

But-for causation is a hypothetical construct. In determining whether a particular factor was a but-for cause of a given event, we begin by assuming that that factor was present at the time of the event, and then ask whether, even if that factor had been absent, the event nevertheless would have transpired in the same way. The present, active tense of the operative verbs of § 703(a)(1)("to fail or refuse"), in contrast, turns our attention to the actual moment of the event in question, the adverse employment decision. The critical inquiry, the one commanded by the words of § 703(a)(1), is whether gender was a factor in the employment decision *at the moment it was made*. Moreover, since we know that the words "because of" do not mean "*solely* because of,"[7] we also know that Title VII meant to condemn even those decisions based on a mixture of legitimate and illegitimate considerations. When, therefore, an employer considers both gender and legitimate factors at the time of making a decision, that decision was "because of" sex and the other, legitimate considerations—even if we may say later, in the context of litigation, that the decision would have been the same if gender had not been taken into account.

To attribute this meaning to the words "because of" does not, as the dissent asserts, * * * divest them of causal significance. A simple example illustrates the point. Suppose two physical forces act upon and move an object, and suppose that either force acting alone would have moved the object. As the dissent would have it, *neither* physical force was a "cause" of the motion unless we can show that but for one or both of them, the object would not have moved; to use the dissent's terminology, both forces were simply "in the air" unless we can identify at least one of them as a but-for cause of the object's movement. * * * Events that are causally overdetermined, in other words, may not have any "cause" at all. This cannot be so.

We need not leave our common-sense at the doorstep when we interpret a statute. It is difficult for us to imagine that, in the simple words "because of," Congress meant to obligate a plaintiff to identify the precise causal role played by legitimate and illegitimate motivations in the employment decision she challenges. We conclude, instead, that Congress meant to obligate her to prove that the employer relied upon sex-based considerations in coming to its decision.

6. We made passing reference to a similar question in *McDonald v. Santa Fe Trail Transportation Co.*, 427 U.S. 273, 282, n. 10, 96 S.Ct. 2574, 2580, n. 10, 49 L.Ed.2d 493 (1976), where we stated that when a Title VII plaintiff seeks to show that an employer's explanation for a challenged employment decision is pretextual, "no more is required to be shown than that race was a 'but for' cause." This passage, however, does not suggest that the plaintiff *must* show but-for cause; it indicates only that if she does so, she prevails. More important,

McDonald dealt with the question whether the employer's stated reason for its decision was *the* reason for its action; unlike the case before us today, therefore, *McDonald* did not involve mixed motives. This difference is decisive in distinguishing this case from those involving "pretext." * * *

7. Congress specifically rejected an amendment that would have placed the word "solely" in front of the words "because of." 110 Cong. Rec. 2728, 13837 (1964).

Our interpretation of the words "because of" also is supported by the fact that Title VII does identify one circumstance in which an employer may take gender into account in making an employment decision, namely, when gender is a "bona fide occupational qualification [(BFOQ)] reasonably necessary to the normal operation of th[e] particular business or enterprise." * * * The only plausible inference to draw from this provision is that, in all other circumstances, a person's gender may not be considered in making decisions that affect her. Indeed, Title VII even forbids employers to make gender an indirect stumbling block to employment opportunities. An employer may not, we have held, condition employment opportunities on the satisfaction of facially neutral tests or qualifications that have a disproportionate, adverse impact on members of protected groups when those tests or qualifications are not required for performance of the job. See *Watson v. Fort Worth Bank & Trust,* * * *; *Griggs v. Duke Power Co.,* * * *.

To say that an employer may not take gender into account is not, however, the end of the matter, for that describes only one aspect of Title VII. The other important aspect of the statute is its preservation of an employer's remaining freedom of choice. We conclude that the preservation of this freedom means that an employer shall not be liable if it can prove that, even if it had not taken gender into account, it would have come to the same decision regarding a particular person. The statute's maintenance of employer prerogatives is evident from the statute itself and from its history, both in Congress and in this Court.

To begin with, the existence of the BFOQ exception shows Congress' unwillingness to require employers to change the very nature of their operations in response to the statute. And our emphasis on "business necessity" in disparate-impact cases, see *Watson* and *Griggs,* and on "legitimate, nondiscriminatory reason[s]" in disparate-treatment cases, see *McDonnell Douglas Corp. v. Green,* * * *; *Texas Dept. of Community Affairs v. Burdine,* * * * results from our awareness of Title VII's balance between employee rights and employer prerogatives. In *McDonnell Douglas,* we described as follows Title VII's goal to eradicate discrimination while preserving workplace efficiency: "The broad, overriding interest, shared by employer, employee, and consumer, is efficient and trustworthy workmanship assured through fair and racially neutral employment and personnel decisions. In the implementation of such decisions, it is abundantly clear that Title VII tolerates no racial discrimination, subtle or otherwise." * * *

When an employer ignored the attributes enumerated in the statute, Congress hoped, it naturally would focus on the qualifications of the applicant or employee. The intent to drive employers to focus on qualifications rather than on race, religion, sex, or national origin is the theme of a good deal of the statute's legislative history. * * *

* * * The central point is this: while an employer may not take gender into account in making an employment decision (except in those very narrow circumstances in which gender is a BFOQ), it is free to decide against a woman for other reasons. We think these principles require that, once a plaintiff in a Title VII case shows that gender played a motivating part in an employment decision, the defendant may avoid a finding of liability[10] only by

10. Hopkins argues that once she made this showing, she was entitled to a finding that Price Waterhouse had discriminated against her on the basis of sex; as a consequence, she

proving that it would have made the same decision even if it had not allowed gender to play such a role. This balance of burdens is the direct result of Title VII's balance of rights.

Our holding casts no shadow on *Burdine,* in which we decided that, even after a plaintiff has made out a prima facie case of discrimination under Title VII, the burden of persuasion does not shift to the employer to show that its stated legitimate reason for the employment decision was the true reason. * * * We stress, first, that neither court below shifted the burden of persuasion to Price Waterhouse on this question, and in fact, the District Court found that Hopkins had not shown that the firm's stated reason for its decision was pretextual. * * * Moreover, since we hold that the plaintiff retains the burden of persuasion on the issue whether gender played a part in the employment decision, the situation before us is not the one of "shifting burdens" that we addressed in *Burdine.* Instead, the employer's burden is most appropriately deemed an affirmative defense: the plaintiff must persuade the factfinder on one point, and then the employer, if it wishes to prevail, must persuade it on another. See *NLRB v. Transportation Management Corp.,* 462 U.S. 393, 400, 103 S.Ct. 2469, 2473, 76 L.Ed.2d 667 (1983).[11]

says, the partnership's proof could only limit the relief she received. She relies on Title VII's § 706(g), which permits a court to award affirmative relief when it finds that an employer "has intentionally engaged in or is intentionally engaging in an unlawful employment practice," and yet forbids a court to order reinstatement of, or backpay to, "an individual * * * if such individual was refused * * * employment or advancement or was suspended or discharged *for any reason other than* discrimination on account of race, color, religion, sex, or national origin." 42 U.S.C. § 2000e–5(g)(emphasis added). We do not take this provision to mean that a court inevitably can find a violation of the statute without having considered whether the employment decision would have been the same absent the impermissible motive. That would be to interpret § 706(g)—a provision defining *remedies*—to influence the substantive commands of the statute. We think that this provision merely limits courts' authority to award affirmative relief in those circumstances in which a violation of the statute is not dependent upon the effect of the employer's discriminatory practices on a particular employee, as in pattern-or-practice suits and class actions. "The crucial difference between an individual's claim of discrimination and a class action alleging a general pattern or practice of discrimination is manifest. The inquiry regarding an individual's claim is the reason for a particular employment decision, while 'at the liability stage of a pattern-or-practice trial the focus often will not be on individual hiring decisions, but on a pattern of discriminatory decisionmaking.'" *Cooper v. Federal Reserve Bank of Richmond,* 467 U.S. 867, 876, 104 S.Ct. 2794, 2799–2800, 81 L.Ed.2d 718 (1984), quoting *Teamsters v.*

United States, 431 U.S. 324, 360, n. 46, 97 S.Ct. 1843, 1867, n. 46, 52 L.Ed.2d 396 (1977).

Without explicitly mentioning this portion of § 706(g), we have in the past held that Title VII does not authorize affirmative relief for individuals as to whom, the employer shows, the existence of systemic discrimination had no effect. See *Franks v. Bowman Transportation Co.,* 424 U.S. 747, 772, 96 S.Ct. 1251, 1268, 47 L.Ed.2d 444 (1976); *Teamsters v. United States,* 431 U.S. 324, 367–371, 97 S.Ct. 1843, 1870–1873, 52 L.Ed.2d 396 (1977); *East Texas Motor Freight System, Inc. v. Rodriguez,* 431 U.S. 395, 404, n. 9, 97 S.Ct. 1891, 1897, n. 9, 52 L.Ed.2d 453 (1977). These decisions suggest that the proper focus of § 706(g) is on claims of systemic discrimination, not on charges of individual discrimination. Cf. *NLRB v. Transportation Management Corp.,* 462 U.S. 393, 103 S.Ct. 2469, 76 L.Ed.2d 667 (1983)(upholding the National Labor Relations Board's identical interpretation of § 10(c) of the National Labor Relations Act, 29 U.S.C. § 160(c), which contains language almost identical to § 706(g)).

11. Given that both the plaintiff and defendant bear a burden of proof in cases such as this one, it is surprising that the dissent insists that our approach requires the employer to bear "the ultimate burden of proof." It is, moreover, perfectly consistent to say *both* that gender was a factor in a particular decision when it was made *and* that, when the situation is viewed hypothetically and after the fact, the same decision would have been made even in the absence of discrimination. Thus, we do not see the "internal inconsistency" in our opinion that the dissent perceives. Finally, where liability is imposed because an employer is unable to prove that it would have made the

Price Waterhouse's claim that the employer does not bear any burden of proof (if it bears one at all) until the plaintiff has shown "substantial evidence that Price Waterhouse's explanation for failing to promote Hopkins was not the 'true reason' for its action" * * * merely restates its argument that the plaintiff in a mixed-motives case must squeeze her proof into *Burdine's* framework. Where a decision was the product of a mixture of legitimate and illegitimate motives, however, it simply makes no sense to ask whether the legitimate reason was "*the* 'true reason' " * * * for the decision—which is the question asked by *Burdine.* See *Transportation Management, supra,* * * *.[12] Oblivious to this last point, the dissent would insist that *Burdine's* framework perform work that it was never intended to perform. It would require a plaintiff who challenges an adverse employment decision in which both legitimate and illegitimate considerations played a part to pretend that the decision, in fact, stemmed from a single source—for the premise of *Burdine* is that *either* a legitimate *or* an illegitimate set of considerations led to the challenged decision. To say that *Burdine's* evidentiary scheme will not help us decide a case admittedly involving *both* kinds of considerations is not to cast aspersions on the utility of that scheme in the circumstances for which it was designed.

<h3 style="text-align:center">B</h3>

In deciding as we do today, we do not traverse new ground. We have in the past confronted Title VII cases in which an employer has used an illegitimate criterion to distinguish among employees, and have held that it is the employer's burden to justify decisions resulting from that practice. When an employer has asserted that gender is a bona fide occupational qualification within the meaning of § 703(e), for example, we have assumed that it is the employer who must show why it must use gender as a criterion in employment. See *Dothard v. Rawlinson,* * * *. In a related context, although the Equal Pay Act expressly permits employers to pay different wages to women where disparate pay is the result of a "factor other than sex," see 29 U.S.C. § 206(d)(1), we have decided that it is the employer, not the employee, who must prove that the actual disparity is not sex-linked. See *Corning Glass Works v. Brennan,* * * *. As these examples demonstrate, our assumption

same decision even if it had not discriminated, this is not an imposition of liability "where sex made no difference to the outcome." In our adversary system, where a party has the burden of proving a particular assertion and where that party is unable to meet its burden, we assume that that assertion is inaccurate. Thus, where an employer is unable to prove its claim that it would have made the same decision in the absence of discrimination, we are entitled to conclude that gender *did* make a difference to the outcome.

12. Nothing in this opinion should be taken to suggest that a case must be correctly labeled as either a "pretext" case or a "mixed motives" case from the beginning in the District Court; indeed, we expect that plaintiffs often will allege, in the alternative, that their cases are both. Discovery often will be necessary before the plaintiff can know whether both legitimate and illegitimate considerations played a part in the decision against her. At some point in the proceedings, of course, the District Court must decide whether a particular case involves mixed motives. If the plaintiff fails to satisfy the factfinder that it is more likely than not that a forbidden characteristic played a part in the employment decision, then she may prevail only if she proves, following *Burdine,* that the employer's stated reason for its decision is pretextual. The dissent need not worry that this evidentiary scheme, if used during a jury trial, will be so impossibly confused and complex as it imagines. Juries long have decided cases in which defendants raise affirmative defenses. The dissent fails, moreover, to explain why the evidentiary scheme that we endorsed over ten years ago in *Mt. Healthy* has not proved unworkable in that context but would be hopelessly complicated in a case brought under federal antidiscrimination statutes.

always has been that if an employer allows gender to affect its decisionmaking process, then it must carry the burden of justifying its ultimate decision. We have not in the past required women whose gender has proved relevant to an employment decision to establish the negative proposition that they would not have been subject to that decision had they been men, and we do not do so today.

We have reached a similar conclusion in other contexts where the law announces that a certain characteristic is irrelevant to the allocation of burdens and benefits. In *Mt. Healthy City School Dist. Board of Education v. Doyle,* 429 U.S. 274, 97 S.Ct. 568, 50 L.Ed.2d 471 (1977), the plaintiff claimed that he had been discharged as a public school teacher for exercising his free-speech rights under the First Amendment. Because we did not wish to "place an employee in a better position as a result of the exercise of constitutionally protected conduct than he would have occupied had he done nothing," we concluded that such an employee "ought not to be able, by engaging in such conduct, to prevent his employer from assessing his performance record and reaching a decision not to rehire on the basis of that record." We therefore held that once the plaintiff had shown that his constitutionally protected speech was a "substantial" or "motivating factor" in the adverse treatment of him by his employer, the employer was obligated to prove "by a preponderance of the evidence that it would have reached the same decision as to [the plaintiff] even in the absence of the protected conduct." A court that finds for a plaintiff under this standard has effectively concluded that an illegitimate motive was a "but-for" cause of the employment decision. * * *

In *Transportation Management,* we upheld the NLRB's interpretation of § 10(c) of the National Labor Relations Act, which forbids a court to order affirmative relief for discriminatory conduct against a union member "if such individual was suspended or discharged for cause." * * * The Board had decided that this provision meant that once an employee had shown that his suspension or discharge was based in part on hostility to unions, it was up to the employer to prove by a preponderance of the evidence that it would have made the same decision in the absence of this impermissible motive. In such a situation, we emphasized, "[t]he employer is a wrongdoer; he has acted out of a motive that is declared illegitimate by the statute. It is fair that he bear the risk that the influence of legal and illegal motives cannot be separated, because he knowingly created the risk and because the risk was created not by innocent activity but by his own wrongdoing." * * *

We have, in short, been here before. Each time, we have concluded that the plaintiff who shows that an impermissible motive played a motivating part in an adverse employment decision has thereby placed upon the defendant the burden to show that it would have made the same decision in the absence of the unlawful motive. Our decision today treads this well-worn path.

C

In saying that gender played a motivating part in an employment decision, we mean that, if we asked the employer at the moment of the decision what its reasons were and if we received a truthful response, one of those reasons would be that the applicant or employee was a woman.[13] In the

---

13. After comparing this description of the plaintiff's proof to that offered by the concur- ring opinion, * * * we do not understand why the concurrence suggests that they are mean-

specific context of sex stereotyping, an employer who acts on the basis of a belief that a woman cannot be aggressive, or that she must not be, has acted on the basis of gender.

Although the parties do not overtly dispute this last proposition, the placement by Price Waterhouse of "sex stereotyping" in quotation marks throughout its brief seems to us an insinuation either that such stereotyping was not present in this case or that it lacks legal relevance. We reject both possibilities. As to the existence of sex stereotyping in this case, we are not inclined to quarrel with the District Court's conclusion that a number of the partners' comments showed sex stereotyping at work. * * * As for the legal relevance of sex stereotyping, we are beyond the day when an employer could evaluate employees by assuming or insisting that they matched the stereotype associated with their group, for " '[i]n forbidding employers to discriminate against individuals because of their sex, Congress intended to strike at the entire spectrum of disparate treatment of men and women resulting from sex stereotypes.' " *Los Angeles Dept. of Water & Power v. Manhart,* * * * quoting *Sprogis v. United Air Lines, Inc.,* * * *. An employer who objects to aggressiveness in women but whose positions require this trait places women in an intolerable and impermissible Catch–22: out of a job if they behave aggressively and out of a job if they don't. Title VII lifts women out of this bind.

Remarks at work that are based on sex stereotypes do not inevitably prove that gender played a part in a particular employment decision. The plaintiff must show that the employer actually relied on her gender in making its decision. In making this showing, stereotyped remarks can certainly be *evidence* that gender played a part. In any event, the stereotyping in this case did not simply consist of stray remarks. On the contrary, Hopkins proved that Price Waterhouse invited partners to submit comments; that some of the comments stemmed from sex stereotypes; that an important part of the Policy Board's decision on Hopkins was an assessment of the submitted comments; and that Price Waterhouse in no way disclaimed reliance on the sex-linked evaluations. This is not, as Price Waterhouse suggests, "discrimination in the air"; rather, it is, as Hopkins puts it, "discrimination brought to ground and visited upon" an employee. By focusing on Hopkins' specific proof, however, we do not suggest a limitation on the possible ways of proving that stereotyping played a motivating role in an employment decision, and we refrain from deciding here which specific facts, "standing alone," would or would not establish a plaintiff's case, since such a decision is unnecessary in this case. *But see post,* (JUSTICE O'CONNOR, concurring in judgment).

As to the employer's proof, in most cases, the employer should be able to present some objective evidence as to its probable decision in the absence of an impermissible motive.[14] Moreover, proving "that the same decision would

---

ingfully different from each other * * *. Nor do we see how the inquiry that we have described is "hypothetical," * * *. It seeks to determine the content of the entire set of reasons for a decision, rather than shaving off one reason in an attempt to determine what the decision would have been in the absence of that consideration. The inquiry that we de-

scribe thus strikes us as a distinctly non-hypothetical one.

14. Justice White's suggestion, that the employer's own testimony as to the probable decision in the absence of discrimination is due special credence where the court has, contrary to the employer's testimony, found that an

have been justified * * * is not the same as proving that the same decision would have been made." * * * An employer may not, in other words, prevail in a mixed-motives case by offering a legitimate and sufficient reason for its decision if that reason did not motivate it at the time of the decision. Finally, an employer may not meet its burden in such a case by merely showing that at the time of the decision it was motivated only in part by a legitimate reason. The very premise of a mixed-motives case is that a legitimate reason was present, and indeed, in this case, Price Waterhouse already has made this showing by convincing Judge Gesell that Hopkins' interpersonal problems were a legitimate concern. The employer instead must show that its legitimate reason, standing alone, would have induced it to make the same decision.

III

The courts below held that an employer who has allowed a discriminatory impulse to play a motivating part in an employment decision must prove by clear and convincing evidence that it would have made the same decision in the absence of discrimination. We are persuaded that the better rule is that the employer must make this showing by a preponderance of the evidence.

Conventional rules of civil litigation generally apply in Title VII cases, * * * and one of these rules is that parties to civil litigation need only prove their case by a preponderance of the evidence. * * * Exceptions to this standard are uncommon, and in fact are ordinarily recognized only when the government seeks to take unusual coercive action—action more dramatic than entering an award of money damages or other conventional relief—against an individual. * * * Only rarely have we required clear and convincing proof where the action defended against seeks only conventional relief, * * * and we find it significant that in such cases it was the defendant rather than the plaintiff who sought the elevated standard of proof—suggesting that this standard ordinarily serves as a shield rather than, as Hopkins seeks to use it, as a sword.

Although Price Waterhouse does not concretely tell us how its proof was preponderant even if it was not clear and convincing, this general claim is implicit in its request for the less stringent standard. Since the lower courts required Price Waterhouse to make its proof by clear and convincing evidence, they did not determine whether Price Waterhouse had proved by *a preponderance of the evidence* that it would have placed Hopkins' candidacy on hold even if it had not permitted sex-linked evaluations to play a part in the decisionmaking process. Thus, we shall remand this case so that that determination can be made.

IV

The District Court found that sex stereotyping "was permitted to play a part" in the evaluation of Hopkins as a candidate for partnership. * * * Price Waterhouse disputes both that stereotyping occurred and that it played any part in the decision to place Hopkins' candidacy on hold. In the firm's view, in other words, the District Court's factual conclusions are clearly erroneous. We do not agree.

illegitimate factor played a part in the decision, is baffling.

In finding that some of the partners' comments reflected sex stereotyping, the District Court relied in part on Dr. Fiske's expert testimony. Without directly impugning Dr. Fiske's credentials or qualifications, Price Waterhouse insinuates that a social psychologist is unable to identify sex stereotyping in evaluations without investigating whether those evaluations have a basis in reality. This argument comes too late. At trial, counsel for Price Waterhouse twice assured the court that he did not question Dr. Fiske's expertise * * * and failed to challenge the legitimacy of her discipline. Without contradiction from Price Waterhouse, Fiske testified that she discerned sex stereotyping in the partners' evaluations of Hopkins and she further explained that it was part of her business to identify stereotyping in written documents. * * * We are not inclined to accept petitioner's belated and unsubstantiated characterization of Dr. Fiske's testimony as "gossamer evidence" * * * based only on "intuitive hunches" * * * and of her detection of sex stereotyping as "intuitively divined" * * *. Nor are we disposed to adopt the dissent's dismissive attitude toward Dr. Fiske's field of study and toward her own professional integrity, * * *.

Indeed, we are tempted to say that Dr. Fiske's expert testimony was merely icing on Hopkins' cake. It takes no special training to discern sex stereotyping in a description of an aggressive female employee as requiring "a course at charm school." Nor, turning to Thomas Beyer's memorable advice to Hopkins, does it require expertise in psychology to know that, if an employee's flawed "interpersonal skills" can be corrected by a soft-hued suit or a new shade of lipstick, perhaps it is the employee's sex and not her interpersonal skills that has drawn the criticism.[15]

Price Waterhouse also charges that Hopkins produced no evidence that sex stereotyping played a role in the decision to place her candidacy on hold. As we have stressed, however, Hopkins showed that the partnership solicited evaluations from all of the firm's partners; that it generally relied very heavily on such evaluations in making its decision; that some of the partners' comments were the product of stereotyping; and that the firm in no way disclaimed reliance on those particular comments, either in Hopkins' case or in the past. Certainly a plausible—and, one might say, inevitable—conclusion to draw from this set of circumstances is that the Policy Board in making its decision did in fact take into account all of the partners' comments, including the comments that were motivated by stereotypical notions about women's proper deportment.[16]

* * *

15. We reject the claim, advanced by Price Waterhouse here and by the dissenting judge below, that the District Court clearly erred in finding that Beyer was "responsible for telling [Hopkins] what problems the Policy Board had identified with her candidacy." * * * This conclusion was reasonable in light of the testimony at trial of a member of both the Policy Board and the Admissions Committee, who stated that he had "no doubt" that Beyer would discuss with Hopkins the reasons for placing her candidacy on hold and that Beyer "knew exactly where the problems were" regarding Hopkins.

16. We do not understand the dissenters' dissatisfaction with the District Judge's statements regarding the failure of Price Waterhouse to "sensitize" partners to the dangers of sexism. * * * Made in the context of determining that Price Waterhouse had not disclaimed reliance on sex-based evaluations, and following the judge's description of the firm's history of condoning such evaluations, the judge's remarks seem to us justified.

Nor is the finding that sex stereotyping played a part in the Policy Board's decision undermined by the fact that many of the suspect comments were made by supporters rather than detractors of Hopkins. A negative comment, even when made in the context of a generally favorable review, nevertheless may influence the decisionmaker to think less highly of the candidate; the Policy Board, in fact, did not simply tally the "yes's" and "no's" regarding a candidate, but carefully reviewed the content of the submitted comments. The additional suggestion that the comments were made by "persons outside the decisionmaking chain" * * *—and therefore could not have harmed Hopkins—simply ignores the critical role that partners' comments played in the Policy Board's partnership decisions.

Price Waterhouse appears to think that we cannot affirm the factual findings of the trial court without deciding that, instead of being overbearing and aggressive and curt, Hopkins is in fact kind and considerate and patient. If this is indeed its impression, petitioner misunderstands the theory on which Hopkins prevailed. The District Judge acknowledged that Hopkins' conduct justified complaints about her behavior as a senior manager. But he also concluded that the reactions of at least some of the partners were reactions to her as a *woman* manager. Where an evaluation is based on a subjective assessment of a person's strengths and weaknesses, it is simply not true that each evaluator will focus on, or even mention, the same weaknesses. Thus, even if we knew that Hopkins had "personality problems," this would not tell us that the partners who cast their evaluations of Hopkins in sex-based terms would have criticized her as sharply (or criticized her at all) if she had been a man. It is not our job to review the evidence and decide that the negative reactions to Hopkins were based on reality; our perception of Hopkins' character is irrelevant. We sit not to determine whether Ms. Hopkins is nice, but to decide whether the partners reacted negatively to her personality because she is a woman.

V

We hold that when a plaintiff in a Title VII case proves that her gender played a motivating part in an employment decision, the defendant may avoid a finding of liability only by proving by a preponderance of the evidence that it would have made the same decision even if it had not taken the plaintiff's gender into account. Because the courts below erred by deciding that the defendant must make this proof by clear and convincing evidence, we reverse the Court of Appeals' judgment against Price Waterhouse on liability and remand the case to that court for further proceedings.

It is so ordered.

JUSTICE WHITE, concurring in the judgment.

In my view, to determine the proper approach to causation in this case, we need look only to the Court's opinion in *Mt. Healthy City School District Bd. of Ed. v. Doyle,* * * *.

It is not necessary to get into semantic discussions on whether the *Mt. Healthy* approach is "but for" causation in another guise or creates an affirmative defense on the part of the employer to see its clear application to the issues before us in this case. As in *Mt. Healthy,* the District Court found that the employer was motivated by both legitimate and illegitimate factors.

And here, as in *Mt. Healthy,* and as the Court now holds, Hopkins was not required to prove that the illegitimate factor was the only, principal, or true reason for the petitioner's action. Rather, as Justice O'Connor states, her burden was to show that the unlawful motive was a *substantial* factor in the adverse employment action. The District Court, as its opinion was construed by the Court of Appeals, so found, * * * and I agree that the finding was supported by the record. The burden of persuasion then should have shifted to Price Waterhouse to prove "by a preponderance of the evidence that it would have reached the same decision * * * in the absence of" the unlawful motive. * * *

I agree with Justice Brennan that applying this approach to causation in Title VII cases is not a departure from and does not require modification of the Court's holdings in * * * *Burdine* and *McDonnell Douglas* * * *. The Court has made clear that "mixed motive" cases, such as the present one, are different from pretext cases such as *McDonnell Douglas* and *Burdine*. In pretext cases, "the issue is whether either illegal or legal motives, but not both, were the 'true' motives behind the decision." * * * In mixed motive cases, however, there is no one "true" motive behind the decision. Instead, the decision is a result of multiple factors, at least one of which is legitimate. It can hardly be said that our decision in this case is a departure from cases that are "inapposite." I also disagree with the dissent's assertion that this approach to causation is inconsistent with our statement in *Burdine* that "[t]he ultimate burden of persuading the trier of fact that the defendant intentionally discriminated against the plaintiff remains at all times with the plaintiff." * * * As we indicated in *Transportation Management Corp.,* the showing required by *Mt. Healthy* does not improperly shift from the plaintiff the ultimate burden of persuasion on whether the defendant intentionally discriminated against him or her. * * *

Because the Court of Appeals required Price Waterhouse to prove by clear and convincing evidence that it would have reached the same employment decision in the absence of the improper motive, rather than merely requiring proof by a preponderance of the evidence as in *Mt. Healthy,* I concur in the judgment reversing this case in part and remanding. With respect to the employer's burden, however, the plurality seems to require, at least in most cases, that the employer submit objective evidence that the same result would have occurred absent the unlawful motivation. * * * In my view, however, there is no special requirement that the employer carry its burden by objective evidence. In a mixed motive case, where the legitimate motive found would have been ample grounds for the action taken, and the employer credibly testifies that the action would have been taken for the legitimate reasons alone, this should be ample proof. This would even more plainly be the case where the employer denies any illegitimate motive in the first place but the court finds that illegitimate, as well as legitimate, factors motivated the adverse action.**

JUSTICE O'CONNOR, concurring in the judgment.

** I agree with the plurality that if the employer carries this burden, there has been no violation of Title VII.

I agree with the plurality that on the facts presented in this case, the burden of persuasion should shift to the employer to demonstrate by a preponderance of the evidence that it would have reached the same decision concerning Ann Hopkins' candidacy absent consideration of her gender. I further agree that this burden shift is properly part of the liability phase of the litigation. I thus concur in the judgment of the Court. My disagreement stems from the plurality's conclusions concerning the substantive requirement of causation under the statute and its broad statements regarding the applicability of the allocation of the burden of proof applied in this case. The evidentiary rule the Court adopts today should be viewed as a supplement to the careful framework established by our unanimous decisions in *McDonnell Douglas Corp.* * * * and *Burdine,* * * * for use in cases such as this one where the employer has created uncertainty as to causation by knowingly giving substantial weight to an impermissible criterion. I write separately to explain why I believe such a departure from the *McDonnell Douglas* standard is justified in the circumstances presented by this and like cases, and to express my views as to when and how the strong medicine of requiring the employer to bear the burden of persuasion on the issue of causation should be administered.

I

* * * The legislative history of Title VII bears out what its plain language suggests: a substantive violation of the statute only occurs when consideration of an illegitimate criterion is the "but-for" cause of an adverse employment action. The legislative history makes it clear that Congress was attempting to eradicate discriminatory actions in the employment setting, not mere discriminatory thoughts. Critics of the bill that became Title VII labeled it a "thought control bill," and argued that it created a "punishable crime that does not require an illegal external act as a basis for judgment." * * * Senator Case, whose views the plurality finds so persuasive elsewhere, responded:

"The man must do or fail to do something in regard to employment. There must be some specific external act, more than a mental act. Only if he does the act because of the grounds stated in the bill would there be any legal consequences."

Thus, I disagree with the plurality's dictum that the words "because of" do not mean "but-for" causation; manifestly they do. * * * We should not, and need not, deviate from that policy today. The question for decision in this case is what allocation of the burden of persuasion on the issue of causation best conforms with the intent of Congress and the purposes behind Title VII.

* * *

Like the common law of torts, the statutory employment "tort" created by Title VII has two basic purposes. The first is to deter conduct which has been identified as contrary to public policy and harmful to society as a whole. As we have noted in the past, the award of backpay to a Title VII plaintiff provides "the spur or catalyst which causes employers and unions to self-examine and to self-evaluate their employment practices and to endeavor to eliminate, so far as possible, the last vestiges" of discrimination in employment. * * * The second goal of Title VII is "to make persons whole for injuries suffered on account of unlawful employment discrimination." * * *

Both these goals are reflected in the elements of a disparate treatment action. There is no doubt that Congress considered reliance on gender or race in making employment decisions an evil in itself. * * * Reliance on such factors is exactly what the threat of Title VII liability was meant to deter. While the main concern of the statute was with employment opportunity, Congress was certainly not blind to the stigmatic harm which comes from being evaluated by a process which treats one as an inferior by reason of one's race or sex. * * * At the same time, Congress clearly conditioned legal liability on a determination that the consideration of an illegitimate factor *caused* a tangible employment injury of some kind.

Where an individual disparate treatment plaintiff has shown by a preponderance of the evidence that an illegitimate criterion was a *substantial* factor in an adverse employment decision, the deterrent purpose of the statute has clearly been triggered. More importantly, as an evidentiary matter, a reasonable factfinder could conclude that absent further explanation, the employer's discriminatory motivation "caused" the employment decision. The employer has not yet been shown to be a violator, but neither is it entitled to the same presumption of good faith concerning its employment decisions which is accorded employers facing only circumstantial evidence of discrimination. Both the policies behind the statute, and the evidentiary principles developed in the analogous area of causation in the law of torts, suggest that at this point the employer may be required to convince the factfinder that, despite the smoke, there is no fire.

We have given recognition to these principles in our cases which have discussed the "remedial phase" of class action disparate treatment cases. Once the class has established that discrimination against a protected group was essentially the employer's "standard practice," there has been harm to the group and injunctive relief is appropriate. But as to the individual members of the class, the liability phase of the litigation is not complete. * * * Because the class has already demonstrated that, as a rule, illegitimate factors were considered in the employer's decisions, the burden shifts to the employer "to demonstrate that the individual applicant was denied an employment opportunity for legitimate reasons." *Teamsters v. United States,* * * *.

The individual members of a class action treatment case stand in much the same position as Ann Hopkins here. There has been a strong showing that the employer has done exactly what Title VII forbids, but the connection between the employer's illegitimate motivation and any injury to the individual plaintiff is unclear. At this point calling upon the employer to show that despite consideration of illegitimate factors the individual plaintiff would not have been hired or promoted in any event hardly seems "unfair" or contrary to the substantive command of the statute. In fact, an individual plaintiff who has shown that an illegitimate factor played a substantial role in the decision in her case has proved *more* than the class member in a *Teamsters* type action. The latter receives the benefit of a burden shift to the defendant based on the *likelihood* that an illegitimate criterion was a factor in the individual employment decision.

* * *

II

The dissent's summary of our individual disparate treatment cases to date is fair and accurate, and amply demonstrates that the rule we adopt today is at least a change in direction from some of our prior precedents. * * * We have indeed emphasized in the past that in an individual disparate treatment action the plaintiff bears the burden of persuasion throughout the litigation. Nor have we confined the word "pretext" to the narrow definition which the plurality attempts to pin on it today. * * * *McDonnell Douglas* and *Burdine* clearly contemplated that a disparate treatment plaintiff could show that the employer's proffered explanation for an event was not "the true reason" either because it *never* motivated the employer in its employment decisions or because it did not do so in a particular case. *McDonnell Douglas* and *Burdine* assumed that the plaintiff would bear the burden of persuasion as to both these attacks, and we clearly depart from that framework today. Such a departure requires justification, and its outlines should be carefully drawn.

First, *McDonnell Douglas* itself dealt with a situation where the plaintiff presented no direct evidence that the employer had relied on a forbidden factor under Title VII in making an employment decision. The prima facie case established there was not difficult to prove, and was based only on the statistical probability that when a number of potential causes for an employment decision are eliminated an inference arises that an illegitimate factor was in fact the motivation behind the decision. * * * In the face of this inferential proof, the employer's burden was deemed to be only one of production; the employer must articulate a legitimate reason for the adverse employment action. * * * The plaintiff must then be given an "opportunity to demonstrate by competent evidence that the presumptively valid reasons for his rejection were in fact a coverup for a racially discriminatory decision." * * * As the discussion of *Teamsters* and *Arlington Heights* indicates, I do not think that the employer is entitled to the same presumption of good faith where there is direct evidence that it has placed substantial reliance on factors whose consideration is forbidden by Title VII.

The only individual treatment case cited by the dissent which involved the kind of direct evidence of discriminatory animus with which we are confronted here is *United States Postal Service Bd. of Governors v. Aikens,* 460 U.S. 711, 713–714, n. 2, * * * (1983). The question presented to the Court in that case involved only a challenge to the elements of the prima facie case under *McDonnell Douglas* and *Burdine,* see Pet. for Cert. in *United States Postal Service Bd. of Governors v. Aikens,* O.T.1981, No. 1044, and the question we confront today was neither briefed nor argued to the Court. As should be apparent, the entire purpose of the *McDonnell Douglas* prima facie case is to compensate for the fact that direct evidence of intentional discrimination is hard to come by. That the employer's burden in rebutting such an inferential case of discrimination is only one of production does not mean that the scales should be weighted in the same manner where there *is* direct evidence of intentional discrimination. * * *

Second, the facts of this case, and a growing number like it decided by the Courts of Appeals, convince me that the evidentiary standard I propose is necessary to make real the promise of *McDonnell Douglas* that "[i]n the implementation of [employment] decisions, it is abundantly clear that Title VII tolerates no * * * discrimination, subtle or otherwise." * * * In this case, the District Court found that a number of the evaluations of Ann Hopkins submitted by partners in the firm overtly referred to her failure to conform to certain gender stereotypes as a factor militating against her election to the partnership. * * * The District Court further found that these evaluations were given "great weight" by the decisionmakers at Price Waterhouse. * * * In addition, the District Court found that the partner responsible for informing Hopkins of the factors which caused her candidacy to be placed on hold, indicated that her "professional" problems would be solved if she would "walk more femininely, talk more femininely, wear make-up, have her hair styled, and wear jewelry." * * * As the Court of Appeals characterized it, Ann Hopkins proved that Price Waterhouse "permitt[ed] stereotypical attitudes towards women to play a significant, though unquantifiable, role in its decision not to invite her to become a partner." * * *

At this point Ann Hopkins had taken her proof as far as it could go. She had proved discriminatory input into the decisional process, and had proved that participants in the process considered her failure to conform to the stereotypes credited by a number of the decisionmakers had been a substantial factor in the decision. It is as if Ann Hopkins were sitting in the hall outside the room where partnership decisions were being made. As the partners filed in to consider her candidacy, she heard several of them make sexist remarks in discussing her suitability for partnership. As the decisionmakers exited the room, she was *told* by one of those privy to the decision-making process that her gender was a major reason for the rejection of her partnership bid. If, as we noted in *Teamsters,* "[p]resumptions shifting the burden of proof are often created to reflect judicial evaluations of probabilities and to conform with a party's superior access to the proof," * * * one would be hard pressed to think of a situation where it would be more appropriate to require the defendant to show that its decision would have been justified by wholly legitimate concerns.

Moreover, there is mounting evidence in the decisions of the lower courts that respondent here is not alone in her inability to pinpoint discrimination as the precise cause of her injury, despite having shown that it played a significant role in the decisional process. Many of these courts, which deal with the evidentiary issues in Title VII cases on a regular basis, have concluded that placing the risk of nonpersuasion on the defendant in a situation where uncertainty as to causation has been created by its consideration of an illegitimate criterion makes sense as a rule of evidence and furthers the substantive command of Title VII. * * * Particularly in the context of the professional world, where decisions are often made by collegial bodies on the basis of largely subjective criteria, requiring the plaintiff to prove that *any* one factor was the definitive cause of the decisionmakers' action may be tantamount to declaring Title VII inapplicable to such decisions. See, *e.g., Fields v. Clark University,* 817 F.2d 931, 935–937 (C.A.1 1987)(where plaintiff produced "strong evidence" that sexist attitudes infected faculty tenure decision burden properly shifted to defendant to show that it would have reached the same decision absent discrimination); *Thompkins v. Morris Brown College,* 752 F.2d 558, 563 (C.A.11 1985)(direct evidence of discriminatory animus in decision to discharge college professor shifted burden of persuasion to defendant).

Finally, I am convinced that a rule shifting the burden to the defendant where the plaintiff has shown that an illegitimate criterion was a "substantial factor" in the employment decision will not conflict with other congressional policies embodied in Title VII. Title VII expressly provides that an employer need not give preferential treatment to employees or applicants of any race, color, religion, sex, or national origin in order to maintain a work force in balance with the general population. * * * The interpretive memorandum, whose authoritative force is noted by the plurality, * * * specifically provides: "There is no requirement in title VII that an employer maintain a racial balance in his work force. On the contrary, any deliberate attempt to maintain a racial balance, whatever such a balance may be, would involve a violation of title VII because maintaining such a balance would require an employer to hire or refuse to hire on the basis of race." * * *

Last Term, in *Watson* * * * the Court unanimously concluded that the disparate impact analysis first enunciated in *Griggs* * * * should be extended to subjective or discretionary selection processes. At the same time a plurality of the Court indicated concern that the focus on bare statistics in the disparate impact setting could force employers to adopt "inappropriate prophylactic measures" in violation of § 2000e–2(j). The plurality went on to emphasize that in a disparate impact case, the plaintiff may not simply point to a statistical disparity in the employer's work force. Instead, the plaintiff must identify a particular employment practice and "must offer statistical evidence of a kind and degree sufficient to show that the practice in question has caused the exclusion of applicants for jobs or promotions because of their membership in a protected group." * * * The plurality indicated that "the ultimate burden of proving that discrimination against a protected group has been caused by a specific employment practice remains with the plaintiff at all times." * * *

I believe there are significant differences between shifting the burden of persuasion to the employer in a case resting purely on statistical proof as in the disparate impact setting and shifting the burden of persuasion in a case like this one, where an employee has demonstrated by direct evidence that an illegitimate factor played a substantial role in a particular employment decision. First, the explicit consideration of race, color, religion, sex, or national origin in making employment decisions "was the most obvious evil Congress had in mind when it enacted Title VII." *Teamsters,* * * *. While the prima facie case under *McDonnell Douglas* and the statistical showing of imbalance involved in an impact case may both be indicators of discrimination or its "functional equivalent," they are not, in and of themselves, the evils Congress sought to eradicate from the employment setting. Second, shifting the burden of persuasion to the employer in a situation like this one creates no incentive to preferential treatment in violation of § 2000e–2(j). To avoid bearing the burden of justifying its decision, the employer need not seek racial or sexual balance in its work force; rather, all it need do is avoid substantial reliance on forbidden criteria in making its employment decisions.

While the danger of forcing employers to engage in unwarranted preferential treatment is thus less dramatic in this setting than in the situation the Court faced in *Watson,* it is far from wholly illusory. Based on its misreading of the words "because of" in the statute, * * * the plurality appears to conclude that if a decisional process is "tainted" by awareness of sex or race in any way, the employer has violated the statute, and Title VII thus *commands* that the burden shift to the employer to justify its decision. * * * The plurality thus effectively reads the causation requirement out of the statute, and then replaces it with an "affirmative defense." * * *

In my view, in order to justify shifting the burden on the issue of causation to the defendant, a disparate treatment plaintiff must show by direct evidence that an illegitimate criterion was a substantial factor in the decision. * * * Requiring that the plaintiff demonstrate that an illegitimate factor played a substantial role in the employment decision identifies those employment situations where the deterrent purpose of Title VII is most clearly implicated. As an evidentiary matter, where a plaintiff has made this type of strong showing of illicit motivation, the factfinder is entitled to presume that the employer's discriminatory animus made a difference to the outcome, absent proof to the contrary from the employer. Where a disparate treatment plaintiff has made such a showing, the burden then rests with the employer to convince the trier of fact that it is more likely than not that the decision would have been the same absent consideration of the illegitimate factor. The employer need not isolate the sole cause for the decision, rather it must demonstrate that with the illegitimate factor removed from the calculus, sufficient business reasons would have induced it to take the same employment action. This evidentiary scheme essentially requires the employer to place the employee in the same position he or she would have occupied absent discrimination. Cf. *Mt. Healthy* * * *. If the employer fails to carry this burden, the factfinder is justified in concluding that the decision was made "because of" consideration of the illegitimate factor and the substantive standard for liability under the statute is satisfied.

Thus, stray remarks in the workplace, while perhaps probative of sexual harassment, see *Meritor Savings Bank v. Vinson,* * * * cannot justify requiring the employer to prove that its hiring or promotion decisions were based on legitimate criteria. Nor can statements by nondecisionmakers, or statements by decisionmakers unrelated to the decisional process itself suffice to satisfy the plaintiff's burden in this regard. In addition, in my view testimony such as Dr. Fiske's in this case, standing alone, would not justify shifting the burden of persuasion to the employer. Race and gender always "play a role" in an employment decision in the benign sense that these are human characteristics of which decisionmakers are aware and may comment on in a perfectly neutral and nondiscriminatory fashion. For example, in the context of this case, a mere reference to "a lady candidate" might show that gender "played a role" in the decision, but by no means could support a rational factfinder's inference that the decision was made "because of" sex. What is required is what Ann Hopkins showed here: direct evidence that decisionmakers placed substantial negative reliance on an illegitimate criterion in reaching their decision.

It should be obvious that the threshold standard I would adopt for shifting the burden of persuasion to the defendant differs substantially from that proposed by the plurality, the plurality's suggestion to the contrary notwithstanding. See *ante*, at * * * n. 13. The plurality proceeds from the premise that the words "because of" in the statute do not embody any causal requirement at all. Under my approach, the plaintiff must produce evidence sufficient to show that an illegitimate criterion was a substantial factor in the particular employment decision such that a reasonable factfinder could draw an inference that the decision was made "because of" the plaintiff's protected status. Only then would the burden of proof shift to the defendant to prove that the decision would have been justified by other, wholly legitimate considerations. See also *ante*, * * * (WHITE, J., concurring in judgment).

In sum, because of the concerns outlined above, and because I believe that the deterrent purpose of Title VII is disserved by a rule which places the burden of proof on plaintiffs on the issue of causation in all circumstances, I would retain but supplement the framework we established in *McDonnell Douglas* and subsequent cases. The structure of the presentation of evidence in an individual treatment case should conform to the general outlines we established in *McDonnell Douglas* and *Burdine*. First, the plaintiff must establish the *McDonnell Douglas* prima facie case by showing membership in a protected group, qualification for the job, rejection for the position, and that after rejection the employer continued to seek applicants of complainant's general qualifications. * * * The plaintiff should also present any direct evidence of discriminatory animus in the decisional process. The defendant should then present its case, including its evidence as to legitimate, nondiscriminatory reasons for the employment decision. As the dissent notes, under this framework, the employer "has every incentive to convince the trier of fact that the decision was lawful." * * * Once all the evidence has been received, the court should determine whether the *McDonnell Douglas* or *Price Waterhouse* framework properly applies to the evidence before it. If the plaintiff has failed to satisfy the *Price Waterhouse* threshold, the case should be decided under the principles enunciated in *McDonnell Douglas* and *Burdine*, with the plaintiff bearing the burden of persuasion on the ultimate issue whether the employment action was taken because of discrimination. In my view, such a system is both fair and workable and it calibrates the evidentiary requirements demanded of the parties to the goals behind the statute itself.

I agree with the dissent, see *post*, at * * * n. 4, that the evidentiary framework I propose should be available to all disparate treatment plaintiffs where an illegitimate consideration played a substantial role in an adverse employment decision. The Court's allocation of the burden of proof in *Johnson v. Transportation Agency*, * * * rested squarely on "the analytical framework set forth in *McDonnell Douglas*," * * * which we alter today. It would be odd to say the least if the evidentiary rules applicable to Title VII actions were themselves dependent on the gender or the skin color of the litigants.

In this case, I agree with the plurality that petitioner should be called upon to show that the outcome would have been the same if respondent's professional merit had been its only concern. On remand, the District Court should determine whether Price Waterhouse has shown by a preponderance of the evidence that if gender had not been part of the process, its employment decision concerning Ann Hopkins would nonetheless have been the same.

Justice Kennedy, with whom the Chief Justice and Justice Scalia join, dissenting.

Today the Court manipulates existing and complex rules for employment discrimination cases in a way certain to result in confusion. Continued adherence to the evidentiary scheme established in *McDonnell Douglas* and *Burdine* is a wiser course than creation of more disarray in an area of the law already difficult for the bench and bar, and so I must dissent.

* * *

I

The plurality describes this as a case about the standard of *causation* under Title VII, but I respectfully suggest that the description is misleading. Much of the plurality's rhetoric is spent denouncing a "but-for" standard of causation. The theory of Title VII liability the plurality adopts, however, essentially incorporates the but-for standard. The importance of today's decision is not the standard of causation it employs, but its shift to the defendant of the burden of proof. The plurality's causation analysis is misdirected, for it is clear that, whoever bears the burden of proof on the issue, Title VII liability requires a finding of but-for causation. See also *ante,* * * * (opinion of O'Connor, J.); *ante,* * * * (opinion of White, J.).

* * *

By any normal understanding, the phrase "because of" conveys the idea that the motive in question made a difference to the outcome. We use the words this way in everyday speech. * * * Congress could not have chosen a clearer way to indicate that proof of liability under Title VII requires a showing that race, color, religion, sex, or national origin caused the decision at issue.

* * *

What we term "but-for" cause is the least rigorous standard that is consistent with the approach to causation our precedents describe. If a motive is not a but-for cause of an event, then by definition it did not make a difference to the outcome. The event would have occurred just the same without it. Common law approaches to causation often require proof of but-for cause as a starting point toward proof of legal cause. The law may require more than but-for cause, for instance proximate cause, before imposing liability. Any standard less than but-for, however, simply represents a decision to impose liability without causation. As Dean Prosser puts it, "[a]n act or omission is not regarded as a cause of an event if the particular event would have occurred without it." W. Keeton, D. Dobbs, R. Keeton, & D. Owen, Prosser and Keeton on Law of Torts 265 (5th ed. 1984).

One of the principal reasons the plurality decision may sow confusion is that it claims Title VII liability is unrelated to but-for causation, yet it adopts a but-for standard once it has placed the burden of proof as to causation upon the employer. This approach conflates the question whether causation must be shown with the question of how it is to be shown. Because the plurality's theory of Title VII causation is ultimately consistent with a but-for standard, it might be said that my disagreement with the plurality's comments on but-for cause is simply academic. See *ante,* * * * (opinion of White, J.). But since those comments seem to influence the decision, I turn now to that part of the plurality's analysis.

The plurality begins by noting the quite unremarkable fact that Title VII is written in the present tense. * * * This observation, however, tells us nothing of particular relevance to Title VII or the cause of action it creates. I am unaware of any federal prohibitory statute that is written in the past tense. Every liability determination, including the novel one constructed by the plurality, necessarily is concerned with the examination of a past event.[1] The plurality's analysis of verb tense serves only to divert attention from the causation requirement that is made part of the statute by the "because of" phrase. That phrase, I respectfully submit, embodies a rather simple concept that the plurality labors to ignore.[2]

We are told next that but-for cause is not required, since the words "because of" do not mean "*solely* because of." * * * No one contends, however, that sex must be the sole cause of a decision before there is a Title VII violation. This is a separate question from whether consideration of sex must be *a* cause of the decision. Under the accepted approach to causation that I have discussed, sex is a cause for the employment decision whenever, either by itself or in combination with other factors, it made a difference to the decision. Discrimination need not be the sole cause in order for liability to arise, but merely a necessary element of the set of factors that caused the decision, *i.e.*, a but-for cause. * * * The plurality seems to say that since we know the words "because of" do not mean "solely because of," they must not mean "because of" at all. This does not follow, as a matter of either semantics or logic.

The plurality's reliance on the "bona fide occupational qualification" (BFOQ) provisions of Title VII, is particularly inapt. The BFOQ provisions allow an employer, in certain cases, to make an employment decision of which it is conceded that sex is the cause. That sex may be the legitimate cause of an employment decision where gender is a BFOQ is consistent with the opposite command that a decision caused by sex in any other case justifies the imposition of Title VII liability. This principle does not support, however, the novel assertion that a violation has occurred where sex made no difference to the outcome.

The most confusing aspect of the plurality's analysis of causation and liability is its internal inconsistency. The plurality begins by saying: "When * * * an employer considers both gender and legitimate factors at the time of making a decision, that decision was 'because of' sex and the other, legitimate

---

1. The plurality's description of its own standard is both hypothetical and retrospective. The inquiry seeks to determine whether "if we asked the employer at the moment of decision what its reasons were and if we received a truthful response, one of those reasons would be that the applicant or employee was a woman."

2. The plurality's discussion of overdetermined causes only highlights the error of its insistence that but-for is not the substantive standard of causation under Title VII. The opinion discusses the situation where two physical forces move an object, and either force acting alone would have moved the object. Translated to the context of Title VII, this situation would arise where an employer took an adverse action in reliance both on sex and on legitimate reasons, and *either* the illegitimate or the legitimate reason standing alone would have produced the action. If this state of affairs is proved to the factfinder, there will be no liability under the plurality's own test, for the same decision would have been made had the illegitimate reason never been considered.

considerations—even if we may say later, in the context of litigation, that the decision would have been the same if gender had not been taken into account." Yet it goes on to state that "an employer shall not be liable if it can prove that, even if it had not taken gender into account, it would have come to the same decision."

Given the language of the statute, these statements cannot both be true. Title VII unambiguously states that an employer who makes decisions "because of" sex has violated the statute. The plurality's first statement therefore appears to indicate that an employer who considers illegitimate reasons when making a decision is a violator. But the opinion then tells us that the employer who shows that the same decision would have been made absent consideration of sex is *not* a violator. If the second statement is to be reconciled with the language of Title VII, it must be that a decision that would have been the same absent consideration of sex was not made "because of" sex. In other words, there is no violation of the statute absent but-for causation. The plurality's description of the "same decision" test it adopts supports this view. The opinion states that "[a] court that finds for a plaintiff under this standard has effectively concluded that an illegitimate motive was a 'but-for' cause of the employment decision," * * * and that this "is not an imposition of liability 'where sex made no difference to the outcome,' * * *."

The plurality attempts to reconcile its internal inconsistency on the causation issue by describing the employer's showing as an "affirmative defense." This is nothing more than a label, and one not found in the language or legislative history of Title VII. Section 703(a)(1) is the statutory basis of the cause of action, and the Court is obligated to explain how its disparate treatment decisions are consistent with the terms of § 703(a)(1), not with general themes of legislative history or with other parts of the statute that are plainly inapposite. While the test ultimately adopted by the plurality may not be inconsistent with the terms of § 703(a)(1), * * * the same cannot be said of the plurality's reasoning with respect to causation. As Justice O'Connor describes it, the plurality "reads the causation requirement out of the statute, and then replaces it with an 'affirmative defense.'" * * * Labels aside, the import of today's decision is not that Title VII liability can arise without but-for causation, but that in certain cases it is not the plaintiff who must prove the presence of causation, but the defendant who must prove its absence.

II

We established the order of proof for individual Title VII disparate treatment cases in *McDonnell Douglas* * * * and reaffirmed this allocation in * * * *Burdine.* * * * I would adhere to this established evidentiary framework, which provides the appropriate standard for this and other individual disparate treatment cases. Today's creation of a new set of rules for "mixed-motive" cases is not mandated by the statute itself. The Court's attempt at refinement provides limited practical benefits at the cost of confusion and complexity, with the attendant risk that the trier of fact will misapprehend the controlling legal principles and reach an incorrect decision.

* * *

Our opinions make plain that *Burdine* applies to all individual disparate treatment cases, whether the plaintiff offers direct proof that discrimination motivated the employer's actions or chooses the indirect method of showing that the employer's proffered justification is false, that is to say, a pretext. * * * The plurality is mistaken in suggesting that the plaintiff in a so-called "mixed motives" case will be disadvantaged by having to "squeeze her proof into *Burdine's* framework." * * * *Burdine* compels the employer to come forward with its explanation of the decision and permits the plaintiff to offer evidence under either of the logical methods for proof of discrimination. This is hardly a framework that confines the plaintiff; still less is it a justification for saying that the ultimate burden of proof must be on the employer in a mixed motives case. *Burdine* provides an orderly and adequate way to place both inferential and direct proof before the factfinder for a determination whether intentional discrimination has caused the employment decision. Regardless of the character of the evidence presented, we have consistently held that the ultimate burden "remains at all times with the plaintiff." * * *

Aikens illustrates the point. There, the evidence showed that the plaintiff, a black man, was far more qualified than any of the white applicants promoted ahead of him. More important, the testimony showed that "the person responsible for the promotion decisions at issue had made numerous derogatory comments about blacks in general and Aikens in particular." 460 U.S., at 713–714, n. 2, 103 S.Ct., at 1481, n. 2. Yet the Court in *Aikens* reiterated that the case was to be tried under the proof scheme of *Burdine*. JUSTICE BRENNAN and JUSTICE BLACKMUN concurred to stress that the plaintiff could prevail under the *Burdine* scheme in either of two ways, one of which was directly to persuade the court that the employment decision was motivated by discrimination. * * * *Aikens* leaves no doubt that the so-called "pretext" framework of *Burdine* has been considered to provide a flexible means of addressing all individual disparate treatment claims.

Downplaying the novelty of its opinion, the plurality claims to have followed a "well-worn path" from our prior cases. The path may be well-worn, but it is in the wrong forest. The plurality again relies on Title VII's BFOQ provisions, under which an employer bears the burden of justifying the use of a sex-based employment qualification. See *Dothard v. Rawlinson,* * * *. In the BFOQ context this is a sensible, indeed necessary, allocation of the burden, for there by definition sex is the but-for cause of the employment decision and the only question remaining is how the employer can justify it. * * *

Closer analogies to the plurality's new approach are found in *Mt. Healthy Board of Education* * * * and *NRLB v. Transportation Management Corp.,* * * * but these cases were decided in different contexts. *Mt. Healthy* was a First Amendment case involving the firing of a teacher, and *Transportation Management* involved review of the NLRB's interpretation of the National Labor Relations Act. The *Transportation Management* decision was based on the deference that the Court traditionally accords NLRB interpretations of the statutes it administers. Neither case therefore tells us why the established *Burdine* framework should not continue to govern the order of proof under Title VII.

In contrast to the plurality, Justice O'Connor acknowledges that the approach adopted today is a "departure from the *McDonnell Douglas* standard." * * * Although her reasons for supporting this departure are not without force, they are not dispositive. As Justice O'Connor states, the most that can be said with respect to the Title VII itself is that "nothing in the language, history, or purpose of Title VII *prohibits* adoption" of the new approach. * * * Justice O'Connor also relies on analogies from the common law of torts, other types of Title VII litigation, and our equal protection cases. These analogies demonstrate that shifts in the burden of proof are not unprecedented in the law of torts or employment discrimination. Nonetheless, I believe continued adherence to the *Burdine* framework is more consistent with the statutory mandate. Congress' manifest concern with preventing imposition of liability in cases where discriminatory animus did not actually cause an adverse action, see *ante,* * * * (opinion of O'Connor, J.), suggests to me that an affirmative showing of causation should be required. And the most relevant portion of the legislative history supports just this view. * * * The limited benefits that are likely to be produced by today's innovation come at the sacrifice of clarity and practical application.

The potential benefits of the new approach, in my view, are overstated. First, the Court makes clear that the *Price Waterhouse* scheme is applicable only in those cases where the plaintiff has produced direct and substantial proof that an impermissible motive was relied upon in making the decision at issue. The burden shift properly will be found to apply in only a limited number of employment discrimination cases. The application of the new scheme, furthermore, will make a difference only in a smaller subset of cases. The practical importance of the burden of proof is the "risk of nonpersuasion," and the new system will make a difference only where the evidence is so evenly balanced that the factfinder cannot say that either side's explanation of the case is "more likely" true. This category will not include cases in which the allocation of the burden of proof will be dispositive because of a complete lack of evidence on the causation issue, cf. *Summers v. Tice,* 33 Cal.2d 80, 199 P.2d 1 (1948)(allocation of burden dispositive because no evidence of which of two negligently fired shots hit plaintiff). Rather, *Price Waterhouse* will apply only to cases in which there is substantial evidence of reliance on an impermissible motive, as well as evidence from the employer that legitimate reasons supported its action.

Although the *Price Waterhouse* system is not for every case, almost every plaintiff is certain to ask for a *Price Waterhouse* instruction, perhaps on the basis of "stray remarks" or other evidence of discriminatory animus. Trial and appellate courts will therefore be saddled with the task of developing standards for determining when to apply the burden shift. One of their new tasks will be the generation of a jurisprudence of the meaning of "substantial factor." Courts will also be required to make the often subtle and difficult distinction between "direct" and "indirect" or "circumstantial" evidence. Lower courts long have had difficulty applying *McDonnell Douglas* and *Burdine.* Addition of a second burden-shifting mechanism, the application of which itself depends on assessment of credibility and a determination whether evidence is sufficiently direct and substantial, is not likely to lend clarity to the process. The presence of an existing burden-shifting mechanism distinguishes the individual disparate treatment case from the tort, class action discrimination, and equal protection cases on which Justice O'Connor relies. The distinction makes Justice White's assertions that one "need look only to" *Mt. Healthy* and *Transportation Management* to resolve this case, and that our Title VII cases in this area are "inapposite," * * * at best hard to understand.

* * *

I do not believe the minor refinement in Title VII procedures accomplished by today's holding can justify the difficulties that will accompany it. Rather, I "remain confident that the *McDonnell Douglas* framework permits the plaintiff meriting relief to demonstrate intentional discrimination." * * * Although the employer does not bear the burden of persuasion under *Burdine*, it must offer clear and reasonably specific reasons for the contested decision, and has every incentive to persuade the trier of fact that the decision was lawful. * * * Further, the suggestion that the employer should bear the burden of persuasion due to superior access to evidence has little force in the Title VII context, where the liberal discovery rules available to all litigants are supplemented by EEOC investigatory files. * * * In sum, the *Burdine* framework provides a "sensible, orderly way to evaluate the evidence in light of common experience as it bears on the critical question of discrimination," * * * and it should continue to govern the order of proof in Title VII disparate treatment cases.[4]

III

The ultimate question in every individual disparate treatment case is whether discrimination caused the particular decision at issue. Some of the plurality's comments with respect to the District Court's findings in this case, however, are potentially misleading. As the plurality notes, the District Court based its liability determination on expert evidence that some evaluations of respondent Hopkins were based on unconscious sex stereotypes,[5] and

4. The plurality states that it disregards the special context of affirmative action. It is not clear that this is possible. Some courts have held that in a suit challenging an affirmative action plan, the question of the plan's validity need not be reached unless the plaintiff shows that the plan was a but-for cause of the adverse decision. See *McQuillen v. Wisconsin Education Association Council*, 830 F.2d 659, 665 (C.A.7 1987), cert. denied, 485 U.S. 914, 108 S.Ct. 1068, 99 L.Ed.2d 248 (1988). Presumably it will be easier for a plaintiff to show that consideration of race or sex pursuant to an affirmative action plan was a substantial factor in a decision, and the court will need to move on to the question of a plan's validity. Moreover, if the structure of the burdens of proof in Title VII suits is to be consistent, as might be expected given the identical statutory language involved, today's decision suggests that plaintiffs should no longer bear the burden of showing that affirmative action plans are illegal. See *Johnson v. Transportation Agency*, 480 U.S. 616, 626–627, 107 S.Ct. 1442, 1449, 94 L.Ed.2d 615 (1987).

5. The plaintiff who engages the services of Dr. Susan Fiske should have no trouble show-

ing that sex discrimination played a part in any decision. Price Waterhouse chose not to object to Fiske's testimony, and at this late stage we are constrained to accept it, but I think the plurality's enthusiasm for Fiske's conclusions unwarranted. Fiske purported to discern stereotyping in comments that were gender neutral—*e.g.*, "overbearing and abrasive"—without any knowledge of the comments' basis in reality and without having met the speaker or subject. "To an expert of Dr. Fiske's qualifications, it seems plain that no woman could *be* overbearing, arrogant, or abrasive: any observations to that effect would necessarily be discounted as the product of stereotyping. If analysis like this is to prevail in federal courts, no employer can base any adverse action as to a woman on such attributes." 263 U.S.App.D.C. 321, 825 F.2d 458, 477 (1987)(Williams, J., dissenting). Today's opinions cannot be read as requiring factfinders to credit testimony based on this type of analysis. See also *ante,* * * * (opinion of O'Connor, J.).

on the fact that Price Waterhouse failed to disclaim reliance on these comments when it conducted the partnership review. The District Court also based liability on Price Waterhouse's failure to "make partners sensitive to the dangers [of stereotyping], to discourage comments tainted by sexism, or to investigate comments to determine whether they were influenced by stereotypes." * * *

Although the District Court's version of Title VII liability is improper under any of today's opinions, I think it important to stress that Title VII creates no independent cause of action for sex stereotyping. Evidence of use by decisionmakers of sex stereotypes is, of course, quite relevant to the question of discriminatory intent. The ultimate question, however, is whether discrimination caused the plaintiff's harm. Our cases do not support the suggestion that failure to "disclaim reliance" on stereotypical comments itself violates Title VII. Neither do they support creation of a "duty to sensitize." As the dissenting judge in the Court of Appeals observed, acceptance of such theories would turn Title VII "from a prohibition of discriminatory conduct into an engine for rooting out sexist thoughts." * * *

Employment discrimination claims require factfinders to make difficult and sensitive decisions. Sometimes this may mean that no finding of discrimination is justified even though a qualified employee is passed over by a less than admirable employer. In other cases, Title VII's protections properly extend to plaintiffs who are by no means model employees. As Justice Brennan notes, * * * courts do not sit to determine whether litigants are nice. In this case, Hopkins plainly presented a strong case both of her own professional qualifications and of the presence of discrimination in Price Waterhouse's partnership process. Had the District Court found on this record that sex discrimination caused the adverse decision, I doubt it would have been reversible error. Cf. *Aikens,* 460 U.S., at 714, n. 2, 103 S.Ct., at 1481, n. 2. That decision was for the finder of fact, however, and the District Court made plain that sex discrimination was not a but-for cause of the decision to place Hopkin's partnership candidacy on hold. Attempts to evade tough decisions by erecting novel theories of liability or multitiered systems of shifting burdens are misguided.

IV

The language of Title VII and our well-considered precedents require this plaintiff to establish that the decision to place her candidacy on hold was made "because of" sex. Here the District Court found that the "comments of the individual partners and the expert evidence of Dr. Fiske do not prove an intentional discriminatory motive or purpose," * * * and that "[b]ecause plaintiff has considerable problems dealing with staff and peers, the Court cannot say that she would have been elected to partnership if the Policy Board's decision had not been tainted by sexually based evaluations," * * *. Hopkins thus failed to meet the requisite standard of proof after a full trial. I would remand the case for entry of judgment in favor of Price Waterhouse.

***Notes on* Hopkins**

1. What, exactly, distinguishes a "mixed motive" case from a "pretext" case? Compare the views of the plurality and Justice O'Connor on this point.

Why does Justice Kennedy resist the recognition of a category of mixed motive cases under Title VII? Do you agree with Justice Kennedy when he says on p. 690 supra that the shifting of burdens "will be found to apply in only a limited number" of cases? In upper level or professional jobs, aren't most employment decisions the result of "mixed motives?" When complex and subjective judgments are involved, it will be the rare plaintiff who will be able to establish that all of the employer's legitimate business reasons are "unworthy of credence." If one or more legitimate reasons articulated by the employer survive plaintiff's proof of pretext, the trier of fact will be required to sort out the remaining "mixed motives."

2. In the Civil Rights Act of 1991, Congress endorsed part and overruled part of Justice Brennan's plurality opinion. Congress agreed with Justice Brennan that in a "mixed motive" case, the plaintiff must prove gender, or another protected status, played only a "motivating part" in the adverse employment decision. It added the following provision to § 703 of Title VII:

> (m) Except as otherwise provided in this title, an unlawful employment practice is established when the complaining party demonstrates that race, color, religion, sex, or national origin was a motivating factor for any employment practice, even though other factors also motivated the practice.

Pub.L. 102–166, § 107, 105 Stat. 1075 (Nov. 21, 1991)(adding a new subsection (m) to Section 703 of the Civil Rights Act of 1964 (42 U.S.C. § 2000e–2)).

On the other hand, Congress reversed that part of Justice Brennan's opinion allowing the employer to present an affirmative defense to any liability. Instead, Congress allowed the employer to present this *Mt. Healthy* affirmative defense during the remedy phase, to limit the relief available to plaintiff in such a "mixed motive" case. Consequently, Congress amended the remedy provisions of Title VII, adding a new section to § 706(g)(2):

> (B) On a claim in which an individual proves a violation under section 703(m) and a respondent demonstrates that the respondent would have taken the same action in the absence of the impermissible motivating factor, the court—

>> (i) may grant declaratory relief, injunctive relief (except as provided in clause (ii)), and attorney's fees and costs demonstrated to be directly attributable only to the pursuit of a claim under section 703(m); and

>> (ii) shall not award damages or issue an order requiring any admission, reinstatement, hiring, promotion, or payment, described in subparagraph (A).

Pub.L. 102–166, § 107, 105 Stat. 1075–76 (Nov. 21, 1991)(amending Section 706(g)) of the Civil Rights Act of 1964 (42 U.S.C. § 2000e–5(g)). In adopting the *Mt. Healthy* affirmative defense as a limitation on available remedies, rather than as a limitation on liability, Congress followed the position taken by at least two circuits, Bibbs v. Block, 778 F.2d 1318 (8th Cir.1985), and Fadhl v. City and Co. of San Francisco, 741 F.2d 1163 (9th Cir.1984). District Judge Gesell in *Hopkins* also allowed this defense to limit relief, not liability, but he would have required the employer to prove the defense by "clear and convincing evidence." 618 F.Supp. 1109, 1120 (D.D.C.1985). How will this legislative compromise work in practice? A plaintiff who proves intentional discrimination cannot be defeated by a defendant who proves it would have taken the same action absent the discrimination, but plaintiff cannot win either damages or a job. What relief is available?

A declaration that defendant has violated the Act, together with attorney fees and costs. Why should plaintiff bother to sue at all? Or is that the point?

3. Although Price Waterhouse was successful in obtaining a lower standard of proof on its affirmative defense, that it would have made the same decision even if intentional discrimination had been absent, it did not secure ultimate victory for its cause. On remand, Judge Gesell announced that he was not persuaded that non-discriminatory factors alone justified the decision to put Hopkin's candidacy on hold:

> Although the Supreme Court's decision lowered the standard of proof, it did not shift the burden of proof. Price Waterhouse, having permitted discriminatory comments to be weighed in the hold decision when appraising Ms. Hopkins, was required to separate the good from the bad. As Justice Brennan's plurality opinion states, where the proof shows that the employer acted with an illegitimate motive, " '[i]t is fair that he bear the risk that the inference of illegal and legal motives cannot be separated, because he knowingly created the risk and because the risk was created not by innocent activity but by his own wrongdoing.' " * * * Price Waterhouse had the burden to prove something; it had to persuade the Court. This it has failed to do.

Hopkins v. Price Waterhouse, 737 F.Supp. 1202, 1206 (D.D.C.), affirmed 920 F.2d 967 (D.C.Cir.1990). In addition to back pay, Judge Gesell ordered Price Waterhouse to admit Ann Hopkins to partnership, effective July 1, 1990.

4. Suppose Price Waterhouse had made Ann Hopkins a partner, only to expel her from the firm six months later because she was considered too aggressive and unlady-like in the partners' meetings. Can Hopkins sue her partners for sex discrimination under Title VII? The United States Supreme Court has held that, under appropriate circumstances, the right to be considered for partnership status in a law firm may constitute a term, condition, or privilege of a law associate's employment under Title VII. See Hishon v. King & Spalding, 467 U.S. 69, 76–78, 104 S.Ct. 2229, 2234–35, 81 L.Ed.2d 59, 67–69 (1984). The Court did not, however, reach the further question of the application of Title VII to the partners themselves. How should Title VII be read in a case where a female partner claims sex discrimination? In Wheeler v. Main Hurdman, 825 F.2d 257 (10th Cir.1987), cert. denied 484 U.S. 986, 108 S.Ct. 503, 98 L.Ed.2d 501 (1987), Marilyn Wheeler claimed that her expulsion as a general partner in the accounting firm of Main Hurdman violated Title VII, the Age Discrimination in Employment Act (29 U.S.C.A. §§ 621–634), and the Equal Pay Act. In April 1982, when Wheeler became a partner, Main Hurdman's personnel roster included 3570 persons, of whom 502 were partners. She argued that, as a matter of "economic reality," her work remained unchanged after she became a partner: she had the same client load, the same duties and responsibilities, the same support staff, and continued to be supervised by the same department head. The Tenth Circuit rejected both the "economic realities" and "control" tests developed to distinguish between employees and independent contractors as inapplicable to bona fide general partners. It held that general partners are not employees within the meaning of the anti-discrimination statutes. Judge Anderson reasoned that Wheeler's own situation illustrated the difference between an employee and a general partner:

> Her participation in profits and losses, exposure to liability, investment in the firm, partial ownership of firm assets, and her voting rights—plus her position under the partnership agreement and partnership laws—clearly

placed her in a different economic and legal category. Evidence of that conclusion is found in the fact that only a small percentage of Main Hurdman personnel were admitted to the partnership.

Id., 825 F.2d at 276. Do you agree with this analysis? Wheeler's initial contribution to the firm's capital was $4000, a sum said to represent a .000058 share of the firm's total capital account. Would *Wheeler* have been decided differently if 75% of the firm's accounting personnel had been partners?

5. In discrimination litigation, the problem of stereotyping affects both employers and the judges who decide the cases. Compare Barbano v. Madison County, 922 F.2d 139 (2d Cir.1990), a "mixed motive" case in which the defendants selected Alan Wagner instead of plaintiff Maureen E. Barbano for the position of Director of the Madison County Veterans Service Agency. Plaintiff's job interview featured questions by Donald Greene, one member of the interviewing committee, concerning why plaintiff thought she was qualified for the job when she was not a veteran; what her plans were for having a family (followed, when plaintiff objected to this question as discriminatory, by the comment that the interviewer did not want to hire a woman who would get pregnant and quit); and whether her husband would object to her transporting male veterans around the country. The district court found that these questions, which were not objected to by other members of the committee, showed that the Board discriminated on the basis of sex in making the hiring decision; placed on defendants the burden of showing that they would have not hired plaintiff absent the discrimination; and found for plaintiff when defendants failed to satisfy that burden. The Second Circuit, relying on *Price Waterhouse,* affirmed. It noted that the Board relied on the Committee's recommendations in choosing Wagner rather than plaintiff, despite her charge of discrimination made at the Board's public meeting when it voted to appoint him, and thus failed either to investigate the possibility of improprieties or to disclaim any reliance upon the discrimination, concluding that "[i]n short, the circumstances show the Board was willing to rely on the Committee's recommendation even if Barbano had been discriminated against during her interview." Id., at 144. The court held that Judge McAvoy's finding that the defendants failed to prove by a preponderance of the evidence that they would not have hired Barbano even if they had not discriminated against her was not clearly erroneous.

Judge Van Graafeiland, concurring in part and dissenting in part, saw the interview very differently. He accepted the testimony of committee members who stated that plaintiff came to the interview with a chip on her shoulder (Judge McAvoy had found these assertions "frivolous"), and observed that "[p]laintiff was not preparing for a job interview; she was preparing for a fight." Id., at 150. He went on to say:

> I am not at all sure that Mr. Greene's question concerning the reaction of plaintiff's husband to the duties of the proposed employment was indicative of sexual bias. If a man applied for a job that required him to run around the countryside with a bunch of women, he might very well be asked what his wife's reaction would be. Family discord that is job related has an inevitable deleterious effect on employee performance, regardless of whether the employee is a man or a woman. Whether or not the question was proper, the fact remains that plaintiff was seeking employment, not carrying on a battle for women's rights. Plaintiff stated in her deposition that the newspapers accused her of being abrasive in the interview, and she did not dispute the characterization. She said that if she was abrasive it was because she was

> antagonized. However, regardless of the cause, abrasiveness does not win offers of employment.

Id., at 151 (opinion of Judge Van Graafeiland, concurring in part and dissenting in part). What do you suppose is the sexual composition of the interview committee that Judge Van Graafeiland imagines might ask a male candidate whether his wife would object to his taking a job that required him to transport a bunch of women around the countryside? What do you think of his advice to women candidates?

6. Does the Court adopt the view that sex stereotyping *per se* constitutes a violation of Title VII? If not, what weight do the individual Justices give to that concept? Do you agree with Justice O'Connor that a "mere reference" to Ann Hopkins as "a lady candidate" is insufficient to support a finding that the decision not to make her a partner was made "because of sex"? Would the Price Waterhouse partners have spoken of a "gentleman candidate"? See generally, Mary F. Radford, Sex Stereotyping and the Promotion of Women to Positions of Power, 41 Hastings L.J. 471 (1990). In *Hopkins*, Judge Gesell found that Price Waterhouse intentionally discriminated against Hopkins because the firm did not disavow the sex stereotypes implicit in various partners' comments, but, in fact, relied on them in making its decision. The Supreme Court affirmed this finding of intentional discrimination. Requiring proof of intentional discriminatory motivation is one of the major limitations of the disparate treatment theory of discrimination. Sex stereotyping may not rise to a conscious level in the decision-maker's mind. Is Title VII violated when employers act on the basis of unconscious attitudes about women? Judge Gesell sought to fill this logical gap by noting that "[a]lthough the stereotyping by individual partners may have been unconscious on their part, the maintenance of a system that gave weight to such biased criticisms was a conscious act of the partnership as a whole." Id., 618 F.Supp. at 1119. Is this explanation sufficient?

In 1980, Professor Nadine Taub proposed a Title VII theory of liability based on stereotyping *per se* because none of the existing theories seemed to cover the situation, Stereotyping Per Se as a Form of Employment Discrimination, 21 B.C.L. Rev. 345 (1980). As she observed,

> In sum, to fit the case of stereotyping *per se,* the original concept of discrimination as adverse acts motivated by class-based animus must be expanded to include benevolent, as well as malevolent, acts, and unconscious, as well as conscious, acts.

Taub, id., 21 B.C.L.Rev. at 402. But has Taub sold her case short? Are unconscious acts necessarily unintentional ones? See generally Charles R. Lawrence, The Id, the Ego, and Equal Protection: Reckoning with Unconscious Racism, 39 Stan.L.Rev. 317, 322 (1987)(arguing that because of our common historical and cultural heritage in which racism has played and continues to play a dominant role, and because most Americans are unaware of the extent to which that heritage has made all of us racists, "a large part of the behavior that produces racial discrimination is influenced by unconscious racial motivation"). Lawrence does not explore the role of the unconscious in sex discrimination. Is his argument consistent with Taub's proposal?

7. As the disparate treatment model of discrimination has evolved under Title VII from "pretext" to "mixed motive," it has come under increasing attack as an inaccurate and simplistic approach to the problem of prejudice or bias. The intent or motivational component of Title VII jurisprudence is intimately connected with the Court's imposition of an intent requirement under the Fourteenth Amendment's equal protection clause. See Washington v. Davis, 426 U.S. 229

(1976), set forth at p. 972 infra. The number of scholars disputing the Court's use of intent in constitutional litigation continues to grow. See Charles Lawrence, Note 6, supra; Barbara Flagg, "Was Blind, But Now I See": White Race Consciousness and the Requirement of Discriminatory Intent, 91 Mich. L. Rev. 953 (1993). Similarly, Title VII scholars have been suggesting that the Court alter its approach to disparate treatment analysis. Professor Martha Chamallas has attacked the "motivational" explanation for both decisionmakers' biased acts and for the supposed "choices" women make to remain in female-dominated occupations or jobs: "the motivational orientation is so deeply embedded in discussions of workplace equality and discrimination that it is often invisible." Chamallas, Structuralist and Cultural Domination Theories Meet Title VII: Some Contemporary Influences, 92 Mich. L. Rev. 2370, 2377 (1994). She emphasized the need to incorporate elements of the structuralist approach to discrimination, locating bias outside of the "minds of individuals who make discrete decisions" and focusing on the organizational impacts of "tokenism" and "skewed" groups. Id. at 2378–79. She also explored the contributions that cultural domination theorists have made to the discussion of workplace equality, the theory that dominant groups will continually find ways to maintain their societal position, with the law failing to address these "culturally ingrained responses." Id. at 2385, citing Derrick Bell's two books, And We Are Not Saved: The Elusive Quest for Racial Justice (1987) and Faces at the Bottom of the Well: The Permanence of Racism (1992).

The assumptions behind the concept of intentional discrimination have been further undermined by Linda Krieger's work on Title VII, The Content of Our Categories: A Cognitive Bias Approach to Discrimination and Equal Employment Opportunity, 47 Stanford L. Rev. 1161 (1995). Drawing upon principles of social cognition theory in psychology, she has argued that the Court's basic premises about why discrimination occurs and how prejudice operates are erroneous, rooted in obsolete notions of social psychology developed from the 1920s to the 1960s. Id. at 1174–76. Krieger explained that both Justices Brennan and O'Connor in *Hopkins* share the view that discrimination occurs because the decision maker had an intention to harm a member of a particular category of persons at the "moment" he made the adverse employment decision, and that this decision maker is aware of this discriminatory motivation, if only he would be truthful. Id. at 1181–1186. Current social cognitive theory tells us that the basic mental process of categorizing and processing information results in stereotyping and other forms of biased judgments, which lead to negative behavior previously attributed to prejudicial motivation. Id. at 1187. Through the process of categorization, people come to believe that members of certain groups will behave in a certain way; our stereotypes about people are imbedded in the very way we process information. Id. at 1199. Because social cognition theory has substantially eroded the notion that disparate treatment results from discriminatory motive or intent, Krieger has suggested that we replace the disparate treatment "pretext" model with a modified version of the "mixed motive" approach:

> * * * a Title VII plaintiff would simply be required to prove that his group status *played a role* in causing the employer's action or decision. Causation would no longer be equated with intentionality. The critical inquiry would be whether the applicant or employee's group status "made a difference" * * *, not whether the decisionmaker intended that it make a difference. * * *

Disparate treatment jurisprudence has long treated the nondiscrimination principle as a *proscriptive* duty not to discriminate. However, social cognition theory suggests that the nondiscrimination principle would be more effective in reducing intergroup bias were it understood as *prescriptive* duty to identify and control for errors in social perception and judgment which inevitably occur, even among the well-intended.

Id. at 1242, 1245. For an alternative approach to a nonintentional reformulation of Title VII theory, see David Oppenheimer, Negligent Discrimination, 141 U. Penn. L. Rev. 899 (1993).

c. Systemic Disparate Treatment

OTTAVIANI v. STATE UNIVERSITY OF NEW YORK AT NEW PALTZ

United States Court of Appeals, Second Circuit, 1989
875 F.2d 365

Before VAN GRAAFEILAND, CARDAMONE and PIERCE, CIRCUIT JUDGES.

PIERCE, CIRCUIT JUDGE:

This is an appeal from a judgment of the United States District Court for the Southern District of New York, [Shirley] Kram, J., in which the court found in favor of defendants on all of the Title VII claims asserted by individual faculty members and a class of similarly situated plaintiffs, following a lengthy bench trial. The decision of the district court is published in a thorough and lengthy opinion at 679 F.Supp. 288 (S.D.N.Y.1988), familiarity with which is assumed herein. Appellants contend the district court erred in its decision and principally attack the district court's treatment of the evidence presented in support of their Title VII claims. For the reasons that follow, we affirm.

BACKGROUND

This complicated Title VII suit was commenced by and on behalf of full-time, academic rank female faculty members at the State University of New York ("SUNY") at New Paltz ("the University") who were employed in the University's Division of Liberal Arts and Sciences at any time between academic years 1973 and 1984. The plaintiffs alleged that between 1973 and 1984, the University discriminated against female members of its faculty on the basis of gender in three separate categories: (1) placement in initial faculty rank at the University, (2) promotion into higher rank, and (3) salary. Judge Kram conducted a bench trial which extended over nine months on all of the plaintiffs' claims, and both parties presented extensive evidence to the court. For the sake of brevity, we will discuss only so much of the proceedings below as is relevant to our discussion of the key issues raised on appeal. During the trial, the district court basically considered two types of evidence—objective statistical evidence and extensive "anecdotal" evidence. The statistical evidence presented by both sides consisted primarily of data produced by means of various "multiple regression analyses." Depending upon the party presenting the statistical evidence, the data was intended to either demonstrate or rebut the plaintiffs' claim of a pattern of ongoing discrimination against women within the University in all three of the contested categories.

A. The Statistical Evidence

Multiple regression analysis is a statistical tool commonly used by social scientists to determine the influence that various independent, predetermined factors (so-called "independent variables") have on an observed phenomenon (the so-called "dependent variable"). See Eastland v. Tennessee Valley Auth. 704 F.2d 613, 621 (11th Cir.1983), cert. denied, 465 U.S. 1066, 104 S.Ct. 1415, 79 L.Ed.2d 741 (1984); Fisher, Multiple Regression in Legal Proceedings, 80 Colum.L.Rev. 702, 702, 705–06 (1980). In disparate treatment cases involving claims of gender discrimination, plaintiffs typically use multiple regression analysis to isolate the influence of gender on employment decisions relating to a particular job or job benefit, such as salary. See, e.g., Sobel v. Yeshiva Univ., 839 F.2d 18, 21–22 (2d Cir.1988); EEOC v. Sears, Roebuck & Co., 839 F.2d 302, 324–25 & n. 22 (7th Cir.1988); Palmer v. Shultz, 815 F.2d 84, 90–91 (D.C.Cir.1987).

The first step in such a regression analysis is to specify all of the possible "legitimate" (i.e., nondiscriminatory) factors that are likely to significantly affect the dependent variable and which could account for disparities in the treatment of male and female employees. See Sobel, 839 F.2d at 20–21; Segar v. Smith, 738 F.2d 1249, 1261 (D.C.Cir.1984), cert. denied, 471 U.S. 1115, 105 S.Ct. 2357, 86 L.Ed.2d 258 (1985); Fisher, supra, at 713–14. By identifying those legitimate criteria that affect the decision making process, individual plaintiffs can make predictions about what job or job benefits similarly situated employees should ideally receive, and then can measure the difference between the predicted treatment and the actual treatment of those employees. If there is a disparity between the predicted and actual outcomes for female employees, plaintiffs in a disparate treatment case can argue that the net "residual" difference represents the unlawful effect of discriminatory animus on the allocation of jobs or job benefits. See Palmer, 815 F.2d at 90–91; D. Baldus & J. Cole, Statistical Proof of Discrimination § 3.2, at 94 (1980); id. § 8.02[1], at 245–46.[2]

In this case, the parties' statistical experts each determined what factors they thought were relevant to the setting of salaries and rank at the University, and used those factors as independent variables in their multiple regression analyses. By accounting for all of the "legitimate" factors that could affect salary and rank in general, the plaintiffs hoped to prove that there was a net "residual" difference or disparity between the predicted and actual salaries and rank of female faculty members that could only be attributed to ongoing gender discrimination within the University. Conversely, the defendants sought to attribute observed disparities in the pay and rank of male versus female faculty members to "legitimate" factors such as unequal job qualifications.

1. *Plaintiffs' Proof of Salary Discrimination*

a. *Plaintiffs' Main Salary Study*

The plaintiffs' main salary study was contained in Trial Exhibit 882 and purported to demonstrate the difference in salaries between male and female

---

2. Another way in which statisticians can measure the influence of gender on a particular employment decision is by using gender as one of the independent variables in a regression analysis. For each independent variable in a multiple regression analysis, the statistician calculates a coefficient, which is a measure of the effect that the variable has on the dependent variable being examined. If the regression coefficient for gender is sufficiently large, then it is probative of the impact that gender has on the employment decision at issue. D. Baldus & J. Cole, supra, §§ 8.01 to 8.02[1], at 240–45; see, e.g., Segar, 738 F.2d at 1261–62.

faculty members at New Paltz. According to the plaintiffs' statistical expert, Dr. Mary Gray, women actually earned from $1,036 to $2,277 less than their predicted salaries in each year of the class period. The defendants challenged these findings on several grounds, but principally attacked the plaintiffs' study for its failure to include certain independent variables which the defendants claimed were influential in the setting of faculty salaries at the University.

The plaintiffs' main salary study incorporated the following independent variables: (1) number of years of full time teaching experience prior to hire at New Paltz; (2) number of years' teaching experience in academic rank at New Paltz; (3) possession of a doctorate degree; (4) number of years since obtaining the doctorate degree; (5) number of publications; (6) other experience prior to hire at New Paltz; and (7) years of full-time high school teaching experience. The plaintiffs' statistical expert, however, did not include academic rank variables in her main salary study such as prior rank, current rank, and years in current rank. Although Dr. Gray conceded that these three factors may influence salary decisions, she maintained that academic rank itself was subject to discrimination at New Paltz, and that the use of rank variables would therefore be inappropriate.

In connection with this assertion, the plaintiffs attempted to demonstrate that female faculty members were placed in lower academic ranks at New Paltz than their male counterparts, and promoted more slowly into higher academic ranks than their male counterparts, solely because of their gender.[3] The defendants' statistical expert, Dr. Judith Stoikov, responded by attempting to prove that rank at New Paltz was not discriminatory. After considering all the evidence as to rank, the district court rejected plaintiffs' proof as "unpersuasive," and concluded that plaintiffs had "failed to prove that rank at New Paltz was discriminatory." Ottaviani, 679 F.Supp. at 306.

The district court's rejection of plaintiffs' claims as to discrimination in rank at New Paltz had two important consequences for the plaintiffs' case. First, the court's ruling eliminated two of the contested categories of discrimination at New Paltz, and left the salary discrimination claim as plaintiffs' only remaining Title VII claim. Second, and equally important from the plaintiffs' perspective, the court's ruling "validated" academic rank as one of the legitimate factors to consider in accounting for salary disparities between male and female faculty members. Since the court considered the academic rank of faculty members to be a legitimate influencing factor on faculty salaries at New Paltz, and since the plaintiffs' main salary study failed to include academic rank variables, the court found the plaintiffs' principal study to be fundamentally flawed and less probative of discrimination than it otherwise might have been.

b. Plaintiffs' Other Salary Studies

Apart from their main salary study, the plaintiffs had also performed salary regressions which did include rank variables. Since these other studies did include what the court considered to be most of the relevant legitimate factors which could influence salary at New Paltz, the court accordingly

3. There are four types of "academic rank" at New Paltz: (1) professor, (2) associate professor, (3) assistant professor, and (4) instructor. Faculty members in one of these academic ranks either hold tenure or are on a "tenure track."

looked primarily to these studies to determine whether the plaintiffs had made out a prima facie case of gender discrimination. After considering and weighing all the evidence presented, the district court reached certain conclusions with respect to both the plaintiffs' and the defendants' statistical evidence. While the district judge found some of the plaintiffs' statistical evidence "persuasive," she thought that it was insufficient to establish a prima facie case of gender discrimination. On the other hand, the district judge did not believe that defendants' statistical evidence was sufficient to rebut the plaintiffs' discrimination claims altogether. Since the judge found the statistical evidence to be inconclusive one way or the other, she ruled that whether or not the plaintiffs could prevail on their discrimination claims would depend upon whether the totality of the evidence adduced at trial supported a finding of discrimination. Accordingly, the district judge next considered whether the extensive anecdotal evidence proffered by plaintiffs supported their claims of discrimination.

B. The Anecdotal Evidence

The anecdotal evidence at trial consisted of various narrative descriptions of events at the University which the plaintiffs contended illustrated or proved that the University had discriminated against its female faculty members. Specifically, the plaintiff class members sought to establish that: (1) the University did not have a viable affirmative action program; (2) New Paltz's methods for identifying and correcting existing salary inequities from 1973 to 1984 were either flawed or non-existent; (3) the University either retrenched or eliminated faculty positions to the detriment of its female faculty members; and (4) the University demonstrated a disdain for women's issues through its handling of the Women's Studies Program at New Paltz. Eleven witnesses also testified about individual instances of alleged salary discrimination at New Paltz, which the plaintiffs contended were illustrative of the administration's policies toward women as a whole.[4]

On rebuttal, the defendants sought to negate the plaintiffs' claims through the specific testimony of University administrators and faculty members, and other types of anecdotal evidence. The defendants contended that such evidence demonstrated that there were nondiscriminatory reasons for all of the actions taken by the University during the period in question which negatively affected its female faculty members, and that none of the employment practices at issue were motivated by discriminatory animus.

After reviewing the anecdotal evidence, the district judge held that the plaintiffs had not proven their Title VII claims against the University. Although she found that the anecdotal evidence supported an inference of prima facie discrimination in a few of the individual class members' cases, in each of those cases she either accepted the defendants' explanations for the pay disparities, or found that the isolated incidents of discrimination were insufficient to support the class' claim of a pattern or practice of gender

4. The plaintiffs presented testimonial evidence of discrimination against: three New Paltz faculty members who were neither class members nor individual plaintiffs (i.e., Nancy Schniedewind, Susan Puretz, and Sheila Schwartz); four individual members of the class who had not brought individual Title VII claims (i.e., Susan Lehrer, Barbara Scott, Johanna Sayre, and Samantha Joe Mullen), and four members of the class who had asserted individual Title VII claims as well (i.e., Roberta Ottaviani, Dorothy Jessup, Joan Marie de la Cova, and Carolee Schneemann).

discrimination. Accordingly, the district court entered judgment in favor of defendants on all of the Title VII claims.

On appeal, the appellants contend that the district court erred in its treatment and analysis of the evidence in several key respects, and that as a result, the court's finding of no discrimination was erroneous. First, appellants challenge the district court's determination that the statistical evidence was inconclusive. Appellants contend that the statistical evidence adduced at trial was more than sufficient to establish a prima facie case of gender discrimination as a matter of law. Moreover, they also contend that the district judge's decision to allow allegedly "tainted" variables such as "rank" to be used in the multiple regression analyses minimized the overall impact of defendants' alleged discriminatory treatment of female faculty members, and resulted in weaker statistical proof. Appellants also take issue with the district court's rejection of the proffered anecdotal evidence of discrimination. Finally, appellants contend that the district court erroneously excluded or ignored evidence of pre-Title VII discrimination, in contravention of the Supreme Court's decision in Bazemore v. Friday, 478 U.S. 385, 106 S.Ct. 3000, 92 L.Ed.2d 315 (1986).

For the reasons that follow, we hold that Judge Kram did not clearly err in finding in favor of the defendants, and we affirm the decision of the district court.

DISCUSSION

We begin by noting that the district court correctly stated the familiar legal standards to be applied in Title VII cases. Since the plaintiff class herein had raised a "disparate treatment" claim under Title VII, the claimants bore the burden of not only establishing discriminatory intent on the part of SUNY administrators, but that "unlawful discrimination [was] a regular procedure or policy followed by [the University]." International Bhd. of Teamsters v. United States, 431 U.S. 324, 360 * * * (1977); see Coser v. Moore, 739 F.2d 746, 749 (2d Cir.1984)("In order to prevail on their claim of a pattern and practice of discrimination, plaintiffs had to show by a preponderance of the evidence that [the defendant]'s 'standard operating procedure—the regular rather than the unusual practice' is to discriminate on the basis of sex.")(quoting Teamsters, 431 U.S. at 336, 97 S.Ct. at 1855).

The Supreme Court has established a three-step process for evaluating disparate treatment claims brought pursuant to Title VII. McDonnell Douglas Corp. v. Green, 411 U.S. 792 * * *. First, the plaintiffs bear the burden of establishing a prima facie case of discrimination by a preponderance of the evidence, McDonnell Douglas Corp., 411 U.S. at 802, 93 S.Ct. at 1824, which gives rise to a rebuttable presumption of unlawful discrimination, Texas Dep't of Community Affairs v. Burdine, 450 U.S. 248, 254 & n. 7 * * *. Once they have done so, the burden of production shifts to the defendants to "articulate some legitimate, nondiscriminatory reason" for the challenged employment practice. McDonnell Douglas Corp., 411 U.S. at 802, 93 S.Ct. at 1824. In cases where the plaintiff has relied on statistical evidence to establish a prima facie case of discrimination, the defendants may also attempt to undermine the plaintiffs' prima facie case by attacking the validity of that statistical evidence, or by introducing statistical evidence of their own showing that the challenged practice did not result in disparate treatment. See Berger v. Iron

Workers Reinforced Rodmen Local 201, 843 F.2d 1395, 1412 (D.C.Cir.1988)(citing Teamsters, 431 U.S. at 360 * * *). If the defendants meet this burden, the plaintiffs must then show either that the defendants' statistical proof is inadequate, or that the defendants' explanation for the challenged practice is merely a pretext for discrimination. See Zahorik v. Cornell Univ., 729 F.2d 85, 92 (2d Cir.1984).

Even though the burden of production shifts to the defendants during the second stage of the process, the ultimate burden of persuasion rests always with the plaintiffs to prove their claims of discrimination. See United States Postal Serv. Bd. of Governors v. Aikens, 460 U.S. 711, 716 * * *.[5] As stated earlier, appellants contend herein that they met their burden of proof, and that the evidence at trial clearly established a pattern and practice of discrimination by University administrators with respect to faculty rank and salary. We will consider plaintiffs' principal claims of error seriatim, beginning with the district court's treatment of the statistical evidence adduced at trial.

A. Significance of Plaintiffs' Statistical Evidence

At trial, the plaintiffs herein contended that the statistical evidence alone was sufficient to establish a prima facie case of discrimination. According to plaintiffs, female faculty members were clearly treated less favorably than their male counterparts, and that unfavorable, disparate treatment was due solely to gender bias. The district court, however, found that the plaintiffs' statistical evidence was not "statistically significant" enough to establish a prima facie case of discrimination. For the reasons that follow, we conclude that the district court did not clearly err in ruling that the plaintiffs' proffered statistical evidence was not dispositive of their Title VII claims.

As discussed earlier, plaintiffs in a disparate treatment case frequently rely on statistical evidence to establish that there is a disparity between the predicted and actual treatment of employees who are members of a disadvantaged group, and to argue that such disparities exist because of an unlawful bias directed against those employees. Not all disparities, however, are probative of discrimination. Before a deviation from a predicted outcome can be considered probative, the deviation must be "statistically significant."

Statistical significance is a measure of the probability that a disparity is simply due to chance, rather than any other identifiable factor. See Segar, 738 F.2d at 1282; see also Castaneda v. Partida, 430 U.S. 482, 496 n. 17 * * *. Because random deviations from the norm can always occur, * * * statisticians do not consider slight disparities between predicted and actual results to be statistically significant. * * * As the disparity between predicted and actual results becomes greater, however, it becomes less likely that the deviation is a random fluctuation. When the probability that a disparity is due to chance sinks to a certain threshold level, statisticians can then infer from the statistical evidence, albeit indirectly, that the deviation is attributable to some other cause unrelated to mere chance. * * *

---

5. The Supreme Court's recent decision in Price Waterhouse v. Hopkins, 490 U.S. 228, 109 S.Ct. 1775, 104 L.Ed.2d 268 (1989), does not affect our analysis of these plaintiffs' claims. See ___ U.S. at ___, 109 S.Ct. at 1788 ("the situation before us is not the one of 'shifting burdens' that we addressed in Burdine").

One unit of measurement used to express the probability that an observed result is merely a random deviation from a predicted result is the "standard deviation." * * * The standard deviation "is a measure of spread, dispersion or variability of a group of numbers." D. Baldus & J. Cole, supra, at 359. Generally, the fewer the number of standard deviations that separate an observed from a predicted result, the more likely it is that any observed disparity between predicted and actual results is not really a "disparity" at all but rather a random fluctuation. Conversely, "[t]he greater the number of standard deviations, the less likely it is that chance is the cause of any difference between the expected and observed results." * * * A finding of two standard deviations corresponds approximately to a one in twenty, or five percent, chance that a disparity is merely a random deviation from the norm, and most social scientists accept two standard deviations as a threshold level of "statistical significance." See Castaneda, 430 U.S. at 496 n. 17 * * *. When the results of a statistical analysis yield levels of statistical significance at or below the 0.05 level, chance explanations for a disparity become suspect, and most statisticians will begin to question the assumptions underlying their predictions.

Cognizant of the important role that statistics play in disparate treatment cases, the Supreme Court has held that "[w]here gross statistical disparities can be shown, they alone may in a proper case constitute prima facie proof of a pattern or practice of discrimination." Hazelwood School Dist. v. United States, 433 U.S. 299, 307–08 * * * (1977). The threshold question in disparate treatment cases, then, is: "[A]t what point is the disparity in selection rates * * * sufficiently large, or the probability that chance was the cause sufficiently low, for the numbers alone to establish a legitimate inference of discrimination [?]" Palmer, 815 F.2d at 92 (emphasis added); see Frazier, 851 F.2d at 1452. In answer to this question, "most courts follow the conventions of social science which set 0.05 as the level of significance below which chance explanations become suspect." D. Baldus & J. Cole, supra, s 9.02, at 291; see, e.g., Castenada, 430 U.S. at 496 n. 17 * * *. The existence of a 0.05 level of statistical significance indicates that it is fairly unlikely that an observed disparity is due to chance, and it can provide indirect support for the proposition that disparate results are intentional rather than random.[6] By no means, however, is a five percent probability of chance (or approximately two standard deviations) considered an "exact legal threshold." Palmer, 815 F.2d at 92.

In the present case, the three salary studies which the district court considered most probative of a pattern or practice of discrimination produced a range of standard deviations between approximately one and five, and of the total thirty-three standard deviation measures cited, twenty-four exceeded two standard deviations.[7] Significantly, however, nine of the measures cited

---

6. The commentators are careful to point out, however, that no matter how great the number of standard deviations is, statistical tests can never entirely rule out the possibility that chance caused the disparity. See Palmer, 815 F.2d at 91; D. Baldus & J. Cole, supra, s 9.42, at 191–93 (Supp.1987).

7. As discussed supra, two standard deviations corresponds roughly to a 1 in 20 chance

that the outcome is a random fluctuation. Three standard deviations corresponds to approximately a 1 in 384 chance of randomness. Finally, a range of four to five standard deviations corresponds to a probability range of 1 chance in 15,786 to 1 chance in 1,742,160. M. Abramowitz & I. Steigan, Handbook of Mathematical Functions, National Bureau of Standards, U.S. Government Printing Office, Ap-

fell below two standard deviations. Also, the negative residuals associated with being female were not significant in every year of the liability period.

Given the range of standard deviations associated with their salary regressions, the plaintiffs contended that the statistical evidence clearly gave rise to a presumption of discrimination. As discussed earlier herein, however, although the district judge found the studies to be "persuasive," she nevertheless held that these levels of "statistical significance" alone were "not sufficiently high to support a prima facie claim of salary discrimination." Ottaviani, 679 F.Supp. at 309.

On appeal, appellants argue inter alia that, as a matter of law, a finding of two standard deviations should be equated with a prima facie case of discrimination. According to appellants, the district court therefore erred in finding that they had not met their burden of establishing a prima facie case. In support of this argument, appellants point out that several courts have accepted two standard deviations as prima facie proof of discrimination. See, e.g., Berger, 843 F.2d at 1412 ("if the likelihood that a fluctuation from expected results occurred by chance is five percent or less, a statistically significant difference is proved, and a prima facie case of discrimination is established")(citing Segar, 738 F.2d at 1282–83); Eldredge v. Carpenters 46 N. Cal. Counties JATC, 833 F.2d 1334, 1340 n. 8 (9th Cir.1987)(.045 level of statistical significance (approximately two standard deviations or 1 chance in 22) sufficient to give rise to an inference that discriminatory system rather than chance is responsible for women's lower admission rates to apprenticeship program), cert. denied, 487 U.S. 1210, 108 S.Ct. 2857, 101 L.Ed.2d 894 (1988); Dalley v. Michigan Blue Cross/Blue Shield, Inc., 612 F.Supp. 1444, 1451 n. 18 (E.D.Mich.1985)("Most courts and commentators have accepted the .05 level," or 1 in 20 probability, as indicative of statistical significance). While appellants' argument that a finding of two standard deviations should be equated with a prima facie case of discrimination under Title VII is not without initial appeal, we are constrained to reject such a formal "litmus" test for assessing the legitimacy of Title VII claims.

It is certainly true that a finding of two to three standard deviations can be highly probative of discriminatory treatment. See Segar, 738 F.2d at 1282–83. As tempting as it might be to announce a black letter rule of law, however, recent Supreme Court pronouncements instruct that there simply is no minimum threshold level of statistical significance which mandates a finding that Title VII plaintiffs have made out a prima facie case. See, e.g., Watson v. Fort Worth Bank & Trust, 487 U.S. 977, 108 S.Ct. 2777, 2789 n. 3, 101 L.Ed.2d 827 (1988)("We have emphasized the useful role that statistical methods can have in Title VII cases, but we have not suggested that any particular number of 'standard deviations' can determine whether a plaintiff has made out a prima facie case in the complex area of employment discrimination."); see also Palmer, 815 F.2d at 92 (noting that Supreme Court has not established "an exact legal threshold at which statistical evidence, standing alone, establishes an inference of discrimination"); Coser v. Moore, 739 F.2d at 754 n. 3 (a significance level of 5% probability of chance "has no talismanic importance"); EEOC v. American Nat'l Bank, 652 F.2d 1176, 1192 (4th Cir.1981)("courts of law should be extremely cautious in drawing any

plied Mathematics Series No. 55 (1966)(Tables 26.1, 26.2).

conclusions from standard deviations in the range of one to three"), cert. denied, 459 U.S. 923, 103 S.Ct. 235, 74 L.Ed.2d 186 (1982); D. Baldus & J. Cole, supra, s 9.4, at 188–89 (Supp.1987)(courts should use tests of statistical significance only as "an aid to interpretation" and not as a "rule of law"). Accordingly, in accordance with Supreme Court pronouncements, we must reject appellants' suggestion that this court announce a rule of law with respect to what level of statistical significance automatically gives rise to a rebuttable presumption of discrimination.

Moreover, as a practical matter, the issue of whether or not two or more standard deviations establish a prima facie case of discrimination is not pivotal in this case. It is well-established that "once a Title VII case has been 'fully tried on the merits,' the question whether the plaintiff has established a prima facie case 'is no longer relevant.' " Mitchell v. Baldrige, 759 F.2d 80, 83 (D.C.Cir.1985)(quoting Aikens, 460 U.S. at 714 15, 103 S.Ct. at 1481–82). As the Supreme Court stated in Bazemore v. Friday, "the only issue to be decided at that point is whether the plaintiffs have actually proved discrimination." 478 U.S. at 398, 106 S.Ct. at 3008 (emphasis added). Despite appellants' efforts to deemphasize on appeal what transpired at trial, the district court herein actually proceeded as though the plaintiffs had made out a prima facie case of discrimination, and it cannot be gainsaid that the plaintiffs' claims were fully litigated on the merits. At the close of the plaintiffs' case-in-chief, the defendants moved to dismiss the action specifically on the grounds that plaintiffs had not met their burden of establishing a prima facie case. The court denied the motion without explanation, however, and directed the defendants to proceed with their case. Later, at the close of defendants' rebuttal case, the court also allowed the plaintiffs to respond to the defendants' rebuttal evidence. Accordingly, the question remaining for the district court at the close of the entire trial was whether the plaintiffs should ultimately prevail on their Title VII claims. See Bazemore, 478 U.S. at 398, 106 S.Ct. at 3008. Since the plaintiffs fully litigated those claims, any arguments on appeal directed at whether or not plaintiffs established a prima facie case are arguably misleading and misplaced. See EEOC v. Sears, Roebuck & Co., 839 F.2d at 312 n. 9.

The net import of Judge Kram's rulings regarding the significance of plaintiffs' statistical evidence is that she found the evidence to be "persuasive" but not dispositive. Contrary to appellants' assertions, it is clear from the district judge's rulings that she did not simply ignore the statistical evidence of discrimination presented by plaintiffs. The court found this evidence sufficient to cause her to deny the defendants' motion to dismiss at the end of plaintiffs' case, and to accept rebuttal evidence from the defendants. On rebuttal, however, the defendants were able to successfully undermine the plaintiffs' case by attacking the validity of the plaintiffs' statistical evidence, and by introducing statistical evidence of their own to negate the inference of discrimination that had been raised. Cf. Berger, 843 F.2d at 1416 ("Mere conjecture or general assertions of inadequacies in the opponent's statistical case, without demonstrating their effect on the results, will not suffice."); Sobel, 839 F.2d at 34 (same).

Specifically, the defendants criticized the plaintiffs' most probative studies for excluding one factor which they claimed exerted a "highly significant positive influence on current salary," namely, whether a faculty member had held a prior, full-time administrative position at SUNY New Paltz before returning to full-time teaching. The defendants also criticized these studies because the salary regressions were "fitted" only to male faculty members, i.e., they used independent variables that were derived only from the male population. The district court noted in its opinion that a "males only regression" based exclusively on values existing only in the male population might have tended to overestimate the predicted salaries of certain female faculty members, because it might not have taken into account legitimate factors existing solely in the female population which could have affected the rate of pay for women teachers at the University. See Ottaviani, 679 F.Supp. at 307. If the predicted salary for a female faculty member was overestimated, this type of regression arguably would have overestimated the discrepancies between male and female salaries at the University. Finally, the defendants criticized these studies because they inappropriately aggregated Instructors and Assistant Professors into a single "rank." The defendants pointed out at trial that when the two ranks were combined into a single rank, the predicted salary of a female Instructor would essentially be based on the higher salary of an Assistant Professor, and hence the net residual difference between the predicted and actual salaries of a female Instructor would be overstated. Apart from these criticisms of plaintiffs' statistical evidence, the defendants also offered persuasive anecdotal evidence to negate the plaintiffs' claims of discriminatory animus. After considering all of the evidence presented, both statistical and anecdotal, the district court simply found that plaintiffs had failed to preponderate on their claims.

Recent Supreme Court precedent has made it clear that this court can reverse such a factual determination "only if it is clearly erroneous in light of all the evidence in the record or if it rests on legal error." Palmer, 815 F.2d at 101 (citing, inter alia, Bazemore, 478 U.S. 385, 106 S.Ct. 3000). Especially in cases where statistical evidence is involved, " 'great deference is due the district court's determination of whether the resultant numbers are sufficiently probative of the ultimate fact in issue.' " EEOC v. Sears, Roebuck & Co., 839 F.2d at 310 (citation omitted); see Griffin v. Board of Regents of Regency Univ., 795 F.2d 1281, 1289–90 (7th Cir.1986). As the Supreme Court cautioned in the Teamsters case, "statistics are not irrefutable; they come in infinite variety and, like any other kind of evidence, they may be rebutted. In short, their usefulness depends on all of the surrounding facts and circumstances." 431 U.S. at 340, 97 S.Ct. at 1857. The district judge herein gave due consideration to all of the evidence presented, and after reviewing the record, we do not perceive a convincing basis for finding her interpretation of that evidence to be clearly erroneous. Accordingly, we affirm her rulings with respect to the statistical evidence presented.

B.   Use of Rank Variables

In conjunction with their attack on the district court's assessment of the sufficiency of plaintiffs' statistical evidence, appellants also challenge the district court's determination that "rank" was an appropriate factor to consider in assessing pay disparities between male and female faculty members. According to appellants, if the court had rejected the rank variables and considered only those salary studies which excluded rank, then the number of standard deviations associated with their findings of discrimination would have been much greater, and their statistical proof would have been even more probative.

Although we recognize that the use of rank variables in testing for salary discrimination against women faculty members is not universally accepted, see Finkelstein, The Judicial Reception of Multiple Regression Studies in Race and Sex Discrimination Cases, 80 Colum.L.Rev. 737, 741–42 (1980); D. Baldus & J. Cole, supra, § 8.23, at 113–14 (Supp.1987), in Sobel v. Yeshiva University, this court specifically upheld the use of rank variables in a multiple regression analysis, stating that rank could be used as a legitimate factor in explaining pay disparities so long as rank itself was clearly not tainted by discrimination, 839 F.2d at 35. As the plaintiffs' statistical expert, Dr. Mary Gray, explained in her own report: "In a bias-free system, one could use rank as a measure of productivity since the review process for promotion or hire should evaluate teaching, scholarship and service." (Emphasis added). See D. Baldus & J. Cole, supra, § 8.2, at 114. The question to be resolved, then, in cases involving the use of academic rank factors, is whether rank is tainted by discrimination at the particular institution charged with violating Title VII. Although appellants reiterate on appeal their claim that rank at New Paltz was tainted, it is clear that the district judge accepted and considered evidence from the parties on both sides of this issue, and that she rejected the plaintiffs' contentions on this point.

At trial, the plaintiffs failed to adduce any significant statistical evidence of discrimination as to rank. As the district court stated in its opinion, the plaintiffs' studies of rank, rank at hire, and waiting time for promotion "were mere compilations of data" which neither accounted for important factors relevant to assignment of rank and promotion, "nor demonstrated that observed differences were statistically significant." Ottaviani, 679 F.Supp. at 306. The defendants, on the other hand, offered persuasive objective evidence to demonstrate that there was no discrimination in either placement into initial rank or promotion at New Paltz between 1973 and 1984, and the district court chose to credit the defendants' evidence. Upon review of the record, we cannot state that the court's rulings in this regard were clearly erroneous. Accordingly, the district court's decision to focus primarily on those studies which included rank as an essential independent variable was not improper, and appellants' contentions to the contrary must be rejected. See Presseisen v. Swarthmore College, 442 F.Supp. 593, 614, 619 (E.D.Pa.1977)(inclusion of rank variable appropriate when evidence showed no discrimination with respect to hiring and promotion), aff'd mem., 582 F.2d 1275 (3d Cir.1978); see also EEOC v. Sears, Roebuck & Co., 839 F.2d at 327 (court's decision to focus generally on those regression analyses which did not omit "major factors" was proper); Rossini v. Ogilvy & Mather, Inc., 798 F.2d 590, 603–04 (2d Cir.1986)(trial court's reliance on studies which incorporated controversial variables not clearly erroneous, where court's decision came after "extensive testimony from experts on both sides of the issue").

C. Anecdotal Evidence

Appellants also contend on appeal that the district court did not give sufficient weight to the anecdotal evidence adduced at trial, and that the court should have rejected the explanations proffered by University administrators to explain pay and rank inequities as "pretextual." Our review of the anecdotal evidence, however, is limited to ascertaining whether the district judge committed clear error in making her findings. See Anderson v. City of Bessemer, 470 U.S. 564, 573 * * * (1985); Pullman–Standard v. Swint, 456 U.S. 273, 287 * * * (1982). It is not the function of this court to reweigh the evidence anew, particularly when findings by a district court are based on in-court credibility determinations. Anderson, 470 U.S. at 575. Rather, under the clearly erroneous standard, we may only reject findings by the trial court when we are left with the "definite and firm conviction that a mistake has been committed." United States v. United States Gypsum Co., 333 U.S. 364, 395 * * * (1948).

In this case, the district court found that the defendants had successfully rebutted the plaintiffs' anecdotal proof, and that, in any event, the anecdotal evidence on its face was too limited to prove class-wide discrimination. After reviewing the entire record, we do not think that the court's decision to credit the testimony of the defendants rather than that of the plaintiffs was clearly erroneous. Since the district court's "account of the evidence is plausible in light of the record viewed in its entirety," we may not overturn the findings of the court even if we might "have weighed the evidence differently," had we been sitting as the trier of fact. Anderson, 470 U.S. at 573–74, 105 S.Ct. at 1510–11. Accordingly, we affirm the findings of the district court with respect to the anecdotal evidence presented.

D. Bazemore Claim

In Bazemore v. Friday, 478 U.S. 385 * * * (1986), the Supreme Court held that employers have an obligation to eradicate employment discrimination that began prior to the effective date of Title VII (1972), if the discrimination continues into the post–1972 liability period. Id. at 397. The Supreme Court also stated that statistical evidence of pre-Act discrimination can be probative of ongoing, post-Act discrimination. Id. at 402.

On appeal, appellants contend that the district court erroneously excluded evidence of pre-Act discrimination in violation of the Supreme Court's dictates in Bazemore. In particular, appellants claim that the district judge improperly excluded Exhibit 990, which purported to document statistically significant evidence of discrimination as to initial faculty rank. This claim is without merit, however. At trial, the defendants objected to the admission of Exhibit 990 not because it was offered to prove pre-Act discrimination, but because it was unreliable and incomplete. While the weakness of statistical evidence should not ordinarily preclude its admission, see Bazemore, 478 U.S. at 400, the Supreme Court has recognized that some statistical evidence may be so unreliable as to be irrelevant, see id. at 400 n. 10, 106 S.Ct. at 3009 n. 10; see also Penk v. Oregon State Bd. of Higher Educ., 816 F.2d 458, 465 (9th Cir.)("Bazemore * * * does not give blanket approval to the introduction of all evidence derived from multiple regression analyses."), cert. denied, 484 U.S. 853, 108 S.Ct. 158, 98 L.Ed.2d 113 (1987). Apparently the district judge herein thought that to be the case with respect to this particular exhibit, because she sustained the defendants' objection to its admission on the grounds that it was irrelevant and unduly confusing. Upon review of the record, we do not find the district court's decision to exclude the study to be clearly erroneous, and therefore we affirm the evidentiary ruling.

Moreover, we note that appellant's reliance on this court's decision in *Sobel v. Yeshiva University* as support for their more generalized, Bazemore-type claims is misplaced. In *Sobel*, the plaintiffs introduced evidence specifically designed to prove that women were discriminated against prior to the effective date of Title VII, and argued that "Yeshiva had a legal obligation to equalize women's salaries immediately upon application of Title VII to universities." 839 F.2d at 27. In the present case, even though the Supreme Court handed down its decision in *Bazemore* the same month that plaintiffs' trial was commenced, the plaintiffs did not introduce any statistical evidence of substance to prove that there was discrimination at New Paltz prior to the effective date of Title VII. Instead, nearly all of the plaintiffs' studies focused on the class liability period, which covered the years 1973 to 1984. This is in marked contrast to *Sobel* and *Bazemore*, wherein the plaintiffs offered direct, independent proof of pre-Act discrimination. See *Bazemore*, 478 U.S. at 401; *Sobel*, 839 F.2d at 30. Accordingly, we find appellants' arguments on this point generally to be without merit.

CONCLUSION

In sum, the burden of persuasion was on the plaintiffs to prove by a preponderance of the evidence that there was a pattern or practice of discrimination at SUNY New Paltz, and they failed to meet that burden. We have considered all of the arguments presented on appeal, and find them to be without merit. For the reasons stated above, the judgment of the district court is affirmed.

***Notes on* Ottaviani**

1. The *Ottaviani* case is an example of a "pattern or practice" lawsuit with plaintiffs seeking to prove that the employer's entire system of employment intentionally discriminates against women on the basis of sex. In *Ottaviani*, plaintiffs presented several individual disparate treatment cases, which the court labeled "anecdotal" evidence, along with their statistical case of differential treatment. In systemic disparate treatment litigation, plaintiffs must demonstrate that discrimination based on sex is the employer's "standard operating procedure," a difficult standard to meet. The interaction between proof of the individual cases and the statistical case is difficult to measure. If plaintiffs had been successful in proving some of the individual cases, would they have been more successful in proving intentional discrimination overall? If intentional discrimination had been shown by the statistical analysis, would plaintiffs have been successful in their individual cases?

Compare *Ottaviani* with EEOC v. Sears, Roebuck & Co., 628 F.Supp. 1264, 1277 (N.D.Ill.1986), affirmed 839 F.2d 302 (7th Cir.1988). In *Sears*, despite voluminous statistical evidence supporting the EEOC's claim of discrimination, the district court ruled in favor of defendants, stating:

> Notably absent from EEOC's presentation was the testimony of any witness who could credibly claim that Sears discriminated against women by refusing to hire or promote women into commission sales. It is almost inconceivable that, in a nationwide suit alleging a pattern and practice of intentional discrimination for at least 8 years involving more than 900 stores, EEOC would be unable to produce even one witness who could credibly testify that Sears discriminated against her. EEOC's total failure to produce any alleged

victim of discrimination serves only to confirm the court's conclusions that no reasonable inference of sex discrimination can be drawn from EEOC's statistical evidence regarding hiring into commission sales.

Id. at 1324–25. The Seventh Circuit affirmed, finding EEOC's statistical case "questionable." 839 F.2d at 309. Concluding that deficiencies in statistical evidence are best remedied by anecdotal evidence, the court chastised the EEOC for refusing to bring forward individual witnesses, particularly in light of the fact that the lawsuit had gone on for 10 years and that 47,000 hires and promotions were at issue. The court stated that individual victim testimony is useful to bring " 'cold numbers convincingly to life.' " Id. at 311 (quoting International Bhd. of Teamsters v. United States, 431 U.S. 324, 339 (1977)). In Hazelwood School District v. U.S., 433 U.S. 299 (1977), the Supreme Court said that "gross statistical disparities" alone may be sufficient to prove intentional discrimination in a proper case, discussed in Note 2 infra, but such cases are so rare that convincing individual disparate treatment cases must be regarded as essential in contemplating a possible systemic disparate treatment case.

2. The first Title VII systemic disparate treatment case decided by the Supreme Court was International Brotherhood of Teamsters v. United States, 431 U.S. 324 (1977). The Court stated that in such a case the plaintiff must show that the employer "regularly and purposefully treated" persons of color less favorably than white persons. 431 U.S. at 335. "Proof of discriminatory motive is critical, although it can in some situations be inferred from the mere fact of differences in treatment." Id. at 336 fn. 15. The *Teamsters* case was discussed in Note 3 at p. ___ supra. The statistical evidence of intentional discrimination in *Teamsters* did not involve calculations of statistical significance or multiple regression analysis, only raw data. Among the trucking company's 6,472 employees, 5% were African American and 4% were Spanish-surnamed Americans. Among the company's 1,828 high-paid long distance drivers, however, only 8 employees (0.4%) were African American and 5 employees (0.3%) were Spanish-surnamed. No African American had been employed as a long-distance driver until 1969, after the litigation began. Id. at 337. In addition to the statistics, individual employees testified about 40 specific instances of alleged discrimination.

The Court commented on the significance of the statistical evidence:

> [O]ur cases make it unmistakably clear that "[s]tatistical analyses have served and will continue to serve an important role" in cases in which the existence of discrimination is a disputed issue. * * * We have repeatedly approved the use of statistical proof where it reached proportions comparable to those in this case, to establish a prima facie case of racial discrimination in jury selection cases * * *. Statistics are equally competent in proving employment discrimination.[20]

---

20. [T]he statistical evidence [in this case] was not offered or used to support an erroneous theory that Title VII requires an employer's work force to be racially balanced. Statistics showing racial or ethnic imbalance are probative in a case such as this one only because such imbalance is often a telltale sign of purposeful discrimination; absent explanation, it is ordinarily to be expected that nondiscriminatory hiring practices will in time result in a work force more or less representative of the racial and ethnic composition of the population in the community from which employees are hired. Evidence of longlasting and gross disparity between the composition of a work force and that of the general population thus may be significant even though § 703(j) makes clear that Title VII imposes no requirement that a work force mirror the general population. * * * Consideration such as small sample size may, of course, detract from the value of such evidence, * * * and evidence showing that the figures for the general population might not accurately reflect the pool of qualified job applicants would also be relevant. * * *

We caution only that statistics are not irrefutable; they come in infinite variety and, like any other kind of evidence, they may be rebutted. In short, their usefulness depends on all of the surrounding facts and circumstances.

Id. at 339–340.

Once plaintiffs presented a prima facie case that purposeful discrimination was the employer's regular practice, then "the burden shifts" to the company to demonstrate that the plaintiffs' statistical proof is "either inaccurate or insignificant." Id. at 360. The Court noted that the employer may also rebut the prima facie case by providing a "nondiscriminatory explanation for the apparently discriminatory result." Id. at 360 fn. 46. The most common nondiscriminatory explanation for a racially-skewed workforce has been a collectively-bargained seniority system, which the Court accepted in *Teamsters* as an adequate justification for some of the alleged discriminatory effects of the company's employment system. Id. at 355.

The Supreme Court first accepted proof of intentional discrimination by use of standard deviation calculations indicating statistical significance in Castaneda v. Partida, 430 U.S.482 (1977), a constitutional equal protection case where plaintiff argued that county officials intentionally discriminated against Mexican Americans in selecting members of the grand jury that indicted the plaintiff. The census data showed that 79% of the county's population was Mexican American; the average composition of grand juries over a ten-year period was 39% Mexican American. The binomial distribution statistical method, used to calculate standard deviations, measures observed fluctuations in selecting persons from a targeted group and compares them to the expected number based on the composition of the available pool from which selections are made. Calculation of standard deviations gives the observer a method to decide if the results observed were the product of chance, rather than intentional decision making. In *Castaneda*, the Court found that the number of Mexican Americans on grand juries resulted in a calculation of 29 standard deviations. Using the binomial distribution formula, the size of the chance variable was 12 persons: any random selection of Mexican Americans for jury service could have varied by 12 persons based solely on chance. The actual selection, however, differed from chance 29 times, or, in other words, by 29 standard deviations. "As a general rule for such large samples, if the difference between the expected value and the observed number is greater than two or three standard deviations, then the hypothesis that the jury drawing was random would be suspect to a social scientist." Id. at 496–97 fn. 17. The Court held that the data in *Castaneda* was sufficient to present a prima facie case of intentional discrimination.

Three months after the *Castaneda* decision, the Court overturned and remanded a finding of racial discrimination based on statistical evidence in a second Title VII systemic disparate treatment case, Hazelwood School District et al. v. United States, 433 U.S. 299 (1977). The district court had ruled that the federal government as plaintiff had not presented a prima facie case of racial discrimination in hiring teachers, but the Eighth Circuit reversed. The Court of Appeals held that the percentage of African Americans among public school teachers in the St. Louis metropolitan area, 15.4%, should have been used as the basis for deciding whether the suburban school district's 1.4% to 1.8% of African American

"Since the passage of the Civil Rights Act of 1964, the courts have frequently relied upon statistical evidence to prove a violation * * *. In many cases the only available avenue of proof is the use of racial statistics to uncover clandestine and covert discrimination by the employer or union involved." * * *

teachers was the result of intentional discrimination. In addition, the Eighth Circuit found that 16 of the 55 alleged individual instances of discriminatory hiring had been proven under the *McDonnell Douglas v. Green* structure, which cases "buttressed" the statistical proof. Id. at 306. On appeal from the Eighth Circuit, the Supreme Court noted the importance of the statistical evidence: "Where gross statistical disparities can be shown, they alone may in a proper case constitute prima facie proof of a pattern or practice of discrimination." Id. at 307–08. The Supreme Court agreed with the Eighth Circuit that the district court had improperly compared the percentage of Hazelwood's black teachers to its black students, just over 2%. Instead the trial court should have compared the percentage of Hazelwood's black teachers to the percentage in the qualified labor pool from which Hazelwood hired. The Court, however, suggested that perhaps the suburban percentage of 5.7% black teachers may be the correct comparison figure, not the metropolitan area figure of 15.4%. The Court commented that even using the suburban base figure, the number of black teachers on Hazelwood's staff would differ from the number expected by more than five or six standard deviations:

> A precise method of measuring the significance of such statistical disparities was explained in *Castaneda* * * *. It involves calculation of the "standard deviation" as a measure of predicted fluctuations from the expected value of a sample. * * * The Court in *Castaneda* noted that "[a]s a general rule for such large samples, if the difference between the expected value and the observed number is greater than two or three standard deviations," then the hypothesis that teachers were hired without regard to race would be suspect.

433 U.S. at 309 fn. 14. On the other hand, if one examined only the actual hires the school district made during the two years at issue, and not the total teaching staff, then the number of standard deviations would drop below 2 standard deviations if the 5.7% suburban figure on the available labor pool was used. Id. at 311 fn. 17. The Court remanded the case for further evaluation of the statistical proof by the trial court. Only Justice Stevens dissented, noting that the evidence established that one-third of Hazelwood's teachers resided in St. Louis at the time they were hired. "After Title VII became applicable [to the school district in 1972], only 3.7% of the new teachers hired by Hazelwood were black. Proof of these gross disparities was in itself sufficient to make out a prima facie case of discrimination." Id. at 316.

Since these early cases, proof in systemic disparate treatment cases has become much more complicated, using multiple regression analysis where an expert statistician can control for a variety of factors, in order to isolate the influence of the one prohibited factor, sex or race. For further discussion of multiple regression techniques, see Catherine Connolly, "The Use of Multiple Regression Analysis in Employment Discrimination Cases," 10 Population Res. and Pol. Rev. 117 (1991); Thomas J. Campbell, Regression Analysis in Title VII Cases—Minimum Standards, Comparable Worth, and Other Issues Where Law and Statistics Meet, 36 Stan. L. Rev. 1299 (1984); Franklin M. Fisher, Multiple Regression in Legal Proceedings, 80 Colum. L. Rev. 702 (1980); and Michael O. Finkelstein, The Judicial Reception of Multiple Regression Studies in Race and Sex Discrimination Cases, 80 Colum. L. Rev. 737 (1980).

Regardless of the statistical method employed to prove systemic disparate treatment, the evaluation of statistics remains a judgment call for the trier of fact. As one federal judge commented at the end of a very lengthy opinion, occupying 165 pages in the Federal Supplement:

To place the court's findings in perspective, an additional observation is required. Despite their recent recognition, the econometric techniques employed in this case are not discrimination CAT scanners—ready to detect alien discrimination in corporate bodies. It may reveal shadows but its resolution is seldom more precise.

Ultimately the findings of fact here are not numerical products and sums but a human judgment that the facts found are more likely true than not true.

Remarks of District Judge Patrick Higginbotham in Vuyanich v. Republic National Bank of Dallas, 505 F.Supp. 224, 394 (N.D.Tex.1980), vacated on other grounds 723 F.2d 1195 (5th Cir.)(en banc), cert. denied 469 U.S. 1073 (1984).

3. Statistical evidence is crucial in both a systemic disparate treatment case and a disparate impact case, but the statistics are used in a systemic disparate treatment case to prove a different type of prima facie case. A systemic disparate treatment case differs from a disparate impact case in that it looks for a pattern of discrimination among the actual hiring, salary, or promotion decisions made by an employer over a substantial period of time. A disparate impact case focuses on a facially neutral policy or practice, a specific employment barrier, such as standardized tests or a prior-experience requirement, that may have a differential impact on a protected group. The statistics used in an impact case calculate the success rates of the members of each ethnic or gender group in jumping over the particular barrier under examination. The success rates of each group are then compared to the success rate of the most successful group. For example, in Connecticut v. Teal, 457 U.S. 440 (1982), a disparate impact case, 79% of white applicants for promotion passed a written qualifying exam, but only 54% of the black applicants passed the exam. Id. at 443. Because the black success rate was significantly below the white pass rate, the Court held that the written exam had a disparate impact on black applicants. Id. at 451. Conversely, in a systemic disparate treatment case, the statistics focus on the end result of a decision-making system that may include many separate barriers or facially neutral job requirements. If one were to bring an impact case against an entire subjective evaluation system where one could *not* measure the impact of each barrier separately, the statistics in a disparate impact case would begin to look almost identical to those in a systemic disparate treatment case. See Watson v. Fort Worth Bank & Trust, 487 U.S. 977 (1988), discussed in Note 5, p. 588 supra.

2. SPECIFIC APPLICATIONS OF TITLE VII TO SEX DISCRIMINATION

a. *Classifications Based on Sex*

PHILLIPS v. MARTIN MARIETTA CORPORATION

Supreme Court of the United States, 1971.
400 U.S. 542, 91 S.Ct. 496, 27 L.Ed.2d 613.

PER CURIAM.

Petitioner Mrs. Ida Phillips commenced an action in the United States District Court for the Middle District of Florida under Title VII of the Civil Rights Act of 1964 alleging that she had been denied employment because of her sex. The District Court granted summary judgment for Martin Marietta Corp. (Martin) on the basis of the following showing: (1) in 1966 Martin informed Mrs. Phillips that it was not accepting job applications from women with pre-school-age children; (2) as of the time of the motion for summary judgment, Martin employed men with pre-school-age children; (3) at the time Mrs. Phillips applied 70–75% of the applicants for the position she sought were women; 75–80% of those hired for the position, assembly trainee, were women, hence no question of bias against women as such was presented.

The Court of Appeals for the Fifth Circuit affirmed, 411 F.2d 1, and denied a rehearing *en banc,* 416 F.2d 1257 (1969). We granted certiorari. * * *

Section 703(a) of the Civil Rights Act of 1964 requires that persons of like qualifications be given employment opportunities irrespective of their sex. The Court of Appeals therefore erred in reading this section as permitting one hiring policy for women and another for men—each having pre-school-age children. The existence of such conflicting family obligations, if demonstrably more relevant to job performance for a woman than for a man, could arguably be a basis for distinction under § 703(e) of the Act. But that is a matter of evidence tending to show that the condition in question "is a bona fide occupational qualification reasonably necessary to the normal operation of that particular business or enterprise." The record before us, however, is not adequate for resolution of these important issues. See Kennedy v. Silas Mason Co., 334 U.S. 249, 256, 257, 68 S.Ct. 1031, 1034, 92 L.Ed. 1347 (1948). Summary judgment was therefore improper and we remand for fuller development of the record and for further consideration.

Vacated and remanded.

MR. JUSTICE MARSHALL, concurring.

While I agree that this case must be remanded for a full development of the facts, I cannot agree with the Court's indication that a "bona fide occupational qualification reasonably necessary to the normal operation of" Martin Marietta's business could be established by a showing that some women, even the vast majority, with pre-school-age children have family responsibilities that interfere with job performance and that men do not usually have such responsibilities. Certainly, an employer can require that all of his employees, both men and women, meet minimum performance standards, and he can try to insure compliance by requiring parents, both mothers and fathers, to provide for the care of their children so that job performance is not interfered with.

But the Court suggests that it would not require such uniform standards. I fear that in this case, where the issue is not squarely before us, the Court has fallen into the trap of assuming that the Act permits ancient canards about the proper role of women to be a basis for discrimination. Congress, however, sought just the opposite result.

By adding the prohibition against job discrimination based on sex to the 1964 Civil Rights Act Congress intended to prevent employers from refusing "to hire an individual based on stereotyped characterizations of the sexes." [Citations omitted.] Even characterizations of the proper domestic roles of the sexes were not to serve as predicates for restricting employment opportunity. The exception for a "bona fide occupational qualification" was not intended to swallow the rule.

That exception has been construed by the Equal Employment Opportunity Commission, whose regulations are entitled to "great deference," Udall v. Tallman, 380 U.S. 1, 16, 85 S.Ct. 792, 801, 13 L.Ed.2d 616 (1965), to be applicable only to job situations that require specific physical characteristics necessarily possessed by only one sex. Thus the exception would apply where necessary "for the purpose of authenticity or genuineness" in the employment of actors or actresses, fashion models, and the like. If the exception is to be limited as Congress intended, the Commission has given it the only possible construction.

When performance characteristics of an individual are involved, even when parental roles are concerned, employment opportunity may be limited only by employment criteria that are neutral as to the sex of the applicant.

Notes on Phillips

1. *Phillips* was the first Title VII case to reach the Court. The issue it presented was appropriately important: is an employer's rule, barring the hire of some women, but not most women, a classification based on sex in violation of the Act? Martin Marietta's argument that its policy of refusing to hire women with pre-school age children did not constitute discrimination based on sex was accepted by the District Court and the Fifth Circuit. Passages from the latter opinion reveal the conceptual confusion surrounding the meaning of Title VII:

> A per se violation of the Act can only be discrimination based solely on one of the categories, i.e., in the case of sex; women vis-a-vis men. When another criterion of employment is added to one of the classifications listed in the Act, there is no longer apparent discrimination based solely on race, color, religion, sex or national origin. * * *

411 F.2d 1, 3–4 (5th Cir.1969).

In his dissent from the Fifth Circuit's refusal to grant a rehearing en banc, Chief Judge Brown gave this reasoning the treatment it deserved:

> The case is simple. A woman with pre-school children may not be employed, a man with pre-school children may. The distinguishing factor seems to be motherhood versus fatherhood. The question then arises: Is this sex-related? To the simple query the answer is just as simple: Nobody—and this includes Judges, Solomonic or life tenured—has yet seen a male mother. A mother, to oversimplify the simplest biology, must then be a woman.
>
> It is the fact of the person being a mother—i.e., a woman—not the age of the children, which denies employment opportunity to a woman which is open to a man.

416 F.2d 1257, 1259 (5th Cir.1969).

2. Can Martin Marietta cure its Title VII problem by refusing to hire all persons who are parents of pre-school age children? What about only those parents who have the primary obligation of care for young children? In the case of a married couple living together, who decides which parent has the primary child care responsibility? The couple, between themselves, or the employer? See generally, Mary Joe Frug, Securing Job Equality for Women: Labor Market Hostility to Working Mothers, 59 B.U.L.Rev. 55 (1979). See also Nancy E. Dowd, Work and Family: The Gender Paradox and the Limitations of Discrimination Analysis in Restructuring the Workplace, 24 Harv. Civ. Rts. Civ. Lib. L. Rev. 79 (1989).

3. Could Martin Marietta choose to hire single men with no family responsibilities rather than married women with children? No? Is the situation different when the job that is available is the Directorship of a teacher's center, and the School District Superintendent, who interviewed the two final candidates for the job, asked the female candidate about her attendance record, the days she had missed because of illness in her family, the ages of her children, and whether she could handle the long hours associated with the job? Are these questions improper? The Superintendent, who selected the male candidate for the position, informed the female candidate at a subsequent deselection interview that he had chosen the male because he was more "available" and "dedicated" than she; the Superintendent also noted that the male was not married and had no immediate family. Reviewing this record, the Eighth Circuit concluded that the employment decision had been made largely on the basis of a sexual stereotype, and reversed the district court's judgment for the school district. Coble v. Hot Springs School District No. 6, 682 F.2d 721, 727 (8th Cir.1982). Was that the right conclusion? Compare Anderson v. City of Bessemer City, 470 U.S. 564, 105 S.Ct. 1504, 84 L.Ed.2d 518 (1985), set forth at p. 637, supra.

WILLINGHAM v. MACON TELEGRAPH PUB. CO.

United States Court of Appeals, Fifth Circuit, 1975.
507 F.2d 1084.

SIMPSON, CIRCUIT JUDGE.

Alan Willingham, plaintiff-appellant, applied for employment with defendant-appellee Macon Telegraph Publishing Co., Macon, Georgia (Macon Telegraph) as a display or copy layout artist on July 28, 1970. Macon Telegraph refused to hire Willingham. The suit below alleged that the sole basis for refusal to hire was objection to the length of his hair. On July 30, 1970, he filed a complaint with the Equal Employment Opportunity Commission (E.E.O.C.), asserting discrimination by Macon in its hiring policy based on sex, and therefore in violation of Sec. 703(a), Civil Rights Act of 1964, Title 42, U.S.C.A., § 2000e–2(a).

[The EEOC found reasonable cause to believe that a violation of Title VII had occurred and issued a right to sue letter. Willingham lost on summary judgment in the district court, 352 F.Supp. 1018 (M.D.Ga.1972), but a panel of the Fifth Circuit, 482 F.2d 535 (5th Cir.1973) reversed and remanded.]

Upon en banc consideration, we vacate the remand order * * * and affirm the district court.

* * *

The factual background of this case is set forth in the district court opinion and in the majority and dissenting opinion of the original panel. There is no substantial dispute between the parties as to the facts the more important of which we repeat here for convenience. Willingham was 22 years of age when he applied for work with Macon Telegraph in late July, 1970. Shortly before, during the Fourth of July holidays, an "International Pop Festival" was held at Byron, Georgia, a village about 15 miles from Macon. This event, attended by hundreds of thousands of young people, is described in footnote 3 to the dissenting opinion, 482 F.2d at 539:

The record shows that Macon community disapproval of long-haired males had been recently exacerbated by an "International Pop Festival" on July 3, 4, 5, 1970, at Byron, Georgia, a small community 15 miles from Macon. The crowds attracted to Byron were variously estimated at between 400,000 and 500,000 people. Bearded and long-haired youths and scantily dressed young women flooded the countryside. Use of drugs and marijuana was open. Complete nudity by both sexes, although not common was frequently observed. Of course the managing officials of the Macon Telegraph Publishing Company were peculiarly aware of community indignation over excesses during the Byron Pop Festival because of the wide publicity in its own daily newspaper. The appellee was entitled to consider that the business community of Macon, including its own advertisers, was particularly sour on youthful long-haired males at the time of Willingham's application of July 28, 1970. It was a fair inference on the part of company officials that advertisers would share an attitude not significantly different from that of the community in general.

In short, Macon Telegraph's management believed that the entire business community it served—and depended upon for business success—associated long hair on men with the counter-culture types who gained extensive unfavorable national and local exposure at the time of the festival. Therefore the newspaper's employee grooming code, which required employees (male and female) who came into contact with the public to be neatly dressed and groomed in accordance with the standards customarily accepted in the business community, was interpreted to exclude the employing of men (but not women) with long hair. Willingham's longer than acceptable shoulder length hair was thus the grooming code violation upon which Macon Telegraph based its denial of employment.

* * * Willingham's argument is that Macon Telegraph discriminates amongst employees based upon their sex, in that female employees can wear their hair any length they choose, while males must limit theirs to the length deemed acceptable by Macon Telegraph. He asserts therefore that he was denied employment because of his sex: were he a girl with identical length hair and comparable job qualifications, he (she) would have been employed. * * *

Although our judicial inquiry necessarily focuses upon the proper statutory construction to be accorded Sec. 703, it is helpful first to define narrowly the precise issue to be considered. * * * [W]e are not concerned with discrimination based upon sex alone. That situation obtains when an employer refuses to hire, promote, or raise the wages of an individual solely because of sex, as, for instance, if Macon Telegraph had refused to hire any women for the job of copy layout artist because of their sex.

Willingham relies on a more subtle form of discrimination, one which courts and commentators have often characterized as "sex plus." In general, this involves the classification of employees on the basis of sex *plus* one other ostensibly neutral characteristic. The practical effect of interpreting Sec. 703 to include this type of discrimination is to impose an equal protection gloss upon the statute, i.e. similarly situated individuals of either sex cannot be discriminated against vis à vis members of their own sex unless the same distinction is made with respect to those of the opposite sex. Such an interpretation may be necessary in order to counter some rather imaginative efforts by employers to circumvent Sec. 703.

Inclusion of "sex plus" discrimination within the proscription of Sec. 703 has legitimate legislative and judicial underpinning. An amendment which would have added the word "solely" to the bill, modifying "sex", was defeated on the floor in the House of Representatives. 110 Cong.Rec. 2728 (1964). Presumably, Congress foresaw the debilitating effect such a limitation might have upon the sex discrimination amendment. Further, the Supreme Court, in Phillips v. Martin Marietta Corp., 1971, 400 U.S. 542, 91 S.Ct. 496, 27 L.Ed.2d 613, found expressly that "sex plus" discrimination violates the Civil Rights Act. The employer in *Phillips* refused to accept job applications from women with pre-school age children, but had no such policy with respect to male applicants. The defendant argued that it was not discriminating between men and women, but only amongst women, and then only with respect to a neutral fact—pre-school age children. In a short per curiam decision, the Supreme Court held that if the legislative purpose of giving persons of like qualifications equal employment opportunity irrespective of sex were to be effected, employers could not have one hiring policy for men and another for women. Thus "sex plus" discrimination against being a woman *plus* having pre-school age children, was under the facts of that case just as unlawful as would have been discrimination based solely upon sex.

In this analytical context, then, the single issue in this case is precisely drawn: Does a particular grooming regulation applicable to men only constitute "sex plus" discrimination within the meaning of Sec. 703, as construed by the Supreme Court? Willingham and numerous amici curiae have advanced several arguments supporting an affirmative answer to the question. We proceed to consider these arguments.

The primary premise of Willingham's position is that "sex plus" must be read to intend to include "sex plus any sexual stereotype" and thus, since short hair is stereotypically male, requiring it of all male applicants violates Sec. 703. While the Supreme Court did not explicate the breadth of its rationale in *Phillips,* it seems likely that Mr. Justice Marshall at least might agree with Willingham. In his special concurrence he noted that any hiring distinction based upon stereotyped characterizations of the sexes violates the Act, and went on to say that such discrimination could never be a BFOQ exception, an issue expressly left open in the majority's per curiam opinion.
* * *

Willingham finds further comfort in Sprogis v. United Air Lines, Inc., 7 Cir.1971, 444 F.2d 1194. Plaintiff there was a female stewardess who challenged an airline rule that stewardesses were not allowed to marry, but with no such provision for male stewards or other employees. The *Sprogis* court found the rule to be an unlawful form of "sex plus" discrimination, relying in part on *Phillips.* * * *

The beginning (and often the ending) point of statutory interpretation is an exploration of the legislative history of the Act in question. * * *

We discover, as have other courts earlier considering the problem before us, that the meager legislative history regarding the addition of "sex" in Sec. 703(a) provides slim guidance for divining Congressional intent. The amendment adding "sex" was passed one day before the House of Representatives approved Title VII of the Civil Rights Act and nothing of import emerged from the limited floor discussion. Diaz v. Pan American World Airways, 5 Cir. 1971, 442 F.2d 385, 386. Ironically, the amendment was introduced by Representative Howard Smith of Virginia, who had opposed the Civil Rights Act, and was accused by some of wishing to sabotage its passage by his proposal of the "sex" amendment. Note, Employer Dress and Appearance Codes and Title VII of the Civil Rights Act of 1964, 46 So.Cal.L.Rev. 965, 968; Note, Developments in the Law–Employment Discrimination and Title VII of the Civil Rights Act of 1964, 84 Harv.L.Rev. 1109, 1167 (1971). And while it is argued that a lack of change in this section in the 1972 amendments to the Act evidences Congressional agreement with the position of the E.E.O.C., it may be argued with equal force that the law was insufficiently developed at the time the amendments were considered to support any change. We find the legislative history inconclusive at best and draw but one conclusion, and that by way of negative inference. Without more extensive consideration, Congress in all probability did not intend for its proscription of sexual discrimination to have significant and sweeping implications. We should not therefore extend the coverage of the Act to situations of questionable application without some stronger Congressional mandate.

We perceive the intent of Congress to have been the guarantee of equal job opportunity for males and females. Providing such opportunity is where the emphasis rightly lies. This is to say that the Act should reach any device or policy of an employer which serves to deny acquisition and retention of a job or promotion in a job to an individual *because* the individual is either male or female. * * *

Juxtaposing our view of the Congressional purpose with the statutory interpretations advanced by the parties to this action elucidates our reasons for adopting the more narrow construction. Equal employment *opportunity* may be secured only when employers are barred from discriminating against employees on the basis of immutable characteristics, such as race and national origin. Similarly, an employer cannot have one hiring policy for men and another for women *if* the distinction is based on some fundamental right. But a hiring policy that distinguishes on some other ground, such as grooming codes or length of hair, is related more closely to the employer's choice of how to run his business than to equality of employment opportunity. In *Phillips,* supra, the Supreme Court condemned a hiring distinction based on having pre-school age children, an existing condition not subject to change. In Sprogis v. United Air Lines, supra, the Seventh Circuit reached a similar result with respect to marital status. We have no difficulty with the result reached in those cases; but nevertheless perceive that a line must be drawn between distinctions grounded on such fundamental rights as the right to have children or to marry and those interfering with the manner in which an employer exercises his judgment as to the way to operate a business. Hair length is not immutable and in the situation of employer vis à vis employee enjoys no constitutional protection. If the employee objects to the grooming code he has the right to reject it by looking elsewhere for employment, or alternatively he may choose to subordinate his preference by accepting the code along with the job.

* * *

We adopt the view, therefore, that distinctions in employment practices between men and women on the basis of something other than immutable or protected characteristics do not inhibit employment *opportunity* in violation of Sec. 703(a). Congress sought only to give all persons equal access to the job market, not to limit an employer's right to exercise his informed judgment as to how best to run his shop.

We are in accord also with the alternative ground mentioned in both the District of Columbia Circuit cases and relied upon by Judge Bootle in his memorandum decision in *Willingham:* "From all that appears, equal job opportunities are available to both sexes. It does not appear that defendant fails to impose grooming standards for female employees; thus in this respect each sex is treated equally." * * * 352 F.Supp. at 1020. * * * This frame of analysis removes Willingham's complaint completely from the Sec. 703(a) "sex plus" category, because both sexes are being screened with respect to a neutral fact, i.e., grooming in accordance with generally accepted community standards of dress and appearance. Since Macon Telegraph applies this criterion to male and female applicants (see the original record at 17, Response of Defendant to Plaintiff's Request for Admissions), the equal protection gloss has no applicability.

Nothing that we say should be construed as disparagement of what many feel to be a highly laudable goal—maximizing individual freedom by eliminating sexual stereotypes. We hold simply that such an objective may not be read into the Civil Rights Act of 1964 without further Congressional action. Private employers are prohibited from using different hiring policies for men and women only when the distinctions used relate to immutable characteristics or legally protected rights. While of course not impervious to judicial scrutiny, even those distinctions do not violate Sec. 703(a) if they are applied to both sexes.

WISDOM, CIRCUIT JUDGE, joined by TUTTLE, GOLDBERG and GODBOLD, CIRCUIT JUDGES, dissenting.

I dissent for the reasons stated in the original opinion of the panel. Willingham v. Macon Telegraph Pub. Co., 5 Cir.1973, 482 F.2d 535.

Notes on Willingham

1. Does Judge Simpson hold that Alan Willingham was not rejected as a potential employee because of his sex? But if an employer objects to long hair only when it grows on the heads of men, how is it possible to deny that Willingham was rejected because of his sex? Judge Wisdom, who authored the panel opinion, thought Phillips v. Martin Marietta furnished the appropriate standard:

> Applying this standard to the present case, we find that a grooming code requiring different hair lengths for male and female job applicants discriminates on the basis of sex within the meaning of section 703. Such a code treats applicants differently because of a sex stereotype: only males are prohibited from wearing their hair long. Section 703 does not permit one standard for men and another for women, where both are similarly situated.

Willingham, 482 F.2d at 538. Was Judge Wisdom's interpretation the preferable one? Was it the one Congress intended?

2. Between 1969 and 1975, the Fifth Circuit reversed itself on the concept of "sex plus" discrimination. Originally, the employer in Phillips v. Martin Marietta tried to use the concept of "sex plus" as a defense to a Title VII sex discrimination claim. The employer argued that even though it did not hire women with preschool age children, 75–80% of its employees in the relevant jobs were women. Consequently, it claimed that it did not discriminate against women within the meaning of Title VII. In 1969 both the trial court and the Fifth Circuit agreed with this argument. 411 F.2d 1, rehearing *en banc* denied, 416 F.2d (1969). After the Supreme Court's 1971 opinion in *Phillips* rejected "sex plus" as a defense, however, it became one avenue to prove a violation of Title VII.

In *Willingham*, in 1975, when the Fifth Circuit had a chance to revisit the issue of "sex plus" discrimination, it agreed with the Supreme Court that "inclusion of 'sex plus' discrimination within the proscription of Sec. 703 has legitimate legislative and judicial underpinning." Supra at p. 719. While accepting "sex plus" as a basis for proving sex discrimination, the Fifth Circuit limited its use to any sexual stereotype involving a fundamental right or an immutable characteristic. Since wearing long hair did not involve either an immutable characteristic or a fundamental right, the Fifth Circuit concluded that this claim was not the type of "sex plus" which would violate Title VII. The Fifth Circuit's limitations have been both accepted and modified over time by a variety of cases litigating a variety of issues as discussed in the notes below.

3. Sprogis v. United Air Lines, 444 F.2d 1194 (7th Cir.1971), cert. denied 404 U.S. 991, 92 S.Ct. 536, 30 L.Ed.2d 543, cited by the court in *Willingham*, measured United's no-marriage rule against Title VII and found it wanting:

Viewing the class of United's married employees, it is clear that United has contravened Section 703(a)(1) by applying one standard for men and one for women. Cf. Phillips v. Martin Marietta Corp., supra. Concededly, the marital status rule applicable to stewardesses has been applied to no male employee, whatever his position. More pointedly, no male flight personnel, including male flight cabin attendants or stewards, have been subject to that condition of hiring or continued employment.

It is irrelevant to this determination of discrimination that the no-marriage rule has been applied only to female employees falling into the single, narrowly drawn "occupational category" of stewardess. Disparity of treatment violative of Section 703(a)(1) may exist whether it is universal throughout the company or confined to a particular position. Nor is the fact of discrimination negated by United's claim that the female employees occupy a unique position so that there is no distinction between members of opposite sexes within the job category. Considerations of the peculiar characteristics of the position only pertain to the claim of a bona fide occupational qualification under Section 703(e)(1). See 29 CFR § 1604.3(b); cf. Phillips v. Martin Marietta Corp., supra.

Id., 444 F.2d at 1198. The case features a dissent by Justice Stevens, then sitting as a Circuit Judge. In his view,

If, except for his sex, plaintiff's husband had precisely the same job qualifications as plaintiff, he would not have been eligible for employment as her replacement. United's requirements for employment as a flight cabin attendant simultaneously discriminated against Mr. Sprogis because of his sex and against Mrs. Sprogis because of her sex.

Since there are only two sexes, a reading of § 703(a)(1) of the Civil Rights Act of 1964 which leads to such an anomalous result cannot be correct. * * *

When plaintiff's marriage made her ineligible for continued employment as a stewardess, she was offered, and rejected, an opportunity to remain in United's employ in an available ground capacity in accordance with her seniority and qualifications. Neither plaintiff's marriage nor her sex disqualified her from employment by United.

The no marriage rule was only one of several requirements for the position of stewardess. Each of the requirements, whether rational or irrational, was an impediment to employment as a stewardess. All of the requirements discriminated against stewardesses as opposed to other females. None, however, discriminated against females as opposed to males because no male was eligible for employment in the position of stewardess.

Id., 444 F.2d at 1202–05. Is there something wrong with this analysis? Compare Stroud v. Delta Air Lines, Inc., 544 F.2d 892 (5th Cir.1977), rehearing denied en banc 548 F.2d 356, cert. denied 434 U.S. 844, 98 S.Ct. 146, 54 L.Ed.2d 110, declining to follow *Sprogis* and upholding the no-marriage rule where only women were hired as flight attendants. The fact that Delta did not apply its no-marriage rule to men and women working in other job classifications was deemed irrelevant: the other employees were not competing for positions as flight attendants.

The exclusion of men from jobs as flight attendants was invalidated under Title VII in Diaz v. Pan American World Airways, 442 F.2d 385 (5th Cir.1971), cert. denied 404 U.S. 950, 92 S.Ct. 275, 30 L.Ed.2d 267, and again in Wilson v. Southwest Airlines Co., 517 F.Supp. 292 (N.D.Tex.1981). Both cases are discussed at pp. 785–787, infra, in the context of the bona fide occupational qualification (BFOQ) defense.

4. *Willingham* has carried the day on the long hair question. In accord are Barker v. Taft Broadcasting Co., 549 F.2d 400 (6th Cir.1977); Earwood v. Continental Southeastern Lines, Inc., 539 F.2d 1349 (4th Cir.1976); Longo v. Carlisle DeCoppet & Co., 537 F.2d 685 (2d Cir.1976); Knott v. Missouri Pacific Railroad Co., 527 F.2d 1249 (8th Cir.1975); Baker v. California Land Title Co., 507 F.2d 895 (9th Cir.1974) cert. denied 422 U.S. 1046, 95 S.Ct. 2664, 45 L.Ed.2d 699 (1975); and Dodge v. Giant Food, Inc., 488 F.2d 1333 (D.C.Cir.1973).

Moreover, *Willingham's* sex-neutral "grooming code" approach has been extended to other aspects of personal appearance required for the job by the employer. See Bellissimo v. Westinghouse Elec. Corp., 764 F.2d 175, 181 (3d Cir.1985), cert. denied 475 U.S. 1035, 106 S.Ct. 1244, 89 L.Ed.2d 353 (1986)(Title VII not violated where female attorney was asked to "tone down" her "flashy" attire; male attorneys were also advised not to wear sport jackets or slacks to the office and to keep their jackets on during meetings); Fountain v. Safeway Stores, Inc., 555 F.2d 753 (9th Cir.1977)(neckties required for male clerks in supermarket).

Constitutional challenges to grooming codes by public employees in the 1970's did not fare any better. See Kelley v. Johnson, 425 U.S. 238, 96 S.Ct. 1440, 47 L.Ed.2d 708 (1976)(hair length rule for men in police department upheld); East Hartford Educ. Ass'n v. Board of Educ., 562 F.2d 838 (2d Cir.1977), opinion on rehearing en banc, 562 F.2d at 856 (1977)(ties for male high school teachers while in classroom upheld).

Although the federal courts have permitted employers to maintain most grooming codes as sex-neutral classifications, the courts have struck down requirements under Title VII where the grooming requirement has created a greater burden on one sex than the other. See Carroll v. Talman Fed. Sav. and Loan Ass'n of Chicago, 604 F.2d 1028 (7th Cir.1979), cert. denied 445 U.S. 929, 100 S.Ct. 1316, 63 L.Ed.2d 762 (1980), invalidating under Title VII an employer's requirement that its female employees wear a uniform while permitting its male employees to wear customary business attire. Judge Cummings, author of the majority opinion in *Sprogis*, discussed in Note 3, supra, offered this distinction of *Carroll* from the other grooming cases:

> So long as they find some justification in commonly accepted social norms and are reasonably related to the employer's business needs, such regulations are not necessarily violations of Title VII even though the standards prescribed differ somewhat for men and women. However, the situation is different where, as here, two sets of employees performing the same functions are subjected on the basis of sex to two entirely separate dress codes—one including a variety of normal business attire and the other requiring a clearly identifiable uniform * * * Moreover, the disparate treatment is demeaning to women. While there is nothing offensive about uniforms *per se*, when some employees are uniformed and others not there is a natural tendency to assume that the uniformed women have a lesser professional status than their male colleagues attired in normal business clothes.

Id., 604 F.2d at 1032–33. Judge Pell, dissenting, charged that the majority had ignored the extent to which "men's customary business attire has never really advanced beyond the status of being a uniform." Id., 604 F.2d at 1034.

Similarly, in O'Donnell v. Burlington Coat Factory Warehouse, Inc., 656 F.Supp. 263 (S.D.Ohio 1987), the court granted summary judgment to female sales clerks who challenged a retail store's practice requiring female sales clerks to wear a "smock" while male sales clerks were only required to wear "business attire" (slacks, shirt, and necktie). The female clerks reported for work wearing a blouse and tie and were suspended as a result. The defendant retail store argued that the smock was not a "uniform," that the smock was required to identify the female sales clerks, not demean them. The court rejected defendant's arguments, agreeing with *Carroll*: "it is demeaning for one sex to wear a uniform when members of the other sex holding the same positions are allowed to wear normal business attire." Id. at 266.

An airline rule that male stewards could wear glasses, but female stewardesses had to wear contacts was struck down by the court in Laffey v. Northwest Airlines, Inc., 366 F.Supp. 763, 774 (D.D.C.1973), affirmed in part, reversed in part 567 F.2d 429 (D.C.Cir.1976), cert. denied 434 U.S. 1086 (1978), finding that contacts were substantially more expensive than glasses. For further discussion of gender stereotypes, business attire, and grooming standards, see Peter Brandon Bayer, Mutable Characteristics & the Definition of Discrimination, 20 UCD L.Rev. 769 (1987). Other issues of appearance and required costumes or uniforms that are sexually revealing are often litigated as part of Title VII's prohibition of sexual harassment. See pp. 824–825 infra.

The airlines' weight restrictions for flight attendants have continued to cause difficulty under Title VII. In Gerdom v. Continental Airlines, Inc., 692 F.2d 602 (9th Cir.1982)(en banc), certiorari petition dismissed 460 U.S. 1074, 103 S.Ct. 1534, 75 L.Ed.2d 954 (1983), the Ninth Circuit held that Continental's policy of requiring female flight attendants, but not male directors of passenger service who also provided in-flight service, to adhere to weight restrictions constituted discriminatory treatment based on sex in violation of Title VII. For the court en banc,

Judge Schroeder distinguished the "grooming" cases as applicable only when the employer's rule does not significantly deprive either sex of employment opportunities and when it is applied even-handedly to employees of both sexes. In *Gerdom,* by contrast, only women were subjected to the weight requirement. Turning to Continental's argument that slender flight attendants helped it to compete with other airlines, the court found this policy not to be sex neutral: the pretextual quality of the argument was shown by the presence of the male directors of passenger service who, like the flight attendants, served the flying public but who were not required to be slender. Female flight attendants successfully challenged Pan American's weight policy in Independent Union of Flight Attendants v. Pan America World Airways, Inc., 1987 WL 246612 (N.D.Cal.1987). The district court cited the "well-established body of law" on weight control policies: while weight restrictions are not per se unlawful, weight restrictions, arbitrarily applied to or unequally enforced against females, violate Title VII. The court found "Pan Am's weight policy [was] designed to perpetuate sexual stereotypes that encourage the public to think of female flight attendants as slim-bodied, attractive women as opposed to competent employees:"

> "all flight attendants * * * [were] subject to an appearance checklist, which required them to undergo a program of weight checks if they 'appeared' overweight to supervisory personnel. The Appearance Check List specified that 'unsatisfactory appearance characteristics' are '[d]isproportionate weight or flabbiness in the areas of the chin, upper arms, waistline, hips, thighs, or legs/ankles.' " * * *

> "The flight attendant's supervisor rated the following check list items either 'satisfactory' or 'unsatisfactory': upper arms, waistline, thighs/hips, and legs/ankles. The application of the appearance check list was, by definition, subjective."

Id. at 1701–2. For discussion of cases on airline appearance standards finding that even nondiscriminatory policies will be "easily defeated" if applied unequally to one sex, see generally Lynne D. Mapes–Riordan, Sex Discrimination and Employer Weight and Appearance Standards, 16 Employee Rel. L.J. 493, 499–505 (1991).

Other flaws have been incorporated into airlines' sex-based weight tables. Airlines have calculated men's weight based on a "large frame," and women's weight based on a "medium frame." Before 1991, a 5′ 5″ American Airlines female flight attendant had a choice: weigh 129 pounds or less, or be suspended. American loses weighty case, USA Today, August 29, 1991, at 2B. Often, age has not been factored into permissible weight standards. The weight tables "played on the old image of stewardesses' and the 'fly-me, sky-girl stereotype,' * * *. [They were] a form of age and sex discrimination, especially hard on women over 40 and those returning from pregnancy." Carol Kleiman, Flight Attendants Win Fight Over Weight Rules, Chi. Trib., March 13, 1991, at C1. In 1991, American agreed to relax its weight standards and to allow the weight limits to increase with age. USAir did not agree to abandon its traditional weight rules until 1994. Tamar Lewin, USAir Agrees To Lift Rules On the Weight of Attendants, N.Y. Times, April 8, 1994, at A12.

Do the cases represent a sensible accommodation between an employer's right to decide how to run the business and an employee's right to be free from discrimination based on sex? Our grooming codes and appearance standards keep changing over time. A definition of appropriate business attire is not the same today as it was yesterday, nor is it the same in Los Angeles as in Chicago or

Hawaii. Even the airlines have responded to protests. In 1991 when Continental Airlines adopted a new rule requiring women ticket agents to wear makeup, they rescinded it within a month, rehired and apologized to a woman employee who had contacted the ACLU. Airline Retracts Rule Requiring Makeup Use, N.Y. Times, May 16, 1991, at A19. On the other hand, some employers have remained inflexible in adhering to old ways. In response, the California legislature enacted a statute in 1994 giving women employees the right to wear pants to work. Cal. Gov't Code § 12947.5 (West Supp. 1995).

5. The appearance issue surfaced once again in Craft v. Metromedia, Inc., 572 F.Supp. 868 (W.D.Mo.1983), affirmed in part and reversed in part 766 F.2d 1205 (8th Cir.1985) cert. denied 475 U.S. 1058, 106 S.Ct. 1285, 89 L.Ed.2d 592 (1986). Christine Craft, hired as a female co-anchor of KMBC's evening news in Kansas City in 1980, resigned in 1981 after the station proposed to reassign her to work as a reporter, following indications of negative audience reaction to her dress and appearance. Charging that the news director, Ridge Shannon, had told her she was being removed because she was "too old, too unattractive, and not deferential enough to men," Craft filed suit alleging sex discrimination under Title VII, as well as violations of the Equal Pay Act and intentional fraud and misrepresentation. After winning compensatory and punitive damage awards on her fraud claim in two jury trials, despite losing the sex discrimination charge after findings by the court that Shannon never uttered the words quoted above, Craft lost her case on appeal. The trial court's conclusion that the station had imposed the same on-air "business-like appearance" standard on both males and females, id., 572 F.Supp. at 877, was upheld.

Would Craft have fared better if, instead of claiming disparate treatment in makeup and dress requirements, she had charged discrimination on the basis of sex plus age-related appearance? How would such a cause of action be established under Title VII? See Note, Title VII Limits on Discrimination Against Television Anchorwomen on the Basis of Age–Related Appearance, 85 Colum.L.Rev. 190 (1985). See also Note, Sex Discrimination in Newscasting, 84 Mich.L.Rev. 443 (1985)(arguing that Title VII prohibits use of viewer surveys that do not compensate for sex bias among viewers). A New York Times article published the week Craft's trial went to the jury in 1983 noted: "Perhaps the most troublesome aspect of the concern about the way women are judged on the air is the question of age—as evidenced by the paucity of women over the age of 40 now on camera." Sally B. Smith, TV Newswoman's Suit Stirs A Debate On Values In Hiring, N.Y. Times, Aug. 6, 1993, § 1 at 1. The article cites a news consulting company's survey showing that "of 1,200 local news anchors around the country, 48 percent of the men, and only 3 percent of the women, were over the age of 40. No women in local anchor jobs were over 50, although 16 percent of the men were." Id. Does this concern indicate disparate treatment of men and women regarding age in the media industry? Sex plus age?

Craft left the television industry for a medium of communication, radio, where she "[n]o longer fac[ed] the stinging judgment of wardrobe consultants and makeup experts." In 1993 she spoke "reverentially" of her new medium: "Radio is of the mind and of the voice * * *. You have the opportunity to express a point of view and argue a point." Jane Gross, Conversations/Christine Craft; Revenge of a Former Talking Head: Seen Less but Heard More, N.Y. Times, Aug. 15, 1993, § 4 at 7. In September 1993, Craft surfaced in the news again, this time for being fired from her job as a radio personality. Craft appeared on " 'Good Morning America', and ma[de] the startling pronouncement that too many radio talk-show hosts were conservative white males * * *. Just after her national TV appearance, station KFBK in Sacramento fired her. The station alleg[ed] there was no connection between the two events * * * ." John Carroll, Christine Craft Gets the Boot Again, S.F. Chron., Sept. 3, 1993, at C16.

Studies of comparative attractiveness of job candidates in other industries reveal interesting results. A 1985 study by two New York University psychologists showed that in managerial jobs, attractive men were viewed as more capable than unattractive ones, whereas attractive women were viewed as less capable than unattractive ones. In high-level jobs, predominantly filled by men, the more an individual is viewed as having masculine attributes, the more competent they seem to others. Consequently, being attractive for women has negative consequences because attractiveness emphasizes femininity. Attractive men were thought of as more masculine and, therefore, more competent. Madeline Heilman and Melanie Stopeck, Attractiveness and Corporate Success: Different Causal Attributions for Males and Females, 70 J. of App. Psych. 379 (1985).

A 1993 study, however, analyzing broad-based household and worker surveys from 1971, 1977 and 1981, found that both men and women rated below average in attractiveness by survey interviewers typically earned 10 to 20 percent less than those rated above average. Both men and women rated attractive earned about 5% more per hour than those with average looks. Men with below average looks suffered a greater drop in earnings than women: unattractive men earned 10% below those with average looks, whereas unattractive women suffered only a 5% decrease in earnings compared to those with average appearances. Daniel Hamermesh and Jeff Biddle, Beauty and the Labour Market, Nat. Bureau of Econ. Res., Working Paper #4518 (1993).

Other studies have reached similar results, showing obese women are at a considerable earnings disadvantage. Peter Passell, Economic Scene; An Ugly Subject: the Prejudice Against Hiring Homely People, N.Y. Times, Jan. 24, 1994, at D2. These survey results seem to indicate that attractiveness is a factor for both sexes. Does it help or hinder a claim of sex-based appearance discrimination or age-based discrimination? Or sex plus age discrimination?

Some courts have found sex discrimination against older women as a violation of Title VII, even though these women would also have a possible claim under the Age Discrimination in Employment Act (ADEA), 29 U.S.C. § 621 et seq. (1990). In Arnett v. Aspin, 846 F.Supp. 1234 (E.D.Pa.1994), the woman plaintiff applied for two advertised positions for an equal employment specialist with the defendant employer. The defendant hired a 30 year-old woman for the first job, and a 29 year-old woman for the second job. The plaintiff showed that every woman selected for the position had been under forty, whereas every male equal employment specialist selected had been over forty. The employer argued that Title VII does not allow sex plus age discrimination claims. It urged the court to separate the plaintiff's claim into one claim for age discrimination under the ADEA, and one claim for sex discrimination under Title VII. Relying on Phillips, Willingham, and Jefferies v. Harris, 615 F.2d 1025 (5th Cir.1980), supra at pp. 628–629, the district court found that "what has emerged from Phillips and its progeny is a rule which allows plaintiffs to bring a Title VII claim for sex discrimination if they can demonstrate that the defendant discriminated against a subclass of women (or men) based on either (1) an immutable characteristic or (2) the exercise of a fundamental right." The court denied defendant's motion for summary judgment, concluding that the plaintiff was a member of a protected subclass of women over forty. 846 F.Supp. at 1239.

6. Does an employer grooming policy that prohibits employees from appearing at work with their hair dressed in "corn rows" discriminate on the basis of sex or race? Or on the basis of a combination of sex and race? See Rogers v. American Airlines, Inc., 527 F.Supp. 229 (S.D.N.Y.1981)(dismissing claims of sex and race discrimination by black woman plaintiff but permitting proof on the question whether the policy had been applied to plaintiff in a discriminatory manner). For a discussion of cases raising the issue of sex plus race, or ethnicity, see Note 7, p. 628, supra.

CITY OF LOS ANGELES, DEPT. OF WATER AND POWER v. MANHART

Supreme Court of the United States, 1978.
435 U.S. 702, 98 S.Ct. 1370, 55 L.Ed.2d 657.

MR. JUSTICE STEVENS delivered the opinion of the Court.

As a class, women live longer than men. For this reason, the Los Angeles Department of Water and Power required its female employees to make larger contributions to its pension fund than its male employees. We granted certiorari to decide whether this practice discriminated against individual female employees because of their sex in violation of § 703(a)(1) of the Civil Rights Act of 1964, as amended.

For many years the Department has administered retirement, disability, and death benefit programs for its employees. Upon retirement each employee is eligible for a monthly retirement benefit computed as a fraction of his or her salary multiplied by years of service. The monthly benefits for men and women of the same age, seniority, and salary are equal. Benefits are funded entirely by contributions from the employees and the Department, augmented by the income earned on those contributions. No private insurance company is involved in the administration or payment of benefits.

Based on a study of mortality tables and its own experience, the Department determined that its 2,000 female employees, on the average, will live a few years longer than its 10,000 male employees. The cost of a pension for the average retired female is greater than for the average male retiree because more monthly payments must be made to the average woman. The Department therefore required female employees to make monthly contributions to the fund which were 14.84% higher than the contributions required of comparable male employees.[4] Because employee contributions were withheld from pay checks, a female employee took home less pay than a male employee earning the same salary.[5]

Since the effective date of the Equal Employment Opportunity Act of 1972, the Department has been an employer within the meaning of Title VII of the Civil Rights Act of 1964. See 42 U.S.C.A. § 2000e. In 1973, respondents brought this suit in the United States District Court for the Central District of California on behalf of a class of women employed or formerly employed by the Department. They prayed for an injunction and restitution of excess contributions.

4. The Department contributes an amount equal to 110% of all employee contributions.

5. The significance of the disparity is illustrated by the record of one woman whose contributions to the fund (including interest on the amount withheld each month) amounted to $18,171.40; a similarly situated male would have contributed only $12,843.53.

While this action was pending, the California Legislature enacted a law prohibiting certain municipal agencies from requiring female employees to make higher pension fund contributions than males. The Department therefore amended its plan, effective January 1, 1975. The current plan draws no distinction, either in contributions or in benefits, on the basis of sex. On a motion for summary judgment, the District Court held that the contribution differential violated § 703(a)(1) and ordered a refund of all excess contributions made before the amendment of the plan.[9] The United States Court of Appeals for the Ninth Circuit affirmed.[10]

The Department and various *amici curiae* contend that: (1) the differential in take-home pay between men and women was not discrimination within the meaning of § 703(a)(1) because it was offset by a difference in the value of the pension benefits provided to the two classes of employees; (2) the differential was based on a factor "other than sex" within the meaning of the Equal Pay Act and was therefore protected by the so-called Bennett Amendment; (3) the rationale of General Electric Co. v. Gilbert, 429 U.S. 125, 97 S.Ct. 401, 50 L.Ed.2d 343, requires reversal; and (4) in any event, the retroactive monetary recovery is unjustified. We consider these contentions in turn.

I

There are both real and fictional differences between women and men. It is true that the average man is taller than the average woman; it is not true that the average woman driver is more accident-prone than the average man. Before the Civil Rights Act of 1964 was enacted, an employer could fashion his personnel policies on the basis of assumptions about the differences between men and women, whether or not the assumptions were valid.

It is now well recognized that employment decisions cannot be predicated on mere "stereotyped" impressions about the characteristics of males or females.[13] Myths and purely habitual assumptions about a woman's inability to perform certain kinds of work are no longer acceptable reasons for refusing to employ qualified individuals, or for paying them less. This case does not, however, involve a fictional difference between men and women. It involves a generalization that the parties accept as unquestionably true: Women, as a class, do live longer than men. The Department treated its women employees differently from its men employees because the two classes are in fact different. It is equally true, however, that all individuals in the respective classes do not share the characteristic which differentiates the average class representatives. Many women do not live as long as the average man and many men outlive the average woman. The question, therefore, is whether

9. The Court had earlier granted a preliminary injunction. Manhart v. City of Los Angeles, Department of Water and Power, 387 F.Supp. 980 (C.D.Cal.1975).

10. Manhart v. City of Los Angeles, Department of Water and Power, 553 F.2d 581 (1976). Two weeks after the Ninth Circuit decision, this Court decided General Electric Co. v. Gilbert, 429 U.S. 125, 97 S.Ct. 401, 50 L.Ed.2d 343. In response to a petition for rehearing, a majority of the panel concluded that its original decision did not conflict with

Gilbert. Id., at 592 (1977). Judge Kilkenny dissented. Id., at 594.

13. "In forbidding employers to discriminate against individuals because of their sex, Congress intended to strike at the entire spectrum of disparate treatment of men and women resulting from sex stereotypes. Section 703(a)(1) subjects to scrutiny and eliminates such irrational impediments to job opportunities and enjoyment which have plagued women in the past." Sprogis v. United Air Lines, Inc., 444 F.2d 1194, 1198 (C.A.7 1971).

the existence or nonexistence of "discrimination" is to be determined by comparison of class characteristics or individual characteristics. A "stereotyped" answer to that question may not be the same as the answer which the language and purpose of the statute command.

The statute makes it unlawful "to discriminate against any *individual* with respect to his compensation, terms, conditions or privileges of employment, because of such *individual's* race, color, religion, sex, or national origin." 42 U.S.C.A. § 2000e–2(a)(1)(emphasis added). The statute's focus on the individual is unambiguous. It precludes treatment of individuals as simply components of a racial, religious, sexual, or national class. If height is required for a job, a tall woman may not be refused employment merely because, on the average, women are too short. Even a true generalization about the class is an insufficient reason for disqualifying an individual to whom the generalization does not apply.

That proposition is of critical importance in this case because there is no assurance that any individual woman working for the Department will actually fit the generalization on which the Department's policy is based. Many of those individuals will not live as long as the average man. While they were working, those individuals received smaller paychecks because of their sex, but they will receive no compensating advantage when they retire.

It is true, of course, that while contributions are being collected from the employees, the Department cannot know which individuals will predecease the average woman. Therefore, unless women as a class are assessed an extra charge, they will be subsidized, to some extent, by the class of male employees.[14] It follows, according to the Department, that fairness to its class of male employees justifies the extra assessment against all of its female employees.

But the question of fairness to various classes affected by the statute is essentially a matter of policy for the legislature to address. Congress has decided that classifications based on sex, like those based on national origin or race, are unlawful. Actuarial studies could unquestionably identify differences in life expectancy based on race or national origin, as well as sex.[15] But a statute which was designed to make race irrelevant in the employment market, see Griggs v. Duke Power Co., * * * could not reasonably be construed to permit a take-home pay differential based on a racial classification.[16]

Even if the statutory language were less clear, the basic policy of the statute requires that we focus on fairness to individuals rather than fairness to classes. Practices which classify employees in terms of religion, race, or sex tend to preserve traditional assumptions about groups rather than thoughtful

---

14. The size of the subsidy involved in this case is open to doubt, because the Department's plan provides for survivors' benefits. Since female spouses of male employees are likely to have greater life expectancies than the male spouses of female employees, whatever benefits men lose in "primary" coverage for themselves, they may regain in "secondary" coverage for their wives.

15. For example, the life expectancy of a white baby in 1973 was 72.2 years; a nonwhite baby could expect to live 65.9 years, a difference of 6.3 years. See Public Health Service, IIA Vital Statistics of the United States 1973 Table 5–3.

16. Fortifying this conclusion is the fact that some States have banned higher life insurance rates for blacks since the 19th century. See generally M. James, The Metropolitan Life—A Study in Business Growth 338–339.

scrutiny of individuals. The generalization involved in this case illustrates the point. Separate mortality tables are easily interpreted as reflecting innate differences between the sexes; but a significant part of the longevity differential may be explained by the social fact that men are heavier smokers than women.[17]

Finally, there is no reason to believe that Congress intended a special definition of discrimination in the context of employee group insurance coverage. It is true that insurance is concerned with events that are individually unpredictable, but that is characteristic of many employment decisions. Individual risks, like individual performance, may not be predicted by resort to classifications proscribed by Title VII. Indeed, the fact that this case involves a group insurance program highlights a basic flaw in the department's fairness argument. For when insurance risks are grouped, the better risks always subsidize the poorer risks. Healthy persons subsidize medical benefits for the less healthy; unmarried workers subsidize the pensions of married workers;[18] persons who eat, drink, or smoke to excess may subsidize pension benefits for persons whose habits are more temperate. Treating different classes of risks as though they were the same for purposes of group insurance is a common practice which has never been considered inherently unfair. To insure the flabby and the fit as though they were equivalent risks may be more common than treating men and women alike;[19] but nothing more than habit makes one "subsidy" seem less fair than the other.[20]

An employment practice that requires 2,000 individuals to contribute more money into a fund than 10,000 other employees simply because each of them is a woman, rather than a man, is in direct conflict with both the language and the policy of the Act. Such a practice does not pass the simple test of whether the evidence shows "treatment of a person in a manner which but for the person's sex would be different."[21] It constitutes discrimination

17. See R. Retherford, The Changing Sex Differential in Mortality 71–82 (1975). Other social causes, such as drinking or eating habits—perhaps even the lingering effects of past employment discrimination—may also affect the mortality differential.

18. A study of life expectancy in the United States for 1949–1951 showed that 20–year-old men could expect to live to 60.6 years of age if they were divorced. If married, they could expect to reach 70.9 years of age, a difference of more than 10 years. R. Retherford, The Changing Sex Differential In Mortality 93 (1975).

19. The record indicates, however, that the Department has funded its death benefit plan by equal contributions from male and female employees. A death benefit—unlike a pension benefit—has less value for persons with longer life expectancies. Under the Department's concept of fairness, then, this neutral funding of death benefits is unfair to women as a class.

20. A variation on the Department's fairness theme is the suggestion that a gender-neutral pension plan would itself violate Title VII because of its disproportionately heavy impact on male employees. Cf. Griggs v. Duke Power Co., 401 U.S. 424, 91 S.Ct. 849, 28 L.Ed.2d 158. This suggestion has no force in the sex discrimination context, because each retiree's total pension benefits is ultimately determined by his *actual life span;* any differential in benefits paid to men and women in the aggregate is thus "based on [a] factor other than sex," and consequently immune from challenge under the Equal Pay Act, 29 U.S.C. § 206(d); cf. n. 24, infra. Even under Title VII itself—assuming disparate impact analysis applies to fringe benefits, cf. Nashville Gas Co. v. Satty, 434 U.S. 136, 144–145, 98 S.Ct. 347 at 352, 54 L.Ed.2d 356—the male employees would not prevail. Even a completely neutral practice will inevitably have *some* disproportionate impact on one group or another. *Griggs* does not imply, and this Court has never held, that discrimination must always be inferred from such consequences.

21. Developments in the Law: Employment Discrimination in Title VII of the Civil Rights Act of 1964, 84 Harv.L.Rev. 1109, 1170; see also Sprogis v. United Air Lines, Inc., 444 F.2d 1194, 1205 (C.A.7 1971)(Stevens, J., dissenting).

and is unlawful unless exempted by the Equal Pay Act or some other affirmative justification.

II

Shortly before the enactment of Title VII in 1964, Senator Bennett proposed an amendment providing that a compensation differential based on sex would not be unlawful if it was authorized by the Equal Pay Act, which had been passed a year earlier.[22] The Equal Pay Act requires employers to pay members of both sexes the same wages for equivalent work, except when the differential is pursuant to one of four specified exceptions.[23] The Department contends that the fourth exception applies here. That exception authorizes a "differential based on any other factor other than sex."

The Department argues that the different contributions exacted from men and women were based on the factor of longevity rather than sex. It is plain, however, that any individual's life expectancy is based on a number of factors, of which sex is only one. The record contains no evidence that any factor other than the employee's sex was taken into account in calculating the 14.84% differential between the respective contributions by men and women. We agree with Judge Duniway's observation that one cannot "say that an actuarial distinction based entirely on sex is 'based on any other factor other than sex'. Sex is exactly what it is based on." 553 F.2d, at 588.[24]

* * *

III

* * *

In essence, the Department is arguing that the prima facie showing of discrimination based on evidence of different contributions for the respective sexes is rebutted by its demonstration that there is a like difference in the cost of providing benefits for the respective classes. That argument might prevail if Title VII contained a cost justification defense comparable to the affirmative defense available in a price discrimination suit. But neither Congress nor the courts have recognized such a defense under Title VII.

Although we conclude that the Department's practice violated Title VII, we do not suggest that the statute was intended to revolutionize the insurance and pension industries. All that is at issue today is a requirement that men and women make unequal contributions to an employer-operated pension

22. The Bennett Amendment became part of § 703(h) * * *.

23. We need not decide whether retirement benefits or contributions to benefit plans are "wages" under the Act, because the Bennett Amendment extends the Act's four exceptions to all forms of "compensation" covered by Title VII. See n. 22, supra. The Department's pension benefits, and the contributions that maintain them, are "compensation" under Title VII. Cf. Peters v. Missouri–Pacific R. Co., 483 F.2d 490, 492 n. 3 (C.A.5 1973), cert. denied 414 U.S. 1002, 94 S.Ct. 356, 38 L.Ed.2d 238.

24. The Department's argument is specious because its contribution schedule distinguished

only imperfectly between long-lived and short-lived employees, while distinguishing precisely between male and female employees. In contrast, an entirely gender-neutral system of contributions and benefits would result in differing retirement benefits precisely "based on" longevity, for retirees with long lives would always receive more money than comparable employees with short lives. Such a plan would also distinguish in a crude way between male and female pensioners, because of the difference in their average life spans. It is this sort of disparity—and not an explicitly gender-based differential—that the Equal Pay Act intended to authorize.

fund. Nothing in our holding implies that it would be unlawful for an employer to set aside equal retirement contributions for each employee and let each retiree purchase the largest benefit which his or her accumulated contributions could command in the open market.[33] Nor does it call into question the insurance industry practice of considering the composition of an employer's work force in determining the probable cost of a retirement or death benefit plan.[34] Finally, we recognize that in a case of this kind it may be necessary to take special care in fashioning appropriate relief.

[Part IV of the Court's opinion, which carefully preserves the presumption favoring retroactive relief in Title VII cases created by Albermarle Paper Co. v. Moody, discussed at p. 883, infra, while determining that retroactive relief was not proper on the facts in *Manhart,* is omitted.]

MR. JUSTICE BRENNAN took no part in the consideration or decision of this case.

[MR. JUSTICE BLACKMUN's concurring opinion is omitted.]

MR. CHIEF JUSTICE BURGER, with whom MR. JUSTICE REHNQUIST joins, concurring in part and dissenting in part.

I join Part IV of the Court's opinion; as to Parts I, II, and III, I dissent.

Gender-based actuarial tables have been in use since at least 1843,[1] and their statistical validity has been repeatedly verified.[2] The vast life insurance, annuity and pension plan industry is based on these tables. As the Court recognizes, it is a fact that "women, as a class, do live longer than men." It is equally true that employers cannot know in advance when individual members of the classes will die. Yet, if they are to operate economically workable group pension programs, it is only rational to permit them to rely on statistically sound and proven disparities in longevity between men and women. Indeed, it seems to me irrational to assume Congress intended to outlaw use of the fact that, for whatever reasons or combination of reasons, women as a class outlive men.

* * *

The reality of differences in human mortality is what mortality experience tables reflect. The difference is the added longevity of women. All the reasons why women statistically outlive men are not clear. But categorizing people on the basis of sex, the one acknowledged immutable difference between men and women, is to take into account all of the unknown reasons, whether biologically or culturally based, or both, which give women a significantly greater life expectancy than men. It is therefore true as the Court says, "that any individual's life expectancy is based on a number of factors, of

33. Title VII and the Equal Pay Act govern relations between employees and their employer, not between employees and third parties. * * *

34. Title VII bans discrimination against an "individual" because of "such individual's" sex. 42 U.S.C.A. § 2000e–2(a)(1). The Equal Pay Act prohibits discrimination "within any establishment," and discrimination is defined as "paying wages to employees * * * at a rate less than the rate at which [the employer] pays

employees of the opposite sex" for equal work. 29 U.S.C.A. § 206(d)(1). Neither of these provisions makes it unlawful to determine the funding requirements for an establishment's benefit plan by considering the composition of the entire force.

1. See H. Moir, Sources and Characteristics of the Principal Mortality Tables 10, 14 (1919).

2. See, e.g., 1970 Demographic Yearbook, United Nations, 710–729 (1971).

which sex is only one." But it is not true that by seizing upon the only constant, "measurable" factor, no others were taken into account. All other factors, whether known but variable—or unknown—are the elements which automatically account for the actuarial disparity. And all are accounted for when the constant factor is used as a basis for determining the costs and benefits of a group pension plan.

* * *

This is in no sense a failure to treat women as "individuals" in violation of the statute, as the Court holds. It is to treat them as individually as it is possible to do in the face of the unknowable length of each individual life. Individually, every woman has the same statistical possibility of outliving men. It is the essence of basing decisions on reliable statistics when individual determinations are infeasible or, as here, impossible.

* * *

MR. JUSTICE MARSHALL, concurring in part and dissenting in part.

I agree that Title VII of the Civil Rights Act of 1964, as amended, forbids petitioners' practice of requiring female employees to make larger contributions to a pension fund than do male employees. I therefore join all of the Court's opinion except Part IV.

[The remainder of Justice Marshall's opinion is omitted.]

Notes on Manhart

1. Is the discrimination at issue in *Manhart* based on sex or longevity? Does the result reached by the Court compel the employer to discriminate against men? Is it possible to protect each woman, as an individual, from making higher monthly contributions without requiring the employer to donate a larger amount on account of its female employees to cover the higher cost of their pension package? If it costs more to hire women than men, will employers find ways to prefer men? See Michael Evan Gold, Of Giving and Taking: Applications and Implications of City of Los Angeles Department of Water and Power v. Manhart, 65 Va.L.Rev. 663 (1979), arguing that, if normal market conditions are allowed to operate, *Manhart* will lead to a sex-segregated work force.

If the Court had allowed the employer to continue to calculate pensions using sex-based actuarial tables, how could it have distinguished this practice from the generally prohibited use of race-based actuarial tables? Race may be a better predictor of longevity than gender, but as the Court indicates, use of race-based tables has never been acceptable. Isn't this one example where the prohibition of sex discrimination in the same statute as that prohibiting race discrimination mandates the outcome?

2. What is the impact of *Manhart* on a plan that differs from that of the Los Angeles Department of Water and Power in two respects: (a) it provides for equal treatment of women and men at the pay-in stage, but not at the pay-out stage; and (b) the coverage is provided by an independent insurance carrier, rather than the employer? The coverage provided by TIAA–CREF to the bulk of academic and staff employees of institutions of higher education featured equal contributions by or on behalf of similarly-situated employees regardless of sex. Prior to 1980, however, upon retirement a woman choosing a "single life annuity" would

be paid a lower monthly amount than a man with an identical credit to his account who chose the same option, based on her longer life expectancy.

In Arizona Governing Committee for Tax Deferred Annuity and Deferred Compensation Plans v. Norris, 463 U.S. 1073, 103 S.Ct. 3492, 77 L.Ed.2d 1236 (1983), the United States Supreme Court held that Title VII forbade sex discrimination at the pay-out stage as well as at the pay-in stage. It endorsed the Second Circuit's reasoning on this point in Spirt v. Teachers Insurance & Annuity Association, 691 F.2d 1054 (2d Cir.1982), vacated and remanded in light of *Norris*, 463 U.S. 1223, 103 S.Ct. 3565, 77 L.Ed.2d 1406 (1983), which had held that Long Island University's selection of TIAA–CREF as the carrier for its mandatory employee retirement benefit program could not be isolated from TIAA–CREF's decision to use sex-segregated mortality tables. *Norris* involved yet another factual variation: the State of Arizona made no employer contribution to the voluntary deferred compensation plan created by its employees, and merely offered the employees a choice of carriers as funding agents. Since all the carriers used sex-segregated mortality tables, however, the Arizona plan violated Title VII. In announcing its decision in *Norris,* the High Court issued a terse per curiam opinion announcing that five Justices had held that the employer's practice of offering its employees the option of receiving retirement benefits from one of several companies selected by the employer, all of which paid a woman lower monthly benefits than a man who had made the same contributions, violated Title VII; and that five Justices had voted to apply this holding prospectively only, thus permitting benefits derived from contributions made prior to August 1, 1983 (the effective date of the decision in *Norris)* to be calculated under the Arizona plan as it existed prior to *Norris.* The per curiam opinion was followed by two opinions, each justifying part of the Court's holding. The first, written by Justice Marshall and joined by Justices Brennan, White, Stevens, and in part by Justice O'Connor, based the Title VII holding squarely on *Manhart:*

> We have no hesitation in holding, as have all but one of the lower courts that have considered the question, that the classification of employees on the basis of sex is no more permissible at the pay-out stage of a retirement plan than at the pay-in stage. We reject petitioners' contention that the Arizona plan does not discriminate on the basis of sex because a woman and a man who defer the same amount of compensation will obtain upon retirement annuity policies having approximately the same present actuarial value. Arizona has simply offered its employees a choice among different levels of annuity benefits, any one of which, if offered alone, would be equivalent to the plan at issue in *Manhart,* where the employer determined both the monthly contributions employees were required to make and the level of benefits that they were paid. If a woman participating in the Arizona plan wishes to obtain monthly benefits equal to those obtained by a man, she must make greater monthly contributions than he, just as the female employees in *Manhart* had to make greater contributions to obtain equal benefits. For any particular level of benefits that a woman might wish to receive, she will have to make greater monthly contributions to obtain that level of benefits than a man would have to make. The fact that Arizona has offered a range of discriminatory benefit levels, rather than only one such level, obviously provides no basis whatsoever for distinguishing *Manhart.*

> In asserting that the Arizona plan is nondiscriminatory because a man and a woman who have made equal contributions will obtain annuity policies of roughly equal present actuarial value, petitioners incorrectly assume that Title VII permits an employer to classify employees on the basis of sex in

predicting their longevity. Otherwise there would be no basis for postulating that a woman's annuity policy has the same present actuarial value as the policy of a similarly situated man even though her policy provides lower monthly benefits. This underlying assumption—that sex may properly be used to predict longevity—is flatly inconsistent with the basic teaching of *Manhart:* that Title VII requires employers to treat their employees as *individuals,* not "as simply components of a racial, religious, sexual, or national class." 435 U.S., at 708. *Manhart* squarely rejected the notion that, because women as a class live longer than men, an employer may adopt a retirement plan that treats every individual woman less favorably than every individual man.

Id., 463 U.S. at 1081–1083, 103 S.Ct. at 3497–3498, 77 L.Ed.2d at 1246–1248.

3. Do you agree with the Supreme Court's refusal to apply *Norris* retroactively? This part of the Court's per curiam holding was explained in an opinion authored by Justice Powell and joined by Chief Justice Burger, Justices Blackmun and Rehnquist, and in part by Justice O'Connor. It disapproved the District Court's order requiring that future payments to retired female employees be increased to equal those paid to retired men who had made the same contributions. Declaring that "[t]o approve this award would be both unprecedented and manifestly unjust"—because the employer could reasonably have assumed that *Manhart* allowed it to set aside equal contributions for men and women employees and then make available to them annuities offered by insurance companies "on the open market"—these Justices held that the liability imposed by *Norris* should be prospective only.

The Powell group, minus Justice O'Connor, dissented from the Court's judgment on the Title VII point, arguing that *Manhart* was limited to employer-operated pension plans and asserting that Title VII was not intended to revolutionize the insurance industry. In response, Justice Marshall pointed out in footnote seventeen of his opinion that "* * * our judgment will in no way preclude any insurance company from offering annuity benefits that are calculated on the basis of sex-segregated actuarial tables. All that is at issue in this case is *an employment practice:* the practice of offering a male employee the opportunity to obtain greater monthly annuity benefits than could be obtained by a similarly situated female employee." Id., 463 U.S. at 1087, n. 17.

Justice O'Connor filed a separate opinion explaining her agreement with the Marshall group that *Manhart* was indistinguishable from *Norris* on the liability issue, but at the same time noting her concurrence with the Powell group that the holding should be made prospective in order to avoid bankrupting pension funds. She stressed that the holding in *Norris* did not necessarily affect "* * * the larger issue of whether considerations of sex should be barred from all insurance plans, including individual purchases of insurance, an issue that Congress is currently debating. See S. 372, 98th Cong., 1st Sess. (1983); H.R. 100, 98th Cong., 1st Sess. (1983)." Id., 463 U.S. at 1107, 103 S.Ct. at 3511, 77 L.Ed.2d at 1263. Neither of the bills cited by Justice O'Connor was enacted by Congress, but the matter continued to be debated. See generally Leah Wortham, Insurance Classification: Too Important to be Left to the Actuaries, 19 U. Mich. J.L. Ref. 349 (1986); Robert H. Jerry and Kyle B. Mansfield, Justifying Unisex Insurance: Another Perspective, 34 Am. U. L. Rev. 329 (1985).

On remand in *Norris,* the Ninth Circuit affirmed the District Court's order granting prospective relief only and refusing to "top up" the level of women's prospective benefits to the level paid to men prior to *Norris.* The District Court ordered Arizona to calculate annuity benefits derived from contributions made after August 1, 1983 (the date the judgment in *Norris* was transmitted to the District Court) without regard to the sex of the employee. In complying with this order, the state used a gender-neutral actuarial table: a method that raised the women's benefits slightly and lowered the men's benefits slightly, but did not increase the benefits paid to women to the level of those previously paid to men. Judge Pregerson reasoned that the District Court's refusal to "top up" the women's prospective benefits was not inconsistent with that part of the *Norris* opinion invalidating retroactive relief, that "topping up" was not necessary to achieve equal benefits for all employees, and was not an abuse of discretion. Norris v. Arizona Governing Committee, 796 F.2d 1119, 1121–22 (9th Cir.1986). Do you agree?

4. The discrimination against women challenged in *Manhart* and *Norris* resulted from the lower benefits paid to women under single-life annuity options, where retired female employees received lower monthly payments because of their assumed greater longevity than male employees. When a joint life-survivor option is chosen, however, a male employee who designates a female beneficiary will receive lower monthly payments during their joint lives because of his assumed shorter life expectancy. This discrimination against men has also been invalidated under Title VII. See, e.g., Probe v. State Teachers' Retirement System, 780 F.2d 776, 781–83 (9th Cir.1986), cert. denied 476 U.S. 1170, 106 S.Ct. 2891, 90 L.Ed.2d 978; Long v. State of Florida, 805 F.2d 1542, 1547–48 (11th Cir.1986), cert. granted in part 484 U.S. 814, 108 S.Ct. 65, 98 L.Ed.2d 29 (1987) and denied in part 484 U.S. 820, 108 S.Ct. 78, 98 L.Ed.2d 41 (1987). *Long* and *Probe* are in conflict over when employers were put on notice that optional pension pay-out plans using sex-based mortality tables violated Title VII, thus differing on the date that relief should be commenced: *Probe* chose the date *Norris* was decided, while *Long* opted for the date of *Manhart*. The Supreme Court sided with *Probe*, holding that *Norris*, not *Manhart*, required pension benefits to be nondiscriminatory as to sex. Florida v. Long, 487 U.S. 223, 108 S.Ct. 2354, 101 L.Ed.2d 206 (1988), rehearing denied 487 U.S. 1263, 109 S.Ct. 25, 101 L.Ed.2d 975 (1988).

5. The *Manhart* decision has left in its wake a swirl of controversy. Those who view the problem from traditional actuarial perspectives believe that the Court's chosen solution constitutes reverse discrimination against men. See Richard A. Miller, How to Discriminate by Sex: Federal Regulation of the Insurance Industry, 17 Conn.L.Rev. 567 (1985); Spencer L. Kimball, Reverse Sex Discrimination: Manhart, 1979 American Bar Foundation Research Journal 83, 97–103. Those who view the question from the perspective of the traditional civil rights commitment to achieve equal rights for the individual regardless of race or sex support the Court's result and its reasoning, for they interpret Title VII as placing the eradication of discriminatory treatment of individuals ahead of the goal of achieving equality for groups. See Lea Brilmayer, Richard W. Hekeler, Douglas Laycock & Teresa A. Sullivan, Sex Discrimination in Employer–Sponsored Insurance Plans: A Legal and Demographic Analysis, 47 U.Chi.L.Rev. 505 (1980). Compare George J. Benston, The Economics of Gender Discrimination in Employee Fringe Benefits: *Manhart* Revisited, 49 U.Chi.L.Rev. 489 (1982), disagreeing with Brilmayer and her co-authors and arguing that when men and women are different, a practice that treats them as if they were alike violates the Equal Pay Act and Title VII. The debate is continued in Brilmayer, Laycock & Sullivan, The Efficient Use of Group Averages as Nondiscrimination: A Rejoinder to Professor Benston, 50 U.Chi.L.Rev. 222 (1983); Benston, Discrimination and Economic Efficiency in Employee Fringe Benefits: A Clarification of Issues and a

Response to Professors Brilmayer, Laycock and Sullivan, 50 U.Chi.L.Rev. 250 (1983). And those who would prefer to treat the social problems caused by sex and race discrimination differently find themselves in support of the Court's approach, not on the basis of principle, but because any other solution necessary to guarantee equal treatment of men and women would be unduly cumbersome. See George Rutherglen, Sexual Equality in Fringe–Benefit Plans, 65 Va.L.Rev. 199, 248–255 (1979).

6. Would your assessment of *Manhart* change if it could be shown that the conventional association between sex and mortality is neither stable nor uniform, but instead exhibits substantial variation over time and place and is heavily influenced by environmental and behavioral factors? See Brilmayer, Hekeler, Laycock & Sullivan, supra Note 5, at 539–59. The exchange is continued in Spencer L. Kimball, Reprise on *Manhart,* 1980 Am.B.F.Res.J. 915; Laycock & Sullivan, Sex Discrimination as "Actuarial Equality": A Rejoinder to Kimball, 1981 Am.B.F.Res.J. 221.

NEWPORT NEWS SHIPBUILDING & DRY DOCK CO. v. EEOC

Supreme Court of the United States, 1983.
462 U.S. 669, 103 S.Ct. 2622, 77 L.Ed.2d 89.

JUSTICE STEVENS delivered the opinion of the Court.

In 1978 Congress decided to overrule our decision in General Electric Co. v. Gilbert, 429 U.S. 125, 97 S.Ct. 401, 50 L.Ed.2d 343 (1976), by amending Title VII of the Civil Rights Act of 1964 "to prohibit sex discrimination on the basis of pregnancy." On the effective date of the act, petitioner amended its health insurance plan to provide its female employees with hospitalization benefits for pregnancy-related conditions to the same extent as for other medical conditions. The plan continued, however, to provide less favorable pregnancy benefits for spouses of male employees. The question presented is whether the amended plan complies with the amended statute.

Petitioner's plan provides hospitalization and medical-surgical coverage for a defined category of employees[3] and a defined category of dependents. Dependents covered by the plan include employees' spouses, unmarried children between 14 days and 19 years of age, and some older dependent children.[4] Prior to April 29, 1979, the scope of the plan's coverage for eligible dependents was identical to its coverage for employees.[5] All covered males, whether employees or dependents, were treated alike for purposes of hospitalization coverage. All covered females, whether employees or dependents, also were treated alike. Moreover, with one relevant exception, the coverage for males and females was identical. The exception was a limitation on hospital

---

3. On the first day following three months of continuous service, every active, full-time, production, maintenance, technical, and clerical area bargaining unit employee becomes a plan participant. App. to Pet. for Cert. 29a.

4. For example, unmarried children up to age 23 who are full-time college students solely dependent on an employee and certain mentally or physically handicapped children are also covered. Id., at 30a.

5. An amount payable under the plan for medical expenses incurred by a dependent does, however, take into account any amounts payable for those expenses by other group insurance plans. An employee's personal coverage is not affected by his or her spouse's participation in a group health plan. Id., at 34a–36a.

coverage for pregnancy that did not apply to any other hospital confinement.[6]

After the plan was amended in 1979, it provided the same hospitalization coverage for male and female employees themselves for all medical conditions, but it differentiated between female employees and spouses of male employees in its provision of pregnancy-related benefits.[7] In a booklet describing the plan, petitioner explained the amendment that gave rise to this litigation in this way:

> "B. Effective April 29, 1979, maternity benefits for female employees will be paid the same as any other hospital confinement as described in question 16. This applies only to deliveries beginning on April 29, 1979 and thereafter.

> "C. Maternity benefits for the wife of a male employee will continue to be paid as described in part 'A' of this question." App. to Pet. for Cert. 37a.

In turn, Part A stated, "The Basic Plan pays up to $500 of the hospital charges and 100% of reasonable and customary for delivery and anesthesiologist charges." Ibid. As the Court of Appeals observed, "To the extent that the hospital charges in connection with an uncomplicated delivery may exceed $500, therefore, a male employee receives less complete coverage of spousal disabilities than does a female employee." 667 F.2d 448, 449 (C.A.4 1982).

After the passage of the Pregnancy Discrimination Act, and before the amendment to petitioner's plan became effective, the Equal Opportunity Employment Commission issued "interpretive guidelines" in the form of questions and answers. Two of those questions, numbers 21 and 22, made it clear that the EEOC would consider petitioner's amended plan unlawful. Number 21 read as follows:

> "21. Q. Must an employer provide health insurance coverage for the medical expenses of pregnancy-related conditions of the spouses of male employees? Of the dependents of all employees?

> "A. Where an employer provides no coverage for dependents, the employer is not required to institute such coverage. However, if an employer's insurance program covers the medical expenses of spouses of female employees, then it must equally cover the medical expenses of spouses of male employees, including those arising from pregnancy-related conditions.

> "But the insurance does not have to cover the pregnancy-related conditions of non-spouse dependents as long as it excludes the pregnancy-

---

6. For hospitalization caused by uncomplicated pregnancy, petitioner's plan paid 100% of the reasonable and customary physicians' charges for delivery and anesthesiology, and up to $500 of other hospital charges. For all other hospital confinement, the plan paid in full for a semi-private room for up to 120 days and for surgical procedures; covered the first $750 of reasonable and customary charges for hospital services (including general nursing care, X-ray examinations, and drugs) and other necessary services during hospitalization;

and paid 80% of the charges exceeding $750 for such services up to a maximum of 120 days. Id., at 31a–32a (question 16); see id., at 44a–45a (same differentiation for coverage after the employee's termination).

7. Thus, as the EEOC found after its investigation, "the record reveals that the present disparate impact on male employees had its genesis in the gender-based distinction accorded to female employees in the past." App. 37.

related conditions of such non-spouse dependents of male and female employees equally." 44 Fed.Reg. 23807 (April 20, 1979).[9]

On September 20, 1979, one of petitioner's male employees filed a charge with the EEOC alleging that petitioner had unlawfully refused to provide full insurance coverage for his wife's hospitalization caused by pregnancy * * *.

Ultimately the question we must decide is whether petitioner has discriminated against its male employees with respect to their compensation, terms, conditions, or privileges of employment because of their sex within the meaning of § 703(a)(1) of Title VII. Although the Pregnancy Discrimination Act has clarified the meaning of certain terms in this section, neither that Act nor the underlying statute contains a definition of the word "discriminate." In order to decide whether petitioner's plan discriminates against male employees because of *their* sex, we must therefore go beyond the bare statutory language. Accordingly, we shall consider whether Congress, by enacting the Pregnancy Discrimination Act, not only overturned the specific holding in General Electric v. Gilbert, supra, but also rejected the test of discrimination employed by the Court in that case. We believe it did. Under the proper test petitioner's plan is unlawful, because the protection it affords to married male employees is less comprehensive than the protection it affords to married female employees.

I

At issue in General Electric v. Gilbert was the legality of a disability plan that provided the company's employees with weekly compensation during periods of disability resulting from nonoccupational causes. Because the plan excluded disabilities arising from pregnancy, the District Court and the Court of Appeals concluded that it discriminated against female employees because of their sex. This Court reversed.

After noting that Title VII does not define the term "discrimination," the Court applied an analysis derived from cases construing the Equal Protection Clause of the Fourteenth Amendment to the Constitution. 429 U.S., at 133, 97 S.Ct., at 406. The *Gilbert* opinion quoted at length from a footnote in Geduldig v. Aiello, 417 U.S. 484, 94 S.Ct. 2485, 41 L.Ed.2d 256 (1974), a case which had upheld the constitutionality of excluding pregnancy coverage under California's disability insurance plan. "Since it is a finding of sex-based discrimination that must trigger, in a case such as this, the finding of an unlawful employment practice under § 703(a)(1)," the Court added, "*Geduldig* is precisely in point in its holding that an exclusion of pregnancy from a

---

9. Question 22 is equally clear. It reads:

"22. Q. Must an employer provide the same level of health insurance coverage for the pregnancy-related medical conditions of the spouses of male employees as it provides for its female employees?

"A. No. It is not necessary to provide the same level of coverage for the pregnancy-related medical conditions of spouses of male employees as for female employees. However, where the employer provides coverage for the medical conditions of the spouses of its employees, then the level of coverage for pregnancy-related medical conditions of the spouses of male employees must be the same as the level of coverage for all other medical conditions of the spouses of female employees. For example, if the employer covers employees for 100 percent of reasonable and customary expenses sustained for a medical condition, but only covers dependent spouses for 50 percent of reasonable and customary expenses for their medical conditions, the pregnancy-related expenses of the male employee's spouse must be covered at the 50 percent level." 44 Fed.Reg., at 23807–23808.

disability-benefits plan providing general coverage is not a gender-based discrimination at all." 429 U.S., at 136, 97 S.Ct., at 408.

The dissenters in *Gilbert* took issue with the majority's assumption "that the Fourteenth Amendment standard of discrimination is coterminous with that applicable to Title VII." Id., at 154, n. 6, 97 S.Ct., at 417, n. 6 (Brennan, J., dissenting); id., at 160–161, 97 S.Ct., at 420. (Stevens, J., dissenting). As a matter of statutory interpretation, the dissenters rejected the Court's holding that the plan's exclusion of disabilities caused by pregnancy did not constitute discrimination based on sex. As Justice Brennan explained, it was facially discriminatory for the company to devise "a policy that, but for pregnancy, offers protection for all risks, even those that are 'unique to' men or heavily male dominated." Id., at 160, 97 S.Ct., at 420. It was inaccurate to describe the program as dividing potential recipients into two groups, pregnant women and non-pregnant persons, because insurance programs "deal with future *risks* rather than historic facts." Rather, the appropriate classification was "between persons who face a risk of pregnancy and those who do not." Id., at 161–162, n. 5, 97 S.Ct., at 421, n. 5 (Stevens J., dissenting). The company's plan, which was intended to provide employees with protection against the risk of uncompensated unemployment caused by physical disability, discriminated on the basis of sex by giving men protection for all categories of risk but giving women only partial protection. Thus, the dissenters asserted that the statute had been violated because conditions of employment for females were less favorable than for similarly situated males.

When Congress amended Title VII in 1978, it unambiguously expressed its disapproval of both the holding and the reasoning of the Court in the *Gilbert* decision. It incorporated a new subsection in the "definitions" applicable "[f]or the purposes of this subchapter." 42 U.S.C. § 2000e–2 (1976 ed., Supp. V.). The first clause of the Act states, quite simply: "The terms 'because of sex' or 'on the basis of sex' include, but are not limited to, because of or on the basis of pregnancy, childbirth, or related medical conditions." § 2000e–(k).[14] The House Report stated, "It is the Committee's view that the dissenting Justices correctly interpreted the Act." Similarly, the Senate Report quoted passages from the two dissenting opinions, stating that they "correctly express both the principle and the meaning of title VII." Proponents of the bill repeatedly emphasized that the Supreme Court had erroneously interpreted Congressional intent and that amending legislation was necessary to reestablish the principles of Title VII law as they had been understood prior to the *Gilbert* decision. Many of them expressly agreed with the views of the dissenting Justices.

As petitioner argues, congressional discussion focused on the needs of female members of the work force rather than spouses of male employees. This does not create a "negative inference" limiting the scope of the act to the specific problem that motivated its enactment. * * * Congress apparently assumed that existing plans that included benefits for dependents typically provided no less pregnancy-related coverage for the wives of male employees than they did for female employees.[19] When the question of differential

---

14. The meaning of the first clause is not limited by the specific language in the second clause, which explains the application of the general principle to women employees.

19. This, of course, was true of petitioner's

coverage for dependents was addressed in the Senate Report, the Committee indicated that it should be resolved "on the basis of existing title VII principles." The legislative context makes it clear that Congress was not thereby referring to the view of Title VII reflected in this Court's *Gilbert* opinion. Proponents of the legislation stressed throughout the debates that Congress had always intended to protect *all* individuals from sex discrimination in employment—including but not limited to pregnant women workers. Against this background we review the terms of the amended statute to decide whether petitioner has unlawfully discriminated against its male employees.

II

Section 703(a) makes it an unlawful employment practice for an employer to "discriminate against any individual with respect to his compensation, terms, conditions, or privileges of employment, because of such individual's race, color, religion, sex, or national origin. * * *" 42 U.S.C. § 2002e–2(a)(1976). Health insurance and other fringe benefits are "compensation, terms, conditions, or privileges of employment." Male as well as female employees are protected against discrimination. Thus, if a private employer were to provide complete health insurance coverage for the dependents of its female employees, and no coverage at all for the dependents of its male employees, it would violate Title VII. Such a practice would not pass the simple test of Title VII discrimination that we enunciated in Los Angeles Department of Water & Power v. Manhart, 435 U.S. 702, 711, 98 S.Ct. 1370, 1377, 55 L.Ed.2d 657 (1978), for it would treat a male employee with dependents "in a manner which but for that person's sex would be different." The same result would be reached even if the magnitude of the discrimination were smaller. For example, a plan that provided complete hospitalization coverage for the spouses of female employees but did not cover spouses of male employees when they had broken bones would violate Title VII by discriminating against male employees.

Petitioner's practice is just as unlawful. Its plan provides limited pregnancy-related benefits for employees' wives, and affords more extensive coverage for employees' spouses for all other medical conditions requiring hospitalization. Thus the husbands of female employees receive a specified level of hospitalization coverage for all conditions; the wives of male employees receive such coverage except for pregnancy-related conditions.[24] Although *Gilbert* concluded that an otherwise inclusive plan that singled out pregnancy-related benefits for exclusion was nondiscriminatory on its face, because only women can become pregnant, Congress has unequivocally rejected that reasoning. The 1978 Act makes clear that it is discriminatory to treat pregnancy-related conditions less favorably than other medical conditions. Thus petitioner's plan unlawfully gives married male employees a benefit package

---

plan prior to the enactment of the statute. See p. 2, supra. See S.Rep. No. 95–331, supra n. 15, at 6, Leg.Hist. at 43 ("Presumably because plans which provide comprehensive medical coverage for spouses of women employees but not spouses of male employees are rare, we are not aware of any Title VII litigation concerning such plans. It is certainly not this committee's desire to encourage the institution of such plans."); 123 Cong.Rec. 29,663

(1977)(remarks of Senator Cranston); Brief for the Equal Employment Opportunity Commission 31–33, n. 31.

24. This policy is analogous to the exclusion of broken bones for the wives of male employees, except that both employees' wives and employees' husbands may suffer broken bones, but only employees' wives can become pregnant.

for their dependents that is less inclusive than the dependency coverage provided to married female employees.

There is no merit to petitioner's argument that the prohibitions of Title VII do not extend to discrimination against pregnant spouses because the statute applies only to discrimination in employment. A two-step analysis demonstrates the fallacy in this contention. The Pregnancy Discrimination Act has now made clear that, for all Title VII purposes, discrimination based on a woman's pregnancy is, on its face, discrimination because of her sex. And since the sex of the spouse is always the opposite of the sex of the employee, it follows inexorably that discrimination against female spouses in the provision of fringe benefits is also discrimination against male employees. Cf. Wengler v. Druggists Mutual Ins. Co., 446 U.S. 142, 147, 100 S.Ct. 1540, 1543, 64 L.Ed.2d 107 (1980).[25] By making clear that an employer could not discriminate on the basis of an employee's pregnancy, Congress did not erase the original prohibition against discrimination on the basis of an employee's sex.

In short, Congress' rejection of the premises of General Electric v. Gilbert forecloses any claim that an insurance program excluding pregnancy coverage for female beneficiaries and providing complete coverage to similarly situated male beneficiaries does not discriminate on the basis of sex. Petitioner's plan is the mirror image of the plan at issue in *Gilbert*. The pregnancy limitation in this case violates Title VII by discriminating against male employees.[26]

The judgment of the Court of Appeals is

Affirmed.

JUSTICE REHNQUIST, with whom JUSTICE POWELL joins, dissenting.

In General Electric Co. v. Gilbert, 429 U.S. 125, 97 S.Ct. 401, 50 L.Ed.2d 343 (1976), we held that an exclusion of pregnancy from a disability-benefits plan is not discrimination "because of [an] individual's * * * sex" within the meaning of Title VII of the Civil Rights Act of 1964, § 703(a)(1), 78 Stat. 255, 42 U.S.C. § 2000e–2(a)(1). In our view, therefore, Title VII was not violated by an employer's disability plan that provided all employees with nonoccupa-

---

25. * * * This reasoning does not require that a medical insurance plan treat the pregnancies of employees' wives the same as the pregnancies of female employees. For example, as the EEOC recognizes, see n. 9 supra (Question 22), an employer might provide full coverage for employees and no coverage at all for dependents. Similarly, a disability plan covering employees' children may exclude or limit maternity benefits. Although the distinction between pregnancy and other conditions is, according to the 1978 Act, discrimination "on the basis of sex," the exclusion affects male and female *employees* equally since both may have pregnant dependent daughters. The EEOC's guidelines permit differential treatment of the pregnancies of dependents who are not spouses. See 44 Fed.Reg. 23804, 23805, 23807 (1979).

26. Because the 1978 Act expressly states that exclusion of pregnancy coverage is gender-based discrimination on its face, it eliminates any need to consider the average monetary value of the plan's coverage to male and female employees. Cf. *Gilbert*, 429 U.S., at 137–140, 97 S.Ct., at 408–410.

The cost of providing complete health insurance coverage for the dependents of male employees, including pregnant wives, might exceed the cost of providing such coverage for the dependents of female employees. But although that type of cost differential may properly be analyzed in passing on the constitutionality of a State's health insurance plan, see Geduldig v. Aiello, supra, no such justification is recognized under Title VII once discrimination has been shown. *Manhart*, supra, 435 U.S. at 716–717, 98 S.Ct., at 1379; 29 CFR § 1604.9(e)(1982)("It shall not be a defense under Title VII to a charge of sex discrimination in benefits that the cost of such benefits is greater with respect to one sex than the other.")

tional sickness and accident benefits, but excluded from the plan's coverage disabilities arising from pregnancy. Under our decision in *Gilbert*, petitioner's otherwise inclusive benefits plan that excludes pregnancy benefits for a male employee's spouse clearly would not violate Title VII. For a different result to obtain, *Gilbert* would have to be judicially overruled by this Court or Congress would have to legislatively overrule our decision in its entirety by amending Title VII.

Today, the Court purports to find the latter by relying on the Pregnancy Discrimination Act of 1978, Pub.L. 95–555, 92 Stat. 2076, 42 U.S.C. § 2000e(k), a statute that plainly speaks only of female employees affected by pregnancy and says nothing about spouses of male employees. Congress, of course, was free to legislatively overrule *Gilbert* in whole or in part, and there is no question but what the Pregnancy Discrimination Act manifests congressional dissatisfaction with the result we reached in *Gilbert*. But I think the Court reads far more into the Pregnancy Discrimination Act than Congress put there, and that therefore it is the Court, and not Congress, which is now overruling *Gilbert*.

In a case presenting a relatively simple question of statutory construction, the Court pays virtually no attention to the language of the Pregnancy Discrimination Act or the legislative history pertaining to that language. The Act provides in relevant part:

> "The terms 'because of sex' or 'on the basis of sex' include, but are not limited to, because of or on the basis of pregnancy, childbirth, or related medical conditions; and women affected by pregnancy, childbirth, or related medical conditions shall be treated the same for all employment-related purposes, including receipt of benefits under fringe benefit programs, as other persons not so affected but similar in their ability or inability to work. * * *"

Pub.L. 95–555, 92 Stat. 2076, 42 U.S.C. § 2000e(k).

The Court recognizes that this provision is merely definitional and that "[u]ltimately the question we must decide is whether petitioner has discriminated against its male employees * * * because of their sex within the meaning of § 703(a)(1)" of Title VII. Ante, at 675, 103 S.Ct. at 2626. * * * It is undisputed that in § 703(a)(1) the word "individual" refers to an employee or applicant for employment. As modified by the first clause of the definitional provision of the Pregnancy Discrimination Act, the proscription in § 703(a)(1) is for discrimination "against any individual * * * *because of such individual's* * * * *pregnancy*, childbirth, or related medical conditions." This can only be read as referring to the pregnancy of an *employee*.

That this result was not inadvertent on the part of Congress is made very evident by the second clause of the Act, language that the Court essentially ignores in its opinion. When Congress in this clause further explained the proscription it was creating by saying that "women affected by pregnancy * * * shall be treated the same * * * as other persons not so affected but *similar in their ability or inability to work*" it could only have been referring to *female employees*. The Court of Appeals below stands alone in thinking otherwise.[3]

---

3. See EEOC v. Joslyn Manufacturing & Supply Co., 706 F.2d 1469, 1479 (C.A.7 1983); EEOC v. Lockheed Missiles & Space Co., 680 F.2d 1243, 1245 (C.A.9 1982).

The Court concedes that this is a correct reading of the second clause. Ante, at 678, n. 14, 103 S.Ct. at 2628, n. 14. Then in an apparent effort to escape the impact of this provision, the Court asserts that "[t]he meaning of the first clause is not limited by the specific language in the second clause." Ibid. I do not disagree. But this conclusion does not help the Court, for as explained above, when the definitional provision of the first clause is inserted in § 703(a)(1), it says the very same thing: the proscription added to Title VII applies only to female employees.

The plain language of the Pregnancy Discrimination Act leaves little room for the Court's conclusion that the Act was intended to extend beyond female employees. The Court concedes that "congressional discussion focused on the needs of female members of the work force rather than spouses of male employees." Ante, at 679, 103 S.Ct. at 2629. In fact the singular focus of discussion on the problems of the *pregnant worker* is striking.

* * *

Under our decision in General Electric Co. v. Gilbert petitioner's exclusion of pregnancy benefits for male employee's spouses would not offend Title VII. Nothing in the Pregnancy Discrimination Act was intended to reach beyond female employees. Thus, *Gilbert* controls and requires that we reverse the Court of Appeals. But it is here, at what should be the stopping place, that the Court begins. * * * It would seem that the Court has refuted its own argument by recognizing that the Pregnancy Discrimination Act only clarifies the meaning of the phrases "because of sex" and "on the basis of sex," and says nothing concerning the definition of the word "discriminate."[8] Instead the Court proceeds to try and explain that while Congress said one thing, it did another.

The crux of the Court's reasoning is that even though the Pregnancy Discrimination Act redefines the phrases "because of sex" and "on the basis of sex" only to include discrimination against female employees affected by pregnancy, Congress also expressed its view that in *Gilbert* "the Supreme Court * * * erroneously interpreted Congressional intent." Ante, at 679, 103 S.Ct. at 2628. See also ante, at 684, 103 S.Ct. at 2631. Somehow the Court then concludes that this renders all of *Gilbert* obsolete.

In support of its argument, the Court points to a few passages in Congressional Reports and several statements by various Members of the 95th Congress to the effect that the Court in *Gilbert* had, when it construed Title VII, misperceived the intent of the 88th Congress. Ante, at 679, and n. 17, 103 S.Ct. at 2629 and n. 17. The Court also points out that "[m]any of [the

---

The Court of Appeals' majority, responding to the dissent's reliance on this language, excused the import of the language by saying: "The statutory reference to 'ability or inability to work' denotes disability and does not suggest that the spouse must be an employee of the employer providing the coverage. In fact, the statute says 'as other persons not so affected'; it does not say 'as other *employees* not so affected.'" 667 F.2d 448, 450–451 (C.A.4 1982). This conclusion obviously does not comport with a commonsense understanding of

the language. The logical explanation for Congress' reference to "persons" rather than "employees" is that Congress intended that the amendment should also apply to applicants for employment.

8. The Court also concedes at one point that the Senate Report on the Pregnancy Discrimination Act "acknowledges that the new definition [in the Act] does not itself resolve the question" presented in this case. Ante, at 680, 103 S.Ct. at 2629 n. 20.

Members of 95th Congress] expressly agreed with the views of the dissenting Justices." Ante, at 679, 103 S.Ct. at 2629. Certainly *various Members of Congress* said as much. But the fact remains that *Congress as a body* has not expressed these sweeping views in the Pregnancy Discrimination Act.

Under our decision in General Electric Co. v. Gilbert, petitioner's exclusion of pregnancy benefits for male employees' spouses would not violate Title VII. Since nothing in the Pregnancy Discrimination Act even arguably reaches beyond female employees affected by pregnancy, *Gilbert* requires that we reverse the Court of Appeals. Because the Court concludes otherwise, I dissent.

Notes on Newport News

1. *Newport News* marks the culmination of the effort to obtain Title VII coverage for pregnant workers. Ironically, the victory came in a case brought by male workers to secure their equal treatment with females in the provision of fringe benefits for their dependents. Is the issue in *Newport News* distinguishable from that decided under the constitution in Frontiero v. Richardson, 411 U.S. 677, 93 S.Ct. 1764, 36 L.Ed.2d 583 (1973), set forth at p. 31, supra? Could an employer, after *Newport News,* exclude all health care coverage for the spouses of employees from its medical plan?

2. The Supreme Court's consideration of the rights of pregnant workers began with two cases questioning whether an employer's practices met constitutional standards. Cleveland Bd. of Educ. v. LaFleur, 414 U.S. 632, 94 S.Ct. 791, 39 L.Ed.2d 52 (1974), struck down as violative of due process mandatory maternity leave provisions affecting school teachers; Geduldig v. Aiello, 417 U.S. 484, 94 S.Ct. 2485, 41 L.Ed.2d 256 (1974), upheld against an equal protection challenge California's disability insurance system which excluded coverage for disability accompanying normal pregnancy and childbirth. In *LaFleur,* the decision was rested on "conclusive presumption" due process analysis, despite the fact that equal protection had been the sole constitutional rubric in the lower court opinions and the dominant theme in the presentations to the Supreme Court. In *Aiello,* where equal protection was the decisional basis, the High Court focused its attention on the risks that were covered rather than, as the lower court had done, on the persons who were at risk. Its entire analysis of the gender discrimination problem is contained in its cryptic footnote 20, which asserted that the relevant distinction was between "pregnant women and nonpregnant persons," rather than between men and women. One commentator has suggested that "[t]he conclusion that pregnancy-based classifications are not in themselves sex-based suggests an exceedingly formalistic view of the problem." The Supreme Court, 1976 Term, 91 Harv.L.Rev. 1, 244 (1977). Both cases indicate the Court's unwillingness to undertake a searching analysis of the unique employment problems faced by all women who plan to be both mothers and workers. See generally Katharine T. Bartlett, Pregnancy and the Constitution: The Uniqueness Trap, 62 Calif.L.Rev. 1532 (1974). The fuzzy line between the two opinions was illustrated in the per curiam opinion in Turner v. Dep't of Employment Sec., 423 U.S. 44, 96 S.Ct. 249, 46 L.Ed.2d 181 (1975), invalidating on the authority of *LaFleur* a provision of Utah law that made pregnant women ineligible for unemployment benefits for a period extending from 12 weeks before the expected date of childbirth until a date six weeks after birth. *Aiello* was distinguished: neither respondents' argument nor the opinion of the Utah Supreme Court had suggested that the coverage limitations in the statute were based on insurance principles

rather than arbitrary presumptions about the woman's ability to work late in her pregnancy.

3. Did *Aiello* survive the pregnancy amendment to Title VII? Title VII was amended in 1972 to apply to state employees, so the issue raised in *Aiello* would now be decided under Title VII, rather than the constitution. Prior to 1991, congressional employees were not covered by Title VII, but were entitled to constitutional protection. See Davis v. Passman, 442 U.S. 228, 99 S.Ct. 2264, 60 L.Ed.2d 846 (1979)(recognizing a cause of action under the Fifth Amendment for a female plaintiff who had been fired by Congressman Passman because it was "essential" that the understudy to his Administrative Assistant "be a man.") If Shirley Davis had been terminated, not because she was a woman, but because she was pregnant, how would the case have been decided?

The House of Representatives extended Title VII to itself in the Civil Rights Act of 1991. See Pub.L. 102–166, § 117, 105 Stat. 1080 (Nov. 21, 1991), codified at 2 U.S.C.A. § 60*l* (1995). The Senate created its own law, The Government Employee Rights Act of 1991, Pub.L. 102–166, §§ 301–325, 105 Stat. 1088 (Nov. 21, 1991), codified at 2 U.S.C.A. §§ 1201–1224 (1995), to protect its employees from job discrimination. Both provisions establish internal grievance procedures, with the final determination made subject to review in the appellate courts. Neither provision extends to Congressional employees the right, enjoyed by other employees covered by Title VII, to bring a civil suit in a federal district court.

4. How should the following case be decided under the Pregnancy Discrimination Act? A stewardess is required by her employer to give notice as soon as she learns that she is pregnant. Upon giving notice, she is immediately placed on unpaid maternity leave for the duration of her pregnancy and for a short time following its termination by childbirth, miscarriage, or abortion. Does the employer's practice constitute a *per se* violation of Title VII? After *Gilbert,* but before the Pregnancy Discrimination Act, arguably not: the discrimination was against pregnant persons, not women. None of the cases decided during that period, however, were willing to take *Gilbert* that literally. All allowed the plaintiffs to sue, most on the basis that the challenged discrimination was a pretext for gender discrimination. See, e.g., In re National Airlines, 434 F.Supp. 249, 255–59 (S.D.Fla.1977), in which the court reasoned that National's policy deprived females of the opportunity to work, and thus of a means of support, during pregnancy. Since no other medical condition automatically results in a similar deprivation, and since pregnancy is an exclusively female condition, National's policy inevitably had a disproportionate impact on females. Moreover, since in many cases the need to earn a living would necessitate the postponement of pregnancy, National's policy also impinged on the woman's constitutionally-protected choice of whether to bear children. See also Harriss v. Pan American World Airways, Inc., 649 F.2d 670 (9th Cir.1980), following the prior decision in deLaurier v. San Diego Unified Sch. Dist., 588 F.2d 674, 677 (9th Cir.1978)(invalidating a mandatory pregnancy leave for schoolteachers after *Gilbert*), to hold that Pan American's "stop policy" had a discriminatory impact on women and therefore constituted a prima facie violation of Title VII. Accord, Burwell v. Eastern Air Lines, Inc., 458 F.Supp. 474 (E.D.Va.1978), affirmed on this point 633 F.2d 361 (4th Cir.1980), cert. denied 450 U.S. 965, 101 S.Ct. 1480, 67 L.Ed.2d 613 (1981); cf. EEOC v. Delta Air Lines, Inc., 485 F.Supp. 1004 (N.D.Ga.1980)(refusing to hold that Delta's "stop work" policy is *per se* proper under Title VII).

If these cases had arisen after the effective date of the Pregnancy Discrimination Act, would the disparate impact analysis have been necessary? Is it clear, after 1978, that the policy of forcing pregnant stewardesses to stop flying constitutes a *per se* violation of Title VII? It is clear to the Ninth Circuit; see *Harriss*, supra, 649 F.2d at 676. See also Nancy S. Erickson, Pregnancy Discrimination: An Analytical Approach, 5 Women's Rights L.Rep. 83, 104 (1979). Whether the employer can justify its practices under a bona fide occupational qualification defense will be explored at pp. 805–807, infra.

5. In Pallas v. Pacific Bell, 940 F.2d 1324 (9th Cir.1991), certiorari denied 502 U.S. 1050, 112 S.Ct. 916, 116 L.Ed.2d 815 (1992), Lana Pallas challenged defendant's denial to her of a retirement benefit instituted in 1987, the "Early Retirement Opportunity," under the Pregnancy Discrimination Act, ERISA, and the California Fair Employment and Housing Law. Pallas began working for Pacific Bell and its predecessor companies in 1967. The defendant calculated her eligibility for the benefit by using its "net credited service" system, which denied service credit for personal leaves but granted credit for disability leaves. Prior to the enactment of the PDA, the company required employees disabled by pregnancy to take personal leaves; after 1979, the company changed its policy to permit pregnant workers to take disability leaves. Pallas had taken a personal leave, as required by company policy, for her pregnancy in 1972. The company excluded that period from her service credits, and found that she was three to four days short of the necessary amount of service credit to qualify for the Early Retirement Opportunity. The District Court dismissed her claim on the ground that it was not timely filed under two Supreme Court cases, Lorance v. AT & T Technologies, Inc., 490 U.S. 900, 109 S.Ct. 2261, 104 L.Ed.2d 961 (1989), and United Air Lines, Inc. v. Evans, 431 U.S. 553, 97 S.Ct. 1885, 52 L.Ed.2d 571 (1977), holding that the statute of limitations for challenges to facially neutral bona fide seniority systems under Title VII begins to run from the time the system is adopted. On appeal, Judge Mary Schroeder held that these cases were "inapposite" for two reasons. First, Pallas was not challenging the discriminatory impact of a pre-PDA program, but rather the criteria for determining eligibility for the 1987 early retirement benefit; and second, the net credit system was not facially neutral because it "distinguishes between similarly situated employees: female employees who took leave prior to 1979 due to a pregnancy-related disability and employees who took leave prior to 1979 for other temporary disabilities." Id., 940 F.2d at 1327. She went on to explain:

> In 1987, Pacific Bell instituted a program that adopted, and thereby perpetuated, acts of discrimination which occurred prior to enactment of the Pregnancy Discrimination Act. While the act of discriminating against Pallas in 1972 is not, itself, actionable, Pacific Bell is liable for its decision to discriminate against Pallas in 1987 on the basis of pregnancy. Pallas's complaint states a valid claim under Title VII.

Id. The court also upheld the complaint as timely under the California statute and as proper under ERISA. What is the potential impact of *Pallas*? How many companies do you think treated pregnancy as a temporary disability before 1979? Congress has endorsed the result in *Pallas* by repudiating *Lorance* and *Evans* in the Civil Rights Act of 1991:

> (2) For purposes of this section, an unlawful employment practice occurs, with respect to a seniority system that has been adopted for an intentionally discriminatory purpose in violation of this title (whether or not that discriminatory purpose is apparent on the face of the seniority provision), when the seniority system is adopted, when an individual becomes subject to the

seniority system, or when a person aggrieved is injured by the application of the seniority system or provision of the system.

Pub.L. 102–166, § 112, 105 Stat. 1078 (Nov. 21, 1991)(amending section 706(e)) of the Civil Rights Act of 1964 (42 U.S.C. § 2000e–5(e)).

6.   As women enter non-traditional jobs in increasing numbers, the possibility of conflicts between federal laws, such as the Occupational Safety and Health Act, 29 U.S.C.A. §§ 651–78 (OSHA), designed to protect workers against hazards of the workplace, and Title VII, designed to protect workers against job discrimination, has become apparent.   One set of problems arises out of the special threat to persons of childbearing age from toxic substances found in the work environment.   The issue of "fetal protection" policies is explored in International Union, UAW v. Johnson Controls, 499 U.S. 187 (1991), set out at p. 790, infra, discussing the bona fide occupational qualification (BFOQ) defense.

CALIFORNIA FEDERAL SAV. AND LOAN ASS'N v. GUERRA

Supreme Court of the United States, 1987.
479 U.S. 272, 107 S.Ct. 683, 93 L.Ed.2d 613.

JUSTICE MARSHALL delivered the opinion of the Court.

The question presented is whether Title VII of the Civil Rights Act of 1964, as amended by the Pregnancy Discrimination Act of 1978, pre-empts a state statute that requires employers to provide leave and reinstatement to employees disabled by pregnancy.

I

California's Fair Employment and Housing Act (FEHA), Cal.Gov't Code Ann. § 12900 *et seq.* (West 1980 and Supp.1986), is a comprehensive statute that prohibits discrimination in employment and housing.   In September 1978, California amended the FEHA to proscribe certain forms of employment discrimination on the basis of pregnancy.   See Cal.Labor Code Ann. § 1420.35, 1978 Cal.Stats. ch. 1321, § 1, p. 4320–4322, now codified at Cal.Gov't Code Ann. § 12945(b)(2)(West 1980).[1]   Subdivision (b)(2)—the provision at issue here—is the only portion of the statute that applies to

---

1.   Section 12945(b)(2) provides, in relevant part:

"It shall be an unlawful employment practice unless based upon a bona fide occupational qualification:

"(b) For any employer to refuse to allow a female employee affected by pregnancy, childbirth, or related medical conditions. * * *"

"(2) To take a leave on account of pregnancy for a reasonable period of time; provided, such period shall not exceed four months. * * * Reasonable period of time means that period during which the female employee is disabled on account of pregnancy, childbirth, or related medical conditions. * * *"

"An employer may require any employee who plans to take a leave pursuant to this section to give reasonable notice of the date such leave shall commence and the estimated duration of such leave."

Originally, the statute was intended to reverse, as to California employers, the rule established by this Court's decision in *General Electric Co. v. Gilbert,* 429 U.S. 125, 97 S.Ct. 401, 50 L.Ed.2d 343 (1976).   At the time, California law prohibited school districts from discriminating on the basis of pregnancy, see former Cal.Labor Code Ann. § 1420.2 (1977), now codified at Cal.Gov't Code Ann. § 12943 (West 1980).   The first version of § 12945 simply imposed this requirement on all California employers with five or more employees.   As a result of employer opposition, however, the measure was changed to its present form.

employers subject to Title VII. See § 12945(e).[2] It requires these employers to provide female employees an unpaid pregnancy disability leave of up to four months. Respondent Fair Employment and Housing Commission, the state agency authorized to interpret the FEHA, has construed § 12945(b)(2) to require California employers to reinstate an employee returning from such pregnancy leave to the job she previously held, unless it is no longer available due to business necessity. In the latter case, the employer must make a reasonable, good faith effort to place the employee in a substantially similar job. The statute does not compel employers to provide *paid* leave to pregnant employees. Accordingly, the only benefit pregnant workers actually derive from § 12945(b)(2) is a qualified right to reinstatement.

Title VII of the Civil Rights Act of 1964, 42 U.S.C. § 2000e *et seq.*, also prohibits various forms of employment discrimination, including discrimination on the basis of sex. However, in *General Electric Co. v. Gilbert*, 429 U.S. 125 * * * (1976), this Court ruled that discrimination on the basis of pregnancy was not sex discrimination under Title VII. In response to the *Gilbert* decision, Congress passed the Pregnancy Discrimination Act of 1978 (PDA), 42 U.S.C. § 2000e(k). The PDA specifies that sex discrimination includes discrimination on the basis of pregnancy.

II

Petitioner California Federal Savings and Loan Association (Cal Fed) is a federally chartered savings and loan association based in Los Angeles; it is an employer covered by both Title VII and § 12945(b)(2). Cal Fed has a facially neutral leave policy that permits employees who have completed three months of service to take unpaid leaves of absence for a variety of reasons, including disability and pregnancy. Although it is Cal Fed's policy to try to provide an employee taking unpaid leave with a similar position upon returning, Cal Fed expressly reserves the right to terminate an employee who has taken a leave of absence if a similar position is not available.

Lillian Garland was employed by Cal Fed as a receptionist for several years. In January 1982, she took a pregnancy disability leave. When she was able to return to work in April of that year, Garland notified Cal Fed, but was informed that her job had been filled and that there were no receptionist or similar positions available. Garland filed a complaint with respondent Department of Fair Employment and Housing, which issued an administrative accusation against Cal Fed on her behalf.[7] Respondent charged Cal Fed with violating § 12945(b)(2) of the FEHA. Prior to the scheduled hearing before respondent Fair Housing and Employment Commission, Cal Fed, joined by

2. Aware that legislation on this subject was pending before Congress, the State Legislature added the following section:

"In the event Congress enacts legislation amending Title VII of the Civil Rights Act of 1964 to prohibit sex discrimination on the basis of pregnancy, the provisions of this act, except paragraph (2) of subdivision (b) * * * shall be inapplicable to any employer subject to such federal law. * * *" 1978 Cal.Stats. ch. 1321, § 4, p. 4322.

When Congress passed the Pregnancy Discrimination Act of 1978, this section rendered the state law, except subdivision (b)(2), invalid as applied to all employers covered by Title VII. California subsequently adopted subdivision (e), which provides:

"The provisions of this section, except paragraph (2) of subdivision (b), shall be inapplicable to any employer subject to Title VII of the federal Civil Rights Act of 1964."

7. Cal Fed reinstated Garland in a receptionist position in November 1982, seven months after she first notified it that she was able to return to work.

petitioners Merchants and Manufacturers Association and the California Chamber of Commerce, brought this action in the United States District Court for the Central District of California. They sought a declaration that § 12945(b)(2) is inconsistent with and pre-empted by Title VII and an injunction against enforcement of the section. The District Court granted petitioners' motion for summary judgment.

* * *

The United States Court of Appeals for the Ninth Circuit reversed. 758 F.2d 390 (1985). * * *

We * * * now affirm.

III

A

In determining whether a state statute is pre-empted by federal law and therefore invalid under the Supremacy Clause of the Constitution, our sole task is to ascertain the intent of Congress. [citations omitted.] Federal law may supersede state law in several different ways. First, when acting within constitutional limits, Congress is empowered to pre-empt state law by so stating in express terms. [citations omitted.] Second, congressional intent to pre-empt state law in a particular area may be inferred where the scheme of federal regulation is sufficiently comprehensive to make reasonable the inference that Congress "left no room" for supplementary state regulation. [citations omitted.] Neither of these bases for pre-emption exists in this case. Congress has explicitly disclaimed any intent categorically to pre-empt state law or to "occupy the field" of employment discrimination law. See 42 U.S.C. §§ 2000e–7 and 2000h–4.

As a third alternative, in those areas where Congress has not completely displaced state regulation, federal law may nonetheless pre-empt state law to the extent it actually conflicts with federal law. Such a conflict occurs either because "compliance with both federal and state regulations is a physical impossibility," *Florida Lime & Avocado Growers, Inc. v. Paul,* 373 U.S. 132, 142–143 * * * (1963), or because the state law stands "as an obstacle to the accomplishment and execution of the full purposes and objectives of Congress." *Hines v. Davidowitz,* 312 U.S. 52, 67 * * * (1941). [citations omitted.] Nevertheless, pre-emption is not to be lightly presumed. See *Maryland v. Louisiana,* 451 U.S. 725, 746 * * * (1981).

This third basis for pre-emption is at issue in this case. In two sections of the 1964 Civil Rights Act, §§ 708 and 1104, Congress has indicated that state laws will be pre-empted only if they actually conflict with federal law. Section 708 of Title VII provides:

> "Nothing in this title shall be deemed to exempt or relieve any person from any liability, duty, penalty, or punishment provided by any present or future law of any State or political subdivision of a State, other than any such law which purports to require or permit the doing of any act which would be an unlawful employment practice under this title." § 2000e–7.

Section 1104 of Title XI, applicable to all titles of the Civil Rights Act, establishes the following standard for pre-emption:

"Nothing contained in any title of this Act shall be construed as indicating an intent on the part of Congress to occupy the field in which any such title operates to the exclusion of State laws on the same subject matter, nor shall any provision of this Act be construed as invalidating any provision of State law unless such provision is inconsistent with any of the purposes of this Act, or any provision thereof." § 2000h–4.

Accordingly, there is no need to infer congressional intent to pre-empt state laws from the substantive provisions of Title VII; these two sections provide a "reliable indicium of congressional intent with respect to state authority" to regulate employment practice. *Malone v. White Motor Corp., supra,* 435 U.S. at 505, 98 S.Ct., at 1190.

Sections 708 and 1104 severely limit Title VII's pre-emptive effect. Instead of pre-empting state fair employment laws, § 708 " 'simply left them where they were before the enactment of title VII.' " [citations omitted.] Similarly, § 1104 was intended primarily to "assert the intention of Congress to preserve existing civil rights laws." 110 Cong.Rec. 2788 (1964)(remarks of Rep. Meader). * * * The narrow scope of pre-emption available under §§ 708 and 1104 reflects the importance Congress attached to state antidiscrimination laws in achieving Title VII's goal of equal employment opportunity. [citations omitted.] The legislative history of the PDA also supports a narrow interpretation of these provisions, as does our opinion in *Shaw v. Delta Air Lines, Inc., supra.*[15]

In order to decide whether the California statute requires or permits employers to violate Title VII, as amended by the PDA, or is inconsistent with the purposes of the statute, we must determine whether the PDA prohibits the States from requiring employers to provide reinstatement to pregnant workers, regardless of their policy for disabled workers generally.

B

Petitioners argue that the language of the federal statute itself unambiguously rejects California's "special treatment" approach to pregnancy discrimination, thus rendering any resort to the legislative history unnecessary. They contend that the second clause of the PDA forbids an employer to treat pregnant employees any differently than other disabled employees. Because "[t]he purpose of Congress is the ultimate touchstone" of the pre-emption inquiry, *Malone v. White Motor Corp.,* 435 U.S., at 504, 98 S.Ct., at 1189 (quoting *Retail Clerks v. Schermerhorn,* 375 U.S. 96, 103, 84 S.Ct. 219, 222, 11 L.Ed.2d 179 (1963)), however, we must examine the PDA's language against the background of its legislative history and historical context. As to the language of the PDA, "[i]t is a 'familiar rule, that a thing may be within the letter of the statute and yet not within the statute, because not within its spirit, nor within the intention of its makers.' " *Steelworkers v. Weber,* 443 U.S. 193, 201, 99 S.Ct. 2721, 2726, 61 L.Ed.2d 480 (1979) [citations omitted.]

It is well established that the PDA was passed in reaction to this Court's decision in *General Electric Co. v. Gilbert* * * *. "When Congress amended Title VII in 1978, it unambiguously expressed its disapproval of both the

---

15. In *Shaw v. Delta Air Lines, Inc.,* 463 U.S. 85, 100–104, 103 S.Ct. 2890, 2901–2903, 77 L.Ed.2d 490 (1983), we concluded that Title VII did not pre-empt a New York statute which proscribed discrimination on the basis of pregnancy as sex discrimination at a time when Title VII did not equate the two.

holding and the reasoning of the Court in the *Gilbert* decision." *Newport News Shipbuilding & Dry Dock Co. v. EEOC*, 462 U.S., at 678, 103 S.Ct., at 2628. By adding pregnancy to the definition of sex discrimination prohibited by Title VII, the first clause of the PDA reflects Congress' disapproval of the reasoning in *Gilbert. Newport News, supra*, at 678–679, 103 S.Ct., at 2628, and n. 17 (citing legislative history). Rather than imposing a limitation on the remedial purpose of the PDA, we believe that the second clause was intended to overrule the holding in *Gilbert* and to illustrate how discrimination against pregnancy is to be remedied. Cf. 462 U.S., at 678, n. 14, 103 S.Ct., at 2628, n. 14 ("The meaning of the first clause is not limited by the specific language in the second clause, which explains the application of the general principle to women employees"); see also *id.*, at 688, 103 S.Ct., at 2633 (Rehnquist, J., dissenting).[16] Accordingly, subject to certain limitations,[17] we agree with the Court of Appeals' conclusion that Congress intended the PDA to be "a floor beneath which pregnancy disability benefits may not drop—not a ceiling above which they may not rise." 758 F.2d, at 396.

The context in which Congress considered the issue of pregnancy discrimination supports this view of the PDA. Congress had before it extensive evidence of discrimination *against* pregnancy, particularly in disability and health insurance programs like those challenged in *Gilbert* and *Nashville Gas Co. v. Satty*, 434 U.S. 136, 98 S.Ct. 347, 54 L.Ed.2d 356 (1977). The reports, debates, and hearings make abundantly clear that Congress intended the PDA to provide relief for working women and to end discrimination against pregnant workers. In contrast to the thorough account of discrimination against pregnant workers, the legislative history is devoid of any discussion of preferential treatment of pregnancy,[20] beyond acknowledgments of the existence of state statutes providing for such preferential treatment. See *infra* this page. Opposition to the PDA came from those concerned with the cost of including pregnancy in health and disability benefit plans and the application of the bill to abortion, not from those who favored special accommodation of pregnancy.

In support of their argument that the PDA prohibits employment practices that favor pregnant women, petitioners and several *amici* cite statements in the legislative history to the effect that the PDA does not *require* employers to extend any benefits to pregnant women that they do not already provide to other disabled employees. For example, the House Report explained that the proposed legislation "does not require employers to treat pregnant employees in any particular manner. * * * H.R. 6075 in no way requires the institution of any new programs where none currently exist." We do not interpret these references to support petitioners' construction of the statute. On the contrary, if Congress had intended to *prohibit* preferen-

---

16. Several commentators have construed the second clause of the PDA in this way. See, *e.g.*, Note, Employment Equality Under The Pregnancy Discrimination Act of 1978, 94 Yale L.J. 929, 937 (1985); Note, Sexual Equality Under the Pregnancy Discrimination Act, 83 Colum.L.Rev. 690, 696, and n. 26 (1983).

17. For example, a State could not mandate special treatment of pregnant workers based on stereotypes or generalizations about their needs and abilities. See *infra*, at 694–695.

20. The statement of Senator Brooke, quoted in the dissent, *post*, at 699, merely indicates the Senator's view that the PDA does not *itself* require special disability benefits for pregnant workers. It in no way supports the conclusion that Congress intended to prohibit the *States* from providing such benefits for pregnant workers. See n. 29, *infra*.

tial treatment, it would have been the height of understatement to say only that the legislation would not *require* such conduct. It is hardly conceivable that Congress would have extensively discussed only its intent not to require preferential treatment if in fact it had intended to prohibit such treatment.

We also find it significant that Congress was aware of state laws similar to California's but apparently did not consider them inconsistent with the PDA. In the debates and reports on the bill, Congress repeatedly acknowledged the existence of state antidiscrimination laws that prohibit sex discrimination on the basis of pregnancy. Two of the States mentioned then required employers to provide reasonable leave to pregnant workers.[24] After citing these state laws, Congress failed to evince the requisite "clear and manifest purpose" to supersede them. See *Pacific Gas & Electric Co. v. State Energy Resources Conservation and Development Comm'n*, 461 U.S. 190, 206, 103 S.Ct. 1713, 1723, 75 L.Ed.2d 752 (1983). To the contrary, both the House and Senate Reports suggest that these laws would continue to have effect under the PDA.[25]

Title VII, as amended by the PDA, and California's pregnancy disability leave statute share a common goal. The purpose of Title VII is "to achieve equality of employment opportunities and remove barriers that have operated in the past to favor an identifiable group of * * * employees over other employees." *Griggs v. Duke Power Co.*, 401 U.S. 424, 429–430 * * * (1971). * * * Rather than limiting existing Title VII principles and objectives, the PDA extends them to cover pregnancy.[26] As Senator Williams, a sponsor of the Act, stated: "The entire thrust * * * behind this legislation is to guarantee women the basic right to participate fully and equally in the workforce, without denying them the fundamental right to full participation in family life." 123 Cong.Rec. 29658 (1977).

24. See, *e.g.*, Conn.Gen.Stat. § 31–126(g)(1977), now codified at § 46a–60(a)(7)(1985); Mont.Rev.Codes § 41–2602 (Smith Supp.1977), now codified at Mont.Code Ann. §§ 49–2–310 and 49–2–311 (1986). The Connecticut statute provided, in relevant part:

"It shall be an unfair employment practice

"(g) For an employer * * * (ii) to refuse to grant to [a pregnant] employee a reasonable leave of absence for disability resulting from such pregnancy. * * * (iii) Upon signifying her intent to return, such employee shall be reinstated to her original job or to an equivalent position with equivalent pay and accumulated seniority, retirement, fringe benefits and other service credits unless, in the case of a private employer, the employer's circumstances have so changed as to make it impossible or unreasonable to do so." Conn.Gen. Stat. § 31–126(g)(1977).

The Montana statute in effect in 1977 was virtually identical. Both have been recodified in current statutory compilations, but the leave and reinstatement requirements are unchanged. See also Mass.Gen.Laws ch. 149, § 105D (1985)(providing up to eight weeks maternity leave).

The dissent suggests that the references to the Connecticut and Montana statutes should be disregarded, because Congress did not expressly state that it understood that "these statutes required anything more than equal treatment." *Post*, at 700. However, we are not as willing as the dissent to impute ignorance to Congress. Where Congress has cited these statutes in the House and Senate Reports on the PDA, we think it fair to assume that it was aware of their substantive provisions.

25. For example, the Senate Report states: "Since title VII does not pre-empt State laws which would not require violating title VII * * *, these States would continue to be able to enforce their State laws if the bill were enacted." S.Rep. No. 95–331, *supra*, at 3, n. 1, Leg.Hist. 40.

26. "Proponents of the bill repeatedly emphasized that the Supreme Court had erroneously interpreted congressional intent and that the amending legislation was necessary to reestablish the principles of Title VII law as they had been understood prior to the *Gilbert* decision." *Newport News Shipbuilding & Dry Dock Co. v. EEOC*, 462 U.S., at 679, 103 S.Ct., at 2628.

Section 12945(b)(2) also promotes equal employment opportunity. By requiring employers to reinstate women after a reasonable pregnancy disability leave, § 12945(b)(2) ensures that they will not lose their jobs on account of pregnancy disability.[27] California's approach is consistent with the dissenting opinion of Justice Brennan in *General Electric Co. v. Gilbert,* which Congress adopted in enacting the PDA. Referring to *Lau v. Nichols,* 414 U.S. 563, 94 S.Ct. 786, 39 L.Ed.2d 1 (1974), a Title VI decision, Justice Brennan stated:

> "[D]iscrimination is a social phenomenon encased in a social context and, therefore, unavoidably takes its meaning from the desired end products of the relevant legislative enactment, end products that may demand due consideration of the uniqueness of the 'disadvantaged' individuals. A realistic understanding of conditions found in today's labor environment warrants taking pregnancy into account in fashioning disability policies." 429 U.S., at 159, 97 S.Ct., at 419 (footnote omitted).

By "taking pregnancy into account," California's pregnancy disability leave statute allows women, as well as men, to have families without losing their jobs.

We emphasize the limited nature of the benefits § 12945(b)(2) provides. The statute is narrowly drawn to cover only the period of *actual physical disability* on account of pregnancy, childbirth, or related medical conditions. Accordingly, unlike the protective labor legislation prevalent earlier in this century,[28] § 12945(b)(2) does not reflect archaic or stereotypical notions about pregnancy and the abilities of pregnant workers. A statute based on such stereotypical assumptions would, of course, be inconsistent with Title VII's goal of equal employment opportunity. See, *e.g., Los Angeles Dept. of Water and Power v. Manhart* * * *; *Phillips v. Martin Marietta Corp.,* * * * (Marshall, J., concurring).

C

Moreover, even if we agreed with petitioners' construction of the PDA, we would nonetheless reject their argument that the California statute requires employers to violate Title VII.[29] Section 12945(b)(2) does not prevent employers from complying with both the federal law (as petitioners construe it) and the state law. This is not a case where "compliance with both federal and

---

27. As authoritatively construed by respondent Commission, the provision will "insure that women affected by pregnancy, childbirth or related medical conditions have equal employment opportunities as persons not so affected." California Fair Employment and Housing Commission's Proposed Regulation, see App. 49.

28. See generally B. Brown, A. Freedman, H. Katz & A. Price, Women's Rights and the Law 209–210 (1977). In the constitutional context, we have invalidated on equal protection grounds statutes designed "to exclude or 'protect' members of one gender because they are presumed to suffer from an inherent handicap or to be innately inferior." *Mississippi University for Women v. Hogan,* 458 U.S. 718, 725, 102 S.Ct. 3331, 3336, 73 L.Ed.2d 1090 (1982).

29. Petitioners assert that even if § 12945(b)(2) does not *require* employers to treat pregnant employees differently from other disabled employees, it *permits* employers to do so because it does not specifically prohibit different treatment. Of course, since the PDA does not itself prohibit different treatment, it certainly does not require the States to do so. Moreover, if we were to interpret the term "permit" as expansively as petitioners suggest, the State would be required to incorporate every prohibition contained in Title VII into its state law, since it would otherwise be held to "permit" any employer action it did not expressly prohibit. We conclude that "permit" in § 708 must be interpreted to pre-empt only those state laws that expressly *sanction* a practice unlawful under Title VII; the term does not pre-empt state laws that are silent on the practice.

state regulations is a physical impossibility," *Florida Lime & Avocado Growers, Inc. v. Paul,* 373 U.S. 132, 142–143, 83 S.Ct. 1210, 1217, 10 L.Ed.2d 248 (1963), or where there is an "inevitable collision between the two schemes of regulation." *Id.,* at 143, 83 S.Ct., at 1217.[30] Section 12945(b)(2) does not compel California employers to treat pregnant workers *better* than other disabled employees; it merely establishes benefits that employers must, at a minimum, provide to pregnant workers. Employers are free to give comparable benefits to other disabled employees, thereby treating "women affected by pregnancy" no better than "other persons not so affected but similar in their ability or inability to work." Indeed, at oral argument, petitioners conceded that compliance with both statutes "is theoretically possible." Tr. of Oral Arg. 6.

Petitioners argue that "extension" of the state statute to cover other employees would be inappropriate in the absence of a clear indication that this is what the California Legislature intended. They cite cases in which this Court has declined to rewrite underinclusive state statutes found to violate the Equal Protection Clause. See, *e.g., Wengler v. Druggists Mutual Insurance Co.,* 446 U.S. 142, 152–153, 100 S.Ct. 1540, 1546, 64 L.Ed.2d 107 (1980); *Caban v. Mohammed,* 441 U.S. 380, 392–393, n. 13, 99 S.Ct. 1760, 1768, n. 13, 60 L.Ed.2d 297 (1979). This argument is beside the point. Extension is a remedial option to be exercised by a court once a statute is found to be invalid.[31] See, *e.g., Califano v. Wescott,* 443 U.S. 76, 89, 99 S.Ct. 2655, 2663, 61 L.Ed.2d 382 (1979)(quoting *Welsh v. United States,* 398 U.S. 333, 361, 90 S.Ct. 1792, 1807, 26 L.Ed.2d 308 (1970)(Harlan, J., concurring in the result)).

IV

Thus, petitioners' facial challenge to § 12945(b)(2) fails. The statute is not pre-empted by Title VII, as amended by the PDA, because it is not inconsistent with the purposes of the federal statute, nor does it require the doing of an act which is unlawful under Title VII.[32]

The judgment of the Court of Appeals is

Affirmed.

JUSTICE STEVENS, concurring in part, and concurring in the judgment.

The Pregnancy Discrimination Act of 1978 (PDA) does not exist in a vacuum. As Justice White recognizes in his dissent, Congress did not intend to "put pregnancy in a class by itself within Title VII," and the enactment of

---

30. Indeed, Congress and the California Legislature were each aware in general terms of the regulatory scheme adopted by the other when they enacted their legislation. California recognized that many of its provisions would be pre-empted by the PDA and, accordingly, exempted employers covered by Title VII from all portions of the statute except those guaranteeing unpaid leave and reinstatement to pregnant workers. Congress was aware that some state laws mandated certain benefits for pregnant workers, but did not indicate that they would be pre-empted by federal law. See *supra,* at 692–693.

31. We recognize that, *in cases where a state statute is otherwise invalid,* the Court

must look to the intent of the state legislature to determine whether to extend benefits or nullify the statute. By arguing that extension would be inappropriate in this case, however, post, at 701, and citing this as a basis for pre-emption, the dissent simply ignores the prerequisite of invalidity.

32. Because we conclude that in enacting the PDA Congress did not intend to prohibit all favorable treatment of pregnancy, we need not decide and therefore do not address the question whether § 12945(b)(2) could be upheld as a legislative response to leave policies that have a disparate impact on pregnant workers.

the PDA "did not mark a departure from Title VII principles." *Post*, at 698. But this realization does not lead me to support Justice White's position; rather, I believe that the PDA's posture as part of Title VII compels rejection of his argument that the PDA mandates complete neutrality and forbids all beneficial treatment of pregnancy.[1]

In *Steelworkers v. Weber*, 443 U.S. 193, 99 S.Ct. 2721, 61 L.Ed.2d 480 (1979), the Court rejected the argument that Title VII prohibits all preferential treatment of the disadvantaged classes that the statute was enacted to protect. The plain words of Title VII, which would have led to a contrary result, were read in the context of the statute's enactment and its purposes.[2] In this case as well, the language of the Act seems to mandate treating pregnant employees the same as other employees. I cannot, however, ignore the fact that the PDA is a definitional section of Title VII's prohibition against gender-based discrimination. Had *Weber* interpreted Title VII as requiring neutrality, I would agree with Justice White that the PDA should be interpreted that way as well. But since the Court in *Weber* interpreted Title VII to draw a distinction between discrimination *against* members of the protected class and special preference *in favor of* members of that class, I do not accept the proposition that the PDA requires absolute neutrality.

I therefore conclude that Justice Marshall's view, which holds that the PDA allows some preferential treatment of pregnancy, is more consistent with our interpretation of Title VII than Justice White's view is. This is not to say, however, that all preferential treatment of pregnancy is automatically beyond the scope of the PDA.[3] Rather, as with other parts of Title VII,

1. Because I agree with the Court that the California statute does not conflict with the purposes of the PDA, and does not purport to "require or permit" action inconsistent with the PDA, I do not reach the question whether § 1104 of the Civil Rights Act of 1964, 42 U.S.C. § 2000h–4, is applicable to Title VII, or whether, as Justice Scalia suggests, § 708, 42 U.S.C. § 2000e–7, is the only provision governing Title VII's preemptive scope. Even if § 1104 applies, the California statute would not be preempted in this case. Since Section IIIA of Justice Marshall's opinion does not make it clear whether it decides this issue, or whether it only assumes for the purposes of the decision that § 1104 applies, I do not join that section. I do, however, join the remainder of the Court's opinion.

The choice between disposing of the case through interpreting the preemption provisions of Title VII and Title XI as Justice Scalia does, or through interpreting the substance of the PDA and thus obviating the need to decide the Title XI question, is a choice between two grounds of statutory construction. Neither approach is inherently narrower than the other. Given the value of having an opinion for the Court, I have therefore concluded that I should choose between the conflicting views of the PDA expressed by Justice Marshall and Justice White, even though Justice Scalia may be correct in arguing that this case could be decided without reaching that issue.

2. There is a striking similarity between the evidence about the enactment of Title VII that was available in *Steelworkers v. Weber*, * * *, and the evidence available regarding the enactment of the PDA. First, the plain language in both cases points to neutrality, see *ante*, at 692–693; 443 U.S., at 201, 99 S.Ct., at 2726, although, if anything, that language was even less equivocal in *Weber* than it is here. See *ante*, at 691. Second, in both cases the records are replete with indications that Congress' goal was to bar discrimination against the disadvantaged class or classes at issue. * * * Third, in neither case was there persuasive evidence that Congress considered the ramifications of a rule mandating complete neutrality. * * * Finally, there were statements in the legislative histories of both provisions stressing that Congress did not intend to *require* preferential treatment, statements that undermine the conclusion that Congress indeed intended to *prohibit* such treatment. * * *

3. I do not read the Court's opinion as holding that Title VII presents no limitations whatsoever on beneficial treatment of pregnancy. Although the opinion does make some mention of the "floor" but "not a ceiling" language employed by the Court of Appeals, see *ante*, at 691, the Court also points out that there are limitations on what an employer can do, even when affording "preferential" treat-

preferential treatment of the disadvantaged class is only permissible so long as it is consistent with "accomplish[ing] the goal that Congress designed Title VII to achieve." *Weber, supra,* at 204, 99 S.Ct., at 2727.[4] That goal has been characterized as seeking "to achieve equality of employment opportunities and to remove barriers that have operated in the past to favor an identifiable group of * * * employees over other employees." *Griggs v. Duke Power Co.,* 401 U.S. 424, 429–430, 91 S.Ct. 849, 852–853, 28 L.Ed.2d 158 (1971).

It is clear to me, as it is to the Court, and was to the Court of Appeals, that the California statute meets this test. Thus, I agree that a California employer would not violate the PDA were it to comply with California's statute without affording the same protection to men suffering somewhat similar disabilities.

JUSTICE SCALIA, concurring in the judgment.

The only provision of the Civil Rights Act of 1964 whose effect on pre-emption need be considered in the present case is § 708 of Title VII, 42 U.S.C. § 2000e–7.

* * *

Section 708 narrows the pre-emptive scope of the PDA so that it pre-empts only laws which "purpor[t] to require or permit the doing of any act which would be an unlawful employment practice" under the title. 42 U.S.C. § 2000e–7. Thus, whether or not the PDA prohibits discriminatorily favorable disability treatment for pregnant women, § 12945(b)(2) of the California Code cannot be pre-empted, since it does not remotely purport to require or permit any refusal to accord federally mandated equal treatment to others similarly situated. No more is needed to decide this case. * * *

I am fully aware that it is more convenient for the employers of California and the California Legislature to have us interpret the PDA prematurely. It has never been suggested, however, that the constitutional prohibition upon our rendering of advisory opinions is a doctrine of convenience. I would affirm the judgment of the Court of Appeals on the ground that § 12945(b)(2) of the California Code does not purport to require or permit any act that would be an unlawful employment practice under any conceivable interpretation of the PDA, and therefore, by virtue of § 708, cannot be pre-empted.

JUSTICE WHITE, with whom THE CHIEF JUSTICE and JUSTICE POWELL join, dissenting.

I disagree with the Court that Cal.Gov't Code Ann. § 12945(b)(2)(West 1980) is not pre-empted by the Pregnancy Discrimination Act of 1978 (PDA), 92 Stat. 2076, codified at 42 U.S.C. § 2000e(k), and § 708 of Title VII. Section 703(a) of Title VII, 78 Stat. 255, 42 U.S.C. § 2000e–2(a), forbids

ment to pregnancy. See *ante,* at 691, n. 17; *ante,* at 694. Indeed, the Court of Appeals also subjected California's statute to the test of "whether the policy furthers 'Title VII's prophylactic purpose of achieving "equality of employment opportunities."'" 758 F.2d 390, 396 (1985)(quoting *EEOC v. Puget Sound Log Scaling & Grading Bureau,* 752 F.2d 1389, 1392 (C.A.9 1985)(quoting *Griggs v. Duke Power Co.,* * * * (1971)).

4. The Court has not yet had occasion to explore the exact line of demarcation between permissible and impermissible preferential treatment under Title VII. The factors discussed in *Weber* are, in my view, merely exemplary, and do not necessarily define the outer limits of what a private employer or a State may do to in an attempt to effectuate the goals of Title VII.

discrimination in the terms of employment on the basis of race, color, religion, sex, or national origin. The PDA gave added meaning to discrimination on the basis of sex * * *.

The second clause * * * could not be clearer: it mandates that pregnant employees "shall be treated the same for all employment-related purposes" as non-pregnant employees similarly situated with respect to their ability or inability to work. This language leaves no room for preferential treatment of pregnant workers. The majority would avoid its plain meaning by misapplying our interpretation of the clause in *Newport News Shipbuilding & Dry Dock Co. v. EEOC* * * *. *Ante,* at 691. The second clause addresses only female employees and was not directly implicated in *Newport News* because the pregnant persons at issue in that case were spouses of male employees. We therefore stated in *Newport News* that the second clause had only explanatory or illustrative significance. We did not indicate in any way, however, that the second clause does not mean exactly what it says in a situation where it is directly implicated.

Contrary to the mandate of the PDA, California law requires every employer to have a disability leave policy for pregnancy even if it has none for any other disability. An employer complies with California law if it has a leave policy for pregnancy but denies it for every other disability. On its face, § 12945(b)(2) is in square conflict with the PDA and is therefore pre-empted. Because the California law permits employers to single out pregnancy for preferential treatment and therefore to violate Title VII, it is not saved by § 708 which limits pre-emption of state laws to those that require or permit an employer to commit an unfair employment practice.[1]

The majority nevertheless would save the California law on two grounds. First, it holds that the PDA does not require disability from pregnancy to be treated the same as other disabilities; instead, it forbids less favorable, but permits more favorable, benefits for pregnancy disability. The express command of the PDA is unambiguously to the contrary, and the legislative history casts no doubt on that mandate.

The legislative materials reveal Congress' plain intent not to put pregnancy in a class by itself within Title VII, as the majority does with its "floor * * * not a ceiling" approach. *Ante,* at 691. The Senate Report clearly stated:

> "By defining sex discrimination to include discrimination against pregnant women, the bill rejects the view that employers may treat pregnancy and its incidents as *sui generis,* without regard to its functional comparability to other conditions. Under this bill, the treatment of pregnant women in covered employment must focus not on their condition alone but on the actual effects of that condition on their ability to work. Pregnant women who are able to work must be permitted to work on the same conditions as other employees; and when they are not able to work for medical reasons, they must be accorded the same rights, leave

---

1. The same clear language preventing preferential treatment based on pregnancy forecloses respondents' argument that the California provision can be upheld as a legislative response to leave policies that have a disparate impact on pregnant workers. Whatever remedies Title VII would otherwise provide for victims of disparate impact, Congress expressly ordered pregnancy to be treated in the same manner as other disabilities.

privileges and other benefits, as other workers who are disabled from working."[2]

The House Report similarly stressed that the legislation did not mark a departure from Title VII principles:

> "It must be emphasized that this legislation, *operating as part of Title VII,* prohibits only discriminatory treatment. Therefore, it does not require employers to treat pregnant employees in any particular manner with respect to hiring, permitting them to continue working, providing sick leave, furnishing medical and hospital benefits, providing disability benefits, or any other matter. H.R. 6075 in no way requires the institution of any new programs where none currently exist. The bill would simply require that pregnant women be treated the same as other employees on the basis of their ability or inability to work."[3]

The majority correctly reports that Congress focused on discrimination against, rather than preferential treatment of, pregnant workers. There is only one direct reference in the legislative history to preferential treatment. Senator Brooke stated during the Senate debate: "I would emphasize most strongly that S. 995 in no way provides special disability benefits for working women. They have not demanded, nor asked, for such benefits. They have asked only to be treated with fairness, to be accorded the same employment rights as men." Given the evidence before Congress of the wide-spread discrimination against pregnant workers, it is probable that most Congresspersons did not seriously consider the possibility that someone would want to afford preferential treatment to pregnant workers. The parties and their *amici* argued vigorously to this Court the policy implications of preferential treatment of pregnant workers. In favor of preferential treatment it was urged with conviction that preferential treatment merely enables women, like men, to have children without losing their jobs. In opposition to preferential treatment it was urged with equal conviction that preferential treatment represents a resurgence of the 19th century protective legislation which perpetuated sex-role stereotypes and which impeded women in their efforts to take their rightful place in the workplace. See, *e.g., Muller v. Oregon,* 208 U.S. 412, 421–423, 28 S.Ct. 324, 326–327, 52 L.Ed. 551 (1908); *Bradwell v. Illinois,* 16 Wall. 130, 141, 21 L.Ed. 442 (1872) (Bradley, J., concurring). It is not the place of this Court, however, to resolve this policy dispute. Our task is to interpret Congress' intent in enacting the PDA. Congress' silence in its consideration of the PDA with respect to preferential treatment of pregnant workers cannot fairly be interpreted to abrogate the plain statements in the

---

2. S.Rep. No. 95–331, p. 4 (1977), Legislative History of the Pregnancy Discrimination Act of 1978 for the Senate Committee on Labor and Human Resources 41 (1980)(Leg.Hist.).

3. H.R.Rep. No. 95–948, p. 4 (1978), Leg. Hist. 150 (emphasis added), U.S.Code Cong. & Admin.News 1978, p. 4752. The same theme was also expressed repeatedly in the floor debates. Senator Williams, for example, the Chairman of the Senate Committee on Labor and Human Resources and a sponsor of the Senate bill, described the bill as follows in his introduction of the bill to the Senate:

"The central purpose of the bill is to require that women workers be treated equally with other employees on the basis of their ability or inability to work. The key to compliance in every case will be equality of treatment. In this way, the law will protect women from the full range of discriminatory practices which have adversely affected their status in the work force." 123 Cong.Rec. 29385 (1977), Leg.Hist. 62–63.

legislative history, not to mention the language of the statute, that equality of treatment was to be the guiding principle of the PDA.

Congress' acknowledgment of state antidiscrimination laws does not support a contrary inference. *Ante,* at 692–693. The most extensive discussion of state laws governing pregnancy discrimination is found in the House Report. It was reported that six States, Alaska, Connecticut, Maryland, Minnesota, Oregon and Montana, and the District of Columbia specifically included pregnancy in their fair employment practices laws. In 12 additional States, Illinois, Indiana, Iowa, Kansas, Massachusetts, Michigan, Missouri, New York, Pennsylvania, South Dakota, Washington, and Wisconsin, the prohibition on sex discrimination in the state fair employment practices law had been interpreted, either by a state court or the state enforcement agency, to require equal treatment of pregnant workers. Finally, five States, California, Hawaii, New Jersey, New York, and Rhode Island, had included pregnancy in their temporary disability laws under which private employers are required to provide partial wage replacement for temporary disabilities. The Report noted, however, that whereas California, New Jersey, and New York covered complications from pregnancy on the same basis as other disabilities, California, New Jersey, New York, and Rhode Island set maximum limits on the coverage required for disability associated with normal childbirth. The Report did not in any way set apart the Connecticut and Montana statutes, on which the majority relies, from the other state statutes. The House Report gave no indication that these statutes required anything more than equal treatment. Indeed, the state statutes were considered, not in the context of pre-emption, but in the context of a discussion of health insurance costs. The House Report expressly stated that "[t]he significance of this State coverage" is that "many employers are *already* under a State law obligation to provide benefits to pregnant disabled workers. Passage of the bill thus has little or no economic impact on such employers."

Nor does anything in the legislative history from the Senate side indicate that it carefully considered the state statutes, including those of Connecticut and Montana, and expressly endorsed their provisions. The Senate Report noted that "25 States presently interpret their own fair employment practices laws to prohibit sex discrimination based on pregnancy and childbirth," and Senator Williams presented during the Senate debate a list of States which required coverage for pregnancy and pregnancy-related disabilities, but there was no analysis of their provisions. The majority seems to interpret Senator Javits' acknowledgment that several state legislatures, including New York, his own State, had mandated certain benefits for pregnant employees as an unqualified endorsement of those state statutes. *Ante,* at 693, n. 23. Later, however, when pressed by Senator Hatch about the fact that the New York statute limited the required coverage of disability caused by pregnancy to eight weeks, Senator Javits had no hesitation in expressing his disagreement with the New York statute. Passing reference to state statutes without express recognition of their content and without express endorsement is insufficient in my view to override the PDA's clear equal-treatment mandate, expressed both in the statute and its legislative history.

The Court's second, and equally strange, ground is that even if the PDA does prohibit special benefits for pregnant women, an employer may still comply with both the California law and the PDA: it can adopt the specified leave policies for pregnancy and at the same time afford similar benefits for all other disabilities. This is untenable. California surely had no intent to require employers to provide general disability leave benefits. It intended to prefer pregnancy and went no farther. Extension of these benefits to the entire work force would be a dramatic increase in the scope of the state law and would impose a significantly greater burden on California employers. That is the province of the California Legislature. See *Wengler v. Druggists Mutual Insurance Co.*, 446 U.S. 142, 152–153, 100 S.Ct. 1540, 1546, 64 L.Ed.2d 107 (1980); *Caban v. Mohammed,* 441 U.S. 380, 392–393, n. 13, 99 S.Ct. 1760, 1768, n. 13, 60 L.Ed.2d 297 (1979); *Craig v. Boren,* 429 U.S. 190, 210, n. 24, 97 S.Ct. 451, 463, n. 24, 50 L.Ed.2d 397 (1976). Nor can § 12945(b)(2) be saved by applying Title VII in tandem with it, such that employers would be required to afford reinstatement rights to pregnant workers as a matter of state law but would be required to afford the same rights to all other workers as a matter of federal law. The text of the PDA does not speak to this question but it is clear from the legislative history that Congress did not intend for the PDA to impose such burdens on employers. As recognized by the majority, opposition to the PDA came from those concerned with the cost of including pregnancy in health and disability benefit plans. *Ante,* at 692. The House Report acknowledged these concerns and explained that the bill "in no way requires the institution of any new programs where none currently exist." The Senate Report gave a similar assurance. In addition, legislator after legislator stated during the floor debates that the PDA would not require an employer to institute a disability benefits program if it did not already have one in effect. Congress intended employers to be free to provide any level of disability benefits they wished—or none at all—as long as pregnancy was not a factor in allocating such benefits. The conjunction of § 12945(b)(2) and the PDA requires California employers to implement new minimum disability leave programs. Reading the state and federal statutes together in this fashion yields a result which Congress expressly disavowed.

In sum, preferential treatment of pregnant workers is prohibited by Title VII, as amended by the PDA. Section 12945(b)(2) of the California Gov't Code, which extends preferential benefits for pregnancy, is therefore pre-empted. It is not saved by § 708 because it purports to authorize employers to commit an unfair employment practice forbidden by Title VII.[12]

Notes on Cal Fed

1. The issue presented by *Cal Fed* touched off an intense dispute among feminist lawyers, usually referred to as the "equal treatment/special treatment" debate. That debate, and some of its broader implications for the meaning of equality between women and men, will be explored in Text Note, Ensuring Non-Discrimination, at p. 767, infra. The *Cal Fed* opinion itself, however, found wide-

12. Section 12945(b)(2) does not *require* employers to treat pregnant employees better than other disabled employees; employers are free voluntarily to extend the disability leave to all employees. But if this is not a statute which "purports to * * * permit the doing of any act which would be an unlawful employ- ment practice" under Title VII, I do not know what such a statute would look like. See, *ante,* at 694, n. 29.

Neither is § 12945(b)(2) saved by § 1104 of the Civil Rights Act since it is inconsistent with the equal-treatment purpose and provisions of Title VII.

spread acceptance among feminist groups. Even the National Organization for Women, which had filed an *amicus* brief urging extension or invalidation of the California statute, hailed Justice Marshall's opinion as a "clear and crucial victory for women". See National NOW TIMES, Winter 1987, at 6, col. 1. How do you explain NOW's attitudes?

2. The Montana statute cited in *Cal Fed* was challenged in Miller–Wohl Co., Inc. v. Commissioner of Labor and Industry, 692 P.2d 1243 (Mont.1984), vacated and remanded 479 U.S. 1050, 107 S.Ct. 919, 93 L.Ed.2d 972 (1987), opinion reinstated on remand 744 P.2d 871 (Mont.1987). In *Miller–Wohl,* Tamara Buley was hired on August 1, 1979 as a sales clerk by Miller–Wohl to work in its clothing store in Great Falls, Montana. Between August 1 and August 27, Buley was absent from work for several days and was unable to perform her job on other days because of pregnancy-related illness. She was terminated on August 27, 1979. Miller–Wohl had no policy of sick leave, leave of absence for protracted illness, or temporary disability plan for any employee with less than one year's seniority. After her discharge, Buley filed a complaint with the Montana Commissioner of Labor and Industry alleging that the employer's action violated the Montana Maternity Leave Act, which provided in part that

It shall be an unlawful employment practice for an employer or his agent to:

(1) terminate a woman's employment because of her pregnancy;

(2) refuse to grant to the employee a reasonable leave of absence for such pregnancy.

Montana Code Ann. §§ 39–7–203(1), 39–7–203(2). The Commissioner held that Buley's discharge for missing work due to "morning sickness" violated these provisions.

Like the employer in *Cal Fed,* the Miller–Wohl Company argued that Title VII preempted the Montana statute. In addition, however, Miller–Wohl argued that the statute violated the due process and equal protection clauses of the federal constitution. Since these arguments were not raised in *Cal Fed,* nor addressed by the Montana Supreme Court on remand in *Miller–Wohl,* they remain open. How should the constitutional questions be resolved?

3. In Troupe v. May Dept. Stores, 20 F.3d 734 (7th Cir.1994), the court held that the Pregnancy Discrimination Act does not protect a woman who was fired one day before her scheduled maternity leave after repeated tardiness resulting from morning sickness. She had been a "satisfactory" employee prior to her pregnancy. Judge Posner, complaining of the lack of any showing that the employer had treated plaintiff less favorably than other employees who were late to work for health reasons unrelated to pregnancy and who were about to take a protracted sick leave at the employer's expense, observed that:

The Pregnancy Discrimination Act does not, despite the urgings of feminist scholars, e.g., Herma Hill Kay, "Equality and Difference: The Case of Pregnancy," 1 Berkeley Women's L.J. 1, 30–31 (1985), require employers to offer maternity leave or take other steps to make it easier for pregnant women to work, cf. California Federal Savings & Loan Ass'n v. Guerra * * *; Barrash v. Bowen * * *; (EEOC Guidelines on Discrimination Because of Sex; Questions and Answers on the Pregnancy Discrimination Act)—to make it as easy, say, as it is for their spouses to continue working during pregnancy. Employers can treat pregnant women as badly as they treat similarly affected but nonpregnant employees, even to the point of "conditioning the availability of an employment benefit on an employee's decision to return to work after the end of the medical disability that pregnancy causes." Maganuco v. Leyden Community High School Dist. 212, 939 F.2d 440, 445 (7th Cir.1991).

Is that your understanding of Cal.Fed.? Look again at part III–B of Justice Marshall's opinion, especially the quotation from Senator Williams on p. 754. Does Judge Posner's approach to pregnancy discrimination "* * * guarantee women the basic right to participate fully and equally in the workplace, without denying them the fundamental right to full participation in family life"? What impact, if any, does *Cal Fed* have on the exclusion of fertile women from toxic workplaces? See the discussion of this question in the *Notes* on *Johnson Controls* at p. 805, infra.

4. In Wimberly v. Labor & Indus. Rel. Com'n., 479 U.S. 511, 107 S.Ct. 821, 93 L.Ed.2d 909 (1987), a unanimous Supreme Court held that a Missouri statute which denied unemployment benefits to a claimant who "has left his work voluntarily without good cause attributable to his work or to his employer" could be applied to deny benefits to workers who had quit because they were pregnant without violating the Federal Unemployment Tax Act, 26 U.S.C. § 3304(a)(12), which mandates that "no person shall be denied compensation under such State law solely on the basis of pregnancy or termination of pregnancy." Linda Wimberly had worked for the J.C. Penney Company for approximately three years when she became pregnant. She requested maternity leave in August, 1980, and received the employer's normal leave without guarantee of reinstatement. She gave birth on November 5, 1980, and notified the employer on December 1, 1980, that she was ready to return to work. She was told that no positions were then open, and she applied for unemployment benefits. Her claim was denied because, in the view of the Missouri Division of Employment Security, she had left work voluntarily and without good cause attributable to her work or to her employer. The Missouri Supreme Court upheld the Division's view of the state statute, and further held that it was not in conflict with the Federal Act. Justice O'Connor's opinion for the Court sustained Missouri's freedom to adopt its chosen policy toward pregnant workers, and disapproved a contrary interpretation of the Federal Act put forward by Brown v. Porcher, 660 F.2d 1001 (4th Cir.1981), cert. denied 459 U.S. 1150, 103 S.Ct. 796, 74 L.Ed.2d 1000 (1983). She reasoned that:

> The treatment of pregnancy-related terminations is a matter of considerable disparity among the States. Most States regard leave on account of pregnancy as a voluntary termination for good cause. Some of these States have specific statutory provisions enumerating pregnancy-motivated termination as good cause for leaving a job, while others, by judicial or administrative decision, treat pregnancy as encompassed within larger categories of good cause such as illness or compelling personal reasons. A few States, however, like Missouri, have chosen to define "leaving for good cause" narrowly. In these States, all persons who leave their jobs are disqualified from receiving benefits unless they leave for reasons directly attributable to the work or to the employer.

> Petitioner does not dispute that the Missouri scheme treats pregnant women the same as all other persons who leave for reasons not causally connected to their work or their employer, including those suffering from other types of temporary disabilities. [Citations omitted.] She contends, however, that § 3304(a)(12) is not simply an antidiscrimination statute, but rather that it mandates preferential treatment for women who leave work because of pregnancy. According to petitioner, § 3304(a)(12) affirmatively requires States to provide unemployment benefits to women who leave work

because of pregnancy when they are next available and able to work, regardless of the State's treatment of other similarly situated claimants. See Brief for Petitioner 19–25.

Contrary to petitioner's assertions, the plain import of the language of § 3304(a)(12) is that Congress intended only to prohibit States from singling out pregnancy for unfavorable treatment. The text of the statute provides that compensation shall not be denied under state law "solely on the basis of pregnancy." The focus of this language is on the basis for the State's decision, not the claimant's reason for leaving her job. Thus, a State could not decide to deny benefits to pregnant women while at the same time allowing benefits to persons who are in other respects similarly situated: the "sole basis" for such a decision would be on account of pregnancy. On the other hand, if a State adopts a neutral rule that incidentally disqualifies pregnant or formerly pregnant claimants as part of a larger group, the neutral application of that rule cannot readily be characterized as a decision made "solely on the basis of pregnancy." For example, under Missouri law, *all* persons who leave work for reasons not causally connected to the work or the employer are disqualified from receiving benefits. To apply this law, it is not necessary to know that petitioner left because of pregnancy: all that is relevant is that she stopped work for a reason bearing no causal connection to her work or her employer. Because the State's decision could have been made without ever knowing that petitioner had been pregnant, pregnancy was not the "sole basis" for the decision under a natural reading of § 3304(a)(12)'s language.

* * *

Even petitioner concedes that § 3304(a)(12) does not prohibit States from denying benefits to pregnant or formerly pregnant women who fail to satisfy neutral eligibility requirements such as ability to work and availability for work. See Brief for Petitioner 24. See also S.Rep. No. 94–1265, p. 21 (1976), U.S.Code Cong. & Admin.News 1976, pp. 5997, 6015 ("Pregnant individuals would * * * continue to be required to meet generally applicable criteria of availability for work and ability to work"); H.R.Rep. No. 94–755, p. 50 (1975). Nevertheless, she contends that the statute prohibits the application to pregnant women of neutral *disqualification* provisions. Reply Brief for Petitioner 8–9. But the statute's plain language will not support the distinction petitioner attempts to draw. The statute does not extend only to disqualification rules. It applies, by its own terms, to any decision to deny compensation. In both instances, the scope of the statutory mandate is the same: the State cannot single out pregnancy for disadvantageous treatment, but it is not compelled to afford preferential treatment.

Id., 479 U.S. at 515–518, 107 S.Ct. at 824–26, 93 L.Ed.2d at 914–16. Was *Wimberly* decided correctly? Is it consistent with *Cal Fed?* Does it ensure that pregnant workers are treated equally? Is the Missouri statute vulnerable to a challenge on due process grounds? See Sokol v. Smith, 671 F.Supp. 1243 (W.D.Mo.1987)(holding the statute does not force women to choose between bearing children and accepting employment). Is it vulnerable to challenge on disparate impact grounds? See Washington v. Davis, set forth at p. 972 infra.

5. Judge Hawkins, the district court judge in Brown v. Porcher, cited in Note 4, supra, thus summarized his reasons for reading the federal act broadly:

The problem addressed by the statute under scrutiny was that the period of unemployment (and attendant wage loss), which necessarily accompanies pregnancy, can serve to force otherwise employable women out of the job market. Like all other unemployed workers, women who have stopped working to have a child can readily remain effective participants in the economy only if assistance is provided to encourage their return to work when they are physically able to do so. By providing partial wage replacement for pregnancy-related periods of actual unemployment, Congress sought to facilitate the process of seeking reemployment. Absent some assistance, many women would be hampered in their effort to rejoin the work force. Absent, for example, some income to pay for child care expenses while looking for work, a woman cannot effectively compete in the employment process with others. If the statute is to fulfill the remedial purpose of encouraging a woman's search for a suitable job after having a child, it must be read to forbid the policies and practices complained of in this case. For it was those very policies which were used to deny plaintiffs the partial wage replacement that would have facilitated their job hunting efforts.

Brown v. Porcher, 502 F.Supp. 946, 956 (D.S.C.1980), affirmed with modifications 660 F.2d 1001 (4th Cir.1981), cert. denied 459 U.S. 1150, 103 S.Ct. 796, 74 L.Ed.2d 1000 (1983), disapproved, Wimberly v. Labor & Indus. Rel. Com'n., 479 U.S. 511, 107 S.Ct. 821, 93 L.Ed.2d 909 (1987). Whose approach do you prefer? That taken by Justice O'Connor or Judge Hawkins?

6. When is it permissible for an employer to fire an employee because of her pregnancy? See Chambers v. Omaha Girls Club, 629 F.Supp. 925 (D.Neb.1986), affirmed 834 F.2d 697 (8th Cir.1987), rehearing denied 840 F.2d 583 (8th Cir.1988), rejecting the claim of a black female that the Girls Club violated Title VII, among other laws, when it fired her from its staff because she was unmarried and pregnant. The employer persuaded Chief Judge Beam that its "Negative Role Model Policy" which declared single parent pregnancies to be negative role modeling for the predominantly black teenagers who were members of the Girls Club did not discriminate on the basis of sex, race, or a combination of both sex and race.

7. Does *Cal Fed* mean that Title VII permits employers to limit childrearing leave, as distinguished from childbearing leave, to mothers? In Schafer v. Board of Public Education, 903 F.2d 243 (3d Cir.1990), the Pittsburgh Board of Education argued that a provision in its collective bargaining agreement which expressly limited maternity leave to female teachers was a "permissible accommodation to females" under *Cal Fed* that justified its denial of an unpaid leave for the 1981–1982 school year to Gerald Schafer for the purpose of caring for his son. Judge A. Leon Higginbotham, Jr., rejected this interpretation of *Cal Fed,* holding that under Title VII the provision was "per se void for any leave granted beyond the period of actual physical disability on account of pregnancy, childbirth or related medical conditions." Id., 903 F.2d at 248.

8. On February 5, 1993, President Clinton signed into law the Family and Medical Leave Act of 1993 (FMLA), P.L. 103–3, codified at 29 U.S.C. §§ 2601–2654, which took effect August 5, 1993. The Act provides for unpaid leave of up to 12 weeks in any 12–month period for the birth or adoption of a child, or to care for a child, spouse, or parent with a serious health condition, or for the employee's own serious health condition. The Act only applies to employers with 50 or more employees. To be eligible, an employee must have worked at least one year, and

must have worked for a minimum total of 1,250 hours over that year (an average of 25 hours per week). FMLA provides that the employer must return the employee to her/his old job or to an equivalent position at the end of the 12–week leave. The employer must also continue any health care benefits it currently provides during the leave, but if the employee does not return to work when the leave ends, the employee can be required to repay the cost of any employer-paid health-care premiums. FMLA permits the employer to require medical opinions and certifications in support of the employee's request for the unpaid leave.

The FMLA was passed by Congress in 1990 and 1992, but vetoed both times by President Bush. Members of the women's movement had lobbied for this type of legislation for many years. It was eventually enacted with the strong support of the powerful lobby for retired persons, due to its provision of leave for an employee to take care of seriously ill parents, in addition to child care leave. The major limitation of FMLA is its lack of paid leave; only those workers who can otherwise financially support their households during a leave can take advantage of this statute. For a critical analysis of FMLA and suggested alternative approaches, see Nancy Dowd, Family Values and Valuing Family: A Blueprint for Family Leave, 30 Harv. J. on Legis. 335 (1993). Despite its limitations, Martin Malin argues that FMLA is useful in encouraging fathers to take parental leave. M. Malin, Fathers and Parental Leave, 72 Tex. L. R. 1047 (1994).

Text Note
Ensuring Non–Discrimination

Most of the constitutional challenges to classifications based on sex considered in Chapter I, as well as the Title VII statutory challenges considered in Chapter III, were brought by plaintiffs seeking access to opportunities or entitlements available to members of the other sex. The litigation was designed to remove barriers preventing entry or possession. The legal theory underlying these cases is based on the assumption that men and women are similarly situated with respect to the matter in dispute, and that the sex-based restriction is invalid, either because the line drawn was arbitrary,[1] failed to reflect a substantial relationship to an important governmental purpose,[2] or violated the statutory antidiscrimination principle contained in Title VII.[3] That legal theory was modeled on the successful strategy used earlier to attack race discrimination: the demonstration that there are few, if any, differences between blacks (or members of other minority groups) and whites that can be used as the basis for legal classifications. As we have seen,[4] in philosophical terms the model is an assimilationist one: it asserts that racial differences are irrelevant to the public order. The assimilationist model is a powerful one that ultimately became symbolic of the national resolve to overcome the institutional racism that had been built into the very fabric of American society.[5]

1. Reed v. Reed, 404 U.S. 71, 92 S.Ct. 251, 30 L.Ed.2d 225 (1971), set out at p. 23, supra.

2. Mississippi University for Women v. Hogan, 458 U.S. 718, 102 S.Ct. 3331, 73 L.Ed.2d 1090 (1982), set out at p. 137, supra; Craig v. Boren, 429 U.S. 190, 97 S.Ct. 451, 50 L.Ed.2d 397 (1976), set out at p. 41, supra.

3. Phillips v. Martin Marietta Corp., 400 U.S. 542, 91 S.Ct. 496, 27 L.Ed.2d 613 (1971), set out at p. 714, supra.

4. See Introduction: What is Equality Between the Sexes?, at p. 1 supra.

5. See generally, Richard Kluger, Simple Justice: The History of *Brown v. Board of*

We have questioned the limitations of the analogy between race and sex discrimination for constitutional purposes.[6] Here, we will broaden that inquiry by noting that women and men display characteristic and undeniable sex differences along a broad spectrum ranging from the biological reproductive sex differences that define male and female to the social and psychological gender characteristics based on cultural norms that comprise our notions of masculinity and femininity.[7] According legal significance to many of these differences led an earlier generation to produce the protective labor laws that are rightly characterized today as having restricted women's opportunities by excluding them from the marketplace.[8] That earlier experience counsels against modern attempts to justify sex-based classifications on the need of members of one sex or the other for special protections.[9] But it may also be a mistake to deny that sex differences have any legal relevance. Such a position may hamper women's struggle for equality today by conditioning their full participation in the work force upon their willingness to conform to a male norm, thereby confirming the conventional view that the primary labor force should be restricted to males and to females who behave like males.[10] The antidiscrimination principle embodied in the assimilationist model, in other words, can prevent discrimination only to the extent the disadvantaged group is similar to the advantaged group.[11] The larger task of ensuring non-discrimination by providing equal opportunity to dissimilar groups is beyond its ken. Because it may be necessary to take account of some sex differences in order to provide equal opportunity to both women and men, a theory of equality between the sexes must confront the question of difference.

Feminist legal theorists were forced to confront that question by the Supreme Court's approach to the first round of pregnancy cases, which denied benefits to pregnant workers.[12] Their initial response was to seek an amendment to Title VII to correct the Court's mistaken holding in General Electric Co. v. Gilbert[13] that an employer's exclusion of pregnancy from its temporary disability package did not constitute discrimination based on sex. That amendment, the Pregnancy Discrimination Act, was drafted to require that "* * * women affected by pregnancy * * * shall be treated the same for all employment-related purposes, including receipt of benefits under fringe benefit programs, as other persons not so affected but similar in their ability or inability to work, * * *."[14] This second clause of the Pregnancy Discrimination Act was specifically designed to overrule *Gilbert*. It did not purport to be a comprehensive effort to deal with all sex differences that might be relevant in the employment context. Indeed, such an effort would have been inconsistent with the purpose of the Act, which was designed to conceal, rather than to identify, the differences between pregnancy and other disabilities.

Education and Black America's Struggle for Equality (1976).

6. See generally Herma Hill Kay, Models of Equality, 1985 U.Ill.L.Rev. 39.

7. See generally, Anne Fausto–Sterling, Myths of Gender: Biological Theories About Women and Men (1985). For a humorous alphabetical catalogue of various statements about male-female differences, see Jane Barr Stump, What's the Difference? How Men and Women Compare (1985).

8. See generally, Judith Baer, The Chains of Protection (1978).

9. See Wendy Williams, The Equality Crisis: Some Reflections on Culture, Courts, and Feminism, 7 Women's Rights L.Rep. 175, 196 (1982).

10. See Christine Littleton, Reconstructing Sexual Equality, 75 Calif.L.Rev. 1279, 1320–22 (1987).

11. See Kay, supra note 6, at 78–81.

12. See General Electric Co. v. Gilbert, 429 U.S. 125, 97 S.Ct. 401, 50 L.Ed.2d 343 (1976)(private employer's refusal to cover pregnancy under temporary disability package did not violate Title VII); Geduldig v. Aiello, 417 U.S. 484, 94 S.Ct. 2485, 41 L.Ed.2d 256 (1974)(public employer's refusal to cover pregnancy under temporary disability package did not violate the equal protection clause).

13. 429 U.S. 125, 97 S.Ct. 401, 50 L.Ed.2d 343 (1976).

14. Pub.L. No. 95–555, 92 Stat. 2076, codified at 42 U.S.C. § 2000e(k)(1982).

The first clause of the Act, however, specified that "[t]he terms 'because of sex' or 'on the basis of sex' include, but are not limited to, because of or on the basis of pregnancy, * * *."[15] In the second round of pregnancy cases, employers invoked this clause to invalidate state laws in Montana and California that were designed to benefit pregnant workers, arguing that these laws discriminated against men.[16]

The employers' claims, asserted first in Miller–Wohl v. Commissioner of Labor & Industry,[17] were an unanticipated interpretation of the PDA that split the feminist legal community. Professor Wendy Williams, whose testimony[18] had been influential in securing the passage of the PDA, expressed the dilemma best:[19]

> [T]he same doctrinal approach that permits pregnancy to be treated *worse* than other disabilities is the same one that will allow the state constitutional freedom to create special *benefits* for pregnant women. The equality approach to pregnancy (such as that embodied in the PDA) necessarily creates not only the desired floor under the pregnant woman's rights but also the ceiling which the *Miller–Wohl* case threw into relief. If we can't have it both ways, we need to think carefully about which way we want to have it.

In the years that have elapsed since Williams challenged feminists in 1982 to "think carefully about which way we want to have it," several writers have offered responses not only to the specific question of pregnancy, but also to the general problem of equality and difference. Williams herself has ably defended what she calls the "equal treatment" position, stressing the similarities between women and men rather than their differences and urging that overt sex-based classifications should be generally impermissible, while facially neutral laws that have a disproportionately negative effect upon one sex should be justified by their proponents under an elevated burden.[20] More recently, writing in collaboration with Professor Nadine Taub,[21] Williams has acknowledged that an assimilation model is inadequate to produce equality. The authors observe that "[w]e have accomplished relatively little, it seems to us, if all we can claim is that we have guaranteed for women born tall as the average man or willing and able to adopt traditional male life patterns and habits the right to move into the male world."[22] They propose to enlarge the concept of formal equality by bringing in the doctrine that employment discrimination may also result from an employer's use of a facially-neutral rule or practice that has a disparate impact on protected groups of employees such as women.[23] The disparate impact doctrine was first recognized for Title VII purposes by the United States Supreme Court in Griggs v. Duke Power Company,[24] set out at p. 580, infra.

15. Ibid.

16. See Herma Hill Kay, Equality and Difference: The Case of Pregnancy, 1 Berkeley Women's L.J. 1, 15 & nn. 80–81 (1985).

17. 214 Mont. 238, 692 P.2d 1243 (Mont. 1984), vacated 479 U.S. 1050, 107 S.Ct. 919, 93 L.Ed.2d 972 (1987), opinion reinstated on remand 228 Mont. 505, 744 P.2d 871 (Mont. 1987).

18. See Discrimination on the Basis of Pregnancy, 1977: Hearings Before the Subcommittee on Labor of the Senate Committee on Human Resources, 95th Cong., 1st Sess. 113–48 (1977)(Testimony of Wendy Webster Williams).

19. Williams, supra note 9, at 196 (emphasis in original).

20. Williams, Equality's Riddle: Pregnancy and the Equal Treatment/Special Treatment Debate, 13 N.Y.U.Rev.L. & Soc. Change 325 (1984–85).

21. Taub & Williams, Will Equality Require More Than Assimilation, Accommodation or Separation From The Existing Social Structure?, 37 Rutgers L.Rev./Civ.Rits.Devs. 825, 830 (1985).

22. Id., at 832.

23. Id., at 836–44.

24. 401 U.S. 424, 91 S.Ct. 849, 28 L.Ed.2d 158 (1971).

Professor Ann Scales initially proposed an "incorporationist" approach that would recognize special rights for women only with respect to unique sex characteristics, such as pregnancy and breastfeeding.[25] Linda Krieger and Patricia Cooney drew on Scales's approach, among others, to defend the Montana statute in *Miller–Wohl* as an example of the type of "positive action" necessary to "facilitate substantive, rather than merely formalistic, equality between men and women."[26] Professor Sylvia Law proposed that laws regulating reproductive biology be removed from the comparative antidiscrimination principle, and that their validity be judged instead under a two-part test that would first determine whether such laws significantly perpetuate either "the oppression of women or culturally imposed sex-role constraints on individual freedom" and, if so, would apply a strict scrutiny standard to determine whether the law serves a compelling state interest.[27] Professor Stephanie Wildman also wished to discard the antidiscrimination principle, with its mandatory comparison between women and men; instead, she proposed a "participatory perspective" to ensure full societal participation by women, thus ending sex discrimination.[28]

Dean Herma Hill Kay has proposed that biological reproductive sex differences should be relevant for legal purposes only during those discrete episodes when they are being exercised, and should not be relevant before or after those episodes.[29] She has argued that this "episodic analysis" may serve as a way of harmonizing some of the views of the participants in the "equal treatment/special treatment" debate: it accepts Williams's view that the assimilationist approach has worked well as a tool against sex discrimination in those cases where the two groups being compared are not different in any relevant way, but it insists that during the episode of pregnancy a woman's body functions in a unique way that must be recognized in order to prevent penalizing her for exercising her reproductive capacity.[30] She concluded that, "[i]f confined in this way, the recognition of pregnancy as 'unique' will enable the law to treat women differently than men during a limited period when their needs may be greater than those of men as a way of ensuring that women will be equal to men with respect to their overall employment opportunities."[31]

Professor Lucinda Finley also sought to transcend the equal treatment/special treatment debate by examining the ways in which equality analysis allows participants on both sides of the argument to avoid an examination of gender hierarchy.[32] She characterized the debate as essentially one "between two strands of traditional liberal equality theory—formal versus substantive equality, or equal opportunity versus equal outcomes."[33] She asserted that both strands of equality theory are subject to criticism for indeterminacy, the use of a male norm as the standard against which similarity and difference are measured, and a focus on individual autonomy and rights analysis.[34] She focused instead on the meaning and significance of an attribution of difference, and on the interconnections

25. Scales, Towards a Feminist Jurisprudence, 56 Ind.L.Rev. 375 (1980–81).

26. Krieger & Cooney, The Miller–Wohl Controversy: Equal Treatment, Positive Action and the Meaning of Women's Equality, 13 Golden Gate U.L.Rev. 513, 572 (1983).

27. Law, Rethinking Sex and the Constitution, 132 U.Pa.L.Rev. 955, 1008–12 (1984).

28. Wildman, The Legitimation of Sex Discrimination: A Critical Response to Supreme Court Jurisprudence, 63 Or.L.Rev. 265, 304–07 (1984).

29. Kay, supra note 16, at 21–28.

30. Id., at 32–37.

31. Id., at 34 (footnote omitted).

32. Finley, Transcending Equality Theory: A Way Out of the Maternity and the Workplace Debate, 86 Colum.L.Rev. 1118, 1121 (1986).

33. Id., at 1144.

34. Id., at 1148–63.

between aspects of difference.[35] She suggested that such a focus can help prevent the attribution of difference from being experienced as stigmatizing or seen as hierarchical.[36] She also proposed to supplement the notion of rights with the conception of responsibility.[37] Taking such a dual approach, she concluded, will enable "both women and men to combine their work lives with involvement in the family."[38]

Professor Nancy Dowd advocated that "a wholesale restructuring and reexamination of the workplace is needed" to achieve true equal employment opportunity for women.[39] She went on to state that:[40]

The existing employment structure must ensure actual, not merely formal equality of employment opportunity. This requires not only eliminating facially neutral practices that disadvantage pregnant women, but also implementing affirmative policies that redress the disproportionate impact of the existing structure on pregnant women. Even more fundamentally, the underlying assumptions of the structure of the workplace must be examined, particularly assumptions concerning the relationship between work and family responsibilities.

She suggested that the sex differences approach used by the United States Supreme Court should be refined to limit the definition of "sex differences" narrowly, so that it would include only "biological, definitional differences" and exclude "social and cultural stereotypes"; laws or policies that take account of such stereotypes in order to remedy the current effects of historical discrimination, however, are permissible.[41] If the doctrine is so refined, she concluded, "[t]he incorporation of a sex differences approach in the definition of sex discrimination and the concept of equality ultimately is justified on the basis of public policy, as an essential means to achieve the goal of equal opportunity."[42]

Professor Christine Littleton has boldly taken a broader approach to the question of difference and offered a model of "equality as acceptance," by which she means "simply that *difference between human beings, whether perceived or real, and whether biologically or socially based, should not be permitted to make a difference in the lived-out equality of those persons.*"[43] She suggested that such an encompassing principle is required to overcome an insidious and complex form of male domination, which she called "phallocentrism," and defined as "a self-referencing system by which those things culturally identified as 'male' are more highly valued than those identified as 'female,' even when they appear to have little or nothing to do with either biological sex."[44] She thus summarized the feminist critique of equality analysis:[45]

* * * current equality analysis is phallocentrically biased in three respects: (1) it is inapplicable once it encounters "real" difference; (2) it locates difference in women, rather than in relationships; and (3) it fails to question the assumptions that social institutions are gender-neutral, and that women and men are therefore similarly related to those institutions.

35. Id., at 1167–70.

36. Id., at 1163–67.

37. Id., at 1171–79.

38. Id., at 1182.

39. Dowd, Maternity Leave: Taking Sex Differences into Account, 54 Fordham L.Rev. 699 (1986).

40. Id., at 699–700.

41. Id., at 762–64.

42. Id., at 764.

43. Littleton, supra note 10, at 1284–85.

44. Id., at 1280.

45. Id., at 1308.

Littleton rejected the position taken by adherents of the special treatment view (which she terms "asymmetrical" theories) that male institutions should take account of, and make accommodations for, women's differences because that position implicitly accepts the prevailing norm as generally legitimate. She proposed instead a model of acceptance, not accommodation, and offered the following illustration:[46]

> The distinction between accommodation and acceptance may be illustrated by a rather commonplace example. I remember a feminist lawyer walking up to a podium to deliver a speech. The podium was high enough that she could not reach the microphone. While arrangements were being modified, she pointedly noted, "Built for a man!" Accommodation is a step platform brought for her to stand on. Acceptance is a podium whose height is adjustable.

She concluded by summarizing the major points in her argument on behalf of the acceptance model:[47]

> (1) in order to be faithful to feminist critique, a reconstructed equality norm must be capable of application across or beyond difference; (2) although no reconstruction undertaken under conditions of inequality can claim to be completely free from phallocentric bias, a reconstruction can increase equality and invite later, freer reconstructions by shifting the frame and moving the margin into the picture; (3) making difference costless (or even cost less) will shift the frame, allowing us to see ever more subtle forms of phallocentric bias while reducing the danger that difference will be used to recreate inequality; (4) the model of costless difference can be applied *within* contexts without impeding later efforts to apply it *across* contexts; and (5) much of the model's usefulness can be realized now, without waiting for major legislative or cultural change.

Modifying her earlier view, Professor Ann Scales decided that the effort to "arrive at a definitive list of differences" was not helpful. Instead, she later urged that:[48]

> Our aim must be to affirm differences as emergent and infinite. We must seek a legal system that works and, at the same time, makes differences a cause for celebration, not classification.

In this essay, Scales accepted an approach advocated by Professor Catharine MacKinnon:[49]

> Law must embrace a version of equality that focuses on the real issues— domination, disadvantage and disempowerment—instead of on the interminable and diseased issue of differences between the sexes. I endorse the definition of equality proposed by Professor Catharine MacKinnon in 1979: The test in any challenge should be "whether the policy or practice in question integrally contributes to the maintenance of an underclass or a deprived position because of gender status." MacKinnon contrasts this to the "differences approach," calling it the "inequality approach." I would call the former "thinking like a lawyer;" the latter, "thinking like a person."

46. Id., at 1314.

47. Id., at 1337.

48. Scales, The Emergence of Feminist Jurisprudence: An Essay, 95 Yale L.J. 1373, 1376 (1986).

49. Id., at 1394 (footnotes omitted; citing C. MacKinnon, Sexual Harassment of Working Women 110 (1979)).

Do you detect an emerging consensus among feminist legal theorists to the problem of equality and difference?[50] Feminist writers continue to explore the practical and theoretical dimensions of equality and difference.[51] A distinctive minority voice is emerging that focuses on the confluence of race and sex in feminist legal theory.[52]

How do you think the question of difference should be resolved in specific cases of employment discrimination? Consider the following examples of cases raising aspects of this question in contexts other than pregnancy:

1. Lynch v. Freeman, 817 F.2d 380 (6th Cir.1987). Plaintiff Eileen Lynch, a carpenter apprentice working for the Construction Service Branch of the Tennessee Valley Authority, was fired for "unsatisfactory conduct in work area." Her conduct consisted of unauthorized use of a restroom located indoors in the powerhouse rather than the portable toilets provided for construction workers. She argued in part that the employer's provision of portable toilets that were dirty, often had only soiled toilet paper or no paper at all, lacked running water, and were not equipped with sanitary napkins had a disparate impact on women employees by subjecting them to health hazards not experienced by men. In order to avoid using the portable toilets, Ms. Lynch began holding her urine until she left work, a practice that could cause bladder infection. Ms. Lynch did contract cystitis, a type of urinary tract infection. She was advised that the use of soiled toilet paper, as well as holding her urine, could cause this condition. She began using the powerhouse indoor restroom, and her infection disappeared.

50. See, generally, Martha Minow, Foreword: Justice Engendered, 101 Harv.L.Rev. 10 (1987)(exploring broadly the dilemma of difference reflected in Supreme Court adjudication during the 1986 Term); John D. Gibson, Note, Childbearing and Childrearing: Feminists and Reform, 73 Va.L.Rev. 1145 (1987)(reviewing the equal treatment/special treatment debate in the context of existing employee leave policies and practices, and supporting parental and nurturing leave policies in part because such policies would "formally end the liberal state's endorsement of the 'cult' of motherhood and the nuclear family").

51. See, e.g., Martha Minow, Making All The Difference (1990); Deborah Rhode, Justice and Gender 274–321 (1990); Joan Williams, Dissolving the Sameness/Difference Debate: A Post–Modern Path Beyond Essentialism in Feminist and Critical Race Theory, 1991 Duke L.J. 296 (1991); Deborah Rhode, The "No–Problem" Problem: Feminist Challenges and Cultural Change, 100 Yale L.J. 1731 (1991); Feminist Jurisprudence Symposium, 24 Ga. L.Rev. 759 (1990); Symposium, Feminism in the Law: Theory, Practice and Criticism, 1989 University of Chicago Legal Forum; Symposium, Voices of Experience: New Responses to Gender Discourse, 24 Harv.Civ.Rts.Civ.Lib. L.Rev. 1–172 (1989); Robin West, Jurisprudence and Gender, 55 U.Chi.L.Rev. 1 (1988); Mary Becker, Prince Charming: Abstract Equality, 1987 Supreme Court Review 201 (1988); Judith Brown, Wendy Parmet & Phyllis Barmann, The Failure of Gender Equality: An Essay in Constitutional Dissonance, 36 Buf.

L.Rev. 573 (1987). Some writers are beginning to examine feminist methodology in its own right. See, e.g., Katharine T. Bartlett, Feminist Legal Methods, 103 Harv.L.Rev. 829 (1990); Deborah Rhode, Feminist Critical Theories, 42 Stan.L.Rev. 617 (1990); Pat Cain, Feminist Jurisprudence: Grounding The Theories, 4 Berkeley Wom.L.J. 191 (1989–90); Mari Matsuda, When The First Quail Calls: Multiple Consciousness as Jurisprudential Method, 11 Wom.Rts.L.Rptr. 7 (1989).

52. See, e.g., Patricia Williams, The Alchemy of Race and Rights: Diary of a Law Professor (1991); Symposium: Black Women Law Professors, Building a Community at the Intersection of Race and Gender, 6 Berkeley Wom. L.J. (1990–91); Paulette Caldwell, A Hair Piece: Perspectives on the Intersection of Race and Gender, 1991 Duke L.J. 365 (1991); Angela Harris, Race and Essentialism in Feminist Legal Theory, 42 Stan.L.Rev. 581 (1990); Kimberle Crenshaw, Demarginalizing the Intersection of Race and Sex: A Black Feminist Critique of Antidiscrimination Doctrine, Feminist Theory and Antiracist Politics, 1989 U.Chi. Leg.F. 139; Judy Scales–Trent, Black Women and the Constitution: Finding Our Place, Asserting Our Rights, 42 Harv.Civ.Rts.Civ.Lib. L.Rev. 9 (1989); Regina Austin, Sapphire Bound!, 1989 Wis.L.Rev. 539 (1989); Mari Matsuda, Looking To The Bottom: Critical Legal Studies and Reparations, 22 Harv.Civ. Rts.Civ.Lib.L.Rev. 323 (1987).

Defendant TVA argued that since the portable toilet facilities for men and women are the same, the sexes were being treated equally. It characterized plaintiff's argument as a plea for preferential treatment for women, not required by Title VII.

Judge John T. Nixon, Jr., the district court judge, found that women were placed at a higher risk of urinary tract infection than men, who were not exposed to the same dangers because of "anatomical differences between the sexes." He nevertheless concluded that plaintiff had not made out a prima facie case of sex discrimination, noting that she and other women construction workers could avoid the increased danger to their health by taking the following "simple measures": bringing their own toilet paper to work; refraining from sitting on the dirty toilet seats; using the waterless hand cleaner provided by the employer; and seeking permission to use the indoor restroom during their menstrual periods.

The Sixth Circuit, reversing, held that Judge Nixon had erred as a matter of law in concluding that plaintiff had not made out a prima facie case. Noting that "[a]ny employment practice that adversely affects the health of female employees while leaving male employees unaffected has a significantly discriminatory impact," Chief Judge Lively held that plaintiff was entitled to judgment on her disparate impact claim. Judge Boggs, in dissent, objected that the majority had confused Title VII with the Occupational Safety and Health Act, and observed that "I see nothing [in the legislative history of Title VII], or in the whole movement toward sexual equality in the workplace embodied in Title VII, to enact a requirement that working conditions for all must be upgraded to some unstated standard before women can have full access to the workplace."

2. EEOC v. Sears, Roebuck & Co., 628 F.Supp. 1264 (N.D.Ill.1986), affirmed 839 F.2d 302 (7th Cir.1988). Charged by the EEOC with practicing nationwide discrimination against women in violation of Title VII and the Equal Pay Act, Sears chose to rely on an asserted difference between the interests of women and men in certain types of jobs. Specifically, Sears defended against the allegation that it intentionally discriminated against women in hiring and promotion into commission sales jobs by showing that, although it had made repeated good faith efforts to recruit women for such jobs, women had little interest in commission sales jobs. To prove this defense, Sears offered testimony from its store managers, personnel managers, and other officials regarding their efforts to recruit women into commission sales jobs as part of a company-wide voluntary affirmative action program. In addition, Sears presented an expert witness, Dr. Rosalind Rosenberg, a specialist in American Women's History at Barnard College. Judge Nordberg, who found Dr. Rosenberg to be "a highly credible witness," thus summarized her testimony:[53]

> [W]omen generally prefer to sell soft-line products, such as apparel, housewares or accessories sold on a noncommission bases, and are less interested in selling products such as fencing, refrigeration equipment and tires. Women tend to be more interested than men in the social and cooperative aspects of the workplace. Women tend to see themselves as less competitive. They often view noncommission sales as more attractive than commission sales, because they can enter and leave the job more easily, and because there is more social contact and friendship, and less stress in noncommission selling.

---

53. EEOC v. Sears, Roebuck & Co., 628 F.Supp. 1264, 1308 & n. 42 (N.D.Ill.1986), af- firmed 839 F.2d 302 (7th Cir.1988).

Sears also offered the testimony of Dr. Irving Crespi, a prominent consultant specializing in public opinion polling and market research. He drew the following conclusions from national surveys and polls taken from the mid–1930s through 1983 relating to the changing status of women in American society:[54]

> Dr. Crespi found that: (1) men were more likely than women to be interested in working at night or on weekends, (2) women were more likely than men to be interested in regular daytime work; (3) men were more likely than women to be interested in sales jobs involving a high degree of competition among salespersons; (4) men were more likely to be interested in jobs where there was a chance of making more money, even though it involved a risk of losing the job if they did not sell enough; and (5) men were more likely than women to be motivated by the pay of a job than by the nature of the job and whether they like it.

To rebut these points, the EEOC offered the testimony of Dr. Alice Kessler–Harris, Professor of History at Hofstra University, Dr. Janice Fanning Madden, Associate Professor of Regional Science at the University of Pennsylvania, and Ms. Eileen Applebaum. As his opinion shows, Judge Nordberg was not impressed by their presentation:[55]

> These witnesses described the general history of women in the workforce, and contend essentially that there are no significant differences between the interests and career aspirations of men and women. They assert that women are influenced only by the opportunities presented to them, not by their preferences. They often focused on small segments of women, rather than the majority of women, in giving isolated examples of women who have seized opportunities for greater income in nontraditional jobs when they have arisen.

> However, these experts provided little persuasive authority to support their theories. The particular examples of unknown numbers and proportions of women in history to which they refer generally focus on small groups

---

54. Id., at 1308.

55. Id., at 1314. The expert testimony offered at the *Sears Roebuck* trial touched off a debate among feminist scholars every bit as intense as that generated among feminist legal practitioners and scholars by the *Miller–Wohl* and *Cal Fed* cases. See Archives, Women's History Goes to Trial: EEOC v. Sears, Roebuck and Company, 11 SIGNS 751 (1986)(setting forth the Offer of Proof Concerning the Testimony of Dr. Rosalind Rosenberg and the Written Testimony of Dr. Alice Kessler–Harris, and noting that "[t]his turn of events—a courtroom confrontation between feminist scholars offering antithetical interpretations of the new scholarship in women's history—holds an obvious potential for animosity. Instead, we hope it can serve as a catalyst for fruitful debate"). See also Milkman, Women's History and the Sears Case, 12 Feminist Studies 375, 394–95 (No. 2, Summer 1986)(giving an account of the case and the dispute between Rosenberg and Kessler–Harris and warning feminist scholars "that we must be self-conscious in our formulations, keeping firmly in view the ways in which our work can be exploited politically").

Judge Cudahy, dissenting from the affirmance of *Sears,* charged that the majority's acceptance of this expert testimony was like agreeing with the proposition "that women are by nature happier cooking, doing the laundry and chauffeuring the children to softball games than arguing appeals or selling stocks." EEOC v. Sears, Roebuck & Co., 839 F.2d 302, 361 (7th Cir.1988)(dissenting opinion of Judge Cudahy). Is this an appropriate analogy?

See Thomas Haskel & Sanford Levinson, Academic Freedom and Expert Witnessing: Historians and the *Sears* case, 66 Tex.L.Rev. 1629, 1635, 1638 (1988), denouncing the criticism of Rosenberg's testimony as a violation of her academic freedom while criticizing Kessler–Harris's testimony for its "obvious exaggeration" and dismissing the EEOC's trial strategy in *Sears* as "bewilderingly wrongheaded." The piece is followed by a response from Kessler–Harris and a reply from the authors: see Alice Kessler–Harris, Response, 67 Tex.L.Rev. 429 (1988); Haskell & Levinson, Reply, 67 Tex.L.Rev. 1951 (1989).

of unusual women and their demonstrated abilities in various historical contexts, not on the majority of women or their interests at the time of this case. The sweeping generalizations these witnesses sought to make are not supported by credible evidence. [In footnote 63, Judge Nordberg rejected Dr. Kessler–Harris's conclusion that "numerical differences between men and women within jobs in the workforce can only be explained by sex discrimination by employers."] * * *

More convincing testimony in this area was offered by Sears expert Dr. Rosalind Rosenberg. Dr. Rosenberg testified that, although differences between men and women have diminished in the past two decades, these differences still exist and may account for different proportions of men and women in various jobs. She offered the more reasonable conclusion that differences in the number of men and women in a job could exist without discrimination by an employer.

How would the feminist legal theorists cited above resolve these cases? How would you?

Does this exploration of equality and difference in the context of sex and gender carry implications for the continued acceptance of the assimilation model in the context of racial discrimination? Black scholar William Wilson, Professor of Sociology and Public Policy at the University of Chicago, has recently questioned the efficacy of that model to achieve racial equality.[56] Wilson points out that neither the traditional civil rights model of nondiscrimination directed at eliminating barriers to individual access posed by racial bias nor the newer focus on group entitlements reflected in affirmative action programs designed to increase the numbers of ethnic and minority group members in preferred positions has had much success in addressing the problems of the truly disadvantaged. This is true, Wilson argues, because both equal treatment and preferential treatment approaches benefit primarily those blacks who come from advantaged family backgrounds and are therefore best qualified for the positions made available on a preferential basis. He advocates instead what James Fishkin[57] has called the "principle of equality of life chances." Wilson explains that "[t]he major factor that distinguishes the principle of equality of life chances from the principles of equality of individual opportunity and equality of group opportunity is the recognition that the problems of truly disadvantaged individuals—class background, low income, a broken home, inadequate housing, poor education, or cultural or linguistic differences—may not be clearly related to the issue of previous discrimination."[58] He goes on to propose that:[59]

> Under the principle of equality of life chances, efforts to correct family background disadvantages through such programs as income redistribution, compensatory job training, compensatory schooling, special medical services and the like would not "require any reference to past discrimination as the basis for justification." All that would be required is that the individuals targeted for preferred treatment by [sic] objectively classified as disadvantaged in terms of the competitive resources associated with their economic-class background.

56. W. Wilson, The Truly Disadvantaged: The Inner City, the Underclass, and Public Policy 109–118 (1987).

57. J. Fishkin, Justice, Equal Opportunity, and the Family 30–35 (1983).

58. Wilson, supra note 54, at 117.

59. Ibid.

Ironically, the shift from preferential treatment for those with certain racial or ethnic characteristics to those who are truly disadvantaged in terms of their life chances would not only help the white poor, but would also address more effectively the problems of the minority poor. * * *

Do you agree with this analysis? Is it also applicable to the situation of females in poverty? Does it transcend both sex and race differences? To rephrase the implicit question posed by Taub and Williams,[60] if all we have accomplished is to improve the situation of those women who are most like men and those blacks who are most like whites, have we gone very far toward the achievement of social justice? Which, if any, of the theories discussed in this Text Note addresses this question?

b. The BFOQ Defense to Sex–Based Classifications

DOTHARD v. RAWLINSON

Supreme Court of the United States, 1977.
433 U.S. 321, 97 S.Ct. 2720, 53 L.Ed.2d 786.

MR. JUSTICE STEWART delivered the opinion of the Court.

[Dianne Rawlinson established that the refusal of the Alabama Board of Corrections to consider her application as a prison guard and that of similarly-situated females based on minimum height and weight requirements violated Title VII because of the disparate impact on women. See discussion at p. 586 supra. While the suit was pending, the Board of Corrections adopted Administrative Regulation 204, which established a gender criterion for assigning prison guards (called "correctional counselors" in Alabama) to maximum security institutions for positions requiring continuous close physical proximity to inmates. The district court found that the regulation excluded women from 75% of the jobs in the Alabama prison system. Appellants sought to justify Regulation 204 under the BFOQ exception.]

III

Unlike the statutory height and weight requirements, Regulation 204 explicitly discriminates against women on the basis of their sex. In defense of this overt discrimination, the appellants rely on § 703(e) of Title VII, which permits sex-based discrimination "in those certain instances where * * * sex * * * is a bona fide occupational qualification reasonably necessary to the normal operation of that particular business or enterprise."

The District Court rejected the bona fide occupational qualification (bfoq) defense, relying on the virtually uniform view of the federal courts that § 703(e) provides only the narrowest of exceptions to the general rule requiring equality of employment opportunities. This view has been variously formulated. In Diaz v. Pan American World Airways, 442 F.2d 385, 388, the Court of Appeals for the Fifth Circuit held that "discrimination based on sex is valid only when the *essence* of the business operation would be undermined by not hiring members of one sex exclusively." (Emphasis in original.) In an earlier case, Weeks v. Southern Bell Telephone and Telegraph Co., 5 Cir., 408 F.2d 228, 235, the same court said that an employer could rely on the bfoq exception only by proving "that he had reasonable cause to believe, that is, a

---

60. Taub & Williams, supra note 21, at 830 (quoted in text at n. 22, supra).

factual basis for believing, that all or substantially all women would be unable to perform safely and efficiently the duties of the job involved." See also Phillips v. Martin Marietta Corp., 400 U.S. 542, 91 S.Ct. 496, 27 L.Ed.2d 613. But whatever the verbal formulation, the federal courts have agreed that it is impermissible under Title VII to refuse to hire an individual woman or man on the basis of stereotyped characterizations of the sexes, and the District Court in the present case held in effect that Regulation 204 is based on just such stereotypical assumptions.

We are persuaded—by the restrictive language of § 703(e), the relevant legislative history, and the consistent interpretation of the Equal Employment Opportunity Commission—that the bfoq exception was in fact meant to be an extremely narrow exception to the general prohibition of discrimination on the basis of sex.[20] In the particular factual circumstances of this case, however, we conclude that the District Court erred in rejecting the State's contention that Regulation 204 falls within the narrow ambit of the bfoq exception.

The environment in Alabama's penitentiaries is a peculiarly inhospitable one for human beings of whatever sex. Indeed, a federal district court has held that the conditions of confinement in the prisons of the State, characterized by "rampant violence" and a "jungle atmosphere," are constitutionally intolerable. James v. Wallace, 406 F.Supp. 318, 325 (M.D.Ala.). The record in the present case shows that because of inadequate staff and facilities, no attempt is made in the four maximum security male penitentiaries to classify or segregate inmates according to their offense or level of dangerousness—a procedure that, according to expert testimony, is essential to effective penalogical administration. Consequently, the estimated 20% of the male prisoners who are sex offenders are scattered throughout the penitentiaries' dormitory facilities.

In this environment of violence and disorganization, it would be an oversimplification to characterize Regulation 204 as an exercise in "romantic paternalism." Cf. Frontiero v. Richardson, 411 U.S. 677, 684, 93 S.Ct. 1764, 1769, 36 L.Ed.2d 583. In the usual case, the argument that a particular job is too dangerous for women may appropriately be met by the rejoinder that it is the purpose of Title VII to allow the individual woman to make that choice for herself. More is at stake in this case, however, than an individual woman's decision to weigh and accept the risks of employment in a "contact" position in a maximum security male prison.

The essence of a correctional counselor's job is to maintain prison security. A woman's relative ability to maintain order in a male, maximum security, unclassified penitentiary of the type Alabama now runs could be directly reduced by her womanhood. There is a basis in fact for expecting that sex offenders who have criminally assaulted women in the past would be moved to do so again if access to women were established within the prison. There would also be a real risk that other inmates, deprived of a normal

---

20. In the case of a state employer, the bfoq exception would have to be interpreted at the very least so as to conform to the Equal Protection Clause of the Fourteenth Amendment. The parties do not suggest, however, that the Equal Protection Clause requires more rigorous scrutiny of a State's sexually discriminatory employment policy than does Title VII. There is thus no occasion to give independent consideration to the District Court's ruling that Regulation 204 violates the Fourteenth Amendment as well as Title VII.

heterosexual environment, would assault women guards because they were women.[22] In a prison system where violence is the order of the day, where inmate access to guards is facilitated by dormitory living arrangements, where every institution is understaffed, and where a substantial portion of the inmate population is composed of sex offenders mixed at random with other prisoners, there are few visible deterrents to inmate assaults on women custodians.

The plaintiffs' own expert testified that dormitory housing for aggressive inmates poses a greater security problem than single-cell lockups, and further testified that it would be unwise to use women as guards in a prison where even 10% of the inmates had been convicted of sex crimes and were not segregated from the other prisoners. The likelihood that inmates would assault a woman because she was a woman would pose a real threat not only to the victim of the assault but also to the basic control of the penitentiary and protection of its inmates and the other security personnel. The employee's very womanhood would thus directly undermine her capacity to provide the security that is the essence of a correctional counselor's responsibility.

There was substantial testimony from experts on both sides of this litigation that the use of women as guards in "contact" positions under the existing conditions in Alabama maximum security male penitentiaries would pose a substantial security problem, directly linked to the sex of the prison guard. On the basis of that evidence, we conclude that the District Court was in error in ruling that being male is not a bona fide occupational qualification for the job of correctional counselor in a "contact" position in an Alabama male maximum security penitentiary.

The judgment is accordingly affirmed in part and reversed in part, and the case is remanded to the District Court for further proceedings consistent with this opinion.

MR. JUSTICE REHNQUIST, with whom THE CHIEF JUSTICE and MR. JUSTICE BLACKMUN join, concurring in the result and concurring in part.

I agree with, and join, Parts I and III of the Court's opinion in this case and with its judgment. * * *

MR. JUSTICE MARSHALL, with whom MR. JUSTICE BRENNAN joins, concurring in part and dissenting in part.

I agree entirely with the Court's analysis of Alabama's height and weight requirements for prison guards, and with its finding that these restrictions discriminate on the basis of sex in violation of Title VII. Accordingly, I join Parts I and II of the Court's opinion. I also agree with much of the Court's general discussion in Part III of the bona fide occupational qualification exception contained in § 703(e) of Title VII. The Court is unquestionably correct when it holds "that the bfoq exception was in fact meant to be an extremely narrow exception to the general prohibition of discrimination on the basis of sex." See Phillips v. Martin Marietta Corp., 400 U.S. 542, 544, 91 S.Ct. 496, 497, 27 L.Ed.2d 613 (1971)(Marshall, J., concurring). I must,

---

22. The record contains evidence of an attack on a female clerical worker in an Alabama prison, and of an incident involving a woman student who was taken hostage during a visit to one of the maximum security institutions.

however, respectfully disagree with the Court's application of the bfoq exception in this case.

The Court properly rejects two proffered justifications for denying women jobs as prison guards. It is simply irrelevant here that a guard's occupation is dangerous and that some women might be unable to protect themselves adequately. Those themes permeate the testimony of the state officials below, but as the Court holds, "the argument that a particular job is too dangerous for women" is refuted by the "purpose of Title VII to allow the individual woman to make that choice for herself." Some women, like some men, undoubtedly are not qualified and do not wish to serve as prison guards, but that does not justify the exclusion of all women from this employment opportunity. Thus, "[i]n the usual case," ibid., the Court's interpretation of the bfoq exception would mandate hiring qualified women for guard jobs in maximum security institutions. The highly successful experiences of other States allowing such job opportunities, see Briefs *amicus curiae* of the States of California and Washington, confirm that absolute disqualification of women is not, in the words of Title VII, "reasonably necessary to the normal operation" of a maximum security prison.

What would otherwise be considered unlawful discrimination against women is justified by the Court, however, on the basis of the "barbaric and inhumane" conditions in Alabama prisons, conditions so bad that state officials have conceded that they violate the Constitution. See James v. Wallace, 406 F.Supp. 318, 329, 331 (M.D.Ala.1976). To me, this analysis sounds distressingly like saying two wrongs make a right. It is refuted by the plain words of § 703(e). The statute requires that a bfoq be "reasonably necessary to the normal operation of that particular business or enterprise." But no governmental "business" may operate "normally" in violation of the Constitution. Every action of government is constrained by constitutional limitations. While those limits may be violated more frequently than we would wish, no one disputes that the "normal operation" of all government functions takes place within them. A prison system operating in blatant violation of the Eighth Amendment is an exception that should be remedied with all possible speed, as Judge Johnson's comprehensive order in James v. Wallace, supra, is designed to do. In the meantime, the existence of such violations should not be legitimatized by calling them "normal." Nor should the Court accept them as justifying conduct that would otherwise violate a statute intended to remedy age-old discrimination.

The Court's error in statutory construction is less objectionable, however, than the attitude it displays toward women. Though the Court recognizes that possible harm to women guards is an unacceptable reason for disqualifying women, it relies instead on an equally speculative threat to prison discipline supposedly generated by the sexuality of female guards. There is simply no evidence in the record to show that women guards would create any danger to security in Alabama prisons significantly greater than already exists. All of the dangers—with one exception discussed below—are inherent in a prison setting whatever the gender of the guards.

The Court first sees women guards as a threat to security because "there are few visible deterrents to inmate assaults on women custodians." In fact, any prison guard is constantly subject to the threat of attack by inmates and "invisible" deterrents are the guard's only real protection. No prison guard relies primarily on his or her ability to ward off an inmate attack to maintain order. Guards are typically unarmed and sheer numbers of inmates could overcome the normal complement. Rather, like all other law enforcement officers, prison guards must rely primarily on the moral authority of their office and the threat of future punishment for miscreants. As one expert testified below, common sense, fairness, and mental and emotional stability are the qualities a guard needs to cope with the dangers of the job. App. 81. Well qualified and properly trained women, no less than men, have these psychological weapons at their disposal.

The particular severity of discipline problems in the Alabama maximum security prisons is also no justification for the discrimination sanctioned by the Court. The District Court found in James v. Wallace, supra, that guards "must spend all their time attempting to maintain control or to protect themselves." 406 F.Supp., at 325. If male guards face an impossible situation, it is difficult to see how women could make the problem worse, unless one relies on precisely the type of generalized bias against women that the Court agrees Title VII was intended to outlaw. For example, much of the testimony of appellants' witnesses ignores individual differences among members of each sex and reads like "ancient canards about the proper role of women." Phillips v. Martin Marietta Corp., supra, 400 U.S., at 545, 91 S.Ct., at 498. The witnesses claimed that women guards are not strict disciplinarians; that they are physically less capable of protecting themselves and subduing unruly inmates; that inmates take advantage of them as they did their mothers, while male guards are strong father figures who easily maintain discipline, and so on.[2] Yet the record shows that the presence of women guards has not led to a single incident amounting to a serious breach of security in any Alabama institution.[3] And in any event, "Guards rarely enter the cell blocks and dormitories," James v. Wallace, supra, 406 F.Supp., at 325, where the danger of inmate attacks is the greatest.

2. * * * The State Commissioner of Corrections summed up these prejudices in his testimony:

"Q Would a male that is 5'6", 140 lbs., be able to perform the job of Correctional Counselor in an all male institution?

* * *

"A Well, if he qualifies otherwise, yes.

"Q But a female 5'6", 140 lbs., would not be able to perform all the duties?

"A No.

"Q What do you use as a basis for that opinion?

"A The innate intention between a male and a female. The physical capabilities, the emotions that go into the psychic make-up of a female vs. the psychic make-up of a male. The attitude of the rural type inmate we have vs. that of a woman. The superior feeling that a man has, historically, over that of a female." App. 153.

Strikingly similar sentiments were expressed a century ago by a justice of this Court in a case long since discredited:

"I am not prepared to say that it is one of [women's] fundamental rights and privileges to be admitted into every office and position, including those which require highly special qualifications and demanding special responsibilities * * *. [I]n my opinion, in view of the particular characteristics, destiny, and mission of woman, it is within the province of the legislature to ordain what offices, positions, and callings shall be filled and discharged by men, and shall receive the benefit of those energies and responsibilities, and that decision and firmness which are presumed to dominate in the sterner sex." Bradwell v. Illinois, 16 Wall. 130, 139, 142, 21 L.Ed. 442 (1872)(Bradley, J., concurring).

3. The Court refers to two incidents involving potentially dangerous attacks on women in prisons. Ante, at n. 22. But these did not involve trained corrections officers; one victim was a clerical worker and the other a student visiting on a tour.

It appears that the real disqualifying factor in the Court's view is "[t]he employee's very womanhood." The Court refers to the large number of sex offenders in Alabama prisons, and to "the likelihood that inmates would assault a woman because she was a woman." In short, the fundamental justification for the decision is that women as guards will generate sexual assaults. With all respect, this rationale regrettably perpetuates one of the most insidious of the old myths about women—that women, wittingly or not, are seductive sexual objects. The effect of the decision, made I am sure with the best of intentions, is to punish women because their very presence might provoke sexual assaults. It is women who are made to pay the price in lost job opportunities for the threat of depraved conduct by prison inmates. Once again, "[t]he pedestal upon which women have been placed has * * *, upon closer inspection, been revealed as a cage." Sail'er Inn, Inc. v. Kirby, 5 Cal.3d 1, 20, 95 Cal.Rptr. 329, 341, 485 P.2d 529, 541 (1971). It is particularly ironic that the cage is erected here in response to feared misbehavior by imprisoned criminals.[4]

The Court points to no evidence in the record to support the asserted "likelihood that inmates would assault a woman because she was a woman." Perhaps the Court relies upon common sense, or "innate recognition." Brief for Appellants, at 51. But the danger in this emotionally laden context is that common sense will be used to mask the "romantic paternalism" and persisting discriminatory attitudes that the Court properly eschews. To me, the only matter of innate recognition is that the incidence of sexually motivated attacks on guards will be minute compared to the "likelihood that inmates will assault" a *guard* because he or she is a *guard*.

The proper response to inevitable attacks on both female and male guards is not to limit the employment opportunities of law-abiding women who wish to contribute to their community, but to take swift and sure punitive action against the inmate offenders. Presumably, one of the goals of the Alabama prison system is the eradication of inmates' antisocial behavior patterns so that prisoners will be able to live one day in free society. Sex offenders can begin this process by learning to relate to women guards in a socially acceptable manner. To deprive women of job opportunities because of the threatened behavior of convicted criminals is to turn our social priorities upside down.[5]

---

4. The irony is multiplied by the fact that enormous staff increases are required by the District Court's order in James v. Wallace, supra. This necessary hiring would be a perfect opportunity for appellants to remedy their past discrimination against women, but instead the Court's decision permits that policy to continue. Moreover, once conditions are improved in accordance with the *James* order, the problems that the Court perceives with women guards will be substantially alleviated.

5. The appellants argue that restrictions on employment of women are also justified by consideration of inmates' privacy. It is strange indeed to hear state officials who have for years been violating the most basic principles of human decency in the operation of their prisons suddenly become concerned about in-

mate privacy. It is stranger still that these same officials allow women guards in contact positions in a number of non-maximum security institutions, but strive to protect inmates' privacy in the prisons where personal freedom is most severely restricted. I have no doubt on this record that appellants' professed concern is nothing but a feeble excuse for discrimination.

As the District Court suggested, it may well be possible, once constitutionally adequate staff is available, to rearrange work assignments so that legitimate inmate privacy concerns are respected without denying jobs to women. Finally, if women guards behave in a professional manner at all times, they will engender reciprocal respect from inmates, who will recognize that their privacy is being invad-

Although I do not countenance the sex discrimination condoned by the majority, it is fortunate that the Court's decision is carefully limited to the facts before it. I trust the lower courts will recognize that the decision was impelled by the shockingly inhuman conditions in Alabama prisons, and thus that the "extremely narrow [bfoq] exception" recognized here will not be allowed "to swallow the rule" against sex discrimination. See Phillips v. Martin Marietta Corp., supra, 400 U.S., at 545, 91 S.Ct., at 498. Expansion of today's decision beyond its narrow factual basis would erect a serious roadblock to economic equality for women.

[MR. JUSTICE WHITE's dissenting opinion is omitted.]

Notes on Dothard

1. The BFOQ exception in section 703(e) of Title VII applies only to discrimination based on religion, sex and national origin—not to that based on race or color. A similar exception appears in the Age Discrimination in Employment Act of 1967. 29 U.S.C.A. § 623(f). What is the rationale for the exception? Indications of congressional intent are sparse. When the BFOQ exception was initially considered by the House, it merely applied to discrimination based on religion and national origin. Representative Goodell asked Representative Bolton whether she would consider adding "sex" as a BFOQ, saying:

There are so many instances where the matter of sex is a bona fide occupational qualification. For instance, I think of an elderly woman who wants a female nurse. There are many things of this nature which are bona fide occupational qualifications, and it seems to me they would be properly considered here as an exception.

110 Cong.Rec. 2718 (1964).

Representative Bolton replied:

I have not studied that. It was not brought to my attention by the staff. But if that is the sense of the House, I will be very glad to accept it.

110 Cong.Rec. 2718 (1964).

During consideration of Title VII by the Senate, its floor managers, Senators Clark and Case, offered an interpretative memorandum discussing its provisions. The BFOQ exception, according to the memorandum, creates

a limited right to discriminate on the basis of religion, sex or national origin where the reason for the discrimination is a bona fide occupational qualification. Examples of such legitimate discrimination would be the preference of a French restaurant for a French cook, the preference of a professional baseball team for male players, and the preference of a business which seeks the patronage of members of particular religious groups for a salesman of that religion.

110 Cong.Rec. 7213 (1964).

In discussing why no BFOQ exception was permitted for race or color, Senator Clark said in response to questions submitted by Senator Dirksen that certain discretion nevertheless remained to employers:

ed no more than if a woman doctor examines them. The suggestion implicit in the privacy argument that such behavior is unlikely on either side is an insult to the professionalism of guards and the dignity of inmates.

[A] director of a play or movie who wished to cast an actor in the role of a Negro, could specify that he wished to hire someone with the physical appearance of a Negro—but such a person might actually be a non-Negro. Therefore, the act would not limit the director's freedom of choice.

110 Cong.Rec. 7217 (1964). Yet the EEOC's guidelines indicate that where authenticity or genuineness is required—as in the case of an actor or actress—sex will be considered a bona fide occupational qualification. 29 C.F.R. § 1604.2(a)(2). Why should not the employer be required to hire someone with the "physical appearance" of a man or woman—but who "might actually be" a member of the opposite sex? Don't you think Dame Judith Anderson was a convincing Hamlet? The authors of the Harvard Developments Note on Title VII are of the opinion that the inclusion of sex as a BFOQ "seems to have been more intuitively felt than explained by the Act's draftsmen." 84 Harv.L.Rev. 1109, 1176 (1971). Do you agree? Does the inclusion of sex, but not race, as a BFOQ exception mean that the policy of ending discrimination in employment based on race represents a stronger national commitment than the policy of eradicating sex-based discrimination? The House made short shrift of an amendment proposed by Representative Williams of Mississippi that would have added "race or color" as BFOQ exceptions, despite the solicitous remarks by him and other Southern Representatives protesting that the amendment was necessary to permit black businessmen in the South to exclude whites as employees. 110 Cong.Rec. 2550–51 (1964). Does the discussion of sex as a BFOQ merely reflect the back-handed way in which sex was added to Title VII in the first place? See Caroline Bird's account of "Ladies Day in the House," in Born Female 1–15 (1969).

2. Early interpretation of the BFOQ exception came in the context of cases involving the impact of Title VII on state protective laws. In Rosenfeld v. Southern Pac. Co., 444 F.2d 1219 (9th Cir.1971), the employer refused to assign Leah Rosenfeld to the position of agent-telegrapher solely because of her sex, arguing in part that her appointment would violate California laws limiting the hours women were allowed to work and restricting the weight they were permitted to lift. This potential conflict between state and federal law might be resolved, the company suggested, by holding that the state protective laws created a BFOQ. Instead, the Ninth Circuit held that Title VII superseded the state protective laws, a position that became generally accepted. See Joseph P. Kennedy, Sex Discrimination: State Protective Laws Since Title VII, 47 Notre Dame L. 514 (1972). Should protective laws be invalidated in light of Title VII, or should they be extended to men? See Barbara A. Brown, Thomas I. Emerson, Gail Falk & Ann E. Freedman, The Equal Rights Amendment: A Constitutional Basis for Equal Rights for Women, 80 Yale L.J. 871, 936 (1971), suggesting that under both Title VII and the ERA,

[i]n general, labor legislation which confers clear benefits upon women would be extended to men. Laws which are plainly exclusionary would be invalidated. Laws which restrict or regulate working conditions would probably be invalidated, leaving the process of general or functional regulation to the legislatures.

Despite this analysis, however, several courts declined to extend overtime pay laws created for women to men. See, e.g., Homemakers, Inc. v. Division of Indus. Welfare, 509 F.2d 20 (9th Cir.1974), cert. denied 423 U.S. 1063, 96 S.Ct. 803, 46 L.Ed.2d 655 (1976); State v. Fairfield Communities Land Co., 260 Ark. 277, 538 S.W.2d 698 (1976), cert. denied 429 U.S. 1004, 97 S.Ct. 538, 50 L.Ed.2d 617; Idaho Trailer Coach Ass'n v. Brown, 95 Idaho 910, 523 P.2d 42 (1974).

3. Unable to rely on state protective laws, other employers sought to exclude women from "strenuous" jobs, such as that of a telephone switchman. In Weeks v. Southern Bell Tel. & Tel. Co., 408 F.2d 228, 235–36 (5th Cir.1969), the court gave that argument short shrift:

> We conclude that the principle of nondiscrimination requires that we hold that in order to rely on the bona fide occupational qualification exception an employer has the burden of proving that he had reasonable cause to believe, that is, a factual basis for believing, that all or substantially all women would be unable to perform safely and efficiently the duties of the job involved.
>
> Southern Bell has clearly not met that burden here. They introduced no evidence concerning the lifting abilities of women. Rather, they would have us "assume," on the basis of a "stereotyped characterization" that few or no women can safely lift 30 pounds, while all men are treated as if they can. While one might accept, *arguendo,* that men are stronger on the average than women, it is not clear that any conclusions about relative lifting ability would follow. This is because it can be argued tenably that technique is as important as strength in determining lifting ability. Technique is hardly a function of sex. What does seem clear is that using these class stereotypes denies desirable positions to a great many women perfectly capable of performing the duties involved.
>
> Southern Bell's remaining contentions do not seem to be advanced with great seriousness. The emergency work which a switchman allegedly must perform consists primarily in the handling of a 34–pound extinguisher in the event of fire. A speculative emergency like that could be used as a smoke screen by any employer bent on discriminating against women. It does seem that switchmen are occasionally subject to late hour call-outs. Of course, the record also reveals that other women employees are subject to call after midnight in emergencies. Moreover, Title VII rejects just this type of romantic paternalism as unduly Victorian and instead vests individual women with the power to decide whether or not to take on unromantic tasks. Men have always had the right to determine whether the incremental increase in remuneration for strenuous, dangerous, obnoxious, boring or unromantic tasks is worth the candle. The promise of Title VII is that women are now to be on equal footing. We cannot conclude that by including the bona fide occupational qualification exception Congress intended to renege on that promise.
>
> Having concluded that Southern Bell has not satisfied its burden of proving that the job of switchman is within the bona fide occupational qualification exception, we must reverse the District Court on this issue and hold that Southern Bell has violated 42 U.S.C.A. Sec. 2000e–2(a). This case is remanded to the District Court for determination of appropriate relief under the provisions of 42 U.S.C.A. Sec. 2000e–5(g).

The test announced in *Weeks*—that an employer must show a factual basis for believing that "all or substantially all" women would be unable to perform safely and efficiently the duties of the job—has been widely followed.

4. An additional element was added to the *Weeks* BFOQ test by the Fifth Circuit in Diaz v. Pan American World Airways, Inc., 442 F.2d 385 (5th Cir.1971), cert. denied 404 U.S. 950, 92 S.Ct. 275, 30 L.Ed.2d 267 (1971). The court rejected Pan American's argument that the BFOQ exception justified its refusal to hire men as flight attendants. Pan Am attempted to use a customer preference rationale to support its BFOQ defense. The following evidence persuaded the

lower court in *Diaz* that airline passengers generally prefer females as flight attendants (311 F.Supp. 559, 565–66 (S.D.Fla.1970)):

> Pan Am sought, through a psychiatrist, Dr. Eric Berne, author of the "Structure and Dynamics of Organizations and Groups", to explain in psychological terms why, as the other evidence indicated, most airline passengers of both sexes prefer to be served by female stewardesses. There was no challenge to Dr. Berne's qualifications as an expert, and the Court found a considerable part of his testimony persuasive. Dr. Berne explained that the cabin of a modern airliner is, for passengers, a special and unique psychological environment ("sealed enclave"), characterized by the confinement of a number of people together in an enclosed and limited space, by their being subjected to the unusual physical experience of being levitated off the ground and transported through the atmosphere at high speed, by their being substantially out of touch with their accustomed world, and by their own inability to control events. That environment, said Dr. Berne, creates three typical passenger emotional states with which the air carrier must deal; first and most important, a sense of apprehension; second, a sense of boredom; and third, a feeling of excitement. Dr. Berne expressed the opinion that female stewardesses, because of the nature of their psychological relationship as females to persons of both sexes, would be better able to deal with each of these psychological states. He specially emphasized, however, that the relief of passenger anxiety, due to apprehended but non-imminent dangers, represents the most important psychological factor to be dealt with by airlines, and that females are themselves psychologically better suited for that role than males because passengers of both sexes would, in this context, respond better to the presence of females than males. He explained that many male passengers would subconsciously resent a male flight attendant perceived as more masculine than they, but respond negatively to a male flight attendant perceived as less masculine, whereas male passengers would generally feel themselves more masculine and thus more at ease in the presence of a young female attendant. He further explained that female passengers might consider personal overtures by male attendants as intrusive and inappropriate, while at the same time welcoming the attentions and conversation of another woman. He concluded that there are sound psychological reasons for the general preference of airline passengers for female flight attendants.

The Fifth Circuit did not reject this evidence, but found that this type of customer preference would not support a BFOQ for hiring only women:

> [U]se of the word 'necessary in section 703(e) requires that we apply a business *necessity* test, not a business *convenience* test. * * * [D]iscrimination based on sex is valid only when the *essence* of the business operation would be undermined by not hiring members of one sex exclusively.

> The primary function of an airline is to transport passengers safely from one point to another.

442 F.2d at 388. The court found that despite women's apparent ability to perform the "non-mechanical functions" of the job more effectively than most men, these functions were tangential to the essence of the business. Thus, for a BFOQ to be upheld, an employer must not only show that "all or substantially all" persons of the excluded sex cannot perform the job functions at issue, but these job functions must be "reasonably necessary," and go to the "essence" of the business.

For a reprise of the customer preference rationale in the airline industry, with a different and humerous twist, see Wilson v. Southwest Airlines Co., 517 F.Supp. 292 (N.D.Tex.1981). Southwest Airlines contended that being a woman was a BFOQ for both flight attendant and ticket agent jobs, because its marketing campaign emphasized the sex appeal of these women employees, a marketing strategy necessary to attract the businessmen who made up the bulk of its customers. The district court found that the airline's widely marketed "love" personality, while contributing to the company's competitive success, did not go to the essence of its business. 517 F.Supp. at 302–303.

5. Customer preference of a somewhat different kind was relied on by the district court in Fernandez v. Wynn Oil Co., 20 F.E.P. 1162 (C.D.Cal.1979). The district court accepted the company's argument that it could not promote women into its international marketing positions, conducting overseas business, because its Latin American and Southeast Asian clients would feel uncomfortable or refuse to do business with women. The lower court accepted the employer's testimony that "a woman would not be accepted * * * because of the prevalent mores relating to the proper roles of men and women in those countries. * * * [A] female simply could not perform the job of attracting, and doing business with, potential customers[.]" In the court's view, customer preference here was not a matter merely of convenience, but hiring women in these international oil marketing positions "would have totally subverted any business Wynn hoped to accomplish in those areas of the world." 20 F.E.P. at 1164–1165. Do you agree that the employer in *Fernandez* should have been able to rely on the BFOQ exception?

The Ninth Circuit did not. On appeal, it affirmed the district court's judgment on the basis that plaintiff had not made out a prima facie case of disparate treatment, but rejected the BFOQ holding:

> * * * *Diaz,* supra, held that customer preference based on sexual stereo-type cannot justify discriminatory conduct. The court below relied on these cases, yet found that customer preference which prevents customers from dealing with the employer does qualify as a BFOQ. Nothing in those cases justifies this distinction.

> Wynn attempts to distinguish *Diaz* by asserting that a separate rule applies in international contexts. Such a distinction is unfounded. Though the United States cannot impose standards of non-discriminatory conduct on other nations through its legal system, the district court's rule would allow other nations to dictate discrimination in this country. No foreign nation can compel the non-enforcement of Title VII here.

Fernandez v. Wynn Oil Co., 653 F.2d 1273, 1277 (9th Cir.1981). Does *Fernandez* mean that staying in business isn't a business necessity? Or only that defendant did not prove that sex neutral hiring would put it out of business? Can you imagine a case in which such a defense would be accepted? See Mark S. Brodin, Costs, Profits, and Equal Employment Opportunity, 62 Notre Dame L.Rev. 318 (1987), noting that, while courts have typically rejected a cost defense in Title VII disparate treatment exclusionary cases, like *Fernandez* or *Wilson,* such a defense has been accepted in disparate impact cases, particularly when used in connection with public safety concerns.

6. What view of the BFOQ exception did the Court adopt in *Dothard* ? Is Justice Marshall's understanding of the narrowness of the test the same as the Court's? Should lower courts read the decision as limited to the special situation of prisons characterized by a "jungle atmosphere"? *Dothard* was so distinguished

in Gunther v. Iowa State Men's Reformatory, 612 F.2d 1079, 1085 (8th Cir.1980), cert. denied 446 U.S. 966, 100 S.Ct. 2942, 64 L.Ed.2d 825, the court noting that Anamosa, the medium security institution where plaintiff wished to work as a correctional officer II, "is no rose garden; neither is it the stygian spectre which faced the Supreme Court in *Dothard.*" See also Manley v. Mobile County, Alabama, 441 F.Supp. 1351 (S.D.Ala.1977)(plaintiff's position as an Identification Assistant Officer in an all-male county jail was not a "contact" position; her chief duties would be to fingerprint and photograph inmates); State Div. of Human Rights v. New York State Dept. of Correctional Serv's, 61 A.D.2d 25, 401 N.Y.S.2d 619 (1978)(sex is not a BFOQ for the position of cook in a minimum security correctional facility for males).

Are the privacy rights of male inmates violated by the presence of female guards? The court in *Gunther* suggested, without deciding, that

> [a] proper classification narrowly drawn indicating that most of the duties of that classification would involve shower and toilet surveillance, strip searches and related duties necessary to inmate privacy may satisfy a bfoq for males at Anamosa, or females at a women's institution.

Id., 612 F.2d at 1087. Do you agree? See Deborah M. Tharnish, Comment, Sex Discrimination in Prison Employment: The Bona Fide Occupational Qualification and Prisoners' Privacy Rights, 65 Iowa L.Rev. 428 (1980). This matter is explored further in Chapter Five.

7. Representative Goodell's view that the BFOQ exception would be broad enough to protect the wishes of "an elderly woman who wants a female nurse", see Note 1 supra, was tested and upheld in Fesel v. Masonic Home of Delaware, Inc., 447 F.Supp. 1346 (D.Del.1978), affirmed mem. 591 F.2d 1334 (3d Cir.1979). Fesel, a male nurse's aide, was rejected because of his sex. The court found that a BFOQ exception was proper because of the objections of the Home's female guests, nine of whom signed an affidavit stating that they objected "most strenuously" to the employment of male nurses or nurses' aides. Selective job assignments of the type discussed in *Gunther,* Note 6 supra, were not feasible in *Fesel* due to the small size of the nursing staff. Was *Fesel* correctly decided? The female guests of the Home did not object to being treated by male physicians, nor did the male guests object to female nurses. *Fesel* is sharply criticized in Kenneth W. Kingma, Comment, Sex Discrimination Justified Under Title VII: Privacy Rights in Nursing Homes, 14 Valparaiso U.L.Rev. 577, 589 (1980)("By honoring the individual privacy interest of the Home's female guests, the court in *Fesel* indirectly attacked the integrity of the medical profession, undermined the EEOC guidelines on sex discrimination, and yielded to existing social prejudices which Title VII intended to eliminate."). Do cases like *Fesel* and *Dothard* reflect a modern "pragmatic" paternalism that is just as restrictive in its own way as the 19th century "romantic" paternalism ever was? Professor Kathryn Powers thinks so. See Powers, The Shifting Parameters of Affirmative Action: "Pragmatic" Paternalism in Sex–Based Employment Discrimination Cases, 26 Wayne L.Rev. 1281, 1293–1307 (1980).

Fesel was followed by Backus v. Baptist Medical Center, 510 F.Supp. 1191 (E.D.Ark.1981), vacated and dismissed as moot 671 F.2d 1100 (8th Cir.1982)(female sex is a BFOQ for the position of nurse in an OB–GYN unit). Compare Brooks v. ACF Industries, Inc., 537 F.Supp. 1122 (S.D.W.Va.1982)(male sex is a BFOQ for the job of janitor assigned under the plant's seniority system to clean the male bathhouses). Other courts have rejected the application of the BFOQ exception where the employer appeared to be using sexual stereotypes as the basis of its practices. See, e.g., Jatczak v. Ochburg, 540 F.Supp. 698 (E.D.Mich. 1982)(male sex not a BFOQ for position of child care worker for mentally ill young adults, most of whom were black males; employer urged that a male role model was needed); EEOC v. Spokane Concrete Products, Inc., 534 F.Supp. 518 (E.D.Wash.1982)(male sex not a BFOQ for position of truck driver). Was *Jatczak* decided correctly? Is it relevant that the sheltered workshop already had a female child care worker on its staff and the job opening was created by the departure of a male child care worker?

Professor Carolyn S. Bratt suggests a distinction be drawn in the privacy BFOQ cases based on whether the person asserting a right of privacy is located in a coercive or a noncoercive environment. Coercive environments include prisons and hospitals or nursing homes, where the occupant's presence is compelled by judicial sentence or illness. Noncoercive environments are primarily commercial settings where the customer voluntarily chooses to transact business. Bratt would reject the privacy BFOQ defense entirely in the latter case; otherwise, "customers' preferences and social prejudices will determine not only whether sex discrimination is valid but also whether employment patterns will change." Bratt, Privacy and the Sex BFOQ: An Immodest Proposal, 48 Albany L.Rev. 923, 944 (1984). In coercive environments, the occupant has not waived the right of privacy. Accordingly, Bratt proposes a two-step test to resolve the conflict between the right of privacy and the right to be free of discrimination in employment. First, she would have the courts determine whether the act complained of (such as a body cavity search of a prison inmate or a physical examination of a hospital patient) is an infringement of the right of privacy. If so, she would then ask whether the invasion of privacy is nevertheless justified by other competing interests, such as the need for security. She would, however, exclude the factor of the sex of the employee and that of the occupant from the competing considerations. If privacy must be invaded in the name of some overriding interest, she contends, the sex of the person who performs the invasion is irrelevant. Id., at 942–49. Do you find this approach a promising one?

Not surprisingly, courts have accorded greater weight to the privacy interests of hospital patients than prisoners. In Jennings v. New York State Office of Mental Health, 786 F.Supp. 376 (S.D.N.Y.1992), judgment affirmed per curiam 977 F.2d 731, (2d Cir.1992), the district court commented:

> [A mental patient's] right to privacy may not be abrogated by virtue of their confinement in a state-run facility unlike a prison inmate who has forfeited some rights in repayment to society.

786 F.Supp. at 384. In *Jennings*, mental health assistants alleged that their right to bid for positions in the hospital was limited and they were denied overtime on the basis of their sex due to a staffing policy designed to protect the privacy interest of the patients. The hospital required that at least one assistant of the same gender as the patients be on a ward at all times. The court held this was a permissible BFOQ. Because "a person of the opposite gender would be unable to adequately perform some of the duties * * * which affect the privacy rights of the patient and successfully respect those rights," the court found the hospital's policy was the least restrictive method to safeguard the privacy rights of the patients. Id. at 383. Mental health patients present a particularly sympathetic group; the court accepted the rationale that these patients were "vulnerable and mentally ill. Basic decency demands that their privacy be respected to whatever degree feasible." Id. at 384.

INTERNATIONAL UNION, UAW v.
JOHNSON CONTROLS, INC.

Supreme Court of the United States, 1991.
499 U.S. 187, 111 S.Ct. 1196, 113 L.Ed.2d 158.

JUSTICE BLACKMUN delivered the opinion of the Court.

In this case we are concerned with an employer's gender-based fetal-protection policy. May an employer exclude a fertile female employee from certain jobs because of its concern for the health of the fetus the woman might conceive?

I

Respondent Johnson Controls, Inc., manufactures batteries. In the manufacturing process, the element lead is a primary ingredient. Occupational exposure to lead entails health risks, including the risk of harm to any fetus carried by a female employee.

Before the Civil Rights Act of 1964, 78 Stat. 241, became law, Johnson Controls did not employ any woman in a battery-manufacturing job. In June 1977, however, it announced its first official policy concerning its employment of women in lead-exposure work:

"[P]rotection of the health of the unborn child is the immediate and direct responsibility of the prospective parents. While the medical profession and the company can support them in the exercise of this responsibility, it cannot assume it for them without simultaneously infringing their rights as persons.

* * *

"* * * Since not all women who can become mothers wish to become mothers (or will become mothers), it would appear to be illegal discrimination to treat all who are capable of pregnancy as though they will become pregnant." App. 140.

Consistent with that view, Johnson Controls "stopped short of excluding women capable of bearing children from lead exposure," *id.,* at 138, but emphasized that a woman who expected to have a child should not choose a job in which she would have such exposure. The company also required a woman who wished to be considered for employment to sign a statement that she had been advised of the risk of having a child while she was exposed to lead. The statement informed the woman that although there was evidence "that women exposed to lead have a higher rate of abortion," this evidence was "not as clear * * * as the relationship between cigarette smoking and cancer," but that it was, "medically speaking, just good sense not to run that risk if you want children and do not want to expose the unborn child to risk, however small * * *." *Id.,* at 142–143.

Five years later, in 1982, Johnson Controls shifted from a policy of warning to a policy of exclusion. Between 1979 and 1983, eight employees became pregnant while maintaining blood lead levels in excess of 30 micrograms per deciliter. Tr. of Oral Arg. 25, 34. This appeared to be the critical level noted by the Occupational Health and Safety Administration (OSHA) for a worker who was planning to have a family. See 29 CFR § 1910.1025 (1989). The company responded by announcing a broad exclusion of women from jobs that exposed them to lead:

"* * * [I]t is [Johnson Controls'] policy that women who are pregnant or who are capable of bearing children will not be placed into jobs involving lead exposure or which could expose them to lead through the exercise of job bidding, bumping, transfer or promotion rights." App. 85–86.

The policy defined "women * * * capable of bearing children" as "[a]ll women except those whose inability to bear children is medically documented." *Id.*, at 81. It further stated that an unacceptable work station was one where, "over the past year," an employee had recorded a blood lead level of more than 30 micrograms per deciliter or the work site had yielded an air sample containing a lead level in excess of 30 micrograms per cubic meter. *Ibid.*

II

In April 1984, petitioners filed in the United States District Court for the Eastern District of Wisconsin a class action challenging Johnson Controls' fetal-protection policy as sex discrimination that violated Title VII of the Civil Rights Act of 1964, as amended, 42 U.S.C. § 2000e *et seq.* Among the individual plaintiffs were petitioners Mary Craig, who had chosen to be sterilized in order to avoid losing her job, Elsie Nason, a 50–year–old divorcee, who had suffered a loss in compensation when she was transferred out of a job where she was exposed to lead, and Donald Penney, who had been denied a request for a leave of absence for the purpose of lowering his lead level because he intended to become a father. Upon stipulation of the parties, the District Court certified a class consisting of "all past, present and future production and maintenance employees" in United Auto Workers bargaining units at nine of Johnson Controls' plants "who have been and continue to be affected by [the employer's] Fetal Protection Policy implemented in 1982." Order of Feb. 25, 1985.

The District Court granted summary judgment for defendant-respondent Johnson Controls. 680 F.Supp. 309 (1988). * * *

The Court of Appeals for the Seventh Circuit, sitting en banc, affirmed the summary judgment by a 7–to–4 vote. 886 F.2d 871 (1989). * * *

With its ruling, the Seventh Circuit became the first Court of Appeals to hold that a fetal-protection policy directed exclusively at women could qualify as a BFOQ. We granted certiorari, * * * to resolve the obvious conflict between the Fourth, Seventh, and Eleventh Circuits on this issue, and to address the important and difficult question whether an employer, seeking to protect potential fetuses, may discriminate against women just because of their ability to become pregnant.

III

The bias in Johnson Controls' policy is obvious. Fertile men, but not fertile women, are given a choice as to whether they wish to risk their reproductive health for a particular job. Section 703(a) of the Civil Rights Act of 1964, 78 Stat. 255, as amended, 42 U.S.C. § 2000e–2(a), prohibits sex-based classifications in terms and conditions of employment, in hiring and discharging decisions, and in other employment decisions that adversely affect an employee's status. Respondent's fetal-protection policy explicitly discriminates against women on the basis of their sex. The policy excludes women with childbearing capacity from lead-exposed jobs and so creates a facial classification based on gender. Respondent assumes as much in its brief before this Court. * * *

Nevertheless, the Court of Appeals assumed, as did the two appellate courts who already had confronted the issue, that sex-specific fetal-protection policies do not involve facial discrimination. 886 F.2d, at 886–887; *Hayes [v. Shelby Memorial Hospital,* 726 F.2d 1543 (C.A.11 1984)], 726 F.2d, at 1547; [and] *Wright [v. Olin Corp.,* 697 F.2d 1172 (C.A.4 1982),] 697 F.2d, at 1190. These courts analyzed the policies as though they were facially neutral, and had only a discriminatory effect upon the employment opportunities of women. Consequently, the courts looked to see if each employer in question had established that its policy was justified as a business necessity. The business necessity standard is more lenient for the employer than the statutory BFOQ defense. The Court of Appeals here went one step further and invoked the burden-shifting framework set forth in *Wards Cove Packing Co. v. Atonio,* 490 U.S. 642, 109 S.Ct. 2115, 104 L.Ed.2d 733 (1989), thus requiring petitioners to bear the burden of persuasion on all questions. 886 F.2d, at 887–888. The court assumed that because the asserted reason for the sex-based exclusion (protecting women's unconceived offspring) was ostensibly benign, the policy was not sex-based discrimination. That assumption, however, was incorrect.

First, Johnson Controls' policy classifies on the basis of gender and childbearing capacity, rather than fertility alone. Respondent does not seek to protect the unconceived children of all its employees. Despite evidence in the record about the debilitating effect of lead exposure on the male reproductive system, Johnson Controls is concerned only with the harms that may befall the unborn offspring of its female employees. Accordingly, it appears that Johnson Controls would have lost in the Eleventh Circuit under *Hayes* because its policy does not "effectively and equally protec[t] the offspring of all employees." 726 F.2d, at 1548. This Court faced a conceptually similar situation in *Phillips v. Martin Marietta Corp.,* 400 U.S. 542, 91 S.Ct. 496, 27 L.Ed.2d 613 (1971), and found sex discrimination because the policy established "one hiring policy for women and another for men—each having preschool-age children." *Id.,* at 544, 91 S.Ct., at 498. Johnson Controls' policy is facially discriminatory because it requires only a female employee to produce proof that she is not capable of reproducing.

Our conclusion is bolstered by the Pregnancy Discrimination Act of 1978 (PDA), 92 Stat. 2076, 42 U.S.C. § 2000e(k), in which Congress explicitly provided that, for purposes of Title VII, discrimination "on the basis of sex" includes discrimination "because of or on the basis of pregnancy, childbirth, or related medical conditions." "The Pregnancy Discrimination Act has now made clear that, for all Title VII purposes, discrimination based on a woman's pregnancy is, on its face, discrimination because of her sex." *Newport News Shipbuilding & Dry Dock Co. v. EEOC,* 462 U.S. 669, 684, 103 S.Ct. 2622, 2631, 77 L.Ed.2d 89 (1983). In its use of the words "capable of bearing children" in the 1982 policy statement as the criterion for exclusion, Johnson Controls explicitly classifies on the basis of potential for pregnancy. Under the PDA, such a classification must be regarded, for Title VII purposes, in the same light as explicit sex discrimination. Respondent has chosen to treat all its female employees as potentially pregnant; that choice evinces discrimination on the basis of sex.

We concluded above that Johnson Controls' policy is not neutral because it does not apply to the reproductive capacity of the company's male employees in the same way as it applies to that of the females. Moreover, the absence of a malevolent motive does not convert a facially discriminatory policy into a neutral policy with a discriminatory effect. Whether an employment practice involves disparate treatment through explicit facial discrimination does not depend on why the employer discriminates but rather on the explicit terms of the discrimination. In *Martin Marietta, supra,* the motives underlying the employers' express exclusion of women did not alter the intentionally discriminatory character of the policy. Nor did the arguably benign motives lead to consideration of a business necessity defense. The question in that case was whether the discrimination in question could be justified under § 703(e) as a BFOQ. The beneficence of an employer's purpose does not undermine the conclusion that an explicit gender-based policy is sex discrimination under § 703(a) and thus may be defended only as a BFOQ.

* * *

In sum, Johnson Controls' policy "does not pass the simple test of whether the evidence shows 'treatment of a person in a manner which but for that person's sex would be different.'" *Los Angeles Dept. of Water & Power v. Manhart,* 435 U.S. 702, 711, 98 S.Ct. 1370, 1377, 55 L.Ed.2d 657 (1978), quoting Developments in the Law, Employment Discrimination and Title VII of the Civil Rights Act of 1964, 84 Harv.L.Rev. 1109, 1170 (1971). We hold that Johnson Controls' fetal-protection policy is sex discrimination forbidden under Title VII unless respondent can establish that sex is a "bona fide occupational qualification."

IV

Under § 703(e)(1) of Title VII, an employer may discriminate on the basis of "religion, sex, or national origin in those certain instances where religion, sex, or national origin is a bona fide occupational qualification reasonably necessary to the normal operation of that particular business or enterprise." 42 U.S.C. § 2000e–2(e)(1). We therefore turn to the question whether Johnson Controls' fetal-protection policy is one of those "certain instances" that come within the BFOQ exception.

The BFOQ defense is written narrowly, and this Court has read it narrowly. * * * Our emphasis on the restrictive scope of the BFOQ defense is grounded on both the language and the legislative history of § 703.

The wording of the BFOQ defense contains several terms of restriction that indicate that the exception reaches only special situations. The statute thus limits the situations in which discrimination is permissible to "certain instances" where sex discrimination is "reasonably necessary" to the "normal operation" of the "particular" business. Each one of these terms—certain, normal, particular—prevents the use of general subjective standards and favors an objective, verifiable requirement. But the most telling term is "occupational"; this indicates that these objective, verifiable requirements must concern job-related skills and aptitudes.

The concurrence defines "occupational" as meaning related to a job. * * * According to the concurrence, any discriminatory requirement imposed by an employer is "job-related" simply because the employer has chosen to make the requirement a condition of employment. In effect, the concurrence argues that sterility may be an occupational qualification for women because Johnson Controls has chosen to require it. This reading of "occupational" renders the word mere surplusage. "Qualification" by itself would encompass an employer's idiosyncratic requirements. By modifying "qualification" with "occupational," Congress narrowed the term to qualifications that affect an employee's ability to do the job.

Johnson Controls argues that its fetal-protection policy falls within the so-called safety exception to the BFOQ. Our cases have stressed that discrimination on the basis of sex because of safety concerns is allowed only in narrow circumstances. In *Dothard v. Rawlinson,* this Court indicated that danger to a woman herself does not justify discrimination. 433 U.S., at 335, 97 S.Ct. at 2729–2730. We there allowed the employer to hire only male guards in contact areas of maximum-security male penitentiaries only because more was at stake than the "individual woman's decision to weigh and accept the risks of employment." *Ibid.* We found sex to be a BFOQ inasmuch as the employment of a female guard would create real risks of safety to others if violence broke out because the guard was a woman. Sex discrimination was tolerated because sex was related to the guard's ability to do the job— maintaining prison security. We also required in *Dothard* a high correlation between sex and ability to perform job functions and refused to allow employers to use sex as a proxy for strength although it might be a fairly accurate one.

Similarly, some courts have approved airlines' layoffs of pregnant flight attendants at different points during the first five months of pregnancy on the ground that the employer's policy was necessary to ensure the safety of passengers. See *Harriss v. Pan American World Airways, Inc.,* 649 F.2d 670 (C.A.9 1980); *Burwell v. Eastern Air Lines, Inc.,* 633 F.2d 361 (C.A.4 1980), cert. denied, 450 U.S. 965, 101 S.Ct. 1480, 67 L.Ed.2d 613 (1981); *Condit v. United Air Lines, Inc.,* 558 F.2d 1176 (C.A.4 1977), cert. denied, 435 U.S. 934, 98 S.Ct. 1510, 55 L.Ed.2d 531 (1978); *In re National Airlines, Inc.,* 434 F.Supp. 249 (S.D.Fla.1977). In two of these cases, the courts pointedly indicated that fetal, as opposed to passenger, safety was best left to the mother. *Burwell,* 633 F.2d at 371; *National Airlines,* 434 F.Supp., at 259.

We considered safety to third parties in *Western Airlines, Inc. v. Criswell, supra,* in the context of the ADEA. We focused upon "the nature of the flight engineer's tasks," and the "actual capabilities of persons over age 60" in relation to those tasks. 472 U.S., at 406, 105 S.Ct., at 2747. Our safety concerns were not independent of the individual's ability to perform the assigned tasks, but rather involved the possibility that, because of age-connected debility, a flight engineer might not properly assist the pilot, and might thereby cause a safety emergency. Furthermore, although we considered the safety of third parties in *Dothard* and *Criswell,* those third parties were indispensable to the particular business at issue. In *Dothard,* the third parties were the inmates; in *Criswell,* the third parties were the passengers on the plane. We stressed that in order to qualify as a BFOQ, a job qualification must relate to the "essence," *Dothard,* 433 U.S., at 333, 97 S.Ct., at 2751, or to the "central mission of the employer's business," *Criswell,* 472 U.S., at 413, 105 S.Ct., at 2751.

The concurrence ignores the "essence of the business" test and so concludes that "the safety to fetuses in carrying out the duties of battery manufacturing is as much a legitimate concern as is safety to third parties in guarding prisons (*Dothard*) or flying airplanes (*Criswell*)." * * * By limiting its discussion to cost and safety concerns and rejecting the "essence of the business" test that our case law has established, the concurrence seeks to expand what is now the narrow BFOQ defense. Third-party safety considerations properly entered into the BFOQ analysis in *Dothard* and *Criswell* because they went to the core of the employee's job performance. Moreover, that performance involved the central purpose of the enterprise. *Dothard,* 433 U.S., at 335, 97 S.Ct., at 2729–2730 ("The essence of a correctional counselor's job is to maintain prison security"); *Criswell,* 472 U.S., at 413, 105 S.Ct., at 2751 (the central mission of the airline's business was the safe transportation of its passengers). The concurrence attempts to transform this case into one of customer safety. The unconceived fetuses of Johnson Controls' female employees, however, are neither customers nor third parties whose safety is essential to the business of battery manufacturing. No one can disregard the possibility of injury to future children; the BFOQ, however, is not so broad that it transforms this deep social concern into an essential aspect of batterymaking.

Our case law, therefore, makes clear that the safety exception is limited to instances in which sex or pregnancy actually interferes with the employee's ability to perform the job. This approach is consistent with the language of the BFOQ provision itself, for it suggests that permissible distinctions based on sex must relate to ability to perform the duties of the job. Johnson Controls suggests, however, that we expand the exception to allow fetal-protection policies that mandate particular standards for pregnant or fertile women. We decline to do so. Such an expansion contradicts not only the language of the BFOQ and the narrowness of its exception but the plain language and history of the Pregnancy Discrimination Act.

The PDA's amendment to Title VII contains a BFOQ standard of its own: unless pregnant employees differ from others "in their ability or inability to work," they must be "treated the same" as other employees "for all employment-related purposes." 42 U.S.C. § 2000e(k). This language clearly sets forth Congress' remedy for discrimination on the basis of pregnancy and potential pregnancy. Women who are either pregnant or potentially pregnant must be treated like others "similar in their ability * * * to work." *Ibid.* In other words, women as capable of doing their jobs as their male counterparts may not be forced to choose between having a child and having a job.

The concurrence asserts that the PDA did not alter the BFOQ defense. * * * The concurrence arrives at this conclusion by ignoring the second clause of the Act which states that "women affected by pregnancy, childbirth, or related medical conditions shall be treated the same for all employment-related purposes * * * as other persons not so affected but similar in their ability or inability to work." 42 U.S.C. § 2000e(k). Until this day, every Member of this Court had acknowledged that "[t]he second clause [of the PDA] could not be clearer: it mandates that pregnant employees 'shall be treated the same for all employment-related purposes' as nonpregnant employees similarly situated with respect to their ability or inability to work." *California Federal S. & L. Assn. v. Guerra,* 479 U.S. 272, 297, 107 S.Ct. 683, 698, 93 L.Ed.2d 613 (1987)(White, J., dissenting). The concurrence now seeks to read the second clause out of the Act.

The legislative history confirms what the language of the Pregnancy Discrimination Act compels. Both the House and Senate Reports accompanying the legislation indicate that this statutory standard was chosen to protect female workers from being treated differently from other employees simply because of their capacity to bear children. * * *

This history counsels against expanding the BFOQ to allow fetal-protection policies. The Senate Report quoted above states that employers may not require a pregnant woman to stop working at any time during her pregnancy unless she is unable to do her work. Employment late in pregnancy often imposes risks on the unborn child, see Chavkin, Walking a Tightrope: Pregnancy, Parenting, and Work, in Double Exposure 196, 196–202 (W. Chavkin ed. 1984), but Congress indicated that the employer may take into account only the woman's ability to get her job done. See Becker, From *Muller v. Oregon* to Fetal Vulnerability Policies, 53 U.Chi.L.Rev. 1219, 1255–1256 (1986). With the PDA, Congress made clear that the decision to become pregnant or to work while being either pregnant or capable of becoming pregnant was reserved for each individual woman to make for herself.

We conclude that the language of both the BFOQ provision and the PDA which amended it, as well as the legislative history and the case law, prohibit an employer from discriminating against a woman because of her capacity to become pregnant unless her reproductive potential prevents her from performing the duties of her job. We reiterate our holdings in *Criswell* and *Dothard* that an employer must direct its concerns about a woman's ability to perform her job safely and efficiently to those aspects of the woman's job-related activities that fall within the "essence" of the particular business.[4]

V

We have no difficulty concluding that Johnson Controls cannot establish a BFOQ. Fertile women, as far as appears in the record, participate in the manufacture of batteries as efficiently as anyone else. Johnson Controls' professed moral and ethical concerns about the welfare of the next generation do not suffice to establish a BFOQ of female sterility. Decisions about the welfare of future children must be left to the parents who conceive, bear, support, and raise them rather than to the employers who hire those parents.

---

4. The concurrence predicts that our reaffirmation of the narrowness of the BFOQ defense will preclude considerations of privacy as a basis for sex-based discrimination. *Post,* at n. 8. We have never addressed privacy-based sex discrimination and shall not do so here because the sex-based discrimination at issue today does not involve the privacy interests of Johnson Controls' customers. Nothing in our discussion of the "essence of the business test," however, suggests that sex could not constitute a BFOQ when privacy interests are implicated. See, *e.g., Backus v. Baptist Medical Center,* 510 F.Supp. 1191 (E.D.Ark.1981), vacated as moot, 671 F.2d 1100 (C.A.8 1982)(essence of obstetrics nurse's business is to provide sensitive care for patient's intimate and private concerns).

Congress has mandated this choice through Title VII, as amended by the Pregnancy Discrimination Act. Johnson Controls has attempted to exclude women because of their reproductive capacity. Title VII and the PDA simply do not allow a woman's dismissal because of her failure to submit to sterilization.

Nor can concerns about the welfare of the next generation be considered a part of the "essence" of Johnson Controls' business. Judge Easterbrook in this case pertinently observed: "It is word play to say that 'the job' at Johnson [Controls] is to make batteries without risk to fetuses in the same way 'the job' at Western Air Lines is to fly planes without crashing." 886 F.2d, at 913.

Johnson Controls argues that it must exclude all fertile women because it is impossible to tell which women will become pregnant while working with lead. This argument is somewhat academic in light of our conclusion that the company may not exclude fertile women at all; it perhaps is worth noting, however, that Johnson Controls has shown no "factual basis for believing that all or substantially all women would be unable to perform safely and efficiently the duties of the job involved." *Weeks v. Southern Bell Tel. & Tel. Co.*, 408 F.2d 228, 235 (C.A.5 1969), quoted with approval in *Dothard*, 433 U.S., at 333, 97 S.Ct., at 2751. Even on this sparse record, it is apparent that Johnson Controls is concerned about only a small minority of women. Of the eight pregnancies reported among the female employees, it has not been shown that any of the babies have birth defects or other abnormalities. The record does not reveal the birth rate for Johnson Controls' female workers but national statistics show that approximately nine percent of all fertile women become pregnant each year. The birthrate drops to two percent for blue collar workers over age 30. See Becker, 53 U.Chi.L.Rev., at 1233. Johnson Controls' fear of prenatal injury, no matter how sincere, does not begin to show that substantially all of its fertile women employees are incapable of doing their jobs.

VI

A word about tort liability and the increased cost of fertile women in the workplace is perhaps necessary. One of the dissenting judges in this case expressed concern about an employer's tort liability and concluded that liability for a potential injury to a fetus is a social cost that Title VII does not require a company to ignore. 886 F.2d, at 904–905. It is correct to say that Title VII does not prevent the employer from having a conscience. The statute, however, does prevent sex-specific fetal-protection policies. These two aspects of Title VII do not conflict.

More than 40 States currently recognize a right to recover for a prenatal injury based either on negligence or on wrongful death. See, *e.g.*, *Wolfe v. Isbell*, 291 Ala. 327, 333–334, 280 So.2d 758, 763 (1973); *Simon v. Mullin*, 34 Conn.Sup. 139, 147, 380 A.2d 1353, 1357 (1977). See also Note, 22 Suffolk U.L.Rev. 747, 754–756, and nn. 54, 57, and 58 (1988)(listing cases). According to Johnson Controls, however, the company complies with the lead standard developed by OSHA and warns its female employees about the damaging effects of lead. It is worth noting that OSHA gave the problem of lead lengthy consideration and concluded that "there is no basis whatsoever for the claim that women of childbearing age should be excluded from the workplace in order to protect the fetus or the course of pregnancy." 43 Fed.Reg. 52952, 52966 (1978). See also *id.,* at 54354, 54398. Instead, OSHA established a series of mandatory protections which, taken together, "should effectively minimize any risk to the fetus and newborn child." *Id.,* at 52966. See 29 CFR § 1910.125(k)(ii)(1989). Without negligence, it would be difficult for a court to find liability on the part of the employer. If, under general tort principles, Title VII bans sex-specific fetal-protection policies, the employer fully informs the woman of the risk, and the employer has not acted negligently, the basis for holding an employer liable seems remote at best.

Although the issue is not before us, the concurrence observes that "it is far from clear that compliance with Title VII will preempt state tort liability." * * *

If state tort law furthers discrimination in the workplace and prevents employers from hiring women who are capable of manufacturing the product as efficiently as men, then it will impede the accomplishment of Congress' goals in enacting Title VII. Because Johnson Controls has not argued that it faces any costs from tort liability, not to mention crippling ones, the pre-emption question is not before us. We therefore say no more than that the concurrence's speculation appears unfounded as well as premature.

The tort-liability argument reduces to two equally unpersuasive propositions. First, Johnson Controls attempts to solve the problem of reproductive health hazards by resorting to an exclusionary policy. Title VII plainly forbids illegal sex discrimination as a method of diverting attention from an employer's obligation to police the workplace. Second, the spectre of an award of damages reflects a fear that hiring fertile women will cost more. The extra cost of employing members of one sex, however, does not provide an affirmative Title VII defense for a discriminatory refusal to hire members of that gender. See *Manhart,* 435 U.S., at 716–718, and n. 32, 98 S.Ct., at 1379–1380, and n. 32. Indeed, in passing the PDA, Congress considered at length the considerable cost of providing equal treatment of pregnancy and related conditions, but made the "decision to forbid special treatment of pregnancy despite the social costs associated therewith." * * *

We, of course, are not presented with, nor do we decide, a case in which costs would be so prohibitive as to threaten the survival of the employer's business. We merely reiterate our prior holdings that the incremental cost of hiring women cannot justify discriminating against them.

VII

Our holding today that Title VII, as so amended, forbids sex-specific fetal-protection policies is neither remarkable nor unprecedented. Concern for a woman's existing or potential offspring historically has been the excuse for denying women equal employment opportunities. See, *e.g., Muller v. Oregon,* 208 U.S. 412, 28 S.Ct. 324, 52 L.Ed. 551 (1908). Congress in the PDA prohibited discrimination on the basis of a woman's ability to become pregnant. We do no more than hold that the Pregnancy Discrimination Act means what it says.

It is no more appropriate for the courts than it is for individual employers to decide whether a woman's reproductive role is more important to herself and her family than her economic role. Congress has left this choice to the woman as hers to make.

The judgment of the Court of Appeals is reversed and the case is remanded for further proceedings consistent with this opinion.

It is so ordered.

JUSTICE WHITE with whom THE CHIEF JUSTICE and JUSTICE KENNEDY join, concurring in part and concurring in the judgment.

The Court properly holds that Johnson Controls' fetal protection policy overtly discriminates against women, and thus is prohibited by Title VII unless it falls within the bona fide occupational qualification (BFOQ) exception, set forth at 42 U.S.C. § 2000e–2(e). The Court erroneously holds, however, that the BFOQ defense is so narrow that it could never justify a sex-specific fetal protection policy. I nevertheless concur in the judgment of reversal because on the record before us summary judgment in favor of Johnson Controls was improperly entered by the District Court and affirmed by the Court of Appeals.

I

In evaluating the scope of the BFOQ defense, the proper starting point is the language of the statute. * * * For the fetal protection policy involved in this case to be a BFOQ, therefore, the policy must be "reasonably necessary" to the "normal operation" of making batteries, which is Johnson Controls' "particular business." Although that is a difficult standard to satisfy, nothing in the statute's language indicates that it could *never* support a sex-specific fetal protection policy.[1]

On the contrary, a fetal protection policy would be justified under the terms of the statute if, for example, an employer could show that exclusion of women from certain jobs was reasonably necessary to avoid substantial tort liability. Common sense tells us that it is part of the normal operation of business concerns to avoid causing injury to third parties, as well as to employees, if for no other reason than to avoid tort liability and its substantial costs. This possibility of tort liability is not hypothetical; every State currently allows children born alive to recover in tort for prenatal injuries caused by third parties, see W. Keeton, D. Dobbs, R. Keeton, & D. Owen, Prosser and Keeton on Law of Torts § 55 p. 368 (5th ed. 1984), and an increasing number of courts have recognized a right to recover even for prenatal injuries caused by torts committed prior to conception, see 3 F. Harper, F. James, & O. Gray, Law of Torts § 18.3, pp. 677–678, n. 15 (2d ed. 1986).

The Court dismisses the possibility of tort liability by no more than speculating that if "Title VII bans sex-specific fetal-protection policies, the

---

1. The Court's heavy reliance on the word "occupational" in the BFOQ statute, * * * is unpersuasive. *Any* requirement for employment can be said to be an occupational qualification, since "occupational" merely means related to a job. See Webster's Third New International Dictionary 1560 (1976). Thus, Johnson Controls' requirement that employees engaged in battery manufacturing be either male or non-fertile clearly is an "occupational qualification." The issue, of course, is whether the qualification is "reasonably necessary to the normal operation" of Johnson Controls' business. It is telling that the Court offers no case support, either from this Court or the lower Federal Courts, for its interpretation of the word "occupational."

employer fully informs the woman of the risk, and the employer has not acted negligently, the basis for holding an employer liable seems remote at best." * * * Such speculation will be small comfort to employers. First, it is far from clear that compliance with Title VII will pre-empt state tort liability, and the Court offers no support for that proposition. Second, although warnings may preclude claims by injured *employees,* they will not preclude claims by injured children because the general rule is that parents cannot waive causes of action on behalf of their children, and the parents' negligence will not be imputed to the children. Finally, although state tort liability for prenatal injuries generally requires negligence, it will be difficult for employers to determine in advance what will constitute negligence. Compliance with OSHA standards, for example, has been held not to be a defense to state tort or criminal liability. * * * Moreover, it is possible that employers will be held strictly liable, if, for example, their manufacturing process is considered "abnormally dangerous." See Restatement (Second) of Torts § 869, comment *b* (1979).

Relying on *Los Angeles Dept. of Water and Power v. Manhart,* 435 U.S. 702, 98 S.Ct. 1370, 55 L.Ed.2d 657 (1978), the Court contends that tort liability cannot justify a fetal protection policy because the extra costs of hiring women is not a defense under Title VII. * * * This contention misrepresents our decision in *Manhart.* * * * We did not in that case address in any detail the nature of the BFOQ defense, and we certainly did not hold that cost was irrelevant to the BFOQ analysis. Rather, we merely stated in a footnote that "there has been no showing that sex distinctions are reasonably necessary to the normal operation of the Department's retirement plan." *Id.,* at 716, n. 30, 98 S.Ct., at 1379, n. 30. We further noted that although Title VII does not contain a "cost-justification defense comparable to the affirmative defense available in a price discrimination suit," "no defense based on the *total* cost of employing men and women was attempted in this case." *Id.,* at 716–717, and n. 32, 98 S.Ct., at 1379–1380, and n. 32.

Prior decisions construing the BFOQ defense confirm that the defense is broad enough to include considerations of cost and safety of the sort that could form the basis for an employer's adoption of a fetal protection policy. * * *

Dothard and *Criswell* make clear that avoidance of substantial safety risks to third parties is *inherently* part of both an employee's ability to perform a job and an employer's "normal operation" of its business. Indeed, in both cases, the Court approved the statement in *Weeks v. Southern Bell Telephone & Telegraph Co.,* 408 F.2d 228 (C.A.5 1969), that an employer could establish a BFOQ defense by showing that "all or substantially all women would be unable to perform *safely and efficiently* the duties of the job involved." *Id.,* at 235 (emphasis added). See *Criswell,* 472 U.S., at 414, 105 S.Ct., at 2751–52; *Dothard, supra,* 433 U.S., at 333, 97 S.Ct., at 2728–29. The Court's statement in this case that "the safety exception is limited to instances in which sex or pregnancy actually interferes with the employee's ability to perform the job," * * * therefore adds no support to its conclusion that a fetal protection policy could never be justified as a BFOQ. On the facts of this case, for example, protecting fetal safety while carrying out the duties of battery manufacturing is as much a legitimate concern as is safety to third parties in guarding prisons (*Dothard*) or flying airplanes (*Criswell*).

Dothard and *Criswell* also confirm that costs are relevant in determining whether a discriminatory policy is reasonably necessary for the normal operation of a business. In *Dothard,* the safety problem that justified exclusion of women from the prison guard positions was largely a result of inadequate staff and facilities. See 433 U.S., at 335, 97 S.Ct., at 2729–30. If the cost of employing women could not be considered, the employer there should have been required to hire more staff and restructure the prison environment rather than exclude women. Similarly, in *Criswell* the airline could have been required to hire more pilots and install expensive monitoring devices rather than discriminate against older employees. The BFOQ statute, however, reflects "Congress' unwillingness to require employers to change the very nature of their operations." *Price Waterhouse v. Hopkins,* 490 U.S. 228, 242, 109 S.Ct. 1775, 1786, 104 L.Ed.2d 268 (1989)(plurality opinion).

The Pregnancy Discrimination Act (PDA), 42 U.S.C. § 2000e(k), contrary to the Court's assertion, * * * did not restrict the scope of the BFOQ defense. The PDA was only an amendment to the "Definitions" section of Title VII, 42 U.S.C. § 2000e, and did not purport to eliminate or alter the BFOQ defense. Rather, it merely clarified Title VII to make it clear that pregnancy and related conditions are included within Title VII's antidiscrimination provisions. * * *

This interpretation is confirmed by the PDA's legislative history. * * * [T]he PDA was designed to overrule the decision in *General Electric Co. v. Gilbert,* 429 U.S. 125, 97 S.Ct. 401, 50 L.Ed.2d 343 (1976), where the Court had held that "an exclusion of pregnancy from a disability benefits plan providing general coverage is not a gender-based discrimination at all." * * * The PDA thus "makes clear that it is discriminatory to treat pregnancy-related conditions less favorably than other medical conditions." *Newport News, supra,* 462 U.S., at 684, 103 S.Ct., at 2631. It does not, however, alter the standards for employer *defenses.* The Senate Report, for example, stated that the PDA "defines sex discrimination, as proscribed in the existing statute, to include these physiological occurrences [pregnancy, childbirth, and related medical conditions] peculiar to women; *it does not change the application of Title VII to sex discrimination in any other way.*" S.Rep. No. 95–331, pp. 3–4 (1977)(emphasis added). Similarly, the House Report stated that "[p]regnancy-based distinctions will be subject to the same scrutiny *on the same terms* as other acts of sex discrimination proscribed in the existing statute." H.R.Rep. No. 95–948, p. 4 (1978), U.S.Code Cong. & Admin.News 1978, p. 4752 (emphasis added).[7]

In enacting the BFOQ standard, "Congress did not ignore the public interest in safety." *Criswell, supra,* 472 U.S., at 419, 105 S.Ct., at 2754. The Court's narrow interpretation of the BFOQ defense in this case, however, means that an employer cannot exclude even *pregnant* women from an environment highly toxic to their fetuses. It is foolish to think that Congress intended such a result, and neither the language of the BFOQ exception nor

---

7. Even if the PDA *did* establish a separate BFOQ standard for pregnancy-related discrimination, if a female employee could only perform the duties of her job by imposing substantial safety and liability risks, she would not be "similar in [her] ability or inability to work" as a male employee, under the terms of the PDA. See 42 U.S.C. § 2000e(k).

our cases require it.[8]

II

Despite my disagreement with the Court concerning the scope of the BFOQ defense, I concur in reversing the Court of Appeals because that court erred in affirming the District Court's grant of summary judgment in favor of Johnson Controls. First, the Court of Appeals erred in failing to consider the level of risk-avoidance that was part of Johnson Controls' "normal operation." Although the court did conclude that there was a "substantial risk" to fetuses from lead exposure in fertile women, 886 F.2d 871, 879–883, 898 (C.A.7 1989), it merely meant that there was a high risk that *some* fetal injury would occur absent a fetal protection policy. That analysis, of course, fails to address the *extent* of fetal injury that is likely to occur. If the fetal protection policy insists on a risk-avoidance level substantially higher than other risk levels tolerated by Johnson Controls such as risks to employees and consumers, the policy should not constitute a BFOQ.[10]

Second, even without more information about the normal level of risk at Johnson Controls, the fetal protection policy at issue here reaches too far. This is evident both in its presumption that, absent medical documentation to the contrary, all women are fertile regardless of their age, see *id.,* at 876, n. 8, and in its exclusion of presumptively fertile women from positions that might result in a promotion to a position involving high lead exposure, *id.,* at 877. There has been no showing that either of those aspects of the policy is reasonably necessary to ensure safe and efficient operation of Johnson Controls' battery-manufacturing business. Of course, these infirmities in the company's policy do not warrant invalidating the entire fetal protection program.

Third, it should be recalled that until 1982 Johnson Controls operated without an exclusionary policy, and it has not identified any grounds for believing that its current policy is reasonably necessary to its normal operations. Although it is now more aware of some of the dangers of lead exposure, *id.,* at 899, it has not shown that the risks of fetal harm or the costs

---

8. The Court's cramped reading of the BFOQ defense is also belied by the legislative history of Title VII, in which three examples of permissible sex discrimination were mentioned—a female nurse hired to care for an elderly woman, an all-male professional baseball team, and a masseur. See 110 Cong.Rec. 2718 (1964)(Rep. Goodell); *id.,* at 7212–7213 (interpretive memorandum introduced by Sens. Clark and Case); *id.,* at 2720 (Rep. Multer). In none of those situations would gender "actually interfer[e] with the employee's ability to perform the job," as required today by the Court.

The Court's interpretation of the BFOQ standard also would seem to preclude considerations of privacy as a basis for sex-based discrimination, since those considerations do not relate directly to an employee's physical ability to perform the duties of the job. The lower federal courts, however, have consistently recognized that privacy interests may justify sex-based requirements for certain jobs. See, *e.g.,*

Fesel v. Masonic Home of Delaware, Inc., 447 F.Supp. 1346 (D.Del.1978), aff'd, 591 F.2d 1334 (C.A.3 1979)(nurse's aide in retirement home); *Jones v. Hinds General Hospital,* 666 F.Supp. 933 (S.D.Miss.1987)(nursing assistant); *Local 567 American Federation of State, County, and Municipal Employees, AFL–CIO v. Michigan Council 25, American Federation of State, County, and Municipal Employees, AFL–CIO,* 635 F.Supp. 1010 (E.D.Mich.1986)(mental health workers); *Norwood v. Dale Maintenance System, Inc.,* 590 F.Supp. 1410 (N.D.Ill.1984)(washroom attendant); *Backus v. Baptist Medical Center,* 510 F.Supp. 1191 (E.D.Ark.1981), vacated as moot, 671 F.2d 1100 (C.A.8 1982)(nursing position in obstetrics and gynecology department of hospital).

10. It is possible, for example, that alternatives to exclusion of women, such as warnings combined with frequent bloodtestings, would sufficiently minimize the risk such that it would be comparable to other risks tolerated by Johnson Controls.

associated with it have substantially increased. Cf. *Manhart,* 435 U.S., at 716, n. 30, 98 S.Ct., at 1379, n. 30, in which we rejected a BFOQ defense because the employer had operated prior to the discrimination with no significant adverse effects.

Finally, the Court of Appeals failed to consider properly petitioners' evidence of harm to offspring caused by lead exposure in males. The court considered that evidence only in its discussion of the business necessity standard, in which it focused on whether *petitioners* had met their burden of proof. 886 F.2d, at 889–890. The burden of proving that a discriminatory qualification is a BFOQ, however, rests with the employer. See, *e.g., Price Waterhouse,* 490 U.S., at 248, 109 S.Ct., at 1789; *Dothard,* 433 U.S., at 333, 97 S.Ct., at 2728–29. Thus, the court should have analyzed whether the evidence was sufficient for petitioners to survive summary judgment in light of *respondent's* burden of proof to establish a BFOQ. Moreover, the court should not have discounted the evidence as "speculative," 886 F.2d, at 889, merely because it was based on animal studies. We have approved the use of animal studies to assess risks, * * * and OSHA uses animal studies in establishing its lead control regulations, * * * It seems clear that if the Court of Appeals had properly analyzed that evidence, it would have concluded that summary judgment against petitioners was not appropriate because there was a dispute over a material issue of fact.

* * *

JUSTICE SCALIA, concurring in the judgment.

I generally agree with the Court's analysis, but have some reservations, several of which bear mention.

First, I think it irrelevant that there was "evidence in the record about the debilitating effect of lead exposure on the male reproductive system," * * *. Even without such evidence, treating women differently "on the basis of pregnancy" constitutes discrimination "on the basis of sex," because Congress has unequivocally said so. Pregnancy Discrimination Act of 1978, 92 Stat. 2076, 42 U.S.C. § 2000e(k).

Second, the Court points out that "Johnson Controls has shown no factual basis for believing that all or substantially all women would be unable to perform safely * * * the duties of the job involved," * * * In my view, this is not only "somewhat academic in light of our conclusion that the company may not exclude fertile women at all," *ibid.;* it is entirely irrelevant. By reason of the Pregnancy Discrimination Act, it would not matter if all pregnant women placed their children at risk in taking these jobs, just as it does not matter if no men do so. As Judge Easterbrook put it in his dissent below, "Title VII gives parents the power to make occupational decisions affecting their families. A legislative forum is available to those who believe that such decisions should be made elsewhere." *International Union, UAW v. Johnson Controls, Inc.,* 886 F.2d 871, 915 (C.A.7 1989)(Easterbrook, J., dissenting).

Third, I am willing to assume, as the Court intimates, * * * that any action required by Title VII cannot give rise to liability under state tort law. That assumption, however, does not answer the question whether an action *is* required by Title VII (including the BFOQ provision) even if it is subject to liability under state tort law. It is perfectly reasonable to believe that Title VII has *accommodated* state tort law through the BFOQ exception. However, all that need be said in the present case is that Johnson has not demonstrated a substantial risk of tort liability—which is alone enough to defeat a tort-based assertion of the BFOQ exception.

Last, the Court goes far afield, it seems to me, in suggesting that increased cost alone—short of "costs * * * so prohibitive as to threaten survival of the employer's business," * * *—cannot support a BFOQ defense. * * * I agree with Justice White's concurrence, * * * that nothing in our prior cases suggests this, and in my view it is wrong. I think, for example, that a shipping company may refuse to hire pregnant women as crew members on long voyages because the on-board facilities for foreseeable emergencies, though quite feasible, would be inordinately expensive. In the present case, however, Johnson has not asserted a cost-based BFOQ.

I concur in the judgment of the Court.

Notes on Johnson Controls

1. Judge Easterbrook, dissenting from the Seventh Circuit's judgment, remarked that *Johnson Controls* "is likely the most important sex-discrimination case in any court since 1964, when Congress enacted Title VII", adding that if the majority decision stood, "by one estimate 20 million industrial jobs could be closed to women". International Union, UAW v. Johnson Controls, Inc., 886 F.2d 871, 920 (7th Cir.1989), reversed 499 U.S. 187, 111 S.Ct. 1196, 113 L.Ed.2d 158 (1991). Is the Supreme Court's decision in *Johnson Controls* a victory for women? As Judge Johnson observed in one of the earliest cases interpreting the BFOQ exception, "Men have always had the right to determine whether the incremental increase in remuneration for strenuous, dangerous, obnoxious, boring or unromantic tasks is worth the candle. The promise of Title VII is that women are now to be on equal footing." Weeks v. Southern Bell Tel. & Tel. Co., 408 F.2d 228, 236 (5th Cir.1969). Does that logic apply to toxic workplaces? Judge Easterbrook thought so: "No legal or ethical principle compels or allows Johnson to assume that women are less able than men to make intelligent decisions about the welfare of the next generation, that the interests of the next generation always trump the interests of living women, and that the only acceptable level of risk is zero." Id., 886 F.2d at 913 (dissenting opinion). Do you agree?

2. The reactions of notewriters to *Johnson Controls* are something of a mixed bag. A Harvard notewriter applauded the outcome, but felt that the Court should have explored the policy reasons for rejecting fetal protection plans, explaining that "[i]n addition to violating the letter of Title VII, fetal protection policies that exclude women from the work force undermine the goals embodied in Title VII—work force integration, pay equality, and equal opportunity." The Supreme Court, 1990 Term, Leading Cases, 105 Harv.L.Rev. 177, 380 (1991). A Virginia notewriter described the outcome as "a feminist victory of sorts," but she found the theoretical basis for the opinion "seriously flawed." See Alison E. Grossman, Note, Striking Down Fetal Protection Policies: A Feminist Victory?, 77 Va.L.Rev. 1607, 1624 (1991). She would rather ground *Johnson Controls* and other BFOQ decisions in feminist theory—preferably MacKinnon's inequality theory—but recognizes that there is a "real risk" that judges might misapply this theory. How does she think inequality theory, correctly applied, would decide the validity of fetal protection policies? While noting that her conclusion is not

"absolute," the notewriter answers that "[i]nequality theory chooses against allowing the exclusion of women with fetal protection policies because such policies reinforce economic subordination and shape reality to conform to sex differences, the source of much sexual inequality in the first instance." Id., 77 Va. at 1634 & n. 124. Is this consistent with Judge Easterbrook's view, quoted in Note 1, supra?

3. A California appellate court had come earlier to the same conclusion under state law about the validity of Johnson's fetal protection policy. In Johnson Controls, Inc. v. California Fair Employment and Housing Comm'n, 218 Cal.App.3d 517, 267 Cal.Rptr. 158 (1990), opinion modified and rehearing denied, petition for review denied, California Supreme Court Minutes (May 17, 1990), real party in interest Queen Elizabeth Foster applied for work at Johnson's Globe Automotive Battery Plant in Fullerton, California. She was rejected because she declined to show medical evidence of infertility. She filed a complaint with the Commission, which found that the employer's refusal to hire Foster constituted unlawful sex discrimination under California law and was not justified by proof of a BFOQ defense. It also found that the business necessity defense was available only to excuse a facially neutral practice having only an incidental adverse affect on women. On review, the Court of Appeals sustained the Commission's order and declined to follow the Seventh Circuit decision in *Johnson Controls*. The Court noted that the decision "has been recently reviewed and sharply criticized by the federal Equal Employment Opportunity Commission in the policy guidance rules issued by that administrative body" going on to point out that the Commission concluded that "Commission field offices should not rely on the Johnson Controls decision as guidance for processing 'fetal hazards' charges." Id., 218 Cal.App.3d at 547, 267 Cal.Rptr. at 174–75.

4. What position should those who are concerned with equality for working women take concerning fetal protection policies? Does *Cal Fed*, supra at p. 749, provide a foundation for framing employer policies or state legislation that will enable women "to have families without losing their jobs"—or risking damage to their future children? Professor Furnish believes it does. She argues that *Cal Fed* would permit fetal protection policies that meet two standards: (1) the policy is based on an actual physical difference between men and women, rather than on a stereotype about pregnancy; and (2) the policy is consistent with the overall purpose of Title VII as elaborated by the PDA to achieve equal employment opportunity. She concludes that policies that protect pregnant workers plainly meet both tests, for "only the pregnant woman clearly runs the risk that toxins will affect her fetus' health" and such preferential treatment "is completely consistent with the PDA's goal of placing and keeping women in the work force's mainstream and not penalizing them for pregnancy." She concedes that affording protection to fertile women but not to fertile men is more difficult, but may nevertheless be nonstereotypic and therefore possible if the preference is "based on the fact that fetal harm may occur in the early stages of pregnancy, in some cases before the woman knows she is pregnant." Hannah Arterian Furnish, Beyond Protection: Relevant Difference and Equality in the Toxic Work Environment, 21 U.C. Davis L.Rev. 1, 18–20 (1988). Do you agree that *Cal Fed* can or should be extended in this manner?

5. The pregnant stewardess cases, discussed at p. 747, supra, treated the BFOQ exception in a particularly confusing manner. Defendant airlines sought to justify their policy of requiring stewardesses to give notice and stop flying upon learning of the pregnancy by relying upon the BFOQ exception: they argued that a stewardess who continues to fly while pregnant is potentially dangerous to the

safety of passengers. Reliance was placed on FAA requirements that a plane must be evacuated of passengers in 90 seconds under emergency conditions. To satisfy this demand, stewardesses must be able to inflate life rafts weighing between 125 and 130 pounds; push open doors requiring 70 to 100 pounds of force to move; and generally be agile and quick in helping passengers down the emergency chutes and dragging them away from the vicinity of the aircraft. Medical testimony was introduced dealing with the potentially disabling complications of pregnancy that might render the stewardess less capable of performing her duties safely, including fatigue, nausea and vomiting, the danger of spontaneous abortion in early pregnancy, and increasing girth and disturbance of balance as the pregnancy advances. In most of the cases, the litigation centered on the conclusions to be drawn from the medical testimony; frequently, plaintiffs conceded that if defendants could establish that a pregnant flight attendant was unable to perform her safety functions as effectively in an emergency, a BFOQ defense would be made out. Plaintiffs urged that Title VII required individualized testing to determine when each pregnant stewardess should stop flying.

The reported decisions were in conflict. Some held that the mandatory grounding policy was essential to passenger safety and was justified as a BFOQ defense. E.g., Condit v. United Air Lines, Inc., 558 F.2d 1176 (4th Cir.1977), cert. denied 435 U.S. 934, 98 S.Ct. 1510, 55 L.Ed.2d 531 (1978); EEOC v. Delta Air Lines, Inc., 441 F.Supp. 626 (S.D.Tex.1977). Others held that the BFOQ defense was not available during the early stages of pregnancy, and permitted pregnant stewardesses to continue flying for a period of time upon consultation with their physicians. E.g., Maclennan v. American Airlines, Inc., 440 F.Supp. 466 (E.D.Va. 1977)(through the 26th week of pregnancy); In re Nat'l Airlines, Inc., 434 F.Supp. 249 (S.D.Fla.1977)(no mandatory grounding during first trimester of pregnancy; individual testing during second trimester; mandatory grounding permitted during third trimester); Burwell v. Eastern Air Lines, 633 F.2d 361 (4th Cir.1980)(en banc)(mandatory grounding permissible after first trimester), cert. denied 450 U.S. 965, 101 S.Ct. 1480, 67 L.Ed.2d 613 (1981).

What was the impact of the Pregnancy Discrimination Act on pregnant stewardesses? As we have seen, the 1978 amendment did not simply add "pregnancy discrimination" as a new category to the Act; rather, it stated that the term "sex" includes "pregnancy." Congress made it clear that disparate treatment of pregnant workers is sex discrimination under Title VII. It follows, then, that the BFOQ exception is applicable if what the employer wants to do is to exclude pregnant workers from the job category of flight attendant. But does the BFOQ exception operate the same way where the disparate treatment is based on pregnancy as it does in other sex discrimination cases?

This problem was discussed in Harriss v. Pan American World Airways, 649 F.2d 670 (9th Cir.1980). Since the case involved both a request for back pay as well as an injunction, the court felt itself bound to determine the legality of Pan American's "stop policy" both before and after the 1978 Amendment. The court held that prior to the PDA, Pan American's policy, under *Gilbert*, did not constitute *per se* sex discrimination, but that the policy did have a disparate impact on women. Applying the business necessity defense, the court affirmed the trial court's finding that Pan American had shown a sufficient correlation between its policy and passenger safety to satisfy an "appropriately narrow" definition of the defense. The trial court's finding was based on the following factors:

1) "[t]he ability of each flight attendant to perform at full capacity is vital to emergency management"; 2) a flight attendant's ability to perform her emergency functions might be impaired by fatigue, nausea and vomiting, or spontaneous abortion, all of which occur with some regularity during the first two trimesters of pregnancy; and 3) the gravity of the safety risk, measured by the likelihood of harm and the probable severity of harm, was great enough to warrant the imposition of a stringent personnel policy for flight attendants.

Id., 649 F.2d at 675.

Turning to the impact of the 1978 Amendment, the *Harriss* court recognized that its terms required a holding that discrimination based on pregnancy constituted a *per se* violation of the Act. It further held that the BFOQ exception was the standard against which the employer's defenses must be measured. Using the definitions of the BFOQ defense developed in *Diaz* and *Weeks,* discussed in Notes 3 and 4, supra at p. 785, the court concluded that Pan American must show that its policy of grounding pregnant stewardesses was "reasonably necessary" to the essence of its business, namely, safely transporting passengers from one place to another. This test, it concluded, had been satisfied: in light of the trial court's findings quoted above concerning the significance of the risk to passengers involved in allowing pregnant stewardesses to continue flying, Pan American's policy was "reasonably necessary" to passenger safety. The court further accepted the trial court's finding that individualized testing would be impractical.

Can you see any difference between the court's application, as distinguished from its phrasing, of the business necessity test and the BFOQ exception in *Harriss* ? Are the two tests the same in practical effect in pregnancy discrimination cases? As we have seen, courts disagree about the exact point at which pregnancy disables a stewardess from performing the duties of her job. The cases are in agreement that she is disabled after the 28th week of pregnancy; a narrow majority believe that she is disabled prior to the end of the first trimester. What about the second trimester? Is individualized testing required under the BFOQ exception after the 1978 Amendment, despite what *Harriss* says? Judge Mary M. Schroeder, dissenting in *Harriss,* urged that Pan American was required to

> design procedures, reviews, and tests which measure the ability of all flight attendants who have medical conditions which might affect their performance in an emergency situation

instead of just singling pregnancy out as a disabling condition. Id., 649 F.2d at 680. Isn't she right? But see Levin v. Delta Air Lines, 730 F.2d, 994 (5th Cir.1984), affirming district court finding that airline is unable to predict in advance which pregnant flight attendants may become disabled, rejecting individualized testing requirement.

In contrast to the pregnant flight attendant cases, the Eighth Circuit in Carney v. Martin Luther Home, Inc., 824 F.2d 643 (8th Cir.1987), found discrimination based on pregnancy and rejected defendant's BFOQ defense. Plaintiff, a houseparent/adult services trainer in an intermediate care facility for mentally retarded persons, experienced some lightheadedness and dizziness during her pregnancy. Her physician advised her to refrain from pushing or lifting without assistance, but did not advise her to stop working. Defendant forced her to take an unpaid leave of absence, and to be reconsidered for employment after giving birth. Judge Larson rejected defendant's claim that its decision was based on plaintiff's medical condition, rather than her pregnancy *per se,* and was therefore not in violation of Title VII. Pointing to the statutory phrase "on the basis of pregnancy, childbirth, or related medical conditions," he agreed with plaintiff that

> she presented direct evidence of discrimination by establishing that the defendant placed her on unpaid medical leave as a result of a "related medical condition," and we find that the district court erred in applying the *McDonnell Douglas* test under these circumstances.

Id., 824 F.2d at 648. Moreover, defendant failed to establish a BFOQ, and in fact conceded on appeal that plaintiff could perform her job without difficulty. Judge Larson concluded:

> While we have no doubt that the Home harbors no ill motive against plaintiff or other pregnant women, history reveals that women have consistently been denied equal opportunities based on a professed concern for their well-being and/or unfounded notions about their capabilities. [citations omitted.] The PDA was enacted to ensure that pregnant women are judged on their actual ability and willingness to work, and although the Home had no mandatory leave policy, its decision as to the plaintiff in effect forced her from the workplace at a time when she was willing and able to perform her job successfully. * * *

Id., 824 F.2d at 649.

c. *Sexual Harassment*

[The EEOC Guidelines on Sexual Harassment appear
in the Statutory Appendix]

MERITOR SAVINGS BANK, FSB v. VINSON

Supreme Court of the United States, 1986.
477 U.S. 57, 106 S.Ct. 2399, 91 L.Ed.2d 49.

Justice Rehnquist delivered the opinion of the Court.

This case presents important questions concerning claims of workplace "sexual harassment" brought under Title VII of the Civil Rights Act of 1964, 78 Stat. 253, as amended, 42 U.S.C. § 2000e *et seq.*

I

In 1974, respondent Mechelle Vinson met Sidney Taylor, a vice president of what is now petitioner Meritor Savings Bank (the bank) and manager of one of its branch offices. When respondent asked whether she might obtain employment at the bank, Taylor gave her an application, which she completed and returned the next day; later that same day Taylor called her to say that she had been hired. With Taylor as her supervisor, respondent started as a teller-trainee, and thereafter was promoted to teller, head teller, and assistant branch manager. She worked at the same branch for four years, and it is undisputed that her advancement there was based on merit alone. In September 1978, respondent notified Taylor that she was taking sick leave for an indefinite period. On November 1, 1978, the bank discharged her for excessive use of that leave.

Respondent brought this action against Taylor and the bank, claiming that during her four years at the bank she had "constantly been subjected to sexual harassment" by Taylor in violation of Title VII. She sought injunctive relief, compensatory and punitive damages against Taylor and the bank, and attorney's fees.

At the 11–day bench trial, the parties presented conflicting testimony about Taylor's behavior during respondent's employment. Respondent testified that during her probationary period as a teller-trainee, Taylor treated her in a fatherly way and made no sexual advances. Shortly thereafter, however, he invited her out to dinner and, during the course of the meal, suggested that they go to a motel to have sexual relations. At first she refused, but out of what she described as fear of losing her job she eventually agreed. According to respondent, Taylor thereafter made repeated demands upon her for sexual favors, usually at the branch, both during and after business hours; she estimated that over the next several years she had intercourse with him some 40 or 50 times. In addition, respondent testified that Taylor fondled her in front of other employees, followed her into the women's restroom when she went there alone, exposed himself to her, and even forcibly raped her on several occasions. These activities ceased after 1977, respondent stated, when she started going with a steady boyfriend.

Respondent also testified that Taylor touched and fondled other women employees of the bank, and she attempted to call witnesses to support this charge. But while some supporting testimony apparently was admitted without objection, the District Court did not allow her "to present wholesale evidence of a pattern and practice relating to sexual advances to other female employees in her case in chief, but advised her that she might well be able to present such evidence in rebuttal to the defendants' cases." *Vinson v. Taylor,* 22 EPD ¶ 30708, pp. 14688–14689, 23 FEP Cases 37, 38–39, n. 1 (D.D.C.1980). Respondent did not offer such evidence in rebuttal. Finally, respondent testified that because she was afraid of Taylor she never reported his harassment to any of his supervisors and never attempted to use the bank's complaint procedure.

Taylor denied respondent's allegations of sexual activity, testifying that he never fondled her, never made suggestive remarks to her, never engaged in sexual intercourse with her and never asked her to do so. He contended instead that respondent made her accusations in response to a business-related dispute. The bank also denied respondent's allegations and asserted that any sexual harassment by Taylor was unknown to the bank and engaged in without its consent or approval.

The District Court denied relief, but did not resolve the conflicting testimony about the existence of a sexual relationship between respondent and Taylor. It found instead that

> "If [respondent] and Taylor did engage in an intimate or sexual relationship during the time of [respondent's] employment with [the bank], that relationship was a voluntary one having nothing to do with her continued employment at [the bank] or her advancement or promotions at that institution." *Id.,* at 42 (footnote omitted).

The court ultimately found that respondent "was not the victim of sexual harassment and was not the victim of sexual discrimination" while employed at the bank. *Id.,* 43.

Although it concluded that respondent had not proved a violation of Title VII, the District Court nevertheless went on to address the bank's liability. After noting the bank's express policy against discrimination, and finding that neither respondent nor any other employee had ever lodged a complaint about sexual harassment by Taylor, the court ultimately concluded that "the bank was without notice and cannot be held liable for the alleged actions of Taylor." *Id.,* at 42.

The Court of Appeals for the District of Columbia Circuit reversed. 243 U.S.App.D.C. 323, 753 F.2d 141 (1985). Relying on its earlier holding in *Bundy v. Jackson,* 205 U.S.App.D.C. 444, 641 F.2d 934 (1981), decided after the trial in this case, the court stated that a violation of Title VII may be predicated on either of two types of sexual harassment: harassment that involves the conditioning of concrete employment benefits on sexual favors, and harassment that, while not affecting economic benefits, creates a hostile or offensive working environment. The court drew additional support for this position from the Equal Employment Opportunity Commission's Guidelines on Discrimination Because of Sex, 29 CFR § 1604.11(a)(1985), which set out these two types of sexual harassment claims. Believing that "Vinson's grievance was clearly of the [hostile environment] type," 243 U.S.App.D.C., at 327, 753 F.2d, at 145, and that the District Court had not considered whether a violation of this type had occurred, the court concluded that a remand was necessary.

The court further concluded that the District Court's finding that any sexual relationship between respondent and Taylor "was a voluntary one" did not obviate the need for a remand. "[U]ncertain as to precisely what the [district] court meant" by this finding, the Court of Appeals held that if the evidence otherwise showed that "Taylor made Vinson's toleration of sexual harassment a condition of her employment," her voluntariness "had no materiality whatsoever." *Id.,* at 328, 753 F.2d, at 146. The court then surmised that the District Court's finding of voluntariness might have been based on "the voluminous testimony regarding respondent's dress and personal fantasies," testimony that the Court of Appeals believed "had no place in this litigation." *Id.,* at 328, 753 F.2d, at 146, n. 36.

As to the bank's liability, the Court of Appeals held that an employer is absolutely liable for sexual harassment practiced by supervisory personnel, whether or not the employer knew or should have known about the misconduct. The court relied chiefly on Title VII's definition of "employer" to include "any agent of such a person," 42 U.S.C. § 2000e(b), as well as on the EEOC guidelines. The court held that a supervisor is an "agent" of his employer for Title VII purposes, even if he lacks authority to hire, fire, or promote, since "the mere existence—or even the appearance—of a significant degree of influence in vital job decisions gives any supervisor the opportunity to impose on employees." 243 U.S.App.D.C., at 332, 753 F.2d, at 150.

In accordance with the foregoing, the Court of Appeals reversed the judgment of the District Court and remanded the case for further proceedings. A subsequent suggestion for rehearing en banc was denied, with three judges dissenting. 245 U.S.App.D.C. 306, 760 F.2d 1330 (1985). We granted certiorari, 474 U.S. 815, 106 S.Ct. 57, 88 L.Ed.2d 46 (1985), and now affirm but for different reasons.

II

Title VII of the Civil Rights Act of 1964 makes it "an unlawful employment practice for an employer * * * to discriminate against any individual with respect to his compensation, terms, conditions, or privileges of employment, because of such individual's race, color, religion, sex, or national origin." 42 U.S.C. § 2000e–2(a)(1). The prohibition against discrimination based on sex was added to Title VII at the last minute on the floor of the House of Representatives. 110 Cong.Rec. 2577–2584 (1964). The principal argument in opposition to the amendment was that "sex discrimination" was sufficiently different from other types of discrimination that it ought to receive separate legislative treatment. See *id.*, at 2577 (Statement of Rep. Celler quoting letter from United States Department of Labor); *id.*, at 2584 (statement of Rep. Green). This argument was defeated, the bill quickly passed as amended, and we are left with little legislative history to guide us in interpreting the Act's prohibition against discrimination based on "sex."

Respondent argues, and the Court of Appeals held, that unwelcome sexual advances that create an offensive or hostile working environment violate Title VII. Without question, when a supervisor sexually harasses a subordinate because of the subordinate's sex, that supervisor "discriminate[s]" on the basis of sex. Petitioner apparently does not challenge this proposition. It contends instead that in prohibiting discrimination with respect to "compensation, terms, conditions, or privileges" of employment, Congress was concerned with what petitioner describes as "tangible loss" of "an economic character," not "purely psychological aspects of the workplace environment." Brief for Petitioner 30–31, 34. In support of this claim petitioner observes that in both the legislative history of Title VII and this Court's Title VII decisions, the focus has been on tangible, economic barriers erected by discrimination.

We reject petitioner's view. First, the language of Title VII is not limited to "economic" or "tangible" discrimination. The phrase "terms, conditions, or privileges of employment" evinces a congressional intent "'to strike at the entire spectrum of disparate treatment of men and women' "in employment. *Los Angeles Department of Water and Power v. Manhart*, 435 U.S. 702, 707, n. 13 * * * (1978), quoting *Sprogis v. United Air Lines, Inc.*, 444 F.2d 1194, 1198 (C.A.7 1971). Petitioner has pointed to nothing in the Act to suggest that Congress contemplated the limitation urged here.

Second, in 1980 the EEOC issued guidelines specifying that "sexual harassment," as there defined, is a form of sex discrimination prohibited by Title VII. As an "administrative interpretation of the Act by the enforcing agency," *Griggs v. Duke Power Co.*, * * * these guidelines, " 'while not controlling upon the courts by reason of their authority, do constitute a body of experience and informed judgment to which courts and litigants may properly resort for guidance,' " *General Electric Co. v. Gilbert*, 429 U.S. 125, 141–142 * * * (1976), quoting *Skidmore v. Swift & Co.*, 323 U.S. 134, 140, 65 S.Ct. 161, 164, 89 L.Ed. 124 (1944). The EEOC guidelines fully support the view that harassment leading to noneconomic injury can violate Title VII.

In defining "sexual harassment," the guidelines first describe the kinds of workplace conduct that may be actionable under Title VII. These include "[u]nwelcome sexual advances, requests for sexual favors, and other verbal or physical conduct of a sexual nature." 29 CFR § 1604.11(a)(1985). Relevant to the charges at issue in this case, the guidelines provide that such sexual misconduct constitutes prohibited "sexual harassment," whether or not it is directly linked to the grant or denial of an economic *quid pro quo,* where "such conduct has the purpose or effect of unreasonably interfering with an individual's work performance or creating an intimidating, hostile, or offensive working environment." § 1604.11(a)(3).

In concluding that so-called "hostile environment" (*i.e.,* non *quid pro quo*) harassment violates Title VII, the EEOC drew upon a substantial body of judicial decisions and EEOC precedent holding that Title VII affords employees the right to work in an environment free from discriminatory intimidation, ridicule, and insult. See generally 45 Fed.Reg. 74676 (1980). *Rogers v. EEOC,* 454 F.2d 234 (C.A.5 1971), cert. denied, 406 U.S. 957, 92 S.Ct. 2058, 32 L.Ed.2d 343 (1972), was apparently the first case to recognize a cause of action based upon a discriminatory work environment. In *Rogers,* the Court of Appeals for the Fifth Circuit held that a Hispanic complainant could establish a Title VII violation by demonstrating that her employer created an offensive work environment for employees by giving discriminatory service to its Hispanic clientele. The court explained that an employee's protections under Title VII extend beyond the economic aspects of employment:

> "[T]he phrase 'terms, conditions or privileges of employment' in [Title VII] is an expansive concept which sweeps within its protective ambit the practice of creating a working environment heavily charged with ethnic or racial discrimination. * * * One can readily envision working environments so heavily polluted with discrimination as to destroy completely the emotional and psychological stability of minority group workers. * * *" 454 F.2d, at 238.

Courts applied this principle to harassment based on race, *e.g., Firefighters Institute for Racial Equality v. St. Louis,* 549 F.2d 506, 514–515 (CA8), cert. denied *sub nom. Banta v. United States,* 178 U.S.App.D.C. 91, 98, 434 U.S. 819, 98 S.Ct. 60, 54 L.Ed.2d 76 (1977); *Gray v. Greyhound Lines, East,* 178 U.S.App.D.C. 91, 98, 545 F.2d 169, 176 (1976), religion, *e.g., Compston v. Borden, Inc.,* 424 F.Supp. 157 (S.D.Ohio 1976), and national origin, *e.g., Cariddi v. Kansas City Chiefs Football Club,* 568 F.2d 87, 88 (C.A.8 1977). Nothing in Title VII suggests that a hostile environment based on discriminatory *sexual* harassment should not be likewise prohibited. The guidelines thus appropriately drew from, and were fully consistent with, the existing caselaw.

Since the guidelines were issued, courts have uniformly held, and we agree, that a plaintiff may establish a violation of Title VII by proving that discrimination based on sex has created a hostile or abusive work environment. As the Court of Appeals for the Eleventh Circuit wrote in *Henson v. Dundee,* 682 F.2d 897, 902 (1982):

> "Sexual harassment which creates a hostile or offensive environment for members of one sex is every bit the arbitrary barrier to sexual equality at the workplace that racial harassment is to racial equality. Surely, a requirement that a man or woman run a gauntlet of sexual abuse in return for the privilege of being allowed to work and make a

living can be as demeaning and disconcerting as the harshest of racial epithets.''

Accord, *Katz v. Dole,* 709 F.2d 251, 254–255 (C.A.4 1983); *Bundy v. Jackson,* 205 U.S.App.D.C. 444, 641 F.2d at 934–944 (1981); *Zabkowicz v. West Bend Co.,* 589 F.Supp. 780 (ED Wisc.1984).

Of course, as the courts in both *Rogers* and *Henson* recognized, not all workplace conduct that may be described as "harassment" affects a "term, condition, or privilege" of employment within the meaning of Title VII. See *Rogers v. EEOC, supra,* at 238 ("mere utterance of an ethnic or racial epithet which engenders offensive feelings in an employee" would not affect the conditions of employment to a sufficiently significant degree to violate Title VII); *Henson, supra,* at 904 (quoting same). For sexual harassment to be actionable, it must be sufficiently severe or pervasive "to alter the conditions of [the victim's] employment and create an abusive working environment." *Ibid.* Respondent's allegations in this case—which include not only pervasive harassment but also criminal conduct of the most serious nature—are plainly sufficient to state a claim for "hostile environment" sexual harassment.

The question remains, however, whether the District Court's ultimate finding that respondent "was not the victim of sexual harassment," 22 EPD ¶ 30708, at 14692–14693, 23 FEP Cases, at 43, effectively disposed of respondent's claim. The Court of Appeals recognized, we think correctly, that this ultimate finding was likely based on one or both of two erroneous views of the law. First, the District Court apparently believed that a claim for sexual harassment will not lie absent an *economic* effect on the complainant's employment. See *ibid.* ("It is without question that sexual harassment of female employees in which they are asked or required to submit to sexual demands as a *condition to obtain employment or to maintain employment or to obtain promotions* falls within protection of Title VII.") (emphasis added). Since it appears that the District Court made its findings without ever considering the "hostile environment" theory of sexual harassment, the Court of Appeals' decision to remand was correct.

Second, the District Court's conclusion that no actionable harassment occurred might have rested on its earlier "finding" that "[i]f [respondent] and Taylor did engage in an intimate or sexual relationship * * *, that relationship was a voluntary one." *Id.,* at 14692, 23 FEP cases, at 42. But the fact that sex-related conduct was "voluntary," in the sense that the complainant was not forced to participate against her will, is not a defense to a sexual harassment suit brought under Title VII. The gravamen of any sexual harassment claim is that the alleged sexual advances were "unwelcome." 29 CFR § 1604.11(a)(1985). While the question whether particular conduct was indeed unwelcome presents difficult problems of proof and turns largely on credibility determinations committed to the trier of fact, the District Court in this case erroneously focused on the "voluntariness" of respondent's participation in the claimed sexual episodes. The correct inquiry is whether respondent by her conduct indicated that the alleged sexual advances were unwelcome, not whether her actual participation in sexual intercourse was voluntary.

Petitioner contends that even if this case must be remanded to the District Court, the Court of Appeals erred in one of the terms of its remand.

Specifically, the Court of Appeals stated that testimony about respondent's "dress and personal fantasies," 243 U.S.App.D.C. at 328, n. 36, 753 F.2d, at 146, n. 36, which the District Court apparently admitted into evidence, "had no place in this litigation." *Ibid.* The apparent ground for this conclusion was that respondent's voluntariness *vel non* in submitting to Taylor's advances was immaterial to her sexual harassment claim. While "voluntariness" in the sense of consent is not a defense to such a claim, it does not follow that a complainant's sexually provocative speech or dress is irrelevant as a matter of law in determining whether he or she found particular sexual advances unwelcome. To the contrary, such evidence is obviously relevant. The EEOC guidelines emphasize that the trier of fact must determine the existence of sexual harassment in light of "the record as a whole" and "the totality of circumstances, such as the nature of the sexual advances and the context in which the alleged incidents occurred." 29 CFR § 1604.11(b)(1985). Respondent's claim that any marginal relevance of the evidence in question was outweighed by the potential for unfair prejudice is the sort of argument properly addressed to the District Court. In this case the District Court concluded that the evidence should be admitted, and the Court of Appeals' contrary conclusion was based upon the erroneous, categorical view that testimony about provocative dress and publicly expressed sexual fantasies "had no place in this litigation." 243 U.S.App.D.C., at 328, n. 36, 753 F.2d, at 146, n. 36. While the District Court must carefully weigh the applicable considerations in deciding whether to admit evidence of this kind, there is no *per se* rule against its admissibility.

III

Although the District Court concluded that respondent had not proved a violation of Title VII, it nevertheless went on to consider the question of the bank's liability. Finding that "the bank was without notice" of Taylor's alleged conduct, and that notice to Taylor was not the equivalent of notice to the bank, the court concluded that the bank therefore could not be held liable for Taylor's alleged actions. The Court of Appeals took the opposite view, holding that an employer is strictly liable for a hostile environment created by a supervisor's sexual advances, even though the employer neither knew nor reasonably could have known of the alleged misconduct. The court held that a supervisor, whether or not he possesses the authority to hire, fire, or promote, is necessarily an "agent" of his employer for all Title VII purposes, since "even the appearance" of such authority may enable him to impose himself on his subordinates.

The parties and *amici* suggest several different standards for employer liability. Respondent, not surprisingly, defends the position of the Court of Appeals. Noting that Title VII's definition of "employer" includes any "agent" of the employer, she also argues that "so long as the circumstance is work-related, the supervisor is the employer and the employer is the supervisor." Brief for Respondent 27. Notice to Taylor that the advances were unwelcome, therefore, was notice to the bank.

Petitioner argues that respondent's failure to use its established grievance procedure, or to otherwise put it on notice of the alleged misconduct, insulates petitioner from liability for Taylor's wrongdoing. A contrary rule would be unfair, petitioner argues, since in a hostile environment harassment case the employer often will have no reason to know about, or opportunity to cure, the alleged wrongdoing.

The EEOC, in its brief as *amicus curiae,* contends that courts formulating employer liability rules should draw from traditional agency principles. Examination of those principles has led the EEOC to the view that where a supervisor exercises the authority actually delegated to him by his employer, by making or threatening to make decisions affecting the employment status of his subordinates, such actions are properly imputed to the employer whose delegation of authority empowered the supervisor to undertake them. Brief for United States and Equal Employment Opportunity Commission as *Amicus Curiae* 22. Thus, the courts have consistently held employers liable for the discriminatory discharges of employees by supervisory personnel, whether or not the employer knew, should have known, or approved of the supervisor's actions. *E.g., Anderson v. Methodist Evangelical Hospital, Inc.,* 464 F.2d 723, 725 (C.A.6 1972).

The EEOC suggests that when a sexual harassment claim rests exclusively on a "hostile environment" theory, however, the usual basis for a finding of agency will often disappear. In that case, the EEOC believes, agency principles lead to

"a rule that asks whether a victim of sexual harassment had reasonably available an avenue of complaint regarding such harassment, and, if available and utilized, whether that procedure was reasonably responsive to the employee's complaint. If the employer has an expressed policy against sexual harassment and has implemented a procedure specifically designed to resolve sexual harassment claims, and if the victim does not take advantage of that procedure, the employer should be shielded from liability absent actual knowledge of the sexually hostile environment (obtained, *e.g.,* by the filing of a charge with the EEOC or a comparable state agency). In all other cases, the employer will be liable if it has actual knowledge of the harassment or if, considering all the facts of the case, the victim in question had no reasonably available avenue for making his or her complaint known to appropriate management officials." Brief for United States and Equal Opportunity Employment Commission as *Amici Curiae,* 26.

As respondent points out, this suggested rule is in some tension with the EEOC guidelines, which hold an employer liable for the acts of its agents without regard to notice. 29 CFR § 1604.11(c)(1985). The guidelines do require, however, an "examin[ation of] the circumstances of the particular employment relationship and the job [f]unctions performed by the individual in determining whether an individual acts in either a supervisory or agency capacity." *Ibid.*

This debate over the appropriate standard for employer liability has a rather abstract quality about it given the state of the record in this case. We do not know at this stage whether Taylor made any sexual advances toward respondent at all, let alone whether those advances were unwelcome, whether they were sufficiently pervasive to constitute a condition of employment, or whether they were "so pervasive and so long continuing * * * that the employer must have become conscious of [them]," *Taylor v. Jones,* 653 F.2d

1193, 1197–1199 (C.A.8 1981)(holding employer liable for racially hostile working environment based on constructive knowledge).

We therefore decline the parties' invitation to issue a definitive rule on employer liability, but we do agree with the EEOC that Congress wanted courts to look to agency principles for guidance in this area. While such common-law principles may not be transferable in all their particulars to Title VII, Congress' decision to define "employer" to include any "agent" of an employer, 42 U.S.C. § 2000e(b), surely evinces an intent to place some limits on the acts of employees for which employers under Title VII are to be held responsible. For this reason, we hold that the Court of Appeals erred in concluding that employers are always automatically liable for sexual harassment by their supervisors. See generally Restatement (Second) of Agency §§ 219–237 (1958). For the same reason, absence of notice to an employer does not necessarily insulate that employer from liability. *Ibid.*

Finally, we reject petitioner's view that the mere existence of a grievance procedure and a policy against discrimination, coupled with respondent's failure to invoke that procedure, must insulate petitioner from liability. While those facts are plainly relevant, the situation before us demonstrates why they are not necessarily dispositive. Petitioner's general nondiscrimination policy did not address sexual harassment in particular, and thus did not alert employees to their employer's interest in correcting that form of discrimination. App. 25. Moreover, the bank's grievance procedure apparently required an employee to complain first to her supervisor, in this case Taylor. Since Taylor was the alleged perpetrator, it is not altogether surprising that respondent failed to invoke the procedure and report her grievance to him. Petitioner's contention that respondent's failure should insulate it from liability might be substantially stronger if its procedures were better calculated to encourage victims of harassment to come forward.

IV

In sum, we hold that a claim of "hostile environment" sex discrimination is actionable under Title VII, that the District Court's findings were insufficient to dispose of respondent's hostile environment claim, and that the District Court did not err in admitting testimony about respondent's sexually provocative speech and dress. As to employer liability, we conclude that the Court of Appeals was wrong to entirely disregard agency principles and impose absolute liability on employers for the acts of their supervisors, regardless of the circumstances of a particular case.

Accordingly, the judgment of the Court of Appeals reversing the judgment of the District Court is affirmed, and the case is remanded for further proceedings consistent with this opinion.

It is so ordered.

JUSTICE MARSHALL, with whom JUSTICE BRENNAN, JUSTICE BLACKMUN, and JUSTICE STEVENS join, concurring in the judgment.

I fully agree with the Court's conclusion that workplace sexual harassment is illegal, and violates Title VII. Part III of the Court's opinion, however, leaves open the circumstances in which an employer is responsible under Title VII for such conduct. Because I believe that question to be properly before us, I write separately.

The issue the Court declines to resolve is addressed in the EEOC Guidelines on Discrimination Because of Sex, which are entitled to great deference. See *Griggs v. Duke Power Co.*, 401 U.S. 424, 433–434, 91 S.Ct. 849, 854–55, 28 L.Ed.2d 158 (1971)(EEOC Guidelines on Employment Testing Procedures of 1966) * * *. [Excerpt from 29 CFR §§ 1604.11(c), (d)(1985), p. 1254 infra, omitted.].

The Commission, in issuing the Guidelines, explained that its rule was "in keeping with the general standard of employer liability with respect to agents and supervisory employees. * * * [T]he Commission and the courts have held for years that an employer is liable if a supervisor or an agent violates the Title VII, regardless of knowledge or any other mitigating factor." 45 Fed.Reg. 74676 (1980). I would adopt the standard set out by the Commission.

An employer can act only through individual supervisors and employees; discrimination is rarely carried out pursuant to a formal vote of a corporation's board of directors. Although an employer may sometimes adopt company-wide discriminatory policies violative of Title VII, acts that may constitute Title VII violations are generally effected through the actions of individuals, and often an individual may take such a step even in defiance of company policy. Nonetheless, Title VII remedies, such as reinstatement and backpay, generally run against the employer as an entity.[1] The question thus arises as to the circumstances under which an employer will be held liable under Title VII for the acts of its employees.

The answer supplied by general Title VII law, like that supplied by federal labor law, is that the act of a supervisory employee or agent is imputed to the employer.[2] Thus, for example, when a supervisor discriminatorily fires or refuses to promote a black employee, that act is, without more, considered the act of the employer. The courts do not stop to consider whether the employer otherwise had "notice" of the action, or even whether the supervisor had actual authority to act as he did. *E.g., Flowers v. Crouch–Walker Corp.*, 552 F.2d 1277, 1282 (C.A.7 1977); *Young v. Southwestern Savings and Loan Assn.*, 509 F.2d 140 (C.A.5 1975); *Anderson v. Methodist Evangelical Hospital, Inc.*, 464 F.2d 723 (C.A.6 1972). Following that approach, every Court of Appeals that has considered the issue has held that sexual harassment by supervisory personnel is automatically imputed to the employer when the harassment results in tangible job detriment to the subordinate employee. See *Horn v. Duke Homes, Div. of Windsor Mobile Homes, Inc.* 755 F.2d 599, 604–606 (C.A.7 1985); *Vinson v. Taylor,* 243 U.S.App.D.C. 323, 329–334, 753 F.2d 141, 147–152 (1985); *Craig v. Y & Y Snacks, Inc.*, 721 F.2d 77, 80–81 (C.A.3 1983); *Katz v. Dole,* 709 F.2d 251, 255, n. 6 (C.A.4 1983); *Henson v. City of Dundee,* 682 F.2d 897, 910 (C.A.11 1982); *Miller v. Bank of America,* 600 F.2d 211, 213 (C.A.9 1979).

---

1. The remedial provisions of Title VII were largely modeled on those of the National Labor Relations Act (NLRA). See *Albemarle Paper Co. v. Moody,* 422 U.S. 405, 419, and n. 11, 95 S.Ct. 2362, 2372, and n. 11 (1975); see also *Franks v. Bowman Transportation Co.,* 424 U.S. 747, 768–770, 96 S.Ct. 1251, 1266–67, 47 L.Ed.2d 444 (1976).

2. For NLRA cases, see, *e.g., Graves Trucking, Inc. v. NLRB,* 692 F.2d 470 (C.A.7 1982); *NLRB v. Kaiser Agricultural Chemicals, Division of Kaiser Aluminum & Chemical Corp.,* 473 F.2d 374, 384 (C.A.5 1973); *Amalgamated Clothing Workers of America v. NLRB,* 124 U.S.App.D.C. 365, 377, 365 F.2d 898, 909 (1966).

The brief filed by the Solicitor General on behalf of the EEOC in this case suggests that a different rule should apply when a supervisor's harassment "merely" results in a discriminatory work environment. The Solicitor General concedes that sexual harassment that affects tangible job benefits is an exercise of authority delegated to the supervisor by the employer, and thus gives rise to employer liability. But, departing from the EEOC Guidelines, he argues that the case of a supervisor merely creating a discriminatory work environment is different because the supervisor "is not exercising, or threatening to exercise, actual or apparent authority to make personnel decisions affecting the victim." Brief for United States and EEOC as *Amici Curiae* 24. In the latter situation, he concludes, some further notice requirement should therefore be necessary.

The Solicitor General's position is untenable. A supervisor's responsibilities do not begin and end with the power to hire, fire, and discipline employees, or with the power to recommend such actions. Rather, a supervisor is charged with the day-to-day supervision of the work environment and with ensuring a safe, productive, workplace. There is no reason why abuse of the latter authority should have different consequences than abuse of the former. In both cases it is the authority vested in the supervisor by the employer that enables him to commit the wrong: it is precisely because the supervisor is understood to be clothed with the employer's authority that he is able to impose unwelcome sexual conduct on subordinates. There is therefore no justification for a special rule, to be applied *only* in "hostile environment" cases, that sexual harassment does not create employer liability until the employee suffering the discrimination notifies other supervisors. No such requirement appears in the statute, and no such requirement can coherently be drawn from the law of agency.

Agency principles and the goals of Title VII law make appropriate some limitation on the liability of employers for the acts of supervisors. Where, for example, a supervisor has no authority over an employee, because the two work in wholly different parts of the employer's business, it may be improper to find strict employer liability. See 29 CFR § 1604.11(c)(1985). Those considerations, however, do not justify the creation of a special "notice" rule in hostile environment cases.

Further, nothing would be gained by crafting such a rule. In the "pure" hostile environment case, where an employee files an EEOC complaint alleging sexual harassment in the workplace, the employee seeks not money damages but injunctive relief. See *Bundy v. Jackson,* 205 U.S.App.D.C. 444, 446, 641 F.2d 934, 936, n. 12 (1981). Under Title VII, the EEOC must notify an employer of charges made against it within 10 days after receipt of the complaint. 42 U.S.C. § 2000e–5(b). If the charges appear to be based on "reasonable cause," the EEOC must attempt to eliminate the offending practice through "informal methods of conference, conciliation, and persuasion." *Ibid.* An employer whose internal procedures assertedly would have redressed the discrimination can avoid injunctive relief by employing these procedures after receiving notice of the complaint or during the conciliation period. Cf. Brief for United States and EEOC as *Amici Curiae* 26. Where a complainant, on the other hand, seeks backpay on the theory that a hostile work environment effected a constructive termination, the existence of an internal complaint procedure may be a factor in determining not the employer's liability but the remedies available against it. Where a complainant without good reason bypassed an internal complaint procedure she knew to be effective, a court may be reluctant to find constructive termination and thus to award reinstatement or backpay.

I therefore reject the Solicitor General's position. I would apply in this case the same rules we apply in all other Title VII cases, and hold that sexual harassment by a supervisor of an employee under his supervision, leading to a discriminatory work environment, should be imputed to the employer for Title VII purposes regardless of whether the employee gave "notice" of the offense.

JUSTICE STEVENS, concurring.

Because I do not see any inconsistency between the two opinions, and because I believe the question of statutory construction that JUSTICE MARSHALL has answered is fairly presented by the record, I join both the Court's opinion and JUSTICE MARSHALL's opinion.

HARRIS v. FORKLIFT SYSTEMS, INC.

Supreme Court of the United States, 1993.
510 U.S. 17, 114 S.Ct. 367, 126 L.Ed.2d 295.

JUSTICE O'CONNOR delivered the opinion of the Court.

In this case we consider the definition of a discriminatorily "abusive work environment" (also known as a "hostile work environment") under Title VII of the Civil Rights Act of 1964, * * *.

I

Teresa Harris worked as a manager at Forklift Systems, Inc., an equipment rental company, from April 1985 until October 1987. Charles Hardy was Forklift's president.

The Magistrate found that, throughout Harris' time at Forklift, Hardy often insulted her because of her gender and often made her the target of unwanted sexual innuendos. Hardy told Harris on several occasions, in the presence of other employees, "You're a woman, what do you know" and "We need a man as the rental manager"; at least once, he told her she was "a dumb ass woman." * * * Again in front of others, he suggested that the two of them "go to the Holiday Inn to negotiate [Harris] raise." * * * Hardy occasionally asked Harris and other female employees to get coins from his front pants pocket. * * * He threw objects on the ground in front of Harris and other women, and asked them to pick the objects up. * * * He made sexual innuendos about Harris' and other women's clothing. * * *

In mid-August 1987, Harris complained to Hardy about his conduct. Hardy said he was surprised that Harris was offended, claimed he was only joking, and apologized. * * * He also promised he would stop, and based on this assurance Harris stayed on the job. * * * But in early September, Hardy began anew: While Harris was arranging a deal with one of Forklift's customers, he asked her, again in front of other employees, "What did you do, promise the guy * * * some [sex] Saturday night?" * * * On October 1, Harris collected her paycheck and quit.

Harris then sued Forklift, claiming that Hardy's conduct had created an abusive work environment for her because of her gender. The United States District Court for the Middle District of Tennessee, adopting the report and recommendation of the Magistrate, found this to be "a close case," * * * but held that Hardy's conduct did not create an abusive environment. The court found that some of Hardy's comments "offended [Harris], and would offend the reasonable woman," * * * but that they were not

> "so severe as to be expected to seriously affect [Harris'] psychological well-being. A reasonable woman manager under like circumstances would have been offended by Hardy, but his conduct would not have risen to the level of interfering with that person's work performance.
>
>   "Neither do I believe that [Harris] was subjectively so offended that she suffered injury * * *. Although Hardy may at times have genuinely offended [Harris], I do not believe that he created a working environment so poisoned as to be intimidating or abusive to [Harris]." * * *

In focusing on the employee's psychological well-being, the District Court was following Circuit precedent. See *Rabidue v. Osceola Refining Co.,* 805 F.2d 611, 620 (C.A.6 1986), cert. denied, 481 U.S. 1041, 107 S.Ct. 1983, 95 L.Ed.2d 823 (1987). The United States Court of Appeals for the Sixth Circuit affirmed in a brief unpublished decision, 976 F.2d 733 (CA6 1992).

We granted certiorari, * * * to resolve a conflict among the Circuits on whether conduct, to be actionable as "abusive work environment" harassment (no *quid pro quo* harassment issue is present here), must "seriously affect [an employee's] psychological well-being" or lead the plaintiff to "suffe[r] injury." Compare *Rabidue* (requiring serious effect on psychological well-being); *Vance v. Southern Bell Telephone & Telegraph Co.,* 863 F.2d 1503, 1510 (C.A.11 1989)(same); and *Downes v. FAA,* 775 F.2d 288, 292 (C.A.Fed.1985)(same), with *Ellison v. Brady,* 924 F.2d 872, 877–878 (C.A.9 1991)(rejecting such a requirement).

II

Title VII of the Civil Rights Act of 1964 makes it "an unlawful employment practice for an employer * * * to discriminate against any individual with respect to his compensation, terms, conditions, or privileges of employment, because of such individual's race, color, religion, sex, or national origin." * * * As we made clear in *Meritor Savings Bank v. Vinson,* 477 U.S. 57, 106 S.Ct. 2399, 91 L.Ed.2d 49 (1986), this language "is not limited to 'economic' or 'tangible' discrimination. The phrase 'terms, conditions, or privileges of employment' evinces a congressional intent 'to strike at the entire spectrum of disparate treatment of men and women' in employment," which includes requiring people to work in a discriminatorily hostile or abusive environment. *Id.,* at 64, 106 S.Ct., at 2404, quoting *Los Angeles Dept. of Water and Power v. Manhart* * * *. * * * When the workplace is permeated with "discriminatory intimidation, ridicule, and insult," 477 U.S., at 65, 106 S.Ct., at 2405, that is "sufficiently severe or pervasive to alter the conditions of the victim's employment and create an abusive working environment," *id.,* at 67, 106 S.Ct., at 2405, * * * Title VII is violated.

This standard, which we reaffirm today, takes a middle path between making actionable any conduct that is merely offensive and requiring the conduct to cause a tangible psychological injury. As we pointed out in *Meritor*, "mere utterance of an * * * epithet which engenders offensive feelings in a employee," * * * does not sufficiently affect the conditions of employment to implicate Title VII. Conduct that is not severe or pervasive enough to create an objectively hostile or abusive work environment—an environment that a reasonable person would find hostile or abusive—is beyond Title VII's purview. Likewise, if the victim does not subjectively perceive the environment to be abusive, the conduct has not actually altered the conditions of the victim's employment, and there is no Title VII violation.

But Title VII comes into play before the harassing conduct leads to a nervous breakdown. A discriminatorily abusive work environment, even one that does not seriously affect employees' psychological well-being, can and often will detract from employees' job performance, discourage employees from remaining on the job, or keep them from advancing in their careers. Moreover, even without regard to these tangible effects, the very fact that the discriminatory conduct was so severe or pervasive that it created a work environment abusive to employees because of their race, gender, religion, or national origin offends Title VII's broad rule of workplace equality. The appalling conduct alleged in *Meritor*, and the reference in that case to environments " 'so heavily polluted with discrimination as to destroy completely the emotional and psychological stability of minority group workers,' " *supra*, at 66, 106 S.Ct., at 2405, quoting *Rogers v. EEOC*, 454 F.2d 234, 238 (C.A.5 1971), cert. denied, 406 U.S. 957, 92 S.Ct. 2058, 32 L.Ed.2d 343 (1972), merely present some especially egregious examples of harassment. They do not mark the boundary of what is actionable.

We therefore believe the District Court erred in relying on whether the conduct "seriously affect[ed] plaintiff's psychological well-being" or led her to "suffe[r] injury." Such an inquiry may needlessly focus the factfinder's attention on concrete psychological harm, an element Title VII does not require. Certainly Title VII bars conduct that would seriously affect a reasonable person's psychological well-being, but the statute is not limited to such conduct. So long as the environment would reasonably be perceived, and is perceived, as hostile or abusive, *Meritor, supra,* 477 U.S., at 67, 106 S.Ct., at 2405, there is no need for it also to be psychologically injurious.

This is not, and by its nature cannot be, a mathematically precise test. We need not answer today all the potential questions it raises, nor specifically address the EEOC's new regulations on this subject, see 58 Fed.Reg. 51266 (1993)(proposed 29 CFR §§ 1609.1, 1609.2);* see also 29 CFR § 1604.11 (1993). But we can say that whether an environment is "hostile" or "abusive" can be determined only by looking at all the circumstances. These may include the frequency of the discriminatory conduct; its severity; whether it is physically threatening or humiliating, or a mere offensive utterance; and whether it unreasonably interferes with an employee's work performance. The effect on the employee's psychological well-being is, of course, relevant to determining whether the plaintiff actually found the environment abusive.

---

* Ed. Note—These proposed regulations were withdrawn by the EEOC in October 1994.   59 Fed. Reg. 51396 (Oct. 11, 94).

But while psychological harm, like any other relevant factor, may be taken into account, no single factor is required.

III

Forklift, while conceding that a requirement that the conduct seriously affect psychological well-being is unfounded, argues that the District Court nonetheless correctly applied the *Meritor* standard. We disagree. Though the District Court did conclude that the work environment was not "intimidating or abusive to [Harris]," * * * it did so only after finding that the conduct was not "so severe as to be expected to seriously affect plaintiff's psychological well-being," * * * and that Harris was not "subjectively so offended that she suffered injury," * * *. The District Court's application of these incorrect standards may well have influenced its ultimate conclusion, especially given that the court found this to be a "close case," * * *.

We therefore reverse the judgment of the Court of Appeals, and remand the case for further proceedings consistent with this opinion.

So ordered.

JUSTICE SCALIA, concurring.

Meritor * * * held that Title VII prohibits sexual harassment that takes the form of a hostile work environment. The Court stated that sexual harassment is actionable if it is "sufficiently severe or pervasive 'to alter the conditions of [the victim's] employment and create an abusive work environment.'" * * * (quoting *Henson v. Dundee*, 682 F.2d 897, 904 (C.A.11 1982)). Today's opinion elaborates that the challenged conduct must be severe or pervasive enough "to create an objectively hostile or abusive work environment—an environment that a reasonable person would find hostile or abusive." * * *

"Abusive" (or "hostile," which in this context I take to mean the same thing) does not seem to me a very clear standard—and I do not think clarity is at all increased by adding the adverb "objectively" or by appealing to a "reasonable person's" notion of what the vague word means. Today's opinion does list a number of factors that contribute to abusiveness, * * * but since it neither says how much of each is necessary (an impossible task) nor identifies any single factor as determinative, it thereby adds little certitude. As a practical matter, today's holding lets virtually unguided juries decide whether sex-related conduct engaged in (or permitted by) an employer is egregious enough to warrant an award of damages. One might say that what constitutes "negligence" (a traditional jury question) is not much more clear and certain than what constitutes "abusiveness." Perhaps so. But the class of plaintiffs seeking to recover for negligence is limited to those who have suffered harm, whereas under this statute "abusiveness" is to be the test of whether legal harm has been suffered, opening more expansive vistas of litigation.

Be that as it may, I know of no alternative to the course the Court today has taken. One of the factors mentioned in the Court's nonexhaustive list—whether the conduct unreasonably interferes with an employee's work performance—would, if it were made an absolute test, provide greater guidance to juries and employers. But I see no basis for such a limitation in the language of the statute. Accepting *Meritor*'s interpretation of the term "conditions of employment" as the law, the test is not whether work has been impaired, but whether working conditions have been discriminatorily altered. I know of no test more faithful to the inherently vague statutory language than the one the Court today adopts. For these reasons, I join the opinion of the Court.

JUSTICE GINSBURG, concurring.

Today the Court reaffirms the holding of *Meritor:* * * * "[A] plaintiff may establish a violation of Title VII by proving that discrimination based on sex has created a hostile or abusive work environment." The critical issue, Title VII's text indicates, is whether members of one sex are exposed to disadvantageous terms or conditions of employment to which members of the other sex are not exposed. See 42 U.S.C. § 2000e–2(a)(1)(declaring that it is unlawful to discriminate with respect to, *inter alia,* "terms" or "conditions" of employment). As the Equal Employment Opportunity Commission emphasized, see Brief for United States and Equal Employment Opportunity Commission as *Amici Curiae* 9–14, the adjudicator's inquiry should center, dominantly, on whether the discriminatory conduct has unreasonably interfered with the plaintiff's work performance. To show such interference, "the plaintiff need not prove that his or her tangible productivity has declined as a result of the harassment." *Davis v. Monsanto Chemical Co.,* 858 F.2d 345, 349 (C.A.6 1988). It suffices to prove that a reasonable person subjected to the discriminatory conduct would find, as the plaintiff did, that the harassment so altered working conditions as to "ma[k]e it more difficult to do the job." *Davis* concerned race-based discrimination, but that difference does not alter the analysis; except in the rare case in which a bona fide occupational qualification is shown, see *Automobile Workers v. Johnson Controls, Inc.,* 499 U.S. 187, 200–207, 111 S.Ct. 1196, 1204–08, 113 L.Ed.2d 158 (1991)(construing 42 U.S.C. § 2000e–2(e)(1)), Title VII declares discriminatory practices based on race, gender, religion, or national origin equally unlawful.*

The Court's opinion, which I join, seems to me in harmony with the view expressed in this concurring statement.

Notes on Vinson *and* Harris

1. The notion that sexual harassment on the job might constitute sex discrimination under Title VII came slowly to most courts. All the early cases asserting this legal theory were dismissed at the trial court level. A variety of judicial reasoning supported the lower court results: the supervisor who demanded sexual favors was merely attempting to satisfy his personal urges, e.g., Corne v. Bausch & Lomb, Inc., 390 F.Supp. 161 (D.Ariz.1975), vacated 562 F.2d 55 (9th Cir.1977); the employer could not be held liable for unauthorized sexual misconduct on the job, e.g., Barnes v. Train, 13 Fair Empl.Prac.Cas. 123 (D.D.C.1974), reversed sub nom. Barnes v. Costle, 561 F.2d 983 (D.C.Cir.1977); the incident was not job-related, even though it had happened at work, e.g., Tomkins v. Public Serv. Elec. & Gas Co., 422 F.Supp. 553 (D.N.J.1976), reversed 568 F.2d 1044 (3d Cir.1977).

---

* Indeed, even under the Court's equal protection jurisprudence, which requires "an exceedingly persuasive justification" for a gender-based classification, *Kirchberg v. Feenstra,* 450 U.S. 455, 461, 101 S.Ct. 1195, 1199, 67 L.Ed.2d 428 (1981)(internal quotation marks omitted), it remains an open question whether "classifications based upon gender are inherently suspect." See *Mississippi Univ. for Women v. Hogan,* 458 U.S. 718, 724, 102 S.Ct. 3331, 3336, 73 L.Ed.2d 1090, and n. 9 (1982).

By 1976, the tide had begun to turn. Judge Richey held in Williams v. Saxbe, 413 F.Supp. 654 (D.C.Cir.1976), reversed on other grounds sub nom. Williams v. Bell, 587 F.2d 1240 (D.C.Cir.1978), that Diane Williams would establish a cause of action under Title VII if she could prove that her termination had resulted from her supervisor's retaliation following her rejection of his sexual advances. Opinion on remand sustaining plaintiff's claim Williams v. Civiletti, 487 F.Supp. 1387 (D.D.C.1980). Subsequently, as the citations following the cases mentioned above disclose, the earlier lower court decisions were reversed or vacated on appeal.

In 1980, the EEOC issued its guidelines on sexual harassment, in effect, "codifying" the law as it had developed. See the Guidelines at p. 1253 infra.

2. Catharine A. MacKinnon helped develop the legal theory supporting a sexual harassment cause of action and identified two different forms of sexual harassment that occur in the workplace. The first, which she termed the "quid pro quo" variety, is a more or less explicit exchange in which the woman's sexual compliance is proposed by her male supervisor to be exchanged for an employment opportunity, be it a raise, a promotion, or simple retention of her job. The second category, which MacKinnon called the "condition of work" variety (and which most courts term "hostile" work environment), describes a situation in which the woman is perpetually made aware of her body and its uses in the fantasies of her coworkers or supervisors. As MacKinnon put it, the woman

> may be constantly felt or pinched, visually undressed and stared at, surreptitiously kissed, commented upon, manipulated into being found alone, and generally taken advantage of at work—but never promised or denied anything explicitly connected with her job.

C. MacKinnon, Sexual Harassment of Working Women 40 (1979). The quid pro quo type of sexual harassment could also apply to the case of a female boss and a male employee. Are males subjected to hostile environment sexual harassment by females?

The cases cited in Note 1, supra, are all examples of the quid pro quo type of sexual harassment. The first case to recognize a Title VII cause of action for hostile environment harassment was also initially lost at the trial court level. In Bundy v. Jackson, 19 F.E.P.Cas. 828 (D.D.C.1979), reversed and remanded 641 F.2d 934 (D.C.Cir.1981), cited in Vinson, at p. 527, supra, plaintiff had been subjected to sexual propositions by five of her supervisors over a two and one-half year period. Because she was unable to show that her rejection of their advances had resulted in loss of job benefits or promotions, she lost below. Reversing, Judge Wright held that an employer violates Title VII merely by subjecting female employees to sexual harassment even in the absence of the deprivation of tangible job benefits. See Note, Sexual Harassment Claims of Abusive Work Environment Under Title VII, 97 Harv.L.Rev. 1449 (1984).

3. Vinson was the first sexual harassment case to reach the Supreme Court. The Court clearly recognized both varieties of sexual harassment—quid pro quo and hostile environment—as appropriate Title VII claims, and held that a hostile environment claim may be established even in the absence of economic injury to the plaintiff. What do you make of Justice Rehnquist's treatment of the defendant's argument that plaintiff's "voluntary" participation in a sexual relationship with her supervisor is a defense to Title VII liability? In rejecting this argument, Justice Rehnquist says that the proper question is whether the plaintiff indicated that the alleged sexual advances were "unwelcome." What does this mean? Who has the burden of proof on this issue? Do you agree with Rehnquist that a plaintiff's "sexually provocative speech or dress" is "obviously relevant" to this

inquiry? Should a court use a subjective or objective standard to determine whether a particular outfit is "sexually provocative"?

How will this standard affect women who are required to wear costumes designed to be sexually provocative as part of their job? See, e.g., EEOC v. Newtown Inn Associates, 647 F.Supp. 957 (E.D.Va.1986) involving a claim by two women cocktail servers who were asked to wear "revealing, thematic attire for events such as 'Bikini Night', 'P.J. Night', and 'Whips and Chains Night'." The women alleged that "[a]s a consequence [they] were subjected to unwelcome sexual proposals and both verbal and physical abuse of a sexual nature." Does Justice Rehnquist have something a bit less lurid in mind? And is his inquiry limited to costumes chosen by the employee, rather than those imposed by the employer?

Susan Estrich, in Sex at Work, 43 Stan.L.Rev. 813, 826–43 (1991), argues that the "unwelcomeness" requirement imports "some of the most pernicious doctrines of rape law into Title VII cases" and is an unnecessary element of the cause of action either for quid pro quo or hostile environment claims of sexual harassment. Do you agree?

4. In between the *Vinson* and *Harris* cases came the Senate Judiciary Committee's hearings on Clarence Thomas's confirmation to the U.S. Supreme Court. Although Justice Thomas was confirmed on October 15, 1991, by a vote of 52 to 48, The Thomas Confirmation, N.Y. Times, October 16, 1991, at A19, Professor Anita Hill's testimony of sexual harassment by Thomas when she worked under his supervision made the issue of sexual harassment one of national concern. Since 1991 the number of sexual harassment complaints and lawsuits has continued to increase, with sizeable damage verdicts awarded to women. Perhaps the largest damage award was secured under California state law by legal secretary Rena Weeks, when a jury awarded her $7.1 million in punitive damages against the law firm of Baker & McKenzie for failing to protect her from sexual harassment by one of its partners. ABA Journal, Award a Lesson for Firms, Nov. 1994 at 19. Although the judge later reduced the award to $3.5 million, representing 5% of the firm's net worth, such monetary awards have continued to focus employers' attention on the need to prevent sexual harassment from occurring.

On remand in *Harris*, itself, Teresa Harris received a substantial back pay award for her hostile environment and constructive discharge claims against Forklift Systems: $151,435 and interest, plus attorney's fees and costs. 1994 WL 792661, 66 FEP Cases 1886 (M.D.Tenn. 1994).

5. The *Harris* test on hostile environment was applied in Saxton v. American Telephone and Telegraph Company, 10 F.3d 526 (7th Cir.1993), a case in which plaintiff Marcia Saxton's supervisor, Jerome Richardson, made sexual overtures to her over a period of time. Richardson invited Saxton to accompany him to a nightclub for drinks after work and then to a jazz club. During the evening, he put his hand on her leg above the knee several times, and kissed her briefly once. Each time, Saxton told him not to do those things again, and he agreed. About three weeks later, Richardson was driving Saxton back to her car after a work-related lunch, when he detoured to a park (the Morton Arboretum), got out of the car and walked away. Saxton also took a walk, and was surprised when Richardson "lurched" at her from behind some bushes. She dashed away to avoid him. When they returned to the car, Saxton again told Richardson that his conduct was inappropriate, and he became sullen. No further sexual overtures occurred, but plaintiff perceived a change in the supervisor's attitude toward her. He became condescending, cancelled meetings with her, refused to speak to

her, and teased her about a romantic interest in a coworker. After some months, plaintiff became concerned that her work environment had deteriorated and complained to a different supervisor. The company investigated, and found the evidence of sexual harassment inconclusive, but ultimately separated the supervisor from plaintiff's vicinity by transferring him to another department housed in a different building about one-half mile away. Plaintiff, who had been allowed to work at home during the investigation, never returned to work and ultimately filed a sexual harassment charge against the company.

The district court granted defendant's motion for summary judgment, see Saxton v. American Tel. & Tel. Co., 785 F.Supp. 760 (N.D.Ill.1992), and the Seventh Circuit affirmed. Measuring the facts against the *Harris* standard, Judge Ilana Diamond Rovner concluded that Saxton had not been subjected to a hostile work environment (10 F.3d at 534–35):

> We evaluate these factors from both a subjective and an objective viewpoint—that is, we consider not only the effect the discriminatory conduct actually had on the plaintiff, but also the impact it likely would have had on a reasonable employee in her position. * * *[13] Here, even if we assume that the conduct at issue had a sufficiently adverse effect on Saxton, her claim must still fail, as the objective prong of the inquiry is not satisfied.

> Although Richardson's conduct was undoubtedly inappropriate, it was not so severe or pervasive as to create an objectively hostile work environment. Certainly any employee in Saxton's position might have experienced significant discomfort and distress as the result of her superior's uninvited and unwelcome advances. At the same time, Richardson's offensive behavior was relatively limited, presumably because Saxton was forthright and persistent in making clear that the advances were unwelcome. And although there were two instances of sexual misconduct rather than one, it simply did not rise to the level of pervasive harassment as that term has been defined by this court. See *Weiss*, 990 F.2d at 337 (no actionable harassment where plaintiff's supervisor asked plaintiff out on dates, called her a "dumb blond," placed his hand on her shoulder several times, placed "I love you" signs in her work area, and attempted to kiss her on one or more occasions). Indeed, after the Morton Arboretum incident, Richardson made no further advances toward Saxton. Compare Dockter v. Rudolf Wolff Futures, Inc., 913 F.2d 456, 461 (7th Cir.1990)(multiple incidents of sexual misconduct during plaintiff's first two weeks of work did not support hostile environment claim where they ceased after plaintiff reprimanded the aggressor), with *King*, 898 F.2d at 534–35, 538 (repeated verbal assaults and physical harassment that continued despite plaintiff's objections were sufficient to support a hostile environment claim).

> Moreover, even if we assume that Richardson turned a particularly cold shoulder to Saxton after she rebuffed his advances, the evidence does not suggest that this behavior rendered her environment hostile. Saxton has offered no evidence that Richardson's conduct was frequent or severe, that it interfered with her work,[14] or that it otherwise created an abusive work

13. We are not called upon to decide here whether it might be more appropriate to evaluate the plaintiff's work environment from the perspective of a reasonable *woman* as opposed to a genderless reasonable person. See Burns v. McGregor Elec. Indus., Inc., 989 F.2d 959, 962 n. 3 (8th Cir.1993); Ellison v. Brady, 924 F.2d 872, 879–80 (9th Cir.1991). The result of our analysis would be the same under either standard.

14. Title VII, as interpreted by *Harris*, does not require proof that the harassment interfered with the plaintiff's work performance.

environment. Thus, although it might be reasonable for us to assume that Richardson's inaccessibility, condescension, impatience, and teasing made Saxton's life at work subjectively unpleasant, the evidence fails to demonstrate that his behavior was not "merely offensive," *Harris,* ___ U.S. at ___, 114 S.Ct. at 370, but instead was "sufficiently severe or pervasive to alter the conditions of [her] employment and create an abusive working environment." *Vinson,* 477 U.S. at 67, 106 S.Ct. at 2405. Even if, as Saxton contends, questions of fact remain as to how difficult the work environment became for her, Saxton Br. at 16, that is not enough to avoid summary judgment in the absence of evidence suggesting that a reasonable person would have found the environment to be hostile.

Is this a correct application of the *Harris* standard as phrased by Justice O'Connor? If so, does it satisfy Justice Ginsburg's test? If not, is the Court's opinion truly "in harmony" with Ginsburg's concurring opinion? Would you say that one is more stringent than the other? Which one?

6. Although Judge Keith, dissenting in Rabidue v. Oseola Refining Co., 805 F.2d 611, 626 (6th Cir.1986), cert. denied 481 U.S. 1041, 107 S.Ct. 1983, 95 L.Ed.2d 823 (1987), had suggested the use of a "reasonable woman" standard in sexual harassment claims, the Ninth Circuit was the first court to hold that sexual harassment claims should be examined from the victim's perspective. In Ellison v. Brady, 924 F.2d 872, 878–81 (9th Cir.1991), Judge Beezer reasoned as follows:

> * * * we believe that in evaluating the severity and pervasiveness of sexual harassment, we should focus on the perspective of the victim. King, 898 F.2d at 537; EEOC Compliance Manual (CCH) § 615, ¶ 3112, C at 3242 (1988)(courts "should consider the victim's perspective and not stereotyped notions of acceptable behavior.") If we only examined whether a reasonable person would engage in allegedly harassing conduct, we would run the risk of reinforcing the prevailing level of discrimination. Harassers could continue to harass merely because a particular discriminatory practice was common, and victims of harassment would have no remedy.
>
> We therefore prefer to analyze harassment from the victim's perspective. A complete understanding of the victim's view requires, among other things, an analysis of the different perspectives of men and women. Conduct that many men consider unobjectionable may offend many women. See, e.g., Lipsett v. University of Puerto Rico, 864 F.2d 881, 898 (1st Cir.1988)("A male supervisor might believe, for example, that it is legitimate for him to tell a female subordinate that she has a 'great figure' or 'nice legs.' The female subordinate, however, may find such comments offensive"); *Yates,* 819 F.2d at 637, n. 2 ("men and women are vulnerable in different ways and offended

---

See ___ U.S. at ___, 114 S.Ct. at 371 ("no single factor is required"); see also id. ___ U.S. at ___, 114 S.Ct. at 372 (Scalia, J., concurring)("the test is not whether work has been impaired, but whether working conditions have been discriminatorily altered"). But see id., ___ U.S. at ___, 114 S.Ct. at 372 (Ginsburg, J., concurring):

[T]he adjudicator's inquiry should center, dominantly, on whether the discriminatory conduct has unreasonably interfered with the plaintiff's work performance. To show such interference, "the plaintiff need not prove that his or her tangible productivity

has declined as a result of the harassment." Davis v. Monsanto Chemical Co., 858 F.2d 345, 349 (C.A.6 1988). It suffices to prove that a reasonable person subjected to the discriminatory conduct would find, as the plaintiff did, that the harassment so altered working conditions as to "make it more difficult to do the job." See ibid.

Justice Ginsburg's concurrence suggests that although proof of an adverse impact on the plaintiff's work performance is not required, it remains a particularly important factor in the hostile environment analysis.

by different behavior"). *See also* Ehrenreich, Pluralist Myths and Powerless Men: The Ideology of Reasonableness in Sexual Harassment Law, 99 Yale L.J. 1177, 1207–1208 (1990)(men tend to view some forms of sexual harassment as "harmless social interactions to which only overly-sensitive women would object"); Abrams, Gender Discrimination and the Transformation of Workplace Norms, 42 Vand.L.Rev. 1183, 1203 (1989)(the characteristically male view depicts sexual harassment as comparatively harmless amusement).

We realize that there is a broad range of viewpoints among women as a group, but we believe that many women share common concerns which men do not necessarily share. For example, because women are disproportionately victims of rape and sexual assault, women have a stronger incentive to be concerned with sexual behavior. Women who are victims of mild forms of sexual harassment may understandably worry whether a harasser's conduct is merely a prelude to violent sexual assault. Men, who are rarely victims of sexual assault, may view sexual conduct in a vacuum without a full appreciation of the social setting or the underlying threat of violence that a woman may perceive.

In order to shield employers from having to accommodate the idiosyncratic concerns of the rare hyper-sensitive employee, we hold that a female plaintiff states a prima facie case of hostile environment sexual harassment when she alleges conduct which a reasonable woman would consider sufficiently severe or pervasive to alter the conditions of employment and create an abusive working environment.

* * *

We adopt the perspective of a reasonable woman primarily because we believe that a sex-blind reasonable person standard tends to be male-biased and tends to systematically ignore the experiences of women. The reasonable woman standard does not establish a higher level of protection for women than men. Cf. Rosenfeld v. Southern Pacific Co., 444 F.2d 1219, 1225–1227 (9th Cir.1971)(invalidating under Title VII paternalistic state labor laws restricting employment opportunities for women). Instead, a gender-conscious examination of sexual harassment enables women to participate in the workplace on an equal footing with men. By acknowledging and not trivializing the effects of sexual harassment on reasonable women, courts can work towards ensuring that neither men nor women will have to "run a gauntlet of sexual abuse in return for the privilege of being allowed to work and make a living." Henson v. Dundee, 682 F.2d 897, 902 (11th Cir.1982).

We note that the reasonable victim standard we adopt today classifies conduct as unlawful sexual harassment even when harassers do not realize that their conduct creates a hostile working environment. Well-intentioned compliments by co-workers or supervisors can form the basis of a sexual harassment cause of action if a reasonable victim of the same sex as the plaintiff would consider the comments sufficiently severe or pervasive to alter a condition of employment and create an abusive working environment. That is because Title VII is not a fault-based tort scheme. "Title VII is aimed at the consequences or effects of an employment practice and not at the * * * motivation" of co-workers or employers. Rogers, 454 F.2d at 239; see also Griggs v. Duke Power Co., 401 U.S. 424, 432, 91 S.Ct. 849, 854, 28 L.Ed.2d 158 (1971)(the absence of discriminatory intent does not redeem an otherwise unlawful employment practice). To avoid liability under Title VII, employers may have to educate and sensitize their workforce to eliminate conduct which a reasonable victim would consider unlawful sexual harassment. See 29 C.F.R. § 1604.11(f)("Prevention is the best tool for the elimination of sexual harassment.")

* * *

Sexual harassment is a major problem in the workplace. Adopting the victim's perspective ensures that courts will not "sustain ingrained notions of reasonable behavior fashioned by the offenders." *Lipsett,* 864 F.2d at 898, quoting, *Rabidue,* 805 F.2d at 626 (Keith, J., dissenting). Congress did not enact Title VII to codify prevailing sexist prejudices. To the contrary, "Congress designed Title VII to prevent the perpetuation of stereotypes and a sense of degradation which serve to close or discourage employment opportunities for women." *Andrews,* 895 F.2d at 1483. We hope that over time both men and women will learn what conduct offends reasonable members of the other sex. When employers and employees internalize the standard of workplace conduct we establish today, the current gap in perception between the sexes will be bridged.

Is the "reasonable woman" standard a victory for women in sexual harassment cases? The *Harris* court was not required to and did not address the appropriateness of such a standard, preferring to phrase the objective prong of its test as whether a "reasonable person" would find the work environment hostile or abusive, and the *Saxton* case, cited in Note 5, supra, similarly avoided the issue, see 10 F.3d at 534 n. 13 ("We are not called upon to decide here whether it might be more appropriate to evaluate the plaintiff's work environment from the perspective of a reasonable woman as opposed to a genderless reasonable person"). Feminists disagree. Professor Susan Estrich observes that the dispositive question in determining whether hostile environment harassment in the workplace is "based on sex" may be simply a question of whose perspective should govern. She adds that "* * * if that is the right question, the male perspective is not necessarily the right answer." Susan Estrich, Sex at Work, 43 Stan.L.Rev. 813, 841 (1991). Nancy Ehrenreich is less certain: she provides a detailed critique of the interplay between reasonableness and pluralism in the opinions in *Rabidue* and concludes that even the use of a "reasonable woman" standard allows courts to retreat to a stance of neutrality that masks the political necessity of limiting the freedom of men to exercise their sexual domination over women in the workplace as a necessary consequence of protecting the freedom of women to work without harassment. Ehrenreich, Pluralist Myths and Powerless Men: The Ideology of Reasonableness in Sexual Harassment Law, 99 Yale L.J. 1177 (1990).

7. In Robinson v. Jacksonville Shipyards, Inc., 760 F.Supp. 1486 (M.D.Fla.1991)(appeal still pending), Lois Robinson testified that the "circumstances" of her work environment as one of the few female craftworkers employed by the defendant between 1977 and 1988 featured "extensive, pervasive posting of pictures depicting nude women, partially nude women, or sexual conduct" as well as "harassing behavior perpetrated by her male coworkers and supervisors." Id., 760 F.Supp. at 1494. Judge Melton found that her testimony provided "a vivid description of a visual assault on the sensibilities of female workers at JSI that did not relent during working hours." Id., 760 F.Supp. at 1495 (Robinson's testimony is detailed at 1495–99). He found a "reasonable woman" standard appropriate (id., at 1524–25):

A reasonable woman would find that the working environment at JSI was abusive. This conclusion reaches the totality of the circumstances, including the sexual remarks, the sexual jokes, the sexually-oriented pictures of women, and the non-sexual rejection of women by coworkers. The testimony of Dr. Fiske [Dr. Susan Fiske, Professor of Psychology at the University of Massachusetts at Amherst, and a specialist in sexual stereotyping] and Ms. Wagner [Ms. K.C. Wagner, a consultant on women and the work environment, whose specialty is the prevention of sexual harassment on the job] provides a reliable basis upon which to conclude that the cumulative, corrosive effect of this work environment over time affects the psychological well-being of a reasonable woman placed in these conditions. This corollary conclusion holds true whether the concept of psychological well-being is measured by the impact of the work environment on a reasonable woman's work performance or more broadly by the impact of the stress inflicted on her by the continuing presence of the harassing behavior. The fact that some female employees did not complain of the work environment or find some behaviors objectionable does not affect this conclusion concerning the objective offensiveness of the work environment as a whole.

Would an order telling Lois Robinson's co-workers to knock it off violate the First Amendment? See Marcy Strauss, Sexist Speech in the Workplace, 25 Harv. Civ. Rts.-Civ. Lib. L. Rev. 1 (1990); Amy Horton, Comment, Of Supervision, Centerfolds, and Censorship: Sexual Harassment, the First Amendment, and the Contours of Title VII, 46 U.Miami L.Rev. 403 (1991).

One commentator suggests a distinction between *"directed* speech—speech that is aimed at a particular employee because of her race, sex, religion, or national origin—and *undirected* speech, speech between other employees that is overheard by the offended employee, or printed material, intended to communicate to the other employees in general, that is seen by the offended employee." The argument is that the state's "interest in assuring equality in the workplace would justify restricting directed speech, but not undirected speech." Eugene Volokh, Freedom of Speech and Workplace Harassment, 39 U.C.L.A. L.Rev. 1791, 1846 (1992). How would this distinction apply to the *Jacksonville Shipyards* posters? The author suggests that "if a male employee intentionally leaves an offensive poster (pornographic or merely bigoted) on a coworker's desk, this would be directed speech; but if the employee puts the poster up on the walls where coworkers might see it, it would not be." Id., at 1868. Do you agree that posters on walls commonly used by all employees constitute "undirected speech"? Is the standard subjective or objective? What if there are only a handful of female employees in a traditionally male workplace? Is this the right place to draw the first amendment line?

8. What impact, if any, does Title VII have on mutual sexual attraction between co-workers? What impact does it have on competition between co-workers? If a female employee is carrying on a sexual relationship with her male supervisor, should her male co-workers be allowed to sue for the loss of "the extraordinary opportunities offered the woman"? See Note, Sexual Harassment and Title VII: The Foundation for the Elimination of Sexual Cooperation as an Employment Condition, 76 Mich.L.Rev. 1007, 1032 (1978). The EEOC Guidelines under the tactful heading "other related practices," recognize in section (g) that

[w]here employment opportunities or benefits are granted because of an individual's submission to the employer's sexual advances or requests for sexual favors, the employer may be held liable for unlawful sex discrimination against other persons who were qualified for but denied that employment opportunity or benefit.

See p. 1254 infra. What does that mean? In DeCintio v. Westchester County Medical Center, 807 F.2d 304 (2d Cir.1986), cert. denied 484 U.S. 825, 108 S.Ct. 89, 98 L.Ed.2d 50 (1987), plaintiffs were seven male respiratory therapists who alleged that they had been unfairly disqualified from promotion to the position of Assistant Chief Respiratory Therapist because James Ryan, the Program Administrator, imposed a new requirement that the Assistant Chief be registered with the National Board of Respiratory Therapists in order to be able to select Jean Guagenti, the woman with whom he had been engaged in a romantic relationship, for the position. Accepting these allegations as true, the court held that plaintiffs had not set forth a cognizable Title VII claim. It reasoned as follows:

> Ryan's conduct, although unfair, simply did not violate Title VII. Appellees were not prejudiced because of their status as males; rather, they were discriminated against because Ryan preferred his paramour. Appellees faced exactly the same predicament as that faced by any woman applicant for the promotion: No one but Guagenti could be considered for the appointment because of Guagenti's special relationship to Ryan. That relationship forms the basis of appellees' sex discrimination claims. Appellees' proffered interpretation of Title VII prohibitions against sex discrimination would involve the EEOC and federal courts in the policing of intimate relationships. Such a course, founded on a distortion of the meaning of the word "sex" in the context of Title VII, is both impracticable and unwarranted.

Id., at 308. The court had earlier read the EEOC Guideline quoted above as limited to situations involving an element of coercion and as inapplicable to personal, social relationships. Do you agree with this interpretation? Do you think plaintiffs were discriminated against on the basis of their sex? Anthony DeCintio was subsequently fired; his Title VII claim for retaliation is reported in DeCintio v. Westchester County Medical Center, 821 F.2d 111 (2d Cir.1987), cert. denied 484 U.S. 965, 108 S.Ct. 455, 98 L.Ed.2d 395.

The Second Circuit in *DeCintio* declined to follow King v. Palmer, 778 F.2d 878 (D.C.Cir.1985), in which the parties agreed that Title VII covered plaintiff Mable King's contention that she was denied promotion to the position of supervisory forensic/clinical nurse because of the sexual relationship between the successful candidate, Norma Jean Grant, and Dr. Francis Smith, the Chief Medical Officer at the District of Columbia Jail where all parties worked. The District Court's judgment against Ms. King was reversed in part because it had erroneously required that King prove the sexual relationship between Grant and Smith had been consummated by sexual intercourse. Judge Edwards found sufficient basis to sustain plaintiff's case in the District Court's finding "that there was direct evidence of a sexual relationship, i.e., kisses, embraces and other amorous behavior, which concededly played a substantial role in Ms. Grant's selection for promotion." Id., at 882. In his opinion filed with the *per curiam* order denying a suggestion for rehearing *en banc*, Judge Bork emphasized that, because of the parties' agreement, the question of whether Title VII "affords a claim for relief for sex-based discrimination to a woman who alleges that she was denied a promotion in favor of another woman who had a sexual relationship with their supervisor" had not been raised before the panel on appeal and therefore was not a proper matter for rehearing *en banc*. Id., at 883. Does this mean that Judge Edwards's statement in *King* is dicta? Do you think Mable King's complaint is covered by Title VII?

DeCintio was followed in Candelore v. Clark County Sanitation District, 752 F.Supp. 956 (D.Nev.1990), affirmed 975 F.2d 588 (9th Cir.1992), to deny Elaine

Candelore's § 1983 complaint that a newly-arrived younger woman was given preferential treatment including a lighter work load, longer lunch hours, and new office furniture because she was having an affair with the District Director. Citing *DeCintio,* Judge Pro disagreed:

> The Court * * * concludes that preferential treatment of a paramour, while perhaps unfair, is not discrimination on the basis of sex in violation of Title VII or, in this case, the Equal Protection Clause of the Constitution. No term or condition of employment was conditioned on submission to unwelcome advances; rather, nobody but the one woman allegedly engaged in the affair could have received special treatment. This is not "quid pro quo" sexual harassment.

Id., 752 F.Supp. at 961. Judge Pro also rejected plaintiff's claim of hostile environment harassment on the ground that she had not shown the "kind of statements and actions that would establish a hostile or offensive environment" for herself. Id. Would you call this a narrow interpretation of the claim?

See Mary C. Manemann, Comment, The Meaning of "Sex" in Title VII: Is Favoring an Employee Lover a Violation of the Act?, 83 Nw.U.L.Rev. 612, 657–64 (1989), proposing that plaintiffs like Mable King and the male therapists in *DeCintio* should be able to make out a prima facie case of sex discrimination, provided they are able to prove that the person hired or promoted was substantially less qualified than they. Do you agree?

9. Is Title VII violated by a gay supervisor who demands sexual favors from an employee of his or her same gender? Is Title VII violated by a bisexual supervisor who demands sexual favors from both male and female workers? In Barnes v. Costle, 561 F.2d 983, 990 & n. 55 (D.C.Cir.1977) a quid pro quo case in which a supervisor abolished plaintiff's job in retaliation for her refusal to grant his demands for sexual favors, Judge Robinson suggested that a bisexual supervisor would not be covered by Title VII:

> The District Court felt, however, that appellant's suit amounted to no more than a claim "that she was discriminated against, not because she was a woman, but because she refused to engage in a sexual affair with her supervisor." In similar vein, appellee has argued that "[a]ppellant was allegedly denied employment enhancement not because she was a woman, but rather because she decided not to furnish the sexual consideration claimed to have been demanded." We cannot accept this analysis of the situation charged by appellant. But for her womanhood, from aught that appears, her participation in sexual activity would never have been solicited. To say, then, that she was victimized in her employment simply because she declined the invitation is to ignore the asserted fact that she was invited only because she was a woman subordinate to the inviter in the hierarchy of agency personnel.[55] Put another way, she became the target of her superior's sexual desires because she was a woman, and was asked to bow to his demands as the price for holding her job. The circumstance imparting high visibility to the role of

---

55. It is no answer to say that a similar condition could be imposed on a male subordinate by a heterosexual female superior, or upon a subordinate of either gender by a homosexual superior of the same gender. In each instance, the legal problem would be identical to that confronting us now—the exaction of a condition which, but for his or her sex, the employee would not have faced. These situations, like that at bar, are to be distinguished from a bisexual superior who conditions the employment opportunities of a subordinate of either gender upon participation in a sexual affair. In the case of the bisexual superior, the insistence upon sexual favors would not constitute gender discrimination because it would apply to male and female employees alike.

gender in the affair is that no male employee was susceptible to such an approach by appellant's supervisor. Thus gender cannot be eliminated from the formulation which appellant advocates, and that formulation advances a prima facie case of sex discrimination within the purview of Title VII.

Would the *Barnes* court allow a complaint under Title VII if a male supervisor demanded a cash payoff from male, but not female, employees as the price of promotion?

Although research indicates that 90% of workplace sexual harassment cases arise from men harassing women, 9% do arise from same-sex harassment. See Ellen Bravo and Ellen Cassedy, the 9to5 Guide to Combating Sexual Harassment: Candid Advice from 9to5, the National Association for Working Women 64 (1992). (The remaining 1% arise from women harassing men.) The federal courts are split over whether Title VII protects victims of same-sex harassment. If the harassment is of the quid pro quo variety, courts are more likely to find a Title VII cause of action. In Wright v. Methodist Youth Services, Inc., 511 F.Supp. 307 (N.D.Ill.1981), the district court relied on the above language from *Barnes v. Costle* to hold that plaintiff, a man, stated a cause of action under Title VII when he alleged he was terminated for refusing the homosexual advances of his gay male supervisor. A good discussion of intervening case law on this issue is found in EEOC v. Walden Book Co., 885 F.Supp. 1100, 67 FEP Cases 1446 (M.D.Tenn. 1995), where the district court held that plaintiff's claim of sexual harassment by his gay male supervisor stated a cause of action under Title VII. Just as "reverse" discrimination suits are allowed in those rare instances where the defendant is "that unusual employer who discriminates against the majority," same-sex sexual harassment suits may proceed in those circumstances "where, but for the subordinate's sex, he would not be subject to that treatment." Id. at 1449. See also Raney v. District of Columbia, 892 F.Supp. 283 (D.C.Cir. 1995), where the district court relied in part on the EEOC's Compliance Manual for its position that Title VII protects employees from same-sex discrimination: "the victim [of harassment] does not have to be of the opposite sex from the harasser." Id. In dicta, the Seventh Circuit has commented:

> The concept of sexual harassment is designed to protect working women from the kind of male attention that can make the workplace hellish for women. (Sexual harassment of women by men is the most common kind, but we do not mean to exclude the possibility that sexual harassment of men by women, or men by other men, or women by other women would not also be actionable in appropriate cases.)

Baskerville v. Culligan International Co., 50 F.3d 428, 430 (7th Cir.1995).

Courts have been more reluctant to recognize hostile environment sexual harassment claims based on same-sex interactions. See Garcia v. Elf Atochem N. America, 28 F.3d 446 (5th Cir.1994)(male employee whose supervisor grabbed his crotch area from behind and made sexual motions had no cause of action under Title VII, notwithstanding evidence that the employer had received two prior complaints about the supervisor's conduct; harassment by a male supervisor against a male subordinate "does not state a claim under Title VII even though the harassment has sexual overtones. Title VII addresses gender discrimination."); Hopkins v. Baltimore Gas & Elec. Co., 871 F.Supp. 822 (D.Md.1994)(male employee's male supervisor repeatedly made unwelcome sexual jokes, comments, and gestures of a sexual nature; court followed *Garcia*, holding no Title VII claim for hostile environment harassment by supervisor of same sex); Fleenor v. Hewitt Soap Co., 1995 WL 386793, 67 FEP Cases 1625 (S.D.Ohio 1994) (rejecting same sex hostile environment claim by male co-worker against other co-workers). In Goluszek v. Smith, 697 F.Supp. 1452 (N.D.Ill.1988), the district court held that heterosexual male-to-male harassment involving sexual horseplay did not create a hostile environment cause of action under Title VII. Plaintiff was teased because he had no wife or girlfriend, lived with his mother, and was "unsophisticated," with "little or no sexual experience." Id. at 1453. The *Goluszek* court asserted that "the discrimination Congress was concerned about when it enacted Title VII is one stemming from an imbalance of power and an abuse of that imbalance by the powerful which results in discrimination against a discrete and vulnerable group." Id. at 1456, citing Note, Sexual Harassment Claims of Abusive Work Environment Under Title VII, 97 Harv.L.Rev. 1449, 1451–52 (1984). "Actionable sexual-harassment fosters a sense of degradation in the victim by attacking their sexuality. * * * In effect, the offender is saying by words or actions that the victim is inferior because of the victim's sex." Id. at 1456. While the court found that "if Goluszek were a women, [the employer] would have taken action to stop the harassment, * * * and that the harassment was pervasive and continuous from the time Goluszek began until he was fired," the court held that "[s]imply stated, the defendant's conduct was not the type of conduct Congress intended to sanction when it enacted Title VII." Id.

One commentator calls the present Title VII sexual harassment paradigm "defective," and warns against the danger of "inject[ing] male abuse of power and economic privilege into the very definition of sexual harassment:"

> Incorporating abuse of power into the definition [of sexual harassment] seems unduly limiting. While it mirrors accurately what transpires in the classic quid pro quo situation, it reflects only uneasily hostile environment sexual harassment by co-workers.

Ellen Frankel Paul, Sexual Harassment as Sex Discrimination: A Defective Paradigm, 8 Yale Law & Policy Rev. 333, 334–35 (1990). Paul "questions the assumptions" behind inclusion of sexual harassment under Title VII, and concludes that the defective Title VII paradigm should be replaced with a "new tort remedy for sexual harassment." Id. at 346–353, 335. She also discusses the "perplexing doctrinal anomaly" of the bisexual supervisor:

> The identical offense is sex discrimination under Title VII when perpetrated by a man against a women, by a man against a man, by a woman against a woman; yet, if a bisexual of either sex preys equally on men and women, he (or she) is beyond the reach of Title VII. The law is supposed to look to acts, whether criminal or tortious, to determine culpability and not to the individual characteristics of the perpetrators. * * * Yet, if sexual harassment is sexual discrimination under Title VII, why are some perpetrators insulated? A savy harasser need only note this anomaly and become an equal opportunity harasser.

Id. at 351.

In Chiapuzio v. BLT Operating Corp., 826 F.Supp. 1334, (D.Wyo.1993), however, the district court found that an "equal-opportunity harasser," who created a hostile environment by sexually harassing both men and women, could not escape the male plaintiffs' Title VII claim where the harasser, in fact, intended to demean, and therefore harm plaintiffs because they were men.

Should Title VII protect workers from same-sex harassment? Do we need further legislative clarification of what "discrimination based on sex" means? For further discussion of claims of both heterosexual and homosexual harassment, see

Michelle Ridgeway Peirce, Sexual Harassment and Title VII—A Better Solution, 30 B.C. L.Rev. 1071 (1989), advocating new legislation with "primary purpose of combating sexual harassment." Id. at 1100. For discussion of social science research aiding understanding of sexual behavior in the workplace as it relates to sexual harassment, see Barbara A. Gutek, Understanding Sexual Harassment at Work, 6 Notre Dame J. L. Ethics, & Pub. Policy 335 (1992). For further discussion of congressional intent and Title VII sexual harassment cases, see Susan Estrich, Sex at Work, 43 Stanford L. Rev. 813, 818–19 (1991): "the early [sexual harassment cases] focused on a rather standard set of arguments. One argument frequently heard was 'Congress never intended such a cause of action.' Certainly this was true, but then Congress barely intended that sex discrimination be prohibited in employment at all." Id. at 818.

10. Employers are responding to the increased volume of sexual harassment litigation by taking strong action against employees found to have committed sexual harassment. Some men, either accused or found "guilty" by their employers, have sought relief in the courts, with mixed results. In Castleberry v. Boeing Co., 880 F.Supp. 1435 (D.Kan. 1995), two male managers sued Boeing for sex discrimination because they were terminated for a prank involving the purchase of a dildo and its presentation to an employee at her birthday party. The woman employee who initiated the dildo purchase was merely disciplined, receiving a 5–day suspension without pay. The men complained that this difference constituted sex discrimination. The district court granted summary judgment for Boeing, finding that the men received the highest level of discipline, termination, because they were managers, they had recently attended a mandatory sexual harassment prevention training program, and Boeing had a right to expect a higher level of conduct from management than from nonmanagement personnel. Therefore, the court held the two men were not similarly situated to the woman subordinate, and consequently, were not discriminated against because of their sex. Id. at 1441–1442. For additional cases filed by men accused of or dismissed for sexually harassing women subordinates or co-workers, see, e.g., Chalmers v. Quaker Oats Co., 61 F.3d 1340 (7th Cir.1995)(denial of severance pay for "gross misconduct" was not arbitrary or capricious under the Employee Retirement Income Security Act, even though employer's policy against sexual harassment was more stringent than Title VII); Garziano v. E.I. Du Pont De Nemours & Co., 818 F.2d 380 (5th Cir.1987)(Company's issuance of Bulletin on Sexual Harassment which described the reasons for male employee's dismissal, although it did not mention his name, was protected against his libel and slander action by a qualified privilege); Huff v. County of Butler, 524 F.Supp. 751 (W.D.Pa.1981)(cause of action available under 42 U.S.C.A. § 1983 for male supervisor who was forced to resign without a hearing allegedly because of his sexual harassment of female employees; plaintiff also alleged that his former employer spread gossip throughout the community about his "immoral" activities); EEOC v. Levi Strauss & Co., 515 F.Supp. 640 (N.D.Ill.1981)(refusing to dismiss EEOC charge that a male supervisor who filed a defamation suit in state court against female employee who complained of his sexual harassment had filed the suit with intent to retaliate against her in violation of Title VII); Barnes v. Oody, 514 F.Supp. 23 (E.D.Tenn.1981)(holds defamation suit filed by male co-worker against female who complained of sexual harassment barred by finding of administrative tribunal that investigated the claim that the allegations were true; suit was filed in state court and removed to federal court).

In Anderson v. Hewlett–Packard, 694 F.Supp. 1294 (N.D.Ohio 1988), Edgar Anderson, dismissed by Hewlett–Packard as personnel manager of its Cleveland office, sued the employer for breach of contract and promissory estoppel. Hewlett–Packard claimed that Anderson had been fired for gross misconduct, namely, the sexual harassment of women employees working under his supervision. District Judge Ann Aldrich found for the employer and dismissed Anderson's complaint, noting sharply that:

> It is clear to the Court that Anderson's constant sexual remarks, innuendos, insinuations and suggestions made life completely unbearable for the women working for him, as did the childish punishments he inflicted upon them when they would not accede to his demands.

* * *

> It should be clear to corporate America, by now, that the law does not tolerate the type of behavior Anderson exhibited. The termination of employees who behave as Anderson did is justified and lawful. In fact, the only troublesome part of this case is that it took H–P as long as it did to fire Anderson. * * *

Id. at 1303–04. It is clear, however, that not everyone in "corporate America" has gotten the message. See, e.g., Jones v. Wesco Investments, Inc., 846 F.2d 1154 (8th Cir.1988), a sexual harassment case in which Senior Judge Bright affirmed a judgment for the plaintiff based on a showing of "repeated sexual advances, request for sexual favors, and other verbal or physical contact of a sexual nature" on the part of the President of the Company, Benjamin B. Rose. Noting that "any other result would have been a miscarriage of justice," Judge Bright quoted the following passage from defendant's brief, adding that the argument "accords neither with the facts nor the law in the present case":

> Any argument in this type of case on this issue is bound to sound sexist, but it is important to point out that one of the traditional places where man meets woman is at the work place. Such meetings often result in dating, blossom into love, and eventually into marriage. Not always are both parties in this cycle unmarried. If civil liability is implanted on an employer for its employees natural interaction between the genders, either the collapse of our commercial system or the end of the human race can be foreseen. No employer could safely employ both males and females, and the number of marriages with children will be substantially decreased. There should be nothing wrong with a man, even a supervisor, telling a female that she looks nice. Nor can there be anything wrong with a man, even a supervisor, asking a female our of [sic] a date. In doing so the man should not have to gamble civil liability upon her "yes" response. Where is the line between these instances and those held to be actionable in *Meritor* * * *?

Id., at 1156–57 & n. 6. On second thought, maybe it's legal America that hasn't gotten the message. See generally Michael D. Vhay, Comment, The Harms of Asking: Towards a Comprehensive Treatment of Sexual Harassment, 55 U.Chi. L.Rev. 328 (1988).

11. In an effort to broaden Title VII's coverage of sexual harassment, California Senator Dianne Feinstein introduced S.B. 1864, the "Harassment–Free Work Place Act of 1994" on February 23, 1994. The bill would have extended Title VII's protection to cover workers in businesses with fewer than 15 employees. In her remarks on the floor, Senator Feinstein noted that the bill was modeled on California law, which similarly prohibits sexual harassment by all employers with one or more employees. See West's Ann.Cal.Gov.Code § 12940(h).

California has recently extended the concept of sexual harassment beyond the employment context and into the world of professional and business relationships. Under California law, effective January 1, 1995, a person may be liable for sexual harassment if "(1) there is a business, service, or professional relationship" between plaintiff and defendant, such as patients or clients with physicians, psychotherapists, dentists, attorneys, counselors, real estate agents, accountants, and so forth, or between tenants and landlords, students and teachers, and any other similar relationships. Sexual harassment has occurred if:

(2) The defendant has made sexual advances, solicitations, sexual requests, or demands for sexual compliance by the plaintiff that were unwelcome and persistent or severe, continuing after a request by the plaintiff to stop.

(3) There is an inability by the plaintiff to easily terminate the relationship without tangible hardship.

(4) The plaintiff has suffered or will suffer economic loss or disadvantage or personal injury as a result of the conduct described in paragraph (2).

Unruh Civil Rights Act, § 51.9, Calif. Civil Code, as amended by Ch. 710, L. 1994. Plaintiffs may recover damages under this statute.

12. Do you agree with Justice Rehnquist that a different standard of employer liability should apply in quid pro quo and hostile environment sexual harassment claims? What justification does he provide for this distinction? Is Justice Marshall's view that the employer should be held to the same high standard in both cases better grounded in the statute? Early notewriters agreed that the distinction is not convincing. See, e.g, The Supreme Court—Leading Cases, 100 Harv.L.Rev. 1, 280 (1986) (concluding that *Vinson* "should have held employers strictly liable for *all* sexual harassment perpetrated by their supervising employees" because "[o]nly this firm rule—and nothing else—will prod employers into developing effective grievance procedures"); Christopher P. Barton, Note, Between the Boss and a Hard Place: A Consideration of Meritor Savings Bank, FSB v. Vinson and the Law of Sexual Harassment, 67 B.U.L.Rev. 445, 462 (1987)("It is unfortunate that the Court did not adopt a unified rule of employer liability of the sort proposed by Justice Marshall"). Applying *Vinson* to a case involving an employer's liability for the actions of a male supervisor "who harassed women on a daily basis in the course of his supervision of them" in the context of a "policy of not placing documentation of sexual harassment in personnel files [which] seems to protect only Avco and the harasser, rather than the affected employee," a panel of the Sixth Circuit had no trouble imposing liability even though the employer may not have had actual notice of the supervisor's behavior prior to the plaintiffs' complaints. In Yates v. Avco Corp., 819 F.2d 630 (6th Cir.1987), the court concluded that the finding that Avco "knew, or upon reasonably diligent inquiry should have known, that Sanders was sexually harassing the plaintiffs and other females" was not clearly erroneous. It distinguished *Rabidue,* discussed in *Harris,* supra, on the ground that the plaintiff and her harasser were "peers," whereas in *Yates,* a supervisor was involved. Why should that make a difference? Does *Yates* satisfy the criticisms of the Notewriters cited above?

In a more recent case, the D.C. Circuit held that an employer was not liable under common law agency principles for a Title VII hostile environment sexual harassment claim filed by a woman against one of her supervisors. In Gary v. Long, 59 F.3d 1391 (D.C.Cir.1995), the court found that the employer had a well-publicized policy against sexual harassment. Therefore, the plaintiff "knew or should have known that the employer did not tolerate such conduct [including an alleged rape] and that she could report it to the employer without fear of adverse consequences." Id. at 1398. Accordingly, under common law agency principles, she could not have believed that the supervisor was acting within the scope of his employment, "within the color of his authority:"

> "It is a general principle of agency law that '[i]f a person has information which would lead a reasonable man [sic] to believe that the agent is violating the orders of the principal or that the principal would not wish the agent to act under the circumstances known to the agent, he cannot subject the principal to liability.' "

Id. at 1398, quoting from the Restatement (Second) of Agency § 166 cmt. a. One wonders what kind of working world these federal judges think employees experience. Under this kind of approach, perhaps testimony from co-workers about their fears of adverse consequences will become crucial. After ruling that plaintiff could not hold her employer liable, the appellate court also affirmed the district court's finding that the supervisor was not individually liable under Title VII because he was not an "employer" within the meaning of the Act. Id. at 1399. Does this mean plaintiffs will have a sexual harassment hostile environment claim against no one?

d. Women in Upper Level Jobs

BROWN v. TRUSTEES OF BOSTON UNIVERSITY

United States Court of Appeals, First Circuit, 1989.
891 F.2d 337, cert. denied 496 U.S. 937, 110 S.Ct. 3217, 110 L.Ed.2d 664 (1990).

Before CAMPBELL, CHIEF JUDGE, BREYER and TORRUELLA, CIRCUIT JUDGES.

LEVIN H. CAMPBELL, CHIEF JUDGE.

Julia Prewitt Brown, an assistant professor of English at Boston University sued in the Massachusetts Superior Court after she was denied tenure by defendants, the Trustees of Boston University ("University"). The University removed the case to the District Court for the District of Massachusetts. Alleging that she had been refused tenure because of her sex, Professor Brown contended that denying her tenure for that reason violated an anti-discrimination clause in the University's collective bargaining agreement with its faculty. A jury found in her favor on this contract claim; it awarded her $200,000 damages for the breach. Brown also brought claims for the alleged sex-based denial of tenure under Title VII of the Civil Rights Act of 1964, 42 U.S.C. § 2000e et seq. (1982), and under the Massachusetts anti-discrimination statute, Mass.Gen.L. ch. 151B, § 4 (1982). Applying to these other claims the finding of sex discrimination made by the jury in the contract action, the district court ordered the University to pay Brown $15,000 in damages for emotional distress, enjoined the University from further sex discrimination against Brown and other faculty members, and ordered the University to grant to Brown the position of Associate Professor with tenure. Boston University appeals from the jury verdict, the award of tenure, and the injunction from further sex discrimination. We affirm the findings of liability and the tenure award, but slightly modify the anti-discrimination injunction.

I. BACKGROUND

In the fall of 1974, plaintiff Brown began working at Boston University as an Assistant Professor of English Literature, on the tenure track. Tenure candidates had to teach for six years before being eligible for tenure. During the sixth year the candidate was evaluated in three areas: scholarship, teaching, and service to the university. Excellence had to be demonstrated in two of the three areas.

Brown came up for tenure in the academic year 1979–80. At this time the ground rules for tenure review were spelled out in a recently negotiated collective bargaining agreement ("Agreement" or "Contract") between the Boston University Chapter of the American Association of University Professors ("Chapter") and Boston University. The process was to last the entire academic year, progressing through a series of committee and individual reviews culminating in a review by the President of the University, who then made a recommendation to the Trustees. The Trustees made the final decision to grant or deny tenure.

Brown prepared a dossier describing her accomplishments. Under the heading "Research and Publication," she listed a book, Jane Austen's Novels: Social Change and Literary Form, a revision of her Ph.d dissertation that had been published by the Harvard University Press, and three book reviews or review essays. Brown listed "all reviews, discussions and major citations" of her book, which included a review in the New York Times Sunday Book Review, four other reviews, two "readers' reports" from Harvard University Press and a letter from Harvard University Press concerning a second printing of the book. Under "work in progress" Brown listed a proposed book about Oscar Wilde. During academic years 1979–80, the year of her tenure review, she had received a Mellon grant to research and write this book, as well as to teach at Harvard University. Brown attached to her tenure dossier the six page prospectus describing her planned study of Oscar Wilde that had earned her the $16,000 Mellon grant.

Under the category of teaching, Brown listed the courses she had taught at Boston University, including two she had developed, "Fiction and National Character" and "Freud and the Victorian Novel." In respect to advising, she stated that she advised 15–20 undergraduates in composing their class schedules, spending about an hour per year with each student. She also described her activities on a committee that assisted undergraduate English majors in choosing a graduate school, and noted that, in 1977–78, she conducted a "woman's literature discussion group for graduate students which met informally once every two weeks." In the category of service to the University, Brown noted that she had been asked to assist in editing the "Partisan Review" for 1979–80, and listed service on various Boston University committees.

The first stop for Brown's file was a committee composed of all the tenured professors in the English department. The department committee voted unanimously, by a vote of 22–0, to promote her to Associate Professor with tenure. The department chairman's rationale included high praise for Brown's teaching and scholarship. On September 14, 1979, the chairman wrote, "[a]s a teacher, Judy Brown has two talents in rare combination. She has a very detailed and exact grasp of works of literature and she is able to see them in a larger cultural and historical perspective." The chairman stated that Brown's book on Jane Austen had been widely recognized by noted critics. He opined that "[i]t is rare for an older, let alone a younger, critic to write an important book on a major writer ... but Judy Brown has done so." In describing the book, the chairman noted Brown's "sensitivity to the fact that Jane Austen was a female novelist." The recommendation continued, "Professor Brown has the requisite literary tact to write about Jane Austen as a female writer without the ideological distortion and special pleading that sometimes mar such criticism."

The next review was by the Appointments, Promotions and Tenure Committee ("APT") of the College of Liberal Arts (CLA). This committee also recommended tenure, again unanimously. The committee's report described her as an "excellent teacher" and "a first rank ... scholar," saying that "she is bound to become a most distinguished and nationally recognized critic and scholar." On December 7, 1979 the APT sent its report to the Dean of the CLA. Before making his own recommendation, the Dean met with Brown. At that meeting, the Dean gave Brown the opportunity to answer criticism received in a letter solicited from an outside scholar in Brown's field. The Dean also asked Brown about the amount of time she spent advising students. After this meeting, the Dean recommended promotion and tenure. However, the Dean's report contained reservations about Brown's "historical scholarship," citing certain negative comments in a review and in the outside scholar's letter. The Dean recommended that subsequent reviewers solicit the view of an historian from Harvard University. He suggested that if the criticisms of the historical scholarship in Brown's book proved to be valid, the University should offer Brown a three year extension of her probationary period, so that her work on Oscar Wilde could be evaluated.[1] The Dean also characterized Brown's teaching as "fine," but expressed concern that she did not spend enough time advising students. The Dean sent a letter to Brown informing her that he had recommended her for tenure, but not mentioning the reservations he had expressed or his recommendation of a possible three year extension.

The week after the Dean completed his evaluation, Brown sent him a letter, along with additional material for her file. The letter dealt with the amount of time Brown spent advising students, saying that in addition to helping her advisees to prepare their schedules, she had office hours for four hours per week, of which most of her advisees took advantage. She included in the letter the names of three former advisees who would speak on her behalf. Brown also informed the Dean that her book had been nominated by the Harvard University Press, along with four others, for the James Russell Lowell Award, sponsored by the Modern Language Association.[2]

Notwithstanding the Dean's reservations, Brown received a further positive vote at the next level of review, a University-wide APT, which recommended tenure and promotion by a vote of 9–2. The committee report to the Provost concluded that "Dr. Brown is a serious and committed teacher-scholar who at a very early age has already made her imprint in one of the

---

1. While professors who were not granted tenure ordinarily had to leave after one more year, the Agreement allowed a three-year extension of the normal six-year probationary period "in occasional cases of substantial merit where a faculty member is potentially tenurable, but where further scholarly work is expected to be completed in short order." Such an extension required the agreement of the candidate and the various university groups and officials who passed on tenure. See n.3, infra.

2. Brown testified that "[t]he award is given to the work of literary criticism judged most distinguished by a group of scholars every year."

toughest and most competitive of fields * * *." Next, at the level of the Provost's review, an Assistant Provost, Simon Parker, evaluated Brown's candidacy. Parker's memo to the Provost expressed concern about the quality of Brown's book, although he praised the book generally. Parker recommended a three year extension, stating that "Brown's publishing achievements are limited in quantity to a revised dissertation and three book reviews * * *. The three year extension will enable her to finish this major independent work [the Oscar Wilde book], and prove whether she is able to sustain and improve the quality of her work as a maturing humanist."

Soon after the Assistant Provost completed his assessment, Brown requested from her department head a maternity leave of absence for the upcoming semester, which was granted. Next, the Provost concurred with Parker's assessment and advised Brown that he had recommended to the University's President, Dr. John Silber, that she be given a three year extension. Since the three year extension clause of the agreement required the concurrence of Brown and all three committees, her candidacy was again put to a vote. The 23 tenured members of the English department sent a letter to the Provost stating that "[i]t is the unanimous view of the Department that your recommendation * * * does not take into account the substance of the case for Professor Brown made by the Department and Faculty Committees" and urging the Provost to make a recommendation of tenure. The College APT sent a brief memo stating that it "wish[ed] to reaffirm our original unanimous recommendation for tenure and promotion for Professor Brown." The University APT, which originally had voted 9–2 for tenure, wrote that its members agreed Brown's scholarship "had reached sufficient maturity to warrant our recommendation." The minutes of the Committee's meeting reveal that the "Committee unanimously (10/0) agreed to reaffirm its original positive recommendation. The members did not wish to reject the extension in the event that Professor Brown agreed to it." Another exchange of letters between the Provost and the Department resulted in the unequivocal statement of the Department Chairman that "the [Department] Committee * * * refused to assent to a three year extension for [Brown] by a unanimous vote." On the same date, Professor Brown wrote to the Provost indicating that she did "not accept the recommendation of a three year extension."

In response, the Provost informed Brown that he had recommended against tenure. Because the Provost's recommendation was not in accordance with the judgments of the College and University APTs, Brown's case was forwarded to a three-member ad hoc Tenure Review Committee. The Agreement provided that the ad hoc Committee

> shall be composed of three impartial persons from outside of Boston University who shall be acknowledged authorities in the candidate's field or academic specialty. One of these three persons shall be designated by the Provost, one by the University APT, and one by mutual agreement between the two persons already designated.

The ad hoc committee voted for tenure by a margin of 2–1. The committee's report stated that the committee

> found Professor Brown's book on Jane Austen to be a substantial contribution to Austen studies * * *. [W]e evaluated the book as useful and

sometimes brilliant; we were not much impressed by its historical dimensions and found the statements about historicity a bit misleading. We agreed that the mind behind the book was a first-rate one, one that perhaps still had some maturing to do, but one that was capable of excellent original critical thinking.

The report also stated, "[w]e all regretted that we had no further work on which to judge Professor Brown; one committee member felt that such a lack of evidence of wider commitment was crucial * * *."

Upon receipt of the ad hoc committee's report, the Provost reported to President Silber that "[t]he report does not give a strong, unqualified endorsement of the candidate's work. Rather it confirms my earlier judgment that Professor Brown has not yet established a sufficiently strong scholarly record to merit tenure at Boston University." President Silber then informed Brown that "I shall recommend to the Trustees that tenure not be granted."

Brown subsequently wrote to ask President Silber to reconsider her case, making several charges of unfair treatment and irregularities over the course of her tenure candidacy. Brown raised the issue of sex discrimination, telling President Silber that "[o]ne of the main problems that women in my profession have is that they are frequently put under the microscope, in a way that men often are not, when seeking promotion." Brown compared her qualifications to those of several men who had been granted tenure in her department and in the year of her candidacy, saying that both the Dean and the Provost may have held women to higher standards than those imposed on men who had been granted tenure. The Dean, Brown said, singled her out for unusual treatment, recommending that her work be reviewed by someone outside her field, a historian, when he made no such recommendation concerning the candidacies of several men who were up for tenure. Brown also suggested that the Provost's treatment of her case had been more exacting than his treatment of men candidates. Brown asserted that although the Provost's expressed concern was with the quantity of Brown's scholarly work, the Provost had recommended tenure for another man in Brown's department who had produced a smaller amount of scholarly work. President Silber responded that he had reviewed Brown's case as she requested, but that he would stand by his earlier decision. On President Silber's recommendation, the Trustees denied Professor Brown tenure.

Soon after receiving President Silber's final letter, Brown brought suit in the Massachusetts Superior Court, alleging that Boston University had violated the Agreement by discriminating against her on the basis of her sex.[4] Boston University removed the suit to the United States District Court for the District of Massachusetts, alleging subject matter jurisdiction under Section 301(a) of the Labor Management Relations Act ("Act"), 29 U.S.C. s

4. Brown's complaint also alleged that Boston University had violated the terms of a settlement agreement entered into at the time the Agreement was negotiated, which provided that "there shall be no reprisals or abuse, either institutional or personal, against any member of the University community for his/her actions during the strike." Prior to the Agreement's execution, the Boston University faculty had engaged in a labor strike. Brown participated in the strike, picketing in front of President Silber's office and in front of an office of one of the University's Trustees. At trial, the jury found that Boston University had not discriminated against Brown on the basis of her strike activity. Brown has not appealed from that finding. Therefore, we address only the issues raised as a result of the jury's finding that Boston University discriminated against Brown because of her sex.

185(a)(1982), which confers federal jurisdiction over "[s]uits for violation of contracts between an employer and a labor organization representing employees * * *." After completing the required administrative procedures, Brown amended her complaint to include claims that the University's actions violated Title VII of the Civil Rights Act of 1964, 42 U.S.C. § 2000e–2, and the Massachusetts anti-discrimination statute, Mass.Gen.L. ch. 151B § 4.

Prior to trial, the University moved for summary judgment as to Brown's contract claims and for denial of Brown's jury demand as to all counts. The district court refused to grant summary judgment against Brown on her claim that the University had violated the Agreement. The court ruled that Brown was entitled to a jury trial on the contract claim, because "[a] complaint which alleges a breach by an employer of a collective bargaining agreement in which the plaintiff seeks back pay states a claim for legal damages, and the plaintiff has a right to trial by jury on that claim." Recognizing that Brown had no right to a jury trial on either the Title VII or the Chapter 151B claims, the court ruled that Brown's right to a jury trial on her contract claim extended to all issues common to the three separate claims. See Curtis v. Loether, 415 U.S. 189, 94 S.Ct. 1005, 39 L.Ed.2d 260 (1974). The most important factual issue common to the three claims was whether Boston University had denied Brown tenure because of her sex.

Brown's evidence at the trial compared her qualifications, including her published writing, with those of others, particularly males, in English and related fields who had been granted tenure. She placed in evidence the voluminous tenure files of herself and of the allegedly "similarly situated" faculty members. She called as witnesses several Boston University professors, including two former heads of the English Department, who had participated in her own tenure review as well as the tenure reviews of others during this period. Several witnesses interpreted scholarly reviews and gave their opinions on how to compare the various files. The thrust of Brown's comparative evidence was that she had been held to a stricter standard than her male peers.[6]

---

6. Brown introduced evidence showing that over the six year period prior to the time the University denied her tenure no single tenure candidate in the English department had a second published book, and that all the books published by tenure candidates in the department were based on the candidates' dissertations. (This contrasts with testimony from the President suggesting that Brown's qualifications were inadequate because she had published only one book, and that was based on her dissertation.) One male English teacher who was granted tenure shortly after the President made his final decision to deny Brown tenure had not written any book, and while he had written several articles, none of them had received reviews. The evidence also showed that during this time Brown was the only candidate in the English department to be denied tenure after having published a book and having it reviewed. There was evidence that Brown's publisher, the Harvard University Press, had very high standards.

In addition, Brown's evidence showed that her support from the various tenure committees was quite high when compared to the votes on English professors who received tenure around the time of Brown's candidacy. While a couple of successful candidates received support comparable to Brown's, including unanimous votes from the English Department, there were others with much less support who nonetheless received tenure. The male English professor who received tenure shortly after Brown was denied tenure received a 16–6 vote in favor of tenure from the English Department; a 2–5 vote against tenure from the College APT committee; and an 8–3 vote in favor of tenure from the University APT committee. A male English professor who received tenure before Brown's review period had received a vote of 10–4 in favor of tenure from the English Department.

Brown also presented evidence of alleged irregularities in her tenure review, particularly with regard to the inclusion of the single dissenter on the ad hoc committee, whom Brown sought to show was a long-time associate of President Silber's, had previously clashed with faculty in Boston University's English Department, and was not, in Brown's view, an "acknowledged authority" within Brown's academic specialty, as required by the Agreement. Brown also introduced evidence from which she argued the jury could infer that President Silber and the Dean of the CLA harbored discriminatory attitudes towards women.

The University called as witnesses Geoffrey Bannister, the Dean of the College of Liberal Arts; Simon Parker, the Assistant Provost; and John Silber, the President of the University. They testified that Brown was denied tenure and instead offered a three year extension, because of good- faith, non-discriminatory concerns regarding the adequacy of her scholarship.

The district court told the jury to decide whether Brown had met her burden of persuading them that the reason offered by the University for denying her tenure was a pretext for discrimination based on her sex. A special verdict form was handed to the jury. Among the questions on the form was "Do you find that the Trustees at Boston University refused to grant tenure to the plaintiff because of her sex?" The jury answered this question "yes," and found damages in the amount of $200,000 as a consequence of the breach of contract.

Although recognizing that Brown's claims under federal and state civil rights statutes were not, by themselves, triable to a jury, the court held that the jury's finding of sex discrimination under the contract claim was determinative of the University's liability under the two statutes. The district court determined that under those statutes, Brown was entitled to $15,000 for emotional distress and reinstatement to the position of associate professor with tenure.[7] The district court also enjoined the University "from discrimination on the basis of sex with respect to the appointment, promotion and tenure of faculty members, and in particular with respect to the promotion, salary or other benefits to which the plaintiff may become entitled," and awarded Brown her reasonable attorneys' fees and expenses of suit. The district court denied the University's subsequent motions for judgment notwithstanding the verdict and for a new trial.

On appeal, the University alleges error in the court's evidentiary rulings and in the jury charge. The University also contends that the district court lacked jurisdiction over the contract claim, hence erred in applying the jury's sex discrimination finding to the federal statutory claims. Further, the University contends that the district court's award of tenure impermissibly intruded into the operations of the University, and that the anti- discrimination injunction is overbroad.

II. APPLICABLE LAW

* * * When Title VII originally was enacted, Congress exempted from it educational institutions. In 1972, however, Congress removed this exemp-

---

7. The district court ruled that damages for emotional distress may be recovered under Massachusetts civil rights law. * * *

tion, in response to widespread concern about employment discrimination in educational institutions. See H.R.Rep. No. 238, 92d Cong., 2d Sess., reprinted in 1972 U.S.Code Cong. & Admin.News 2137, 2154–55 ("Discrimination against minorities and women in the field of education is as pervasive as discrimination in any other area of employment. * * * [W]omen have long been invited to participate as students in the academic process, but without the prospect of gaining employment as serious scholars. * * * The committee cannot imagine a more sensitive area than educational institutions where the Nation's youth are exposed to a multitude of ideas that will strongly influence their future development. To permit discrimination here would, more than in any other area, tend to promote misconceptions leading to future patterns of discrimination."); H.R.Rep. No. 554, 92d Cong., 2d Sess., reprinted in 1972 U.S.Code Cong. & Admin.News 2462, 2511–12 (noting that female faculty at institutions of higher learning were, in 1972, much less likely to be associate or full professors and that in 1965–66 the median salary of female full professors was $11,649 compared with $12,758 for men).

Title VII strikes a balance between protecting employees from unlawful discrimination and preserving for employers their remaining freedom of choice. Price Waterhouse v. Hopkins, 490 U.S. 228, 109 S.Ct. 1775, 1785–86, 104 L.Ed.2d 268 (1989). In tenure cases, courts must take special care to preserve the University's autonomy in making lawful tenure decisions.

> [C]ourts must be extremely wary of intruding into the world of university tenure decisions. These decisions necessarily hinge on subjective judgments regarding the applicant's academic excellence, teaching ability, creativity, contributions to the university community, rapport with students and colleagues, and other factors that are not susceptible of quantitative measurement. Absent discrimination, a university must be given a free hand in making such tenure decisions.

Kumar v. Board of Trustees, University of Massachusetts, 774 F.2d 1, 12 (1st Cir.1985)(Campbell, C.J., concurring), cert. denied, 475 U.S. 1097, 106 S.Ct. 1496, 89 L.Ed.2d 896 (1986). At the same time, however, an employee's right not to be denied tenure for discriminatory reasons prevents insulating the tenure process from any judicial review. As in other forms of employment, an inference of discrimination can be derived from a showing that a university's given reasons for denying tenure to the plaintiff were "obviously weak or implausible," or that the tenure standards for prevailing at the tenure decisions were "manifestly unequally applied." Id. at 15. The essential words here are "obviously" and "manifestly." A court may not simply substitute its own views concerning the plaintiff's qualifications for those of the properly instituted authorities; the evidence must be of such strength and quality as to permit a reasonable finding that the denial of tenure was "obviously" or "manifestly" unsupported. In this case, Brown's burden was to show that the University *manifestly* applied an unequal standard to her tenure application.

III. EVIDENTIARY ISSUES

A. *Testimony of Professors Goodheart, Craddock, Vendler and Speisman and excluded testimony of Professor Clarke*

The University protests permitting four professors—Professor Goodheart, who served as Chairman of the English department at the time of Brown's tenure candidacy, Professor Craddock, Professor Speisman, and Professor Vendler—to compare Brown's qualifications with those of other faculty members considered for tenure at Boston University. The University also complains that the district court erred in excluding the testimony of Professor Clarke, who chaired the College APT. Clarke would have testified that his vote for Brown was premised on a misperception of her progress on the Wilde book. We do not find prejudicial error.

The University contends that the four professors' testimony should have been excluded both because the testimony invited the jury to substitute its own tenure judgment for that of the University, and because these professors' testimony had not, as such, appeared in Brown's tenure file and, therefore, was unavailable to the University when it decided Brown's case.[10]

Federal Rule of Evidence 402 allows the admission of all relevant evidence and prohibits the admission of irrelevant evidence. Rule 403 permits the exclusion of relevant evidence of its probative value is outweighed by the danger of unfair prejudice or comparable factors. "A trial judge has much latitude in these matters." Dente v. Riddell, Inc., 664 F.2d 1, 5 (1st Cir.1981)(citations omitted). "A district court's ultimate determination in such a situation is reviewed on appeal only for abuse of discretion." United States v. Gonsalves, 668 F.2d 73, 75 (1st Cir.), cert. denied, 456 U.S. 909, 102 S.Ct. 1759, 72 L.Ed.2d 168 (1982).

We see no abuse of discretion in admitting this evidence. Insofar as the four professors' testimony tended to show that the qualifications of others granted tenure were beneath Brown's known qualifications, it was relevant to create an inference that the University's criticisms of Brown's scholarship were pretextual. A sex discrimination plaintiff

> may attack the motive advanced by the university in one of two ways: she may try to show that the motive is not worthy of belief; or she may try to show that in fact some other motive explains the university's action better than the motive offered. * * * To prove the proffered motive is not worthy of belief, evidence of a comparative sort is appropriate: if others were hired or promoted though by the same reasoning they ought to have been excluded, then the motive is a "pretext."

Namenwirth v. Board of Regents of University of Wisconsin System, 769 F.2d 1235 at 1240 (7 Cir.1985)(citations omitted).

To be sure, in balancing the probativeness of evidence like this against its danger for unfair prejudice, a court should realize that comparing the qualifications of others granted tenure with those of plaintiff presents the risk of improperly substituting a judicial tenure decision for a university one. To admit such comparative evidence, the trial court must be satisfied, and we must later be satisfied on appeal, that the evidence is so compelling as to permit a reasonable finding of one-sidedness going beyond a mere difference in judgment.

---

10. It is not denied that the four testifying professors had taken part in Brown's tenure review. As English Chairman, Professor Goodheart had written the English Department's favorable evaluation and the others had voted for tenure. The University's point is that the express reasoning in Brown's favor set forth in their testimony, had never gone to the President, Provost, Dean and other evaluators at the time she was turned down.

That criterion was met here. The English Department voted 22–0 for tenure; the CLA APT was unanimous; the University-wide APT was almost unanimous at first and was unanimous a second time. The outside Tenure Review Committee favored tenure 2–1. The witnesses whose testimony is challenged included two former department heads who were well acquainted with the tenure process and with those who had been tenured or rejected around Brown's time. They testified that Brown was either superior or equal to the other candidates who had received tenure. They testified that none of these others had been required to write a second book. The first book of the others, rewritten from a thesis, had sufficed. One had not written any book. Yet notwithstanding acceptance and publication of Brown's book by a leading university press, the Assistant Provost and President, while acknowledging Brown's promise, insisted that she needed to do more to qualify for tenure. The court was entitled to conclude that a reasonable jury might in these circumstances properly find that the denial of tenure to Brown was "manifestly" unequal.

* * *

Professor Goodheart and Professor Craddock compared Brown's qualifications with other members of the English department who were reviewed for tenure within a few years before and after Brown's review. While their specific testimony had not, of course, been presented to those who considered Brown at an earlier time, it rested upon, and evaluated, the contents of the relevant tenure files. Those files had been before the reviewing authorities and were in evidence at trial. The University was free to present, and did present, evidence of contrary opinions as to Brown's comparative qualifications.

* * *

Professor Vendler's testimony similarly rested upon information that was available to the University at the time it evaluated Brown. In addition to comparing Brown's qualifications with those of others in the English Department, Vendler gave her opinion to the jury as to how to interpret the various scholarly reviews of the candidates' books. Both the reviews and publications were in evidence and had been before the persons evaluating the different applicants. Whether the reviews were "good" or "bad" was a disputed point. Evaluating them depended to some degree on the reputation of the reviewer in the field of the publication. It was within the court's discretion to allow expert opinion on this subject.

The University contends that the exclusion of Professor Clarke's testimony was prejudicial error. The University sought to have Clarke, the chair of the College APT, testify that he and other members of the committee were under the mistaken impression that Brown's book about Oscar Wilde was "forthcoming," and that this influenced the vote in Brown's favor. The district court excluded this testimony, ruling that Clarke's thoughts, other than his "yes" or "no" vote, were not available to the University at the time it made the decision regarding Brown's tenure.

We believe that Clarke should probably have been permitted to so testify, although the University was less than clear as to the purpose for which it was offering the testimony. The court understood that the University was offering Clarke's testimony merely to impeach his previous affirmative vote for Brown. Why Clarke voted as he did was irrelevant, since only the vote appears in the tenure file, and there was no reason to let Clarke impeach the vote. A proper reason to have accepted Clarke's testimony, however, was that it demonstrated Clarke's opinion that progress on the Wilde piece was important. President Silber and Assistant Provost Simon later testified that one reason for withholding tenure for three more years was to await Brown's work on the Wilde piece. Clarke's testimony would have tended to show that their judgment in this regard was a reasonable one. Assuming, without deciding that the district court abused its discretion in not permitting Clarke's testimony for this purpose, we do not find that the ruling prejudiced the University. * * *

B. Evidence of Remarks by President Silber

The University challenges admission of remarks made by President Silber in 1982 and 1983, after Brown's tenure candidacy, relative to another female tenure candidate, Bonnie Costello. While being considered for tenure, Professor Costello was offered a tenured position at another university. As permitted by a provision in the collective bargaining agreement, Costello had asked President Silber to expedite her Boston University tenure review so that she could more intelligently deal with the other offer. Initially, Professor Craddock, then Chairman of the English Department, met with President Silber to discuss Costello's situation. Silber refused to speed up the process, although he did say that, when the file came to his desk, he would act on it swiftly. Professor Craddock testified that President Silber remarked that Costello was an outstanding scholar, saying "I don't see what a good woman in your department is worrying about. The place is a damn matriarchy." A few months later, Costello herself met with President Silber. Silber again refused to intervene in the tenure review process, telling Costello that a person with her credentials would do well "and anyway, I never worried about job security, and your husband is a parachute, so why are you worried[?]". Professor Costello rejected the outside offer and later in the year was granted tenure at Boston University. Brown also presented evidence that President Silber and the administration had expedited review in the case of a male professor who had received an outside offer.

Admission of evidence of these matters was not an abuse of the district court's discretion. Other courts have held that prior discriminatory conduct is recognized as probative in an employment discrimination case on the issue of motive or intent. See Fed.R.Evid. 404(b). The Seventh Circuit has remarked, "[g]iven the difficulty of proving employment discrimination—the employer will deny it, and almost every worker has some deficiency on which the employer can plausibly blame the worker's troubles—a flat rule that evidence of other discriminatory acts * * * can never be admitted without violating Rule 403 would be unjustified." Hunter v. Allis–Chalmers Corp., Engine Div., 797 F.2d 1417, 1423 (7th Cir.1986). Accordingly, "[t]he question of the legitimacy of the employer's motivation in firing the employee * * * is one upon which past acts of the employer has some bearing." Morris v. Washington Metropolitan Area Transit, 702 F.2d 1037, 1045 (D.C.Cir.1983). See also Hunter, 797 F.2d at 1423–24 (in an employment discrimination action, evidence of harassment against other black workers besides plaintiff was admissible to show that defendant "condoned racial harassment by its workers and [to] rebut [ ] [defendant's] defense that it had fired [plaintiff] for cause"); Scaramuzzo v. Glenmore Distilleries, Co., 501 F.Supp. 727, n. 7 (N.D.Ill.1980)("Evidence of past discrimination of an employer may in some circumstances support the inference that such discrimination continued. * * *"). Cf. Jay Edwards, Inc. v. New England Toyota Distributor, Inc., 708 F.2d 814, 824 (1st Cir.)(in dealer's action against distributor claiming bad faith actions on the part of distributor, evidence of distributor's actions with other dealers was admissible on the issue of distributor's intent regarding its dealings with plaintiff), cert. denied, 464 U.S. 894, 104 S.Ct. 241, 78 L.Ed.2d 231 (1983).

Derogatory remarks indicative of a discriminatory attitude are also admissible in a proper case. See Hunter, 797 F.2d at 1423 (in employment discrimination action, evidence that supervisor called blacks "niggers" was admissible to show what supervisor's racial attitudes were). Cf. Carson v. Polley, 689 F.2d 562, 571–73 (5th Cir.1982)(performance evaluation report stating that defendant had a bad temper was admissible to show intent in action for assault and battery).

President Silber's conduct and comments were far weaker as indicative of a discriminatory attitude than those we have mentioned. While Silber did not expedite review in Costello's case, he did offer her tenure. Still, his comments reflected a patronizing attitude toward women—an attitude that might possibly have affected his earlier decision in Brown's case. At the time Silber called the English Department a "damn matriarchy," it had a female chairman and six other tenured female professors from among a total of 26 tenured English professors. That so small a proportion of women could provoke this comment suggests that the President might not be indifferent to the gender of a tenure applicant. Silber's "parachute" remark, especially when made in an official setting, likewise suggested a preoccupation with gender in a context where both the contract and the law would expect a sex-blind approach.

To be sure, it is a tremendous leap to infer from remarks such as these that President Silber denied Brown tenure because of her gender. Besides recommending tenure for Costello, the evidence showed that President Silber had recommended tenure for many women. Nonetheless, the court correctly left the significance of the remarks to the jury. A judge should not exclude evidence which a reasonable jury might find relevant unless its probative value is substantially outweighed by the danger of unfair prejudice. Fed. R.Evid. 403.

That the remarks occurred subsequent, rather than prior, to the allegedly discriminatory conduct does not alter their admissibility. The jury was entitled to infer that any discriminatory animus toward women manifested in 1982 and 1983 would have existed in 1980 and 1981, when President Silber acted on Brown's case. Evidence of a discriminatory cast to the views of one person in a university community might not, of course, be probative if the individual's role in the tenure decision were minor. President Silber's recommendation, however, was the final and most important one in the chain of tenure recommendations. He provided leadership to the University community. The jury could have inferred that the Provost and Dean, the other administrators who expressed doubts about Brown's suitability, would have been sensitive to the President's attitudes concerning tenure candidates.

The reason given by the Provost and President for withholding tenure went not to Brown's teaching ability nor to any deficiencies in her service to the university community, but to her lack of academic excellence. Yet Brown was recommended for tenure by virtually all of her academic peers, both in her own department and outside. It could be concluded that her academic reputation was superior to many who were tenured. In such circumstances, the district court was entitled to permit plaintiff to focus on the personality and predilections of the President, insofar as these suggested that he held a more traditional view of the woman's place.

While we thus uphold evidence of the Costello interchanges, we do not sustain the court's admission of a portion of a speech given by President Silber at a Freedoms Foundation Symposium on Citizen Responsibilities in 1984. In the speech, Silber discussed the decline of the traditional family and the consequential deterioration of children's education. He stated,

> the number of working mothers—that is, the proportion of children who do not have even one parent at home during the day—has increased sharply. * * * [T]he number of working wives—as opposed to working mothers with children under 1 rose from 26 percent to 46 percent. Lack of parental supervision associated with both parents working explains in part that children typically watch 24 hours of television a week.

Brown asserts that this speech was relevant to show President Silber's view of working women, possibly explaining his motive in denying Brown tenure, especially in view of Brown's pregnancy and the birth of her first child during her tenure review. To our minds, this evidence is far afield. While evidence of closely related discriminatory conduct and remarks may be admissible in a case like this, it does not follow that plaintiffs may present ambivalent evidence. President Silber did not denigrate women in his speech. He did not say that women should not work; least of all did he suggest that professional women or others who might be able to obtain child care elsewhere should be denied promotion on merit. He merely quoted statistics showing the dimensions of a social problem that few people would deny exists, whatever the proper solution may be. It is an untenable leap from such a speech to the inference that the author would deliberately deny tenure to a qualified faculty member. Its relevance, if not quite zero, is close to that. While one would hope that jurors would see them for what they are, there is the danger such red-herrings, skillfully manipulated, could cause a jury to stray. We fear, moreover, the chilling effect that admission of such remarks could have on academic freedom. Use of such evidence in a court of law could cause a university president, dean or teacher to avoid topics of this kind altogether for fear that one or two sentences might later be used as evidence of alleged discriminatory animus. It was error to admit these remarks.

While we hold that the evidence should have been excluded, we do not believe that it effected the outcome of the trial. As we have said, the evidence is without probative value of sex discrimination. That children watch television because their mothers are not at home is a position commonly advocated in the press (and on television itself). To be sure, the matter was mentioned by plaintiff's counsel in closing argument. Nonetheless, while we find the error regrettable, we think it highly unlikely that these remarks, in a trial of this complexity and length, would have had an effect on the outcome. We, therefore, do not find the improper admission of this evidence to be prejudicial error.

C. *Evidence of the Dean's Attitude Toward the Women's Studies Program*

The University next challenges the district court's admission of a letter written by the Dean concerning a Women's Studies Program. Boston University offered a minor in Women's Studies, for which students were required to take a core course and a number of courses from a list of approved electives. Professor Brown never taught Women's Studies, but some of her courses were included on the list of electives. In 1978, the Dean of the CLA, who was the first to express reservations about Brown's scholarship, wrote a letter responding negatively to a request for funding for a half-time director for the Women's Studies program.

The University argues that the Dean's letter should not have been admitted, because Brown failed to show how the Dean's views on the Women's Studies Program had any bearing on her tenure. Brown argues that the evidence at trial showed that the approach in Brown's book was characterized by many as "a feminist interpretation" of Jane Austen. Brown further argues that the Dean's reservations about Brown's historical scholarship may have resulted from his general doubts about feminist scholarship.

For the same reasons given as to the President's speech, we hold that the district court erred in admitting this evidence. A panel of the Ninth Circuit has held that evidence of contempt for women's issues generally may in some circumstances be probative of a discriminatory attitude. See Lynn v. Regents of the University of California, 656 F.2d 1337, 1343 & n. 5 (9th Cir.1981)("A disdain for women's issues, and a diminished opinion of those [including men] who concentrate on those issues, is evidence of a discriminatory attitude towards women."), cert. denied, 459 U.S. 823, 103 S.Ct. 53, 74 L.Ed.2d 59 (1982). But whether or not this is so in proper circumstances, we do not see how the Dean's expression of reservations about a particular academic department had, by itself, any tendency to show a discriminatory animus against women. * * * Still, when read in the context of this particular trial, we are not persuaded that the outcome was affected by the admission this evidence. We hold that the admission of this improper evidence was harmless error.

In addition to challenging the admission of much of Brown's evidence, the University argues that "the relevant, properly admitted, evidence is insufficient as a matter of law to support a finding of sex discrimination against the University." As we interpret this argument, the University is contending that if we remove the evidence discussed above, the remaining evidence is insufficient to support the verdict. Since we rule today that the district court made no prejudicial error in admitting the evidence at issue here, we need not address this argument. Moreover, we need not consider the issue of the sufficiency of the evidence generally, for the University has not properly raised this issue. See Fed.R.App.P. 28(a)(brief must contain statement of issues presented for review and argument with respect to such issues) * * *.

IV. JURY INSTRUCTIONS

A. *Causation*

The University's next argument is that the district court, in its jury charge, improperly defined the required connection between an employer's discriminatory motive and the action taken against its employee. The relevant statutory language provides that it is unlawful for an employer to take an adverse employment action "because of" an individual's sex. 42 U.S.C. s 2000e–2; Mass.Gen.L. ch. 151B, s 4. In a "pretext" case, such as here, a plaintiff who has shown that her sex was a "but for" cause of an adverse employment action has satisfied the statutory requirement of showing that the decision was "because of" her sex. Price Waterhouse v. Hopkins, 490 U.S. 228, 109 S.Ct. 1775, 1785 n. 6, 104 L.Ed.2d 268 (1989). See also Fields v. Clark University, 817 F.2d 931, 935 (1st Cir.1987)(mixed motive case)(citing McDonald v. Santa Fe Trail Transportation Co., 427 U.S. 273, 282 n. 10, 96 S.Ct. 2574, 2580 n. 10, 49 L.Ed.2d 493 (1976)).[13]

The district court's jury instruction on causation included the following:

> Now, when I say in these questions [the special interrogatories]: Do you find that the Trustees refused to grant tenure *because of* sex or *because of* strike participation, or *because of* some combination of the above, I mean did that factor that I referred to *affect the result*? *Would the result have been different* if there had been no sex discrimination or no retaliation or no combination of the above procedure? That is to say, *did it bring about a difference in the resulting decision*?

(Emphasis added.) This instruction properly informed the jury that the plaintiff must show that but for the impermissible motive, the University would have granted tenure. See, e.g., Geller v. Markham, 635 F.2d 1027, 1035 (2d Cir.1980)(age discrimination)("If age discrimination was a 'factor * * * [which] made a difference,' then the employee's fortunes would have been 'different' without the discriminatory action and * * * discrimination was therefore a 'but for' cause of the result that did take place.").

The University has no quarrel with the above-quoted portion of the court's instruction. Instead, they direct our attention to a later portion of the instruction, in which the court said:

> Now, the law gives a great deal of discretion to the people in charge of a university. That is part of academic freedom also, that * * * we do not interfere in the freedom of the university as an institution, and that means the universities have the right to exercise independent judgment in choosing faculty and its decision must be respected unless *tainted* by

---

13. Justice Brennan's recent plurality opinion in Price Waterhouse v. Hopkins, 490 U.S. 228, 109 S.Ct. 1775, 104 L.Ed.2d 268 (1989), which addressed the proper causation standard in a "mixed motive" case, casts some doubt on the appropriate interpretation of McDonald v. Santa Fe Trail Transportation Co., 427 U.S. 273, 96 S.Ct. 2574, 49 L.Ed.2d 493 (1976). In McDonald, the Court stated, in the context of a "pretext" case, that "no more is required to be shown than that race was a 'but for' cause." 427 U.S. at 282 n. 10, 96 S.Ct. at 2580 n. 10. Subsequent decisions of this court have read McDonald to hold that an employee must prove "but for" causation. See Loeb v. Textron, Inc., 600 F.2d 1003, 1019 (1st Cir.1979)(age discrimination)(followed in Freeman v. Package Machinery Co., 865 F.2d 1331, 1335 (1st Cir.1988) and Menard v. First Security Ser-

vices Corp., 848 F.2d 281, 285 (1st Cir.1988)). The plurality opinion in Price Waterhouse says, however,

> [t]his passage [in McDonald] * * * does not suggest that the plaintiff must show but-for cause; it indicates only that if she does so, she prevails. More important, McDonald dealt with the question whether the employer's stated reason for its decision was the reason for its action; unlike the case before us today, therefore, McDonald did not involve mixed motives.

Price Waterhouse, 109 S.Ct. at 1785 n. 6. Because it is not necessary to our decision in this case, we do not inquire whether, under Price Waterhouse, there are circumstances in which a "pretext" plaintiff could prevail if she proved something less than "but for" causation.

one or more or both of the illegal reasons asserted by the plaintiff. * * * The university has the right to be wrong except in those two respects. They can make any kind of mistake except a decision that is *tainted* by sex discrimination or retaliation for strike activity, and your disagreement in general terms is not a basis for a finding for the plaintiff unless you find that the decision was effectively *tainted* by those two illegal considerations.

(Emphasis added.) The University asserts that the court's use of the word "taint" renders this portion of the instruction erroneous and prejudicial. The University claims that rather than describing a "but for" standard of causation, the district court's use of "taint" three times suggested to the jury that it could find for Brown if the University's tenure decision was "affected slightly" with sex discrimination.

"Our principal focus in reviewing jury instructions is to determine whether they tended to confuse or mislead the jury on the controlling issues." Service Merchandise Company v. Boyd Corporation, 722 F.2d 945, 950 (1st Cir.1983) * * *. "On appeal, the charge must be examined as a whole; portions of it are not to be treated in isolation." Id. We agree with the University that a "tainted" decision is not necessarily one that would have been different "but for" the taint.[14] We do not think that in the context of the jury instruction as a whole, however, the district court's "taint" remarks confused the jury. First, the court correctly instructed the jury that the words "because of" in the special interrogatories meant that the impermissible factors must have brought about "a difference in the resulting decision." Then, the court reiterated that "the plaintiff's burden here is that she has to prove—has to persuade you that it is more likely true than not true that she was denied tenure because of her sex or because of her strike activity or because of some combination of the two." (Emphasis added). The three "taint" remarks were contained in two paragraphs immediately following the above, which discussed not the meaning of "because of," but described the university's prerogative to make bad, but not illegal, decisions.

Later in the instruction, in describing the law about "pretext," the court also stated three times that the jury's function was to determine whether the University's reason was so unworthy of belief that it was probable that one or more of the illegal reasons were the "true reasons" or "real reasons" for denying Brown tenure. The concept of a "true" or "real" reason suggests "but for" causation. The jury could not have decided that discrimination was the "true" reason for the University's decision without concluding that but for discriminatory animus the University would have made a different decision regarding tenure for Professor Brown.

---

14. "Taint" means "to touch or affect slightly with something bad or undesirable" or "to contaminate morally." Webster's Third New International Dictionary (1971). An employment decision impermissibly motivated by discrimination proscribed by Title VII can accurately be described as "tainted" or "infected" with discrimination. See, e.g., Fields v. Clark University, 817 F.2d 931, 932–33 (1st Cir.1987)("The [district] court found that the process by which plaintiff was denied tenure at Clark University was tainted with sexual discrimination"; also found decision was "impermissibly infected with sexual discrimination"). But an employment decision can be "tainted" with discrimination without the "taint" making a difference in the outcome. See Price Waterhouse, 109 S.Ct. at 1804 (O'Connor, J., concurring in judgment)(criticizing plurality opinion for appearing "to conclude that if a decisional process is 'tainted' by awareness of sex or race in any way, the employer has violated" Title VII).

The "taint" remarks were thus sandwiched between several statements which accurately defined the meaning of the words "because of" on the special interrogatory forms and several statements that sex must be the "true" or "real" reason for discrimination. In that context, we do not see a likelihood that the three references to "taint" confused or misled the jury with respect to the applicable causation standard.

B. Jury's Role

The University also complains that the district court's instructions encouraged the jurors to substitute their own judgment about the merit of Brown's tenure candidacy, in contravention of *Kumar*, instead of merely deciding whether the University impermissibly discriminated against Brown. The University complains both that the jury charge implied that the jury was to determine whether Brown deserved tenure, and that the court refused to give a requested instruction which would have made clear for the jury its role in reviewing the evidence. We see no merit to either of these arguments. First, the University complains about a portion of the jury instruction which included the following:

> Whether the plaintiff deserves tenure or not is not the test here, either. I would suppose that deserving people are sometimes awarded tenure and sometimes not. Certainly, before you get—that is not the full test; that is certainly one thing you have to consider. Obviously, if she didn't deserve tenure on any kind of objective basis, the university was quite right in turning her down. *If you find that she did deserve tenure*, she was qualified on an equal basis, then you have the question of whether she was turned down for one or two of these illegal reasons that I have mentioned. That is the key to the case.

(Emphasis added.) We agree that the court would have erred had it told the jury that it should find for Brown if it found that she deserved tenure. But this instruction did no such thing. On the contrary, it specifically states that "whether the plaintiff deserves tenure or not is not the test." The emphasized portion reinforces this by informing the jury that it is not enough to find that she deserved tenure, but rather the jury must find that she was denied tenure because of her sex and not simply because the University made a mistake. We think this instruction correctly stated the law.

V. THE CONTRACT CLAIM

The University next argues that the district court erred in denying the University's motion to dismiss Brown's contract claim for lack of subject matter jurisdiction and in ruling that the contract gave Brown a judicially enforceable right to a discrimination-free tenure decision.

[discussion of this issue omitted]

VI. THE ORDER TO GRANT TENURE

We turn now to the matter of the district court's order that the University reinstate Brown with tenure. Courts have quite rarely awarded tenure as a remedy for unlawful discrimination, and those that have, have done so under circumstances distinguishable from those here.[21] The University ar-

---

21. There are no cases, however, *denying* an award of tenure to a professor who has been found to be the victim of a discriminatory tenure decision.

gues that tenure is a significantly more intrusive remedy than remedies ordinarily awarded in Title VII cases, such as reinstatement or seniority, because a judicial tenure award mandates a lifetime relationship between the University and the professor. The University further contends that due to the intrusiveness of tenure awards and the First Amendment interest in academic freedom, a court should not award tenure unless there is no dispute as to a professor's qualifications. Thus, the University concludes, the district court should not have awarded tenure to Brown, because there existed a dispute as to her qualifications.

We agree that courts should be "extremely wary of intruding into the world of university tenure decisions," Kumar, 774 F.2d at 12, (Campbell, C.J., concurring). However, once a university has been found to have impermissibly discriminated in making a tenure decision, as here, the University's prerogative to make tenure decisions must be subordinated to the goals embodied in Title VII. The Supreme Court has ruled that the remedial provision of Title VII, 42 U.S.C. § 2000e–5 (1982),[22] requires courts to fashion the most complete relief possible for victims of discriminatory employment decisions. Albemarle Paper Co. v. Moody, 422 U.S. 405, 421, 95 S.Ct. 2362, 2373, 45 L.Ed.2d 280 (1975). Once Title VII liability has been imposed, a court should deny "make whole" relief "only for reasons which, if applied generally, would not frustrate the central statutory purposes of eradicating discrimination throughout the economy and making persons whole for injuries suffered through past discrimination." Id.

We see no reason to deny Brown such "make whole" relief here. We disagree with the University's characterization of the tenure award as an infringement on its First Amendment right to determine for itself who may teach. In often- quoted language, Justice Frankfurter defined academic freedom as " 'an atmosphere in which there prevail the four essential freedoms of a university—to determine for itself *on academic grounds* who may teach, what may be taught, how it shall be taught, and who may be admitted to study.' " Sweezy v. New Hampshire, 354 U.S. 234, 263, 77 S.Ct. 1203, 1218, 1 L.Ed.2d 1311 (1957)(Frankfurter, J., concurring in result)(emphasis

---

Courts of appeals have upheld judicial tenure awards in two instances. In 1980, the Third Circuit upheld a conditional tenure award in Kunda v. Muhlenberg College, 621 F.2d 532 (3d Cir.1980). The district court in Kunda had found that the college discriminated on the basis of sex against a female professor by denying her tenure because she did not have a master's degree, without telling her in advance that she needed one. The court of appeals upheld the district court's order that the professor be granted tenure if she obtained a master's degree within two years. In 1984, the Sixth Circuit upheld an order reinstating a professor, with tenure, to an institution which automatically awarded tenure after five years of successful teaching. Ford v. Nicks, 741 F.2d 858 (6th Cir.1984). The professor in Ford had been discharged, after four years, in retaliation for helping his wife file a sex discrimination claim against the school. The University ar-

gues that Kunda and Ford are distinguishable on their facts from this case, because there was no dispute over the professors' qualifications, as there was over Brown's.

22. The statute provides:

If the court finds that the respondent has intentionally engaged in * * * an unlawful employment practice * * *, the court may * * * order such affirmative action as may be appropriate, which may include, but is not limited to, reinstatement or hiring of employees, with or without back pay * * *, or any other equitable relief as the court deems appropriate * * *. No order of the court shall require the admission or reinstatement of an individual * * * if such individual was * * * refused advancement * * * for any reason other than discrimination on account of race, color, religion, sex or national origin * * *. 42 U.S.C. § 2000e–5(g).

added). * * * Academic freedom does not include the freedom to discriminate against tenure candidates on the basis of sex or other impermissible grounds. See Powell v. Syracuse University, 580 F.2d 1150, 1154 (2d Cir. 1978). Our decisions in this area have formulated a university's prerogatives similarly. While we have been and remain hesitant to interfere with universities' independent judgment in choosing their faculty, we have said that we will respect universities' judgment only "so long as they do not discriminate." Kumar, 774 F.2d at 12, (Campbell, C.J., concurring).

The University also argues that the special needs of academic institutions counsel imposition of less restrictive alternative remedies. However, the University suggests none. Some *amici* suggest that Brown be reinstated for a three year probationary period, or be subjected to a non- discriminatory tenure decision. Aside from the impracticality of the latter, well over eight years after the original decision, these suggestions fall far short of remedies which will make Brown whole. According to the jury's verdict, she was offered the three year extension *because* of discrimination. The jury found that, "but for" sex discrimination, Brown would immediately have been granted tenure. Awarding her tenure is the only way to provide her the most complete relief possible. See Albemarle Paper Co., 422 U.S. at 421, 95 S.Ct. at 2373.

The conclusion that tenure is an appropriate Title VII remedy is borne out by the statute's legislative history. In 1972, Congress both amended the remedial portion of Title VII, granting courts broad discretion to fashion "make whole" remedies, and removed the then-existing Title VII exemption for educational institutions. A Congressional report notes, "women have long been invited to participate in the academic process, but without the prospect of gaining employment as serious scholars." H.R.Rep. No. 238, 92d Cong., 2d Sess., reprinted in 1972 U.S.Code Cong. & Admin.News 2137, 2154–55. The process of becoming a "serious scholar" necessarily includes a fair opportunity to become tenured, because tenure serves to ensure academic freedom, by allowing " 'a faculty member to teach, study, and act free from a large number of restraints and pressures which otherwise would inhibit independent thought and action.' " Note, Tenure and Partnership As Title VII Remedies, 94 Harv.L.Rev. 457, 474 & n. 104 (1980)(quoting C. Byse & L. Joughin, Tenure in American Higher Education 2 (1959)). Thus, to deny tenure because of the intrusiveness of the remedy and because of the University's interest in making its own tenure decisions would frustrate Title VII's purpose of "making persons whole for injuries suffered through past discrimination." Albemarle Paper Co., 422 U.S. at 421, 95 S.Ct. at 2373. We add that Brown's near unanimous endorsement by colleagues within and without her department suggest strongly that there are no issues of collegiality or the like which might make the granting of tenure inappropriate.

VII. THE INJUNCTION AGAINST FURTHER DISCRIMINATION

The final issue raised on appeal regards the district court's order that "[t]he defendant is enjoined from discrimination on the basis of sex with respect to the appointment, promotion and tenure of faculty members, and in particular with respect to the promotion, salary or other benefits to which the plaintiff may become entitled." The University argues that the injunction is overbroad insofar as it enjoins the University from sex discrimination against faculty other than Professor Brown, because it is tantamount to an injunction to "obey the statute," which the Supreme Court rejected as too broad in N.L.R.B. v. Express Publishing Co., 312 U.S. 426, 61 S.Ct. 693, 85 L.Ed. 930 (1941). The hazard of such an injunction, warns the University, is that the order has the potential to further embroil the courts in the University's internal affairs, allowing faculty members to circumvent administrative procedures by simply invoking the contempt jurisdiction of the district court whenever a dispute arises.

We agree. An injunction should be narrowly tailored to give only the relief to which plaintiffs are entitled. See Califano v. Yamasaki, 442 U.S. 682, 702, 99 S.Ct. 2545, 2558, 61 L.Ed.2d 176 (1979). Ordinarily, classwide relief, such as the injunction here which prohibits sex discrimination against the class of Boston University faculty, is appropriate only where there is a properly certified class. See Zepeda v. United States I.N.S., 753 F.2d 719, 727–28 & n. 1 (9th Cir.1983). Of course, "[a]n injunction * * * is not necessarily made overbroad by extending benefit or protection to persons other than prevailing parties in * * * [a] lawsuit—even if it is not a class action—if such breadth is necessary to give prevailing parties the relief to which they are entitled." Professional Association of College Educators, TSTA/NEA v. El Paso County Community College District, 730 F.2d 258, 273–74 (5th Cir.) * * *. But there is no such reason here for an injunction running to the benefit of nonparties. Professor Brown's case established that she alone had been the victim of sex discrimination. The only permissible focus of the injunctive relief, therefore, would be on protecting her from further instances of sex discrimination or retaliation. That portion of the injunction which provides that "[t]he defendant is enjoined from discrimination on the basis of sex with respect to * * * promotion, salary or other benefits to which the plaintiff may become entitled" provides her with the outer limit of the relief to which she is entitled. That portion of the injunction which provides that the University "is enjoined from discrimination on the basis of sex with respect to the appointment, promotion and tenure of faculty members" is overbroad, and is vacated.

Conclusion

The jury's finding of liability and the district court's order that Boston University reinstate Julia Prewitt Brown as an associate professor with tenure are affirmed. That part of the injunction which ran to the benefit of Boston University faculty other than Professor Brown is vacated, but the portion prohibiting sex discrimination against Professor Brown is affirmed.

Notes on **Brown**

1. *Brown* was tried as a disparate treatment case ala *Burdine* and *Hopkins*, with the need to prove discriminatory motivation: denial of tenure "because of" plaintiff's sex, as recently emphasized by *Hicks*. Although using Title VII law as developed in a variety of cases, the First Circuit articulated the special standard of deference that the federal courts have developed in discrimination cases brought against colleges and universities. Chief Judge Campbell quotes himself from Kumar v. Board of Trustees, U. of Mass, 774 F.2d 1, 12 (1st Cir.1985): "[C]ourts must be extremely wary of intruding into the world of university tenure decisions." *Brown*, supra at p. 845. An inference of discrimination is permissible

only if the university's asserted reasons for denial of tenure were "obviously weak or implausible," or the prevailing tenure standards were "manifestly unequally applied." "The essential words here are 'obviously' and 'manifestly.' * * * the evidence must be of such strength and quality as to permit a reasonable finding that the denial of tenure was 'obviously' or 'manifestly' unsupported." Supra at p. 845. On the issue of admitting comparative evidence that men were treated more favorably than plaintiff, Judge Campbell would require that the evidence regarding the men's qualifications for tenure "is so compelling as to permit a reasonable finding of one-sidedness going beyond a mere difference in judgment." Supra at p. 846. Judge Campbell then points out how overwhelming the evidence in plaintiff's favor was in this case: the department vote was 22–0 in favor of tenure, the college-level committee vote was unanimous in support, the university-wide committee first voted 9–2 in her favor and then 10–0 in her favor. The professors who testified all agreed that no one else had ever been required to write a second book in order to receive tenure. If this is the kind of evidence of "onesidedness" one needs to meet the standard of deference granted to universities by federal judges, then it is no surprise that such successful tenure cases are rarely found. How does this standard of proof differ from the factual basis supporting the finding of discrimination in *Hopkins*?

The case presented below, University of Pennsylvania v. EEOC, infra p. 861, further illustrates the strength of academic institutions in protecting themselves from lawsuits claiming discrimination. Under principles of "academic freedom," which no other Title VII employer can claim, colleges and universities have prevented full disclosure of relevant evidence of discriminatory motivation or intent, the very evidence essential to proving a Title VII case.

2. In addition to the deferential standard used to examine academic employment decisions under Title VII, women in upper level jobs have a difficult time proving sex discrimination because evaluation of professional competence is highly subjective. In upper level jobs, the greater the subjectivity involved the more difficult it is to prove discrimination. Subjective evaluation of professional ability is illustrated by *Burdine*, p. 617 supra. See Note 5 on p. 626 supra. In one court's view of academia, proof of discrimination is difficult, unless plaintiff is fortunate enough to be able to persuade the court that "[t]he selection process was a charade:" see Greer v. University of Arkansas Board of Trustees, 544 F.Supp. 1085, 1102 (E.D.Ark.1982) affirmed as to this part, vacated and remanded on award of damages for harassment, sub nom. Behlar v. Smith, 719 F.2d 950, 952 (8th Cir.1983), certiorari denied sub nom. University of Arkansas Board of Trustees v. Greer, 466 U.S. 958, 104 S.Ct. 2169, 80 L.Ed.2d 552 (1984)(holding that male selected for position of Director of Student Teaching and Clinical Experiences was preselected for the job, and that requirements specified in the vacancy notice had been tailored to his background).

For an example of how insulated subjective evaluations can be, see Grano v. Department of Development of City of Columbus, 699 F.2d 836 (6th Cir.1983). Plaintiff Barbara Grano alleged that defendant's failure to promote her was based on her sex. In particular, she cited the decision of her supervisor, Jack Huddle, to hire a man, Richard McClure, for the newly-created position of Public Information Specialist II, rather than herself. Grano had worked for the defendant for nearly two years at the time the Public Information position was created, and had helped to define the duties of the job, many of which she had been performing. Huddle testified that he was familiar with Grano's qualifications and that he did not consider her qualified for the new position, which he felt required three years of experience. He did not inform Grano that the new position had been created, nor did he interview her for the job. The district court found that Grano was qualified for the new position. After initially placing an unduly heavy burden of rebuttal on the defendant at the second stage and being reversed on this point, see Grano v. Department of Development of City of Columbus, 637 F.2d 1073, 1079–80 (6th Cir.1980), the district court held on remand that although "plaintiff Grano was in fact qualified for the disputed position, the * * * defendants' articulated belief in the inferiority of plaintiff's qualifications is sufficient to satisfy their burden in Burdine." Grano v. Department of Development of City of Columbus, 699 F.2d at 836. It further held that plaintiff had not proved pretext, and entered judgment for defendant. The Sixth Circuit affirmed this judgment per curiam as not clearly erroneous, but made clear its misgivings about the subjective nature of Huddle's decision. After reviewing the cases that had dealt with subjective decision making, the court concluded that:

> [s]ubjective employment evaluations, however, are not illegal per se. The ultimate issue in each case is whether the subjective criteria were used to disguise discriminatory action.

Id., 699 F.2d at 837. Is this a classic case of a male supervisor undervaluing a female subordinates' potential for promotion? Should Huddle have been required at least to interview Grano? Or would this place an unduly onerous burden on employers? Compare Burrus v. United Telephone Co. of Kansas, Inc., 683 F.2d 339 (10th Cir.1982), certiorari denied 459 U.S. 1071, 103 S.Ct. 491, 74 L.Ed.2d 633, a case in which the female plaintiff established that she possessed the objective qualifications for several promotions that nevertheless went to men, and thus was held to have made out a prima facie case of sex discrimination, but in which she was rejected based on the subjective evaluation that she lacked the necessary ability to get along with others. The court reasoned,

> Where applicants for a position have objective qualifications that are equal, it is within the employer's discretion to choose among them so long as the decision is not based on unlawful criteria. Texas Department of Community Affairs, 450 U.S. at 259, 101 S.Ct. at 1096. We have reviewed the entire record in this case and we do not have a definite and firm conviction that the trial court was mistaken in finding no discrimination. There is evidence that two of the promoted males were more qualified than Burrus because of education, experience, or both. The other males were at least as well qualified as Burrus. Several employees of UTC, including Burrus' direct supervisor and a female employee, testified that Burrus did not get along or communicate well with other UTC employees. Adequate evidence supports the trial court's ultimate conclusion that Burrus was not discriminated against on the basis of her sex.

Id., 683 F.2d at 343. Plaintiff's claim of retaliation for filing charges of sex discrimination was also rejected.

Plaintiffs' proof problem is eased somewhat if the issue of subjective qualifications is not evaluated at the prima facie case stage, but considered either as part of the employer's evidence of a legitimate reason or the plaintiff's showing of pretext. See, e.g., Jayasinghe v. Bethlehem Steel Corp., 760 F.2d 132 (7th Cir.1985), where Bethlehem Steel defended its decision to promote two women chemists to supervisory positions instead of plaintiff, a male chemist from Sri Lanka who had superior objective qualifications, because of his "secretive, asocial, and occasionally quarrelsome" personality. The trial court erred in including in plaintiff's prima facie case these subjective "personality" qualifications, but its error was harmless because its ultimate judgment that Bethlehem did not intentionally discriminate against plaintiff was not clearly erroneous. Judge Swygert noted that "forcing the plaintiff at the outset to prove subjective qualifications subverts the indirect method of proof by requiring, in turn, proof of the subjective standards and motives of the employer." He added that, "[t]he purpose of the indirect method of proof is precisely to escape the necessity of showing direct subjective intent." Id., at 135.

Despite the subjective nature of partnership decisions in law firms or accounting firms, Ms. Hopkins was successful against Price Waterhouse, in part, because the number of women partners was so very small, but also because the firm collected written evaluations and comments from all the partners, creating a record of "direct evidence" available for trial, a rare occurrence. In contrast to *Hopkins*, however, *Ottaviani* illustrates how difficult it is to break down the complicated decision making process of an academic institution to try and isolate that component or series of components that lead to continuing and persistent disparities between women and men in academic jobs.

3. The *Brown* case was unique at that time because it was tried to a jury. It is a rare example of appellate review of jury instructions in a Title VII case. The right to jury trial was granted to Title VII plaintiffs by the 1991 Civil Rights Act. See Note 2 on p. 645 supra. Julia Brown obtained a jury trial in 1987 under her federal claim involving breach of the collective bargaining agreement between the faculty and Boston University. Would the jury instructions used in *Brown* need to be rewritten in light of *Hicks*?

Although *Brown* was tried as a "pretext" case, not a "mixed motive" case, if tried under the standards of Justice O'Connor's opinion in *Hopkins*, what would you use as "direct evidence" of sex discrimination? Compare the facts of *Brown* with the facts of Jackson v. Harvard University, 721 F.Supp. 1397 (D.Mass.1989), affirmed 900 F.2d 464 (1st Cir.), cert. denied 498 U.S. 848, 111 S.Ct. 137, 112 L.Ed.2d 104 (1990). In *Jackson*, plaintiff alleged that the Harvard Business School held her to a higher standard of "creativity" than male tenure candidates. In analyzing her sex discrimination claim, the First Circuit agreed with the trial court that there was no "direct evidence" of discrimination which it required to trigger a mixed motive analysis. In fact, the trial court found there was virtually no evidence of any kind showing discriminatory motivation in her denial of tenure. 721 F.Supp. at 1401. In addition, the plaintiff had received a final department vote that split 29 to 35 against her tenure. 721 F.Supp. at 1420. After this vote, the Harvard Business School extended her tenure review period for another three years, but at the end of that time, she received only a slim majority vote of the full faculty. 900 F.2d at 465–66. Finally, the trial court's finding of no sex discrimination may have been influenced by the fact that plaintiff left her $43,000 Harvard faculty position a year *before* her extended contract expired to accept an $80,000 job with a business consulting firm. 721 F.Supp. at 1428.

For an amazing example of "direct evidence" of race discrimination in a tenure case, see Clark v. Claremont University Center, 6 Cal.App.4th 639, 8 Cal.Rptr.2d 151 (Cal.App.2d Dist.1992). During the tenure review process, Reginald Clark, African American, happened to overhear loud voices coming from a room in the building. It turned out it was the tenured faculty discussing his own tenure file. Among the comments he overheard were, "Who the hell does he think he is anyway. * * * I mean, us [sic] white people have rights too." "I don't know how I would feel working on a permanent base [sic] with a black man." As Clark listened outside the door, he began taking notes and heard the next professor say, "Well, we are not under any obligation to have any blacks because we are a private college." 8 Cal.Rptr.2d at 157–158. This conversation took place among highly educated professors of education at the Claremont Graduate School in 1984. Id. at 151–152. Had he been granted tenure, he would have been the first tenured faculty member of color in the school's history. Id. at 160. The jury awarded Professor Clark $1 million in compensatory damages, $16,300 in punitive damages, and attorney's fees of $420,000. The verdict was upheld on appeal. Id.

UNIVERSITY OF PENNSYLVANIA v. E.E.O.C.

Supreme Court of the United States, 1990.
493 U.S. 182, 110 S.Ct. 577, 107 L.Ed.2d 571.

JUSTICE BLACKMUN delivered the opinion of the Court.

In this case we are asked to decide whether a university enjoys a special privilege, grounded in either the common law or the First Amendment, against disclosure of peer review materials that are relevant to charges of racial or sexual discrimination in tenure decisions.

I

The University of Pennsylvania, petitioner here, is a private institution. It currently operates 12 schools, including the Wharton School of Business, which collectively enroll approximately 18,000 full-time students.

In 1985, the University denied tenure to Rosalie Tung, an associate professor on the Wharton faculty. Tung then filed a sworn charge of discrimination with respondent Equal Employment Opportunity Commission (EEOC or Commission). * * * As subsequently amended, the charge alleged that Tung was the victim of discrimination on the basis of race, sex, and national origin, in violation of § 703(a) of Title VII * * *.

In her charge, Tung stated that the Department Chairman had sexually harassed her and that, in her belief, after she insisted that their relationship remain professional, he had submitted a negative letter to the University's Personnel Committee which possessed ultimate responsibility for tenure decisions. She also alleged that her qualifications were "equal to or better than" those of five named male faculty members who had received more favorable treatment. Tung noted that the majority of the members of her Department had recommended her for tenure, and stated that she had been given no reason for the decision against her, but had discovered of her own efforts that the Personnel Committee had attempted to justify its decision "on the ground that the Wharton School is not interested in China-related research." * * * This explanation, Tung's charge alleged, was a pretext for discrimination: "simply their way of saying they do not want a Chinese–American, Oriental, woman in their school." * * *

The Commission undertook an investigation into Tung's charge, and requested a variety of relevant information from petitioner. When the University refused to provide certain of that information, the Commission's Acting District Director issued a subpoena seeking, among other things, Tung's tenure-review file and the tenure files of the five male faculty members identified in the charge. * * * Petitioner refused to produce a number of the tenure-file documents. It applied to the Commission for modification of the subpoena to exclude what it termed "confidential peer review information," specifically, (1) confidential letters written by Tung's evaluators; (2) the Department Chairman's letter of evaluation; (3) documents reflecting the internal deliberations of faculty committees considering applications for tenure, including the Department Evaluation Report summarizing the deliberations relating to Tung's application for tenure; and (4) comparable portions of the tenure-review files of the five males. The University urged the Commission to "adopt a balancing approach reflecting the constitutional and societal interest inherent in the peer review process" and to resort to "all feasible methods to minimize the intrusive effects of its investigations." * * *

The Commission denied the University's application. It concluded that the withheld documents were needed in order to determine the merit of Tung's charges. The Commission found: "There has not been enough data supplied in order for the Commission to determine whether there is reasonable cause to believe that the allegations of sex, race and national origin discrimination is true." * * * The Commission rejected petitioner's contention that a letter, which set forth the Personnel Committee's reasons for denying Tung tenure, was sufficient for disposition of the charge. "The Commission would fall short of its obligation" to investigate charges of discrimination, the EEOC's order stated, "if it stopped its investigation once [the employer] has * * * provided the reasons for its employment decisions, without verifying whether that reason is a pretext for discrimination." * * * The Commission also rejected petitioner's proposed balancing test, explaining that "such an approach in the instant case * * * would impair the Commission's ability to fully investigate this charge of discrimination." * * * The Commission indicated that enforcement proceedings might be necessary if a response was not forthcoming within 20 days. * * *

The University continued to withhold the tenure-review materials. The Commission then applied to the United States District Court for the Eastern District of Pennsylvania for enforcement of its subpoena. The court entered a brief enforcement order. * * *

The Court of Appeals for the Third Circuit affirmed the enforcement decision. 850 F.2d 969 (1988).[2] Relying upon its earlier opinion in *EEOC v. Franklin and Marshall College,* 775 F.2d 110 (1985), cert. denied, 476 U.S. 1163, 106 S.Ct. 2288, 90 L.Ed.2d 729 (1986), the court rejected petitioner's claim that policy considerations and First Amendment principles of academic freedom required the recognition of a qualified privilege or the adoption of a balancing approach that would require the Commission to demonstrate some particularized need, beyond a showing of relevance, to obtain peer review materials. Because of what might be thought of as a conflict in approach with the Seventh Circuit's decision in *EEOC v. University of Notre Dame Du Lac,* 715 F.2d 331, 337 (1983), and because of the importance of the issue, we granted certiorari limited to the compelled-disclosure question. * * *

2. The Court of Appeals did not rule on the question whether the Commission's subpoena permits petitioner to engage in any redaction of the disputed records before producing them, because the District Court had not fully considered that issue. The Third Circuit therefore ordered that the case be remanded for further consideration of possible redaction. See 850 F.2d, at 982.

II

As it had done before the Commission, the District Court, and the Court of Appeals, the University raises here essentially two claims. First, it urges us to recognize a qualified common-law privilege against disclosure of confidential peer review materials. Second, it asserts a First Amendment right of "academic freedom" against wholesale disclosure of the contested documents. With respect to each of the two claims, the remedy petitioner seeks is the same: a requirement of a judicial finding of particularized necessity of access, beyond a showing of mere relevance, before peer review materials are disclosed to the Commission.

A

Petitioner's common-law privilege claim is grounded in Federal Rule of Evidence 501. This provides in relevant part:

> "Except as otherwise required by the Constitution * * * or provided by Act of Congress or in rules prescribed by the Supreme Court * * *, the privilege of a witness * * * shall be governed by the principles of the common law as they may be interpreted by the courts of the United States in the light of reason and experience."

The University asks us to invoke this provision to fashion a new privilege that it claims is necessary to protect the integrity of the peer review process, which in turn is central to the proper functioning of many colleges and universities. These institutions are special, observes petitioner, because they function as "centers of learning, innovation and discovery." * * *

[W]e cannot accept the University's invitation to create a new privilege against the disclosure of peer review materials. We begin by noting that Congress, in extending Title VII to educational institutions and in providing for broad EEOC subpoena powers, did not see fit to create a privilege for peer review documents.

When Title VII was enacted originally in 1964, it exempted an "educational institution with respect to the employment of individuals to perform work connected with the educational activities of such institution." * * * Eight years later, Congress eliminated that specific exemption by enacting § 3 of the Equal Employment Opportunity Act of 1972, 86 Stat. 103. This extension of Title VII was Congress' considered response to the widespread and compelling problem of invidious discrimination in educational institutions. The House Report focused specifically on discrimination in higher education, including the lack of access for women and minorities to higher ranking (*i.e.,* tenured) academic positions. * * * Significantly, opponents of the extension claimed that enforcement of Title VII would weaken institutions of higher education by interfering with decisions to hire and promote faculty members. Petitioner therefore cannot seriously contend that Congress was oblivious to concerns of academic autonomy when it abandoned the exemption for educational institutions.

The effect of the elimination of this exemption was to expose tenure determinations to the same enforcement procedures applicable to other employment decisions. * * *

On their face, § 2000e–8(a) and § 2000e–9 do not carve out any special privilege relating to peer review materials, despite the fact that Congress undoubtedly was aware, when it extended Title VII's coverage, of the potential burden that access to such material might create. Moreover, we have noted previously that when a court is asked to enforce a Commission subpoena, its responsibility is to "satisfy itself that the charge is valid and that the material requested is 'relevant' to the charge * * * and more generally to assess any contentions by the employer that the demand for information is too indefinite or has been made for an illegitimate purpose." It is not then to determine "whether the charge of discrimination is 'well founded' or 'verifiable.'" *EEOC v. Shell Oil Co.*, 466 U.S., at 72, n. 26, 104 S.Ct., at 1632, n. 26.

The University concedes that the information sought by the Commission in this case passes the relevance test set forth in *Shell Oil.* Tr. of Oral Arg. 6. Petitioner argues, nevertheless, that Title VII affirmatively grants courts the discretion to require more than relevance in order to protect tenure-review documents. Although petitioner recognizes that Title VII gives the Commission broad "power to *seek* access to all evidence that may be 'relevant to the charge under investigation,'" * * * it contends that Title VII's subpoena enforcement provisions do not give the Commission an unqualified right to *acquire* such evidence. * * * This interpretation simply cannot be reconciled with the plain language of the text of § 2000e–8(a), which states that the Commission "*shall * * * have* access" to "relevant" evidence (emphasis added). The provision can be read only as giving the Commission a right to obtain that evidence, not a mere license to seek it.

Although the text of the access provisions thus provides no privilege, Congress did address situations in which an employer may have an interest in the confidentiality of its records. The same § 2000e–8 which gives the Commission access to any evidence relevant to its investigation also makes it "unlawful for any officer or employee of the Commission to make public in any manner whatever any information obtained by the Commission pursuant to its authority under this section prior to the institution of any proceeding" under the Act. A violation of this provision subjects the employee to criminal penalties. * * * To be sure, the protection of confidentiality that § 2000–8(e) provides is less than complete.[5] But this, if anything, weakens petitioner's argument. Congress apparently considered the issue of confidentiality, and it provided a modicum of protection. Petitioner urges us to go further than Congress thought necessary to safeguard that value, that is, to strike the balance differently from the one Congress adopted. Petitioner, however, does not offer any persuasive justification for that suggestion.

We readily agree with petitioner that universities and colleges play significant roles in American society. Nor need we question, at this point, petitioner's assertion that confidentiality is important to the proper functioning of the peer review process under which many academic institutions operate. The costs that ensue from disclosure, however, constitute only one side of the balance. As Congress has recognized, the costs associated with racial and sexual discrimination in institutions of higher learning are very substantial. Few would deny that ferreting out this kind of invidious discrimination is a great if not compelling governmental interest. Often, as even

---

5. The prohibition on Commission disclosure does not apply, for example, to the charging party. See *EEOC v. Associated Dry Goods* *Corp.,* 449 U.S. 590, 598–604, 101 S.Ct. 817, 822–825, 66 L.Ed.2d 762 (1981).

petitioner seems to admit, * * * disclosure of peer review materials will be necessary in order for the Commission to determine whether illegal discrimination has taken place. Indeed, if there is a "smoking gun" to be found that demonstrates discrimination in tenure decisions, it is likely to be tucked away in peer review files. * * *

Moreover, we agree with the EEOC that the adoption of a requirement that the Commission demonstrate a "specific reason for disclosure," * * * beyond a showing of relevance, would place a substantial litigation-producing obstacle in the way of the Commission's efforts to investigate and remedy alleged discrimination. * * * A university faced with a disclosure request might well utilize the privilege in a way that frustrates the EEOC's mission. We are reluctant to "place a potent weapon in the hands of employers who have no interest in complying voluntarily with the Act, who wish instead to delay as long as possible investigations by the EEOC." * * *

Acceptance of petitioner's claim would also lead to a wave of similar privilege claims by other employers who play significant roles in furthering speech and learning in society. What of writers, publishers, musicians, lawyers? It surely is not unreasonable to believe, for example, that confidential peer reviews play an important part in partnership determinations at some law firms. We perceive no limiting principle in petitioner's argument. Accordingly, we stand behind the breakwater Congress has established: unless specifically provided otherwise in the statute, the EEOC may obtain "relevant" evidence. Congress has made the choice. If it dislikes the result, it of course may revise the statute.

Finally, we see nothing in our precedents that supports petitioner's claim. * * *

B

As noted above, petitioner characterizes its First Amendment claim as one of "academic freedom." Petitioner begins its argument by focusing our attention upon language in prior cases acknowledging the crucial role universities play in the dissemination of ideas in our society and recognizing "academic freedom" as a "special concern of the First Amendment." *Keyishian v. Board of Regents,* 385 U.S. 589, 603, 87 S.Ct. 675, 683, 17 L.Ed.2d 629 (1967). In that case the Court said: "Our Nation is deeply committed to safeguarding academic freedom, which is of transcendent value to all of us and not merely to the teachers concerned." See also *Adler v. Board of Education,* 342 U.S. 485, 511, 72 S.Ct. 380, 394, 96 L.Ed. 517 (1952)(academic freedom is central to "the pursuit of truth which the First Amendment is designed to protect" (dissenting opinion of Douglas, J.)). Petitioner places special reliance on Justice Frankfurter's opinion, concurring in the result, in *Sweezy v. New Hampshire,* 354 U.S. 234, 263, 77 S.Ct. 1203, 1218, 1 L.Ed.2d 1311 (1957), where the Justice recognized that one of "four essential freedoms" that a university possesses under the First Amendment is the right to "determine for itself on academic grounds *who may teach* "(emphasis added).

Petitioner contends that it exercises this right of determining "on academic grounds who may teach" through the process of awarding tenure. A tenure system, asserts petitioner, determines what the university will look like over time. "In making tenure decisions, therefore, a university is doing nothing less than shaping its own identity." * * *

Petitioner next maintains that the peer review process is the most important element in the effective operation of a tenure system. A properly functioning tenure system requires the faculty to obtain candid and detailed written evaluations of the candidate's scholarship, both from the candidate's peers at the university and from scholars at other institutions. These evaluations, says petitioner, traditionally have been provided with express or implied assurances of confidentiality. It is confidentiality that ensures candor and enables an institution to make its tenure decisions on the basis of valid academic criteria.

Building from these premises, petitioner claims that requiring the disclosure of peer review evaluations on a finding of mere relevance will undermine the existing process of awarding tenure, and therefore will result in a significant infringement of petitioner's First Amendment right of academic freedom. As more and more peer evaluations are disclosed to the EEOC and become public, a "chilling effect" on candid evaluations and discussions of candidates will result. And as the quality of peer review evaluations declines, tenure committees will no longer be able to rely on them. "This will work to the detriment of universities, as less qualified persons achieve tenure causing the quality of instruction and scholarship to decline." * * * Compelling disclosure of materials "also will result in divisiveness and tension, placing strain on faculty relations and impairing the free interchange of ideas that is a hallmark of academic freedom." * * * The prospect of these deleterious effects on American colleges and universities, concludes petitioner, compels recognition of a First Amendment privilege.

In our view, petitioner's reliance on the so-called academic freedom cases is somewhat misplaced. In those cases government was attempting to control or direct the *content* of the speech engaged in by the university or those affiliated with it. In *Sweezy,* for example, the Court invalidated the conviction of a person found in contempt for refusing to answer questions about the content of a lecture he had delivered at a state university. Similarly, in *Keyishian,* the Court invalidated a network of state laws that required public employees, including teachers at state universities, to make certifications with respect to their membership in the Communist Party. When, in those cases, the Court spoke of "academic freedom" and the right to determine on "academic grounds who may teach" the Court was speaking in reaction to content-based regulation. See *Sweezy v. New Hampshire,* 354 U.S., at 250, 77 S.Ct., at 1211 (plurality opinion discussing problems that result from imposition of a "strait jacket upon the intellectual leaders in our colleges and universities"); *Keyishian v. Board of Regents,* 385 U.S., at 603, 87 S.Ct., at 683 (discussing dangers that are present when a "pall of orthodoxy" is cast "over the classroom").

Fortunately, we need not define today the precise contours of any academic-freedom right against governmental attempts to influence the content of academic speech through the selection of faculty or by other means, because petitioner does not allege that the Commission's subpoenas are intended to or will in fact direct the content of university discourse toward or away from particular subjects or points of view. Instead, as noted above, petitioner claims that the "quality of instruction and scholarship [will] decline" as a result of the burden EEOC subpoenas place on the peer review process.

Also, the cases upon which petitioner places emphasis involved *direct* infringements on the asserted right to "determine for itself on academic grounds who may teach." In *Keyishian,* for example, government was attempting to *substitute* its teaching employment criteria for those already in place at the academic institutions, directly and completely usurping the discretion of each institution. In contrast, the EEOC subpoena at issue here effects no such usurpation. The Commission is not providing criteria that petitioner *must* use in selecting teachers. Nor is it preventing the University from using any criteria it may wish to use, except those—including race, sex, and national origin—that are proscribed under Title VII.[7] In keeping with Title VII's preservation of employers' remaining freedom of choice, see *Price Waterhouse v. Hopkins,* 490 U.S. 228, 109 S.Ct. 1775, 104 L.Ed.2d 268 (1989)(plurality opinion), courts have stressed the importance of avoiding second-guessing of legitimate academic judgments. This Court itself has cautioned that "judges * * * asked to review the substance of a genuinely academic decision * * * should show great respect for the faculty's professional judgment." *Regents of University of Michigan v. Ewing,* 474 U.S. 214, 225, 106 S.Ct. 507, 513, 88 L.Ed.2d 523 (1985). Nothing we say today should be understood as a retreat from this principle of respect for *legitimate* academic decisionmaking.

That the burden of which the University complains is neither content-based nor direct does not necessarily mean that petitioner has no valid First Amendment claim. Rather, it means only that petitioner's claim does not fit neatly within any right of academic freedom that could be derived from the cases on which petitioner relies. In essence, petitioner asks us to recognize an *expanded* right of academic freedom to protect confidential peer review materials from disclosure. Although we are sensitive to the effects that content-neutral government action may have on speech, see, *e.g., Heffron v. International Society for Krishna Consciousness, Inc.,* 452 U.S. 640, 647–648, 101 S.Ct. 2559, 2563–2564, 69 L.Ed.2d 298 (1981), and believe that burdens that are less than direct may sometimes pose First Amendment concerns, see, *e.g., NAACP v. Alabama ex rel. Patterson,* 357 U.S. 449, 78 S.Ct. 1163, 2 L.Ed.2d 1488 (1958), we think the First Amendment cannot be extended to embrace petitioner's claim.

First, by comparison with the cases in which we have found a cognizable First Amendment claim, the infringement the University complains of is extremely attenuated. To repeat, it argues that the First Amendment is infringed by disclosure of peer review materials because disclosure undermines the confidentiality which is central to the peer review process, and this in turn is central to the tenure process, which in turn is the means by which petitioner seeks to exercise its asserted academic-freedom right of choosing who will teach. To verbalize the claim is to recognize how distant the burden is from the asserted right.

Indeed, if the University's attenuated claim were accepted, many other generally applicable laws might also be said to infringe the First Amendment. In effect, petitioner says no more than that disclosure of peer review materials

7. Petitioner does not argue in this case that race, sex, and national origin constitute "academic grounds" for the purposes of its claimed First Amendment right to academic freedom. Cf. *Regents of the University of California v. Bakke,* 438 U.S. 265, 312–313, 98 S.Ct. 2733, 2759–2760, 57 L.Ed.2d 750 (1978)(opinion of Powell, J.).

makes it more difficult to acquire information regarding the "academic grounds" on which petitioner wishes to base its tenure decisions. But many laws make the exercise of First Amendment rights more difficult. For example, a university cannot claim a First Amendment violation simply because it may be subject to taxation or other government regulation, even though such regulation might deprive the university of revenue it needs to bid for professors who are contemplating working for other academic institutions or in industry. We doubt that the peer review process is any more essential in effectuating the right to determine "who may teach" than is the availability of money. Cf. *Buckley v. Valeo,* 424 U.S. 1, 19, 96 S.Ct. 612, 634, 46 L.Ed.2d 659 (1976)(discussing how money is sometimes necessary to effectuate First Amendment rights).

In addition to being remote and attenuated, the injury to academic freedom claimed by petitioner is also speculative. As the EEOC points out, confidentiality is not the norm in all peer review systems. See, *e.g.,* G. Bednash, The Relationship Between Access and Selectivity in Tenure Review Outcomes (1989)(unpublished Ph.D. Dissertation, University of Maryland). Moreover, some disclosure of peer evaluations would take place even if petitioner's "special necessity" test were adopted. Thus, the "chilling effect" petitioner fears is at most only incrementally worsened by the absence of a privilege. Finally, we are not so ready as petitioner seems to be to assume the worst about those in the academic community. Although it is possible that some evaluators may become less candid as the possibility of disclosure increases, others may simply ground their evaluations in specific examples and illustrations in order to deflect potential claims of bias or unfairness. Not all academics will hesitate to stand up and be counted when they evaluate their peers.

* * *

Because we conclude that the EEOC subpoena process does not infringe any First Amendment right enjoyed by petitioner, the EEOC need not demonstrate any special justification to sustain the constitutionality of Title VII as applied to tenure peer review materials in general or to the subpoena involved in this case. Accordingly, we need not address the Commission's alternative argument that any infringement of petitioner's First Amendment rights is permissible because of the substantial relation between the Commission's request and the overriding and compelling state interest in eradicating invidious discrimination.[9]

The judgment of the Court of Appeals is affirmed.

It is so ordered.

Notes on University of Pennsylvania

1. A notewriter, commenting on Namenwirth v. Board of Regents of the University of Wisconsin System, 769 F.2d 1235 (7th Cir.1985), certiorari denied 474 U.S. 1061, 106 S.Ct. 807, 88 L.Ed.2d 782 (1986), a case holding that an academic plaintiff had failed to prove that her tenure denial was based on sex

---

9. We also do not consider the question, not passed upon by the Court of Appeals, whether the District Court's enforcement of the Commission's subpoena will allow petitioner to redact information from the contested materials before disclosing them. See n. 2, *supra.*

discrimination, ventured the opinion that "[f]ifteen years of Title VII litigation seems to have had no great effect on the way academic institutions make their tenure decisions." Christopher H. Kallaher, Note, Namenwirth v. Board of Regents of the University of Wisconsin System: Proving Pretext in a Title VII Tenure Denial Case, 1987 Wis.L.Rev. 1041, 1059 (1987). Will the unanimous decision in *University of Pennsylvania* make it any easier for academic plaintiffs to win tenure cases?

2. In footnote 9, the Court reserved the question of whether plaintiff is entitled to nonredacted files. What kind of information do you imagine a University would like to be able to conceal from plaintiffs in Title VII tenure cases? The names of faculty members at other institutions who acted as "external reviewers" of plaintiff's scholarly or creative work? The identity of faculty members appointed to serve on internal *ad hoc* review committees charged with making recommendations concerning plaintiff's tenure? In a university with several levels of review, such as that described in Brown v. Boston University, p. 838, supra, the precise level at which the negative recommendation or decision was made? Given the Court's approach to the First Amendment claim in *University of Pennsylvania*, which, if any, of these crucial bits of information can the university hope to conceal?

The issue of redaction has generated a mixed response from the federal courts. In Schneider v. Northwestern University, 151 F.R.D. 319 (N.D.Ill.1993), the university refused to reveal the identity of plaintiff's ad hoc tenure committee members from the School of Education and of plaintiff's outside reviewers, as well as the identity of those same persons in the tenure files of five comparative male candidates. In suing for sex discrimination in denial of tenure, plaintiff alleged, in part, that the ad hoc committee had not honored her selection of outside reviewers, whereas the ad hoc committees for the male candidates had honored their selections. The trial court ordered disclosure of the identity of plaintiff's outside reviewers. The trial court found that not only was this information relevant to plaintiff's case, but that, apparently, the outside reviewers did not object to the disclosure of their names. In regard to the comparative male candidates, the trial court ordered the disclosure of the list of names of outside reviewers requested by the candidates, and the list of names of those chosen by the committees, without identifying the particular author of any outside evaluation letter. The trial court, however, refused to order the university to disclose the identity of plaintiff's ad hoc tenure committee members, finding that "compelled disclosure * * * potentially undermines the working relationship plaintiff might have with faculty members if she prevails in this lawsuit and is granted tenure." Id. at 324. Small consolation for plaintiff, who at that point was probably a long way from winning and obtaining tenure. Hasn't plaintiff already "undermined" working relationships by suing in the first place? The trial court did say that if plaintiff at a later time made a stronger showing of "particularized need" for the information, such as evidence of discriminatory animus, the court would consider ordering disclosure. At the time of this decision, plaintiff "has pointed to no bias or evidence of discrimination in particular reports." Id. at 323. After this narrow reading of *University of Pennsylvania*, the plaintiff must have asked herself how she would be able to gather any evidence of bias, if she did not know the identity of the faculty members on the ad hoc committee.

Contrary to *Schneider*, a district court magistrate in Weinstock v. Columbia University, 1995 WL 567399 (S.D.N.Y. 1995) ordered Columbia to turn over plaintiff's own tenure file to plaintiff's attorney, as well as the files of 43 other faculty considered for tenure in the hard sciences at Columbia since 1985, plus the names of the ad hoc committee members who considered plaintiff for tenure. The magistrate recognized the relevance of plaintiff's discovery requests, finding the other faculty files necessary for plaintiff to do a comparative evaluation to determine if the tenure standards applied to her were the same as those applied to male faculty. Furthermore, the identity of the ad hoc committee members was relevant to plaintiff's need to show illegal motivation or intent under Title VII in her denial of tenure. The magistrate cited the Second Circuit's opinion in Fisher v. Vassar College, 66 F.3d 379, 68 FEP Cases 1537, 1546 (2d Cir.1995), where the appellate panel held that it "was appropriate for the district court to consider plaintiff's record and to compare it with the records of other Vassar professors."

In response to *University of Pennsylvania*, the University of California amended its faculty personnel policies in 1992 to provide for increased access by faculty to their personnel files. Instead of receiving only summaries of documents, candidates for promotion are now entitled, upon request, to complete unredacted copies of review letters from departments, administrative officers, and school or campus personnel committees. The identity of the authors of these documents are already known to the candidate, so no redaction is allowed. For those evaluation documents where the authors' identities are secret, such as those from individual reviewers or ad hoc committees, candidates are entitled to redacted copies of the letters. Redaction is limited, however, to removing only the name, title, and institutional affiliation, the information which would disclose the identity of the author. See UC Academic Personnel Manual, § APM–160.

3. Did Justice Blackmun give a satisfactory rationale for the Court's rejection of the University of Pennsylvania's claim that, without assurances of confidentiality, reviewers would refuse to provide candid examinations of a tenure candidate's work, thus undercutting the academic quest for excellence? As you might expect, reaction to the decision by some University spokespersons expressed fear that the frankness of reviewers would be inhibited. Law Professor William Van Alstyne commented that, "To operate in a fishbowl is necessarily to inhibit candor." In his view, the EEOC should be required to prove sufficient cause before files are released. The Chronicle of Higher Education, Jan. 17, 1990, at A–1, A–17 at col. 1–2. Professor Michael Olivas, an expert in higher education law and author of *The Law and Higher Education: Cases and Materials on Colleges in Court* (Carolina Academic Press, Durham, No.Car.1989), was of the opinion that the case "should encourage the fair treatment of all individuals, encourage institutions to keep records more carefully, and help faculty members who were planning to pursue discrimination claims to prove their cases." Ibid. Others, however, believe that the decision will have no impact on tenure decisions. The New York Times, January 10, 1990, at A16, col. 4. If the latter observers are correct, why did the University make such a fuss? The American Association of University Professors, the American Council on Education, Harvard University, and Stanford University all filed amicus briefs in support of the University's position in *University of Pennsylvania*.

4. Rosalie Tung, the real party in interest in *University of Pennsylvania*, now holds a tenured professorship at the University of Wisconsin, Milwaukee, where she also acts as Director of the International Business Center. The Chronicle of Higher Education, Jan. 17, 1990, p. A1, at col. 4.

5. When does the time for filing a Title VII charge begin to run in academic cases? In Delaware State College v. Ricks, 449 U.S. 250, 101 S.Ct. 498, 66 L.Ed.2d 431, the Court held that plaintiff's cause of action accrued "at the time the tenure decision was made and communicated to Ricks," not when his

employment actually added at the end of his "terminal" year. Id. at 258. Although the Court agreed there were a variety of possible dates to choose from, because of the complex nature of academic decisionmaking, all of these dates had occurred outside the applicable statute of limitations. Thus, the Court reversed the 3rd Circuit and affirmed the original decision of the district court. Id. at 262. The parties in Lever v. Northwestern University, 979 F.2d 552 (7th Cir.1992), certiorari denied 508 U.S. 951, 113 S.Ct. 2443, 124 L.Ed.2d 661 (1993), spent eleven years litigating whether the time began to run on May 5, 1980, when the Dean of the College of Arts and Sciences notified plaintiff Janet Lever that "I shall not recommend to the Provost that you be promoted to the rank of associate professor" and offering her a terminal year appointment, or on February 12, 1981, when the Provost notified her that "I do not feel that I am justified in reversing the decision of the Dean not to recommend your promotion to tenure at North-western University." Plaintiff filed her Title VII complaint with the EEOC on June 15, 1981. Judge Easterbrook affirmed the district court's determination that because the Dean's letter constituted the alleged discriminatory act, the claim was time barred, noting that, despite ambiguity in the university's faculty hand-book, "the Dean's decision is final in the same sense as a judgment of a district court: it is self-effectuating and stands unless reversed, which can occur only on a request for review." Id., at 555.

Text Note
Proving Discrimination: Title VII in Academe

As originally enacted, Title VII did not apply to educational institutions "with respect to the employment of individuals to perform work connected with the educational activities of that institution."[1] In 1972 Congress simultaneously amended Title VII to cover academic employees,[2] enacted Title IX of the Education Amendments to prohibit sex discrimination in certain education programs or activities receiving federal assistance,[3] and extended the Equal Pay Act to academic and professional employees.[4] Antedating these developments was the use of Executive Order 11246 of 1965, expanded to include sex discrimination by Executive Order 11375 in 1967, to require colleges and universities, in their role as federal contractors, to undertake affirmative action with respect to the employment of women.[5] Developments under these other provisions will be noted elsewhere;[6] here, the focus is on the efficacy of Title VII to identify and rectify discrimination in academic employment.

As we have seen, from 1964 until 1972, Title VII law was developed largely in the industrial setting. The *Griggs* and *McDonnell Douglas* standards, moreover, arose from the context of race, not sex, discrimination. The earliest Title VII case law on sex discrimination was concerned with determining what constituted sex discrimination and the scope of the BFOQ exception. Academic cases had vastly different overtones. They called into question the judgments of highly educated and well respected individuals, who had chosen to pursue a life of scholarship and instruction. The judgments themselves, concerning as they did subtle questions

---

1. Pub.L. No. 88–352, § 702, 78 Stat. 255 (1964).

2. Pub.L. No. 92–261, § 3, amending § 702, 86 Stat. 103 (1972).

3. Pub.L. No. 92–318, Title IX, § 901, 86 Stat. 373 (1972).

4. Pub.L. No. 92–318, Title IX, § 906(b)(1), 86 Stat. 375 (1972).

5. See Text Note: Room at the Top: Affirmative Action at Colleges and Universities, at p. 1110, infra.

6. Title IX and the use of the Executive Orders in academic settings are considered in Chapter Four; the Equal Pay Act is considered in Chapter Three at Subsection B.

of quality and the prediction of future achievement, were subjective ones. And, in the most bitterly fought cases, what was at stake was the collective judgment of the plaintiff's peers about her academic excellence as represented in the decision whether to award tenure: a decision rationalized as necessary to protect the academic freedom of the institution itself.

Given these considerations, it is perhaps not surprising that many courts initially were reluctant to adopt any attitude except one of extreme deference in reviewing academic cases. Judge Moore's opinion for the Second Circuit in Faro v. New York Univ.[7] is frequently cited as typical of the noninterventionist position:

> Dr. Faro, in effect, envisions herself as a modern Jeanne d'Arc fighting for the rights of embattled womanhood on an academic battlefield, facing a solid phalanx of men and male faculty prejudice. She would compare herself and her qualifications with all recent appointees to the NYU medical faculty and asserts that she is just as competent as they are. In particular, she selects three doctors for comparison. She states that she was offered $4,000 for the same job for which a Dr. Alves was paid $23,000. Of course, as the district court found and the record substantiates, it was not the same job. Analysis of the proof clearly shows that the experience possessed by such male professors as have been hired is not comparable to the limited teaching and research background of Dr. Faro.

* * *

> Of all fields, which the federal courts should hesitate to invade and take over, education and faculty appointments at a University level are probably the least suited for federal court supervision.[8]

Faced with this judicial attitude, individual plaintiffs charging disparate treatment in academic cases under Title VII have almost uniformly been unsuccessful. George LaNoue and Barbara Lee, who studied academic cases litigated in the federal courts between 1971 and 1984, found that plaintiffs won only 34 of 160, 21% of the cases that were decided on the merits.[9]

Kunda v. Muhlenberg College,[10] was the first case to order that plaintiff, an instructor in the Department of Physical Education at Muhlenberg College, be granted tenure over the college's objection. In affirming this judgment, the Third Circuit was able to distinguish the other academic cases on the ground that "Kunda's achievements, qualifications, and prospects were not in dispute. She was considered qualified by the unanimous vote of both faculty committees which evaluated her teaching, research, and creative work, and college and public service."[11] The major impediment to plaintiff's promotion to tenure was her lack of an advanced degree. Accordingly, the court affirmed the lower court's order that she "be permitted the opportunity to complete the requirements for a

---

7. 502 F.2d 1229 (2d Cir.1974).

8. 502 F.2d at 1231–32.

9. George R. LaNoue & Barbara A. Lee, Academics in Court: The Consequences of Faculty Discrimination Litigation 23–34 (1987). The authors studied only those cases litigated under Title VII, the Equal Pay Act, the Age Discrimination in Employment Act, and the Rehabilitation Act that ended in a published

opinion by a federal court between 1971 and 1984. They count 156 such decisions on procedural or jurisdictional issues, and 160 decisions that reached the merits of the plaintiff's claim. Id., at 27.

10. 463 F.Supp. 294 (E.D.Pa.1978), affirmed 621 F.2d 532 (3d Cir.1980).

11. 621 F.2d at 548 (3d Cir.1980).

masters degree within two full school years * * * and, upon successful achievement of the masters degree, be awarded tenure effective September 1, 1975."[12] In defending its decision in *Kunda,* the Third Circuit observed that,

> [t]he fact that the discrimination in this case took place in an academic rather than commercial setting does not permit the court to abdicate its responsibility to insure the award of a meaningful remedy. Congress did not intend that those institutions which employ persons who work primarily with their mental faculties should enjoy a different status under Title VII than those which employ persons who work primarily with their hands.[13]

A handful of other cases in the 1970s awarded tenure or a promotion to full professorship as a remedy for academic discrimination. In Sweeney v. Board of Trustees of Keene State College,[14] plaintiff Christine M. Sweeney had been awarded tenure in 1972. She applied for promotion to full professor in 1974, but was rejected. She brought suit, alleging sex discrimination, and applied again for promotion in 1975. This time she was successful. The First Circuit affirmed the district court's order holding that the College's refusal to promote her in 1974 was in violation of Title VII. Judge Campbell, who viewed the case as "close" but not as clearly erroneous, was persuaded that the evidence showed that the College's reasons for refusing to promote Sweeney were either insubstantial or fictitious, and that in general "women at Keene State were evaluated by a stricter standard than their male colleagues, and that the institution generally was unresponsive to the concerns of its female faculty."[15] In light of the College's decision to promote Sweeney in 1975, does the case involve anything more than a year's back pay?

It was, perhaps, a measure of the relative imperviousness to individual legal onslaught of academic hiring and promotion procedures that *Kunda, Sweeney,* and two cases in which the defendants entered into consent settlements in class action suits[16] were taken to herald a new trend of judicial activism in academic cases.[17] In view of the limited holdings in *Kunda* and *Sweeney,* and the individual burden placed on those seeking to benefit from one of the class action settlements,[18] this conclusion appeared unjustified. Moreover, cases in the 1980s negated this view. In Lieberman v. Gant,[19] which affirmed the dismissal of the plaintiff's claim that she had been denied tenure in the English Department of the University of Connecticut because of sex discrimination, Judge Friendly expressly limited an

---

12. Kunda v. Muhlenberg College, 463 F.Supp. at 315. Kunda was promoted to full professor in 1987. See G.R. LaNoue & B.A. Lee, supra note 9, at 109. The authors recount the details of Connie Rae Kunda's case at 89–113.

13. Kunda v. Muhlenberg College, 621 F.2d at 550. See generally, Note, Tenure and Partnership as Title VII Remedies, 94 Harv.L.Rev. 457 (1980).

14. 604 F.2d 106 (1st Cir.1979), certiorari denied 444 U.S. 1045, 100 S.Ct. 733, 62 L.Ed.2d 731 (1980).

15. Id., 604 F.2d at 112–13.

16. Lamphere v. Brown University and Rajender v. University of Minnesota. The consent decree in *Lamphere* is set out at 491 F.Supp. 238–262, in an Appendix to Lamphere v. Brown Univ., 491 F.Supp. 232 (D.R.I.1980). The consent decree in *Rajender* was approved

by the district court in August, 1980. See Rajender v. University of Minn., 563 F.Supp. 401 (D.Minn.1983), reversed in part, vacated in part, remanded 730 F.2d 1110 (8th Cir.1984). *Rajender* is discussed in LaNoue & Lee, supra note 9, at 177–219.

17. See News and Comment, Ending Sex Discrimination in Academia, 208 Science 1120 (June 6, 1980); Kleiman, Female Academics Show Gains in Combating Sex Discrimination, The New York Times, July 15, 1980, at 1, col. 3.

18. Lamphere v. Brown Univ., 491 F.Supp. 232 (D.R.I.1980). Compare Lamphere v. Brown University (Appeal of Ann Seidman), 798 F.2d 532 (1st Cir.1986)(explaining the similarities and differences between a Title VII suit and a proceeding under the consent decree).

19. 630 F.2d 60 (2d Cir.1980).

earlier Second Circuit opinion in Powell v. Syracuse Univ.[20] that contained language supporting an activist stance in academic cases:[21]

> Although the *Powell* court upheld the dismissal of Ms. Powell, it did so on the ground that the university had successfully rebutted the *prima facie* case she had made out. It made clear that Faro v. New York University, 502 F.2d 1229, 1231–33 (2d Cir.1974), which it characterized as a "common-sense position", was not to be read as a "policy of self-abnegation where colleges are concerned."

> We think the judge may have somewhat overread *Powell,* which concerned renewal of a teaching contract rather than appointment to tenure. In contrast to an ordinary teaching position, terminable at the end of any academic year, and in still greater contrast to employment as a bricklayer as in Flowers v. Crouch–Walker Corp., 552 F.2d 1277, 1283 (7th Cir.1977), on which the *Powell* court relied, advancement to tenure entails what is close to a life-long commitment by a university, and therefore requires much more than the showing of performance "of sufficient quality to merit continued employment" which the Seventh Circuit held enough in the case of the bricklayer in *Flowers.* The policies of the University of Connecticut, like those of most universities, prescribe qualifications for tenure that are considerably higher than those for the making or renewal of an appointment. * * *

As Vice President Wilson explained in an April 21, 1969 memorandum to the faculty long before Dr. Lieberman's case arose:

> *When in doubt, don't.* Since the tenure decision is a commitment by the University to twenty or thirty years of support and several hundred thousand dollars of salary, from which there can be no turning back, we have felt that if we must err, we ought to err on the side of caution; we ought not to gamble widely. (PX–66 p. 3)(emphasis in original).

Under such appropriately rigorous standards, a candidate for tenure does not make out the elements needed for a *prima facie* case merely by showing qualifications for continuation as an untenured faculty member; indeed to hold that he did would be in effect to negate the requirements beyond minimally satisfactory performance properly entering into the tenure decision.

In Zahorik v. Cornell University,[22] the Second Circuit reaffirmed its position in *Lieberman,* noting that courts are "understandably reluctant to review the merits of a tenure decision,"[23] and holding that four women who were denied

---

20. 580 F.2d 1150 (2d Cir.1978). Judge Moore, who authored the *Faro* opinion, concurred in *Powell,* noting that "[a]ny reluctance of the federal courts to interfere with the decision-making process of universities does not come from an interest in promoting discrimination. Rather, such reluctance reflects the inability of the courts to perform 'a discriminating analysis of the qualifications of each candidate for hiring or advancement, taking into consideration his or her educational experience, the specifications of the particular position open and, of great importance, the personality of the candidate.' " Id., 580 F.2d at 1157.

21. Lieberman v. Gant, 630 F.2d at 64. *Lieberman* is discussed in LaNoue & Lee, supra note 9, at 51–88. Compare Davis v. Weid-

ner, 596 F.2d 726, 731–32 (7th Cir.1979), where the court, although affirming the dismissal of a female plaintiff's claim that the termination of her position was due to sex discrimination, espoused an active standard of review. See also Smith v. University of North Carolina, 632 F.2d 316, 345–46 (4th Cir.1980), rejecting plaintiff's claims of discrimination based on age, sex, and religion, and acknowledging that "[u]niversity employment cases have always created a decisional dilemma for the courts."

22. 729 F.2d 85 (2d Cir.1984).

23. 729 F.2d at 93.

tenure in four different departments over a four-year period had failed to prove sex discrimination. See also Langland v. Vanderbilt University,[24] holding that the denial of tenure to a female assistant professor of English was based on "deficient scholarship" rather than sex discrimination. Elizabeth Langland's department recommended her for tenure by a vote of 15–5; she was denied tenure when the Dean of the College of Arts and Science refused to concur in the departmental recommendation. Langland sought and received the personnel files of 40 candidates for tenure who had been reviewed by the Dean during his term of office. After making what it accurately described as "an exhaustive comparison of [plaintiff's] file to those of male professors", the court determined that "she was held to the same standard they were."[25]

Under these deferential standards of federal court review, women who have won Title VII claims have presented overwhelming evidence of differential treatment, or of harassment, leading to findings of sex discrimination. Julia Brown was a "superstar" in the eyes of her colleagues, one of few faculty at Boston University to have her Ph.D. dissertation published as a book by Harvard University Press to overwhelmingly positive reviews. Unanimous support by her colleagues provided a solid foundation for her successful claim of sex discrimination against the University.[26] To understand how strong a factual foundation is necessary for a successful federal suit, read the egregious fact pattern of Jew v. University of Iowa.[27] Jean Jew, an associate professor in the College of Medicine, successfully sued for sexual harassment and failure to promote after the university took no corrective action against her male colleagues who conducted a twelve-year smear campaign against her, referring to her as a "whore" and a "chink," despite her repeated complaints. A comparable case is Austen v. University of Hawaii,[28] where the plaintiff suffered years of arbitrary treatment and antagonism from her department chair, who blocked her grant of tenure. In granting judgment for Austen on her sex discrimination claim, the federal judge found that university officials supported the department chair's sabotage of her career, until she was finally forced out by stress-related disability.[29]

Despite the formidable obstacles presented by lawsuits, some women continue to win cases against universities, but more often in state courts than in federal courts. Professor Antoinette Gomes won a $1.1 million *jury* verdict in Los Angeles Superior Court under California law in February 1995 for sex discrimination in the failure of the UCLA Medical School to promote her to full professor.[30] (At this time, the University of California's appeal is pending.) Other women have won tenure through settlements of their sex discrimination claims, either during university grievance procedures or during the course of lengthy litigation.

Professor Eleanor Swift was awarded tenure at the University of California Berkeley Law School (Boalt Hall) as the result of a successful internal grievance process. She was denied tenure by the Boalt Hall faculty in 1987. In February 1988 she filed a grievance with the UC Berkeley Privilege and Tenure Committee of the campus Academic Senate. She alleged sex discrimination, contending that the law faculty applied different and more onerous standards to her tenure file

24. 589 F.Supp. 995 (M.D.Tenn.1984), affirmed without opinion 772 F.2d 907 (6th Cir. 1985).

25. 589 F.Supp. at 1017.

26. Brown v. Trustees of Boston University, 891 F.2d 337 (1st Cir.1989), supra at p. 838.

27. 749 F.Supp. 946, 949–57 (S.D.Iowa 1990).

28. 759 F.Supp. 612, 613–29 (D.Haw.1991), affirmed 967 F.2d 583 (9th Cir.1992).

29. 759 F.Supp. at 627.

30. L. A. Times, Part B, p. 15, col. 6, Feb. 25, 1995.

than it had applied to men who had obtained tenure during the 1980s. After a preliminary investigation, the campus committee, for the first time in a gender case, found enough evidence for a "prima facie" case of sex discrimination and "sufficient reason" to conduct a full hearing on her grievance.[31] In December 1988, on the eve of the full grievance hearing, the university settled with Professor Swift, agreeing to resubmit her tenure file to a new committee wholly outside the faculty of the Boalt Hall Law School. In addition, the university agreed that her tenure file would not be evaluated under some theoretically objective standard of "academic excellence," but would be evaluated under a comparative standard based on the files of the men who had received tenure during the previous 10 years. The outside committee recommended that Professor Swift be granted tenure, which UC Berkeley did in August 1989.[32] The resolution of Professor Swift's case came after only two years, a relatively short time for a dispute over tenure.

The 1993 settlement in Professor Jenny Harrison's tenure case against the UC Berkeley Math Department is one example of a favorable court settlement, but only after years of internal review and legal negotiations. Professor Harrison was denied tenure by the Math Department in 1986. She filed a grievance with the Campus Privilege and Tenure Committee, which finally held a full hearing in 1989. When the committee ruled against her, Professor Harrison filed suit in state court. In 1991, the court granted Professor Harrison and her lawyer access to the tenure files of eight men who had previously been granted tenure by the Math Department. In March 1993, Professor Harrison and the university reached a settlement after months of mediation.[33] The structure of the settlement was similar to the settlement Professor Swift negotiated prior to her committee hearing. The university agreed to have Professor Harrison's tenure file reevaluated by a new outside committee. As in Professor Swift's case, the outside committee recommended tenure for her. The committee also recommended advancement to the full professor level, urging the university to waive any years for her as associate professor. In July 1993, Professor Harrison received tenure as a full professor.[34]

In January 1996, a third UC Berkeley plaintiff, alleging both sex and national origin discrimination in denial of tenure, obtained a settlement of $1 million from the University of California. Marcy Wong was denied tenure by the School of Architecture in 1985. After 10 years of both internal reviews and pre-trial litigation, the university settled the case short of trial. Ms. Wong did not seek reinstatement or tenure because she had established her own private architecture practice after leaving the university in 1988, upon exhaustion of her internal appeals.[35] What lessons, if any, has the university learned from this sequence of successful grievances and lawsuits?

Even when a woman wins a judgment of sex discrimination under Title VII, her victory at trial can be nullified on appeal. Judge Constance Baker Motley ruled in May 1994 that Vassar College had violated Title VII in 1985 by denying tenure to Cynthia J. Fisher, an assistant professor of biology, in part because she was married and had spent eight years away from work rearing two daughters

31. Eleanor Swift, Becoming a Plaintiff, 4 Berkeley Women's L.J., 245 (1990).

32. Id. at 250.

33. Margy Rochlin, The Mathematics of Discrimination, L.A. Times Mag., May 2, 1993, at 29, 30, 60, 62.

34. Elaine Herscher, UC Grants Tenure in Lawsuit Settlement, San Francisco Chron., July 8, 1993, at A17.

35. San Francisco Chronicle, January 9, 1996, A15.

before she was hired by Vassar.[36] In an exhaustive opinion with 111 paragraphs of findings of fact, Judge Motley found that the Vassar tenure committee's conclusions regarding Fisher's scholarship "were made in bad faith, were pretextual, and represented the application of patently discriminatory standards."[37] Judge Motley proceeded to find that Vassar had discriminated against Fisher on the basis of "sex plus," because she was a married woman who had taken time out from her career to raise children:

> The persistent fixation of the Biology Department's senior faculty on a married woman's pre-Vassar family choices reflects the acceptance of a stereotype and bias: that a married woman with an active and on-going family life cannot be a productive scientist and, therefore, is not one despite much evidence to the contrary.[38]

Despite detailed findings of intentional discrimination, a panel of the Second Circuit reversed.[39] The Second Circuit upheld Judge Motley's findings of pretext, but reversed her findings of intentional sex discrimination, finding that the Vassar faculty members involved simply did not like Fisher.[40] Contrary to Judge Motley, Judge Dennis Jacobs[41] wrote that Fisher's gap in her career to raise a family from 1965–1974 was a "tenure-relevant" factor when she went up for tenure in 1985:

> In making tenure decisions, it is perfectly reasonable to consider as a factor the candidate's prolonged absence from academia. The law does not prevent employers from considering such things. * * * A policy may discriminate between those employees who take off long periods of time in order to raise children and those who either do not have children or are able to raise them without an appreciable career interruption. That is not inherently sex specific and does not give rise to a claim under Title VII.[42]

Does this sound like a variation of the Geduldig v. Aiello conclusion that distinguishing between pregnant persons and non-pregnant persons does not involve a classification based on sex? Judge Jacobs also failed to mention that Fisher's time off was before Vassar hired her. Despite the protection that a trial court's findings of intent as a factual matter are supposed to enjoy under the "clearly erroneous" standard of Federal Rule 52, the Second Circuit panel reversed the trial judge's factual inferences of sex discrimination and dismissed Fisher's claims in their entirety. In February 1996, however, the Second Circuit granted Fisher's petition for rehearing en banc.

Finally, in pursuing sex discrimination claims against universities, the financial and emotional toll paid by women plaintiffs and their supporters is enormous. Professor Martha Chamallas has written a comprehensive and disturbing account of the impact of Jean Jew's lawsuit on the University of Iowa community.[43] Eleanor Swift has recounted her successful pursuit of tenure through the Univer-

---

36. Fisher v. Vassar College, 852 F.Supp. 1193 (S.D.N.Y.1994).

37. 852 F.Supp. at 1209.

38. Id. at 1216.

39. Fisher v. Vassar College, 70 F.3d 1420 (2d Cir.1995).

40. Id. at 1436.

41. Dennis Jacobs, a member of the Federalist Society, was appointed to the Second Circuit by President Bush in 1992, with some of the "strongest conservative credentials on the appellate bench." By 1994, he had the *lowest* rate of reversal of district court opinions among the Second Circuit. Almanac of the Federal Judiciary, vol. 2, 2nd Circuit, at 7 (1995).

42. 70 F.3d at 1448.

43. M. Chamallas, Jean Jew's Case: Resisting Sexual Harassment in the Academy, 6 Yale Journal of Law and Feminism 71 (1994).

sity of California grievance process, describing the essential but difficult transition from being a "tenure victim" to becoming a "discrimination plaintiff."[44]

Can anything be done to better adjust Title VII to the academic setting so that the institutional values at stake can be preserved without sacrificing the protection against discrimination that the Act was intended to provide? George LaNoue and Barbara Lee do not offer proposals for legal change based on their examination of academic litigation. Instead, they suggest that academic plaintiffs and institutional employers can educate themselves about the impact of academic litigation as a result of the authors' study and perhaps be in a better position to make informed choices about alternatives to litigation. LaNoue and Lee conclude that "[a]lthough there are substantial differences in degree, most of the impacts of the litigation process were negative for most parties."[45]

Consistent with LaNoue and Lee's conclusion on the negative impact of litigation, Professor Martha West has described in detail how the Supreme Court's interpretations of Title VII in *Burdine*, *Aikens*, *Hopkins*, and now *Hicks*, have made it even more unlikely that women will be able to prove intentional sex discrimination under federal law.[46] In addition to the subjective nature of academic decision making, and the very high standard of federal court deference to the institutions, Professor West discusses three additional problems women encounter in these cases:[47]

1. Decision-making by committee: Whose intent does plaintiff have to prove?

2. A belief in the myth of meritocracy; and

3. The subconscious nature of bias.

1. Decision-making by committee: Whose intent does plaintiff have to prove?

One of the biggest obstacles under the disparate treatment theory of Title VII in the professional setting is a committee decision-making system. Whose intent does a plaintiff need to prove? A committee system of decision-making does not easily fit under the Title VII theory or structure.

To make the situation more complicated, the academic context usually involves more than one committee. In the University of California faculty personnel process, there are three, four, or five different committees. Depending on the number of faculty in a department, over thirty or forty people could be participating in a single personnel decision. How many of the participants must harbor illegal intent for any one decision to violate Title VII?

Of course, the answer depends on the facts of the case. If a plaintiff can show purposeful discrimination by the top man,[48] the president or chancellor, she has the best chance of winning. He is the final decision-maker and is not insulated from scrutiny as a member of any committee. Thus, in Brown v. Trustees of Boston University, testimony about President Silber's sexist remarks was particularly crucial to plaintiff's proof of her case. On the other hand, in Kumar v.

---

44. Swift, supra note 31.

45. LaNoue & Lee, supra note 9, at 248–49.

46. Martha S. West, Gender Bias in Academic Robes: the Law's Failure to Protect Women Faculty, 67 Temple Law Review 67 (1994).

47. Id. at 125–127, 139–145. The following section is adapted from her article.

48. Eighty-five to 90% of students attend colleges or universities whose top three executive officers are male. In addition, nearly 90% of the full professors at their institutions are male. Sherry H. Penney & Nancy Kelly, Why Not a Fifty–Fifty Goal? Increasing Female Leadership in Higher Education, 6 New Eng. J. Pub. Pol'y 39, 41 (1990).

Board of Trustees, University of Massachusetts[49] even though the trial judge found that the chancellor was not sincere and was not a credible witness, the chancellor had made no overt prejudicial remarks. The appellate court reversed the credibility findings of the trial court and found that the chancellor had acted in good faith.[50] If the final decision-maker is also the person that reverses a departmental or committee recommendation in favor of a plaintiff and makes the decision adverse to the plaintiff, it becomes essential for the plaintiff to show illegal intent on the part of this last decision-maker to win her case.

If the adverse decision begins with a negative recommendation from plaintiff's department or from a review committee, then plaintiff has an almost impossible job of proving purposeful discrimination. Under current case law, prejudicial remarks from several faculty or committee members have not been enough to prove illegal intent on the part of the university. In Lam v. University of Hawaii,[51] the court found that one of the search committee members "had difficulty dealing with women" and that several faculty members resented the plaintiff's prior criticism of their search procedures. The court held, however, that this was not enough to taint the entire search process.[52] Similarly, in Brousard-Norcross v. Augustana College Ass'n[53] the United States Court of Appeals for the Eighth Circuit affirmed a trial court's grant of summary judgment against the plaintiff, even though two of the three men opposing the plaintiff had allegedly made sexist remarks about her and had previously warned the plaintiff that they would retaliate against her.[54] In another case, the First Circuit held that one biased member of a tenure subcommittee was not enough to show illegal intent because the court considered his role in the decision-making process to be "de minimis."[55] Finally, even in a small academic department with only six faculty members, a district court ruled that one faculty member's remark, indicating gender bias and desire to retaliate against the plaintiff, was insufficient to have infected the department's denial of tenure.[56] These academic cases indicate how difficult it is for a plaintiff to attribute the prejudice shown by the remarks of one member of a decision-making committee to the decision of the committee as a whole, or to the eventual adverse action against the plaintiff.

2. The myth of merit.

The courts refuse to look behind the criteria of "academic excellence" because judges believe these standards are based on merit and that the procedures used by faculty personnel systems create a legitimate meritocracy. American academics, for the most part, also believe we function under a fair and rational system. Most faculty seem to believe that we really do choose new ladder-rank faculty members on the basis of merit; that we really are able to determine who is the "best" candidate; that we really do promote and reward our present colleagues on the basis of "academic excellence." Some of us, however, are beginning to recognize or acknowledge publicly that our assumption of a functioning meritocracy may be a myth.

49. 774 F.2d 1 (1st Cir.1985), cert. denied 475 U.S. 1097, 106 S.Ct. 1496, 89 L.Ed.2d 896 (1986).

50. Id. at 2, 10.

51. 1991 WL 490015, 59 Fair Empl. Prac. Cas. (BNA) 113 (D.Haw. 1991), reversed in part 40 F.3d 1551 (9th Cir.1994).

52. 59 F.E.P. Cas. 113 at 117, 120.

53. 935 F.2d 974 (8th Cir.1991).

54. Id. at 980–81 (Heaney, Jr., dissenting).

55. Jackson v. Harvard Univ., 900 F.2d 464, 467 (1st Cir.1990).

56. Fields v. Clark Univ. (Field III), 1991 WL 349620, 59 Fair Empl. Prac. Case. (BNA) 124, 127 (D. Mass. 1991), affirmed 966 F.2d 49 (1st Cir.1992), cert. denied 506 U.S. 1052, 113 S.Ct. 976, 122 L.Ed.2d 130 (1993).

In hiring new faculty, traditional academic criteria of excellence in teaching and research are useful as a sorting function in the search process to winnow down the number of candidates to a relatively short list for any given academic position. Once a list of three or four candidates is created, however, final choices between the top candidates, particularly after the typical two days of interviews with departmental faculty, are based on highly subjective and personally idiosyncratic criteria. Final votes in department meetings reflect highly personal choices.[57] Votes based on how faculty members react to candidates allow for gender, race, and ethnicity to be determining factors in close ballot tallies without conscious awareness on anyone's part. In faculty hiring, our merit system functions as a broad screening device; it does not determine ultimate faculty hires.

The merit system works even worse in the promotion process. In surveys of faculty on the tenure review criteria, many faculty report that the criteria are unclear, inappropriate, or unrealistic. Some faculty also perceive the undue influence of personality traits or conflicts in review systems. Candidates for tenure are in a very precarious position. If there is a factional split in a department, among areas of specialization, over attitudes toward teaching or research, or run-of-the-mill but not infrequent personality conflicts, the tenure candidate will sometimes lose votes based on who her mentor is and/or which faculty colleagues are her friends or enemies. In small departments, alliances formed out of past or current fights among the tenured faculty can determine the vote on a candidate. Sometimes university administrators are aware of these departmental problems and can correct for them. Sometimes they cannot or do not. This is hardly a description of a merit process.

Some will argue that these scenarios only occur occasionally. Those of us who have served in administration know, however, whether or not we voice our concerns, that such problems are all too common. A conspiracy of silence settles over a campus in regard to divisive departments; it seems like we have all agreed to pretend to the outside world that university faculties operate on a rational basis. Furthermore, personal contacts and influence, "who you know," are just as important in the university world as they are in the business world. To be prudent, we must cultivate contacts and influence not only among ourselves on campus, but among those in our fields nationwide. Because letters of outside review take on enormous importance in the tenure and promotion process, it is very important that faculty, particularly senior members of a department, are well-known across the country so they can obtain favorable letters of review for the junior colleagues they want to protect, or the reverse for those they do not.

Yes, our academic world is based, in part, on merit, but also on race, gender, class, and a variety of miscellaneous attributes not related to academic qualifica-

---

57. Professor Julius Getman, in his recent book, In the Company of Scholars, describes faculty meetings from various law schools where he has taught, commenting that faculty hiring meetings are the worst:

Faculty meetings * * * are where the least rational aspects of academic life most frequently arise * * * [F]aculty meetings quickly disabused me of the expectation that reason held sway in academic life. The issues were often petty, the arguments irrational, and the exchanges marked by anger or discontent. * * * On almost all faculties, the most competitive, emotion-laden, acrimonious, lengthy, and pretentious debates are about faculty appointments. Questioning the ability of the candidate is often an indirect way of asserting the speaker's superiority and usually of simultaneously insulting someone currently on the faculty.

Debate at faculty meetings often resembles one-on-one schoolyard basketball more than it does serious academic discussion.

Julius Getman, In the Company of Scholars 91–92 (1992).

tions. For example, Professors Merritt, Reskin, and Fondell found that after controlling for academic credentials, men with unemployed partners were hired by law schools into their first tenure track jobs at two-thirds of a rank higher than single men.[58] [See further discussion of law faculty at p. 1125 infra.]

Many women are particularly sensitive to these aspects of academic life that are not based on merit, but on academic politics, including previous advantages, personal influence, and academic alliances. As outsiders in the academy, women have not been in the best position to use favoritism, prestige, or academic status to advance themselves or others. Furthermore, one study found that even when women know how to play the game of politics in the academy, they may not be willing to participate.[59] These women recognized that their colleagues were consciously manipulating images, "posturing" and "politicking," "all of it heavily disguised with he language of the academic world." Some wanted to believe, however, that a "true" merit system could or should exist in an academic institution and, consequently, they eschewed academic politics to pursue their own "dream" of merit.[60] Many women in academic life have found it disappointing that the academic world is *not* that different from the business world; that their academic results are trivialized by the need to find publication in the right journals or within the right time frame; and that academic research and writing is, in fact, treated like commercial products. It is ironic that many women continue to believe in a true merit system that does not exist, while at the same time, losing out to the game of academic politics, a reality that does exist but which federal courts ignore. If the proper academic language is used, the right committee reports are written, adequate letters of review are solicited, and no high level dean or chancellor is overheard making explicit biased remarks, an academic hire or promotion decision will most likely stand. As long as the academic game is properly played, no one will acknowledge that it is a game at all.

3. The subconscious of bias.

Just as the theory and structure of a Title VII disparate treatment case are too limited to expose illegal bias in a committee decision-making system based on subjective evaluations, Title VII litigation has not been capable of dealing with subconscious racial or gender prejudice. It is difficult to meet the Supreme Court's intent requirement when a large part of the exclusionary behavior of decision-makers is unconscious and therefore "unintentional," the result of unacknowledged bias that is part of the culture in which we live.[61] Much of the gender bias that continues to hamper women's progress in academia is unconscious or

---

58. Deborah Merritt et al., Family, Place, and Career: The Gender Paradox in Law School Hiring, 1993 Wis. L. Rev. 395 (1993), at 432.

59. Nadya Aisenberg & Mona Harrington, Women of Academe: Outsiders in the Sacred Grove (1988) at 51–58.

60. Id. at 54.

61. As Professor Charles Lawrence has written in regard to racial prejudices:

Americans share a common historical and cultural heritage in which racism has played and still plays a dominant role. Because of this shared experience, we also inevitably share many ideas, attitudes, and beliefs that attach significance to an individual's race and induce negative feelings and opinions about nonwhites. To the extent that this

cultural belief system has influenced all of us, we are all racists. At the same time, most of us are unaware of our racism. We do not recognize the ways in which our cultural experience has influenced our beliefs about race or the occasions on which those beliefs affect our actions. In other words, a large part of the behavior that produces racial discrimination is influenced by unconscious racial motivation.

Charles R. Lawrence II, The Id, the Ego and Equal Protection; Reckoning with Unconscious Racism, 39 Stan. L. Rev. 317, 322 n.22 (1987). For his full discussion of the unconscious nature of racial prejudice, see id. at 328–44.

subconscious. Because stereotyped notions about women are so much a part of our society, women as well as men harbor subconscious assumptions about women's lack of ability or professional competence. Yet the requirement imposed by the Court mandating a showing of purposeful discrimination operates to make this unconscious bias invisible.

The intent requirement in discrimination law is one way of maintaining and justifying the present myth of meritocracy. By pretending that discrimination results only from decisions made by people with prejudicial motives, and because most of us think we do not operate with such motives, we can continue to believe that those of us who have succeeded in this system have done so by our own meritorious performance. In Professor Charles Lawrence's view, the intent requirement imposed by the Supreme Court on the constitutional law of equal protection does not serve the interests of blacks, but the interests of white elites, allowing white men in positions of power to theorize that they operate with benign motives. It was the Court's imposition of the intent requirement under the equal protection clause of the Fourteenth Amendment in 1976 which led to its inclusion in Title VII litigation. Just as the intent requirement has been used in constitutional litigation to avoid confronting the problem of unconscious racial prejudice, so it serves to prevent the exposure of subconscious gender or racial bias under employment discrimination law.

* * *

Because Professor West concludes that Title VII litigation for women faculty is so problematic, she proposes alternatives to litigation, focusing on the need to organize women faculty and redirect university policy from within the institution.[62] Specifically, in order to increase the number of women on faculties, she suggests that universities restrict or eliminate their hiring of new faculty with tenure and hire new faculty at the assistant professor level, where the pool of qualified women is greatest.[63] She agrees with Professor Herma Hill Kay that departments must undertake "vigorous and determined searches for qualified candidates"[64] in order to meet voluntary affirmative action goals for faculty hiring or goals set under written affirmative action plans mandated by federal executive order.

The possibilities offered by affirmative action in education will be explored further in Chapter Four, but it is appropriate to note here that at least in one academic setting, the law schools, affirmative action efforts have been successful in recruiting women and minority group faculty members. In presenting the results of the American Bar Foundation's first major study of law teachers, Donna Fossum[65] noted that almost 90 percent of women and minority faculty in law schools entered tenure track teaching after affirmative action programs were instituted.

62. 67 Temple L. Rev. at 155–178.

63. 38% of new faculty hires within the University of California system since 1984 have been hired with tenure at the associate or full professor level. Among American Ph.D. recipients, women accounted for 45% of Americans completing doctoral degrees in 1993. When foreign citizens receiving American Ph. D.s are included, women received 38% of American doctorates in 1993. Delores H. Thurgood & Julie E. Clarke, Summary Report 1993: Doctorate Recipients from U.S. Universities, Table B–2 (1995).

64. Herma Hill Kay, Commentary: The Need for Self–Imposed Quotas in Academic Employment, 1979 Wash. U.L.Q. 137, 138 145 (1979).

65. Fossum, Law Professors: A Profile of the Teaching Branch of the Legal Profession, 1980 A.B.F. Research J. 501, 532–33 (1980).

3. TITLE VII REMEDIES

a. *Introductory Note*

Section 706(g) of Title VII, 42 U.S.C. § 2000e–5(g), permits a court that has made a finding of intentional discrimination to grant injunctive relief and to order affirmative action including, but not limited to, "reinstatement or hiring of employees, with or without back pay * * * or any other equitable relief as the court deems appropriate." Prior to the 1991 amendments, only "equitable," not legal relief, was available under Title VII. Back pay awards are regarded as part of equitable relief.

The Civil Rights Act of 1991 amended the remedy provision of Title VII by adding a new section to Title 42 of the U.S. Code. Section 1981A authorizes the award of legal relief, compensatory and punitive damages, in actions brought under Title VII by "a complaining party" who cannot recover under 42 U.S.C. § 1981, "in addition to any relief authorized by section 706(g) of the Civil Rights Act of 1964 * * *." See p. 1247 in the Statutory Appendix. Compensatory and punitive damages are available only for intentional discrimination, not unlawful discrimination resulting from disparate impact. Damages authorized by this section are capped at $50,000 for employers with more than 14 and fewer than 101 employees; $100,000 for those with more than 100 and fewer than 201 employees; $200,000 for those with more than 200 and fewer than 501 employees; and $300,000 for those with more than 500 employees. Which "complaining parties" are affected by this provision? See discussion of the coverage of section 1981 infra at p. 985. If compensatory or punitive damages are sought under this provision, any party may demand a jury trial, but the jury is not to be informed of the limitations on damages.

Attorney fees are available to a "prevailing party" under Title VII and expert fees may also be included as part of the costs. 42 U.S.C. § 2000e–5(k); section 706(k) of Title VII.

The United States Supreme Court has interpreted Title VII's provision for back pay awards quite liberally, stating in Albemarle Paper Co. v. Moody, 422 U.S. 405, 421, 95 S.Ct. 2362, 2373, 45 L.Ed.2d 280, 298–99 (1975), that

> It follows that, given a finding of unlawful discrimination, backpay should be denied only for reasons which, if applied generally, would not frustrate the central statutory purposes of eradicating discrimination throughout the economy and making persons whole for injuries suffered through past discrimination.

Albemarle's central importance was underscored by a note-writer in 54 N.C.L.R. 196, 202 (1976), who saw the opinion as resolving prior judicial uncertainty

> in favor of a consistently liberal approach toward the award of back pay. Evident throughout the opinion is the proposition that a denial of back pay should be the exception rather than the rule, once a finding of discrimination and economic loss by the discriminatee has been made.

To what extent has *Albemarle* been limited by the Court's subsequent decision in Ford Motor Co. v. EEOC, 458 U.S. 219, 102 S.Ct. 3057, 73 L.Ed.2d 721 (1982), holding that, absent special circumstances, "the ongoing accrual of back pay liability is tolled when a Title VII claimant rejects the job he originally sought"? Id., 458 U.S. at 238–239, 102 S.Ct. at 3069, 73 L.Ed.2d at 737. Judy Gaddis and Rebecca Starr applied for jobs at a Ford parts warehouse in June and July 1971. At that time, Ford had never hired any women to work as "picker-packers" in the warehouse. In January 1973, both women were recalled to their former positions as picker-packers at the GM warehouse. In July 1973, after the EEOC had filed a sex discrimination charge against the company, Ford offered a job, first to Gaddis, then to Starr, without including in its offer seniority retroactive to the date she was rejected in 1971. At trial, Ford's warehouse operations manager testified that he had offered the job because the EEOC claim had been filed and "we wanted to give one of them an opportunity to go to work for us". Id., 458 U.S. at 246 n. 4, 102 S.Ct. at 3073 n. 4, 73 L.Ed.2d at 742 n. 4 (dissenting opinion). (When making the offers, the warehouse manager warned first Gaddis and then Starr she might be subjected to sexual harassment because she would be the first woman in the warehouse. See the Fourth Circuit's opinion, 645 F.2d 183, 193 fn. 10 (4th Cir.1981).) Both women declined the job, as the District Court found, because neither wanted to lose the seniority she had earned at GM and neither wished to be the only woman working in the Ford warehouse. Both women were laid off in 1974 when GM closed its warehouse; neither was able to find work until September 1975, when both entered a government training program for the unemployed. The EEOC filed suit against Ford in July 1975; the District Court found that Ford had discriminated against the women on the basis of their sex and awarded backpay in an amount equal to the difference between the amount they would have earned had they been hired in August 1971 until the date of the court's order in 1977, and the amounts they actually earned or reasonably could have earned between those dates.

The Supreme Court overturned the back pay awards, holding that Ford's liability for backpay terminated when it offered jobs to Gaddis and Starr in July 1973: "[A]n employer charged with unlawful discrimination often can toll the accrual of backpay liability by unconditionally offering the claimant the job he sought and thereby providing him with an opportunity to minimize damages." 458 U.S. at 232. By "unconditional," the Court meant the employer cannot require the employee to settle her claim, but the employee must remain free to pursue her case against the employer in court and seek full relief. How likely a prospect is this?

Justices Blackmun, Brennan and Marshall charged in dissent that the Court's approach permitted employers to make "cheap offers" to victims of discrimination, by extending "offers they cannot reasonably accept." Id., 458 U.S. at 249, 102 S.Ct. at 3075, 73 L.Ed.2d at 744. Do you agree that *Ford Motor Co.* undercuts the "make whole" purpose of Title VII emphasized in *Albemarle?* See also Morris v. American National Can Corporation, 952 F.2d 200 (8th Cir.1991), tolling award of backpay to Jacqueline Morris on her sexual harassment claim after the employer made an unconditional offer of reinstatement. Morris proved that she had been subjected to "ongoing and pervasive acts of sexual harassment" from the time she was hired as a machinist in 1984 to the time she resigned on March 30, 1987. She declined to accept defendant's offer of reinstatement on September 8, 1987 because she did not believe the company's assurances that it would protect her from further sexual harassment. Judge Gibson stated that:

In light of the egregious conduct that occurred here, we sympathize with Morris's statement that she reasonably refused to accept American Can's offer of reinstatement. Nevertheless, a plaintiff's refusal of a reinstatement offer is measured by an objective standard: "Generally, it is the duty of the trier of fact to weigh the evidence to determine whether a reasonable person would refuse the offer of reinstatement." Fiedler [v. Indianhead Truck Line, Inc.,] 670 F.2d [806] at 808 [(8th Cir.1982)]. We have reviewed the correspondence between American Can and Morris regarding the terms of her reinstatement, as well as the testimony of company representatives and we are satisfied that this evidence shows that American Can was sincere in its claim that it was prepared to protect Morris from any further sexual harassment. We also view Morris's ultimate return to her position as evidence that the company was prepared to protect Morris from any further sexual harassment. Although we may have viewed the evidence differently, we cannot conclude that the district court clearly erred in tolling American Can's offer of backpay on September 8, 1987. Anderson v. City of Bessemer City, 470 U.S. 564, 574–75, 105 S.Ct. 1504, 1511–12, 84 L.Ed.2d 518 (1985).

Id., 952 F.2d at 203.

A Title VII plaintiff is expected to minimize the back pay award by diligently seeking other suitable employment, but this duty does not require the plaintiff to remain permanently in an unsuitable job she may have accepted pending litigation. See Sellers v. Delgado Community College, 839 F.2d 1132 (5th Cir.1988), reversing as "clearly erroneous" the trial court's tolling of a back pay award during the periods plaintiff Mary Juanita Sellers worked as a secretary or a "biscuit instructor" because these two jobs were not comparable to her position as defendant's coordinator of public relations.

Identifiable victims of discrimination may also be granted retroactive seniority, see Franks v. Bowman Transportation Co., Inc., 424 U.S. 747, 96 S.Ct. 1251, 47 L.Ed.2d 444 (1976)(rejecting the argument that an award of "competitive" seniority, rather than "benefit" seniority is unfair to other employees). "Competitive" seniority consists of credits used to determine the right, as between employees, to job-related values that cannot be supplied equally to all employees, such as priority in bidding for specific jobs or in resisting lay-off. "Benefit" seniority, on the other hand, consists of credits used in computing fringe benefits, such as pensions, vacation time, and unemployment insurance.

A court may also order affirmative race-conscious relief as a remedy for past discrimination that benefits members of the groups protected by Title VII even if they have not themselves been identified as victims of discrimination; such relief is appropriate where an employer or labor union has engaged in persistent or egregious discrimination. See Local 28, Sheet Metal Workers' International Association v. Equal Employment Opportunity Commission, 478 U.S. 421, 106 S.Ct. 3019, 92 L.Ed.2d 344 (1986)(upholding district court's imposition of a 29% nonwhite membership goal in a case where the union had "consistently and egregiously violated Title VII"). See also United States v. Paradise, 480 U.S. 149, 107 S.Ct. 1053, 94 L.Ed.2d 203 (1987)(district court's order requiring a one-black-for-one-white promotion ratio as an interim measure for state trooper promotions in the Alabama Department of Public Safety did not violate the equal protection clause where Department had engaged in egregious discriminatory conduct that had excluded blacks from all positions). The implementation of race-conscious relief, however, may be a lengthy and frustrating process for all concerned, including the federal judiciary. See United States v. City of Chicago, 894 F.2d 943, 948–49 (7th Cir.1990)(concurring opinion of Judge Easterbrook).

Reinstatement may be a controversial remedy when higher-level jobs are at stake. See the Text Note on Proving Discrimination: Title VII in Academe, at p. 872, supra, for a discussion of tenure as a remedy in academic litigation. Compare EEOC v. Kallir, Philips, Ross, Inc., 420 F.Supp. 919, 926–27 (S.D.N.Y.1976), affirmed 559 F.2d 1203 (2d Cir.1977), certiorari denied 434 U.S. 920, 98 S.Ct. 395, 54 L.Ed.2d 277 (1977), denying reinstatement to female senior account executive with an advertising agency because

> * * * in this case the job from which plaintiff was discharged required a close working relationship between plaintiff and top executives of defendant. It also involved frequent personal contact with defendant's clients, with plaintiff acting as defendant's representative. Lack of complete trust and confidence between plaintiff and defendant could lead to misunderstandings, misrepresentations and mistakes, and could seriously damage defendant's relationship with its clients. The situation here is quite unlike that presented when reinstatement is sought for an assembly line or clerical worker, or even for an executive whose job is not as sensitive for his employer's interests as is plaintiff's job here. The Court is convinced that after three and a half years of bitter litigation the necessary trust and confidence can never exist between plaintiff and defendant. To order reinstatement on the facts of this case would merely be to sow the seeds of future litigation, and would unduly burden the defendant.

But see Sebastian v. Texas Department of Corrections, 541 F.Supp. 970, 976 (S.D.Tex.1982)(ordering plaintiff reinstated in her former position as Administrator of Medical Support Services, restored to her former office, and credited with lost vacation and holiday time; commenting that "[a]ntagonism between parties occurs as the natural bi-product of any litigation * * *. The evidence indicates that the discord, at least in part, was generated by the very fact that plaintiff is a female, that the male counterparts resented her and wanted her out. This is the very reason to reinstate her. Further, any injury done to the harmony of defendants working atmosphere is certainly outweighed by the great harm done to plaintiff in terms of her professional career and her reputation in general."). See Joan D. McMullen, Note, Employment Discrimination Suits by Professionals: Should the Reinstatement Remedy Be Granted? 39 U.Pitt.L.Rev. 103 (1977).

In Hopkins v. Price Waterhouse, 737 F.Supp. 1202 (D.D.C.), affirmed 920 F.2d 967 (D.C.Cir.1990), Judge Gesell ordered that Ann Hopkins be admitted to partnership in the firm, despite his clear recognition that "Price Waterhouse plainly does not want her and would not voluntarily admit her." Id., at

1210–11. In doing so, he reasoned in part that controlling law required that Title VII victims should be made "whole" as near as may be; that Price Waterhouse is a national firm with approximately 900 partners spread over some 90 offices nationwide; and that for non-accountant management consultant partners, such as Ann Hopkins would be, partnership is more like a promotion carrying increased pay and greater opportunity than a recognition of increased status within the firm. Id., at 1209–10. For her part, Ann Hopkins declared herself "tough-minded" and ready to go back to Price Waterhouse's Washington office, where, she noted, many of the people who criticized her are no longer working. New York Times, May 19, 1990, at 7, col. 1.

Front pay is an alternative to reinstatement where hostility or other factors make reinstatement inappropriate. See, e.g., Goss v. Exxon Office Systems Co., 747 F.2d 885, 890 (3d Cir.1984)(affirming order granting front pay to plaintiff, a sales representative for Exxon, who was removed from her lucrative sales territory after she had suffered two miscarriages, but missed only six days of work, because her supervisor had doubts about her ability to combine motherhood and a career); compare Shore v. Federal Express Corp., 777 F.2d 1155, 1160 (6th Cir.1985)(reversing trial court's order awarding plaintiff five years front pay following her discharge when her male supervisor terminated their sexual relationship, and refusing to accept the cost of a college education as a basis for the award, noting that "[t]he front pay award is limited to the amount required to place the plaintiff in the position she would have occupied in the absence of the discrimination. However desirable a college education may be, we cannot impose this cost on the defendant in this case.")

In contrast to Title VII, unlimited damages are available under other statutes that forbid discrimination, such as 42 U.S.C.A. §§ 1981 and 1983, discussed at p. 984, infra. Immediately after the 1991 Civil Rights Act was enacted, Senator Ted Kennedy introduced a bill, The Equal Remedies Act of 1991, S.2062, to remove the caps on damages under Title VII, and make its relief parallel to that available for race discrimination under 42 U.S.C. § 1981. Some state statutes also authorize legal as well as equitable relief. In California, a court may award punitive damages in a civil suit for employment discrimination brought pursuant to the California Fair Employment and Housing Act; see Commodore Home Systems, Inc. v. Superior Court, 32 Cal.3d 211, 185 Cal.Rptr. 270, 649 P.2d 912 (1982).

For further information on remedies, see generally, Barbara Lindemann Schlei & Paul Grossman, Employment Discrimination Law (2d Ed., 1983), Chapters 37–38 (on remedies) and 39 (on attorney's fees).

A more controversial question than the scope of statutory relief has been the issue of what voluntary measures are available to an employer to combat job discrimination in the absence of a court finding of actual discrimination. This question is confronted in the materials that follow.

b. *Voluntary Affirmative Action: Reverse Discrimination Under Title VII?*

JOHNSON v. TRANSPORTATION AGENCY, SANTA CLARA COUNTY

Supreme Court of the United States, 1987.
480 U.S. 616, 107 S.Ct. 1442, 94 L.Ed.2d 615.

JUSTICE BRENNAN delivered the opinion of the Court.

Respondent, Transportation Agency of Santa Clara County, California, unilaterally promulgated an Affirmative Action Plan applicable, *inter alia,* to promotions of employees. In selecting applicants for the promotional position of road dispatcher, the Agency, pursuant to the Plan, passed over petitioner Paul Johnson, a male employee, and promoted a female employee applicant, Diane Joyce. The question for decision is whether in making the promotion the Agency impermissibly took into account the sex of the applicants in violation of Title VII of the Civil Rights Act of 1964, * * * The District Court for the Northern District of California, in an action filed by petitioner following receipt of a right-to-sue letter from the Equal Employment Opportunity Commission (EEOC), held that respondent had violated Title VII. * * * The Court of Appeals for the Ninth Circuit reversed. * * *

We affirm.[2]

I

A

In December 1978, the Santa Clara County Transit District Board of Supervisors adopted an Affirmative Action Plan (Plan) for the County Transportation Agency. The Plan implemented a County Affirmative Action Plan, which had been adopted, declared the County, because "mere prohibition of discriminatory practices is not enough to remedy the effects of past practices and to permit attainment of an equitable representation of minorities, women and handicapped persons." * * * Relevant to this case, the Agency Plan provides that, in making promotions to positions within a traditionally segregated job classification in which women have been significantly underrepresented, the Agency is authorized to consider as one factor the sex of a qualified applicant.

In reviewing the composition of its work force, the Agency noted in its Plan that women were represented in numbers far less than their proportion of the county labor force in both the Agency as a whole and in five of seven job categories. Specifically, while women constituted 36.4% of the area labor market, they composed only 22.4% of Agency employees. Furthermore, women working at the Agency were concentrated largely in EEOC job categories traditionally held by women: women made up 76% of Office and Clerical Workers, but only 7.1% of Agency Officials and Administrators, 8.6%

---

2. No constitutional issue was either raised or addressed in the litigation below. See 748 F.2d 1308, 1310, n. 1 (1984). We therefore decide in this case only the issue of the prohibitory scope of Title VII. Of course, where the issue is properly raised, public employers must justify the adoption and implementation of a voluntary affirmative action plan under the Equal Protection Clause. See *Wygant v. Jackson Board of Education,* 476 U.S. 267, 106 S.Ct. 1842, 90 L.Ed.2d 260 (1986).

of Professionals, 9.7% of Technicians, and 22% of Service and Maintenance workers. As for the job classification relevant to this case, none of the 238 Skilled Craft Worker positions was held by a woman. * * * The Plan noted that this underrepresentation of women in part reflected the fact that women had not traditionally been employed in these positions, and that they had not been strongly motivated to seek training or employment in them "because of the limited opportunities that have existed in the past for them to work in such classifications." * * * The Plan also observed that, while the proportion of ethnic minorities in the Agency as a whole exceeded the proportion of such minorities in the county work force, a smaller percentage of minority employees held management, professional, and technical positions.[4]

The Agency stated that its Plan was intended to achieve "a statistically measurable yearly improvement in hiring, training and promotion of minorities and women throughout the Agency in all major job classifications where they are underrepresented." * * * As a benchmark by which to evaluate progress, the Agency stated that its long-term goal was to attain a work force whose composition reflected the proportion of minorities and women in the area labor force. * * * Thus, for the Skilled Craft category in which the road dispatcher position at issue here was classified, the Agency's aspiration was that eventually about 36% of the jobs would be occupied by women.

The Plan acknowledged that a number of factors might make it unrealistic to rely on the Agency's long-term goals in evaluating the Agency's progress in expanding job opportunities for minorities and women. Among the factors identified were low turnover rates in some classifications, the fact that some jobs involved heavy labor, the small number of positions within some job categories, the limited number of entry positions leading to the Technical and Skilled Craft classifications, and the limited number of minorities and women qualified for positions requiring specialized training and experience. * * * As a result, the Plan counselled that short-range goals be established and annually adjusted to serve as the most realistic guide for actual employment decisions. Among the tasks identified as important in establishing such short-term goals was the acquisition of data "reflecting the ratio of minorities, women and handicapped persons who are working in the local area in major job classifications relating to those utilized by the County Administration," so as to determine the availability of members of such groups who "possess the desired qualifications or potential for placement." * * * These data on qualified group members, along with predictions of position vacancies, were to serve as the basis for "realistic yearly employment goals for women, minorities and handicapped persons in each EEOC job category and major job classification." * * *

The Agency's Plan thus set aside no specific number of positions for minorities or women, but authorized the consideration of ethnicity or sex as a factor when evaluating qualified candidates for jobs in which members of such groups were poorly represented. One such job was the road dispatcher position that is the subject of the dispute in this case.

---

4. While minorities constituted 19.7% of the county labor force, they represented 7.1% of the Agency's Officials and Administrators, 19% of its Professionals, and 16.9% of its Technicians. *Id.*, at 48.

B

On December 12, 1979, the Agency announced a vacancy for the promotional position of road dispatcher in the Agency's Roads Division. Dispatchers assign road crews, equipment, and materials, and maintain records pertaining to road maintenance jobs. * * * The position requires at minimum four years of dispatch or road maintenance work experience for Santa Clara County. The EEOC job classification scheme designates a road dispatcher as a Skilled Craft worker.

Twelve County employees applied for the promotion, including Joyce and Johnson. Joyce had worked for the County since 1970, serving as an account clerk until 1975. She had applied for a road dispatcher position in 1974, but was deemed ineligible because she had not served as a road maintenance worker. In 1975, Joyce transferred from a senior account clerk position to a road maintenance worker position, becoming the first woman to fill such a job. * * * During her four years in that position, she occasionally worked out of class as a road dispatcher.

Petitioner Johnson began with the county in 1967 as a road yard clerk, after private employment that included working as a supervisor and dispatcher. He had also unsuccessfully applied for the road dispatcher opening in 1974. In 1977, his clerical position was downgraded, and he sought and received a transfer to the position of road maintenance worker. * * * He also occasionally worked out of class as a dispatcher while performing that job.

Nine of the applicants, including Joyce and Johnson, were deemed qualified for the job, and were interviewed by a two-person board. Seven of the applicants scored above 70 on this interview, which meant that they were certified as eligible for selection by the appointing authority. The scores awarded ranged from 70 to 80. Johnson was tied for second with score of 75, while Joyce ranked next with a score of 73. A second interview was conducted by three Agency supervisors, who ultimately recommended that Johnson be promoted. Prior to the second interview, Joyce had contacted the County's Affirmative Action Office because she feared that her application might not receive disinterested review.[5] The Office in turn contacted the Agency's Affirmative Action Coordinator, whom the Agency's Plan makes responsible for, *inter alia,* keeping the Director informed of opportunities for the Agency to accomplish its objectives under the Plan. At the time, the Agency employed no women in any Skilled Craft position, and had never

---

5. Joyce testified that she had had disagreements with two of the three members of the second interview panel. One had been her first supervisor when she began work as a road maintenance worker. In performing arduous work in this job, she had not been issued coveralls, although her male co-workers had received them. After ruining her pants, she complained to her supervisor, to no avail. After three other similar incidents, ruining clothes on each occasion, she filed a grievance, and was issued four pair of coveralls the next day. * * * Joyce had dealt with a second member of the panel for a year and a half in her capacity as chair of the Roads Operations Safety Committee, where she and he "had sev-

eral differences of opinion on how safety should be implemented." * * * In addition, Joyce testified that she had informed the person responsible for arranging her second interview that she had a disaster preparedness class on a certain day the following week. By this time about ten days had passed since she had notified this person of her availability, and no date had yet been set for the interview. Within a day or two after this conversation, however, she received a notice setting her interview at a time directly in the middle of her disaster preparedness class. * * * This same panel member had earlier described Joyce as a "rebel-rousing, skirt-wearing person," * * *

employed a woman as a road dispatcher. The Coordinator recommended to the Director of the Agency, James Graebner, that Joyce be promoted.

Graebner, authorized to choose any of the seven persons deemed eligible, thus had the benefit of suggestions by the second interview panel and by the Agency Coordinator in arriving at his decision. After deliberation, Graebner concluded that the promotion should be given to Joyce. As he testified: "I tried to look at the whole picture, the combination of her qualifications and Mr. Johnson's qualifications, their test scores, their expertise, their background, affirmative action matters, things like that * * * I believe it was a combination of all those." * * *

The certification form naming Joyce as the person promoted to the dispatcher position stated that both she and Johnson were rated as well-qualified for the job. The evaluation of Joyce read: "Well qualified by virtue of 18 years of past clerical experience including 3–1/2 years at West Yard plus almost 5 years as a [road maintenance worker]." * * * The evaluation of Johnson was as follows: "Well qualified applicant; two years of [road maintenance worker] experience plus 11 years of Road Yard Clerk. Has had previous outside Dispatch experience but was 13 years ago." * * * Graebner testified that he did not regard as significant the fact that Johnson scored 75 and Joyce 73 when interviewed by the two-person board. * * *

Petitioner Johnson filed a complaint with the EEOC alleging that he had been denied promotion on the basis of sex in violation of Title VII. * * *

II

As a preliminary matter, we note that petitioner bears the burden of establishing the invalidity of the Agency's Plan. Only last term in *Wygant v. Jackson Board of Education,* 476 U.S. 267, 277–278, 106 S.Ct. 1842, 1848, 90 L.Ed.2d 260 (1986), we held that "[t]he ultimate burden remains with the employees to demonstrate the unconstitutionality of an affirmative-action program," and we see no basis for a different rule regarding a plan's alleged violation of Title VII. This case also fits readily within the analytical framework set forth in *McDonnell Douglas Corp. v. Green,* 411 U.S. 792, 93 S.Ct. 1817, 36 L.Ed.2d 668 (1973). Once a plaintiff establishes a prima facie case that race or sex has been taken into account in an employer's employment decision, the burden shifts to the employer to articulate a nondiscriminatory rationale for its decision. The existence of an affirmative action plan provides such a rationale. If such a plan is articulated as the basis for the employer's decision, the burden shifts to the plaintiff to prove that the employer's justification is pretextual and the plan is invalid. As a practical matter, of course, an employer will generally seek to avoid a charge of pretext by presenting evidence in support of its plan. That does not mean, however, as petitioner suggests, that reliance on an affirmative action plan is to be treated as an affirmative defense requiring the employer to carry the burden of proving the validity of the plan. The burden of proving its invalidity remains on the plaintiff.

The assessment of the legality of the Agency Plan must be guided by our decision in [*Steelworkers v. Weber,* 443 U.S. 193, 99 S.Ct. 2721, 61 L.Ed.2d 480 (1979)] *supra.*[6] In that case, the Court addressed the question whether the

---

6. The dissent maintains that the obligations of a public employer under Title VII   must be identical to its obligations under the Constitution, and that a public employer's

employer violated Title VII by adopting a voluntary affirmative action plan designed to "eliminate manifest racial imbalances in traditionally segregated job categories." *Id.,* 443 U.S., at 197, 99 S.Ct. at 2724. The respondent employee in that case challenged the employer's denial of his application for a position in a newly established craft training program, contending that the employer's selection process impermissibly took into account the race of the applicants. The selection process was guided by an affirmative action plan, which provided that 50% of the new trainees were to be black until the percentage of black skilled craftworkers in the employer's plant approximated the percentage of blacks in the local labor force. Adoption of the plan had been prompted by the fact that only 5 of 273, or 1.83%, of skilled craftworkers at the plant were black, even though the work force in the area was approximately 39% black. Because of the historical exclusion of blacks from craft positions, the employer regarded its former policy of hiring trained outsiders as inadequate to redress the imbalance in its work force.

We upheld the employer's decision to select less senior black applicants over the white respondent, for we found that taking race into account was consistent with Title VII's objective of "break[ing] down old patterns of racial segregation and hierarchy." *Id.,* at 208, 99 S.Ct., at 2730. As we stated:

> "It would be ironic indeed if a law triggered by a Nation's concern over centuries of racial injustice and intended to improve the lot of those who had 'been excluded from the American dream for so long' constituted the first legislative prohibition of all voluntary, private, race-conscious efforts to abolish traditional patterns of racial segregation and hierar-

adoption of an affirmative action plan therefore should be governed by *Wygant.* This rests on the following logic: Title VI embodies the same constraints as the Constitution; Title VI and Title VII have the same prohibitory scope; therefore, Title VII and the Constitution are coterminous for purposes of this case. The flaw is with the second step of the analysis, for it advances a proposition that we explicitly considered and rejected in *Weber.* As we noted in that case, Title VI was an exercise of federal power "over a matter in which the Federal Government was already directly involved," since Congress "was legislating to assure federal funds would not be used in an improper manner." 443 U.S., at 206 n. 6, 99 S.Ct., at 2729 n. 6. "Title VII, by contrast, was enacted pursuant to the commerce power to regulate purely private decisionmaking and was not intended to incorporate and particularize the commands of the Fifth and Fourteenth Amendments. Title VII and Title VI, therefore, cannot be read *in pari materia.*" *Ibid.* This point is underscored by Congress' concern that the receipt of any form of financial assistance might render an employer subject to the commands of Title VI rather than Title VII. As a result, Congress added § 604 to Title VI, 42 U.S.C. § 2000d–3, which provides:

"Nothing contained in this subchapter shall be construed to authorize action under this subchapter by any department or agency with respect to any employment practice of any employer, employment agency, or labor organization except where a primary objective of the Federal financial assistance is to provide employment."

The sponsor of this section, Senator Cooper, stated that it was designed to clarify that "it was not intended that [T]itle VI would impinge on [T]itle VII." 110 Cong.Rec. 11615 (1964).

While public employers were not added to the definition of "employer" in Title VII until 1972, there is no evidence that this mere addition to the definitional section of the statute was intended to transform the substantive standard governing employer conduct. Indeed, "Congress expressly indicated the intent that the same Title VII principles be applied to governmental and private employers alike." *Dothard v. Rawlinson,* 433 U.S. 321, 332 n. 14, 97 S.Ct. 2720, 2728 n. 14, 53 L.Ed.2d 786 (1977). The fact that a public employer must also satisfy the Constitution does not negate the fact that the *statutory* prohibition with which that employer must contend was not intended to extend as far as that of the Constitution.

chy." *Id.*, at 204, 99 S.Ct., at 2728 (quoting remarks of Sen. Humphrey, 110 Cong.Rec. 6552 (1964)).[7]

We noted that the plan did not "unnecessarily trammel the interests of the white employees," since it did not require "the discharge of white workers and their replacement with new black hirees." *Ibid.* Nor did the plan create "an absolute bar to the advancement of white employees," since half of those trained in the new program were to be white. *Ibid.* Finally, we observed that the plan was a temporary measure, not designed to maintain racial balance, but to "eliminate a manifest racial imbalance." *Ibid.* As Justice Blackmun's concurrence made clear, *Weber* held that an employer seeking to justify the adoption of a plan need not point to its own prior discriminatory practices, nor even to evidence of an "arguable violation" on its part. *Id.*, at 212, 99 S.Ct., at 2731. Rather, it need point only to a "conspicuous * * * imbalance in traditionally segregated job categories." *Id.*, at 209, 99 S.Ct., at 2730. Our decision was grounded in the recognition that voluntary employer action can play a crucial role in furthering Title VII's purpose of eliminating the effects of discrimination in the workplace, and that Title VII should not be read to thwart such efforts. *Id.*, at 204, 99 S.Ct. at 2727–28.[8]

---

7. The dissent maintains that *Weber*'s conclusion that Title VII does not prohibit voluntary affirmative action programs "rewrote the statute it purported to construe." * * * *Weber*'s decisive rejection of the argument that the "plain language" of the statute prohibits affirmative action rested on (1) legislative history indicating Congress' clear intention that employers play a major role in eliminating the vestiges of discrimination, 443 U.S., at 201–204, 99 S.Ct., at 2726–28, and (2) the language and legislative history of § 703(j) of the statute, which reflect a strong desire to preserve managerial prerogatives so that they might be utilized for this purpose. *Id.*, at 204–207, 99 S.Ct. at 2727–29. As Justice Blackmun said in his concurrence in *Weber*, "[I]f the Court has misperceived the political will, it has the assurance that because the question is statutory Congress may set a different course if it so chooses." *Id.*, at 216, 99 S.Ct., at 2734. Congress has not amended the statute to reject our construction, nor have any such amendments even been proposed, and we therefore may assume that our interpretation was correct.

The dissent faults the fact that we take note of the absence of Congressional efforts to amend the statute to nullify *Weber*. It suggests that Congressional inaction cannot be regarded as acquiescence under all circumstances, but then draws from that unexceptional point the conclusion that *any* reliance on Congressional failure to act is necessarily a "canard." * * * The fact that inaction may not always provide crystalline revelation, however, should not obscure the fact that it may be probative to varying degrees. *Weber*, for instance, was a widely-publicized decision that addressed a prominent issue of public debate. Legislative inattention thus is not a plausible explanation for Congressional inaction. Fur-

thermore, Congress not only passed no contrary legislation in the wake of *Weber*, but not one legislator even proposed a bill to do so. The barriers of the legislative process therefore also seem a poor explanation for failure to act. By contrast, when Congress has been displeased with our interpretation of Title VII, it has not hesitated to amend the statute to tell us so. For instance, when Congress passed the Pregnancy Discrimination Act of 1978, 42 U.S.C. § 2000e(k), "it unambiguously expressed its disapproval of both the holding and the reasoning of the Court in [*General Electric v. Gilbert*, 429 U.S. 125, 97 S.Ct. 401, 50 L.Ed.2d 343 (1976)]." *Newport News Shipbuilding & Dry Dock v. EEOC*, 462 U.S. 669, 678, 103 S.Ct. 2622, 2628, 77 L.Ed.2d 89 (1983). Surely, it is appropriate to find some probative value in such radically different Congressional reactions to this Court's interpretations of the same statute.

As one scholar has put it, "When a court says to a legislature: 'You (or your predecessor) meant X,' it almost invites the legislature to answer: 'We did not.' " G. Calabresi, A Common Law for the Age of Statutes 31–32 (1982). Any belief in the notion of a dialogue between the judiciary and the legislature must acknowledge that on occasion an invitation declined is as significant as one accepted.

8. See also *Firefighters v. Cleveland*, 478 U.S. 501, 515, 106 S.Ct. 3063, 3072, 92 L.Ed.2d 405 (1986)("We have on numerous occasions recognized that Congress intended for voluntary compliance to be the preferred means of achieving the objectives of Title VII"); *Alexander v. Gardner–Denver*, 415 U.S. 36, 44, 94 S.Ct. 1011, 1017, 39 L.Ed.2d 147 (1974)("Cooperation and voluntary compliance were selected as the preferred means for achieving [Title

In reviewing the employment decision at issue in this case, we must first examine whether that decision was made pursuant to a plan prompted by concerns similar to those of the employer in *Weber*. Next, we must determine whether the effect of the plan on males and non-minorities is comparable to the effect of the plan in that case.

The first issue is therefore whether consideration of the sex of applicants for skilled craft jobs was justified by the existence of a "manifest imbalance" that reflected underrepresentation of women in "traditionally segregated job categories." *Id.*, at 197, 99 S.Ct., at 2724. In determining whether an imbalance exists that would justify taking sex or race into account, a comparison of the percentage of minorities or women in the employer's work force with the percentage in the area labor market or general population is appropriate in analyzing jobs that require no special expertise, see *Teamsters v. United States*, 431 U.S. 324, 97 S.Ct. 1843, 52 L.Ed.2d 396 (1977)(comparison between percentage of blacks in employer's work force and in general population proper in determining extent of imbalance in truck driving positions), or training programs designed to provide expertise, see *Weber, supra* (comparison between proportion of blacks working at plant and proportion of blacks in area labor force appropriate in calculating imbalance for purpose of establishing preferential admission to craft training program). Where a job requires special training, however, the comparison should be with those in the labor force who possess the relevant qualifications. See *Hazelwood School District v. United States*, 433 U.S. 299, 97 S.Ct. 2736, 53 L.Ed.2d 768 (1977)(must compare percentage of blacks in employer's work ranks with percentage of qualified black teachers in area labor force in determining underrepresentation in teaching positions). The requirement that the "manifest imbalance" relate to a "traditionally segregated job category" provides assurance both that sex or race will be taken into account in a manner consistent with Title VII's purpose of eliminating the effects of employment

VII's] goal"). The dissent's suggestion that an affirmative action program may be adopted only to redress an employer's past discrimination * * * was rejected in *Steelworkers v. Weber*, 443 U.S. 193, 99 S.Ct. 2721, 61 L.Ed.2d 480 (1979), because the prospect of liability created by such an admission would create a significant disincentive for voluntary action. As Justice Blackmun's concurrence in that case pointed out, such a standard would "plac[e] voluntary compliance with Title VII in profound jeopardy. The only way for the employer and the union to keep their footing on the 'tightrope' it creates would be to eschew all forms of voluntary affirmative action." 443 U.S., at 210, 99 S.Ct., at 2731. Similarly, Justice O'Connor has observed in the constitutional context that "[t]he imposition of a requirement that public employers make findings that they have engaged in illegal discrimination before they engage in affirmative action programs would severely undermine public employers' incentive to meet voluntarily their civil rights obligations." *Wygant, supra*, at 290, 106 S.Ct., at 1855 (O'Connor, J., concurring in part and concurring in the judgment).

Contrary to the dissent's contention, * * * our decisions last term in *Firefighters, supra*, and *Sheet Metal Workers v. EEOC*, 478 U.S. 421, 106 S.Ct. 3019, 92 L.Ed.2d 344 (1986), provide no support for a standard more restrictive than that enunciated in *Weber*. *Firefighters* raised the issue of the conditions under which parties could enter into a consent decree providing for explicit numerical quotas. By contrast, the affirmative action plan in this case sets aside no positions for minorities or women. * * * In *Sheet Metal Workers*, the issue we addressed was the scope of judicial remedial authority under Title VII, authority that has not been exercised in this case. The dissent's suggestion that employers should be able to do no more voluntarily than courts can order as remedies * * * ignores the fundamental difference between volitional private behavior and the exercise of coercion by the state. Plainly, "Congress' concern that federal courts not impose unwanted obligations on employers and unions," *Firefighters, supra*, 478 U.S., at 524, 106 S.Ct., at 3077, reflects a desire to preserve a relatively large domain for voluntary employer action.

discrimination, and that the interests of those employees not benefitting from the plan will not be unduly infringed.

A manifest imbalance need not be such that it would support a prima facie case against the employer, as suggested in Justice O'Connor's concurrence, *post,* since we do not regard as identical the constraints of Title VII and the federal constitution on voluntarily adopted affirmative action plans. Application of the "prima facie" standard in Title VII cases would be inconsistent with *Weber*'s focus on statistical imbalance,[10] and could inappropriately create a significant disincentive for employers to adopt an affirmative action plan. See *Weber, supra,* 443 U.S., at 204, 99 S.Ct., at 2727–28 (Title VII intended as a "catalyst" for employer efforts to eliminate vestiges of discrimination). A corporation concerned with maximizing return on investment, for instance, is hardly likely to adopt a plan if in order to do so it must compile evidence that could be used to subject it to a colorable Title VII suit.[11]

It is clear that the decision to hire Joyce was made pursuant to an Agency plan that directed that sex or race be taken into account for the purpose of remedying underrepresentation. The Agency Plan acknowledged the "limited opportunities that have existed in the past," * * *, for women to find employment in certain job classifications "where women have not been traditionally employed in significant numbers."[12] * * * As a result, observed

10. The difference between the "manifest imbalance" and "prima facie" standards is illuminated by *Weber*. Had the Court in that case been concerned with past discrimination by the employer, it would have focused on discrimination in hiring skilled, not unskilled, workers, since only the scarcity of the former in Kaiser's work force would have made it vulnerable to a Title VII suit. In order to make out a prima facie case on such a claim, a plaintiff would be required to compare the percentage of black skilled workers in the Kaiser work force with the percentage of black skilled craft workers in the area labor market.

Weber obviously did not make such a comparison. Instead, it focused on the disparity between the percentage of black skilled craft workers in Kaiser's ranks and the percentage of blacks in the area labor force. 443 U.S., at 198–199, 99 S.Ct., at 2724–2725. Such an approach reflected a recognition that the proportion of black craft workers in the local labor force was likely as miniscule as the proportion in Kaiser's work force. The Court realized that the lack of imbalance between these figures would mean that employers in precisely those industries in which discrimination has been most effective would be precluded from adopting training programs to increase the percentage of qualified minorities. Thus, in cases such as *Weber,* where the employment decision at issue involves the selection of unskilled persons for a training program, the "manifest imbalance" standard permits comparison with the general labor force. By contrast, the "prima facie" standard would require comparison with the percentage of minorities or women qualified for the job for which the trainees are

being trained, a standard that would have invalidated the plan in *Weber* itself.

11. In some cases, of course, the manifest imbalance may be sufficiently egregious to establish a prima facie case. However, as long as there is a manifest imbalance, an employer may adopt a plan even where the disparity is not so striking, without being required to introduce the non-statistical evidence of past discrimination that would be demanded by the "prima facie" standard. See, *e.g., Teamsters v. United States,* 431 U.S. 324, 339, 97 S.Ct. 1843, 1856, 52 L.Ed.2d 396 (1977)(statistics in pattern and practice case supplemented by testimony regarding employment practices). Of course, when there is sufficient evidence to meet the more stringent "prima facie" standard, be it statistical, non-statistical, or a combination of the two, the employer is free to adopt an affirmative action plan.

12. For instance, the description of the Skilled Craft Worker category, in which the road dispatcher position is located, is as follows:

"Occupations in which workers perform jobs which require special manual skill and a thorough and comprehensive knowledge of the process involved in the work which is acquired through on-the-job training and experience or through apprenticeship or other formal training programs. Includes: mechanics and repairmen; electricians, heavy equipment operators, stationary engineers, skilled machining occupations, carpenters, compositors and typesetters and kindred workers." App. 108.

As the Court of Appeals said in its decision below, "A plethora of proof is hardly necessary

the Plan, women were concentrated in traditionally female jobs in the Agency, and represented a lower percentage in other job classifications than would be expected if such traditional segregation had not occurred. Specifically, 9 of the 10 Para–Professionals and 110 of the 145 Office and Clerical Workers were women. By contrast, women were only 2 of the 28 Officials and Administrators, 5 of the 58 Professionals, 12 of the 124 Technicians, none of the Skilled Craft Workers, and 1—who was Joyce—of the 110 Road Maintenance Workers. * * * The Plan sought to remedy these imbalances through "hiring, training and promotion of * * * women throughout the Agency in all major job classifications where they are underrepresented." * * *

As an initial matter, the Agency adopted as a benchmark for measuring progress in eliminating underrepresentation the long-term goal of a work force that mirrored in its major job classifications the percentage of women in the area labor market.[13] Even as it did so, however, the Agency acknowledged that such a figure could not by itself necessarily justify taking into account the sex of applicants for positions in all job categories. For positions requiring specialized training and experience, the Plan observed that the number of minorities and women "who possess the qualifications required for entry into such job classifications is limited." * * * The Plan therefore directed that annual short-term goals be formulated that would provide a more realistic indication of the degree to which sex should be taken into account in filling particular positions. * * * The Plan stressed that such goals "should not be construed as 'quotas' that must be met," but as reasonable aspirations in correcting the imbalance in the Agency's work force. * * * These goals were to take into account factors such as "turnover, layoffs, lateral transfers, new job openings, retirements and availability of minorities, women and handicapped persons in the area work force who possess the desired qualifications or potential for placement." * * * The Plan specifically directed that, in establishing such goals, the Agency work with the County Planning Department and other sources in attempting to compile data on the percentage of minorities and women in the local labor force that were actually working in the job classifications comprising the Agency work force. From the outset, therefore, the Plan sought annually to develop even more refined measures of the underrepresentation in each job category that required attention.

As the Agency Plan recognized, women were most egregiously underrepresented in the Skilled Craft job category, since *none* of the 238 positions was occupied by a woman. In mid–1980, when Joyce was selected for the road dispatcher position, the Agency was still in the process of refining its short-term goals for Skilled Craft Workers in accordance with the directive of the Plan. This process did not reach fruition until 1982, when the Agency established a short-term goal for that year of three women for the 55 expected openings in that job category—a modest goal of about 6% for that category.

We reject petitioner's argument that, since only the long-term goal was in place for Skilled Craft positions at the time of Joyce's promotion, it was

to show that women are generally underrepresented in such positions and that strong social pressures weigh against their participation." 748 F.2d, at 1313.

13. Because of the employment decision at issue in this case, our discussion henceforth

refers primarily to the Plan's provisions to remedy the underrepresentation of women. Our analysis could apply as well, however, to the provisions of the plan pertaining to minorities.

inappropriate for the Director to take into account affirmative action considerations in filling the road dispatcher position. The Agency's Plan emphasized that the long-term goals were not to be taken as guides for actual hiring decisions, but that supervisors were to consider a host of practical factors in seeking to meet affirmative action objectives, including the fact that in some job categories women were not qualified in numbers comparable to their representation in the labor force.

By contrast, had the Plan simply calculated imbalances in all categories according to the proportion of women in the area labor pool, and then directed that hiring be governed solely by those figures, its validity fairly could be called into question. This is because analysis of a more specialized labor pool normally is necessary in determining underrepresentation in some positions. If a plan failed to take distinctions in qualifications into account in providing guidance for actual employment decisions, it would dictate mere blind hiring by the numbers, for it would hold supervisors to "achievement of a particular percentage of minority employment or membership * * * regardless of circumstances such as economic conditions or the number of qualified minority applicants * * *" *Sheet Metal Workers' v. EEOC,* 478 U.S. 421, 106 S.Ct. 3019, 92 L.Ed.2d 344 (1986)(O'Connor, J., concurring in part and dissenting in part).

The Agency's Plan emphatically did *not* authorize such blind hiring. It expressly directed that numerous factors be taken into account in making hiring decisions, including specifically the qualifications of female applicants for particular jobs. Thus, despite the fact that no precise short-term goal was yet in place for the Skilled Craft category in mid–1980, the Agency's management nevertheless had been clearly instructed that they were not to hire solely by reference to statistics. The fact that only the long-term goal had been established for this category posed no danger that personnel decisions would be made by reflexive adherence to a numerical standard.

Furthermore, in considering the candidates for the road dispatcher position in 1980, the Agency hardly needed to rely on a refined short-term goal to realize that it had a significant problem of underrepresentation that required attention. Given the obvious imbalance in the Skilled Craft category, and given the Agency's commitment to eliminating such imbalances, it was plainly not unreasonable for the Agency to determine that it was appropriate to consider as one factor the sex of Ms. Joyce in making its decision.[14] The promotion of Joyce thus satisfies the first requirement enunciated in *Weber,* since it was undertaken to further an affirmative action plan designed to eliminate Agency work force imbalances in traditionally segregated job categories.

We next consider whether the Agency Plan unnecessarily trammeled the rights of male employees or created an absolute bar to their advancement. In contrast to the plan in *Weber,* which provided that 50% of the positions in the craft training program were exclusively for blacks, and to the consent decree

---

14. In addition, the Agency was mindful of the importance of finally hiring a woman in a job category that had formerly been all-male. The Director testified that, while the promotion of Joyce "made a small dent, for sure, in the numbers," nonetheless "philosophically it made a larger impact in that it probably has encouraged other females and minorities to look at the possibility of so-called 'non-traditional' jobs as areas where they and the agency both have samples of a success story." * * *

upheld last term in *Firefighters v. Cleveland,* 478 U.S. 501, 106 S.Ct. 3063, 92 L.Ed.2d 405 (1986), which required the promotion of specific numbers of minorities, the Plan sets aside no positions for women. The Plan expressly states that "[t]he 'goals' established for each Division should not be construed as 'quotas' that must be met." * * * Rather, the Plan merely authorizes that consideration be given to affirmative action concerns when evaluating qualified applicants. As the Agency Director testified, the sex of Joyce was but one of numerous factors he took into account in arriving at his decision. * * * The Plan thus resembles the "Harvard Plan" approvingly noted by Justice Powell in *University of California Regents v. Bakke,* 438 U.S. 265, 316–319, 98 S.Ct. 2733, 2761–63, 57 L.Ed.2d 750 (1978), which considers race along with other criteria in determining admission to the college. As Justice Powell observed, "In such an admissions program, race or ethnic background may be deemed a 'plus' in a particular applicant's file, yet it does not insulate the individual from comparison with all other candidates for the available seats." *Id.,* at 317, 98 S.Ct., at 2762. Similarly, the Agency Plan requires women to compete with all other qualified applicants. *No* persons are automatically excluded from considerations; *all* are able to have their qualifications weighed against those of other applicants.

In addition, petitioner had no absolute entitlement to the road dispatcher position. Seven of the applicants were classified as qualified and eligible, and the Agency Director was authorized to promote any of the seven. Thus, denial of the promotion unsettled no legitimate firmly rooted expectation on the part of the petitioner. Furthermore, while the petitioner in this case was denied a promotion, he retained his employment with the Agency, at the same salary and with the same seniority, and remained eligible for other promotions.[15]

Finally, the Agency's Plan was intended to *attain* a balanced work force, not to maintain one. The Plan contains ten references to the Agency's desire to "attain" such a balance, but no reference whatsoever to a goal of maintaining it. The Director testified that, while the "broader goal" of affirmative action, defined as "the desire to hire, to promote, to give opportunity and training on an equitable, non-discriminatory basis," is something that is "a permanent part" of "the Agency's operating philosophy," that broader goal "is divorced, if you will, from specific numbers or percentages." Tr. 48–49.

The Agency acknowledged the difficulties that it would confront in remedying the imbalance in its work force, and it anticipated only gradual increases in the representation of minorities and women.[16] It is thus unsur-

---

15. Furthermore, from 1978 to 1982 Skilled Craft jobs in the Agency increased from 238 to 349. The Agency's personnel figures indicate that the Agency fully expected most of these positions to be filled by men. Of the 111 new Skilled Craft jobs during this period, 105, or almost 95%, went to men. As previously noted, the Agency's 1982 Plan set a goal of hiring only three women out of the 55 new Skilled Craft positions projected for that year, a figure of about 6%. While this degree of employment expansion by an employer is by no means essential to a plan's validity, it underscores the fact that the Plan in this case in no way significantly restricts the employment prospects of such persons. Illustrative of this is the fact that an additional road dispatcher position was created in 1983, and petitioner was awarded the job. Brief for Respondent Transportation Agency 36, n. 35.

16. As the Agency Plan stated, after noting the limited number of minorities and women qualified in certain categories, as well as other difficulties in remedying underrepresentation:

"As indicated by the above factors, it will be much easier to attain the Agency's employment goals in some job categories than

prising that the Plan contains no explicit end date, for the Agency's flexible, case-by-case approach was not expected to yield success in a brief period of time. Express assurance that a program is only temporary may be necessary if the program actually sets aside positions according to specific numbers. See, *e.g.*, *Firefighters, supra,* 478 U.S., at 510, 106 S.Ct., at 3069 (four-year duration for consent decree providing for promotion of particular number of minorities); *Weber,* 443 U.S., at 199, 99 S.Ct., at 2725 (plan requiring that blacks constitute 50% of new trainees in effect until percentage of employer work force equal to percentage in local labor force). This is necessary both to minimize the effect of the program on other employees, and to ensure that the plan's goals "[are] not being used simply to achieve and maintain * * * balance, but rather as a benchmark against which" the employer may measure its progress in eliminating the underrepresentation of minorities and women. *Sheet Metal Workers, supra,* 478 U.S., at 477–478, 106 S.Ct., at 3051. In this case, however, substantial evidence shows that the Agency has sought to take a moderate, gradual approach to eliminating the imbalance in its work force, one which establishes realistic guidance for employment decisions, and which visits minimal intrusion on the legitimate expectations of other employees. Given this fact, as well as the Agency's express commitment to "attain" a balanced work force, there is ample assurance that the Agency does not seek to use its Plan to maintain a permanent racial and sexual balance.

III

In evaluating the compliance of an affirmative action plan with Title VII's prohibition on discrimination, we must be mindful of "this Court's and Congress' consistent emphasis on 'the value of voluntary efforts to further the objectives of the law.'" *Wygant,* 476 U.S., at 290, 106 S.Ct., at 1855 (O'Connor, J., concurring in part and concurring in judgment)(quoting *Bakke, supra,* 438 U.S., at 364, 98 S.Ct., at 2785–86). The Agency in the case before us has undertaken such a voluntary effort, and has done so in full recognition of both the difficulties and the potential for intrusion on males and non-minorities. The Agency has identified a conspicuous imbalance in job categories traditionally segregated by race and sex. It has made clear from the outset, however, that employment decisions may not be justified solely by reference to this imbalance, but must rest on a multitude of practical, realistic factors. It has therefore committed itself to annual adjustment of goals so as to provide a reasonable guide for actual hiring and promotion decisions. The Agency earmarks no positions for anyone; sex is but one of several factors that may be taken into account in evaluating qualified applicants for a position.[17] As both the Plan's language and its manner of operation attest,

in others. It is particularly evident that it will be extremely difficult to significantly increase the representation of women in technical and skilled craft job classifications where they have traditionally been greatly underrepresented. Similarly, only gradual increases in the representation of women, minorities or handicapped persons in management and professional positions can realistically be expected due to the low turnover that exists in these positions and the small numbers of persons who can be expected to compete for available openings." * * *

17. The dissent predicts that today's decision will loose a flood of "less qualified" minorities and women upon the workforce, as employers seek to forestall possible Title VII liability. The first problem with this projection is that it is by no means certain that employers could in every case necessarily avoid liability for discrimination merely by adopting an affirmative action plan. Indeed, our unwillingness to require an admission of discrimination as the price of adopting a plan has been premised on concern that the potential liability to which such an admission would expose an employer

the Agency has no intention of establishing a work force whose permanent composition is dictated by rigid numerical standards.

We therefore hold that the Agency appropriately took into account as one factor the sex of Diane Joyce in determining that she should be promoted to the road dispatcher position. The decision to do so was made pursuant to an affirmative action plan that represents a moderate, flexible, case-by-case approach to effecting a gradual improvement in the representation of minorities and women in the Agency's work force. Such a plan is fully consistent with Title VII, for it embodies the contribution that voluntary employer action can make in eliminating the vestiges of discrimination in the workplace. Accordingly, the judgment of the Court of Appeals is

Affirmed.

JUSTICE STEVENS, concurring.

While I join the Court's opinion, I write separately to explain my view of this case's position in our evolving antidiscrimination law and to emphasize that the opinion does not establish the permissible outer limits of voluntary programs undertaken by employers to benefit disadvantaged groups.

I

Antidiscrimination measures may benefit protected groups in two distinct ways. As a sword, such measures may confer benefits by specifying that a person's membership in a disadvantaged group must be a neutral, irrelevant factor in governmental or private decisionmaking or, alternatively, by compelling decisionmakers to give favorable consideration to disadvantaged group status. As a shield, an antidiscrimination statute can also help a member of a protected class by assuring decisionmakers in some instances that, when they elect for good reasons of their own to grant a preference of some sort to a minority citizen, they will not violate the law. The Court properly holds that the statutory shield allowed respondent to take Diane Joyce's sex into account in promoting her to the road dispatcher position.

Prior to 1978 the Court construed the Civil Rights Act of 1964 as an absolute blanket prohibition against discrimination which neither required nor permitted discriminatory preferences for any group, minority or majority. The Court unambiguously endorsed the neutral approach, first in the context of gender discrimination and then in the context of racial discrimination against a white person. As I explained in my separate opinion in *University of California Regents v. Bakke,* 438 U.S. 265, 412–418, 98 S.Ct. 2733, 2810–

would serve as a disincentive for creating an affirmative action program. See *supra,* n. 6.

A second, and more fundamental, problem with the dissent's speculation is that it ignores the fact that

"[i]t is a standard tenet of personnel administration that there is rarely a single, 'best qualified' person for a job. An effective personnel system will bring before the selecting official several fully-qualified candidates who each may possess different attributes which recommend them for selection. Especially where the job is an unexceptional, middle-level craft position, without the need for unique work experience or educational at-

tainment and for which several well-qualified candidates are available, final determinations as to which candidate is 'best qualified' are at best subjective." Brief for American Society for Personnel Administration as *Amicus Curiae* 9.

This case provides an example of precisely this point. Any differences in qualifications between Johnson and Joyce were minimal, to say the least. * * * The selection of Joyce thus belies the dissent's contention that the beneficiaries of affirmative action programs will be those employees who are merely not "utterly unqualified." * * *

2813, 57 L.Ed.2d 750 (1978), and as the Court forcefully stated in *McDonald v. Santa Fe Trail Transportation Co.,* 427 U.S. 273, 280, 96 S.Ct. 2574, 2578, 49 L.Ed.2d 493 (1976), Congress intended " 'to eliminate all practices which operate to disadvantage the employment opportunities of any group protected by Title VII including Caucasians.' " (citations omitted). If the Court had adhered to that construction of the Act, petitioner would unquestionably prevail in this case. But it has not done so.

In the *Bakke* case in 1978 and again in *Steelworkers v. Weber,* 443 U.S. 193, 99 S.Ct. 2721, 61 L.Ed.2d 480 (1979), a majority of the Court interpreted the antidiscriminatory strategy of the statute in a fundamentally different way. The Court held in the *Weber* case that an employer's program designed to increase the number of black craftworkers in an aluminum plant did not violate Title VII. It remains clear that the Act does not *require* any employer to grant preferential treatment on the basis of race or gender, but since 1978 the Court has unambiguously interpreted the statute to *permit* the voluntary adoption of special programs to benefit members of the minority groups for whose protection the statute was enacted. Neither the "same standards" language used in *McDonald,* nor the "color blind" rhetoric used by the Senators and Congressmen who enacted the bill, is now controlling. Thus, as was true in *Runyon v. McCrary,* 427 U.S. 160, 189, 96 S.Ct. 2586, 2603, 49 L.Ed.2d 415 (1976)(Stevens, J., concurring), the only problem for me is whether to adhere to an authoritative construction of the Act that is at odds with my understanding of the actual intent of the authors of the legislation. I conclude without hesitation that I must answer that question in the affirmative, just as I did in *Runyon. Id.,* at 191–192, 96 S.Ct., at 2604–05.

Bakke and *Weber* have been decided and are now an important part of the fabric of our law. This consideration is sufficiently compelling for me to adhere to the basic construction of this legislation that the Court adopted in *Bakke* and in *Weber.*

* * *

As construed in *Weber* and in *Firefighters, [v. Cleveland,* 478 U.S. 501, 516, 106 S.Ct. 3063, 3072, 92 L.Ed.2d 405 (1986)]the statute does not absolutely prohibit preferential hiring in favor of minorities; it was merely intended to protect historically disadvantaged groups *against* discrimination and not to hamper managerial efforts to benefit members of disadvantaged groups that are consistent with that paramount purpose. The preference granted by respondent in this case does not violate the statute as so construed; the record amply supports the conclusion that the challenged employment decision served the legitimate purpose of creating diversity in a category of employment that had been almost an exclusive province of males in the past. Respondent's voluntary decision is surely not prohibited by Title VII as construed in *Weber.*

II

Whether a voluntary decision of the kind made by respondent would ever be prohibited by Title VII is a question we need not answer until it is squarely presented. Given the interpretation of the statute the Court adopted in *Weber,* I see no reason why the employer has any duty, prior to granting a preference to a qualified minority employee, to determine whether his past conduct might constitute an arguable violation of Title VII. Indeed, in some instances the employer may find it more helpful to focus on the future. Instead of retroactively scrutinizing his own or society's possible exclusions of minorities in the past to determine the outer limits of a valid affirmative-action program—or indeed, any particular affirmative-action decision—in many cases the employer will find it more appropriate to consider other legitimate reasons to give preferences to members of underrepresented groups. Statutes enacted for the benefit of minority groups should not block these forward-looking considerations.

* * *

The Court today does not foreclose other voluntary decisions based in part on a qualified employee's membership in a disadvantaged group. Accordingly, I concur.

JUSTICE O'CONNOR, concurring in the judgment.

In *Steelworkers v. Weber,* 443 U.S. 193, 99 S.Ct. 2721, 61 L.Ed.2d 480 (1979), this Court held that § 703(d) of Title VII does not prohibit voluntary affirmative action efforts if the employer sought to remedy a "manifest * * * imbalanc[e] in traditionally segregated job categories." *Id.,* at 197, 99 S.Ct., at 2724. As Justice Scalia illuminates with excruciating clarity, § 703 has been interpreted by *Weber* and succeeding cases to permit what its language read literally would prohibit. * * *

None of the parties in this case have suggested that we overrule *Weber* and that question was not raised, briefed, or argued in this Court or in the courts below. If the Court is faithful to its normal prudential restraints and to the principle of *stare decisis* we must address once again the propriety of an affirmative action plan under Title VII in light of our precedents, precedents that have upheld affirmative action in a variety of circumstances. This time the question posed is whether a public employer violates Title VII by promoting a qualified woman rather than a marginally better qualified man when there is a statistical imbalance sufficient to support a claim of a pattern or practice of discrimination against women under Title VII.

I concur in the judgment of the Court in light of our precedents. I write separately, however, because the Court has chosen to follow an expansive and ill-defined approach to voluntary affirmative action by public employers despite the limitations imposed by the Constitution and by the provisions of Title VII, and because the dissent rejects the Court's precedents and addresses the question of how Title VII should be interpreted as if the Court were writing on a clean slate. The former course of action gives insufficient guidance to courts and litigants; the latter course of action serves as a useful point of academic discussion, but fails to reckon with the reality of the course that the majority of the Court has determined to follow.

In my view, the proper initial inquiry in evaluating the legality of an affirmative action plan by a public employer under Title VII is no different from that required by the Equal Protection Clause. In either case, consistent with the congressional intent to provide some measure of protection to the interests of the employer's nonminority employees, the employer must have had a firm basis for believing that remedial action was required. An employer would have such a firm basis if it can point to a statistical disparity sufficient to support a prima facie claim under Title VII by the employee beneficiaries of the affirmative action plan of a pattern or practice claim of discrimination.

In *Weber,* this Court balanced two conflicting concerns in construing § 703(d): Congress' intent to root out invidious discrimination against *any* person on the basis of race or gender, *McDonald v. Santa Fe Transp. Co.,* 427 U.S. 273, 96 S.Ct. 2574, 49 L.Ed.2d 493 (1976), and its goal of eliminating the lasting effects of discrimination against minorities. Given these conflicting concerns, the Court concluded that it would be inconsistent with the background and purpose of Title VII to prohibit affirmative action in all cases. As I read *Weber,* however, the Court also determined that Congress had balanced these two competing concerns by permitting affirmative action only as a remedial device to eliminate actual or apparent discrimination or the lingering effects of this discrimination.

* * *

The *Weber* view of Congress' resolution of the conflicting concerns of minority and nonminority workers in Title VII appears substantially similar to this Court's resolution of these same concerns in *Wygant v. Jackson Board of Education, supra,* which involved the claim that an affirmative action plan by a public employer violated the Equal Protection Clause. In *Wygant,* the Court was in agreement that remedying past or present racial discrimination by a state actor is a sufficiently weighty interest to warrant the remedial use of a carefully constructed affirmative action plan. The Court also concluded, however, that "[s]ocietal discrimination, without more, is too amorphous a basis for imposing a racially classified remedy." *Id.,* at 276, 106 S.Ct., at 1848. Instead, we determined that affirmative action was valid if it was crafted to remedy past or present discrimination by the employer. Although the employer need not point to any contemporaneous findings of actual discrimination, I concluded in *Wygant* that the employer must point to evidence sufficient to establish a firm basis for believing that remedial action is required, and that a statistical imbalance sufficient for a Title VII prima facie case against the employer would satisfy this firm basis requirement:

* * *

Unfortunately, the Court today gives little guidance for what statistical imbalance is sufficient to support an affirmative action plan. Although the Court denies that the statistical imbalance need be sufficient to make out a prima facie case of discrimination against women, * * * the Court fails to suggest an alternative standard. Because both *Wygant* and *Weber* attempt to reconcile the same competing concerns, I see little justification for the adoption of different standards for affirmative action under Title VII and the Equal Protection Clause.

* * * Evidence sufficient for a prima facie Title VII pattern or practice claim against the employer itself suggests that the absence of women or minorities in a work force cannot be explained by general societal discrimination alone and that remedial action is appropriate.

In applying these principles to this case, it is important to pay close attention to both the affirmative action plan, and the manner in which that plan was applied to the specific promotion decision at issue in this case.

* * * At the time the plan was adopted, not one woman was employed in respondents' 238 skilled craft positions, and the plan recognized that women "are not strongly motivated to seek employment in job classifications where they have not been traditionally employed because of the limited opportunities that have existed in the past for them to work in such classifications." * * *

The long-term goal of the plan was "to attain a work force whose composition in all job levels and major job classifications approximates the distribution of women * * * in the Santa Clara County work force." * * * If this long-term goal had been applied to the hiring decisions made by the Agency, in my view, the affirmative action plan would violate Title VII. "[I]t is completely unrealistic to assume that individuals of each [sex] will gravitate with mathematical exactitude to each employer * * * absent unlawful discrimination." *Sheet Metal Workers, supra,* 478 U.S., at 494, 106 S.Ct., at 3060 (O'Connor, J., concurring in part and dissenting in part). Thus, a goal that makes such an assumption, and simplistically focuses on the proportion of women and minorities in the work force without more, is not remedial. Only a goal that takes into account the number of women and minorities qualified for the relevant position could satisfy the requirement that an affirmative action plan be remedial.

* * *

The ultimate decision to promote Joyce rather than petitioner was made by James Graebner, the Director of the Agency. As Justice Scalia views the record in this case, the Agency Director made the decision to promote Joyce rather than petitioner solely on the basis of sex and with indifference to the relative merits of the two applicants. * * * In my view, however, the record simply fails to substantiate the picture painted by Justice Scalia. The Agency Director testified that he "tried to look at the whole picture, the combination of [Joyce's] qualification's and Mr. Johnson's qualifications, their test scores, their experience, their background, affirmative action matters, things like that." * * * Contrary to Justice Scalia's suggestion, * * * the Agency Director knew far more than merely the sex of the candidates and that they appeared on a list of candidates eligible for the job. The Director had spoken to individuals familiar with the qualifications of both applicants for the promotion, and was aware that their scores were rather close. Moreover, he testified that over a period of weeks he had spent several hours making the promotion decision, suggesting that Joyce was not selected solely on the basis of her sex. * * * Additionally, the Director stated that had Joyce's experience been less than that of petitioner by a larger margin, petitioner might have received the promotion. * * * As the Director summarized his decision to promote Joyce, the underrepresentation of women in skilled craft positions was only one element of a number of considerations that led to the promotion of Ms. Joyce. While I agree with the dissent that an affirmative action program that automatically and blindly promotes those marginally qualified candidates falling within a preferred race or gender category, or that can be equated with a permanent plan of "proportionate representation by race and sex" would violate Title VII, I cannot agree that this is such a case. Rather, as the Court demonstrates, Joyce's sex was simply used as a "plus" factor. * * *

In sum, I agree that the respondents' affirmative action plan as implemented in this instance with respect to skilled craft positions satisfies the requirements of *Weber* and of *Wygant*. Accordingly, I concur in the judgment of the Court.

JUSTICE WHITE, dissenting.

I agree with Parts I and II of Justice Scalia's dissenting opinion. Although I do not join Part III, I also would overrule *Weber*. My understanding of *Weber* was, and is, that the employer's plan did not violate Title VII because it was designed to remedy intentional and systematic exclusion of blacks by the employer and the unions from certain job categories. That is how I understood the phrase "traditionally segregated jobs" we used in that case. The Court now interprets it to mean nothing more than a manifest imbalance between one identifiable group and another in an employer's labor force. As so interpreted, that case, as well as today's decision, as Justice Scalia so well demonstrates, is a perversion of Title VII. I would overrule *Weber* and reverse the judgment below.

JUSTICE SCALIA, with whom THE CHIEF JUSTICE joins, and with whom JUSTICE WHITE joins in Parts I and II, dissenting.

With a clarity which, had it not proven so unavailing, one might well recommend as a model of statutory draftsmanship, Title VII of the Civil Rights Act of 1964 declares:

"It shall be an unlawful employment practice for an employer—

"(1) to fail or refuse to hire or to discharge any individual, or otherwise to discriminate against any individual with respect to his compensation, terms, conditions, or privileges of employment, because of such individual's race, color, religion, sex, or national origin; or

"(2) to limit, segregate, or classify his employees or applicants for employment in any way which would deprive or tend to deprive any individual of employment opportunities or otherwise adversely affect his status as an employee, because of such individual's race, color, religion, sex, or national origin." 42 U.S.C. § 2000e–2(a).

The Court today completes the process of converting this from a guarantee that race or sex will *not* be the basis for employment determinations, to a guarantee that it often *will*. Ever so subtly, without even alluding to the last obstacles preserved by earlier opinions that we now push out of our path, we effectively replace the goal of a discrimination-free society with the quite incompatible goal of proportionate representation by race and by sex in the workplace. Part I of this dissent will describe the nature of the plan that the Court approves, and its effect upon this petitioner. Part II will discuss prior holdings that are tacitly overruled, and prior distinctions that are disregarded. Part III will describe the engine of discrimination we have finally completed.

I

On October 16, 1979, the County of Santa Clara adopted an Affirmative Action Program (County plan) which sought the "attainment of a County work force whose composition * * * includes women, disabled persons and ethnic minorities in a ratio in all job categories that reflects their distribution in the Santa Clara County area work force." * * *

Several salient features of the plan should be noted. Most importantly, the plan's purpose was assuredly not to remedy prior sex discrimination by the Agency. It could not have been, because there was no prior sex discrimination to remedy. The majority, in cataloging the Agency's alleged misdeeds, *ante,* at n. 5, neglects to mention the District Court's finding that the Agency "has not discriminated in the past, and does not discriminate in the present against women in regard to employment opportunities in general and promotions in particular." * * * This finding was not disturbed by the Ninth Circuit.

Not only was the plan not directed at the results of past sex discrimination by the Agency, but its objective was not to achieve the state of affairs that this Court has dubiously assumed would result from an absence of discrimination—an overall work force "more or less representative of the racial and ethnic composition of the population in the community." *Teamsters v. United States,* 431 U.S. 324, 340, n. 20, 97 S.Ct. 1843, 1856, n. 20, 52 L.Ed.2d 396 (1977). Rather, the oft-stated goal was to mirror the racial and sexual composition of the entire county labor force, not merely in the Agency work force as a whole, but in each and every individual job category at the Agency. In a discrimination-free world, it would obviously be a statistical oddity for every job category to match the racial and sexual composition of even that portion of the county work force *qualified* for that job; it would be utterly miraculous for each of them to match, as the plan expected, the composition of the *entire* work force. Quite obviously, the plan did not seek to replicate what a lack of discrimination would produce, but rather imposed racial and sexual tailoring that would, in defiance of normal expectations and laws of probability, give each protected racial and sexual group a governmentally determined "proper" proportion of each job category.

* * *

The petitioner in the present case, Paul E. Johnson, had been an employee of the Agency since 1967, coming there from a private company where he had been a road dispatcher for seventeen years. He had first applied for the position of Road Dispatcher at the Agency in 1974, coming in second. Several years later, after a reorganization resulted in a downgrading of his Road Yard Clerk II position, in which Johnson "could see no future," * * * he requested and received a voluntary demotion from Road Yard Clerk II to Road Maintenance Worker, to increase his experience and thus improve his chances for future promotion. When the Road Dispatcher job next became vacant, in 1979, he was the leading candidate—and indeed was assigned to work out of class full-time in the vacancy, from September of 1979 until June of 1980. There is no question why he did not get the job.

* * *

After a two-day trial, the District Court concluded that Diane Joyce's gender was *"the determining factor,"* * * * in her selection for the position. Specifically, it found that "[b]ased upon the examination results and the departmental interview, [Mr. Johnson] was more qualified for the position of Road Dispatcher than Diane Joyce," * * * that "[b]ut for [Mr. Johnson's] sex, male, he would have been promoted to the position of Road Dispatcher," * * * and that "[b]ut for Diane Joyce's sex, female, she would not have been appointed to the position * * *". * * * The Ninth Circuit did not reject these factual findings as clearly erroneous, nor could it have done so on the record before us. We are bound by those findings under Federal Rule of Civil Procedure 52(a).

II

The most significant proposition of law established by today's decision is that racial or sexual discrimination is permitted under Title VII when it is intended to overcome the effect, not of the employer's own discrimination, but of societal attitudes that have limited the entry of certain races, or of a particular sex, into certain jobs. Even if the societal attitudes in question consisted exclusively of conscious discrimination by other employers, this holding would contradict a decision of this Court rendered only last Term. *Wygant v. Jackson Board of Education,* 476 U.S. 267, 106 S.Ct. 1842, 90 L.Ed.2d 260 (1986), held that the objective of remedying societal discrimination cannot prevent remedial affirmative action from violating the Equal Protection Clause. * * * While Mr. Johnson does not advance a constitutional claim here, it is most unlikely that Title VII was intended to place a *lesser* restraint on discrimination by public actors than is established by the Constitution. The Court has already held that the prohibitions on discrimination in Title VI, 42 U.S.C. § 2000d, are at least as stringent as those in the Constitution. See *Regents of the University of California v. Bakke,* 438 U.S. 265, 286–287, 98 S.Ct. 2733, 2746–2747, 57 L.Ed.2d 750 (1978)(opinion of Powell, J.)(Title VI embodies constitutional restraints on discrimination); *id.,* at 329–340, 98 S.Ct. at 2768 (opinion of Brennan, White, Marshall, and Blackmun, JJ.) (same); *id.,* at 416, 98 S.Ct., at 2812 (opinion of Stevens, J., joined by Burger, C.J., and Stewart and Rehnquist, JJ.)(Title VI "has independent force, with language and emphasis *in addition to* that found in the Constitution")(emphasis added). There is no good reason to think that Title VII, in this regard, is any different from Title VI. Because, therefore, those justifications (*e.g.,* the remedying of past societal wrongs) that are inadequate to insulate discriminatory action from the racial discrimination prohibitions of the Constitution are also inadequate to insulate it from the racial discrimination prohibitions of Title VII; and because the portions of Title VII at issue here treat race and sex equivalently; *Wygant,* which dealt with race discrimination, is fully applicable precedent, and is squarely inconsistent with today's decision.[4]

* * *

4. Justice O'Connor's concurrence at least makes an attempt to bring this term into accord with last. Under her reading of Title VII, an employer may discriminate affirmatively, so to speak, if he has a "firm basis" for believing that he might be guilty of (nonaffirmative) discrimination under the Act, and if his action is designed to remedy that suspected prior discrimination. * * * This is something of a half-way house between leaving employers scot-free to discriminate against disfavored groups, as the majority opinion does, and prohibiting discrimination, as do the words of Title VII. In the present case, although the District Court found that in fact no sex dis-

crimination existed, Justice O'Connor would find a "firm basis" for the agency's *belief* that sex discrimination existed in the "inexorable zero": the complete absence, prior to Diane Joyce, of any women in the Agency's skilled positions. There are two problems with this: First, even posting a "firm basis" for the Agency's belief in prior discrimination, as I have discussed above the plan was patently not *designed to remedy* that prior discrimination, but rather to establish a sexually representative work force. Second, even an absolute zero is not "inexorable." While it may inexorably provide "firm basis" for belief in the mind of an outside observer, it cannot conclusively es-

In fact, however, today's decision goes well beyond merely allowing racial or sexual discrimination in order to eliminate the effects of prior societal *discrimination*. The majority opinion often uses the phrase "traditionally segregated job category" to describe the evil against which the plan is legitimately (according to the majority) directed. As originally used in *Steelworkers v. Weber*, 443 U.S. 193, 99 S.Ct. 2721, 61 L.Ed.2d 480 (1979), that phrase described skilled jobs from which employers and unions had systematically and intentionally excluded black workers—traditionally segregated jobs, that is, in the sense of conscious, exclusionary discrimination. See *id.*, at 197–198, 99 S.Ct., at 2724–2725. But that is assuredly not the sense in which the phrase is used here. It is absurd to think that the nationwide failure of road maintenance crews, for example, to achieve the Agency's ambition of 36.4% female representation is attributable primarily, if even substantially, to systematic exclusion of women eager to shoulder pick and shovel. It is a "traditionally segregated job category" *not* in the *Weber* sense, but in the sense that, because of longstanding social attitudes, it has not been regarded *by women themselves* as desirable work. Or as the majority opinion puts the point, quoting approvingly the Court of Appeals: "'A plethora of proof is hardly necessary to show that women are generally underrepresented in such positions and that strong social pressures weigh against their participation.'" * * * Given this meaning of the phrase, it is patently false to say that "[t]he requirement that the 'manifest imbalance' relate to a 'traditionally segregated job category' provides assurance that sex or race will be taken into account in a manner consistent with Title VII's purpose of eliminating the effects of employment discrimination." * * * There are, of course, those who believe that the social attitudes which cause women themselves to avoid certain jobs and to favor others are as nefarious as conscious, exclusionary discrimination. Whether or not that is so (and there is assuredly no consensus on the point equivalent to our national consensus against intentional discrimination), the two phenomena are certainly distinct. And it is the alteration of social attitudes, rather than the elimination of discrimination, which today's decision approves as justification for state-enforced discrimination. This is an enormous expansion, undertaken without the slightest justification or analysis.

III

I have omitted from the foregoing discussion the most obvious respect in which today's decision o'erleaps, without analysis, a barrier that was thought still to be overcome. In *Weber*, this Court held that a private-sector affirmative-action training program that overtly discriminated against white applicants did not violate Title VII. However, although the majority does not advert to the fact, until today the applicability of *Weber* to public employers remained an open question. * * * This distinction between public and private employers has several possible justifications. *Weber* rested in part on the assertion that the 88th Congress did not wish to intrude too deeply into

tablish such a belief *on the employer's part,* since he may be aware of the particular reasons that account for the zero. That is quite likely to be the case here, given the nature of the jobs we are talking about, and the list of *"Factors Hindering Goal Attainment"* recited by the Agency plan. * * * The question is in any event one of fact, which, if it were indeed relevant to the outcome, would require a remand to the District Court rather than an affirmance.

private employment decisions. * * * Whatever validity that assertion may have with respect to private employers (and I think it negligible), it has none with respect to public employers or to the 92d Congress that brought them within Title VII. * * * Another reason for limiting *Weber* to private employers is that state agencies, unlike private actors, are subject to the Fourteenth Amendment. As noted earlier, it would be strange to construe Title VII to permit discrimination by public actors that the Constitution forbids.

In truth, however, the language of 42 U.S.C. § 2000e–2 draws no distinction between private and public employers, and the only good reason for creating such a distinction would be to limit the damage of *Weber*. It would be better, in my view, to acknowledge that case as fully applicable precedent, and to use the Fourteenth Amendment ramifications—which *Weber* did not address and which are implicated for the first time here—as the occasion for reconsidering and overruling it. It is well to keep in mind just how thoroughly *Weber* rewrote the statute it purported to construe. * * * *Weber* disregarded the text of the statute, invoking instead its " 'spirit,' " * * * and "practical and equitable [considerations] only partially perceived, if perceived at all, by the 88th Congress," 443 U.S., at 209, 99 S.Ct., at 2730 (Blackmun, J., concurring). It concluded, on the basis of these intangible guides, that Title VII's prohibition of intentional discrimination on the basis of race and sex does not prohibit intentional discrimination on the basis of race and sex, so long as it is "designed to break down old patterns of racial [or sexual] segregation and hierarchy," "does not unnecessarily trammel the interests of the white [or male] employees," "does not require the discharge of white [or male] workers and their replacement with new black [or female] hirees," "does [not] create an absolute bar to the advancement of white [or male] employees," and "is a temporary measure * * * not intended to maintain racial [or sexual] balance, but simply to eliminate a manifest racial [or sexual] imbalance." * * * In effect, *Weber* held that the legality of intentional discrimination by private employers against certain disfavored groups or individuals is to be judged not by Title VII but by a judicially crafted code of conduct, the contours of which are determined by no discernible standard, aside from (as the dissent convincingly demonstrated) the divination of congressional "purposes" belied by the face of the statute and by its legislative history. We have been recasting that self-promulgated code of conduct ever since—and what it has led us to today adds to the reasons for abandoning it.

* * *

JUSTICE STEVENS' concurring opinion emphasizes "the underlying public interest in 'stability and orderly development of the law,' " * * * that often requires adherence to an erroneous decision. As I have described above, however, today's decision is a demonstration not of stability and order but of the instability and unpredictable expansion which the substitution of judicial improvisation for statutory text has produced. For a number of reasons, *stare decisis* ought not to save *Weber*. First, this Court has applied the doctrine of *stare decisis* to civil rights statutes less rigorously than to other laws. See *Maine v. Thiboutot*, 448 U.S. 1, 33, 100 S.Ct. 2502, 2519, 65 L.Ed.2d 555 (1980)(Powell, J., dissenting); *Monroe v. Pape, supra*, 365 U.S., at 221–222, 81 S.Ct., at 502–503 (Frankfurter, J., dissenting in part). Second, as Justice

Stevens acknowledges in his concurrence, * * * *Weber* was itself a dramatic departure from the Court's prior Title VII precedents, and can scarcely be said to be "so consistent with the warp and woof of civil rights law as to be beyond question." *Monell v. New York City Dept. of Social Services, supra,* 436 U.S., at 696, 98 S.Ct., at 2039. Third, *Weber* was decided a mere seven years ago, and has provided little guidance to persons seeking to conform their conduct to the law, beyond the proposition that Title VII does not mean what it says. Finally, "even under the most stringent test for the propriety of overruling a statutory decision * * *—'that it appear beyond doubt * * * that [the decision] misapprehended the meaning of the controlling provision,'" 436 U.S., at 700, 98 S.Ct., at 2040 (quoting *Monroe v. Pape,* 365 U.S., at 192, 81 S.Ct., at 486–87 (Harlan, J., concurring)), *Weber* should be overruled.

In addition to complying with the commands of the statute, abandoning *Weber* would have the desirable side-effect of eliminating the requirement of willing suspension of disbelief that is currently a credential for reading our opinions in the affirmative action field—from *Weber* itself, which demanded belief that the corporate employer adopted the affirmative action program "voluntarily," rather than under practical compulsion from government contracting agencies, see 443 U.S., at 204, 99 S.Ct., at 2727–28; to *Bakke,* a Title VI case cited as authority by the majority here, * * * which demanded belief that the University of California took race into account as merely one of the many diversities to which it felt it was educationally important to expose its medical students, see 438 U.S., at 311–315, 98 S.Ct., at 2759–61, to today's opinion, which—in the face of a plan obviously designed to force promoting officials to prefer candidates from the favored racial and sexual classes, warning them that their "personal commitment" will be determined by how successfully they "attain" certain numerical goals, and in the face of a particular promotion awarded to the less qualified applicant by an official who "did little or nothing" to inquire into sources "critical" to determining the final candidates' relative qualifications other than their sex—in the face of all this, demands belief that we are dealing here with no more than a program that "merely authorizes that consideration be given to affirmative action concerns when evaluating qualified applicants." * * * Any line of decisions rooted so firmly in naivete must be wrong.

The majority emphasizes, as though it is meaningful, that "*No* persons are automatically excluded from consideration; *all* are able to have their qualifications weighed against those of other applicants." * * * One is reminded of the exchange from Shakespeare's King Henry the Fourth, Part I: "GLENDOWER: I can call Spirits from the vasty Deep. HOTSPUR: Why, so can I, or so can any man. But will they come when you do call for them?" Act III, Scene I, lines 53–55. Johnson was indeed entitled to have his qualifications weighed against those of other applicants—but more to the point, he was virtually assured that, after the weighing, if there was any minimally qualified applicant from one of the favored groups, he would be rejected.

Similarly hollow is the Court's assurance that we would strike this plan down if it "failed to take distinctions in qualifications into account," because that "would dictate mere blind hiring by the numbers." * * * For what the Court means by "taking distinctions in qualifications into account" consists of no more than eliminating from the applicant pool those who are not even *minimally qualified* for the job. Once that has been done, once the promoting officer assures himself that all the candidates before him are "M.Q.s" (minimally qualifieds), he can then ignore, as the Agency Director did here, how much better than minimally qualified some of the candidates may be, and can proceed to appoint from the pool solely on the basis of race or sex, until the affirmative action "goals" have been reached. The requirement that the employer "take distinctions in qualifications into account" thus turns out to be an assurance, not that candidates' comparative merits will always be considered, but only that none of the successful candidates selected over the others solely on the basis of their race or sex will be utterly unqualified. That may be of great comfort to those concerned with American productivity; and it is undoubtedly effective in reducing the effect of affirmative-action discrimination upon those in the upper strata of society, who (unlike road maintenance workers, for example) compete for employment in professional and semiprofessional fields where, for many reasons, including most notably the effects of past discrimination, the numbers of "M.Q." applicants from the favored groups are substantially less. But I fail to see how it has any relevance to whether selecting among final candidates solely on the basis of race or sex is permissible under Title VII, which prohibits discrimination on the basis of race or sex.[5]

Today's decision does more, however, than merely reaffirm *Weber,* and more than merely extend it to public actors. It is impossible not to be aware that the practical effect of our holding is to accomplish *de facto* what the law—in language even plainer than that ignored in *Weber,* see 42 U.S.C. § 2000e–2(j)—forbids anyone from accomplishing *de jure:* in many contexts it effectively *requires* employers, public as well as private, to engage in intentional discrimination on the basis of race or sex. This Court's prior interpretations of Title VII, especially the decision in *Griggs v. Duke Power Co.,* 401 U.S. 424, 91 S.Ct. 849, 28 L.Ed.2d 158 (1971), subject employers to a potential Title VII suit whenever there is a noticeable imbalance in the representation of minorities or women in the employer's work force. Even the employer who is confident of ultimately prevailing in such a suit must contemplate the expense and adverse publicity of a trial, because the extent of the imbalance, and the "job relatedness" of his selection criteria, are questions of fact to be explored through rebuttal and counter-rebuttal of a "prima facie case" consisting of no more than the showing that the employer's selection process "selects those from the protected class at a 'significantly' lesser rate than their counterparts." B. Schlei & P. Grossman, Employment Discrimination Law 91 (2d ed. 1983). If, however, employers are free to discriminate through affirmative action, without fear of "reverse discrimination" suits by their nonminority or male victims, they are offered a threshold defense against

---

5. In a footnote purporting to respond to this dissent's (nonexistent) "predict[ion]" that today's decision will loose a flood of 'less qualified' minorities and women upon the workforce," * * * the majority accepts the contention of the American Society for Personnel Administration that there is no way to determine who is the best qualified candidate for a job such as Road Dispatcher. This effectively constitutes appellate reversal of a finding of fact by the District Court in the present case ("plaintiff was more qualified for the position of Road Dispatcher than Diane Joyce," App. to Pet. for Cert. 12a). More importantly, it has staggering implications for future Title VII litigation, since the most common reason advanced for failing to hire a member of a protected group is the superior qualification of the hired individual. I am confident, however, that the Court considers this argument no more enduring than I do.

Title VII liability premised on numerical disparities. Thus, after today's decision the *failure* to engage in reverse discrimination is economic folly, and arguably a breach of duty to shareholders or taxpayers, wherever the cost of anticipated Title VII litigation exceeds the cost of hiring less capable (though still minimally capable) workers. (This situation is more likely to obtain, of course, with respect to the least skilled jobs—perversely creating an incentive to discriminate against precisely those members of the nonfavored groups *least* likely to have profited from societal discrimination in the past.) It is predictable, moreover, that this incentive will be greatly magnified by economic pressures brought to bear by government contracting agencies upon employers who refuse to discriminate in the fashion we have now approved. A statute designed to establish a color-blind and gender-blind workplace has thus been converted into a powerful engine of racism and sexism, not merely *permitting* intentional race- and sex-based discrimination, but often making it, through operation of the legal system, practically compelled.

It is unlikely that today's result will be displeasing to politically elected officials, to whom it provides the means of quickly accommodating the demands of organized groups to achieve concrete, numerical improvement in the economic status of particular constituencies. Nor will it displease the world of corporate and governmental employers (many of whom have filed briefs as *amici* in the present case, all on the side of Santa Clara) for whom the cost of hiring less qualified workers is often substantially less—and infinitely more predictable—than the cost of litigating Title VII cases and of seeking to convince federal agencies by nonnumerical means that no discrimination exists. In fact, the only losers in the process are the Johnsons of the country, for whom Title VII has been not merely repealed but actually inverted. The irony is that these individuals—predominantly unknown, unaffluent, unorganized—suffer this injustice at the hands of a Court fond of thinking itself the champion of the politically impotent. I dissent.

Notes on Johnson

1. As you can infer from the opinions in *Johnson,* the Court was sharply divided in United Steelworkers of America v. Weber, 443 U.S. 193, 99 S.Ct. 2721, 61 L.Ed.2d 480 (1979), the case that upheld Kaiser Aluminum's voluntary affirmative action plan undertaken as part of its collective bargaining agreement with the Steelworkers. Justice Brennan, for the majority, and then-Justice Rehnquist, dissenting, offered conflicting views of the legislative history to sustain their opposite positions. Professor Boyd thinks both accounts left something to be desired:

> A conclusion that Congress intended title VII to bar such racially preferential plans as that adopted by Kaiser does seem more compelling than the Brennan majority admits. Although the Court's decision in *McDonald* [v. Santa Fe Trail Transp. Co., 427 U.S. 273, 96 S.Ct. 2574, 49 L.Ed.2d 493 (1976)] explicitly reserved the issue of the effect of title VII upon affirmative action plans, it clearly held that the statute protects white as well as black employees. Moreover, Congress was concerned about the impact of racial preferences on both blacks and whites; it certainly was not oblivious to the problem of potential discrimination against whites. Consequently, the majority's argument is less than flawless. On the other hand, the dissenters' criticisms are probably overstated.

William E. Boyd, Affirmative Action in Employment—The *Weber* Decision, 66 Iowa L.Rev. 1, 7 (1980). See also George Schatzki, United Steelworkers of America v. Weber: An Exercise in Understandable Indecision, 56 Wash.L.Rev. 51, 66–67 (1980)("In my judgment, both the majority and the dissent missed the mark. The truth is, I believe, whether or not the members of Congress thought of voluntary affirmative action, they did not discuss the issue. That being so, it is difficult for me to understand how either the majority or the dissent found much solace in the history.").

Other observers are less equivocal. Barbara Lerner, for example, thinks that "[t]he *Weber* decision is a gross and blatant refusal by the Court to enforce the legislative will." Lerner, Employment Discrimination: Adverse Impact, Validity, and Equality, 1979 Supreme Court Review 17, 45 (1980).

2. Commentators speculated about the circumstances under which a private employer might implement a voluntary affirmative action plan after *Weber*. Professor Boyd proposed this formulation:

> Voluntary private affirmative action undertaken by an employer in collaboration with a union is not barred by title VII even where the plan is racially preferential, indeed even if the preference is accomplished through the device of a quota, so long as the plan is directed to eliminating conspicuous racial imbalance in traditionally segregated job categories.

Boyd, supra Note 1, at 9. Was this statement unduly cautious? Did *Johnson* show that *Weber* is not limited to plans jointly negotiated between labor and management? What job categories are "traditionally" segregated? Boyd suggests that the term be used descriptively, not analytically, to mean "historically true." This interpretation would apply *Weber* to cases where the disparity among workers in a given job category is conspicuous and persistent—in other words, to societal discrimination. Boyd, id., at 10–17. Since *Weber* allowed the use of an explicit quota, Boyd concludes that voluntary remedial quotas aimed at eliminating past societal discrimination are valid, at least where they do not involve the discharge of white workers or create an absolute bar to their advancement, and are temporary in duration—all characteristics of the Kaiser plan. Are these limitations essential? What impact does *Johnson* have on Boyd's analysis?

3. Should Justice Brennan have explained in *Johnson* why he thought *Weber* applied to affirmative action plans designed to benefit women? Commenting on *Weber*, Professor Edmund Kitch noted that the legislative "spirit" invoked by the majority arose from a congressional purpose to end race discrimination, not discrimination directed against other groups. He nevertheless concluded that the logic of the *Weber* opinion would result in its application to all the proscribed classifications under Title VII. Kitch, The Return of Color–Consciousness to the Constitution: Weber, Dayton, and Columbus, 1979 Supreme Court Review 1, 5 (1980). He did not appear entirely pleased with the prospect:

> Indeed, one could imagine that under the Court's logic, the statute may be converted into a pervasive dispersion program. In any occupation where a group has been underrepresented, the statute would permit affirmative action to increase that group's representation. Thus affirmative action for men would be appropriate in the flight attendant, telephone operator, and elementary school teacher classifications, while affirmative action for women would be appropriate in the airlines maintenance, line repairman, and university teaching fields. Affirmative action for blacks would be appropriate in crafts, professional, and management fields, while affirmative action for whites would be appropriate for urban hotel services, urban bus drivers, parts of the

postal service, and so on.   But it would be difficult to reconcile such a
sweeping program of social dispersion with the Court's emphasis in *Weber* on
blacks as special beneficiaries of the statutory program.

Id., at 6.   Compare Boyd, supra Note 1, at 52–58.   On what basis could the Court
restrict affirmative action to only one of the groups protected by Title VII?   The
legislative history accompanying the Equal Employment Opportunity Act of 1972
expressly indicated that the eradication of sex discrimination carries a priority
equal to that of eliminating other forms of discrimination.   See H.R.Rep. No. 92–
238, 92nd Cong., 2d Sess. 2, reprinted in [1972] U.S.Code, Cong. & Ad.News 2137,
2141: "Discrimination against women is no less serious than other forms of
prohibited employment practices and is to be accorded the same degree of social
concern given to any type of unlawful discrimination."   Do all members of the
Court share that view?

4. *Johnson* settles one question left open in *Weber*: whether a public
employer would violate Title VII by adopting a voluntary affirmative action plan.
It did not settle another question: whether such action would be unconstitutional.
As Justice Brennan points out in footnote 2 to his opinion, the parties in *Johnson*
did not raise the constitutional question.   How should that question be decided?
Rutherglen and Ortiz argue that the relevant distinction is not between constitu-
tional and statutory claims of reverse discrimination, but rather between volun-
tary and court-ordered preferences.   See George Rutherglen & Daniel R. Ortiz,
Affirmative Action Under the Constitution and Title VII: From Confusion to
Convergence, 35 U.C.L.A. L.Rev. 467 (1988).

Writing before the decision in *Johnson,* Dean Jesse H. Choper speculated
about the position held by each individual Justice.   See Choper, Continued
Uncertainty as to the Constitutionality of Remedial Racial Classifications: Identi-
fying the Pieces of the Puzzle, 72 Iowa L.Rev. 255, 271–74 (1987).   Now that
Justice Powell has been replaced by Justice Kennedy, has the uncertainty been
increased or decreased?   See also the two comments on Choper's paper by former
Solicitor General Rex E. Lee, Missing Pieces: A Commentary on Choper, 72 Iowa
L.Rev. 275 (1987), and Dean Paul Brest, Affirmative Action and the Constitution:
Three Theories, 72 Iowa L.Rev. 281 (1987).

Beginning in 1989, the Court has acted to limit the use of affirmative action
plans, focusing on statutory affirmative action requirements in awarding governmental contracts.   For the first time, a majority of the United States Supreme
Court held in City of Richmond v. J.A. Croson Co., 488 U.S. 469, 109 S.Ct. 706,
102 L.Ed.2d 854 (1989) that affirmative action plans creating set-asides favoring
minority business enterprises promulgated by states or their political subdivisions
must be tested under the Equal Protection Clause by a strict scrutiny standard,
rather than an intermediate standard.   A 6–3 majority, including Justice Stevens,
voted to invalidate the Richmond plan, which mandated a 30% set-aside favoring
minority business enterprises in city-awarded construction contracts for businesses owned and controlled by "citizens of the United States who are Blacks,
Spanish-speaking, Orientals, Indians, Eskimos, or Aleuts."   Only Chief Justice
Rehnquist and Justice White joined Part II of Justice O'Connor's plurality opinion
explaining why a strict scrutiny standard was appropriate to measure set-asides
established by states and municipalities, but not to test similar plans adopted by
the United States Congress.   Both Justices Kennedy and Scalia, however, separately indicated their agreement with the use of a strict scrutiny standard.
Justice Kennedy would limit the standard to racial preferences, while Justice
Scalia would apply it to all race-based governmental classification.   Justice Mar-

shall, joined in dissent by Justices Brennan and Blackmun, restated his belief that an intermediate standard was the appropriate vehicle for testing race-conscious classifications designed to further remedial goals. Professor Michel Rosenfeld argues that the "seeming order emerging from *Croson's* embrace of the strict scrutiny test" is achieved only by a process of "decontextualization" that leaves in place "the same turmoil and uncertainty that have previously thwarted the Court's efforts to overcome conflict and fragmentation." Michael Rosenfeld, Decoding *Richmond:* Affirmative Action and the Elusive Meaning of Constitutional Equality, 87 Mich.L.Rev. 1729, 1732 (1989).

In 1995, in Adarand Constructors, Inc. v. Pena, 515 U.S. ___, 115 S.Ct., 2097, 132 L.Ed.2d 158 (1995) a new majority on the Supreme Court extended *Croson* and applied the strict scrutiny standard to a federal government contracting provision giving prime contractors a monetary incentive to subcontract with "socially and economically disadvantaged" small businesses. Small businesses, 51% owned by Black Americans, Hispanic Americans, Asian Americans, or Native Americans were presumed to be disadvantaged under the federal Small Business Act, 15 U.S.C. §§ 637(d)(2),(3). In applying a strict scrutiny standard under the Fifth Amendment to a federal minority set-aside provision, a majority of the Court questioned or overruled two prior opinions upholding federal contracting provisions under more lenient standards. In Fullilove v. Klutznick, 448 U.S. 448, 100 S.Ct. 2758, 65 L.Ed.2d 902 (1980), the Court had previously ruled that a 10% set-aside for minority owned businesses was a "limited use of racial and ethnic criteria," and, in the context presented, was a permissible means for achieving legislative objectives with the power of Congress. Similarly, in 1990, a year after *Croson* and on a 5 to 4 vote, the Court ruled in Metro Broadcasting, Inc. v. FCC, 497 U.S. 547, 110 S.Ct. 2997, 111 L.Ed.2d 445 (1990), that "benign" federal racial classifications need only satisfy intermediate scrutiny, were constitutionally permissible if they served important governmental objectives within the power of Congress, and were substantially related to achievement of those objectives. The *Adarand* Court found the *Fullilove* and *Metro Broadcasting* results at odds with a long history of congruence between the equal protection obligations of the Fourteenth and Fifth Amendments:

> Accordingly, we hold today that all racial classifications, imposed by whatever federal, state, or local governmental actor, must be analyzed by a reviewing court under strict scrutiny. In other words, such classifications are constitutional only if they are narrowly tailored measures that further compelling governmental interests.

115 S.Ct. at 2113. The Court remanded the case to the lower courts to determine if the presumption of disadvantage based on race or ethnicity was, in fact, a narrowly tailored provision supported by a compelling governmental interest, commenting "We wish to dispel the notion that strict scrutiny is 'strict in theory, but fatal in fact.'" Id. at 2117. *Adarand* involved a racial classification. What will the Court do with a sex-based classification setting aside a certain percentage of government contracts for women-owned businesses? See Subsection D for further discussion of the government contracting issues, *Croson* and *Adarand* at pp. 994, 1005 infra.

5. Those who question the use of affirmative action plans or preferences to redress past societal discrimination object that it is unfair to require the present members—themselves blameless of discriminatory conduct—of groups favored in prior years to pay the cost of social reparations through their own loss of

employment and academic opportunities. See Kitch, supra Note 3, at 12–13, who queries,

> [w]ill those who are asked to step aside for the benefit of blacks not harbor ill will against them? Will this not be a particular problem for the young, who, having grown up on this side of the civil rights revolution, disassociate themselves from the racism of the old America, and may be surprised to learn that they are asked to pay for it?

The point is pressed especially strongly by Professor (now Justice) Scalia, who notes the existence of

> many white ethnic groups that came to this country in great numbers relatively late in its history—Italians, Jews, Irish, Poles—who not only took no part in, and derived no profit from, the major historic suppression of the currently acknowledged minority groups, but were, in fact, themselves the object of discrimination by the dominant Anglo–Saxon majority. * * * Yet curiously enough, we find that in the system of restorative justice established by the Wisdoms and the Powells and the Whites, it is precisely *these* groups that do most of the restoring. It is they who, to a disproportionate degree, are the competitors with the urban blacks and Hispanics for jobs, housing, education—all those things that enable one to scramble to the top of the social heap where one can speak eloquently (and quite safely) of restorative justice.

Antonin Scalia, The Disease as Cure, 1979 Wash.U.L.Q. 147, 152. Is there a satisfactory response to these objections? See J. Skelly Wright, Color–Blind Theories and Color–Conscious Remedies, 47 U.Chi.L.Rev. 231 (1980); Harry T. Edwards, Preferential Remedies and Affirmative Action in Employment in the Wake of *Bakke,* 1979 Wash.U.L.Q. 113, 133–35.

> Professor Robert Sedler does not rest his case for racial preferences on the need to make reparations for past societal discrimination or on a desire to ensure that each minority group receive a proportional share of society's benefits. Rather, he suggests

> that there is a strong societal interest in the equal participation of blacks in all aspects of American life, and that this being so, the government can give racial preference to advance this interest, even though by doing so it causes "racial detriment" to individual whites.

Sedler, Racial Preference and the Constitution: The Societal Interest in the Equal Participation Objective, 26 Wayne L.Rev. 1227, 1236 (1980). See also Kathleen M. Sullivan, The Supreme Court 1985 Term, Comment: Sins of Discrimination: Last Term's Affirmative Action Cases, 100 Harv.L.Rev. 78 (1986), arguing that the Court should uphold affirmative action plans by examining their future potential for promoting a variety of goals dependent on racial balance, ranging from securing workplace peace to eliminating workplace caste. Can this analysis be applied to women?

> Professor Roy Brooks argues powerfully that the public policy of formal equal opportunity established in Brown v. Board of Education, 347 U.S. 483, 74 S.Ct. 686, 98 L.Ed. 873 (1954) has failed to cure the American race problem; he urges the current generation of civil rights scholars and policymakers to fashion a new approach, that will meet three conditions: come to grips with the existence of class stratification in Black society; avoid new forms of racial subordination; and be reconcilable with the existing liberal democratic state. See Brooks, Racial

Subordination Through Formal Equal Opportunity, 25 San Diego L.Rev. 881 (1988).

B. WAGE DISCRIMINATION

1. THE EQUAL PAY ACT OF 1963

[The text of the Act appears in the Statutory Appendix]

a. *Equal Work*

SHULTZ v. WHEATON GLASS CO.

United States Court of Appeals, Third Circuit, 1970.
421 F.2d 259, cert. denied 398 U.S. 905, 90 S.Ct. 1696, 26 L.Ed.2d 64.

FREEDMAN, CIRCUIT JUDGE. This appeal presents important problems in the construction of the Equal Pay Act of 1963 (29 U.S.C.A. § 206(d)), which was added as an amendment to the Fair Labor Standards Act of 1938, (29 U.S.C.A. §§ 201 et seq.).

The Equal Pay Act prohibits an employer from discriminating "between employees on the basis of sex by paying wages to employees * * * at a rate less than the rate at which he pays wages to employees of the opposite sex * * * for equal work on jobs the performance of which requires equal skill, effort, and responsibility, and which are performed under similar working conditions, except where such payment is made pursuant to * * * (IV) a differential based on any other factor other than sex * * *."

Invoking the enforcement provisions of the Fair Labor Standards Act the Secretary of Labor brought this action against Wheaton Glass Co., claiming that it discriminated against its "female selector-packers" on the basis of sex by paying them at an hourly rate of $2.14, which is 10% less than the $2.355 rate it pays to its "male selector-packers." The Secretary sought an injunction against future violations and the recovery of back pay for past violations. The company denied that the female selector-packers perform equal work within the terms of the Act and claimed that in any event the 10% pay differential is within exception (IV) of the Act because it is based on a "factor other than sex."

After an extensive trial the district court entered judgment for the defendant, holding that the Secretary had failed to carry his burden of proving that the wage differential was based upon sex discrimination and that the company had discharged the burden of establishing the exception that the wage differential was based on a factor other than sex. Wirtz v. Wheaton Glass Co., 284 F.Supp. 23 (D.N.J.1968). The Secretary has appealed.

The company is one of the largest manufacturers of glass containers in the United States. Its plant at Millville, New Jersey, which is here involved, is called a "job shop" plant and manufactures glass containers to special order. Unlike the usual modern plants in the glass industry which make standard items in large quantities and employ automatic machinery, the company's job shop operation requires manual handling and visual inspection of the product.

Selector-packers are employed in the Bottle Inspection Department. They work at long tables and visually inspect the bottles for defects as they emerge on a conveyor from the oven, or "lehr." The defective products are discarded into waste containers. Those which meet the specifications are packed in cardboard cartons on a stand within arm's reach of the selector-packers and then lifted onto an adjacent conveyor or rollers and sent off to the Quality Control Department for further examination and processing. In the Bottle Inspection Department is another category of employees known as "snap-up boys," who crate and move bottles and generally function as handymen, sweeping and cleaning and performing other unskilled miscellaneous tasks. They are paid at the hourly rate of $2.16.

Prior to 1956, the company employed only male selector-packers. In that year, however, the shortage of available men in the Millville area forced the company to employ for the first time female selector-packers. On the insistence of the Glass Bottle Blowers Association of the United States and Canada, AFL–CIO, Local 219, with which the company had a collective bargaining agreement, there was, in the language of the district court, "carved out of the total job of selector-packer * * * a new role of female selector-packer." This new classification was written into the collective bargaining agreement, and pursuant to it female selector-packers were not to lift bulky cartons or cartons weighing more than 35 pounds. At the union's insistence a provision was added to the collective bargaining agreement that no male selector-packer was to be replaced by a female selector-packer except to fill a vacancy resulting from retirement, resignation, or dismissal for just cause.

On its face the record presents the incongruity that because male selector-packers spend a relatively small portion of their time doing the work of snap-up boys whose hourly rate of pay is $2.16, they are paid $2.355 per hour for their own work, while female selector-packers receive only $2.14. This immediately casts doubt on any contention that the difference in the work done by male and female selector-packers, which amounts substantially to what the snap-up boys do, is of itself enough to explain the difference in the rate of pay for male and female selector-packers on the grounds other than sex.

The district court explored this difference in some detail. The court found that while male and female selector-packers perform substantially identical work at the ovens, the work of the male selector-packers is substantially different because they perform sixteen additional tasks. These consist of lifting packages weighing more than 35 pounds;[4] lifting cartons which, regardless of weight, are bulky or difficult to handle; stacking full cartons; tying stacks of cartons; moving wooden pallets fully loaded with stacks of cartons; moving and placing empty pallets for later use; operating hand trucks near the ovens; positioning and adjusting portable roller conveyors

---

4. For a discussion of the effect of weight-lifting restrictions under the Equal Pay Act, see H.R.Rep. No. 309, to accompany H.R. 6060, at p. 3, 88th Cong. 1st Sess.1963, p. 687. See also comments of Rep. Thompson of New Jersey, 109 Cong.Rec. 9198 (1963). Weight-lifting restrictions on females similar to those imposed by Wheaton Glass have been held illegal under the Civil Rights Act of 1964, 42 U.S.C.A. § 2000e et seq. Bowe v. Colegate–Palmolive Co., 416 F.2d 711 (7 Cir.1969); Weeks v. Southern Bell Tel. & Tel. Co., 408 F.2d 228 (5 Cir.1969).

and packing stands holding empty cartons for filling; collecting dump trays and tubs of rejected glassware; sweeping and cleaning work areas near the ovens; fitting and attaching metal clips to glass containers at the ovens; unjamming overhead carton conveyors and automatic belts; occasionally reinspecting, repacking and restacking glassware already delivered to the premises of customers; locating glassware in the warehouse, at times involving climbing over palletized cartons; and voluntarily working, when necessary, in excess of ten hours per day or of 54 hours per week.[5] The district court also found that the training period for men was six months, whereas the training period for women was three months.[6]

The district court pointed to evidence submitted by the company that the male selector-packers spent an average of approximately 18 percent of their total time on this work, which was forbidden to women. It made no finding, however, that this was a fact, nor did it make any finding as to what percentage of time was spent by male selector-packers either on the average or individually in performing this different work. Indeed, it made no finding that all male selector-packers performed this extra work, but only that the extra work when not performed by snap-up boys was done by male selector-packers. There is, therefore, no basis for an assumption that all male selector-packers performed any or all of these 16 additional tasks.

Even if there had been a finding that all the male selector-packers performed all of the 16 additional tasks and that these consumed a substantial amount of their time, there would still be lacking an adequate basis for the differential in wages paid to male and female selector-packers. For there would be no rational explanation why men who at times perform work paying two cents per hour more than their female counterparts should for that reason receive 21-1/2 cents per hour more than females for the work they do in common.

The district court, therefore, placed its conclusion on a factor of "flexibility." The company's job shop requires frequent shutdowns of the ovens when a customer's order is completed and before the run of a new order is begun. During such shutdowns the idled female selector-packers are assigned to what is known as the "Resort" area, where they inspect and pack glassware rejected by the Quality Control Inspection Department. Idled male selector-packers are similarly reassigned to the Resort area, but some of them are assigned to do work which otherwise would be done by snap-up boys.

The district court found that this availability of male selector-packers to perform the work of snap-up boys during shutdowns was an element of flexibility and deemed it to be of economic value to the company in the operation of its unique, customized plant. It is on this element of flexibility that the judgment of the district court ultimately rests.

5. It is argued that under New Jersey law, women are barred from working double shifts. But see Wirtz v. Rainbo Baking Co. of Lexington, 303 F.Supp. 1049 (E.D.Ky.1967), holding that such a statutory restriction on the number of hours a female employee can work will not justify payment of lower wages. To the same effect as *Rainbo,* see the applicable regulation, 29 C.F.R. § 800.163.

6. A similar difference in training was recently held not to constitute a defense to a claim of discrimination under the Equal Pay Act. Shultz v. First Victoria National Bank, 420 F.2d 648 (5 Cir.1969).

Under the collective bargaining agreement the company could at any time assign selector-packers to perform the work of snap-up boys, although they would continue to receive their regular rate of pay. While this explains why male selector-packers would not have their pay reduced in performing work of snap-up boys, it does not run the other way and explain why their performance of the work of snap-up boys who receive only two cents per hour more than female selector-packers justifies their being paid 21–1/2 cents per hour more than female selector-packers for performing selector-packer work.

* * *

An even more serious imperfection in the claim of flexibility is the absence, as we have already indicated, of any finding or explanation why availability of men to perform work which pays two cents per hour more than women receive should result in overall payment to men of 21–1/2 cents more than women for their common work. A 10% wage differential is not automatically justified by showing that some advantage exists to the employer because of a flexibility whose extent and economic value is neither measured nor determined and which is attained by the performance of work carrying a much lower rate of pay. In short, there is no finding of the economic value of the element of flexibility on which the district court justified the 10% discrimination in pay rate between male and female selector-packers.

There is, moreover, an additional element of significance with which the district court did not deal. * * * There is an absence of any finding on the ability of any female selector-packers to perform the work of snap-up boys. The fact that some female selector-packers, unlike some male selector-packers, may have been unwilling or unable to do the work of snap-up boys might justify a wage differential between them. But it would still leave open the question why the company did not include under its flexibility requirement the female selector-packers who are both able and willing to do the work of snap-up boys. There may have been some male selector-packers who were unwilling or even incompetent to do the work of snap-up boys. Yet because some of the class was willing and available to do the work of snap-up boys, all of the class received 21–1/2 cents per hour more than all females * * *.

These disparities in rates of pay under which snap-up boys performing physical labor receive a higher rate than female selector-packers while male selector-packers receive a much higher rate because they are available also to do some of the work of snap-up boys, take on an even more discriminatory aspect when viewed in the light of their history. For as the district court indicated, the classification of female selector-packers at the lowest rate of pay of these three categories was made at a time of labor shortage when the company was forced to hire women and the union insisted on conditions which would minimize their future competition against the men with whom they would now be working. The motive, therefore, clearly appears to have been to keep women in a subordinate role rather than to confer flexibility on the company and to emphasize this subordination by both the 10% differential between male and female selector-packers and the two cents difference between snap-up boys and female selector-packers.

The effect of such a motive and the evaluation of the distinction in the work done by male and female selector-packers requires us to turn to the construction of the Equal Pay Act of 1963. The Act was the culmination of many years of striving to eliminate discrimination in pay because of sex. Similar bills were before Congress for many years before the Act ultimately was adopted, and in its final form it bears evidence of the competing tendencies which surrounded its birth. There are problems of construction which leap up from the reading of its language. It has not been authoritatively construed by the Supreme Court and a study of its legislative history and the bills which preceded it yields little guidance in the construction of its provisions in concrete circumstances.

In adopting the Act, Congress chose to specify equal pay for "equal" work. In doing so, Congress was well aware of the experience of the National War Labor Board during World War II and its regulations requiring equal pay for "comparable" work. Under these regulations the National War Labor Board made job evaluations to determine whether inequities existed within a plant even between dissimilar occupations. Since Congress was aware of the Board's policy and chose to require equal pay for "equal" rather than "comparable" work, it is clear that the references in the legislative history to the Board's regulations were only to show the feasibility of administering a federal equal pay policy and do not warrant use of the Board's decisions as guiding principles for the construction of the Equal Pay Act.

On the other hand, Congress in prescribing "equal" work did not require that the jobs be identical, but only that they must be substantially equal. Any other interpretation would destroy the remedial purposes of the Act.

The Act was intended as a broad charter of women's rights in the economic field. It sought to overcome the age-old belief in women's inferiority and to eliminate the depressing effects on living standards of reduced wages for female workers and the economic and social consequences which flow from it.

Differences in job classifications were in general expected to be beyond the coverage of the Equal Pay Act. This was because in the case of genuine job classifications the differences in work necessarily would be substantial and the differences in compensation therefore would be based on the differences in work which justified them. Congress never intended, however, that an artificially created job classification which did not substantially differ from the genuine one could provide an escape for an employer from the operation of the Equal Pay Act.[12] This would be too wide a door through which the content of the Act would disappear.

This view is strengthened by the subsequent adoption of Title VII of the Civil Rights Act of 1964 which prohibits discrimination because of sex in the classification of employees as well as in their employment and compensation. Although the Civil Rights Act is much broader than the Equal Pay Act, its provisions regarding discrimination based on sex are in pari materia with the Equal Pay Act. This is recognized in the provision of § 703(h) of the Civil Rights Act (42 U.S.C.A. § 2000e–2(h)) that an employer's differentiation upon

---

12. The committee report accompanying the final version of the Act stated the effect of its language as it bore on job classification as follows: "This language recognizes that there are many factors which may be used to measure the relationships between jobs and which establish a valid basis for a difference in pay. These factors will be found in a majority of the job classification systems. Thus, it is anticipated that a *bona fide* job classification program *that does not discriminate on the basis of sex* will serve as a valid defense to a charge of discrimination." [Emphasis supplied.] H.R.Rep. No. 309, May 20, 1963.

the basis of sex in determining wages or compensation shall not be an unlawful employment practice under the Civil Rights Act if the differentiation is authorized by the Equal Pay Act. Since both statutes serve the same fundamental purpose against discrimination based on sex, the Equal Pay Act may not be construed in a manner which by virtue of § 703(h) would undermine the Civil Rights Act.

It is not necessary here, however, to delineate the precise manner in which these two statutes must be harmonized to work together in service of the underlying Congressional objective. For even if the Civil Rights Act is put aside, the Equal Pay Act alone does not permit artificial classification to prevent inquiry whether there exists a difference in pay for substantially equal work.

The district court held that the Secretary failed to carry his burden of proof that the company's wage differential is based on sex discrimination. In view of the facts which the district court found, we hold this conclusion to be erroneous. The Secretary met his burden of proof when he showed that male selector-packers received a pay rate 10% higher than female selector-packers although both performed identical work and that the additional work of snap-up boys which male selector-packers also performed was work which carried virtually the same rate of pay as that done by women. When to these circumstances are added the origin of the classification of female selector-packers and their reduced pay even below that paid to snap-up boys, the Secretary clearly established his prima facie case that the wage differential was based on sex and therefore discriminated against women.

Under the statute, the burden of proof thereupon fell on the company to prove its claim that it came within exception (IV). This burden the district court held the company had successfully met.

There is no finding, nor indeed evidence in the record on which a finding could be based, of the economic value of the labor of snap-up boys performed by male selector-packers. Nor is there any finding or evidence from which adequate findings could be made to support the claim that flexibility justifies the 10% wage differential. More significantly, there is nothing in the record to show the amount of any savings which the company effected by being able to use male selector-packers to help out in the work of snap-up boys or that the element of flexibility bore any relation to the 10% wage differential between male and female selector-packers. Nor are there any findings that all members of the class of male selector-packers were able and available to do the work of snap-up boys whereas no members of the class of female selector-packers were so available.

The burden of showing this properly rested on the company, for it invoked the defense that the differential was based on a factor other than sex. In cases such as this, where the justification for the differential rests on economic benefit, the company has peculiarly within its knowledge the means of proof, and the burden therefore is one which cannot be satisfied by general or conclusory assertions.

The district court held that the company met its burden of proving that it came within the exception because "the acceptable proof convincingly demonstrates that the defendant's disparity in wages is based upon factors other than sex * * *." It also stated that "substantial differences exist, in fact, in the full job cycles between the sexes, thereby justifying the disparity in their wages." These, however, are statements of ultimate conclusions for which there is no adequate support either in findings of fact or in the record.

We are, of course, bound by findings of fact unless they are clearly erroneous. Federal Rule of Civil Procedure 52(a). See Speyer, Inc. v. Humble Oil and Refining Co., 403 F.2d 766, 770 (3 Cir.1968). We are not, however, bound by evidence which has not reached the status of a finding of fact, nor by conclusions which are but legal inferences from facts. Baumgartner v. United States, 322 U.S. 665, 670–671, 64 S.Ct. 1240, 88 L.Ed. 1525 (1944); Lehmann v. Acheson, 206 F.2d 592, 594 (3 Cir.1953); and cases cited 2B Barron & Holtzoff, Federal Practice and Procedure § 1137, n. 12 (Wright ed. 1961).

Since the Secretary established his prima facie case and the company failed to prove that the discrimination in wages paid to female selector-packers was based on any factor other than sex, the claim of the Secretary was established and an appropriate judgment should have been entered in his favor.

The judgment of the district court, therefore, will be reversed with direction to enter an appropriate judgment in favor of plaintiff.

Notes on Wheaton Glass

1. *Wheaton Glass* has been regarded as a decision of central importance which immeasurably aided the Government in enforcing the Equal Pay Act. As stated in Thomas E. Murphy, Female Wage Discrimination: A Study of the Equal Pay Act 1963–1970, 39 U.Cin.L.Rev. 615, 626 (1970), the decision

> not only involves a clear holding that "equal" means "substantially equal," and that the performance of certain physical duties by males does not render the jobs unequal, but also involves a more than implicit view that even the additional duties performed by males must, in themselves, require greater skill or responsibility in order to justify a differential. * * *

> * * * [Moreover, the decision completely rejected] generalized male and female characteristics as they relate to job performance or capability.

See also Caruthers G. Berger, Equal Pay, Equal Employment Opportunity and Equal Enforcement of the Law for Women, 5 Val.L.Rev. 326, 339–40 (1971).

2. If it had been shown in *Wheaton Glass* that all the men performed some duties that women did not perform, would the court have had authority under the Act to shift the burden of proof to the employer? Upon what basis does the element of flexibility become a matter for the defense? How would an economic value be assigned to the element of flexibility? See Goodrich v. International Brotherhood of Electrical Workers, AFL–CIO, 815 F.2d 1519 (D.C.Cir.1987), holding that plaintiff Bernice P. Goodrich did not perform equal work to that performed by five male IBEW members who worked with her in the Agreement Approval Department because the men had work responsibilities that extended beyond analyzing agreements and encompassed duties that called on their prior union experience and that the union deemed significant in its ongoing mission.

3. As *Wheaton Glass* demonstrates, the "equal work" component of the Equal Pay Act requires a close comparison of the duties performed by female and male workers. Few guiding principles have emerged to shape this inquiry; as the

Second Circuit put it, "[s]ince job content is a matter determined by the particular employer, whether two job classifications entail 'equal work' under the Act necessarily must be decided on a case-by-case basis," Usery v. Columbia Univ., 568 F.2d 953, 958 (2d Cir.1977). It is not surprising, then, that courts come to different conclusions about whether the equal work requirement has been met in cases involving common job classifications where the traditional assignment of women to the lower paying of two closely similar positions seems clearly based on sex stereotypes. Two different sets of cases, one involving women working as maids and men as janitors, the other concerning nurses' aides and orderlies, offer conflicting results that turn on judicial comparison of the duties assigned. See, e.g., EEOC v. State of Rhode Island, 549 F.Supp. 60, 66 (D.R.I.1982), affirmed 720 F.2d 658 (1st Cir.1983)(female "cleaners" perform essentially the same work as male "janitors"; court notes that "[i]n the style of Gertrude Stein, dusting is dusting is dusting, and though there may be some differences in cleaning tasks and in the use of certain equipment to maintain the various buildings, cleaning is cleaning is cleaning"). Marshall v. Kent State Univ., 589 F.2d 255 (6th Cir.1978)(custodial workers I and custodial workers II performed equal work); Marshall v. Building Maintenance Corp., 587 F.2d 567, 569 (2d Cir.1978)("Additional or different tasks assigned to male employees which require more effort than tasks done in common will justify a pay differential only if the additional tasks consume a significant amount of all of the male employees' time."). Contra, Marshall v. Dallas Indep. Sch. Dist., 605 F.2d 191 (5th Cir.1979), rehearing en banc denied 608 F.2d 1373 (Helpers I, nearly all males, do heavier work and work year-round; Helpers II, all females, do lighter work during school year and do not work during the summers); Marshall v. School Bd., Hermitage Sch. Dist., 599 F.2d 1220 (3d Cir.1979)(work done by maintenance men and cleaning women is not equal, but two women who worked as maintenance men had to be paid at the higher rate); Usery v. Columbia Univ., 568 F.2d 953 (2d Cir.1977)(heavy cleaners, all men, required to exert greater effort on the job than light cleaners, all women).

On nurses' aides and orderlies, see, e.g., Brennan v. South Davis Community Hosp., 538 F.2d 859 (10th Cir.1976)(female aides and male orderlies do equal work); Brennan v. Owensboro–Daviess County Hosp., 523 F.2d 1013 (6th Cir. 1975), cert. denied 425 U.S. 973, 96 S.Ct. 2170, 48 L.Ed.2d 796 (1976)(same); Brennan v. Prince William Hosp. Corp., 503 F.2d 282 (4th Cir.1974), cert. denied 420 U.S. 972, 95 S.Ct. 1392, 43 L.Ed.2d 652 (1975)(same). Contra, Marshall v. St. John Val. Sec. Home, 560 F.2d 12 (1st Cir.1977)(ambulance attendants and orderlies do different work than nurses' aides); Secretary of Labor v. Washington Hosp., 475 F.Supp. 1242 (W.D.Pa.1979), affirmed sub nom. EEOC v. Washington Hosp., 615 F.2d 1353 (3d Cir.1980)(training for male orderlies differs from that given nurses' aides; the men also perform cystoscopies and catheterizations).

4. Does "equal work" refer to the job done or the skills needed to perform it? See Forsberg v. Pacific Northwest Bell Telephone Co., 840 F.2d 1409 (9th Cir.1988), permitting a company to pay its predominantly female Maintenance Administrators less than it previously had paid its predominantly male Test Desk Technicians, even though both groups diagnosed malfunctions in customer telephone lines. While the MAs could rely on computers for the diagnosis, the TDTs had to use their own analytical, "puzzle-solving" skills to get the same job done. The majority was not persuaded that its logic would allow a bus driver operating a vehicle equipped with an automatic transmission to be paid less than a driver using a manual gear shift. Are you?

CORNING GLASS WORKS v. BRENNAN

Supreme Court of the United States, 1974.
417 U.S. 188, 94 S.Ct. 2223, 41 L.Ed.2d 1.

MR. JUSTICE MARSHALL delivered the opinion of the Court.

These cases arise under the Equal Pay Act of 1963, 29 U.S.C.A. § 206(d)(1), which added to the Fair Labor Standards Act the principle of equal pay for equal work regardless of sex. The principal question posed is whether Corning Glass Works violated the Act by paying a higher base wage to male night shift inspectors than it paid to female inspectors performing the same tasks on the day shift, where the higher wage was paid in addition to a separate night shift differential paid to all employees for night work. In No. 73–29, the Court of Appeals for the Second Circuit, in a case involving several Corning plants in Corning, New York, held that this practice violated the Act. 474 F.2d 226 (1973). In No. 73–695, the Court of Appeals for the Third Circuit, in a case involving a Corning plant in Wellsboro, Pennsylvania, reached the opposite conclusion. 480 F.2d 1254 (1973). We granted certiorari and consolidated the cases to resolve this unusually direct conflict between two circuits. 414 U.S. 1110, 94 S.Ct. 839, 38 L.Ed.2d 737. Finding ourselves in substantial agreement with the analysis of the Second Circuit, we affirm in No. 73–29 and reverse in No. 73–695.

I

Prior to 1925, Corning operated its plants in Wellsboro and Corning only during the day, and all inspection work was performed by women. Between 1925 and 1930, the company began to introduce automatic production equipment which made it desirable to institute a night shift. During this period, however, both New York and Pennsylvania law prohibited women from working at night.[2] As a result, in order to fill inspector positions on the new night shift, the company had to recruit male employees from among its male day workers. The male employees so transferred demanded and received wages substantially higher than those paid to women inspectors engaged on the two day shifts.[3] During this same period, however, no plant-wide shift differential existed and male employees working at night, other than inspectors, received the same wages as their day shift counterparts. Thus a situation developed where the night inspectors were all male,[4] the day

---

2. New York prohibited the employment of women between 10 p.m. and 6 a.m. See 1927 N.Y.Laws, c. 453; 1930 N.Y.Laws, c. 868. Pennsylvania prohibited them from working between midnight and 6 a.m. See Act of July 25, 1913, Pub.L. 1024.

3. Higher wages were demanded in part because the men had been earning more money on their day shift jobs than women were paid for inspection work. Thus, at the time of the creation of the new night shift, female day shift inspectors received wages ranging from 20 to 30 cents per hour. Most of the men designated to fill the newly created night shift positions had been working in the blowing room where the lowest wage rate was 48 cents

per hour and where additional incentive pay could be earned. As night shift inspectors these men received 53 cents per hour. There is also some evidence in the record that additional compensation was necessary because the men viewed inspection jobs as "demeaning" and as "women's work."

4. A temporary exception was made during World War II when manpower shortages caused Corning to be permitted to employ women on the steady night shift inspection jobs at both locations. It appears that women night inspectors during this period were paid the same higher night shift wages earned by the men.

inspectors all female, and the male inspectors received significantly higher wages.

In 1944, Corning plants at both locations were organized by a labor union and a collective-bargaining agreement was negotiated for all production and maintenance employees. This agreement for the first time established a plant-wide shift differential,[5] but this change did not eliminate the higher base wage paid to male night inspectors. Rather, the shift differential was superimposed on the existing difference in base wages between male night inspectors and female day inspectors.

Prior to the June 11, 1964, effective date of the Equal Pay Act, the law in both Pennsylvania and New York was amended to permit women to work at night. It was not until some time after the effective date of the Act, however, that Corning initiated efforts to eliminate the differential rates for male and female inspectors. Beginning in June 1966, Corning started to open up jobs on the night shift to women. Previously separate male and female seniority lists were consolidated and women became eligible to exercise their seniority, on the same basis as men, to bid for the higher paid night inspection jobs as vacancies occurred.

On January 20, 1969, a new collective-bargaining agreement went into effect, establishing a new "job evaluation" system for setting wage rates. The new agreement abolished for the future the separate base wages for day and night shift inspectors and imposed a uniform base wage for inspectors exceeding the wage rate for the night shift previously in effect. All inspectors hired after January 20, 1969, were to receive the same base wage, whatever their sex or shift. The collective-bargaining agreement further provided, however, for a higher "red circle" rate for employees hired prior to January 20, 1969, when working as inspectors on the night shift. This "red circle" rate served essentially to perpetuate the differential in base wages between day and night inspectors.

The Secretary of Labor brought these cases to enjoin Corning from violating the Equal Pay Act and to collect back wages allegedly due female employees because of past violations. Three distinct questions are presented: (1) Did Corning ever violate the Equal Pay Act by paying male night shift inspectors more than female day shift inspectors? (2) If so, did Corning cure its violation of the Act in 1966 by permitting women to work as night shift inspectors? (3) Finally, if the violation was not remedied in 1966, did Corning cure its violation in 1969 by equalizing day and night inspector wage rates but establishing higher "red circle" rates for existing employees working on the night shift?

II

Congress' purpose in enacting the Equal Pay Act was to remedy what was perceived to be a serious and endemic problem of employment discrimination in private industry—the fact that the wage structure of "many segments of American industry has been based on an ancient but outmoded belief that a man, because of his role in society, should be paid more than a woman, even

5. The shift differential was originally three cents an hour for the afternoon shift and five cents an hour for the night shift. It has been increased to 10 and 16 cents per hour respectively.

though his duties are the same." S.Rept. No. 176, 88th Cong., 1st Sess. (1963), at 1. The solution adopted was quite simple in principle: to require that "equal work be rewarded by equal wages." Ibid.

* * *

* * * [O]nce the Secretary has carried his burden of showing that the employer pays workers of one sex more than workers of the opposite sex for equal work, the burden shifts to the employer to show that the differential is justified under one of the Act's four exceptions. All of the many lower courts that have considered this question have so held, and this view is consistent with the general rule that the application of an exemption under the Fair Labor Standards Act is a matter of affirmative defense on which the employer has the burden of proof.

The contentions of the parties in this case reflect the Act's underlying framework. Corning argues that the Secretary has failed to prove that Corning ever violated the Act because day shift work is not "performed under similar working conditions" as night shift work. The Secretary maintains that day shift and night shift work are performed under "similar working conditions" within the meaning of the Act. Although the Secretary recognizes that higher wages may be paid for night shift work, the Secretary contends that such a shift differential would be based upon a "factor other than sex" within the catch-all exception to the Act and that Corning has failed to carry its burden of proof that its higher base wage for male night inspectors was in fact based on any factor other than sex.

The courts below relied in part on conflicting statements in the legislative history having some bearing on this question of statutory construction. * * *

The most notable feature of the history of the Equal Pay Act is that Congress recognized early in the legislative process that the concept of equal pay for equal work was more readily stated in principle than reduced to statutory language which would be meaningful to employers and workable across the broad range of industries covered by the Act. As originally introduced, the Equal Pay bills required equal pay for "equal work on jobs the performance of which requires equal skills." There were only two exceptions—for differentials "made pursuant to a seniority or merit increase system which does not discriminate on the basis of sex * * *."

In both the House and Senate committee hearings, witnesses were highly critical of the Act's definition of equal work and of its exemptions. Many noted that most of American industry used formal, systematic job evaluation plans to establish equitable wage structures in their plants. Such systems, as explained coincidentally by a representative of Corning Glass Works who testified at both hearings, took into consideration four separate factors in determining job value—skill, effort, responsibility and working conditions— and each of these four components was further systematically divided into various subcomponents. Under a job evaluation plan, point values are assigned to each of the subcomponents of a given job, resulting in a total point figure representing a relatively objective measure of the job's value.

In comparison to the rather complex job evaluation plans used by industry, the definition of equal work used in the first drafts of the Equal Pay Act was criticized as unduly vague and incomplete. Industry representatives feared that as a result of the Act's definition of equal work, the Secretary of Labor would be cast in the position of second-guessing the validity of a company's job evaluation system. They repeatedly urged that the bill be amended to include an exception for job classification systems, or otherwise to incorporate the language of job evaluation into the bill. Thus Corning's own representative testified:

"Job evaluation is an accepted and tested method of obtaining equity in wage relationship.

"A great part of industry is committed to job evaluation by past practice and by contractual agreement as the basis for wage administration.

" 'Skill' alone, as a criterion, fails to recognize other aspects of the job situation that affect job worth.

"We sincerely hope that this committee in passing language to eliminate wage differences based on sex alone, will recognize in its language the general role of job evaluation in establishing equitable rate relationships."

We think it plain that in amending the Act's definition of equal work to its present form, the Congress acted in direct response to these pleas. * * * Indeed, the most telling evidence of congressional intent is the fact that the Act's amended definition of equal work incorporated the specific language of the job evaluation plan described at the hearings by Corning's own representative—that is, the concepts of "skill," "effort," "responsibility," and "working conditions."

Congress' intent, as manifested in this history, was to use these terms to incorporate into the new federal act the well-defined and well-accepted principles of job evaluation so as to ensure that wage differentials based upon bona fide job evaluation plans would be outside the purview of the Act. * * *

While a layman might well assume that time of day worked reflects one aspect of a job's "working conditions," the term has a different and much more specific meaning in the language of industrial relations. As Corning's own representative testified at the hearings, the element of working conditions encompasses two subfactors: "surroundings" and "hazards." "Surroundings" measure the elements, such as toxic chemicals or fumes, regularly encountered by a worker, their intensity, and their frequency. "Hazards" take into account the physical hazards regularly encountered, their frequency, and the severity of injury they can cause. This definition of "working conditions" is not only manifested in Corning's own job evaluation plans but is also well accepted across a wide range of American industry.

Nowhere in any of these definitions is time of day worked mentioned as a relevant criterion. The fact of the matter is that the concept of "working conditions," as used in the specialized language of job evaluation systems, simply does not encompass shift differentials. Indeed, while Corning now argues that night inspection work is not equal to day inspection work, all of its own job evaluation plans, including the one now in effect, have consistently treated them as equal in all respects, including working conditions. And Corning's Manager of Job Evaluation testified in No. 73–29 that time of day worked was not considered to be a "working condition." Significantly, it is not the Secretary in this case who is trying to look behind Corning's bona fide job evaluation system to require equal pay for jobs which Corning has historically viewed as unequal work. Rather, it is Corning which asks us to differentiate between jobs which the company itself has always equated. We agree with the Second Circuit that the inspection work at issue in this case, whether performed during the day or night, is "equal work" as that term is defined in the Act.

This does not mean, of course, that there is no room in the Equal Pay Act for nondiscriminatory shift differentials. Work on a steady night shift no doubt has psychological and physiological impacts making it less attractive than work on a day shift. The Act contemplates that a male night worker may receive a higher wage than a female day worker, just as it contemplates that a male employee with 20 years seniority can receive a higher wage than a woman with two years seniority. Factors such as these play a role under the Act's four exceptions—the seniority differential under the specific seniority exception, the shift differential under the catch-all exception for differentials "based on any other factor other than sex."

The question remains, however, whether Corning carried its burden of proving that the higher rate paid for night inspection work, until 1966 performed solely by men, was in fact intended to serve as compensation for night work, or rather constituted an added payment based upon sex. We agree that the record amply supported the District Court's conclusion that Corning had not sustained its burden of proof. As its history revealed, "the higher night rate was in large part the product of the generally higher wage level of male workers and the need to compensate them for performing what were regarded as demeaning tasks." 474 F.2d, at 233. The differential in base wages originated at a time when no other night employees received higher pay than corresponding day workers and it was maintained long after the company instituted a separate plant-wide shift differential which was thought to compensate adequately for the additional burdens of night work. The differential arose simply because men would not work at the low rates paid women inspectors, and it reflected a job market in which Corning could pay women less than men for the same work. That the company took advantage of such a situation may be understandable as a matter of economics, but its differential nevertheless became illegal once Congress enacted into law the principle of equal pay for equal work.

III

We now must consider whether Corning continued to remain in violation of the Act after 1966 when, without changing the base wage rates for day and night inspectors, it began to permit women to bid for jobs on the night shift as vacancies occurred. It is evident that this was more than a token gesture to end discrimination, as turnover in the night shift inspection jobs was rapid. The record in No. 73–29 shows, for example, that during the two-year period after June 1, 1966, the date women were first permitted to bid for night inspection jobs, women took 152 of the 278 openings, and women with very little seniority were able to obtain positions on the night shift. Relying on these facts, the company argues that it ceased discriminating against women in 1966, and was no longer in violation of the Equal Pay Act.

But the issue before us is not whether the company, in some abstract sense, can be said to have treated men the same as women after 1966. Rather, the question is whether the company remedied the specific violation of the Act which the Secretary proved.   * * *

The Equal Pay Act is broadly remedial, and it should be construed and applied so as to fulfill the underlying purposes which Congress sought to achieve. If, as the Secretary proved, the work performed by women on the day shift was equal to that performed by men on the night shift, the company became obligated to pay the women the same base wage as their male counterparts on the effective date of the Act. To permit the company to escape that obligation by agreeing to allow some women to work on the night shift at a higher rate of pay as vacancies occurred would frustrate, not serve, Congress' ends. * * *

The company's final contention—that it cured its violation of the Act when a new collective-bargaining agreement went into effect on January 20, 1969—need not detain us long. While the new agreement provided for equal base wages for night or day inspectors hired after that date, it continued to provide unequal base wages for employees hired before that date, a discrimination likely to continue for some time into the future because of a large number of laid-off employees who had to be offered re-employment before new inspectors could be hired. * * * We therefore conclude that on the facts of this case, the company's continued discrimination in base wages between night and day workers, though phrased in terms of a neutral factor other than sex, nevertheless operated to perpetuate the effects of the company's prior illegal practice of paying women less than men for equal work. Cf. Griggs v. Duke Power Co., 401 U.S. 424, 430, 91 S.Ct. 849, 853, 28 L.Ed.2d 158 (1971).

                                   * * *

Mr. Justice Stewart took no part in the consideration or decision of these cases.

The Chief Justice, Mr. Justice Blackmun, and Mr. Justice Rehnquist dissent and would affirm the judgment of the Court of Appeals for the Third Circuit and reverse the judgment of the Court of Appeals for the Second Circuit for the reasons stated by Judge Adams in his opinion for the Court of Appeals in Brennan v. Corning Glass Works, 480 F.2d 1254 (C.A.3).

Notes on Corning Glass

1. Do faculty members who teach in such different fields as Business Administration, English and Humanities, Physical Education, Mathematics, and Psychology have different working conditions? One court has held that the job of teaching in all academic fields requires the same or similar effort and responsibility, and that only those who teach physical education work under dissimilar working conditions. See Marshall v. Georgia Southwestern College, 489 F.Supp. 1322, 1330 (M.D.Ga.1980), affirmed in part and remanded in part 765 F.2d 1026, 1027 (11th Cir.1985)(noting with approval that all of the teachers compared "were within the same academic division, taught students of approximately the same level, * * * and had course loads of approximately fifteen hours per week, with the exception of physical education teachers who carried slightly more hours"). Does that mean that physical education teachers can be paid more or less than teachers who work in academic fields?

2. The Equal Pay Act requires that the work claimed to be equal must be performed within a single "establishment". What does this mean? In Bartelt v. Berlitz School of Languages of America, Inc., 698 F.2d 1003 (9th Cir.1983), certiorari denied 464 U.S. 915, 104 S.Ct. 277, 78 L.Ed.2d 257 (1983), a case brought under both Title VII and the Equal Pay Act, two women directors of Berlitz's schools alleged that they were paid lower salaries, commissions, and bonuses than either former male directors at their respective schools or male directors currently employed at other Berlitz schools. The court agreed that a comparison of the plaintiffs' salaries with those of male directors at other Berlitz schools did not meet the "single establishment" requirement of the Equal Pay Act. It went on to hold, however, that the Supreme Court's interpretation of Title VII's Bennett amendment in County of Washington v. Gunther, 452 U.S. 161, 101 S.Ct. 2242, 68 L.Ed.2d 751 (1981)(set out at p. 949 infra), meant that the "single establishment" requirement was not necessary for a Title VII wage discrimination claim.

3. Does the Equal Pay Act always prohibit reducing the pay of males to that of females as a remedy for inequity in pay? In Cayce v. Adams, 439 F.Supp. 606 (D.D.C.1977), the court found that two employees of the Federal Aviation Administration, one male and the other female, sat at adjoining desks performing substantially equal work, from August 1975 to the female's retirement in December 1976. The male was classified as a GS–11 under the Civil Service System; the female was classified as a GS–9. Efforts by her supervisor to have her reclassified as a GS–11 proved unavailing. A violation of the Equal Pay Act was found to exist since the Civil Service System, a "bona fide classification system" under the Act, had in this instance been improperly applied. Judge Gesell suggested that the disparity could have been terminated by reducing the male to a GS–9. He added in a footnote that this action would not have violated the Equal Pay Act:

> The proper course in this case would have been promptly to downgrade the male GS–11 in accordance with classification standards (although even this might not have prevented a recovery for the interim period). * * * Plaintiff argues that such downgrading to eliminate a disparity would violate the plain language of the proviso to the Equal Pay Act, * * *. The argument is not well taken. In downgrading, the FAA would simply be adhering to the objective dictates of the bona fide classification scheme and thus would be exempt from the operation of the Equal Pay Act. Indeed it is only defendants' failure to reclassify the men down to their proper levels that warrants a finding that the system did not operate in a bona fide manner. Legal arguments aside, it simply cannot be maintained that Congress intended to remedy every sex-based Civil Service misclassification by upgrading all those with the lower grade even when, as here, the classification standards indicate that the lower grade is the correct one. Such a practice would result in widespread grade inflation and thus threaten the integrity of the entire Civil Service system.

Id., 439 F.Supp. at 609 n. 3. Does this opinion mean that, in a University setting where salary is tied to rank and step, disparities between the pay of male and female professors can be remedied by lowering the rank of more highly-paid males? Why not?

EEOC v. MADISON COMM. UNIT SCHOOL DIST. NO. 12

United States Court of Appeals, Seventh Circuit, 1987.
818 F.2d 577.

POSNER, CIRCUIT JUDGE.

The Equal Employment Opportunity Commission brought this suit against the school district of Madison, Illinois, charging that the district was paying female athletic coaches in its high school and junior high school less than male coaches, in violation of the Equal Pay Act of 1963. * * *

The trial brought out the following facts:

Long was paid substantially less for coaching girls' track than Steptoe, a man, was paid for coaching boys' track. Although the boys' track program included more students and had more meets than the girls', Steptoe had two assistant coaches compared to Long's one, and as a result Long and Steptoe devoted approximately equal time to their coaching jobs. Long also coached the girls' tennis team, and Jakich, a man, the boys' tennis team; and Jakich was paid more than Long even though there were no significant differences between the teams in number of students, length of season, or number of practice sessions; however, the boys' team played almost twice as many matches as the girls' team. Long was also assistant coach of the girls' basketball team one year and received lower pay than Tyus, the male assistant coach of the boys' track team. The district judge found that the work of the two assistant coaches was substantially equal and required the same skill, effort, and responsibility—except that Long worked longer hours than Tyus.

Cole, who coached the girls' volleyball, girls' basketball, and girls' softball teams, was paid less for coaching volleyball than the male coach of the boys' soccer team, less for coaching basketball than the male coach of the boys' soccer team, and less for coaching softball than the male coach of the boys' baseball team. Also, as assistant coach of the girls' track team she was paid less than the assistant coach of the boys' track team. In all of these cases the judge found that the work of the female coach and her male counterpart was the same in skill, effort (including time), and responsibility. Any potential differences in effort and responsibility stemming from the fact that the boys' teams were sometimes larger and played longer seasons were, he found, offset by the fact that the head coaches of the boys' teams had more assistants than their female counterparts.

The picture with respect to the other two female coaches on whose behalf the EEOC sued is similar.

The first question we must decide is whether the pairs of jobs that the district judge compared in finding unequal pay are sufficiently similar to be "equal work" within the meaning of the Equal Pay Act. The Act is not a general mandate of sex-neutral compensation. It does not enact "comparable worth"—the principle that wages should be based on "objective" factors, rather than on market conditions of demand and supply which may depress wages in jobs held mainly by women relative to wages in jobs held mainly by men. See *American Nurses' Ass'n v. Illinois*, 783 F.2d 716, 718–20 (7th Cir.1986). [set forth at p. 959, infra] A female secretary paid less than a male janitor cannot complain under the Equal Pay Act that the disparity in their wages is not justified by "objective" factors such as differences in skill, responsibility, and effort. "We do not expect the Labor Department people to go into an establishment and attempt to rate jobs that are not equal. We do not want to hear the Department say, 'Well, they amount to the same thing,' and evaluate them so they come up to the same skill or point. We expect this to apply only to jobs that are substantially identical or equal." 109 Cong.Rec. 9197 (1963)(remarks of Congressman Goodell, one of the Act's sponsors). Cf. *Lemons v. City & County of Denver,* 620 F.2d 228, 229 (10th Cir.1980). The Act requires equal pay only when men and women are performing "equal work on jobs the performance of which requires equal skill, effort, and responsibility, and which are performed under similar working conditions." 29 U.S.C. § 206(d)(1). The working conditions of a janitor are different from those of a secretary, and so are the skills and responsibilities of the two jobs. The Act does not prohibit paying different wages even if the result is to pay a woman less than a man and by doing so "underpay" her because the difference in the wage rate is greater than necessary to compensate the male for any greater skill, effort, or responsibility required by, or any inferior working conditions encountered in, his job.

Thus the jobs that are compared must be in some sense the same to count as "equal work" under the Equal Pay Act; and here we come to the main difficulty in applying the Act: whether two jobs are the same depends on how fine a system of job classifications the courts will accept. If coaching an athletic team in the Madison, Illinois school system is considered a single job rather than a congeries of jobs, the school district violated the Equal Pay Act prima facie by paying female holders of this job less than male holders, and the only question is whether the district carried its burden of proving that the lower wages which the four female coaches received were lower than the wages of their male counterparts because of a factor other than sex. If on the other hand coaching the girls' tennis team is considered a different job from coaching the boys' tennis team, and *a fortiori* if coaching the girls' volleyball or basketball team is considered a different job (or jobs) from coaching the boys' soccer team, there is no prima facie violation. So the question is how narrow a definition of job the courts should be using in deciding whether the Equal Pay Act is applicable.

We can get some guidance from the language of the Act. The Act requires that the jobs compared have "similar working conditions," not the same working conditions. This implies that some comparison of different jobs is possible. It is true that similarity of working conditions between the jobs being compared is not enough to bring the Act into play—the work must be "equal" and the jobs must require "equal" skill, effort, and responsibility, as well as similar working conditions. But since the working conditions need not be "equal," the jobs need not be completely identical.

Estimating and comparing the skill, effort, responsibility, and working conditions in two jobs are factual determinations. See, e.g., *Epstein v. Secretary, U.S. Dept. of Treasury,* 739 F.2d 274, 277–78 (7th Cir.1984). We can overturn them, therefore, only if they are clearly erroneous. See Fed. R.Civ.P. 52(a); cf. *Wright v. United States,* 809 F.2d 425, 428 (7th Cir.1987). The district judge found (among other things) that coaching a girls' tennis team is sufficiently like coaching a boys' tennis team, coaching a girls' softball team is sufficiently like coaching a boys' hardball team, and, indeed, coaching a girls' volleyball or basketball team is sufficiently like coaching a boys' soccer team, to allow each pair of jobs to be described as involving equal work, as requiring equal skill, effort, and responsibility, and as being performed under similar working conditions. If these assessments are not clearly erroneous, we must uphold them, regardless of what we might think the correct assessment as an original matter.

There are pitfalls in allowing *any* comparisons between different jobs, and they are illustrated by this case. One is a tendency to focus entirely on the measurable differences and ignore the equally or more important but less readily measurable ones. The witnesses in this case concentrated on the amount of skill and time required for coaching girls' and boys' teams and paid little attention to responsibility. It may be true that because the boys' teams tend to have more assistant coaches than the girls' teams, the head coaches of the boys' teams put in no more time than the head coaches of the girls' teams even when the boys' teams are larger and play more matches. But normally there is greater responsibility (one of the dimensions in which the statute requires equality between the jobs compared) if you have a staff than if you don't. That is one reason why the president of a company is paid more than a junior executive who, lacking staff assistance, may work longer hours. "Direction of others as well as value of commodity worked upon and overall importance of assignment may be considered as part of an employees' [sic] job responsibility." 109 Cong.Rec. 9209 (1963)(remarks of Congressman Goodell).

Another difference tends to be ignored when effort, which is hard to measure, is equated to time, which is easy to measure. Boys and girls differ on average in strength, speed, and perhaps other dimensions of athletic ability; there may also be important differences in their attitudes toward athletic competition. See, besides the extensive scholarly literature on this subject illustrated by Lever, *Sex Differences in the Games Children Play*, 23 Soc.Probs. 478 (1976), and by Gilligan, *In a Different Voice: Psychological Theory and Women's Development* 9–11 (1982), the deposition of coach Michael Lasiter in the present case. The differences between boys and girls in athletic aptitude and interest may make coaching a boys' team harder—or easier—than coaching a girls' team; there can be no confidence that the two jobs require equal effort. The district judge set aside this consideration by ruling that a difference in the sex of students, customers, etc. can't be used to justify a pay difference under the Equal Pay Act. But this is wrong. The reference to "factor other than sex" refers to the sex of the employee, not the sex of the employer's customers, clients, or suppliers. See *Kenneweg v. Hampton Township School Dist.*, 438 F.Supp. 575, 577 (W.D.Pa.1977); 29 U.S.C. §§ 206(d), 203(e); 109 Cong.Rec. 9206 (1963)(remarks of Representative Goodell); cf. *Hodgson v. Robert Hall Clothes, Inc.*, 473 F.2d 589 (3d Cir.1973). Suppose that the school district happened to have just male, or just female, coaches and paid coaches more for coaching boys' teams than girls' teams. Men paid less than other men for coaching, or women paid less than other women, could not complain of a violation of the Equal Pay Act. The Act was passed early in the history of public regulation of sex discrimination—so early that a principal sponsor, Congressman Goodell, could quote with approval the following evaluation of the woman's position in American life:

> The emancipation of women was an achievement of the 19th century and the early decades of the 20th. * * * With emancipation the feminist movement came to an end. The victory was so complete that any girl who now doubts the equality of the sexes probably assumes the natural superiority of women. Having achieved emancipation and equality of opportunity, women did a sharp about-face and during the 1950's "the thundering hoofs of women stampeding back to the nest" were heard.

109 Cong.Rec. 9208 (1963). The Act did not seek to eliminate whatever differences between the sexes might make it harder to coach a boys' team than a girls' team. If it is harder (we are not saying it is harder—we are just discussing possibilities), the statutory requirement of equal effort is not met and the differential in pay is outside the scope of the Act.

Nevertheless, we are unwilling to hold that coaches of girls' and boys' teams can never be found to be doing equal work requiring equal skill, effort, and responsibility and performed under similar working conditions. Above the lowest rank of employee, every employee has a somewhat different job from every other one, even if the two employees being compared are in the same department. So if "equal work" and "equal skill, effort, and responsibility" were taken literally, the Act would have a minute domain. Of course, opponents of an equal pay act may have been strong enough to block the passage of a strong bill—and, to some extent, they were. Remarkably, considering that the Act was enacted almost a quarter of a century ago, its proponents wanted to enact the principle of "comparable worth." See, e.g., 109 Cong.Rec. 9200 (1963)(remarks of Congressman Dent). But they were beaten back. In the words of Congressman Goodell, "Last year when the House changed the word 'comparable' to 'equal' the clear intention was to narrow the whole concept. We went from 'comparable' to 'equal' meaning that the jobs involved should be virtually identical, that is, they would be very much alike or closely related to each other." *Id.* at 9197.

But the words "very much alike," "closely related," or, as the cases sometimes say, "substantially equal"—even the words "virtually identical"— are not synonymous with "identical." See, e.g., *Horner v. Mary Institute,* 613 F.2d 706, 713 (8th Cir.1980); *Marshall v. Building Maintenance Corp.,* 587 F.2d 567, 569 (2d Cir.1978)(per curiam); *Brennan v. City Stores, Inc.,* 479 F.2d 235, 238–41 (5th Cir.1973). There is a gray area, which we must be vigilant to police, between "very much alike," which is within the scope of the Act, and "comparable," which is outside; for it is plain that Congress did not want to enact comparable worth as part of the Equal Pay Act of 1964. "Differences in pay between groups or categories of employees that contain both men and women within the group or category are not covered by this act." 109 Cong.Rec. 9209 (1963)(remarks of Congressman Goodell). "Congress did not intend to put either the Secretary [of Labor, the original enforcer of the Act] or the courts in the business of evaluating jobs and determining what constituted a proper differential for unequal work." *Hodgson v. Corning Glass Works,* 474 F.2d 226, 231 (2d Cir.1973)(Friendly, J.), aff'd under the name *Corning Glass Works v. Brennan,* 417 U.S. 188, 94 S.Ct. 2223, 41 L.Ed.2d 1 (1974).

The courts have thus had to steer a narrow course. The cases do not require an absolute identity between jobs, but do require substantial identity. The line is a fine, perhaps imperceptible, one. Compare *Marshall v. Dallas Independent School Dist.*, 605 F.2d 191 (5th Cir.1979)(heavy and light custodial jobs not equal within meaning of Act); *Marshall v. Building Maintenance Corp.*, 587 F.2d 567 (2d Cir.1978)(per curiam)(light-duty and heavy-duty cleaning—ditto), and *Angelo v. Bacharach Instrument Co.*, 555 F.2d 1164 (3d Cir.1977)(light and heavy assembling—ditto), with *Brock v. Georgia Southwestern College*, 765 F.2d 1026, 1033–36 (11th Cir.1985)(teaching different subjects, and teaching physical education but with different coaching duties—intramural athletics program versus intercollegiate basketball team—held to be equal within meaning of Act), and *Thompson v. Sawyer*, 678 F.2d 257, 274–76 (D.C.Cir.1982)(different bindery jobs—ditto).

Whatever answer we might give, if we were the finders of fact, to the question whether coaching a girl's tennis team and coaching a boy's tennis team are sufficiently alike to be equal work within the meaning of the Act, we cannot, on the record compiled in this case (a potentially important qualification), deem the district court's determination clearly erroneous. His error in thinking that a difference in the sex of the teams could not be used to ground a difference in the pay of their coaches is immaterial. The record contains no evidence that the sex of the team affects the skill, effort, responsibility, or working conditions of coaching. And while it is odd that the greater number of assistant coaches of boys' compared to girls' teams should be thought a factor tending to equate the jobs of the head coaches of boys' and girls' teams rather than to show that coaching a boys' team is a more responsible position, there is also no evidence that—in the Madison school system, anyway—having an assistant coach is viewed as anything more than a timesaver for the head coach. And there is evidence that head coaches of boys' teams have more assistants in relation to the number of boys on the team than head coaches of girls' teams have in relation to the number of girls.

Boys' teams might of course be greater revenue producers than girls' teams. *Jacobs v. College of William & Mary*, 517 F.Supp. 791, 797 (E.D.Va. 1980), aff'd without opinion, 661 F.2d 922 (4th Cir.1981), relied on this factor; see also *Hodgson v. Robert Hall Clothes, Inc., supra.* But *Jacobs* involved college teams. Madison has only one revenue-producing team, the boys' high-school basketball team, and the plaintiffs do not complain about the higher wage that the head coach of that team received—they acknowledge that his job is not the same as that of any female coach. Concerning the coaching jobs that were compared, male and female coaches alike testified that the skill, effort, and responsibility required were the same and the working conditions also the same—not merely similar, which is all the Act requires. Some of the boys' teams were larger than the girls' teams with which they were compared, and competed more often, but apparently any additional effort or responsibility involved in coaching a larger team or one that competes more often was cancelled out by a combination of more assistant coaches for the larger teams and more practice sessions (requiring the same time and effort) for teams that compete less often.

For those of us whose knowledge of athletic coaching is confined to newspaper and television accounts of the travails of professional and college coaches, the idea of homogenizing the coaching profession in the manner attempted by the plaintiffs and accepted by the district judge is discordant. But we must, by an effort of imagination, place ourselves in a different world, that of small-town high-school and junior-high-school athletics, where the coach's task is not to compete for money in a high-pressure environment but to impart elementary athletic skills and norms of sportsmanship to adolescents. Given these modest goals, a finding that the coaching of boys' and of girls' tennis involves inconsequential differences in skill, effort, responsibility, and working conditions is not so improbable that we can set it aside, under the deferential clear-error standard that governs appellate review of findings of fact, by substituting our personal impressions for the evidence introduced at trial. Compare *Horner v. Mary Institute, supra,* 613 F.2d at 714, where the evidence showed that a male physical education teacher had a different job from a female physical education teacher because he was responsible for curricular development and she was not, with *Brock v. Georgia Southwestern College, supra,* 765 F.2d at 1035, where the evidence showed that two physical education teachers, one of whom also coached the intramural athletics program and the other the intercollegiate basketball team, nevertheless had substantially equal jobs.

Although we conclude that there is no objection in principle to comparing different coaching jobs, the record of the present case does require us to distinguish between coaching boys' and girls' teams of the same sport and coaching boys' and girls' teams of different sports. The judge equated coaching girls' basketball and girls' volleyball to coaching boys' soccer (and, in the assistant-coach comparisons, girls' basketball with boys' track), without regard for the fact that Madison treats coaching a different sport as a different coaching job irrespective of the sex of either the coach or the team. In the 1980 academic year, for example, the boys' track coach received $1,140 each while the boys' soccer coach received only $840 and the boys' tennis coach even less—$780. (These are head-coach salaries; the salary for the assistant coach of the boys' track team was $835 and for the assistant coach of the boys' soccer team $600; there was no assistant tennis coach.) In other words, there is not a single job classification such as "head coach" or "assistant coach"; the wage varies by the sport. The judge was therefore arbitrary in assuming that if the coach of the girls' volleyball team or basketball team had been male, he would have been paid as much as the boys' soccer coach. (The plaintiffs concede, as we said, that coaching the boys' basketball team is not comparable to coaching the girls' basketball team.) We are willing to assume that hardball and fast-pitch softball—similar sports played under similar rules—are the same sport for purposes of the Equal Pay Act. See *Brennan v. Woodbridge School District,* 74 Labor Cases ¶ 33,121, at p. 46,627 (D.Del.1974). But given the wage differentials among the male coaches, we cannot make this assumption for volleyball and soccer, or for basketball and soccer. Another consideration is the arbitrariness of the particular comparisons suggested by the plaintiffs. In 1980 Long, as girls' track coach, received the same wage as the male coach of the boys' soccer team. How was the school district to know that a court would think basketball and soccer or volleyball and soccer a closer pair than track and soccer? We vacate the findings of the district judge with respect to a violation of the Equal Pay Act in the comparison between boys' soccer and girls' volleyball, boys' soccer and girls' basketball, and boys' track and girls' basketball.

[The second part of this case, dealing with the employer's defense, is set forth at p. 944, infra.]

Notes on Madison School District

1. What do you make of Judge Posner's discussion of the equal work issue in *Madison School District*? Why did the plaintiffs concede that the job of the head coach of the boys' basketball team was not the same as that of any female coach? Why did Judge Posner reject the district court's findings that the School District had violated the Act with respect to the salaries it paid to the women who coached girls' volleyball and girls' basketball when compared to those paid to the men who coached boys' soccer? What about his rejection of the comparison between the coaching of girls' basketball and boys' track? Were the plaintiffs actually relying on the concept of "comparable" worth? Reconsider after reading Judge Posner's opinion in *American Nurses' Association*, at p. 959 infra.

2. Male faculty members have challenged the efforts of academic employers to redress past wage discrimination against women as violations of the Equal Pay Act in several cases. Thus, in Board of Regents of Univ. of Nebraska v. Dawes, 522 F.2d 380 (8th Cir.1975), cert. denied 424 U.S. 914, 96 S.Ct. 1112, 47 L.Ed.2d 318 (1976), a University had been found to have paid women faculty members less than it paid men. In order to bring itself into compliance with the law, the University devised a formula that compared the salaries of females with a hypothetical average male salary based only on education, specialization, experience and merit. The salaries of 33 females were found to be below the formula salary and these salaries were raised to match the formula salary. Suit was then brought under the Equal Pay Act by 92 male faculty members whose salaries were also below the hypothetical formula salary, but whose salaries were not raised. The court held that refusal to pay the males the formula salary constituted a violation of the Equal Pay Act.

Contrary to this result, the Seventh Circuit in Ende v. Bd. of Regents of Regency Universities, 757 F.2d 176 (7th Cir.1985), held on similar facts that Northern Illinois University did not violate the Equal Pay Act when it disbursed $150,000 on a yearly basis to women faculty to remedy prior salary discrimination against them and bring their salaries into line with male faculty salaries. Again, a multiple regression formula was devised to measure the impact of sex discrimination, and the resulting aggregate monetary amount was distributed to women based on a point system, taking into account any below-average salary, above-average years without promotion, and longevity at the university. After the women received adjustments, male faculty sued, alleging that using the point system applied to the women, they would be eligible for adjustments also. The Seventh Circuit rejected the men's argument, ruling that

> an increase which restores a victim of past discrimination to the salary level he/she would have enjoyed in the absence of the discrimination qualifies as a defense [of "any factor other than sex"] even where the discrimination itself was based on sex. To conclude otherwise would create a wholly unnecessary tension between compliance with the anti-discrimination provisions of Title VII (and of the Equal Pay Act itself) with the Equal Pay Act.

757 F.2d at 182–83. The Seventh Circuit distinguished *Dawes* on the basis that the previous existence of sex discrimination against the women faculty had not

been established in *Dawes* and its formula was not tailored to correspond to the measure of past discrimination.

Similarly, in Winkes v. Brown University, 747 F.2d 792 (1st Cir.1984), the First Circuit reversed a district court judgment in favor of a male faculty member, who sued under the Equal Pay Act when his female departmental colleague received a substantial salary increase in response to an outside offer from another university. The First Circuit noted that at the time Brown matched the outside offer for the woman, the university was operating under a consent decree resulting from a Title VII case filed by women faculty charging Brown with sex discrimination in failing to tenure women professors. On the Equal Pay Act claim itself, the First Circuit ruled that the university successfully rebutted the male plaintiff's prima facie case by proving that matching outside offers was a regular practice of the university, a defense under the Act of "any factor other than sex." In fact, the department chair testified that matching outside offers was "about the only way * * * substantial merit increases were ever allocated to [the] faculty." 747 F.2d at 795. The court pointed out that had the university not matched the woman faculty member's outside offer, it would have found itself in violation of its consent decree as well as Title VII for not following normal university policy.

For further information on faculty pay equity studies, see Elizabeth L. Scott, Higher Education Salary Evaluation Kit (AAUP, 1977); Mary W. Gray & Elizabeth L. Scott, A "Statistical" Remedy for Statistically Identified Discrimination, 66 Academe 174 (AAUP, 1980).

3. Do men who work in predominantly female jobs have standing to complain of sex discrimination in pay directed against women? The Ninth Circuit thinks not. In Spaulding v. University of Washington, 740 F.2d 686 (9th Cir.1984), certiorari denied 469 U.S. 1036, 105 S.Ct. 511, 83 L.Ed.2d 401 (1984), the nursing faculty of women plus one man sued for sex discrimination on several theories, including the Equal Pay Act and Title VII. The Ninth Circuit held that the Equal Pay claim failed because the plaintiffs had not shown that the actual day-to-day responsibilities, skill, and effort required of predominantly male medical faculties were substantially equal to those of the nursing faculty. It also rejected the Title VII claim of sex-based wage discrimination. It went on to reject the claim of the male plaintiff:

> The nursing faculty next asserts that Reg Williams, the male faculty member, has a valid claim for discrimination because he received a salary "infected" by the discrimination the female faculty members suffered. However, even where the female faculty members are able to frame a cognizable Title VII or Equal Pay Act claim, it does not allow the male employees "to bootstrap their job grievances * * * into an employment discrimination claim rooted in federal law." (Ruffin v. County of Los Angeles, 607 F.2d 1276, 1281 (9th Cir.)), cert. denied, 445 U.S. 951, 100 S.Ct. 1600, 63 L.Ed.2d 786 (1980)(sex-based wage discrimination suit brought by male officers dismissed on summary judgment). * * * Williams makes no claim that he received a lower wage because of his sex.

Id., 740 F.2d at 709. See also Patee v. Pacific Northwest Bell Telephone Co., 803 F.2d 476 (9th Cir.1986)(applying *Spaulding* to reject claim of male employees under Title VII who were paid a higher wage when they were classified as Test Desk Technicians, a predominantly male category, than they are currently paid for doing the same work after their reclassification as Maintenance Administrators, a predominantly female category). Are *Spaulding* and *Patee* correctly decided? Should the result necessarily be the same under the Equal Pay Act and

Title VII? Professor Christine Littleton points out that the male nursing faculty member in Spaulding was discriminated against because of his sex: he was sociologically female. See Littleton, Reconstructing Sexual Equality, 75 Calif.L.Rev. 1279, 1308–1309 (1987).

4. A useful guide to the law and practice concerning wage discrimination is found in Diana L. Stone, Pay Equity Sourcebook (Equal Rights Advocates and the National Committee on Pay Equity, 1988)(available from Equal Rights Advocates, Inc., San Francisco, California).

b. Differentials Based On Any Other Factor Other Than Sex

HODGSON v. ROBERT HALL CLOTHES, INC.

United States Court of Appeals, Third Circuit, 1973.
473 F.2d 589, cert. denied 414 U.S. 866, 94 S.Ct. 50, 38 L.Ed.2d 85.

JAMES HUNTER, III, CIRCUIT JUDGE. This case involves the application of the Equal Pay Act of 1963, 29 U.S.C.A. § 206(d)(1). * * *

The Robert Hall store in question is located in Wilmington, Delaware. It sells clothing, and contains a department for men's and boys' clothing and another department for women's and girls' clothing. The store is a one-floor building, and the departments are in separate portions of it.

The merchandise in the men's department was, on the average, of higher price and better quality than the merchandise in the women's department; and Robert Hall's profit margin on the men's clothing was higher than its margin on the women's clothing. Consequently, the men's department at all times showed a larger dollar volume in gross sales, and a greater gross profit. Breaking this down, the salespeople in the men's department, on the average, sold more merchandise in terms of dollars and produced more gross profit than did the people in the women's department per hour of work.

The departments are staffed by full and part-time sales personnel. At all times, only men were permitted to work in the men's department and only women were permitted to work in the women's department. The complaint is not addressed to the propriety of such segregated employment.

The salespeople receive a base salary and can earn additional incentive payments. Various factors relating to the garment sold determine the amount of incentive payments.[3] At all times, the salesmen received higher salaries than the saleswomen. Both starting salaries and periodic increases were higher for the males. The amount of incentive compensation was very slightly greater for the men.[4]

* * *

"ANY OTHER FACTOR OTHER THAN SEX"

The initial question facing us is one raised by the Secretary. He contends that economic benefit to the employer cannot be used to justify a wage differential under § 206(d)(1)(iv).

3. These factors included style, quality, price, mark-up, and ease of selling specific merchandise involved. Hodgson v. Robert Hall, Inc., [326 F.Supp. 1264] at 1272, 1278.

4. "The net effect of the incentive system, however, resulted in a ratio of incentive pay to gross sales which was approximately .2% more in the case of men than women." Hodgson v. Robert Hall, Inc., supra at 1272.

He argues that "any other factor" does not mean *any* other factor. Instead he claims it means any other factor other than sex which "is related to job performance or is typically used in setting wage scales." He contends that economic benefits to an employer do not fall within this exception.

He recognizes that the men's department produces a greater profit for Robert Hall. His contention is that the salesmen have nothing to do with producing this benefit since the district court found that the salesmen and saleswomen performed equal work. Since the saleswomen cannot sell the higher-priced clothing sold in the men's department, this cannot be used as a factor on which to base a wage differential. Otherwise, "the exception could swallow the rule." Shultz v. First Victoria National Bank, 420 F.2d 648 (5th Cir.1969).

Robert Hall does not argue that "any other" means "any other" either. It claims that a wage differential is permissible if based on a legitimate business reason. As the district court found, economic benefits could justify a wage differential. We need go no further than to say the district court was correct to hold in this case that economic benefits to an employer can justify a wage differential.

The Secretary's argument is incorrect for several reasons. It ignores the basic finding of the district court that Robert Hall's segregation of its work force was done for legitimate business purposes. [The District Court found that, unless the sales persons and the customers were of the same sex, the necessity for physical contact between them would create embarrassment and inhibit sales.] It is also inconsistent with the wording of the statute.

In providing for exceptions, the statute states that they will apply when the males and females are doing equal work. Congress thus intended to allow wage differentials even though the contrasted employees were performing equal work. However, two of the examples given as exceptions, (§§ 206(d)(1)(ii) and (iii)), may be read to say that the contrasted employees really are not performing equal work. If, for example, some employees produce a greater quantity of work than others, pursuant to § 206(d)(1)(iii), they may receive greater compensation.

The Secretary's test might be acceptable if §§ 206(d)(1)(ii) and (iii) stood alone. However, §§ 206(d)(1)(i) and (iv) indicate that there must be some factors upon which an employer may base a wage differential which are not related to job performance. We must point to the plain wording of the clause. It reads "*any* other factor * * *." While the examples preceding § 206(d)(1)(iv) necessarily qualify it to some extent, they do not narrow it to the degree for which the Secretary contends.

The Secretary recognizes this reasoning in § 800.116(e) of his Wage-Hour Administrator's Interpretative Bulletin and § 34d07 of his Field Office Handbook. In both of these the Secretary approves a commission system in which the amount of compensation is determined by the type of article sold. The stated hypothesis is that the *sales people are performing equal work*. Since this is given, the only basis for approving such a system has to be that the economic benefit to the employer is greater. As the Field Office Handbook states, "Such a difference in commission rates might be based on many factors such as sales volume, markup, cost of the items sold, type of merchandise sold, turnover in merchandise, and the ease of selling merchandise in each particular department." These are all factors of value to the employer. It might take no more effort or skill to sell two different pairs of ten dollar shoes; but if the employer makes a four dollar profit on one pair as opposed to a two dollar profit on the other, the Secretary apparently allows a higher commission rate. That the salary in this case is a base salary rather than a commission is not a significant distinction. The principle remains the same: the compensation is based on economic benefit to the employer, and the work performed is equal.

This would make good business sense. The saleswomen are paid less because the commodities which they sell cannot bear the same selling costs that the commodities sold in the men's department can bear. Without a more definite indication from Congress, it would not seem wise to impose the economic burden of higher compensation on employers. It could serve to weaken their competitive position. If anything, the legislative history supports a broader reading of § 206(d)(1)(iv) than that proposed by the Secretary. * * *

Our decision in Shultz v. Wheaton Glass Co., 421 F.2d 259 (3d Cir.1970), cert. denied 398 U.S. 905, 90 S.Ct. 1696, 26 L.Ed.2d 64 (1970) also lends support to this result. In discussing whether the employer had met his burden of proving an exception to this act, we held against the employer partly because the record did not show that he had realized any greater economic benefits from certain additional activities allegedly performed by the male employees. While we did not specifically consider the issue of whether "economic benefit" falls under the act, the decision implicitly accepts the fact that it does. Shultz v. Wheaton Glass Co., supra at 267.

In addition, this case comes to us on a finding by the district court that "the jobs performed by salesmen and salesladies, respectively, are not reasonably susceptible of performance by both sexes because of the nature of the jobs." * * * Although the fact that the jobs in question require employment of one sex exclusively may not alone justify a wage differential, it does seem to be a factor that can be considered in evaluating the employer's justification for his differential.

* * *

BURDEN OF PROOF

The next question is whether Robert Hall proved that it received the economic benefits upon which it claimed it based its salary differentials. It is well-settled that the employer has the burden of proof on this issue. * * *

Robert Hall introduced evidence to show that for every year of the store's operation, the men's department was substantially more profitable than the women's department. * * *

Robert Hall contends that this greater profitability is a sufficient reason to justify paying the sales people in its men's department more than it pays the sales people in its women's department. It does not have to tie its compensation scheme into the performance of the individual sales person, and this is what the district court implicitly required.

We agree that the district court's opinion implies that such a correlation is necessary. It compared the individual performances of the full-time male and the full-time female. It also compared the individual performances of the part-time workers. * * * As we have mentioned, it was not Robert Hall's practice to retain records of individual performance. * * * The question is whether the Equal Pay Act requires the employer to justify his base salary by correlating it to individual performance.

The overwhelming evidence which showed that the men's department was more profitable than the women's was sufficient to justify the differences in base salary. These statistics proved that Robert Hall's wage differentials were not based on sex but instead fully supported the reasoned business judgment that the sellers of women's clothing could not be paid as much as the sellers of men's clothing. Robert Hall's executives testified that it was their practice to base their wage rates on these departmental figures.

While no business reason could justify a practice clearly prohibited by the act, the legislative history set forth above indicates a Congressional intent to allow reasonable business judgments to stand. It would be too great an economic and accounting hardship to impose upon Robert Hall the requirement that it correlate the wages of each individual with his or her performance. This could force it toward a system based totally upon commissions, and it seems unwise to read such a result into § 206(d)(1)(iv). Robert Hall's method of determining salaries does not show the "clear pattern of discrimination," (Rep. Goodell, 109 Cong.Rec. 9203), that would be necessary for us to make it correlate more precisely the salary of each of its employees to the economic benefit which it receives from them. Robert Hall introduced substantial evidence. This is not a case where if we sustain the proof as justification for a wage differential "the exception will swallow the rule." Shultz v. First Victoria National Bank, 420 F.2d 648, 656, 657 (5th Cir.1969).

The Secretary contends that our decision in Shultz v. Wheaton Glass Company, supra, supports the district court's decision not to rely on group averages to justify the wage differential. * * * We do not agree that *Wheaton* supports the district court. In that case the question, in part, was whether additional duties allegedly performed by certain males would justify paying males more than females. The courts held that the employers had failed to show that all of the males performed the additional duties. Here all of the salesmen perform the same duties. One could analogize to *Wheaton Glass* and say that as the alleged justification there was the additional duties, the alleged justification here is the economic benefits. And as the employer there did not prove that each individual performed the duties here Robert Hall did not prove that each individual provided economic benefits. However, the nature of the proof required distinguishes the two cases. It would not have been difficult in *Wheaton* for the employer to have proved that each or most male workers performed the additional duties. That is not the case here.

Also, in *Wheaton Glass,* the court relied on the fact that there had been no finding that the women workers could not perform the additional duties allegedly performed by the men. Here there was a specific finding by the district court, unchallenged by the Secretary, that the women could not perform the work done by the men.

Since we have determined that Robert Hall has not violated § 206(d)(1), we find it unnecessary to reach the question of whether the district court was correct in not awarding interest in this case.

The decision of that court will be affirmed as to the full-time personnel and reversed as to the part-time personnel.

EEOC v. MADISON COMM. UNIT SCHOOL DIST. NO. 12

United States Court of Appeals, Seventh Circuit, 1987.
818 F.2d 577.

[The first part of this case, dealing with the "equal work"
issue, is set forth at p. 932, supra.]

With this exception we conclude that the plaintiffs did establish a prima facie case of violation of the Equal Pay Act, and we move on to consider defenses, of which only one ("factor other than sex") is relevant. Madison argues that the sex *of the teams* is a factor other than sex, and though the district court thought this wrong, we disagree as we have said; the factor other than sex to which the Act refers is a factor other than the *employee's* sex. But this point cannot help Madison. We do not understand it to be arguing that it has carried its burden of proving "factor other than sex" as an affirmative defense. Its quarrel is with the district court's suggestion that the sex of the teams can't be taken into account in determining whether the coaching jobs are equal work; it can be. Furthermore, the language of the statute ("except where such payment is made pursuant to * * * a differential based on any factor other than sex") makes clear that the pay differential must be caused by the other factor, and not by the sex of the employees who receive the different pay. See generally *Covington v. Southern Illinois University,* 816 F.2d 317, 321–325 (7th Cir.1987). If Madison, having decided for reasons unrelated to the sex of the coaches that coaches of male teams should be paid more than coaches of female teams, neither prohibited nor even discouraged women from coaching male teams, the difference in pay between male coaches of boys' teams and female coaches of girls' teams would be due to a decision unrelated to the sex of the coaches. But Madison discouraged women, including Cole and Long, from applying to coach boys' teams, which not only adds a reason related to the sex of the coaches for a difference in pay between men and women to a reason related solely to the sex of the team members, but also casts doubt on the bona fides of the school district's claim to have based the difference in the pay of coaches of male and of female teams solely on the sex of the team members. Cf. *Bence v. Detroit Health Corp.,* 712 F.2d 1024, 1029–31 (6th Cir.1983); *id.* at 1032–33 (dissenting opinion). There was contrary evidence: a woman once was hired to coach the boys' tennis team and was paid the same as her male predecessor; several times men were hired to coach girls' teams and paid the same as female coaches of those teams. But such job offers were very rare prior to the EEOC's investigation, and the district judge was entitled to find their evidentiary significance outweighed by the evidence that women were discouraged from applying to coach boys' teams.

The reason for discouraging women from coaching boys' teams was that the school authorities were concerned about the "locker room problem." This may or may not be a good reason (a question touched on later), but it does suggest that women receive less pay than men for doing what the district court found was equal work within the meaning of the Equal Pay Act because they are women; their sex makes them ineligible to receive the higher wage that men receive for equal work. Even if the school district is entitled to insist that coaches and coached be of the same sex, if the work of each coach is the same and the reason for the difference in pay is the difference in the sex of the coach, the Equal Pay Act is violated. An employer cannot divide equal work into two job classifications that carry unequal pay, forbid women to compete for one of the classifications, and defend the resulting inequality in pay between men and women by reference to a "factor other than [the] sex" of the employees. Cf. 29 C.F.R. § 800.114(a). It would not be the sexual segregation that had caused the inequality in pay, but a decision to pay men more for doing the same work as women (albeit with a "clientele" of a different sex from the women's "clientele").

Another subsection of the Equal Pay Act, 29 U.S.C. § 206(d)(1)(i), not in issue in this case, allows a pay difference pursuant to a bona fide seniority scheme. If the employer prevents a woman from obtaining additional seniority, for no other reason than that she is a woman, then the difference in pay between her and more senior men is due not to the seniority scheme but to her sex, and the defense fails. That is analogous to the present case.

So the school district violated the Equal Pay Act; the next question is whether the violation was willful, which would extend the period of back pay from two to three years. A violation is "willful" under the Act if the defendant either knew he was violating the Act or was indifferent to whether he was violating it or not (and therefore "reckless"). *Trans World Airlines, Inc. v. Thurston,* 469 U.S. 111, 125–29, 105 S.Ct. 613, 623–26, 83 L.Ed.2d 523 (1985), and *Walton v. United Consumers Club, Inc.,* 786 F.2d 303, 310–11 (7th Cir.1986), so hold, and though neither of these cases involved a suit under the Equal Pay Act, this doesn't matter. The Age Discrimination in Employment Act, under which *Thurston* was decided, incorporates (see 29 U.S.C. § 626(b)) the remedial provisions of the Fair Labor Standards Act, 29 U.S.C. §§ 201 *et seq.* The Equal Pay Act is an amendment to the Fair Labor Standards Act, and hence is subject to the same remedial provisions. See 29 U.S.C. §§ 206(d), 216(b). *Walton* was decided under a different substantive provision of the Fair Labor Standards Act, so again the same remedial provisions were involved as in this case.

The district judge said that "Madison was aware of the requirements of the Equal Pay Act at the time it set the wages of the female coaches," and "aware that its conduct was governed by the Equal Pay Act." This might mean only that Madison knew it was subject to the Act, which is not the same thing as knowing it was violating the Act or not caring whether it was or not. Elsewhere in his opinion the judge found that Madison had a policy (as we have said) of hiring only male coaches to teach male teams, that the female coaches had complained about their lower pay, and that after the EEOC began its investigation in 1980, Madison had—in order to "muddy the waters," as the court put it—hired male coaches to coach girls' teams. None of this is evidence of willfulness. Until today, the law in this or any circuit was foggy on whether the Equal Pay Act can reach pay disparities between coaches of boys' and of girls' teams. Maintaining a defensible view of what a statute requires is not the same thing as willfully violating the statute; and Madison was not required to abandon its view merely because the female coaches challenged it and persuaded the EEOC to conduct an investigation. After the investigation began, the school district began appointing more men to coach girls' teams for the same pay as the women coaches received, and maybe this was done to strengthen the school district's case that it was not discriminating between male and female coaches of the same teams. But efforts to bring one's conduct into conformity with one's litigating posture are not evidence of willful noncompliance with the law. Here they are evidence of compliance with a defensible although in our judgment incorrect conception of what a less than perfectly clear law required.

The judge also made a finding that Madison had "willfully deemphasized the girls' sports." The Equal Pay Act does not require school districts to give girls' sports equal prominence with boys'. The failure to do so might violate another statute, but the Equal Pay Act does not require employers to equalize the work performed by their male and female employees; it just forbids employers to pay women less than men for the same work.

Although the judge found that Madison's violation of the Equal Pay Act had been willful, he refused to award double damages. As the plaintiffs point out, this conclusion is inconsistent with our recent holding that it is easier to get double damages under the Act than to extend the statute of limitations. *Walton v. United Consumers Club, Inc., supra,* 786 F.2d at 312. To extend the statute of limitations a plaintiff must prove a willful violation; to avoid double damages the defendant must prove that he was acting in the sincere and reasonably grounded belief that his conduct was lawful, and if he proves this the district court "may, in its sound discretion"—not must—award only single damages. 29 U.S.C. § 260. If Madison was acting reasonably and in good faith, it could hardly be guilty of violating the law either intentionally or with reckless disregard for the legality of its conduct. It is not easy to figure out how the district judge resolved this paradox in his mind. He gave no reason for declining to award double damages, and the statute gives him no discretion to "dedouble" unless the defendant proves that it was acting reasonably and in good faith. Probably the judge misunderstood the statutory standard of willfulness (as the passages we quoted earlier from his opinion suggest) but was persuaded that the defendants had acted reasonably and in good faith in the sense relevant to the double-damages provision and that he should exercise his discretion not to double. The judge's comment about "muddy[ing] the waters" may seem to negate reasonableness but apparently was not intended to do so, or the judge would have awarded double damages; in any event, it has no basis, and there is no other evidence of bad faith or unreasonable conduct. Madison resisted the women's demands for higher pay on the basis of a sincerely held and reasonable, though ultimately rejected, interpretation of the Equal Pay Act.

* * *

The case must be remanded to recompute back pay (not only because of the shorter statute of limitations, but also because we have vacated some of the district court's findings of violation) and attorney's fees in accordance with this opinion; otherwise the decision of the district court is affirmed. No costs shall be awarded in this court.

Affirmed in Part, Reversed in Part, and Remanded With Directions.

Notes on Robert Hall and Madison School District

1. Compare with *Robert Hall* the result in Hodgson v. City Stores, Inc., 332 F.Supp. 942 (M.D.Ala.1971), affirmed 479 F.2d 235 (5th Cir.1973). In both cases (a) the wage differential was between women selling women's and children's clothing and men selling men's clothing in the same store; (b) there was a finding that the work was equal, so that a prima facie violation of the Act occurred. In *City Stores,* however, the employer lost because it failed to persuade the court that its wage differential was based on "any other factor other than sex." While claiming generally that a wide range of wage rates existed throughout the store based on "the individual employee, the department to which the employee is assigned, and the product sold" (332 F.Supp. at 945), defendant in *City Stores* did not allege that it made a higher profit on men's clothes than on women's and children's clothes. The employer's attempts to base its wage differential on factors other than sex were summarily rejected by the district court (332 F.Supp. at 949–50):

> * * * [D]efendant has advanced several arguments seeking to establish that its wage scale has been based on factors other than sex. Its chief contention is that any differential has resulted from traditional and historical differences in job content, the scale prevalent in the labor market and the customer following of certain male salespersons.

> The Court having determined that the male and female sales positions are substantially similar, it is unnecessary to discuss the defendant's first point. The fact that women tend to receive less from the labor market as a whole also carries no weight since defendant may not justify its discrimination by pointing to the conduct of others. The fact that the defendant has succeeded in paying a low, labor market rate does not authorize that which the Act seeks to end: wage differentials within its store between equivalent jobs. Finally, the evidence reflects, and the Court so finds, that certain of the women salespersons also maintained customer followings. Thus, the Court is compelled to the conclusion that the wage differential is a product of sexual discrimination and that the defendant is unable to avail itself of exception (iv) of § 206(d)(1).

See also 479 F.2d at 241 n. 12.

2. Is *Madison School District* inconsistent with *Robert Hall*? Didn't Robert Hall do exactly what Judge Posner says an employer cannot do: divide equal work into two job classifications that carry unequal pay, forbid women to compete for one of the classifications, and then defend the resulting inequity in pay between men and women as a "factor other than sex"?

3. Do you agree with Judge Posner that Madison School District could decide to pay the coaches of male teams more than coaches of female teams so long as it hired men and women for both jobs without discrimination based on the sex of the coaches?

4. Both *City Stores* and *Robert Hall* assume that it is permissible to hire only males to sell men's clothes and only females to attend the fitting of women's clothes. Does your understanding of Title VII support this assumption? If so, can the holding in *Robert Hall* be limited to cases where sex is a BFOQ for the job? But if the jobs are not interchangeable, how can they be compared for purposes of the Equal Pay Act? Compare Laffey v. Northwest Airlines, Inc., 567 F.2d 429 (D.C.Cir.1976), cert. denied 434 U.S. 1086, 98 S.Ct. 1281, 55 L.Ed.2d 792

(1978), where Northwest's stewardesses charged violation of both Title VII and the Equal Pay Act resulting from the defendant's initial refusal and subsequent discouragement of their applications for positions as pursers. Conceding a violation of Title VII in excluding the female stewardesses from the higher-paying male purser position, the company nevertheless argued that plaintiffs could not have it both ways. As the court summarized the argument (567 F.2d at 444–45):

> NWA further contends that * * * [i]f the purser and stewardess jobs are "equal," and thus support the court's holding of an Equal Pay Act violation, the company's refusal to permit women to become pursers does not deprive them of advancement opportunities—because the jobs are equal—and thus there can be no encroachment upon Title VII. Conversely, if the purser job is superior, there is no infringement of the Equal Pay Act although access to that position has unlawfully been denied to women under Title VII.

Affirming the district court's decision that both statutes had been violated, the court observed (567 F.2d at 445):

> Nor do we doubt that the same set of facts may form the basis for redress under both Title VII and the Equal Pay Act if the requirements of each are separately satisfied and the claimant does not reap overlapping relief for the same wrong.

Since the effect of the judgment was to equalize the pay and perquisites of the two positions and to enjoin future discrimination based on sex in the employment of cabin attendants, would it violate Title VII if the company continued to call its male cabin attendants "pursers" and dress them in uniforms resembling that of the pilots, while calling its female cabin attendants "stewardesses" and dressing them in short skirts? Recall the discussion of dress codes under Title VII, p. 724 supra. Should the union, which had insisted on retaining the pay premium for pursers in the collective bargaining agreement, bear any responsibility for the back pay award assessed against the company? See Text Note, The Role of Unions in Employment Discrimination, at p. 1015, infra.

On appeal from the district court's final adjudication in *Laffey,* the Court of Appeals for the District of Columbia Circuit reaffirmed the original finding that Northwest Airlines had violated both the Equal Pay Act and Title VII in paying stewardesses less than pursers. Northwest's argument that the Supreme Court's interpretation of the Bennett Amendment in County of Washington v. Gunther, set forth at p. 949, infra, had enlarged the "factor other than sex" defense in Equal Pay Act cases was brushed aside. Northwest asserted that an employer who believed in good faith that the two jobs were different should not be liable under the Equal Pay Act, after *Gunther,* even if it should turn out that the employer was mistaken. The court disagreed, finding Northwest's position incompatible with the statutory design, which takes account of an employer's good faith only on the issue of disallowing double damages, and not supported by the *Gunther* opinion. Laffey v. Northwest Airlines, Inc., 740 F.2d 1071, 1077–81 (D.C.Cir.1984), certiorari denied 469 U.S. 1181, 105 S.Ct. 939, 83 L.Ed.2d 951 (1985).

5. Given the persistent wage gap between men and women, can an employer who hires a man and a woman for the same job description, setting their current salaries based in part on their wages in a prior job, escape Equal Pay Act liability if it turns out that the man is paid more than the woman? What about the validity of continuing to pay the higher salary earned by a male employee elsewhere to get him to transfer into a job where the women already working there are being paid a lower amount? Do the first "previous employer salary"

cases raise the same issues under the Equal Pay Act as the second "salary retention plan" cases do? Can the employer justify either practice as a "factor other than sex" under the Act? See Kouba v. Allstate Ins. Co., 691 F.2d 873 (9th Cir.1982) discussed at p. 971, infra. See also Jeanne M. Hamburg, Note, When Prior Pay Isn't Equal Pay: A Proposed Standard for the Identification of "Factors Other Than Sex" Under the Equal Pay Act, 89 Colum.L.Rev. 1085 (1989). See generally, Symposium: The Gender Gap in Compensation, 82 Geo.L.J. 27 (1993).

2. INCORPORATION OF THE EQUAL PAY ACT INTO TITLE VII

COUNTY OF WASHINGTON v. GUNTHER

Supreme Court of the United States, 1981.
452 U.S. 161, 101 S.Ct. 2242, 68 L.Ed.2d 751.

JUSTICE BRENNAN delivered the opinion of the Court.

The question presented is whether § 703(h) of Title VII of the Civil Rights Act of 1964, 78 Stat. 257, 42 U.S.C.A. § 2000e–2(h), restricts Title VII's prohibition of sex-based wage discrimination to claims of equal pay for equal work.

I

This case arises over the payment by petitioner, the County of Washington, Ore., of substantially lower wages to female guards in the female section of the county jail than it paid to male guards in the male section of the jail.[1] Respondents are four women who were employed to guard female prisoners and to carry out certain other functions in the jail.[2] In January 1974, the county eliminated the female section of the jail, transferred the female prisoners to the jail of a nearby county, and discharged respondents.　* * *

Respondents filed suit against petitioner in Federal District Court under Title VII, 42 U.S.C.A. § 2000e et seq., seeking backpay and other relief.[3] They alleged that they were paid unequal wages for work substantially equal to that performed by male guards, and in the alternative, that part of the pay differential was attributable to intentional sex discrimination. The latter allegation was based on a claim that, because of intentional discrimination, the county set the pay scale for female guards, but not for male guards, at a level lower than that warranted by its own survey of outside markets and the worth of the jobs.

After trial, the District Court found that the male guards supervised more than 10 times as many prisoners per guard as did the female guards, and that

---

1. Prior to February 1, 1973, the female guards were paid between $476 and $606 per month, while the male guards were paid between $668 and $853. Effective February 1, 1973, the female guards were paid between $525 and $668, while salaries for male guards ranged from $701 to $940. Gunther v. County of Washington, 20 FEP Cases 788, 789 (Ore. 1976).

2. Oregon requires that female inmates be guarded solely by women, Ore.Rev.Stat. §§ 137.350, 137.360, and the District Court opinion indicates that women had not been employed to guard male prisoners. 20 FEP Cases, at 789, 792, nn. 8–9. For purposes of

this litigation, respondents concede that gender is a bona fide occupational qualification for some of the female guard positions. See 42 U.S.C.A. § 2000e–2(e)(1); Dothard v. Rawlinson, 433 U.S. 321 (1977).

3. Respondents could not sue under the Equal Pay Act because the Equal Pay Act did not apply to municipal employees until passage of the Fair Labor Standards Amendments of 1974, 88 Stat. 55, 58–62. Title VII has applied to such employees since passage of the Equal Employment Opportunity Act of 1972, § 2(1), 86 Stat. 103.

the females devoted much of their time to less-valuable clerical duties. It therefore held that respondents' jobs were not substantially equal to those of the male guards, and that respondents were thus not entitled to equal pay. 20 FEP Cases 788, 791 (Ore.1976). The Court of Appeals affirmed on that issue, and respondents do not seek review of the ruling.

The District Court also dismissed respondents' claim that the discrepancy in pay between the male and female guards was attributable in part to intentional sex discrimination. It held as a matter of law that a sex-based wage discrimination claim cannot be brought under Title VII unless it would satisfy the equal work standard of the Equal Pay Act, 29 U.S.C.A. § 206(d), 20 FEP Cases, at 791. The Court therefore permitted no additional evidence on this claim, and made no findings on whether petitioner's pay scales for female guards resulted from intentional sex discrimination.

The Court of Appeals reversed, holding that persons alleging sex discrimination "are not precluded from suing under Title VII to protest * * * discriminatory compensation practices" merely because their jobs were not equal to higher-paying jobs held by members of the opposite sex. 602 F.2d 882, 891 (C.A.9 1979), supplemental opinion on denial of rehearing, 623 F.2d 1303, 1317 (1980). We * * * affirm.

We emphasize at the outset the narrowness of the question before us in this case. Respondents' claim is not based on the controversial concept of "comparable worth,"[6] under which plaintiffs might claim increased compensation on the basis of a comparison of the intrinsic worth or difficulty of their job with that of other jobs in the same organization or community.[7] Rather, respondents seek to prove, by direct evidence, that their wages were depressed because of intentional sex discrimination, consisting of setting the wage scale for female guards, but not for male guards, at a level lower than its own survey of outside markets and the worth of the jobs warranted. The narrow question in this case is whether such a claim is precluded by the last sentence of § 703(h) of Title VII, called the "Bennett Amendment."[8]

II

Title VII makes it an unlawful employment practice for an employer "to discriminate against any individual with respect to his compensation, terms,

6. The concept of "comparable worth" has been the subject of much scholarly debate, as to both its elements and its merits as a legal or economic principle. See e.g., E. Livernash, Comparable Worth: Issues and Alternatives (1980); Blumrosen, Wage Discrimination, Job Segregation, and Title VII of the Civil Rights Act of 1964, 12 U.Mich.J.L.Ref. 397 (1979); Nelson, Opton & Wilson, Wage Discrimination and the "Comparable Worth" Theory in Perspective, 13 U.Mich.J.L.Ref. 231 (1980). The Equal Employment Opportunity Commission has conducted hearings on the question, see BNA Daily Labor Report Nos. 83–85 (February 30, 1999), and has commissioned a study of job evaluation systems, see D. Treiman, Job Evaluation: An Analytic Review (1979)(interim report).

7. Respondents thus distinguish Lemons v. City and County of Denver, 620 F.2d 228

(C.A.10), cert. denied 449 U.S. 888 (1980), on the ground that the plaintiffs, nurses employed by a public hospital, sought increased compensation on the basis of a comparison with compensation paid to employees of comparable value—other than nurses—in the community, without direct proof of intentional discrimination.

8. We are not called upon in this case to decide whether respondents have stated a prima facie case of sex discrimination under Title VII, cf. Christensen v. Iowa, 563 F.2d 353 (C.A.8 1977), or to lay down standards for the further conduct of this litigation. The sole issue we decide is whether respondents' failure to satisfy the equal work standard of the Equal Pay Act in itself precludes their proceeding under Title VII.

conditions, or privileges of employment, because of such individual's * * * sex * * *." 42 U.S.C.A. § 2000e–2(a). The Bennett Amendment to Title VII, however, provides:

> "It shall not be an unlawful employment practice under this subchapter for any employer to differentiate upon the basis of sex in determining the amount of the wages or compensation paid or to be paid to employees of such employer if such differentiation is authorized by the provisions of section 206(d) of title 29." 42 U.S.C.A. § 2000e–2(h).

To discover what practices are exempted from Title VII's prohibitions by the Bennett Amendment, we must turn to § 206(d) of title 29—the Equal Pay Act * * *. On its face, the Equal Pay Act contains three restrictions pertinent to this case. First, its coverage is limited to those employers subject to the Fair Labor Standards Act. S.Rep. No. 176, 88th Cong., 1st Sess., 2 (1963). Thus, the Act does not apply, for example, to certain businesses engaged in retail sales, fishing, agriculture, and newspaper publishing. See 29 U.S.C.A. §§ 203(s), 213(a). Second, the Act is restricted to cases involving "equal work on jobs the performance of which requires equal skill, effort, and responsibility, and which are performed under similar working conditions." 29 U.S.C.A. § 206(d). Third, the Act's four affirmative defenses exempted any wage differentials attributable to seniority, merit, quantity or quality of production, or "any other factor other than sex." Ibid.

Petitioner argues that the purpose of the Bennett Amendment was to restrict Title VII sex-based wage discrimination claims to those that could also be brought under the Equal Pay Act, and thus that claims not arising from "equal work" are precluded. Respondents, in contrast, argue that the Bennett Amendment was designed merely to incorporate the four affirmative defenses of the Equal Pay Act into Title VII for sex-based wage discrimination claims. Respondents thus contend that claims for sex-based wage discrimination can be brought under Title VII even though no member of the opposite sex holds an equal but higher-paying job, provided that the challenged wage rate is not based on seniority, merit, quantity or quality of production, or "any other factor other than sex." The Court of Appeals found respondents' interpretation the "more persuasive." 623 F.2d at 1311. While recognizing that the language and legislative history of the provision are not unambiguous, we conclude that the Court of Appeals was correct.

A

The language of the Bennett Amendment suggests an intention to incorporate only the affirmative defenses of the Equal Pay Act into Title VII. The Amendment bars sex-based wage discrimination claims under Title VII where the pay differential is "authorized" by the Equal Pay Act. Although the word "authorize" sometimes means simply "to permit," it ordinarily denotes affirmative enabling action. * * * The question, then, is what wage practices have been affirmatively authorized by the Equal Pay Act.

The Equal Pay Act is divided into two parts: a definition of the violation, followed by four affirmative defenses. The first part can hardly be said to "authorize" anything at all: it is purely prohibitory. The second part, however, in essence "authorizes" employers to differentiate in pay on the basis of seniority, merit, quantity or quality of production, or any other factor other than sex, even though such differentiation might otherwise violate the

Act. It is to these provisions, therefore, that the Bennett Amendment must refer.

Petitioner argues that this construction of the Bennett Amendment would render it superfluous. * * * Petitioner claims that the first three affirmative defenses are simply redundant of the provisions elsewhere in § 703(h) of Title VII that already exempt bona fide seniority and merit systems and systems measuring earnings by quantity or quality of production,[10] and that the fourth defense—"any other factor other than sex"—is implicit in Title VII's general prohibition of sex-based discrimination.

We cannot agree. The Bennett Amendment was offered as a "technical amendment" designed to resolve any potential conflicts between Title VII and the Equal Pay Act. * * * Thus, with respect to the first three defenses, the Bennett Amendment has the effect of guaranteeing that courts and administrative agencies adopt a consistent interpretation of like provisions in both statutes. Otherwise, they might develop inconsistent bodies of case law interpreting two sets of nearly identical language.

More importantly, incorporation of the fourth affirmative defense could have significant consequences for Title VII litigation. Title VII's prohibition of discriminatory employment practices was intended to be broadly inclusive, proscribing "not only overt discrimination but also practices that are fair in form, but discriminatory in operation." Griggs v. Duke Power Co., 401 U.S. 424, 431 (1971). The structure of Title VII litigation, including presumptions, burdens of proof, and defenses, has been designed to reflect this approach. The fourth affirmative defense of the Equal Pay Act, however, was designed differently, to confine the application of the Act to wage differentials attributable to sex discrimination. H.R.Rep. No. 309, 88th Cong., 1st Sess., 3 (1963). Equal Pay Act litigation, therefore, has been structured to permit employers to defend against charges of discrimination where their pay differentials are based on a bona fide use of "other factors other than sex." Under the Equal Pay Act, the courts and administrative agencies are not permitted "to substitute their judgment for the judgment of the employer * * * who [has] established and employed a bona fide job rating system," so long as it does not discriminate on the basis of sex. 109 Cong.Rec. 9209 (statement of Rep. Goodell, principal exponent of the Act). Although we do not decide in this case how sex-based wage discrimination litigation under Title VII should be structured to accommodate the fourth affirmative defense of the Equal Pay Act, see supra, n. 8, we consider it clear that the Bennett Amendment, under this interpretation, is not rendered superfluous.

We therefore conclude that only differentials attributable to the four affirmative defenses of the Equal Pay Act are "authorized" by that Act within the meaning of § 703(h) of Title VII.

---

10. Section 703(h) provides in relevant part:

"Notwithstanding any other provision of this subchapter, it shall not be an unlawful employment practice for an employer to apply different standards of compensation, or different terms, conditions, or privileges of employment *pursuant to a bona fide seniority or merit system, or a system which measures earnings by quantity or quality of production* * * * provided that such differences are not the result of an intention to discriminate because of * * * sex * * *." 42 U.S.C.A. § 2000e–2(h)(emphasis added).

B

The legislative background of the Bennett Amendment is fully consistent with this interpretation.

* * *

D

Our interpretation of the Bennett Amendment draws additional support from the remedial purposes of Title VII and the Equal Pay Act. Section 703(a) of Title VII makes it unlawful for an employer "to fail or refuse to hire or to discharge any individual, or *otherwise to discriminate* against any individual with respect to his compensation, terms, conditions, or privileges of employment" because of such individual's sex. 42 U.S.C.A. § 2000e–2(a)(emphasis added). As Congress itself has indicated, a "broad approach" to the definition of equal employment opportunity is essential to overcoming and undoing the effect of discrimination. S.Rep. No. 867, 88th Cong., 2d Sess., 12 (1964). We must therefore avoid interpretations of Title VII that deprive victims of discrimination of a remedy, without clear congressional mandate.

Under petitioner's reading of the Bennett Amendment, only those sex-based wage discrimination claims that satisfy the "equal work" standard of the Equal Pay Act could be brought under Title VII. In practical terms, this means that a woman who is discriminatorily underpaid could obtain no relief—no matter how egregious the discrimination might be—unless her employer also employed a man in an equal job in the same establishment, at a higher rate of pay. Thus, if an employer hired a woman for a unique position in the company and then admitted that her salary would have been higher had she been male, the woman would be unable to obtain legal redress under petitioner's interpretation. Similarly, if an employer used a transparently sex-biased system for wage determination, women holding jobs not equal to those held by men would be denied the right to prove that the system is a pretext for discrimination. Moreover, to cite an example arising from a recent case, Los Angeles Department of Water & Power v. Manhart, 435 U.S. 702 (1978), if the employer required its female workers to pay more into its pension program than male workers were required to pay the only women who could bring a Title VII action under petitioner's interpretation would be those who could establish that a man performed equal work: a female auditor thus might have a cause of action while a female secretary might not. Congress surely did not intend the Bennett Amendment to insulate such blatantly discriminatory practices from judicial redress under Title VII.[19]

Moreover, petitioner's interpretation would have other far-reaching consequences. Since it rests on the proposition that any wage differentials not prohibited by the Equal Pay Act are "authorized" by it, petitioner's interpretation would lead to the conclusion that discriminatory compensation by employers not covered by the Fair Labor Standards Act is "authorized"— since not prohibited—by the Equal Pay Act. Thus it would deny Title VII protection against sex-based wage discrimination by those employers not

---

19. The dissent attempts to minimize the significance of the Title VII remedy in these cases on the ground that the Equal Pay Act already provides an action for sex-based wage discrimination by women who hold jobs not *currently* held by men. * * * But the dissent's position would still leave remediless all victims of discrimination who hold jobs *never* held by men.

subject to the Fair Labor Standards Act but covered by Title VII.   * * * There is no persuasive evidence that Congress intended such a result, and the EEOC has rejected it since at least 1965. See 29 CFR § 1604.7 (1966). Indeed, petitioner itself apparently acknowledges that Congress intended Title VII's broader coverage to apply to equal pay claims under Title VII, thus impliedly admitting the fallacy in its own argument.   * * *

Petitioner's reading is thus flatly inconsistent with our past interpretations of Title VII as "prohibit[ing] all practices in whatever form which create inequality in employment opportunity due to discrimination on the basis of race, religion, sex, or national origin." Franks v. Bowman Transportation Co., 424 U.S. 747, 763 (1976). As we said in Los Angeles Department of Water & Power v. Manhart, 435 U.S., at 707, n. 13: "In forbidding employers to discriminate against individuals because of their sex, Congress intended to strike at the *entire spectrum* of disparate treatment of men and women resulting from sex stereotypes." (Emphasis added.) We must therefore reject petitioner's interpretation of the Bennett Amendment.

III

Petitioner argues strenuously that the approach of the Court of Appeals places "the pay structure of virtually every employer and the entire economy * * * at risk and subject to scrutiny by the federal courts." * * * It raises the spectre that "Title VII plaintiffs could draw any type of comparison imaginable concerning job duties and pay between any job predominantly performed by women and any job predominantly performed by men." * * * But whatever the merit of petitioner's arguments in other contexts, they are inapplicable here, for claims based on the type of job comparisons petitioner describes are manifestly different from respondents' claim. Respondents contend that the County of Washington evaluated the worth of their jobs; that the county determined that they should be paid approximately 95% as much as the male correctional officers; that it paid them only about 70% as much, while paying the male officers the full evaluated worth of their jobs; and that the failure of the county to pay respondents the full evaluated worth of their jobs can be proven to be attributable to intentional sex discrimination. Thus, respondents' suit does not require a court to make its own subjective assessment of the value of the male and female guard jobs, or to attempt by statistical technique or other method to quantify the effect of sex discrimination on the wage rates.[20]

We do not decide in this case the precise contours of lawsuits challenging sex discrimination in compensation under Title VII. It is sufficient to note that respondents' claims of discriminatory undercompensation are not barred by § 703(h) of Title VII merely because respondents do not perform work equal to that of male jail guards. The judgment of the Court of Appeals is therefore

Affirmed.

---

20. See D. Treiman, Job Evaluation: An Analytic Review 35–36 (1979)(interim report to the EEOC); Fisher, Multiple Regression in Legal Proceedings, 80 Colum.L.Rev. 702, 721–725 (1980); Nelson, Opton & Wilson, Wage Discrimination and the "Comparable Worth" Theory in Perspective, 13 U. of Mich.J. of Law Reform 231, 278–288 (1980); Schwab, Job Evaluation and Pay Setting: Concepts and Practices, printed in Livernash, Comparable Worth: Issues and Alternatives 49, 52–70 (1980).

JUSTICE REHNQUIST, with whom THE CHIEF JUSTICE, JUSTICE STEWART, and JUSTICE POWELL join dissenting.

The Court today holds a plaintiff may state a claim of sex-based wage discrimination under Title VII without even establishing that she has performed "equal or substantially equal work" to that of males as defined in the Equal Pay Act. Because I believe that the legislative history of both the Equal Pay Act and Title VII clearly establish that there can be no Title VII claim of sex-based wage discrimination without proof of "equal work," I dissent.

I

Because the Court never comes to grips with petitioners' argument, it is necessary to restate it here. Petitioners argue that Congress in adopting the Equal Pay Act of 1963 specifically addressed the problem of sex-based wage discrimination and determined that there should be a remedy for claims of unequal pay for equal work, but not for "comparable" work. Petitioners further observe that nothing in the legislative history of Title VII, enacted just one year later in 1964, reveals an intent to overrule that determination. Quite the contrary, petitioner notes that the legislative history of Title VII, including the adoption of the so-called Bennett Amendment, demonstrates Congress' intent to require all sex-based wage discrimination claims, whether brought under the Equal Pay Act or under Title VII, to satisfy the "equal work" standard. Because respondents have not satisfied the "equal work" standard, petitioners conclude that they have not stated a claim under Title VII.

In rejecting that argument, the Court ignores traditional canons of statutory construction and relevant legislative history. Although I had thought it well settled that the legislative history of a statute is a useful guide to the intent of Congress, the Court today claims that the legislative history "has no bearing on the meaning of the Act," * * * "does not provide a solution to our present problem," * * * and is simply of "no weight." * * * Instead, the Court rests its decision on its unshakable belief that any other result would be unsound public policy. It insists that there simply *must* be a remedy for wage discrimination *beyond* that provided in the Equal Pay Act. The Court does not explain *why* that must be so, nor does it explain *what* that remedy might be. And, of course, the Court cannot explain why it and not Congress is charged with determining what is and what is not sound public policy.

* * *

The Court blithely ignores all of this legislative history and chooses to interpret the Bennett Amendment as incorporating only the Equal Pay Act's four affirmative defenses, and not the equal work requirement. That argument does not survive scrutiny. In the first place, the language of the amendment draws no distinction between the Equal Pay Act's standard for liability—equal pay for equal work—and the Act's defenses. Nor does any Senator or Congressman even come close to suggesting that the Amendment incorporates the Equal Pay Act's affirmative defenses into Title VII, but not the equal work standard itself. Quite the contrary, the concern was that Title VII would render the Equal Pay Act a nullity. It is only too obvious that reading just the four affirmative defenses of the Equal Pay Act into Title VII does not protect the careful draftsmanship of the Equal Pay Act. We must examine statutory words in a manner that "reconstitutes the gamut of values current at the time when the words were uttered." Woodwork Manufacturers v. NLRB, 386 U.S. 612, 620 (1967)(quoting L. Hand, J.). In this case, it stands Congress' concern on its head to suppose that Congress sought to incorporate the affirmative defenses, but not the equal work standard. It would be surprising if Congress in 1964 sought to reverse its decision in 1963 to require a showing of "equal work" as a predicate to an equal pay claim and at the same time carefully preserve the four affirmative defenses.

Moreover, even on its own terms the Court's argument is unpersuasive. The Equal Pay Act contains four statutory defenses * * *. The flaw in interpreting the Bennett Amendment as incorporating only the four defenses of the Equal Pay Act into Title VII is that Title VII, even without the Bennett Amendment, contains those very same defenses. The opening sentence of § 703(h) protects differentials and compensation based on seniority, merit, or quantity or quality of production. These are three of the four EPA defenses. The fourth EPA defense, "a factor other than sex," is already implicit in Title VII because the statute's prohibition of sex discrimination applies only if there is discrimination on the basis of sex. Under the Court's interpretation, the Bennett Amendment, the second sentence of § 703(h), is mere surplusage. * * * The Court's answer to this argument is curious. It suggests that repetition ensures that the provisions would be consistently interpreted by the courts. * * * But that answer only speaks to the purpose for incorporating the defenses in each statute, not for stating the defenses twice in the same statute. Courts are not quite as dense as the majority assumes.

In sum, Title VII and the Equal Pay Act, read together, provide a balanced approach to resolving sex-based wage discrimination claims. Title VII guarantees that qualified female employees will have access to all jobs, and the Equal Pay Act assures that men and women performing the same work will be paid equally. Congress intended to remedy wage discrimination through the Equal Pay Act standards, whether suit is brought under that statute or under Title VII. What emerges is that Title VII would have been construed *in pari materia* even without the Bennett Amendment, and that the Amendment serves simply to insure that the equal work standard would be the standard by which all wage compensation claims would be judged.

III

Perhaps recognizing that there is virtually no support for its position in the legislative history, the Court rests its holding on its belief that any other holding would be unacceptable public policy. * * * It argues that there must be a remedy for wage discrimination beyond that provided for in the Equal Pay Act. Quite apart from the fact that that is an issue properly left to Congress and not the Court, the Court is wrong even as a policy matter. The Court's parade of horribles that would occur absent a distinct Title VII remedy simply do not support the result it reaches.

First, the Court contends that a separate Title VII remedy is necessary to remedy the situation where an employer admits to a female worker, hired for a unique position, that her compensation would have been higher had she been male. * * * Stated differently, the Court insists that an employer could isolate a predominantly female job category and arbitrarily cut its wages because no men currently perform equal or substantially equal work. But a Title VII remedy is unnecessary in these cases because an Equal Pay Act remedy is available. Under the Equal Pay Act, it is not necessary that every Equal Pay Act violation be established through proof that members of the opposite sex are *currently* performing equal work for greater pay. However unlikely such an admission might be in the bullpen of litigation, an employer's statement that "if my female employees performing a particular job were males, I would pay them more simply because they are males" would be admissible in a suit under that Act. Overt discrimination does not go unremedied by the Equal Pay Act. * * * In addition, insofar as hiring or placement discrimination caused the isolated job category, Title VII already provides numerous remedies (such as back-pay, transfer and constructive seniority) without resort to job comparisons. In short, if women are limited to low paying jobs against their will, they have adequate remedies under Title VII for denial of job opportunities even under what I believe is the correct construction of the Bennett Amendment.

The Court next contends that absent a Title VII remedy women who work for employers exempted from coverage of the Equal Pay Act would be wholly without a remedy for wage discrimination. * * * The Court misapprehends petitioners' argument. As Senator Clark explained in his memorandum, * * * Congress sought to incorporate into Title VII the substantive standard of the Equal Pay Act—the "equal work" standard—not the employee coverage provisions. * * * Thus, to say that the "equal pay for equal work" standard is incorporated into Title VII does not mean that employees are precluded from bringing compensation discrimination claims under Title VII. It means only that if employees choose to proceed under Title VII, they must show that they have been deprived of "equal pay for equal work."

There is of course a situation in which petitioners' position *would* deny women a remedy for claims of sex-based wage discrimination. A remedy would not be available where a lower paying job held primarily by women is "comparable," but not substantially equal to, a higher paying job performed by men. That is, plaintiffs would be foreclosed from showing that they received unequal pay for work of "comparable worth" or that dissimilar jobs are of "equal worth." The short, and best, answer to that contention is that Congress in 1963 explicitly chose not to provide a remedy in such cases. And contrary to the suggestion of the Court, it is by no means clear that Title VII was enacted to remedy *all* forms of alleged discrimination. We recently emphasized for example, that "Title VII could not have been enacted into law without substantial support from legislators in both Houses who traditionally resisted federal regulation of private business. Those legislators demanded as a price for their support that 'management prerogative, and union freedoms * * * be left undisturbed to the greatest extent possible.'" United Steelworkers v. Weber, 443 U.S. 193 (1979). See Mohasco Corp. v. Silver, 100 S.Ct. 2486 (1980)(a 90–day statute of limitations may have "represented a necessary sacrifice of the rights of some victims in order that a civil rights bill could be enacted"). Congress balanced the need for a remedy for wage discrimination against its desire to avoid the burdens associated with governmental intervention into wage structures. The Equal Pay Act's "equal pay for equal work" formula reflects the outcome of this legislative balancing. In construing Title VII, therefore, the courts cannot be indifferent to this sort of political compromise.

IV

Even though today's opinion reaches what I believe to be the wrong result, its narrow holding is perhaps its saving feature. The opinion does not endorse the so-called "comparable worth" theory; though the Court does not indicate how a plaintiff might establish a prima facie case under Title VII, the Court does suggest that allegations of unequal pay for unequal, but comparable, work will not state a claim on which relief may be granted. The Court, for example, repeatedly emphasizes that this is not a case where plaintiffs ask the court to compare the value of dissimilar jobs or to quantify the effect of sex discrimination on wage rates. * * * Indeed, the Court relates, without criticism, respondents' contention that Lemons v. City and County of Denver, 620 F.2d 228 (C.A.10), cert. denied, 449 U.S. 888 (1980), is distinguishable. * * * There the court found that Title VII did not provide a remedy to nurses who sought increased compensation based on a comparison of their jobs to dissimilar jobs of "comparable" value in the community. See also Christensen v. Iowa, 563 F.2d 353 (C.A.8 1977)(no prima facie case under Title VII when plaintiffs, women clerical employees of a university, sought to compare their wages to the employees in the physical plant).

Given that implied repeals of legislation are disfavored, TVA v. Hill, 437 U.S. 153, 189 (1978), we should not be surprised that the Court disassociates itself from the entire notion of "comparable worth." In enacting the Equal Pay Act in 1963, Congress specifically prohibited the courts from comparing the wage rates of dissimilar jobs: there can only be a comparison of wage rates where jobs are "equal or substantially equal." Because the legislative history of Title VII does not reveal an intent to overrule that determination, the courts should strive to harmonize the intent of Congress in enacting the Equal Pay Act with its intent in enacting Title VII. Where, as here, the policy of prior legislation is clearly expressed, the Court should not "transfuse the successor statute with a gloss of its own choosing." De Sylva v. Ballentine, 351 U.S. 570, 579 (1956).

Because there are no logical underpinnings to the Court's opinion, all we may conclude is that even absent a showing of equal work, there is a cause of action under Title VII where there is direct evidence that an employer has *intentionally* depressed a woman's salary because she is a woman. The decision today does not approve a cause of action based on a *comparison* of the wage rates of dissimilar jobs.

For the foregoing reasons, however, I believe that even that narrow holding cannot be supported by the legislative history of the Equal Pay Act and Title VII. This is simply a case where the Court has superimposed upon Title VII a "gloss of its own choosing."

AMERICAN NURSES' ASSOCIATION
v. STATE OF ILLINOIS

United States Court of Appeals, Seventh Circuit, 1986.
783 F.2d 716.

POSNER, CIRCUIT JUDGE.

This class action charges the State of Illinois with sex discrimination in employment, in violation of Title VII of the Civil Rights Act of 1964, 42 U.S.C. § 2000e, and the equal protection clause of the Fourteenth Amendment. The named plaintiffs are two associations of nurses plus 21 individuals, mostly but not entirely female, who work for the state in jobs such as nursing and typing that are filled primarily by women. The suit is on behalf of all state employees in these job classifications. The precise allegations of the complaint will require our careful attention later, but for now it is enough to note that they include as an essential element the charge that the state pays workers in predominantly male job classifications a higher wage not justified by any difference in the relative worth of the predominantly male and the predominantly female jobs in the state's roster. * * * In April 1985 the district judge dismissed the complaint * * *. The ground for dismissal was that the complaint pleaded a comparable worth case and that a failure to pay employees in accordance with comparable worth does not violate federal antidiscrimination law. The plaintiffs appeal. They argue that their case is not (or perhaps not just) a comparable worth case and that in characterizing the complaint as he did the district judge terminated the lawsuit by a semantic manipulation. The state both defends the judge's ground for dismissal and argues that we can equally well affirm on the ground that the state's motion for summary judgment should have been granted.

Comparable worth is not a legal concept, but a shorthand expression for the movement to raise the ratio of wages in traditionally women's jobs to wages in traditionally men's jobs. Its premises are both historical and cognitive. The historical premise is that a society politically and culturally dominated by men steered women into certain jobs and kept the wages in those jobs below what the jobs were worth, precisely because most of the holders were women. The cognitive premise is that analytical techniques exist for determining the relative worth of jobs that involve different levels of skill, effort, risk, responsibility, etc. These premises are vigorously disputed on both theoretical and empirical grounds. Economists point out that unless employers forbid women to compete for the higher-paying, traditionally men's jobs—which would violate federal law—women will switch into those jobs until the only difference in wages between traditionally women's jobs and traditionally men's jobs will be that necessary to equate the supply of workers in each type of job to the demand. Economists have conducted studies which show that virtually the entire difference in the average hourly wage of men and women, including that due to the fact that men and women tend to be concentrated in different types of job, can be explained by the fact that most women take considerable time out of the labor force in order to take care of their children. As a result they tend to invest less in their "human capital" (earning capacity); and since part of any wage is a return on human capital, they tend therefore to be found in jobs that pay less. Consistently with this hypothesis, the studies find that women who have never married earn as much as men who have never married. To all this the advocates of comparable worth reply that although there are no longer explicit barriers to women's entering traditionally men's jobs, cultural and psychological barriers remain as a result of which many though not all women internalize men's expectations regarding jobs appropriate for women and therefore invest less in their human capital.

On the cognitive question economists point out that the ratio of wages in different jobs is determined by the market rather than by any a priori conception of relative merit, in just the same way that the ratio of the price of caviar to the price of cabbage is determined by relative scarcity rather than relative importance to human welfare. Upsetting the market equilibrium by imposing such a conception would have costly consequences, some of which might undercut the ultimate goals of the comparable worth movement. If the movement should cause wages in traditionally men's jobs to be depressed below their market level and wages in traditionally women's jobs to be jacked above their market level, women will have less incentive to enter traditionally men's fields and more to enter traditionally women's fields. Analysis cannot stop there, because the change in relative wages will send men in the same direction: fewer men will enter the traditionally men's jobs, more the traditionally women's jobs. As a result there will be more room for women in traditionally men's jobs and at the same time fewer opportunities for women in traditionally women's jobs—especially since the number of those jobs will shrink as employers are induced by the higher wage to substitute capital for labor inputs (e.g., more word processors, fewer secretaries). Labor will be allocated less efficiently; men and women alike may be made worse off.

Against this the advocates of comparable worth urge that collective bargaining, public regulation of wages and hours, and the lack of information and mobility of some workers make the market model an inaccurate description of how relative wages are determined and how they influence the choice of jobs. The point has particular force when applied to a public employer such as the State of Illinois, which does not have the same incentives that a private firm would have to use labor efficiently.

It should be clear from this brief summary that the issue of comparable worth (on which see the discussion and references in Paul Weiler, The Uses and Limits of Comparable Worth in the Pursuit of Pay Equity for Women, Discussion Paper No. 15, Program in Law and Economics, Harvard Law School, November 1985) is not of the sort that judges are well equipped to resolve intelligently or that we should lightly assume has been given to us to resolve by Title VII or the Constitution. An employer (private or public) that simply pays the going wage in each of the different types of job in its establishment, and makes no effort to discourage women from applying for particular jobs or to steer them toward particular jobs, would be justifiably surprised to discover that it may be violating federal law because each wage rate and therefore the ratio between them have been found to be determined by cultural or psychological factors attributable to the history of male domination of society; that it has to hire a consultant to find out how it must, regardless of market conditions, change the wages it pays, in order to achieve equity between traditionally male and traditionally female jobs; and that it must pay backpay, to boot. We need not tarry over the question of law presented by this example because as we understand the plaintiffs' position it is not that a mere failure to rectify traditional wage disparities between predominantly male and predominantly female jobs violates federal law. The circuits that have considered this contention have rejected it, see *Spaulding v. University of Washington*, 740 F.2d 686, 706–07 (9th Cir.1984); *Lemons v. City & County of Denver*, 620 F.2d 228 (10th Cir.1980); *Christensen v. Iowa*, 563 F.2d 353 (8th Cir.1977), and the *AFSCME* case discussed below; we shall see shortly that this rejection may be compelled by the Supreme Court's decisions in the *Davis* and *Feeney* cases.

The next question is whether a failure to achieve comparable worth—granted that it would not itself be a violation of law—might permit an inference of deliberate and therefore unlawful discrimination, as distinct from passive acceptance of a market-determined disparity in wages. The starting point for analyzing this question must be *County of Washington v. Gunther*, 452 U.S. 161, 101 S.Ct. 2242, 68 L.Ed.2d 751 (1981). * * *

* * * The relevance of a comparable worth study in proving sex discrimination is that it may provide the occasion on which the employer is forced to declare his intentions toward his female employees. In *Gunther* the county accepted (it was alleged) the recommendation of its comparable worth consultant regarding the male guards—decided to pay them "the full evaluated worth of their jobs"—but then rejected the recommendation regarding the female guards and did so because of "intentional sex discrimination," that is, because they were female, not because they had easier jobs or jobs that, for any reason, the market valued below the guarding of male prisoners (however a comparable worth consultant might value them).

The State of Illinois asks us to limit the teaching of *Gunther* to cases where the employer has accepted the recommendation of the comparable worth consultant with respect to the male job classifications. But that would be to take undue liberties with the Supreme Court's decision. The dissenting Justices pointed out that in limiting the Equal Pay Act to cases of equal work Congress had deliberately rejected liability based on the concept of comparable worth, and they argued that Congress had not intended to reverse field on the issue when it enacted Title VII a year later. The majority rejected this argument but left open "the precise contours of lawsuits challenging sex discrimination in compensation under Title VII." 452 U.S. at 181, 101 S.Ct. at 2254. It used the facts alleged in the case to argue that the dissenting Justices were exaggerating the impact of the decision on employers, but did not suggest that its holding was limited to cases with the same facts. So limited, its only effect would be to discourage employers from commissioning comparable worth studies.

Gunther suggests the type of evidence that is sufficient but perhaps not necessary to establish sex discrimination in wages for different work. A more recent case out of the State of Washington, *American Federation of State, County & Municipal Employees (AFSCME) v. Washington*, 770 F.2d 1401 (9th Cir.1985), suggests the type of evidence that is insufficient. The state's traditional policy had been to pay state employees the prevailing market rates of pay. Beginning in 1974, however, the state commissioned a series of comparable worth studies, each of which found that employees in predominantly female job classifications were paid about 20 percent less than employees in predominantly male job classifications judged to be of comparable worth. Eventually the state passed legislation providing for the phasing in over a decade of a wage system based on comparable worth. The suit charged that the state's failure to act sooner was a form of discrimination. The case was tried and the plaintiffs won in the district court, but the Ninth Circuit reversed. It held that a decision to pay market wages is not discriminatory, that "comparable worth statistics alone are insufficient to establish the requisite inference of discriminatory motive," *id.* at 1407, and that "isolated incidents" (*id.*) of intentional discrimination in the form of help-wanted ads specifying the sex of the applicant were not enough to convert the case into one of wage discrimination across different jobs.

The *AFSCME* case resembles our hypothetical case of the firm accused of sex discrimination merely because it pays market wages. *AFSCME* shows that such a case is not actionable under Title VII even if the employer is made aware that its pattern of wages departs from the principle of comparable worth to the disadvantage of women (plus the occasional male occupant of a traditionally woman's job) and even if the employer is not so much a prisoner of the market that it cannot alter its wages in the direction of comparable worth, as eventually the State of Washington did. The critical thing lacking in *AFSCME* was evidence that the state decided not to raise the wages of particular workers *because* most of those workers were female. Without such evidence, to infer a violation of Title VII from the fact that the state had conducted a comparable worth study would, again, just discourage such studies.

The plaintiffs can get no mileage out of casting a comparable worth case as an equal protection case. The Supreme Court held in *Washington v. Davis,* 426 U.S. 229, 96 S.Ct. 2040, 48 L.Ed.2d 597 (1976), that the equal protection clause is violated only by intentional discrimination; the fact that a law or official practice adopted for a lawful purpose has a racially differential impact is not enough. The Court applied this principle to sex discrimination in *Personnel Administrator v. Feeney,* 442 U.S. 256, 99 S.Ct. 2282, 60 L.Ed.2d 870 (1979). Massachusetts had a law giving preference in state employment to veterans. The preference was applicable to female as well as male veterans but of course most veterans are male. But as the purpose of the law was to benefit veterans of either sex rather than to favor men over women, the plaintiff's constitutional challenge failed. " '[D]iscriminatory purpose' * * * implies more than intent as volition or intent as awareness of consequences. It implies that the decisionmaker * * * selected or reaffirmed a particular course of action at least in part 'because of,' not merely 'in spite of,' its adverse effects upon an identifiable group." *Id.* at 279, 99 S.Ct. at 2296 (citation and footnotes omitted).

These holdings cast additional light on the contention that intentional discrimination can be inferred from the state's failure to eliminate wage disparities shown by the comparable worth report. Knowledge of a disparity is not the same thing as an intent to cause or maintain it; if for example the state's intention was to pay market wages, its knowledge that the consequence would be that men got higher wages on average than women and that the difference might exceed any premium attributable to a difference in relative worth would not make it guilty of intentionally discriminating against women. Similarly, even if the failure to act on the comparable worth study could be regarded as "reaffirming" the state's commitment to pay market wages, this would not be enough to demonstrate discriminatory purpose. To demonstrate such a purpose the failure to act would have to be motivated at least in part by a desire to benefit men at the expense of women.

Neither *Davis* nor *Feeney* were Title VII cases, a point emphasized in *Davis*. See 426 U.S. at 238–39, 96 S.Ct. at 2046–47. But when intentional discrimination is charged under Title VII the inquiry is the same as in an equal protection case. The difference between the statutory and constitutional prohibitions becomes important only when a practice is challenged not because it is intended to hurt women (say), but because it hurts them inadvertently and is not justified by the employer's needs—when, in short, the challenge is based on a theory of "disparate impact," as distinct from "disparate treatment" (= intentional discrimination). The plaintiffs in this case, however, have said that they are proceeding on the basis of disparate treatment rather than disparate impact. Their decision is understandable. In the usual disparate-impact case the plaintiff challenges some job qualification—for example, that the applicant have a high-school diploma, or pass an entrance exam—as disproportionately excluding blacks or some other protected group, and the issue is whether the qualification is reasonably necessary for the job, in which event it is lawful notwithstanding its exclusionary effect. See, e.g., *Aguilera v. Cook County Police & Corrections Merit Bd.*, 760 F.2d 844, 846–47 (7th Cir.1985), and cases cited there. It is not apparent what the analogy to an exclusionary job qualification would be in this case.

Another point is that the Bennett Amendment to Title VII (the last sentence in 42 U.S.C. § 2000e–2(h)) authorizes employers to pay different wages to men and women provided that the difference would be lawful under the Equal Pay Act, which allows unequal pay for equal work if the inequality results from "any * * * factor other than sex," 29 U.S.C. § 206(d)(1)(iv). The Supreme Court in *Gunther* assumed without quite deciding that the Bennett Amendment allows an employer charged (necessarily under Title VII rather than the Equal Pay Act) with paying unequal wages for unequal work to defend by showing that the inequality is based on something other than sex, even if the result is a disparate impact. See 452 U.S. at 171, 101 S.Ct. at 2249. This reading would confine the scope of Title VII in a case such as the present to intentional discrimination.

So if all that the plaintiffs in this case are complaining about is the State of Illinois' failure to implement a comparable worth study, they have no case and it was properly dismissed. We must therefore consider what precisely they are complaining about. * * *

* * *

The key paragraph of the complaint is paragraph 9, * * *.

* * *

If this were the entire charging part of the complaint, there would be no question of dismissing it for failure to state a claim. The paragraph initially charges the state with intentional discrimination against its female employees, because of their sex; and this, standing alone, would be quite enough to state a claim under Title VII. It continues, "and because of their employment in historically female-dominated sex-segregated job classifications," and then adds a claim on behalf of male employees in those classifications. The continuation could be interpreted as an allegation that the state's failure to adopt a wage scale based on the principle of comparable worth violates Title VII, and if so fails to state a claim. But the mention of "sex-segregated" blurs the picture. If the state has deliberately segregated jobs by sex, it has violated Title VII. Anyway a complaint cannot be dismissed merely because it includes invalid claims along with a valid one. Nothing is more common.

Subparagraphs (a) through (g) present a list of particular discriminatory practices; and since they are merely illustrative ("not limited to"), the complaint would not fail even if none of them were actionable. Some are, some aren't. If (a), the "use of a sex-biased system for pay and classification which results in and perpetuates discrimination in compensation against women employed in historically female-dominated sex-segregated job classifications," just means that the state is paying wages determined by the market rather than by the principle of comparable worth, it states no claim. But if it means to allege that the state has departed from the market measure on grounds of sex—not only paying higher than market wages in predominantly male job classifications and only market wages in predominantly female classifications, but keeping women from entering the predominantly male jobs ("sex-segregated")—it states a claim. * * *

* * *

Maybe the allegations in paragraph 9 are illuminated by subsequent paragraphs of the complaint. Paragraph 10, after summarizing the comparable worth study, says, "Defendants knew or should have known of the historical and continuing existence of patterns and practices of discrimination in compensation and classification, as documented at least in part by the State of Illinois Study."   All that the study "documents," however, is that 28 percent of the employees subject to the state's personnel code are employed in 24 job classifications, in each of which at least 80 percent of the employees are of the same sex, and that based on the principles of comparable worth the 12 predominantly female job classifications are underpaid by between 29 and 56 percent. For example, an electrician whose job is rated in the study at only 274 points in skill, responsibility, etc. has an average monthly salary of $2,826, compared to $2,104 for a nurse whose job is rated at 480 points. These disparities are consistent, however, with the state's paying market wages, and of course the fact that the state knew that market wages do not always comport with the principles of comparable worth would not make a refusal to abandon the market actionable under Title VII. But at the very end of paragraph 10 we read, "Moreover, defendants have knowingly and *willfully* failed to take any action to correct such discrimination" (emphasis added), and in the word "willfully" can perhaps be seen the glimmerings of another theory of violation that could survive a motion to dismiss. Suppose the state has declined to act on the results of the comparable worth study not because it prefers to pay (perhaps is forced by labor-market or fiscal constraints to pay) market wages but because it thinks men deserve to be paid more than women. Cf. *Crawford v. Board of Education,* 458 U.S. 527, 539 n. 21, 102 S.Ct. 3211, 3218 n. 21, 73 L.Ed.2d 948 (1982). This would be the kind of deliberate sex discrimination that Title VII forbids, once the statute is understood to allow wage disparities between dissimilar jobs to be challenged (*Gunther*).

"Willfully" is, however, a classic legal weasel word. Sometimes it means with wrongful intent but often it just means with knowledge of something or other. Willful evasion of taxes means not paying when you know you owe tax. After reading the comparable worth study the responsible state officials knew that the state's compensation system might not be consistent with the principles of comparable worth ("might" because there has been no determination that the comparable worth study is valid even on its own terms—maybe it's a lousy comparable worth study). But it would not follow that their failure to implement the study was willful in a sense relevant to liability under Title VII. They may have decided not to implement it because implementation would cost too much or lead to excess demand for some jobs and insufficient demand for others. The only thing that would make the failure a form of intentional and therefore actionable sex discrimination would be if the motivation for not implementing the study was the sex of the employees—if for example the officials thought that men ought to be paid more than women even if there is no difference in skill or effort or in the conditions of work.

We have said that a plaintiff can plead himself right out of court. * * * As we said earlier, if the plaintiff, though not required to do so, pleads facts, and the facts show that he is entitled to no relief, the complaint should be dismissed. There would be no point in allowing such a lawsuit to go any further; its doom is foretold. But this is not such a case. Although the complaint tries to make too much out of a comparable worth study that, standing alone, cannot provide a basis for a claim under Title VII—although the complaint appears to include the theory of violation that the Ninth Circuit later and rightly rejected—a complaint cannot be dismissed merely because one of the theories on which it proceeds, and the facts alleged in support of that theory, do not make out a claim for relief. A complaint that alleges intentional sex discrimination, which *Gunther* makes actionable even though the discrimination is between different job classifications rather than within the same classification, cannot be dismissed just because one of the practices, indeed the principal practice, instanced as intentional sex discrimination—the employer's failure to implement comparable worth—is lawful.

Furthermore, a complaint is not required to allege all, or any, of the facts logically entailed by the claim. If Illinois is overpaying men relative to women, this must mean—unless the market model is entirely inapplicable to labor markets—that it is paying women at least their market wage (and therefore men more), for women wouldn't work for less than they could get in the market; and if so the state must also be refusing to hire women in the men's jobs, for above-market wages in those jobs would be a magnet drawing the women from their lower-paying jobs. Maybe the references in the complaint to the segregation of jobs by sex are meant to allege such refusals but if not this pleading omission would not be critical. A plaintiff does not have to plead evidence. If these plaintiffs admitted or the defendants proved that there was no steering or other method of segregating jobs by sex, the plaintiffs' theory of discrimination might be incoherent, and fail. But a complaint does not fail to state a claim merely because it does not set forth a complete and convincing picture of the alleged wrongdoing. So the plaintiffs do not have to allege steering even if it is in some sense implicit in their claim.

* * *

The state asks us, finally, to uphold dismissal on the ground that the difficulties of remedying wage discrimination between different jobs are insuperable. It points out that the district court would have to decide what the wages in the different jobs would have been but for discrimination in order to know how much backpay to award. But if difficulties of remedy, unless completely insurmountable, were a proper reason for throwing out a complaint at the pleading stage, *Brown v. Board of Education,* 347 U.S. 483, 74 S.Ct. 686, 98 L.Ed. 873 (1954), would have been decided in favor of allowing public schools to continue to segregate the races. Even if, as the state argues, a court could not reasonably impose comparable worth on an employer even as a remedy for blatant discrimination, except in a case such as *Gunther* (or indeed *AFSCME,* had the plaintiffs there prevailed) where the employer has in some sense approved a plan for comparable worth, this would just mean that some other, though perhaps less effective, remedy would have to be substituted. Maybe the plaintiffs would have to be content with an injunction that would knock down any barriers to women's being hired in the traditionally men's jobs, thus allowing the market to eliminate any sex-linked wage differential not justified by a difference in demand and supply, as women gravitated into the higher-paying men's jobs. It is premature to conclude that there is *no* worthwhile remedy for the intentional discrimination that consists of overpaying workers in predominantly male jobs because most of those workers are male. We emphasize, however, that proof of this causality is essential and is not to be inferred merely from the results of a comparable worth study and from the refusal of the employer to implement the study's recommendations. We do not want to arouse false hopes; the plaintiffs have a tough row to hoe. They may lose eventually on summary judgment if discovery yields no more evidence than is contained in the unsupported assertions and stale and seemingly isolated incidents in the plaintiffs' exhibits. But the plaintiffs are entitled to make additional efforts to prove a case of intentional discrimination within the boundaries sketched in this opinion.

Reversed and Remanded.

Notes on Gunther and American Nurses' Ass'n

1. The continued existence of a wage gap between men and women, despite the enactment of legislation forbidding sex discrimination in employment, fuels the search for additional solutions. Even though its size varies depending on which groups of women and men are being compared, a residual earnings gap persists. Thus, Professor Paul Weiler offers the following analysis of the relevant measurements: if the average earnings of all working women and men are compared, the women's wages are only about fifty percent of those earned by men; if the comparison groups are limited to full-time, year-round workers, then the wage gap is closer to sixty percent; if one adjusts the usual annual or weekly earnings ratios by an estimate of the difference in actual hours worked (taking account of overtime and second jobs), the ratio is reduced to seventy-five percent; and, finally, "[i]f we take into consideration all three factors that should and do

influence earnings—the hours of work on the job, the length of experience in the labor force, and the location, hazards, and other conditions of work—then the maximum level of wage gap to be explained by sex discrimination * * * is on the order of ten to fifteen percent." Weiler, The Wages of Sex: The Uses and Limits of Comparable Worth, 99 Harv.L.Rev. 1728, 1779–84 (1986). Weiler adds that even the smallest estimate of the gap "implies a substantial injustice."

Ruth Blumrosen offers one possible explanation of the persistence of the male-female wage gap: men and women work at different jobs; the jobs open to men pay more than those open to women. She elaborates,

> [i]t is the thesis of this article that job segregation and wage discrimination are not separate problems, but rather are intimately related. Whenever there is job segregation, the same forces which determine that certain jobs or job categories will be reserved for women or minorities also and simultaneously determine that the economic value of those jobs is less than if they were "white" or "male" jobs. Thus, those women and minorities who are channelled into segregated jobs are not only deprived of initial hiring opportunities in other jobs and meaningful transfer opportunities, but are also paid wages for the jobs that they get which are discriminatorily depressed.

R. Blumrosen, Wage Discrimination, Job Segregation, and Title VII of the Civil Rights Act of 1964, 12 U.Mich.J.L.Reform 397 (1979). Since Title VII prohibits all racial job segregation and permits only that sexual job segregation subject to the BFOQ exception, see pp. 594–622 supra, what are the "forces" that, in Blumrosen's view, determine that certain jobs will be segregated factually? She points to the lingering imprint on present job patterns of pre-Act intentional job segregation; social stereotypes of work that is appropriate for women; and the relatively small number of women entering nontraditional employment. Id., at 402–08. Psychological and anthropological data are relied on to establish that division of labor by sex is a cross-cultural phenomenon and that whatever work is assigned to women carries with it a lower social value. Id., at 415–20. Finally, she notes the overt wage discrimination between men and women that preceded the enactment of the Equal Pay Act in 1963. Id., at 421–28. She then argues that wage setting mechanisms, such as job evaluation systems, the use of "prevailing" or "community" wage rates, collective bargaining, and the market rate relied on by classical economic theory all operate to translate job segregation into wage discrimination:

> The conclusion to be drawn from the totality of the evidence discussed above conforms to a common sense understanding of the way in which discrimination works and to a review of the facts concerning patterns of discrimination which have been developed in cases decided under Title VII. It is not only that the jobs into which women and minorities have been traditionally segregated are lower paying jobs, but it is that they are lower paying, in part at least, because they are the jobs which have been reserved for minorities and women. The social, historical, and economic studies have demonstrated the high degree of likelihood that the jobs of minorities and women are considered to be of lesser worth because they are female or minority jobs, and the analysis of both job evaluation and the general method of setting wages has established how this value judgment is applied in the setting of wages.

Id., at 455–57.

Blumrosen next applies her theory to Title VII. She argues that:

where a plaintiff has established that jobs have been segregated in the past or present, that jobs are identified as female or minority jobs, that a wage rate structure exists for segregated jobs which is low in the employer's overall structure, or that a job is traditionally reserved for minorities or women throughout the labor force, the inference that segregation influenced the pay rate is sufficient to require the employer to present evidence as to how the wages were set.

Id., at 468. It is not necessary to the prima facie case, says Blumrosen, to show "pure" job segregation; it is enough if the occupants of a particular job are 70 to 80 percent minorities or women. Id., at 461. Blumrosen here speaks of disparate impact discrimination; she acknowledges that individual plaintiffs seeking to prove discrimination on a theory of disparate treatment would be required to show "that the depressed wage was racially or sexually motivated." Id., at 460. The burden that shifts to employer under Blumrosen's theory cannot be discharged by a showing that it has simply paid the "market rate" for the segregated job. In her view, the market rate itself reflects discriminatory factors and cannot be used as a defense. Unfortunately, Blumrosen's theory has not been accepted in court. See Briggs v. City of Madison, 536 F.Supp. 435 (W.D.Wis.1982)(lower pay of public health nurses, who were women, paid less than sanitarians, all men, did not violate Title VII). More recently, she has offered additional suggestions that courts or employers might use to remedy systemic undervaluation of job categories traditionally occupied by women and minorities. See Ruth Blumrosen, Remedies for Wage Discrimination, 20 U.Mich.J.L.Ref. 99 (1986).

2. Why is Justice Brennan so careful to refrain from endorsing the "comparable worth" doctrine in *Gunther*? Does the majority opinion cast doubt on that doctrine, or simply leave it for decision at another time? Does Justice Rehnquist's statement in part IV of his dissenting opinion, that "the Court does suggest that allegations of unequal pay for unequal, but comparable, work will not state a claim on which relief may be granted" exaggerate what the Court held in *Gunther*?

3. Judge Posner congratulates the plaintiffs in *American Nurses' Association* for their decision not to try to make out a disparate impact case under Title VII. Noting that "[i]t is not apparent what the analogy to an exclusionary job qualification would be in this case", Posner suggests that comparable worth claims do not fit the traditional disparate impact model. Elsewhere in his opinion, Posner cites two Ninth Circuit cases that rejected comparable worth claims on both disparate impact and disparate treatment theories, *Spaulding* and *AFSCME*. *AFSCME* is discussed on p. 587 supra. Does the Supreme Court's application of disparate impact analysis to subjective decisionmaking systems in *Watson*, p. 588, supra, affect this analysis?

Courts have continued to require a showing of intentional discrimination in Title VII pay claims. For example, see California State Employees' Ass'n. v. State of California, 724 F.Supp. 717 (N.D.Cal.1989), where Judge Marilyn Patel, acting under compulsion of the Ninth Circuit's requirement in *AFSCME*, 770 F.2d 1401 (9th Cir.1985) that intentional discrimination be shown in disparate treatment cases involving wage discrimination, held that plaintiffs had failed to show that the defendant had intentionally discriminated against women state workers in the 1930s and that such discrimination carried over to present wage structures.

4. Despite the failure of comparable worth as a litigation strategy, an intense debate over the concept continues unabated in the journals. As Judge Posner notes in *American Nurses' Association*, the core of the controversy is about

economic theory. Thus, Fischel and Lazear draw on neo-classical economic theory for the proposition that "comparable worth is *never* the correct remedy, even if wage differentials and job segregation are the product of discrimination against women." Daniel R. Fischel & Edward P. Lazear, Comparable Worth and Discrimination in Labor Markets, 53 U.Chi.L.Rev. 891, 894 (1986). The authors state the essence of their argument as follows:

> The essence of our argument is as follows. Assume that women are discriminated against and wrongfully denied entry into a male-dominated occupation, say, electronics. Women prevented from becoming electricians will flood other occupations such as nursing. The increased supply of women in nursing and other female-dominated occupations may well have the effect of depressing wages. The proper solution, however, is not to raise the wage of nurses while doing nothing about barriers to entry in electronics. Such a remedy would merely combat one inefficiency in the economy (barriers to entry in electronics) by creating a second inefficiency (a minimum wage in nursing). Yet this is precisely the effect of comparable worth.

> We then discuss the moral argument that comparable worth is compelled by the need for pay equity for women. We argue that the attempt to justify comparable worth on moral grounds only serves to obscure the effects of comparable worth on various groups. In fact, many women may be hurt by comparable worth. If a consensus exists that women should be compensated for the effects of past discrimination, such compensation should be in the form of a direct public subsidy rather than comparable worth.

> Finally, we assess the argument that comparable worth is simply an extension of existing anti-discrimination legislation. Because comparable worth imposes a minimum wage but does nothing about discrimination in the economy, we argue that it is fundamentally inconsistent with, rather than an extension of, existing anti-discrimination legislation. In practice, however, existing anti-discrimination legislation may have the same perverse effects as comparable worth. But even if we assume that Title VII and the Equal Pay Act are beneficial, they still provide no support for comparable worth.

Id., at 894–95. This thesis is attacked by James Holzhaur on economic grounds, and by Mary Becker on social and cultural ones. See Holzhaur, The Economic Possibilities of Comparable Worth, 53 U.Chi.L.Rev. 919 (1986)(arguing that the economic case against comparable worth is not as simple and clear-cut as Fischel and Lazear claim); Becker, Barriers Facing Women in the Wage–Labor Market and the Need for Additional Remedies: A Reply to Fischel and Lazear, 53 U.Chi.L.Rev. 934 (1986)(arguing that neoclassical economic models are inherently incapable of describing many of the barriers women face in the wage-labor market; citing, among others, such factors as the ideology of gender and sexual identity; unconscious bias in valuing the work of women; unconscious use of stereotypes to fill information gaps; and sex-linked external and internal barriers to women's advancement in non-traditional jobs). See also Fischel & Lazear, Comparable Worth: A Rejoinder, 53 U.Chi.L.Rev. 950 (1986).

Other commentators have tried to focus the debate more narrowly. Thus, Weiler concludes after canvassing the argument on both sides that "[t]he principle of comparable worth implies only that whatever valuation a particular employer happens to place upon the factor for which it rewards the male or integrated jobs in its operation (and this could even include a factor for shortages in supply), the employer should apply those values uniformly in setting the pay for positions filled primarily by women." Weiler, supra Note 1, at 1777–78. He is doubtful, however, whether comparable worth, as an implemented legal policy, is capable of making more than a relatively small dent in the overall gender gap in earnings. He proposes, instead, other avenues to secure pay equity for women: equal employment policies that will ensure equal access to higher paying jobs; collective bargaining; and voluntary affirmative action by individual employers, especially by the Government implemented through Executive Order 11,246. See also Judith Olans Brown, Phyllis Tropper Baumann & Elaine Millar–Melnick, Equal Pay for Jobs of Comparable Worth: An Analysis of the Rhetoric, 21 Harv.Civ.Rts./ Civ.Lib.L.Rev. 127 (1986) arguing that three inter-related factors explain the lack of litigational success in comparable worth cases: first, a misunderstanding of the dimensions of comparable worth—the legal doctrine should properly be limited to claims against a common employer, not to randomly selected job categories such as nurses and truck drivers; second, an extremely narrow definition of what constitutes sex discrimination in employment—the courts have limited plaintiffs to a showing of intentional discrimination by their rejection of disparate impact approaches; and third, judicial fear of the remedial implications of comparable worth doctrine—the courts have accepted the "market rate" defense too readily. If these are indeed the factors preventing comparable worth strategies from succeeding in the courtroom, what can be done to eliminate them?

5. What about state comparable worth legislation as an additional avenue toward pay equity? See Tina L. Speiser, Note, The Future of Comparable Worth: Looking in New Directions, 37 Syracuse L.Rev. 1189, 1214–17 (1987). At least thirteen states have passed some form of legislation mandating use of the comparable worth principle in setting wages: Alaska, California (for public employees only), Idaho, Iowa (state employees), Kentucky, Maine, Maryland, Massachusetts, North Dakota, Oklahoma, Oregon, South Dakota, and West Virginia. In addition, in 1986, the state of Ohio began implementing a pay equity study to eliminate gender bias from state employees' salaries, projecting a cost estimate of 4.5 million dollars per year for two to four years. The Ohio study found that women working for state agencies earned an average 13% less than men. 121 Labor Relations Reporter 243 (BNA, Apr. 7, 1986).

Public sector employees have also successfully used comparable worth principles to obtain pay equity adjustments through collective bargaining. New York state employees began receiving some 37.8 million dollars in pay equity adjustments in 1987, five years after the state agreed in collective bargaining with its state employee unions to conduct a comparable worth study. Pay adjustments were recommended for 35,000 women workers and 17,000 minority workers. 124 Labor Relations Reporter 250 (BNA, Ap. 20, 1987). Even the state of Washington, after the failure of the American Federation of State Court & Municipal Employees (AFSCME) litigation, agreed with the union to make pay equity adjustments in the wages of its women workers. Over a four year period, new pay levels at above-market rates were set for 62,000 women employees. Peter T. Kilborn, "Wage Gap Between Sexes Is Cut in Test, But At a Price," New York Times, Sec. A., p. 1, col. 1, May 31, 1990. One of the noted effects of raising the pay of female-dominated job categories by an average of 20% has been to reinforce women's attachment to those jobs and deter their entry into now equally-paid male-dominated job categories, a problem anticipated by Judge Posner in *American Nurses*. Clerk typists in Washington state received a 27% raise in pay but are locked into a dead-end job series. Prior to the pay equity adjustments, many were anxious to seek promotion to a fiscal technician job, which could eventually lead to a higher level accountant job. Now, clerk typists are paid more than fiscal technicians; relatively few women are accepting transfers to the lower paid technician jobs, even though eventually they could seek promotion to the higher paid accountant job. Id.

6. What is the proper allocation of burdens of proof in a claim of sex discrimination in compensation brought under Title VII after *Gunther?* At least two different approaches have been sketched out in the cases. A bold tack was adopted by Judge Karlton in Kouba v. Allstate Insurance Co., 523 F.Supp. 148 (E.D.Cal.1981), reversed and remanded on other grounds, 691 F.2d 873 (9th Cir.1982). Reasoning that the four defenses available to the employer under the Equal Pay Act are affirmative defenses, Judge Karlton decided that the employer's burden of rebuttal in Title VII wage discrimination cases based on sex cannot be the slight "burden of production" identified as appropriate in *Burdine.* Instead, after the plaintiff has persuaded the trier of fact that she is paid less than men doing the same work, the burden of persuasion shifts to the employer to establish one of the four affirmative defenses made part of Title VII by the Bennett Amendment. In Judge Karlton's words,

> Consistent with the statutory language then, plaintiff establishes her liability case by proffering evidence and persuading the trier of fact that she is paid less than men doing the same work. Once the plaintiff has done so, defendant must then shoulder its burden of proffering evidence and persuading the trier of fact that the unequal pay is an "authorized differentiation", that is one permitted by the Equal Pay Act.

Id., 523 F.Supp. at 157. This allocation of the burden of proof was upheld on appeal. Kouba v. Allstate Insurance Co., 691 F.2d 873, 875 (9th Cir.1982). Under this approach, the employer's burden is heavier in a sex discrimination case charging wage discrimination than one charging discriminatory failure to hire or promote under Title VII. Is the employer's burden also heavier in a case charging wage discrimination based on sex than it is in a case charging wage discrimination based on race? If so, does the enactment of the Bennett Amendment indicate that Congress intended unequal pay cases affecting women to be treated differently under Title VII than those affecting male minority group members?

On its facts, *Kouba* was a case challenging the employer's practice of setting the entry level pay (called the "monthly minimum") for newly hired insurance sales agents based on a combination of four factors: ability, education, experience, and prior salary. The fourth factor was alleged to constitute sex discrimination because of the generally depressed level of women's wages. In fact, the use of this formula produced a monthly minimum for women that was lower than that of men for the years 1973 through 1979. The employer argued that the prior salary factor was a "factor other than sex" and thus an available defense existed under the Bennett Amendment. This argument was rejected as a matter of law by the district court, but the Ninth Circuit reversed the judgment on this point and remanded the case for trial on the validity of the two "business reasons" for using the prior salary offered by defendant: namely, that tying current salary to prior salary acts as a sales-incentive program to stimulate greater effort to surpass the prior salary by earning commissions; and that prior salary is used as a rough predictor of ability and therefore of sales performance. Are either of these justifications convincing? *Kouba* was settled on October 1, 1984, when Allstate agreed to pay $5 million to 3100 current or former women sales agents. EEOC Chairman Clarence Thomas hailed the settlement as one of "historic proportions" that will have "significant impact on salary setting practices nationwide." San Francisco Chronicle, Oct. 2, 1984, at p. 1, col. 1.

Compare Boyd v. Madison County Mutual Insurance Co., 653 F.2d 1173 (7th Cir.1981), certiorari denied 454 U.S. 1146, 102 S.Ct. 1008, 71 L.Ed.2d 299 (1982), a Title VII wage discrimination claim brought by a male claims superintendent who alleged that he was treated unequally because the attendance bonuses given to the clerical staff for excellent attendance records were not available to him. The court noted that the "equal work" standards of the Equal Pay Act did not apply to the case because of *Gunther's* interpretation of the Bennett Amendment. It went on to conclude that "classic Title VII analysis"—i.e., the *McDonnell–Douglas–Burdine* order of proof rules—applied to the case. A prima facie case was made out by showing that women (the clerical staff) were eligible for bonuses, but that men (the four management personnel) were not. The defendant was held only to *Burdine's* burden of production of a legitimate, nondiscriminatory reason for its action. This was satisfied by showing that the policy was instituted in response to a serious absenteeism problem with the clerical staff. Plaintiff was unable to prove that this explanation was pretextual, and lost his case. Would the result have been different if the employer had been given the burden of proving, as an affirmative defense, that its policy was based on a factor other than sex?

The *Kouba* approach was questioned in Marcoux v. Maine, 797 F.2d 1100 (1st Cir.1986), a Title VII wage discrimination case in which a class of female corrections officers who worked at the Maine Correctional Center claimed they perform work substantially equal to that of the predominantly male guards who worked at the Maine State Prison, but receive less favorable retirement benefits than the guards. The district court, using the *Kouba* burden of proof allocation, had ruled in favor of the plaintiffs. Noting that the *Kouba* approach had been "severely criticized" in EEOC v. Sears, Roebuck & Co., 628 F.Supp. 1264, 1328–32 (N.D.Ill.1986), affirmed 839 F.2d 302 (7th Cir.1988), discussed at p. 573, infra, the *Marcoux* court declined to determine whether the district court had erred because the defendants did not object to the use of the *Kouba* analysis. In affirming the judgment, the *Marcoux* court reserved for future decision the correctness of the *Kouba* analysis.

See generally, Edith Barnett, Comparable Worth and the Equal Pay Act—Proving Sex–Based Wage Discrimination Claims After County of Washington v. Gunther, 28 Wayne L.Rev. 1669 (1982); Barbara A. Norris, Comment, Comparable Worth, Disparate Impact, and the Market Rate Salary Problem: A Legal Analysis and Statistical Application, 71 Calif.L.Rev. 730 (1983).

C. CONSTITUTIONAL PROHIBITIONS AGAINST INTENTIONAL DISCRIMINATION IN EMPLOYMENT

WASHINGTON v. DAVIS

Supreme Court of the United States, 1976.
426 U.S. 229, 96 S.Ct. 2040, 48 L.Ed.2d 597.

MR. JUSTICE WHITE delivered the opinion of the Court.

[This case involved challenges under the Federal Constitution and the District of Columbia Code to the validity of a written personnel test ("Test 21") used generally throughout the federal service and administered here to applicants for positions as police officers in the District of Columbia Metropolitan Police Department. The test, which excluded four times as many blacks as whites, had not been validated to establish its reliability for measuring subsequent job performance, but was shown to be directly relevant to the requirements of the police recruit training program. It had been developed by the Civil Service Commission to test verbal ability, vocabulary, reading, and comprehension. On cross motions for summary judgment, the test was sustained by the District Court but invalidated by the Court of Appeals.]

II

Because the Court of Appeals erroneously applied the legal standards applicable to Title VII cases in resolving the constitutional issue before it, we reverse its judgment in respondents' favor. Although the petition for certiorari did not present this ground for reversal, our Rule 40(1)(d)(2) provides that we "may notice a plain error not presented"; and this is an appropriate occasion to invoke the rule.

As the Court of Appeals understood Title VII,[10] employees or applicants proceeding under it need not concern themselves with the employer's possibly discriminatory purpose but instead may focus solely on the racially differential impact of the challenged hiring or promotion practices. This is not the constitutional rule. We have never held that the standard for adjudicating claims of invidious racial discrimination is identical to the standards applicable under Title VII, and we decline to do so today.

The central purpose of the Equal Protection Clause of the Fourteenth Amendment is the prevention of official conduct discriminating on the basis of race. It is also true that the Due Process Clause of the Fifth Amendment contains an equal protection component prohibiting the United States from invidiously discriminating between individuals or groups. Bolling v. Sharpe, 347 U.S. 497, 74 S.Ct. 693, 98 L.Ed. 884 (1954). But our cases have not embraced the proposition that a law or other official act, without regard to whether it reflects a racially discriminatory purpose, is unconstitutional *solely* because it has a racially disproportionate impact.

Almost 100 years ago, Strauder v. West Virginia, 100 U.S. 303, 25 L.Ed. 664 (1879), established that the exclusion of Negroes from grand and petit juries in criminal proceedings violated the Equal Protection Clause, but the fact that a particular jury or a series of juries does not statistically reflect the racial composition of the community does not in itself make out an invidious discrimination forbidden by the Clause. "A purpose to discriminate must be present which may be proven by systematic exclusion of eligible jurymen of the prescribed race or by an unequal application of the law to such an extent as to show intentional discrimination." Akins v. Texas, 325 U.S. 398, 403–404, 65 S.Ct. 1276, 1279, 89 L.Ed. 1692, 1696 (1945). A defendant in a criminal case is entitled "to require that the State not deliberately and systematically deny to the members of his race the right to participate as jurors in the administration of justice." See also Carter v. Jury Commission, 396 U.S. 320, 335–337, 339, 90 S.Ct. 518, 526–528, 529, 24 L.Ed.2d 549, 560–

---

10. Although Title VII standards have dominated this case, the statute was not applicable to federal employees when the complaint was filed; and although the 1972 amendments extending the title to reach government employees were adopted prior to the District Court's judgment, the complaint was not amended to state a claim under that title, nor did the case thereafter proceed as a Title VII case. Respondents' motion for partial summary judgment, filed after the 1972 amendments, rested solely on constitutional grounds; and the Court of Appeals ruled that the motion should have been granted.

* * *

561, 562 (1970); Cassell v. Texas, 339 U.S. 282, 287–290, 70 S.Ct. 629, 631–633, 94 L.Ed. 839, 847–849 (1950); Patton v. Mississippi, 332 U.S. 463, 468–469, 68 S.Ct. 184, 187, 92 L.Ed. 76, 80 (1947).

The rule is the same in other contexts. Wright v. Rockefeller, 376 U.S. 52, 84 S.Ct. 603, 11 L.Ed.2d 512 (1964), upheld a New York congressional apportionment statute against claims that district lines had been racially gerrymandered. The challenged districts were made up predominantly of whites or of minority races, and their boundaries were irregularly drawn. The challengers did not prevail because they failed to prove that the New York legislature "was either motivated by racial considerations or in fact drew the districts on racial lines"; the plaintiffs had not shown that the statute "was the product of a state contrivance to segregate on the basis of race or place of origin." 376 U.S., at 56, 58, 84 S.Ct., at 605, 11 L.Ed.2d, at 515. The dissenters were in agreement that the issue was whether the "boundaries * * * were purposefully drawn on racial lines." 376 U.S., at 67, 84 S.Ct., at 611, 11 L.Ed.2d, at 522.

The school desegregation cases have also adhered to the basic equal protection principle that the invidious quality of a law claimed to be racially discriminatory must ultimately be traced to a racially discriminatory purpose. That there are both predominantly black and predominantly white schools in a community is not alone violative of the Equal Protection Clause. The essential element of *de jure* segregation is "a current condition of segregation resulting from intentional state action * * * the differentiating factor between *de jure* segregation and so-called *de facto* segregation * * * is *purpose* or *intent* to segregate." Keyes v. School District No. 1, 413 U.S. 189, 205, 208, 93 S.Ct. 2686, 2696, 37 L.Ed.2d 548, 561 (1973). See also *id.,* at 199, 211, 213, 93 S.Ct. at 2692, 2698, 2699, 37 L.Ed.2d, at 558, 564, 566. The Court has also recently rejected allegations of racial discrimination based solely on the statistically disproportionate racial impact of various provisions of the Social Security Act because "the acceptance of appellant's constitutional theory would render suspect each difference in treatment among the grant classes, however lacking the racial motivation and however otherwise rational the treatment might be." Jefferson v. Hackney, 406 U.S. 535, 548, 92 S.Ct. 1724, 1732, 32 L.Ed.2d 285, 297 (1972). And compare Hunter v. Erickson, 393 U.S. 385, 89 S.Ct. 557, 21 L.Ed.2d 616 (1969), with James v. Valtierra, 402 U.S. 137, 91 S.Ct. 1331, 28 L.Ed.2d 678 (1971).

This is not to say that the necessary discriminatory racial purpose must be express or appear on the face of the statute, or that a law's disproportionate impact is irrelevant in cases involving Constitution-based claims of racial discrimination. A statute, otherwise neutral on its face, must not be applied so as invidiously to discriminate on the basis of race. Yick Wo v. Hopkins, 118 U.S. 356, 6 S.Ct. 1064, 30 L.Ed. 220 (1886). It is also clear from the cases dealing with racial discrimination in the selection of juries that the systematic exclusion of Negroes is itself such an "unequal application of the law * * * as to show intentional discrimination." Akins v. Texas, supra, 325 U.S., at 404, 65 S.Ct., at 1279, 89 L.Ed., at 1696. Smith v. Texas, 311 U.S. 128, 61 S.Ct. 164, 85 L.Ed. 84 (1940); Pierre v. Louisiana, 306 U.S. 354, 59 S.Ct. 536, 83 L.Ed. 757 (1939); Neal v. Delaware, 103 U.S. 370, 26 L.Ed. 567 (1881). A prima facie case of discriminatory purpose may be proved as well by the absence of Negroes on a particular jury combined with the failure of the jury commissioners to be informed of eligible Negro jurors in a community, Hill v. Texas, 316 U.S. 400, 404, 62 S.Ct. 1159, 1161, 86 L.Ed. 1559, 1562 (1942), or with racially non-neutral selection procedures, Alexander v. Louisiana, 405 U.S. 625, 92 S.Ct. 1221, 31 L.Ed.2d 536 (1972); Avery v. Georgia, 345 U.S. 559, 73 S.Ct. 891, 97 L.Ed. 1244 (1953); Whitus v. Georgia, 385 U.S. 545, 87 S.Ct. 643, 17 L.Ed.2d 599 (1967). With a prima facie case made out, "the burden of proof shifts to the State to rebut the presumption of unconstitutional action by showing that permissible racially neutral selection criteria and procedures have produced the monochromatic result." *Alexander,* supra, 405 U.S., at 632, 92 S.Ct., at 1226, 31 L.Ed.2d, at 542. See also Turner v. Fouche, 396 U.S. 346, 361, 90 S.Ct. 532, 540, 24 L.Ed.2d 567, 579 (1970); Eubanks v. Louisiana, 356 U.S. 584, 587, 78 S.Ct. 970, 973, 2 L.Ed.2d 991, 994 (1958).

Necessarily, an invidious discriminatory purpose may often be inferred from the totality of the relevant facts, including the fact, if it is true, that the law bears more heavily on one race than another. It is also not infrequently true that the discriminatory impact—in the jury cases for example, the total or seriously disproportionate exclusion of Negroes from jury venires—may for all practical purposes demonstrate unconstitutionality because in various circumstances the discrimination is very difficult to explain on nonracial grounds. Nevertheless, we have not held that a law, neutral on its face and serving ends otherwise within the power of government to pursue, is invalid under the Equal Protection Clause simply because it may affect a greater proportion of one race than of another. Disproportionate impact is not irrelevant, but it is not the sole touchstone of an invidious racial discrimination forbidden by the Constitution. Standing alone, it does not trigger the rule, McLaughlin v. Florida, 379 U.S. 184, 85 S.Ct. 283, 13 L.Ed.2d 222 (1964), that racial classifications are to be subjected to the strictest scrutiny and are justifiable only by the weightiest of considerations.

There are some indications to the contrary in our cases. In Palmer v. Thompson, 403 U.S. 217, 91 S.Ct. 1940, 29 L.Ed.2d 438 (1971), the city of Jackson, Miss., following a court decree to this effect, desegregated all of its public facilities save five swimming pools which had been operated by the city and which, following the decree, were closed by ordinance pursuant to a determination by the city council that closure was necessary to preserve peace and order and that integrated pools could not be economically operated. Accepting the finding that the pools were closed to avoid violence and economic loss, this Court rejected the argument that the abandonment of this service was inconsistent with the outstanding desegregation decree and that the otherwise seemingly permissible ends served by the ordinance could be impeached by demonstrating that racially invidious motivations had prompted the city council's action. The holding was that the city was not overtly or covertly operating segregated pools and was extending identical treatment to both whites and Negroes. The opinion warned against grounding decision on legislative purpose or motivation, thereby lending support for the proposition that the operative effect of the law rather than its purpose is the paramount factor. But the holding of the case was that the legitimate purposes of the ordinance—to preserve peace and avoid deficits—were not open to impeachment by evidence that the councilmen were actually motivated by racial considerations. Whatever dicta the opinion may contain, the decision did not involve, much less invalidate, a statute or ordinance having neutral purposes but disproportionate racial consequences.

Wright v. Council of City of Emporia, 407 U.S. 451, 92 S.Ct. 2196, 33 L.Ed.2d 51 (1972), also indicates that in proper circumstances, the racial impact of a law, rather than its discriminatory purpose, is the critical factor. That case involved the division of a school district. The issue was whether the division was consistent with an outstanding order of a federal court to desegregate the dual school system found to have existed in the area. The constitutional predicate for the District Court's invalidation of the divided district was "the enforcement until 1969 of racial segregation in the public school system of which Emporia had always been a part." Id., at 459, 92 S.Ct., at 2202, 33 L.Ed.2d, at 60. There was thus no need to find "an independent constitutional violation." Ibid. Citing Palmer v. Thompson, we agreed with the District Court that the division of the district had the effect of interfering with the federal decree and should be set aside.

That neither *Palmer* nor *Wright* was understood to have changed the prevailing rule is apparent from Keyes v. School District No. 1, supra, where the principal issue in litigation was whether and to what extent there had been purposeful discrimination resulting in a partially or wholly segregated school system. Nor did other later cases, Alexander v. Louisiana, supra, and Jefferson v. Hackney, supra, indicate that either *Palmer* or *Wright* had worked a fundamental change in equal protection law.[11]

Both before and after Palmer v. Thompson, however, various Courts of Appeals have held in several contexts, including public employment, that the substantially disproportionate racial impact of a statute or official practice standing alone and without regard to discriminatory purpose, suffices to prove racial discrimination violating the Equal Protection Clause absent some justification going substantially beyond what would be necessary to validate most other legislative classifications.[12] The cases impressively demonstrate

11. To the extent that *Palmer* suggests a generally applicable proposition that legislative purpose is irrelevant in constitutional adjudication, our prior cases—as indicated in the text—are to the contrary; and very shortly after *Palmer,* all Members of the Court majority in that case joined the Court's opinion in Lemon v. Kurtzman, 403 U.S. 602, 91 S.Ct. 2105, 29 L.Ed.2d 745 (1971), which dealt with the issue of public financing for private schools and which announced, as the Court had several times before, that the validity of public aid to church-related schools includes close inquiry into the purpose of the challenged statute.

12. Cases dealing with public employment include: Chance v. Board of Examiners, 458 F.2d 1167, 1176–1177 (C.A.2 1972); Castro v. Beecher, 459 F.2d 725, 732–733 (C.A.1 1972); Bridgeport Guardians v. Bridgeport Civil Service Comm'n, 482 F.2d 1333, 1337 (C.A.2 1973); Harper v. Mayor of Baltimore, 359 F.Supp. 1187, 1200 (D.Md.), aff'd in pertinent part sub nom. Harper v. Kloster, 486 F.2d 1134 (C.A.4 1973); Douglas v. Hampton, 168 U.S.App.D.C. 62, 512 F.2d 976, 981 (1975); but cf. Tyler v. Vickery, 517 F.2d 1089, 1096–1097

(C.A.5 1975), petition for certiorari pending, No. 75–1026 O.T.1975. There are also District Court cases: Wade v. Mississippi Cooperative Extension Service, 372 F.Supp. 126, 143 (N.D.Miss.1974); Arnold v. Ballard, 390 F.Supp. 723, 736, 737 (N.D.Ohio 1975); United States v. City of Chicago, 385 F.Supp. 543, 553 (N.D.Ill.1974); Fowler v. Schwarzwalder, 351 F.Supp. 721, 724 (D.Minn.1972), reversed on other grounds 498 F.2d 143 (C.A.8 1974).

In other contexts there are Norwalk CORE v. Norwalk Redevelopment Agency, 395 F.2d 920 (C.A.2 1968)(urban renewal); Kennedy Park Homes Assn., Inc. v. City of Lackawanna, 436 F.2d 108, 114 (C.A.2 1970), cert. denied, 401 U.S. 1010, 91 S.Ct. 1256, 28 L.Ed.2d 546 (1971)(zoning); Southern Alameda Spanish Speaking Organization v. Union City, 424 F.2d 291 (C.A.9 1970)(dictum)(zoning); Metropolitan H.D. Corp. v. Village of Arlington Heights, 517 F.2d 409 (C.A.7 1975), cert. granted December 15, 1975, 423 U.S. 1030, 96 S.Ct. 560, 46 L.Ed.2d 404 (zoning); Gautreaux v. Romney, 448 F.2d 731, 738 (dictum)(C.A.7 1971)(public housing); Crow v. Brown, 332

that there is another side to the issue; but, with all due respect, to the extent that those cases rested on or expressed the view that proof of discriminatory racial purpose is unnecessary in making out an equal protection violation, we are in disagreement.

As an initial matter, we have difficulty understanding how a law establishing a racially neutral qualification for employment is nevertheless racially discriminatory and denies "any person equal protection of the laws" simply because a greater proportion of Negroes fail to qualify than members of other racial or ethnic groups. Had respondents, along with all others who had failed Test 21, whether white or black, brought an action claiming that the test denied each of them equal protection of the laws as compared with those who had passed with high enough scores to qualify them as police recruits, it is most unlikely that their challenge would have been sustained. Test 21, which is administered generally to prospective government employees, concededly seeks to ascertain whether those who take it have acquired a particular level of verbal skill; and it is untenable that the Constitution prevents the government from seeking modestly to upgrade the communicative abilities of its employees rather than to be satisfied with some lower level of competence, particularly where the job requires special ability to communicate orally and in writing. Respondents, as Negroes, could no more successfully claim that the test denied them equal protection than could white applicants who also failed. The conclusion would not be different in the face of proof that more Negroes than whites had been disqualified by Test 21. That other Negroes also failed to score well would, alone, not demonstrate that respondents individually were being denied equal protection of the laws by the application of an otherwise valid qualifying test being administered to prospective police recruits.

Nor on the facts of the case before us would the disproportionate impact of Test 21 warrant the conclusion that it is a purposeful device to discriminate against Negroes and hence an infringement of the constitutional rights of respondents as well as other black applicants. As we have said, the test is neutral on its face and rationally may be said to serve a purpose the government is constitutionally empowered to pursue. Even agreeing with the District Court that the differential racial effect of Test 21 called for further inquiry, we think the District Court correctly held that the affirmative efforts of the Metropolitan Police Department to recruit black officers, the changing racial composition of the recruit classes and of the force in general, and the relationship of the test to the training program negated any inference that the Department discriminated on the basis of race or that "a police officer qualifies on the color of his skin rather than ability." 348 F.Supp., at 18.

Under Title VII, Congress provided that when hiring and promotion practices disqualifying substantially disproportionate numbers of blacks are challenged, discriminatory purpose need not be proved, and that it is an insufficient response to demonstrate some rational basis for the challenged practices. It is necessary, in addition, that they be "validated" in terms of job performance in any one of several ways, perhaps by ascertaining the mini-

F.Supp. 382, 391 (N.D.Ga.1971), aff'd 457 F.2d 788 (C.A.5 1972)(public housing); Hawkins v. Town of Shaw, 437 F.2d 1286 (C.A.5 1971), aff'd on rehearing en banc 461 F.2d 1171 (1972)(municipal services).

mum skill, ability or potential necessary for the position at issue and determining whether the qualifying tests are appropriate for the selection of qualified applicants for the job in question.[13] However this process proceeds, it involves a more probing judicial review of, and less deference to, the seemingly reasonable acts of administrators and executives than is appropriate under the Constitution where special racial impact, without discriminatory purpose, is claimed. We are not disposed to adopt this more rigorous standard for the purposes of applying the Fifth and the Fourteenth Amendments in cases such as this.

A rule that a statute designed to serve neutral ends is nevertheless invalid, absent compelling justification, if in practice it benefits or burdens one race more than another would be far reaching and would raise serious questions about, and perhaps invalidate, a whole range of tax, welfare, public service, regulatory, and licensing statutes that may be more burdensome to the poor and to the average black than to the more affluent white.

Given that rule, such consequences would perhaps be likely to follow. However, in our view, extension of the rule beyond those areas where it is already applicable by reason of statute, such as in the field of public employment, should await legislative prescription.

As we have indicated, it was error to direct summary judgment for respondents based on the Fifth Amendment.

* * *

The judgment of the Court of Appeals accordingly is reversed.

Mr. Justice Stewart joins Parts I and II of the Court's opinion.

Mr. Justice Stevens, concurring.

While I agree with the Court's disposition of this case, I add these comments on the constitutional issue discussed in Part II * * *.

The requirement of purposeful discrimination is a common thread running through the cases summarized in Part II. These cases include criminal convictions which were set aside because blacks were excluded from the grand jury, a reapportionment case in which political boundaries were obviously influenced to some extent by racial considerations, a school desegregation case, and a case involving the unequal administration of an ordinance purporting to prohibit the operation of laundries in frame buildings. Although it

---

13. It appears beyond doubt by now that there is no single method for appropriately validating employment tests for their relationship to job performance. Professional standards developed by the American Psychological Association in its Standards for Educational and Psychological Tests and Manuals (1966), accept three basic methods of validation: "empirical" or "criterion" validity (demonstrated by identifying criteria that indicate successful job performance and then correlating test scores and the criteria so identified), "construct" validity (demonstrated by examinations structured to measure the degree to which job applicants have identifiable characteristics that have been determined to be im-portant in successful job performance), and "content" validity (demonstrated by tests whose content closely approximates tasks to be performed on the job by the applicant). These standards have been relied upon by the Equal Employment Opportunity Commission in fashioning its Guidelines on Employment Selection procedures, 29 CFR pt. 1607, and have been judicially noted in cases where validation of employment tests has been in issue. See, e.g., Albemarle Paper Co. v. Moody, 422 U.S. 405, 431, 95 S.Ct. 2362, 2378, 45 L.Ed.2d 280, 304 (1975); Douglas v. Hampton, 168 U.S.App.D.C. 62, 512 F.2d 976, 984 (1975); Vulcan Society v. Civil Service Comm'n, 490 F.2d 387, 394 (C.A.2 1973).

may be proper to use the same language to describe the constitutional claim in each of these contexts, the burden of proving a prima facie case may well involve differing evidentiary considerations. The extent of deference that one pays to the trial court's determination of the factual issue, and indeed, the extent to which one characterizes the intent issue as a question of fact or a question of law, will vary in different contexts.

Frequently the most probative evidence of intent will be objective evidence of what actually happened rather than evidence describing the subjective state of mind of the actor. For normally the actor is presumed to have intended the natural consequences of his deeds. This is particularly true in the case of governmental action which is frequently the product of compromise, of collective decisionmaking, and of mixed motivation. It is unrealistic, on the one hand, to require the victim of alleged discrimination to uncover the actual subjective intent of the decisionmaker or, conversely, to invalidate otherwise legitimate action simply because an improper motive affected the deliberation of a participant in the decisional process. A law conscripting clerics should not be invalidated because an atheist voted for it.

My point in making this observation is to suggest that the line between discriminatory purpose and discriminatory impact is not nearly as bright, and perhaps not quite as critical, as the reader of the Court's opinion might assume. I agree, of course, that a constitutional issue does not arise every time some disproportionate impact is shown. On the other hand, when the disproportion is as dramatic as in Gomillion v. Lightfoot, 364 U.S. 339, 81 S.Ct. 125, 5 L.Ed.2d 110 or *Yick Wo,* it really does not matter whether the standard is phrased in terms of purpose or effect. Therefore, although I accept the statement of the general rule in the Court's opinion, I am not yet prepared to indicate how that standard should be applied in the many cases which have formulated the governing standard in different language.*

My agreement with the conclusion reached in Part II of the Court's opinion rests on a ground narrower than the Court describes. I do not rely at all on the evidence of good-faith efforts to recruit black police officers. In my judgment, neither those efforts nor the subjective good faith of the District administration, would save Test 21 if it were otherwise invalid.

* * *

On the understanding that nothing which I have said is inconsistent with the Court's reasoning, I join the opinion of the Court except to the extent that it expresses an opinion on the merits of the cases cited in n. 12.

[The dissenting opinion of JUSTICE BRENNAN and JUSTICE MARSHALL is omitted.]

PERSONNEL ADM'R OF MASSACHUSETTS v. FEENEY

Supreme Court of the United States, 1979.
442 U.S. 256, 99 S.Ct. 2282, 60 L.Ed.2d 870.

[This case is set forth at p. 94, supra.]

---

* Specifically, I express no opinion on the merits of the cases listed in n. 12 of the Court's opinion.

Notes on Washington v. Davis *and* Feeney

1. What must a plaintiff show to establish discriminatory intent? Further light on this matter was provided in Arlington Heights v. Metropolitan Housing Development Corp., 429 U.S. 252, 97 S.Ct. 555, 50 L.Ed.2d 450 (1977), which held that the action of the Village's Board of Trustees in refusing to grant a rezoning request would not be held unconstitutional solely because it resulted in a racially disproportionate impact. *Davis* had established that "proof of racially discriminatory intent or purpose" must be shown to establish a denial of equal protection. The Court then summarized illustrative "subjects of proper inquiry in determining whether racially discriminatory intent existed" (429 U.S. at 266–68, 97 S.Ct. at 564–65, 50 L.Ed.2d at 465–66):

> Determining whether invidious discriminatory purpose was a motivating factor demands a sensitive inquiry into such circumstantial and direct evidence of intent as may be available. The impact of the official action—whether it "bears more heavily on one race than another," Washington v. Davis, 426 U.S., at 242, 96 S.Ct., at 2049—may provide an important starting point. Sometimes a clear pattern, unexplainable on grounds other than race, emerges from the effect of the state action even when the governing legislation appears neutral on its face. Yick Wo v. Hopkins, 118 U.S. 356, 6 S.Ct. 1064, 30 L.Ed. 220 (1886); Guinn v. United States, 238 U.S. 347, 35 S.Ct. 926, 59 L.Ed. 1340 (1915); Lane v. Wilson, 307 U.S. 268, 59 S.Ct. 872, 83 L.Ed. 1281 (1939); Gomillion v. Lightfoot, 364 U.S. 339, 81 S.Ct. 125, 5 L.Ed.2d 110 (1960). The evidentiary inquiry is then relatively easy.[13] But such cases are rare. Absent a pattern as stark as that in *Gomillion* or *Yick Wo,* impact alone is not determinative,[14] and the Court must look to other evidence.[15]
>
> The historical background of the decision is one evidentiary source, particularly if it reveals a series of official actions taken for invidious purposes. See Lane v. Wilson, supra; Griffin v. County School Board, 377 U.S. 218, 84 S.Ct. 1226, 12 L.Ed.2d 256 (1964); Davis v. Schnell, 81 F.Supp. 872 (S.D.Ala.), aff'd per curiam 336 U.S. 933, 69 S.Ct. 749, 93 L.Ed. 1093 (1949); cf. Keyes v. School District No. 1, 413 U.S., at 207, 93 S.Ct., at 2696. The specific sequence of events leading up to the challenged decision also may shed some light on the decisionmaker's purposes. Reitman v. Mulkey, 387 U.S. 369, 373–376, 87 S.Ct. 1627, 1629–1631, 18 L.Ed.2d 830 (1967); Grosjean v. American Press, 297 U.S. 233, 250, 56 S.Ct. 444, 449, 80 L.Ed. 660 (1936). For example, if the property involved here always had been zoned R–

---

13. Several of our jury selection cases fall into this category. Because of the nature of the jury selection task, however, we have permitted a finding of constitutional violation even when the statistical pattern does not approach the extremes of *Yick Wo* or *Gomillion.* See, e.g., Turner v. Fouche, 396 U.S. 346, 359, 90 S.Ct. 532, 539, 24 L.Ed.2d 567 (1970); Sims v. Georgia, 389 U.S. 404, 407, 88 S.Ct. 523, 525, 19 L.Ed.2d 634 (1967).

14. This is not to say that a consistent pattern of official racial discrimination is a necessary predicate to a violation of the equal protection clause. A single invidiously discriminatory governmental act—in the exercise

of the zoning power as elsewhere—would not necessarily be immunized by the absence of such discrimination in the making of other comparable decisions. See City of Richmond v. United States, 422 U.S. 358, 378, 95 S.Ct. 2296, 2307, 45 L.Ed.2d 245 (1975).

15. In many instances, to recognize the limited probative value of disproportionate impact is merely to acknowledge the "heterogeneity" of the nation's population. Jefferson v. Hackney, 406 U.S. 535, 548, 92 S.Ct. 1724, 1732, 32 L.Ed.2d 285 (1972); see also Washington v. Davis, 426 U.S., at 248, 96 S.Ct., at 2051.

5 but suddenly was changed to R–3 when the town learned of MHDC's plans to erect integrated housing,[16] we would have a far different case. Departures from the normal procedural sequence also might afford evidence that improper purposes are playing a role. Substantive departures too may be relevant, particularly if the factors usually considered important by the decisionmaker strongly favor a decision contrary to the one reached.[17]

The legislative or administrative history may be highly relevant, especially where there are contemporary statements by members of the decisionmaking body, minutes of its meetings, or reports. In some extraordinary instances the members might be called to the stand at trial to testify concerning the purpose of the official action, although even then such testimony frequently will be barred by privilege. See Tenney v. Brandhove, 341 U.S. 367, 71 S.Ct. 783, 95 L.Ed. 1019 (1951); United States v. Nixon, 418 U.S. 683, 705, 94 S.Ct. 3090, 3106, 41 L.Ed.2d 1039 (1974); 8 Wigmore, Evidence § 2371 (McNaughton rev.ed. 1961).[18]

The case was remanded for consideration of whether the Village's action violated the Fair Housing Act, Title VIII of the Civil Rights Act of 1968. On remand, the Seventh Circuit determined that an official action taken without discriminatory intent but which produced a discriminatory effect might violate the Act under stated circumstances. The court carefully noted that Washington v. Davis, while announcing an intent requirement for equal protection cases, had at the same time reaffirmed the viability of *Griggs* for Title VII cases, so that "a prima facie case of employment discrimination can still be established under Title VII by statistical evidence of discriminatory impact, without a showing of discriminatory intent." Metropolitan, Etc. v. Village of Arlington Heights, 558 F.2d 1283, 1289 (7th Cir.1977), cert. denied 434 U.S. 1025, 98 S.Ct. 752, 54 L.Ed.2d 772 (1978). On remand a consent decree was approved, allowing building to proceed on a new site adjacent to Arlington Heights. See Metropolitan Housing Development Corp. v. Village of Arlington Heights, 469 F.Supp. 836 (N.D.Ill.1979), affirmed 616 F.2d 1006 (7th Cir.1980).

16. See, e.g., Progress Development Corp. v. Mitchell, 286 F.2d 222 (C.A.7 1961)(park board allegedly condemned plaintiffs' land for a park upon learning that the homes plaintiffs were erecting there would be sold under a marketing plan designed to assure integration); Kennedy Park Homes Association, Inc. v. City of Lackawanna, 436 F.2d 108 (C.A.2 1970), cert. denied 401 U.S. 1010, 91 S.Ct. 1256, 28 L.Ed.2d 546 (1971)(town declared moratorium on new subdivisions and rezoned area for park land shortly after learning of plaintiffs' plans to build low income housing). To the extent that the decision in *Kennedy Park Homes* rested solely on a finding of discriminatory impact, we have indicated our disagreement. Washington v. Davis, 426 U.S., at 244–245, 96 S.Ct., at 2050.

17. See Dailey v. City of Lawton, 425 F.2d 1037 (C.A.10 1970). The plaintiffs in *Dailey* planned to build low income housing on the site of a former school that they had purchased. The city refused to rezone the land from PF, its public facilities classification, to R–4, high-density residential. All the surrounding area was zoned R–4, and both the present and the former planning director for the city testified that there was no reason "from a zoning standpoint" why the land should not be classified R–4. Based on this and other evidence, the Court of Appeals ruled that "the record sustains the [District Court's] holding of racial motivation and of arbitrary and unreasonable action." Id., at 1040.

18. This Court has recognized, ever since Fletcher v. Peck, 10 U.S. (6 Cranch) 87, 130–131, 3 L.Ed. 162 (1810), that judicial inquiries into legislative or executive motivation represent a substantial intrusion into the workings of other branches of government. Placing a decisionmaker on the stand is therefore "usually to be avoided." Citizens to Preserve Overton Park v. Volpe, 401 U.S. 402, 420, 91 S.Ct. 814, 825, 28 L.Ed.2d 136 (1971). The problems involved have prompted a good deal of scholarly commentary. See Tussman & tenBroek, The Equal Protection of the Laws, 37 Calif.L.Rev. 341, 356–361 (1949); A. Bickel, The Least Dangerous Branch, 208–221 (1962); Ely, Legislative and Administrative Motivation in Constitutional Law, 79 Yale L.J. 1205 (1970); Brest, [Palmer v. Thompson: An Approach to the Problem of Unconstitutional Motive, 1971 Sup.Ct.Rev. 95, 116–118.]

Does the opinion in *Feeney* further clarify the nature of plaintiff's burden?

2. In Hunter v. Underwood, 471 U.S. 222, 105 S.Ct. 1916, 85 L.Ed.2d 222 (1985), the Court invalidated as a violation of equal protection a provision of the Alabama Constitution of 1901, which disenfranchised persons convicted of any of a list of offenses, including any "crime involving moral turpitude." Carmen Edwards, a black voter, challenged his removal from the voter rolls after conviction of the misdemeanor of presenting a worthless check, a crime determined by the county registrar to involve moral turpitude. Justice Rehnquist, writing for the Court, accepted the finding of the Court of Appeals that the provision had a disparate impact on blacks, disenfranchising approximately ten times as many black voters as whites within two years of its operative date, and 1.7 times as many in modern times. The Court reaffirmed its holdings in Mt. Healthy City Board of Education v. Doyle, 429 U.S. 274, 287, 97 S.Ct. 568, 576, 50 L.Ed.2d 471, 484 (1977); Arlington Heights v. Metropolitan Housing Development Corp., 429 U.S. 252, 264–265, 97 S.Ct. 555, 563, 50 L.Ed.2d 450, 464 (1977); and Washington v. Davis, 426 U.S. 229, 239, 96 S.Ct. 2040, 2047, 48 L.Ed.2d 597, 607 (1976), that proof of the racially disproportionate impact of a neutral state law or official action is insufficient, without more, to support an equal protection violation. Proof of racially discriminatory intent or purpose is required as well. The Court made clear, however, that

> [o]nce racial discrimination is shown to have been a "substantial" or "motivating" factor behind enactment of the law, the burden shifts to the law's defenders to demonstrate that the law would have been enacted without this factor.

471 U.S. at 228, 105 S.Ct. at 1920, 85 L.Ed.2d at 228. The State's effort to meet that burden, by arguing that the Alabama constitutional convention delegates had intended to disenfranchise poor whites as well as blacks, failed because

> an additional purpose to discriminate against poor whites would not render nugatory the purpose to discriminate against all blacks, and it is beyond peradventure that the latter was a "but-for" motivation for the enactment of § 182.

Id., 471 U.S. at 232, 105 S.Ct. at 1922, 85 L.Ed.2d at 231. Would the *Hunter* test have made Helen Feeney's task any easier? Was the virtual elimination of women from high-level state jobs a "but-for motivation for the enactment" of the Massachusetts veterans' preference statute? But since Feeney was unable to show that sex discrimination was a "substantial or motivating factor" behind the veterans' preference, she never reached the point at which the *Hunter* test would shift the burden to the law's defenders, did she?

3. Does the *Washington v. Davis* intent requirement apply to Title VII cases? What about Title VII cases brought against public employers? The 1972 amendments, which extended Title VII to public employment, were expressly based on the Congressional power to implement the Fourteenth Amendment. The 1972 amendments, however, were not interpreted to impose the same burden of proof on plaintiffs suing under the statute that they are required to bear when suing under the constitution. In Connecticut v. Teal, 457 U.S. 440, 102 S.Ct. 2525, 73 L.Ed.2d 130 (1982), the Supreme Court ruled that the legislative history of the 1972 amendments to Title VII "demonstrate that Congress recognized and endorsed the disparate-impact analysis employed by the Court in *Griggs*." 457 U.S. at 447 n. 8. Congress intended to provide state and municipal employees the same protection under Title VII as that provided to employees in the private

sector. Id. at 449. See also the Court's discussion of the Title VII/Equal Protection contrast in Johnson v. Transportation Agency, at p. 891 n. 6 supra.

4. Was *Washington v. Davis* correctly decided? Judge Skelly Wright has made plain his concern that an interpretation of the equal protection clause that requires a showing of intentional discrimination unduly limits the effectiveness of the clause in protecting disadvantaged minority groups against race discrimination. Wright, Judicial Review and the Equal Protection Clause, 15 Harv.Civ.Rts.–Civ.Lib.L.Rev. 1, 20–27 (1980). Professor Charles R. Lawrence III agrees with the critics of *Washington v. Davis*, but he has proposed a different way of thinking about racial discrimination that may transform the very definition of "discriminatory intent." He argues that "a large part of the behavior that produces racial discrimination is influenced by unconscious racial motivation" and he proposes "a new test to trigger judicial recognition of race-based behavior":

> I propose a test that would look to the "cultural meaning" of an allegedly racially discriminatory act as the best available analogue for and evidence of the collective unconscious that we cannot observe directly. This test would evaluate governmental conduct to see if it conveys a symbolic message to which the culture attaches racial significance. The court would analyze governmental behavior much like a cultural anthropologist might: by considering evidence regarding the historical and social context in which the decision was made and effectuated. If the court determined by a preponderance of the evidence that a significant portion of the population thinks of the governmental action in racial terms, then it would presume that socially shared, unconscious racial attitudes made evident by the action's meaning had influenced the decisionmakers. As a result, it would apply heightened scrutiny.

> The unconscious racial attitudes of individuals manifest themselves in the cultural meaning that society gives their actions in the following way: In a society that no longer condones overt racist attitudes and behavior, many of these attitudes will be repressed and prevented from reaching awareness in an undisguised form. But as psychologists have found, repressed wishes, fears, anger, and aggression continue to seek expression, most often by attaching themselves to certain symbols in the external world. Repressed feelings and attitudes that are commonly experienced are likely to find common symbols particularly fruitful or productive as a vehicle for their expression. Thus, certain actions, words, or signs may take on meaning within a particular culture as a result of the collective use of those actions, words, or signs to represent or express shared but repressed attitudes. The process is cyclical: The expression of shared attitudes through certain symbols gives those symbols cultural meaning, and once a symbol becomes an enduring part of the culture, it in turn becomes the most natural vehicle for the expression of those attitudes and feelings that caused it to become an identifiable part of the culture.

Lawrence III, The Id, the Ego, and Equal Protection: Reckoning with Unconscious Racism, 39 Stan.L.Rev. 317, 322, 324, 355–56 (1987)(footnotes omitted). What was the "cultural meaning" of the government's use of the civil service examination in *Washington v. Davis*? Lawrence suggests that there are two elements in the historical and cultural context of the case that cause us to interpret the government's action—at least intuitively—in racial terms:

> The first involves the nature of the work or activity from which blacks have been excluded: the job of police officer in a predominantly but not

entirely black community. The second relates to the reason given for their exclusion: that they failed to demonstrate sufficient proficiency in verbal and written language skills.

It is significant that the challenged action in *Davis* excluded blacks from working as police officers and not as mail carriers or bus drivers. The occupation of police officer has symbolic meaning within our culture. Police officers represent the law as well as enforce it. They are armed and have discretionary authority to use violence. They are charged with protecting the lives and property of some individuals within society and controlling the violent and unlawful behavior of others. If history—the accumulated meaningful behavior of our culture—has taught us to attach significance to race in considering these elements of the job of police officer—authority, control, protection, and sanctioned violence—then an action that determines the racial composition of a police force also has racial meaning.

* * *

The cultural meaning test would require the plaintiffs to produce evidence that a substantial part of the population will interpret the disproportionate results of "Test 21" not as the product of random selection or the differential educational background or socioeconomic status of the test takers but as testimony to the inherent intellectual abilities of the racial groups to which the test takers belong. In other words, the government's use of the test has racial meaning if our culture has taught us to believe that blacks that fail the test have done so because they are black.

* * *

Plaintiffs trying *Davis* under the test proposed in this article would present evidence detailing both the history and the contemporary manifestations of this myth. They would seek to convince the court that most people in our culture believe that the average white person is inherently smarter than the average black person and that whites will interpret the racially selective impact of "Test 21" as a confirmation of that belief. If the culture gives the governmental action this kind of racial meaning, the action constitutes a direct racial stigmatization. Like the segregated beach and the Memphis wall, it conveys a message that has its origins in a pervasive and mutually reinforcing pattern of racially stigmatizing actions, and it adds one more stigmatizing action to that pattern. Presumably, the decisionmakers who chose to use "Test 21" were aware of that message and were influenced by it, whether consciously or unconsciously.

Id., at 370, 373, 375. Do you agree that this analysis will enable equal protection doctrine to come to grips with unconscious racism, as Lawrence hopes?

Does Lawrence's analysis apply to sex discrimination? He implies in n. 22, at p. 322, that *Feeney* may be a case of unconscious sexism. What do you think?

Text Note
The Post Civil War Civil Rights Acts:
42 U.S.C.A. §§ 1981 and 1983

[The text of these provisions appears in the Statutory Appendix.]

Although neither of these provisions expressly prohibit discrimination in employment, both have been held to provide remedies for employment discrimination in at least some situations. Of the two, only § 1983 applies to sex-based discrimination.

Section 1981

This statute guarantees to "all persons" specified rights "enjoyed by white citizens." It has been construed to cover private discrimination,[1] and has been widely used in employment discrimination cases.[2] Although § 1981 has been held to protect white persons against racial discrimination in employment,[3] it has not been extended to sex discrimination.[4] Women can, of course, sue under § 1981 charging racial discrimination in a proper case.[5] A showing of intentional discrimination is required in § 1981 suits.[6] Compensatory and punitive damages are available.[7]

The Supreme Court severely limited § 1981's application to employment disputes in Patterson v. McLean Credit Union,[8] but Congress overrode *Patterson* with the 1991 Civil Rights Act's amendments to § 1981. In *Patterson*, a majority of the Supreme Court held that Brenda Patterson's claim of racial harassment in employment was not actionable under section 1981. Justice Kennedy, speaking for the Court, reasoned that:

> Section 1981 cannot be construed as a general proscription of racial discrimination in all aspects of contract relations, for it expressly prohibits discrimination only in the making and enforcement of contracts * * *.
>
> By its plain terms, the relevant provision in § 1981 protects two rights: "the same right * * * to make * * * contracts" and "the same right * * * to * * * enforce contracts." The first of these protections extends only to the formation of a contract, but not to problems that may arise later from the conditions of continuing employment. The statute prohibits, when based on race, the refusal to enter into a contract with someone, as well as the offer to make a contract only on discriminatory terms. But the right to make contracts does not extend, as a matter of either logic or semantics, to conduct by the employer after the contract relation has been established, including breach of the terms of the contract or imposition of discriminatory working conditions. Such postformation conduct does not involve the right to make a contract, but rather implicates the performance of established contract obligations and the conditions of continuing employment, matters more naturally governed by state contract law and Title VII.

---

1. Jones v. Alfred H. Mayer Co., 392 U.S. 409, 88 S.Ct. 2186, 20 L.Ed.2d 1189 (1968)(private owner's refusal to sell a house to petitioner because of his race violated 42 U.S.C.A. § 1982). Runyon v. McCrary, 427 U.S. 160, 96 S.Ct. 2586, 49 L.Ed.2d 415 (1976)(extending analysis of § 1982 in *Jones* to § 1981 and holding that § 1981 covers claims of racial discrimination in admission to private schools).

2. See generally, Comment, Developments in the Law—Section 1981, 15 Harv.Civ.Rts.– Civ.Lib.L.Rev. 29 (1980).

3. McDonald v. Santa Fe Trail Transp. Co., 427 U.S. 273, 96 S.Ct. 2574, 49 L.Ed.2d 493 (1976).

4. See Comment, supra note 2, at 98–99. But see Stanley, Sex Discrimination and Section 1981, 1 Women's Rights Law Reporter 2

(No. 4, Spring 1973)(arguing that § 1981 should be construed to protect the employment rights of women).

5. See, e.g., Fisher v. Dillard University, 499 F.Supp. 525 (E.D.La.1980)(white woman charges race discrimination under Title VII and 42 U.S.C.A. § 1981).

6. General Building Contractors Ass'n, Inc. v. Pennsylvania, 458 U.S. 375, 102 S.Ct. 3141, 73 L.Ed.2d 835 (1982).

7. See, e.g., Williamson v. Handy Button Machine Co., 817 F.2d 1290 (7th Cir. 1987)(black woman awarded $150,000 compensatory and $100,000 punitive damages for racial discrimination in employment under § 1981).

8. 491 U.S. 164, 109 S.Ct. 2363, 105 L.Ed.2d 132 (1989).

The second of these guarantees, "the same right * * * to * * * enforce contracts * * * as is enjoyed by white citizens," embraces protection of a legal process, and of a right of access to legal process, that will address and resolve contract-law claims without regard to race. In this respect, it prohibits discrimination that infects the legal process in ways that prevent one from enforcing contract rights, by reason of his or her race, and this is so whether this discrimination is attributed to a statute or simply to existing practices. It also covers wholly *private* efforts to impede access to the courts or obstruct nonjudicial methods of adjudicating disputes about the force of binding obligations, as well as discrimination by private entities, such as labor unions, in enforcing the terms of a contract * * *. The right to enforce contracts does not, however, extend beyond conduct by a employer which impairs an employee's ability to enforce through legal process his or her established contract rights * * *.[9]

Justices Brennan, Marshall and Blackmun, dissenting from this interpretation of section 1981, argued in part that:

* * * [T]he language of § 1981 is quite naturally read as extending to cover postformation conduct that demonstrates that the contract was not really made on equal terms at all. It is indeed clear that the statutory language of § 1981 imposes some limit upon the type of harassment claims that are cognizable under § 1981, for the statute's prohibition is against discrimination in the making and enforcement of contracts; but the Court mistakes the nature of that limit. In my view, harassment is properly actionable under the language of § 1981 mandating that all persons "shall have the same right * * * to make * * * contracts * * * as is enjoyed by white citizens" if it demonstrates that the employer has in fact imposed discriminatory terms and hence has not allowed blacks to make a contract on an equal basis.[10]

Congress negated *Patterson*'s holding and restored the employment coverage of section 1981 in the Civil Rights Act of 1991 by adding new subsection (b):

(b) For purposes of this section, the term "make and enforce contracts" includes the making, performance, modification, and termination of contracts, and the enjoyment of all benefits, privileges, terms, and conditions of the contractual relationship.

The *Patterson* Court also reaffirmed its decision in Runyon v. McCrary,[11] that section 1981 prohibits racial discrimination in the making and enforcement of private contracts. Congress amended the statute to reflect that interpretation in new subsection (c):

(c) The rights protected by this section are protected against impairment by nongovernmental discrimination and impairment under color of State law.[12]

See Statutory Appendix at p. 1247 infra.

Plaintiff Brenda Patterson also alleged that the defendant failed to promote her from a teller and file coordinator to an intermediate accounting clerk position because of her race in violation of section 1981. That part of the Court's opinion dealing with the promotion claim is set out below.

9. Id., 491 U.S. at 176–78, 109 S.Ct. at 2372–73, 105 L.Ed.2d at 150–51.

10. Id., 491 U.S. at 207–08, 109 S.Ct. at 2388–89, 105 L.Ed.2d at 170 (dissenting opinion of Justice Brennan).

11. 427 U.S. 160, 96 S.Ct. 2586, 49 L.Ed.2d 415 (1976).

12. Pub.L. 102–166, § 101, 105 Stat. 1071 (Nov. 21, 1991)(amending 42 U.S.C. § 1981).

PATTERSON v. McLEAN CREDIT UNION

Supreme Court of the United States, 1989.
491 U.S. 164, 109 S.Ct. 2363, 105 L.Ed.2d 132.

JUSTICE KENNEDY delivered the opinion of the Court.

In this case, we consider important issues respecting the meaning and coverage of one of our oldest civil rights statutes, 42 U.S.C. § 1981.

I

Petitioner Brenda Patterson, a black woman, was employed by respondent McLean Credit Union as a teller and a file coordinator, commencing in May 1972. In July 1982, she was laid off. After the termination, petitioner commenced this action in District Court. She alleged that respondent, in violation of 42 U.S.C. § 1981, had * * * failed to promote her to an intermediate accounting clerk position, and then discharged her, all because of her race.
* * *

* * *

We granted certiorari to decide * * * whether the jury instruction given by the District Court on petitioner's § 1981 promotion claim was error.
* * *

* * *

IV

Petitioner's claim that respondent violated § 1981 by failing to promote her, because of race, to a position as an intermediate accounting clerk is a different matter. * * * Because respondent has not argued at any stage that petitioner's promotion claim is not cognizable under § 1981, we need not address the issue further here.

This brings us to the question of the District Court's jury instructions on petitioner's promotion claim. We think the District Court erred when it instructed the jury that petitioner had to prove that she was better qualified than the white employee who allegedly received the promotion. In order to prevail under § 1981, a plaintiff must prove purposeful discrimination. General Building Contractors Assn., Inc. v. Pennsylvania, 458 U.S. 375, 391, 102 S.Ct. 3141, 3150, 73 L.Ed.2d 835 (1982). We have developed, in analogous areas of civil rights law, a carefully designed framework of proof to determine, in the context of disparate treatment, the ultimate issue of whether the defendant intentionally discriminated against the plaintiff. See Texas Dept. of Community Affairs v. Burdine * * *; McDonnell Douglas Corp. v. Green * * *. We agree with the Court of Appeals that this scheme of proof, structured as a "sensible, orderly way to evaluate the evidence in light of common experience as it bears on the critical question of discrimination," Furnco Construction Corp. v. Waters, 438 U.S. 567, 577, 98 S.Ct. 2943, 2949–50, 57 L.Ed.2d 957 (1978), should apply to claims of racial discrimination under § 1981.

Although the Court of Appeals recognized that the *McDonnell Douglas/Burdine* scheme of proof should apply in § 1981 cases such as this one, it erred in describing petitioner's burden. Under our well-established framework, the plaintiff has the initial burden of proving, by the preponderance of the evidence, a prima facie case of discrimination. *Burdine* * * *. The burden is not onerous. Id. * * * Here, petitioner need only prove by a preponderance of the evidence that she applied for and was qualified for an available position, that she was rejected, and that after she was rejected respondent either continued to seek applicants for the position, or, as is alleged here, filled the position with a white employee. * * * *McDonnell Douglas, supra.*

Once the plaintiff establishes a prima facie case, an inference of discrimination arises. * * * In order to rebut this inference, the employer must present evidence that the plaintiff was rejected, or the other applicant was chosen, for a legitimate nondiscriminatory reason. * * * Here, respondent presented evidence that it gave the job to the white applicant because she was better qualified for the position, and therefore rebutted any presumption of discrimination that petitioner may have established. At this point, as our prior cases make clear, petitioner retains the final burden of persuading the jury of intentional discrimination. * * *

Although petitioner retains the ultimate burden of persuasion, our cases make clear that she must also have the opportunity to demonstrate that respondent's proffered reasons for its decision were not its true reasons. * * * In doing so, petitioner is not limited to presenting evidence of a certain type. This is where the District Court erred. The evidence which petitioner can present in an attempt to establish that respondent's stated reasons are pretextual may take a variety of forms. * * * Indeed, she might seek to demonstrate that respondent's claim to have promoted a better-qualified applicant was pretextual by showing that she was in fact better qualified than the person chosen for the position. The District Court erred, however, in instructing the jury that in order to succeed petitioner was *required* to make such a showing. There are certainly other ways in which petitioner could seek to prove that respondent's reasons were pretextual. Thus, for example, petitioner could seek to persuade the jury that respondent had not offered the true reason for its promotion decision by presenting evidence of respondent's past treatment of petitioner, including the instances of the racial harassment which she alleges and respondent's failure to train her for an accounting position. * * * While we do not intend to say this evidence necessarily would be sufficient to carry the day, it cannot be denied that it is one of the various ways in which petitioner might seek to prove intentional discrimination on the part of respondent. She may not be forced to pursue any particular means of demonstrating that respondent's stated reasons are pretextual. It was, therefore, error for the District Court to instruct the jury that petitioner could carry her burden of persuasion only by showing that she was in fact better qualified than the white applicant who got the job.

V

The law now reflects society's consensus that discrimination based on the color of one's skin is a profound wrong of tragic dimension. Neither our words nor our decisions should be interpreted as signaling one inch of retreat from Congress' policy to forbid discrimination in the private, as well as the public, sphere. Nevertheless, in the area of private discrimination, to which the ordinance of the Constitution does not directly extend, our role is limited to interpreting what Congress may do and has done. * * *

* * * The Court of Appeals erred, however, in holding that petitioner could succeed in her discriminatory promotion claim under § 1981 only by proving that she was better qualified for the position of intermediate accounting clerk than the white employee who in fact was promoted. The judgment of the Court of Appeals is therefore vacated insofar as it relates to petitioner's discriminatory promotion claim, and the case is remanded for further proceedings consistent with this opinion.

It is so ordered.

Note on Patterson

Brenda Patterson argued on remand that the 1991 Civil Rights Act should be applied retroactively to her case. She lost.[13] The Supreme Court subsequently held in Rivers v. Roadway Express, Inc.,[14] that the amendment to section 1981 did not apply to a case that arose before the Civil Rights Act of 1991 was enacted. In a companion case, Landgraf v. USI Film Products,[15] the Court also held that the right conferred by the Civil Rights Act of 1991 to recover compensatory and punitive damages and the accompanying right to demand a trial by jury if such damages are sought do not apply to a Title VII case that was pending on appeal when the statute was enacted.

Section 1983

This statute, although not itself the source of substantive rights,[16] provides a remedy against deprivation of rights secured by the Constitution or federal law by persons acting under color of state law.[17] Just as a law forbidding the publication of newspapers would be invalidated as violating the first amendment, so under § 1983 a state official who closed down a newspaper would be subject to suit for injunctive relief and damages. Similarly, just as a state law forbidding the hiring of women would be invalidated under the equal protection clause, so a state official who refused to hire on the basis of sex would be subject to suit for injunctive relief and damages.[18] Before Title VII was extended to public employment in 1972, suits alleging unconstitutional discrimination in employment based on sex or race were brought under § 1983. Differences in procedure and remedies available under the two statutes continue to make it attractive in appropriate cases to join charges under both in a single suit.[19]

---

13. See Patterson v. McLean Credit Union, 784 F.Supp. 268 (M.D.N.C.1992).

14. ___ U.S. ___, 114 S.Ct. 1510, 128 L.Ed.2d 274 (1994).

15. ___ U.S. ___, 114 S.Ct. 1483, 128 L.Ed.2d 229 (1994).

16. Chapman v. Houston Welfare Rights Organization, 441 U.S. 600, 617–18, 99 S.Ct. 1905, 1915–16, 60 L.Ed.2d 508, 522–23 (1979).

17. See, e.g., Frazier v. Board of Trustees of Northwest Mississippi Regional Medical Center, 765 F.2d 1278, 1283–88 (5th Cir.1985), rehearing denied 777 F.2d 329, certiorari denied 476 U.S. 1142, 106 S.Ct. 2252, 90 L.Ed.2d 697 (1986)(holding that the decision of a private company that operated a public hospital's

respiratory therapy department in demoting plaintiff Dorothy Frazier from her former position as respiratory therapist to that of technician did not constitute state action for purposes of § 1983).

18. See, e.g., Riordan v. Kempiners, 831 F.2d 690 (7th Cir.1987)(reversing entry of directed verdict on plaintiff Mary Riordan's § 1983 claim of sex-based wage discrimination).

19. See generally, Bill W. Bristow, § 1983: An Analysis and Suggested Approach, 29 Ark. L.Rev. 255 (1975). The burden of proof carried by a plaintiff claiming both disparate treatment under Title VII and a violation of § 1983 is essentially the same: intentional discrimination must be shown. See Grano v.

The Supreme Court, reversing earlier precedent,[20] held in 1980 that municipalities are not immune from damages under § 1983, even if their actions were taken in good faith.[21] In recent years, however, § 1983 litigation against governmental entities has become more confused. In 1989 the Supreme Court held in Will v. Michigan Department of State Police,[22] that neither a state nor a state official acting in his or her official capacity may be sued for damages under § 1983 because neither is a "person" within the meaning of that statute. The majority claimed that its analysis did not affect Monell v. New York City Department of Social Services.[23] Do you agree? You might also want to consult Jett v. Dallas Independent School District.[24] In 1991, Justice O'Connor attempted to clarify the holding in *Will* to make plain that "state officials, sued in their personal capacities, are 'persons' within the meaning of § 1981" even though the acts complained of were undertaken in their official capacity.[25] Got it?

D. OBLIGATIONS OF GOVERNMENT CONTRACTORS

1. EXECUTIVE ORDER 11246

Notes on the Executive Order

1. President Roosevelt first exercised executive authority in the field of fair employment practices when he signed Executive Order 8802 on June 25, 1941. Described as action necessary to the successful conduct of the national defense production effort, this Order established in the Office of Production Management a Committee on Fair Employment Practice, and required the inclusion in defense contracts of a covenant not to discriminate against any worker because of race, creed, color, or national origin. President Truman continued the Committee's existence in Executive Order 9664, signed on December 18, 1945, relying on the National War Agencies Appropriation Act of 1946. For the first time in Executive Order 10479, signed on August 13, 1953, President Eisenhower continued the Committee's functions without reference to defense production.

As the civil rights movement grew in strength, President Kennedy imposed the obligation on federal contractors to "take affirmative action to ensure that applicants are employed, and that employees are treated during employment, without regard to their race, creed, color, or national origin" by Executive Order 10925, signed March 6, 1961; this obligation was extended to all federally assisted construction contracts by Executive Order 11114, signed on June 22, 1963. By Executive Order 11246, signed September 24, 1965, President Johnson continued both the affirmative action requirement and the coverage of federally assisted construction contracts. In 1967, Executive Order 11246 was amended by Executive Order 11375, signed October 13, 1967, to include sex.

Department of Development of the City of Columbus, 637 F.2d 1073, 1080–82 (6th Cir. 1980). Only if a plaintiff's Title VII claim is based on a disparate impact theory are the two burdens different.

20. Monroe v. Pape, 365 U.S. 167, 81 S.Ct. 473, 5 L.Ed.2d 492 (1961), which had held that local governments were not "persons" within the meaning of § 1983, was overruled in Monell v. New York City Dept. of Social Servs., 436 U.S. 658, 98 S.Ct. 2018, 56 L.Ed.2d 611 (1978).

21. Owen v. City of Independence, Missouri, 445 U.S. 622, 100 S.Ct. 1398, 63 L.Ed.2d 673 (1980).

22. 491 U.S. 58, 109 S.Ct. 2304, 105 L.Ed.2d 45 (1989).

23. 436 U.S. 658, 98 S.Ct. 2018, 56 L.Ed.2d 611 (1978).

24. 491 U.S. 701, 109 S.Ct. 2702, 105 L.Ed.2d 598 (1989).

25. Hafer v. Melo, 502 U.S. 21, 112 S.Ct. 358, 365, 116 L.Ed.2d 301, 313 (1991).

2. In 1969, the Secretary of Labor implemented the affirmative action requirement of the Order as to race by promulgating the so-called Philadelphia Plan, which required that bidders on any federal or federally assisted construction contract for projects in a five-county area around Philadelphia, the estimated total cost of which exceeded $500,000, include with the bid an affirmative action program containing specific goals for the utilization of minority workers in six skilled crafts: ironworkers, plumbers and pipefitters, steamfitters, sheetmetal workers, electrical workers, and elevator construction workers. The validity of this plan was challenged by a group of contractors as violative of due process; as beyond the authority of the Executive branch; and as inconsistent with Titles VI and VII of the Civil Rights Act of 1964 and the National Labor Relations Act. The Philadelphia Plan, and with it the President's authority to redress employment discrimination by federal contractors, was upheld in Contractors Ass'n of Eastern Pennsylvania v. Secretary of Labor, 442 F.2d 159 (3d Cir.1971), cert. denied 404 U.S. 854, 92 S.Ct. 98, 30 L.Ed.2d 95. In rejecting the argument that the affirmative action requirement of the Order violated Title VII, the court said in part:

The order of September 23, 1969 contained findings that although overall minority group representation in the construction industry in the five-county Philadelphia area was thirty per cent, in the six trades representation was approximately one per cent. It found, moreover, that this obvious underrepresentation was due to the exclusionary practices of the unions representing the six trades. It is the practice of building contractors to rely on union hiring halls as the prime source for employees. The order made further findings as to the availability of qualified minority tradesmen for employment in each trade, and as to the impact of an affirmative action program with specific goals upon the existing labor force. The Department of Labor found that contractors could commit to the specific employment goals "without adverse impact on the existing labor force." Some minority tradesmen could be recruited, in other words, without eliminating job opportunities for white tradesmen.

To read § 703(a) in the manner suggested by the plaintiffs we would have to attribute to Congress the intention to freeze the status quo and to foreclose remedial action under other authority designed to overcome existing evils. We discern no such intention either from the language of the statute or from its legislative history. Clearly the Philadelphia Plan is color-conscious. Indeed the only meaning which can be attributed to the "affirmative action" language which since March of 1961 has been included in successive Executive Orders is that Government contractors must be color-conscious. Since 1941 the Executive Order program has recognized that discriminatory practices exclude available minority manpower from the labor pool. In other contexts color-consciousness has been deemed to be an appropriate remedial posture. Porcelli v. Titus, 302 F.Supp. 726 (D.N.J.1969), aff'd, 431 F.2d 1254 (3d Cir.1970); Norwalk CORE v. Norwalk Redevelopment Agency, 395 F.2d 920, 931 (2d Cir.1968); Offermann v. Nitkowski, 378 F.2d 22, 24 (2d Cir. 1967). It has been said respecting Title VII that "Congress did not intend to freeze an entire generation of Negro employees into discriminatory patterns that existed before the Act." Quarles v. Philip Morris, Inc., supra, 279 F.Supp. at 514. The *Quarles* case rejected the contention that existing, nondiscriminatory seniority arrangements were so sanctified by Title VII that the effects of past discrimination in job assignments could not be overcome. We reject the contention that Title VII prevents the President acting through the Executive Order program from attempting to remedy the absence from the Philadelphia construction labor of minority tradesmen in key trades.

Id., 442 F.2d at 173. Would *Contractors Association* be decided the same way today? Do the decisions in United Steelworkers of America v. Weber and Johnson v. Transportation Agency, Santa Clara County, discussed at p. 888, supra, reaffirm the holding in *Contractors Association* as far as Title VII is concerned?

3. Executive Order 11246 as amended applies to all those who have a federally assisted contract for over $10,000 or who operate programs that receive grants from the federal government. The regulations implementing the Executive Order require that a written affirmative action plan be adopted by any employer with 50 or more employees and a federal contract of $50,000 or more. 41 C.F.R. § 60–1.40 (1980). When the Executive Order was first issued in 1965, it exempted public institutions from the requirement of developing a written affirmative action plan. This exemption was deleted in January, 1973. The authority for enforcing the Executive Order lies with the Office of Federal Contract Compliance Programs (OFCCP) in the Department of Labor. The legal requirements governing affirmative action plans are set forth in the OFCCP's Revised Order no. 4, Affirmative Action Guidelines, 41 C.F.R. §§ 60–2–60.2.32 (1980). Under these guidelines, an employer with federal contracts must annually survey its current workforce, and the geographical area from which it hires, to determine if any racial or ethnic group, or women, are underrepresented in any portion of its workforce. If the employer finds "underutilization," then the employer must develop a plan to reduce that underrepresentation and set goals and timetables for doing so. The goals must be "significant, measurable and attainable," and the contractor must make "every good faith effort" to "achieve prompt and full utilization of minorities and women at all levels and in all segments of its work force where deficiencies exist." 41 C.F.R. § 60–2.10. The sanction for failure to comply with the Executive Order is debarment from receipt of federal contracts.

4. Despite the requirement for "goals" and "timetables" in construction industry affirmative action plans since 1969, efforts to end discrimination in the building trades in Philadelphia have not been successful. In 1961, Local 542 of the International Union of Operating Engineers and four construction trade associations entered into a collective bargaining agreement establishing a hiring hall system of referring workers to employers. By 1971, suit had been filed by the Commonwealth of Pennsylvania and twelve black plaintiffs representing a proposed class of minority group members residing within the jurisdiction of Local 542 who alleged violation of numerous state and federal laws prohibiting employment discrimination, including Title VII and 42 U.S.C.A. § 1981, by the Union and the Joint Apprenticeship and Training Committee, which administered the apprenticeship program. In 1978, the district court found Local 542 liable for intentional, class wide discrimination against minority workers in violation of Title VII and 42 U.S.C.A. § 1981. Commonwealth of Pennsylvania v. Local Union 542, Intern. Union of Operating Engineers, 469 F.Supp. 329 (E.D.Pa.1978), affirmed 648 F.2d 922 (3d Cir.1981)(en banc). Efforts to hold the contractors liable for this discrimination, based on their use of the hiring hall system, failed, however, because of the plaintiffs' inability to prove that the contractors themselves had engaged in intentional discrimination—a standard imposed under § 1981 by the Supreme Court in the parallel case against the trade association and individual employers, General Building Contractors Association, Inc. v. Pennsylvania, 458 U.S. 375, 102 S.Ct. 3141, 73 L.Ed.2d 835 (1982).

The Union met neither the referral nor the hours-worked specifications of the initial decree, nor did it comply with the integrated membership and validation requirements. In 1985 the Master appointed to oversee implementation of the decree, recommended that the time period covered by the decree be extended. The district court entered its order on August 1, 1985, extending the injunctive decree for two years, to August 31, 1987. This order was affirmed in Commonwealth of Pennsylvania v. Local Union 542, Intern. Union of Operating Engineers, 807 F.2d 330 (3d Cir.1986). Judge Stapleton, writing for the panel, noted that

> In 1961, the Union insisted upon and won a hiring hall system which forced the channeling of all employment opportunities with contractors in the industry through the hands of the Union. The record in this case shows that the Union has deliberately manipulated that system to the plaintiffs' detriment for over two decades during which period the white members of the Union have received far more than their fair share of working hours and wages.

Id., at 338.

For further discussion of affirmative action under the Executive Order in higher education, se the Text Note on Room at the Top: Affirmative Action in Colleges and Universities, p. 1110 infra.

2. OPPORTUNITIES FOR WOMEN–OWNED BUSINESSES

Notes on Set–Aside Provisions for Government Contractors

1. Parallel to the development of written affirmative action plans by government contractors under the Executive Order, Congress added a series of provisions to public works authorization legislation, and other government procurement bills, mandating that a certain percentage of government contracts be awarded to businesses owned by members of minority groups. Eventually, set-aside provisions were also created to assist women-owned businesses in obtaining government contracts. Many of these statutes, reserving a certain percentage of contracts for enterprises owned by members of "disadvantaged" groups, came under legal attack.

The first Supreme Court decision on such a set-aside provision, Fullilove v. Klutznick, 448 U.S. 448, 100 S.Ct. 2758, 65 L.Ed.2d 902 (1980), involved an amendment to the Public Works Employment Act of 1977, initially offered from the floor by Congressman Mitchell of Maryland. Pointing out that less than 1% of government contracts go to minority businesses in any fiscal year, Congressman Mitchell asked for a "targeting" for minority enterprises in the Act. 123 Cong.Rec. H1437–38 daily ed. Feb. 24, 1977. The Act, which provided additional funding for projects authorized by the Local Public Works Act of 1976, had as its primary purposes the alleviation of nationwide unemployment in the construction industry and stimulation of the national economy by assisting state and local governments to build necessary public facilities. The amendment proposed by Congressman Mitchell was not the subject of committee deliberation. As enacted, it reads (P.L. 95–28, 91 Stat. 117, § 103(f)(2)):

> Except to the extent that the Secretary determines otherwise, no grant shall be made under this chapter for any local public works project unless the applicant gives satisfactory assurance to the Secretary that at least 10 per centum of the amount of each grant shall be expended for minority business enterprises. For purposes of this paragraph, the term "minority business enterprise" means a business at least 50 per centum of which is owned by

minority group members or, in case of publicly owned business, at least 51 per centum of the stock of which is owned by minority group members. For the purposes of the preceding sentence, minority group members are citizens of the United States who are Negroes, Spanish-speaking, Orientals, Indians, Eskimos and Aleuts.

This provision was attacked by several associations of construction contractors and subcontractors on the basis that it conflicted with the Equal Protection Clause and with several statutes, including Title VI and Title VII.

In *Fullilove*, the Court upheld the so-called MBE provision as facially valid. Although no majority opinion could be produced, seven members of the Court upheld the use by Congress of racial classifications and racial quotas to redress past societal discrimination. Only Justices Stewart and Rehnquist espoused the view that the Constitution forbids the government, as distinguished from private employers, from acting "to the detriment of a person solely because of that person's race." Id., 448 U.S. at 525, 100 S.Ct. at 2799, 65 L.Ed.2d at 954. Justice Stevens, who dissented in *Fullilove* essentially because Congress had failed to tailor its remedy to the goal of redressing past discrimination by creating what he called "a grant of privilege", expressly rejected the view of Stewart and Rehnquist that the equal protection clause contains "an absolute prohibition against any statutory classification based on race." Id., 448 U.S. at 548, 100 S.Ct. at 2811, 65 L.Ed.2d at 969.

One commentator saw the case as a definitive ruling on affirmative action:

> *Fullilove* confirms indications in [Regents of the University of California v. Bakke, 438 U.S. 265, 98 S.Ct. 2733, 57 L.Ed.2d 750 (1978)] that the government's interest in remedying present effects of past discrimination is sufficiently compelling to allow appropriately tailored racial classifications to survive an equal protection challenge. More important, *Fullilove* breaks new ground on many disputed affirmative action issues: (a) the permissible *means* of remedying past discrimination—validating the use of quotas; (b) the requisite *findings*—sanctioning race-conscious action predicated upon findings of past societal discrimination; (c) the *power* of governmental bodies to take race-conscious action—confirming congressional authority, opening the door to actions by other bodies; and (d) the *scope* of permissible remedial action—upholding the set-aside, laying the analytical groundwork for action of greater magnitude.

The Supreme Court, 1979 Term, 94 Harv.L.Rev. 1, 127–28 (1980).

2. Nine years later, however, a set-aside for minority business enterprises adopted by the City of Richmond and modeled on the Public Works Employment Act of 1977 upheld in *Fullilove* did not pass constitutional muster. A majority of the Court held in City of Richmond v. J.A. Croson Co., 488 U.S. 469, 109 S.Ct. 706, 102 L.Ed.2d 854 (1989) that a 30% set-aside favoring minority businesses owned and controlled by "Blacks, Spanish-speaking, Orientals, Indians, Eskimos, or Aleuts" impermissibly discriminated against other contractors on the basis of their race. In Part III–A of her opinion, which was joined only by Chief Justice Rehnquist and Justices White and Kennedy, Justice O'Connor noted that blacks composed approximately 50% of the Richmond City Council. Why is this fact relevant to an assessment of the plan's validity? See The Supreme Court— Leading Cases, 103 Harv.L.Rev. 137, 227 (1989), arguing that the plurality's focus on the racial composition of the Richmond City Council is "misleading" because "[d]ue to their monopoly on the attributes of wealth and power and their dominance at the state and national levels, whites simply do not require extraordi-

nary protection from majoritarian politics at the local level." Do you agree with this analysis?

Speaking for the Court in Part III–B of her opinion, Justice O'Connor wrote:

In sum, none of the evidence presented by the city points to any identified discrimination in the Richmond construction industry. We, therefore, hold that the city has failed to demonstrate a compelling interest in apportioning public contracting opportunities on the basis of race. To accept Richmond's claim that past societal discrimination alone can serve as the basis for rigid racial preferences would be to open the door to competing claims for "remedial relief" for every disadvantaged group. The dream of a Nation of equal citizens in a society where race is irrelevant to personal opportunity and achievement would be lost in a mosaic of shifting preferences based on inherently unmeasurable claims of past wrongs. "Courts would be asked to evaluate the extent of the prejudice and consequent harm suffered by various minority groups. Those whose societal injury is thought to exceed some arbitrary level of tolerability then would be entitled to preferential classifications * * *." *Bakke,* 438 U.S., at 296–297, 98 S.Ct., at 2751 (Powell, J.). We think such a result would be contrary to both the letter and spirit of a constitutional provision whose central command is equality.

The foregoing analysis applies only to the inclusion of blacks within the Richmond set-aside program. There is *absolutely no evidence* of past discrimination against Spanish-speaking, Oriental, Indian, Eskimo, or Aleut persons in any aspect of the Richmond construction industry. The District Court took judicial notice of the fact that the vast majority of "minority" persons in Richmond were black. * * * It may well be that Richmond has never had an Aleut or Eskimo citizen. The random inclusion of racial groups that, as a practical matter, may never have suffered from discrimination in the construction industry in Richmond, suggests that perhaps the city's purpose was not in fact to remedy past discrimination.

If a 30% set-aside was "narrowly tailored" to compensate black contractors for past discrimination, one may legitimately ask why they are forced to share this "remedial relief" with an Aleut citizen who moves to Richmond tomorrow? The gross overinclusiveness of Richmond's racial preference strongly impugns the city's claim of remedial motivation. See *Wygant,* 476 U.S., at 284, n. 13, 106 S.Ct., at 1852, n. 13 (haphazard inclusion of racial groups "further illustrates the undifferentiated nature of the plan") * * *.

In dissent, Justice Marshall warned that:

A majority of this Court holds today, however, that the Equal Protection Clause of the Fourteenth Amendment blocks Richmond's initiative. The essence of the majority's position is that Richmond has failed to catalogue adequate findings to prove that past discrimination has impeded minorities from joining or participating fully in Richmond's construction contracting industry. I find deep irony in second-guessing Richmond's judgment on this point. As much as any municipality in the United States, Richmond knows what racial discrimination is; a century of decisions by this and other federal courts has richly documented the city's disgraceful history of public and private racial discrimination. In any event, the Richmond City Council has supported its determination that minorities have been wrongly excluded from local construction contracting. Its proof includes statistics showing that minority-owned businesses have received virtually no city contracting dollars and rarely if ever belonged to area trade associations; testimony by municipal officials that discrimination has been widespread in the local construction industry; and the same exhaustive and widely publicized federal studies relied on in *Fullilove,* studies which showed that pervasive discrimination in the Nation's tight-knit construction industry had operated to exclude minorities from public contracting. These are precisely the types of statistical and testimonial evidence which, until today, this Court had credited in cases approving of race-conscious measures designed to remedy past discrimination.

More fundamentally, today's decision marks a deliberate and giant step backward in this Court's affirmative action jurisprudence. Cynical of one municipality's attempt to redress the effects of past racial discrimination in a particular industry, the majority launches a grapeshot attack on race-conscious remedies in general. The majority's unnecessary pronouncements will inevitably discourage or prevent governmental entities, particularly States and localities, from acting to rectify the scourge of past discrimination. This is the harsh reality of the majority's decision, but it is not the Constitution's command.

In an effort to avert the wholesale dismantling of municipal affirmative action plans, Professor Laurence Tribe convened an unprecedented Constitutional Scholars' Conference on Affirmative Action at the African Meeting House in Boston on March 30, 1989. The resulting "Constitutional Scholars' Statement on Affirmative Action After City of Richmond v. J.A. Croson Co." was subsequently published in 98 Yale L.J. 1711 (1989). Its message, that "[i]t would deny not only the Supreme Court's decisions but the fundamental purposes of the equal protection clause to conclude that the Constitution forbids all such inclusive remedial measures, or requires that such measures be treated in exactly the same way as the invidious discrimination of the nation's past" was in turn sharply disputed by former Solicitor General Charles Fried in "A Response to the Scholars' Statement," 99 Yale L.J. 155 (1989). See also the "Scholars' Reply to Professor Fried," 99 Yale L.J. 163 (1989). What do you suppose motivated the convening of the Conference?

3. The defense of a local government set-aside program was more successful in San Francisco than in Richmond. In Associated General Contractors of California, Inc. v. Coalition for Economic Equity, 950 F.2d 1401 (9th Cir.1991), certiorari denied 503 U.S. 985, 112 S.Ct. 1670, 118 L.Ed.2d 390 (1992), the Ninth Circuit affirmed Judge Thelton Henderson's order denying a preliminary injunction enjoining the enforcement of San Francisco's Minority/Woman/Local Business Utilization Ordinance insofar as it applies to prime construction contracts. The Ordinance, which became effective on July 1, 1989, gives a five percent bid preference for local business enterprises (LBEs), woman-owned or controlled business enterprises (WBEs), and minority-owned or controlled business enterprises (MBEs)(minorities are defined to include Asians, Blacks and Latinos). The LBE bid preferences can also be invoked by local WBEs and MBEs, for a total bid preference of ten percent. Non–MBEs and non-WBEs who engage in a joint venture with a local MBE or WBE also obtain a five percent bid preference if the MBE's or WBE's participation is between 35% and 51%.

Plaintiff AGCC challenged the preferences given to both WBEs and MBEs, but its constitutional challenge was limited to MBEs. Testing that aspect of the Ordinance against *Croson,* Judge Betty Fletcher found it satisfied both prongs of the strict scrutiny test there announced: that a municipality's classifications based on race must serve a compelling state interest and must be narrowly tailored to further that interest. Addressing the compelling state interest prong, she reasoned in part that:

> * * * In contrast to the "mere recitation of a 'benign' or legitimate purpose" criticized in *Croson,* * * * the record in this case discloses that the Board made detailed findings of prior discrimination in construction and building within the City's borders. Based on testimony taken at more than ten public hearings and on numerous written submissions from the public, the Board found that City departments continued to discriminate against MBEs and WBEs and continued to operate under the "old boy network" in awarding contracts, thereby disadvantaging MBEs and WBEs. Furthermore, it found that large statistical disparities existed between the percentage of contracts awarded to MBEs and the percentage of available MBEs.

* * *

> * * * Unlike the exceedingly sparse foundation for the City of Richmond's findings of discrimination, the record in this case indicates that San Francisco is likely to demonstrate a "strong basis in evidence" supporting its decision to adopt a race-conscious plan.

Id., 950 F.2d at 1413–16. On the question of whether the race-conscious remedy was narrowly tailored to redress the consequences of the discrimination, Judge Fletcher pointed out that the City had attempted to use race-neutral means to address the problem of discrimination, and that it continued to make efforts to enforce its anti-discrimination ordinance. She observed that the race-conscious ordinance used "a more modest system * * * of bid preferences" rather than "the rigid quota system found faulty in *Croson.*" And she noted that:

> * * * Moreover, the plan remedies only specifically identified discrimination: the City provides preferences only to those minority groups found to have previously received a lower percentage of specific types of contracts than their availability to perform such work would suggest. For example, Black-owned medical services firms do not receive preferences because they have not been disadvantaged in the past with respect to the award of these contracts. For the same reasons, San Francisco's program does not provide for a bid preference for Asian- or Latino-owned architectural/engineering or computer system firms. In addition, since the Ordinance confines the preference to those who are economically disadvantaged, MBEs are prevented from using the preferences to obtain windfalls.

Id., 950 F.2d at 1416–18. Do you think that Judge Fletcher has successfully distinguished the San Francisco Ordinance from that invalidated in *Croson?*

4. Despite the results in *Croson,* a narrow majority of the Court continued to review federal set-aside programs under a more lenient constitutional standard. Metro Broadcasting, Inc. v. FCC, 497 U.S. 547, 110 S.Ct. 2997, 111 L.Ed.2d 445 (1990), involved a constitutional challenge to FCC policies designed to promote diversity in programming by increasing the number of broadcast license holders who are members of minority groups. Two FCC policies were at issue: the "distress sale" program, which, according to the agency's 1978 Policy Statement, permits

> licensees whose licenses have been designated for revocation hearing, or whose renewal applications have been designated for hearing on basic qualification issues * * * to transfer or assign their licenses at a "distress sale" price to applicants with a significant minority ownership interest, assuming the proposed assignee or transferee meets our other qualifications.

The second FCC policy is that of granting qualitative enhancements to minority applicants for new licenses in comparative hearings. Both policies also contain sex preferences, but those preferences were not before the Court in *Metro Broadcasting.*

Justice Brennan aligned the legal problem in *Metro Broadcasting* with that presented in *Fullilove* rather than *Croson,* pointing out the "overriding significance" of the fact that the FCC's minority ownership programs had been "specifically approved—indeed, mandated—by Congress" and going on to "hold that benign race-conscious measures mandated by Congress—even if those measures are not 'remedial' in the sense of being designed to compensate victims of past governmental or societal discrimination—are constitutionally permissible to the extent that they serve important governmental objectives within the power of Congress and are substantially related to achievement of those objectives." Id., 497 U.S. at 563–65, 110 S.Ct. at 3008–09, 111 L.Ed.2d at 462–63. The Court limited *Croson* to minority set-aside programs adopted by a municipality, noting that the case does not control the level of scrutiny applied to a "benign racial classification employed by Congress." Id., 497 U.S. at 565, 110 S.Ct. at 3009, 111 L.Ed.2d 463. Applying this newly-adopted intermediate level of scrutiny, the Court held that the FCC minority ownership policies served the important governmental objective of broadcast diversity, and that those policies are substantially related to the achievement of that objective. In announcing the Court's position on the latter point, Justice Brennan reaffirmed and expanded Justice Powell's approach to educational diversity in University of California Regents v. Bakke, 438 U.S. 265, 311–15, 98 S.Ct. 2733, 2759–61, 57 L.Ed.2d 750, 785–86 (1978)(opinion of Powell, J.), as follows:

C

The judgment that there is a link between expanded minority ownership and broadcast diversity does not rest on impermissible stereotyping. Congressional policy does not assume that in every case minority ownership and management will lead to more minority-oriented programming or to the expression of a discrete "minority viewpoint" on the airwaves. Neither does it pretend that all programming that appeals to minority audiences can be labeled "minority programming" or that programming that might be described as "minority" does not appeal to nonminorities. Rather, both Congress and the FCC maintain simply that expanded minority ownership of broadcast outlets will, in the aggregate, result in greater broadcast diversity. A broadcasting industry with representative minority participation will produce more variation and diversity than will one whose ownership is drawn from a single racially and ethnically homogeneous group. The predictive judgment about the overall result of minority entry into broadcasting is not a rigid assumption about how minority owners will behave in every case but rather is akin to Justice Powell's conclusion in *Bakke* that greater admission of minorities would contribute, on average, "to the 'robust exchange of ideas.' " * * * To be sure, there is no ironclad guarantee that each minority owner will contribute to diversity. But neither was there an assurance in *Bakke* that minority students would interact with nonminority students or that the particular minority students admitted would have typical or distinct "minority" viewpoints. See id., * * * (opinion of Powell, J.)(noting only that educational excellence is "*widely believed* to be promoted by a diverse student body")(emphasis added); *id.,* * * * (" 'In the nature of things, it is hard to know how, and when, and even if, this informal "learning through diversity" actually occurs' ")(citation omitted).

Although all station owners are guided to some extent by market demand in their programming decisions, Congress and the Commission have determined that there may be important differences between the broadcasting practices of minority owners and those of their nonminority counterparts. This judgment—and the conclusion that there is a nexus between minority ownership and broadcasting diversity—is corroborated by a host of empirical evidence. * * *

Id., 497 U.S. at 577–80, 110 S.Ct. at 3016–17, 111 L.Ed.2d at 472–73.

Justice Stevens, concurring, welcomed the Court's new approach to affirmative action:

Today the Court squarely rejects the proposition that a governmental decision that rests on a racial classification is never permissible except as a remedy for a past wrong. * * * I endorse this focus on the future benefit, rather than the remedial justification, of such decisions.

I remain convinced, of course, that racial or ethnic characteristics provide a relevant basis for disparate treatment only in extremely rare situations and that it is therefore "especially important that the reasons for any such classification be clearly identified and unquestionably legitimate." Fullilove v. Klutznick, * * * (dissenting opinion). The Court's opinion explains how both elements of that standard are satisfied. Specifically, the reason for the classification—the recognized interest in broadcast diversity—is clearly identified and does not imply any judgment concerning the abilities of owners of different races or the merits of different kinds of programming. Neither the favored nor the disfavored class is stigmatized in any way. In addition, the Court demonstrates that this case falls within the extremely narrow category of governmental decisions for which racial or ethnic heritage may provide a rational basis for differential treatment. The public interest in broadcast diversity—like the interest in an integrated police force, diversity in the composition of a public school faculty or diversity in the student body of a professional school—is in my view unquestionably legitimate.

Therefore, I join both the opinion and the judgment of the Court.

Id., 497 U.S. at 601, 110 S.Ct. at 3028, 111 L.Ed.2d at 486.

Justice O'Connor, joined in dissent by the Chief Justice and Justices Scalia and Kennedy, strongly protested the Court's "renewed toleration of racial classifications and [its] repudiation of our recent affirmation that the Constitution's equal protection guarantees extend equally to all citizens." Id., 497 U.S. at 602, 110 S.Ct. at 3029, 111 L.Ed.2d at 487. Justices Kennedy and Scalia dissenting separately, scathingly compared the Court's opinion to the decision in Plessy v. Ferguson, 163 U.S. 537, 16 S.Ct. 1138, 41 L.Ed. 256 (1896), which they characterized as having upheld "a government-sponsored race-conscious measure" designed to serve "the governmental interest of increasing the riding pleasure of railroad passengers." Id., 497 U.S. at 630, 110 S.Ct. at 3044, 111 L.Ed.2d at 505–06. They concluded by repeating Justice Harlan's warning:

Though the racial composition of this Nation is far more diverse than the first Justice Harlan foresaw, his warning in dissent is now all the more apposite: "The destinies of the two races, in this country, are indissolubly linked together, and the interests of both require that the common government of all shall not permit the seeds of race hate to be planted under the sanction of law." Plessy, * * * (dissenting opinion). Perhaps the Court can succeed in its assumed role of case-by-case arbiter of when it is desirable and

benign for the Government to disfavor some citizens and favor others based
on the color of their skin. Perhaps the tolerance and decency to which our
people aspire will let the disfavored rise above hostility and the favored escape
condescension. But history suggests much peril in this enterprise, and so the
Constitution forbids us to undertake it. I regret that after a century of
judicial opinions we interpret the Constitution to do no more than move us
from "separate but equal" to "unequal but benign."

Id., 497 U.S. at 637, 110 S.Ct. at 3047, 111 L.Ed.2d at 509–10.

5. The Supreme Court has yet to rule on the validity of set-aside provisions
for women-owned businesses. In a sign of further changes to come, however, the
United States Court of Appeals for the District of Columbia Circuit in Lamprecht
v. FCC, 958 F.2d 382 (D.C.Cir.1992), held that the FCC policy favoring female
applicants in order to achieve diversity in broadcasting violates the equal protection component of the Fifth Amendment. Justice Clarence Thomas authored the
lead opinion; Judge Buckley concurred, and Judge Mikva dissented. Excerpts
from Justice Thomas's opinion follow.

Metro Broadcasting confirms that although we are "to give 'great weight
to the decisions of Congress and to the experience of the Commission,'" 110
S.Ct., at 3011 (citation omitted), we are still obliged in the end to review the
government's policy—both the judgment of law that the policy is constitutional and the findings of fact that underlie it. The Court explained: "[W]e do
not '"defer" to the judgment of the Congress and the Commission on a
constitutional question,' and would not 'hesitate to invoke the Constitution
should we determine that the Commission has not fulfilled its task with
appropriate sensitivity' to equal protection principles." * * * We examine,
then, the relationship between achieving diversity on the airwaves and the
Commission's policy of preferring women owners, and in doing so we bear in
mind Justice O'Connor's warning for the Court in Mississippi University for
Women: "Although the test for determining the validity of a gender-based
classification is straightforward, it must be applied free of fixed notions
concerning the roles and abilities of males and females." 458 U.S., at 724–25.

In applying that test, the Supreme Court has repeatedly denounced
"unsupported generalizations about the relative interests and perspectives of
men and women," Roberts v. United States Jaycees, 468 U.S. 609, 628 (1984),
regardless of which sex the generalizations purport to favor. See, e.g.,
Mississippi Univ. for Women * * *; Caban v. Mohammed * * *; Craig v.
Boren * * *; Weinberger v. Wiesenfeld * * *. As the Court has recognized
time and again, "[D]iscrimination based on archaic and overbroad assumptions about the relative needs and capacities of the sexes forces individuals to
labor under stereotypical notions that often bear no relationship to their
actual abilities." Jaycees, 468 U.S., at 625; see also Orr v. Orr * * *;
Frontiero v. Richardson * * *.

Applying its standard of intermediate scrutiny, the Court has therefore
required not only that sex-based generalizations be "supported," but that the
support be strong enough to advance "substantially" the legitimating governmental interest. * * *

* * * [I]n Weinberger v. Wiesenfeld, the Court reviewed the constitutionality of an act of Congress that gave to widows Social Security benefits not
available to widowers. Congress had proceeded on the presumption that
women are less likely than men to be the family breadwinners, and the Court
acknowledged that Congress's presumption was "not entirely without empiri-

cal support." Nevertheless, as Justice Brennan explained for the Court, "such a gender-based generalization cannot suffice to justify the denigration of the efforts of women who do work and whose earnings contribute significantly to their families' support." 420 U.S., at 645 * * *. Cf. Arizona Governing Comm. v. Norris, 463 U.S. 1073 (1983)(holding that title VII of the Civil Rights Act of 1964 prohibits differences in the amount of pension benefits paid to men and women, even though sex-based actuarial tables show that women in the aggregate live longer than men).

Metro Broadcasting thus reinforces the lessons of cases such as *Craig* and *Wiesenfeld:* Any "predictive judgments" concerning group behavior and the differences in behavior among different groups must at the very least be sustained by meaningful evidence.[3] In concluding in *Metro Broadcasting* that the government's race-based predictions were "a product of 'analysis' rather than a 'stereotyped reaction' based on '[h]abit,'" the Supreme Court examined a "host" of studies supporting the government's judgment that diversity of viewpoints increases substantially when station owners are selected in part on the basis of race or ethnicity. See 110 S.Ct., at 3018 (citation omitted and internal quotation marks amended). We now examine, in light of these principles, the evidence supporting the government's judgment that diversity increases substantially when owners are selected in part on the basis of sex.

(3)

Implicit in the government's judgment are at least three assumptions: first, that there exists such a thing as "women's programming" (or "Alaskan programming," say, or "suburban teenage easy listener programming"); second, that these distinct types of programming are underrepresented on the airwaves; and third, that women who own radio or television stations are likelier than white men to broadcast these distinct types of programming. Lamprecht challenges each of these assumptions.

We decline to address Lamprecht's first argument. The Supreme Court assumed in *Metro Broadcasting* that there are such things as "minority programming" of different kinds, and we assume the same with respect to "women's programming" and other distinct programming types. We also decline to address Lamprecht's second argument. Although the Commission might risk raising other constitutional questions if it tried to set out some

---

3. Our dissenting colleague asserts that a sex-based classification might survive intermediate scrutiny even if it rests upon unsupported generalizations about men or women as a group. * * * He notes correctly that "the purpose of intermediate scrutiny" is to ensure that sex-based classifications are based on "reasoned analysis" rather than "archaic stereotypes," * * * possibilities that he appears rightly to regard as mutually exclusive. But an "analysis" that rests upon unsupported factual premises cannot possibly be "reasoned," and an untrue and widely-held generalization about men or women is by definition a "stereotype." See, e.g., U.S. Civil Rights Comm'n, Characters in Textbooks 5 (1980)(explaining that a member of a group is "stereotyped" when she is "portrayed in a stylized manner that conforms to widely accepted, but often untrue, ideas of what members of the group

are like"). More to the point, unless a generalization about men or women asserted in defense of a sex-based classification is grounded in some degree of fact, the classification cannot possibly advance *any* legitimate state interest, much less an important one. Our dissenting colleague, however, insists that a relevant generalization is presumed true (even if unsupported) unless proved otherwise. * * * On this point, our colleague is mistaken—for it is a "firmly established principle[ ]" that "the burden of showing an 'exceedingly persuasive justification'" falls on "the party seeking to uphold a statute that classifies individuals on the basis of their gender." Mississippi Univ. for Women, 458 U.S., at 723–24 (citation omitted); see also Heckler v. Mathews, 465 U.S. 728, 744–45 (1984)(imposing the same burden with respect to federal statutes). * * *

"correct" mix of information or viewpoints, we follow the Supreme Court's lead and assume that all the types of programming that women might put on the air are underrepresented. We assess, then, the last of the assumptions implicit in the Commission's sex-conscious policy. But having considered the evidence offered to demonstrate a link between ownership by women and any type of underrepresented programming, we are left unconvinced.[4]

The Commission's brief cites nothing that might support its predictive judgment that women owners will broadcast women's or minority or any other underrepresented type of programming at any different rate than will men. Nor is there any proof in the administrative record, a point that the Commission's lawyer confirmed repeatedly at oral argument. We consider then the only study, so far as we know, either inside or outside the legislative record, that actually did examine the possibility: the Congressional Research Service report, *Minority Broadcast Station Ownership and Broadcast Programming: Is There a Nexus?*

Whatever the study's methodological flaws,[8] it does answer its own question, at least with respect to women. The answer it gives is "no." Consider the following facts, which we summarize in text and show in tables in the appendix.

* Of stations owned primarily by women, slightly more than a third, or 35%, broadcast what the study calls "women's programming." Of stations owned entirely by "non-women," a slightly lower portion, or 28%, broadcast women's programming. For others given preferences in comparative licensing, the difference is dramatic. Of stations owned primarily by Blacks, 79% broadcast Black programming, while of stations owned entirely by people who are not Black, 20% broadcast Black programming; of stations owned primarily by Hispanics, nearly three-quarters, or 74%, broadcast Hispanic programming, while of stations owned entirely by people who are not Hispanic, 10% broadcast Hispanic programming; of stations owned primarily by Asians or Pacific Islanders, 25% broadcast Asian or Pacific Islander programming, while of stations owned entirely by people who are not Asians or Pacific Islanders, 3% broadcast Asian or Pacific Islander programming; of stations owned primarily by Indians or Alaskans, 46% broadcast Indian or Alaskan programming, while of stations owned entirely by people who are not Indian or Alaskan, 4% broadcast Indian or Alaskan programming. To put it another way: Stations owned primarily by Indians or Alaskans are more than eleven

4. Our dissenting colleague tells us that we identify "women's or minority programming" as "programming specifically targeted at women or minorities," * * * We do not. Neither "women's viewpoint" nor "women's programming" necessarily means viewpoints or programming targeted to women or of special interest to women or concerning subjects that some may suppose women are likely to put on the airwaves, and the same is true for "minority viewpoint" or "minority programming." Rather than presume to give content to these terms, * * * (calling "innocuous to the point of being obvious" the assumption that "some female programmers will choose to emphasize different subjects—breast cancer, say, or glass ceilings in the workplace"); infra note 8, we remain agnostic. We do assume, however, as did Congress, that these terms necessarily have *some* meaning—but whatever "women's programming" and "minority programming" are, there is no evidence showing that women owner/managers are substantially likelier to program them than are men.

8. Unfortunately, *Minority Programming* does not define terms such as "women's programming" (or "minority programming," for that matter), but rather, relied on the reporting stations to characterize themselves. The study itself warns readers of this and other problems. See *Minority Programming* at 1–8; see also Spitzer, Justifying Minority Preferences in Broadcasting, 64 S.Cal.L.Rev. 293, 342–45, 345–46 (1991); *Winter Park,* 873 F.2d, at 358–61 (Williams, J., concurring in part and dissenting in part).

times as likely to broadcast Indian or Alaskan programming as are stations with no Indian or Alaskan owners. For Asians or Pacific Islanders, the comparable multiplier is more than eight; for Hispanics, more than seven; for Blacks, almost four. In contrast, stations owned primarily by women are just one and one quarter times as likely to broadcast women's programming as are stations owned entirely by men. See app. table 1, at 35.

  * Stations in which women own anywhere from 1% to 50% of the equity are just as likely to broadcast women's programming as are stations owned principally or entirely by women. In contrast, stations in which Indians or Alaskans own from 1% to 50% are only half as likely to broadcast Indian or Alaskan programming as are stations owned principally by Indians or Alaskans. See app. table 2, at 36.

  * In five large cities, New York, Los Angeles, Chicago, Dallas, and Atlanta, stations with any owners of Black, American Indian, Alaskan, Hispanic, Asian, or Pacific Islander heritage are likelier to broadcast women's programming than are stations with any owners who are women: Only one-third of stations with any women owners broadcast women's programming, while almost three-fifths of stations with Hispanic owners, half of stations with Asian, Pacific Islander, Indian, or Alaskan owners, and more than two-fifths of stations with Black owners, broadcast women's programming. In all cities combined, barely more than one-third of stations with women owners broadcast women's programming, while half of stations with Indian or Alaskan owners, and more than 40% of stations with Hispanic or Black owners, do so. For stations in which the relevant group holds between one and fifty percent ownership interests, women are less likely to broadcast women's programming than are Indians, Alaskans, Hispanics, Blacks, Asians, and Pacific Islanders. See app. table 3, at 37; app. table 4, at 37; app. table 5, at 38.

  * Of the ten most-used programming formats, nine are as popular in almost precisely the same order for stations owned by "non-minorities" (again, that could include both women and men) as they are for stations owned by women. See app. table 10, at 40.

  * Nor are stations owned by women much likelier to engage in *minority* programming than are stations owned by men, as *Minority Programming* reveals. Stations with women owners are barely, if at all, likelier to broadcast assorted types of minority programming than are stations owned by anyone else, and are in fact much less likely to broadcast minority programming than members of most of the relevant minority groups. Of stations owned in any part by women, just 5% broadcast Asian or Pacific Islander programming, for example, while of stations owned by "non-Asian/Pacific Islanders" (which may or may not include women) only 3% broadcast Asian or Pacific Islander programming. Stations with Hispanic owners, in contrast, are three times as likely to broadcast Asian or Pacific Islander programming as are stations with any women owners, and stations with Black owners are more than twice as likely to broadcast Asian or Pacific Islander programming as are stations with any owners who are women. The data show similar results for Hispanic programming: stations with Hispanic owners are nearly five times as likely, and stations with Asian or Pacific Islander owners more than twice as likely, to broadcast Hispanic programming as are stations owned in any part by women. Of stations with women owners, only 5% broadcast Indian or Alaskan programming, barely a higher proportion than

the 4% of stations owned entirely by "non-Indian/Alaskans" that do so. For Black programming the comparable percentages are 26% for stations with women owners and 20% for stations owned by non-Blacks. See app. table 6, at 38; app. table 7, at 39; app. table 8, at 39; app. table 9, at 40.

To summarize: The data in *Minority Programming* fail to establish any statistically meaningful link between ownership by women and programming of any particular kind. The study, in short, highlights the hazards associated with government endeavors like this one. As Justice Brennan has written for the Court, "[P]roving broad sociological propositions by statistics is a dubious business, and one that inevitably is in tension with the normative philosophy that underlies the Equal Protection Clause." Craig v. Boren, 429 U.S., at 204.[9]

When the government treats people differently because of their sex, equal-protection principles at the very least require that there be a meaningful factual predicate supporting a link between the government's means and its ends. In this case, the government has failed to show that its sex-preference policy is substantially related to achieving diversity on the air-waves. We therefore hold that the policy violates the Constitution.

958 F.2d at 391–98.

Chief Judge Mikva thus summarized his dissent:

When the Supreme Court decided *Metro Broadcasting* in 1990, the opinion was criticized vigorously for its indulgent approval of an affirmative action program adopted by the FCC and approved by Congress. * * *

The Supreme Court, of course, may now decide to overrule *Metro Broadcasting* and to require strict scrutiny of Congress's affirmative action policies, as the four dissenters urged. But as appellate judges, our duty is to follow Supreme Court precedents, not to anticipate them. And it strikes me as impossible to reconcile the Supreme Court's decision in *Metro Broadcasting* with my colleagues' decision today.

The Supreme Court held that Congress may require the FCC to make certain broadcasting licenses available only to minorities; yet this Court reaches the surprising conclusion that Congress may *not* require the FCC to adopt a far milder and far less discriminatory preference program for women. Although they pay lip service to Justice Brennan's majority opinion, my

---

9. Our dissenting colleague declares that "judges have no basis, except their own policy preferences," for concluding that the degree of correlation shown here is not "enough," since the Fifth Amendment does not identify the "mystical" point at which a correlation satisfies the dictates of equal protection. * * * Our colleague is not the first to criticize the intermediate-scrutiny test for its indeterminacy. See Craig v. Boren, 429 U.S., at 221 (Rehnquist, J., dissenting)("[T]he phrases used are so diaphanous and elastic as to invite subjective judicial preferences or prejudices relating to particular types of legislation masquerading as judgments whether such legislation is directed at 'important' objectives or whether the relationship to those objectives is 'substantial.' "). While rational basis or strict scrutiny review would make for fewer close cases, how-

ever, we have no authority for departing from the Supreme Court's decision to follow the middle course. Intermediate scrutiny, then, which *Metro Broadcasting* requires of us, calls for judgment—for drawing a line. The line we necessarily draw today, holding that the degree of correlation in this case is not enough, is different from the line drawn in *Metro Broadcasting* (that a much stronger degree of correlation was enough), the line drawn in *Craig* (that an arguably weaker degree of correlation was not enough), and the line proposed today by our colleague in dissent (that the degree of correlation in this case is enough). Despite what our colleague states, the line that we draw is neither more nor less principled than the line that he draws; our lines are merely grounded in different exercises of judgment.

colleagues apply in practice the more exacting scrutiny of Justice O'Connor's dissent.

My colleagues point to only one difference between this case and *Metro*: the statistics in one report showed a greater correlation between minority ownership and programming diversity than between female ownership and programming diversity. This poses an interesting question for social scientists, but not for judges. The study that my colleagues invoke to strike down the preference explicitly concluded that there *is* a link between female ownership and programming diversity. The study showed that stations owned by women are 20% more likely than stations owned by men to broadcast "women's programming," and about 30% more likely than stations owned by non-minorities to broadcast "minority programming." My colleagues do not share with us the text or history of the Equal Protection clause that tells them that a 20% or 30% increase is unconstitutional, while a larger increase is not. And even though the Supreme Court in *Metro* cited empirical studies offered by amicus groups rather than by the FCC or Congress, my colleagues ignore similar studies that provide more of the statistics they require.

In striking down the preference policy, my colleagues have done precisely what the Supreme Court forbids them to do: they have rejected Congress's conclusion that more female owners of broadcast stations will lead to more diverse programming, even though *Metro* says repeatedly that courts should *defer* to Congress's conclusions about the link between ownership and programming, as long as the conclusions reflect reasoned analysis rather than archaic stereotypes. *Metro* 's holding is consistent with a long line of gender cases; and this, after all, is a case about gender, not race. Applying the Supreme Court's test, I think Congress clearly used reasoned analysis when it concluded that increasing the number of women who own and manage television and radio stations will increase programming diversity. And it would be hard to conclude that the gender preference *reflects* outdated stereotypes, since the FCC and Congress designed it to *reduce* outdated stereotypes. My colleagues are free to question the wisdom of the gender preference, but the Supreme Court forbids them (for now) from striking the policy down.

I cannot join them, and respectfully dissent.

958 F.2d at 404.

6. Justice Thomas was joining the Supreme Court just as the *Lamprecht* opinion was being issued. The next time the Court considered a federally-mandated set-aside provision, Justice Thomas was part of the majority undercutting *Fullilove* and overruling *Metro Broadcasting* by applying the strict scrutiny test of *Croson* to a federal set-aside program. In Adarand Constructors, Inc. v. Pena, 515 U.S. ___, 115 S.Ct. 2097, 132 L.Ed.2d 158 (1995), Justice O'Connor announced the 5 to 4 judgment of the Court, and wrote an opinion, joined by Justice Kennedy, and by Chief Justice Rehnquist, Thomas, and Scalia in all but one section. *Adarand* involved a provision of the Small Business Act, 15 U.S.C. § 637(d), creating a presumption that "Black Americans, Hispanic Americans, Native Americans, Asian Pacific Americans, and other minorities, or any other individual found to be disadvantaged by the [Small Business] Administration pursuant to section 8(a) of the Small Business Act" are "socially and economically disadvantaged individuals," whose businesses are entitled to preferential treatment by prime contractors in awarding subcontracts. 115 S.Ct. at 2102. After

comparing the treatment of race-based equal protection claims under the differing commands of the Fourteenth and Fifth Amendments, Justice O'Connor concluded that the weight of precedent required the Court to apply the same strict scrutiny standard to federal racial classifications under the Fifth Amendment, as it does to state action under the Fourteenth Amendment:

     * * * The various opinions in Frontiero v. Richardson * * *, which concerned sex discrimination by the Federal Government, took their equal protection standard of review from Reed v. Reed * * *, a case that invalidated sex discrimination by a State, without mentioning any possibility of a difference between the standards applicable to state and federal action. * * * Thus, in 1975, the Court stated explicitly that "[t]his Court's approach to Fifth Amendment equal protection claims has always been precisely the same as to equal protection claims under the Fourteenth Amendment." Weinberger v. Wisenfeld * * * ; see also Buckley v. Valeo, 424 U.S. 1, 93, 96 S.Ct. 612, 670, 46 L.Ed.2d 659 (1976)("Equal protection analysis in the Fifth Amendment area is the same as that under the Fourteenth Amendment"). United States v. Paradise, 480 U.S. 149, 166, n. 16, 107 S.Ct. 1053, 1064, n. 16, 94 L.Ed.2d 203 (1987)(plurality opinion of Brennan, J.)("[T]he reach of the equal protection guarantee of the Fifth Amendment is coextensive with that of the Fourteenth"). We do not understand a few contrary suggestions appearing in cases in which we found special deference to the political branches of the Federal Government to be appropriate, e.g., Hampton v. Mow Sun Wong, 426 U.S. 88, 100, 101–102 n. 21, 96 S.Ct. 1895, 1903, 1904–1905, n. 21, 48 L.Ed.2d 495 (1976)(federal power over immigration), to detract from this general rule.

B

     Most of the cases discussed above involved classifications burdening groups that have suffered discrimination in our society. In 1978, the Court confronted the question whether race-based governmental action designed to *benefit* such groups should also be subject to "the most rigid scrutiny." Regents of Univ. of California v. Bakke, 438 U.S. 265, 98 S.Ct. 2733, 57 L.Ed.2d 750, involved an equal protection challenge to a state-run medical school's practice of reserving a number of spaces in its entering class for minority students. The petitioners argued that "strict scrutiny" should apply only to "classifications that disadvantage 'discrete and insular minorities.'" Id., at 287–288, 98 S.Ct., at 2747 (opinion of Powell, J.). * * * *Bakke* did not produce an opinion for the Court, but Justice Powell's opinion announcing the Court's judgment rejected the argument. In a passage joined by Justice White, Justice Powell wrote that "[t]he guarantee of equal protection cannot mean one thing when applied to one individual and something else when applied to a person of another color." 438 U.S., at 289–290, 98 S.Ct., at 2748. He concluded that "[r]acial and ethnic distinctions of any sort are inherently suspect and thus call for the most exacting judicial examination." Id., at 291, 98 S.Ct., at 2748. * * *

     With *Croson,* the Court finally agreed that the Fourteenth Amendment requires strict scrutiny of all race-based action by state and local governments. But *Croson* of course had no occasion to declare what standard of review the Fifth Amendment requires for such action taken by the Federal Government. * * *

     A year later, however, the Court took a surprising turn [in] Metro Broadcasting, Inc. v. FCC. * * *

By adopting intermediate scrutiny as the standard of review for congressionally mandated "benign" racial classifications, *Metro Broadcasting* departed from prior cases in two significant respects. First, it turned its back on *Croson's* explanation of why strict scrutiny of all governmental racial classifications is essential:

> "Absent searching judicial inquiry into the justification for such race-based measures, there is simply no way of determining what classifications are 'benign' or 'remedial' and what classifications are in fact motivated by illegitimate notions of racial inferiority or simple racial politics. Indeed, the purpose of strict scrutiny is to 'smoke out' illegitimate uses of race by assuring that the legislative body is pursuing a goal important enough to warrant use of a highly suspect tool. The test also ensures that the means chosen 'fit' this compelling goal so closely that there is little or no possibility that the motive for the classification was illegitimate racial prejudice or stereotype." *Croson,* supra, at 493, 109 S.Ct. at 721 (plurality opinion of O'Connor, J.).

We adhere to that view today, despite the surface appeal of holding "benign" racial classifications to a lower standard, because "it may not always be clear that a so-called preference is in fact benign," *Bakke,* supra, at 298, 98 S.Ct., at 2752 (opinion of Powell, J.). "[M]ore than good motives should be required when government seeks to allocate its resources by way of an explicit racial classification system." Days, Fullilove, 96 Yale L.J. 453, 485 (1987).

Second, *Metro Broadcasting* squarely rejected one of the three propositions established by the Court's earlier equal protection cases, namely, congruence between the standards applicable to federal and state racial classifications, and in so doing also undermined the other two—skepticism of all racial classifications, and consistency of treatment irrespective of the race of the burdened or benefited group. * * *

* * *

D

Our action today makes explicit what Justice Powell thought implicit in the *Fullilove* lead opinion: federal racial classifications, like those of a State, must serve a compelling governmental interest, and must be narrowly tailored to further that interest. * * *

Finally, we wish to dispel the notion that strict scrutiny is "strict in theory, but fatal in fact." *Fullilove,* supra, at 519, 100 S.Ct. at 2795 (Marshall, J., concurring in judgment). The unhappy persistence of both the practice and the lingering effects of racial discrimination against minority groups in this country is an unfortunate reality, and government is not disqualified from acting in response to it. As recently as 1987, for example, every Justice of this Court agreed that the Alabama Department of Public Safety's "pervasive, systematic, and obstinate discriminatory conduct" justified a narrowly tailored race-based remedy. See United States v. Paradise, 480 U.S., at 167, 107 S.Ct., at 1064 (plurality opinion of Brennan, J.); id., at 190, 107 S.Ct., at 1076 (Stevens, J.)., (concurring in judgment); id., at 196, 107 S.Ct., at 1079–1080 (O'Connor, J., dissenting). When race-based action is necessary to further a compelling interest, such action is within constitutional constraints if it satisfies the "narrow tailoring" test this Court has set out in previous cases.

IV

Because our decision today alters the playing field in some important respects, we think it best to remand the case to the lower courts for further consideration in light of the principles we have announced. * * *

Id. at 2107–2118.

Justice Stevens in dissent pointed out that despite the majority's insistence on "consistency" in treating benign racial classifications under the same strict scrutiny standard that applied to invidious racial discrimination, the majority's position will create additional problems of "consistency:"

Moreover, the Court may find that its new "consistency" approach to race-based classifications is difficult to square with its insistence upon rigidly separate categories for discrimination against different classes of individuals. For example, as the law currently stands, the Court will apply "intermediate scrutiny" to cases of invidious gender discrimination and "strict scrutiny" to cases of invidious race discrimination, while applying the same standard for benign classifications as for invidious ones. If this remains the law, then today's lecture about "consistency" will produce the anomalous result that the Government can more easily enact affirmative-action programs to remedy discrimination against women than it can enact affirmative-action programs to remedy discrimination against African Americans—even though the primary purpose of the Equal Protection Clause was to end discrimination against the former slaves. See Associated General Contractors of Cal., Inc. v. San Francisco, 813 F.2d 922 (C.A.9 1987)(striking down racial preference under strict scrutiny while upholding gender preference under intermediate scrutiny). When a court becomes preoccupied with abstract standards, it risks sacrificing common sense at the altar of formal consistency.

Id. at 2122.

Although Justice Ginsburg joined both Justice Steven's and Justice Souter's dissents, she also wrote separately to emphasize the common ground she shared with the majority opinion:

* * * I write separately to underscore not the differences the several opinions in this case display, but the considerable field of agreement—the common understandings and concerns—revealed in opinions that together speak for a majority of the Court.

I

The statutes and regulations at issue, as the Court indicates, were adopted by the political branches in response to an "unfortunate reality": "[t]he unhappy persistence of both the practice and the lingering effects of racial discrimination against minority groups in this country." Ante, at 2117 (lead opinion). The United States suffers from those lingering effects because, for most of our Nation's history, the idea that "we are just one race," ante, at 2119 (Scalia, J., concurring in part and concurring in judgment), was not embraced. For generations, our lawmakers and judges were unprepared to say that there is in this land no superior race, no race inferior to any other. In Plessy v. Ferguson, 163 U.S. 537, 16 S.Ct. 1138, 41 L.Ed. 256 (1896), not only did this Court endorse the oppressive practice of race segregation, but even Justice Harlan, the advocate of a "color-blind" Constitution, stated:

The white race deems itself to be the dominant race in this country. And so it is, in prestige, in achievements, in education, in wealth and in power. So, I doubt not, it will continue to be for all time, if it remains true to its great heritage and holds fast to the principles of constitutional liberty. Id., at 559, 16 S.Ct., at 1146 (Harlan, J., dissenting).

Not until Loving v. Virginia, 388 U.S. 1, 87 S.Ct. 1817, 18 L.Ed.2d 1010 (1967), which held unconstitutional Virginia's ban on interracial marriages, could one say with security that the Constitution and this Court would abide no measure "designed to maintain White Supremacy." Id., at 11, 87 S.Ct., at 1823.[2]

The divisions in this difficult case should not obscure the Court's recognition of the persistence of racial inequality and a majority's acknowledgement of Congress's authority to act affirmatively, not only to end discrimination, but also to counteract discrimination's lingering effects. * * * Those effects, reflective of a system of racial caste only recently ended, are evident in our workplaces, markets, and neighborhoods. Job applicants with identical resumes, qualifications, and interview styles still experience different receptions, depending on their race.[3] White and African–American consumers still encounter different deals.[4] People of color looking for housing still face discriminatory treatment by landlords, real estate agents, and mortgage lenders.[5] Minority entrepreneurs sometimes fail to gain contracts though they are the low bidders, and they are sometimes refused work even after winning contracts.[6] Bias both conscious and unconscious, reflecting traditional and unexamined habits of thought, keeps barriers that must come down if equal opportunity and nondiscrimination are ever genuinely to become this country's law and practice.

Given this history and its practical consequences, Congress surely can conclude that a carefully designed affirmative action program may help to

2. The Court, in 1955 and 1956, refused to rule on the constitutionality of antimiscegenation laws; it twice declined to accept appeals from the decree on which the Virginia Supreme Court of Appeals relied in *Loving.* * * *

3. See, e.g., H. Cross, et al., Employer Hiring Practices: Differential Treatment of Hispanic and Anglo Job Seekers 42 (Urban Institute Report 90–4, 1990)(e.g., Anglo applicants sent out by investigators received 52% more job offers than matched Hispanics); M. Turner, et al., Opportunities Denied, Opportunities Diminished: Racial Discrimination in Hiring xi (Urban Institute Report 91–9, 1991)('In one out of five audits, the white applicant was able to advance farther through the hiring process than his black counterpart. In one out of eight audits, the white was offered a job although his equally qualified black partner was not. In contrast, black auditors advanced farther than their white counterparts only 7 percent of the time, and received job offers while their white partners did not in 5 percent of the audits.').

4. See, e.g., Ayres, Fair Driving: Gender and Race Discrimination in Retail Car Negotiations, 104 Harv.L.Rev. 817, 821–822, 819 828 (1991)('blacks and women simply cannot buy the same car for the same price as can white men using identical bargaining strategies'; the final offers given white female testers reflected

40 percent higher markups than those given white male testers; final offer markups for black male testers were twice as high, and for black female testers three times as high as for white male testers).

5. See e.g., A Common Destiny: Blacks and American Society 50 (G. Jaynes & R. Williams eds. 1989) '([I]n many metropolitan areas one-quarter to one-half of all [housing] inquiries by blacks are met by clearly discriminatory responses.'); M. Turner, *et al.*, U.S. Department of Housing and Urban Development, Housing Discrimination Study: Synthesis i–vii (1991)(1989 audit study of housing searches in 25 metropolitan areas; over half of African–American and Hispanic testers seeking to rent or buy experienced some form of unfavorable treatment compared to paired white testers); Leahy Are Racial Factors Important for the Allocation of Mortgage Money?, 44 Am.J.Econ. & Soc. 185, 193 (1985)(controlling for socioeconomic factors, and concluding that 'even when neighborhoods appear to be similar on every major mortgage-lending criterion except race, mortgage-lending outcomes are still unequal').

6. See, e.g., Associated General Contractors v. Coalition for Economic Equity, 950 F.2d 1401, 1415 (C.A.9 1991)(detailing examples in San Francisco).

realize, finally, the "equal protection of the laws" the Fourteenth Amendment has promised since 1968.[8]

II

The lead opinion uses one term, "strict scrutiny," to describe the standard of judicial review for all governmental classifications by race. Ante, at 2117–2118. But that opinion's elaboration strongly suggests that the strict standard announced is indeed 'fatal' for classifications burdening groups that have suffered discrimination in our society. That seems to me, and, I believe, to the Court, the enduring lesson one should draw from Korematsu v. United States * * * ; for in that case, scrutiny the Court described as "most rigid," * * * nonetheless yielded a pass for an odious, gravely injurious racial classification. * * * A *Korematsu*-type classification, as I read the opinions in this case, will never again survive scrutiny: such a classification, history and precedent instruct, properly ranks as prohibited.

For a classification made to hasten the day when "we are just one race," ante, at 2119 (Scalia, J., concurring in part and concurring in judgment), however, the lead opinion has dispelled the notion that "strict scrutiny" is "fatal in fact." * * * Properly, a majority of the Court calls for review that is searching, in order to ferret out classifications in reality malign, but masquerading as benign. * * * The Court's once lax review of sex-based classifications demonstrates the need for such suspicion. See, e.g., Hoyt v. Florida, 368 U.S. 57, 60, 82 S.Ct. 159, 161–162, 7 L.Ed.2d 118 (1961)(upholding women's "privilege" of automatic exemption from jury service); Goesaert v. Cleary, 335 U.S. 464, 69 S.Ct. 198, 93 L.Ed. 163 (1948)(upholding Michigan law barring women from employment as bartenders); see also Johnston & Knapp, Sex Discrimination by Law: A Study in Judicial Perspective, 46 N.Y.U.L.Rev. 675 (1971). Today's decision thus usefully reiterates that the purpose of strict scrutiny "is precisely to distinguish legitimate from illegitimate uses of race in governmental decisionmaking," ante, at 2112 (lead opinion), "to 'differentiate between' permissible and impermissible governmental use of face," id., at 2113, to distinguish "between a 'No Trespassing' sign and a welcome mat." Id., at 2114.

Close review also is in order for this further reason. As Justice Souter points out, ante, at 2133–2134 (dissenting opinion), and as this very case shows, some members of the historically favored race can be hurt by catch-up mechanisms designed to cope with the lingering effects of entrenched racial subjugation. Court review can ensure that preferences are not so large as to trammel unduly upon the opportunities of others or interfere too harshly with legitimate expectations of persons in once-preferred groups. * * *

While I would not disturb the programs challenged in this case, and would leave their improvement to the political branches, I see today's decision as one that allows our precedent to evolve, still to be informed by and responsive to changing conditions.

---

8. On the differences between laws designed to benefit an historically disfavored group and laws designed to burden such a group, see, e.g., Carter, When Victims Happen To Be Black, 97 Yale L.J. 420, 433–434 (1988)('[W]hatever the source of racism, to count it the same as racialism, to say that two centuries of struggle for the most basic of civil rights have been mostly about freedom from racial categorization rather than freedom from racial oppression, is to trivialize the lives and deaths of those who have suffered under racism. To pretend * * * that the issue presented in *Bakke* was the same as the issue in *Brown* is to pretend that history never happened and that the present doesn't exist.').

Id. at 2134–2136.

Adarand leaves several questions open: Will some contract set-aside pro-grams using racial preferences survive the courts' strict scrutiny? Equally interesting are the questions *Adarand* raises relating to women-owned businesses. First, will set-aside provisions for women's businesses survive constitutional review? Second, exactly what standard of scrutiny will the Court use in reviewing such provisions? As Justice Stevens has pointed out, it would indeed be ironic if affirmative action programs for women, primarily white women, were upheld, but not affirmative action programs for people of color. Will the Court's review of affirmative action under strict scrutiny lead, indirectly, to its eventual adoption of the strict scrutiny standard when reviewing sex-based classifications?

E. TEXT NOTE: THE ROLE OF UNIONS IN EMPLOYMENT DISCRIMINATION

In unionized workplaces, often the union is sued along with the employer as a co-defendant in both race and sex discrimination cases. In an important book on the history and future prospects of women working within the labor movement, *Women and Unions,*[1] Professor Dorothy Sue Cobble writes:[2]

> Historically, working women and unions have been at odds. The majori-ty of international unions in the nineteenth century, for example, forbade female membership in their written constitutions. Formal barriers fell in the early twentieth century, but many unions remained skeptical or at best indifferent to the organization of women. In the 1930s and 1940s, women were swept into the newly emerging CIO unions—in large measure because of "the logic of industrial unionism" that included all workers at a particular worksite regardless of job title, race, or gender—but, even so, the primary objective of the CIO remained organizing the male-dominated mass produc-tion industries (auto, steel, rubber). Moreover, gender prejudice at times triumphed over industrial inclusiveness: Sharon Strom, for example, has documented instances in which every occupational group within an industry organized with the exception of the clerical sector, the one female-dominated unit. When the dust settled in the late 1940s, virtually every major industry had unionized, boosting the proportion of organized workers to a high-water mark of one in every three workers in 1954. Nonetheless, until the last decade, the male work force consistently enjoyed unionization rates more than double those of female: in 1920, 26 percent of men were organized, 7 percent of women. In the late 1970s, 29 percent of men and 12 percent of women belonged to unions. Only in the 1980s did the gender gap in union membership close significantly. By 1990, unions represented 21.4 percent of men and 14.5 percent of women.
>
> The record of union action and inaction toward women workers partially reflected the economic competition between men and women, competition fostered by employers concerned with boosting their profitability and authori-ty at the workplace. Male unionists as well sought the exclusion of women from their trades and the continuation of sex-segregated workplaces in order to secure better jobs and working conditions. Psychological concerns, howev-er, undergirded the economic. Frequently, men desired separation from

---

1. Women and Unions: Forging a Partner-ship, Dorothy S. Cobble, ed. (ILR Press, Cor-nell: 1993).

2. Cobble, "Introduction: Remaking Un-ions for the New Majority," id. at 5–10 (refer-ences omitted).

women to retain their status in the eyes of a society that devalued jobs held by women and to sustain their sense of masculinity—an identity that, Nancy Chodorow and others have argued, rested in large part on the definition of women as other and as inferior. Lastly, male unionists viewed women as marginal, temporary interlopers in the waged work world and sought (often with the support of women) to enhance the earning capacities of men so that women could return to their duties in the domestic sphere.

The attitudes and actions of women also shaped the nature of their relationship with organized labor. As soon as they entered wage work, women began to form separate-sex unions as well as demand access to the existing male-dominated labor institutions. Yet even in the instances in which the doors of unionism swung open, fewer women (proportionately) than men crossed the threshold. The poor bargaining position of women as "unskilled" workers and the intense opposition they faced from employers dependent on their low wages inhibited union formation and longevity among women. Union membership also lagged because women themselves made other choices. Some wage-earning women viewed their labor force partic- ipation as temporary or as secondary to the problems they faced fulfilling their home responsibilities. * * *

Long-term economic and social changes have now dramatically altered the situation of both women and unions and created the basis for a new relationship. Women can no longer be considered a supplemental, temporary work force. In 1992, three out of four women between the ages of twenty-five and fifty-four were in the work force, women work nearly as many years as men, and the pattern of women's labor force participation increasingly resembles that of men. They begin work early, drop out for only a few years at most, and work into their sixties and seventies.

In addition, by the 1990s, fewer women qualified as "secondary" workers in an economic sense. The rise of single female-headed families and the overall decline in real wages since 1973 have increased the economic pres- sures on women wage earners. The majority of U.S. families in the 1990s *require* at least two incomes to maintain what they perceive as an adequate standard of living; only one family in five has an adult devoted full-time to unwaged household tasks. * * *

Attitudinal shifts among women have been equally dramatic. The wom- en's movement of the 1960s and 1970s helped move U.S. society toward a new consensus regarding the status of wage-earning women. It became legitimate for married women and even women with children to work outside the home and to expect equal treatment while on the job. The longstanding division of the work world into men's jobs and women's jobs also appeared increasingly indefensible both legally and in the eyes of the public.

In particular, women rejected the notion that their identity and sense of fulfillment should come solely (and in some cases primarily) from the domes- tic sphere. * * * Married working-class women as well as "career women" and single heads of household now talk about waged work as central to their identity and essential to the economic well-being of their family.

By the 1980s, it was clear that women would not be returning to the home and that the 1950s ideal of the family would never again be the dominant reality. Yet what kind of family structure and what status in the waged sphere did women want? How would the competing demands of work and family be resolved. * * *

* * * Survey research inevitably reveals that the majority of women still identify with the historic goals of the feminist movement for job equality and equal opportunity. In addition, however, they want their desires for a life outside of work to be an important part of that movement. *Newsweek,* for example, found in 1986 that most of the women they polled wanted *neither* full-time jobs *nor* full-time housework; they wanted a reasonable balance—an alternative our society has yet to offer. The new generation of women demands not only "equal treatment" and "opportunity," but a work world responsive to their desires for family, community, and leisure.

Thus, women are concerned with creating new workplace options, and increasingly, I would argue, they are recognizing that these changes will only come about through collective power, whether it be political or economic. Significantly, there is now a gender gap in union sentiment paralleling the oft-cited gender gap in political attitudes. Countering the conventional wisdom that women are less "organizable" than men, research in the last decade consistently has shown that women workers are more interested in unions than men and, when given the actual choice, are more likely to vote for unionization. Thomas Kochan's 1979 findings that 40 percent of women would vote for a union if given the chance (as compared to only 33 percent for all nonunion workers) have been confirmed by Freeman and Medoff as well as others. Indeed, AFL–CIO organizing survey data for 1986–87 revealed that unions won 57 percent of all campaigns conducted in female-dominated workplaces (units with 75 percent or more women) as compared to 33 percent in those with a majority of men.

In part, women are more responsive to unions because the labor movement itself has changed. The feminization of the work force and the unionization in the 1960s and 1970s of female-dominated sectors of the economy—education; federal, state, and municipal government; the health care industry—altered the gender composition of organized labor. In 1954, 17 percent of organized workers were women; by 1988, the figure had climbed to 37 percent. By 1990, women constituted a majority (or close to a majority) of members in the newer international unions that had emerged in the 1960s—the American Federation of State, County and Municipal Employees (AFSCME), the Service Employees International Union (SEIU), and the teacher unions. Women also numerically dominated in such older internationals as the United Food and Commercial Workers (UFCW), The Communications Workers of America (CWA), and the garment unions. * * *

Many of the most powerful and vocal internationals within the labor movement are now unions with large female constituencies. * * * [I]t has been these unions that have provided national leadership on a wide range of women's concerns, from pay equity to parental leave, devising what sociologist Ruth Milkman has called a new "gender politics."

As Cobble points out, women have joined unions in significant numbers in the public sector as teachers and government employees. It is the private sector world of blue-collar work, still unionized to a significant degree, that has been the most difficult area for women workers to integrate. In *Women and Unions,* Brigid O'Farrell and Suzanne Moore discuss the realities of the 1980's and 1990's:[3]

---

3. B. O'Farrell & S. Moore, "Unions, Hard Hats, and Women Workers," id. at 70–72 (references omitted).

Data collected from 1979 to 1989 provide concrete evidence that women can enter and remain in blue-collar jobs historically done by men, even under very difficult circumstances. Occupational segregation among blue-collar jobs, however, remains virtually intact. Similarly, economic equity is still elusive and patterns of segregation are emerging in new occupations and industries.

There are only token levels of female participation within the best craft jobs, even in categories where there has been some growth in the total number of jobs. For example, the number of painters increased 12 percent, from 483,000 to 543,000 while the number of women who are painters increased 35 percent, from 24,150 to 32,580. Yet women are only 6 percent of all painters. The *percentage* of women carpenters actually *declined* from 1.3 to 1.2 percent, despite an increase in the total number of carpenters. The percentage of women increased in several machine and production jobs, such as telephone installer, but the number of women declined due to the overall loss of jobs in the industries.

There are some differences within occupations and industries, however. Women have made more progress among light truck driving than heavy truck driving jobs, and bus driver is now an occupation that is more than 50 percent women, one of the resegregation patterns discussed by Reskin and Roos. Women have made the most progress in the entry-level laborer categories where the heaviest, dirtiest work is found. Some of these jobs are important, however, as possible routes to the more skilled jobs in both the production and construction trades. Still, 20 percent of the laborers in production are women, compared with just 3 percent in construction. * * *

Despite declining national memberships, workers in blue-collar jobs are more likely to be union members or represented by unions than those in other occupations. Although 16 percent of all wage and salary workers are union members, over 25 percent of blue-collar workers belong to unions. Blue-collar jobs are also found in the public sector, where 44 percent of employed wage and salary workers are represented by unions.

Although some white male unions have been in the forefront of the legal attacks on affirmative action by filing "reverse discrimination" lawsuits, many unions and union leaders have been in the driving force behind the issue of pay equity and comparable worth. The AFSCME v. State of Washington case is a good example.[4] Professor Carrie Donald in *Women and Unions* sheds light on why the union movement has been more willing to take on the pay equity issue:[5]

Obviously, the few unions that opposed affirmative action have not acted alone. They have acted in concert with employers and in conformity to the invidious attitudes of a large segment of the general public. Nevertheless, such unions have failed to show positive leadership on this issue and have sought to preserve an economic spoils system for white males. Indeed, affirmative action has flourished more as a government requirement than as an issue championed by unions. In contrast, the gains made in the pay equity movement can, in large part, be credited to union leadership and involvement.

4. 770 F.2d 1401 (9th Cir.1985), discussed at p. 587 supra.

5. C. Donald, "Comments," Women and Unions, supra note 1, at 103 (references omitted).

What explains this divergence in union responses to affirmative action and pay equity? First, affirmative action followed shortly after the passage of Title VII in 1964; the concept that women and minorities had equal rights, let alone the idea of providing preferential treatment to secure those job rights, had not gained public acceptance. Pay equity, however, emerged as an issue in the late 1970s, when equal employment rights were more accepted and women and minorities represented a growing percentage of the work force. Second, affirmative action programs place women in direct competition with men for jobs. As O'Farrell and Moore observe, white males, especially in the blue-collar sector, are concerned about job deskilling and security. Affirmative action threatens job opportunities for men whereas pay equity potentially endangers *only* their level of pay increases and job status vis-à-vis other positions.

Professor Cobble and the contributors to *Women and Unions* make a strong case for the opportunities for women to create a new labor movement by the next century. In the meantime, unions remain liable for sex discrimination in a variety of contexts and are expressly included in the anti-discrimination prohibitions of both the Equal Pay Act[6] and Title VII.[7] Obvious discriminatory practices such as maintaining sex-segregated locals[8] or refusing to refer for employment a qualified heavy truck driver because of her sex,[9] have been held to be *per se* violations of Title VII. A union that insists on dividing among all its members a back pay award intended to compensate women workers for the employer's past violation of the Equal Pay Act can itself be held liable in damages by the Secretary of Labor.[10]

Unions may be liable under Title VII if a collective bargaining agreement jointly negotiated with the employer is held to violate the Act.[11] Federal courts have held that when negotiating a new contract to replace an expired one, the union must at least make a good faith effort to eliminate the discriminatory provision at issue.[12]

Most collective bargaining agreements today include a clause prohibiting both the employer and the union from discriminating against employee on the basis of race, ethnicity, religion, or sex. What liability does the union have under such a contract for continuing discrimination by the employer? In 1987, the Supreme Court had the opportunity to address this issue in Goodman v. Lukens Steel Company.[13] The courts below found that despite an express clause in the collective bargaining agreement prohibiting race discrimination by both employer

6. 29 U.S.C.A. § 206(d)(2).

7. Section 703(c), codified at 42 U.S.C.A. § 2000e–2(c).

8. E.g., Evans v. Sheraton Park Hotel, 5 F.E.P.Cas. 393 (D.D.C.1972), remanded on other grounds 503 F.2d 177 (D.C.Cir.1974), noted in Edward Matson Sibble, Comment, Remedies for Labor Union Sex Discrimination, 63 Geo. L.J. 939 (1975). The same result applies in cases of racially segregated locals. See United States v. International Longshoremen's Ass'n, 460 F.2d 497 (4th Cir.1972), cert. denied 409 U.S. 1007, 93 S.Ct. 439, 34 L.Ed.2d 300.

9. Mills v. International Broth. of Teamsters, 634 F.2d 282 (5th Cir.1981).

10. Hodgson v. Sagner, Inc., 326 F.Supp. 371 (D.Md.1971), affirmed mem. Hodgson v. Baltimore Regional Joint Bd., Amalgamated

Clothing Workers, AFL–CIO, 462 F.2d 180 (4th Cir.1972).

11. E.g., Jackson v. Seaboard Coast Line R.R. Co. 678 F.2d 992 (11th Cir.1982); Myers v. Gilman Paper Corp., 544 F.2d 837 (5th Cir. 1977), modified 556 F.2d 758, cert. dismissed 434 U.S. 801, 98 S.Ct. 28, 54 L.Ed.2d 59. See generally, Note, Union Liability for Employer Discrimination, 93 Harv.L.Rev. 702 (1980).

12. See Terrell v. United States Pipe & Foundry Co., 644 F.2d 1112 (5th Cir.1981); Martinez v. Oakland Scavenger Co., 680 F.Supp. 1377 (N.D.Ca.1987).

13. 482 U.S. 656, 107 S.Ct. 2617, 96 L.Ed.2d 572 (1987).

and union, the employer discriminated against blacks in discharging probationary employees. The union was aware of this practice, but refused to do anything about it. Furthermore, the union ignored grievances based on incidents of racial harassment and refused to include allegations of race discrimination in grievances which also asserted other contract violations.[14] The Court agreed with the Third Circuit that the union's deliberate choice not to assert racially-based grievances against the employer violated the command of § 703(c)(1) of Title VII, 42 U.S.C. § 2000e–2(c)(3), making it an unlawful practice for a union to "* * * otherwise to discriminate against" any individual because of her race. Six members of the Court joined this part of Justice White's opinion:[15]

> As we understand it, there was no suggestion below that the Unions held any racial animus against or denigrated blacks generally. Rather, it was held that a collective-bargaining agent could not, without violating Title VII and § 1981, follow a policy of refusing to file grievable racial discrimination claims however strong they might be and however sure the agent was that the employer was discriminating against blacks. The Unions, in effect, categorized racial grievances as unworthy of pursuit and, while pursuing thousands of other legitimate grievances, ignored racial discrimination claims on behalf of blacks, knowing that the employer was discriminating in violation of the contract. Such conduct, the courts below concluded, intentionally discriminated against blacks seeking a remedy for disparate treatment based on their race and violated both Title VII and § 1981. * * *

> The courts below, in our view, properly construed and applied Title VII and § 1981. Those provisions do not permit a union to refuse to file any and all grievances presented by a black person on the ground that the employer looks with disfavor on and resents such grievances. It is no less violative of these laws for a union to pursue a policy of rejecting disparate-treatment grievances presented by blacks solely because the claims assert racial bias and would be very troublesome to process.

Although no similar case has been presented raising the issue of sex discrimination, the same reasoning would apply to a union which routinely refused to process grievances raising sex discrimination issues under a collective bargaining agreement.

What is the relationship between a worker's rights under the collective bargaining agreement and her rights under Title VII? A worker who believes that she has been subjected to an employer practice that violates the collective bargaining agreement will normally proceed to obtain relief by using the grievance machinery established in the contract.[16] But if the employer practice is also a violation of Title VII, the worker is not precluded from pursuing her remedies under the Act, even if she had elected to proceed first through the contract's grievance and arbitration route and lost. In Alexander v. Gardner–Denver Co.,[17] the Supreme Court rejected the argument that use of the grievance machinery constituted either an election of remedies or a waiver of the employee's Title VII rights. The two remedies are independent of each other, the first based on the collective bargaining agreement, which constitutes the "law of the shop", the

---

14. Id. at 666.

15. Id. at 668–669.

16. See David E. Feller, A General Theory of the Collective Bargaining Agreements, 61 Calif. L. Rev. 663, 740–45 (1973).

17. 415 U.S. 36, 94 S.Ct. 1011, 39 L.Ed.2d 147 (1974).

second on the law of the land. The Court thus summarized its holding in its final paragraph:[18]

> We think, therefore, that the federal policy favoring arbitration of labor disputes and the federal policy against discriminatory employment practices can best be accommodated by permitting an employee to pursue fully both his remedy under the grievance-arbitration clause of a collective-bargaining agreement and his cause of action under Title VII. The federal court should consider the employee's claim *de novo*. The arbitral decision may be admitted as evidence and accorded such weight as the court deems appropriate.

Because of a union's exclusive right to represent workers included within the bargaining unit, the union has been held to a judicially-created duty of fair representation[19] that prevents it from treating its members in ways that are "arbitrary, discriminatory, or in bad faith."[20] A breach of the duty of fair representation based on evidence that the union took action or refused to take action because of the union member's race or sex may also constitute a violation of Title VII by the union.[21] See Farmer v. ARA Services, Inc.,[22] in which plaintiffs sued both their employer and their Union, Local 1064, United Catering, Bar and Hotel Workers, alleging that the Union had violated both its duty of fair representation and Title VII by negotiating and entering into collective bargaining agreements which perpetuated sexually discriminatory hiring and work assignment patterns, and which resulted in compensating women at a lower rate than men for comparable work. The district court's order awarding backpay and damages for emotional and mental distress was upheld against the union, but its award of punitive damages was reversed.

What are the rights of an employer if an employee, having the opportunity to sue both her employer and her union, singles out the employer as the sole defendant? The general question was raised in Northwest Airlines, Inc. v. Transport Workers Union,[23] a suit in which the employer sought to compel the union to contribute to a $37 million back pay award arising out of a complaint filed against the employer under both Title VII and the Equal Pay Act. Northwest's stewardesses, who had brought the underlying suit, Laffey v. Northwest Airlines, Inc.,[24] had not named the union as a co-defendant. After judgment had been entered in *Laffey,* and nearly one and one-half years after trial had been completed, the employer sought to amend its answer to assert a counterclaim for contribution or indemnification against the union. When its motion was denied,[25] Northwest Airlines sought to proceed by asserting a right to contribution against the union arising under federal common law.[26]

18. Id., 415 U.S. at 59–60, 94 S.Ct. at 1025, 39 L.Ed.2d at 164–65.

19. Steele v. Louisville & Nashville R.R., 323 U.S. 192, 65 S.Ct. 226, 89 L.Ed. 173 (1944).

20. Vaca v. Sipes, 386 U.S. 171, 190, 87 S.Ct. 903, 916, 17 L.Ed.2d 842, 857 (1967). See also Bowen v. United States Postal Service, 459 U.S. 212, 103 S.Ct. 588, 74 L.Ed.2d 402 (1983), apportioning backpay liability between an employer which wrongfully discharged an employee and a union which breached its duty of fair representation by failing to take the matter to arbitration. See generally, Feller, supra note 16.

21. E.g., Martin v. Local 1513, 859 F.2d 581 (8th Cir.1988).

22. 660 F.2d 1096 (6th Cir.1981).

23. 451 U.S. 77, 101 S.Ct. 1571, 67 L.Ed.2d 750 (1981).

24. 366 F.Supp. 763 (D.D.C.1973) and 374 F.Supp. 1382 (1974), affirmed in part and vacated in part 567 F.2d 429 (D.C.Cir.1976), cert. denied 434 U.S. 1086, 98 S.Ct. 1281, 55 L.Ed.2d 792 (1978).

25. Id., 567 F.2d at 476–78.

26. Northwest Airlines, Inc. v. T.W.U., 606 F.2d 1350, 1352 (D.C.Cir.1979), affirmed in part and vacated in part 451 U.S. 77, 101 S.Ct. 1571, 67 L.Ed.2d 750 (1981).

The United States Supreme Court held[27] that neither the Equal Pay Act nor Title VII conferred an implied right to contribution upon an employer. It also concluded[28] that, in the face of the comprehensive legislative scheme for combatting employment discrimination represented by those two statutes, the Court should not exercise its common law power to create an additional right of contribution. In reaching these decisions, the Court expressly assumed that the plaintiffs in the *Laffey* litigation could have asserted a claim against either their unions or their employer under both the Equal Pay Act and Title VII.

Although her Title VII rights may be pursued independently of her rights under a collective bargaining agreement, the woman worker should not ignore the advantages to be gained on the job by union membership. Today's unions have frequently supported Title VII suits charging sex discrimination in employment at the behest of their women members.[29] As we have seen, the needs of women workers are not limited to the absence of discrimination based on sex. Because women may choose to be mothers as well as workers, and because pregnancy is uniquely disabling for women workers either because of personal disability or workplace hazards threatening to the fetus, the concerns of women in unions go beyond those traditionally considered at the bargaining table. The issues raised by women in unions are likely to be social problems that fall more heavily on women than men. Although these issues are new ones for many unions, they may be resolved more easily by agreement than by litigation. It is therefore of particular importance that women have effective ways of presenting their views to the union membership. The success of the United Steelworkers and the aluminum industry in bargaining for affirmative action for black workers sets an encouraging precedent for what unions and employers, working together, can do for women.[30]

27. Northwest Airlines, Inc. v. T.W.U., 451 U.S. 77, 101 S.Ct. 1571, 67 L.Ed.2d 750 (1981).

28. Id., 451 U.S. at 98, 101 S.Ct. at 1581, 67 L.Ed.2d at 764.

29. Plaintiffs in General Elec. Co. v. Gilbert, 429 U.S. 125, 97 S.Ct. 401, 50 L.Ed.2d 343 (1976), the Title VII pregnancy discrimination case, included seven female employees and the International Union of Electrical, Radio and Machine Workers, AFL–CIO (IUE) and the latter's affiliate, Local 161. Id., 429 U.S. at 129 n. 5, 97 S.Ct. at 405, 50 L.Ed.2d at 350. The litigation against "fetal protection" policies was brought by the United Auto Workers (UAW). See International Union, UAW v. Johnson Controls, 499 U.S. 187, 111 S.Ct. 1196, 113 L.Ed.2d 158 (1991) at p. 790 supra.

30. See United Steelworkers of America v. Weber, 443 U.S. 193, 99 S.Ct. 2721, 61 L.Ed.2d 480 (1979). Women were covered by the Kaiser plan, but this fact was not stressed by counsel nor mentioned by the Court. See Brief for Appellant at 6, n. 18. See generally, Seymour Moskowitz, New Opportunities for Unions to Foster Equal Employment Opportunity, 15 Val.U.L.Rev. 1 (1980).

Chapter IV

EDUCATIONAL OPPORTUNITY

Introductory Note

Consider the following assessments of the opportunities available to women in education:

Slowly but surely, the overt discrimination is ending. We are now fighting the subtle forms of discrimination, and these are harder to identify, far harder to prove, and much harder to deal with and remedy. Moreover, men and women often view the subtle forms of discrimination very differently. Too often, many find it easier to acknowledge and understand overt, intentional discrimination. For example, when overt barriers are dismantled, such as when a department chair no longer excludes women from his department, some men assume the problem is fully solved. Many women, on the other hand, often view discrimination as being more than just the formal barriers; they see a whole host of subtle behaviors that have a discriminatory effect. Women may view social behavior, such as male faculty always having lunch together, as having a discriminatory effect, because women are excluded from such informal sources of information and the subsequent opportunity to learn more about their profession. Thus, many men tend to overestimate the progress which has been made; many women tend to understate the progress. Many men often think in terms of how far we have come; many women in terms of how far we have yet to go.[1]

Sitting in the same classroom, reading the same textbook, listening to the same teacher, boys and girls receive very different educations. From grade school through graduate school female students are more likely to be invisible members of classrooms. Teachers interact with males more frequently, ask them better questions, and give them more precise and helpful feedback. Over the course of years the uneven distribution of teacher time, energy, attention, and talent, with boys getting the lion's share, takes its toll on girls. Since gender bias is not a noisy problem, most people are unaware of the secret sexist lessons and the quiet losses they engender.

Girls are the majority of our nation's schoolchildren, yet they are second-class educational citizens. The problems they face—loss of self-esteem, decline in achievement, and elimination of career options—are at the heart of

---

1. Bernice Sandler, Editorial: Women on Campus: A Ten–Year Retrospect, 26 On Cam- pus With Women 3 (Association of American Colleges, Spring 1980).

the educational process. Until educational sexism is eradicated, more than half of our children will be shortchanged and their gifts lost to society.[2]

In 1920, when women won the right to vote, 26% of full-time faculty in American higher education were women. In 1995, 31% of full-time faculty in American higher education are women: an increase of 5% over seventy-five years! Looking back over the last seventy-five years, the status of women on higher education faculties appears to be frozen in time.

Women's exceedingly slow integration of the faculty ranks, particularly during more recent times, is most distressing given the rapid increase in the percentages of American PhDs obtained by women in the 1970s and 1980s. Women earned 30% of American doctorates in 1980. By 1993, women were earning 38% of our PhDs.

Broad national numbers obscure the wide variation in women's faculty participation depending on the type of academic institution where they teach. As the prestige of an institution increases, the percentage of women on the faculty decreases. In 1987, 38% of full-time faculty at public 2–year colleges were women; 27% to 29% at private and public non-research universities were women, but only 19.5% to 21% of faculty at private and public research universities were women.

Where are all the women recently earning PhDs going? Not into the tenured ranks. In 1975, 46% of women in full-time teaching in higher education had tenure. In 1992, this number was *exactly* the same: 46%. In contrast to women, the male faculty have consistently improved their tenured rates over this same time period: 64% of faculty men had tenure in 1975, 70% in 1982, and now 72% in 1994–95. Because we find relatively few women in the tenured ranks, it should be no surprise that we find an increasing percentage of women in the lower status, less prestigious, and less secure ranks of instructor and lecturer. In fact, the percentage of women among those classified as full-time instructors keeps increasing, from 52% in 1983 to 59% in 1994–95. Similarly, among full-time lecturers, women's percentage grew from 47.5% in 1983 to 56.5% today. Clearly, women with PhDs are being "steered," either consciously or unconsciously, into non-research academic institutions and/or into lower status jobs at the more prestigious research institutions.[3]

A. CONSTITUTIONAL CHALLENGES TO SEX SEGREGATION IN EDUCATION

1. ADMISSION BARRIERS: SINGLE–SEX SCHOOLS

MISSISSIPPI UNIVERSITY FOR WOMEN v. HOGAN

Supreme Court of the United States, 1982.
458 U.S. 718, 102 S.Ct. 3331, 73 L.Ed.2d 1090.

[This case is set forth at p. 137, supra.]

2. Myra and David Sadker, Failing at Fairness: How America's Schools Cheat Girls at 1 (1994).

3. Adapted from Martha West, Women Faculty: Frozen in Time, ACADEME, July/August 1995, at 26–27 (American Association of University Professors).

VORCHHEIMER v. SCHOOL DIST. OF PHILADELPHIA

United States Court of Appeals, Third Circuit, 1976.
532 F.2d 880 affirmed by equally divided Court, 430
U.S. 703, 97 S.Ct. 1671, 51 L.Ed.2d 750 (1977).

JOSEPH F. WEIS, JR., CIRCUIT JUDGE.

Do the Constitution and laws of the United States require that every public school, in every public school system in the Nation, be coeducational? Stated another way, do our Constitution and laws forbid the maintenance by a public school board, in a system otherwise coeducational, of a limited number of single-sex high schools in which enrollment is voluntary and the educational opportunities offered to girls and boys are essentially equal? This appeal presents those questions and, after careful consideration, we answer negatively. Accordingly, we vacate the district court's judgment which held that the school board policy was impermissible.[1]

Plaintiff is a teen-age girl who graduated with honors from a junior high school in Philadelphia. She then applied to Central High School, a public school in the city, but was refused admission because that institution is restricted to male students. After that setback, she filed this class action in the United States District Court seeking relief under 42 U.S.C.A. § 1983 from alleged unconstitutional discrimination. After a trial, the district court granted an injunction, ordering that she and other qualified female students be admitted to Central.

The Philadelphia School District offers four types of senior high schools: academic, comprehensive, technical and magnet. Although this suit is aimed at only an academic school, it is necessary to review the roles of other schools as well.

Comprehensive schools provide a wide range of courses, including those required for college admission, and offer advanced placement classes for students who are intellectually able to progress at a faster than average rate. The criterion for enrollment in the comprehensive schools is residency within a designated area. Although most of these schools are co-ed, two admit only males and one is restricted to female students. At the time the injunction was granted, plaintiff was enrolled at George Washington High School, a coeducational comprehensive school.

Academic high schools have high admission standards and offer only college preparatory courses. There are but two such schools in Philadelphia, and they accept students from the entire city rather than operating on a neighborhood basis. Central is restricted to males, and Girls High School, as the name implies, admits only females.

Central High School was founded in 1836 and has maintained a reputation for academic excellence. For some years before 1939, it was designated a comprehensive rather than an academic high school as it is presently. Its

---

1. The district court's opinion is published at 400 F.Supp. 326 (E.D.Pa.1975).

graduates both before and after 1939 have made notable contributions to the professions, business, government and academe.

Girls High has also achieved high academic standing. It was founded in 1848 and became an academic school in 1893. Its alumnae have compiled enviable records and have distinguished themselves in their chosen diverse fields. It now has a faculty of more than 100 and a student body of approximately 2,000, about the same as those of Central.

Enrollment at either school is voluntary and not by assignment. Only 7% of students in the city qualify under the stringent standards at these two schools, and it is conceded that plaintiff met the scholastic requirements of both. The Philadelphia school system does not have a co-ed academic school with similar scholastic requirements for admission.

The courses offered by the two schools are similar and of equal quality. The academic facilities are comparable, with the exception of those in the scientific field where Central's are superior. The district court concluded "that [generally] the education available to the female students at Girls is comparable to that available to the male students at Central." Moreover, "[g]raduates of both Central and Girls High, as well as the other senior high schools of Philadelphia," have been and are accepted by the most prestigious universities.

The plaintiff has stipulated that "the practice of educating the sexes separately is a technique that has a long history and worldwide acceptance." Moreover, she agrees that "there are educators who regard education in a single-sex school as a natural and reasonable educational approach." In addition to this stipulation, the defendants presented the testimony of Dr. J. Charles Jones, an expert in the field of education. Dr. Jones expressed a belief, based on his study of New Zealand's sex-segregated schools, that students in that educational environment had a higher regard for scholastic achievement and devoted more time to homework than those in co-ed institutions. The district judge commented that even had the parties not stipulated to the educational value of the practice, "this Court would probably have felt compelled to validate the sex-segregated school on the basis of Dr. Jones' hypotheses concerning the competition for adolescent energies in a coed school and its detrimental effect on student learning and academic achievement."[2]

Before deciding which school she wished to attend, the plaintiff visited a number of them and developed some definite opinions. As to Girls High, she commented, "I just didn't like the impression it gave me. I didn't think I would be able to go there for three years and not be harmed in any way by it." As to Central, she said, "I liked it there. I liked the atmosphere and also what I heard about it, about its academic excellence." She was somewhat dissatisfied with her education at George Washington High School because of her belief that the standards which the teacher set for the students were not high enough.[3]

2. 400 F.Supp. at 335. The defendants also relied on the testimony of Dr. M. Elizabeth Tidball who studied the educational background of those recognized in Who's Who of American Women. She found that the percentage of those listed was higher for graduates of women's colleges than for those of co-ed schools.

3. In an affidavit accompanying a Motion to Dissolve Stay Pending Appeal, the plaintiff

The trial judge found the gender based classification of students at the two schools to lack a "fair and substantial relationship to the School Board's legitimate interest" and enjoined the practice.

The court's factual finding that Girls and Central are academically and functionally equivalent establishes that the plaintiff's desire to attend Central is based on personal preference rather than being founded on an objective evaluation.

A fair summary of the parties' positions, therefore, is that:

1. the local school district has chosen to make available on a voluntary basis the time honored educational alternative of sexually-segregated high schools;

2. the schools for boys and girls are comparable in quality, academic standing, and prestige;

3. the plaintiff prefers to go to the boys' school because of its academic reputation and her personal reaction to Central. She submitted no factual evidence that attendance at Girls High would constitute psychological or other injury;

4. the deprivation asserted is that of the opportunity to attend a specific school, not that of an opportunity to obtain an education at a school with comparable academic facilities, faculty and prestige.

With this factual background, we now turn to a review of the legal issues. We look first to federal statutory law to determine if it resolves the question raised here.

* * *

[The Court's discussion of the Equal Educational Opportunities Acts of 1972 and 1974 is omitted.]

We conclude the legislation is so equivocal that it cannot control the issue in this case. Our research into the legislative history reveals no indication of Congressional intent to order that every school in the land be coeducational and that educators be denied alternatives. That drastic step should require clear and unequivocal expression. Judicial zeal for identity of educational methodology should not lead us to presume that Congress would impose such limitations upon the nationwide teaching community by equivocation or innuendo. Congress spoke clearly enough on single-sex schools in 1972 when it chose to defer action in order to secure the data needed for an intelligent judgment. We do not believe that the ambiguous wording of the Equal Educational Opportunities Act of 1974 represented an abandonment of the clearly expressed desire to wait for more information before making a decision. Since no such data were produced, a realistic and, in our view, inescapable interpretation is that Congress deliberately chose not to act and to leave open the question of single-sex schools. We thus have no need to consider the extent to which the legislative body may determine what activity constitutes a violation of the Equal Protection Clause of the Fourteenth Amendment. See Katzenbach v. Morgan, 384 U.S. 641, 86 S.Ct. 1717, 16

stated that at the end of the eleventh grade at George Washington, she would qualify for early admission to college.

L.Ed.2d 828 (1966). Cf. Oregon v. Mitchell, 400 U.S. 112, 91 S.Ct. 260, 27 L.Ed.2d 272 (1970).

Finding no Congressional enactments which authoritatively address the problem, we must consider the constitutional issues which provided the impetus for issuance of the injunction.

The district court reviewed the line of recent cases dealing with sex discrimination, beginning with Reed v. Reed * * *. As a result of that analysis, the district judge reasoned that, while the Supreme Court has not held sex to be a suspect classification, a stricter standard than the rational relationship test applies and is denominated "fair and substantial relationship."

In each of the cases cited, however, there was an actual deprivation or loss of a benefit to a female which could not be obtained elsewhere. * * *

In each instance where a statute was struck down, the rights of the respective sexes conflicted, and those of the female were found to be inadequate. None of the cases was concerned with a situation in which equal opportunity was extended to each sex or in which the restriction applied to both. And, significantly, none occurred in an educational setting.

The nature of the discrimination which the plaintiff alleges must be examined with care. She does not allege a deprivation of an education equal to that which the school board makes available to boys. Nor does she claim an exclusion from an academic school because of a quota system, cf. Berkelman v. San Francisco Unified School District, 501 F.2d 1264 (9th Cir.1974), or more stringent scholastic admission standards. Cf. Bray v. Lee, 337 F.Supp. 934 (D.Mass.1972). Moreover, enrollment at the single-sex schools is applicable only to high schools and is voluntary, not mandatory. The plaintiff has difficulty in establishing discrimination in the school board's policy. If there are benefits or detriments inherent in the system, they fall on both sexes in equal measure.

Plaintiff cites Sweatt v. Painter, 339 U.S. 629, 70 S.Ct. 848, 94 L.Ed. 1114 (1950), and Brown v. Board of Education, 347 U.S. 483, 74 S.Ct. 686, 98 L.Ed. 873 (1954), which prohibit racial segregation in the educational process. Those cases are inapplicable here. Race is a suspect classification under the Constitution, but the Supreme Court has declined to so characterize gender. We are committed to the concept that there is no fundamental difference between races and therefore, in justice, there can be no dissimilar treatment. But there are differences between the sexes which may, in limited circumstances, justify disparity in law. As the Supreme Court has said: "[g]ender has never been rejected as an impermissible classification in all instances." Kahn v. Shevin, supra, 416 U.S., at 356 n. 10, 94 S.Ct. at 1738, 40 L.Ed.2d at 194.

Equal educational opportunities should be available to both sexes in any intellectual field. However, the special emotional problems of the adolescent years are matters of human experience and have led some educational experts to opt for one-sex high schools. While this policy has limited acceptance on its merits, it does have its basis in a theory of equal benefit and not discriminatory denial.

The only occasion on which the Supreme Court ruled upon a gender classification in school admissions policy was in Williams v. McNair, 316 F.Supp. 134 (D.S.C.1970), aff'd, 401 U.S. 951, 91 S.Ct. 976, 28 L.Ed.2d 235 (1971), a case which was decided many years after *Sweatt,* supra, and *Brown,* supra. *Williams* was a summary affirmance of a three-judge district court, and we do not have the benefit of the Supreme Court's reasoning. Yet, the result does have precedential weight for us. Hicks v. Miranda, 422 U.S. 332, 95 S.Ct. 2281, 45 L.Ed.2d 223 (1975). The district court's opinion details a fact situation quite similar to that confronting us here, except that the plaintiffs were males who sought admission to a girls' state college. Reed v. Reed, supra, had not yet been decided and the district court therefore had no reason to discuss a substantial relationship test. Rather, it applied the traditional rational relationship guidelines. The court said:

> "While history and tradition alone may not support a discrimination, the Constitution does not require that a classification 'keep abreast of the latest' in educational opinion, especially when there remains a respectable opinion to the contrary; it only demands that the discrimination not be wholly wanting in reason." 316 F.Supp. at 137.

Believing the problem could not be considered in isolation, the court noted that the school involved was only one in an extensive state system which included several co-ed schools as well as an all male one.

We may not cavalierly disregard *Williams* although it predated *Reed* by a few months.[8] Indeed, the two cases are not inconsistent because the state schools' restrictive admissions policy applied to both sexes, a significant difference from the preferential statutory procedure in *Reed.* This distinction is enough to justify the use of the rational relationship test in *Williams* even though it is likely that the result would have been the same under the substantial relationship formula.

We do not accept *Williams* as being inapplicable merely because males were barred rather than females, as in the case *sub judice.* We are aware of the suggestion that disparity is likely to be favorably considered when it confers on the female some benefit tending to rectify the effects of past discrimination. For example, in Kahn v. Shevin, supra, a widow's tax exemption was permissible although no such benefit was provided for a widower. See also, 1975 Duke L.J. 163, 179; Note, The Supreme Court 1973 Term, 88 Harv.L.Rev. 129 (1974). But we have no such exempting qualification here because there is no evidence of past deprivation of educational opportunities for women in the Philadelphia School District. Indeed, the factual findings establish that, for many years past and at the present, excellent educational facilities have been and are available to both sexes.[9]

Since there is no remedial measure at stake, we see no basis for differentiation between *Williams,* and the case at bar. Consequently, we differ with the district court's opinion that *Williams* has only a tenuous applicability here. In our view it is strong, if not controlling authority for denial of an injunction.

---

8. Probable jurisdiction was noted in Reed v. Reed on March 1, 1971. Williams was affirmed on March 8, 1971.

9. This fact, in addition to others, distinguishes the case of Kirstein v. Rector and Visitors of the University of Virginia, 309 F.Supp. 184 (E.D.Va.1970).

The record does contain sufficient evidence to establish that a legitimate educational policy may be served by utilizing single-sex high schools. The primary aim of any school system must be to furnish an education of as high a quality as is feasible. Measures which would allow innovation in methods and techniques to achieve that goal have a high degree of relevance. Thus, given the objective of a quality education and a controverted, but respected theory that adolescents may study more effectively in single-sex schools, the policy of the school board here does bear a substantial relationship.

We need not decide whether this case requires application of the rational or substantial relationship tests because, using either, the result is the same. We conclude that the regulations establishing admission requirements to Central and Girls High School based on gender classification do not offend the Equal Protection Clause of the United States Constitution.

The gravamen of plaintiff's case is her desire to attend a specific school based on its particular appeal to her. She believes that the choice should not be denied her because of an educational policy with which she does not agree.

We are not unsympathetic with her desire to have an expanded freedom of choice, but its cost should not be overlooked. If she were to prevail, then all public single-sex schools would have to be abolished. The absence of these schools would stifle the ability of the local school board to continue with a respected educational methodology. It follows too that those students and parents who prefer an education in a public, single-sex school would be denied their freedom of choice. The existence of private schools is no more an answer to those people than it is to the plaintiff.

It is not for us to pass upon the wisdom of segregating boys and girls in high school. We are concerned not with the desirability of the practice but only its constitutionality. Once that threshold has been passed, it is the school board's responsibility to determine the best methods of accomplishing its mission.

The judgment of the district court will be reversed.

GIBBONS, CIRCUIT JUDGE (dissenting).

The majority opinion may be briefly summarized as follows:

> The object of the [14th] Amendment was undoubtedly to enforce the * * * equality of the two [sexes] before the law, but in the nature of things it could not have been intended to abolish distinctions based upon [sex], or to enforce social, as distinguished from political equality, or a commingling of the two [sexes] upon terms unsatisfactory to either. Laws permitting, and even requiring, their separation in places where they are liable to be brought into contact with each other do not necessarily imply the inferiority of either [sex] to the other, and have been generally, if not universally, recognized as within the competency of the state legislatures in the exercise of their police power. The most common instance of this is connected with the establishment of separate schools for [male] and [female] children, which has been held to be a valid exercise of the legislative power even by courts of States where the political rights of [women] have been longest and most earnestly enforced.

The quotation, with appropriate substitutions, will be recognized immediately as the analysis of Justice Brown, for the majority of the Supreme Court, in Plessy v. Ferguson, 163 U.S. 537, 544, 16 S.Ct. 1138, 1140, 41 L.Ed. 256, 258 (1896). No doubt had the issue in this case been presented to the Court at any time from 1896 to 1954, a "separate but equal" analysis would have carried the day. I was under the distinct impression, however, that "separate but equal" analysis, especially in the field of public education, passed from the fourteenth amendment jurisprudential scene over twenty years ago. See, e.g., Brown v. Board of Education, 347 U.S. 483, 74 S.Ct. 686, 98 L.Ed. 873 (1954). The majority opinion, in establishing a twentieth-century sexual equivalent to the *Plessy* decision, reminds us that the doctrine can and will be invoked to support sexual discrimination in the same manner that it supported racial discrimination prior to *Brown*.

But the resurrection of the "separate but equal" analysis is not my most serious quarrel with the majority opinion. What I find most disturbing is the majority's deliberate disregard of an express Congressional finding that the maintenance of dual school systems in which students are assigned to schools solely on the basis of sex violates the equal protection clause of the fourteenth amendment. § 203(a)(1), Equal Educational Opportunities Act of 1974, 20 U.S.C.A. § 1702(a)(1)(Supp.1976). So long as Congress has acted within the sphere of its legislative competence in making such a finding, I submit, we are not free to substitute a "separate but equal" legislative judgment of our own. Because I conclude that Congress has acted to prohibit the maintenance of single-sex public schools pursuant to its powers under § 5 of the fourteenth amendment, I dissent from the majority's substitution of a "separate but equal" legislative judgment. I would affirm the decision below.

* * *

Notes on Hogan *and* Vorchheimer

1. *Vorchheimer* was decided by the Third Circuit before the Supreme Court heard oral argument in Craig v. Boren, set forth at p. 41, supra. If the *Craig* "intermediate standard" of equal protection analysis had been applied in *Vorchheimer,* would the case have been decided differently? Note that *Vorchheimer* was affirmed by an equally-divided Supreme Court. Justice Rehnquist did not participate. Had he been available, how do you think the case would have been decided? In footnote 1 of her *Hogan* opinion, Justice O'Connor sets aside for another day "the question of whether States can provide 'separate but equal' undergraduate institutions for males and females." Does her opinion give you any clues about how that question might be decided? Can either *Vorchheimer* or Williams v. McNair, 316 F.Supp. 134 (D.S.C.1970), affirmed mem. 401 U.S. 951, 91 S.Ct. 976, 28 L.Ed.2d 235 (1971), on which *Vorchheimer* relies, stand after *Hogan?*

2. How would *Vorchheimer* be decided under the Pennsylvania state equal rights amendment? Vorchheimer's attorneys sought to rely on the state ERA in federal court, but the district court refused to hear the argument on the ground that not enough case law existed interpreting the state provision for it to proceed. In a subsequent case, three female plaintiffs who were denied admission to Central High successfully challenged their rejection under the Pennsylvania Equal Rights Amendment and the Fourteenth Amendment to the United States Constitution. After the trial court entered a permanent injunction preventing defen-

dants from refusing to admit females to Central, and after the Board of Education had chosen not to appeal the order, a group of students and graduates of Central and Girls' High sought to appeal the judgment. They were not allowed to do so, nor were they granted permission to intervene in order to present arguments that the judgment should be reversed. See Newberg by Newberg v. Board of Public Education, 330 Pa.Super. 65, 478 A.2d 1352 (1984).

3. Many of the earlier cases resolving challenges to discriminatory admissions policies are discussed in the *Vorchheimer* opinion. Bray v. Lee, 337 F.Supp. 934 (D.Mass.1972), challenged differing admission requirements to Boys Latin School and Girls Latin School in Boston for the seventh grade class in September 1970. The building in which Boys Latin was housed had a seating capacity of approximately 3,000; that for Girls Latin had only 1,500. In evaluating the number of seats available in each building, the School Board took the number of boys scoring highest on the common entrance examination to fill the vacant seats in the Boys Latin building and the number of girls scoring highest for the Girls Latin building. The result was that all boys who scored 120 points or higher (up to a possible 200 points) were admitted in 1970, while girls needed to score at least 133 points to succeed. The court held that the use of separate and different admission standards for boys and girls violated the equal protection clause. The School Department determined that if a separate cut-off mark had not been used for the two groups, a score of 127 would have been required to gain admission. The 47 girls who had scored 127 or better were then ordered admitted without further examination as ninth graders. Under this decision, may Boston admit separately to Boys Latin and Girls Latin so long as it uses the same standard for admission?

Compare Berkelman v. San Francisco Unified Sch. Dist., 501 F.2d 1264 (9th Cir.1974), where the District's policies governing admission to San Francisco's academic high school, Lowell High, were challenged. In 1970, the District had adopted a policy that the Lowell student body should be divided 50–50 between boys and girls. To achieve this ratio, it was found necessary to set a higher admission standard for girls than for boys. The entrance requirement for boys in 1970 and 1971 was a grade point average of 3.25 on a 4 point scale; for girls, it was a 3.50 average. Applying a middle tier equal protection test, the court said:

> An unsupported notion that an equal number of male and female students is an essential element in a good high-school education was apparently the justification for the school district's policy * * *. While that policy is not based upon an invidious stereotype such as was present in *Reed* and *Frontiero,* we do not read those cases so narrowly as to sanction all other sex discrimination. No actual proof that a balance of the sexes furthers the goal of better academic education was offered by the school district.

Id., 501 F.2d at 1269. The court also noted that the district's evidence on an alternate justification "—that females got better grades in their early school years but that males catch up with females at the high-school level—was inconclusive." 501 F.2d at 1269 n. 8.

Would the District's policy have fared better if it had been tested, not against the equal protection clause, but against the Washington state equal rights amendment as it was interpreted in Marchioro v. Chaney, set out at p. 178, supra?

Lowell High School's troubles aren't over. A group of Chinese–American students and parents have brought a class action suit against the district, California's State Department of Education, and the NAACP. At issue is the legality of a 1983 consent decree in a desegregation case brought by the NAACP that caps Chinese–American enrollment in Lowell High School at 40%. The consent decree provided that no ethnic or racial group's enrollment should exceed 40% at Lowell. Although African–American and Latino students combined make up 36% of San Francisco's students, they constitute only 14% of Lowell's 2,700 students. The current lawsuit alleges that the cap on Chinese–Americans primarily benefits white students, now 16% of the student body, not other students of color. The effect of the enrollment cap on Chinese–American students is that they must score 63 (out of a possible 69) based on tests and prior GPAs to gain admittance to Lowell while whites and other Asian Americans need score only 60. African Americans, Latinos and Native Americans need a score of 50. For the 1995–96 school year, 94 Chinese–American students were denied admission to Lowell who scored between 60 and 62. Nanette Asimov, A Hard Lesson in Diversity: Chinese–Americans Fight Lowell's Admissions Policy, S.F. Chron., June 19, 1995, at A1; Lora Jo Foo and Laura L. Ho, Caps, Caps and Gowns, and Changing Demographics, The Recorder, June 21, 1995, at 6. How much weight should a court give to the argument about balance or proportionality in this context? Are there alternative approaches the court should consider?

4. The male plaintiffs in Williams v. McNair, 316 F.Supp. 134 (D.S.C.1970), affirmed mem. 401 U.S. 951, 91 S.Ct. 976, 28 L.Ed.2d 235 (1971), sought admission to Winthrop College—a school for girls that was part of the South Carolina state system of higher education. The district court thus described Winthrop's unique place within the system:

> The several institutions so established vary in purpose, curriculum, and location. Some are limited to undergraduate programs; others extend their offerings into the graduate field. With two exceptions, such institutions are co-educational. Two, by law, however, limit their student admissions to members of one sex. Thus the Citadel restricts its student admission to males and Winthrop, the college involved in this proceeding, may not admit as a regular degree candidate males. There is an historical reason for these legislative restrictions upon the admission standards of these two latter institutions. The first, the Citadel, while offering a full range of undergraduate liberal arts courses and granting degrees in engineering as well, is designated as a military school, and apparently, the Legislature deemed it appropriate for that reason to provide for an all-male student body. Winthrop, on the other hand, was designed as a school for young ladies, which, though offering a liberal arts program, gave special attention to many courses thought to be specially helpful to female students.

Id., 316 F.Supp. at 136. The court detailed in a footnote the courses thought to be "specially helpful" to women: stenography, typewriting, telegraphy, bookkeeping, drawing (freehand, mechanical, architectural, etc.), designing, engraving, sewing, dress-making, millinery, art, needlework, cooking, housekeeping, and "such other industrial arts as may be suitable to their sex and conducive to their support and usefulness." Id., 316 F.Supp. at 136 n. 3. The court was unable to find the legislative decision to reserve Winthrop for young ladies "without any rational justification and violative of the Equal Protection Clause." Id., 316 F.Supp. at 138. Do you agree? Compare the assessment of Professors John Johnston & Charles Knapp:

> [S]uppose that South Carolina, in addition to operating one or more racially mixed institutions, should maintain two other colleges. One, Dred Scott Institute, would offer degrees in agriculture, music, dance and physical education; it would accept only black students. The other, Calhoun College,

would offer degrees in nuclear physics, medicine, law, engineering and business administration; only whites need apply. Even assuming that all of these studies were available at a biracial institution in the state, would such a scheme survive constitutional scrutiny?

It is difficult to see how; indeed, any other answer is unthinkable. And yet, maintenance of two institutions for the sexes in South Carolina, one for male warriors and the other for female domestics, is different only in that the assumptions it reflects about individual capabilities and aspirations are more widely shared. The role of a housewife or a secretary is an honorable and productive one; so of course is the role of a champion athlete or tenant farmer. To attack the attitudes reflected in the *Williams* decision is not to denigrate the individuals for whom such stereotypes happen to be accurate; it is to attack the arrogant assumption that merely because these stereotypes are accurate for some individuals the state has a right to apply them to all individuals—and, indeed, to shape its official policy toward the end that they shall *continue* to be accurate * * *.

Johnston & Knapp, Sex Discrimination by Law: A Study in Judicial Perspective, 46 N.Y.U.L.Rev. 675, 725–26 (1971). Winthrop College became coeducational in 1974, and women are now seeking admission to The Citadel. For the status of litigation involving The Citadel, see Faulkner v. Jones, 858 F.Supp. 552 (D.S.C. 1994), affirmed 51 F.3d 440 (4th Cir.1995), discussed in Note 2, p. 1049 infra.

5. Note that Winthrop College was originally established only for "white girls." Williams v. McNair, 316 F.Supp. 134, 136 n. 3 (D.S.C.1970). In some southern communities sex separation was instituted or planned when race desegregation in the public schools became imminent. Smith v. Concordia Parish Sch. Bd., Civ. No. 11,577 (W.D.La.September 30, 1970), declared unconstitutional sex separation in a system that had been coeducational until racial integration was required. The Court found that the design was to isolate and "protect" white girls from black boys. Concluding that the arrangement was a facade for perpetuation of race discrimination, the court left unresolved the alternate issue raised by plaintiffs: is "separate but equal" viable as applied to males and females. See generally Note, The Constitutionality of Sex Separation in School Desegregation Plans, 37 U.Chi.L.Rev. 296 (1970); Note, Single–Sex Public Schools: The Last Bastion of "Separate but Equal"?, 1977 Duke L.J. 259.

UNITED STATES v. COMMONWEALTH OF VIRGINIA (VMI I)*

United States Court of Appeals, Fourth Circuit, 1992.
976 F.2d 890, cert. denied, sub. nom. V.M.I. v. United States,
___ U.S. ___, 113 S.Ct. 2431, 124 L.Ed.2d 651 (1993).

NIEMEYER, CIRCUIT JUDGE:

The male-only admissions policy of Virginia Military Institute (VMI), a state institution of higher education located in Lexington, Virginia, is challenged by the federal government under the Equal Protection Clause of the Fourteenth Amendment and the jurisprudence of Mississippi Univ. for Women v. Hogan, 458 U.S. 718, 102 S.Ct. 3331, 73 L.Ed.2d 1090 (1982). The government contends that the school's policy discriminates against women and is not substantially related to the achievement of an important governmental objective.

Following a six-day trial and extensive findings of fact, the district court concluded that VMI's male-only policy "is fully justified" by a generally

* The Supreme Court's opinion in U.S. v. Commonwealth of Va. (VMI) is set forth in the Appendix at p. 1257 infra.

accepted benefit of single-sex education, and that the admission of women would "significantly" change the "methods of instruction and living conditions" at VMI. Having concluded that "diversity in education" was a legitimate state interest, the district court summarized, "I find that both VMI's single-sex status and its distinctive educational method represent legitimate contributions to diversity in the Virginia higher education system, and that excluding women is substantially related to this mission." 766 F.Supp. 1407, 1411–13 (W.D.Va.1991).

The United States contends on appeal that enhancing diversity by offering a distinctive single-sex education to men only is not a legitimate state objective and that the Commonwealth and VMI have not established a sufficient justification for VMI's male-only admissions policy.

For the reasons that we give more fully below, we accept the district court's factual determinations that VMI's unique methodology justifies a single-gender policy and material aspects of its essentially holistic system would be substantially changed by coeducation. Moreover, all parties appear to acknowledge, as did the district court, the positive and unique aspects of the program. The Commonwealth of Virginia has not, however, advanced any state policy by which it can justify its determination, under an announced policy of diversity, to afford VMI's unique type of program to men and not to women.

Because Virginia has failed to articulate an important objective which supports the provision of this unique educational opportunity to men only, we vacate the judgment of the district court and remand the case to the district court to require the Commonwealth of Virginia to formulate, adopt, and implement a plan that conforms to the principles of equal protection discussed herein. We do not, however, order that women be admitted to VMI if adequate alternatives are available.

I

VMI was established by the Virginia legislature in 1839 as a four-year military college, and its graduates have distinguished themselves in the 150 years since. A VMI professor, Thomas "Stonewall" Jackson, achieved notoriety as a confederate general during the Civil War. The VMI cadet corps fought Union troops at New Market, Virginia, and almost 1800 alumni (constituting 94% of all VMI graduates at the time) fought in the Civil War. Among the thousands of alumni who have served this country during war is General of the Army George C. Marshall, and six have been awarded the Congressional Medal of Honor. VMI graduates have achieved similarly in civilian life. The school's success and reputation are uncontroverted in this case. Indeed, it is apparently that very success in producing leaders that has made admission to VMI desirable to some women, prompting the government to challenge the policy of excluding women.

* * *

The mission of VMI is to produce "citizen-soldiers, educated and honorable men who are suited for leadership in civilian life and who can provide military leadership when necessary."[2]   Focusing primarily on character development and leadership training through a unique and intense process, characterized as an "adversative" educational model drawn from earlier military training and English public schools, VMI's educational method emphasizes physical rigor, mental stress, absolute equality of treatment, absence of privacy, minute regulation of behavior, and indoctrination of values.   The process is designed to foster in VMI cadets doubts about previous beliefs and experiences and to instill in cadets new values which VMI seeks to impart. The model employs a hostile, spartan environment that is characterized by six interrelated components—the "rat line," the class system, the "dyke" system, the honor code, the barracks life, and the military system.

The *rat line* refers to the harsh orientation process to which all new cadets ("rats") are subjected during their first seven months at VMI.   Designed to be comparable to the Marine Corps' boot camp in terms of physical rigor and mental stress, the rat line includes indoctrination, minute regulation of individual behavior, frequent punishments, rigorous physical education, and military drills.   The *class system* entails the peer assignment of privileges and responsibilities, including supervisory roles, to classes of cadets based on rank.   The *dyke system,* which is "closely linked" with the rat line, assigns each rat to a first classman, who acts as a mentor ("dyke") to relieve some of the stress generated from the rat line.   The dyke system aims to create cross-class bonding and provide a model for leadership and support. The *honor code,* that a cadet "does not lie, cheat, steal nor tolerate those who do," is a stringently enforced code of conduct applying to all aspects of life at VMI and providing the single penalty of expulsion for its violation.   The *barracks life,* described as important to VMI's ethos of egalitarianism, is dictated by the nature and functioning of the barracks.   Each class is assigned to one floor of the four-story barracks structure and three to five cadets are assigned to a room.   The rooms are stark and unattractive.   There are no locks on the doors and windows are uncovered.   Access to bathrooms is provided by outside corridors visible to the quadrangle, and there is a total lack of privacy in the barracks, where cadets are subjected to constant scrutiny and minute regulation, all intended to foster cadet equality and to induce stress.   Finally, the *military system,* providing regulation, etiquette, and drill, pervades life at VMI.   As part of the military system each cadet must participate in an ROTC program throughout his four years.   The district court found that the various systems in place at VMI are integrated and interdependent, and several of them cannot be changed without materially affecting others.

2. As stated in the final report of the Mission Study Committee of the VMI Board of Visitors, dated May 16, 1986:

The Virginia Military Institute believes that the measure of a college lies in the quality and performance of its graduates and their contributions to society.

Therefore, it is the mission of the Virginia Military Institute to produce educated and honorable men, prepared for the varied work of civil life, imbued with love of learning, confident in the functions and attitudes of leadership, possessing a high sense of public service, advocates of the American Democracy and free enterprise system, and ready as citizen-soldiers to defend their country in time of national peril.

To accomplish this result, the Virginia Military Institute shall provide to qualified young men undergraduate education of highest quality—embracing engineering, science, and the arts—conducted in, and facilitated by, the unique VMI system of military discipline.

VMI, with approximately 1,300 male students, has never accepted applications from women. During the two years preceding the filing of this action, it did, however, receive over 300 inquiries from women. Today, VMI is the only state-supported, single-sex college in Virginia, although historically most of Virginia's 15 public colleges were at one time single-sex institutions.

The government instituted this action on March 1, 1990, under Title IV of the Civil Rights Act of 1964, 42 U.S.C. § 2000c–6, on behalf of a female high school student who desired admission to VMI, contending that VMI's male-only admissions policy violates the Equal Protection Clause of the Fourteenth Amendment. * * *

II

The district court began its opinion by noting that in May 1864, during the Civil War, VMI cadets bravely fought Union troops at New Market, Virginia. The court continued, "the combatants have again confronted each other, but this time the venue is in this court." What was not said is that the outcome of each confrontation finds resolution in the Equal Protection Clause. When the Civil War was over, to assure the abolition of slavery and the federal government's supervision over that policy, *all* states, north and south, yielded substantial sovereignty to the federal government in the ratification of the Fourteenth Amendment, and every state for the first time was expressly directed by federal authority not to deny any *person* within the state's jurisdiction "equal protection of the laws." U.S. Const. amend. XIV, § 1. The government now relies on this clause to attack VMI's admissions policy.

* * *

* * * to conduct the appropriate Fourteenth Amendment analysis in this case, we must determine whether the state policy of excluding women from admission to VMI is substantially related to an important policy or objective of Virginia.

III

VMI argues that its own admissions policy is the state's policy because the admissions policy is by statute delegated to each state institution. The code provisions establishing VMI provide that its Board of Visitors "shall prescribe the terms upon which cadets may be admitted, their number, the course of their instruction, the nature of their service, and the duration thereof." Va.Code Ann. § 23–104. And this delegation of admissions policy-making is confirmed by the language of Va.Code Ann. § 23–9.6:1(2), which provides that the Council of Higher Education is not empowered to affect "the standards and criteria for admission of any public institution, whether related to academic standards, residence or other criteria, it being the intention of this section that * * * student admission policies shall remain a function of the individual institutions." VMI thus contends that its admissions policy becomes the state policy so that, as its admissions policy is justified by the mission of developing citizen soldiers, a legitimate and important state purpose is served.

To address VMI's argument, we must first decide whether VMI's male-only admissions policy, maintained pursuant to state-delegated authority, is a classification justified by a fair and substantial relationship with the institution's mission of developing citizen soldiers, and this in turn leads to an examination of whether VMI's mission would be materially altered by the admission of women.

Much of the debate between the parties relates to the physiological differences between men and women and the question of a woman's ability to perform and endure the physical training included in VMI's program. While it is agreed by the parties that *some* women can meet the physical standards now imposed on men, it is also agreed that a smaller percentage of women can do so. Based on evidence about the experience of the service academies and the Marine Corps, the district court was justified in finding that if women were to be admitted, VMI would have to convert to a dual-track physical training program in order to subject women to a program equal in effect to that of men, and that, as found by a study conducted at West Point, cadets of both sexes would nevertheless perceive the treatment of them as unequal, leading to jealousy and resentment.

All the parties also agree that men and women would and should be entitled to some degree of privacy, at least to the extent that men and women not, in all respects, be exposed to each other. While again there was much debate among the parties as to the changes that might be required to accommodate this at VMI with the admission of women, all agreed that some accommodation would be necessary.

Finally, the parties have debated extensively the effect of cross-sexual confrontations that the adversative program would produce. Testimony was received that the deliberate harassment that upperclassmen give to "rats" would play out differently when the upperclassman is of one sex and the "rat" another. While the government attributed the predicted effect of this as stereotyping, the evidence supported the district court's finding that cross-sexual confrontation and interaction introduces additional elements of stress and distraction which are not accommodated by VMI's methodology. The court relied on testimony by experts and similar such observations made in the West Point study.

The sum of the changes that could be expected prompted the district court to conclude that if VMI became coeducational, it would offer "neither males nor females the VMI education that now exists." The court observed that "equal treatment would necessarily give way to fair treatment, thus undermining egalitarianism," which is a critical characteristic that now pervades several aspects of VMI's methodology. And the record supports the district court's findings that at least these three aspects of VMI's program— physical training, the absence of privacy, and the adversative approach— would be materially affected by coeducation, leading to a substantial change in the egalitarian ethos that is a critical aspect of VMI's training.

The district court's conclusions that VMI's mission can be accomplished only in a single-gender environment and that changes necessary to accommodate coeducation would tear at the fabric of VMI's unique methodology are adequately supported. And the district court was not clearly erroneous in concluding that if a court were to require the admission of women to VMI to give them access to this unique methodology, the decision would deny those women the very opportunity they sought because the unique characteristics of

VMI's program would be destroyed by coeducation. The Catch–22 is that women are denied the opportunity when excluded from VMI and cannot be given the opportunity by admitting them, because the change caused by their admission would destroy the opportunity.

It is not the maleness, as distinguished from femaleness, that provides justification for the program. It is the homogeneity of gender in the process, regardless of which sex is considered, that has been shown to be related to the essence of the education and training at VMI.

The argument by the government that VMI's existing program is maintained as the result of impermissible stereotyping and overly broad generalizations, without a more detailed analysis, might lead, if accepted, to a finding that would impose a conformity that common experience rejects. Men and women are different, and our knowledge about the differences, physiological and psychological, is becoming increasingly more sophisticated. Indeed the evidence in this case amply demonstrated that single-genderedness in education can be pedagogically justifiable.

For instance, in a ten-year empirical study reported by Alexander W. Astin in *Four Critical Years: Effects of College on Beliefs, Attitudes, and Knowledge* (San Francisco: Jossey–Bass 1977), it was found that single-sex colleges have advantages over coeducational colleges in numerous areas. A summary of the report provided by the parties in this case states:

> Single-sex colleges show a pattern of effects on both sexes that is almost uniformly positive. Students of both sexes become more academically involved, interact with faculty frequently, show large increases in intellectual self-esteem, and are more satisfied with practically all aspects of college experience (the sole exception is social life) compared with their counterparts in coeducational institutions.

* * *

Thus, while the data support a pedagogical justification for a single-sex education, they do not materially favor either sex. Both men *and* women appear to have benefited from single-sex education in a materially similar manner. * * *

In summary, the record supports the conclusion that single-sex education is pedagogically justifiable, and VMI's system, which the district court found to include a holistic formula of training, even more so. It is not remarkable therefore that the government in its brief conceded, "[I]t is not our position that the Fourteenth Amendment embodies a per se bar to public single-sex education."

IV

While this conclusion answers the question of whether VMI's male-only policy is justified by its institutional mission, the argument does not answer the larger question of whether the unique benefit offered by VMI's type of education can be denied to women by the state under a policy of diversity, which has been advanced as the justification and which was relied on by the district court.

* * * While VMI's institutional mission justifies a single-sex program, the Commonwealth of Virginia has not revealed a policy that explains why it offers the unique benefit of VMI's type of education and training to men and not to women. Although it is readily apparent from the evidence that the rigor of the physical training at VMI is tailored to males, in the context of a single-sex female institution, it could be adjusted without detrimental effect. No other aspect of the program has been shown to depend upon maleness rather than single-genderedness.

Virginia has committed the development of its educational policy in the first instance to the State Council of Higher Education for Virginia, but affords each institution of higher learning significant autonomy. * * * To oversee and coordinate the several state-supported institutions of higher education, * * * the Council of Higher Education is charged with the responsibility of preparing plans, which it has done biennially. These plans articulate "access, excellence and accountability" as an overriding goal of Virginia's system of higher education, and they reaffirm a policy of *autonomy and diversity* to provide a variety of choice. * * *

Announcing a similar policy, a special commission legislatively established to chart the future goals of higher education in Virginia, the Commission on the University of the 21st Century, reported to the Governor and the General Assembly of Virginia in 1990 that the hallmarks of Virginia higher education, "autonomy and diversity," should be maintained. Within its report, the Commission indirectly reaffirmed the earlier stated policy of affording broad access to higher education in Virginia, and also observed:

> Because colleges and universities provide opportunities for students to develop values and learn from role models, it is extremely important that they deal with faculty, staff, and students *without regard to sex, race, or ethnic origin.*

(Emphasis added.) That statement is the only explicit one that we have found in the record in which the Commonwealth has expressed itself with respect to gender distinctions. Our inability to find a stated policy justifying single-sex education in state-supported colleges and universities is confirmed by the Virginia Attorney General's statement about the absence of such a state policy: "In the *absence* of a statute explicitly expressing the General Assembly's view on the policy issue, [the Governor's] statement of the Commonwealth's policy [that 'no person should be denied admittance to a State supported school because of his or her gender'] is persuasive." (Emphasis added.)

The lack of a state-announced policy to justify gender classifications is aggravated by the reluctance of the Commonwealth, as a party, and its governor to participate in this case and in this appeal. To the extent that the Governor's view represents state policy, VMI's single-sex admissions policy violates state policy.

If VMI's male-only admissions policy is in furtherance of a state policy of "diversity," the explanation of how the policy is furthered by affording a unique educational benefit only to males is lacking. A policy of diversity which aims to provide an array of educational opportunities, including single-gender institutions, must do more than favor one gender. Moreover, if responsibility for implementing diversity has somehow been delegated to an individual institution, no explanation is apparent as to how one institution with autonomy, but with no authority over any other state institution, can give effect to a state policy of diversity among institutions.

On a more empirical level, we have been given no explanation for the movement away from gender diversity in Virginia by public colleges and universities. At one time most of Virginia's institutions of higher learning were single-sex, including four all-female institutions. Today, all but VMI are coeducational. If VMI thus remains male in furtherance of the state's policy of diversity, which includes diversity in gender, did the decisions of the other institutions violate state policy by moving uniformly to coeducation? * * * [T]hat randomness has fortuitously resulted in 14 coeducational institutions and VMI, an all-male institution.

In short, VMI has adequately defended a single-gender education and training program to produce "citizen soldiers," but it has not adequately explained how the maintenance of one single-gender institution gives effect to, or establishes the existence of, the governmental objective advanced to support VMI's admissions policy, a desire for educational diversity.

V

We are thus left with three conclusions: (1) single-gender education, and VMI's program in particular, is justified by a legitimate and relevant institutional mission which favors neither sex; (2) the introduction of women at VMI will materially alter the very program in which women seek to partake; and (3) the Commonwealth of Virginia, despite its announced policy of diversity, has failed to articulate an important policy that substantially supports offering the unique benefits of a VMI-type of education to men and not to women.

* * * In the proceedings below, Virginia had the opportunity to meet its burden of demonstrating that it had made an important and meaningful distinction in perpetuating this condition. *See* Kirchberg v. Feenstra, 450 U.S. 455, 461, 101 S.Ct. 1195, 1199, 67 L.Ed.2d 428 (1981). As the record stands, however, evidence of a legitimate and substantial state purpose is lacking.

In light of our conclusions and the generally recognized benefit that VMI provides, we do not order that women be admitted to VMI if alternatives are available. But VMI's continued status as a state institution is conditioned on the Commonwealth's satisfactorily addressing the findings we affirm and bringing the circumstances into conformity with the Equal Protection Clause of the Fourteenth Amendment. * * * [W]e do not mean to suggest the specific remedial course that the Commonwealth should or must follow hereafter. Rather, we remand the case to the district court to give to the Commonwealth the responsibility to select a course it chooses, so long as the guarantees of the Fourteenth Amendment are satisfied. Consistent therewith, the Commonwealth might properly decide to admit women to VMI and adjust the program to implement that choice, or it might establish parallel institutions or parallel programs, or it might abandon state support of VMI, leaving VMI the option to pursue its own policies as a private institution. While it is not ours to determine, there might be other more creative options or combinations.

Accordingly, we vacate the judgment and remand the case to the district court: (1) to require the defendants to formulate, adopt, and implement a plan that conforms with the Equal Protection Clause of the Fourteenth Amendment, (2) to establish appropriate timetables, and (3) to oversee the implementation of the plan.

VACATED AND REMANDED FOR FURTHER PROCEEDINGS.

UNITED STATES v. COMMONWEALTH OF VIRGINIA (VMI II)

United States Court of Appeals, Fourth Circuit, 1995.
44 F.3d 1229, cert. granted, ___ U.S. ___, 116 S.Ct. 281, 133 L.Ed.2d 201 (1995).

NIEMEYER, CIRCUIT JUDGE:

At issue is the important question of whether a state may sponsor single-gender education without violating the Equal Protection Clause of the Fourteenth Amendment.

In United States v. Commonwealth of Virginia, (VMI I), 976 F.2d 890 (4th Cir.1992), we concluded that single-gender education was "pedagogically justifiable," id. at 897, and the United States has acknowledged in this case that state sponsorship of single-gender education, if provided to both genders, is not per se a denial of equal protection. * * *

We must decide now whether the Commonwealth of Virginia's proposal (1) to continue to provide a single-gender military-type college education for men at the Virginia Military Institute (VMI), (2) to provide, beginning in 1995, a single-gender education with special leadership training for women at Mary Baldwin College, and (3) to continue to provide other forms of college education, including military training, for both men and women at other colleges and universities in the state is constitutionally permissible. After applying a heightened intermediate scrutiny test specially tailored to the circumstances before us and imposing specific performance criteria on the implementation of Virginia's proposal, we affirm the district court's judgment approving the proposal.

* * *

On remand [from VMI I], Virginia designed a proposal to implement a parallel program at Mary Baldwin College providing women with single-gender education, coupled with special leadership training. Following a trial on the appropriateness of the remedy, the district court approved the plan and directed Virginia "to proceed with all deliberate speed in implementing the Plan and to have the Plan operational for the academic year commencing in the Fall of 1995." United States v. Commonwealth of Virginia, 852 F.Supp. 471, 485 (W.D.Va.1994). The court retained jurisdiction to supervise implementation of the plan and required a status report every six months.

The plan approved by the district court provides for Virginia to establish with state funds the Virginia Women's Institute for Leadership (VWIL) as part of the undergraduate program at the otherwise privately funded Mary Baldwin College, a women's liberal arts college founded in 1842 in Staunton, Virginia, about 35 miles from VMI. The plan is the product of a task force, chaired by Dr. James D. Lott, Dean of Mary Baldwin College, which set as its goal the task of designing a program at Mary Baldwin College to produce "citizen-soldiers who are educated and honorable women, prepared for varied work of civil life, qualified to serve in the armed forces, imbued with love of learning, confident in the functions and attitudes of leadership, and possessing a high sense of public service." Because its mission is similar to VMI's mission, VWIL would have its students pursue the same five goals as those pursued at VMI: education, military training, mental and physical discipline, character development, and leadership development. In designing the program at Mary Baldwin College, however, the task force concluded that aspects of VMI's military model, especially the adversative method, would not be effective for women as a group, even though the task force concluded that some women would be suited to and interested in experiencing a "women's VMI." The task force concluded instead that its mission and goals could better be achieved by designing a program which deemphasized the military methods associated with the "rat line," see VMI I, 976 F.2d at 893, utilizing instead a structured environment emphasizing leadership training.

In addition to the standard bachelor of arts program offered at Mary Baldwin College, VWIL students would be required to complete, as a "minor," core and elective courses in leadership. * * * Outside of the classroom, students would be required to complete a leadership externship during which they would work off campus in the public or private sector for up to one semester and to participate in a speaker series in which each VWIL class would be responsible for bringing outstanding leaders to speak on campus. Finally, all VWIL students would be required to organize and carry out community service projects.

While students at VWIL would be required to participate in four years of ROTC and in an ROTC summer camp, VWIL would not be organized under the pervasive military regimen that exists at VMI. Nevertheless, in addition to standard ROTC training, the students would conduct "leadership laboratory activities" which might incorporate aspects of military training, and they would participate in a newly-established Virginia Corps of Cadets, a uniformed military corps comprised of the all-female VWIL, the all-male VMI, and the coeducational Virginia Tech ROTC corps. The Virginia Corps of Cadets would be largely ceremonial.

Finally, VWIL students would be required to take and pass eight semesters of physical education, a portion of which would be devoted to health education courses. These programs would include athletics, physical training and a "cooperative confidence building program" to be held twice a week.

The VWIL program would be implemented at Mary Baldwin College with its faculty, although VMI faculty would conduct some ROTC training and teach some ROTC courses at Mary Baldwin College. The program would be funded by the Commonwealth of Virginia, providing a per student payment equal to the current annual appropriation paid per cadet at VMI. The program, which task force members expect would have about 25 to 30 students in the first year, would also be given a permanent endowment of $5.46 million. The out-of-pocket expenses for students to attend VWIL is expected to be no greater than those of students attending VMI, and VWIL students would be eligible for the same financial aid programs as are available to VMI cadets.

The experts for both sides acknowledge that the proposed VWIL program differs from VMI in methodology since VWIL would not rely on the pervasive military life and adversative methods to achieve its goals. Members of the task force, who are professionals in education, testified that the different approach was selected principally to address the different educational needs of most women. Dr. Heather Anne Wilson, a member of the task force, summarized the thinking, stating that "the VMI model is based on the premise that young men come with [an] inflated sense of self-efficacy that must [be] knocked down and rebuilt * * *. What [women] need is a system that builds their sense of self-efficacy through meeting challenges, developing self-discipline, meeting rigor and dealing with it, and having successes." * * *

II

The United States contends that the remedial program offered by the Commonwealth of Virginia does not meet the requirements of the Fourteenth Amendment's Equal Protection Clause. It states that "[the proposed remedy] does not correct the constitutional violation, i.e., the denial to women of VMI's unique educational methodology. As the district court recognized, the program 'differs substantially' from the educational program offered at VMI." At oral argument the United States argued that any parallel program would have to be "identical" in substance and methodology to that of VMI. The United States maintains further that by not offering coeducation at VMI, the Commonwealth of Virginia is relying on false stereotypes and generalizations "that women are not tough enough to succeed in VMI's rigorous, military-style program." * * * The United States urges that we enter an order directing Virginia to admit women to VMI as the only remedy for correcting the past constitutional violation.

III

Equal protection of the law requires that persons similarly circumstanced be treated alike, Reed v. Reed, 404 U.S. 71, 76 (1971), but equal protection does not deny states the power "to treat different classes of persons in different ways." * * *

In [Mississippi Univ. for Women v.] *Hogan* the Court outlined a two-step process that inquires (1) whether the state's objective is "legitimate and important," and (2) whether "the requisite direct, substantial relationship between objective and means is present." Id. at 725. The Court explained that tailoring the means to fit the legitimate and important purpose is necessary to assure that the classification is the product of "reasoned analysis" rather than the "mechanical application of traditional, often inaccurate, assumptions about the proper roles of men and women." * * * The Court in *Hogan* did not decide, however, and indeed appears deliberately to have left open, the question of whether states could provide single-gender education in other circumstances. See 458 U.S. at 720 n. 1.

In undertaking the first step of the *Hogan* analysis to determine whether the state's objective is "legitimate and important," a court should not substitute its priorities of value over those established by the democratically chosen branch. * * *

Accordingly, under the intermediate level of scrutiny of a statute or program that classifies by gender, the analysis begins with the limited inquiry into whether the state objective is both consistent with a legitimate governmental role and important in serving that role. Thereafter it must shift to an inquiry of heightened scrutiny into whether the classification "substantially and directly furthers" that objective.

Application of this traditional test, however, to a case where the classification is not directed per se at men or women, but at homogeneity of gender, presents a unique problem, because once the state's objective is found to be an important one, the classification by gender is by definition necessary for accomplishing the objective and might thereby bypass any equal protection scrutiny. The second prong of the test thus would provide little or no scrutiny of the effect of a classification directed at homogeneity of gender. Thus, in order to measure the legitimacy of a classification based on homogeneity of gender against the Equal Protection Clause, we conclude that we must take the additional step of carefully weighing the alternatives available to members of each gender denied benefits by the classification.

To achieve the equality of treatment demanded by the Equal Protection Clause, the alternatives left available to each gender by a classification based on a homogeneity of gender need not be the same, but they must be substantively comparable so that, in the end, we cannot conclude that the value of the benefits provided by the state to one gender tends, by comparison to the benefits provided to the other, to lessen the dignity, respect, or societal regard of the other gender. We will call this third step an inquiry into the substantive comparability of the mutually exclusive programs provided to men and women.

Therefore, in this case we will examine a state-sponsored educational scheme offered by the Commonwealth of Virginia, under which the state provides a single-gender military-type college education to men and a single-gender college education with special leadership training to women, and determine (1) whether the state's objective of providing single-gender education to its citizens may be considered a legitimate and important governmental objective; (2) whether the gender classification adopted is directly and substantially related to that purpose; and (3) whether the resulting mutual exclusion of women and men from each other's institutions leaves open opportunities for those excluded to obtain substantively comparable benefits at their institution or through other means offered by the state. This is the special intermediate scrutiny test that we shall apply in deciding this case.*

IV

Turning to Virginia's proposed VWIL program, we begin with the first part of the test and inquire into whether single-gender education constitutes a legitimate and important governmental objective, remembering that deference

---

* The dissenting opinion has improperly characterized this test as one for "allowable separate-but-equal state-supported educational institutions." This misunderstands the standard we utilize. As a general principle of equal protection jurisprudence, when there is no meaningful and relevant difference between two classes of persons for purposes of a given state regulation, equality is demanded, and "separate but equal" does not fulfill the demand. When there is a difference between two classes of persons, then separate and different facilities for each class may satisfy equal protection if the difference in facilities is sufficiently related to the nature of the difference between the classes. In this case, we do not espouse a "separate-but-equal" test and never discuss "separate-but-equal facilities." Rather, the test we utilize would allow separate and substantively comparable facilities where a state justifies its offering of single gender education as a legitimate governmental objective.

is to be accorded the state's legislative will so long as the purpose is not pernicious and does not violate traditional notions of the role of government.

The provision of education is considered one of the most important functions of state and local government. * * *

As important as education is thought to be to the welfare of the people, it is nevertheless not a right secured to the people by the Constitution, see San Antonio School District v. Rodriguez, 411 U.S. 1, 35 (1973), and following from that reality, a citizen does not, in the absence of legislative will, have a right to demand a publicly financed education. * * *

When a state chooses to support college education, it need not provide all types of education, all disciplines, all methods, or all courses. * * * When a state narrows the range of its educational offerings, a narrowing of the class of those appropriately benefited is a necessary consequence. But a state may not establish a classification for admission, for example, to a medical school unrelated to its purpose of providing a medical education. Thus, we would expect judicial approval of an admissions classification based on intellectual capability, but not on race or national origin. * * *

Turning to this case, providing the option of a single-gender college education may be considered a legitimate and important aspect of a public system of higher education. That single-gender education at the college level is beneficial to both sexes is a fact established in this case. See United States v. Commonwealth of Virginia, 766 F.Supp. 1407, 1411–12 (W.D.Va.1991). Indeed, the briefs submitted in this case by the parties and amici curiae list a multitude of professional articles describing the benefits of single-gender education, especially for late adolescents coming out of high school. This should not be surprising in light of common experience that a sex-neutral atmosphere can be less distracting to late adolescents in an educational setting where the focus is properly on matters other than relationships between the sexes. Moreover, it is not surprising that the public, increasingly seeking admission to single-gender colleges, finds this objective to be important. * * *

Just as a state's provision of publicly financed education to its citizens is a legitimate and important governmental objective, so too is a state's opting for single-gender education as one particular pedagogical technique among many. * * * Thus, we should defer to a state's selection of educational techniques when we conclude, as we do here, that the purpose of providing single-gender education is not pernicious and falls within the range of the traditional governmental objective of providing citizens higher education. Accordingly, we conclude that Virginia has met the first part of our intermediate scrutiny test.

V

When applying the special intermediate scrutiny test for classifications based on homogeneity of gender in the context of higher education, we next consider whether that classification is substantially related to the state's purpose. When combined with the third part of the test, i.e., the inquiry into whether excluded men and women have opportunities to obtain substantively comparable benefits, this inquiry scrutinizes the means by which the state chooses to obtain its objective.

* * * Even though it may be offered to both genders through separate institutions, separate campuses, or even separate classrooms, a single-gender educational program necessarily excludes members of the gender not included in that institution, campus, or classroom. The importance of the classification is not the fact that the student body is male or female, but that it is of the same gender, whichever is chosen for the particular program. But the only way to realize the benefits of homogeneity of gender is to limit admission to one gender. Thus, the means of classifying by gender are focused on the single-gender educational purpose as directly as the nature of the objective allows.

The classification for single-gender education at VMI is also directly related to achieving the results of an adversative method in a military environment. The adversative method was not designed to exclude women, but seized on the possibility, in a sexually homogeneous environment, of grating egos and setting the aggressiveness of one person against another through conflict, egalitarianism, lack of privacy, and stress—both physical and mental. The adversative method is intended to break down individualism and to instill the uniform values espoused by the institution. The methodology described, however, has never been tolerated in a sexually heterogeneous environment; indeed, we condemn it for good reason. If we were to place men and women into the adversative relationship inherent in the VMI program, we would destroy, at least for that period of the adversative training, any sense of decency that still permeates the relationship between the sexes.

Accordingly, to preserve the benefits of single-gender education, * * * men must be excluded from the women's program and women from the men's.

While we are satisfied that a classification for homogeneity of gender is necessary to provide single-gender education, at whatever level of separation, we must nevertheless, under the special intermediate scrutiny test that we are applying for such classification, be satisfied that both excluded men and excluded women have reasonable opportunities to obtain benefits substantively comparable to those they are denied. That brings us to the final inquiry of this intermediate scrutiny test.

VI

In determining the substantive comparability of benefits, we are faced with at least two questions: how are the benefits from which one gender is excluded to be defined, and on what level and to what degree must other benefits be comparable.

The United States notes that VMI affords a unique type of military training as part of its educational program which cannot be duplicated in another institution. * * *

* * * If we ordered VMI to admit women, the program would be irrevocably altered, forever denying its unique methodology to both women and men. Changes would have to be made to the adversative method, to the absence of privacy, and to the physical requirements of the program, all of which are part of VMI's unique methodology. Certainly military training could be provided for women at VMI, but it would be substantially different from the training

VMI cadets currently receive and would be closer to the programs offered by the U.S. military academies, which are already open to women. Thus, neither gender would experience the unique type of adversative military training now utilized at VMI if VMI were to become coeducational.

* * * In considering the level of detail for any comparison of the two programs, we must, to achieve a meaningful comparison of substance, do more than simply recognize that both programs provide higher education leading to an undergraduate degree. But we should not reject programs that are aimed at achieving similar results, not generally available from other institutions of higher learning, simply because they differ in approach. * * *

* * * The possibility of adapting the adversative methodology to women, setting woman against woman with the intended purpose of breaking individual spirit and instilling values, could succeed only if it is true that women, subjected to the same grating of mind and body, respond in the same way men do, and only then if a sufficient number of women necessary to make such a program work desired to participate in the program. Educational experts for the Commonwealth testified that women may not respond similarly and that if the state were to establish a women's VMI-type program, the program would attract an insufficient number of participants to make the program work. * * * This is the type of ongoing debate that is to be expected among substantively comparable institutions, and it reveals a vitality of professional concern which can lead to institutional betterment through adjustments down the road. In this case, the mission and goals are the same, and the methodologies for attaining the goals, while different, nevertheless are reasonably calculated to succeed at each institution. Those differences that do exist do not require that the important state purpose of providing single-gender education for both sexes be defeated in this case.

It is true that VWIL is at its incipiency, and the VWIL degree from Mary Baldwin College lacks the historical benefit and prestige of a degree from VMI. But such intangible benefits can never be created on command—they must be the byproduct of a longer-term effort. Moreover, to some extent, we compensate for this deficiency in the remedy section, below. For purposes of the Equal Protection Clause, however, we are satisfied that the programs to be offered at both institutions can be substantively comparable if VWIL is undertaken with a persistently high level of commitment by Virginia and that men and women mutually excluded by the two programs will not be denied the opportunity for an undergraduate education with discipline and special training in leadership. * * *

In this case, we conclude that if the conditions that we impose below are fulfilled, the opportunities that would be open both to men and women are sufficiently comparable. We therefore are satisfied that the special intermediate scrutiny test defined for this case has been met, insofar as a proposed program can meet this test, by the VWIL program proposed at Mary Baldwin College.

VII

* * *

In this case, however, there is an added element created by the *presence now* of VMI as an ongoing and successful institution with a long history and the *absence now* of a comparable single-gender women's institution. Virginia's proposal for Mary Baldwin College is just that—a proposal. Virginia has undertaken what appears to be a serious effort at developing a plan to meet this historic deficiency. * * * [G]overnmental officials in Virginia seem to be supporting the new program at every level. In our earlier opinion we noted some ambivalence in that regard. Then–Governor Douglas Wilder had favored coeducation at VMI in the face of no other alternative, and state education officials favored a separate program, or some other course, leading the state, as a party, to bow out of the liability phase of the litigation as a house divided. Governor Wilder is now firmly behind the VWIL program as is current Governor George Allen. Moreover, the Virginia legislature has supported the program by providing what appears to be adequate funding and by promising to increase the level of funding, should the response require it.

Nevertheless, a state's response to a court ordered correction of a Fourteenth Amendment violation is given under command and therefore must be viewed with some skepticism. While the court was assured at oral argument that the program proposed at Mary Baldwin College was serious and had the full support of the state, the important question remains whether Virginia will implement the program with the intensity and perseverance necessary to provide a substantively comparable opportunity for women, so that when VWIL is established we will not conclude that the value of the benefits provided by that program, when compared to VMI, tends "to lessen the dignity, respect, or societal regard" of women. To allay any skepticism and assure eradication of the constitutional violation, we therefore find it essential, during the early stage of VWIL's history, to be assured affirmatively that a high level of state support continues.

Accordingly, while we affirm the judgment of the district court, which has issued an injunction mandating implementation of the plan and retaining jurisdiction to oversee the implementation, we are remanding the case with instructions that the court include, as part of its oversight of the plan's implementation, a specific review to ensure that (1) the program is headed by a well-qualified, motivated administrator, attracted by a level of compensation suited for the position; (2) the program is well-promoted to potentially qualified candidates; (3) the program includes a commitment for adequate funding by the state for the near term; and (4) the program includes a mechanism for continuing review by qualified professional educators so that its elements may be adjusted as necessary to keep the program aimed not only at providing a quality bachelor's degree but also at affording the additional element of taught discipline and leadership training for women.

AFFIRMED AND REMANDED.

PHILLIPS, SENIOR CIRCUIT JUDGE, dissenting:

* * * I do not believe the proposed remedial plan, whose judicial adoption in unrealized form obviously does not bring Virginia into present compliance with equal protection guarantees, has any real and effectively measurable capacity to do so over foreseeable time.

* * *

When Virginia Military Institute was founded in 1839 as a state-supported military school for men only, it is inconceivable that any thought was given by the founders to the possibility that women should not be denied its intended benefits. No conscious governmental choice between alternatives therefore dictated the original men-only policy; it simply reflected the un-questioned general understanding of the time about the distinctively different roles in society of men and women. See Mississippi Univ. for Women v. Hogan, 458 U.S. 718, 725 n. 10 (1982)(noting numerous examples from that era of "legislative attempts to exclude women from particular areas simply because legislators believed women were less able than men to perform a particular function"). Since that time and until this litigation (so far as anything before us reveals) no conscious governmental choice had ever been made by the Commonwealth of Virginia to reexamine that original policy. So far as can be told, the gender-role premises of its origins were those that continued over time to sustain it as official state policy.

It is clear then that it was this litigation that prompted the Common-wealth's first official re-examination of the policy and its underlying premises in light of the Fourteenth Amendment's requirement that the states provide the equal protection of their laws to all persons subject to them. That obligation, as imposed in 1868, has from earliest times been understood by the courts to expose gender-classifications to equal protection judicial scrutiny. Early on, that scrutiny was almost completely deferential to the legislative prerogative, asking only whether the classification served any reasonably conceivable, legitimate governmental purpose. See, e.g., Bradwell v. Illinois * * * (1872) * * *.

Several important things emerge from [VMI I]. The first is that the remedial plan proposed by the Commonwealth and adopted as remedy by the district court simply involves a new gender-classification which now has become the proper subject of the heightened scrutiny mandated by *Craig* and its progeny. * * *

The next point of importance is that this new gender-classification (in its projected form) is of a type that has not yet been definitively subjected to equal protection scrutiny: it involves a state's provision of separate single-gender educational institutions for men and women which it is claimed will meet equal protection requirements by providing substantially equal, though separately administered, benefits. This could raise a threshold question whether separate state-supported educational facilities for men and women, like those for white and black students, are so "inherently unequal," by reason of their stigmatic implications, see Brown v. Bd. of Educ., 347 U.S. 483, 495 (1954), that the new classification violates equal protection per se and warrants no further scrutiny.

If the answer to that threshold question is, however, "no", so that intermediate scrutiny must proceed in detail, a final point of importance about the new classification must be faced. It is that one of the two critical elements in its separate-but-equal arrangement, the women-only program at Mary Baldwin, is only a plan and not a present reality. This creates a difficult problem for Equal Protection analysis. Must we assume, without question, that the stated goals of the women's program are actually achievable and that the fact of their achievement is subject to judicial verification when it occurs, so that we should, on that assumption, (though conditionally) assess the plan in its proposed ultimate form? Or may we, in intermediate scrutiny, question either or both the achievability of the program's stated objectives and the ability of the courts effectively to assess their achievement? * * *

* * *

The first step * * * is to identify the precise governmental objective(s) the Commonwealth asserts to be the "important" one(s) justifying the proposed double gender-classification under which women will continue to be denied admission to VMI and men to VWIL. * * *

* * * We are entitled at the outset to inquire as to whether the "governmental objectives" now asserted are the "actual purposes," and to reject them if the record draws their reality as the true motivations for the policy sufficiently in doubt. * * *

I believe that a comparable inquiry here could properly support a like rejection of the various governmental objectives suggested by the Commonwealth—on the basis that they demonstrably are rationalizations compelled by the exigencies of this litigation rather than the actual overriding purpose of the proposed separate-but-equal arrangement. Such an inquiry—looking realistically to the historical record, taking judicial notice of much of relevance that is known to the whole world and of which we are not compelled to feign ignorance, see Watts v. Indiana, 338 U.S. 49, 52 (1948), and holding the Commonwealth to its appropriate stringent burden of justification, see Hogan, 458 U.S. at 724 (must be "exceedingly persuasive") would, I believe, reveal a quite different actual purpose. Specifically, I think it would support a confident and fair conclusion that the primary, overriding purpose is not to create a new type of educational opportunity for women, nor to broaden the Commonwealth's educational base for producing a special kind of citizen-soldier leadership, nor to further diversify the Commonwealth's higher education system—though all of these might result serendipitously from the arrangement—but is simply by this means to allow VMI to continue to exclude women in order to preserve its historic character and mission as that is perceived and has been primarily defined in this litigation by VMI and directly affiliated parties.

* * *

What is the "substantial and direct relationship"—the "fit"—between means and asserted ends for which we search in intermediate scrutiny, and how do we look for it—in general, and particularly in this case? * * *

* * * no such arrangement could be found substantially related to any conceivable governmental objective unless the benefits to be separately distributed by the arrangement were substantially equal across the board of the relevant criteria for evaluating educational institutions. * * * Certainly, when separate-but-equal educational arrangements for the races were considered to be tolerable under the Equal Protection Clause, a basic prerequisite was that they be truly, substantially equal in all the relevant criteria, tangible and intangible, by which educational institutions are evaluated. See e.g., Sweatt v. Painter, 339 U.S. 629, 633–34 (1950)(requiring "substantial equality in educational opportunities" to justify separate state-supported law schools for white and black students, and not finding it upon considering both tangible resources such as "scope of library" and intangible resources such as "position and influence of the alumni," "traditions and prestige"). Though

race is a "suspect" classification and gender so far is not, I see no reason why the same requirement of substantial equality of benefits that was thought at one time to justify separate-but-equal schools for the different races should not apply to separate schools for men and women if that classification now does, as race formerly but no longer does, permit separate-but-equal arrangements. * * *

* * * Without denigrating in any way the proposed VWIL program, nor certainly Mary Baldwin, the contrast between the two on all the relevant tangible and intangible criteria is so palpable as not to require detailed recitation. * * *

The district court and the majority apparently seek to avoid the insurmountable problem of finding substantial equality of benefits by narrowly defining the relevant range of those to be considered. * * * But that, of course, won't do. The proper perspective from which to measure substantial equality of available benefits is that of the potential student who could be admitted to either school and has a choice. As was said in *Sweatt*, "[i]t is difficult to believe that one who had a free choice between [these] schools would consider the question close."

* * *

Notes on VMI I and II

1. The Supreme Court heard oral argument on *VMI I* and *VMI II* on January 17, 1996. In April, 1995, a request for rehearing en banc had been denied in *VMI II*, 52 F.3d 90 (4th Cir.1995). Six judges voted to rehear the case en banc, and only 4 voted not to rehear the case. Three judges, however, disqualified themselves. The Fourth Circuits' local rule requires a majority vote among all the judges in active service, without regard to whether a judge is disqualified, in order to rehear a case. Consequently, seven votes were needed. See the opinion of Judge Diana Gibbon Motz, dissenting from denial of rehearing en banc, id. at n. 1. Judge Motz, joined in dissent by Judges Hall, Murnaghan, and Michael, questions whether any proposed program for women could be regarded as "substantially comparable" to VMI:

> Even leaving aside "adversative" training, how can a degree from a yet to be implemented supplemental program at Mary Baldwin be held "substantively comparable" to a degree from a venerable Virginia military institution that was established more than 150 years ago? As the majority acknowledges, in almost epic understatement, the alternative degree from Mary Baldwin "lacks the historical benefit and prestige of a degree from VMI." VMI II, 44 F.3d at 1241. People do not seek to attend VMI only for the course work or the citizenship and military training. At least as important is VMI's reputation, the opportunity to know and learn from other students, faculty, and graduates, and the ability to rely on those connections and friendships in later life. The proposed alternative program offers no remotely similar, let alone "substantively comparable," experience. * * * No one is arguing that women or men should be forced to attend VMI. The question is can they constitutionally be denied that opportunity when the Commonwealth—with tax dollars from men and women—supports the institution. Recently the United States eliminated its rule excluding women from combat duty, explaining that the rule was an "armour-plated ceiling" preventing the

advancement of women in the military. Several months ago, one of the first women fighter pilots was killed during a practice run. Anyone who is prepared to do combat for her country—indeed, to be killed in preparation for that combat—should be eligible to apply for what she perceives to be the best possible training. As long as the Commonwealth provides support for VMI, women should be given the opportunity to attend.

Id. at 93–94.

2. Shannon R. Faulkner applied and was conditionally admitted to The Citadel, the South Carolina equivalent of VMI. The Citadel's application form did not ask candidates to disclose their sex, and Faulkner chose not to volunteer that information. When her femaleness was discovered, The Citadel withdrew its acceptance. Throughout its 150 year history, The Citadel has admitted only men to its Corps of Cadets. It has, however, admitted women to its other educational programs. Faulkner filed suit to compel her admission to the Corps, and sought a preliminary injunction to permit her to attend day classes with the Corps pending the litigation. The district court granted the injunction, and the Fourth Circuit, in an opinion by Judge Niemeyer, affirmed. Acknowledging that *VMI I* was directly on point, the court nevertheless pointed out that the plaintiff in *VMI* had not sought a preliminary injunction. It noted that the district court's order did not require structural changes to The Citadel's program, did not order her actual admission to the Corps, so was not tantamount to integrating the institution. It agreed that Faulkner would suffer irreparable injury if she were forced to await the outcome of her litigation, while the injury to The Citadel was "minimal at best." It concluded that "[t]he most telling aspect of this case, and that which distinguishes this case from *VMI*, is the presence of this time pressure, combined with an absence of present opportunity for Faulkner." Faulkner v. Jones, 10 F.3d 226, 233 (4th Cir.1993), motion to stay mandate denied 14 F.3d 3 (4th Cir.1994), motion to stay mandate denied ____ U.S. ____, 114 S.Ct. 872, ____ L.Ed.2d ____ (1994).

In January, 1994, Shannon Faulkner became the first female to attend day classes with cadets at The Citadel in 151 years. She was initially allowed to attend class, but not live, march or eat with cadets while her lawsuit proceeded. Shannon's case went to trial in May 1994. In July 1994, the District Court found that The Citadel's refusal to admit Shannon to its Corps of Cadets violated the Equal Protection Clause. Faulkner v. Jones, 858 F.Supp. 552 (D.S.C.1994). The Citadel maintained that although all parties were bound by the Fourth Circuit's holdings in *VMI I*, it could provide new justification for South Carolina's provision of military-style education to men, but not women. According to District Judge Houck, the only new justification The Citadel offered was its argument that in South Carolina there was insufficient demand for single-sex public education for women:

> * * * This justification is very appealing to those who sincerely revere The Citadel and its rich traditions, to those who determine where the scarce resources of this state will be placed, and to the many people, men and women, who live in this state and in undesignated places elsewhere who do not want to see The Citadel change. In a referendum the state's policy may be approved by a landslide, or it may fail. The problem is, this is not a referendum where the emotions and likes and dislikes of the plurality carry the day. It also is not an occasion where one judge votes his will. In this matter the Constitution of the United States alone speaks and determines the outcome of this controversy.

The defendants have called the court's attention to no case that supports the proposition that lack of demand is a sufficient justification for the State of South Carolina providing single-sex education to men but not to women. A thorough search by this court has also failed to find any such precedent. * * * To suggest that a lack of demand for a certain type of equal protection can somehow justify the denial of another person's constitutional right thereto undermines the express intent of the Fourteenth Amendment.

858 F.Supp. at 564. In turning to the issue of proper remedy, the District Court noted:

* * * [T]he primary difference in this case and [VMI I] is that we have a real, live plaintiff here who wants to be admitted to the Corps of Cadets whereas in VMI the Department of Justice was the only plaintiff. Because of that difference, the matter of remedy must be looked at from the standpoint of Faulkner and also from the standpoint of other women similarly situated who may seek to join the Corps of Cadets at some future date.

* * * The Citadel has made no secret of the fact that its primary goal in this case is to keep Faulkner out of the Corps of Cadets, and the State of South Carolina appears ready to give its support in that cause. Not once has a defendant done anything to indicate that it is sincerely concerned to any extent whatsoever about Faulkner's constitutional rights. The most reveal-ing fact of all, however, is that the defendants have continued to defend this case at a cost of millions of dollars to the taxpayers of South Carolina when they do not have a single case to offer in support of their position that a lack of demand for single-sex education on the part of women justifies its provid-ing such an education only for men.

Time is not on the side of Faulkner. She is now a rising sophomore and cannot become a member of the corps of Cadets after the beginning of her junior year. * * * [T]here remain only three avenues through which Faulk-ner can receive the rights guaranteed to her under the Equal Protection Clause. Admittedly, the Citadel cannot go private, [because the cost is prohibitive,] and that leaves only two options remaining. One of those is a parallel institution or program, and the other is admission to the Corps of Cadets.

The defendants have almost total control over the development and implementation of a parallel institution or program. They alone can develop it, and they alone can fund it. In addition, it is clear that they can easily delay that process beyond the point in time that Faulkner would ever benefit from such a program. * * *

858 F.Supp. at 566–568. The court had previously found that it could take South Carolina up to 10 years to create a new single-sex college for women. Id. at 561. Consequently, the court ordered that Shannon be admitted to the Corps immedi-ately and that The Citadel develop, adopt, and implement a plan by the 1995–96 school year to accommodate any additional qualified women who may wish to attend The Citadel. Id. at 569.

The Fourth Circuit modified the remedy on appeal, staying Shannon's imme-diate admission to the Corps, and giving South Carolina and The Citadel until August 1995 to provide a parallel program that meets the criteria of VMI II, or adopts another acceptable option as discussed in VMI I, 51 F.3d 440, 450 (4th Cir.1995). In concurring with the Fourth Circuit, Judge Hall reluctantly felt bound by the *VMI* precedent, but concluded any attempt to maintain publicly-supported single-sex education was ultimately misguided:

> I choose to write separately because I am convinced that we have embarked on a path that will inevitably fall short of providing women their deserved equal access to important avenues of power and responsibility. * * *
>
> Our failure became apparent in *VMI II*, long after the time had passed to ask the only question that matters: "Why has the state decided to create or maintain this institution for the benefit of only one gender?" Instead, we were constrained to ask a wholly irrelevant one: "Does the state offer a 'substantively comparable' educational option to the other gender?" * * *
>
> In fact, though VMI, The Citadel, and their advocates have ceaselessly insisted that education is at the heart of this debate, I suspect that these cases have very little to do with education. They instead have very much to do with wealth, power, and the ability of those who have it now to determine who will have it later. The daughters of Virginia and South Carolina have every right to insist that their tax dollars no longer be spent to support what amount to fraternal organizations whose initiates emerge as full-fledged members of an all-male aristocracy. Though our nation has, throughout its history, discounted the contributions and wasted the abilities of the female half of its population, it cannot continue to do so. As we prepare, together to face the twenty-first century, we simply cannot afford to preserve a relic of the nineteenth.

51 F.3d at 450–451.

Neither The Citadel nor the State of South Carolina developed a constitutional alternative by August 1995. Consequently, Shannon Faulkner began training with the Corps of Cadets in early August. Unfortunately, she became sick and, after the stress of two and one-half years of litigation and one year of ostracism as a day student, decided to withdraw at the end of the first week. Within two weeks, another woman, Nancy Mellette, a high-school senior at a North Carolina military boarding school, was seeking to intervene in Faulkner's place and asking for admission to The Citadel in the fall of 1996. Nancy's father is a Citadel graduate and her brother a senior at The Citadel. The New York Times, Sept. 10, 1995, p. 37, col. 1. In the meantime, South Carolina is busy setting up its Institute of Leadership for Women, admitting 22 students to this new special program at Converse College, a private women's college, with the state providing each South Carolina woman a $10,175 scholarship. Women in Higher Education Newsletter, October 1995, p. 2.

3. In its brief before the Supreme Court in *VMI I* and *II*, the Department of Justice is asking the Court to declare sex a suspect class:

> Sex, like race, is an immutable and highly visible characteristic that frequently bears no relation to ability to perform or contribute to society. * * * To remove any remaining ambiguity about the general illegitimacy of classifications * * * based solely on sex, this court should now hold that such classifications are inherently suspect and subject to strict scrutiny.

Quotation from U.S. Solicitor General Drew Days III and Deval Patrick, Assistant Attorney General for civil rights, David Savage, Women Divided Over All–Male Academy, San Francisco Chronicle, p. A4, col. 1, January 2, 1996. Some feminist scholars, however, have filed briefs in opposition to this position, and in support of VMI. Professor Susan Estrich, among others, argues that the Court should not outlaw separate programs for women. If the Court declares sex classifications unconstitutional, she argues, even private women's colleges could be threatened because they receive federal funds. Estrich, a Wellesley graduate, states that single-sex education plays an important role for women. "* * * if you believe that, then you have to ask yourself: 'Why shouldn't boys have the same option?'" Id. Is she correct? Can an argument be made that separate schools for men are unconstitutional, but not separate schools for women? What about sex-separate programs or classes within public schools? What about special all-girl classes in math, or summer programs to interest high school girls or college women in engineering careers? For further discussion, see Text Note: Is There a Place for Women's Colleges?, p. 1054 infra.

Regardless of the outcome in *VMI I* and *II*, the debate will continue over both public and private single-sex education. For examples of differing viewpoints, see Kristin S. Caplice, The Case for Public Single Sex Education, 18 Harv. Journal of Law & Pub. Policy 227, 267 (1994)("states have legitimate and important interests in * * * maintenance of systemwide education diversity * * *. Single sex education, when offered for both male and female students ads a voluntary alternative to coeducation, should not contravene the mandates of the Equal Protection Clause * * *"). See also William A. DeVan, Note, Toward a New Standard in Gender Discrimination: The Case of Virginia Military Institute, 33 William & Mary L.Rev. 489, 540–42 (1992), defending *VMI I* on the ground that "[t]he sexual attractions and physical and emotional differences between the sexes distinguish gender discrimination from racial discrimination" and arguing for preservation of the diversity represented by single sex military education while compensating the women excluded from participation through common law damages.

For the proposition that coeducation provides "intangible benefits" that "separate but equal" learning environments cannot provide, and that single sex institutions can be "ideologically denigrating" and perpetrate paternalistic stereotypes for women, see Julie M. Amstein, United States v. Virginia: The Case of Coeducation at Virginia Military Institute, 3 Am. U.J. Gender & L.69, 99–108 (1994) See also Juliette Kayyem, The Search for Citizen–Soldiers: Female Cadets and the Campaign Against the Virginia Military Institute—*United States v. Commonwealth of Virginia*, Recent Developments, 30 Harv. Civ. Rights–Civ. Liberties L. Rev. 247 (1995), (criticizing the Fourth Circuit's "outcome based" analysis in *VMI II* "overlooking both the tangible and intangible qualitative differences between the VMI and VWIL programs," as well as overlooking "stigmatic effects that state-supported programs based on gender stereotypes have on potential female applicants." Id. at 261.); Lucille M. Ponte, *Waldie* Answered: Equal Protection and the Admissions of Women to Military Colleges and Academies, 25 New England L.Rev. 1137 (1991)(arguing that single-sex admissions policies in military schools violate Equal Protection). See generally, VMI Essays, 50 Wash. & Lee L.Rev. 15 (1993).

4. The City of Detroit also attempted to invoke the benefits of single-sex education as a justification for opening three all-male academies for 250 boys in preschool through fifth grade in the fall of 1991. The academies were designed to address the high unemployment rates, school dropout levels and homicide among urban males by offering a special program featuring a class entitled "Rites of Passage," an Afrocentric curriculum, futuristic lessons in preparation for 21st century careers, an emphasis on male responsibility, mentors, individualized counseling, extended classroom hours including Saturday classes, and student uniforms. A group of female students enrolled in the Detroit schools and their

parents challenged the School District's plan on constitutional and statutory grounds. Judge George Woods granted the plaintiffs' motion for a preliminary injunction, ruling both that defendants' rationale for the Academies was weak and that defendants had failed to meet the burden of showing that the creation of male academies was substantially related to the asserted state interest. He observed in part:

> * * * The primary rationale for the Academies is simply that co-educational programs aimed at improving male performance have failed.
>
> The Court is wary of accepting such a rationale. Although co-educational programs have failed, there is no showing that it is the co-educational factor that results in failure. Even more dangerous is the prospect that should the male academies proceed and succeed, success would be equated with the absence of girls rather than any of the educational factors that more probably caused the outcome.

* * *

> None of [the Board of Education's] findings meet the defendant's burden of showing how the exclusion of females from the Academies is necessary to combat unemployment, dropout and homicide rates among urban males. There is no evidence that the educational system is failing urban males because females attend schools with males. In fact, the educational system is also failing females * * *.

Garrett v. Board of Education of School District of City of Detroit, 775 F.Supp. 1004, 1007–08 (E.D.Mich.1991). Would Judge Niemeyer have come to this result? What about Justice Powell? After Judge Woods issued the injunction, the school board and the plaintiffs reached a tentative agreement to admit girls to the academies. New York Times, August 26, 1991, p. A9, at cols. 1–2. Is there any way, consistent with the constitution, that the School District could have achieved its original aim? Easy, says one notewriter: the district could have provided *three* schools: one for males, one for females, and a co-educational alternative school. See Note, Inner–City Single–Sex Schools: Educational Reform or Invidious Discrimination? 105 Harv.L.Rev. 1741 (1992). The school district's lawyers might like that solution; what about its fiscal officers? See also, for a compelling defense of immersion schools, Kevin Brown, "Do African–Americans Need Immersion Schools?: The Paradoxes Created by Legal Conceptualization of Race and Public Education," 78 Iowa L.Rev. 813 (1993).

School reform efforts have continued to address the needs of urban children. As of 1992, school boards in Baltimore, Chicago, the District of Columbia, New Orleans, New York, and San Diego had proposed or were in various stages of implementing separate schools or classes for black males. Note, Creating Space for Racial Difference: The Case for African–American Schools, 27 Harv. Civil Rights–Civil Liberties L.Rev. 187, 187 (1992). To avoid race and sex discrimination claims, school districts modified their original plans to provide their "Afrocentric curriculum" only to males. Milwaukee developed a pilot program involving two "African–American immersion schools." These schools use district curriculum but infuse African–American history and culture where possible. The schools are open to any student, male or female, of any race. As of 1993, the enrollment of both schools was more than 95% African–American, about the same percentage as before the immersion programs began. The Columbus Dispatch, Oct. 18, 1993, at 1C.

The issue of sex discrimination is especially troubling in the ongoing debate:

[T]he crisis facing black girls is as severe as that facing boys. According to Detroit's proposal for its Male Academy, forty-five percent of girls in the public schools dropped out in the 1989–90 school year, with approximately forty percent of these girls dropping out because of pregnancy or parenting duties.

Note, supra, at 200–01. This commentator argues that any schools that focus solely on the needs of African–American boys reinforces and perpetuates a myth that African–American girls represent the paradigm of what is wrong with the African–American community, and it is up to the men to take charge, dominate, and instill the values necessary to repair the social structure.

For commentary on both sides of the African–American school and single gender education debate, see generally, Kristin S. Caplice, The Case For Public Single–Sex Education, 18 Harv. Journal of Law & Pub. Policy, 227, 275–92 (1994)(arguing for flexibility in allowing educators to implement single-sex educational programs as part of school reform efforts); Joshua E. Kimerling, Black Male Academies: Re–Examining the Strategy of Integration, 42 Buffalo L. Rev. 829, 840–850, 855–858 (1994)(Afrocentric schools are a response to the failure of courts to follow through on desegregation and integration mandates, and a flexible policy re-adopting integration programs would best provide students with access to better education); Daniel Gardenswartz, Public Education: An Inner City Crisis! Single–Sex Schools: An Inner–City Answer? 42 Emory L.J. 591, 632–646 (1993)(arguing for flexibility for states to adopt creative educational solutions crafted towards specific community problems, but noting that the needs of "at risk" females must be met as well).

Text Note
Is There A Place For Women's Colleges?

In a letter prepared for inclusion in these materials, David B. Truman[1] states the case for single-sex education for women:

The case rests, in my view, on two propositions, one dealing with the learning process and the other deriving from the process of socialization. The two are distinguishable, but they are related to one another, and their effects are joint ones.

Although theories of the learning process differ, they all accept the view that, whatever may be the stages through which the individual normally passes, the rates of learning differ quite widely among individuals. Whether because of differences in genetic endowment or in consequence of variations in the environment, no two persons of the same chronological age can be assumed to be at the same stage of learning. Persons of equal intelligence, however that may be measured, and of the same age are not necessarily equally ready to gain from a given educational experience. In maturity they may, and probably do, end up at essentially the same intellectual level, other things being equal, but in the process of learning, of development, they are not necessarily at the same point in any given year.

1. Letter from David B. Truman to Herma Hill Kay (December 12, 1980). Dr. Truman was President of Mount Holyoke College from 1969–1978; Vice–President and Provost of Columbia University from 1967–1969; and Dean of Columbia College from 1963–1967. He was Professor of Government at Columbia from 1951–1969, and has taught at a variety of other institutions, including Bennington, Cornell, Harvard, Yale and Williams.

See also Kaplan, Women's Education: The Case for the Single–Sex College, H. Astin & W. Hirsch, eds., The Higher Education of Women: Essays in Honor of Rosemary Park, at 53–67 (1978).

The general meaning of this proposition is that no single curriculum, standardized by age level, is the right one for every individual. Every experienced teacher knows this and attempts, within the limits imposed by the educational system, to reach the individual student where she (or he) is at the moment.

By easy extension, the proposition also means that no one type of educational setting or environment is the right one for all students of a given age. Schools (and colleges) have hidden curricula that do not appear in their catalogues. A product of atmosphere and tradition, the hidden curriculum of any institution is contributed to by the unarticulated assumptions of teachers (and administrators) and especially by the norms and expectations that are, in effect, set by the students themselves. The latter are unconscious standard-setters, drawing upon their perceptions of the ways of the larger, adult society and particularly upon the norms of the typically quite different adolescent society. This hidden curriculum may be for any individual student stimulating and constructive or restrictive and destructive (rarely neutral), depending on the stage of intellectual and emotional development that the individual has reached. It follows that no one type of institutional environment, no one form of the hidden curriculum, is appropriate for every student of a given age.

Taken by itself, this proposition about the learning process is simply an argument for institutional and curricular diversity and for pedagogical adaptability. We do not know enough about education to insist that all schools (and colleges) should follow a single pattern. Put more positively, we do know enough to be certain that uniformity of pattern would ill serve the healthy development of large numbers of students. The proposition alone, therefore, has no special bearing on the education of women or, for that matter, on that of any conventionally defined sector of the population.

If, however, it is evident that the members of such a sector—all, most, or a substantial number—bring a distinctive set of experiences and problems to the learning process, then the proposition about that process has a special significance for the type of educational program and setting that will be most appropriate for them. This is where the second proposition, about socialization and especially differential socialization, comes in. Women do belong to such a sector because, despite recent and slowly accelerating changes, the socialization of females is different, distinctive, and fraught with implications for their educational and personal development.

This is not the place to attempt to specify all the elements of this socialization process. I shall rely on a quick sketch, I hope not a caricature, the essence of which is familiar to you.

Typically in American society young females are given quite restricted role options. That society's many devices for providing inducements and assigning rewards and penalties are different for females and males is perhaps not itself astonishing. The problems arise because the range is much narrower for females. A boy or young man can receive approval for a very wide range of sometimes contradictory behaviors—scholar, athlete, gentleman, roughneck, loner, good mixer, and so on. Development and achievement in a wide range of areas are offered to him, and his initiatives are encouraged and rewarded. By contrast a girl, especially as she approaches adolescence, is subject to a narrower and more consistent range of behavioral pressures. She is rewarded for good grades (but not too good) and for being pretty, especially in the eyes of males, on whose approval she is taught to depend for her estimate of herself. Her initiatives outside such areas are viewed with concern, if not alarm, and she is expected to show promise in the nurturing, mothering roles and, at least implicitly, as a desirable sexual partner.

The impact of these differences often becomes heavy and destructive during adolescence. Essentially what occurs is that, as the girl begins to approach the stage of maximum physical appeal to the opposite sex, she is faced—or feels faced—with the choice, false but no less real for her, between being a woman and being a person. Especially for the intellectually able young woman, this can be damagingly restrictive. She must moderate her visible academic accomplishments, notably her school grades, if in competing with males she is not to lose out in the competition with females for male attention. More subtly, her intellectual horizons tend to be limited as she learns from the hidden curriculum that some subjects—especially quantitative and scientific ones—not only are difficult but are not the things that "successful" girls are interested in. It is no accident in this country that females show accomplishment equal to males in scientific and quantitative areas up to the onset of puberty and from there on show a marked and steady decline. The loss to the intellectually able young woman and to the society is appalling.

The educational implications of this situation seem to me clear. The young woman needs a school environment in which such stereotyping by sex is minimized, where the boy-girl game is not played as constantly as it is in the usual coeducational setting. Above all she needs an environment in which she can find herself as a person, measuring her strengths and talents by real criteria and securing confidence in her choices, before she is required to decide how she will live and perform as an adult woman. She needs to learn that her options are set by her talents and preferences, not by her sex, and that her value is to be measured by how she exercises those options and not by her willingness or ability to conform to the conventional expectations of society and of male contemporaries.

This is the strongest case for the element of diversity in the educational system that is provided by single-sex schools and colleges for young women. The case is, by the way, not a hypothetical one. It is a fact, for example, that many women's colleges over the past three-quarters of a century have produced more graduates, absolutely and not merely in proportion to their size, who have secured advanced degrees, especially in scientific fields, than comparable male or coeducational colleges or major, large coeducational universities.

At what level is single-sex education most needed? We do not know, but, on the basis of the proposition about the learning process, certainly at both the secondary and the collegiate levels. A given young woman may not require both but will likely benefit from either, depending on where she is in the learning process.

For how long shall we need single-sex education? Given the subtlety of socialization processes, their consequent slow rate of change, and their reinforcement by the adolescent culture, for as long as I can see into the future.

Is Dr. Truman's defense of single-sex education as valid today as when it was written in 1980? Does Dr. Truman's defense of single-sex education extend to men's colleges? Jencks and Reisman,[2] who tend to agree on the whole with Truman's position, emphatically would not extend the argument to men's colleges. They note,[3]

> [t]he pluralistic argument for preserving all-male colleges is uncomfortably similar to the pluralistic argument for preserving all-white colleges * * *. The all-male college would be relatively easy to defend if it emerged from a world in which women were established as fully equal to men. But it does not. It is therefore likely to be a witting or unwitting device for preserving tacit assumptions of male superiority—assumptions for which women must eventually pay.

Is it constitutional, in a state system of higher education, to provide a range of coeducational institutions and a women's college but not a male college? Recall that in Williams v. McNair, discussed in Note 4, supra, p. 1029, South Carolina's decision to exclude men from Winthrop College was justified in part because there also existed The Citadel for men as well as several coeducational institutions. Would it have been constitutional for South Carolina to admit women to The Citadel but at the same time exclude men from Winthrop? Does Dr. Truman's argument support a characterization of state-supported women's colleges as a form of affirmative action required to overcome societal discrimination?

What is the other side to the argument about single-sex education for women? That coeducational institutions, particularly the major research universities, offer a higher quality of education ranked on the scale of facilities, faculty, and courses than the often financially troubled women's colleges are able to provide?[4] That since women must compete with men in the work force, their association with men in the educational arena is a better preparation than the temporary and artificial separation offered by women's colleges? That, in any event, societal discrimination against women is so pervasive that the lesson taught subliminally in single-sex colleges—that women can succeed by virtue of their talent—is ultimately a false and misleading one?

Is it possible to dilute the impact of coeducational stress upon women through the development of women's studies courses? The Report of the Carnegie Commission,[5] while approving the introduction of women's courses and women's study programs on a transitional basis, warned that these courses should not be offered through separate departments on women's studies, lest they come to be viewed as second-class programs. Is this objection limited to coeducational institutions? Is it constitutional, in a coeducational institution supported by a state government, to exclude male students from women's studies courses? Can female teachers be required?

After reviewing the history of single-sex education in the United States and discussing the cases included in these materials, Professor Deborah Rhode offers the following alternative approach to sex segregated education:[6]

> In the long run, however, the role of separatist education requires reexamination. Responding to problems in mixed institutions by perpetuating segregated alternatives is at best a palliative. In all-female settings, it is

---

2. Christopher Jencks & David Reisman, The Academic Revolution 298 (1968).

3. Id., at 297–98.

4. See Jeffrey M. Shaman, Commentary: College Admission Policies Based on Sex and the Equal Protection Clause, 20 Buffalo L.Rev. 609, 613–14 (1971).

5. Report of the Carnegie Commission on Higher Education, Opportunities for Women in Higher Education, 78 (September 1973).

6. Rhode, Association and Assimilation, 81 Nw.U.L.Rev. 106, 144–45 (1986)(footnotes omitted).

more difficult to challenge the underlying cultural attitudes that perpetuate subordination; by definition, many of those most in need of such challenge are absent. Moreover, as noted earlier, the strongest arguments for all-women's institutions raise obvious problems of asymmetry. It is difficult to defend women's separate culture while demanding entry into men's. As an interim measure, this dual approach appears essential. But as the remedial role of all-female schools becomes less necessary, their status becomes more problematic. One goal of contemporary women's schools should be to create a society in which their compensatory function no longer is required. To the extent that women's institutions have been especially supportive for women, by providing role models, leadership opportunities, and positive faculty/student interaction, such characteristics should become more dominant in coeducational environments as well.

It is not only those characteristics that require attention. To make educational structures truly coeducational will entail commitments affecting not just admissions policies but also institutional priorities. Although women by no means speak with one voice on matters of institutional structure, there are certain concerns that large constituencies share. A school genuinely hospitable to such concerns, for example, would have different relationships with its internal and surrounding communities than those typical of existing institutions. Its working environment would have a less hierarchical and sex-segregated structure than the prevailing norm, in which female clerical and support staffs dominate the lower reaches and male tenured professors and senior administrators occupy the upper tier. Its student body would include a broader cross-section of American society, including greater representation of older and part-time women students with interrupted career patterns and competing family responsibilities. Its curricula and classroom climate would be more responsive to the experiences of subordinate groups and to the need for challenging as well as transmitting dominant intellectual paradigms. And its wage scales, working hours, promotion policies, and child-care commitments would reflect greater sensitivity to the needs of working parents. The objective, as Virginia Woolf emphasized, is not for women simply to "join the [academic] procession." It is rather that both women and men rethink the direction of that procession and the terms on which they are prepared to enter.

Regardless of your own conclusions about the merits of single-sex education for women at the college level, that option exists for very few women. The Carnegie Commission reported in 1973 that the total number of women's colleges was down to 146, and they enrolled less than 10 percent of all female students.[7] A new interest, however, in women's colleges has emerged in the 1990s. By 1995, the number of women's colleges had declined to 84, but enrollment increased by 19% in the 1990s, going from 85,000 in 1991 to 105,000 in 1995.[8] An example of this revived interest is the battle to keep Mills College for women only.[9]

---

7. Report of the Carnegie Commission, supra note 5, at 70. Rhode reports that by the mid–1980s, single-sex schools accounted for only 2.3 percent of all college women and a much smaller percentage of men, and that the trend was similar in secondary schools. Rhode, supra note 6, at 136. See also Deborah Rhode, Justice and Gender 288–98 (1989).

8. Ben Gose, Second Thoughts at Women's Colleges, The Chronicle of Higher Education, Feb. 10, 1995, at A22.

9. On May 3, 1990, The Board of Trustees of Mills College voted to admit men as undergraduates, beginning in 1991. Women students shaved their heads, shut down classes, and demonstrated in T-shirts reading "Better dead than co-ed." Chair Warren Hellman ex-

2.   THE RIGHT TO EQUAL PLAY: SEX SEGREGATION IN ATHLET-IC PROGRAMS

CLARK v. ARIZONA INTERSCHOLASTIC ASSOCIATION

United States Court of Appeals, Ninth Circuit, 1982.
695 F.2d 1126, certiorari denied, 464 U.S. 818, 104 S.Ct. 79, 78 L.Ed.2d 90 (1983).

NELSON, CIRCUIT JUDGE:

Appellants seek review of the district court's judgment dismissing their claim that Appellees' policy of precluding boys from playing on girls' interscholastic volleyball teams in Arizona high schools violates the equal protection clause. The district court held that the policy was a permissible means of attempting to insure equality of opportunity for girls in Arizona interscholastic sports and of redressing past discrimination. We affirm.

FACTUAL AND PROCEDURAL BACKGROUND

The Appellants, plaintiffs below, are students in Arizona High Schools, and have demonstrated their prowess in volleyball by participating on national championship teams sponsored by the Amateur Athletic Union. The plaintiffs have not, however, been able to participate on their high school volleyball teams. Their schools only sponsor interscholastic volleyball teams for girls, and a policy of the Arizona Interscholastic Association (the AIA) has been interpreted to preclude boys from playing on girls' teams, even though girls are permitted to participate on boys' athletic teams. The AIA's policy on matters relating to gender discrimination is set forth in its resolution of October 19, 1981:

> 2.   That the present rules regarding volleyball are silent as to whether or not boys['] volleyball is permitted, and that should sufficient interest on the part of the AIA members be evinced so that the Legislative Council finds it desirable to prepare rules for and sanction interscholastic competition in volleyball for boys, that such action would certainly be permissible under the current Constitution and Bylaws of the AIA;

> 3.   That the nondiscrimination policy of the AIA permits participation by girls on boys['] teams in non-contact sports in order to compensate for the girls['] historical lack of opportunity in interscholastic athletics, however, boys are not allowed to play on girls['] teams in non-contact sports since boys historically have had ample opportunity for participation and currently have available to them sufficient avenues for interscholastic participation, and since to allow boys to play on girls['] teams in non-contact

plained that "Mills needs at least 1,000 undergraduates in order to secure a strong future." Mills currently enrolls 777 women undergraduates; tuition is $17,000 per year. San Francisco Chronicle, May 4, 1990, at A1, col. 1.

The students' tactics were successful. On May 18, 1990, the Mills Trustees reversed their decision as faculty, alumnae, and staff dedicated themselves to resolve the school's financial problems by 1995. President Mary Metz, who had voted to admit men, declared, "A passion for women's education has made history."

New York Times, May 19, 1990, at 1, col. 1. Metz herself, however, will not be available to lead the five-year effort at student recruitment and fund-raising necessary to translate the new decision into reality. On June 22, 1990, she resigned as President, effective immediately. New York Times, June 23, 1990, at 7, col. 4. The new president, Janet Holmgren McKay, former vice provost of Princeton, has vowed to carry on the mission. San Francisco Chronicle, March 5, 1991, p. A3.

sports would displace girls from those teams and further limit their opportunities for participation in interscholastic athletics.

The following stipulation was presented at trial:

> Generally, high school males are taller, can jump higher and are stronger than high school females. There are six basic skills necessary in volleyball—serving, passing, setting, digging, hitting and blocking. Of these skills, hitting and blocking are enhanced by physical size, strength and vertical jump. Males generally have the potential to be better hitters and blockers than females and thus may dominate these two skills in volleyball.

A second stipulation indicates that these physiologically-derived differences in athletic potential have real impact on the game of volleyball. Under the rules of the AIA, girls' volleyball teams use a net that is substantially lower than that used by boys' teams. According to the stipulated facts there seems to be no question, then, that boys will on average be potentially better volleyball players than girls.

The plaintiffs brought this action in September, 1981, seeking to enjoin the AIA from enforcing its policy which prevents boys from playing on girls' volleyball teams. After preliminary relief was denied, the parties submitted the case for judgment on stipulated facts. The district court entered final judgment denying the plaintiffs relief, and this timely appeal was taken.

The trial court found that the rules and regulations of the AIA do not violate the equal protection clause of the fourteenth amendment. It held that the maintenance of a girls-only volleyball team "is substantially related to and serves the achievement of the important governmental objective" of: 1) promoting equal athletic opportunities for females in interscholastic sports, and 2) redressing the effects of past discrimination. Specifically, the court held:

> [M]ore favorable treatment for females is permissible if such treatment redresses society's longstanding disparate treatment of women. [Citation omitted]. Precluding male students from becoming members of the girls' volleyball team is a permissible means of redressing the past discrimination against females in high school interscholastic athletic programs.

Discussion

The only issue presented on appeal is whether the trial court was correct in holding that the AIA's policy of prohibiting boys from playing on girls' volleyball teams did not deprive plaintiffs of equal protection under the fourteenth amendment.

* * *

The equal protection clause of the fourteenth amendment is implicated only when a classification treats persons similarly situated in different ways. Reed v. Reed * * *. A gender based discrimination is subject to a level of scrutiny somewhere between the level of "traditional" equal protection analysis (minimal scrutiny), Frontiero v. Richardson * * *, and the highest level of scrutiny (strict scrutiny), Graham v. Richardson, 403 U.S. 365, 375–76, 91 S.Ct. 1848, 1854, 29 L.Ed.2d 534, 544 (1971). This intermediate level of scrutiny which applies to gender classifications is clearly set forth in Craig v. Boren * * *.

This standard continues to be the Supreme Court standard for testing gender based classifications. Mississippi University for Women v. Hogan * * *. Rephrased, then, the issue in this case is whether the AIA's policy regarding boys not playing volleyball on the girls' team fails substantially to further an important governmental objective.

In applying this standard, the Supreme Court is willing to take into account actual differences between the sexes, including physical ones. In Michael M. v. Sonoma County Superior Court, 450 U.S. 464, 468–69, 101 S.Ct. 1200, 1204, 67 L.Ed.2d 437, 442 (1981), Justice Rehnquist, writing for a plurality noted that the "Court has consistently upheld statutes where the gender classification is not invidious, but rather realistically reflects the fact that the sexes are not similarly situated in certain circumstances." 450 U.S. at 469 * * *. The Court reasoned that the legislature could punish the participant (the male) who would suffer few of the consequences of his conduct while the woman suffered virtually all the harmful consequences.

In Kahn v. Shevin, 416 U.S. 351, 94 S.Ct. 1734, 40 L.Ed.2d 189 (1974), the Court upheld a property tax exemption for widows but not widowers, recognizing the different financial opportunities available to men and women. Id. at 353, 94 S.Ct. at 1736. * * *

On the other hand, the Supreme Court has soundly disapproved of classifications that reflect " 'archaic and overbroad' generalizations, Schlesinger v. Ballard, [419 U.S. 498, 508, 95 S.Ct. 572, 577, 42 L.Ed.2d 610], or ' "old notions," ' Stanton v. Stanton, 421 U.S. 7, 14, 95 S.Ct. 1373, 1377, 43 L.Ed.2d 688 (1975)." Califano v. Goldfarb, 430 U.S. 199, 207, 97 S.Ct. 1021, 1027, 51 L.Ed.2d 270, 276 (1977)(plurality opinion). Most recently, in Mississippi University for Women v. Hogan, 458 U.S. 718, 102 S.Ct. 3331, 73 L.Ed.2d 1090 (1982), the Court struck down a gender based admissions policy when the policy's proposed compensatory objective was without factual justification.

The courts have had little trouble with the situation converse to the one at bar, where females are excluded from participation in a sport. In Brenden v. Independent School District 742, 477 F.2d 1292 (8th Cir.1973), the Eighth Circuit held that schools could not prohibit girls from playing on a boys' team, at least in non-contact sports.[1]

When schools have offered separate teams for boys and girls, courts have generally approved prohibitions of girls' participation on boys' teams. In O'Conner v. Board of Education, 645 F.2d 578 (7th Cir.), *cert. denied,* 454 U.S. 1084, 102 S.Ct. 641, 70 L.Ed.2d 619 (1981), the court held that plaintiff could not demonstrate a reasonable likelihood of success on the merits of her claim that she be allowed to participate on a boys' basketball team when "separate but equal" teams were provided for boys and girls.

---

1. A number of state and federal courts have reached a similar result. *See, e.g.,* Morris v. Michigan State Board of Education, 472 F.2d 1207 (6th Cir.1973); Hoover v. Meiklejohn, 430 F.Supp. 164 (D.Col.1977)(disapproving rule that prohibited girls from playing on boys' soccer team—a contact sport team); Reed v. Nebraska School Activities Association, 341 F.Supp. 258 (D.Neb.1972); Haas v. South Bend Community School Corporation, 259 Ind. 515, 289 N.E.2d 495 (1972).

The courts' treatment of the issue here is not as well settled as in the two related situations discussed above. Some recent cases, however, although all in inferior state courts, have upheld the exclusion of boys from girls' teams in situations such as the one at bar.[2] In Petrie v. Illinois High School Athletic Association, 75 Ill.App.3d 980, 31 Ill.Dec. 653, 394 N.E.2d 855 (1979), the Appellate Court of Illinois concluded that even under a strict scrutiny analysis, the exclusion was a legitimate means of providing athletic opportunities for girls. The court noted that the classification of teams based on sex was "based on the innate physical differences between the sexes, [rather than on] generalizations that are 'archaic' (Schlesinger v. Ballard (1975), 419 U.S. 498, 508, 95 S.Ct. 572, 577, 42 L.Ed.2d 610, 618), [or attitudes of] romantic paternalism (Frontiero v. Richardson (1973), 411 U.S. 677, 684, 93 S.Ct. 1764, 1769, 36 L.Ed.2d 583, 590)." 75 Ill.App.3d at 989, 31 Ill.Dec. at 660, 394 N.E.2d at 862. The court acknowledged that the sexual classification could be avoided by classifying directly on the basis of physical differences such as height or weight, but concluded that such classifications would be "too difficult to devise," 75 Ill.App.3d at 988, 31 Ill.Dec. at 660, 394 N.E.2d at 862, primarily because of strength differentials between the sexes. Handicapping competitions, the court concluded, would be difficult and contrary to the interest of achieving the best competition possible. Other schemes, such as multi-tiered teams (for example, with varsity and junior varsity squads), or having a separate boys' team were rejected by the court as being too expensive to impose on the schools. Finally, the court concluded that sex was "the only feasible classification to promote the legitimate and substantial state interest of providing for interscholastic athletic opportunities for girls." 75 Ill.App.3d at 989, 31 Ill.Dec. at 660, 394 N.E.2d at 862.

Another case reaching the same result is Mularadelis v. Haldane Central School Board, 74 A.D.2d 248, 255–57, 427 N.Y.S.2d 458, 463–64 (N.Y.App.Div. 1980). In that case, the Appellate Division of the Supreme Court of New York held that if overall athletic opportunities for males were equal, the equal protection clause was not violated by exclusion of boys from any particular team.

While *Mularadelis*, 74 A.D.2d at 255–57, 427 N.Y.S.2d at 463–64, says that only *overall* athletic opportunities must be equal, most cases such as Mass. Interscholastic Athletic Ass'n, 378 Mass. 342, 393 N.E.2d 284, conclude that the denial of an opportunity in a specific sport, even when overall opportunities are equal, can be a violation of the equal protection clause. We believe that while a lack of overall equality of athletic opportunity certainly raises its own problems, the presence of such equality cannot by itself justify specific inequality of opportunity in any given sport. The question, then, is

---

2. *See* Hoover v. Meiklejohn, 430 F.Supp. at 170 (The court noted):

> Given the lack of athletic opportunity for females in past years, the encouragement of female involvement in sports is a legitimate objective and separation of teams [by sex] may promote that purpose. [Citations omitted]. It may also justify the sanction of some sports only for females, of which volleyball may be an example.

But see Gomes v. Rhode Island Interscholastic League, 469 F.Supp. 659 (D.R.I.), *vacated as*

moot, 604 F.2d 733 (1st Cir.1979)(exclusion of boys from girls' volleyball team prohibited when no boys' team offered); Attorney General v. Massachusetts Interscholastic Athletic Association, 378 Mass. 342, 393 N.E.2d 284 (1979)(exclusion of boys from girls' teams prohibited under strict scrutiny mandated by state's equal rights amendment; in dictum court added that exclusion could not withstand even minimal scrutiny, 378 Mass. at 356, 393 N.E.2d at 292).

whether denying boys the particular opportunity to compete on a girls' volleyball team, even when boys' overall opportunity is not inferior to girls', can be justified as substantially related to an important governmental interest.

As discussed above, the governmental interest claimed is redressing past discrimination against women in athletics and promoting equality of athletic opportunity between the sexes. There is no question that this is a legitimate and important governmental interest. *Petrie*, 75 Ill.App.3d at 989, 31 Ill.Dec. at 660, 394 N.E.2d at 862.

The only question that remains, then, is whether the exclusion of boys is substantially related to this interest. The question really asks whether any real differences exist between boys and girls which justify the exclusion; i.e. are there differences which would prevent realization of the goal if the exclusion were not allowed.

The record makes clear that due to average physiological differences, males would displace females to a substantial extent if they were allowed to compete for positions on the volleyball team. Thus, athletic opportunities for women would be diminished. As discussed above, there is no question that the Supreme Court allows for these average real differences between the sexes to be recognized or that they allow gender to be used as a proxy in this sense if it is an accurate proxy. *See, e.g.* Kahn v. Shevin * * *; Michael M. v. Sonoma County Superior Court * * *. This is not a situation where the classification rests on " 'archaic and overbroad' generalizations [citation omitted]," Califano v. Goldfarb * * * or "the baggage of sexual stereotypes," Orr v. Orr * * *. Nor is this a situation involving invidious discrimination against women, *Michael M.,* 450 U.S. at 475, 101 S.Ct. at 1207, 67 L.Ed.2d at 446, or stigmatization of women. The AIA is simply recognizing the physiological fact that males would have an undue advantage competing against women for positions on the volleyball team. *Petrie,* 75 Ill.App.3d at 988–89, 31 Ill.Dec. at 660, 394 N.E.2d at 862. The situation here is one where there is clearly a substantial relationship between the exclusion of males from the team and the goal of redressing past discrimination and providing equal opportunities for women.

We recognize that specific athletic opportunities could be equalized more fully in a number of ways. For example, participation could be limited on the basis of specific physical characteristics other than sex, a separate boys' team could be provided[3], a junior varsity squad might be added, or boys' participation could be allowed but only in limited numbers.[4] The existence of these alternatives shows only that the exclusion of boys is not *necessary* to achieve the desired goal.[5] It does not mean that the required substantial relationship does not exist. Cases such as *Kahn v. Shevin* show that absolute necessity is

---

3. This would be constitutionally permissible. *Gomes,* 469 F.Supp. at 664; *See* Vorchheimer v. School District of Philadelphia, 532 F.2d 880 (3d Cir.1976), *aff'd mem.,* 430 U.S. 703, 97 S.Ct. 1671, 51 L.Ed.2d 750 (1977)(separate boys' and girls' *schools* permissible).

4. All of these alternatives were rejected by the *Petrie* court as either too impractical or otherwise unnecessary to the constitutionality of the exclusion alternative. * * * *But see,* Mass. Interscholastic Athletic Ass'n, 393 N.E.2d at 295.

5. The *Petrie* court, however, did conclude that the problems with the various other alternatives were enough to create a "substantial element of necessity" for the exclusion of boys. 75 Ill.App.3d at 990, 31 Ill.Dec. at 661, 394 N.E.2d at 863.

not required before a gender based classification can be sustained. In *Kahn,* the tax credit could have been determined on the basis of actual need rather than on females' tendency on average to have a greater need. Nevertheless, the court allowed the classification.

In this case, the alternative chosen may not maximize equality, and may represent trade-offs between equality and practicality. But since absolute necessity is not the standard, and absolute equality of opportunity in every sport is not the mandate, even the existence of wiser alternatives than the one chosen does not serve to invalidate the policy here since it is substantially related to the goal. That is all the standard demands. Kahn v. Shevin, 416 U.S. at 356 n. 10, 94 S.Ct. at 1737–38 n. 10, 40 L.Ed.2d at 193–94 n. 10. While equality in specific sports is a worthwhile ideal, it should not be purchased at the expense of ultimate equality of opportunity to participate in sports. As common sense would advise against this, neither does the Constitution demand it.

Affirmed.

LANTZ BY LANTZ v. AMBACH

United States District Court, Southern District of New York, 1985.
620 F.Supp. 663.

STANTON, DISTRICT JUDGE.

Plaintiff Jacqueline Lantz, a 16–year–old healthy female student in her junior year at Lincoln High School, Yonkers, New York wants to play football. Lincoln High School has no girls' football team, so she attempted to try out for the junior varsity football squad. Her attempts were blocked by a regulation promulgated by the defendant Commissioner of the New York State Department of Education under the authority of the defendant members of the New York State Board of Regents, and applied by defendants The Board of Education of Yonkers, New York and The New York State Public High School Athletic Association. The regulation, 8 N.Y.C.R.R. § 135.4(c)(7)(ii)(c)(2) states:

> "There shall be no mixed competition in the following sports: basketball, boxing, football, ice hockey, rugby and wrestling."

[P]laintiff claims the regulation violates * * * her right to equal protection of the laws as guaranteed by the Fourteenth Amendment to the United States Constitution. She seeks a declaratory judgment that the regulation as written violates that statute and that clause of the Fourteenth Amendment, and an injunction requiring the defendants to delete the regulation and permit her to try out for the junior varsity squad, and an award of attorney's fees. Under Fed.R.Civ.P. 65(a)(2) the trial of the action on the merits has been advanced and consolidated with the hearing of the application for a preliminary injunction.

* * *

The Supreme Court has stated that discrimination among applicants on the basis of their gender is subject to scrutiny under the Equal Protection clause of the Fourteenth Amendment, and will be upheld only where there is "exceedingly persuasive justification" showing at least that the classification serves "important governmental objectives and that the discriminatory means employed are substantially related to the achievement of those objectives." *See* Mississippi University for Women v. Hogan (quoting Kirchberg v. Feenstra * * * and Wengler v. Druggists Mutual Ins. Co. * * *). Here the governmental objective is to protect the health and safety of female students, and there is no quarrel with the importance of that objective. To demonstrate that the regulation is substantially related to that objective, the Commissioner and the Board of Regents have offered data establishing that "as a general rule, senior high school students (age 15 through 18) are more physically developed, stronger, more agile, faster and have greater muscular endurance than their female counterparts" (Atty Genl's brief at 6–18), medical opposition to girls' participation on boys' teams in such contact sports as football (which Dr. Falls described as a "collision" sport) because of the risk of injury in such participation, and the testimony of Dr. Willie to the effect, among other points, that the present regulation enhances safety by permitting simple and uniform administration across the state.

But these data, however refined, inevitably reflect averages and generalities. The Commissioner and the Regents say (Atty Genl's brief at 19), "It makes no difference that there might be a few girls who wish to play football who are more physically fit than some of the boys on the team." Yet it does make a difference, because the regulation excludes all girls. No girl—and simply because she is a girl—has the chance to show that she is as fit, or more, to be on the squad as the weakest of its male members. Where such cases exist, the regulation has no reasonable relation to the achievement of the governmental objective. In such a case, the effect of the regulation is to exclude qualified members of one gender "because they are presumed to suffer from an inherent handicap or to be innately inferior." *See* Mississippi University for Women v. Hogan, 458 U.S. 718, 725, 102 S.Ct. 3331, 3336, 73 L.Ed.2d 1090 (1982). Thus the regulation's operation is too broad, and must give way to the facts in particular cases.

Applying the language of Force v. Pierce City R–VI School District, 570 F.Supp. 1020, 1031 (W.D.Mo.1983), to this case, Jacqueline Lantz "obviously has no legal entitlement to a starting position" on the Lincoln High School Junior Varsity football squad, "since the extent to which she plays must be governed solely by her abilities, as judged by those who coach her. But she seeks no such entitlement here.

"Instead she seeks simply a chance, like her counterparts, to display those abilities. She asks, in short, only the right to try."

To the extent that the challenged regulation deprives her of the opportunity to try out for the junior varsity football squad, it operates to abridge her right under Section 1 of the Fourteenth Amendment to the Constitution of the United States, and the defendants will be enjoined from complying with it or enforcing it.

Notes on Clark *and* Lantz

1. Do you agree with the reasoning in *Clark?* Does Judge Dorothy Nelson place too much weight on *Kahn?* Is the United States Supreme Court still in sympathy with the *Kahn* approach to "benign discrimination" as a means of compensating women for past disadvantages? Look again at Mississippi University for Women v. Hogan, set out at p. 137, supra, and the notes following that case.

Judge Nelson cites the *Petrie* case in support of her reasoning. Compare the dissent filed in that case by Justice Craven:

> Surely, not even the majority here, nor society generally, would condone the exclusion of blacks from an all-white basketball team on the grounds that blacks generally are more skilled at the game than whites and might tend to dominate it. Nor would we tolerate an exclusion of Catholics from an all-Protestant high school soccer team on the grounds that Catholic elementary schools have traditionally emphasized that sport so as to give their graduates an unfair advantage. Yet the constitutional prohibition against sex discrimination in Illinois is *more specific* than that against either racial or religious discrimination. There are legally tolerable means of categorizing athletes by size, strength, and ability. To adopt sex as a proxy for more precisely defined means of leveling off competition is both illegal and irrational. It is simply foolish to perpetuate the fear of equality between sexes. It is more than foolish to justify discrimination upon the asserted basis of protection and allowing "catch up" time.

> This litigation started to see whether Trent Petrie could play volleyball when the only volleyball team available was one limited to girls. Ironically, the majority opinion of Mr. Justice Green recognizes that some girls may be better volleyball players than some boys, and indeed on this particular team such may be the fact. Trent Petrie may not have made the team based upon criteria unrelated to sex. The majority opinion is but a labored effort to defend and approve a classification that is proscribed.

* * *

> Finally, the ultimate cruel element in the discrimination approved is that the majority seeks to "protect" females because of an implied conclusion that "they" are again to be classified as weak and inferior. Because females are deemed to be weak and inferior, the majority concludes that they need to be special wards protected by this misplaced, gratuitous, judicial benevolence. I prefer to be identified with such reasoning only in dissent.

Id., 75 Ill.App.3d at 996–97, 31 Ill.Dec. at 665–66, 394 N.E.2d at 867–68. Whose view of affirmative action do you prefer, Nelson's or Craven's? One notewriter denounced *Clark* in no uncertain terms: "[T]he holding in *Clark* was the product of 'archaic and overbroad generalizations,' and such generalizations violate equal protection." Barbara L. Pryor, Comment, Equal Protection Scrutiny of High School Athletics, 72 Ky.L.J. 935, 950 (1983–84). Do you agree?

The Ninth Circuit adhered to its position in Clark v. Arizona Interscholastic Association, 886 F.2d 1191 (9th Cir.1989)(Clark II), an identical challenge to the AIA rule restricting interscholastic competition in volleyball to single-sex teams brought by Wade Clark, the younger brother of the named plaintiff in the class action suit considered in *Clark I*, Gregory Clark. Wade argued in part that because the social attitudes contributing to women's unequal participation in sports "may persist forever," the chosen remedy of excluding males from volleyball did not qualify as a narrowly drawn, constitutional affirmative action plan permissible under City of Richmond v. J.A. Croson Co., discussed supra at p. 994. The court rejected this argument on the ground that, as Clark conceded, female athletes within AIA's jurisdiction presently suffer the effects of past discrimination, and that the AIA's rule protecting them against being displaced is substantially related to the goal of redressing past discrimination. Is that sufficient under *Croson?* See also Rowley v. Board of Education of St. Vrain Valley School

District, 863 F.2d 39 (10th Cir.1988), reversing a district court's preliminary injunction ordering that a male be allowed to try out for the girls' volleyball team, provided he did not displace any member of the Varsity team, on the ground that the court had used an equal protection standard more stringent than that approved in Craig v. Boren, p. 41, supra.

2. Does *Lantz* reach the right result? Can it be reconciled with *Clark?* Why does the equal protection clause require that a girl be allowed to try out for the boys' football team, but not that a boy be allowed to try out for the girls' volleyball team? Is the constitutional standard different in the two situations? Should the courts be influenced by the possibility that boys might take over the volleyball team, while girls may face strong competition for places on the football team? As you might imagine, the cases in which a female plaintiff has sought to play football have not been very numerous. One of the early cases was brought under the Washington Equal Rights Amendment. In Darrin v. Gould, 85 Wash.2d 859, 540 P.2d 882 (1975), two girls wanted to play on the Wishkah Valley High School football team. In the fall term of 1973, when they applied, Carol Darrin was a junior, 16 years of age, 5 feet 6 inches tall, who weighed about 170 pounds. Delores Darrin was a freshman, 14 years of age, 5 feet 9 inches tall, who weighed about 212 pounds. The high school football coach found that both girls qualified for the team and had allowed them to play in practice sessions. A rule of the Washington Interscholastic Activities Association prevented them from playing in competition games. The Washington Supreme Court concluded that the WIAA rule violated the Equal Rights Amendment, based on the following reasoning:

> Boys as well as girls run the risk of physical injury in contact football games. The risk of injury to "the average boy" is not used as a reason for denying boys the opportunity to play on the team in interscholastic competition. Moreover, the fact that some boys cannot meet the team requirements is not used as a basis of disqualifying those boys that do meet such requirements. Instead, WIAA expressly permitted small, slightly built young boys, prone to injury, to play football without proper training to prevent injury.

* * *

> Findings Nos. 9 and 10 dealing with the possible disruption of the girls' athletic programs if girls are permitted to play on boys contact football teams in interscholastic competition is based on opinion testimony necessarily conjectural in character as to what might happen. There is no such evidence based on experience of Wishkah Valley High School because that school has never had any girls contact football team. Finding No. 8. Furthermore, the possibility of disruption has not prevented WIAA from approving boy-girl participation in noncontact sports.

* * *

> In sum, the WIAA rule discriminating against girls on account of their sex violates Const. art. 31, if not the Equal Protection Clause of the Fourteenth Amendment, Const. art. 1, § 12 and Const. art. 9, § 1. No compelling state interest requires a holding to the contrary. The overriding compelling state interest as adopted by the people of this state in 1972 is that: "Equality of rights and responsibility under the law shall not be denied or abridged on account of sex." See also RCW 49.60.010 and .030. We agree with the rationale of Commonwealth v. Pennsylvania Interscholastic Athletic Ass'n, supra, that under our ERA discrimination on account of sex is forbidden. The WIAA rule forbidding qualified girls from playing on the high school

football team in interscholastic competition cannot be used to deny the Darrin girls, and girls like them, the right to participate as members of that team. This is all the more so when the school provides no corresponding girls' football team on which girls may participate as players.

Id., 85 Wash.2d at 876–78, 540 P.2d at 892–93. How would the Washington Supreme Court have decided *Clark?* See also Croteau v. Fair, 686 F.Supp. 552 (E.D.Va.1988), dismissing Nancy Croteau's claim that she was not allowed to play on the varsity baseball team after passing the first cut because of her sex. Judge Ellis was not persuaded that Nancy was eliminated because of her sex: "[r]ather, the Court is convinced that plaintiff received a fair tryout and that the decision to cut her was made in good faith and for reasons unrelated to gender." The judge pointed out that plaintiff had no constitutional or statutory right to play baseball, only a right "to compete for such a position on equal terms and to be free from sex discrimination in state action." Did Nancy Croteau compete on equal terms?

3. A more recent examination of the cases decided under state equal rights amendments in Washington and Pennsylvania concludes that either "separate but equal" teams—if they can be made truly "equal"—or mixed teams is consistent with the equality principle. But Susan Jewett rejects the result obtained by combining the approaches in *Clark* and *Lantz:*

> One alternative would be to require that girls be allowed to compete for positions on the boys' teams but not vice-versa. * * * A one-way protection means that the policy of the Amendment is such that affirmative action to protect the oppressed group is a valid state interest, justifying classification by sex.

> The legality of affirmative action preferences has not yet been decided, but if they are permissible, it is only as temporary measures to achieve actual equality. In this situation, it does not seem that this "preference" is going to bring about actual equality, and it may in fact increase the problems of women who remain on female teams. * * * [U]nder a system where successful female athletes are allowed to compete on the men's team, the women's team will be drained of its best talent, and the remaining team will be of even poorer quality than that of current women's teams. The image of the athletes on these teams will be even worse than that of current women athletes, and the benefit of this less than second class status is doubtful, even where the alternative is no interscholastic competition for some women.

> To provide women with special teams may give them some opportunity to compete that they would not otherwise have, but to do so is to treat the effect of discrimination in a way which will continue the cause of the discrimination.
> * * *

Jewett, The Equal Rights Amendment and Athletics, 1 Harv.Wom.L.J. 53, 71–72 (1978). She is also critical of the combined-team approach:

> Another alternative that has been suggested is a system where the school "team" is made up of components, one male and one female, and the success of the "team" depends on the combined success of the components in each competition. Again, in the important area of the intangible quality of the athletic experience, it seems unlikely that this system would overcome the "stigma" which women's sports carries. Although it would be important to have a good girls' team, it would undoubtedly still be considered a team of secondary importance in terms of prestige and seriousness. In addition, it is

unlikely that many schools could afford to have such teams in more than a few sports.

Jewett, id., at 73.

Professor Karen Tokarz also rejects the "separate but equal" approach to educational athletic programs. Her thesis is that:

> [S]egregation in educational sports programs, based on average or stereotyped physical sex differences, is constitutionally impermissible under the equal protection clause. Without the separate but equal doctrine as its foundation, sex segregation in educational sports programs cannot survive the intermediate standard of review for sex-based classifications. Students, male and female, must be provided with the opportunity to compete in educational sports on the basis of their individual athletic abilities.

Tokarz, Separate But Unequal Educational Sports Programs: The Need for a New Theory of Equality, 1 Berkeley Wom.L.J. 201, 205–06 (1985). Tokarz goes on to analyze the asserted governmental interests supporting, and the challengers' interests opposing, sex segregation in educational sports programs.

4. How would you decide a complaint by a female high school basketball player who plays as a "guard" in one of the few states where girls play under "half-court" rules that she is disadvantaged because of her sex in competing for college athletic scholarships awarded most frequently to women with "full court" experience? The boys' team plays under full court rules; but plaintiff doesn't want to play on the boys' team: she just wants the girls' team to play under the boys' rules. The cases are in conflict. In Cape v. Tennessee Secondary Sch. Athletic Ass'n, 563 F.2d 793 (6th Cir.1977), the court held that half-court rules for girls enforced by public school officials did not violate equal protection. Although it found that the different rules for boys' and girls' teams were legitimately based on "distinct differences in physical characteristics and capabilities between the sexes," the court noted that the plaintiff did not complain of "the most apparent sex-based classification in [the] case," the "[e]ntirely separate basketball leagues for males and females." Id., 563 F.2d at 795. Accord, Jones v. Oklahoma Secondary Sch. Activities Ass'n., 453 F.Supp. 150 (W.D.Okl.1977).

The opposite result was reached in Dodson v. Arkansas Activities Ass'n, 468 F.Supp. 394 (E.D.Ark.1979), noted 65 Iowa L.Rev. 766 (1980). Applying the equal protection standard first announced in Craig v. Boren, set forth at p. ___, supra, the Dodson court concluded that no "important governmental objective" had been shown to justify the difference in treatment: the defendant had merely suggested that the girls' game had traditionally been played under half-court rules, and it had continued the tradition. The court commented, "[s]imply doing things the way they've always been done is not an 'important governmental objective,' if indeed it is a legitimate objective at all." Id., 468 F.Supp. at 398. How would these cases be decided under an equal rights provision? If separate teams are permissible, does the use of different rules make them unequal?

5. Is a "separate but equal" approach permissible in Olympic competition? How should a court respond to a suit brought by women runners and runners' organizations seeking to compel the addition of two events, a 5,000 meter and 10,000 meter track event, to the program of the 1984 Summer Olympic Games? The district court denied their motion for a preliminary injunction, and the Ninth Circuit affirmed. See Martin v. International Olympic Committee, 740 F.2d 670 (9th Cir.1984). The suit was based on state and federal law. The Ninth Circuit

majority found itself uncomfortable with the argument based on West's Ann.Cal. Civ.Code § 51 (the so-called "Unruh Civil Rights Act"):

> [W]e have difficulty with the theory advanced by the women runners. The women runners clearly are not seeking an opportunity to compete against men in the existing men's 5,000 meter and 10,000 meter races. Thus, they do not attempt to invoke the Act as a means of removing arbitrary barriers to their use or enjoyment of existing "accommodations, advantages, facilities, privileges or services." Yet a challenge to the total exclusion of women from these races would appear to be the most logical application of the Act. Instead, the women runners claim that the Act requires the creation of new competitive opportunities for them, through the use of this court's equitable powers, to remedy the allegedly unequal results that have obtained under, as we hold below, the facially neutral test of rule 32 [which establishes procedures for determining what events will be included in each sport—Ed.]. We express no view on whether the Act would apply to a direct challenge to the men's events. We do conclude that it may not be used as argued by the women runners. We simply do not read the Act to compel the creation of separate but equal events for women.

Id., at 676. Do you agree with this reasoning? Why do you suppose the women did not seek admission to the men's events?

6. Where do commercial sports fit into this analysis? Would a Title VII suit lie against, say, the San Francisco 49ers, or the New York Yankees, to compel either team to hire a qualified female football or baseball player? If the changes in educational sports programs at the grammar school and high school level discussed here eventually help to produce competitive female athletes, is such a Title VII suit a likely possibility? See generally, Karen Tokarz, Women, Sports, and the Law: A Comprehensive Research Guide to Sex Discrimination in Sports (1986).

B. TITLE IX OF THE EDUCATION AMENDMENTS OF 1972

[Selections from Title IX appear in the Statutory Appendix.]

Text Note
Overview of Title IX

Legal tools available for combatting sex discrimination in education include the same familiar ones we have encountered in earlier Chapters: constitutional challenge; statutory attack; and, because of the heavy infusion of federal money into education, Executive Order 11246. As we have already seen, Title VII applies to employment discrimination by educational institutions.[1] In 1972, Congress added a new and potentially powerful tool. Title IX of the Education Amendments of 1972 explicitly prohibits sex discrimination in admissions, educational programs and educational activities of institutions receiving federal financial assistance.[2] Title IX has also been interpreted to prohibit sex discrimination in employment by such institutions.[3]

---

1. See Text Note on Proving Discrimination: Title VII in Academe, at p. 871, supra.
2. The text of Title IX appears at pp. 1250, infra.

3. North Haven Board of Education v. Bell, 456 U.S. 512, 102 S.Ct. 1912, 72 L.Ed.2d 299 (1982), discussed at p. 1075, infra.

Title IX applies to all educational institutions that receive federal funding. As Margaret Dunkle and Bernice Sandler[4] note,

> [t]his includes all schools: kindergartens, preschools, elementary and secondary schools, vocational schools, junior and community colleges, four-year colleges, universities and graduate and professional schools.

Only two types of institutions have been given blanket exemptions from Title IX: schools controlled by religious organizations, if the application of the statute "would not be consistent with the religious tenets of such organization",[5] and military schools whose "primary purpose is the training of individuals for the military services of the United States, or the merchant marine."[6] In addition, certain types of institutions are exempt from the requirement of non-discrimination in admissions policies. These include private undergraduate institutions; single-sex public undergraduate institutions; and preschools and elementary and secondary schools (but not vocational schools).[7] What is the rationale for these exceptions?

As applied to public institutions, of course, these exceptions can be tested under the Constitution. In Mississippi University for Women v. Hogan,[8] the University relied on § 901(a)(5), which exempts from the admissions requirement "any public institution of undergraduate higher education which is an institution that traditionally and continually from its establishment has had a policy of admitting only students of one sex". This exception, argued MUW, expressly "permits the institution to exist as it has in the past." Justice O'Connor made short shrift of this argument:[9]

> The argument is based upon the language of § 901(a) in Title IX of the Education Amendments of 1972, 20 U.S.C. § 1681(a). Although § 901(a) prohibits gender discrimination in education programs that receive federal financial assistance, subsection 5 exempts the admissions policies of undergraduate institutions "that traditionally and continually from [their] establishment [have] had a policy of admitting only students of one sex" from the general prohibition. See n. 5, supra. Arguing that Congress enacted Title IX in furtherance of its power to enforce the Fourteenth Amendment, a power granted by § 5 of that Amendment, the State would have us conclude that § 901(a)(5) is but "a congressional limitation upon the broad prohibitions of the Equal Protection Clause of the Fourteenth Amendment."

> The argument requires little comment. Initially, it is far from clear that Congress intended, through § 901(a)(5), to exempt MUW from any constitutional obligation. Rather, Congress apparently intended, at most, to exempt MUW from the requirements of Title IX.

> Even if Congress envisioned a constitutional exemption, the State's argument would fail. Section 5 of the Fourteenth Amendment gives Congress

4. Dunkle & Sandler, Sex Discrimination Against Students: Implications of Title IX of the Education Amendments of 1972, 18 Inequality in Education 12, 14 (1974).

5. Pub.L. No. 92–318, Title IX, § 901(a)(3), 86 Stat. 373 (June 23, 1972).

6. Id., § 901(a)(4).

7. Id., § 901(a)(1); § 901(a)(5).

8. 458 U.S. 718, 102 S.Ct. 3331, 73 L.Ed.2d 1090 (1982), set out at p. ___, supra.

9. Id., 458 U.S. at 732–33, 102 S.Ct. at 3340–41, 73 L.Ed.2d at 1103–04. Does this reasoning undercut the arguments of the antiabortionists who urge that Congressional enactment of a "Human Life Bill" affirming that human life begins at conception would be proper under § 5 of the Fourteenth Amendment, and that such Congressional action should prompt the Supreme Court to reconsider its holding in Roe v. Wade, 410 U.S. 113, 93 S.Ct. 705, 35 L.Ed.2d 147 (1973)(set out at p. 414, supra)? Or is this reasoning limited to Title IX?

broad power indeed to enforce the command of the Amendment and "to secure to all persons the enjoyment of perfect equality of civil rights and the equal protection of the laws against State denial or invasion. * * *" Ex parte Virginia, 100 U.S. (10 Otto) 339, 346, 25 L.Ed. 676 (1879). Congress' power under § 5, however, "is limited to adopting measures to enforce the guarantees of the Amendment; § 5 grants Congress no power to restrict, abrogate, or dilute these guarantees." Katzenbach v. Morgan, 384 U.S. 641, 651 n. 10, 86 S.Ct. 1717, 1724 n. 10, 16 L.Ed.2d 828 (1966). Although we give deference to congressional decisions and classifications, neither Congress nor a State can validate a law that denies the rights guaranteed by the Fourteenth Amendment. See, e.g., Califano v. Goldfarb, 430 U.S. 199 at 210, 97 S.Ct. 1021 at 1028, 51 L.Ed.2d 270; Williams v. Rhodes, 393 U.S. 23, 29, 89 S.Ct. 5, 9, 21 L.Ed.2d 24 (1968).

The fact that the language of § 901(a)(5) applies to MUW provides the State no solace: "[A] statute apparently governing a dispute cannot be applied by judges, consistently with their obligations under the Supremacy Clause, when such an application of the statute would conflict with the Constitution. Marbury v. Madison, 1 Cranch 137 [2 L.Ed. 60] (1803)." Younger v. Harris, 401 U.S. 37, 52, 91 S.Ct. 746, 754, 27 L.Ed.2d 669 (1971).

To these exclusions, which were contained in the original version of Title IX, Congress added others by subsequent amendment. In 1974,[10] the membership practices of social sororities and fraternities were excluded as were those of such organizations as the YWCA, YMCA, Girl Scouts, Boy Scouts, Camp Fire Girls, and other "voluntary youth service organizations." In 1976,[11] such traditional events as Boys State, Girls State, Boys Nation and Girls Nation were exempted from coverage as were practices such as mother-daughter and father-son events. The awarding of scholarships as prizes in beauty pageants was also the subject of special exception.[12] Do these exceptions seriously weaken the effect of Title IX in eliminating sex discrimination in education? As applied to public institutions, are they constitutional?[13]

Title IX's application to athletics has been perhaps the most controversial aspect of its coverage. The legislative history surrounding enactment of Title IX contains practically no mention of athletic programs. Senator Birch Bayh, the principal sponsor of the legislation, commented briefly while discussing the scope of the Act, that "[w]e are not requiring that intercollegiate football be desegregated."[14] The 1975 regulations included "interscholastic, intercollegiate, club or intramural athletics offered by a recipient", as being within Title IX's coverage, but separate teams for men and women are expressly permitted "where selection for such teams is based upon competitive skill or the activity involved is a contact sport." Contact sports are defined to include "boxing, wrestling, rugby, ice hockey, football, basketball, and other sports the purpose or major activity of which involves bodily contact."[15] That section also provides that "where a recipient operates or sponsors a team in a particular sport for members of one sex but operates or sponsors no such team for members of the other sex, and athletic

---

10. Pub.L. No. 93–568, § 3(a), adding subsection (6), 88 Stat. 1862 (Dec. 31, 1974).

11. Pub.L. No. 94–482, Title IV, § 412(a), adding subsections (7), (8) and (9), 90 Stat. 2234 (Oct. 12, 1976).

12. Ibid.

13. See generally, Daniel L. Schwartz, Comment, Sex Discrimination on Campus: A Critical Examination of Single–Sex College Social Organizations, 75 Calif.L.Rev. 2117 (1987).

14. 117 Cong.Rec. 30407 (1971). See generally, Note, Title IX and Intercollegiate Athletics: HEW Gets Serious About Equality in Sports? 15 New England L.Rev. 573 (1980).

15. 45 C.F.R. § 86.41(b).

opportunities for members of that sex have previously been limited, members of the excluded sex must be allowed to try-out for the team offered unless the sport involved is a contact sport." Is this proviso limited to girls excluded from boys' teams?[16]

The really controversial aspect of the 1975 regulations, however, concerned funding and proportionate participation. Section 86.41(c) provides that "[u]nequal aggregate expenditures for members of each sex or unequal expenditures for male and female teams if a recipient operates or sponsors separate teams will not constitute non-compliance with this section, but the Director may consider the failure to provide necessary funds for teams for one sex in assessing equality of opportunity for members of each sex." HEW has issued two sets of policy interpretations to help resolve ambiguities and respond to criticisms of this provision. The 1978 proposed policy interpretation required that "[s]ubstantially equal average per capita funds [be] allocated to participating male and female athletes" in three areas: scholarships; recruitment; and "[a]ll other readily financially measurable benefits and opportunities."[17] After receiving substantial criticism of this interpretation, HEW revised it substantially before promulgating the policy interpretation in its final form.[18] Only in the provision of scholarship aid is funding required to be substantially proportional to the number of male and female athletes in the recipient's program. Elsewhere, "equivalent treatment" is the rule of thumb. In 1979, the then newly-created Department of Education took over Title IX enforcement, adopting as its own the 1975 HEW Title IX regulations and policy interpretations.[19] See subsection on Title IX and College Athletics, p. 1092, infra, for discussion of the expanding litigation over the meaning of equal opportunity for women in sports.

The remaining coverage of Title IX is impressively broad. It is said to include such diverse topics as recruitment of students; admission to programs; financial aid; rules governing dress codes,[20] curfews, and the participation of unwed mothers in extracurricular activities; housing rules and facilities; graduation requirements; physical education and athletics; health care and insurance; employment opportunities; extracurricular activities; textbooks and curricula; counseling of students; single-sex courses and programs; vocational education programs; women's studies and women's centers; flexible programs; continuing education programs; and child care facilities.[21]

Not all of these topics, however, were included in the 1975 regulations to Title IX. A notable exception is the failure of the regulations to cover school textbooks or curricular materials,[22] ostensibly for fear of encountering first amendment

---

16. See Petrie v. Illinois High School Ass'n, 75 Ill.App.3d 980, 31 Ill.Dec. 653, 394 N.E.2d 855 (1979) discussed at p. 1066, supra.

17. 43 Fed.Reg. 58070, 58072 (Dec. 11, 1978).

18. See 44 Fed.Reg. 71413–71423 (December 11, 1979).

19. See generally Ann M. Seha, The Administrative Enforcement of Title IX in Intercollegiate Athletics, 2 Law & Inequality 121 (1984)(examining in detail the enforcement efforts of the Department of Education's Office of Civil Rights in the area of intercollegiate athletic programs).

20. The Secretary of Education revoked § 106.31(b)(5) of the Title IX Regulations,

which had prohibited discrimination in the application of dress codes. See 47 Federal Register 32526 (July 28, 1982). In explaining its action, the Department stated that it agreed with those commentators who believed that appearance codes should be left to local determination. Opponents had objected that dress codes could encourage restrictive stereotyped roles for male and female students and might foster an atmosphere unconducive to equal educational opportunity. Which of these positions do you prefer?

21. Margaret C. Dunkle & Bernice Sandler, supra note 1, at 15–29.

22. 45 C.F.R. § 86.42 provides: "[n]othing in this regulation shall be interpreted as requiring or prohibiting or abridging in any way

problems.[23] Yet many believe that the most troubling problems of sex stereotyping lie precisely in this area. Traditional attitudes concerning appropriate sex roles are mirrored in courses of study, textbooks and counseling in school systems throughout the country.[24] Despite the many reports and recommendations made in the 1970s to eliminate sex-based stereotypes in education,[25] problems persist. In its 1992 report on girls in school,[26] the AAUW Educational Foundation cited a 1989 study of high school English courses, finding that among the ten books assigned most frequently, only one was written by a woman, and none by a person of color.[27] Using studies from 1963 and 1907 as a base line, the authors concluded there had been little change in the mix of readings from similar lists 25 or 80 years ago.[28] What legal measures, if any, would you consider appropriate in working toward solution of these problems?

The question whether a private cause of action exists under Title IX was resolved affirmatively in Cannon v. University of Chicago.[29] The decision left many other questions unanswered, including the relevant burden of proof and the range of appropriate remedies. Is a distinction between disparate treatment and disparate impact akin to that drawn in Title VII cases likely to develop under Title IX? Or will a showing of intentional discrimination similar to that required under the Equal Protection Clause be necessary? The Court in Cannon recognized that Title IX was patterned after Title VI of the Civil Rights Act of 1964 and that the

the use of particular textbooks or curricular materials."

23. See generally, Carol Amyx, Comment, Sex Discrimination: The Textbook Case, 62 Calif.L.Rev. 1312 (1974)(arguing that the First Amendment does not prevent elimination of sex stereotypes from textbooks).

24. See the AAUW report, How Schools Shortchange Girls, AAUW Educational Foundation (1992)(vocational education, in particular, continues to prepare girls for sex-stereotyped jobs. Id. at 42–44.). See also A Look at Women in Education: Issues and Answers for HEW 2–8 (Report of the Commissioner's Task Force on the Impact of Office of Education Programs on Women, November 1972); Sandra L. Bem & Daryl Bem, Training the Woman to Know Her Place: The Social Antecedents of Women in the World of Work (Pennsylvania Department of Education 1973).

25. The dimensions of the problem were explored in a 1971 report, updated in 1972 and 1973, Let Them Aspire! A Plea and Proposal for Equality of Opportunity for Males and Females in the Ann Arbor (Michigan) Public Schools, prepared by the Committee to Eliminate Sexual Discrimination, Marcia Federbush, Chairwoman. With respect to textbooks, for example, the report identified the following problems:

Elementary mathematics books present sets grouping people in rigidly defined sex roles, for example, all doctors are male, all nurses female. Elementary school readers exhibit similar sex-typed illustrations: all mothers are housewives (many of the children assigned these readers come from homes in which a woman is head of household, and others come from two-earner families); boys

are active, girls are not. History books contain few references to women.

The report proposed the following solutions:

Ask textbook publishers to avoid stereotyping (as they now attempt to do in depicting members of minority groups), and to portray women and girls, as well as men and boys, in a variety of occupational roles and physically active situations. Purchase books in which sex stereotyping has been eliminated and history texts detailing accomplishments of women.

Similar reports proliferated elsewhere. See Memorandum of the Citizens' Advisory Committee on the Status of Women, Need for Studies of Sex Discrimination in Public Schools (1972). A project on non-sexist programs at the pre-school level was launched by the Women's Action Alliance in 1972, encompassing curriculum development and the preparation of equipment, teaching materials and records for use in classrooms and at home. On pre-school book fare, see Weitzman, Eifler, Hokada & Ross, Sex–Role Socialization in Picture Books for Pre–School Children, 77 Am.J.Soc. 1125 (1972). On elementary readers and books for children generally, see Judith Hole & Ellen Levine, Rebirth of Feminism 333–37 (1973).

26. How Schools Shortchange Girls, American Association of University Women (AAUW) Educational Foundation (1992).

27. Id. at 62

28. Id.

29. 441 U.S. 677, 99 S.Ct. 1946, 60 L.Ed.2d 560 (1979). Plaintiff in Cannon alleged that she had been denied admission to defendant's medical school because of her sex.

statutes have much in common.[30] In University of California Board of Regents v. Bakke,[31] five members of the Court concluded that Title VI incorporated the constitutional standard. If that position is adhered to in future cases, will it be extended to Title IX as well?

In the early 1980s, the Supreme Court resolved two questions of Title IX's coverage, but in the process, significantly restricted the reach of the statute. The Court held that Title IX covered the employment practices of educational institutions, but then limited its application to those specific programs receiving federal funds. Thus, in North Haven Board of Education v. Bell,[32] the majority sustained the validity of regulations promulgated by the Department of Education that prohibited federally funded education programs from discriminating on the basis of sex in employment, but in reaching its result, the majority called attention to the "program-specific" nature of Title IX. It concluded that "an agency's authority under Title IX both to promulgate regulations and to terminate funds is subject to the program-specific limitation of §§ 901 and 902."[33] The Court expanded on this point in Grove City College v. Bell,[34] holding that Grove City's enrollment of students who receive Basic Educational Opportunity Grants (BEOG's) was sufficient to subject it to Title IX, even though no other federal funding was accepted by the college as a matter of principle, but limiting Title IX's application to the college's financial aid program. The majority specifically rejected the argument that the college as a whole was the "program" covered by Title IX.[35]

In 1988 Congress enacted, over President Reagan's veto, The Civil Rights Restoration Act of 1987 designed to overrule *Grove City*. The bill provides that Title IX applies to a college, university, or other postsecondary institution, "any part of which is extended Federal financial assistance."[36]

In the 1990s, Title IX has taken on new importance with the Supreme Court's decision in the following case.

1. COVERAGE AND REMEDIES UNDER TITLE IX

FRANKLIN v. GWINNETT COUNTY PUBLIC SCHOOLS

Supreme Court of the United States, 1992.
503 U.S. 60, 112 S.Ct. 1028, 117 L.Ed.2d 208.

JUSTICE WHITE delivered the opinion of the Court.

This case presents the question whether the implied right of action under Title IX of the Education Amendments of 1972, 20 U.S.C. § 1681–1688 (Title IX), which this Court recognized in Cannon v. University of Chicago, 441 U.S. 677 (1979), supports a claim for monetary damages.

---

30. Id., 441 U.S. at 694–703, 99 S.Ct. at 1956–61, 60 L.Ed.2d at 574–79.

31. 438 U.S. 265, 98 S.Ct. 2733, 57 L.Ed.2d 750 (1978)(the five Justices were Powell, Brennan, White, Marshall, and Blackmun).

32. 456 U.S. 512, 102 S.Ct. 1912, 72 L.Ed.2d 299 (1982).

33. 456 U.S., at 538, 102 S.Ct. at 1926, 72 L.Ed.2d at 318.

34. 465 U.S. 555, 104 S.Ct. 1211, 79 L.Ed.2d 516 (1984).

35. Id., 465 U.S. at 570–574, 104 S.Ct. at 1220–1222, 79 L.Ed.2d at 530–32.

36. Pub.L. 100–259, Sec. 3(a)(adding Sec. 908 to Title IX)(March 22, 1988)(set forth at p. 1252, infra). See generally, Barrie L. Brejcha, Note, Grove City College v. Bell: Restricting The Remedial Reach of Title IX, 16 Loyola U. of Chi.L.J. 319 (1985); Andrew S. Love, Note, Undermining Civil Rights Enforcement in Education: Grove City College v. Bell, 19 U.San Francisco L.Rev. 53 (1984).

I

Petitioner Christine Franklin was a student at North Gwinnett High School in Gwinnett County, Georgia, between September 1985 and August 1989. Respondent Gwinnett County School District operates the high school and receives federal funds. According to the complaint filed on December 29, 1988 in the United States District Court for the Northern District of Georgia, Franklin was subjected to continual sexual harassment beginning in the autumn of her tenth grade year (1986) from Andrew Hill, a sports coach and teacher employed by the district. Among other allegations, Franklin avers that Hill engaged her in sexually-oriented conversations in which he asked about her sexual experiences with her boyfriend and whether she would consider having sexual intercourse with an older man, * * * that Hill forcibly kissed her on the mouth in the school parking lot, * * * that he telephoned her at her home and asked if she would meet him socially, * * * and that, on three occasions in her junior year, Hill interrupted a class, requested that the teacher excuse Franklin, and took her to a private office where he subjected her to coercive intercourse. * * * The complaint further alleges that though they became aware of and investigated Hill's sexual harassment of Franklin and other female students, teachers and administrators took no action to halt it and discouraged Franklin from pressing charges against Hill. * * * On April 14, 1988, Hill resigned on the condition that all matters pending against him be dropped. * * * The school thereupon closed its investigation. * * *

In this action,[3] the District Court dismissed the complaint on the ground that Title IX does not authorize an award of damages. The Court of Appeals affirmed. Franklin v. Gwinnett Cty. Public Schools, 911 F.2d 617 (C.A.11 1990). The court noted that analysis of Title IX and Title VI of the Civil Rights Act of 1964, 42 USC § 2000d et seq. (Title VI), has developed along similar lines. Citing as binding precedent Drayden v. Needville Independent School Dist., 642 F.2d 129 (C.A.5 1981), a decision rendered prior to the division of the Fifth Circuit, the court concluded that Title VI did not support a claim for monetary damages. * * * As a second basis for its holding that monetary damages were unavailable, the court reasoned that Title IX was enacted under Congress' Spending Clause powers and that "[u]nder such statutes, relief may frequently be limited to that which is equitable in nature, with the recipient of federal funds thus retaining the option of terminating such receipt in order to rid itself of an injunction." Franklin, 911 F.2d, at 621.[4]

Because this opinion conflicts with a decision of the Court of Appeals for the Third Circuit, see Pfeiffer v. Marion Center Area School Dist., 917 F.2d 779, 787–789 (1990), we granted certiorari, 501 U.S. __ (1991). We reverse.

---

3. Prior to bringing this lawsuit, Franklin filed a complaint with the Office of Civil Rights of the United States Department of Education (OCR) in August 1988. After investigating these charges for several months, OCR concluded that the school district had violated Franklin's rights by subjecting her to physical and verbal sexual harassment and by interfering with her right to complain about conduct proscribed by Title IX. OCR determined, however, that because of the resignations of Hill and respondent William Prescott and the implementation of a school grievance procedure, the district had come into compliance with Title IX. It then terminated its investigation. First Amended Complaint, Exh. A, pp. 7–9.

4. The court also rejected an argument by Franklin that the terms of outright prohibition of Title VII, 42 USC §§ 2000e to 2000e–17, apply by analogy to Title IX's antidiscriminatory provision, and that the remedies available under the two statutes should also be the same. Franklin, 911 F.2d, at 622. Because Franklin does not pursue this contention here, we need not address whether it has merit.

II

In Cannon v. University of Chicago, 441 U.S. 677 (1979), the Court held that Title IX is enforceable through an implied right of action. We have no occasion here to reconsider that decision. Rather, in this case we must decide what remedies are available in a suit brought pursuant to this implied right. As we have often stated, the question of what remedies are available under a statute that provides a private right of action is "analytically distinct" from the issue of whether such a right exists in the first place. Davis v. Passman, 442 U.S. 228, 239 (1979). Thus, although we examine the text and history of a statute to determine whether Congress intended to create a right of action, Touche Ross & Co. v. Redington, 442 U.S. 560, 575–576 (1979), we presume the availability of all appropriate remedies unless Congress has expressly indicated otherwise. *Davis, supra,* at 246–247. This principle has deep roots in our jurisprudence.

A

"[W]here legal rights have been invaded, and a federal statute provides for a general right to sue for such invasion, federal courts may use any available remedy to make good the wrong done." Bell v. Hood, 327 U.S. 678, 684 (1946). The Court explained this longstanding rule as jurisdictional, and upheld the exercise of the federal courts' power to award appropriate relief so long as a cause of action existed under the Constitution or laws of the United States. *Ibid.*

* * *

B

Respondents and the United States as *amicus curiae,* however, maintain that whatever the traditional presumption may have been when the Court decided *Bell v. Hood,* it has disappeared in succeeding decades. We do not agree. In J.I. Case Co. v. Borak, 377 U.S. 426 (1964), the Court adhered to the general rule that all appropriate relief is available in an action brought to vindicate a federal right when Congress has given no indication of its purpose with respect to remedies. Relying on *Bell v. Hood,* the *Borak* Court specifically rejected an argument that a court's remedial power to redress violations of the Securities Exchange Act of 1934 was limited to a declaratory judgment.
* * *

The United States contends that the traditional presumption in favor of all appropriate relief was abandoned by the Court in Davis v. Passman, 442 U.S. 228 (1979), and that the *Bell v. Hood* rule was limited to actions claiming constitutional violations. The United States quotes language in *Davis* to the effect that "the question of who may enforce a *statutory* right is fundamentally different from the question of who may enforce a right that is protected by the Constitution." *Davis,* 442 U.S., at 241. The Government's position, however, mirrors the very misunderstanding over the difference between a cause of action and the relief afforded under it that sparked the confusion we attempted to clarify in *Davis.* Whether Congress may limit the class of persons who have a right of action under Title IX is irrelevant to the issue in this lawsuit. To reiterate, "the question whether a litigant has a 'cause of action' is analytically distinct and prior to the question of what relief, if any, a litigant may be entitled to receive." *Id.,* at 239. *Davis,* therefore, did nothing to interrupt the long line of cases in which the Court has held that if a right of action exists to enforce a federal right and Congress is silent on the question of remedies, a federal court may order any appropriate relief. * * *

* * *

The general rule, therefore, is that absent clear direction to the contrary by Congress, the federal courts have the power to award any appropriate relief in a cognizable cause of action brought pursuant to a federal statute.

III

We now address whether Congress intended to limit application of this general principle in the enforcement of Title IX. See Bush v. Lucas, 462 U.S. 367, 378 (1983); Wyandotte Transp. Co. v. United States, 389 U.S. 191, 200 (1967). Because the cause of action was inferred by the Court in *Cannon,* the usual recourse to statutory text and legislative history in the period prior to that decision necessarily will not enlighten our analysis. Respondents and the United States fundamentally misunderstand the nature of the inquiry, therefore, by needlessly dedicating large portions of their briefs to discussions of how the text and legislative intent behind Title IX are "silent" on the issue of available remedies. Since the Court in *Cannon* concluded that this statute supported no express right of action, it is hardly surprising that Congress also said nothing about the applicable remedies for an implied right of action.

During the period prior to the decision in *Cannon,* the inquiry in any event is *not* "'basically a matter of statutory construction,' "as the United States asserts. Brief for United States as *Amicus Curiae* 8 (quoting Transamerica Mortgage Advisors, Inc. v. Lewis, 444 U.S. 11, 15 (1979)). Rather, in determining Congress's intent to limit application of the traditional presumption in favor of all appropriate relief, we evaluate the state of the law when the legislature passed Title IX. Cf. Merrill Lynch, Pierce, Fenner & Smith, Inc. v. Curran, 456 U.S. 353, 378 (1982). In the years before and after Congress enacted this statute, the Court "follow[ed] a common-law tradition [and] regarded the denial of a remedy as the exception rather than the rule." *Id.,* at 375 (footnote omitted). As we outlined in Part II, this has been the prevailing presumption in our federal courts since at least the early nineteenth century. In *Cannon,* the majority upheld an implied right of action in part because in the decade immediately preceding enactment of Title IX in 1972, this Court had found implied rights of action in six cases. In three of those cases, the Court had approved a damages remedy. See, *e.g.,* J.I. Case Co., 377 U.S., at 433, Wyandotte Transp. Co., *supra,* at 207; Sullivan v. Little Hunting Park, Inc., 396 U.S. 229 (1969). Wholly apart from the wisdom of the *Cannon* holding, therefore, the same contextual approach used to justify an implied right of action more than amply demonstrates the lack of any legislative intent to abandon the traditional presumption in favor of all available remedies.

In the years *after* the announcement of *Cannon,* on the other hand, a more traditional method of statutory analysis is possible, because Congress was legislating with full cognizance of that decision. Our reading of the two amendments to Title IX enacted after *Cannon* leads us to conclude that Congress did not intend to limit the remedies available in a suit brought under Title IX. In the Civil Rights Remedies Equalization Amendment of

1986, 42 U.S.C. § 2000d–7, Congress abrogated the States' Eleventh Amendment immunity under Title IX, Title VI, § 504 of the Rehabilitation Act of 1973, and the Age Discrimination Act of 1975. This statute cannot be read except as a validation of *Cannon's* holding. A subsection of the 1986 law provides that in a suit against a State, "remedies (including remedies both at law and in equity) are available for such a violation to the same extent as such remedies are available for such a violation in the suit against any public or private entity other than a State." 42 U.S.C. § 2000d–7(a)(2). While it is true that this savings clause says nothing about the nature of those other available remedies, cf. Milwaukee v. Illinois, 451 U.S. 304, 329, n. 22 (1981), absent any contrary indication in the text or history of the statute, we presume Congress enacted this statute with the prevailing traditional rule in mind.

In addition to the Civil Rights Remedies Equalization Amendment of 1986, Congress also enacted the Civil Rights Restoration Act of 1987, Pub.L. 100–259, 102 Stat. 28 (1988). Without in any way altering the existing rights of action and the corresponding remedies permissible under Title IX, Title VI, § 504 of the Rehabilitation Act, and the Age Discrimination Act, Congress broadened the coverage of these antidiscrimination provisions in this legislation. In seeking to correct what it considered to be an unacceptable decision on our part in Grove City College v. Bell, 465 U.S. 555 (1984), Congress made no effort to restrict the right of action recognized in *Cannon* and ratified in the 1986 Act or to alter the traditional presumption in favor of any appropriate relief for violation of a federal right. We cannot say, therefore, that Congress has limited the remedies available to a complainant in a suit brought under Title IX.

IV

Respondents and the United States nevertheless suggest three reasons why we should not apply the traditional presumption in favor of appropriate relief in this case.

A

First, respondents argue that an award of damages violates separation of powers principles because it unduly expands the federal courts' power into a sphere properly reserved to the Executive and Legislative Branches. Brief for Respondents 22–25. In making this argument, respondents misconceive the difference between a cause of action and a remedy. Unlike the finding of a cause of action, which authorizes a court to hear a case or controversy, the discretion to award appropriate relief involves no such increase in judicial power. * * *

B

Next, consistent with the Court of Appeals's reasoning, respondents and the United States contend that the normal presumption in favor of all appropriate remedies should not apply because Title IX was enacted pursuant to Congress's Spending Clause power. In Pennhurst State School and Hospital v. Halderman, 451 U.S. 1, 28–29 (1981), the Court observed that remedies were limited under such Spending Clause statutes when the alleged violation was *unintentional*. Respondents and the United States maintain that this presumption should apply equally to *intentional* violations. We disagree.

The point of not permitting monetary damages for an unintentional violation is that the receiving entity of federal funds lacks notice that it will be liable for a monetary award. See *id.* at 17. This notice problem does not arise in a case such as this, in which intentional discrimination is alleged. Unquestionably, Title IX placed on the Gwinnett County Schools the duty not to discriminate on the basis of sex, and "when a supervisor sexually harasses a subordinate because of the subordinate's sex, that supervisor 'discriminate[s]' on the basis of sex." Meritor Savings Bank, FSB v. Vinson, 477 U.S. 57, 64 (1986). We believe the same rule should apply when a teacher sexually harasses and abuses a student. Congress surely did not intend for federal monies to be expended to support the intentional actions it sought by statute to proscribe. Moreover, the notion that Spending Clause statutes do not authorize monetary awards for intentional violations is belied by our unanimous holding in *Darrone*. See 465 U.S., at 628. Respondents and the United States characterize the backpay remedy in *Darrone* as equitable relief, but this description is irrelevant to their underlying objection: that application of the traditional rule in this case will require state entities to pay monetary awards out of their treasuries for intentional violations of federal statutes.[8]

C

Finally, the United States asserts that the remedies permissible under Title IX should nevertheless be limited to backpay and prospective relief. In addition to diverging from our traditional approach to deciding what remedies are available for violation of a federal right, this position conflicts with sound logic. First, both remedies are equitable in nature, and it is axiomatic that a court should determine the adequacy of a remedy in law before resorting to equitable relief. * * * Moreover, in this case the equitable remedies suggested by respondent and the Federal Government are clearly inadequate. Backpay does nothing for petitioner, because she was a student when the alleged discrimination occurred. Similarly, because Hill—the person she claims subjected her to sexual harassment—no longer teaches at the school and she herself no longer attends a school in the Gwinnett system, prospective relief accords her no remedy at all. The government's answer that administrative action helps other similarly-situated students in effect acknowledges that its approach would leave petitioner remediless.

V

In sum, we conclude that a damages remedy is available for an action brought to enforce Title IX. The judgment of the Court of Appeals, therefore, is reversed and the case is remanded for further proceedings consistent with this opinion.

So ordered.

JUSTICE SCALIA, with whom the CHIEF JUSTICE and JUSTICE THOMAS join, concurring in the judgment.

---

8. Franklin argues that, in any event, Title IX should not be viewed solely as having been enacted under Congress' Spending Clause powers and that it also rests on powers derived from § 5 of the Fourteenth Amendment. See Brief for Petitioner 19, n. 10. Because we conclude that a money damages remedy is available under Title IX for an intentional violation irrespective of the constitutional source of Congress' power to enact the statute, we need not decide which power Congress utilized in enacting Title IX.

The substantive right at issue here is one that Congress did not expressly create, but that this Court found to be "implied." See Cannon v. University of Chicago, 441 U.S. 677 (1979). Quite obviously, the search for what was Congress's *remedial* intent as to a right whose very existence Congress did not expressly acknowledge is unlikely to succeed, * * * it is "hardly surprising," as the Court says, *ibid.,* that the usual sources yield no explicit answer.

The Court finds an implicit answer, however, in the legislators' presumptive awareness of our practice of using "any available remedy" to redress violations of legal rights. Bell v. Hood, 327 U.S. 678, 684 (1946) * * *. This strikes me as question-begging. We can plausibly assume acquiescence in our *Bell v. Hood* presumption when the legislature says nothing about remedy in expressly creating a private right of action; perhaps even when it says nothing about remedy in creating a private right of action by clear textual implication; but not, I think, when it says nothing about remedy in a statute in which the courts divine a private right of action on the basis of "contextual" evidence such as that in *Cannon,* which charged Congress with knowledge of a court of appeals' creation of a cause of action under a similarly worded statute. See *Cannon, supra,* at 696–698. Whatever one thinks of the validity of the last approach, it surely rests on attributed rather than actual congressional knowledge. It does not demonstrate an explicit legislative decision to create a cause of action, and so could not be expected to be accompanied by a legislative decision to alter the application of *Bell v. Hood.* Given the nature of *Cannon* and some of our earlier "implied right of action" cases, what the Court's analytical construct comes down to is this: Unless Congress expressly legislates a more limited remedial policy with respect to rights of action it does not know it is creating, it intends the full gamut of remedies to be applied.

In my view, when rights of action are judicially "implied," categorical limitations upon their remedial scope may be judicially implied as well. Cf. Cort v. Ash, 422 U.S. 66, 84–85. Although we have abandoned the expansive rights-creating approach exemplified by *Cannon,* see Touche Ross & Co. v. Redington, 442 U.S. 560, 575–576 (1979); Transamerica Mortgage Advisors, Inc. v. Lewis, 444 U.S. 11, 18, 23–24 (1979)—and perhaps ought to abandon the notion of implied causes of action entirely, see Thompson v. Thompson, 484 U.S. 174, 191 (1988)(Scalia, J., concurring in judgment)—causes of action that came into existence under the *ancien regime* should be limited by the same logic that gave them birth. To require, with respect to a right that is not consciously and intentionally created, that any limitation of remedies must be express, is to provide, in effect, that the most questionable of private rights will also be the most expansively remediable. As the United States puts it, "[w]hatever the merits of 'implying' rights of action may be, there is no justification for treating [congressional] silence as the equivalent of the broadest imaginable grant of remedial authority." Brief for United States as *Amicus Curiae* 12–13.

I nonetheless agree with the Court's disposition of this case. Because of legislation enacted subsequent to *Cannon,* it is too late in the day to address whether a judicially implied exclusion of damages under Title IX would be appropriate. The Civil Rights Remedies Equalization Amendment of 1986, 42 U.S.C. § 2000d–7(a)(2), must be read, in my view, not only "as a validation of *Cannon's* holding," *ante,* at 11, but also as an implicit acknowledgment that damages are available. See 42 U.S.C. § 2000d–7(a)(1)(withdrawing the States' Eleventh Amendment immunity); § 2000d–7(a)(2)(providing that, in suits against States, "remedies (including remedies both at law and in equity) are available for [violations of Title IX] to the same extent as such remedies are available for such a violation in the suit against any public or private entity other than a State"). I therefore concur in the judgment.

Notes on Franklin

1. The Civil Rights Act of 1991 authorized compensatory and punitive damages in Title VII cases, but imposed a cap on recovery for "complaining parties" not covered by 42 U.S.C.A. § 1981: that is, white women. See section on Title VII Remedies, p. 883, supra. Since Title IX also covers employment discrimination in academic institutions per North Haven Board of Education v. Bell, 456 U.S. 512, 102 S.Ct. 1912, 72 L.Ed.2d 299 (1982), will *Franklin* give a better deal to white women who work in academic institutions than is available to other white women plaintiffs who complain of discrimination against their employers?

2. Academic women employees claiming sexual harassment have heretofore commonly used Title VII and/or Section 1983 as the basis for their claims. See, e.g., King v. Board of Regents of University of Wisconsin System, 898 F.2d 533 (7th Cir.1990)(upholding plaintiff Katherine King's jury verdict on her claim of sexual harassment by a fellow professor, Stephen A. Sonstein, who repeatedly verbally assaulted her, fondled her, and on one occasion physically attacked her; his defense against the § 1983 claim—that his conduct was not sex-based because it was directed toward King as a person to whom he was sexually attracted, not as a woman—was laughed out of court on appeal; he did not bother to defend the Title VII claim); Jew v. University of Iowa, 749 F.Supp. 946 (S.D.Iowa 1990)(false rumors that Dr. Jean Jew had been treated favorably because she had engaged in a sexual affair with her department head created a hostile work environment for Title VII purposes that had adversely affected a term of her employment, namely her promotion from associate professor to full professor; she won promotion to full professor and back pay); see also Austen v. State of Hawaii, 759 F.Supp. 612 (D.Hawai'i 1991)(plaintiff Kay Austen, described as "an active promoter of women's rights" proved a claim under Title VII for harassment, discrimination, and retaliation; the court applied the "reasonable woman" standard announced in Ellison v. Brady, 924 F.2d 872 (9th Cir.1991), discussed at p. 827, supra). After *Franklin,* would you advise plaintiffs like these to add a count under Title IX to their existing claims under Title VII and/or § 1983?

3. Is it possible for an academic employer to argue convincingly that *Franklin* is limited to claims of sexual harassment by students and that the holding does not extend to claims of employment discrimination?

4. Will *Franklin* motivate educational institutions to take more aggressive steps to end sexual harassment against female students and teachers? It is reported that sexual harassment is widespread in high schools and junior high schools: see The New York Times, March 11, 1992, p. A1, at col. 1. Moreover, a report released in June, 1993, by the American Association of University Women Educational Foundation cites sexual harassment of girls by their classmates as one of the reasons why girls get less out of the public schools than boys. See Hostile Hallways: the AAUW Survey on Sexual Harassment in America's Schools (1993).

5. Is sexual harassment the same thing under Title IX and Title VII? Will one legal definition, standard of conduct, and burden of proof suffice under both statutes? Professor Ronna Greff Schneider points out that, while the two claims are analogous, the analogy is not perfect and should be used with caution. In particular, she argues that in cases where the plaintiff alleges the creation or maintenance of an environment hostile to women, a higher standard should be imposed on faculty members than on employers, because "the student-faculty relationship encompasses a trust and dependency that does not inherently exist between parties involved in a sexual harassment claim under Title VII." Schneider, Sexual Harassment and Higher Education, 65 Tex.L.Rev. 525, 551 (1987). How high should the standard be? Schneider suggests a fiduciary standard that requires a professor to act in scrupulous good faith toward his students would be appropriate. Id., at 552. Do you agree?

What about the liability of the institution for the actions of employees or third parties toward students? In Murray v. New York University College of Dentistry, 57 F.3d 243 (2d Cir.1995), Patricia Murray, a student, sued for hostile environment sexual harassment arising from unwanted sexual attention, including stalking incidents, from a clinic patient. The Second Circuit acknowledged that courts, in reviewing claims of discrimination by employees under Title IX, generally adopted the same legal standards applied to such claims under Title VII. "Whether Title VII standards should also be applied in determining a Title IX sexual harassment claim by a student has not been directly addressed." Id. at 248. Relying on the Supreme Court's use of *Meritor Savings & Vinson* in support of *Franklin's* central holding, "an educational institution may be held liable under standards similar to those applied in cases under Title VII." Id. at 249. The Second Circuit proceeded to uphold the district court's dismissal of Murray's Title IX claim, however, on the basis that neither NYU nor its agents "knew or should have known" of the harassment. Murray had not complained to school officials or given NYU sufficient notice of the patient's offensive behavior. Id. at 250. The Second Circuit based its holding on the EEOC's standard of liability for harassment by co-workers or third parties set forth in its Title VII Sexual Harassment Guidelines.

6. Are hostile environment sexual harassment claims by women students actionable under Title IX? In Bougher v. University of Pittsburgh, 713 F.Supp 139 (W.D.Pa.1989), affirmed 882 F.2d 74 (3d Cir.1989), the court flatly rejected in scathing terms a plaintiff's effort to build on a Title VII model to establish a cla of "hostile environment" sexual harassment under Title IX.

> Plaintiff does not state, nor do the facts allege, a Title IX claim a
> Pitt. Even accepting plaintiff's uncorroborated allegations as tru
> leaving aside such overwrought prose as "instead of being her me
> Melia became her tormentor"[3]), she does not allege the denial of a
> by Pitt to her on the basis of sex. For that matter, she does
> defendant Melia discriminated in any respect either. There is t
> *quid pro quo* claim. The plaintiff's complaint and evidence b
> with an alleged consensual sexual relationship which began in
> was over twenty-one years old and ended at the latest in 1983
> years prior to the filing of this complaint.

3. This is only a sample of what is submitted by way of legal memorandum. We exhort the trial bar to leave the writing of romantic prose to those who are qualified for it, and

remember that nouns an
conclusory adjectives, are
clear thought and pers
made.

An extensive recital of plaintiff's evidence is not necessary. She portrays herself as the victim of a lecherous professor[4] from whom she took a single course in rhetoric in 1976. She does not assert that her association and alleged sexual relationship caused her to be denied any academic benefit unless she agreed to have a continuing relationship with him. She complains rather that the relationship which in retrospect was "unwelcome" and "violative" but which at all times was consensual, "went sour" after she called defendant Melia at his family residence, but that defendant, though now cold and distant emotionally, still intruded on her life.

For this intrusion, she seeks to hold Pitt responsible.

Defendant Melia is not alleged at any point after 1976 to have had any official role as plaintiff's advisor or teacher. At most, he is alleged to have abandoned a paper that Melia and plaintiff were co-authoring, forcing plaintiff to complete it at some inconvenience to her Christmas vacation.

Melia's work on the paper is not alleged to be in any way related to any duty or office held by him.

Plaintiff, desirous of stating a claim, ignores judicial precedent and blandly blurs fundamental distinctions between Title VII of the Civil Rights Act of 1964, an exercise by Congress of its power under the Commerce Clause to regulate employment conditions, and Title IX of the Education Amendments of 1972, an exercise by Congress under the Spending Clause to eliminate the use of federal funds in certain discriminatory educational programs. * * *

Plaintiff begins by assuming her conclusions—that what defendant Melia was allegedly guilty of is sexual harassment for which Pitt is responsible, and that sexual harassment, construed as any sexual involvement between a Pitt employee and a student, violates Title IX. Both assumptions are incorrect. Under Title VII, the Equal Employment Opportunity Commission of the Department of Labor, as an exercise of its agency expertise in interpreting and administratively enforcing Title VII, has promulgated * * * guidelines for defining sexual discrimination in employment [including] the "hostile environment" definition of sexual harassment * * *. 29 C.F.R. § 1604.11(a)(3)(1988). Plaintiff, aside from asking the Court to interpret the meaning of "unwelcome" to include "it used to be welcome, but now it's not", is also asking the court to transfer wholesale the EEOC guidelines into an area for which they were not drafted, for enforcement directly by the judiciary without administrative review by the OCR, and in ignorance of Title VI, 42 U.S.C. § 2000d, after which Title IX was patterned, Cannon v. University of Chicago, supra, and the procedural provisions of which Title IX adopts. 34 C.F.R. § 106.71.

Title IX prevents gender discrimination in a federal program's distribution of benefits. It also clearly reaches what has been defined as *quid pro quo* sexual harassment by a recipient of Federal funds, since without administrative interpretation this clearly violates Title IX by conditioning benefits on the basis of impermissible criteria. But to suggest, as plaintiff must, that unwelcome sexual advances, from *whatever* source, official or unofficial, constitute Title IX violations is a leap into the unknown which, whatever its wisdom, is the duty of Congress or an administrative agency to take. Title IX

---

4. "The Lecherous Professor" is the title of a book co-authored by an expert witness proffered by plaintiff. It is an anecdotal account of the author's research into sexual relationships between male faculty members and female students.

simply does not permit a "hostile environment" claim as described for the workplace by 29 C.F.R. § 1604.11(a)(3).

* * *

Id., at 144–45. On appeal, the Third Circuit found it "unnecessary" to reach the question whether evidence of a hostile environment is sufficient to sustain a claim of sexual discrimination in education in violation of Title IX, holding instead that most of the alleged events plaintiff cited to establish her case occurred prior to the applicable limitations period and those few that fell within the 180 day period prior to the filing date were insufficient to create a cause of action. Bougher v. University of Pittsburgh, 882 F.2d 74, 77 (3d Cir.1989).

In Patricia H. v. Berkeley Unified School District, 830 F.Supp. 1288 (N.D.Cal. 1993), Judge Orrick refused, in light of the Third Circuit's basis for affirmance in *Bougher,* to adopt the reasoning of the district court. Instead, he held, in what may be a case of first impression, that a claim for hostile environment sexual harassment could be established under Title IX. Following Ellison v. Brady, 924 F.2d 872 (9th Cir.1991), discussed on p. 827 supra, he used the perspective of a "reasonable victim" to determine whether as a matter of law plaintiffs had stated a claim under Title IX. The complaint alleged that plaintiff Patricia H., the mother of three daughters who attended school in the defendant school district, and Charles Hamilton, who teaches band at various schools in the district, had been involved in a romantic relationship. While on a trip to Lake Tahoe with plaintiff and two of her daughters, then aged 10 and 12, Hamilton had allegedly molested the 12 year old, Jackie H. Plaintiffs allege that Hamilton also molested both girls on later occasions in the family home by unwanted and improper touching, but they sought summary judgment only on Jackie H.'s claim. They allege that the mere presence of Hamilton as a teacher, a figure of authority and respect, in the schools the two girls attended (or would have attended, but for his presence), created a hostile environment that deprived them of full enjoyment of their education. Judge Orrick agreed with the logic of this argument:

> The very severity of the molestation, and the grave disparity in age and power between the girls and Hamilton, suggests that a reasonable student, having experienced such an assault, would be intimidated and fearful of Hamilton's presence at her school, so much so that her fear would interfere with her ability to learn, and to enjoy all aspects of her education fully, even though the alleged molestations were isolated in time and occurred outside of the school setting.

Id., 830 F.Supp. at 1297. He remanded for jury determination the question whether a reasonable female student of Jackie H.'s age would find that Hamilton's mere presence at Berkeley High School created a hostile environment. The jury must also determine whether defendant BUSD is liable for its alleged failure to take reasonable steps necessary under Title IX to remedy the situation. What sort of evidence would be persuasive on these questions?

In 1994, the Berkeley school district settled the case with the plaintiffs for $800,000. Equal Rights Advocates, a public interest advocacy organization specializing in sex discrimination issues, filed an amicus brief in the case and later reported the settlement, commenting that this large settlement should serve "as a warning to school districts that sexual harassment of students must be taken seriously." Equal Rights Advocates Newsletter, October 1994.

The circuits are split on whether or not school districts are liable under Title IX for failing to eliminate a hostile environment created by sexual harassment of students by other students. In Davis v. Monroe County Bd. of Educ., 74 F.3d 1186 (11th Cir.1996), the Eleventh Circuit held districts liable under Title IX if school "authorities knowingly fail to act to eliminate the harassment." 74 F.3d at 1193. In contrast, the Fifth Circuit held in Rowinski v. Bryan Indep. Sch. Dist., 80 F.3d 1006 (5th Cir.1996), that the school district was not liable under Title IX for junior high boys' sexual harassment of eighth grade girls on the school bus. The federal appeals court construed the language of Title IX to impose liability only for the acts of the recipient of federal funds, not for the acts of third parties. In the view of Judges Smith and Garwood, the school district would be liable under Title IX only if it directly discriminated based on sex, for example, "if it treated sexual harassment of boys more seriously than sexual harassment of girls." Id. at 2640. Judge Dennis dissented, stating that Title IX imposed a duty on recipients of federal funds to take appropriate measures to protect students from sexual harassment in the school environment. How should peer sexual harassment be handled under Title IX? What steps should a school district be required to take?

7. Should the sexual harassment of students constitute a proper basis for discharging a tenured professor? See Levitt v. Monroe, 590 F.Supp. 902 (W.D.Tex.1984), affirmed sub nom. Levitt v. University of Texas, 759 F.2d 1224 (5th Cir.1985), certiorari denied 474 U.S. 1034, 106 S.Ct. 599, 88 L.Ed.2d 578 (1985), sustaining the action of the University of Texas at El Paso in terminating a tenured professor of Chemistry because he made improper sexual advances on several occasions toward female students enrolled in his classes. See Monroe H. Freedman, The Professional Responsibility of the Law Professor: Three Neglected Questions, 39 Vanderbilt L.Rev. 275, 277–80 (1986), arguing that the practice of sexually exploiting students is unprofessional conduct that is adequate cause for dismissal of a tenured professor. See generally, Billie Wright Dziech, The Lecherous Professor (1984).

8. Do male professors take the problem of sexual harassment of students very seriously? On May 6, 1986, the Systemwide Assembly of the Academic Senate of the University of California rejected the proposal of the University Committee on Privilege and Tenure to include the following new item on the list of unacceptable faculty conduct contained in the Faculty Code of Conduct:

A. Teaching and Students

Types of unacceptable conduct:

* * *

A–6. Engaging in a romantic or sexual relationship with a student under circumstances which compromise student-faculty relationships.

The vote was 19 opposed, 6 in favor of the proposal. The debate suggested that the opponents of the measure saw little harm in "romance" between faculty members and students. The Daily Californian, May 7, 1986, p. 1, col. 5. Do those opposing this proposal share Schneider's characterization of a faculty member's relationship toward students as a "fiduciary" one? Do you? See generally, Peter DeChiara, The Need for Universities to Have Rules on Consensual Sexual Relationships Between Faculty Members and Students, 21 Col.J.L. & Soc.Probs. 137 (1988).

In 1989, the Association of American Law Schools adopted a "Statement of Good Practices by Law Professors in the Discharge of Their Ethical and Professional Responsibilities." The following two paragraphs are included in the Section titled "Responsibilities to Students:"

Discriminatory conduct based on such factors as race, color, religion, national origin, sex, sexual orientation, disability or handicap, age, or political beliefs is unacceptable in the law school community. Law professors should seek to make the law school a hospitable community for all students and should be sensitive to the harmful consequences of professorial or student conduct or comments in classroom discussions or elsewhere that perpetuate stereotypes or prejudices involving such factors. Law professors should not sexually harass students and should not use their role or position to induce a student to enter into a sexual relationship, or to subject a student to a hostile academic environment based on any form of sexual harassment.

Sexual relationships between a professor and a student who are not married to each other or who do not have a preexisting analogous relationship are inappropriate whenever the professor has a professional responsibility for the student in such matters as teaching a course or in otherwise advising a student as part of a school program. Even when a professor has no professional responsibility for a student, the professor should be sensitive to the perceptions of other students that a student who has a sexual relationship with a professor may receive preferential treatment from the professor or the professor's colleagues. A professor who is closely related to a student by blood or marriage, or who has a preexisting analogous relationship with a student, normally should eschew roles involving a professional responsibility for the student.

Are these guidelines enforceable? Should they be?

9. Has the feminist critique of sexual conduct given rise to a new societal and legal approach to such conduct? Professor Martha Chamallas thinks so. She identifies three overarching views of sexual conduct in American society: the traditional view that sex is permissible only in marriage; the liberal view that sexual conduct is a private matter that should be free of legal regulation; and the egalitarian view that seeks to empower women to form and maintain noncoercive sexual relationships both within and outside marriage. After examining criminal laws on rape and prostitution, civil rights laws on sexual harassment and amorous relationships, and tort actions governing deception in sexual relationships, she concludes that a new, positive ideal of mutual sexual conduct is emerging, one that regards sex as inappropriate if acquiescence is induced by physical force, economic pressure, or deception. Under such an egalitarian view, "sexual conduct is mutual and acceptable when animating inducements are the parties' desires for sexual pleasure or for intimacy." Chamallas, Consent, Equality, and the Legal Control of Sexual Conduct, 61 So.Cal.L.Rev. 777, 862 (1988).

10. What about sexual harassment of junior women faculty by senior male faculty? The University of California definition of sexual harassment includes the following provision:

Unwelcome sexual advances, requests for sexual favors, and other verbal or physical conduct of a sexual nature constitute sexual harassment when:

* * *

2. submission to or rejection of such conduct by an individual is used as a basis for evaluation in making academic or personnel decisions affecting an individual; * * *.

University of California, Faculty Handbook, at p. 46 (1986). Is this policy adequate to protect nontenured women faculty members from sexual harassment?

11. Can an educational institution be in violation of Title IX for the discriminatory activities of a student organization? The question was presented, but ultimately not decided on the merits, in Iron Arrow Honor Society v. Hufstedler, 499 F.Supp. 496 (S.D.Fla.1980), affirmed 652 F.2d 445 (5th Cir.1981), vacated and remanded in light of North Haven, 458 U.S. 1102, 102 S.Ct. 3475, 73 L.Ed.2d 1363 (1982), affirmed 702 F.2d 549 (5th Cir.), dismissed as moot sub nom. Iron Arrow Honor Society v. Heckler, 464 U.S. 67, 104 S.Ct. 373, 78 L.Ed.2d 58 (1983). The Iron Arrow Honor Society is an all-male student recognition society established in 1926 by the first President of the University of Miami, and maintained with the "substantial assistance" of the University since that time. The University, under threat of the termination of its federal funds, prohibited the Society from performing its "tapping ceremony", that identified the new members, on campus. The Society sought an injunction to prevent the Secretary of Education from applying the Title IX Regulations so as to interfere with the conduct of its functions on campus. Both the district court and the Fifth Circuit were in agreement that the Regulations under which the Secretary acted were within the scope of the statute: when a recipient of federal funds gives substantial assistance to an "outside" organization that discriminates on the basis of sex, and when that organization's activities relate so closely to the recipient's educational program that these activities can be considered as activities of the recipient itself, the Regulations correctly permit the termination of federal funds to the recipient. Both courts also held that the University of Miami did actually contribute "substantial assistance" to the Society, both indirectly in terms of prestige gained through association with the campus, and directly through tangible support such as secretarial service, alumni mailings, and the use of meeting rooms. The case was ultimately dismissed as moot because of a letter written to Iron Arrow by President Foote of the University of Miami, stating the University's "unequivocal position that Iron Arrow cannot return to campus as a University organization nor conduct its activities on campus until it discontinues its discriminatory membership policy", and indicating that the University intended to adhere to the stated position regardless of the outcome of the lawsuit. Id., 464 U.S. at 69–70, 104 S.Ct. at 374, 78 L.Ed.2d at 61. How should the case have been decided on the merits, absent the President's letter? What if that office received no federal funds? Does the 1987 Restoration Act amending Title IX mean that Iron Arrow's membership practices could put all of Miami's federal funds in jeopardy?

What about the Whiffenpoofs who sing at Yale? In 1987, for the first time since the group was formed in 1909 when Yale was an all-male college, women auditioned for admission to the group of fourteen "gentlemen songsters." No women, however, were chosen during the midnight tapping ceremonies held on the Yale campus. President Benno C. Schmidt, Jr., issued a statement deploring sex discrimination, but noting that the Whiffenpoofs, although registered with the University, were not an official student organization. New York Times, April 20, 1987, p. Y17, col. 1.

Skull and Bones, a secret all-male club founded at Yale in 1832, finally admitted women by a vote of the entire membership held on October 24, 1991, after a protracted and highly publicized struggle between the 1991 delegation who had tapped six women and nine men for the 1992 delegation in April, only to find themselves locked out of their meeting place, "The Tomb," by irate alumni. One of the newly-tapped women was reported to have commented when she learned of the vote, "It's great, but it's a little overdue." The New York Times, October 27, 1991, p. 16, at col. 1.

12. Are tests which show a disparate impact based on sex illegal under Title IX? In Sharif by Salahuddin v. New York State Educ. Dept., 709 F.Supp. 345 (S.D.N.Y.1989), plaintiffs relied on Title IX and its implementing regulations as well as the Equal Protection Clause to challenge defendants' practice of using Scholastic Aptitude Test (SAT) scores as the sole basis for awarding Regents College Scholarships and Empire State Scholarships of Excellence to high school students. Plaintiffs did not allege intentional discrimination; rather, they argued that the practice had a disparate impact on females. Plaintiffs presented the following showing of statistical impact:

3. Statistical Impact on Men and Women Statewide

Males have outscored females on the verbal portion of the SAT since 1972, with an average score differential of at least 10 points since 1981. Males have also consistently outscored females on the mathematics portion, with an average differential of at least 40 points since 1967. In 1988, for example, girls scored 56 points lower than boys on the test. The probability that these score differentials happened by chance is approximately about one in a billion and the probability that the result could consistently be so different is essentially zero. * * *

Statisticians have attempted to explain the score differentials between males and females by removing the effect of "neutral" variables, such as ethnicity, socioeducational status (parental education), high school classes, and proposed college major. However, under the most conservative studies presented in evidence, even after removing the effect of these factors, at least a 30 point combined differential remains unexplained.

As a result of the State's practice of basing scholarship awards solely upon SAT scores, males have consistently received substantially more scholarships than females. In 1987 for example, males were 47 percent of the scholarship competitors, but received 72 percent of the Empire State Scholarships and 57 percent of the Regents Scholarships. For Empire State Scholarships, these results represent 15.8 standard deviations from the mean; for Regents Scholarships, the difference represents 31.7 standard deviations. In other words, the probability that the Empire Scholarship results would occur by chance is less than one in a billion, and the probability of the Regents Scholarship results would occur by chance is even less.

Id., 709 F.Supp. at 355–56.

Judge Walker ruled that the Title IX claim could proceed without a showing of intentional discrimination, and granted a preliminary injunction based on plaintiff's showing of disparate impact. He also held that the challenged practice could not survive even the minimal scrutiny required by the rational relationship standard. Excerpts from his opinion follow.

2. Likelihood of Success on Merits

a. Title IX

Plaintiffs invoke the protections provided by Title IX, which prohibits sex discrimination in federally-funded educational programs. Plaintiffs do not claim that defendants have intentionally discriminated against them based on their sex. Rather, they claim that defendants' practice of sole reliance upon SAT scores to award prestigious state scholarships disparately impacts female students. To this Court's knowledge, this is the first disparate impact case challenging educational testing practices under Title IX.

Neither the Supreme Court nor any court in the Second Circuit has determined whether intent must be shown in Title IX cases. This Court, however, is not without substantial guidance. Recognizing that "Title IX was patterned after Title VI of the Civil Rights Act of 1964," Grove City College v. Bell, 465 U.S. 555, 566, 104 S.Ct. 1211, 1218, 79 L.Ed.2d 516 (1984), courts examining Title IX questions have looked to the substantial body of law developed under Title VI, 42 U.S.C. § 2000d, which prohibits race discrimination in federally-funded programs, and Title VII, 42 U.S.C. § 2000e, which prohibits discrimination in employment. See, e.g., Mabry v. State Board of Community Colleges and Occupational Education, 813 F.2d 311, 317 (10th Cir.), cert. denied, 484 U.S. 849, 108 S.Ct. 148, 98 L.Ed.2d 104 (1987); Haffer v. Temple University, 678 F.Supp. 517, 539 (E.D.Pa.1987).

In Guardians Association v. Civil Service Commission, 463 U.S. 582, 103 S.Ct. 3221, 77 L.Ed.2d 866 (1983), the Supreme Court held that a violation of Title VI itself requires proof of discriminatory intent. However, a majority also agreed that proof of discriminatory effect suffices to establish liability when a suit is brought to enforce the regulations promulgated under Title VI, rather than statute itself. See also Alexander v. Choate, 469 U.S. 287, 293–294, 105 S.Ct. 712, 716, 83 L.Ed.2d 661 (1985); Latinos Unidos De Chelsea v. Secretary of Housing, 799 F.2d 774, 785 n. 20 (1st Cir.1986).

Plaintiffs' amended complaint explicitly alleges both violations of Title IX and its implementing regulations. This Court finds no persuasive reason not to apply Title VI's substantive standards to the present Title IX suit. * * *

The Title IX implementing regulations, like the regulations promulgated under Title VI, to which Title IX is frequently compared, are consistent with this interpretation of the comprehensive reach of the statute. Several Title IX regulations specifically prohibit facially neutral policies. * * *

Based upon a reading of the Title IX regulations, as well as the decisions that apply them, the Court finds that Title IX regulations, like the Title VI regulations at issue in *Guardians,* prohibit testing practices with a discriminatory *effect* on one sex. Consequently, plaintiffs need not prove intentional discrimination.

* * *

Applying the Title VII formulations to this Title IX case as modified to take into account "educational necessity," this Court finds that plaintiffs have demonstrated a likelihood of success on the merits. Plaintiffs have met their burden of establishing a *prima facie* case through persuasive statistical evidence and credible expert testimony that the composition of scholarship winners tilted decidedly toward males and could not have occurred by a random distribution. * * * Defendants have failed to attack plaintiffs' evidence of statewide disparate impact but have instead focused in an *ad hoc* fashion on individual schools and counties. In a case alleging statewide discrimination, such a focus does not rebut plaintiffs' statewide *prima facie* case.

Plaintiffs, moreover, have established that the probability, absent discriminatory causes, that women would consistently score 60 points less on the SAT than men is nearly zero. * * * Defendants concede that at least half of this differential cannot be explained away by "neutral" variables. Based upon the totality of evidence, then, this Court finds that plaintiffs have demonstrated that the State's practice of sole reliance upon the SAT disparately impacts young women.

Thus, to prevail, defendants must show a manifest relationship between use of the SAT and recognition and award of academic achievement in high school. The Court finds that defendants have failed to show even a reasonable relationship between their practice and their conceded purpose. The SAT was not designed to measure achievement in high school and was never validated for that purpose. * * *

* * *

Plaintiffs have offered an alternative to sole reliance upon the SAT: a combination of GPAs and SATs. The SED's use of this alternative in 1988 sharply reduced the disparate impact against females caused by the use of the SAT alone. A significantly greater number of female students received scholarships in 1988 than in each prior year in which the SED relied solely upon the SAT. * * * Defendants concede that females had a greater opportunity to receive scholarships under the combination system. Defendants also concede that grades are the best measure of high school achievement within the walls of a single school. Instead, they argue that since there is a disparity among schools and their grading systems it is both unfair and impossible to use grades as part of the scholarship eligibility determination. Defendants plan instead to develop a statewide achievement test. While this Court does not dispute the apparent advantages of a statewide achievement test—if indeed a valid test can be developed—it does not agree that pending the implication of such a test, use of grades would be either unfair or infeasible.

While a combination system—using both GPAs and SATs—is not a perfect alternative, it is the best alternative presently available. The SED is concerned that students in academically superior high schools not be disadvantaged by the use of GPAs. This concern is addressed by the combination system because in effect grades would be weighted by SATs. The SAT component which cannot properly itself measure achievement serves to balance the grade component that does. In this way, the SED's concern that use of grades alone will deprive good students in superior high schools of scholarships is ameliorated. * * * More importantly, the combination system would be "fair" in the larger sense of the word, because it would better advance the state's goal of awarding high school performance and would better provide *all* students—not just male students or students from selective schools—with an equal opportunity to compete for prestigious state scholarships.

* * *

Faced with a conflict between the SED's administrative concerns on the one hand, and the risk of substantial discriminatory harm to plaintiffs on the other, the Court has little difficulty in concluding that the balance of hardships tips decidedly in plaintiffs' favor. See Mitchell v. Cuomo, 748 F.2d 804, 808 (2d Cir.1984). The Court finds that plaintiffs have offered a feasible alternative to sole reliance upon SATs. Accordingly, the Court finds that plaintiffs have demonstrated a likelihood of success on the merits of their Title IX claim and, thus, a preliminary injunction is warranted.

b. Equal Protection

Alternatively, a preliminary injunction is warranted because plaintiffs also have established a likelihood that they will succeed on their equal protection claim. The classification of scholarship applicants solely on the basis of SAT scores violates the equal protection clause of the Fourteenth Amendment because this method is not rationally related to the state's goal of rewarding students who have demonstrated academic achievement.

Under the lowest standard of equal protection review—the "rational relationship standard"—"[t]he State may not rely on a classification whose relationship to an asserted goal is so attenuated as to render the distinction arbitrary or irrational." City of Cleburne v. Cleburne Living Center, 473 U.S. 432, 446, 105 S.Ct. 3249, 3257, 87 L.Ed.2d 313 (1985). Although considerable deference is given to the decisions of legislators and state administrators under the rational basis test, the test "is not a toothless one." * * * In a long line of cases, the Supreme Court has applied rational basis scrutiny to strike down legislation where the permissible bounds of rationality were exceeded. * * *

For the reasons stated above, the SED's use of the SAT as a proxy for high school achievement is too unrelated to the legislative purpose of awarding academic achievement in high school to survive even the most minimal scrutiny. The evidence is clear that females score significantly below males on the SAT while they perform equally or slightly better than males in high school. Therefore, the SED's use of the SAT as the sole criterion for awarding Regents and Empire Scholarships discriminates against females and, since such a practice is not rationally related to the legislative purpose, it unconstitutionally denies young women equal protection of the laws and must be enjoined on that ground as well.

* * *

Id., 709 F.Supp. at 360–64. In footnote 39 of his opinion, Judge Walker brushed aside the defendants' reliance on Justice O'Connor's opinion in Watson v. Fort Worth Bank & Trust, excerpted at p. 588, concerning the quantum of proof needed for disparate impact cases, on the ground that she spoke only for a plurality of the Court. After her opinion was accepted by a majority of the Court in Wards Cove Packing Co. v. Atonio, set forth at p. 596, supra, the question arose whether *Sharif* was still good law. A notewriter answered affirmatively, arguing that although *Sharif* significantly expanded Title IX, *Wards Cove* did not impair the holding. See Recent Cases, 103 Harv.L.Rev. 806 (1990). Do you agree? At any event, the Civil Rights Act of 1991 makes the question moot, doesn't it?

2. TITLE IX AND COLLEGE ATHLETICS

COHEN v. BROWN UNIVERSITY

United States Court of Appeals, First Circuit, 1993.
991 F.2d 888.

Before SELYA, CYR and STAHL, CIRCUIT JUDGES.

SELYA, CIRCUIT JUDGE.

In this watershed case, defendants-appellants Brown University * * * appeal from the district court's issuance of a preliminary injunction ordering

Brown to reinstate its women's gymnastics and volleyball programs to full intercollegiate varsity status pending the resolution of a Title IX claim. See Cohen v. Brown Univ., 809 F.Supp. 978 (D.R.I.1992). After mapping Title IX's rugged legal terrain and cutting a passable swath through the factual thicket that overspreads the parties' arguments, we affirm.

I. Brown Athletics: An Overview

College athletics, particularly in the realm of football and basketball, has traditionally occupied a prominent role in American sports and American society. For college students, athletics offers an opportunity to exacuate leadership skills, learn teamwork, build self-confidence, and perfect self-discipline. In addition, for many student-athletes, physical skills are a passport to college admissions and scholarships, allowing them to attend otherwise inaccessible schools. These opportunities, and the lessons learned on the playing fields, are invaluable in attaining career and life successes in and out of professional sports.

The highway of opportunity runs in both directions. Not only student-athletes, but universities, too, benefit from the magic of intercollegiate sports. Successful teams generate television revenues and gate receipts which often fund significant percentages of a university's overall athletic program, offering students the opportunity to partake of sports that are not financially self-sustaining. Even those institutions whose teams do not fill the grandstands of cavernous stadiums or attract national television exposure benefit from increased student and alumni cohesion and the support it engenders. Thus, universities nurture the legends, great or small, inhering in their athletic past, polishing the hardware that adorns field-house trophy cases and reliving heroic exploits in the pages of alumni magazines.

In these terms, Brown will never be confused with Notre Dame or the more muscular members of the Big Ten. Although its football team did play in the 1916 Rose Bowl and its men's basketball team won the Ivy League championship as recently as 1986, Brown's athletic program has only occasionally achieved national prominence or, for that matter, enjoyed sustained success.[2] Moreover, at Brown, as at most schools, women are a relatively inconspicuous part of the storied athletic past. Historically, colleges limited athletics to the male sphere, leaving those few women's teams that sprouted to scrounge for resources.

The absence of women's athletics at Brown was, until 1970, an ineluctable consequence of the absence of women; Brown sponsored a women's college—Pembroke—but did not itself admit women. In 1971, Brown subsumed Pembroke. Brown promptly upgraded Pembroke's rather primitive athletic offerings so that by 1977 there were fourteen women's varsity teams. In subsequent years, Brown added only one distaff team: winter track. Hence, in the 1991–92 academic year, Brown fielded fifteen women's varsity teams—one fewer than the number of men's varsity teams.

---

2. We note, not without a certain irony, that the now-demoted women's volleyball and gymnastics teams won Ivy League championships in 1988 and 1990, respectively.

II. THE PLAINTIFF CLASS

In the spring of 1991, Brown announced that it, like many other schools, was in a financial bind, and that, as a belt-tightening measure, it planned to drop four sports from its intercollegiate varsity athletic roster: women's volleyball and gymnastics, men's golf and water polo. The University permitted the teams to continue playing as "intercollegiate clubs," a status that allowed them to compete against varsity teams from other colleges,[3] but cut off financial subsidies and support services routinely available to varsity teams (e.g., salaried coaches, access to prime facilities, preferred practice time, medical trainers, clerical assistance, office support, admission preferences, and the like). Brown estimated that eliminating these four varsity teams would save $77,813 per annum, broken down as follows: women's volleyball, $37,-127; women's gymnastics, $24,901; men's water polo, $9,250; men's golf, $6,545.

Before the cuts, Brown athletics offered an aggregate of 328 varsity slots for female athletes and 566 varsity slots for male athletes. Thus, women had 36.7% of the athletic opportunities and men 63.3%. Abolishing the four varsity teams took substantially more dollars from the women's athletic budget than from the men's budget, but did not materially affect the athletic opportunity ratios; women retained 36.6% of the opportunities and men 63.4%. At that time (and for a number of years prior thereto), Brown's student body comprised approximately 52% men and 48% women.

Following Brown's announcement of the cutbacks, disappointed members of the women's volleyball and gymnastics teams brought suit. They proceeded on an implied cause of action under Title IX, 20 U.S.C. §§ 1681–1688 (1988). See Franklin v. Gwinnett County Pub. Sch. * * * (1992) * * *. The plaintiffs charged that Brown's athletic arrangements violated Title IX's ban on gender-based discrimination, a violation that was allegedly exacerbated by Brown's decision to devalue the two women's programs without first making sufficient reductions in men's activities or, in the alternative, adding other women's teams to compensate for the loss.

On plaintiffs' motion, the district court certified a class of "all present and future Brown University women students and potential students who participate, seek to participate, and/or are deterred from participating in intercollegiate athletics funded by Brown." And, after hearing fourteen days of testimony from twenty witnesses, the judge granted a preliminary injunction requiring Brown to reinstate the two women's teams pending the outcome of a full trial on the merits. * * * We stayed execution of the order and expedited Brown's appeal.

III. TITLE IX AND COLLEGIATE ATHLETICS

Title IX prohibits gender-based discrimination by educational institutions receiving federal financial support—in practice, the vast majority of all accredited colleges and universities. The statute sketches wide policy lines, leaving the details to regulating agencies. Since this appeal demands that we

---

3. As a practical matter, many schools with varsity squads are reluctant to compete against club teams. This case aptly illustrates the point. As soon as Brown demoted its women's volleyball team from varsity to club status, Northeastern University and West Point declined to include Brown on future volleyball schedules. * * *

invade terra incognita,[4] we carefully recount the developments leading to the present version of Title IX and then examine the pertinent statutory and regulatory language.

A. Scope of Title IX.

At its inception, the broad proscriptive language of Title IX caused considerable consternation in the academic world. The academy's anxiety chiefly centered around identifying which individual programs, particularly in terms of athletics, might come within the scope of the discrimination provision, and, relatedly, how the government would determine compliance. The gridiron fueled these concerns: for many schools, the men's football budget far exceeded that of any other sport, and men's athletics as a whole received the lion's share of dedicated resources—a share that, typically, was vastly disproportionate to the percentage of men in the student body.

Part of the confusion about the scope of Title IX's coverage and the acceptable avenues of compliance arose from the absence of secondary legislative materials. Congress included no committee report with the final bill and there were apparently only two mentions of intercollegiate athletics during the congressional debate. See 118 Cong.Rec. 5,807 (1972) (statement of Sen. Bayh on privacy in athletic facilities); 117 Cong.Rec. 30,407 (1971)(statement of Sen. Bayh noting that proposed Title IX will not require gender-blended football teams). Nevertheless, under congressional direction to implement Title IX, the Secretary of Health, Education and Welfare (HEW) promulgated regulations in 1975 which included specific provisions for college athletics. Four years later, HEW's Office of Civil Rights (OCR) added another layer of regulatory exegesis when, after notice and comment, it published a "Policy Interpretation" that offered a more detailed measure of equal athletic opportunity.

In 1984, the Supreme Court radically altered the contemporary reading of Title IX. The Court held that Title IX was "program-specific," so that its tenets applied only to the program(s) which actually received federal funds and not to the rest of the university. Grove City College v. Bell, 465 U.S. 555, 574 * * * (1984). Because few athletic departments are direct recipients of federal funds—most federal money for universities is channelled through financial aid offices or invested directly in research grants—Grove City cabined Title IX and placed virtually all collegiate athletic programs beyond its reach.[5]

In response to Grove City, Congress scrapped the program-specific approach and reinstated an institution-wide application of Title IX by passing

---

4. Although there has been a spate of sports-related Title IX suits during the last two years, see Andrew Blum, Athletics in the Courts, Nat'l L.J., Apr. 5, 1993, at 1, few have been fully litigated. See, e.g., Carol Herwig, Massachusetts Reinstates Women's Sports, USA Today, Oct. 22, 1992, at 14C (announcing agreement to reinstate three women's teams at the University of Massachusetts and reporting the school's intention to become "the first university in the country to come into full compliance with Title IX"). While the case we decide today is apparently the first of these to reach the courts of appeals, others are pending. See,

e.g., Roberts v. Colorado State Univ., No. 93–1052 (10th Cir.1993)(not yet argued); Cook v. Colgate Univ., No. 92–9175 (2d Cir.1993)(argued Feb. 26, 1993).

5. Following the Court's decision in Grove City, the United States Department of Education (which by then had been spun off from HEW, see infra Part III(C)) dropped or curtailed seventy-nine ongoing Title IX cases. See Statements on Civil Rights Restoration Act, Daily Lab. Rep. (BNA) No. 53, at D1 (Mar. 20, 1981).

the Civil Rights Restoration Act of 1987, 20 U.S.C. s 1687 (1988). * * * Although the Restoration Act does not specifically mention sports, the record of the floor debate leaves little doubt that the enactment was aimed, in part, at creating a more level playing field for female athletes. See, e.g., 130 Cong.Rec. S12,642 (daily ed. Oct. 2, 1984)(statement of Sen. Byrd decrying past discrimination against female athletes); 130 Cong.Rec. S11,253 (daily ed. Sept. 17, 1984)(statement of Sen. Hatch regarding importance of Title IX to ensuring development of women athletes); 130 Cong.Rec. S2,267 (daily ed. Mar. 2, 1984)(statement of Sen. Riegle noting extensive evidence of sex discrimination in education and athletics).

The appellants do not challenge the district court's finding that, under existing law, Brown's athletic department is subject to Title IX. Accordingly, we devote the remainder of Part III to deterrating the meaning of Title IX, looking first at the statute and then at the regulations.

B. Statutory Framework.

Title IX, like the Restoration Act, does not explicitly treat college athletics. Rather, the statute's heart is a broad prohibition of gender- based discrimination in all programmatic aspects of educational institutions * * *. After listing a number of exempt organizations, section 1681 makes clear that, while Title IX prohibits discrimination, it does not mandate strict numerical equality between the gender balance of a college's athletic program and the gender balance of its student body. Thus, section 1681(a) shall not

> be interpreted to require any educational institution to grant preferential or disparate treatment to the members of one sex on account of an imbalance which may exist with respect to the total number or percentage of persons of that sex participating in or receiving the benefits of any federally supported program or activity, in comparison with the total number or percentage of persons of that sex in any community, State, section, or other area * * *.

20 U.S.C. § 1681(b)(1988). Put another way, a court assessing Title IX compliance may not find a violation solely because there is a disparity between the gender composition of an educational institution's student constituency, on the one hand, and its athletic programs, on the other hand.

That is not to say, however, that evidence of such a disparity is irrelevant. Quite the contrary: under the proviso contained in section 1681(b), a Title IX plaintiff in an athletic discrimination suit must accompany statistical evidence of disparate impact with some further evidence of discrimination, such as unmet need amongst the members of the disadvantaged gender.

C. Regulatory Framework.

As we mentioned above, the Secretary of HEW, following Congress's instructions, promulgated regulations implementing Title IX in the pre-Grove City era. See 40 Fed.Reg. 24,128 (1975). Thereafter, in 1979, Congress split HEW into the Department of Health and Human Services (HHS) and the Department of Education (DED). See 20 U.S.C. §§ 3401–3510 (1988). In a wonderful example of bureaucratic muddle, the existing Title IX regulations were left within HHS's arsenal while, at the same time, DED replicated them as part of its own regulatory armamentarium. Compare 45 C.F.R. § 86 (1992)(HHS regulations) with 34 C.F.R. § 106 (1992)(DED regulations).

Both sets of regulations were still in effect when the Restoration Act passed. They are identical, save only for changes in nomenclature reflecting the reorganization of the federal bureaucracy.

In short, like pretenders to the emirate of a deceased sheik, both HHS and DED lay an hereditary claim to this oasis which arises from the regulatory desert, asserting authority to enforce Title IX. Nevertheless, DED is the principle locus of ongoing enforcement activity. See 20 U.S.C. § 3441(a)(1)(transferring all education functions of HEW to DED); see also 20 U.S.C. § 3441(a)(3)(transferring education-related OCR work to DED). Therefore, like the parties, we treat DED, acting through its OCR, as the administrative agency charged with administering Title IX.

Recognizing the agency's role has important practical and legal consequences. Although DED is not a party to this appeal, we must accord its interpretation of Title IX appreciable deference. * * * The degree of deference is particularly high in Title IX cases because Congress explicitly delegated to the agency the task of prescribing standards for athletic programs under Title IX. See Pub.L. No. 93–380, § 844, 88 Stat. 612 (1974); see also *Chevron*, 467 U.S. at 844, 104 S.Ct. at 2782 (holding that where Congress has explicitly delegated responsibility to an agency, the regulation deserves "controlling weight") * * *.

It is against this backdrop that we scrutinize the regulations and the Policy Interpretation.

1. The Regulations. DED's regulations begin by detailing Title IX's application to college athletics.[8] The regulations also recognize, however, that an athletic program may consist of gender- segregated teams as long as one of two conditions is met: either the sport in which the team competes is a contact sport or the institution offers comparable teams in the sport to both genders. See 34 C.F.R. § 106.41(b).

Finally, whether teams are segregated by sex or not, the school must provide gender-blind equality of opportunity to its student body. The regulations offer a non-exclusive compendium of ten factors which OCR will consider in assessing compliance with this mandate:

(1) Whether the selection of sports and levels of competition effectively accommodate the interests and abilities of members of both sexes;

(2) The provision of equipment and supplies;

(3) Scheduling of games and practice time;

(4) Travel and per diem allowance;

(5) Opportunity to receive coaching and academic tutoring;

(6) Assignment and compensation of coaches and tutors;

(7) Provision of locker rooms, practice and competitive facilities;

(8) Provision of medical and training facilities and services;

---

8. The regulations provide: No person shall, on the basis of sex, be excluded from participation in, be denied the benefits of, be treated differently from another person or otherwise be discriminated against in any inter- scholastic, intercollegiate, club or intramural athletics offered by a recipient, and no recipient shall provide any such athletics separately on such basis. 34 C.F.R. § 106.41(a)(1992).

(9) Provision of housing and dining facilities and services;

(10) Publicity.

34 C.F.R. § 106.41(c)(1992).[9] The district court rested its preliminary injunction on the first of these ten areas of inquiry: Brown's failure effectively to accommodate the interests and abilities of female students in the selection and level of sports. * * * Hence, this area is the most critical in terms of evaluating the charges against Brown (although it is also the most difficult to measure).

2. The Policy Interpretation. In the three years next following the initial issuance of the regulations, HEW received over one hundred discrimination complaints involving more than fifty schools. In order to encourage self-policing and thereby winnow complaints, HEW proposed a Policy Interpretation. See 43 Fed.Reg. 58,070 (1978). It then promulgated the Policy Interpretation in final form, see 44 Fed.Reg. 71,413 (1979), a matter of months before the effective date of the statute through which Congress, emulating King Solomon, split HEW. The parties are in agreement that, at DED's birth, it clutched the Policy Interpretation, and, as a practical matter, that appears to be the case. * * * Although we can find no record that DED formally adopted the Policy Interpretation, we see no point to splitting the hair, particularly where the parties have not asked us to do so. Because this document is a considered interpretation of the regulation, we cede it substantial deference. * * *

In line with the Supreme Court's direction that, "if we are to give [Title IX] the scope that its origins dictate, we must accord it a sweep as broad as its language," North Haven Bd. of Educ. v. Bell, 456 U.S. 512, 521 * * * the Policy Interpretation limns three major areas of regulatory compliance: "Athletic Financial Assistance (Scholarships)," * * * "Equivalence in Other Athletic Benefits and Opportunities," * * * and "Effective Accommodation of Student Interests and Abilities" * * *. The court below * * * and a number of other district courts, see, e.g., Roberts v. Colorado State Univ., 814 F.Supp. 1507, 1510–11 (D.Colo.1993); Favia v. Indiana Univ. of Pa., 812 F.Supp. 578, 584–85 (W.D.Pa.1993), have adopted this formulation and ruled that a university violates Title IX if it ineffectively accommodates student interests and abilities regardless of its performance in other Title IX areas.

Equal opportunity to participate lies at the core of Title IX's purpose. Because the third compliance area delineates this heartland, we agree with the district courts that have so ruled and hold that, with regard to the effective accommodation of students' interests and abilities, an institution can violate Title IX even if it meets the "financial assistance" and "athletic equivalence" standards. In other words, an institution that offers women a smaller number of athletic opportunities than the statute requires may not rectify that violation simply by lavishing more resources on those women or achieving equivalence in other respects.[12]

9. The same regulation also stipulates that: Unequal aggregate expenditures for members of each sex or unequal expenditures for male and female teams if a recipient operates or sponsors separate teams will not constitute noncompliance with this section, but [DED] may consider the failure to provide necessary funds for teams for one sex in assessing equality of opportunity for members of each sex. 34 C.F.R. § 106.41(c)(1992).

12. In any event, both the financial assistance and athletic equivalence standards are inapposite for present purposes. As to the

3. Measuring Effective Accommodation. The parties agree that the third compliance area is the field on which this appeal must be fought. In surveying the dimensions of this battleground, that is, whether an athletic program effectively accommodates students' interests and abilities, the Policy Interpretation maps a trinitarian model under which the university must meet at least one of three benchmarks:

(1) Whether intercollegiate level participation opportunities for male and female students are provided in numbers substantially proportionate to their respective enrollments; or

(2) Where the members of one sex have been and are underrepresented among intercollegiate athletes, whether the institution can show a history and continuing practice of program expansion which is demonstrably responsive to the developing interest and abilities of the members of that sex; or

(3) Where the members of one sex are underrepresented among intercollegiate athletes, and the institution cannot show a continuing practice of program expansion such as that cited above, whether it can be demonstrated that the interests and abilities of the members of that sex have been fully and effectively accommodated by the present program.

44 Fed.Reg. at 71,418. The first benchmark furnishes a safe harbor for those institutions that have distributed athletic opportunities in numbers "substantially proportionate" to the gender composition of their student bodies. Thus, a university which does not wish to engage in extensive compliance analysis may stay on the sunny side of Title IX simply by maintaining gender parity between its student body and its athletic lineup.

The second and third parts of the accommodation test recognize that there are circumstances under which, as a practical matter, something short of this proportionality is a satisfactory proxy for gender balance. For example, so long as a university is continually expanding athletic opportunities in an ongoing effort to meet the needs of the underrepresented gender, and persists in this approach as interest and ability levels in its student body and secondary feeder schools rise, benchmark two is satisfied and Title IX does not require that the university leap to complete gender parity in a single bound. Or, if a school has a student body in which one sex is demonstrably less interested in athletics, Title IX does not require that the school create teams for, or rain money upon, otherwise disinterested students; rather, the third benchmark is satisfied if the underrepresented sex's discernible interests are fully and effectively accommodated.[13]

former, Brown does not confer athletic scholarships and the plaintiffs do not allege that Brown has discriminated by gender in distributing other financial aid. As to the latter, the district court made only preliminary findings, see Cohen, 809 F.Supp. at 994–97, on the explicit understanding that it would revisit compliance vel non with the athletic equivalence standard at trial. Id. at 997.

13. OCR also lists a series of illustrative justifications for the disparate treatment of men's and women's athletic teams, including (1) sports that require more resources because of the nature of the game (e.g., contact sports generally require more equipment), (2) special circumstances, such as an influx of first-year players, that may require an extraordinary infusion of resources, (3) special operational expenses (e.g., crowd control at a basketball tournament), as long as special operational expense needs are met for both genders and (4) affirmative measures to remedy past limitations on athletic opportunities for one gender. 44 Fed. Reg. at 71,415–16.

It seems unlikely, even in this day and age, that the athletic establishments of many coeducational universities reflect the gender balance of their student bodies.[14] Similarly, the recent boom in Title IX suits suggests that, in an era of fiscal austerity, few universities are prone to expand athletic opportunities. It is not surprising, then, that schools more often than not attempt to manage the rigors of Title IX by satisfying the interests and abilities of the underrepresented gender, that is, by meeting the third benchmark of the accommodation test. Yet, this benchmark sets a high standard: it demands not merely some accommodation, but full and effective accommodation. If there is sufficient interest and ability among members of the statistically underrepresented gender, not slaked by existing programs, an institution necessarily fails this prong of the test.

Although the full-and-effective-accommodation standard is high, it is not absolute. Even when male athletic opportunities outnumber female athletic opportunities, and the university has not met the first benchmark (substantial statistical proportionality) or the second benchmark (continuing program expansion) of the accommodation test, the mere fact that there are some female students interested in a sport does not ipso facto require the school to provide a varsity team in order to comply with the third benchmark. Rather, the institution can satisfy the third benchmark by ensuring participatory opportunities at the intercollegiate level when, and to the extent that, there is "sufficient interest and ability among the members of the excluded sex to sustain a viable team and a reasonable expectation of intercollegiate competition for that team * * *. " 44 Fed.Reg. at 71,418. Staying on top of the problem is not sport for the short-winded: the institution must remain vigilant, "upgrading the competitive opportunities available to the historically disadvantaged sex as warranted by developing abilities among the athletes of that sex," id., until the opportunities for, and levels of, competition are equivalent by gender.[15]

Brown argues that DED's Policy Interpretation, construed as we have just outlined, goes so far afield that it countervails the enabling legislation. Brown suggests that, to the extent students' interests in athletics are disproportionate by gender, colleges should be allowed to meet those interests incompletely as long as the school's response is in direct proportion to the comparative levels of interest. Put bluntly, Brown reads the "full" out of the duty to accommodate "fully and effectively." It argues instead that an institution satisfactorily accommodates female athletes if it allocates athletic opportunities to women in accordance with the ratio of interested and able

14. Success in this regard is, however, attainable. After Washington State University was ordered to increase participation opportunities for women to a level equivalent with the percentage of female undergraduates, see Blair v. Washington State Univ., 108 Wash.2d 558, 740 P.2d 1379 (1987), the University experienced considerable success in meeting court-ordered goals. See Mary Jordan, Only One School Meets Gender Equity Goal, Wash. Post, June 21, 1992, at D1.

15. If in the course of adding and upgrading teams, a university attains gender parity

between its athletic program and its student body, it meets the first benchmark of the accommodation test. But, Title IX does not require that a school pour ever-increasing sums into its athletic establishment. If a university prefers to take another route, it can also bring itself into compliance with the first benchmark of the accommodation test by subtraction and downgrading, that is, by reducing opportunities for the overrepresented gender while keeping opportunities stable for the underrepresented gender (or reducing them to a much lesser extent).

women to interested and able men, regardless of the number of unserved women or the percentage of the student body that they comprise.

Because this is mountainous terrain, an example may serve to clarify the distinction between Brown's proposal and our understanding of the law. Suppose a university (Oooh U.) has a student body consisting of 1,000 men and 1,000 women, a one to one ratio. If 500 men and 250 women are able and interested athletes, the ratio of interested men to interested women is two to one. Brown takes the position that both the actual gender composition of the student body and whether there is unmet interest among the underrepresented gender are irrelevant; in order to satisfy the third benchmark, Oooh U. must only provide athletic opportunities in line with the two to one interested athlete ratio, say, 100 slots for men and 50 slots for women. Under this view, the interest of 200 women would be unmet—but there would be no Title IX violation.

We think that Brown's perception of the Title IX universe is myopic. The fact that the overrepresented gender is less than fully accommodated will not, in and of itself, excuse a shortfall in the provision of opportunities for the underrepresented gender. Rather, the law requires that, in the absence of continuing program expansion (benchmark two), schools either meet benchmark one by providing athletic opportunities in proportion to the gender composition of the student body (in Oooh U.'s case, a roughly equal number of slots for men and women, as the student body is equally divided), or meet benchmark three by fully accommodating interested athletes among the underrepresented sex (providing, at Oooh U., 250 slots for women).[16]

In the final analysis, Brown's view is wrong on two scores. It is wrong as a matter of law, for DED's Policy Interpretation, which requires full accommodation of the underrepresented gender, draws its essence from the statute. Whether Brown's concept might be thought more attractive, or whether we, if writing on a pristine page, would craft the regulation in a manner different than the agency, are not very important considerations. Because the agency's rendition stands upon a plausible, if not inevitable, reading of Title IX, we are obligated to enforce the regulation according to its tenor. See Chevron, 467 U.S. at 843 n. 11, 104 S.Ct. at 2782 n. 11 (holding that a "court need not conclude that the agency construction was the only one it permissibly could have adopted to uphold [it]")(collecting cases); Massachusetts v. Secretary of Agric., 984 F.2d 514, 522 (1st Cir.1993)(similar).

Brown's reading of Title IX is legally flawed for yet another reason. It proceeds from the premise that the agency's third benchmark countervails Title IX. But, this particular imprecation of the third benchmark overlooks the accommodation test's general purpose: to determine whether a student has been "excluded from participation in, [or] denied the benefits of" an athletic program "on the basis of sex * * *." 20 U.S.C. s 1681(a). While any single element of this tripartite test, in isolation, might not achieve the goal set by the statute, the test as a whole is reasonably constructed to implement the statute. * * *

16. Of course, if Oooh U. takes the benchmark three route, it will also have to provide at least the same number of slots for men; but, so long as women remain the underrepresented gender and their interests are fully accommodated, the university can provide as many (or as few) additional slots for men as it sees fit.

As it happens, Brown's view is also poor policy for, in the long run, a rule such as Brown advances would likely make it more difficult for colleges to ensure that they have complied with Title IX. Given that the survey of interests and abilities would begin under circumstances where men's athletic teams have a considerable head start, such a rule would almost certainly blunt the exhortation that schools should "take into account the nationally increasing levels of women's interests and abilities" and avoid "disadvantag [ing] members of an underrepresented sex * * *." 44 Fed.Reg. at 71,417.

Brown's proposal would also aggravate the quantification problems that are inevitably bound up with Title IX. Student plaintiffs, who carry the burden of proof on this issue, as well as universities monitoring self-compliance, would be required to assess the level of interest in both the male and female student populations and determine comparatively how completely the university was serving the interests of each sex. By contrast, as we read the accommodation test's third benchmark, it requires a relatively simple assessment of whether there is unmet need in the underrepresented gender that rises to a level sufficient to warrant a new team or the upgrading of an existing team. We think the simpler reading is far more serviceable.

Furthermore, by moving away from OCR's third benchmark, which focuses on the levels of interest and ability extant in the student body, Brown's theory invites thorny questions as to the appropriate survey population, whether from the university, typical feeder schools, or the regional community. In that way, Brown's proposal would do little more than overcomplicate an already complex equation.

We will not paint the lily. Brown's approach cannot withstand scrutiny on either legal or policy grounds. We conclude that DED's Policy Interpretation means exactly what it says. This plain meaning is a proper, permissible rendition of the statute.

IV. THE CONSTITUTIONAL CHALLENGE

We turn now to a series of case-specific issues, starting with Brown's constitutional challenge to the statutory scheme.

A. *Equal Protection.*

Brown asseverates that if the third part of the accommodation test is read as OCR wrote it—to require full and effective accommodation of the underrepresented gender—the test violates the Fifth Amendment's Equal Protection Clause. We think not.

Brown assumes that full and effective accommodation disadvantages male athletes.[17] While it might well be that more men than women at Brown are currently interested in sports, Brown points to no evidence in the record that men are any more likely to engage in athletics than women, absent socialization and disparate opportunities. In the absence of any proof supporting Brown's claim, and in view of congressional and administrative urging that

---

17. In characterizing Title IX as benefitting only women, Brown takes a rather isthmian view of the world at large. After all, colleges that have converted from exclusively female enrollment to coeducational enrollment face situations inverse to Brown's. In such a setting, the men's athletic program may well be underdeveloped, or underfunded, or both, while fiscal retrenchment offers no reprieve. Under these circumstances, Title IX would protect the athletic interests of men as the underrepresented sex.

women, given the opportunity, will naturally participate in athletics in numbers equal to men, we do not find that the regulation, when read in the common-sense manner that its language suggests, see supra Part III(C)(3), offends the Fifth Amendment.

What is more, even if we were to assume, for argument's sake, that the regulation creates a gender classification slanted somewhat in favor of women, we would find no constitutional infirmity. It is clear that Congress has broad powers under the Fifth Amendment to remedy past discrimination. See, e.g., Metro Broadcasting, Inc. v. FCC, 497 U.S. 547, 565–66, 110 S.Ct. 2997, 3009, 111 L.Ed.2d 445 (1990)(noting that Congress need not make specific findings of discrimination to grant race-conscious relief); Califano v. Webster, 430 U.S. 313, 317, 97 S.Ct. 1192, 1195, 51 L.Ed.2d 360 (1977)(upholding social security wage law that benefitted women in part because its purpose was "the permissible one of redressing our society's longstanding disparate treatment of women"). Despite the little legislative history regarding discrimination in collegiate athletics that emerged during the consideration of Title IX, Congress did hold "extensive hearings on higher education" when Title IX was pending, in the course of which "much testimony was heard with respect to discrimination against women in our institutions of higher education." H.R.Rep. No. 554, 92d Cong., 2d Sess. (1972), reprinted in 1972 U.S.C.C.A.N. 2462, 2511. Athletics featured even more prominently in Congress's decision to reverse the *Grove City* rule. * * * Under these circumstances, we find Brown's plaint unbecoming.

B. Affirmative Action.

Brown rehashes its equal protection argument and serves it up as a nominally different dish, arguing that the district court's preliminary injunction constitutes "affirmative action" and violates the Equal Protection Clause because the court lacked a necessary factual predicate to warrant such a step. It is, however, established beyond peradventure that, where no contrary legislative directive appears, the federal judiciary possesses the power to grant any appropriate relief on a cause of action appropriately brought pursuant to a federal statute. See Franklin, ___ U.S. at ___, 112 S.Ct. at 1035 * * *; see also Fed.R.Civ.P. 54(c). Hence, this initiative, too, is bootless.

V. BURDEN OF PROOF

In addition to its constitutional challenges, Brown questions the district court's allocation of the burden of proof. * * * [I]n the Title IX milieu, the controlling statutes and regulations are clear. To invoke the prophylaxis of Title IX, the statute, 20 U.S.C. § 1681(b), and the regulations, read together, require a Title IX plaintiff to show disparity between the gender composition of the institution's student body and its athletic program, thereby proving that there is an underrepresented gender. Then, the plaintiff must show that a second element—unmet interest—is present. In other words, the plaintiff must prove that the underrepresented gender has not been "fully and effectively accommodated by the present program." 44 Fed.Reg. at 71,418. If the plaintiff carries the devoir of persuasion on these two elements, she has proven her case unless the university shows, as an affirmative defense, "a history and continuing practice of program expansion which is demonstrably responsive to the developing interests and abilities of the members" of the underrepresented gender. Id.

Over and beyond the express dictates of the applicable statute and regulations, there is another valid reason for eschewing the Title VII paradigm in most Title IX cases. The scope and purpose of Title IX, which merely conditions government grants to educational institutions, are substantially different from those of Title VII, which sets basic employment standards. See Franklin v. Gwinnett County Pub. Sch., 911 F.2d 617, 622 (11th Cir.1990)(declining to apply Title VII analysis to Title IX litigation), aff'd, 503 U.S. 60, 112 S.Ct. 1028, 117 L.Ed.2d 208 (1992). Title IX, while it applies only to schools that receive federal funds, influences almost all aspects of educational management. In contrast, Title VII applies to a much wider range of institutions—virtually all employers—but targets only employment-related matters. Moreover, Title IX is largely aspirational—on the whole, affected institutions choose how to accomplish the statutory goal—whereas Title VII is largely peremptory—covered employers must adhere to statutorily prescribed standards. * * *

We conclude, therefore, that excepting perhaps in the employment discrimination context, see Lipsett v. University of P.R., 864 F.2d 881, 897 (1st Cir.1988)(applying Title VII standards in Title IX case, but explicitly limiting the crossover to the employment context), the Title VII burden-of-proof rules do not apply in Title IX cases. Consequently, a Title IX plaintiff makes out an athletic discrimination case by proving numerical disparity, coupled with unmet interest, each by a fair preponderance of the credible evidence, so long as the defendant does not rebut the plaintiff's showing by adducing preponderant history-and-practice evidence.

VI. THE PRELIMINARY INJUNCTION

* * *

Here, the district court found that the [preliminary injunction standards] favored plaintiffs' position. * * *

A. Likelihood of Success.

It is old hat, but still very much in fashion, that a movant's likelihood of success at trial is particularly influential in the preliminary injunction calculus. * * * In this case, the district court paid meticulous attention to the parties' prospects for success over the long haul. * * * It held a lengthy adversary hearing and reviewed voluminous written submissions. And at journey's end, it correctly focused on the three-part accommodation test. * * *

* * * [T]he court below found that, although Brown could point to "impressive growth" in its women's athletic program in the 1970s, the school had not continued filling the gap during the next two decades. * * * We find no error, therefore, in the district court's resolution of the second aspect of the accommodation test.

The third benchmark presents a more problematic scenario. The district court incorrectly held that Brown bore the burden of showing that it had fully and effectively accommodated the interests and abilities of its women athletes. * * * Section 1681(b) requires that the plaintiffs, rather than the University, prove a shortfall in the full and effective accommodation of interested female athletes by showing, initially, both numerical disparity and unmet interest.

See supra Part V. Nonetheless, we do not think that the court's bevue is fatal. Even when a trial court has misconstrued the law, an appellate tribunal may avoid remanding if the record is sufficiently developed and the facts necessary to shape the proper legal matrix are sufficiently clear.   * * *

* * *

In this instance, the district court's subsidiary findings of fact render it beyond cavil that the plaintiffs carried their burden of proof. The court found, for example, that there was "great interest and talent" amongst Brown's female undergraduates which, following the cuts, would go unserved. * * * Of particular moment, the court also found the interest and talent on campus ample to support women's varsity volleyball and gymnastics teams, * * * a finding that is hardly surprising in view of the teams' robust health before the budget-cutters arrived on the scene. The court proceeded to note that, while club teams can be equivalent to intercollegiate teams when they regularly participate in varsity competition, see 44 Fed.Reg. at 71,413 n. 1, the teams that Brown downgraded would not regularly be competing against varsity teams and would suffer a diminution of status in a wide range of other significant respects. * * *

* * * Because the record contains nothing that would allow a trier to find that Brown's athletic agenda reflects the makeup of its student body or that the plaintiff class is so poorly populated as to warrant a reduction in women's sports, the court's error was harmless. In a nutshell, the plaintiffs met their challenge on parts one and three of the accommodation test. This conclusion, in partnership with the district court's supportable finding that Brown did not satisfactorily demonstrate a continuing expansion of its women's athletic lineup, strikes the gold. The court's prediction of plaintiffs' probable success was, therefore, adequately grounded.

B. Irreparable Injury.

The next area of inquiry is irreparable harm. The district court heard from a variety of athletic administration experts. The court concluded that, absent judicial intervention, the plaintiffs would suffer irremediable injury in at least three respects: competitive posture, recruitment, and loss of coaching. As club teams, the district court thought women's volleyball and gymnastics would increasingly become less competitive, have fewer players, be unable to schedule varsity teams from other schools, become unattractive to potential stars making college choices, and suffer stagnation in the growth of individual talent due to the absence of coaching. * * * We will not second-guess the district court's finding of irreparable injury.

C. The Balance of Harms.

Finally, the district court found that the competing equities weighed in favor of granting the injunction. After hearing testimony from Brown's Financial Vice–President and its Associate Athletic Director, the district court concluded that the cost of the interim injunction would be relatively slight; and that, in view of discretionary funds already contained in the Athletic Department budget and a presidential "contingency fund," Brown possessed the wherewithal to defray the costs without undue hardship. * * * On balance, the court determined that the financial burden on Brown was tolerable, and, in any event, was overbalanced by the potential harm to the plaintiff class if the court took no action.

D. Summing Up.

We summarize succinctly, beginning with the probability of plaintiffs' success. In an era where the practices of higher education must adjust to stunted revenues, careening costs, and changing demographics, colleges might well be obliged to curb spending on programs, like athletics, that do not lie at the epicenter of their institutional mission. Title IX does not purport to override financial necessity. Yet, the pruning of athletic budgets cannot take place solely in comptrollers' offices, isolated from the legislative and regulatory imperatives that Title IX imposes.

This case aptly illustrates the point. Brown earnestly professes that it has done no more than slash women's and men's athletics by approximately the same degree, and, indeed, the raw numbers lend partial credence to that characterization.[23] But, Brown's claim overlooks the shortcomings that plagued its program before it took blade in hand. If a school, like Brown, eschews the first two benchmarks of the accommodation test, electing to stray from substantial proportionality and failing to march uninterruptedly in the direction of equal athletic opportunity, it must comply with the third benchmark. To do so, the school must fully and effectively accommodate the underrepresented gender's interests and abilities, even if that requires it to give the underrepresented gender (in this case, women) what amounts to a larger slice of a shrinking athletic-opportunity pie.

The record reveals that the court below paid heed to these realities. It properly recognized that even balanced use of the budget-paring knife runs afoul of Title IX where, as here, the fruits of a university's athletic program remain ill-distributed after the trimming takes place. Because the district court understood this principle, and because its findings of fact as to the case's probable outcome are based on substantial evidence, the court's determination that plaintiffs are likely to succeed on the merits is inexpugnable.

* * *

VII. REMEDIATION

After applying the preliminary injunction standard, the district court ordered relief pendente lite, temporarily reinstating the women's volleyball and gymnastics teams. Brown argues that such specific relief is inappropriate because it intrudes on Brown's discretion. The point has some cogency. We are a society that cherishes academic freedom and recognizes that universities deserve great leeway in their operations. See, e.g., Wynne v. Tufts Univ. Sch. of Med., 976 F.2d 791, 795 (1st Cir.1992), petition for cert. filed (Feb. 3, 1993); Lamphere v. Brown Univ., 875 F.2d 916, 922 (1st Cir.1989). In addition, Title IX does not require institutions to fund any particular number or type of athletic opportunities—only that they provide those opportunities in a nondiscriminatory fashion if they wish to receive federal funds.

---

23. We note, however, that while the cuts proposed by Brown eliminate a roughly equal number of athletic opportunities for women as for men, those cuts subtract roughly four times more money from the budget for female pancratiasts than from the budget for their male counterparts. See supra pp. 892–93. And, as a noted playwright once observed, "where there is no money, there is no change of any kind." Moss Hart, Act One (1959).

Nonetheless, the district court has broad discretionary power to take provisional steps restoring the status quo pending the conclusion of a trial. See Ricci v. Okin, 978 F.2d 764, 767 (1st Cir.1992); Guilbert, 934 F.2d at 7 & n. 3. Considering the district court's proper estimation and deft application of the preliminary injunction standard, see supra Part VI, we think that requiring Brown to maintain the women's volleyball and gymnastics teams in varsity status for the time being is a remedial choice within the district court's discretion. * * *

* * *

The preliminary injunction is affirmed, the temporary stay is dissolved, and the cause is remanded to the district court for further proceedings. Costs to appellees.

Notes on Cohen

1. After a 30–day trial on the merits, District Judge Raymond Pettine found that Brown University had violated Title IX by not "fully and effectively accommodating "the interests and ability of women to the extent necessary to provide "equal opportunity" within the meaning of Title IX regulations. Cohen v. Brown University, 879 F.Supp. 185 (D.R.I.1995). "There are interested women able to compete at the university-funded varsity level in gymnastics, fencing, skiing and water polo." 879 F.Supp. at 212. Therefore, Brown violated Title IX by demoting gymnastics from university-funded varsity level to club status, and by not elevating the remaining teams from the lower level donor-funded status to university-funded status. Stating that he has no desire to "micromanage" Brown's athletic program, Judge Pettine did not tell Brown what it had to do to come into compliance with Title IX. Instead, he ordered Brown to submit a comprehensive compliance plan to the court within 120 days, commenting:

> Brown may achieve compliance with Title IX in a number of ways. It may eliminate its athletic program altogether, it may elevate or create the requisite number of women's positions, it may demote or eliminate the requisite number of men's positions, or it may implement a combination of these remedies. I leave it entirely to Brown's discretion to decide how it will balance its program to provide equal opportunities for its men and women athletes. I recognize the financial constraints Brown faces; however, its own priorities will necessarily determine the path to compliance it elects to take.

Id. at 214. The order was stayed pending appeal; meanwhile the original preliminary injunction remained in effect.

2. Following the First Circuit's opinion in Cohen, interpreting Title IX in the context of college athletics, four additional circuit courts have reached similar results. In Favia v. Indiana University of Pennsylvania, 7 F.3d 332 (3d Cir.1993), plaintiffs, former members of the women's gymnastics and field hockey teams who had obtained a preliminary injunction in 1992 to save these programs from being cut for budgetary reasons, went back to court to prevent the University from substituting a soccer program for the gymnastics program. The substitution would have increased the total number of women participating in athletics from 159 (38.97% of the student-athlete population) to 188 (43.02% of the student-athlete population), but would have decreased the total funds devoted to women's athletics from $150,000 to $50,000. The District Court denied the University's motion to amend the preliminary injunction and the Third Circuit affirmed,

observing that it was not clear that the substitution would substantially ameliorate the University's likely violation of Title IX.

In Horner v. Kentucky High School Athletic Ass'n, 43 F.3d 265 (6th Cir. 1994), female high school athletes sued the athletic association (KHSAA) for refusing to offer competition in fast-pitch softball for girls, the equivalent of boys' baseball. Although girls' slow-pitch softball was offered, the girls could not compete for college scholarships because the National Collegiate Athletic Association (NCAA) does not offer slow-pitch softball, only women's fast-pitch. The appellate court reversed the district court's grant of summary judgment in favor of the KHSAA, relying on Title IX's policy interpretation requiring full and effective accommodation of girls' interests and abilities. For similar results, see Kelley v. Board of Trustees, 35 F.3d 265 (7th Cir.1994)(male swimmers sued for "reverse discrimination" after U. of Illinois cut 3 men's teams, swimming, diving and fencing, but only one women's team, diving; appellate court affirmed district court's rejection of men's claims under Title IX and equal protection, holding that even after eliminating men's swim team, men's athletic participation remained proportionately higher than women's compared to the student body); and Roberts v. Colorado State Bd. of Agriculture, 998 F.2d 824 (10th Cir.1993)(women's softball team at Colorado State sought reinstatement after it was eliminated along with men's baseball team; applying the "effective accommodation" test, appellate court affirmed trial court that university was not in compliance with Title IX, despite only a 10.5% disparity between women's enrollment and athletic participation).

3. Title IX regained its vitality at the same time as colleges and universities began experiencing financial difficulties and budget-cutting. Consequently, the impact on men's athletics has been more severe than expected. As a result, coaches of men's teams, particularly football, have become quite alarmed. See Martha Burk, Why Football Coaches Are Trying to Sack Title IX, Ms. Magazine, July/August 1995 at 93, discussing the American Football Coaches' Association's efforts to convince Congress to exempt football from Title IX. She points out that the coaches' association membership includes professional football coaches:

> College football amounts to a taxpayer-subsidized farm system for the pros, and sports corporations no doubt have an interest in short-changing women to maintain football in high style. If football programs were cut down to size, the National Football League might have to pay for training future players on its own—an expensive proposition.

Id. Editors at Sports Illustrated have labeled football the "third sex," criticizing the football coaches and their allies for seeking preferential status under Title IX. See Scorecard, The Third Sex, Sports Illustrated, Feb. 6, 1995 at 15. The editors take issue with the myth that football revenues underwrite women's sports: "In fact, only about one fifth of the NCAA's 554 football teams even pay for themselves; one third of the programs in Division I–A are running an annual deficit that averages more than $1 million." Id.

The Washington Supreme Court rejected an argument that football should be exempt from gender equity reviews of college athletics. In Blair v. Washington State University, 108 Wash.2d 558, 740 P.2d 1379 (1987), female athletes filed a sex discrimination action against Washington State University under the state Equal Rights Amendment. The state supreme court overturned the trial court's exemption of football from its calculation of proportional participation. The supreme court held:

The exclusion of football would prevent sex equity from ever being achieved since men would always be guaranteed many more participation opportunities than women, despite any efforts by the teams, the sex equity committee, or the program to promote women's athletics under the injunction.

740 P.2d at 1383. Despite this conclusion, the supreme court upheld that portion of the trial court's injunction which allowed each sport to retain the revenue it generated, effectively excluding football from the financial calculation. The appellate court found this provision to be gender-neutral, and would encourage women's sports to increase their own revenue. The court noted that sports such as football are certainly not prohibited from sharing revenue. In fact, the football program had been transferring $150,000 per year to the women's program. Id. at 1384. This limitation on sharing revenue has apparently not impeded the growth of women's athletics at Washington State. See footnote 14 in the *Cohen* opinion, congratulating Washington State on its gender equity achievements.

Meanwhile, the Chronicle of Higher Education's survey of college athletics in 1994 showed slow change since 1990 in the proportion of male to female athletes or women's share of scholarship money. See Debra Blum, Slow Progress on Equity, The Chronicle of Higher Education, Oct. 26, 1994 at A45. In 1990–91, among Division I schools, women made up 30.9% of varsity athletes and received 30.4% of scholarship money. In 1993–94, women were 33.6% of varsity athletes, receiving 35.7% of the scholarship money. Id. It is ironic that universities will spend thousands of dollars on litigation to defend their right to cut women's sports programs because of budget constraints. Given that Title IX plaintiffs can be awarded damages in addition to injunctive relief, one commentator suggests that universities analyze their compliance with Title IX under the three-part test specified in *Cohen* before making any program cuts in order to avoid costly litigation. Jill K. Johnson, Title IX and Intercollegiate Athletics: Current Judicial Interpretation of the Standards for Compliance, 74 Boston University Law Review 553 (1994).

4. One ironic consequence of Title IX was a significant decline in the percentage of coaches who were women. In 1972 when Title IX was passed, 90% of the coaches and administrators of women's college teams were women. By 1992 women accounted for only 48% of the coaches and 17% of administrators. Alexander Wolff, The Slow Track, Sports Illustrated, Sept. 28, 1992, p. 53, 62. After the NCAA took over collegiate women's sports in 1982, the pay for coaching women's teams went up significantly, so men started to apply for these jobs. Meanwhile, colleges merged their men's and women's athletic departments and male athletic directors took over women's sports. Men continue to occupy 99% of the coach and administrative jobs in men's college sports. Id. Donna Lopiano, Executive Director of the Women's Sports Foundation and former director of women's athletics at University of Texas at Austin, presented the following data at a 1993 hearing on intercollegiate sports before a committee of the House of Representatives:

Percent of Women Coaching Women's Sports

	1978	1992
Basketball	79.4%	63.5%
Cross Country	35.2%	20.1%
Softball	83.5%	63.7%
Tennis	72.9%	48.0%
Track & Field	52.0%	20.4%
Volleyball	86.6%	78.7%

Title IX Impact on Women's Participation in Intercollegiate Athletics and Gender Equity, Hearing before the Subcommittee on Commerce, Consumer Protection, and Competitiveness of the Committee on Energy and Commerce, House of Representatives, February 17, 1993, at p. 27 (citing R. Vivian Acosta and Linda Jean Carpenter). In 1982, about 5,140 jobs existed as head coaches of women's teams. The number of these jobs increased by 812 to 5,952 jobs in 1992. Women held only 181 more coaching jobs in 1992 than in 1982, while men coaching women's teams increased by 631 during the same period. Id. at p. 21. Employment discrimination remains a serious problem for women who want to coach college athletics, with a virtually all-male pool considered for those seeking jobs coaching revenue-producing men's sports, but a mixed pool of men and women applying for jobs coaching women's sports and nonrevenue-producing men's sports. Id. at p. 27.

In response to the continuing inequities in women's college sports, Congress passed the Equity in Athletics Disclosure Act in October 1994, Pub. L. 103–382, codified at 20 U.S.C.A. § 1092 (g)(1995), requiring college athletic programs to report annually to the public on the gender breakdown of athletes, staff, and expenditures by sport. The first reports will be due in October 1996. 20 U.S.C.A. § 1092 (g)(5).

Race discrimination remains a problem as well in college athletics. African American women coaches, administrators, or officials were non-existent in 1992. Testimony of Donna Lopiano in Hearings, supra, at 21. Title IX has done little to help African American women who continue to comprise a disproportionately small percentage of college athletes and are usually "typecast" into only track and basketball. Moreover, Title IX has not eased the prejudice that lesbian athletes experience nor the practice of pejoratively labeling women athletes as lesbians. Wendy Olson, Beyond Title IX: Toward an Agenda for Women and Sports in the 1990s, 3 Yale Journal of Law and Feminism 105, 127–134 (1991) Olson has called for a stronger alliance between the women's sports movement and the broader feminist movement, emphasizing the important role that sports plays in contemporary American culture. Id. at 136. She cites sociologist Harry Edwards, Desegregating Sexist Sport, in Out of the Bleachers (S. Twin, ed. 1979), for the proposition that sports has replaced formal religion as a dominant force in the lives of many Americans, mostly male: "The women's movement cannot afford to ignore such a pervasive social institution, even if the institution seems to want to ignore the women's movement." Id.

C. AFFIRMATIVE ACTION

Text Note
Room at the Top: Affirmative Action at Colleges and Universities

Federal legislation enacted in the 1960s to prevent discrimination in the workplace did not initially apply to academic employment. The 1963 Equal Pay Act did not extend to academic or professional employees.[1] Title VII of the 1964 Civil Rights Act did not cover state agencies or educational institutions.[2] Only the

---

1. Pub.L. 92–318 Sec. 906(b)(1), 86 Stat. 375, amended the Fair Labor Standards Act to extend the provisions of the Equal Pay Act to employees "employed in a bona fide executive, administrative, or professional capacity," * * *.

2. As originally enacted, Title VII contained specific exemptions in section 702. Among

constitutional clauses guaranteeing due process and equal protection were available at the national level to serve as the basis for a legal attack on the discriminatory policies of educational employers.[3]

In 1967, however, Executive Order 11246, issued in 1965 and initially applicable to discrimination by federal contractors based on race, religion, color, or national origin, was amended by Executive Order 11375 to apply to sex discrimination. The Order requires federal contractors to adopt and implement "affirmative action programs" to promote attainment of equal employment objectives.[4] Late in 1969 a small and relatively unknown women's civil rights organization, the Women's Equity Action League (WEAL), "discovered" Executive Order 11375, and realized that it could provide a potential weapon against sex discrimination at schools that hold federal contracts: a group estimated to include more than 80 percent of the nation's institutions of higher education.

Under the supervision of Dr. Bernice Sandler,[5] WEAL filed scores of complaints with the Department of Labor, and later with the Department of Health, Education and Welfare, when HEW's Office for Civil Rights was assigned responsibility for Executive Order compliance at universities and colleges. An initial complaint charging the entire academic community with an "industry-wide" pattern of sex discrimination was accompanied by substantial documentation. But most of the complaints filed against particular institutions took the form of a brief letter calling for comprehensive investigation. A sample follows.[6]

The Honorable Elliot Richardson

Secretary

Department of Health, Education and Welfare

Washington. D.C. 20201

Dear Mr. Secretary:

Please consider this letter as a formal charge of sex discrimination against _____ University. These charges are filed under Executive Order 11246 as amended, which forbids *all* federal contractors from discriminating on the basis of sex.

The charges are based on information attached to this letter giving the number of women in various units of the University. The figures detail a consistent pattern of discrimination against women at _____. For example, of 172 faculty in the College of Liberal Arts, not one woman is a full professor.

---

these exemptions was "an educational institution with respect to the employment of individuals to perform work connected with the educational activities of such institution." This exemption was removed from Section 702 by the Equal Employment Opportunity Act of 1972, Pub.L. 261 Sec. 3, 86 Stat. 103.

3. The early cases brought by pregnant schoolteachers to challenge mandatory maternity leave policies that forced them out of the classroom were brought under 42 U.S.C.A. § 1983. See, e.g., Cohen v. Chesterfield County School Board, 474 F.2d 395 (4th Cir. 1973)(en banc), reversed sub nom. Cleveland Bd. of Educ. v. LaFleur 414 U.S. 632, 94 S.Ct. 791, 39 L.Ed.2d 52 (1974).

4. 39 C.F.R. 173. When the WEAL effort began, the Executive Order had been enforced primarily with respect to access by minorities to construction work. Sex discrimination guidelines had not yet been issued by the Department of Labor, and the Department's Order No. 4, detailing affirmative action plan requirements for federal contractors, then applied only to minorities, not to women.

5. Among her many early comments on Executive Order potential, see The Day WEAL Opened Pandora's Box, Chronicle of Higher Education, January 22, 1973, p. 8; Male vs. Female: A Bread-and-Butter Issue, Chronicle of Higher Education, February 5, 1973, p. 4; Affirmative Action is Still Very Much Alive, Chronicle of Higher Education, April 9, 1973, p. 7.

6. Sample supplied by Dr. Bernice Sandler.

Only two are associate professors. The remaining 44 women are in the lower ranks, without tenure. In the Psychology Department, where one would expect a substantial number of women because 23% of the doctorates awarded nationally go to women, there were no women on the faculty of 12. In the College of Education where one would also expect to find substantial numbers of women, only 5 of the 48 assistant, associate and full professors are women, although at the lowest level, fully half of the instructors are women (4 out of 8). In administration, women are present but mainly at the lower levels. There are no women deans, nor are any of the officers of the University female.

The Women's Equity Action League requests an immediate full scale compliance review, and that such review include an investigation of admission policies, financial aid to women students, placement of graduates, recruiting, hiring and promotion policies for all women staff and faculty, and salary inequities. We also ask that all current contract negotiations be suspended until such time as all inequities are eliminated and an acceptable plan of affirmative action is implemented. Please notify us when the compliance review begins.

Sincerely,

Other women's organizations, campus groups and commissions or caucuses in various professions joined the effort in 1970 and 1971. By the end of 1971, complaints had been filed against over 350 institutions, compliance reviews, varying considerably in style and vigor from one campus to another, had been initiated at an estimated 200 institutions, and receipt of contract funds had been delayed at approximately 40 institutions.

For a time, it appeared that the Executive Order had a "bite" more intimidating than any other remedy against employment discrimination. Unlike Title IX of the Education Amendments of 1972, which, until its amendment in 1988, provided for sanctions limited to the noncomplying unit or program, Executive Order sanctions may be directed to the university or college as a whole. Thus noncompliance by the Philosophy Department could lead to termination of a contract to be performed at the university's School of Engineering. In practice, however, delayed funding has been the sole coercive measure. In no case to date has any contract been terminated, nor has the ultimate sanction—debarment from federal contracts—been invoked against any school. Non-application of the more drastic sanctions is at least in part a reflection of the manner in which the Order is enforced. Although women and minorities are the beneficiaries of the Order, the only direct participants in the compliance review procedure are the institution under investigation, and the reviewing agency.[7] Private suits for violations of the Order have not been permitted.[8] However, the remedial gap for academic employees or applicants for employment was closed in 1972 when Title VII

7. Affected groups have been permitted to sue the agency charged with enforcing the Order to compel it to abide by its own regulations. See Legal Aid Soc'y of Alameda County v. Brennan, 608 F.2d 1319, 1328–36 (9th Cir. 1979).

8. E.g., Cohen v. Illinois Institute of Technology, 524 F.2d 818, 822 n. 4 (7th Cir.1975), cert. denied 425 U.S. 943, 96 S.Ct. 1683, 48 L.Ed.2d 187 (1976). But see Lewis v. Western Airlines, Inc., 379 F.Supp. 684 (N.D.Cal.1974)(recognizing a private cause of action under the Order by an employee against the federal contractor; decision came prior to the Ninth Circuit's opinion in *Legal Aid Society of Alameda County,* supra note 7).

coverage was extended to educational institutions.[9] As a result of that extension, individual complaints under the Executive Order were no longer handled by HEW's Office for Civil Rights, but were referred to the Equal Employment Opportunity Commission. As we have seen, the Supreme Court interpreted Title IX to apply to academic employment in 1982.[10]

The initial HEW contract compliance investigations were hampered by inadequate staffing and, until October 1972, the absence of guidelines defining "affirmative action" and appropriate modes of implementation in an academic setting. Lack of uniform policies and procedures among regional offices engaged in compliance reviews, and insufficient notice at the start and throughout the review process were principal criticisms raised by schools as well as women's groups.[11]

Some of the investigators approached their work with a notable lack of enthusiasm. For example, the head of HEW's regional Office for Civil Rights in Chicago was quoted in the July 16, 1971 issue of Science as follows: "* * * if we acted on these [complaints of sex discrimination] there would be a flood * * *. If the women see that we're effective, they will file more charges. If they see that we aren't, they won't bother."[12] On the university side, officials sometimes spoke intemperately about investigations thought to be overzealous. The Human Relations Director at the University of Michigan was quoted in the March 20, 1971 issue of the New Republic for the remark: "Once you let women know they've got you over a barrel, they'll take everything they can get from you."[13] The same article attributes to a vice president of the University the comment: "We just want to get these bastards at HEW off our back."[14] A professor at Columbia was quoted in the December 4, 1972 issue of Newsweek for the comment: "We haven't had this kind of intervention since the days of Joe McCarthy."[15] Not surprisingly, women university officials and professors took a different view. Martha E. Peterson, the president of Barnard College, regarded affirmative action as a disgrace for a different reason. She viewed the hostile reaction to women's demands for equal treatment as a prime example of the academic community's lack of internal leadership. Federal intervention occurred, she observed, because "the higher education community seemed unable to recognize and to take action in correcting injustices until forced to do so * * *. The disgrace of 'affirmative action' is that HEW had to get into it at all."[16] Professor Gertrude Ezorsky noted

9. Pub.L. 92–261, 86 Stat. 103 (1972), amending former 42 U.S.C.A. §§ 2000e–1 and 2000e(b). The first order granted to an academic woman under Title VII was made on May 29, 1973, when the Federal District Court for the Western District of Pennsylvania issued a preliminary injunction restraining the University of Pittsburgh from terminating the employment of Dr. Sharon Johnson, an assistant professor at the University's Medical School. Johnson v. University of Pittsburgh, 359 F.Supp. 1002 (W.D.Pa.1973). Dr. Johnson subsequently lost on the merits. Johnson v. University of Pittsburgh, 435 F.Supp. 1328 (W.D.Pa.1977). See Text Note on Proving Discrimination: Title VII in Academe, at p. 871, supra.

10. North Haven Board of Education v. Bell, 456 U.S. 512, 102 S.Ct. 1912, 72 L.Ed.2d 299 (1982).

11. See Bernice Sandler & Steinbach, HEW Contract Compliance—Major Concerns of Institutions, in American Council on Education

Special Report on Sex Discrimination and Contract Compliance 5 (April 1972).

12. At p. 215.

13. Zwerdling, Sex Discrimination on Campus, The Womanpower Problem, at p. 11.

14. Id. at 12. For a later account of developments at Michigan, see Women in Michigan: Academic Sexism under Siege, Science, November 24, 1972, p. 841.

15. At p. 127. See also Seabury, HEW and the Universities, Commentary, February 1972, at 38; The Idea of Merit, Commentary, December 1972, at 41.

16. Keynote address of Martha E. Peterson at October 1972 annual meeting of American Council on Education, as reported in Chronicle of Higher Education, October 16, 1972, p. 3. The theme of the meeting was "Women in Higher Education." Background papers appear in Women in Higher Education (American Council on Education 1972).

that if the universities had truly been following a merit system in hiring and promotion, "academic women wouldn't have found it necessary to call in the law."[17] A similar position was taken at the University of Pennsylvania when, despite the absence of charges against it, a plan to reduce barriers to equal opportunity for women was made public. Announcing the plan in January 1971, the University's president said: "Our action is less because of the Federal Government pressing us, but more because of the humaneness that universities stand for. We should be concerned not just with half of humanity but with all of it."[18]

Indicative of the ambivalence displayed by many university leaders are the following excerpts from an address by President William J. McGill of Columbia University at the University of Michigan commencement ceremonies, May 6, 1972. Columbia and Michigan had experienced compliance reviews that attracted considerable media coverage. President McGill entitled his address: "A New Problem in Academic Freedom"; he defined the problem as the "conflict between affirmative action for removing discrimination and the criteria of excellence in faculty appointments":

* * *

In many respects universities need to concede the necessity for accepting this new idea of non-discrimination. For too long we have been content with appointment practices at faculty level that have produced relatively few women faculty members, fewer blacks, very few orientals and almost no Puerto Ricans and Chicanos. We can take no pride in such a performance. Moreover, it is no longer satisfactory to claim that our standards of excellence preclude the appointment of significant numbers of women or ethnic minorities merely because they are underrepresented in the academic population. If that is true we must begin to turn our attention to eliminating such underrepresentation by concentrating our efforts on graduate and professional training. This is one of the historic avenues for social mobility provided by American society. We must also recognize that it is a solemn obligation of universities to take the leadership in society in this vital area. Thus we can have no quarrel with the principle of affirmative action, or with its objectives. Women, blacks, and latins are crying out for their full rights in our society and there is no excuse for pious or sanctimonious explanations of why these rights cannot be granted in 1972. We are past all that.

Nevertheless, many of us, my own university included, are experiencing serious problems with the government over issues of affirmative action. In the first place, the statistics describing availability of qualified minorities and women at faculty levels are a morass of confusion. * * * Moreover, such statistics are contaminated by the question of levels of ability of quality, and this, as you might imagine, is an extraordinarily sensitive issue.

Many universities, for example, have been criticized for turning out a certain fraction of women Ph.D.'s and then employing a much smaller fraction. The discrepancy is interpreted as evidence of a bias against the employment of women and indeed it may be. That is just the conclusion drawn by militant feminists groups pressing for their rights. There is, however, another explanation which may govern at least some of the observed

17. Ezorsky, The Fight Over University Women, The New York Review of Books, May 16, 1974, at 32, 35.

18. Pennsylvania Gazette, March 1971, at 7.

discrepancies. Research by sociologists has confirmed an apparent sex bias favoring males in appointments to academic departments of major universities. However, studies of appointment statistics to science departments also show that when quality and quantity of publications are taken into account, sex status has very little effect on the prestige rank of a scientist's academic affiliation, nor does it influence the professional age at which women are promoted to tenured positions. Accordingly, the observed first order statistics suggesting bias against women at faculty levels, may be due to an artifact caused by an artificial relation between sex and quality in our current production of Ph.D.'s. If such a relation does exist, we need to determine its cause and root it out. The point is that no one knows with any precision what biases exist in our faculty appointment procedures because of the high levels of ability required for appointment at universities such as Michigan and Columbia and because of the wide dispersion in ability between the best and the worst Ph.D.'s. Most university people recognize that these are matters of the utmost subtlety. They need to be handled with great restraint by government officials seeking to end discrimination at universities. * * *

Other academics were more sanguine about the compatibility of affirmative action and quality standards. Christopher Jencks and David Reisman considered the problem before the Executive Order arrived on campus:[19]

> The professions may have very narrow assumptions about what kinds of work are valuable and what kinds are not * * *. Suppose, for example, that a man gets a Ph.D. and becomes a scholar at a leading university, while his equally talented wife gets a Ph.D. and teaches at a small women's college nearby. We would argue that the wife may well make more of a contribution to the general welfare through her teaching than her husband makes by writing for the *Publications of the Modern Language Association* or the *Physical Review*. In saying this we do not mean to prejudge the debate over teaching versus research, which must be looked at on a case-by-case basis. The problem is that graduate admissions committees *do* prejudge the debate, taking it for granted that a "serious scholar" who publishes is *automatically* doing more for the world than a more brilliant woman who "dissipates" her energies teaching irregularly at local colleges. We have noticed, however, that it is often precisely the part-time female practitioner who is most available for professional innovation, such as the medical and legal programs sponsored by the Office of Economic Opportunity. Men with families to support are less free to heed their consciences and imaginations when asked to work on such ventures.

The Carnegie Commission on Higher Education, after a comprehensive study of the problem, concluded that fears of dilution of academic excellence were not supported by the evidence regarding women's potential:[20]

> We do not share the views of some male academic critics of affirmative action for women whose writings imply that increasing the number of women on faculties will inevitably lower quality. Such views are inconsistent with the evidence we have presented relating to the relative ability of women holding doctor's degrees. We do believe, however, that some of this criticism has arisen because departments or schools have unwisely explained the rejection of particular white male candidates on the ground that their institu-

19. C. Jencks & D. Reisman, The Academic Revolution 299 (1968).

20. Report of the Carnegie Commission on Higher Education, Opportunities for Women in Higher Education (Sept. 1973), at 138–39.

tion's policies force them to hire women or members of minority groups. We believe that such explanations often provide a convenient way out of informing a particular candidate that he is not the most qualified applicant for a position. * * *

Sensitive to the threat to university autonomy that President McGill and many others have noted, Alan Pifer, President of the Carnegie Corporation, said of the dilemma:[21]

> * * * I regret that it has become necessary, because of intransigence, or at least a lack of perceptiveness, on the part of higher education, for government to take coercive action [through Executive Order affirmative action requirements]. Measures such as these seem to me to constitute an invasion of campus autonomy and an abridgement of academic freedom. On the other hand, government has a basic obligation to protect the rights of its citizens— yes, even women—and without the threat of coercion it seems unlikely higher education would have budged an inch on the issue. Certainly it had every chance to do so and failed.

In October, 1972, HEW's Office for Civil Rights issued the long-awaited Higher Education Guidelines for application of the Executive Order.[22] The Guidelines were expected to eliminate some of the diversity in compliance review standards that drew criticism from women's organizations as well as institutions. They emphasized the distinction between nondiscrimination—"the elimination of all existing discriminatory conditions, whether purposeful or inadvertent * * * on grounds of race, color, religion, sex or national origin"—and affirmative action,[23] which

> requires the contractor to do more than ensure employment neutrality. As the phrase implies, affirmative action requires the employer to make additional efforts to recruit, employ and promote qualified members of groups formerly excluded * * *. The premise of the affirmative action concept * * * is that unless positive action is undertaken to overcome the effects of systemic institutional forms of exclusion and discrimination, a benign neutrality in employment practices will tend to perpetuate the *status quo ante* indefinitely.

The Guidelines instructed institutions to undertake job analyses to identify "underutilization," as determined by the availability of qualified women. On the basis of these analyses, the institution must develop a plan setting numerical goals and timetables consistent with the availability of qualified women and the projected turnover in employment. Underscored in the Guidelines was the distinction between goals established as a target to aim at, and inflexible quotas that must be filled even to the detriment of academic standards: "[W]hile goals are required, quotas are neither required nor permitted by the Executive Order.

---

21. Speech Before the Southern Association of Colleges and Schools, November 29, 1971.

22. The Guidelines were reprinted in 37 Fed.Reg. 24686–24696 (November 18, 1972). They were designed to interpret the meaning of Order No. 4 on affirmative action, issued by the Office of Federal Contract Compliance Programs (OFCCP), Department of Labor, and to apply the affirmative action requirements to higher education. Lenore Weitzman, Legal Requirements * * *, Women in Academia (Elga Wasserman et al. eds., 1975) at 46. The Guidelines were never codified in the Code of Federal Regulations. The current Affirmative

Action Guidelines, Revised Order No. 4, are codified at 41 C.F.R. §§ 60–2 60.2.32 (1980).

23. The affirmative action requirements in the Guidelines related to women and "minorities," defined by the Department of Labor as "Negroes, Spanish-surnamed, American Indians and Orientals." Some of the Guidelines reflected differences in the character of problems encountered by women and minorities; for example, the guidelines on maternity and parental leaves and on amendment of antinepotism policies dealt with issues of special concern to women. Guidelines at 2–3.

When used correctly, goals are an indicator of probable compliance and achievement, not a rigid or exclusive measure of performance."[24]

The Guidelines called for "reasonably explicit" criteria for hiring and promotion, drawn by the institution and made available to applicants and employees. The Guidelines further stipulated that institutions should use search committees that include women, draw on data provided by women's groups, and advertise openings through channels that will reach women; eliminate salary and fringe benefit differentials not based on qualifications and merit; amend antinepotism rules that in practice operate to deny opportunity to a wife rather than to a husband; revise policies on employment of the institution's own graduates so that they do not work to deny opportunities to women; provide maternity leave for women and child rearing leave for both sexes;[25] encourage child care programs; develop sound internal grievance procedures; and publish the affirmative action plan.

The anticipated improvement in agency-campus interaction over affirmative action as a result of the Guidelines did not, however, materialize. Examining the results in 1976, Lewis Solomon and Judith Heeter concluded:[26]

> Today, after nearly four years under the Guidelines, affirmative action is more than ever a hotly contested policy. Rather than inducing dramatic changes in the composition of faculties, it has instead proved to be more a case study of how difficult it is to force profound change in an institution as complex, prestigious, slow-moving, and sensitive to the economy as a college or university.

Dr. Bernice Sandler,[27] looking back in 1980 over ten years of effort to obtain compliance with the Order in the wake of WEAL's initial charges filed on January 31, 1970, gave this assessment:

> The past decade has been one of paradox. On the one hand, hundreds of institutions were charged with sex discrimination. More than twelve hundred pages of congressional hearings documented a pattern of discrimination throughout academe, and in response, the Congress shaped a new national policy to prohibit sex discrimination on campus. Title VII of the 1964 Civil Rights Act was amended to cover employment in educational institutions. The Equal Pay Act was amended to cover executives, administrators and professionals, which included faculty women. Title IX of the Education Amendments of 1972 was also enacted to cover students in all federally assisted educational programs. Women were energized; women's organiza-

24. Guidelines at 4. See also id. at 8: "Statements [that the Executive Order requires preferential treatment regardless of merit] constitute either a misunderstanding of the law or a willful distortion of it. In either case, where they actually reflect decisions not to employ or promote on grounds of race, color, sex, religion or national origin, they constitute a violation of the Executive Order and other Federal laws."

25. A number of affirmative action plans provide for part-time full faculty status appointments and extension of the period in which tenure determinations are made for parents of young children whose family commitments require reduced teaching schedules. The Guidelines took no position on part-time

appointments and delayed tenure decisions, but both were covered in Recommendations of the American Association of University Women, Standards for Women in Higher Education: Affirmative policy in achieving sex equality in the academic community (1972). See also Joint Statement on Women in Higher Education (American Association of University Women 1973).

26. Solomon & Heeter, Affirmative Action in Higher Education: Towards A Rationale For Preference, 52 Notre Dame Law. 41, 49 (1976).

27. Sandler, Editorial: Women on Campus: A Ten-Year Retrospect, 26 On Campus With Women 2–3 (Association of American Colleges, Spring 1980).

tions and caucuses proliferated; more charges of sex discrimination were filed against institutions of higher education than against any other industry in the country. As a result of all this activity, the number and proportion of women students increased substantially at all levels; women's studies courses increased from a mere handful to over 15,000; innumerable campuses have "women's committees," and written affirmative action plans.

On the other hand, the more things change, the more they remain the same:

- Most women continue to major in the traditional female fields such as education.

- The salaries of women in academe are still lower than those of men with comparable training and experience at every age, every degree level, every field, and every type of institution.

- Despite an increase in the number of women assistant professors, these gains were not matched by gains in promotions; there has been no comparable gain in the tenured ranks.

- The unemployment rate for women Ph.D.'s in the sciences and social sciences is two to four times that of men.

- More than 90 percent of all college students attend institutions where all three of the top administrative positions—president, chief academic officer, and dean—are held by men.

The general pattern of women employed in post-secondary institutions is as distressingly the same as it was in 1970:

- The higher the rank, the fewer the women.

- The more prestigious the field or the school, the fewer the women.

- The higher the prestige of the job, the fewer women (only 6.8 percent of college presidents are female, and most of them are at women's colleges).

* * * Notwithstanding myths to the contrary, not one penny of federal dollars has ever been taken away because of sex discrimination. In fact, the few times that federal dollars have been temporarily delayed has usually occurred because an institution did not have a written affirmative action plan, not because of sex discrimination. * * *

Nevertheless, there has been some progress. One of the most important changes in the past decade has been the legitimatization of women's issues as an area of concern in higher education. Throughout the educational community, women have joined together to press for better policies and programs. There are more than 100 women's caucuses or committees in the various academic and professional organizations. In several states women have organized statewide networks of academic women. Most campuses, as mentioned earlier, have a committee or commission to deal with women's issues. Although women students have been somewhat less active, they too have pressed for change in such areas as athletics, health services, and the elimination of sexual harassment by male faculty. Still another area of progress lies in the marked increase of women at the graduate level, and in medicine, science and law.

Most important, perhaps, is that a national policy is now in place and that is a major accomplishment. It is probably the most comprehensive national policy in the world regarding discrimination against women in the workplace, and women and girls in the schoolroom. Although there have been continued attempts to chip parts of it away, it is unlikely that Congress would ever overturn all of the legislation.

* * *

Most of Bernice Sandler's observations are still true in the 1990s. As Professor Martha West has observed, universities continue to maintain affirmative action plans as required by federal order, but virtually no effort is made to enforce them in regard to discrimination against academic women.[28]

As we have seen, the Executive Order is by no means the only tool for remedying employment discrimination in higher education. The Sloan Commission on Government and Higher Education[29] counted seventeen different legal provisions, including constitutional provisions, executive orders, and federal laws, administered by eight different government agencies, that bear on equal opportunity in higher education. It found this diversity an impediment to a coordinated enforcement effort. Moreover, because of the collegial nature of academic employment, the Commission believed that litigation may be counterproductive:[30]

> In the final analysis, faculty status is not won in the courtroom. Remedies that compel employment or tenure ignore the sociology of the collegial structure. Less drastic remedies, such as ordering back-pay, may recoup financial loss, but litigiousness is not an attribute that enhances standing with colleagues. An individual litigant may win the immediate battle at great emotional and economic cost, only to lose the academic war.

But the Commission recognized that past discrimination has existed in higher education, and it was convinced that the regulatory effort has produced improvements and that such efforts continue to be necessary.[31] Although the Sloan Commission's proposals for changes in enforcement mechanisms were not implemented, its core insight that the faculty must become "seriously involved" in affirmative action programs if such programs are to have "lasting impact",[32] however, is a sound one. In most colleges and universities, the initial hiring decisions are made at the departmental level. Accordingly, it is at that level that a commitment to affirmative action efforts will have the greatest impact. A departmental decision to hold open available faculty positions while a serious search for women and minority candidates is undertaken is perhaps the single most effective way to diversify faculty composition.[33] Beyond that, as a University of California study confirmed in 1987, faculty members must become aware that "actions they take in relation to undergraduates, graduates, junior and senior faculty colleagues, all affect the 'pipeline' and its ability to attract, prepare and promote minority and women along an academic career trajectory."[34]

The moment is at hand for building diversity in the professorial ranks. The

---

28. Martha S. West, Gender Bias in Academic Robes: The Law's Failure to Protect Women Faculty, 67 Temple L. Rev. 67, 161–165 (1994).

29. Report of the Sloan Commission on Government and Higher Education, A Program for Renewed Partnership, at 63 (1980).

30. Id., at 61.

31. Id., at 56–57.

32. Id., at 11.

33. See Herma Hill Kay, The Need for Self–Imposed Quotas in Academic Employment, 1979 Wash.U.L.Q. 137.

34. The University of California in the Twenty–First Century: Successful Approaches to Faculty Diversity, p. 69 (Office of the President, Spring 1987).

University of California study made this point well:[35]

> Like many research institutions across the U.S., the University of California
> faces a high rate of turnover in its faculty between now—and especially after
> 1989—and the early 2000s. In this period, it is projected that approximately
> 40% of the current ladder rank faculty members will retire; simultaneously,
> enrollments are projected to increase, indicating further demands for addi-
> tional faculty. At this rate, the University may need to hire about 6,000 new
> ladder rank faculty by the year 2000, or somewhat over 400 per year,
> compared to a present rate of approximately 300 per year[.] * * * Thus, the
> next two decades present an unusual opportunity for the University to
> improve dramatically the representation of women and minorities on its
> faculty.

The University of California, in response to budget problems, offered three
generous early retirement options to its faculty from 1991 through 1994. As a
result, 25% of the faculty retired, over 90% of them white men. Consequently,
the percentage of women on the UC system's ladder rank faculty increased from
17% in 1990 to 22% in 1994, not as the result of new hires, but because of male
attrition.[36] On July 20, 1995, the Regents of the University of California attempted to abolish affirmative action within the university by passing resolutions
prohibiting the university from using "race, religion, sex, color, ethnicity, or
national origin as criteria" for admission, employment, and in contracting.[37] The
resolution on employment and contracting, however, specified that no actions
would be prohibited that were necessary to maintain eligibility for federal or state
programs or funds.[38] Because the university's affirmative action plans for employment are mandated by Executive Order 11246, the university must continue
to make "every good faith effort" to cure the "underutilization" of women and
people of color in its faculty ranks.[39] The practical impact of the Regents' action
falls on its admission programs, not its employment practices, but the political
impact will cast a wider shadow. Strong efforts will be necessary to maintain
diversity in faculty hiring.

So far, the greatest impact of affirmative action efforts has been in increasing
the number of newly hired women and minority group faculty members at the
entry level. For most, the tenure decision is yet to come. That process, requiring
as it does the evaluation of one's colleagues at the departmental level, followed in
most institutions by *ad hoc* peer review committees, and marked by subjective
judgments at all levels, can easily be contaminated by a distaste for affirmative
action requirements. Judge Higginbotham's comment that "it is better for
victims to endure the emotional and economic cost of litigation than to win
neither the 'immediate battle' nor the academic war"[40] reflects a choice between
harsh alternatives. The support of sympathetic colleagues is vitally important to
many.

---

35. Id., at 31. The impact on such projections of the elimination of mandatory retirement laws affecting tenured employees in 1994
is uncertain, and few college officials have formulated plans to deal with the issue. The
Chronicle of Higher Education, Jan. 6, 1988, at
p. A11, col. 2.

36. Martha West, Women Faculty: Frozen
in Time, Academe, July/August 1995 at 28
(Am. Assn. of Univ. Profs.).

37. University of California Board of Regents, Resolutions SP–1 and SP–2, July 20,
1995.

38. Regents Resolution SP–2, Section 3,
July 20, 1995.

39. See Affirmative Action Guidelines, Revised Order No. 4, 41 C.F.R. § 60–2.10 (1980).

40. Report of the Sloan Commission, supra
note 29, at 91–92.

D. LAW SCHOOLS

Introductory Note
Women as Law Students and Professors

The spectacular rise in women's enrollment in law schools in the 1970s is a prime indicator of the impact of the women's movement on the career aspirations of female students. For both sexes, a declining market for Ph.D.s and the appeal of a profession that deals with important social problems contributed to the application boom. But these factors alone cannot account for the readiness of increasing numbers of women to prepare for a profession that, perhaps more than any other in the United States, has been sex-typed as male.

As Justice Bradley's concurring opinion in Bradwell[1] graphically illustrates, "the concepts of 'woman' and 'lawyer' have historically been incompatible."[2] A 1922 Barnard graduate recalled:[3]

> At the time I was ready to enter law school, women were looked upon as people who should not be in law schools. * * * I wanted very much to go to Columbia, but I couldn't get in. I went over to see Harlan Stone, Dean Stone, who was later Chief Justice, and asked him to open the law school [to women] and he said no. * * * I asked why * * * and he said "We don't because we don't." That was final.

Other prestigious law schools continued not to reason why long after the general pattern of exclusion had ended, most conspicuously, Harvard Law School, which remained off limits to women until the 1950s. But practices once largely unchallenged even by women professionals[4] were subjected to critical appraisal in the late 1960s as the idea of equal opportunity for men and women began to take hold. Women law students organized and made demands for equal treatment in classrooms and in access to law school facilities and placement services.[5] Faculty members, many of them prominent in efforts to reduce racial, religious, economic and political discrimination, began to assess student complaints and evidence of prejudice among legal employers.[6]

On December 30, 1970, the Association of American Law Schools (AALS) became one of the first national academic associations to prohibit sex discrimination in admissions, employment and placement at member schools. AALS adoption of a ban on sex discrimination was preceded by a survey on the status of women in law schools; covering the period 1966–1970, the survey was conducted

---

1. Bradwell v. Illinois, 83 U.S. (16 Wall.) 130, 21 L.Ed. 442 (1873)(discussed in the Text Note on Legislative and Judicial Perspectives on American Womanhood at p. 11, supra).

2. Bradley Soule & Kay Standley, Lawyers' Perceptions of Sex Discrimination in Their Profession, 59 A.B.A.J. 1144 (1973).

3. Cynthia Fuchs Epstein, Women in Law 51 (reporting an interview with Frances Marlatt). See generally, Karen Berger Morello, The Invisible Bar: The Woman Lawyer in America: 1638 to the Present (1986).

4. See C. Epstein, supra, note 3 at 37. For an indication of conditions and lawyers' attitudes at the turn of the century, see Isabella Mary Pettus, The Legal Education of Women, 61 Alb.L.J. 325 (1900). See also D. Kelly Weis-

berg, Barred From the Bar: Women and Legal Education in the United States 1870–1890, 28 J.Leg.Ed. 485 (1977).

5. E.g., Statement of Women's Rights Committee of New York University Law School, in Discrimination Against Women, Hearings on Section 805 of H.R. 16098 Before the Special Subcomm. on Education of the House Comm. on Education and Labor, 91st Cong., 2d Sess. 584 (1970); Dorothy J. Glancy, Women in Law: The Dependable Ones, 21 Harv.L.S.Bull. 22 (1970).

6. See James F. White, Women in the Law, 65 Mich.L.Rev. 1051 (1967); Ruth Bader Ginsburg, Treatment of Women by the Law: Awakening Consciousness in the Law Schools, 5 Val.L.Rev. 480 (1971).

by the Association's newly formed Committee on Women in Legal Education.[7] A follow-up survey, conducted by the Committee in 1972, indicated distinct improvement, although still a distance to go, particularly in the placement field.[8] To a considerable extent, complaints about sex discrimination by law firms that use law school placement facilities reflected traditional attitudes still prevalent in the profession. A 1972 social scientists' report based on interview and questionnaire responses by women and men in the fields of law, medicine and architecture, concluded:[9]

> Sex discrimination as perceived by male and female professionals is common in law, medicine, and architecture but is a significantly accentuated characteristic of law. While lawyers may have a special skill in discerning these attitudes, sex discriminatory action seems characteristic of the profession and appears to be accepted by a number of its professionals.

But if lawyers have a special skill in discerning discriminatory attitudes they are also specially attuned to legal requirements. Discrimination made illegal by Title VII was unlikely to remain overt in law firms. The percent of women lawyers and judges rose from 4.7 in 1970 to 19.7 in 1987.[10] Cynthia Epstein[11] put the number of women partners in the 32 largest New York City law firms at 3 in 1968, 29 in 1977, and 41 in 1980. The number of women serving as federal judges was increased from 5 to 46 by President Carter's appointments between 1976 and 1980.[12] President Reagan appointed the first woman, Justice Sandra Day O'Connor, to the Supreme Court in 1981, an event she modestly attributed to having been in the right place at the right time.[13] When President Clinton took office, 92 of the 721 sitting federal judges (13%) were women.[14] By 1995, 126 of 823 federal judges (15%) were women.[15]

Despite this progress, women remain a minority of the legal profession. An ABA survey of lawyers conducted in May, 1983, found that 65 percent of male lawyers had no female colleagues at work.[16] Women have not integrated the partnership ranks at corporate firms, despite their increasing presence among law graduates and in the practicing bar.[17] A 1995 study of women lawyers at Wall Street firms reported that among the associates who began working at top-grossing firms in 1987, 94% of the women had left their jobs, compared with 72%

7. See Frank T. Read & Elizabeth S. Petersen, Sex Discrimination in Law School Placement, 18 Wayne L.Rev. 639, 639–40, nn. 4, 5, 652–56 (1972). (Shortly after the Read & Petersen article went to press, the Equal Employment Opportunity Act of 1972 settled the question concerning application of Title VII to the law school placement office: Title VII applies.)

8. See Shirley R. Bysiewicz, 1972 AALS Questionnaire on Women in Legal Education, 25 J.Legal Ed. 503 (1973); Joan Baker, The Impact of Title VII of the 1964 Civil Rights Act on Employment Discrimination Against Women Lawyers, 59 A.B.A.J. 1029 (1973).

9. Soule & Standley, supra note 2, at 1147.

10. Employment and Earnings, Table 22, at p. 181 (U.S. Department of Labor, Bureau of Labor Statistics, January 1988).

11. Epstein, supra, note 3, at 179.

12. Sarah Weddington, The Carter Administration's Accomplishments for Women, 10 Women Today 223 (December 26, 1980).

13. Laurence Bodine, Sandra Day O'Connor, 69 A.B.A.J. 1394 (October 1983).

14. Martha West, Gender Bias in Academic Robes: The Law's Failure to Protect Women Faculty, 67 Temple L. Rev. 67, 120 n. 209 (1994).

15. Reynolds Holding, Sitting in Judgment, San Fran. Chronicle, Sunday Section, October 29, 1995, at 1, 4.

16. Bill Winter, Survey: Women Lawyers Work Harder, Are Paid Less, but They're Happy, 69 A.B.A.J. 1384 (October 1983). In late 1987, the ABA Board of Governors established an eleven-member Commission on Women in the Profession to make a study and develop recommendations regarding issues affecting women in the legal profession. The Commission scheduled hearings in 1988.

17. See Mona Harrington, Women Lawyers: Rewriting the Rules (1993).

of the men.[18] A survey of 570 firms nationwide found that in 1995, 13.4% partners are women and 2.8% of partners are members of minority groups.[19] Social scientists predict that lawyers will continue, for the immediate future, to have to cope with the problems that confront women in male-dominated professions.[20]

1. Law Students

Slowly at first, then more rapidly as the young women who had been active in the civil rights and women's movement in the 1960s focused their heightened aspirations on the legal profession, the law schools began admitting women in ever-increasing numbers. The ratio of women J.D. enrollment to total J.D. enrollment rose from 4 percent in 1965, to 8.6% in 1970, doubling to 16% in 1973, further increasing to 23% in 1975, 34% in 1980, 40% in 1985, 42.5% in 1990, and 43.3% in 1994.[21]

As women law students approach parity of numbers with men in the classroom, however, evidence grows that their experience as law students is very different from that of men.[22] In part, that difference may be explained by the still relatively small numbers of women in positions of authority in the law school world—as tenured law professors or as Deans.

2. Law Professors

The first woman law professor in the United States to teach at an ABA-approved law school, Barbara Nachtrieb Armstrong, was appointed at the University of California, Berkeley, in 1919 as a lecturer in law and economics.[23] She became a full-time member of the law faculty in 1928 and attained the full professorship in 1935. Her primary fields of interest were social insurance—she helped to draft the Social Security Act—and family law. Professor Armstrong

---

18. Amy Bach, Nolo Contendere, New York Magazine, p. 49 (Dec. 11, 1995). The partnership rate for women in New York City has gone down in recent years: a study by the N.Y. City Bar Association showed 21.5% of male associates hired between 1973–1981 have made partner, compared to 15.25% of the women. For associates hired after 1981, 17% of the men have made partner, compared to 5% of the women. Id. at 50.

19. 1995 survey by National Association for Law Placement, New York Law Journal, p. 1, col. 1 (Dec. 7, 1995).

20. See generally, C. Epstein, supra note 3, at 265–302; Rosabeth Moss Kanter, Reflections on Women and the Legal Profession: A Sociological Perspective, 1 Harv.Wom.L.J. 1 (1978). See also Linda Leifland, Career Patterns of Male and Female Lawyers, 35 Buffalo L.Rev. 601 (1986).

21. ABA Section of Legal Education and Admissions to the Bar, A Review of Legal Education in the United States, Fall, 1994, at p. 67 (1994).

22. See Lani Guinier, Michelle Fine et al, Becoming Gentlemen: Women's Experience at One Ivy League Law School, 143 U. of Penn. L. Rev. 1 (1994) (documenting the negative impact of the grading system and Socratic method on women law students); Catherine Weiss & Louise Melling, The Legal Education of Twenty Women, 40 Stanford L. Rev. 1299 (1988)(the experience of 20 women in the Yale class of 1987. See also Linda B. Klein, The View From My Corner of The World: A Personal Comment on the Process of Becoming a Lawyer, 22 Akron L. Rev. 471 (1989); J.R. Elkins, ed., Worlds of Silence: Women in Law School, 8 ALSA Forum 1 (No. 1, 1984)(accounts by women students at West Virginia University Law School of their experiences as law students); Meredith Gould, The Paradox of Teaching Feminism and Learning Law, 7 ALSA Forum 270 (Special Double Issue on Women & Law, Nos. 2–3, 1983)(suggesting a feminist approach to pedagogy); Barbara Kass, A Woman's View of Law School, 15 Student Lawyer Journal 4 (November 1969); see also Alice D. Jacobs, Women in Law School: Structural Constraint and Personal Choice in the Formation of Professional Identity, 24 J.Leg. Ed. 462 (1972). This matter is explored further in the Text Note on Feminist Jurisprudence, at p. 1127, infra.

23. In Memoriam: Barbara Nachtrieb Armstrong, 65 Calif.L.Rev. 920–36 (1977). See Herma Hill Kay, The Future of Women Law Professors, Iowa L. Rev. 5 (1991)(describing her research on Armstrong as the first of 13 early women law professors).

retired in 1961; she died in 1976, having left a lasting imprint on her many students, her colleagues, and the law itself.

The ABA Section of Legal Education and Admissions to the Bar released the following figures in 1994:[24]

NUMBERS OF TEACHERS IN APPROVED LAW SCHOOLS, 1994

	Total	Women	Minorities
Full–Time	5,052	1,325 (26%)	614 (12%)
Part–Time	4,237	1,951 (46%)	677 (16%)

As Elyce Zenoff and Kathryn Lorio note, however, such figures need qualification. They point out, for example, that the number of women with tenure-track titles listed in the AALS Directory is consistently smaller than the total number of women listed as teachers by the ABA.[25] The number of women who are Deans of law schools continues to slowly rise. The authors counted three women deans in 1983, nine in 1987; by November 1995, fifteen of 179 ABA approved law schools (8.4%) were headed by women.

Kelly Weisberg,[26] examining the distribution of women law professors through the 1975–76 academic year, found that women were concentrated in "primarily progressive institutions, newly accredited law schools and some schools which may be labelled as 'non-prestigious' law schools." The so-called "top ten" law schools, at that time, employed fewer women than the national average.[27] These early findings were confirmed by Richard Chused's study of law faculties sponsored by the Society of American Law Teachers in 1988.[28] As the prestige of the law school increases, the percentage of women on the faculty decreases.[29]

The American Bar Foundation study[30] of law professors shows that the women entering law teaching resemble their male colleagues in educational credentials and early career experiences. Like the men, most of the women were trained at one of the twenty law schools (called "producer schools" in the study) that have trained nearly 60% of all law professors.[31] The women were as likely as the men to have held judicial clerkships. More women than men, however, had

---

24. See note 21, supra.

25. Zenoff & Lorio, What We Know, What We Think We Know, and What We Don't Know About Women Law Professors, 25 Ariz. L.Rev. 869, 872 (1984).

26. Weisberg, Women in Law School Teaching: Problems and Progress, 30 J.Leg. Ed. 226, 229 (1979).

27. Id. New York University Law School, because of its special efforts to recruit women faculty, was exempted from this statement.

28. Richard H. Chused, The Hiring and Retention of Minorities and Women on American Law School Faculties, 137 U. Pa. L. Rev. 537, 549, tbls. 9, 16 (1988). See also Marina Angel, Women in Legal Education: What It's Like to be Part of a Perpetual First Wave or the Case of the Disappearing Women, 61 Temple L. Rev. 799 (1988).

29. Robert J. Borthwick & Jordan R. Schau, Gatekeepers of the Profession: An Em- pirical Profile of the Nation's Law Professors, 25 U. Mich. J. L. Ref. 191 (1991). In 1988, women comprised 11% of the ladder faculty at the top seven law schools, approximately 17% of faculty at law schools ranked from eight to 60, 22% at schools ranked from 61 to 120, and 26% at the remaining law schools ranked from 121 to 175. Id. at tbl. 5.

30. Donna Fossum, Law Professors: A Pro- file of the Teaching Branch of the Legal Pro- fession, 1980 A.B.F.Res.J. 501.

31. Id., at 533–34. The 20 producer schools are identified as Harvard, Yale, Colum- bia, Michigan, Chicago, N.Y.U., Georgetown, Texas, Virginia, Berkeley, Pennsylvania, Wis- consin, Northwestern, Stanford, Iowa, Illinois, Minnesota, Cornell, Duke, and George Wash- ington. Id., at 507, Table 2. The schools are listed in descending order of the number of their graduates in law teaching. Thirty-three percent of all full-time law teachers graduated from the top five of these schools.

entered law teaching at a non-tenured level.[32] Donna Fossum concludes from this data that, even though the law teaching profession has changed considerably in its demographic characteristics in recent years,[33] the influx of women and minority group teachers "has not injected diversity into the group."[34]

Again, more recent studies confirm these earlier results. Professors Deborah Merritt and Barbara Reskin surveyed all law faculty hired into tenure-track positions between 1986 and 1991. The first part of their analysis focused on men and women of color.[35] They discovered that, among faculty of color, women of color were hired at lower ranks, by less prestigious schools, and given lower-status courses to teach than men of color.[36] These gender differences persisted even when the authors controlled for a variety of factors influencing teaching qualifications, such as prestige of undergraduate and law schools, service on law journals during law school, judicial clerkships after graduation, and type of law practice.[37] Using multiple regression analysis and controlling for other variables, the authors found that gender was significant in predicting hiring outcomes: being a woman was associated with teaching at a lower prestige law school and predictive of whether one taught a skills course. Finally, gender alone was a more important predictor of these hiring decisions than any of the other credential-based variables.[38] The authors concluded that the differences between minority women and men in law faculty hiring are startling: "Minority women suffer a pervasive disadvantage in the job market that cannot be explained by differences in their credentials or personal constraints."[39]

In their second study, Professors Merritt and Reskin, with Michelle Fondell, examined the effects of family ties and geographical constraints on entry into the professorate.[40] Contrary to prevailing assumptions, they found that almost as many men as women were part of dual-career couples.[41] Moreover, a significant

32. Id., at 535.

33. Id., at 532.

34. Id., at 538.

35. Deborah J. Merritt & Barbara F. Reskin, The Double Minority: Empirical Evidence of a Double Standard in Law School Hiring of Minority Women, 65 S. Cal. L. Rev. 2299 (1992).

36. Out of the 1105 faculty hired by American Bar Association accredited law schools between 1986 and 1991, 181 were faculty of color: 84 women and 97 men. Among the faculty of color, 44% of the women began their teaching careers in nontenure-track positions, compared to only 28.9% of the minority men. Id. at 2317. At the other end of the academic scale, 30.9% of the men of color began teaching at the rank of associate professor, whereas only 16.7% of the minority women began at that rank. Id. at 2318. Merritt and Reskin also found that minority women tended to be hired by less prestigious schools than minority men. Id. at 2320. Finally, more minority women than men were required to teach courses like legal writing and research, clinicals, and trial or appellate advocacy—skills courses regarded as less prestigious than the more traditional academic courses. Only 18.6% of the minority men listed one of these courses as part of their assigned teaching load, whereas 34.5% of the

women of color taught one or more. Id. at 2321.

37. Similar percentages went to elite law schools: 28.4% of the men and 29.3% of the women graduated from either Harvard or Yale Law Schools. Id. at 2323. Similar percentages of both minority men and women obtained LLM degrees or non-law masters prior to teaching (39.2% of men and 35% of women). Id. at 2325. After law school, 28.6% of the women and 29.9% of the men served as judicial clerks.

38. Id. at 2347–48.

39. Id. at 2356–57.

40. Deborah J. Merritt et al., Family, Place and Career: The Gender Paradox in Law School Hiring, 1993 Wis. L. Rev. 395 (1993). They received completed survey forms from 738 of the 1094 faculty hired between the fall of 1986 and the spring of 1991, and still in teaching in 1991. Among the respondents, 41% were women (302) and 59% (436) were men. 15.6% (115) were faculty of color. Id. at 400, 412 n.57.

41. Over half (54%) of the men and almost two-thirds (63%) of the women had an employed partner when they began their first tenure-track job. Id. at 417. Among the men in dual-career couples, 86% of their partners were attorneys, academics, or had other profes-

number of men imposed geographic limitations on their job searches.[42]   When the authors used multiple regression analysis to control for hiring credentials and to measure the effects of these family and geographic limitations on hiring outcomes, they were surprised by their results.   They found that family ties tended to affect men's job outcomes in a positive way, while having only limited impact on the job rank or the type of law school where women began teaching.[43]   For a man, having a partner, whether employed or unemployed, significantly *enhanced* the rank of his first teaching job, after controlling for academic credentials.   Having a partner turned out to be one of the most important variables in determining initial rank for men, more important than graduating from a prestigious law school or clerking for a judge.[44]   In addition, a man with an unemployed partner secured a tenure-track job at a rank about two-thirds higher than the rank of an unpartnered man, whereas if the man's partner was employed, the man's first tenure-track job was at a rank four-tenths higher than that of a single man.[45]   The impact of geographical limitations on a man's job search was even more surprising.   Men's job prospects at more prestigious schools were significantly *improved* by their imposition of geographic constraints, whereas women's job outcomes were significantly impaired by similar constraints.[46]   The authors have carefully documented this gender paradox: while family ties and limited geographic mobility affected the placement of women law professors less often than commonly believed, the same ties affected men more often and with surprisingly beneficial results.

The examination of problems women encounter in legal education continues. In January 1996, the ABA's Commission on Women in the Profession issued its latest report, titled "Elusive Equality," noting that although women now constitute 23% of the profession, "[t]he hope that gender bias [in law schools] would have disappeared with the increasing number of women faculty and students was not realized."[47]   The Commission reported that some observers believe overt

sional or managerial careers. Id. at 419 n.69. Although these dual-career couple rates were not radically different between men and women, the partnership status of the remaining men and women faculty diverged significantly from each other. Of the 46% of men who were not part of a dual-career couple, 28% had spouses who were homemakers (77), students (28), or seeking work (9). The remaining men, 18%, were not in a partner relationship. In contrast to the men, over 34% of the women were not in a partner relationship when they began they first tenure-track job, leaving only 3% with partners who were not employed in the labor force. Among the total sample, the partnership status of 23 men and 12 women was unknown. Id. at 417 and tbl. 5.

42. The authors divided geographical constraints into two types: major, limiting one's search to an area containing 15 or less law schools; or minor, a limitation that included more than 15 schools. Id. at 404. Among the men, 21.5% imposed a major constraint on their search for their first tenure-track job and 24% imposed a minor geographical limitation. Among the women, 43% imposed a major geographical constraint, and 24% imposed a minor one. Id. at 419. The reasons for the limitations differed significantly by gender. Among

the women, 41.5% limited their search because of family-related reasons, whereas only 24% of the men did so. Id. at 420.

43. Women with partners or with children were just as likely to obtain an initial law school job at each rank, or a tenure-track job, as women without any family ties. Id. at 425, 435. Furthermore, family ties did not diminish the prestige of the school where women began teaching. Id. at 429. In fact, women with children may have obtained tenure-track positions at somewhat more prestigious schools than childless women with similar credentials and geographic constraints. Id. at 436.

44. Id. at 425–26.

45. Id. at 432.

46. When men imposed a major geographical limitation on their job search, the prestige of the school where they obtained their initial teaching job increased. For women who imposed a major geographical constraint, the prestige of the school where they were first hired declined. Id. at 430.

47. Am. Bar Assn. Commission on Women in the Profession, Elusive Equality: The Experiences of Women in Legal Education, Executive Summary 2 (1996).

hostility, particularly from young white male students, was more common in the 1990s than when women were present in smaller numbers in law schools. On the other hand, changes at many law schools have helped create climates more conducive to equal participation of women as students and on the faculty.[48] The Commission made specific recommendations focused on equalizing the classroom experience of women, as well as increasing the percentage of women on the faculty. In addition, creation of both national-level and law school-level permanent committees on gender issues would assist law schools in gathering information and ideas about how to improve the educational environment for women.[49]

Other members of the professorate have focused on the difficulties faced by faculty of color. Richard Delgado and Derrick Bell have presented a disturbing picture of the quality of life experienced by law professors of color, both men and women, in American law schools.[50] Black women are beginning to tell their own stories.[51]

The struggle continues to integrate law faculties by sex, race and ethnicity, but the results of greater equality are worth the price. It is important to diversify faculty ranks because as the composition of the faculty changes, the decisions of the faculty change. In analyzing the hiring and retention of minorities and women at law schools from 1980–1987, Professor Richard Chused found that at law schools where over 12% of the tenured faculty were women, women tenure candidates were more successful than at schools with lower percentages of tenured women faculty. If the tenured faculty were more than 12% women, 64% of the women tenure candidates received tenure. At the "laggard" schools with less than 12% women on the tenured faculty, only 40.5% of the women received tenure. The rates for tenuring men were similar at both categories of schools; 49.6% and 51.3%, respectively received tenure.[52] Professor Chused concluded, "The presence of a certain size core of tenured women on a faculty significantly improves the likelihood that junior level women will successfully leap the tenure hurdle."[53]

Another striking indication of the benefits of diversifying law faculties by sex is the appearance of courses dealing with women and the law or sex-based discrimination in the law school curriculum. A second and related indication is the emergence of feminist jurisprudence as a field of scholarly research. It is too early to tell what the long-range effect on women students presently in law school of having significant numbers of women professors as role models may be. There is, however, room to hope that an atmosphere more conducive to the intellectual growth and professional development of women lawyers can be created than has yet been attained.

Text Note
Feminist Jurisprudence:
What Is It? When Did It Start? Who Does It?
By Herma Hill Kay and Christine A. Littleton

The necessary conditions for the development of feminist jurisprudence arose when women began entering the law schools in large numbers in the late 1960s.

---

48. Id. at 2–3.

49. Id. a 6.

50. See Delgado & Bell, Minority Law Professors' Lives: The Bell–Delgado Survey, 24 Harv. Civ. Rts. Civ. Lib. L. Rev. 349 (1989).

51. See Patricia J. Williams Alchemy of Race and Rights: Diary of a Law Professor

(1991); Symposium, Black Women Law Professors: Building a Community at the Intersection of Race and Gender, 6 Berkeley Women's L.J. 1 (1990–91).

52. Chused, note 28 supra, tbl. 18, at 550–52.

53. Id. at 550.

The presence of these women, and the questions they asked posed significant challenges to formerly all- or predominantly-male bastions.

In particular, female law students asked why the curriculum was so silent on issues that mattered deeply to them as women—unequal pay and job opportunities; rape and sexual assault; battering of wives; reproduction. The women themselves organized to "fill in" the gaps in their legal education, forming the National Conference on Women and the Law in 1970.[1] And the law schools responded, at varying rates, by creating the first courses in "Women and the Law," many of which were later renamed "Sex–Based Discrimination" to reflect the coming of age in the mid–1970s of new legal avenues of redress for women's unequal situation.

As these women became lawyers, and especially law professors, they began writing about their concrete experiences as women in, around, and with the law. The subjects they chose arose from their own interests in particular areas of law, and from their unique methodology of acquiring knowledge. This method was rooted in the consciousness-raising groups that provided the grass-roots base of the second wave of feminism, the modern women's movement. It is a process of identifying, of naming, women's concrete experience. Taking women's experience seriously, indeed even listening to women at all, was a radical act then, and remains an unfortunately uncommon enterprise in law schools today. Feminist legal scholars and lawyers began using the fruits of this process to build legal theory and to inform litigation strategies.

The method itself was liberating and empowering. It combatted the isolation that individual women had felt in their law school classrooms and interactions with law school classmates. It allowed us the recognition that the personal is the political; that while we occasionally faced individual hostility and personal foibles, we more often faced a political structure that oppressed us *as women*. This structure practically guaranteed that we would study law as women, work as women, and even teach and write as women. But our insights into the political nature of the law also indicated that we could organize as women, describe and analyze as women, and in fact, challenge and change as women the political structure that oppressed us as women.

Insights gained through this methodology were refined by women active in the Critical Legal Studies movement, and much feminist jurisprudence makes use of the deconstructionist strategies developed by CLS scholars,[2] particularly the technique of using ostensibly justificatory arguments as the ground for new challenges to the obstacles that confront oppressed people. They were also used and refined by feminist lawyers making concrete claims on the legal system on behalf of real women. These twin refinements—one theoretical and one intensely practical—form much of the basis of feminist jurisprudence. Another important

---

1. The Conference was organized each year by local law students, bringing together women law students, faculty, and practitioners. It held its 20th anniversary conference in 1989 before disbanding in 1992. Elizabeth M. Schneider, Feminist Lawmaking and Historical Consciousness: Bringing the Past into the Future, 2 Vir. J. of Soc. Pol. & L. 1–5 (1994); Patricia A. Cain, Lesbian Perspective, Lesbian Experience, and the Risk of Essentialism, 2 Vir. J. of Soc. Pol. & L. 43 (1994).

2. "Deconstruction" in Critical Legal Studies circles denotes a method of analyzing legal materials. Using the internal contradictions within legal texts and between the texts and their referents, the analyst can demonstrate either intellectual incoherence, see, e.g., Clare Dalton, An Essay in the Deconstruction of Contract Doctrine, 94 Yale L.J. 997 (1985)(discussing indeterminacy of contract rules), or political bias, see, e.g., Karl Klare, Judicial Deradicalization of the Wagner Act and the Origins of Modern Legal Consciousness, 1937–1941, 62 Minn.L.Rev. 265 (1978)(discussing the judicial impact upon organized labor and its consequences).

refinement is the work of feminist theorists from disciplines outside law—feminist anthropologists, biologists, physiologists, psychologists, educators, social scientists, literary critics, philosophers, and historians—as well as feminist activists in all walks of life. The interdisciplinary flavor of feminist jurisprudence is a necessary component of a form of legal theory and critique that seeks to build on the experience of women.[3]

The emerging body of feminist jurisprudence already reflects the richness and diversity of women's experience and perspectives. Some theorists have developed accounts of women's experience in specific situations, giving voice to the silence so long imposed by the confusion of male experience with *human* experience. Examples include Fran Olsen's[4] and Carrie Menkel–Meadow's[5] descriptions of women in the Critical Legal Studies movement, Lucinda Finley's account of women's experience as law students,[6] and Carrie Menkel–Meadow's story about how particular groups have been excluded from the making and practice of law.[7] Others have used feminist methodology to inform their critical analysis of existing legal structures and doctrine. Susan Estrich[8] begins a recent article by presenting rape as a concrete personal experience rather than merely a legal category, while Mary Jo Frug[9] uncovers sexism in the keystone of legal education—the first year casebook. Still other scholars use the tools of feminist method in reconstruction of small and large areas of the law. Consider Catharine MacKinnon's[10] controversial re-interpretation of pornography as a violation of women's civil rights; Wendy Williams's,[11] Sylvia Law's,[12] and Herma Hill Kay's[13] varying approaches to sex equality in reproductive activity; Christine Littleton's[14] reconstruction of general equality norms as requiring "equal acceptance" of biologically and socially female attributes; Elizabeth Schneider's[15] analysis of the transformation of rights rheto-

3. Deborah Rhode aptly observes that:

A research agenda sensitive to feminist values would * * * reflect not a common theory but rather certain common commitments. Central among them would be commitments to gender as a category of analysis and to equality between the sexes as a societal objective. Such an agenda would remain attentive both to women's concrete experience, and to the ways that such experience varies across race, class, ethnicity, age, sexual orientation, and so forth. Its stance would remain self-critical, but without the kind of slide into absolute relativism that would undercut its own legitimacy.

Rhode, Gender and Jurisprudence: An Agenda for Research, 56 U.Cin.L.Rev. 521, 523 (1987). See also Katharine Bartlett, Feminist Legal Methods, 103 Harv. L. Rev. 829 (1990); Patricia Cain, Feminist Jurisprudence: Grounding the Theories, 4 Berkeley Wom. L. J. 191 (1989–90).

4. Frances Olsen, Transcript of presentation at keynote panel on Feminist Perspectives on Law, sponsored by the European Conference on Critical Legal Studies, University College, London, April 3–5, 1986.

5. Menkel–Meadow, Feminist Legal Theory, Critical Legal Studies, and Legal Education or "The Fem–Crits Go To Law School," 38 J.Leg.Ed. 61 (1988).

6. Lucinda Finley, Learning from Women's Silence: A Feminist Critique of Legal Education (1987)(manuscript on file with the authors).

7. Menkel–Meadow, Excluded Voices: New Voices in the Legal Profession Making New Voices in the Law, 42 U. Miami L.Rev. 29 (1987).

8. Estrich, Rape, 95 Yale L.J. 1097 (1986). See also S. Estrich, Real Rape (1987).

9. Frug, Re–Reading Contracts: A Feminist Analysis of Contracts Casebook, 34 Am. U.L.Rev. 1065 (1985).

10. E.g., MacKinnon, Not a Moral Issue, 2 Yale L. & Policy Rev. 321 (1984).

11. Williams, Equality's Riddle: Pregnancy and the Equal Treatment/Special Treatment Debate, 13 N.Y.U.Rev.L. & Soc. Change 325 (1984/85).

12. Law, Rethinking Sex and the Constitution, 132 U.Pa.L.Rev. 955 (1984).

13. Kay, Equality and Difference: The Case of Pregnancy, 1 Berkeley Wom.L.J. 1 (1985).

14. Littleton, Reconstructing Sexual Equality, 75 U.Calif.L.Rev. 1279 (1987).

15. Schneider, The Dialectic of Rights and Politics: Perspectives from the Women's Movement, 61 N.Y.U.L.Rev. 589 (1986).

ric through litigation on behalf of women; and Martha Minow's[16] unpacking of the various themes and perspectives of "difference."

We do not seek to define feminist jurisprudence further, or to exclude other strands that are continually emerging within the general field.[17] The silence of women in the law has only begun to be broken,[18] and therefore much of our work as feminist legal scholars must be devoted to the continuing task of listening for, articulating and learning from the voices of women. No introductory statement such as this can define the boundaries or set the directions of feminist jurisprudence,[19] nor does it attempt to do so. Only the gradually swelling chorus that is the voice of women, in all our richness, complexity, commonality, and difference, can provide the compass.

16. Minow, The Supreme Court 1986 Term, Foreward: Justice Engendered, 101 Harv.L.Rev. 10 (1987).

17. Other attempts have been made to describe (although rarely to define completely) the field of feminist jurisprudence. See, e.g., Christine Littleton, In Search of a Feminist Jurisprudence, 10 Harv.Wom.L.J. 1 (1987); Clare Dalton, Where We Stand: Observations on the Situation of Feminist Legal Thought, 3 Berkeley Wom.L.J. 1 (1987–88); Ann Scales, The Emergence of Feminist Jurisprudence: An Essay, 95 Yale L.J. 1373 (1986); Heather Ruth Wishik, To Question Everything: The Inquiries of Feminist Jurisprudence, 1 Berkeley Wom.L.J. 64 (1985).

Textbooks on feminist legal theory include Katharine T. Bartlett, Gender and Law (1993) and Mary Becker et al., Feminist Jurisprudence (1994).

18. See generally, Symposium on Civic and Legal Education, Part One: Legal Education, Feminist Values, and Gender Bias, 45 Stan. L. Rev. 1525–80 (1993); Symposium: The Voices of Women: A Symposium on Women in Legal Education, 77 Iowa L. Rev. 1 (1991). See also Symposium on Women and Legal Education— Pedagogy, Law, Theory, and Practice, 38 J. Leg. Ed. 1 (1988); Morrison Torrey, Jackie Casey & Karin Olson, Teaching Law in a Feminist Manner: A Commentary From Experience, 13 Harv. Wom. L.J. 87 (1990).

19. Robin West has argued powerfully that feminist jurisprudence is a conceptual anomaly so long as legal doctrine does not take women's humanity seriously. She concludes that "[t]he virtual abolition of patriarchy is the necessary political condition for the creation of non-masculine feminist jurisprudence," adding that what is presently taken for feminist jurisprudence is really two discrete projects of feminist legal theory. The first project is "the unmasking and critiquing of the patriarchy behind purportedly ungendered law and theory," while the second is "reconstructive jurisprudence" that consists of feminist law reform in areas such as rape, sexual harassment, reproductive freedom, and rights for pregnant workers. West, Jurisprudence and Gender, 55 U.Chi.L.Rev. 1, 60–61 (1988).

Chapter V

WOMEN AND CRIME

A. RAPE

1. STATUTORY RAPE

MICHAEL M. v. SUPERIOR COURT

Supreme Court of the United States, 1981.
450 U.S. 464, 101 S.Ct. 1200, 67 L.Ed.2d 437.

Justice Rehnquist announced the judgment of the Court and delivered an opinion in which The Chief Justice, Justice Stewart, and Justice Powell joined.

The question presented in this case is whether California's "statutory rape" law, § 261.5 of the California Penal Code, violates the Equal Protection Clause of the Fourteenth Amendment. Section 261.5 defines unlawful sexual intercourse as "an act of sexual intercourse accomplished with a female not the wife of the perpetrator, where the female is under the age of 18 years." The statute thus makes men alone criminally liable for the act of sexual intercourse.

In July 1978, a complaint was filed in the Municipal Court of Sonoma County, Cal., alleging that petitioner, then a 17½ year old male, had had unlawful sexual intercourse with a female under the age of 18, in violation of § 261.5. The evidence adduced at a preliminary hearing showed that at approximately midnight on June 3, 1978, petitioner and two friends approached Sharon, a 16½ year old female, and her sister as they waited at a bus stop. Petitioner and Sharon, who had already been drinking, moved away from the others and began to kiss. After being struck in the face for rebuffing petitioner's initial advances, Sharon submitted to sexual intercourse with petitioner. Prior to trial, petitioner sought to set aside the information on both state and federal constitutional grounds, asserting that § 261.5 unlawfully discriminated on the basis of gender. The trial court and the California Court of Appeal denied petitioner's request for relief and petitioner sought review in the Supreme Court of California.

The Supreme Court, 25 Cal.3d 608, 159 Cal.Rptr. 340, 601 P.2d 572, held that "Section 261.5 discriminates on the basis of sex because only females may be victims, and only males may violate the section." The court then subjected the classification to "strict scrutiny," stating that it must be justified by a compelling state interest. It found that the classification was "supported not by mere social convention but by the immutable physiological fact that it is the female exclusively who can become pregnant." Canvassing "the tragic human cost of illegitimate teenage pregnancies," including the large number of teenage abortions, the increased medical risk associated with teenage pregnancies, and the social consequences of teenage child bearing, the court concluded that the state has a compelling interest in preventing such pregnancies. Because males alone can "physiologically cause the result which the law properly seeks to avoid" the court further held that the gender classification was readily justified as a means of identifying offender and victim. For the reasons stated below, we affirm the judgment of the California Supreme Court.[1]

As is evident from our opinions, the Court has had some difficulty in agreeing upon the proper approach and analysis in cases involving challenges to gender-based classifications. The issues posed by such challenges range from issues of standing, see Orr v. Orr, 440 U.S. 268, 99 S.Ct. 1102, 59 L.Ed.2d 306 (1979), to the appropriate standard of judicial review for the substantive classification. Unlike the California Supreme Court, we have not held that gender-based classifications are "inherently suspect" and thus we do not apply so-called "strict scrutiny" to those classifications. See Stanton v. Stanton, 421 U.S. 7, 95 S.Ct. 1373, 43 L.Ed.2d 688 (1975). Our cases have held, however, that the traditional minimum rationality test takes on a somewhat "sharper focus" when gender-based classifications are challenged. See Craig v. Boren, 429 U.S. 190, 210 n. * 97 S.Ct. 451, 464, 50 L.Ed.2d 397 (1976)(Powell, J., concurring). In Reed v. Reed, 404 U.S. 71, 92 S.Ct. 251, 30 L.Ed.2d 225 (1971), for example, the Court stated that a gender-based classification will be upheld if it bears a "fair and substantial relationship" to legitimate state ends, while in Craig v. Boren, supra, 429 U.S., at 197, 97 S.Ct., at 457, the Court restated the test to require the classification to bear a "substantial relationship" to "important governmental objectives."

Underlying these decisions is the principle that a legislature may not "make overbroad generalizations based on sex which are entirely unrelated to any differences between men and women or which demean the ability or social status of the affected class." Parham v. Hughes, 441 U.S. 347, 354, 99 S.Ct. 1742, 60 L.Ed.2d 269 (1979)(Stewart, J. plurality). But because the Equal Protection Clause does not "demand that a statute necessarily apply equally to all persons" or require "things which are different in fact * * * to be treated in law as though they were the same," Rinaldi v. Yeager, 384 U.S. 305, 309, 86 S.Ct. 1497, 1499, 16 L.Ed.2d 577 (1966), quoting Tigner v. Texas, 310 U.S. 141, 147, 60 S.Ct. 879, 882, 84 L.Ed. 1124 (1940), this Court has consistently upheld statutes where the gender classification is not invidious, but rather realistically reflects the fact that the sexes are not similarly situated in certain circumstances. Parham v. Hughes, supra; Califano v. Webster, 430 U.S. 313, 97 S.Ct. 1192, 51 L.Ed.2d 360 (1977); Schlesinger v. Ballard, 419 U.S. 498, 95 S.Ct. 572, 42 L.Ed.2d 610 (1975); Kahn v. Shevin, 416 U.S. 351, 94 S.Ct. 1734, 40 L.Ed.2d 189 (1974). As the Court has stated, a legislature may "provide for the special problems of women." Weinberger v. Wiesenfeld, 420 U.S. 636, 653, 95 S.Ct. 1225, 1236, 43 L.Ed.2d 514 (1975).

---

1. The lower federal courts and state courts have almost uniformly concluded that statuto-ry rape laws are constitutional [citations omitted].

Applying those principles to this case, the fact that the California Legislature criminalized the act of illicit sexual intercourse with a minor female is a sure indication of its intent or purpose to discourage that conduct. Precisely why the legislature desired that result is of course somewhat less clear. This Court has long recognized that "inquiries into congressional motives or purposes are a hazardous matter," United States v. O'Brien, 391 U.S. 367, 383–384, 88 S.Ct. 1673, 1682–1683, 20 L.Ed.2d 672 (1968); Palmer v. Thompson, 403 U.S. 217, 224, 91 S.Ct. 1940, 1944, 29 L.Ed.2d 438 (1971), and the search for the "actual" or "primary" purpose of a statute is likely to be elusive. Arlington Heights v. Metropolitan Housing Corp., 429 U.S. 252, 265 (1977); McGinnis v. Royster, 410 U.S. 263, 276–277, 93 S.Ct. 1055, 1062–1063, 35 L.Ed.2d 282 (1973). Here, for example, the individual legislators may have voted for the statute for a variety of reasons. Some legislators may have been concerned about preventing teenage pregnancies, others about protecting young females from physical injury or from the loss of "chastity," and still others about promoting various religious and moral attitudes towards premarital sex.

The justification for the statute offered by the State, and accepted by the Supreme Court of California, is that the legislature sought to prevent illegitimate teenage pregnancies. That finding, of course, is entitled to great deference. Reitman v. Mulkey, 387 U.S. 369, 373–374, 87 S.Ct. 1627, 1629–1630, 18 L.Ed.2d 830 (1967). And although our cases establish that the State's asserted reason for the enactment of a statute may be rejected, "if it could not have been a goal of the legislation," Weinberger v. Wiesenfeld, supra, 420 U.S., at 648, n. 16, 95 S.Ct., at 1233, this is not such a case.

We are satisfied not only that the prevention of illegitimate pregnancy is at least one of the "purposes" of the statute, but that the State has a strong interest in preventing such pregnancy. At the risk of stating the obvious, teenage pregnancies, which have increased dramatically over the last two decades,[3] have significant social, medical and economic consequences for both the mother and her child, and the State.[4] Of particular concern to the State is that approximately half of all teenage pregnancies end in abortion.[5] And of those children who are born, their illegitimacy makes them likely candidates to become wards of the State.[6]

3. In 1976 approximately one million 15–19 year olds became pregnant, one-tenth of all women in that age group. Two-thirds of the pregnancies were illegitimate. Illegitimacy rates for teenagers (births per 1,000 unmarried females ages) increased 75% for 14–17 year olds between 1961 and 1974 and 33% for 18–19 year olds. Alan Guttmacher Institute, 11 Million Teenagers 10, 13 (1976); C. Chilman, Adolescent Sexuality In A Changing American Society, 195 (NIH Pub. No. 80–1426, 1980).

4. The risk of maternal death is 60% higher for a teenager under the age of 15 than for a woman in her early twenties. The risk is 13% higher for 15–19 year olds. The statistics further show that most teenage mothers drop out of school and face a bleak economic future. See, e.g., 11 Million Teenagers, supra, at 23, 25; Bennett & Bardon, The Effects of a School

Program On Teenage Mothers And Their Children, 47 Am.J. of Orthopsychiatry 671 (1977); Phipps–Yonas, Teenage Pregnancy and Motherhood, 50 Am.J. of Orthopsychiatry 403, 414 (1980).

5. This is because teenagers are disproportionately likely to seek abortions. Center for Disease Control, Abortion Surveillance 1976, 22–24 (1978). In 1978, for example, teenagers in California had approximately 54,000 abortions and 53,800 live births. California Center for Health Statistics, Reproductive Health Status of California Teenage Women 1, 23 (1980).

6. The policy and intent of the California Legislature evinced in other legislation buttresses our view that the prevention of teenage pregnancy is a purpose of the statute. The preamble to the "Pregnancy Freedom of Choice Act," for example, states "The legisla-

We need not be medical doctors to discern that young men and young women are not similarly situated with respect to the problems and the risks of sexual intercourse. Only women may become pregnant and they suffer disproportionately the profound physical, emotional, and psychological consequences of sexual activity. The statute at issue here protects women from sexual intercourse at an age when those consequences are particularly severe.[7]

The question thus boils down to whether a State may attack the problem of sexual intercourse and teenage pregnancy directly by prohibiting a male from having sexual intercourse with a minor female.[8] We hold that such a statute is sufficiently related to the State's objectives to pass constitutional muster.

Because virtually all of the significant harmful and inescapably identifiable consequences of teenage pregnancy fall on the young female, a legislature acts well within its authority when it elects to punish only the participant who, by nature, suffers few of the consequences of his conduct. It is hardly

ture finds that pregnancy among unmarried persons under 21 years of age constitutes an increasing social problem in California." Cal.Welfare & Inst.Code § 16145 (West 1980).

Subsequent to the decision below, the California Legislature considered and rejected proposals to render § 261.5 gender neutral, thereby ratifying the judgment of the California Supreme Court. That is enough to answer petitioner's contention that the statute was the "accidental byproduct of a traditional way of thinking about women." Califano v. Webster, 430 U.S. 313, 320, 97 S.Ct. 1192, 1196, 51 L.Ed.2d 360 (1977)(quoting Califano v. Goldfarb, 430 U.S. 199, 223, 97 S.Ct. 1021, 1035, 51 L.Ed.2d 270 (1977)(Stevens, J., concurring)). Certainly this decision of the California Legislature is as good a source as is this Court in deciding what is "current" and what is "outmoded" in the perception of women.

7. Although petitioner concedes that the State has a "compelling" interest in preventing teenage pregnancy, he contends that the "true" purpose of § 261.5 is to protect the virtue and chastity of young women. As such, the statute is unjustifiable because it rests on archaic stereotypes. What we have said above is enough to dispose of that contention. The question for us—and the only question under the Federal Constitution—is whether the legislation violates the Equal Protection Clause of the Fourteenth Amendment, not whether its supporters may have endorsed it for reasons no longer generally accepted. Even if the preservation of female chastity were one of the motives of the statute, and even if that motive be impermissible, petitioner's argument must fail because "it is a familiar practice of constitutional law that this court will not strike down an otherwise constitutional statute on the basis of an alleged illicit legislative motive." United States v. O'Brien, 391 U.S. 367, 383, 88 S.Ct. 1673, 1682, 20 L.Ed.2d 672 (1968). In Orr v. Orr, 440 U.S. 268, 99 S.Ct. 1102, 59

L.Ed.2d 306 (1979), for example, the Court rejected one asserted purpose as impermissible, but then considered other purposes to determine if they could justify the statute. Similarly, in Washington v. Davis, 426 U.S. 229, 243, 96 S.Ct. 2040, 2049, 48 L.Ed.2d 597 (1976) the Court distinguished Palmer v. Thompson, 403 U.S. 217, 91 S.Ct. 1940, 29 L.Ed.2d 438 (1971) on the grounds that the purposes of the ordinance there were not open to impeachment by evidence that the legislature was actually motivated by an impermissible purpose. See also Arlington Heights v. Metropolitan Housing Corp., 429 U.S. 252, 270, n. 21, 97 S.Ct. 555, 566, 50 L.Ed.2d 450 (1977); Mobile v. Bolden, 446 U.S. 55, 91, 100 S.Ct. 1490, 1508, 64 L.Ed.2d 47 (1980)(Stevens, J., concurring).

8. We do not understand petitioner to question a state's authority to make sexual intercourse among teenagers a criminal act, at least on a gender-neutral basis. In Carey v. Population Services International, 431 U.S. 678, 694, n. 17, 97 S.Ct. 2010, 2021, 52 L.Ed.2d 675 (1977)(Brennan, J., plurality), four Members of the Court assumed for the purposes of that case that a State may regulate the sexual behavior of minors, while four other Members of the Court more emphatically stated that such regulation would be permissible. Id., at 702, 703 (White, J., concurring); Id., at 705–707, 709, 97 S.Ct. at 2026–2028, 2029 (Powell, J., concurring); Id., at 713 (Stevens, J., concurring); Id., at 718, 97 S.Ct., at 2033 (Rehnquist, J., dissenting). The Court has long recognized that a State has even broader authority to protect the physical, mental, and moral well-being of its youth, than of its adults. See, e.g., Planned Parenthood of Missouri v. Danforth, 428 U.S. 52, 72–74, 96 S.Ct. 2831, 2842–2843, 49 L.Ed.2d 788 (1976); Ginsberg v. New York, 390 U.S. 629, 639–640, 88 S.Ct. 1274, 1280–1281, 20 L.Ed.2d 195 (1968); Prince v. Massachusetts, 321 U.S. 158, 170, 64 S.Ct. 438, 444, 88 L.Ed. 645 (1944).

unreasonable for a legislature acting to protect minor females to exclude them from punishment. Moreover, the risk of pregnancy itself constitutes a substantial deterrence to young females. No similar natural sanctions deter males. A criminal sanction imposed solely on males thus serves to roughly "equalize" the deterrents on the sexes.

We are unable to accept petitioner's contention that the statute is impermissibly underinclusive and must, in order to pass judicial scrutiny, be *broadened* so as to hold the female as criminally liable as the male. It is argued that this statute is not *necessary* to deter teenage pregnancy because a gender-neutral statute, where both male and female would be subject to prosecution, would serve that goal equally well. The relevant inquiry, however, is not whether the statute is drawn as precisely as it might have been, but whether the line chosen by the California Legislature is within constitutional limitations. Kahn v. Shevin, 416 U.S., at 356, n. 10, 94 S.Ct., at 1737–1738.

In any event, we cannot say that a gender-neutral statute would be as effective as the statute California has chosen to enact. The State persuasively contends that a gender-neutral statute would frustrate its interest in effective enforcement. Its view is that a female is surely less likely to report violations of the statute if she herself would be subject to criminal prosecution.[9] In an area already fraught with prosecutorial difficulties, we decline to hold that the Equal Protection Clause requires a legislature to enact a statute so broad that it may well be incapable of enforcement.[10]

9. Petitioner contends that a gender-neutral statute would not hinder prosecutions because the prosecutor could take into account the relative burdens on females and males and generally only prosecute males. But to concede this is to concede all. If the prosecutor, in exercising discretion, will virtually always prosecute just the man and not the woman, we do not see why it is impermissible for the legislature to enact a statute to the same effect.

10. The question whether a statute is *substantially* related to its asserted goals is at best an opaque one. It can be plausibly argued that a gender-neutral statute would produce fewer prosecutions than the statute at issue here. See Stewart, J., concurring. The dissent argues, on the other hand, that

"even assuming that a gender neutral statute would be more difficult to enforce * * *, [c]ommon sense * * * suggests that a gender-neutral statutory rape law is potentially a greater deterrent of sexual activity than a gender-based law, for the simple reason that a gender-neutral law subjects both men and women to criminal sanctions and thus arguably has a deterrent effect on twice as many potential violators."

Where such differing speculations as to the effect of a statute are plausible, we think it appropriate to defer to the decision of the California Supreme Court, "armed as it was with the knowledge of the facts and the circumstances concerning the passage and poten-

tial impact of [the statute], and familiar with the milieu in which that provision would operate." Reitman v. Mulkey, 387 U.S. 369, 378–379, 87 S.Ct. 1627, 1633, 18 L.Ed.2d 830 (1967).

It should be noted that two of the three cases relied upon by the dissent are readily distinguishable from the instant one. See n. 3. In both Navedo v. Preisser, 630 F.2d 636 (C.A.8 1980), and Meloon v. Helgemoe, 564 F.2d 602 (C.A.1 1977), cert. denied, 436 U.S. 950, 98 S.Ct. 2858, 56 L.Ed.2d 793 (1978), the respective governments asserted that the purpose of the statute was to protect young women from physical injury. Both courts rejected the justification on the grounds that there had been no showing that young females are more likely than males to suffer physical injury from sexual intercourse. They further held, contrary to our decision, that pregnancy prevention was not a "plausible" purpose of the legislation. Thus neither court reached the issue presented here, whether the statute is substantially related to the prevention of teenage pregnancy. Significantly, *Meloon* has been severely limited by Rundlett v. Oliver, 607 F.2d 495 (C.A.1 1979), where the court upheld a statutory rape law on the ground that the State had shown that sexual intercourse physically injures young women more than males. Here, of course, even the dissent does not dispute that young women suffer disproportionately the deleterious consequences of illegitimate pregnancy.

We similarly reject petitioner's argument that § 261.5 is impermissibly overbroad because it makes unlawful sexual intercourse with prepubescent females, who are, by definition, incapable of becoming pregnant. Quite apart from the fact that the statute could well be justified on the grounds that very young females are particularly susceptible to physical injury from sexual intercourse, see Rundlett v. Oliver, 607 F.2d 495 (C.A.1 1979), it is ludicrous to suggest that the Constitution requires the California Legislature to limit the scope of its rape statute to older teenagers and exclude young girls.

There remains only petitioner's contention that the statute is unconstitutional as it is applied to him because he, like Sharon, was under 18 at the time of sexual intercourse. Petitioner argues that the statute is flawed because it presumes that as between two persons under 18, the male is the culpable aggressor. We find petitioner's contentions unpersuasive. Contrary to his assertions, the statute does not rest on the assumption that males are generally the aggressors. It is instead an attempt by a legislature to prevent illegitimate teenage pregnancy by providing an additional deterrent for men. The age of the man is irrelevant since young men are as capable as older men of inflicting the harm sought to be prevented.

In upholding the California statute we also recognize that this is not a case where a statute is being challenged on the grounds that it "invidiously discriminates" against females. To the contrary, the statute places a burden on males which is not shared by females. But we find nothing to suggest that men, because of past discrimination or peculiar disadvantages, are in need of the special solicitude of the courts. Nor is this a case where the gender classification is made "solely * * * for administrative convenience," as in Frontiero v. Richardson, 411 U.S. 677, 690, 93 S.Ct. 1764, 1772, 36 L.Ed.2d 583 (1973) or rests on "the baggage of sexual stereotypes" as in Orr v. Orr, 440 U.S. 268, 283, 99 S.Ct. 1102, 1114, 59 L.Ed.2d 306 (1979). As we have held, the statute instead reasonably reflects the fact that the consequences of sexual intercourse and pregnancy fall more heavily on the female than on the male.

Accordingly, the judgment of the California Supreme Court is affirmed.

Affirmed.

JUSTICE STEWART, concurring.

Section 261.5, on its face, classifies on the basis of sex. A male who engages in sexual intercourse with an underage female who is not his wife violates the statute; a female who engages in sexual intercourse with an underage male who is not her husband does not. The petitioner contends that this state law, which punishes only males for the conduct in question, violates his Fourteenth Amendment right to the equal protection of the law. The Court today correctly rejects that contention.

A

At the outset, it should be noted that the statutory discrimination, when viewed as part of the wider scheme of California law, is not as clearcut as might at first appear. Females are not freed from criminal liability in California for engaging in sexual activity that may be harmful. It is unlawful, for example, for any person, of either sex, to molest, annoy, or contribute to the delinquency of anyone under 18 years of age. All persons are prohibited from committing "any lewd or lascivious act," including consensual inter-course, with a child under 14. And members of both sexes may be convicted for engaging in deviant sexual acts with anyone under 18. Finally, females may be brought within the proscription of § 261.5 itself, since a female may be charged with aiding and abetting its violation.

Section 261.5 is thus but one part of a broad statutory scheme that protects all minors from the problems and risks attendant upon adolescent sexual activity. To be sure, § 261.5 creates an additional measure of punish-ment for males who engage in sexual intercourse with females between the ages of 14 and 17. The question then is whether the Constitution prohibits a state legislature from imposing this *additional* sanction on a gender-specific basis.

B

The Constitution is violated when government, state or federal, invidious-ly classifies similarly situated people on the basis of the immutable character-istics with which they were born. Thus, detrimental racial classifications by government always violate the Constitution, for the simple reason that, so far as the Constitution is concerned, people of different races are always similarly situated. See Fullilove v. Klutznick, 448 U.S. 448, 522, 100 S.Ct. 2758, 2797, 65 L.Ed.2d 902 (dissenting opinion); McLaughlin v. Florida, 379 U.S. 184, 198, 85 S.Ct. 283, 13 L.Ed.2d 222 (concurring opinion); Brown v. Board of Educ., 347 U.S. 483, 74 S.Ct. 686, 98 L.Ed. 873; Plessy v. Ferguson, 163 U.S. 537, 552, 16 S.Ct. 1138, 1144, 41 L.Ed. 256 (dissenting opinion). By contrast, while detrimental gender classifications by government often violate the Constitution, they do not always do so, for the reason that there are differ-ences between males and females that the Constitution necessarily recognizes. In this case we deal with the most basic of these differences: females can become pregnant as the result of sexual intercourse; males cannot.

As was recognized in Parham v. Hughes, 441 U.S. 347, 354, 99 S.Ct. 1742, 1747, 60 L.Ed.2d 269, "a State is not free to make overbroad generalizations based on sex which are entirely unrelated to any differences between men and women or which demean the ability or social status of the protected class." Gender-based classifications may not be based upon administrative conve-nience, or upon archaic assumptions about the proper roles of the sexes. Craig v. Boren, 429 U.S. 190, 97 S.Ct. 451, 50 L.Ed.2d 397; Frontiero v. Richardson, 411 U.S. 677, 93 S.Ct. 1764, 36 L.Ed.2d 583; Reed v. Reed, 404 U.S. 71, 92 S.Ct. 251, 30 L.Ed.2d 225. But we have recognized that in certain narrow circumstances men and women are *not* similarly situated, and in these circumstances a gender classification based on clear differences between the sexes is not invidious, and a legislative classification realistically based upon those differences is not unconstitutional. See Parham v. Hughes, supra; Califano v. Webster, 430 U.S. 313, 316–317, 97 S.Ct. 1192, 1194–1195, 51 L.Ed.2d 360; Schlesinger v. Ballard, 419 U.S. 498, 95 S.Ct. 572, 42 L.Ed.2d 610; cf. San Antonio School Dist. v. Rodriguez, 411 U.S. 1, 59, 93 S.Ct. 1278, 1310, 36 L.Ed.2d 16 (concurring opinion) "[G]ender-based classifications are not invariably invalid. When men and women are not in fact similarly situated in the area covered by the legislation in question, the Equal Protec-tion Clause is not violated." Caban v. Mohammed, 441 U.S. 380, 398, 99 S.Ct. 1760, 1771, 60 L.Ed.2d 297 (dissenting opinion).

Applying these principles to the classification enacted by the California Legislature, it is readily apparent that § 261.5 does not violate the Equal Protection Clause. Young women and men are not similarly situated with respect to the problems and risks associated with intercourse and pregnancy, and the statute is realistically related to the legitimate state purpose of reducing those problems and risks.

C

As the California Supreme Court's catalogue shows, the pregnant unmarried female confronts problems more numerous and more severe than any faced by her male partner. She alone endures the medical risks of pregnancy or abortion. She suffers disproportionately the social, educational, and emotional consequences of pregnancy. Recognizing this disproportion, California has attempted to protect teenage females by prohibiting males from participating in the act necessary for conception.[10]

The fact that males and females are not similarly situated with respect to the risks of sexual intercourse applies with the same force to males under 18 as it does to older males. The risk of pregnancy is a significant deterrent for unwed young females that is not shared by unmarried males, regardless of their age. Experienced observation confirms the commonsense notion that adolescent males disregard the possibility of pregnancy far more than do adolescent females. And to the extent that § 261.5 may punish males for intercourse with prepubescent females, that punishment is justifiable because of the substantial physical risks for prepubescent females that are not shared by their male counterparts.

D

The petitioner argues that the California Legislature could have drafted the statute differently, so that its purpose would be accomplished more precisely. "But the issue, of course, is not whether the statute could have been drafted more wisely, but whether the lines chosen by the * * * [l]egislature are within constitutional limitations." Kahn v. Shevin, 416 U.S. 351, 356, n. 10, 94 S.Ct. 1734, 1738, 40 L.Ed.2d 189. That other States may have decided to attack the same problems more broadly, with gender-neutral statutes, does not mean that every State is constitutionally compelled to do so.[13]

10. Despite the increased availability of contraceptives and sex education, the pregnancy rates for young women are increasing. See Alan Guttmacher Institute, 11 Million Teenagers 12 (1976). See generally C. Chilman, Adolescent Sexuality in a Changing American Society (NIH Pub. No. 89–1426)(1980).

The petitioner contends that the statute is overinclusive because it does not allow a defense that contraceptives were used, or that procreation was for some other reason impossible. The petitioner does not allege, however, that he used a contraceptive, or that pregnancy could not have resulted from the conduct with which he was charged. But even assuming the petitioner's standing to raise the claim of overbreadth, it is clear that a statute recognizing

the defenses he suggests would encounter difficult if not impossible problems of proof.

13. The fact is that a gender-neutral statute would not necessarily lead to a closer fit with the aim of reducing the problems associated with teenage pregnancy. If both parties were equally liable to prosecution, a female would be far less likely to complain; the very complaint would be self-incriminating. Accordingly, it is possible that a gender-neutral statute would result in fewer prosecutions than the one before us.

In any event, a state legislature is free to address itself to what it believes to be the most serious aspect of a broader problem. "[T]he Equal Protection Clause does not require that a State must choose between attacking every

E

In short, the Equal Protection Clause does not mean that the physiological differences between men and women must be disregarded. While those differences must never be permitted to become a pretext for invidious discrimination, no such discrimination is presented by this case. The Constitution surely does not require a State to pretend that demonstrable differences between men and women do not really exist.

JUSTICE BLACKMUN, concurring in the judgment.

It is gratifying that the plurality recognizes that "[a]t the risk of stating the obvious, teenage pregnancies * * * have increased dramatically over the last two decades" and "have significant social, medical and economic consequences for both the mother and her child, and the State." There have been times when I have wondered whether the Court was capable of this perception, particularly when it has struggled with the different but not unrelated problems that attend abortion issues [citations omitted]. * * *

I, however, cannot vote to strike down the California statutory rape law, for I think it is a sufficiently reasoned and constitutional effort to control the problem at its inception. For me, there is an important difference between this state action and a State's adamant and rigid refusal to face, or even to recognize, the "significant * * * consequences"—to the woman—of a forced or unwanted conception. * * *

Craig v. Boren, 429 U.S. 190, 97 S.Ct. 451, 50 L.Ed.2d 397 (1976), was an opinion which, in large part, I joined, id., at 214. The plurality opinion in the present case points out, * * * the Court's respective phrasings of the applicable test in Reed v. Reed, 404 U.S. 71, 76, 92 S.Ct. 251, 254, 30 L.Ed.2d 225 (1971), and in Craig v. Boren, 429 U.S., at 197, 97 S.Ct., at 466. I vote to affirm the judgment of the Supreme Court of California and to uphold the State's gender-based classification on that test and as exemplified by those two cases and by Schlesinger v. Ballard, 419 U.S. 498, 95 S.Ct. 572, 42 L.Ed.2d 610 (1975); Weinberger v. Wiesenfeld, 420 U.S. 636, 95 S.Ct. 1225, 43 L.Ed.2d 514 (1975); and Kahn v. Shevin, 416 U.S. 351, 94 S.Ct. 1734, 40 L.Ed.2d 189 (1974).

* * *

I think, too, that it is only fair, with respect to this particular petitioner, to point out that his partner, Sharon, appears not to have been an unwilling participant in at least the initial stages of the intimacies that took place the night of June 3, 1978.* Petitioner's and Sharon's nonacquaintance with each other before the incident; their drinking; their withdrawal from the others of

aspect of a problem or not attacking the problem at all." Dandridge v. Williams, 397 U.S. 471, 486–487, 90 S.Ct. 1153, 1162–1163, 25 L.Ed.2d 491; see also Williamson v. Lee Optical Co., 348 U.S. 483, 75 S.Ct. 461, 99 L.Ed. 563.

* Sharon at the preliminary hearing testified as follows:

"Q. [by the Deputy District Attorney]. On June the 4th, at approximately midnight—midnight of June the 3rd, were you in Rohnert Park?

"A. [by Sharon]. Yes.

"Q. Is that in Sonoma County?

"A. Yes.

"Q. Did anything unusual happen to you that night in Rohnert Park?

"A. Yes.

"Q. Would you briefly describe what happened that night? Did you see the defendant that night in Rohnert Park?

"A. Yes.

"Q. Where did you first meet him?

the group; their foreplay, in which she willingly participated and seems to have encouraged; and the closeness of their ages (a difference of only one year and 18 days) are factors that should make this case an unattractive one to prosecute at all, and especially to prosecute as a felony, rather than as a misdemeanor chargeable under § 261.5. But the State has chosen to prosecute in that manner, and the facts, I reluctantly conclude, may fit the crime.

"A. At a bus stop.

"Q. Was anyone with you?

"A. My sister.

"Q. Was anyone with the defendant?

"A. Yes.

"Q. How many people were with the defendant?

"A. Two.

"Q. Now, after you met the defendant, what happened?

"A. We walked down to the railroad tracks.

"Q. What happened at the railroad tracks?

"A. We were drinking at the railroad tracks and we walked over to this bush and he started kissing me and stuff, and I was kissing him back, too, at first. Then, I was telling him to stop—

"Q. Yes.

"A. —and I was telling him to slow down and stop. He said, 'Okay, okay.' But then he just kept doing it. He just kept doing it and then my sister and two other guys came over to where we were and my sister said— told me to get up and come home. And then I didn't—

"Q. Yes.

"A. —and then my sister and—

"Q. All right.

"A. —David, one of the boys that were there, started walking home and we stayed there and then later—

"Q. All right.

"A. —Bruce left Michael, you know.

"The Court: Michael being the defendant?

"The Witness: Yeah. We was laying there and we were kissing each other, and then he asked me if I wanted to walk him over to the park; so we walked over to the park and we sat down on a bench and then he started kissing me again and we were laying on the bench. And he told me to take my pants off.

"I said, 'No,' and I was trying to get up and he hit me back down on the bench and then I just said to myself, 'Forget it,' and I let him do what he wanted to do and he took my pants off and he was telling me to put my legs around him and stuff—

"Q. Did you have sexual intercourse with the defendant?

"A. Yeah.

"Q. He did put his penis into your vagina?

"A. Yes.

"Q. You said that he hit you?

"A. Yeah.

"Q. How did he hit you?

"A. He slugged me in the face.

"Q. With what did he slug you?

"A. His fist.

"Q. Where abouts in the face?

"A. On my chin.

"Q. As a result of that, did you have any bruises or any kind of an injury?

"A. Yeah.

"Q. What happened?

"A. I had bruises.

"The Court: Did he hit you one time or did he hit you more than once?

"The Witness: He hit me about two or three times.

* * *

CROSS-EXAMINATION

"Q. Did you go off with Mr. *M.* away from the others?

"A. Yeah.

"Q. Why did you do that?

"A. I don't know. I guess I wanted to.

* * *

"Q. So your sister and the other two boys came over to where you were, you and Michael were, is that right?

"A. Yeah.

"Q. What did they say to you, if you remember?

"A. My sister didn't say anything. She said, 'Come on, Sharon, let's go home.'

"Q. She asked you to go home with her?

"A. (Affirmative nod.)

"Q. Did you go home with her?

"A. No.

"Q. You wanted to stay with Mr. *M.?*

"A. I don't know.

"Q. Was this before or after he hit you?

"A. Before.

JUSTICE BRENNAN, with whom JUSTICES WHITE and MARSHALL join, dissenting.

I

It is disturbing to find the Court so splintered on a case that presents such a straightforward issue: whether the admittedly gender-based classification in Cal.Penal Code § 261.5 bears a sufficient relationship to the State's asserted goal of preventing teenage pregnancies to survive the "mid-level" constitutional scrutiny mandated by Craig v. Boren, 429 U.S. 190, 97 S.Ct. 451, 50 L.Ed.2d 397 (1976). Applying the analytical framework provided by our precedents, I am convinced that there is only one proper resolution of this issue: the classification must be declared unconstitutional. I fear that the plurality and Justices Stewart and Blackmun reach the opposite result by placing too much emphasis on the desirability of achieving the State's asserted statutory goal—prevention of teenage pregnancy—and not enough emphasis on the fundamental question of whether the sex-based discrimination in the California statute is *substantially* related to the achievement of that goal.[2]

II

After some uncertainty as to the proper framework for analyzing equal protection challenges to statutes containing gender-based classifications, this Court settled upon the proposition that a statute containing a gender-based classification cannot withstand constitutional challenge unless the classification is substantially related to the achievement of an important governmental objective [citations omitted]. This analysis applies whether the classification discriminates against males or against females [citations omitted]. The burden is on the government to prove both the importance of its asserted objective and the substantial relationship between the classification and that objective [citations omitted]. And the State cannot meet that burden without showing that a gender-neutral statute would be a less effective means of

---

2. None of the three opinions upholding the California statute fairly applies the equal protection analysis this Court has so carefully developed since Craig v. Boren. The plurality, for example, focusing on the obvious and uncontested fact that only females can become pregnant, suggests that the statutory gender discrimination, rather than being invidious, actually ensures equality of treatment. Since only females are subject to a risk of pregnancy, the plurality concludes that "[a] criminal sanction imposed solely on males * * * serves to roughly 'equalize' the deterrents on the sexes." Justice Stewart adopts a similar approach. Recognizing that "females can become pregnant as the result of sexual intercourse; males cannot," Justice Stewart concludes that "[y]oung women and men are not similarly situated with respect to the problems and risks associated with intercourse and pregnancy," and therefore § 261.5 "is *realistically* related to the legitimate state purpose of reducing those problems and risks" (emphasis added). Justice Blackmun, conceding that some limits must be placed on a State's power to regulate

"the control and direction of young people's sexual activities," also finds the statute constitutional. He distinguishes the State's power in the abortion context, where the pregnancy has already occurred, from its power in the present context, where the "problem [is] at its inception." He then concludes, without explanation, that "the California statutory rape law * * * is a sufficiently reasoned and constitutional effort to control the problem at its inception."

All three of these approaches have a common failing. They overlook the fact that the State has not met its burden of proving that the gender discrimination in § 261.5 is *substantially* related to the achievement of the State's asserted statutory goal. My Brethren seem not to recognize that California has the burden of proving that a gender-neutral statutory rape law would be less effective than § 261.5 in deterring sexual activity leading to teenage pregnancy. Because they fail to analyze the issue in these terms, I believe they reach an unsupportable result.

achieving that goal [citations omitted].[3] The State of California vigorously asserts that the "important governmental objective" to be served by § 261.5 is the prevention of teenage pregnancy. It claims that its statute furthers this goal by deterring sexual activity by males—the class of persons it considers more responsible for causing those pregnancies.[4] But even assuming that prevention of teenage pregnancy is an important governmental objective and that it is in fact an objective of § 261.5, * * * California still has the burden of proving that there are fewer teenage pregnancies under its gender-based statutory rape law than there would be if the law were gender-neutral. To meet this burden, the State must show that because its statutory rape law punishes only males, and not females, it more effectively deters minor females from having sexual intercourse.

* * * However, a State's bare assertion that its gender-based statutory classification substantially furthers an important governmental interest is not enough to meet its burden of proof under Craig v. Boren. Rather, the State must produce evidence that will persuade the Court that its assertion is true. See Craig v. Boren, supra, 429 U.S., at 200–204, 97 S.Ct., at 458–460.

The State has not produced such evidence in this case. Moreover, there are at least two serious flaws in the State's assertion that law enforcement problems created by a gender-neutral statutory rape law would make such a statute less effective than a gender-based statute in deterring sexual activity.

First, the experience of other jurisdictions, and California itself, belies the plurality's conclusion that a gender-neutral statutory rape law "may well be incapable of enforcement." There are now at least 37 States that have enacted gender-neutral statutory rape laws. Although most of these laws protect young persons (of either sex) from the sexual exploitation of older individuals, the laws of Arizona, Florida, and Illinois permit prosecution of both minor females and minor males for engaging in mutual sexual conduct. California has introduced no evidence that those states have been handicapped by the enforcement problems the plurality finds so persuasive.[7] Surely, if those States could provide such evidence, we might expect that California would have introduced it.

In addition, the California Legislature in recent years has revised other sections of the Penal Code to make them gender-neutral. For example, Cal.Penal Code §§ 286(b)(1) and 288a(b)(1), prohibiting sodomy and oral copulation with a "person who is under 18 years of age," could cause two minor homosexuals to be subjected to criminal sanctions for engaging in mutually consensual conduct. Again, the State has introduced no evidence to

3. Gender-based statutory rape laws were struck down in Navedo v. Preisser, 630 F.2d 636 (C.A.8 1980), United States v. Hicks, 625 F.2d 216 (C.A.9 1980), and Meloon v. Helgemoe, 564 F.2d 602 (C.A.1 1977), cert. denied, 436 U.S. 950, 98 S.Ct. 2858, 56 L.Ed.2d 793 (1978), precisely because the government failed to meet this burden of proof.

4. In a remarkable display of sexual stereotyping, the California Supreme Court stated:

"The Legislature is well within its power in imposing criminal sanctions against males, alone, because they are the *only* persons who may physiologically cause the re-

sult which the law properly seeks to avoid." 25 Cal.3d 608, 613, 159 Cal.Rptr. 340, 601 P.2d 572 (1979)(emphasis in original).

7. There is a logical reason for this. In contrast to laws governing forcible rape, statutory rape laws apply to consensual sexual activity. Force is not an element of the crime. Since a woman who consents to an act of sexual intercourse is unlikely to report her partner to the police—whether or not she is subject to criminal sanctions—enforcement would not be undermined if the statute were to be made gender-neutral.

explain why a gender-neutral statutory rape law would be any more difficult to enforce than those statutes.

The second flaw in the State's assertion is that even assuming that a gender-neutral statute would be more difficult to enforce, the State has still not shown that those enforcement problems would make such a statute less effective than a gender-based statute in deterring minor females from engaging in sexual intercourse.[8] Common sense, however, suggests that a gender-neutral statutory rape law is potentially a *greater* deterrent of sexual activity than a gender-based law, for the simple reason that a gender-neutral law subjects both men and women to criminal sanctions and thus arguably has a deterrent effect on twice as many potential violators. Even if fewer persons were prosecuted under the gender-neutral law, as the State suggests, it would still be true that twice as many persons would be *subject* to arrest. The State's failure to prove that a gender-neutral law would be a less effective deterrent than a gender-based law, like the State's failure to prove that a gender-neutral law would be difficult to enforce, should have led this Court to invalidate § 261.5.

III

Until very recently, no California court or commentator had suggested that the purpose of California's statutory rape law was to protect young women from the risk of pregnancy. Indeed, the historical development of § 261.5 demonstrates that the law was initially enacted on the premise that young women, in contrast to young men, were to be deemed legally incapable of consenting to an act of sexual intercourse.[9] Because their chastity was

8. As it is, § 261.5 seems to be an ineffective deterrent of sexual activity. Cf. Carey v. Population Services Int'l, supra, 431 U.S., at 695, 97 S.Ct., at 2021 (1977)(substantial reason to doubt that limiting access to contraceptives will substantially discourage early sexual behavior). According to statistics provided by the State, an average of only 61 juvenile males and 352 adult males were arrested for statutory rape each year between 1975 and 1978. Brief for Respondent, at 19. During each of those years there were approximately one million Californian girls between the ages of 13–17. California Dept. of Finance, Population Projections for California Counties, 1975–2020, with Age/Sex Detail to 2000, Series E–150 (1977). Although the record in this case does not indicate the incidence of sexual intercourse involving those girls during that period, the California State Department of Health estimates that there were almost 50,000 pregnancies among 13–17–year-old girls during 1976. State of California, Department of Health, Birth and Abortion Records, and Physician Survey of Office Abortions, 1976. I think it is fair to speculate from this evidence that a comparison of the number of arrests for statutory rape in California with the number of acts of sexual intercourse involving minor females in that State would likely demonstrate to a male contemplating sexual activity with a minor female that his chances of being arrested are reassuringly low. I seriously question,

therefore, whether § 261.5 as enforced has a substantial deterrent effect. See Craig v. Boren, supra, 429 U.S., at 214, 97 S.Ct., at 465 (Stevens, J., concurring).

9. California's statutory rape law had its origins in the Statutes of Westminster enacted during the reign of Edward I at the close of the 13th century (3 Edw. 1, ch. 13 (1275); 13 Edw. 1, ch. 34 (1285)). The age of consent at that time was 12 years, reduced to 10 years in 1576 (18 Eliz. 1, ch. 7, § 4). This statute was part of the common law brought to the United States. Thus, when the first California penal statute was enacted, it contained a provision (Stats.1850, ch. 99, § 47, p. 234) that proscribed sexual intercourse with females under the age of 10. In 1889, the California statute was amended to make the age of consent 14 (Stats.1889, ch. 191, § 1, p. 223). In 1897, the age was advanced to 16 (Stats.1897, ch. 139, § 1, p. 201). In 1913 it was fixed at 18, where it now remains (Stats.1913, ch. 122, § 1, p. 212).

Because females generally have not reached puberty by the age of 10, it is inconceivable that a statute designed to prevent pregnancy would be directed at acts of sexual intercourse with females under that age.

The only legislative history available, the draftsmen's notes to the Penal Code of 1872, supports the view that the purpose of Califor-

considered particularly precious, those young women were felt to be uniquely in need of the State's protection.[10] In contrast, young men were assumed to be capable of making such decisions for themselves; the law therefore did not offer them any special protection.

It is perhaps because the gender classification in California's statutory rape law was initially designed to further these outmoded sexual stereotypes, rather than to reduce the incidence of teenage pregnancies, that the State has been unable to demonstrate a substantial relationship between the classification and its newly asserted goal. Cf. Califano v. Goldfarb, supra, 430 U.S., at 223, 97 S.Ct., at 1035 (Stevens, J., concurring). But whatever the reason, the State has not shown that Cal.Penal Code § 261.5 is any more effective than a gender-neutral law would be in deterring minor females from engaging in sexual intercourse. It has therefore not met its burden of proving that the statutory classification is substantially related to the achievement of its asserted goal.

I would hold that § 261.5 violates the Equal Protection Clause of the Fourteenth Amendment and I would reverse the judgment of the California Supreme Court.

JUSTICE STEVENS, dissenting.

Local custom and belief—rather than statutory laws of venerable but doubtful ancestry—will determine the volume of sexual activity among unmarried teenagers. The empirical evidence cited by the plurality demonstrates the futility of the notion that a statutory prohibition will significantly affect the volume of that activity or provide a meaningful solution to the problems created by it. Nevertheless, as a matter of constitutional power, unlike my Brother Brennan, * * * I would have no doubt about the validity of a state law prohibiting all unmarried teenagers from engaging in sexual

nia's statutory rape law was to protect those who were too young to give consent. The draftsmen explained that the "[statutory rape] provision embodies the well settled rule of the existing law; that a girl under ten years of age is incapable of giving any consent to an act of intercourse which can reduce it below the grade of rape." Code Commissioners' note, subd. 1, foll. Pen.Code, § 261 (1st ed. 1872, p. 111). There was no mention whatever of pregnancy prevention. See also Note, Forcible and Statutory Rape: An Explanation of the Operation and Objectives of the Consent Standard, 62 Yale L.J. 55, 74–76 (1952).

10. Past decisions of the California courts confirm that the law was designed to protect the State's young females from their own uninformed decisionmaking. In People v. Verdegreen, 106 Cal. 211, 214–215, 39 P. 607, 608–609 (1895), for example, the California Supreme Court stated:

"The obvious purpose of [the statutory rape law] is the protection of society by protecting from violation the virtue of young and unsophisticated girls. * * * It is the insidious approach and vile tampering with their persons that primarily undermines the virtue of young girls, and eventually destroys it; and

the prevention of this, as much as the principal act, must undoubtedly have been the intent of the legislature."

As recently as 1964, the California Supreme Court decided People v. Hernandez, supra, 61 Cal.2d, at 531, 39 Cal.Rptr., at 362, 393 P.2d, at 674, in which it stated that the under-age female

"is presumed too innocent and naive to understand the implications and nature of her act. * * * The law's concern with her capacity or lack thereof to so understand is explained in part by a popular conception of the social, moral and personal values which are preserved by the abstinence from sexual indulgence on the part of a young woman. An unwise disposition of her sexual favor is deemed to do harm both to herself and the social mores by which the community's conduct patterns are established. Hence the law of statutory rape intervenes in an effort to avoid such a disposition."

It was only in deciding Michael M. that the California Supreme Court decided, for the first time in the 130–year history of the statute, that pregnancy prevention had become one of the purposes of the statute.

intercourse. The societal interests in reducing the incidence of venereal disease and teenage pregnancy are sufficient, in my judgment, to justify a prohibition of conduct that increases the risk of those harms.

My conclusion that a nondiscriminatory prohibition would be constitutional does not help me answer the question whether a prohibition applicable to only half of the joint participants in the risk-creating conduct is also valid. It cannot be true that the validity of a total ban is an adequate justification for a selective prohibition; otherwise, the constitutional objection to discriminatory rules would be meaningless. The question in this case is whether the difference between males and females justifies this statutory discrimination based entirely on sex.[4]

The fact that the Court did not immediately acknowledge that the capacity to become pregnant is what primarily differentiates the female from the male[5] does not impeach the validity of the plurality's newly-found wisdom. I think the plurality is quite correct in making the assumption that the joint act that this law seeks to prohibit creates a greater risk of harm for the female than for the male. But the plurality surely cannot believe that the risk of pregnancy confronted by the female—any more than the risk of venereal disease confronted by males as well as females—has provided an effective deterrent to voluntary female participation in the risk-creating conduct. Yet the plurality's decision seems to rest on the assumption that the California Legislature acted on the basis of that rather fanciful notion.

In my judgment, the fact that a class of persons is especially vulnerable to a risk that a statute is designed to avoid is a reason for making the statute applicable to that class. The argument that a special need for protection provides a rational explanation for an exemption is one I simply do not comprehend.[6]

---

4. Equal protection analysis is often said to involve different "levels of scrutiny." It may be more accurate to say that the burden of sustaining an equal protection challenge is much heavier in some cases than in others. Racial classifications, which are subjected to "strict scrutiny," are presumptively invalid because there is seldom, if ever, any legitimate reason for treating citizens differently because of their race. On the other hand, most economic classifications are presumptively valid because they are a necessary component of most regulatory programs. In cases involving discrimination between men and women, the natural differences between the sexes are sometimes relevant and sometimes wholly irrelevant. If those differences are obviously irrelevant, the discrimination should be treated as presumptively unlawful in the same way that racial classifications are presumptively unlawful. Cf. Califano v. Goldfarb, 430 U.S. 199, 223, 97 S.Ct. 1021, 1035, 51 L.Ed.2d 270 (1977)(Stevens, J., concurring in the judgment). But if, as in this case, there is an apparent connection between the discrimination and the fact that only women can become pregnant, it may be appropriate to presume that the classification is lawful. This presumption, however, may be overcome by a demon-

stration that the apparent justification for the discrimination is illusory or wholly inadequate. Thus, instead of applying a "mid-level" form of scrutiny in all sex discrimination cases, perhaps the burden is heavier in some than in others. Nevertheless, as I have previously suggested, the ultimate standard in these, as in all other equal protection cases, is essentially the same. See Craig v. Boren, 429 U.S. 190, 211–212, 97 S.Ct. 451, 464–465, 50 L.Ed.2d 397 (1976)(Stevens, J., concurring). Professor Cox recently noted that however the level of scrutiny is described, in the final analysis, "the Court is always deciding whether in its judgment the harm done to the disadvantaged class by the legislative classification is disproportionate to the public purposes the measure is likely to achieve." Cox, Book Review, 94 Harv. L.Rev. 700, 706 (1981).

5. See General Electric Co. v. Gilbert, 429 U.S. 125, 162, 97 S.Ct. 401, 421, 50 L.Ed.2d 343 (1976)(Stevens, J., dissenting).

6. A hypothetical racial classification will illustrate my point. Assume that skin pigmentation provides some measure of protection against cancer caused by exposure to certain chemicals in the atmosphere and, therefore,

In this case, the fact that a female confronts a greater risk of harm than a male is a reason for applying the prohibition to her—not a reason for granting her a license to use her own judgment on whether or not to assume the risk. Surely, if we examine the problem from the point of view of society's interest in preventing the risk-creating conduct from occurring at all, it is irrational to exempt 50% of the potential violators. See Dissent of Justice Brennan * * *. And, if we view the government's interest as that of a *parens patriae* seeking to protect its subjects from harming themselves, the discrimination is actually perverse. Would a rational parent making rules for the conduct of twin children of opposite sex simultaneously forbid the son and authorize the daughter to engage in conduct that is especially harmful to the daughter? That is the effect of this statutory classification.

If pregnancy or some other special harm is suffered by one of the two participants in the prohibited act, that special harm no doubt would constitute a legitimate mitigating factor in deciding what, if any, punishment might be appropriate in a given case. But from the standpoint of fashioning a general preventive rule—or, indeed, in determining appropriate punishment when neither party in fact has suffered any special harm—I regard a total exemption for the members of the more endangered class as utterly irrational.

In my opinion, the only acceptable justification for a general rule requiring disparate treatment of the two participants in a joint act must be a legislative judgment that one is more guilty than the other. The risk-creating conduct that this statute is designed to prevent requires the participation of two persons—one male and one female.[7] In many situations it is probably true that one is the aggressor and the other is either an unwilling, or at least a less willing, participant in the joint act. If a statute authorized punishment of only one participant and required the prosecutor to prove that that participant had been the aggressor, I assume that the discrimination would be valid. Although the question is less clear, I also assume, for the purpose of deciding this case, that it would be permissible to punish only the male participant, if one element of the offense were proof that he had been the aggressor, or at least in some respects the more responsible participant in the joint act. The statute at issue in this case, however, requires no such proof. The question raised by this statute is whether the State, consistently with the Federal Constitution, may always punish the male and never the female when they are equally responsible or when the female is the more responsible of the two.

that white employees confront a greater risk than black employees in certain industrial settings. Would it be rational to require black employees to wear protective clothing but to exempt whites from that requirement? It seems to me that the greater risk of harm to white workers would be a reason for including them in the requirement—not for granting them an exemption.

7. In light of this indisputable biological fact, I find somewhat puzzling the California Supreme Court's conclusion, quoted by the plurality, * * * that males "are the *only* per-

sons who may physiologically cause the result which the law properly seeks to avoid." 25 Cal.3d 608, 612, 159 Cal.Rptr. 340, 601 P.2d 572, 575 (1979)(emphasis in original). Presumably, the California Supreme Court was referring to the equally indisputable biological fact that only females may become pregnant. However, if pregnancy results from sexual intercourse between two willing participants— and the California statute is directed at such conduct—I would find it difficult to conclude that the pregnancy was "caused" solely by the male participant.

It would seem to me that an impartial lawmaker could give only one answer to that question. The fact that the California Legislature has decided to apply its prohibition only to the male may reflect a legislative judgment that in the typical case the male is actually the more guilty party. Any such judgment must, in turn, assume that the decision to engage in the risk-creating conduct is always—or at least typically—a male decision. If that assumption is valid, the statutory classification should also be valid. But what is the support for the assumption? It is not contained in the record of this case or in any legislative history or scholarly study that has been called to our attention. I think it is supported to some extent by traditional attitudes toward male-female relationships. But the possibility that such an habitual attitude may reflect nothing more than an irrational prejudice makes it an insufficient justification for discriminatory treatment that is otherwise blatantly unfair. For, as I read this statute, it requires that one, and only one, of two equally guilty wrongdoers be stigmatized by a criminal conviction.

I cannot accept the State's argument that the constitutionality of the discriminatory rule can be saved by an assumption that prosecutors will commonly invoke this statute only in cases that actually involve a forcible rape, but one that cannot be established by proof beyond a reasonable doubt. That assumption implies that a State has a legitimate interest in convicting a defendant on evidence that is constitutionally insufficient. Of course, the State may create a lesser-included offense that would authorize punishment of the more guilty party, but surely the interest in obtaining convictions on inadequate proof cannot justify a statute that punishes one who is equally or less guilty than his partner.

Nor do I find at all persuasive the suggestion that this discrimination is adequately justified by the desire to encourage females to inform against their male partners. Even if the concept of a wholesale informant's exemption were an acceptable enforcement device, what is the justification for defining the exempt class entirely by reference to sex rather than by reference to a more neutral criterion such as relative innocence? Indeed, if the exempt class is to be composed entirely of members of one sex, what is there to support the view that the statutory purpose will be better served by granting the informing license to females rather than to males? If a discarded male partner informs on a promiscuous female, a timely threat of prosecution might well prevent the precise harm the statute is intended to minimize.

Finally, even if my logic is faulty and there actually is some speculative basis for treating equally guilty males and females differently, I still believe that any such speculative justification would be outweighed by the paramount interest in even-handed enforcement of the law. A rule that authorizes punishment of only one of two equally guilty wrongdoers violates the essence of the constitutional requirement that the sovereign must govern impartially.

I respectfully dissent.

STATE v. STEVENS

Supreme Judicial Court of Maine, 1986.
510 A.2d 1070.

WATHEN, JUSTICE.

The State appeals, pursuant to 15 M.R.S.A. § 2115–A (1980), from an order of the Superior Court (Kennebec County) dismissing an indictment that charged defendant Sandra Stevens with the rape of a thirteen year-old boy. *See* 17–A M.R.S.A. § 252(a)(A)(1983). The Superior Court ruled that section 252 does not encompass males as victims of rape. We conclude that section 252 is gender-neutral, contemplating male as well as female victims. Accordingly, we vacate the order of the Superior Court.

Maine's rape statute provides in relevant part:

A person is guilty of rape if he engages in sexual intercourse:

With any person, not his spouse, who has not in fact attained his 14th birthday * * *[1]

17–A M.R.S.A. § 252(1)(A). Sexual intercourse is defined as "any penetration of the female sex organ by the male sex organ." 17–A M.R.S.A. § 251(1)(B)(1983). The Superior Court found that section 252, together with the definition of sexual intercourse, sets forth the offense of rape in gender-neutral terms. The court held, however, that the comments prepared by the drafters of the criminal code demonstrated the Legislature's intent to confine the protection afforded by section 252 to females only. Specifically, the court noted that the comment to section 252 reflects an intent to carry forward, without alteration, Maine's former statutory rape law, which was explicitly confined to female victims. *See* 17 M.R.S.A. § 3151 (1964); *State v. Rundlett*, 391 A.2d 815, 817 (Me. 1978). In addition, the court pointed to the comment to section 253, gross sexual misconduct, which refers to the victims of rape as female. *See* 17–A M.R.S.A. § 253 (1983) comment.

We agree with the Superior Court that the statutory language in question is gender-neutral, and thus, on its face applies equally to male victims as well as female victims.[2] Given the statute's plain language, we must faithfully apply it to both male and female victims unless the context of the statute's enactment manifestly reveals a contrary legislative intent. *Anderson v. Cape Elizabeth School Board*, 472 A.2d 419, 421 (Me.1984). In the present case, the comments relied upon by the Superior Court do not provide a reason for disregarding the plain language chosen by the Legislature.

The comments to section 252 and 253 were prepared by the Criminal Law Revision Commission to accompany an initial proposed draft of Maine's Criminal Code. Commission to Prepare Revision of the Criminal Laws, *Draft Criminal Code*, ch. 23, §§ 2, 3 comments (February 9, 1973). In that initial draft, the section creating the offense of rape explicitly referred to females as victims. *Id.* § 2. Before submitting the proposed draft to the Legislature, the Commission altered the rape section to define the offense in gender-

---

1. Under 17–A M.R.S.A. § 2(14), the personal pronouns he and she are made interchangeable. The text of the substantive offense uses only the male form of the personal pronoun.

2. On appeal, defendant argues that the definition of sexual intercourse connotes the male as actor, thereby restricting the victims of offenses involving sexual intercourse to females. We disagree. The definition reflects the biological reality that during intercourse

the male sex organ penetrates the female sex organ, but we do not interpret that definition as determining the sex of the perpetrator of crimes involving sexual intercourse. Our conclusion is bolstered by the Criminal Code's use of the same definition with regards to prostitution, an offense traditionally associated with female offenders. *See* 17–A M.R.S.A. § 851 (1983).

neutral terms. The comments, however, were never amended to reflect the incorporation of gender-neutral language into the final draft. *Compare id.* §§ 2, 3 comments *with* 17–A M.R.S.A. §§ 252, 253 comments (1983). In these circumstances, the comments create no contextual impediment to an application of the plain language adopted by the Legislature.

When viewed in light of the evil the Legislature sought to remedy and in conjunction with accompanying provisions, our construction of section 252 is confirmed. Section 252 was enacted as part of a comprehensive codification of Maine's criminal laws, in the process of which the laws governing sex offenses were revised and consolidated into four sections. *See* 17–A M.R.S.A. §§ 252–255 (1983 & Supp.1985–1986). Each of the four sections is drafted in gender-neutral language, and each contains a provision criminalizing sexual conduct based strictly on the age of the participants. *Id.* §§ 252(1)(A), 253(1)(B), 254(1), 255(1)(C). Taken together, these statutes represent a comprehensive effort on behalf of the Legislature to outlaw the sexual exploitation of children, whether male or female. We conclude that the plain language of section 252(1)(A) must be construed in harmony with this comprehensive legislative scheme to encompass both male and female victims.

The entry is:

Order dismissing indictment vacated. Remanded for further proceedings consistent with the opinion herein.

All concurring.

Notes on Michael M. *and* Stevens

1. Did the five Justices who voted to sustain California's statutory rape law in *Michael M.* do so for the same reasons? Why does Justice Blackmun find it relevant that Sharon "appears not to have been an unwilling participant" in the events leading up to her consensual intercourse with Michael? After reading the excerpt from Sharon's testimony, do you agree with his interpretation? Do you agree with the plurality that California sufficiently established that the purpose of the statute is to prevent teenage pregnancy? How does that argument square with the legislative history cited in footnote 9 of Justice Brennan's dissenting opinion?

2. Note that the California Supreme Court upheld the validity of its statutory rape law while using the strict scrutiny standard adopted for sex discrimination cases in Sail'er Inn v. Kirby, 5 Cal.3d 1, 485 P.2d 529, 95 Cal.Rptr. 329 (1971), discussed at p. 28, supra. Its decision was affirmed by the United States Supreme Court under an intermediate scrutiny standard. If the United States Supreme Court had also been using strict scrutiny, would the case have been reversed? Is there any answer to Justice Brennan's contention, in footnote 2 of his dissenting opinion, that the Justices voting to sustain the California statute are waffling on the *Craig* standard? What is to be said for the California Supreme Court? Has it abandoned strict scrutiny in gender discrimination cases? See Rita Eidson, Comment, The Constitutionality of Statutory Rape Laws, 27 U.C.L.A.L.Rev. 757, 784–87 (1980).

In 1993, California joined other states in making its statutory rape law gender neutral; punishment differs according to whether or not the perpetrator is more than three years older than the minor, or whether the perpetrator is over 21 years of age and the minor is under 16 years of age. Cal. Penal Code § 261.5 (1994).

3. How, exactly, does a statutory rape law punishing only males prevent pregnancy? In January 1996, California Governor Pete Wilson called for aggressive prosecution of statutory rape cases in order to reduce the number of teen mothers on welfare, based on the fact that two-thirds of the fathers of babies born to teen mothers are adult men, 18 years of age or older. Kathryn Dorè Perkins, Wilson's War on Teen Pregnancy * * *, Sacramento Bee, Jan. 10, 1996, p. A1, A10. How effective as a welfare reform strategy will this be?

4. If Sharon had become pregnant as a result of her intercourse with Michael M., and if she had then decided to give birth to the child and surrender it for adoption, would Michael M.'s consent to the adoption be necessary? Does the Supreme Court's decision in Caban v. Mohammed, discussed at p. 413, supra, cover the relative constitutional rights of the natural parents in a case where the pregnancy has resulted from statutory rape? Would Justice Stevens hold that the father's rights to participate in the adoption decision should be recognized here because both parties were equally responsible for the act? Would you? If so, what about the rights of the natural father in a case where the conception resulted from forcible rape?

5. Do you prefer the reasoning in *Stevens* to that in *Michael M.?* Professor Arnold Loewy criticized the California statute because it "demeans all of California's young women by forbidding their sexual experimentation while allowing their younger brothers to experiment whenever they can find a willing older woman." Loewy, Returned to the Pedestal—The Supreme Court and Gender Classification Cases: 1980 Term, 60 No.Car.L.Rev. 87, 98 (1981). The interpretation of the Maine statute in *Stevens* forecloses that inequity, doesn't it? Does it do so at the price of forbidding "sexual experimentation" to young people of both sexes? Do statutory rape laws perform a useful social function?

Professor Frances Olsen explores the conflict between the right to privacy and the right to be protected against harm from others that is illustrated by statutory rape laws. Using those laws as the basis for a critique of rights analysis, she identifies several ways the statutory rape laws could be changed to free young women from state-enforced sexual restraint or to help them overcome debilitating stereotypes. She concludes, however, that rights analysis provides little guidance in choosing among those possible alternatives, because "[e]very effort to protect young women against private oppression by individual men risks subjecting women to state oppression, and every effort to protect them against state oppression undermines their power to resist individual oppression." Olsen, Statutory Rape: A Feminist Critique of Rights Analysis, 63 Tex.L.Rev. 387, 412 (1984). Her own critique of *Michael M.* suggests that the Supreme Court should have used the case "to examine conditions of sexuality in a society of gender hierarchy." Id., at 428. What would you expect such an examination to disclose?

2. FORCIBLE RAPE

WITHERS v. LEVINE

United States Court of Appeals, Fourth Circuit, 1980.
615 F.2d 158.

HAYNSWORTH, CHIEF JUDGE:

In this § 1983 action, the district court granted declaratory and injunctive relief, requiring prison officials to devise a procedure to provide inmates with reasonable protection from aggressive sexual assaults. The findings of fact are fully supported in the record, and, since we approve the court's legal reasoning, we affirm. See Withers v. Levine, 449 F.Supp. 473 (D.Md.1978).

In the Maryland House of Corrections, a medium security institution for males, some homosexual rapes are reported annually. There was evidence, however, that many more such assaults go unreported because the victim is usually threatened with violence or death should the incident be reported. Typically, the attacks are upon younger prisoners, and a young, white, slightly built man is at the greatest risk of all. Withers, although black, otherwise fits this description. Moreover, it appears that once a prisoner has been thus victimized, word spreads throughout the prison and he becomes a special target for subsequent attacks.

Newly arriving prisoners at MHC are placed on an "idle tier" where they remain from sixty to ninety days, pending assignment to a prison job and regular housing. Prisoners were assigned to two-man cells, largely on the basis of space availability and without regard to considerations of safety.

When Withers first arrived at MHC he got into an altercation with his cellmate who attempted a sexual assault. As a result of the altercation, each of them was put in solitary confinement, but Withers requested a transfer to another institution. He reported that he had been the victim of a similar assault three years earlier while in the Baltimore City Jail. Because of his age and his victimization by sexually aggressive prisoners, he was transferred to the Maryland Correctional Institute at Hagerstown. Approximately one and one-half years later, however, he was transferred back to MHC despite the fact that the classification team which ordered the transfer had reviewed his base file which contained information about the sexual assaults upon him. No effort was made to alert the cell assignment officials at MHC to any need of special care for Withers.

When he arrived at MHC the second time, the cell assignment official placed him in a cell with a prisoner named Redd. The base file goes with the prisoner, but it goes to the records office and was unavailable to the cell assigning official. Had it been available and had that official consulted it, he would have learned of Withers' earlier victimizations. Had he reviewed Redd's file, he would have learned that Redd, a large man, had a history of violent, aggressive, sexual assaults.

On his second night in the cell with Redd, threatened by a razor and pressed with Redd's greater weight and strength, Withers again became the victim of a sexual assault.

* * *

II.

In Woodhous v. Virginia, 487 F.2d 889 (4th Cir.1973), we held that a prisoner has a constitutional right "to be reasonably protected from the constant threat of violence and sexual assault from his fellow inmates * * *." To obtain relief, he must show "a pervasive risk of harm to inmates from other prisoners" and that the prison officials have failed to exercise reasonable care to prevent prisoners from intentionally inflicting harm or creating unreasonable risks of harm to other prisoners.

A.

A pervasive risk of harm may not ordinarily be shown by pointing to a single incident or isolated incidents, but it may be established by much less than proof of a reign of violence and terror in the particular institution. The defendants seized upon that explanatory phrase from *Woodhous* to contend that something approaching anarchy must be proven before a cause of action under *Woodhous* may be made out, but conditions need not deteriorate to that extent before the constitutional right to protection arises. It is enough that violence and sexual assaults occur on the idle tier at MHC with sufficient frequency that the younger prisoners, particularly those slightly built, are put in reasonable fear for their safety and to reasonably apprise prison officials of the existence of the problem and the need for protective measures. The proof in this case and the findings of the district court fully meet those requirements.

It is not necessary to show that all prisoners suffer a pervasive risk of harm. It is enough that an identifiable group of prisoners do, if the complainant is a member of that group. It is irrelevant that larger, older men need experience no such fear, when younger and smaller men are frequently victimized and each such person has a reasonable basis for fearing that he will become a victim or will be victimized again. The analysis in the opinion of the district court, while showing that sexual assault was not rampant at MHC or on its idle tiers, amply demonstrates that the risk of sexual assault was a serious problem of substantial dimensions, particularly for younger prisoners. It surely was enough to require the prison officials to take reasonable precautions to provide reasonable protection for such prisoners.

* * *

V.

Agreeing with the district court's findings and conclusions, the judgment is affirmed in all respects.

AFFIRMED.

PEOPLE v. LIBERTA
Court of Appeals of New York, 1984.
64 N.Y.2d 152, 474 N.E.2d 567, 485 N.Y.S.2d 207, certiorari denied
471 U.S. 1020, 105 S.Ct. 2029, 85 L.Ed.2d 310 (1985).

WACHTLER, JUDGE.

The defendant, while living apart from his wife pursuant to a Family Court order, forcibly raped and sodomized her in the presence of their 2½ year old son. Under the New York Penal Law a married man ordinarily cannot be prosecuted for raping or sodomizing his wife. The defendant, however, though married at the time of the incident, is treated as an unmarried man under the Penal Law because of the Family Court order. On this appeal, he contends that because of the exemption for married men, the statutes for rape in the first degree (Penal Law, § 130.35) and sodomy in the first degree (Penal Law, § 130.50), violate the equal protection clause of the Federal Constitution (U.S.Const., 14th Amdt.). The defendant also contends that the rape statute violates equal protection because only men, and not women, can be prosecuted under it.

I

Defendant Mario Liberta and Denise Liberta were married in 1978. Shortly after the birth of their son, in October of that year, Mario began to beat Denise. In early 1980 Denise brought a proceeding in the Family Court in Erie County seeking protection from the defendant. On April 30, 1980 a temporary order of protection was issued to her by the Family Court. Under this order, the defendant was to move out and remain away from the family home, and stay away from Denise. The order provided that the defendant could visit with his son once each weekend.

On the weekend of March 21, 1981, Mario, who was then living in a motel, did not visit his son. On Tuesday, March 24, 1981 he called Denise to ask if he could visit his son on that day. Denise would not allow the defendant to come to her house, but she did agree to allow him to pick up their son and her and take them both back to his motel after being assured that a friend of his would be with them at all times. The defendant and his friend picked up Denise and their son and the four of them drove to defendant's motel.

When they arrived at the motel the friend left. As soon as only Mario, Denise, and their son were alone in the motel room, Mario attacked Denise, threatened to kill her, and forced her to perform fellatio on him and to engage in sexual intercourse with him. The son was in the room during the entire episode, and the defendant forced Denise to tell their son to watch what the defendant was doing to her.

The defendant allowed Denise and their son to leave shortly after the incident. Denise, after going to her parents' home, went to a hospital to be treated for scratches on her neck and bruises on her head and back, all inflicted by her husband. She also went to the police station, and on the next day she swore out a felony complaint against the defendant. On July 15, 1981 the defendant was indicted for rape in the first degree and sodomy in the first degree.

II

Section 130.35 of the Penal Law provides in relevant part that "A male is guilty of rape in the first degree when he engages in sexual intercourse with a female * * * by forcible compulsion". "Female", for purposes of the rape statute, is defined as "any female person who is not married to the actor" (Penal Law, § 130.00, subd. 4). Section 130.50 of the Penal Law provides in relevant part that "a person is guilty of sodomy in the first degree when he engages in deviate sexual intercourse with another person * * * by forcible compulsion". "Deviate sexual intercourse" is defined as "sexual conduct between persons not married to each other consisting of contact between the penis and the anus, the mouth and penis, or the mouth and the vulva" (Penal Law, § 130.00, subd. 2). Thus, due to the "not married" language in the definitions of "female" and "deviate sexual intercourse", there is a "marital exemption" for both forcible rape and forcible sodomy. The marital exemption itself, however, has certain exceptions. For purposes of the rape and sodomy statutes, a husband and wife are considered to be "not married" if at the time of the sexual assault they "are living apart * * * pursuant to a valid and effective: (i) order issued by a court of competent jurisdiction which by its terms or in its effect requires such living apart, or (ii) decree or judgment of separation, or (iii) written agreement of separation" (Penal Law, § 130.00, subd. 4).

* * *

IV

The defendant's constitutional challenges to the rape and sodomy statutes are premised on his being considered "not married" to Denise and are the same challenges as could be made by any unmarried male convicted under these statutes. The defendant's claim is that both statutes violate equal protection because they are underinclusive classifications which burden him, but not others similarly situated (see Tribe, American Constitutional Law, p. 997).

* * *

A. THE MARITAL EXEMPTION

As noted above, under the Penal Law a married man ordinarily cannot be convicted of forcibly raping or sodomizing his wife. This is the so-called marital exemption for rape (see 1881 Penal Code, tit. X, ch. II, § 278). Although a marital exemption was not explicit in earlier rape statutes (see 1863 Rev.Stats. part 4, ch. I, tit. 2, art. 2, § 22), an 1852 treatise stated that a man could not be guilty of raping his wife (Barbour, Criminal Law of State of New York [2d ed.], p. 69). The assumption, even before the marital exemption was codified, that a man could not be guilty of raping his wife, is traceable to a statement made by the 17th century English jurist Lord Hale, who wrote: "[T]he husband cannot be guilty of a rape committed by himself upon his lawful wife, for by their mutual matrimonial consent and contract the wife hath given up herself in this kind unto her husband, which she cannot retract" (1 Hale, History of Pleas of the Crown, p. 629). Although Hale cited no authority for his statement it was relied on by State Legislatures which enacted rape statutes with a marital exemption and by courts which established a common-law exemption for husbands.[4]

The first American case to recognize the marital exemption was decided in 1857 by the Supreme Judicial Court of Massachusetts, which stated in dictum that it would always be a defense to rape to show marriage to the victim (Commonwealth v. Fogerty, 74 Mass. 489). Decisions to the same effect by other courts followed, usually with no rationale or authority cited other than Hale's implied consent view.[5] In New York, a 1922 decision noted the marital exemption in the Penal Law and stated that it existed "on account of the matrimonial consent which [the wife] has given, and which she cannot retract" (People v. Meli, 193 N.Y.S. 365, 366 [Sup.Ct.]).

4. The influence of Hale's statement, despite its failure to cite any authority has been discussed by several courts and commentators (see *State v. Smith,* 85 N.J. 193, 199, 426 A.2d 38; *Commonwealth v. Chretien,* 383 Mass. 123, 124, n. 1, 417 N.E.2d 1203; *State v. Rider,* 449 So.2d 903, 904 (Fla.App.); Note, Abolishing The Marital Exemption For Rape: A Statutory Proposal, 1983 U. of Ill.L.Rev. 201, 202 [hereafter cited as "Abolishing the Marital Exemption"]; Note, Spousal Exemption To Rape, 65 Marq.L.Rev. 120, 121 [hereafter cited as "Spousal Exemption"]). Interestingly, Hale's statement has not been fully accepted in England (see *Weishaupt v. Commonwealth,* 227 Va. 389, 315 S.E.2d 847, 850–852).

5. See, generally, *State v. Smith,* 85 N.J. at p. 200, 426 A.2d 38; "Spousal Exemption", *supra,* at n. 4, at pp. 129–130; Note, Marital Rape Exemption, 52 N.Y.U.L.Rev. 306, 309 (hereafter cited as "Marital Rape Exemption").

Presently, over 40 States still retain some form of marital exemption for rape.[6] While the marital exemption is subject to an equal protection challenge, because it classifies unmarried men differently than married men, the equal protection clause does not prohibit a State from making classifications, provided the statute does not arbitrarily burden a particular group of individuals (Reed v. Reed, 404 U.S. 71, 75–76, 92 S.Ct. 251, 253–254, 30 L.Ed.2d 225). Where a statute draws a distinction based upon marital status, the classification must be reasonable and must be based upon "some ground of difference that rationally explains the different treatment" (Eisenstadt v. Baird, 405 U.S. 438, 447, 92 S.Ct. 1029, 1035, 31 L.Ed.2d 349; People v. Onofre, 51 N.Y.2d 476, 491, 434 N.Y.S.2d 947, 415 N.E.2d 936, cert. den. 451 U.S. 987, 101 S.Ct. 2323, 68 L.Ed.2d 845).

We find that there is no rational basis for distinguishing between marital rape and nonmarital rape. The various rationales which have been asserted in defense of the exemption are either based upon archaic notions about the consent and property rights incident to marriage or are simply unable to withstand even the slightest scrutiny. We therefore declare the marital exemption for rape in the New York statute to be unconstitutional.

Lord Hale's notion of an irrevocable implied consent by a married woman to sexual intercourse has been cited most frequently in support of the marital exemption ("Equal Protection Considerations", *supra,* n. 6, 16 N.Eng.L.Rev., at p. 21). Any argument based on a supposed consent, however, is untenable. Rape is not simply a sexual act to which one party does not consent. Rather, it is a degrading, violent act which violates the bodily integrity of the victim and frequently causes severe, long-lasting physical and psychic harm (see Coker v. Georgia, 433 U.S. 584, 597–598, 97 S.Ct. 2861, 2868–2869, 53 L.Ed.2d 982; Note, Rape Reform and a Statutory Consent Defense, 74 J. of Crim.L. & Criminology 1518, 1519, 1527–1528). To ever imply consent to such an act is irrational and absurd. Other than in the context of rape statutes, marriage has never been viewed as giving a husband the right to coerced intercourse on demand (see De Angelis v. De Angelis, 54 A.D.2d 1088, 388 N.Y.S.2d 744; "Abolishing the Marital Exemption", *supra,* at n. 4, 1983 U. of Ill.L.Rev., at p. 207; "Marital Rape Exemption", *supra,* at n. 5, 52 N.Y.U.L.Rev., at pp. 311–312). Certainly, then, a marriage license should not be viewed as a license for a husband to forcibly rape his wife with impunity. A married woman has the same right to control her own body as does an

---

6. Statutes in nine States provide a complete exemption to rape as long as there is a valid marriage (Alabama, Arkansas, Kansas, Montana, South Dakota, Texas, Vermont, Washington, West Virginia). In 26 other States, statutes provide for a marital exemption but with certain exceptions, most typically where the spouses are living apart pursuant to either a court order or a separation agreement (Alaska, Arizona, Colorado, Idaho, Indiana, Kentucky, Louisiana, Maine, Maryland, Michigan, Minnesota, Missouri, Nevada, New Mexico, New York, North Carolina, North Dakota, Ohio, Oklahoma, Pennsylvania, Rhode Island, South Carolina, Tennessee, Utah, Wyoming, Wisconsin). In three other States (Georgia, Mississippi, Nebraska) and the District of Co-

lumbia the exemption appears to still exist as a common-law doctrine, and it may still have a limited application in Virginia (see Weishaupt v. Commonwealth, 227 Va. 389, 315 S.E.2d 847). Finally, in Connecticut, Delaware, Hawaii, and Iowa, there is a marital exemption for some, but not all degrees of forcible rape (see, generally, for statutory references, Schwartz, Spousal Exemption for Criminal Rape Prosecution, 7 Vt.L.Rev. 33, 38–41 [hereafter cited as "Rape Prosecution"]; Note, Clancy, Equal Protection Considerations of the Spousal Sexual Assault Exclusion, 16 N.Eng. L.Rev. 1, 2–3, n. 4 [hereafter cited as "Equal Protection Considerations"]; "Abolishing the Marital Exemption", *supra,* at n. 4, at pp. 203–205).

unmarried woman ("Equal Protection Considerations", *supra*, n. 6, 16 N.Eng. L.Rev., at pp. 19–20; cf. Planned Parenthood v. Danforth, 428 U.S. 52, 96 S.Ct. 2831, 49 L.Ed.2d 788). If a husband feels "aggrieved" by his wife's refusal to engage in sexual intercourse, he should seek relief in the courts governing domestic relations, not in "violent or forceful self-help" (State v. Smith, 85 N.J. 193, 206, 426 A.2d 38).

The other traditional justifications for the marital exemption were the common-law doctrines that a woman was the property of her husband and that the legal existence of the woman was "incorporated and consolidated into that of the husband" (1 Blackstone's Commentaries [1966 ed.], p. 430; see State v. Smith, supra, at pp. 204–205, 426 A.2d 38; "Marital Rape Exemption", *supra*, n. 5, 52 N.Y.U.L.Rev., at pp. 309–310). Both these doctrines, of course, have long been rejected in this State. Indeed, "[n]owhere in the common-law world—[or] in any modern society—is a woman regarded as chattel or demeaned by denial of a separate legal identity and the dignity associated with recognition as a whole human being" (Trammel v. United States, 445 U.S. 40, 52, 100 S.Ct. 906, 913, 63 L.Ed.2d 186).

Because the traditional justifications for the marital exemption no longer have any validity, other arguments have been advanced in its defense. The first of these recent rationales, which is stressed by the People in this case, is that the marital exemption protects against governmental intrusion into marital privacy and promotes reconciliation of the spouses, and thus that elimination of the exemption would be disruptive to marriages. While protecting marital privacy and encouraging reconciliation are legitimate State interests, there is no rational relation between allowing a husband to forcibly rape his wife and these interests. The marital exemption simply does not further marital privacy because this right of privacy protects consensual acts, not violent sexual assaults (see Griswold v. Connecticut, 381 U.S. 479, 485–486, 85 S.Ct. 1678, 1682–1683, 14 L.Ed.2d 510; "Equal Protection Considerations", *supra*, n. 6, 16 N.Eng.L.Rev., at p. 23). Just as a husband cannot invoke a right of marital privacy to escape liability for beating his wife,[7] he cannot justifiably rape his wife under the guise of a right to privacy.

Similarly, it is not tenable to argue that elimination of the marital exemption would disrupt marriages because it would discourage reconciliation. Clearly, it is the violent act of rape and not the subsequent attempt of the wife to seek protection through the criminal justice system which "disrupts" a marriage (Weishaupt v. Commonwealth, 227 Va. 389, 315 S.E.2d 847, at p. 855). Moreover, if the marriage has already reached the point where intercourse is accomplished by violent assault it is doubtful that there is anything left to reconcile (see Trammel v. United States, 445 U.S. 40, 52, 100 S.Ct. 906, 913, 63 L.Ed.2d 186, *supra*; "Marital Rape Exemption", *supra*, n. 5, 52 N.Y.U.L.Rev., at p. 315). This, of course, is particularly true if the wife is willing to bring criminal charges against her husband which could result in a lengthy jail sentence.

Another rationale sometimes advanced in support of the marital exemption is that marital rape would be a difficult crime to prove. A related

7. A wife may sue her husband for torts he commits against her, including assault and bat- tery (General Obligations Law, § 3–313).

argument is that allowing such prosecutions could lead to fabricated complaints by "vindictive" wives. The difficulty of proof argument is based on the problem of showing lack of consent. Proving lack of consent, however, is often the most difficult part of any rape prosecution, particularly where the rapist and the victim had a prior relationship (see "Spousal Exemption to Rape", *supra,* at n. 4, 65 Marq.L.Rev., at p. 125; "Marital Rape Exemption", *supra,* n. 5, 52 N.Y.U.L.Rev., at p. 314). Similarly, the possibility that married women will fabricate complaints would seem to be no greater than the possibility of unmarried women doing so ("Marital Rape Exemption", *supra,* n. 5, 52 N.Y.U.L.Rev., at p. 314; "Equal Protection Considerations", *supra,* n. 6, 16 N.Eng.L.Rev., at p. 24).[8] The criminal justice system, with all of its built-in safeguards, is presumed to be capable of handling any false complaints. Indeed, if the possibility of fabricated complaints were a basis for not criminalizing behavior which would otherwise be sanctioned, virtually all crimes other than homicides would go unpunished.

The final argument in defense of the marital exemption is that marital rape is not as serious an offense as other rape and is thus adequately dealt with by the possibility of prosecution under criminal statutes, such as assault statutes, which provide for less severe punishment. The fact that rape statutes exist, however, is a recognition that the harm caused by a forcible rape is different, and more severe, than the harm caused by an ordinary assault (see "Marital Rape Exemption", *supra,* n. 5, 52 N.Y.U.L.Rev., at p. 316; "Abolishing the Marital Exemption", *supra,* n. 4, 1983 U. of Ill.L.Rev., at p. 208). "Short of homicide, [rape] is the 'ultimate violation of self' "(Coker v. Georgia, 433 U.S. 584, 597, 97 S.Ct. 2861, 2869, 53 L.Ed.2d 982 [citation omitted], *supra*). Under the Penal Law, assault is generally a misdemeanor unless either the victim suffers "serious physical injury" or a deadly weapon or dangerous instrument is used (Penal Law, §§ 120.00, 120.05, 120.10). Thus, if the defendant had been living with Denise at the time he forcibly raped and sodomized her he probably could not have been charged with a felony, let alone a felony with punishment equal to that for rape in the first degree.

Moreover, there is no evidence to support the argument that marital rape has less severe consequences than other rape. On the contrary, numerous studies have shown that marital rape is frequently quite violent and generally has *more* severe, traumatic effects on the victim than other rape (see, generally, Russell, Rape In Marriage, pp. 190–199; "Rape Prosecution", *supra,* at n. 6, 7 Vt.L.Rev., at pp. 45–46; "Abolishing the Marital Exemption", *supra,* at n. 4, 1983 U. of Ill.L.Rev., at p. 209).

Among the recent decisions in this country addressing the marital exemption, only one court has concluded that there is a rational basis for it (see People v. Brown, 632 P.2d 1025 [Col.]).[10] We agree with the other courts

8. The stigma and other difficulties associated with a woman reporting a rape and pressing charges probably deter most attempts to fabricate an incident; rape remains a grossly under-reported crime (see Note, Rape Reform and a Statutory Consent Defense, 74 J. of Crim.L. & Criminology 1518, 1519, n. 7; "Marital Rape Exemption", *supra,* n. 5, 52 N.Y.U.L.Rev., at pp. 314–315; "Spousal Exemption", *supra,* n. 4, 65 Marq.L.Rev., at p. 126).

10. The Colorado Supreme Court, relying on a 1954 Law Review comment, stated that the marital exemption "may remove a substantial obstacle to the resumption of normal marital relations" and "averts difficult emotional issues and problems of proof inherent in this

which have analyzed the exemption, which have been unable to find any present justification for it (see People v. De Stefano, 121 Misc.2d 113, 467 N.Y.S.2d 506; Commonwealth v. Chretien, 383 Mass. 123, 417 N.E.2d 1203; State v. Smith, 85 N.J. 193, 426 A.2d 38, *supra;* Weishaupt v. Commonwealth, 227 Va. 389, 315 S.E.2d 847, *supra;* State v. Rider, 449 So.2d 903 [Fla.App.]; State v. Smith, 401 So.2d 1126 [Fla.App.]). Justice Holmes wrote: "It is revolting to have no better reason for a rule of law than that so it was laid down in the time of Henry IV. It is still more revolting if the grounds upon which it was laid down have vanished long since, and the rule simply persists from blind imitation of the past" (Holmes, The Path of the Law, 10 Harv.L.Rev. 457, 469). This statement is an apt characterization of the marital exemption; it lacks a rational basis, and therefore violates the equal protection clauses of both the Federal and State Constitutions (U.S. Const., 14th Amdt., § 1; N.Y. Const., art. I, § 11).

B. The Exemption for Females

Under the Penal Law only males can be convicted of rape in the first degree.[11] Insofar as the rape statute applies to acts of "sexual intercourse", which, as defined in the Penal Law (see Penal Law, § 130.00) can only occur between a male and a female, it is true that a female cannot physically rape a female and that therefore there is no denial of equal protection when punishing only males for forcibly engaging in sexual intercourse with females.[12] The equal protection issue, however, stems from the fact that the statute applies to males who forcibly rape females but does not apply to females who forcibly rape males.

Rape statutes historically applied only to conduct by males against females, largely because the purpose behind the proscriptions was to protect the chastity of women and thus their property value to their fathers or husbands (see State v. Smith, 85 N.J. at p. 204, 426 A.2d 38, *supra;* 2 Burdick, Law of Crime, pp. 218–225; Comment, Rape Laws, Equal Protection, and Privacy Rights, 54 Tulane L.Rev. 456, 457 [hereafter cited as "Rape Laws"]). New York's rape statute has always protected only females, and has thus applied only to males (see Penal Law, § 130.35; 1909 Penal Law, § 2010; 1881 Penal Code, tit. X, ch. II, § 278). Presently New York is one of only 10 jurisdictions that does not have a gender-neutral statute for forcible rape.[13]

A statute which treats males and females differently violates equal protection unless the classification is substantially related to the achievement of an important governmental objective (Caban v. Mohammed, 441 U.S. 380, 388, 99 S.Ct. 1760, 1766, 60 L.Ed.2d 297; Craig v. Boren, 429 U.S. 190, 197, 97 S.Ct. 451, 457, 50 L.Ed.2d 397; People v. Whidden, 51 N.Y.2d 457, 460,

---

sensitive area" (632 P.2d at p. 1027). We have considered, and rejected, both of these arguments.

11. The sodomy statute applies to any "person" and is thus gender neutral. Defendant's gender-based equal protection challenge is therefore addressed only to the rape statute.

12. A female can, however, be convicted under the present statute as an accomplice to a forcible rape of a female (Penal Law, §§ 20.00,

20.05, subd. 3; *People v. Evans,* 58 A.D.2d 919, 396 N.Y.S.2d 727).

13. The other nine jurisdictions are Alabama, Delaware, District of Columbia, Georgia, Idaho, Kansas, Mississippi, Oregon, and Virginia. Some of these other States, like New York (see Penal Law, § 130.65), have other statutes which proscribe conduct including the forcible rape of a male by a female and which have less severe punishments than for forcible rape of a female by a male.

434 N.Y.S.2d 936, 415 N.E.2d 927, app.dsmd. 454 U.S. 803, 102 S.Ct. 75, 70 L.Ed.2d 72). This test applies whether the statute discriminates against males or against females (Caban v. Mohammed, 441 U.S. at p. 394, 99 S.Ct. at p. 1769, *supra;* Orr v. Orr, 440 U.S. 268, 279, 99 S.Ct. 1102, 1111, 59 L.Ed.2d 306, *supra;* People v. Whidden, *supra*). The People bear the burden of showing both the existence of an important objective and the substantial relationship between the discrimination in the statute and that objective (Wengler v. Druggists Mut. Ins. Co., 446 U.S. 142, 151–152, 100 S.Ct. 1540, 1545–1546, 64 L.Ed.2d 107; Caban v. Mohammed, 441 U.S. at p. 393, 99 S.Ct. at p. 1768, *supra*). This burden is not met in the present case, and therefore the gender exemption also renders the statute unconstitutional.

The first argument advanced by the People in support of the exemption for females is that because only females can become pregnant the State may constitutionally differentiate between forcible rapes of females and forcible rapes of males. This court and the United States Supreme Court have upheld statutes which subject males to criminal liability for engaging in sexual intercourse with underage females without the converse being true (People v. Whidden, *supra;* Michael M. v. Sonoma County Superior Ct., 450 U.S. 464, 101 S.Ct. 1200, 67 L.Ed.2d 437, *supra*). The rationale behind these decisions was that the primary purpose of such "statutory rape" laws is to protect against the harm caused by teenage pregnancies, there being no need to provide the same protection to young males (see Michael M. v. Sonoma County Superior Ct., 450 U.S. at pp. 470–473, 101 S.Ct. at pp. 1204–1207, *supra;* People v. Whidden, 51 N.Y.2d at p. 461, 434 N.Y.S.2d 936, 415 N.E.2d 927, *supra*).

There is no evidence, however, that preventing pregnancies is a primary purpose of the statute prohibiting forcible rape, nor does such a purpose seem likely (see "Rape Laws", *op. cit.,* 54 Tulane L.Rev., at p. 467). Rather, the very fact that the statute proscribes "forcible compulsion" shows that its overriding purpose is to protect a woman from an unwanted, forcible, and often violent sexual intrusion into her body (cf. Ballard v. United States, 430 A.2d 483 [D.C.App.]; "Rape Laws", *op. cit.,* at p. 468).[14] Thus, due to the different purposes behind forcible rape laws and "statutory" (consensual) rape laws, the cases upholding the gender discrimination in the latter are not decisive with respect to the former, and the People cannot meet their burden here by simply stating that only females can become pregnant.

The People also claim that the discrimination is justified because a female rape victim "faces the probability of medical, sociological, and psychological problems unique to her gender". This same argument, when advanced in support of the discrimination in the statutory rape laws, was rejected by this court in People v. Whidden (51 N.Y.2d at p. 461, 434 N.Y.S.2d 936, 415 N.E.2d 927, *supra*), and it is no more convincing in the present case. "[A]n ' "archaic and overbroad" generalization' * * * which is evidently grounded in long-standing stereotypical notions of the differences between the sexes, simply cannot serve as a legitimate rationale for a penal provision that is addressed only to adult males" (*id.,* quoting Craig v. Boren, 429 U.S. at p.

14. In at least two States there is a specific statute which states that "[t]he essential guilt of rape consists in the outrage to the person and feelings of the female" (Okla.Stats.Ann., tit. 21, § 1113; Idaho Code Ann, § 18–6103).

198, 97 S.Ct. at p. 457, *supra;* cf. Orr v. Orr, 440 U.S. at p. 283, 99 S.Ct. at p. 1114, *supra;* Tribe, Constitutional Law, p. 1066).

Finally, the People suggest that a gender-neutral law for forcible rape is unnecessary, and that therefore the present law is constitutional, because a woman either cannot actually rape a man or such attacks, if possible, are extremely rare. Although the "physiologically impossible" argument has been accepted by several courts (see People v. Reilly, 85 Misc.2d 702, 706–707, 381 N.Y.S.2d 732; Brooks v. State, 24 Md.App. 334, 330 A.2d 670; Finley v. State, 527 S.W.2d 553 [Tex.Crim.App.]), it is simply wrong. The argument is premised on the notion that a man cannot engage in sexual intercourse unless he is sexually aroused, and if he is aroused then he is consenting to intercourse. "Sexual intercourse" however, "occurs upon any penetration, however slight" (Penal Law, § 130.00); this degree of contact can be achieved without a male being aroused and thus without his consent.

As to the "infrequency" argument, while forcible sexual assaults by females upon males are undoubtedly less common than those by males upon females this numerical disparity cannot by itself make the gender discrimination constitutional. Women may well be responsible for a far lower number of all serious crimes than are men, but such a disparity would not make it permissible for the State to punish only men who commit, for example, robbery (cf. Craig v. Boren, 429 U.S. at pp. 200–204, 97 S.Ct. at pp. 458–461, *supra*).

To meet their burden of showing that a gender-based law is substantially related to an important governmental objective the People must set forth an " 'exceedingly persuasive justification' " for the classification (Mississippi Univ. for Women v. Hogan, 458 U.S. 718, 724, 102 S.Ct. 3331, 3336, 73 L.Ed.2d 1090; Kirchberg v. Feenstra, 450 U.S. 455, 461, 101 S.Ct. 1195, 1199, 67 L.Ed.2d 428), which requires, among other things, a showing that the gender-based law serves the governmental objective better than would a gender-neutral law (Orr v. Orr, 440 U.S. at pp. 281–282, 99 S.Ct. at pp. 1112–1113, *supra;* "Rape Laws", *op. cit.,* 54 Tulane L.Rev., at p. 468; cf. Michael M. v. Sonoma County Superior Ct., 450 U.S. at p. 464, 101 S.Ct. at p. 1201, *supra*). The fact that the act of a female forcibly raping a male may be a difficult or rare occurrence does not mean that the gender exemption satisfies the constitutional test. A gender-neutral law would indisputably better serve, even if only marginally, the objective of deterring and punishing forcible sexual assaults. The only persons "benefitted" by the gender exemption are females who forcibly rape males. As the Supreme Court has stated, "[a] gender-based classification which, as compared to a gender-neutral one, generates additional benefits only for those it has no reason to prefer cannot survive equal protection scrutiny" (Orr v. Orr, 440 U.S. at pp. 282–283, 99 S.Ct. at pp. 1113–1114, *supra*).

Accordingly, we find that section 130.35 of the Penal Law violates equal protection because it exempts females from criminal liability for forcible rape.

V

Having found that the statutes for rape in the first degree and sodomy in the first degree are unconstitutionally underinclusive, the remaining issue is the appropriate remedy for these equal protection violations. When a statute is constitutionally defective because of underinclusion, a court may either strike the statute, and thus make it applicable to nobody, or extend the coverage of the statute to those formerly excluded * * *.

* * *

Accordingly we choose the remedy of striking the marital exemption from sections 130.35 and 130.50 of the Penal Law and the gender exemption from section 130.35 of the Penal Law, so that it is now the law of this State that any person who engages in sexual intercourse or deviate sexual intercourse with any other person by forcible compulsion is guilty of either rape in the first degree or sodomy in the first degree. Because the statutes under which the defendant was convicted are not being struck down, his conviction is affirmed.

* * *

Notes on Withers *and* Liberta

1. Although women are the primary victims of forcible rape, *Withers* shows that some men also become targets for sexual assault, particularly in the prison setting. A report on 16 males who sexually assaulted other males in a community setting and on 6 additional males who were victims of rape concludes that several parallels exist between male and female rape. The age of the offender, the methods used to gain control over the victim, and the fact that sexual gratification is not the primary motivation for the assault are typical of both kinds of rape. Male victims, like female victims, find that rape is stressful; that it is difficult to report the attack; and that one's lifestyle is disrupted by the attack. See Groth and Burgess, Male Rape: Offenders and Victims, 137 Am.J.Psych. 806 (July, 1980). Compare Carroll M. Brodsky, Rape at Work, in (Marcia J. Walker & Stanley L. Brodsky, eds.) Sexual Assault: The Victim and the Rapist 35, 45–46 (1976), noting that the reactions of males who are mugged are similar to those of females who are raped at work.

2. Constitutional attacks on statutes that define forcible rape in terms of gender, punishing only males, have generally been rejected. See e.g., Country v. Parratt, 684 F.2d 588 (8th Cir.1982), certiorari denied 459 U.S. 1043, 103 S.Ct. 461, 74 L.Ed.2d 612, rejecting the argument that the legislative purpose of a forcible rape statute was to prevent unwanted pregnancy as a "dangerously broad rationalization" in view of the state's failure to present any evidence of the legislative intent, but upholding the constitutionality of a forcible rape law that punished only men on the ground that only a man can impose the fear of an unwanted pregnancy with its physical, emotional, ethical, and financial consequences, upon a woman through a sexual attack upon her person; Lamar v. State, 243 Ga. 401, 402, 254 S.E.2d 353, 355 (1979), appeal dismissed 444 U.S. 803, 100 S.Ct. 23, 62 L.Ed.2d 16 (1979) holding a forcible rape law constitutional because "[t]he difference recognized by the statute is a physiological reality, and the objective serves a public purpose in preventing sexual attacks upon women, with the resulting physical injury, psychological trauma, and possible pregnancy." Is the argument that rape laws are designed to prevent pregnancy more persuasive in the context of forcible rape than in statutory rape cases?

3. As the *Liberta* court notes, the traditional definition of forcible rape has excluded the wife of the perpetrator, apparently on the theory that a married woman cannot refuse her husband's sexual overtures. The *Liberta* court disposes of that argument rather easily doesn't it? How well does it deal with the marital

privacy argument? See generally, Frances E. Olsen, The Myth of State Intervention in the Family, 18 U.Mich.J.L.Reform 835 (1985). See also Judith A. Lincoln, Comment, Abolishing the Marital Rape Exemption: The First Step in Protecting Married Women From Spousal Rape, 35 Wayne L.Rev. 1219 (1989).

Rape by an intimate partner can also be a form of woman abuse. One study found that 37% of battered wives had also been raped by their husbands. See Diana E.H. Russel, Rape in Marriage 87–101 (1990). For further discussion of issues surrounding abuse of women, see subsection on Woman Abuse, p. 1181 infra.

4. What punishment is appropriate for forcible rape? Immediately prior to the Supreme Court's reappraisal of the constitutional standards governing the imposition of capital punishment in Furman v. Georgia, 408 U.S. 238, 92 S.Ct. 2726, 33 L.Ed.2d 346 (1972), sixteen states and the Federal Government authorized capital punishment for the rape of an adult female. In the wake of legislative activity that followed *Furman,* only three states reinstated capital punishment as the penalty for rape in such cases. In Coker v. Georgia, 433 U.S. 584, 97 S.Ct. 2861, 53 L.Ed.2d 982 (1977), the Court held that imposition of the death penalty for rape of an adult woman constituted cruel and unusual punishment in violation of the Eighth Amendment. This result had been supported in an amici curiae brief filed in *Coker* on behalf of several legal organizations devoted to equal rights for women, who urged that the death penalty for rape was

> a vestige of an ancient, patriarchal view of women as the property of men, * * * a reflection of societal ambivalence toward the woman victim, and * * * a barrier to proper and vigorous enforcement of rape laws.

Brief Amici Curiae of the American Civil Liberties Union, the Center for Constitutional Rights, the National Organization for Women Legal Defense and Education Fund, the Women's Law Project, the Center for Women Policy Studies, the Women's Legal Defense Fund, and Equal Rights Advocates, Inc., at 9. In justifying its decision, the Court said in part:

> We do not discount the seriousness of rape as a crime. It is highly reprehensible, both in a moral sense and in its almost total contempt for the personal integrity and autonomy of the female victim and for the latter's privilege of choosing those with whom intimate relationships are to be established. Short of homicide, it is the "ultimate violation of self." It is also a violent crime because it normally involves force, or the threat of force or intimidation, to overcome the will and the capacity of the victim to resist. Rape is very often accompanied by physical injury to the female and can also inflict mental and psychological damage. Because it undermines the community's sense of security, there is public injury as well.

> Rape is without doubt deserving of serious punishment; but in terms of moral depravity and of the injury to the person and to the public, it does not compare with murder, which does involve the unjustified taking of human life. Although it may be accompanied by another crime, rape by definition does not include the death of or even the serious injury to another person. The murderer kills; the rapist, if no more than that, does not. Life is over for the victim of the murderer; for the rape victim, life may not be nearly so happy as it was, but it is not over and normally is not beyond repair. We have the abiding conviction that the death penalty, which "is unique in its severity and irrevocability," Gregg v. Georgia, 428 U.S., at 187, 96 S.Ct., at 2931, is an excessive penalty for the rapist who, as such, does not take human life.

Id., 433 U.S. at 597–98, 97 S.Ct. at 2869, 53 L.Ed.2d at 992–93 (footnotes omitted). Do you agree with this reasoning?

What about "date" rape? Should it be treated any differently than any other type of forcible rape? See also Lois Pineau, Date Rape: A Feminist Analysis, 8 Law & Philosophy 217 (1989), making the point that in cases of date rape, "what is really sexual assault is often mistaken for seduction."

5. Civil remedies also exist for the victims of rape. Women employees raped at work may claim worker's compensation for their injuries in California. See Carroll Brodsky, supra Note 1, at 35–51. Damages have been awarded against a mass transit carrier that failed to provide adequate lighting and insufficient employee oversight of conditions at one of its train stations where plaintiff was raped. See Kenny v. Southeastern Pennsylvania Transp. Auth., 581 F.2d 351 (3d Cir.1978), certiorari denied 439 U.S. 1073, 99 S.Ct. 845, 59 L.Ed.2d 39 (1979). A female tenant raped in her apartment stated a legally sufficient claim against her landlord for failing to warn her that several other tenants had been raped in the apartment complex, and for failing to provide adequate security against attack. See O'Hara v. Western Seven Trees Corp. Intercoast Management, 75 Cal.App.3d 798, 142 Cal.Rptr. 487 (1977). Actions in tort are also available in proper cases against the rapist. For an excellent discussion of the theoretical and practical aspects of such litigation, see Camille LeGrand and Frances Leonard, Civil Suits for Sexual Assault: Compensating Rape Victims, 8 Golden Gate Univ.L.Rev. 479 (Women's Law Forum, 1979); Gail M. Ballou, Note, Recourse For Rape Victims: Third Party Liability, 4 Harv.Wom.L.J. 105 (1981).

In states where workers' compensation is the exclusive remedy for a work-related injury, the existence of a workers' compensation claim for forcible rape may preclude a suit in tort against the employer. See, e.g., Williams v. Munford, Inc., 683 F.2d 938 (5th Cir.1982), holding that the Mississippi workers' compensation laws prevented recovery by an 18 year old convenience store clerk who was raped at 4:00 a.m. during a robbery of the store. Plaintiff's argument that her employer had breached the contract of employment by failing to provide her a safe place to work was rejected as an attempt to circumvent the policy underlying the workers' compensation laws.

But see Doe v. United States, 718 F.2d 1039 (11th Cir.1983)(reversing judgment awarding $70,000 damages to a woman raped in a Post Office located in a high crime area in North Miami Beach; trial court erred in excluding evidence that post office itself was in a low crime area, hence the rape was not sufficiently "forseeable" to make defendant's acts the proximate cause of plaintiff's injury); Wright v. City of Ozark, 715 F.2d 1513 (11th Cir.1983)(woman's claim under 42 U.S.C.A. §§ 1983 and 1985(3) that city and its officials had deliberately suppressed information of prior rapes in Ozark in order not to jeopardize business and commercial activity failed to state a cause of action, at least in the absence of a special relationship between the victim and the criminal or between the victim and the state).

In Mary M. v. City of Los Angeles, 54 Cal.3d 202, 285 Cal.Rptr. 99, 814 P.2d 1341 (1991), the California Supreme Court upheld a jury verdict of $150,000 awarded to Mary M. after she had been raped by a police officer, Sergeant Leigh Schroyer, who had stopped her at 2:30 a.m. for erratic driving. When she pleaded with him not to arrest her, he drove her to her home, where the following events occurred:

After entering the house with plaintiff, Sergeant Schroyer told her that he expected "payment" for taking her home instead of to jail. Plaintiff tried to run away, but Schroyer grabbed her hair and threw her on the couch. When plaintiff screamed, Schroyer put his hand over her mouth and threatened to take her to jail. Plaintiff stopped struggling, and Schroyer raped her. He then left the house.

From his police car, Sergeant Schroyer sent a radio message that he was returning from a "lunch" break. The radio operator questioned this, because Schroyer had previously reported that he was conducting an investigation. Schroyer did not respond to the question, and returned to the police station.

Id., 54 Cal.3d at 207, 285 Cal.Rptr. at 100–101, 814 P.2d at 1342. Rejecting the City's argument that the officer was not acting within the scope of his employment when he raped Mary M., Justice Joyce Kennard reasoned in part as follows:

As noted previously, society has granted police officers great power and control over criminal suspects. Officers may detain such persons at gunpoint, place them in handcuffs, remove them from their residences, order them into police cars and, in some circumstances, may even use deadly force. The law permits police officers to ensure their own safety by frisking persons they have detained, thereby subjecting detainees to a form of nonconsensual touching ordinarily deemed highly offensive in our society. (Terry v. Ohio (1968) 392 U.S. 1, 88 S.Ct. 1868, 20 L.Ed.2d 889.) In view of the considerable power and authority that police officers possess, it is neither startling nor unexpected that on occasion an officer will misuse that authority by engaging in assaultive conduct. The precise circumstances of the assault need not be anticipated, so long as the risk is one that is reasonably foreseeable. Sexual assaults by police officers are fortunately uncommon; nevertheless, the risk of such tortious conduct is broadly incidental to the enterprise of law enforcement, and thus liability for such acts may appropriately be imposed on the employing public entity.

Id., 54 Cal.3d at 217–18, 285 Cal.Rptr. at 107–08, 814 P.2d at 1349–50. Justice Arabian, concurring, traced the history of rape reform in California and observed that "[o]ur holding today advances the cause of reform by providing a meaningful civil remedy to the victims of those who exploit unique institutional prerogatives to facilitate a sexual assault." Id., 54 Cal.3d at 224, 285 Cal.Rptr. at 112, 814 P.2d at 1354. Justices Baxter and Chief Justice Lucas concurred in the result on the basis that Los Angeles had invited error by its request for a jury instruction on the vicarious liability issue, but dissented from the opinion on the ground that the City's liability could not easily be limited: "In sum, the principles espoused by the majority have the potential to convert blameless public agencies into liability insurers for much, if not all, of the intentional misconduct committed by peace officers in their employ." Id., 54 Cal.3d at 242, 285 Cal.Rptr. at 125, 814 P.2d at 1367. So?

See also Doe v. Dominion Bank of Washington, 963 F.2d 1552 (D.C.Cir.1992), where a secretary was forced off an office building elevator at 9:20 a.m., dragged to an unlocked office on a vacant floor and raped and robbed. Then–Judge Ginsburg cited "the thrust of evolving D.C. precedent" for the proposition that a commercial landlord, as well as a residential landlord, must exercise reasonable care to protect tenants from foreseeable criminal conduct occurring in common areas within the landlord's control. The matter was remanded for trial.

Text Note
Rape Reform Statutes

Feminists[1] have been in the forefront of efforts to reform the rape laws, having recognized that traditional social attitudes toward rape victims and entrenched practices in the investigation and prosecution of the relatively few cases brought to trial actually deterred victims from seeking legal retribution through the criminal law. Attention has been focused on the rejection or substantial modification of the corroboration requirement and restraints on admissibility of the victim's past sexual behavior to prove consent or to impeach credibility.[2] Accompanying the legal effort has been the drive to establish rape crisis centers, domestic violence counselling units, and specially trained task forces in hospitals and police stations to deal with rape victims.

The response to these efforts has been massive, in part because the women's groups pressing for change were joined by other special interest groups, including those interested in the codification of state criminal laws and others whose primary motivation was crime control.[3] Michigan[4] enacted the first comprehensive rape reform law in 1974: it was drafted in sex-neutral terms and covered a variety of conduct, including sexual contact as well as sexual penetration. The Michigan statute has been viewed as a model by other states. Virtually every American state has modified or reformed its rape laws in recent years.[5]

It goes without saying that changes of this magnitude have not been unaccompanied by controversy. Thus, the rape victim shield laws, which restrict the defendant's ability to disclose the victim's prior sexual history to the jury, have been attacked as violative of the Sixth Amendment.[6] Others[7] have seen the new laws as relatively ineffective, leaving untouched as they do underlying attitudes within the criminal justice system about rape and rape victims that conspire to prevent effective investigation, prosecution, and trial of the rapist.

In cases where the defendant asserts that the plaintiff consented to sexual intercourse, a conflict exists over whether expert testimony is admissible to show that plaintiff suffered a form of post traumatic stress disorder, known in the literature as "rape trauma syndrome." The dispute is over whether the testimony tends to invade the province of the jury to decide whether a rape has in fact

1. See, e.g., Camille LeGrand, Rape and Rape Laws: Sexism in Society and Law, 61 Calif.L.Rev. 919 (1973). Compare Karen De-Crow, Sexist Justice 209–215 (1974); see generally, Susan Brownmiller, Against Our Will: Men, Women and Rape (1975).

2. See, e.g., Vivian Berger, Man's Trial, Woman's Tribulation: Rape Cases in the Courtroom, 77 Colum.L.Rev. 1 (1977).

3. Wallace D. Loh, The Impact of Common Law and Reform Rape Statutes on Prosecution: An Empirical Study, 55 Wash.L.Rev. 543, 567–76 (1980).

4. Mich.Comp.Laws §§ 750.520(a)–(l)(1980–81 Supp.)

5. See generally, Camille LeGrand, J. Reich, and D. Chappell, Forcible Rape: An Analysis of Legal Issues (Battelle Law and Justice Study Center, 1977).

6. See, e.g., Alexander Tanford & Anthony J. Bocchino, Rape Victim Shield Laws and the Sixth Amendment, 128 U.Pa.L.Rev. 544 (1980). Cases upholding rape shield laws against con-

stitutional attack include Bell v. Harrison, 670 F.2d 656 (6th Cir.1982)(court refused to permit defense counsel to ask the prosecutrix "what men she has gone out with and how long she has gone with them"; such "fishing expeditions" are no longer allowed); Moore v. Duckworth, 687 F.2d 1063 (7th Cir.1982)(in order to prevent jury from discovering that prosecutrix was pregnant by her boyfriend, she was not allowed to stand up in presence of the jury and was told by the judge to keep her coat in her lap and her hands in a certain position; reviewing court sustained defendant's conviction because he was unable to prove that the jury learned that prosecutrix was pregnant and believed that her pregnancy was the result of the rape).

7. See, e.g., Kathleen Quenneville, Will Rape Ever Be A Crime of The Past? : A Feminist View of Societal Factors & Rape Law Reforms, 9 Golden Gate Univ.L.Rev. 581 (Women's Law Forum 1978–1979).

occurred, and is therefore unduly prejudicial to the defendant. Kansas has held such testimony admissible;[8] other states have rejected such testimony.[9] Which view is preferable? One writer argues that, even if evidence of rape trauma syndrome is not admissible to prove that a rape occurred, such evidence should be acceptable as proper rehabilitation matter to rebut defendant's assertion that the victim's conduct was not consistent with her claim of rape.[10]

Professor Susan Estrich doubts whether tinkering with the statutory language is a profitable way for feminists to spend their time. She notes that:[11]

> [T]he answer is not to write the perfect statute. While some statutes invite a more restrictive application than others, there is no "model statute" solution to rape law, because the problem has never been the words of the statutes as much as our interpretation of them. A typical statute of the 1890's—punishing a man who engages in sexual intercourse "by force" and "against the will and without the consent" of the woman—may not be all that different from the "model" statute we will enforce in the 1990's. The difference must come in our understanding of "consent" and "will" and "force."
>
> Some of those who have written about rape from a feminist perspective intimate that nothing short of political revolution can redress the failings of the traditional approach to rape, that most of what passes for "sex" in our capitalist society is coerced, and that no lines can or should be drawn between rape and what happens in tens of millions of bedrooms across America.
>
> So understood, this particular feminist vision of rape shares one thing with the most traditional sexist vision: the view that non-traditional rape is not fundamentally different from what happens in tens of millions of bedrooms across America. According to the radical feminist, all of it is rape; according to the traditionalist, it is all permissible sex and seduction. In policy terms, neither is willing to draw lines between rape and permissible sex. As a result, the two visions, contradictory in every other respect, point to the same practical policy implications.
>
> My own view is different from both of these. I recognize that both men and women in our society have long accepted norms of male aggressiveness and female passivity which lead to a restricted understanding of rape. And I do not propose, nor do I think it feasible, to punish all of the acts of sexual intercourse that could be termed coerced. But lines can be drawn between these two alternatives. The law should be understood to prohibit claims and threats to secure sex that would be prohibited by extortion law and fraud or false pretenses law as a means to secure money. The law should evaluate the conduct of "reasonable" men, not according to a *Playboy*-macho philosophy that says "no means yes," but by according respect to a woman's words. If in 1986 silence does not negate consent, at least crying and saying "no" should.

8. State v. Marks, 231 Kan. 645, 647 P.2d 1292 (1982).

9. See, e.g., People v. Bledsoe, 36 Cal.3d 236, 203 Cal.Rptr. 450, 681 P.2d 291 (1984)(rejecting analogy to battered child syndrome and declining to follow *Marks,* supra note 8, because the rape trauma syndrome was developed as a method of treatment, not as a scientifically reliable means of proving that a rape occurred); State v. Taylor, 663 S.W.2d 235 (Mo.1984)(probative value of expert testimony is outweighed by possible prejudice and confusion of jury).

10. Toni M. Massaro, Experts, Psychology, Credibility, and Rape: The Rape Trauma Syndrome Issue and Its Implications for Expert Psychological Testimony, 69 Minn.L.Rev. 395 (1985).

11. Susan Estrich, Rape, 95 Yale L.J. 1087, 1093 (1986)(footnotes omitted). A popularized version of this article appears in book form in Susan Estrich, REAL RAPE (1987).

How are the new laws working in practice? Wallace Loh[12] studied 445 rape complaints filed by the King County (Seattle) Prosecuting Attorney's office between 1972 and 1977, including 208 cases filed under the old Washington law and 237 filed under the reform law. The statistical profiles of the victim, the suspect, and the circumstances of the rape of that group of cases arising under the new law were as follows: the victims had a median age of 17.5 years, with a range of 4 to 61 years; they were predominantly (80%) white and unmarried (82%). Suspects had a median age of 25, with a range of 15 to 73 years; about one-half (53%) were white, while the rest were either black (38%) or members of another minority group (9%). Most (83%) were unemployed or in low occupational groups, were unmarried (71%), and had adult arrest records (66%). In the majority of these cases (61%) the victim and suspect were socially acquainted or belonged to the same family; only slightly over a third (39%) were strangers. In a majority (68%) of the cases, the victim had agreed to a date with the suspect, while in one-fourth of the cases there had been no prior social contact, and a small minority of the victims had been hitchhiking (7%). About one-half of the cases involved only whites, 17% involved only minority persons (mostly black), while close to a third (31%) of the cases involved white victims and black suspects. The rape occurred most often in the suspect's residence or car (44%) or in the victim's residence or car (27%). When the crime took place in the victim's home, the suspect had been invited to enter in 38% of the cases, had been uninvited but had entered without the use of force in 33% of the cases, and had gained entry by force or deception in 20% of the cases. No physical force, other than the sexual penetration itself, was used in about one-fourth of the cases. Greater force was used in the stranger rape cases: here force was used in 28% of attacks, compared to 17% of rapes by casual acquaintances, and 14% by close acquaintances. The victims resisted in one-half of the attacks by strangers, but only in about one-third of assaults by close acquaintances or relatives. Three-quarters of the victims reported the crime to the police within 24 hours, if at all. Most tend to report the act first to friends or relatives (64%).

Loh found that the conviction rate for rape increased 19% under the reform statute, but that the overall conviction rate remained the same: under the old law, only 37% of the suspects were convicted of rape or carnal knowledge, as compared to 56% under the reform statute, but 35% were convicted under the old law for lesser charges such as assault or indecent liberties, whereas only 15% of the charges brought under the reform statute resulted in convictions for other offenses.[13] He concludes[14]

> [i]ncreasing rape convictions was one of the principal motivations of law reform advocates. This objective has been achieved. However, this does not mean that the total pool of offenders has expanded, only that within it there is more precise labelling. The new statute, then, is not a bigger mousetrap, only a better mousetrap. The symbolic significance of calling a convicted defendant a "rapist" rather than "assaulter" should not be underestimated.

Loh also found, however, that "[t]he impact of Washington's reform legislation on the charging process has been negligible."[15] Prosecutors still rely primarily on five factors in deciding whether to present a charge of forcible rape: the presence of physical force, social interaction between suspect and victim prior to

---

12. Loh, supra note 3, at 585–91.

13. Id., at 591–93. The overall conviction rate under the old law was 72% (37% + 35%) and under the reform statute 71% (56% + 15%).

14. Id., at 593.

15. Id., at 613. The five factors are identified at 604–06.

the alleged rape, the existence of corroborative evidence, the credibility of the victim, and the race of the victim and suspect. Speculating about the implications to be drawn for future reform from his study, Loh comments,[16]

> [t]he effectiveness of rape law enforcement will depend, ultimately, on official and lay attitudes toward the crime. Those attitudes influence the will of victims to prosecute, of prosecutors to file, and of juries to convict.

Compare Kathleen Quenneville's assessment:[17]

> Legislative reform must be accompanied by changes in attitude and behavior of both men and women. Because the omnipresence of rape directly affects women, and because few men have taken the initiative to change their own behavior or the attitudes of others, women must press those changes on men and our male-dominated society. Women need to monitor each step of the legal process—police, medical personnel, prosecutors, judges, and juries. When the legal system ineffectively responds to the problem of rape, strong objections should be voiced—whether it be voting judges out of office, bringing public pressure on prosecutors and police or leafletting outside courtrooms where trials are being conducted in a sexist manner. * * *

Do you agree that these tactics should be considered? How do you assess their effectiveness?

THE FLORIDA STAR v. B.J.F.

Supreme Court of the United States, 1989.
491 U.S. 524, 109 S.Ct. 2603, 105 L.Ed.2d 443.

JUSTICE MARSHALL delivered the opinion of the Court.

Florida Stat. § 794.03 (1987) makes it unlawful to "print, publish, or broadcast * * * in any instrument of mass communication" the name of the victim of a sexual offense.[1] Pursuant to this statute, appellant The Florida Star was found civilly liable for publishing the name of a rape victim which it had obtained from a publicly released police report. The issue presented here is whether this result comports with the First Amendment. We hold that it does not.

I

The Florida Star is a weekly newspaper which serves the community of Jacksonville, Florida, and which has an average circulation of approximately 18,000 copies. A regular feature of the newspaper is its "Police Reports" section. That section, typically two to three pages in length, contains brief articles describing local criminal incidents under police investigation.

On October 20, 1983, appellee B.J.F.[2] reported to the Duval County, Florida, Sheriff's Department (the Department) that she had been robbed and

---

16. Id., at 624. See also Hubert S. Field & Leigh B. Bienen, Jurors and Rape (1980).

17. Quenneville, supra note 7, at 606.

1. The statute provides in its entirety:

"Unlawful to publish or broadcast information identifying sexual offense victim.— No person shall print, publish, or broadcast, or cause or allow to be printed, published, or broadcast, in any instrument of mass com-

munication the name, address, or other identifying fact or information of the victim of any sexual offense within this chapter. An offense under this section shall constitute a misdemeanor of the second degree, punishable as provided in § 775.082, § 775.083, or § 775.084." Fla.Stat. § 794.03 (1987).

2. In filing this lawsuit, appellee used her full name in the caption of the case. On appeal, the Florida District Court of Appeal

sexually assaulted by an unknown assailant. The Department prepared a report on the incident which identified B.J.F., by her full name. The Department then placed the report in its press room. The Department does not restrict access either to the press room or to the reports made available therein.

A Florida Star reporter-trainee sent to the press room copied the police report verbatim, including B.J.F.'s full name, on a blank duplicate of the Department's forms. A Florida Star reporter then prepared a one-paragraph article about the crime, derived entirely from the trainee's copy of the police report. The article included B.J.F.'s full name. It appeared in the "Robberies" subsection of the "Police Reports" section on October 29, 1983, one of fifty-four police blotter stories in that day's edition. The article read:

> "[B.J.F.] reported on Thursday, October 20, she was crossing Brentwood Park, which is in the 500 block of Golfair Boulevard, enroute to her bus stop, when an unknown black man ran up behind the lady and placed a knife to her neck and told her not to yell. The suspect then undressed the lady and had sexual intercourse with her before fleeing the scene with her 60 cents, Timex watch and gold necklace. Patrol efforts have been suspended concerning this incident because of a lack of evidence."

In printing B.J.F.'s full name, The Florida Star violated its internal policy of not publishing the names of sexual offense victims.

On September 26, 1984, B.J.F. filed suit in the Circuit Court of Duval County against the Department and The Florida Star, alleging that these parties negligently violated § 794.03. * * * Before trial, the Department settled with B.J.F. for $2,500. The Florida Star moved to dismiss, claiming, *inter alia,* that imposing civil sanctions on the newspaper pursuant to § 794.03 violated the First Amendment. The trial judge rejected the motion. * * *

At the ensuing day-long trial, B.J.F. testified that she had suffered emotional distress from the publication of her name. She stated that she had heard about the article from fellow workers and acquaintances; that her mother had received several threatening phone calls from a man who stated that he would rape B.J.F. again; and that these events had forced B.J.F. to change her phone number and residence, to seek police protection, and to obtain mental health counseling. In defense, The Florida Star put forth evidence indicating that the newspaper had learned B.J.F.'s name from the incident report released by the Department, and that the newspaper's violation of its internal rule against publishing the names of sexual offense victims was inadvertent.

At the close of B.J.F.'s case, and again at the close of its defense, The Florida Star moved for a directed verdict. On both occasions, the trial judge denied these motions. He ruled from the bench that § 794.03 was constitutional because it reflected a proper balance between the First Amendment and privacy rights, as it applied only to a narrow set of "rather sensitive * * * criminal offenses." * * * At the close of newspaper's defense, the judge

sua sponte revised the caption, stating that it would refer to the appellee by her initials, "in order to preserve [her] privacy interests." 499 So.2d 883, 883, n. * (1986). Respecting those interests, we, too, refer to appellee by her initials, both in the caption and in our discussion.

granted B.J.F.'s motion for a directed verdict on the issue of negligence, finding the newspaper *per se* negligent based upon its violation of § 794.03. * * * This ruling left the jury to consider only the questions of causation and damages. The judge instructed the jury that it could award B.J.F. punitive damages if it found that the newspaper had "acted with reckless indifference to the rights of others." * * * The jury awarded B.J.F. $75,000 in compensatory damages and $25,000 in punitive damages. Against the actual damage award, the judge set off B.J.F's settlement with the Department.

The First District Court of Appeal affirmed in a three-paragraph *per curiam* opinion. 499 So.2d 883 (1986). * * *

The Florida Star appealed to this Court. We noted probable jurisdiction, * * * and now reverse.

II

The tension between the right which the First Amendment accords to a free press, on the one hand, and the protections which various statutes and common-law doctrines accord to personal privacy against the publication of truthful information, on the other, is a subject we have addressed several times in recent years. Our decisions in cases involving government attempts to sanction the accurate dissemination of information as invasive of privacy, have not, however, exhaustively considered this conflict. On the contrary, although our decisions have without exception upheld the press' right to publish, we have emphasized each time that we were resolving this conflict only as it arose in a discrete factual context.

The parties to this case frame their contentions in light of a trilogy of cases which have presented, in different contexts, the conflict between truthful reporting and state-protected privacy interests. In Cox Broadcasting Corp. v. Cohn, 420 U.S. 469, 95 S.Ct. 1029, 43 L.Ed.2d 328 (1975), we found unconstitutional a civil damages award entered against a television station for broadcasting the name of a rape-murder victim which the station had obtained from courthouse records. In Oklahoma Publishing Co. v. District Court, 430 U.S. 308, 97 S.Ct. 1045, 51 L.Ed.2d 355 (1977), we found unconstitutional a state court's pretrial order enjoining the media from publishing the name or photograph of an 11–year–old boy in connection with a juvenile proceeding involving that child which reporters had attended. Finally, in Smith v. Daily Mail Publishing Co., 443 U.S. 97, 99 S.Ct. 2667, 61 L.Ed.2d 399 (1979), we found unconstitutional the indictment of two newspapers for violating a state statute forbidding newspapers to publish, without written approval of the juvenile court, the name of any youth charged as a juvenile offender. The papers had learned about a shooting by monitoring a police band radio frequency, and had obtained the name of the alleged juvenile assailant from witnesses, the police, and a local prosecutor.

Appellant takes the position that this case is indistinguishable from *Cox Broadcasting*. * * * Alternatively, it urges that our decisions in the above trilogy, and in other cases in which we have held that the right of the press to publish truth overcame asserted interests other than personal privacy, can be distilled to yield a broader First Amendment principle that the press may never be punished, civilly or criminally, for publishing the truth. * * * Appellee counters that the privacy trilogy is inapposite, because in each case the private information already appeared on a "public record," * * * and because the privacy interests at stake were far less profound than in the present case. * * * In the alternative, appellee urges that *Cox Broadcasting* be overruled and replaced with a categorical rule that publication of the name of a rape victim never enjoys constitutional protection. * * *

We conclude that imposing damages on appellant for publishing B.J.F.'s name violates the First Amendment, although not for either of the reasons appellant urges. Despite the strong resemblance this case bears to *Cox Broadcasting,* that case cannot fairly be read as controlling here. The name of the rape victim in that case was obtained from courthouse records that were open to public inspection, a fact which Justice White's opinion for the Court repeatedly noted. * * * Significantly, one of the reasons we gave in *Cox Broadcasting* for invalidating the challenged damages award was the important role the press plays in subjecting trials to public scrutiny and thereby helping guarantee their fairness. * * * That role is not directly compromised where, as here, the information in question comes from a police report prepared and disseminated at a time at which not only had no adversarial criminal proceedings begun, but no suspect had been identified.

Nor need we accept appellant's invitation to hold broadly that truthful publication may never be punished consistent with the First Amendment. Our cases have carefully eschewed reaching this ultimate question, mindful that the future may bring scenarios which prudence counsels our not resolving anticipatorily. See, *e.g.,* Near v. Minnesota ex rel. Olson, 283 U.S. 697, 716, 51 S.Ct. 625, 75 L.Ed. 1357 (1931)(hypothesizing "publication of the sailing dates of transports or the number and location of troops"); see also Garrison v. Louisiana, 379 U.S. 64, 72, n. 8, 74, 85 S.Ct. 209, 215, n. 8, 216, 13 L.Ed.2d 125 (1964)(endorsing absolute defense of truth "where discussion of public affairs is concerned," but leaving unsettled the constitutional implications of truthfulness "in the discrete area of purely private libels"); * * *. Indeed, in *Cox Broadcasting,* we pointedly refused to answer even the less sweeping question "whether truthful publications may ever be subjected to civil or criminal liability" for invading "an area of privacy" defined by the State. * * * Respecting the fact that press freedom and privacy rights are both "plainly rooted in the traditions and significant concerns of our society," we instead focused on the less sweeping issue of "whether the State may impose sanctions on the accurate publication of the name of a rape victim obtained from public records—more specifically, from judicial records which are maintained in connection with a public prosecution and which themselves are open to public inspection." * * * We continue to believe that the sensitivity and significance of the interests presented in clashes between First Amendment and privacy rights counsel relying on limited principles that sweep no more broadly than the appropriate context of the instant case.

In our view, this case is appropriately analyzed with reference to such a limited First Amendment principle. It is the one, in fact, which we articulated in *Daily Mail* in our synthesis of prior cases involving attempts to punish truthful publication: "[I]f a newspaper lawfully obtains truthful information about a matter of public significance then state officials may not constitutionally punish publication of the information, absent a need to further a state interest of the highest order." * * * According the press the ample protection provided by that principle is supported by at least three separate considerations, in addition to, of course, the overarching " 'public interest, secured by the Constitution, in the dissemination of truth.' " * * *

First, because the *Daily Mail* formulation only protects the publication of information which a newspaper has "lawfully obtain[ed]," * * * the government retains ample means of safeguarding significant interests upon which publication may impinge, including protecting a rape victim's anonymity. To the extent sensitive information rests in private hands, the government may under some circumstances forbid its nonconsensual acquisition, thereby bringing outside of the *Daily Mail* principle the publication of any information so acquired. To the extent sensitive information is in the government's custody, it has even greater power to forestall or mitigate the injury caused by its release. The government may classify certain information, establish and enforce procedures ensuring its redacted release, and extend a damages remedy against the government or its officials where the government's mishandling of sensitive information leads to its dissemination. Where information is entrusted to the government, a less drastic means than punishing truthful publication almost always exists for guarding against the dissemination of private facts. * * *

A second consideration undergirding the *Daily Mail* principle is the fact that punishing the press for its dissemination of information which is already publicly available is relatively unlikely to advance the interests in the service of which the State seeks to act. It is not, of course, always the case that information lawfully acquired by the press is known, or accessible, to others. But where the government has made certain information publicly available, it is highly anomalous to sanction persons other than the source of its release. * * *

A third and final consideration is the "timidity and self-censorship" which may result from allowing the media to be punished for publishing certain truthful information. * * * *Cox Broadcasting* noted this concern with over-deterrence in the context of information made public through official court records, but the fear of excessive media self-suppression is applicable as well to other information released, without qualification, by the government. A contrary rule, depriving protection to those who rely on the government's implied representations of the lawfulness of dissemination, would force upon the media the onerous obligation of sifting through government press releases, reports, and pronouncements to prune out material arguably unlawful for publication. This situation could inhere even where the newspaper's sole object was to reproduce, with no substantial change, the government's rendition of the event in question.

Applied to the instant case, the *Daily Mail* principle clearly commands reversal. The first inquiry is whether the newspaper "lawfully obtain[ed] truthful information about a matter of public significance." * * * It is undisputed that the news article describing the assault on B.J.F. was accurate. In addition, appellant lawfully obtained B.J.F.'s name. Appellee's argument to the contrary is based on the fact that under Florida law, police reports which reveal the identity of the victim of a sexual offense are not among the matters of "public record" which the public, by law, is entitled to inspect. * * * But the fact that state officials are not required to disclose such reports does not make it unlawful for a newspaper to receive them when furnished by the government. Nor does the fact that the Department apparently failed to fulfill its obligation under § 794.03 not to "cause or allow to be * * * published" the name of a sexual offense victim make the newspaper's ensuing receipt of this information unlawful. Even assuming the Constitution permitted a State to proscribe *receipt* of information, Florida has not taken this step. It is, clear, furthermore, that the news article concerned "a matter of public significance," * * * in the sense in which the *Daily Mail* synthesis of prior cases used that term. That is, the article generally, as opposed to the specific identity contained within it, involved a matter of paramount public import: the commission, and investigation, of a violent crime which had been reported to authorities. * * *

The second inquiry is whether imposing liability on appellant pursuant to § 794.03 serves "a need to further a state interest of the highest order." * * * Appellee argues that a rule punishing publication furthers three closely related interests: the privacy of victims of sexual offenses; the physical safety of such victims, who may be targeted for retaliation if their names become known to their assailants; and the goal of encouraging victims of such crimes to report these offenses without fear of exposure. * * *

At a time in which we are daily reminded of the tragic reality of rape, it is undeniable that these are highly significant interests, a fact underscored by the Florida Legislature's explicit attempt to protect these interests by enacting a criminal statute prohibiting much dissemination of victim identities. We accordingly do not rule out the possibility that, in a proper case, imposing civil sanctions for publication of the name of a rape victim might be so overwhelmingly necessary to advance these interests as to satisfy the *Daily Mail* standard. For three independent reasons, however, imposing liability for publication under the circumstances of this case is too precipitous a means of advancing these interests to convince us that there is a "need" within the meaning of the *Daily Mail* formulation for Florida to take this extreme step. * * *

First is the manner in which appellant obtained the identifying information in question. As we have noted, where the government itself provides information to the media, it is most appropriate to assume that the government had, but failed to utilize, far more limited means of guarding against dissemination than the extreme step of punishing truthful speech. That assumption is richly borne out in this case. B.J.F.'s identity would never have come to light were it not for the erroneous, if inadvertent, inclusion by the Department of her full name in an incident report made available in a press room open to the public. Florida's policy against disclosure of rape victims' identities, reflected in § 794.03, was undercut by the Department's failure to abide by this policy. Where, as here, the government has failed to police itself in disseminating information, it is clear under *Cox Broadcasting, Oklahoma Publishing,* and *Landmark Communications* that the imposition of damages against the press for its subsequent publication can hardly be said to be a narrowly tailored means of safeguarding anonymity. * * * Once the government has placed such information in the public domain, "reliance must rest upon the judgment of those who decide what to publish or broadcast," *Cox Broadcasting,* * * * and hopes for restitution must rest upon the willingness of the government to compensate victims for their loss of privacy, and to protect them from the other consequences of its mishandling of the information which these victims provided in confidence.

That appellant gained access to the information in question through a government news release makes it especially likely that, if liability were to be imposed, self-censorship would result. Reliance on a news release is a paradigmatically "routine newspaper reporting techniqu[e]." *Daily Mail,* * * *. The government's issuance of such a release, without qualification, can only convey to recipients that the government considered dissemination lawful, and indeed expected the recipients to disseminate the information further. Had appellant merely reproduced the news release prepared and released by the Department, imposing civil damages would surely violate the First Amendment. The fact that appellant converted the police report into a news story by adding the linguistic connecting tissue necessary to transform the report's facts into full sentences cannot change this result.

A second problem with Florida's imposition of liability for publication is the broad sweep of the negligence *per se* standard applied under the civil cause of action implied from § 794.03. Unlike claims based on the common law tort of invasion of privacy, see Restatement (Second) of Torts § 652D (1977), civil actions based on § 794.03 require no case-by-case findings that the disclosure of a fact about a person's private life was one that a reasonable person would find highly offensive. On the contrary, under the *per se* theory of negligence adopted by the courts below, liability follows automatically from publication. This is so regardless of whether the identity of the victim is already known throughout the community; whether the victim has voluntarily called public attention to the offense; or whether the identity of the victim has otherwise become a reasonable subject of public concern—because, perhaps, questions have arisen whether the victim fabricated an assault by a particular person. Nor is there a scienter requirement of any kind under § 794.03, engendering the perverse result that truthful publications challenged pursuant to this cause of action are less protected by the First Amendment than even the least protected defamatory falsehoods: those involving purely private figures, where liability is evaluated under a standard, usually applied by a jury, of ordinary negligence. * * * We have previously noted the impermissibility of categorical prohibitions upon media access where important First Amendment interests are at stake. * * * More individualized adjudication is no less indispensable where the State, seeking to safeguard the anonymity of crime victims, sets its face against publication of their names.

Third, and finally, the facial underinclusiveness of § 794.03 raises serious doubts about whether Florida is, in fact, serving, with this statute, the significant interests which appellee invokes in support of affirmance. Section 794.03 prohibits the publication of identifying information only if this information appears in an "instrument of mass communication," a term the statute does not define. Section 794.03 does not prohibit the spread by other means of the identities of victims of sexual offenses. An individual who maliciously spreads word of the identity of a rape victim is thus not covered, despite the fact that the communication of such information to persons who live near, or work with, the victim may have consequences equally devastating as the exposure of her name to large numbers of strangers. See Tr. of Oral

Arg. 49–50 (appellee acknowledges that § 794.03 would not apply to "the backyard gossip who tells 50 people that don't have to know").

When a State attempts the extraordinary measure of punishing truthful publication in the name of privacy, it must demonstrate its commitment to advancing this interest by applying its prohibition evenhandedly, to the smalltime disseminator as well as the media giant. Where important First Amendment interests are at stake, the mass scope of disclosure is not an acceptable surrogate for injury. A ban on disclosures effected by "instrument[s] of mass communication" simply cannot be defended on the ground that partial prohibitions may effect partial relief. * * * Without more careful and inclusive precautions against alternative forms of dissemination, we cannot conclude that Florida's selective ban on publication by the mass media satisfactorily accomplishes its stated purpose.

III

Our holding today is limited. We do not hold that truthful publication is automatically constitutionally protected, or that there is no zone of personal privacy within which the State may protect the individual from intrusion by the press, or even that a State may never punish publication of the name of a victim of a sexual offense. We hold only that where a newspaper publishes truthful information which it has lawfully obtained, punishment may lawfully be imposed, if at all, only when narrowly tailored to a state interest of the highest order, and that no such interest is satisfactorily served by imposing liability under § 794.03 to appellant under the facts of this case. The decision below is therefore

Reversed.

JUSTICE SCALIA, concurring in part and concurring in the judgment.

I think it sufficient to decide this case to rely upon the third ground set forth in the Court's opinion, * * * that a law cannot be regarded as protecting an interest "of the highest order," * * * and thus as justifying a restriction upon truthful speech, when it leaves appreciable damage to that supposedly vital interest unprohibited. In the present case, I would anticipate that the rape victim's discomfort at the dissemination of news of her misfortune among friends and acquaintances would be at least as great as her discomfort at its publication by the media to people to whom she is only a name. Yet the law in question does not prohibit the former in either oral or written form. Nor is it at all clear, as I think it must be to validate this statute, that Florida's general privacy law would prohibit such gossip. Nor, finally, is it credible that the interest meant to be served by the statute is the protection of the victim against a rapist still at large—an interest that arguably would extend only to mass publication. There would be little reason to limit a statute with that objective to rape alone; or to extend it to all rapes, whether or not the felon has been apprehended and confined. In any case, the instructions here did not require the jury to find that the rapist was at large.

This law has every appearance of a prohibition that society is prepared to impose upon the press but not upon itself. Such a prohibition does not protect an interest "of the highest order." For that reason, I agree that the judgment of the court below must be reversed.

JUSTICE WHITE, with whom THE CHIEF JUSTICE and JUSTICE O'CONNOR join, dissenting.

"Short of homicide, [rape] is the 'ultimate violation of self.'" Coker v. Georgia, 433 U.S. 584, 597, 97 S.Ct. 2861, 2869, 53 L.Ed.2d 982 (1977)(opinion of WHITE, J.). For B.J.F., however, the violation she suffered at a rapist's knifepoint marked only the beginning of her ordeal. A week later, while her assailant was still at large, an account of this assault—identifying by name B.J.F. as the victim—was published by The Florida Star. As a result, B.J.F. received harassing phone calls, required mental health counseling, was forced to move from her home, and was even threatened with being raped again. Yet today, the Court holds that a jury award of $75,000 to compensate B.J.F. for the harm she suffered due to the Star's negligence is at odds with the First Amendment. I do not accept this result.

The Court reaches its conclusion based on an analysis of three of our precedents and a concern with three particular aspects of the judgment against appellant. I consider each of these points in turn, and then consider some of the larger issues implicated by today's decision.

I

The Court finds its result compelled, or at least supported in varying degrees, by three of our prior cases: * * *. I disagree. None of these cases requires the harsh outcome reached today.

Cox Broadcasting reversed a damage award entered against a television station, which had obtained a rape victim's name from public records maintained in connection with the judicial proceedings brought against her assailants. While there are similarities, critical aspects of that case make it wholly distinguishable from this one. First, in *Cox Broadcasting,* the victim's name had been disclosed in the hearing where her assailants pled guilty; and, as we recognized, judicial records have always been considered public information in this country. * * * In fact, even the earliest notion of privacy rights exempted the information contained in judicial records from its protections. See Warren & Brandeis, The Right to Privacy, 4 Harv.L.Rev. 193, 216–217 (1890). Second, unlike the incident report at issue here, which was meant by state law to be withheld from public release, the judicial proceedings at issue in *Cox Broadcasting* were open as a matter of state law. Thus, in *Cox Broadcasting,* the State-law scheme made public disclosure of the victim's name almost inevitable; here, Florida law forbids such disclosure. See Fla.Stat. § 794.03 (1987).

These facts—that the disclosure came in judicial proceedings, which were open to the public—were critical to our analysis in *Cox Broadcasting.* The distinction between that case and this one is made obvious by the penultimate paragraph of *Cox Broadcasting:*

"We are reluctant to embark on a course that would make *public records generally available to the media* but would forbid their publication if offensive * * *. [T]he First and Fourteenth Amendments will not allow exposing the press to liability for truthfully publishing information *released to the public in official court records. If there are privacy interests to be protected in judicial proceedings, the States must respond by means which avoid public documentation or other exposure of private* *information * * *.* Once true information is disclosed in *public court documents open to public inspection,* the press cannot be sanctioned for publishing it." * * *

Cox Broadcasting stands for the proposition that the State cannot make the press its first line of defense in withholding private information from the public—it cannot ask the press to secrete private facts that the State makes no effort to safeguard in the first place. In this case, however, the State has undertaken "means which avoid [but obviously, not altogether prevent] public documentation or other exposure of private information." No doubt this is why the Court frankly admits that *"Cox Broadcasting * * * cannot fairly be read as controlling here."* * * *

Finding *Cox Broadcasting* inadequate to support its result, the Court relies on *Smith v. Daily Mail Publishing Co.* as its principal authority.[1] * * *

More importantly, at issue in *Daily Mail* was the disclosure of the name of the perpetrator of an infamous murder of a 15–year–old student. * * * Surely the rights of those accused of crimes and those who are their victims must differ with respect to privacy concerns. That is, whatever rights alleged criminals have to maintain their anonymity pending an adjudication of guilt— and after *Daily Mail,* those rights would seem to be minimal—the rights of crime victims to stay shielded from public view must be infinitely more substantial. *Daily Mail* was careful to state that the "holding in this case is narrow * * * *there is no issue here of privacy."* * * * But in this case, there is an issue of privacy—indeed, that is the principal issue—and therefore, this case falls outside of *Daily Mail's* "rule" (which, as I suggest above, was perhaps not even meant as a rule in the first place).

Consequently, I cannot agree that *Cox Broadcasting,* or *Oklahoma Publishing,* or *Daily Mail* require—or even substantially support—the result reached by the Court today.

II

We are left, then, to wonder whether the three "independent reasons" the Court cites for reversing the judgment for B.J.F. support its result. * * *

The first of these reasons relied on by the Court is the fact "appellant gained access to [B.J.F.'s name] through a government news release." * * * "The government's issuance of such a release, without qualification, can only convey to recipients that the government considered dissemination lawful," the Court suggests. * * * So described, this case begins to look like the situation in *Oklahoma Publishing,* where a judge invited reporters into his courtroom, but then tried to forbid them from reporting on the proceedings they observed. But this case is profoundly different. Here, the "release" of information provided by the government was not, as the Court says, "without qualification." As the Star's own reporter conceded at trial, the crime incident report that inadvertently included B.J.F.'s name was posted in a

---

1. The second case in the "trilogy" which the Court cites is *Oklahoma Publishing Co. v. District Court, * * *.* But not much reliance is placed on that case, and I do not discuss it with the degree of attention devoted to *Cox Broadcasting* or *Daily Mail.*

As for the support *Oklahoma Publishing* allegedly provides for the Court's result here, the reasons that distinguish *Cox Broadcasting* and *Daily Mail* from this case are even more apt in the case of *Oklahoma Publishing.* Probably that is why the Court places so little weight on this middle leg of the three.

room that contained signs making it clear that the names of rape victims were not matters of public record, and were not to be published. * * * The Star's reporter indicated that she understood that she "[was not] allowed to take down that information" (*i.e.*, B.J.F.'s name) and that she "[was] not supposed to take the information from the police department." * * * Thus, by her own admission the posting of the incident report did not convey to the Star's reporter the idea that "the government considered dissemination lawful"; the Court's suggestion to the contrary is inapt.

Instead, Florida has done precisely what we suggested, in *Cox Broadcasting,* that States wishing to protect the privacy rights of rape victims might do: "respond [to the challenge] by means which *avoid* public documentation or other exposure of private information." * * * By amending its public records statute to exempt rape victims' names from disclosure, Fla.Stat. § 119.07(3)(h)(1983), and forbidding its officials from releasing such information, Fla.Stat. § 794.03 (1983), the State has taken virtually every step imaginable to prevent what happened here. This case presents a far cry, then, from *Cox Broadcasting* or *Oklahoma Publishing,* where the State asked the news media not to publish information it had made generally available to the public: here, the State is not asking the media to do the State's job in the first instance. Unfortunately, as this case illustrates, mistakes happen: even when States take measures to "avoid" disclosure, sometimes rape victims' names are found out. As I see it, it is not too much to ask the press, in instances such as this, to respect simple standards of decency and refrain from publishing a victim's name, address, and/or phone number.[2]

Second, the Court complains that appellant was judged here under too strict a liability standard. The Court contends that a newspaper might be found liable under the Florida courts' negligence *per se* theory without regard to a newspaper's scienter or degree of fault. * * * The short answer to this complaint is that whatever merit the Court's argument might have, it is wholly inapposite here, where the jury found that appellant acted with "reckless indifference towards the rights of others," * * * a standard far higher than the *Gertz* standard the Court urges as a constitutional minimum today. * * * B.J.F. proved the Star's negligence at trial—and, actually, far more than simple negligence; the Court's concerns about damages resting on a strict liability or mere causation basis are irrelevant to the validity of the judgment for appellee.

---

2. The Court's concern for a free press is appropriate, but such concerns should be balanced against rival interests in a civilized and humane society. An absolutist view of the former leads to insensitivity as to the latter.

This was evidenced at trial, when the Florida Star's lawyer explained why the paper was not to blame for any anguish caused B.J.F. by a phone call she received, the day after the Star's story was published, from a man threatening to rape B.J.F. again. Noting that the phone call was received at B.J.F.'s home by her mother (who was baby-sitting B.J.F.'s children while B.J.F. was in the hospital), who relayed the threat to B.J.F., the Star's counsel suggested:

"[I]n reference to the [threatening] phone call, it is sort of blunted by the fact that [B.J.F.] didn't receive the phone call. Her mother did. And if there is any pain and suffering in connection with the phone call, it has to lay in her mother's hands. I mean, my God, she called [B.J.F.] up at the hospital to tell her [of the threat]—you know, I think that is tragic, but I don't think that is something you can blame the Florida Star for." * * *

While I would not want to live in a society where freedom of the press was unduly limited, I also find regrettable an interpretation of the First Amendment that fosters such a degree of irresponsibility on the part of the news media.

But even taking the Court's concerns in the abstract, they miss the mark. Permitting liability under a negligence *per se* theory does not mean that defendants will be held liable without a showing of negligence, but rather, that the standard of care has been set by the legislature, instead of the courts. The Court says that negligence *per se* permits a plaintiff to hold a defendant liable without a showing that the disclosure was "of a fact about a person's private life * * * that a reasonable person would find highly offensive." * * * But the point here is that the legislature—reflecting popular sentiment—has determined that disclosure of the fact that a person was raped is categorically a revelation that reasonable people find offensive. And as for the Court's suggestion that the Florida courts' theory permits liability without regard for whether the victim's identity is already known, or whether she herself has made it known—these are facts that would surely enter into the calculation of damages in such a case. In any event, none of these mitigating factors was present here; whatever the force of these arguments generally, they do not justify the Court's ruling against B.J.F. in this case.

Third, the Court faults the Florida criminal statute for being underinclusive: § 794.03 covers disclosure of rape victims' names in "instrument[s] of mass communication," but not other means of distribution, the Court observes. * * * But our cases which have struck down laws that limit or burden the press due to their underinclusiveness have involved situations where a legislature has singled out one segment of the news media or press for adverse treatment, see, *e.g., Daily Mail* (restricting newspapers and not radio or television), or singled out the press for adverse treatment when compared to other similarly situated enterprises, * * *. Here, the Florida law evenhandedly covers all "instrument[s] of mass communication" no matter their form, media, content, nature or purpose. It excludes neighborhood gossips, * * * because presumably the Florida Legislature has determined that neighborhood gossips do not pose the danger and intrusion to rape victims that "instrument[s] of mass communication" do. Simply put: Florida wanted to prevent the widespread distribution of rape victims' names, and therefore enacted a statute tailored almost as precisely as possible to achieving that end.

Moreover, the Court's "underinclusiveness" analysis itself is "underinclusive." After all, the lawsuit against the Star which is at issue here is not an action for violating the statute which the Court deems underinclusive, but is, more accurately, for the negligent publication of appellee's name. * * * The scheme which the Court should review, then, is not only § 794.03 (which, as noted above, merely provided the standard of care in this litigation), but rather, the whole of Florida privacy tort law. As to the latter, Florida does recognize a tort of publication of private facts. Thus, it is quite possible that the neighborhood gossip whom the Court so fears being left scot-free to spread news of a rape victim's identity would be subjected to the same (or similar) liability regime under which appellant was taxed. The Court's myopic focus on § 794.03 ignores the probability that Florida law is more comprehensive than the Court gives it credit for being.

Consequently, neither the State's "dissemination" of B.J.F.'s name, nor the standard of liability imposed here, nor the underinclusiveness of Florida tort law require setting aside the verdict for B.J.F. And as noted above, such a result is not compelled by our cases. I turn, therefore, to the more general principles at issue here to see if they recommend the Court's result.

III

At issue in this case is whether there is any information about people, which—though true—may not be published in the press. By holding that only "a state interest of the highest order" permits the State to penalize the publication of truthful information, and by holding that protecting a rape victim's right to privacy is not among those state interests of the highest order, the Court accepts appellant's invitation, * * * to obliterate one of the most note-worthy legal inventions of the 20th–Century: the tort of the publication of private facts. W. Prosser, J. Wade, & V. Schwartz, Torts 951–952 (8th ed. 1988). Even if the Court's opinion does not say as much today, such obliteration will follow inevitably from the Court's conclusion here. If the First Amendment prohibits wholly private persons (such as B.J.F.) from recovering for the publication of the fact that she was raped, I doubt that there remain any "private facts" which persons may assume will not be published in the newspapers, or broadcast on television.

Of course, the right to privacy is not absolute. Even the article widely relied upon in cases vindicating privacy rights, Warren & Brandeis, The Right to Privacy, 4 Harv.L.Rev., at 193, recognized that this right inevitably conflicts with the public's right to know about matters of general concern—and that sometimes, the latter must trump the former. * * * Resolving this conflict is a difficult matter, and I do not fault the Court for attempting to strike an appropriate balance between the two, but rather, for according too little weight to B.J.F.'s side of equation, and too much on the other.

I would strike the balance rather differently. * * *

I do not suggest that the Court's decision today is radical departure from a previously charted course. The Court's ruling has been foreshadowed. In *Time, Inc. v. Hill*, 385 U.S. 374, 383–384, n. 7, 87 S.Ct. 534, 539–540, n. 7, 17 L.Ed.2d 456 (1967), we observed that—after a brief period early in this century where Brandeis' view was ascendant—the trend in "modern" jurisprudence has been to eclipse an individual's right to maintain private any truthful information that the press wished to publish. More recently, in *Cox Broadcasting,* * * * we acknowledged the possibility that the First Amendment may prevent a State from ever subjecting the publication of truthful but private information to civil liability. Today, we hit the bottom of the slippery slope.

I would find a place to draw the line higher on the hillside: a spot high enough to protect B.J.F.'s desire for privacy and peace-of-mind in the wake of a horrible personal tragedy. There is no public interest in publishing the names, addresses, and phone numbers of persons who are the victims of crime—and no public interest in immunizing the press from liability in the rare cases where a State's efforts to protect a victim's privacy have failed. Consequently, I respectfully dissent.

Notes on **B.J.F.**

1. Did Justice Marshall give adequate weight to B.J.F.'s privacy claim? A notewriter argues that "[a]lthough the majority * * * appeared to balance the

claims of privacy and press freedom, it undercut the evenhandedness of its balancing test by giving little weight to interests other than those of the press." The Supreme Court—Leading Cases, 103 Harv.L.Rev. 137, 265 (1989). What approach would have been better? The notewriter suggests that "[a]n approach that gave more weight to the state's interests in protecting rape victims' privacy and safety, and in encouraging victims to report rapes to the police, would have set a better standard for the future." Ibid.

2. But what if the rape victim wants to tell her story to the public? Nancy Ziegenmeyer, a rape victim, sought out Geneva Overholser, editor of The Des Moines Register, to disclose the details of her experience. The story, which ran on the front page of the Register for five consecutive days, attracted national attention and has been widely praised. Said Overholser, "I think Nancy Ziegenmeyer will help make the day come sooner that we will treat rape more like other crimes." The New York Times, March 25, 1990, at A1, col. 1.

B. WOMAN ABUSE

1. PROSECUTING WOMAN ABUSE

[This section was written by Nicole G. Berner for inclusion here.]

THURMAN v. CITY OF TORRINGTON

U.S. District Court, District of Connecticut, 1984.
595 F.Supp. 1521.

BLUMENFELD, SENIOR DISTRICT JUDGE

The plaintiffs have brought this action pursuant to 42 U.S.C. §§ 1983, 1985, 1986 and 1988, as well as the fifth, ninth, and fourteenth amendments to the Constitution, alleging that their constitutional rights were violated by the nonperformance or malperformance of official duties by the defendant police officers. In addition, the plaintiffs seek to hold liable the defendant City of Torrington (hereinafter, the "City"). The defendant City has filed a motion to dismiss the plaintiffs' complaint, or various claims therein, pursuant to Rule 12(b) of the Federal Rules of Civil Procedure.

* * *

Between early October 1982 and June 10, 1983, the plaintiff, Tracey Thurman, a woman living in the City of Torrington, and others on her behalf, notified the defendant City through the defendant police officers of the City of repeated threats upon her life and the life of her child, the plaintiff Charles J. Thurman, Jr., made by her estranged husband, Charles Thurman. Attempts to file complaints by plaintiff Tracey Thurman against her estranged husband in response to his threats of death and maiming were ignored or rejected by the named defendants and the defendant City.

An abbreviated chronology of the plaintiff's attempted and actual notifications of the threats made against her and her son by her estranged husband to the defendant City and police officers is appropriate for consideration of this motion.

In October 1982, Charles Thurman attacked plaintiff Tracey Thurman at the home of Judy Bentley and Richard St. Hilaire in the City of Torrington. Mr. St. Hilaire and Ms. Bentley made a formal complaint of the attack to one of the unnamed defendant police officers and requested efforts to keep the plaintiff's husband, Charles Thurman, off their property.

On or about November 5, 1982, Charles Thurman returned to the St. Hilaire–Bentley residence and using physical force took the plaintiff Charles J. Thurman, Jr. from said residence. Plaintiff Tracey Thurman and Mr. St. Hilaire went to Torrington police headquarters to make a formal complaint. At that point, unnamed defendant police officers of the City of Torrington refused to accept a complaint from Mr. St. Hilaire even as to trespassing.

On or about November 9, 1982, Charles Thurman screamed threats at Tracey while she was sitting in her car. Defendant police officer Neil Gemelli stood on the street watching Charles Thurman scream threats at Tracey until Charles Thurman broke the windshield of plaintiff Tracey Thurman's car while she was inside the vehicle. Charles Thurman was arrested after he broke the windshield, and on the next day, November 10, 1982, he was convicted of breach of peace. He received a suspended sentence of six months and a two-year "conditional discharge," during which he was ordered to stay completely away from the plaintiff Tracey Thurman and the Bentley–St. Hilaire residence and to commit no further crimes. The court imposing probation informed the defendants of this sentence.

On December 31, 1982, while plaintiff Tracey Thurman was at the Bentley–St. Hilaire residence, Charles Thurman returned to said residence and once again threatened her. She called the Torrington Police Department. One of the unnamed police officer defendants took the call, and, although informed of the violation of the conditional discharge, made no attempt to ascertain Charles Thurman's whereabouts or to arrest him.

Between January 1, 1983 and May 4, 1983, numerous telephone complaints to the Torrington Police Department were taken by various unnamed police officers, in which repeated threats of violence to the plaintiffs by Charles Thurman were reported and his arrest on account of the threats and violation of the terms of his probation was requested.

On May 4 and 5, 1983, the plaintiff Tracey Thurman and Ms. Bentley reported to the Torrington Police Department that Charles Thurman had said that he would shoot the plaintiffs. Defendant police officer Storrs took the written complaint of plaintiff Tracey Thurman who was seeking an arrest warrant for her husband because of his death threat and violation of his "conditional discharge." Defendant Storrs refused to take the complaint of Ms. Bentley. Plaintiff Tracey Thurman was told to return three weeks later on June 1, 1983 when defendant Storrs or some other person connected with the police department of the defendant City would seek a warrant for the arrest of her husband.

On May 6, 1983, Tracey filed an application for a restraining order against Charles Thurman in the Litchfield Superior Court. That day, the court issued an ex parte restraining order forbidding Charles Thurman from assaulting, threatening, and harassing Tracey Thurman. The defendant City was informed of this order.

On May 27, 1983, Tracey Thurman requested police protection in order to get to the Torrington Police Department, and she requested a warrant for her husband's arrest upon her arrival at headquarters after being taken there by one of the unnamed defendant police officers. She was told that she would have to wait until after the Memorial Day holiday weekend and was advised to call on Tuesday, May 31, to pursue the warrant request.

On May 31, 1983, Tracey Thurman appeared once again at the Torrington Police Department to pursue the warrant request. She was then advised by one of the unnamed defendant police officers that defendant Schapp was the only policeman who could help her and that he was on vacation. She was told that she would have to wait until he returned. That same day, Tracey's brother-in-law, Joseph Kocsis, called the Torrington Police Department to protest the lack of action taken on Tracey's complaint. Although Mr. Kocsis was advised that Charles Thurman would be arrested on June 8, 1983, no such arrest took place.

On June 10, 1983, Charles Thurman appeared at the Bentley–St. Hilaire residence in the early afternoon and demanded to speak to Tracey. Tracey, remaining indoors, called the defendant police department asking that Charles be picked up for violation of his probation. After about 15 minutes, Tracey went outside to speak to her husband in an effort to persuade him not to take or hurt Charles Jr. Soon thereafter, Charles began to stab Tracey repeatedly in the chest, neck and throat.

Approximately 25 minutes after Tracey's call to the Torrington Police Department and after her stabbing, a single police officer, the defendant Petrovits, arrived on the scene. Upon the arrival of Officer Petrovits at the scene of the stabbing, Charles Thurman was holding a bloody knife. Charles then dropped the knife and, in the presence of Petrovits, kicked the plaintiff Tracey Thurman in the head and ran into the Bentley–St. Hilaire residence. Charles returned from within the residence holding the plaintiff Charles Thurman, Jr. and dropped the child on his wounded mother. Charles then kicked Tracey in the head a second time. Soon thereafter, defendants DeAngelo, Nukirk, and Columbia arrived on the scene but still permitted Charles Thurman to wander about the crowd and to continue to threaten Tracey. Finally, upon approaching Tracey once again, this time while she was lying on a stretcher, Charles Thurman was arrested and taken into custody.

It is also alleged that at all times mentioned above, except for approximately two weeks following his conviction and sentencing on November 10, 1982, Charles Thurman resided in Torrington and worked there as a counterman and short order cook at Skie's Diner. There he served many members of the Torrington Police Department including some of the named and unnamed defendants in this case. In the course of his employment Charles Thurman boasted to the defendant police officer patrons that he intended to "get" his wife and that he intended to kill her.

I. Motion to Dismiss the Claims of Tracey Thurman

The defendant City now brings a motion to dismiss the claims against it. The City first argues that the plaintiff's complaint should be dismissed for failure to allege the deprivation of a constitutional right. Though the complaint alleges that the actions of the defendants deprived the plaintiff Tracey Thurman of her constitutional right to equal protection of the laws, the defendant City argues that the equal protection clause of the fourteenth amendment "does not guarantee equal application of social services." * * *

Rather, the defendant City argues that the equal protection clause "only prohibits intentional discrimination that is racially motivated" citing Arlington Heights v. Metropolitan Housing Dev. Corp., 429 U.S. 252, 50 L.Ed.2d 450, 97 S.Ct. 555 (1977) and Washington v. Davis, 426 U.S. 229, 48 L.Ed.2d 597, 96 S.Ct. 2040 (1976).

The defendant City's argument is clearly a misstatement of the law. The application of the equal protection clause is not limited to racial classifications or racially motivated discrimination. The equal protection clause will be applied to invalidate state laws which classify on the basis of alienage for the purpose of the distribution of economic benefits unless that law is necessary to promote a compelling or overriding state interest. Graham v. Richardson, 403 U.S. 365, 29 L.Ed.2d 534, 91 S.Ct. 1848 (1971); In re Griffiths, 413 U.S. 717, 37 L.Ed.2d 910, 93 S.Ct. 2851 (1973). The equal protection clause will be applied to strike down classifications based on legitimacy at birth if they are not related to a legitimate state interest. Pickett v. Brown, 462 U.S. 1, 76 L.Ed.2d 372, 103 S.Ct. 2199 (1983); Mills v. Habluetzel, 456 U.S. 91, 97–99, 71 L.Ed.2d 770, 102 S.Ct. 1549 (1982). Classifications on the basis of gender will be held invalid under the equal protection clause unless they are substantially related to an important governmental objective, Craig v. Boren * * *. And lastly, the equal protection clause will be applied to strike down classifications which are not rationally related to a legitimate governmental purpose. San Antonio School Dist. v. Rodriguez, 411 U.S. 1, 55, 36 L.Ed.2d 16, 93 S.Ct. 1278, reh'g denied, 411 U.S. 959, 36 L.Ed.2d 418, 93 S.Ct. 1919 (1973).

In the instant case, the plaintiffs allege that the defendants use an administrative classification that manifests itself in discriminatory treatment violative of the equal protection clause. Police protection in the City of Torrington, they argue, is fully provided to persons abused by someone with whom the victim has no domestic relationship. But the Torrington police have consistently afforded lesser protection, plaintiffs allege, when the victim is (1) a woman abused or assaulted by a spouse or boyfriend, or (2) a child abused by a father or stepfather. The issue to be decided, then, is whether the plaintiffs have properly alleged a violation of the equal protection clause of the fourteenth amendment.

Police action is subject to the equal protection clause and section 1983 whether in the form of commission of violative acts or omission to perform required acts pursuant to the police officer's duty to protect. Smith v. Ross, 482 F.2d 33, 36–37 (6th Cir.1973)("law enforcement officer can be liable under § 1983 when by his inaction he fails to perform a statutorily imposed duty to enforce the laws equally and fairly, and thereby denies equal protection.") Byrd v. Brishke, 466 F.2d 6, 11 (7th Cir.1972)(police officer liable under section 1983 for failing to prevent beating of plaintiff by other officers); Azar v. Conley, 456 F.2d 1382, 1387 (6th Cir.1972). See also Cooper v. Molko, 512 F.Supp. 563, 567 (N.D.Cal.1981), and Huey v. Barloga, 277 F.Supp. 864, 872–73 (N.D.Ill.1967)(failure of city officials and police officers to perform their duty of taking reasonable measures to protect personal safety of persons whom they know may be attacked is a denial of equal protection of the laws and is actionable under section 1983). City officials and police officers are under an affirmative duty to preserve law and order, and to protect the personal safety of persons in the community. Id. at 872. This duty applies equally to women whose personal safety is threatened by individuals with whom they have or have had a domestic relationship as well as to all other persons whose personal safety is threatened, including women not involved in domestic relationships. If officials have notice of the possibility of attacks on women in domestic relationships or other persons, they are under an affirmative duty to take reasonable measures to protect the personal safety of such persons in the community. Failure to perform this duty would constitute a denial of equal protection of the laws.

Although the plaintiffs point to no law which on its face discriminates against victims abused by someone with whom they have a domestic relationship, the plaintiffs have alleged that there is an administrative classification used to implement the law in a discriminatory fashion. It is well settled that the equal protection clause is applicable not only to discriminatory legislative action, but also to discriminatory governmental action in administration and enforcement of the law. See Yick Wo v. Hopkins, 118 U.S. 356, 30 L.Ed. 220, 6 S.Ct. 1064 (1886); Britton v. Rogers, 631 F.2d 572, 577 (8th Cir.1980), cert. denied, 451 U.S. 939, 68 L.Ed.2d 327, 101 S.Ct. 2021 (1981); and Flipside, Hoffman Estates, Inc. v. Village of Hoffman Estates, 485 F.Supp. 400, 409 (1980)(administrative classifications can give rise to an equal protection claim), order rev'd on other grounds, 639 F.2d 373 (7th Cir.1981); rev'd on other grounds, 455 U.S. 489, 71 L.Ed.2d 362, 102 S.Ct. 1186, reh'g denied, 456 U.S. 950, 72 L.Ed.2d 476, 102 S.Ct. 2023 (1982). Here the plaintiffs were threatened with assault in violation of Connecticut law. Over the course of eight months the police failed to afford the plaintiffs protection against such assaults, and failed to take action to arrest the perpetrator of these assaults. The plaintiffs have alleged that this failure to act was pursuant to a pattern or practice of affording inadequate protection, or no protection at all, to women who have complained of having been abused by their husbands or others with whom they have had close relations. * * * Such a practice is tantamount to an administrative classification used to implement the law in a discriminatory fashion.

If the City wishes to discriminate against women who are the victims of domestic violence, it must articulate an important governmental interest for doing so. Craig v. Boren * * *; Reed v. Reed * * *. In its memorandum and at oral argument the City has failed to put forward any justification for its disparate treatment of women.[1] Such a practice was at one time sanctioned by law:

> English common law during the eighteenth century recognized the right of husbands to physically discipline their wives. Subsequently, American common law in the early nineteenth century permitted a man to chastise his wife " 'without subjecting himself to vexatious prosecutions for assault and battery, resulting in the discredit and shame of all parties concerned.' " Some restrictions on the right of chastisement

---

1. It may develop that the classification in the instant case is not one based on gender, but instead consists of all spouses who are victims of domestic violence—male and female. At this stage of the proceedings, however, plaintiffs' allegations of gender-based discrimination will be taken as true. In one study of interspousal abuse it is claimed that "in 29 out of every 30 such cases the husband stands accused of abusing his wife." Leeds, Family Offense Cases in the Family Court System: A Statistical Description, Henry Street Settlement Urban Life Center, Nov. 1978, p. ii, cited in Bruno v. Codd, 47 N.Y.2d 582, 419 N.Y.S.2d 901, 902 n. 2, 393 N.E.2d 976.

evolved through cases which defined the type, severity, and timing of permissible wifebeating * * *.

B. Finesmith, Police Response to Battered Women: Critique and Proposals for Reform, 14 Seton Hall L. Rev. 74, 79 (1983)(citations omitted).

> In our own country a husband was permitted to beat his wife so long as he didn't use a switch any bigger around than his thumb. In 1874 the Supreme Court of North Carolina nullified the husband's right to chastise his wife "under any circumstances." But the court's ruling became ambiguous when it added, "If no permanent injury has been inflicted, nor malice, cruelty, nor dangerous violence shown by the husband, it is better to draw the curtain, shut out the public gaze, and leave the parties to forgive and forget."

Del Martin, "Scope of the Problem," Battered Women: Issues of Public Policy (1978)(Consultation Sponsored by the United States Commission on Civil Rights)(hereinafter "Consultation") at 6.

> Today, however, any notion of a husband's prerogative to physically discipline his wife is an "increasingly outdated misconception." Craig v. Boren, 429 U.S. at 198–99. As such it must join other "archaic and over-broad" premises which have been rejected as unconstitutional. Crawford v. Cushman, 531 F.2d 1114 (2d Cir.1976)(rejecting the notion that pregnancy renders servicewomen unfit and requires discharge); Weinberger v. Wiesenfeld, 420 U.S. 636, 643, 43 L.Ed.2d 514, 95 S.Ct. 1225 (1975)(rejecting proposition that the earnings of female wage earners do not significantly contribute to their families' support); Frontiero v. Richardson, 411 U.S. 677, 689, 36 L.Ed.2d 583, 93 S.Ct. 1764 (1973)(rejecting assertion that female spouses of servicemen would normally be dependent upon their husbands while male spouses of servicewomen would not be dependent upon their wives); Stanton v. Stanton, 421 U.S. 7, 14–15, 43 L.Ed.2d 688, 95 S.Ct. 1373 (1975)(rejecting "old notion" that the female is destined solely for the home and the rearing of the family and the male only for the marketplace and the world of ideas).

> A man is not allowed to physically abuse or endanger a woman merely because he is her husband. Concomitantly, a police officer may not knowingly refrain from interference in such violence, and may not "automatically decline to make an arrest simply because the assaulter and his victim are married to each other." Bruno v. Codd, 90 Misc.2d 1047, 1049, 396 N.Y.S.2d 974, 976 (1977), rev'd on other grounds, 64 App. Div. 2d 582, 407 N.Y.S.2d 165 (1978), aff'd, 47 N.Y.2d 582, 419 N.Y.S.2d 901, 393 N.E.2d 976 (1979). Such inaction on the part of the officer is a denial of the equal protection of the laws.

> In addition, any notion that defendants' practice can be justified as a means of promoting domestic harmony by refraining from interference in marital disputes, has no place in the case at hand.[2] Rather than evidencing a

---

2. See Finesmith, supra, at 82 (referring to the factor of "Lack of Social/Legal Resources" as one of the variety of factors which combine to support the maintenance of violent households—"the societal and prosecutorial view that domestic abuse is a minor problem best handled in the home"). Cf. id. at 80, citing Eisenberg & Micklow, The Assaulted Wife: Catch 22 Revisited, 3 Women's Rights L. Rep. 138, 146 (1977). The "banner of supporting the marital relationship and domestic harmony" has also been seen as a justification for

desire to work out her problems with her husband privately, Tracey pleaded with the police to offer her at least some measure of protection. Further, she sought and received a restraining order to keep her husband at a distance. Finally, it is important to recall here the Supreme Court's dictum in Reed v. Reed, 404 U.S. at 77, that "whatever may be said as to the positive values of avoiding intrafamily controversy, the choice in this context may not lawfully be mandated solely on the basis of sex." Accordingly, the defendant City of Torrington's motion to dismiss the plaintiff Tracey Thurman's complaint on the basis of failure to allege violation of a constitutional right is denied.

[The court upheld the dismissal of the child's claims against the City of Torrington because, unlike his mother, Charles Thurman, Jr. did not suffer from a "continuous failure of the police to provide him protection."]

* * *

III.   Have the Plaintiffs Properly Alleged a Custom or Policy on the Part of the City of Torrington?

The plaintiffs have alleged in paragraph 13 of their complaint as follows:

> During the period of time described herein, and for a long time prior thereto, the defendant City of Torrington acting through its Police Department, condoned a pattern or practice of affording inadequate protection, or no protection at all, to women who have complained of having been abused by their husbands or others with whom they have had close relations. Said pattern, custom or policy, well known to the individual defendants, was the basis on which they ignored said numerous complaints and reports of threats to the plaintiffs with impunity.

While a municipality is not liable for the constitutional torts of its employees on a respondeat superior theory, a municipality may be sued for damages under section 1983 when "the action that is alleged to be unconstitutional implements or executes a policy statement, ordinance, regulation, or decision officially adopted and promulgated by the body's officers" or is "visited pursuant to governmental 'custom' even though such a custom has not received formal approval through the body's official decisionmaking channels." Monell v. New York City Department of Social Services, 436 U.S. 658, 690, 98 S.Ct. 2018, 56 L.Ed.2d 611 (1978).[3]

Some degree of specificity is required in the pleading of a custom or policy on the part of a municipality. Mere conclusory allegations devoid of factual content will not suffice. See Schramm v. Krischell, 84 F.R.D. 294 (D.Conn. 1979). As this court has pointed out, a plaintiff must typically point to facts outside his own case to support his allegation of a policy on the part of a municipality. Appletree v. City of Hartford, 555 F.Supp. 224, 228 (D.Conn. 1983).

In the instant case, however, the plaintiff Tracey Thurman has specifically alleged in her statement of facts a series of acts and omissions on the part

interspousal tort immunity. According to one commentator, that doctrine "appeared in court decisions of the early 1900's to prevent battered wives from bringing actions in tort against their abusing spouses."

3. Such a custom or policy, if found to exist in the instant case, would not be unique. See Finesmith, supra, at 84–101, where the author outlines the official police guidelines for dealing with domestic disputes in 30 major American cities.

of the defendant police officers and police department that took place over the course of eight months. From this particularized pleading a pattern emerges that evidences deliberate indifference on the part of the police department to the complaints of the plaintiff Tracey Thurman and to its duty to protect her. Such an ongoing pattern of deliberate indifference raises an inference of "custom" or "policy" on the part of the municipality. See Estelle v. Gamble, 429 U.S. 97, 106, 50 L.Ed.2d 251, 97 S.Ct. 285 (1976), reh'g denied, 429 U.S. 1066, 50 L.Ed.2d 785, 97 S.Ct. 798 (1977) and Turpin v. Mailet, 619 F.2d 196, 201–02 (2d Cir.), cert. denied, 449 U.S. 1016, 66 L.Ed.2d 475, 101 S.Ct. 577 (1980). Furthermore, this pattern of inaction climaxed on June 10, 1983 in an incident so brutal that under the law of the Second Circuit that "single brutal incident may be sufficient to suggest a link between a violation of constitutional rights and a pattern of police misconduct." Owens v. Haas, 601 F.2d 1242, 1246 (2d Cir.), cert. denied, 444 U.S. 980, 100 S.Ct. 483, 62 L.Ed.2d 407 (1979). Finally, a complaint of this sort will survive dismissal if it alleges a policy or custom of condoning police misconduct that violates constitutional rights and alleges "that the City's pattern of inaction caused the plaintiffs any compensable injury." Batista v. Rodriguez, 702 F.2d 393, 397–98 (2d Cir.1983); Escalera v. New York City Housing Authority, 425 F.2d 853, 857 (2d Cir.), cert. denied, 400 U.S. 853, 27 L.Ed.2d 91, 91 S.Ct. 54 (1970)("an action, especially under the Civil Rights Act, should not be dismissed at the pleadings stage unless it appears to a certainty that plaintiffs are entitled to no relief under any state of the facts, which could be proved in support of their claims"). Accordingly, defendant City of Torrington's motion to dismiss the plaintiffs claims against it, on the ground that the plaintiffs failed to properly allege a custom or policy on the part of the municipality, is denied.

* * *

For the reasons stated above, the City's motion to dismiss the complaint for failure to allege the deprivation of a constitutional right is denied. * * *

So ordered.

Notes on Thurman

1. The *Thurman* court ostensibly concluded that failure to intervene in domestic violence settings constitutes impermissible sex-based discrimination. Does the opinion adequately articulate this rationale? For an argument in favor of applying equal protection analysis to cases of police failure to intervene see Carolyne R. Hathaway, Case Comment: Gender Based Discrimination in Police Reluctance to Respond to Domestic Assault Complaints, 75 Geo. L. Rev. 667 (1986).

2. The possibility of suing police for inadequate response to domestic violence was subsequently severely undercut by the Supreme Court in DeShaney v. Winnebago County Department of Social Services, 489 U.S. 189, 109 S.Ct. 998 (1989). In *DeShaney*, a mother brought suit against the Department of Social Services for failing to protect her son from abuse of which they had extensive knowledge. The Court held that, except where a citizen is in police custody, the state has no affirmative constitutional duty under the due process clause to protect a citizen from private violence.

Does the holding in *DeShaney* foreclose a due process claim to battered women against police for failure to intervene? Is a sex discrimination equal protection claim still available? The Court suggested as much in footnote 3:

> The State may not, of course, selectively deny its protective services to certain disfavored minorities without violating the Equal Protection Clause. See *Yick Wo v. Hopkins*, 118 U.S. 356 (1886). But no such argument has been made here.

489 U.S. at 197, 109 S.Ct. at 1004. What about an equal protection claim based on discrimination against victims of domestic violence? See Pinder v. Cambridge, 821 F.Supp. 376 (D.Md. 1993)(applying rational basis scrutiny to police failure to protect battered woman). What about other avenues for suing police specifically left open in *DeShaney*, such as "failure to train" or "policy or custom"? Or a state tort claim? See Leonard Karp & Cheryl L. Karp, Beyond the Normal Ebb and Flow * * * Infliction of Emotional Distress in Domestic Violence Cases, 28 Fam. L. Q. 389 (1994); See also, Laura S. Harper, Note: Battered Women Suing Police for Failure to Intervene: Viable Legal Avenues After Deshaney v. Winnebago County Department of Social Services, 75 Cornell L. Rev. 1393 (1990).

3. *Thurman* received widespread publicity, in both popular and professional press, in part because of the large liability award. The jury awarded Thurman $2.3 million in damages against individual police officers; the parties settled for $1.9 million. See Note: Battered Women and the Equal Protection Clause: Will the Constitution Help Them When the Police Won't?, 95 Yale L.J. 788, 795 n. 31 (1986). It was even the subject of a television movie: A Cry for Help: The Tracey Thurman Story (1989). The notoriety of the case pushed many police departments and local governments to improve their policies toward battered women. Eve S. Buzawa & Carl G. Buzawa, Domestic Violence: The Criminal Justice Response 74–75 (1990).

More recently, the O.J. Simpson "trial of the century" further pushed the abuse of women into the public eye and placed pressure on legislatures to enact measures to protect women from their lovers, husbands or ex-husbands. The Simpson trial influenced the California legislature to propose new laws which eliminate counseling programs for batterers in lieu of jail sentences, require police officers to take courses in domestic violence, and prohibit health plans from canceling or denying coverage to battered women. San Francisco Chronicle, Dec. 30, 1995, A11, Col. 6.

Is proper police response sufficient? What steps can or should the state take to end domestic violence? Is it simply enough to remove sexist biases in existing laws or should legislatures take affirmative steps to confront the problem? Heightened societal awareness about the problem of domestic violence has led to increased services for battered women and their children as well as improvements in the legal system. The Harvard Law Review surveyed the changes in mechanisms for responding to battered women, as well as proposed state and federal responses in Developments in the Law—Legal Responses to Domestic Violence, 106 Harv. L. Rev. 1498, 1499–1573 (1993).

4. Is it possible for state response to domestic violence to go too far? For example, many states require health and social service practitioners to report cases of suspected domestic violence. What are the risks of such laws to battered women? Do these laws once again place a battered woman in a position of having someone else control her destiny? What about professional ethical obligations of confidentiality? See Ariella Hyman, Dean Schillinger and Bernard Lo, Laws Mandating Reporting of Domestic Violence: Do They Promote Patient Well-

being?, 273 J. Am. Med. Assn. 1781 (1994)(arguing against mandatory reporting laws).

5. The court in footnote 1 suggests that although Mrs. Thurman had not shown that sex-based classification existed in this case it was likely that she would be able to do so at trial. Most studies conclude that, although men can also be abused in both heterosexual and homosexual relationships, the overwhelming majority (90–95%) of domestic violence victims are women. U.S. Dep't of Just., Bureau of Justice Stat., Selected Findings, Domestic Violence: Violence Between Intimates. 2–3 (Nov. 1994). For this reason, the term "woman abuse" is preferable to the term "domestic violence" which erases the gendered nature of the problem and includes a broader range of issues not discussed here, such as child abuse and elder abuse.

> "Domestic violence is one of those gray phrases * * * designed to give people a way of talking about a topic without seeing what's really going on. Like 'repatriation' or 'ethnic cleansing,' it's a euphemistic abstraction that keeps us at a dispassionate distance, far removed from the repugnant spectacle of human beings in pain."

Ann Jones, Next Time She'll be Dead 81 (1994).

6. Most explanations of woman abuse are gendered. Feminist theorists explain woman abuse as resulting from disparities of power between men and women and a manifestation of male control over women. Feminist discussion of this topic is extensive. The most influential is Dr. Lenore Walker's The Battered Woman Syndrome (1984). See also, Susan Schechter, Women and Male Violence, (1982). Given these gendered understandings, how can one explain the phenomenon of intra-lesbian abuse? Does the fact that women also beat other women undermine feminist theories about woman abuse? See generally Naming the Violence: Speaking Out About Lesbian Battering (Kerry Lobel, ed. 1986). For specific discussion of treatment of intra-lesbian violence in the legal system see Ruthann Robson, Lavender Bruises: Intra–Lesbian Violence, Law and Lesbian Legal Theory, 20 Golden Gate U. L. Rev. 567 (1990).

7. In cases of woman abuse, it is becoming increasingly common for defendants, particularly new immigrants, to present a "cultural defense" as an attempt to negate or mitigate criminal liability. Should a batterer be exonerated because his background and beliefs permit, or sometimes encourage, such acts? For a discussion of particular cases employing the "cultural defense" see Alice J. Gallin, Note: The Cultural Defense: Undermining the Policies Against Domestic Violence, 35 B.C. L. Rev. 723 (1994); see also, People v. Aphaylath, 68 N.Y.2d 945, 510 N.Y.S.2d 83, 502 N.E.2d 998 (Ct. of App. N.Y. 1986). For an excellent discussion of Asian immigrants' use of cultural defenses see Leti Volpp, (Mis)identifying Culture: Asian Women and the "Cultural Defense," 17 Harv. Women's L.J. 57 (1994).

Is it possible to respect different cultures and at the same time condemn violence against women? This issue has placed feminist and multiculturalist legal theorists on opposite sides of a difficult debate. One theorist attempts to reconcile the two seemingly divergent perspectives. Holly Maguigan, Cultural Evidence and Male Violence: Are Feminist and Multiculturalist Reformers on a Collision Course in Criminal Courts?, 70 N.Y.U. L. Rev. 36 (1995).

8. Should women who are persecuted by their husbands in foreign countries be eligible for asylum in the United States? For powerful anecdotal evidence and

an argument for asylum under current human rights law, see Pamela Goldberg, Anyplace But Home: Asylum in the United States for Women Fleeing Intimate Violence, 26 Cornell Int'l. L. J. 565 (1993). Until recently, woman abuse was not considered a human rights issues. Increasingly, however, international human rights organizations are recognizing that "women's rights are human rights." Dorothy Q. Thomas and Michele E. Beasley document this change and suggest that the human rights paradigm also has limitations in Domestic Violence as a Human Rights Issue, 58 Alb. L. Rev. 1119 (1995).

Text Note
Woman Abuse

Though disturbing, the facts in *Thurman* are not unique. Woman abuse is the single largest cause of injury to women in the United States.[1] The problem exists in families of all racial and socioeconomic backgrounds.[2] Estimates of the number of women who are battered by husbands or boyfriends vary; between twenty[3] and fifty[4] percent of all American women will experience violence in an intimate relationship. However, documentation is difficult because survivors are reluctant to disclose.[5]

Batterers generally believe that they have the right to control their female partners. Violence is a way for batterers to assert power and control. Battering often begins or increases when a woman becomes pregnant.[6] When a battered woman challenges this control, or tries to break free of the relationship, battering often becomes more severe. Cases when women are murdered by their current or former partners occur most frequently when the woman attempted to leave an abusive relationship.[7]

The impact of woman abuse resonates beyond the lives of the battered women and their partners. Without intervention the cycle of violence recreates itself across generations and throughout society. Children whose mothers are battered are more likely to experience child abuse.[8] Even when not abused themselves, children who witness violence often evidence the same symptoms as those evidenced by abused children.[9] Boys who witness their fathers' abuse of their mothers are more likely to become batterers, just as girls who grow up in violent homes are more likely to tolerate abuse as adults.[10] Domestic violence is thought to be a major cause of homelessness among women and children.[11] One study showed that over eighty-five percent of federal offenders in prison for violent

1. Antonia C. Novello, The Domestic Violence Issue: Hear Our Voices, Am. Med. News, Mar. 23/30, 1992, 25 ("Domestic violence is the leading cause of injury to women ages 15–44. More common than automobile accidents, muggings and [nonmarital] rapes combined.")

2. Catherine F. Klein & Leslye E. Orloff, Providing Legal Protection for Battered Women: An Analysis of State Statutes and Case Law, 21 Hofstra L. Rev. 801, 807 (1993).

3. Murray Straus et al., Behind Closed Doors: A Survey of Family Violence in America 40 (1980).

4. National Clearinghouse of the Defense of Battered Women, Statistic Packet 104–06 (3d ed. 1994).

5. Id. at 35.

6. Lenore E. Walker, The Battered Woman 106–09 (1979).

7. Id. at 7.

8. Evan Stark & Anne H. Flitcraft, Woman–Battering, Child Abuse and Social Heredity: What is the Relationship? in Marital Violence 147–71 (Johnson ed., 1985).

9. Peter G. Jaffe et. al, Children of Battered Women (1990).

10. Id.

11. Division of Policy Studies, U.S. Dep't of Housing and Urban Development, Report on the 1988 National Survey of Shelters for the Homeless 14 (Mar. 1988); Joan Zorza, Woman Battering: A Major Cause of Homelessness, 25 Clearinghouse Review 421 (1991).

crimes either witnessed, or were victims of, domestic violence as children.[12]

Although woman abuse is not a new problem, it was rarely discussed until feminists began speaking out about violence in the family in the late 1960s.[13] Before that time, most people viewed woman abuse as a private matter not to be interfered with by outsiders, and victims of such abuse had few legal remedies available to them.[14] Battered women's activists began by setting up support centers, shelters and hot lines for women in crisis and their children.[15] They also pressed for a series of legal reforms at all levels of government.

Since the 1970s, significant legal developments in the area of domestic violence transformed the law into a protective tool for battered women.[16] These changes emerged in many areas of law. Perhaps the most useful law, adopted in every state, is the civil protection order which grants immediate and accessible relief to victims of domestic violence.[17] Where evidence of abuse is shown, most states permit restraining orders, eviction of the perpetrator from the abused partner's home, no-contact mandates, child custody provisions, counseling and attorney's fees. Criminal and family laws have also been made more sensitive to the problem of domestic violence. In most states, police may now make warrantless arrests for misdemeanor crimes of domestic violence; some even require police to arrest the perpetrator when they determine a crime of domestic violence was committed.[18] A majority of states enacted legislation which requires history of domestic violence to be taken into consideration in custody determinations or exempts victims of domestic violence from compulsory divorce and custody mediation.[19]

Legislation has also been enacted on the federal level. In 1994 Congress passed the federal Violence Against Women Act (VAWA).[20] Recognizing that violence against women has reached epidemic levels, the VAWA requires states to grant full faith and credit to civil protection orders issued in other states. The Act further discourages the use and recognition of mutual protection orders, those where the batterer cross-claims against the victim of battering, by limiting the full faith and credit granted such orders and providing funding to states which prohibit their issuance except under limited circumstances. Additional federal domestic violence crimes were created under the VAWA which open up new legal avenues for protection of abused women. For example, the VAWA makes it a federal crime to cross state lines and violate a valid protection order or injure an intimate partner.[21]

12. Elana Salzman, Note: The Quincy District Court Domestic Violence Prevention Program, 74 B.U. L. R. 329, 329 (1994).

13. For a personal account of feminist activism in the battered women's movement see Karen Bernstein, Naming the Violence: Destroying the Myth, 58 Alb. L. Rev. 961 (1995).

14. Ann Jones, Next Time She'll be Dead 18–27 (1994).

15. See Susan Schechter, Women and Male Violence, 53–156 (1982)(documenting history of battered women's movement).

16. See American Responses to Domestic Violence: Selected Policies from the United States of America (1994).

17. Peter Finn & Sarah Colson, Civil Protection Orders: Legislation, Current Court Practice, and Enforcement, Issues and Practices in Criminal Justice (1990).

18. Joan Zorza, Mandatory Arrest Summary Chart. New York: National Center on Women and Family Law (1991).

19. See The Family Violence Project of the National Council of Juvenile and Family Court Judges, Family Violence in Child Custody Statutes: An Analysis of State Codes and Legal Practice, 29 Fam. L. Q. 197 (1995).

20. The Violence Against Women Act of 1994, Pub. L. No. 103–322, Title IV, 108 Stat. 1902–55 (codified in sections of 8 U.S.C.A., 18 U.S.C.A., & 42 U.S.C.A.).

21. See Catherine F. Klein, Full Faith and Credit: Interstate Enforcement of Protection Orders Under the Violence Against Women Act of 1994, 29 Fam. L. Q. 253 (1995).

Because, in most cases, the implementation of these laws is discretionary, popular stereotypes and misconceptions about battered women influence treatment of domestic violence cases within the justice system.[22] As Chief Justice Wilentz pointed out in State v. Kelly,[23] "[s]ome popular misconceptions about battered women include the beliefs that they are masochistic and actually enjoy their beatings, that they purposely provoke their husbands into violent behavior, and, most critically * * * that women who remain in battering relationships are free to leave their abusers at any time." Prosecutors, police, judges and juries, all charged with enforcing protections of battered women, often harbor these inaccurate and damaging notions. Hence, despite legal changes, battered women continue to be blamed for their abuse and batterers continue to be treated leniently.

In addition to legal changes, copious sociological and psychological research about woman abuse has emerged since the 1970s. These studies attempt to understand battered women within the context of the cycle of violence in abusive homes as well as gender inequities in society generally. The New Jersey Supreme Court described this research and the so-called "battered women's syndrome" in State v. Kelly:

> As the problem of battered women has begun to receive more attention, sociologists and psychologists have begun to focus on the effects a sustained pattern of physical and psychological abuse can have on a woman. The effects of such abuse are what some scientific observers have termed "the battered-woman's syndrome," a series of common characteristics that appear in women who are abused physically and psychologically over an extended period of time by the dominant male figure in their lives. Dr. Lenore Walker, a prominent writer on the battered-woman's syndrome, defines the battered woman as one who is repeatedly subjected to any forceful physical or psychological behavior by a man in order to coerce her to do something he wants her to do without concern for her rights. Battered women include wives or women in any form of intimate relationships with men. Furthermore, in order to be classified as a battered woman, the couple must go through the battering cycle at least twice. Any woman may find herself in an abusive relationship with a man once. If it occurs a second time, and she remains in the situation, she is defined as a battered woman. [L. Walker, supra, at xv].

> According to Dr. Walker, relationships characterized by physical abuse tend to develop battering cycles. Violent behavior directed at the woman occurs in three distinct and repetitive stages that vary both in duration and intensity depending on the individuals involved. L. Walker, supra, at 55–70.

> Phase one of the battering cycle is referred to as the "tension-building stage," during which the battering male engages in minor battering incidents and verbal abuse while the woman, beset by fear and tension, attempts to be as placating and passive as possible in order to stave off more serious violence. Id. at 56–59.

> Phase two of the battering cycle is the "acute battering incident." At some point during phase one, the tension between the battered woman and the batterer becomes intolerable and more serious violence inevitable. The

---

22. See Martha R. Mahoney, Legal Images of Battered Women: Redefining the Issue of Separation, 90 Mich. L. Rev. 1 (1991). See also, Jones, supra note 14, at 143. ("A recent study in Milwaukee found that 95 percent of assaultive men arrested were not prosecuted, and only 1 percent were convicted.")

23. State v. Kelly, 97 N.J. 178, 192, 478 A.2d 364, 370 (1984).

triggering event that initiates phase two is most often an internal or external event in the life of the battering male, but provocation for more severe violence is sometimes provided by the woman who can no longer tolerate or control her phase-one anger and anxiety. Id. at 59–65.

Phase three of the battering cycle is characterized by extreme contrition and loving behavior on the part of the battering male. During this period the man will often mix his pleas for forgiveness and protestations of devotion with promises to seek professional help, to stop drinking,[5] and to refrain from further violence. For some couples, this period of relative calm may last as long as several months, but in a battering relationship the affection and contrition of the man will eventually fade and phase one of the cycle will start anew. Id. at 65–70.

The cyclical nature of battering behavior helps explain why more women simply do not leave their abusers. The loving behavior demonstrated by the batterer during phase three reinforces whatever hopes these women might have for their mate's reform and keeps them bound to the relationship. R. Langley & R. Levy, Wife Beating: The Silent Crisis 112–14 (1977).

Some women may even perceive the battering cycle as normal, especially if they grew up in a violent household. Battered Women, A Psychosociological Study of Domestic Violence 60 (M. Roy ed. 1977); D. Martin, Battered Wives, 60 (1981). Or they may simply not wish to acknowledge the reality of their situation. T. Davidson, Conjugal Crime, at 50 (1978)("The middle-class battered wife's response to her situation tends to be withdrawal, silence and denial * * *").

Other women, however, become so demoralized and degraded by the fact that they cannot predict or control the violence that they sink into a state of psychological paralysis and become unable to take any action at all to improve or alter the situation. There is a tendency in battered women to believe in the omnipotence or strength of their battering husbands and thus to feel that any attempt to resist them is hopeless. L. Walker, supra, at 75.

In addition to these psychological impacts, external social and economic factors often make it difficult for some women to extricate themselves from battering relationships. A woman without independent financial resources who wishes to leave her husband often finds it difficult to do so because of a lack of material and social resources.

Even with the progress of the last decade, women typically make less money and hold less prestigious jobs than men, and are more responsible for child care. Thus, in a violent confrontation where the first reaction might be to flee, women realize soon that there may be no place to go. Moreover, the stigma that attaches to a woman who leaves the family unit without her children undoubtedly acts as a further deterrent to moving out.

In addition, battered women, when they want to leave the relationship, are typically unwilling to reach out and confide in their friends, family, or the

5. Alcohol is often an important component of violence toward women. Evidence points to a correlation between alcohol and violent acts between family members. In one British study, 44 of 100 cases of wife abuse occurred when the husband was drunk. Gayford, "Wife Battering: A Preliminary Survey of 100 Cases," British Medical Journal 1:194–197 (1975). Gelles, in The Violent Home: A Study of Physical Aggression between Husbands and Wives (1979), found that in 44 families where violence had occurred, drinking accompanied the violence in 21 of the cases. He also posited that alcohol and family violence are more closely related than alcohol and other types of violence.

police, either out of shame and humiliation, fear of reprisal by their husband, or the feeling they will not be believed.

Dr. Walker and other commentators have identified several common personality traits of the battered woman: low self-esteem, traditional beliefs about the home, the family, and the female sex role, tremendous feelings of guilt that their marriages are failing, and the tendency to accept responsibility for the batterer's actions. L. Walker, supra, at 35–36.

Finally, battered women are often hesitant to leave a battering relationship because, in addition to their hope of reform on the part of their spouse, they harbor a deep concern about the possible response leaving might provoke in their mates. They literally become trapped by their own fear. Case histories are replete with instances in which a battered wife left her husband only to have him pursue her and subject her to an even more brutal attack. D. Martin, supra, at 76–79.

The combination of all these symptoms—resulting from sustained psychological and physical trauma compounded by aggravating social and economic factors—constitutes the battered-woman's syndrome. Only by understanding these unique pressures that force battered women to remain with their mates, despite their long-standing and reasonable fear of severe bodily harm and the isolation that being a battered woman creates, can a battered woman's state of mind be accurately and fairly understood.

State v. Kelly, 97 N.J. 178, 190–196, 478 A.2d 364, 371–372 (1984).

Thus, the past quarter of a century witnessed both improved legal response mechanisms and heightened social consciousness about woman abuse, yet women continue to be abused in many American families. If the problem of battered women emanates from deep-seated societal beliefs about the appropriate roles of men and women, can anything be done to change these beliefs?

2. USE OF SELF DEFENSE BY WOMEN

STATE v. WANROW

Supreme Court of Washington, 1977.
88 Wash.2d 221, 559 P.2d 548.

UTTER, ASSOCIATE JUSTICE.

Yvonne Wanrow was convicted by a jury of second-degree murder and first-degree assault. * * *

We order a reversal of the conviction on two grounds. * * * The second ground is error committed by the trial court in improperly instructing the jury on the law of self-defense as it related to the defendant.

On the afternoon of August 11, 1972, defendant's (respondent's) two children were staying at the home of Ms. Hooper, a friend of defendant. Defendant's son was playing in the neighborhood and came back to Ms. Hooper's house and told her that a man tried to pull him off his bicycle and drag him into a house. Some months earlier, Ms. Hooper's 7-year-old daughter had developed a rash on her body which was diagnosed as venereal disease. Ms. Hooper had been unable to persuade her daughter to tell her who had molested her. It was not until the night of the shooting that Ms. Hooper discovered it was William Wesler (decedent) who allegedly had violated her daughter. A few minutes after the defendant's son related his story to Ms. Hooper about the man who tried to detain him, Mr. Wesler appeared on the porch of the Hooper house and stated through the door, "I didn't touch the kid, I didn't touch the kid." At that moment, the Hooper girl, seeing Wesler at the door, indicated to her mother that Wesler was the man who had molested her. Joseph Fah, Ms. Hooper's landlord, saw Wesler as he was leaving and informed Shirley Hooper that Wesler had tried to molest a young boy who had earlier lived in the same house, and that Wesler had previously been committed to the Eastern State Hospital for the mentally ill. Immediately after this revelation from Mr. Fah, Ms. Hooper called the police who, upon their arrival at the Hooper residence, were informed of all the events which had transpired that day. Ms. Hooper requested that Wesler be arrested then and there, but the police stated, "We can't, until Monday morning." Ms. Hooper was urged by the police officer to go to the police station Monday morning and "swear out a warrant." Ms. Hooper's landlord, who was present during the conversation, suggested that Ms. Hooper get a baseball bat located at the corner of the house and "conk him over the head" should Wesler try to enter the house uninvited during the weekend. To this suggestion, the policeman replied, "Yes, but wait until he gets in the house." (A week before this incident Shirley Hooper had noticed someone prowling around her house at night. Two days before the shooting someone had attempted to get into Ms. Hooper's bedroom and had slashed the window screen. She suspected that such person was Wesler.)

That evening, Ms. Hooper called the defendant and asked her to spend the night with her in the Hooper house. At that time she related to Ms. Wanrow the facts we have previously set forth. The defendant arrived sometime after 6 p.m. with a pistol in her handbag. The two women ultimately determined that they were too afraid to stay alone and decided to ask some friends to come over for added protection. The two women then called the defendant's sister and brother-in-law, Angie and Chuck Michel. The four adults did not go to bed that evening, but remained awake talking and watching for any possible prowlers. There were eight young children in the house with them. At around 5 a.m., Chuck Michel, without the knowledge of the women in the house, went to Wesler's house, carrying a baseball bat. Upon arriving at the Wesler residence, Mr. Michel accused Wesler of molesting little children. Mr. Wesler then suggested that they go over to the Hooper residence and get the whole thing straightened out. Another man, one David Kelly, was also present, and together the three men went over to the Hooper house. Mr. Michel and Mr. Kelly remained outside while Wesler entered the residence.

The testimony as to what next took place is considerably less precise. It appears that Wesler, a large man who was visibly intoxicated, entered the home and when told to leave declined to do so. A good deal of shouting and confusion then arose, and a young child, asleep on the couch, awoke crying. The testimony indicates that Wesler then approached this child, stating, "My what a cute little boy," or words to that effect, and that the child's mother, Ms. Michel, stepped between Wesler and the child. By this time Hooper was screaming for Wesler to get out. Ms. Wanrow, a 5'4" woman who at the time had a broken leg and was using a crutch, testified that she then went to the front door to enlist the aid of Chuck Michel. She stated that she shouted for him and, upon turning around to reenter the living room, found Wesler standing directly behind her. She testified to being gravely startled by this situation and to having then shot Wesler in what amounted to a reflex action.

* * *

Reversal of respondent's conviction is also required by a second serious error committed by the trial court. Instruction No. 10, setting forth the law of self-defense, incorrectly limited the jury's consideration of acts and circumstances pertinent to respondent's perception of the alleged threat to her person. An examination of the record of the testimony and of the colloquies which took place with regard to the instructions on self-defense indicate the critical importance of these instructions to the respondent's theory of the case. Based upon the evidence we have already set out, it is obviously crucial that the jury be precisely instructed as to the defense of justification.

In the opening paragraph of instruction No. 10, the jury, in evaluating the gravity of the danger to the respondent, was directed to consider only those acts and circumstances occurring "at or immediately before the killing * * * ".[7] This is not now, and never has been, the law of self-defense in Washington. On the contrary, the justification of self-defense is to be evaluated in light of *all* the facts and circumstances known to the defendant, including those known substantially before the killing.

* * *

As shown by the discussion above, instruction No. 10 erred in limiting the acts and circumstances which the jury could consider in evaluating the nature of the threat of harm as perceived by respondent. Under the well-established rule, this error is presumed to have been prejudicial. Moreover, far from affirmatively showing that the error was harmless, the record demonstrates the limitation to circumstances "at or immediately before the killing" was of crucial importance in the present case. Respondent's knowledge of the victim's reputation for aggressive acts was gained many hours before the killing and was based upon events which occurred over a period of years. Under the law of this state, the jury should have been allowed to consider this information in making the critical determination of the " 'degree of force which * * * a reasonable person in the same situation * * * seeing what [s]he sees and knowing what [s]he knows, then would believe to be necessary.' " * * *

The second paragraph of instruction No. 10 contains an equally erroneous and prejudicial statement of the law. That portion of the instruction reads:

7. Instruction No. 10 reads:

"To justify killing in self-defense, there need be no actual or real danger to the life or person of the party killing, but there must be, or reasonably appear to be, at or immediately before the killing, some overt act, or some circumstances which would reasonably indicate to the party killing that the person slain, is, at the time, endeavoring to kill him or inflict upon him great bodily harm.

"However, when there is no reasonable ground for the person attacked to believe that his person is in imminent danger of death or great bodily harm, and it appears to him that only an ordinary battery is all that is intended, and all that he has reasonable grounds to fear from his assailant, he has a right to stand his ground and repel such threatened assault, yet he has no right to repel a threatened assault with naked hands, by the use of a deadly weapon in a deadly manner, unless he believes, and has reasonable grounds to believe, that he is in imminent danger of death or great bodily harm."

However, when there is no reasonable ground for the person attacked to believe that *his* person is in imminent danger of death or great bodily harm, and it appears to *him* that only an ordinary battery is all that is intended, and all that *he* has reasonable grounds to fear from *his* assailant, *he* has a right to stand *his* ground and repel such threatened assault, yet *he* has no right to repel a threatened assault with naked hands, by the use of a deadly weapon in a deadly manner, unless *he* believes, *and has reasonable grounds* to believe, that *he* is in imminent danger of death or great bodily harm.

(Italics ours.) In our society women suffer from a conspicuous lack of access to training in and the means of developing those skills necessary to effectively repel a male assailant without resorting to the use of deadly weapons.[8] Instruction No. 12 does indicate that the "relative size and strength of the persons involved" may be considered; however, it does not make clear that the defendant's actions are to be judged against her own subjective impressions and not those which a detached jury might determine to be objectively reasonable. State v. Miller, supra; State v. Tyree, supra; State v. Dunning, supra. The applicable rule of law is clearly stated in *Miller,* at page 105, 250 P. at page 645:

> If the appellants, at the time of the alleged assault upon them, as reasonably and ordinarily cautious and prudent men, honestly believed that they were in danger of great bodily harm, they would have the right to resort to self-defense, and their conduct is to be judged by the condition appearing to them at the time, not by the condition as it might appear to the jury in the light of testimony before it.

The second paragraph of instruction No. 10 not only establishes an objective standard, but through the persistent use of the masculine gender leaves the jury with the impression the objective standard to be applied is that applicable to an altercation between two men. The impression created—that a 5'4" woman with a cast on her leg and using a crutch must, under the law, somehow repel an assault by a 6'2" intoxicated man without employing weapons in her defense, unless the jury finds her determination of the degree of danger to be objectively reasonable—constitutes a separate and distinct misstatement of the law and, in the context of this case, violates the respondent's right to equal protection of the law. The respondent was entitled to have the jury consider her actions in the light of her own perceptions of the situation, including those perceptions which were the product of our nation's "long and unfortunate history of sex discrimination." Frontiero v. Richardson, 411 U.S. 677, 684, 93 S.Ct. 1764, 1769, 36 L.Ed.2d 583 (1973). Until such time as the effects of that history are eradicated, care must be taken to assure that our self-defense instructions afford women the right to have their conduct judged in light of the individual physical handicaps which are the product of sex discrimination. To fail to do so is to deny the right of the individual woman involved to trial by the same rules which are applicable to male defendants. See Lamb v. Brown, 456 F.2d 18 (10th Cir.1972); see also Reed v. Reed, 404 U.S. 71, 92 S.Ct. 251, 30 L.Ed.2d 225

---

8. See B. Babcock, A. Freedman, E. Norton and S. Ross, Sex Discrimination and the Law: Causes and Remedies 943–1070 (1975); S. Brownmiller, Against our Will: Men, Women and Rape (1975).

(1971); Darrin v. Gould, 85 Wash.2d 859, 540 P.2d 882 (1975). The portion of the instruction above quoted misstates our law in creating an objective standard of "reasonableness." It then compounds that error by utilizing language suggesting that the respondent's conduct must be measured against that of a reasonable male individual finding himself in the same circumstances.

We conclude that the instruction here in question contains an improper statement of the law on a vital issue in the case, is inconsistent, misleading and prejudicial when read in conjunction with other instructions pertaining to the same issue, and therefore is a proper basis for a finding of reversible error.

Finally, we agree with the conclusion of the Court of Appeals that the trial court cannot be said to have abused its discretion in this case in declining to allow defendant's counsel to call an expert witness to present opinion evidence on the effects of defendant's Indian culture upon her perception and actions. We also find the remaining contentions advanced by the respondent in support of the reversal of her conviction to be without merit.

In light of the errors in admission of evidence and instruction of the jury, the decision of the Court of Appeals is affirmed, the conviction reversed, and the case remanded for a new trial.

HUNTER, BRACHTENBACH and HOROWITZ, JJ., concur.

WRIGHT, ASSOCIATE JUSTICE (concurring).

[JUSTICE WRIGHT'S concurring opinion on a different ground is omitted.]

HAMILTON, ASSOCIATE JUSTICE (dissenting).

I dissent, for I * * * do not feel that the jury instructions were so prejudicial that a new trial must be granted.

* * *

I also do not believe that the defendant is entitled to a new trial because of the jury instructions. Although instruction No. 10 did not direct the jury to consider *all of the surrounding circumstances,* see State v. Miller, 141 Wash. 104, 250 P. 645 (1926), and State v. Lewis, 6 Wash.App. 38, 491 P.2d 1062 (1971), this deficiency was corrected by the giving of instruction No. 12.[3] Instructions must be considered as a whole and if, when so considered, they properly state the law, they are sufficient. See State v. Stafford, 44 Wash.2d 353, 355, 267 P.2d 699 (1954); State v. Refsnes, 14 Wash.2d 569, 572, 128 P.2d 773 (1942); State v. Smith, 196 Wash. 534, 83 P.2d 749 (1938). The trial court instructed the jury to "consider the instructions as a whole and * * * not place undue emphasis on any particular instruction or part there-

---

3. Instruction No. 12 reads:

"In connection with the defense of justification, you are instructed that you may consider the words and actions of the deceased prior to the homicide, the relative size and strength of the persons involved, *together with any and all factors which in your judgment may bear upon your determination as to whether the defendant reasonably believed herself in danger of grievous bodily harm at*

the time in question. But a person who is attacked has no right to use greater force than he or she honestly believes is necessary, or has reasonable grounds to believe is necessary for self-defense.

"There is no legal justification or excuse for a private person to deliberately assault another as a result of anger or to inflict vengeance."

of." In my view, the instructions were not so prejudicial so as to require a new trial for the defendant.

For the above reasons, I would conclude that the defendant received a fair trial and that the decision of the Court of Appeals should be reversed and the judgment of the trial court upon the jury verdict reinstated.

STAFFORD, C.J., and ROSELLINI, J., concur.

STATE v. ANAYA

Supreme Judicial Court of Maine, 1981.
438 A.2d 892.

WATHEN, JUSTICE.

In the Superior Court (Cumberland County), defendant Linda Anaya was found guilty of manslaughter, 17–A M.R.S.A. § 203 (Supp.1981). Her appeal from this jury verdict assigns numerous claims of error. Since we find that the presiding justice committed reversible error in excluding testimony relating to the "battered wife syndrome," we sustain the appeal and vacate the judgment of conviction.

I.

On April 9, 1980, shortly after midnight, Brunswick Police responded to a report of a stabbing at the defendant's apartment. They found Frank Williams, defendant's lover, lying on the floor unconscious while defendant stroked his head and talked to him. He died shortly thereafter. The cause of death was determined to be a knife wound in the back which severed the aorta. The evidence proving that defendant stabbed the deceased was overwhelming and she has not contested this fact on appeal.

Frank Williams moved into defendant's apartment in mid-November, 1979, approximately five months before his death. In December, soon after Williams moved out of the apartment, Linda Anaya cut her wrists and was treated at the local hospital. Williams returned to the apartment the next day.

On February 7, 1980, defendant's roommate, Pam Davis, called the police twice to intervene in domestic problems. First, Frank Williams cut his wrists and Davis called for help, but he refused it, saying "Aren't I cute?" Later on during that evening, Davis apparently called the police again because Williams had pushed and kicked the defendant and held a knife to defendant's throat, threatening to kill her. He had also chased Davis while threatening her with a hammer. At some point, Williams received a knife wound in the back and claimed that defendant had stabbed him. Defendant received some bruises and, according to Davis, had to be treated for a concussion.

In March, 1980, defendant was treated for face and head injuries caused by Frank Williams. Life at the apartment was "like a madhouse" at this time. Williams had threatened to kill defendant if she left him and she appeared to be frightened. At the end of March, defendant attempted to commit suicide. On April 5, 1980, Williams and the defendant sustained cuts on their arms from a chisel. Defendant received a deep wound inflicted by Williams. During these months there were many fights and usually Williams was the aggressor.

Pam Davis was in the apartment on the night of Williams' death. She testified that Williams was quite intoxicated, that the couple argued, and that Williams pushed the defendant around. After five or ten minutes of fighting, Davis heard nothing. Twenty minutes later she heard Williams leave the kitchen and go to the bedroom where he and the defendant were found by the police.

An indictment against the defendant was returned by the grand jury (Cumberland County) on May 6, 1980, charging defendant with the murder of Frank Williams. * * *

Trial began on December 1, 1980, in Superior Court, Cumberland County. Defendant's motions for judgment of acquittal entered after the State rested and again after the defendant rested were denied. The jury returned a verdict of guilty of manslaughter on December 8, 1980. Defendant's timely motion for a new trial, alleging seven errors, was denied on January 29, 1981, and this appeal followed seasonably.

II.

At trial, defendant called to the stand Dr. John Bishop, an experienced and qualified psychologist. After an extensive voir dire conducted in the absence of the jury, the trial justice ruled that although Dr. Bishop was qualified to testify about the "battered wife syndrome," the evidence would be excluded as irrelevant, prejudicial, and confusing to the jury. The doctor's testimony would have described his profession's analysis of the behavior and emotional patterns of women suffering from repeated physical abuse inflicted by their husbands or lovers. He characterized abuse as a cyclical process involving three phases: (1) a build-up of tension in the relationship, (2) the occurrence of violent acts, and (3) a reduction in tension. Dr. Bishop also discussed the psychological and environmental factors which contribute to the individual male's disposition towards abuse.

Defendant, later on during the trial, attempted to introduce evidence that she was a victim of the battered wife syndrome. Dr. Myron Krueger, a specialist in internal medicine, testified that he had treated the defendant at least five times for injuries which included a concussion, a black eye, and a laceration in her arm. The presiding justice refused to allow defense counsel to question the doctor about the battered wife syndrome, stating that the evidence was irrelevant and without foundation. The record shows that Dr. Krueger would have stated that he had occasionally seen persons he believed to be victims of the battered wife syndrome and that in his opinion defendant was one of these victims. Defense counsel again moved to introduce Dr. Bishop's testimony unsuccessfully.

Although the defendant did not testify, the record clearly shows that she was relying on a theory of self-defense or provocation[1] to mitigate or justify her conduct. In closing argument, defense counsel admitted that Linda Anaya killed Frank Williams intentionally or knowingly but asserted that defendant acted reasonably to protect herself from another beating. The State's closing argument focused on the "bizarre" behavior of the victim and

---

1. The admissibility of preceding events on the issue of provocation and the reasonableness of the actor's reaction of extreme anger or fear presents the problem addressed in State v.   Flick, Me., 425 A.2d 167 (1981). On this appeal we are concerned only with admissibility on the issue of self-defense.

the defendant, implying that defendant could not have been fearful of Williams since she never attempted to leave him, and suggesting that the injuries received by defendant over the course of several months were part of a loving game, not attempts to commit suicide or the result of physical abuse. Thus, the jury's characterization of the evidence concerning their relationship would have been a crucial factor in deciding whether defendant was guilty of murder or manslaughter or not guilty because her acts were committed in self-defense.

On appeal, we will reverse a decision based on M.R.Evid. 403 to exclude evidence only if the trial justice abused his discretion in so deciding, State v. Hinds, Me., 437 A.2d 191 (1981). Interpreting the decision below as one based on Rule 403, we find such an abuse of discretion. Both Dr. Bishop's and Dr. Krueger's testimonies were highly probative and more helpful than confusing to the jury. The record shows that Dr. Bishop would have testified that abused women often continue to live with their abusers even though beatings continue, and that a certain substrata of abused women perceive suicide and/or homicide to be the only solutions to their problems. This evidence would have given the jury reason to believe that the defendant's conduct was, contrary to the State's assertions, consistent with her theory of self-defense. We agree with the District of Columbia Court of Appeals, and various commentators,[2] that where the psychologist is qualified to testify about the battered wife syndrome, and the defendant establishes her identity as a battered woman, expert evidence on the battered wife syndrome must be admitted since it "may have * * * a substantial bearing on her perceptions and behavior at the time of the killing, * * * [and is] central to her claim of self defense." Ibn–Tamas v. United States, 407 A.2d 626, 639 (D.C.1979). Since we cannot say beyond the reasonable doubt required to make the error harmless that this evidence would not have affected the jury's consideration of the self-defense claim, State v. True, Me., 438 A.2d 460 (1981), defendant is entitled to a new trial.

* * *

In light of defendant's attempted evidentiary showing, we find error in the trial court's decision to deny defendant expert assistance. Defendant made a timely request for reasonably necessary expert services under circumstances "in which a reasonable attorney would engage such services for a client having the independent financial means to pay for them." United States v. Bass, 477 F.2d 723, 725 (9th Cir.1973)(interpreting a federal statute defining indigent defendant's right to expert assistance).

On remand, defendant may be tried only upon a charge of manslaughter since the conviction for manslaughter "acts as an acquittal of the charge of murder." State v. Chaplin, Me., 286 A.2d 325 (1972).

The entry is:

Judgment vacated.

---

2. See Eber, "The Battered Wife's Dilemma: To Kill or Be Killed," 32 Hast.L.J. 895 (1981); Schneider, "Equal Rights to Trial for Women: Sex Bias in the Law of Self Defense", 15 Harv.C.R.C.L.L.Rev. 673 (1980); Note, "The Battered Wife Syndrome: A Potential Defense to a Homicide Charge," 6 Pepperdine L.Rev. 213 (1978).

Remanded to the Superior Court for further proceedings consistent with the opinion herein.

All concurring.

Notes on Wanrow and Anaya

1. Does Justice Utter's plurality opinion in *Wanrow* establish different standards for male and female defendants who claim that they acted in self-defense? Are all women defendants, simply because of their gender, to be viewed by future Washington juries as disabled by the "long and unfortunate" national "history of sex discrimination"? If so, is it open to the prosecution to show that a particular female defendant, whatever the impact of such discrimination on the rest of her sex, had a personal history of combative, aggressive, self-reliant action in the face of danger? Or does the plurality intend only to require juries faced with female defendants to look more closely at the ways in which individual women may be impaired in their ability to withstand attack, including the handicapping effect of their own psycho-social upbringing? If the latter interpretation is accurate, why did the court uphold the lower court's decision to exclude expert testimony concerning the impact of Yvonne Wanrow's Indian background upon her actions?

Professor Elizabeth M. Schneider tells the story of how the appellate strategy in *Wanrow* was hammered out. See Schneider, The Dialectic of Rights and Politics: Perspectives From the Women's Movement, 61 N.Y.U.L.Rev. 589, 604–610 (1986). She uses the experience as an illustration of feminist theory in practice:

> The legal theory emerged from political experience; the legal theory in turn served to refine and sharpen political insights and to clarify tensions in the political struggle; the political struggle was reassessed in light of the legal theory; and, finally, experience reshaped the legal theory.

Id., at 610.

2. If the Washington legislature were to enact a statute defining self-defense in gender-based terms, attributing to women, but not to men, a tendency to resort to the use of weapons rather than to rely on personal strength when threatened with attack, would the statute survive scrutiny under either the Equal Protection Clause or the Washington state Equal Rights Amendment? *Wanrow* is discussed in Jennifer Marsh, Recent Development, Women's Self Defense Under Washington Law, 54 Wash.L.Rev. 221 (1978), and W.J. Roarty, Recent Decisions, Self–Defense, 13 Gonzaga L.Rev. 278 (1977).

3. *Wanrow* was followed in State v. Crigler, 23 Wash.App. 716, 598 P.2d 739 (1979), in which the conviction of a woman for the first-degree murder of a male companion was reversed on the ground that the jury had not been properly instructed in the law of self-defense. The facts, as reported by Judge Petrie, were as follows:

> If believed by a jury, the following fact pattern supportive of her theory of the case would emerge. Ms. Crigler, age 21, and the victim, Keith Rolland, age 24, had lived together in an apartment for several months prior to May 10, 1977. Their life together was often stormy; and, when provoked, he brutally beat her on several occasions. On May 10, following one of the more stormy occasions in which he punched her repeatedly about the mouth, he moved into another apartment complex several miles away.

On May 13, ostensibly to effect a reconciliation, she went to his apartment, found another woman in his bed, and, in his absence, stuck her foot through one of his paintings, flipped his stereo set upside down, and dumped garbage on the floor. Ms. Crigler then returned to her apartment. She notified the police that Rolland was about to assault her, that he had a gun, and the warrants for his arrest on traffic violations were outstanding. The police arrested Rolland; he bailed out; and, she testified, the police told her they did not find his gun. Shortly after 2 a.m. on May 14, he obtained keys to Crigler's apartment from the apartment manager and was attempting to unlock the door when she shouted, "Keith, if it's you, get away, back off." Hearing no response, she shot blindly through the door. The projectile passed through his aorta and he died of acute hemorrhage within minutes.

Id., 23 Wash.App. at 718, 598 P.2d at 740. The instructions given to the jury stressed that self-defense was not available unless at or immediately before the killing, the decedent committed some overt act that would reasonably suggest to the accused that he was attempting to inflict great bodily harm upon her. The court held that this instruction was erroneous under *Wanrow;* the gravity of the danger to defendant Crigler must be measured by all the surrounding circumstances which had occurred during the several months preceding the slaying.

Would the defense of self-defense have been available to Keith Rolland if he had shot Sharon Josie Crigler as she stood outside his apartment door fumbling with a key in the lock? Does the answer to that question depend on the sex of the parties or on whether Sharon had been the aggressor in the domestic violence that characterized their relationship?

4. Was *Anaya* correctly decided? On remand, Linda Anaya was again convicted of manslaughter; this time her conviction was affirmed on appeal. The court upheld the admissibility of the testimony of Patricia Williams, the victim's sister-in-law, that the victim had shown her a small cut on his back and had told her, in Anaya's presence, that Anaya had cut him. Williams then testified that, in response to the charge, Anaya "just laughed and said she would do a better job next time". Williams also testified that the victim held no steady job throughout the time he lived with defendant. The court concluded that this testimony tended to refute the battered-wife defense and so was admissible as rebuttal evidence. State v. Anaya, 456 A.2d 1255, 1265–66 (Me.1983). Do you agree?

Is the battered woman syndrome an independent defense available only to women, an indication of impaired mental state, such as insanity or diminished capacity, or a mitigating factor in sentencing? One observer asserts that it is none of the above: rather, properly understood, the battered woman's syndrome is used in connection with a plea of self-defense, as a way of explaining the reasonableness of the woman's perception of imminent danger. See Roberta K. Thyfault, Comment, Self–Defense: Battered Woman Syndrome on Trial, 20 Cal.Western L.Rev. 485, 495 (1984). In State v. Kelly, 97 N.J. 178, 478 A.2d 364 (1984), supra at p. 1193, the Supreme Court of New Jersey held expert testimony of the battered woman syndrome admissible and relevant both to the defendant's state of mind, to show that she honestly believed she was in imminent danger of death from her husband, and relevant to the reasonableness of her belief that she was in imminent danger of death or serious injury. See also State v. Allery, 101 Wash.2d 591, 682 P.2d 312 (1984), relying on *Wanrow* and *Anaya* to support the admissibility of expert testimony on the battered woman syndrome, and explaining that:

> [In *Wanrow*] we held that the jury must consider all the facts and circumstances known to the woman at the time of the killing in evaluating her claim of self-defense. To effectively present the situation as perceived by the defendant, and the reasonableness of her fear, the defense has the option to explain her feelings to enable the jury to overcome stereotyped impressions about women who remain in abusive relationships. It is appropriate that the jury be given a professional explanation of the battering syndrome and its effects on the woman through the use of expert testimony.

Id., 101 Wn.2d at 597, 682 P.2d at 316. See also, collecting cases, Cynthia L. Coffee, Note, A Trend Emerges: A State Survey on the Admissibility of Expert Testimony Concerning the Battered Woman Syndrome, 25 J.Fam.L. 373 (1986–1987)(trend favors admissibility).

Should the jury in *Crigler*, discussed in Note 3, supra, be instructed, under the *Wanrow* approach, that women are the primary victims of domestic violence and that the defendant, because of her sex, was more likely to fear abuse at the hands of her companion?

Should the defense be conceptualized in criminal law theory as a justification or as an excuse? Feminists disagree. See Phyllis L. Crocker, The Meaning of Equality for Battered Women Who Kill Men in Self–Defense, 8 Harv.Wom.L.J. 121, 130–32 (1985)(justification); contra, Cathryn Jo Rosen, The Excuse of Self–Defense: Correcting A Historical Accident on Behalf of Battered Women Who Kill, 36 Am.U.L.Rev. 11 (1986) (excuse).

What can the law do to prevent battering, beyond the recognition of the battered woman syndrome as relevant to the defense of self-defense when the victim herself ends the battering cycle by killing her tormentor? Professor Kathleen Waits proposes a program for dealing with battering, which includes both protecting the victim and deterring the batterer. See Waits, The Criminal Justice System's Response to Battering: Understanding the Problem, Forging the Solutions, 60 Wash.L.Rev. 267 (1985). See also Christine Littleton, Women's Experience and the Problem of Transition: Perspectives on Male Battering of Women, 1989 University of Chicago Legal Forum 23, asking (and beginning to answer) the very complex and dangerous question: "What would legal doctrine and practice look like if it took seriously a mandate to make women safer *in* relationships, instead of offering separation as the *only* remedy for violence against women?" Id., at 52. See also Holly Maguigan, Battered Women and Self–Defense: Myths and Misconceptions in Current Reform Proposals, 140 U.Pa. L.Rev. 379 (1991); Martha Mahoney, Legal Images of Battered Women: Redefining the Issue of Separation, 90 Mich.L.Rev. 1 (1991).

What do you think of the approach taken to deterring male batterers by a trial court judge in Maine, who stated, upon sentencing defendant Brian Houston for assault upon Amy Stocks, that, "I generally give a short jail sentence when men are convicted of beating women or hitting women because I take a very dim view of men hitting women * * * ". Accordingly, he added two or three days of jail time to Houston's sentence, to teach the defendant that he "can't go around hitting women." The Supreme Court of Maine was not impressed with this practice. It held that the sentence violated the equal protection clauses of the United States and Maine constitutions. Chief Justice McKusick reasoned in part as follows:

> The equal protection clauses of the United States and Maine Constitutions "prohibit[] selective enforcement [of criminal laws] 'based upon an unjustifiable standard such as race, religion or other arbitrary classifica-

tion.' "   State v. Pickering, 462 A.2d 1151, 1161 (Me.1983)(quoting State v. Heald, 382 A.2d 290, 301 (Me.1978)).   Cf. McCleskey v. Kemp, 481 U.S. 279, 107 S.Ct. 1756, 1765, 95 L.Ed.2d 262, 278 (1987)(Court recognized that equal protection clause would be violated by sentencing purposefully on the basis of racial considerations); Zant v. Stephens, 462 U.S. 862, 886, 103 S.Ct. 2733, 2747, 77 L.Ed.2d 235 (1983)("race, religion, or political affiliation of the defendant" termed "constitutionally impermissible or totally irrelevant to the sentencing process").   Furthermore, one of the declared purposes of the Criminal Code is to "eliminate inequalities in sentences that are unrelated to legitimate criminological goals."   17–A.M.R.S.A. § 1151(5)(1983).   In other contexts we have required that sex-based statutory classifications, in order to withstand equal protection challenge, must advance "an important governmental objective" and be "substantially related" to achieving that objective. State v. Rundlett, 391 A.2d 815, 818 (Me.1978)(quoting Craig v. Boren, 429 U.S. 190, 197, 97 S.Ct. 451, 456, 50 L.Ed.2d 397 (1976)).

In the case now before us, the sentencing justice, by starting with a minimum jail term of two days for any male convicted of assaulting a female, relied improperly upon a gender-based classification that is not substantially related to any important governmental objective.   There exists no sound reason for punishing more harshly a man's unprovoked assault upon a woman than a similar attack upon a victim who is an equally defenseless male.   This unconstitutional gender-based classification requires that we vacate the sentencing based upon it.

State v. Houston, 534 A.2d 1293, 1296–97 (Me.1987).

5.   Premenstrual Syndrome, defined by its leading medical proponent, Dr. Katherina Dalton, as "the presence of monthly recurrent symptoms in the premenstruum or early menstruation with a complete absence of symptoms after menstruation" (see K. Dalton, The Premenstrual Syndrome and Progesterone Therapy 3 (2d Ed. 1984)), has been accepted by some English courts as a mitigating factor in criminal cases.   See Lillian Apodaca and Lori Fink, Note, Criminal Law: Premenstrual Syndrome in the Courts, 24 Washburn L.J. 54, 62–64 (1984)(discussing three unreported cases, two involving the same defendant). PMS was offered as a defense to a charge of assault in the second degree, but was withdrawn after plea bargaining in a New York case, *People v. Santos,* No. 1Ko46229 (N.Y.Kings County Crim.Ct.1981; plea entered Nov. 3, 1982).   The District Attorney whose office prosecuted *Santos,* Elizabeth Holtzman, is convinced that "[t]here is no scientific evidence that a condition called 'premenstrual syndrome' exists, or that it has anything to do with crimes committed by women." Holtzman, Premenstrual Syndrome: The Indefensible Defense, 7 Harvard Women's L.J. 1 (1984).   The *Washburn* notewriters, while cautious in their appraisal of PMS, nevertheless conclude that it may offer a productive strategy for women criminal defendants who suffer from PMS as a mitigating factor at the charging or sentencing stage rather than as an insanity or diminished capacity defense.   Note, id., 24 Washburn L.J. at 76–77.   Another commentator is persuaded that PMS "can be used to aid women who suffer from the worst effects of the syndrome in a way that does not necessarily harm the cause of women's rights"—i.e., by acting as a "humanizing factor" that can tailor a particular woman's sentence to her individual condition, rather than labeling all women who have PMS as "violent and crazy".   Nora Mulligan, Recent Developments, Premenstrual Syndrome, 6 Harvard Women's L.J. 219, 227 (1983).   Do you agree?

In 1994, the American Psychiatric Association (APA) added premenstrual dysphoric disorder (PMDD), a severe form of PMS, to its Diagnostic and Statistical Manual (DSM–IV), the basic diagnostic reference tool used by mental health professionals, insurance companies, and courts to identify and define mental illness. The APA took this action despite significant opposition from many feminists. See Lee Solomon, Premenstrual Syndrome: The Debate Surrounding Criminal Defense, 54 Maryland L. Rev. 571, 576–578 (1995). Solomon suggests that this formal acknowledgement of one extreme form of PMS will lead to greater and more effective use of it as a legal defense, assisting those women who suffer from its impact. Critics, however, charge that this official classification is not based on sufficient medical evidence and will further stereotype and stigmatize women. Id. at 578–581, 596–599. Are both positions correct?

6. The female criminal, long neglected in studies of criminal behavior by social and behavioral scientists, has become a subject of interest, discussed in symposia and collected readings. See, e.g., S. Datesman and F. Scarpitti, Women, Crime & Justice (1980); Women, Crime and Criminology, 8 Issues in Criminology No. 2, pp. 1–162 (Fall 1973); Symposium, Women and the Criminal Law, 11 American Criminal Law Review 291–510 (1973). The subject is worthy of study, says Professor Barbara Babcock,

> because it lends insight to basic problems in a context where new solutions may feasibly be tried; because there is a fresh feminist perspective from which to make analysis; and because the form and administration of criminal laws affecting women is a measure of how far we are from realizing an egalitarian society.

Babcock, Introduction: Women and the Criminal Law, 11 American Criminal Law Review, 291, 294 (1973).

C. PROSTITUTION

PLAS v. STATE

Supreme Court of Alaska, 1979.
598 P.2d 966.

CONNOR, JUSTICE.

This opinion arises from a petition for review and a criminal appeal that were consolidated for review by this court. The facts are uncontested. On June 19, 1976, appellant Debbie Plas was charged by an Alaska State Trooper with soliciting for the purpose of prostitution in violation of AS 11.40.230 which reads:

> "It is unlawful within the state to procure or solicit, or to offer to procure or solicit for the purpose of prostitution."

A preceding section, AS 11.40.210 states:

> "Prostitution includes the giving or receiving of the body by a female for sexual intercourse for hire."[1]

It is this statutory language which is at issue in this appeal.

* * *

---

1. AS 11.40.220 states: "It is unlawful to engage in prostitution in
                                                      the state."

On April 20, 1977, appellants Farrell and Ross were charged by an Alaska State Trooper with soliciting for the purpose of prostitution in violation of AS 11.40.230. A motion to dismiss on the ground that the statute was unconstitutional was denied by the district court. Farrell and Ross unsuccessfully sought reversal in the superior court, and then petitioned us for review, which we have granted. The questions presented are (1) whether AS 11.40.210–230 is unconstitutional, * * *

Two provisions of the Alaska Constitution bear upon our decision:

Article I, section 1, provides:

"Inherent Rights. This constitution is dedicated to the principles that all persons have a natural right to life, liberty, the pursuit of happiness, and the enjoyment of the rewards of their own industry; that all persons are equal and entitled to equal rights, opportunities, and protection under the law; and that all persons have corresponding obligations to the people and to the State."

Article I, section 3, provides:

"Civil Rights. No person is to be denied the enjoyment of any civil or political right because of race, color, creed, sex, or national origin. The legislature shall implement this section."

It is significant that the category "sex" was added to article I, section 3, of the Alaska Constitution by amendment in 1972.[3] We must thus consider the statute in the light of this constitutional prohibition, and the guarantee of equal rights and protection under the law contained in article I, section 1, of the Alaska Constitution.

As we stated in *State v. Erickson,* 574 P.2d 1 (Alaska 1978), we must assess equal protection claims under the Alaska Constitution by considering the purpose of the statute, the legitimacy of that purpose, the means used to accomplish the legislative objective, and "then determine whether the means chosen substantially further the goals of the enactment." *Id.* at 12. We must also balance the state interest in the chosen means against the nature of the constitutional right which is at issue. *Id.* at 12.

It is apparent that the statute invidiously discriminates against females. The offense of prostitution is capable of being committed by a male,[4] but is nowhere made criminal by the statute. In striking at prostitution the legislation singles out only the female body as the critical physical element of the crime. In view of gender neutrality required by article I, section 3, of the Alaska Constitution, the means used to accomplish the legislative end lacks rational justification. In creating criminal offenses it is particularly important that any distinctions as to gender rest upon some logical justification

---

3. It appears that at least one woman member of the Alaska Constitutional Convention, Delegate Hermann, argued strenuously against the inclusion of that word in this section, on the ground that it was unnecessary. 2 Proceedings of the Alaska Constitutional Convention 1296 (Jan. 5, 1956).

4. We find unpersuasive the state's argument that the definition section of the statute, AS 11.40.210, is ambiguous, and that when taken with the general prohibitory section, AS 11.40.220, and the punishment section, AS 11.40.250, which applies to a "person" convict-

having a basis in the actual conditions of human life.[5] In our view the statute is unconstitutional insofar as it limits its operation to selling of only a female body.[6] This does not, however, end our task.

The language which presents the constitutional difficulty here is the phrase "by a female" contained in AS 11.40.210. We must consider whether the statute, with that offending language stricken, can still accomplish its general intended purpose, and thus be saved from total nullity through the operation of the severability clause of this statute.[7] We think that the statute can be so sustained, with the mentioned words omitted. For the provision would then read:

> "Prostitution includes the giving or receiving of the body for sexual intercourse for hire."

It would then be neutral as to gender, it would accomplish the broad aim of the statute, and would not unreasonably distort the legislative intent. We believe that this is the proper solution to the problem.

We hold that the clause "by a female" is invalid for violating article I, section 3, of the Alaska Constitution, but that the balance of the statute remains legally intact.

* * *

AFFIRMED.

PEOPLE v. SUPERIOR COURT (HARTWAY)

Supreme Court of California, 1977.
19 Cal.3d 338, 138 Cal.Rptr. 66, 562 P.2d 1315.

CLARK, J.

The People petition for a writ of prohibition to prevent respondent superior court from enforcing its order directing that a peremptory writ of prohibition issue restraining the Municipal Court for the Oakland–Piedmont Judicial District from proceeding with prosecution of defendants, real parties in interest herein.

Defendants are women charged with soliciting or engaging in prostitution.[1] Pen.Code, § 647, subd. (b).[2] They moved in municipal court for

---

ed, the definition can be read to contain an implied prohibition of male prostitution.

5. For example, in *Lamb v. Brown,* 456 F.2d 18 (10th Cir.1972), the court struck down an Oklahoma statute which allowed females under the age of 18 years to be proceeded against under the juvenile code rather than by a criminal proceeding, but entitled males to such benefits only if they were under the age of 16 years. See also *Craig v. Boren,* 429 U.S. 190, 97 S.Ct. 451, 50 L.Ed.2d 397 (1976); *Reed v. Reed,* 404 U.S. 71, 92 S.Ct. 251, 30 L.Ed.2d 225 (1971).

6. As Judge Cates put it, concurring in *Holloway v. City of Birmingham,* 55 Ala.App. 568, 574, 317 So.2d 535, 541 (1975), "[O]ur society, either in asepsis or asceticism, should be evenhanded."

7. Chapter 104, § 6, SLA 1955 provides:

"If any portion of this Act shall be declared unconstitutional, such decision shall not affect the validity of the remaining portions or sections of this Act."

1. Approximately 252 individual actions are joined in this proceeding.

2. Penal Code section 647 provides: "Every person who commits any of the following acts is guilty of disorderly conduct, a misdemeanor:

"* * *

"(b) Who solicits or who engages in any act of prostitution. As used in this subdivision, 'prostitution' includes any lewd act between persons for money or other consideration.

dismissal of the charges on the grounds that section 647, subdivision (b), is unconstitutional on its face and as applied by the Oakland Police Department. The principal questions presented by the motion were: (1) whether the term "solicit" as used in the statute is unconstitutionally vague; and (2) whether the Oakland Police Department deliberately discriminates against women in enforcing the statute. After a thorough evidentiary hearing into the latter question, the municipal court filed comprehensive findings of fact and conclusions of law, resolving both questions against defendants, and denied the motion.

Upon application by defendants, respondent superior court then issued its writ restraining trial proceedings. Disagreeing with the trial court on both questions, respondent held: (1) section 647, subdivision (b), is unconstitutional on its face insofar as it prohibits soliciting an act of prostitution. The term "solicit" is too vague to provide fair notice of offending conduct, a requisite of due process under the federal and California Constitutions. However, the invalid solicitation provision is severable from the remainder of the statute, leaving intact the prohibition against engaging in an act of prostitution. (2) Section 647, subdivision (b), is also unconstitutional as applied by the Oakland Police Department. That department systematically discriminates against women in enforcing the statute, denying them equal protection of the law. The municipal court's contrary conclusion is not supported by the record.

Like the municipal court, and unlike respondent superior court, we find the challenged statute to be constitutional both on its face and as applied. Accordingly, we grant the People's petition for a peremptory writ of prohibition.

<small>VAGUENESS</small>

The solicitation provision of section 647, subdivision (b), is not so vague as to deny an accused due process of law under the federal or California Constitutions.

The federal due process standard was recently restated in Rose v. Locke (1975) 423 U.S. 48 [46 L.Ed.2d 185, 96 S.Ct. 243]. Rejecting the contention that a statute prohibiting a "crime against nature" was unconstitutionally vague, the high court observed: "It is settled that the fair-warning requirement embodied in the Due Process Clause prohibits the States from holding an individual 'criminally responsible for conduct which he could not reasonably understand to be proscribed.' But this prohibition against excessive vagueness does not invalidate every statute which a reviewing court believes could have been drafted with greater precision. Many statutes will have some inherent vagueness for '[i]n most English words and phrases there lurk uncertainties.' Even trained lawyers may find it necessary to consult legal dictionaries, treatises, and judicial opinions before they may say with any certainty what some statutes may compel or forbid. All the Due Process Clause requires is that the law give sufficient warning that men may conduct themselves so as to avoid that which is forbidden." (*Id.*, at pp. 49–50 [46 L.Ed.2d at p. 188], citations omitted.)

"* * *"

Similarly, under California law, " 'Reasonable certainty is all that is required. A statute will not be held void for uncertainty if any reasonable and practical construction can be given its language.' It will be upheld if its terms may be made reasonably certain by reference to other definable sources." [citations omitted.]

"Solicit" was defined in a related context—soliciting for a prostitute, i.e., pimping (Pen.Code, § 266h)—in People v. Phillips (1945) 70 Cal.App.2d 449 [160 P.2d 872]. " 'To tempt (a person); to lure on, esp. into evil, * * * to bring about, forth, on, etc., by gentle or natural operations; to seek to induce or elicit; * * * ['] (Webster's New International Dictionary (2d ed.) [.)] 'To appeal to (for something); to apply to for obtaining something; to ask earnestly; to ask for the purpose of receiving; to endeavor to obtain by asking or pleading; to entreat, implore, or importune; to make petition to; to plead for; to try to obtain. * * * While it does imply a serious request, it requires no particular degree of importunity, entreaty, imploration or supplication. * * *' (58 C.J. 804–805.)" (70 Cal.App.2d at p. 453.)

* * *

Amici are critical of a portion of the *Phillips* definition which this court deleted in quoting from that case in *Aetna*. The passage in question defines "solicit" as: " 'To tempt (a person); to lure on, esp. into evil, * * * to bring about, forth, on, etc., by gentle or natural operations; to seek to induce or elicit; * * * [']" (People v. Phillips, supra, 70 Cal.App.2d at p. 453.) If merely "tempting" a person to engage in an act of prostitution constitutes solicitation within the meaning of section 647, subdivision (b), then, amici contend, one could be convicted for "waving to a passing vehicle, nodding to a passing stranger, or standing on a street corner in a miniskirt."

We agree that such conduct, per se, should not be deemed a violation of the statute. However, there is no evidence in this record that anyone has been arrested for, much less convicted of, soliciting an act of prostitution on the basis of such ambiguous conduct. To the contrary, the evidence indicates that persons arrested for this crime not only make their entreaties verbally, but, assuming one is familiar with their jargon, express themselves in language of brutal clarity.

Although most solicitations are verbal, we are not prepared to accept amici's suggestion that the concept be limited, for the purposes of this statute, to "verbal offers." If we so held, well-advised prostitutes would immediately enroll in sign language courses. Nor are we willing to accept another of amici's suggestions—that solicitations be limited to offers specifying both price and services. There is a significant difference between avoiding the prohibited and evading the prohibition. The statute now satisfies due process by giving the innocent sufficient warning of that which is prohibited that they may avoid it. The "clarifications" sought by amici would simply give the guilty means of evading the prohibition.

"The root of the vagueness doctrine is a rough idea of fairness. It is not a principle designed to convert into a constitutional dilemma the practical difficulties in drawing criminal statutes both general enough to take into account a variety of human conduct and sufficiently specific to provide fair warning that certain kinds of conduct are prohibited." (Colten v. Kentucky

(1972) 407 U.S. 104, 110 [32 L.Ed.2d 584, 590, 92 S.Ct. 1953].) The challenged statute, insofar as it prohibits soliciting an act of prostitution, satisfies this standard.

DISCRIMINATORY ENFORCEMENT

The Oakland Police Department, in enforcing section 647, subdivision (b), does not deliberately discriminate against women and thereby deny them equal protection of the law.

The Fourteenth Amendment to the United States Constitution and article I, section 7, subdivision (a), of the California Constitution prohibit all state action denying any person "equal protection of the laws."

In Murgia v. Municipal Court (1975) 15 Cal.3d 286, 124 Cal.Rptr. 204, 540 P.2d 44, this court pointed out that although the great bulk of litigation under these constitutional provisions has recently focused upon the propriety of classifications in statutory enactments, this contemporary emphasis on the application of the equal protection doctrine to legislation should not obscure the fact that from the very inception of the Fourteenth Amendment, courts have recognized that the equal protection clause safeguards individuals from invidiously discriminatory acts of all branches of government, including the executive. We noted that as early as 1886, in Yick Wo v. Hopkins (1886) 118 U.S. 356, 6 S.Ct. 1064, 30 L.Ed. 220, the United States Supreme Court had applied the principles of the equal protection clause to the discriminatory enforcement of a San Francisco ordinance by administrative or executive officials. We rejected the People's contention that the rationale of *Yick Wo* did not extend to the enforcement of penal statutes. We held that a criminal defendant may object to the maintenance of a prosecution on the ground of deliberate invidious discrimination in the enforcement of the law and we further held that the objection should be raised, as it has been here, in a pretrial motion to dismiss. (Murgia v. Municipal Court, supra, 15 Cal.3d at pp. 293–301, 124 Cal.Rptr. 204, 540 P.2d 44.) We did not in *Murgia* have occasion to consider all of the classifications that may be arbitrary for the purposes of a discriminatory enforcement claim, but it is clear that in California sex is such a classification (see Sail'er Inn, Inc. v. Kirby (1971) 5 Cal.3d 1, 20, 95 Cal.Rptr. 329, 485 P.2d 529), and we do not understand the People to contend otherwise.

Like the ordinance in *Yick Wo,* the statute challenged here is "fair on its face and impartial in appearance." (Yick Wo v. Hopkins, supra, 118 U.S. at p. 373, 6 S.Ct. at p. 1073). Section 647, subdivision (b), by its terms applies to "*Every person* * * * [w]ho solicits or who engages in any act of prostitution." (Italics added.) The statute is clearly designed to punish specific acts without reference to the sex of the perpetrator. (Leffel v. Municipal Court (1976) 54 Cal.App.3d 569, 575, 126 Cal.Rptr. 773.) However, equal protection of the law may be denied by a statute fair on its face and impartial in appearance if it is applied "with an evil eye and an unequal hand." (Yick Wo v. Hopkins, supra, 118 U.S. at pp. 373–374, 6 S.Ct. at p. 1073; see Murgia v. Municipal Court, supra, 15 Cal.3d at p. 295, 124 Cal.Rptr. 204, 540 P.2d 44.) Defendants contend that the Oakland Police Department so applies this statute.

Because of the presumption that official duty has been properly, hence constitutionally, performed (Evid.Code, § 664), the defendant has the burden of proof in establishing the defense of discriminatory enforcement of the law.

(Murgia v. Municipal Court, supra, 15 Cal.3d at p. 305, 124 Cal.Rptr. 204, 540 P.2d 44; People v. Sperl (1976) 54 Cal.App.3d 640, 657, 126 Cal.Rptr. 907; People v. Gray (1967) 254 Cal.App.2d 256, 265, 63 Cal.Rptr. 211.)

The elements of the defense of discriminatory enforcement were set forth in Murgia v. Municipal Court, supra. To establish the defense, the defendant must prove: (1) "that he has been deliberately singled out for prosecution on the basis of some invidious criterion;" and (2) that "the prosecution would not have been pursued except for the discriminatory design of the prosecuting authorities." (15 Cal.3d at p. 298, 124 Cal.Rptr. 204, 540 P.2d 44.)

Defendants allege that the Oakland Police Department engages in the following practices which, defendants contend, manifest a policy of deliberate discrimination against women in enforcing section 647, subdivision (b).

1. More men than women are employed as "decoys" for solicitation of acts of prostitution with the result that more female prostitutes than male customers are arrested for that crime.

2. In "trick" cases, the female prostitute, but not the male customer, is arrested even if his culpability is as great as, or greater than, hers.[4]

3. If the man is arrested in a trick case, he is merely cited, i.e., released with a written notice to appear in court, whereas the woman is subjected to custodial arrest.

4. Female prostitutes are quarantined when arrested whereas their male customers are not so restrained.

Decoy Cases

The record establishes that the Oakland Police Department does employ more men than women as decoys for solicitation of acts of prostitution and that, as a result of this practice, the department does arrest more female prostitutes than male customers for this crime.[5] The critical question is whether the department adopted this practice—employing more men than women as decoys—with intent to discriminate against women. After a thorough evidentiary hearing into this matter of fact, the municipal court found that the practice was not adopted with such intent. It found, instead, that the practice is a consequence of the department's sexually unbiased policy of concentrating its enforcement effort on the "profiteer," rather than the customer of commercial vice. This dispositive finding of fact is amply supported by substantial evidence. Therefore, under settled principles of review, neither the superior court nor this court may reweigh the evidence in order to come to the contrary conclusion.

The subdivision of the Oakland Police Department having special responsibility for the enforcement of section 647, subdivision (b), is the vice control unit; this unit is also responsible for combatting illegal narcotics and gambling. For the purposes of this discussion, each of these criminal subcultures—prostitution, narcotics and gambling—may be thought of as pyramidal

---

4. "Trick" may refer to either the act of prostitution or the customer. Trick cases are to be distinguished from decoy cases. In decoy cases, one of the parties to a solicitation, either the apparent prostitute or the apparent customer, is an undercover vice officer. In trick cases, neither party is an undercover vice officer.

5. In 1973 and 1974, 1,160 women were arrested by means of male decoys and 57 men were arrested by means of female decoys.

in structure. In narcotics, for example, the base of the pyramid is formed by users of illicit narcotics. The remainder of the structure is composed of providers of the contraband. The providers, from the major distributor at the apex of the triangle to the street dealer, are "profiteers" in the parlance of the vice control unit, i.e., they profit financially from the illicit commerce. An analogous structure can be perceived in prostitution. The customer forms the base of the triangle; the prostitute, male or female, constitutes the largest class of profiteers; and at the apex are the pimp, the panderer, and the bar, restaurant, hotel and motel proprietors who knowingly derive profit from the vicious trade.

In order to most efficiently utilize its limited resources, the vice control unit concentrates on the profiteers in each vice with special emphasis on those at the apex of the illicit commerce. It is a matter of common knowledge of which we may take judicial notice that most law enforcement agencies— federal, state and local—endorse this approach with respect to narcotics. Although both parties to an illicit narcotics transaction break the law, as do both parties to an act of prostitution, no one seriously suggests that it is inappropriate for a law enforcement agency to concentrate on the profiteer and to carry out this policy by, among other things, using its undercover officers as decoys to arrest sellers rather than buyers. The record supports the municipal court's conclusion that the Oakland Police Department adopted a profiteer-oriented approach to prostitution in good faith and not as a smokescreen for deliberate discrimination against women.

In terms of personnel hours expended, 60 percent of the time allotted to prostitution is devoted to investigating pimps, panderers, and bar, restaurant, motel and hotel proprietors. Prostitutes, male and female, receive 30 percent of the unit's attention and customers are the subject of the remaining 10 percent. Because 95 percent of the pimps, etc., are male, as are 10 percent of the prostitutes and all of the customers, it is clear that the vice control unit devotes at least half of its resources to prosecuting men.

It is by no means certain that employing more male than female under- cover officers as decoys for solicitation is the most efficient use of this limited resource in fighting prostitution. However, on the available evidence, the Oakland Police Department could in good faith come to this conclusion. Prostitutes, the municipal court found, average five customers per night; thc average customer does not patronize prostitutes five times a year. Because of an effective grapevine, arrest of one prostitute by an undercover officer will deter others, at least for a time. Customers, on the other hand, are usually unknown to one another. Therefore, in the absence of widespread publicity, arrest of one customer will not deter others. Finally, using female decoys is twice as "expensive" as using males because an additional officer is required under current practice to ensure the female's safety.

Even assuming arguendo that using more male than female decoys is a manifestation of a policy of deliberate discrimination against women, defen- dants have not established the other element of a discriminatory enforcement defense—that they would not have been arrested but for this policy. To the contrary, substantial evidence supports the municipal court's conclusion that "[t]he Oakland Police Department made arrests for violations of section 647 [subdivision] (b) Penal Code based upon probable cause to believe the arrestee has committed the offense and not on the basis of the sex of the arrestee."

TRICK CASES

In trick cases, defendants allege, the Oakland Police Department arrests the woman, but not the man, even if his culpability is as great as or greater than, hers.

In support of this allegation, defendants introduced evidence of six trick cases in which the woman was arrested for solicitation while the man was set free. In rebuttal, the People introduced evidence of four trick cases in which the man was arrested.[8] Having judged the credibility of the witnesses, resolved any conflicts in their testimony, weighed the evidence and drawn factual conclusions, the municipal court found there was "absolutely no [sexual] discrimination whatsoever." As to one of defendants' six cases, the court did find there was probable cause to arrest the man as well as the woman. However, the court found that failure to arrest the man in this case was not a manifestation of a policy of deliberate discrimination against women. To the contrary, as has been stated, the court found that "[t]he Oakland Police Department made arrests for violations of section 647 [subdivision] (b) Penal Code based upon probable cause to believe the arrestee has committed the offense and not on the basis of the sex of the arrestee." Having carefully reviewed the record, we conclude that ample evidence supports this conclusion.

ARREST PROCEDURES

Prior to 29 March 1975, the customary practice of the Oakland Police Department was to custodially arrest the prostitute—male and female alike— and cite the customer, i.e., release him with a written notice to appear in court pursuant to section 853.6 of the Penal Code. Since 29 March 1975, all prostitution arrests have been custodial.[9]

The municipal court concluded that the previous practice was not a manifestation of a policy of deliberate discrimination against women. The most obvious ground for this conclusion is that male and female prostitutes were treated alike in this regard. However, the court also based its conclusion on a finding that prostitutes, unlike their customers, did not ordinarily satisfy the standards for release pursuant to section 853.6. This finding is amply supported by the evidence. The criteria for releasing a misdemeanor arrestee pursuant to section 853.6 are set forth in subdivisions (i) and (j) of that section. Under subdivision (j), if he does not cite and release the arrestee, the officer is to indicate, on a form provided for that purpose, the reason or reasons for maintaining custody. The standard reasons include: "The person could not provide satisfactory evidence of personal identification." (Id.) Under subdivision (i), if a misdemeanor arrestee is not released prior to booking, a "background" investigation is then to be conducted into his eligibility for release. The pertinent information includes "name, address, length of residence at that address, length of residence within this state,

---

8. In two of the four cases, both the man and the woman were arrested for engaging in an act of prostitution. In the remaining two cases, the man was arrested for soliciting an act of prostitution while the woman was set free.

9. This change in practice was, apparently, in response to a court order in another case.

marital and family status, employment, length of that employment, prior arrest record." (Id.) Between 26 February 1975 and 23 April 1975, 109 female prostitutes were arrested. Of the 109, 20 had no identification or refused to identify themselves, 13 had aliases or suspect identification, 29 had no permanent address, 30 were not permanent residents of the area, 34 had no relatives in the area, 74 were not regularly employed, and 50 had prior arrests or convictions for prostitution. During the same period, 24 male customers were arrested. Of the 24, all had reliable identification, only one had no permanent address, only two were not permanent residents of the area, only two had no relatives in the area, all were regularly employed, and only one had a prior criminal history indicating that he was a poor citation risk.

QUARANTINE

In the ordinary course of events, when weekends and holidays did not intervene, a female prostitute was tested for gonorrhea and syphilis the morning after her arrest. The result of the gonorrhea test was available the following morning. If the test was negative, she was released from quarantine. If the test was positive, she was given penicillin and then released from quarantine. In either case she was encouraged to return voluntarily to a clinic in a few days to obtain the result of the syphilis test. The procedure was the same for a male prostitute except that he was released from quarantine earlier because the test for gonorrhea in the male yields results more quickly. Customers were not quarantined. The quarantine procedure was discontinued on 21 April 1975 because of a significant decline in the gonorrhea infectivity rate among female prostitutes and because voluntary programs had become the preferred alternative among California public health officials.

The municipal court concluded that the previous practice—quarantining prostitutes while not so restraining their customers—was not a manifestation of a policy of deliberate discrimination against women by the Oakland Police Department. This conclusion was based on a finding that female prostitutes were more likely than their male customers to communicate venereal diseases. This finding was amply supported by the following evidence: Whereas the venereal disease rate for the general population was 4 percent, the infectivity rate among quarantined female prostitutes was 22 percent for gonorrhea alone. A female prostitute has a greater number of sexual contacts than does her male customer. Because females are more likely to be asymptomatic for gonorrhea, they are less likely to seek treatment for it.

However, the most obvious ground for the trial court's conclusion that the quarantine procedure was not a manifestation of a policy of deliberate discrimination against women is, again, that male and female prostitutes were, essentially, treated alike under the program. The distinction was not between male and female, but between prostitute and customer.

Finally, the quarantine procedure was the responsibility—not of the police or of the prosecutor—but of the public health officials. (See Health & Saf.Code, § 3195.) Therefore, its relevance to a claim of deliberate discrimination on the part of the police is highly questionable.

Let the peremptory writ of prohibition issue as prayed.

Mosk, J., Richardson, J., and Sullivan, J., concurred.

Tobriner, Acting C.J.

I dissent. Despite the clear language of Penal Code section 647, subdivision (b), prohibiting the solicitation of acts of prostitution by both men and women, customers and prostitutes, the majority today holds that the Oakland police may effectively ignore a sex-neutral statutory mandate by directing its enforcement effort primarily against women. The deliberate failure to enforce the law against male customers cuts the intended coverage of section 647, subdivision (b) in half. In my view, the superior court properly found that the challenged enforcement policy constitutes invidious sex-based discrimination in violation of the equal protection guarantees of the United States and California Constitutions.

* * *

In the instant case, defendants presented a wealth of statistical evidence which established beyond question that the procedures employed by the Oakland police in enforcing the prostitution solicitation law have resulted in the arrest of a significantly disproportionate number of women, as compared to men. Indeed, the police do not deny that by consciously choosing to employ primarily male decoys, they virtually assured that most of the law violators apprehended would be women, not men. The superior court concluded that this practice constituted invidious, constitutionally proscribed discrimination.

The majority argue, however, that the real parties have failed to demonstrate that the challenged police enforcement policies were motivated by "an intent to discriminate against women." According to the majority, the disparate treatment of the sexes is simply "a consequence of the department's sexually unbiased policy of concentrating its enforcement effort on the 'profiteer' rather than the customer of commercial vice." (Ante, p. 349.)

In reaching this conclusion, I believe that the majority err in two respects. First, the majority mistakenly equate concentration of law enforcement efforts on sellers of illegal narcotics with the similar focus of enforcement procedures on the "profiteer" in prostitution transactions. In the case of narcotics transactions the Legislature itself has drawn a distinction between buyers and sellers, and has endorsed the policy of concentrating police resources on the apprehension of sellers. (See Health & Saf.Code, §§ 11350 (possession); 11351 (possession for sale); and 11352 (sale).)

But the Legislature specifically refused to draw such a distinction between prostitutes and their customers in defining the offense of solicitation. * * *

Despite the clear legislative mandate to arrest and prosecute customers as well as prostitutes, the Oakland police have adopted an enforcement policy that directly contravenes the judgment of the Legislature. Although the police unquestionably may exercise discretion in the allocation of scarce resources, such discretion is not so unbridled as to permit the police to carve out invidious exceptions to a statutory prohibition, exceptions which the Legislature has specifically declined to enact. * * *

In addition to drawing an inappropriate analogy to the enforcement of drug laws, the majority err in accepting at face value the People's contention that the challenged "profiteer-oriented" enforcement policy bears no relation to traditional sex-based stereotypes but instead simply represents the most efficient means of reducing the incidence of prostitution. (Cf. Castaneda v. Partida (1977) 430 U.S. 482, 492, 97 S.Ct. 1272, 51 L.Ed.2d 498.) Several centuries of law enforcement history belie any claim that a "profiteer"–directed enforcement program is an effective means of eliminating prostitution, and the record in the instant case demonstrates quite unmistakenly that the arrest of male customers in addition to female prostitutes is a singularly more effective law enforcement strategy than the approach traditionally employed by the police.

From February 26, 1975, through April 22, 1975, the Oakland police were compelled by order of the Alameda County Superior Court to employ female decoys and to arrest male customers guilty of section 647, subdivision (b) violations. (Riemer v. Jensen, No. 455371–9.) During this brief period of even-handed enforcement, the arrest of male customers coupled with newspaper publicity surrounding the sex-neutral police procedures, resulted, according to the testimony of the senior vice squad officer, in a "devastating" reduction in observed levels of prostitution related offenses. Similar results have been achieved in other jurisdictions in which enforcement efforts have been directed at male customers as well as female prostitutes. (See, e.g., United States v. Moses (D.C.App.1975) 339 A.2d 46; Kanowitz, Women and the Law (1969) p. 17. See generally Jennings, The Victim as Criminal: A Consideration of California's Prostitution Law (1976) 64 Cal.L.Rev. 1235.)

In light of the demonstrated success of an enforcement policy which encompasses both customers and prostitutes, I cannot accept the suggestion that the police department's resumption of its traditional enforcement policy, directed primarily at women, is explicable by reference to legitimate law enforcement objectives. Although the majority discern no discriminatory intent in the action of the Oakland police, I agree with the American Bar Association's section of Individual Rights and Responsibilities which has characterized such police practices as "one of the most direct forms of discrimination against women in this country today. In accordance with society's double standard of sexual morality, the woman who sells her body is punished criminally and stigmatized socially while her male customer * * * is left unscathed." (ABA Section of Individual Rights and Responsibilities, Rep. to House of Delegates, Rep. No. 101B, p. 1 (1974).)

More than a half century ago, a New York court observed: "The men create the market, and the women who supply the demand pay the penalty. It is time this unfair discrimination and injustice should cease." (People v. Edwards (N.Y.Co.Ct.1920) 180 N.Y.S. 631, 634–635). Hopefully, it will not be yet another half century before this discriminatory practice is eliminated.

I would deny the requested writ.

WRIGHT, J., concurred.

Notes on Plas *and* Hartway

1. Did *Plas* reach the right result as a matter of constitutional analysis? Was the Alaska court applying the state or federal constitution? Does extension of prostitution laws to men exhaust the possibilities for reform in this area? Who are the patrons of male prostitutes?

2. Did *Hartway* reach the right result as a matter of constitutional analysis? Did the California Supreme Court do more than pay lip service to the strict scrutiny standard imposed under the California state constitution in sex discrimination cases? Or does Justice Clark believe that no sex discrimination has occurred?

3. The court order referred to in footnote 9 of the *Hartway* opinion was a preliminary injunction issued in Reimer v. Jensen, No. 455371–9 (Superior Court of California, Alameda County, April 1, 1975), a taxpayers' suit brought to prevent named county officials and agencies, including the Oakland Police Department, from spending public funds for the enforcement of Penal Code § 647(b) in a discriminatory manner. One immediate effect of Judge Avakian's order in *Reimer* was the departure of many of Oakland's prostitutes to the sea-side community of Monterey, much to the discomfiture of local officials. In response, the Monterey police department announced that it, too, would arrest the male clients along with the prostitutes. San Francisco Chronicle, March 4, 1975, at 3, col. 1. Does this suggest that non-discriminatory enforcement of the prostitution laws is also the most effective means of enforcement?

4. Do prostitutes enjoy a right to privacy? Or, if they are arrested for public solicitation rather than for the performance of a sexual act for money in private, does their potential privacy claim disappear? It has been argued that this distinction is inadequate:

> Defendants in these cases, however, did not claim any constitutionally protected right to solicit in public; rather, they claimed that the right of privacy encompassed an individual's decision to engage in private, consensual, commercial sexual activities. Had these courts recognized that argument, it would have been necessary for them to consider whether defendants were soliciting for an act that the state could validly criminalize. Following the reasoning of these courts, however, no defendant charged with soliciting for prostitution would be able to raise a right of privacy challenge. Yet, the validity of a defendant's solicitation charge is dependent on the constitutionality of the state's criminalization of the acts solicited. Quite obviously, a state may prohibit solicitation of a crime. A state may also place an absolute ban on advertisement of illegal products or services. Either precept would allow a state to prohibit solicitation for prostitution if the underlying prohibition of prostitution were constitutional. If, however, criminalization of commercial sex is not constitutionally valid, then the state may ban solicitation only as a reasonable time, place, and manner regulation of public advertising.

Note, Right of Privacy Challenges to Prostitution Statutes, 58 Wash.U.L.Q. 439, 465–66 (1980). Does the right to privacy encompass the decision of an adult to engage in private, consensual, sexual activity outside of marriage? Does Bowers v. Hardwick, 478 U.S. 186, 106 S.Ct. 2841, 92 L.Ed.2d 140 (1986), set out at p. 371, supra, resolve this question? For both homosexuals and heterosexuals? See The Supreme Court, 1985 Term, 100 Harv.L.Rev. 1, 210–220 (1986).

5. If one wanted to reform the prostitution laws, what approach should be followed? Decriminalization? Licensing? Zoning of prostitutes into "red light" districts? These and other alternatives are considered in light of an investigation of how, if at all, prostitution harms society (with special emphasis on Boston) by Barbara Milman. She concludes:

It would be premature at this point to recommend detailed laws for the control of prostitution. Circumstances may vary greatly from city to city, and some experimentation with different forms of regulation seems desirable. It may be that what works best in one city will be entirely inappropriate for another. Yet even if details of better prostitution laws must wait to be developed, some promising directions for change can be identified. From the point of view of this author, initial changes in prostitution laws should include:

(1) Decriminalization of private, adult prostitution;

(2) Regulation, by geographical zoning and licensing of business premises, of public places where solicitation for prostitution would be permitted;

(3) Regulation, by geographical zoning and licensing of premises, of houses of prostitution;

(4) Regulation, by general zoning, public nuisance and disturbing the peace statutes, of prostitution either within or without areas zoned for public solicitation;

(5) Modification of existing laws against pimping and living off the earnings of a prostitute to permit legitimate business arrangements relating to prostitution;

(6) Modification of existing laws against living off the earnings of a prostitute to permit prostitutes freely to choose relationships with members of the opposite sex;

(7) Modification of existing criminal laws to permit adults to patronize or solicit prostitutes wherever prostitution or solicitation is permitted;

(8) Modification of existing criminal laws to provide equal criminal penalties for prostitutes and customers who solicit or engage in acts of prostitution in areas or premises where prostitution is prohibited;

(9) Modification of existing laws to permit solicitation for prostitution through newspaper and magazine advertisements;

(10) Retention of present criminal laws against enticing, aiding or encouraging minors to engage in prostitution, or forcing adults or minors to become or remain prostitutes;

(11) Development of medical services designed primarily for prostitutes to diagnose and treat, and to provide education about venereal disease.

Milman, New Rules for the Oldest Profession: Should We Change Our Prostitution Laws?, 3 Harv.Wom.L.J. 1, 63–64 (1980). Professor Margaret Jane Radin, on the other hand, concludes after an intensive analysis of nonsalability, a species of inalienability that she calls "market-inalienability," that prostitution should be governed by a regime of incomplete commodification. Radin, Market–Inalienability, 100 Harv.L.Rev. 1849, 1921 (1987). She explains:

The issue thus becomes how to structure an incomplete commodification that takes account of our nonideal world, yet does not foreclose progress to a better world of more equal power (and less susceptibility to the domino effect of market rhetoric). I think we should now decriminalize the sale of sexual services in order to protect poor women from the degradation and danger either of the black market or of other occupations that seem to them less desirable. At the same time, in order to check the domino effect, we should prohibit the capitalist entrepreneurship that would operate to create an organized market in sexual services even though this step would pose enforcement difficulties. It would include, for example, banning brokerage (pimping) and recruitment. It might also include banning advertising. Trying to keep commodification of sexuality out of our discourse by banning advertising does have the double bind effect of failing to legitimate the sales we allow, and hence it may fail to alleviate significantly the social disapproval suffered by those who sell sexual services. It also adds "information costs" to their "product," and thus fails to yield them as great a "return" as would the full-blown market. But these nonideal effects must be borne if we really accept that extensive permeation of our discourse by commodification-talk would alter sexuality in a way that we are unwilling to countenance.

Id., at 1924–25 (footnotes omitted). How do you compare these approaches to prostitution? See also Jennings, The Victim as Criminal: A Consideration of California's Prostitution Law, 64 Calif.L.Rev. 1235 (1976). See also Note, Men Who Own Women: A Thirteenth Amendment Critique of Forced Prostitution, 103 Yale L.J. 791 (1993).

D. WOMEN AS OFFICERS IN THE CRIMINAL JUSTICE SYSTEM

JOHNSON v. PHELAN

United States Court of Appeals, Seventh Circuit, 1995.
69 F.3d 144.

EASTERBROOK, CIRCUIT JUDGE.

Albert Johnson brought this suit under 42 U.S.C. § 1983. According to his complaint, which the district court dismissed for failure to state a claim on which relief may be granted, female guards at the Cook County Jail are assigned to monitor male prisoners' movements and can see men naked in their cells, the shower, and the toilet. Johnson sought damages * * *. The district court * * * properly rejected Johnson's argument that different monitoring patterns in different cellblocks within the Jail violate the equal protection clause of the fourteenth amendment. Johnson has abandoned on appeal any contention that monitoring in the local courthouse lockup's bathroom violates the Constitution. But his argument that cross-sex monitoring in the Jail violates the due process clause requires additional discussion in light of Canedy v. Boardman, 16 F.3d 183 (7th Cir.1994), which holds that a right of privacy limits the ability of wardens to subject men to body searches by women, or the reverse. Our case involves visual rather than tactile inspections, and we must decide whether male prisoners are entitled to prevent female guards from watching them while undressed.

Observation is a form of search, and the initial question therefore is whether monitoring is "unreasonable" under the fourth amendment. So the

Supreme Court conceived the issue in Bell v. Wolfish, 441 U.S. 520, 60 L.Ed.2d 447, 99 S.Ct. 1861 (1979), where a pretrial detainee argued that routine inspections of his body cavities violated the Constitution. * * * The Court held that these searches are "reasonable" because they are prudent precautions against smuggling drugs and other contraband into prison. 441 U.S. at 558–60. Prisoners argued that metal detectors plus supervision of inmates' contacts with outsiders would be superior to body-cavity inspections. The Court replied that prisons need not adopt the best alternatives. * * *

Wolfish assumed without deciding that prisoners retain some right of privacy under the fourth amendment. Five years later the Court held that they do not. Hudson v. Palmer, 468 U.S. 517, 526–30, 82 L.Ed.2d 393, 104 S.Ct. 3194 (1984), observes that privacy is the thing most surely extinguished by a judgment committing someone to prison. Guards take control of where and how prisoners live; they do not retain any right of seclusion or secrecy against their captors, who are entitled to watch and regulate every detail of daily life. After *Wolfish* and *Hudson* monitoring of naked prisoners is not only permissible—wardens are entitled to take precautions against drugs and weapons (which can be passed through the alimentary canal or hidden in the rectal cavity and collected from a toilet bowl)—but also sometimes mandatory. Inter-prisoner violence is endemic, so constant vigilance without regard to the state of the prisoners' dress is essential. Vigilance over showers, vigilance over cells—vigilance everywhere, which means that guards gaze upon naked inmates.

Johnson mentions the fourth amendment but ignores *Wolfish* and *Hudson*. His principal argument uses the due process clause * * *. Under the due process clause the question is whether the regulation is "reasonably related to legitimate penological interests." Turner v. Safley, 482 U.S. 78, 89, 96 L.Ed.2d 64, 107 S.Ct. 2254 (1987). Surveillance of prisoners is essential, as *Wolfish* establishes. Observation of cells, showers, and toilets is less intrusive than the body-cavity inspections *Wolfish* held permissible. Guards do the surveillance. Male guards and female guards too—for Title VII of the Civil Rights Act of 1964 opens prisons to women and requires states to hire them unless sex is a bona fide occupational qualification, a high standard of necessity. Dothard v. Rawlinson, 433 U.S. 321, 53 L.Ed.2d 786, 97 S.Ct. 2720 (1977); United States v. Gregory, 818 F.2d 1114 (4th Cir.1987)(rejecting an argument that a desire to curtail cross-sex monitoring of naked prisoners makes sex a bona fide occupation qualification for prison guards); see also United Auto. Workers v. Johnson Controls, Inc., 499 U.S. 187, 113 L.Ed.2d 158, 111 S.Ct. 1196 (1991). Unless female guards are shuffled off to back office jobs, itself problematic under Title VII, they are bound to see the male prisoners in states of undress. Frequently. Deliberately. Otherwise they are not doing their jobs. Smith v. Fairman, 678 F.2d 52 (7th Cir.1982), puts two and two together, holding that in light of Title VII female guards are entitled to participate in the normal activities of guarding, including pat-down searches of male inmates. We held in Torres v. Wisconsin Department of Health & Social Services, 859 F.2d 1523 (7th Cir.1988)(en banc), a case filed by guards under Title VII, that a state could exclude men from one of its four prisons, in order to promote the female prisoners' rehabilitation. *Torres* did not say that the Constitution requires this exclusion; instead we deferred to the judgment of prison administrators that they needed to limit cross-sex monitoring to achieve penological objectives. Today deference leads to the opposite result: Cook County does not believe that cross-sex monitoring imperils its mission, and evenhanded willingness to accept prison administrators' decisions about debatable issues means that Johnson cannot prevail under the due process clause.

After holding in *Hudson* that prisoners lack any reasonable expectation of privacy under the fourth amendment, the Court remarked that a prisoner could use the eighth amendment to overcome "calculated harassment unrelated to prison needs." 468 U.S. at 530. Similarly, the Court observed in *Graham* that the eighth amendment offers some protection supplementary to the fourth. 490 U.S. at 392, 394. We therefore think it best to understand the references to "privacy" in *Canedy* and similar cases as invocations of the eighth amendment's ban on cruel and unusual punishments. See Jordan v. Gardner, 986 F.2d 1521 (9th Cir.1993)(en banc), which makes explicit the role of that provision.

Johnson's complaint (and the brief filed on his behalf in this court by a top-notch law firm) do not allege either particular susceptibility or any design to inflict psychological injury. A prisoner could say that he is especially shy—perhaps required by his religion to remain dressed in the presence of the opposite sex—and that the guards, knowing this, tormented him by assigning women to watch the toilets and showers. So, too, a prisoner has a remedy for deliberate harassment, on account of sex, by guards of either sex. Johnson does not allege this or anything like it. His case therefore does not present the sort of claim that *Hudson* holds in reserve. It does not satisfy the more general requirements of the eighth amendment either.

One who makes a claim under the cruel and unusual punishments clause must show that the state has created risk or inflicted pain pointlessly. "After incarceration, only the unnecessary and wanton infliction of pain * * * constitutes cruel and unusual punishment forbidden by the Eighth Amendment." Whitley v. Albers, 475 U.S. 312, 319, 89 L.Ed.2d 251, 106 S.Ct. 1078 (1986)(internal quotations omitted). See also Rhodes v. Chapman, 452 U.S. 337, 69 L.Ed.2d 59, 101 S.Ct. 2392 (1981); Wilson v. Seiter, 501 U.S. 294, 298–300, 115 L.Ed.2d 271, 111 S.Ct. 2321 (1991); Helling v. McKinney, 125 L.Ed.2d 22, 113 S.Ct. 2475 (1993). Does cross-sex monitoring serve a function beyond the infliction of pain? Monitoring is vital, but how about the cross-sex part? For this there are two justifications.

First, it makes good use of the staff. It is more expensive for a prison to have a group of guards dedicated to shower and toilet monitoring (equivalently, a group that can do every function except this) than to have guards all of whom can serve each role in the prison. If only men can monitor showers, then female guards are less useful to the prison; if female guards can't perform this task, the prison must have more guards on hand to cover for them. It is a form of featherbedding. O'Lone v. [Estate of Shabazz, 482 U.S. 342 (1987)] held that an interest in the efficient deployment of the staff permits the prison to block inmates from attending religious services, although religion has powerful protection in the first amendment. Similarly, an interest in efficient deployment of the staff supports cross-sex monitoring. See Timm v. Gunter, 917 F.2d 1093, 1102 (8th Cir.1990), which concludes that "opposite-sex surveillance of male inmates, performed on the same basis as same-sex surveillance," is constitutionally permissible. By the same token, the prison may assign homosexual male guards to monitor male prisoners, heterosexual male guards to monitor effeminate male homosexual prisoners, and so on. There are too many permutations to place guards and prisoners into multiple classes by sex, sexual orientation, and perhaps other criteria, allowing each group to be observed only by the corresponding groups that occasion the least unhappiness.

Second, cross-sex monitoring reduces the need for prisons to make sex a criterion of employment, and therefore reduces the potential for conflict with Title VII and the equal protection clause. Cells and showers are designed so that guards can see in, to prevent violence and other offenses. Prisoners dress, undress, and bathe under watchful eyes. Guards roaming the corridors are bound to see naked prisoners. A prison could comply with the rule Johnson proposes, and still maintain surveillance, only by relegating women to the administrative wing, limiting their duties (thereby raising the cost of the guard complement), or eliminating them from the staff.

To the riposte that Title VII and the equal protection clause can't authorize a violation of the eighth amendment, we rejoin: True enough, but not pertinent. A warden must accommodate conflicting interests—the embarrassment of reticent prisoners, the entitlement of women to equal treatment in the workplace. A state may reject the prisoner's claim if it has a reason, as *Wolfish* establishes for a substantially greater intrusion. The interest of women in equal treatment is a solid reason, with more secure footing in American law than prisoners' modesty, leading to the conclusion that there is no violation of the eighth amendment. * * * When interests clash, a judge must prefer those based on legislative decisions over those that reflect their own views of sound policy. The premise of judicial review is that the Constitution is an authoritative decision binding on all branches of government; when it has only such substance as judges pour into it themselves, the decisions of the elected branches prevail. *Canedy* accordingly avowed reluctance to do more than forbid cross-sex body searches, 16 F.3d at 187, which it conceived as pointless debasement. Anonymous visual inspections from afar are considerably less intrusive and carry less potential for "the unnecessary and wanton infliction of pain". To the extent incautious language in *Canedy* implies that deliberate visual inspections are indistinguishable from physical palpitations, its discussion is dictum. Further reflection leads us to conclude that it should not be converted to a holding.

How odd it would be to find in the eighth amendment a right not to be seen by the other sex. Physicians and nurses of one sex routinely examine the other. In exotic places such as California people regularly sit in saunas and hot tubs with unclothed strangers. Cf. Miller v. South Bend, 904 F.2d 1081 (7th Cir.1990)(en banc)(holding that there is a constitutional right to dance nude in public), reversed under the name Barnes v. Glen Theatre, Inc., 501 U.S. 560, 115 L.Ed.2d 504, 111 S.Ct. 2456 (1991). Most persons' aversion to public nudity pales compared with the taboo against detailed inspections of body cavities, yet the Court found no constitutional obstacle to these in *Wolfish*; the Constitution does not require prison managers to respect the social conventions of free society. Drug testing is common, although this often requires observation of urination. Vernonia School District 47J v. Acton, 132 L.Ed.2d 564, 115 S.Ct. 2386 (1995)(drug testing of seventh grade boy as condition of participation in sports is "reasonable" under the fourth amendment); see also Dimeo v. Griffin, 943 F.2d 679, 682–83 (7th Cir. 1991)(en banc), in which this court treated the imposition on privacy as slight. More to the point, the clash between modesty and equal employment opportunities has been played out in sports. Women reporters routinely enter locker rooms after games. How could an imposition that male athletes tolerate be deemed cruel and unusual punishment?

Some cases say that the Constitution forbids deliberate cross-sex monitoring (as opposed to infrequent or accidental sightings). See Cornwell v. Dahlberg, 963 F.2d 912, 916–17 (6th Cir.1992)(basing this conclusion on the fourth amendment, but without mentioning *Hudson*); Lee v. Downs, 641 F.2d 1117, 1120 (4th Cir.1981)(decided three years before *Hudson*). Decisions such as *Timm* and Grummett v. Rushen, 779 F.2d 491 (9th Cir.1985), * * * hold that cross-sex monitoring is constitutional * * *. Each emphasized that the female guards' views were not universally unobstructed. But if this is important (and we do not think it is), Johnson's own complaint brings the case within the scope of *Timm*. Johnson alleges that

> when a female correctional officer is assigned to work a dorm it is her duty and responsibility to make counts, also to constantly supervise all inmates in the dorms, making periodic, unannounced spot checks of inmates in their living area, and surveying in the remainder of the area such as the general toilet, and shower facilities, which is in an open unobstructed area, except by a thin sheet that can be seen through.

Thus Johnson tells us that the Jail offers some, but imperfect, shielding from guards' observation, exactly the situation that the eighth circuit held permissible in *Timm*. We agree with that conclusion. See also Jordan v. Gardner, 986 F.2d at 1545–67 (Wallace, Wiggins, Trott & Kleinfeld, JJ., dissenting).

Any practice allowed under the due process analysis of *Turner* is acceptable under the eighth amendment too—not only because the objective component of cruel and unusual punishment is more tolerant toward wardens, but also because the eighth amendment has a demanding mental state component. Farmer v. Brennan, 128 L.Ed.2d 811, 114 S.Ct. 1970 (1994), holds that the standard is criminal recklessness. The guard or warden must want to injure the prisoner or must know of and disregard a substantial risk that harm will befall the prisoner. Johnson does not allege that any of the defendants sought to humiliate him. * * *

Put the eighth amendment aside for a moment and consider the question whether a "deliberate" decision—that is, a considered choice with knowledge of the consequences—establishes "intent" for purposes of constitutional provisions containing a mental-state ingredient. That question has been before the Supreme Court many times, and the answer is "no." A good example is Personnel Administrator of Massachusetts v. Feeney, 442 U.S. 256, 60 L.Ed.2d 870, 99 S.Ct. 2282 (1979), apropos because it deals with sex discrimination. Massachusetts decided to give military veterans an absolute, lifetime preference in employment. Approximately 98 percent of veterans are male, and as a result the bureaucracy is overwhelmingly male. A three-judge district court held the preference unconstitutional. Recognizing that the equal protection clause forbids only disparate treatment, and not disparate impact, see Washington v. Davis, 426 U.S. 229, 48 L.Ed.2d 597, 96 S.Ct. 2040

(1976), the district court observed that people are deemed to intend the natural and probable consequences of their acts. Massachusetts adopted the preference deliberately, and it maintained the preference after recognizing that it excluded many qualified women from the civil service. The Supreme Court acknowledged all of this but held that deliberate acts, with knowledge of the consequences, do not establish "intent" in the constitutional sense—for, if they did, then the distinction between disparate treatment and disparate impact would collapse as soon as anyone informed the decisionmaker of the impact. After a canvass of its cases, the Court concluded:

> "Discriminatory purpose" * * * implies more than intent as volition or intent as awareness of consequences. It implies that the decisionmaker * * * selected or reaffirmed a particular course of action at least in part "because of," not merely "in spite of," its adverse effects upon an identifiable group.

442 U.S. at 279 (citation and footnotes omitted). Since *Feeney* the distinction between choices made "because" the decisionmaker wants to achieve particular consequences, and those "in spite of" unwelcome effects, has been a staple of constitutional law. See, e.g., Miller v. Johnson, 132 L.Ed.2d 762, 115 S.Ct. 2475, 2488 (1995).

Wardens make many choices that have unpleasant consequences for prisoners, and frequently wardens wish that they could do things differently. Budgetary shortfalls may dictate that prisoners live in cramped conditions, even though wardens know that penological purposes would be better served by additional space. The question whether a deliberate choice to put two prisoners in a cell with only 100 square feet of space satisfied the intent component of the eighth amendment came up in Wilson v. Seiter. Prisoners alleged that the dilapidated facility had "overcrowding, excessive noise, insufficient locker storage space, inadequate heating and cooling, improper ventilation, unclean and inadequate restrooms, unsanitary dining facilities and food preparation, and housing ith mentally and physically ill inmates." 501 U.S. at 296. The warden knew all about this, and official decisions led to the problems—for example, the state spent money on guards' salaries rather than better food facilities. The Court assumed that conditions at the prison fell below objectively permissible standards but held that the prisoners had not demonstrated the essential mental state.

* * *

Where does this leave us? The fourth amendment does not protect privacy interests within prisons. Moving to other amendments does not change the outcome. Cross-sex monitoring is not a senseless imposition. As a reconciliation of conflicting entitlements and desires, it satisfies the *Turner* standard. It cannot be called "inhumane" and therefore does not fall below the floor set by the objective component of the eighth amendment. And Johnson does not contend that his captors adopted their monitoring patterns because of, rather than in spite of, the embarrassment it causes some prisoners. He does not submit that the warden ignored his sensibilities; he argues only that they received too little weight in the felicific calculus. Like the district court, therefore, we conclude that the complaint fails to state a claim on which relief may be granted.

AFFIRMED

POSNER, CHIEF JUDGE, concurring and dissenting.

I agree with the district judge and my colleagues that Johnson's equal protection claim has no possible merit, that there is no possible basis for imputing liability to the president of the Cook County Board of Commissioners, and that the claims against the defendants in their official capacities must be dismissed as unauthorized suits against the State of Illinois. That is where my agreement ends.

The cruel and unusual punishments clause of the Eighth Amendment to the United States Constitution, like so much in the Bill of Rights, is a Rohrschach test. What the judge sees in it is the reflection of his or her own values, values shaped by personal experience and temperament as well as by historical reflection, public opinion, and other sources of moral judgment. No other theory of constitutional interpretation can explain the elaborate edifice of death-penalty jurisprudence that the Supreme Court has erected in the name of the Eighth Amendment. Or the interpretation of the amendment as a charter, however limited, of the rights of prisoners. The limitations imposed by the amendment might be thought, indeed were thought for more than 150 years after the amendment was adopted, to end with the sentence, leaving the management of prisons, the informal "punishment" meted out by brutal guards, constitutionally unregulated.

The critical values, in giving content to the Eighth Amendment, are those of the Justices of the Supreme Court. My colleagues believe that the Justices have spoken to the issue presented by this case. I think that they have not, and I shall try to show this. But I want first to lay out the essential background of facts and values on which I believe the judgment in this case must ultimately turn.

There are different ways to look upon the inmates of prisons and jails in the United States in 1995. One way is to look upon them as members of a different species, indeed as a type of vermin, devoid of human dignity and entitled to no respect; and then no issue concerning the degrading or brutalizing treatment of prisoners would arise. In particular there would be no inhibitions about using prisoners as the subject of experiments, including social experiments such as the experiment of seeing whether the sexes can be made interchangeable. The parading of naked male inmates in front of female guards, or of naked female inmates in front of male guards, would be no more problematic than "cross-sex surveillance" in a kennel.

I do not myself consider the 1.5 million inmates of American prisons and jails in that light. This is a nonnegligible fraction of the American population. And it is only the current inmate population. The fraction of the total population that has spent time in a prison or jail is larger, although I do not know how large. A substantial number of these prison and jail inmates, including the plaintiff in this case, have not been convicted of a crime. They are merely charged with crime, and awaiting trial. Some of them may actually be innocent. Of the guilty, many are guilty of sumptuary offenses, or of other victimless crimes uncannily similar to lawful activity (gambling offenses are an example), or of esoteric financial and regulatory offenses (such as violation of the migratory game laws) some of which do not even require a guilty intent. It is wrong to break even foolish laws, or wise laws that should carry only civil penalties. It is wrongful to break the law even when the lawbreaker is flawed, weak, retarded, unstable, ignorant, brutalized, or profoundly disadvantaged, rather than violent, vicious, or evil to the core. But we should have a realistic conception of the composition of the prison and jail population before deciding that they are a scum entitled to nothing better than what a vengeful populace and a resource-starved penal system choose to give them. We must not exaggerate the distance between "us," the lawful ones, the respectable ones, and the prison and jail population; for such exaggeration will make it too easy for us to deny that population the rudiments of humane consideration.

The nudity taboo retains great strength in the United States. It should not be confused with prudery. It is a taboo against being seen in the nude by strangers, not by one's intimates. Ours is a morally diverse populace and the nudity taboo is not of uniform strength across it. It is strongest among professing Christians, because of the historical antipathy of the Church to nudity; and as it happens the plaintiff alleges that his right "to practice Christian modesty is being violated." The taboo is particularly strong when the stranger belongs to the opposite sex. There are radical feminists who regard "sex" as a social construction and the very concept of "the opposite sex," implying as it does the dichotomization of the "sexes" (the "genders," as we are being taught to say), as a sign of patriarchy. For these feminists the surveillance of naked male prisoners by female guards and naked female prisoners by male guards are way stations on the road to sexual equality. If prisoners have no rights, the reconceptualization of the prison as a site of progressive social engineering should give us no qualms. Animals have no right to wear clothing. Why prisoners, if they are no better than animals? There is no answer, if the premise is accepted. But it should be rejected, and if it is rejected, and the duty of a society that would like to think of itself as civilized to treat its prisoners humanely therefore acknowledged, then I think that the interest of a prisoner in being free from unnecessary cross-sex surveillance has priority over the unisex-bathroom movement and requires us to reverse the judgment of the district court throwing out this lawsuit.

I have been painting in broad strokes, and it is time to consider the particulars of this case and the state of the precedents. Albert Johnson, a pretrial detainee in the Cook County Jail, complains that female guards were allowed to watch his naked body while he showered and used the toilet. All we have is the complaint, which my colleagues want to dismiss without giving Johnson a chance to develop the facts. The main issue raised by the appeal is whether a prisoner has an interest that the Constitution protects in hiding his naked body from guards of the opposite sex. A subordinate issue is whether, if so, the complaint—which Johnson drafted without assistance of counsel—sufficiently alleges deliberate as distinct from merely accidental exposure to survive dismissal.

The parties have confused the first issue by describing it as the extent of a prisoner's "right of privacy." They cannot be criticized too harshly for this. Countless cases, including our own Canedy v. Boardman, 16 F.3d 183 (7th Cir.1994), have done the same thing. E.g., Cornwell v. Dahlberg, 963 F.2d 912, 916–17 (6th Cir.1992); Cookish v. Powell, 945 F.2d 441, 446 (1st Cir.1991)(per curiam); Cumbey v. Meachum, 684 F.2d 712 (10th Cir. 1982)(per curiam). The problem is that the term "right of privacy" bears meanings in law that are remote from its primary ordinary-language meaning, which happens to be the meaning that a suit of this sort invokes. One thing it means in law is the right to reproductive autonomy; another is a congeries of tort rights only one of which relates to the naked body; still another is the right to maintain the confidentiality of certain documents and conversations. Another and overlapping meaning is the set of interests protected by the Fourth Amendment, which prohibits unreasonable searches and seizures. It has been held to be inapplicable to searches and seizures within prisons, Hudson v. Palmer, 468 U.S. 517, 526, 82 L.Ed.2d 393, 104 S.Ct. 3194 (1984), and if applicable to jails housing pretrial detainees as distinct from convicted defendants—an unsettled question—is only tenuously so, Bell v. Wolfish, 441 U.S. 520, 556–57, 60 L.Ed.2d 447, 99 S.Ct. 1861 (1979); Brothers v. Klevenhagen, 28 F.3d 452, 457 and n. 6 (5th Cir.1994); Valencia v. Wiggins, 981 F.2d 1440 (5th Cir.1993); United States v. Willoughby, 860 F.2d 15, 21 (2d Cir.1988), though this may depend on the precise invasion complained of. A unanimous Supreme Court held in Winston v. Lee, 470 U.S. 753, 84 L.Ed.2d 662, 105 S.Ct. 1611 (1985), that forcing a pretrial detainee to undergo surgery violates the Fourth Amendment. * * *

* * * "Disclosure" of the person's naked body might be argued to violate a cognate right to the concealment of the body. In this way a right to "privacy" in the rather literal sense in which it is invoked here might laboriously be extracted from constitutional precedent.

I consider this too tortuous and uncertain a route to follow in the quest for constitutional limitations on the infliction of humiliation on prison inmates. The Eighth Amendment forbids the federal government (and by an interpretation of the due process clause of the Fourteenth Amendment the states as well) to inflict cruel and unusual punishments. The due process clause has been interpreted to lay a similar prohibition on the infliction of cruel and unusual punishments on pretrial detainees who, like Johnson, not having been convicted, are not formally being "punished." Bell v. Wolfish, supra, 441 U.S. at 534–35; City of Revere v. Massachusetts General Hospital, 463 U.S. 239, 244, 77 L.Ed.2d 605, 103 S.Ct. 2979 (1983). I take it that purely psychological punishments can sometimes be deemed cruel and unusual. * * * The question is then whether exposing naked prisoners to guards of the opposite sex can ever be deemed one of these cruel and unusual psychological punishments. The Sixth Circuit held in Kent v. Johnson, 821 F.2d 1220, 1227 (6th Cir.1987), that it can be, and did not retract the holding in its order on rehearing, although it did retract any suggestion that cross-sex surveillance was unconstitutional per se. See id. at 1229. My colleagues do not suggest that recasting Johnson's right of privacy claim as a claim under the Eighth Amendment can prejudice the state. The substance of the analysis is unchanged, and the parties in their briefs cite Eighth Amendment cases interchangeably with right of privacy cases.

I have no patience with the suggestion that Title VII of the Civil Right Act of 1964 forbids a prison or jail to impede, however slightly, the career opportunities of female guards by shielding naked male prisoners from their eyes. It is true that since the male prison population is vastly greater than the female, female guards would gain no corresponding advantage from being allowed to monopolize the surveillance of naked female prisoners. But Title VII cannot override the Constitution. There cannot be a right to inflict cruel and unusual punishments in order to secure a merely statutory entitlement to equal opportunities for women in the field of corrections. Although the equal protection clause of the Fourteenth Amendment has been held to protect women against sex discrimination by a state, Trigg v. Fort Wayne Community Schools, 766 F.2d 299, 302 (7th Cir.1985); Gray v. Lacke, 885 F.2d 399, 414 (7th Cir.1989); Day v. Wayne County Board of Auditors, 749 F.2d 1199, 1205 (6th Cir.1984), and the Cook County jail is an arm of the State of Illinois, the clause is not plausibly interpreted to license the infliction of cruel and unusual punishments. Just as it would not be a defense to a charge that the rack and thumbscrew are forms of cruel and unusual punishment to demonstrate that they are cheaper than imprisonment, so it is not a defense to the infliction of cruel and unusual psychological punishments that they advance women's career opportunities. And this is assuming that the interests of women would be advanced by a rule, implicit in my colleagues' decision, that gave no legal protection to female prisoners from the prying eyes of male guards; for Title VII and the equal protection clause are considered to protect men as well as women from sex discrimination.

This is not to say that exposing the naked male body to women's eyes constitutes cruel and unusual punishment in all circumstances. A male prisoner has no constitutional right to be treated by a male doctor. Cf. Dothard v. Rawlinson, 433 U.S. 321, 346 n. 5, 53 L.Ed.2d 786, 97 S.Ct. 2720 (1977)(separate opinion); Gargiul v. Tompkins, 704 F.2d 661 (2d Cir.1983), vacated on other grounds, 465 U.S. 1016 (1984). Men have long been attended in hospitals by female nurses, and latterly by female doctors as well. Even the "right of privacy" cases reject the suggestion that any time a female guard glimpses a naked male prisoner his rights have been invaded. See, e.g., Michenfelder v. Sumner, 860 F.2d 328, 335 (9th Cir.1988); Grummett v. Rushen, 779 F.2d 491, 494–95 (9th Cir.1985). Not only is the injury from an occasional glimpse slight; but in addition, as we can see when the "right of privacy" cases are reclassified under the proper constitutional rubrics, neither the Eighth Amendment nor the counterpart protections of pretrial detainees under the due process clauses extend to unintentional wrongs. * * * Deliberately to place male prisoners under continuous visual surveillance by female guards, however, so that whenever the prisoner dresses or undresses, takes a shower, or uses the toilet, a woman is watching him, gives even my colleagues pause.

Ours is the intermediate case, where the prison or jail makes no effort, or a patently inadequate effort, to shield the male prisoners from the gaze of female guards when the prisoners are nude. No case holds that the surveillance of naked inmates by guards of the opposite case is lawful per se—not Timm v. Gunter, 917 F.2d 1093, 1101–02 (8th Cir.1990), and not Hudson v. Palmer, supra, which held only that the right of privacy protected by the Fourth Amendment does not extend to prisoners, and not, as I shall show, Bell v. Wolfish. I infer from their discussion of Torres v. Wisconsin Dept. of Health & Social Services, 859 F.2d 1523 (7th Cir.1988)(en banc), that my colleagues believe that female inmates have no constitutionally protected interest in not being seen in the nude by male guards. This surprises me. Jordan v. Gardner, 986 F.2d 1521 (9th Cir.1993)(en banc) is against this view, and no case supports it.

I have stated the interest at issue in this case as not being seen nude by a guard of the opposite sex, not only because most people are more embarrassed in that situation but also because the right of prisons and jails to maintain visual surveillance of potentially dangerous prisoners even when naked cannot be doubted in light of the serious security problems in many American prisons and jails today. What is in question is the right of prison officials to entrust the surveillance of naked prisoners to guards of the opposite sex from the prisoners. Bell v. Wolfish, supra, holds that pretrial detainees may be subjected to digital and visual inspection of the rectum for concealed weapons or other contraband. It does not follow that no constitutional issue is raised if the search is performed by a male guard on a female prisoner, or a female guard on a male prisoner; or if the search is visual rather than digital (it was both in Bell v. Wolfish); or if what is being watched is the prisoner's genitalia rather than the interior of his rectum. Jordan v. Gardner, supra, 986 F.2d at 1522, holds that "a policy that requires male guards to conduct random, non-emergency, suspicionless clothed body searches on female prisoners," violates the Eighth Amendment. What Johnson alleges is worse, albeit with the sexes reversed.

The Eighth Amendment requires in my view that reasonable efforts be made to prevent frequent, deliberate, gratuitous exposure of nude prisoners of one sex to guards of the other sex. I doubt that any more precise statement of the proper constitutional test is feasible. It is precise enough to show that my colleagues indulge in hyperbole when they say that a decision for Johnson would mean that "female guards are shuffled off to back office jobs." They would not be, but that is not the most important point. The most important point is that sexual equality may not be pursued with no regard to competing interests, and with an eye blind to reality. The reality is that crime is gendered, and the gender is male. Stephen J. Schulhofer, "The Feminist Challenge in Criminal Law," 143 University of Pennsylvania Law Review 2151 (1995). The vast majority of criminals are male. The vast majority of their victims are male. The vast majority of police and correctional officers are male. These are inescapable realities in the design of penal institutions and the validation of penal practices.

My colleagues toy with the idea that unless the intentions of the prison officials are in some sense punitive, there can be no liability under the cruel and unusual punishments clause, whatever the psychological impact of the prison's actions. There is support for this suggestion in language of some lower-court cases quoted in Wilson v. Seiter, supra, 501 U.S. at 300. But I do not think that that language was intended to override the distinction between motive and intent. The cruel and unusual punishments clause is not limited to sadistic inflictions, or, as my colleagues put it, to cases in which "the state has created risk or inflicted pain pointlessly" (my emphasis). The motives of prison officials and guards are in fact irrelevant. The relevant deliberateness is the deliberate adoption of a measure that constitutes cruel and unusual punishment. If prison officials use the thumbscrew and rack to discipline unruly prisoners, it is immaterial that their motive is not to punish but merely to maintain good order in the prison, or to save money. Id. at 301–02. The public beheadings of murderers by Saudi Arabia are, I imagine, motivated not by sadism but rather (to the extent that they have any secular motivation) by a belief that the public infliction of cruel punishments minimizes the crime rate. If prison officials deliberately expose male prisoners to the gaze of female guards, or female prisoners to the gaze of male guards, it should be irrelevant that the motive of the officials may have been merely to avoid sorting custodial tasks by gender.

The distinction between motive and intent runs all through the law. If someone plants a bomb in an airplane, his intent in the eyes of the law is to kill, though his motive might be to intimidate political opponents, obtain publicity, demonstrate skill with explosives, collect life insurance on a passenger, or distract the police from his other criminal activities. United States v. McAnally, 666 F.2d 1116, 1119 (7th Cir.1981). More to the point, the distinction that I am emphasizing between motive and intent is implicit in the standard of "deliberate indifference" which the courts use to determine whether the state of mind requirement of the Eighth Amendment has been satisfied. See, e.g., Wilson v. Seiter, supra, 501 U.S. at 303; Ivey v. Harney, supra, 47 F.3d at 182. That standard is satisfied by proof of "actual knowledge of impending harm easily preventable," Duckworth v. Franzen, supra, 780 F.2d at 653—a formulation that dispenses entirely with any investigation of motive. If prison officials know that they are subjecting male prisoners to gratuitous humiliation, the infliction is deliberate, even if the officials are not actuated by any punitive purpose and are not even certain that humiliation will result. "An eighth amendment complainant need not show that a prison official acted or failed to act believing that harm actually would befall an inmate; it is enough that the official acted or failed to act despite his knowledge of a substantial risk of serious harm." Farmer v. Brennan, supra, 114 S.Ct. at 1981. The principal application of the standard of deliberate indifference is to cases of medical care. If prison officials, knowing that an inmate is seriously ill, refuse to provide him with any treatment, the fact that their motive is not to punish him but merely to save time and money is not a defense to his Eighth Amendment claim. Estelle v. Gamble, 429 U.S. 97, 50 L.Ed.2d 251, 97 S.Ct. 285 (1976); see also Wilson v. Seiter, supra, 501 U.S. at 302.

I turn now to the question whether the complaint states a claim for the infringement of the right that I have sketched. * * * The defendants fasten on the allegation in the complaint that there was a "sheet" between the bathroom (containing both showers and toilets) used by Johnson and other male inmates and the area in which the guards are stationed. In fact what Johnson alleged was that

> when a female correctional officer is assigned to work a dorm it is her duty and responsibility to make counts, also to constantly supervise all inmates in the dorms, making periodic, unannounced spot checks of inmates in their living area, and surveying in the remainder of the area such as the general toilet, and shower facilities, which is in an open unobstructed area, except by a thin sheet that can be seen through.

This can fairly be read to allege that female guards assigned to Johnson's dorm are responsible for maintaining visual surveillance of the bathroom, which they are able to do because it is separated from the part of the dorm in which the guards are stationed by a transparent "sheet," perhaps a kind of shower curtain. So read, the complaint is consistent with a form of cross-sex surveillance sufficiently frequent, gratuitous, and deliberate to withstand dismissal on the pleadings. A further factual inquiry is necessary to determine whether Johnson's constitutional rights have been violated.

My colleagues say that we must respect "the hard choices made by prison administrators." I agree. There is no basis in the record, however, for supposing that such a choice was made here, or for believing that an effort to limit cross-sex surveillance would involve an inefficient use of staff—"featherbedding," as my colleagues put it. There is no record. The case was dismissed on the complaint. We do not know whether the Cook County Jail cannot afford a thicker sheet or, more to the point, cannot feasibly confine the surveillance of naked male prisoners to male guards and naked female prisoners to female guards. We do not even know what crime [Johnson] is charged with. My colleagues urge deference to prison administrators, but at the same time speak confidently about the costs of redeploying staff to protect Johnson's rights. It would be nice to know a little more about the facts before making a judgment that condones barbarism.

Notes on Johnson

1. The *Johnson* majority says that cross-sex monitoring is justified because it "makes good use of the staff" and "reduces the need for prisons to make sex a criterion of employment." The court notes that "[t]he interest of women in equal treatment is a solid reason, with more secure footing in American law than prisoners' modesty, leading to the conclusion that there is no violation of the eighth amendment." Is the majority's summary of the issues in this case oversimplified? If a prisoner "lack(s) any reasonable expectation of privacy under the fourth amendment," how far can a prison administration go before a prisoner's rights under the Eighth Amendment are violated?

2. Compare with *Johnson* the Ninth Circuit's opinion in Jordan v. Gardner, 986 F.2d 1521 (9th Cir.1993)(en banc), on the issue of body searches at a women's prison by male guards. In *Jordan*, inmates at Washington Corrections Center for Women (WCCW) sued prison officials to enjoin a policy requiring male guards to perform random, non-emergency, suspicionless, clothed body searches on female prisoners. Before the new policy was instituted, these searches were routinely performed only at fixed checkpoints by female guards. Male guards had been permitted to search inmates only in emergency situations. The search policy was instituted by a new superintendent, Eldon Vail, in response to a grievance filed by female guards who were unhappy that their meal breaks were occasionally interrupted to conduct searches at the fixed checkpoints. The new policy was designed to control the flow of contraband within the prison by introducing uncertainty in the time and place of the clothed-body searches. The new policy was put into effect on July 5, 1989, and caused severe distress to some inmates. Later that same day, inmates filed suit under 42 U.S.C.A. § 1983, and obtained a preliminary injunction prohibiting the practice. After a seven day trial, the district court issued an order permanently enjoining the searches. A three-judge panel reversed the district court, Jordan v. Gardner, 953 F.2d 1137 (9th Cir.1992), but that decision was vacated and rehearing en banc granted, Jordan v. Gardner, 968 F.2d 984 (9th Cir.1992), which resulted in a judgment upholding the injunction. The Ninth Circuit held that these searches violated the Eight Amendment's prohibition of cruel and unusual punishment.

The inmates challenged the searches under the First, Fourth, and Eighth Amendments. The en banc opinion was badly split. Judge O'Scannlain commanded a majority of the court for the proposition that the Eighth Amendment was violated, but only a plurality for the decision not to invoke the Fourth Amendment. Judges Reinhardt and Canby, concurring, would have held that the practice violated both the Fourth and Eighth Amendments. Judge Noonan concurred separately. Judge Trott, Wiggins and Kleinfeld dissented from the Eighth Amendment holding and expressed disagreement with Judge Reinhardt's Fourth Amendment analysis. Chief Judge Wallace, the author of the panel opinion, dissented separately and would have adhered to the panel majority opinion.

The disputed practice, termed a "pat-down search" by the prison officials and the dissent, was renamed a "clothed body search" by the district court and the majority. Judge O'Scannlain described it as follows:

> During the cross-gender clothed body search, the male guard stands next to the female inmate and thoroughly runs his hands over her clothed body starting with her neck and working down to her feet. According to the prison training material, a guard is to "[u]se a flat hand and pushing motion across the [inmate's] crotch area." * * * The guard must "[p]ush inward and upward when searching the crotch and upper thighs of the inmate." All seams in the leg and the crotch area are to be "squeez[ed] and knead[ed]." Using the back of the hand, the guard also is to search the breast area in a sweeping motion, so that the breasts will be "flattened."

Id., 985 F.2d at 1523. 85% of the inmates at WCCW had reported a history of abuse to prison counselors, including rape, molestation, beatings, and slavery. One of the inmates searched on the only day this policy was in force had a long history of sexual abuse by men. She "unwillingly submitted to a cross-gender clothed body search and suffered severe distress: she had to have her fingers pried loose from bars she had grabbed during the search, and she vomited after returning to her cell block." Id., at 1523.

Judge O'Scannlain agreed with the district court that the searches inflicted "pain." He also determined that the pain inflicted was "unnecessary," since the Superintendent was able to continue the clothed-body searches by using female guards to perform them. The question of whether the pain was inflicted wantonly was closer, but Judge O'Scannlain decided that the proper standard was whether the Superintendent's decision displayed "deliberate indifference" to the inmate's suffering, not the more rigorous standard whether the force was applied "maliciously and sadistically for the very purpose of causing harm."

The majority in *Jordan* declined to reach the Fourth Amendment privacy claims:

> Whether such rights exist—whether the inmates possess privacy interests that could be infringed by the cross-gender aspect of otherwise constitutional searches—is a difficult and novel question, and one that cannot be dismissed lightly. But we cannot assume from the fact that the searches cause immense anguish that they therefore violate protected Fourth Amendment interests. Far from it, our prior case law suggests that prisoners' legitimate expectations of bodily privacy from persons of the opposite sex are extremely limited.

Id. at 1524. Because they affirmed the district court on Eighth Amendment grounds, they did not decide the Fourth Amendment issues.

Judge Reinhardt, concurring, would have found a violation of the Fourth Amendment: "* * * prison inmates have a right of privacy and dignity in their persons." In a footnote he explains:

> The precise fourth amendment interest that is violated is "[t]he right of people to be secure in their persons * * * against unreasonable searches." Moreover, while privacy is the primary interest underlying the fourth amendment, that amendment also protects persons against infringements of bodily integrity, and personal dignity. The Court refers to these interests together as "dignitary interests." It is the privacy and dignitary interests of the female inmates that are violated here.

Id. at 1534 n.7 (citations omitted).

In the first part of his dissent, Judge Trott thus characterized the case:

> The facts of this case are these: Some women in prison with histories of sexual and physical abuse by men will have their external private parts periodically searched through their clothing by the hands of male corrections officers. This touching may cause them considerable distress; a distress which those of us who have not experienced it may not fully appreciate. Nevertheless, these women are in prison because they committed serious felony offenses, thus forfeiting their liberty. Prisons are difficult places, but we must deal with the way things are, not the way we would like them to be.

Id., 986 F.2d at 1546 (dissenting opinion). Judge Trott disagreed with the majority on the standard to be applied to judge whether the infliction of pain was "wanton." In his judgment, the higher standard must be used: whether the conduct complained of must have been pursued "maliciously and sadistically for the very purpose of causing harm." Quoting at length from Superintendent Vail's testimony, Judge Trott concluded that the standard had not been met.

Judge Noonan's separate concurring opinion went beyond the specific question at issue to challenge the legal framework of gender neutrality within which it arose:

> How did a civilized country and a civilized state like Washington get into this fix where it takes federal judges to tell a responsible state official to stop his approval of indecency because he is violating the Constitution? By blindly going down an egalitarian path premised on the belief that there are no real differences between the sexes, that we must march to a unisex world. In the necessary effort to eliminate discrimination based on gender there has been a simpleminded effort to eliminate gender. But we are en-gendered persons.
>
> There should not be male guards at a women's prison. There should not be a male superintendent of a women's prison. Our statutes should not be construed to require such mechanical suppression of the recognition that in our culture such a relation between men in power and women in prison leads to difficulties, temptations, abuse, and finally to cruel and unusual punishment. That is the broader context of this case.

Id., 986 F.2d at 1544–45 (concurring opinion). What is your response? Chief Judge Wallace had indicated in the vacated panel opinion that he could find no principled basis for distinguishing *Jordan* from Grummett v. Rushen, 779 F.2d 491 (9th Cir.1985), where the court had rejected a constitutional challenge to a prison policy that allowed female guards to perform pat-down searches on male prisoners. He added this statement in his dissent in the en banc case:

It would, in my judgment, be far better not to permit cross-gender searches on men or women prisoners which involve physical contact or unclothed prisoner viewing. I believe this policy is misguided and hope it will be changed.

Id., 986 F.2d at 1566 (dissenting opinion). Is there any way this policy can be changed without undermining the Constitution and Title VII?

In the principal case *Johnson*, Judge Posner discusses Jordan v. Gardner and then comments, "What Johnson alleges is worse, albeit with the sexes reversed." Supra at p. 1231. Do you agree?

3. While "privacy" has been rejected by many courts as a legitimate basis for excluding corrections officers of one gender from all or parts of correctional facilities, "rehabilitation" was an acceptable rationale to the Seventh Circuit in Torres v. Wisconsin Dept. of Health & Soc. Services, 859 F.2d 1523 (7th Cir. 1988)(en banc), cert. denied 489 U.S. 1017 and 1082 (1989). In *Torres*, the male correctional officers at Taycheedah Correctional Institution (TCI), a women's maximum security prison, challenged an administration policy that employed only female correctional officers in the prison's living quarters, on the basis that being a woman was a bona fide occupational qualification (BFOQ) for these security positions. The prison administration presented three grounds for the policy: inmate rehabilitation, inmate privacy, and prison security. The BFOQ was initially struck down on all three grounds by the district court. Judge Robert Warren examined TCI's asserted rehabilitation policy and found it lacking:

* * * a large number of inmates at TCI (approximately 60%) had been physically or sexually abused by males. Because of this abuse, the theory continues, female inmates are uncomfortable with the presence of males in the housing units, which presence thereby deters their rehabilitation. * * *

Defendants offered only a theory of rehabilitation as a justification for the BFOQ plan. They offered no objective evidence.

639 F.Supp. 271, 280 (E.D.Wis.1986). The Court of Appeals, en banc, took a different view, reversed and remanded for reconsideration of the rehabilitation justification. The court found that the need to deal with difficult sociological problems and implement asserted goals of the penal system leads to a need to "innovate and experiment." Torres, 859 F.2d at 1529. The District Court's demand for empirical studies and objective evidence showing the validity of TCI's rehabilitation policy created "an unrealistic, and therefore unfair burden" on prison authorities. Id. at 1532. The prison's policy was based on Superintendent Nona Switala's "interviews and daily contact with female prisoners" at TCI, her "professional judgment that giving women prisoners a living environment free from the presence of males in a position of authority was necessary to foster the goal of rehabilitation," taking into account that sixty percent of TCI's inmates had been sexually abused prior to incarceration. Id. at 1530. Again, this court did not find a BFOQ justified on prisoners' privacy interests, but on the basis of deference to the prison administration's policy grounds.

4. As Judge Posner pointed out in *Johnson*, the world of prisons in the United States is an overwhelmingly male world. Women have struggled for years to gain access to the relatively well-paid and increasingly numerous correctional officer jobs. The first attempt to integrate prison guard jobs ultimately failed. See Dothard v. Rawlinson, 433 U.S. 321 (1977), set forth at p. 777 supra. See also Notes 3 and 6 on pp. 586, 591 supra. But Cynthia Gunther was ultimately more successful in Gunther v. Iowa State Men's Reformatory, 462 F.Supp. 952

(N.D.Iowa 1979), affirmed 612 F.2d 1079 (8th Cir.), cert. denied 446 U.S. 966, 100 S.Ct. 2942, 64 L.Ed.2d 825 (1980). Cynthia Gunther's legal battle went on for years to achieve promotion from a Correctional Officer I at the Anamosa Reformatory in Iowa to Correctional Officer II. CO I is an entry-level classification; incumbents rotate through various tasks on a limited basis and have little contact with inmates. CO II's perform all the duties of CO I's and, in addition, are responsible for riot control, patrol of cell blocks, and superintending inmates in the bath and shower room. They conduct frequent pat searches and strip searches; they can and do view the inmates' toilet. CO II's may advance to CO III and CO IV, with increasing authority and pay. Some CO II's, because of advancing age or fear, choose voluntary demotion to CO I to avoid frequent inmate contact and to have a relatively safe job sitting it out on the tower before retirement.

Gunther, who was qualified for promotion to CO II, requested the advancement, but was denied because of her sex. On May 21, 1975, she filed grievances with the Iowa Merit Employment Commission and with the EEOC. The state agency found that plaintiff was entitled to the promotion. Its ruling was sustained by the state trial court, which ordered that Gunther be promoted to CO II, but that she be excused from the performance of duties that could reasonably be expected to violate the prisoners' rights of privacy. The Supreme Court of Iowa reversed. Applying Iowa law, it held that the duties that plaintiff could not perform constituted the "very core and substance of the CO II classification", and that the prison authorities were not required to readjust their procedures and classifications to accommodate plaintiff. The Bona Fide Occupational Qualification (BFOQ) exception to Iowa's anti-discrimination law prevented plaintiff from serving as a CO II. Iowa Dept. of Social Servs. v. Iowa Merit Employment Dept., 261 N.W.2d 161 (Iowa 1977).

Plaintiff, who had not cross-appealed from the Iowa state trial court decision, pressed her claim in federal court instead. In October, 1977, before the Iowa Supreme Court decision was announced, she filed a complaint in the federal district court under Title VII. That court rejected the BFOQ argument under Title VII, and ordered the defendants to promote plaintiff to CO II, while making such scheduling adjustments as were required to protect the plaintiff's interest in equal employment opportunity, the state's interest in prison security and order and the prisoners' interest in preserving their privacy. 462 F.Supp. 952.

In affirming the district court's decision, the Eighth Circuit did not hold that the prison authorities could not create a job available only to men in men's prisons and to women in women's prisons that would consist of "shower and toilet surveillance, strip searches and related duties necessary to inmate privacy". *Gunther,* id., 612 F.2d at 1087. Instead, it held that the defendant had not shown that it could not modify the current classification in less discriminatory ways in order to avoid restricting the advancement of women from CO I to CO II. It noted that female CO II's at Fort Madison, the maximum security men's penitentiary, performed limited duties such as those plaintiff sought for herself at Anamosa. It also pointed out that Anamosa adjusted its work schedules for certain male CO II's, permitting them to perform a single job function for as long as three years. It concluded that "[i]f these job functions and procedures have not undermined the goals and functions of the reformatory at Anamosa, there is little reason to suggest that scheduling to avoid the invasion of inmate privacy rights by female officers would give rise to undue hardship on the prison administration." Id., 612 F.2d at 1087. The two Iowa cases were discussed in Deborah M. Tharnish, Comment, Sex Discrimination in Prison Employment: The

Bona Fide Occupational Qualification and Prisoners' Privacy Rights, 65 Iowa L.Rev. 428 (1980).

5. Did the decision in *Gunther* require reverse discrimination against male prison guards? Defendants so argued in *Gunther:*

> Anamosa additionally argues that any functional assignment would require men to perform all of the high risk duties at Anamosa while women would perform only low risk duties, with both being compensated at the CO II level. It argues that this would be sex discrimination against male CO II's.

Gunther v. Iowa State Men's Reformatory, supra Note 3, at 1086. The findings of fact of the Commissioner in the Iowa state proceedings had included this item:

> g. It would be economically unsound, would present serious scheduling problems, would destroy essential flexibility in the assignment of CO II's *and cause discontent among male CO II's to limit the functions of a female CO II.*

Iowa Department of Social Services v. Iowa Merit Employment Department, supra Note 3, at 166 (emphasis supplied). Is there a satisfactory answer to this argument? Has the fuller integration of jobs, as required by *Johnson* eliminated this problem? But at the cost of male inmates' privacy?

6. Is the "discontent" among male CO II's mentioned in Note 5, supra, likely to impair the ability of female CO II's to perform well on the job? A review of the studies done in several American cities to discover the effectiveness of women police officers assigned to patrol duties concluded that

> [t]here were three areas of agreement within the literature. The studies show that citizen attitudes toward female patrol officers are favorable. In most instances, citizens were as satisfied with the performance of female officers as with male officers; the New York City and Newton [Massachusetts] data showed citizens consistently more satisfied with female officers than male officers. Although the studies show the public supportive of women in law enforcement, they also showed that the greatest resistance to the use of women on patrol still comes from male officers. * * * Although there is disagreement concerning various components of performance, the studies concur in the observation that female officers are generally competent on patrol. A major issue, that of female officers' response to violent and/or dangerous situations needs more research before any conclusive judgments can be made.

Silbert, Women in Policing 26–27 (Report of the San Francisco Police Department, 1980). Silbert also conducted an attitudinal survey of 267 San Francisco Police officers from Recruit Classes 126 through 131. The first 60 women hired to be trained for patrol duty were part of the group that entered Recruit Classes 126 and 127 in the summer and fall of 1975. The sample of 267 officers included 81% males and 19% females; they were 67% white, 14% black, 9% Asian; 8% Latin; and 3% other minority groups. The mean age of the sample was 28; their mean height was 5' 10"; their mean weight 172 pounds; and their mean education 14.4 years.

The officers were questioned on a variety of items, including training issues, general issues in policing, and women in policing. The San Francisco study is consistent with earlier studies in finding that male police officers have a negative attitude about women police officers, both as to their performance and as to the appropriateness of their presence on the force. For example, although all the women thought it was a good idea to have women regularly assigned to patrol duty, most men disagreed. In rating themselves on specific patrol tasks, men rated women higher than they rated themselves on only one item: questioning rape victims. The men saw women as nearly as competent as they in handling traffic accidents and writing reports; women were rated lowest by men in their ability to handle situations involving violence. In choosing a patrol partner, male officers preferred a male partner, while women showed no preference but slightly leaned toward having a male partner. Black and Asian officers were significantly more supportive of women officers than were White or Latin officers. The opposition to women on patrol appears to increase with height: the taller the officers, the more strongly they opposed women on patrol, thought the community also opposed such assignments, preferred male partners, and, in general, believed that the attempt to obtain equal rights for women had gone too far. Silbert concludes:

> [M]ale officers' responses to women in policing appear to be based on cultural stereotypes regarding male and female attributes and on a particular understanding of police work which centers around traits culturally viewed as male traits: physical strength, forcefulness, and aggressiveness. Although women in all of the studies including this one are confident of their abilities to do all aspects of police work, they too are influenced by cultural stereotypes, particularly when assessing men's capabilities. For example, in the current study women rated men *higher* than men rated themselves on the following traits: aggressiveness, physical strength, and good leadership. They also indicated that a higher percentage of men than women possess courage and persuasiveness. * * *

Silbert, id., at 100–101. See generally, Lynn Etta Zimmer, Women Guarding Men (1986).

Statutory Appendix

SELECTIONS FROM TITLE VII OF THE CIVIL RIGHTS ACT OF 1964*

42 U.S.C. § 2000e et seq.

DEFINITIONS

Sec. 2000e [§ 701]. For the purposes of this subchapter—

(a) The term "person" includes one or more individuals, governments, governmental agencies, political subdivisions, labor unions, partnerships, associations, corporations, legal representatives, mutual companies, joint-stock companies, trusts, unincorporated organizations, trustees, trustees in cases under Title 11, or receivers.

(b) The term "employer" means a person engaged in an industry affecting commerce who has fifteen or more employees for each working day in each of twenty or more calendar weeks in the current or preceding calendar year, and any agent of such a person, but such term does not include (1) the United States, a corporation wholly owned by the Government of the United States, an Indian tribe, or any department or agency of the District of Columbia subject by statute to procedures of the competitive service (as defined in section 2102 of Title 5 of the United States Code), or (2) a bona fide private membership club (other than a labor organization) which is exempt from taxation under section 501(c) of Title 26, except that during the first year after March 24, 1972, persons having fewer than twenty-five employees (and their agents) shall not be considered employers.

(c) The term "employment agency" means any person regularly undertaking with or without compensation to procure employees for an employer or to procure for employees opportunities to work for an employer and includes an agent of such a person.

(d) The term "labor organization" means a labor organization engaged in an industry affecting commerce, and any agent of such an organization, and includes any organization of any kind, any agency, or employee representation

---

* Provisions in italics were added by the Civil Rights Act of 1991.

committee, group, association, or plan so engaged in which employees participate and which exists for the purpose, in whole or in part, of dealing with employers concerning grievances, labor disputes, wages, rates of pay, hours, or other terms or conditions of employment, and any conference, general committee, joint or system board, or joint council so engaged which is subordinate to a national or international labor organization.

(e) A labor organization shall be deemed to be engaged in an industry affecting commerce if (1) it maintains or operates a hiring hall or hiring office which procures employees for an employer or procures for employees opportunities to work for an employer, or (2) the number of its members (or, where it is a labor organization composed of other labor organizations or their representatives, if the aggregate number of the members of such other labor organization) is (A) twenty-five or more during the first year after March 24, 1972, or (B) fifteen or more thereafter, and such labor organization—

(1) is the certified representative of employees under the provisions of the National Labor Relations Act, as amended, or the Railway Labor Act, as amended;

(2) although not certified, is a national or international labor organization or a local labor organization recognized or acting as the representative of employees of an employer or employers engaged in an industry affecting commerce; or

(3) has chartered a local labor organization or subsidiary body which is representing or actively seeking to represent employees of employers within the meaning of paragraph (1) or (2); or

(4) has been chartered by a labor organization representing or actively seeking to represent employees within the meaning of paragraph (1) or (2) as the local or subordinate body through which such employees may enjoy membership or become affiliated with such labor organization; or

(5) is a conference, general committee, joint or system board, or joint council subordinate to a national or international labor organization, which includes a labor organization engaged in an industry affecting commerce within the meaning of any of the preceding paragraphs of this subsection.

(f) The term "employee" means an individual employed by an employer, except that the term "employee" shall not include any person elected to public office in any State or political subdivision of any State by the qualified voters thereof, or any person chosen by such officer to be on such officer's personal staff, or an appointee on the policy making level or an immediate adviser with respect to the exercise of the constitutional or legal powers of the office. The exemption set forth in the preceding sentence shall not include employees subject to the civil service laws of a State government, governmental agency or political subdivision. *With respect to employment in a foreign country, such term includes an individual who is a citizen of the United States.*

(g) The term "commerce" means trade, traffic, commerce, transportation, transmission, or communication among the several States; or between a State and any place outside thereof; or within the District of Columbia, or a possession of the United States; or between points in the same State but through a point outside thereof.

(h) The term "industry affecting commerce" means any activity, business, or industry in commerce or in which a labor dispute would hinder or obstruct commerce or the free flow of commerce and includes any activity or industry "affecting commerce" within the meaning of the Labor–Management Reporting and Disclosure Act of 1959, and further includes any governmental industry, business, or activity.

(i) The term "State" includes a State of the United States, the District of Columbia, Puerto Rico, the Virgin Islands, American Samoa, Guam, Wake Island, the Canal Zone, and Outer Continental Shelf lands defined in the Outer Continental Shelf Lands Act.

(j) The term "religion" includes all aspects of religious observance and practice, as well as belief, unless an employer demonstrates that he is unable to reasonably accommodate to an employee's or prospective employee's religious observance or practice without undue hardship on the conduct of the employer's business.

(k) The terms "because of sex" or "on the basis of sex" include, but are not limited to, because of or on the basis of pregnancy, childbirth, or related medical conditions; and women affected by pregnancy, childbirth, or related medical conditions shall be treated the same for all employment-related purposes, including receipt of benefits under fringe benefit programs, as other persons not so affected but similar in their ability or inability to work, and nothing in section 2000e–2(h) of this title shall be interpreted to permit otherwise. This subsection shall not require an employer to pay for health insurance benefits for abortion, except where the life of the mother would be endangered if the fetus were carried to term, or except where medical complications have arisen from an abortion: *Provided,* That nothing herein shall preclude an employer from providing abortion benefits or otherwise affect bargaining agreements in regard to abortion.

(l) The term "complaining party" means the Commission, the Attorney General, or a person who may bring an action or proceeding under this title.

(m) The term "demonstrates" means meets the burdens of production and persuasion.

(n) The term "respondent" means an employer, employment agency, labor organization, joint labor-management committee controlling apprenticeship or other training or retraining program, including an on-the-job training program, or Federal entity subject to section 717.

EXEMPTIONS

Sec. 2000e–1 [§ 702]. *(a)* This subchapter shall not apply to an employer with respect to the employment of aliens outside any State, or to a religious corporation, association, educational institution, or society with respect to the employment of individuals of a particular religion to perform work connected with the carrying on by such corporation, association, educational institution, or society of its activities.

(b) and (c) [Provisions of 1991 Act on American employees working in foreign countries omitted.]

UNLAWFUL EMPLOYMENT PRACTICES

Sec. 2000e–2 [§ 703]. (a) It shall be an unlawful employment practice for an employer—

(1) to fail or refuse to hire or to discharge any individual, or otherwise to discriminate against any individual with respect to his compensation, terms, conditions, or privileges of employment, because of such individual's race, color, religion, sex, or national origin; or

(2) to limit, segregate, or classify his employees or applicants for employment in any way which would deprive or tend to deprive any individual of employment opportunities or otherwise adversely affect his status as an employee, because of such individual's race, color, religion, sex, or national origin.

(b) It shall be an unlawful employment practice for an employment agency to fail or refuse to refer for employment, or otherwise to discriminate against, any individual because of his race, color, religion, sex, or national origin, or to classify or refer for employment any individual on the basis of his race, color, religion, sex, or national origin.

(c) It shall be an unlawful employment practice for a labor organization—

(1) to exclude or to expel from its membership, or otherwise to discriminate against, any individual because of his race, color, religion, sex, or national origin;

(2) to limit, segregate, or classify its membership or applicants for membership, or to classify or fail or refuse to refer for employment any individual, in any way which would deprive or tend to deprive any individual of employment opportunities, or would limit such employment opportunities or otherwise adversely affect his status as an employee or as an applicant for employment, because of such individual's race, color, religion, sex, or national origin; or

(3) to cause or attempt to cause an employer to discriminate against an individual in violation of this section.

(d) It shall be an unlawful employment practice for any employer, labor organization, or joint labor-management committee controlling apprenticeship or other training or retraining, including on-the-job training programs to discriminate against any individual because of his race, color, religion, sex, or national origin in admission to, or employment in, any program established to provide apprenticeship or other training.

(e) Notwithstanding any other provision of this subchapter, (1) it shall not be an unlawful employment practice for an employer to hire and employ employees, for an employment agency to classify, or refer for employment any individual, for a labor organization to classify its membership or to classify or refer for employment any individual, or for an employer, labor organization, or joint labor-management committee controlling apprenticeship or other training or retraining programs to admit or employ any individual in any such program, on the basis of his religion, sex, or national origin in those certain instances where religion, sex, or national origin is a bona fide occupational qualification reasonably necessary to the normal operation of that particular business or enterprise, and (2) it shall not be an unlawful employment practice for a school, college, university, or other educational institution or institution of learning to hire and employ employees of a particular religion if such school, college, university, or other educational institution or institution of learning is, in whole or in substantial part, owned, supported, controlled, or managed by a particular religion or by a particular religious corporation, association, or society, or if the curriculum of such school, college, university, or other educational institution or institution of learning is directed toward the propagation of a particular religion.

(f) As used in this subchapter, the phrase "unlawful employment practice" shall not be deemed to include any action or measure taken by an employer, labor organization, joint labor-management committee, or employment agency with respect to an individual who is a member of the Communist Party of the United States or of any other organization required to register as a Communist-action or Communist-front organization by final order of the Subversive Activities Control Board pursuant to the Subversive Activities Control Act of 1950.

(g) Notwithstanding any other provision of this subchapter, it shall not be an unlawful employment practice for an employer to fail or refuse to hire and employ any individual for any position, for an employer to discharge any individual from any position, or for an employment agency to fail or refuse to refer any individual for employment in any position, or for a labor organization to fail or refuse to refer any individual for employment in any position, if—

(1) the occupancy of such position, or access to the premises in or upon which any part of the duties of such position is performed or is to be performed, is subject to any requirement imposed in the interest of the national security of the United States under any security program in effect pursuant to or administered under any statute of the United States or any Executive order of the President; and

(2) such individual has not fulfilled or has ceased to fulfill that requirement.

(h) Notwithstanding any other provision of this subchapter, it shall not be an unlawful employment practice for an employer to apply different standards of compensation, or different terms, conditions, or privileges of employment pursuant to a bona fide seniority or merit system, or a system which measures earnings by quantity or quality of production or to employees who work in different locations, provided that such differences are not the result of an intention to discriminate because of race, color, religion, sex, or national origin, nor shall it be an unlawful employment practice for an employer to give and to act upon the results of any professionally developed ability test provided that such test, its administration or action upon the results is not designed, intended or used to discriminate because of race, color, religion, sex or national origin. It shall not be an unlawful employment practice under this subchapter for any employer to differentiate upon the basis of sex in determining the amount of the wages or compensation paid or to be paid to employees of such employer if such differentiation is authorized by the provisions of section 206(d) of Title 29 [the Equal Pay Act].

(i) Nothing contained in this subchapter shall apply to any business or enterprise on or near an Indian reservation with respect to any publicly announced employment practice of such business or enterprise under which a preferential treatment is given to any individual because he is an Indian living on or near a reservation.

(j) Nothing contained in this subchapter shall be interpreted to require any employer, employment agency, labor organization, or joint labor-management committee subject to this subchapter to grant preferential treatment to any individual or to any group because of the race, color, religion, sex, or national origin of such individual or group on account of an imbalance which may exist with respect to the total number or percentage of persons of any race, color, religion, sex, or national origin employed by any employer, referred or classified for employment by any employment agency or labor organization, admitted to membership or classified by any labor organization, or admitted to, or employed in, any apprenticeship or other training program, in comparison with the total number or percentage of persons of such race, color, religion, sex, or national origin in any community, State, section, or other area, or in the available work force in any community, State, section, or other area.

(k)(1)(A) An unlawful employment practice based on disparate impact is established under this title only if—

(i) a complaining party demonstrates that a respondent uses a particular employment practice that causes a disparate impact on the basis of race, color, religion, sex, or national origin and the respondent fails to demonstrate that the challenged practice is job related for the position in question and consistent with business necessity; or

(ii) the complaining party makes the demonstration described in subparagraph (C) with respect to an alternative employment practice and the respondent refuses to adopt such alternative employment practice.

(B)(i) With respect to demonstrating that a particular employment practice causes a disparate impact as described in subparagraph (A)(i), the complaining party shall demonstrate that each particular challenged employment practice causes a disparate impact, except that if the complaining party can demonstrate to the court that the elements of a respondent's decisionmaking process are not capable of separation for analysis, the decisionmaking process may be analyzed as one employment practice.

(ii) If the respondent demonstrates that a specific employment practice does not cause the disparate impact, the respondent shall not be required to demonstrate that such practice is required by business necessity.

(C) The demonstration referred to by subparagraph (A)(ii) shall be in accordance with the law as it existed on June 4, 1989, with respect to the concept of "alternative employment practice".

(2) A demonstration that an employment practice is required by business necessity may not be used as a defense against a claim of intentional discrimination under this title.

(3) Notwithstanding any other provision of this title, a rule barring the employment of an individual who currently and knowingly uses or possesses a controlled substance, as defined in schedules I and II of section 102(6) of the Controlled Substances Act (21 U.S.C. 802(6)), other than the use or possession of a drug taken under the supervision of a licensed health care professional, or

any other use or possession authorized by the Controlled Substances Act or any other provision of Federal law, shall be considered an unlawful employment practice under this title only if such rule is adopted or applied with an intent to discriminate because of race, color, religion, sex, or national origin.

(l) It shall be an unlawful employment practice for a respondent, in connection with the selection or referral of applicants or candidates for employment or promotion, to adjust the scores of, use different cutoff scores for, or otherwise alter the results of, employment related tests on the basis of race, color, religion, sex, or national origin.

(m) Except as otherwise provided in this title, an unlawful employment practice is established when the complaining party demonstrates that race, color, religion, sex, or national origin was a motivating factor for any employment practice, even though other factors also motivated the practice.

(n) [Provision of 1991 Act on challenging consent decrees is omitted.]

OTHER UNLAWFUL EMPLOYMENT PRACTICES

Sec. 2000e–3 [§ 704].   (a) It shall be an unlawful employment practice for an employer to discriminate against any of his employees or applicants for employment, for an employment agency, or joint labor-management committee controlling apprenticeship or other training or retraining, including on-the-job training programs, to discriminate against any individual, or for a labor organization to discriminate against any member thereof or applicant for membership, because he has opposed any practice made an unlawful employment practice by this title, or because he has made a charge, testified, assisted, or participated in any manner in an investigation, proceeding, or hearing under this subchapter.

(b) It shall be an unlawful employment practice for an employer, labor organization, employment agency, or joint labor-management committee controlling apprenticeship or other training or retraining, including on-the-job training programs, to print or publish or cause to be printed or published any notice or advertisement relating to employment by such an employer or membership in or any classification or referral for employment by such a labor organization, or relating to any classification or referral for employment by such an employment agency, or relating to admission to, or employment in, any program established to provide apprenticeship or other training by such a joint labor-management committee, indicating any preference, limitation, specification, or discrimination, based on race, color, religion, sex, or national origin, except that such a notice or advertisement may indicate a preference, limitation, specification, or discrimination based on religion, sex, or national origin when religion, sex, or national origin is a bona fide occupational qualification for employment.

* * *

POST CIVIL WAR CIVIL RIGHTS ACTS
Civil Rights Act of 1870, as amended
by the Civil Rights Act of 1991
42 U.S.C.

§ 1981. Equal rights under the law

(*a*) All persons within the jurisdiction of the United States shall have the same right in every State and Territory to make and enforce contracts, to sue, be parties, give evidence, and to the full and equal benefit of all laws and proceedings for the security of persons and property as is enjoyed by white citizens, and shall be subject to like punishment, pains, penalties, taxes, licenses, and exactions of every kind, and to no other.

(*b*) *For purposes of this section, the term "make and enforce contracts" includes the making, performance, modification, and termination of contracts, and the enjoyment of all benefits, privileges, terms, and conditions of the contractual relationship.*

(*c*) *The rights protected by this section are protected against impairment by nongovernmental discrimination and impairment under color of State law.*

§ 1981A. *Damages in Cases of Intentional Discrimination in Employment*

(*a*) *Right of Recovery—*

(1) *Civil rights.—In an action brought by a complaining party under section 706 or 717 of the Civil Rights Act of 1964 (42 U.S.C. 2000e–5) against a respondent who engaged in unlawful intentional discrimination (not an employment practice that is unlawful because of its disparate impact) prohibited under section 703, 704, or 717 of the Act (42 U.S.C. 2000e–2 or 2000e–3), and provided that the complaining party cannot recover under section 1977 of the Revised Statutes (42 U.S.C. 1981), the complaining party may recover compensatory and punitive damages as allowed in subsection (b), in addition to any relief authorized by section 706(g) of the Civil Rights Act of 1964, from the respondent.*

(2) *and* (3) *[Provisions on Disability Omitted.]*

(*b*) *Compensatory and Punitive Damages.—*

(1) *Determination of punitive damages.—A complaining party may recover punitive damages under this section against a respondent (other than a government, government agency or political subdivision) if the complaining party demonstrates that the respondent engaged in a discriminatory practice or discriminatory practices with malice or with reckless indifference to the federally protected rights of an aggrieved individual.*

(2) *Exclusions from compensatory damages.—Compensatory damages awarded under this section shall not include backpay, interest on backpay, or any other type of relief authorized under section 706(g) of the Civil Rights Act of 1964.*

(3) *Limitations.—The sum of the amount of compensatory damages awarded under this section for future pecuniary losses, emotional pain, suffering, inconvenience, mental anguish, loss of enjoyment of life, and*

other nonpecuniary losses, and the amount of punitive damages awarded under this section, shall not exceed, for each complaining party—

(A) in the case of a respondent who has more than 14 and fewer than 101 employees in each of 20 or more calendar weeks in the current or preceding calendar year, $50,000;

(B) in the case of a respondent who has more than 100 and fewer than 201 employees in each of 20 or more calendar weeks in the current or preceding calendar year, $100,000; and

(C) in the case of a respondent who has more than 200 and fewer than 501 employees in each of 20 or more calendar weeks in the current or preceding calendar year, $200,000; and

(D) in the case of a respondent who has more than 500 employees in each of 20 or more calendar weeks in the current or preceding calendar year, $300,000.

(4) Construction.—Nothing in this section shall be construed to limit the scope of, or the relief available under, section 1977 of the Revised Statutes (42 U.S.C. 1981).

(c) Jury Trial.—If a complaining party seeks compensatory or punitive damages under this section—

(1) any party may demand a trial by jury; and

(2) the court shall not inform the jury of the limitations described in subsection (b)(3).

(d) Definitions.—As used in this section:

(1) Complaining party.—The term 'complaining party' means—

(A) in the case of a person seeking to bring an action under subsection (a)(1), the Equal Employment Opportunity Commission, the Attorney General, or a person who may bring an action or proceeding under title VII of the Civil Rights Act of 1964 (42 U.S.C. 2000e et seq.); or

(B) [provision on disability omitted]

(2) Discriminatory practice.—The term "discriminatory practice" means the discrimination described in paragraph (1), or the discrimination or the violation described in paragraph (2), of subsection (a).

Civil Rights Act of 1871.
42 U.S.C.

§ 1983. Civil action for deprivation of rights

Every person who, under color of any statute, ordinance, regulation, custom, or usage, of any State or Territory or the District of Columbia, subjects, or causes to be subjected, any citizen of the United States or other person within the jurisdiction thereof to the deprivation of any rights, privileges, or immunities secured by the Constitution and laws, shall be liable to the party injured in an action at law, suit in equity, or other proper proceeding for redress. For the purposes of this section, any Act of Congress applicable exclusively to the District of Columbia shall be considered to be a statute of the District of Columbia.

§ 1985.　Conspiracy to interfere with civil rights—Preventing officer from performing duties

* * *

Depriving persons of rights or privileges

(3) If two or more persons in any State or Territory conspire or go in disguise on the highway or on the premises of another, for the purpose of depriving, either directly or indirectly, any person or class of persons of the equal protection of the laws, or of equal privileges and immunities under the laws; or for the purpose of preventing or hindering the constituted authorities of any State or Territory from giving or securing to all persons within such State or Territory the equal protection of the laws; or if two or more persons conspire to prevent by force, intimidation, or threat, any citizen who is lawfully entitled to vote, from giving his support or advocacy in a legal manner, toward or in favor of the election of any lawfully qualified person as an elector for President or Vice President, or as a Member of Congress of the United States; or to injure any citizen in person or property on account of such support or advocacy; in any case of conspiracy set forth in this section, if one or more persons engaged therein do, or cause to be done, any act in furtherance of the object of such conspiracy, whereby another is injured in his person or property, or deprived of having and exercising any right or privilege of a citizen of the United States, the party so injured or deprived may have an action for the recovery of damages, occasioned by such injury or deprivation, against any one or more of the conspirators.

THE EQUAL PAY ACT OF 1963

29 U.S.C.

Sec. 206.

* * *

(d)(1) No employer having employees subject to any provisions of this section shall discriminate, within any establishment in which such employees are employed, between employees on the basis of sex by paying wages to employees in such establishment at a rate less than the rate at which he pays wages to employees of the opposite sex in such establishment for equal work on jobs the performance of which requires equal skill, effort, and responsibility, and which are performed under similar working conditions, except where such payment is made pursuant to (i) a seniority system; (ii) a merit system; (iii) a system which measures earnings by quantity or quality of production; or (iv) a differential based on any other factor other than sex: *Provided,* That an employer who is paying a wage rate differential in violation of this subsection shall not, in order to comply with the provisions of this subsection, reduce the wage rate of any employee.

(2) No labor organization, or its agents, representing employees of an employer having employees subject to any provisions of this section shall

cause or attempt to cause such an employer to discriminate against an employee in violation of paragraph (1) of this subsection.

(3) For purposes of administration and enforcement, any amounts owing to any employee which have been withheld in violation of this subsection shall be deemed to be unpaid minimum wages or unpaid overtime compensation under this Act.

(4) As used in this subsection, the term "labor organization" means any organization of any kind, or any agency or employee representation committee or plan, in which employees participate and which exists for the purpose, in whole or in part, of dealing with employers concerning grievances, labor disputes, wages, rates of pay, hours of employment, or conditions of work.

EDUCATION AMENDMENTS OF 1972

20 U.S.C. § 1681 et seq.

TITLE IX—PROHIBITION OF SEX DISCRIMINATION

Sex Discrimination Prohibited

Sec. 1681 [§ 901]. (a) No person in the United States shall, on the basis of sex, be excluded from participation in, be denied the benefits of, or be subjected to discrimination under any education program or activity receiving Federal financial assistance, except that:

(1) in regard to admissions to educational institutions, this section shall apply only to institutions of vocational education, professional education, and graduate higher education, and to public institutions of undergraduate higher education;

(2) in regard to admissions to educational institutions, this section shall not apply (A) for one year from June 23, 1972, nor for six years after June 23, 1972, in the case of an educational institution which has begun the process of changing from being an institution which admits only students of one sex to being an institution which admits students of both sexes, but only if it is carrying out a plan for such a change which is approved by the Secretary of Education or (B) for seven years from the date an educational institution begins the process of changing from being an institution which admits only students of only one sex to being an institution which admits students of both sexes, but only if it is carrying out a plan for such a change which is approved by the Secretary of Education, whichever is the later;

(3) this section shall not apply to an educational institution which is controlled by a religious organization if the application of this subsection would not be consistent with the religious tenets of such organization;

(4) this section shall not apply to an educational institution whose primary purpose is the training of individuals for the military services of the United States, or the merchant marine;

(5) in regard to admissions this section shall not apply to any public institution of undergraduate higher education which is an institution that

traditionally and continually from its establishment has had a policy of admitting only students of one sex;

(6) this section shall not apply to membership practices—

(A) of a social fraternity or social sorority which is exempt from taxation under section 501(a) of Title 26, the active membership of which consists primarily of students in attendance at an institution of higher education, or

(B) of the Young Men's Christian Association, Young Women's Christian Association, Girl Scouts, Boy Scouts, Camp Fire Girls, and voluntary youth service organizations which are so exempt, the membership of which has traditionally been limited to persons of one sex and principally to persons of less than nineteen years of age;

(7) this section shall not apply to—

(A) any program or activity of the American Legion undertaken in connection with the organization or operation of any Boys State conference, Boys Nation conference, Girls State conference, or Girls Nation conference; or

(B) any program or activity of any secondary school or educational institution specifically for—

(i) the promotion of any Boys State conference, Boys Nation conference, Girls State conference, or Girls Nation conference; or

(ii) the selection of students to attend any such conference;

(8) this section shall not preclude father-son or mother-daughter activities at an educational institution, but if such activities are provided for students of one sex, opportunities for reasonably comparable activities shall be provided for students of the other sex; and

(9) this section shall not apply with respect to any scholarship or other financial assistance awarded by an institution of higher education to any individual because such individual has received such award in any pageant in which the attainment of such award is based upon a combination of factors related to the personal appearance, poise, and talent of such individual and in which participation is limited to individuals of one sex only, so long as such pageant is in compliance with other nondiscrimination provisions of Federal law.

(b) Nothing contained in subsection (a) of this section shall be interpreted to require any educational institution to grant preferential or disparate treatment to the members of one sex on account of an imbalance which may exist with respect to the total number or percentage of persons of that sex participating in or receiving the benefits of any federally supported program or activity, in comparison with the total number or percentage of persons of that sex in any community, State, section, or other area: *Provided,* That this subsection shall not be construed to prevent the consideration in any hearing or proceeding under this chapter of statistical evidence tending to show that such an imbalance exists with respect to the participation in, or receipt of the benefits of, any such program or activity by the members of one sex.

(c) For purposes of this chapter an educational institution means any public or private preschool, elementary, or secondary school, or any institution of vocational, professional, or higher education, except that in the case of an educational institution composed of more than one school, college, or department which are administratively separate units, such term means each such school, college, or department.

* * *

Effect on Other Laws

Sec. 1685 [§ 905]. Nothing in this chapter shall add to or detract from any existing authority with respect to any program or activity under which Federal financial assistance is extended by way of a contract of insurance or guaranty.

Interpretation With Respect to Living Facilities

Sec. 1686 [§ 906]. Notwithstanding anything to the contrary contained in this chapter, nothing contained herein shall be construed to prohibit any educational institution receiving funds under this Act, from maintaining separate living facilities for the different sexes.

* * *

CIVIL RIGHTS RESTORATION ACT OF 1987
(P.L. 100–259)

* * *

EDUCATION AMENDMENTS AMENDMENT

SEC. 3. (a) Title IX of the Education Amendments of 1972 is amended by adding at the end of the following new sections:

"INTERPRETATION OF 'PROGRAM OR ACTIVITY' "

[Sec. 1687] "SEC. 908. For the purposes of this title, the term 'program or activity' and 'program' mean all of the operations of—

"(1)(A) a department, agency, special purpose district, or other instrumentality of a State or of a local government; or

"(B) the entity of such State or local government that distributes such assistance and each such department or agency (and each other State or local government entity) to which the assistance is extended, in the case of assistance to a State or local government;

"(2)(A) a college, university, or other postsecondary institution, or a public system of higher education; or

"(B) a local educational agency (as defined in section 198(a)(10) of the Elementary and Secondary Education Act of 1965), system of vocational education, or other school system;

"(3)(A) an entire corporation, partnership, or other private organization, or an entire sole proprietorship—

"(i) if assistance is extended to such corporation, partnership, private organization, or sole proprietorship as a whole; or

"(ii) which is principally engaged in the business of providing education, health care, housing, social services, or parks and recreation; or

"(B) the entire plant or other comparable, geographically separate facility to which Federal financial assistance is extended, in the case of any other corporation, partnership, private organization, or sole proprietorship; or

"(4) any other entity which is established by two or more of the entities described in paragraph (1), (2), or (3);

any part of which is extended Federal financial assistance, except that such term does not include any operation of an entity which is controlled by a religious organization if the application of section 901 to such operation would not be consistent with the religious tenets of such organization."

(b) Notwithstanding any provision of this Act or any amendment adopted thereto:

"NEUTRALITY WITH RESPECT TO ABORTION"

[Sec. 1688] "SEC. 909. Nothing in this title shall be construed to require or prohibit any person, or public or private entity, to provide or pay for any benefit or service, including the use of facilities, related to an abortion. Nothing in this section shall be construed to permit a penalty to be imposed on any person or individual because such person or individual is seeking or has received any benefit or service related to a legal abortion."

* * *

EQUAL EMPLOYMENT OPPORTUNITY COMMISSION GUIDELINES ON DISCRIMINATION BECAUSE OF SEX
29 C.F.R. § 1604 et seq.

* * *

§ 1604.11   Sexual harassment.

(a) Harassment on the basis of sex is a violation of Sec. 703 of Title VII.[1] Unwelcome sexual advances, requests for sexual favors, and other verbal or physical conduct of a sexual nature constitute sexual harassment when (1) submission to such conduct is made either explicitly or implicitly a term or condition of an individual's employment, (2) submission to or rejection of such conduct by an individual is used as the basis for employment decisions affecting such individual, or (3) such conduct has the purpose or effect of unreasonably interfering with an individual's work performance or creating an intimidating, hostile, or offensive working environment.

(b) In determining whether alleged conduct constitutes sexual harassment, the Commission will look at the record as a whole and at the totality of the circumstances, such as the nature of the sexual advances and the context

---

1. The principles involved here continue to apply to race, color, religion or national origin.

in which the alleged incidents occurred. The determination of the legality of a particular action will be made from the facts, on a case by case basis.

(c) Applying general Title VII principles, an employer, employment agency, joint apprenticeship committee or labor organization (hereinafter collectively referred to as "employer") is responsible for its acts and those of its agents and supervisory employees with respect to sexual harassment regardless of whether the specific acts complained of were authorized or even forbidden by the employer and regardless of whether the employer knew or should have known of their occurrence. The Commission will examine the circumstances of the particular employment relationship and the job junctions performed by the individual in determining whether an individual acts in either a supervisory or agency capacity.

(d) With respect to conduct between fellow employees, an employer is responsible for acts of sexual harassment in the workplace where the employer (or its agents or supervisory employees) knows or should have known of the conduct, unless it can show that it took immediate and appropriate corrective action.

(e) An employer may also be responsible for the acts of non-employees, with respect to sexual harassment of employees in the workplace, where the employer (or its agents or supervisory employees) knows or should have known of the conduct and fails to take immediate and appropriate corrective action. In reviewing these cases the Commission will consider the extent of the employer's control and any other legal responsibility which the employer may have with respect to the conduct of such non-employees.

(f) Prevention is the best tool for the elimination of sexual harassment. An employer should take all steps necessary to prevent sexual harassment from occurring, such as affirmatively raising the subject, expressing strong disapproval, developing appropriate sanctions, informing employees of their right to raise and how to raise the issue of harassment under Title VII, and developing methods to sensitize all concerned.

(g) Other related practices: Where employment opportunities or benefits are granted because of an individual's submission to the employer's sexual advances or requests for sexual favors, the employer may be held liable for unlawful sex discrimination against other persons who were qualified for but denied that employment opportunity or benefit.

TITLE II [OF THE CIVIL RIGHTS ACT OF 1991]—GLASS CEILING

Sec. 201. Short Title

This title may be cited as the "Glass Ceiling Act of 1991".

Sec. 202. Findings and Purpose

(a) Findings.—Congress finds that—

(1) despite a dramatically growing presence in the workplace, women and minorities remain underrepresented in management and decision-making positions in business;

(2) artificial barriers exist to the advancement of women and minorities in the workplace;

(3) United States corporations are increasingly relying on women and minorities to meet employment requirements and are increasingly aware of the advantages derived from a diverse work force;

(4) the "Glass Ceiling Initiative" undertaken by the Department of Labor, including the release of the report entitled "Report on the Glass Ceiling Initiative", has been instrumental in raising public awareness of—

(A) the underrepresentation of women and minorities at the management and decisionmaking levels in the United States work force;

(B) the underrepresentation of women and minorities in line functions in the United States work force;

(C) the lack of access for qualified women and minorities to credential-building developmental opportunities; and

(D) the desirability of eliminating artificial barriers to the advancement of women and minorities to such levels;

(5) the establishment of a commission to examine issues raised by the Glass Ceiling Initiative would help—

(A) focus greater attention on the importance of eliminating artificial barriers to the advancement of women and minorities to management and decisionmaking positions in business; and

(B) promote work force diversity;

(6) a comprehensive study that includes analysis of the manner in which management and decisionmaking positions are filled, the developmental and skill-enhancing practices used to foster the necessary qualifications for advancement, and the compensation programs and reward structures utilized in the corporate sector would assist in the establishment of practices and policies promoting opportunities for, and eliminating artificial barriers to, the advancement of women and minorities to management and decisionmaking positions; and

(7) a national award recognizing employers whose practices and policies promote opportunities for, and eliminate artificial barriers to, the advancement of women and minorities will foster the advancement of women and minorities into higher level positions by—

(A) helping to encourage United States companies to modify practices and policies to promote opportunities for, and eliminate artificial barriers to, the upward mobility of women and minorities; and

(B) providing specific guidance for other United States employers that wish to learn how to revise practices and policies to improve the access and employment opportunities of women and minorities.

(b) Purpose.—The purpose of this title is to establish—

(1) a Glass Ceiling Commission to study—

(A) the manner in which business fills management and decisionmaking positions;

(B) the developmental and skill-enhancing practices used to foster the necessary qualifications for advancement into such positions; and

(C) the compensation programs and reward structures currently utilized in the workplace; and

(2) an annual award for excellence in promoting a more diverse skilled work force at the management and decisionmaking levels in business.

Sec. 203. Establishment of Glass Ceiling Commission

(a) In General.—There is established a Glass Ceiling Commission (referred to in this title as the "Commission"), to conduct a study and prepare recommendations concerning—

(1) eliminating artificial barriers to the advancement of women and minorities; and

(2) increasing the opportunities and developmental experiences of women and minorities to foster advancement of women and minorities to management and decisionmaking positions in business.

Appendix

UNITED STATES v. VIRGINIA et al.

Supreme Court of the United States, 1996.
__ U.S. __, __ S.Ct. __, __ L.Ed.2d __, 1996 WL 345786.

[This opinion affirms in part and overrules in part the Fourth Circuit's VMI opinions on pp. 1030 and 1038.]

Justice Ginsburg delivered the opinion of the Court.

Virginia's public institutions of higher learning include an incomparable military college, Virginia Military Institute (VMI). The United States maintains that the Constitution's equal protection guarantee precludes Virginia from reserving exclusively to men the unique educational opportunities VMI affords. We agree.

I

Founded in 1839, VMI is today the sole single-sex school among Virginia's 15 public institutions of higher learning. VMI's distinctive mission is to produce "citizen-soldiers," men prepared for leadership in civilian life and in military service. VMI pursues this mission through pervasive training of a kind not available anywhere else in Virginia. Assigning prime place to character development, VMI uses an "adversative method" modeled on English public schools and once characteristic of military instruction. VMI constantly endeavors to instill physical and mental discipline in its cadets and impart to them a strong moral code. The school's graduates leave VMI with heightened comprehension of their capacity to deal with duress and stress, and a large sense of accomplishment for completing the hazardous course.

VMI has notably succeeded in its mission to produce leaders; among its alumni are military generals, Members of Congress, and business executives. The school's alumni overwhelmingly perceive that their VMI training helped them to realize their personal goals. VMI's endowment reflects the loyalty of its graduates; VMI has the largest per-student endowment of all undergraduate institutions in the Nation.

Neither the goal of producing citizen-soldiers nor VMI's implementing methodology is inherently unsuitable to women. And the school's impressive record in producing leaders has made admission desirable to some women. Nevertheless, Virginia has elected to preserve exclusively for men the advantages and opportunities a VMI education affords.

II

A

From its establishment in 1839 as one of the Nation's first state military colleges, see 1839 Va. Acts, ch. 20, VMI has remained financially supported by Virginia and "subject to the control of the [Virginia] General Assembly,"

Va.Code Ann. § 23–92 (1993). First southern college to teach engineering and industrial chemistry, see H. Wise, Drawing Out the Man: The VMI Story 13 (1978)(The VMI Story), VMI once provided teachers for the State's schools, see 1842 Va. Acts, ch. 24, § 2 (requiring every cadet to teach in one of the Commonwealth's schools for a 2–year period).[1] Civil War strife threatened the school's vitality, but a resourceful superintendent regained legislative support by highlighting "VMI's great potential[,] through its technical know-how," to advance Virginia's postwar recovery. The VMI Story 47.

VMI today enrolls about 1,300 men as cadets.[2] Its academic offerings in the liberal arts, sciences, and engineering are also available at other public colleges and universities in Virginia. But VMI's mission is special. It is the mission of the school

> " 'to produce educated and honorable men, prepared for the varied work of civil life, imbued with love of learning, confident in the functions and attitudes of leadership, possessing a high sense of public service, advocates of the American democracy and free enterprise system, and ready as citizen-soldiers to defend their country in time of national peril.' " 766 F.Supp. 1407, 1425 (W.D.Va.1991)(quoting Mission Study Committee of the VMI Board of Visitors, Report, May 16, 1986).

In contrast to the federal service academies, institutions maintained "to prepare cadets for career service in the armed forces," VMI's program "is directed at preparation for both military and civilian life"; "[o]nly about 15% of VMI cadets enter career military service." 766 F.Supp., at 1432.

VMI produces its "citizen-soldiers" through "an adversative, or doubting, model of education" which features "[p]hysical rigor, mental stress, absolute equality of treatment, absence of privacy, minute regulation of behavior, and indoctrination in desirable values." Id., at 1421. As one Commandant of Cadets described it, the adversative method "dissects the young student," and makes him aware of his "limits and capabilities," so that he knows "how far he can go with his anger, . . . how much he can take under stress, . . . exactly what he can do when he is physically exhausted." Id., at 1421–1422 (quoting Col. N. Bissell).

VMI cadets live in spartan barracks where surveillance is constant and privacy nonexistent; they wear uniforms, eat together in the mess hall, and regularly participate in drills. Id., at 1424, 1432. Entering students are incessantly exposed to the rat line, "an extreme form of the adversative model," comparable in intensity to Marine Corps boot camp. Id., at 1422. Tormenting and punishing, the rat line bonds new cadets to their fellow

---

1. During the Civil War, school teaching became a field dominated by women. See A. Scott, The Southern Lady: From Pedestal to Politics, 1830–1930, p. 82 (1970).

2. Historically, most of Virginia's public colleges and universities were single-sex; by the mid–1970's, however, all except VMI had become coeducational. 766 F.Supp. 1407, 1418–1419 (W.D.Va.1991). For example, Virginia's legislature incorporated Farmville Female Seminary Association in 1839, the year VMI opened. 1839 Va. Acts, ch. 167. Originally providing instruction in "English, Latin, Greek, French, and piano" in a "home atmosphere," R. Sprague, Longwood College: A History 7–8, 15 (1989)(Longwood College), Farmville Female Seminary became a public institution in 1884 with a mission to train "white female teachers for public schools," 1884 Va. Acts, ch. 311. The school became Longwood College in 1949, Longwood College 136, and introduced coeducation in 1976, id., at 133.

sufferers and, when they have completed the 7–month experience, to their former tormentors. Ibid.

VMI's "adversative model" is further characterized by a hierarchical "class system" of privileges and responsibilities, a "dyke system" for assigning a senior class mentor to each entering class "rat," and a stringently enforced "honor code," which prescribes that a cadet " 'does not lie, cheat, steal nor tolerate those who do.' " Id., at 1422–1423.

VMI attracts some applicants because of its reputation as an extraordinarily challenging military school, and "because its alumni are exceptionally close to the school." Id., at 1421. "[W]omen have no opportunity anywhere to gain the benefits of [the system of education at VMI]." Ibid.

B

In 1990, prompted by a complaint filed with the Attorney General by a female high-school student seeking admission to VMI, the United States sued the Commonwealth of Virginia and VMI, alleging that VMI's exclusively male admission policy violated the Equal Protection Clause of the Fourteenth Amendment. Id., at 1408. Trial of the action consumed six days and involved an array of expert witnesses on each side. Ibid.

In the two years preceding the lawsuit, the District Court noted, VMI had received inquiries from 347 women, but had responded to none of them. Id., at 1436. "[S]ome women, at least," the court said, "would want to attend the school if they had the opportunity." Id., at 1414. The court further recognized that, with recruitment, VMI could "achieve at least 10% female enrollment"—"a sufficient 'critical mass' to provide the female cadets with a positive educational experience." Id., at 1437–1438. And it was also established that "some women are capable of all of the individual activities required of VMI cadets." Id., at 1412. In addition, experts agreed that if VMI admitted women, "the VMI ROTC experience would become a better training program from the perspective of the armed forces, because it would provide training in dealing with a mixed-gender army." Id., at 1441.

The District Court ruled in favor of VMI, however, and rejected the equal protection challenge pressed by the United States. That court correctly recognized that Mississippi Univ. for Women v. Hogan, 458 U.S. 718 (1982), was the closest guide.   * * *

The District Court reasoned that education in "a single-gender environment, be it male or female," yields substantial benefits. 766 F.Supp., at 1415. VMI's school for men brought diversity to an otherwise coeducational Virginia system, and that diversity was "enhanced by VMI's unique method of instruction." Ibid. If single-gender education for males ranks as an important governmental objective, it becomes obvious, the District Court concluded, that the only means of achieving the objective "is to exclude women from the all-male institution—VMI." Ibid.

"Women are [indeed] denied a unique educational opportunity that is available only at VMI," the District Court acknowledged. Id., at 1432. But "[VMI's] single-sex status would be lost, and some aspects of the [school's] distinctive method would be altered" if women were admitted, id., at 1413: "Allowance for personal privacy would have to be made," id., at 1412; "[p]hysical education requirements would have to be altered, at least for the women," id., at 1413; the adversative environment could not survive unmodified, id., at 1412–1413. Thus, "sufficient constitutional justification" had been shown, the District Court held, "for continuing [VMI's] single-sex policy." Id., at 1413.

The Court of Appeals for the Fourth Circuit disagreed and vacated the District Court's judgment. The appellate court held: "The Commonwealth of Virginia has not ... advanced any state policy by which it can justify its determination, under an announced policy of diversity, to afford VMI's unique type of program to men and not to women." 976 F.2d 890, 892 (1992).

* * *

The parties agreed that "*some* women can meet the physical standards now imposed on men," id., at 896, and the court was satisfied that "neither the goal of producing citizen soldiers nor VMI's implementing methodology is inherently unsuitable to women," id., at 899. The Court of Appeals, however, accepted the District Court's finding that "at least these three aspects of VMI's program—physical training, the absence of privacy, and the adversative approach—would be materially affected by coeducation." Id., at 896–897. Remanding the case, the appeals court assigned to Virginia, in the first instance, responsibility for selecting a remedial course. The court suggested these options for the State: Admit women to VMI; establish parallel institutions or programs; or abandon state support, leaving VMI free to pursue its policies as a private institution. Id., at 900. In May 1993, this Court denied certiorari. See 508 U.S. 946; see also ibid. (opinion of SCALIA, J., noting the interlocutory posture of the litigation).

C

In response to the Fourth Circuit's ruling, Virginia proposed a parallel program for women: Virginia Women's Institute for Leadership (VWIL). The 4–year, state-sponsored undergraduate program would be located at Mary Baldwin College, a private liberal arts school for women, and would be open, initially, to about 25 to 30 students. Although VWIL would share VMI's mission—to produce "citizen-soldiers"—the VWIL program would differ, as does Mary Baldwin College, from VMI in academic offerings, methods of education, and financial resources. See 852 F.Supp. 471, 476–477 (W.D.Va. 1994).

The average combined SAT score of entrants at Mary Baldwin is about 100 points lower than the score for VMI freshmen. See id., at 501. Mary Baldwin's faculty holds "significantly fewer Ph.D.'s than the faculty at VMI," id., at 502, and receives significantly lower salaries, see Tr. 158 (testimony of James Lott, Dean of Mary Baldwin College), reprinted in 2 App. in Nos. 94–1667 and 94–1717(CA4)(hereinafter Tr.). While VMI offers degrees in liberal arts, the sciences, and engineering, Mary Baldwin, at the time of trial, offered only bachelor of arts degrees. See 852 F.Supp., at 503. A VWIL student seeking to earn an engineering degree could gain one, without public support, by attending Washington University in St. Louis, Missouri, for two years, paying the required private tuition. See ibid.

Experts in educating women at the college level composed the Task Force charged with designing the VWIL program; Task Force members were drawn from Mary Baldwin's own faculty and staff. Id., at 476. Training its attention on methods of instruction appropriate for "most women," the Task Force determined that a military model would be "wholly inappropriate" for VWIL. Ibid.; see 44 F.3d 1229, 1233 (C.A.4 1995).

VWIL students would participate in ROTC programs and a newly established, "largely ceremonial" Virginia Corps of Cadets, id., at 1234, but the VWIL House would not have a military format, 852 F.Supp., at 477, and VWIL would not require its students to eat meals together or to wear uniforms during the school day, id., at 495. In lieu of VMI's adversative method, the VWIL Task Force favored "a cooperative method which reinforces self-esteem." Id., at 476. In addition to the standard bachelor of arts program offered at Mary Baldwin, VWIL students would take courses in leadership, complete an off-campus leadership externship, participate in community service projects, and assist in arranging a speaker series. See 44 F.3d, at 1234.

Virginia represented that it will provide equal financial support for instate VWIL students and VMI cadets, 852 F.Supp., at 483, and the VMI Foundation agreed to supply a $5.4625 million endowment for the VWIL program, id., at 499. Mary Baldwin's own endowment is about $19 million; VMI's is $131 million. Id., at 503. Mary Baldwin will add $35 million to its endowment based on future commitments; VMI will add $220 million. Ibid. The VMI Alumni Association has developed a network of employers interested in hiring VMI graduates. The Association has agreed to open its network to VWIL graduates, id., at 499, but those graduates will not have the advantage afforded by a VMI degree.

D

Virginia returned to the District Court seeking approval of its proposed remedial plan, and the court decided the plan met the requirements of the Equal Protection Clause. Id., at 473. The District Court again acknowledged evidentiary support for these determinations: "[T]he VMI methodology could be used to educate women and, in fact, some women ... may prefer the VMI methodology to the VWIL methodology." Id., at 481. But the "controlling legal principles," the District Court decided, "do not require the Commonwealth to provide a mirror image VMI for women." Ibid. The court anticipated that the two schools would "achieve substantially similar outcomes." Ibid. It concluded: "If VMI marches to the beat of a drum, then Mary Baldwin marches to the melody of a fife and when the march is over, both will have arrived at the same destination." Id., at 484.

A divided Court of Appeals affirmed the District Court's judgment. 44 F.3d 1229 (C.A.4 1995). This time, the appellate court determined to give "greater scrutiny to the selection of means than to the [State's] proffered objective." Id., at 1236. The official objective or purpose, the court said, should be reviewed deferentially. Ibid. Respect for the "legislative will," the court reasoned, meant that the judiciary should take a "cautious approach," inquiring into the "legitima[cy]" of the governmental objective and refusing approval for any purpose revealed to be "pernicious." Ibid.

"[P]roviding the option of a single-gender college education may be considered a legitimate and important aspect of a public system of higher education," the appeals court observed, id., at 1238; that objective, the court added, is "not pernicious," id., at 1239. Moreover, the court continued, the adversative method vital to a VMI education "has never been tolerated in a sexually heterogeneous environment." Ibid. The method itself "was not designed to exclude women," the court noted, but women could not be accommodated in the VMI program, the court believed, for female participation in VMI's adversative training "would destroy . . . any sense of decency that still permeates the relationship between the sexes." Ibid.

Having determined, deferentially, the legitimacy of Virginia's purpose, the court considered the question of means. Exclusion of "men at Mary Baldwin College and women at VMI," the court said, was essential to Virginia's purpose, for without such exclusion, the State could not "accomplish [its] objective of providing single-gender education." Ibid.

The court recognized that, as it analyzed the case, means merged into end, and the merger risked "bypass[ing] any equal protection scrutiny." Id., at 1237. The court therefore added another inquiry, a decisive test it called "substantive comparability." Ibid. The key question, the court said, was whether men at VMI and women at VWIL would obtain "substantively comparable benefits at their institution or through other means offered by the [S]tate." Ibid. Although the appeals court recognized that the VWIL degree "lacks the historical benefit and prestige" of a VMI degree, it nevertheless found the educational opportunities at the two schools "sufficiently comparable." Id., at 1241.

Senior Circuit Judge Phillips dissented. * * * The Fourth Circuit denied rehearing en banc. * * *

III

The cross-petitions in this case present two ultimate issues. First, does Virginia's exclusion of women from the educational opportunities provided by VMI—extraordinary opportunities for military training and civilian leadership development—deny to women "capable of all of the individual activities required of VMI cadets," 766 F.Supp., at 1412, the equal protection of the laws guaranteed by the Fourteenth Amendment? Second, if VMI's "unique" situation, id., at 1413—as Virginia's sole single-sex public institution of higher education—offends the Constitution's equal protection principle, what is the remedial requirement?

IV

We note, once again, the core instruction of this Court's pathmarking decisions in J.E.B. v. Alabama ex rel. T. B., 511 U.S. 127, 136–137, and n. 6, 114 S.Ct. 1419, 128 L.Ed.2d 89 (1994), and Mississippi Univ. for Women, 458 U.S., at 724 (internal quotation marks omitted): Parties who seek to defend gender-based government action must demonstrate an "exceedingly persuasive justification" for that action.

Today's skeptical scrutiny of official action denying rights or opportunities based on sex responds to volumes of history. As a plurality of this Court acknowledged a generation ago, "our Nation has had a long and unfortunate history of sex discrimination." Frontiero v. Richardson, 411 U.S. 677, 684, 93 S.Ct. 1764, 36 L.Ed.2d 583 (1973). Through a century plus three decades and more of that history, women did not count among voters composing "We the

People";[5] not until 1920 did women gain a constitutional right to the franchise. Id., at 685. And for a half century thereafter, it remained the prevailing doctrine that government, both federal and state, could withhold from women opportunities accorded men so long as any "basis in reason" could be conceived for the discrimination. See, e.g., Goesaert v. Cleary, 335 U.S. 464, 467, 69 S.Ct. 198, 93 L.Ed. 163 (1948)(rejecting challenge of female tavern owner and her daughter to Michigan law denying bartender licenses to females—except for wives and daughters of male tavern owners; Court would not "give ear" to the contention that "an unchivalrous desire of male bartenders to ... monopolize the calling" prompted the legislation).

In 1971, for the first time in our Nation's history, this Court ruled in favor of a woman who complained that her State had denied her the equal protection of its laws. Reed v. Reed, 404 U.S. 71, 73, 92 S.Ct. 251, 30 L.Ed.2d 225 (holding unconstitutional Idaho Code prescription that, among " 'several persons claiming and equally entitled to administer [a decedent's estate], males must be preferred to females' "). Since Reed, the Court has repeatedly recognized that neither federal nor state government acts compatibly with the equal protection principle when a law or official policy denies to women, simply because they are women, full citizenship stature—equal opportunity to aspire, achieve, participate in and contribute to society based on their individual talents and capacities. See, e.g., Kirchberg v. Feenstra, 450 U.S. 455, 462–463, 101 S.Ct. 1195, 67 L.Ed.2d 428 (1981)(affirming invalidity of Louisiana law that made husband "head and master" of property jointly owned with his wife, giving him unilateral right to dispose of such property without his wife's consent); Stanton v. Stanton, 421 U.S. 7, 95 S.Ct. 1373, 43 L.Ed.2d 688 (1975)(invalidating Utah requirement that parents support boys until age 21, girls only until age 18).

Without equating gender classifications, for all purposes, to classifications based on race or national origin,[6] the Court, in post-Reed decisions, has carefully inspected official action that closes a door or denies opportunity to women (or to men). See J.E. B., 511 U.S., at 152 (KENNEDY, J., concurring in judgment)(case law evolving since 1971 "reveal[s] a strong presumption that gender classifications are invalid"). To summarize the Court's current directions for cases of official classification based on gender: Focusing on the differential treatment or denial of opportunity for which relief is sought, the reviewing court must determine whether the proffered justification is "exceedingly persuasive." The burden of justification is demanding and it rests entirely on the State. See Mississippi Univ. for Women, 458 U.S., at 724. The State must show "at least that the [challenged] classification serves 'important governmental objectives and that the discriminatory means employed' are 'substantially related to the achievement of those objectives.' "

---

5. As Thomas Jefferson stated the view prevailing when the Constitution was new:

"Were our State a pure democracy ... there would yet be excluded from their deliberations ... women, who, to prevent depravation of morals and ambiguity of issue, should not mix promiscuously in the public meetings of men." Letter from Thomas Jefferson to Samuel Kercheval (Sept. 5, 1816), in 10 Writings of Thomas Jefferson 45–46, n. 1 (P. Ford ed. 1899).

6. The Court has thus far reserved most stringent judicial scrutiny for classifications based on race or national origin, but last Term observed that strict scrutiny of such classifications is not inevitably "fatal in fact." Adarand Constructors, Inc. v. Pena, 515 U.S. __, __ (1995)(slip op., at 35)(internal quotation marks omitted).

Ibid. (quoting Wengler v. Druggists Mutual Ins. Co., 446 U.S. 142, 150, 100 S.Ct. 1540, 64 L.Ed.2d 107 (1980)). The justification must be genuine, not hypothesized or invented post hoc in response to litigation. And it must not rely on overbroad generalizations about the different talents, capacities, or preferences of males and females. See Weinberger v. Wiesenfeld, 420 U.S. 636, 643, 648, 95 S.Ct. 1225, 43 L.Ed.2d 514 (1975); Califano v. Goldfarb, 430 U.S. 199, 223–224, 97 S.Ct. 1021, 51 L.Ed.2d 270 (1977)(STEVENS, J., concurring in judgment).

The heightened review standard our precedent establishes does not make sex a proscribed classification. Supposed "inherent differences" are no longer accepted as a ground for race or national origin classifications. See Loving v. Virginia, 388 U.S. 1, 87 S.Ct. 1817, 18 L.Ed.2d 1010 (1967). Physical differences between men and women, however, are enduring: "[T]he two sexes are not fungible; a community made up exclusively of one [sex] is different from a community composed of both." Ballard v. United States, 329 U.S. 187, 193, 67 S.Ct. 261, 91 L.Ed. 181 (1946).

"Inherent differences" between men and women, we have come to appreciate, remain cause for celebration, but not for denigration of the members of either sex or for artificial constraints on an individual's opportunity. Sex classifications may be used to compensate women "for particular economic disabilities [they have] suffered," Califano v. Webster, 430 U.S. 313, 320, 97 S.Ct. 1192, 51 L.Ed.2d 360 (1977)(per curiam), to "promot[e] equal employment opportunity," see California Federal Sav. & Loan Assn. v. Guerra, 479 U.S. 272, 289, 107 S.Ct. 683, 93 L.Ed.2d 613 (1987), to advance full development of the talent and capacities of our Nation's people.[7] But such classifications may not be used, as they once were, see *Goesaert*, 335 U.S., at 467, to create or perpetuate the legal, social, and economic inferiority of women.

Measuring the record in this case against the review standard just described, we conclude that Virginia has shown no "exceedingly persuasive justification" for excluding all women from the citizen-soldier training afforded by VMI. We therefore affirm the Fourth Circuit's initial judgment, which held that Virginia had violated the Fourteenth Amendment's Equal Protection Clause. Because the remedy proffered by Virginia—the Mary Baldwin VWIL program—does not cure the constitutional violation, i.e., it does not provide equal opportunity, we reverse the Fourth Circuit's final judgment in this case.

7. Several *amici* have urged that diversity in educational opportunities is an altogether appropriate governmental pursuit and that single-sex schools can contribute importantly to such diversity. Indeed, it is the mission of some single-sex schools "to dissipate, rather than perpetuate, traditional gender classifications." See Brief for Twenty–Six Private Women's Colleges as *Amici Curiae* 5. We do not question the State's prerogative evenhandedly to support diverse educational opportunities. We address specifically and only an educational opportunity recognized by the District Court and the Court of Appeals as "unique," see 766 F.Supp., at 1413, 1432, 976 F.2d, at 892, an opportunity available only at Virginia's premier military institute, the State's sole single-sex public university or college. Cf. Mississippi Univ. for Women v. Hogan, 458 U.S. 718, 720, n. 1, 102 S.Ct. 3331, 73 L.Ed.2d 1090 (1982)("Mississippi maintains no other single-sex public university or college. Thus, we are not faced with the question of whether States can provide 'separate but equal' undergraduate institutions for males and females.").

V

The Fourth Circuit initially held that Virginia had advanced no state policy by which it could justify, under equal protection principles, its determination "to afford VMI's unique type of program to men and not to women." 976 F.2d, at 892. Virginia challenges that "liability" ruling and asserts two justifications in defense of VMI's exclusion of women. First, the Commonwealth contends, "single-sex education provides important educational benefits," Brief for Cross–Petitioners 20, and the option of single-sex education contributes to "diversity in educational approaches," id., at 25. Second, the Commonwealth argues, "the unique VMI method of character development and leadership training," the school's adversative approach, would have to be modified were VMI to admit women. Id., at 33–36. We consider these two justifications in turn.

A

Single-sex education affords pedagogical benefits to at least some students, Virginia emphasizes, and that reality is uncontested in this litigation.[8] Similarly, it is not disputed that diversity among public educational institutions can serve the public good. But Virginia has not shown that VMI was established, or has been maintained, with a view to diversifying, by its categorical exclusion of women, educational opportunities within the State. In cases of this genre, our precedent instructs that "benign" justifications proffered in defense of categorical exclusions will not be accepted automatically; a tenable justification must describe actual state purposes, not rationalizations for actions in fact differently grounded. See *Wiesenfeld*, 420 U.S., at 648, and n. 16 ("mere recitation of a benign [or] compensatory purpose" does not block "inquiry into the actual purposes" of government-maintained gender-based classifications); Goldfarb, 430 U.S., at 212–213 (rejecting government-proffered purposes after "inquiry into the actual purposes")(internal quotation marks omitted).

Mississippi Univ. for Women is immediately in point. There the State asserted, in justification of its exclusion of men from a nursing school, that it was engaging in "educational affirmative action" by "compensat[ing] for discrimination against women." 458 U.S., at 727. Undertaking a "searching analysis," id., at 728, the Court found no close resemblance between "the alleged objective" and "the actual purpose underlying the discriminatory classification," id., at 730. Pursuing a similar inquiry here, we reach the same conclusion.

Neither recent nor distant history bears out Virginia's alleged pursuit of diversity through single-sex educational options. In 1839, when the State established VMI, a range of educational opportunities for men and women was

---

8. On this point, the dissent sees fire where there is no flame. See post, at 33–34, 35–37. "Both men and women can benefit from a single-sex education," the District Court recognized, although "the beneficial effects" of such education, the court added, apparently "are stronger among women than among men." 766 F.Supp., at 1414. The United States does not challenge that recognition. Cf. C. Jencks & D. Riesman, The Academic Revolution 297–298 (1968):

"The pluralistic argument for preserving all-male colleges is uncomfortably similar to the pluralistic argument for preserving all-white colleges. . . . The all-male college would be relatively easy to defend if it emerged from a world in which women were established as fully equal to men. But it does not. It is therefore likely to be a witting or unwitting device for preserving tacit assumptions of male superiority—assumptions for which women must eventually pay."

scarcely contemplated. Higher education at the time was considered dangerous for women;[9] reflecting widely held views about women's proper place, the Nation's first universities and colleges—for example, Harvard in Massachusetts, William and Mary in Virginia—admitted only men. See E. Farello, A History of the Education of Women in the United States 163 (1970). VMI was not at all novel in this respect: In admitting no women, VMI followed the lead of the State's flagship school, the University of Virginia, founded in 1819.

"[N]o struggle for the admission of women to a state university," a historian has recounted, "was longer drawn out, or developed more bitterness, than that at the University of Virginia." 2 T. Woody, A History of Women's Education in the United States 254 (1929)(History of Women's Education). In 1879, the State Senate resolved to look into the possibility of higher education for women, recognizing that Virginia " 'has never, at any period of her history,' " provided for the higher education of her daughters, though she " 'has liberally provided for the higher education of her sons.' " Ibid. (quoting 10 Educ. J. Va. 212 (1879)). Despite this recognition, no new opportunities were instantly open to women.[10]

Virginia eventually provided for several women's seminaries and colleges. Farmville Female Seminary became a public institution in 1884. See supra, at 3, n. 2. Two women's schools, Mary Washington College and James Madison University, were founded in 1908; another, Radford University, was founded in 1910. 766 F.Supp., at 1418–1419. By the mid–1970's, all four schools had become coeducational. Ibid.

Debate concerning women's admission as undergraduates at the main university continued well past the century's midpoint. Familiar arguments were rehearsed. If women were admitted, it was feared, they "would encroach on the rights of men; there would be new problems of government, perhaps scandals; the old honor system would have to be changed; standards would be lowered to those of other coeducational schools; and the glorious reputation of the university, as a school for men, would be trailed in the dust." 2 History of Women's Education 255.

Ultimately, in 1970, "the most prestigious institution of higher education in Virginia," the University of Virginia, introduced coeducation and, in 1972, began to admit women on an equal basis with men. See Kirstein v. Rector and Visitors of Univ. of Virginia, 309 F.Supp. 184, 186 (E.D.Va.1970). A

---

9. Dr. Edward H. Clarke of Harvard Medical School, whose influential book, Sex in Education, went through 17 editions, was perhaps the most well-known speaker from the medical community opposing higher education for women. He maintained that the physiological effects of hard study and academic competition with boys would interfere with the development of girls' reproductive organs. See E. Clarke, Sex in Education 38–39, 62–63 (1873); id., at 127 ("identical education of the two sexes is a crime before God and humanity, that physiology protests against, and that experience weeps over"); see also H. Maudsley, Sex in Mind and in Education 17 (1874)("It is not that girls have not ambition, nor that they fail generally to run the intellectual race [in coeducational settings], but it is asserted that they do it at a cost to their strength and health

which entails life-long suffering, and even incapacitates them for the adequate performance of the natural functions of their sex."); C. Meigs, Females and Their Diseases 350 (1848)(after five or six weeks of "mental and educational discipline," a healthy woman would "lose ... the habit of menstruation" and suffer numerous ills as a result of depriving her body for the sake of her mind).

10. Virginia's Superintendent of Public Instruction dismissed the coeducational idea as " 'repugnant to the prejudices of the people' " and proposed a female college similar in quality to Girton, Smith, or Vassar. 2 History of Women's Education 254 (quoting 1 Report of the Commissioner of Education, H.R. Doc. No. 5, 58th Cong., 2d Sess., 438 (1904)).

three-judge Federal District Court confirmed: "Virginia may not now deny to women, on the basis of sex, educational opportunities at the Charlottesville campus that are not afforded in other institutions operated by the [S]tate." Id., at 187.

Virginia describes the current absence of public single-sex higher education for women as "an historical anomaly." Brief for Cross–Petitioners 30. But the historical record indicates action more deliberate than anomalous: First, protection of women against higher education; next, schools for women far from equal in resources and stature to schools for men; finally, conversion of the separate schools to coeducation. The state legislature, prior to the advent of this controversy, had repealed "[a]ll Virginia statutes requiring individual institutions to admit only men or women." 766 F.Supp., at 1419. And in 1990, an official commission, "legislatively established to chart the future goals of higher education in Virginia," reaffirmed the policy "of affording broad access" while maintaining "autonomy and diversity." 976 F.2d, at 898–899 (quoting Report of the Virginia Commission on the University of the 21st Century). Significantly, the Commission reported:

" 'Because colleges and universities provide opportunities for students to develop values and learn from role models, it is extremely important that they deal with faculty, staff, and students without regard to sex, race, or ethnic origin.' " Id., at 899 (emphasis supplied by Court of Appeals deleted).

This statement, the Court of Appeals observed, "is the only explicit one that we have found in the record in which the Commonwealth has expressed itself with respect to gender distinctions." Ibid.

Our 1982 decision in *Mississippi Univ. for Women* prompted VMI to reexamine its male-only admission policy. See 766 F.Supp., at 1427–1428. Virginia relies on that reexamination as a legitimate basis for maintaining VMI's single-sex character. See Reply Brief for Cross–Petitioners 6. A Mission Study Committee, appointed by the VMI Board of Visitors, studied the problem from October 1983 until May 1986, and in that month counseled against "change of VMI status as a single-sex college." See 766 F.Supp., at 1429 (internal quotation marks omitted). Whatever internal purpose the Mission Study Committee served—and however well-meaning the framers of the report—we can hardly extract from that effort any state policy evenhandedly to advance diverse educational options. As the District Court observed, the Committee's analysis "primarily focuse[d] on anticipated difficulties in attracting females to VMI," and the report, overall, supplied "very little indication of how th[e] conclusion was reached." Ibid.

In sum, we find no persuasive evidence in this record that VMI's male-only admission policy "is in furtherance of a state policy of 'diversity.' " See 976 F.2d, at 899. No such policy, the Fourth Circuit observed, can be discerned from the movement of all other public colleges and universities in Virginia away from single-sex education. See ibid. That court also questioned "how one institution with autonomy, but with no authority over any other state institution, can give effect to a state policy of diversity among institutions." Ibid. A purpose genuinely to advance an array of educational options, as the Court of Appeals recognized, is not served by VMI's historic and constant plan—a plan to "affor[d] a unique educational benefit only to males." Ibid. However "liberally" this plan serves the State's sons, it makes no provision whatever for her daughters. That is not *equal* protection.

B

Virginia next argues that VMI's adversative method of training provides educational benefits that cannot be made available, unmodified, to women. Alterations to accommodate women would necessarily be "radical," so "drastic," Virginia asserts, as to transform, indeed "destroy," VMI's program. See Brief for Cross–Petitioners 34–36. Neither sex would be favored by the transformation, Virginia maintains: Men would be deprived of the unique opportunity currently available to them; women would not gain that opportunity because their participation would "eliminat[e] the very aspects of [the] program that distinguish [VMI] from ... other institutions of higher education in Virginia." Id., at 34 (internal quotation marks omitted).

The District Court forecast from expert witness testimony, and the Court of Appeals accepted, that coeducation would materially affect "at least these three aspects of VMI's program—physical training, the absence of privacy, and the adversative approach." 976 F.2d, at 896–897. And it is uncontested that women's admission would require accommodations, primarily in arranging housing assignments and physical training programs for female cadets. See Brief for Cross–Respondent 11, 29–30. It is also undisputed, however, that "the VMI methodology could be used to educate women." 852 F.Supp., at 481. The District Court even allowed that some women may prefer it to the methodology a women's college might pursue. See ibid. "[S]ome women, at least, would want to attend [VMI] if they had the opportunity," the District Court recognized, 766 F.Supp., at 1414, and "some women," the expert testimony established, "are capable of all of the individual activities required of VMI cadets," id., at 1412. The parties, furthermore, agree that "*some* women can meet the physical standards [VMI] now impose[s] on men." 976 F.2d, at 896. In sum, as the Court of Appeals stated, "neither the goal of producing citizen soldiers," VMI's raison d'etre, "nor VMI's implementing methodology is inherently unsuitable to women." Id., at 899.

In support of its initial judgment for Virginia, a judgment rejecting all equal protection objections presented by the United States, the District Court made "findings" on "gender-based developmental differences." 766 F.Supp., at 1434–1435. These "findings" restate the opinions of Virginia's expert witnesses, opinions about typically male or typically female "tendencies." Id., at 1434. For example, "[m]ales tend to need an atmosphere of adversativeness," while "[f]emales tend to thrive in a cooperative atmosphere." Ibid. "I'm not saying that some women don't do well under [the] adversative model," VMI's expert on educational institutions testified, "undoubtedly there are some [women] who do"; but educational experiences must be designed "around the rule," this expert maintained, and not "around the exception." Ibid. (internal quotation marks omitted).

The United States does not challenge any expert witness estimation on average capacities or preferences of men and women. Instead, the United States emphasizes that time and again since this Court's turning point decision in Reed v. Reed, 404 U.S. 71, 92 S.Ct. 251, 30 L.Ed.2d 225 (1971), we have cautioned reviewing courts to take a "hard look" at generalizations or "tendencies" of the kind pressed by Virginia, and relied upon by the District

Court. See O'Connor, Portia's Progress, 66 N.Y.U.L.Rev. 1546, 1551 (1991). State actors controlling gates to opportunity, we have instructed, may not exclude qualified individuals based on "fixed notions concerning the roles and abilities of males and females." *Mississippi Univ. for Women*, 458 U.S., at 725; see J.E. B., 511 U.S., at 139, n. 11 (equal protection principles, as applied to gender classifications, mean state actors may not rely on "overbroad" generalizations to make "judgments about people that are likely to ... perpetuate historical patterns of discrimination").

It may be assumed, for purposes of this decision, that most women would not choose VMI's adversative method. As Fourth Circuit Judge Motz observed, however, in her dissent from the Court of Appeals' denial of rehearing en banc, it is also probable that "many men would not want to be educated in such an environment." 52 F.3d, at 93. (On that point, even our dissenting colleague might agree.) Education, to be sure, is not a "one size fits all" business. The issue, however, is not whether "women—or men—should be forced to attend VMI"; rather, the question is whether the State can constitutionally deny to women who have the will and capacity, the training and attendant opportunities that VMI uniquely affords. Ibid.

The notion that admission of women would downgrade VMI's stature, destroy the adversative system and, with it, even the school,[11] is a judgment hardly proved,[12] a prediction hardly different from other "self-fulfilling prophec[ies]," see *Mississippi Univ. for Women*, 458 U.S., at 730, once routinely used to deny rights or opportunities. When women first sought admission to the bar and access to legal education, concerns of the same order were expressed. For example, in 1876, the Court of Common Pleas of Hennepin County, Minnesota, explained why women were thought ineligible for the practice of law. Women train and educate the young, the court said, which

> "forbids that they shall bestow that time (early and late) and labor, so essential in attaining to the eminence to which the true lawyer should ever aspire. It cannot therefore be said that the opposition of courts to the admission of females to practice ... is to any extent the outgrowth of ... 'old fogyism[.]' ... [I]t arises rather from a comprehension of the magnitude of the responsibilities connected with the successful practice of

11. See post, at 1, 35, 40. Forecasts of the same kind were made regarding admission of women to the federal military academies. See, e.g., Hearings on H.R. 9832 et al. before Subcommittee No. 2 on Military Personnel of the House Committee on Armed Services, 93d Cong., 2d Sess., 137 (1975)(statement of Lt. Gen. A.P. Clark, Superintendent of U.S. Air Force Academy)("It is my considered judgment that the introduction of female cadets will inevitably erode this vital atmosphere."); id., at 165 (statement of Hon. H.H. Callaway, Secretary of the Army)("Admitting women to West Point would irrevocably change the Academy.... The Spartan atmosphere—which is so important to producing the final product— would surely be diluted, and would in all probability disappear.").

12. See 766 F.Supp., at 1413 (describing testimony of expert witness David Riesman: "[I]f VMI were to admit women, it would even-

tually find it necessary to drop the adversative system altogether, and adopt a system that provides more nurturing and support for the students."). Such judgments have attended, and impeded, women's progress toward full citizenship stature throughout our Nation's history. Speaking in 1879 in support of higher education for females, for example, Virginia State Senator C.T. Smith of Nelson recounted that legislation proposed to protect the property rights of women had encountered resistance. 10 Educ. J. Va. 213 (1879). A Senator opposing the measures objected that "there [was] no formal call for the [legislation]," and "depicted in burning eloquence the terrible consequences such laws would produce." Ibid. The legislation passed, and a year or so later, its sponsor, C.T. Smith, reported that "not one of [the forecast "terrible consequences"] has or ever will happen, even unto the sounding of Gabriel's trumpet." Ibid. See also supra, at 20.

law, and a desire to grade up the profession." In re Application of Martha Angle Dorsett to Be Admitted to Practice as Attorney and Counselor at Law (Minn. C.P. Hennepin Cty., 1876), in The Syllabi, Oct. 21, 1876, pp. 5, 6 (emphasis added).

A like fear, according to a 1925 report, accounted for Columbia Law School's resistance to women's admission, although

"[t]he faculty ... never maintained that women could not master legal learning.... No, its argument has been ... more practical. If women were admitted to the Columbia Law School, [the faculty] said, then the choicer, more manly and red-blooded graduates of our great universities would go to the Harvard Law School!" The Nation, Feb. 18, 1925, p. 173.

Medical faculties similarly resisted men and women as partners in the study of medicine. See R. Morantz–Sanchez, Sympathy and Science: Women Physicians in American Medicine 51–54, 250 (1985); see also M. Walsh, "Doctors Wanted: No Women Need Apply" 121–122 (1977)(quoting E. Clarke, Medical Education of Women, 4 Boston Med. & Surg. J. 345, 346 (1869)(" 'God forbid that I should ever see men and women aiding each other to display with the scalpel the secrets of the reproductive system....' ")); cf. supra, at 18–19, n. 9. More recently, women seeking careers in policing encountered resistance based on fears that their presence would "undermine male solidarity," see F. Heidensohn, Women in Control? 201 (1992); deprive male partners of adequate assistance, see id., at 184–185; and lead to sexual misconduct, see C. Milton et al., Women in Policing 32–33 (1974). Field studies did not confirm these fears. See Women in Control? supra, at 92–93; P. Bloch & D. Anderson, Policewomen on Patrol: Final Report (1974).

Women's successful entry into the federal military academies,[13] and their participation in the Nation's military forces,[14] indicate that Virginia's fears for the future of VMI may not be solidly grounded.[15] The State's justification for excluding all women from "citizen-soldier" training for which some are qualified, in any event, cannot rank as "exceedingly persuasive," as we have explained and applied that standard.

Virginia and VMI trained their argument on "means" rather than "end," and thus misperceived our precedent. Single-sex education at VMI serves an "important governmental objective," they maintained, and exclusion of wom-

---

13. Women cadets have graduated at the top of their class at every federal military academy. See Brief for Lieutenant Colonel Rhonda Cornum et al. as *Amici Curiae* 11, n. 25; cf. Defense Advisory Committee on Women in the Services, Report on the Integration and Performance of Women at West Point 64 (1992).

14. Brief for Lieutenant Colonel Rhonda Cornum, supra, at 5–9 (reporting the vital contributions and courageous performance of women in the military); see J. Mintz, President Nominates 1st Woman to Rank of Three–Star General, Washington Post, Mar. 27, 1996, p. A19, col. 1 (announcing President's nomination of Marine Corps Major General Carol Mutter to rank of Lieutenant General; Mutter will

head Corps manpower and planning); M. Tousignant, A New Era for the Old Guard, Washington Post, Mar. 23, 1996, p. C1, col. 2 (reporting admission of Sergeant Heather Johnsen to elite Infantry unit that keeps round-the-clock vigil at Tomb of the Unknowns in Arlington National Cemetery).

15. Inclusion of women in settings where, traditionally, they were not wanted inevitably entails a period of adjustment. As one West Point cadet squad leader recounted: "[T]he classes of '78 and '79 see the women as women, but the classes of '80 and '81 see them as classmates." U.S. Military Academy, A. Vitters, Report of Admission of Women (Project Athena II) 84 (1978)(internal quotation marks omitted).

en is not only "substantially related," it is essential to that objective. By this notably circular argument, the "straightforward" test *Mississippi Univ. for Women* described, see 458 U.S., at 724–725, was bent and bowed.

The State's misunderstanding and, in turn, the District Court's, is apparent from VMI's mission: to produce "citizen-soldiers," individuals

> " 'imbued with love of learning, confident in the functions and attitudes of leadership, possessing a high sense of public service, advocates of the American democracy and free enterprise system, and ready . . . to defend their country in time of national peril.' " 766 F.Supp., at 1425 (quoting Mission Study Committee of the VMI Board of Visitors, Report, May 16, 1986).

Surely that goal is great enough to accommodate women, who today count as citizens in our American democracy equal in stature to men. Just as surely, the State's great goal is not substantially advanced by women's categorical exclusion, in total disregard of their individual merit, from the State's premier "citizen-soldier" corps.[16] Virginia, in sum, "has fallen far short of establishing the 'exceedingly persuasive justification,' " *Mississippi Univ. for Women*, 458 U.S., at 731, that must be the solid base for any gender-defined classification.

VI

In the second phase of the litigation, Virginia presented its remedial plan—maintain VMI as a male-only college and create VWIL as a separate program for women. The plan met District Court approval. The Fourth Circuit, in turn, deferentially reviewed the State's proposal and decided that the two single-sex programs directly served Virginia's reasserted purposes: single-gender education, and "achieving the results of an adversative method in a military environment." See 44 F.3d, at 1236, 1239. Inspecting the VMI and VWIL educational programs to determine whether they "afford[ed] to both genders benefits comparable in substance, [if] not in form and detail," id., at 1240, the Court of Appeals concluded that Virginia had arranged for men and women opportunities "sufficiently comparable" to survive equal protection evaluation, id., at 1240–1241. The United States challenges this "remedial" ruling as pervasively misguided.

A

A remedial decree, this Court has said, must closely fit the constitutional violation; it must be shaped to place persons unconstitutionally denied an opportunity or advantage in "the position they would have occupied in the absence of [discrimination]." See *Milliken v. Bradley*, 433 U.S. 267, 280, 97 S.Ct. 2749, 53 L.Ed.2d 745 (1977)(internal quotation marks omitted). The constitutional violation in this case is the categorical exclusion of women from

---

16. VMI has successfully managed another notable change. The school admitted its first African–American cadets in 1968. See The VMI Story 347–349 (students no longer sing "Dixie," salute the Confederate flag or the tomb of General Robert E. Lee at ceremonies and sports events). As the District Court noted, VMI established a Program on "retention of black cadets" designed to offer academic and social-cultural support to "minority members of a dominantly white and tradition-oriented student body." 766 F.Supp., at 1436–1437. The school maintains a "special recruitment program for blacks" which, the District Court found, "has had little, if any, effect on VMI's method of accomplishing its mission." Id., at 1437.

an extraordinary educational opportunity afforded men. A proper remedy for an unconstitutional exclusion, we have explained, aims to "eliminate [so far as possible] the discriminatory effects of the past" and to "bar like discrimination in the future." Louisiana v. United States, 380 U.S. 145, 154, 85 S.Ct. 817, 13 L.Ed.2d 709 (1965).

Virginia chose not to eliminate, but to leave untouched, VMI's exclusionary policy. For women only, however, Virginia proposed a separate program, different in kind from VMI and unequal in tangible and intangible facilities.[17] Having violated the Constitution's equal protection requirement, Virginia was obliged to show that its remedial proposal "directly address[ed] and relate[d] to" the violation, see *Milliken*, 433 U.S., at 282, i.e., the equal protection denied to women ready, willing, and able to benefit from educational opportunities of the kind VMI offers. Virginia described VWIL as a "parallel program," and asserted that VWIL shares VMI's mission of producing "citizen-soldiers" and VMI's goals of providing "education, military training, mental and physical discipline, character ... and leadership development." Brief for Respondents 24 (internal quotation marks omitted). If the VWIL program could not "eliminate the discriminatory effects of the past," could it at least "bar like discrimination in the future"? See *Louisiana*, 380 U.S., at 154. A comparison of the programs said to be "parallel" informs our answer. * * *

VWIL affords women no opportunity to experience the rigorous military training for which VMI is famed. * * * Instead, the VWIL program "deemphasize[s]" military education, 44 F.3d, at 1234, and uses a "cooperative method" of education "which reinforces self-esteem," 852 F.Supp., at 476.

* * * Virginia deliberately did not make VWIL a military institute. The VWIL House is not a military-style residence and VWIL students need not live together throughout the 4–year program, eat meals together, or wear uniforms during the school day. * * * "[T]he most important aspects of the VMI educational experience occur in the barracks," the District Court found, id., at 1423, yet Virginia deemed that core experience nonessential, indeed inappropriate, for training its female citizen-soldiers.

VWIL students receive their "leadership training" in seminars, externships, and speaker series, see 852 F.Supp., at 477, episodes and encounters lacking the "[p]hysical rigor, mental stress, ... minute regulation of behavior, and indoctrination in desirable values" made hallmarks of VMI's citizen-soldier training, see 766 F.Supp., at 1421. Kept away from the pressures, hazards, and psychological bonding characteristic of VMI's adversative training, see id., at 1422, VWIL students will not know the "feeling of tremendous

---

17. As earlier observed, see supra, at 11–12, Judge Phillips, in dissent, measured Virginia's plan against a paradigm arrangement, one that "could survive equal protection scrutiny": single-sex schools with "substantially comparable curricular and extra-curricular programs, funding, physical plant, administration and support services, ... faculty [,] and library resources." 44 F.3d, at 1250. Cf. Bray v. Lee, 337 F.Supp. 934 (D.Mass.1972)(holding inconsistent with the Equal Protection Clause admission of males to Boston's Boys Latin School with a test score of 120 or higher (up to a top score of 200) while requiring a score, on the same test, of at least 133 for admission of females to Girls Latin School, but not ordering coeducation). Measuring VMI/VWIL against the paradigm, Judge Phillips said, "reveals how far short the [Virginia] plan falls from providing substantially equal tangible and intangible educational benefits to men and women." 44 F.3d, at 1250.

accomplishment" commonly experienced by VMI's successful cadets, id., at 1426.

Virginia maintains that these methodological differences are "justified pedagogically," based on "important differences between men and women in learning and developmental needs," "psychological and sociological differences" Virginia describes as "real" and "not stereotypes." Brief for Respondents 28 (internal quotation marks omitted). The Task Force charged with developing the leadership program for women, drawn from the staff and faculty at Mary Baldwin College, "determined that a military model and, especially VMI's adversative method, would be wholly inappropriate for educating and training *most women*." * * * (noting Task Force conclusion that, while "some women would be suited to and interested in [a VMI-style experience]," VMI's adversative method "would not be effective for *women as a group* ") * * *.

As earlier stated, * * * generalizations about "the way women are," estimates of what is appropriate for *most women*, no longer justify denying opportunity to women whose talent and capacity place them outside the average description. Notably, Virginia never asserted that VMI's method of education suits *most men*. It is also revealing that Virginia accounted for its failure to make the VWIL experience "the entirely militaristic experience of VMI" on the ground that VWIL "is planned for women who do not necessarily expect to pursue military careers." 852 F.Supp., at 478. By that reasoning, VMI's "entirely militaristic" program would be inappropriate for men in general or *as a group*, for "[o]nly about 15% of VMI cadets enter career military service." See 766 F.Supp., at 1432.

In contrast to the generalizations about women on which Virginia rests, we note again these dispositive realities: VMI's "implementing methodology" is not "inherently unsuitable to women," 976 F.2d, at 899; "some women . . . do well under [the] adversative model," 766 F.Supp., at 1434 (internal quotation marks omitted); "some women, at least, would want to attend [VMI] if they had the opportunity," id., at 1414; "some women are capable of all of the individual activities required of VMI cadets," id., at 1412, and "can meet the physical standards [VMI] now impose[s] on men," 976 F.2d, at 896. It is on behalf of these women that the United States has instituted this suit, and it is for them that a remedy must be crafted,[19] a remedy that will end their exclusion from a state-supplied educational opportunity for which they are fit, a decree that will "bar like discrimination in the future." *Louisiana*, 380 U.S., at 154.

B

In myriad respects other than military training, VWIL does not qualify as VMI's equal. VWIL's student body, faculty, course offerings, and facilities

---

19. Admitting women to VMI would undoubtedly require alterations necessary to afford members of each sex privacy from the other sex in living arrangements, and to adjust aspects of the physical training programs. See Brief for Petitioner 27–29; cf. note following 10 U.S.C. § 4342 (academic and other standards for women admitted to the Military, Naval, and Air Force Academies "shall be the same as those required for male individuals, except for those minimum essential adjust- ments in such standards required because of physiological differences between male and female individuals"). Experience shows such adjustments are manageable. See U.S. Military Academy, A. Vitters, N. Kinzer, & J. Adams, Report of Admission of Women (Project Athena I–IV)(1977–1980)(4–year longitudinal study of the admission of women to West Point); Defense Advisory Committee on Women in the Services, Report on the Integration and Performance of Women at West Point 17–18 (1992).

hardly match VMI's. Nor can the VWIL graduate anticipate the benefits associated with VMI's 157–year history, the school's prestige, and its influential alumni network.

* * * The Mary Baldwin faculty holds "significantly fewer Ph.D.'s," id., at 502, and receives substantially lower salaries, see Tr. 158 (testimony of James Lott, Dean of Mary Baldwin College), than the faculty at VMI.

Mary Baldwin does not offer a VWIL student the range of curricular choices available to a VMI cadet. * * * VWIL students attend a school that "does not have a math and science focus," 852 F.Supp., at 503; they cannot take at Mary Baldwin any courses in engineering or the advanced math and physics courses VMI offers, see id., at 477.

For physical training, Mary Baldwin has "two multi-purpose fields" and "[o]ne gymnasium." Id., at 503. VMI has "an NCAA competition level indoor track and field facility; a number of multi-purpose fields; baseball, soccer and lacrosse fields; an obstacle course; large boxing, wrestling and martial arts facilities; an 11–laps-to-the-mile indoor running course; an indoor pool; indoor and outdoor rifle ranges; and a football stadium that also contains a practice field and outdoor track." Ibid.

Although Virginia has represented that it will provide equal financial support for in-state VWIL students and VMI cadets, * * * the difference between the two schools' financial reserves is pronounced. Mary Baldwin's endowment, currently about $19 million, will gain an additional $35 million based on future commitments; VMI's current endowment, $131 million—the largest per-student endowment in the Nation—will gain $220 million. Id., at 503.

The VWIL student does not graduate with the advantage of a VMI degree. Her diploma does not unite her with the legions of VMI "graduates [who] have distinguished themselves" in military and civilian life. See 976 F.2d, at 892–893. "[VMI] alumni are exceptionally close to the school," and that closeness accounts, in part, for VMI's success in attracting applicants. See 766 F.Supp., at 1421. A VWIL graduate cannot assume that the "network of business owners, corporations, VMI graduates and non-graduate employers ... interested in hiring VMI graduates," 852 F.Supp., at 499, will be equally responsive to her search for employment, see 44 F.3d, at 1250 (Phillips, J., dissenting)("the powerful political and economic ties of the VMI alumni network cannot be expected to open" for graduates of the fledgling VWIL program).

Virginia, in sum, while maintaining VMI for men only, has failed to provide any "comparable single-gender women's institution." Id., at 1241. Instead, the Commonwealth has created a VWIL program fairly appraised as a "pale shadow" of VMI in terms of the range of curricular choices and faculty stature, funding, prestige, alumni support and influence. See id., at 1250 (Phillips, J., dissenting).

Virginia's VWIL solution is reminiscent of the remedy Texas proposed 50 years ago, in response to a state trial court's 1946 ruling that, given the equal protection guarantee, African Americans could not be denied a legal education at a state facility. See Sweatt v. Painter, 339 U.S. 629, 70 S.Ct. 848, 94 L.Ed. 1114 (1950). Reluctant to admit African Americans to its flagship University of Texas Law School, the State set up a separate school for Herman Sweatt and other black law students. Id., at 632. As originally opened, the new school had no independent faculty or library, and it lacked accreditation. Id., at 633. Nevertheless, the state trial and appellate courts were satisfied that the new school offered Sweatt opportunities for the study of law "substantially equivalent to those offered by the State to white students at the University of Texas." Id., at 632 (internal quotation marks omitted).

Before this Court considered the case, the new school had gained "a faculty of five full-time professors; a student body of 23; a library of some 16,500 volumes serviced by a full-time staff; a practice court and legal aid association; and one alumnus who ha[d] become a member of the Texas Bar." Id., at 633. This Court contrasted resources at the new school with those at the school from which Sweatt had been excluded. The University of Texas Law School had a full-time faculty of 16, a student body of 850, a library containing over 65,000 volumes, scholarship funds, a law review, and moot court facilities. Id., at 632–633.

More important than the tangible features, the Court emphasized, are "those qualities which are incapable of objective measurement but which make for greatness" in a school, including "reputation of the faculty, experience of the administration, position and influence of the alumni, standing in the community, traditions and prestige." Id., at 634. Facing the marked differences reported in the *Sweatt* opinion, the Court unanimously ruled that Texas had not shown "substantial equality in the [separate] educational opportunities" the State offered. Id., at 633. Accordingly, the Court held, the Equal Protection Clause required Texas to admit African Americans to the University of Texas Law School. Id., at 636. In line with *Sweatt*, we rule here that Virginia has not shown substantial equality in the separate educational opportunities the State supports at VWIL and VMI.

C

When Virginia tendered its VWIL plan, the Fourth Circuit did not inquire whether the proposed remedy, approved by the District Court, placed women denied the VMI advantage in "the position they would have occupied in the absence of [discrimination]." *Milliken*, 433 U.S., at 280 (internal quotation marks omitted). Instead, the Court of Appeals considered whether the State could provide, with fidelity to the equal protection principle, separate and unequal educational programs for men and women.

The Fourth Circuit acknowledged that "the VWIL degree from Mary Baldwin College lacks the historical benefit and prestige of a degree from VMI." 44 F.3d, at 1241. The Court of Appeals further observed that VMI is "an ongoing and successful institution with a long history," and there remains no "comparable single-gender women's institution." Ibid. Nevertheless, the appeals court declared the substantially different and significantly unequal VWIL program satisfactory. The court reached that result by revising the applicable standard of review. The Fourth Circuit displaced the standard developed in our precedent, * * * and substituted a standard of its own invention.

We have earlier described the deferential review in which the Court of Appeals engaged * * *. [T]he Court of Appeals candidly described its own analysis as one capable of checking a legislative purpose ranked as "pernicious," but generally according "deference to [the] legislative will."   44 F.3d, at 1235, 1236.   Recognizing that it had extracted from our decisions a test yielding "little or no scrutiny of the effect of a classification directed at [single-gender education]," the Court of Appeals devised another test, a "substantive comparability" inquiry, id., at 1237, and proceeded to find that new test satisfied, id., at 1241.

The Fourth Circuit plainly erred in exposing Virginia's VWIL plan to a deferential analysis, for "all gender-based classifications today" warrant "heightened scrutiny."   See J.E. B., 511 U.S., at 136.   Valuable as VWIL may prove for students who seek the program offered, Virginia's remedy affords no cure at all for the opportunities and advantages withheld from women who want a VMI education and can make the grade.   * * *[20] In sum, Virginia's remedy does not match the constitutional violation; the State has shown no "exceedingly persuasive justification" for withholding from women qualified for the experience premier training of the kind VMI affords.

VII

A generation ago, "the authorities controlling Virginia higher education," despite long established tradition, agreed "to innovate and favorably entertain [ed] the [then] relatively new idea that there must be no discrimination by sex in offering educational opportunity."   *Kirstein*, 309 F.Supp., at 186.   Commencing in 1970, Virginia opened to women "educational opportunities at the Charlottesville campus that [were] not afforded in other [State-operated] institutions."   Id., at 187; see supra, at 20.   A federal court approved the State's innovation, emphasizing that the University of Virginia "offer[ed] courses of instruction ... not available elsewhere."   309 F.Supp., at 187. The court further noted: "[T]here exists at Charlottesville a 'prestige' factor [not paralleled in] other Virginia educational institutions."   Ibid.

VMI, too, offers an educational opportunity no other Virginia institution provides, and the school's "prestige"—associated with its success in developing "citizen-soldiers"—is unequaled.   Virginia has closed this facility to its daughters and, instead, has devised for them a "parallel program," with a

---

20. Virginia's prime concern, it appears, is that "plac[ing] men and women into the adversative relationship inherent in the VMI program ... would destroy, at least for that period of the adversative training, any sense of decency that still permeates the relationship between the sexes."   44 F.3d, at 1239; see supra, at 22–27.   It is an ancient and familiar fear.   Compare In re Lavinia Goodell, 39 Wis. 232, 246 (1875)(denying female applicant's motion for admission to the bar of its court, Wisconsin Supreme Court explained: "Discussions are habitually necessary in courts of justice, which are unfit for female ears.   The habitual presence of women at these would tend to relax the public sense of decency and propriety."), with Levine, Closing Comments, 6 Law & Inequality 41, 41 (1988)(presentation at Eighth Circuit Judicial Conference, Colorado Springs, Colorado, July 17, 1987)(footnotes omitted): "Plato questioned whether women should be afforded equal opportunity to become guardians, those elite Rulers of Platonic

society.   Ironically, in that most undemocratic system of government, the Republic, women's native ability to serve as guardians was not seriously questioned.   The concern was over the wrestling and exercise class in which all candidates for guardianship had to participate, for rigorous physical and mental training were prerequisites to attain the exalted status of guardian.   And in accord with Greek custom, those exercise classes were conducted in the nude.   Plato concluded that their virtue would clothe the women's nakedness and that Platonic society would not thereby be deprived of the talent of qualified citizens for reasons of mere gender."

For Plato's full text on the equality of women, see 2 The Dialogues of Plato 302–312 (B. Jowett transl., 4th ed.1953).   Virginia, not bound to ancient Greek custom in its "rigorous physical and mental training" programs, could more readily make the accommodations necessary to draw on "the talent of [all] qualified citizens."   Cf. supra, at 34, n. 19.

faculty less impressively credentialed and less well paid, more limited course offerings, fewer opportunities for military training and for scientific specialization. Cf. *Sweatt*, 339 U.S., at 633. VMI, beyond question, "possesses to a far greater degree" than the VWIL program "those qualities which are incapable of objective measurement but which make for greatness in a ... school," including "position and influence of the alumni, standing in the community, traditions and prestige." Id., at 634. Women seeking and fit for a VMI-quality education cannot be offered anything less, under the State's obligation to afford them genuinely equal protection.

A prime part of the history of our Constitution, historian Richard Morris recounted, is the story of the extension of constitutional rights and protections to people once ignored or excluded.[21] VMI's story continued as our comprehension of "We the People" expanded. * * * There is no reason to believe that the admission of women capable of all the activities required of VMI cadets would destroy the Institute rather than enhance its capacity to serve the "more perfect Union."

* * *

For the reasons stated, the initial judgment of the Court of Appeals, 976 F.2d 890 (C.A.4 1992), is affirmed, the final judgment of the Court of Appeals, 44 F.3d 1229 (C.A.4 1995), is reversed, and the case is remanded for further proceedings consistent with this opinion.

It is so ordered.

JUSTICE THOMAS took no part in the consideration or decision of this case.

CHIEF JUSTICE REHNQUIST, concurring in judgment.

The Court holds first that Virginia violates the Equal Protection Clause by maintaining the Virginia Military Institute's (VMI's) all-male admissions policy, and second that establishing the Virginia Women's Institute for Leadership (VWIL) program does not remedy that violation. While I agree with these conclusions, I disagree with the Court's analysis and so I write separately.

I

Two decades ago in Craig v. Boren, 429 U.S. 190, 197, 97 S.Ct. 451, 50 L.Ed.2d 397 (1976), we announced that "[t]o withstand constitutional challenge, ... classifications by gender must serve important governmental objectives and must be substantially related to achievement of those objectives." We have adhered to that standard of scrutiny ever since. * * * While the majority adheres to this test today, * * * it also says that the State must demonstrate an " 'exceedingly persuasive justification' " to support a gender-

---

21. R. Morris, The Forging of the Union, 1781–1789, p. 193 (1987); see id., at 191, setting out letter to a friend from Massachusetts patriot (later second President) John Adams, on the subject of qualifications for voting in his home state: "[I]t is dangerous to open so fruitful a source of controversy and altercation as would be opened by attempting to alter the qualifications of voters; there will be no end of it. New claims will arise; women will demand a vote; lads from twelve to twenty-one will think their rights not enough attended to; and every man who has not a farthing, will demand an equal voice with any other, in all acts of state. It tends to confound and destroy all distinctions, and prostrate all ranks to one common level." Letter from John Adams to James Sullivan (May 26, 1776), in 9 Works of John Adams 378 (C. Adams ed. 1854).

based classification. * * * It is unfortunate that the Court thereby introduces an element of uncertainty respecting the appropriate test.

While terms like "important governmental objective" and "substantially related" are hardly models of precision, they have more content and specificity than does the phrase "exceedingly persuasive justification." That phrase is best confined, as it was first used, as an observation on the difficulty of meeting the applicable test, not as a formulation of the test itself. See, e.g., *Feeney*, supra, at 273 ("[T]hese precedents dictate that any state law overtly or covertly designed to prefer males over females in public employment require an exceedingly persuasive justification"). To avoid introducing potential confusion, I would have adhered more closely to our traditional, "firmly established," *Hogan*, supra, at 723; *Heckler*, supra, at 744, standard that a gender-based classification "must bear a close and substantial relationship to important governmental objectives." *Feeney*, supra, at 273.

Our cases dealing with gender discrimination also require that the proffered purpose for the challenged law be the actual purpose. See ante, at 15, 18. It is on this ground that the Court rejects the first of two justifications Virginia offers for VMI's single-sex admissions policy, namely, the goal of diversity among its public educational institutions. While I ultimately agree that the State has not carried the day with this justification, I disagree with the Court's method of analyzing the issue.

VMI was founded in 1839, and, as the Court notes, ante, at 18–19, admission was limited to men because under the then-prevailing view men, not women, were destined for higher education. However misguided this point of view may be by present-day standards, it surely was not unconstitutional in 1839. The adoption of the Fourteenth Amendment, with its Equal Protection Clause, was nearly 30 years in the future. The interpretation of the Equal Protection Clause to require heightened scrutiny for gender discrimination was yet another century away.

Long after the adoption of the Fourteenth Amendment, and well into this century, legal distinctions between men and women were thought to raise no question under the Equal Protection Clause. The Court refers to our decision in Goesaert v. Cleary, 335 U.S. 464 (1948). Likewise representing that now abandoned view was Hoyt v. Florida, 368 U.S. 57, 82 S.Ct. 159, 7 L.Ed.2d 118 (1961), where the Court upheld a Florida system of jury selection in which men were automatically placed on jury lists, but women were placed there only if they expressed an affirmative desire to serve. The Court noted that despite advances in women's opportunities, the "woman is still regarded as the center of home and family life." Id., at 62.

Then, in 1971, we decided Reed v. Reed, 404 U.S. 71, 92 S.Ct. 251, 30 L.Ed.2d 225, which the Court correctly refers to as a seminal case. But its facts have nothing to do with admissions to any sort of educational institution. * * * The brief opinion in *Reed* made no mention of either *Goesaert* or *Hoyt*.

Even at the time of our decision in *Reed v. Reed*, therefore, Virginia and VMI were scarcely on notice that its holding would be extended across the constitutional board. They were entitled to believe that "one swallow doesn't make a summer" and await further developments. Those developments were 11 years in coming. In Mississippi Univ. for Women v. Hogan, 458 U.S. 718,

102 S.Ct. 3331, 73 L.Ed.2d 1090 (1982), a case actually involving a single-sex admissions policy in higher education, the Court held that the exclusion of men from a nursing program violated the Equal Protection Clause. This holding did place Virginia on notice that VMI's men-only admissions policy was open to serious question.

The VMI Board of Visitors, in response, appointed a Mission Study Committee to examine "the legality and wisdom of VMI's single-sex policy in light of" *Hogan.* 766 F.Supp. 1407, 1427 (W.D.Va.1991). But the committee ended up cryptically recommending against changing VMI's status as a single-sex college. After three years of study, the committee found " 'no information' " that would warrant a change in VMI's status. Id., at 1429. Even the District Court, ultimately sympathetic to VMI's position, found that "[t]he Report provided very little indication of how [its] conclusion was reached" and that "the one and one-half pages in the committee's final report devoted to analyzing the information it obtained primarily focuses on anticipated difficulties in attracting females to VMI." Ibid. The reasons given in the report for not changing the policy were the changes that admission of women to VMI would require, and the likely effect of those changes on the institution. That VMI would have to change is simply not helpful in addressing the constitutionality of the status after *Hogan.*

Before this Court, Virginia has sought to justify VMI's single-sex admissions policy primarily on the basis that diversity in education is desirable, and that while most of the public institutions of higher learning in the State are coeducational, there should also be room for single-sex institutions. I agree with the Court that there is scant evidence in the record that this was the real reason that Virginia decided to maintain VMI as men only.* But, unlike the majority, I would consider only evidence that postdates our decision in *Hogan,* and would draw no negative inferences from the State's actions before that time. I think that after *Hogan,* the State was entitled to reconsider its policy with respect to VMI, and to not have earlier justifications, or lack thereof, held against it.

Even if diversity in educational opportunity were the State's actual objective, the State's position would still be problematic. The difficulty with its position is that the diversity benefited only one sex; there was single-sex public education available for men at VMI, but no corresponding single-sex public education available for women. When *Hogan* placed Virginia on notice that VMI's admissions policy possibly was unconstitutional, VMI could have dealt with the problem by admitting women; but its governing body felt strongly that the admission of women would have seriously harmed the institution's educational approach. Was there something else the State could

---

* The dissent equates our conclusion that VMI's "asserted interest in promoting diversity" is not " 'genuine,' " with a "charge" that the diversity rationale is "a pretext for discriminating against women." Post, at 15, 15–16. Of course, those are not the same thing. I do not read the Court as saying that the diversity rationale is a pretext for discrimination, and I would not endorse such a proposition. We may find that diversity was not the State's real reason without suggesting, or having to show, that the real reason was "antifemin- ism," post, at 16. Our cases simply require that the proffered purpose for the challenged gender classification be the actual purpose, although not necessarily recorded. See ante, at 15, 18. The dissent also says that the interest in diversity is so transparent that having to articulate it is "absurd on its face." Post, at 29. Apparently, that rationale was not obvious to the Mission Study Committee which failed to list it among its reasons for maintaining VMI all-men admission policy.

have done to avoid an equal protection violation? Since the State did nothing, we do not have to definitively answer that question.

I do not think, however, that the State's options were as limited as the majority may imply. The Court cites, without expressly approving it, a statement from the opinion of the dissenting judge in the Court of Appeals, to the effect that the State could have "simultaneously opened single-gender undergraduate institutions having substantially comparable curricular and extra-curricular programs, funding, physical plant, administration and support services, and faculty and library resources." Ante, at 11–12 (internal quotation marks omitted). If this statement is thought to exclude other possibilities, it is too stringent a requirement. VMI had been in operation for over a century and a half, and had an established, successful and devoted group of alumni. No legislative wand could instantly call into existence a similar institution for women; and it would be a tremendous loss to scrap VMI's history and tradition. In the words of Grover Cleveland's second inaugural address, the State faced a condition, not a theory. And it was a condition that had been brought about, not through defiance of decisions construing gender bias under the Equal Protection Clause, but, until the decision in *Hogan*, a condition which had not appeared to offend the Constitution. Had Virginia made a genuine effort to devote comparable public resources to a facility for women, and followed through on such a plan, it might well have avoided an equal protection violation. I do not believe the State was faced with the stark choice of either admitting women to VMI, on the one hand, or abandoning VMI and starting from scratch for both men and women, on the other.

But, as I have noted, neither the governing board of VMI nor the State took any action after 1982. If diversity in the form of single-sex, as well as coeducational, institutions of higher learning were to be available to Virginians, that diversity had to be available to women as well as to men.

The dissent criticizes me for "disregarding the four all-women's private colleges in Virginia (generously assisted by public funds)." Post, at 32. The private women's colleges are treated by the State *exactly* as all other private schools are treated, which includes the provision of tuition-assistance grants to Virginia residents. Virginia gives no special support to the women's single-sex education. But obviously, the same is not true for men's education. Had the State provided the kind of support for the private women's schools that it provides for VMI, this may have been a very different case. For in so doing, the State would have demonstrated that its interest in providing a single-sex education for men, was to some measure matched by an interest in providing the same opportunity for women.

Virginia offers a second justification for the single-sex admissions policy: maintenance of the adversative method. I agree with the Court that this justification does not serve an important governmental objective. A State does not have substantial interest in the adversative methodology unless it is pedagogically beneficial. While considerable evidence shows that a single-sex education is pedagogically beneficial for some students, see 766 F.Supp., at 1414, and hence a State may have a valid interest in promoting that methodology, there is no similar evidence in the record that an adversative method is pedagogically beneficial or is any more likely to produce character traits than other methodologies.

II

The Court defines the constitutional violation in this case as "the categorical exclusion of women from an extraordinary educational opportunity afforded to men." Ante, at 30. By defining the violation in this way, and by emphasizing that a remedy for a constitutional violation must place the victims of discrimination in " 'the position they would have occupied in the absence of [discrimination],' " ibid., the Court necessarily implies that the only adequate remedy would be the admission of women to the all-male institution. As the foregoing discussion suggests, I would not define the violation in this way; it is not the "exclusion of women" that violates the Equal Protection Clause, but the maintenance of an all-men school without providing any—much less a comparable—institution for women.

Accordingly, the remedy should not necessarily require either the admission of women to VMI, or the creation of a VMI clone for women. An adequate remedy in my opinion might be a demonstration by Virginia that its interest in educating men in a single-sex environment is matched by its interest in educating women in a single-sex institution. To demonstrate such, the State does not need to create two institutions with the same number of faculty PhD's, similar SAT scores, or comparable athletic fields. See ante, at 34–35. Nor would it necessarily require that the women's institution offer the same curriculum as the men's; one could be strong in computer science, the other could be strong in liberal arts. It would be a sufficient remedy, I think, if the two institutions offered the same quality of education and were of the same overall calibre.

If a state decides to create single-sex programs, the state would, I expect, consider the public's interest and demand in designing curricula. And rightfully so. But the state should avoid assuming demand based on stereotypes; it must not assume *a priori*, without evidence, that there would be no interest in a women's school of civil engineering, or in a men's school of nursing.

In the end, the women's institution Virginia proposes, VWIL, fails as a remedy, because it is distinctly inferior to the existing men's institution and will continue to be for the foreseeable future. VWIL simply is not, in any sense, the institution that VMI is. In particular, VWIL is a program appended to a private college, not a self-standing institution; and VWIL is substantially underfunded as compared to VMI. I therefore ultimately agree with the Court that Virginia has not provided an adequate remedy.

JUSTICE SCALIA, dissenting.

Today the Court shuts down an institution that has served the people of the Commonwealth of Virginia with pride and distinction for over a century and a half. To achieve that desired result, it rejects (contrary to our established practice) the factual findings of two courts below, sweeps aside the precedents of this Court, and ignores the history of our people. As to facts: it explicitly rejects the finding that there exist "gender-based developmental differences" supporting Virginia's restriction of the "adversative" method to only a men's institution, and the finding that the all-male composition of the Virginia Military Institute (VMI) is essential to that institution's character.

As to precedent: it drastically revises our established standards for reviewing sex-based classifications. And as to history: it counts for nothing the long tradition, enduring down to the present, of men's military colleges supported by both States and the Federal Government.

Much of the Court's opinion is devoted to deprecating the closed-mindedness of our forebears with regard to women's education, and even with regard to the treatment of women in areas that have nothing to do with education. Closed-minded they were—as every age is, including our own, with regard to matters it cannot guess, because it simply does not consider them debatable. The virtue of a democratic system with a First Amendment is that it readily enables the people, over time, to be persuaded that what they took for granted is not so, and to change their laws accordingly. That system is destroyed if the smug assurances of each age are removed from the democratic process and written into the Constitution. So to counterbalance the Court's criticism of our ancestors, let me say a word in their praise: they left us free to change. The same cannot be said of this most illiberal Court, which has embarked on a course of inscribing one after another of the current preferences of the society (and in some cases only the counter-majoritarian preferences of the society's law-trained elite) into our Basic Law. Today it enshrines the notion that no substantial educational value is to be served by an all-men's military academy—so that the decision by the people of Virginia to maintain such an institution denies equal protection to women who cannot attend that institution but can attend others. Since it is entirely clear that the Constitution of the United States—the old one—takes no sides in this educational debate, I dissent.

I

I shall devote most of my analysis to evaluating the Court's opinion on the basis of our current equal-protection jurisprudence, which regards this Court as free to evaluate everything under the sun by applying one of three tests: "rational basis" scrutiny, intermediate scrutiny, or strict scrutiny. These tests are no more scientific than their names suggest, and a further element of randomness is added by the fact that it is largely up to us which test will be applied in each case. Strict scrutiny, we have said, is reserved for state "classifications based on race or national origin and classifications affecting fundamental rights," Clark v. Jeter, 486 U.S. 456, 461, 108 S.Ct. 1910, 100 L.Ed.2d 465 (1988)(citation omitted). It is my position that the term "fundamental rights" should be limited to "interest[s] traditionally protected by our society," Michael H. v. Gerald D., 491 U.S. 110, 122, 109 S.Ct. 2333, 105 L.Ed.2d 91 (1989)(plurality opinion of SCALIA, J.); but the Court has not accepted that view, so that strict scrutiny will be applied to the deprivation of whatever sort of right we consider "fundamental." We have no established criterion for "intermediate scrutiny" either, but essentially apply it when it seems like a good idea to load the dice. So far it has been applied to content-neutral restrictions that place an incidental burden on speech, to disabilities attendant to illegitimacy, and to discrimination on the basis of sex. See, e.g., Turner Broadcasting System, Inc. v. FCC, 512 U.S. ___, ___ (1994)(slip op., at 38); Mills v. Habluetzel, 456 U.S. 91, 98–99, 102 S.Ct. 1549, 71 L.Ed.2d 770 (1982); Craig v. Boren, 429 U.S. 190, 197, 97 S.Ct. 451, 50 L.Ed.2d 397 (1976).

I have no problem with a system of abstract tests such as rational-basis, intermediate, and strict scrutiny (though I think we can do better than applying strict scrutiny and intermediate scrutiny whenever we feel like it). Such formulas are essential to evaluating whether the new restrictions that a changing society constantly imposes upon private conduct comport with that "equal protection" our society has always accorded in the past. But in my view the function of this Court is to *preserve* our society's values regarding (among other things) equal protection, not to *revise* them; to prevent backsliding from the degree of restriction the Constitution imposed upon democratic government, not to prescribe, on our own authority, progressively higher degrees. For that reason it is my view that, whatever abstract tests we may choose to devise, they cannot supersede—and indeed ought to be crafted *so as to reflect*—those constant and unbroken national traditions that embody the people's understanding of ambiguous constitutional texts. More specifically, it is my view that "when a practice not expressly prohibited by the text of the Bill of Rights bears the endorsement of a long tradition of open, widespread, and unchallenged use that dates back to the beginning of the Republic, we have no proper basis for striking it down." Rutan v. Republican Party of Ill., 497 U.S. 62, 95, 110 S.Ct. 2729, 111 L.Ed.2d 52 (1990)(SCALIA, J., dissenting). The same applies, *mutatis mutandis*, to a practice asserted to be in violation of the post-Civil War Fourteenth Amendment. See, e.g., Burnham v. Superior Court of Cal., County of Marin, 495 U.S. 604, 110 S.Ct. 2105, 109 L.Ed.2d 631 (1990)(plurality opinion of SCALIA, J.)(Due Process Clause); J.E.B. v. Alabama ex rel. T. B., 511 U.S. 127, 156–163, 114 S.Ct. 1419, 128 L.Ed.2d 89 (SCALIA, J., dissenting)(Equal Protection Clause); Planned Parenthood of S.E. Pa. v. Casey, 505 U.S. 833, 979–984, 1000–1001, 112 S.Ct. 2791, 120 L.Ed.2d 674 (1992)(SCALIA, J., dissenting)(various alleged "penumbras").

The all-male constitution of VMI comes squarely within such a governing tradition. Founded by the Commonwealth of Virginia in 1839 and continuously maintained by it since, VMI has always admitted only men. And in that regard it has not been unusual. For almost all of VMI's more than a century and a half of existence, its single-sex status reflected the uniform practice for government-supported military colleges. Another famous Southern institution, The Citadel, has existed as a state-funded school of South Carolina since 1842. And all the federal military colleges—West Point, the Naval Academy at Annapolis, and even the Air Force Academy, which was not established until 1954—admitted only males for most of their history. Their admission of women in 1976 (upon which the Court today relies, see ante, at 27–28, nn. 13, 15), came not by court decree, but because the people, through their elected representatives, decreed a change. See, e.g., Pub.L. 94–106, § 803(a), 89 Stat. 537–538 (1975). In other words, the tradition of having government-funded military schools for men is as well rooted in the traditions of this country as the tradition of sending only men into military combat. The people may decide to change the one tradition, like the other, through democratic processes; but the assertion that either tradition has been unconstitutional through the centuries is not law, but politics-smuggled-into-law.

And the same applies, more broadly, to single-sex education in general, which, as I shall discuss, is threatened by today's decision with the cut-off of all state and federal support. Government-run *non*military educational institutions for the two sexes have until very recently also been part of our national tradition. "[It is] [c]oeducation, historically, [that] is a novel educational theory. From grade school through high school, college, and graduate and professional training, much of the Nation's population during much of our history has been educated in sexually segregated classrooms." Mississippi Univ. for Women v. Hogan, 458 U.S. 718, 736, 102 S.Ct. 3331, 73 L.Ed.2d 1090 (1982)(Powell, J., dissenting); see id., at 736–739. These traditions may of course be changed by the democratic decisions of the people, as they largely have been.

Today, however, change is forced upon Virginia, and reversion to single-sex education is prohibited nationwide, not by democratic processes but by order of this Court. Even while bemoaning the sorry, bygone days of "fixed notions" concerning women's education, see ante, at 18–19, and n. 10, 20–21, 25–27, the Court favors current notions so fixedly that it is willing to write them into the Constitution of the United States by application of custom-built "tests." This is not the interpretation of a Constitution, but the creation of one.

II

To reject the Court's disposition today, however, it is not necessary to accept my view that the Court's made-up tests cannot displace longstanding national traditions as the primary determinant of what the Constitution means. It is only necessary to apply honestly the test the Court has been applying to sex-based classifications for the past two decades. It is well settled, as Justice O'connor stated some time ago for a unanimous Court, that we evaluate a statutory classification based on sex under a standard that lies "[b]etween th [e] extremes of rational basis review and strict scrutiny." Clark v. Jeter, 486 U.S., at 461. We have denominated this standard "intermediate scrutiny" and under it have inquired whether the statutory classification is "substantially related to an important governmental objective." * * *

Before I proceed to apply this standard to VMI, I must comment upon the manner in which the Court avoids doing so. Notwithstanding our above-described precedents and their " 'firmly established principles,' "*Heckler*, supra, at 744 (quoting *Hogan*, supra, at 723), the United States urged us to hold in this case "that strict scrutiny is the correct constitutional standard for evaluating classifications that deny opportunities to individuals based on their sex." Brief for United States in No. 94–2107, p. 16. (This was in flat contradiction of the Government's position below, which was, in its own words, to "stat[e] *unequivocally* that the appropriate standard in this case is 'intermediate scrutiny.' " 2 Record, Doc. No. 88, p. 3 (emphasis added).) The Court, while making no reference to the Government's argument, effectively accepts it.

Although the Court in two places recites the test as stated in *Hogan*, see ante, at 6, 15, which asks whether the State has demonstrated "that the classification serves important governmental objectives and that the discriminatory means employed are substantially related to the achievement of those objectives," 458 U.S., at 724 (internal quotation marks omitted), the Court never answers the question presented in anything resembling that form. When it engages in analysis, the Court instead prefers the phrase "exceedingly persuasive justification" from *Hogan.* The Court's nine invocations of that phrase, see ante, at 6, 11, 12, 13, 15, 16, 28, 29, 39, and even its fanciful description of that imponderable as "the core instruction" of the Court's decisions in J.E.B. v. Alabama ex rel. T. B., 511 U.S. 127, 114 S.Ct. 1419, 128 L.Ed.2d 89 (1994), and *Hogan,* supra, see ante, at 13, would be unobjectionable if the Court acknowledged that *whether* a "justification" is "exceedingly persuasive" must be assessed by asking "[whether] the classification serves important governmental objectives and [whether] the discriminatory means employed are substantially related to the achievement of those objectives." Instead, however, the Court proceeds to interpret "exceedingly persuasive justification" in a fashion that contradicts the reasoning of *Hogan* and our other precedents.

That is essential to the Court's result, which can only be achieved by establishing that intermediate scrutiny is not survived if there are *some* women interested in attending VMI, capable of undertaking its activities, and able to meet its physical demands. Thus, the Court summarizes its holding as follows:

"In contrast to the generalizations about women on which Virginia rests, we note again these *dispositive* realities: VMI's implementing methodology is not *inherently* unsuitable to women; *some* women do well under the adversative model; *some* women, at least, would want to attend VMI if they had the opportunity; *some* women are capable of all of the individual activities required of VMI cadets and can meet the physical standards VMI now imposes on men." Ante, at 33 (internal quotation marks, citations, and punctuation omitted, emphasis added).

Similarly, the Court states that "[t]he State's justification for excluding all women from 'citizen-soldier' training for which some are qualified ... cannot rank as 'exceedingly persuasive'...." Ante, at 28.

Only the amorphous "exceedingly persuasive justification" phrase, and not the standard elaboration of intermediate scrutiny, can be made to yield this conclusion that VMI's single-sex composition is unconstitutional because there exist several women (or, one would have to conclude under the Court's reasoning, a single woman) willing and able to undertake VMI's program. Intermediate scrutiny has never required a least-restrictive-means analysis, but only a "substantial relation" between the classification and the state interests that it serves. Thus, in Califano v. Webster, 430 U.S. 313, 97 S.Ct. 1192, 51 L.Ed.2d 360 (1977) (per curiam), we upheld a congressional statute that provided higher Social Security benefits for women than for men. We reasoned that "women ... as such have been unfairly hindered from earning as much as men," but we did not require proof that each woman so benefited had suffered discrimination or that each disadvantaged man had not; it was sufficient that even under the former congressional scheme "women *on the average* received lower retirement benefits than men." Id., at 318, and n. 5 (emphasis added). The reasoning in our other intermediate-scrutiny cases has similarly required only a substantial relation between end and means, not a perfect fit. In Rostker v. Goldberg, 453 U.S. 57, 101 S.Ct. 2646, 69 L.Ed.2d 478 (1981), we held that selective-service registration could constitutionally exclude women, because even "assuming that a small number of women could be drafted for noncombat roles, Congress simply did not consider it worth the added burdens of including women in draft and registration plans." Id., at 81. In Metro Broadcasting, Inc. v. FCC, 497 U.S. 547, 579, 582–583, 110 S.Ct. 2997, 111 L.Ed.2d 445 (1990), overruled on other grounds, Adarand Constructors, Inc. v. Pena, 515 U.S. ___, ___ (1995)(slip op., at 25–26), we held that a classification need not be accurate "in every case" to survive intermediate scrutiny so long as, "in the aggregate," it advances the underlying objective. There is simply no support in our cases for the notion that a sex-based classification is invalid unless it relates to characteristics that hold true in every instance.

Not content to execute a *de facto* abandonment of the intermediate scrutiny that has been our standard for sex-based classifications for some two decades, the Court purports to reserve the question whether, even in principle, a higher standard (i.e., strict scrutiny) should apply. "The Court has," it says, "*thus far* reserved most stringent judicial scrutiny for classifications based on race or national origin ...," ante, at 14, n. 6 (emphasis added); and it describes our earlier cases as having done no more than decline to "equat[e] gender classifications, *for all purposes*, to classifications based on race or national origin," ante, at 14 (emphasis added). The wonderful thing about these statements is that they are not actually false—just as it would not be actually false to say that "our cases have thus far reserved the 'beyond a reasonable doubt' standard of proof for criminal cases," or that "we have not equated tort actions, for all purposes, to criminal prosecutions." But the statements are misleading, insofar as they suggest that we have not already categorically held strict scrutiny to be inapplicable to sex-based classifications. * * * And the statements are irresponsible, insofar as they are calculated to destabilize current law. Our task is to clarify the law—not to muddy the waters, and not to exact over-compliance by intimidation. The States and the Federal Government are entitled to know *before they act* the standard to which they will be held, rather than be compelled to guess about the outcome of Supreme Court peek-a-boo.

The Court's intimations are particularly out of place because it is perfectly clear that, if the question of the applicable standard of review for sex-based classifications were to be regarded as an appropriate subject for reconsideration, the stronger argument would be not for elevating the standard to strict scrutiny, but for reducing it to rational-basis review. The latter certainly has a firmer foundation in our past jurisprudence: Whereas no majority of the Court has ever applied strict scrutiny in a case involving sex-based classifications, we routinely applied rational-basis review until the 1970's, see, e.g., Hoyt v. Florida, 368 U.S. 57, 82 S.Ct. 159, 7 L.Ed.2d 118 (1961); Goesaert v. Cleary, 335 U.S. 464, 69 S.Ct. 198, 93 L.Ed. 163 (1948). And of course normal, rational-basis review of sex-based classifications would be much more in accord with the genesis of heightened standards of judicial review, the famous footnote in United States v. Carolene Products Co., 304 U.S. 144, 58 S.Ct. 778, 82 L.Ed. 1234 (1938), which said (intimatingly) that we did not have to inquire in the case at hand

> "whether prejudice against discrete and insular minorities may be a special condition, which tends seriously to curtail the operation of those political processes ordinarily to be relied upon to protect minorities, and which may call for a correspondingly more searching judicial inquiry." Id., at 152–153, n. 4.

It is hard to consider women a "discrete and insular minorit[y]" unable to employ the "political processes ordinarily to be relied upon," when they constitute a majority of the electorate. And the suggestion that they are incapable of exerting that political power smacks of the same paternalism that the Court so roundly condemns. See, e.g., ante, at 18–20, 25–28 (and accompanying notes). Moreover, a long list of legislation proves the proposition false. See, e.g., Equal Pay Act of 1963, 29 U.S.C. § 206(d); Title VII of the Civil Rights Act of 1964, 42 U.S.C. § 2000e–2; Title IX of the Education Amendments of 1972, 20 U.S.C. § 1681; Women's Business Ownership Act of 1988, Pub.L. 100–533, 102 Stat. 2689; Violence Against Women Act of 1994, Pub.L. 103–322, Title IV, 108 Stat.1902.

III

With this explanation of how the Court has succeeded in making its analysis seem orthodox—and indeed, if intimations are to be believed, even overly generous to VMI—I now proceed to describe how the analysis should have been conducted. The question to be answered, I repeat, is whether the exclusion of women from VMI is "substantially related to an important governmental objective."

A

It is beyond question that Virginia has an important state interest in providing effective college education for its citizens. That single-sex instruction is an approach substantially related to that interest should be evident enough from the long and continuing history in this country of men's and women's colleges. But beyond that, as the Court of Appeals here stated: "That single-gender education at the college level is beneficial to both sexes is a *fact established in this case*." 44 F.3d 1229, 1238 (C.A.4 1995)(emphasis added).

The evidence establishing that fact was overwhelming—indeed, "virtually uncontradicted" in the words of the court that received the evidence, 766 F.Supp. 1407, 1415 (W.D.Va.1991). As an initial matter, Virginia demonstrated at trial that "[a] substantial body of contemporary scholarship and research supports the proposition that, although males and females have significant areas of developmental overlap, they also have differing developmental needs that are deep-seated." * * * "[I]n the light of this very substantial authority favoring single-sex education," the District Court concluded that "the VMI Board's decision to maintain an all-male institution is fully justified even without taking into consideration the other unique features of VMI's teaching and training." Id., at 1412. This finding alone, which even this Court cannot dispute, see ante, at 17, should be sufficient to demonstrate the constitutionality of VMI's all-male composition.

But besides its single-sex constitution, VMI is different from other colleges in another way. It employs a "distinctive educational method," sometimes referred to as the "adversative, or doubting, model of education." * * * No one contends that this method is appropriate for all individuals; education is not a "one size fits all" business. Just as a State may wish to support junior colleges, vocational institutes, or a law school that emphasizes case practice instead of classroom study, so too a State's decision to maintain within its system one school that provides the adversative method is "substantially related" to its goal of good education. Moreover, it was uncontested that "if the state were to establish a women's VMI-type [i.e., adversative] program, the program would attract an insufficient number of participants to make the program work," 44 F.3d, at 1241; and it was found by the District Court that if Virginia were to include women in VMI, the school "would eventually find it necessary to drop the adversative system altogether," 766 F.Supp., at 1413. Thus, Virginia's options were an adversative method that excludes women or no adversative method at all.

There can be no serious dispute that, as the District Court found, single-sex education and a distinctive educational method "represent legitimate contributions to diversity in the Virginia higher education system." * * *

Virginia did not make this determination regarding the make-up of its public college system on the unrealistic assumption that no other colleges exist. Substantial evidence in the District Court demonstrated that the Commonwealth has long proceeded on the principle that " '[h]igher education resources should be viewed as a whole—public and private' "—because such an approach enhances diversity and because " 'it is academic and economic waste to permit unwarranted duplication.' " Id., at 1420–1421 (quoting 1974 Report of the General Assembly Commission on Higher Education to the General Assembly of Virginia). It is thus significant that, whereas there are "four all-female private [colleges] in Virginia," there is only "one private all-male college," which "indicates that the private sector is providing for th[e] [former] form of education to a much greater extent that it provides for all-male education." 766 F.Supp., at 1420–1421. In these circumstances, Virginia's election to fund one public all-male institution and one on the adversative model—and to concentrate its resources in a single entity that serves both these interests in diversity—is substantially related to the State's important educational interests.

B

The Court today has no adequate response to this clear demonstration of the conclusion produced by application of intermediate scrutiny. Rather, it relies on a series of contentions that are irrelevant or erroneous as a matter of law, foreclosed by the record in this case, or both.

1. I have already pointed out the Court's most fundamental error, which is its reasoning that VMI's all-male composition is unconstitutional because "some women are capable of all of the individual activities required of VMI cadets," 766 F.Supp., at 1412, and would prefer military training on the adversative model. See supra, at 6–9. This unacknowledged adoption of what amounts to (at least) strict scrutiny is without antecedent in our sex-discrimination cases and by itself discredits the Court's decision.

2. The Court suggests that Virginia's claimed purpose in maintaining VMI as an all-male institution—its asserted interest in promoting diversity of educational options—is not "genuin[e]," but is a pretext for discriminating against women. * * * To support this charge, the Court would have to impute that base motive to VMI's Mission Study Committee, which conducted a 3–year study from 1983 to 1986 and recommended to VMI's Board of Visitors that the school remain all-male. The Committee, a majority of whose members consisted of non-VMI graduates, "read materials on education and on women in the military," "made site visits to single-sex and newly coeduca-

tional institutions" including West Point and the Naval Academy, and "considered the reasons that other institutions had changed from single-sex to coeducational status"; its work was praised as "thorough" in the accreditation review of VMI conducted by the Southern Association of Colleges and Schools. * * * The Court states that "[w]hatever internal purpose the Mission Study Committee served—and however well-meaning the framers of the report—we can hardly extract from that effort any state policy evenhandedly to advance diverse educational options." Ante, at 22. But whether it is part of the evidence to prove that diversity was the Commonwealth's objective (its short report said nothing on that particular subject) is quite separate from whether it is part of the evidence to prove that anti-feminism was not. The relevance of the Mission Study Committee is that its very creation, its sober 3–year study, and the analysis it produced, utterly refute the claim that VMI has elected to maintain its all-male student-body composition for some misogynistic reason.

The Court also supports its analysis of Virginia's "actual state purposes" in maintaining VMI's student body as all-male by stating that there is no explicit statement in the record " 'in which the Commonwealth has expressed itself' " concerning those purposes. Ante, at 18, 21 (quoting 976 F.2d 890, 899 (C.A.4 1992)); see also ante, at 7. That is wrong on numerous grounds. First and foremost, in its implication that such an explicit statement of "actual purposes" is needed. The Court adopts, in effect, the argument of the United States that since the exclusion of women from VMI in 1839 was based on the "assumptions" of the time "that men alone were fit for military and leadership roles," and since "[b]efore this litigation was initiated, Virginia never sought to supply a valid, contemporary rationale for VMI's exclusionary policy," "[t]hat failure itself renders the VMI policy invalid." Brief for United States in No. 94–2107, at 10. This is an unheard-of doctrine. Each state decision to adopt or maintain a governmental policy need not be accompanied—in anticipation of litigation and on pain of being found to lack a relevant state interest—by a lawyer's contemporaneous recitation of the State's purposes. The Constitution is not some giant Administrative Procedure Act, which imposes upon the States the obligation to set forth a "statement of basis and purpose" for their sovereign acts, see 5 U.S.C. § 553(c). The situation would be different if what the Court assumes to have been the 1839 policy *had* been enshrined *and remained enshrined* in legislation—a VMI charter, perhaps, pronouncing that the institution's purpose is to keep women in their place. But since the 1839 policy was no more explicitly recorded than the Court contends the present one is, the mere fact that *today's* Commonwealth continues to fund VMI "is enough to answer [the United States'] contention that the [classification] was the 'accidental by-product of a traditional way of thinking about females.' " *Michael M.*, 450 U.S., at 471, n. 6 (plurality opinion)(quoting Califano v. Webster, 430 U.S. 313, 320, 97 S.Ct. 1192, 51 L.Ed.2d 360 (1977))(internal quotation marks omitted).

It is, moreover, not true that Virginia's contemporary reasons for maintaining VMI are not explicitly recorded. It is hard to imagine a more authoritative source on this subject than the 1990 Report of the Virginia Commission on the University of the 21st Century to the Governor and General Assembly (1990 Report). As the parties stipulated, that report "notes that the hallmarks of Virginia's educational policy are 'diversity and autonomy.'" Stipulations of Fact, at 37, reprinted in Lodged Materials from the Record 64 (Lodged Materials). It said: "The formal system of higher education in Virginia includes a great array of institutions: state-supported and independent, two-year and senior, research and highly specialized, traditionally black *and single-sex*." 1990 Report, quoted in relevant part at Lodged Materials 64–65 (emphasis added).[2] The Court's only response to this is repeated reliance on the Court of Appeals' assertion that " 'the only explicit [statement] that we have found in the record in which the Commonwealth has expressed itself with respect to gender distinctions'" (namely, the statement in the 1990 Report that the Commonwealth's institutions must "deal with faculty, staff, and students without regard to sex") had nothing to do with the purpose of diversity. Ante, at 7, 21 (quoting 976 F.2d, at 899). This proves, I suppose, that the Court of Appeals did not find a statement dealing with sex and diversity in the record; but the pertinent question (accepting the need for such a statement) is *whether it was there*. And the plain fact, which the Court does not deny, is that it *was*.

The Court contends that "[a] purpose genuinely to advance an array of educational options . . . is not served" by VMI. Ante, at 22. It relies on the fact that all of Virginia's *other* public colleges have become coeducational. Ibid.; see also ante, at 3, n. 2. The apparent theory of this argument is that unless Virginia pursues a great deal of diversity, its pursuit of some diversity must be a sham. This fails to take account of the fact that Virginia's resources cannot support all possible permutations of schools, * * * and of the fact that Virginia coordinates its public educational offerings with the offerings of in-state private educational institutions that the Commonwealth provides money for its residents to attend and otherwise assists—which include four women's colleges.[3]

Finally, the Court unreasonably suggests that there is some pretext in Virginia's reliance upon decentralized decisionmaking to achieve diversity—its granting of substantial autonomy to each institution with regard to student-body composition and other matters, see 766 F.Supp., at 1419. The Court adopts the suggestion of the Court of Appeals that it is not possible for "one institution with autonomy, but with no authority over any other state institution, [to] give effect to a state policy of diversity among institutions."

2. * * * It should be noted (for this point will be crucial to our later discussion) that these official reports quoted here, in text and footnote, regard the Commonwealth's educational system—public *and private*—as a unitary one.

3. The Commonwealth provides tuition assistance, scholarship grants, guaranteed loans, and work-study funds for residents of Virginia who attend private colleges in the Commonwealth. * * * These programs involve substantial expenditures: for example, Virginia appropriated $4,413,750 (not counting federal funds it also earmarked) for the College Scholarship Assistance Program for both 1996 and 1997, and for the Tuition Assistance Grant Program appropriated $21,568,000 for 1996 and $25,842,000 for 1997. See 1996 Va. Ap-

propriations Act, ch. 912, pt. 1, § 160. In addition, as the parties stipulated in the District Court, the Commonwealth provides other financial support and assistance to private institutions—including single-sex colleges—through low-cost building loans, state-funded services contracts, and other programs. See, e.g., Va.Code Ann. §§ 23–30.39 to 23.30.58 (Educational Facilities Authority Act). The State Council of Higher Education for Virginia, in a 1989 document not created for purposes of this litigation but introduced into evidence, has described these various programs as a "means by which the Commonwealth can provide funding to its independent institutions, thereby helping to maintain a diverse system of higher education." Budget Initiatives, p. 10.

Ante, at 22 (internal quotation marks omitted). If it were impossible for individual human beings (or groups of human beings) to act autonomously in effective pursuit of a common goal, the game of soccer would not exist. And where the goal is diversity in a free market for services, that tends to be achieved even by autonomous actors who act out of entirely selfish interests and make no effort to cooperate. Each Virginia institution, that is to say, has a natural incentive to make itself distinctive in order to attract a particular segment of student applicants. And of course none of the institutions is *entirely* autonomous; if and when the legislature decides that a particular school is not well serving the interest of diversity—if it decides, for example, that a men's school is not much needed—funding will cease.[4]

3. In addition to disparaging Virginia's claim that VMI's single-sex status serves a state interest in diversity, the Court finds fault with Virginia's failure to offer education based on the adversative training method to women. It dismisses the District Court's " 'findings' on 'gender-based developmental differences' " on the ground that "[t]hese 'findings' restate the opinions of Virginia's expert witnesses, opinions about typically male or typically female 'tendencies.' " Ante, at 23 (quoting 766 F.Supp., at 1434–1435). How remarkable to criticize the District Court on the ground that its findings rest on the evidence (i.e., the testimony of Virginia's witnesses)! That is what findings are supposed to do. It is indefensible to tell the Commonwealth that "[t]he burden of justification is demanding and it rests entirely on [you]," ante, at 15, and then to ignore the District Court's findings because they rest on the evidence put forward by the Commonwealth—particularly when, as the District Court said, "[t]he evidence in the case . . . is *virtually uncontradicted*," 766 F.Supp., at 1415 (emphasis added).

Ultimately, in fact, the Court does not deny the evidence supporting these findings. See ante, at 24–29. It instead makes evident that the parties to this case could have saved themselves a great deal of time, trouble, and expense by omitting a trial. The Court simply dispenses with the evidence submitted at trial—it never says that a single finding of the District Court is clearly erroneous—in favor of the Justices' own view of the world, which the Court proceeds to support with (1) references to observations of someone who is not a witness, nor even an educational expert, nor even a judge who reviewed the record or participated in the judgment below, but rather a judge who merely dissented from the Court of Appeals' decision not to rehear this case en banc, see ante, at 24, (2) citations of nonevidentiary materials such as amicus curiae briefs filed in this Court, see ante, at 27, nn. 13, 14, and (3)

---

4. The Court, unfamiliar with the Commonwealth's policy of diverse and independent institutions, and in any event careless of state and local traditions, must be forgiven by Virginians for quoting a reference to "the Charlottesville campus" of the University of Virginia. See ante, at 20. The University of Virginia, an institution even older than VMI, though not as old as another of the Commonwealth's universities, the College of William and Mary, occupies the portion of Charlottesville known, not as the "campus," but as "the grounds." More importantly, even if it were a "campus," there would be no need to specify "the Charlottesville campus," as one might refer to the Bloomington or Indianapolis campus of Indiana University. Unlike university systems with which the Court is perhaps more familiar, such as those in New York (e.g., the State University of New York at Binghamton or Buffalo), Illinois (University of Illinois at Urbana-Champaign or at Chicago), and California (University of California, Los Angeles or University of California, Berkeley), there is only one University of Virginia. It happens (because Thomas Jefferson lived near there) to be located at Charlottesville. To many Virginians it is known, simply, as "the University" * * *.

various historical anecdotes designed to demonstrate that Virginia's support for VMI as currently constituted reminds the Justices of the "bad old days," see ante, at 25–28.

It is not too much to say that this approach to the case has rendered the trial a sham. But treating the evidence as irrelevant is absolutely necessary for the Court to reach its conclusion. Not a single witness contested, for example, Virginia's "substantial body of 'exceedingly persuasive' evidence . . . that some students, both male and female, benefit from attending a single-sex college" and "[that] [f]or those students, the opportunity to attend a single-sex college is a valuable one, likely to lead to better academic and professional achievement." 766 F.Supp., at 1411–1412. Even the United States' expert witness "called himself a 'believer in single-sex education,' "although it was his "personal, philosophical preference," not one "born of educational-benefit considerations," "that single-sex education should be provided only by the private sector." Id., at 1412.

4. The Court contends that Virginia, and the District Court, erred, and "misperceived our precedent," by "train[ing] their argument on 'means' rather than 'end,' " ante, at 28. The Court focuses on "VMI's mission," which is to produce individuals "imbued with love of learning, confident in the functions and attitudes of leadership, possessing a high sense of public service, advocates of the American democracy and free enterprise system, and ready . . . to defend their country in time of national peril." 766 F.Supp., at 1425 (quoting Mission Study Committee of the VMI Board of Visitors, Report, May 16, 1986). "Surely," the Court says, "that goal is great enough to accommodate women." Ante, at 28.

This is law-making by indirection. What the Court describes as "VMI's mission" is no less the mission of *all* Virginia colleges. * * * It can be summed up as "learning, leadership, and patriotism." To be sure, those general educational values are described in a particularly martial fashion in VMI's mission statement, in accordance with the military, adversative, and all-male character of the institution. But imparting those values *in that fashion*—i.e., in a military, adversative, all-male environment—is the *distinctive* mission of VMI. And as I have discussed (and both courts below found), *that* mission is *not* "great enough to accommodate women."

The Court's analysis at least has the benefit of producing foreseeable results. Applied generally, it means that whenever a State's ultimate objective is "great enough to accommodate women" (as it always will be), then the State will be held to have violated the Equal Protection Clause if it restricts to men even one means by which it pursues that objective—no matter how few women are interested in pursuing the objective by that means, no matter how much the single-sex program will have to be changed if both sexes are admitted, and no matter how beneficial that program has theretofore been to its participants.

5. The Court argues that VMI would not have to change very much if it were to admit women. See, e.g., ante, at 22–25. The principal response to that argument is that it is irrelevant: If VMI's single-sex status is substantially related to the government's important educational objectives, as I have demonstrated above and as the Court refuses to discuss, that concludes the inquiry. There should be no debate in the federal judiciary over "how much"

VMI would be required to change if it admitted women and whether that would constitute "too much" change.

But if such a debate were relevant, the Court would certainly be on the losing side. The District Court found as follows: "[T]he evidence establishes that key elements of the adversative VMI educational system, with its focus on barracks life, would be fundamentally altered, and the distinctive ends of the system would be thwarted, if VMI were forced to admit females and to make changes necessary to accommodate their needs and interests." 766 F.Supp., at 1411. Changes that the District Court's detailed analysis found would be required include new allowances for personal privacy in the barracks, such as locked doors and coverings on windows, which would detract from VMI's approach of regulating minute details of student behavior, "contradict the principle that everyone is constantly subject to scrutiny by everyone else," and impair VMI's "total egalitarian approach" under which every student must be "treated alike"; changes in the physical training program, which would reduce "[t]he intensity and aggressiveness of the current program"; and various modifications in other respects of the adversative training program which permeates student life. See id., at 1412–1413, 1435–1443. As the Court of Appeals summarized it, "the record supports the district court's findings that at least these three aspects of VMI's program—physical training, the absence of privacy, and the adversative approach—would be materially affected by coeducation, leading to a substantial change in the egalitarian ethos that is a critical aspect of VMI's training." 976 F.2d, at 896–897.

In the face of these findings by two courts below, amply supported by the evidence, and resulting in the conclusion that VMI would be fundamentally altered if it admitted women, this Court simply pronounces that "[t]he notion that admission of women would downgrade VMI's stature, destroy the adversative system and, with it, even the school, is a judgment hardly proved." Ante, at 25 (footnote omitted). The point about "downgrad[ing] VMI's stature" is a strawman; no one has made any such claim. The point about "destroy[ing] the adversative system" is simply false; the District Court not only stated that "[e]vidence supports this theory," but specifically concluded that while "[w]ithout a doubt" VMI could assimilate women, "it is equally without a doubt that VMI's present methods of training and education would have to be changed" by a "move away from its adversative new cadet system." 766 F.Supp., at 1413, and n. 8, 1441. And the point about "destroy[ing] the school," depending upon what that ambiguous phrase is intended to mean, is either false or else sets a standard much higher than VMI had to meet. It sufficed to establish, as the District Court stated, that VMI would be "significantly different" upon the admission of women, 766 F.Supp., at 1412, and "would eventually find it necessary to drop the adversative system altogether," id., at 1413.[5]

5. The Court's do-it-yourself approach to factfinding, which throughout is contrary to our well-settled rule that we will not "undertake to review concurrent findings of fact by two courts below in the absence of a very obvious and exceptional showing of error," Graver Tank & Mfg. Co. v. Linde Air Products Co., 336 U.S. 271, 275, 69 S.Ct. 535, 93 L.Ed. 672 (1949)(and cases cited), is exemplified by its invocation of the experience of the federal military academies to prove that not much change would occur. * * * In fact, the District Court noted that "the West Point experience" supported the theory that a coeducational VMI would have to "adopt a [different] system," for West Point found it necessary upon becoming coeducational to "move away" from its adversative system. 766 F.Supp., at 1413, 1440.

6. Finally, the absence of a precise "all-women's analogue" to VMI is irrelevant. In Mississippi Univ. for Women v. Hogan, 458 U.S. 718, 102 S.Ct. 3331, 73 L.Ed.2d 1090 (1982), we attached no constitutional significance to the absence of an all-male nursing school. As Virginia notes, if a program restricted to one sex is necessarily unconstitutional unless there is a parallel program restricted to the other sex, "the opinion in *Hogan* could have ended with its first footnote, which observed that 'Mississippi maintains no other single-sex public university or college.'" Brief for Cross–Petitioners in No. 94–2107, at 38 (quoting Mississippi Univ. for Women v. Hogan, supra, at 720, n. 1).

Although there is no precise female-only analogue to VMI, Virginia has created during this litigation the Virginia Women's Institute for Leadership (VWIL), a state-funded all-women's program run by Mary Baldwin College. I have thus far said nothing about VWIL because it is, under our established test, irrelevant, so long as VMI 's all-male character is "substantially related" to an important state goal. But VWIL now exists, and the Court's treatment of it shows how far-reaching today's decision is.

VWIL was carefully designed by professional educators who have long experience in educating young women. The program *rejects* the proposition that there is a "difference in the respective spheres and destinies of man and woman," Bradwell v. State, 16 Wall. 130, 141, 21 L.Ed. 442 (1872), and is designed to "provide an all-female program that will achieve substantially similar outcomes [to VMI's] in an all-female environment," 852 F.Supp. 471, 481 (W.D.Va.1994). After holding a trial where voluminous evidence was submitted and making detailed findings of fact, the District Court concluded that "there is a legitimate pedagogical basis for the different means employed [by VMI and VWIL] to achieve the substantially similar ends." Ibid. The Court of Appeals undertook a detailed review of the record and affirmed. 44 F.3d 1229 (C.A.4 1995).[6] * * * It is worth noting that none of the United States' own experts in the remedial phase of this case was willing to testify that VMI's adversative method was an appropriate methodology for educating women. This Court, however, does not care. Even though VWIL was carefully designed by professional educators who have tremendous experience in the area, and survived the test of adversarial litigation, the Court simply declares, with no basis in the evidence, that these professionals acted on " 'overbroad' generalizations," ante, at 24, 33.

"Without a doubt ... VMI's present methods of training and education would have to be changed as West Point's were." Id., at 1413, n. 8; accord, 976 F.2d, at 896–897 (upholding District Court's findings that "the unique characteristics of VMI's program," including its "unique methodology," "would be destroyed by coeducation").

6. The Court is incorrect in suggesting that the Court of Appeals applied a "deferential" "brand of review inconsistent with the more exacting standard our precedent requires." Ante, at 38. That court "inquir[ed] (1) whether the state's objective is 'legitimate and important,' and (2) whether 'the requisite direct,

substantial relationship between objective and means is present,'" 44 F.3d, at 1235 (quoting *Hogan*, 458 U.S., at 725). To be sure, such review is "deferential" to a degree that the Court's new standard is not, *for it is intermediate scrutiny.* (The Court cannot evade this point or prove the Court of Appeals too deferential by stating that that court "devised another test, a 'substantive comparability' inquiry," ante, at 38 (quoting 44 F.3d, at 1237), for as that court explained, its "substantive comparability" inquiry was an *"additional* step" that it engrafted on "th[e] traditional test" of intermediate scrutiny, 44 F.3d, at 1237 (emphasis added).)

C

A few words are appropriate in response to the concurrence, which finds VMI unconstitutional on a basis that is more moderate than the Court's but only at the expense of being even more implausible. The concurrence offers three reasons: First, that there is "scant evidence in the record," ante, at 5, that diversity of educational offering was the real reason for Virginia's maintaining VMI. "Scant" has the advantage of being an imprecise term. I have cited the clearest statements of diversity as a goal for higher education in the 1990 Report of the Virginia Commission on the University of the 21st Century to the Governor and General Assembly, the 1989 Virginia Plan for Higher Education, the Budget Initiatives prepared in 1989 by the State Council of Higher Education for Virginia, the 1974 Report of the General Assembly Commission on Higher Education, and the 1969 Report of the Virginia Commission on Constitutional Revision. See supra, at 14, 17–18, and n. 2, 19–20, n. 3. There is *no* evidence to the contrary, once one rejects (as the concurrence rightly does) the relevance of VMI's founding in days when attitudes towards the education of women were different. Is this conceivably not enough to foreclose rejecting as clearly erroneous the District Court's determination regarding "the Commonwealth's objective of educational diversity"? 766 F.Supp., at 1413. Especially since it is absurd on its face even to *demand* "evidence" to prove that the Commonwealth's reason for maintaining a men's military academy is that a men's military academy provides a distinctive type of educational experience (i.e., fosters diversity). What other purpose *would* the Commonwealth have? One may argue, as the Court does, that this *type* of diversity is designed only to indulge hostility towards women—but that is a separate point, explicitly rejected by the concurrence, and amply refuted by the evidence I have mentioned in discussing the Court's opinion.[7] What is now under discussion—the concurrence's making central to the disposition of this case the supposedly "scant" evidence that Virginia maintained VMI in order to offer a diverse educational experience—is rather like making crucial to the lawfulness of the United States Army record "evidence" that its purpose is to do battle. A legal culture that has forgotten the concept of *res ipsa loquitur* deserves the fate that it today decrees for VMI.

Second, the concurrence dismisses out of hand what it calls Virginia's "second justification for the single-sex admissions policy: maintenance of the adversative method." Ante, at 7. The concurrence reasons that "this justification does not serve an important governmental objective" because, whatever the record may show about the pedagogical benefits of single-sex education, "there is no similar evidence in the record that an adversative method is pedagogically beneficial or is any more likely to produce character traits than other methodologies." Ante, at 7–8. That is simply wrong. * * * In reality, the pedagogical benefits of VMI's adversative approach were not only proved, but were a given in this litigation. The reason the woman applicant who

---

7. The concurrence states that it "read[s] the Court" not "as saying that the diversity rationale is a pretext" for discriminating against women, but as saying merely that the diversity rationale is not genuine. Ante, at 5, n. *. The Court itself makes no such disclaimer, which would be difficult to credit inasmuch as the foundation for its conclusion that the diversity rationale is not "genuin[e]," ante, at 22, is its antecedent discussion of Virginia's "deliberate" actions over the past century and a half, based on "[f]amiliar arguments," that sought to enforce once "widely held views about women's proper place," ante, at 17–22.

prompted this suit wanted to enter VMI was assuredly not that she wanted to go to an all-male school; it would cease being all-male as soon as she entered. She wanted the distinctive adversative education that VMI provided, and the battle was joined (in the main) over whether VMI had a basis for excluding women from that approach. The Court's opinion recognizes this, and devotes much of its opinion to demonstrating that " 'some women ... do well under [the] adversative model' " and that "[i]t is on behalf of these women that the United States has instituted this suit." Ante, at 33–34 (quoting 766 F.Supp., at 1434). Of course, in the last analysis it does not matter whether there are any benefits to the adversative method. The concurrence does not contest that there are benefits to *single-sex* education, and that alone suffices to make Virginia's case, since admission of a woman will even more surely put an end to VMI's single-sex education than it will to VMI's adversative methodology.

A third reason the concurrence offers in support of the judgment is that the Commonwealth and VMI were not quick enough to react to the "further developments" in this Court's evolving jurisprudence. Ante, at 4. Specifically, the concurrence believes it should have been clear after *Hogan* that "[t]he difficulty with [Virginia's] position is that the diversity benefited only one sex; there was single-sex public education available for men at VMI, but no corresponding single-sex public education available for women." Ante, at 6. If only, the concurrence asserts, Virginia had "made a genuine effort to devote comparable public resources to a facility for women, and followed through on such a plan, it might well have avoided an equal protection violation." Ante, at 7. That is to say, the concurrence believes that after our decision in *Hogan* * * *, the Commonwealth should have known that what this Court expected of it was ... yes!, the creation of a state all-women's program. Any lawyer who gave that advice to the Commonwealth ought to have been either disbarred or committed. (The proof of that pudding is today's 6–Justice majority opinion.) And any Virginia politician who proposed such a step when there were already 4 4–year women's colleges in Virginia (assisted by state support that may well exceed, in the aggregate, what VMI costs, see n. 3, supra)ought to have been recalled.

In any event, "diversity in the form of single-sex, as well as coeducational, institutions of higher learning," *is* "available to women as well as to men" in Virginia. Ante, at 7. The concurrence is able to assert the contrary only by disregarding the four all-women's private colleges in Virginia (generously assisted by public funds) and the Commonwealth's longstanding policy of coordinating public with private educational offerings * * *. According to the concurrence, the reason Virginia's assistance to its four all-women's private colleges does not count is that "[t]he private women's colleges are treated by the State *exactly* as all other private schools are treated." Ante, at 7. But if Virginia cannot get *credit* for assisting women's education if it only treats women's private schools as it does all other private schools, then why should it get *blame* for assisting men's education if it only treats VMI as it does all other public schools? This is a great puzzlement.

IV

As is frequently true, the Court's decision today will have consequences that extend far beyond the parties to the case. What I take to be the Court's unease with these consequences, and its resulting unwillingness to acknowledge them, cannot alter the reality.

A

Under the constitutional principles announced and applied today, single-sex public education is unconstitutional. By going through the motions of applying a balancing test—asking whether the State has adduced an "exceedingly persuasive justification" for its sex-based classification—the Court creates the illusion that government officials in some future case will have a clear shot at justifying some sort of single-sex public education. Indeed, the Court seeks to create even a greater illusion than that: It purports to have said nothing of relevance to *other* public schools at all. "We address specifically and only an educational opportunity recognized ... as 'unique'...." Ante, at 16, n. 7.

The Supreme Court of the United States does not sit to announce "unique" dispositions. Its principal function is to establish *precedent*—that is, to set forth principles of law that every court in America must follow. As we said only this Term, we expect both ourselves and lower courts to adhere to the "*rationale* upon which the Court based the results of its earlier decisions." Seminole Tribe of Fla. v. Florida, 517 U.S. ___, ___ (1996)(slip op., at 21)(emphasis added). That is the principal reason we publish our opinions.

And the rationale of today's decision is sweeping: for sex-based classifications, a redefinition of intermediate scrutiny that makes it indistinguishable from strict scrutiny. See supra, at 6–9. Indeed, the Court indicates that if any program restricted to one sex is "uniqu[e]," it must be opened to members of the opposite sex "who have the will and capacity" to participate in it. Ante, at 25. I suggest that the single-sex program that will not be capable of being characterized as "unique" is not only unique but nonexistent.[8]

In any event, regardless of whether the Court's rationale leaves some small amount of room for lawyers to argue, it ensures that single-sex public education is functionally dead. The costs of litigating the constitutionality of a single-sex education program, and the risks of ultimately losing that litigation, are simply too high to be embraced by public officials. Any person with standing to challenge any sex-based classification can haul the State into federal court and compel it to establish by evidence (presumably in the form of expert testimony) that there is an "exceedingly persuasive justification" for the classification. Should the courts happen to interpret that vacuous phrase as establishing a standard that is not utterly impossible of achievement, there is considerable risk that whether the standard has been met will not be determined on the basis of the record evidence—indeed, that will necessarily be the approach of any court that seeks to walk the path the Court has trod today. No state official in his right mind will buy such a high-cost, high-risk lawsuit by commencing a single-sex program. The enemies of single-sex

---

8. In this regard, I note that the Court—which I concede is under no obligation to do so—provides no example of a program that *would* pass muster under its reasoning today: not even, for example, a football or wrestling program. On the Court's theory, any woman ready, willing, and physically able to participate in such a program would, *as a constitutional matter*, be entitled to do so.

education have won; by persuading only seven Justices (five would have been enough) that their view of the world is enshrined in the Constitution, they have effectively imposed that view on all 50 States.

This is especially regrettable because, as the District Court here determined, educational experts in recent years have increasingly come to "suppor[t][the] view that substantial educational benefits flow from a single-gender environment, be it male or female, *that cannot be replicated in a coeducational setting.*" 766 F.Supp., at 1415 (emphasis added). "The evidence in th[is] case," for example, "is virtually uncontradicted" to that effect. Ibid. Until quite recently, some public officials have attempted to institute new single-sex programs, at least as experiments. In 1991, for example, the Detroit Board of Education announced a program to establish three boys-only schools for inner-city youth; it was met with a lawsuit, a preliminary injunction was swiftly entered by a District Court that purported to rely on *Hogan*, see Garrett v. Board of Education of School Dist. of Detroit, 775 F.Supp. 1004, 1006 (E.D.Mich.1991), and the Detroit Board of Education voted to abandon the litigation and thus abandon the plan, see Detroit Plan to Aid Blacks with All–Boy Schools Abandoned, Los Angeles Times, Nov. 8, 1991, p. A4, col. 1. Today's opinion assures that no such experiment will be tried again.

B

There are few extant single-sex public educational programs. The potential of today's decision for widespread disruption of existing institutions lies in its application to *private* single-sex education. Government support is immensely important to private educational institutions. Mary Baldwin College—which designed and runs VWIL—notes that private institutions of higher education in the 1990–1991 school year derived approximately 19 percent of their budgets from federal, state, and local government funds, *not including financial aid to students*. See Brief for Mary Baldwin College as Amicus Curiae 22, n. 13 (citing U.S. Dept. of Education, National Center for Education Statistics, Digest of Education Statistics, p. 38 and Note (1993)). Charitable status under the tax laws is also highly significant for private educational institutions, and it is certainly not beyond the Court that rendered today's decision to hold that a donation to a single-sex college should be deemed contrary to public policy and therefore not deductible if the college discriminates on the basis of sex. See Note, The Independent Sector and the Tax Laws: Defining Charity in an Ideal Democracy, 64 S. Cal. L.Rev. 461, 476 (1991). See also Bob Jones Univ. v. United States, 461 U.S. 574, 103 S.Ct. 2017, 76 L.Ed.2d 157 (1983).

The Court adverts to private single-sex education only briefly, and only to make the assertion (mentioned above) that "[w]e address specifically and only an educational opportunity recognized by the District Court and the Court of Appeals as 'unique.'" Ante, at 16, n. 7. As I have already remarked, see supra, at 32–33, that assurance assures nothing, unless it is to be taken as a promise that in the future the Court will disclaim the reasoning it has used today to destroy VMI. The Government, in its briefs to this Court, at least purports to address the consequences of its attack on VMI for public support of private single-sex education. It contends that private colleges which are the direct or indirect beneficiaries of government funding are not thereby necessarily converted into state actors to which the Equal Protection Clause is then applicable.   See Brief for United States in No. 94–2107, at 35–37 (discussing Rendell–Baker v. Kohn, 457 U.S. 830, 102 S.Ct. 2764, 73 L.Ed.2d 418 (1982), and Blum v. Yaretsky, 457 U.S. 991, 102 S.Ct. 2777, 73 L.Ed.2d 534 (1982)).   That is true.   It is also virtually meaningless.

The issue will be not whether government assistance turns private colleges into state actors, but whether the government itself would be violating the Constitution by providing state support to single-sex colleges.   For example, in Norwood v. Harrison, 413 U.S. 455, 93 S.Ct. 2804, 37 L.Ed.2d 723 (1973), we saw no room to distinguish between state operation of racially segregated schools and state support of privately run segregated schools. "Racial discrimination in state-operated schools is barred by the Constitution and '[i]t is also axiomatic that a state may not induce, encourage or promote private persons to accomplish what it is constitutionally forbidden to accomplish.'"   Id., at 465 (quoting Lee v. Macon County Bd. of Ed., 267 F.Supp. 458, 475–476 (M.D.Ala.1967));   see also Cooper v. Aaron, 358 U.S. 1, 19, 78 S.Ct. 1401, 3 L.Ed.2d 5 (1958) ("State support of segregated schools through any arrangement, management, funds, or property cannot be squared with the [Fourteenth] Amendment's command that no State shall deny to any person within its jurisdiction the equal protection of the laws");   Grove City College v. Bell, 465 U.S. 555, 565, 104 S.Ct. 1211, 79 L.Ed.2d 516 (1984)(case arising under Title IX of the Education Amendments of 1972 and stating that "[t]he economic effect of direct and indirect assistance often is indistinguishable").   When the Government was pressed at oral argument concerning the implications of these cases for private single-sex education if government-provided single-sex education is unconstitutional, it stated that the implications will not be so disastrous, since States *can* provide funding to *racially* segregated private schools, "depend[ing] on the circumstances," Tr. of Oral Arg. 56.   I cannot imagine what those "circumstances" might be, and it would be as foolish for private-school administrators to think that that assurance from the Justice Department will outlive the day it was made, as it was for VMI to think that the Justice Department's "unequivoca[l]" support for an intermediate-scrutiny standard in this case would survive the Government's loss in the courts below.

The only hope for state-assisted single-sex private schools is that the Court will not apply in the future the principles of law it has applied today. That is a substantial hope, I am happy and ashamed to say.   After all, did not the Court today abandon the principles of law it has applied in our earlier sex-classification cases?   And does not the Court positively invite private colleges to rely upon our ad-hocery by assuring them this case is "unique"?   I would not advise the foundation of any new single-sex college (especially an all-male one) with the expectation of being allowed to receive any government support; but it is too soon to abandon in despair those single-sex colleges already in existence.   It will certainly be possible for this Court to write a future opinion that ignores the broad principles of law set forth today, and that characterizes as utterly dispositive the opinion's perceptions that VMI was a uniquely prestigious all-male institution, conceived in chauvinism, etc., etc.   I will not join that opinion.

* * *

Justice Brandeis said it is "one of the happy incidents of the federal system that a single courageous State may, if its citizens choose, serve as a laboratory; and try novel social and economic experiments without risk to the rest of the country." New State Ice Co. v. Liebmann, 285 U.S. 262, 311, 52 S.Ct. 371, 76 L.Ed. 747 (1932)(dissenting opinion). But it is one of the unhappy incidents of the federal system that a self-righteous Supreme Court, acting on its Members' personal view of what would make a "more perfect Union," ante, at 41 (a criterion only slightly more restrictive than a "more perfect world"), can impose its own favored social and economic dispositions nationwide. As today's disposition, and others this single Term, show, this places it beyond the power of a "single courageous State," not only to introduce novel dispositions that the Court frowns upon, but to reintroduce, or indeed even adhere to, disfavored dispositions that are centuries old. See, e.g., BMW of North America, Inc. v. Gore, 517 U.S. ___ (1996); Romer v. Evans, 517 U.S. ___ (1996). The sphere of self-government reserved to the people of the Republic is progressively narrowed.

In the course of this dissent, I have referred approvingly to the opinion of my former colleague, Justice Powell, in Mississippi Univ. for Women v. Hogan, 458 U.S. 718, 102 S.Ct. 3331, 73 L.Ed.2d 1090 (1982). Many of the points made in his dissent apply with equal force here—in particular, the criticism of judicial opinions that purport to be "narro[w]" but whose "logic" is "sweepin[g]." Id., at 745–746, n. 18. But there is one statement with which I cannot agree. Justice Powell observed that the Court's decision in *Hogan*, which struck down a single-sex program offered by the Mississippi University for Women, had thereby "[l]eft without honor ... an element of diversity that has characterized much of American education and enriched much of American life." Id., at 735. Today's decision does not leave VMI without honor; no court opinion can do that.

In an odd sort of way, it is precisely VMI's attachment to such old-fashioned concepts as manly "honor" that has made it, and the system it represents, the target of those who today succeed in abolishing public single-sex education. The record contains a booklet that all first-year VMI students (the so-called "rats") were required to keep in their possession at all times. Near the end there appears the following period-piece, entitled "The Code of a Gentleman":

> "Without a strict observance of the fundamental Code of Honor, no man, no matter how 'polished,' can be considered a gentleman. The honor of a gentleman demands the inviolability of his word, and the incorruptibility of his principles. He is the descendant of the knight, the crusader; he is the defender of the defenseless and the champion of justice ... or he is not a Gentleman.

> A Gentleman ...

> Does not discuss his family affairs in public or with acquaintances.

> Does not speak more than casually about his girl friend.

> Does not go to a lady's house if he is affected by alcohol. He is temperate in the use of alcohol.

> Does not lose his temper; nor exhibit anger, fear, hate, embarrassment, ardor or hilarity in public.

Does not hail a lady from a club window.

A gentleman never discusses the merits or demerits of a lady.

Does not mention names exactly as he avoids the mention of what things cost.

Does not borrow money from a friend, except in dire need. Money borrowed is a debt of honor, and must be repaid as promptly as possible. Debts incurred by a deceased parent, brother, sister or grown child are assumed by honorable men as a debt of honor.

Does not display his wealth, money or possessions.

Does not put his manners on and off, whether in the club or in a ballroom. He treats people with courtesy, no matter what their social position may be.

Does not slap strangers on the back nor so much as lay a finger on a lady.

Does not 'lick the boots of those above' nor 'kick the face of those below him on the social ladder.'

Does not take advantage of another's helplessness or ignorance and assumes that no gentleman will take advantage of him.

A Gentleman respects the reserves of others, but demands that others respect those which are his.

A Gentleman can become what he wills to be ... "

I do not know whether the men of VMI lived by this Code; perhaps not. But it is powerfully impressive that a public institution of higher education still in existence sought to have them do so. I do not think any of us, women included, will be better off for its destruction.

*

Index

References are to Pages

†

0–314–09633–7

90000

9 780314 096333